# THE

# HANDBOOK

# OF

# SCHOOL
# PSYCHOLOGY

## THIRD EDITION

*Editors*

**CECIL R. REYNOLDS, PH.D.**
**Department of Educational Psychology**
**Texas A & M University**

**TERRY B. GUTKIN, PH.D.**
**Department of Educational Psychology**
**University of Nebraska-Lincoln**

**JOHN WILEY & SONS, INC.**

NEW YORK • CHICHESTER • WEINHEIM •
BRISBANE • SINGAPORE • TORONTO

| | |
|---|---|
| *Acquisitions Editor* | Christopher J. Rogers |
| *Marketing Manager* | Bonnie Cabot |
| *Senior Production Editors* | Jeanie Berke and Deborah Herbert |
| *Book Designer* | Karin Gerdes Kincheloe |
| *Illustration Editor* | Anna Melhorn |

This book was set in 9.5/11.5 Janson Text by Digitype and printed and bound by Hamilton Printing. The cover was stamped by Hamilton Printing.

This book is printed on acid-free paper. ∞

The paper in this book was manufactured by a mill whose forest management programs include sustained yield harvesting of its timberlands. Sustained yield harvesting principles ensure that the numbers of trees cut each year does not exceed the amount of new growth.

***Library of Congress Cataloging-in-Publication Data:***
The handbook of school psychology / editors, Cecil R. Reynolds, Terry
  B. Gutkin,—3rd ed.
     p.    cm.
  Includes bibliographical references.
  ISBN 0-471-12205-X (cloth : alk. paper)
    1. Educational psychology—Handbooks, manuals, etc.  2. School
psychology—Handbooks, manuals, etc.    I. Reynolds, Cecil R., 1952–
  II. Gutkin, Terry B., 1947–
LB1051.H2356    1998
370. 15—dc21                            98-17618
                                            CIP

Printed in the United States of America.

10  9  8  7  6  5  4  3  2

# LIST OF CONTRIBUTORS

**THOMAS M. ACHENBACH**
Department of Psychiatry
University of Vermont • Burlington, Vermont

**PATRICIA A. ALEXANDER**
Department of Human Development
University of Maryland • College, Park, Maryland

**DAVID W. BARNETT**
Teachers College
University of Cincinnati • Cincinnati, Ohio

**DONALD N. BERSOFF**
Haverford, Pennsylvania

**WILLIAM E. BICKEL**
Department of Educational Administration
University of Pittsburgh • Pittsburgh, Pennsylvania

**CHRISTINE E. BORGELT**
Department of Educational Psychology
University of Nebraska • Lincoln, Nebraska

**RONALD T. BROWN**
Medical University of South Carolina
Department of Pediatrics
Division of Genetics and Child Development
Charleston, South Carolina

**MICHAELANTHONY BROWN-CHEATHAM**
(deceased)
Graduate School of Professional Studies
San Diego State University • San Diego, California

**KARLA BUERKLE**
University of Minnesota
Minneapolis, Minnesota

**R. T. BUSSE**
Department of Psychology
University of Wisconsin • Whitewater, Wisconsin

**THOMAS P. CAFFERTY**
Department of Psychology
University of South Carolina • Columbia, South Carolina

**JOHN CARLSON, M.S.**
School of Applied Health and
Educational Psychology
Oklahoma State University • Stillwater, Oklahoma

**SANDRA L. CHRISTENSON**
University of Minnesota • Minneapolis, Minnesota

**JANE CLOSE CONOLEY**
College of Education
Texas A&M University • College Station, Texas

**JACQUELINE CUNNINGHAM**
Department of Behavioral Science
Children's Hospital National Medical Center •
Washington, District of Columbia

**MICHAEL J. CURTIS**
Department of Psychology and
Social Foundations
University of South Florida • Tampa, Florida

**EDWARD J. DALY III**
College of Eduction
University of Cinncinati • Cinncinati, Ohio

**RIK D'AMATO**
Division of Professional Psychology
University of Northern Colorado • Greeley, Colorado

**JOAN E. DONEGAN**
Department of Pediatrics
Division of Child and Adolescent Psychiatry
Emory University School of Medicine • Atlanta, Georgia

107846

**JUDY ELLIOTT**
National Center on Educational Outcomes
College of Education and Human Development
University of Minnesota • Minneapolis,
Minnesota

**STEPHEN N. ELLIOTT**
Department of Educational Psychology
University of Wisconsin • Madison, Wisconsin

**TOM FAGAN**
Department of Psychology
University of Memphis • Memphis, Tennessee

**STEVEN R. FORNESS**
Department of Curriculum and Instruction
University of Iowa • Iowa City, Iowa

**MARIBETH GETTINGER**
Department of Educational Psychology
University of Wisconsin • Madison, Wisconsin

**YVONNE L. GODDARD**
School of Physical Activity and
Educational Services
Ohio State University • Columbus, Ohio

**TODD GRAVOIS**
College of Education
Counseling and Personnel Service
University of Maryland • College Park, Maryland

**BARRY C. GRIBBONS**
Division of Counseling and Educational Psychology
University of Southern California–University Park •
Los Angeles, California

**TERRY B. GUTKIN**
Department of Educational Psychology
University of Nebraska • Lincoln, Nebraska

**RONALD K. HAMBLETON**
School of Education
University of Massachusetts • Amherst,
Massachusetts

**MARY HENNING-STOUT**
Graduate School of Professional Studies
Lewis and Clark College • Portland, Oregon

**TIMOTHY E. HERON**
School of Physical Activity and Educational Services
Ohio State University • Columbus, Ohio

**JAN N. HUGHES**
Department of Educational Psychology
Texas A&M University • College Station, Texas

**ROBERT J. ILLBACK**
R.E.A.C.H. of Louisville, Inc.
Louisville, Kentucky

**CAROLYN IMPERATO-MCCAMMON**
Educational Psychology Department
University of Georgia • Athens, Georgia

**JAMES W. KALAT**
Department of Psychology
North Carolina State University • Raleigh, North
Carolina

**RANDY W. KAMPHAUS**
Department of Educational Psychology
University of Georgia • Athens, Georgia

**ALAN S. KAUFMAN**
Stamford, Connecticut

**KENNETH A. KAVALE**
Department of Curriculum and Instruction
University of Iowa • Iowa City, IA

**TIMOTHY Z. KEITH**
Division of School Psychology
Alfred University • Alfred, New York

**JOHN H. KRANZLER**
Foundations of Education
University of Florida • Gainesville, Florida

**THOMAS R. KRATOCHWILL**
Department of Educational Psychology
University of Wisconsin • Madison, Wisconsin

**DANIEL A. KRAUSS**
Department of Psychology
University of Arizona • Tucson, Arizona

**NADINE M. LAMBERT**
School of Education
University of California • Berkeley, California

**KIM L. LASECKI, M.S.**
Educational Psychology Department
University of Utah • Salt Lake City, Utah

**DOUGLAS LEE, M.D.**
Department of Pediatrics
Division of Child and Adolescent Psychiatry
Emory University School of Medicine • Atlanta,
Georgia

**ELIZABETH O. LICHTENBERGER**
Laboratory for Cognitive Neuroscience
The Salk Institute • La Jolla, California

**PATRICIA A. LOWE**
Educational Psychology Department
Texas A&M University • College Station, Texas

**GREGG M. MACMANN**
University of Kentucky College of Education
Department of Educational and Counseling
Psychology • Lexington, Kentucky

**CHARLES A. MAHER**
Graduate School of Applied and Professional
Psychology
Rutgers University • Piscataway, New Jersey

**BRIAN K. MARTENS**
Department of Psychology
Syracuse University • Syracuse, New York

**STEPHANIE H. MCCONAUGHY**
Psychiatry Department
University of Vermont • Burlington, Vermont

**FREDERIC J. MEDWAY**
Department of Psychology
University of South Carolina • Columbia, South
Carolina

**Joel Meyers**
Department of Counseling and
Psychological Services
Georgia State University • Atlanta, Georgia

**Dwight Morrison**
Independent School District 709 • Duluth,
Minnesota

**P. Karen Murphy**
Department of Human Development
University of Maryland • College Park, Maryland

**Jack A. Naglieri**
Education Service and Research
Ohio State University • Columbus, Ohio

**Bonnie K. Nastasi**
Programs in School Psychology
SUNY–Albany • Albany, New York

**Thomas D. Oakland**
Department of Educational Psychology
University of Florida • Gainesville, Florida

**Thomas D. Overcast**
Attorney at Law • Edmonds, Washington

**Kathleen D. Paget**
The Center for Child and Family Studies
College of Social Work
University of South Carolina • Columbia, South
Carolina

**Beeman N. Phillips**
Department of Educational Psychology
University of Texas at Austin • Austin, Texas

**Donald E. Polkinghorne**
Division of Counseling and
Educational Psychology
University of Southern California–University Park •
Los Angeles, California

**Frances F. Prevatt**
Department of Educational Psychology
Texas A&M University • College Station, Texas

**Walter B. Pryzwansky**
School of Education
University of North Carolina • Chapel Hill, North
Carolina

**Dorrie L. Rapp**
White River Junction, Vermont

**Daniel J. Reschly**
Peabody College of Education and
Human Development
Vanderbilt University • Nashville, Tennessee

**Cecil R. Reynolds**
Department of Educational Psychology
Texas A&M University • College Station, Texas

**Sylvia Rosenfield**
College of Education
Counseling and Personnel Service
University of Maryland • College Park, Maryland

**Barbara A. Rothlisberg**
Educational Psychology Department
Ball State University • Muncie, Indiana

**Donal M. Sacken**
Department of Psychology
University of Arizona • Tucson, Arizona

**Adam L. Saenz**
Educational Psychology Department
Texas A&M University • College Station, Texas

**Bruce D. Sales**
Department of Psychology
University of Arizona • Tucson, Arizona

**Edward S. Shapiro**
College of Education
Lehigh University • Bethlehem, Pennsylvania

**Susan M. Sheridan**
Department of Educational Psychology
University of Nebraska • Lincoln, Nebraska

**Karen Callan Stoiber**
Department of Educational Psychology
University of Wisconsin • Madison, Wisconsin

**Robert D. Tennyson**
Department of Educational Psychology
University of Minnesota • Minneapolis, Minnesota

**Deborah J. Tharinger**
Department of Educational Psychology
University of Texas at Austin • Austin, Texas

**Timothy R. Vollmer**
School of Medicine
University of Pennsylvania • Philadelphia,
Pennsylvania

**Dorlene Walker**
Department of Educational Psychology
University of Utah • Salt Lake City, Utah

**Joseph C. Witt**
Psychology Department
Louisiana State University • Baton Rouge,
Louisiana

**Patricia H. Leu Work**
Division of Professional Psychology
University of Northern Colorado • Greeley,
Colorado

**Tracie Wurm**
Department of Psychology
North Carolina State University • Raleigh, North
Carolina

**James E. Ysseldyke**
National Center on Educational Outcomes
College of Education and Human Development
University of Minnesota • Minneapolis, Minnesota

**Joseph E. Zins, Ph.D.**
Teachers College
University of Cincinnati • Cincinnati, Ohio

· DEDICATION ·

To the legacy of *Jack Bardon*, mentor, scholar, and exemplar extraordinaire.

# FOREWORD

JOHN H. JACKSON, PH.D.
*The Wisconsin School of Professional Psychology*

The Third Edition of *The Handbook of School Psychology*, edited by Terry B. Gutkin and Cecil R. Reynolds, is testimony that the volume in its first and second editions has been useful to the specialty of school psychology, as well as to others. The *Handbook* has been current for 16 years, and with the third edition it will be current into the twenty-first century—a period of almost three decades. This is an enviable record for any scientifically based publication, and it is the successive editions that have kept it up to date. Its influence has been felt by waves of graduate students and by many practicing school psychologists for the better part of their professional careers. Its service to the specialty of school psychology is unmeasured, but it can be realistically estimated as profound.

Any handbook of a psychological specialty that is as dynamic as school psychology faces major challenges. The first challenge is that of adequately serving a specialty in which practice is dependent on a slowly developing underlying science as fluid as that in school psychology. When the *Handbook* was first published, school psychology as a field of practice was considered sufficiently fluid that APA accreditation of its internships was seen as impractical and was not encouraged. What, if any, impact did the earlier editions have on helping the specialty gain the degree of concordant crystalization necessary to achieve the APA accreditation that came later?

Reaching its third edition is evidence that *The Handbook of School Psychology* has satisfactorily met a second challenge, that of remaining on the cutting edge of the specialty. New chapters have been included here on topics that have become well established since the second edition, including "Secondary Prevention: Applications Through Intervention Assistance Programs and Inclusive Education," "Psychopharmacotherapy with School-aged Children," and "Implications of Recent Research in Biological Psychology for School Psychology." Many chapters have been reconceptualized and given new foci, such as "Child Psychotherapy." Others have been updated, like "Ten Years Later: Trends in the Assessment of Infants, Toddlers, Preschoolers, and Their Families." Many new authors and fresh voices in a number of areas have been added.

By succeeding in these two challenges, this third edition satisfies what I see as a third challenge. That is, it remains relevant to new or evolving practice models at the edge of mainstream practice in the specialty of school psychology. As with other clinical specialties in the profession of psychology, for some time academics and researchers and practitioners have not always shared similar perspectives, with each side emphasizing different priorities. The organization of the *Handbook* provides a basis for bringing these two sides together. Section 2 sets forth the scientific foundations of professional practice and functional theory in the specialty. The remaining sections focus on an array of practices in the profession, providing insights into how practices can put science to work for the benefit of clients. Juxtaposing science and practice in a nonconfrontational manner can be a useful way of assisting scientists and practitioners to be open to each others' perceptions of the developing field of school psychology.

School psychology has been moving forward on a broad front, steadily pursuing a variety of professional activities despite differing opinions concerning what is acceptable in practicing in the schools and, indeed, in educational settings everywhere. These differing opinions are suggested by varying responses to often-posed and debated questions. Is individual psychological counseling or psychotherapy in the schools appropriate in view of the large number of schoolchildren needing psychotherapeutic intervention? Can group psychological processes effectively confront deep-seated problems in children, adolescents, and young adults? Because projective tests are lacking norms and depend on clinical interpretation, can they yield valid, reliable, and useful information about students? Are objective personality tests too vulnerable to faking to yield valid information? Should school psychologists focus on the academic success or the mental health of troubled children, adolescents, and young adults? Does the school psychologist work with the individual child or the child together with members of the family? Can we afford to provide direct services to children in schools, given the limited resources for service delivery? Are behavioral techniques capable of producing real change in a democratic society? Are psychodynamic interventions practical? The practitioner in school psychology who uses an unbiased resource such as the *Handbook* has the opportunity to maintain an open perspective in providing professional interventions with school clients through adaptive applications of the many approaches and tools available.

In the varied positions in which I have served the profession in recent years, I have become aware of a pattern of practice among school psychologists who have been board-certified or who have received diplomas in school psychology from the American Board of Professional Psychology, as well as some school psychologists who have obtained doctoral degrees. They have tended to practice in whole or in part outside of the school. Their practices are very clinical in terms of the services they provide. That is, they are not limited to the range of professional activities used in the school. The activities of these psychologists are taking place in private clinics, hospitals, and private professional offices, as well as in correctional and other institutions. Although the *Handbook* does not speak directly to practice in these institutions, it does address the full range of activities in which the school psychologist engages.

The relevance of the *Handbook* to these newer modalities of school psychology practice may be the realization of the view that the editors revealed in their preface to the second edition. They saw the volume as a bridge between what school psychology was at the time and its future potential. Section 1 of this edition conceptualizes this view rather well. Here, the editors include a historical perspective of where the specialty has been and where it is now. Here, too, is a discussion of where the specialty might go in the twenty-first century.

*The Handbook of School Psychology* addresses school psychology, and to a lesser degree the delivery of school psychological services. But let us look at the relationship between school psychology and service delivery. With many contending forces (both centripetal and centrifugal) operating within the specialty of school psychology, it is important for it to be organized. It must be clear in its purposes within a given school district and within an individual school or program. In other words, a program of school psychological services must be deliberately designed and guided.

The organization needed is that organization that is forged in the school psychological services administrative unit, whether it is designated as a psychological services department, a program, an office, or a bureau. In the psychological services unit, the types of possible services to be offered to the schools are determined, as are the models of service delivery, the limits of service responsibilities, the nature of overseeing the quality of services offered, the identity of the personnel from whom service requests and instructions are received, recognition of who is responsible for formal evaluations, and numerous other functions that proceed from the organization.

Management of the unit requires certain positions that are crucial. These are unit leadership positions, including the unit administrators and an appropriate number of supervisors. When these positions or roles do not exist, even though the staff is well trained and materials are abundant, school psychological services do not ordinarily reach their potential. School psychologists function in a setting that has the primary function of educating or training, that is, a setting devoted to addressing the public agenda of transmitting the cultural heritage to oncoming generations. School psychologists, with their emphasis on the private agenda of the learner (the psychologist's client) find themselves in an environment that does not fully understand them or their roles. Therefore, whole school populations need to be educated about who school psychologists are, what their education and training are, what they are capable of doing, and what their ethical limits are. Unit administrative and supervisory leaders, working with the psychological services staff, make these decisions and communicate them to the leaders of the educational enterprise. Leaders are also responsible for much of the continuing education that is required to maintain and improve the knowledge, skills, and attitudes of the psychological services staff.

The importance of school psychological leadership positions or roles is acknowledged in the professional literature and emphasized on the front lines of service delivery. Nevertheless, there continues to be insufficient research to determine the efficacy of leadership models on resultant outcomes of service delivery. Such research would inform future choices among leadership styles. It would also facilitate training options for present and future leaders. As research in administration and supervision of school psychological services develops and provides scientific underpinnings of role models, a scientific rationale for their inclusion in the *Handbook* will have been met. This is important because the nature of the delivery of services may be the difference between success and failure of what is brought to bear on a specific case or situation. There is much opportunity for professional activity in this context.

The editors should take satisfaction from the contribution they have made to their profession through the publication of the *Handbook* and for their sustained scholarly efforts through the succeeding editions. The publication, which they hoped would be a bridge to the future of school psychology, begins to look like a broad avenue at the entrance of the twenty-first century.

J.H.J.

# PREFACE

In the 20 years since we first conceptualized what became the first edition of this work, school psychology has continued to grow and to change, and to do so rapidly. The content of *The Handbook of School Psychology* thus changes, but our vision for this work has not. We began with the intent to provide a comprehensive treatment of the body of knowledge on which school psychology was founded and on which it continues to grow. Although politics, social policy, and economic policy influence schools, schoolings and those who serve these processes and entities, we continue to hold to the belief that "school psychology must first and foremost be built on the foundations of scientific psychology" (from the second edition, p. xiii). This Rubicon has been the forefront of our efforts in developing this and former editions.

As school psychology has broadened its service domain, at times by design and at times by legislative fiat, and as social and public policy also alters our perceptions, the *Handbook* continues to change in its specific content and organization. There are many new chapters, new authors, and some alteration of the overall organization of the work, but all represent the cutting edge of research and profitable perspectives on the science and the practice of school psychology. Chapters retained from the second edition have all been completely revised to provide the most up-to-date knowledge base and cogent thought in the various fields represented.

We continue to endorse the scientist-practitioner model and the behavior and philosophy it implies. As Cecil R. Reynolds has espoused here and in the first two volumes, "In God we Trust; all others must have data." We must be guided by empirical research and the heuristic of strong and tested theories in our practice. To this, we add our endorsement of the inescapable conclusion that school psychologists are health service providers, working at the level of systems (large and small) that affect learners of all ages and at the level of individuals within those systems. The American Psychological Association, in its approval of the Petition for Reaffirmation of the Specialty of School Psychology continues to recognize school psychology not only as a distinct professional discipline in psychology but also as one of the specialties providing health services. With health being defined as mental health, wellness, resiliency, stress management, coping, and the development of a healthy lifestyle, it is clear that school psychologists pervasively affect the health of their clients both in and out of schools.

The profession thus continues to expand and to accept new challenges, even as the oldest problems of schools, children, teachers, and parents persist, and in an ever more rapidly changing environment. With this expansion, the *Handbook* has grown and evolved as well. There is no other single source with the breadth and depth of coverage of topics vital to school psychology, ranging from theory-based presentation to scholarly reviews of research to more directive, or how-to, chapters. We hope we have helped to meet some of the challenges of the profession and to shape its immediate future.

We continue to be indebted to an enormous number of people in the derivation and production of this work. Our authors, past and present, are the most crucial, and to them go our first and greatest thanks. We trust that this edition, as did the first two, embodies the best thinking abut science and issues important to the development and delivery of school psychological services. We continue to be pleased, excited, and honored that so many of our colleagues have worked so hard to contribute to this work. Thanks go to our own mentors, Alan S. Kaufman and Beeman N. Phillips, who provided such excellent models of scholarship for us, and to our respective universities, Texas A&M University and the University of Nebraska–Lincoln, for their encouragement of the scholarly activities represented in this work. We also express our appreciation to the staff and development team at John Wiley & Sons, headed by our editor, Chris Rogers, who have done an excellent job in producing this volume (Jeanie Berke/Deborah Herbert, Karin Gerdes Kincheloe, Anna Melhorn, and Caroline Ryan).

Our families continue to provide a source of support and refuge in our pursuit of this edition of the *Handbook*. We are especially indebted to our wives, Julia Hickman and Barbara Gutkin. Thank you, once again.

As we have said before and continue to believe, because of its primary focus and the nature of its clientele, school psychology may have the greatest impact of all psychological specialties on the future of the mental health of our nation. School psychology also faces the most difficult challenges where it is most often practiced, the public schools, where politics and policy often override science. It is our fervent hope that this edition of *The Handbook of School Psychology* will help the practitioner, the scholar, the teacher, and the student to overcome the obstacles in delivering the best available health services and in improving practice skills, research, and thinking in and about school psychology.

CECIL R. REYNOLDS
TERRY B. GUTKIN

# CONTENTS

# CURRENT PERSPECTIVES IN SCHOOL PSYCHOLOGY

## CHAPTER 1

# TRAINING SCHOOL PSYCHOLOGISTS BEFORE THERE WERE SCHOOL PSYCHOLOGIST TRAINING PROGRAMS: A HISTORY, 1890–1930[1]

THOMAS K. FAGAN
*University of Memphis*

## INTRODUCTION AND METHODOLOGY

Until recent years there were few historical accounts of the field of school psychology. Collectively, earlier sources surveyed the major developments in school psychology during the period referred to as the hybrid years, 1890–1970 (Cutts, 1955; Fagan, 1990b; Hildreth, 1930; Symonds, 1942; Wallin, 1914; Wallin & Ferguson, 1967). Since the 1970s, several historical items have provided more in-depth discussion of school psychology's history and have extended the analyses into the period referred to as the thoroughbred years (Fagan 1990b, 1990c, 1992, 1995; Fagan & Wise, 1994; French, 1984, 1988, 1990). While a general history of school psychology is now available, few historical analyses have focused on the training of school psychologists. Considerable descriptive literature has appeared in the past 30

[1] I wish to express my appreciation to the archivists at the Archives of the History of American Psychology, Bobst Library of New York University, Clark University, The Library of Congress, Milbank Memorial Library at Teachers College–Columbia University (Archives of the New York City Board of Education), Mount Holyoke College, Okmulgee (Oklahoma) Public Schools, University of Illinois, University of Pennsylvania, and Yale University. I also thank Joseph French, Paul McReynolds, Ludy Benjamin, Gil Trachtman, Dawn Wells, and Patti Wilson for their assistance with the manuscript.

years: the number and location of programs; enrollment and graduation data; financial aid; program content; and comparative data over time, including comparisons of training models (e.g., Bardon, Costanza, & Walker, 1971; Brown & Minke, 1986; Cardon & French, 1968–1969; French, 1966; French & McCloskey, 1979; Goh, 1977; Knoff, 1986; Lambert, 1993; Prout, Toler, & Eklund, 1976; Reschly & Wilson, 1995). In recent decades, directories of school psychology programs and internships and several personalized accounts of specific training programs have been published. Collectively, these sources detail the nature of contemporary training in school psychology. However, there have been no in-depth histories of how school psychologists were trained in this century. A review by Fagan (1986b) focuses on the quantitative growth of programs that spanned most of the twentieth century but contains only brief discussions of program content or models. In response to this void, this chapter explores the development of the preparation of school psychologists from approximately 1890 to 1930—the period up to and including the first training program specifically for school psychologists.

The current status of training in school psychology is substantially different from that of earlier times. As of 1992–1993 there were between 208 and 215 institutions that offered masters, specialist, and doctoral degree programs (Carey & Wilson, 1995; Reschly, 1995; Smith & Fagan,

1995). The institutions were unevenly distributed across the United States, although consistent with the distribution of the population of school psychologists and the schoolchildren served (Smith & Fagan, 1995). The typical length of these programs was 67.3 semester hours at the specialist level and 101.5 semester hours at the doctoral level. Combining specialist and doctoral data, we see that in 1992–1993 there were 1,615 graduates and a total enrollment of 8,678. The number of primary faculty in the training was 869, with a full-time equivalent of 649.

Guided by national-level standards of the American Psychological Association (APA) and the National Association of School Psychologists (NASP), as well as by state-level requirements of state boards of education or boards of examiners in psychology, school psychology programs currently include a combination of foundation requirements in psychology and education, specialty courses, and field experiences. The field experience requirements include several practica and an internship of at least 1,500 hours for doctoral programs; nondoctoral programs typically offer at least one practicum and an internship of 1,200 hours. At least half of these internship hours must be in schools. Programs that are not in compliance with the APA or NASP standards usually offer less didactic training and fewer field experiences. More detailed discussions of the status of training in recent years appear in Carey and Wilson (1995), Fagan (1986b, 1990a), Fagan and Wise (1994), and Reschly (1995). The current status of the field is also shown by the school psychology category among the specialties listed in *U.S. News & World Report*'s ranking of the best doctoral programs in the country (see the March 20, 1995, edition).

In stark contrast, for most of the period discussed here (1890–1930), there were no state or national standards for training or practice and no state associations of school psychologists, although there were a few local or regional groups in large cities (e.g., Chicago Psychological Association, 1984). The APA was available, but because of stringent membership requirements, it had a regular membership of only about 500 by 1930 and about the same number of associate members (Fernberger, 1932); nor was there an institution of higher learning that offered a training program specifically for school psychology. The number of persons practicing something like school psychology was probably fewer than 500, even late in the period. Only after the middle of this period did

practitioners begin using standardized, published tests of ability and achievement. Few districts offered special educational services, and their range of services was much narrower than in recent times (Fagan, 1995; Van Sickle, Witmer, & Ayers, 1911; Wallin, 1914).

Among the characteristics of the hybrid years (approximately 1890–1970) was a diversity of practitioner backgrounds and preparation necessitated by a lack of consensus regarding the preferred nature of preparation and any enforceable set of standards; the vehicles for enforcing standards of training as we know them today were largely absent. Most practitioners were emerging as school psychologists from a variety of backgrounds and rallying around specific roles and functions rather than a specific training identity. I have referred to this period of training as "diversity of necessity" to distinguish it from a later period of training I refer to as "restriction for identity," which occurred in the thoroughbred years and was characterized by increasing regulation of training (Fagan, 1993b).

Perhaps the simplest method for studying early training would be to trace backward from the present to the origins of existing training programs. Unfortunately, this would lead to blind alleys in some cases since most programs have no history of school psychology training before 1950, even though their administrative departments date to early in the century. It is believed that the earliest program was in the late 1920s at New York University. Because tracing backward would provide only limited information and virtually nothing before 1930, the present research draws on several sources that reveal different aspects of preparation during the early hybrid years. The research questions are (a) where was the training of school psychologists being conducted? and (b) what were the characteristics of that training? The answer to the first question can be found in a historical analysis of the growth of training programs, which includes a chronological sequence (Fagan, 1986b). As for formal preparation programs for school psychologists, there were none until the late 1920s.

The focus of the present research is on question b, the general content of training, and was approached by several methods. First, a review of the literature was conducted to determine what had been written about early training practices and expectations. Second, specific program histories were reviewed—some that had been published and others that were archival in nature.

Third, biographical and autobiographical accounts and selected archival sources were reviewed, including those of several well-known early practitioners; these included transcripts to determine the specific types and content of the courses taken. Fourth, the earliest certification standards of state departments of education and the recommendations of available organizations were reviewed; some were not in effect during this period but reflected emerging training expectations. Finally, personal correspondence and communications were employed, despite the limitations inherent in this method. From these vantage points, several perspectives have been developed from which conclusions can be drawn about the early training of school psychologists.

Throughout the discussion I use the term *school psychologist* liberally to mean a person trained in a variety of ways to provide psychological services in public, private, or institutional schools. In fact, most practitioners in this era were generically referred to as applied or clinical psychologists, psychotechnicians, or psychological examiners (Fagan, 1985). Although the term *school psychologist* was introduced and used in practice by the middle of the period (Gesell, 1952; Stern, 1911), it was not used widely until the end. Thus, in many respects, this analysis could be generalized from school psychology to clinical psychology, especially child clinical psychology.

## PRACTICE PREDATING FORMAL PREPARATION

The origins of school psychological services were related to a cluster of circumstances and conditions in the late nineteenth century (Fagan & Wise, 1994). Central to these circumstances were the changing status of children in America, the subsequent focus on developmental stages and child study and the need for formal and compulsory schooling (Fagan, 1992; Hiner & Hawes, 1985; Wortham, 1992). Child study preceded the formal study of children by practicing psychologists, and although advocated by many, including G. Stanley Hall, child study required little or no formal academic training. The study of children by psychologists in schools grew, in part, out of the child study movement but embraced formal preparation as a prerequisite to practice. Although early practice was far narrower in conceptualization than it is today, it employed a problem-solving approach that changed with the

changing perspectives of influences on child behavior (Fagan, 1995).

One might think that the period of origin for psychological services to schoolchildren, approximately 1890–1920, would be closely accompanied in time by fairly specific training. Ironically, it was several years after the emergence of practice that specific training emerged, and then it was not formal or based on any national consensus. The first training program clearly identified for school psychologists appears to have been given in 1929 at New York University (Fagan, 1985). Thus, practice preceded formal training by about three decades, although practice was occurring concurrently with less formal avenues of training.

## LIGHTNER WITMER

A logical starting point is to inquire about the nature of training received by Lightner Witmer (1867–1956), considered a father of school psychology and perhaps its earliest practitioner. Thanks to the scholarly research and writing of Paul McReynolds (1997), we have a more thorough understanding of Witmer's education than simply where he went to school and when he received his degrees. After completing his secondary education at the Episcopal Academy in Philadelphia, Witmer entered the University of Pennsylvania in 1884. To be admitted, he was required to pass examinations in Greek, Latin, English, geography, history, and mathematics.

> In his first year, Witmer, as required, studied Greek, Latin, English, history, and mathematics (algebra, geometry, and trigonometry). During his sophomore year he completed the required courses in Greek language and literature, Latin language and literature, rhetoric and the English language, English composition and declamation, higher mathematics, and chemistry, as well as an elective in German. . . . During his junior year, Witmer took work in ethics, logic and philosophy, physics, American history, constitutional law, political science, political economy, mercantile practice, and declamation (p. 20).

According to McReynolds, the intellectual and moral philosophy and the ethics courses, taught by Professor George S. Fullerton, were up-to-date introductions to the study of psychology at that time. Although senior-year records are not available, it is known that Witmer took courses in finance and political economy in the recently founded Wharton School of Finance and Economy. The mixture of courses reflect the strong classical tradition of the period as well as Lightner's early interests in business and law. Although it is not listed among his courses, it is known that Witmer had sufficient mastery of German to later study with Wundt and to publish his dissertation in German (Witmer, 1894b).

Witmer's freshman class had only 24 male students (women were not admitted at that time) in the arts program; university enrollment was 380 (McReynolds, 1997, p. 20). An exceptionally talented student, Witmer received his A.B. degree at age 21 in 1888 and then "took a position teaching English and history at the Rugby Academy for Boys, a preparatory school in Philadelphia" (p. 24). According to McReynolds, the teaching position was possibly taken because Lightner did not have clear future goals and was "marking time." Within two years, Witmer was enrolled in Penn's Department of Philosophy, working toward an advanced degree in political science. Like many contemporary students, he began graduate studies while working as a teacher. At Rugby Academy, Witmer encountered a student with special problems for whom he provided tutoring. This, in addition to some of his undergraduate training, may have piqued his interest in the psychological applications that would later characterize his career.

This orientation was further stimulated by James McKeen Cattell, who joined Penn's faculty as professor of psychology in 1889 in the Department of Philosophy. Witmer was quickly encouraged to change from political science to experimental psychology and became Cattell's assistant for the 1890–1891 year; this may be the first instance of someone holding a psychology assistantship rather than a fellowship (McReynolds, 1997). According to McReynolds, "Witmer was one of four students in the new graduate program in psychology at the University of Pennsylvania and the only one primarily interested in psychology (two of the four were clergymen, and the other was a student of philosophy)." The psychology faculty, though few in number, and the psychological laboratory at Penn were among the strongest in the country at that time. Since Cattell's work was greatly influenced by Galton, the study of individual differences was a major aspect of Witmer's work as Cattell's assistant (see Cattell, 1890). According to McReynolds, in addition to his assistant duties, Witmer's courses under

Cattell in 1890–1891 probably included scientific methods in psychology, experimental psychology, special psychological problems, and advanced psychology. He also completed four semesters of work in philosophy under George Fullerton, four in political science with Edmund James, and two in physiology with Edward Reichert who was on the medical faculty (pp. 36–37).

When Cattell left for a position at Columbia in 1891, Witmer agreed to go to Germany and study with Wundt. Witmer's assistantship at Penn was continued at an annual salary of $800, even while he was studying in Germany (McReynolds, 1997, p. 37). Starting in the summer of 1891, Witmer took seminars in experimental psychology, history of educational theory and pedagogy, and courses on introduction to experimental psychology, history of monarchy, aristocracy and democracy, aesthetics, and psychology (p. 40). In his second semester, he enrolled in Wundt's history of modern philosophy, the psychological laboratory, two courses in education, one on psychology, and one on philosophy of law. While working on his dissertation, he took one course in his third and final semester in the summer of 1892, Wundt's introduction to philosophy and logic (pp. 40–41). His dissertation, "On the Experimental Aesthetics of Simple Spatial Relationships of Form" (Witmer, 1894a) is described by McReynolds. Witmer, at age 25, completed both the A.M. and Ph.D. degrees from Leipzig in 1892.

Witmer returned to Penn, where he took over Cattell's laboratory.[2] In 1892–1893 he offered courses on mental measurements, experimental psychology, and experimental aesthetics, each having lectures and lab demonstrations. In the next year he added two undergraduate courses on experimental psychology (physiology of nervous system and sensation; perception). In 1894–1895 the Department of Philosophy, with three faculty members (Fullerton, Newbold, and Witmer), offered courses in general psychology and experimental psychology (basic and advanced), special topics for class experimentation, a seminar for the study of child psychology, and individual laboratory work (McReynolds, 1997). It appears that the child psychology seminar was

---

[2]His title in 1892–1893 was lecturer in experimental psychology and, within a few years, assistant professor of psychology. His salary for 1893–1894 was $1,500 (McReynolds, 1997).

"for teachers and others who have special opportunities of observing children" (p. 60). Topics of importance to "pedagogical psychology" were to be used in the work with children, either in school or in the laboratory. The University of Pennsylvania, largely under Witmer's direction, was reaching out to Philadelphia-area schoolteachers even before the first psychological clinic was added to Cattell's former laboratory.

In "The Organization of Practical Work in Psychology," Witmer (1897) spoke of adapting instruction in psychology to meet the wants of two classes of teachers:

a. The common school teacher of all grades from the kindergarten to the university, who needs, above all else, courses in the practical study of children.

b. The psychological expert who is capable of treating the many difficult cases that resist the ordinary methods of the school room. The pedagogical or psychological expert requires thorough courses in some branches of medicine and in practical psychology (p. 117).

At least originally, Witmer (1896) had intended the "psychological expert" to be a teacher specially trained to deal with school-related problems: "The regular practitioners of psychology are the teachers" (p. 462). By 1907, however, he stated that "we must look forward to the training of men to a new profession which will be exercised more particularly in connection with educational problems, but for which the training of the psychologist will be a prerequisite" (1907a, p. 7). The psychological expert would not necessarily be a teacher or perhaps even have the benefit of teacher training. Nevertheless, Witmer's expert continued to be trained especially for psychological applications in the schools. Witmer had predicted the "training of students for a new profession—that of the psychological expert, who should find his career in connection with the school system, through the examination and treatment of mentally and morally retarded children, or in connection with the practice of medicine" (p. 5). An orientation to children and their educational needs would dominate the training and practice of school psychologists throughout this period.

Among Witmer's contributions was the practicum aspects of his instruction. His frequent clinics were demonstration diagnostic teaching sessions that served as a prototype for incorporating practicum components in training courses.

Witmer established his clinical training program in connection with his clinic (Fagan, 1996), and the demonstration approach was employed by others, including Wallin, in preparing special education teachers (Wallin, 1927). Witmer also used students in training. According to Fernberger (1931), clinic policies allowed "qualified graduate students to assist in the routine examination work, and for qualified graduate and even psychology major undergraduate students to assist in the activities of the social service and clinic teaching departments" (p. 21).

According to Reisman (1976, p. 76), Witmer began offering his summer clinics in 1897 and formal training in clinical psychology in 1904–1905, with courses for credit in psychiatry and neuropathology in the medical school. We gain a better understanding of the nature of the training he developed for others from his course descriptions, published in *The Psychological Clinic* (Witmer, 1907b, 1911). In 1907, Witmer identified eight courses of study that could be taken by either college or graduate students in psychology. There appears to have been little or no distinction between these courses as graduate or undergraduate. Witmer was also more concerned about the proper sequencing of work than who was enrolled.[3] With only minor modifications in sequencing, summer offerings (which appear to have been popular) were the same as those during the regular academic year.

Witmer conceived the unique mark of the psychology program at the University of Pennsylvania to be its clinical method, in contrast to Hall's syllabus (questionnaire) methods at Clark University and Cattell's statistical method at Columbia University. However, students were exposed to the clinical method only after the foundation work of experimental psychology, which included analytical psychology and physiological psychology in the first year, each including one hour per week of lecture and two hours of laboratory work. The second-year courses were in synthetic and genetic psychology, also with lectures and labs. With these foundation courses completed, the student progressed to the "most important single field of work comprehended within the general field of psychology . . . child

---

[3]The courses were considered useful for many persons, including undergraduate or graduate students of psychology, physicians, medical students, social workers, teachers of backward children, and superintendents of schools.

psychology" (Witmer, 1907b, p. 29). Child psychology consisted of lectures on special methods and results (Course 2: Child Psychology); a seminar on research into "problems connected with the psychology of education" (p. 30) (Course 4: Educational Psychology; then Course 7: Advanced Educational Psychology); and Course 8: The Psychological Clinic. The description for Course 8 reads as follows:

> Children will be examined in the presence of the students taking this course. The object of the course is to illustrate various mental and physical defects found in school children, to discuss the causes, to point out the nature of the consequent retardation and to propose the appropriate treatment. The course will also serve to make the student acquainted with the methods of examination. A daily clinic will be conducted by Professor Witmer and his assistants or by medical specialists for the eye, the ear, the nose and throat, the nervous system, orthopedics, and internal medicine.
>
> A training school for backward and defective children will also be in daily session. One or more classes will be taught by competent instructors. Clinical study will also be carried on through visits to neighboring institutions for the training of special classes of children—The Pennsylvania Training School for Feeble-Minded Children at Elwyn, the House of Refuge, and the Pennsylvania Institutions for the Instruction of the Blind and Deaf (p. 35).

The summer clinics were for one hour daily for five weeks (early July to mid-August). In addition to Witmer, courses were taught by E. B. Twitmeyer of the department, Herbert Stotesbury from Temple College, and several lecturers from area schools and agencies.[4] The program of studies in child psychology was strongly applied and was oriented toward both research and practice. Although Witmer insisted that a sound basis in experimental psychology, including training in introspection, is necessary for clinical work (Popplestone & McPherson, 1984), his didactic supervision was highly practical.

By 1911, the university's summer school announcement (Witmer, 1911) indicated A.B., B.S., M.A., and Ph.D. degrees in psychology and in pedagogy. The recommended basic psychological preparation for teachers was similar to that of 1907 (three hours weekly for two years or three hours daily for two summer sessions). The number of courses had increased to 13, and many had changed title. The courses were in three groups: practical (educational psychology, clinical psychology, abnormal psychology, mental and physical defects of schoolchildren, and social aspects of school work); systematic (general psychology, genetic psychology, and two laboratory courses; and advanced (experimental psychology, child psychology, social research in clinical psychology, and tests and measurements of children). The systematic courses were considered prerequisite to the practical or advanced courses, and the program of studies was considered appropriate for a variety of practitioners, including "those who will become clinical psychologists in institutions for the insane and the feebleminded, or psychological experts for the public schools and in special training schools" (p. 257).

Lengthy descriptions of each course were provided, including photographs of laboratory and clinical methods. The clinical psychology course is akin to contemporary courses on mental retardation in that it dealt with backward and mentally defective children. In fact, much of the curriculum was oriented toward defective children and their education. Witmer also insisted that students study normal child development before abnormal aspects. The content of the earlier course on the psychological clinic appears to have been spread over several new courses, including clinical psychology and tests and measurements of children. The latter included traditional experimental instrumentation and "anthropometric measurements and mental tests of various kinds, including the Binet system" (Witmer, 1911, p. 273).[5]

Witmer earned the title "father of clinical psychology" in the United States, and many consider him to be among the fathers in school psychology history as well (Fagan, 1992, 1996; McReynolds, 1996). His introduction of clinical and school psychology blended his training in

---

[4]Witmer employed area school superintendents and other staff in the educational psychology courses to discuss research and direct sessions. Some lecturers were former students (e.g., Margaret Maguire and Clara Town).

[5]The *Oral History of Gertha Williams* (1965) gives an interesting account of instruction with the Seguin Form Board in which a chimpanzee completed the board more quickly than most of the children.

experimental psychology, including introspection but especially individual differences, with his experience and preparation in pedagogy. He succeeded in blending these areas along idiographic lines of child study, as opposed to the nomothetic blending characteristics of the contributions of Granville Stanley Hall (Fagan, 1992).

## TEACHER TRAINING

Because most early and many later school psychology practitioners had teacher training and/or experience, exploring the nature of that training is important. Some practitioners must have come from normal school backgrounds or from teacher preparation in private or public colleges and universities. Teachers of the elementary grades often had little more than a formal elementary school education and were often ineligible for admission to state colleges and universities (Armstrong, 1964; Spring, 1990). By 1905 only 22% of normal schools required a high school diploma for admission (Spring, 1990, p. 253). Secondary teachers, although often better qualified, were usually exposed to much less specific and intensive training. Normal schools and teacher colleges focused curricula and resources on teacher preparation, while suffering a lack of breadth in curriculum. Cremin (1988) distinguished between colleges and universities and normal schools according to the emphasis on scholarship in an academic discipline versus the emphasis on preparation for teaching. According to Armstrong (1964), as late as 1930 "only 12% of elementary teachers in service held Bachelor's degrees" (p. 52), and at the turn of the century the situation was as follows:

> At that time nearly all elementary teachers received two years or fewer of college preparation. . . . The curriculum did little to increase the knowledge of the students in such subjects as mathematics, music, English, and history. The mathematics was largely a review of arithmetic mixed with the methods that the teacher would need in teaching practically the same content to children. Music had some content suitable for adults but largely it consisted of children's songs with much attention to the methods of teaching them. And so on for the other subjects in the curriculum. At the end of the two-year normal school the prospective elementary teacher knew a little about the nature of children and learning and much more about the materials and methods she would use in teaching children. She had not become much better educated as a person and as a result in no position to help children beyond the rudimentary skills. And as a source of help on broader community problems, her two-year normal preparation gave her little equipment (pp. 50–51).

The deemphasis on broader community problems may have been an intentional goal of the early normal school and its predecessor, the teaching institute, in which preparation for such matters was limited. Discussing the role of women in the nineteenth century, Spring (1990) states, "The proper role for women was to connect with the public sphere by nurturing moral character in the family and the school. Thus, both in the common school and in teacher-training institutions, there was little discussion of the major social, economic, and political problems confronting society. Discussion was limited to individual motives and desires" (pp. 126–127). Of course, there were exceptions. Later, as teacher training expanded to state colleges, a broader curriculum would emerge that was matched by a growing range of women's opportunities and ideas about their status.

Armstrong (1964) stated that by the turn of the century, secondary school teachers "were prepared largely by universities and liberal arts colleges. Many began to teach with less than college degrees but those who advanced that far usually took regular academic majors supplemented by some philosophy of education and specific methods. By 1930 at least 75% of the high school teachers held Bachelor's degrees" (p. 52).

The academic preparation of teachers gained acceptance in the late nineteenth century, and by 1899 "departments or chairs of education had been established at 244 American universities" (Spring, 1990, p. 253). By the 1920s it was generally agreed that more preparation for all teachers was desirable, and between 1920 and 1933 the number of normal schools in the United States decreased from 137 to 30 while the number of teachers colleges increased from 46 to 146. In several cases, the normal schools were upgraded to state teachers colleges. Even at smaller institutions, the transition was accompanied by expanded psychology offerings for teacher trainees (Hanson, 1990; Litton, 1986).

In rural areas, the circumstances were often worse than in cities. According to Cubberley (1914), the average rural teacher was

*a mere slip of a girl, often almost too young to have formed as yet any conception of the problem of rural life and needs; that she knows little as to the nature of children or the technique of instruction; that her education is very limited and confined largely to the old traditional school-subjects, while of the great and important fields of science she is almost entirely ignorant; and that she not infrequently lacks in those qualities of leadership which are so essential for rural progress" (p. 283).*

Whereas the city district might expect as a prerequisite to employment a "good high-school education, followed by normal school training or by an apprenticeship in the country," the rural school might settle for "sixteen or seventeen years of age and a third grade county teacher's certificate, obtained by coaching up on and passing an examination on the old common-school subjects, plus the good will of some district trustee" (p. 288).

Another characteristic of the teaching force was the strong presence of women. The proportion of women varied from 65% in 1890 to 83% in 1930, achieving a high of 86% in 1919–1920 (Grant & Snyder, 1986). Women teachers often had limited educational and employment opportunities, worked with children who were required to attend school, were increasingly in public (common) schools, and were often paid lower salaries. Their annual salaries in rural areas were below that of young girls employed in other fields and appear to have been in the range of $200 to $1,000.[6] Usually greater preparation meant better salaries in urban districts, but even principals were paid in the range of $1,000 to $3,500 per year during this period (Marden et al., 1913).

Teachers working with exceptional children could expect a supplement to their salaries within a range of $50 to $300, and in some districts a supplement of 50% was offered (Wallin, 1914). There was little formal training of special education teachers in this period. Such training could include "corrective or remedial pedagogy of the

subnormal . . . theoretical foundations of educational psychology, and the psychology of subnormality, so that they may be able independently to psychologize each child and thereby continuously to modify and adapt the training to meet the changing requirements of the individual" (Wallin, 1921, p. 325). Wallin's preferred training for special education teachers and psychological examiners echos Witmer's early descriptions of the clinical psychologist (Fagan, 1996). The salary supplements probably reflected the difficulty of attracting teachers to these positions rather than the additional training the teacher may have had. While teaching was a readily available and respected field for women, its academic and financial status was low. These circumstances combined to create an image of low status for women and the field of education. Since many went into school psychological work, the image spread to those services as well, especially in comparison to other psychology specialties.

The early distinctions between normal schools and teachers colleges and other institutions of higher education blurred for a while as teacher training moved into the private and state colleges and universities. The controversy over professional preparation versus academic content has reemerged with the establishment of Master of Arts in Teaching (MAT) programs, which provide an avenue into the teaching profession after completing a regular liberal arts or science degree (Spring, 1989). From these historical descriptions, it is not difficult to identify the origin of persistent biases toward teacher education on many campuses and their spinoff to school psychology programs. Despite the lack of identifiable differences between school psychology programs located in education or psychology academic units in recent decades (Fagan & Wise, 1994; Goh, 1977; Reschly, 1995; Reschly & McMaster-Beyer, 1991), such biases are still observed. A relevant historical analysis of this phenomenon can be gained from Goodlad's (1990) discussion of education as the "not-quite" profession (see pp. 69–107).

Today, many practitioners continue to receive training in school psychology, as well as teacher preparation. However, the nature of teacher training now is vastly different from that earlier in the century. During the period 1890–1930, teacher education was much less relevant to later preparation for school psychology practice. It often lacked empirically based, theo-

---

[6]Wallin (1955b) mentions having been paid only $35 per month for teaching in Montgomery County, Iowa, in 1899.

retical preparation in child and adolescent development, tests and measurements, instructional methods and technology, and human learning. These contributions would emerge later in the period, as clinical and educational psychology offerings became more widely available.

Since World War II, almost all teachers have been prepared in private or state colleges and universities, some that have evolved from former normal schools (Armstrong, 1964), and the four-year teaching degree has become standard. The shift of teacher education to four-year and graduate institutions is important in understanding the preparation of school psychologists. Many psychology departments emerged in schools of education and later sought independence from them; at other institutions the psychology department emerged independent of, but in proximity to, the teacher education unit. In still other places the psychology department has remained in the education unit. In all cases, school psychology programs have been influenced by the relative availability of education and psychology courses.

Thus, during the period 1890–1930, teacher education was very limited, and while it might have sensitized some to seek further training in psychological services, it was seldom an adequate prerequisite. Nevertheless, some school psychologists must have come from such backgrounds, and some had only modest training in psychological examination in addition to their teacher training. As will be discussed, these persons provided services in relatively large numbers during this period.

## CONTRIBUTIONS OF TECHNICAL WRITING

Additional insight into the training of school psychologists comes from reviewing the content of selected texts. The works of E. L. Thorndike provide topics that would be considered in an educational psychology course. In addition to his "Law of Effect", Thorndike's (1912) *Education* included "Situation and Response as the Elements in Human Behavior," "The Physiological Basis of Human Behavior," "Individual Differences and Their Causes," "The Laws of Habit Formation," and "Methods in Education" (including "Habituation and Methods for Analysis," "Inductive Methods," "Expressive Methods," "The Method of Discovery," and "Methods in Moral Education"). The text builds on his *Princi-*

*ples of Teaching Based on Psychology* (Thorndike, 1906). Although acknowledging that "present knowledge of psychology is nearer to zero than to complete perfection, and its applications to teaching must therefore be often incomplete, indefinite and insecure" (p. 9), Thorndike makes a case for the scientific study of education, and he has a chapter on the importance of measuring teaching effectiveness. Stressing the importance of education for building character, as well as knowledge, the book also discusses moral training and formal discipline, attention, association, analysis, reasoning, feeling, motor expression, and motor education. By contemporary standards, these texts dispense more advice than generalizable scientific facts.

William James (1899/1939) acknowledges this fact in his popular *Talks to Teachers:* "The worst thing that can happen to a good teacher is to get a bad conscience about her profession because she feels herself hopeless as a psychologist. . . . The best teacher may be the poorest contributor of child-study material, and the best contributor may be the poorest teacher. No fact is more palpable than this" (pp. 13–14). James's remarks continue to be relevant in the ongoing debate about whether school psychologists need teacher training and experience to function effectively. I believe that James's answer would be no, based on a contention he shared with his colleague Munsterberg that the teacher's attitude toward the child is concrete and ethical, whereas that of the psychological observer is abstract and analytic (p. 13). Munsterberg's (1909) *Psychology and the Teacher* was an attempt to bring the science of psychology to the practice of teaching and is also replete with cautions about the limitations of psychological science and the growing demand for training in educational psychology. Toward the end of the period, Pillsbury's (1925) *Education as the Psychologist Sees It* continues to have traditional psychological content but is based on more empirical information and has greater emphasis on individual differences and testing in school subjects.

Introductory textbooks on psychology from this period (Angell, 1906; Baldwin, 1893; James, 1892/1948; Ladd, 1898; McDougall, 1928; Titchener, 1919; Wundt, 1912) reveal a consensus that psychology was the study of consciousness and a natural science with strong connections to philosophy and physiology. With introspection and observation as basic methodologies, the definition of psychology was far less concerned with behavior than in later historical periods (Henley, Johnson, Jones, & Herzog, 1989). Topical coverage was much less comprehensive than in contemporary introductory textbooks and included such topics as attention, sensation, perception, reasoning, instincts, emotion, volition, and will. Abnormal psychology is seldom discussed in these texts, although examples (e.g., feeble-mindedness and alternating personality) are identified as psychological phenomena; nor are children given much attention in comparison to work done with adults.

Aspiring school psychologists would have had to seek in-depth treatments of applied topics from other works. Several books on mental deficiency, giftedness, special learning problems, and delinquency were available (e.g., Bronner, 1917; Gesell, 1921; Goddard, 1914a, 1921, 1928; Hollingworth, 1920; Holmes, 1912; Wallin, 1914, 1921). Watsonian behaviorism is discussed toward the end of this period in McDougall's text. Watson's work, linked to the earlier work of Thorndike, helped to shift the focus of psychological study to specific behavioral responses and found considerable receptivity among educators (Behavioristic psychology, 1920). Methodology was shifting from internal to external perceptions of phenomena and from mental states to observable behavior. Many books toward the end of the period were relevant to the practice of school psychology, with such topics as clinical psychology, intelligence testing, exceptional children, special education, educational research, and reading.[7]

An abundance of material was available on the mainstay of applied psychology—mental testing. The Binet–Simon Scales, with several revisions in the United States (Goddard, 1911; Kuhlmann, 1922; Terman, 1916), along with the success of group tests in World War I, launched the field of mental and academic measurement into public awareness for many decades to come (Anastasi, 1993). There was little distinction between the experimental laboratory study of children with these scales and their use in the field by practitioners. The strength of the testing movement can be seen in the manuals that describe available tests for use in the laboratory or the school (Bronner, Healy, Lowe, & Shimberg, 1927; Goodenough, 1926; Stern, 1914; Whipple, 1914, 1915), perhaps prototypes of the later *Mental Measurements Yearbooks*. The number of available tests was surprisingly large, and considerable academic and practicum study would have been needed to master them. Terman's (1919) *The Intelligence of School Children* is an example of how research and service could be brought together for application to schoolchildren. Texts on exceptional children focused heavily on children with intellectual problems and related conditions, reflecting the impact of the new measurement technology. Among the few comprehensive attempts to connect experimental to applied psychology was Munsterberg's (1914) *Psychology: General and Applied*, which included educational, legal, economic, medical, and cultural psychology. Munsterberg's failure to mention Witmer or clinical psychology reveals the nomothetic approach taken in his book.

There was no text specifically about school psychology until Hildreth's (1930) *Psychological Service for School Problems*. As the first text in school psychology, it complemented a growing but small school psychological literature scattered among various education and psychology journals, as well as Witmer's journal, *The Psychological Clinic* (Fagan, 1986a; French, 1986). Despite the relatively small amount of professional literature, compared to recent decades, there was sufficient literature in experimental, clinical, and exceptional child psychology to support a program of studies relevant to school psychologists. Perhaps the greatest difference from contemporary times is the lack of alternative sources on similar topics. In recent years we see not only a breadth of topics but also a breadth of literary selections in them.

## CONTRIBUTION OF CLINICS

Many clinics, including Witmer's, participated in the preparation of persons who would provide psychological services in schools. Among the more prominent clinics that supervised field experiences was the research department established under the supervision of Henry H. Goddard in 1908 at the Vineland Training School in New Jersey. According to Morrow (1946), Vineland was the earliest setting to offer formal and paid internships in clinical psychology, and the nature of these experiences was more akin to what later became school psychology. The internships appeared as early as 1908 and were systematically organized by 1912. "Under fairly close supervision the intern engaged in psychometrics, interviewing, research, clerical, library, and statistical

---

[7]A comprehensive list appears in Fagan et al. (1986).

work and attended seminars and courses. University credit for the internship could be obtained by application" (p. 168).

Other internship sites before 1930 included state hospitals and prisons, which were less likely settings for potential school psychologists. The New York Institute for Child Guidance had more potential, and according to Tulchin (cited in Morrow, 1946),

> During its existence, 1927–1933, the Institute granted three paid fellowships in psychology per year. The fellows were required to put in full time. They were supervised in a testing program, attended staff conferences, worked on a research project, did tutoring, made a complete study of a case including social history and psychiatric examination, etc. No university credit was given. They were permitted to carry one or two university courses.

Paid assistants and graduate students were also used in the psychological laboratory for the Vocational Bureau, founded in 1911 in the Cincinnati public schools (see Veatch, 1978, pp. 31–39), and in a psychological clinic that evolved between 1912 and 1917 in the Cleveland (Ohio) public schools (*Psychological Clinic*, n.d.). The Cincinnati assistants studied working and non-working youths in the early years and then in 1916 expanded to more typical psychological services in programs for the mentally defective. Veatch also indicates the presence of graduate students from the University of Cincinnati. The number of assistants were few in its early years, but by 1922–1923 Cincinnati reported 20 assistants; the Cleveland school clinic reported only 3 (Martens, 1924). About 50 cities had research bureaus in their school system, and although some had many assistants, the median number was only 1. The functions of research bureaus were different from but overlapped those of traditional psychological clinics, and many later evolved into school psychological services.

By the late 1920s, the personnel in the Cleveland clinic included four psychologists with a Ph.D., three with an M.A., "one examiner with general psychological training, one assistant and a secretary" (*Psychological Clinic*, n.d., p. 2). At least some of the assistants used their employment as a field experience in addition to or concurrent with academic training. The descriptions of Vineland and the New York Institute indicate a clear orientation toward training and suggest at least some

arrangement for credit from an academic institution. Since the amount of applied psychology training in colleges and universities was very limited, the "internship" (apparently under various titles) appears to have served as the practical applications component of training for many students with undergraduate or graduate degrees.

The university-based clinic was a special version of emerging psychological clinics. Although not formal internships, Witmer's students were engaged in supervised experiences from the early years of the clinic's establishment. There were several university-based clinics during this period, as observed in the data gathered by Wallin (1914) and a listing published in *The Psychological Clinic* (Report of Committee of Clinical Section of American Psychological Association, 1935). With a focus on training, as well as service, university clinics engaged in the supervised practice of students and assistants; that is, the faculty were often not the direct service providers. Comparing supervised child study that employed paid assistants to the work of ghost writers, Hollingworth (1933) decried studying the child in absentia (i.e., by faculty who supervised case studies but had no direct involvement with the client). An earlier criticism of this practice was mentioned by Wallin in describing the need for clinical trainers to "have actual, first-hand clinical experience" (Gesell, Goddard, & Wallin, 1919, p. 92). The practice of supervision was in vogue in off-campus agencies as well, and supervision also extended to research in what Hollingworth described as a rush to gather data and to get something published. Even in these early years we can detect tension between academic instructors and practitioners of clinical methods. The tension could be observed in the politics of the American Association of Applied Psychologists, (founded in 1937); and later, when a division of school psychologists was established within the reorganized APA of 1945, it would refuse membership to academics unless they were engaged in practical work in schools.

## SELECTED SCHOOL PSYCHOLOGISTS

Information on training can also be ascertained from academic backgrounds. Although French's (1988) study of eminent women concentrated on their contributions, his research revealed their presence in school psychology and their representation among those having a doctorate. Whereas French contended that Witmer's clinic and training program produced few school-based psychological practitioners, Witmer's efforts had a strong influence on psychological and special education services to children generally. Several Witmer graduates became directors of special education or held other school posts. From personal records and other sources, I can provide the following information on training of several practitioners in the early history of school psychology. Space does not permit description of their subsequent contributions to the field. Suggested references are provided, and brief descriptions and additional references may be found in the *Historical Encyclopedia of School Psychology* (Fagan & Warden, 1996).

## Norma Cutts

Among the early trainees at Vineland was Norma E. Cutts, following the completion of her B.A. degree at Mt. Holyoke College in 1913.[8] During her "internship," she is identified in a Vineland publication as "Research Student." She was supervised by Goddard while also working under the supervision of Edgar A. Doll, the assistant psychologist. From a description of the staff in 1913–1914, Cutts is identified as the only "student," although probably other "assistants" were listed who were also interns (Goddard, 1914b; Morrow, 1946).[9] The work of the institute, including anthropometric and Binet assessments, is described by Goddard. The work was a blend of the psychological and physiological study of feeble-mindedness.

At Mount Holyoke College (1909–1913), Cutts took courses in chemistry, English, German, Latin, mathematics, physical training, history, zoology, biblical history, art and archaeology, economics, and sociology.[10] Her junior and seniors years were concentrated on courses in education (Principles of Education and Teachers' Course in English) and in philosophy and psychology (General Psychology, Psychological Classics, Ethics, Modern Philosophy, Experimental Psychology, Genetic Psychology,[11] Modern Philosophy Since Kant, and Problems of Philosophy). With a double major in English literature and philosophy and psychology, Cutts was well prepared for an internship; her English preparation would serve her well later when she wrote or edited several books, including the Thayer Conference proceedings (Cutts, 1955).[12] Instruction in the Department of Philosophy and Psychology consisted of lectures, textbooks, library readings, experiments in the psychological laboratory,[13] considerable classroom discussion, and preparation of papers (Talbot, 1918). It appears that some of the instruction in the laboratory concentrated on introspection as a means of gaining personal insight and attempting to make rudimentary applications of scientific psychology. Instruction in mental testing (probably with translations and adaptations of the Binet–Simon Scales) was undertaken for the demonstration of individual differences (Hayes, 1918).

Although not a teacher training institution, Mount Holyoke was an opportunity for Cutts to pursue teaching and child study. Her experiences at Vineland provided additional preparation for work as a psychological examiner or special class teacher. At Vineland she gained extensive experience in testing feeble-minded children with the

---

[8]For a description of Cutts's career see Fagan (1989).

[9]A photograph in the Vineland publication contains 17 people, including Cutts, Doll, and Goddard. The publication also has photographs of the tests administered and a list of persons previously affiliated with The Training School.

[10]Among the courses she completed in this subject, the description of one reads, "Charities and Corrections. A general introductory course during the first semester, treating of the following topics: causes of poverty, methods of caring for destitute and defective adults and children, penal institutions, treatment of adults and juvenile offenders, constructive work, including a study of the principles and methods of relief, reform, and prevention" (Mount Holyoke College, 1912–1913). Following graduation, Cutts mentions how valuable it would be to have this course taught on the grounds of The Vineland Training School.

[11]The course description was this: "The course will include the study of mental development in the lower animals, and the psychology of the child." Something like an introductory course in psychology was required of each student.

[12]It was common for psychology and philosophy to be offered in the same department. At many institutions, psychology departments emerged from philosophy departments, faculty held appointments in both philosophy and psychology, and departmental courses were offered in both subjects. According to the college catalogue for her freshman year, the total semester hours required for graduation was 120, with 30 hours given to a major subject. Work in the first two years was prescribed (including general psychology and an elective in that department), and in the last two years, courses were elective.

[13]The psychological laboratory was established in 1901–1902 by Helen B. Thompson, who would later be among the first employees of the Cincinnati Public Schools Vocational Bureau, founded in 1911.

Binet and form board tests and in the development of specialized academic and vocational instruction. There were also weekly staff meetings for discussion of unusual cases and no doubt ample opportunities for discussion in the "Keller cottage, an old farmhouse on the edge of the grounds, where a number of the laboratory assistants live" (Cutts, 1914, p. 36).[14] The assistants also helped in the preparation of Goddard's (1914a) book on feeble-mindedness and conducted tours of the facilities for its many visitors. Late in the year she gained experience in using the Rosanoff Association Tests at the New Jersey State Home for Girls, and she attended lectures in Philadelphia on the treatment of speech defects. The testing was part of a research project for publication (letter from Cutts to Gesell, May 9, 1914).

Like contemporary interns, she sought employment that would utilize her skills, and having a mentor who was "well connected" proved helpful. In a letter to Arnold Gesell, Goddard recommended Cutts for employment, mentioning that she was seeking a special class teaching position but that "she will be too valuable to be used simply as a teacher" (letter from Goddard to Gesell, December 4, 1913).[15] The record suggests that she was able to get a special class teaching position in New Haven and a part-time examiner position with Gesell. The special class teaching position was offered at an annual salary of only $600 (letter from Cutts to Gesell, May 19, 1914). Thus, Norma Cutts initiated her career in school psychology with a B.A. degree and an internship that provided practical training to supplement her college work. Later she would complete her M.A. (Yale, 1922) and Ph.D. (Yale, 1933), which would broaden her training and open avenues for college teaching and school administration.[16] She served for many years in special education administrative positions and was active in the APA division of school psychology.

## Arnold Gesell

Gesell graduated in 1899 from Stevens Point (Wisconsin) Normal School and worked for two years at the Stevens Point High School, "teaching U.S. history, ancient history, German, accounting, commercial geography, and coaching and refereeing football" (Gesell, 1952, p. 125). He earned a Ph.B. in 1903 at the University of Wisconsin, worked as a high school principal, and then completed his Ph.D. with G. Stanley Hall at Clark University (Worcester, Massachusetts).

Few specifics are available about Gesell's study at Clark (September 1904 to June 1906), where he was appointed a fellow in pedagogy, with an initial stipend of $100 and remission of all fees (letter from Hall to Edgar Swift, May 6, 1904).[17] His Ph.D. included a major in psychology and a minor in pedagogy.[18] The course of study was designed to be two to three years in length. The subjects then available from Hall, and probably completed by Gesell, included the History of Philosophy During the Nineteenth Century; Development of Mind in Animals, Children, and the Race; Psychology of Religion and of Christianity; Education; and Abnormal, which provided field experiences in local hospitals and institutions with the assistance of Dr. Adolf Meyer and Dr. Cowles. Gesell also participated in Hall's often acclaimed seminary, taught "at his home, three hours every Monday evening, throughout the year" (*Clark University Register*, February 1904, p. 59). Gesell's minor in pedagogy, a common connection with the psychology program, probably included the following subjects: child study; educational psychology; school hygiene; principles of education; history of education and reforms; methods, devices, and apparatus; organization of schools in different countries; the teaching profession; motor education; moral and religious education; and ideals. Several courses were available in experimental psychology, and the psychological laboratory was described as "one of the most favorably placed in the world" (p. 58), with a photographic dark room, library, lecture and demonstration rooms, apparatus and testing rooms, and other facilities.

---

[14]In a letter to her fellow graduates, she describes what would now be called a case of fetal alcohol syndrome (Mount Holyoke College, 1914).

[15]Cutts wrote to Gesell the next day, requesting consideration for employment. See the Gesell Papers, Library of Congress.

[16]Unfortunately, I am unable to describe the nature of her graduate work.

[17]The Clark University register of February 1904 identifies both fellows in pedagogy and fellows in psychology.

[18]According to Dorothy Mosakowski, coordinator of archives at Clark, the files on Gesell do not have any information about his specific courses. However, she was able to provide a copy of the results of his oral examination and a university register that described the course of study in psychology and in education (c. 1904).

During the oral examination for Gesell's Ph.D., the examining committee (five faculty members and President Hall) accepted his dissertation on jealousy and questioned him in the following areas: biology (10 minutes), psychology (32 minutes), library research (9 minutes), anthropology (23 minutes), philosophy and psychology (38 minutes), and pedagogy (43 minutes). The time in each subject probably reflects the relative weights of his training and interests at Clark. Following graduation, he held several positions, including settlement worker while teaching German in the New York City public schools; normal school instructor in Platteville, Wisconsin; and professor at Los Angeles State Normal School. He then returned to the University of Wisconsin to study medicine in 1910, finally completing his medical degree while an assistant professor of education at Yale (1911–1915) (Fagan, 1987). He then continued his employment at Yale while serving part time as a school psychologist for the state of Connecticut from 1915 to 1919.

Gesell came into school psychology from several avenues: coaching, psychology and education (child study), rural and urban living, teaching experiences, and medicine. At least in terms of credentials, he was among the best-trained persons in school psychology in this period. His preparation was closer to Wallin's (1919) preferences than perhaps anyone else at that time. Unlike Witmer and most other practitioners of the period, for several years he used the title of "school psychologist."

It seems ironic that Gesell, along with Goddard, would offer summer courses (c. 1910–1915) for teachers in New York (Randall's Island), where they could learn to use the Binet scales, as well as characteristics and methods, with defective children. These courses were under the auspices of New York University's summer school. It is likely that many of these students went on to use the scales in schools and probably were among the "amateurs" often scorned by those who were better trained. This discrepancy in training attitudes is explained by Gesell's and Goddard's belief in two levels of practice: the technician (trained in short courses like these), who was expected only to administer scales, and the clinician (with much greater training), who was expected to provide diagnoses and interpretations. However, in most schools this two-tier approach to training and supervision was not widely practiced.

## Gertrude Hildreth

Gertrude Howell Hildreth received preparatory training at Garfield High School (Terre Haute, Indiana); an A.B. degree from North Central College; an M.A. in education from the University of Illinois (1921); and a Ph.D. in educational psychology at Teachers College, Columbia University (1925). After receiving her M.A. she was a school psychologist in the Okmulgee, Oklahoma, schools until June 1923, with an initial salary of $1,850; this was perhaps the first such appointment in that state (Fagan, 1988). Archival materials reveal that she had taken 19 credit hours in "strictly pedagogical work" as part of her A.B. and M.A. degrees.

Her university of Illinois transcript shows the following courses:

*1st Semester, 1920–1921* Seminar in Education Theory, Research in History of American Education, Problems in Educational Psychology, Thesis

*2nd Semester, 1920–1921* Research in History of American Education, Seminar in Educational Administration, Mental Tests, Educational Psychology, Thesis Summer Session, 1921: Seminar in Educational Psychology

All her courses were from those assigned for advanced undergraduates and graduates, and her selections amount to almost half those available in graduate education. In addition, all graduate education majors attended a departmental conference with the staff on the second and fourth Mondays of each month from 7:00-9:00 P.M., both semesters, for no credit (*Annual Register 1920–1921*, p. 313).

Her educational psychology course was described as the "psychology of school subjects," which was close to the title of a recent book by her instructor (Cameron, 1921). Cameron also taught the mental test course, described as "laboratory drill in the technic of mental tests, including tests of sensory capacities; attention; memory; learning; suggestibility; inventiveness; systems of tests for diagnosis of mental age; general intellectual status; mental retardation" (*Annual Register 1920–1921*, p. 312).

Her performance in Cameron's courses secured his recommendation for employment in Oklahoma. Another letter of recommendation indicates that "she is well qualified to teach English, mathematics, and public speaking," having an undergraduate major in English (26 hours), 21 hours of mathematics, and 4 hours of public speaking. Although she had no teaching experience, she was nevertheless considered to have the appropriate qualities of a teacher. Her Okmulgee, Oklahoma, personnel records reveal that she had read Dewey's *Democracy and Education* and Terman's *Measurement of Intelligence* and regularly read the journals *Education* and *School and Society*. She had an eminent career in clinical, school, and educational psychology (see Saretzky & Davis, 1986).

## Leta Stetter Hollingworth

Leta Stetter attended the University of Nebraska–Lincoln. Hoping to find a career in writing, she nevertheless acquired teaching credentials and took some psychology courses before graduating in 1906. She had little success in writing short stories while teaching high school in Nebraska. After moving to New York City to marry Harry Hollingworth in 1908, she learned that as a married woman she was prohibited by law from teaching in the New York City schools. Following several years of dissatisfaction with her status as a housewife, she completed an M.A. and a Master's Diploma in Education in 1913 at Columbia University. She continued her studies, supported in part by Binet testing work at the Clearing-House for Mental Defectives, and completed her Ph.D. in educational psychology at Columbia University (1916), working under E. L. Thorndike. She worked at Bellevue Hospital before accepting a position at Columbia, where she remained for the rest of her career. Although never a school-based psychologist, her research on women, adolescence, mental testing, and giftedness were significant to those who were (Hollingworth, 1933).[19]

Among her contributions was her service as secretary pro-tem for the American Association of Clinical Psychologists (AACP). A 1917 AACP charter membership roster identified 48 persons, most of whom were affiliated in some way with the practice or preparation of clinical psychologists, some practicing in clinics and others in schools. Everyone on the list had a Ph.D. and/or M.D. degree; in fact, the group required members to have a Ph.D. degree in psychology or in educational psychology or its equivalent (letter from Hollingworth to Arnold Gesell, January 15, 1918).

## Marie Skodak

Another picture is provided by the descriptions of Marie Skodak Crissey. Marie Skodak received a B.S. in education and an M.A. in clinical psychology in 1931 from Ohio State University, then a Ph.D. in developmental psychology at the University of Iowa in 1938. In her autobiographical account (Crissey, 1983), she describes a program at Ohio State University in the late 1920s that was not a prescribed set of courses, nor was it called "school psychology" per se (letter from Crissey to Thomas Fagan, November 30, 1982): "It was a freedom to choose those courses, in those departments, which seemed vocationally relevant" (p. 164). Although not required, most persons entering the program were previously trained in elementary or secondary education and some had had teaching experience. "Typically they began graduate work in summer school, and more often did not continue for a Ph.D., but took specialized courses in clinical psychology, school administration, or social work" (pp. 164–165). According to her account (Crissey, 1983),

> the courses in the psychology department most frequently selected were in clinical work (Francis Maxfield, H. H. Goddard), educational psychology (Sidney Pressey), counseling (Emily Stogdill, Mervin Durea), and theory (Robert Williams). The experimental, general, and animal psychology departments tended to be less attractive to school psychology aspirants and were usually in another building. Supplemental or minor sequence courses could be selected in a variety of departments or schools. For instance, Child Development in Home Economics in the School of Agriculture or Social Work in Liberal Arts were among the options. Departmental liaison with Social Work was very close and the offerings in "Social Agencies," "Social Case Work," and "Interviewing" were most frequently selected (p. 165).

Regarding field experiences, she stated,

> the opportunities for what are now called clerkships or internships were particularly broad. For example, for practicum (credit)

---

[19]For a discussion of Hollingworth's influence on the psychology of women and the general status of educated women in the early twentieth century, see Benjamin and Shields (1990) and Rosenberg (1982).

or volunteer service, I had substantial experience in testing, counseling, and recreation in the State Institution for the Feeble Minded, the State Hospital for the Insane, a community recreation center in a slum area, a residential school for delinquent girls, and the local juvenile detention facility. To round out the prevocational experience, I did a master's thesis on the study of habits of gifted girls in a private school for affluent students. (p. 165)

## T. Ernest Newland

Considered the founder of one of the first clearly specified doctoral-level school psychology programs at the University of Illinois in the early 1950s, T. Ernest Newland received his B.A. in Foreign Languages in 1925 from Wittenburg College (Ohio) and his M.A. (1929) and Ph.D. (1931) in general psychology from Ohio State University. Trained at Ohio State in part by Francis Maxfield, a former Witmer student—and therefore later dubbed his grandchild by Witmer—Newland had courses in individual testing (Binet and Herrick Scales) and experience in testing juvenile delinquents and preschoolers, although never directly employed by the schools throughout his career (Newland, 1981). Newland had a strong allegiance to blending general psychology with special education in the creation of his training program at Illinois.[20] At least some of his graduate courses were the same as those taken by Skodak at Ohio State. His background reflects that of many others in that he chose to pursue psychology only late in his college work. Field experiences after his degree appear to have supplemented course work.

## Wilda Rosebrook

Wilda Rosebrook earned a B.A. at Ohio Wesleyan in 1917 and was an English teacher from 1918 to 1925. Attending Ohio State University during the same period as T. E. Newland, she completed her M.A. in 1926 and Ph.D. in clinical psychology in 1931. Later she would return to

Ohio State's faculty and assist in its clinic, which provided district-level services on a regional basis (Rosebrook, 1942). After getting a master's degree she worked for the Michigan Home and Training School and then served a fellowship at Boston Psychopathic Hospital (letter from Rosebrook to Joseph French, February 2, 1986).

## Frances Mullen

In her autobiographical account, Mullen (1981) gives only a brief description of the training she received in this period. We learn that she entered the University of Chicago "at age 16 on a mathematics scholarship and graduated four years later with a hodge podge of courses" (p. 104). She specifically mentions "Psych 101," taught by a graduate student, and social psychology. Having earned a Ph.B. in mathematics in 1923, she taught in Chicago high schools while completing an M.A. in education (1927) and a Ph.D. in educational psychology (1939) at Chicago. Her work for the M.A. degree included courses on curriculum construction, psychology of secondary education, junior high school teaching problems, two courses on statistical methods and educational problems, methods of teaching ideas, investigations in arithmetic, mental tests, teaching techniques in high school, educational research, elementary school mathematics, and historical geology. Her doctoral coursework included experimental education, additional courses on teaching arithmetic, several courses on school administration, psychology of social groups, school social work, research methods and statistics, psychiatric problems in education, mathematics, junior college, the school in the social order, educational psychology, history of educational thought, psychology of learning, educational psychology, economics, mental growth, and factor theory (Fagan & Wells, 1998). As did others of her time, she came from a teaching background and got into school psychology from indirect routes, primarily educational psychology.

## Morris and Judith Krugman

The first elected president of APA's Division of School Psychology (1945–1946), Morris Krugman originally prepared to become a rabbi, graduating from Jewish Theological Seminary of America in 1917. Concurrently studying at Brooklyn Polytechnic Institute, he earned a B.S. in chemical engineering in 1919. Following a short business career in chemistry, he worked as a high school teacher in New York City; along the

---

[20]For a brief overview of his career, see Fagan, McCoy, and McCoy (1993). Newland (1981) lists his various jobs, including being the first psychologist at the U.S. Military Academy at West Point. Since he was involved in the planning of the Thayer Conference, it may be that his experience at West Point introduced him to the Thayer Hotel and encouraged him to recommend that site for the 1954 conference.

way he earned an M.A. in educational psychology in 1925 and a Ph.D. in clinical psychology in 1928 at New York University. His interest in psychological work came from his experiences in school guidance with delinquents and dropouts. He went on to become a high-level administrator in psychological services and school administration with the New York City Board of Education.

Krugman's wife, Judith Israelite Krugman, whose career took place largely after 1930, completed her B.A. in history at Hunter College (1928), M.A. in general psychology at Columbia University (1931), and Ph.D. in clinical psychology at New York University (1941). In the 1930s, she worked at the Judge Baker Foundation Child Guidance Clinic in Boston; at Worcester State Hospital; and at Caswell Training School in Kinston, North Carolina. She never worked as a schoolteacher before becoming a clinical and school psychologist (Fagan, 1994).

## Wallin's Survey

A broader picture is provided by Wallin's (1914) survey, which identified clinic locations, dates of origins, types of examinations conducted, and a general idea of the preparation of those conducting examinations of "feeble-minded and backward children" in 103 cities. Reporting data from 84 school systems, Wallin found that 57% gave educational tests and 81% psychological tests, "either by employees of the school boards or by outside agencies" (p. 393). There were 19 school-based clinic facilities. Wallin's Table III indicates that all providers of services in the largest cities (over 500,000) had a Ph.D. or M.D. degree. In cities of 250,000 and fewer than 500,000, some had a Ph.D. or M.D. but others were identified as assistants, with training in mental tests or subnormal children; normal school and college graduates; or special training at summer schools, preparing techniques for defectives. In cities of 100,000 or fewer than 250,000, there were a few practitioners with M.D.s, others with graduate degrees, and several with summer course preparation on subnormal children. The category of cities with fewer than 100,000 was dominated by persons with summer course preparation on subnormal children; there were few doctoral personnel.[21]

---

[21]Wallin (1914) is especially critical of the summer school preparation of many examiners and explains his own practices for admitting students to training (pp. 210–215). He was also critical of the skills of school medical inspectors.

The availability of services corresponded positively to the size of the school district and suggested that the better-trained examiners, as was the case with teachers, were in urban settings. Nevertheless, Wallin (1914) expressed dissatisfaction with the credentials of the practitioners:

> The psychological testing in most of the cities is exceedingly meager and crude, being conducted by teachers, principals, educators, psychologists, and physicians who are not specialists on the physiology, psychology and pedagogy of feeble-minded, backward or other types of mentally abnormal children (p. 393).

Wallin described many of the responses to his question about examiner training as "ambiguous, evasive or unsatisfactory" (p. 394). Emphasizing the importance of the preparation of the examiner as "the man behind the gun," Wallin stated that of the 115 examiners,

> 52 are special class teachers, 11 supervisors of special classes or principals, 4 superintendents of schools, 5 alienists or neurologists, 22 medical inspectors or physicians, 8 psychologists and 13 clinical psychologists (restricting the application of the latter term to those only who are trained experts on the psychology and pedagogy of mentally unusual children) (p. 394).

Referring to them as "amateurs," Wallin (1914) stated that in "the vast majority of cases the psychological testing (and possibly also the diagnoses) of mentally exceptional children in the schools is made by Binet testers," whom he believed performed "74% of the testing being done" (p. 395). He described the preparation of "the great majority of the Binet testers" as follows:

> [It] consists in having taken normal school, college or university courses in the usual branches of education and psychology, and a summer course on mental tests and on feeble-minded children; or in having taken a regular medical course and then reading literature on feeble-minded and backward children, learning to give the Binet system, or paying a visit to a psychological clinic. Even if we concede that it is possible thus to prepare psycho-educational testers, the conclusion remains true: that such testers are not expert psychoeducational

diagnosticians, and that to prepare expert psycho-educational diagnosticians requires three or four years of technical training and clinical experience (p. 395).

Wallin (1914) also concluded that the "vast majority of psychological examiners are educators" (p. 396) and not properly trained. However, he was sensitive to the lack of available trained practitioners and training programs and the financial plight of rural areas, and he condoned having "the psychological testing done by school teachers who have learned to administer various tests," but not as a diagnostic function (Wallin, 1921, p. 274). The statement reflects the recognition of two levels of training and practice—testing by psychological examiners and diagnostic functions by better-trained practitioners preferably who held doctoral degrees.

A similar survey conducted in 1948 by Wallin (1955) reported that school psychologists and teachers were administering educational tests in 22% and 39%, respectively, of the districts reporting; "psychological examinations were conducted most frequently by the school psychologist or psychoeducational examiner (47%), mental hygiene clinic (30%), teacher (9%), principal (8%), and supervisor (6%)" (p. 108).[22] Of the 138 cities responding to the question, 106 (77%) employed a psychoeducational examiner or psychologist and 84% required certification of the psychologist. The shift toward much better-trained personnel reflects acceptance of school psychology, certification standards of several states, and the greater availability of training programs in both school and clinical psychology (Cutts, 1955).

## TRAINING EXPECTATIONS

An additional perspective is gained from viewpoints about what training levels and content *should* be. One set of viewpoints can be seen in the membership requirements of the American Psychological Association (APA); the short-lived American Association of Clinical Psychologists (AACP); and the Division of Clinical Psychology of the APA, founded in 1919. Each of these organizations, representing clinical and applied psy-

chologists, required a doctoral degree for regular membership throughout the period under study, although some recognition for practice as examiners was given to persons with master's and bachelor's degrees (Fagan, 1993a). Only after 1926 did the APA allow associate members, which could include nondoctoral practitioners, graduate students, and those who had not published any research (Fernberger, 1932; Wallin, 1960).

During its brief existence (1917–1919), the AACP had a Committee on the Qualifications of Psychological Examiners and Other Psychological Experts. Among its recommendations for certification (Committee Report of December 1917 meeting) are the following training and qualifications, which were thought to approximate the requirements for a Ph.D. in psychology plus an apprenticeship in practical work:

1. introductory (elementary or general) psychology, 45 class room hours, minimum.
2. experimental (or laboratory) psychology (drill in technique of experimentation), 70 class hours, minimum.
3. mental testing, including the statistical handling of data, 70 class hours, minimum.
4. applications of psychology to medicine, education, industry, commerce, law, etc.; 40 class room hours minimum.
5. 400 class room hours from among: psychology of individual differences, genetic (developmental) psychology, abnormal psychology, social psychology, psychology of learning, psychology of higher mental processes, advanced systematic psychology, educational psychology, minor laboratory problems, psychology of business, criminal psychology, history of psychology.
6. 300 class room hours from among: economics, sociology, anthropology, biology, psychology, neurology, embryology, statistics, education, business administration.
7. At least 400 chronological (135 class room) hours on a research problem or other form of intensive study of a special field.
8. Evidence of experience in the practical application of psychology in relation to medicine, education, industry, or other recognized spheres of practical psychology (p. 4).

Another perspective on training is provided by Wallin (1919), who had earlier criticized the

---

[22]I do not know of any other publication that contains these data. Wallin (1955) also provides data on the most frequently administered group and individual tests.

use of the title clinical psychologist by inadequately prepared people in summer courses, medical inspectors, or "expert experimental, educational, or genetic psychologists" (1914, p. 216). In his 1919 article on training, Wallin identifies the "kind of courses which should be pursued and not the amount of time which should be devoted to each course" (p. 469):

1. Undergraduate courses in general, functional, genetic educational, physiological and experimental psychology, mental and anthropometric tests, child study, biology, human anatomy, physiology and hygiene.
2. Clinical psychology including methods of examination, and practical examination of at least 200 cases, and an institutional internship of at least one year.
3. Pedagogical courses (educational tests and scores, methods of teaching, especially reading, spelling, and number, and the methods of the kindergarten, and courses in school supervision and educational sociology).
4. Courses on the psychology and pedagogy of various types of mental deviation or anomalies of school children, including observation and teaching.
5. Social pathology
6. A minimum amount of medical work in physical diagnosis, pediatrics, EENT, etc.

Moreover, Wallin stated, "If the student begins to specialize in his senior year in college, he should easily find it possible to complete the above outline of work in the time now required to take the Ph.D. degree, with the possible exception of the year's internship" (p. 470). Wallin insisted on making the requirements comparable to those of physicians.

The qualifications necessary to take the examination for license as a psychologist were announced for the first time in 1925 by the New York City Board of Education's Board of Examiners. The written examination would be given on Monday, February 15, 1926, with later examinations to include "oral and practical tests which will include an oral interview, an examination on psychological diagnosis and a clinical test" (Announcement, Examination for License as a Psychologist, December 29, 1925). The written examination was on content that would most likely have been learned from didactic study, whereas other aspects would have necessitated some field experience. The primary qualifications were a master's degree in psychology and one year's experience in mental measurement.[23]

Recommended for approval in 1933, the first Pennsylvania State Department of Education certification requirements applied to two levels: public school psychologists and public school psychological examiners. The overall requirements were "the completion of an approved college or university curriculum" and additional semester hours of study and practicum distributed across several areas (48 hours for the school psychologist and 36 hours for the examiner). Since the only difference in the requirements was 12 semester hours of experience, only the school psychologist requirements are here described:

*Part I.* Theory or content (24 semester hours): Twenty hours were required in courses on educational psychology (4 hours in lab work and 2 in lecture courses); clinical psychology, abnormal psychology, psychology of atypical children, psychology of exceptional children, psychology of abnormal children, and psychology and education of atypical or subnormal children (4 hours); psychology of childhood and adolescence (4 hours); tests and measurements (4 hours, to include individual and group tests, theory and application, and interpretation); and statistical methods (2 hours). Four hours were for unassigned courses from mental hygiene, social psychology, psychology of personality, "and courses usually classified as sociological, studying the causes of poverty, dependence and delinquency" (State Council on Education records, p. 25).

**Part II.** Laboratory and practice (12 semester hours): Clinical methods, practice, and diagnosis (4 hours); diagnostic teaching (2 hours); individual research in educational psychology (4 hours including individual case research work); social service and field work (2 hours).

**Part III.** Experience (12 semester hours): "Experience in recognized and approved psychological work, including diagnosis and recommendation for care and remedial

---

[23]These were tenure-track positions with a salary of $2,200 per year. Applicants could be men or women, "over 25 and under 46 years of age" (not applicable to already employed New York City teachers), with U.S. citizenship or application for such, and who had in writing and speech a "satisfactory command of English."

treatment shall be required. Equivalent— 216 clock hours" (p. 25).

The Pennsylvania expectations were revised in 1937 and included much greater distinction between the two levels in five areas: general and theoretical psychology, psychometric techniques, other specialized techniques, related courses, and clinical practice (under supervision and allowable in several settings in addition to schools).

The New York certification requirements, adopted in 1934 and effective "on or after September 1, 1935" (Cooper, 1935, p. 6) provided for provisional and permanent certificates. The provisional certificate requirements included a four-year B.A. or B.S. curriculum "offered by a recognized institution of higher education, and in addition 30 semester hours in approved graduate courses leading to the master's degree with a major in psychology or approved equivalent preparation; said preparation shall have included 52 semester hours in appropriate courses distributed according to the following schedule" (p. 15):

General psychology (6 hours)

Education and educational psychology (21 hours), to include at least one course in each of the following areas: Group 1—methods of teaching, psychology of school subjects, remedial methods, guidance or similar courses; Group 2—history principles or philosophy of education, educational sociology, or similar courses; Group 3—educational measurements and statistics; Group 4—psychology of childhood, adolescence, learning, child development, or similar courses.

Clinical psychology (12 hours) may include individual psychology, abnormal psychology, psychiatry, social psychology, psychology of subnormal, psychology of superior children, delinquency, mental hygiene, mental adjustment, and social casework.

Clinical tests and procedures (3 hours). No description is given.

"Supervised practice in the giving of individual tests and in making reports involving interpretation and recommendation" (4 hours) (p. 15).

Applied anatomy and physiology (6 hours) may include neuroanatomy, neuropathology, hygiene, and speech development.

The permanent certificate had additional expectations: "The psychologist shall have prepared 50 case reports which have been submitted to and approved by the State Education Department" and "shall have completed five years of appropriate experience, three of which, during the preceding five-year period, shall have been as a student psychologist in the public schools of New York State" (p. 16).

From the Pennsylvania and New York requirements, it appears that the expectations in the early to mid-1930s were rapidly being increased to the graduate level, allowing a mixture of undergraduate and graduate courses to meet the overall requirements. It is noteworthy that both mention approved or recognized institutions and programs and considerable supervised field experience, suggesting a new form of oversight developing in the training-credentialing arena for school practice. However, the expectations of experts, agencies, and organizations provide only a picture of the ideology of the period, not the practice. It would be decades before the typical level of training for school psychologists approached these expectations.

# NEW YORK UNIVERSITY

The preceding information suggests that inevitably a program of studies specific to school psychology would be founded. Based on its annual bulletins and historical data from Fagan (1986b), Hug (n.d.), and Trachtman (1987), it is believed that the first training program designated for school psychology appeared at New York University (NYU) in 1929. According to Elsie Hug, the School of Pedagogy in its first year (1890) offered a course entitled The Practical Applications of the Psychology of Expressional Activities; by 1910, "25% of the School's program consisted of courses in psychology"; and in 1915, the following courses were listed: Childhood and Adolescent Psychology, Physiological and Experimental Psychology, and Elementary and Advanced Psychoanalysis. References to special education were also in the course listings. Psychology courses (not necessarily different courses) increased throughout this period from 9 (1921–1922) to 29 (1929–1930), when the school psychology program was begun.[24] The

---

[24]The nine courses in 1921–1922 were Outlines of Psychology, Problems of Psychology, Psychology of the High School Age, Educational Psychology (Principles), Educational Psychology (Problems), Laboratory Psychology, Applied Psychology, Systematic Psychology, and Psychological Seminar (Social Psychology).

new Department of Educational Psychology's courses in 1929, presumably a few for under-graduate- but most for graduate-level credit (points in parenthesis) were as follows:

*100 Number Courses*
Elements of Psychology for Teachers (4)
Psychology of Secondary Education (2)
Psychology of High School Subjects (2)
Experimental Introduction to the Learning Process (2)
Summary of Experiments in Learning (unspecified; not offered until 1930–1931)
Genetic Psychology: Mental Development in the Individual (unspecified; not offered until 1930–1931)
Principles of Educational Psychology (I, II) (2 each)
Applied Psychology (4)
Psychology of Childhood (2)
Psychology of Adolescence (2)
Psychology for Teachers of Backward and Defective Children (2)*[25]
The Psychology of Problem Children (2)*
The Psychological Foundations of Method (unspecified; not offered until 1930–1931)
Psychology of Elementary-School Subjects (2)
Clinical Psychology (4)*
Mental Tests (Intelligence Tests) (2)*
Psychology of Character (4)
Principles of Mental Hygiene (4)*
Psychology of Religion (4)

*200 and 300 Number Courses:*
Social Psychology (6)
Educational Psychology (Advanced Course) (6)
Mental Hygiene (Advanced Course) (6)
Practicum in Educational Psychology (6)
Seminar: Educational Psychology (6)

Course descriptions indicate that what is now termed a course on intellectual assessment (administration and interpretation) was taught in the clinical psychology course; the mental tests course was more like a contemporary course in tests and measurements. The mental hygiene courses were geared to prevention, "to study the various factors involved in keeping the normal individual normal" (*School of Education Bulletin, Part II*, 1929–1930, p. 25).

The Practicum in Educational Psychology was a critical review of literature and not a field

experience. It appears that any field experiences were gained as components of testing courses or from available agencies. Although Trachtman (1987) and Hug (n.d.) indicate that a psychoedu-cational clinic was opened in connection with the department in 1930 to foster school and later clinical psychology, several other settings in the New York City area were available for field expe-rience at and before that time. A listing pub-lished in 1935 identified 15 clinics, including 1 in Brooklyn and 1 in White Plains (Report of Com-mittee of Clinical Section of American Psycho-logical Association, 1935).[26] Thus, several agen-cies could have supported an academic sequence of training or a more formal program in applied psychology before the opening of a "school psy-chologist" program in 1929 and the psychoedu-cational clinic in 1930. That is, the formal school psychology program of 1929 was doubtless pre-ceded by a less formal arrangement of courses from which students sought field experiences and employment. The program, therefore, evolved from a long history of applied psychology offer-ings. It is likely that students in the 1929 pro-gram found practical experience in several New York City area settings. Nevertheless, specific reference to field experiences (e.g., practicum or internship as we now know them) was lacking in the first official program description and depart-ment offerings.

The 1929–1930 *School of Education Bulletin, Part I*, identified the requirements for a "school psychologists" program (Curriculum 35) leading to B.S., A.M., and Ph.D. degrees.[27] The pro-grams were geared to six functions of a school psychologist: mental testing, interpretation of the intelligence rating, placement of pupils ac-cording to mental ability, helping "problem" children in their adjustment to society, educa-tional and vocational guidance, and advising

---

[25]Asterisks denote the required courses for Group III.

[26]Earlier listings of clinics appear on a charter membership list for the AACP, December 28, 1917 (Gesell Papers, Library of Congress) and in Wallin (1914).

[27]All graduate degrees required a B average for graduation. The point scale for undergraduate and graduate grades was A = 90–100, B = 80–89, C = 70–79 and D = 60–69. Tuition was only $.50 per point to a maximum of $6.00 a term, or $12.00 a year. An additional tuition fee of $9.00 per point was charged. Thus, at $9.50 per point, the A.M. degree of 28–36 points would have cost roughly $250–350. The 1995–1996 cost per point would place a 32-point degree at about $18,000.

teachers and administrators on the modern problems involved in learning and in the integration of experiences of children (p. 88). The orientation was remarkably similar to the definitions of clinical psychology by Gesell, Goddard, and Wallin (1919).

A B.S. degree required a total of 128 points from four groups:

**Group I.** Courses required in common of all candidates for the degree of bachelor of science—28 points.

**Group II.** Courses required in common of all persons contemplating service as school psychologists—10 or 14 points.

**Group III.** Courses offered to provide the student an opportunity to make the special preparation needed in subject matter, methods, supervision, and administration of work as a school psychologist—60 points.

**Group IV.** Unrestricted electives to bring the total from I-II-III-IV to 128 points.

Group I requirements were actually the curriculum for "prospective teachers of elementary grades," leading to a B.S. degree. The curriculum described could be completed over eight semesters (four years), by taking 16 points each semester. It appears that the student could adapt the program to some extent for secondary school, but observation and supervised student teaching were required in both elementary and secondary schools. Given the amount of flexibility in choosing with one's program director the subject matter and methods courses and the unrestricted electives, it seems that the B.S. degree for school psychologists could be squeezed into that for the elementary grades curriculum without too much difficulty.

Group II is what would now be considered professional foundations courses in teacher education—principles of elementary and secondary education, tests and measurements for both levels, statistics, and observation and supervised student teaching, unless one already had a "certified record of successful teaching experience" (*Bulletin*, Part I, p. 88). Teacher preparation was clearly required for the degree in school psychology, and Group II requirements overlapped heavily with those of the elementary teacher preparation, as in Group I.

The required courses in Group III are marked with an asterisk plus the Social Background of the School Child (4), Woodwork for Teachers of Defective Children (two courses, 2 points each), Industrial Arts in the Lower Elementary Grades (4), and Teacher as Adviser (2); these were apparently not offered by the Department of Educational Psychology, or at least not in that year. Students could add to this cluster of 28 points electives from other departments with approval by Dr. Charles Benson, program director. Overall, the undergraduate degree in school psychology was actually an elementary teaching degree with certain substitutions and electives. The curriculum had little required liberal arts and sciences content except for courses in spoken and written English, problems of government and politics, types of literature, and a survey of the development of civilization; courses in biology, general science, American history, and geography were all listed for teachers (e.g., General Biology for Teachers).

As in the earlier normal schools and teachers colleges, the NYU program in school psychology appears to have been long on methods and specific practical applications and short on content from the liberal arts and sciences. It must be added, however, that elsewhere in the NYU *School of Education Bulletin, Part I* (see pp. 99–101) a Washington Square College of Education Curriculum for B.A. or B.S. degrees contains considerable required content from the liberal arts and sciences, although it is not mentioned in the school psychology requirements. It seems that the Washington Square requirements were beefed up to ensure that the degree met the teacher certification expectations of New York City and the "college graduate certificate" requirements of New York State. The impression given is that the regular teaching degree was considered more of a professional degree and not a regular college degree.

The specific content of the A.M. and Ph.D degrees are only vaguely described; courses and research were determined in consultation with the faculty and program director. At a minimum, the master of arts degree required six full courses, "of which at least two must be numbered above 200 and of which at least two must be taken in the same department of instruction. At least three courses were to be selected from the following group (if they had not already been credited toward the bachelor's degree): (a) educational psychology; (b) educational sociology; (c) history of education; (d) principles or philosophy of education; (e) educational administration"

(*School of Education Bulletin, Part I*, p. 139).[28] In addition, at least four of the required courses had to be taken at NYU and "at least one year must elapse between the conferring of the bachelor's degree and the conferring of the master's degree" (p. 139).

All of the degree requirements could be met during summer school. A thesis was required and "must not be a mere essay; it must present evidence of a thorough acquaintance with some limited special field, obtained by recourse to original sources" (*School of Education Bulletin, Part I*, p. 140). To avoid penalty, the student had to complete the thesis within one year of completing all course work. Since the thesis was to be written in connection with a 200-level or higher course, it presumably carried academic credit. In graduate studies, 200-level and higher courses meeting for two hours per week for a year (i.e., "full courses") carried 6 points, whereas lower-numbered courses carried 4. Thus, the number of points for the A.M. degree would have been in the range of 28 to 36 points.

The Ph.D. degree required a thesis of independent research and scholarly technique, usually requiring one year to complete. In addition, 12 full courses beyond the bachelor's degree were required, with at least half above the 200 level and at least 5 taken at NYU. Four full courses could be taken in one's area of specialization. A "preliminary oral examination" preceded a "preliminary written examination," after which a student could become a candidate for the degree. The written examinations were comprehensive and covered four subjects, including at least two "which are basal to education as a science," one or two in "special fields," and one related to the "major field in which the thesis is to be written" *School of Education Bulletin, Part I*, (pp. 142–143). Considered separate from the course requirements was "a reading knowledge of two foreign languages or of one modern foreign language and the ability to use statistical methods for purposes of research" (p. 142). The degree was not to be conferred until at least seven months after the written examinations. The thesis requirement was followed by a "final oral examination" of about two hours, covering the area of the thesis "though [the candidate]

may also be questioned concerning any aspect of education" (p. 147).[29]

The graduate and undergraduate curricula overlapped, and many graduate requirements were met by undergraduate offerings. The graduate program was essentially a specialization built on an undergraduate teacher education foundation. Nevertheless, the kind of preparation provided at the graduate level was much more akin to contemporary school psychologist training than that of the NYU undergraduate program.

Why did the first program start at NYU? Why not Teachers College, Columbia University (TCCU), which had a long-standing faculty of reknown in psychology and educational psychology, including Thorndike, Hollingworth, Hildreth, Norsworthy, and Pintner? Perhaps the TCCU orientation and tradition were less practical and applied and more scientific. It was more in the camp of educational psychology than clinical psychology, that is, less idiographic and more nomothetic.

The NYU School of Education had a tradition dating to 1890 (called the School of Pedagogy until 1921) and was more service-oriented toward public education. It opened its Department of Educational Psychology in 1929 and appointed its first chair, Dr. Charles Benson, who intended to build a strong faculty and develop specific professional programs (Hug, n.d.). Benson had a long history of service in public schools and in higher education and, no doubt, a strong educational psychology background with degrees from the University of Nebraska (A.B. and A.M.) and Columbia University (Ph.D., 1922). He served as director of the school psychology program from 1929 to 1943.

In addition, the timing for a formal program was right: the faculty of educational psychology was growing; the department was getting a new facility, with a psychoeducational clinic (opening in 1930); the New York Board of Education had

---

[28]A full course meant that the class met for at least two hours per week for a period of 30 weeks or its equivalent; this was essentially a two-semester sequence.

[29]Perhaps related to the impact of heavy immigration during this period, all thesis requirements include this statement: "No thesis will be read irrespective of any other consideration unless the English is technically accurate" (p. 144). In addition, the thesis committee was made up of three faculty members, including a faculty sponsor. The thesis, anticipated to be between 5,000 and 30,000 words, was expected to be original in nature and show independent research skills as a contribution to education. The final oral examination was open to the entire faculty.

established formal examinations and credentials for the hiring of its psychologists in 1925 and had intended to expand its staff considerably (letter from David Ment to Thomas Fagan, July 31, 1984); and there was no doubt a natural rivalry between NYU and other New York area institutions that also had clinic facilities. The NYU department also had a long history of offering educational and applied psychology courses that rivaled those of other institutions.[30] Sooner or later an institution was going to start a formal program in school psychology. The history of applied psychology is centered in the Northeast, especially New York City, and NYU appears to have simply answered the call of several influences that were operating at that time. By 1930–1931, the department was offering programs to prepare "the school psychologist, the school psychiatrist, the mental hygienist, and the research expert in educational psychology" *School of Education Bulletin, Part I*, 1930–1931, p. 99).

Finally, by the mid-1920s, separate departments of psychology were established at the Washington Square and the University Heights campuses of NYU. Their psychology offerings were mixed with those of the philosophy and pedagogy departments, often sharing faculty (Stout, 1954). Graduate offerings were initiated in the late 1920s, but distinct graduate-level psychology programs were not available until the late 1940s (Silverman, c. 1971). School psychology remained within the School of Education, whereas clinical psychology emerged later in the College of Arts and Sciences. At the time the school psychology program was established, there was no formal clinical psychology training at NYU.

By the end of the training period reviewed here, it was recognized that the "problems confronting the school psychologist make demands upon him which necessitate specialized training and the possession of distinctive qualifications for successful work" (Hildreth, 1930, p. 21). In the first book specifically about school psychology, Hildreth lists the academic courses in the Columbia University bulletin that were "suitable for the training of school psychologists":

Teaching in special classes
Field work with special classes
Administration of special classes
Psychology of exceptional children
Mental adjustments
Vocational tests
Statistical methods
Mental and educational tests
Measurement in elementary education
Mental testing of the young child
Clinical work with young children
Measurement in kindergarten and first grade
Measurement in secondary education
Tests and measurement in music education
Tests and measurement in physical education
Methods of research
Clinical psychology
Diagnosis and remedial treatment in elementary subjects
Research in intelligence testing

In addition to these courses, which provided technical background, educational and psychological background would be provided by courses in the theory and history of education, administration and methods in general, and educational psychology. Hence, by the late 1920s there was formal training at NYU and known sequences of training at other institutions like the University of Illinois, Columbia University, and Ohio State University.[31] No doubt other examples could be uncovered. Although many institutions would join in the training of school psychologists after 1960, until then these institutions dominated the production of practitioners and leadership in the field (Ferguson, 1963).

## OVERALL CONCLUSIONS:

1. The practice of school psychology, including the title "school psychologist," predated formal preparation programs. The chronological sequence of professional development was from perception of need for services to their provision and later to the preparation of providers. Thus, training practices

---

[30]A "News and Comment" item in *The Psychological Clinic*, Vol. 1, pp. 39–40, mentions a series of lectures on the education of defectives started by the NYU School of Pedagogy and names several well-known people from area school districts, institutions, and hospitals who would deliver the lectures.

[31]The broader nature of psychological course work in the United States can be judged from the fact that many of the courses listed were also taught at James Madison University (Hanson, 1990) and the Kansas State Teachers College of Pittsburg (Litten, 1986).

emerged from needs and from on-the-job practices. It is doubtful that this direction has persisted throughout the history of training. Once training programs were established, they began to influence the nature of practice through increasingly diverse courses and experiences adapted to practice settings. The limits of this influence are unclear. For decades there has been a concern that practice was not following training or that training was not adequate to the needs of practice. Narrow practitioner roles and functions in contemporary practice continue to be criticized despite the fact that training requirements are more than double those of the early 1970s. The training-into-practice dilemma appears to have increased since the earliest period, when training seems to have emerged from practice.

There also appears to have been a directional shift in the influence of training on credentials. Although certification requirements of state departments of education are now a primary influence on training requirements, the reverse appears to have been the case earlier in the century. Authoritative opinion, organizations' membership requirements, work experience, and a mixture of training approaches collectively influenced the development of the earliest certification requirements of New York and Pennsylvania (Cornell, 1941). Once in place, these requirements began to reverse the process of influence to a point where now many training programs follow a pragmatic model geared almost entirely to state certification and licensure requirements (Fagan & Wise, 1994). The conflicting responsibilities of training programs and certification agencies would eventually complicate efforts to raise the quality of professional training (Ferguson, 1963).

2. The formal training of school psychologists was initiated with undergraduate and graduate programs at NYU in 1929. Previous approaches to preparation were informal and allied to experimental and applied psychology or teacher education; field experiences were obtained from a variety of sources not necessarily connected to an academic program. From such varied backgrounds at least three types of practitioners emerged. The first were persons trained as teachers (often without a college degree) who completed lit-

tle formal psychological training and were pressed into service with little more than a crash course in using the new Binet scales. These "amateurs," "Binet testers," or "tyros" were a source of scorn and embarrassment to the better-trained practitioners and encouraged a call for improved training (Luckey, 1920, 1921; Whipple, 1913).[32] The second was a psychological examiner who completed training in education, psychology, or educational psychology at the undergraduate and/or graduate level, often holding a master's degree, and obtained practical experience as part of or following the degree. The third type of practitioner usually held a doctoral degree in psychology or education and had more extensive training and practical experience than the psychological examiner.[33]

In 1914, Wallin had stated, "Until recently it was impossible to obtain adequate training in clinical psychology except through an apprenticeship with one of the few experts in the field. Now a few universities—although very few—are able to offer satisfactory didactic and clinical courses in the psychological and educational examination of children" (pp. 115–116). The improvement of training by the end of this period is witnessed in Hildreth's (1930) survey, revealing that "psychologists in the larger school systems almost invariably hold the M.A. or Ph.D. degree, chiefly in education" (p. 22). More than half the respondents reported five or more years of experience as psychologists and more than three as teachers. In contrast to the overall dismal assessment of practitioner training by Wallin (1914), Hildreth concluded "that in the large majority of cases psychologists at present actively engaged in their work are well prepared" (p. 23). The NYU program, formally established in 1929, and the presence of other recommended training sequences symbolized the beginning of a new era in

---

[32]To some extent, these people may have been encouraged by expert testimony regarding the simplicity of the Binet scales and their value even in the hands of untrained examiners (see, e. g., Goddard, 1913; Wallin, 1911).

[33]A list of those with early Ph.D. training and employment as clinical psychologists appears in Wallin (1961).

which school psychologists would be formally prepared and then credentialed for their work. Although it would take the remainder of the century to spread this practice to most corners of the country, the new era was at least initiated by 1930.

3. The formal preparation of school psychologists was often appended to or blended with training in clinical psychology and teacher education. Clinical psychology was considered a method, not necessarily a distinct field, and its primary characteristic was the application of tests and other methods to individuals. Teacher education was considered important in understanding the setting in which the individual clients of the school psychologist were enrolled. Thus, school psychology emerged as a version of applying a clinical method to children and others in educational settings. The work of guidance personnel with groups and group tests would later blend into school psychologist training and vice versa. This was nurtured by the fact that training for both fields took place in connection with a department, school, or college of education. For all practical purposes, much of clinical psychology was school psychology in the early part of the century, and applied psychology had, at least temporarily, found a welcome home in many education administrative units for training and in the schools for practice. The cooperative involvement of education and psychology departments in the training of school psychologists would be a persistent struggle despite being advocated by Witmer and Wallin in their earliest discussions of training (Ferguson, 1963). Nevertheless, in the early part of the century, the history of training in both school and clinical psychology was dominated by an education, special education, and experimental educational psychology-orientation (including mental tests).

   A related aspect of the training of this early period is the overlap of school psychologist training with that of clinical psychologists, educational psychologists, physicians, school administrators, social workers, special educators, speech therapists, and vocational counselors. Although core specialty training that is restricted to school psychology students has been evident for several decades, much of contemporary and certainly early training is a selective use of courses, concepts, and materials from related fields. It is still common to see school psychology curricula that include courses from several other educational or psychological fields. This psychological and educational diversity has been a strength in the history of school psychology training.

4. The earliest trainers in a training program for school psychologists were among the faculty at NYU, including Charles Benson, Charles Skinner, Paul West, and Andrew Wylie, as well as several adjunct faculty members from regional agencies (e.g., Meta Anderson from Newark, New Jersey). While Lightner Witmer appears to have been largely self-trained in what he called clinical psychology, he was not a school psychologist by title, nor did he prepare others specifically as school psychologists in any formal program specifically for them. French (1988) even contends that few Witmer graduates practiced as school psychologists in schools. It must be noted, however, that Witmer, Cameron, Hildreth, Hollingworth, Goddard, Maxfield, and many others were among the earliest trainers of school psychologists by way of less formal programs of study. Indeed, had Witmer referred to his clinical psychology as essentially school psychology, he would be a strong candidate for the first official program trainer.

5. The structure of school psychologist preparation had three basic elements. First, the content of training included educational preparation, psychological preparation, and field experiences. All are still evident in contemporary training practices and standards. The second basic element is that preparation was increasingly provided in institutions of higher education. In the earliest part of this period, normal-school and undergraduate-level preparation were observed; later the training expectations evolved to the master's and doctoral levels. Third, the nature of this training took place through traditional didactic, classroom methodology, where an instructor provided information to a group of students, and in on-campus or off-campus field placements, where supervision of practical tasks was given independent of or in some relationship to the instruction at the institution of higher learning. In many instances, however, school psy-

chologists were trained on the job by better-educated supervisors—a mentorial approach—or self-trained in this era of minimal regulation. The importance of the field experiences cannot be overestimated. Even in 1937, Hildreth pointed out that "at the present time experience in actual clinic situations may be more important than academic course work" (Louttit, 1939, p. 377). The use of campus psychological clinics for supervised work in relationship to didactic work was still observed in almost half the institutions with school psychology programs in the mid-1980s (Hughes & Benson, 1986).

6. At least for the period under study (1890–1930), the mental testing movement in American psychology had a strong impact on the model and content of training. Whatever else programs chose to include in the preparation of school psychologists, one or more courses in mental testing and achievement testing (and later in personality testing) were typical. The new mental tests, especially those of the Binet type, freed training programs from the necessity of having expensive, cumbersome experimental laboratory equipment for judging mental ability based on reaction time, sensation, perception, and anthropometric measurements. The lab was now in a test kit that allowed school and clinical psychology a portability it had not previously enjoyed. To the extent that training programs serve to shape a field's identity, it is little wonder that the psychometric and psychodiagnostic tradition has been so strong in school psychology.

7. Interventions, both psychological and educational, are observed in training programs throughout much of our history. According to Sandoval (1993), during the first several decades of school psychologist training, interventions were primarily along the lines of academic instruction, including direct remediation, process- and ability-based interventions, or alterations of the curriculum. Nonacademic interventions were most often concerned with "moral deficiency," especially truancy and delinquency, and schools collaborated closely with other community agencies (e.g., police and courts) for their alleviation. The courses taught by Witmer and those in several other institutions reveal what we would now consider a strong remedial and special education content (including diagnostic teaching). Counseling and psychotherapeutic interventions, individual or group, were present in this period but emerged more visibly after World War II. Thus, guidance, vocational counseling, and special instruction were the most visible intervention aspects in early school psychologist training.

8. Among the observed curricula and experiences of this era are courses on educational sociology, poverty, delinquency, and urban and rural characteristics, which denote a sensitivity to the environmental circumstances of many families and their impact on schooling. Field experiences were often in agencies that worked with immigrant and poor children. Gesell's year of experience in the East Side Settlement House in New York City appears to have been a fairly common type of experience for new graduates. The sensitivity is also observed in the blending of undergraduate and graduate work for school practitioners of psychology or social work. The emphasis is reminiscent of the 1960s and 1970s, when many graduate programs were offering courses on culturally and/or linguistically disadvantaged children. More recently we see specific courses on multiculturalism and diversity.

9. The application of models of training as we recognize them today seems to have been nonexistent. Although rudimentary elements of a scientist-practitioner model or a professional model could be observed in early training expectations, those models would formally emerge much later from the Boulder Conference in 1949 (Raimy, 1950) and the Vail Conference in 1973 (Korman, 1973). A model could have been contrived from the research conducted, but there was almost no discussion of models at that time. As acceptance of applied psychology increased, we can observe a decrease in the classical and philosophical aspects of graduate work and an increase in psychological and applied psychology courses.

10. The dual influences of educational and psychological training and practice, still characteristic of school psychology in the thoroughbred years (see, e.g., Fagan, 1986c), are consistently observed in the preparation

characteristics of the early hybrid years. Every area reveals the influences in clinical and school psychological training from both education and psychology. It is observed in the location of training programs, the title and content of courses, the mixture of field experiences, the backgrounds of the trainers, and the backgrounds and employment of practitioners.

The study of early training practices reveals the importance of historical analysis to our understanding of contemporary issues and practices in school psychologist preparation. The history of school psychology, especially in the first half of the twentieth century, was blended with the history of other applied psychology specialties. While we can detect early signs of the specializations that would dominate the development of psychology in the second half of the century, we share considerable commonality in our origins. It is not surprising that we find a sharing of clients, settings, and training as well. Among the training challenges of the future is preserving a common psychological identity as we grow further and further apart through specialization and subspecialization.

## REFERENCES

Anastasi, A. (1993). A century of psychological testing: Origins, problems, and progress. In T. K. Fagan & G. R. VandenBos (Eds.), *Exploring applied psychology: Origins and critical analyses* (pp. 9–36). Washington, DC: American Psychological Association.

Angell, J. R. (1906). *Psychology.* New York: Henry Holt.

*Annual Register 1920–1921.* Urbana: University of Illinois.

Armstrong, W. E. (1964). *The education of teachers: Retrospect and prospect.* Kirksville: Northeast Missouri State Teachers College.

Baldwin, J. M. (1893). *Elements of psychology.* New York: Henry Holt.

Bardon, J. I., Costanza, L. J., & Walker, N. W. (1971). Institutions offering graduate training in school psychology 1970–71. *Journal of School Psychology, 9,* 252–260.

Behavioristic psychology. (1920, March 4). *Journal of Education, 91,* 266.

Benjamin, L. T., & Shields, S. A. (1990). Leta Stetter Hollingworth (1886–1939). In A. N. O'Connell & N. F. Russo (Eds.), *Women in psychology: a bio-bibliographic source book* (pp. 173–183). Westport, CT: Greenwood Press.

Bronner, A. (1917). *The psychology of special abilities and disabilities.* Boston: Little, Brown.

Bronner, A. F., Healy, W., Lowe, G. M., & Shimberg, M. E. (1927). *A manual of individual mental tests and testing.* Boston: Little, Brown.

Brown, D. T., & Minke, K. M. (1986). School psychology graduate training: A comprehensive analysis. *American Psychologist, 41,* 1328–1338.

Cameron, E. H. (1921). *Psychology and the school.* New York: Century.

Cardon, B. W., & French, J. L. (1968–1969). Organization and content of graduate programs in school psychology. *Journal of School Psychology, 7*(2), 28–32.

Carey, K. T., & Wilson, M. S. (1995). Best practices in training school psychologists. In A. Thomas & J. Grimes (Eds.), *Best practices in school psychology—III* (pp. 171–178). Washington, DC: National Association of School Psychologists.

Cattell, J. McK. (1890). Mental tests and measurement. *Mind, 15,* 373–380.

Chicago Psychological Association. (1984). *History of the Chicago Psychological Association 1924–1984.* Chicago: Clark University. (1904, February). *Register.* Worcester, MA: Author.

Cooper, H. (1935). *Certification bulletin no. 3, Certification for school services. Laws, rules, regulations, and information.* Albany: University of the State of New York.

Cornell, E. (1941). Certification of specialized groups of psychologists (school psychologists). *Journal of Consulting Psychology, 5*(2), 62–65.

Cremin, L. A. (1988). *American education: The metropolitan experience 1876–1980.* New York: Harper & Row.

Crissey, M. S. (1983). School psychology: Reminiscences of earlier times. *Journal of School Psychology, 21,* 163–177.

Cubberley, E. P. (1914). *Rural life and education.* Boston: Houghton Mifflin.

Cutts, N. (1914, May). Letter while at The Training School, Vineland, N.J. In, Mount Holyoke College (Ed.), *First class letter of the class of 1913.* South Hadley, MA: Mount Holyoke College.

Cutts, N. E. (Ed.). (1955). *School psychologists at mid-century.* Washington, DC: American Psychological Association.

Fagan, T. K. (1985). Sources for the delivery of school psychological services during 1890–1930. *School Psychology Review, 14,* 378–382.

Fagan, T. K. (1986a). The evolving literature of school psychology. *School Psychology Review, 15,* 430–440.

Fagan, T. K. (1986b). The historical origins and growth of programs to prepare school psychologists in the United States. *Journal of School Psychology, 24,* 9–22.

Fagan, T. K. (1986c). School psychology's dilemma: Reappraising solutions and directing attention to the future. *American Psychologist, 41,* 851–861. See also *School Psychology Review, 16*(1).

Fagan, T. K. (1987). Gesell: The first school psychologist, Part I. The road to Connecticut. *School Psychology Review, 16,* 103–107.

Fagan, T. K. (1988). The first school psychologist in Oklahoma. *Communique, 17*(3), 19.

Fagan, T. K. (1989). Obituary: Norma Estelle Cutts. *American Psychologist, 44,* 1236.

Fagan, T. K. (1990a). Best practices in the training of school psychologists: Considerations for trainers, prospective entry-level and advanced students. In A. Thomas & J. Grimes (Eds.), *Best practices in school psychology—II* (pp. 723–741).

Fagan, T. K. (1990b). A brief history of school psychology in the United States. In A. Thomas & J. Grimes (Eds.), *Best practices in school psychology—II* (pp. 913–929). Washington, DC: National Association of School Psychologists.

Fagan, T. K. (1990c). Research on the history of school psychology: Recent developments, significance, resources, and future directions. In T. R. Kratochwill (Ed.), *Advances in school psychology* (Vol. 7, pp. 151–182). Hillsdale, NJ: Erlbaum.

Fagan, T. K. (1992). Compulsory schooling, child study, clinical psychology, and special education: Origins of school psychology. *American Psychologist, 47,* 236–243.

Fagan, T. K. (1993a). Separate but equal: School psychology's search for organizational identity. *Journal of School Psychology, 31,* 3–90.

Fagan, T. K. (1993b, April). Toward a diversified future for training school psychologists. Trainers of School Psychologists Annual Meeting, Washington, DC.

Fagan, T. K. (1994). Morris and Judith Krugman: Division-16's only spousal presidents. *The School Psychologist, 48*(3), 8, 14–15.

Fagan, T. K. (1995). Trends in the history of school psychology in the United States. In A. Thomas & J. Grimes (Eds.), *Best practices in school psychology—III* (pp. 59–67). Washington, DC: National Association of School Psychologists.

Fagan, T. K. (1996). Witmer's contributions to school psychological services. *American Psychologist, 51,* 241–243.

Fagan, T. K., Delugach, F. J., Mellon, M., & Schlitt, P. (1986). *A bibliographic guide to the literature of professional school psychology 1890–1985.* Washington, DC: National Association of School Psychologists.

Fagan, T. K., McCoy, G., & McCoy, S. (1993). Obituary: T. E. Newland (1903–1992). *American Psychologist, 48,* 988.

Fagan, T. K., & Warden, P. (Eds.). (1996). *Historical encyclopedia of school psychology.* Westport, CT: Greenwood Press.

Fagan, T. K., & Wells, P. D. (1998). Frances Mullen: Her life and contributions to school psychology.

Unpublished paper.

Fagan, T. K., & Wise, P. S. (1994). *School psychology: Past, present, and future.* White Plains, NY: Longman.

Ferguson, D. G. (1963). Training programs in school psychology. In M. G. Gottsegen & G. B. Gottsegen (Eds.), *Professional school psychology* (Vol. II, pp. 287–305). New York: Grune & Stratton.

Fernberger, S. W. (1931). The history of the psychological clinic. In R. A. Brotemarkle (Ed.), *Clinical psychology: Studies in honor of Lightner Witmer to commemorate the thirty-fifth anniversary of the founding of the first psychological clinic* (pp. 10–36). Philadelphia: University of Pennsylvania Press.

Fernberger, S. W. (1932). The American Psychological Association: A historical summary. *Psychological Bulletin, 29,* 1–89.

French, J. (1966). Financial assistance for graduate students in school psychology training programs. *The School Psychologist* (Division-16 newsletter), *20,* 80–82.

French, J. L. (1984). On the conception, birth, and early development of school psychology: With special reference to Pennsylvania. *American Psychologist, 39,* 976–987.

French, J. L. (1986). Books in school psychology: The first forty years. *Professional School Psychology, 1,* 267–277.

French, J. L. (1988). Grandmothers I wish I knew: Contributions of women to the history of school psychology. *Professional School Psychology, 3,* 51–68.

French, J. L. (1990). History of school psychology. In T. B. Gutkin & C. R. Reynolds (Eds.), *Handbook of school psychology* (pp. 3–20). New York: Wiley.

French, J. L., & McCloskey, G. (1979). Characteristics of school psychology program directors and program production. *American Psychologist, 34,* 710–714.

Gesell, A. (1921). *Exceptional children and public school policy.* New Haven, CT: Yale University Press.

Gesell, A. (1952). Autobiography. In E. G. Boring, H. S. Langfeld, & R. M. Yerkes (Eds.), *A history of psychology in autobiography* (Vol. IV, pp. 123–142). Worcester, MA: Clark University Press.

Gesell, A., Goddard, H. H., & Wallin, J. E. W. (1919). The field of clinical psychology as an applied science. *Journal of Applied Psychology, 3,* 81–95.

Goddard, H. H. (1911). The Binet-Simon Measuring Scale for Intelligence, revised. *Training School Bulletin, 8,* 56–42.

Goddard, H. H. (1913). The Binet tests and the inexperienced teacher. *Training School Bulletin, 10,* 9–11.

Goddard, H. H. (1914a). *Feeble-Mindedness: Its causes and consequences.* New York: Macmillan.

Goddard, H. H. (1914b, May). *The research department: What it is, what it is doing, what it hopes to do.* Vineland, NJ: The Training School.

Goddard, H. H. (1921). *Juvenile delinquency.* New York: Dodd, Mead.

Goddard, H. H. (1928). *School training of gifted children.* Yonkers-on-Hudson, NY: World Book.

Goh, D. S. (1977). Graduate training in school psychology. *Journal of School Psychology, 15,* 207–218.

Goodenough, F. L. (1926). *Measurement of intelligence by drawings.* Yonkers-on-Hudson, NY: World Book.

Goodlad, J. I. (1990). *Teachers for our nation's schools.* San Francisco: Jossey-Bass.

Grant, W. V., & Snyder, T. D. (1986). *Digest of education statistics 1985–86.* Washington, DC: U.S. Government Printing Office.

Hanson, D. P. (1990). *A study in development: A history of psychology at James Madison University 1908–1990.* Harrisonburg, VA: Author.

Hayes, S. P. (1918). The psychological laboratory. *Mount Holyoke Alumnae Quarterly, 2*(2), 95–100.

Henley, T. B., Johnson, M. G., Jones, E. M., & Herzog, H. A. (1989). Definitions of psychology. *The Psychological Record, 39,* 143–152.

Hildreth, G. H. (1930). *Psychological service for school problems.* Yonkers-on-Hudson, NY: World Book.

Hiner, N. R., & Hawes, J. M. (Eds.). (1985). *Growing up in America: Children in historical perspective.* Urbana: University of Illinois Press.

Hollingworth, L. S. (1920). *The psychology of subnormal children.* New York: Macmillan.

Hollingworth, L. S. (1933). Psychological service for public schools. *Teachers College Record, 34,* 368–379.

Holmes, A. (1912). *The conservation of the child: A manual of clinical psychology presenting the examination and treatment of backward children.* Philadelphia: Lippincott.

Hug, E. A. (n.d., c. 1970s). *The Department of Educational Psychology: A partial review 1929–1970.* New York: New York University, School of Education.

Hughes, J. N., & Benson, A. J. (1986). University clinics as field placements in school psychology training: A national survey. *Professional School Psychology, 1,* 131–142.

James, W. (1892/1948). *Psychology* (Intro. Ralph Barton Perry). New York: World Publishing.

James, W. (1899/1939). *Talks to teachers on psychology* (Intro. John Dewey and William H. Kilpatrick). New York: Henry Holt.

Knoff, H. M. (1986). *Graduate training in school psychology: A national survey of professional coursework.* Washington, DC: National Association of School Psychologists.

Korman, M. (Ed.). (1973). *Levels and patterns of professional training in psychology.* Washington, DC: American Psychological Association.

Kuhlmann, F. (1922). *A handbook of mental tests* (a further revision and extension of the Binet-Simon Scale). Baltimore, MD: Warwick & York.

Ladd, G. T. (1898). *Outlines of descriptive psychology.* New York: Scribner.

Lambert, N. M. (1993). Historical perspective on school psychology as a scientist-practitioner specialization in school psychology. *Journal of School Psychology, 31,* 163–193.

Litton, M. J. (1986). *The history of the Department of Psychology and Counseling 1905–1986.* Pittsburg, KS: Pittsburg State University Alumni Foundation.

Louttit, C. M. (1939). The nature of clinical psychology. *Psychological Bulletin, 36,* 361–389.

Luckey, G. W. A. (1920). The psychological clinic in practise. *School and Society, 12*(288), 6–12.

Luckey, G. W. A. (1921). The services of the clinical psychologist. *School and Society, 13*(318), 135–137.

Marden, O. S., Merrill, J. B., Lindsey, B. B., Northrop, A. R., Blumenthal, G. A., & Weaver, E. W. (1913). *The uplift book of child culture.* Philadelphia: Uplift Publishing.

Martens, E. H. (1924). *Organization of research bureaus in city school systems* (City School Leaflet No. 14). Washington, DC: U.S. Government Printing Office.

McDougall, W. (1928). *An outline of psychology.* London: Methuen.

McReynolds, P. (1996). Lightner Witmer, Father of clinical psychology. In G. A. Kimble, C. A. Boneau, & M. Wertheimer (Eds.), *Portraits of pioneers in psychology* (Vol. 2, pp. 62–71). Washington, DC: American Psychological Association.

McReynolds, P. (1997). *Lightner Witmer: His life and times.* Washington, DC: American Psychological Association.

Morrow, W. R. (1946). The development of psychological internship training. *Journal of Consulting Psychology, 10,* 165–183.

Mount Holyoke College. (1912–1913). *Catalogue of Mount Holyoke College.* South Hadley, MA: Author.

Mount Holyoke College. (1914, May). *First class letter of the class of 1913.* South Hadley, MA: Author.

Mullen, F. A. (1981). School psychology in the USA: Reminiscences of its origins. *Journal of School Psychology, 19,* 103–119.

Munsterberg, H. (1909). *Psychology and the teacher.* New York: Appleton.

Munsterberg, H. (1914). *Psychology: General and applied.* New York: Appleton.

Newland, T. E. (1981). School psychology-observation and reminiscence. *Journal of School Psychology, 19,* 4–20.

New York University (1929). *NYU bulletin, School of Education, Part I: Curricula and Schedule of courses; 1929–1930,* and *Part II.* New York, NY: Author.

Oral history of Gertha Williams. (1965, September 18). Akron, OH: Archives of the History of American Psychology.

Pillsbury, W. B. (1925). *Education as the psychologist sees it*. New York: Macmillan.

Popplestone, J. A., & McPherson, M. W. (1984). Pioneer psychology laboratories in clinical settings. In J. Brozek (Ed.), *Explorations in the history of psychology in the United States* (pp. 196–272). Cranbury, NJ: Associated University Presses.

Prout, H. T., Toler, K. C., & Eklund, S. J. (1976). Textbook preferences among trainers of school psychologists. *Journal of School Psychology, 14*, 346–354.

*Psychological clinic: Brief survey.* (n.d., c. 1928). Cleveland, OH: Cleveland Public Schools.

Raimy, V. C. (1950). *Training in clinical psychology*. New York: Prentice-Hall.

Reisman, J. R. (1976). *A history of clinical psychology*. New York: Irvington.

Report of Committee of Clinical Section of American Psychological Association (1935). *The Psychological Clinic, 23*(1–2), 1–140.

Reschly, D. J. (1995, August 10). *Characteristics of school psychology graduate education and school-based practice: Implications for doctoral specialty definition*. Paper presented at the Second Annual School Psychology Training Conference, New York.

Reschly, D. J., & McMaster-Beyer, M. (1991). Influences of degree level, institutional orientation, college affiliation, and accreditation status on school psychology graduate education. *Professional Psychology: Research and Practice, 22*, 368–374.

Reschly, D. J., & Wilson, M. S. (1995). School psychology practitioners and faculty: 1986 to 1991–92 trends in demographics, roles, satisfaction, and system reform. *School Psychology Review, 24*, 62–80.

Rosebrook, W. M. (1942). Psychological service for schools on a regional basis. *Journal of Consulting Psychology, 6*, 196–200.

Rosenberg, R. (1982). *Beyond separate spheres: Intellectual roots of modern feminism*. New Haven, CT: Yale University Press.

Sandoval, J. (1993). The history of interventions in school psychology. *Journal of School Psychology, 31*, 195–217.

Saretzky, G. D., & Davis, J. E. (1986). *A guide to the Gertrude Hildreth Papers and Test Collection*. Princeton, NJ: Educational Test Service Archives.

Silverman, R. E. (c. 1971). *History of the Department of Psychology at University College*. New York: New York University (available from archivist at Bobst Library).

Smith, D. K., & Fagan, T. K. (1995). Resources on the training of school psychologists. In A. Thomas & J. Grimes (Eds.), *Best practices in school psychology—III* (pp. 1257–1271). Washington, DC: National Association of School Psychologists.

Spring, J. (1989). *American education: An introduction to social and political aspects*. White Plains, NY: Longman.

Spring, J. (1990). *The American school 1642–1990*. White Plains, NY: Longman.

Stern, W. (1911). The supernormal child II (Trans. Lucy Day). *Journal of Educational Psychology, 2*, 181–190.

Stern, W. (1914). *The psychological methods of testing intelligence* (Trans. Guy Montrose Whipple). Baltimore, MD: Warwick & York.

Stout, P. D. (1954, Dec.). The Department of Psychology at New York University. *The New York State Psychologist, 7*(3), 3–4.

Symonds, P. M. (Ed.). (1942). *Journal of Consulting Psychology, 6*(4). (This issue is devoted almost entirely to school psychology.)

Talbot, E. B. (1918). History and scope of the department. *Mount Holyoke Alumnae Quarterly, 2*(2), 92–95.

Terman, L. M. (1916). *The measurement of intelligence*. Boston: Houghton Mifflin.

Terman, L. M. (1919). *The intelligence of school children*. Boston: Houghton Mifflin.

Thorndike, E. L. (1906). *The principles of teaching based on psychology*. New York: A. G. Seiler.

Thorndike, E. L. (1912). *Education: A first book*. New York: Macmillan.

Titchener, E. B. (1919). *A textbook of psychology*. New York: Macmillan.

Trachtman, G. M. (1987). Bootstrapping it in the Big Apple: A history of school psychology at New York University. *Professional School Psychology, 2*, 281–296.

Van Sickle, J. H., Witmer, L., & Ayres, L. P. (1911). *Provision for exceptional children in the public schools* (U.S. Bureau of Education Bulletin No. 14). Washington, DC: U.S. Government Printing Office.

Veatch, B. A. (1978). *Historical and demographic influences in the development of a situation specific model of school psychological services*. University of Cincinnati, Dissertation Abstracts Intl., *39*(09), Sec. A, 5423.

Wallin, J. E. W. (1911). The new clinical psychology and the psycho-clinicist. *Journal of Educational Psychology, 2*, 191–210.

Wallin, J. E. W. (1914). *The mental health of the school child*. New Haven, CT: Yale University Press.

Wallin, J. E. W. (1919). The field of the clinical psychologist and the kind of training needed by the psychological examiner. *School and Society, 9*(225), 463–470.

Wallin, J. E. W. (1921). *Problems of subnormality*. Yonkers-on-Hudson, NY: World Book.

Wallin, J. E. W. (1927). *Clinical and abnormal psychology*. Boston: Houghton Mifflin.

Wallin, J. E. W. (1955a). *Education of mentally handicapped children*. New York: Harper & Brothers.

Wallin, J. E. W. (1955b). *The odyssey of a psychologist: Pioneering experiences in special education, clinical psychology, and mental hygiene with a comprehensive bibliography of the author's publications.* Wilmington, DE: Author.

Wallin, J. E. W. (1960). History of the struggles within the American Psychological Association to attain membership requirements, test standardization, certification of psychological practitioners, and professionalization. *Journal of General Psychology, 63,* 287–308.

Wallin, J. E. W. (1961). PhDs in psychology who functioned as clinical psychologists between 1896 and 1910. *The Psychological Record, 11,* 339–341.

Wallin, J. E. W., & Ferguson, D. G. (1967). The development of school psychological services. In J. R. Magary (Ed.), *School psychological services in theory and practice, a handbook* (pp. 1–29). Englewood Cliffs, NJ: Prentice-Hall.

Whipple, G. M. (1913). Amateurism in Binet testing once more. *Journal of Educational Psychology, 4,* 301–302.

Whipple, G. M. (1914). *Manual of mental and physical tests: Part I: Simpler processes.* Baltimore, MD: Warwick & York.

Whipple, G. M. (1915). *Manual of mental and physical tests: Part II: Complex processes,* Baltimore, MD: Warwick & York.

Witmer, L. (1894a). Aesthetics of form. *Psychological Review, 1,* 205–208.

Witmer, L. (1894b). Zur experimentellen Aesthetik einfacher raumlicher Formverhaltnisse (On the experimental aesthetics of simple spatial relations of form). *Philosophische Studien, 9,* 96–144, 209–263.

Witmer, L. (1896). Practical work in psychology. *Pediatrics, 2,* 462–471.

Witmer, L. (1897). The organization of practical work in psychology. *Psychological Review, 4,* 116–117.

Witmer, L. (1907a). Clinical psychology. *The Psychological Clinic, 1,* 1–9.

Witmer, L. (1907b). University courses in psychology. *The Psychological Clinic, 1,* 25–35.

Witmer, L. (1911). Courses in psychology at the summer school of the University of Pennsylvania. *The Psychological Clinic, 4,* 245–273.

Wortham, S. C. (1992). *Childhood 1892–1992.* Wheaton, MD: Association for Childhood Education International.

Wundt, W. (1912). *An introduction to psychology* (Trans. Rudolf Pintner). London: George Allen & Unwin.

## CHAPTER 2

# THE FUTURES OF SCHOOL PSYCHOLOGY: CONCEPTUAL MODELS FOR ITS DEVELOPMENT AND EXAMPLES OF THEIR APPLICATIONS

THOMAS OAKLAND
*University of Florida*
JACQUELINE CUNNINGHAM
*Wilmington, DE*

This chapter discusses issues important to descriptions of the futures of school psychology. Attempts to foresee these futures require, minimally, knowledge of the past and current status together with the current and emerging conditions that may influence future trajectories. These conditions are internal to and under some control of school psychology, as well as external to and largely beyond its control. Readers are encouraged to consult other sources for a more complete review of school psychology's rich history and current status (e.g., this edition of the *Handbook on School Psychology; Journal of School Psychology,* 1993, *31*(1)). Those interested in additional views on the futures of school psychology are encouraged to consult the following: Bickman and Ellis (1990); *Journal of School Psychology,* 1995, *33*(3); Phillips (1990); *School Psychology Quarterly,* 1995, *10*(3); and *School Psychology Review,* 1994, *23*(4).

Attempts to foresee the futures also require suitable conceptual models. Three models commonly used to forecast the futures of school psychology (i.e., stage, linear trends, and contextual) are reviewed and evaluated. The chapter concludes by identifying some issues that affect the futures of school psychology.

## MODELS FOR UNDERSTANDING PSYCHOLOGY'S DEVELOPMENT AND FUTURE TRENDS

Approaches to understanding school psychology's development have been based on lineal and contextual models of disciplinary development (Cunningham, 1994). Lineal approaches, including stage models, are unidirectional and deterministic and are concerned with the effects particular variables (e.g., a country's level of economic development) have in producing progressive change within a discipline or profession; contextual models are concerned with examining relationships between a discipline or profession and its environment, and they try to explain changes within them as the world in which they exist is changing (Furomoto, 1989; Minton, 1992).

One stage model (Catterall, 1979), one lineal trend model (Ogilvy, 1982), and two contextual models (Altman, 1987; Fagan, 1986) are critically reviewed for their heuristic value in explaining the mechanisms that underlie the growth of school psychology. Conclusions are drawn about the usefulness of these models in helping us improve knowledge of how growth trends for school psychology and other specialties may be optimized.

## Lineal Approaches
### *Catterall's Four Levels of Development Model*

Interest in the development of school psychology gained impetus through the publications of *Psychology in the Schools in International Perspectives* by Catterall in 1977, 1978, and 1979. The three-volume work culminated efforts initiated by one of the founders of the international school psychology movement (Oakland, 1993) to promote understanding of the ways in which economic and social factors contribute to growth in the field (Catterall, 1979). Because Catterall's model has an international focus, it offers broader perspectives than those confined to only one nation. His work is largely a compendium of first-hand reports on the status of school psychology by international experts, each representing 1 of more than 40 countries throughout the world. In summarizing and integrating this information, Catterall drew the following conclusions.

Four factors broadly relate a country's level of development to the impact on school psychology: its general levels of economic development, programs of educational development (including its status on the training and use of teachers), provisions for children needing special education, and development of psychology and psychological organizations. Specific social, cultural, geographic, and linguistic factors, mainly associated with northern European traditions, also are strongly related to school psychology's development.

In adopting a stage model, Catterall's (1979) conception of development in school psychology reflected a view that progress in a discipline is sequential and directed toward a predetermined goal. His descriptions of the important status characteristics of countries at four consecutive levels of development in school psychology are summarized as follows.

### *Characteristics of Countries at Level IV (Lowest Level)*
Countries at this level generally have an agricultural economy. Publicly supported schools are not well developed, and there is no compulsory education. Elementary school teachers tend to have less formal training and to come from families of lower socioeconomic status than secondary school teachers. Only extreme cases of physical handicap and/or mental retardation are identified for treatment, and interventions, if available, are provided in residential institutions. Psychological organizations do not exist. Applied psychologists tend to work in residential schools for the physically handicapped. An occasional undergraduate university program in psychology is typically taught as an academic subject, often within education or philosophy.

### *Characteristics of Countries at Level III*
Countries at this level have begun to develop an industrial economy. There are compulsory attendance laws for students 7 to 14 or 15 years old. Emphasis is placed on teaching the hypothetical normal student, and there is little or no individualization of instruction. Experimental classes for the less severely handicapped have begun. Advocacy groups are formed to educate the public on the need for these classes. Psychological organizations have begun to exist, primarily to advocate the legal protection of psychological practice. The specialty of clinical psychology has begun to emerge. School psychologists often are former teachers who return to school to obtain minimum training for this profession.

### *Characteristics of Countries at Level II*
Industrial development is at a high level, and employment is fairly high. Educational programs prosper at all levels, from preschool through postsecondary. The goal is to educate all children and youths. There is no differentiation in training requirements for elementary and secondary school teachers, although there is increasing specialization in the teaching profession. A wide range of interventions, involving combinations of special class, resource class, and regular class placements, are available to meet the needs of students with increasingly recognized complex learning problems. A psychological organization is well established, and psychology is held in high esteem by other professions. School psychologists pioneer in developing curricula that facilitate improved psychological skills in students. School psychology continues to function predominantly at just below the doctoral level. One or more associations exclusively for school psychologists form as the belief mounts that the traditional academic or clinical psychological associations do not meet the needs of these professionals.

### *Characteristics of Countries at Level I*
The nation begins to value the quality of life over the production of material goods. Education begins to take on a new dimension of helping people learn how to live more effectively in the present and how to make better use of their leisure time. The unique needs of the learner are fitted to a given kind of curriculum that is under the direction of a teaching staff that functions best in a particular type of setting. The gap between regular and special education begins to close. Services that have been "special" in the past are seen as extensions of the individualization that characterizes the overall education program.

Psychology demonstrates the following six characteristics: (1) the discipline facilitates international communication as these countries become increasingly committed to the ideal of fostering the maximum development of all nations; (2) psychological organizations continue to strengthen professionally; (3) many older legal issues in psychology begin to be resolved or to be regulated by larger social agencies; (4) rivalries among psychological specialties begin to diminish; (5) specialization in psychology continues; (6) school psychology, per se, reflects greater diversity in roles and functions. Increases in differentiation within the profession among level I countries result in greater energy increasingly directed toward individualization of education in regular education, not just special education.

### Strengths and Limitations of Catterall's Model

Catterall's (1979) stage model represents a significant and original attempt to relate the development of school psychology on an international scale to structural (e.g., economic) factors that create the bases for stability and change in a country in general, and in a profession in particular. The model identifies several national conditions that vary synchronously with advancement through levels of development in school psychology; among the most potent factors is a country's ability to individualize education for all of its children and youths, including those who have handicapping conditions. The model is well supported. Structural factors identified as significant to school psychology's status on an international basis overlap those identified by Russell (1984) as influencing the development of psychology more generally.

While seemingly valid, the model embodies shortcomings inherent to all stage models. It implies that progress in a field is sequential, even, and directed toward a predetermined goal. As such, it cannot account for the uneven quality of development, particular that seen in developing countries (Moghaddam, 1987; Moghaddam & Taylor, 1985). According to Moghaddam and Taylor, psychology develops largely because of fortuitous circumstances, such as local political perceptions of need for particular psychological services, or the alliance of a local university with a major university in the West.

Catterall's (1979) stage model bears the shortcomings of deterministic approaches in understanding development in psychology. As such, it is not particularly helpful in understanding problems generated by rapid economic development and social change which create demands for appropriate school psychological services in diverse regions throughout the world (Oakland & Saigh, 1989).

Therefore, the model has limited applications, especially since interest in understanding psychology's development here and abroad focuses to a large extent on uneven development in an attempt to identify options available for improving the relevance of psychological theory and practice in specific contexts (e.g., Connolly, 1985; Durojaiye, 1984; Nixon, 1990; Oakland & Saigh, 1989; Salazar, 1984). Approaches that can guide the discipline are better able to answer ecologically based questions on the perceptions and needs of persons who sustain particular roles and models of practice for psychologists in given national contexts (Nixon, 1990). Stage models, including Catterall's (1979) model, are insufficient in this regard because they do not consider the probabilistic and multidirectional nature of change that characterizes many aspects of development in psychology's diverse contexts (Moghaddam & Taylor, 1985) or the serendipitous events that affect a profession.

For example, Phillips (1990) reports that development in school psychology is best viewed as fairly chancy and probabilistic rather than linear and deterministic. Social, personalistic (e.g., perceptions of leaders), and even fortuitous contributions provide stability and change in the field. Change in school psychology often is paradoxical and circular (e.g., the tendency of rigid role identification to be transformed into role diffusion). Bardon (1979) presented a dramatic illustration of this situation when, as the expert representing the United States in Catterall's (1979) research, he reported that school psychologists in this country no longer are known as school psychologists when they assume administrative roles in a school system. Despite its limitations, Catterall's model accurately underscores particular social conditions, especially a country's ability to individualize education, as being strongly associated with the development of school psychology.

Within a historical framework, Catterall's (1979) scholarship has significant implications for understanding the history of school psychology because it provides international accounts that tend to support the assumption that school psychology focuses primarily on the individual (Cushman, 1990, 1991; Hermans, Kempen, & von Loon, 1992; Howard, 1991; Sampson, 1989; Sarason, 1988; Schneider, 1990; Triandis, 1989) rather than, more comprehensively, on schooling. School psychology's mission, wherever found in the world, has focused more or less exclusively on individual differences and insufficiently on environments in its efforts to apply psychology to optimize the effects of education. Some believe (Phillips, 1990) that the specialty's goal of contributing psychological insight to the individualization of education will not be fulfilled until school psychology adopts models of practice that extend its concern for individual differences to a broadened involvement with schools, schooling, and society.

School psychology's mission could have been considerably different. For example, there were possibilities during psychology's formative period for the adoption of an applied educational psychology model (Binet, 1908; Binet & Simon, 1911), a school-consultative model (James, 1899/1983), or a social-environmental model (Mead, 1899).

## Ogilvy's Trend Analyses for the 1980s

Having examined some advantages and disadvantages of one stage model, we now turn to Ogilvy's (1982) trend analyses for the 1980s. Although it offers considerable appeal, limitations demonstrated in stage models also characterize trend analyses.

Ogilvy's (1982) trend analyses were proposed at the 1980 Olympia Conference on the Future of School Psychology to highlight critical factors believed likely to influence the development of school psychology in the United States during the 1980s. At this conference, economic, geopolitical, and social trends, evident for at least a decade, were graphically described by Ogilvy, who utilized actuarial data published by credible sources. The information indicated that the 1980s would be a period of a national economic restructuring, supplanting the long postwar era that included vigorous economic growth. During the 1980s the world would become more dangerous and competitive. Postwar optimism would turn toward pessimism and fear of the future.

During the decade, radical changes in economic, geopolitical, and cultural forces were expected to characterize the nation in various ways. The growing economy of the postwar period was expected to become stagnant because of high debt and decreased manufacturing productivity. A work force formerly based on manufacturing would be replaced by one based on information technology.

The economic dominance of the United States in the world would be replaced by global economic interdependence. Low postwar constraints on resource utilization and costs would turn to high constraints, seen particularly in rising energy costs. The high population growth rate would shift to a decreasing growth rate. There would be a change from a homogeneous to a multiethnic and diverse society. Postwar faith in institutions would turn to cynicism and distrust, and the crime rate would rise significantly.

While Ogilvy (1982) focused on structural factors (e.g., economic change) that would produce trends toward social diversity, his main interest was in the political reactions these trends would be apt to generate. Accordingly, he presented a functional analysis of trends he believed would result from problems prevalent since the 1970s. He reasoned that a positive trend during the following decade would be a return to moderate conservatism, whereas a negative one would be a persistent lack of political consensus and absence of core social values (e.g., values pertaining to saving, hard work, family, community, basic education).

Ogilvy (1982) speculated that high stress, diversity, complexity, and intolerable tradeoffs would be engendered by these prevailing forces and would lead either to political and social conservatism within the country or, conversely, to greater diversity, threats of reactionary authoritarianism in government, and the likelihood of a major war. Either set of alternatives was possible. However, he noted that a consensus in favor of political and social conservatism had begun to form to support an integrated agenda for decreasing government spending; increasing military strength; and returning to core values centered on saving, hard work, family, neighborhood, community, basic education, and vocational education.

The main implications of Ogilvy's (1982) trend analyses for the future course of school psychology during the 1980s were that problems would be imposed by decreased federal funding and federal responsibility for education, coexisting with increased demands to deliver appropriate services to a multiethnic student population with special needs. Furthermore, progress during this period was expected to rest primarily on the development and implementation of public policies that would ameliorate the loss of stability and the threat of disintegration, which were apparent in many societal institutions involved with economic, business, government, cultural, educational, and other domains (Ogilvy, 1979, 1982).

### Strengths and Limitations of Ogilvy's Trend Analyses

Ogilvy's (1982) trend analyses have merit in their timely identification of national and international conditions. However, their descriptive value is constrained by overgeneralization of relationships between macrolevel (e.g., sociopolitical trends toward diversity) and microlevel (e.g., individual political behavior) variables that are expected to cause change in the field; their prescriptive value for guiding school psychology's development is even more limited. In addressing these issues, Alpert (1985) noted that trend analysis has three major drawbacks. First, the method is dependent on one's ability to predict the future of one's environment. Second, the method focuses on what one thinks the field will become rather than on what one thinks it should become. Thus, the method implies that professions will take a passive rather than a proactive stance. Third, data trends are frequently misinterpreted. Predictions are reasoned and data-based and thus assumed to be objective, reliable, and valid. Research is not as trustworthy as is often believed. Social scientists are inclined to select theories consistent with personal values and attitudes and then seek data that validate their beliefs, ignoring contradictory data. The futurist can attend to some trends and not to others. The predictions follow logically and thus are credible. However, had other trends been considered, other predictions would have followed.

There were many examples in the 1980s of how trends toward both political consensus and diversity balance one another, a process that is described more fully later. Whereas a shift to moderate conservatism, predicated by Ogilvy (1982), was seen during the Reagan years, those years also accentuated a shift to individualism that discouraged, rather than supported, a consensus on traditional values, centered on concern for community (Smith, 1990).

However, Ogilvy's (1982) expectations of a conservative consensus in the face of rising social diversity were commonly held. For example, books that encouraged the development of a shared public philosophy (Bellah, Madsen, Sullivan, Swidler, & Tipton, 1985; Bloom, 1987) were widely read and persuasive (Smith, 1990). However, expressions of cohesiveness were fragmentary, with centrifugal trends characterizing

the decade (Altman, 1987; Odegaard, 1987; Smith, 1990).

Also in opposition to Ogilvy's (1982) speculations, political conservatism tended to heighten rather than lessen problems associated with diversity in education. For example, increased individualism led to decreased support of equal rights for the underprivileged (Rokeach & Ball-Rokeach, 1989); this in turn intensified problems associated with meeting the special needs of a multiethnic and heterogeneous school population (Oakland, 1985).

Ogilvy's pessimism about the nation's future, including the future of school psychology, was reasonable if diversity and lack of faith in government were to remain unabated. For example, attempts in school psychology for national education reform (National Association of School Psychologists/National Coalition of Advocates for Students, 1985) lacked coherent conceptual and research bases (Oakland & Cunningham, 1990). A consensus about the identification of problems were missing (Rosenfield, 1990), and solutions were even more elusive.

Some psychologists believe that centrifugal trends promote positive consequences (Altman, 1987; Kukla, 1992; McNally, 1992; Phillips, 1990). For example, some think that the impetus for competing internationally and assimilating international perspectives is an important challenge for the future development of psychology (Oakland, 1985; Rosenzweig, 1984).

Ogilvy's (1982) predictions seemed vapid to participants at Olympia for the same reasons that Catterall's (1979) stage model offers insufficiently substantive explanations of disciplinary development. Both view change as externally imposed and along too narrow a continuum. While the ubiquity of centrifugal trends was well reported by Ogilvy in his conference address, his analyses lacked specific and concrete explanations of discipline-environment interrelationships that reflected the pervasiveness of these trends. Therefore, opportunities were missed for construing viable ways of alleviating negative aspects of centrifugalism that occurred within school psychology's organizational, professional, cultural, or other contexts.

In contrast, a cogent grasp of the meaningfulness of centrifugal trends for psychology's development was conveyed by Altman (1987) at the Utah Conference on Graduate Education in 1987 (Bickman, 1987). Altman demonstrated the efficacy of nonlinear perspectives, emphasizing multiplicity and wholeness, and his contextual analysis provided salient understandings of the historical events in which psychology's development is embedded. These analyses enabled conference participants to weigh options on which policies for graduate education could be decided (Bickman, 1987).

Thus, lineal trend analyses are limited in understanding national conditions that contribute to disciplinary development. Contextual approaches may be better suited for this purpose. Two are considered.

## Contextual Approaches

### *Fagan's Contextual Analysis of School Psychology's Dilemma*

Fagan's (1986) analysis of school psychology's emerging identity considered the complex interplay of variables, including accreditation and credentialing mechanisms, students' perceptions of needs for training, public perceptions of needs for services, and developments in the fields of education and psychology. He believed that the years between 1955 and 2050 comprise the temporal context within which a structure of school psychological practice is emerging from an interplay of historical and contemporary forces. The analysis is a good example of a diachronic (uneven) and contextual (transactional), rather than synchronic and lineal approach to understanding disciplinary development (Altman & Rogoff, 1987) in that it defines development as continuously changing relationships among personalistic (e.g., public perception of needs) and environmental (e.g., accreditation mechanisms) aspects of a total pattern of disciplinary growth that characterizes school psychology (Fagan, 1986).

The analysis was offered by Fagan to clarify issues that were creating an enduring area of conflict, frequently termed "school psychology's dilemma" (Bardon, 1982, 1983; Bardon, Brown, & Hyman, 1979; Phillips, 1981, 1985a, 1985b; Trachtman, 1981). This dilemma is associated with the different groups that advocate two different sets of standards for credentialing school psychologists and accrediting their professional preparation programs.

Rather than attempting to understand these issues through stage theory or lineal trend analyses, Fagan (1986) utilized holistic and historical perspectives. He underscored the importance of the nature of quality control mechanisms in promoting an understanding of a whole system of interrelated variables that create conditions for change in school psychology.

Mechanisms for credentialing and accreditation are based in the fields of education and psychology, respectively, and stem from relatively weak positions of power rather than from a uniform position of authority. No authoritative agency can direct a specific change throughout one aspect of the system without upsetting other aspects of the system. The system as a whole functions as an intricate network of social and political interrelationships.

Historically, accreditation of training programs had been granted by authority of the Council on Postsecondary Accreditation (COPA), which had superseded both the power of accreditation agencies in education—that is, the National Council for Accreditation of Teacher Education (NCATE) and the National Association of School Psychologists (NASP)—and that in psychology, that is, the American Psychological Association (APA). Thus, COPA had the power to determine who accredits; once a determination had been made, the power to accredit was given solely to the designated agency.

However, COPA's authority always was limited to accreditation and had not extended to credentialing because the credentialing of professionals for practice is the legal right of the 50 states, and their power is associated with state-level professional associations in both education and psychology. Therefore, COPA had been encouraged to support these associations in their efforts at quality control through a reciprocal accreditation mechanism under its national purview. Since professional associations in psychology and education historically have opposed one another on the doctoral issue, COPA had necessarily accredited training in accordance with two separate sets of standards. These differences had reinforced a bifurcation of school psychology (Fagan, 1986). Although COPA has been replaced recently by CORPA (Committee on Recognition of Postsecondary Accreditation), the bifurcated standards in school psychology still remain.

Approaches to resolving this dilemma have spanned broad parameters (Bardon, 1982; Phillips, 1985a, 1985b; Trachtman, 1981), including advocacy for two types of practice—a psychology of schooling that is controlled by doctoral-level practice in psychology and a traditional form of school psychology that is controlled by education and nondoctoral practice (Bardon, 1982, 1983). Simultaneously, there are recurring requests that NASP join with APA in requiring the doctorate as the entry-level degree for school psychological practice on the premise that most states will accept this criterion and find mechanisms to implement it (Brown, 1987).

According to Fagan (1986), any of these alternative courses of action probably would be aborted through the workings of a whole system of interrelated influences by which school psychology's status is defined. For example, were NASP and APA to join forces in requiring a doctorate, the education community is likely to maintain its present functioning by a variety of reactions, which include the following.

Roles of school psychologists would be taken over by nondoctoral professionals already working in the schools (e.g., psychoeducational diagnosticians). A new national organization for nondoctoral practitioners would be established. Most state school psychology associations, made up of non–doctoral degree holders, would affiliate with this new national organization. Almost all the nondoctoral training programs would continue to operate and be recognized by NCATE. Certification standards would change little.

Change in school psychology is thought to occur multidirectionally (Fagan, 1986). The opposing forces that create bifurcation in school psychology need to be mediated in ways conducive to systemic, rather than unilateral, change. To this end, communication, mediation, and cooperation within relevant professional communities at the local, state, and national levels are important sources of influence because they can contribute the improved public and professional relations needed to further the natural evolution of school psychology. Accordingly, those who want to resolve the thorny issues of entry-level training and title standards must be content to let the field progress toward its natural maturation and a time when these issues will be less threatening; the issues then may be resolvable at the national level through joint agreement by agencies in education and psychology.

In support of this position, Fagan (1986) directs our attention to inevitable outcomes that presently result either from exerting strong doctoral-licensing control over school psychologists, training programs, and state association activity or from the presence of educational examiners-diagnosticians. In Fagan's judgment, the full maturation of school psychology and its representation as a doctoral-level specialty are dependent on the complex workings of interre-

lated factors such as perceptions by students and practitioners that advanced training is an avenue to improved practice, employment opportunity, and mobility; public support of educational excellence and teacher competency; and willingness by other specialties to accord the field reasonable opportunity to continue as part of professional psychology. While Fagan believes that the historical setting in which school psychology is developing favors a robust vitality, he nonetheless speculates that the level of professional autonomy and capacity for comprehensive service envisioned at the Thayer conference in 1955 (Cutts, 1955) will not be practical on a national basis until around 2050, or nearly 100 years after the conference.

### Strengths and Limitations of Fagan's Contextual Analysis

Although the United States has one of the most favorable ratios of school psychologists-to-pupils in the world (Oakland & Cunningham, 1989), Fagan's (1986) cogent analysis of the drawbacks experienced by school psychology in seeking professional maturity in this country is a dramatic example of the complexity of social forces in the evolution of a field. Fagan's analysis identifies problems that transcend entry-level training and title issues. He convincingly states that arbitrary agreements on these matters would do little to liberate school psychology of restrictions placed on professional functioning. Moreover, since role restrictions are felt in sectors more strongly affiliated with education (i.e., with NASP), as well as those strongly affiliated with psychology (i.e., with APA), his views are pragmatic in suggesting that appropriate directions for the future need to address areas of mutual concern in the delivery of school psychology services.

In directing our attention to the bifurcated system that characterizes school psychology's organization, Fagan (1986) encourages a proactive rather than a passive stance. His contextual analysis identifies and evaluates the political implications of specific courses of action. The key to school psychology's progress will be the extent to which APA and NASP collaborate on issues of service provision without getting bogged down on entry-level and title issues. The main thrust of this plan is focused on expediency and the reconciliation of political concerns.

Conflicts in education and psychology need to be defined not mainly by the political necessities they engender but also, and more importantly, in ways that promote institutional innovation and intellectual change. Fagan's (1986) analysis is heuristic because it identifies important interrelationships that should be monitored in the attempt to guide the development of school psychology. For example, perceptions by school psychology students of the advantages of obtaining a doctoral degree should be studied along with indexes of public support for education as a way of tracking conditions that favor change in the profession.

However, the analysis ignores other variables that are difficult to assess for their relevance to improved practice; these variables relate to difficulties practitioners have in internalizing new ideas when the ideas compete with tacit understandings they have acquired as part of their socialization into a profession (Alpert, 1985). Before political issues can be meaningfully resolved, tacit, taken-for-granted, collective responses to conflicts among differing traditions in education and psychology need to be examined to see how they impede prospects for change. Conceivably, a prevalence in psychology of decontextualized views of the person (i.e., those based too narrowly on individual qualities) hampers school psychologists from acquiring the judgmental and inferential skills needed for broadened diagnostic and intervention activities in schools and for a deepened involvement with schooling (Phillips, 1990).

Because accepted theories and practices are inextricably embedded in social contexts (Kuhn, 1970), methods for creating change in a profession are elusive. Although Fagan (1986) emphasizes the importance of communication among members of the intraprofessional community in response to pressures from outside of it, he gives little attention to the communication that also must occur concerning insufficiently examined philosophies of practice that emanate from school psychology itself. Thus, further analysis is needed to see how conflict over entry-level and title issues reflects the more essential problem of conceptualizing the requirements of socially meaningful practices. Ultimately, a contextual model is needed that will relate the social, cultural, historical, and moral dimensions of scientific psychological knowledge to the development of a science of psychological practice (Hoshmand & Polkinghorne, 1992; Phillips, 1987).

Additional development of social-contextual thought for representing and guiding psychology's development is found in Altman's (1987) model. Here, the confluence of extraprofessional and in-traprofessional forces that are shaping the discipline's evolution is further explained by principles of transactionalism and contextualism (Dewey & Bentley, 1949; Gergen, 1982; Pepper, 1942, 1967; Rosnow, 1981; Stokols, 1987; Wapner, 1987) and dialectics (Altman, 1975; Brent, 1978).

## Altman's Transactional-Contextual and Dialectic Model of Disciplinary Development

Contextual models focus on the political aspects of disciplinary growth and closely link progress in a profession with changes in social perceptions rather than stages of development. The difference is confronted directly and obliquely in Altman's (1987) model.

Altman's consideration of opposing trends in psychology's history from the 1900s to the present led to his dialectic view of the discipline's patterns of change. During this period, broad trends toward conformity and independence in the field were associated with similar trends in larger sociopolitical contexts, creating cycles of centripetalism and centrifugalism both intraprofessionally and extraprofessionally. The cyclical nature of these trends contributed to Altman's holistic conception of the social influences that affect the growth of the discipline.

A circumplex model of Altman's analysis is shown in Figure 2.1. The model depicts the contextual and dialectic bases of Altman's conceptualizations. Two central dimensions of cohesion (unity, affiliation, and centripetalism) and independence (disunity and centrifugalism) are represented on two central axes: from extreme unity (i.e., centripetal) to extreme disunity (i.e., centrifugal) of intraprofessional (vertical axis) and extraprofessional foci (horizontal axis). The area between the four poles displays the varying degrees of unity or disunity observed in the predominating trends from the pre-1900s to the present.

The pre-1900 years are unified extraprofessionally (socially and politically) but diversified intraprofessionally. The period from the 1900s to 1960s is depicted as strongly unified, both extraprofessionally and intraprofessionally, with intermittent extraprofessional centrifugal trends that have little effect on intraprofessional cohesion. Conversely, the period from the 1960s to the present is depicted as strongly diversified, both intraprofessionally and extraprofessionally. That is, trends toward centripetalism have evolved into opposing centrifugal trends to the

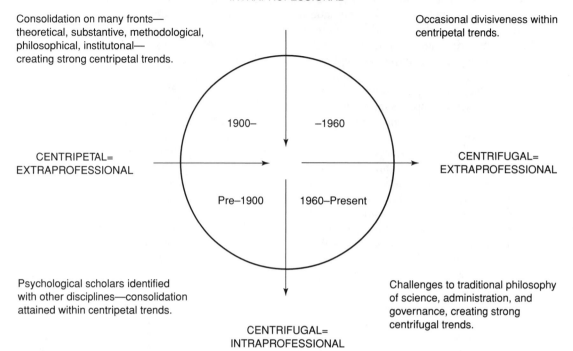

FIGURE 2.1  Circumplex Model of Altman's analysis of centripetal-centrifugal trends in extraprofessional and intraprofessional contexts of psychology's development in the United States.

Adapted from Altman (1987). Reproduced with permission.

extent that centrifugalism strongly characterizes American society and psychology at present. True to a dialectic model, *complementarity* and *opposition* on two orthogonal dimensions form the basis of this analysis.

### Dialectic Complementarity

Centripetal and centrifugal trends in intraprofessional domains have tended to complement similar trends in extraprofessional contexts. Beginning around the turn of the twentieth century and continuing to the 1960s, centripetalism characterized American psychology as it consolidated on many fronts. Psychological theorizing and research were increasingly cohesive, as the field set down its substantive theories and topics and defined its content and approach to psychological phenomena. The result was a powerful centripetal trend that unified psychology around a normative and idealized methodological strategy and a logical, positivist philosophy of science that emphasized operational definition; analysis; and the search for antecedent-consequent relationships as a basis for inferences about causation, for discovery of uni-

versal and generalizable laws of behavior, and for the sharp separation between the behaving organism and its environment (Altman, 1987).

An educational infrastructure that reinforced centripetal trends also evolved gradually during the 1900–1960 period in that graduate education was more general and less specialized in comparison with the expansion years of the 1960s and beyond. This made it possible for psychologists to be more easily identified with general psychology yet affiliate with psychological specialties.

In addition to its supportive educational infrastructure, psychology's institutional infrastructure during this period also contributed to a sense of cohesion. The APA served as the primary and strong centripetal force for the discipline during the 1900–1960 period by seeking to establish a consolidated base for a unified profession.

During that period, centripetal trends complementary to those in psychology furnished consensual views within social and political contexts. Strong centripetal qualities in American society were reflected in the citizenry's fundamental faith in the democratic system, the presidency, and the governing structure. These expectations for strong leadership were boosted in a post-World War II boom in the economy which brought prosperity for many Americans. Nonetheless, despite the ubiquity of centripetal trends, the clarity of purpose and direction that was seen in American society and psychology during this period gave way to divisive forces, both extraprofessionally and intraprofessionally, beginning in the mid-1960s (Altman, 1987).

Socially and politically, trends toward unification evolved into disunity as the average citizen's knowledge, expectations, and values changed because of events in the 1960s and 1970s. Social upheavals with regard to civil rights, the quagmire of Vietnam, and a presidential resignation after a loss of faith in leadership divided the citizenry into irreconcilable constituencies whose viewpoints tended to erode fundamental social values that previously had bound the American people together in at least a loose way.

Centrifugal trends in social and political contexts were complemented by similar trends in higher education. The dramatic changes in American society beginning in the 1960s had counterparts in higher education in the form of protest movements, students' participation in governance, and new attitudes toward undergraduate and graduate curriculums. Also, lessened financial support exacerbated centrifugal trends by encouraging academic departments to become increasingly insular, self-protective, and adversarial. Institutional needs to generate external economic support favored the technical-professional components of universities—engineering, science, medicine, business, law, pharmacy, and computer science—departments that have a direct bearing on economic progress. They fared better than others in securing the resource commitments of their states and universities (Altman, 1987). Education and psychology did not appear on this list.

Paralleling the sociopolitical and educational contexts, centrifugal trends emerged in psychology, provoking new curriculum and training orientations, broadened theoretical and methodological perspectives, and changes in the regulating influences of institutional and educational structures. Beginning in the 1970s, increasing specialization in psychology was associated with a downturn in the economy. Whereas psychologists traditionally had been commonly employed in academic settings, with basic research and teaching the main focus of their work,

a paucity of new academic positions led psychology students to prepare for nonacademic employment in selected specialties. A tight job market had graduates seeking nonacademic positions in state, local, and federal agencies and in industry. The growth of the private practice of psychology was most noticeable. In response to these trends, students did practica or internships in settings other than universities, and control of graduate and postgraduate training extended beyond psychology departments into freestanding medical and business schools. Nontraditional training experiences, alongside increasing specialization in the curriculum, contributed to the students' development of identities and affiliations outside of psychology in general. In addition, emphasis on the history and values of their current discipline of psychology waned.

The centrifugal pattern of psychology's current educational structures is reflected in its institutional infrastructure, notably the APA. Increasing specialization is represented in the expansion of APA divisions, which designate the new interests of the membership, as well as the creation of the rival American Psychological Society. Divergent interests are associated with a widening split between academic and professional parts of the discipline, most notably between clinical and nonclinical groups. As psychologists identify with division and state associations, the APA tends to lose the ability it once had to consolidate the field as a whole (Altman, 1987).

Table 2.1 summarizes the various aspects of centripetal and centrifugal trends in extraprofessional and intraprofessional contexts in light of Altman's (1987) analysis. Centrifugal and centripetal trends in psychology have been associated with complementary trends in social and political contexts. Change in the direction of these trends can be explained by using the concept of dialectic opposition.

### Dialectic Opposition

Viable systems of development, including those that guide the development of disciplines and professions, are dynamic, open systems engaged in continual exchange with their environment, according to Altman (1987). As such, they possess several important properties that relate to their potential for change. First, they are made up of oppositional features that exist in a dynamic condition of tension (e.g., conflict and harmony, interpersonal openness and closedness, conformity and independence, unification and

TABLE 2.1    Centripetal and Centrifugal Trends
             in Extraprofessional and Intraprofessional Contexts

| Centripetal Trends in Extraprofessional Contexts | Centripetal Trends in Intraprofessional Contexts |
|---|---|
| Fundamental faith in democratic system | Consolidation on many fronts—theoretical, |
| Clarity of purpose and consensus of direction in | substantive, methodological, philosophical, |
| government | institutional |
| Unified citizenry | Unified national organization |
| Sacrifices readily accepted by citizenry | Key role in accreditation and standards of |
| Government concerns for citizens in social | national organization |
| welfare programs | Need to present a unified face to the world |
| "Melting pot" ideal with regard to racial and | General core education |
| ethnic integration | |
| Mass education | More generalization, less specialization |
| Boom in industry | Psychologists easily identified with the field as |
| Boom in economy | a whole |
| Material prosperity for citizens | Rare socially active directions |

*Social Political Context*

| | |
|---|---|
| Erosion of confidence in a national sense of | Proliferation of specialties |
| unity and purpose | Loss of a common core of ideas |
| Lack of strength, common direction, and | Increased role of single-issue interest groups |
| national purpose | Decline of financial support |
| Lack of respect in presidency as a symbol of the | Diversity of settings for graduate and |
| unity of the nation | postdoctoral education (e.g., medical school) |
| Changing lifestyles | Freestanding professional schools |
| "Pluralism" as ideal with regard to racial and | Affiliations with new primary reference groups |
| ethnic minorities | |

*Higher Education*

| | |
|---|---|
| Curriculum unhinged from its traditional | Widening split between academic and |
| structure | professional parts of the discipline |
| Protest movements | Interdisciplinary organizations |
| Focus by departments on their own | (e.g., Neurosciences Society) |
| development without regard to the institution | Movement away from some of the context, |
| as a whole | theory, methods, and traditional values of |
| "Multiversity" | psychology |
| Mobile faculty | Cross-disciplinary approaches |
| Lessened student commitment to a university | Challenges to traditional philosophy of science, |
| Part-time students | administration, and governance |
| Faltering national and state economic support | Large and complex national organization (APA) |
| Decline in student financial aid | Lessened affiliation and identification with |
| Salary discrepancies among faculty | national organization |
| Focus on economic development | Emerging professional practitioner activities in |
| Deemphasis of traditional arts, letters, and basic | many fields of psychology |
| sciences at public institutions | Shortage of high-quality graduate students |

Based on Altman's (1987) analysis.

diversification, and consolidation and separation). Second, their oppositional processes form a unity or whole, with each pole in the system lending meaning to the other and with the whole dependent on the existence of some amount of the opposite. Accordingly, centripetal and centrifugal trends have formed psychology's disciplinary profile historically. Third, their oppositional processes display dynamic, changing relationships with their polar opposites, assuming different strengths with regard to one another at different times. Accordingly, centripetal trends have prevailed in psychology, universities, and society at certain times in history, and centrifugal factors have dominated at other times. Fourth, although one pole of the system may predominate at a given time, both oppositional processes are operative at all times. Thus, centripetal and centrifugal forces in psychology always are present to one degree or another even though one or the other pole may be stronger momentarily. Fifth, both polar positions in the system have potentially positive or negative attributes. According to Altman (1987), "Centripetal qualities are unifying and provide organization and structure, but they are also potentially stagnating and resistant to adaptive change. Similarly, centrifugal qualities can result in new ideas and creative change, but can also be divisive" (p. 1059). In sum, dialectic opposition conceptualizes the forces in psychology that attempt to abate threats to stagnation or divisiveness.

Principles of dialectic complementarity and dialectic opposition underlie Altman's belief that present-day centrifugal trends need to be abated. However, such trends cannot be averted because of their social embeddedness and their multifaceted qualities. Arbitrary attempts to control them inevitably will be ineffective; for example, attempts to revamp undergraduate education with throwbacks to the curricula of the 1940s and 1950s ignore the unsuitability of traditional curricula for new cohorts of students. Because centrifugal trends are ubiquitous, they are subject mainly to intervention by being diagnosed, understood, and capitalized on. For example, understanding the needs of a diverse population of students can reshape the educational system in a cohesive way (Altman, 1987).

Centrifugal trends are affected positively by promoting the view that the study of psychological phenomena is enhanced by drawing on the strengths of other fields. A shared commitment to this ideal encourages integration of psychology's history and present status with plans of action that

can consolidate aspects of the discipline. Altman believes that this is both possible and inevitable. His model predicts that the developmental course of psychology eventually will come full circle as the broad psychological viewpoints shared by scholars from philosophy, biology, medicine, and other fields in the pre-1900s are transformed into newly evolving multidisciplinary perspectives for understanding psychological phenomena. Such integration and transformation represent the full synthesis and further maturation of the field, which will allow psychology to accommodate the needs of a global society.

### Strengths and Limitations of Altman's Model

The drama and reality of events that have led to psychology's preeminence and simultaneous threat of decline, in a country in which the field has prospered throughout most of the twentieth century, are well captured in Altman's contextual model. His transactional and dialectical perspectives heuristically represent a pattern of development that is rich in its complexity and yet predictable in some of its trajectories.

Altman attains breadth in his conceptualizations by focusing on the dynamics that contribute to change in one of the world's most economically advantaged countries. Using the pattern of psychology's development in the United States as a historical event (Pepper, 1942), he is able to identify social, educational, and disciplinary interrelationships that are critical to psychology's establishment as a profession and science.

Socioeconomic factors figure prominently in the discipline's evolution. Their role is associated not only with the status characteristics identified in Catterall's (1979) stage model—such as the presence of an educational infrastructure that supports graduate education in psychology and an institutional infrastructure represented by a progressive national organization (e.g., APA) that secures the legitimacy of the field—but also the philosophies of science likely to thrive in particular social contexts (Altman, 1987; Danziger, 1990). A favorable economy generally is associated with trust in government and public institutions, which favors traditionalism, whereas the pressures of an unfavorable economy heighten decentralization of the educational enterprise and subsequent diversity in orientations to knowledge (Altman, 1987). When these basic processes are identified, patterns of discipline-environmental interactions emerge that are subterfuged in unidirectional models of progress.

The need to better understand these social

processes is clear from a review of the status of school psychology in developed and developing countries. In reviewing school psychology practices in the latter, including Russia, Brazil, and China, Oakland (1992) concluded that the field can be strengthened through diversity: "Countries in which school psychology services are emerging are likely to have fewer regulations governing services and fewer resources to utilize in providing services. Thus, they are better able to use creative approaches to address their needs. . . . School psychologists in all nations can benefit from knowledge of creative solutions found to be useful in the developing countries" (p. 173). The proposition that diversity can contribute to the growth of psychology and its specialties is upheld by most international investigators (Blackler, 1983; Catterall, 1979; Ching, 1984; Gilgen & Gilgen, 1987; Rosenzweig, 1992a, 1992b; Saigh & Oakland, 1989; Schwendler, 1984; Serpell, 1984; Sexton & Hogan, 1992; Sexton & Misiak, 1987; Sinha & Holtzman, 1984). Implicity to this position is a view of disciplinary progress within a social-contextual (i.e., transactional, holistic, and systemic) framework.

Because complex social systems are better understood contextually than linearly (Giddens, 1984; Parson, 1951), Altman's (1987) holistic model of the social influencies that affect psychology is heuristic for the study of disciplinary development. However, the model is complex and not easily understood. In addition, its value has been insufficiently evaluated. Altman's contextual-dialectical analysis has been referred to in discussions on the development of psychology and its specialties (Bardon, 1988; Hoshmand & Polkinghorne, 1992; Phillips, 1990), and its analysis has been used to examine the development of school psychology internationally (Cunningham, 1994). However, it has not been used to examine the development of school psychology or other specialty areas of psychology in the United States. Therefore, the model's primary limitation is the incompleteness due to its infrequent application.

## Summary of Models to Forecast Future Developments

Three models have been reviewed: stage, linear, and contextual. This review suggests that among the three, contextual methods are most useful in forecasting a profession's futures.

Methods for estimating change are not well established. Those who attempt to forecast the future often rely on linear methods, which logically extend current trends into the future. However, growth is uneven, nonlinear, and often affected by serendipitous events. Thus, methods that utilize only logic and multiple, linear approaches, while helpful, are incomplete and yield inaccurate forecasts. In addition, the use of contextual models to forecast the future is both complex and largely untested.

Despite these and other methodological limitations, attempts to forecast the future of school psychology must occur inasmuch as forecasts are tied inextricably to attempts toward stability, self-control, and therefore planning. When planning and forecasting, one must consider various qualities that are internal to and under the control of school psychology, as well as those external to and largely beyond its direct control.

## SOME QUALITIES AND RESOURCES THAT WILL AFFECT SCHOOL PSYCHOLOGY

### Those Over Which School Psychology Has Most Control

School psychology is not without resources which, when used well, can strongly affect its futures. These include but are not limited to its history, membership, professional associations, literature, standards, current certification and licensure provisions, models for and nature of graduate preparation, and professional and political relationships with others.

### Those Over Which School Psychology Has Some Control

School psychology also has various resources over which it has some control inasmuch as they are generally shared with others. They include but are not limited to the quality of and financial support for schools; state and federal statutes that govern services; the nature of the psychological services provided in the schools; the extent to which school psychologists can provide services outside of the schools (e.g., in hospitals or through private practice); the numbers of professional programs, of students preparing for the profession, and of professionals who want employment as school psychologists; the public's image of and perceived needs for school psychological services; the technology and knowledge from other sources; and the bifurcation of psychological science and practice. Its willingness and ability to resolve sources of tension and disputes will also affect its future.

## Those Over Which School Psychology Has Little Direct Control

The futures of school psychology are also affected by various conditions beyond its direct control. These include but are not limited to cultural, economic, historical, political, philosophical, and social components of the settings in which school psychologists work; conditions that arise that affect the need for professional services; knowledge produced from unrelated disciplines; and serendipitous events.

# SOURCES OF TENSION AND THEIR RESOLUTIONS THAT MAY AFFECT PSYCHOLOGY'S FUTURES

Various tensions exist within school psychology (e.g., the entry level for practice), as well as between school psychology and various external conditions (e.g., the desire to provide a full range of psychological services vs. a school district's resources for only assessment services). The types of methods utilized to resolve tensions (e.g., withdrawal, confrontation, cooperation, or mediation) will strongly affect its futures. Six sources of tension are briefly identified as examples of those facing school psychology, and one is discussed more extensively. Whether these and other sources of tensions are resolved and the nature of their resolution will strongly affect school psychology's future.

## Unity Versus Plurality in School Psychology

Until recently, school psychology was fairly uniform in the nature of its preparation, services, and locations. This unity is undergoing change. School psychologists are preparing to work with a broader age range of persons (many of whom are not students), interning in nontraditional settings (e.g., hospitals and other nonschool settings), establishing practices outside of schools (e.g., private or agency-related), and providing a broader range of services (e.g., neuropsychology, forensic psychology, consultation, and research). This growing plurality poses problems in defining the specialty to the public and other professionals, as well as to those responsible for credentialling and licensing psychologists. In addition, those who work in nontraditional ways often disassociate themselves from the profession of school psychology and form associations with others who have similar interests.

## Brevity Versus Completeness of Professional Preparation

Most full-time school psychology students spend an average of three and one-half to six years in their graduate preparation. This length of time exceeds averages in other professionals (e.g., law), is very expensive to students and universities, and often does not reflect the level of remuneration they will receive once they begin their work. In contrast, given the expanding nature of social and psychological problems of children and youths, pressures are being exerted to further extend the professional preparation of school psychologists.

## Thoroughness Versus Economy

School psychologists generally are personally committed and professionally prepared to provide thorough and high-quality services. Moreover, the number of students in need of psychological services is increasing dramatically. However, the length and nature of the services as well as the services provided by other professionals are increasingly guided by diminishing financial factors. School psychologists are being asked to provide more services with the same or diminished resources.

## Services Needed Versus Ability to Deliver Them

Schools are being required to take responsibility for addressing academic, social, and psychological problems that are increasing in number, range, and severity. In addition, schools often are held responsible for ensuring that students' academic development shows continuous growth and that their social and emotional problems are abated. These requirements often go far beyond the professional and managerial resources available. Schools are often being asked to deliver services at an unattainable level. School psychologists frequently feel considerable tension, wanting to make a positive impact on students' behaviors yet lacking the knowledge and managerial resources to do so. Given their inability to address psychological needs effectively, other professionals may be employed in their place.

## Remediation Versus Prevention Programs

School psychologists often feel considerable tension over the narrowness of their roles. Their work typically focuses on resolving academic, emotional, or social difficulties manifested by individual students. But many school psychologists believe that their efforts could be utilized more effectively by emphasizing prevention through their work with groups (e.g., teachers, parents, administrators) and through helping to restructure schools.

## Special Education Versus General Education

School psychologists often have divided feelings about their work in special and general education. They recognize that special education's financial resources often support services and that their work in special education is important. However, many want to have a broader impact by working with general education students and their parents, teachers, and administrators. Many believe that their working environments do not permit them to utilize the full range of services they are prepared and want to offer.

## Traditional Versus Emerging Assessment Practices

School psychologists, along with others in education, are being asked to rethink certain premises that have guided their work (Oakland, 1995). Proposed changes may affect the nature of assessment services, an arena central to the livelihood of school psychologists. Given their importance, some emerging trends in education and their implications for education are reviewed in some detail (Table 2.2).

Consistent with a contextual model of development, school psychology is likely to maintain a central role in assessment by actively engaging in the constructive resolution of tensions associated with proposed changes. Leadership begins by conducting research to determine the viability of these changes, reviewing the impact they will have on other critical elements in the system, and helping to implement those changes that seem both viable and achievable. Changes, if implemented, will require school psychologists to expand their repertoire of services, a condition needed for professions to survive.

School psychology is likely to become increasingly useful to education by providing leadership in implementing the following changes. School psychologists are being asked to expand their repertoire of services through these methods, not to totally abandon the use of traditional methods. School psychology has been poised and desirous to move in these directions for years yet

restrained from doing so by being required to use traditional medical-model methods of assessment.

*Focus more on behaviors that can change, not only on those that are permanent.* Psychology and education typically have placed considerable emphasis on behaviors thought to be relatively stable. Constructs important in defining intelligence, language, adaptive behaviors, and personality are examples of those thought to be quite stable, often having a biological basis and thus typically modified largely by maturation. For example, research that helps to define the construct of intelligence and leads to reliable measures to assess it clearly represents one of psychology's major contributions during the last century. Intelligence accounts for the largest student-related source of variance associated with achievement and figures importantly in understanding affective, cognitive, and neuropsychological disorders.

Despite these presumed benefits, psychology is being asked to develop new concepts of cognition and academic aptitudes (Snow, 1992) that identify qualities that have two characteristics: they need to be modifiable, and they need to have a direct influence on learning and other important developmental areas. In contrast with the first of these two desired qualities, intelligence is relatively permanent and nonmodifiable; few if any methods are known that advance its development in school-age children and youths. However, it does meet the second standard. As a result, school psychology is being asked to place greater emphasis on learning and study strategies, learning potential, and similar qualities thought to be modifiable and to affect learning outcomes directly.

*Involve students as active participants throughout the teaching and learning process.* Education has been guided by various assumptions about teaching and learning. Teachers have been solely responsible for guiding instruction. Teachers first instruct and then assess the degree to which students have learned, largely emphasizing attainment of knowledge or learned abilities.

New models of teaching broaden responsibility by including students and parents along with teachers; peer groups are added to this team when utilizing cooperative learning. Each person has an important and unique role in helping to determine the nature of what is learned and who is responsible for learning. Greater self-regulation of learning is encouraged. Emphasis is placed on developing learning abilities, understanding the process of learning, developing abilities that fur-

**TABLE 2.2** **Some Differences Between Traditional and Emerging Trends in Student Assessment**

| Assessment Strategies | |
|---|---|
| **Traditional** | **Possibly Emerging** |
| **Assumptions About Academic Behavior** | |
| Promote stable behavior | Allow changable behavior |
| **Assumptions About Teaching** | |
| Precede testing with instruction | Precede instruction with testing |
| Let only teachers be responsible for guiding instruction | Let pupil, peers, parents, and teachers be responsible for guiding instruction |
| Promote ability to solve problems | Promote ability to demonstrate suitable problem-solving methods |
| Emphasize learned abilities | Emphasize learning abilities |
| Emphasize assessment of memorized knowledge | Emphasize assessment of higher-order cognitive applications |
| Rely on external regulation of achievement | Promote self-regulation of achievement |
| **Assumptions About Learning** | |
| Let teachers and tests evaluate degree of attainment | Let students, along with other sources, evaluate degree of attainment |
| Reward attainment at high levels | Reward attainment at or above potential |
| Reward convergent thinking | Promote divergent thinking |
| **Traditional** | **Emerging** |
| **Assumptions About the Purposes of Testing** | |
| Assess outcomes or products | Assess the process used to achieve the product |
| Focus evaluation on past and present | Focus evaluation on present and future |
| Test to inform professionals | Test to inform students |
| Diagnose and label permanent barriers that restrict attainment | Identify (without labeling) temporary and improvable barriers to attainment |
| **Assumptions About the Testing Process** | |
| Assess achievement separately in content areas | Assess achievement across content areas |
| Exclude assessment of feelings and personal attitudes | Include assessment of feelings and personal attitudes |
| Use paper-and-pencil methods | Use multisources and multimethods to measure multitraits |
| Test simulated outcomes | Test authentic outcomes |
| Score tests quantitatively | Score tests qualitatively |
| Establish external standards | Promote internal standards |
| Judge attainment in light of behavioral objectives | Judge attainment in light of developmental outcomes |
| Rely on norm-referenced standards | Rely on criterion-referenced standards |
| Emphasize summative evaluation | Emphasize formative evaluation |

ther learning in other contexts, and promoting problem solving together with self-regulation and self-motivation.

*Involve students as active participants in the assessment process.* Practices that govern the assessment of educational achievement typically have emphasized the use of tests to evaluate degrees of attainment, relying on standards set by teachers when using classroom tests or by national norms when using standardized tests. Convergent thinking and high levels of attainment typically are rewarded.

Psychologists and educators are asked to help create conditions that involve students directly as active participants in the evaluation process. Students, along with others, should help set standards for their performance. In addition, rewards are contingent on attaining these or higher standards. Moreover, assessment methods include the use of divergent production as well as risk taking. Information provided should promote self-regulation and self-motivation.

*Utilize tests to help create pathways to success.* Psychoeducational assessments as performed by school psychologists have been guided by various assumptions about the purpose of testing. The purpose usually is to provide a retrospective analysis of students' qualities to determine, in part, the legitimacy of assigning diagnostic labels for processes that pose as permanent barriers in attaining important school outcomes, given the resources typically available only in regular education. Such information usually is given to professionals and, in a summary form, to parents.

New assessment methods that have different purposes are being requested. These include those that provide a prospective focus, emphasize possible future attainments, and identify (without labeling) temporary barriers to attainment that are penetrable or avoidable. Results of these assessments are conveyed to students in ways that promote self-understanding, self-regulation, and self-motivation.

*Examine skills in an integrated fashion.* Achievement domains (e.g., reading, math, social studies, and sciences) typically have been assessed separately by content areas through paper-and-pencil measures, containing items that are based on behavioral objectives and that simulate important learned outcomes. Feelings and attitudes are not assessed. Test data in quantitative form are interpreted by using external and norm-referenced standards to make summative evaluations.

New methods are beginning to guide the assessment process. Achievement is being assessed by combining content across domains of study through tests that use more authentic settings when measuring important developmental outcomes. This assessment process is broader in focus and includes information from various sources beyond students and relevant traits (e.g., feelings, personal attitudes, and preferences) when appropriate. Test data in quantitative and qualitative forms are interpreted by using internal and external standards to make formative evaluations.

*Use technology.* The use of word processors and other technology to assist in learning and assessment processes has become standard in some school districts and will be so in almost all by 2010. In special education, technology can be expected to be used routinely as an aide in learning to read, write, acquire math skills, and gain knowledge in many other critical areas.

School psychologists are being asked to identify desired technology, to assess students' abilities to benefit from their use, to estimate levels of achievement when students are provided with these resources, to make recommendations of the best conditions for students to acquire needed skills and abilities, and to prepare students to make optimal use of this technology. This process again underscores the importance of providing a prospective focus, one that emphasizes possible future attainments and identifies, without labeling, temporary barriers to attainment that are penetrable or avoidable through the use of technology. Information is conveyed to students in ways that promote self-understanding, self-regulation, and self-motivation.

Word processors also are being used routinely in assessment, both for classroom criterion-referenced measures and nationally standardized norm-referenced measures. The use of computers, when combined with scanners, promotes flexibility and economy and enables educators to retain and retrieve large amounts of student data easily and to analyze data in ways that provide more detailed and comprehensive descriptions of current qualities, as well as suggested directions for future attainment. Again, school psychologists could be at the forefront of this development and use of technology.

## CONCLUSION

The futures of school psychology cannot be forecast reliably. They will be determined, in part, by conditions over which it has considerable control, some control, and no control. Broad swings and major changes in a profession are uncommon, particularly in those that are well established, such as school psychology. Professional stability is promoted by the long-standing presence of infrastructures that both define and delimit its nature. Thus, a retrospective view of school psychology in 10 years is likely to find the number of significant changes to be far less than its consistencies over this period.

# REFERENCES

Alpert, J. (1985). Change within a profession: Change, future, prevention, and school psychology. *American Psychologist, 40,* 1112–1121.

Altman, I. (1975). *Environment and social behavior: Privacy, personal space, territory and crowding.* New York: Cambridge University Press.

Altman, I. (1987). Centripetal and centrifugal trends in psychology. *American Psychologist, 42,* 1058–1069.

Altman, I., & Rogoff, B. (1987). World views in psychology: Trait, interactional, organismic, and transactional perspectives. In D. Stokols & I. Altman (Eds.), *Handbook of environmental psychology* (pp. 1–40). New York: Wiley

Bardon, J. I. (1979). School psychology in the United States. In C. D. Catterall (Ed.), *Psychology in the schools in international perspective* (Vol. 2, pp. 183–210). Columbus, OH: International School Psychology Steering Committee.

Bardon, J. I. (1982). School psychology's dilemma: A proposal for its resolution. *Professional Psychology, 13,* 955–968.

Bardon, J. I. (1983). Psychology applied to education: A specialty in search of an identity. *American Psychologist, 38,* 185–196.

Bardon, J. I. (1988). Alternative delivery approaches: Implications for school psychology. In J. L. Graden, J. E. Zins, & M. J. Curtis (Eds.), *Alternative educational delivery systems: Enhancing instructional options for all students* (pp. 563–571). Washington, DC: National Association of School Psychologists.

Bardon, J. I., Brown, D. T., & Hyman, I. P. (1979). Debate: Will the real school psychologist please stand up? *School Psychology Digest, 8,* 162–186.

Bellah, R., Madsen, R., Sullivan, W. M., Swidler, A., & Tipton, S. M. (1985). *Habits of the heart: Individualism and commitment in American life.* Berkeley: University of California Press.

Bickman, L. (Ed.). (1987). Proceedings of the National Conference on Graduate Education in Psychology, University of Utah, Salt Lake City, June 13–19, 1987. *American Psychologist* (Special Issue), *42* (12).

Bickman, L., & Ellis, H. (1990). *Preparing psychologists for the 21st century.* Hillsdale, NJ: Erlbaum.

Binet, A. (1908). Un livre récent de William James sur l'éducation: *Causeries pédagogiques.* [A recent book by William James on education: *Talks to teachers.*] *L'Année Psychologique, 17,* 270–277.

Binet, A., & Simon, T. (1911). Réponse à quelques critiques (Reply to certain criticisms). *L'Année Psychologique, 17,* 270–277.

Blackler, F. (Ed.). (1983). *Social psychology and developing countries.* Chichester, Eng.: Wiley.

Bloom, A. (1987). *The closing of the American mind.* New York: Simon & Schuster.

Brent, S. B. (1978). Prigogine's model for self-organization in nonequilibrium systems: Its relevance for developmental psychology. *Human Development, 21,* 374–387.

Brown, D. T. (1987). Comment on Fagan's "School Psychology's Dilemma." *American Psychologist, 42,* 755–756.

Catterall, C. D. (Ed.). (1977–1979). *Psychology in the schools in international perspective* (Vols. 1–3). Columbus, OH: International School Psychology Steering Committee.

Ching, C. A. (1984). Psychology and the four modernizations in China. *International Journal of Psychology, 14,* 57–63.

Connolly, K. (1985). Can there be a psychology for the third world? *Bulletin of the British Psychological Society, 38,* 249–257.

Cunningham, J. (1994). A contextual investigation of the international development of psychology in the schools. Doctoral dissertation, University of Texas, Austin.

Cushman, P. (1990). Why the self is empty: Toward a historically situated psychology. *American Psychologist, 45,* 599–611.

Cushman, P. (1991). Ideology obscured: Political uses of the self in Daniel Stern's infant. *American Psychologist, 46,* 206–219.

Cutts, N. E. (Ed.). (1955). *School psychologists at mid-century.* Washington, DC: American Psychological Association.

Danziger, K. (1990). *Constructing the subject: Historical origins of psychological research.* New York: Cambridge University Press.

Dewey, J., & Bentley, A. F. (1949). *Knowing and the known.* Boston: Beacon.

Durojaiye, M. O. A. (1984). The impact of psychological testing on educational and personnel selection in Africa. *International Journal of Psychology, 19,* 135–144.

Fagan, T. K. (1986). School psychology's dilemma: Reappraising solutions and directing attention to the future. *American Psychologist, 41,* 851–861.

Furomoto, L. (1989). The new history of psychology. In I. S. Cohen (Ed.), *The G. Stanley Hall Lecture Series* (pp. 9–34). Washington, DC: American Psychological Association.

Gergen, K. (1982). *Toward transformation in social knowledge.* New York: Springer-Verlag.

Giddens, A. (1984). *The constitution of society.* Cambridge: Polity Press.

Gilgen, A. R., & Gilgen, C. K. (1987). *International handbook of psychology.* New York: Greenwood Press.

Hermans, H. J. M., Kempen, H. J. G., & von Loon, R. J. P. (1992). The dialogical self: Beyond individualism and rationalism. *American Psychologist, 47,* 23–33.

Hoshmand, L. T., & Polkinghorne, D. E. (1992). Redefining the science-practice relationship and professional training. *American Psychologist, 47,* 55–66.

Howard, G. S. (1991). Culture tales: A narrative approach to thinking, cross-cultural psychology, and psychotherapy. *American Psychologist, 46,* 187–197.

James, W. (1899/1983). *Talks to teachers on psychology: And to students on some of life's ideals.* Cambridge, MA: Harvard University Press.

Kuhn, T. S. (1970). The structure of scientific revolutions. Chicago: University of Chicago Press.

Kukla, A. (1992). Unification as a goal for psychology. *American Psychologist, 47,* 1054–1055.

McNally, R. J. (1992). Disunity in psychology: Chaos or speciation? *American Psychologist, 47,* 1054.

Mead, G. H. (1899). The working hypothesis in social reform. *American Journal of Sociology, 5,* 367–371.

Minton, H. L. (1992). Root metaphors and the evolution of American social psychology. *Canadian Psychology, 33,* 547–553.

Moghaddam, F. M. (1987). Psychology in the three worlds: As reflected by the crisis in the social psychology and the move toward indigenous third-world psychology. *American Psychologist, 42,* 912–920.

Moghaddam, F. M., & Taylor, D. M. (1985). Psychology in the developing world: An evaluation through the concepts of "dual perception" and "parallel growth." *American Psychologist, 40,* 1144–1146.

National Association of School Psychologists/National Coalition of Advocates for Students. (1985). *Advocacy for the appropriate educational services for all children. A position statement adopted by the Executive Board Delegate Assembly of the National Association of School Psychologists.* Washington, DC: Author.

Nixon, M. (1990). Professional training in psychology: Quest for international standards. *American Psychologist, 45,* 1257–1262.

Oakland, T. (1985). Selected current trends in the United States, implications for education and possible futures for school psychology. *School Psychology International, 6,* 1–4.

Oakland, T. D. (1992). Formulating priorities for international school psychology toward the turn of the twentieth century. *School Psychology International, 13,* 171–177.

Oakland, T. (1993). A brief history of international school psychology. *Journal of School Psychology, 31,* 109–122.

Oakland, T. (1995). Test use with children and youth internationally. In T. Oakland & R. Hambleton (Eds.), *International perspectives on academic assessment.* Boston: Kluwer Academic Publishers.

Oakland, T., & Cunningham, J. (1989, November). Brief report on the status of school psychology in the world. *World-Go-Round,* p. 4.

Oakland, T., & Cunningham, J. L. (1990). Advocates for educational services for all children need improved research and conceptual bases. *School Psychology Quarterly, 5,* 66–77.

Oakland, T., & Saigh, P. A. (1989). Psychology in the schools: An introduction to international perspectives. In P. A. Saigh & T. Oakland (Eds.), *International perspectives on psychology in the schools* (pp. 1–23). Hillsdale, NJ: Erlbaum.

Odegaard, C. E. (1987). A historical perspective on the dilemmas confronting psychology. *American Psychologist, 42,* 1048–1051.

Ogilvy, J. (1979). *Many dimensional man.* New York: Harper & Row.

Ogilvy, J. (1982). The forces shaping the 1980s. *School Psychology Review, 11,* 112–126.

Parsons, T. (1951). *The social system.* New York: Free Press.

Pepper, S. C. (1942). *World hypotheses: A study in evidence.* Berkeley: University of California Press.

Pepper, S. C. (1967). *Concept and quality: A world hypothesis.* La Salle, IL: Open Court Publishing.

Phillips, B. N. (1981). School psychology in the 1980s: Some critical issues related to practice. In T. R. Kratochwill (Ed.), *Advances in school psychology* (Vol. 1, pp. 19–43). Hillsdale, NJ: Erlbaum.

Phillips, B. N. (1985a). Reminiscences of things past. *Journal of School Psychology, 22,* 119–130.

Phillips, B. N. (1985b). Toward an empirically derivable definition of entry level. *Professional Psychology: Research and Practice, 16,* 138–147.

Phillips, B. N. (1987). On science, mirrors, lamps, and professional practice. *Professional School Psychology, 24,* 222–229.

Phillips, B. N. (1990). *School psychology at a turning point: Ensuring a bright future for the profession.* San Francisco: Jossey-Bass.

Rokeach, M., & Ball-Rokeach, S. J. (1989). Stability and change in American value priorities, 1968–1981. *American Psychologist, 44,* 775–784.

Rosenfield, S. (1990). Taking a position on "Appropriate Educational Services." *School Psychology Quarterly, 5,* 46.

Rosenzweig, M. R. (1984). U.S. psychology and world psychology. *American Psychologist, 39,* 877–884.

Rosenzweig, M. R. (1992a). (Ed.). *International psychological science: Progress, problems, and prospects.*

Washington, DC: American Psychological Association.

Rosenzweig, M. R. (1992b). Psychological science around the world. *American Psychologist, 47,* 718–722.

Rosnow, R. L. (1981). *Paradigms in transition: The methodology of social inquiry.* New York: Oxford University Press.

Russell, R. (1984). Psychology in its world context. *American Psychologist, 39,* 1017–1025.

Saigh, P. A., & Oakland, T. (Eds.). (1989). *International perspectives on psychology in the schools.* Hillsdale, NJ: Erlbaum.

Salazar, J. M. (1984). The use and impact of psychology in Venezuela: Two examples. *International Journal of Psychology, 19,* 113–122.

Sampson, E. E. (1989). The challenge of social change for psychology: Globalization and psychology's theory of the person. *American Psychologist, 44,* 914–921.

Sarason, S. B. (1988). *The making of an American psychologist.* San Francisco: Jossey-Bass.

Schneider, S. F. (1990). Psychology at a crossroads. *American Psychologist, 45,* 521–529.

Schwendler, W. (1984). UNESCO's project on the exchange of knowledge for endogenous development. *International Journal of Psychology, 19,* 3–16.

Serpell, R. (1984). Commentary: The impact of psychology on third world development. *International Journal of Psychology, 19,* 179–192.

Sexton, V. S. & Hogan, J. (Eds.). (1992). *International psychology: Views from around the world* (2nd ed.). Lincoln, NE: University of Nebraska Press.

Sexton, V. S. & Misiak, H. (Eds.). (1987). *Psychology around the world.* Monterey, CA: Brooks/Cole.

Sinha, D., & Holtzman, W. H. (Eds.). (1984). The impact of psychology on third world development. *International Journal of Psychology* (special issue), *19* (1/2).

Smith, M. B. (1990). Psychology in the public interest: What have we done? What can we do? *American Psychologist, 45,* 530–536.

Snow, R. (1992). Aptitude theory: Yesterday, today, and tomorrow. *Educational Psychologist, 27,* 5–32.

Stokols, D. (1987). Scientific and policy challenges of contextually oriented psychology. In D. Stokols & I. Altman (Eds.), *Handbook of environmental psychology* (pp. 41–70). New York: Wiley.

Trachtman, G. (1981). On such a full sea. *School Psychology Review, 10,* 138–181.

Triandis, H. C. (1989). Individualism and social psychological theory. In C. Kagitcibasi (Ed.), *Growth and progress in cross-cultural psychology* (pp. 78–83). Lisse, Neth.: Swets & Zeitlinger.

Wapner, S. (1987). A holistic developmental, systems-oriented environmental psychology: Some beginnings. In D. Stokols and I. Altman (Eds.), *Handbook of environmental psychology* (pp. 1433–1466). New York: Wiley.

# SCHOOL PSYCHOLOGY AND THE SCIENTIFIC STUDY OF BEHAVIOR: CONTRIBUTIONS TO THEORY AND PRACTICE

•

## CHAPTER 3

# STRENGTHENING THE LINKS BETWEEN SCIENCE AND PRACTICE: READING, EVALUATING, AND APPLYING RESEARCH IN SCHOOL PSYCHOLOGY[1]

BEEMAN N. PHILLIPS
*University of Texas at Austin*

Exploring the interaction between science and practice in school psychology is the central focus of this chapter. The need to join science and practice has been a concern of school psychology since its founding. But science and practice are still not joined in the most meaningful and significant sense, and if future efforts are to be more successful, both the science and the practice of school psychology must be changed, even transformed, in important ways.

At the core of this chapter is the central belief that science can significantly contribute to practice, directly and indirectly, and that its contribution will be greatest where researchers adjust their priorities to reflect practice-oriented issues. Such readjustment should reduce the disaffection of practitioners with research and increase the proportion of researchers who are concerned and interested in matters of practice.

To apply this core belief to school psychology, it should be noted that school psychological practice is broad and not precisely definable and that it is similarly difficult to define psychological research in any precise way. In this connection, it is also important to take into account the meaning of the term *relevance* as it applies to the relationship between science and practice. This term can be used to identify areas of psychological re-

search that bear an obvious relation to professional practice. It must be recognized, however, that basic and applied research constitute a continuum and that, in an important sense, all psychological research is relevant, although the relevance of some research is more apparent than that of others. It would be a mistake, therefore, for school psychologists to construe the relevance of research narrowly or to overlook the avenues through which school psychological practice can have an impact on research.

The bidirectionality of the relationship between psychological research and professional practice is another significant point. A useful approach for construing this bidirectionality is to consider the origins of psychological research and professional practice. Basic research, for example, is endogenous. It is knowledge-driven and formulated in terms of contemporary theory and research on questions, issues, and hypotheses important to the discipline, with little regard for societal or practice ramifications (Masters, 1984). Applied psychological research, on the other hand, is exogenous, stemming from a consideration of societal issues, technological problems, or practice matters.

In a similar vein, one can trace the source of some professional practice to the direct or indirect influence of basic and applied research. That is, some aspects of practice are exogenous, being the product of applied, as well as basic, research.

---

[1]Portions of this chapter are based on my chapter in *The Handbook of School Psychology* (Phillips, 1990a).

In contrast, other aspects of practice have endogenous origins. In these instances, professional practice arises out of practice goals and conditions, training and experience, professional practice norms, and characteristics of the practitioner.

Those who would explore ways to apply science to practice more effectively also face a dilemma. Despite a strong commitment to this endeavor, practical application itself is not fully understood. For some, practical application entails applied research carried out in natural rather than laboratory settings. For others, it means addressing the questions generated by those working directly with children, youths, schools, and families. For still others, practical application consists of interpreting basic theory or research, as in the question, "What does B. F. Skinner have to say to school psychologists?" Finally, there are those who view practical application primarily in terms of communication between researchers and those responsible for formulating public policy.

In addressing this dilemma, it is also necessary to take into account the predicament of the practitioner, which is that in the variations of professional practice there is the "high, hard ground," where the practitioner can more readily make use of research findings, and there is the "swampy lowland," where situations are perplexing, messy, and incapable of straightforward technical solutions (Schon, 1983). The problem for the school psychologist, therefore, is to practice good psychological science in the swamp, as well as on the high, hard ground.

To more fully understand these propositions, I discuss the nature of psychological science, arguing for the need to augment the traditional view of science and detailing central themes in the social constructionist view of science. Then I examine important aspects of the science-practice relationship, including the need to legitimize practice as a source of knowledge. In the next section, I describe research roles for school psychologists, including that of "secondary" researcher. Then, I present considerations involved in the evaluation of a research study's scientific merit and practical significance. This is followed by a discussion of criteria for identifying model school intervention programs. Finally, I offer observations about ethical and legal aspects of research and conclusions about the need for a better partnership between researchers and practitioners in school psychology.

# NATURE OF PSYCHOLOGICAL SCIENCE

A full understanding of the relationship between science and practice turns on fundamental philosophical issues. Of central importance in this regard is the philosophy of science revolution that is brewing in psychology and has led to a war of words between the experimentalists and the social constructionists. The following are some of the questions this debate raises for school psychologists (B. N. Phillips, 1993, pp. 30–31): do the social constructionists who challenge what they claim is the privileged position of experimentalism claim the same privilege for social constructionism? Is both experimentalism and social constructionism historically relative or universal and transhistorical? Are all scientific theories politically dangerous precisely when they claim to transcend history and culture? Are both the experimentalists and the social constructionists trying to put forward a political agenda as the cure for American society's educational and other ills? Are the social constructionists now advocating a politically correct view of psychological science?

In a brief response to these questions and related issues, one might argue that it is important to recognize that ideology is imbedded in all views of psychological science. One might also conclude that the arguments of the experimentalists and social constructionists do not boil down to choosing between ideologies and claiming a privileged position for the one chosen. It should also be noted that social constructionists have played an important role in pointing out the limitations of the traditional ideological view of psychological science, in part because experimentalists usually do not expressly acknowledge their ideological stance.

## Role of Ideology in Applying Science to Practice

In moving beyond such bald, perhaps bold, questions and assertions, a further point needs to be made, which is that no science-practice relationship is ever free from the shaping force of one particular ideology or another (Bevan, 1991; Bevan & Kessel, 1994). Ideology is centrally involved in the science-practice relationship because, in Bevan's view, psychology is fundamentally a socially constructed activity. However, in emphasizing the important influences of sociopolitical and other ideological factors, Bevan is not saying that all of the issues resident in the science-practice relationship are ideological. Rather, he is saying that the efforts of scientists and practitioners to apply science to practice are always influenced by their personal experiences, intentions, values, and worldviews.

The "bell curve" controversy created by Hernstein and Murray (1994) illustrates this point. As Frisby (1995) has noted, some attempts to explain racial differences in scholastic achievement by deemphasizing the role of intelligence have continued to thrive despite being decisively refuted by empirical evidence (as in the case of the test bias "explanation"). He has further observed that the implicit emotional themes imbedded in such alternative explanations have overridden an objective and dispassionate consideration of the scientific evidence. With the passage of time, such explanations have evolved into social ideologies and orthodox ways of thinking about racial differences in scholastic achievement.

The science and politics of race-norming of psychological tests is another example of the influence of ideology (Gottfredson, 1994). Scientists and professionals who criticize score adjustment have argued that such adjustments are not scientifically justified and that technical expertise has been turned by supporters of score adjustment to disguise a serious social problem as a technical one and a particular political solution as a scientific necessity. On the other hand, scientists and professionals who support score adjustment have argued that such adjustments are scientifically justified, although their position might best be described as a value judgment that is informed only by scientific data. In essence, they have attempted to usurp a fundamentally political decision by transforming it into a seemingly technical, scientific issue over which scientists could claim special authority.

A more extreme example is the facilitated communication (FC) movement (Jacobson, Mulick, & Schwartz, 1995). Introduced into the United States in the 1980s without any scientific evidence of its validity and effectiveness, FC has become ubiquitous in special education. In recent years, controlled research, using single and double-blind procedures in laboratories and natural settings, not only has shown that FC does not unlock hidden intellectual competence but also that there is widespread, systematic facilitator control of the typed content in communications generated with facilitation. Despite this damning evidence, there is continuing acceptance of FC by the public and segments of the professional community.

In the context of school psychology, this means that sociopolitical and other ideological factors are like sand at a picnic: they get into all aspects of the science-practice relationship (Minogue, 1985). It is important, therefore, that school psychologists try to understand the application of science as a human social enterprise. Such understanding will underscore the dangers inherent in promoting a scientific theory to further a particular educational philosophy or sociopolitical agenda. It also will lead to greater realization that school psychologists who are the most motivated to provide the best services they can may also be the most vulnerable to the false promise of dubious assessment and intervention procedures. As an additional benefit, such understanding will help school psychologists to become more fully aware of their obligation, in their relationship to society at large, to vigorously oppose the misuse of science by advocates of educational or social causes and proposals.

## Realities of Doing Actual Research: Emergence of a Pluralistic Perspective on Psychological Science

In recent years, there have been an increasing number of psychologists who have realized that a variety of compromises must occur in psychological science that take into account the realities of actual research, especially in applied settings. For them, the traditional model of research is plainly in need of augmentation. If one asks school psychologists, for example, what it means to be scientific, their answers will range along a continuum—from views that reflect the traditional norms of a unified science, in which there is only one kind of psychological science and only one way to do it, to views that reflect a pluralistic perspective on psychological science, in which there is a diversity of scientific methods. In addition to implications for the scientific enterprise in school psychology, those who take the unified-science perspective are likely to be pessimistic about the promise and contributions of psychological science to school psychology, whereas those who take the plurality-of-science perspective are likely to be more optimistic. Fortunately, the majority of school psychologists seem to take a pluralistic view of psychological science.

A pluralistic perspective is also prevalent in the broader context of the social sciences. As I noted earlier (B. N. Phillips, 1990b), this point is made by the well-known methodologists Lee J. Cronbach, Paul Meehl, and Donald Campbell in their contributions to the volume edited by Fiske and Shweder (1986). They agree that logical positivism has been discredited in the social sciences generally and that the model of scientific method usually taught in graduate education programs in psychology is inappropriate for the study of human behavior. This traditional model, they emphasize, is not even used in the hard sciences. They also wonder why psychologists continue to criticize it since logical positivism and the scientific method it generated is history. They further note that scientists have rarely agreed about the meaning of the term *scientific*, and that "knowledge gained through any form of scholarly inquiry can be valid and indeed can constitute a privileged kind of knowledge when it is pursued on the basis of special training and experience" (p. 276). They also believe that social scientists are unduly defensive about the lack of rigor in their research, in comparison to that of the hard sciences, because, they maintain, the differences between the social sciences and the hard sciences are not as great as imagined. In both areas, researchers conduct a wide variety of equally valid disciplined activities that seek information about the world.

In support of these contentions, Prigogine (Prigogine & Stengers, 1984), who won a Nobel Prize in chemistry in 1977, says that modern science "is truly an art—that is, it is based on special skills and not general rules" (p. 42). Experimental method, in his view, "is the art of choosing an interesting question and scanning all the consequences of the theoretical framework thereby implied, all the ways nature could answer in the theoretical language chosen" (p. 42). Nature questioned in this way is, of course, simplified, for "amid the concrete complexity of natural phenomena, one phenomenon has to be selected as the most likely to embody the theory's implications in an unambiguous way. This phenomenon will then be abstracted from the environment and 'staged' to allow the theory to be tested in a reproducible and communicable way. The experimental dialogue thus corresponds to a highly specific procedure in which nature is cross-examined, as if in a court of law" (p. 42). In Prigogine's view, all measurements, all experiments, and all observations are only truths within situations.

Another good account of these modern developments is provided by Scarr (1985). In selectively adopting constructionist ideas, she posits that social constructionism is a means for better understanding the processes of psychological science. For example, one of the tenets of constructionism is that scientific facts do not exist independently but rather are created within the theoretical systems. Theory not only guides inquiry through the questions raised, it also influences the framework of research studies and interpretations of results. In doing research, psychologists seek to find "facts" to assimilate into their own worldviews and are biased toward "facts" that are concurrent with their prior beliefs. There is the further realization that reality is a construction of the researcher's mind and that no one set of facts, theory-guided in their invention, is absolute and real. In addition, there is the realization that the real world is a "cloud of correlated events" and interacting persons and environments. As researchers, psychologists can only construct theories about relations among these events, persons, and environments, then select a few elements, put them into studies, and in doing so eliminate other potentially important variables a priori from analysis. This view also highlights the problems of causal inference because behaviors in the real world are intrinsically confounded.

## Social Constructionism: More of a Bane than a Boon for Psychology?

With this background, we turn now to the full reality of social constructionism. Kvale (1992) raises the question of "whether the modern science of psychology can be developed and enriched by drawing on postmodern knowledge" (p. 1). Or, he goes on to ask, "Does postmodern thought radically undermine, or transform, the concept of scientific psychology as developed during the modern age?" (p. 1). To understand the nature of the impact alluded to in those questions, it is useful to identify social constructionism's central themes, as they relate to psychology as a science. In essence, social constructionism turns nearly every aspect of scientific psychology on its head. Gone is the faith in an objectively knowable universe and with it the hope that elimination of human bias, adherence to canons of methodology, and reliance on a pure language of observation can yield a true human science, mirroring psychological reality without distortion. Gone, too, is the modern notion of an essentialized self, an individual ego who is the locus of choice, action, and rational self-appraisal.

In their place is a panoply of perspectives whose common threads include an acknowledgement of multiple realities, socially constituted and historically situated, that defy adequate comprehension in objectivist terms. Language, in this view, actually constitutes the structures of social reality, so that new approaches (e.g., hermeneutic, narrative, deconstructionist, rhetorical, and discursive) appropriate in analyzing the "text" of human experience in social context need to be cultivated. The resulting image of psychological "science" is in some respects more humble (aiming only for the production of "local knowledges" that are more bounded and closer to the domain of practice). It is also a more disquieting image, holding out the promise of only a shifting, fragmentary, and constructed knowledge, without the bedrock certainty of firm (logical and empirical) foundations.

In this image of psychological "science," even the self is dethroned from a position of agency and conscious self-determination, vanishing into a proliferation of social roles on the interpersonal and cultural stage. Nowhere is this "death of the self" theme more explicit than in Shotter and Gergen (1989), where the self is viewed as continually defined and redefined through linguistic and cultural practices. It is argued that because forms of social discourse provide their "inhabitants" with the fundamental resources for defining the self, personal identity can be understood by way of a contextual analysis distinct from the person's self-understanding.

One implication of this dispersion of the self is a fundamental redefinition of such traditional concepts as motivation, emotion, learning, perception, and cognition, all of which are reconstituted in terms of social roles, competencies, or formative actions rather than individualized states, structures, or processes. As one example of such redefinition, the contributors to Middleton and Edwards (1990) develop the hypothesis that not only is memory a function of social context but also the process and organization of remembering and forgetting are social in nature. Left implicit is the bolder claim that individual consciousness is essentially socially constituted.

Such conceptual redefinition also lays the groundwork for important alternative approaches to research practice. To illustrate this point, the social constructionistic perspective raises the issue of what is the appropriate unit of analysis for research. For example, if instruction is communication among group members and cognition is socially shared and does not necessarily exist inside the head, the individual is no longer the focus of research; the situation or context becomes the most important aspect. Although there is not yet a good synthesis to such opposing views about the role of the individual and the context, there are a number of positive developments in that direction. As one example, Snow (1989) in the cognitive domain and Lazarus (1991) in the affective domain proposed the unit "persons-in-situations" to capture the dialectical nature of the interactions between individuals and situations. In the social and personality area, self-schemas (Markus & Nurius, 1986) and life tasks (Cantor & Kihlstrom, 1987) are relevant examples.

Efforts also are underway to explore more directly the implications of social constructionism for psychology in the schools. The *Educational Researcher* has been the main focus of such discourse up to now (e.g., Miller & Fredericks, 1991), although there have been other such endeavors. Prawatt and Floden's (1994) examination of constructionist views of learning and D. C. Phillips's (1994) critical analysis of narrative research methods are two good examples. The general conclusion one is left with is that social constructionist ideas have won a place in the intellectual agenda of psychologists who work in schools or who have an interest in schooling. Still, the practical payoffs of these endeavors are yet to be demonstrated.

# GROUNDING PRACTICE IN SCIENCE: THE PROBLEMS AND PROMISE

Psychological science and professional practice have long had a problematic relationship, in part because the primary purpose of psychological science is the development of theory, whereas the primary purpose of professional practice is the prevention and remediation of individual and group problems. Nevertheless, many psychologists believe it is important to consider the ways in which theory and research can guide practice, as well as the ways in which knowledge of professional practice can inform theory and research.

## Compatibility of Scientific and Practical Activities

Some psychologists, however, have disputed the claim that the science and practice of psychology are compatible and have tried to demonstrate that these two kinds of activities are done by psychologists who are as different as opposite poles of a magnet (B. N. Phillips, 1989). Supporters of this view seem to suggest that psychologists naturally gravitate, as a result of their personalities, to one pole or the other and that these different traits cannot coexist harmoniously because of an invisible but powerful repelling force between these two extremes of psychologists: the scientist and practitioner. Frank's (1984) review of studies, for example, suggests that researchers are more introverted, autonomous, creative, logical, field-independent, and technically oriented, whereas practitioners tend to be more intraverted, altruistic, intuitive, field-dependent, and service-oriented.

Others, however, do not feel that these differences are that serious or even that distinct. For example, Kimble (1984) found differences in value systems between researchers and practitioners but noted that the separation does not seem as clear-cut as is often thought. Krasner and Houts (1984) share his view, stating that insofar as psychology has one cultural heritage, different groups within that culture will have similar value systems. Matarazzo (1987) made an even stronger claim, pointing out that "there is only one psychology" and that all psychologists share a common frame of reference and core of knowledge.

## Research Activities of Practitioners

In an attempt to understand and, consequently, bridge the gap between science and practice, other researchers have studied the research activities of professional psychologists. Typically, this has been done by assessing both their utilization of research (willingness to conduct research and publish results and attitudes toward involvement in research) and their consumption of research (willingness to consult existing literature). According to summaries of this literature (e.g., Barlow, 1981; Shinn, 1987), the typical professional psychologist does not engage in research, publishes little or nothing, is unwilling to participate in research projects, and has a negative attitude toward research and research training.

So why are practitioners so unwilling to participate in research and consume existing literature? Utilizing information from the reports just cited, we can see that some of the major causes are these: (1) questions addressed in the research literature are not relevant to practice; (2) variables in studies are not representative of situations and populations that occur in actual practice; (3) treatments used are not adequately described, standardized, or selected and, therefore, not useful to the practitioner; (4) data analyses overemphasize group statistics and statistical significance, which often obscure information about individual differences and interaction effects; (5) researchers make little attempt to communicate their findings in a way that practitioners can use; and (6) there are limitations for practitioners themselves, including limited graduate school training in research activities, busy work schedules, and lack of personal motivation.

Thus, if researchers are to become more relevant to practitioners, they must, first and foremost, answer the questions practitioners are asking; cover topics that are currently popular; speak the language of practice as it is done in the schools rather than as they would like to see it; and emphasize group results and probability statistics less and case studies and other qualitative research more. However, while a cogent case can be made for practice-relevant research, a balancing caveat is in order. Research does not exist solely for the practitioner but is needed also for the advancement of knowledge. Research may be immediately practical, but it is a dangerous step to assume that demonstrable practicality is the acid test of its worth.

## Blurring the Distinction Between Basic and Applied Research

In the larger sense, this means that the distinction between basic and applied research in school psychology is becoming blurred. Traditionally, basic research has been distinguished from applied research by purported goals. Basic research sought knowledge for knowledge's sake and established general relations among theoretical constructs with no regard to practicality. Applied research, ideally, drew from these theoretical relations to address immediate problems.

It also means that we no longer have the luxury in school psychology of adhering to this traditional definition of basic research. When establishing general theoretical relations, our eyes must also focus on the implications for solving school problems. In fact, basic researchers in school psychology sometimes find themselves in the position of testing basic research questions in schools. In such cases, the conclusions drawn are susceptible to overinterpretation toward application rather than remaining in the basic research paradigm.

Societal demands for answers to school problems also place increased pressures on researchers to find not only statistically significant but also practically significant research findings. Unfortunately, as the distinction between basic and applied research is necessarily obscured in school psychology, the tendency for statistically significant relationships between theoretical constructs to be interpreted as practically significant relationships has increased. But never has the need to link theory and practice been greater in school psychology. This link, however, can only be as strong as the foundations on which crucial theoretical relations have been built. To rush in and implement school interventions with a weak theoretical basis is impractical. It is necessary, therefore, to spur research in the direction of demanding rigorous tests of purported theoretical relations before moving forward.

## Legitimizing Practice as a Source of Knowledge

A recurrent theme in social constructionist writings (e.g., Kvale, 1992), is a distrust of academic theory and a concomitant elevation of the local knowledge revealed in practice. One detailed treatment of this point appears in Semin and Gergen (1990), which surveys a variety of knowledge domains. One issue addressed by the contributors is the relationship of understanding at the practice level with that of the scientist. Although some of the contributors accord a special status to the scientist, others accord a special status to the practitioner, which is more in keeping with a social constructionist stance. For the most part, social constructionists argue that scientists draw roughly on the same regions of understanding as practitioners, thereby reducing the traditional boundaries that have kept the two distinct.

Another potentially far-reaching effort to integrate science and practice focuses on the process of knowledge generation. A necessity, in this approach, is the reconceptualization of the relationship between science and practice. This can be accomplished, according to Hoshmand and Polkinghorne (1992), by reframing the science-practice relationship from two separate activities based on disparate modes of reasoning and knowledge-generating procedures into a unified, interactive system of purposeful inquiry and action in which practice is legitimized as a source of knowledge.

However, granting a role for knowledge generated through practice does not mean the abandonment of disciplined inquiry. There must be appropriate standards for judging practice-based inquiry and the experiential knowledge of practitioners. It is fortunate, therefore, that some steps in depicting knowledge processes in professional practice have been taken (e.g., Dreyfus & Dreyfus, 1986). The study of performance in different domains of expertise also has potential relevance for understanding the acquisition of expertise in professional practice (e.g., Ericsson & Smith, 1991; Morrison, 1991).

## Going Beyond "Main Effects" Research Strategies

Assessing the boundaries of the theory and research that can contribute to school psychology is another difficult issue. The main reason for this is that the knowledge base of school psychology has greatly expanded over the years, in part because of the expanded role and responsibilities of school psychologists. As a consequence, a way to prioritize a potentially vast body of relevant theory and research is needed.

In responding to this situation, it is important to recognize the intrinsic limitations of different research paradigms and the knowledge they generate. For example, although "main effects" research constitutes one useful basis for practice, there are factors that limit the usefulness of this strategy. To illustrate, using an example provided by Rorer and Widiger (1983), in the prototypical experiment, one group is subjected to an experimental manipulation and another (the control group) is not. At the end of the experiment, the mean scores of the two groups are compared, and if they differ in a statistically significant sense (with the mean for the experimental group being higher), it is concluded that the intervention caused changes in the participants—in the predicted direction—in the outcome measured.

However, several things should be noted about this prototypical experiment and the conclusion reached. The intervention is applied to the *group as a whole*, and results *for the group* are used to infer a *within-individual effect*. The inference involved here is questionable, of course, because in the treated group some participants' scores were significantly higher, others did not significantly increase or decrease, and a few were significantly lower. As a consequence, there is no uniform effect on participants for which the intervention can be said to be the cause. One can only say that the intervention caused some scores of individuals to increase, a few to decrease, and most to stay the same on the outcome measure. To extract further information from such research, one would need to examine more closely those individual differences.

Such efforts rest on an important assumption, which is that interactions between personal characteristics and characteristics of interventions do exist and are important to researchers and practitioners. In addition, in going beyond main effects and attending to interactions, the analysis of behavior would be considerably extended and the process of conceptualizing and operationalizing individual differences and intervention variables would become crucial. It should not be surprising, therefore, that theories that guide such research, including conceptions of intervention, have been inadequate; that such research has often been methodologically weak, so that the presence of interactions could not be determined fully; and that few reliable interactions have been demonstrated up to now (Corno & Snow, 1986; Cronbach & Snow, 1977; B. N. Phillips, 1985).

## Practitioners as "Lamps" Rather than "Mirrors"

In contrast, some suggest that there is a more basic issue that should be confronted, namely the need for a better description of practitioners' roles in the application of science to practice (B. N. Phillips, 1987). One of the essential elements of the marriage of science and practice is for the practitioner to blend the desire to understand scientific theories, principles, and facts and the desire to *use them* to shape practice. For this to be possible, it is not enough merely for the practitioner to understand scientific knowledge. Applying science to practice involves active rather than passive understanding. What must be done is to "manipulate" scientific theories, principles, and facts and to "stage" them in such a way that they conform as closely as possible to the requirements of the practice situation and the purposes of the practitioner.

It is for such distinctions that an enlarged view of practitioners' roles should be introduced. For this purpose, two metaphors can be used as a frame of reference, one comparing the practitioner to a mirror or reflector, the other to a lamp or radiant projector (B. N. Phillips, 1987). The first presents the practitioner as a passive, imitative mirror of scientific truths; that is, the practitioner is assigned the role of holding up a mirror to scientific truths, to reflect them into his or her practice. The other envisions the practitioner as an active, expressive lamp that projects a light on such scientific truths, so that they are arranged in the colors and seen through the "sights and sounds" of practice and are fused and remolded in the crucible of practice. Thus, the practitioner is pictured not only as active, rather than merely passive, but also as contributing to science in the very process of using its theories and facts. In actuality, practitioners are discovering, in this process, what they have themselves partly made.

Nevertheless, we must not lose sight of the fact that in applying science to practice, there is no independent certainty (B. N. Phillips, 1989). Variations in professional practice are influenced by the conditions and goals of practice, and successful applications of science to practice are context- and situation-specific. In essence, professional practice is relativistic, with no absolutes. Uncertainty, therefore, is always a condition of applying science to practice. Accepting uncertainty as a given, practitioners also accept the fact that scientists can describe for them the world of their practice, not as they would like to see it, but only as scientists are able to see it through the combined impact of research results and theoretical concepts. In full realization of the import of this situation, practitioners accept not only the fact that they must learn from researchers and research findings but also the fact that they must learn from other practitioners. As a further necessity, practitioners see their efforts to improve practice as ways of exploring, rather than controlling, the unknown and realize they therefore open themselves to risks and take ultimate responsibility for the results of their practice.

## Functions of Theory and Research in Practice

Another challenge in understanding the relationship of science to practice is the need to develop a broader conception of the role of theory and research in professional practice. To appreciate this point more fully, it should be realized that practitioners construct their own practice and approach practice problems with particular viewpoints that implicitly influence the questions they raise about practice problems, the framework of their subsequent inquiries, and their interpretation and application of relevant theory and research. Although these may be personal idiosyncrasies, more often they are preferred ways of looking at practice issues and problems that are widely shared by colleagues. As a case in point, many school psychologists see the causes of classroom learning and behavior problems in child-centered terms and have a preference for child-changing interventions, in contrast to a systemic focus and a preference for system-changing interventions (B. N. Phillips, 1990b). Such differences in the level of analysis and the approach to practice issues and problems need to be taken into account, of course, in applications of theory and research to practice.

In addition, philosophical, value, and attitudinal differences divide researchers from practitioners (e.g., Frank, 1984; Kimble, 1984), although there is more shared experience and similarity of views when practitioners are part of a highly professionalized field. In psychology, for example, many practitioners have doctoral degrees and training in universities, where they were exposed to theory and research and did some research of their own. For them, scientific concepts and research methods have been a language of discourse and a way to define and resolve practice issues and problems. Yet, even under the more promising conditions, there still is a difference in definition of the usefulness of theory and research in practice. Many scientists see scientific research as providing *prescriptions* for practice. In contrast, practitioners see theory and research as contributing in more diverse ways to practice. For example, theory and research that raise new practice issues are a highly important aspect of usefulness. Overall, the practitioner's view of usefulness includes the scientists' prescriptive definition, but it extends to the more comprehensive range of functions that follow (see B. N. Phillips, 1986):

1.  Professional knowledge, that is, keeping up with developments and literature in areas related to one's work;

2.  Definition of practice problems and professional issues, that is, framing or conceptualizing problems and issues in psychological terms;

3.  Advocacy, that is, lobbying for new programs, attacking established policies, legitimizing budget allocations, and bringing new ideas to public attention; and

4.  Problem solving, that is, providing prescriptive information for on-the-job actions and decisions.

In summary, practitioners rarely use research directly and instrumentally, as the basis for making specific practice decisions. They believe that this is only one of the several ways in which research evidence and scientific ideas can contribute to practice.

## Role of Research Training Environments

The low utilization of theory and research by practitioners is often cited as evidence that our research training practices have had major deficiencies (e.g., Barlow, 1981; Shinn, 1987). The situation in most graduate education programs in professional psychology is that although students enter with a strong service commitment and a sense of efficacy regarding service, they tend to be ambivalent about their interest and capabilities to be researchers (Gelso, 1993). The effective graduate research environment, therefore, not only needs to teach research knowledge and skills but also must motivate its students. Although these programs offer a standard fare of required research courses and experiences (O'Sullivan & Quevillon, 1992; Wampold, 1986), few of them emphasize the enhancement of students' research attitudes as a training goal (Frank, 1984; Gelso, 1979; Shinn, 1987). Even the research experiences that are offered or required (dissertations, research seminars, statistics, etc.) can have negative effects on students' attitudes.

Despite these problems, studies of the research interests of students in professional psychology programs indicate that attitudes toward research do strengthen during the course of training, although increases are modest. It is important to note, moreover, that there is substantial between-program variability in the impact of these programs (Perl & Kahn, 1986; Royalty, Gelso, Mallinckrodt, & Garrett, 1992).

Given such deficiencies in research training, Gelso (1993) has attempted to revise and update a theory about the research training environment. His overall aim is to facilitate the development of research training experiences that will result in more and better utilization and production of research in professional psychology. In pursuit of this objective, Gelso has identified six ingredients (p. 470) that he hypothesizes will influence positively the research interests and activity of students. There is a need, he argues, for the following:

1.  Faculty to more adequately model scientific behavior and attitudes;

2. Scientific activity to be more positively reinforced, both formally and informally, in the education and training environment;

3. Students to be involved in research earlier in their training, and in a more nonthreatening way;

4. Training to emphasize that all research studies are limited and flawed in one way or another;

5. Varied approaches to research to be taught and valued; and

6. Students to be more regularly shown how science and practice can be wedded.

Gelso (1993) does note, however, that each ingredient has not received uniform research support. He further points out that linkages of these factors to the research training environment can be quite complex. The importance of such theory development and related research to the future success of research training environments in influencing the role of the scientist-practitioner in professional practice is also emphasized.

# EMERGING RESEARCH ROLES FOR SCHOOL PSYCHOLOGISTS: A BRIDGE FOR JOINING SCIENCE AND PRACTICE

Conducting and utilizing research in school systems is an old dilemma that needs frequent revisiting. Although the problem is not new, it is increasingly important. In this era of limits, funding and support for research logically depend on building bridges between the needs and interests of schools and those of school researchers. To be successful, essential distinctions also need to be made between a by-the-book model of research and approaches in which methods and methodology are less rigid and views of what is scientifically acceptable are more pragmatic. There also must be a shift in the focus of inquiry, from the desire to know to the desire to solve practical problems.

The politics of school systems is another consideration. Researchers need to understand the sources of power and influence in their school system, so they can create opportunities for research practice. School psychologists, in applying research findings, are also agents of change. This means that when research-based recommendations would change school policies or procedures or would upset deeply rooted beliefs and opinions or social and professional habits, they will activate defense mechanisms (Levy-Leboyer, 1988). The research findings then may be ignored or the scientific quality of the research studies questioned. Although school psychologists may rightly complain about such resistance, they may sometimes be partly to blame because they forgot to apply what they know about the psychology of change.

## Limitations of Science in the Formulation of Educational Policy

What is the role of science in the formulation of educational policy? Kendler (1993) argues that it is clearly in the scientific realm to comment on the likely consequences of competing educational policies. Judging the value, as opposed to the costs, of such policies is, however, a matter of political rather than scientific discourse.

The review of research on class size by Glass, Cahen, Smith, and Filby (1982) is a case in point. In their widely publicized review, which has been critically evaluated by Cooper (1989) and Slavin (1989), the research question was this: Does class size affect pupils' achievement and pupils' and teachers' attitudes? They located and analyzed the results for 77 studies on class size and pupils' achievement and 59 studies of affective and instructional effects of class size. Then they synthesized and summarized this accumulated knowledge through meta-analysis. In the meta-analysis, they used 725 statistical comparisons from the 77 studies and 371 comparisons from the 59 studies. In all analyses, they compared very small versus small classes, small versus medium classes, medium versus large classes, and large versus very large classes.

What Glass et al. (1982) found, for pupil achievement especially, is that (1) very small classes are much better than small classes, (2) small classes are better than large classes, and (3) large classes are better than very large classes. They also suggest a plausible explanation for the effect of class size, which is that teachers are better able to monitor individual pupils, keep them on task, and provide effective feedback when class size is substantially reduced.

But let us now take a closer look at their results (1) to see whether the impression created in the public eye was fully justified, and (2) to give additional meaning to, and a better understanding of, their major finding (Glass et al., 1982). To do so, we need to closely scrutinize Figure 2.1 (on p. 42) and Table A.1 (on p. 141). What should be noted, first, is that the authors assumed that class size and achievement are exponentially related; that is, the drop in learning as class size goes from 1 to 2 is greater than from 2 to 3 and so on. Also, a substantial number of the studies used to construct Figure 2.1 compared a class size of 1 pupil with class sizes of 20 to 35 pupils. In addition, the effects of class size on achievement are scaled in terms of percentile ranks. Although these conceptual and design decisions potentially limit the meaning of the data, if we take the overall result at face value it is obvious, in examining Figure 2.1, that most of the effect of class size occurs between class sizes of 1 to 10 and that for class sizes above 20 to 25 there is little effect. The most reasonable interpretation of this finding, therefore, is that significant improvement in achievement occurs only when class sizes are *drastically reduced*, to fewer than 10, and that increases in class size beyond 20 to 25 have little negative impact on achievement.

Taking this matter further, we see that the research question should not simply be whether reducing class size improves achievement. Two additional questions need to be addressed. First, does class size affect achievement enough to justify the cost? Second, are there better ways to obtain the same end? To answer the first question, greatly reducing the average class size (i.e., to 10 or fewer) would significantly affect achievement but greatly increase costs (for additional classrooms and teachers), whereas substantially increasing the average class size would have little impact on achievement but significant impact on lowering costs over time. The issue, however, needs to be considered in the larger context of how the educational dollar is spent. For example, Odden, Monk, Nakib, and Picus (1995) point out that 40% of the educational dollar is spent on nondirect instructional purposes. They also note that 25% is consumed by special education, where the teacher-student ratio is considerably smaller than that for regular classes.

To answer the second question, assume, for example, that one's goal is to increase the achievement of low-income pupils; a comparison would then be needed between the effects of using other educational resources, such as teacher aides, or spending the same amount of money on reducing the size of the classes. Clearly, educational decisions are not based simply on what works. Even if there is agreement on the importance of a goal, there is still the economic question of which of several alternative uses of limited resources will achieve the end most efficiently. In a larger sense, the overriding issue is how to restructure the system to make the use of educational dollars more productive.

There also are other factors to consider beyond the question of what works and how cost-effective it is. Making educational policy involves the agendas of stakeholder groups, as well as different personal opinions and perspectives on schools and schooling. Therefore, claims about what research can provide directly for the implementation of educational policy must be made cautiously.

## School Psychologists as "Knowledge Brokers" and "Melders"

Despite these acknowledged limitations, growing interaction between school psychology and educational policy needs special attention. Broadly defined, educational policy includes the development, execution, and assessment of educational programs. One might also argue that psychological science is inherently relevant to policy deliberations. The key question for school psychologists, therefore, is how the interaction between school psychology and educational policy can best be nurtured. Some school psychologists, of course, are conducting research that has obvious relevance to educational policy. Their research is decision-driven; that is, they take an educationally relevant question and design research to answer it. Others are involved in more basic research, that is, research that is knowledge-driven and not designed to shape educational policy but rather seeks answers relevant to psychological science. There is a place, however, for a new job description for some school psychologists, that of *knowledge broker* (using the term coined by Masters, 1984). This is a school psychologist who has a solid understanding of the research literature, knows how to evaluate research articles, and can communicate findings effectively to educational policymakers. The most important function of knowledge brokers is to demonstrate the relevance of research, especially when "face relevance" is not apparent to policymakers.

On a broader level, there is a continuum of involvement in educational policymaking by school psychologists, who function as scientist-practitioners, from knowledge-driven to decision-driven researchers. Turning again to Masters (1984), on the knowledge-driven end are the knowledge-producers, school psychologists who are involved in the production of knowledge for its own sake. While they have no aversion to applied science, their primary interest is in production rather than application. Next along Masters's continuum are the "melders." They are the knowledge-driven researchers, school psychologists who are beginning to make some effort to emphasize applications in their published articles' discussions and methodologies, for example, by putting in extra variables and demographic data. In the middle of Masters' continuum are the problem solvers. They find themselves attracted to research questions that policymakers want answered. Finally on the other end of Masters' continuum are the application specialists, who are driven only by policy considerations with little or no emphasis on basic research. Above the continuum stands the "spokesperson," who has such an interest in policy that he or she ceases to be a researcher and becomes more of a knowledge broker.

To follow up on Masters's (1984) views, what is needed in school psychology, in addition to more knowledge brokers, is a move toward more melding in school psychologists' research activities. What this means is that school psychologists would reflect more on the relevance of their research to educational policy. This does not mean, however, that school psychologists should all become application specialists. A continuum of involvement would be healthy for the field. Nonetheless, a greater appreciation of school psychologists' potential influence on educational policy is certainly in order. As for how this can be accomplished, school psychologists' understanding of methodologies that explain schools and schooling is an asset for educational policymaking, and this is something that school psychologists should recognize. For example, they need to emphasize ecological validity, as this can enhance the applicability of psychological research (e.g., McKee, Witt, Elliott, Pardue, & Judycki, 1987). School psychologists can also add educationally relevant factors to their research designs.

One may argue further that seeing educational relevance is an acquired skill that typically is not taught well in graduate training programs in school psychology. Therefore, greater emphasis needs to be placed on educational relevance in research components of graduate programs. There should also be more emphasis on the development of policy literacy. In essence, what is called for is a broad integration of psychological science and educational policy.

## School Psychologists as Secondary Researchers

To understand the full range of potential research roles for the school psychologist is a matter that turns on other developments in psychology. Of special note is the possibility that psychological science will become a two-tiered research enterprise (Schmidt, 1992). Applied to school psychology, this would mean that there would be one group of researchers who would specialize in individual empirical studies and who would be known as "primary" researchers. There would also be another group of researchers who would apply meta-analytic methods to cumulations of those individual empirical studies and who would be known as "secondary" researchers.

According to Schmidt (1992), the foundation for such developments is the continuing disappointment in the progress that psychology has made over the years. Although numerous reasons have been advanced for why progress has been slow (e.g., faulty assumptions in the philosophy of science and the negative influence of behaviorism), Schmidt focuses on the methods that psychologists have traditionally used to analyze and interpret data, both in individual empirical studies and in the research literature. He further argues that meta-analytic techniques provide a better way to think about the meaning of data, that the use of meta-analysis methods requires a change in the way we view individual empirical studies, and that they may even lead to changes in our views of the nature of scientific discovery.

In explaining his views, Schmidt (1992) points out that the development of theory is the major task of psychological science; he further notes that a theory is simply an "explanation of the processes that actually take place in a phenomenon" (p. 1177). In addition, he says that a theory is a causal explanation, which is important because the goal of psychological science is explanation, and explanation is always causal. The researcher is, in many ways, a detective whose "job is to find out why and how things happen the way they do" (p. 1177). But "to construct theories, one must first know some of the basic facts, such as the empirical relations among variables," and "these relations are the building blocks of theory" (p. 1177).

Schmidt (1992) later discusses the broader impact of meta-analysis, using as a starting point what he considers to be the unwarranted "faith in data as the direct source of scientific truths" and "the commonly held belief that research progress will be made if only we let the data speak" (p. 1179). In opposition to such views, Schmidt argues that "it would be more accurate to say that data come to us encrypted, and to understand their meaning we must break the code. Doing this requires meta-analysis" (p. 1179). As a consequence, the scientific status and value of individual empirical studies are, in his view, necessarily reduced.

The increasing status of meta-analytic reviews, in comparison to the status of narrative-subjective reviews, is a related development. Journals that formerly published only primary empirical studies are now publishing meta-analytic reviews. But a far more important development, according to Schmidt (1992), is that discoveries and advances in cumulative knowledge are increasingly being made by those who use meta-analytic techniques. They have been increasingly successful in discovering the latent meaning of research literature. It is even possible for the meta-analyst to make important scientific discoveries and contributions without doing any primary empirical studies. This process of mining the information in accumulated research literature is well underway today in some fields of psychology, and such efforts need to become a more important part of the research enterprise in school psychology. It should be noted, however, that there are issues and problems relevant to school practice that have not been well researched; that is, the needed primary empirical studies have not been done. In such areas, meta-analysis would be less useful.

Accepting Schmidt's (1992) position in school psychology would require a major change in the way school psychologists view the research process. Moreover, views of the scientific value of the individual empirical study, and even the fundamental nature of scientific discovery, may also need to change. It also would mean that school psychology would be more of a two-tiered research enterprise. Although there would continue to be a need for primary researchers, who would specialize in conducting individual empirical studies, the field would also need to develop a cadre of secondary researchers, who would apply complex and sophisticated meta-analysis methods to those cumulative studies.

Such a structure would also raise some troubling questions. What would be the relative status of the two groups of researchers in the overall school psychology research enterprise? In this division of labor, would the primary researchers be considered the "experimental" school psychologists, and the secondary researchers the "theoretical" school psychologists? What might happen, of course, with an increased emphasis on meta-analysis, is that the primary researchers in school psychology would also conduct the meta-analyses. But mastering a particular area of research often requires all of a researcher's time and effort. Meta-analytic methods, as they are refined and improved, are also becoming increasingly elaborate, complex, and abstract. Thus they are likely to be increasingly forbidding to all but the most statistically knowledgeable primary researchers. For these reasons, it is unlikely that these two roles will be combined, so a better solution would seem to be the development of a cadre of meta-analysts in school psychology who would work with the field's primary researchers. Such a collaborative approach is necessary because expert knowledge of the primary research area is desirable, and often indispensable, in applying meta-analysis optimally.

## School Psychologists as Disseminators of Their Own Research

The extent to which school psychologists disseminate the findings of their own studies in venues other than refereed research journals is unknown. Yet it is important that they make the findings they believe are relevant to the real world known to those who would apply them. Some of the modalities available to school psychologists for communicating research to potential users are: giving lectures to laypersons, consulting with school systems and community agencies and organizations, presenting workshops, publishing in a popular journal or magazine, preparing press releases, and communicating with legislators or the judiciary.

Academic school psychologists are the most involved in research and therefore are of special concern. Unfortunately, only a few of them will venture to bring their research findings to the attention of policymakers. This may reflect a lack of support by academic institutions or a lack of motivation, perhaps because this is seen as an inappropriate activity for school psychologists in their university roles. It may also reflect a lack of skill in the use of available venues for disseminating research. Nonetheless, such dissemination by academic school psychologists is a critical aspect of applying science to practice.

## JUDGING THE SCIENTIFIC MERIT AND PRACTICAL SIGNIFICANCE OF RESEARCH

Criteria for evaluating a research study are limited by how unchartable are the seas of discovery. In Szent-Gyorgi's (1971) words, "Research means going out into the unknown with the hope of finding something new to bring home" (p. 1). At the end of such a journey, there usually is a written report that shares the results with others. There are different kinds of research journeys, of course, and therefore empirical and other types of reports need to be evaluated by appropriate criteria. Some approaches are presented here for evaluating reports of empirical research journeys. For this purpose, it is assumed that both the form and the content of the report are important; that is, they are not mutually exclusive considerations.

### Criteria for Evaluating the Form and Content of an Empirical Research Report

The primary criteria for good scientific writing are accuracy and clarity (Bem, 1987). The first step toward clarity is organization, and the second is writing that is simple and direct. That is, it is succinct, concise, and to the point. If it is interesting and written with style, that is a plus, but these are only subsidiary virtues of the written report. In a more general sense, good scientific writing is good teaching. In essence, the report should be written to be comprehensible to the widest possible audience.

The written report also reflects the consensual image of the research process in psychology. As a result, there are guidelines for organizing the report and for evaluating each of its components (e.g., American Psychological Association, 1994). The first section will be an introduction that sets out the general research area in ordinary language, and the major question here is whether the basic idea of the study is clear. The report will next review the important research and scholarship on the issue and formulate the specific questions or hypotheses that will be addressed in the study. Two questions that arise in this connection are, first, how adequate the theory is, and second, whether there are close links to past related research. After this, the general

way in which the research will attack the problem will be described. One evaluation issue here relates to the adequacy of the information provided on the design, the nature of the participants and the setting, and other important matters. Another concerns whether there are methodological ambiguities. And a third involves the question of whether there are clear-cut links between the theory and research planned. Data analysis procedures are described next. The general issue here is whether the procedures are clearly presented, although the appropriateness of the data analysis will be the major concern. Following this, results will be presented. Here the important question is the extent to which the results are made clear. Finally, there will be a discussion section. In evaluating this section, the overriding issue will be whether the results are well summarized and related to the conclusions.

### Causal Implications of the Study

The causal implications of a study deserve special attention. Often when researchers discuss their results, they fall into a casual, sometimes careless, use of the words *cause* and *effect*. This is particularly the case when they are presenting interpretations of data and pointing to the need to rule out alternative explanations. As a consequence, especially in field research, they encounter the full range of problems associated with causation, problems philosophers of science have encountered for centuries.

Although there are several notions of causation (see Cook & Campbell, 1979, Chap. 1), most are similar to one another and to ordinary research usage.[2] The concept of cause implicit in many of these conceptions of a causal relationship is that the manipulation of a cause will result in the manipulation of an effect; that is, causation implies that by varying one factor, one can usually vary another.

Knowledge of what is likely to happen if something is deliberately varied has great practical value, of course, to school psychology. Without causal knowledge, one cannot easily bring

---

[2]It should be noted that these notions of causality are challenged by nonlinear dynamical systems theory, also popularly known as chaos theory (see Barton, 1994). However, at the present time it would not be fruitful to align causal models in school psychology with this perspective. Nonlinear dynamical data-analytic techniques are scarce and would prove difficult to apply and interpret in school psychology research.

about desired changes in practice, and even tentative, partial, and probabilistic causal knowledge can help to improve practice. For this reason, it is important to evaluate empirical research studies in terms of their causal implications.

In addressing causal implications, we are considering the question of validity. It is a question, however, that cannot be answered directly; we can only look at the study's vulnerabilities or potential sources of invalidity. Generally, studies that are true experiments are least vulnerable, and quasi-experimental studies (e.g., equivalent groups) are next in line. Others, including one-group, causal modeling, and case studies, are most vulnerable.

Although we can invoke many types of validity in developing a framework for evaluating causal implications, the four kinds of validity in Cook and Campbell's model (1979, Chap. 2) seem most useful because they correspond to the four major questions that a researcher or practitioner needs to ask in doing a technical analysis of a research study. These questions are as follows:

1. Is there a *relationship* between the variables? (statistical conclusion validity)
2. Is it a *causal* relationship? (internal validity)
3. Is there a *good fit* between the variables and the constructs they represent? (construct validity)
4. Is the relationship *generalizable?* (external validity)

Cook and Campbell (1979) provide answers to these questions by listing and discussing (in Chapter 2) some of the major threats to each kind of validity. They realize, of course, that no list of threats is perfect. Nor do they believe that each threat operates with equal frequency or that each affects the outcomes of applied research to the same degree. Their examples of each threat and their brief discussion of some of the critiques of their conceptualization of validity give additional meaning to this aspect of the scientific evaluation process.

## Special Challenges in Evaluating an ATI Study

Special problems with the dominant style of past aptitude-treatment interaction, or ATI, research (see Cronbach & Snow, 1977; B. N. Phillips, 1985) need to be taken into account in evaluating such a study. For example, we cannot place the usual emphasis on statistical significance. Confidence limits do preserve researchers and practitioners from premature closure, but closure in the end has to come from the theoretical coherence of results rather than from statistical significance alone. The costs of ATI experimentation and the need for replication and generalization also make it impossible to rely on statistics alone.

Past ATI research typically has regarded individuals as independent and ignored sociopsychological effects. For example, individual difference effects have been used to match individual students and treatments, in contrast to the determination of classroom-based interaction effects and matching classes to treatments.

Most intervention studies using the ATI paradigm have also been too brief. Complex school-related skills, such as those in reading, take years to acquire. Such studies, therefore, have educational significance only if their results apply throughout an extended period. There has also been too much emphasis on learning through practice rather than learning through instruction. That is, "repeated trials" has been the typical approach in ATI studies of school learning, so that learning outcomes are based on practice rather than on instructional effects. The need to find out what actually happens in the course of intervention is also important, as is the need for more educationally realistic interventions.

The demographic variables often used in ATI research need to be augmented with process-oriented variables (Snow, 1989). Age, sex, socioeconomic status (SES), and so on should not be thought of as the major individual difference variables. Variability within a demographic subgroup is enormous, and such variables might better be considered as only proxies for more meaningful ATI research variables.

Two other methodological factors also need special attention. Samples in ATI research are generally too small. For example, Cronbach and Snow (1977) recommend a sample size of 100 as a minimum. They also advocate the use of regression rather than analysis-of-variance models for ATI research.

## Significance of the Study for the Discipline

There are two levels of scientific evaluation. In the first, formative evaluation, a research study is evaluated as a process and product, using psychological science's agreed-on set of criteria. In this situation, which was described previously, the evaluator concentrates on the way a research study was given form and shape and was conducted and written up.

In the second level, the significance of a study for the discipline is assessed. This amounts to summative evaluation, or a summing up of a study's probable impact on the field. It is also important to note that this advanced level of evaluation does not compete with or supplant formative evaluation. That is, formative evaluation is an important constituent of the higher level but can in no way account for it.

Although there are no ready-made sources of criteria for this higher level of evaluation, one good source is the expert who evaluates manuscripts on a regular basis for research-oriented journals. From research on this manuscript review process (see Fiske & Fogg, 1990; Gottfredson, 1978), we know that reviewers as a group are highly credible, visible experts. We also know a good deal about the things reviewers consider in evaluating manuscripts. Of particular importance is the high priority assigned to a manuscript's significance for the field. As evidence of such probable impact, reviewers note such features as these (Gottfredson, 1978): it makes the reader think about something in a different way; it offers a new perspective on an old problem; it speaks to central problems that are facing the discipline; it provokes much useful controversy; it attempts to unify important aspects of the field; it deals with an important topic; it outlines implications for future work; and, it integrates findings from diverse sources into a coherent framework.

## Evaluation of the Practical Usefulness of Research Reports

The criteria for scientific evaluation that are included in the previous sections are of primary concern to the research psychologist. In contrast, research reports that are to be shown to practitioners must be useful, as well as scientifically meritorious. However, the usefulness of a research report involves a number of considerations. A research report is useful only if it is judged to be high on both the dimensions of scientific generality and ecological validity. For example, in evaluating the usefulness of a report of experimental research, we would realize that the report's findings cannot be presumed to be relevant to the real world of schools and schooling. We would, instead, look for evidence that this presumption of relevance to schools and schooling had been demonstrated.

Another consideration is that if we take into account the limited access of practitioners to the research literature, its usefulness depends on its accessibility and dissemination. In addition, research reports that include direct implications for action are more useful. That is, to be useful in this sense, the meaning of research results needs to be readily grasped. In writing up research results, therefore, it is important for researchers to make the meaning clear.

To sum up these and other considerations, research reports that are useful to practitioners are understandably written and not overly technical, have clear relevance to a practical problem or issue, sample a population of practical interest, make practice recommendations supported by the data, provide adequate replication or follow-up of results, and add to practical knowledge.

## Value of Integrated Knowledge Bases in School Psychology

Individual research studies have an important place in the research enterprise. Yet knowledge of their results offers little power to the school psychologist because, contrary to widespread belief, no single study can resolve a practice issue or answer a school policy question. Called on to assume many roles and perform myriad tasks, the school psychologist also needs cumulative knowledge, and that requires literature reviews. In essence, the school psychologist needs to mine the information in accumulated research literature.

As a case in point, the school psychologist needs systematic knowledge about the *efficacy* of educational and psychological interventions for individual students and schools. However, in any given intervention, the relevant research often yields an ambiguous mix of positive, suggestive, and null results. School psychologists must then pick through these results with the hope of finding a preponderance of evidence that supports a conclusion about efficacy.

Fortunately, meta-analysis is an alternative approach to integrating and interpreting a body of research. Although meta-analytic methods have limitations, there are good reasons to believe that their results on the efficacy of educational and psychological interventions are more credible than those of conventional reviews. There have also been many meta-analyses of intervention effectiveness, as evidenced by Lipsey and Wilson's (1993) compilation of the results of

302 meta-analyses of psychological, educational, and behavioral interventions.

To put the results of these meta-analyses in context, and thus enhance their usability in the schools, it is necessary to define the level or scope of actually existing and projected educational, psychological, and behavioral interventions. At one end of such a continuum, we can distinguish intervention techniques, such as the use of advance organizers in teaching lesson plans or self-disclosure by school psychologists in counseling sessions. At the other end are broad policy-based initiatives that combine many intervention elements, organizational arrangements, and so forth, for example, mainstreaming handicapped children or school desegregation efforts.

In the Lipsey and Wilson (1993) survey, both ends of this continuum were excluded. They focused instead on mid-range interventions, including psychotherapy, parent effectiveness training, student tutoring, and intervention programs for kindergarten children (see their Table 1, pp. 1183–1191, for the complete list of intervention categories and subcategories for which they provided meta-analytic results). It is also noteworthy that Lipsey and Wilson concluded, from their broad review of all the meta-analytic evidence, that educational, psychological, and behavioral interventions generally have meaningful positive effects on intended outcomes. The number and scope of effective interventions covered by this conclusion is impressive. Of additional importance to the practitioner, Lipsey and Wilson also concluded that effect sizes in general are large enough to support the claim that educational, psychological, and behavioral intervention generally is efficacious in practical, as well as statistical, terms. This is good news, of course, for the practicing school psychologist.

# IDENTIFYING MODEL SCHOOL INTERVENTION PROGRAMS

School psychologists need to evaluate intervention *programs*. These are programmatic efforts that include intervention strategies as critical ingredients, that can be adopted in school systems, and that can be made part of the practice of school psychologists. What is needed for this purpose is a set of criteria that has a discernable orientation that practitioners would use in making such decisions. For example, these criteria

need to be conditioned by the systemic character of school-based intervention. They are, therefore, necessarily grounded in contextual information, and they should be ecologically oriented.

## Quantitative Versus Qualitative Evaluation

In evaluating an intervention program, the initial question is whether it has made contributions that are enduring rather than ephemeral. That is, the prime concern is how to determine whether the intervention program has worked. One extreme would be to rely entirely on rigorous empirical data to decide the question. From this perspective, an intervention program would have produced irrefutable scientific evidence of its capacity to produce projected outcomes. At the other extreme is reliance on school acceptance. From this perspective, evidence that the program worked would be reflected in the positive responses of those who provided and received the intervention. Little emphasis would be placed on the outcomes of formal evaluations on the assumption that those charged with the allocation of scarce educational resources would have examined program outcomes according to their own norms, and they would have concluded that their expectations had been met. The perspective taken here, however, is that evaluation of an intervention program should be based on quantitative outcomes, although consideration should also be given to desired outcomes, setting conditions, local norms, and other consumer-oriented factors.

## Criteria for Identifying Model School Intervention Programs

In taking on this evaluative task, the school psychologist needs a way to identify *model* programs. For this purpose, multiple criteria such as the following, which are partly derived from Price, Cowen, Lorion, and Ramos-McKay (1988), would be helpful:

1. Description of the target of the intervention program, that is, characteristics of recipients and the nature of their problems.
2. Description of the steps to be taken to recruit intervention recipients.
3. Description of the skills (and personnel) necessary to conduct the intervention program.
4. Statement of the rationale for and research evidence that directly or indirectly supports

the expected efficacy of the intervention program.

5. Specification of measurable program objectives.
6. Detailed description of the actual interventions.
7. Description of evaluation procedures, instruments, follow-up data, and program monitoring.
8. Description of how the intervention program is related to the school as an organization and to other groups and agencies in the community.
9. Recognition of ethical and potential legal issues and a description of their resolution.
10. Description of factors that would influence the transferability of the intervention program to other school systems.

Unfortunately, few intervention programs that might be used in school systems will survive such scrutiny. As evidence, Price et al. (1988) examined approximately 300 programs used in schools and other community settings and analyzed detailed materials on a further screened sample of 52. Of these, only 14 were found to have sufficiently met the criteria for model programs. One reason for such high attrition is that only one-third of the 300 submitted programs had systematically evaluated their efforts. A significant number also lacked program manuals or other means of documenting their efforts. Because of these vaguely defined procedures, they would have little chance of successful replication in other settings. A number of others appeared to have methodologically flawed evaluations that cast a shadow on outcome findings. In still others, the program's value was accepted without question by its adherents, so there was no perceived need to evaluate it.

Nevertheless, many intervention programs out there work, and the prime concern is to identify the ones that have been used successfully or that have good potential. The previously listed criteria will help the school psychologist do this.

## The ISA-SPS School Intervention Program as an Exemplary Model

One good example of a school intervention program that meets the criteria is the Improving Social Awareness–Social Problem Solving (ISA-SPS) program, initiated and carried out by Elias

and associates (see, especially, Elias & Clabby, 1989, 1991). A strength of their comprehensive intervention is that it approached the problem of transition to middle school, and the related stress on students, from an ecological perspective. In addition to uncovering over 20 discrete stressors, ranging from remembering one's locker combination to resisting peer pressure to use alcohol or drugs, they found that there were two focal points for most of the students' difficulties: initial transition difficulties, centering around adaptation to many new routines, and longitudinal problems, centering around peer pressure and acculturation into the social system of the middle school.

Based on an analysis of problems from a child and systems perspective, a three-part strategy for developing students' social competence was designed. The first component focused on the development of skills in self-control, group participation, and social awareness. It emphasized such things as the students' ability to follow directions; calm themselves when upset; start and maintain a conversation without being provoked by others to lose self-control (or provoking others to do so); give, receive, and obtain help; and build trusting and caring friendships. The second strategy concerned the development of skills in social decision making and problem solving, and in this phase of the intervention the students learned an eight-step affective and cognitive strategy to use when under stress and when they faced problems for which they had to make choices or decisions. In fulfilling the third goal of the intervention, promoting skill acquisition and application in the environment, teachers and other school personnel and parents were trained in techniques to elicit students' thoughts about decision making in social and academic situations and to cue and prompt students to use specific self-control and group participation skills.

Results of this intervention have also been evaluated. On a key measure that included 28 middle school stressors, covering conflicts with authority and older students, academic pressure, peer relationships and peer pressure for substance abuse, and logistical difficulties, significant differences occurred between students who received the intervention and no-intervention controls (Elias, Gara, & Ubriaco, 1985). In additional analyses, there was evidence that students' levels of social decision-making and problem-solving skills mediated intervention outcomes.

As for generalization of the intervention

program at other environmental levels, guidance contacts and disciplinary records show that students used their social decision-making and problem-solving skills when prompted by the guidance counselor or school administrator, but their spontaneous use of these skills appeared to diminish over time. To overcome this problem, a middle school "survival skills" program was developed over a period of years that included an organizational and study skills component and an infusion of social decision making into the social studies curriculum. From the results of these further endeavors, it would appear to be necessary to complement a skills-focused intervention with supportive changes in the middle school environment if the stress of the transition process is to be minimized (Elias & Clabby, 1991).

Another, more general finding was that efforts to obtain and maintain the support of parents, administrators and school board members, and the teachers and students most closely involved in the intervention program were of utmost importance. The convergence of the interests and synergistic actions of multiple constituencies and systems is an implicit principle of all successful school intervention programs.

To sum up, Elias and his associates, in articulating their conceptual and operational approach for their intervention work, have provided descriptions of the key tasks in the development of a successful and enduring intervention that also track the criteria previously identified. But other good examples of this comprehensive approach to school intervention are available in the literature. To mention only one, Rosenfield (1992) describes a program for developing school-based consultation teams that includes a design for organizational change consisting of three major stages—initiation, implementation, and institutionalization. She recognizes, among other important factors, that innovative change in schools is a developmental process and that development activities must be integrated with efforts to change the school culture and structures. The importance of evaluation at all stages of the innovation and change process is also emphasized.

# ETHICAL AND LEGAL ASPECTS OF RESEARCH

Psychology's concern with ethical issues in research, especially those involving human participants, is long-standing. The basic consideration,

in such concerns, is whether ethical and methodological issues are inextricably linked (Sieber, 1992a). Ethically sensitive research is more likely than ethically questionable research to produce valid results because participants are more likely to be cooperative with and trusting of the researcher and research process.

One goal of planning ethically sensitive research, of course, is to meet federal legal requirements and avoid problems with institutional review boards. A more important goal, however, is to deal concretely with such ethical and legal issues as privacy and confidentiality, deception, informed consent, assessment of potential research risks and benefits, and problems with vulnerable populations.

To address these and other issues, ethical and legal aspects of research are receiving increasing attention. It is of special note, for example, that codes of ethics have been regularly revised in recent years, to reflect more adequately current ethical issues in research, and that the federal government and the judiciary have stepped up efforts to set up guidelines and regulations and to establish legal principles that promote ethically and legally sensitive research practices. The consensus at the present time among psychologists about the ethics of research is represented by *Ethical Principles in the Conduct of Research with Human Participants* (American Psychological Association, 1982). In addition, the more general and comprehensive *Ethical Principles of Psychologists and Code of Conduct* (American Psychological Association, 1992) includes a number of sections on research. To give critical consideration to legal aspects of research, we should also be familiar with the National Research Act of 1974 (Public Law 93–348), which outlines federal policies for research with human participants. Regulations implementing this act are issued through the U.S. Department of Health and Human Services. In general, these regulations reflect prevailing legal opinion about appropriate conduct in research activity.

Questions have been raised, however, about the helpfulness of the new APA codes for dealing with research ethics. For example, Sieber (1992b) believes that deficiencies are particularly evident in the following areas: privacy and confidentiality, institutional review boards, deception, debriefing, and data sharing, as well as research on children and adolescents and marginalized populations and research in organizational contexts. To help researchers, she provides bibliographic resources and other suggestions for dealing with these problematic situations.

There are also increasing numbers of scholarly and empirical investigations of ethical and legal aspects of research practice. A good example is the book by Diener and Crandall (1978) in which the ethical dilemmas that arise in research are thoroughly discussed. The interdisciplinary volume edited by Stanley and Sieber (1992), which emphasizes children's rights, the consent process, and ethical and legal guidelines for research on high-risk behaviors, and Chapter 9 of Jacob-Timm and Hartshorne (1995), which emphasizes ethical and legal issues in doing research in the schools, are two other good examples. Other authors (e.g., Adair, Dushenko, & Lindsay, 1985; Baumrind, 1985) have reviewed research that documents the impact of ethical procedures on research results. According to the *Publication Manual of the American Psychological Association*, ethical practices should be reported and described; but as these authors point out, detailed descriptions of ethical practices are generally not included in published research reports (although some journals require a written statement from authors that they have complied with APA ethical standards). This impedes knowing the effects of ethical procedures on research results and makes it more difficult to take ethical considerations into account in applying research to practice.

## ACADEMICIANS AND PRACTITIONERS: A VITAL BUT DIFFICULT PARTNERSHIP IN SCHOOL PSYCHOLOGY

All previous discussion in this chapter implies that there is also a need to overcome attitudes that tend to justify and reinforce the isolation of the academic community, on the one hand, and the practitioner community, on the other. Today, when psychological science and practice in the schools are moving at a rapid pace, new questions and new interests in both psychological science and professional practice require academicians and practitioners to enter into new dialogues and to look for a new coherence between the science and practice of school psychology. In such collaboration, the practicing school psychologist can provide the insight, wisdom, judgment, and experience possible only from one who interacts daily with school issues and problems.

This form of collaboration also has other benefits. Practitioners keep one foot in the world of practice, whereas academicians sometimes are diverted by the theoretically elegant. This is not necessarily bad, of course, from the perspective of psychology as a discipline, although it is important to keep the focus of the collaborative enterprise on the important issues and problems of school practice. Having practitioners as collaborators also lends authority to research on problems in school practice and to the application of research findings. Collaboration is also likely to make practicing school psychologists more receptive to scientific ideas and more analytic in assessing their value. Increased feelings of professional confidence and a strengthened commitment to the improvement of school psychological practice may be another result.

To make such a partnership work, new operational strategies are needed. Although it is difficult to say with precision what the new arrangements would be, if they are to work they will have to serve the psychological ends of the greater community. There is an acronym that makes this point, the three C's—communication, collaboration, and colleagueship (Bevan, 1991). Neither university training programs in school psychology as they are now constituted nor scholarly and professional societies that serve school psychology as they now operate provide a climate suitable for what must evolve. More than ever before, training programs and organizational experiments must somehow be directed toward integrating science and practice themes and strategies. It will take time and great patience, of course, for academicians and practitioners in school psychology to learn to talk, think, and act together.

## REFERENCES

Adair, J. G., Dushenko, T. W., & Lindsay, R. C. L. (1985). Ethical regulations and their impact on research practice. *American Psychologist, 40,* 59–72.

American Psychological Association (1982). *Ethical principles in the conduct of research with human participants.* Washington, DC: Author.

American Psychological Association (1992). *Ethical principles of psychologists and code of conduct.* Washington, DC: Author.

American Psychological Association (1994). *Publication manual of the American Psychological Association.* (4th ed.). Washington, DC: Author.

Barlow, D. H. (1981). On the relation of clinical research to clinical practice: Current issues, new directions. *Journal of Consulting and Clinical Psychology, 49,* 147–155.

Barton, S. (1994). Chaos, self-organization, and psychology. *American Psychologist, 49,* 5–14.

Baumrind, D. (1985). Research using intentional deception: Ethical issues revisited. *American Psychologist, 40,* 165–174.

Bem, D. J. (1987). Writing the empirical journal article. In M. P. Zanna and J. M. Darley (Eds.), *The compleat academic: A practical guide for the beginning social scientist.* New York: Random House.

Bevan, W. (1991). Contemporary psychology: A tour inside the onion. *American Psychologist, 46,* 475–483.

Bevan, W., & Kessel, F. (1994). Plain truths and home cooking: Thoughts on the making and remaking of psychology. *American Psychologist, 49,* 505–509.

Cantor, N., & Kihlstrom, J. (1987). *Personality and social intelligence.* Englewood Cliffs, NJ: Prentice-Hall.

Cook, T. D., & Campbell, D. T. (1979). *Quasi-experimentation: Design & analysis issues for field settings.* Chicago: Rand McNally.

Cooper, H. M. (1989). Does reducing student-to-instructor ratios affect achievement? *Educational Psychologist, 24,* 79–98.

Corno, L., & Snow, R. E. (1986). Adapting teaching to individual differences among learners. In M. C. Wittrock (Ed.), *Handbook of research on teaching* (3rd ed., pp. 605–629). New York: Macmillan.

Cronbach, L. J., & Snow, R. E. (1977). *Aptitude and instructional methods: Handbook for research on interactions.* New York: Irvington.

Diener, E., & Crandall, R. (1978). *Ethics in social and behavioral research.* Chicago: University of Chicago Press.

Dreyfus, H. L., & Dreyfus, S. E. (1986). *Mind over machine.* New York: Free Press.

Elias, M. J., & Clabby, J. F. (1989). *Social decision making skills: A curriculum guide for the elementary grades.* Rockville, MD: Aspen.

Elias, M. J., & Clabby, J. R. (1991). *School-based enhancement of children and adolescents' social problem solving skills.* San Francisco: Jossey-Bass.

Elias, M. J., Gara, M., & Ubriaco, M. (1985). Sources of stress and support in children's transition to middle school: An empirical analysis. *Journal of Clinical Child Psychology, 14,* 112–118.

Ericsson, K. A., & Smith, J. (Eds.). (1991). *Toward a general theory of expertise: Prospects and limits.* Cambridge: Cambridge University Press.

Fiske, D. W., & Fogg, L. (1990). But the reviewers are making different criticisms of my paper: Diversity and uniqueness in reviewer comments. *American Psychologist, 45,* 591–598.

Fiske, D. W., & Shweder, R. A. (Eds.). (1986). *Metatheory in social science: Pluralisms and subjectivities.* Chicago: University of Chicago Press.

Frank, B. (1984). The Boulder model: History, rationale, and critique. *Professional Psychology: Research and Practice, 15,* 417–435.

Frisby, C. L. (1995). When facts and orthodoxy collide: *The Bell Curve* and the robustness criterion. *School Psychology Review, 24,* 12–19.

Gelso, C. J. (1979). Research in counseling: Methodological and professional issues. *The Counseling Psychologist, 8,* 7–35.

Gelso, C. J. (1993). On the making of a scientist-practitioner: A theory of research training in professional psychology. *Professional Psychology: Research and Practice, 24,* 468–476.

Glass, G. V., Cahen, L. S., Smith, M. L., & Filby, N. N. (1982). *School class size: Research and policy.* Beverly Hills, CA: Sage.

Gottfredson, L. S. (1978). Evaluating psychological research reports: Dimensions, reliability, and correlates of quality judgments. *American Psychologist, 33,* 920–934.

Gottfredson, L. S. (1994). The science and politics of race-norming. *American Psychologist, 49,* 955–963.

Hernstein, R. J., & Murray, C. (1994). The Bell Curve:*Intelligence and class structure in American life.* New York: Free Press.

Hoshmand, L. T., & Polkinghorne, D. E. (1992). Redefining the science-practice relationship and professional training. *American Psychologist, 47,* 55–66.

Jacobson, J. W., Mulick, J. A., & Schwartz, A. A. (1995). A history of facilitated communication. *American Psychologist, 50,* 750–765.

Jacob-Timm, S., & Hartshorne, T. (1995). *Ethics and law for school psychologists* (2nd ed.). Brandon, VT: Clinical Psychology Publishing.

Kendler, H. H. (1993). Psychology and the ethics of social policy. *American Psychologist, 48,* 1046–1053.

Kimble, G. A. (1984). Psychology's two worlds. *American Psychologist, 39,* 833–839.

Krasner, L., & Houts, A. (1984). A study of the "value" systems of behavioral scientists. *American Psychologist, 39,* 840–850.

Kvale, S. (1992). *Psychology and postmodernism.* Newbury Park, CA: Sage.

Lazarus, R. (1991). *Emotion and adaptation.* New York: Oxford University Press.

Levy-Leboyer, C. (1988). Success and failure in applying psychology. *American Psychologist, 43,* 779–785.

Lipsey, M. W., & Wilson, D. B. (1993). The efficacy of psychological, educational, and behavioral interventions: Confirmation from meta-analysis. *American Psychologist, 48,* 1181–1209.

Markus, H., & Nurius, P. (1986). Possible selves. *American Psychologist, 41,* 954–969.

Masters, J. C. (1984). Psychology, research, and social policy. *American Psychologist, 39,* 851–862.

Matarazzo, J. D. (1987). There is only one psychology, no specialties, but many applications. *American Psychologist, 42,* 893–903.

McKee, W. T., Witt, J. C., Elliott, S. N., Pardue, M., & Judycki, A. (1987). Practice informing research: A survey of research dissemination and knowledge utilization. *School Psychology Review, 16*, 338–347.

Middleton, D., & Edwards, D. (Eds.). (1990). *Collective remembering.* Newbury Park, CA: Sage.

Miller, S. I., & Fredericks, M. (1991). Postpositivistic assumptions and educational research: Another view. *Educational Researcher, 20*, 2–8.

Minogue, K. (1985). *Alien powers: The pure theory of ideology.* New York: St. Martin's Press.

Morrison, J. E. (Ed.). (1991). *Training for performance: Principles of applied human learning.* New York: Wiley.

Odden, A., Monk, D., Nakib, Y., & Picus, L. (1995). The story of the education dollar. *Phi Delta Kappan, 77*, 161–168.

O'Sullivan, J. J., & Quevillon, R. P. (1992). Forty years later: Is the Boulder model still alive? *American Psychologist, 47*, 67–70.

Perl, K. G., & Kahn, M. W. (1983). Psychology graduate students' attitudes toward research: A national survey. *Teaching of Psychology, 10*, 139–143.

Phillips, B. N. (1985). New directions in ATI research: Concepts and methods. In C. R. Reynolds and V. L. Wilson (Eds.), *Methodological and statistical advances in the study of individual differences* (pp. 92–115). Hillsdale, NJ: Erlbaum.

Phillips, B. N. (1986). The impact of education and training on school psychological services. In S. N. Elliott & J. C. Witt (Eds.), *The delivery of psychological services in schools: Concepts, processes, and issues* (pp. 329–348). Hillsdale, NJ: Erlbaum.

Phillips, B. N. (1987). On science, mirrors, lamps, and professional practice. *Professional School Psychology, 2*, 221–229.

Phillips, B. N. (1989). Role of the practitioner in applying science to practice. *Professional Psychology: Research and Practice, 20*, 3–8.

Phillips, B. N. (1990a). Reading, evaluating, and applying research in school psychology. In T. B. Gutkin and C. R. Reynolds (Eds.), *The handbook of school psychology* (2nd ed., pp. 53–73). New York: Wiley.

Phillips, B. N. (1990b). *School Psychology at a turning point: Ensuring a bright future for the profession.* San Francisco: Jossey-Bass.

Phillips, B. N. (1993). Challenging the stultifying bonds of tradition: Some philosophical, conceptual, and methodological issues in applying the scientist-practitioner model. *School Psychology Quarterly, 8*, 27–37.

Phillips, D. C. (1994). Telling it straight: Issues in addressing narrative research. *Educational Psychologist, 29*, 13–21.

Prawatt, R. S., & Floden, R. E. (1994). Philosophical perspectives on constructivist views of learning. *Educational Psychologist, 29*, 37–48.

Price, R. H., Cowen, E. L., Lorion, R. P., & Ramos-McKay, J. (1988). *14 ounces of prevention: A casebook for practitioners.* Washington, DC: American Psychological Association.

Prigogine, I., & Stengers, I. (1984). *Order out of chaos.* New York: Bantam.

Rorer, L. G., & Widiger, T. A. (1983). Personality structure and assessment. *Annual Review of Psychology, 34*, 431–463.

Rosenfield, S. (1992). Developing school-based consultation teams: A design for organizational change. *School Psychology Quarterly, 7*, 27–46.

Royalty, G. M., Gelso, C. J., Mallinckrodt, B., & Garrett, K. (1986). The environment and the student in counseling psychology: Does the research training environment influence graduate students' attitudes toward research? *The Counseling Psychologist, 14*, 9–30.

Scarr, S. (1985). Constructing psychology: Making facts and fables for our times. *American Psychologist, 40*, 499–512.

Schmidt, F. L. (1992). What do data really mean? Research findings, meta-analysis, and cumulative knowledge in psychology. *American Psychologist, 47*, 1173–1181.

Schon, D. A. (1983). *The reflective practitioner.* New York: Basic Books.

Semin, G. R., & Gergen, K. J. (Eds.). (1990). *Everyday understanding: Social and scientific implications.* Newbury Park, CA: Sage.

Shinn, M. R. (1987). Research by practicing school psychologists: The need for fuel for the lamp. *Professional School Psychology, 2*, 235–243.

Shotter, J., & Gergen, K. J. (1989). *Texts of identity.* Newbury Park, CA: Sage.

Sieber, J. E. (1992a). *Planning ethically responsible research: A guide for students and internal review boards.* Newbury Park, CA: Sage.

Sieber, J. E. (1992b). Will the new code help researchers to be more ethical? *Professional Psychology: Research and Practice. 25*, 369–375.

Slavin, R. E. (1989). Class size and student achievement: Small effects of small classes. *Educational Psychologist, 24*, 99–110.

Snow, R. (1989). Cognitive-conative aptitude interactions in learning. In R. Kanfer, P. Ackerman, & R. Cudeck (Eds.), *Abilities, motivation, and methodology: The Minnesota symposium on learning and individual differences* (pp. 435–474). Hillsdale, NJ: Erlbaum.

Stanley, B., & Sieber, J. E. (Eds.). (1992). *Social research on children and adolescents: Ethical issues.* Newbury Park, CA: Sage.

Szent-Gyorgi, A. (1971). Looking back. *Perspectives in Biology and Medicine, 15*, 1–6.

Wampbold, B. E. (1986). Toward quality research in counseling psychology: What the professionals say. *The Counseling Psychologist, 14*, 37–48.

## CHAPTER 4

# STRUCTURAL EQUATION MODELING IN SCHOOL PSYCHOLOGY

TIMOTHY Z. KEITH
*Alfred University*

The purpose of this chapter is to provide an overview of the use of structural equation modeling, with a special emphasis on the kinds of research problems of interest to school psychologists. Structural equation modeling (SEM) is a multivariate method for determining the magnitude of influence of one or several presumed causes on one or several presumed effects. It is built on the specification of a model—often in the form of a drawing—of cause and effect, and this model may be thought of as the researcher's informal theory of the influence of one variable on another. Used primarily in nonexperimental research in which neither the independent nor the dependent variables are manipulated, SEM also offers a powerful method for the analysis of experimental, quasi-experimental, and psychometric research.

Structural equation modeling goes by a variety of names; it is also referred to as analysis-of-covariance structures, latent variable analysis, and causal analysis. Path analysis and confirmatory factor analysis are subsumed under the more general approach of SEM. Linear structural relations, or LISREL (Jöreskog & Sörbom, 1993) was the first and is still the most widely known computer program for conducting SEM, and the term LISREL is sometimes used interchangeably with SEM.

In this chapter the term SEM will be used to refer to all types of structural equation modeling, with and without latent variables. The term *path*

*analysis* will be used to refer to a subtype of SEM that uses only *measured* variables, whereas *latent variable* SEM will be used to refer to the subtype of SEM in which models include latent or unmeasured variables. These terms will be explained as the chapter progresses.

A number of computer programs are designed to conduct SEM, along with path analysis and confirmatory factor analysis. In addition to LISREL, other common programs include EQS (Bentler, 1995) and CALIS, a part of the SAS statistical program (Hartmann, 1995). The analyses in this chapter were conducted by using Amos (Analysis of Moment Structures), which includes both a drawing program and pictorial input and output of models (Arbuckle, 1997). Amos is available both as a stand-alone program and as a part of the SPSS program (SPSS, Inc. 1990). The journal *Structural Equation Modeling* publishes reviews of these and other SEM programs (e.g., Hox, 1995).

This chapter will present SEM as a nonexperimental method with importance for school psychology. Path analysis will be presented as one of the most valuable methods for the analysis of nonexperimental data, and SEM with latent variables will be presented as a more complete and elegant method for the analysis of these same kinds of problems. Confirmatory factor analysis (CFA) will be touched on briefly, but only as a stepping-stone to understanding SEM (for a more detailed discussion of CFA, see Keith

1997). Several examples of SEM from the school psychology literature will be discussed, and examples will be presented of potential SEM studies that would be useful in the field.

# NONEXPERIMENTAL RESEARCH

## What Is Nonexperimental Research?

Many school psychologists were trained in the experimental method: research was done properly by random assignment of subjects to groups. Those groups were then given different treatments (e.g., children taught with different math curricula), and after a given period of time, dependent measures were collected (e.g., performance on a math test). The data were analyzed by using some variation of analysis of variance (ANOVA). This true experiment was the ideal in psychological and educational research.

Unfortunately, experimental research is not always possible, especially in applied settings. Complete experimental control is not always possible; a school administrator may be interested in the effects of different math curricula on math learning but will not allow the random assignment of students to different curricula. The administrator may allow the random assignment of classes or schools to different curricula, however, and the researcher thus has *partial* experimental control. Different methods of quasi-experimental research are useful when partial experimental control is possible (for a more complete discussion of research design as applied to school psychology, see Keith, 1988b).

In many cases, however, even partial experimental control is not feasible. The question of the effects of ability grouping on student learning, motivation, and self-concept continues to be an important educational issue (e.g., National Association of School Psychologists 1993/1995). And although students certainly can be randomly assigned to homogeneously grouped versus heterogeneously grouped classes, few parents or school administrators would support that kind of manipulation for the sake of research. Thus, although it is possible to experimentally manipulate ability grouping, it may not be feasible to do so in practice. For other variables, experimental manipulation is not even possible. We may be interested in the effects of educational motivation on learning, but we cannot assign students to levels of motivation. In these cases, nonexperimental research can be used to estimate the effects of the independent on the dependent variable in the absence of experimental manipulation.

In nonexperimental research, there is no manipulation of the independent variable; instead, existing variation is studied to estimate the effects of one variable on another. In other words, the nonexperimental researcher investigates explanatory or causal hypotheses (the presumed effects of one variable on another) without manipulating the presumed cause. Nonexperimental research is sometimes referred to as correlational research. I believe this is sloppy nomenclature because it confuses a research design with a statistical method; it is like calling experimental research ANOVA research. In addition, nonexperimental research can be analyzed in a number of ways, just as experimental research can be analyzed through a variety of methods (including correlational analysis). As this chapter will show, SEM is a particularly powerful and appropriate method for the analysis of nonexperimental data. Although it can be used profitably in the analysis of other types of research (e.g., it may be the best method for analysis of many quasi-experiments), this chapter will focus primarily on nonexperimental research.

## Why Should School Psychologists Understand Nonexperimental Research?

School psychologists need to be familiar with nonexperimental research because it is quite common in psychology and education and in school psychology in particular. Education and psychology journals of interest to school psychologists commonly report the results of nonexperimental research, often—but not always—by using SEM. Nonexperimental research is quite common in school psychology journals as well. For example, a review of the last two years of the *Journal of School Psychology* and *School Psychology Review* shows that of the articles that reported research findings and in which the researchers argued for the effects of one variable on another, between approximately one-third and one-half of those articles were nonexperimental in nature.[1] Nonexperimental research is common in school psychology, but is not always recognized as being nonexperimental and is often improperly analyzed.

---

[1] I am grateful to Michelle DeGraff for conducting this review.

# Analyzing Nonexperimental Research

Those raised in the experimental tradition will be tempted to analyze the results of nonexperimental research by using those methods—such as ANOVA—with which they are familiar. Unfortunately, ANOVA methods are generally a poor choice for the analysis of nonexperimental research. In the real world our influences are rarely categorical (nominal) in nature. ANOVA analyzes the effects of a categorical variable (treatment 1 vs. treatment 2 vs. control) on a continuous dependent variable. If we are studying the effects of social skills on learning, however, social skills is a continuous independent variable; to fit it into an ANOVA analysis, we have to turn the continuous independent variable into a categorical one, a process that discards variance and results in a weaker statistical test (Cohen, 1983; Humphreys & Fleishman, 1974). Furthermore, if we recode the continuous variable into several categories (e.g., high, medium, and low social skills), ANOVA will not naturally take into account the ordered nature of the independent variable; again, power is lost.

Even if the problem of continuous variables is overcome, other problems remain. Nonexperimental research invariably deals with multiple independent variables because the variables of interest cannot be isolated from other possible causes of the dependent variable. In ANOVA terminology, a *factorial* analysis is needed. But ANOVA assumes that independent variables are uncorrelated with one another, an assumption that is almost never met in nonexperimental research. If students are assigned randomly to one of two types of mathematics instruction (e.g., new math vs. old math) and to one of two types of practice (e.g., computer assisted vs. worksheets), the two independent variables (math instruction and math practice) are uncorrelated. In the real world, however, independent variables are rarely uncorrelated. We may be interested in the effects of sex and sports participation on students' homework completion. Both the independent variables are categorical, so ANOVA may seem workable. But sex and sports participation are very likely correlated, and thus ANOVA will provide inexact estimates of their effects.

Multiple regression analysis (MR) is a better method for the analysis of nonexperimental data. With MR, the independent variables may be continuous or categorical or a mix of the two. Any number of independent variables may be included in the analysis, and there is no assumption that the independent variables are uncorrelated. In fact, ANOVA is a special case of MR; MR is a more general technique with fewer assumptions. Many modern textbooks discuss ANOVA as part of the general linear model; those familiar with this presentation will have no difficulty in switching to MR, which is virtually a direct implementation of the general linear model (Cohen, 1968; Cohen & Cohen, 1983).

The chief problem with MR as a method for the analysis of nonexperimental data is that there are several different methods, each focusing on somewhat different statistics. With *hierarchical* MR, variables are entered into the regression equation one at a time, and their significance is evaluated by testing the increase in $R^2$ associated with each variable. The significance of each variable may depend on its order of entry in the equation, so an orderly, theoretically driven approach is needed. In *forced entry* regression, all variables are entered simultaneously, and the resulting regression coefficients (understandardized $b$'s or standardized $\beta$'s) are tested for significance. With either approach, the primary question of interest will be which variables have significant effects on the outcome. Unfortunately, hierarchical MR and forced entry MR can give different answers to that question. Keith and Reynolds (1990) presented an example in which the two approaches were used to analyze the same data and resulted in different conclusions about the importance of influences.

*Stepwise* regression is common in school psychological research but should be avoided for explanatory research, research in which we want to know the extent of the influence of one variable on another. In stepwise regression, variables enter the equation according to the degree to which they increase the predictive power of the equation ($R^2$). The single best predictor enters first, followed by the next best predictor (after the variance due to the first predictor is removed), and so on. Variables that do not improve prediction are not included in the equation. Thus decisions concerning the relative importance of variables are statistical; theory and judgment are not considered. A variable may be important in one prediction, but when a new set of predictors is used it may appear unimportant. Stepwise regression is appropriate as a *predictive* method, for determining which subset of predictors is most efficient; it is not appropriate for explanatory research. Wolfle (1980) was blunter: "Stepwise regression suffers even more; variables mindlessly enter into the analysis in the absence of theory and the results, therefore, are theoretical garbage" (p. 206). For further discussion of the difference between prediction and explanation, see Pedhazur (1997); for other problems with stepwise methods, see Willson and Reynolds (1982).

In this chapter I argue that SEM is an especially appropriate method for analysis of nonexperimental data. In its simplest form (path analysis), SEM uses MR, but in a structured, theoretically driven manner, and it captures the information highlighted by both forced entry and hierarchical MR. More complex forms of SEM address problems long plaguing social science and other research and allow the estimation of complex, theory-derived hypotheses.

## PATH ANALYSIS
### A Simple Model

Suppose a researcher is interested in the effects of academic motivation on student achievement. Although motivation may indeed be manipulable—presumably, well-designed interventions devised to raise motivation are often effective—it is certainly not randomly assignable. The researcher cannot assign students at random to high and low motivation groups to study the effects of motivation on subsequent achievement. Thus, nonexperimental research—and path analysis—may be the best method. Figure 4.1 illustrates the data collected: students' level of motivation, measured by the composite of several questionnaire items (students' ratings of their interest in school, willingness to work hard in school, and plans for college), and achievement, measured by the composite of achievement tests in reading, math, science, civics, and writing.[2] The researcher has also collected information about the parents' family background (or socioeconomic status, a composite of measures of parental occupational status, education level, family income, and possessions in the home) in the belief that it might affect both a student's level of motivation and his or her subsequent achievement and thus should be controlled in the

_____
[2]These data are from Keith and Cool (1992).

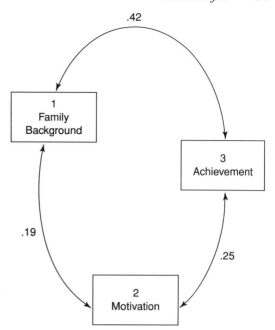

**FIGURE 4.1** **Correlations among three variables. No cause and effect are inferred.**

research. The curved lines in the figure represent the correlations among the three variables; the correlation between motivation and achievement is .25, for example.

Although all correlations are significant, the correlations tell little about the effect of motivation on achievement (although they tell us as much or more than a one-way ANOVA). No cause and effect are inferred in the figure; we may term this figure, then, an "agnostic" model.

Yet the researcher wants to make a causal interpretation of the data; the entire purpose in conducting the research was to determine the effects of motivation on achievement, a causal question. Thus in Figure 4.2 the researcher makes the bold step of inferring causality by drawing arrows from the presumed causes to the presumed effects. The purpose of the research was to determine the *effects* of motivation on achievement, so it makes sense to draw the arrow, or path, from motivation to achievement. Moreover, the researcher included family background in the research in the belief that family background might affect *both* motivation and achievement; the paths from family background

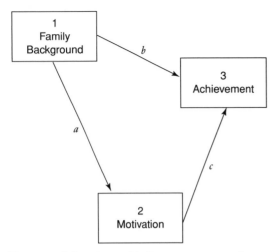

FIGURE 4.2 Causal inferences are made. Arrows are drawn from presumed causes to presumed effects.

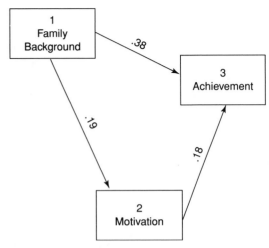

FIGURE 4.3 The data are used to estimate the magnitude of the influence of family background and motivation on achievement.

to motivation and achievement simply make this assumption explicit. So this drawing of paths is not such a bold step, after all, but rather simply a figural representation of the research design.

The paths drawn in the figure assert what is called a weak causal ordering. As such, the paths do not assert that motivation, for example, directly causes achievement but rather that *if* the two variables are causally related, the cause is in the direction of the arrow rather than the reverse. It is important to note that it was at this point, and based on thought, that the inference of cause and effect was made; the data (the correlations) did not inform that decision one whit.

Figure 4.2 thus shows the researcher's "model" of the nature of the relations among the three variables, and Figure 4.1 shows the data. It is possible to use the data—the correlations—to solve for the three paths in Figure 4.2. The researcher does so by using the "tracing rule": the correlation between two variables $x$ and $z$ is equal to the sum of the product of all paths from each possible tracing between $x$ and $z$. These tracings include all possible routes between $x$ and $z$, with the exceptions that (1) the same variable is not entered twice per tracing and (2) a variable is not both entered and exited through an arrowhead (Kenny, 1979, p. 30). Thus the correlation between family background and motivation ($r_{12}$) is equal to path $a$. The possible tracing of $bc$ violates the second exception (a path is entered and exited through an arrowhead) and thus is not included. We can also apply the tracing rule to the other correlations and develop three equations:

(1) $r_{12} = a$

(2) $r_{13} = b + ac$

(3) $r_{23} = c + ab$

With three equations and three unknowns, the researcher can use simple algebra to solve for the paths:

(4) $a = r_{12} = .19$

(5) $b = (r_{13} - r_{12}r_{23})/(1 - r_{12}^2) = .38$

(6) $c = (r_{23} - r_{12}r_{13})/(1 - r_{12}^2) = .18$

and can then insert the solved paths into the model in Figure 4.3.[3]

Figure 4.3 may be interpreted straightforwardly as demonstrating the effects of family background and motivation on achievement (along with the effects of family background on motivation). The (standardized) path coefficients are in-

[3]For a more detailed explanation of solving the paths by algebra, see Keith (1988a). The tracing rule does not work with all models. In particular, it does not work with nonrecursive models, those with paths drawn in two directions. Another method of developing equations, the "first law" of path analysis, works for all models. The first law is explained in Keith (1988a), Kenny (1979), and many other explanations of path analysis and structural equation modeling.

terpreted in standard deviation (SD) units: the path of 0.18 from motivation to achievement suggests that—given the adequacy of the model—each standard deviation change in motivation will result in .18 SD increase in achievement. Unstandardized paths may also be calculated and may provide more direct interpretations in some instances. The researcher can also calculate the statistical significance of the paths or, for more complete interpretation, confidence intervals around the paths, using the standard errors of the path coefficients.

In fact, it is not necessary to use algebra to solve the paths. Readers familiar with multiple regression will recognize equations (5) and (6) as those used to solve for standardized regression coefficients (the betas, or $\beta$'s) from multiple regression analysis (e.g., Pedhazur, 1997, p. 102). Indeed, given the adherence to several assumptions, the paths in path analysis are equal to the $\beta$'s from multiple regression. Thus paths $b$ and $c$ are the respective $\beta$'s from the regression of achievement on family background and motivation. Path $a$ is equal to the $\beta$ from the regression of motivation on family background (and with only one predictor, $\beta$ is equal to $r$). Unstandardized paths are equal to the $b$'s from multiple regression.

The model shown in Figure 4.3 is not quite complete. It is obvious—given the path of .19—that family background is not the only influence on motivation and that motivation and family background are not the only causes of achievement. Figure 4.4 shows a more complete model. The small circle labeled $d1$ represents all other causes of motivation not included in the model (i.e., all causes except family background); $d2$ represents all other causes of achievement. These "disturbances" are enclosed in circles or ellipses to signify that they are not measured by the researcher. Later sections of this chapter will discuss these and other unmeasured variables in more detail. The disturbances are estimated by the square root of the unexplained variance ($\sqrt{1 - R^2}$). Thus the path from $d2$ to achievement is the square root of 1 minus the $R^2$ from the regression of achievement on family background and motivation ($\sqrt{1 - .206} = .891$).

## The Inference of Cause and Effect

It would appear, then, that path analysis commits what we all learned as the first deadly sin in introductory statistics: it infers causality from correlations. Astute readers will note,

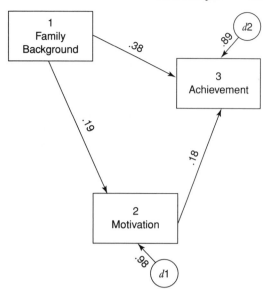

**FIGURE 4.4** Disturbances, representing all other causes besides those in the model, are added to the path model.

however, that the correlations had nothing to do with the inference of cause and effect. That inference was made before the researcher even gathered the data, and it was made explicit in drawing the model in Figure 4.2. The magnitude and direction of the correlations had nothing to do with the inference of cause and effect.

How then did the researcher make the inference of cause and effect? Several lines of evidence were used: formal and informal theory, previous research, time precedence, and logic. Both formal and informal theory are useful. For example, the researcher was justified in drawing a path from motivation to achievement, based on school learning theories, virtually all of which list motivation as an influence on learning (Walberg, 1986). Theories are often not as explicit and well defined as in this example, however, and "informal" theory will need to be used. For example, Keith, Harrison, and Ehly (1987) used informal theory to develop a model of the effects of adaptive behavior on achievement. They noted that definitions of adaptive behavior and mental retardation, along with federal law, make the assumption that adaptive behavior should affect learning, thus providing an informal theory of adaptive behavior and achievement.

Precedence in time also provides support for the inference of cause and effect because cause does not operate backward in time. Longitudinal data are useful in SEM (and much other research) because if one variable is measured before another, the fact of time precedence bolsters our confidence in assigning cause from time 1 to time 2.[4] It is also possible to establish *logical* time precedence with cross-sectional data. So, for example, it is easy to draw the paths from family background to motivation and achievement because the parents' level of socioeconomic status is largely in place before children even start school.

Likewise, previous research can assist in inferring causal direction. But none of these aides can replace simple logic; there is no substitute for sitting down and puzzling over the plausibility of cause and effect. I find it useful to first imagine the conditions under which cause could operate in one direction and then to imagine the opposite. Often these mental exercises will make it obvious that one direction is overwhelmingly more plausible than the other.

### Logical Requirements

At a more formal level, three conditions must be met to make a valid inference of causality. First, there must be some sort of relation between the two variables. If two variables are unrelated, it makes no sense to argue that one causes the other. This requirement may be satisfied in SEM by the presence of a correlation between the two variables. Second, there must be time precedence of the cause over the effect. Again, cause does not operate backward in time. Third, the relation between the two variables must be a *true* relation rather than a spurious relation. This condition is the hardest to satisfy and has thus received considerable attention in the SEM literature; indeed, Herbert Simon (1954) long ago explained the nature of spurious correlation by using path models. A spurious relation, or correlation, exists when the correlation between two variables (*x* and *y*) is the result of some other variable (*z*) jointly causing both *x* and *y*. A common example will help illustrate the problem (cf. Keith, 1988a).

---

[4]Longitudinal data are no panacea, however. Imagine measuring self-concept in 1994 and sex in 1995. Although our data are longitudinal, few would argue that the causal direction is from self-concept to gender. Logical time precedence goes in the other direction.

### The Danger of Omitted Common Causes

If a researcher were to measure the shoe size and the reading proficiency (e.g., through the number of words read correctly from the Dolch list) of all the children in any elementary school, he or she would find that the two variables—shoe size and reading skill—were substantially correlated. This correlation is illustrated graphically at the top of Figure 4.5 by the curved line between shoe size and reading skill. Despite the relation between the two variables, the researcher would be foolish to assume that shoe size causes reading skill (as in the middle of the figure) or that reading skill causes shoe size. The reason it would be foolish to make this inference is that the correlation is spurious; there is another variable—growth, maturation, or age—that causes, in part, both shoe size and reading skill. Other things being

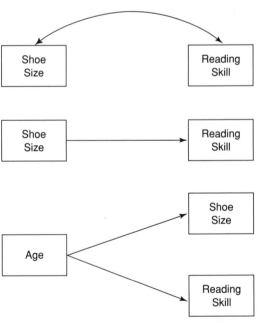

**FIGURE 4.5   The nature of common causes. Shoe size and reading skill are correlated, but it would be foolish to assume that shoe size affects reading skill. Instead, age is a common cause of both reading skill and shoe size; once it is controlled, the apparent connection between shoe size and reading skill disappears.**

equal, older children both have larger feet and are better readers. As shown in the bottom of the figure, the correlation between shoe size and reading skill is simply a result of growth influencing both variables rather than shoe size and reading skill being related to each other in any causal fashion. In the jargon of SEM, growth is a *common cause* of both shoe size and reading skill. A model that neglects a common cause is *misspecified* and will provide misleading estimates of influences.

The models used to illustrate SEM (Figures 4.1–4.4) are misspecified because a common cause of motivation and achievement—ability or previous achievement—was not included in the model. Models of school learning and previous research both suggest that students who are more able or who have a history of high achievement will also have higher levels of motivation than less able students (e.g., Keith & Cool, 1992), and ability and previous achievement also affect current achievement. For the models to provide valid estimates of the effects of motivation on achievement, this common cause of motivation and achievement must be included in the model.[5]

Figure 4.6 shows a more properly identified model; ability (as measured by a short vocabulary test) is included and is specified as affecting both motivation and achievement. The substantial and significant paths from ability to motivation (.15) and achievement (.67) support ability as a common cause of these two variables. (The coefficients associated with the disturbances are not included in this and subsequent figures to simplify the figures.) What is most interesting, however, is the effect of the including ability in the model on the path from motivation to achievement: the path diminishes from .18 (Figure 4.4) to .10 in Figure 4.6. The analysis still suggests that motivation has an influence on achievement, but that effect is considerably smaller than initially estimated. The neglect of common causes often has this effect of inflating estimates of the influence of the presumed cause on the presumed effect (see Page & Keith, 1981, for a real-

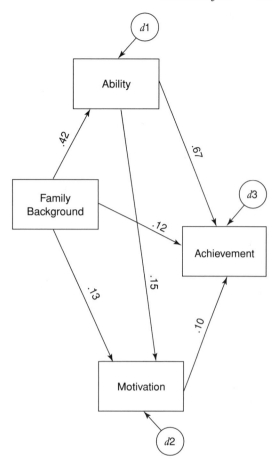

**FIGURE 4.6 Ability is a probable common cause of motivation and achievement. When added to the model, the apparent effects of motivation on achievement diminish.**

world example with important policy implications).

Obviously it is very important to include any common causes of the presumed cause and presumed effect in path and structural equation models. Researchers guard against the omission of common causes by a thorough understanding of theory and previous research. Suspected common causes can be measured and included in models.

It follows that readers of research who doubt the results of a structural equations analysis should first check for omitted common causes. The omission of well-established, important common causes is reason to question the findings. Those common causes should be important; trivial common causes will make no substantive difference if

---

[5]Ability and previous achievement function somewhat interchangeably in school learning models. However, when previous achievement is used in a model that includes current achievement as the outcome, the model becomes one of change, that is, one that examines the influences on *change* in achievement over some time period.

inserted in a model. Of course, as in other research, armchair analysis (e.g., "What about self-concept as a common cause of motivation and achievement?") will generally prove unreliable. If you question the existence of an omitted common cause, you should marshal substantive theory, previous research, or data to support your claims. As Reynolds (Chapter 22) reminds us, "In God we trust; all others must have data."

It should be obvious that path analysis and SEM do not prove or even test causality per se. Instead, SEM provides estimates of the magnitude of the effect of the one variable on another, given the causal model. Cause and effect are inferred by the researcher, not proven by the analysis. The validity of those inferences depends on the quality of the research design, as manifested in the accuracy of the researcher's model in reflecting reality.

What may be surprising to those still squeamish about inferring cause and effect is that the previous paragraph applies *to any causal research*, experimental or nonexperimental, ANOVA-based or SEM-based; ANOVA neither proves nor tests causality either. A researcher makes the same inference of cause and effect in experimental research, and the validity of that inference depends on the research design (cf. Hoyle, 1995a).

The same *logical* requirements for inferring causality apply in any causal research as well. There must be a relation between the variables. In experimental research, for example, that condition is often satisfied by the demonstration of a significant *F* ratio. There must be time precedence; in experimental research that condition is met by the experimental manipulation that precedes the measurement of the outcome. Finally, the control of common causes is critical in experimental research, although common causes generally go by a different name in experiments—threats to internal validity (Campbell & Stanley, 1963). Indeed, the beauty and power of a true experiment is that all possible common causes are controlled through the simple act of random assignment. If subjects are randomly assigned to treatment groups (the independent variable), there should be no causes of the independent variable other than chance (see Keith, 1988a).

## A Path Analytic Example: The Effects of Homework on Grades

Another example will help illustrate the method and provide a comparison for more complex methods. Figure 4.7 shows a model designed to test the influence of time spent on homework on high school grade point average (GPA). The data

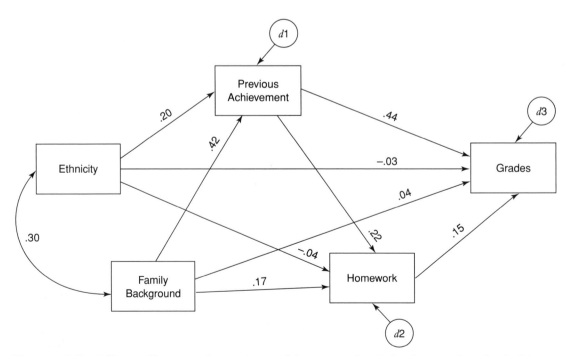

**FIGURE 4.7** **Effects of homework, previous achievement, family background, and ethnicity on students' grades in high school.**

are from the National Education Longitudinal Study (NELS); subjects include more than 16,000 students nationwide (see National Center for Education Statistics, 1990, or Keith, Troutman, Bickley, Trivette, & Singh, 1993, for more information). Ethnicity is a categorical variable coded 1 for white and Asian-American students and 0 for students from other ethnic backgrounds (see Pedhazur, 1997, Part 2, or any standard multiple regression text for an explanation of the proper analysis of categorical variables). Family background is defined in similar fashion as in the previous example. Previous achievement is a composite of scores on short achievement tests in reading, math, science, and social studies. Homework is a composite of student reports of the number of hours of homework completed per week in each academic area, and grades is a composite of students' GPA in English, math, science, and history. The model is longitudinal in nature: ethnicity, family background, and previous achievement were measured in 1988, when the students were in eighth grade. Grades were measured in 1990; homework was a composite of 1988 and 1990 reports and was thus designed to estimate *average* homework over a two-year period.[6]

The model could be analyzed by multiple regression analysis. The paths to grades are the $\beta$'s from the forced entry regression of grades on homework, previous achievement, family background, and ethnicity; the paths to homework are the $\beta$'s from the regression of homework on previous achievement, family background, and ethnicity; and so on. The model can also be analyzed by using a SEM program such as Amos or LISREL.

The results suggest that—given the accuracy of the model and other things being equal—each SD unit change in homework will result in a .15 SD change in GPA. The path is statistically significant; with an $N$ of 16,000, even tiny paths are statistically significant. Thus further qualitative interpretation is also needed: is this path of .15 important? Standardized paths ($\beta$'s) may be thought of as similar to effect sizes in experi-

mental research (Hoyle, 1995a). One common rule of thumb is that a path less than .05 is too small to be considered meaningful, even if it is significant (e.g., Pedhazur, 1997, Chap. 18). I have suggested that for manipulable influences on learning, paths above .05 may be considered small but meaningful influences, paths above .10–.15 may be considered moderate influences, and paths above .25 may be considered large effects (Keith, 1993, p. 26). Using these rules of thumb, it appears that time spent on homework has a moderate influence on students' tenth-grade GPA. Further interpretation suggests that the strongest influence on GPA is previous achievement (.44). Ethnicity (−.03) and family background (.04) have little influence on students' grades once previous achievement and homework are controlled.

## Direct, Indirect, and Total Effects

The previous interpretation focuses only on direct effects. Inspection of the model should also suggest the possibility of indirect effects, however. For example, in addition to affecting grades directly, previous achievement also affects homework (.22), which in turn affects grades (.15). Such indirect effects, also important to evaluate, are easily calculated by multiplying paths (and if there is more than one indirect route, by summing the products). There is only one indirect effect of previous achievement on grades—through homework—and the indirect effect is calculated as .22 × .15 = .03. It is also possible to calculate total effects by summing the direct effects and indirect effects (.44 + .03 = .47). The process of multiplying and summing paths can get quite complex as one moves backward in the model—from proximal to distal influences—but there are other, easier methods for calculating indirect and total effects when multiple regression is used to solve a model (e.g., Alwin & Hauser, 1975). Most SEM programs can provide a table of total and indirect effects.

The ability to calculate all three types of effects is one of the major advantages of SEM over other methods of analyzing nonexperimental data. Forced entry regression, for example, focuses only on direct effects; hierarchical regression focuses on something similar to total effects. Table 4.1 shows the direct, indirect, and total effects of each variable in the model on grades. The effect of homework is completely direct because there are no intervening variables between homework and grades. Previous achievement has

---

[6]The grades variable was designed to get at ninth- and tenth-grade GPA by asking students to "mark the statement that best describes your grades from the beginning of ninth grade until now" (National Center for Education Statistics, 1992, App. O, p. 16) in each subject area. Because homework represents an average of eighth- to tenth-grade homework, and grades an average of ninth- to tenth-grade grades, time precedence is from homework to grades.

TABLE 4.1 **Direct, Indirect, and Total Effects of Ethnicity, Family Background, Previous Achievement, and Homework on Tenth-Grade GPA: Path Analysis Model**

| Variable | Direct | Indirect | Total |
|---|---|---|---|
| Ethnicity | −.03 | .09 | .05 |
| Family background | .04 | .22 | .26 |
| Previous achievement | .44 | .03 | .47 |
| Homework | .15 | | .15 |

This table corresponds to Figure 4.7. Total = direct + indirect. Any inconsistencies are due to errors of rounding.

primarily direct effects on grades. But ethnicity and family background primarily affect grades indirectly rather than directly. Students from more advantaged backgrounds (higher family background), for example, have higher previous achievement and do more homework, and these variables, in turn, affect grades.

The examination of indirect effects is an excellent method for examining possible mechanisms by which one variable influences another. We might wonder, for example, if one way in which homework affects grades is by displacing other time-consuming activities, such as viewing television and spending time with friends. We could test those hypotheses by placing variables that represent these constructs between homework and grades. If television and time with friends helped explain the effect of homework, if they were important *intervening* variables, some of the direct effect of homework shown in Figure 4.7 would become an indirect effect through TV and Time with Friends. The total effect of homework on grades, however, would remain unchanged. Thus the comparison of direct, indirect, and total effects is an excellent method for testing the importance of intervening variables.

## Identification and Estimation

In the jargon of SEM, all of the models shown so far are recursive and just-identified. Recursive means that the paths point in only one direction; the model does not recognize the possibility of reciprocal causation. Just-identified means that we have just enough information to solve for the paths and no more. As a general rule, for a just-identified model, the number of correlations among variables will be equal to the number of paths and other parameters; for the model in

Figure 4.7, there were 10 correlations in the original matrix, and there are 10 parameters to solve for in the model (9 paths and the correlation between ethnicity and family background).

Figure 4.8 shows a *nonrecursive, underidentified* model. The model is nonrecursive because it assumes that not only does homework affect grades but also grades affect homework. However, now the model is also *under*identified, meaning that there are more paths than correlations, so that we cannot solve for the paths without modifying the model. For the model to be estimated, it must be identified (just-identified or overidentified). We could accomplish identification by making additional assumptions (e.g., paths *a* and *b* are equal), by deleting other paths, or by adding additional variables to the model.[7] Underidentified models cannot be estimated; nonrecursive models (as long as they are identified) can be estimated, but not through multiple regression analysis.

Figure 4.9 shows an *overidentified* model. The model is overidentified because it estimates only 8 parameters from the 10 correlations; we have more information than is needed to solve for the paths. To return to the notion of solving for paths by algebra, with the model in Figure 4.9 we can develop more than one equation— and therefore more than one estimate—for several of the paths in the model. This may seem a

---

[7] I have oversimplified a complex topic. With complex models it is possible to have portions of a model underidentified and other portions overidentified. Empirical underidentification is another possibility. Any standard SEM text will discuss the issue of identification in more detail. My nonrecursive model is invalid because at least a portion of the homework variable occurs before GPA, and thus GPA cannot cause homework.

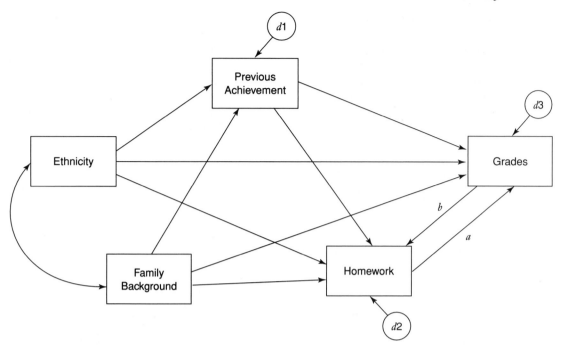

**FIGURE 4.8   A nonrecursive, underidentified model, which cannot be estimated.**

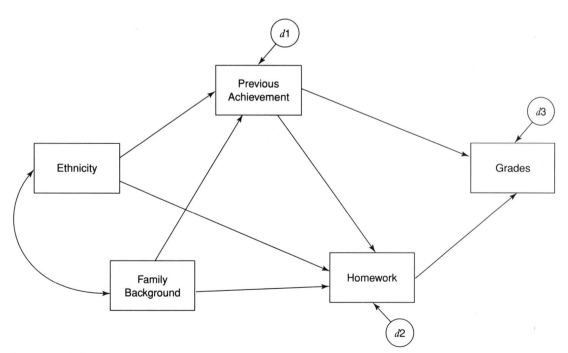

**FIGURE 4.9   An overidentified model. No paths are drawn from ethnicity and family background to grades.**

disadvantage of overidentified models, but as we will see when we discuss latent variable models, it can actually be an advantage. Intuitively, it seems obvious that a model in which the different estimates of the same paths were quite similar would be "better" than a model in which the different estimates of the same paths were very far apart. Thus overidentified models can provide some information concerning the "goodness" or "badness" of a model.

Should researchers, therefore, strive for overidentified models? In my opinion, the answer to that question depends on the method used for estimation. If one is using multiple regression to estimate paths, there is little advantage of overidentified as opposed to just-identified models. Instead, I recommend drawing all paths but making a priori predictions about which paths should approach zero and which should be positive versus negative. The accuracy of these predictions then provides informal feedback about the adequacy of the model. So, for example, it makes sense that ethnicity and family background should affect grades only by affecting previous achievement, and we might expect the paths from ethnicity and family background to be close to zero. That they are close to zero (Figure 4.7) gives us confidence in our model.

Any SEM program (e.g., LISREL or Amos) can also be used to estimate path models such as those shown in the figures. The results of these analyses generally will be the same as if regression were used, but SEM programs also have a number of advantages over ordinary MR analysis. First, with overidentified models, SEM programs provide feedback, in the form of fit indexes, concerning the adequacy of the model. These fit indexes will be discussed later in this chapter. Thus, if a SEM program is being used to estimate a path model, I urge the researcher to strive to develop, before estimation, overidentified models. Second, SEM programs generally can provide tables of indirect or total effects, thus saving sometimes cumbersome and error-prone calculations. Such tables are often in the original (unstandardized) metric, but conversion to standardized indirect and total effects is no different than conversion of $b$ to $\beta$ [$\beta = b(SD_x/SD_y)$]. Third, SEM programs can analyze nonrecursive models (if they are identified).

## Assumptions

It should not be surprising that several assumptions underlie the causal interpretation of the path coefficients. First, if multiple regression is used to estimate paths, there can be no reverse causation (no nonrecursive models). Multiple regression will provide inaccurate estimates of paths in nonrecursive models. This assumption does not apply when a SEM program is used. Second, all common causes of the presumed cause and the presumed effect must be included in the model. This assumption, the effects of its violation, and methods to ensure its satisfaction have already been discussed in some detail. Third, the variables in the model—and especially the presumed causes—should be measured with near-perfect reliability and validity. Obviously, this third requirement is rarely met in practice.

## Error: The Scourge of Research

Just how serious is the violation of this final assumption? Few social science measures have near-perfect reliability or validity; how does this unreliability and invalidity affect our research? We will turn first to the problem of unreliability.

The model shown in Figure 4.7 assumes that all of the variables in the model are error-free (completely reliable). That assumption is, of course, fallacious. For example, homework is measured by self-report via several questions that ask for the approximate amount of time students spend on homework in a subject each week. The variable is undoubtedly error-laden, but what effect does that error have on estimates of the effects of homework on grades? Figure 4.10 shows a model in which it is assumed that 30% of the variation in homework is due to error (.70 reliability). The most obvious change in the model from Figure 4.7 is that the path from homework to grades has increased from .15 to .19. The paths to homework have also increased—some slightly, some substantially—and there are minor changes in the paths from other variables in the model to grades. Apparently, the assumption of perfect reliability should not be taken lightly.

Homework, of course, is not the only unreliable variable in the model. Grades are also based on students' self-report and are subject to forgetfulness, rose-colored glasses, and various other inaccuracies (for analyses of the accuracy of such self-report items, see Fetters, Stowe, & Owings, 1984, or National Center for Education Statistics, 1991). An estimate of 20% error in grades might also be reasonable (cf. Fetters et al.). Indeed, a case can be made for the unreliability of every variable in the model. Even ethnicity, while undoubtedly quite reliable, is not without error, if

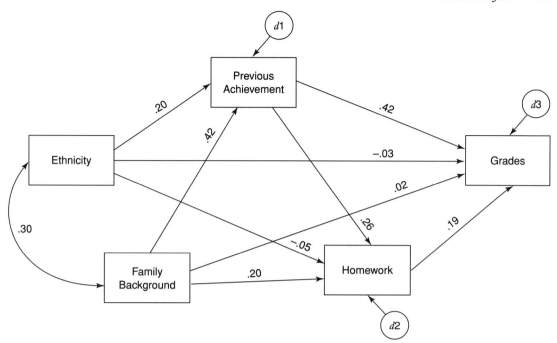

**FIGURE 4.10** **The effects of error. When the model takes into account the unreliability of homework, the apparent effect of homework on grades increases.**

for no other reason than errors in reading, transcription errors, or uncertainty about how students whose parents are from two different ethnic groups should answer such a question. Figure 4.11 shows a model in which the various probable reliabilities are taken into account. I have assumed reliabilities of .80 for grades, .70 for homework, .85 for previous achievement, .80 for family background, and .99 for ethnicity. With these assumptions, there are changes from Figure 4.7 in the magnitude of every path in the model. Some are substantial (the effect of previous achievement on Grades increased from .44 to .53), and some are minor (ethnicity to grades increased from −.03 to −.05). In most cases, the apparent effects increase when this complex pattern of reliabilities is taken into account, but in several cases the estimates decrease (family background to grades dropped from .04 to 0). Indeed, this is a common finding: path analysis with unreliable variables will generally, but not always, *underestimate* the effects of one variable on another.

It would seem, then, that we should steer clear of path analysis; unreliability in the variables can severely threaten our causal conclusions. But these problems with unreliability affect *all social science research*. In a true experiment, the independent variable may be measured perfectly (because it is as-

signed), but the dependent variable rarely is, and an unreliable dependent variable can make an important treatment appear insignificant. Furthermore, in applied settings, even a randomly assigned treatment may not be perfectly reliable. Consider students assigned to different types of mathematics instruction. Even though students in different classes may be assigned to the same supposed treatment, their actual instruction may vary considerably. And in a factorial design in which one independent variable is active and another is a control or subject variable (e.g., level of self-concept), the control variable may be quite error-laden. The most common effect of error will be to reduce the apparent effects of the independent on the dependent variables, but in complex designs with different degrees of error, the opposite could occur.[8] Error affects and confounds all social science research, indeed, all research. In a recent commentary on progress in gene mapping, for example, Goffeau (1995) questioned the effects of error in that field.

---

[8]The similarities in assumptions and requirements of these different types of research is no coincidence: ANOVA is simply a special case of structural equation modeling (Hoyle, 1995a). Put another way, multiple regression subsumes ANOVA, and SEM subsumes multiple regression.

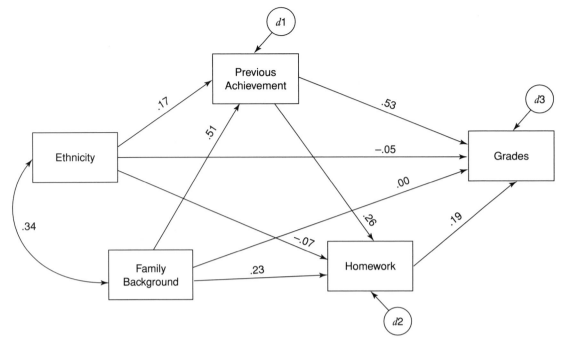

FIGURE 4.11 The effects of error. This model attempts to account for unreliability in all of the variables. Again, the estimates of effects change with this recognition.

Figure 4.11 might suggest that the way to deal with error in SEM is to correct the correlations for attenuation and conduct the path analysis with the corrected correlation matrix, or somehow to build in estimates of unreliability into the estimation of the model. Although such a procedure may be warranted in some cases (cf. Anderson & Keith, 1997; Hayduk, 1987, Chap. 7), it is generally not the best solution. First, it is inelegant, and the correction of correlations and their subsequent analysis smacks of voodoo. It is possible, however, to do the correction and analysis in one step by using SEM programs (Amos was used for the analyses of Figures 4.10 and 4.11). Second, the results will differ, depending on the reliability estimates used, and there easily may be several estimates from which to choose. Finally, although this procedure takes into account unreliability, it does not deal with the problem of invalidity.

## Invalidity

Fortunately, there is a common method for isolating the reliable and valid portion of the variation in a set of measures: factor analysis. Theoretically, the factors derived from factor analysis are perfectly valid and therefore perfectly reliable (since validity is a subset of reliability) estimates of the

constructs underlying our measures (Keith & Reynolds, 1990). One possible solution to the problem of unreliability and invalidity might then be to collect multiple measures of the poorly measured constructs, factor-analyze each construct, and then use the factor scores in subsequent analyses (path analysis, regression, ANOVA, etc.).

Although this solution to measurement problems is possible, it, too, is inelegant. It may indeed remove unreliability and invalidity from the estimates of the effects of one variable on another, but it is a multiple-step solution. The estimation of each construct is separate from all others, and the estimation of the constructs is separate from the estimation of the effects of one construct on another.

Latent variable structural equation modeling (latent variable SEM) provides a more elegant solution to the problem of poorly measured constructs. Conceptually, latent variables are the constructs we are interested in, the constructs that underlie the variables that we actually measure in our research. Researchers and practitioners alike are invariably more interested in the constructs that underlie their measures than in the measures themselves, but they are generally forced to infer the construct from the measure. Intelligence is a construct, a latent variable, and a

Wechsler Intelligence Scale for Children-III (WISC-III) Full Scale IQ (FSIQ) is a measure of that construct. A psychologist who administers a WISC-III is more interested in a child's *true* intelligence than in the child's FSIQ but must simply infer the former from the latter. If the FSIQ is a valid measure of intelligence, the psychologist can make that inference comfortably.

Practically, latent variables—constructs—are operationalized through factors in factor analysis. Latent variable SEM conducts confirmatory factor analysis and path analysis of those factors in one step rather than in several. Thus, the chief advantage of the method is that the simultaneous factor and path analysis accounts for unreliability and invalidity in estimating the effects of one variable on another. In addition, latent variable SEM can provide a test of the degree to which

the variables measure the constructs (the measurement model) and the degree to which the path analysis explains the relations among the constructs (the structural model). Latent variable SEM is thus a very powerful method for the analysis of nonexperimental data.

# LATENT VARIABLE STRUCTURAL EQUATION MODELING

## A Latent Variable Homework Model

Figure 4.12 shows a latent variable version of the homework path model tested previously. Most of the variables in the previous analyses were composites of several measures. Grades in Figures 4.7–4.11, for example, was a mean of grades in English, math, science, and history. In the latent

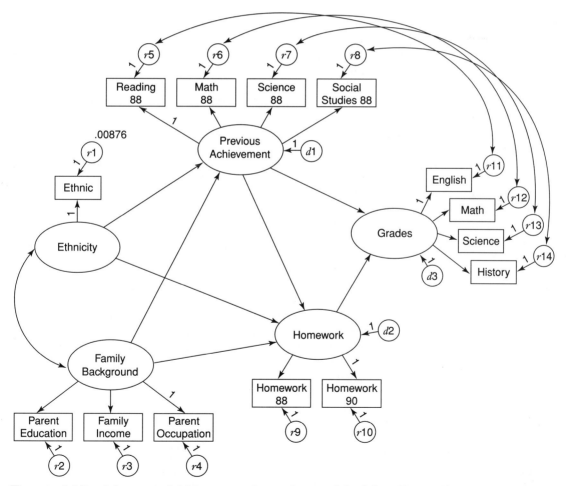

**FIGURE 4.12    A latent variable structural equation model of the effects of homework on grades. The variables enclosed in rectangles are measured variables; those enclosed in ovals and circles are unmeasured variables.**

variable model, these components of the previous composites are shown in rectangles. These variables are the *measured variables* (or manifest variables) in the latent variable analysis. The large variables in ellipses are the *latent variables* (or unmeasured variables) that are estimated from the measured variables. Unlike in previous analyses, these variables are not composites but are *factors* estimated from the measured variables.

The paths from the latent to measured variables constitute the *measurement model*, a joint confirmatory factor analysis of all of the latent variables; the numbers associated with those paths (in subsequent figures) are factor loadings. The paths from one latent variable to another constitute the *structural model*, a path analysis of the latent variables. As before, the small circles labeled $d1$ through $d3$ are the disturbances, the effects on the latent variables of all variables not included in the model. The small circles labeled $r1$ through $r14$ (for residual) represent the combined unique (invalidity) and error (unreliability) variances of the measured variables. Like the disturbances, the residuals can be thought of as all other influences on the measured variable in addition to the latent variable. For example, $r6$ represents all other influences on the 1988 Math Achievement tests beyond the construct general 1988 achievement. These influences include error and specific math achievement.

Some of the paths in the figure have the value 1 beside them. The measured variables in the model have a defined scale. English grades, for example, ranged from 1 (mostly below D) to 8 (mostly A's). But none of the unmeasured variables (not the factors, disturbances, or residuals) has a set scale. The 1's beside the paths simply serve to set the scale to be the same as that of the variable to which the arrow points. The value of 1 for the path from grades to English, for example, sets the scale of the latent grades variable to be the same as that of the measured English grades variable. The use of 1 is arbitrary, any value could be used. Once the model has been estimated by using these constrained values (called the unstandardized or metric solution), all values in the model are restandardized (the standardized solution). Finally, the variance of $r1$ has been set to .00876. The latent variable ethnicity has a single indicator, ethnic. With single indicator measured variables, the residual variance must also be set to some value or that portion of the model will be underidentified. The common choices for setting the residual variance are zero

(which, like the path analysis models, assumes the variable is perfectly reliable and valid) or 1 minus the variable's reliability (this is how the models in Figures 4.10 and 4.11 were analyzed). I chose the latter approach and estimated the reliability of ethnic at .95 {.00876 = [(1 − $r_{tt}$) × (variance of ethnic)] = .05 × .175}.

The model shown also includes several less-common features as well. The curved lines between $r5$–$r8$ and $r11$–$r14$ represent correlations between the residuals of the eighth-grade tests and the tenth-grade grades. It seems likely that math achievement test scores and later math grades will have more in common than the effect of previous general achievement on subsequent general GPA. That additional something, of course, is specific math achievement; the correlated residual from $r6$ to $r12$ builds recognition of this specific math achievement into the model. This ability of latent variable SEM to model such complex relations is another of its advantages over other methods.

To reiterate, by examining the effects of latent rather than measured variables on one another, latent variable SEM more closely approaches the constructs of interest. Thus, the model shown is designed to test the effects of "true" homework time on "true" grades, rather than the effects of an error-laden measure of homework on an error-laden measure of grades. Latent variable SEM does so by taking unreliability and invalidity into account and by separating such measurement error from the estimation of the magnitude of the influence of one variable on another.

The model shown is overidentified. There are 14 measured variables in the model, and thus 91 moments in the correlation matrix and 105 in the variance-covariance matrix.[9] In comparison,

---

[9]Why have I suddenly switched from correlation matrices to covariance matrices? Although for many SEM analyses the analysis of covariance and correlation matrices will produce the exact same results, in some cases they will not. Some models must be based on the analysis of covariance matrices to produce accurate estimates of effects, standard errors, and so on (e.g., multigroup analyses). In addition, the analysis of covariance matrices allows the estimation of unstandardized or metric effects, which are often important, despite my lack of coverage in this chapter. For these reasons most methodologists recommend the routine analysis of covariance matrices. Most SEM programs allow the input of a correlation matrix and standard deviations, which will recover the covariance matrix to be used in analyses. This is the approach used for the examples in this chapter (cf. Hoyle & Panter, 1995).

only 39 parameters are estimated in the model: 16 paths (9 factor loadings and 7 paths from 1 latent variable to another), 5 correlations/covariances (between ethnicity and family background and between *r5–r8* and *r11–r14*), and 18 variances (*r2–r14*, *d1–d3*, ethnicity, and family background). Because there are more covariances than there are parameters to be estimated, the model is overidentified. As noted earlier, with overidentified models it is possible to estimate some of the paths in more than one way, and if the various estimates of the paths are close to one another, we can conclude that the model does a good job of explaining the data; that is, the model "fits" the data.

Although it would be possible to solve every possible permutation of each parameter, there is a more efficient method of doing the same thing.

Just as we estimate the parameters in the model from the covariance matrix, it is also possible to do the reverse—to use the estimated model (e.g., Figure 4.13) to estimate the covariance matrix. If the model is overidentified, the matrix implied by the model will be different from the actual matrix, with the degree of that difference providing evidence of the degree to which the model provides a good explanation of the data. This is what the various "fit indexes" do in SEM (and CFA): They compare the actual with the implied matrix to assess the degree to which the model fits the data.

The estimated model is shown in Figure 4.13. Five fit indexes are shown in the lower right of the figure, although there are dozens of possible indexes from which to choose. Chi-square ($\chi^2$) is the most commonly reported index. It has

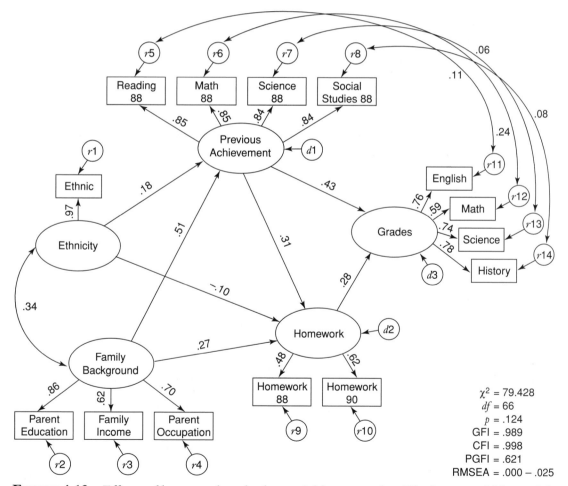

**FIGURE 4.13   Effects of homework and other variables on grades. The latent variable model recognizes that variables are not measured without error, and it thus provides more accurate estimates of the effects of one construct on another.**

the advantage of allowing a statistical test of the fit of the model; it can be used with the degrees of freedom (*df*) to determine the probability that the model is "correct."[10] Thus, a large $\chi^2$ in relation to the *df* and a small probability ($p < .05$) suggest that the implied covariance matrix is significantly different from the actual matrix, that the model provides a poor fit to the data, and that the model could not have produced the data. The relatively small $\chi^2$ [$\chi^2(66, N = 1000) = 79.428$, $p > .05$] in Figure 4.13 suggests that the model does provide a good explanation of the data.

Although $\chi^2$ is the most ubiquitous fit index, it also has well-known shortcomings. In particular, $\chi^2$ is directly related to sample size, so that with large samples, trivial deviations of the implied from the actual matrix will produce a significant $\chi^2$ and thus lead to the rejection of a good model (see Bentler & Bonett, 1980, or Tanaka, 1993, among others, for further discussion); for this reason all sample sizes in this and subsequent models have been set to a maximum of 1,000, even when the true sample sizes are much larger. With small samples, even badly misspecified models may produce insignificant chi-squares, thus leading to the acceptance of a poor model. A variety of other fit indexes have been developed to deal with these and other problems; the ones shown in Figure 4.13 highlight different dimensions of fit (Tanaka, 1993). The goodness of fit index (GFI) is analogous to $R^2$ in multiple regression analysis; it provides an estimate of the total variance and covariance accounted for by the model (Tanaka, 1993). The comparative fit index (CFI) compares the model to a null, or independence, model, one in which the measured variables are assumed to be unrelated. The CFI provides a population estimate of the improvement in fit over the null model (although null models are the most common comparison, the CFI can also be calculated with more restricted but substantive models). Although neither the GFI nor the CFI is independent of sample size (Tanaka, 1993), they are much less affected by it than is $\chi^2$. For both indexes, values approaching 1.0 suggest a better fit; common rules of thumb suggest that values over .9 represent an adequate fit (although .95 or greater is a better cutoff).

One problem with all of the fit indexes discussed so far is that they are affected by model complexity: complex models will always fit better than less complex models (although sometimes the difference is trivial). The parsimony GFI (PGFI) adjusts the GFI by the degrees of freedom to take into account model complexity and reward more parsimonious models. Larger values (closer to 1.0) of the PGFI are also better, but this and other parsimony fit indexes are more useful for comparing competing models.

Another problem with $\chi^2$ and its associated probability is that *p* is the probability that a model fits perfectly in the population, even though most researchers would argue that a model is only designed to approximate reality. The root mean square error of approximation (RMSEA) is designed to assess the approximate fit of a model. Those below .05 suggest a "close fit of the model in relation to the degrees of freedom" (Browne & Cudeck, 1993, p. 144). Shown in Figure 4.13 is the 90% confidence interval for the RMSEA. It, like all of the other fit indexes, suggests a good fit of the model to the data.

Given a good fit, the next step is the substantive interpretation of the model.[11] The most striking finding in Figure 4.13 is the path from homework to grades ($\beta = .28$), suggesting that the amount of time students spend on homework has a powerful effect on their GPA, even after previous achievement and other background characteristics are controlled. Even more interesting for the present discussion is the comparison of this path with that shown in Figure 4.7. The two analyses used the same data, but the apparent effects of homework increased from .15 in Figure 4.7 to .28 in Figure 4.13. The latent variable analysis, by taking into account errors in measurement, demonstrated a more powerful effect. Or, more properly, the path analysis (Figure 4.7) ignored errors in measurement and thus masked a substantial portion of the true effect of homework on grades.

---

[10]Recall that there were 105 moments in the variance-covariance matrix and that 39 parameters were estimated. The *df* = 105 − 39 = 66; the *df* are not related to sample size.

[11]In fact, the assessment of fit continues beyond that discussed here. Paths, factor loadings, $R^2$'s, and other parameter estimates should be reasonable (e.g., no standardized paths > 1.0), and should be in the direction expected (e.g., a path expected to be positive should not be negative). If these expectations are not fulfilled, researchers should be suspicious of their findings. The examination of modification indexes and residuals (the actual matrix minus the implied matrix) is also useful in evaluating fit and in helping to rectify a lack of fit.

There are several other interesting interpretive aspects of the model. Previous achievement had a strong effect on homework ($\beta = .31$), suggesting that high achievement results in increased homework, which in turn results in continued high achievement. Stated differently, a portion of the effect of previous achievement on grades is indirect through homework ($.31 \times .28 = .09$), or homework *mediates* the effect of previous achievement on grades. Ethnicity had a negative direct effect on homework, meaning—since majority students were coded 1 and minority students 0—that minority students report spending more time on homework than do white and asian students, once family background and previous achievement are controlled. Furthermore, a portion of the indirect effect of ethnicity on grades is positive (through previous achievement), and a portion of it is negative (through homework), thus resulting in a small total effect for ethnicity on grades (.06). A summary of all direct, indirect, and total effects on grades is shown in Table 4.2.

## Testing Alternative Models

In addition, SEM can be used to test competing models, and thus test specific hypotheses about those models. Such model comparisons also strengthen the conclusions we can make from SEM research: "The fact that one model fits the data reasonably well does not mean that there could not be other, different models that fit better. At best, a given model represents a tentative explanation of the data. The confidence with which one accepts such an explanation depends, in part, on whether other, rival explanations have been tested and found wanting" (Loehlin, 1992, p. 65).

There are no paths in Figure 4.13 from ethnicity or family background to grades (or, alternatively, these paths are constrained to a value of zero). Substantively, the model asserts that ethnicity and family background characteristics have no direct effect on subsequent GPA, but they affect GPA only by affecting previous achievement and homework. The viability of these assertions can be tested by comparing the fit of that model with one in which the paths are estimated (unconstrained). The fit of this less-constrained model is shown in Table 4.3, where it is labeled the direct effects model. As shown in the table, this model also provides a good fit to the data [e.g., $\chi^2(64) = 77.51$; GFI = .989].

Of more interest is the comparison of the direct effects model with the initial model (Figure 4.13). Despite the problem associated with $\chi^2$ as a "stand-alone" index of fit, it can be quite effective for comparing the fit of competing models. If the two models are nested, meaning that one model is a more constrained version of the other, the *difference* between the two $\chi^2$'s (the $\chi^2$ change, or $\Delta\chi^2$) is also distributed as $\chi^2$ and can be used to determine whether the change in the model significantly improves or damages the fit. The direct effects model represents a relaxation of the initial model (two additional paths were estimated), and thus both the $\chi^2$ and the *df* will decrease. The question of interest is whether the decrease is significant, a finding that would suggest that the relaxation in the model resulted in a significant improvement in the fit of the model.

Information about change in $\chi^2$ is shown in the fourth and fifth columns of Table 4.3. Freeing the two extra paths in the direct effects model resulted in a decrease in $\chi^2$ of 1.917, along with 2 less degrees of freedom. This value is insignificant ($p > .05$), suggesting that allowing these two paths to be estimated does not improve the fit of the model. Since parsimony is valued in

**TABLE 4.2** **Direct, Indirect, and Total Effects of Ethnicity, Family Background, Previous Achievement, and Homework on Tenth-Grade GPA: Latent Variable Model**

| Variable | Direct | Indirect | Total |
|---|---|---|---|
| Ethnicity | 0 | .06 | .06 |
| Family background | 0 | .34 | .34 |
| Previous achievement | .43 | .09 | .52 |
| Homework | .28 | | .28 |

This table corresponds to Figure 4.13.

TABLE 4.3   **Comparison of Alternative Models of the Effects of Homework Time on Grade Point Average**

| Models | $\chi^2(df)$ | $p$ | $\Delta\chi^2(df)$[a] | $\Delta p$ | GFI | CFI | PGFI | RMSEA |
|---|---|---|---|---|---|---|---|---|
| 1. Initial | 79.428(66) | .12 | | | .989 | .998 | .621 | .000–.025 |
| 2. Direct effects | 77.511(64) | .12 | 1.917(2) | .38 | .989 | .998 | .603 | .000–.025 |
| 3. No correlated errors | 140.389(70) | <.01 | 60.961(4) | <.01 | .979 | .988 | .653 | .024–.039 |
| 4. No homework effects | 108.827(67) | <.01 | 29.409(1) | <.01 | .984 | .993 | 628 | .016–.033 |
| 5. Nonrecursive | 79.421(65) | .11 | 0.007(1) | .93 | .989 | .997 | .612 | .000–.025 |

[a]Each model is compared to the initial model.

science, and since the initial model fits as well as the direct effects model but is more parsimonious, I accept the initial model over the direct effects model. As a result, I therefore conclude that ethnicity and family background indeed appear to affect grades only indirectly, through previous achievement and homework. The GFI, CFI, and similar indexes are not as useful for comparing competing models (Hoyle & Panter, 1995), and they changed little from one model to the next. Like the $\chi^2$, the RMSEA did not improve with the addition of the direct effects. As might be expected, however, the PGFI decreased slightly (from .621 to .603) as the model became less parsimonious, although the fit did not improve.

The initial model makes another key assumption that should be tested: that the unique variances of the tests and grades are correlated. To test this assumption, I removed the correlated errors (or set them to the default value of zero) and reestimated the model. The fit indexes for this "no correlated errors" model are also shown in Table 4.3. This change in the model requires additional constraints, and thus the $\chi^2$ for the model (and the $df$) will both get larger (and the fit worse); the question, of course, is whether this change is significant. As shown in Table 4.3, the change is indeed significant [$\Delta\chi^2 = 60.96(4)$; $p < .001$]; the model provides a worse fit to the data, and the assumption of correlated errors of measurement indeed appears to be viable. The RMSEA also became larger (indicating a worse fit), but because of the increase in parsimony, the PFGI was slightly improved.

These two alternative models tested important assumptions about the initial model but did not really test any substantive questions. The key question in these models is the extent of the influence of homework on grades. If this path is removed, asserting that homework has no effect on GPA, what then will happen to the fit of the model? The fit statistics for this "no homework effects" model are also shown in Table 4.3. This change in the model required one additional constraint (and thus resulted in 1 additional $df$) but resulted in a large and significant increase in $\chi^2$. There were, again, minor changes in the other fit indexes. The comparison of models suggests that homework indeed affects grades. (Of course, with this univariate test, I would have come to the same conclusion by examining the $t$ value associated with the path from homework to grades in the initial model: $t = 4.645$; $p < .001$.)

## More Complex Models

The SEM programs can also model and estimate more complex hypotheses about the relations among constructs. We might suspect, for example, that GPA and homework were causally related in a reciprocal fashion, so that homework affected grades, and grades, in turn, affected homework, even after previous achievement was controlled. This possibility is illustrated by the nonrecursive model shown in Figure 4.14. Of course the model is impossible—1989–1990 grades cannot cause 1988 homework—but is used to illustrate the estimation of nonrecursive models.

It is somewhat reassuring to see that the nonrecursive model—with one additional free parameter—led to no improvement in the fit (see Table 4.3) over the initial model and that the path representing the reverse causation (from grades to homework) is both tiny and insignificant. It appears, then, that allowing for reciprocal causation does not help explain the relation between grades and homework.

We might also wonder whether the effects of homework on grades—and indeed, the entire

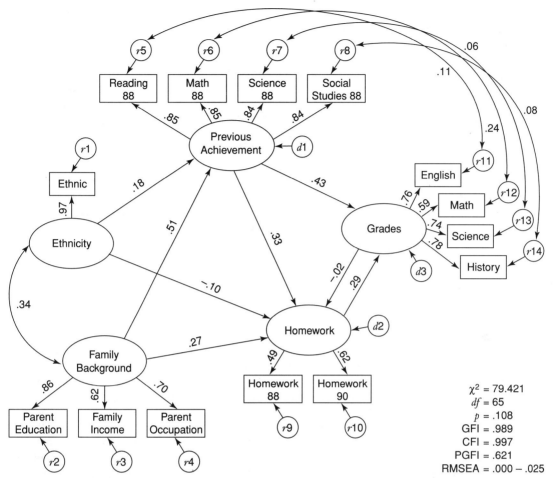

**FIGURE 4.14   A nonrecursive model. Homework is assumed to both affect and be affected by grades.**

model of homework and grades—is the same for boys and girls. Perhaps girls use their time more wisely, so that two hours of study has a greater effect on the grades of girls than of boys. Or perhaps boys are more attuned to the feedback provided by previous achievement and respond accordingly, in which case the effect of previous achievement on homework might be stronger for boys than for girls. This type of question—is the magnitude of influence larger for one group than another?—is, in fact, a question of interaction. Does, for example, gender interact with homework in its effects on grades?

One obvious way to test for such interactions would be to analyze the model shown in Figure 4.13 separately for boys and girls and then examine the paths in the model to look for differences. The problem with this approach is

that it is generally unclear whether differences in the paths across groups are trivial or significant. It is also possible to add interaction terms to the model (Kenny & Judd, 1984), but this approach can quickly become quite cumbersome. An alternative is the use of a multisample analysis, in which the model is fit to several groups simultaneously. Any or all aspects of the model can be specified as invariant across groups. So for example, all paths and factor loadings might be specified as invariant for boys and girls, or only the path from homework to grades might be specified as invariant. The fit for these various specifications can then be compared to determine whether the model differs significantly across groups and, if so, where those differences occur.

I conducted a multisample analysis of the homework model used throughout this chapter.

The model shown in Figure 4.12 was estimated separately for boys and girls, but with the stipulation that all factor loadings and all paths were identical for both groups. The fit indexes for this analysis are shown in Table 4.4. The model provided a good fit to the data [$\chi^2(149, N = 1000) = 91.526$; $p = 1.00$; GFI = .987, etc]. The RMSEA is not included in this table because its 90% confidence interval was .000–.000; it is replaced by the common Tucker-Lewis index (TLI), which, as does the CFI, approaches 1.00 as the fit improves.

Although this "all-invariant" model provided a good fit, what is most important is the comparison of this model with models in which the equality constraints are gradually relaxed. For the second analysis, the path from homework to grades was allowed to vary across groups. That is, the path from homework to grades was estimated separately for boys and girls, while all other constraints were kept in place. The decrease in $\chi^2$—the improvement of fit of this model over the all-invariant model—was insignificant. This finding suggests that the influence of homework on grades is the same for boys as for girls; there is no interaction between homework and gender in their influence on GPA. For the third model ("all paths vary"), all paths were estimated separately for boys and girls, while the factor loadings were constrained to be invariant. Again, there was no significant improvement in fit; none of the variables in the model seem to interact with gender in influencing grades. The fourth and final model tested the equivalence of the factors across groups by removing the requirement that the factor loadings be equal for boys and girls. The lack of improvement of fit suggests that the factors or constructs of interest in the model are the same for boys and girls. In summary, this set of model compar-

isons suggests that the constructs in the model are equivalent for girls and boys and that the influences of the constructs on each other are the same. In other words, the same model (i.e., the one shown in Figure 4.12) applies equally well for girls as for boys. For further illustration of the method, see Keith (1993), Keith and Benson (1992), or Marsh (1993).

## Estimating Models

My advice to those conducting path analyses by multiple regression is to estimate just-identified models, examining results to make sure that paths expected to be zero are indeed close to zero. In contrast, with latent variable SEM (and with path analyses conducted by using SEM programs), I recommend developing overidentified models with paths set to zero a priori. The viability of the hypotheses embodied by the constraint of these paths to zero can then be tested by comparing subsequent models, as illustrated previously in this chapter.

The example used in this chapter is fairly simple, the constructs used are well defined, and the estimation of the model is straightforward. For more complex models, however, additional steps may be useful. With more complex or more exploratory models, the fit of the initial model is often poor, and it is unclear whether the poor fit is the result of problems with the measurement or with the structural model. One useful method is to first test and fit a measurement model, working out any kinks before imposing a structural model (James, Mulaik, & Brett, 1982). The fit of the two models (measurement vs. measurement + structural models) can be compared to determine the fit of the structural model as separate from the measurement model. Using the present example, we would have a model with

## TABLE 4.4  Comparison of the Influences on GPA for Girls and Boys

| Models | $\chi^2(df)$ | $p$ | $\Delta\chi^2(df)$[a] | $\Delta p$ | GFI | TLI | CFI | PGFI |
|---|---|---|---|---|---|---|---|---|
| **1.** All invariant | 91.526(149) | 1.0 | | | .987 | 1.013 | 1.00 | .700 |
| **2.** Path from homework varies | 91.518(148) | 1.0 | 0.008(1)[a] | .93 | .987 | 1.012 | 1.00 | .696 |
| **3.** All paths vary | 89.078(141) | 1.0 | 2.448(8)[a] | .96 | .987 | 1.012 | 1.00 | .663 |
| **4.** All loadings and paths vary | 80.411(132) | 1.0 | 11.115(17)[a] | .85 | .988 | 1.013 | 1.00 | .621 |
| | | | 8.667(9)[b] | .47 | | | | |

[a]Model is compared to the all-invariant model.

[b]Model is compared to the preceding model.

the same latent variables shown in Figure 4.13 but with correlations among all of them. Note that the measurement model is statistically indistinguishable from the model in which the structural model is just-identified (e.g., the direct effects model in Table 4.3), so that this method assumes that the structural model will be over-identified (for a discussion of indistinguishable models, see Stelzl, 1986).

The model used in this chapter, and the modifications of it, were also developed a priori; there was little modification based on the results of the analysis. The method of comparing alternative, competing models is sometimes termed an alternative models (Jöreskog & Sörbom, 1993, p. 115) or model comparison (MacCallum, 1995, p. 31) strategy, and it is an excellent approach to SEM. Often, however, especially in earlier stages of research, a more exploratory approach is needed, one in which models are adjusted and respecified to improve fit, delete insignificant paths, and so on. This model-generating strategy is common and useful but can lead to erroneous conclusions, especially with smaller samples (MacCallum, 1986, 1995). The process is data-driven and can capitalize on chance, and it is logically suspect to use the same data both to develop and to test the model. A more powerful method for model generation is to divide a large sample at random into smaller calibration and validation samples. The model is fit to the calibration sample, modified, fit again, and so on until one or several good models are developed. These final models are then cross-validated by using the validation sample (for more information, see Jöreskog & Sörbom, 1993, Chapter 4; for an example, see Keith, Keith, Quirk, Sperduto, Santillo, & Killings, in press).

## Dangers

Latent variable SEM is effective in dealing with one of the problems of nonexperimental, as well as all other, research—measurement error in the variables used. But what about the other dangers and difficulties of nonexperimental research? Do the fit statistics and other exciting features of SEM tell us when we have neglected an important common cause of our presumed cause and our presumed effect? Do they warn us when we have drawn a path in the wrong direction? In a word, no. No warning bells go off when we omit a common cause nor when we draw a path in the wrong direction.

In Figure 4.15, previous achievement, an important common cause of homework and grades, was omitted from the model and the model was reestimated. The fit of the model did not degrade—no warning bells went off; in fact, by most criteria the fit improved. Figure 4.16 shows a model in which grades are assumed to affect homework rather than the reverse. Since homework 88 (one of the measured homework variables) occurred before any of the grades, this model is clearly wrong; the path is drawn in the wrong direction. But again, the fit of the model in Figure 4.16 is no worse than that in Figure 4.13 (and if we had compared two models in which the structural model was just-identified, the fit would have been identical). The best protection against these specification errors in SEM is the same as for any other type of nonexperimental research: a solid understanding of theory and previous research, actual or logical time precedence, and careful thought and observation. Again, the solution is one of design, not statistics. "Good ideas do not come out of computer packages, but from people's heads" (Kenny, 1979, p. 8).

Often SEM novices generalize from the admonition that all *common* causes must be included in a model to the frightening conclusion that *all* causes of the cause and the effect must be included in the model. If this requirement were accurate, it would of course mean that all models would include many dozens of variables, and models would quickly become unmanageable. Fortunately, the admonition pertains only to common causes of the presumed cause and presumed effect. If a variable that affected only grades but not homework were included in the model in Figure 4.13, the estimate of the effect of homework on grades would remain unchanged.

Intervening variables are also puzzling: must mediating variables be included in a model for it to be valid? Again, the answer is no. Homework, for example, is an intervening variable between previous achievement and grades. Yet the *total* effect of previous achievement on grades would be the same whether homework were included in the model or not. What an intervening variable does is to help explain how an influence operates. Previous achievement affects grades, in part, because students with high achievement study more, and that extra study improves their grades. Keith et al. (1993) provided a useful example;

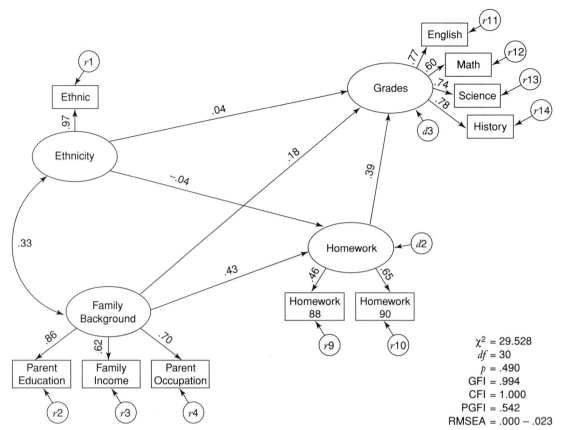

**FIGURE 4.15** **A common cause of both homework and grades is omitted from the model.**

they found a powerful effect for parental involvement on student achievement; subsequent analysis suggested that the effect of parental involvement on achievement was partially explained by homework. Students whose parents were more involved spent more time on homework, and that homework, in turn, improved their achievement. Homework was an intervening or mediating variable between parental involvement and achievement.

SEM is a complex method and, like all complex methods, is open to abuse. It is not an easy method to learn, and those new to the method will make mistakes. At the same time, fewer readers of research will be able to spot errors in an article based on SEM than in one based on a simple ANOVA. Others, "seduced by sophistication" (Wampold, 1987, p. 311), may suspend critical judgment when reviewing the results of SEM studies. The answer to these dangers, both for those who conduct and those who consume

SEM research, is education in the method of SEM, its appropriate use, its strengths and weaknesses, and its proper interpretation. As with other complex methods, "the manipulation of statistical formulas is no substitute for knowing what one is doing" (Blalock, 1972, p. 448). I hope that this chapter will serve as a useful introduction to both consumers and conductors of SEM research.

## Advantages

There are also advantages to the use of SEM over other methods for the analysis of nonexperimental data. As noted, the dangers of excluded third variables and causal misdirection are equally applicable for all nonexperimental research, no matter how analyzed. Nevertheless, I believe that SEM better guards against these dangers through the simple requirement of a visual model of presumed cause and effect. When the researcher's theory of cause and effect are displayed visually,

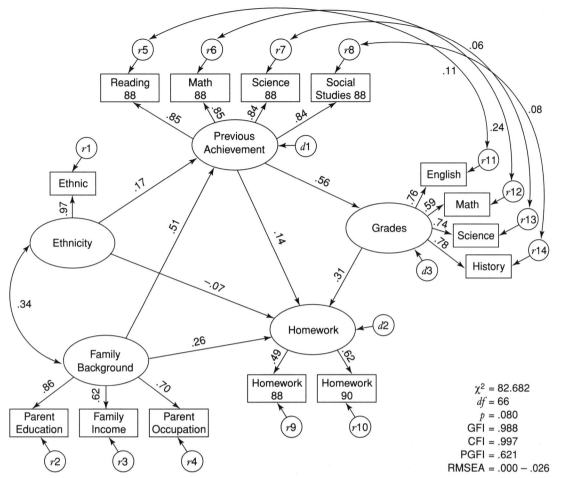

**FIGURE 4.16** **The path between grades and homework is drawn in the wrong direction.**

in the form of a path model, its shortcomings are much more obvious than when described in the text of an article. Both omitted common causes and mistakes in assumptions of causal direction become more obvious with visual display. Indeed, I recommend that readers of nonexperimental research that does not use a visual model draw the model as outlined by the researchers; the researchers' assumptions, and errors, will become much more obvious.

A chief advantage of latent variable SEM has already been discussed but bears repeating: latent variable SEM, by estimating and dealing with errors of measurement separately from the structural model, provides more stable, more accurate measures of the effects of one variable on another. This ability to remove the effects of error

in the estimation of the model is an advantage over other methods of analysis of both nonexperimental and experimental research.

Latent variable SEM's ability to model complex structural and measurement relations is another advantage of the method over other analytic techniques. The ability to model reciprocal causation, correlated errors of measurement, and both direct and indirect effects makes latent variable SEM a powerful and flexible method of data analysis. This flexibility means that latent variable SEM can model and test the assumptions of other methods. Sörbom (1978), for example, demonstrated a SEM alternative to traditional analysis of covariance that allows the testing of assumptions underlying that analysis (see also Arbuckle, 1997).

## Applications

The SEM method has been used to study a variety of problems of interest to school psychologists. It has been used to test the relative influence of different definitions of parental involvement on student learning (Singh, Bickley, Trivette, Keith, & Anderson, 1995), to test Carroll's (1963) model of school learning (Gettinger, 1984), and to test other school learning models (Keith & Cool, 1992). Engagement has been compared with other possible influences on achievement by using SEM (Greenwood, Terry, Marquis, & Walker, 1994), and SEM has been used to study the social acceptance of handicapped children (Morrison, Forness, & MacMillan, 1983). Thus SEM methods are becoming increasingly common in school psychology research, and related journals outside the field of school psychology routinely publish SEM articles. Much school psychology research that has not used SEM could benefit from its methods.

SEM would be an appropriate choice for studying many research questions of interest to school psychologists. Which is more important for effective consultation: that the consultant have good interpersonal skills or good problem-solving skills? Or is the time spent on problem definition more important still? Consultation research is plagued, or blessed, with a myriad of important possible influences on the effectiveness of consultation, and it is difficult to deal with even a portion of those influences in any experimental study. However, SEM offers an excellent method for sorting out the importance of these influences, as well as for studying the extent to which these variables affect one another (cf. Gresham & Kendell, 1987).

The recent statement by NASP (1993/1995) on ability grouping suggests that research on this issue is clear-cut; it is not. The effects of ability grouping on students' learning, self-concept, and aspirations are still hotly debated, and SEM offers an important method for helping to resolve these questions. In particular, SEM would be useful in understanding the longitudinal effects—if any—of ability grouping.

The importance of phonemic awareness as a precursor to reading is becoming increasingly apparent in reading research (cf. Snider, 1995). Yet research has not delineated the relative importance of phonemic awareness and a host of other important skills, such as orthography, exposure to print, vocabulary development, or verbal expression. It is also important to understand the influences on phonemic awareness and the methods by which phonemic awareness affects beginning reading skills (indirect effects) if we are to use such reading research to develop interventions to improve this skill. Again, SEM offers a powerful method for testing complex models of the reading process (e.g., Shanahan & Lomax, 1986).

Which aspects of psychologists' everyday functioning leads to more effective service delivery? Numerous studies have asked how school psychologists spend their time, and some have even asked psychologists and others their perceptions of which of these duties make for more effective service delivery. What is now needed is research that assesses the relative importance of these duties on stakeholders' (e.g., teachers, administrators, and parents) ratings of effectiveness of and satisfaction with psychological services, and SEM would be an excellent method for testing the influences on effectiveness.

The issue of test bias continues to be important in school psychology (Reynolds, Chapter 22). Again, SEM is a powerful method for testing for bias in tests and other assessments and in the uses of those assessments. Stone (1993) used SEM to determine whether placement decisions are biased against minority children; Keith, Fugate, DeGraff, Diamond, Shadrach, and Stevens (1995) demonstrated the use of CFA to assess construct bias. Multisample SEM is also an excellent method for testing for predictive bias (e.g., McArdle, 1994).

School psychologists continue to debate the importance of general versus specific abilities, along with their relative influence on students' learning (e.g., Kaufman, 1994; Keith, 1994; Macmann & Barnett, 1994). SEM provides a more powerful method than has previous research for determining the extent of the influence, if any, of specific abilities on learning (McGrew, Flanagan, Keith, & Vanderwood, 1997).

*The Bell Curve* (Hernstein & Murray, 1994) has caused much controversy in and out of school psychology (see, for example, Frisby, 1995). Those wishing to dispute, support, or test the findings reported in the book could do so more powerfully, in many cases, by using SEM. Does, for example, parental intelligence affect a child's environment and development? Does intelligence affect civic responsibility? These questions are tailor-made for SEM.

# CONCLUSIONS

This chapter is an introduction to structural equation modeling, with an emphasis on the kinds of research problems of interest to school psychologists. Structural equation modeling was presented as a research method especially appropriate for the analysis of nonexperimental data. Nonexperimental research is quite common in school psychology but is often poorly or inappropriately analyzed, thus threatening the causal conclusions drawn. However, SEM is an excellent method for analyzing such data.

This chapter demonstrated the development and analysis of a simple SEM, commonly called path analysis. Path analysis was used to demonstrate many of the critical issues in SEM and in nonexperimental research. Latent variable SEM was illustrated by using the same example as in path analysis to demonstrate the continuity in approaches that use measured and latent variables. Errors of measurement (unreliability and invalidity) confound the results of all social science research and, indeed, all research. A chief advantage of the latent variable approach is that it takes into account errors of measurement (unreliability and invalidity) and, as a result, gets closer to the *constructs* of true interest in our research. Alternative models were developed and compared to illustrate the use of SEM to test specific hypotheses and alternative theories. More complex relations were modeled as well. Finally, several applications of SEM to research of interest to school psychologists were mentioned, and several other potential applications with interest to the field were discussed.

This chapter is, at best, only a cursory overview of SEM; I have neglected important issues in an effort to cover the most critical topics. I have also endeavored to present a conceptual, rather than a numerical, overview of the method. Fortunately, there are many excellent books on SEM for those who wish to know more. Loehlin (1992) presents an excellent introduction, one that integrates path analysis, factor analysis, and latent variable SEM (1992); Hoyle (1995b) provides another excellent introduction, which discusses many of the important issues by the leading methodologists in the field. Kenny's (1979) book also provides a gentle, entertaining introduction to SEM but is, sadly, out of print. There are also a number of excellent texts available for those who wish to go beyond these introductions (e.g., Bollen, 1989; Bollen & Long, 1993; Byrne, 1994; Hayduk, 1987, 1996).

This chapter also has not discussed the nitty-gritty details of estimating models because they vary according to the SEM program being used. Fortunately, the user's guides that accompany most SEM programs provide numerous examples and are extremely helpful for learning the method. Many of those manuals also use the same examples, so it is easy to see similarities and differences across programs.

The use of SEM has shown explosive growth in other areas of psychology; it should experience similar growth in school psychology. School psychologists who conduct nonexperimental research should become familiar with the method because it provides a powerful, flexible, and theoretically driven method of analysis. Likewise, psychologists who read and consume research should become familiar with the method so that they can understand what they read and the strengths and weaknesses of the method. Structural equation modeling can and should become an important method in school psychological research.

# REFERENCES

Alwin, D. F., & Hauser, R. M. (1975). The decomposition of effects in path analysis. *American Sociological Review, 40*, 37–47.

Anderson, E. S., & Keith, T. Z. (1997). A longitudinal test of a model of academic success for at-risk high school students. *The Journal of Educational Research, 90*, 259–268.

Arbuckle, J. L. (1997). *Amos user's guide version 3.6.* Chicago: SmallWaters.

Bentler, P. M., & Bonett, D. G. (1980). Significance tests and goodness of fit in the analysis of covariance structures. *Psychological Bulletin, 88*, 588–606.

Bentler, P. M. (1995). *EQS structural equations program manual.* Encino, CA: Multivariate Software.

Blalock, H. M. (1972). *Social statistics* (2nd ed.). New York: McGraw-Hill.

Bollen, K. A. (1989). *Structural equations with latent variables.* New York: Wiley.

Bollen, K. A., & Long, J. S. (Eds.). (1993). *Testing structural equation models.* Newbury Park, CA: Sage.

Browne, M. W., & Cudeck, R. (1993). Alternative ways of assessing model fit. In K. A. Bollen & J. S. Long (Eds.), *Testing structural equation models* (pp. 136–162). Newbury Park, CA: Sage.

Byrne, B. M. (1994). *Structural equation modeling with EQS and EQS/Windows: Basic concepts, applications, and programming.* Newbury Park, CA: Sage.

Campbell, D. T., & Stanley, J. C. (1963). *Experimental and quasi-experimental designs for research.* Chicago: Rand McNally.

Carroll, J. B. (1963). A model for school learning. *Teachers College Record, 64,* 723–733.

Cohen, J. (1968). Multiple regression as a general data-analytic system. *Psychological Bulletin, 70,* 426–443.

Cohen, J. (1983). The cost of dichotomization. *Applied Psychological Measurement, 7,* 249–253.

Cohen, J., & Cohen, P. (1983). *Applied multiple regression/correlation analysis for the behavioral sciences* (2nd ed.). Hillsdale, NJ: Erlbaum.

Fetters, W. B., Stowe, P. S., & Owings, J. A. (1984). *Quality of responses of high school students to questionnaire items* (NCES 84-216). Washington, DC: U.S. Government Printing Office.

Frisby, C. L. (Ed.). (1995). Commentaries on *The Bell Curve. School Psychology Review, 24,* 9–44.

Gettinger, M. (1984). Achievement as a function of time spent in learning and time needed for learning. *American Educational Research Journal, 21,* 617–628.

Goffeau, A. (1995). Life with 482 genes. *Science, 270,* 445–446.

Greenwood, C. R., Terry, B., Marquis, J., & Walker, D. (1994). Confirming a performance-based instructional model. *School Psychology Review, 23,* 652–668.

Gresham, F. M., & Kendell, G. K. (1987). School consultation research: Methodological critique and future research directions. *School Psychology Review, 16,* 306–316.

Hartmann, W. M. (1995). *The CALIS procedure release 6.11 extended user's guide.* Cary, NC: SAS Institute.

Hayduk, L. A. (1987). *Structural equation modeling with LISREL: Essentials and advances.* Baltimore, MD. Johns Hopkins University Press.

Hayduk, L. A. (1996). *LISREL issues, debates, and strategies.* Baltimore, MD: Johns Hopkins University Press.

Hernstein, R. J., & Murray, C. (1994). *The bell curve.* New York: Free Press.

Hox, J. J. (1995). Amos, EQS, and LISREL for Windows: A comparative review. *Structural Equation Modeling, 2,* 79–91.

Hoyle, R. H. (1995a). The structural equation modeling approach: Basic concepts and fundamental issues. In R. H. Hoyle (Ed.), *Structural equation modeling: Concepts, issues, and applications* (pp. 1–15). Thousand Oaks, CA: Sage.

Hoyle, R. H. (Ed.). (1995b). *Structural equation modeling: Concepts, issues, and applications.* Thousand Oaks, CA: Sage.

Hoyle, R. H., & Panter, A. T. (1995). Writing about structural equation models. In R. H. Hoyle (Ed.), *Structural equation modeling: Concepts, issues, and applications* (pp. 158–176). Thousand Oaks, CA: Sage.

Humphreys, L. G., & Fleishman, A. (1974). Pseudo-orthogonal and other analysis of variance designs involving individual difference variables. *Journal of Educational Psychology, 66,* 464–472.

James, L. R., Mulaik, S. A., & Brett, J. M. (1982). *Causal analysis: Assumptions, models, and data.* Beverly Hills, CA: Sage.

Jöreskog, K. G., & Sörbom, D. (1993). *LISREL 8: Structural equation modeling with the SIMPLIS command language.* Chicago: Scientific Software.

Kaufman, A. S. (1994). A reply to Macmann and Barnett: Lessons from the blind man and the elephant. *School Psychology Quarterly, 9,* 199–207.

Keith, T. Z. (1988a). Path analysis: An introduction for school psychologists. *School Psychology Review, 17,* 343–362.

Keith, T. Z. (1988b). Research methods in school psychology: An overview. *School Psychology Review, 17,* 502–520.

Keith, T. Z. (1993). Causal influences on school learning. In H. J. Walberg (Ed.), *Analytic methods for educational productivity* (pp. 21–47). Greenwich, CT: JAI Press.

Keith, T. Z. (1994). Intelligence *is* important, intelligence *is* complex. *School Psychology Quarterly, 9,* 209–221.

Keith, T. Z. (1997). Using confirmatory factor analysis to aid in understanding the constructs measured by intelligence tests. In D. P. Flanagan, J. L. Genshaft, & P. L. Harrison (Eds.), *Contemporary intellectual assessment: Theories, tests, and issues* (pp. 373–402). New York: Guilford.

Keith, T. Z., & Benson, M. J. (1992). Effects of manipulable influences on high school grades across five ethnic groups. *Journal of Educational Research, 86,* 85–93.

Keith, T. Z., & Cool, V. A. (1992). Testing models of school learning: Effects of quality of instruction, motivation, academic coursework, and homework on academic achievement. *School Psychology Quarterly, 7,* 207–226.

Keith, T. Z., Fugate, M. H., DeGraff, M., Diamond, C. M., Shadrach, E. A., & Stevens, M. L. (1995). Using multi-sample confirmatory factor analysis to test for construct bias: An example using the K-ABC. *Journal of Psychoeducational Assessment, 13,* 347–364.

Keith, T. Z., Harrison, P. L., & Ehly, S. W. (1987). Effects of adaptive behavior on achievement: Path analysis of a national sample. *Professional School Psychology, 2,* 205–215.

Keith, T. Z., Keith, P. B., Quirk, K. J., Sperduto, J., Santillo, S., & Killings, S. (in press). Longitudinal effects of parent involvement on high school grades: Similarities and differences across gender and ethnic groups. *Journal of School Psychology.*

Keith, T. Z., Keith, P. B., Troutman, G. C., Bickley, P. G., Trivette, P. S., & Singh, K. (1993). Does parental involvement affect eighth grade student achievement? Structural analysis of national data. *School Psychology Review, 22,* 472–494.

Keith, T. Z., & Reynolds, C. R. (1990). Measurement and design issues in child assessment research. In C. R. Reynolds & R. W. Kamphaus (Eds.), *Handbook of psychological and educational assessment of children: Vol. 1, Intelligence and achievement* (pp. 29–61). New York: Guilford.

Kenny, D. A. (1979). *Correlation and causality.* New York: Wiley.

Kenny, D. A., & Judd, C. M. (1984). Estimating the nonlinear and interactive effects of latent variables. *Psychological Bulletin, 96,* 201–210.

Loehlin, J. C. (1992). *Latent variable models: An introduction to factor, path, and structural analysis* (2nd ed.). Hillsdale, NJ: Erlbaum.

MacCallum, R. (1986). Specification searches in covariance structure modeling. *Psychological Bulletin, 100,* 107–120.

MacCallum, R. C. (1995). Model specification: Procedures, strategies, and related issues. In R. H. Hoyle (Ed.), *Structural equation modeling: Concepts, issues, and applications* (pp. 16–36). Thousand Oaks, CA: Sage.

Macmann, G. M., & Barnett, D. W. (1994). Structural analysis of correlated factors: Lessons from the verbal-performance dichotomy of the Wechsler Scales. *School Psychology Quarterly, 9,* 161–197.

Marsh, H. W. (1993). The multidimensional structure of academic self-concept: Invariance over gender and age. *American Educational Research Journal, 30,* 841–860.

McArdle, J. J. (1994, September). *Contemporary statistical models for examining test bias.* Paper presented at the conference on Human Cognitive Abilities in Theory and Practice, Charlottesville, VA.

McGrew, K. S., Flanagan, D. P., Keith, T. Z., & Vanderwood, M. (1997). Beyond *g:* The impact of *Gf-Gc* specific abilities research on the future use and interpretation of intelligence test batteries in the schools. *School Psychology Review, 26,* 189–210.

Morrison, G. M., Forness, S. R., & MacMillan, D. L. (1983). Influences on the sociometric ratings of mildly handicapped children: A path analysis. *Journal of Educational Psychology, 75,* 63–74.

National Association for School Psychologists (1993/1995). NASP position statements: Ability grouping. In A. Thomas & J. Grimes (Eds.), *Best practices in school psychology—III* (pp. 1201–1202). Washington, DC: Author.

National Center for Education Statistics (1990). *National Education Longitudinal Study of 1988: Base year: Student component data file user's manual* (NCES 90-464). Washington, DC: U.S. Government Printing Office.

National Center for Education Statistics (1991). *Quality of the responses of eighth-grade students in NELS-88* (NCES 91-487). Washington, DC: U.S. Department of Education.

National Center for Education Statistics (1992).

*National Education Longitudinal Study of 1988: First follow-up: Student component data file user's manual* (Vol. 1); NCES 92-030. Washington, DC: U.S. Government Printing Office.

Page, E. B., & Keith, T. Z. (1981). Effects of U.S. private schools: A technical analysis of two recent claims. *Educational Researcher, 10*(7), 7–17.

Pedhazur, E. J. (1997). *Multiple regression in behavioral research: Explanation and prediction* (3rd ed.). New York: Harcourt Brace.

Reynolds, C. R. (in press). Bias in psychological assessment. In C. R. Reynolds & T. B. Gutkin (Eds.), *The handbook of school psychology.* New York: Wiley.

Shanahan, T., & Lomax, R. G. (1986). An analysis and comparison of theoretical models of the reading-writing relationship. *Journal of Educational Psychology, 78,* 116–123.

Simon, H. A. (1954). Spurious correlation: A causal interpretation. *Journal of the American Statistical Association, 48,* 467–479.

Singh, K., Bickley, P. G., Trivette, P. S., Keith, T. Z., Keith, P. B., & Anderson, E. S. (1995). The effects of four components of parental involvement on eighth grade student achievement: Structural analysis of NELS-88 data. *School Psychology Review, 24,* 299–317.

Snider, V. E. (1995). A primer on phonological awareness: What it is, why it's important, and how to teach it. *School Psychology Review, 24,* 443–455.

Sörbom, D. (1978). An alternative to the methodology for analysis of covariance. *Psychometrika, 43,* 381–396.

SPSS, Inc. (1990). *SPSS reference guide.* Chicago: Author.

Stelzl, I. (1986). Changing a causal hypothesis without changing the fit: Some rules for generating equivalent path models. *Multivariate Behavioral Research, 21,* 309–331.

Stone, B. J. (1993). Bias in learning disabilities placement. *Psychological Reports, 72,* 1243–1247.

Tanaka, J. S. (1993). Multifaceted conceptions of fit in structural equation models. In K. S. Bollen & J. S. Long (Eds.), *Testing structural equation models* (pp. 10–39). Newbury Park, CA: Sage.

Walberg, H. J. (1986). Synthesis of research on teaching. In M. C. Wittrock (Ed.), *Handbook of research on teaching* (3rd ed., pp. 214–229). New York: Macmillan.

Wampold, B. E. (1987). Covariance structures analysis: Seduced by sophistication? *The Counseling Psychologist, 15,* 311–315.

Willson, V. L., & Reynolds, C. R. (1982). Methodological and statistical problems in determining membership in clinical populations. *Clinical Neuropsychology, 4,* 134–138.

Wolfle, L. M. (1980). Strategies in path analysis. *American Educational Research Journal, 17,* 183–209.

## CHAPTER 5

# APPLICATIONS OF QUALITATIVE RESEARCH STRATEGIES TO SCHOOL PSYCHOLOGY RESEARCH PROBLEMS

DONALD E. POLKINGHORNE
BARRY C. GRIBBONS
*University of Southern California*

Chapters in handbooks often provide a distillation or synthesis of the existing literature in a field. Articles that report research generated through qualitative strategies have rarely appeared in the school psychology literature. Thus, instead of a retrospective consolidation of how qualitative strategies have been used in school psychology research, this chapter offers a prospective look at how qualitative approaches might be used. The chapter proposes that an expansion of school psychology's methodological repertoire to include qualitative procedures will positively extend the profession's body of knowledge. Contemporary qualitative procedures are grounded in an enlarged notion of what constitutes trustworthy knowledge. It yields understandings of individual people and particular situations in place of information about aggregates and their probabilistic relation to other aggregates. By augmenting its traditional aggregate-based methods with situation-based qualitative methods, school psychologists will have more comprehensive knowledge for the clients they serve.

Psychology, as a discipline, has lagged behind other disciplines that study the human realm. The first section of this chapter reviews the use of qualitative procedures by the other disciplines and the renewed interest in these procedures by psychology in general and school psychology in particular. The next section provides a discussion of the theory and practice of qualitatively based research. The final section describes

possible formal and informal applications of qualitative approaches to knowledge in areas of concern for school psychology, such as consultation, assessment, and evaluation.

## BACKGROUND

*Qualitative research* is an umbrella term under which is included the multiple research approaches that employ qualitative procedures for analyzing data. Although qualitative-like procedures have been used in the biological sciences (e.g., ornithology) to classify species (Lakoff, 1987), their use is most closely associated with the disciplines whose objects of study are part of the human realm. Tesch (1990) has identified 46 types of qualitative research employed in the human disciplines, of which 13 have been used in psychology. Some of these are ethnography, ethnomethodology, naturalistic inquiry, grounded theory, phenomenological psychology, case studies, and life histories. Denzin and Lincoln (1994b), in the preface to their valuable *Handbook of Qualitative Research* state that the "field of qualitative research is far from a unified set of principles promulgated by networked groups of scholars" (p. ix).

There are tensions, disagreements, and contradictions among those engaged in qualitative research about its appropriate epistemological bases, methodological procedures, and reporting forms. Yet within this diversity, there is what might be termed *mainstream* positions, which inform most of the contemporary research in this field. These mainstream positions are linked to the traditions of qualitative strategies and to the principles of empirically based knowledge development. In addition, these positions are grouped around an "illusive center," which Lincoln and Denzin (1994) describe as lying "in the humanistic commitment of the qualitative researcher to study the world always from the perspective of the interacting individual" (p. 575). The focus of this chapter is on the mainstream positions in qualitative research, and thus it presents a more unified view than actually holds in the field.

## The Tradition

Historically, qualitative research has been most closely identified with anthropology and its ethnographic field studies of foreign cultures (Stocking, 1983). Franz Boas, at the turn of this century (Roberts, 1976), laid out an approach termed *interpretative anthropology*, in which researchers were to study how a culture was understood by its own members rather than how it appears through a Western framework (Bogdan & Biklen, 1992). Malinowski's (1922) study of the Trobriand Islanders is often recognized as the beginning of the systematic use of qualitative research procedures (Easthope, 1974). Another early application of qualitative procedures was made by sociologists of the symbolic interactionist tradition at the University of Chicago in the 1920s and 1930s (Meltzer, Petras, & Reynolds, 1975). They used qualitative community-based field studies to investigate life in local settings (e.g., Wirth's 1928 study of an urban ghetto).

Before the early 1970s, little literature was produced that attempted to clarify and systematically describe the employment of qualitative procedures. The approach and methods of individual researchers were passed on informally to their students. It wasn't until the 1970s that a critically reflective literature on qualitative procedures began to appear. Examples of this literature include Bogdan and Taylor's (1975) *Introduction to Qualitative Research Methods;* Filstead's (1970) edited collection, *Qualitative Methodology;* Lazarsfeld's (1972) *Qualitative Analysis;* Lofland's (1971) *Analyzing Social Settings;* and Pelto's (1970) *Anthropological Research.* These texts continue to exert an influence on the implementation of qualitative procedures and form the backdrop to a more recent effusion of literature about qualitative research. Sage Publications is producing the bulk of this new work. Its series of monographs, begun in 1986 and edited by John Van Maanen, is entitled *Qualitative Research Methods* (1986–1997) and now includes more than 40 volumes. As part of its *Applied Social Research* series, Sage has also published books on qualitative methodology (Denzin, 1989; Fetterman, 1989; Jorgensen, 1989; Marshall and Rossman, 1989; and Yin, 1984). Examples of other important texts in the recent surge of literature on qualitative methods are Erlandson et al. (1993) *Doing Naturalistic Inquiry*, Goetz and LeCompte's (1984) *Ethnography and Qualitative Design in Educational Research*, Miles and Huberman's (1994) *Qualitative Data Analysis*, and Strauss and Corbin's (1990) *Basics of Qualitative Research.* Two impressive handbooks have been published—*Handbook of Qualitative Research* (Denzin & Lincoln, 1994a) and *The Handbook of Qualitative Research in Education* (LeCompte, Millroy, & Preissle, 1992). Three journals devoted to qualitative research are now being published—the *International Journal of Qualitative Studies in Education, Qualitative Inquiry,* and *Journal of Life History and Narrative.* The literature addressing issues in the use of qualitative methods has become so extensive in the last decade that it is beyond the scope of this chapter to do more than note a sample of what is available.

Qualitative research has remained the mainstay of anthropological research (e.g., Geertz, 1973; Turner & Brunner, 1986). Sociological research has, in the main, adapted quantitative methods; however, the influence of symbolic interactionism and its use of qualitative procedures has continued as part of the discipline (e.g., Filstead, 1970; Manis & Meltzer, 1978). Nursing, which has in the last decades instituted research training at the doctoral level, has developed a strong literature on the use of qualitative methods (e.g., Chenitz & Swanson, 1986a; Morse, 1991, 1994).

School psychology programs are most often housed in schools of education, a discipline that makes extensive use of qualitative strategies in its research. In recent years, education's primary research journal, *American Education Research Journal,* has consistently published articles in which qualitative methods were employed. The journal featured a special section on qualitative methodology, including criteria it uses to judge the scholarly adequacy of articles with qualitative procedures (Richardson-Koehler, 1987). Also, the *Educational Researcher,* a publication sent to all the American Educational Research Association (AERA) members, has regularly contained articles that address current issues in qualitative strategies. Texts on educational research usually include chapters on qualitative procedures (e.g., Borg & Gall, 1989; Fraenkel & Wallen, 1990; Hopkins & Antes, 1990), the *Handbook of Research on Teaching* has a chapter called "Qualitative Methods in Research on Teaching" (Erickson, 1986), and the *Handbook in Research and Evaluation* (Isaac & Michael, 1995) includes a qualitative research chapter. LeCompte et al. (1992) were able to report in their preface to the recently published *Handbook of Qualitative Research in Education*, "In the less than thirty years since qualitative research emerged as a serious approach to inquiry in education, its status has evolved from that of an upstart, marginal, and often pariah stepchild to a respected member of the research community" (p. xvi).

## Qualitative Research in Psychology and School Psychology

An early definition of the school psychologist by Walter (1925) states that he or she is one who brings "to bear upon educational problems the knowledge and technique which have been developed by the science of psychology" (p. 167). Bardon and Bennett (1974) also identify school psychology as a psychological specialty that "brings psychological knowledge, skills, and techniques to bear on the problems presented by the school" (p. 8). School psychology is one of the professional areas of psychology, along with clinical and counseling psychology. Unlike the other social and behavioral sciences, psychology has been slow to add qualitative procedures to its methodological repertoire.

### *Psychology*

Within psychology, counseling psychology, a sister practice to school psychology, has shown the most interest in qualitative methods. Discussions about the importance of qualitative methods appeared in its literature for 20 years (e.g., Goldman, 1976; Hoshmand, 1989; Howard, 1983; Neimeyer & Resnikoff, 1982; Polkinghorne, 1984). In 1991, Watkins and Schneider published a collection of essays on procedures for counseling research in which they included a chapter on qualitative methods (Polkinghorne, 1991). Until recently, however, very few studies that actually used qualitative methods have been published. In 1992, Toukmanian and Rennie (1992) published the first collection of qualitative studies in counseling psychology, but the number of such studies has remained small. Hill and Corbett (1993) could say about

qualitative studies of the counseling process, "Few examples of how to use them exist in therapy research" (p. 16). The first research article using qualitative methods (Reed, Patton, & Gold, 1993) to be published in the *Journal of Counseling Psychology*, an American Psychological Association (APA) journal, appeared in the April 1993 issue. The Fall 1994 issue contained a special section on qualitative research in the counseling process and outcomes. The eight studies of this special section make up the most extensive publication of qualitative research in an APA journal.

Psychology has had other research programs that used qualitative methods, for example, ecological (Barker, 1963) and phenomenological psychology (Giorgi, Fischer, & Von Eckartsberg, 1971; Polkinghorne, 1989b). Phenomenological psychology was developed at Duquesne University under Amedo Giorgi and produced an extensive literature, including the *Journal of Phenomenological Psychology*, now publishing its twenty-fourth volume, and four collections of articles published under the title of *Duquesne Studies in Phenomenological Psychology*. The products of these qualitatively based research programs did not become part of mainstream psychology in the way that the more recent publications in counseling psychology have. Thus, although research with qualitative procedures has for the past decade become a part of the disciplinary literature of most of the human sciences, it has only begun to make its appearance in the contemporary psychological literature. The reasons for this late interest are complex and outside the focus of this chapter. A contributing factor may have been, as Koch (1959) commented, the psychology defined itself by its adherence to a particular methodology instead of by its subject matter.

At times in its past, before committing itself completely to a natural science program, psychology had been more open to alternate approaches to research. Wilhelm Wundt, who was identified by Boring as the father of experimental and formal psychology, suggested that another, practical psychology be created alongside the study of mental structures (Leahey, 1980). This practical study, which he called *characterology*, would investigate the basic and typical forms of individual character, aided by principles derived from a general theoretical psychology.

Henry A. Murray, director of the Psychological Clinic at Harvard, emphasized the study of the individual case and the notion of the organic, or whole, character of human behavior. Murray's

(1938) book, *Explorations in Personality,* called for an intensive study of individual subjects. He pointed to the limits of the usual large-scale studies of human behavior in which the findings consisted of group tendencies or overall relations and did not characterize any single individual. Murray proposed that an adequate understanding of behavior could come only from a complete and detailed study of individuals. He held that group studies were important only when accompanied by careful inquiry into subjects who represented exceptions to the group norms.

Gordon Allport (1942) supported the idea that the human disciplines should use multiple approaches. He believed that investigators may choose to study the human realm in terms of general principles and universal variables, using a large number of subjects, or they may focus on the individual case, using methods and variables that are adequate to the uniqueness of each person. Allport, who had studied in Europe, borrowed from Windelband the team *nomothetic* to designate universal studies and the term *ideographic* to designate individual studies. (Later he substituted new terms for these designations, *dimensional* and *morphogenic,* respectively.) Allport acknowledged that there was a place for more than one kind of approach, but because American studies had so overwhelmingly emphasized nomothetic, or formal, science, he felt that a drastic reorientation was necessary. He emphasized the uniqueness of each person and urged the investigator to select methods of study that did not conceal this individuality. As part of his efforts to develop such methods, Allport proposed the importance of personal documents as information for understanding individuals.

The focus of these early qualitative programs in psychology was the study of the individual person. Qualitative methods were held to be supplemental to the quantitative methods used to study large-scale groups. Large scale studies focused on a single dimension, such as intelligence, and established norms to which individual performance could be compared. The qualitative programs used qualitative strategies to understand the complexity of the individual person and how the intersection of the multiplicity of psychological and environmental dimensions would be manifest in the individual (Greene, 1994).

### School Psychology

Whereas the literature of school psychology has not included much discussion of qualitative

methods in the past, in recent years there has been interest in qualitative research as an adjunct to its traditional research approaches. Bardon (1987) noted that research methods in school psychology had been overly traditional, and he recommended that it give consideration to qualitative methods. However, Keith's (1988) overview of school psychology research methods did not include qualitative research. His article is the first of a six-part series in *School Psychology Review* on research methods; the series emphasizes quantitative methods that could be used to study interventions and services to regular education students. Medway and Skedsvold (1992), in a chapter on school-based research and evaluation in *School Psychology: A Social Psychological Perspective* (Medway & Cafferty, 1992), include a section on naturalistic inquiry.

The journals of school psychology, although showing editorial interest in publishing research with qualitative procedures, have not yet published qualitatively based articles. In our review of the last 10 years of school psychology journals, we did not come across an article that explicitly used qualitative methods. However, Joel Meyers (1993), at the beginning of his editorship of the *Journal of School Psychology* (*JSP*), wrote, "Another goal is to broaden the research methodologies that are accepted for publication in JSP. . . . There are . . . descriptive methodologies, such as those that rely on observational and interview procedures, that can contribute to the literature, and there will be a systematic effort to attract manuscripts that focus on a range of populations of concern to school psychologists." (p. 238) Two years later he repeated his intention of broadening the research methodologies: "Another goal was to broaden the approaches to research published in JSP and a particular goal was to publish strong examples of qualitative methodology. To date we have received no examples of strong research using qualitative methodology, other than one special theme section focused on qualitative methods that is currently in preparation. This is another area in which authors are strongly encouraged to submit their research." (p. 2)

## THE THEORY AND PRACTICE OF QUALITATIVE RESEARCH

The contemporary practice of qualitative research is not method-driven. The validity of its findings is not dependant on following a methodological algorithm or set of rules. It generates a different kind of knowledge than the customary quantitative methods. Patton (1990) writes, "It is important to understand that the interpretive explanation of qualitative analysis does not yield knowledge in the same sense as quantitative explanation. The emphasis is on illumination, understanding, and extrapolation rather than causal determination, prediction, and generalization" (p. 424). Qualitative research is informed by a different view of science and knowledge. These differences make qualitative research appear to psychologists, who receive extensive training in quantitative methods, to be lacking in rigor and precision. The kind of knowledge quantitative researchers seek to establish is an accurate description of the general or probable relationships that actually exist in the world. This kind of knowledge can predict where members of a group will probably score on an index if one knows their scores on other indexes or their group membership. The kind of knowledge produced by qualitative strategies is more akin to a lens that brings aspects of a complex flux into focus. It is not meant as a description of how things "really are" but a useful cognitive frame that draws attention to significant aspects of the object of study.

When viewed from the perspective of quantitative criteria for judging research designs and their results, qualitative research studies do not use enough subjects to warrant generalization from a sample to a population. They lack the use of control groups necessary for critically evaluating the efficacy of interventions. Because their analytic procedures rely on human judgments instead of objective mathematical calculations, they may be susceptible to researchers' bias. Quantitative designs have been developed to ensure the production of knowledge that is internally and externally valid while minimizing researchers' effects. Because qualitative strategies develop a different kind of knowledge and are informed by a different view of science, it is inappropriate to judge their productions as if they were intended to be simply a softer approach to generating the customary quantitative type of knowledge. To determine the value of qualitative results and to distinguish the "stronger" and worthwhile qualitative products from the weaker and less useful ones, it is important to address the theoretical orientations that inform the qualitative field. This background sets a context for explaining the data production and analytic procedures used in the practice of qualitative research.

# The Theory of Qualitative Research

Early qualitative researchers attempted to revise and bend traditional positivistic approaches to knowledge to substantiate their work within the bounds of mainstream science. Contemporary qualitative researchers, however, have been influenced by recent philosophical developments, for example, critical theory, with its concern about inequality and the effect of ideological beliefs on human behavior (Carspecken & Apple, 1992); feminist theory, with its awareness of the subordinate positions assigned to people according to their sex, race, class, and age (Roman, 1992); and the poststructural approach to human knowledge (Rosenau, 1992). These developments challenge the notion that there is only one legitimate way to develop knowledge (Hempel, 1965) and provide qualitative research with an epistemological position that is more in tune with its actual practice. The poststructural view, which overlaps and shares many of the suppositions of the experientialist, constructivist, and postmodern ideas, disputes the traditional notions about the known, the knower, and the relation between them.

The strategies of qualitative research are intended for the study of the human realm, the realm of concern for school psychology. The methods used in traditional psychological research were first developed to study the physical realm and then adapted for application to the human realm (Polkinghorne, 1983). Because the human realm has characteristics not found in the physical realm, it is difficult for traditional methods alone to understand the full range and depth of the human domain.

## Investigation of the Human Realm

The argument in current philosophical and scientific circles for the distinctiveness of human beings centers on the notion of emergence (J. Margolis, 1986). Emergence refers to the idea that as organizational complexity is increased in entities, it is possible for new properties to appear that were not present in the less complex forms (Miller, 1978). In many cases the emerged novel and innovative characteristics could not have been predicted from knowledge of the less complex levels. Thus, explanations of the actions of the more complex levels cannot be reduced to the characteristics of the less complex levels. In discussions of the unique attributes of human beings, distinctions are often made among three supralevels of organization—the physical realm, the biological realm, and the human realm.

1. ***The Physical Realm.*** The attributes of the physical realm are characterized by the constancy and invariance of relationships that hold among its elements. The composites of the physical realm can be broken into their parts (analysis), and the separate parts studied in isolation from the whole. The findings of such studies are thought to hold in different spatial and temporal contexts. For example, the law of gravitational attraction does not vary because of a change in location, nor does it change over time. Except in the area of subatomic particles, the laws or relationship in the physical realm are exact. This invariance in the physical realm is such that if an observer's report varies from that which the knowledge of relationships would predict (e.g., the position of a planet), it is assumed that the variation is the result of statistically expected observer error, not probabilities in the physical realm itself.

Because of the spatial and temporal consistency of the relationships in the physical realm, it is possible to develop knowledge statements that are general and universal. One can have foreknowledge of what the relationship will be in the future (prediction), as well as knowledge of what they have been in the past (explanation). By knowing the tensile strength of a type of metal and the weight it supports, one can be assured that in the future metals of this type will have this strength, and this knowledge can be used in the construction of bridges with the confidence that the strength will not vary according to where the bridge is constructed or when it is constructed.

Because psychology has identified itself with the methods of the physical sciences, its customary approach to objectivity has inappropriately assumed that procedures designed to promote objectivity in the physical realm are applicable in the human realm. The principle of agreement among judges, although suitable for a realm in which the relations among the objects under scrutiny are stable and regular, is not as suitable for producing objective results in a realm whose relations are variant and context-sensitive.

2. ***The Biological Realm.*** Because biological entities have emerged attributes, such as context sensitivity and change through time, they need to be studied as units rather than as isolated parts. The study of biological entities requires researchers to focus their attention on the relationships that hold within a systemic structure. In the biological realm, the characteristics of an entity are influenced by and influence the system of which it is a part. In addition, biological systems interact with and adjust to the environments in which they are situated. Because of the variability of internal and external environmental conditions, biological systems of the same kind do not respond in the same way. Thus, knowledge of the biological realm cannot be universal (predictive of how each system will respond) but must be distributive (what the mean response in a group of biological systems will be to a range of environmental conditions). For example, the height a corn plant will reach cannot be determined by examining a single plant. Because the environmental conditions in a field vary—some plants receive more shade; some, on a lower part of the field, receive more water; and some are in a more nutrient-rich part of the soil—knowledge statements need to be in the form of the central tendencies and variations of the individual plants considered as group.

Biological systems are not static but undergo developmental changes in their structural characteristics over time. The rate and type of changes the systems undergo are the result of genetic information and environmental interactions. Because of the changing nature of biological systems, they do not respond to the same stimulus in the same way throughout their development. Procedures designed to promote greater objectivity in the biological realm need to be amended to take into account the fact that two judges who are observing the same system and responding to the same stimuli at different times may not observe the same response. To objectively describe biological systems requires that knowledge statements differ from those used to describe aspects of the physical realm. Statements about the biological realm need to recognize the variations that occur throughout the development of biological systems, as well as the limitations in understanding how individual biological systems will respond when knowledge is based on the study of aggregates of biological systems.

3. **The Human Realm.** The emerged properties of the human realm center on the capacity for conceptual thought and the consequential discontinuity between environmental stimuli and bodily response. The distinctiveness of human beings has been an important theme throughout the history of psychology (Reisman, 1991). Humans can design abstract strategies for achieving goals, and they can anticipate the effect of a possible action. They can conceptualize themselves as continuous beings, different from all others, and the authors of the thoughts they experience and the actions they perform. Humans have created a linguistic environment in which sounds and marks stand for ideas, and they can manipulate and communicate these ideas. Because of the languaged environment, they can be influenced by the thoughts of others, as well as by the actions of others. Language allows them to be affected by cultural traditions and stories of people who have lived in the past, contemporaries whom they have not met, and imagined people created by novelists and screen writers. These emerged capacities produce inconsistent patterns of response across individuals and promote within the same person innovative and creative responses over time to the same stimulus.

Human beings are embedded in all three realms—the physical, biological, and human. Each less complex realm is necessary for the functions of the more complex realm. For example, the physical stratum is a necessary but not sufficient condition for the emergence of the innovative properties of the biological realm, and the biological stratum is necessary for the emergence of human attributes. People do not inhabit merely the human realm, nor are their actions always conceptually guided. They are embodied beings (Merleau-Ponty, 1945/1962; Varela, Thompson, & Rosch, 1991), and there is an interactive relationship between their biological attributes and human attributes (e.g., the influence of human attributes on biological responses in placeboes and psychosomatic illnesses).

## Qualitative Knowledge Claims

The focus of qualitative research is the study of the human realm, and because of the properties of this realm, the results of qualitative research are expressed in substantially different kinds of knowledge statements than those appropriate in the physical and biological sciences. It is possible to produce knowledge about the physical and biological strata of human beings (studies of the physics of joint movements or the effect of certain drugs on the cells). Such knowledge can be expressed in the forms appropriate for describing the physical or biological realms independently of their connection to the human realm. In general, the production of research findings in psychology has retained three assumptions from the physical and biological sciences: (1) one can know what holds for populations on the bases of samples; (2) one can know what will hold for people on the bases of examinations of past actions; and (3) one can know the uninterpreted, actual reasons people act in the way they do.

Qualitative research does not make use of these assumptions in the development of results. It does not produce knowledge that is an accurate description of the way things are. Instead its productions are suggested cognitive maps, which can guide those who use them in understanding the investigated situation. The results are claimed to have only limited validity in the clarity they display about a predicament. They are asserted to hold for the particular situation at the time of the investigation and are based on interpretations of what participants said and did.

1. **Claims About Particular and Local Situations.** The findings produced by the customary approach to social science research are knowledge statements that claim to hold for people who were not examined during the research project. The assumptions about the distribution of human responses are drawn from the biological realm and the properties of aggregates. Biological properties of humans, such as weight, are distributed across populations, either normally or with skewing, and knowledge of the properties of a sample aggregate can be used to infer knowledge of the population aggregate. However, people's actions which incorporate the characteristics of the human realm, are dependent on the history and experiences of the individual actors and do not necessarily conform to the characteristics of a normal

population distribution. The imposition of aggregate properties on a collection of information about individual actions constrains findings by treating the individual actions as if they were merely variations of a general type of response. Qualitative claims are limited to descriptions of the people actually studied and are not extended through probability inferences to populations.

2. *Retrospective Claims About Situations.* The findings produced by the customary approach to research do not include temporal limits, and they imply that findings hold for future human responses, as well as for the examined past actions. The assumption of stability across time of people's behavior is an inference that goes beyond the collected data. What have been examined are the actions of a number of particular people at a particular time. The extension of the information gained from these people to claims about how people will behave in the future is based on a presupposition about the stability over time of human characteristics. Because of the capacity of the individual to change responses over time and because of the changes in influential social values and directives over time, qualitative research limits its claims about the future behavior of people by examination of past behaviors. Although qualitative researchers recognize the relative stability of personality traits across time (McCrae, 1992), their focus is on the expression of this trait in a particular situation (Cantor & Zirkel, 1990). The data collected in the psychological research concern people's past actions. In this sense, all psychological research is historical: it concerns what people have done in the past. Popper (1961) criticized attempts to identify laws of history in which a type of event was thought to be regularly followed by a particular type of response, and he concluded that one cannot predict the future course of history. Using these historical data to infer knowledge claims about how people will act in the future manifests the assumption that people's responses to stimuli will remain the same across time. Although qualitative findings are not predictive of future behavior, the patterns they describe may be useful in understanding future behaviors and situations. In qualitative research, claims are limited to retrospective descriptions of how and why people responded as they did in the past. In adopting this type of claim, the knowledge statements of qualitative research resemble those of its sister inquiry, history, which also focuses its investigations on human experiences and actions.

3. *Claims Are Interpretations.* Knowledge statements that claim to explain human actions need to include the reasons and motivations of the person who undertook the action. Human actions, unlike physical objects, cannot be understood simply by examining their relationship to observable variables. Researchers' access to a people's reasons for their actions is problematic on two counts: (a) people do not have access to all the reasons for their actions, and (b) people's reasons are usually multiple and complex and are difficult to translate into propositional statements. On the one hand, the purposes and motivations for people's actions are often not available to their reflective thought. Unconscious processes, as well as complex experiential processes (Epstein, 1993), are inaccessible to awareness. Thus, answers to questionnaires or interview questions about why a person acted as he or she did are not complete descriptions of the multiple and many-leveled reasons that affected the decision to act. On the other hand, people's presentation in language of the portion of experience of which they can become aware is not a transparent representation. Language, to serve its communicative function, is more highly organized grammatically and conceptually than is experience (Gendlin, 1991). To communicate the felt meaning of their purposes and motives, people often use metaphoric, analogic, and narrative forms of expression (Ricoeur, 1976).

Although these limits diminish the power of qualitative research to provide knowledge that allows for the governance of human behavior, they generate findings that are consistent with the belief that humans are agents who are capable of willful choices and innovative responses to environmental cues. This is the belief that underlies the goals and values of personal change and empowerment that inform the work of school psychologists. The kind of findings produced by qualitative research are similar in form to the experiential and practical knowledge developed by practitioners (Lave & Wenger, 1991).

The findings provide an informed display of a situation that practitioners can use to supplement their experience and general knowledge in deciding which course of action to undertake.

## The Application of Qualitative Research Results in Practice

The usefulness of the kind of knowledge that qualitative research produces derives from an understanding that human actions are informed by interpretative schemes people use to make sense of their experiences. In the British empirical tradition, which had served as the philosophical base for traditional research, the mind was conceived of as basically passive, a blank tablet on which experience writes. Kant offered a different conception, one in which the mind actively constructs experience from sensual cues. Qualitative research is aligned with the Kantian notion that experience is a product of a person's mapping strategies in interaction with the fragments of sensation, emotion, memory, and thought (H. Margolis, 1987). For Kant, experience is not a mere passive reception of impressions: it is the active grasping and comprehensions of perceptions; and without the concepts and categories through which people order and understand perceptions, experience would be formless and meaningless. Qualitative research does not share Kant's belief that the constructive patterns are universal; instead, it holds a more contemporary constructivist-constructionist view. This view accepts both the constructivist ideas of Piaget (1952), that cognitive structuring patterns are developed by individuals through feedback from their actions in the world, and the social constructionist ideas (Gergen, 1992), that structuring patterns are passed on to individuals through the conceptual models inherent in their culture's language.

Qualitative research procedures are based on these processes of ordinary comprehension, and they mimic constructive processes that humans ordinarily use to understand their experience. However, in the practice of qualitative research, these processes are elevated through deliberation and reflection. Through concentrated examination of a situation and through the process of abduction (Williams, 1985), people devise structural descriptions to display the dimensions of the situation in an insightful way. These descriptions are tested against the data of the situation and undergo rounds of revision until the data fit and are meaningfully displayed by the evolved structural description.

The products of research, as are the products of everyday experience, are not mirrored reflections of an external reality (Rorty, 1979) but rather the reflections of human structuring operations (Neimeyer & Mahoney, 1995). Because actions proceed from a person's interpretation of a situation (Combs & Syngg, 1959), the structures derived through qualitative study bring into focus aspects of a complex human situation to make it more understandable and thereby assist practitioners in their deliberation about what would be an appropriate response to the problem. The task of qualitative research in school psychology is to generate interpretative schemes that display educational predicaments in ways that usefully contribute to the practitioners' decisions about what actions to undertake. A strong result of a qualitative research effort will promote from the background of a problem those figures and dimensions that are significant for recognizing a successful solution.

As occurs in ordinary experience, once an interpretive structure has served to meaningfully order a situation, it becomes part of a person's conceptual repertoire and can be used for understanding other situations. However, given that each situation has unique historical and contextual differences, the successful transfer of a conceptual scheme to new situations (generalization) is problematic. The situation may be similar enough to be assimilated by the scheme, or the difference may be sufficient to "make a difference" and require the structure to be revised to accommodate it. Lincoln and Guba (1985) warn that although qualitative findings might be transferred to other settings, "the burden of proof [of the transferability of findings] lies less with the original investigator than with the person seeking to make an application elsewhere" (p. 298). The transferability of a qualitative finding to a different setting can be established only after testing the new situation to determine whether or not the interpretive structure can display the new setting usefully in spite of its differences.

## The Practice of Qualitative Research

Qualitative research is empirically grounded in that it collects and generates data about the situations it studies. These data are carefully analyzed to produce structural descriptions of the data's themes and their relationships. Which procedures are used and how they are employed depends on the situation under study and the researchers' experienced and informed judgment. The practice of qualitative research resembles the trial-and-error learning process of everyday problem solving rather than a step-by-step walk through a set of predetermined fixed method. In this, the type of reasoning employed in its practice has a different tone from the formal logic of quantitative designs. Thus, qualitative practice is analogous to the production of a picture by an artist who is knowledgeable and experienced in the properties of paint and skilled in the use of brushes and who can creatively solve the problems related to light and perspective to produce a painting that displays his or her ideas. This kind of production requires different skills than those necessary to complete a paint-by-numbers portrait.

To produce strong results with qualitative strategies requires a significant investment in training and experience with their procedures. It also requires the researcher to have sufficient ability in pattern recognition to abstract significant themes from a bulk of data fragments. Eisner (1991) writes that people with this ability are said to be perceptive: "Experience—our consciousness of some aspect of the world—is an achievement. And, to my mind, it is a cognitive achievement. We *learn* to see, or at least we learn to see those aspects of the world that are subtle and complex. When we think about people we regard as expert in some field . . . it is clear that they hear and see more than we do. At the most sophisticated level we call these people 'connoisseurs'" (p. 17). Early examples of qualitative research in education were sometimes produced by people who lacked sufficient training and experience in the process. Hoshmand (1989) proposed a graduate curriculum for training in qualitative methods, and many schools of education offer basic and advanced courses in qualitative research and have faculty skilled in supervising dissertation research that uses these strategies. Qualitative research is not an alternative for those simply wanting to avoid statistics; the proper use of its strategies requires high levels of training and the development of a researcher's perceptive abilities.

The strength of the results of a qualitative project is not determined by whether or not the researcher accurately followed a prescribed design but by the pragmatic criteria of the power of the structural description to provide insight into the investigated situation. However, judgment can be made about the process through which the researcher reached his or her results. Researchers need to provide a clear description about how and why they chose to produce particular data about the situation and to give a complete account of how they produced a thematic description that fit these data.

The basic procedures used in qualitative research are production of the data, analysis of the data, and production of a research report. These procedures are common to all qualitative projects; however, they can be used to produce different kinds of structural descriptions. For example, they can generate results in the form of mid-level models of human activity (grounded theory), structural descriptions of concepts (phenomenological research), thematic descriptions of people's responses to a program or intervention (qualitative evaluation studies), and histories of people's lives or life episodes (case studies).

## Qualitative Procedures

Most of the descriptions in the educational literature (see the section on tradition) about how to do qualitative research contain chapters devoted to data production, data analysis, and communication of results. The content of these chapters is in the form of advice rather than instructions on what to do. Suggestions about how to conduct research are drawn from the authors' experience and exemplar studies. Advances in the literature on the practice of qualitative research are the consequence of the accumulation of experience with the strategy.

Although data production and data analysis are presented as sequential chapters in the literature, in conducting qualitative studies researchers move recursively from data collection to analysis and back to data collection to further analysis and so on. This is a significant and crucial departure from the process of quantitative research, in which all the data are collected before performing the analysis. The development of qualitative results evolves during the research process. After the initial collection of data, a first analytic effort produces a prototypic structural description. Then, to test the prototypic description, more data are produced. From the situation under study, sources of data are selected that appear to call into question the adequacy of the prototypic structure to display the essential themes and relationships in the whole situation. Most often structural description has to be revised to accommodate these additional data and is followed by the production of additional data, which leads to further revisions. After each recursive cycle, the description should become more adequate in displaying the accumulated data. At times, however, the outlines of the emerging description cannot account for themes that appear in the newly produced data. When this occurs, major revisions in the thematic structure are often required so that the complexity and variation in all the situation's produced data are exhibited. The process can be visualized as a downward helix in which each turn produces a deeper and more adequate structural description. The process continues until newly produced data do not force revisions in the emerged description but continue to be accommodated by it; that is, the emerged description is completely saturated by all the produced data. This final saturated description is the finding of the research.

Hans Reichenbach (1938) proposed that research consists of two separated phases—the *context of discovery* and the *context of justification*. The context of discovery refers to the process of creating or developing hypotheses, and the context of justification to the process of testing hypotheses. Reichenbach held that the methods of science were applicable only to the context of justification that these two phases of research should be separated, and that epistemology was concerned only with the context of justification. Once a hypothesis had been proposed, scientific procedures could determine if the hypothesis were false (Popper, 1972). The creation of hypotheses requires a different type of thinking, called *abduction* by Peirce (1955) (Buchler, 1955), which differs from the formal logic used in justifying them. It involves the use of the Gestalt part-whole and systemic process.

Qualitative research combines the context of discovery and the context of justification, and its procedures both create and refine hypotheses within a single research project (Borgen, 1992). In the traditional approach to research, the design functions as a one-shot test of the proposed hypothesis. Evolution of hypotheses occurs historically as answers are accumulated from a succession of singular tests of each new hypothesis revision. Reichenbach's (1938) limitation of science to the justification of hypotheses is overly narrow. Qualitative research provides a scientifically responsible approach to the development and testing of hypotheses concerning the thematic structures of a situation. From its data-based formulations of hypothesized structural descriptions to their data-based revisions, the process is deliberative, methodical, and subject to public scrutiny. Its proposed research conclusions are tested against data that are intentionally selected to show their inadequacies, and the analysis used to obtain them are submitted to the community of scholars for critique and judgment.

Three basic procedures are used in qualitative research projects—data production, data analysis, and communication of results. Because these procedures are discussed in detail elsewhere, they will be treated only briefly here, highlighting general principles and providing references to more detailed presentations.

### Data Production

Qualitative researchers are interested in any data that contribute to knowledge of the situation they are studying. They both gather and produce data. They make use of documents, such as letters (Allport, 1942), printed announcements, classroom papers, teachers' reports, and so on. They produce data through interviews with the people involved in the situation. Because researchers are concerned with understanding a situation completely, they seek out data that are rich and deep in description (Geertz, 1973). No single source of information can be trusted to provide a comprehensive view of the situation under investigation. Goetz and LeCompte (1984) write, "A distinguishing characteristic of ethnographic research is the fluid, developmental process through which [the] means of collecting data are chosen and constructed" (p. 107).

Research data can be categorized into three basic forms—short answer, numerical, and natural language. A data-generating questionnaire illustrates these categories. Respondents can be asked to provide data in a short-answer format (e.g., name, nationality, areas of interest), in a numerical format (e.g., choosing a number on a Likert scale to indicate level of interest in a topic), and in natural language format (e.g., writing several paragraphs on why they are interested in a position). Although qualitative research can use all three forms of data, it is primarily characterized by its use of natural language.

Because qualitative analytic procedures are designed to work directly with data in the form of natural language, the researcher is not required to use instruments designed to create data in a numeric form nor to translate natural language data into nominal or ranked data before analyzing them. To submit data to statistical analysis, they must end up in a numerical form; however, qualitative analysis requires data of sufficient complexity and variation to display a situation's structure. The qualitative researcher's concern is for context. The focus in producing data moves between figure and ground—like a zoom lens on a camera—to catch the fine detail of what is happening in a situation and to keep a perspective on its context.

*The Function of Participants.* The primary function of participants in qualitative research is to serve as sources of rich data. The choice of participants is not guided by the need to produce a random selection to conform to the requirements of statistical probability theory. Participants are chosen purposefully to fulfill the two requirements of an adequate qualitative data base: intense descriptions of the situation under investigation and enough variation in the data to develop a comprehensive structural description (Chenitz & Swanson, 1986b). The rationale for selecting participants is that they have a particularly useful perspective about the situation and are able to articulate it.

*Intermittent Selection of Subjects.* As mentioned, the selection of participants continues throughout the investigation (Glaser & Strauss, 1967); it is informed by the need to test the limits of the emerging description. To produce a saturated description, qualitative researchers select participants on the basis of the contribution they might make toward its ongoing development (Woods, 1992). In place of looking for additional participants who will confirm the emerging description, the researcher seeks out participants whose experience in the situation is atypical and might disconfirm the description. Glaser and Strauss refer to this iterative process of participant selection as *theoretical sampling*. They note that an "inadequate theoretical sample is easily spotted, since the theory associated with it is usually thin and not well integrated, and has too many obvious unexplained exceptions" (p. 63). The process of qualitative investigation calls for an oscillation between data gathering and analysis, and it reaches completion when the data saturate the description.

*The Number of Participants.* A researcher cannot know in advance how many participants will be required before an evolving description becomes saturated. The often-asked question of how many participants are needed for a qualitative study is a holdover from quantitative research and misses the essential thrust of the role participants play in the development of qualitative findings, which do not refer to a situation other than the one studied. The question about the number of subjects and the process by which they were randomly selected is related to the requirements of inferential statistics and the move to generalize findings to populations or situations beyond those participants who were the actual sources of data. A qualitative researcher cannot know in advance how many participants must be interviewed nor how much documental data must be gathered. The amount of data needed depends on the complexity of the examined situation and the skill and fortune involved in devising a structural description that is revealing enough to pass the tests of disconfirmation and reach saturation.

The logic of qualitative analysis makes it inappropriate to suppose that a characteristic or theme is more significant because it appears often in the data. Analyses uncover what kinds of themes or structures make up a situation, not their levels in a frequency distribution. For example, if a qualitative study found that newspapers receive four kinds of letters in response to published articles and that one kind appeared only once among 30 examined letters and another kind 20 times, there is no basis for assertions about the probable distribution of the kinds of letters received. The statistical logic required to derive such a conclusion requires a randomly chosen or representative selection. However, participants in qualitative studies are chosen because they have experienced a situation from a unique perspective and are able to give detailed and extensive descriptions of their experience; they are not selected as random members of a population or because they make up a representative sample.

*Interviews.* Skillfully conducted interviews can provide the most authentic and complete descriptions of subjects' experiences (Mishler, 1986). The intensive interview allows researchers and participants to establish a level of trust and openness in their relationship (Ely, Anzul, Friedman, Garner & Steinmetz, 1991). This closeness can lessen the biasing effects that derive from participants' need to manage the impressions they give and can permit the exploration of aspects of their experiences not available at first recall. Seidman (1991) suggests that a one-time interview with a participant is not adequate to produce the depth and breadth of information most useful in developing structural descriptions. Although some qualitative researchers produce data by requesting participants to respond to questions in writing, this procedure does not allow for the kind of exploration that is possible in face-to-face interviews and is dependent on the subjects' ability for written expression. Written responses often "yield responses of a distant and highly reflective nature" (Stevick, 1971, p. 135). Nevertheless, logistical considerations often determine the type of data collection that can be used in a qualitative study. Within practical limits, the goal is to preserve the narrative richness of the subjects' experience.

Descriptions produced in interviews do not necessarily depict events accurately as they occurred. Memory is a reconstructive process in which fragments are pieced together and gaps are filled in so that the memory makes sense (Loftus, Donders, Hoffman, & Schooler, 1989). Coercive and leading interviews can produce data that are primarily reflections of the researcher's biases. Children are particularly vulnerable to interviewers' suggestions (Underwager & Wakefield, 1990). School psychologists are often interested in situations that involve children. Special care and skill are required in gaining an understanding of their experiences. In a normal interview with adults, the interviewer and the participant sit down and engage in conversation. This practice is not very productive with young children (Mahoney, 1995). Several short discussions within a context of play held in a familiar environment will be more productive. Access to children's understanding of a situation requires observations of their behavior, as well as attention to what they say (Fine & Sandstrom, 1988).

Whether produced by observation or interviews, data must be reduced to written form to be analyzed. Before analysis, interviews are most often audio-recorded and then transcribed and observations are recorded in written form. As the data are accumulated, they are analyzed and re-analyzed.

### Data Analysis

The primary outcome of a qualitative analytic process is the integration of information from multiple sources and disparate personal descriptions. The kinds of data that might appear in a school psychology study include (1) transcripts of interviews with a child and his or her playmates, family members (including siblings), and present and past teachers; (2) notes from observing the child's interactions in the classroom, playground, and home; (3) descriptions from community members of the social environment; and (4) scores from various assessment instruments. The purpose of an analysis is to synthesize these data into a general structural description that exhibits the situation's various "forces" and their vectors (Lewin, 1951). The outcome might consist of a model of the interplay among the family members' expectations; the child's self-understanding, aspirations, interpersonal patterns, and motivations; the cultural and institutional context; the availability of resources; and the child's range of capacities and performances.

Several excellent texts are available to assist qualitative researchers in the analysis of data, for example, Dey (1993), Miles and Huberman (1994), Strauss and Corbin (1990), and Wolcott (1994). These texts depict qualitative analytic work, drawing on a researcher's capacity to identify patterns in an apparently disconnected set of personal descriptions. By studying and comparing the descriptions, common themes and relationships emerge as identifiable figures out of the complex data set. The emergence takes place as a cognitive negotiation with the data in which the processes of assimilation and accommodation form a set of concepts that makes a situation more understandable. The researcher plays an active role in conceptually organizing the data into themes and relationships. Thus, the analytic work is more than a discovery; it is a construction that, in interaction with the data, shows off certain consistencies and patterns.

Analysis usually begins with reading the data, during which sentences or meaning units are identified as instances of a category. In research into the human realm, most of the analytical categories are artifactual rather than natural. Natural categories are those that are held to exist in nature, for example, male and female, and artifactual categories are distinctions created by humans, for example, social classes (Rothbart & Taylor, 1992). The statement "The child said he didn't have any playmates and no one pays attention to me" might be identified as an instance of the artifactual category "isolation." These category identifications are often written in the left margin of the transcript. To save time and space, they are usually abbreviated; for example, "ISO" could be used for "isolation." The abbreviations are referred to as codes, and the process of identifying elements of the transcript is called coding.

Contemporary qualitative researchers usually use computer programs to manage their data. Most computer programs provide a way to mark off and to assign a code to sections of text.

The programs will also gather into a text file all the sections that have been assigned the same code. The computer programs do not actually analyze the data, as is the case with statistical software. Programs for qualitative analysis merely make working with data less labor-intensive. Weitzman and Miles (1995) have produced an excellent text in which they review the available qualitative analysis software; one of the more helpful programs is NUD-IST (Nonnumerical Unstructured Data Indexing Searching and Theorizing) which is now available from Sage Publications, (Qualitative Solutions and Research, 1994).

The coding process is designed to separate the data into groups of like items. The grouped items are inspected to identify the common attributes that define them as members of a category (Strauss, 1987). Most qualitative analytic procedures emphasize a recursive movement between the data and the emerging categorical definitions during the process of producing classifications that organize the data. The analysis builds the categorical definitions by continually testing their power to order the data. The categories are revised and retested until they provide the best fit of a categorical scheme for the data set. Although the general practice of qualitative analysis follows this description of developing a categorical schematic out of the data, Strauss and Corbin (1994) believe that it is acceptable to begin with a predetermined network of themes and their relationships (e.g., psychoanalytic theory) and to use them for scrutiny of data. Glaser (1992), Strauss's early collaborator, is strongly opposed to the use of predetermined categories in data analysis. He argues that their use can prevent the researcher from discovering the unique themes and structural organization present in the situation under study.

In building a structural description of an investigated situation, qualitative analysis is not content to simply identify a set of categories that identifies the particular elements of the data base. Analysis also seeks structural relations that hold among the categorical themes. This second phase of analysis, which Glaser (1978) calls *theoretical coding*, tries to show how the categories are linked to one another: "Theoretical codes conceptualize how the substantive codes [categorization] may relate to each other" (p. 72). Glaser presents 18 examples of ways in which categorical themes might be related, including stages, chains, cycles, polarities, elements, facets, parts, causes, contexts, contingencies, consequences, covariances, and conditions.

Unlike quantitative research, in which the analysis itself is conducted by computerized mathematical operations, qualitative analysis is steeped in researchers' judgments. To lessen the threat of bias, several procedures are usually performed. The first check is internal to the research process—the deliberate search for instances in the data that do not fit into the structural description. This search is supplemented by the use of outside auditors, who examine the data to see if the description actually displays their full range. Qualitative researchers often form groups in which members serve as auditors for one another's work (Strauss, 1987). Also some researchers present their descriptions to participants from whom the data were gained (member checks), asking them if the descriptions accurately display the themes and relations in their situations. As a final procedure, qualitative reports include a recounting of the analytic process used in producing the structural description. The recounting is expected to include discussions of early attempts at descriptions that were altered as additional data were analyzed.

The final product of qualitative analysis is a structural description that shows the thematic relationships in the studied situation. The question "Are the findings true" misses the different kind of knowledge produced by qualitative analysis. In traditional terminology, findings are true or valid if they correspond to the reality they are intended to describe (Altheide & Johnson, 1994). Qualitative results are not valid in this sense; it may be more appropriate to ask, "Is the model trustworthy" (Lincoln & Guba, 1985). It is possible to generate more than one trustworthy model of the same situation, although there are a limited number of models that can fit the data. For example, the structure of a deck of playing cards can be described as having two different colors, four different symbols, or numbers and letters. Whether or not the model is useful depends on the question asked.

An initial criterion for rigor in quantitative methods is consistency, or reliability. The consistency can be assessed for items (internal consistency), responses on occasions (test-retest reliability), or different raters (interrater reliability). Lincoln and Guba (1985) describe dependability as analogous to reliability. In qualitative methods, an audit performed by an external person or agency on the process of data collection can establish the dependability of the data. When school psychologists do an assessment, it is important to report the methods by which the data were gathered and analyzed.

Another issue related to the production of research findings is validity. Validity has a long history in quantitative measurement. Boring (1945) is often quoted as stating, "Intelligence is what the tests test" (p. 244). Actually, Boring said, "If intelligence is what the tests test, it is possible to ask whether what the tests test is neural speed or normal education or something else" (p. 244). This statement calls into question assumptions about the measurements labeled as intelligence. Similarly, in qualitative methods the meaning of the information can still be questioned. Techniques for supporting the ascribed meaning are called credibility. This construct closely corresponds to the construct of validity (Lincoln & Guba, 1985). Techniques for establishing the credibility or trustworthiness of data include prolonged engagement, triangulation with multiple sources of information, member checks, persistent observation, peer debriefing, and negative case analysis. If prolonged engagement is avoided and the school psychologist has only one conversation with the student or only observes the student once, the credibility of the data is subject to criticism. Another method for establishing the credibility of qualitative data is triangulation, in which multiple sources of information are used in the production of data. This method has also been recommended for school psychology assessments (Carroll, Gurski, Hinsdale & McIntyre, 1977; Hyman & Kaplinski, 1994; Jones, 1988; Miller-Jones, 1989).

Another technique for assessing the trustworthiness of qualitative analysis is member checks. School psychologists should request feedback from participants on whether or not the structural description includes their point of view. Young children are likely to be rather limited in the feedback they provide. However, teachers and parents can offer important suggestions for revisions in the descriptive analysis. Soliciting feedback from parents and teachers might also have other desired effects. Although PL 94-142 requires that parents be involved in the assessment process, the extent to which they have been actively involved is suspect (Jones, 1988). Although not discussing assessment, Lincoln and Guba (1985) identify the characteristics necessary for negotiating recommendations, such as being explicit and open about information and facilitating a common understanding among stakeholders.

### Communication of Results

In qualitative research, writing the report is a continuation of the analytic process. The document is expected to include citations from the data to illustrate and clarify the thematic descriptions and structural model. During composition, the researcher reviews the data set to gather the illustrative material. During this review, the terms used to identify the themes may be revised and new insights about the fit between the structural description and the situation appear. Strauss (1987) relates that while writing the report, "researchers always find themselves discovering something that tightens up or extends the total analysis" (p. 212).

The purpose of the report is to make public (publish) the structural description of the situation studied. The report must give a full account of (1) how the data were collected and why the researcher chose to gather them and (2) why decisions about themes and their structural relations were made. Readers of a qualitative report can expect to follow and understand the judgments made by the researchers as they evolved their version of a structural model. The point of the report is not to demonstrate that because the researcher followed an established design, the results must be legitimate, but rather to allow the reader to see that the process that led to the result was reasonable.

Qualitative results are not intended to add to a discipline's body of knowledge in the same way that quantitative results are. The latter are intended to be general truths about a discipline's object of study. Once the knowledge claim is established, other researchers expect to be able to cite it as evidence on which they can ground their studies. Qualitative results are not intended to be general truths but structural descriptions of particular situations. It does not follow from the logic of qualitative research that the structure developed to display a particular situation will hold for any other situation. Researchers can, however, use previously developed themes and models as possibilities for the situations they are studying. Thus, qualitative results add to a discipline's body of knowledge by contributing innovations in the dimensions and structures through which the discipline understands and approaches its objects of study.

# APPLICATIONS OF QUALITATIVE RESEARCH IN SCHOOL PSYCHOLOGY

Psychology has followed the pattern of other disciplines in creating a division of labor in which some (primarily situated in the academy) serve as researchers, developing the discipline's body of knowledge, and others (primarily working in the field) serve as practitioners, applying the developed body of knowledge. School psychologists, along with clinical and counseling (and industrial-organizational) psychologists, serve as psychology's practitioners, who have been expected only to apply the findings developed by the academic researchers. They were understood as the "appliers" of knowledge and were considered to have lesser standing than the researchers who actually developed the knowledge. In other words, the activity of science produced knowledge of laws and general principles that could be translated into techniques for use by practitioners in specific situations. Practitioners were to be trained in research so that as consumers of research, they could read the research journals and keep themselves up to date on the latest findings produced in the academy. They were not to trust as reliable the experiential understandings that they derived from their practice. Because these understandings, which were derived from trial and error or anecdotal experience, had not yet been tested by the rigorous methods used by the academic scientists, they were not considered appropriate to guide the practitioners' actions and interventions. Practice based on personal experience was unsystematic and held to produce unpredictable results (Polkinghorne, 1992).

Because qualitative research produces knowledge about particular situations, rather than general, lawlike knowledge, it does not fit the traditional model of application. Qualitative knowledge helps in the solution of a specific problem, and it is expected to be directly, not generally, relevant to decision making. Qualitative research can be undertaken by research consultants to a school psychologist or by the school psychologists themselves.

1. ***The Qualitative Researcher as Consultant.*** When confronted with an assessment or intervention, an experienced qualitative researcher could be called on to study the situation and produce a structural map of it for the school psychologist and other members of the decision team. The map should provide the team with a clear and new understanding of the problem. It should highlight the interplay of the various factors or themes in such a way that the team is able to come to a productive decision. Because of their training and focus and because they have not been directly involved in the history or politics of the situation, consultants can produce a fresh way of viewing the problem. The results of a consultative research intervention need to be presented in language and with a format that speak directly to those who will use the information as part of their decision-making process. Thus, the form will not be governed by a publication's style requirements (Bazerman, 1987) but will be guided by the principles of psychological report writing (Tallent, 1988). The duties of the researcher as consultant closely resemble the assessment role of the school psychologist.

2. ***The School Psychologist as Qualitative Researcher.*** Fagan and Wise (1994), in their recent text on the function and training of school psychologists, list assessment as the primary role and list consultation as the secondary role. Research is listed under the heading "additional roles and functions." Administrative priorities and time constraints limit traditional research by school psychologists, especially when it appears not to relate directly to the task of specifically serving the psychological needs of the unit's children. However, school psychologists with skill and training in qualitative methods can directly contribute more considered decisions in their educational services to students. If school psychologists were to function as qualitative researchers, training programs would have to include courses to prepare them for this new role. Education in qualitative research would not replace the study of psychometrics but could be offered as an extension of the problem-solving model of assessment and consultation. Time constraints may not allow school psychologists to regularly expend the time and effort required to conduct a formal qualitative investigation. Nevertheless, the principles of gathering data from multiple sources and skills in interviewing, plus the understanding of how to produce structural models

from data, can be used informally in the normal course of the school psychologist's daily tasks.

## Qualitative Research and Assessment

A large number of qualitative studies have investigated how children experience life in schools. LeCompte and Preissle (1992) conducted an examination of over 100 qualitative studies of children in preschool, elementary, and secondary schools. Their examination found that the topics of these studies could be divided into five categories: (1) students' perceptions of their participation in schools and classrooms, (2) students' behaviors as structured by teachers, (3) students' behavior as a function of cultural congruity, (4) students' behavior as a function of links between the school and larger society, and (5) students' behavior and learning as a social construction.

The qualitative study of children focuses on a particular child or group of children (e.g., children in a specific classroom). The tradition of studying individual children goes back to Lightner Witmer at the beginning of this century (Brotemarkle, 1931). When the situation studied by qualitative researchers is an individual child or group of children, the study is referred to as a case study. A case study uses multiple data sources that exhibit various themes and trajectories found in an individual person or group. Case studies most often employ a narrative structure (Zeller, 1995), which extends the analysis beyond a cross section of the present to include past life events and future possibilities (Polkinghorne, 1995). Case studies can limit the time span of the inquiry to an episode or study the full life of a person. Full-life studies employ the biographical method, which Denzin (1989) describes as "the studied use and collection of life documents which describe turning-point moments in an individual's life" (p. 7). Life documents include autobiographies, dairies, letters, life stories, personal experience stories, and oral histories (Denzin, 1989). Stake (1988, 1994, 1995) gives qualitative researchers a useful approach to conducting case studies of individuals and groups, and Yin (1984, 1993) provides a model for case studies of organizations.

Case studies can be used for two purposes: (1) as an information source for consideration in an assessment decision and (2) as a report on a completed assessment process. A case study of a child can assist in team judgment by providing the context of a unique life whose present circum-stances result from the confluence of interrelated purposive, situational, and historical events. Reports of completed assessments (e.g., Cervantees, 1988; Morrison, 1988; Scott & Fisher, 1988), provide examples of processes, which can inform other school psychologists of alternate methods. Studies of completed assessments allow for the inclusion of the consequences (Moss, 1992).

The primary role of school psychologists is assessment (Fagan & Wise, 1994). The notion of assessment has changed from a concentration on psychometric testing to an emphasis on problem solving that may or may not include the use of tests. Test data now need to be integrated into other sources of information, and qualitative research provides a method for doing so. Assessment help in negotiations that lead to solving the problems of an individual child. Guba and Lincoln (1989) suggest that evaluation has changed over generations. Previous generations could be characterized as measurement-oriented, description-oriented, and judgment-oriented; the present, fourth generation, is negotiation-oriented. One of the properties of fourth-generation evaluations is as follows:

> Evaluation outcomes are not descriptions of the "way things really are" or "really work," or of some "true" state of affairs, but instead represent meaningful constructions that individual actors or groups of actors form to "make sense" of the situations in which they find themselves. The findings are not "facts" in some ultimate sense but are, instead, literally *created* through an interactive process that *includes* the evaluator . . . as well as the many stakeholders that are put at some risk by the evaluation. What emerges from this process is one of more *constructions* that *are* the realities of the case. (p. 8)

Qualitative research provides a strategy for identifying the values, hopes, and views of a child so that one perspective is not emphasized at the expense of others. Test data and their assumptions and values provide one point of view in arriving at a negotiated decision on how the student's educational needs can best be served.

Historically, the assessment process has emphasized quantitative information. In previous generations of assessment, a standardized instrument might have been developed that purported to measure an attribute or characteristic of the student. Alternatively, observations of classroom behavior might have been made through a structured format. The responses to the instrument or observations were converted to numbers, assuming that they represented a set of mathematical properties. The set of numbers might have been used descriptively or interpreted through a comparison with norms. To the extent that the instrument measured meaningful characteristics or constructs and observations or responses corresponded to a set of mathematical properties, the measurements would have yielded useful information (Cliff, 1973; Krantz, Luce, Suppes, & Tversky, 1971; Stevens, 1951). The earlier model of assessment was testing-based and reflected a medical model of learning problems. The diagnosis of a problem involved noting the extent to which a student's scores deviated from the norm established from the sample used in developing the instrument. In this tradition, the scores were viewed as "real" facts and learning problems were also "real" and existed with the individual. This view no longer conforms to the current ideas of learning, cognition, and literacy. The traditional approach to assessment has had unfortunate consequences for minority students, as well as for others, and these have been litigated extensively in the courts.

## Context for Change in Assessment

Assessment procedures have undergone significant criticism in past years, especially in relation to the disproportionate placement of minority children in educable mentally retarded (EMR) classes (Mercer, 1973). These criticisms are reflected in numerous court cases and legislation (Jones, 1988; Valdez & Figueroa, 1994). Although not directly addressing assessment, *Brown v. Board of Education* (1954), which concerned the desegregation of schools, can be considered to be the initial case that affected later legal views about assessment. A few years later, *Hobson v. Hansen* (1967) readdressed segregation. In this case, however, aptitude or intelligence tests were directly involved. Students were tracked, or segregated, on the basis of test scores, which were confounded with ethnicity. As a result of this case, several problems with aptitude tests were identified, including the use of inappropriate norms, lack of predictive validity, and use of standard English only.

A few years later, a similar case *Diana v. State Board of Education* (1970), which involved Latin-American students, was contested. Again, the primary issue was the use of intelligence tests to place minority children in "special" programs such as EMR classes. As a result, both parties agreed to the following: (1) students should be tested in their primary language (such as Spanish) and English; (2) nonverbal intelligence tests scores should be used for Latin-American children already placed in EMR classes, (3) retesting should be undertaken in which the focus would be on nonverbal scores; and (4) the proportion of EMR students who are Latin-American should be monitored. Mercer (1973), in a study responding to the final agreement, concluded that a disproportionate number of Hispanic children were placed in EMR classes.

While *Diana v. State Board of Education* concerned Latin-American students, *Larry P. v. Riles* (1979) addressed testing issues as they related to the placement of black children in EMR classes. As a result of this case, intelligence tests were banned from use for the placement of black children in California unless specific court approval could be obtained for a given case. It is interesting to note that in the Order Modifying Judgment (1986), assessment procedures were formally extended beyond standardized testing to include personal histories, assessment of adaptive behavior, classroom performance, academic achievement, and assessment of specific academic abilities.

Two other court cases supported the use of standardized tests for minority children. In *Parents in Action for Special Education (PASE) v. Hannon* (1980), items from the WISC, WISC-R, and Stanford-Binet tests were reviewed. Only a few items were considered to be biased against minority children. The other case that supporting the use of intelligence tests in assessment was *Crawford v. Honig* (1988); in this case, the parents requested the testing of their child.

These court cases as a whole indicate growing concerns about assessment of minority children through standardized intelligence or aptitude tests. Specifically, issues of bias and segregation, based on these tests, were at issue. The results of the court cases or of a concurrent interest was to determine the underlying purpose of testing and question the use of these tests as the primary means of assessment.

## Uses of Qualitative Research in Assessment

Assessment based on a qualitative research model offers a possible solution to the problems inherent in the testing model. As previously described, qualitative research understands that human performance is highly sensitive to context. A student's performance cannot be understood simply as a characteristic of the individual but rather as a characteristic of the individual in interaction with others in a specific activity; that is, a problem in performance or a learning "disability" is socially constructed. Thus, assessment requires mapping the interaction of multiple dimensions, contexts, and social processes that are involved in a child's performance. This approach differs from the physical science model of law-governed behavior acts, which was the basis for the traditional view of testing.

In general, a problem-solving model of assessment includes three steps: initial assessment, diagnosis, and treatment (Hyman & Kaplinski, 1994; Kehle, Clark, & Jensen, 1993). Synthesizing several elaborations on this model, Jones (1988) presents six stages of problem-solving assessment:

1. Problem identification
2. Obtaining parental permission
3. Gathering assessment data including testing
4. Drawing conclusions on the data and formulating recommendations
5. Development of an individual education plan (IEP) by a team
6. Follow-up

Not all assessments follow these stages in sequence, although these processes are typically involved in most assessments. The initial stage, problem identification or initiation of the assessment process, is discussed next, followed by selecting types of assessment information; other stages are discussed in the context of assessment authenticity.

### Initiating the Assessment Process

Referrals should not be seen as an identification of the problem; they are an indication that someone believes the child is not achieving satisfactory academic success. Educational researchers (Craig, Kaskowitz, & Malgoire, 1978; Tomlinson et al., 1977; Zucker, Prieto, & Rutherford, 1979) have investigated teachers' referrals for EMR placement, although these studies focused only on the degree to which the referrals were biased, based on proportions of ethnic or economic groups. Underlying social processes, including personal beliefs of the teachers and students, institutional goals of schooling in the United States and other countries, and referrals that resulted from legal activity have not been adequately studied.

Qualitative inquiries could assist in understanding a specific referral or a collection of referrals in a school. Interviews with a teacher could include queries about the specific behaviors or characteristics of the student that led the referral. What was perceived by the teacher as problematic and why? A teacher's beliefs about schooling and the role he or she played in the referral could be investigated. The interviews would allow the teachers to express the intuitive elements of their decision, as well as the institutionally approved ones. An analysis of the interplay of the themes that contributed to the decision can provide a rich and nuanced understanding of the particular referral. The analysis of interviews with several teachers in a school might uncover conflicting thematic patterns, as well as socially grounded views of what kinds of behavior lead to a referral.

### Selecting Types of Assessment Information

Following referrals of students, assessment information, which should elucidate the nature of the academic problem, is collected. The information is presented in two categories—the object of inquiry and the student and the classroom. These two categories do not capture all types of information that may be relevant to the assessment. For example, Ogbu (1992) addresses cultural and institutional factors in students' success. Omission of these and other relevant factors could have a strong negative impact on the quality of a qualitative assessment.

***Student Characteristics.*** Traditional assessment has focused on standardized measures of cognitive functioning, especially intelligence. These tests have received considerable attack, as is evident from numerous court cases. Intelligence is typically conceptualized as a fixed trait of an individual. Although the trait can change over an individual's lifetime, it is believed to be relatively stable. This fixed trait presumably measures some ability of the student to perform well in school. A low score on an intelligence-measuring instrument would indicate the need for special placement. This approach to determining the student's problem in school is characteristic of traditional assessment. The construct, intelligence, was identified, and then measures of the construct were developed. The validity of the assessment information focuses on correlations with school success. Having found that correlations exist, school psychologists might infer that students with low scores on intelligence instruments need alternative educational placements.

There are, of course, many other conceptualizations of intelligence (Kehle et al., 1993), including Piaget's (1952) stage sequential theory, Gardner's (1983) theory of multiple, independent intelligences, and Sternberg's (1985) triarchic theory of intelligence. Using instruments in the assessment process that are based on one of these conceptualizations of intelligence would yield different information than measurements based on such conceptualizations as Spearman's (1923) *g*.

A variety of other characteristics believed to influence students' performance has also been measured. For example, dynamic assessment (Feurstein, Rand, & Hoffman, 1979; Haywood, 1977, 1988) purports to assess students' potential for obtaining skills or cognitive structures, for learning effectively. Although the characteristics measured are not thought to be fixed traits of ability such as those measured by traditional intelligence tests (WISC-R and Stanford-Binet), they are still characteristics possessed by an individual. Other forms of measurement have focused on behaviors that occur in a particular setting (Anderson, 1988), adaptive behavior (Scott & Fisher, 1988), or a combination of several types of information (Cervantees, 1988; Hyman & Kaplinski, 1994; Mercer & Lewis, 1979; Morrison, 1988). These approaches assess students in a particular context, either a testing situation or some other.

The System of Multicultural Pluralistic Assessment, or SOMPA (Mercer & Lewis, 1979; Morrison, 1988), is a measurement-based approach to assessment that acknowledges the multidimensionality of children. As a consequence, it addresses three aspects of students—medical, social, and cultural. Examination of each aspect yields different types of information and interpretations of a problem. Measurements related to the medical aspect give scores related to the diagnosis and screening of neurological problems. Measurements related to the social system give scores related to a child's functioning in the school and home. The SOMPA acknowledges that American society consists of a dominant Anglo culture and many other unique cultural groups. Thus, measurements related to the pluralistic cultural aspect call for the use of local norms for the appropriate sociocultural group. The interpretations of scores from all three aspects are combined to yield a comprehensive measurement-based evaluation of a problem to provide an integrated set of recommendations. No single source of scores is considered to give an accurate account of the problem.

School psychologists have many options for the types of measurement-generated information they gather, including standardized tests of intelligence, other standardized tests, adaptive behaviors, classroom behaviors, and classroom interactions. Although scores from these measuring instruments are useful for making decisions about an individual student, they retain the limitations inherent in probability correlations among aggregate groups. Their information is based on how scores of previously examined groups of representative students related to scores on criteria measures. Even if the instruments are reliable and valid, they only indicate the likelihood that a child with a particular score will perform in a certain way in the future. Even in combinations, such as the SOMPA model, they may not yield an adequate understanding of how a particular child will perform. Information about the unique circumstances of a particular child needs to be understood and taken into account in making a decision about his or her placement. The purpose of qualitative research is to give decision-makers a thematic and structural description about a particular child. Analysis of data, whether collected through participant observation, historical documents, unstructured interviews, or traditional psychoeducational tests, attempts to identify the issues relevant and meaningful to the students, teachers, parents, and other stakeholders in child's education.

### Characteristics of the Classroom

Although it is not the primary concern of school psychologists, others have focused on issues of the classroom to illuminate academic problems. Vygotskian and neo-Vygotskian researchers have assessed interactions in particular settings (Moll & Greenberg, 1990; Tharp & Gallimore, 1988; Valdez & Figueroa, 1994; Vygotsky, 1978, 1987). From this perspective, teaching is simply assisting performance within the child's zone of proximal development. The child might be at a certain competency on some specific task within a specific context. The teacher can help the child develop his or her competency by questioning, instructing, cognitive structuring, modeling, contingency management, or feedback. If learning fails to occur, it implies that the teacher-student interaction failed. Perhaps there was no assistance or it was inappropriate. In either case, the interaction failed to achieve the desired outcome—learning. This failure involves the teacher, the student, the context, and most importantly, their interaction. Assessment of academic problems from this perspective requires the school psychologist to be present during the interaction. Merely assessing the child in a testing setting would not necessarily provide useful information.

### Authentic Assessment

The strength of a qualitative research project's contribution to an assessment decision is related to the authenticity of the resulting decision. Several categories of authenticity have been identified, including ontological, educative, catalytic, and tactical (Lincoln & Guba, 1985, 1986). Ontological authenticity reduces discrepancies between various people's conscious realities. Previously, parents' roles in assessment were involved negotiating recommendations. To the extent that efforts are made to help parents understand the role of the school in educating the child and to help the school personnel understand the student and parents, ontological authenticity is achieved.

Closely related to ontological authenticity is educative authenticity. Assessments should promote an understanding of the child's learning, the teacher's instructional strategies, school resources, and parental resources. Catalytic authenticity concerns the degree to which assessment information produces change. If assessment information is not utilized, the assessment may not have been worthwhile. The final form of authenticity is tactical. For change to occur, stakeholders must be empowered to produce it. Delgado-Gaitan (1991) provides an example of parents who are involved in children's schooling before and after problems arise. As previous noted, parents can provide useful assessment information pertaining to the child's history. Parents can also facilitate utilization of assessment information if the school considers home resources in designing the child's instructional plan. Before the parental involvement can be fruitful, however, the parents must be empowered. Delgado-Gaitan describes a community in which parents were empowered through knowledge of the school's activities, roles, responsibilities, and resources.

## Qualitative Research and Evaluation

The assessment function performed by school psychologists is most often concerned with evaluating the performance of an individual child and participating in a problem-solving consultation about what actions to take. A recent survey by Reschly & Wilson (1995) supports previous indications that school psychologists clearly pre-

fer to be engaged in additional roles, such as direct intervention and consultation (Costenbader, Swartz, & Petrix, 1992; Meyers, 1993, 1995; Reschly & Wilson, 1995), and they believe that the consultation model will result in better delivery of services than the medical model (Hyman & Kaplinski, 1994). A consultative role school psychologists can perform for their educational units is program and intervention evaluation. Qualitative-based program evaluation involves the application of the skills and procedures used in individual qualitative assessment to programs. Qualitative research first made an impact in education as an evaluation strategy (Guba, 1978; Lincoln & Guba, 1985; Patton, 1980). A number of worthwhile sources on making qualitative evaluations are available (Green, 1994; Guba & Lincoln, 1981, 1989; Herman, 1987; Pitman & Maxwell, 1992), including Patton's (1990) important work.

### Kinds of Educational Evaluation

Several approaches to educational evaluation have been proposed. Although a complete discussion is beyond the scope of this chapter, several major approaches are briefly presented. (For a thorough discussion see the *Program Evaluation Kit*, edited by Joan Herman (1987). Morris and Fitz-Gibbon (1978) classified evaluations according to six categories: goals-oriented, decision-oriented, transactional, research, goals-free, and adversary.

Goals-oriented evaluation has also been described as objectives-oriented (Worthen & Sanders, 1987). Some advocates of this approach include Bloom, Hastings, and Maduas (1971), Metfessel and Michael (1967), and Provus (1971). Its principal purpose is to assess the degree to which the stated objectives or goals have been met. In implementing this approach, one compares measurements of a student's performance with criteria stated in the objectives or in pretest measurements.

In evaluation research, explanations of academic performance are sought. Its principal proponents include Campbell (1969) and Cooley and Lohnes (1976). Traditionally, this approach, as well as goals-oriented evaluation, were dominated by positivistic or postpositivistic philosophies and relied on quantitative measurements.

Goals-free evaluation (Scriven, 1974) is described by Worthen and Sanders (1987) as consumer-oriented. In this approach, information pertaining to the program's or educational product's worth is assessed independently of stated goals or objectives. Adversary-oriented evaluations (Levine, 1973; Owens, 1973), strongly resemble a judicial approach to evaluation. Opposing sides to the evaluation are given equal access to program information, and they then present their interpretation.

Another type of evaluation is decision-oriented. The focus of this approach is to generate information that can facilitate decisions about the program. Evaluation decisions are divided into four categories: context, input, process, and product (CIPP). Stufflebeam's CIPP (Stufflebeam et al., 1971) is a leading model. This approach is not limited to either qualitative or quantitative methods. Rather, any method that generates useful information for the various decisions is considered appropriate. Conversely, methods can be evaluated by the degree to which the information generated is useful in a given educational decision-making process.

The final approach to be discussed is transactional evaluation (Rippey, 1973; Stake, 1975). This approach focuses on the processes involved in the program and the perspectives of stakeholders. Naturalistic (Lincoln & Guba, 1985) and later constructivist (Guba & Lincoln, 1994) approaches to evaluation evolved from this perspective and are described as qualitative methods.

## Qualitative Evaluation

Qualitative evaluation can be undertaken either post hoc, that is, after the intervention or program is completed, or as action research, that is, as an adjunct to the development and delivery of the program. A post hoc evaluation would engage all the stakeholders in the program's outcome. The evaluation of an intervention program would produce most of its data from interviews with family members, teachers, children, and administrators. Other data, such as pretest and posttest scores, reports from outside observers, and community members, might be included. The analysis of these data would produce a report of the positive and negative outcomes of the program as experienced by those affected. It would draw attention to the multiple values of the different stakeholders and the various perspectives from which they judged the effectiveness of the intervention.

Qualitative action research is an active intervention in program development and delivery. It assists those responsible by providing information throughout the program's formation and delivery

as it is needed. The purpose of this research is not simply to gather information about the successes and failures of a program but also to facilitate an understanding by all stakeholders of the decisions made. During the formative stages of a program, qualitative research can gather and analyze opinions about the needs the program is to meet. It can assist in the development of the intervention by accumulating relevant information about the expected effects of possible designs. This phase involves the identification of those whose lives will be affected by the designs, including the child's parents and home life (Black, 1995; Sheridan & Kratochwill, 1992). For example, in one project, teachers are trained to use qualitative methods to study children's homes and communities and to identify "funds of knowledge" (Diaz, Mool, & Mehan, 1986). This information is then used by the teachers in designing thematic units in the classroom. Regardless of the specific strategy employed, continued involvement of relevant stakeholders, including the parents, teachers, and students, in design decisions is an important factor in the reception and cooperation chosen interventions will receive.

Once an intervention is designed, its implementation is assessed on a regular basis. Early assessment of the program gives stakeholders the kind of information that allows them to implement useful changes along the way. Stakeholders can be interviewed to determine how the program is being implemented and the degree to which it is producing the expected results (Galloway & Sheridan, 1994). Directors and teachers engaged in the delivery of the program are themselves a rich source of data about how the intervention is progressing.

Qualitative action research continues its consultation to the completion of the program, when it performs a post hoc evaluation. However, because it has been involved with the program from the beginning, it is able to provide a historical dimension to its assessment. It can include the unintended consequences of earlier decisions and unexpected effects, such as changes in parents' or teachers' attitudes toward the child. Although its outcomes would probably include typical measures of school achievement, including standardized achievement test scores and classroom-developed tests, other outcomes that involve changes in attitudes, motivation, and expectations would be sought in the production of data.

# CONCLUSION

Skovholt and Rønnestad (1992) conducted a qualitative study of the professional development of practicing psychologists. It concluded that as practitioners gain experience in the field, they rely less on generalized knowledge and more on the unique aspects of each person. They also come to appreciate the great complexity of the people they serve and abandon the more simple models that they had been taught during their training. Qualitative research allows its results to reflect the interwoven complex of themes that function in a person's life at a particular time. This type of knowledge differs from and is supplemental to the type of knowledge generated by quantitative research. Quantitative and qualitative methods are not oppositional; they are merely different. They share a commitment to the generation of knowledge proposals through a reasoned and reflective examination of empirical data and the submission of those proposals to the community of scholars for criticism and testing.

When done well, qualitative research produces descriptions that display a situation in an innovative manner, allowing school psychologists to recognize aspects and to notice relationships and organizational patterns that were not readily evident to them before the research was conducted. Sometimes the results bring about a Gestalt shift in the practitioner's understanding of the situation in which new solutions to a problem become apparent. Qualitative methods are crafted to work with data that retain the multiple levels of meaning of ordinary language. Their analytic procedures are designed to identify the patterns and relationships that organize various themes in a situation.

The implementation of qualitative research by school psychologists will require doctoral training programs to modify their curricula and their notions of acceptable methods for dissertations. Faculty members who are skilled in qualitative research are needed to teach courses and supervise dissertations, and they would have to be hired or trained. As a temporary measure, students could take the courses in other departments in schools of education. There is also the difficulty of finding room in the already full curriculum for qualitative research courses. Instruction sufficient to prepare a student to begin a doctoral dissertation by using these methods requires as much time as does the present instruction in quantitative methods. By extending the repertoire of research approaches, school psychology can increase its understanding of the range of human experience and action and thereby better serve its students.

Perhaps the most important contribution qualitative research can make to the practice of school psychology occurs at the level of conceptual utilization. Because the analytic tools of qualitative research are directed at uncovering themes and structures of meaning in ordinary language data, they overlap the assessment task of understanding a child's interpretive patterns. Schön (1983) proposes that the judgments of practitioners do not consist of the simple application of research findings. Rather, their judgments are the result of a complex process, involving the consolidation of background knowledge, awareness of the salient characteristics of the particular situation, recollections drawn from experience of patterns of action that might have a bearing on the situation, and evaluative reflection on possible responses. If this description is accurate, neither training in quantitative and qualitative methods nor reading research articles is simply and directly applied in interventions. Rather, they add to the school psychologist's body of background knowledge, patterns of understanding, and suggestions for possible actions. Furthermore, they help equip the practitioner with the evaluative and conceptual understandings needed for skilled reflection.

# REFERENCES

Allport, G. W. (1942). *The use of personal documents in psychological science* (Bulletin No. 49). New York: Social Science Research Council.

Altheide, D. L., & Johnson, J. M. (1994). Criteria for assessing interpretive validity in qualitative research. In N. K. Denzin & Y. S. Lincoln (Eds.), *Handbook of qualitative research* (pp. 485–499). Thousand Oaks, CA: Sage.

Anderson, W. A., Jr. (1988). The behavioral assessment of conduct disorders in a black child. In R. L. Jones (Ed.), *Psychoeducational assessment of minority group children: A casebook* (pp. 193–223). Berkeley, CA: Cobb & Henry.

Bardon, J. I. (1987). The translation of research into practice in school psychology. *School Psychological Review, 16*, 317–328.

Bardon, J. I., & Bennett, V. C. (1974). *School Psychology.* Englewood Cliffs, NJ: Prentice Hall.

Barker, R. G. (1963). *Ecological psychology: Concepts and methods for studying the environment of human behavior.* Stanford: Stanford University Press.

Bazerman, C. (1987). Codifying the social scientific

style: The APA Publication Manual as a behavioristic rhetoric. In J. S. Nelson, A. Megill, & D. N. McCloskey (Eds.), *The rhetoric of the human sciences: Language and argument in scholarship and public affairs* (pp. 125–144). Madison: University of Wisconsin Press.

Black, M. M. (1995). Failure to thrive: Strategies for evaluation and intervention. *School Psychological Review, 24*(2), 171–185.

Bloom, B. S., Hastings, J. T., & Maduas, G. F. (1971). *Handbook of formative and summative evaluation of student learning.* New York: McGraw-Hill.

Bogdan, R. C., & Biklen, S. K. (1992). *Qualitative research for education: An introduction to theory and methods* (2nd ed.). Boston: Allyn & Bacon.

Bogdan, R., & Taylor, S. J. (1975). *Introduction to qualitative research methods: A phenomenological approach to the social sciences.* New York: John Wiley.

Borg, W. R., & Gall, M. D. (1989). *Educational research: An introduction.* (5th ed.). New York: Longman.

Borgen, F. N. (1992). Expanding scientific paradigms in counseling psychology. In S. D. Brown & R. W. Lent (Eds.), *Handbook of counseling psychology* (2nd ed., pp. 111–139). New York: Wiley.

Boring, E. G. (1945). The use of operational definitions in science. *Psychological Review, 52,* 243–245.

Brotemarkle, R. A. (Ed.). (1931). *Clinical psychology: Studies in honor of Lightner Witmer to commemmorate the thirty-fifth anniversary of the founding of the first psychological clinic.* Philadelphia: University of Pennsylvania Press.

Buchler, J. (Ed.). (1955). *Philosophical writings of Peirce.* New York: Dover.

Campbell, D. (1969). Reforms as experiments. *American Psychologist, 24,* 409–429.

Cantor, N., & Zirkel, S. (1990). Personality, cognition, and purposive behavior. In L. Pervin (Ed.), *Handbook of personality theory and research* (pp. 135–164). New York: Guilford.

Carroll, A., Gurski, G., Hinsdale, K., & McIntyre, K. (1977). *Culturally appropriate assessment. A source book for practitioners.* Los Angeles: Regional Resource Center.

Carspecken, P. F., & Apple, M. (1992). Critical qualitative research: Theory, methodology, and practice. In M. D. LeCompte, W. L. Millroy, & J. Preissle (Eds.), *The handbook of qualitative research in education* (pp. 507–553). San Diego: Academic Press.

Cervantees, H. T. (1988). Nondiscriminatory assessment and informal data gathering: The case of Gonzaldo L. In R. L. Jones (Ed.), *Psychoeducational assessment of minority group children: A casebook* (pp. 239–256). Berkeley, CA: Cobb & Henry.

Chenitz, W. C., & Swanson, J. M. (Eds.). (1986a). *From practical to grounded theory: Qualitative research in nursing.* Menlo Park, CA: Addison-Wesley.

Chenitz, W. C., & Swanson, J. M. (1986b). Qualitative research using grounded theory. In W. C. Chenitz & J. M. Swanson (Eds.), *From practice to grounded theory* (pp. 3–15). Menlo Park, CA: Addison-Wesley.

Cliff, N. (1973). Psychometrics. In B. B. Wolman (Ed.), *Evaluation research in education* (pp. 67–89). New York: Irvington.

Combs, A. W., & Syngg, D. (1959). *Individual behavior: A perceptual approach to behavior* (rev.ed.). New York: Harper & Brothers.

Cooley, W. W., & Lohnes, P. R. (1976). *Evaluation research education.* New York: Irvington.

Costenbader, V., Swartz, J., & Petrix, L. (1992). Consultation in the schools: The relationship between preservice training, perception of consultative skills, and actual time spent in consultation. *School Psychology Review, 21*(1), 95–108.

Craig, P. A., Kaskowitz, D. H., & Malgoire, M. A. (1978). *Teacher identification of handicapped pupils (ages 6–11) compared with identification using other indictors* (Vol. II). Menlo Park, CA: Educational Policy Research Center, Stanford Research Institute.

Delgado-Gaitan, C. (1991). Involving parents in schools: A process of empowerment. *American Journal of Education, 100*(1), 20–46.

Denzin, N. K. (1989) *Interpretive biography.* Newbury Park, CA: Sage.

Denzin, N. K., & Lincoln, Y. S. (Eds.). (1994a). *Handbook of qualitative research.* Thousand Oaks, CA: Sage.

Denzin, N. K., & Lincoln, Y. S. (1994b). Preface. In N. K. Denzin & Y. S. Lincoln (Eds.), *Handbook of qualitative research* (pp. ix–xii). Thousand Oaks, CA: Sage.

Dey, I. (1993). *Qualitative data analysis: A user-friendly guide for social scientists.* New York: Routledge.

Diaz, S., Mool, L. C., & Mehan, H. (1986). Sociocultural resources in instruction: A context-specific approach. In *Beyond language: Social and cultural factors in schooling language minority students* (pp. 187–230). Los Angeles: Evaluation, Dissemination, and Assessment Center, California State University at Los Angeles.

Easthope, G. (1974). *A history of social research methods.* London: Longman.

Eisner, E. W. (1991). *The enlightened eye: Qualitative inquiry and the enhancement of educational practice.* New York: Macmillan.

Ely, M., Anzul, M., Friedman, T., Garner, D., & Steinmetz, A. M. (1991). *Doing qualitative research: Circles within circles.* London: Falmer.

Epstein, S. (1993). Implications of cognitive-experiential self-theory for personality and development. In D. C. Funder, R. D. Parke, C. Tomlinson-Keasey, & K. Widaman (Eds.), *Studying lives through time: Personality and development* (pp. 399–434). Washington, DC: American Psychological Association.

Erickson, F. (1986). Qualitative methods in research on teaching. In M. C. Wittrock (Ed.), *Handbook of research on teaching* (3rd ed., pp. 119–161). New York: Macmillan.

Erlandson, D. A. Harris, E. L., Skipper, B. L., & Allen, S. D. (1993). *Doing naturalistic inquiry: A guide to methods.* Newbury Park, CA: Sage.

Fagan, T. K., & Wise, P. S. (1994). *School psychology: Past, present, and future.* New York: Longman.

Fetterman, D. M. (1989). *Ethnography: Step by step.* Beverly Hills, CA: Sage.

Feurstein, R., Rand, Y., & Hoffman, M. B. (1979). *The dynamic assessment of retarded performers: The learning potential assessment devise, theory, instruments, and techniques.* Glenview, IL: Scott, Foresman.

Filstead, W. J. (Ed.). (1970). *Qualitative methodology: Firsthand involvement with the social world.* Chicago: Markham.

Fine, G. A., & Sanstrom, K. L. (1988). *Knowing children: Participant observation with minors.* Newbury Park, CA: Sage.

Fraenkel, J. R. (1990). *How to design and evaluate research in education.* New York: McGraw-Hill.

Galloway, J., & Sheridan, S. M. (1994). Scientific practitioner: Implementing scientific practices through case studies: Examples using home-school interventions and consultation. *Journal of School Psychology, 32*(4), 385–413.

Gardner, H. (1983). *Frames of mind: The theory of multiple intelligences.* New York: Basic Books.

Geertz, C. (1973). *Interpretation of cultures.* New York: Basic Books.

Gendlin, E. T. (1991). Thinking beyond patterns: Body, language, and situations. In B. den Ouden & M. Moen (Eds.), *The presence of feeling in thought* (pp. 22–151). New York: Peter Lang.

Gergen, K. J. (1992). The social constructionist movement in modern psychology. In R. S. Miller (Ed.), *The restoration of dialogue: Readings in the philosophy of clinical psychology* (pp. 556–569). Washington, DC: American Psychological Association.

Giorgi, A., Fischer, W. F., & Eckartsberg, R. v. (Eds.). (1971). *Duquesne studies in phenomenological psychology.* (Vol. 1). Pittsburgh: Duquesne University Press.

Glaser, B. G. (1978). *Theoretical sensitivity: Advances in the methodology of grounded theory.* Mill Valley, CA: Sociology Press.

Glaser, B. G. (1992). *The basics of grounded theory analysis.* Mill Valley, CA: Sociology Press.

Glaser, B. G., & Strauss, A. L. (1967). *The discovery of grounded theory: Strategies for qualitative research.* New York: Aldine de Gruyter.

Goetz, J. P., & LeCompte, M. D. (1984). *Ethnography and qualitative design in educational research.* New York: Academic Press.

Goldman, L. (1976). A revoltuion in counseling psychology. *Journal of Counseling Psychology, 23,* 543–552.

Greene, J. C. (1994). Qualitative program evaluation: Practice and promise. In N. K. Denzin & Y. S. Lincoln (Eds.), *Handbook of qualitative research* (pp. 530–544). Thousand Oaks, CA: Sage.

Guba, E. G. (1978). *Toward a methodology of naturalistic inquiry in educational evaluation. Monograph 8.* Los Angeles: UCLA Center for the Study of Evaluation.

Guba, E. G., & Lincoln, Y. S. (1981). *Effective evaluation.* San Francisco: Jossey-Bass.

Guba, E. G., & Lincoln, Y. S. (1989). *Fourth generation evaluation.* Newbury Park, CA: Sage.

Guba, E. G., & Lincoln, Y. S. (1994). Competing paradigms in qualitative research. In N. K. Denzin & Y. S. Lincoln (Eds.), *Handbook of qualitative research* (pp. 105–117). Thousand Oaks, CA: Sage.

Haywood, H. C. (1977). Alternatives to normative assessment. In P. Mittler (Ed.), *Research to practice in mental retardation: Proceedings of the 4th Congress of IASSMD: Vol 2. Education and training.* Baltimore, MD: University Park Press.

Haywood, H. C. (1988). Dynamic assessment: The learning potential assessment device. In R. L. Jones (Ed.), *Psychoeducational assessment of minority group children: A casebook* (pp. 39–63). Berkeley, CA: Cobb & Henry.

Hempel, C. G. (1965). *Aspects of scientific explanation and other essays in the philosophy of science.* New York: Free Press.

Herman, J. L. (Ed.). (1987). *Program evaluation kit* (2nd ed.). Newbury Park, CA: Sage.

Hill, C. E., & Corbett, M. M. (1993). A perspective on the history of process and outcome research in counseling psychology. *Journal of Counseling Psychology, 40*(1), 3–24.

Hopkins, C. D., & Antes, R. L. (1990). *Educational research: A structure for inquiry* (3rd ed.). Itasca, IL: F. E. Peacock.

Hoshmand, L. L. T. (1989). Alternative research paradigms: A review and teaching proposal. *The Counseling Psychologist, 17*(1), 3–79.

Howard, G. S. (1983). Toward methodological pluralism. *Journal of Counseling Psychology, 30,* 19–21.

Hyman, I. A., & Kaplinski, K. (1994). Will the real school psychologist please stand up: Is the past a prologue for the future of school psychology. *School Psychology Review, 23*(4), 564–583.

Isaac, S., & Michael, E. G. (1995). *Handbook in research and evaluation. A collection of principles, methods, and* strategies useful in the planning, design, and evaluation of studies in education and the behavioral sciences (3rd ed.). San Diego: EdITS.

Jones, R. L. (1988). Psychoeducational assessment of minority group children: Issues and perspectives. In R. L. Jones (Ed.), *Psychoeducational assessment of minority group children: A casebook* (pp. 13–35). Berkeley, CA: Cobb & Henry.

Jorgensen, D. L. (1989). *Participant observation: A methodology for human studies.* Beverly Hills, CA: Sage.

Kehle, T. J., Clark E., & Jensen, W. R. (1993). Development of testing as applied to school psychology. *Journal of School Psychology, 31,* 143–161.

Keith, T. Z. (1988). Research methods in school psychology: An overview. *School Psychology Review, 17*(3), 502–520.

Koch, S. (1959). Epilogue. In S. Koch (Ed.), *Psychology, a study of a science* (pp. 729–788). New York: McGraw-Hill.

Krantz, D. H., Luce, R. D., Suppes, P., & Tversky, A. (1971). *Foundations of measurement.* New York: Academic Press.

Lakoff, G. (1987). *Women, fire, and dangerous things: What categories reveal about the mind.* Chicago: University of Chicago Press.

Lave, J., & Wenger, E. (1991). *Situated learning: Legitimate peripheral participation.* Cambridge: Cambridge University Press.

Lazarsfeld, P. F. (1972). *Qualitative analysis: Historical and critical essays.* Boston: Allyn & Bacon.

Leahey, T. H. (1980). *A history of psychology: Main currents in psychological thought.* Englewood Cliffs, NJ: Prentice Hall.

LeCompte, M. D., Millroy, W. L., & Preissle, J. (Eds.). (1992). *The handbook of qualitative research in education.* San Diego: Academic Press.

LeCompte, M. D., & Preissle, J. (1992). Toward an ethnology of student life in schools and classrooms: Synthesizing the qualitative research tradition. In M. D. LeCompte, W. L. Millroy, & J. Preissle (Eds.), *The handbook of qualitative research in education* (pp. 815–859). San Diego: Academic Press.

Levine, M. (1973). Scientific method and the adversary model: Some preliminary suggestions. *Evaluations Comment, 4*(2), 1–3.

Lewin, K. (1951). *Field theory in social science.* New York: Harper.

Lincoln, Y. S., & Denzin, N. K. (1994). The fifth movement. In N. K. Denzin & Y. S. Lincoln (Eds.), *Handbook of qualitative research* (pp. 575–586). Thousand Oaks, CA: Sage.

Lincoln, Y. S., & Guba, E. G. (1985). *Naturalistic inquiry.* Newbury Park, CA: Sage.

Lincoln, Y., & Guba, E. G. (1986). But is it rigorous? Trustworthiness and authenticity in naturalistic evaluation. In D. D. Williams (Ed.), *Naturalistic evaluation* (pp. 73–84). San Francisco: Jossey-Bass.

Lofland. (1971). *Analyzing social settings: A guide to qualitative observation and analysis.* Belmont, WA: Wadsworth.

Loftus, E. F., Donders, K., Hoffman, H. G., & Schooler, J. W. (1989). Creating new memories that are quickly assessed and confidently held. *Memory and Cognition, 17,* 607–616.

Mahoney, J. R. (1995). Interviews with children: How they perceive psychotherapy. Doctoral dissertation, University of Southern California, Los Angeles.

Malinowski, B. (1922). *Argonauts of the Western Pacific: An account of native enterprise and adventure in the Melanesian New Guinea.* New York: Dutton.

Manis, J. G., & Meltzer, B. N. (1978). *Symbolic interaction* (3rd ed.). Boston: Allyn & Bacon.

Margolis, H. (1987). *Patterns, thinking, and cognition: A theory of judgment.* Chicago: University of Chicago Press.

Margolis, J. (1986). Psychology and its methodological options. In J. Margolis, P. T. Manicas, R. Harré, & P. F. Secord (Eds.), *Psychology: Designing the discipline* (pp. 12–51). New York: Basil Blackwell.

Marshall, C., & Rossman, G. B. (1989). *Designing Qualitative research.* Newbury Park, CA: Sage.

McCrae, R. R. (Ed.). (1992). *The five-factor model: A special issue of the* Journal of Personality. Durham, NC: Duke University Press.

Medway, F. J., & Cafferty, T. P. (Eds.). (1992). *School psychology: A social psychological perspective.* Hillsdale, NJ: Erlbaum.

Medway, F. J., & Skedsvold, P. (1992). Contributions of school psychology to school-based research and evaluation. In F. J. Medway & T. P. Cafferty (Eds.), *School psychology: A social psychological perspective* (pp. 193–225). Hillsdale, NJ: Erlbaum.

Meltzer, B. N., Petras, J. W., & Reynolds, L. T. (1975). *Symbolic interactionism: Genesis, varieties, and criticism.* London: Routledge & Kegan Paul.

Mercer, J. R. (1973). *Labeling the mentally retarded.* Berkeley: University of California Press.

Mercer, J. R., & Lewis, J. F. (1979). *Technical manual for the System of Multicultural Pluralistic Assessment.* San Antonio, TX: Psychological Corporation.

Merleau-Ponty, M. (1945/1962). *Phenomenology of perception* (Trans. C. Smith). New York: Humanities.

Metfessel, J. R., & Michael, W. B. (1967). A paradigm involving multiple criterion measures for the evaluation of the effectiveness of school programs. *Educational and Psychological Measurement, 27,* 931–943.

Meyers, J. (1993). Editorial statement. *Journal of School Psychology, 31,* 237–239.

Meyers, J. (1995). Editorial statement. *Journal of School Psychology, 33,* 1–3.

Miles, M. B., & Huberman, A. M. (1994). *Qualitative data analysis* (2nd ed.). Thousand Oaks, CA: Sage.

Miller, J. G. (1978). *Living systems.* New York: McGraw-Hill.

Miller-Jones, D. (1989). Culture and testing. *American Psychologist, 44*(2), 360–366.

Mishler, E. G. (1986). *Research interviewing: Context and narrative.* Cambridge, MA: Harvard University Press.

Moll, L., & Greenberg, J. (1990). Creating zones of possibilities: Combining social contexts for instruction. In L. Moll (Ed.), *Vygotsky and education: Instructional implications and application of sociohistorical psychology* (pp. 319–348). New York: Cambridge University Press.

Morris, L. L., & Fitz-Gibbon, C. T. (1978). *Evaluator's handbook.* Newbury Park, CA: Sage.

Morrison, J. A. (1988). Rudy Garcia: A SOMPA case study. In R. L. Jones (Ed.), *Psychoeducational assessment of minority group children: A casebook* (pp. 79–107). Berkeley, CA: Cobb & Henry.

Morse, J. M. (Ed.). (1991). *Qualitative nursing research: A contemporary dialogue* (rev. ed.). Newbury Park, CA: Sage.

Morse, J. M. (Ed.). (1994). *Critical issues in qualitative research methods.* Thousand Oaks, CA: Sage.

Moss, P. A. (1992). Shifting conceptions of validity in educational measurement: Implications for performance assessment. *Review of Educational Research, 363*(3), 229–258.

Murray, H. A. (1938). *Explorations in personality: A clinical and experimental study of fifty men of college age.* New York: Oxford Unversity Press.

Neimeyer, R. A., & Mahoney, M. J. (1995). *Constructivism in psychotherapy.* Washington, DC: American Psychological Association.

Neimeyer, G., & Resnikoff, A. (1982). Qualitative strategies in counseling research. *The Counseling Psychologist, 10*(4), 75–85.

Ogbu, J. (1992). Understanding cultural diversity and learning. *Educational Research, 21*(8), 5–14.

Owens, T. R. (1973). Educational evaluations by adversary proceedings. In E. R. House (Ed.), *School evaluation: The politics and process* (pp. 295–307). Berkeley, CA: McCutchan.

Patton, M. Q. (1980). *Qualitative evaluation methods.* Beverly Hills, CA: Sage.

Patton, M. Q. (1990). *Qualitative evaluation and research* (2nd ed.). Newbury Park, CA: Sage.

Peirce, C. S. (Ed.). (1955). *Philosophical writings of Peirce.* New York: Dover.

Pelto, P. J. (1970). *Anthropological research: The structure of inquiry.* New York: Harper & Row.

Piaget, J. (1952). *The origins of intelligence in children.* New York: International Universities Press.

Pitman, M. A., & Maxwell, J. A. (1992). Qualitative approaches to evaluation: Models and methods. In M. D. LeCompte, W. L. Millroy, & J. Preissle (Eds.), *The handbook of qualitative research in education* (pp. 729–770). San Diego: Academic Press.

Polkinghorne, D. E. (1983). *Methodology for the human sciences: Systems of inquiry.* Albany: State University of New York Press.

Polkinghorne, D. E. (1984). Further extensions of methodological diversity of counseling psychology. *Journal of Counseling Psychology, 31*(4), 416–429.

Polkinghorne, D. E. (1989). Phenomenological research methods. In R. S. Valle & S. Halling (Eds.), *Existential-phenomenological perspectives in psychology* (pp. 41–60). New York: Plenum Press.

Polkinghorne, D. E. (1991). Qualitative procedures for counseling research. In C. E. Watkins & L. J. Schneider (Eds.), *Research in counseling* (pp. 163–207). Hillsdale, NJ: Erlbaum.

Polkinghorne, D. E. (1992). Postmodern epistemology of practice. In S. Kvale (Ed.), *Psychology and postmodernism* (pp. 146–165). London: Sage.

Polkinghorne, D. E. (1995). Narrative configurations in qualitative analysis. *International Journal of Qualitative Studies in Education, 8*(1), 8–25.

Popper, K. R. (1961). *The poverty of historicism* (3rd ed.). New York: Harper & Row.

Popper, K. R. (1972). *Objective knowledge.* Oxford: Clarendon.

Provus M. (1971). *Discrepancy evaluation for educational program improvement and assessment.* Berkeley, CA: McCutchan.

Qualitative Solutions and Research. (1994). *Q.S.R. NUD-IST* (Version 3.0). Victoria, Aust.: Author.

Reed, J. R., Patton, M. J., & Gold, P. B. (1993). Effects of turn-taking sequences in vocational test interpretation interviews. *Journal of Counseling Psychology, 40*(2), 144–155.

Reichenbach, H. (1938). *Experience and prediction.* Chicago: University of Chicago Press.

Reisman, J. M. (1991). *A history of clinical psychology* (2nd ed.). New York: Hemisphere.

Reschly, D. J., & Wilson, M. S. (1995). School psychology practitioners and faculty: 1986 to 1991–92. Trends in demographics, roles, satisfaction, and system reform. *School Psychology Review, 24*(1), 62–80.

Richardson-Koehler. (1987). Editor's Statement. *American Educational Research Journal, 24*(2), 171–172.

Ricoeur, P. (1976). *Interpretation theory: Discourse and the surplus of meaning.* Fort Worth, TX: Texas Christian University Press.

Rippey, R. M. (Ed.). (1973). *Studies in transactional evaluation.* Berkeley, CA: McCutchan.

Roberts, J. (1976). An overview of anthropology and education. In J. Roberts & S. Akinsanya (Eds.), *Educational patterns and cultural configurations* (pp. 1–20). New York: David McKay.

Roman, L. G. (1992). The political significance of other ways of narrating ethnography: A feminist material approach. In M. D. LeCompte, W. L. Millroy, & J. Preissle (Eds.), *The handbook of qualitative research in education* (pp. 555–594). San Diego: Academic Press.

Rorty, R. (1979). *Philosophy and the mirror of nature.* Princeton, NJ: Princeton University Press.

Rosenau, P. M. (1992). *Post-modernism and the social sciences: Insights, inroads, and intrusions.* Princeton, NJ: Princeton University Press.

Rothbart, M., & Taylor, M. (1992). Category labels and social reality: Do we view social categories as natural kinds? In G. R. Semin & K. Fiedler (Eds.), *Language, Interaction, and social cognition.* Thousand Oaks, CA: Sage.

Schön, D. A. (1983). *The reflective practitioner.* New York: Basic Books.

Scott, L. S., & Fisher, A. T. (1988). The Texas environmental adaptation measure: Test development and standardization, a case study. In R. L. Jones (Ed.), *Psychoeducational assessment of minority group children: A casebook* (pp. 109–189). Berkeley, CA: Cobb & Henry.

Scriven, M. (1974). Pros and cons about goal free evaluations. In W. J. Popham (Ed.), *Evaluation in education: Current applications* (pp. 34–43). Berkeley, CA: McCutchan.

Seidman, I. E. (1991). *Interviewing as qualitative research.* New York: Teachers College Press.

Sheridan, S. M., & Kratochwill, T. R. (1992). Behavioral parent-teacher consultation: Conceptual and research considerations. *Journal of School Psychology, 30,* 117–139.

Skovholt, T. M., & Rønnestad, M. H. (1992). *The evolving professional self: Stages and themes in therapist and counselor development.* New York: Wiley.

Spearman, C. E. (1923). *The nature of "intelligence" and the principles of cognition.* London: Macmillan

Stake, R. E. (1975). *Evaluating the arts in education: A responsive approach.* Columbus, OH: Merrill.

Stake, R. E. (1988). Case study methods in educational research: Seeking sweet water. In R. M. Jaeger (Ed.), *Complementary methods for research in education* (pp. 253–300). Washington, DC: American Educational Research Association.

Stake, R. E. (1994). Case studies. In N. K. Denzin & Y. S. Lincoln (Eds.), *Handbook of qualitative research* (pp. 236–247). Thousand Oaks, CA: Sage.

Stake, R. E. (1995). *The art of case study research.* Thousand Oaks, CA: Sage.

Sternberg, R. J. (1985). *Beyond IQ: A triarchic theory of human intelligence.* Cambridge: Cambridge University Press.

Stevens, S. S. (1951). Mathematics, measurement, and psychophysics. In S. S. Stevens (Ed.), *Handbook in experimental psychology* (pp. 1–49). New York: Wiley.

Stevick, E. L. (1971). An empirical investigation of the experience of anger. In A. Giorgi, W. F. Fischer,

& R. v. Eckartsberg (Eds.) *Duquesne studies in phenomenological psychology* (Vol. 1, pp. 132–148). Pittsburgh, PA: Duquesne University Press.

Stocking, G. W. (Ed.). (1983). *Observers observed: Essays on ethnographic fieldwork.* Madison: University of Wisconsin Press.

Strauss, A. (1987). *Qualitative analysis for social scientists.* Cambridge: Cambridge University Press.

Strauss, A., & Corbin, J. (1990). *Basics of qualitative research: Grounded theory procedures and techniques.* Newbury Park, CA: Sage.

Strauss, A., & Corbin, J. (1994). Grounded theory methodology. In N. K. Denzin & Y. S. Lincoln (Eds.), *Handbook of qualitative research* (pp. 273–285). Thousand Oaks, CA: Sage.

Stufflebeam, D. L., Foley, W. J., Gephart, W. J., Guba, E. G., Hammond, H. O., Merriman, H. O., & Provus, M. M. (1971). *Educational evaluation and decision making.* Itasca, IL: Peacock.

Tallent, N. (1988). *Psychological report writing* (3rd ed.). Englewood Cliffs, NJ: Prentice Hall.

Tesch, R. (1990). *Qualitative research: Analysis types and software tools.* New York: Falmer.

Tharp, R. G., & Gallimore, R. (1988). *Rousing minds to life: Teaching, learning, and schooling in social contexts.* New York: Cambridge University Press.

Tomlinson, J. R., Acker, N., Conter, A., & Lindborg, S. (1977). Minority status and school psychological services. *Psychology in the Schools, 14,* 456–460.

Toukmanian, S. G., & Rennie, D. L. (Eds.). (1992). *Psychotherapy process research: Paradigmatic and narrative approaches.* Newbury Park, CA: Sage.

Turner, V. W., & Brunner, E. M. (Eds.). (1986). *The anthropology of experience.* Urbana: University of Illinois Press.

Underwager, R., & Wakefield, H. (1990). *The real world of child interrogations.* Springfield, IL: Thomas.

Valdez, G., & Figueroa, R. A. (1994). *Bilingualism and testing: A special case of bias.* Norwood, NJ: Ablex.

Van Maanen, J. (Ed.). (1986–1997). *Qualitative research methods series.* Newbury Park, CA: Sage.

Varela, F. J., Thompson, E., & Rosch, E. (1991). *The embodied mind: Cognitive science and human experience.* Cambridge, MA: MIT Press.

Vygotsky, L. S. (1978). *Mind in society: The development of higher psychological processes.* Cambridge, MA: Harvard University Press.

Vygotsky, L. S. (1987). Speech and thinking. In R. R. A. Carton (Ed.), *L. S. Vygotsky: Collected works.* New York: Plenum.

Walter, R. (1925). The functions of a school psychologist. *American Education, 29,* 167–170.

Watkins, C. E., Jr., & Schneider, L. J. (Eds.). (1991). *Research in counseling.* Hillsdale, NJ: Erlbaum.

Weitzman, E. A., & Miles, M. B. (1995). *Computer programs for qualitative data analysis.* Thousand Oaks, CA: Sage.

Williams, W. J. (1985). *The miracle of abduction: Applied*

*epistemology as a method of inquiry.* Los Angeles: Epistemics Institute Press.

Wirth, L. (1928). *The ghetto.* Chicago: University of Chicago Press.

Wolcott, H. F. (1994). *Transforming qualitative data.* Thousand Oaks, CA: Sage.

Woods, P. (1992). Symbolic interactionism: Theory and method. In M. D. LeCompte, W. L. Millroy, & J. Preissle (Eds.), *The handbook of qualitative research in education* (pp. 337–404). San Diego: Academic Press.

Worthen, B. R., & Sanders, J. R. (1987). *Educational evaluation: Alternative approaches and practical guidelines.* New York: Longman.

Yin, R. K. (1984). *Case study research: Design and methods.* Beverly Hills, CA: Sage.

Yin, R. K. (1993). *Applications of case study research.* Newbury Park, CA: Sage.

Zeller, N. (1995). Narrative strategies for case reports. *International Journal of Qualitative Studies in Education, 8*(1), 5–24.

Zucker, S. H., Prieto, A. G., & Rutherford, R. B. (1979). Racial determinants of teacher's perceptions of placement of the educable mentally retarded (ERIC Document Reproduction Service No. ED 191 015). Paper presented at the meeting of the Council for Exceptional Children, Dallas, TX.

## CHAPTER 6

# THE APPLICATION OF DEVELOPMENTAL PSYCHOLOGY TO SCHOOL PSYCHOLOGY PRACTICE: INFORMING ASSESSMENT, INTERVENTION, AND PREVENTION EFFORTS

DEBORAH J. THARINGER
*University of Texas at Austin*
NADINE M. LAMBERT
*University of California–Berkeley*

## INTRODUCTION

The theoretical and empirical knowledge base of developmental psychology, in combination with the emerging field of developmental psychopathology, is essential to the practice of professional psychology in the schools, particularly in the areas of assessment, intervention, and prevention. Developmental psychology and developmental psychopathology contribute to school psychology at three different levels. At the first level, understanding the theories and research findings of developmental psychology and developmental psychopathology enables the school psychologist *to describe* the level of cognitive, social, and personal development of a particular child; to make inferences about the child's prior developmental achievements; to specify the next developmental hurdles to be mounted; to depict how the child's prior developmental accomplishments may affect competence with a next task; and to be informed about the environmental circumstances that may promote or hinder the child's development. At a second and higher level, knowledge of developmental theories and research empowers the school psychologist *to explain* behavior within a developmental framework and to inform others of the probable reasons for a child's particular behavior at a given time. At the third and highest level, school psychologists

who have integrated theories of development and research findings into a conceptual framework for understanding behavior can develop comprehensive assessment plans to appraise the developmental characteristics of a child and can collaborate with teachers, parents, and other professionals to design interventions to further the child's developmental progress; thus they can attempt *to predict* what the child needs to foster his or her development and can test out the predictions.

The status of developmental psychology and developmental psychopathology as a means to describe, explain, and predict children's behavior—as well as to inform interventions to promote children's academic, social, and personal development and, in turn, children's mental health—has evolved concomitantly with school psychologists' role evolution from efforts to measure and describe individual differences, to offer reasons for children's behavior, and to intervene comprehensively to promote the effective educational and behavioral functioning of the children in school. The applicability of theory and research from the field of developmental psychology to the practice of school psychology seems so obvious that for some the bridge is a given. That is, it makes implicit sense that a specialty that has systematically studied the development of the individual, specifically the child, and has had as its overall goal the description, explanation, and prediction of the developmental process, would be invaluable to an applied specialty that has as its goal promoting the educational development and mental health of children in the schools. However, although some practicing school psychologists and school psychology training programs adhere to a developmental perspective formally and some intuitively, others do not and may not realize the potential to be gained from such an approach. Thus, although most school psychologists have acquired a variety of methods for understanding and describing children's behavior, and many rely on a developmental framework in describing their psychological knowledge of children to others, fewer use a developmental perspective to apply developmental knowledge differentially to explanations of children's behavior and interventions predicted to promote the educational and psychological needs of children. Obstacles to this integration and application are presented in an upcoming section.

Throughout this chapter the position is taken that a developmental perspective is necessary but not sufficient for functioning competently as a school psychologist. The information here is designed to educate and encourage school psychologists and educators of school psychologists to integrate a developmental perspective into their practice, and into their education and training models. Furthermore, as school psychologists function in emerging models for the delivery of school-based and school-linked health and mental health services and expand their roles in the schools in relation to health and educational reforms (Carlson, Tharinger, Bricklin, DeMers, & Paavola, 1996; Tharinger et al., 1996), the understanding and application of developmental knowledge and principles will be even more essential.

The goal of this chapter is to demonstrate the applicability of theory, empirical knowledge, and principles of developmental psychology and developmental psychopathology to assessment, intervention, and prevention efforts that are designed to enhance health, mental health, and educational attainment of children and adolescents in the schools. Considering the increased knowledge about the interaction of health, mental health, and educational attainment—as well as developmental variation in the presentation of different types of educational, health, and mental

health problems—a multifaceted approach to promoting school success and decreasing school failure by assessing and responding to children's and adolescent's health and mental health needs, in combination with responding to their educational needs, is warranted. The schools in many communities are, or will be, a central site for the provision or coordination of educational, health, and mental health services.

To address and illustrate the contributions of developmental psychology to school psychology practice in this chapter, we first present the parameters of developmental psychology and the new field of developmental psychopathology. Next, we discuss historic and current obstacles to the integration of school psychology practice and developmental psychology, followed by a brief review of the history of developmental psychology. We then discuss the usefulness of theory and give a succinct review of seven major developmental theories, including key contributions from each theory for practice. Following that, we present an integrated, contemporary view of the developing child, highlighting six principles of development that should be useful to the school psychologist. Finally, we discuss the contributions of developmental psychology to school psychology practice, specifically assessment, intervention, and prevention, giving illustrations of developmentally informed (1) psychological assessments, (2) psychotherapeutic interventions (with an emphasis on working with adolescents), and (3) prevention efforts (utilizing the example of school-linked services to prevent aggression and antisocial behavior during childhood and adolescence).

# DEVELOPMENTAL PSYCHOLOGY

Developmental psychology is the scientific study of how individuals change over time and of the factors that produce those changes. Development implies "systematic and successive changes over time in an organism" (Lerner, 1986, p. 41). The basic task of developmental psychology is to describe and explain change. Developmentalists trace the transformations that take place in an individual through the periods of childhood, adolescence, and adulthood and characterize the manner in which people remain identifiably the same but also change radically as they grow older. Changes that occur at an early age have an impact on subsequent development. At the least, the diversity of changes possible at a later time is constrained by those that occur at an earlier time (Lerner, 1986).

According to Edelbrock (1984), the developmental point of view can best be described as a normative-developmental perspective because it involves two basic principles. According to the normative principle, it is helpful to evaluate children's behavior with respect to appropriate reference groups, most generally, involving children of the same age. Ideally, normative information related to gender, socioeconomic status (SES), ethnicity, and culture would also be available. The developmental principle calls attention to the importance of accounting for quantitative and qualitative changes that occur with development. These changes are usually systemic, successive, orderly, and build on one another. Yet, at other times, these changes may be rapid and uneven. The developmental principle suggests that current behavior should be viewed in a context that includes consideration of events preceding and following it. Thus, the normative-developmental perspective emphasizes the central importance of change over time and the need for relevant norms against which children can be compared.

Whereas developmentalists have historically centered their attention on normal development and the bulk of their research has addressed age-normative behavior of children, the current interests of developmental psychology are much broader. The maturity of the field has allowed the emergence of the discipline of developmental psychopathology, which has placed development in context and onto the continuum of health and pathology. This continuum necessitates a focus on both intervention and prevention and health promotion. Thus, school psychologists need to be prepared to work with children who are atypical from a health, mental health, and/or educational perspective (this is probably where the bulk of their time will be spent), as well as those who are at risk of being atypical. Many children and adolescents who school psychologists serve will be experiencing only educational difficulties, many will be experiencing both educational and health or mental health difficulties, and some will be experiencing only mental health or health difficulties. A developmental approach and the theory and research from the new field of developmental psychopathology offers a useful and needed perspective.

# DEVELOPMENTAL PSYCHOPATHOLOGY

Developmental psychopathology is rapidly emerging as the organizational framework for the study of behavior problems in children and adolescents, and it has as its goal the understanding of psychopathology in the full context of human development (Masten & Braswell, 1991). Furthermore, it provides a framework for looking at the manifestation and process of "abnormal development" in relation to normal development and vice versa. The term *developmental psychopathology* highlights the value of studying psychopathology in relation to the major changes that typically occur across the life cycle (Achenbach, 1990). According to Kazdin (1985), developmental psychopathology refers to the study of clinical dysfunction over the course of development. In that light, the developmental psychopathologist is concerned with the origins and time course of a given disorder, its varying manifestations with development, its precursors and sequels, and its relation to nondisordered patterns of behavior. Kazdin notes that although the interaction of development, maturation, and adjustment is relevant over the entire life span, developmental psychopathology has usually involved the study of childhood and adolescence. Furthermore, "a developmental perspective on the study of psychopathology takes in account the continuities and discontinuities between normal growth and psychological disorder, age-related changes in modes of adaptation and symptom expression, behavioral reorganizations that occur around salient developmental challenges, internal and external sources of competence and vulnerability, and the effects of development on pathology and of pathology on development" (Attie, Brooks-Gunn, & Peterson, 1990, p. 409). As Sroufe (1989), a prominent figure in the field of developmental psychopathology has stated so well,

> Developmental psychopathologists are interested in those individuals who consistently follow a pathway leading to disorder. But they are just as interested in those individuals who, having deviated from normal developmental pathways, ultimately resume normal development and achieve adequate adaptation and those who resist stresses that usually lead to developmental

deviation. Such a dual focus on competence in the face of early adversity, on the one hand, and continuity in maladaptation in other cases is the essence of risk research. Such comparative studies will provide important clues for prevention and intervention. (p. 13)

# OBSTACLES IN INTEGRATED DEVELOPMENTAL PSYCHOLOGY AND SCHOOL PSYCHOLOGY PRACTICE

School and developmental psychology share common ground, both in placing their professional and scientific origins at the establishment of the Lightner Witmer clinic and in being influenced by events in the general history of the field of psychology. Most importantly, they both focus primarily on children—developmental from a theoretical and research perspective, and school from an applied practice perspective. Even with these commonalities, the relationship between developmental and school psychology continues to be underdeveloped and discontinuous. Obstacles to effective integration have included unique perspectives of researchers and clinicians, distinct views of human nature, the dominance of behavioral approaches in school psychology, the phenomena of adult-morphizing children in professional practice, and the misunderstanding of the application of Piagetian theory and research findings to practice.

## Unique Perspectives of Psychological Researchers and Clinicians

A major factor in the delay of the productive integration of a developmental approach and school psychology practice has been the lack of an effective bridge between science and practice, as well as lack of attention to developmental principles in the education and training of school psychologists and other professional psychologists. As Shirk (1988) has noted;

> Researchers and clinicians often find themselves speaking different languages. For the clinicians, group averages and significant statistical effects pale in comparison to the unique histories of individual children and significant therapeutic effects. For the researcher, narrative accounts of therapeutic progress, case summaries, and clinical impressions often represent sources of

frustration rather than sources of insight. As a result, the boundary between developmental research and clinical-child practice has remained rather impermeable for some time. (p. 1)

Although these comments were directed at child clinical practice, they apply as well to school psychology practice. Initial efforts to integrate developmental theory and research and the practice of child professional psychology have focused on the relationship between typical and atypical development. The emergence of developmental psychopathology represents the fruits of this initial cross-fertilization. Much work remains to be done in bringing developmental theory and research into the actual practice of assessment, intervention, and prevention. This chapter aims to provide some of the connections needed between developmental and school psychology practice.

## Distinct Views of Human Nature

Another factor that affects the delayed interaction between developmental psychology as a field and school psychology practice is that they have been guided by distinct roles in their efforts to understand human nature. Developmentalists primarily have taken an organismic view of human nature, with the exception of the period in history when behaviorism dominated child psychology. From the organismic view, the child is seen as an active, organized whole who is changing constantly, and self-initiated behavior and thought lead to changes in both the structure and content of the child's behavior and thought (Scarr, 1985). Many, though not all, school psychologists have been influenced by a mechanistic view, partially because of the dominant historical influence of behaviorism and learning theory in the practice of school psychology and education. In the mechanistic view, development is caused by external forces and events that act on the passive, machinelike mind of the child (Scarr, 1985). A mechanistic view of the child's development has been quite prominent in American education, and school psychologists have undoubtedly been attracted by the promise of finding answers to children's problems in environmental contingencies.

The mechanistic view has been appealing because it has offered the psychologist a great deal of control over explaining the behavior of the child and developing behavioral assessment and intervention techniques, which have met with moderate success, although a behavioral perspective has led to the exclusion of other equally valuable theoretical frameworks. However, few contemporary school psychology practitioners today are radical behaviorists. Recent additions to the social learning perspective have caused many practitioners of the behavioral persuasion to adopt a view of the child as active and interactive with the environment and to acknowledge that a child's behavior is organized. But viewing the child only from interactions with the environment provides only part of the story. The rest comes from determining how the child views the situation, how the child reasons about his or her behavior, and the social context and environmental circumstances. Thus, the school psychologist who is open to an organismic view of child development and who integrates this perspective in practice has the opportunity to select from many rich assessment, intervention, and prevention alternatives.

## Historic Dominance of Behavioral and Learning Theories

The view of human nature reflected in mechanistically driven behavioral approaches to assessment, observation, interviews, consultation, and direct intervention with children based on classical, operant, and social learning principles has impeded the integration of a developmental approach to school psychology practice. From the perspective of the learning theorist, learning accounts for development, but for a developmentalist, developmental change allows for learning. As discussed earlier, these are two very distinct points of view with very different implications for educational and psychological intervention. Learning theorists historically were not interested in developmental principles. The objective of learning theorists has been to discover general principles of behavior that hold across ages. The behavioral approach has yielded moderately impressive techniques for managing the behavior of children with serious problems with aggression, impulsivity, autism, and mental retardation. In 1938, Skinner argued that "the basic premise of behavioral psychology (was) that all organisms, human and subhuman, young and old, were subject to the same law of effect (principle of reinforcement) and could be studied in the same basic manner" (Gelfand & Peterson, 1985, p. 27), and therefore, developmental processes were viewed as unimportant. Gelfand and Peterson have further noted that "because developmental

level could not be manipulated, it was not viewed (by early behaviorists) as an independent variable worthy of research attention" (p. 27). Similarly, Rutter (1986) has maintained that the notion of the child as a developing organism "has always received lip service and often much more than in psychodynamic therapies, but until very recently it has been steadfastly ignored by many behavior therapists" (p. 144).

Although there is still an appreciable lack of interaction between developmental psychology and clinical assessment and treatment of children and adolescents, a merger of the developmental and behavioral perspectives is occurring, making a rapprochement between the developmental and behavioral perspectives increasingly more likely (Ollendick & King, 1991). Many contemporary learning theorists and behaviorists are beginning to recognize the importance of a child's developmental level and underlying developmental processes. Behaviorists have suggested that developmental theory and empirical findings make potentially important contributions to behavioral psychology (Hartman, Roper, & Bradford, 1979; Kazdin, 1985; Mash & Terdal, 1981), specifically in the formulation of behavioral assessment and intervention. Behaviorists have begun to acknowledge that developmental norms and processes must be considered when judging whether a behavior's frequency is excessive or deficient. A particular type and rate of behavior may well be normal at one age but abnormal at another. In addition, it has been suggested that a complete behavioral assessment must consider the child's developmental history (Ross, 1978) and that it is impossible to judge the adequacy of a child's social skills without taking the child's developmental level into account (Hops & Greenwood, 1981). Some cognitive behaviorists have called for the adoption of an underlying developmental, process-oriented conceptualization for cognitive-behavioral approaches to children's problems (Mahoney & Nezworski, 1985). Thus, behavioral approaches, which have been among the most resistant to a developmental perspective, have begun to integrate developmental findings and to acknowledge that developmental considerations have an important place in assessment and intervention. The question remains, however, about the extent to which the child and his or her developmental perspective is considered a fundamental source of information in planning assessment and intervention from a behavioral perspective.

## Adult-morphizing Children

A further obstacle to the integration of developmental and school psychology, and related to the distinct view of human nature and dominance of behavioral and learning theories already discussed, has been the tendency for some school psychologists to adult-morphize children (Garber, 1984; Gefland & Peterson, 1985). That is, children are viewed as if they are little adults, especially in terms of psychopathology and direct intervention. Adult-morphizing has been supported tacitly by the two grand psychological theories, psychoanalytic theory and learning theory. Early psychoanalytic writings did not stress the uniqueness of children and some practitioners formed the idea that an in-depth understanding of child development was not necessary because the same knowledge and techniques that are used with adults could be applied to children and adolescents. Furthermore, as discussed earlier, learning and behavioral theories historically were not developmentally oriented. In addition, until recently, many school psychologists, along with clinical psychologists, have been content to use theories of adult psychopathology and adult research findings to understand children's disorders and to apply techniques developed with adults to intervene with children.

Fortunately, adult-morphizing is becoming a phenomenon of the past. There is a considerable literature about the application of psychoanalytic methods to therapy with children and more and more behaviorists are calling for the integration of a developmental perspective when applying learning principles to the understanding of childhood disorders and to intervention with children (Kazdin, 1985; Kendall, 1985; Mahoney & Nezworski, 1985). Cognitive developmental theory and research findings have much to offer to the practitioner concerning schoolwork, peer interactions, reasoning about expected social behavior and attitudes, and the stages of self-development, as well as interventions that are appropriate to the child's developmental status. Furthermore, the field of developmental psychopathology asks questions and sets up research endeavors that should make adult-morphizing totally extinct. Although developmental psychopathology has borrowed the methodology and rigor of developmental psychology, it differs from the study of normal child development in its strong focus on individual differences. Developmental psychopathologists ask about variations in the course of development and about individual differences in the developmental process (Rutter & Garmezy, 1983). Finally, the change in thinking, away from applying adult methods to children, has also been influenced by recent classification systems that utilize categories specific to the child's developmental level, for example, the *Diagnostic and Statistical Manual* of the American Psychiatric Association (1980, 1987, 1994) and the child behavior checklist system (Achenbach & Edelbrock, 1983).

## Misunderstanding the Piagetian Perspective

The dominance of Piagetian theory from 1960 to the late 1970s in developmental psychology may be viewed by some as having presented an obstacle to the application of developmental psychology to school psychology. The dominance of learning theories in developmental psychology and an overemphasis on behavior, with a neglect of cognitive and emotional factors, characterize the years from 1940 to 1960. In contrast, research during the Piagetian era can be characterized as overemphasizing cognition, with the neglect of emotion and behavior. Because behavior problems bring most children to the attention of school psychologists, the dominance of a Piagetian approach, with its focus on reasoning and cognitive stages (even though Piaget acknowledged the importance of emotion and the social context in development) may have frustrated practitioners, whose goal was behavior change rather than understanding its meaning for the child. If practitioners were looking to Piagetian theory and research findings for exact methods for changing the behavior of children in the classroom, such as the behavioral theories attempted to offer, it follows that they were disappointed because Piaget focused on the importance of the child's interactions with the environment in the construction of cognitive structures and on universal stage sequences of cognitive development. Piaget did not focus on how the environment affects the individual child or on individual differences.

Furthermore, if practitioners were looking to Piagetian theory and research to understand more fully the workings of the unconscious and of emotions, that is, to add a cognitive component to the contributions of psychoanalytic theorists, it again follows that they would be disappointed. Piaget's work was concentrated on the physical and logical-mathematical domains. He himself focused very little on the social, emotional, and behavioral domains of development, which are of primary interest to many school psychologists. Although Piaget (1970) stressed the importance of peer interaction for cognitive development and described affectivity as the motivation for cognition, he did not develop these ideas extensively. Developmental psychologists who have been influenced by Piaget and interested in the social and emotional domains have studied social, moral, and psychological reasoning (Kohlberg, 1969; Selman, 1980; Turiel, 1983), which is cognition about social and individual phenomena. These researchers have not focused on behavior but rather on the essential relationship among cognition, emotion, and behavior.

When Piagetian theory did not generate specific answers to such questions as how to get a child to behave in the classroom, many practitioners were unconvinced of its value. This is unfortunate, as Piagetian theory is the most purely developmental theory of all and offers much to school psychology practice. Cognitive developmental theory proposes general mechanisms of change, and Piagetian research findings offer universal descriptions of development. The Piagetian-oriented school psychologist knows that children think, perceive, organize, and understand their physical, social, and personal worlds very differently at different stages in their development. In terms of assessment and intervention, this simple statement has profound implications for practice. The Piagetian view of development offers a way of understanding children's thoughts that has useful implications for assessment and intervention in the cognitive domain, as well as in the social, emotional, and behavioral domains (see Rosen, 1984). Particular assessment methods, for example, structured and unstructured interviews, reflect increasing sensitivity to cognitive developmental theory. A child's interview can be very useful if it is structured with the child's developmental level in mind (Goodman, 1972; Greenspan, 1981; Reisman, 1973), and research findings on cognitive development provides many helpful guidelines for interviewing children (Bierman, 1983; Kanfer, Eyberg, and Krahn, 1983). Excellent suggestions about the implications of developmental changes in cognitive development, language competence, psychosocial development, and social reasoning for interviewing and intervening

with children and adolescents are offered by Hughes (1986) and Worchel (1986). In addition, Rosen's (1984) work on Piagetian perspectives on psychopathology and psychotherapy is extremely valuable for the practitioner who wants an in-depth understanding of dysfunction.

## Summary

School psychologists will be well prepared to integrate and embrace a developmental orientation if they can build a working, two-way bridge between science and practice; adopt an organismic view of development; be open to the challenge of integrating this theoretical orientation to practice; recognize the unique developmental features, tasks, and stages of childhood; and understand how a child's level of cognition impacts on and informs assessment, intervention, and prevention strategies. Having examined the obstacles to this integration, we should now examine the history of developmental psychology and then turn to the contributions of major developmental theories to school psychology practice.

## HISTORY OF DEVELOPMENTAL PSYCHOLOGY

It is informative to examine the periods when certain developmental theories and research findings became available for the practitioner and to chart the rise and fall of major theoretical perspectives. Cairns (1983) describes 100 years of developmental psychology, subdivided into the formative period (1882–1912), the period of fragmentation (1913–1946), and the period of modern growth and expansion (1947–1982). His review is summarized here. The 15 years since his review, which have been dominated by refinements in the study of cognitive, social, and emotional development of children, as well as the emphasis on the emergence of developmental psychopathology, is also discussed.

During the formative years, the field of child development was a vigorous, multidisciplinary undertaking with new ideas, fresh approaches, and novel methods, involving European and American psychologists, anatomists, pediatricians, child guidance workers, and statisticians. During the 1890s, the first developmental journal was published, the first research institute was established, the first developmental textbooks were published, the first professional organizations were begun, and the first psychological clinic for children was set up by Lightner Witmer at the University of Pennsylvania, referred to as the first child guidance clinic in America. It is noteworthy that developmental psychology, school psychology, and child clinical psychology see the establishment of the Witmer clinic as part of their birthright. Famous figures during the formative period included Alfred Binet, G. Stanley Hall, James Mark Baldwin, and Sigmund Freud. The major contributions of this early period included the study of the ontogeny of consciousness and intelligence; the development of volition and intentionality; the study of moral development; the relations between ontogeny and phylogeny; nature versus nurture; the question of the enduring effects of early experience; and such social policy issues as the application of developmental principles to child-rearing practices, passage of child labor laws, and revision of school curricula.

During the middle period (1913–1946) and the prosperous years of the 1920s, there was strong support for research in psychology. For developmental psychology, in particular, there was an immediate need to extend its methodological boundaries to permit systematic observation of social, cognitive, language, and moral development, as well as psychobiologic changes over time. There also was an explosion in empirical research. The enterprise of child and developmental psychology evolved into separate arenas, topics, and theories. It was readily apparent that no single theoretical model was broad enough to encompass the interests of the field. During this middle period, child development institutes were established at Iowa University; Merrill Palmer Institute, University of Minnesota; and the University of California, Berkeley, for the study and improvement of child rearing. The Society for Research in Child Development was established in 1933, along with its journal, Child Development. The study of intellectual development, the pursuit of longitudinal studies, the examination of children's fears (e.g., Jersild, Markey, & Jersild, 1933), and the documentation of growth and physical maturation from a maturational-unfolding perspective (Gesell, 1928, 1940) were prominent research themes. Research methods included the use of systematic observation, drawings, and interviews. Studies of social and personality development examined size and gender composition of groups by age, natural occurrence of aggression, and social exchange. Honesty, prosocial behavior, and

moral development were pursued, for example, in Hartshorne and May's (1928) studies of experimentally manipulated groups and Piaget's (1932) documentation of the natural occurrence of rule making and moral judgments. The development of, and relationship between, language and thought was explored by Piaget (1926) and by Vygotsky (1939). Developmental psychobiology and ethology were investigated (Lorenz, 1935), resulting in the origins of the systems approach that is influential in psychology today. In addition, Biber (1934) proposed the application of developmental psychology as an essential framework for the emerging nursery school programs. In-depth perspectives on theory and research in child and adolescent psychology available at the end of this period are provided by Barker, Kounin, and Wright (1943) and Carmichael (1946).

Although the grand theories of child psychology were vigorously studied and applied during this middle period, they evolved basically independently of each other and the distinctiveness of developmental and behavioral approaches became more definitive. Each new theory challenged a previous one and proposed an attractive alternative conception of development more than it refined the earlier theory. By the end of the middle period, there was a large body of empirical work on many domains of child development that can be depicted as description of the normal course of development. But there was also much fragmentation, and because of the competition among theories, there was no overall theoretical integration and no overall theory to account for development. Concurrent theoretical trends during this middle period included classical psychoanalysis, post- and neo-Freudian formulations, and behaviorism that reinterpreted psychoanalytic concepts—the original social learning theory (Dollard, Miller, Doob, Mowrer, & Sears, 1939). Of broad significance, behaviorism became rooted in research and practice during this time with J. B. Watson (1914, 1928), an experimental child psychologist, sprouting the "modern" scientific approach to child rearing of the 1920s and 1930s. Piaget's (1950) theory of cognitive development, symbolic interactionism (Mead, 1934), Lewin's (1931) field theory, and ethology (Lorenz, 1935) continued to guide competing explanations of children's behavior and development.

The modern era (1947–1982) can be characterized by expansion, invention, and maturation.

During the first half (1947–1962), the most visible theoretical trend was the rise, domination, and passing of the general learning theories. Until their grip began to weaken during the 1960s, the behavioral model of learning was equivalent to American psychology, and aspects of child behavior and development were couched in behavioristic terms. Social learning theory was prominent. Sears (1944) explored psychoanalytic learning theory from a social learning perspective, looking at aggression and dependency, but he abandoned it to pursue bidirectionality and social interactions in families, a pursuit that remains active in the field today. Operant conditioning models were prominent. Modeling and vicarious reinforcement were introduced by Bandura (1969), and cognitive reformulations of learning theories and principles were proposed (Kendler & Kendler, 1962). The extensive work in the behavioral tradition laid the foundation for school psychology's current use of behavioral measures, behavior modification, and behavioral consultation. Although the practice of many school psychologists continued to be dominated by behavioral approaches, the developmental researchers of this period were not swayed by the potential of operant and social learning principles, and with the fall of behaviorism and mechanistic models in the 1960s, dynamic and developmental models again gained prominence in the child behavior and development literature.

The second half of the modern era (1962–1982) saw the reemergence of Piagetian theory as a central focus for thinking about and researching cognitive development (Flavell, 1963). Investigations of children's language development, thinking, sensation, and information processing flourished. The barrier between social development and cognitive development was transcended, as evidenced by the study of social cognition (Shantz, 1975). There also was a fresh look at the major issues of psychobiological and behavioral development, including the effects of early experience, whether the infant is especially sensitive or invulnerable, and the importance of attachment, represented by the work of Harlow (Harlow, 1958; Harlow & Harlow, 1965), Bowlby (1958, 1969), and Ainsworth (1969). In addition, there was a surge of interest in the study of infant development and in the view of the infant as an adaptive and adapting organism. Organismic models predominated in the second half of the modern era and continue to do so today.

Developmental psychology in the 1980s and first half of the 1990s can be described by five conceptual features: (1) concern with explanations of developmental change, that is, with the specification of the causes, antecedents, and mechanisms of development as opposed to just the description of development; (2) attention to theory or model testing as opposed to mere generation of developmental norms; (3) emphasis on and concern with continual, reciprocal relations between active organisms and active contexts, that is, a dialectical, transactional view; (4) predominance of theoretical pluralism, or multiplicity of reasonable theoretical alternatives; and (5) attention to the understanding of maladaptive development, the interaction of normal and atypical development, and variables that help place children at risk developmentally (e.g., maltreatment and pathological parenting), reflected by the field of developmental psychopathology. Understanding the history of developmental psychology sets the stage for appreciating the prominence of major developmental theories, as well as their implications for practice.

## DEVELOPMENTAL THEORIES

Theory is a prerequisite for the advancement of science because it organizes and gives meaning to facts, provides a framework for them, and assigns more importance to some facts than to others. In addition, a theory serves as a heuristic device, a process that raises questions, guides observations, and generates new information. Psychological theory guides the behavior of psychologists who are doing research. It helps them formulate questions, choose what to study, and decide how to study a problem. Theory is useful to the practitioner because it provides a framework to guide problem solving. Unique to psychological theories, developmental theory focuses on qualitative, structural, and internal changes over time. This concern with change has presented developmental theorists and researchers with the tasks of describing changes in one or several areas of behavior, describing changes in the relationships among several areas of behavior, and explaining the course of development (Miller, 1989). Although much of the early work in child psychology was concerned with description, including description of the change process, recent work in developmental psychology attempts to explain and even predict change.

To account for developmental change, most

theories offer a set of general principles or rules for change. These specify necessary and sufficient antecedents for change and identify variables that modify or modulate the rate or nature of each change. These processes have been as diverse as dynamic equilibration in Piaget's theory, physical maturation in Freudian and ethological theory, and vicarious reinforcement and modeling in social learning theory. No one developmental theory has satisfactorily handled both description and explanation (Miller, 1989), partly because the various theories have considered different phenomena. The phenomena studied and the methods of investigation employed are tied to the level of analysis undertaken, a focus on structure (organization) or process (dynamic, functioning aspects of the system), what content is emphasized, (e.g., personality or cognition), and whether overt behavior or covert thought and personality is emphasized. The various theories attend to very different levels of behavior and select different content. The stage theories look at stage-defining characteristics and thus operate at a very general level. In their view, the most important developments are cognitive or personality structures. Other theorists focus on more specific acquisitions that are often limited to certain situations or types of stimulation. The theories range in content from social behaviors and personality to cognitive and metacognitive processes. Some theories focus on universal change and some on individual differences. For example, Piaget emphasized cognitive concepts acquired in all cultural groups, and Freud described universal psychosexual development. Social cognitive development models focus on the levels of reasoning children use to explain why their behavior and that of others is appropriate. These diverse emphases illustrate why an integration of developmental theories is so difficult.

However, even without a workable integration of developmental approaches, a knowledge of the key developmental theories prevents tunnel vision among practitioners (Miller, 1989). A rigid perspective can be avoided if one incorporates several theories in an attempt to understand children's behavior. In addition, as cultural conditions change and new information about development comes to light, practitioners must select what is useful from the various theories and research findings and ignore the aspects that are no longer applicable. Combining and integrating Freud's concern with underlying motivations and emotions, Erikson's concern with the mastery of psychosocial crises, Piaget's concern with cognitive structures, Bowlby's concern with the quality of attachment and the impact of separation, and Bronfenbrenner's framework for considering transactions between the child and multiple environmental systems—all produce a powerful perspective for understanding children's behavior. Seven major developmental theories are described briefly, with an emphasis on what develops, the principles or mechanisms of development, and key contributions to practice.

## Freud's Psychoanalytic Theory

Psychoanalytic theory focuses on the motivational forces underlying behavior, emotional aspects of the personality, and the development of the psyche (the self). In this perspective, development is the process by which the child copes with an invariant sequence of conflicts or psychological disturbances. Development occurs because of disturbances or conflicts between a child's drives at different stages of maturation and the social environment. The tension-reduction equilibration process that occurs results from the child's subsequent attempt to restore calm. What develops is the emergence and balance of psychological structures that channel, repress, and transform psychosexual energy. These structures—id, ego, and superego—mediate between the drives and the behavior. The child's development through the psychosexual stages early in life lays the foundation of personality.

### Principles of Development

Freud's theory is a "trouble" theory of development; that is, development proceeds because of disturbances or perturbations to the system. The factors that initiate change include maturation, external frustrations, internal conflicts, personal inadequacies, and anxieties (Hall, 1954). Maturational changes both propel children into activity as they try to satisfy the drives and move them from stage to stage as the bodily site of pleasure changes. External frustrations come from people or events that do not allow for the immediate expression of needs. These frustrations cause a painful buildup of tension and force children to delay and detour their discharge of energy. Internal conflicts arise from battle among the id, ego, and superego, or more specifically, between drives and forces of repression. Personal inadequacies refer to certain skills, knowledge, expertise, or experience that the child needs but may lack. Anxieties are unpleasant feelings that occur when the child anticipates physical or psychological pain. It is the ego that has the primary responsibility for guiding the course of change initiated by the disturbances, and it strives to maintain a balance between the needs of the id and the superego.

## Key Contributions for Practice

Knowledge about the unconscious, defense mechanisms, transference, countertransference, and the effects of early experiences are important for school psychology practice. Psychoanalytic theory is widely recognized for acknowledging and promoting the unconscious as a powerful shaper of development. The belief is that the antecedents of daily behavior are often beyond the realm of conscious awareness. Behavior is seen as neither haphazard nor random but the result of determinable causes and goals, although on the surface it may appear irrational. Today many psychologists accept that behavior is directed by powerful unconscious drives. Another major contribution of psychoanalytic theory comes from defense mechanisms. As the ego develops, it evolves techniques for accommodating the conflicting demands made on it. A strong, mature ego uses direct means to accomplish this. It admits the nature of the demands and proposes forthright, reasoned ways to effect a solution that satisfies each to an acceptable degree. But a less mature ego uses defense mechanisms because it cannot solve the conflicts among the demands that confront it. The function of a defense mechanism is to avoid or terminate anxiety, and defenses are not necessarily pathological. They are a necessary means of control, and some are characteristic of the mature adult. The extensive use of defense mechanisms to control inadequate psychological adjustment, however, can result in rigid adaptation and possibly psychological disturbance.

The concept of transference is also of use to the practitioner. Children transfer feelings and reactions that they have had to other important figures in the past onto current important figures, such as a school counselor or classroom teacher. Although the interpretation of the transference may be reserved for in-depth psychoanalytic treatment, understanding the dynamics of how the child acts with key adults at school provides diagnostic information. The concept of countertransference is also of key importance.

Countertransference involves the practitioners' reactions to a child's behavior, feelings, thoughts, appearance, or history that may remind them of some aspect of their own life or experience that makes it difficult for them to respond appropriately to the child with whom they are working. For example, a school psychologist with a history of childhood abuse that has not been resolved may be unable to recognize or appropriately respond to the child's depiction of abuse and current reactions. The clinicians may under- or overreact because of their own countertransference. Finally, Freud developed the idea, so widely accepted today, that early experience is crucial to later development. According to Freud, a behavior can be understood only if one knows how it developed in the person's early history. Both normal and abnormal behavior have their roots in the early years, when the basic structure of the personality is laid down. The early interactions between children's drives and their social environment set the pattern for later learning, social adjustment, and coping with anxiety. Although today this notion has been broadened to include the cumulative effects of early experience and to recognize mediators that may buffer or challenge these effects, the influence of early experience remains a central construct in developmental psychology and is crucial to the practitioner.

## Erickson's Psychosocial Theory

Psychosocial theory focuses on the development of ego identity and the healthy personality (Erikson, 1950) and reflects a "normal" developmental framework, in which people move from nonego identity to ego identity. Erikson is one of the founders of ego psychology. This movement in psychoanalysis reaffirms the importance of the ego in everyday behavior and recognizes not only that overt behavior is the direct result of unconscious forces but also that consciousness and the successful resolution of ego developmental milestones greatly affect one's behavior and personality. Ego psychology focuses on adaptation in the normal course of development. These psychologists give the environment and culture a greater role in the shaping of personality and postulate that the ego did not originate from the id but had its own autonomous development. Ego psychology has affected therapeutic methods in that focus of attention is on ego defenses against instinctual forces rather than on only the expression of the id.

## Principles of Development

According to Erikson's psychosocial theory, the mechanism of development is equated with the epigenetic principle; that is, physical maturation writes the general timetable for development, and within these parameters the child's culture pushes, pulls, nurtures, and harms. In Erikson's view, society exerts its influence on the developing child at many levels, ranging from abstract ideology to a parent's caress. Development is a result of the resolution of conflict from opposing forces. Erikson's picture of the process features a description of conflicts, inner and outer, which the vital personality weathers, reemerging from each crisis with an increased sense of inner unity, good judgment, and the capacity "to do well" according to the individual's own standards and those people who are significant to that person. Erikson (1977) also elaborates on play as a specific mechanism of development. He uses *play* in a broad sense to mean the use of imagination to try out ways of mastering and adapting to the world, to express emotions, to re-create past situations or imagine future situations, and to develop new models of existence.

## Key Contributions for Practice

Erikson's (1950) best-known contribution is his model of the eight psychosocial stages of development. Each stage centers on a psychosocial crisis that involves the interaction of maturational and societal expectations and must be resolved if the child is to move constructively and effectively to the next stage. Over the developmental progressions of the eight stages, there is an expansion of the radius of significant relationships, from the maternal person at the Trust versus Mistrust stage to the basic family at the Initiative versus Guilt stage to peer groups at the Identity versus Identity Diffusion stage. At each stage, the individual struggles with the question "Who am I?" and reworks the answer. Although each crisis is most evident at a particular stage in the life cycle, each earlier crisis appears in some form throughout development. Each stage builds on the previous stages and influences the form of the later stages, but it also adds a new dimension to the person's interactions with the self and the environment. If a stage is not handled satisfactorily, the person continues to fight earlier battles in later life. Erikson optimistically claims, however, that it is never too late to resolve any of the crises. Additional contributions from Erikson that are useful for practice include a focus on the

fit between the child and the culture at different stages of development and the need to look at the structure of the social organization surrounding each child, as the child is a life cycle in a community of life cycles.

## Social Learning Theory

It is beyond the scope of this chapter to review learning theories, which traditionally emphasize learned behaviors, the environment's control of behavior, a breakdown of behavior into simple units, observable behavior, and rigorous experimental methodology (Miller, 1989). As already mentioned, learning theories historically have not been developmentally oriented or open to developmental principles. However, a contemporary view of social learning theory, which is the most developmental of the learning theories, merits attention.

Social learning theory began as an attempt to explain systematically psychoanalytic constructs (Dollard et al., 1939; Sear, 1944), but soon after it began to focus on the process of socialization and how children learn social behaviors in a social context. Bandura (1969) introduced the concept of learning complex repertoires of behaviors through observation or modeling, imitation, and vicarious reinforcement. His later work (Bandura, 1977) depicts the child as an active participant in learning, with the child's cognition as a central mediator and organizer. To Bandura, the entire learning context consists of the characteristics of the child, the child's specific behavior, the environment, and the resulting interactions. He called this process "reciprocal determinism." The result of these interactions is new behavior and information that is the outcome of a new organization of behavior learned earlier. Bandura does not propose an underlying cognitive structure, as does Piaget. It is interesting that whereas other theories have as their aim of development the acquisition or resolution of higher stages of development, such as Piaget, Freud, and Erikson, there is no universal goal or end point to development from a social learning perspective. What is universally developed is a skilled ability to learn by observing or listening, which allows the child to acquire large chunks of new behavior.

## Principles of Development

There is currently considerable controversy about whether social learning theory or any current learning theory is truly a developmental theory. Questions that remain unanswered include the following: Are developmental changes the same as short-term changes accumulated over a longer period of time? Are the central laws of learning the same regardless of the child's cognitive level? Social learning theory focuses on processes of change, in contrast to Piaget and Freud, who focus on structural changes as the child goes through the stages. However, Bandura's (1977) current model of observational learning, which proposes attentional, retention, motor, and motivational processes, identifies a number of developmental variables: physical maturation, experience with the social world, and cognitive development. Physical maturation is relevant in that a child may not have the physical maturity to reproduce certain observed motor patterns. Experience with the social world causes development in two ways: the child, with increasing age, has a larger and increasingly differentiated set of social behaviors, and as children get older they face different social environments. The child's attention, memory, and cognitive organization undergo dramatic changes during development.

## Key Contributions for Practice

Social learning theory goes beyond the associational principle of classical conditioning and the reinforcement, punishment, and extinction principles of operant conditioning and, as a result, offers much to the practitioner who works with children in complex social contexts. Social learning theory has demonstrated systematically that children learn by observation, imitation, and vicarious reinforcement. Learning can occur without reinforcement, direct or vicarious, but it does have a powerful effect on performance. The child is seen as an active organism, who interacts with the environment and whose processing of the environment is dependent on the cognitive abilities of attention and retention. An explicit integration of developmental principles and learning is lacking, however. For example, little attention has been given to how the developmental level affects the acquisition of social skills in research, although many practitioners are likely to keep such a limitation in mind.

## Piaget's Theory of Cognitive Development

Piaget spent a lifetime in the study of genetic epistemology—that is, the development of the construction of knowledge—to answer the question "How do we come to know?" He put the construct of constructivism in a central position; that is, the child actively constructs knowledge, has an active part in the process of knowing, and contributes to the form knowledge takes (Piaget, 1950, 1970). Piaget also proposed the construct of structuralism: the development of the underlying organizational properties of knowledge. Piaget is best known for his stage approach to cognitive development. A stage is a period of time in which a child's thinking and behavior in a variety of situations reflect a particular type of underlying logical structure, and cognitive development proceeds through a series of stages. Various cognitive levels provide different ways of adapting to the environment.

## Principles of Development

Piaget, who was educated as a biologist, takes the position that living things, by definition, require active interaction with the environment or they will die. For Piaget (1950, 1970), intelligence means adaptation to the environment, and one essential aspect of interaction is the processing of information. The child is kept in intellectual interaction with the environment in order to survive, and in the process the self-regulating balance (equilibration) between assimilation and accommodation produces intellectual growth. Assimilation is the process of fitting one's understanding of reality into one's current cognitive organization. Children apply what they know to understand properties and relationships between properties and events. Accommodation refers to adjustments in the cognitive organization as a result of the demands of reality. Accommodation occurs because of the failure of the current structures to interpret a particular object or event satisfactorily. The resulting reorganization of thought leads to a different and more satisfactory assimilation of the experience. Assimilation and accommodation are closely intertwined in every cognitive activity from birth to death. Attempts to assimilate reality necessarily involve slight changes in the cognitive structures as they adjust to the new elements. Assimilation and accommodation are so related that Piaget sometimes defines adaptation as equilibrium between assimilation and accommodation. In a state of equilibrium, neither assimilation nor accommodation dominates. An excessive predominance of one over the other can result in grossly dysfunctional behavior.

Piaget (1950, 1970) defines the developmental process as the result of physical maturation, plus experience with the physical environment and plus social experience, regulated by the process of equilibration. For Piaget, equilibration is the critical mechanism for change and growth. With each newly achieved equilibrated balance, a wider perspective is attained, the ability to coordinate more perspectives is possible, and a new view of the old perspective is acquired. Reequilibration occurs when the current structural organization is no longer adequate to its task: it cannot assimilate or resolve the problem at the current level of development. The individual is stuck in a state of disequilibrium, and in moving beyond the impasse structural modification or the invention of new structure (accommodation) will occur. The varying degrees of discrepancy between the current organizational structures and the experience at hand raise the issue of what the limitations mean to accommodations. Piaget's answer, which has implications for educational and therapeutic practice, is that only moderately discrepant events or characteristics can be accommodated; great leaps are not possible. If the reality being presented or perceived is too different from the child's current level of understanding, the child cannot bridge the gap. There can never be radical departures from the old. Thus, development necessarily proceeds in small steps.

## *Key Contributions for Practice*

Piaget's (1950, 1970) theory has many implications for practice (see Cowan, 1978; Rosen, 1984). Piaget has described the child as an active constructor of knowledge, one who takes an active role in her or his development and learning. Also, knowledge is biased: experience is always filtered through the child's current ways of understanding, which are determined by the child's stage, or level of cognitive development, and its underlying structure of logic. In addition, the child is motivated to seek equilibrium when disequilibrated, which results in change. The role of the teacher and the counselor is to promote moderate disequilibrium in the child by presenting ideas that are slightly above the current conceptual level. But the activities presented cannot be at too difficult a level for the child or development and learning will not occur. Furthermore, social interaction is key to the construction of knowledge, as it helps relinquish egocentrism, forcing the child to define, justify, and clarify her or his thoughts. Finally, assessment and intervention activities must be matched to the cognitive developmental level of the child.

## Bowlby's Attachment Theory

Bowlby's (1980) theory of attachment incorporates a great deal from psychoanalytic thinking but also adopts principles from ethological and cognitive theory. His theory provides a way to conceptualize the propensity of human beings to make strong affectional bonds to significant others and to explain many forms of emotional distress and personality disturbance, including anxiety, anger, depression, and emotional detachment, which are a result of unwilling separation and loss. According to Bowlby (1969, 1980), attachment behaviors are innate and promote survival of the species because they allow adaptation of the environment. In addition, adults are biologically predisposed to develop attachment, giving children a secure base from which to explore, safety when threats are encountered, and opportunity to learn to regulate their level of stress. Attachment behavior is any form of behavior that results in attaining or retaining proximity to some other differentiated and preferred individual. It contributes to individuals' survival by keeping them in touch with care-givers, thereby reducing the risk of harm. During the course of healthy development, attachment behaviors lead to the development of attachments that are present and active throughout the life cycle. How these behaviors develop and the patterns they take affect the patterns of affectional bonds throughout one's lifetime.

## *Principles of Development*

Bowlby (1979) specifically claims that there is a strong causal relationship between an individuals' experiences with one's parents and the later capacity to make affectional bonds. Variations in this capacity result from variations in the ways that parents perform their roles. Parents need to give their children a secure base and encourage them to explore from it. Children then grow up to be secure and self-reliant and to be trusting, cooperative, and helpful toward others. In contrast, children who experience pathogenic parenting may become anxious and insecure and are usually described as overly dependent or overly independent. Under stress, these individuals are more at risk for developing neurotic symptoms, depression, or phobias than securely attached individuals. Thus, anxious attachment is not necessarily a cause of subsequent pathology but rather a risk factor that tends to predict behavioral problems when it occurs in conjunction with other risk factors.

Children with parents who had an anxious

attachment relationship to their own parents or their spouses are, according to Bowlby (1979), even more at risk for pathogenic parenting. These children have parents who are persistently unresponsive to their care-eliciting behavior or are actively rejecting; the children experience the discontinuities of parenting (sometimes leading to hospitalization), including persistent denials of love, threats of abandonment, threats of suicide, and guilt inducements (claims that the child's behavior is or will be responsible for the parent's death or illness). In addition, if young children's attachment behaviors are continually aroused but not responded to, they eventually exclude from their awareness the sights, thoughts, or feelings that would normally activate attachment behaviors. This process is called defensive exclusion, and it probably interferes with a child's emotional and social development. Thus, from this theoretical perspective, the effects of parental behaviors on the next generation are very powerful. For example, an abused child, who has not resolved the abuse, is more likely to abuse his or her own children or fail to protect them from abuse than is a child who was not abused (Bowlby, 1982).

## *Key Contributions for Practice*

There is a growing body of evidence to support Bowlby's theory of personality and emotional development. Abnormal infant attachment experiences have been linked to adult depression and loneliness, character disorders, and phobias (Bowlby, 1982). In addition, there is strong evidence that children who experience secure attachment as infants become more competent cognitively, emotionally, and socially (Campos, Barrett, Lamb, Goldsmith, & Stenberg, 1983) than do infants who have anxious and insecure attachment relationships. According to Bowlby, adverse childhood experiences, such as insecure attachment, can have at least two kinds of effects. They make the individual more vulnerable to later adverse experiences, and they make it more likely that the individual will meet with further such experiences. Later adverse experiences are likely to be partially the consequences of the child's own actions, actions that spring from those disturbances of personality to which the earlier experiences have given rise. However, there is also some evidence that secure attachment relationships in childhood and adolescence can offset adverse earlier experiences (Rutter, 1981). Child practitioners need to recognize the

importance of early and ongoing attachment relationships, the possible adverse consequences of separation and loss, the negative effects of pathogenic parenting, the need to intervene with parents and families who have negative relational patterns, the importance of promoting positive peer interactions, and the necessity of providing a secure base in counseling from which the child can explore the self and make changes.

## Bronfenbrenner's Ecological Theory

Bronfrenbrenner (1979) provides a framework for viewing the development of the child in context. His notions of the ecology of human development lie at a point of convergence among the biological, psychological, and social sciences as they bear on the evolution of the individual in society. Bronfenbrenner describes the ecological environment as a set of nested structures, each contained within the next, the innermost level being the developing child. These structures include the microsystem, which is defined as the complex of relations between the developing person and the environment in an immediate setting (e.g., home or school); the mesosystem, which is defined as the interrelations among major settings at a particular point in the developing person's life (e.g., the relations between home and school); the exosystem, which is defined as an extension of the mesosystem that embraces other specific social structures that do not themselves contain the developing person but impinge on or encompass the immediate settings in which he or she is found and thereby influence or delimit what goes on there (e.g., the parent's work setting or the school board); and the macrosystem, which is defined as the overarching institutional patterns of the culture or subculture, such as the economic, social, educational, legal, and political systems, of which micro-, meso-, and exosystems are the concrete manifestations. Development is defined as a lasting change in the way in which a person perceives and deals with the environment. The study of development focuses on what the person perceives, desires, fears, and thinks about and how the nature of this psychological material changes as a function of a person's exposure and interaction in the environment. Development is viewed as the person's evolving conception of the ecological environment and one's relation to it, as well as the person's growing capacity to discover, sustain, or alter its properties.

## Principles of Development

Bronfenbrenner's (1979) theory is concerned with the progressive accommodation between a growing human organism and its immediate environment and the ways in which these relations are mediated by forces that emanate from more remote regions in the larger physical and social milieu. This is a theory of environmental interconnections and their impact on the forces that directly affect the child's psychological growth: "The ecology of human development involves the scientific study of the progressive, mutual accommodation between an active, growing human being and the changing properties of the immediate settings in which the developing person lives, as this process is affected by relations between these settings, and by the larger contexts in which the settings are embedded" (p. 21).

## Key Contributions for Practice

An ecological perspective provides a useful overall model for planning assessment and intervention activities. It also provides a helpful orientation from which to conceptualize emotional disturbance and behavior or conduct disorders (Apter & Conoley, 1984; Hobbs 1966, 1982; Swap, 1974). Most children who are judged to be "normal" are operating in a behavioral ecology that can be defined as congruent. That is, the individual's behavior is in harmony with the social norms of the environment. When such congruence does not exist, the child is likely to be considered deviant or incompetent. From an ecological approach, emotional disturbance and behavior disorders reside in the interaction between a child and critical aspects of the surrounding environment. Disturbance is viewed not as a disease located within the child but rather as discordance, a lack of balance in the system, a failure to achieve a match between the child and the child's systems. The disturbance lies in the area of functional maladaptation between the individual and the environment. The disturbance is a reciprocal disruptive exchange between the child and the environment—most critically, the child's significant others. It follows from this view of disturbance that the environment must be given intervention attention equal to that shown to the individual who has been singled out as "disturbed." That is, assessment and interventions must focus on these points of discordance and the resulting failure to match. Problems belong to a system, not to an individual child. The goal of intervention is to make the system function in a way that enhances the development and well-being of all its members.

## An Organismic, Transactional Theory of Development

The organismic, transactional theory of development (Cicchetti & Sroufe, 1978; Sroufe, 1979a, 1979b)—also sometimes referred to as the organizational or structural approach—consists of a set of regulative principles that can guide theorizing about and research into human behavior (Santostefano, 1978; Sroufe & Rutter, 1984). This view is congruent with the theoretical conceptualization of organismic theorists (Piaget, 1970; Reese & Overton, 1970; Sroufe, 1979a; Werner, 1948; White, 1976). According to the organizational approach, development may be conceived of as a series of qualitative reorganizations among and within behavioral systems, which take place through differentiation and hierarchical integration. Variables at many levels of analysis determine the character of these organizations: genetic, constitutional, neurobiological, biochemical, behavioral, psychological, environmental, and sociological. Moreover, these variables are conceived as being in dynamic transaction with one another.

## Principles of Development

The organismic transactional model conceptualizes the environment and the child as mutually influencing each other. This perspective makes it plausible to view, for example, maltreatment phenomena as expressions of underlying dysfunction in the parent-child-environment rather than as solely the result of aberrant parental personality traits, environmental stress, or deviant characteristics in the child. Since the child and the environment are seen as reciprocal influences, it follows that behavior at a later point reflects not only the quality or earlier adaptation but also the intervening environmental inputs and supports. As the child develops, the match between child and parent, as well as their salient characteristics, may change. If a child demonstrates deviant development across time, it is assumed that the child has been involved in a continuous maladaptive process. The continued manifestation of maladaptation depends on environmental support, while the child's characteristics, reciprocally, partially determine the nature of the environment. Thus, maladapted children contribute to their own environment and may contribute to their own psychopathology.

## Key Contributions for Practice

This perspective offers a useful conceptualization of healthy and pathological development. Normal or healthy development is defined as fostering structural changes among the child's behavioral systems that reflect the dynamic interactions of changing familial, social, and environmental variables and that allow the child to attain competence (Cicchetti & Schneider-Rosen, 1986). The competent child is defined as one who is able to use internal and external resources to attain a satisfactory developmental adaptation. Internal resources include both specific skills and broad characteristics of an individual, which would be subsumed under general constructs, such as self-esteem. External resources include anything else that may serve to help the developing child coordinate affect, cognition, and behavior to attain short- and long-term adaptation (e.g., relations with others or appropriate imitation of models). Adaptation at a particular developmental level implies the successful resolution of the developmental tasks most salient for that period. It is part of Waters and Sroufe's conception of competence that early competence predicts later competence, given no irregularities in development (e.g., changes in the quality of care the child receives or increased stress in the environment). Pathological development, in contrast, is a lack of effective integration and organization of the social, emotional, and cognitive competencies that are important in achieving adaptation at a particular developmental level (Cicchetti & Schneider-Rosen, 1986). Pathological development leads to personal distress and cognitive, affective, or social incompetence. Because early structures are often incorporated into later structures, an early deviation or disturbance in functioning may ultimately cause a much larger disturbance to emerge later.

## Summary and Integration—A Developmental Perspective for Practice

It is apparent from this historical review and discussion of seven theoretical orientations that there has never been a unitary view of the content, process, or context of children's development. However, by focusing on how developmental theorists have studied change over time and factors that produce change, a developmental perspective, useful to the practitioner, can be described.

A developmental approach poses questions about the developmental course of adaptive and maladaptive behaviors. Its role is to help explain and change troublesome behavior in light of the developmental tasks, sequences, and processes that characterize human growth (Achenbach, 1982). A developmental perspective requires the continuities and discontinuities among infancy, childhood, and adult life to be taken into account. For example, a developmental approach to understanding the process of schooling helps to frame questions about the opportunities children have to acquire conceptual meaning from the classroom, about peer interactions that promote social development, and about the way children perceive themselves as changing in competence and identity. The adjective *developmental* specifies a concern with the general course of psychological development, with the changes that take place with developmental progression, and with the processes and mechanisms that underlie developmental transitions.

For example, developmentalists interested in the interplay between normal and abnormal development question whether there are age-dependent variations in susceptibility to stress, such as parental divorce; whether the development of depression or delinquent activities at one age is dependent on previous occurrences at an earlier age; and whether there are points in development when qualities of personality become stabilized to the extent that although behavior may change, personality can no longer be transformed totally. Developmentally oriented school psychologists examine the match between the child's stages of development and the content and structure of instructional tasks, study the social environment of the classroom and playground to enhance opportunities for social development, and assess the child's current reasoning about personal experiences to understand changes in self-perception. As noted earlier, a developmental approach can shed light on all phases of the life cycle, but the dramatic changes that occur from birth to maturity make it especially crucial for understanding problems of childhood and adolescence. The dramatic changes in development during childhood present opportunities for promoting positive change, as well as preventing problems that can endure over the life span. A developmental perspective, along with age-related developmental processes and descriptions, theoretical models, research findings, and an understanding of context and the child's culture, gives the school psychologist indispensable tools for assessing and constructing solutions to problems. It is important to highlight the centrality of cultural differences in the developmental process. A developmental perspective that integrates a contemporary view of the developmental process and its implications for practice follows.

## CONTRIBUTIONS OF DEVELOPMENTAL PSYCHOLOGY: AN INTEGRATED, CONTEMPORARY VIEW OF THE DEVELOPMENTAL PROCESS

Our descriptions of the major developmental theories indicate the variety of ways and the richness in which the developmental process has been conceptualized. Each of these theoretical frameworks may be useful to the practitioner in carrying out assessments, planning and implementing interventions, and designing prevention initiatives. It is also heuristic to generate an integrated view of the developing child that draws from the multiple developmental theories. The following six general principles are a conceptualization of a contemporary view of the developing child that may be of particular use to school psychologists in their assessment, intervention, and prevention efforts.

### The Child Is Active and Influences Development

The developmental theories previously reviewed have addressed the basic nature of the child and perceived the child in primarily mechanistic or organismic terms. In the mechanistic view, development is caused by external forces and events that act on the passive, machinelike mind of the child. In the organismic view, the child is an active, organized whole who is changing constantly. Self-initiated behavior and thought lead to changes in both the structure and the content of the child's behavior and thought. Development does not occur as a series of linear additions but rather by reorganization of both old and new elements. Thus reorganized, even previously existing elements are transformed. The "same" behavior may have totally new meaning with development, just as it may have different meanings in different contexts.

Furthermore, although the various theories differ in the degree of organization or structure that underlies development, all contemporary versions of developmental theories portray children as active agents in their own development. The child at birth is active, involved, and competent. In addition, over time the child becomes an increasingly active shaper of the environment (Sroufe, 1979a). Later experience is not a random influence on children because they selectively perceive, respond to, and create experience, based on all that has gone before. Thus, the characteristics of children themselves (e.g., intelligence, temperament, and attractiveness) and the resultant influence they have on others plays a part in their developmental process.

### The Interaction and Transaction Between the Child and the Environment Is Complex (Nature/Nurture)

Each developmental theory has addressed how nature and nurture contribute to development. The basic issue is whether knowledge and behavior are derived from one's genetic endowment or from experience in the world. Today nearly all developmentalists agree that the interaction of innate and environmental factors accounts for both the development of a trait or behavior in an individual and its variations among individuals. Development is viewed as an integrated and complicated process, characterized by multiply determined pathways and outcomes that interact in a complex system of biological, psychological, and environmental factors. Nature and nurture are inextricably intertwined. In addition, a child's developmental outcomes are commonly accepted to have multiple historical and causal determinants rather than single-factor etiologies. It is useful to view development from a transactional model, where the multiple transactions among environmental forces, the care-giver's characteristics, and the child's characteristics are seen as dynamic, reciprocal contributions to the events and outcomes of development. Furthermore, the meaning of a child's behavior can be determined only within the child's total psychological context. The child is embedded in a variety of social systems and settings in which members affect one another's development and behavior. The ecology of the child's development is taken into account, as is the transactional influence of care-takers, peers, and multiple systems (e.g., family, school, neighborhood, and culture) on the child and vice versa. Continuity and discontinuity in development are viewed as complimentary.

## Development Consists of Both Qualitative and Quantitative Change

Each developmental theory has taken a stand on whether development is quantitative or qualitative. Theories that have taken a mechanistic view have emphasized quantitative change, whereas those that have adapted the organismic approach have emphasized qualitative change. Qualitative changes refer to changes in kind or type. New phenomena or characteristics emerge that cannot be reduced to previous elements. Qualitative changes typically involve changes in structure or organization. In contrast, quantitative changes refer to changes in amount, frequency, or degree. In some cases, the behavior becomes more efficient or consistent. The change is gradual and occurs in small increments: bits and pieces of information, habits, and skills are acquired during development. At a general level, the issue of qualitative versus quantitative change becomes an issue of stage versus nonstage. When there are similarities in a number of abilities or behaviors during a period of time, a theorist often infers that the child is in a particular stage, or level of development. Although there is debate about the existence of stages and there is controversy about which developmental changes are qualitative and which are quantitative, most developmentalists agree that both qualitative and quantitative changes occur and are necessary.

## Later Development Depends on Earlier Development

The developmental theories would agree that development proceeds in one direction only, in the sense that what happens at any point in the process is dependent on what has occurred up to that point. Development is viewed as a process whereby each solution of a developmental task is built on successful completion of a previous one. The basic agreement is that the earlier experiences influence, but do not determine, what follows. This assumption raises the issue of the relationship between early competence and later development. The relationship is complex, but in examining the competence of children at various stages of the life span, several principles are germane (Cicchetti & Schneider-Rosen, 1986):

(1) competence at one developmental period exerts a positive influence on achieving competence at the next period; (2) early competence also exerts a subtle influence on adaptation throughout the life span since each developmental issue, although perhaps most salient at one developmental period, is of continuing importance throughout the life cycle; (3) the failure to achieve adaptation at one period makes adaptation more difficult at the next, and to some extent more difficult throughout the life span since each issue continues to assume importance throughout the individual's development; and (4) many factors may mediate between early and later adaptation or maladaptation and may permit alternative outcomes to occur; that is, early problems or deviations in the successful resolution of a developmental task may be countered by major changes in the child's experience that could result in the successful negotiation of subsequent developmental tasks.

Furthermore, in examining mediating variables in the relationship between early events and later adaptation or maladaptation, Rutter (1981, 1986) has proposed a number of ways in which early experience might be connected to later disorder. These include some rather direct connections: (1) experience leads to disorder at the time, which then persists; (2) experience leads to bodily changes that influence later functioning; and (3) experience leads to altered patterns of behavior at the time, which only later take the form of disorder. Other connections are less direct: (4) early experience may change the family circumstances, which in time produce disorder in the individual; (5) early experience leads to sensitivities to stress and the modification of coping styles in the individual, which then later predispose the person to disorder, or buffer the person against stress; (6) experience alters the individual's self-concept or attitudes, which in turn influence the response to later situations; and (7) experience influences behavior through effects on the selection of environments or on the opening or closing down of opportunities.

## Development Is Affected by Risk-Vulnerability and Protective Factors

Of the developmental theories reviewed, most have implicitly suggested the presence of risk and protective factors in the developmental process, although only the organismic, transactional theory of development explicitly introduces this concept (however, attachment theory views secure attachment as a protective factor in development, and insecure or disorganized attachment as a risk factor). Currently, the constructs of risk-vulnerability and protective factors, including those internal and external to the child, are well recognized in the developmental process. As Masten (1989) has stated, "While it has long been recognized that certain experiential hazards place a child at risk for developmental problems or psychopathology, pervasive individual differences in observed adaptational outcomes of children at risk have raised a critical question: How is it that some children experience adversity and successfully negotiate the risks to their development while others fail to do so?" (p. 261). This question has led to more than a decade of research on risk factors that render an individual vulnerable, as well as on resilience and protective factors, the positive side of adaptation under extenuating circumstances.

Vulnerability represents a heightened probability for poor development, ostensibly because of the presence of a single or of multiple risk factors (Garmezy, 1993). Whereas vulnerability provides a singular emphasis on risk elements, resilience is defined by the presence of any or many of these self same risk factors; however, the accompanying adaptive outcomes are presumed to be a function of evident or unidentified positive elements within the individual and external environments that serve a protective function. During the past decade, the concept of protective factors has become firmly established in the field of risk research (Rutter, 1990). There has been an increasing appreciation that resilience is a key topic and that an understanding of the mechanisms involved enhance the understanding of the processes involved in risk itself, as well as having key implications for prevention and intervention. Three core factors that appear to operate as protective factors for individuals whose stressful life situations place them at risk are temperament and personality attributes (activity level, reflectiveness when confronted with new situations, cognitive skills, and positive response to others), family factors (warmth, cohesion, and the presence of some caring adult), and social support (Garmezy, 1993). An understanding of how protective factors affect resiliency also holds great promise for the development of intervention and prevention programs. By examining and understanding the processes and mechanisms that contribute to adaptation in situations that more typically result in maladaptation, as well as the protective factors that can overcome the impact of risk, theoreticians and clinicians will be better able to devise ways of promoting positive outcome in high-risk populations (Cicchetti & Toth, 1992).

## Responding to Opportunities for Developmental Change Is a Complex but Cautiously Optimistic Process

The developmental theories reviewed predict that responding to opportunities for developmental change—whether the opportunity is natural; accidental; or planned by a child, family members, or professionals—is a complex, somewhat unpredictable process that gives rise to cautious optimism. Some of the developmental theories, particularly the stage theories, would argue that there may be optimal times for promoting developmental change. Because of the hierarchical, organized nature of developmental processes, points of reorganization and periods of transition offer optimal opportunities for change. As stated well by Cicchetti and Toth (1992),

> Vulnerability to maladaptation is exacerbated in those who have experienced failure on a previous stage-salient issue. Similarly, individuals with a history of successful resolution of stage-salient issues are more likely to deal adaptively with periods of reorganization. However, regardless of the quality of prior adaptation, an individual's level of functioning can change at any time during the life course. Because periods of transition offer opportunities for change, it might be especially important to target prevention and intervention efforts at these periods of reorganization. The provision of "booster services" during developmental transitions, especially for those individuals with a history of serious difficulties also holds great promise for facilitating positive outcome. (p. 491)

Thus, interventions and, more centrally, prevention efforts may be most effective if planned for times of transition. In addition, the knowledge that a child is about to experience multiple courses of change—for example, during a parental divorce and its aftermath or during academic failure at a school transition point—interventions could be timed to assist with the challenges and to protect against debilitating consequences in perceptions of competence and identity.

# APPLICATION OF DEVELOPMENTAL PSYCHOLOGY AND PSYCHOPATHOLOGY TO ASSESSMENT, INTERVENTION, AND PREVENTION

Developmental theory and a developmental orientation are necessary for school psychologists to optimize their use of assessment, intervention, and prevention efforts with children and adolescents. Fortunately, as suggested by Cicchetti and Toth (1992), the last decade has witnessed an increase in dialogue between basic researchers and those who provide developmentally guided psychological assessment, prevention, and intervention services.

## Developmentally Informed Psychological Assessment

Most school psychologists who provide psychoeducational and psychological assessments utilize developmentally based tests and developmental norms, but many have not integrated a developmental perspective in framing or interpreting their assessment activities. Even behavioral observations can be undertaken from a developmental perspective. Children's classroom work provides essential information about how children understand the classroom program, and interviews with them provide invaluable perspectives about their reasons for classroom and playground transgressions. But to be prepared to utilize a developmental perspective in assessment, practitioners must have had opportunities to be grounded in developmental principles and to construct applications of developmental models and research findings into their assessment practices. As noted by Holmbeck and Kendall (1991), "Knowledge of developmental norms serves as a basis for making sound diagnostic judgments, assessing the need for treatment, and selecting the appropriate treatment. In terms of diagnosis, both over diagnosis and under diagnosis can result from a lack or erroneous knowledge of developmental norms" (p. 82).

The goal of psychoeducational and psychological assessment is to evaluate a child's educational and psychological functioning; determine the child's needs; respond to the referral questions; make recommendations for interventions; and provide feedback to the child and his or her parents and teachers in an understandable, developmentally appropriate manner that functions as a motivator for intervention and as an intervention itself. A developmental perspective offers a conceptual model for the assessment process, including guidelines for planning a developmental and family history.

## Developmental Model of Assessment

The model of assessment that a practitioner adopts profoundly affects the assessment process. A very useful overriding developmental model for assessment for the school psychologist is an ecological model. It emphasizes development in context and the transactions between the child and his or her environment that lead to development in the various domains of functioning. The ecological model allows for the integration of other developmental models. That is, the psychoanalytic, psychosocial, cognitive development, attachment, social learning, and transactional organismic perspective can be utilized under the umbrella of an ecological model. The practitioner does not need to discard useful knowledge from the other approaches but rather can integrate them to understand the process of development.

In evaluating the child's functioning from an ecological perspective, the practitioner must determine (1) the degree of normality of the current functioning in numerous domains—such as intellectual, cognitive, language, physical, academic, behavioral, emotional, and social functioning—and the resulting synchrony or lack of synchrony among them; (2) the factors and events that appear to have contributed positively and negatively to the child's functioning; (3) the current environmental factors that are contributing positively and negatively to the child's functioning; (4) the current health, resourcefulness, expectations, and motivation of the child's environments, especially family members and significant school personnel; (5) the current fit among the child, family, and school; and (6) the child's current educational, psychological, and health needs.

Each child has unique features, and thus every assessment is different. The child brings to the process an individual history and a particular way of responding to the environment. As part of the assessment process, the practitioner explains what the process is about, establishes rapport, conducts an interview, and asks the child to perform a number of tests and other tasks. Each child will respond in her or his own way. It is essential for the practitioner to have available a variety of methods of engaging with children of different ages and developmental levels. Although each child must be understood individually, developmental information and guidelines are useful for asking questions in ways that match the children's developmental level, what toys and games they enjoy, what typically motivates them, the basis of their logic, typical themes in play and conversation, and how they express and censor emotion. Skilled practitioners gain this knowledge through the study of developmental norms and descriptions; experience with and feedback from children; and actively staying in touch with children's worlds through the media, children's literature, parenting experiences, and observing children in natural settings. In addition, naturalistic observation is often undertaken as a beginning step, and observation of the child continues throughout the assessment process. The practitioner strives to observe the child along multiple developmental lines (Greenspan, 1981), keeping in mind age appropriateness, the expectations of the environment, and how the child functions on different tasks and in different settings. The application of developmental principles in assessment engages the school psychologist in constructing ever more elaborate frameworks for understanding normal and abnormal development. In summary, the school psychologist does not fit the child to the assessment process but instead fits the assessment process to the child.

## Developmental and Family History

Research findings have established that earlier events in the child's and family's life and how the child copes with them profoundly affect later functioning. A thorough and accurate developmental and family history enables the practitioner to understand the child's current functioning, to have insight into how the child might respond to intervention, and to help decide what types of intervention would be most effective. In a developmental history, the school psychologist needs information on the child's physical, medical, educational, cognitive, social, and emotional development, including when the child met early developmental milestones; how the child formed early attachments; how the child responded to early separations, losses, and traumas; who the primary parenting figures are; how the child mastered early developmental tasks; how the child has responded to and performed on particular academic tasks in school; and the quality of the child's family and peer relationships. In a family history, information is needed on how the family adjusted to the child's arrival; family

preparation for and expectations in school; changes and significant stresses in the family since the child's birth, such as additional children, marital separation or divorce, economic changes, moves, hospitalizations, substance abuse, and deaths in the family and extended family; how the family has coped positively and negatively with the changes and stresses; and what individuals in the family have been a significant resource for the child.

## Developmentally Informed Direct Intervention Activities

Knowledge of developmental psychology and developmental psychopathology has not been used routinely as a basis of intervention planning for children or adolescents. Although progress has been made in not adult-morphizing children, often insufficient attention has been paid to the developmental characteristics that make children and adolescents unique, as well as individual differences within groups of children at the same age or stage. School psychologists need to consider the course of development, developmental level, and pertinent developmental transitions (Holmbeck & Kendall, 1991), as well as contextual, ecological, gender, and cultural influences.

Knowledge of the developmental level can guide the stages of treatment. Selman (1980), representing a cognitive-developmental perspective, has stated that "what appears to be missing, at least in the case of children, is clear acknowledgement of the important role of developmental level as a foundation for determining how variables interact and what path therapy might most productively follow" (p. 225). Similarly, Kendall, Lerner, and Craighead (1984), representing a cognitive-behavioral perspective, have argued that "development means that the same experience—the same intervention—occurring or implemented at distinct points in the life course will be processed differently and may, as a consequence, have different effects . . . thus, developmental theories and data offer guideposts for the selection of an intervention" (p. 73).

## General Application of a Developmental Perspective to Counseling and Therapy

School psychologists are often called on to offer individual or group counseling and therapy. Group counseling requires the practitioner to consider simultaneously multiple variations in developmental functioning because of the range of children in a given group, although it is tempting to adopt the developmental uniformity myth—that is, the assumption that children and adolescents of different ages and developmental level are more alike than they are different, that all can be handled similarly in the treatment setting, and that all children of a certain age or stage are identical in their response to intervention (Kendall, 1984). The goals of counseling are to alleviate the child's emotional and cognitive distress; to change the child's behavior; to get the child back on track developmentally, that is, to meet successfully the challenges of upcoming developmental tasks; and ultimately, to facilitate a more positive fit between the child and the environment. An integrated developmental perspective specifies models for the process of change, a way to match the focus of the counseling intervention to the developmental level, and a way to set therapeutic goals and evaluate progress.

Models adopted to guide counseling usually correspond to the practitioner's explicit or implicit theories of developmental change. The models must also fit the needs of the child, the needs of significant others, and the relationship between the child and the practitioner. Each of the major developmental theories discussed proposes a model of change that can be applied to the therapeutic process. From the psychoanalytic perspective, the goal is to promote emotional and behavioral change by interpreting the child's defenses to allow unconscious elements that have been impeding development to become conscious. From the psychosocial perspective, the goal is to promote the optimal resolution of psychosocial crisis by supporting the child's struggles and by helping to secure healthy, supportive environments. From the cognitive-developmental perspective, the goal is to promote progression to higher stages of cognitive reasoning, thus allowing the child greater ego flexibility, a wider range of application of the new structural organization, the ability to coordinate more perspectives, and an increased capacity to handle new and previously unfamiliar problems. From the social learning and cognitive-behavioral perspectives, the goal is to promote behavioral change directly by reinforcing the desired behavior, by providing positive models and positive vicarious experiences, and by changing cognitions, for example, by helping a child learn cognitive mediation to control impulsive behavior or by helping a child alter negative self-evaluations. From the

attachment perspective, the goal is to promote interpersonal change by providing a secure base for exploration. From the ecological and the transactional-organismic perspectives, the goal is to promote behavioral, cognitive, emotional, and interpersonal change in the child and in the child's environment, especially in parents, family, teachers, and peers.

Although each of the models of change is applicable with children and adolescents and will promote change if matched with the individual's needs and developmental levels, an integrated perspective provides the most flexible and comprehensive model. The practitioner cannot effect change optimally by focusing on only one domain of functioning, be it emotional, cognitive, or behavioral. In counseling, the school psychologist needs to work simultaneously on current cognitive, emotional, and behavioral change. With few exceptions, work is also needed with significant adults in the child's world, especially parents and teachers. The practitioner must provide a setting that is developmentally appropriate; be aware of the developmental tasks with which the child is struggling and how earlier tasks were mastered; supply developmentally appropriate information, activities, feedback, and reinforcers; respond in ways that are understandable to the child; and proceed at a developmentally and individually appropriate rate. Furthermore, the same child is not at the same developmental level cognitively, socially, and emotionally, and therefore the school psychologist must be able to provide materials and ideas at different levels in different domains and to respond on different levels of the same child.

The developmental approach also offers a general method for setting and evaluating counseling goals. By understanding normal developmental progressions and age and culturally designated developmental tasks, the practitioner can evaluate the child's developmental levels and can set as the goals for counseling progression to higher, more advanced, and more mature levels of functioning and preparation for upcoming developmental tasks.

## Interventions in Adolescence: Unique Characteristics and Needs

As stated in the recent report of the Carnegie Council on Adolescent Development (1995), "Adolescence is one of the most fascinating and complex transitions in the life span: a time of accelerated growth and change second only to infancy; a time of expanding horizons, self-discovery, and emerging independence; and a time of metamorphosis from childhood to adulthood" (p. 12). Health and mental health concerns during the adolescent period include injuries and deaths from motor vehicle accidents, homicide, victimization and assault, use of alcohol and cigarettes, rise in use of marijuana, early sexual experience, increased pregnancy rates, increased incidence of depressive disorders, and an increasing rate of suicide (Millstein & Litt, 1990). Educational risks include academic failure and dropping out of school.

Thus, adolescence is a transitional developmental period between childhood and adulthood that is characterized by more biological, psychological, and social role changes than any other stage of life except infancy (Holmbeck & Updegrove, 1995). Adolescents are undergoing biological changes, psychological and cognitive changes, and social redefinition. There are profound changes in family and peer relationships, in the impact of the school, and as a result of working. Adolescents are also faced with the challenging developmental tasks of identity, achievement, sexuality, intimacy, autonomy, and attachment. Change is the defining feature of the adolescent period, and there is considerable variability in the onset, duration, and intensity of these changes. Despite a vast literature on such changes, and although many scholars have recommended that developmental theory be taken into account when designing treatments (Holmbeck & Updegrove, 1995), there have been few attempts to construct developmentally gauged treatment strategies for adolescents. More generally, there has been a marked lack of attention to developmental issues in the adolescent counseling and intervention literature.

A practitioner who neglects information on normative developmental processes during adolescence is at risk for providing therapeutic interventions that do not match the developmental level of the adolescent. Holmbeck and Updegrove (1995) suggest that intermittent developmentally gauged treatments may be more effective than continuous treatment and that peer-oriented approaches may be useful when working with adolescents who are withdrawn or isolated or when attempting to facilitate social-cognitive development.

Children and adolescents provide insights into their own developmental levels and their reasoning about events and behaviors. Parents and teachers need assistance in using observations and interactions to make an accurate assessment of the age-appropriateness of behaviors; teachers and school administrators need help in gathering developmentally based information from students and need up-to-date information about developmentally based interventions; parents, school personnel, and policymakers need to become more prevention-minded. School psychologists also can help parents become more adaptable and sensitive to the changing developmental needs of their offspring during transitions from home to school, from one level of school to another, and from childhood to adolescence.

## Developmentally Informed Prevention Efforts: Example of Childhood Aggression

An emphasis on the prevention of mental health disorders, through primary and secondary prevention efforts, is one of the legacies of the field of community psychology. Community psychology was very prominent in the late 1960s and developed as a reaction to the individual pathology models that dominated much of clinical psychology in the 1940s and 1950s. Community psychologists advocated a paradigm shift from therapeutic to preventive intervention; they were concerned that mental health resources were insufficient to meet the obvious need, that limited resources were distributed inequitably, and that only the most entrenched dysfunctions were identified and treated (Cowen, Trost, Izzo, Lorion, Dorr, & Isaacson, 1975). They argued that the appropriate approach is to build health or resources into the individual in the first place through the creation of social environments that produce mental health, as well as through early identification and prevention efforts. Primary prevention methods, which are designed to prevent the presentation of a disorder, include judicious application of educational approaches; the constructive modification of systems, settings, and environments; reducing sources of stress and training people to cope more effectively with stress; and promoting psychological health (Cowen, 1982). Secondary prevention methods, which are designed to lessen the presentation and/or severity of a disorder in populations at risk (and thus involve working with a more select population), include similar methods, as well as direct intervention with the population at risk. It readily follows that if early prevention efforts truly are more effective, children are indeed ideal targets for primary prevention programs and much of the work can be done in the schools. Schools provide convenient access to large numbers of children and their families, and education is both the natural vehicle for and backbone of primary prevention programming. Primary and secondary prevention programs conducted in the schools have been demonstrated to be effective (Adelman & Taylor, 1993).

The backbone of effective prevention programs is an understanding of the etiological pathways to disorders, although this does not necessarily or even typically guide treatment. However, without a knowledge of etiology, prevention efforts will be sorely mistargeted, as it is extremely clear that there are multiple and complex routes to health and positive mental health:

> Knowledge of developmental predictors has a number of implications for the treatment of children and adolescents. Developmental predictors are those behaviors at time one that reliably predict behaviors at time two. Knowledge of developmental predictors is of great use in treatment, especially in relation to prevention efforts. If it is known, based on longitudinal studies, that a specific set of behavioral deficits, for example, is related to more serious pathology later in the individual's life, we can treat the antecedent and presumably less severe disturbance and thus prevent the more serious subsequent disturbance. This is the goal of all prevention efforts. Knowledge of developmental antecedents and consequences is critical in establishing coherent prevention efforts. Knowledge of developmental antecedents of later, more maladaptive, behaviors, is useful—especially in regard to prevention efforts. (Holmbeck & Kendall, 1991, p. 86)

## The Development of Childhood Aggression

Serious aggression in childhood and adolescence—labeled delinquency by juvenile justice systems and conduct disorder by mental health systems—has significant individual and societal consequences and severely disrupts the educational environment for the disordered children and those around them. The development of aggression in childhood has been of grave concern to educators, developmentalists, developmental

psychopathologists, parents, health and mental health professionals, and of course school psychologists.

Aggression is seen as relatively stable developmentally, particularly with early onset, and intervention is challenging and often met with limited success. Unfortunately, serious aggression, often originating in childhood and diagnosed as conduct disorder in adolescence, is fairly prominent, with estimates ranging from 4% to 10%, with higher presentation in boys than in girls. The disorder is characterized by antisocial behaviors and constant conflict with others (peers, siblings, parents, and teachers) and in adolescence often results in physical injury, pain, and property damage. With early onset, it is also associated with other mental disorders (particularly depression), learning disabilities, peer difficulties, delinquency, drug and alcohol abuse, dropping out of school, suicide and criminality in adulthood. The etiological picture of the early onset type is complex and implicates the transaction of genetic predisposition, child temperament, disorganized or controlling early attachment patterns, childhood onset Attention Deficit Hyperactivity Disorder (ADHD), conflictual parent-child relationships, aggressive siblings, inconsistent parental management style, and psychopathology in and drug and alcohol misuse by the parents. With advancing age, serious aggression becomes increasingly resistant to change, despite extraordinary efforts in treatment (Kazdin, 1985). Not surprisingly, serious aggression has been depicted as one of the most intractable mental health problems of childhood and adolescence.

Recent developmental conceptualizations that are useful in reducing serious aggression include Moffitt's (1993) documentation of the distinct etiological and development course of early onset versus late onset of aggressive behavior, referred to as adolescent-limited and life-course-persistent antisocial behavior; Patterson, De-Baryshe, and Ramsey's (1989) developmental perspective on antisocial behavior; Caspi, Lynam, Moffit, and Silva's (1993) conceptualization of biological, dispositional, and contextual contributions to adolescent misbehavior in girls, which include early puberty and association with delinquent boys; Lyons-Ruth's (1996) recent review of attachment relationships among children with aggressive behavior problems, which suggests that disorganized or controlling early attachment patterns are precursors to aggression; and Loeber and Hay's (1994) integration of developmental approaches to aggression and conduct problems.

Tolan, Guerra, and Kendall (1995) provide an excellent summary of the current literature and conclude that (1) by the early elementary school years, childhood aggression is predictive of later aggressive and antisocial behavior; (2) even among the most aggressive children, fewer than 50% continue at elevated aggression levels or escalate to serious antisocial behavior; (3) different antisocial outcomes are related to variations in the risk factors; (4) the precise mechanisms and processes implicated in the development of antisocial behavior may vary by gender and ethnicity, as well as by other demographic distinctions; (5) convergent evidence supports the influence of social-cognitive factors, as well as those of parenting and family; and (6) there is an urgent need for multicomponent, multicontext interventions that are sensitive to risk factors and gender and ethnicity, focused on changing individuals, the influence of negative close interpersonal relations, and the contexts of development—particularly family but also school and neighborhood.

### *Prevention of Aggression in Childhood: The FAST Track Program*

We have selected a recent school-linked program to illustrate a prevention program based on developmental principles and research findings on the etiological pathways to aggressive disorders. The program, conducted by the Conduct Problems Prevention Research Group (1992), is entitled FAST Track Program, which stands for Families and Schools Together. It is designed as a developmental and clinical model for the treatment of conduct disorders through preventive intervention. The aim is to promote competence in the family, child, and schools and thus prevent conduct problems, poor social relationships, and school failure. This secondary prevention program targets a sample of first-graders who are identified as high risk because of disruptive behavior both at school and at home. The program provides interventions for a two-year period. The integrated components of the model include parent training, home visiting, social skills training, academic tutoring, and classroom interventions.

The investigators cite six innovations that they believe will contribute to the success of their prevention model; all of them involve principles from developmental psychology and developmental psychopathology: (1) the model is built on a clear developmental conceptualization of the problem of early aggression and its developmental trajectory; (2) the model is based on the belief that combining universal and target interventions at the same time will lead to reciprocal effects; (3) the choice of periods of intensive prevention efforts are defined by important transitions or choice points in which children are most at risk and families are most receptive; (4) the program takes a multisystemic focus by attempting to build appropriate skills, attitudes, and expectancies in each system (family, school, and peers), as well as positive relations among these systems; (5) the intervention is structured in a way that recognizes that this is a developmental problem, one that is unlikely to be solved in a single developmental period; and (6) parents and other family members are treated as collaborative partners in the process of helping their children succeed, and their involvement is central.

### Summary of the Application to Assessment, Intervention, and Prevention

As the interaction between normal and abnormal development has evolved, the application of theory and research findings from developmental psychology and developmental psychopathology to assessment, intervention, and prevention has increased. The results of investigations about the continuities and discontinuities of adaptive and maladaptive early development have underscored the intricacy of the developmental process, highlighted the importance of prevention and early assessment and intervention, and heightened the awareness of positive or negative reorganizations at subsequent developmental periods despite the level of the previous adaptation (Cicchetti & Toth, 1992). Combined with over 100 years of knowledge on the development of the normal child, recent knowledge of risk conditions and disorders, as well as information on the etiology and longitudinal course of high-risk conditions and psychopathological disorders, sets the stage for increasingly powerful action. Etiological models of the development of health and disorders increasingly reflect the true complexity inherent in development, guides prevention efforts, and informs assessment and intervention activities.

## SUMMARY AND CONCLUSIONS

The theoretical and empirical knowledge base of developmental psychology, in combination with the new field of developmental psychopathology, is essential to the practice of school psychology, particularly in psychological assessment, intervention, and prevention. Developmental psychology and developmental psychopathology contribute to school psychology at three levels: descriptive, explanatory, and predictive. To illustrate the contributions of developmental psychology and psychopathology to school practice, we first presented their parameters and then the obstacles to their integration with practice, including the unique perspectives of researchers and clinicians, distinct views of human nature, the dominance of behavioral approaches, the phenomena of adult-morphizing children, and the misunderstanding of the application of Piagetian theory and research findings. We then gave a historical review of the last 100 years of the field of developmental psychology, followed by a presentation of the usefulness of theory and a succinct review of seven major developmental theories: Freud's psychoanalytic theory, Erikson's psychosocial theory, social learning theory, Piaget's theory of cognitive development, Bowlby's attachment theory, Bronfenbrenner's ecological theory, and the organismic-transactional theory of development. We presented an integrated, contemporary view of the developing child, highlighting six principles of development that should be useful to the school psychologist: children are active and influence their development, the interaction and transaction between children and the environment (nature and nurture) is complex, development consists of both qualitative and quantitative change, later development depends on earlier development, development is affected by risk and vulnerability and protective factors, and responding to opportunities for developmental change is a complex but cautiously optimistic process.

We then discussed the usefulness of developmental psychology and psychopathology to practice—specifically, assessment, intervention, and prevention—and gave guidelines for developmentally informed psychological assessment; developmentally informed psychotherapeutic interventions, with a focus on adolescents; and developmentally informed prevention efforts, using the example of school-linked prevention. It is hoped that the information in this chapter encourages school psychologists to integrate a developmental perspective into their thinking and practice and a strong developmental orientation into their training models, and that it produces a next generation of school psychologists that can truly call themselves developmentalists.

# REFERENCES

Achenbach, T. M. (1982). *Developmental psychopathology* (2nd ed.). New York: Wiley.

Achenbach, T. M. (1990). What is "developmental" about developmental psychopathology. In J. Rolf (Ed.), *Risk and protective factors in the development of psychopathology* (pp. 29–48). Cambridge: Press Syndicate of the University of Cambridge.

Achenbach, T. M., & Edelbrock, C. (1983). *Manual for the child behavior checklist and revised child behavior profile.* Burlington: University of Vermont.

Adelman, H. S., & Taylor, L. (1993). School-based mental health: Toward a comprehensive approach. *Journal of Mental Health Administration, 20*(1), 32–45.

Ainsworth, M. D. S. (1969). Object relations, dependency, and attachment: A theoretical review of the infant-mother relationship. *Child Development, 40,* 969–1025.

American Psychiatric Association. (1980). *Diagnostic and statistical manual of mental disorders* (3rd ed.). Washington, DC: Author.

American Psychiatric Association. (1987). *Diagnostic and statistical manual of mental disorders* (3rd ed., rev.). Washington, DC: Author.

American Psychiatric Association. (1994). *Diagnostic and statistical manual of mental disorders* (4th ed.). Washington, DC: Author.

Apter, S. J., & Conoley, J. C. (1984). *Childhood behavior disorders and emotional disturbance.* Englewood Cliffs, NJ: Prentice-Hall.

Attie, I., Brooks-Gunn, J., & Peterson, A. C. (1990). A developmental perspective on eating disorders and eating problems. In M. Lewis & S. M. Miller (Eds.), *Handbook of developmental psychopathology* (pp. 409–420). New York: Plenum.

Bandura, A. (1969). *Principles of behavior modification.* New York: Holt, Rinehart & Winston.

Bandura, A. (1977). *Social learning theory.* Englewood Cliffs, NJ: Prentice-Hall.

Barker, R. G., Kounin, J. S., & Wright, H. F. (1943). *Child behavior development.* New York: McGraw-Hill.

Biber, B. (1934). A nursery school puts psychology to work. *69 Bank Street, 1,* 1–11.

Bierman, K. L. (1983). Cognitive development and clinical interviews with children. In B. B. Lahey & A. E. Kazdin (Eds.), *Advances in clinical child psychology* (Vol. 6). New York: Plenum.

Bowlby, J. (1958). The nature of the child's tie to his mother. *International Journal of Psychoanalysis, 39,* 350–373.

Bowlby, J. (1969). *Attachment and loss: Vol. 1. Attachment,* New York: Basic Books.

Bowlby, J. (1979). *The making and breaking of affectional bonds*. London: Tavistock.

Bowlby, J. (1980). *Attachment and loss: Vol. 3 Loss*. New York: Basic Books.

Bowlby, J. (1982). Attachment and loss: Retrospect and prospect. *American Journal of Orthopsychiatry, 52,* 664–678.

Bronfenbrenner, J. (1979). *The ecology of human development: Experiments by nature and design*. Cambridge, MA: Harvard University Press.

Cairns, R. B. (1983). The emergence of developmental psychology. In P. H. Mussen (Ed.), *Handbook of child psychology: Vol. 1. History, theory, and methods*. New York: Wiley.

Campos, J. J., Barrett, K. C., Lamb, M. E., Goldsmith, H. H., & Stenberg, C. (1983). Socioemotional development. In P. H. Mussen (Ed.), *Handbook of child psychology: Vol. II. Infancy and developmental psychobiology*. New York: Wiley.

Carlson, C. I., Tharinger, D. J., Bricklin, P. M., DeMers, S. T., & Paavola, J. C. (1996). Health care reform and psychological practice in school. *Professional Psychology: Research and Practice, 27,* 14–23.

Carmichael, L. (1946). *Manual of child psychology*. New York: Wiley.

Carnegie Council on Adolescent Development. (1995). *Great transitions: Preparing adolescents for a new century*. New York: Carnegie Corporation.

Caspi, A., Lynam, D., Moffitt, T. E., & Silva, P. A. (1993). Unraveling girls' delinquency: Biological, dispositional, and contextual contributions to adolescent misbehavior. *Developmental Psychology, 29,* 19–30.

Cicchetti, D., & Schneider-Rosen, K. (1986). An organizational approach to childhood depression. In M. Rutter, C. E. Izard, & P. B. Read (Eds.), *Depression in young people: Clinical and developmental perspectives*. New York: Guilford.

Cicchetti, D., & Sroufe, A. L. (1978). An organizational view of affect: Illustration from the study of Down's syndrome infants. In M. Lewis & L. Rosenblum (Eds.), *The development of affect*. New York: Plenum.

Cicchetti, D., & Toth, S. L. (1992). The role of developmental theory in prevention and intervention. *Developmental and Psychopathology, 4,* 489–493.

Conduct Problems Prevention Research Group. (1992). A developmental and clinical model for the prevention of conduct disorder: The FAST Track Program. *Development and Psychopathology, 4,* 509–527.

Cowan, P. (1978). *Piaget with feeling*. New York: Holt, Rinehart & Winston.

Cowen, E. L. (1982). Primary prevention: Children and schools. *Journal of Children in Contemporary Society,* 57–68.

Cowen, E. L., Trost, M. A., Lorion, R. P., Dorr, D.,

Izzo, L. D., & Isaacson, R. V. (1975). *New ways in school mental health: Early detection and prevention of school maladaptation*. New York: Human Services Press.

Dollard, J., Miller, N. E., Doob, L. W., Mowrer, O. H., & Sears R. R. (1939). *Frustration and aggression*. New Haven, CT: Yale University Press.

Dweck, C. S., & Elliot, E. S. (1983). Achievement motivation. In P. H. Mussen (Ed.), *Handbook of child psychology: Vol. IV. Socialization, personality and social development*. New York: Wiley.

Edelbrock, C. S. (1984). Developmental considerations. In T. H. Ollendick & M. Hersen (Eds.), *Child behavioral assessment: Principles and procedures*. Elmsford, NY: Pergamon.

Eisenberg, L. (1977). Development as a unifying concept in psychiatry. *British Journal of Psychiatry, 3,* 225–237.

Erikson, E. (1950). *Childhood and society*. New York: Norton.

Erikson, E. (1977). *Toys and reasons*. New York: Norton.

Flavell, J. (1963). *The developmental psychology of Jean Piaget*. Princeton, NJ: Van Nostrand.

Garber, J. (1984). Classification of child psychopathology: A developmental perspective. *Child Development, 1,* 30–48.

Garmezy, N. (1993). Vulnerability and resilience. In D. Funder, R. Parke, C. Tomlinson-Keasey, & K. Widaman (Eds.). *Studying lives through time: Personality and development* (pp. 377–398). Washington, DC: American Psychological Association.

Gelfand, D. M., & Peterson, L. (1985). *Child development and psychopathology*. Beverly Hills, CA: Sage.

Gesell, A. L. (1928). *Infancy and human growth*. New York: Macmillan.

Gesell, A. L. (1940). *The first five years of life*. New York: Harper & Row.

Goodman, J. D. (1972). The psychiatric interview. In B. B. Wolman (Ed.), *Manual of child psychopathology*. New York: McGraw-Hill.

Greenspan, S. (1981). *The clinical interview of the child*. New York: McGraw-Hill.

Hall, C. S. (1954). *A primer of Freudian psychology*. New York: World Press.

Harlow, H. F. (1958). The nature of love. *American Psychologist, 13,* 673–685.

Harlow, H. F., & Harlow, M. K. (1965). The affectional systems. In A. M. Schier, H. F. Harlow, & F. Stollnitz (Eds.), *Behavior of nonhuman primates: Modern research trends* (Vol. 2). New York: Academic Press.

Hartman, D. P., Roper, B. L., & Bradford, D. C. (1979). Some relationshiips between behavioral and a traditional assessment. *Journal of Behavioral Assessment, 1,* 3–21.

Hartshorne, H., & May, M. S. (1928). *Studies in the nature of character*. New York: Macmillan.

Hobbs, N. (1966). Helping disturbed children:

Psychological and ecological strategies. *American Psychologist, 27,* 1105–1115.

Hobbs, N. (1982). *The troubled and troubling child.* San Francisco: Jossey-Bass.

Holmbeck, G. N., & Kendall, P. C. (1991). Clinical-childhood-developmental interface: Implications for treatment. In P. R. Martin (Ed.), *Handbook of behavioral therapy and psychological science: An integrative approach* (pp. 73–99). New York: Pergamon.

Holmbeck, G. N., & Updegrove, A. L. (1995). Clinical-developmental interface: Implications for developmental research for adolescent psychotherapy. *Psychotherapy, 32,* 16–33.

Hops, H., & Greenwood, G. R. (1981). Social skills deficits. In E. J. Mash & L. G. Terdel (Eds.), *Intellectual and social deficiencies.* New York: Gardner Press.

Hughes, J. N. (1986). Interviewing children. In J. Dillard & R. Reilley, *Interviewing and communication skills.* Columbus, OH: Merrill.

Jersild, A. T., Markey, F. V., & Jersild, C. L. (1933). Children's fears, dreams wishes, daydreams likes dislikes, pleasant and unpleasant memories: A study by the interview method of 400 children aged 5 to 12. *Child Development Monographs* (No. 12). New York: Teachers College Press.

Kanfer, R., Eyberg, S., & Krahn, G. L. (1983). Interviewing strategies in child assessment. In C. E. Walker & M. C. Roberts (Eds.), *Handbook of clinical child psychology.* New York: Wiley.

Kazdin, A. E. (1985). Recent advances in child behavior therapy. In S. I. Pfeiffer (Ed.), *Clinical child psychology.* New York: Grune & Stratton.

Kendall, P. C. (1984). Social cognition and problem solving: A developmental and child-clinical interface. In B. Gholson & T. L. Rosenthal (Eds.), *Applications of cognitive-developmental theory* (pp. 115–148). New York: Academic Press.

Kendall, P. (1985). Toward a cognitive-behavioral model of child psychopathology and a critique of related interventions. *Journal of Abnormal Child Psychology, 13* (3), 357–372.

Kendall, P. C., Lerner, R. M., & Craighead, W. E. (1984). Human development and intervention in childhood psychopathology. 71–82.

Kendler, H. H., & Kendler, T. S. (1962). Vertical and horizontal processes in problem solving. *Psychological Review, 69,* 1–16.

Kohlberg, L. (1969). Stage and sequence: The cognitive developmental approach to socialization. In D. A. Goslin (Ed.), *Handbook of socialization theory.* Skokie, IL: Rand McNally.

Lerner, R. M. (1986). *Concepts and theories of human development* (2nd ed.). New York: Random House.

Lewin, K. (1931). Environmental forces in child behavior and development. In C. Murchison (Ed.), *A handbook of child psychology.* Worcester, MA: Clark University Press.

Loeber, R., & Hay, D. F. (1994). Developmental approaches to aggression and conduct problems. In M. Rutter & D. F. Hay (Eds.), *Development through life: A handbook for clinicians* (pp. 488–516). Boston, Blackwell Scientific.

Lorenz, K. Z. (1935). Der Kumpan in der Umvelt des Vogels. *Journal fur Ornithologie, 83,* 137–213, 289–413.

Lyons-Ruth, K. (1996). Attachment relationships among children with aggressive behavior problems: The role of disorganized early attachment patterns. *Journal of Consulting and Clinical Psychology, 64,* 64–73.

Mahoney, M. J., & Nezworski, M. T. (1985). Cognitive behavioral approaches to children's problems. *Journal of Abnormal Child Psychology, 13*(3), 467–476.

Mash, E. J., & Terdal, L. G. (1981). *Behavioral assessment of childhood disorders.* New York: Guilford.

Masten, A. S. (1989). Resilience in development: Implications of the study of successful adaptation for developmental psychopathology. In D. Cicchetti (Ed.), *The emergence of a discipline: Rochester symposium on developmental psychopathology* (Vol. 1, pp. 261–294).

Masten, A. S., & Braswell, L. (1991). Developmental psychopathology: An integrative framework. In P. R. Martin (Ed.), *Handbook of behavioral therapy and psychological science: An integrative approach* (pp. 35–56).

Mead, G. H. (1934). *Mind, self, and society.* Chicago: University of Chicago Press.

Miller, P. (1989). *Theories of developmental psychology* (2nd ed.). San Francisco: Freeman.

Millstein, S. G., & Litt, I. F. (1990). Adolescent health. In S. Feldman & G. Elliot, *At the threshold* (pp. 431–456). Cambridge: Harvard University Press.

Moffitt, T. E. (1993). Adolescent-limited and life-course-persistent antisocial behavior: A developmental taxonomy. *Psychological Review, 100,* 674–701.

Ollendick, T. H., & King, N. J. (1991). Developmental factors in child behavioral assessment. In P. R. Martin (Ed.), *Handbook of behavioral therapy and psychological science: An integrative approach* (pp. 57–72).

Patterson, G. R., DeBaryshe, B. D., & Ramsey, E. (1989). A developmental perspective on antisocial behavior. *American Psychologist, 44,* 329–335.

Piaget, J. (1926). *The language and thought of the child.* New York: Harcourt, Brace.

Piaget, J. (1932). *The moral judgment of the child.* London: Kegan Paul.

Piaget, J. (1950). *The psychology of intelligence.* New York: Harcourt, Brace.

Piaget, J. (1970). Piaget's theory. In P. H. Mussen (Ed.), *Carmichael's manual of child psychology* (Vol. 1). New York: Wiley.

Reese, H., & Overton, W. (1970). Models of development and theories of development. In L. R. Goulet & P. Baltes (Eds.), *Life span developmental psychology: Research and theory*. New York: Academic Press.

Reisman, J. M. (1973). *Principles of psychotherapy with children*. New York: Wiley.

Rosen, H. (1984). *Piagetian dimensions of clinical relevance*. New York: Columbia University Press.

Ross, A. O. (1978). Behavior therapy with children. In S. L. Garfield & A. E. Bergin (Eds.), *Handbook of psychotherapy and behavior change: An empirical analysis*. New York: Wiley.

Rutter, M. (1981). Stress, coping, and development: Some issues and some questions. *Journal of Child Psychology and Psychiatry, 22*, 323–356.

Rutter, M. (1986). The developmental psychopathology of depression: Issues and perspectives. In M. Rutter, C. E. Izard, & P. B. Read (Eds.), *Depression in young people: Clinical and developmental perspectives*. New York: Guilford.

Rutter, M. (1990). Psychosocial resilience and protective mechanisms. In J. Rolf (Ed.), *Risk and protective factors in the development of psychopathology* (pp. 181–214). Cambridge: Press Syndicate of the University of Cambridge.

Rutter, M., & Garmezy, N. (1983). Developmental psychopathology. In P. H. Mussen (Eds.), *Handbook of child psychology: Vol. IV. Socialization, personality and social development*. New York: Wiley.

Santostefano, S. (1978). *A biodevelopmental approach to clinical child psychology*. New York: Wiley.

Scarr, S. (1985). Constructing psychology: Making facts and fables for our times. *American Psychologist, 40*, 499–512.

Sears, R. R. (1944). Experimental analysis of psychoanalytic phenomena. In J. McV. Hunt (Ed.), *Personality and the behavior disorders* (Vol. 1). New York: Ronald Press.

Selman, R. L. (1980). *The growth of interpersonal understanding: Developmental and clinical analyses*. New York: Academic Press.

Shantz, C. U. (1975). The development of social cognition. In E. M. Hetherington (Ed.), *Review of child development research* (Vol. 5). Chicago: University of Chicago Press.

Shirk, S. (1988). *Cognitive development and child psychotherapy*. New York: Plenum.

Sroufe, L. A. (1979a). The coherence of individual development. *American Psychologist, 34*, 834–841.

Sroufe, L. A. (1979b). Socioemotional development. In J. Osofsky (Ed.), *Handbook of infant development*. New York: Wiley.

Sroufe, L. A. (1989). Resilience in development: Implications of the study of successful adaptation for developmental psychopathology. In D. Cicchetti (Ed.), *The emergence of a discipline: Rochester symposium on developmental psychopathology* (Vol. 1, pp. 13–40).

Sroufe, L. A., & Rutter, M. (1984). The domain of developmental psychopathology. *Child Development, 55*, 17–29.

Swap, S. M. (1974). Disturbing classroom behaviors: A developmental and ecological view. *Exceptional Children, 41*, 163–172.

Tharinger, D. J., Lambert, N. M., Bricklin, P. M., Feshbach, N., Johnson, N. F., Oakland, T. D., Paster, V. S., & Sanchez, W. (1996). Educational reform: Challenges for psychology and psychologists. *Professional Psychology: Research and Practice, 27*, 24–33.

Tolan, P. H., Guerra, N. G., & Kendall, P. C. (1995). A developmental-ecological perspective on antisocial behavior in children and adolescents: Toward a unified risk and intervention framework. *Journal of Consulting and Clinical Psychology, 63*, 579–584.

Turiel, E. (1983). *The development of social knowledge: Morality and convention*. Cambridge: Cambridge University Press.

Vigotsky, L. S. (1939). Thought and speech. *Psychiatry, 2*, 29–54.

Watson, J. B. (1914). *Behavior: An introduction to comparative psychology*. New York: Holt.

Watson, J. B. (1928). *Psychological care of infant and child*. New York: Norton.

Werner, H. (1948). *Comparative psychology of mental development*. New York: International Universities Press.

White, S. H. (1976). The active organism in the theoretical behaviorism. *Human Development, 19*, 99–107.

Worchel, F. (1986). Interviewing adolescents. In J. Dillard & R. Reilley (Eds.), *Interviewing and communication skills*. Columbus, OH: Merrill.

## CHAPTER 7

# WHAT COGNITIVE PSYCHOLOGY HAS TO SAY TO SCHOOL PSYCHOLOGY: SHIFTING PERSPECTIVES AND SHARED PURPOSES

PATRICIA A. ALEXANDER
P. KAREN MURPHY
*University of Maryland*

One need only compare the contents of this chapter to the contribution by Glover and Corkill in the second edition of the *Handbook of School Psychology* (Gutkin & Reynolds, 1990) to recognize that many of the issues central to cognitive psychology at the outset of this decade have been expanded or altered in significant ways. In short, cognitive psychology is no longer equated with the theory of information processing, so prevalent in the 1970s and 1980s. Although many valuable lessons learned from this important branch of cognition have been retained, such as those related to knowledge, memory, and strategic processing, new themes have appeared on the horizon. Specifically, as cognitive psychology moves into the next decade, it will probably focus much more on the thinking, reasoning, and creative processing of individuals as they function within various sociocultural contexts; as they reason, problem-solve, or create with others; and as they self-regulate and self-direct their thoughts and actions. In essence, the picture of cognition will become far more complex and will be frequently linked with noncognitive and contextual factors.

Based on the writings in school psychology (e.g., Bradley-Johnson, Johnson, & Jacob-Timm, 1995; Conoley & Gutkin, 1995; Tapasak & Keller, 1995), it is further evident that this field, perhaps partly because of the inclusion movement, is also undergoing a fairly recent and equally dramatic transformation in its orientation and espoused missions (Fuchs, Fuchs, Phillips, Hamlett, & Karns, 1995). For example, in the school psychology literature, there is enhanced dialogue around such topics as inclusion, outcome-based education, and alternative ecological assessment practices (Bradley-Johnson et al., 1995; Fuchs & Fuchs, 1994). What we will attempt to demonstrate here is that the contemporary themes of cognitive psychology, as well as the sociocultural, educational, and political forces that have been the catalysts for them, bear a striking resemblance to the themes and forces reflected in the expanded scope and mission of school psychology. In many ways, the research and practice in both cognitive psychology and school psychology have been influenced by work in such related fields as cultural anthropology, social psychology, teacher education, and educational policy. The end result is an increasingly interdisciplinary appearance in these two educational domains that succeeds in occasionally blurring the lines of what it means to be a cognitive psychologist or a school psychologist in the educational system.

One positive outcome of this broadened perspective is that cognitive psychology and school psychology have come to share more common ground and, thus, have even more to say to each other. As a means of structuring this conversation, we have chosen five themes that have roots in this common ground: the power and role of knowledge, skillful and strategic processing, the interrelationship of cognition and motivation, the development of academic competence, and the influence of context or situation.

# THE POWER AND ROLE OF KNOWLEDGE

Perhaps the most enduring legacy of cognitive psychology in the last quarter century is the recognition of the significant role that individuals' background or prior knowledge plays in subsequent learning and development. To put it simply, the knowledge that individuals currently possess is a potent force in determining what information they will attend to (e.g., Anderson, Pichert, & Shirey, 1983; Hidi, 1990; Reynolds & Shirey, 1988) and how that information will be perceived (e.g., Gibson, 1966). Background or prior knowledge also influences what people judge as relevant or important information (e.g., Alexander, Jetton, Kulikowich, & Woehler, 1994; Pichert & Anderson, 1977; Schraw & Dennison, 1994) and what they comprehend and remember from what they see or hear (e.g., Alvermann, Smith, & Readence, 1985; Anderson, Reynolds, Schallert, & Goetz, 1977; Pritchard, 1990). In essence, the knowledge base, which has been described as the total of all an individual knows or believes (Alexander, Schallert, & Hare, 1991), is indeed a scaffold that supports the construction of future learning (American Psychological Association Task Force on Psychology in Education, 1993).

While this acknowledgment of the power of knowledge has been retained in cognitive psychology, many notions about the nature and role of knowledge have been modified in this decade. Two emergent qualities of knowledge that we will discuss are its multidimensionality and its imperfect nature. In addition, we will explore the relationship between knowing and believing and its potential implications for school learning.

## Knowledge as a Multidimensional Construct

In previous writings in cognition, the construct of knowledge was often portrayed, intentionally or unintentionally, as a singular entity that consistently exerts a positive force in learning. Further, knowledge has been cast as largely invari-

ant, remaining unchanged from context to context (Glaser, 1984; Sternberg, 1985). What is now evident from the literature is that knowledge can no longer be conceived as a single, unified construct (Alexander, 1996, Murphy & Woods, 1996). Knowledge is not *one* thing, but many things, all intricately and inextricably interwoven in the human mind. That is, since the early information-processing studies, knowledge has come to be viewed as a multifaceted construct that is manifest in diverse forms and that encompasses many interactive knowledge dimensions (Alexander et al., 1991; de Jong & Ferguson-Hessler, 1996).

## *States and Levels of Knowing*

According to the literature, individuals' prior knowledge can exist in at least three states: *declarative, procedural,* and *conditional* (Anderson, 1983; Paris, Lipson, & Wixson, 1983; Ryle, 1949). These three states have been characteristically referred to, respectively, as the "whats," the "how tos" and the "whens and wheres" of our knowledge base. Thus, a sixth-grader may be able to give a workable definition of summarization (declarative knowledge) and may be able to produce an acceptable summary of a reading selection (procedural knowledge). Moreover, this sixth-grader may have acquired some understanding of the conditions under which summarization may prove a useful tactic (conditional knowledge).

One sad commentary on the educational system is its propensity toward the transmission of declarative knowledge without adequate attention to procedural and conditional understandings (Cognition and Technology Group at Vanderbilt, 1990; Reimann & Schult, 1996). Consequently, students often acquire a large body of facts and figures, and even rudimentary procedures, without any well-developed sense of how and why this knowledge can and should be applied. The result is the expansion of inert knowledge (Whitehead, 1929/1957)—knowledge that lies dormant, playing no apparent or significant role in learners' thoughts or deeds. It was Whitehead's judgment that such inert knowledge ultimately leads to "mental dryrot" (p. 2). According to Whitehead and others (e.g., Gelman & Greeno, 1989), students' subsequent growth and development in academic areas would be seriously hampered unless their conceptual understanding extended well beyond the declarative stage, that is, unless they possesses a principled body of relevant knowledge. We will return to this issue again when we discuss the development of academic competence.

Not only does prior knowledge exist in various states, but it can also assume a variety of forms, including sociocultural knowledge (Cole & D'Andrade, 1982; Lipson, 1983), strategy knowledge (Weinstein & Mayer, 1986), and personal beliefs, like self-schema (Garner & Alexander, 1994; Pintrich, 1994). In addition, some of this knowledge operates within the realm of consciousness and can become the object of thought and analysis (Prawat, 1989). This "thought about" knowledge has been referred to as explicit knowledge. In comparison, a large segment of one's knowledge base is tacitly known and, therefore, functions indirectly or subconsciously in human thought and deed (Broadbent, FitzGerald, & Broadbent, 1986; Reber, 1989; Sternberg, Conway, Ketron, & Bernstein, 1981). At times, tacit knowledge, or the implicit theories that emerge from this unconscious body of knowledge, can be resurrected from memory and brought to the level of awareness, where it can be reflected on and communicated. At other times, such understandings, as in the form of implicit theories, remain undiscovered and thus unexamined (Alexander & Dochy, 1994, 1995). The task for cognitivists and school psychologists, in these cases, is to assist in the unearthing of deeply held knowledge that may exert an influence on students' thinking and behaving. Such a task is by no means easy to accomplish, as documented in the writings about verbal report data (Ericsson & Simon, 1984; Garner, 1988; White, 1980).

Consider one's sociocultural knowledge as an illustration. Based on the available evidence, it would seem that much of an individual's sociocultural knowledge lies within the realm of tacit understanding (Cole & D'Andrade, 1982; Greene & Ackerman, 1995; Pritchard, 1990). That is, only certain components of this knowledge exist in a form that can be analyzed and communicated. For instance, a high school student can describe in some detail the holidays and rituals that are aspects of her religion, and she can talk about her family lineage and Italian and Scotch-Irish heritage. However, she is largely unaware of how her religion and heritage intrude themselves into her day-to-day reasoning and behavior.

## Schooled and Nonschooled Understanding

Sometimes the dimensions of one's knowledge base work in concert. At other times, however, these dimensions operate in conflict with one another, as when one's informal knowledge or spontaneous concepts are in opposition to the formal or scientific notions that are the mainstay of the instructional enterprise (e.g., Alexander, 1992; Gardner, 1991; Vygotsky, 1934/1986). We can observe the effects when schooled and nonschooled understandings are discrepant in such fields as physics, where day-to-day observations can mislead or cloud individuals' understanding of fundamental principles. In these cases, students often revert to more primitive or real-world interpretations even after correctly espousing the formal concept in more controlled or structured environments (e.g. Alvermann et al., 1985; Champagne, Kloper, & Anderson, 1980). That is, these students *appear* to understand certain physics principles, but in reality they have perhaps acquired only a superficial understanding that is effectively overridden by out-of-school occurrences (diSessa, 1982, 1989). One typical example is the high school student who conveys an understanding of curvilinear impetus when called on to perform textbook problems in her physics class but miscalculates the pathway of a thrown softball when on the playing field.

One lesson to be learned from this example is that schools, for good or for bad, are not the sole source, and perhaps not even the principal source, of relevant knowledge for students. Academic understandings are, in reality, only a portion of one's knowledge base. Much of what individuals know can have its source in informal, everyday experiences, some of which arise from interactions with significant individuals in the family unit, as well as peer, community, work, or religious groups (Rogoff & Chavajay, 1995). Yet, vicarious or indirect experiences can also be quite influential sources of informal or nonschooled knowledge, particularly in media-driven, information-rich, postindustrial societies, such as our own, where technology is abundant and where information moves with remarkable speed along the information superhighway (Postman, 1992, 1995).

The research community has only recently begun to investigate the differences between formal or schooled knowledge and the knowledge that is acquired from everyday experiences (e.g., Carraher, Carraher, & Schliemann, 1985; Cole, 1990; Saxe, 1992; Stewart, 1987). So much more needs to be learned about the source of students' understanding and its impact on their thoughts and behaviors (Alexander & Murphy, 1998;

Gardner, 1991), particularly if educators are to assist students who have problems learning and functioning in academic contexts.

One other point needs to be stressed in this discussion about schooled versus nonschooled understandings. Despite their power, nonschooled experiences are not always positive. Although the physics example offers evidence of this for a more structured domain, the lessons from multicultural education serve as another powerful testimony. Indeed, from a very young age, children learn about inequality and prejudice by watching the behaviors of those around them—behaviors directed toward individuals who are diverse—and by hearing the messages of distrust, ignorance, and hatred that punctuate their daily lives (Banks, 1989, 1992; Derman-Sparks & Anti-Bias Curriculum Task Force, 1989; Katz, 1982; Sleeter & Grant, 1994).

These actions and messages can frame children's self-images, as well as their perceptions of what is good or positive in others. How are educators to combat the power of everyday experiences that may override the more positive lessons that are formally taught in educational communities? For one, educators must be sure to send clear and consistent messages that reflect their actions. Given the research on social modeling, the old adage of "do as I do" certainly remains viable (Bandura, 1993). Further, those in school psychology or related fields should take advantage of the power of nonschooled experiences by attempting to engage students not only in the classroom but also simultaneously where they live, work, and play. Finally, educators must be proactive in their attempts to change students' thoughts and behaviors by reaching into the social, political, and economic institutions that also play roles in their lives (Ogbu, 1992).

## Imperfect Nature of Knowing

We have already described how knowledge is multifaceted and how it exists and operates in many forms and at many levels. As we have also suggested, knowledge can remain buried in memory, as in the case of tacit notions or implicit theories (e.g., Alexander, 1992; Gardner, 1991; Prawat, 1989). Still another attribute of knowledge is relevant to this discussion, that is, the incomplete and imperfect nature of human knowledge and the consequences that this imperfection holds for learning and development (e.g., Alexander, in press; Guzzetti & Hynd, in press). In truth, most if not all of the concepts in one's realm of knowl-

edge are incomplete or flawed in some way. Even the expert in some designated field cannot be expected to know everything that is possible to be known about any given idea. Research on the incompleteness of human knowledge can be found in the literature on conceptual change, conceptual development, and misconceptions. Because of the differences of opinions on this topic in the literature, perhaps resulting from various theoretical frameworks, it is probably worthwhile for us to start with a brief overview of the assumptions that we hold about concepts and about conceptual change.

First, unlike some who profess more radical constructivist views (e.g., von Glaserfeld, 1991) or those who hold to the tenets of critical theory (Young, 1990), we espouse more moderate social constructivist views of knowledge (Harris & Graham, 1994; Woods & Murphy, 1996). Specifically, it is our belief that the concepts individuals form are truly unique constructions that result from both personal and vicarious experiences. However, we also believe that educators can and should evaluate students' conceptual understandings against accepted, albeit changing and relativistic, standards. For example, whereas no two children will internalize the concept of *dog* in an identical manner, it is still justifiable for educators to intervene when a young child mistakenly identifies a cat as a dog. To do otherwise may be to reinforce a misunderstanding or miss an opportunity to enrich or extend an individual's current understanding.

Second, from the standpoint of academic domains, not all concepts are of equal importance (e.g., Alexander, 1992; diSessa, 1982; Spiro & Jehng, 1990). In biology, for instance, it is critical for students to grasp the distinction between living and nonliving entities if they are to progress further in their learning (Carey, 1985). In other words, some particular concepts are pivotal to the type of principled understanding that makes a learner competent in a specific field (Gelman & Greeno, 1989). When these central concepts are malformed, they can have the serious effect of distorting subsequent notions (West & Pines, 1985). Precisely because of the significant impact these key ideas can have on related learnings, they are what we and West and Pines call misconceptions.

Third, we concur with Rumelhart and Norman (1981) that individuals' understandings can be changed in both subtle and dramatic ways through the processes they have labeled accretion, tuning, or restructuring. *Accretion*, as Rumelhart and Norman describe it, corresponds roughly to Piaget's (1929, 1930) notion of assimilation. In accretion, existing knowledge structures are elaborated on or extended through the subsumption of new information. For example, our young child's limited concept of dog can be modified through accretion when the child discovers that dogs bark rather than purr. Rumelhart and Norman's second mechanism for knowledge change, *tuning*, is similarly related to Piaget's (1929) concept of accommodation. Simply speaking, tuning involves some minor adjustment to one's existing concept as a result of new learning that helps to clarify its parameters or attributes. Let us go back to the young child's attempts to grapple with the concept of dog. This young person's understanding of dog may be "tuned" if the child recognizes that certain dogs, because of their size or appearance, should not be approached or petted as readily as other, smaller or seemingly friendlier dogs.

At other times, development of a particular concept cannot progress solely through accretion or tuning. What is needed is almost a reconfiguration of the relevant knowledge and the construction of a virtually new concept. This form of conceptual change has been called *restructuring* and can be of two types, weak and radical. Weak restructuring takes place more gradually than radical restructuring and may result in a less dramatic shift in prior understanding (Vosniadou & Brewer, 1987). When the young child realizes that a favorite stuffed dog, Woofer, is not a *real* dog, for instance, the child may well have to reform the whole concept of dog to distinguish between real animals and toys. In such an event, the child may experience a weak or radical restructuring, depending on the suddenness or breadth of the transformation.

We introduce this topic of the incompleteness and transformation of knowledge because educators have long been perplexed by the resilience of various academic concepts, even those held by seemingly intelligent and well-educated students (e.g., Chinn & Brewer, 1993; Guzzetti & Hynd, in press; Pintrich, Marx, & Boyle, 1993). As we noted, there is ample evidence that students will demonstrate primitive notions or misconceptions that their teachers believed had long been exorcised or extinguished by effective instruction, especially when those students are asked to perform novel tasks or operate in unfamiliar settings (e.g., Perkins & Simmons, 1988;

Roth, 1990). What might account for such regressions?

Some have put forward a stage development explanation for this seeming immutability. Thus, they have argued that concepts may fail to undergo change because individuals have not achieved the stage of cognitive readiness that would permit them to engage in even modest restructuring (Case, 1985; Piaget, 1929, 1930). For instance, it might be argued that our young child could not grasp the difference between a real dog and a stuffed dog until reaching the stage of concrete operations, which according to Piagetian theory, should occur between the ages of 7 and 11 (Thomas, 1992).

Whereas others acknowledge the capacity of overall cognitive development to influence knowledge development, they also consider the impact of other variables on the change process (e.g., Crick & Dodge, 1994). Among the factors that these individuals credit with fueling or frustrating conceptual change are the nature of the information received, the significance of the information giver, and the strategic abilities of the learner (Alexander, in press; Carey, 1985; Chinn & Brewer, 1993; Karmiloff-Smith, 1984, 1986; Perkins & Simmons, 1988). For example, our young child may be more receptive to new information about the dogs when that information is delivered by a veterinarian who visits the classroom and brings several "living" examples.

Still, others have demonstrated the power that motivational factors, such as goals and interests, play in establishing a context for conceptual change (e.g., Pintrich & Schrauben, 1992; Wentzel, 1993; Wigfield & Harold, 1992). Pintrich et al. (1993), for instance, have made a convincing argument for motivated change: "[C]ognition-only models of student learning do not adequately explain why students who seem to have the requisite prior conceptual knowledge do not activate this knowledge for many school tasks, let alone out-of-school tasks" (p. 167). Our own research into conceptual change, in the form of domain-specific development (Alexander, 1995, 1997; Alexander, Jetton, & Kulikowich, 1995; Alexander, Murphy, Woods, Duhon, & Parker, 1997), tends to favor Pintrich et al.'s multidimensional view of conceptual change. Thus, the change or restructuring of concepts may be best understood as a confluence of cognitive and affective factors that occurs within a particular context or situation. One of those factors is the general body of relevant knowledge to which the target concept relates. Consequently, if we want to understand why a student fails to modify the concept of dog, we might begin with an exploration of the child's background knowledge, strategic capabilities to reason and formulate alternatives, and interest in modifying the existing concept.

## The Relationship Between Knowing and Believing

We have recently become interested in understanding more about the implicit theories that guide individuals' thoughts and behaviors. Specifically, we have set out, with the assistance of others, to explore what people who belong to different educational and cultural communities mean when they use words like *knowledge* and *beliefs* (Alexander & Dochy, 1994, 1995; Murphy & Alexander, 1995; Alexander, Murphy, Guan & Murphy, 1998). As we noted, we feel that implicit theories, even though they remain unexplicated, exert a strong force on how people live their lives. Our goal, therefore, was to find a means of excavating these buried notions, bringing them to the level of consciousness so that they could be examined and discussed.

We also wanted to understand how the respondents perceived the relationship between these two fundamental and potentially intertwined constructs. From a practical standpoint, the notions of knowing and believing punctuate everyday discourse and are intimately aligned with the educational system. Although there may be many purposes of education, it would seem that the aim of transmitting knowledge to the next generation of citizens remains a core rationale. Yet, discussion of these two basic terms have been limited most often to the pages of philosophy texts and have not been interjected into discussions among practicing educators. Thus, we know very little about how educators and those whom they teach view knowledge and beliefs. Do teachers and their students perceive knowledge in the same way? Does continued schooling alter the way individuals come to view knowledge? Is a cultural factor evident? Do those in the United States hold to different conceptions of knowing and believing than those reared in Europe or in the Far East? These are among the questions that we have explored in a series of studies. We relate some of our findings here because of the message they convey about the way knowledge is defined by groups and how the distinction between what one knows and what one believes can have serious implications for schooling.

Before we could examine people's conceptions about knowing and believing, we had to devise a task that would give voice to these broad and often unspecified ideas. What we developed was a questionnaire that began with a graphic catalyst (Alexander & Dochy, 1994). Using a series of Venn diagrams, we asked respondents to choose the depiction that most closely represented their conception of the relationship between knowledge and beliefs or to generate their own representation. Each of these depictions was intended to capture rudimentary relations between knowledge and beliefs. Option 1, for instance, displayed knowledge and beliefs as completely separate, whereas option 2 depicted knowledge as a subset of one's beliefs. In contrast, option 3 conveyed beliefs as a subset of one's knowledge, and option 4 presented them as inseparable. Option 5 displayed some aspect of knowledge and beliefs as overlapping, although aspects of each remained separate.

Following this selection component, we included questions intended to build on the options that people chose or generated. First, respondents were asked to provide a definition of *knowledge* and *beliefs* and then to justify their initial selection. In the third question, participants were asked to provide an example from their own experiences that supported their view of the relationship between knowledge and beliefs. Finally, respondents were asked whether they felt that beliefs were changeable and under what conditions such change might occur.

Over the course of the last three years, this task has been administered to hundreds of individuals in this country and abroad. The educational background of these respondents has ranged from ninth-grade students to international experts in either knowledge or beliefs. The majority of our international students have come from the Netherlands and from Singapore. We have also sampled classes of students in relationship to their teachers to investigate the consistency of perspectives among members of the same classroom communities. Key findings from these various administrations include the following:

- Option 5 was the most commonly chosen representation for every educational and cultural group except for postsecondary students in the Netherlands, who acquire much of their academic content via distance, module-based learning.

- Only in the case of high school students (6%) have any Americans chosen option 1. This suggests that Americans typically conceptualize an interrelationship between knowledge and beliefs.

- American experts were the most variable in their option selection and were more tentative in their descriptions than all other educational and cultural communities explored. The European experts in comparison, conveyed far more similarity in their selection (option 3) and in their explanations.

- Based on the extensiveness of definitions and the frequency of key concepts, *knowledge* seems to be an easier term for individuals to define than *beliefs*.

- Whereas knowledge was often characterized by the words *schooled, learned, information* or *data*, and *proven* or *true*, beliefs were described as more *informally acquired, valued personal* (subjective), *unproven*, and associated with *religion* or *God*.

- American students tended to view knowledge as valueless information that had little impact in their lives, but their own teachers, respondents in the Netherlands and Singapore, and international experts felt otherwise.

- Almost all Americans and the vast majority of European respondents, regardless of educational level, held that beliefs were changeable, whereas 8% of Singaporean students and 9% of their teachers felt that beliefs were unchangeable.

- Both American and Singaporean students and teachers strongly aligned beliefs with religion, although American students spoke more openly about resisting information that might counter their beliefs.

- By and large, teachers and their students conveyed similar patterns in their conceptions of knowledge and beliefs.

- Personal experiences were commonly seen as catalysts for belief change in all educational and cultural groups, with education and other people as additional change agents.

Given these and other findings, several important lessons can be gleaned. First, conceptions of knowledge and beliefs are, to some degree, a reflection of one's culture and level of education. Thus, American students typically conveyed notions that varied from students in the Netherlands and Singapore, but within these cultures, years of education often resulted in responses that were more extensive, somewhat more tenuous, and more diverse. Second, when most people talk about knowledge they are talking in terms of formal or academic learning. Thus, knowledge is associated with the educational system. Yet, the most distressing realization to us was the fact that so many American students characterized their schooled learning as valueless and of little importance in their daily lives. Several students spoke with passion about how their task was to "act" as if they cared about or believed in what they were being taught but to remain strong in character by resisting any message that might conflict with their beliefs. Should we, as educators, be surprised that such students fail to demonstrate conceptual change or seem content with only superficial understandings of academic information? There is much more that could be learned by exploring individuals' conceptions of knowledge and beliefs, as well as other constructs that are central to their learning and development.

# SKILLFUL AND STRATEGIC PROCESSING

Among the hallmarks of those who have achieved recognition as experts in any given field is not only the extensive and coherent body of conceptual knowledge they possess but also their remarkable ability to apply that knowledge skillfully and strategically. Although the terms *skills* and *strategies* are routinely associated with achievement, they convey different but complementary forms of mental processing. Let us first consider the similarities between skills and strategies. To begin with, skills and strategies are both special forms of procedural knowledge (Chi, 1985; Paris, et al., 1983). Whether we are describing step-by-step algorithms, like formulas in science, or are discussing general guidelines or heuristics for completing a task, such as principles for writing a good summary, skills and strategies are essentially "how to" knowledge.

Second, there is no way that learning in science, history, English and language arts, or any other academic domain can be advanced without the attainment of skills and strategies for acquiring, remembering, organizing, or transforming information or without the ability to monitor one's own performance. This unique ability to self-monitor or self-regulate is a special case of strategic processing that has been called metacognition or executive control (Borkowski, Carr, & Pressley, 1987; Brown, Armbruster, & Bakers, 1986; Garner, 1987; Garner & Alexander, 1989). Additional metacognitive strategies include planning, goal setting, and regulating. One thing that cognitive researchers have come to realize is that those who reflect on their performance and who then use that self-knowledge to adjust their behaviors are more likely to outperform or show greater improvement than those who do not engage in such executive processing (e.g., Garner, 1987).

Third, both skills and strategies can vary in terms of their generality. Sometimes skills or strategies have very broad utility, meaning that they can be used with many different subjects (e.g., science or English) or very diverse tasks (e.g., conducting an experiment or analyzing historical documents). When skills and strategies are broadly applicable, we refer to them as general (Alexander & Judy, 1988; Glaser, 1984; Weinstein & Mayer, 1986). The ability to see how some new body of information relates to familiar information is one example of a general cognitive skill or strategy. General cognitive strategies also include such processes as rehearsal, summarization, elaboration, and patterning. In contrast, those working in specific areas, such as science, history, or English and language arts, must also acquire skills and strategies that are particular to that area. These more particular instances of skills and strategies are often labeled domain-specific (Glaser, 1984). When a student in physical science selects a certain formula to calculate the atomic weight of a given substance or when a third-grader figures out the meaning of an unknown word by using knowledge of common prefixes and suffixes, they are applying domain-specific skills or strategies.

Domain-specific skills or strategies can actually be regarded as particularized forms of general skills or strategies. Thus, a list of general cognitive strategies used in organizing or transforming information may include the ability to visually represent information. In science, this visualization may take the form of converting raw data into graphs, whereas in history it may relate to the creation of time lines, which mark significant events during a certain era. In English and language arts, we may see this general strategy particularized in the form of using illustrations to enhance comprehension.

Despite these key similarities, two significant attributes differentiate skills from strategies and give each a unique role in achievement and learning: the *automaticity* of performance and learner *awareness* or *intentionality* (Alexander, et al., 1991; Garner, 1987). In essence, skills are procedures that students hone to a level of automaticity, enabling them to perform a given task fluidly and effectively. A skilled reader, for example, can perform certain procedures that are basic to effective reading, such as decoding or reading, without much cognitive effort or even awareness, and a skilled history student may immediately recognize bias in the presentation of historical evidence. Such skilled performance contributes to learning and development by limiting the demands that basic tasks place on the individual's mental faculties. Thus, one of the goals of education is to provide adequate guidance and meaningful opportunities for repeated practice of these fundamental procedures to maximize fluid performance.

However, all learners encounter barriers to complete understanding when performing all but the most commonplace or routine tasks or when they wish to extend their current understanding. When deep understanding is not achieved or when extension of the knowledge base is sought, learners must be able to draw on general and domain-specific procedures in an effortful and conscious way. When this planful and effortful processing takes place, the learner is performing *strategically*. Skilled readers, for instance, may come across a particularly troublesome word that causes them to consciously consider the sound-symbol relationships that they typically employ spontaneously. The word may also cause them to seek alternative sources of information (e.g., a dictionary). Likewise, history students sometimes have to delve deeper into historical accounts to detect bias. In both cases, the students must have recognized that their comprehension was incomplete (i.e., through self-monitoring or self-regulation), and they must have a repertoire of procedures (i.e., cognitive strategies) that can aid them in their pursuit of understanding. Terms such as *problem solving*, *thinking*, or *reasoning* are frequently used in the literature as indicators of strategic or metacognitive processing (Bereiter & Scardamalia, 1989).

We stated that declarative understanding alone is not enough to ensure the effective implementation of an individual's knowledge. Specifically, since the work of Brown (1975) and Flavell (1977), it has been consistently demonstrated that learners must also possess the ability, along with the willingness, to oversee, evaluate, and remedy errors in their own performance. One critical question that is yet unclear, however, is when, where, and for whom certain types of skills or strategies are more effective for learning and development than others (Schoenfeld, 1988). For instance, there is evidence that learners' strategic processing should vary as their knowledge in a domain grows and develops (Hasselhorn & Körkel, 1986; McCutchen, 1986). McCutchen found that students' writing performance was better when they wrote about familiar or personally interesting topics than when the topics were unfamiliar or impersonal. In essence, self-regulation and strategic processing must, almost by definition, vary as the demands of the task or the nature of the context changes (e.g. Lave, 1988; Resnick, 1991). In addition, research has also shown that students will often use a number of strategies concurrently as a learning tactic when they are engaged in performing a complex or demanding task (Baker & Brown, 1984; Schmeck, 1988).

Another consistent finding is that students do better when they discover or are taught about strategies and when they function in an environment where strategic processing is supported and rewarded (Ames & Archer, 1988; Ceci & Bronfenbrenner, 1985; McCombs, 1988; Paris & Winograd, 1990). Regrettably, students often (a) do not discover critical skills or strategies without guidance, (b) develop procedures that are inadequate or ineffective, and (c) find themselves in learning situations where supports or rewards for being strategic or self-regulating are not present (Garner, 1988). In such cases, achievement is negatively affected. Part of the conducive environment to which we refer relates directly to the support and concern students perceive from their teachers and peers (Fuchs et al., 1995; Wentzel, 1991). Overall, educational researchers and practitioners must begin to tackle the difficult question of how teachers can facilitate students' acquisition of cognitive and metacognitive strategies in ways that are meaningful and realistic. Contrived strategy instruction or a focus on skills or strategies isolated from meaningful content appears to contribute little to sustained efforts toward achievement (Alexander, 1997).

Moreover, because strategic processing is effortful, is goal-directed, and can involve self-regulation, it is directly and strongly linked to motivation (Alexander & Murphy, 1998, Pintrich et al., 1993; Wigfield & Eccles, 1992). Therefore, even if students recognize that they do not understand a given task fully and even if they possess the relevant strategic knowledge, they may merely choose not to exert the additional mental energy required to improve or extend their knowledge. Clearly, much more needs to be understood about this intricate relationship between strategies and motivation if optimal learning is to be realized.

Finally, just as there are various strategies that learners can intentionally use to augment their comprehension, there are instructional strategies (e.g., grouping or cooperative learning techniques) teachers can employ to facilitate students' achievement (Brown & Palincsar, 1989; Collins, Brown, & Newman, 1989; Fantuzzo, King, & Heller, 1992). For an optimal learning environment to be created in the classroom, teachers must be cognizant of the academic needs of students and understand how variations in instructional organization from didactic teaching to discovery learning, place different demands on the learner (Fuchs, Fuchs, & Bishop, 1992). When content is highly unfamiliar, for example, teachers may need to consider an instructional technique that allows for increased student support or ensures greater and more efficient delivery of basic concepts. At other times, the teacher might determine that a guided discovery approach or some form of cooperative learning arrangement might facilitate student processing. Additionally, as teachers observe and evaluate progress under diverse instructional conditions, they can begin to formulate patterns of when and for whom particular strategies function best. In essence, teachers, as well as their students, must acquire both conditional knowledge and procedural knowledge for maximum learning to occur.

This point about conditional knowledge for teachers brings us to our final point under strategic processing. Had this chapter been written just 10 years ago, a central issue in this discussion would have related to the relationship between general and domain-specific strategies. That is, little more than a decade ago, the cognitive literature was witness to a lively debate about when general (including metacognitive) strategies or domain-specific ones were more essential to students' learning and development (e.g., Glaser, 1984; Sternberg, 1985). However, this initial debate has apparently come to some resolution with the understanding that both are requisite for learning (Alexander, 1996; Alexander & Judy,

1988). The leading question has now become when, where, and for whom certain types of strategies are more effective for learning (Schoenfeld, 1988). In addition, there have been continued attempts to clarify the meanings of such fundamental terms as *strategies* (Alexander et al., 1991; Pressley, Goodchild, Fleet, Zajchowski, & Evans, 1989), *metacognition*, and *critical* and *creative thinking* (e.g., Alexander, Parsons, & Nash, 1996; Gardner, 1993; Garner & Alexander, 1989; Paris & Winograd, 1990; Sternberg & Lubart, 1991). This search for greater conceptual clarity in the key terms that frame cognition can only help the field to communicate more effectively to others in the research community, as well as to educators in other domains and to those practicing daily in the classroom.

## INTERRELATIONSHIP BETWEEN COGNITION AND MOTIVATION

In the history of American education, there was a point at which individuals began to realize that meaningful learning and development could not be adequately explained by behavioral notions of conditioning (Skinner, 1953). The conceptualization of human performance as simply the by-product of reinforcement and punishment robbed us of our right to self-determination (Ryan, 1992). Simply stated, what behavioral theories failed to appreciate was the need to interject human agency into any theory of learning (Deci & Ryan, 1985; Dewey, 1913; James; 1890). During the 1970s and into the 1980s, the human presence in learning and development, for most cognitivists, was represented by the computer metaphor, with prior knowledge (stored data) imposing itself on incoming information. Although this model of human thinking did much to spark the resurgence of cognitive psychology within this century, it had at least one serious drawback—it virtually stripped human thoughts and actions of any vestiges of feelings or emotions that are decidedly human. Information-processing, in effect, conveyed human thinking and performance as a "coldly cognitive" enterprise (Pintrich & Schrauben, 1992).

Among the most significant trends in the cognitive literature in the past five years is the attempt to reintroduce the dimensions of affect and motivation into theories and models of human cognition (Alexander, 1997; Pintrich et al., 1993). *Affect* is a term we use here to refer broadly to the feelings or emotions that individuals typically display and which also influence

their thoughts and behaviors (e.g., Ames & Ames, 1985). *Motivation*, a related term, pertains to the general processes by which people's needs and desires are activated (Goetz, Alexander, & Ash, 1992). As with affect, these processes influence individuals' perceptions and ideas, as well as their actions.

Those in cognitive psychology have already learned many valuable lessons from the community of motivation researchers. For instance, these researchers have demonstrated how students' engagement, involvement, intrinsic motivation, and commitment enhance learning (e.g., Ames & Ames, 1985, 1989; Corno, & Rohrkemper, 1985; Dweck & Leggett, 1988; Gottfried, 1985, 1990). Likewise, they have helped us to see how a positive self-concept (e.g., Wigfield & Karpathian, 1991; Wylie, 1974, 1979, 1989), a sense of control or autonomy (e.g., deCharms, 1968; Deci & Ryan, 1985, 1991; Deci et al., 1991), and learning versus performance goals (e.g., Dweck, 1986; Nicholls, 1984) typically translate into better learning or higher achievement. Motivation researchers have also shown educators that when students are able to set appropriate goals for their own learning and find their academic work personally relevant, they are more likely to succeed in school (e.g., Bandura, 1977, 1993; Lepper, 1988; Maehr & Braskamp, 1986; Meece, Blumenfeld, & Hoyle, 1988; Schunk, 1991; Tolman, 1932). Finally, when teachers acknowledge students' goals and interests and when these students see the learning environment as supportive and encouraging, their learning and achievement are facilitated (e.g., Ames, 1992; Newman & Schwager, 1992).

Although much of the literature speaks generally of students' personality traits or global orientation toward school or learning, more recent work considers the variability of affect or motivation according to the situation or context (e.g., Ames, 1992). That is, it is recognized that no individual is equally affected or motivated in all situations or contexts (e.g., Csikszentmihalyi, 1990; Phillips & Zimmerman, 1990; Renninger, 1992; Schiefele & Csikszentmihalyi, 1994, 1995). These variations can be accounted for by a number of factors, including a student's sense of the instructional goals (e.g., Jetton & Alexander, 1994), the teacher's expectations (Wigfield & Harold, 1992), or the perceived climate in the classroom (Schunk & Meece, 1992).

One area where the interrelationship between cognition and motivation is especially apparent is strategic processing which we have already discussed. It is undoubtedly a truism to say that people know more than they do. Part of the gap between understanding and performance can be attributed to a lack of desire or investment in the task or problem at hand. We have all probably been acquainted with students who come to the classroom in some circumstance that complicates the learning process (e.g., the learning-disabled student with a language-specific problem). Yet, through persistence or a deep desire to succeed, these students find ways to compensate for their problems so that they can attain the desired level of understanding.

Similarly, the connections between cognition and motivation are quite evident in the realms of *metacognition* and *self-regulation*. The former term is drawn from the cognitive literature (Flavell, 1977; Garner, 1987), whereas the latter is a common term in the motivation literature (Winne, 1995; Zimmerman, 1989, 1994). However, both terms are concerned with individuals' ability to monitor, evaluate, and control their thoughts and actions. They both reflect the intricate relationship between cognition and motivation because they require much more than a mental analysis and synthesis of current performance. They entail learners' judgments of their general and specific competence, their desired ends, their likelihood of success, and other personal and academic factors (Pintrich & DeGroot, 1991; Pressley, Borkowski, & Schneider, 1989; Zimmerman & Martinez-Pons, 1986, 1988).

We do not wish to leave the reader with the impression that affective or motivational factors are always positive forces in learning and development. Just as knowledge can be misleading or misguiding, so, too, can one's feelings, emotions, interests, and goals inhibit learning. The research on learned helplessness is certainly one potent illustration of how negative self-perceptions and judgments about the lack of self-determination can debilitate individuals and keep them from taking appropriate strategic action (Harter, 1990, 1996). While less severe, the literature on the possible side effects of situational interest provides another illustration of the negative influences of affect and motivation.

Interest comes in many shapes and forms. Two types have garnered much attention in the recent literature—*personal* and *situational* interest. Personal, or individual, interest is the kind of enduring and absorbing involvement often associated with one's vocations and avocations. They

are actively pursued and are linked to one's goals and self-identities. For example, a sixth-grader has been an avid rock collector since the age of three. This interest has given rise to numerous trips to museums, to book collections, and even to thoughts of pursuing a career in geology. In contrast, there are those momentary glimmers of interest, in the form of arousing or attention-getting conditions or elements, that can be found in many situations or contexts. Rarely, however, do these situational factors maintain or carry over into individual interests. The draw of tabloid headlines in the checkout line at the grocery store or the pull of some TV or magazine ads that play on our basic human drives are just two examples of situationally interesting forces in our everyday lives.

Situational interest is not restricted to the grocery store or to the media but is present everywhere. For example, according to common pedagogical practice, teachers should seek to grab their students' attention or arouse their interest at the start of a lesson, perhaps by employing some motivating device or initiating activity. But what is the effect of this arousal? Does it, as thought, result in augmented attention throughout the lesson, so that students learn better? The answer, according to recent research, is maybe not. In some cases, the individuals' arousal or attention to information or factors that are not important or even tangential to academic goals can negatively affect learning (e.g., Garner, Alexander, Gillingham, Kulikowich, Brown, 1991; Garner, Gillingham, & White, 1989; Wade, Schraw, Buxton, & Hayes, 1993). The research on seductive details makes this point very vividly.

*Seductive details* are those highly interesting, but basically unimportant, tidbits that are sometimes sprinkled in textbooks or in lectures (Garner et al., 1989). Science books that include a sentence about Stephen Hawking's wager with a colleague for which the prize is *Penthouse* magazine, the history texts that mention that George Washington had wooden teeth, or the writings that allude to Horatio Nelson's bedroom conquests in the midst of describing his naval feats are illustrations of seductive details. What Garner et al. (1991) discovered was that seductive details (e.g., mention of Hawking's wager) negatively affect students' ability to recall highly important but less interesting content (e.g., Grand Unification Theory).

What this work on seductive details suggests is that educators must consider the ramifications of piquing their students' interest for information that is relatively unimportant to the goals of learning. Although teachers should certainly seek to interest students in the content at hand, they would be far better off to find some connection between students' more deeply held interests and the information. Thus, if they are to optimize learning, teachers need to be aware of their students' personal goals and interests (Dewey, 1913), as well as the relative value of the content (Jetton & Alexander, 1994; Wade et al., 1993). In addition, teachers should try to create learning environments that give students the opportunity to pursue their personal interests in meaningful ways, to experience self-determination or choice, and to be responsible for the self-evaluation and self-regulation of their own learning (e.g., Amabile, 1983, 1990; Corno & Rohrkemper, 1985; deCharms, 1968; Dweck & Leggett, 1988; Pintrich & Schrauben, 1992; Ryan, 1992; Zimmerman & Martinez-Pons, 1992).

## THE INFLUENCE OF CONTEXT OR SITUATION

Schooling is and has always been a social institution, existing within a broader sociocultural, political, and economic context (Bronfenbrenner, 1989; Wentzel, 1991). In many ways, the whole concept of teaching and learning is predicated on social interactions among individuals in a context that is expected to afford academic development (Alexander, Murphy, & Woods, 1996; Bronfenbrenner, 1979, 1989; Palincsar & Perry, 1995). Of all the resources that might be made available by the educational institution, it is perhaps the "human" resource, in the presence of caring and knowledgeable teachers and peers, that constitutes the most critical contextual and situational factor.

Even with this understanding, many in cognitive psychology have only recently reawakened to the force that contextual and situational factors exert on learning and development (Alexander & Murphy, 1998). Indeed, one of the most powerful findings to emerge in the psychological literature in the past decade is the recognition that learning is continuously shaped by its sociocultural context (e.g., Alexander, 1996; Cognition & Technology Group at Vanderbilt, 1990; Lave, 1988; Resnick, Levine, & Teasley, 1991; Rogoff, 1990). This growing recognition is reflected in such programs of research as socially-shared cognition (Resnick et al., 1991), distributed cogni-

tion (Salomon, 1993), distributed intelligence (Pea, 1988, 1989), shared expertise (Brown & Palincsar, 1989), guided participation (Rogoff, 1990), situated action (Greeno & Moore, 1993; Vera & Simon, 1993), and anchored instruction (Cognition and Technology Group at Vanderbilt, 1990). In part, this emphasis on the context or situation of learning has been fueled by the writings in sociocultural history, social cognition, cultural anthropology, and information-based technology.

In many ways, the dimensions we have been discussing (i.e., knowledge, strategic processing, and motivation) center primarily on the internal world of the individual. However, what the extensive writings in the previously mentioned programs of research (e.g., cultural anthropology) remind us is that all individuals, including students who are learning in classrooms, must operate in continual interaction with the external world—a world that involves other humans. In other words, human thought does not occur in a vacuum but rather is mediated by all aspects of the context and situation, most notably the human presence (James, 1890).

Despite the seeming disregard of contextual and situational factors in decades past, the social nature of cognition has long been explored by philosophers intrigued with the duality of mind and society, including Durkheim, James, Dewey, and Vygotsky. Still, during the 1970s and 1980s, cognition seemed far more enamored with studying human learning and development through "context-free" tasks administered within "controlled" environments. The results, according to critics, bore little resemblance to actual tasks people typically perform in their everyday lives (Rogoff & Chavajay, 1995; Saxe, 1991; Scribner & Cole, 1981). Thankfully, under the influence of such researchers as Cole, Lave, Rogoff, and Greeno, there has been a renaissance of sorts in cognition—a rebirth that celebrates the collective mind and embraces the power of the environment.

Perhaps one individual, in particular, deserves mention for this increased sensitivity to the sociocultural context of learning and development, Lev Vygotsky (1934/1986). Vygotsky was a Russian psychologist and philosopher whose writings were not readily available to much of the Western world until the 1960s, long after his death (Kozulin, 1990). He felt strongly that Piaget, his contemporary, had drastically underestimated the social nature of human learning and development. Thus, Vygotsky forwarded the concept of the zone of proximal development. According to this notion, there is a marked difference between individuals' levels of performance when working alone and when they are guided by someone who is more knowledgeable and more skilled. This distance in performance under the two conditions (i.e., independent and aided) represents the learners' zone of proximal development.

This concept, of course, reaches beyond the confines of the classroom. That is, learning, as we discussed previously, does not occur only in schools or classrooms. Radziszewska and Rogoff (1988) make the case for this same guided learning in out-of-school settings. Specifically, these researchers observed errand planning in nine-year-olds who were working with both same-age peers and with adults. In their study, the researchers found that the nine-year-olds gained more skills in errand planning when they participated with an adult rather than a same-age partner. Their conclusion was that the knowledge and skill of those with whom a child collaborates or cooperates may be a significant component in the learning equation, both in and out of school. This conclusion is clearly in keeping with Vygotsky's (1934/1986) theoretical arguments about the zone of proximal development and the essential nature of guided learning.

Although cognitivists are rediscovering the importance of context and situation in learning, this does not discount or discredit the significance or individuality of each person in any collective. Rather, it allows cognitivists to consider both the individual and the social natures of learning and development, which have a fascinating, reciprocal nature. On the one hand, the knowledge students can come to know on a personal level is, in part, a sociocultural construction. That is, an understanding shaped by everyone who has ever entered the stream of human experience (McDermott, 1986). On the other hand, our educational artifacts, especially the language we use to communicate in classrooms, are resources of the culture (Cole & Engeström, 1993; Serpell, 1993; Serpell & Boykin, 1994). Moreover, as we discussed in the section on schooled and nonschooled knowledge, learning takes place when and where the individual interacts with his or her world (e.g., Radziszewska & Rogoff, 1988; Rogoff & Gauvin, 1986).

Still, because no two individuals have the same personal histories or enter the stream of human experience at the same point and time, they cannot perceive of their situation in the same way. Further, each member of a sociocultural group forever changes that group by adding his or her personal histories to the stream. Also, we cannot lose sight of the fact that individuals are more than the sum of their social selves and remain active agents in the construction of their own self-schemas (Deci & Ryan, 1991; Dworkin, 1988; Ryan, 1992). To assume otherwise is to remove the ability of the person to think or behave in ways that deviate from the norm for any sociocultural group, that is, to self-govern or to self-regulate. Thus, given these two orientations, we conclude that cognition must be at once both private and idiosyncratic, as well as social and collective (Toulmin, 1985).

As we see it, two educational issues arise in this discussion of the contextual-situational nature of learning. First, since schools are social institutions in which groups of learners are brought together to share in instructional experiences, students are more or less in continual contact with peers and with other adults. Rather than overlook this fact, various researchers have systematically investigated how this social dimension of learning can be utilized to the advantage of students' learning and development (e.g., Brown & Palincsar, 1989; Collins, Brown, & Newman, 1989; Johnson & Johnson, 1985; Palincsar & Brown, 1984; Resnick et al., 1991; Slavin, 1978, 1987).

We can see the outcome of these research efforts in terms of instructional approaches that seek to enhance cooperative learning (Johnson & Johnson, 1985; Slavin, 1987); foster cognitive processing by reciprocal teaching (Brown & Palincsar, 1989); establish cognitive apprenticeships (Collins et al., 1989); stress meaningful, information-based problem solving through anchored instruction (Cognition and Technology Group at Vanderbilt, 1990); or provide opportunities for deeper conceptual learning through Jigsaw procedures (Aronson, 1978; Brown & Campione, 1990). It should be noted that while the data on these various approaches have generally been favorable (e.g., Palincsar & Brown, 1984; Slavin, 1987), the number of empirical studies on their effectiveness remain limited, particularly for some of the more popular and theoretically appealing techniques (e.g., Rosenshine & Meister, 1994). Therefore, educational researchers and practitioners must continue to test the viability and utility of these socially based instructional programs, and they should do so within the most appropriate setting for such work—the classroom community.

Our second educational issue involves the transfer of learning across contexts. Because the school is, in its own way, a socially, politically, and economically contrived context, there will undoubtedly be cases in which the knowledge, skills, and strategies acquired there do not readily transfer to other situations (e.g., Perret-Claremont, Perret, & Bell, 1980). This probably comes as no surprise to teachers, who assume that students understand something only to see them perform under slightly varied conditions as though the lesson was never taught and never learned. Lave (1988) has argued that this lack of transfer is attributable to the artificial barrier between schooled and nonschooled contexts that inhibits the applicability of formal learning. For example, a second-grade student scores well on a science test that deals with the rotation of the earth, seasons of the years, and the like, but is overheard explaining to a younger brother that days are longer in the summer because the earth is closer to the sun. Or this same child is sometimes careless on her mathematics homework when adding and subtracting but is flawless when it comes to calculating the money owed for a good report card or chores (e.g., Schoenfeld, 1988; Stewart, 1987).

In sum, from the growing body of work dealing with contextual and situational factors, especially the human resources that are available in learning environments, we can say that the place in which learning occurs is clearly nontrivial. The more we understand the nature of contextual and situational factors, particularly human-to-human interactions, and their interrelationship to individuals' thoughts, feelings, and behaviors, the greater we can orchestrate enriching and meaningful environments that promote optimal learning and development for all students.

## THE DEVELOPMENT OF ACADEMIC COMPETENCE

Whether or not educators perceive it to be the primary purpose of formal schooling, most would acknowledge that the acquisition of fundamental knowledge and skills in key central academic domains (e.g., reading/writing, mathematics, science, or history) is one rationale for the existence of the educational system. Given that

assertion, however, it is surprising to realize that even after centuries of philosophical debate and decades of empirical research, we have only a limited understanding of how one is transformed from a fledgling in a specific field to someone who can function competently or, perhaps, even expertly in that same field. Through studies of human development, we are cognizant of theories that help to capture the way in which the human species progresses in cognitive, socioemotional, physical, and moral development (Crick & Dodge, 1994; Gilligan, 1977, 1987; Kohlberg, 1981; Piaget, 1929, 1930). We also have a literature that deals with the transformations that occur in the individuals' conceptual understanding (Carey, 1985; Pintrich et al., 1993). Yet, as educators, we are still novices in our comprehension of the factors and forces that propel one student into competence in history or physics while another student flounders and stalls in the same subjects.

In the last decade, cognitive researchers have shed some light on the question of academic competence by investigating the differences between experts and novices in a wide range of tasks and domains (e.g., Chi, Feltovich, & Glaser, 1981; Chi, Glaser, & Farr, 1988; Ericsson & Smith, 1991). Through well-conceived and well-executed experiments, we learned how the quality and organization of the experts' knowledge structures were vastly superior to those of novices (e.g., Chi, 1985; Naveh-Benjamin, McKeachie, Lin, & Tucker, 1986). The richness of their knowledge base thus allowed experts to perceive problems and tasks at a deeper level and gave them quick access to domain-specific and general cognitive strategies that made their problem solving efficient and elegant. However, during this decade, cognitive researchers have found the expert-novice literature to be wanting for several important reasons.

First, research in this paradigm focused almost exclusively on knowledge factors and failed to consider the motivational dimensions of human performance described in the previous section. Second, much of the research on expert-novice distinctions was carried out in laboratory conditions with experimental tasks that did not always mirror the real-world conditions under which experts and novices function. Third, this literature did little to offer explanations of how individuals actually progressed to the stage of expertise. Rather, it appeared to suggest that by promoting or prompting the type of knowledge structures seen in experts, all novices could be virtually transformed into experts in any domain.

Moreover, little attention in the expertise literature was paid to the important differences between domains of study. It overlooked the form and structure that distinguishes physics, for example, from social studies or from reading (Alexander, 1992; Spiro & Jehng, 1990). Yet, these differences would appear to be highly significant in what individuals strive to achieve or in what they are capable of achieving. Finally, the distinctions between experts and novices failed to consider one critical dimension; that is, most individuals will not attain expertise in any academic domain or will do so in only an extremely limited set (Alexander, 1997; Alexander & Murphy, 1998). For most students in schools, some degree of competent or adequate performance level in their basic subjects, rather than expertise, would certainly be a desirable goal. Given these limitations, some other orientation to the development of academic competence was warranted. The model that we present here is one such alternative.

## Characteristics of the MDL

As we noted, cognitive psychology is becoming increasingly multidimensional in its outlook on learning and development (e.g., Pintrich, 1994; Weinstein & McCombs, in press). The Model of Domain Learning, or the MDL (Alexander, 1997, Alexander, Kulikowich, & Schulze, 1994a, 1994b), which we outline here, exemplifies this multidimensionality and embraces the relationship among the cognitive, strategic, and motivational factors. The MDL differs from other, well-known theories or models of development (e.g., Anderson, 1982; Rumelhart & Norman, 1981; Shuell, 1990) in several basic ways. First, the most noticeable feature of the MDL is that it takes a domain-specific orientation to development rather than a species-specific view (e.g., Case, 1985; Piaget, 1952). Thus, the assumption of the MDL is that the same individual can potentially be found at multiple stages of academic development, depending on the domain. For example, a particular academic may be considered an expert in cognitive psychology but be judged a neophyte in microbiology.

Second, although other models pay homage to noncognitive variables (e.g., Shuell, 1990), the MDL associates transformations in domain learning with particular motivational variables, which are reciprocally linked to concomitant changes in various cognitive factors. Consequently, rises in individual interest are correlated to rises in individuals' subject-matter knowledge, whereas greater domain-specific knowledge is aligned with a decreasing reliance on situational interest. Third, the MDL moves away from a simple expert-novice dichotomy by conceptualizing three stages of academic development (i.e., acclimation, competence, and proficiency or expertise).

Specifically, the MDL depicts learning in terms of changes within and interactions between the components of subject-matter knowledge, learners' interest, and general cognitive and metacognitive strategies, which are positioned in a three-stage framework. *Stages* are the rather durable, long-term characterizations that denote shifts in the association of knowledge, interest, and strategic processing. Further, these stages are essentially nonregressive and nonrecursive (Karmiloff-Smith, 1984, 1986; Shuell, 1990). Therefore, it is unlikely that any individual will regress to a lower stage, barring some catastrophic physical, cognitive, or motivational event or some dramatic shift in the domain.

We have already made the case that the context or situation can strongly affect performance. Therefore, it cannot be assumed that an individual's performance or underlying learning in any domain will be invariant or strictly linear. To make this point, the MDL accounts for the situation-specific relations among knowledge, interest, and strategic processing by its inclusion of phases. *Phases* are the more recurrent, iterative aspects of academic development (Karmiloff-Smith, 1984; 1986). In other words, since learning conditions are always in flux, there is a constant interplay among the forces that shape, form, or transform one's state in an academic field. It is this fluidity that characterizes the phases of learning. However, the phases result in discernible and recurring patterns over time. They, in essence, mirror the broader patterns of change in each of the three proposed developmental stages of domain learning.

Since most of the key components of the MDL have already been defined in this chapter, they will only be mentioned here. However, the model identifies two forms of subject-matter knowledge (i.e., domain knowledge and topic knowledge) that require some delineation. *Subject-matter knowledge* can be broadly described as the knowledge an individual possesses in a specific field of study, such as physics, statistics, or economics (Alexander et al., 1991). *Domain knowledge* represents the breadth or generality of one's subject-specific knowledge, encompassing all the declarative, procedural, and conditional knowledge relative to a designated field (e.g., law or psychology). *Topic knowledge*, in comparison, deals with the individual's knowledge of domain-specific concepts (Alexander et al., 1991). Typically, these two forms of subject-matter knowledge are complementary in that the enhancement of topic knowledge contributes to an increase in domain knowledge or vice versa. However, the MDL distinguishes between them precisely because this relationship is not perfect. For example, in the field of school psychology, graduate students may have a great deal of knowledge about certain standardized intelligence tests but have only limited knowledge about assessment practices. Likewise, a graduate student may have a rich body of general knowledge related to his chosen field of school psychology but have little awareness of current research on inclusion.

Another component in the MDL is learner interest. The two forms of interest, previously defined, are individual interest and situational interest. Unlike the complementary nature of domain and topic knowledge, however, individual and situational interest follow rather different and potentially oppositional paths as students progress from acclimation to proficiency. As we show in the profiles that follow, individual interest manifests an increased presence as one moves into competence and on into proficiency. Situational interest, in contrast, exerts more of a presence in one's performance during acclimation.

The final dimension of the MDL is strategic processing in the form of general cognitive and metacognitive strategies (e.g., Garner & Alexander, 1989; Paris & Winograd, 1990; Weinstein & Mayer, 1986). So defined, the general strategy component of the MDL encompasses tools critical in the acquisition, transformation, and transfer of information (Pintrich et al., 1993). Later, general cognitive and metacognitive strategies become important mechanisms in the generation of new knowledge during the proficiency or expert stage.

## The Stages of Domain Learning

As with various other developmental models or learning theories (e.g., Shuell, 1990; Spiro, Feltovich, Jacobson, & Coulson, 1992), the MDL entails three stages: acclimation, competence, and proficiency or expertise.

### *Acclimation*

Acclimation is the initial or entry point in this stage model where individuals are confronted with a domain for which they possess little relevant knowledge. What domain or topic knowledge acclimated learners do possess is poorly organized or fragmented (Gelman & Greeno, 1989). Because of this fragmentation, memory performance for acclimated learners is hampered (Alexander, Pate, Kulikowich, Farrell, & Wright, 1989), as is their ability to differentiate important from trivial content (Alexander, Jetton, Kulikowich, & Woehler, 1994; Alexander, Kulikowich, & Schulze, 1994b) and to associate topics with their related domains (Alexander et al., 1989). For example, Alexander et al. (1989) found that students might be able to provide some information about the concept of black holes but did not understand the association of this concept to any broader domain, such as astronomy or astrophysics.

Moreover, because their knowledge base is so loosely structured (often around declarative information), acclimated learners operate with few misconceptions (e.g., Pines & West, 1983; West & Pines, 1985). However, because they often rely on their implicit theories and non-schooled knowledge, what misconceptions they do possess are frequently difficult to identify and hard to modify (Alexander, Chinn & Brewer, 1993; Gardner, 1991; Vygotsky, 1934/1986).

Also, since their familiarity with the domain is low, acclimated learners must rely heavily on their general strategic knowledge to build a relevant knowledge base and to achieve greater automaticity with common problems or tasks (Anderson, 1982; Brown & Palincsar, 1989; Glaser, 1984). Even acclimated learners' execution of general strategies is hampered as a result of their limited foundation of domain and topic knowledge (Alexander & Judy, 1988). In other words, during early acclimation, learners may well use strategies in somewhat of a trial-and-error or "brute force" approach to problem solving (Garner, 1987). As a consequence of these conditions, acclimated learners may need to rely heavily on resources or affordance in the learning environment to make progress toward competence.

Situational interest also plays a more predominant role in acclimation than does personal or individual interest. Logically, it is difficult to imagine students being deeply invested in any domain that they know little about. Rather, it makes sense that these novice learners would be more affected by transitory and short-lived conditions within the immediate context. It is, therefore, easy to understand why acclimated learners may be more susceptible to the seductive details that punctuate their learning environments. Therefore, educators must be cautious in the manner in which they arouse students' interest or draw their attention during introductions to new content domains. If they are not careful, they may actually divert their students' attention away from more relevant content (Garner et al., 1989; Wade & Adams, 1990; Wade et al., 1993).

## Competence

To understand the nature of competence, it may be useful to contrast these learners with those in acclimation. Unlike acclimated learners, competent students have more principled, coherent subject-matter knowledge. Not only have competent learners acquired more subject-matter knowledge, but also the association between their topic knowledge and domain knowledge is stronger. In addition, their knowledge base in the domain is made up of increasingly more procedural and conditional, as well as declarative, knowledge. Consequently, these more learned students are better able to differentiate domain-relevant from domain-irrelevant information and more important content from less important content. Also, misconceptions in the competence stage are more apt to have a schooled appearance in that they are rooted in content presented in textbooks or arising from teachers' lectures more than from everyday, out-of-school experiences (Alexander, in press). It is conceivable as well that these learners have experienced some form of restructuring of their knowledge in their progression from acclimation to competence.

With its orientation toward expanding and elaborating on the knowledge base, the stage of competence represents the period of optimal interplay between general strategies and the domain-specific strategies that are aspects of subject-matter knowledge. Problems typical of the domain become more familiar and their solution paths more routinized, which decreases the competent learners' reliance on general cognitive strategies. Still, when they do encounter barriers to comprehension or performance, competent learners have enough domain knowledge to employ general strategies efficiently and effectively. Of course, they must still rely on their metacognitive knowledge to monitor the execution of academic tasks and to optimize their learning in a

given domain. Motivation is also a factor in this improved relationship between strategic processing and subject-matter knowledge in that competent learners, by virtue of their self-efficacy, individual interest, or motivation (Bandura, 1993; Harter, 1990; Schunk & Meece, 1992), may be more willing to exert the effort required to behave strategically.

Although it is possible for students' progression from acclimation to competence to be fueled largely by extrinsic factors, such as grades, approval, or financial security, it is conceivable that their growing competence is associated with an increase in personal interest in the domain. Thus, the rise in domain and topic knowledge characteristic of competent performance should be highly correlated with a rise in students' reported individual interest in the field as well as a decreased dependence on situational interest factors (e.g., Alexander, Kulikowich, & Schulze, 1994b; Renninger, 1992).

## Proficiency or Expertise

As with the earlier expert-novice models, the highest stage in the MDL is proficiency or expertise. Unlike these earlier models, however, the MDL does not hypothesize that most or even many of the students in classrooms will reach this highest stage of academic development. Perhaps this is because proficiency seemingly demands high levels of subject-matter knowledge, a well-developed repertoire of general strategies, *and* a passion or deep investment in the domain (Alexander, Kulikowich, & Schulze, 1994a; Hidi, 1990; Schiefele, Krapp, & Wintler, 1992). Moreover, to achieve proficiency or expertise in a domain, individuals must be willing and able to demonstrate a personal interest and level of effort rarely demanded or encouraged in the educational system (e.g., Ames, 1992; Corno, 1993; Dweck & Leggett, 1988; Kruglanski, 1990a, 1990b; Pintrich & DeGroot, 1990; Pintrich & Garcia, 1991). Perhaps understandably, only situational interest holds at a steady level of involvement during proficiency, whereas other factors show an increased presence. This suggests that experts may well find particular facets of a situation intriguing, yet their attention or performance is not diverted from more relevant goals or more important content (Alexander, Kulikowich, & Schulze, 1994a).

Among proficient learners, there is also a greater likelihood of system-wide misconceptions that have been termed "Gordian concepts"

(Perkins & Simmons, 1988). These pervasive misunderstandings are said to result from paradigmatic shifts in the domain, as when mechanics shifted from Aristotelian to Galilean to Newtonian conceptualizations. Thus, experts holding to Gordian misconceptions tend to operate under a theoretical framework that is seriously flawed. The eradication of this class of misconceptions can require experts to radically restructure their entire base of subject-matter knowledge, abandoning strongly and broadly held notions relative to their chosen fields.

Further, while proficient or expert learners continue their quest for understanding in their domains, they must also assume the role of knowledge creator. That is, proficient individuals are typically expected to add to the very base of knowledge that defines a domain. To do so, these experts must, in effect, create their own asynchronies in an otherwise synchronic environment (Gardner, 1993). Because of the demands of knowledge generation and the complex problem solving that is associated with this final stage of academic development, there is more general strategic processing during proficiency. Unlike the prior stages, however, this rise is not necessarily associated with the acquisition of new general strategies or with the refinement of existing ones, but with a more focused and intense use of cognitive and metacognitive strategies during engagement in knowledge generation or complex problem solving.

## IMPLICATIONS FOR EDUCATIONAL PRACTICE

Our intention in this chapter has been to offer an overview of recent trends in cognitive psychology that we believe can speak to school psychologists in their mission to serve members of the educational community. Toward this end, we have examined research into the nature and role of knowledge, skillful and strategic processing, the interrelationship of cognition and motivation, the influence of contextual and situational factors, and the development of academic competence. As a means of summarizing the research in these areas, we would like to leave the reader with guiding principles that arise from the volumes dedicated to each of these central themes. It is our hope that these principles can be the cornerstone for improved learning and development for all individuals who cross the threshold of educational institutions in pursuit of under-

standing. It is also our hope that these precepts will prove useful to those who have accepted the responsibility of aiding others in their educational pursuits.

- Not only must we come to appreciate the complexity and imperfections of human knowledge, as well as its powerful role in coloring and shaping subsequent learning and development, but we must also find ways of unearthing and analyzing individuals' knowledge without trivializing or oversimplifying its true nature.

- Effective school curricula must be much more than a litany of declarative knowledge delivered in a piecemeal fashion. To quell the epidemic of inert knowledge, students must grasp the value of what they are learning and be equipped with the concomitant procedural and conditional knowledge that is essential for the application of what they know.

- If we are to aid learners in acquiring deeper and richer understandings and if we are to assist them in transferring that knowledge from one context to another, the barriers that exist between schooled and nonschooled knowledge must be bridged in terms of both instruction and assessment.

- If we are to help students to alter their primitive theories or change their misconceptions, we must begin with a clearer sense of what they believe and determine how those beliefs interact with schooled learning.

- Success in learning is predicated on skillful and strategic performance. The former contributes to efficient and facile functioning, and the latter ensures that difficulties encountered on the road to improved learning can be circumvented in a planned and effective manner. Further, those skills and strategies must be aligned with content in realistic and meaningful ways and not disembodied from it.

- Learning environments that support and reward strategic processing are more likely to contribute to academic success.

- It is important for educational researchers and practitioners to ascertain when, where, and for whom particular skills and strategies result in improved learning.

- Individuals must engage in self-monitoring and self-regulation of their thoughts and actions if they are to become independent and fully actualized learners. If not, these individuals must remain dependent on others to tell them what to do and how to think. Also, these learners will be hindered in their ability to gauge the quality of their own work and must, therefore, rely on others to gauge their performance.

- Efforts to facilitate students' learning and development must consider their motivations, including their interests, goals, and self-perceptions, or such efforts are likely to fail.
- Limited academic progress may be associated with a lack of will, direction, or desire rather than with any cognitive shortcoming.
- Individuals' thoughts and actions occur within a particular context or situation and are, consequently, altered by it.
- The educational process is fundamentally a social process in which individuals of varying ages, abilities, aptitudes, interests, and backgrounds interact within an instructional community. By building on this social nature, educators may be able to enhance students' learning and development.
- Of all the resources in any given context or situation, the "human" resource may be the most critical in optimizing the educational experience.
- Teachers must be careful not to confuse temporary arousal or piqued attention with more deep-seated interests and involvements. The former, situational interest, may only misdirect or misguide a learner, especially when it fails to call attention to important principles or salient content. What should be sought in the classroom is rooted relevance, where significant content is linked to students' internal goals and personal interests.
- Competent performance in any academic domain demands not only principled knowledge and a rich repertoire of general cognitive and metacognitive strategies but also a growing interest in the domain. However, the knowledge, strategic ability, and personal investment associated with high competence or expert performance are rarely demanded or encouraged by the educational system.

## Postscript

What we hope has been evident in these pages is that cognitive psychology is a dynamic field that has undergone marked changes in the past decade. Whereas the field was once focused on the nature of information processing and whereas the language of the cognitive psychologist was punctuated with computer terminology, today's cognitive psychologist is more likely to speak of motivation, situation, sociocultural context, or multidimensionality and complexity. It may be that the next volume of this text will find that cognition is pursuing simpler and more traditional pathways than those described here. Such shifts have occurred before and may well occur again.

The emergence of these new themes in cognitive psychology should not suggest that cognitivists have abandoned their past. Rather, as with other fields, including school psychology, cognitive psychology has extended its boundaries in an effort to better understand the nature of learning and teaching and to better assist those on the road to greater competence. Whatever the future, it is critical that educational researchers and practitioners learn the lessons of this decade so that their next steps can be carefully and wisely chosen.

As they have built on the decades of research in knowledge, memory, strategic processing, and the like and have moved into new territories, cognitivists have found themselves on common ground with others who have similar educational missions. Thus, many of the themes we have presented in this chapter have analogues in the literature of school psychology. For that reason, the more that cognitive psychology and school psychology can work together to enrich their common ground, the more likely they are to thrive and to bear the fruit of enriched understandings of learning and development. Should these fields be successful in their goals, many children and youth in our schools would be the beneficiaries of their efforts.

## References

Alexander, P. A. (1992). Domain knowledge: Evolving themes and emerging concerns. *Educational Psychologist, 27*, 33–51.

Alexander, P. A. (1996). The past, present, and future of knowledge research: A reexamination of the role of knowledge in learning and instruction. [Editor's notes]. *Educational Psychologist, 31*(2), 89–92.

Alexander, P. A. (1997). Mapping the multidimensional nature of domain learning: The interplay of cognitive, motivational, and strategic forces. In M. L. Maehr & P. R. Pintrich (Eds.), *Advances in motivation and achievement* (Vol. 10, pp. 213–250). Greenwich, CT: JAI Press.

Alexander, P. A. (in press). Positioning conceptual change within a model of domain literacy. In B. Guzzetti & C. Hynd (Eds.), *Theoretical perspectives on conceptual change.* Mahwah, NJ: Erlbaum.

Alexander, P. A., & Dochy, F. J. R. C. (1994). Adults' views about knowing and believing. In R. Garner & P. A. Alexander (Eds.), *Beliefs about text and about instruction with text* (pp. 223–244). Hillsdale, NJ: Erlbaum.

Alexander, P. A., & Dochy, F. J. R. C. (1995). Conceptions of knowledge and beliefs: A comparison across varying cultural and educational communities. *American Educational Research Journal, 32,* 413–442.

Alexander, P. A., Jetton, T. L., & Kulikowich, J. M. (1995). Interrelationship of knowledge, interest, and recall: Assessing a model of domain learning. *Journal of Educational Psychology, 87,* 559–575.

Alexander, P. A., & Judy, J. E. (1988). The interaction of domain-specific and strategic knowledge in academic performance. *Review of Educational Research, 58,* 375–404.

Alexander, P. A., Jetton, T. L., Kulikowich, J. M., & Woehler, C. (1994). Contrasting instructional and structural importance: The seductive effect of teacher questions. *Journal of Reading Behavior, 26,* 19–45.

Alexander, P. A., Kulikowich, J. M., & Schulze, S. K. (1994a). How subject-matter knowledge affects recall and interest on the comprehension of scientific exposition. *American Educational Research Journal, 31,* 313–337.

Alexander, P. A., Kulikowich, J. M., & Schulze, S. K. (1994b). The influence of topic knowledge, domain knowledge, and interest on the comprehension of scientific exposition. *Learning and Individual Differences, 6,* 379–397.

Alexander, P. A., & Murphy, P. K. (1998). The research base for APA's learner-centered principles. In N. Lambert & B. L. McCombs (Eds.), *Issues in school reform: A sampler of psychological perspectives on learner-centered schools.* (pp. 25–60) Washington, DC: The American Psychological Association.

Alexander, P. A., Murphy, P. K., Woods, B. S., Duhon, K., & Parker, D. (1997). College instruction and concomitant changes in students' knowledge, interest, and strategy use: A study of domain learning. *Contemporary Educational Psychology, 22,* 125–146.

Alexander, P. A., Murphy, P. K., Guan, J., & Murphy, P. A. (1998). Teachers' and students' conceptions of knowledge and beliefs: A cross-cultural perspective. *Learning and Instruction, 8,* 97–116.

Alexander, P. A., Murphy, P. K., & Woods, B. S. (1996). Of squalls and fathoms: Navigating the seas of educational reform. *Educational Researcher, 25*(3), 31–36, 39.

Alexander, P. A., Parsons, J. L., & Nash, W. R. (1996). *Toward a theory of creativity.* Washington, DC: National Association for Gifted Children.

Alexander, P. A., Pate, P. E., Kulikowich, J. M., Farrell, D. M., & Wright, N. L. (1989). Domain-specific and strategic knowledge. Effects of training on students of differing ages or competence levels. *Learning and Individual Differences, 1,* 283–325.

Alexander, P. A., Schallert, D. L., & Hare, V. C. (1991). Coming to terms: How researchers in learning and literacy talk about knowledge. *Review of Educational Research, 61,* 315–343.

Alvermann, D. E., Smith, L. C., & Readence, J. E. (1985). Prior knowledge activation and the comprehension of compatible and incompatible text. *Reading Research Quarterly, 20,* 420–436.

Amabile, T. M. (1983). *The social psychology of creativity.* New York: Springer-Verlag.

Amabile, T. M. (1990). With you, without you: The social psychology of creativity, and beyond. In M. A. Runco & R. S. Albert (Eds.), *Theories of creativity* (pp. 61–91). Newbury Park, CA: Sage.

American Psychological Association Presidential Task Force on Psychology in Education. (1993). *Learner-centered psychological principles: Guidelines for school redesign and reform.* Washington, DC: American Psychological Association.

Ames, C. (1992). Classrooms: Goals, structures, and student motivation. *Journal of Educational Psychology, 84,* 261–271.

Ames, C., & Ames, R. (Eds.). (1985). *Research on motivation in education: The classroom milieu* (Vol. 2). San Diego: Academic Press.

Ames, C., & Ames, R. (Eds.). (1989). *Research on motivation in education: The classroom milieu* (Vol. 3). San Diego: Academic Press.

Ames, C., & Archer, J. (1988). Achievement goals in the classroom: Students' learning strategies and motivation processes. *Journal of Educational Psychology, 80,* 260–267.

Anderson, J. R. (1982). Acquisition of cognitive skill. *Psychological Review, 89,* 260–267.

Anderson, J. R. (1983). *The architecture of cognition.* Cambridge, MA: Harvard University Press.

Anderson, R. C., Pichert, J. W., & Shirey, L. L. (1983). Effects of reader's schema at different points in time. *Journal of Educational Psychology, 75,* 271–279.

Anderson, R. C., Reynolds, R. E., Schallert, D. L., & Goetz, E. T. (1977). Frameworks for comprehending discourse. *American Educational Research Journal, 14,* 367–381.

Aronson, E. (1978). *The jigsaw classroom.* Beverly Hills, CA: Sage.

Baker, L., & Brown, A. L. (1984). Metacognitive skills of reading. In P. D. Pearson (Ed.), *Handbook of reading research* (pp. 353–394). New York: Longman.

Bandura, A. (1977). Self-efficacy: Toward a unifying

theory of behavioral change. *Psychological Review, 84*, 191–215.

Bandura, A. (1993). Perceived self-efficacy in cognitive development and functioning. *Educational Psychologist, 28*, 117–148.

Banks, J. A. (1989). Multicultural education: Characteristics and goals. In J. A. Banks & C. A. McGee-Banks (Eds.), *Multicultural education: Issues and perspectives* (pp. 2–26). Needham Heights, MA: Allyn & Bacon.

Banks, J. A. (1992, January). Multicultural education: For freedom's sake. *Educational Leadership*, pp. 32–35.

Bereiter, C., & Scardamalia, M. (1989). Intentional learning as a goal of instruction. In L. B. Resnick (Ed.), *Knowing, learning, and instruction: Essays in honor of Robert Glaser* (pp. 361–392). Hillsdale, NJ: Erlbaum.

Borkowski, J. G., Carr, M., & Pressley, M. (1987). "Spontaneous" strategy use: Perspectives from metacognitive theory. *Intelligence, 11*, 61–75.

Bradley-Johnson, S., Johnson, C. M., & Jacob-Timm, S. (1995). Where will—where should—changes in education leave school psychology? *Journal of School Psychology, 33*, 187–200.

Broadbent, D. E., FitzGerald, P., & Broadbent, M. H. P. (1986). Implicit and explicit knowledge in the control of complex systems. *British Journal of Psychology, 77*, 33–50.

Bronfenbrenner, J. (1979). *The ecology of human development: Experiments by nature and design.* Cambridge, MA: Harvard University Press.

Bronfenbrenner, J. (1989). Ecological systems theory. In R. Vasta (Ed.), *Annals of child development* (Vol. 16, pp. 187–251). Greenwich, CT: JAI Press.

Brown, A. L. (1975). The development of memory: Knowing, knowing about knowing, and knowing how to know. In H. W. Reese (Ed.), *Advances in child development and behavior* (Vol. 10, pp. 103–152). New York: Academic Press.

Brown, A. L., Armbruster, B., & Baker, L. (1986). The role of metacognition in reading and studying. In J. Oransanu (Ed.), *Reading comprehension: From research to practice* (pp. 49–75). Hillsdale, NJ: Erlbaum.

Brown, A. L., & Campione, J. S. (1990). Communities of learning and thinking, or a context by any other name. *Contributions to Human Development, 21*, 108–126.

Brown, A. L., & Palincsar, A. S. (1989). Guided, cooperative learning and individual knowledge acquisition. In L. B. Resnick (Ed.), *Knowing, learning, and instruction: Essays in honor of Robert Glaser* (pp. 393–451). Hillsdale, NJ: Erlbaum.

Carey, S. (1985). *Conceptual change in childhood.* Cambridge, MA: MIT Press.

Carraher, T. N., Carraher, D. W., & Schliemann, A. D. (1985). Mathematics in the streets and in schools. *British Journal of Developmental Psychology, 3*, 21–29.

Case, R. (1985). *Intellectual development: Birth to adulthood.* New York: Academic Press.

Ceci, S. J., & Bronfenbrenner, U. (1985). "Don't forget to take the cupcakes out of the oven": Prospective, memory, strategic time-monitoring, and context. *Child Development, 56*,152–164.

Champagne, A. B., Kloper, L. E., & Anderson, J. H. (1980). Factors influencing the learning of classical mechanics. *American Journal of Physics, 48*, 1074–1079.

Chi, M. T. H. (1985). Interactive roles of knowledge and strategies in the development of organized sorting and recall. In S. F. Chipman, J. W. Segal, & R. Glaser (Eds.), *Thinking and learning skills: Research and open questions* (Vol. 2, pp. 457–483). Hillsdale, NJ: Erlbaum.

Chi, M. T. H., Feltovich, P., & Glaser, R. (1981). Categorization and representation of physics problems by experts and novices. *Cognitive Science, 5*, 121–152.

Chi, M. T. H., Glaser, R., & Farr, M. J. (1988). *The nature of expertise.* Hillsdale, NJ: Erlbaum.

Chinn, C. A., & Brewer, W. F. (1993). The role of anomalous data in knowledge acquisition: A theoretical framework and implications for science instruction. *Review of Educational Research, 63*, 1–49.

Cognition and Technology Group at Vanderbilt. (1990). Anchored instruction and its relationship to situated cognition. *Educational Researcher, 19*(6), 2–10.

Cole, M. (1990). Cognitive development and formal schooling: The evidence from cross-cultural research. In L. C. Moll (Ed.), *Vygotsky and education* (pp. 89–110). Cambridge: Cambridge University Press.

Cole, M., & D'Andrade, R. (1982). The influence of schooling on concept formation: Some preliminary conclusions: *Quarterly Newsletter of the Laboratory of Comparative Human Cognition, 4*, 19–26.

Cole, M., & Engeström, Y. (1993). A cultural-historical approach to distributed cognition. In G. Salomon (Ed.), *Distributed cognition: Psychological and educational considerations* (pp. 1–46). Cambridge: Cambridge University Press.

Collins, A., Brown, J. S., & Newman, S. E. (1989). Cognitive apprenticeships: Teaching the crafts of reading, writing, and mathematics. In L. B. Resnick (Ed.), *Knowing, learning, and instruction: Essays in honor of Robert Glaser* (pp. 453–494). Hillsdale, NJ: Erlbaum.

Conoley, J. C., & Gutkin, T. B. (1995). Why didn't—why doesn't—school psychology realize its promise? *Journal of School Psychology, 33*, 209–217.

Corno, L. (1993). The best-laid plans. Modern conceptions of volition and educational research. *Educational Researcher, 22*(2), 14–22.

Corno, L., & Rohrkemper, M. (1985). The intrinsic

motivation to learn in classrooms. In C. Ames & R. Ames (Eds.), *Research on motivation in education: The classroom milieu* (Vol. 2, pp. 53–84). New York: Academic Press.

Crick, N. R., & Dodge, A. (1994). A review and reformulation of social-information processing mechanisms in children. *Psychological Bulletin, 115*(1), 74–101.

Csikszentmihalyi, M. (1990). *Flow: The psychology of optimal experience.* New York: Cambridge University Press.

deCharms, R. (1968). *Personal causation: The internal affective determinants of behavior.* New York: Academic Press.

Deci, E. L., & Ryan, R. M. (1985). *Intrinsic motivation and self-determination in human behavior.* New York: Academic Press.

Deci, E. L., & Ryan, R. M. (1991). A motivational approach to self: Integration in personality. In R. Dienstbier (Ed.), *Nebraska symposium on motivation, 1990* (pp. 237–288). Lincoln: University of Nebraska Press.

Deci, E. L., Valleran, R. J., Pelletier, L. G., & Ryan, R. M. (1991). Motivation and education: The self-determination perspective. *Educational Psychologist, 26,* 325–346.

de Jong, T., & Ferguson-Hessler, M. G. M. (1996). Types and qualities of knowledge. *Educational Psychologist, 31,*105–113.

Derman-Sparks, L., & Anti-Bias Curriculum Task Force. (1989). *Anti-bias curriculum: Tools for empowering young children.* Washington, DC: National Association for the Education of Young Children.

Dewey, J. (1913). *Interest and effort in education.* Boston: Riverside.

diSessa, A. A. (1982). Unlearning Aristotelian physics. A study of knowledge-based learning. *Cognitive Science, 6,* 37–75.

diSessa, A. A. (1989). Toward an epistemology of physics. *Cognitive Science, 13,* 145–182.

Dweck, C. S. (1986). Motivational processes affecting learning. *American Psychologist, 10,* 1040–1048.

Dweck, C. S., & Leggett, E. L. (1988). A social-cognitive approach to motivation and personality. *Psychological Review, 95,* 256–273.

Dworkin, G. (1988). *The theory and practice of autonomy.* New York: Cambridge University Press.

Ericsson, K. A., & Simon, H. A. (1984). *Protocol analysis: Verbal report as data.* Cambridge, MA: MIT Press.

Ericsson, K. A., & Smith, J. (1991). *Toward a general theory of expertise: Prospects and limits.* Cambridge: Cambridge University Press.

Fantuzzo, J. W., King, J. A., & Heller, L. R. (1992). Effects of reciprocal peer tutoring on mathematics and school adjustment: A component analysis. *Journal of Educational Psychology, 84,* 331–339.

Flavell, J. H. (1977). *Cognitive development.* Englewood Cliffs, NJ: Prentice-Hall.

Fuchs, D., & Fuchs, D. L. (1994). Inclusive schools movement and the radicalization of special education reform. *Exceptional Children, 31,* 75–103.

Fuchs, L. S., Fuchs, D., & Bishop, N. (1992). Instructional adaptation for students at risk for academic failure. *Journal of Educational Research, 86,* 70–84.

Fuchs, L. S., Fuchs, D., Phillips, N. B., Hamlett, C. L., & Karns, K. (1995). Acquisition and transfer effects of classwide peer-assisted learning strategies in mathematics for students with varying learning histories. *School Psychology Review, 24,* 604–620.

Gardner, H. (1991). *The unschooled mind.* New York: Basic Books.

Gardner, H. (1993). *Creating minds.* New York: Basic Books.

Garner, R. (1987). *Metacognition and reading comprehension.* Norwood, NJ: Ablex.

Garner, R. (1988). Verbal-report data on cognitive and metacognitive strategies. In C. E. Weinstein, E. T. Goetz, & P. A. Alexander (Eds.), *Learning and study strategies: Issues in assessment, instruction, and evaluation* (pp. 63–76). San Diego: Academic Press.

Garner, R., & Alexander, P. A. (1989). Metacognition: Answered and unanswered questions. *Educational Psychologist, 24,* 143–148.

Garner, R., & Alexander, P. A. (Eds.). (1994). *Beliefs about text and about instruction with text.* Hillsdale, NJ: Erlbaum.

Garner, R., Alexander, P. A., Gillingham, M. G., Kulikowich, J. M., & Brown, R. (1991). Interest and learning from text. *American Educational Research Journal, 28,* 643–659.

Garner, R., Gillingham, M. G., & White, C. S. (1989). Effects of "seductive details" on macroprocessing and microprocessing in adults and children. *Cognition and Instruction, 6,* 41–57.

Gelman, R., & Greeno, J. G. (1989). On the nature of competence: Principles for understanding in a domain. In L. B. Resnick (Ed.), *Knowing, learning, and instruction: Essays in honor of Robert Glaser* (pp. 125–186). Hillsdale, NJ: Erlbaum.

Gibson, J. J. (1966). *The senses considered as perceptual systems.* Boston: Houghton-Mifflin.

Gilligan, C. (1977). In a different voice: Women's conceptions of the self and of morality. *Harvard Educational Review, 47,* 481–517.

Gilligan, C. (1987). *In a different voice: Psychological theory and women's development.* Cambridge, MA: Harvard University Press.

Glaser, R. (1984). Education and thinking. The role of knowledge. *American Psychologist, 39,* 93–104.

Goetz, E. T., Alexander, P. A., & Ash, M. J. (1992). *Educational psychology: A classroom perspective.* Columbus, OH: Merrill.

Gottfried, A. E. (1985). Academic intrinsic motivation in elementary and junior high school students. *Journal of Educational Psychology, 20,* 205–215.

Gottfried, A. E. (1990). Academic intrinsic motivation in young elementary school children. *Journal of Educational Psychology, 82,* 525–538.

Greene, S., & Ackerman, J. M. (1995). Expanding the constructivist metaphor. A rhetorical perspective on literacy research and practice. *Review of Educational Research, 65,* 383–420.

Greeno, J. G., & Moore, J. L. (1993). Situativity and symbols: Response to Vera and Simon. *Cognitive Science, 17,* 49–59.

Guthrie, J. T., McCann, A., Hynd, C., & Stahl, S. (in press). Classroom contexts promoting literacy engagement. In J. Flood, S. B. Heath, & D. Lapp (Eds.), *Handbook for literacy educators: Research on teaching the communications and visual arts.* New York: Macmillan.

Gutkin, T. B., & Reynolds, C. R. (Eds.). (1990). *The handbook of school psychology.* New York: Wiley.

Guzzetti, B., & Hynd, C. (Eds.). (in press). *Theoretical perspectives on conceptual change.* Mahwah, NJ: Erlbaum.

Harris, K. R., & Graham, S. (1994). Constructivism: Principles, paradigms, and integration. *Journal of Special Education, 28,* 233–247.

Harter, S. (1990). Identity and self-development. In S. Feldman & G. Eliott (Eds.), *At the threshold: The developing adolescent* (pp. 352–387). Cambridge, MA: Harvard University Press.

Harter, S. (1996). Teacher and classmate influences on scholastic motivation, self-esteem, and level of voice in adolescents. In J. Juvonen & K. Wentzel (Eds.), *Social motivation: Understanding children's school adjustment.* (pp. 11–97) New York: Cambridge University Press.

Hasselhorn, M., & Körkel, J. (1986). Metacognitive versus traditional reading instruction: The mediating role of domain specific knowledge on children's text processing. *Human Learning, 5,* 79–90.

Hidi, S. (1990). Interest and its contribution as a mental resource for learning. *Review of Educational Research, 60,* 549–571.

James. W. (1890). *Principles of psychology* (Vols. 1 & 2). New York: Holt.

Jetton, T. L., & Alexander, P. A. (1997). Instructional importance: What teachers value and what students learn. *Reading Research Quarterly, 32,* 290–308.

Johnson, D. W., & Johnson, R. T. (1985). Motivational processes in cooperative, competitive, and individualistic learning situations. In C. Ames & R. Ames (Eds.), *Research on motivation in education* (Vol. 2, pp. 249–286). Orlando, FL: Academic Press.

Karmiloff-Smith, A. (1984). Children's problem solving. In M. E. Lamb, A. L. Brown, & B. Rogoff (Eds.), *Advances in developmental psychology* (Vol. 3, pp. 39–90). Hillsdale, NJ: Erlbaum.

Karmiloff-Smith, A. (1986). Stage/structure versus phase/process in modeling linguistic and cognitive development. In I. Levin (Ed.), *Stage and structure: Reopening the debate* (pp. 164–190). Norwood, NJ: Ablex.

Katz, L. G. (Ed.). (1982). *Current topics in early childhood education* (Vol. 4). Norwood, NJ: Ablex.

Kohlberg, L. (1981). *The philosophy of moral development.* New York: Harper & Row.

Kozulin, A. (1990). *Vygotsky's psychology: A biography of ideas.* Cambridge, MA: Harvard University Press.

Kruglanski, A. W. (1990a). Lay epistemic theory in social-cognitive psychology. *Psychological Inquiry, 1,* 181–197.

Kruglanski, A. W. (1990b). Motivations for judging and knowing: Implications for causal attribution. In E. T. Higgins & R. M. Sorrentino (Eds.), *Handbook of motivation and cognition* (pp. 333–369). New York: Guilford.

Lave, J. (1988). *Cognition in practice.* Cambridge: Cambridge University Press.

Lepper, M. R. (1988) Motivational considerations in the study of instruction. *Cognition and Instruction, 5,* 289–309.

Lipson, M. Y. (1983). The influence of religious affiliation on children's memory for text information. *Reading Research Quarterly, 18,* 448–457.

Maehr, M. L., & Braskamp, L. A. (1986). *The motivation factor: A theory of personal investment.* Lexington, MA: Heath.

McCombs, B. L. (1988). Motivational skills training: Combining metacognitive, cognitive, and affective learning strategies. In C. E. Weinstein, E. T. Goetz, & P. A. Alexander (Eds.), *Learning and study strategies: Issues in assessment, instruction, and evaluation* (pp. 141–169). San Diego: Academic Press.

McCutchen, D. (1986). Domain knowledge and linguistic knowledge in the development of writing ability. *Journal of Memory and Language, 25,* 431–444.

McDermott, J. J. (1986). *Streams of experience: Reflections on the history and philosophy of American culture.* Amherst: University of Massachusetts Press.

Meece, J. L., Blumenfeld, D. C., & Hoyle, R. H. (1988). Students' goal orientation and cognitive engagement in classroom activities. *Journal of Educational Psychology, 80,* 514–523.

Murphy, P. K., & Alexander, P. A. (1995, April). *Educational foundations: Practitioners' perceptions of the interrelationship of philosophy, psychology, and education.* Paper presented at the American Educational Research Association, San Francisco.

Murphy, P. K., & Woods, B. S. (1996). Situating knowledge in learning and instruction:

Unanswered questions and future directions. *Educational Psychologist, 31*(2), 141–145.

Naveh-Benjamin, M., McKeachie, W. J., Lin, Y. G., & Tucker, D. (1986). Inferring students' cognitive structure and their development using the "ordered-tree technique." *Journal of Educational Psychology, 78,* 130–140.

Newman, R. S., & Schwager, M. T. (1992). Student perceptions and academic help-seeking. In D. H. Schunk & J. L. Meece (Eds.), *Student perceptions in the classroom* (pp. 123–148). Hillsdale, NJ: Erlbaum.

Nicholls, J. G. (1984). Achievement motivation: Conceptions of ability, subjective experience, task choice, and performance. *Psychological Review, 91,* 328–346.

Ogbu, J. U. (1992). Understanding cultural diversity. *Educational Researcher, 21,* 5–14.

Palincsar, A. S., & Brown, A. L. (1984). Reciprocal teaching of comprehension-fostering and comprehension-monitoring activities. *Cognition and Instruction, 2,* 117–175.

Palincsar, A. S., & Perry, N. E. (1995). Developmental, cognitive, and sociocultural perspectives on assessing and instructing reading. *School Psychology Review, 24,* 331–344.

Paris, S. G., Lipson, M. Y., & Wixson, K. K. (1983). Becoming a strategic reader. *Contemporary Educational Psychology, 8,* 293–316.

Paris, S. G., & Winograd, P. (1990). Dimensions of thinking and cognitive instruction. In B. F. Jones & L. Idol (Eds.), *How metacognition can promote academic learning and instruction* (pp. 15–51). Hillsdale, NJ: Erlbaum.

Pea, R. D. (1988). Putting knowledge to use. In R. S. Nickerson & P. P. Zodhiates (Eds.), *Technology in education: Looking toward 2020* (pp. 169–212). Hillsdale, NJ: Erlbaum.

Pea, R. D. (1989). Socializing the knowledge transfer problem. *International Journal of Educational Research, 2,* 639–663.

Perkins, D. N., & Simmons, R. (1988). Patterns of misconceptions: An integrative model for science, math, and programming. *Review of Educational Research, 63,* 167–199.

Perret-Claremont, A., Perret, J., & Bell, N. (1980). The social construction of meaning and cognitive activity in elementary school children. In L. B. Resnick, J. M. Levine, & S. D. Teasley (Eds.), *Perspectives on socially shared cognition* (pp. 41–62). Washington, DC: American Psychological Association.

Phillips, D. A., & Zimmerman, M. (1990). The developmental course of perceived competence and incompetence among component children. In R. J. Sternberg & J. Kolligan (Eds.), *Competence considered* (pp. 41–66). New Haven, CT: Yale University Press.

Piaget, J. (1929). *The child's conception of the world.* Totowa, NJ: Littlefield, Adams.

Piaget, J. (1930). *The child's conception of physical causality.* New York: Harcourt, Brace.

Piaget, J. (1952). *The origins of intelligence in children.* New York: International Universities Press.

Pichert, J. W., & Anderson, R. C. (1977). Taking different perspectives on a story. *Journal of Educational Psychology, 69,* 309–315.

Pines, A. L., & West, L. (1983). A framework for conceptual change with special reference to misconceptions. In H. Helm & J. D. Novak (Eds.), *Proceedings of the international seminar on misconceptions in science and mathematics* (pp. 47–52). Ithaca, NY: Cornell University Press.

Pintrich, P. R. (1994). Continuities and discontinuities. Future directions for research in educational psychology. *Educational Psychologist, 29,* 137–148.

Pintrich, P. R., & DeGroot, E. (1991). Student goal orientation and self-regulation in the college classroom. In M. Maehr & P. R. Pintrich (Eds.), *Advances in motivation and achievement: Goals and self-regulatory processes* (Vol. 7, pp. 371–402). Greenwich, CT: JAI Press.

Pintrich, P. R., & Garcia, T. (1991). Student goal orientation and self-regulation in the classroom. In M. Maehr & P. R. Pintrich (Eds.), *Advances in motivation and achievement: Goals and self-regulatory processes* (Vol. 7, pp. 371–402). Greenwich, CT: JAI Press.

Pintrich, P. R., Marx, R. W., & Boyle, R. A. (1993). Beyond cold conceptual change. The role of motivational beliefs and classroom contextual factors in the process of conceptual change. *Review of Educational Research, 63,* 167–199.

Pintrich, P. R., & Schrauben, B. (1992). Students' motivational beliefs and their cognitive engagement in classroom academic tasks. In D. Schunk & J. Meese (Eds.), *Student perceptions in the classroom* (pp. 149–183). Hillsdale, NJ: Erlbaum.

Postman, N. (1992). *Technopoly.* New York: Knopf.

Postman, N. (1995). *The end of education: Redefining the value of school.* New York: Knopf.

Prawat, R. S. (1989). Promoting access to knowledge, strategy, and disposition in students: A research synthesis. *Review of Educational Research, 59,* 1–41.

Pressley, M., Borkowski, J., & Schneider, W. (1989). Good information processing: What is it and what education can do to promote it. *International Journal of Educational Research, 13,* 857–867.

Pressley, M., Goodchild, F., Fleet, J., Zajchowski, R., & Evans, E. D. (1989). The challenges of classroom strategy instruction. *Elementary School Journal, 89,* 301–342.

Pritchard, R. (1990). The effects of cultural schemata on reading processing strategies. *Reading Research Quarterly, 25,* 273–295.

Radziszewska, B., & Rogoff, B. (1988). Influence of adult and peer collaboration on childrens' planning skills. *Developmental Psychology, 24,* 840–848.

Reber, A. S. (1989). Implicit learning and tacit knowledge. *Journal of Experimental Psychology: General, 118*, 219–235.

Reimann, P., & Schult, T. (1996). Turning examples into cases: Acquiring knowledge structures for analogical problem solving. *Educational Psychologist, 31*, 123–132.

Renninger, K. A. (1992). Individual interest and development: Implications for theory and practice. In K. A. Renninger, S. Hidi, & A. Krapp (Eds.), *The role of interest in learning and development* (pp. 361–395). Hillsdale, NJ: Erlbaum.

Resnick, L. B. (1991). Shared cognition. In L. B. Resnick, J. M. Levine, & S. D. Teasley (Eds.), *Perspectives on socially shared cognition* (pp. 1–20). Washington, DC: American Psychological Association.

Resnick, L. B., Levine, J. M., & Teasley, S. D. (Eds.). (1991). *Perspectives on socially shared cognition.* Washington, DC: American Psychological Association.

Reynolds, R. E., & Shirey, L. L. (1988). The role of attention in studying and learning. In C. E. Weinstein, E. T. Goetz, & P. A. Alexander (Eds.), *Learning and study strategies: Issues in assessment, instruction, and evaluation* (pp. 77–100). San Diego: Academic Press.

Rogoff, B. (1990). *Apprenticeship in thinking: Cognitive development in social context.* New York: Oxford University Press.

Rogoff, B., & Chavajay, P. (1995). What's become of research on the cultural view of cognitive development? *American Psychologist, 50*, 859–877.

Rogoff, B., & Gauvain, M. (1986). A method for the analysis of patterns illustrated with data on mother-child instructional interaction. In J. Valsiner (Ed.), *The role of the individual subject on scientific psychology* (pp. 261–290). New York: Plenum.

Rosenshine, B., & Meister, C. (1994). Reciprocal teaching: A review of the research. *Review of Educational Research, 64*, 479–530.

Roth, K. J. (1990). Developing meaningful conceptual understanding in science. In B. F. Jones & L. Idol (Eds.), *Dimensions of thinking and cognitive instruction.* Hillsdale, NJ: Erlbaum.

Rumelhart, D. E., & Norman, D. A. (1981). Accretion, tuning, and restructuring: Three modes of learning. In J. W. Cotton & R. Klatsky (Eds.), *Semantic factors in cognition* (pp. 37–60). Hillsdale, NJ: Erlbaum.

Ryan, R. M. (1992). Agency and organization: Intrinsic motivation, autonomy, and the self in psychological development. In J. Jacobs (Ed.), *Nebraska symposium on motivation* (Vol. 40). Lincoln: University of Nebraska Press.

Ryle, G. (1949). *The concept of mind.* London: Hutchinson.

Salomon, G. (1993). *Distributed cognition: Psychological and educational considerations.* Cambridge: Cambridge University Press.

Saxe, G. B. (1991). *Culture and cognitive development: Studies in mathematical understanding.* Hillsdale, NJ: Erlbaum.

Saxe, G. B. (1992). Studying children's learning in context: Problems and prospects. *Journal of the Learning Sciences, 2*, 215–234.

Schiefele, U., & Csikszentmihalyi, M. (1994). Interest and the quality of experience in classrooms. *European Journal of Psychology of Education, 9*, 251–270.

Schiefele, U., & Csikszentmihalyi, M. (1995). Motivation and ability in mathematics experience and achievement. *Journal for Research in Mathematics Education, 26*, 163–181.

Schiefele, U., Krapp, A., & Wintler, A. (1992). Interest as a predictor of academic achievement: A meta-analysis of research. In K. A. Renninger, S. Hidi, & A. Krapp (Eds.), *The role of interest in learning and development* (pp. 183–211). Hillsdale, NJ: Erlbaum.

Schmeck, R. R. (1988). Individual differences and learning strategies. In C. E. Weinstein, E. T. Goetz, & P. A. Alexander (Eds.), *Learning and study strategies: Issues in assessment, instruction, and evaluation* (pp. 171–188). San Diego: Academic Press.

Schoenfeld, A. H. (1988). When good teaching leads to bad results: The disasters of "well-taught" mathematics courses. *Educational Psychologist, 23*, 145–166.

Schraw, G., & Dennison, R. S. (1994). The effect of reader purpose on interest and recall. *Journal of Reading Behavior, 26*, 1–18.

Schunk, D. (1991). Self-efficacy and academic motivation. *Educational Psychologist, 26*, 207–231.

Schunk, D. H., & Meece, J. L. (Eds.). (1992). *Student perceptions in the classroom.* Hillsdale, NJ: Erlbaum.

Scribner, S., & Cole, M. (1981). *The psychology of literacy.* Cambridge, MA: Harvard University Press.

Serpell, R. (1993). Interface between sociocultural and psychological aspects of cognition. In E. Farman, N. Minick, & A. Stone (Eds.), *Contexts for learning: Sociocultural dynamics in children's development* (pp. 357–368). New York: Oxford University Press.

Serpell, R., & Boykin, A. W. (1994). Cultural dimensions of cognition: A multiplex, dynamic system of constraints and possibilites. In R. J. Sternberg (Ed.), *Thinking and problem solving* (pp. 369–408). San Diego: Academic Press.

Shuell, T. J. (1990). Phases of meaningful learning. *Review of Educational Research, 60*, 531–547.

Skinner, B. F. (1953). *Science and human behavior.* New York: Macmillan.

Slavin, R. E. (1978). *Effects of student teams and peer tutoring on academic achievement and time on-task* (Tech. Rep. No. 240). Baltimore, MD: Johns

Hopkins University, Center for Social Organization of Schools.

Slavin, R. E. (1987). Development and motivational perspectives on cooperative learning: A reconciliation. *Child Development, 58,* 1161–1167.

Sleeter, C. E., & Grant, C. A. (1994). *Making choices for multicultural education: Five approaches to race, class, and gender* (2nd ed.). New York: Macmillan.

Spiro, R. J., Feltovich, P. J., Jacobson, M. J., & Coulson, R. L. (1992). Cognitive flexibility, constructivism, and hypertext: Random access instruction for advanced knowledge acquisition in ill-structured domains. In T. M. Duffy & D. H. Jonassen (Eds.), *Constructivism and the technology of instruction* (pp. 57–75). Cambridge: Cambridge University Press.

Spiro, R. J., & Jehng, J. C. (1990). Cognitive flexibility and hypertext: Theory and technology for the nonlinear and multidimensional traversal of complex subject matter. In D. Nix & R. J. Spiro (Eds.), *Cognition, education, and multimedia* (pp. 163–205). Hillsdale, NJ: Erlbaum.

Sternberg, R. J. (1985). But it's a sad tale that begins at the end: A reply to Glaser. *American Psychologist, 40,* 571–573.

Sternberg, R. J., Conway, B. E., Ketron, J. L., & Bernstein, M. (1981). People's conceptions of intelligence. *Journal of Personality and Social Psychology, 41,* 37–55.

Sternberg, R. J., & Lubart, T. I., (1991). An investment theory of creativity and its development. *Human Development, 34,* 1–31.

Stewart, I. (1987). *The problems of mathematics.* New York: Oxford University Press.

Tapasak, R. C., & Keller, H. R. (1995). A reaction to "Where will . . . ?" and suggestions for "How to": The need to address systems-level variables in school psychology role/function change efforts. *Journal of School Psychology, 33,* 201–208.

Thomas, R. E. (1992). *Comparing theories of child development* (3rd ed.). Belmont, CA: Wadsworth.

Tolman, E. C. (1932). *Purposive behavior in animals and men.* New York: Appleton-Century-Crofts.

Toulmin, S. E. (1985). *The inner life: The outer mind* (Vol. 15, Heinz Werner Lecture Series). Worchester, MA: Clark University Press.

Vera, A. H., & Simon, H. A. (1993). Situated action: A symbolic interpretation. *Cognitive Science, 17,* 7–48.

von Glaserfeld, E. (1991). *Radical constructivism in mathematics education.* Dordrecht, Neth.: Kluwer Academic Publishers.

Vosniadou, S., & Brewer, W. F. (1987). Theories of knowledge restructuring in development. *Review of Educational Research, 57,* 51–67.

Vygotsky, L. (1934/1986). *Thought and language.* (Trans. A. Kozulin). Cambridge, MA: MIT Press.

Wade, S. E., & Adams, R. B. (1990). Effects of importance and interest on recall of biographical text. *Journal of Reading Behavior, 4,* 331–351.

Wade, S. E., Schraw, G., Buxton, W. M., & Hayes, M. T. (1993). Seduction of the strategic reader: Effects of interest on strategies and recall. *Reading Research Quarterly, 28,* 93–114.

Weinstein, C. E., & Mayer, R. E. (1986). The teaching of learning strategies. In M. C. Wittrock (Ed.), *Handbook of research on teaching* (3rd ed., pp. 315–327). New York: Macmillan.

Wentzel, K. R. (1991). Relations between social competence and academic achievement in early adolescence. *Child Development, 62,* 1066–1078.

Wentzel, K. R. (1993). Social and academic goals at school: Motivation and achievement in early adolescence. *Journal of Early Adolescence, 13,* 4–20.

West, L. H. T., & Pines, A. L. (1985). *Cognitive structures and conceptual change* (pp. 101–115). New York: Academic Press.

White, P. (1980). Limitations on verbal reports on internal: A refutation of Nisbett and Wilson and Bem. *Psychological Review, 87,* 105–112.

Whitehead, A. N. (1929/1957). *The aims of education and other essasys.* New York: Macmillan.

Wigfield, A., & Eccles, J. (1992). The development of achievement task values: A theoretical analysis. *Developmental Review, 12,* 265–310.

Wigfield, A., & Harold, R. D. (1992). Teacher beliefs and children's achievement self-perceptions: A developmental perspective. In D. H. Schunk & J. L. Meece (Eds.), *Student perceptions in the classroom* (pp. 95–121). Hillsdale, NJ: Erlbaum.

Wigfield, A., & Karpathian, M. (1991). Who am I and what can I do? Children's self-concepts and motivation in achievement situations. *Educational Psychologist, 26*(3 & 4), 233–261.

Winne, P. H. (1995). Inherent details in self-regulated learning. *Educational Psychologist, 30,* 173–187.

Woods, B. S., & Murphy, P. K. (1996). *Widening the discussion: Situating constructivism within a Jamesian philosophy.* Manuscript submitted for publication.

Wylie, R. C. (1974). *The self-concept* (Vol. 1). Lincoln: University of Nebraska Press.

Wylie, R. C. (1979). *The self-concept* (Vol. 2). Lincoln: University of Nebraska Press.

Wylie, R. C. (1989). *Measures of the self-concept.* Lincoln: University of Nebraska Press.

Young, R. E. (1990). *A critical theory of education: Habermas and our children's future.* New York: Teachers' College Press.

Zimmerman, B. J. (1989). A social cognitive view of self-regulated academic learning. *Journal of Educational Psychology, 81,* 329–339.

Zimmerman, B. J. (1994). Dimensions of academic self-regulation: A conceptual framework for education. In D. H. Schunk & B. J. Zimmerman (Eds.), *Self-regulation of learning and performance: Issues and educational applications* (pp. 3–21). Hillsdale, NJ: Erlbaum.

Zimmerman, B. J., & Martinez-Pons, M. (1986). Development of a structured interview for assessing student use of self-regulated learning strategies. *American Educational Research Journal*, *23*, 614–628.

Zimmerman, B. J., & Martinez-Pons, M. (1988). Construct validation of a strategy model of student self-regulated learning. *Journal of Educational Psychology*, *80*, 284–290.

Zimmerman, B. J., & Martinez-Pons, M. (1992). Perceptions of efficacy and strategy use in the self-regulation of learning. In D. H. Schunk & J. L. Meece (Eds.), *Student perceptions in the classroom* (pp. 185–207). Hillsdale, NJ: Erlbaum.

## CHAPTER 8

# CONTRIBUTIONS OF SOCIAL PSYCHOLOGY TO SCHOOL PSYCHOLOGY

**FREDERIC J. MEDWAY**
**THOMAS P. CAFFERTY**
*University of South Carolina*

One hundred years ago Triplett (1897) conducted the first experiment in social psychology: Indiana schoolchildren took turns winding fishing reels as fast as they could, either alone or in the company of others who also wound reels. Triplett speculated, and ultimately found, that the presence of others "positively stimulated" or facilitated performance on a simple task. This study not only helped set the course for a century of controlled experimentation on social behavior in general and social facilitation in particular (cf. Sanna, 1992) but also had direct implications for contemporary educational practices. Moreover, had the study been done today, it might have been published in any one of a number of journals that focus on social, educational, developmental, school, or other areas of psychology, illustrating that many of the classifications among these areas are more artificial than real. Increasingly, school psychologists publish in social psychology journals and vice versa (e.g., Eisenberger & Selbst, 1994).

In earlier works we have argued that there is much common ground in social and school psychology and that both fields have been shaped by similar political and social forces (Medway & Cafferty, 1992). Moreover, the basic foundations of both social and school (and clinical) psychology derive from the writings of ancient Greek philosophers, who attempted to apply rational thought rather than religious and supernatural concepts to human behavior. Nor is it coincidental that when Triplett was studying social facilitation, Lightner Witmer, the first architect of clinical and school psychology, was establishing the first psychological clinic for children.

In this chapter we define social psychology, briefly review its historical developments, and discuss selected topics that are particularly relevant. Because of limitations on length, our coverage of the topics will be more cursory than we would like. To remedy this, we have attempted to balance discussion of the classical social psychological literature, major research reviews, and recent empirical studies, all the while attempting to draw various implications for school psychology practice. For more extensive coverage of the applications of social psychology to school psychology, see the edited volume by Medway and Cafferty (1992), in which many basic theories and research findings of social psychology are discussed and several chapters are devoted to the application of these principles to assessment, consultation, therapy, classroom learning, relationships with parents, and various social problems.

## THE FIELD OF SOCIAL PSYCHOLOGY

### What Is Social Psychology?

Most social psychologists would accept G. Allport's (1985) definition of social psychology as "an attempt to understand and explain how the thought, feeling and behavior of individuals are influenced by the actual, imagined, or implied presence of others" (p. 3). As implied by the definition, social psychologists have a potentially unlimited array of topics for study. For a variety of theoretical, historical, and practical reasons (Cartwright, 1979; Hendrick, 1977; Jones, 1985), the actual number of topics studied has been more modest. Since the post–World War II growth period, social psychology has focused heavily on the areas of (1) attitudes and attitude change, (2) attribution, (3) cognitive processes, (4) social and personal development, (5) attraction and affiliation, (6) sex roles, and (7) aggression (Smith, Richardson, & Hendrick, 1980). Most recently, there has been a decrease in attention to group processes and the causes of aggression and an increase in research on personality processes—particularly, stress and coping and mood states (West, Newsom, & Fenaughty, 1992).

In addition to the substantive areas just mentioned, social psychologists have conducted extensive research on methodological issues—including experimental demand characteristics, participants' roles, placebo effects, and experimenters' expectations (see Rosenthal & Rosnow, 1991; Wuebben, Straits, & Schulman, 1974)—and on statistical confounds (Baron & Kenney, 1986). Social psychology is also the discipline that has developed the techniques and procedures used in group dynamics and program evaluation. There are approximately 3,000 members of the Division of Personality and Social Psychology of the American Psychological Association (American Psychological Association Directory, 1993). Although most are employed in higher education and in government, increasingly they find employment in community, medical, and educational fields.

## The Development of Contemporary Social Psychology

Interest in understanding human social behavior can be traced back nearly 2,500 years, initially to early philosophers, later to sociologists, and subsequently to early experimental psychologists. In this section we briefly review the contributions of the various disciplines and consider the various historical events that are shaping the field (see also reviews by G. Allport, 1985; Jones, 1985). Of additional interest is Medway's (1992) work specifically comparing the development of social and school psychology. A historical comparison of significant developments in the fields, taken from Medway, is shown in Table 8.1.

### Contributions of Philosophy

Speculation about the origins and nature of social behavior existed long before the advent of an empirical social psychology. In Greek antiquity, Plato (427–347 B.C.) argued that social behavior was a manifestation of innate physiological characteristics of the members of a society. The type of social structure depended on the part of the body—head (intellect), heart (volition), or stomach (appetite)—that was dominant among the members. Aristole (384–322 B.C.), while also stressing inborn capacities as determinants of social behavior, added environmental determinants (Sahakian, 1974). This nature-nurture or organism-environment dichotomy continues to be debated in the social sciences even in contemporary times, and it appears most strongly in social psychology in alternative views of the bases for altruistic and aggressive behavior (Krebs & Miller, 1985).

The era of social philosophizing that immediately preceded the emergence of modern social psychology was strongly influenced by scientific advances of the eighteenth and nineteenth centuries, especially Darwin's theory of evolution. This was an era marked by what G. Allport (1985) has termed "simple and sovereign theories," explanations for social behavior based on single overarching principles such as hedonism, egoism, and imitation. Hedonism, which holds that individuals act to maximize pleasure and minimize pain, subsequently found expression in the modern social psychological theories of balance theory (Heider, 1958) and dissonance theory (Festinger, 1957). Gabriel Tarde's (1843–1904) writings on imitative behavior (1901/1903) set the stage for modern-day social learning theories. Although these theories continue to influence social psychology indirectly, social psychologists have by and large abandoned them in favor of what Merton (1957) has called "theories of the middle range," developed to deal with specific aspects of behavior or specific circumstances, such as helping behavior, aggression, social learning, social influence, interpersonal relations, and cooperation and competition (Hendrick, 1977).

### Contributions of Sociology

In the latter half of the nineteenth-century, the study of social behavior was advanced by several

**TABLE 8.1**   **Landmarks in Social and School Psychology**

| Social Psychology | | School Psychology | |
| --- | --- | --- | --- |
| | | 2200 B.C. | Chinese initiate testing programs for public officials. |
| 400 BC. | Plato and Aristotle discuss the origins of social behavior. | 400 B.C. | Plato discusses the relationship between ability and employment. |
| 1870s | Tarde discusses imitative learning. | 1869 | Galton studies individual differences and heredity. |
| | | 1888 | Cattell, student of Galton, describes mental test. |
| | | 1891 | Hall commences studies of children and adolescents. |
| | | 1894 | Binet develops modern intelligence test. |
| 1895 | LeBon discusses crowd behavior. | | |
| 1897 | Triplett conducts first social psychology experiment. | 1896 | Lightner Witmer calls for psychologists to work in schools. |
| | | 1899 | Centers for testing and counseling school children developed in Chicago. |
| 1900 | Wundt and Durkheim describe social organization and group mind, respectively. | | |
| | | 1902 | Dewey initiates progressive educational movement. |
| 1908 | McDougall and Ross publish first social psychology texts. | | |
| | | 1909 | Mental health reforms initiated by Beers. |
| 1910–1920 | Nietzsche, Alder, Freud discuss the role of "ego" in psychology. | 1915 | Gesell appointed first school psychologist. |
| | | 1917 | World War I: development of army intelligence tests. |
| 1928 | Thurstone introduces study of attitude measurement. | | |
| | | 1930 | New York University offers first graduate program in school psychology. |
| 1934 | Moreno develops sociometry. | 1935 | State departments of education begin certifying school psychologists. |
| 1936 | Sherif studies group influence. | | |
| 1937 | Whyte studies street corner gangs in Boston, using "participant observation." | | |
| 1939 | Lewin studies leadership atmosphere in school; initiates program of action research. | | |
| 1942–1945 | World War II: social psychology applied to war issues such as attitude change, propaganda, etc. | 1942–1945 | World War II: clinical psychologists recruited for diagnosis and treatment. |
| | | 1940s | Emergence of humanism and behaviorism. |

**TABLE 8.1** *(Continued)*

| Social Psychology | | School Psychology | |
|---|---|---|---|
| 1947 | Clark and Clark publish studies of racial preference in children. | 1947 | Division of School Psychology started in APA. |
| 1949 | Hovland studies mass communication and attitude change | 1949 | Wechsler Intelligence Scale for Children published. |
| 1949–1954 | Sherif studies intergroup relations. | 1954 | Standards for psychological tests developed by APA. |
| 1951 | Asch publishes studies on group pressure. | | |
| 1954 | Festinger develops social comparison theory. | 1954 | Thayer conference on education and training of school psychologists. |
| 1954 | *Handbook of Social Psychology* published. | | |
| 1957 | Festinger develops "cognitive dissonance" theory. | 1957 | Russians launch Sputnik; Cowen introduces primary mental health project in Rochester, New York schools. |
| 1958 | French and Raven describe types of social power. | | |
| 1963 | Milgrim publishes studies on conformity. | 1963 | First issue of *Journal of School Psychology*; Caplan publishes work on consultation. |
| 1965–1970 | Development of "attribution theory." | 1965 | Elementary and Secondary Education Act provides increased school funding and demand for school psychologists. |
| | | 1969 | National Association of School Psychologists formed. |
| 1970s | Calls for more relevance and applied research in light of Vietnam conflict, race relations, women's movement, ecological concerns. | 1970s | Rapid growth in states certifying school psychologists and university training programs; increasing interest in cognitive behaviorism. |
| | | 1975 | Passage of PL 94–142. |
| | | 1975–1980 | Professional "guild issues" dominate school psychology; Calls for social activism, child advocacy, and ethics in school psychology. |
| 1980s | Social psychologists study behavioral aspects of health and medicine. | 1980s | Emergence of accountability in education; minimum competency testing; preschool evaluation; family involvement. |
| | | 1982 | *Handbook of School Psychology* published. |
| | | 1986 | Passage of PL 99–457. |

French social theorists who sought to describe the social behavior emanating from groups, masses, and collectives (Sahakian, 1974). Groups were viewed as "organic wholes" rather than simply a collection of individuals, as exemplified by Durkheim's (1951) views on the social causes of suicide and LeBon's (1896) study of crowd behavior. By the late 1880s, abnormal behavior was studied from both sociological and psychological perspectives. The prevailing sociological view was that groups have a reality apart from the individuals that are in them. In contrast, the emerging social psychological view was that group behavior only exists in the minds of individuals who make up the group. This scientific estrangement between sociology and psychology resulted in a failure among psychologists to appreciate and fully utilize the theoretical contributions of psychologically oriented sociologists such as Simmel (1950), Cooley (1918), and Mead (1934). However, this oversight is rapidly being corrected, particularly as social psychologists revive interest in and acknowledge the contributions of sociologists to social development and the self.

## Emergence of Social Psychology

In the latter half of the 1890s, there was increasing interest in social psychology. Wilhelm Wundt (1832–1921) devoted much of the second half of his career as an experimental psychologist to the social psychology of language, myth, and custom, and in 1892 Witmer received his doctorate under Wundt's direction. Wundt had an interest in criminology and social organization, and Witmer believed that sociology and social psychology contributed much to the diagnosis and treatment of disturbed children. By 1908 two textbooks would appear with the title of *Social Psychology* (McDougall, 1908; E. A. Ross, 1908), although the field did not take on a distinct character until years later when F. Allport (1924) published a strongly behavioristic social psychology text.

During the 1920s and 1930s, social psychology was distinctly an applied field, and there was much cross-fertilization between social and abnormal psychology, much as there is today among social psychologists and personality researchers. In 1921 the name of the *Journal of Abnormal Psychology* was changed to the *Journal of Abnormal and Social Psychology*. Economic depression, waves of European immigrants, and the migration of southern blacks to the North all con-

tributed to the rise of open racial and religious hostilities, leading to the study of race, class, prejudice, and attitudes toward different groups. Many of these studies reflected the sociological tradition, such as Whyte's (1943) study of street gangs and the Italian Community Club. Social psychologists like Jacob Moreno (1889–1974) studied the social networks among children in schools, and Moreno himself was greatly influenced by the writings of John Dewey. Moreno's (1934) development of sociometry helped increase attention to the topics of group structure, group development, and friendship. Yet, during the 1930s, there was a distinct trend among most social psychologists to study group phenomena, not in applied settings, but in a controlled laboratory, following the lead of Sherif (1936), who examined social norms in that context.

Despite a number of significant developments in social psychology from the turn of the century through the 1930s, the greatest impetus to the development of the field were the circumstances leading up to and continuing through World War II (see Cartwright, 1979; Hendrick, 1977; Jones, 1985). The main forces contributing to the upsurge of research in this period included technical advances in the measurement of attitudes through self-report scales (e.g., Thurstone and Likert); Sherif's (1936) investigations of group norms in the laboratory; and an influx of European psychologists, such as Fritz Heider, Solomon Asch (1951), and Kurt Lewin, who initiated the systematic study of group dynamics, field theory, and the interrelationship between person and environment. With the outbreak of World War II, Lewin's (1947) work became directly tied to the war effort, most noticeably in studies of techniques to convince consumers to use cheaper cuts of meat and provide better nutritional care for their children. Social psychology, it was claimed, also thrived because research in communication and attitude change had to be developed, led by such individuals as Carl Hovland, to counter the massive German propaganda machine (Cina, 1981).

Between World War II and the late 1950s, the field was dominated by the study of attitude change, group dynamics, and conformity. The two major theoretical orientations were the S-R tradition of behavioral psychology as noted by the work of Hovland and associates (Hovland, Janis, & Kelley, 1953), and the cognitive-perceptual orientation of the Gestalt psychologists from Europe, which included Heider, Sherif, Asch, and Lewin. Lewin's students included Festinger, Lippitt, Kelley, and Thibaut. In 1957, Festinger published his theory of cognitive dissonance, which although relevant to a variety of judgmental, attitudinal, and behavioral tasks, was applied most strongly to the study of attitude change. Its simplicity and empirical support appealed to many social psychologists and made dissonance phenomena the dominant topic of interest for over a decade.

In the mid-1960s there were several attempts to broaden the research foci of social psychology to address directly more relevant issues than had been studied in the 1950s, when attitude change studies were dominant. The calls for relevance stemmed from a new awareness of social ills in the United States, such as racial injustice, rising crime, public apathy to victims in distress, poverty, environmental concerns, potential overpopulation, the women's movement, and public reaction to the Vietnam War. Grand theories like balance and field theory were replaced by those developed to deal with specific social behaviors such as person perception (Heider, 1958; Jones & Davis, 1965; Kelley, 1967) or imitation (Bandura, 1965). At the same time, the number of social psychological journals grew (see Table 8.2). The last decade has witnessed further expansion of both areas, especially the domination of the cognitive perspective (Fiske & Taylor,

1991), social information processing and relationship development. There are also, however, some areas that appear to be fading in importance, despite the fact that there are still large gaps in our understanding. The study of basic group processes is one such area, as is the study of emotions and nonverbal behavior (Berkowitz & Devine, 1995).

Returning to the origins of empirical psychology, there are three aspects of Triplett's (1897) study that set the stage for the next hundred years. First, it was solidly in the psychological tradition, with its focus on individual behavior in the group rather on the group per se. Second, it used the experimental method, manipulating one variable to assess its impact on another. Social psychology continues to be dominated by the true experimental and quasi-experimental study, typically conducted in the research laboratory and usually with undergraduates (West et al., 1992), which has repeatedly raised questions about the generalizability and utility of research findings (see Elms, 1975; Hovland, 1959; McGuire, 1967; West et al., 1992). From 1968 to 1988 studies with children as participants in the *Journal of Personality and Social Psychology* declined (West et al., 1992), although these studies were probably published in educational and developmental psychology journals. Third, Triplett's study was conducted in the United States. Much of social psychology, then and now, has largely been an American enterprise and has had minimal input from other cultures and diverse socioeconomic groups. Thus, one must use caution in generalizing results from many traditional studies, a problem that limits direct applicability to K–12 (kindergarten through grade 12) populations.

In summary, the social psychologists of the 1930s did not seem to concern themselves with the relevance of research. They worked in applied settings or on applied problems and incorporated the problems into their emerging theories or research programs without much self-consciousness. They worked in schools and therefore dealt with school problems and issues. They took the application of their findings by their colleagues in the applied fields for granted. Despite an increased concern for relevance by social psychologists today, the fragmentation and expansion of the field necessitates the organization and interpretation of advances in its wide array of areas. Several of these are covered in the following sections.

## TABLE 8.2 Major Journals in Personality and Social Psychology

### Major Journals in Personality and Social Psychology

Basic and Applied Social Psychology
British Journal of Social Psychology
European Journal of Social Psychology
Journal of Applied Social Psychology
Journal of Experimental Social Psychology
Journal of Personality
Journal of Personality and Social Psychology
Journal of Research in Personality
Journal of Social Issues
Journal of Social Psychology
Journal of Social and Clinical Psychology
Organizational Behavior and Human Decision Processes
Personality and Social Psychology Bulletin
Social Cognition

# ATTITUDES AND ATTITUDE CHANGE

The study of attitudes has long held a major position in the field of social psychology. Indeed, at one time issues about attitude virtually defined the field (G. Allport, 1935; Jones, 1985). Although this is no longer the case, such research remains popular, in part because there are a number of unresolved theoretical issues but also because the field is so important to applied psychology.

For the school psychologist, attitudes surface in a variety of contexts. For instance, one might be interested in attitudes toward the profession as held by the general public, school administrators, teachers, parents, and students; or one might be interested in the attitudes of these groups toward one another. Alternatively, one might be interested in attitudes toward specific policies and practices of concern to school psychologists such as assessment, placement, consultation, and intervention. At the lowest level one might simply be interested in assessing such attitudes. Often, however, one might be interested in changing them. Consultation and intervention, in fact, are usually believed to involve some level of a client's attitude change (Andrews & Gutkin, 1994; Hughes, 1983, 1992; O'Keefe & Medway, 1997). Whether change is involved or not, most instances of applied attitude research ultimately focus on the behavioral consequences of holding an attitude, with an assumption of correspondence between attitudes toward a person or object and behavior relevant to that person or object. In the following subsections we briefly identify contributions to the study of attitudes that may be of interest to school psychologists: (1) defining them, (2) measuring them, (3) changing them, and (4) determining their relationship to behavior. For readers who want more thorough treatments of attitude theory and research, the current standard in the field is the volume by Eagly and Chaiken (1993), although McGuire's (1985) earlier lengthy review also contains useful historical, theoretical, and empirical material. At a more introductory level, Ajzen and Fishbein (1980), Oskamp (1991), Petty and Cacioppo (1981), and Zimbardo and Leippe (1991) have all offered accessible treatments.

## Definition of Attitudes

On even a brief acquaintance with the literature, one becomes aware of differences and ambiguities in the definition of the term *attitude*. This is more than a minor problem, as Fishbein and Ajzen (1975) point out, since a set of articles purportedly dealing with attitudes toward the same issue may actually be dealing with very different concepts. Much of the confusion arises from the presence of single-component versus multicomponent definitions of attitude. Most theorists agree that the concept involves elements of *affect*, *cognition*, and *behavior* (Eagly & Chaiken, 1993; Fishbein & Ajzen, 1975). However, the nature of the involvement and the elements constitute topics of some controversy. Problems arise when different researchers operate on implicit assumptions about how these components interact. For instance, one study of teachers' attitudes toward an instructional program may focus on whether the teachers like or dislike the program (primarily an affect issue). Another study of the same purported topic may focus on teachers' beliefs about the efficacy of such a program or the ease with which it can be implemented (primarily a cognitive issue). Still another study may focus on whether they intend to implement the program in their classrooms (primarily a behavioral issue). Depending on one's definition, it would be quite possible to come up with different conclusions about teachers' "attitudes" toward this program.

Given these problems, Eagly and Chaiken (1993) argue for a definition of attitude as "a psychological tendency that is expressed by evaluating a particular entity with some degree of favor or disfavor" (p. 1). The key terms in this definition are *tendency* and *evaluating*. The use of *tendency* reflects the view that an attitude is an internal process and thus not directly accessible to measurement. When it is expressed, it takes the form of measurable evaluative response. This response may be affective (i.e., physiological), cognitive, or behavioral.

## Attitude Measurement

The discussion of the definition of attitudes in the preceding section suggests that attitudes may be expressed, and therefore measured, in a variety of ways: by physiological measurement, measures of cognitive processes, and behavioral indicators. A brief overview and evaluation of these techniques can be found in Cafferty (1992); Himmelfarb (1993); and Selltiz, Wrightsman, and Cook (1976). However, from a school psychology point of view, many of these techniques are limited by validity, ethical, or logistical problems. One exception might be the use of nonreactive measures as indicators of group attitudes (Webb, Campbell, Schwartz, Sechrest, & Grove, 1981). For the school psychologist, such measures might include traces of behavior in the school, such as graffiti, litter, classroom decoration, or the condition of playground equipment, as indicating students' or teachers' attitudes toward a class, the school, or school policies.

By far the favored means of measuring attitudes, and the one typically used by school psychologists, is the self-report scale. From a practical viewpoint, two related concerns are usually raised about these scales. The first is whether an adequate scale exists to measure some given attitude of interest. The second is the method of constructing such a scale if one does not exist.

To address the first concern, most attitude scales have been devised for a specific study, and—unlike with other scales used by school psychologists—there is no easily accessible source for them. In addition, reliability and validity data may be inadequate for those scales that can be identified. However, some popular scales in general use have been collected and critiqued in volumes by Robinson and Shaver (1973), Robinson, Shaver, and Wrightsman (1991), and Shaw and Wright (1967).

To address the second concern, there are basically four types of scale construction techniques: (1) Thurstone, (2) Likert, (3) Guttman, and (4) semantic differential. Each technique has been derived from a different definition of attitude and a different set of scaling assumptions. Each produces a quantitative index of the degree of favorable or unfavorable evaluation of an object. Space does not permit a discussion of specific techniques here, but guidelines for the construction and evaluation of scales are contained in a number of sources, including Fishbein (1967); Mueller (1986); Rossi, Wright, and Anderson (1983); Selltiz, Wrightsman, and Cook (1976); and Summers (1970). All of the techniques are well over 40 years old and have undergone relatively few modifications since their development. Evaluations in light of modern scaling theory are found in Dawes and Smith (1985) and Himmelfarb (1993).

## Attitude Change

For school psychologists, and other applied psychologists, the most important question about attitudes is how to change them. Several strategies have been suggested, based on views of the nature of attitudes. In the following discussion,

we suggest some implications for change derived from each strategy.

Perhaps the earliest program of research on attitude change was initiated by Carl Hovland during World War II and later continued by him at Yale University. The basic premise behind the Yale Persuasive Communications Program was that an attitude was a learned response, and a persuasive communication was an attempt to change that response. Thus, a successful persuasive communication would necessarily contain some factors that provided an incentive to change (Hovland, Janis, & Kelley, 1953). Hovland felt that these factors could be conveniently grouped into categories that had been recognized as the components of successful argumentation since antiquity, namely, the source (or communicator), the message (or communication), and the audience. He and his colleagues systematically varied aspects of each of these components and measured the impact on attention, comprehension, and yielding to the message. Although the list of components has been expanded to include other factors, such as those related to the medium of the communication, and the list of impacted variables has become more highly articulated (McGuire, 1985), the early findings remain quite robust. Effective communicators are those who are seen by their audience as being trustworthy and having expertise. A message's effectiveness is often a function of both its construction and the audience to whom it is delivered. The impact of the audience in determining the persuasiveness of the message is a particularly important consideration for school psychologists. For example, a communicator and a message that are effective for adults may not be effective for students.

The interaction of message and audience is also emphasized in a related theory of attitude change, assimilation-contrast theory (Sherif & Hovland, 1961). According to this theory, audience members have not only an existing attitude but also a range of attitude positions that they would consider not too different from their own (latitude of acceptance), as well as a range of positions that they would reject as their own (latitude of rejection). Persuasive communications that fall within the latitude of acceptance are assimilated to people's own position and accepted. Communications that fall in the latitude of rejection are contrasted with people's own position and perceived as even more dissimilar than they are. Thus, an effective persuasive communication must advocate a position in the direction preferred by the communicator but still within the recipient's latitude of acceptance. Otherwise the communication will be rejected. The outcome of a successful communication will be acceptance of the message and movement of the latitude of acceptance in the direction desired, allowing for a subsequent message that is even further in the desired direction. Thus, the theory suggests that the practitioner interested in achieving attitude change must first assess the latitude of acceptance of the recipient.

Another strategy for change is based on the view that humans seek cognitive consistency in their transactions with the world. According to this view, which underlies cognitive dissonance theory (Festinger, 1954), attitude change occurs when one encounters inconsistencies in one's cognitions. The cognitions themselves may refer to behavior or to beliefs. One of the most powerful antecedents of attitude change is a perceived inconsistency between one's behavior and the beliefs salient to it. Children who perceive themselves as honest and who believe honest people do not cheat should experience dissonance if they cheat on a test or assignment. The degree of dissonance or inconsistency should be a function of whether the behavior was seen as volitional and the degree of importance to the children of being honest and not cheating. One brings about attitude change, then, by arranging the environment to create an inconsistency in cognitions for the target.

This last notion has been applied directly to clinical practice by Brehm (1976) and Hughes (1983), who have suggested that in working with clients and consultees, psychologists should ask them to freely choose courses of action with little external compensation, to choose actions that require effort, and to make public their commitment. Such actions are theoretically presumed to increase dissonance and thus result in greater behavioral compliance with therapy or consultation suggestions.

In examining the theoretical and empirical literature on attitude change, we can find approaches that suggest fairly simple processes (e.g., classical and operant conditioning principles) and others that suggest more complex cognitive processes (e.g., reconciliation of inconsistencies). Both types seem to predict change well in some contexts but not in others. In an effort to account for these differences in an integrated approach, Petty and Cacioppo (1981) have sug-

gested a model, called the elaboration-likelihood model, that incorporates both types of processes. Basic to the model is the proposition that attitudes may be changed through either of two mental routes, *central* or *peripheral*. Which route is taken depends on the degree to which a persuasive message is cognitively elaborated by the recipient. If the recipient is motivated and capable of elaborating or thinking about the message, it will be processed through the central route. Acceptance of the message will then depend on a number of conditions, such as the strength of the argument and counterarguments. This central route thus involves controlled attentional processes and reasoning. Change is difficult to bring about through the central route because the subject is likely to marshal his or her cognitive resources to defend the existing position. However, once change is achieved, it is relatively long-lasting since it involves cognitive restructuring.

If, however, the recipient is either unmotivated or incapable of elaborating or thinking about the message, it will be processed through the peripheral route. Acceptance of the message will then depend on the effectiveness of peripheral cues associated with the communicator (e.g., appearance or reputation) and/or the message. The peripheral route involves relatively automatic processes without much conscious reasoning in achieving change. Motivation and capability may be a function of the recipient (e.g., intelligence or interest), or it may be a function of situational constraints (e.g., information overload or time pressure). Change achieved through the peripheral route is of relatively short duration and is relatively superficial. It can serve, however, to orient the recipient positively to further messages and thus facilitate later change through the central route.

Petty and Cacioppo (1981) note that these routes are not mutually exclusive and that both are usually operating to some extent in most persuasive communications. The model's strength is that it specifies the factors that determine the choice of the central or peripheral route and the conditions under which change is likely to occur once a route is activated. Andrews and Gutkin (1994), viewing a psychoeducational placement report as a persuasive communication, have applied the elaboration-likelihood model to an analysis of the factors involved in teachers' acceptance of a report that disagreed with their initial preference.

One important class of theories about attitude change that is receiving renewed attention in the literature is based on the notion that attitudes may fulfill a variety of functions and that different attitudes (or the same attitude among different people) might fulfill different functions (Katz, 1960; Pratkanis, Breckler, & Greenwald, 1989; Smith, Bruner, & White, 1956). For instance, some attitudes may be held because they serve a *utilitarian* function, so that holding the attitude helps one reach desired social goals. An adolescent who wants to be accepted by certain peers might adopt a positive attitude toward drug usage if he or she perceives that these peers hold this attitude. Other attitudes may serve *ego-defensive* functions, protecting the self-esteem of those who hold them. Gordon Allport (1954) argued that prejudicial attitudes held by poor, southern whites against African Americans were in part a response to the need of the whites to protect their own sense of worth. Other functions include *value-expressive* and *knowledge* functions. The main point here is that to change an attitude one must know what function(s) it fulfills. Trying to change an attitude that is based on an ego-defensive function by an appeal constructed around an assumed utilitarian function is likely to be unsuccessful. Chassin et al. (1992) demonstrate the importance of this approach for school psychologists in their evaluation of efforts to change drug abuse patterns in adolescents.

## Attitudes and Behavior

Few issues provoke as much heated discussion as the relationship between attitudes, as measured by typical self-report scales, and actual behavior. Most research has been conducted with the assumption that attitude has some implication for behavior, but a variety of studies demonstrate that the statistical relationship is anything but satisfactory (see Wicker, 1969). Partly in response to these concerns, Fishbein and Ajzen (1974, 1975) suggested some modifications to traditional views of the attitude-behavior relationship that have proven very useful to researchers (Ajzen & Fishbein, 1980).

Perhaps the most important modification was the suggestion that the relationship between attitudes and behavior is mediated by behavioral intentions, which are dispositions to act in favorable or unfavorable ways toward the object. Intentions, in turn, are determined by an individual's (1) attitude toward the behavior and (2) perception of subjective norms

for the behavior and motivation to comply with them. For example, children may have a positive attitude toward studying math, but the behavioral intention may be influenced by what they perceive to be their friends' view of studying and by how important peer influence is to them.

Moreover, behavior is closely, but not perfectly, related to behavioral intentions. A variety of situational or temporal constraints may thwart intended behavior. Fishbein and Ajzen (1974) point out that any given behavior occurs in a specific place, at a specific time, with respect to a specific object, and with a specific action. For instance, children work in their room, after dinner, on a certain page in a math workbook, writing the answer to assigned problems. Behavior can then be generalized over any one or all of these components. According to Fishbein and Ajzen, attitude questionnaires will be more predictive of behavior if one tailors their generality or specificity to the level of generality in the behavior one is trying to predict. For example, if one wants to predict cheating on a math exam from attitudes toward cheating, one will get better prediction from a scale that measures attitudes toward cheating on math exams than from a measure of general attitudes toward dishonest behavior.

The approach of Fishbein and Ajzen (1974) to the attitude-behavior question rests on consideration of methodological and other factors for improving prediction. An alternative approach derived from recent work in social cognition suggests that not all attitudes are equally predictive of behavior and that the same attitude may be differentially predictive of behavior over time. This approach suggests that attitudes that are readily *accessible* are better predictors of behavior than those attitudes that are less accessible (Fazio, 1989). Accessibility refers roughly to the ease with which an attitude comes to mind in a situation that calls for behavior toward an object. The work of Fazio and his colleagues suggests that factors that increase accessibility will increase the correspondence between an attitude and a related behavior. Some of these factors include direct experience with the object and priming of the attitude by some previous exposure. Thus a teacher who has worked with disabled students is likely to show greater attitude-behavior correspondence on issues that involve disability than a teacher who has not directly worked with such students.

# ATTRIBUTION THEORY AND CAUSAL REASONING

Understanding the cognitive and motivational processes used in assigning causes to events and behaviors is the goal of attribution theory (Harvey, Ickes, & Kidd, 1978). Unlike other psychological theories that are relatively well integrated, attribution theory involves a number of different propositions and conceptual frameworks to determine how and why perceivers make causal judgments and attribute stable dispositions to others (rather than attributing behavior to situational and other causes) and to understand what they subsequently do with this information (Ross & Nisbett, 1991; Trope, 1986).

The history of attribution theory begins with Heider's (1958) seminal writings on person perception. Heider believed that ordinary people attempt to make sense of things much like scientists do by explaining another person's action as the result of something about or within the person (personal causes) or something external to the person and associated with the environment (situational causes). For example, a teacher might believe that a child's school performance is due to the child's effort or to the ease of the test.

Jones and Davis (1965) provided another influential attribution statement by describing the conditions under which someone discounts environmental causes in favor of personal or trait explanations; simply, if someone does something unique or something not socially desirable (like resisting strong peer pressure) it tells us something about the person's internal character. Subsequently, Kelley (1967) addressed the nature of cues used in deciding between personal and situational determinants. He noted that perceivers weigh information about an actor's consistency over time, distinctiveness over different circumstances, and consensus with others.

Through the early 1970s, most attribution theorists wrote as if causal attribution depended exclusively on informational cues (e.g., Kelley, 1983). However, Jones and Nisbett (1971) pointed out that often people view events in line with motivational biases or various selfish reasons. One of these biases, known as ego-defensive or egocentric attribution, holds that individuals are motivated to view the world in such a way that their self-image is enhanced or protected from threat. According to this view, people generally see themselves as the causes of positive events but deny personal responsibility for negative events. A related concept that has been identified by Ross (1977; Ross & Nisbett, 1991) is the so-called fundamental attribution error, which involves the tendency for attributors to underestimate the impact of situational factors in controlling others' behavior, in comparison to their own behavior. Such tendencies have been studied in numerous clinical settings relevant to school psychologists, including child abuse (Larrance & Twentyman, 1983) and marital conflict (Kyle & Falbo, 1985). Nevertheless, for more than two decades, the prevailing view of the attribution process has been primarily an information-processing model (Sherman et al., 1995; Trope & Higgins, 1995).

These are the major writings about the general process of causal attribution. In addition, there have been several models dealing with attributions for specific types of events. Three of these extensions of attribution theory hold particular relevance for school psychology and have generated considerable research over the last decade. They are attributional models of achievement behavior (Levesque & Lowe, 1992; Weiner 1972, 1979); research on extrinsic-intrinsic motivation (Deci & Ryan, 1985); and Abramson's (Abramson, Seligman, & Teasdale, 1978) reformulated attributional model of learned helplessness, which emphasizes the role of uncontrollability in individuals' attributions.

## Attributional Models of Achievement Behavior

Weiner (1972, 1979) was the first to offer an analysis of achievement behavior and achievement motivation, which took Heider's personal-environmental causal analysis and expanded it to include dimensions of stability (stable-variable) and controllability (potentially controllable or not). He used this analysis to understand why individuals approach or avoid achievement-related tasks; how they make judgments about achievement outcomes; and how this subsequently affects their affect, expectations, and future behavior. Weiner gives most emphasis to the locus of causality and stability dimensions, noting that people normally ascribe the causes of their achievement behavior to one of four causes: their ability, their effort or motivation, the ease or difficulty of the task, or luck. The former two causes are personal and the latter two are environmental. Ability and task difficulty are stable whereas effort and luck are variable.

An excellent summary of the role of attribution and expectations in understanding academic behavior can be found in Levesque and Lowe (1992), who summarize the research on attributional antecedents and review the relevant research on students' attributions for their own behavior and teachers' attributions for students' behavior. Their model for understanding academic behavior is shown in Figure 8.1. Citing Jones and McGillis (1976), Levesque and Lowe distinguish between category-based and target-based expectations and note the importance of each in the attributional process. The former refers to judgments based on class or reference group such as race, gender, SES, and so on. The latter refers to expectancies for specific performance (e.g., on a test or series of tests) by a particular student. Once a behavior is observed, perceivers assign causation and generally use Kelley's (1967) cues of consensus, distinctiveness, and consistency to assess the degree to which the behavior covaries with certain cues and the extent to which certain cues can be discounted or eliminated. To illustrate, in assigning causation for a student's failure of an oral math exam, if one learns that many others failed, that this student passes all tests in other subjects, and that the student passes all written math tests, one can conclude that there must be something unique about this test that caused the failure (environmental attribution).

The Levesque and Lowe (1992) attribution model can be used to shed light on how children explain their own academic behavior and how teachers understand students' behavior. Young

children tend to have high expectations about their own ability and do not tend to decrease their expectations following failure. For them, more ability means less effort and vice versa. Also, they tend not to make category-based attributions. In contrast, by about age 12, the attributions of children resemble those of adults.

In target-based attributions, high achievers tend to attribute success to ability and failure to lack of effort, whereas low achievers tend to attribute failure to lack of ability, which lowers their expectations for future performance, increases negative affect, and decreases future task persistence. Recent research by Vispoel and Austin (1995) suggests that students' external attributions generalize across various subject areas, whereas internal attributions are specific to the subject-area.

Most school psychologists would acknowledge that it is very important to understand how teachers assign causation for students' learning. This issue has been the focus of several studies, which have asked actual teachers or undergraduates who are role-playing teachers to assign responsibility for the success or failure of a student (Bar-Tal, 1982). In some of these studies, the ratings of the teachers are compared with those of objective observers. The results have not, however, been entirely consistent and clear-cut. Two patterns have been reported. One involves a self-protective or egotistic attributional pattern whereby teachers rate their own teaching as more important in determining students' success and less important in determining failure than student-related factors. If, as some have argued (e.g., Guskey &

| ANTECEDENT | OBSERVATION OF BEHAVIOR | INFERENCES ABOUT COVARIATION | ATTRIBUTION OF CAUSE(S) | CONSEQUENCES |
|---|---|---|---|---|
| *Type of Expectancy* | *Behavioral Criteria* | *Type of Information* | *Locus of Cause* | *Type of Consequence* |
| Category-based<br>–IQ<br>–Gender | Success<br>vs.<br>failure | Consensus<br>Distinctiveness<br>Consistency | Personal forces<br>–Ability<br>–Effort | Affective<br>(feelings) |
| | | Covariation Principles<br>Discounting<br>Augmentation | | Cognitive<br>(expectancies) |
| Target-based<br>–Past performance<br>–Peak performance<br>–Pattern of performance | Expected<br>vs.<br>unexpected | Casual schemata<br>Multiple necessary<br>Multiple sufficient | Environmental forces<br>–Task<br>–Teacher | Behavioral<br>(actions) |

**FIGURE 8.1  An attribution model for understanding academic behavior.**
From Levesque and Lowe (1992). Copyright 1992 by Lawrence Erlbaum Assoc. Reprinted by permission.

Passaro, 1994), these attributions reflect a general sense of teachers' efficacy, an egotistic pattern may not necessarily be a negative one, given related research indicating that teachers who feel control over student problems may be more likely to work (with a consultant) to solve the problems (Gutkin & Ajchenbaum, 1984).

The other pattern found in the literature involves the opposite, or counterdefensive, pattern. This pattern appears to be found more among actual teachers than college students in simulation experiments. However, the issue remains unresolved. Some suggest that if the teacher does not anticipate future interactions with the students, the teacher is more likely to blame them for failure and take credit for success. Medway (1979) found that teachers' attributions were directly related to different teaching strategies. In this study, teachers who attributed students' problems to a lack of motivation criticized the students significantly more than they did comparison children.

## Extrinsic Versus Intrinsic Motivation

Deci and Ryan (1985) have proposed a cognitive evaluation theory that holds that individuals have a need to be competent and self-determining. Events that further personal autonomy promote an intrinsic motivation to pursue these activities and enhance exploration and creativity, whereas externally controlling events undermine this autonomy and reduce intrinsic motivation. A classic finding in social psychology is that a promise for an extrinsic reward for engaging in an interesting activity (one in which there already is high intrinsic motivation) undermines that motivation. This follows from classic attribution theory (Heider, 1958; Jones & Davis, 1965), which holds that the stronger the outside forces to engage in behavior, the weaker is the attribution one makes about stable, dispositional traits to engage in the behavior, whether it is a behavior of another or oneself.

Numerous studies have attempted to extend this basic principle to children's interactions with both their teachers and their parents. Students have been found to enjoy learning less when taught by demanding and controlling teachers (Grolnick & Ryan, 1987) and by paid rather than volunteer teachers (Wild, Enzle, & Hawkins, 1992). Parents who choose encouraging motivational practices and do not rely on rewards or punishments tend to enhance children's intrinsic motivation and achievement (Gottfried, Fleming, & Gottfried, 1994).

## Cognitive Diathesis-Stress Model of Depression

According to cognitive diathesis-stress model, individuals are likely to be depressed when (1) they experience a stressful event, and (2) have a general style of interpreting that event to aspects of the self. One such model of depression is the reformulated learned helplessness and learned hopelessness model of depression of Abramson and colleagues (Abramson et al., 1978; Abramson, Metalsky, & Alloy, 1989). This model holds that people who attribute a negative life event to stable, global, and internal causes are more likely to suffer depression than those with a less negative explanatory style. Such beliefs develop over time and appear to be reinforced by the statements of others, such as friends, teachers, and parents. Because this personal acceptance of failure or defeat resembles the behavior of animals and adults in unavoidable aversive situations, it has been labeled learned helplessness.

Peterson (1992) has argued that learned helplessness can be recognized by three criteria: maladaptive passivity, uncontrollability, and beliefs that personal responses and outcomes are independent. Several empirical studies have noted that hopelessness attributions (the cognitive component) are correlated with depression and low self-esteem in adults. In an interesting application of this model, Hilsman and Garber (1995) found that students with a more negative cognitive style reported more negative affect following the receipt of a poor report card at school or a negative reaction from their parents than children with a more positive explanatory style.

Peterson (1992) has also noted that because learned helplessness is a highly cognitive phenomenon, uncontrollability beliefs can possibly be changed, with the result that passivity can be reduced. According to Peterson, this may involve (1) restructuring the learning environment so that there are clear rewards for learning efforts and teaching would build on students' strengths; (2) applying cognitive therapy, which attempts to substitute a positive explanatory style in place of a negative one; (3) retraining, in which children's attributions are changed so that they view (low) effort rather than low ability as a source of failure, which in turn serves to increase their task persistence and academic performance (Cecil &

Medway, 1986); and (4) intervening with parents who may attribute their children's failure to internal, stable causes and therefore pass these "uncontrollable" and self-defeating attributions on to their children.

## Applications of Attribution Theory to Consultation and Therapy

There are several areas of school psychology to which attribution theory has been applied directly. One area is attributions that occur during school-based consultation. Martin and Curtis (1981) asked a sample of school psychologists to recall their most and least successful consultation cases over a recent five-year period and say why the consultee was successful or not. As predicted by a self-protective bias, consultees were held more responsible for consultation failures than for successes. A follow-up study by Smith and Lyon (1986) indicated that the tendency to blame consultees for failure is much stronger among school consultants than is the tendency to blame oneself. Unfortunately, no study has directly compared teachers' and psychologists' perceptions or related these attributional tendencies to the success or failure of school consultation. Another area is the impact of attributions on clients' change in therapy. Sandoval and Davis (1992) note that many therapy models aim to increase clients' sense of internal causation instead of denial and externalizing blame.

# SOCIAL COGNITION

The treatment of attribution processes leads logically to the area of social psychology identified as social cognition. Whereas attribution emerged out of interest in the way we perceive other people, its heavy reliance on cognitive processes of causal analysis quickly produced interest in how we think about the social information we obtain through perception. In a short time attribution research became incorporated into the rapidly growing and more general area of social cognition, a field that is presently the most active area of research and theory in social psychology. This field draws on a number of older areas of social psychology, as well as on developments in cognitive psychology, in addressing a wide variety of issues of traditional concern (e.g., attitudes, decision making, group processes, and interpersonal relations). The breadth of the field is reflected in the definition offered by Fiske and Taylor (1991). "The study of social cognition concerns how people make sense of other people and themselves" (p. 19). In addition to the review by Fiske and Taylor, technical treatment of a number of issues can be found in Markus and Zajonc (1985) and in the set of volumes edited by Wyer and Srull (1994).

A discussion of some of the key issues and concepts in the field begins with the assumption that social information, like other forms of information, is encoded and stored in memory in meaningful structures. These structures allow access to the information for efficiently handling and responding to new information encountered in social interactions.

## Structures

Although many types of structure have been suggested to capture the way social information is processed, the term *schema* is the most widely accepted. Fiske and Taylor (1991) define a schema as "a cognitive structure that represents knowledge about a concept or type of stimulus, including its attributes and the relations among those attributes" (p. 98). Within this general definition, a number of types of schema have been proposed and studied: schemas about specific persons, about oneself, about the roles people fill, and about events (sometimes called scripts). In addition, there may be content-free schemas, such as the causal schemas used in attribution or the balance schemas used in assessing relationships. Whatever types of schema exist, they have in common the property that they allow one to go beyond the social information given in a specific instance and generate hypotheses and additional items of information that may have important implications for behavior toward a social object.

For example, an area of interest to school psychologists is that of labeling (see Rolison & Medway, 1985). A label (e.g., educably mentally disabled [EMD]) may be said to invoke a schema in one for whom the label has meaning. Although the label may be applied on the basis of a limited series of tests on specific aspects of intellectual functioning, the schema it invokes may have far broader implications. It may focus attention on only certain aspects of a child's behavior that are expected within the schema; it may structure the interpretation of that behavior in ways consistent with the schema; it may influence the retrieval of information from memory when one is subsequently required to make judgments of the child; it may influence the kind of behavior displayed toward the child in such a way that behavior consistent with the schema is elicited from the child.

A schema is invoked whenever a social stimulus is somehow characterized as an instance to which the schema may be appropriate. There may be many ways such categorization could occur, but one of major interest to social psychologists is the operation of prototypes, defined as ideal cases of given social categories (Cantor & Mischel, 1977). A social stimulus will be classified as a member of a category to the extent that its characteristics match those of the prototype for that category. The closer the match, the more quickly and easily the categorization will be made. The concept has considerable relevance to a number of issues in school psychology that involve assessment and placement decisions for children on the basis of an approximate match to various diagnostic categories (McDermott, 1981).

Once evoked, a schema directs attention, facilitates interpretation of events, and affects the way such events are stored and recalled from memory. Thus, labeling a child EMD may initiate an event schema or expected sequence of behaviors pertaining to how the child might handle a challenging school task. To the extent that the child's performance matches the schema, the use of the schema is validated. Deviations from expectation may either trigger a change in the schema for future use or force a change in the judgment of the child as diagnosed. Perhaps more important the existence of the schema may lead the perceiver to overlook important but not necessarily dramatic departures, thus maintaining the original and possibly incorrect judgment. A more formal treatment of these functions of a schema is presented in the following section.

## Functions

A social schema is hypothesized to facilitate a number of functions in the processing of social information (Fiske & Taylor, 1991; Markus & Zajonc, 1985). First, it plays a role in directing *attention* to certain stimuli or aspects of a social situation. For instance, a parent for whom a "disabled child" schema has been invoked regarding their child is likely to be especially alert to aspects of the child's behavior relevant to the schema such as instances of unresponsiveness to parental requests, language difficulties, or problems with peer interaction.

Second, a schema plays a role in the *encoding* of information received. One general finding is that ambiguous information is encoded as consistent with the schema. Inconsistent information may be ignored or reinterpreted or may even induce a revision of the schema, depending on its importance and the level of inconsistency. The operation of this function was displayed clearly in Rosenhan's (1973) famous study of normal adults placed on mental hospital wards following a tentative diagnosis of schizophrenia. Many "normal" behaviors were encoded by hospital staff as "abnormal", consistent with the "schizophrenic patient" schema. Similar encoding issues would be of concern in the interpretation of the ambiguous behavior of children and adolescents in schools.

A third issue involves the storage of encoded information in *memory* and its availability for retrieval. Snyder and Uranowitz (1978) demonstrated the selectivity with which material can be recalled to be consistent with an impression formed after the information has been received initially. Information inconsistent with the schema is forgotten, and information consistent with the schema is recalled to support the current impression. For a school psychologist, such selectivity in recall may be a particular problem when a parent or teacher is reporting recalled behavior of a child about whose diagnosis they have already some suspicion.

Finally, a schema may play a powerful role in *inferences* or evaluations based on the information attended to, encoded, and retrieved from memory. The issues of inference have become a separate area of study in social cognition, to which we now turn.

## Inference Processes

We have indicated that schema is assumed to have an effect on processes of social judgment. These processes have also become issues of research. An excellent and readable summary of work in this area is found in Nisbett and Ross (1980), who contend that people have developed a variety of cognitive strategies to deal with the potentially overwhelming amount of information to which they are exposed. These strategies are normally functional in problem solving and decision making. They filter out unnecessary information and frequently result in efficient and speedy judgments. Sometimes, however, these strategies operate to the detriment of the decision maker, resulting in the loss of or incorrect assimilation of important information, which in turn may lead to a failure to adapt to new circumstances.

Probably the most important of these dynamic concepts is the heuristic, or shortcut decision rule. The study of heuristics in social cognition is heavily based on the work of Tverksy and Kahneman (1974), who suggested several types of heuristics that may be operating in general decision making. Two heuristics that have received attention in the social psychological literature are *representativeness* and *availability* (Nisbett & Ross, 1980). According to the former, people base their judgments (such as diagnoses) on the similarity of some characteristic of the target person to presumed characteristics of the class of interest. For instance, an otherwise normal child who has an undetected hearing disorder may be misjudged intellectually deficient by a teacher because the child exhibits behaviors (poor test performance, inability to follow instructions, etc.) that "fit" the teacher's behavioral expectations for intellectually deficient children.

Chapman and Chapman (1967, 1969) have demonstrated a similar process underlying what they call "illusory correlation" in clinical judgments. In their studies, even experienced clinicians relied on invalid diagnostic signs in projective tests, primarily because the signs (e.g., large eyes in the Draw-A-Person Test) seemed representative of the category of assignment (e.g., paranoia). Furthermore, belief in the validity of the signs was reinforced by selective attention to the co-occurence of such signs and inattention to the occurence of one sign without the other. The role of illusory correlation in school psychologists' diagnoses of learning disabilities was investigated in a study by Guys, Willis, and Faust (1995). They found that although diagnostic decisions were largely based on valid information, there was also illusory correlation in the use of some invalid diagnostic indicators.

The availability heuristic operates when one judges the likelihood of an outcome according to its accessibility in cognition. Accessibility refers to the ease with which such an outcome can be imagined, regardless of how likely it actually is to occur. Accessibility can be affected by such factors as recent experiences with the outcome, the dramatic impact of the outcome, and the personal salience of the outcome. For example, a workshop on a particular behavior disorder may sensitize staff to problems that, although serious, occur with relatively low frequency. After the workshop, participants may be more likely to overestimate the prevalence of the problem and to detect it in children who actually do not have it.

The fundamental concern in this area is that the presence of a schema may induce the selection of a heuristic, instead of a more thorough investigation of the information available, and thus may lead to an incorrect inference or evaluation. The thrust of the literature has demonstrated the operation of such heuristics in laboratory or other constrained situations. Recently, there has been concern that this gives too negative a view of the human decision maker, who functions quite adequately in most circumstances (Fiske, 1992). Accordingly, there has been a growing interest in determining conditions under which decision making results in optimum—or at least adequate—outcomes. This emerging literature should prove valuable to all psychologists, particularly to school psychologists, who are so often engaged in the process of evaluation.

# INTERPERSONAL ATTRACTION

Why do we like some people and not others? And how can we get other people to change how much they like us? These issues are central to understanding human interaction and thus have been at the heart of social psychological research. This research originated with Moreno (1934), who described the techniques of "sociometry" to measure patterns of attraction among group members. These techniques have been integral in measuring social behaviors and liking patterns in the classroom (Schmuck & Schmuck, 1971) and continue to be used in school psychology studies (Middleton, Zollinger & Keene, 1986). Today there continues to be strong interest in the study of interpersonal attraction, its causes, consequences, and antecedents (Berscheid, 1985).

Early studies of attraction conceived of it as a unitary dimension that could be measured by a self-report scale, with a "low" or "no attraction" anchor at one end and a "high attraction" at the other. This approach is commonly used in school psychology studies, such as studies of consumer satisfaction with psychologists and their services. However, some recent theorizing suggests that affective responses may involve both positive and negative components and that the scales should be anchored with negative affect at one end and positive affect at the other. There has also been an increase in the number of attraction studies that employ behavioral measures, such as doing favors and expressing positive nonverbal behavior.

## Theories of Attraction

Several general social psychological theories have been used to explain why people are attracted to one another. The cognitive consistency theories, which include Heider's (1958) balance theory and Festinger's (1957) cognitive dissonance theory, basically hold that we like those who like us and vice versa (although people tend to like others more than to dislike them); that we like others who are similar to us and vice versa; and that if harm befalls another person, people tend to dislike the victim in order to restore consistency between the behavioral act and their attitude. The last notion can be seen in Lerner's (1980) work on "just world" beliefs, namely, that good people deserve good things and bad people bad things. Lerner's work has numerous school applications, helping to explain why, among other things, a person might arrive at the belief that a victimized child deserves his or her fate.

The second group of general attraction theories are the reinforcement theories. The simple idea here is that we like people who reward us in some way. However, since interpersonal relations involve two-way interaction, reinforcement notions of attraction have been modified to take into account how much people perceive that they have been rewarded in comparison to how much they have invested in the relationship (Adams, 1965) and the rewards received compared to other options inherent in terminating the relationship (Kelley & Thibaut, 1978). Kelley and Thibaut's theory has important implications for predicting the dissolution of close relationships, as in divorce and giving up a child for adoption.

Recently, some social psychologists have turned from attraction per se to similarly intense emotions and moods related to relationship functioning. In the last two decades considerable attention has been focused on understanding loneliness among school-aged children and adolescents (Johnson, Rose, & Russell, 1992). In recent years 41 studies on depression have appeared in the *Journal of Personality and Social Psychology* (Tennen, Hall, & Affleck, 1995). Much of this research follows the cognitive model and emphasizes attributions, expectations, and schema. Other researchers (e.g., Hobfoll et al., 1991) have examined both the perception of events and social supports available to moderate stress. Several studies have looked at the relationship between parental stress and de-pression and child psychopathology (e.g., Downey & Coyne, 1990). In one recent study (Medway et al., 1995), a direct relationship was found between the perceived distress of military spouses and the behavior problems of their children during the deployment of fathers to the Persian Gulf.

## Determinants of Attraction

Three factors have been found to be especially important in influencing attraction in initial and brief encounters: the physical attractiveness of the other; the similarity of the other to the individual; and to a lesser extent, social contact.

### Physical Attractiveness

Across race, sex, age, and social class, physically attractive people are liked more than less attractive people. Of particular importance to school psychologists are studies that indicate a relationship between children's popularity and attractiveness (Huston & Levinger, 1978) and show that teachers give attractive children better evaluations, give them more opportunities to perform, and treat them less harshly when they transgress (Berscheid, 1985). To some degree physical attractiveness itself is determined by nonverbal cues such as facial expression and smiling (Mueser et al., 1984).

### Similarity

Aristotle observed, "We like those who resemble us and are engaged in the same pursuits" (Byrne, 1969). Over the last 60 years there has been a host of studies showing that people like others similar to themselves. This basic notion has numerous implications for school psychologists, ranging from understanding the cohesion of groups of similar racial makeup to understanding why it is males who tend to be referred for behavior problems by teachers, especially female teachers.

### Social Contact

Numerous studies have indicated that social conduct, familiarity, and physical proximity increase liking and attraction. Simply put, people tend to like others who live and work near them and with whom they interact frequently. There is, however, one important qualifier: the people involved must be treated as equals.

The social contact research has several important implications for school practices. One is the widely held belief that contact between ethnic groups will reduce prejudice. In 1954 the

Supreme Court in *Brown* v. *Topeka Board of Education* ruled that segregated schools were inherently unequal and unconstitutional. Social psychologists who provided court testimony argued that school integration would raise the self-esteem and school achievement of black children, and reduce racial prejudice (Clark & Clark, 1965). Subsequent research, however, has not indicated clear decreases in interracial prejudice following integration. Stephan (1978) noted that, at best, the existing studies were mixed in finding decreased prejudice; at worst, there was some increase in white prejudice. The picture for improvements in achievement and self-esteem has been even less dramatic. What has appeared to go wrong was the failure to ensure equal status. Cook (1984) has noted that integration will work only if the parties are of equal status, if they are encouraged to cooperate, and if the surrounding community supports integrated schools.

A second important extension of the social contact hypothesis is in the area of mainstreaming. Here the research parallels that on school desegregation in indicating few real effects of this practice (or peer tutoring of the handicapped by the nonhandicapped) on the social acceptance of distinctly different handicapped groups, such as mentally disabled children (Gottlieb, Rose, & Lessen, 1983). Although some have argued that the problems lie with needed curricular changes to support mainstreaming (Madden & Slavin, 1983), total acceptance of the handicapped by the nonhandicapped may be wishful thinking unless the two groups can cooperate on an equal footing. We now explore related extensions of the contact hypothesis.

# INTERGROUP RELATIONS

Intergroup relations are processes of cooperation and competition between groups, including the antecedents and consequences of such processes. Much of the early work on group dynamics analyzed intergroup situations in terms of forces or pressures arising from the pursuit of incompatible goals (e.g., Deutsch, 1968). However, the landmark study is Sherif's examination of conflict and cooperation in a boy's summer camp known as the Robber's Cave (Sherif, Harvey, White, & Sherif, 1961). In this study, the researchers placed boys at a summer camp into one of two groups. They then developed high cohesion within each group (by various cooperative exercises) and high conflict between groups (by competitive events and contrived confrontations). They then attempted to reduce intergroup hostility by encouraging friendly contact—an effort that proved unsuccessful. They eventually brought about a reduction in hostility through the introduction of "superordinate goals," requiring the groups to pool their efforts for the good of the camp (e.g., the formation of a joint baseball team to play another camp and the formation of a bucket brigade to supply water when the camp's system "failed"). The construction of the conflict and the use of superordinate goals to overcome intergroup hostility were major developments in the field and have clear implications for the development of cooperation in schools today.

Despite the success of Sherif's field study (Sherif et al., 1961), there have been relatively few attempts at replication and extension. Instead, much of the research on cooperation and competition has been conducted in the laboratory with mixed-motive games. Many of the principles of cooperation and competition applied to intergroup situations are based largely on this dyadic interaction, which is reviewed by Pruitt and Kimmel (1977).

One aspect of intergroup relations relevant to school psychologists is that concerned with prejudice and discrimination. Prejudice refers to an attitude toward members of another group based solely on their membership in that group, whereas discrimination refers to behaviors based on that attitude. Two themes have been the focus of greatest recent attention. The first concerns the origins of prejudice and discrimination. G. Allport (1954), who identified several personal, social, and economic sources, basically believed that prejudice and discrimination arise from some defect in the person or the social system and that the normal state of affairs is intergroup harmony. More recently, Tajfel offered convincing evidence that ingroup-outgroup distinctions and differences in the allocation of rewards arise whenever humans are divided into groups, no matter how arbitrary the basis of the division (Billig & Tajfel, 1973; Tajfel, 1970). The work of Tajfel and others has led to a revision of the earlier, more simplistic theories of ingroup-outgroup prejudice. The revision focuses on the idea that identification with a preferred ingroup enhances individual social identity and that the need for such enhancement is pervasive, as is the tendency to elevate the ingroup and denigrate the outgroup (Brown, 1986; Tajfel, 1978). Efforts at increasing intergroup harmony must overcome this basic process, as well as deal with the substantive problems that underlie conflict.

The second theme of recent interest is the contact hypothesis, which in its simplest form suggests that one of the ways to reduce intergroup prejudice is by increasing intergroup contact. The early evidence pertaining to the validity of the hypothesis has been reviewed by Amir (1969). The evidence is mixed and shows some studies indicating reduction, some no effect, and some increases in outgroup prejudice as a function of increased contact. A reformulated hypothesis suggests that the effect of increased intergroup contact depends on the social context, the nature of the contact, and the prior status of the participants. Support for this reformulation is found in a series of studies by Cook (1969, 1978). His results led to efforts to apply the techniques developed to multiracial and multiethnic classes. One set of such studies is those utilizing the "jigsaw" method (Aronson & Osherow, 1980; Aronson, Stephan, Sikes, Blaney & Snapp, 1978), which assembles multiracial or multiethnic groups of students from integrated classrooms. The material to be learned is divided into meaningful units, and one unit is assigned to each child. The child must teach the assigned unit to the others in the group. All children are evaluated individually. This cooperative, peer-teaching technique results in improved intergroup attitudes, higher self-esteem, and positive attitudes toward school when the groups are ethnically balanced. Academic achievement does not suffer. Indeed, there is evidence that the students in the jigsaw groups outperform traditional classroom students, particularly minority students (Stephen, 1985).

A second set of studies derived from the contact hypothesis has been conducted by researchers at John Hopkins University, who examined the effectiveness of two cooperative learning techniques (Slavan, Sharan, Kagan, Lazarowitz, Webb, & Schmuck, 1985). The first, student-teams-achievement-division (STAD), involves multiracial peer teaching in small groups. Achievement is assessed in terms of individual prior performance or the performance of comparable students. The teams gain by improvement of members at their own level, thus enhancing cooperation among team members. The second technique, teams-games-tournaments (TGT), also involves multiracial peer teaching, but achievement is assessed in tournaments among students of comparable achievement levels. It appears that these efforts generally decrease ingroup-outgroup hostility while increasing, or at least not affecting, academic achievement. Although these and other cooperative learning techniques were developed to remedy school problems in the racially or ethnically desegregated classroom, the impressive gains in self-esteem and academic achievement in traditionally disadvantaged groups have led to further development of the techniques for a variety of educational settings and with a variety of learners. An excellent overview of recent research on cooperative learning and on practical ways to implement this practice is presented by Nastasi and Clements (1991). Bohlmeyer and Burke (1987) also present a useful classification scheme of cooperative learning techniques. They evaluated nine such techniques on the basis of subject matter, nature of students' interdependence, intergroup interaction (cooperative, competitive, or independent), method of grouping, evaluation and reward system, and demands on the system for implementation.

Cooperative learning techniques are rapidly moving out of controlled laboratories and becoming standard practice in primary and secondary schools, as well as becoming an instructional activity in which school psychologists are playing a major role (Bramlett, 1994). Besides research on the origins of discrimination and ways to reduce prejudice, there is increasing interest on the effects of racism, discrimination, and prejudice on the discriminated group. Some have held that just the threat of prejudice may be enough to be disruptive. Steele and Aronson (1995) have argued that where a negative stereotype exists, the stereotyped group may be at risk of confirming it both to themselves and to others. For African-American students the sheer act of taking a scholastic or achievement test may raise a threat of being stereotyped and that this threat may, by directing attention away from task demands, undermine performance. Steele and Aronson suggest that stereotype threat may be an overlooked cause of the lower standardized test scores of black than those of white students.

## AGGRESSION AND VIOLENCE

Aggression may be defined as behavior with the intention to injure another person. The aggressive act may be primarily a means toward some other end (e.g., a child who hits to get a toy or attention), that is, *instrumental* aggression. Or the aggression may be the end in itself (e.g., a child who strikes another with the sole intent to harm), that is, *angry* aggression. Most violent crime is precipitated by anger (Russell & Fehr, 1994) that occurs during arguments, and in 1990, 45% of all murders were attributed to arguments (Anderson & Morrow, 1995).

## Causes of Aggression

There are three major views about the causes of aggression (Berkowitz, 1965). One is that human aggression results from innate, biologically based instincts. A psychoanalytic view is that aggressive energy is continually being generated and, if not released in some socially acceptable way, results in attacks on others or the self. Other psychoanalysts believe in the instinctual nature of the drive but thought it could be modified by environmental circumstances. Ethologists have also argued that all animal species have an inborn aggressive urge that is simply released by certain environmental conditions.

A second perspective, derived from drive theory, is the frustration-aggression hypothesis (Miller, 1941). Since this theory was first advanced and then modified, considerable research has accumulated, indicating that individuals who are thwarted in reaching goals or placed in competitive settings are often aggressive. It will be recalled that in the Robbers Cave experiment by Sherif (Sherif et al., 1961) two groups of male campers were brought into such competition with each other that fights and destructive raids occurred.

It is the third view, however, derived from Bandura's (1965) social learning theory (Bandura & Walters, 1963), that has the most explanatory power and relevance for school psychologists. This model holds that certain antecedent or situational conditions lead to emotional arousal, which may, because of observational learning, reinforcement, or personality characteristics, lead to aggression or some alternative response. The following describes in some detail the parameters of this model.

## Antecedent Conditions

Several antecedents trigger emotional arousal, including sex-role training that encourages boys to be more aggressive than girls, the presence of others (groups exhibit more aggression than individuals alone), aggressive cues like knives and guns, and characteristics of the target of aggression like gender and potential for retaliation. Some types of people are especially likely to be attacked, such as the handicapped and unattractive. For example, in one study (Berkowitz & Frodi, 1979) participants delivered more punishment to a learner who was "funny looking" and stuttered than another with normal appearance, even though all learners made the same number of mistakes. Certain unpleasant environmental conditions, such as heat, crowding, and invasions of personal space, seem to trigger aggression: for instance, high school males are more competitive with one another in smaller rooms, and certain places in buildings (elevators, stairwells, and hallways) are especially likely vandalism targets. Such findings have implications for limiting school populations according to building size and for building design. Finally, competitive situations can lead to conflict and aggression (Deutsch, 1993).

## Mediating Conditions

According to social learning theory, the major conditions that intervene between a potentially aggressive stimulus and an aggressive response are the degree of emotional arousal, and the anticipated consequences of aggression. Schachter (1964) has argued that individuals cannot clearly differentiate among the causes of arousal; in fact, research suggests that erotic or drug-induced arousal may lead to aggression simply because the person may be unable to distinguish the internal signs of anger. Anticipated consequences refers to the reinforcement the person expects to obtain by being aggressive. This may be direct (e.g., peers who are encouraging two students to fight) or vicarious (e.g., an observation that an aggressive individual is rewarded).

## Responses

Bandura's model holds that arousal (or anger) does not invariably result in aggression (Bandura & Walters, 1963). Frustration and anger often lead to dependency, withdrawal, psychosomatic symptoms, constructive coping, or escape through drugs and alcohol, depending on the personality and learning history of the individual.

## Sexual Aggression

Bandura's (1965) social learning theory has been used as a theoretical framework in understanding the nature of sexual aggression (Marshall & Barbaree, 1984), such as rape between acquaintances (so-called date rape) and child sexual abuse

(Finkelhor, 1984). The importance of these theories for school psychologists rests on the fact that—unlike statements that designate types of people likely to abuse others (e.g., based on a history of abuse—these models stress multiple factors in an additive or interactive fashion. They highlight factors that motivate the act, that reduce aggression inhibitions, and that reinforce opportunity. In one study, Malamuth (1986) showed that high levels of sexual aggression can be predicted from knowledge of males' hostility toward females, desire to dominate them, acceptance of force in sexual relationships, and aggression history. Social psychologists are showing that sexual aggression and child abuse must be conceptualized along a continuum, encompassing a tendency toward aggression rather than an all-or-none phenomenon, and that searching for a primary causal factor or primary treatment strategy for sexual and child abuse is likely to be futile.

## Physical and Psychological Maltreatment

Social psychological models have attempted to understand the nature of childhood abuse and neglect (Belsky, 1984). These models stress the interaction of parent, child, and environmental variables and hold greater promise for intervention effectiveness than models that focus on a single aspect.

## Media Influences

In 1974, a nine-year-old girl was sexually assaulted in an incident similar to one shown days earlier on a TV show called "Born Innocent." In 1977, Ronny Zamora killed his neighbor during a burglary in a manner that resembled a recently watched episode of "Kojak." In 1981, John Hinckley, Jr., shot President Reagan and admitted having identified with a character in the film *Taxi Driver.* And in 1995, the film *Money Train* was blamed for contributing to an attack on a New York City subway station attendant. Beyond the headlines, however, there is strong evidence that youths model aggressive acts that they witness in their environments and through the media. Nearly all the major reviews of this issue have concluded that there is a correlation between TV violence and subsequent aggression (Pearl, Bouthilet, & Lazar, 1982), especially when the viewers are preschool or young children who have difficulty in judging intentionality and mo-

tive. The association is less strong for teenagers but still positive, although some have pointed out that aggressive young adults may favor violent shows (Freedman, 1984). A link between violent video games and subsequent aggression has also been established (Cooper & Mackie, 1986).

As Morrison, Furlong, and Morrison (1994) have pointed out, aggression, violence, and related issues like vandalism and victimization have not traditionally been discussed in the school psychology literature. These topics have primarily attracted the attention of those in the fields of criminal justice, public health, and other areas of psychology, including social psychology. However, the recent rise in school-based violence has made violence and aggression priorities for school psychologists (see Furlong & Morrison, 1994), who must take an active role in preventing and reducing violence in the schools, among children, and against them. This role can include working with children to modify viewing habits or their interpretation of violent events, reducing those conditions that reinforce aggression, supporting national and local organizations that are trying to reduce violence on television, and assisting families to teach children the value of prosocial instead of aggressive behavior.

## ORGANIZATIONAL BEHAVIOR

In accordance with our definition of social psychology, most of the contributions to school psychology discussed thus far have applied to relatively simple social situations and interactions (e.g., student-teacher, teacher-psychologist, and student-student). The school in which these situations and interactions occur, however, is a complex formal organization that to some extent determines and is affected by the interactions that occur. Organizational theory and research is a rapidly expanding interdisciplinary enterprise (Pfeffer, 1985), and a review of this literature is not within the scope of the present chapter. The related area of organizational development and systems intervention in the school is covered in Chapter 40 in this volume, and reviews of developments in several areas of organizational behavior can be found in editions of the *Annual Review of Psychology* (House & Singh, 1987; Schneider, 1985). However, social psychologists have contributed a perspective and research tradition to some aspects of the field and continue to do so, particularly at the level of individual behavior in the organization.

# Leadership

One important tradition originated in the work of Lewin, Lippett, and White (1939) on leadership in groups. Appropriately, this work was largely conducted in schools, with teachers serving in the role of leaders for their classes. The most famous of these studies concerned the role of the leader in creating a "climate" for the group. Autocratic, democratic, and laissez-faire styles of supervision were employed to create a so-called climate in which the groups of students worked. Demonstration that the democratic climate proved superior on overall criteria of performance ushered in a period of active research on leader behavior, which received a considerable boost during World War II in the training of effective leaders in the military.

Subsequent work by Lewin's students and colleagues clarified the dimensions of leader behavior and established the validity of the socioemotional versus task distinction in leader orientations. After a period of research on the characteristics of effective leaders, this tradition culminated in Fiedler's development of the contingency theory of leadership effectiveness. According to Fiedler (1964), there is no one most effective leader across all situations. Instead, situations can be characterized as favorable or unfavorable to the leader based on such features as the structure of the task, the preexisting leader-member relations, and the position power of the leader. For situations characterized as very favorable or unfavorable to the leader, those who are relatively task-oriented are likely to prove most effective; for situations between the extremes, those who are relatively human relations–oriented are likely to prove most effective.

Fiedler and Garcia (1987) have proposed a second contingency-type theory to specify conditions under which a leader's cognitive resources will be utilized effectively in a leadership task. This theory suggests that effective use can be made of cognitive resources when a leader is able to employ directive behavior, has task-relevant knowledge, has good leader-member relations, and is not under stress (House & Singh, 1987). Such contingency notions have important implications for the school environment in both principal-teacher and teacher-class interactions. The suggestion from this literature is that whether a given principal or teacher will be effective in a leadership position depends not only on personal style and resources but also on the environment in which such styles and resources are enacted.

# Group Dynamics and Processes

A second research tradition developed by Lewin (1947, 1951) involves the study of group dynamics, the forces that develop in groups to encourage participation and change in their members, as well as commitment to group decisions. The first major study in this area was Lewin's project to change the shopping habits of midwestern homemakers to buy less desirable cuts of meat. He first analyzed the forces on the homemakers that influenced their current purchase decisions. He then set about to change these forces by a variety of discussion techniques, finding that active participation in discussions and group commitment brought about the greatest reported change. The power of group discussion to change behavior and the effectiveness of participatory management became cornerstones of the group dynamics movement established by Lewin in the Center for Group Dynamics, first located at Massachusetts Institute of Technology and later moved to the University of Michigan. As noted by Ross and Nisbett (1991),

> The basic message of these early studies, however, is quite clear and remains just as relevant now as it was then. First, the provision of information, even highly relevant and seemingly persuasive information, often proves to be a disappointingly weak vehicle for achieving changes in feelings and behavior. Second, freeing individuals from an existing source of group pressures or constraints, especially if they are then exposed to new norms and subjected to new social influences, often proves to be a surprisingly powerful vehicle for accomplishing such changes. (pp. 220–221)

Ironically, Lewin's techniques of participatory management and group-work decision were adopted by the Japanese and, in recent years, exported back to the United States (Ross & Nisbett, 1991). One form of participatory management, Quality Circles, has been shown to produce positive effects on workers in industry and business. Quality Circles are small groups of workers who perform similar organizational tasks. These groups meet to identify and solve work-related problems and recommend solutions to management. This approach has been used successfully with teams of school psychologists (Maher & Kruger, 1992) and appears to be an important, although as yet underutilized, method for enhancing the delivery of a full range of psychological services.

Whereas Lewin (1947, 1951) focused on the group as the unit of analysis for his work, a separate tradition developed from the view of an organization as a product of the interlocked behaviors of its members. Katz and Kahn (1978) argued, in their open-systems approach to organizational functioning, that the system processes of input, throughput, and output are accomplished through the interlocked, role-coordinated behavior of the individual members of the organization. Individual problems such as role strain, developing from competing demands on the occupants of various organizational roles, have been extensively examined in this research tradition.

The applicability of this approach to the school is apparent when the school is seen as an open system, the environment providing inputs from students, teachers, parents, school boards, and other concerns that must be recognized and effectively processed through interlocked behavior patterns. When these concerns demand conflicting behaviors, such as when teachers are faced with the need for collective action as members of a union while remaining concerned about their obligation to teach their students, role strain is likely to occur, with a negative impact on the health and well-being of the teachers.

## Performance Appraisal

A more recent area where interests of social psychologists intersect with those of large organizations involves the process of performance appraisal, that is, the periodic evaluation of an employee's job performance. Organizations use these appraisals to make decisions about raises, promotions, transfers, remedial training, and termination. Performance appraisals usually involve rating scales of traits or behaviors relevant to the position being evaluated, so there has been a long-standing concern about their reliability and validity (Landy & Farr, 1980). Efforts to improve relatively poor reliability focused initially on the scales themselves by incorporating more specific behavioral descriptors. Later, emphasis was placed on the training of raters to avoid common errors in the rating process (Landy & Farr, 1980; Williams & Williams, 1992). Both of these ap-

proaches, which produced improved but far from ideal ratings, assumed that the problems were mainly mechanical in nature. More recent work in social cognition, however, suggests that various rating problems may be the result of inherent information-processing strategies that work quite well in nonrating contexts, in which general impressions of others are sufficient (DeNisi, Cafferty, & Meglino, 1984; Landy & Farr, 1980).

The social cognition approach is derived from the recognition that performance appraisals are usually made from memory and that they cover activities of the subordinate over a relatively long period of time (e.g., a year or six months). Under such conditions, a variety of factors that are now of interest to those in social cognition may play an important role in the appraisal process. For instance, general impressions of the subordinate may be formed early, based on salient behavior and various stereotyped expectations. The early general impression forms the basis for a schema, which in turn directs behavior toward the subordinate and information processing of the subordinate's behavior. Later appraisal of the subordinate is based on recall of information in the context of the schema. That recall of information may be biased in a number of ways; for example, information consistent with the schema may be more readily recalled than inconsistent information, or negative information may be recalled more readily than positive information (DeNisi, Cafferty, & Meglino, 1984). Williams and Williams (1992) point out that in this climate of increased accountability and expanded accreditation requirements, performance appraisal research has much to offer school psychologists.

## CONCLUSION

This chapter presents a broad overview of contemporary social psychology and its applications to school psychology. As described in several texts (e.g., Feldman, 1986; Oskamp, 1984), social psychology has at its roots field studies, survey research, group phenomenon, and action research. However, in recent years it has been heavily influenced by emerging work in cognitive psychology, artificial intelligence, and biopsychology. Also, there have been increasing attempts to extend the boundaries of social psychology beyond the laboratory and beyond theory testing to answer real-world problems in ecology, conflict resolution, health, and education. Although social psychology may be criticized for its historical reliance on homogeneous, college-age participants, this, too, is being corrected. Social psychologists are turning their attention to the impact of culture, ethnicity, race, religion, social class, regionalism, and nationality on social behavior (Ross & Nisbett, 1991), an attention that is bound to have important implications for school psychology.

Although we strongly believe that a survey course in social psychology is a basic prerequisite for any school psychologist, the application of social psychology research findings to school psychology practice must remain a priority (cf. Gutkin, 1997; Medway & Cafferty, 1992). As long as school psychologists are in the business of changing social behavior—of students, teachers, parents, or organizations—social perceptions, social pressures, and social contexts will continue to be enormously powerful forces. Social psychology provides rich theories and methodological tools. Now it is up to school psychology to make the most of them.

# REFERENCES

Abramson, L. Y., Seligman, M. E. P., & Teasdale, J. D. (1978). Learned helplessness in humans: Critique and reformulation. *Journal of Abnormal Psychology*, 87, 49–75.

Abramson, L. Y., Metalsky, G. I., & Alloy, L. B. (1989). The hopelessness theory of depression: Does the research test the theory? In L. Y. Abramson (Ed.), *Social cognition and clinical psychology:* A synthesis (pp. 33–65). New York: Guilford Press.

Adams, J. S. (1965). Inequity in social exchanges. In L. Berkowitz (Ed.), *Advances in experimental social psychology* (Vol. 2, pp. 267–299). New York: Academic Press.

Ajzen, I., & Fishbein, M. (1980). *Understanding attitudes and predicting social behavior.* Englewood Cliffs, NJ: Prentice–Hall.

Allport, F. (1924). *Social psychology.* Boston: Houghton Mifflin.

Allport, G. (1954). *The nature of prejudice.* Reading, MA: Addison-Wesley.

Allport, G. W. (1935). Attitudes. In C. Murchison (Ed.), *Handbook of social psychology* (pp. 798–844). Worcester, MA: Clark University Press.

Allport, G. W. (1985). The historical background of social psychology. In G. Lindzey & E. Aronson (Eds.), *The handbook of social psychology* (3rd ed. Vol. 1, pp. 1–46). Hillsdale, NJ: Erlbaum.

American Psychological Association. (1993). *Biographical directory of the American Psychological Association.* Washington: DC.

Amir, Y. (1969). Contact hypothesis in ethnic relations. *Psychological Bulletin, 71,* 319–342.

Anderson, C. A., & Morrow, M. (1995). Competitive aggression without interaction: Effects of competitive versus cooperative instructions on aggressive behavior in video games. *Personality and Social Psychology Bulletin, 21,* 1020–1030.

Andrews, L. W., & Gutkin, T. B. (1994). Influencing attitudes regarding special class placement using a psychoeducational report: An investigation of the elaboration likelihood model. *Journal of School Psychology, 32,* 321–377.

Aronson, E., & Osherow, N. (1980). Cooperation, prosocial behavior, and academic performance: Experiments in the desegregated classroom. In L. Bickman (Ed.), *Applied social psychology annual* (Vol. 1., pp. 163–196). Beverly Hills, CA: Sage.

Aronson, E., Stephan, C., Sikes, J., Blaney, N., & Snapp, M. (1978). *The jigsaw classroom.* Beverly Hills, CA: Sage.

Asch, S. E. (1951). Effects of group pressure upon the modification and distortion of judgments. In H. Guetzkow (Ed.), *Groups, leadership, and men* (pp. 177–190).

Bandura, A. (1965). Vicarious processes: A case of no-trial learning. In L. Berkowitz (Ed.), *Advances in experimental social psychology* (Vol. 2., pp. 301–329). New York: Academic Press.

Bandura, A., & Walters, R. H. (1963). *Social learning and personality development.* New York: Holt.

Baron, R. M., & Kenny, D. A. (1986). The moderator-mediator variable distinction in social psychological research: Conceptual, strategic, and statistical considerations. *Journal of Personality and Social Psychology, 51,* 1173–1182.

Bar-Tal, D. (1982). The effects of teachers' behavior on pupils' attributions: A review. In C. Antaki & C. Brewin (Eds.), *Attributions and psychological change: Applications of attributional theories to clinical and educational practice* (pp. 177–194). New York: Academic Press.

Belsky, J. (1984). The determinants of parenting: A process model. *Child Development, 55,* 83–96.

Berkowitz, L. (1965). The concept of aggressive drive: Some additional considerations. In L. Berkowitz (Ed.), *Advances in experimental social psychology* (Vol. 2, pp. 301–329). New York: Academic Press.

Berkowitz, L., & Devine, P. G. (1995). Has social psychology always been cognitive? What is "cognitive" anyhow? *Personality and Social Psychology Bulletin, 21,* 696–703.

Berkowitz, L., & Frodi, A. (1979). Reactions to a child's mistakes as affected by his/her looks and speech. *Social Psychology Quarterly, 42,* 420–425.

Bersheid, E. (1985). Interpersonal attraction. In G. Lindzey & E. Aronson (Eds.), *Handbook of social psychology* (3rd ed., Vol. 2, pp. 413–484). Englewood Cliffs, NJ: Prentice-Hall.

Billig, M., & Tajfel, H. (1973). Social categorization and similarity in intergroup behavior. *European Journal of Social Psychology, 3,* 27–52.

Bohlmeyer, E. M., & Burke, J. P. (1987). Selecting cooperative learning techniques: A consultative strategy guide. *School Psychology Review, 16,* 36–49.

Bramlett, R. K. (1994). Implementing cooperative learning: A field study evaluating issues for school-based consultants. *Journal of School Psychology, 32,* 67–84.

Brehm, S. S. (1976). *The application of social psychology to clinical practice.* New York: Wiley.

Brown, R. (1986). *Social psychology: The second edition.* New York: Free Press.

Byrne, D. (1969). Attitudes and attraction. In L. Berkowitz (Ed.), *Advances in experimental social psychology* (Vol. 4, pp. 35–89). New York: Academic Press.

Cafferty, T. P. (1992). Measuring and changing attitudes in educational contexts. In F. J. Medway and T. P. Cafferty (Eds.), *School psychology: A social psychological perspective* (pp. 25–46). Hillsdale, NJ: Erlbaum.

Cantor, N., & Mischel, W. (1977). Prototypes in person perception. In L. Berkowitz (Ed.), *Advances in experimental social psychology* (Vol. 12, pp. 3–52). New York: Academic Press.

Cartwright, D. (1979). Contemporary social psychology in historical perspective. *Social Psychology Quarterly, 42,* 82–93.

Cecil, M. A., & Medway, F. J. (1986). Attribution retaining with low-achieving and learned helpless children. *Techniques, 2,* 173–181.

Chapman, L. J., & Chapman, J. P. (1967). Genesis of popular but erroneous psychodiagnostic observations. *Journal of Abnormal Psychology, 72,* 193–204.

Chapman, L. J., & Chapman, J. P. (1969). Illusory correlation as an obstacle to the use of valid psychodiagnostic signs. *Journal of Abnormal Psychology, 74,* 271–280.

Chassin, L., Presson, C. C., Sherman, S. J., & Curran, P. J. (1992). Social psychological factors in adolescent substance use and abuse. In F. J. Medway and T. P. Cafferty (Eds.), *School psychology: A social psychological perspective* (pp. 397–424). Hillsdale, NJ: Erlbaum.

Cina, C. (1981). Social science for whom? A structural history of social psychology. Doctoral dissertation, State University of New York, Stony Brook.

Clark, K. B., & Clark, M. P. (1965). Racial identification and preference in Negro children. In H. Proshansky & B. Seidenberg (Eds.), *Basic studies in social psychology* (pp. 308–317). New York: Holt, Rinehart & Winston.

Cook, S. W. (1969). Motives in a conceptual analysis of attitude-related behavior. In W. J. Arnold & D. Levine (Eds.), *Nebraska symposium on motivation* (Vol. 17, pp. 179–235). Lincoln: University of Nebraska Press.

Cook, S. W. (1978). Interpersonal and attitudinal outcomes in cooperating interracial groups.

*Journal of Research and Development in Education, 12,* 97–113.

Cook, S. W. (1984). The 1954 social science statement and school desegregation: A reply to Gerard. *American Psychologist, 39,* 819–832.

Cooley, C. H. (1918). *The social process.* New York: Scribner.

Cooper, J., & Mackie, D. (1986). Video games and aggression in children. *Journal of Applied Social Psychology, 16,* 726–744.

Dawes, R. M., & Smith, T. L. (1985). Attitudes and opinion measurement. In G. Lindzey & E. Aronson (Eds.), *Handbook of social psychology* (3rd ed., Vol. 1, pp. 509–566). New York: Random House.

Deci, E. L., & Ryan, R. M. (1985). *Intrinsic motivation and self-determination in human behavior.* New York: Plenum.

DeNisi, A. S., Cafferty, T. P., & Meglino, B. M. (1984). A cognitive view of the performance appraisal process: A model and research propositions. *Organizational Behavior and Human Performance, 33,* 360–396.

Deutsch, M. (1968). The effects of cooperation and competition upon group process. In D. Cartwright & A. Zander (Eds.), *Group dynamics* (3rd ed., pp. 461–482). New York: Harper & Row.

Deutsch, M. (1993). *The resolution of conflict.* New Haven, CT: Yale University Press.

Downey, G., & Coyne, J. C. (1990). Children of depressed parents: An integrative review. *Psychological Bulletin, 108,* 50–76.

Durkheim, E. (1951). *Suicide.* Glencoe, IL: Free Press.

Eagly, A. H., & Chaiken, S. (1993). *The psychology of attitudes.* Fort Worth, TX: Harcourt Brace Jovanovich.

Eisenberger, R., & Selbst, M. (1994). Does reward increase or decrease creativity:? *Journal of Personality and Social Psychology, 66,* 1116–1127.

Elms, A. C. (1975). The crisis of confidence in social psychology. *American Psychologist, 30,* 967–976.

Fazio, R. H. (1989). On the power and functionality of attitudes: The role of attitude accessibility. In A. R. Pratkanis, S. J. Breckler, & A. G. Greenwald (Eds.), *Attitude structure and function* (pp. 153–179). Hillsdale, NJ: Erlbaum.

Feldman, R. S. (1986). *The social psychology of education: Current research and theory.* New York: Cambridge University Press.

Festinger, L. (1954). A theory of social comparison processes. *Human Relations, 7,* 117–140.

Festinger, L. (1957). *A theory of cognitive dissonance.* Stanford, CA: Stanford University Press.

Fiedler, F. E. (1964). A contingency model of leadership effectiveness. In L. Berkowitz (Ed.), *Advances in experimental social psychology* (Vol. 1, pp. 150–190). New York: Academic Press.

Fiedler, F. E., & Garcia, J. E. (1987). *New approaches to*

leadership: Cognitive resources and organizational performance. New York: Wiley.

Finkelhor, D. (1984). *Child sexual abuse: New theory and research*. New York: Free Press.

Fishbein, M. (Ed.). (1967). *Readings in attitude theory and measurement*. New York: Wiley.

Fishbein, M., & Ajzen, I. (1974). Attitudes toward objects as predictors of single and multiple behavioral criteria. *Psychological Review, 81*, 59–74.

Fishbein, M., & Ajzen, I. (1975). *Belief, attitude, intention and behavior*. Reading, MA: Addison-Wesley.

Fiske, S. T. (1992). Thinking is for doing: Portraits of social cognition from daguerreotype to laserphoto. *Journal of Personality and Social Psychology, 63*, 877–889.

Fiske, S. T., & Taylor, S. E. (1991). *Social cognition* (2nd ed.). New York: McGraw-Hill.

Freedman, J. L. (1984). Effects of television violence on aggressiveness. *Psychological Bulletin, 96*, 227–246.

Furlong, M. J., & Morrison, G. M. (1994). (Eds.). *School Psychology Review, 23*, (Whole No. 2).

Gottfried, A. E., Fleming, J. S., & Gottfried, A. W. (1994). Role of parental motivational practices in children's academic instrinsic motivation and achievement. *Journal of Educational Psychology, 86*, 104–113.

Gottlieb, J., Rose, T., & Lessen, E. (1983). Mainstreaming. In K. Kerenau, M. Begab, & R. Edgerton (Eds.), *Environments and behavior: The adaption of mentally retarded persons* (pp. 195–212). Baltimore, MD: University Park Press.

Grolnick, W. S., & Ryan, R. M. (1987). Autonomy in children's learning: An experimental and individual difference investigation. *Journal of Personality and Social Psychology, 52*, 890–898.

Guskey, T. R., & Passaro, P. D. (1994). Teacher efficacy: A study of construct dimensions. *American Educational Research Journal, 31*, 627–643.

Gutkin, T. B. (Ed.). (1997). The social psychology of influence with adults (special mini-issue). *Journal of School Psychology*.

Gutkin, T. B., & Ajchenbaum, M. (1984). Teachers' perceptions of control and preferences for consultative services. *Professional Psychology: Research and Practice, 15*, 565–570.

Guys, J. A., Willis, W. G., & Faust, D. (1995). School psychologists' diagnoses of learning disabilities: A study of illusory correlation. *Journal of School Psychology, 33*, 59–73.

Harvey, J. H., Ickes, W., & Kidd, R. F. (Eds.). (1978). *New directions in attribution research* (Vol. 2). Hillsdale, NJ: Erlbaum.

Heider, F. (1958). *The psychology of interpersonal relations*. New York: Wiley.

Hendrick, C. (1977). Social psychology as an experimental science. In C. Hendrick (Ed.),

Perspectives on social psychology (pp. 1–74). Hillsdale, NJ: Erlbaum.

Hilsman, R., & Garber, J. (1995). A test of the cognitive diathesis-stress model of depression in children: Academic stressors, attributional style, perceived competence, and control. *Journal of Personality and Social Psychology, 69*, 370–380.

Himmelfarb, S. (1993). The measurement of attitudes. In A. H. Eagley & S. Chaiken (Eds.), *The psychology of attitudes* (pp. 23–87). Fort Worth, TX: Harcourt Brace Jovanovich.

Hobfoll, S. E., Spielberger, C. D., Breznitz, S., Figley, C., Lepper-Green, B., Meichenbaum, D., Milgram, N., Sandler, I., Sarason, I., & van der Kolk, B. (1991). War-related stress: Addressing the stress of war and other traumatic events. *American Psychologist, 46*, 848–855.

House, R. J., & Singh, J. V. (1987). Organizational behavior: Some new directions for I/O psychology. *Annual Review of Psychology, 38*, 669–718.

Hovland, C. I. (1959). Reconciling results derived from experimental and survey studies of attitude change. *American Psychologist, 14*, 8–17.

Hovland, C. I., Janis, I. L., & Kelley, H. H. (1953). *Communication and persuasion*. New Haven, CT: Yale University Press.

Hughes, J. N. (1983). The application of cognitive dissonance to consultation. *Journal of School Psychology, 21*, 349–357.

Hughes, J. N. (1992). Social psychological foundations of consultation. In F. J. Medway & T. P. Cafferty (Eds.), *School psychology: A social psychological perspective* (pp. 269–303). Hillsdale, NJ: Erlbaum.

Huston, T. L., & Levinger, G. (1978). Interpersonal attraction and relationships. *Annual Review of Psychology, 29*, 115–156.

Johnston, R. A., Rose, J., & Russell, D. W. (1992). Loneliness and interpersonal relationships across the school years. In F. J. Medway & T. C. Cafferty (Eds.), *School psychology: A social psychological perspective* (pp. 377–396). Hillsdale, NJ: Erlbaum.

Jones, E. E. (1985). Major developments in social psychology during the past five decades. In G. Lindzey & E. Aronson (Eds.), *Handbook of social psychology* (3rd ed., Vol. 1, pp. 47–108). New York: Random House.

Jones, E. E., & Davis, K. E. (1965). From acts to dispositions: The attribution process in person perception. In L. Berkowitz (Ed.), *Advances in experimental social psychology* (Vol. 2, pp. 219–266). New York: Academic Press.

Jones, E. E., & McGillis, D. (1976). Correspondent inferences and the attribution cube: A comparative reappraisal. In J. Harvey, W. Ickes, & R. Kidd (Eds.), *New directions in attribution research* (Vol. 1, pp. 89–420). Hillsdale, NJ: Erlbaum.

Jones, E. E., & Nisbett, R. E. (1971). *The actor and the*

*observer: Divergent perceptions of behavior.* Morristown, NJ: General Learning Press.

Katz, D. (1960). The functional approach to the study of attitudes. *Public Opinion Quarterly, 24,* 163–204.

Katz, D., & Kahn, R. L. (1978). *The social psychology of organizations* (2nd ed.). New York: Wiley.

Kelley, H. H. (1967). Attribution in social psychology. In D. Levine (Ed.), *Nebraska symposium on motivation* (pp. 192–238). Lincoln: University of Nebraska Press.

Kelley, H. H. (1983). Perceived causal structures. In J. M. F. Jaspers, F. D. Finchman, & M. R. C. Hewstone (Eds.), *Attribution theory and research: Conceptual, developmental and social dimensions* (pp. 34–56). London: Academic Press.

Kelley, H. H., & Thibaut, J. W. (1978). *Interpersonal relations: A theory of independence.* New York: Wiley.

Krebs, D. L., & Miller, D. T. (1985). Altruism and aggression. In G. Lindzey & D. Aronson (Eds.), *Handbook of social psychology* (3rd ed., Vol. 2, pp. 1–71). New York: Random House.

Kyle, S. O., & Falbo, T. (1985). Relationships between marital stress and attributional preferences for own and spouse behavior. *Journal of Social and Clinical Psychology, 3,* 339–351.

Landy, F. S., & Farr, J. L. (1980). Performance rating. *Psychological Bulletin, 87,* 72–107.

Larrance, D. F., & Twentyman, C. T. (1983). Maternal attributions and child abuse. *Journal of Abnormal Psychology, 92,* 449–457.

LeBon, G. (1896). *The crowd.* London: T. Fisher Unwin.

Lerner, M. J. (1980). *The belief in a just world: The fundamental illusion.* New York: Plenum.

Levesque, M. J., & Lowe, C. A. (1992). The importance of attributions and expectancies in understanding academic behavior. In F. J. Medway & T. P. Cafferty (Eds.), *School psychology: A social psychological perspective* (pp. 47–81). Hillsdale, NJ: Erlbaum.

Lewin, K. (1947). Group decision and social change. In T. M. Newcomb & E. L. Hartley (Eds.), *Readings in social psychology* (pp. 330–344). New York: Henry Holt.

Lewin, K. (1951). Psychological ecology. In D. Cartwright (Ed.), *Field theory in social science* (pp. 170–187). New York: Harper & Row.

Lewin, K., Lippett, R., & White, R. K. (1939). Patterns of aggressive behavior in experimentally created "social climates." *Journal of Social Psychology, 10,* 271–299.

Madden, N. A., & Slavin, R. E. (1983). Effects of cooperative learning on social acceptance of mainstreamed academically handicapped students. *Journal of Special Education, 17,* 171–182.

Maher, C. A., & Kruger, L. J. (1992). The Quality Circle approach and school psychological services: Description and application. *Special Services in the Schools, 6,* 129–154.

Malamuth, N. M. (1986). Predictors of naturalistic sexual aggression. *Journal of Personality and Social Psychology, 50,* 953–962.

Markus, H., & Zajonc, R. B. (1985). The cognitive perspective in social psychology. In G. Lindzey & E. Aronson (Eds.), *The handbook of social psychology* (3rd ed., Vol. 1., pp. 137–230). Hillsdale, NJ: Erlbaum.

Marshall, W. L., & Barbaree, H. E. (1984). A behavioral view of rape. *International Journal of Law and Psychiatry, 7,* 51–77.

Martin, R. P., & Curtis, M. (1981). Consultant's perceptions of causality for success and failure of consultation. *Professional Psychology, 12,* 671–676.

McDermott, P. A. (1981). Sources of error in the psychoeducational diagnosis of children. *Journal of School Psychology, 19,* 31–44.

McDougall, W. (1908). *An introduction to social psychology.* London: Methuen.

McGuire, W. J. (1967). Some impending reorientations in social psychology: Some thoughts provoked by Kenneth Ring. *Journal of Experimental Social Psychology, 3,* 124–139.

McGuire, W. J. (1985). Attitudes and attitude change. In G. Lindzey & E. Aronson (Eds.), *The handbook of social psychology* (3rd ed., Vol. 2, pp. 233–346). Hillsdale, NJ: Erlbaum.

Mead, G. H. (1934). *Mind, self, and society.* Chicago: University of Chicago Press.

Medway, F. J. (1979). Causal attributions for school-related problems: Teacher perceptions and teacher feedback. *Journal of Educational Psychology, 71,* 809–819.

Medway, F. J. (1992). Rapprochment of social psychology and school psychology: A historical analysis. In F. J. Medway & T. P. Cafferty (Eds.), *School psychology: A social psychological perspective* (pp. 5–23). Hillsdale, NJ: Erlbaum.

Medway, F. J., & Cafferty, T. P. (1992). (Eds.). *School psychology: A social psychological perspective.* Hillsdale, NJ: Erlbaum.

Medway, F. J., Davis, K. E., Cafferty, T. P., Chappell, K. D., & O'Hearn, R. E. (1995). Family disruption and adult attachment correlates of spouse and child reactions to separation and reunion due to Operation Desert Storm. *Journal of Social and Clinical Psychology, 14,* 97–118.

Merton, R. K. (1957). *Social theory and social structure.* New York: Free Press.

Middleton, H., Zollinger, J., & Keene, R. (1986). Population peers as change agents for the socially neglected child in the classroom. *Journal of School Psychology, 24,* 343–350.

Miller, N. E. (1941). The frustration-aggression hypothesis. *Psychological Review, 48,* 337–342.

Moreno, J. L. (1934). *Who shall survive?* (Monograph No. 58). Washington, DC: Nervous and Mental Disease Publishing.

Morrison, G. M., Furlong, M. J., & Morrison, R. L.

(1994). School violence to schools safety: Reframing the issue for school psychologists. *School Psychology Review, 23,* 236–256.

Mueller, D. J. (1986). *Measuring social attitudes: A handbook for researchers and practitioners.* New York: Teachers College Press.

Mueser, K. T., Grau, B. W., Sussman, S., & Rosen, A. J. (1984). You're only as pretty as you feel: Facial expression as a determinant of physical attractiveness. *Journal of Personality and Social Psychology, 46,* 468–478.

Natasi, B. K., & Clements, D. H. (1991). Research on cooperative learning: Implications for practice. *School Psychology Review, 20,* 110–131.

Nisbett, R. E., & Ross, L. (1980). *Human inference: Strategies and shortcomings in social judgment.* Englewood Cliffs, NJ: Prentice Hall.

O'Keefe, D. J., & Medway, F. J. (1997). Application of persuasion research to consultation. *Journal of School Psychology, 35,* 173–193.

Oskamp, S. (1984). *Applied social psychology.* Englewood Cliffs, NJ: Prentice Hall.

Oskamp, S. (1991). *Attitudes and opinions* (2nd ed.). Englewood Cliffs, NJ: Prentice Hall.

Pearl, D., Bouthilet, L., & Lazar, J. (Eds.). (1982). *Television and behavior: Ten years of scientific progress and implications for the eighties.* Washington, DC: U.S. Department of Health and Human Services.

Peterson, C. (1992). Learned helplessness and school problems. In F. J. Medway & T. P. Cafferty (Eds.), *School psychology: A social psychological perspective* (pp. 359–376). Hillsdale, NJ: Erlbaum.

Petty, R. E., & Cacioppo, J. T. (1981). *Attitudes and persuasion: Classic and contemporary approaches.* Dubuque, IA: W. C. Brown.

Pfeffer, J. (1985). Organizations and organization theory. In G. Lindzey & E. Aronson (Eds.), *The handbook of social psychology* (3rd ed., Vol. 1, pp. 379–440). Hillsdale, NJ: Erlbaum.

Pratkanis, A. R., Breckler, S. J., & Greenwald, A. G. (Eds.). (1989). *Attitude structure and function.* Hillsdale, NJ: Erlbaum.

Pruitt, D. G., & Kimmel, M. J. (1977). Twenty years of experimental gaming: Critique, synthesis, and suggestions for the future. *Annual Review of Psychology, 28,* 363–392.

Robinson, J. P., & Shaver, W. (1973). *Measures of social psychological attitudes.* Ann Arbor, MI: Institute of Social Relations.

Robinson, J. P., Shaver, P. R., & Wrightsman, L. S. (1991). *Measures of personality and social psychological attitudes* (Vol. 1). San Diego: Academic Press.

Rolison, M. A., & Medway, F. J. (1985). Teachers' expectations and attributions for student achievement: Effects of label, performance pattern, and special education intervention. *American Educational Research Journal, 22,* 561–573.

Rosenhan, D. L. (1973). On being sane in insane places. *Science, 179,* 250–258.

Rosenthal, R., & Rosnow, R. L. (1991). *Essentials of behavioral research: Methods and data analysis* (2nd ed.). New York: McGraw-Hill.

Ross, E. A. (1908). *Social psychology: An outline and a source book.* New York: Macmillan.

Ross, L. (1977). The intuitive psychologist and his shortcomings. In L. Berkowitz (Ed.), *Advances in experimental social psychology* (Vol. 10, pp. 173–220). Orlando, FL: Academic Press.

Ross, L., & Nisbett, R. E. (1991). *The person and the situation: Perspectives of social psychology.* New York: McGraw-Hill.

Rossi, P. H., Wright, J. D., & Anderson, A. B. (Eds.). (1983). *Handbook of survey research.* New York: Academic Press.

Russell, J. A., & Fehr, B. (1994). Fuzzy concepts in a fuzzy hierarchy: Varieties of anger. *Journal of Personality and Social Psychology, 67,* 186–205.

Sahakian, W. S. (1974). *Systematic social psychology.* New York: Chandler.

Sandoval, J. J., & Davis, J. M. (1992). Applications of social psychology to school counseling and therapy. In F. J. Medway & T. P. Cafferty (Eds.), *School psychology: A social psychological perspective* (pp. 245–268). Hillsdale, NJ: Erlbaum.

Sanna, L. J. (1992). Self-efficacy theory: Implications for social facilitation and social loafing. *Journal of Personality and Social Psychology, 62,* 774–786.

Schachter, S. (1964). The interaction of cognitive and physiological determinants of emotional state. In L. Berkowitz (Ed.), *Advances in experimental social psychology* (Vol. 1, pp. 49–80). New York: Academic Press.

Schmuck, R. A., & Schmuck, P. A. (1971). *Group processes in the classroom.* Dubuque, IA: W. C. Brown.

Schneider, B. (1985). Organizational behavior. *Annual Review of Psychology, 36,* 573–611.

Selltiz, C., Wrightsman, L. C., & Cook, S. W. (1976). *Research methods in social relations* (3rd ed.). New York: Holt, Rinehart & Winston.

Shaw, M. E., & Wright, J. M. (1967). *Scales for the measurement of attitudes.* New York: McGraw-Hill.

Sherif, M. (1936). *The psychology of social norms.* New York: Harper.

Sherif, M., Harvey, O. J., White, B. J., Hood, W. R., & Sherif, C. W. (1961). *Intergroup conflict and cooperation: The Robbers' Cave experiment.* Norman: University of Oklahoma Book Exchange.

Sherif, M., & Hovland, C. I. (1961). *Social judgment: Assimilation and contrast effects in communication and attitude change.* New Haven, CT: Yale University Press.

Sherman, R. C., Lim, K. M., Seidel, S. D., Sinai, K. A., & Newman, K. M. (1995). Processing causally relevant information. *Journal of Personality and Social Psychology, 68,* 365–376.

Simmel, G. (1950). *The sociology of George Simmel.* K. H. Wolf (Ed. and Trans.). New York: Macmillan.

Slavin, R. E., Sharon, S., Kagan, S., Hertz-Lazarowitz, R., Webb, C., & Schmuck, R. (Eds.) (1985). *Learning to cooperate, cooperating to learn.* New York: Plenum.

Smith, D. K., & Lyon, M. A. (1986). School psychologists' attributions for success and failure in consultations with parents and teachers. *Professional Psychology: Research and Practice, 17,* 205–209.

Smith, M. B., Bruner, J. S., & White, R. W. (1956). *Opinions and personality.* New York: Wiley.

Smith, S. S., Richardson, D., & Hendrick, C. (1980). Bibliography of journal articles in personality and social psychology. *Personality and Social Psychology Bulletin, 6,* 606–636.

Snyder, M., & Uranowitz, S. W. (1978). Reconstructing the past: Some cognitive consequences of person perception. *Journal of Personality and Social Psychology, 36,* 941–950.

Steele, C. M., & Aronson, J. (1995). Stereotype threat and the intellectual test performance of African Americans. *Journal of Personality and Social Psychology, 69,* 797–811.

Stephan, W. G. (1978). School desegregation: An evaluation of predictions made in *Brown v. Board of Education. Psychological Bulletin, 85,* 215–238.

Stephan, W. G. (1985). Intergroup relations. In G. Lindzey & E. Aronson (Eds.), *The handbook of social psychology* (3rd ed., Vol. 2, pp. 599–658). Hillsdale, NJ: Erlbaum.

Summers, G. E. (Ed.). (1970). *Attitude measurement.* Skokie, IL: Rand McNally.

Tajfel, H. (1970). Experiments in intergroup discrimination. *Scientific American, 223,* 96–102.

Tajfel, H. (1978). *Differentiation between social groups.* London: Academic Press.

Tarde, G. (1903). *Laws of imitation* (E. C. Parsons, Trans.) New York: Henry Holt. (Original work published 1901).

Tennen, H., Hall, J. A., & Affleck, G. (1995). Depression research methodologies in the *Journal of Personality and Social Psychology:* A review and critique. *Journal of Personality and Social Psychology, 68,* 870–884.

Triplett, N. (1897). The dynamogenic factors in pacemaking and competition. *American Journal of Psychology, 9,* 507–533.

Trope, Y. (1986). Identification and inferential processes in dispositional attribution. *Psychological Bulletin, 93,* 239–257.

Trope, Y., & Higgins, E. T. (1995). The what, when, and how of dispositional inference: New answers and new questions. *Personality and Social Psychology Bulletin, 19,* 493–500.

Tversky, A., & Kahneman, D. (1974). Judgment under uncertainty: Heuristics and biases. *Science, 185,* 1124–1131.

Vispoel, W. P., & Austin, J. R. (1995). Success and failure in junior high: A critical incident approach to understanding students' attributional beliefs. *American Educational Research Journal, 32,* 377–412.

Webb, E. J., Campbell, D. T., Schwartz, R. D., Sechrest, L., & Grove, J. B. (1981). *Nonreactive measures in the social sciences* (2nd ed.). Boston: Houghton Mifflin.

Weiner, B. (1972). Attribution theory, achievement motivation, and the educational process. *Review of Educational Research, 42,* 203–215.

Weiner, B. (1979). A theory of motivation for some classroom experiences. *Journal of Educational Psychology, 71,* 3–25.

West, S. G., Newsom, J. T., & Fenaughty, A. M. (1992). Publication trends in *JPSP:* Stability and change in topics, methods, and theories across two decades. *Personality and Social Psychology Bulletin, 18,* 473–484.

Williams, K. J., & Williams, G. M. (1992). Applications of social psychology to school employee evaluation and appraisal. In F. J. Medway & T. P. Cafferty (Eds.), *School psychology: A social psychological perspective* (pp. 333–354). Hillsdale, NJ: Erlbaum.

Whyte, W. F. (1943). *Street corner society.* Chicago: University of Chicago Press.

Wicker, A. (1969). Attitudes versus actions: The relationship of verbal and overt behavioral responses to attitude objects. *Journal of Social Issues, 25,* 41–78.

Wild, T. C., Enzle, M. E., & Hawkins, W. L. (1992). Effects of perceived extrinsic versus intrinsic teacher motivation on student reactions to skill acquisition. *Personality and Social Psychology Bulletin, 18,* 245–251.

Wuebben, P. L., Straits, B. C., & Schulman, G. I. (Eds.). (1974). *The experiment as a social occasion.* Berkeley, CA: Glendessary Press.

Wyer, R. S., Jr., & Srull, T. K. (1994). *Handbook of social cognition.* Hillsdale, NJ: Erlbaum.

Zimbardo, P. G., & Lieppe, M. R. (1991). *The psychology of attitude change and social influence.* New York: McGraw-Hill.

## CHAPTER 9

# CURRENT CONTRIBUTIONS OF THE PSYCHOLOGY OF INDIVIDUAL DIFFERENCES TO SCHOOL PSYCHOLOGY

JOHN H. KRANZLER
*University of Florida*

Individuals differ on virtually every biological and psychological characteristics that can be measured (Minton & Schneider, 1985). Familiar examples include height and weight, blood type and pressure, body temperature, visual acuity, and eye coloration, as well as general and specific cognitive abilities, academic achievement, temperament, personality, values, and interests, among many others. The empirical study of variability in psychological functioning is known as *differential psychology*. According to Reynolds and Willson (1985), differential psychology "is perhaps the single most important basic psychological science that underlies professional practice in psychology" (p. vii). Indeed, many of the most troubling social and behavioral issues in the United States are essentially those of individual and group differences. Social and economic inequalities across racial and ethnic groups, for example, are a matter of tremendous concern in our society—as was recently reflected in the uproar that followed publication of Herrnstein and Murray's (1994) *The Bell Curve*, which addressed the relationship between individual and group differences in intelligence and important social behaviors in American life.

In schools, where overcrowding and diminishing resources are all too common, individual differences, or the degree to which children and youths deviate from the norm, are becoming an increasingly important consideration. For school psychologists, who rely heavily on normative frames of references for the identification and classification of children and youths with academic or behavior problems, knowledge of contemporary research and theory in differential psychology is particularly crucial. A thorough understanding of individual differences is necessary not only for the optimal conceptualization and explanation of school-related difficulties but for the effective planning and evaluation of school-based interventions as well.

## CHAPTER OVERVIEW

The goals of this chapter are (1) to provide an overview of contemporary research and theory in the rapidly advancing field of differential psychology and (2) to discuss its contributions to the discipline and practice of school psychology. This chapter begins with discussion of some of the basic concepts and research methods in differential psychology, with particular emphasis on the differential model, or quantitative behavioral genetics, for studying environmental and genetic influences on individual differences in psychological functioning. I then review the results of research in major domains of psychological functioning that are relevant to the field of school psychology—general and specific cognitive abilities, academic achievement, learning disabilities and mental retardation, and personality—followed by current contributions of contemporary research and theory to school psychology. This chapter concludes with the description of a model for conceptualizing individual differences in the practice and discipline of school psychology.

## BASIC CONCEPTS AND RESEARCH METHODS

### Describing Variability

The core concept in differential psychology is variability. An initial step in the examination of variability in the measurements of large groups of people is the frequency distribution. Frequency distributions organize and summarize data by displaying in tabular form the frequency with which specific scores were obtained. When scores vary widely, they can be grouped according to class intervals to get a clearer picture of the dispersion. Table 9.1 shows a grouped frequency distribution of scores on the Verbal Scale of the Scholastic Aptitude Test (SAT) for 1,450 university students. Frequency distributions can also be displayed graphically as a histogram (bar graph) or as a frequency polygon (smooth-line curve), as shown in Figure 9.1. A frequency distribution facilitates the identification of patterns that may exist in the data.

Frequency polygons can have almost any shape. The data in Figure 9.1, for example, approximate the so-called normal curve. Figure 9.2 shows several additional types of distribution. These data are from Army Alpha, a group test of reasoning ability that was administered to soldiers during World War I. As is apparent in this figure, distributions can vary in skewness. A distribution is said to be skewed when most of the obtained scores fall at one end of the distribution and relatively few at the other. *Positively skewed*

**FIGURE 9.1   Frequency polygon and histogram of Scholastic Aptitude Test— Verbal scores for 1,450 university students. Data are from Table 9.6.**

*Source:* Minton & Schneider (1985).

TABLE 9.1   Grouped Frequency Distribution of Scholastic Aptitude Test—Verbal Scores for 1,450 University Students

| Class Interval | Frequency |
| --- | --- |
| 750–799 | 5 |
| 700–749 | 55 |
| 650–699 | 119 |
| 600–649 | 223 |
| 550–599 | 291 |
| 500–549 | 330 |
| 450–499 | 257 |
| 400–459 | 128 |
| 350–399 | 34 |
| 300–349 | 5 |
| 250–299 | 2 |
| 200–249 | 1 |
| | $N = 1,450.$ |

From Minton & Schneider (1985).

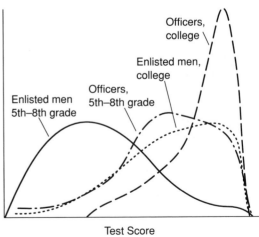

**FIGURE 9.2   Scores on Army Alpha, by level of education.**

*Source:* Cronbach (1990).

distributions have one tail that extends toward the positive, or high, end of the distribution; *negatively skewed* distributions have one tail that extends toward the negative, or low, end of the distribution. Distributions can also vary in their kurtosis, that is, in the flatness or peakness of the distribution. Platykurtic distributions have a wide, broad peak and a large dispersion of scores. Leptokurtic distributions have a relatively sharp peak, with most of the scores clustered around the middle of the distribution. The shape of a distribution is influenced by several factors, including the difficulty of the items for those taking the test (see Jensen, 1980a).

Measures of central tendency and variability can be calculated to quantify certain important characteristics of a distribution. The average, or most typical, score of a distribution can be described in terms of the mean, median, or mode. The mean ($\bar{x}$) is the arithmetical average, obtained by dividing the sum of all scores by the total number of scores. Expressed algebraically, $\bar{x} = \Sigma x/N$, where $\Sigma$ means "the sum of," $x$ refers to each obtained score, and $N$ refers to the total number of scores. The median is the score that divides the frequency distribution in half. Fifty percent of the total number of obtained scores fall above the median and 50% below. The median is a better index of the most typical score in a skewed distribution because the mean will be unduly influenced by the presence of extreme scores in the data. The mode is simply the most commonly obtained score.

Variably in a distribution can be described in terms of the range, semi-interquartile range (SR), variance (SD²), or standard deviation (SD). The range is the distance between the highest and lowest obtained scores. The SR is half the distance between the scores corresponding to the twenty-fifth and seventy-fifth percentiles. The range and SR are relatively unreliable estimates of score dispersion because they are based on only two obtained scores. Since the variance is based on every obtained score, it is a more reliable index of variability than the range or SR. The variance is defined as the average of the squared deviations of every score from the mean of the distribution. The sum of the squared deviations is usually divided by $N-1$ (instead of by $N$) to obtain an unbiased estimate of the population variance. Expressed algebraically, $SD^2 = \Sigma(x - \bar{x})^2/N - 1$, where $\Sigma$ means "the sum of," $x$ refers to each obtained score, $\bar{x}$ is the mean of all scores, and $N$ refers to the total number of scores.

Interpreted as the "amount of information" in a distribution (Cronbach, 1990), variance is an extremely valuable index of variability in differential psychology. Because it is additive, the total amount in a distribution can be partitioned into a number of smaller components. Despite the fact that the variance is easier to work with statistically, its square root—the standard deviation—is more useful in describing the variability in a distribution. The standard deviation reflects the average deviation from the mean in actual units of measurement.

## Explaining Variance

When two variables are measured for each participant in a research study or when the same variable is measured for pairs of participants, the magnitude of the relationship between them can be determined by the methods of correlation. The most widely used measure of correlation is the *Pearson product-moment correlation coefficient* ($r_{xy}$). Like other indexes of correlation, the $r_{xy}$ provides a quantitative index of the strength of association between two variables. The $r_{xy}$ can be calculated by first determining the covariance ($cov_{xy}$), which is defined as the average of the sum of the cross products of deviation scores on two variables. Expressed algebraically, $cov_{xy} = \Sigma(x - \bar{x})(y - \bar{y})/N - 1$, where $\Sigma$ means "the sum of," $x$ refers to the obtained scores on variable $x$, $\bar{x}$ is the mean of the scores on $x$, $y$ refers to the obtained scores on variable $y$, $\bar{y}$ is the mean of the scores on $y$, and $N$ refers to the total number of pairs of scores. The $cov_{xy}$ is divided by the product of the standard deviation of $x$ and the standard deviation of $y$ to obtain the $r_{xy}$. The square of $r_{xy}$ ($r_{xy}^2$) provides an estimate of the proportion of variance on $x$ that is "explained by," "accounted for," or "related to" variance on $y$. The larger the $r_{xy}^2$, the more closely related differences on $x$ are to differences on $y$.

It is important to note that causality is not established by the existence of a correlation between two variables—only the degree to which they covary—regardless of the magnitude of $r_{xy}^2$. Correlation coefficients, however, permit the partitioning of variance on two variables into meaningful shared subcomponents. They can also be used in linear regression, the prediction of one variable from another. Furthermore, correlations provide the foundation for multiple regression, which involves the prediction of one variable from several other variables, and for other, more complex correlational techniques, such as factor analysis and path analysis (see Loehlin, 1992b, for further discussion).

# THE DIFFERENTIAL MODEL

According to Plomin, DeFries, and McClearn (1990), "Quantitative behavioral genetics provides the basis for a general theory of the etiology of individual differences of a scope and power rarely seen in the behavioral sciences" (p. 247). They further state that unlike most other contemporary theories in the social and behavioral sciences, behavioral genetics is not limited to a particular substantive domain. The methods of quantitative behavioral genetics have been effectively applied to the study of individual differences in general and specific cognitive abilities, academic achievement, personality, and temperament, among other domains (for reviews, see Bates & Wachs, 1994; Plomin & McClearn, 1993; Rushton, 1995). In addition, behavioral genetics is a "progressive" scientific theory in that it leads to new, empirically testable predictions (Plomin et al., 1990).

Nevertheless, McClearn (1993) recently argued that the conventional term—*behavioral genetics*—may be misleading. Because quantitative behavioral genetics examines the contributions of genetics and the environment to individual differences in particular traits, a more fitting expression in his view is the *differential model*. McClearn believes that the use of this term may also decrease the frequency with which quantitative behavioral genetics is mistakenly equated with an hereditarian view of individual and group differences. For these reasons, the term *differential model* is used throughout the remainder of this chapter.

## Partitioning Variance

The differential model is perhaps best understood as an attempt to partition variance (Brody, 1992). Underlying this model is the assumption that variance in a *phenotype* ($V_P$)—an observable, measurable characteristic of an individual—can be partitioned into components of variance that reflect the *genotype* ($V_G$)—an individual's genetic composition—and the environment ($V_E$), which can be combined additively. Expressed symbolically, $V_P = V_G + V_E$. The *heritability* ($h^2$) of a particular trait is defined as the proportion of variance in the phenotype that is attributable to variance in the genotype. Heritability (in the broad sense) is expressed by $h^2 = V_G/V_P$. The re-

maining variance (i.e., $1 - h^2$) is known as *environmentality*, which reflects differences in the phenotype that are associated with the environment and with measurement error. The methods of the differential model are thus used to examine the extent to which phenotypic variance reflects differences among the genotypes of individuals or the environments to which they have been exposed (American Psychological Association, 1995).

Table 9.2 summarizes additional components of variance that can be partitioned in the differential model. As is shown, genotypic variance can be further decomposed into *additive* and *nonadditive* components of variance. Additive genetic variance reflects the extent to which genes sum, or "add up," to influence a particular trait. Nonadditive genetic variance reflects the extent to which genes do not add up but are differentially influenced by the effects of dominant genes. Nonadditive genetic variance decreases the resemblance between parents and offspring, or the extent to which genes "breed true" (Plomin et al., 1990). The environmental component of variance can also be partitioned into two subcomponents, *shared* and *nonshared*. Shared environmental influences reflect common experiences that make individuals in the same family similar to one another and different from those in other families. Nonshared, or within-family variance, reflect unique life experiences that make members of the same family different from one another.

In addition to these main effects, phenotypic variance may also result from combined genetic

## TABLE 9.2 Sources of Phenotypic Variation

Genotype
    Additive
    Nonadditive
Environment
    Between family
    Within family
Genotype-environment correlation
    Passive
    Active
    Reactive
Genotype-environment interaction
Error variance
Unexplained variance

and environmental influences, of which there are two kinds—*genotype-environment interaction* and *genotype-environment correlation.* The former refers to the nonlinear combination of genetic and environmental effects on behavior. This occurs when the impact of the environment on a particular trait depends on the genotype. Figure 9.3 illustrates three kinds of genotype-environment interaction. The responses of three hypothetical genotypes (AA, Aa, and aa) are shown in three trait-relevant environments (E1, E2, and E3). Figure 3a shows no interaction effect. The environments and genotypes combine in an additive fashion. In Figure 3b, an ordinal interaction is evident in the differential response of the genotypes across environments, despite the fact that their rank order on the dependent measure remains the same. Figure 3c shows a disordinal interaction—the response of the genotypes are quite different across environments. In this case, the response of a genotype depends on the environment. Other kinds of interaction are also possible.

Few genotype-environment interactions have been discovered in animal or human research that account for more than a negligible portion of phenotypic variance, however (see Loehlin, 1992a). Benson and Weinberg (1990) conjectured that this might be related to ineffectual measurement of environmental factors or to insufficient power in research studies (e.g., small sample $N$'s). Goldsmith (1993) added that the paucity of discovered genetic-environmental interactions may simply stem from the fact that little is known about which environmental and genotypic features might interact.

The genotype-environment correlation "describes the extent to which individuals are exposed to environments as a function of their genetic propensities" (Plomin et al., 1990, p. 251). Plomin, DeFries, and Loehlin (1977) discussed three types of genotype-environment correlation—passive, active, and reactive. A *passive* genotype-environment correlation exists when individuals passively inherit environments that are correlated with their genetic predispositions. Children do not select the environments into which they are born; rather, environments that are favorable or unfavorable to the development of particular traits are imposed on them, for example, when children with superior musical genotypes are born to and raised by parents who provide a musically stimulating environment. This type of correlation also exists when children

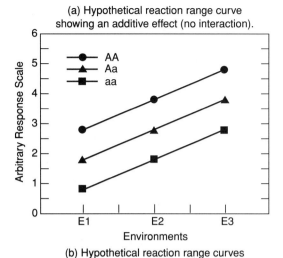

(a) Hypothetical reaction range curve showing an additive effect (no interaction).

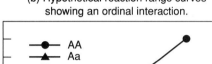

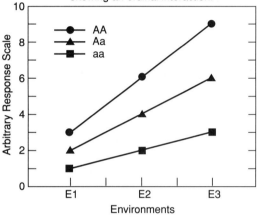

(b) Hypothetical reaction range curves showing an ordinal interaction.

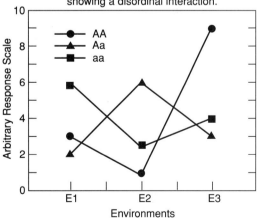

(c) Hypothetical reaction range curves showing a disordinal interaction.

**FIGURE 9.3    Examples of three types of genotype-environment interaction.**
*Source:* Bouchard (1993).

with relatively poor musical genotypes are born to and raised by parents who provide a musically impoverished environment.

A *reactive* genotype-environment correlation refers to environments that are selected or created by others in reaction to an individual's genetic predisposition. A common example in the schools is the identification and placement of children in special classes for the intellectually gifted. In contrast, an *active* genotype-environment correlation occurs when individuals select or create environments that are correlated with their genotypes. For example, children with superior musical genotypes may spend more time listening to, thinking about, and practicing music than other children, regardless of whether anyone wants them to or not (Jensen, 1980b). Passive, active, and reactive genotype-environment correlations increase the phenotypic variance in a trait.

## Common Research Designs

All procedures for estimating the relative contributions of heredity and environment in the differential model involve correlating measurements taken from groups to biologically related and nonbiologically related people and then comparing these correlations with those expected from a purely genetic hypothesis. The expected correlations are called *genetic correlations*, which are derived from principles of Mendelian genetics. They reflect the theoretical correlation between the genotypes of individuals for a particular trait. "Most simply, it can be thought of as the proportion of those genes contributing to the genetic variation that, on the average, are the same in relatives of a given degree of kinship" (Jensen, 1980b, p. 88). Table 9.3 shows the genetic correlations that are expected between various kinships under the assumptions of the simplest genetic model: that there are no dominant or recessive genes and that assortative mating between parents on the trait in question is zero.

Dominance decreases the correlation, on the average, between siblings and between parents and their offspring but not between monozygotic (MZ) twins. The effect of assortative mating increases the correlation between siblings and between more distant relatives, although to a lesser degree. Assortative mating—the tendency for individuals to mate with similar others on certain traits—can be found in many socially important behaviors. Examples of traits on which assorta-

**TABLE 9.3** Genetic Correlation Between Various Kinships Under the Assumptions of the Simplest Genetic Model

| Kinship | Genetic Correlation |
|---|---|
| Monozygotic Twins | 1.00 |
| Dizygotic Twins | 0.50 |
| Full siblings | 0.50 |
| Parent-offspring | 0.50 |
| Grandparent-grandchild | 0.25 |
| Half-siblings | 0.25 |
| Uncle (aunt)–nephew (niece) | 0.25 |
| First cousins | 0.125 |
| Second cousins | 0.0625 |
| Nonbiologically related | 0.00 |

Adapted from Jensen (1980b).

tive mating can be found are shown in Figure 9.4. Between siblings, these two effects on the correlation tend to cancel each other. For more detailed discussion of these and other effects, such as epistasis, see Plomin et al. (1990).

The genetic correlation for identical, or *monozygotic* (MZ), twins is 1.00, because they share 100% of their genetic makeup. Since nontwin offspring receive 50% of their genetic material from each parent, the parent-child genetic correlation is 0.50. The genetic correlation for fraternal, or *dizygotic* (DZ), twins and for full siblings is also 0.50 because they share 50% of their genes as a result of deriving from separate eggs and sperm from the same parents. Given that more distant relatives share even less genetic overlap, the genetic correlations are even lower than 0.50. Nonbiologically related persons have no genes in common—hence the genetic correlation of zero. Obtained correlations for many physical characteristics compare quite well to those expected from a genetic hypothesis, several of which are shown in Table 9.4. Correlations that diverge widely (in either direction) from the expected genetic correlation for a particular kinship do not substantiate a purely genetic hypothesis. If there is no resemblance between family members, the genetic hypothesis is disconfirmed for that particular trait.

*Family, twin,* and *adoption* studies are the three basic research designs used in the differential model. These designs exploit different com-

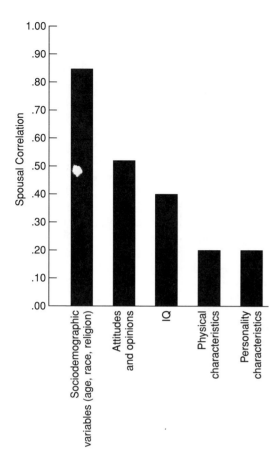

**FIGURE 9.4** **Spousal resemblance on a variety of characteristics. On all dimensions, the similarity between spouses is significantly greater than chance.**
*Source:* Rushton (1995).

**TABLE 9.4** **Median Correlations for Identical and Fraternal Twins for Height, Weight, and Total Ridge Count of Fingerprints**

|  | Correlation | |
| --- | --- | --- |
|  | Identical | Fraternal |
| Height | 0.93 | 0.48 |
| Weight | 0.91 | 0.58 |
| Total ridge count | 0.96 | 0.49 |

Plomin, DeFries, & McClearn (1990).

binations of genotypes and environments that occur naturally in the population (Thompson, 1993). Of particular interest to researchers in the differential model are families in which "(1) genetic influences are controlled or randomized so that the effects of the environment can be studied and (2) environmental influences are controlled so that the effects of genes can be studied" (Plomin et al., 1990, p. 297). In family studies, estimates of $h^2$ are based on comparisons of parents with their offspring and of siblings with each other. Estimates of $h^2$ from family studies are influenced by dominance and by assortative mating. Moreover, because members of the same family share both common genes and environment, evidence of familial similarity is consistent with the genetic hypothesis but cannot confirm it. Estimates of $h^2$ in family studies, therefore, are interpreted as an upper limit of the true $h^2$ for a particular trait. Twin and adoption studies must be used to disentangle the relative contributions of genetics and the environment to phenotypic variance.

Twin studies are one of the most powerful designs in the differential model. If a particular trait is influenced by genetics, the correlation between MZ twins should be greater than the correlation between DZ twins—assuming that the environments of each type of twin are equal—because MZ twins have 100% of their genes in common and DZ twins only 50%, on the average. Correlations for MZ and DZ twins reared together reflect the phenotypic variance accounted for by the *combined* effects of genes and common environment. In twin studies, $h^2$ can be estimated with the following formula: $h^2 = 2 (r_{MZ} - r_{DZ})$, where $r_{MZ}$ is the correlation between MZ twins and $r_{DZ}$ is the correlation between DZ twins. If the correlations for a hypothetical trait are 0.80 for MZ twins and 0.50 for DZ twins, $h^2 = 2 (0.80 - 0.50) = 0.60$, which means that 60% of the phenotypic variance for the trait in this example is accounted for by genetics.

The variance explained by the environment ($e^2$) is estimated by subtracting $h^2$ from 1.00. In this example, the environment accounted for 40% of the phenotypic variance ($e^2 = 1 - h^2 = 1 - 0.60 = 0.40$). The environmental variance can be further partitioned into shared ($e_C^2$) and nonshared ($e_W^2$) environmental components. Given that differences between MZ twins raised in the same family must result from nonshared environmental influences, $e_W^2 = 1.00 - r_{MZ}$. By subtracting $h^2$ from $r_{MZ}$, an estimate of $e_C^2$ can be obtained. For these data, $e_W^2 = 1 - 0.80 = 0.20$, and $e_C^2 = 0.80 - 0.60 = 0.20$. In sum, for this hypothetical trait, genetic factors explain 60% of the phenotypic variance and environmental factors 40%. The total environmental variance is split equally between shared and nonshared environmental influences, each of which account for 20% of the variance, respectively.

Although critics argue that the assumption of equal environments cannot be met in twin studies (e.g., Kamin, 1974), they do not provide empirical evidence in support of this criticism. Rowe (1993) contends that a violation of the assumption of equal environments requires evidence of some form of unequal treatment and a significant relationship between treatment and trait variation. According to Bouchard (1993), the empirical research that has been conducted on this criticism supports the assumption of equal environments (e.g., see Loehlin & Nichols, 1976). Moreover, when differences between the environments of MZ and DZ twins have been found to exist, they tend not to significantly influence measures of personality, cognition, vocational interests, or interpersonal relationships (Plomin et al., 1990). For many important human traits, therefore, the assumption of equal environments seems quite reasonable.

Adoption studies are another invaluable source of information on the relative contributions of genetics and the environment to phenotypic variance because they, too, separate the effects of common genes and common environment. In adoption studies, adoptive parents are compared to their adopted children, with whom they are completely genetically dissimilar, and biological parents are compared to their adopted-away children, with whom they have no environmental experiences in common. Any resemblance between adopted children and their adoptive parents, therefore, can be attributed to the effects of shared environment; conversely, any resemblance between adopted-away children and their biological parents can be attributed to genetics. Pairs of adopted and unadopted children reared together can also be compared to estimate the effects of common environment. Particularly noteworthy are studies in which the adoption and twin methods are combined. In these studies, of which there are relatively few, MZ and DZ twins who have been separated at birth and reared apart are compared.

The age of placement and selective placement are important considerations in adoption studies. For valid results, adopted children should have been placed at birth or shortly thereafter; otherwise, estimates of $h^2$ will be inflated (Thompson, 1993). Selective placement, perhaps the most widely cited criticism of adoption studies (e.g., Kamin, 1974; Lewontin, Rose, & Kamin, 1984; Taylor, 1980), refers to the fact that the homes into which children are adopted are generally better than average. Under conditions of selective placement, both genetic and environmental influences may be overestimated. Bouchard (1993), however, recently demonstrated that the effect of placement bias is less of a problem than many have assumed. He showed that the effect of selective placement on estimates of $h^2$ is rather modest, even on traits that are influenced strongly by the environment and with a relatively high degree of selective placement by current standards.

## Interpreting $h^2$

Plomin et al. (1990) state that a number of important points must be kept in mind when interpreting estimates of $h^2$. First, $h^2$ is simply a statistic that describes the ratio of genotypic variance to phenotypic variance in a population. In other words, $h^2$ describes the extent to which individual differences in a measurable trait can be accounted for by differences in genetics. Specific genetic mechanisms or gene-behavior pathways are *not* implied when $h^2$ is significantly greater than zero. Although heritability does indicate that physiological functioning is related to trait variation, it does not provide information on the specific areas of the brain responsible for that variation or on how they operate (Rowe, 1993).

Second, estimates of $h^2$ refer to populations, not to individuals. An $h^2$ of 0.50 for intelligence, for example, indicates that 50% of the differences in cognitive ability among individuals in a population are associated with differences in genes—not that half of an individual's measured IQ (intelligence quotient) is attributable to genes and half to the environment.

Third, estimates of $h^2$ are not constant. Heritability estimates may vary across different populations at the same time or within the same population at different times, depending on changes in the proportions of genetic and environmental variance. Because estimates of $h^2$ are sensitive to the populations on which they are based, they cannot be generalized to other populations or be used to explain differences between populations (McClearn, 1993).

Fourth, estimates of $h^2$ for a particular trait are just that—estimates. Estimates of $h^2$ involve error, as does all measurement, and they can vary according to the use of different samples, different assessment instruments, and different methods of estimating $h^2$ (Jensen, 1980b).

Fifth, and finally, although a basic assumption underlying the differential model is that differences in genes can lead to differences in phenotypes—even in complex traits such as intelligence—estimates of $h^2$ that are greater than zero do *not* imply biological determinism (Plomin et al., 1990). Genotypes do not directly cause phenotypic expression. Rushton (1995) asserts that "they code for enzymes, which, under the influence of the environment, lay down tracts in the brains and nervous systems of individuals, thus differentially affecting people's minds and the choices they make about behavioral alternatives" (p. 61).

# DOMAINS OF INDIVIDUAL DIFFERENCES

The methods of the differential model have been applied to a number of domains that are relevant to the discipline and practice of school psychology. Results of this research on the etiology of individual differences in the following areas are reviewed next: general cognitive ability, specific cognitive ability, academic achievement, and personality. Learning disabilities and mental disabilities are also discussed within the appropriate domains. The discussion begins with general cognitive ability, or intelligence, because it has been the focus of the vast majority of studies that use the methods of the differential model.

## General Cognitive Ability

What do tests of general cognitive ability, or intelligence measure? According to Jensen (1987), two points are now firmly established in the literature. First, the vast majority of intelligence tests measure, to a large degree, the same source of individual differences. This is evident in the high correlations among scores on tests of general cognitive ability, the average of which is about 0.80 (Jensen, 1980a). The single largest component of variance that underlies tests of cognitive ability is a general factor, or psychometric *g* (see Carroll, 1993). Second, scores on IQ tests correlate more highly with assessments of scholastic performance than any other measurable educational or psychological variable *independent* of IQ (see Jensen, 1980a). These are ro-

bust empirical findings that are rarely disputed today. Their explanation, however, has long been the subject of intense debate.

Given the controversy that has surrounded research on the so-called nature-nurture issue in intelligence over the years, it may come as some surprise to learn that the main focus of research in this area no longer involves the question of whether individual differences in intelligence are related to genetic factors or not (for a detailed review of the nature-nurture issue, see Loehlin, 1984). Most psychologists now believe that *both* genetic and environmental factors are at least partly related to variability in intelligence (Snyderman & Rothman, 1987). As Ceci (1990) stated, "There are so many reports in the behavior-genetics literature of substantial heritability coefficients, calculated from an enormous variety of sources, that it is unlikely they could all be wrong" (p. 130). Current research questions in the differential model involve the "details of genetic architecture and its evolutionary basis, the specific nature of the pathways from genes to behavior, and the forms of interaction and covariance of genetic and environmental factors" (Jensen, 1987, p. 84). Nevertheless, researchers disagree on the exact size of estimates of $h^2$ for intelligence and, more importantly, the meaning attached to them.

Table 9.5 presents results of Bouchard and McGue's (1981) update of Erlenmeyer-Kimling and Jarvik's (1963) review of the world literature on familial studies of the heritability of intelligence. Bouchard and McGue reviewed over 100 independent studies, summarizing over 500 correlations between more than 100,000 family members. As this table shows, the results of these studies are consistent with a genetic hypothesis. Not only are the correlations between MZ twins greater than those between family members with less genetic overlap—even when MZ twins are reared apart—but also the obtained correlations across kinships do not deviate substantially from the expected genetic correlations. Explanations of these results that do not involve genetics must demonstrate that the environments of MZ twins reared apart in different families with different parents are *more* similar than the environments of MZ twins and other siblings reared together in the same family with the same parents. Perhaps it is needless to say that a satisfactory explanation of this pattern of correlations from a purely environmental perspective does not exist. Nevertheless, Bouchard and McGue's (1981)

**TABLE 9.5  Average IQ Correlations Among Family Members**

| Relationship | Average r | Number of Pairs |
|---|---|---|
| **Reared-together biological relatives** | | |
| MZ Twins | 0.86 | 4,671 |
| DZ Twins | 0.60 | 5,533 |
| Siblings | 0.47 | 26,473 |
| Parent-offspring | 0.42 | 8,433 |
| Half-siblings | 0.35 | 200 |
| Cousins | 0.15 | 1.176 |
| **Reared-apart biological relatives** | | |
| MZ twins | 0.72 | 65 |
| Siblings | 0.24 | 203 |
| Parent-offspring | 0.24 | 720 |
| **Reared-together nonbiological relatives** | | |
| Siblings | 0.32 | 714 |
| Parent-offspring | 0.24 | 720 |

MZ = monozygotic; DZ = dizygotic. The sample-size-weighted average of $z$ transformations was used to determine $r$.

Adapted from McGue, Bouchard, Iacono, & Lykken (1993).

A more recent review of the literature by McGue, Bouchard, Iacono, and Lykken (1993), however, incorporated the results of several studies of adult twins published since the 1981 review (Pederson, Plomin, Nesselroade, & McClearn, 1992; Tambs, Sundet, & Magnus, 1984; Vernon, 1989). McGue et al. reached a somewhat different conclusion about the relative contributions of heritability and environmentality to individual differences in general cognitive ability across the life span. Figure 9.5 presents weighted average correlations by age group for MZ and DZ twins reared together. As this figure shows, the correlation between the IQs of MZ twins increases throughout the life span. The correlation between DZ twins, in contrast, although fairly stable between 4 to 20 years of age, decreases dramatically after late adolescence. Figure 9.6 displays components of variance derived from the correlations in Figure 9.5. It is interesting that shared environmental influences account for between 30% to 40% of the variance in IQ until the age of about 20 years, after which the amount of variance explained drops to zero. Nonshared environmental effects, in comparison, remain fairly constant across the life span, explaining somewhere between 10% to 20% of

results also provide substantial support for the significant influence of the environment on individual differences in general mental ability. In addition to the fact that correlations between biological relatives who are reared together are greater than those between individuals of the same degree of kinship who are reared apart, the correlations between nonbiological relatives reared together are substantially greater than zero. Neither of these findings can be explained by genetics alone. Chipeur, Rovine, and Plomin's (1990) biometric analysis of the data presented by Bouchard and McGue yielded an $h^2$ estimate of 0.51 for general mental ability, indicating that slightly more than half of the phenotypic variance is accounted for by genetic factors. Shared environmental influences accounted for 11–35% of the variance, depending on kinship data used in the estimation. Nonshared environmental variance was found to explain 14–38% of the variance. According to Bouchard and McGue's review in 1981, therefore, environment and genetics contribute roughly equally to variability in human intellectual functioning.

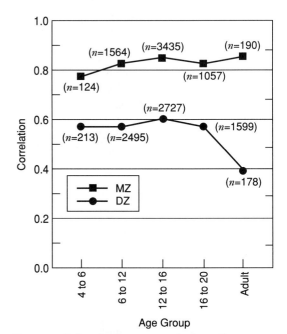

**FIGURE 9.5  Average correlations for monozygotic (MZ) and dizygotic (DZ) twins from published twin studies of intelligence.**

Source: McGue, Bouchard, Iacono, and Lykken (1993).

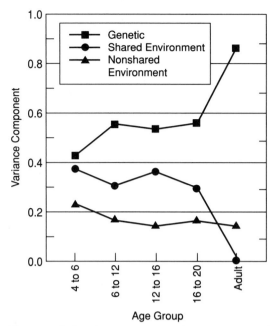

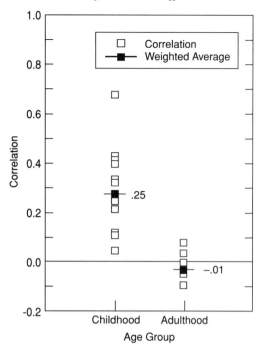

**FIGURE 9.6    Components of environmental and genetic variance from published twin studies of intelligence.**

*Source:* McGue, Bouchard, Iacono, and Lykken (1993).

**FIGURE 9.7    IQ correlations among nonbiologically related but reared-together relatives (both adopted-adopted and adopted-biological pairs) in childhood and adulthood.**

*Source:* McGue, Bouchard, Iacono, and Lykken (1993).

the variance from 4 to 6 years of age into adulthood.

Further substantiation for the postulate that the underlying genetic and environmental determinants of IQ variability change during development comes from adoption studies. Figure 9.7 shows the correlations among nonbiologically related but reared-together relatives (both adopted-adopted and adopted-biological pairs) in childhood and adulthood. As can be seen in this figure, the weighted average correlation (using the Fisher $Z$ transformation method) during childhood is rather substantial, accounting for approximately 25% of the variance in IQ. During adulthood, however, this correlation again decreases to zero. These results indicate that "shared environmental influences may not endure beyond the period of common rearing" (McGue et al., 1993, p. 65). In the long run, declared Plomin and Neiderhiser (1991), the environmental effects that influence variability in general mental ability are nonshared. In addition to the apparent increase in the $h^2$ of general cognitive ability across the life span, Plomin, Pederson, Lichtenstein, and McClearn (1994) found that genetic factors account for approximately 90% of the stability of general cognitive ability later in life (see also Plomin & Thompson, 1987).

Research in the differential model has also recently addressed the question of the etiology of mild mental disabilities. "Although one might expect that very low IQ scores are due to genetic factors . . . the sources of extreme scores can differ from those of individual differences in the middle of the distribution" (Plomin et al., 1990, p. 373). Several recent studies have addressed this question (e.g., Detterman, Thompson, & Plomin, 1990; Saudino, Plomin, Pederson, & McClearn, 1994; Sundet, Eilertsen, Tambs, & Magnus, 1994; Thompson, Detterman, & Plomin, 1993). Detterman et al. analyzed data from 86 pairs of MZ twins and 54 pairs of same-sex DZ twins between 7 and 12 years of age. They found that $h^2$ was related to IQ. Estimates of environmentality were also higher for individuals with low IQs than for those with high IQs. Thompson et al., however, reported no significant difference in $h^2$ between individuals at the high and low ends of the IQ distribution. The effect of shared environment was greater for individuals with low IQs than for those with high IQs. Recent studies by Saudino et al. (1994) and by Sundet et al. (1994) also found no evidence of differential heritability across levels of intelligence. The etiology of mild mental disabilities thus appears to be familial.

Severe mental disabilities, however, appear to result from other causes. Plomin et al. (1990) state that extremely low levels of intelligence tend to be caused by chromosomal abnormalities, such as Down syndrome, or by single-gene defects, such as phenylketonuria (PKU). Additional causes of severe mental disabilities include birth complications (e.g., anoxia), extreme nutritional deficiency, and head injury, among others.

## Specific Cognitive Abilities

Results of Carroll's (1993) reanalysis of over 460 data sets of human abilities substantiated that "there is abundant evidence for a factor of general intelligence" (p. 624), as well as for more than 30 group factors relevant to the study of cognitive abilities. Unlike psychometric g, which enters into all tests, group factors are common

only to certain tests that require similar content (e.g., verbal, numerical, or spatial) or cognitive processes (e.g., memory). Researchers in the differential model have recently begun to investigate the relative contributions of genetics and the environment to individual differences in specific cognitive abilities.

Figure 9.8 presents the results of a large-scale family study of specific cognitive abilities by DeFries et al. (1979). This figure shows the regression of midchild on midparent for 15 cognitive tests and 4 group factors (verbal, spatial, processing speed, and visual memory) in two ethnic groups. As this figure shows, familial resemblance differs across both tests and factors. The verbal and spatial factors tend to show more familial resemblance than the perceptual speed and memory factors. Americans of European ancestry had somewhat higher familial resemblance than those of Japanese descent. DeFries, Vandenberg, and McClearn (1976) and Garfinkle and Vanden-

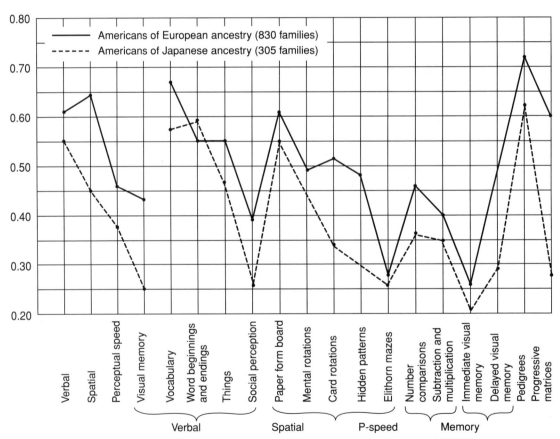

**FIGURE 9.8** **Family study of specific cognitive abilities. Regression of midchild on midparent for four group factors (verbal, spatial, perceptual speed, and memory) and 15 cognitive tests in two ethnic groups.**

*Source:* Plomin, DeFries, and McClearn (1990).

berg (1981) also found greater genetic influences on verbal ability than on other specific abilities, such as memory.

Estimates of the $h^2$ specific cognitive abilities are not as consistent as they are for general cognitive ability, however. Cardon and Fulker (1993) attribute this finding to the use of different samples, different measures of specific cognitive abilities, and different statistical methods. Results of a recent study by Thapar, Petrill, and Thompson (1994) are consistent with this explanation. They found that estimates of the $h^2$ of memory, although generally low, varied according to the instrument used to measure memory. Notwithstanding differences in $h^2$ across studies, Plomin et al. (1990) estimated that the $h^2$ for memory and verbal fluency is approximately 0.30, compared to estimates of $h^2$ in the 0.40–0.50 range for other specific cognitive abilities, such as verbal comprehension, reasoning, and spatial visualization.

Several studies have been conducted on specific cognitive abilities in young children (e.g., LaBuda, DeFries, & Fulker, 1987; Munsinger & Douglass, 1976; Plomin & Vandenberg, 1980; Segal, 1985; Thompson, Detterman, & Plomin,

1991; Wilson, 1975). Table 9.6 presents results of three childhood twin studies of the specific cognitive abilities measured by the Wechsler scales. As shown in this table, estimates of environmental and genetic effects vary not only across subtests within each study but also across studies on the same subtest. These results suggest that there is a greater genetic contribution to variability on the verbal subtests than on the nonverbal subtests. In addition, shared environmental factors generally explain less variance than do genetic factors.

Cyphers, Fulker, Plomin, and DeFries (1989) found similar results in a study of adopted children. In this study, genetic influences were greater for verbal and spatial abilities than for perceptual speed and memory. The influence of shared environment was negligible. Evidently, nonshared environmental effects affect variability in specific cognitive abilities to a greater extent than they do general cognitive ability (Luo, Petrill, & Thompson, 1994). Therefore, "the message is *not* that family experiences are unimportant, but that the relevant environmental influences are specific to each child, not general to an entire family" (Plomin & Neiderhiser, 1991, p. 372; emphasis in original).

**TABLE 9.6   Estimates of Genetic and Shared Family Environmental Influences on Wechsler Subtests**

| | Studies | | | | | |
|---|---|---|---|---|---|---|
| | **WPPSI**[a] | | **WISC-R**[b] | | **WISC-R**[c] | |
| Subtest | $h^2$ | $c^2$ | $h^2$ | $c^2$ | $h^2$ | $c^2$ |
| Information | 0.60 | 0.21 | 0.82 | 0.00 | 0.54 | 0.17 |
| Similarities | 0.31 | 0.43 | 0.94 | 0.00 | 0.33 | 0.14 |
| Arithmetic | 0.26 | 0.39 | 0.80 | 0.00 | 0.43 | 0.04 |
| Vocabulary | 0.42 | 0.29 | 0.72 | 0.06 | 0.51 | 0.10 |
| Comprehension | 0.36 | 0.44 | 0.44 | 0.21 | 0.29 | 0.08 |
| Picture Completion | 0.86 | 0.00 | 0.00 | 0.32 | 0.25 | 0.10 |
| Block Design | 0.50 | 0.18 | 0.84 | 0.00 | 0.24 | 0.43 |
| Picture Arrangement | — | — | 0.16 | 0.17 | 0.26 | 0.14 |
| Object Assembly | — | — | 0.68 | 0.00 | 0.15 | 0.29 |
| Coding | — | — | 0.56 | 0.12 | 0.47 | 0.26 |
| Animal Pegs | 0.84 | 0.00 | — | — | — | — |
| Mazes | 0.32 | 0.29 | — | — | — | — |
| Geometric Design | 0.94 | 0.00 | — | — | — | — |

$h^2$ = heritability; $c^2$ = shared family environment.

[a]Wilson (1975); 50 MZ, 34 DZ twins; estimates from reported twin correlations in study.

[b]Segal (1985); 69 MZ, 35 DZ twins; estimates from reported twin correlations in study.

[c]LaBuda, DeFries, & Fulker (1987); 79 MZ, 64 DZ twins; actual estimates reported in study.

Adapted from Thompson (1993).

Is the heritable portion of specific cognitive abilities related to a general genetic factor? That is, do the same genes that influence general cognitive ability also influence specific cognitive abilities? Several recent studies have addressed this important question (e.g., Cardon, Fulker, DeFries, & Plomin, 1992; Castro, DeFries, & Fulker, 1995; Loehlin, Horn, & Willerman, 1994; Pederson et al., 1992). Pederson et al. analyzed data from a sample of MZ and DZ twins reared together and apart. They found that the $h^2$ of IQ subtests correlated 0.77 with their loadings on psychometric $g$, the general factor of cognitive ability tests.

Castro et al. (1995) investigated the genetic and environmental influences on the verbal comprehension, perceptual organization, and freedom from distractibility factors of the Wechsler Intelligence Scale for Children–Revised (WISC-R). Results of this study are presented in Table 9.7, along with the results of a study on the Wechsler Adult Intelligence Scale (WAIS) by Tambs et al. (1986) for comparison. As Thompson (1993) notes, examination of the covariation among the factors on the two scales leads to somewhat different conclusions. Castor et al. found that both genetic and shared environmental factors are important sources of variance for the WISC-R factors. Between 53% and 58% of the variance on these factors is related to genetic factors; 29% to 32% is explained by shared environmental influences. They also found substantial genetic and environmental specificity for each factor. The nonshared environmental influences result from specific factors. In contrast, Tambs et al. found that most of the covariation among the WAIS factors is accounted for by a common genetic effect.

Results of a recent study by Loehlin et al. (1994) on a different battery of tests, however,

support the hypothesis that independent genetic factors underlie specific cognitive abilities, most clearly with fluid spatial ability. In sum, research appears to suggest that genetic effects on specific cognitive abilities may be related to a general genetic factor but that specific cognitive abilities may be under independent genetic influence as well.

## Academic Achievement

Carroll (1993) defined achievement as "the degree of learning in some procedure intended to produce learning, such as a formal or informal course of instruction, or a period of self-study of a topic, or practice of a skill" (p. 17). Tests of academic achievement are designed to measure the degree of such learning. These tests, however, correlate substantially with tests of general cognitive ability—about 0.50 (Jensen, 1980a)—the heritability of which is substantial (see McGue et al., 1993). Although it may be reasonable to assume that the cause of this overlap is environmental, given education's emphasis on promoting the development of students' abilities and achievements, Cardon, DiLalla, Plomin, DeFries, and Fulker (1990) argue that it is also plausible that the genetic factors underlying individual differences in general cognitive ability influence variability in academic achievement as well. As Thompson (1993) states, understanding the etiology of the relationship between academic achievement and general cognitive ability may have important implications for education.

Table 9.8 presents a summary of a number of twin studies on the heritability of academic achievement. As shown, approximately 46% of the variance in academic achievement is related to genetic factors. In a family study of achievement, Scarr and Carter-Saltzman (1979) report

**TABLE 9.7** **Heritability and Environmentality Estimates for the WISC-R and the WAIS**

| Factor | WISC-R[a] | | | WAIS[b] | | |
|---|---|---|---|---|---|---|
| | $h^2$ | $e_C^2$ | $e_W^2$ | $h^2$ | $e_C^2$ | $e_W^2$ |
| Verbal comprehension | 0.44 | 0.31 | 0.24 | 0.78 | 0.10 | 0.12 |
| Perceptual organization | 0.50 | 0.16 | 0.34 | 0.54 | 0.24 | 0.22 |
| Freedom from distractibility | 0.49 | 0.19 | 0.32 | 0.72 | 0.06 | 0.23 |

$h^2$ is heritability; $e_C^2$ is shared environment, and $e_W^2$ is nonshared environment.

[a]Castro, DeFries, & Fulker (1995).

[b]Tambs, Sundet, & Magnus (1984).

Adapted from Castro, DeFries, & Fulker (1995).

**TABLE 9.8    Twin Correlations and Heritabilities for Academic Achievement**

| Achievement Domain | Median Twin Correlations[a] | | $h^2$ |
|---|---|---|---|
| | Identical | Fraternal | |
| Reading | 0.86 | 0.62 | 0.48 |
| Written language | 0.74 | 0.52 | 0.44 |
| Mathematics | 0.73 | 0.54 | 0.38 |
| Social studies | 0.78 | 0.51 | 0.54 |
| Science | 0.66 | 0.48 | 0.36 |
| Across domains | 0.75 | 0.52 | 0.46 |

[a]Median correlations were obtained from Fischbein (1979), Husén (1959, 1960, 1963), Loehlin & Nichols (1976), Nichols (1965), and Schoenfeldt (1968).

Adapted from Benson & Weinberg (1990).

$h^2$ estimates of 0.26 and 0.53 in reading and mathematics, respectively. These results indicate that the genetic influence on academic achievement is significant but not as substantial as that on general cognitive ability. The results also imply that the heritability of academic achievement varies somewhat across educational domains.

Several studies have examined whether the genetic factors for general cognitive ability and academic achievement are one and the same (e.g., Brooks, Fulker, & DeFries, 1990; Gillis, 1993; Thompson et al., 1991). Brooks et al., for example, analyzed the performance of 86 MZ twins and 60 same-sex DZ twins on the Peabody Individual Achievement Test (PIAT) and the WAIS. Estimates of $h^2$ were 0.57 for IQ and 0.45 for achievement. Shared environmental effects explained only 18% of the variance in IQ and 7% in achievement. Results of multivariate analyses indicated that 59–77% of the phenotypic correlation between Wechsler IQs and the PIAT was due to genetic factors.

Thompson et al. (1991) reported similar results in a study of 146 pairs of MZ twins and 132 pairs of DZ twins with measures of academic achievement in reading, mathematics, and language. In this study, approximately 80% of the covariance between IQ and achievement is explained by genetic factors. Gillis (1993; as cited in Wadsworth, DeFries, Fulker, & Plomin, 1995) analyzed the etiology of the relationship between the verbal comprehension factor of the Wechsler scales and measures of reading, mathematics, and phonological coding with data from 134 MZ pairs of twins and 93 same-sex pairs of DZ twins. Estimates of $h^2$ were 0.28 for verbal comprehension, 0.42 for reading, 0.68 for phonological cod-

ing, and 0.69 for mathematics. Estimates of the shared environmental effects were 0.49 for verbal comprehension, 0.26 for reading, 0.01 for phonological coding, and 0.06 for mathematics. In this study, over 50% of the phenotypic covariation among the verbal comprehension factor of the Wechsler scales and the tests of academic achievement were explained by shared genetic effects.

Cardon et al. (1990) replicated the twin study results in an examination of 119 adoptive and 120 nonadoptive families. They found $h^2$ estimates of 0.38 for reading recognition, 0.36 for verbal IQ, and 0.41 for performance IQ. Substantial commonality was found between measures of cognitive ability and achievement. In this study, 78% of the phenotypic correlation between reading recognition and verbal IQ and 68% of the correlation between reading recognition and performance IQ were explained by genetic factors. Because reading recognition was more closely related to verbal IQ than to performance IQ at the genetic level, Cardon et al. hypothesized that somewhat different genetic mechanisms may underlie individual differences across domains of achievement.

In a study of 198 adoptive and 220 nonadoptive families, Wadsworth et al. (1995) found that genetic factors explained 33–60% of the phenotypic correlations between the verbal comprehension and perceptual organization factors of the WISC-R and measures of reading recognition and mathematics. They also found that almost half of the genetic covariance between reading recognition and mathematics was *independent* of cognitive ability. In their words, "There may be genetic influences on achievement which are not directly related to intellectual performance" (p. 14). The remaining covariance was attributable to nonshared environmental influences. These findings also indicate that the contribution of shared environmental influences to the variance or covariance of these measures was negligible. Similar results were found by Wadsworth, DeFries, Fulker, and Plomin (1995). As Cardon et al. (1990) state, "although substantial heritability does not imply that academic achievement is immutable, these results contradict the notion that tests of achievement reflect only the outcomes of learning; apparently, tests of achievement also reflect important characteristics of the learner."

In addition to these findings, Petrill and Thompson (1992) examined the relative contributions of genetics and the environment on achievement across gender with data from 138 pairs of MZ twins and 125 pairs of DZ twins. Results of their analyses indicate that genetic factors play a relatively larger role in the variability of academic achievement among girls and that shared environmental factors play a relatively larger role among boys. Petrill and Thompson hypothesized that these results may stem from teachers' bias:

> If teachers are more responsive
> environmentally to boys than girls . . .
> common environmental influences would be
> relatively more important in males. In
> contrast, girls would receive a more similar
> (less individually responsive) school
> environment. This additional source of
> common environmental variance in males
> does not necessarily dictate mean differences
> between the sexes, nor is it necessarily
> beneficial to males—this attention may
> involve discipline, etc. However, individual
> differences in girls' performance would be
> more dependent upon genetic differences.
> (p. 638)

Scarr and Weinberg (1994) and Alarcón, DeFries, and Fulker (1995) also found differential effects of genetic factors and the environment on individual differences in academic achievement for male and female students.

Research studies have also examined whether learning disabilities are influenced by genetics (e.g., Bakwin, 1973; DeFries & Gillis, 1993; DeFries, Vogler, & LaBuda, 1986). Central to most definitions of learning disability (LD) is

the concept of discrepancy in general cognitive functioning. In essence, LD is said to exist when a child's performance or rate of skill acquisition in a particular academic area falls far below the level that one would predict for that child's level of general ability, when that discrepancy cannot be explained by other factors, such as cultural differences or lack of educational opportunity. Reading disability (RD) has been the focus of most of this research.

DeFries et al. (1986) examined 1,044 individuals in 125 families (with at least 1 child with RD) and 125 matched control families. Consistent with a genetic hypothesis, siblings and parents of the RD children's families obtained significantly lower scores on reading tests than did the siblings and parents of the control families. In a study of 97 pairs of twins, Bakwin (1973) reported concordance rates for RD of 84% for MZ twins and 29% for DZ twins. Decker and Vandenberg (1985) analyzed data from 40 twin pairs, reporting concordance rates for RD of 80% for MZ twins and 45% for DZ twins. In a study of 133 pairs of MZ twins and 98 pairs of same-sex DZ twins, DeFries and Gillis (1993) found concordance rates for RD of 66% for MZ twins and 43% for DZ twins. These results are generally consistent with the hypothesis that RD is related at least in part to heritable influences.

Differences in the criteria used to define RD is one likely cause of at least some of the variability in the results of these studies. In a study of 285 same-sex twins, Stevenson, Graham, Fredman, and McLoughlin (1984, 1987) reported that concordance rates varied from 33% to 59% for MZ twins and from 29% to 54% for DZ twins as a function of the diagnostic criteria used to determine LD. At present, less is known about the heritability of learning disabilities in other academic areas (e.g., mathematics, spelling, and written expression).

## Personality

Over the past two decades, the etiology of variability in personality has been the focus of a considerable amount of research in the differential model (e.g., see Loehlin, 1992a). Results of these studies strongly indicate (1) that many dimensions of personality are moderately heritable ($h^2 \approx 0.40$–$0.50$) and (2) that the effects of the environment on personality are nonshared rather than shared (Goldsmith, 1993). Table 9.9 shows the variance accounted for by genetic influences and by shared and nonshared environmental ef-

TABLE 9.9    Genetic and Environmental Contributions to Altruism and Aggression in Adults

| | Source of Variance | | |
|---|---|---|---|
| Trait | Additive Genes | Shared Environment | Nonshared Environment |
| Altruism | 0.51 | 0.02 | 0.47 |
| Empathy | 0.51 | 0.00 | 0.49 |
| Nurturance | 0.43 | 0.01 | 0.56 |
| Aggressiveness | 0.39 | 0.00 | 0.61 |
| Assertiveness | 0.53 | 0.00 | 0.47 |

Adapted from Rushton (1995).

fects in two socially relevant personality traits—altruism and aggression—from a study of 573 pairs of MZ and DZ twins (reared together). As shown, approximately half of the variance across traits is attributable to genetic effects and half to nonshared environmental effects. Shared environment explains less than 1% of the variance in these traits. The absence of shared environmental effects on individual differences suggests that the psychological environments of different families may be functionally equivalent for the development of many personality traits (see Rowe, 1993).

An in-depth review of research in the numerous areas of personality and psychopathology that have been found to be influenced by genetics is beyond the scope of this chapter. Interested readers are referred to Loehlin's (1992a) book-length review of research on the "big five" factors of normal variability in personality: surgency, agreeableness, conscientiousness, emotional stability, and culture. Research on the study of early personality, or *temperament*, has also been conducted in the interaction between behavior and biology. Led by Kagan and his colleagues (e.g., Kagan, Arcus, & Snidman, 1993), research in this area suggests that individual and group differences in temperament are at least partially genetically based. See Bates and Wachs (1994) for an extensive review of psychobiological research in temperament. Research on psychopathology has also revealed that many disorders are influenced by genetics. Plomin and McClearn's (1993) book, *Nature, Nurture, and Psychology*, includes excellent reviews of research in the differential model on depression, schizophrenia, alcoholism, autism, and attention-deficit hyperactivity disorder (see also McGuffin & Murray, 1991).

Until quite recently, most of this research has focused on adult populations with self-report instruments. As Benson and Weinberg (1990) stated, "Individual differences in the personalities of children have received less attention in the differential psychology literature than have personality differences in adults" (p. 235). Interest in childhood behavior problems is growing rapidly, however. For example, in an international adoption study, van den Oord, Boomsma, and Verhulst (1994) examined parental ratings on the Child Behavior Checklist (CBCL) for 111 pairs of biological siblings, 221 pairs of nonbiological siblings, and 94 singletons. They found substantial genetic effects for the Externalizing, Social Problems, and Attention Problems scales of the CBCL but not for the Internalizing scale. Estimates of $h^2$ were 0.47 for Attention Problems, 0.65 for Externalizing, and 0.39 for Internalizing.

In a study of 500 pairs of MZ twins and 483 pairs of DZ twins, Hewett, Silberg, Neale, Eaves, and Erickson (1992) found somewhat different results on the CBCL. Strong genetic effects were evident for Internalizing, but shared environmental effects played the larger role for Externalizing. Edelbrock, Rende, Plomin, and Thompson (1992), in a study of 181 pairs of twins (same sex) between the ages of 7 and 15, also found that genetic factors differentially influenced aspects of child behavior on the CBCL. In a study of 229 pairs of twins between 2 and 3 years of age, Schmitz, Cherny, Fulker, and Mrazek (1994) found nonsignificant but possible genetic effects for broad groupings of Externalizing and Internalizing on the CBCL.

The use of parental rating scales is one plausible explanation for these discrepant results. Because parental ratings of child behavior are often used instead of direct observation, self-report, or developmentally appropriate interview methods, these results may be more a reflection of parents' perceptions of their children's behavior than of the behavior itself (Benson & Weinberg, 1990). Another plausible explanation is the use of children of different ages. Although these discrepant results are rather puzzling, inconsistencies in results across studies are not unusual in relatively new areas of research such as this (see Saudino, McGuire, Reiss, Hetherington, & Plomin, 1995).

## IMPLICATIONS OF DIFFERENTIAL PSYCHOLOGY

Turkheimer and Gottesman (1991) contend that $h^2 = 0$ is no longer an interesting hypothesis in differential psychology. According to them, the first law of the differential model should be $h^2 \neq 0$. Plomin and Bergeman (1991) disagreed, asserting that the examination of human behaviors that are under no genetic control would be quite valuable for the development of theory. In any case, research in the differential model strongly supports the important role of *both* genetics and the environment in many domains of psychological functioning relevant to the field of school psychology, including general and specific cognitive abilities, academic achievement, learning disabilities and mental disabilities, and personality and psychopathology. There are a number of contributions of the psychology of individual differences to research and practice in school psychology.

First, the differential model, with its balanced emphasis on both nature and nurture, can contribute significantly to our understanding of environmental influences on behavior (Plomin et al., 1990). As Rowe (1993) stated, "Associations between psychological environments and developmental outcomes may be genetically mediated. Genetic variation can cause variation in psychological environments through its influence on behavioral phenotypes" (p. 187). For example, it is widely known that children with behavior problems tend to come from dysfunctional families. As Braungart-Rieker, Rende, Plomin, DeFries, and Fulker (1995) note, however, the development of behavior problems is often attributed only to environmental influences, such as parental behavior, rather than to the possible joint effects of genes and environment. They maintain that the effects

of the environment and genetics are confounded in most studies of childhood behavior problems because the samples of families mainly consist of biologically related individuals. Rowe states that the results of these studies are "scientifically ambiguous because they merely capitalize on existing genetic variation" (p. 189). Adoption and twin studies have begun to disentangle the effects of genes and the environment on the development of childhood behavior problems.

Second, the methods of the differential model can be used to distinguish between shared and nonshared environmental effects. Shared environmental effects—such as social class and child-rearing practices—appear to contribute relatively little to individual differences in many behaviors, as is evident in the low correlations between biologically unrelated children reared in the same family. Adoptive-nonadoptive siblings reared together correlate about 0.05 on measures of personality, for example (Plomin et al., 1990). For general and specific cognitive abilities and academic achievement, the influence of shared environment on variability is modest. According to Plomin et al.,

> The question becomes: Why are children in the same family so different from one another? The key to unlock this riddle is to study more than one child per family. This permits the study of experiential differences within a family and their association with differences in behavioral outcome. Because heredity contributes to differences between siblings, sibling differences in experiences might reflect rather than affect differences in their behavior. Behavioral genetics methods are useful in addressing this issue. (p. 389)

Understanding the effects of differential experiences between members of the same family can lead to increased knowledge of the causes of individual differences in psychological functioning.

Third, research in differential psychology can be used to clarify the relative roles of heredity and the environment on individual differences in behavior. Proximal and distal dimensions and levels of explanation, as shown in Figure 9.9, may increase understanding of the causes of variability in psychological functioning. It is interesting that when explanations of behavior move from proximal to distal, controversy often ensues (Rushton, 1988). Seldom does this occur when explanations move in the opposite direction, that is, from distal to proximal. In any case, it is im-

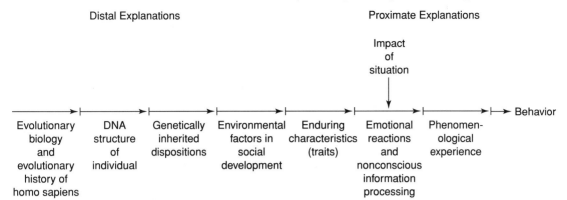

FIGURE 9.9   The distal-proximal dimension and levels of explanation in social behavior.
*Source:* Rushton (1998).

portant to reiterate that *genetic influence* provides a better description of the effects of genetics on individual differences in behavior than *genetic determinism.* The concept of *reaction range* is used to explain the full phenotypic variation that is associated with a particular genotype. A particular genotype does not correlate perfectly with resultant phenotypic expression because phenotypes reflect the combined effects of both genetics and the environment.

Sternberg (1995) notes that even highly heritable traits, such as height and PKU, are susceptible to environmental intervention. Average height, for example, continues to increase each year despite the fact that it is highly heritable (Olivier, 1980). As stated in *Intelligence: Knowns and Unknowns,* the report of a task force established by the Board of Scientific Affairs of the American Psychological Association (1995), "Gene action always involves an environment— at least a biochemical environment, and often an ecological one. (For humans, that ecology is usually interpersonal or cultural.) Thus all genetic effects on the development of observable traits are potentially modifiable by environment input, though the practicability of making such modifications may be another matter" (p. 15).

Over the course of development, environmental effects can give rise to considerable variation in the phenotypic expression of genotypes. In addition, the contributions of genetics and environment to variability in phenotypes can change over the course of development (for reviews, see Fulker, Cherny, & Cardon, 1993; McGue et al., 1993). Nevertheless, "There are probabilistic *limits* to the reaction range, and one

of the tasks of genetic analysis is to explore the extent of those limits in the natural environment and to discover the environmental agents that affect them" (Jensen, 1981, p. 485, emphasis in original). Intelligence, for example, appears to be imperfectly malleable. Based on his review of the results of adoption studies, Locurto (1990) estimates that a gain of about 16 IQ points is the most that can be expected from even dramatic environmental intervention. A threshold model has been proposed to explain the phenotypic expression of particular genotypes (Kimble, 1990).

Fourth, considerable variability should be expected on virtually all school-related behavior. In academic achievement, for example, children are typically grouped "horizontally" by age, not "vertically" by level of scholastic performance. Benson and Weinberg (1990) assert that differences between children of a particular age can be mistakenly attributed to error variance. As Benson and Weinberg noted, normal variation in reading achievement for a seventh-grade classroom may range from the fourth-grade level to the twelfth-grade level. An appreciation of typical and atypical variability is thus required for research and practice in school psychology.

# A MODEL FOR CONCEPTUALIZING INDIVIDUAL DIFFERENCES

Benson and Weinberg (1990) propose a general model for conceptualizing individual differences in psychological functioning (shown in Figure 9.10). In this model, the role of genetics is mediated by broad social contexts and by the family

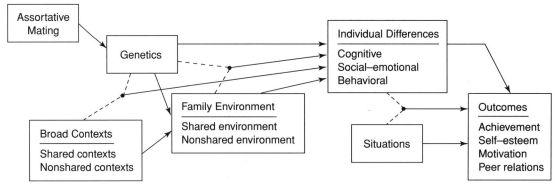

**FIGURE 9.10    Contextual and situational model of individual differences.**
*Source:* Benson & Weinberg (1990).

environment to affect variability in different domains of psychological functioning (cognitive, social-emotional, and behavioral). These individual differences interact with specific situations, leading to outcomes in educationally relevant behaviors, such as achievement, self-esteem, motivation, and peer relations. It is important to emphasize that moderate $h^2$ does not indicate that social influences do not affect the expression of traits as behavioral outcomes (Rowe, 1993). Furthermore, although developmental research has tended to emphasize the role of the family—that is, shared environmental influences—broader social contexts such as the school and community can affect behavior. Research in the differential model suggests that nonshared sources of environmental variance are particularly important for understanding variability in psychological functioning.

Bronfenbrenner and Ceci's (1993) bioecological model of human development is a prime example of a contemporary theory that integrates the effects of genetics, contexts, and situations. In the bioecological model, development is conceptualized as an interaction between the organism and the environment from the moment of conception. According to Bronfenbrenner and Ceci, "Human development takes place through processes of progressively more complex reciprocal interaction between an active evolving biopsychological human organism and the persons, objects, and symbols in its immediate environment" (p. 316). Proximal processes—that is, enduring forms of interaction—are the core of their model. Examples of proximal processes include parent-child and child-child relationships, as well as reading, studying, and learning new skills. Genetic predispositions are seen to be ac-

tively expressed through "selective patterns of attention, action, and response" (p. 316). In this model, therefore, the influences of genetics and the environment (both immediate and remote) are considered jointly to conceptualize development.

Although all of the tenets of the bioecological framework cannot presently be put to formal scientific confirmation or disconfirmation, this model does provide a structure and direction for research on biology-ecology interactionism. Regardless of the model adopted, however, the nature-nurture question must be reframed into new and conceptually different kinds of questions in the field of school psychology. As Horowitz (1993) argues, a "comprehensive environmentalism" is required to explain individual differences in psychological functioning. Genetics and the environment are clearly both involved. The overarching question for future research, therefore, is not *how much* of the variance is attributable to genetic and environmental causes but *how* these causes interact to produce variability in human behavior (Rowe, 1993).

## REFERENCES

Alarcón, M., DeFries, J. C., & Fulker, D. W. (1995). Etiology of individual differences in reading performance: A test of sex limitation. *Behavior Genetics, 25,* 17–23.

American Psychological Association. (1995, August). *Intelligence: Knowns and unknowns.* Washington, DC: Author.

Bakwin, H. (1973). Reading disability in twins. *Developmental Medicine and Child Neurology, 15,* 184–187.

Bates, J. E., & Wachs, T. D. (Eds.). (1994). *Temperament: Individual differences at the interface of biology and behavior.* Washington, DC: American Psychological Association.

Benson, M. J., & Weinberg, R. A. (1990). Contributions of the psychology of individual differences to school psychology: Different drummers—one beat. In T. B. Gutkin & C. R. Reynolds (Eds.), *The handbook of school psychology* (2nd ed., pp. 218–243). New York: Wiley.

Bouchard, T. J., Jr. (1993). The genetic architecture of human intelligence. In P. A. Vernon (Ed.), *Biological approaches to the study of human intelligence* (pp. 33–93). Norwood, NJ: Ablex.

Bouchard, T. J., Jr., & McGue, M. (1981). Familial studies of intelligence: A review. *Science, 250,* 223–238.

Braungart-Rieker, J., Rende, R. D., Plomin, R., DeFries, J. C., & Fulker, D. W. (1995). Genetic mediation of longitudinal associations between family environment and childhood behavior problems. *Development and Psychopathology, 7,* 233–245.

Brody, N. (1992). *Intelligence* (2nd ed.). San Diego: Academic Press.

Bronfenbrenner, U., & Ceci, S. J. (1993). Heredity, environment, and the question "How?"—A first approximation. In R. Plomin & G. E. McClearn (Eds.), *Nature, nurture, and psychology* (pp. 313–324). Washington, DC: American Psychology Association.

Brooks, A., Fulker, D. W., & DeFries, J. C. (1990). Reading performance and general cognitive ability: A multivariate genetic analysis of twin data. *Personality and Individual Differences, 11,* 141–146.

Cardon, L. R., DiLalla, L. F., Plomin, R., DeFries, J. C., & Fulker, D. W. (1990). Genetic correlations between reading performance and IQ in the Colorado Adoption Project. *Intelligence, 14,* 245–257.

Cardon, L. R., & Fulker, D. W. (1993). Genetics of specific cognitive abilities. In R. Plomin & G. E. McClearn (Eds.), *Nature, nurture, and psychology* (pp. 99–120). Washington, DC: American Psychology Association.

Cardon, L. R., Fulker, D. W., DeFries, J. C., & Plomin, R. (1992). Multivariate genetic analysis of specific cognitive abilities in the Colorado Adoption Project at age 7. *Intelligence, 16,* 383–400.

Carroll, J. B. (1993). *Human cognitive abilities: A survey of factor-analytic studies.* New York: Cambridge University Press.

Castro, S. D., DeFries, J. C., & Fulker, D. W. (1995). Multivariate genetic analysis of Wechsler Intelligence Scale for Children–Revised (WISC-R) factors. *Behavior Genetics, 25,* 25–32.

Ceci, S. J. (1990). *On intelligence . . . more or less: A bioecological treatise on intellectual development.* Englewood Cliffs, NJ: Prentice Hall.

Chipeur, H. M., Rovine, M., & Plomin, R. (1990). LISREL modelling: Genetic and environmental influences on IQ revisited. *Intelligence, 14,* 11–29.

Cronbach, L. J. (1990). *Essentials of psychological testing* (5th ed.). New York: Harper & Row.

Cyphers, L. H., Fulker, D. W., Plomin, R., & DeFries, J. C. (1989). Cognitive abilities in the early school years: No effects of shared environment between parents and offspring. *Intelligence, 13,* 369–386.

Decker, S. N., & Vandenberg, S. G. (1985). Colorado Twin Study of Reading Disability. In D. B. Gray & J. F. Kavanagh (Eds.), *Biobehavioral measures of dyslexia* (pp. 123–135). Parkton, MD: York Press.

DeFries, J. C., & Gillis, J. J. (1993). Genetics of reading disability. In R. Plomin & G. E. McClearn (Eds.), *Nature, nurture, and psychology* (pp. 121–145). Washington, DC: American Psychological Association.

DeFries, R. J., Johnson, R. C., Kuse, A. R., McClearn, G. C., Polovina, J., Vandenberg, S. G., & Wilson, J. R. (1979). Familial resemblance for specific cognitive abilities. *Behavior Genetics, 9,* 23–43.

DeFries, R. J., Vandenberg, S. G., McClearn, G. C. (1976). The genetics of specific cognitive abilities. *Annual Review of Genetics, 12,* 179–207.

DeFries, J. C., Vogler, G. P., & LaBuda, M. C. (1986). Colorado Family Reading Study: An overview. In J. Fuller & E. C. Simmel (Eds.), *Perspectives in behavior genetics* (pp. 29–56). Hillsdale, NJ: Erlbaum.

Detterman, D. K., Thompson, L. A., & Plomin, R. (1990). Differences in heritability across groups differing in ability. *Behavior Genetics, 20,* 369–384.

Edelbrock, C., Rende, R. D., Plomin, R., & Thompson, L. A. (1992). A twin study of behavior problems in early adolescence. *Behavior Genetics, 22* (abstract).

Erlenmeyer-Kimling, L., & Jarvik, L. F. (1963). Genetics and intelligence: A review. *Science, 142,* 1477–1478.

Fischbein, S. (1979). *Heredity-environment influences on growth and development during adolescence: A longitudinal study of twins.* Lund, Swed.: CWK/Gleerup.

Fulker, D. W., Cherny, S. S., & Cardon, L. R. (1993). Continuity and change in cognitive development. In R. Plomin & G. E. McClearn (Eds.), *Nature, nurture, and psychology* (pp. 77–97). Washington, DC: American Psychology Association.

Garfinkle, A. S., & Vandenberg, S. G. (1981). Development of Piagetian logico-mathematical concepts and other specific cognitive abilities. In L. Gedda, P. Parsi, & W. E. Nance (Eds.), *Twin research 3: Intelligence, personality, and development* (pp. 51–60). New York: Liss.

Gillis, J. J. (1993). *Comorbidity of reading and mathematics disabilities: Genetic and environmental etiologies.* Doctoral dissertation, University of Colorado, Boulder.

Goldsmith, H. H. (1993). Nature-nurture issues in the behavioral genetics context: Overcoming barriers to communication. In R. Plomin & G. E. McClearn (Eds.), *Nature, nurture, and psychology* (pp. 325–329). Washington, DC: American Psychology Association.

Herrnstein, R. J., & Murray, C. (1994). *The bell curve: Intelligence and class structure in American life.* New York: Free Press.

Hewett, J. K., Silberg, J. L., Neale, M. C., Eaves, L. J., & Erickson, M. (1992). The analysis of parental ratings of children's behavior using LISREL. *Behavior Genetics, 22,* 293–317.

Horowitz, F. D. (1993). The need for a comprehensive new environmentalism. In R. Plomin & G. E. McClearn (Eds.), *Nature, nurture, and psychology* (pp. 341–353). Washington, DC: American Psychology Association.

Husén, T. (1959). *Psychological twin research: A methodological study.* Stockholm: Almqvist & Wiksell.

Husén, T. (1960). Abilities of twins. *Scandinavian Journal of Psychology, 1,* 125–135.

Husén, T. (1963). Intra-pair similarities in the school achievements of twins. *Scandinavian Journal of Psychology, 4,* 108–114.

Jensen, A. R. (1980a). *Bias in mental testing.* New York: Free Press.

Jensen, A. R. (1980b). *Straight talk about mental tests.* New York: Free Press.

Jensen, A. R. (1981). Obstacles, problems, and pitfalls in differential psychology. In S. Scarr (Ed.), *Race, social class, and individual differences in I.Q.* (pp. 483–514). Hillsdale, NJ: Erlbaum.

Jensen, A. R. (1987). The g beyond factor analysis. In J. C. Conoley, J. A. Glover, & R. R. Ronning (Eds.), *The influence of cognitive psychology on testing and measurement.* Hillsdale, NJ: Erlbaum.

Kagan, J., Arcus, D., & Snidman, N. (1993). The idea of temperament: Where do we go from here? In R. Plomin & G. E. McClearn (Eds.), *Nature, nurture, and psychology* (pp. 197–210). Washington, DC: American Psychology Association.

Kamin, L. J. (1974). *The science and politics of IQ.* Potomac, MD: Erlbaum.

Kimble, G. A. (1990). Mother Nature's bag of tricks. *Psychological Science, 1,* 36–41.

LaBuda, M. C., DeFries, J. C., & Fulker, D. W. (1987). Genetic and environmental covariance among WISC-R subtests: A twin study. *Intelligence, 8,* 233–244.

Lewontin, R. C., Rose, S., & Kamin, L. C. (1984). *Not in our genes: Biology, ideology, and human nature.* New York: Pantheon.

Locurto, C. (1990). The malleability of IQ as judged from adoption studies. *Intelligence, 14,* 275–292.

Loehlin, J. C. (1984). Nature/nurture controversy. In R. J. Corsini (Ed.), *Encyclopedia of psychology* (Vol. 2, pp. 418–420). New York: Wiley.

Loehlin, J. C. (1992a). *Genes and environment in personality development.* Newbury Park, CA: Sage.

Loehlin, J. C. (1992b). *Latent variable models: An introduction to factor, path, and structural analysis* (2nd ed.). Hillsdale, NJ: Erlbaum.

Loehlin, J. C., Horn, J. M., & Willerman, L. (1994). Differential inheritance of mental abilities in the Texas Adoption Project. *Intelligence, 19,* 325–336.

Loehlin, J. C., & Nichols, R. C. (1976). *Heredity, environment, and personality.* Austin: University of Texas Press.

Luo, D., Petrill, S. A., & Thompson, L. A. (1994). An exploration of genetic g: Hierarchical factor analysis of cognitive data from the Western Reserve Twin Project. *Intelligence, 18,* 335–347.

McClearn, G. E. (1993). Behavioral genetics: The last century and the next. In R. Plomin & G. E. McClearn (Eds.), *Nature, nurture, and psychology* (pp. 27–54). Washington, DC: American Psychology Association.

McGue, M., Bouchard, T. J., Jr., Iacono, W. G., & Lykken, D. T. (1993). Behavioral genetics of cognitive ability: A life-span perspective. In R. Plomin & G. E. McClearn (Eds.), *Nature, nurture, and psychology* (pp. 59–76). Washington, DC: American Psychology Association.

McGuffin, P., & Murray, R. (Eds.). (1991). *The new genetics of mental illness.* Oxford: Butterworth-Heinemann.

Minton, H. L., & Schneider, F. W. (1985). *Differential psychology.* Prospect Heights, IL: Waveland Press.

Munsinger, H., & Douglass, A. (1976). The syntactic abilities of identical twins, fraternal twins, and their siblings. *Child Development, 47,* 40–50.

Nichols, R. C. (1965). The National Merit Twin Study. In S. G. Vandenberg (Ed.), *Methods and goals in human behavior genetics* (pp. 231–244). New York: Academic Press.

Olivier, G. (1980). The increase of stature in France. *Journal of Human Evolution, 9,* 645–649.

Pederson, N. S., Plomin, R., Nesselroade, J. R., & McClearn, G. E. (1992). A quantitative genetic analysis of cognitive abilities during the second half of the life span. *Psychological Sciences, 3,* 346–353.

Petrill, S. A., & Thompson, L. A. (1994). The effect of gender upon heritability and common environmental estimates in measures of scholastic achievement. *Personality and Individual Differences, 16,* 631–640.

Plomin, R., & Bergeman, C. S. (1991). The nature of nurture: Genetic influences on "environmental" measures. *Behavioral and Brain Sciences, 14,* 373–427.

Plomin, R., DeFries, J. C., & Loehlin, J. C. (1977). Genotype-environment interaction and correlation in the analysis of human behavior. *Psychology Bulletin, 84*, 309–322.

Plomin, R., DeFries, J. C., & McClearn, G. E. (1990). *Behavioral genetics: A primer* (2nd ed.). New York: Freeman.

Plomin, R., & McClearn, G. E. (Eds.). (1993). *Nature, nurture, and psychology*. Washington, DC: American Psychology Association.

Plomin, R., & Neiderhiser, J. (1991). Quantitative genetics, molecular genetics, and intelligence. *Intelligence, 15*, 369–387.

Plomin, R., Pederson, N. L., Lichtenstein, P., & McClearn, G. E. (1994). Variability and stability in cognitive abilities are largely genetic later in life. *Behavior Genetics, 24*, 207–215.

Plomin, R., & Thompson, L. A. (1987). Life-span developmental behavioral genetics. In P. B. Baltes, D. L. Featherman, & R. M. Lerner (Eds.), *Life-span development and behavior* (Vol. 8, pp. 1–31). Hillsdale, NJ: Erlbaum.

Plomin, R., & Vandenberg, S. G. (1980). An analysis of Koch's (1966) Primary Mental Abilities test data for 5- to 7-year-old twins. *Behavior Genetics, 10*, 409–412.

Reynolds, C. R., & Willson, V. L. (Eds.). (1985). *Methodological and statistical advances in the study of individual differences*. New York: Plenum.

Rowe, D. C. (1993). Genetic perspectives on personality. In R. Plomin & G. E. McClearn (Eds.), *Nature, nurture, and psychology* (pp. 179–195). Washington, DC: American Psychology Association.

Rushton, J. P. (1995). *Race, evolution and behavior: A life history perspective*. New Brunswick, NJ: Transaction.

Rushton, J. P. (1998). Race differences in behavior: A review and evolutionary analysis. *Personality and Individual Differences, 9*, 1009–1024.

Saudino, K. J., McGuire, S., Reiss, D., Hetherington, E. M., & Plomin, R. (1995). Parent ratings of EAS temperaments in twins, full siblings, half siblings, and step siblings. *Journal of Personality and Social Psychology, 68*, 723–733.

Saudino, K. J., Plomin, R., Pederson, N. L., & McClearn, G. E. (1994). The etiology of high and low cognitive ability during the second half of the life span. *Intelligence, 19*, 359–371.

Scarr, S., & Carter-Saltzman, L. (1979). Twin method: Defense of a critical assumption. *Behavior Genetics, 9*, 527–542.

Scarr, S., & Weinberg, R. A. (1994). Educational and occupational achievements of brothers and sisters in adoptive and biologically related families. *Behavior Genetics, 24*, 301–325.

Schmitz, S., Cherny, S. S., Fulker, D. W., & Mrazek, D. A. (1994). Genetic and environmental influences on early childhood behavior. *Behavior Genetics, 24*, 25–34.

Schoenfeldt, L. F. (1968). The heredity components of the Project TALENT two-day test battery. *Measurement and Evaluation in Guidance, 1*, 130–140.

Segal, N. L. T. (1985). Monozygotic and dizygotic twins: A comparative analysis of mental ability profiles. *Child Development, 56*, 1051–1058.

Snyderman, M., & Rothman, S. (1987). Survey of expert opinion on intelligence and aptitude testing. *American Psychologist, 42*, 137–144.

Sternberg, R. J. (1995). For whom the bell curve tolls: A review of *The Bell Curve. Psychological Science, 6*, 257–261.

Stevenson, J., Graham, P., Fredman, G., & McLoughlin, V. (1984). The genetics of reading disability. In C. J. Turner & H. B. Miles (Eds.), *The biology of human intelligence* (pp. 85–97). Nafferton, Eng.: Nafferton Books.

Stevenson, J., Graham, P., Fredman, G., & McLoughlin, V. (1987). A twin study of genetic influences on reading and spelling ability and disability. *Journal of Child Psychology and Psychiatry, 28*, 229–247.

Sundet, J. M., Eilertsen, D. E., Tambs, K., & Magnus, P. (1994). No differential heritability of intelligence test scores across ability levels in Norway. *Behavior Genetics, 24*, 337–339.

Tambs, K., Sundet, J. M., & Magnus, P. (1984). Heritability analysis of the WAIS subtests: A study of twins. *Intelligence, 8*, 283–293.

Taylor, H. F. (1980). *The IQ game: A methodological inquiry into the heredity environment controversy*. New Brunswick, NJ: Rutgers University Press.

Thapar, A., Petrill, S. A., & Thompson, L. A. (1994). The heritability of memory in the Western Reserve Twin Project. *Behavior Genetics, 24*, 155–160.

Thompson, L. A. (1993). Genetic contributions to intellectual development in infancy and childhood. In P. A. Vernon (Ed.), *Biological approaches to the study of human intelligence* (pp. 95–138). Norwood, NJ: Ablex.

Thompson, L. A., Detterman, D. K., & Plomin, R. (1991). Scholastic achievement and specific cognitive abilities in 7- to 12-year-old twins. *Psychological Science, 2*, 158–165.

Thompson, L. A., Detterman, D. K., & Plomin, R. (1993). Differences in heritability across groups of differing ability. *Behavior Genetics, 23*, 331–336.

Turkheimer, E., & Gottesman, I. I. (1991). Is $h^2 = 0$ a null hypothesis anymore? *Behavioral and Brain Sciences, 14*, 410–411.

van den Oord, E. J. C. G., Boomsma, D. I., & Verhulst, F. C. (1994). A study of problem behaviors in 10- to 15-year-old biologically related and unrelated international adoptees. *Behavior Genetics, 24*, 193–205.

Vernon, P. A. (1989). The heritability of measures of speed of information-processing. *Personality and Individual Differences, 10*, 573–576.

Wadsworth, S. J., DeFries, J. C., Fulker, D. W., & Plomin, R. (1995). Cognitive ability and academic achievement in the Colorado Adoption Project: A multivariate genetic analysis of parent-offspring and sibling data. *Behavior Genetics*, 25, 1–15.

Wadsworth, S. J., DeFries, J. C., Fulker, D. W., & Plomin, R. (1995). Covariation among measures of cognitive ability and academic achievement in the Colorado Adoption Project: Sibling analysis. *Personality and Individual Differences*. 18, 63–73.

Wilson, R. C. (1975). Twins: Patterns of cognitive development as measured on the WPPSI. *Developmental Psychology*, 11, 126–139.

## CHAPTER 10

# CONTRIBUTIONS OF DEVELOPMENTAL PSYCHOPATHOLOGY TO SCHOOL PSYCHOLOGY[1]

STEPHANIE H. MCCONAUGHY
THOMAS M. ACHENBACH
*University of Vermont*

In this chapter, we discuss developmental psychopathology as a conceptual framework for understanding behavioral, emotional, and learning problems that fall within the purview of school psychologists. We begin by explaining developmental psychopathology as a general approach. We then outline its applications to school psychology in terms of normative-developmental guidelines, concepts of disorders, goals of services, and evaluations of outcomes. Thereafter, we present a model for empirically based assessment, implications for special education, and practical applications to school psychology. For brevity, we use the term *children* to include the ages of 2 to 18 years.

## WHAT IS DEVELOPMENTAL PSYCHOPATHOLOGY?

Developmental psychopathology refers to the study of maladaptive behavioral and emotional deviance in the developmental tasks, sequences, and processes that characterize human growth. It is not a theory or an explanation of *why* specific disorders occur. Instead, it is a way of thinking about problems that arise from many different causes, take different forms at different ages, and have different outcomes.

Children's problems have multiple causes, including constitutional vulnerabilities, temperament, family dynamics, stressful experiences, peer pressures, and cognitive characteristics. It is seldom possible to isolate all the factors contributing to a child's problems and even less possible to undo all the contributing factors. A developmental approach focuses on continuities between past, present, and future functioning. From this perspective, children's functioning is viewed not merely as an outcome of past events but also in relation to current and future developmental tasks, risks, assets, and liabilities. This means that interventions should be oriented more toward helping children master new developmental tasks than toward restoring previous levels of functioning by undoing the past.

School provides an especially crucial sequence of developmental tasks and challenges that must be mastered for successful adaptation in later life. This sequence of tasks is based partly on developmental processes, such as biological and cognitive maturation, and partly on social customs, such as mandatory schooling for ages 6 to 16, the teaching of reading in first grade, and the onset of more specialized teaching around the age of 11 or 12. A developmental perspective compares children's functioning with that of their age-mates to identify areas in which early deviance may be a source of later trouble.

[1]This work was partially supported by research grant 94145892 from the W. T. Grant Foundation, for which we are most grateful.

As applied to school psychology, developmental psychopathology has the following implications:

1. Children's functioning should be evaluated in relation to guidelines derived from normative samples of age-mates.
2. Current maladaptive functioning should be viewed in relation to future developmental needs rather than merely as an outcome of past influences that must be undone.
3. The causes of deviations from normative-developmental guidelines are diverse and can seldom be precisely pinpointed.
4. Interventions should be designed to facilitate mastery of important developmental tasks, especially the acquisition of academic and social skills needed for effective adaptation in later life.
5. The outcome of interventions should be evaluated in terms of improved progress toward specific developmental goals.

## ASSESSMENT MODEL FOR DEVELOPMENTAL PSYCHOLOGY

Standardized measures of ability and achievement have long used age norms for assessing developmental progress. We present an analogous normative-developmental approach to assessing behavioral and emotional problems. We feel that such an approach is especially needed to counteract the current tendency to view these problems as categorical, all-or-none disorders. The tendency to impose categories has been fostered by efforts to make diagnostic criteria more precise, as in the American Psychiatric Association's (1980, 1987, 1994) *Diagnostic and Statistical Manual*, Third Edition, Third Edition–Revised, and Fourth Edition (DSM-III, DSM-III-R, and DSM-IV). In schools, the tendency to view children's problems as categorical entities has been fostered by administrative criteria for special services, such as those required by Public Law 94-142 (1977), the Education of the Handicapped Act (EHA), and its reauthorization in 1990 and 1997 as the Individuals with Disabilities Education Act (IDEA). These criteria stem from regulations for determining eligibility for services, although the administrative criteria do not necessarily reflect the patterns of problems actually found among troubled children.

Administrative criteria may require school psychologists to categorize children by distinctions that fail to serve the children's needs. To receive special education services, for example, a child must meet the criteria for a disability category, such as a specific learning disability or emotional disturbance. Even if the child has problems related to more than one category, it must be determined which disorder is primary and whether the one that is primary meets the criteria for service within that category. Furthermore, the presence of other problems—such as "social maladjustment"—can disqualify the child for services altogether, even though it is clear that the child needs special help, best rendered through the school.

We consider these issues in detail later. The important point here, however, is that administrative categories do not provide comprehensive and accurate pictures of children's problems, strengths, and needs. To provide a better basis for helping troubled children, we outline an approach to assessment based on normative-developmental principles for evaluating behavioral and emotional problems and competencies.

## Multiple Sources of Data

Development proceeds along multiple pathways. Children may be more advanced in one area of functioning, such as cognition, than in another, such as social behavior. Their behavioral competencies and problems also vary from one situation and interaction to another. Because of these variations, it is necessary to draw on multiple sources of data, such as reports by teachers, parents, and observers; self-reports; and psychological tests.

The different sources of data seldom converge on a single diagnostic construct. In fact, meta-analyses of many studies show correlations that average only .28 between different types of informants who rate children's behavioral and emotional problems under different conditions (e.g., teachers versus parents; teachers versus mental health workers; teachers versus observers). Correlations were even lower—averaging only .22—between children's self-ratings and their ratings by others, including teachers, parents, and mental health workers (Achenbach, McConaughy, & Howell, 1987).

Although correlations averaged .60 between similar informants who were seeing the children under generally similar conditions (e.g., pairs of teachers, pairs of parents, and pairs of observers), it is clear that no one informant provides the same data as others would. It is necessary, therefore, to obtain data from multiple informants who interact with the children under different conditions. Furthermore, it is unrealistic to expect that data from different informants will be subsumed by a single diagnostic category. Instead, data obtained from different informants may reflect important variations in the child's functioning, as well as variations between different informants' perceptions of the child.

## Multiaxial Empirically Based Assessment

Because the assessment of children's behavioral and emotional problems depends on data from those who interact with the children, we outline assessment procedures that systematically use such data. These procedures employ *empirically based assessment*, which taps the ways in which the children's functioning is perceived by particular informants.

Rather than imposing a priori categories on the children's problems, empirically based assessment identifies syndromes of problems that actually occur together, as seen by particular informants. Syndromes are identified by factor analyzing the behavioral and emotional problems of disturbed children and adolescents, as reported by parents, teachers, observers, and the subjects themselves. To provide normative-developmental reference points, data obtained for a particular child are compared with those obtained for normative samples of age-mates. The data obtained from each informant are scored on standardized profiles that provide age-based standard scores for each syndrome, as well as for competence and adaptive functioning.

To take account of variations across multiple domains of functioning, different assessment procedures are needed to identify inconsistencies, as well as consistencies. This is especially true in designing the multifaceted interventions that may be needed to help the children. Such interventions can be more effectively designed and evaluated if we document how the child is seen in different contexts than if we depend on a single source of data or view problems only in terms of diagnostic or administrative categories.

To highlight and preserve the variations in assessment data, we have proposed a model called *multiaxial empirically based assessment* (Achenbach & McConaughy, 1997). This model emphasizes the identification of strengths and weaknesses in multiple areas by multiple standardized procedures. Because children's functioning may really differ from one area or situation to another, the goal is to use what each procedure reveals in different contexts. In some cases, multiaxial assessment may reveal that certain interaction partners, such as a parent or teacher, need to change more than the child does. In other cases, multiaxial assessment may show that one type of intervention is needed in one context but a different type is needed in another.

Table 10.1 outlines the following five axes relevant to assessment from preschool through high school: parents' reports, teachers' reports, cognitive assessment, physical assessment, and direct assessment of the child. The examples of assessment procedures have promising reliability, validity, and/or normative data, or such data are potentially available. The numerical ordering of the axes does not imply that the first takes precedence over later ones. Neither does it imply that assessment should always proceed from Axis I to Axis V. In referrals to school psychologists, for example, teachers' reports (Axis II) would often be obtained first. The data to be obtained thereafter would depend on the referral problems and the practices of particular school systems. In some cases, parents' reports (Axis I) or direct observations (Axis V) might be obtained second. In other cases, cognitive assessment (Axis III) or self-reports by the child (Axis V) might follow teachers' reports. The specific procedures would also depend on the age of the child, the nature of the problems, and local conditions. Classroom observations, on the one hand, may be more appropriate for preschool and elementary school levels than for high school. Self-report questionnaires, on the other hand, are more appropriate for adolescents than for younger children.

## EMPIRICALLY BASED PROCEDURES FOR ASSESSING BEHAVIORAL AND EMOTIONAL PROBLEMS

We briefly describe a family of standardized, empirically based instruments for obtaining parents' reports, teachers' reports, self-reports, direct observations, and interview assessments of behavioral and emotional problems. Thereafter, we present applications of these procedures to special education. Details of the development, reliability, validity, and applications of these instruments are presented in manuals, which are cited

**TABLE 10.1 Examples of Multiaxial Assessment Procedures**

| Age Range | Axis I Parents' Reports | Axis II Teachers' Reports | Axis III Cognitive Assessment | Axis IV Physical Assessment | Axis V Direct Assessment of Child |
|---|---|---|---|---|---|
| 2–5 | CBCL/2–3<br>CBCL/4–18<br>Developmental history<br>Parent interview | C-TRF/2–5<br>Preschool records<br>Teacher interview | Ability tests<br>Perceptual-motor tests<br>Language tests | Height, weight<br>Medical exam<br>Neurological exam | Observation during play<br>Interview |
| 6–11 | CBCL/4–18<br>Developmental history<br>Parent interview | TRF<br>School records<br>Teacher interview | Ability tests<br>Achievement tests<br>Perceptual-motor tests<br>Language tests | Height, weight<br>Medical exam<br>Neurological exam | SCICA<br>DOF |
| 12–18 | CBCL/4–18<br>Developmental history<br>Parent interview | TRF<br>School records<br>Teacher interview | Ability tests<br>Achievement tests<br>Language tests | Height, weight<br>Medical exam<br>Neurological exam | SCICA<br>DOF<br>YSR<br>Self-concept measures<br>Personality tests |

CBCL/2–3 = Child Behavior Checklist for Ages 2–3; CBCL/4–18 = Child Behavior Checklist for Ages 4–18; C-TRF = Caregiver-Teacher Report Form for Ages 2–5; TRF = Teacher's Report Form; SCICA = Semistructured Clinical Interview for Children and Adolescents; DOF = Direct Observation Form; YSR = Youth Self-Report.

for each instrument. Hand-scored and com-puter-scored profiles are available for all the in-struments.

## Child Behavior Checklist

The Child Behavior Checklist for Ages 4–18 (CBCL/4–18) is designed to obtain reports of the behavioral and emotional problems and competencies of 4- to 18-year-olds, as seen by their parents and parent surrogates (Achen-bach, 1991b). A version designated as the CBCL/2–3 is also available for 2- and 3-year-olds (Achenbach, 1992). The CBCL/4–18 has 118 problems, plus space to write in additional problems. The parent is asked to score 0 if an item is not true of the child, 1 if it is somewhat or sometimes true, and 2 if it is very true or of-ten true. The standard instructions ask the par-ent to base ratings on the preceding six months, but this interval can be changed to suit the user's aims. Examples of items are "Can't concentrate, can't pay attention for long"; "Gets in many fights"; and "Unhappy, sad, or depressed." The CBCL/4–18 also has 20 com-petence items for reporting the quality and amount of participation in sports, other recre-ational activities, organizations, jobs, and chores; involvement with friends; how well the child gets along with siblings, other children, and parents; how well the child plays and works alone; and school functioning.

The CBCL/4–18 is scored on the Child Behavior Profile, which consists of problem scales derived from principal components analyses of CBCLs completed for 4,455 chil-dren, 4- to 18-years old, referred for mental health services, plus competence scales desig-nated as Activities, Social, and School. The scales are normed on a national sample of 2,368 nonreferred 4- to 18-year-olds. To reflect age and gender differences in the prevalence and patterning of problems, profiles are standard-ized separately for each gender at ages 4 to 11 and 12 to 18. The profiles display scores for in-dividual problem and competence items, scales that comprise multiple competence and prob-lem items, broad-band groupings of problems designated as Internalizing and Externalizing, and total scores for problems and competen-cies. The $T$ scores and percentiles are shown on the profile for various scale scores. $T$ scores are standard scores that have a mean of approxi-mately 50 and standard deviation of approxi-mately 10.

## Teacher's Report Form

The Teacher's Report Form (TRF) for Ages 5–18 has 118 problem items, 93 of which are in the CBCL, plus 25 that are more apt to be ob-served by teachers than by parents (Achenbach, 1991c). Teachers are also asked to rate the pupil's performance in academic subjects, plus four adaptive characteristics; how hard the pupil is working, how appropriately he/she is behaving, how much he/she is learning, and how happy he/she is.

The TRF is scored on the TRF Profile. This profile consists of problem scales derived from principal components analyses of TRFs completed for 2,815 children, 5 to 18 years old, referred for mental health or special school ser-vices for behavioral and emotional problems, plus scales for scoring adaptive functioning. Pro-files are standardized separately for each gender at ages 5 to 11 and 12 to 18, with norms based on a national sample of 1,391 nonreferred children. The profiles display raw scores, $T$ scores, and percentiles for all scales, as well as Internalizing, Externalizing, and total problem and adaptive scores. (A Teacher/Caregiver Report Form for Ages 2–5 is available for assessing preschoolers; Achenbach, 1995).

## Youth Self-Report

The Youth Self-Report (YSR) for Ages 11–18 has most of the same items as the CBCL, but they are worded in the first person and modified where necessary to make them suitable for ado-lescents (Achenbach, 1991d). Sixteen socially de-sirable items encourage adolescents to report their positive characteristics. The YSR Profile consists of problem scales derived from principal components analyses of YSRs completed by 1,272 children, 11- to 18-years old, referred for mental health services, plus competence scales designated as Activities and Social. Profiles dis-playing raw scores, $T$ scores, and percentiles are standardized separately for each gender, with norms based on a national sample of 1,315 non-referred adolescents.

## Coordination of Parent, Teacher, and Self-Reports

To deal with multisource data, it is necessary to have procedures for comparing and contrasting reports from different informants. Thus we have derived cross-informant syndromes from parent, teacher, and self-reports on the CBCL/4–18, TRF, and YSR (Achenbach, 1991a). Principal components analyses of large samples of clinically referred children yielded eight syndromes for both genders and multiple age groups, as rated by different kinds of informants. These syndromes are designated as Aggressive Behavior, Anxious/Depressed, Attention Problems, Delinquent Behavior, Social Problems, Somatic Complaints, Thought Problems, and Withdrawn. (Additional syndromes are specific to particular gender and age groups on single instruments.)

To reflect variations in the problems that are ratable by different kinds of informants, some items are included on a syndrome scale rated by one kind of informant but not on the corresponding syndrome scale rated by other informants. For example, "Hums or makes other odd noises in class" is in the TRF scale for scoring Attention Problems but not in the CBCL/4–18 or YSR scales.

To facilitate comparisons among item scores, syndrome scores, and profile patterns obtained from different informants, a computer program enables the user to enter CBCLs, TRFs, and the YSR obtained for the same child (Arnold & Jacobowitz, 1993). After the data have been entered, the program prints profiles scored from each informant. It can also print side-by-side displays of item scores and scale scores for up to five forms for the same child. In addition, it computes $Q$ correlations, which indicate the degree of agreement between various pairs of informants. (The $Q$ correlations are like Pearson $r$ correlations, except that they reflect agreement between sets of scores obtained from two sources, such as CBCL items rated by a child's parent and the counterpart TRF items rated by the child's teacher.) To aid users in judging whether particular pairs of informants show low, average, or high agreement, the program displays $Q$ correlations for ratings by similar pairs of informants in large reference samples. Users thus have clear-cut documentation for both the similarities and differences among problems reported by different informants and an empirical basis for judging the levels of agreement among informants.

## Semistructured Clinical Interview for Children and Adolescents

The Semistructured Clinical Interview for Children and Adolescents (SCICA) applies empirically based assessment to the interviewing process (McConaughy & Achenbach, 1994b). The SCICA provides a protocol of topics and tasks that guide interviewers in eliciting broad samples of behavior and self-reports from chil-

dren. The SCICA protocol has spaces for noting what the child says and does as a basis for scoring self-report and observational items following the interview. Principal components analyses of item scores for referred children have yielded three syndromes based on children's self-reports and five syndromes based on observations of their behavior during the SCICA. The following syndromes have counterparts that are scored from the CBCL/4–18, TRF, and YSR: Aggressive Behavior, Anxious/Depressed, Attention Problems, and Withdrawn. The other SCICA syndromes are designated as Anxious, Family Problems, Strange, and Resistant.

## Direct Observation Form

The Direct Observation Form (DOF) is designed to score 96 problems similar to those on the TRF from observations of pupils in classrooms and other group settings, such as recess (see Achenbach, 1991b). In using the DOF, an observer writes a narrative description of a 10-minute observational sample of the target child's behavior, while also scoring on-task behavior at 1-minute intervals. At the end of the 10-minute sample, the observer scores the problem items on four-step scales. To obtain representative samples of behavior, the target child should be observed for three to six 10-minute periods on different occasions, such as morning and afternoons on different days. To provide a baseline for the behavior of other children in the same setting, two control children should be observed on the same occasions and their scores averaged for comparison with those of the target child.

Hand-scored and computer-scored profiles can display scores that are averaged from up to six observational sessions for the target child and two control children for on-task, total problems, Internalizing, and Externalizing. The computer-scored DOF profile also scores six syndromes derived from principal components analyses of DOFs for 212 pupils referred for behavioral and emotional problems. Cut points for all problem scales, as well as $T$ scores for the total problem score, are based on 287 randomly selected pupils observed in 45 elementary schools of 23 public and parochial school systems.

## EMPIRICALLY BASED ASSESSMENT AND THE DSM-IV

Several of the empirically based syndromes have approximate counterparts among the child and adolescent disorders of the DSM-IV (American Psychiatric Association, 1994), as summarized in Table 10.2. The similarities lie in the descriptive features found to co-occur in the empirically based syndromes and the descriptive features selected by the committees that constructed the DSM categories. Some empirically based syndromes have no clear counterparts in the DSM, however, while some DSM categories have no counterparts among the empirically based syndromes.

The empirically based syndromes are operationally defined in terms of specific assessment operations and they are scored quantitatively to reflect gradations in the degree to which a child manifests their features. Norms based on randomly selected, general population samples make it possible to quantify the degree of deviance reported for individual children as compared to their age-mates. The DSM categories, in contrast, are not operationally defined in terms of specific assessment procedures. Furthermore, each descriptive feature and diagnosis listed in the DSM must be judged categorically as present versus absent, and there are no norms for determining whether what is reported for a child deviates from what typifies his or her peers.

The DSM diagnostic categories function in some respects like administrative criteria that are used to decide such matters as funding for services but that have not been derived from patterns of problems actually found among samples of troubled children. The DSM recognizes the need for considering multiple aspects of functioning by providing axes for clinical disorders, personality disorders and mental retardation, general medical conditions, psychosocial and environmental problems, and global assessment of functioning. Although the DSM's multiple axes acknowledge that there is more to diagnosis than clinical disorders, the DSM does not provide procedures for obtaining data from multiple sources or for dealing with the variations often found among data from different sources.

# EMPIRICALLY BASED ASSESSMENT AND SPECIAL EDUCATION CLASSIFICATION OF EMOTIONAL DISTURBANCE

With the passage of the EHA/IDEA, assessment of children for special education services became a major function of school psychologists. The IDEA

**TABLE 10.2  Descriptive Relations Between DSM-IV and Empirically Based Syndromes**

| DSM-IV | CBCL/4–18 | TRF/5–18 | YSR/11–18 | SCICA/6–18 | DOF/5–14 |
|---|---|---|---|---|---|
| Attention deficit hyperactivity disorder | Attention Problems | Attention Problems | — | Attention Problems | Hyperactive |
| Conduct disorder | Aggressive Behavior | Aggressive Behavior | Aggressive Behavior | Aggressive Behavior, Resistant | Aggressive |
| Oppositional defiant disorder | Delinquent Behavior | Delinquent Behavior | Delinquent Behavior | | |
| Social phobia | Withdrawn | Withdrawn | Withdrawn | Withdrawn | — |
| Somatization disorder | Somatic Complaints | Somatic Complaints | Somatic Complaints | — | — |
| Major depression dysthymia | Anxious/Depressed | Anxious/Depressed | Anxious/Depressed | Anxious/Depressed | Depressed |
| Generalized anxiety disorder | Anxious/Depressed | Anxious/Depressed | Anxious/Depressed | Anxious/Depressed, Anxious | Nervous-Obsessive |

lists 13 categories of disabilities under which students can be considered eligible for special education services. In the 1992–1993 school year, 5,170,242 individuals from birth to age 21 received special education and related services under the IDEA and Chapter I of the Elementary and Secondary Education Act (state-operated programs), which included 8% of the American population in this age range. Among those 6 to 21 years old who were receiving special education or Chapter I services, 51.1% were classified as having a specific learning disability; 21.6%, speech and language impairments; 11.5%, mental retardation; 8.7%, emotional disturbance; and 6.9%, the remaining nine disabilities (U.S. Department of Education, 1994).

The category of emotional disturbance (ED), which most directly relates to developmental psychopathology, is defined in the EHA/IDEA as follows:

> (i) The term means a condition exhibiting one or more of the following characteristics over a long period of time and to a marked degree, which adversely affects educational performance: (a) an inability to learn which cannot be explained by intellectual, sensory, or other health factors; (b) an inability to build or maintain satisfactory interpersonal relationships with peers and teachers; (c) inappropriate types of behavior or feelings under normal circumstances; (d) a general pervasive mood of unhappiness or depression; or (e) a tendency to develop physical symptoms or fears associated with personal or school problems. (ii) The term includes children who are schizophrenic. The term does not include children who are socially maladjusted, unless it is determined that they have an emotional disturbance. [20 U.S.C. § 1401(a)(1); 34 C.F.R. § 300.7(9); § 602(3)].

To meet the IDEA criteria for ED, a student must exhibit one or more of the five characteristics (a) through (e) or be diagnosed as schizophrenic. In addition, all qualifying conditions listed in paragraph (i) must apply to at least one of the identified characteristics. That is, the characteristic(s) must exist over a long period of time, to a marked degree, and must adversely affect educational performance. A child who exhibits at least one of the characteristics (a)–(e) or schizophrenia, and meets all qualifying conditions, is judged to meet criteria for the disability category of ED. A child who does not meet these criteria may still be eligible for special education under one or more of the remaining categories.

## Variations in State Definitions of ED

As a federal law, the EHA/IDEA outlines the characteristics and qualifying conditions of ED, but states vary considerably in their interpretation of the term and identification rates. (The term *ED* will be used throughout this chapter to cover such labels as "emotionally disturbed," "seriously emotionally disturbed," "socially and emotionally disturbed," "emotionally handicapped," and "behavior disordered," which appear in various state definitions and research studies.) In an early survey of 49 states, Epstein, Cullinan, and Sabatino (1977) found that the majority of states agreed on general criteria for learning, behavioral and emotional, and interpersonal problems, but they were vague and inconsistent in specifying characteristics for ED. A major difference among states was whether externalizing behavior disorders were included in their definition of ED. To address this problem, a special commission was mandated by Congress in 1983 to determine whether a change in terminology was needed. Although the commission found large differences from state to state in the numbers and characteristics of children identified as ED and served under that category, it did not recommend changes in the federal definition (Tallmadge, Gomel, Munson, & Hanley, 1985).

As of the 1992–1993 school year, the percentage of schoolchildren classified as having ED ranged from 0.03% in Mississippi to 1.71% in Connecticut (U.S. Department of Education, 1994). Knitzer, Steinberg, and Fleisch (1990) reported that states that included the term *seriously* in their terminology classified smaller percentages of school-aged children as ED than did states that did not include this qualifier, but they found no significant differences in ED counts among states that used "behavioral" rather than "emotionally disturbed" terminology. Despite variations among the 50 states, the national average for ED has consistently remained near 1% of the school-aged population since implementation of the EHA/IDEA.

## DSM Diagnoses Versus ED Classification

The 1% rate for ED contrasts with prevalence rates of 14% to 20% of children who meet DSM or other criteria for psychiatric disorders in epidemiologic surveys (Brandenburg, Friedman, & Silver, 1990). Some have argued that such differences demonstrate that children with behavioral and emotional problems are underserved in special education (Forness, 1992; Knitzer, Steinberg, & Fleish, 1990). Slenkovich (1983, 1992a, 1992b), however, has argued that the EHA/IDEA definition of ED excludes many DSM diagnoses, particularly those pertaining to externalizing or disruptive behavior disorders, such as oppositional defiant disorder (ODD), conduct disorder (CD), and attention deficit hyperactivity disorder (ADHD). For example, Slenkovich (1983) maintains that the EHA/IDEA ED characteristic of "inappropriate behavior or feelings under normal circumstances" applies only to bizarre or psychotic behavior and not to aggressive or socially unacceptable behavior, typical of ODD or CD, or hyperactive behavior, typical of ADHD. Slenkovich argues further that ODD, CD, and antisocial personality (ASP) are ruled out by the EHA/IDEA stipulation that excludes children who are socially maladjusted. Slenkovich also excludes other disorders from ED, such as dysthymia, major depression–single episode, and adjustment disorders, because they fail to meet the requirement of existing over "a long period of time." Other diagnoses, like eating disorders, are excluded, Slenkovich argues, because they do not "adversely affect educational performance," which she interprets as meaning academic underachievement rather than broader social or developmental advancement.

At least two studies have examined relations between DSM diagnoses and the special education definition of ED. In a survey of 120 school psychologists, Colegrove, Ostrander, Schwartz, and Daniels (1986) found that most adhered to their state definitions of ED and that only about 30% used DSM diagnoses at all. The school psychologists also disagreed on which DSM diagnoses were consistent with ED, largely depending on whether their particular state definition included or excluded disruptive behavior disorders. Tharinger, Laurent, and Best (1986) compared identification rates for disorders based on DSM diagnoses, the EHA definition of ED, and deviance on the pre-1991 version of the TRF (Achenbach & Edelbrock, 1986). In this study, independent raters assigned DSM-III diagnoses to boys 6 to 12 years old who were referred by their teachers for special education evaluations of behavioral and emotional problems.

Tharinger et al. (1986) found that the DSM, EHA, and TRF classified different percentages of the sample as "disturbed," with unanimous agreement on only 29% of the cases as having a disorder and 8% as having no disorder. According to the DSM-III, 82% were classified as having an Axis I disorder, in contrast to 66% classified as deviant on the TRF Internalizing and/or Externalizing scales and 53% classified as having ED according to the EHA criteria. There was slightly higher agreement between the DSM-III and the EHA ED definition (45% of cases) than between the TRF and EHA ED definition (37% of cases). Lower agreement between the TRF and the ED definition, however, was probably due to the researchers' use of a higher cut point for deviance (98th percentile) than the 89th percentile that was recommended for the pre-1991 TRF Internalizing and Externalizing scales. The better agreement between DSM-III and the EHA ED definition also reflected a more liberal interpretation of the ED criteria than Slenkovich's (1983) since 14 out of 20 cases had DSM-III diagnoses that would be excluded according to her interpretation. Other studies have also shown that certain diagnoses excluded by Slenkovich (namely, ADHD, CD, and dysthymia) are among the most common for children with ED (Mattison, Humphrey, & Kales, 1986; Mattison, Humphrey, Kales, Hanford, Finkenbinder, & Hernit, 1986).

Tharinger et al.'s (1986) findings led them to question the validity of the DSM for determining ED for special education. Instead, they recommended the use of empirically based procedures because of their higher reliability and validity, more clearly defined syndromes, normative data, and greater sensitivity and specificity in multimethod approaches to assessment. Similar doubts about the utility of the DSM for determining special education eligibility have since been raised by others (e.g., Gresham & Gansle, 1992; Sinclair & Forness, 1988).

## Social Maladjustment and ED

The EHA/IDEA definition of ED specifically excludes "children who are socially maladjusted" unless they also meet criteria for ED. This exclusionary clause has generated considerable controversy over special education eligibility. According to Cline (1990), the social maladjustment clause was added to the ED definition to impose a fiscal cap on special education services by excluding adjudicated juvenile delinquents (for the history of the federal ED definition, see Cline, 1990; Skiba & Grizzle, 1991). Slenkovich (1983a, 1992a, 1992b) and others (Cheney & Sampson, 1990; Kelly, 1990) extended the interpretation of "social maladjustment" to also exclude children with DSM diagnoses of CD and other forms of externalizing problems. Others have countered that there is no theoretical basis or research evidence for excluding children with externalizing disorders from special education (Forness, 1992; Nelson, Rutherford, Center, & Walker, 1991; Pullis, 1991; Skiba & Grizzle, 1991, 1992).

In a survey of the 50 states plus the District of Columbia, Skiba, Grizzle, and Minke (1994) reported that by 1990, 31 states had explicitly excluded social maladjustment from ED eligibility and 3 additional states had implicitly excluded it. Of these 34 states, however, only 7 had defined social maladjustment in their guidelines, regulations, or supporting materials. The core definitional components of social maladjustment included disregard for commonly held social norms or expectations, behavior acceptable only to a deviant subculture, and specific antisocial behaviors and/or substance abuse. Using the 1990 U.S. Department of Education data, Skiba et al. (1994) found no significant differences in ED prevalence rates between the states with exclusionary clauses and those without them. They concluded that their findings argued against fears that removal of the social maladjustment clause would "open the floodgates" for admitting students with conduct problems into special education.

Evidence on comorbidity between internalizing and externalizing problems also argues against the feasibility and wisdom of excluding externalizing disorders from special education eligibility. The term *comorbidity* refers to the co-occurrence of two or more disorders in the same individual (Caron & Rutter, 1991). Although the DSM defines each disorder as a separate and distinct category, high rates of comorbidity have been found between internalizing and externalizing disorders. For aggregated samples from four general population studies, McConaughy and Achenbach (1994a) reported 21% to 48% comorbidity between DSM-III diagnoses of CD/ODD and affective disorders (e.g., dysthymia and depression) and 25% to 27% comorbidity between CD/ODD and anxiety disorders. Similarly high comorbidity rates have been found for empirically based syndromes. For a large general population sample, McConaughy

and Skiba (1993) reported 28% to 44% co-occurring deviance on the CBCL and TRF Anxious/Depressed and Aggressive Behavior syndromes and 23% to 31% co-occurring deviance on the Anxious/Depressed and Delinquent Behavior syndromes.

Comorbidity rates in clinical samples are likely to be even higher than those in general population samples because individuals with multiple problems are more likely to be referred for treatment, a phenomenon known as Berkson's bias (Berkson, 1946). For example, in a study of 35 psychiatrically hospitalized children, the overlap was 51% for DSM-III-R diagnoses grouped into behavioral disorders rather than affective/anxiety disorders (Woolston, Rosenthal, Riddle, Sparrow, Cicchetti, & Zimmerman, 1989). Similarly, Harrington, Fudge, Rutter, Pickles, and Hill (1991) reported that 46% of their sample of 63 depressed children and adolescents who were inpatients had at least one CD symptom, 25% had one or two CD symptoms, and 21% had three or more CD symptoms. In direct tests of Berkson's bias, McConaughy and Achenbach (1994a) reported significantly higher comorbidity rates in matched clinically referred samples than in general population samples for deviance on pairings of CBCL, TRF, and YSR syndromes.

The high rates of comorbidity suggest that many individuals identified as having ED are likely to exhibit both internalizing and externalizing problems. This was borne out by McConaughy and Skiba's (1993) findings: among 366 students meeting ED criteria, 53% to 55% scored above the borderline clinical cutoffs at the eighty-second percentile on both the CBCL/TRF Internalizing and Externalizing scales. Only 9% to 10% were deviant solely on Internalizing, and 22% to 27% were deviant solely on Externalizing. These results are consistent with other studies, which show that 60% to 80% of students classified as having ED exhibit conduct-related problems (Jennings, Mendelsohn, May, & Brown, 1988; Mattison, Morales, & Bauer, 1992; McGinnis & Forness, 1988; Pullis, 1991). Thus, although the EHA/IDEA and many state definitions of ED exclude "social maladjustment," high comorbidity between externalizing and internalizing suggests that excluding children with conduct problems from special education not only is impractical but also fails to reflect the complex patterns of problem behavior in many children.

# Emotional Disturbance Versus Learning Disabilities

As stated previously, the EHA/IDEA defined ED and learning disabilities (LD) as separate and distinct categories for special education. Yet many children who meet ED criteria may also meet LD criteria, and many children who meet LD criteria may also exhibit behavioral and emotional problems. In an early study, Fabian (1955) found that 83% of problem readers were seriously maladjusted in social and/or personal domains. Since then, many studies have demonstrated behavioral, emotional, and social problems among children with LD (Conolly, 1971; McConaughy, 1986; McConaughy & Ritter, 1986; McKinney, 1989; Meyer, 1983; Michaels & Lewandowski, 1990; Pihl & McLarnon, 1984; Ritter, 1989; Rourke, 1988; Rourke & Fuerst, 1992; Swanson & Malone, 1992). Other studies have documented substantial academic difficulties among children with ED (Fessler, Rosenberg, & Rosenberg, 1991; Forness, Bennett, & Tose, 1983; Friedman, et al., 1988; Kauffman, Cullinan, & Epstein, 1987; Knitzer, Steinberg, & Fleisch, 1990; Wagner, 1989; Wagner & Shaver, 1989).

Since a child's educational performance must be adversely affected to meet ED criteria, it is not surprising to find academic underachievement in children with ED. However, given the overlap between learning and behavioral and emotional problems, researchers have attempted to identify particular characteristics that distinguish children with ED from children with LD and/or children with educable mental retardation (EMR). Several studies, using behavioral rating scales or personality measures, showed that it was easy to distinguish children with EMR or normal children from children with LD or ED but hard to distinguish children with LD from those with ED (e.g., Fuller & Rankin, 1984; Hicks, Johansson, Heinze, & Halscott, 1981). However, Gajar (1980) reported that children with ED scored higher than children with either EMR or LD on behavior rating scales measuring conduct disorder, personality problems, and immaturity/inadequacy. Wynne and Brown (1984) also found that children with ED scored higher than children with LD on ratings of total problems, externalizing, and impulsivity and lower on attention.

Findings may have been mixed for cognitive test differences between children with ED and those with LD. For example, Dean (1978, 1984a) reported that children with LD showed greater perceptual deficits on IQ tests than children with ED, but other researchers have not found much difference on cognitive measures (Coolidge, 1983; Gajar, 1980; Wynne & Brown, 1984).

Two studies used the pre-1991 versions of the CBCL and/or TRF to compare behavioral and emotional problems of children with ED and children with LD. In a study of boys 6 to 12 years old, Harris, King, Reifler, and Rosenberg (1984) found that those with ED scored significantly higher than those with LD on TRF scales for total problems, internalizing, externalizing, social withdrawal, destructiveness, inattention, and overactivity, whereas both groups scored equally high on aggression. The generalizability of these findings was limited, however, because the subjects attended residential schools and had already received extensive special education services. In a study of boys and girls 6- to 11-years old, Costenbader and Keller (1990) found that children with ED (labeled "emotionally handicapped") scored significantly higher than those with LD and nonreferred controls on CBCL and TRF total problems and lower on CBCL total competence. The CBCL and TRF Internalizing and Externalizing scales also classified significantly more children with ED in the "clinical range" than children with LD or nonreferred controls. However, neither the Harris et al. nor the Costenbader and Keller studies could provide direct comparisons on the CBCL and TRF cross-informant syndromes, which first became available in 1991.

Using the 1991 scoring profiles, McConaughy, Mattison, and Peterson (1994) compared CBCL and TRF total problems, Internalizing, Externalizing, and cross-informant syndrome scores obtained by demographically matched children classified as ED, LD, or nonreferred. This study included 366 children aged 5 to 18 in each category. Subjects with ED or LD were drawn from three states (Pennsylvania, Nebraska, and Vermont) that had definitions of ED similar to the IDEA/EHA, although each state labeled the ED category differently. In their definitions of LD, all three states required a discrepancy between ability and achievement on individually administered standardized tests. Nonreferred children were drawn from the CBCL and TRF normative samples.

McConaughy et al. (1994) found significantly higher scores for the ED and LD groups than for the nonreferred group on all CBCL scales and all TRF scales except Somatic Complaints. Children with ED also scored significantly higher than children with LD on all scales except CBCL Somatic Complaints. Since SES was treated as a covariate in analyses, these findings were especially robust because differences in problem scores were not confounded by group differences in parental occupational status. Categorical analyses also revealed significantly higher rates of deviance among children with ED than among children with LD on all CBCL and TRF scales. Among children with ED, 62% to 87% were deviant (≥82nd percentile) on CBCL/TRF total problems, Internalizing, or Externalizing, and 16% to 57% were deviant (≥95th percentile) on at least one of the eight cross-informant syndromes. Among children with LD, 39% to 52% were deviant on the CBCL/TRF broad scales, and 7% to 36% were deviant on the syndrome scales.

Important similarities and differences also emerged in the McConaughy et al. (1994) study. Both the ED and LD groups were more deviant on the CBCL/TRF Social Problems than on other syndromes. On Delinquent Behavior and Aggressive Behavior, however, the ED group was more deviant than on other syndromes, whereas the LD group showed the opposite pattern. Discriminant analyses revealed that the TRF Aggressive Behavior syndrome was the strongest predictor of ED versus LD status for boys and the total sample, whereas the TRF Delinquent Behavior syndrome was the strongest predictor for girls. Other syndromes that predicted classification of children as ED versus LD included CBCL Delinquent Behavior; TRF Social Problems, Attention Problems, and Withdrawn; and the Thought Problems syndrome scored from both the CBCL and TRF.

McConaughy and her colleagues' findings were also consistent with previous research, showing higher scores on the pre-1991 scales of the CBCL and/or TRF for children with LD (McConaughy, 1986; McConaughy & Ritter, 1986; Ritter, 1989) and children with ED (Mattison & Gamble, 1992; Mattison, Humphrey, & Kales, 1986) than normative or nonclinical samples. Their findings were also consistent with the two previous studies that compared children with ED and LD on the pre-1991 CBCL/TRF scales (Costenbader & Keller, 1990; Harris et al., 1984).

In addition, McConaughy and Achenbach (1996) tested the power of a clinical interview, the SCICA, along with the CBCL and TRF, for differentiating among demographically matched children with ED (called EBD in that study), children with LD, and nonreferred children. They found that children with ED or LD scored significantly higher than nonreferred children on several SCICA syndromes, Externalizing, total problems observed during the interview, and total self-reported problems. Children with ED scored significantly higher than children with LD on the SCICA Strange and Resistant syndromes, plus Externalizing and total observed problems. Various combinations of SCICA, CBCL, and TRF scale scores correctly classified 96% to 98% of children with ED versus nonreferred children and 91% to 96% of children with LD versus nonreferred children. Classification rates for discriminating ED from LD cases ranged from 69% to 78%, comparable to rates reported by McConaughy et al. (1994).

The greater severity of problems found for children with ED in these studies was certainly not surprising since, by definition, behavioral and emotional problems determined their eligibility for special education. However, the high rates of aggressive and delinquent behavior reported by parents and teachers add to the evidence previously cited against excluding children with externalizing problems from special education. In addition, the findings revealed high rates of behavioral and emotional problems for many children with LD, even though these problems were not included in the eligibility criteria for LD. Such findings call for multifaceted interventions for many children with ED or LD, rather than restricting services to match one particular category.

## IMPLEMENTING EMPIRICALLY BASED ASSESSMENT

Surveys of school psychologists have documented increasing reliance on behavioral rating scales for assessing children's behavioral and emotional problems. Hutton, Dubes, and Muir (1992) reported that behavioral rating scales ranked third after achievement and intelligence tests as the most frequently used instruments, which represented an increase from their fifth-place ranking 10 years earlier (Goh, Teslow, & Fuller, 1981). Other studies have also documented that school psychologists consider behavioral rating scales among the most useful instruments, along with interviews, for assessing ED (Clarizio & Higgins, 1989; Smith, Frank, & Snider, 1984).

So far, we have focused primarily on the CBCL and related instruments as examples of empirically based assessment. The Behavior Assessment System for Children (BASC) is another empirically based approach for obtaining parents', teachers', and youths' self-ratings of problems and competencies (Reynolds and Kamphaus, 1992). The BASC Parent Rating Scale (PRS) and the Teacher Rating Scale (TRS) each have three separate forms for rating children at ages 4–5, 6–11, and 12–18, with some variation in items for each age range and informant. The scales are scored on 9 empirically derived clinical syndromes: Aggression, Anxiety, Attention Problems, Atypicality, Conduct Problems, Depression, Hyperactivity, Somatization, and Withdrawal. The PRS and TRS are also scored on 3 scales that assess positive traits (Adaptability, Leadership, and Social Skills) and broad scales for Internalizing, Externalizing, and Behavioral Symptoms. The TRS has an additional clinical scale for Learning Problems and a positive scale for Study Skills. The BASC Self-Report of Personality (SRP) is intended for ages 8 to 18. It is scored on the following 14 scales: Anxiety, Atypicality, Locus of Control, Social Stress, Attitude to School, Attitude to Teachers, Depression, Sense of Inadequacy, Relations with Parents, Interpersonal Relations, Self-Esteem, Self-Reliance, Sensation Seeking (ages 12–18 only), and Somatization (ages 12–18 only). SRP composite scores are provided for Clinical Maladjustment, School Maladjustment, Personal Adjustment, and an Emotional Symptoms Index.

Additional examples of empirically based instruments include the Conners Rating Scales (Conners, 1990), Revised Behavior Problem Checklist (RBPC; Quay and Peterson, 1987), and Walker Problem Behavior Identification Checklist (WPBIC; Walker 1983). All these instruments have parents' and/or teachers' rating forms that are scored on syndrome scales derived through statistical procedures like principal components or factor analyses. Other rating forms, such as the Behavior Evaluation Scale–2 (BES-2; McCarney & Leigh, 1990), Behavioral Rating Profile–Second Edition (Brown & Hammill, 1990), and Devereux Behavior Rating Scale–School Form (Naglieri, LeBuffe, & Pfeiffer, 1993), provide quantitative scores for groupings of children's problems, although their scales were not derived empirically from data on referred children.

## Advantages of Empirically Based Assessment

Empirically based assessment has the following advantages for school psychologists:

1. Information obtained on rating scales is quantifiable and amenable to psychometric standards of reliability and validity.
2. Normative data enable users to judge a child's deviance in relation to large samples of age-mates.
3. The large pool of items enables users to assess a broad range of potential problems rather than focusing only on the referral complaints or the most salient problems at the time.
4. Competencies and problems are aggregated into scales, enabling users to organize information in a hierarchical fashion, if desired.
5. Empirically derived syndromes reflect the patterns of problems found to occur among clinically referred children, as reported by particular types of informants.
6. Related instruments for different informants, as well as cross-informant syndromes, enable users to integrate information from multiple informants across a variety of situations.
7. The instruments provide quick and economical means for obtaining information on children's functioning, allowing users to devote more time to aspects of assessment that require more customized tailoring to the idiosyncrasies of each case.

## Empirically Based Assessment of ED

Scores on the empirically based measures can be especially useful for determining whether an individual meets criteria for ED according to the EHA/IDEA and various state definitions. McConaughy (1993) illustrates how scores from the CBCL, TRF, and YSR cross-informant scales can be applied to the IDEA definition of ED. To expand such illustrations, Table 10.3 summarizes relations between the IDEA definition of ED and empirically based assessment by the BASC and five instruments of the CBCL system. The top portion of the table lists the five characteristics of SED outlined in the IDEA definition. Empirically based syndromes from each instru-

TABLE 10.3   Relations Between IDEA Criteria for ED and Empirically Based Assessment

| IDEA Criteria for ED | BASC | CBCL/TRF/YSR | SCICA | DOF |
|---|---|---|---|---|
| Inability to learn | Attention Problems (P,T) Learning Problems (P,T) | Attention Problems | Attention Problems | Withdrawn-Inattentive |
| Inability to build or maintain relationships | Interpersonal Relations (S) Social Skills (P,T) Withdrawal (P,T) | Social Problems Withdrawn | Withdrawn | — |
| Inappropriate types of behavior or feelings | Aggression (P,T) Atypicality (P,T,S) | Aggressive Behavior Thought Problems | Aggressive Behavior Resistant Strange | Nervous-Obsessive Attention-Demanding Aggressive Hyperactive |
| General pervasive mood of unhappiness | Depression (P,T,S) | Anxious/Depressed | Anxious/Depressed | Depressed |
| Tendency to develop physical symptoms or fears | Anxiety (P,T,S) Somatization (P,T,S) | Anxious/Depressed Somatic Complaints | Anxious Anxious/Depressed | — |
| Long period of time Marked degree | Follow-up evaluations Deviant scores for Behavioral Symptoms Index (P,T), Internalizing (P,T), Externalizing (P,T), Emotional Symptoms Index (S), Clinical Maladjustment (S), Personal Maladjustment (S), and/or 10 syndromes | Follow-up evaluations Deviant scores for total problems, Internalizing, Externalizing, and/or 7 syndromes | Follow-up evaluations High scores for total observations, total self-reports, Internalizing, Externalizing, and/or 8 syndromes | Follow-up evaluations Deviant scores for total problems, Internalizing, Externalizing, and/or 6 syndromes |
| Adversely affects educational performance | Deviant scores for School Problems (P,T), Adaptive Skills (P,T), and/or School Maladjustment (S) | Deviant scores for CBCL School, TRF Academic Performance, and/or TRF Adaptive Functioning | Low SCICA achievement test scores | Low on-task score |

BASC = Behavior Assessment System for Children; P = Parent Form; T = Teacher Form; S = Self Form; CBCL = Child Behavior Checklist; TRF = Teacher's Report Form; YSR = Youth Self-Report; SCICA = Semistructured Clinical Interview for Children and Adolescents; DOF = Direct Observation Form ment are listed next to the ED characteristic that they most clearly represent, although some syndromes include behaviors that cover more than one characteristic.

The bottom portion of the table lists the three general conditions for ED and outlines applications of the empirically based scales and scores that document them. The requirement that problems have existed for a "long period of time" is not readily established by the empirically based measures since specific intervals for rating problems do not mean that a problem has been evident over the entire rating period. Further information from parents' and teachers' interviews and school records is required to assess the duration of the problems. The item on the TRF that asks how long the teacher has known the child and a TRF section for adding open-ended comments, however, can elicit information on how long problems have existed. Follow-up evaluations, using one or more of the instruments, are also useful for determining whether problems are continuing.

Norms and clinical cut points for deviance are particularly useful for determining whether reported problems meet the criterion of severity to a "marked degree." The CBCL, TRF, YSR, SCICA, and DOF all provide standard scores and percentiles for comparing an individual to normative samples of peers. The BASC also provides standard scores for both genders within particular age ranges.

The criterion that ED must "adversely affect educational performance" is not so clearly judged from the empirically based measures but instead requires information from other sources, including standardized achievement tests, grades, teachers' reports, and school records. Adverse effects based on the empirically based measures can be indicated by deviant scores on the BASC School Problems, Adaptive Skills, and/or Social Maladjustment scales or the CBCL School and

TRF Academic Performance and Adaptive Functioning scales, as well as low scores on achievement tests administered during the SCICA and low on-task scores obtained on the DOF.

The final determination of whether a child meets ED criteria for special education requires integration of information across multiple data sources. The empirically based measures provide systematic, standardized methods for obtaining information on the nature and severity of behavioral and emotional problems. This information must be integrated with cognitive assessment and other findings, as outlined in the multiaxial approach in Table 10.1. The meta-analyses (Achenbach et al., 1987) previously discussed demonstrate that agreement between ratings of children's behavioral and emotional problems depends on the roles and situations in which the informants interact with the children. The low to moderate correlations among different types of informants reflect variations in children's behavior across diverse situations and in informant's judgments.

## Applications to School Psychology

Having presented the concepts of developmental psychopathology and empirically based assessment, we now illustrate applications to school psychology practice. We outline the roles of empirically based procedures in gathering data, integrating data, developing treatment plans, and evaluating outcomes. A case study of a 12-year-old boy referred to a school psychologist is used to illustrate different types of information obtained in multiaxial assessment.

### *Gathering Data*

#### *Initial Referral*

A typical data-gathering sequence is shown in Figure 10.1 beginning with initial referral. For school-based assessments, the process is often initiated by teachers concerned about a child's

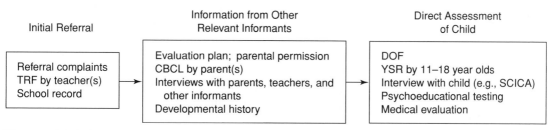

**FIGURE 10.1   Gathering data.**

*Source:* Adapted from Achenbach and McConaughy (1997). Reprinted with permission.

learning or social problems. On the TRF, the following items have been found to discriminate best between referred and nonreferred children: "Difficulty following directions," "Doesn't get along with other pupils," and "Has difficulty learning" (Achenbach, 1991c).

The case of 12-year-old Harold illustrates a typical data-gathering sequence, beginning with a referral to a school psychologist. Harold's teachers referred him for evaluation because he was inattentive and disruptive in class, aggressive, disliked by peers, and off-task much of the time. He was receiving poor or failing grades in several classes, particularly language arts and social studies. As part of the initial referral process, Harold's sixth-grade social studies and language arts teachers completed the TRF. Both teachers rated Harold's academic performance in the clinical range (<10th percentile), with below–grade level performance in language arts, social studies, and math. Harold's TRF score for total adaptive functioning was also in the clinical range on both TRFs, with low ratings for working hard, behaving appropriately, learning, and happiness. On the TRF problem scales, both teachers scored Harold in the clinical range (>90th percentile) for total problems, Internalizing, and Externalizing and in the borderline to clinical range (≥95th percentile) for Anxious/Depressed, Aggressive Behavior, and Social Problems. The social studies teacher also scored Harold in the clinical range for Attention Problems, and the language arts teacher scored him in the clinical range for Thought Problems.

In interviews with the school psychologist, Harold's teachers commented that he seemed anxious and perfectionistic about his schoolwork and, as a result, often failed to complete assignments. They felt he was disorganized, sensitive to any criticism of his written work, and easily frustrated in academic tasks. Teachers also reported that Harold seemed unhappy, had very few friends in school, complained of being teased a lot, and was easily provoked to anger. Fighting with peers during recess led to frequent detentions.

School records revealed similar problems throughout much of Harold's educational history, including poor grades and detentions and suspensions for disruptive behavior. In the early elementary grades, he had received speech and language services and remedial instruction in reading and math. He had changed schools several times because of family moves.

### Information from Other Relevant Informants

Because both TRFs revealed significant deviance, Harold's mother was asked for permission for a comprehensive evaluation. She agreed to complete the CBCL and to be interviewed by the school psychologist. Harold's mother and teachers also completed the parents' and teachers' forms of the Social Skills Rating System (SSRS) to provide further assessment of his social functioning at home and at school (Gresham & Elliott, 1990).

On the CBCL, Harold's total competence score was in the clinical range (<10th percentile). Harold scored in the normal range on the CBCL Activities scale but below the borderline clinical cut point on the Social and School scales (>5th percentile). On the CBCL problem scales, Harold scored in the clinical range (>90th percentile) for total problems, Internalizing, and Externalizing and in the borderline to clinical range (≥95th percentile) for Anxious/Depressed, Aggressive Behavior, Attention Problems, Somatic Complaints, and Thought Problems.

In her interview with the school psychologist, Harold's mother reported that Harold was the older of two children, living with both biological parents. The family had moved several times because of financial difficulties, and Harold's father had some history of domestic violence and alcohol abuse. Harold's mother reported that Harold was delayed in language development and had always been difficult to manage. A state social worker was providing home-based services to help Harold's parents with discipline strategies.

Scores on the SSRS obtained from Harold's mother and the two teachers indicated Harold's low social skills and more behavior problems than reported for normative samples of students his age. Harold obtained particularly low scores on scales that measure self-control and responsibility.

### Direct Assessment of the Child

Direct assessment involves several choices that depend on the reason for referral, the age of the child, and the hypothesized nature of the problems. The DOF can be used for scoring on-task behavior and problems observed in classrooms or other group settings. Norms are provided for classroom observations of children 5- to 14-years old. The YSR can be used to obtain self-ratings from those 11- to 18-years old. An interview with the child is usually included in assessments of behavioral and emotional functioning. The SCICA protocol can be used for interviewing those 6 to 18 years old. For children 6 to 12, the SCICA profile displays separate scales for problems observed by the interviewer and problems reported by the child. (Research is under way to develop a SCICA scoring profile for those aged 13 to 18.) Tests of cognitive ability, academic achievement, physical abnormalities, perceptual-motor skills, and/or speech and language functioning would depend on information already available and the nature of referral complaints.

As part of the direct assessment of Harold, the school psychologist used the DOF to score three 10-minute classroom observations on separate occasions. Observations were also obtained on two randomly selected "control" boys for comparison. The DOF indicated that Harold was on-task only 30% of the time, in contrast to 85% for the two control boys. Harold's DOF total problem, Internalizing, and Externalizing scores fell in the clinical range, whereas scores for the control boys were in the normal range. Harold scored in the clinical range (>98th percentile) on the DOF Withdrawn-Inattentive and Nervous-Obsessive syndromes. The psychologist noted that Harold appeared sad, apathetic, and confused; had difficulty concentrating; and sometimes stared off into space. He also disturbed other students, was restless in his seat, and occasionally disregarded the teacher's directions.

Before meeting with the school psychologist, Harold completed the YSR. His self-ratings produced a total competence score in the normal range, with normal range scores on the Activities and Social scales. His scores on the YSR problem scales were in the borderline to clinical range for total problems, Internalizing, and Externalizing, as well as Attention Problems, Aggressive Behavior, Anxious/Depressed, Social Problems, and Somatic Complaints.

During the SCICA with the school psychologist, Harold was quite open in discussing his own perceptions of his behavior and feelings. He appeared agitated and confused at times, fidgeted occasionally, and had difficulty expressing his ideas. Harold also seemed sad and apathetic, especially when discussing relations with family members and peers. He reported that he had no "real" friends, was teased, and was often left out of things. He acknowledged difficulty in getting along with peers and seemed to have limited

strategies for solving social problems. Harold reported arguing with his parents over rules and routines at home and receiving school detentions for fighting and talking back to teachers. He said he had trouble controlling his temper and felt he was often blamed unfairly for problems at school. Compared to other clinically referred children aged 6 to 12, Harold scored above the seventieth percentile on the SCICA Anxious, Anxious/Depressed, Family Problems, and Aggressive Behavior syndromes and more than 1 standard deviation above the mean for total self-reports, Internalizing, and Externalizing.

Psychoeducational testing indicated average cognitive ability but below average achievement in reading and written language. However, there was no evidence of specific learning disabilities that might account for Harold's poor academic performance.

## Interpreting and Integrating Assessment Data

### Comparing Data and Formulating Conclusions

After the assessment data have been obtained, they must be integrated to form a plan of action, as shown in Figure 10.2. The first step is to compare scores on the different empirically based measures. Actual assessment procedures may vary from one case to the next, depending on the referral questions. Although each instrument is tailored to a different type of informant, overlaps facilitate comparisons between informants in total problems, Internalizing, Externalizing, and syndrome scores. As indicated earlier, the CBCL, TRF, and YSR can also be scored by the cross-informant program, which prints item-by-item comparisons for 89 problem items, the 8 cross-informant syndromes, and broad scale scores that are common to the three instruments. The $Q$ correlations indicate the level of agreement between different informants, such as parent-teacher, parent-youth, and/or teacher-youth. Comparisons across the empirically based measures can reveal similarities and differences in the patterns of problems reported by persons having different perspectives on the child. The findings from the empirically based measures can then be integrated with test results, interviews, the child's history, and relevant aspects of the present environment.

After comparing data from the different sources to determine how the child appears from each perspective, the school psychologist formulates an individualized conception of the child's

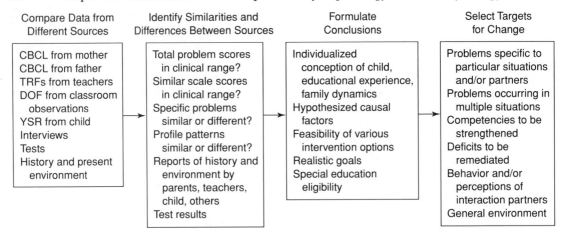

| Compare Data from Different Sources | Identify Similarities and Differences Between Sources | Formulate Conclusions | Select Targets for Change |
|---|---|---|---|
| CBCL from mother<br>CBCL from father<br>TRFs from teachers<br>DOF from classroom observations<br>YSR from child<br>Interviews<br>Tests<br>History and present environment | Total problem scores in clinical range?<br>Similar scale scores in clinical range?<br>Specific problems similar or different?<br>Profile patterns similar or different?<br>Reports of history and environment by parents, teachers, child, others<br>Test results | Individualized conception of child, educational experience, family dynamics<br>Hypothesized causal factors<br>Feasibility of various intervention options<br>Realistic goals<br>Special education eligibility | Problems specific to particular situations and/or partners<br>Problems occurring in multiple situations<br>Competencies to be strengthened<br>Deficits to be remediated<br>Behavior and/or perceptions of interaction partners<br>General environment |

**FIGURE 10.2    Interpreting and integrating data.**
*Source:* Adapted from Achenbach and McConaughy (1997). Reprinted with permission.

functioning in relation to educational experiences, family dynamics, and other important factors. The formulation should include hypotheses about causal factors involved in the case and the feasibility of various interventions. Realistic goals for an intervention plan should emerge from the formulation, along with a determination by a school's basic staffing team about the child's eligibility for special education services.

For Harold, scores on the empirically based measures provided evidence for several IDEA criteria of ED, as summarized in Table 10.4:

1. Inability to learn was suggested by high scores on the CBCL, TRF, and YSR Attention Problems syndromes and the DOF Withdrawn-Inattentive syndrome.

2. Inability to build or maintain relationships was indicated by high scores on the TRF and YSR Social Problems syndromes. Poor peer relationships and low social skills were also evident from the SCICA and from the parents' and teachers' forms of the SSRS.

3. Inappropriate behavior was indicated by high scores on the Aggressive Behavior syndrome, scored from the CBCL, TRF, YSR, and SCICA, as well as on the DOF Nervous-Obsessive syndrome. Inappropriate feelings were also indicated by high scores on the CBCL and TRF Thought Problems syndrome.

4. A general, pervasive mood of unhappiness was indicated by consistently high scores on the Anxious/Depressed syndrome scored from the CBCL, TRF, YSR, and SCICA.

5. A tendency to develop physical symptoms was indicated on the CBCL and YSR Somatic Complaints syndrome, and fears were observed and scored on the SCICA Anxious syndrome.

6. Clinical range scores obtained for CBCL, TRF, and YSR total problems, Internalizing, and Externalizing, as well as five syndromes, indicated problems to a "marked degree," compared to nonreferred normative samples. The SCICA scores for total self-reported problems, Internalizing, Externalizing, and three syndromes were also higher than those of other clinically referred children. Observations scored on the DOF indicated more problems than typically observed for other children, including the controls observed in the same classroom.

7. Low scores on the CBCL school scale and TRF Academic Performance and Adaptive Functioning scales provided evidence of "adverse effects on educational performance." Additional evidence included low standardized achievement test scores, failing grades in several classes, and school detentions.

Further information from the school records and interviews with Harold's parents and teachers indicated poor academic performance and behavior problems since the early elementary grades, demonstrating that his problems had existed for a "long period of time." Despite many attempts at behavior modification programs and prior remedial instruction, Harold was close to failing most of his academic subjects. However, the test results did not meet state criteria for LD classification, and the preponderance of evidence

**TABLE 10.4  Applications of Empirically Based Assessment to ED Criteria for Case of Harold**

| ED Criteria | CBCL | TRF | YSR | SCICA | DOF |
|---|---|---|---|---|---|
| Inability to learn | Attention Problems | Attention Problems (1 TRF) | Attention Problems | — | Withdrawn–Inattentive |
| Inability to build or maintain relationships | — | Social Problems (2 TRFs) | Social Problems | — | — |
| Inappropriate types of behavior or feelings | Aggressive Behavior Thought Problems | Aggressive Behavior (2 TRFs) Thought Problems (1 TRF) | Aggressive Behavior | Aggressive Behavior | Nervous–Obsessive |
| General pervasive mood of unhappiness | Anxious/Depressed | Anxious/Depressed (2 TRFs) | Anxious/Depressed | Anxious/Depressed | — |
| Tendency to develop physical symptoms or fears | Somatic Complaints | — | Somatic Complaints | Anxious | — |
| Long period of time | — | — | — | — | — |
| Marked degree | Total problems, Internalizing, Externalizing, and 5 syndromes for boys ages 12–18 | Total problems, Internalizing, Externalizing, and 5 syndromes for boys ages 12–18 | Total problems, Internalizing, Externalizing, and 5 syndromes for boys ages 11–18 | Total self-reports, Internalizing, Externalizing, and 3 syndromes for children ages 6–12 | Total problems, Internalizing, Externalizing, and 2 syndromes for children ages 5–14 |
| Adversely affects on educational performance | School | Academic Performance and Total Adaptive Functioning | — | — | — |

The table lists scales on which Harold scored in borderline to clinical ranges compared to normative samples for the CBCL, TRF, YSR and DOF. SCICA scores are compared to a clinically referred sample.

pointed toward behavioral and emotional problems. The school psychologist's interviews with Harold and his mother also revealed family problems in addition to Harold's school problems.

### Selecting Targets for Change

Based on the case formulation, the school psychologist selects targets for change, such as problems occurring in relation to specific situations and/or interactions; problems occurring in multiple situations; other people's behavior and/or perceptions that may affect the child; and aspects of the home and school environment; as well as competencies that should be strengthened and deficits to be remediated. In Harold's case, the TRFs, YSR, and SSRS indicated severe social problems and aggressive behavior, combined with anxiety and depression. It was important, therefore, to address both internalizing and externalizing problems in designing school interventions. The CBCL, SCICA, and parent interview also revealed severe problems in family relationships and discipline at home. All of these factors pointed to the need for multifaceted interventions for Harold.

## Implementing Interventions and Evaluating Outcomes

### Designing Interventions

After assessment data are integrated and targets for change are selected, the next step is to design appropriate interventions. Figure 10.3 lists interventions that are typically available to school psychologists, although this is not an exhaustive list. It highlights the fact that empirically based measures do not dictate particular placement decisions or types of interventions. This is an advantage, rather than a disadvantage, because the

results of empirically based assessment can easily lead to different interventions, depending on the needs of the child and the environments in which interventions take place. The systematic selection of interventions is facilitated by empirically based assessment, as well as by advances in knowledge about the efficacy of different interventions for particular types of problems.

For Harold, an individualized education program (IEP) was developed by the school's basic staffing team to address his learning and behavioral and emotional problems in school. The IEP included tutoring in study skills and organization of assignments, especially written work; a behavior modification plan, utilizing a contract system; social skills training, with particular emphasis on problem solving and anger management; weekly consultation among the classroom teachers, special educator, and school psychologist; and home-school collaboration with Harold's parents, the school psychologist, and the family's social worker. Harold was referred to a mental health clinic for individual therapy and further evaluation of ADHD or other psychiatric disorders that might respond to pharmacologic treatment. Home-based services were also continued for the family.

### Monitoring Effects

To monitor the effects of interventions, the empirically based procedures can be repeated over short intervals, such as three to six months, after the interventions have had time to change behavior. More specialized monitoring of academic achievement and specific target behaviors and emotions may also be helpful, such as tabulations of on-task and problem behaviors or use of scales to measure specific problems like hyperactivity,

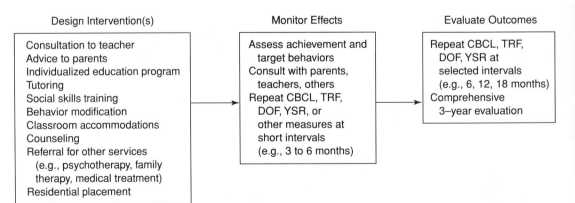

FIGURE 10.3    Implementing interventions and evaluating outcomes.

*Source:* Adapted from Achenbach and McConaughy (1997). Reprinted with permission.

depression, or anxiety. However, if monitoring is confined to only a few target variables, it cannot detect changes for the better or worse in other areas. If the desired improvements do not occur, the interventions may need to be modified and the effects of revised approaches monitored.

### *Evaluating Outcomes*

After the interventions have been tried for a reasonable time or have been completed, evaluations of outcomes can be conducted at intervals, such as 6, 12, and 18 months. This can be done by repeating one or more of the empirically based procedures for comparison with previous assessments. In Harold's case, a follow-up was planned at the end of the school year, including TRFs from the two teachers involved in the initial referral and a newly assigned tutor, along with a CBCL from his mother. Harold's therapist also planned to obtain the YSR at the same time and to provide the school psychologist with the results. Follow-up evaluations are helpful not only to ensure that the student is indeed better off than before the intervention but also to help practitioners determine the typical effects of particular interventions in their caseload. For students in special education placements, the empirically based procedures can easily be incorporated into their required three-year reevaluations for comparison with results from the initial assessment.

## Summary and Conclusions

We have presented a conceptual framework for understanding behavioral, emotional, and learning problems in terms of developmental psychopathology, which is the study of maladaptive deviance in developmental tasks, sequences, and processes. This approach views the children's functioning from the perspective of present and future developmental tasks rather than merely as an outcome of past events. It compares children's functioning with that of their age-mates to identify potential obstacles to development.

We have presented an assessment model for developmental psychopathology that applies normative-developmental principles to the assessment of behavioral and emotional problems and competencies. By focusing on quantitative, developmental, and situational variations in functioning, this model can help to counteract tendencies to view behavioral and emotional problems as disorders that exist in a categorical,

all-or-none form. Designated as *multiaxial empirically based assessment*, the model emphasizes the importance of obtaining standardized data from multiple informants, including parents, teachers, observers, interviewers, and children themselves, as well as from tests and medical procedures. Rather than imposing a priori categories on children's problems, empirically based assessment identifies syndromes of problems that actually occur together, as seen by particular informants. The data obtained from each informant are scored on standardized profiles that provide age-based standard scores for each syndrome, as well as for competencies.

After presenting empirically based procedures for obtaining data from different sources, we have outlined their relations to diagnostic categories of the DSM-IV and the criteria for ED that are prescribed by the EHA/IDEA. We have also considered overlaps between learning disabilities and behavioral and emotional problems. We have demonstrated how empirically based assessment can aid in judging eligibility for special education, as well as in implementing, monitoring, and evaluating the outcomes of interventions. A growing literature indicates that this approach to conceptualizing and assessing problems can improve our ways of helping children and can deal with dilemmas created by administrative criteria for services.

## References

Achenbach, T. M. (1991a). *Integrative guide for the 1991 CBCL, YSR, and TRF profiles.* Burlington: University of Vermont, Department of Psychiatry.

Achenbach, T. M. (1991b). *Manual for the Child Behavior Checklist/4–18 and 1991 Profile.* Burlington: University of Vermont, Department of Psychiatry.

Achenbach, T. M. (1991c). *Manual for the Teacher's Report Form and 1991 Profile.* Burlington: University of Vermont, Department of Psychiatry.

Achenbach, T. M. (1991d). *Manual for the Youth Self-Report and 1991 Profile.* Burlington: University of Vermont, Department of Psychiatry.

Achenbach, T. M. (1992). *Manual for the Child Behavior Checklist/2–3.* Burlington: University of Vermont, Department of Psychiatry.

Achenbach, T. M. (1995). *Caregiver-Teacher Report Form for Ages 2–5.* Burlington: University of Vermont, Department of Psychiatry.

Achenbach, T. M., and Edelbrock, C. (1986). *Manual for the Teacher's Report Form and Teacher Version of the Child Behavior Profile.* Burlington: University of Vermont, Department of Psychiatry.

Achenbach, T. M., & McConaughy, S. H. (1997). *Empirically based assessment of child and adolescent psychopathology: Practical applications* (2 ed.). Newbury Park, CA: Sage.

Achenbach, T. M., McConaughy, S. H., & Howell, C. T. (1987). Child/adolescent behavioral and emotional problems: Implications of cross-informant correlations for situational specificity. *Psychological Bulletin, 101,* 213–232.

American Psychiatric Association. (1980, 1987, 1994). *Diagnostic and statistical manual of mental disorders* (3rd ed., 3rd rev. ed., 4th ed.). Washington, DC: Author.

Arnold, J., & Jacobowitz, D. (1993). *The cross-informant program for the CBCL/4–18, YSR, and TRF.* Burlington: University of Vermont, Department of Psychiatry.

Berkson, J. (1946). Limitations of the application of fourfold table analysis to hospital data. *Biometrics Bulletin, 2,* 47–53.

Brandenburg, N. A., Friedman, R. M., & Silver, S. E. (1990). The epidemiology of childhood psychiatric disorders: Prevalence findings from recent studies. *Journal of the American Academy of Child and Adolescent Psychiatry, 29,* 76–83.

Brown, L., & Hammill, D. D. (1990). *Behavior Rating Profile* (2nd ed.). Austin, TX: PRO-ED.

Caron, C., & Rutter, M. (1991). Co-morbidity in child psychopathology: Concepts, issues, and research strategies. *Journal of Child Psychology and Psychiatry, 132,* 1063–1080.

Cheney, C. O., & Sampson, K. (1990). Issues in identification and service delivery for students with conduct disorders: The "Nevada Solution." *Behavioral Disorders, 15,* 174–179.

Clarizio, H. F., & Higgins, M. M. (1989). Assessment of severe emotional impairment: Practices and problems. *Psychology in the Schools, 26,* 154–162,

Cline, D. H. (1990). A legal analysis of initiatives to exclude handicapped/disruptive students from special education. *Behavioral Disorders, 15,* 159–173.

Colegrove, R., Ostrander, R., Schwartz, N., & Daniels, S. (1986, March). Identification of emotional disturbance in children: A data-based model for schools. Paper presented at the National Association of School Psychologists Conference, Hollywood, FL.

Conners, C. K. (1990). *Conners' rating scales manual.* North Tonawanda, NY: Multi-Health Systems.

Conolly, C. (1971). Social and emotional factors in learning disabilities. In H. R. Myklebust (Ed.), *Progress in learning disabilities* (Vol. 2, pp. 151–178). New York: Grune & Stratton.

Coolidge, F. L. (1983). WISC-R discrimination of learning-disabled and emotionally disturbed children: An intragroup and intergroup analysis.

*Journal of Consulting and Clinical Psychology, 51,* 320.

Costenbader, V. K., & Keller, H. R. (1990). Behavioral ratings of emotionally handicapped, learning disabled, and nonreferred children: Scale and source consistency. *Journal of Psychoeducational Assessment, 8,* 485–496.

Dean, R. S. (1978). Distinguishing learning-disabled and emotionally disturbed children on the WISC-R. *Journal of Consulting and Clinical Psychology, 46,* 381–382.

Dean, R. S. (1984a). Commentary on personality assessment in the schools: The special issue. *School Psychology Review, 13,* 95–98.

Dean, R. S. (1984b). On the multivariate analysis of clinical group profiles: Comment on Coolidge. *Journal of Consulting and Clinical Psychology, 52,* 306.

Education of the Handicapped Act. (1977). *Federal Register, 42,* 42478. Amended in *Federal Register* (1981), *46,* 3866.

Epstein, M., Cullinan, D., & Sabatino, D. (1977). State definitions of behavior disorders. *Journal of Special Education, 11,* 417–425.

Fabian, A. A. (1955). Reading disability: An index of pathology. *American Journal of Orthopsychiatry, 25,* 319–326.

Fessler, M. A., Rosenberg, M. S., & Rosenberg, L. A. (1991). Concomitant learning disabilities and learning problems among students with behavioral/emotional disorders. *Behavioral Disorders, 16,* 97–106.

Forness, S. R. (1992). Legalism versus professionalism in diagnosing SED in the public schools. *School Psychology Review, 21,* 29–34.

Forness, S., Bennett, L., & Tose, J. (1983). Academic deficits in emotionally disturbed children revisited. *Journal of the American Academy of Child Psychiatry, 22,* 140–144.

Friedman, R. M., Silver, S. E., Duchnowski, A. J., Kutash, K., Eisen, M., Brandenburg, N. A., & Prange, M. (1988). *Characteristics of children with serious emotional disturbances identified by public systems as requiring services.* Tampa: Florida Mental Health Institute, University of Southern Florida.

Fuller, G. B., & Rankin, R. E. (1984). Personality differences between learning disabled and emotionally impaired children. *School Psychology Review, 13,* 221–224.

Gajar, A. H. (1980). Characteristics across exceptional categories: EMR, LD, and ED. *The Journal of Special Education, 14,* 165–173.

Goh, D. S., Teslow, C. J., & Fuller, G. B. (1981). The practice of psychological assessment among school psychologists. *Professional Psychology, 12,* 696–706.

Gresham, F. M., & Elliott, S. N. (1990). *Social skills rating system.* Circle Pines, MN: American Guidance System.

Gresham, F. M., & Gansle, K. A. (1992). Misguided assumptions of the DSM-III-R: Implications for school psychological practice. *School Psychology Quarterly*, 7, 79–95.

Harrington, R., Fudge, H., Rutter, M., Pickles, A., & Hill, J. (1991). Adult outcomes of childhood and adolescent depression: II. Links with antisocial disorders. *Journal of the American Academy of Child and Adolescent Psychiatry*, 30, 434–439.

Harris, J. C., King, S. L., Reifler, J. P., & Rosenberg, L. A. (1984). Emotional and learning disorders in 6–12-year-old boys attending special schools. *Journal of the American Academy of Child Psychiatry*, 23, 431–437.

Hicks, M. R., Johansson, C. B., Heinze, A. M., & Halscott, J. F. (1981). Teacher and parent checklist ratings with learning disabled, hyperactive, and emotionally disturbed children. *Journal of Pediatric Psychology*, 6, 43–60.

Hutton, J. B., Dubes, R., & Muir, S. (1992). Assessment practices of school psychologists: Ten years later. *School Psychology Review*, 21, 271–284.

Individuals with Disabilities Education Act. (1990, October). Public Law 101-476. (Reauthorized July, 1997). Public Law 105-17. 20 U.S.C. § 1400 et seq.

Jennings, K. D., Mendelsohn, S. R., May, K., & Brown, G. M. (1988). Elementary students in classes for the emotionally disturbed: Characteristics and classroom behavior. *American Journal of Orthopsychiatry*, 58, 65–76.

Jensen, P., Roper, M., Fisher, P., Piacentini, J., Canino, G., Richters, J., Rubio-Stipec, M., Dulcan, M., Goodman, S., Davies, M., Rae, D., Shaffer, D., Bird, H., Lahey, B., & Schwab-Stone, M. (1995). Test-retest reliability of the Diagnostic Interview Schedule for Children (ver. 2.1): Parent, child, and combined algorithms. *Archives of General Psychiatry*, 52, 61–71.

Kauffman, J. M., Cullinan, D., & Epstein, M. H. (1987). Characteristics of students placed in special programs for the seriously emotionally disturbed. *Behavioral Disorders*, 5, 175–184.

Kelly, E. J. (1990). *The Differential Test of Conduct and Emotional Problems*. Aurora, IL: Slosson.

Knitzer, J., Steinberg, Z., & Fleish, B. (1990). *At the school house door*. New York: Bank Street College of Education.

Mattison, R. E., & Gamble, A. D. (1992). Severity of socially and emotionally disturbed boys' dysfunction at school and home: Comparison with psychiatric and general population boys. *Behavioral Disorders*, 17, 219–224.

Mattison, R. E., Humphrey, F. J., & Kales, S. N. (1986). An objective evaluation of special class placement of elementary schoolboys with behavior problems. *Journal of Abnormal Child Psychology*, 14, 251–262.

Mattison, R. E., Humphrey, R., Kales, S. N., Hanford, H., Finkenbinder, R., & Hernit, R. (1986). Psychiatric background and diagnoses of children evaluated for special class placement. *Journal of the American Academy of Child Psychiatry*, 25, 514–520.

Mattison, R. E., Morales, J., & Bauer, M. A. (1992). Distinguishing characteristics of elementary schoolboys recommended for SED placement. *Behavioral Disorders*, 17, 107–114.

McCarney, S. B., & Leigh, J. E. (1990). *Manual for the Behavior Evaluation Scale–2*. Columbia, MO: Hawthorne.

McConaughy, S. H. (1986). Social competence and behavioral problems of learning disabled boys aged 12–16. *Journal of Learning Disabilities*, 19, 101–106.

McConaughy, S. H. (1993). Evaluating behavioral and emotional disorders with CBCL, TRF, and YSR cross-informant scales. *Journal of Emotional and Behavioral Disorders*, 1, 40–52.

McConaughy, S. H., & Achenbach, T. M. (1994a). Comorbidity of empirically based syndromes in matched general population and clinical samples. *Journal of Child Psychology and Psychiatry*, 35, 1141–1157.

McConaughy, S. H., & Achenbach, T. M. (1994b). *Manual for the Semistructured Clinical Interview for Children and Adolescents*. Burlington: University of Vermont. Department of Psychiatry.

McConaughy, S. H., & Achenbach, T. M. (1996). Contributions of a child interview to multimethod assessment of children with EBD and LD. *School Psychology Review*, 25, 24–39.

McConaughy, S. H., Mattison, R. E., & Peterson, R. (1994). Behavioral/emotional problems of children with serious emotional disturbance and learning disabilities. *School Psychology Review*, 23, 81–98.

McConaughy, S. H., & Ritter, D. (1986). Social competence and behavioral problems of learning disabled boys aged 6–11. *Journal of Learning Disabilities*, 19, 39–45.

McConaughy, S. H., & Skiba, R. (1993). Comorbidity of externalizing and internalizing problems. *School Psychology Review*, 22, 421–436.

McGinnis, E., & Forness, S. R. (1988). Psychiatric diagnosis: A further test of the special education eligibility hypothesis. In R. B. Rutherford, Jr., & J. W. Maag (Eds.), *Severe behavior disorders of children and youth* (Vol. 11, pp. 3–10). Reston, VA: Council for Exceptional Children.

McKinney, J. D. (1989). Longitudinal research on the behavioral characteristics of children with learning disabilities. *Journal of Learning Disabilities*, 22, 141–150.

Meyer, A. (1983). Origins and prevention of emotional disturbances among learning disabled children. *Topics in Learning and Learning Disabilities*, 7, 59–70.

Michaels, C. R., & Lewandowski, L. J. (1990).

Psychological adjustment and family functioning of boys with learning disabilities. *Journal of Learning Disabilities, 23*, 446–450.

Naglieri, J. A., LeBuffe, P. A., & Pfeiffer, S. J. (1993). *Devereux Behavior Rating Scale–School Form.* San Antonio, TX: Psychological Corporation.

National Association of School Psychologists (1993). *Position statement on students with emotional/ behavioral disorders.* Silver Spring, MD: Author.

Nelson, C. M., Rutherford, R. B., Center, D. B., & Walker, H. M. (1991). Do public schools have an obligation to serve troubled children and youth? *Exceptional Children, 57*, 406–414.

Pihl, R. O., & McLarnon, L. D. (1984). Learning disabled children as adolescents. *Journal of Learning Disabilities, 17*, 96–100.

Pullis, M. (1991). Practical considerations of excluding conduct disordered students: An empirical analysis. *Behavioral Disorders, 17*, 9–22.

Quay, H. C., & Peterson, D. R. (1987). *Manual for the Revised Behavior Problem Checklist.* Coral Gables, FL: University of Miami, Department of Psychology.

Reynolds, C. R., & Kamphaus, R. W. (1992). *Behavior Assessment System for Children (BASC).* Circle Pines, MN: American Guidance Service.

Ritter, D. (1989). Social competence and problem behavior of adolescent girls with learning disabilities. *Journal of Learning Disabilities, 22*, 460–461.

Rourke, B. P. (1988). Socioemotional disturbances of learning disabled children. *Journal of Consulting and Clinical Psychology, 56*, 801–810.

Rourke, B. P., & Fuerst, D. R. (1992). Psychosocial dimensions of learning disability subtypes: Neuropsychological studies in the Windsor laboratory. *School Psychology Review, 21*, 361–374.

Sinclair, E., & Forness, S. (1988). Special education classification and its relationship to DSM-III. In E. S. Shapiro & T. R. Kratochwill (Eds.), *Behavioral assessment in schools* (pp. 494–521). New York: Guilford.

Skiba, R., & Grizzle, K. (1991). The social maladjustment exclusion: Issues of definition and assessment. *School Psychology Review, 20*, 577–595.

Skiba, R., & Grizzle, K. (1992). Qualifications v. logic and data: Excluding conduct disorders from the SED definition. *School Psychology Review, 21*, 23–28.

Skiba, R., Grizzle, K., & Minke, K. M. (1994). Opening the floodgates? The social maladjustment exclusion and state SED prevalence rates. *Journal of School Psychology, 32*, 267–282.

Slenkovich, J. (1983). *PL 94-142 as applied to DSM III diagnoses: An analysis of DSM III diagnoses in special education law.* Cupertino, CA: Kinghorn Press.

Slenkovich, J. (1992a). Can the language of "social maladjustment" in the SED definition be ignored? *School Psychology Review, 21*, 21–22.

Slenkovich, J. (1992b). Can the language of "social maladjustment" in the SED definition be ignored? The final words. *School Psychology Review, 21*, 43–44.

Smith, C. R., Frank, A. R., & Snider, B. C. F. (1984). School psychologists' and teachers' perceptions of data used in the identification of behaviorally disordered students. *Behavioral Disorders, 10*, 27–32.

Swanson, H. L., & Malone, S. (1992). Social skills and learning disabilities: A meta-analysis of the literature. *School Psychology Review, 21*, 427–443.

Tallmadge, G. K., Gamel, N. N., Munson, R. G., & Hanley, T. V. (1985). Special study on terminology (Report No. MV-85-01; Contract No. 300-84-0144). Washington, DC: U.S. Department of Education.

Tharinger, D. J., Laurent, J., & Best, L. R. (1986). Classification of children referred for emotional and behavioral problems: A comparison of PL 94-142 SED criteria, DSM III, and the CBCL system. *Journal of School Psychology, 24*, 111–121.

U.S. Department of Education (1994). *16th Annual Report to Congress on the Implementation of the Individuals with Disabilities Education Act.* Washington, DC: Author.

Wagner, M. (1989). *Youth with disabilities during transition: An overview of descriptive findings from the National Longitudinal Study.* Palo Alto, CA: Special Research Institute.

Wagner, M., & Shaver, D. (1989). *Education programs and achievements of secondary special education students: Findings from the national longitudinal transition study.* Palo Alto, CA: Special Research Institute.

Walker, H. M. (1983). *Walker Problem Behavior Identification Checklist.* Los Angeles, CA: Western Psychological Services.

Woolston, J. L., Rosenthal, S. L., Riddle, M., Sparrow, S., Cicchetti, D., & Zimmerman, L. D. (1989). Childhood comorbidity of anxiety/affective disorders and behavior disorders. *Journal of the American Academy of Child and Adolescent Psychiatry, 28*, 707–713.

World Health Organization. (1992). *Mental disorders: Glossary and guide to their classification in accordance with the Tenth Revision of the International Classification of Diseases* (10th ed.). Geneva: Author.

Wynne, M. E., & Brown, R. T. (1984). Assessment of high incidence learning disorders: Isolating measures with high discriminant ability. *School Psychology Review, 13*, 231–237.

## CHAPTER 11

# IMPLICATIONS OF RECENT RESEARCH IN BIOLOGICAL PSYCHOLOGY FOR SCHOOL PSYCHOLOGY

JAMES W. KALAT
TRACIE WURM
*North Carolina State University*

So there you are, trying to assess why an apparently bright third-grader has such trouble reading, meanwhile getting ready for your appointment with a teacher who wants advice on handling an aggressive, sexually precocious fifth-grader, and the main question going through your head is "I wonder what the distribution of NMDA-type glutamate receptors in the dentate gyrus of the hippocampus is?"

And then again, maybe that issue is not your main concern. Research in neuroscience has burgeoned so much in recent decades that it can be quite intimidating to nonspecialists. Nevertheless, a school psychologist needs to stay reasonably conversant with the field to identify children who ought to be referred to a neurologist or other physician and to understand the reports that come back from such specialists (Reynolds, 1989). For purposes of this chapter, we assume that you are aware that major progress has been occurring in neuroscience, that you would like to catch up on some of the relevant findings, and that you do not want to get lost in the details. We begin by introducing some recent advances in our general understanding of the nervous system, concentrating on aspects likely to be interesting or useful to school psychologists. Then we turn to biological aspects of certain types of mental retardation and other conditions that often cause concern in school psychology.

## PROGRESS IN UNDERSTANDING THE BIOLOGY OF BEHAVIOR

We discuss some of the major recent discoveries about genetics, neurons, synapses, brain development, brain functioning, and the physiology of learning and memory.

### Genetics of Behavior and Neural Development

Here is a one-sentence summary of genetics and behavior, as of the mid-1990s: genetic factors contribute to the observed variations in almost all behaviors.

### *Studies of Heritability*

Now, to elaborate: genetic investigators talk about the *heritability* of various traits. A *heritability coefficient* is an estimate that relates differences in some observed trait, such as height or weight, to differences in the genes within a population. A heritability coefficient, which is estimated from twin studies and adoption studies, is a population parameter, not a law of nature. That is, the heritability of a given trait could be high in one population and low or even zero in another, depending on the amount of genetic variation within a population and on the amount of relevant environmental variation.

The evidence suggests a nontrivial positive heritability for virtually every psychological condition that investigators have examined—for example, childhood temperament (Dilalla, Kagan, & Reznick, 1994), alcohol and tobacco use (Cloninger, Bohman, & Sigvardsson, 1981; Pomerleau, 1995; Vaillant & Milofsky, 1982), antisocial behavior (Mason & Frick, 1994), many dimensions of interest and personality (Loehlin, 1992; Viken, Rose, Kaprio, & Koskenvuo, 1994), and a wide range of psychological disorders. The evidence also suggests a positive heritability for certain behaviors we might have assumed to be family-dependent, such as the amount of time spent watching television (Plomin, Corley, DeFries, & Fulker, 1990), degree of religious devoutness (Waller, Kojetin, Bouchard, Lykken, & Tellegen, 1990), and even children's perceptions of how nurturing their families are (Hur & Bouchard, 1995).

We should not, of course, imagine that a particular gene specifically controls television watching or any of these other characteristics. An increase or decrease in any one behavior will indirectly alter many other behaviors. In the case of television watching, for example, we could imagine genes that increase a child's athletic prowess or academic abilities, thereby decreasing the chance that the child will find much time in the day for watching television. No doubt you can imagine additional hypotheses. Similarly in the case of religious devoutness, alcohol use, depression, or anything else, a gene may increase the behavior in question by increasing or decreasing some other behavior that is positively or negatively correlated with it.

Estimates of heritability are often at the center of controversies, such as those concerning the causes of variation in intelligence, mental illness, and criminal behavior. Consider, for example, Herrnstein and Murray's *The Bell Curve* (1994). In such controversies it is important to remember that genetic differences can sometimes affect behavioral development even without any direct effect on the brain. For example, certain genes that influence alcohol consumption act by altering people's ability to metabolize alcohol rather than by any direct influence on the brain (Tu & Israel, 1995). Similarly, a gene linked to obesity in mice produces its effects by increasing the secretion of a protein that is produced by adipose tissue (Zhang, Proenca, Maffai, Barone, Leopold, & Friedman, 1994). In both cases, the genes influence behavior through their effects on the digestive organs, which in turn affect the brain itself. At present, we do not know enough about the genes that supposedly control learning and intelligence to know how they exert their effects.

## Identification of Specific Genes Controlling a Condition

Current technology has enabled investigators to identify the particular genes that are responsible for certain conditions, including Huntington's disease and Alzheimer's disease (Huntington's Disease Collaborative Research Group, 1993; Sherrington et al., 1995). The identification of such a gene has two major benefits: first, the gene provides an accurate presymptomatic test. For example, an individual who has a parent with Huntington's disease can submit to a chromosomal examination to establish whether or not he or she will eventually develop the disease. This information can be valuable to a young adult who is trying to decide whether to have children or who is debating whether or not to enter a professional field that requires many years of education.

Second, investigators can study the protein produced by the identified gene, examine its role in brain development or functioning, and perhaps use this information to design rational treatments to prevent or relieve an undesirable condition. For example, identification of the gene linked to obesity in mice enabled researchers to characterize the protein produced by the normal form of that gene. That protein is found in normal mice (and humans) but not in genetically obese mice. Injections of that protein either into the blood or into the brain itself causes mice to become more active, to eat less, and to lose weight (Campfield, Smith, Guisez, Devos, & Burn, 1995; Halaas et al., 1995; Pellymounter et al., 1995). Eventually, further research may establish some related chemical as a treatment for human obesity. Similarly, the identification of genes responsible for other behavioral abnormalities may lead to new treatments for them; finding the genes is no guarantee of finding an effective treatment, but it certainly facilitates the research.

Because of these potential benefits, researchers have sought to find "the gene" responsible for a number of other medical and psychological conditions. In most cases, however, we cannot expect a quick identification. The search for the Huntington's disease gene, difficult as it was, was facilitated by the fact that all people with the gene get the disease (unless they die young from other causes) and that no people without the gene get the disease. Most psychological disorders, however, probably reflect the combined effects of several genes, not just one. Furthermore, in schizophrenia, depression, and many other conditions, the imperfect concordance between identical twins indicates that the relevant genes merely increase the risk of developing some condition; they do not fully determine the outcome.

Given the current rate of progress in human genetics, we can imagine that someday investigators may be able to use genetic screening as a means of diagnosing many behavioral disorders, perhaps even identifying people at risk for disorders that they have not yet developed. That day is not yet here, however, except for a few disorders like Huntington's disease. For the foreseeable future, school psychologists will have to continue to rely on behavioral methods of diagnosis.

## Brain Development and the Effects of Early Brain Damage

The structure of the brain and its connections is especially plastic early in life; the microscopic structure of individual neurons remains plastic throughout life. Because of a developing axon's dependence on chemical gradients to guide its growth and because a developing neuron depends on trophic factors to sustain its survival, an infant's nervous system is highly vulnerable to a variety of chemical influences that would disturb the mature brain in only temporary or minor ways. For example, thyroid deficiency during early brain development leads to severe mental retardation ("cretinism"); thyroid deficiency in adulthood merely decreases one's mental and physical vigor. A child with phenylketonuria (PKU) must follow a strict low-phenylalanine diet early in life or risk mental retardation; after adolescence, the individual can relax the limits of the diet (except for a woman during pregnancy). For some time, researchers were puzzled because infant animals exposed to low thyroid levels or high phenylalanine levels did not show any impressive deficits in learning. Later research showed that such animals are unimpaired only on very simple learning tasks; on more complex tasks, such as transfer of training from one situation to another, the animals show major deficits (Strupp, Bunsey, Levitsky, & Hamberger, 1994). Similarly, humans suffering from any kind of mental retardation may perform adequately if a task is simple enough; their deficits become more and more apparent as task difficulty increases.

Malnutrition, exposure to alcohol or tobacco, and exposure to toxins are further examples of influences that impair brain functioning much more severely, and much more permanently, in infancy than they do in adulthood. We discuss one environmental toxin, lead, in more detail later. The effects of tobacco are at present suggestive but not conclusive. Children of mothers who smoked cigarettes extensively during pregnancy show a variety of problems in cognitive development and school performance; many also show hyperactivity, attention deficits, and problems of impulse control (Rush & Callahan, 1989). However, these results are strictly correlational; many mothers who smoke during pregnancy also drink alcohol or use other drugs, and a number of them have relatively poor diets for both themselves and their children, both during and after pregnancy. None of the research enables us to separate the effects of smoking during pregnancy from the effects of all the confounding variables.

Research on the effects of alcohol is more extensive and more conclusive. According to animal experiments, exposure of a young adult brain to alcohol produces a minor retraction of dendrites, from which the dendrites recover during a period of abstinence. In contrast, exposure to alcohol at an early stage of brain development can lead to shrunken and disorganized patterns of dendritic branching, which undergo only limited recovery later (West, Hodges, & Black, 1981). Women who drink during pregnancy risk causing fetal alcohol syndrome, characterized by abnormalities of the infant's external appearance, brain development, and behavior. The risk of fetal alcohol syndrome depends on both the amount and the timing of the drinking; it probably also depends on the mother's diet, her smoking habits, and so forth. The safest advice for pregnant women is to avoid alcohol altogether.

Brain development after birth becomes highly sensitive to experiences, as well as to chemicals. After developing axons have followed chemical gradients to their approximate targets, target cells fine-tune the process by selecting combinations of axons that tend to be active in synchrony with one another. A simple summary of that process is this: "axons that fire together, wire together." For example, a cell in the developing visual cortex will strengthen synapses with incoming axons from the left and right eyes, selecting those axons that report information from the same location in the visual field.

The phenomenon of "critical periods" or "sensitive periods" is familiar: an abnormal experience such as restricted or distorted vision can produce much greater effects on brain development at an early age than it would at later ages. In the early stages of development, experience can alter neural anatomy in macroscopic ways. Perhaps the most spectacular example is the phenomenon of absolute pitch—the ability of certain people to identify a tone they have heard, such as C-sharp. Cognitive psychologists have established that absolute pitch is not innate but is instead acquired through extensive practice, beginning in early childhood (Takeuchi & Hulse, 1993). However, people who have developed absolute pitch show identifiable, unusual features in the structure of their auditory cortex (Schlaug, Jäncke, Huang, & Stenimetz, 1995). Evidently, the early experience actually leads to a measurable change in the gross anatomy of the brain. This finding suggests that at least certain kinds of early experience may exert major, long-lasting effects on brain development. The sometimes disappointing effects of Head Start–type programs may indicate only that the particular interventions used were not very powerful, not that other early interventions would have equally modest effects.

At one time, most psychologists and neuroscientists imagined that after early development, the structure of a person's neurons was virtually static, much like a telephone switchboard. We now know that axons and dendrites are forever in flux. By injecting a dye into a neuron and then examining its structure repeatedly, Dale Purves and R. D. Hadley (1985) found that various dendritic branches could grow or retract noticeably over a period of days. Sometimes a neuron would grow new dendritic branches or lose old ones, presumably reflecting the consequences of experience. That is, adult experiences can change neuronal structure in visible, though microscopic, ways—presumably corresponding to the potential for continued learning throughout life.

A school psychologist will periodically encounter a child, or advise others dealing with a child, who is recovering from brain damage. You have probably heard people say that just as the developing brain is more vulnerable than the adult brain in certain ways, it is also more resilient, more capable of reorganizing to recover from brain damage. In fact, however, the al-

legedly superior ability of children to recover from brain damage is not a universal finding. Depending on a child's age and the location of the damage, a child's recovery may be better than, worse than, or about equal to that of adults (Goldman, 1976; Hécaen, Perenin, & Jeannerod, 1984; Kolb & Whishaw, 1989; Stein, Finger, & Hart, 1983). The best documented example in which children recover from brain damage better than adults do is recovery from massive damage to the left hemisphere. Such damage in adults produces a severe or complete loss of language in most cases; even years after the damage, there is little or no recovery. In contrast, children who suffer similar damage before about age two to four years can gain nearly normal use of language through the altered development of the right hemisphere (Satz, Strauss, & Whitaker, 1990). Even in this case, however, recovery comes at a price: a child with early damage to the left hemisphere gains or regains language but generally shows moderate, permanent deficiencies on a variety of visual-spatial tasks. That is, a young right hemisphere that reorganizes to assume some left-hemisphere functions is likely to become deficient in the usual right-hemisphere functions.

## Updates on Neurotransmission

Over the past couple of decades, neuroscientists have enormously increased their understanding of the biochemistry of synapses. A few highlights might be worth knowing, even if only to help you understand some incoming neurological evaluations or to facilitate your conversations with physicians.

Instead of a few transmitter molecules, we now know of dozens of transmitters. Instead of believing that each axon terminal releases only one transmitter, we now understand that many, perhaps most, terminals release combinations of transmitters. The combinations provide for more fine-grained control of the response; for example, one transmitter might quickly excite or inhibit the postsynaptic cell, whereas a cotransmitter might prolong or limit that effect. Researchers now also understand "second messenger" effects in more detail: at certain synapses, the neurotransmitter stimulates a membrane receptor, which activates a protein inside the cell, thereby increasing the concentration of a second messenger like cyclic AMP, which carries out several actions inside the cell. Lithium, which is commonly used for the treatment of patients with bipolar disorder, apparently acts by regulating the activity of second messenger systems (Manji, Potter, & Lenox, 1995). Many other psychotropic drugs probably also act on second messengers.

One exciting finding with far-reaching implications is the discovery that a given neurotransmitter may interact with a great variety of receptors. For example, researchers now believe that the vertebrate brain has at least 10–15 types of serotonin receptors, 9 types of acetylcholine receptors, 5 types of dopamine receptors, and so on. Because of the differences among receptors, a given neurotransmitter may exert relatively brief but rapid effects at some sites and slower but more long-lasting effects at other sites. Furthermore, different receptor types evidently contribute to different aspects of behavior. For example, stimulation of serotonin type 3 receptors leads to nausea; drugs that block those synapses inhibit nausea (Aapro, 1993). Stimulation or blockage of other serotonin receptors has little if any effect on nausea. For another example, drugs that stimulate type 2 or type 3 dopamine receptors have a strong tendency to become addictive; stimulation of type 1 dopamine receptors does not apparently contribute to addiction and may even have contrary, inhibitory effects (Nantwi & Schoener, 1993).

If we assume, as seems likely, that the abundance of various neurotransmitter receptor types varies from one individual to another, we can begin to understand why different drugs have different potencies and side effects for various individuals. For example, a drug that increases activity at serotonin synapses may produce greater amounts of nausea in people with higher abundances of serotonin type 3 receptors. Differences among individuals in their abundance of various receptors may affect whether a prescription drug produces predominantly beneficial effects or predominantly unpleasant side effects. Although at present no one can predict the exact side effects that a drug will produce in different people, one can at least advise parents and teachers to be on the alert for a number of possible outcomes and not to assume that a child who is starting to take a particular drug will experience the same results as some other child who has used that same drug.

## New Methods of Studying Brain Structure and Activity

As in the case of neurons and synapses, research on brain structure and brain damage has grown enormously in recent years. Much of the progress is due to the use of new technologies for examining brain structure and activity in living people, without any need for surgery or anesthesia (Andreasen, 1988). With increasing frequency, such techniques are used for diagnosing certain childhood disorders and injuries, especially with traumatic brain-injured (TBI) children. The following are some terms that you may encounter in neurological reports or in the published literature on certain disorders.

Computerized axial tomography, generally abbreviated CAT scan or CT scan, is a procedure in which one injects a dye into the blood, sends X rays through the body (or specifically the head) at all angles, records the X rays from detectors positioned at all angles around the body, and then uses a computer to reconstruct the three-dimensional anatomy of the body structure. Magnetic resonance imaging (MRI) also produces images of body structure, relying on magnetic fields instead of X rays. The major limitation of MRI has been the need to hold one's head steady for many minutes in order to form one image. Improved techniques, such as echo-planar MRI, can now form images in less than a tenth of a second (Alper, 1993).

Positron-emission tomography (PET) scans enable researchers to measure the relative amounts of neuronal activity in various parts of the brain. The person to be studied first receives an injection of a radioactively labeled chemical like glucose that will be absorbed primarily by the most active areas of the brain. Then detectors around the head measure the amount of radioactivity coming from various locations. Thus PET scans can localize areas of depressed brain activity, such as areas occupied by tumors. They can also determine whether people with a particular psychological disorder have increased or decreased activity in certain brain areas. Regional cerebral blood flow (rCBF) is similar to PET scans except that instead of receiving an injection of a radioactive substance, the person inhales radioactive xenon, an inert gas that simply dissolves in the blood. The rCBF flow takes advantage of the fact that the blood flow to a given brain area increases when neuronal activity increases. Because of the radioactivity, someone should not get a PET or rCBF scan repeatedly.

## Specialized Functions of Various Brain Areas

On occasion, a school psychologist encounters a child who has undergone brain surgery or has been identified as traumatic brain injured (TBI). Although a term like this one may be accurate, it is not especially useful in specifying what to expect from the child. The effects of brain injury vary enormously, depending on the cause, location, and extent of the damage, as well as on the age of the child.

Although almost any brain injury is likely to impair a wide variety of behavioral functions, it is also true that localized brain damage may produce a profound deficit on one task and little apparent deficit on another. According to the "modular" view of brain functioning, the brain consists of a large number of separate modules, each of which performs its own function somewhat independently of other modules. That view cannot be entirely correct; certainly all brain areas communicate constantly with other areas, and no kind of brain damage impairs just one function. Nevertheless, the modular view appears to be at least partly correct; small, localized brain damage can sometimes produce surprisingly specific behavioral deficits. Here are three examples:

- People with damage to certain parts of the temporal lobe become motion blind; although they can see the color and shape of objects, they have trouble distinguishing whether an object is moving or stationary. Even if they determine that it is moving, they cannot determine the speed or direction of movement (Zihl, von Cramon, & Mai, 1983).
- Certain kinds of brain damage impair people's ability to recognize faces, as well as their ability to identify the plants and animals they see, even though the damage spares other aspects of shape perception (Farah, 1990).
- After damage to parts of the prefrontal cortex, monkeys and humans show great impairments on delayed-response tasks, in which they must attend to the location of a signal, wait during a delay after the signal, and then approach the location where the signal had arisen. With very small amounts of damage to these brain areas, monkeys lose the ability to remember the signal in certain locations, although they retain the ability to remember a signal in other locations (Goldman-Rakic, 1994). That is, different frontal cortex areas may be critical for memories of different spatial locations.

The modular view, or any approximation of it, implies that the brain has no "central processor"; the brain conducts many activities in parallel without funneling them all through a single executive. To the extent that this view is correct, it seems at odds with Spearman's *g*—a single, general intellectual ability that underlies performance on a great variety of tasks. How might one reconcile the independence or modularity of intellectual functions with the fact that performance on almost any intellectual function correlates positively with performance on almost any other? The reconciliation is that the growth and development of each brain area is highly correlated with the growth and development of any other area, just as growth of the left hand is correlated with growth of the right hand, the left foot, or the right foot. Although brain damage can impair one behavioral function without much effect on others (just as amputation can damage one hand and not another), under normal circumstances the factors that promote the development of any brain module are the same as those that promote the development of any other brain module—namely, favorable health, good nutrition, general intellectual stimulation, and probably certain genes. In other words, the psychometric reality of *g* is just as compatible with a modular view of the brain and intelligence as it is with a central processor or single executive view.

## The Physiology of Learning and Memory

Researchers in the 1980s and 1990s have made enormous progress in elucidating the physiological mechanisms of learning and memory. Given that learning and memory are certainly topics of great interest to school psychologists, one might imagine that much of the new physiological information would be highly relevant. It is not, however; or, to be more precise, it is not relevant yet. Researchers have learned in detail about certain synaptic processes that probably contribute to learning. For example, we now know that bursts of activity at non-NMDA-type glutamate receptors enables activation of NMDA-type glutamate receptors, which in turn open calcium channels to produce a long-term potentiation of the responsiveness of the non-NMDA receptors (Baudry, Thompson, & Davis, 1993). In the absence of these chemical changes, many kinds of learning are impossible and experiences during an early critical period of development do not produce their usual effects on behavior (Kleinschmidt, Bear, & Singer, 1987). Unfortunately, important as this information is theoretically, it has not yet led to any practical strategies for improving human learning or memory. At some point in the future, this material may become more relevant to the concerns of school psychologists.

Perhaps more immediately useful is an insight that has emerged from studies of brain damage. People have indeed several kinds of memory, and it is possible to damage one type without greatly damaging others (Cohen & Eichenbaum, 1993; Squire, 1992). For example, patients who have suffered damage to the hippocampus of the brain have great difficulty in storing new memories, but they retain old memories. They have severe deficits in learning new factual information, but they learn and retain new motor skills without any apparent difficulty. Finally, they show deficits in explicit memory despite apparently normal performance in implicit memory. Explicit memory includes the ability to answer direct questions, such as "What is the capital of Indonesia?" Implicit memory is the tendency to show some influence of a recent experience, without necessarily realizing that it had an influence. For example, a hippocampus-damaged patient who had just listened to a discussion of Indonesia might not be able to answer any questions about it and might deny even having heard the discussion at all, and yet if asked to name some countries, might begin by saying "Indonesia."

The implication is that when describing someone's learning or memory abilities, one should describe the task or method of measurement as clearly as possible. Someone who performs well or poorly on a given task or with a particular method of measurement may perform quite differently in some other situation.

# CERTAIN CAUSES OF MENTAL RETARDATION

Mental retardation can develop for a great variety of reasons, including brain damage, genetics, malnutrition, psychosocial neglect, hydrocephalus, and exposure to toxins. Here we discuss just a few types of mental retardation and what medical researchers have learned about them. In some cases, a school psychologist may have to explain something about these conditions to parents or teachers; in other cases, the school psychologist may have to un-explain some obsolete or incorrect information that people have heard from ill-informed sources.

## Fragile X Syndrome

A fragile X chromosome is one of the leading hereditary causes of both mental retardation and learning disabilities. At one stretch along a normal X chromosome, there is a series of repetitions of the base sequence cytosine-guanine-guanine. A fragile X chromosome has, instead of the usual 29 or so repetitions, 200 or more. Such a chromosome is likely to snap off somewhere in the midst of that enormous stretch of repeated bases.

In humans, as in other mammals, each male has just one X chromosome per cell; each female, two. Therefore, a male with fragile X chromosomes has nothing but fragile X chromosomes. He will suffer intellectual deficits in proportion to how many of the X chromosomes in his nervous system actually snap. The result generally ranges from moderate to severe mental retardation, with poorly formed dendrites and fewer synapses than normal (Rudelli et al., 1985). Because each female has two X chromosomes per cell, another factor enters the picture: in each of her cells, one of the two X chromosomes is randomly activated, and the other one is randomly inactivated. Depending on how many normal X chromosomes are activated and how many of the activated fragile X chromosomes actually snap, a female with fragile X chromosomes may develop mental retardation, may have learning disabilities, or may even appear intellectually normal. In one reported pair of monozygotic female twins, both twins have fragile X chromosomes but only one twin is mentally retarded, their IQs being 105 and 47, respectively (Mazzocco, Freund, Baumgardner, Forman, & Reiss, 1995). However, even the nonretarded twin has attention problems, conduct problems, and hyperactivity. Thus, the expression of the same genes in two people can vary by a substantial amount.

## Infantile Autism

Infantile autism affects about 1 child in 2,500, with a ratio of about 4 or 5 affected males per female. As a rule, autism is detected no later than age three, and parents frequently report that they suspected something was wrong within the child's first few months of life. The condition is characterized by the following behaviors (Creak, 1961; Kanner, 1943; Ornitz & Ritvo, 1976):

- *Social isolation*, including a failure to take the inititiative in seeking social contact
- *Stereotyped behaviors*, such as repetitive rocking, biting, spinning, or staring

- *Resistance to any change in routine*, including tantrums or other strong emotional responses after a change in schedule or a rearrangement of furniture
- *Abnormal responses to sensory stimuli*, sometimes alternating between periods of excessive startle responses and periods of almost complete unresponsiveness
- *Low sensitivity to pain and excessive heat*, at least at times
- *Inappropriate emotional expressions*, such as bouts of apparently unprovoked crying or laughter
- *Disturbances of movement*, ranging from inactivity to hyperactivity
- *Poor development of speech*, in some cases marked by a parrotlike repetition (echolalia) but very limited use of speech as communication
- *Specialized intellectual abnormalities*, in some cases one or more unusually well-developed skills, contrasted with extremely poor performance on other tasks; intellectual ability difficult to assess because of failure to follow instructions

What (if anything) is the primary behavioral deficit of autism, from which all the other symptoms derive? According to one hypothesis, autistic children focus their attention so tightly on one stimulus or activity that they ignore all other events and all other people (Lovaas, Koegel, & Schreibman, 1979). A related idea is that autistic children sometimes find sensory stimuli so loud or so intense that they retreat into a private world (White & White, 1987). According to another hypothesis, the primary problem is that autistic children fail to identify with other people, that is, fail to understand that other people have their own knowledge and their own perspective (Hobson, 1993).

## Biological Abnormalities in Autistic Children

Autistic children have so many biological abnormalities that it is difficult to identify the original or primary problem. Although most autistic children show no indication of gross brain atrophy, damage, or malformation (Creasey, Rumsey, Schwartz, Duara, Rapoport, & Rapoport, 1986), they do show signs of neurological impairment (Gillberg & Gillberg, 1983), including a very high metabolic rate in some brain regions and a very low rate in others (Rumsey et al., 1985).

Other common biological abnormalities are EEG (electroencephalogram) irregularities, deficient responses to vestibular sensation (Ornitz, Atwell, Kaplan, & Westlake, 1985), irregular waking-sleeping cycles, potentially hallucinogenic chemicals in the blood, and many minor physical anomalies. One puzzling and totally unexplained characteristic of autistic children is that so many of them are unusually good looking. Also surprising is the report that many huddle around radiators or other heat sources as if they feel cold, even in a room that other people consider comfortable (Jeddi, 1970). Moreover, many parents have reported that their autistic children behave more normally when they have a fever, attending to their surroundings and communicating better than they usually do (Sullivan, 1980).

## Possible Causes of Autism

Autism, like most other psychological disorders, is probably the product of somewhat different causes in different individuals. The once-popular view that attributed autism to cold, unemotional parents has been discarded by virtually all researchers in the field. Because of the early onset of the condition, many researchers have assumed that a genetic basis is likely and have sought evidence for it. One study identified 40 pairs of twins that included at least 1 autistic child. The diagnosis of autism was concordant for 22 of 23 pairs of monozygotic twins but only 4 of 17 dizygotic pairs (Ritvo, Freeman, Mason-Brothers, Mo, & Ritvo, 1985). A variety of studies report that only 2% to 8% of the nontwin siblings of an autistic child are themselves autistic. The high concordance between monozygotic twins suggests a genetic basis, but the much lower concordance in dizygotic pairs and nontwin siblings argues against a single gene. Perhaps autism depends on two or more genes that must combine to produce autism.

The greater frequency of autism in males than in females could mean that females need a greater "dose" of the abnormal genes than males do to become autistic. Indeed, female autistic children have more EEG abnormalities, more movement disturbances, poorer bladder and bowel control, and more evidence of brain dysfunction than equally autistic males (Tsai, Stewart, & August, 1981). A family with an autistic daughter has a 14.5% risk of autism in any later children—more than double the risk if the first autistic child had been a son (Ritvo et al., 1989).

One interesting development in genetic research is the discovery that a large number of autistic children have a fragile X chromosome. The fragile X syndrome has also been noted in many mentally retarded people and in the relatives of autistic and mentally retarded children (August & Lockhart, 1984; Gillberg, Wahlström, & Hagberg, 1984). An explanation in terms of a fragile X chromosome might make sense of the disproportionate number of boys with autism: girls have a second X chromosome that can compete with the effects of a defective one. However, because not all autistic children have a fragile X chromosome, it cannot provide a full explanation for autism. That is, evidently a fragile X chromosome sometimes produces autistic symptoms and sometimes produces other disorders; also, some causes other than fragile X can produce autism.

## Possible Role of Endorphins

The low response of autistic children to painful stimuli resembles the behavior of people under the influence of opiate drugs. Opiate users also resemble autistic children in the following behaviors: social withdrawal, repetitive and sometimes stereotyped behaviors, disregard of many sensory stimuli but hallucination of others, periods of either hyperactivity or (more frequently) inactivity, and emotional responses that depend more on an internal state than on external events. Opiate withdrawal is associated with restlessness, anxiety, and a jumpy overresponsiveness to stimulation (Desmond & Wilson, 1975; Glass, Evans, & Rajegowda, 1975; Ream, Robinson, Richter, Hegge, & Holloway, 1975). These similarities suggest a possible link between autism and some disorder of the brain's opiatelike neurotransmitters, known as endorphins (Kalat, 1978; Panksepp, Herman, & Vilberg, 1978).

One opiate receptor in the brain, the zeta ($\zeta$) receptor, is known to modify the growth and development of the central nervous system (Zagon, Goodman, & McLaughlin, 1993). Children who are born to narcotic-addicted mothers suffer many defects in brain development and behavior (Householder, Hatcher, Burns, & Chasnoff, 1982), some of which resembles the behavior of autistic children. The children of addicts have delayed learning and language development and decreased responsiveness to their care-givers.

Do autistic children have some anomaly in their endorphins? Both blood and CSF (cerebrospinal fluid) measures have found elevated endorphin levels in autistic children, especially those with high frequencies of self-injurious behaviors (Gillberg, Terenius, & Lönnerholm, 1985; Sandman, Barron, Demet, Chicz-Demet, Rothenberg, & Zea, 1990). The differences are not trivial; in one study, 11 of 20 autistic children had endorphin levels higher than the highest found in the nonautistic controls (Gillberg, Terenius, & Lönnerholm, 1985). Another study found that the endorphin levels of autistic children could appear to be either normal or extremely elevated, depending on the method the researchers used to measure them. Using an antiserum specific for the *C* terminal of the $\beta$-endorphin molecule, they found that autistic children had endorphin levels almost nine times that of controls. Using an antiserum specific for the *N* terminal (the opposite end of the molecule), they found normal levels of endorphins (Leboyer et al., 1994). Evidently, if autistic children have an endorphin abnormality, it pertains not to the $\beta$-endorphin itself but to either a fragment of the molecule or some other endorphin molecule.

## Therapies for Autism

Autism is generally a lifelong condition, although some individuals become self-sufficient adults. If we take the endorphin hypothesis seriously, we might expect that an opiate-blocking drug, such as naloxone or naltrexone, could help to relieve autism. Several studies with small samples have found that these drugs reduce self-injurious behaviors like hand biting (Sahley & Panksepp, 1987; Sandman et al., 1990); more data are needed, especially on the effects of such drugs at earlier ages. Naltrexone has shown no benefits for mentally retarded adults with autistic or self-injurious behaviors (Willemsen-Swinkels, Buitelaar, Nijhof, & vanEngeland, 1995). Although drugs or other medical interventions may eventually prove helpful in the treatment of autistic children, at present the most successful treatments concentrate on special education rather than on biological interventions (Schopler, 1987).

## Rett Syndrome

Rett syndrome is a type of mental retardation found exclusively or almost exclusively in girls. Girls with Rett syndrome appear nearly normal in infancy, but as they grow older many of their behavioral capacities stop maturing and then regress. The girls gradually lose most of the speech they had developed, lose most useful control of their hands, and develop a number of stereotypic movements (Percy, 1995). Recent research has made Rett syndrome appear even more puzzling than it did a few years ago. Because it occurs early in life and almost exclusively in girls, researchers had originally assumed that it reflected either an X-linked dominant gene or a fragile X chromosome. According to this assumption, Rett syndrome is absent in boys because boys have only one X chromosome per cell and cannot survive with a seriously defective X chromosome.

Research, however, has failed to find any consistent evidence for a defective X chromosome in children with Rett syndrome or in their parents (Migeon, Dunn, Thomas, Schmeckpeper, & Naidu, 1995). Broken chromosomes are indeed more prevalent than average in children with Rett syndrome, but even so, they occur in only a minority of the patients and their occurrence does not correlate well with the severity of the symptoms (Telvi, Leboyer, Chiron, Feingold, & Ponsot, 1994). How, then, might one explain why the condition occurs almost exclusively in girls? One possibility is a sex-limited gene, one that occurs in both sexes but manifests its effects in only one. Most sex-limited genes, however, exert their effects at or after puberty; they are sex-limited because sex hormones trigger their activity. Currently, we have no satisfactory explanation for the sex ratio of Rett syndrome.

Furthermore, the progressive loss of speech and hand function has suggested to many researchers that Rett syndrome is associated with gradual brain degeneration. Not so, say the later studies. Autopsies of the brains girls with Rett syndrome who died at various ages have shown neuronal abnormalities and an overall deficit of brain tissue, but the deficit does not increase over age and researchers do not find proliferations of glia cells, as one ordinarily finds around dead neurons (Percy, 1995). The underlying problem appears to be not a progressive loss of neurons but an abnormality in their development. In particular, neurons in many brain areas have relatively short dendrites with few branches or spines. Many dendrites have long "naked" regions, apparently devoid of synapses (Armstrong, Dunn, Antalffy, & Trivedi, 1995; Belichenko & Dahlström, 1995). Evidently, people with Rett syndrome lack some neurotrophic chemical that is necessary for proper wiring of the synapses in certain parts of the brain. At present, medical science has no means of preventing Rett syndrome and no effective treatment; future exploration of

the neurotrophic factors may lead to some options worth testing.

## Williams Syndrome

Williams syndrome, a relatively recent discovery in neuropsychology, offers another instance in which altered early brain development produces striking and unexpected results. The condition is estimated to affect about 1 child in 25,000—roughly one-tenth the frequency of autism—although we cannot exclude the possibility that many children with this poorly known condition simply escape diagnosis. Children with Williams syndrome are seriously retarded in their motor skills, their ability to care for themselves, and other nonverbal skills; nevertheless, they display remarkable and sometimes even creative use of language (Bellugi, Wang, & Jernigan, 1994). For example, one 18-year-old woman with a measured IQ of 49 had this to say about elephants: "And what an elephant is, it is one of the animals. And what the elephant does, it lives in the jungle. It can also live in the zoo. And what it has, it has long gray ears, fan ears, ears that can blow in the wind. It has a long trunk that can pick up grass, or pick up hay. . . . If they're in a bad mood it can be terrible. . . . If the elephant gets mad it could stomp; it could charge, like a bull can charge. They have long big tusks. They can damage a car. . . . It could be dangerous."

Contrary to what we might expect from studies of lateralization of function in the brain, Williams syndrome is not associated with right-hemisphere damage or any other evidence of impaired lateralization; rather, the origin of the condition apparently lies in an unusual organization of cells and connections at a microscopic level (Jernigan & Bellugi, 1994). Most researchers assume that Williams syndrome has a genetic basis, but its cause is at present uncertain.

## BIOLOGICAL ASPECTS OF CERTAIN BEHAVIORAL PROBLEMS

School psychologists encounter children whose problems stem from a wide variety of sources, ranging from purely biological dysfunctions to the effects of abusive families. Many disorders have a mixture of biological and experiential causes; here we explore what researchers have learned about the biological contributions to a few common problems.

# Attention Deficit Hyperactivity Disorder

One of the most common reasons for referring a child to a school psychologist is attention deficit hyperactivity disorder (ADHD), a condition characterized by persistent patterns of inattention, hyperactivity, and impulsivity that are more severe and frequent than typical for the child's age. The estimated prevalence rate for this disorder is 3%–5%, with as much as a 5:1 ratio of males to females (American Psychiatric Association, 1994). The apparent prevalence may vary, depending on how many borderline cases one includes; still, it is clear that the condition is widespread and that any teacher should be prepared to deal with such children.

School psychologists need to understand the biological bases of the condition for several reasons. First, as Reynolds (1989) has emphasized, they must know when to refer a child to a physician. Second, a grasp of the biological basis of the disorder helps them to "demystify" the disorder for parents and teachers (Levine, 198). Finally, it helps them to diagnose, design, and implement behavior modification techniques; consult with parents and teachers, and apply medication monitoring techniques.

For detailed information about ADHD and its treatment, the reader should consult more specialized sources (e.g., Barkley, 1990). Here we review a few highlights of the etiology, diagnosis, and treatment.

## Genetics

Almost certainly, ADHD is a heterogeneous disorder. Children can become hyperactive, distractible, and impulsive because of temporary problems like inadequate sleep or because of head injuries, exposure to toxins, and other biological events. No one can expect, therefore, to discover "the" cause of ADHD; at most, a researcher can identify factors that contribute to a large number of cases. The research to date indicates that a genetic predisposition contributes to some, probably many, cases of ADHD, although researchers do not yet know which genes are responsible or how they exert their effects. Barkley (1991) cites twin studies that indicate a high concordance rate between identical twins and an estimated heritability of .3 to .5. In one study of adults with persisting ADHD, 84% had at least one child with ADHD and 52% had at least two such children (Biederman et al., 1995a).

Another study examined the DNA of children with ADHD and their parents (Cook et al., 1995). The results suggest a possible association between ADHD and aberrant forms of the gene that controls the dopamine transporter system. If verified by future research, this genetic link might provide an aid to diagnosis and perhaps eventually lead toward more effective treatments.

Although genetic factors may contribute to a child's risk of ADHD, the behavioral outcome clearly depends on environmental influences as well. The risk of ADHD is correlated with severe parental discord, low social class, large family size, paternal criminality, maternal mental disorder, and foster care placement (Biederman et al., 1995b). Other factors implicated as possible contributors to ADHD include exposure to lead and drinking or smoking by the child's mother during pregnancy (Barkley, 1991; Reynolds, 1989).

## Neurology

Although one can find a number of neurological abnormalities in various ADHD children, the most frequent abnormality is a pattern of dysfunction in the frontal lobes and in their connections to other brain regions (Zametkin, 1989). Such a pattern makes sense, given that frontal lobe damage has long been linked with inattentiveness, poor impulse control, and disinhibition. A variety of studies indicate that ADHD children have structural abnormalities in their frontal cortex and elsewhere, that their distractibility and other behaviors are consistent with a hypothesis of frontal lobe dysfunction, and that PET scans and other neuroimaging studies find less than the normal activity level in the frontal lobes of ADHD children (Hynd, Hern, Voeller, & Marshall, 1991). The frontal cortex of ADHD children in MRI scans tend to be bilaterally symmetrical, whereas in most children the right frontal lobe is slightly larger than the left (Castellanos et al., 1994).

Because methylphenidate (Ritalin) and other drugs commonly prescribed for ADHD aim primarily at catecholamine synapses, much speculation has focused on a catecholamine deficit (or possibly excess) as the underlying basis for ADHD (e.g., Shaywitz, Yager, & Klopper, 1976). However, the fact that catecholamine-agonist drugs help to relieve ADHD is not necessarily strong evidence for an underlying catecholamine disorder. One study found that stimulant drugs increase attentiveness and decrease distractibility even in non-

ADHD children (Zahn, Rapoport, & Thompson, 1980). Thus, a test of the catecholamine hypothesis requires a more direct measurement of brain catecholamines. A careful measurement of urine samples found that 35 children with ADHD, aged 6–12 years, had consistently higher than normal levels of catecholamine metabolites, especially norepinephrine metabolites (Pliszka, Maas, Javors, Rogeness, & Baker, 1994).

It is, for many parents, a comfort to be told that their child's impulsive behaviors are a sign of biological problems, not a sign of weak character, being "bad," or even a flaw in how the child was reared. It is, of course, even more of a comfort to be told that professionals are designing a plan to help the child overcome the disorder.

## *Diagnosis*

The fact that ADHD apparently has a neurological basis should not make school psychologists shy away from assessing it. Much of the assessment can, and indeed should, be conducted at school. Diagnostic tools include rating scales to be completed by parents and teachers, various assessment techniques to rule out learning disabilities, and instruments sensitive to frontal lobe damage (Barkley, Grodzinsky, & DuPaul, 1992). Frontal lobe tests include the Stroop Color–Word Test, Hand Movements test, and Go–No Go test, which require the participant to respond to one cue and inhibit response to another. The Continuous Performance Test, a battery of frontal lobe tests, has emerged as a reliable and valid way of distinguishing ADHD children from controls (Gordon, 1983).

## *Treatment*

Although behavior modification programs that provide a highly structured environment and consistent reinforcement consequences can be very helpful to many ADHD children, in many cases medications also appear to be an important supplement. The most commonly used medications are stimulant drugs such as methylphenidate (Ritalin), dextroamphetamine (Dexedrine), and pemoline (Cylert). Each of these drugs acts mostly at dopamine and norepinephrine synapses (Amaya-Jackson, Mesco, McGough, & Cantwell, 1992). Methylphenidate is generally the preferred drug because of its favorable ratio of benefits to side effects (Hutchens & Hynd, 1987). People who take methylphenidate pills as a treatment for ADHD almost never abuse it. Many, in fact, look forward to their "drug holidays," when they can stop tak-

ing it. A realistic problem, however, is that the brothers or sisters of an ADHD child sometimes take some of the prescribed methylphenidate as a drug of abuse. Thus, although ADHD children themselves are not likely to abuse the drug, their siblings and friends should be monitored for possible abuse and even addiction.

Stimulant drugs tend to suppress hyperactive, disruptive, and impulsive behaviors in both adults and children with ADHD (Gadow, Sverd, Sprafkin, Nolan, & Ezor, 1995; Spencer, Wilens, Biederman, Faraone, Ablon, & Lapey, 1995). Side effects vary in both intensity and duration but often include appetite suppression, sleep disturbance, depression and crying, headaches, muscle spasms, stomach upset, or increased activity. Growth suppression sometimes occurs as a long-term effect. Parents, teachers, and physicians should carefully monitor any child taking stimulant medications to determine whether the benefits outweigh the harm.

Many professionals advise against using stimulant drugs for a child who has tics because, in their experience, the drugs aggravate tics. The research indicates, however, that stimulant drugs increase the frequency of some tics and decrease the frequency of others (Gadow et al., 1995). For all children who are using stimulant drugs (especially, but not only, those with tics), it is important for parents and school personnel to monitor both the possible benefits and the side effects. If the side effects pose a serious or lingering problem, those concerned should consider stopping the treatment; decreasing the dose; or at least scheduling drug holidays on weekends, holidays, and vacations. For ADHD individuals who do not respond well to stimulant drugs or who must avoid them because of side effects, tricyclic antidepressants are also frequently helpful (Pliszka, 1987), especially for those with symptoms of both depression and ADHD.

Many people have hoped to deal with ADHD through changes in diet. Benjamin Feingold (1975) claimed that a diet free from additives, dyes, and preservatives could greatly diminish hyperactivity and attention disorders. Many teachers and parents have enthusiastically praised the effects of this diet, although most of its apparent benefits seems to have been the result of selective memory, selective reporting, or self-fulfilling prophecies. Double-blind studies have found few if any benefits from the diet (Harley et al., 1978; Wender, 1986). Similarly, the idea that sugar aggravates hyperactivity continues to be popular among parents, teachers, and even pediatricians, in spite of consistent evidence against it (Milich, Wolraich, & Lindgren, 1986). School psychologists can perform an important service not only by steering parents and teachers toward effective treatments but also by discouraging them from following popular fads that the research does not support.

## Lead Exposure

In a report to Congress, the Agency for Toxic Substances and Disease Registry (1988) stated, "Lead is toxic wherever it is found, and it is found everywhere." Following a flurry of research on lead intoxication in the early 1900s, by 1934 nine countries had banned the use of lead paints. The United States, slower to respond, began phasing out lead-based paints and gasolines gradually between the 1960s and the 1980s.

The near abolition of lead-based paints and lead-based gasoline led many people to believe that the problem has been solved. However, environmental lead is like a sleeping monster, far more dangerous than it appears. In many places, lead-based paint and plaster will continue to chip off for decades to come, sometimes in the presence of small children. Lead from the gasoline of the 1970s and earlier dusted the surrounding countryside and worked its way into the soil, infiltrating it with an estimated 500 million metric tons of lead (Berney, 1993). During new construction, bulldozers can stir up significant amounts of lead. Even remodeling old homes stirs up enough lead to constitute a major hazard to children. People also contact lead by handling fishing weights, making stained glass or pottery, refinishing furniture, burning lead-painted wood, handling certain kinds of ceramics or crystal, using anything that has been soldered, and so forth (Angle, 1993). Clearly, the risk is widespread, almost universal.

According to the U.S. Public Health Services, about one-sixth of all children have had enough contact with lead to pose a serious danger (Dyer, 1993). Studies in several other countries have found that the risks are greatest among active children; among children of low socioeconomic status; and among those who live in old homes, wooden homes, recently remodeled homes, or homes along busy streets (Bergomi et al., 1989; Fergusson, Fergusson, Horwood, & Kinzett, 1988a, 1988b, 1988c; Lyngbye, Hansen, & Grandjean, 1989). Lead exposure tends to be a lingering problem; after initial exposure, blood levels of lead first rise and then fall as the lead leaves the blood and accumulates in the bone, teeth, liver, and muscles. It is gradually released from those stores over a long time, especially in response to infections and sunlight (Dyer, 1993).

Lead that enters the blood has an affinity for entering neurons, where it impairs formation of synapses, interferes with neurotransmission, and damages the myelin covering of motor nerves (Ruff & Bijur, 1989). It impedes learning, particularly through damage to glutamate and dopamine synapses (Coryslechta, 1995). Large doses of lead exposure can produce mental retardation; more commonly, small doses may lead to more modest, subtle effects. Most school psychologists and even most physicians have only limited knowledge of this topic (Bar-on & Boyle, 1994); consequently they can easily overlook mild cases of lead exposure or notice the symptoms but attribute them to other causes.

Children who have been exposed to even modest amounts of lead have lower than average Bayley scores, impaired motor skills, poor school performance, high absenteeism, deviant behavior, and in some cases symptoms that suggest ADHD (Bellinger, Leviton, Waternaux, Needleman, & Rabinowitz, 1987; Dietrich, Berger, & Succop, 1993; Ferguson et al., 1988a, 1988b, 1988c; Needleman, Schell, Bellinger, Leviton, & Allred, 1990; Silva, Hughes, Williams, & Faed, 1988; Thomson, Raab, Hepburn, Hunter, Fulton, & Laxen, 1989; Winneke, Brockhaus, Collet, & Kramer, 1989). Identifying lead exposure as the cause of such problems is, of course, very difficult because so many other factors could be responsible for a similar outcome. However, if behavioral problems seem strikingly prevalent among children from a given neighborhood, one should become suspicious of a toxic basis and should refer the children for medical examinations. Body lead can be measured from blood or urine samples, from deciduous ("baby") teeth, or from X-ray fluorescence of the bones (Angle, 1993; Bergomi et al., 1989; Glotzer, Bauchner, Freedberg, & Palfrey, 1994).

The following is a questionnaire, provided by the Centers for Disease Control (1991), that screens for the probability of lead exposure. If the answer is yes to even one question, that child should be given a blood lead test.

Does your child—

1. Live in or regularly visit a house with peeling or chipping paint built before

1960? This could include a day care center, preschool, the home of a babysitter or a relative, etc.

2. Live in or regularly visit a house built before 1960 with recent, ongoing, or planned renovation or remodeling?

3. Have a brother or sister, housemate, or playmate being followed or treated for lead poisoning (that is, blood lead ≥15 $\mu$g/dL)?

4. Live with an adult whose job or hobby involves exposure to lead?

5. Live near an active lead smelter, battery recycling plant, or other industry likely to release lead?

Excessive lead exposure can be treated by reducing the exposure to lead, increasing the levels of iron and calcium in the diet (because they compete with lead for absorption), and using drugs that chelate lead and remove it through the urine (Angle, 1993).

In short, school psychologists, who have more frequent contact than they probably realize with lead-exposed children, can make an important contribution by calling the attention of parents, teachers, and government officials to possible lead hazards and by referring certain children to medical agencies for testing and possible treatment.

## Dyslexia

Although special educators do not typically use the term *dyslexia*, parents and teachers often refer to it. Dyslexia is a specific reading disability in a person who has adequate vision and reasonably normal performance in academic areas other than reading. Like the terms *headache* or *backache*, *dyslexia* refers to a set of symptoms that may arise for any of a variety of reasons. Future progress in understanding dyslexia will depend in part on distinguishing among its various types and causes.

Many people with dyslexia fail to show the usual left-hemisphere lateralization of language functions. Language-related brain areas that are ordinarily larger in the left hemisphere may be, in people with dyslexia, either equal on both sides or even larger in the right hemisphere (Duara et al., 1991; Hynd & Semrud-Clikeman, 1989). Letter identification, which evokes mostly left-hemisphere activity in normal readers, evokes mostly right-hemisphere activity in dyslexic individuals (Barnea, Lamm, Epstein, & Pratt, 1994). As yet, researchers do not know the links between the impaired lateralization and the observed reading deficits.

A different kind of biological investigation has focused on specific pathways in the visual cortex. Researchers have distinguished between a parvocellular (small-celled) pathway that detects details of objects and a magnocellular (large-celled) pathway that deals more with larger visual patterns. Many dyslexic individuals show signs of decreased responsiveness in the latter (Livingstone, Rosen, Drislane, & Galaburda, 1991). The presumed link is that a magnocellular deficit could impair recognition of large, overall patterns such as words; most dyslexic individuals have trouble reading words and sentences but much less difficulty in identifying an isolated letter.

Still another hypothesis concerns foveal versus parafoveal vision. Try this: focus on the *X* in the center of the following line and try to read other letters to the left and right of that fixation point:

↓

V W C A M P F S X U T B A R G D Y

Most people can easily read the letters nearest the fixation point, but accuracy falls sharply at greater distances. (People who read languages that are printed left to right, such as English, generally can identify more letters to the right of the fixation point; people who read Hebrew, which is printed right to left, can identify more letters to the left.) People with dyslexia are, on the average, slightly worse than ordinary readers at reading letters close to the fixation point but significantly *more* accurate at reading letters far to the right of the fixation point (Geiger, Lettvin, & Zegarra-Moran, 1992). Presumably, this ability interferes with correct identification of the fixated word. Why dyslexic readers develop this tendency is not known; it does, however, appear to be subject to intervention. Both dyslexic children and dyslexic adults have learned to suppress their peripheral attention and thereby to improve their reading skills, according to preliminary studies with small numbers of subjects (Geiger, Lettvin, & Fahle, 1994; Geiger et al., 1992).

## Tourette Syndrome

Although Tourette syndrome, also known as Gilles de la Tourette's syndrome, was first reported in the medical literature in 1885, it languished in obscurity for decades. Typically, an affected child might see a number of specialists over several years until one of them correctly diagnosed the condition; the other specialists were simply unaware of Tourette syndrome or unfamiliar with its manifestations. Therefore, the reputation of Tourette syndrome as a rare disorder had more to do with the knowledge of diagnosticians than it did with the actual prevalence of the disorder. Although the condition is no longer thought to be rare, its exact prevalence remains unknown. Many people with Tourette syndrome, especially those with mild or atypical symptoms, still elude diagnosis today.

Symptoms of Tourette syndrome include repeated movements like facial tics, repetitive touching, repetitive sounds (sometimes, but not necessarily, obscenities or insults), and imitation of other people's words and actions. The condition ordinarily begins in childhood, most frequently around age five to seven and more commonly in boys than in girls. Symptoms may increase or decrease over both short time scales (minute to minute) and long time scales (year to year). Children with Tourette syndrome are disadvantaged in their schoolwork and in their social relationships. The disadvantages stem from a combination of the tics and mannerisms themselves, tic-suppressing medications, other psychological disorders coexisting with Tourette syndrome, and the unfavorable reactions of teachers and fellow students (Singer, Schuerholz, & Denckla, 1995).

Some observers believe that the repetitive movements are involuntary. However, one lifelong sufferer described his movements as not really involuntary but more as the actions of someone scratching an itchy spot: it is possible to inhibit the urge but not easy (Bliss, 1980).

A large percentage of the relatives of someone with Tourette syndrome also suffer from either Tourette or other psychological disorders, such as simple tics, obsessive-compulsive disorder, alcoholism, and affective disorders (Comings, 1994). Several researchers have sought to localize "the" gene for Tourette syndrome, so far without success. A likely interpretation is that Tourette syndrome is a behavioral spectrum disorder, in which an underlying genetic predisposition manifests itself in different ways for different individuals, depending on the effects of other genes and of various environmental influences.

Tourette syndrome often responds favorably to behavioral interventions that decrease emotional tension or to drug therapies, particularly haloperidol and other drugs that block dopamine synapses. The effectiveness of dopamine blockers implies a possible dysfunction at dopamine synapses. However, the research to date has not convincingly demonstrated any significant abnormality at dopamine receptor genes (Gelernter, Pauls, Leckman, Kidd, & Kurlan, 1994) or any impairment in the second-messenger systems of dopamine synapses (Singer, Dickson, Martinie, & Levine, 1995). Measurements of cerebrospinal fluid have found normal levels of dopamine but above-normal levels of norepinephrine (Leckman et al., 1995). The neurochemical correlates of Tourette syndrome are, at present, difficult to explain.

## BIOLOGY AND THE FUTURE OF SCHOOL PSYCHOLOGY

Research in neuroscience and biological psychology continues at an amazing pace. In 1994, one journal alone, *Brain Research*, published 12,500 pages of research articles. Researchers today are answering questions, especially about the genetics and biochemistry of behavior, that they did not know enough to ask even a few years earlier.

We live in an era of increasing specialization, and no one should expect school psychologists to be conversant with all of the literature in neuroscience. However, in the past few years, the National Association of School Psychologists (NASP) has required formal training in the biological bases of behavior for national certification (NCSP). If current trends continue, familiarity with the biology of behavior may become increasingly important in the future. What is most important, however, is that school psychologists serve as a point of referral for children who may have a biological problem and who may benefit from a visit to a neurologist, neuropsychologist, endocrinologist, or other specialist. Thus one should work as part of an interdisciplinary team, and one should know when to call for help from other members.

## REFERENCES

Aapro, M. S. (1993). Review of experience with ondansetron and granisetron. *Annals of Oncology, 4* (Suppl. 3), S9–S14.

Agency for Toxic Substances and Disease Registry (1988). *The nature and extent of lead poisoning in children in the United States: A report to Congress.* Atlanta, GA: Department of Health and Human Services.

Alper, J. (1993). Echo-planar MRI: Learning to read minds. *Science, 261,* 556.

Amaya-Jackson, L., Mesco, R. H., McGough, J. J., & Cantwell, D. P. (1992). Attention Deficit Hyperactivity Disorder. In E. Peschel, R. Peschel, C. W. Howe, & J. W. Howe (Eds.), *Neurobiological disorders in children and adolescents* (pp. 45–57). Ann Arbor, MI: Jossey-Bass.

American Psychiatric Association. (1994). *Diagnostic and statistical manual of mental disorders* (4th ed.). Washington, DC: Author.

Andreasen, N. C. (1988). Brain imaging: Applications in psychiatry. *Science, 239,* 1381–1388.

Angle, C. R. (1993). Childhood lead poisoning and its treatment. *Annual Review of Pharmacology and Toxicology, 33,* 409–434.

Armstrong, D., Dunn, J. K., Antalffy, B., & Trivedi, R. (1995). Selective dendritic alterations in the cortex of Rett syndrome. *Journal of Neuropathology and Experimental Neurology, 54,* 195–201.

August, G. J., & Lockhart, L. H. (1984). Familial autism and the fragile-X chromosome. *Journal of Autism and Developmental Disorders, 14,* 197–204.

Barkley, R. A. (1990). *Attention deficit hyperactivity disorder: A handbook for diagnosis and treatment.* New York: Guilford.

Barkley, R. A. (1991). Attention deficit hyperactivity disorder. *Psychiatric Annals, 21,* 725–733.

Barkley, R. A., Grodzinsky, G., & DuPaul, G. J. (1992). Frontal lobe functions in attention deficit disorder with and without hyperactivity: A review and research report. *Journal of Abnormal Child Psychology, 20,* 163–188.

Barnea, A., Lamm, O., Epstein, R., & Pratt, H. (1994). Brain potentials from dyslexic children recorded during short-term-memory tasks. *International Journal of Neuroscience, 74,* 1–4.

Bar-on, M. E., & Boyle, R. M. (1994). Are pediatricians ready for the new guidelines on lead poisoning? *Pediatrics, 93,* 178–182.

Baudry, M., Thompson, R. F., & Davis, J. L. (Eds.). (1993). *Synaptic plasticity.* Cambridge, MA: MIT Press.

Belichenko, P. V., & Dahlström, A. (1995). Studies on the 3-dimensional architecture of dendritic spines and varicosities in human cortex by confocal laser scanning microscopy and Lucifer Yellow microinjections. *Journal of Neuroscience Methods, 57,* 55–61.

Bellinger, D., Leviton, A., Waternaux, X., Needleman, H., & Rabinowitz, M. (1987). Longitudinal analyses of prenatal and postnatal lead exposure and early cognitive development. *The New England Journal of Medicine, 316,* 1037–1043.

Bellugi, U., Wang, P. P., & Jernigan, T. L. (1994). Williams syndrome: An unusual neuropsychological profile. In S. H. Broman & J. Grafman (Eds.), *Atypical cognitive deficits in developmental disorders* (pp. 23–56). Hillsdale, NJ: Erlbaum.

Bergomi, M., Borella, P., Fanuzzi, G., Vivoli, G., Sturloni, N., Cavazzuti, G., Tampieri, A., & Tartoni, P. L. (1989). Relationship between lead exposure indicators and neuropsychological performance in children. *Developmental Medicine and Child Neurology, 31,* 181–190.

Berney, B. (1993). Round and round it goes: The epidemiology of childhood lead poisoning, 1950–1990. *Milbank Quarterly, 71,* 3–39.

Biederman, J., Faraone, S. V., Mick, E., Spencer, T., Wilens, T., Kiely, K., Guite, J., Ablon, J. S., Reed, E., & Warburton, R. (1995b). High risk for attention deficit hyperactivity disorder among children of parents with childhood onset of the disorder: A pilot study. *American Journal of Psychiatry, 152,* 431–435.

Biederman, J., Milberger, S., Faraone, S. V., Kiely, K., Guite, J., Mick, E., Ablon, S., Warburton, R., & Reed, E. (1995a). Family-environment risk factors for attention-deficit hyperactivity disorder. *Archives of General Psychiatry, 52,* 464–470.

Bliss, J., edited by D. J. Cohen & D. X. Freedman. (1980). Sensory experiences of Gilles de la Tourette syndrome. *Archives of General Psychiatry, 37,* 1343–1347.

Campfield, L. A., Smith, F. J., Guisez, Y., Devos, R., & Burn, P. (1995). Recombinant mouse OB protein: Evidence for a peripheral signal linking adiposity and central neural networks. *Science, 269,* 546–552.

Castellanos, F. X., Giedd, J. N., Eckburg, P., Marsh, W. L., Vaituzis, A. C., Kaysen, D., Hamburger, S. D., & Rapoport, J. L. (1994). Quantitative morphology of the caudate nucleus in attention deficit hyperactivity disorder. *American Journal of Psychiatry, 151,* 1791–1796.

Centers for Disease Control (1991). *Preventing lead poisoning in young children.* Atlanta, GA: U.S. Department of Health and Human Services.

Cloninger, C. R., Bohman, M., & Sigvardsson, S. (1981). Inheritance of alcohol abuse: Cross-fostering analysis of adopted men. *Archives of General Psychiatry, 38,* 861–868.

Cohen, N. J., & Eichenbaum, H. (1993). *Memory, amnesia, and the hippocampal system.* Cambridge, MA: MIT Press.

Comings, D. E. (1994). Tourette syndrome: A hereditary neuropsychiatric spectrum disorder. *Annals of Clinical Psychiatry, 6,* 235–247.

Cook, E. H., Jr., Stein, M. A., Krasowski, M. D., Cox, N. J., Olkon, D. M., Kieffer, J. E., & Leventhal, B. L. (1995). Association of attention-deficit disorder and the dopamine transporter gene. *American Journal of Human Genetics, 56,* 993–998.

Coryslechta, D. A. (1995). Relationships between lead-induced learning impairments and changes in dopaminergic, cholinergic, and glutamatergic neurotransmitter system functions. *Annual Review of Pharmacology and Toxicology, 35,* 391–415.

Creak, M. (1961). Schizophrenic syndrome in childhood. *British Medical Journal, 2,* 889–890.

Creasey, H., Rumsey, J. M., Schwartz, M., Duara, R., Rapoport, J. L., & Rapoport, S. I. (1986). Brain morphometry in autistic men as measured by volumetric computed tomography. *Archives of Neurology, 43,* 669–672.

Desmond, M. M., & Wilson, G. S. (1975). Neonatal abstinence syndrome: Recognition and diagnosis. *Addictive Diseases, 2,* 113–121.

Dietrich, K. N., Berger, O. G., & Succop, P. A. (1993). Lead exposure and the motor developmental status of urban six-year-old children in the Cincinnati prospective study. *Pediatrics, 91,* 301–307.

Dilalla, L. F., Kagan, J., & Reznick, J. S. (1994). Genetic etiology of behavioral-inhibition among 2-year-old children. *Infant Behavior & Development, 17,* 405–412.

Duara, R., Kushch, A., Gross-Glenn, K., Barker, W. W., Jallad, B., Pascal, S., Loewenstein, D. A., Sheldon, J., Rabin, M., Levin, B., & Lubs, H. (1991). Neuroanatomic differences between dyslexic and normal readers on magnetic resonance imaging scans. *Archives of Neurology, 48,* 410–416.

Dyer, F. J. (1993). Clinical presentation of the lead-poisoned child on mental ability tests. *Journal of Clinical Psychology, 49,* 94–101.

Farah, M. (1990). *Visual agnosia.* Cambridge, MA: MIT Press.

Feingold, B. (1975). *Why your child is hyperactive.* New York: Random House.

Fergusson, D. M., Fergusson, J. E., Horwood, L. J., & Kinzett, N. G. (1988a). A longitudinal study of dentine lead levels, intelligence, school performance and behaviour: I. Dentine lead levels and exposure to environmental risk factors. *Journal of Child Psychology and Psychiatry and Allied Disciplines, 29,* 781–792.

Fergusson, D. M., Fergusson, J. E., Horwood, L. J., & Kinzett, N. G. (1988b). A longitudinal study of dentine lead levels, intelligence, school performance and behaviour: II. Dentine lead and cognitive ability. *Journal of Child Psychology and Psychiatry and Allied Disciplines, 29,* 793–809.

Fergusson, D. M., Fergusson, J. E., Horwood, L. J., & Kinzett, N. G. (1988c). A longitudinal study of dentine lead levels, intelligence, school performance and behaviour: III. Dentine lead and exposure to environmental risk factors. *Journal of Child Psychology and Psychiatry and Allied Disciplines, 29,* 811–824.

Gadow, K. D., Sverd, J., Sprafkin, J., Nolan, E. E., & Ezor, S. N. (1995). Efficacy of methylphenidate for attention-deficit hyperactivity disorder in children with tic disorder. *Archives of General Psychiatry, 52,* 444–455.

Geiger, G., Lettvin, J. Y., & Fahle, M. (1994). Dyslexic children learn a new visual strategy for reading: A controlled experiment. *Vision Research, 34,* 1223–1233.

Geiger, G., Lettvin, Y. Y., & Zegarra-Moran, O. (1992). Task-determined strategies of visual process. *Cognitive Brain Research, 1,* 39–52.

Gelernter, J., Pauls, D. L., Leckman, J., Kidd, K. K., & Kurlan, R. (1994). $D_2$ dopamine receptor alleles do not influence severity of Tourette's syndrome. *Archives of Neurology, 51,* 397–400.

Gillberg, C., & Gillberg, I. C. (1983). Infantile autism: A total population study of reduced optimality in the pre-, peri-, and neonatal period. *Journal of Autism and Developmental Disorders, 13,* 153–166.

Gillberg, C., Terenius, L., & Lönnerholm, G. (1985). Endorphin activity in childhood psychosis. *Archives of General Psychiatry, 42,* 780–783.

Gillberg, C., Wahlström, J., & Hagberg, B. (1984). Infantile autism and Rett's syndrome: Common chromosomal denominator? *Lancet, ii,* (8411), 1094–1095.

Glass, L., Evans, H. E., & Rajegowda, B. K. (1975). Neonatal narcotic withdrawal. In R. W. Richter (Ed.), *Medical aspects of drug abuse* (pp. 124–133). Hagerstown, MD: Harper & Row.

Glotzer, D. E., Bauchner, H., Freedberg, K. A., & Palfrey, S. (1994). Screening for childhood lead poisoning: A cost-minimization analysis. *American Journal of Public Health, 84,* 110–112.

Goldman, P. S. (1976). The role of experience in recovery of function following orbital prefrontal lesions in infant monkeys. *Neuropsychologia, 14,* 401–412.

Goldman-Rakic, P. (1994). Specification of higher cortical functions. In S. H. Broman & J. Grafman (Eds.), *Atypical cognitive deficits in developmental disorders* (pp. 3–17). Hillsdale, NJ: Erlbaum.

Gordon, M. (1983). *The Gordon Diagnostic System.* DeWitt, NY: Gordon Systems.

Halaas, J. L., Gajiwala, K. S., Maffei, M., Cohen, S. L., Chair, B. T., Rabinowitz, D., Lallone, R. L., Burley, S. I., & Friedman, J. M. (1995). Weight-reducing effects of the plasma protein encoded by the *obese* gene. *Science, 269,* 543–546.

Harley, J. P., Ray, R. S., Tomasi, L., Eichman, P. L., Mathews, C. G., Chun, R., Cleeland, C. S., & Traisman E. (1978). Hyperkinesis and food additives: Testing the Feingold hypothesis. *Pediatrics, 61,* 818–828.

Hécaen, H., Perenin, M. T., & Jennerod, M. (1984). The effects of cortical lesions in children: Language and visual functions. In C. R. Almli & S. Finger (Eds.), *Early brain damage* (pp. 277–298). Orlando, FL: Academic Press.

Herrnstein, R. J., & Murray, C. (1994). *The bell curve:*

*Intelligence and class structure in American life*. New York: Free Press.

Hobson, R. P. (1993). *Autism and the development of mind*. Hove, Eng.: Erlbaum.

Householder, J., Hatcher, R., Burns, W., & Chasnoff, I. (1982). Infants born to narcotic-addicted mothers. *Psychological Bulletin, 92*, 453–468.

Huntington's Disease Collaborative Research Group (1993). A novel gene containing a trinucleotide repeat that is expanded and unstable on Huntington's disease chromosomes. *Cell, 72*, 971–983.

Hur, Y. M., & Bouchard, T. J. (1995). Genetic influences on perceptions of childhood family environment: A reared apart twin study. *Child Development, 66*, 330–345.

Hutchens, T. A., & Hynd, G. W. (1987). Medications and the school-age child and adolescent: A review. *School Psychology Review, 16*, 527–542.

Hynd, G. W., Hern, K. L., Voeller, K. K., & Marshall, R. M. (1991). Neurobiological basis of attention-deficit hyperactivity disorders (ADHD). *School Psychology Review, 20*, 174–186.

Hynd, G. W., & Semrud-Clikeman, M. (1989). Dyslexia and brain morphology. *Psychological Bulletin, 106*, 447–482.

Jeddi, E. (1970). Confort du contact et thermoregulation comportementale [Contact comfort and behavioral thermoregulation]. *Physiology & Behavior, 5*, 1487–1493.

Jernigan, T. L., & Bellugi, U. (1994). Neuroanatomical distinctions between Williams and Down syndromes. In S. H. Broman & J. Grafman (Eds.), *Atypical cognitive deficits in developmental disorders* (pp. 57–66). Hillsdale, NJ: Erlbaum.

Kalat, J. W. (1978). Letter to the editor: Speculations on similarities between autism and opiate addiction. *Journal of Autism and Childhood Schizophrenia, 8*, 477–479.

Kanner, L. (1943). Autistic disturbances of affective contact. *Nervous Child, 2*, 217–250.

Kleinschmidt, A., Bear, M. F., & Singer, W. (1987). Blockade of "NMDA" receptors disrupts experience-dependent plasticity of kitten striate cortex. *Science, 238*, 355–358.

Kolb, B., & Whishaw, I. Q. (1989). Plasticity in the neocortex: Mechanisms underlying recovery from early brain damage. *Progress in Neurobiology, 32*, 235–276.

Leboyer, M., Bouvard, M. P., Recasens, C., Philippe, A., Guilloud-Bataille, M., Bondoux, D., Tabuteau, F., Dugas, M., Panksepp, J., & Launay, J.-M. (1994). Difference between plasma N- and C-terminally directed β-endorphin immunoreactivity in infantile autism. *American Journal of Psychiatry, 151*, 1797–1801.

Leckman, J. F., Goodman, W. K., Anderson, G. M., Riddle, M. A., Chappell, P. B., McSwiggan-Hardin, M. T., McDougle, C. J., Scahill, L. D.,

Ort, S. I., Pauls, D. L., Cohen, D. J., & Price, L. H. (1995). Cerebrospinal fluid biogenic amines in obsessive compulsive disorder, Tourette's syndrome, and healthy controls. *Neuropsychopharmacology, 12*, 73–86.

Levine, M. D. (1987). Attention deficits: The diverse effects of weak control systems in childhood. *Pediatric annals, 16*, 117–130.

Livingstone, M. S., Rosen, G. D., Drislane, F. W., & Galaburda, A. M. (1991). Physiological and anatomical evidence for a magnocellular defect in developmental dyslexia. *Proceedings of the National Academy of Sciences (U.S.A.), 88*, 7943–7947.

Loehlin, J. C. (1992). *Genes and environment in personality development*. Newbury Park, CA: Sage.

Lovaas, O. I., Koegel, R. L., & Schreibman, L. (1979). Stimulus overselectivity in autism: A review of research. *Psychological Bulletin, 86*, 1236–1254.

Lyngbye, T., Hansen, O. N., & Grandjean, P. (1988). Neurological deficits in children: Medical risk factors and lead exposure. *Neurotoxicology and Teratology, 10*, 531–537.

Manji, H. K., Potter, W. Z., & Lenox, R. H. (1995). Signal transduction pathways. *Archives of General Psychiatry, 52*, 531–543.

Mason, D. A., & Frick, P. J. (1994). The heritability of antisocial behavior: A meta-analysis of twin and adoption studies. *Journal of Psychopathology and Behavioral Assessment, 16*, 301–323.

Mazzocco, M. M. M., Freund, L. S., Baumgardner, T. L., Forman, L., & Reiss, A. L. (1995). Neuropsychological and psychosocial effects of the FMR-1 full mutation: Case report of monozygotic twins discordant for the fragile X syndrome. *Neuropsychology, 9*, 470–480.

Migeon, B. R., Dunn, M. A., Thomas, G., Schmeckpeper, B. J., & Naidu, S. (1995). Studies of X inactivation and isodisomy in twins provide further evidence that the X chromosome is not involved in Rett syndrome. *American Journal of Human Genetics, 56*, 647–653.

Milich, R., Wolraich, M., & Lindgren, S. (1986). Sugar and hyperactivity: A critical review of empirical findings. *Clinical Psychology Review, 6*, 493–513.

Nantwi, K. D., & Schoener, E. P. (1993). Cocaine and dopaminergic actions in rat neostriatum. *Neuropharmacology, 32*, 807–817.

Needleman, H. L., Schell, A., Bellinger, D., Leviton, A., & Allred, E. N. (1990). The long-term effects of exposure to low doses of lead in childhood: An 11-year follow-up report. *New England Journal of Medicine, 322*, 83–88.

Ornitz, E. M., Atwell, C. W., Kaplan, A. R., & Westlake, J. R. (1985). Brain-stem dysfunction in autism. *Archives of General Psychiatry, 42*, 1018–1025.

Ornitz, E. M., & Ritvo, E. R. (1976). Medical assessment. In E. R. Ritvo (Ed.), *Autism* (pp. 7–23). New York: Spectrum.

Panksepp, J., Herman, B., & Vilberg, T. (1978). An opiate excess model of childhood autism. *Neuroscience Abstracts, 4* (Abstract 1601), 500.

Pellymounter, M. A., Cullen, M. J., Baker, M. B., Hecht, R., Winters, D., Boone, T., & Collins, F. (1995). Effects of the *obese* gene product on body weight regulation in *ob/ob* mice. *Science, 269,* 540–543.

Percy, A. K. (1995). Rett syndrome. *Current Opinion in Neurology, 8,* 156–160.

Pliszka, S. R. (1987). Tricyclic antidepressants in the treatment of children with attention deficit disorder. *Journal of the American Academy of Child and Adolescent Psychiatry, 26,* 127–132.

Pliszka, S. R., Maas, J. W., Javors, M. A., Rogeness, G. A., & Baker, J. (1994). Urinary catecholamines in attention-deficit hyperactivity disorder with and without comorbid anxiety. *Journal of the American Academy of Child and Adolescent Psychiatry, 33,* 1165–1173.

Plomin, R., Corley, R., DeFries, J. C., & Fulker, D. (1990). Individual differences in television viewing in early childhood: Nature as well as nurture. *Psychological Science, 1,* 371–377.

Pomerleau, O. F. (1995). Individual differences in sensitivity to nicotine: Implications for genetic research on nicotine dependence. *Behavior Genetics, 25,* 161–177.

Purves, D., & Hadley, R. D. (1985). Changes in the dendritic branching of adult mammalian neurones revealed by repeated imaging *in situ*. *Nature, 315,* 404–406.

Ream, N. W., Robinson, M. G., Richter, R. W., Hegge, F. W., & Holloway, H. C. (1975). Opiate dependence and acute abstinence. In R. W. Richter (Ed.), *Medical aspects of drug abuse* (pp. 81–123). Hagerstown, MD: Harper & Row.

Reynolds, C. R. (1989). Biological bases of behavior and school psychology: Riches or ruin? In M. J. Fine (Ed.), *School psychology: Cutting edges in research and practice* (pp. 54–62). Washington, DC: NEA/NASP.

Ritvo, E. R., Freeman, B. J., Mason-Brothers, A., Mo, A., & Ritvo, A. M. (1985). Concordance for the syndrome of autism in 40 pairs of afflicted twins. *American Journal of Psychiatry, 142,* 74–77.

Ritvo, E. R., Jorde, L. B., Mason-Brothers, A., Freeman, B. J., Pingree, C., Jones, M. B., McMahon, W. M., Petersen, P. B., Jenson, W. R., & Mo, A. (1989). The UCLA-University of Utah epidemiological survey of autism: Recurrence risk estimates and genetic counseling. *American Journal of Psychiatry, 146,* 1032–1036.

Rudelli, R. D., Brown, W. T., Wissniewski, K., Jenkins, E. C., Laure-Kamionowska, M., Connell, F., & Wisniewski, H. M. (1985). Adult fragile X syndrome. Clinico-neuropathologic findings. *Acta Neuropathologica, 67,* 289–295.

Ruff, H. A., & Bijur, P. E. (1989). The effects of low to moderate lead levels on neurobehavioral functioning in children: Toward a conceptual model. *Journal of Developmental and Behavioral Pediatrics, 10,* 103–109.

Rumsey, J. M., Duara, R., Grady, C., Rapoport, J. L., Margolin, R. A., Rapoport, S. I., & Cutler, N. R. (1985). Brain metabolism in autism. *Archives of General Psychiatry, 42,* 448–455.

Rush, D., & Callahan, K. R. (1989). Exposure to passive cigarette smoking and child development: A critical review. *Annals of the New York Academy of Sciences, 562,* 74–100.

Sahley, T. L., & Panksepp, J. (1987). Brain opioids and autism: An updated analysis of possible linkages. *Journal of Autism and Developmental Disorders, 17,* 201–216.

Sandman, C. A., Barron, J. L., Demet, E. M., Chicz-Demet, A., Rothenberg, S. J., & Zea, F. J. (1990). Opioid peptides and perinatal development: Is beta-endorphin a natural teratogen? *Annals of the New York Academy of Sciences, 579,* 91–108.

Satz, P., Strauss, E., & Whitaker, H. (1990). The ontogeny of hemispheric specialization: Some old hypotheses revisited. *Brain and Language, 38,* 596–614.

Schlaug, G., Jäncke, L., Huang, Y., & Steinmetz, H. (1995). In vivo evidence of structural brain asymmetry in musicians. *Science, 267,* 699–701.

Schopler, E. (1987). Specific and nonspecific factors in the effectiveness of a treatment system. *American Psychologist, 42,* 376–383.

Shaywitz, B. A., Yager, R. D., & Klopper, J. H. (1976). Selective brain dopamine depletion in developing rats: An experimental model of minimal brain dysfunction. *Science, 191,* 305–307.

Sherrington, R., Rogaev, E. I., Liang, Y., Rogaeva, E. A., Levesque, G., Ikeda, M., Chi, H., Lin, C., Li, G., Holman, K., Tsuda, T., Mar, L., Focin, J.-F., Bruni, A. C., Montesi, M. P., Sorbi, S., Rainero, I., Pinessi, L., Nee, L., Chumakov, I., Pollen, D., Brookes, A., Sanseau, P., Polinsky, R. J., Wasco, W., DaSilva, H. A. R., Haines, J. L., Pericak-Vance, M. A., Tanzi, R. E., Roses, A. D., Fraser, P. E., Rommens, J. M., & St. George-Hyslop, P. H. (1995). Cloning of a gene bearing missense mutations in early-onset familial Alzheimer's disease. *Nature, 375,* 754–760.

Silva, P. A., Hughes, P., Williams, S., & Faed, J. M. (1988). Blood lead, intelligence, reading attainment, and behaviour in eleven year old children in Dunedin, New Zealand. *Journal of Child Psychology and Psychiatry and Allied Disciplines, 29,* 43–52.

Singer, H. S., Dickson, J., Martinie, D., & Levine, M. (1995). Second messenger systems in Tourette's syndrome. *Journal of the Neurological Sciences, 128,* 78–83.

Singer, H. S., Schuerholz, L. J., & Denckla, M. B. (1995). Learning difficulties in children with

Tourette syndrome. *Journal of Child Neurology, 10* (Suppl. 1), S58–S61.

Spencer, T., Wilens, T., Biederman, J., Faraone, S. V., Ablon, J. S., & Lapey, K. (1995). A double-blind, crossover comparison of methylphenidate and placebo in adults with childhood-onset attention-deficit hyperactivity disorder. *Archives of General Psychiatry, 52,* 434–443.

Squire, L. R. (1992). Memory and the hippocampus: A synthesis from findings with rats, monkeys, and humans. *Psychological Review, 99,* 195–231.

Stein, D. G., Finger, S., & Hart, T. (1983). Brain damage and recovery: Problems and perspectives. *Behavioral and Neural Biology, 37,* 185–222.

Strupp, B. J., Bunsey, M., Levitsky, D. A., & Hamberger, K. (1994). Deficient cumulative learning: An animal model of retarded cognitive development. *Neurotoxicology and Teratology, 16,* 71–79.

Sullivan, R. C. (1980). Why do autistic children? . . . *Journal of Autism and Developmental Disorders, 10,* 231–241.

Takeuchi, A. H., & Hulse, S. H. (1993). Absolute pitch. *Psychological Bulletin, 113,* 345–361.

Telvi, L., Leboyer, M., Chiron, C., Feingold, J., & Ponsot, G. (1994). Is Rett syndrome a chromosome breakage syndrome? *American Journal of Medical Genetics, 51,* 602–605.

Thomson, G. O., Raab, G. M., Hepburn, W. A., Hunter, R., Fulton, M., & Laxen, D. P. (1989). Blood-lead levels and children's behaviour—Results from the Edinburgh lead study. *Journal of Child Psychology and Psychiatry and Allied Disciplines, 30,* 515–528.

Tsai, L., Stewart, M. A., & August, G. (1981). Implication of sex differences in the familial transmission of infantile autism. *Journal of Autism and Developmental Disorders, 11,* 165–173.

Tu, G. C., & Israel, Y. (1995). Alcohol-consumption by Orientals in North America is predicted largely by a single gene. *Behavior Genetics, 25,* 59–65.

Vaillant, G. E., & Milofsky, E. S. (1982). The etiology of alcoholism: A prospective viewpoint. *American Psychologist, 37,* 494–503.

Viken, R. J., Rose, R. J., Kaprio, J., & Koskenvuo, M. (1994). A developmental genetic analysis of adult personality: Extraversion and neuroticism from 18 to 59 years of age. *Journal of Personality and Social Psychology, 66,* 722–730.

Waller, N. G., Kojetin, B. A., Bouchard, T. J., Jr., Lykken, D. T., & Tellegen, A. (1990). Genetic and environmental influences on religious interests, attitudes, and values: A study of twins reared apart and together. *Psychological Science, 1,* 138–142.

Wender, E. H. (1986). The food additive-free diet in the treatment of behavior disorders: A review. *Journal of Developmental and Behavioral Pediatrics, 7,* 35–42.

West, J. R., Hodges, C. A., & Black, A. C., Jr. (1981). Prenatal exposure to ethanol alters the organization of hippocampal mossy fibers in rats. *Science, 211,* 957–959.

White, B. B., & White, M. S. (1987). Autism from the inside. *Medical Hypotheses, 24,* 223–229.

Willemsen-Swinkels, S. H. N., Buitelaar, J. K., Nijhof, G. H., & vanEngeland, H. (1995). Failure of naltrexone hydrochloride to reduce self-injurious and autistic behavior in mentally retarded adults. *Archives of General Psychiatry, 52,* 766–773.

Winneke, G., Brockhaus, A., Collet, W., & Kramer, U. (1989). Modulation of lead-induced performance deficit in children by varying signal rate in a serial choice reaction task. Special issue: Interdisciplinary aspects of neurotoxicity. *Neurotoxicology and Teratology, 11,* 587–592.

Zagon, I. S., Goodman, S. R., & McLaughlin, P. J. (1993). Zeta ($\zeta$), the opioid growth factor receptor: Identification and characterization of binding subunits. *Brain Research, 605,* 50–56.

Zahn, T. P., Rapoport, J. L., & Thompson, C. L. (1980). Autonomic and behavioral effects of dextroamphetamine and placebo in normal and hyperactive prepubertal boys. *Journal of Abnormal Child Psychology, 8,* 145–160.

Zametkin, A. J. (1989). The neurobiology of attention-deficit hyperactivity disorder: A synopsis. *Psychiatric Annals, 19,* 584–586.

Zhang, Y., Proenca, R., Maffei, M., Barone, M., Leopold, L., & Friedman, J. M. (1994). Positional cloning of the mouse *obese* gene and its human homologue. *Nature, 372,* 425–432.

Zihl, J., von Cramon, D., & Mai, N. (1983). Selective disturbance of movement vision after bilateral brain damage. *Brain, 106,* 313–340.

# PSYCHOLOGICAL
# AND
# EDUCATIONAL
# ASSESSMENT

•

## CHAPTER 12

# ROLES OF DIAGNOSIS AND CLASSIFICATION IN SCHOOL PSYCHOLOGY

RANDY W. KAMPHAUS[1]
*University of Georgia*
CECIL R. REYNOLDS
*Texas A & M University*
CAROLYN IMPERATO-MCCAMMON
*University of Georgia*

The classification of children's problems and assets has long been, and is likely to remain, a central function of school psychologists. School psychologists, and in fact all psychologists, are "expected" to provide diagnostic services by their consumers. Witness, for example, the continuing high level of interest in the diagnosis of attention deficit hyperactivity disorder (ADHD) among parents, teachers, adult self-referrals, pediatricians, school administrators, children, and others.

In many ways, the core services provided by psychologists have changed little during the twentieth century. Indeed, the inaugural case of Lightner Witmer's now famous Philadelphia clinic, in March 1896, required a careful diagnosis. According to Witmer (1907), the psychology student evaluating the case, Margaret T. Maquire, "was imbued with the idea that a psychologist should be able, through examination, to ascertain the causes of a deficiency in spelling and to recommend the appropriate pedagogical treatment for its amelioration or cure" (p. 2). In a general

sense, we continue to believe that psychologists ought to be able to recommend treatments based on careful diagnoses that have a better than random chance of success. The probability of success in such endeavors varies as a function of many variables but mostly with regard to the actual disorder itself.

The processes of classification and diagnosis and their many variants represent a complex issue that is deserving of its own volume. The terms *classification* and *diagnosis* are not entirely interchangeable. Psychologists make many classification decisions that would not be considered diagnoses per se, such as "resistant consultee," "uncooperative parent," "overachiever," "performance deficit," and "unsatisfactory classroom climate." Typically, the term *diagnosis* is reserved for classifications that are associated with medical (and medical-like) diagnostic systems.

This is not to say, however, that the two processes differ. One could, for example, "diagnose" a person as a resistant consultee. Classification is an inherent subset in diagnosis, although diagnosis has come to represent a more restrictive term among psychologists and the public. It refers to the process of classifying a child according to popular systems of classifica-

[1]The authors wish to express their gratitude to Nancy Hatcher for making final changes in the manuscript.

tion of psychopathology and/or special education. In this chapter, the terms *diagnosis* and *classification* are used interchangeably, and they are defined as "the process of placing psychological phenomena into distinct categories according to some specified set of rules" (Kamphaus & Frick, 1996).

We also note that diagnosis exists on different levels. The determination of eligibility for participation in a school-based, federally reimbursed program for children with emotional disturbances is a crude form of diagnosis. This type is accomplished more easily and accurately than, for example, a more thorough diagnosis that would provide a detailed picture of the development and nature of the particular form of the emotional disturbance (e.g., distinguishing among an overanxious disorder of childhood, posttraumatic stress disorder, major depressive disorder, and ADHD). The latter leads more readily to differentiated treatments, whereas the former is a simple declaration of eligibility to receive services. Unfortunately, in many school systems, the diagnostic process ends with the diagnosis of eligibility for services. The second form of diagnosis is clearly more in line with the functioning of school psychologists as high-level professionals who are involved with the expectations of the founder of school psychology, Lightner Witmer.

This chapter must of necessity present only a glimpse of selected issues of diagnosis. Accordingly, the discussion focuses on a few key issues that were selected with one objective in mind: to familiarize the school psychologist in training with historical, treatment-related, and other diagnostic issues commonly faced by the school psychologist (and most psychologists). Knowledge of these issues is central to the students' ability to develop an adequate long-term perspective of diagnostic issues. This perspective allows the student to incorporate and respond to new diagnostic knowledge in a more sophisticated manner.

# USES OF DIAGNOSTIC SYSTEMS

Diagnostic systems continue to be widely used for a variety of reasons (Kamphaus & Frick, 1996). First, they remain the most well-developed procedure for determining the need for services. Classification schemes may also be used for related goals such as determining the intensity of treatments. Formal diagnostic systems will probably continue to be used for placement decisions until decision-making systems with better validity, reliability, and practicality are designed.

## Sample Case—Determining Service Need

Marta is a 15-year-old high school sophomore who has a lengthy history of academic underachievement. She has frequently been cited by teachers for failure to work up to her potential. Consequently, she has always had passing grades but few high grades. She occasionally shows evidence of her potential during class discussions and question sessions, when she displays keen insights and an extraordinary memory. If a test is based exclusively on class notes, she does well. In direct contrast, if performance on the test is based on homework assignments, she does poorly. She has been seen by her high school counselor, who reports that Marta is often sad because of family problems. She is also nervous and somewhat shy. Parent conferences have resulted in referrals to her family physician, who has not identified any significant mental health problems.

One day, however, Marta's mother called her homeroom teacher to report that Marta had been hospitalized in a general hospital psychiatric unit for observation because of suicidal threats. The hospital staff completed an evaluation that resulted in the DSM-IV diagnosis of major depression, recurrent and severe.

Because of this diagnosis, school personnel will probably treat Marta differently upon her return to school. First, the diagnosis may or may not make her eligible for special education services, although she would probably receive or be considered for them. She may be required to meet regularly with the school counselor or psychologist to ensure that she is receiving adequate counseling for school problems that may be associated with her depression. She is also now likely to receive additional interventions to improve her homework; for example, her teachers may now be willing to create a reinforcement program. These school-based interventions are mild and relatively noninvasive. Marta may eventually qualify for special education services if the school determines that she has a severe emotional disturbance. The main point in Marta's case is that her ongoing depressive behavior becomes more significant in the eyes of institutions when a diagnostic label is applied, thus making her eligible for services that were heretofore viewed as unnecessary.

Second, the use of a formal, codified system of diagnosis such as the DSM-IV (American Psychiatric Association, 1994) or even the cruder system of diagnosis in the reauthorization of the Individuals with Disabilities Education Act (IDEA) belies the often informal, derogatory labeling that may occur among less informed teachers or other school personnel. Given the most common characteristics of major depressive disorder among children of Marta's age, teachers may have labeled her lazy, disinterested in school, or worse. A considerable body of literature, known for many years (e.g., see Reynolds, 1979), indicates that such informal labeling of children is frequent in educational settings and is most often wrong.

Third, a classification system allows psychologists to communicate more clearly and efficiently with one another, thereby ensuring more efficient delivery of services (Kamphaus & Frick, 1996). It aids communication by providing operational definitions for terms. For example, because of a long history of classification work, psychologists have a relatively consistent understanding of a case of mental retardation. On the other hand, the consistency of our understanding of the "diagnosis" of central auditory processing deficit is not universal at this time.

If a child is being transferred to a new school system, knowledge of previous diagnoses allow the receiving psychologist to begin anticipating needed services. A child who arrives at a new school district with the diagnosis of gifted is going to create different expectations than a child who enters with a diagnosis of dementia subsequent to traumatic brain injury. Of course, such labels can be used to stigmatize a child and deliver inappropriate or inferior services. If, however, a diagnostic category is highly valid, then knowledge of it is more likely to communicate accurate information.

Similarly, a child may be described by a psychologist as shy, a relatively imprecise term that is not a diagnostic label. This description of the child may, therefore, communicate little about a child to another psychologist who will become involved in treatment. When queried, the psychologist may then say that the child is anxious. This label may communicate some additional information about the child's behavior, but we do not yet know if anxious is a symptom or a diagnosis. If, however, the psychologist goes on to say that the child has recently been diagnosed with separation anxiety disorder, early onset, the second psychologist can then make some more specific predictions about the child's behavior. Based on this diagnosis, the new psychologist will be more likely to observe parent and child interactions closely.

## Sample Case—Enhancing Communication

Jorge is a five-year-old male who is entering kindergarten in the fall. He was previously enrolled in a special needs preschool for one year. His preschool director has sent a letter to his new school, describing his behavior during the previous year. Jorge was described as a child with many behavior problems including setting fires, biting other children, and fighting. He had poor peer relationships and some academic delays. A diagnosis, however, was not included.

The detailed information about specific behavior problems in this case is helpful in that the psychologist can develop needed assessment and intervention plans. However, the director omitted some crucial pieces of information. According to the psychologist who assessed him recently, Jorge's development was normal until a few months before being placed in preschool. At that time he saw his mother being shot in an attempted car-jacking. The psychologist made the diagnosis of posttraumatic stress disorder (PTSD). Knowledge of this diagnosis and historical information would almost certainly cause the receiving psychologist to conceptualize this case differently. The psychologist may have initially thought that Jorge was displaying early evidence of a disruptive behavior disorder. The diagnosis of PTSD, however, communicates a different kind of information that is related to special needs and dictates a radically different form of intervention.

Fourth, diagnostic systems allow psychologists to apply research to practice (Kamphaus & Frick, 1996). If each case is evaluated with idiosyncratic methods and classified accordingly, a research base cannot be developed as efficiently. Again, mental retardation serves as an excellent example. As a result of comorbidity research, we now know from the American Association on Mental Retardation (AAMR) that children with a diagnosis of mental retardation are at higher risk (20% to 35%) for other mental health problems than children who do not have this disability (15% to 19%). These children are at increased risk for schizophrenia, personality disorders, depression, ADHD, and other mental health problems. These findings have led to the proscription that all children with this diagnosis should receive a thorough social-emotional evaluation to ensure that they are not also suffering the ill effects of a significant mental health condition (American Association on Mental Retardation, 1992). These comorbidity findings also suggest that psychologists should engage in preventive interventions for children who have been so diagnosed.

Similarly, it is now clear, although perhaps little known, that children with a diagnosis of ADHD are at higher risk for an anxiety disorder at a later point in development (Last, 1993). The diagnosis of ADHD allows the clinician to be vigilant for additional problems that may not be anticipated if based merely on conventional wisdom. Subsequently, because of findings in other areas of educationally handicapping conditions, such as learning disabilities, orthopedic impairments, and the like, IDEA legislation now requires a behavioral assessment as a part of every school-based determination of whether a student has a disability. If research is to guide practice, there must be direct links between the two. Diagnoses provide one way to access research to enlighten practice.

## Sample Case—Applying Research Findings

Ivan is a 12-year-old male who was referred for placement in a special education program. He was evaluated on two previous occasions and did not qualify for special education services. Although below-average academic achievement and intelligence scores were found, they were not low enough to warrant a diagnosis of mild mental retardation. He also showed evidence of hyperactivity and attention problems in previous evaluations, but the symptoms were thought to be subsyndromal. His adjustment to school at that time was poor. He was failing all of his middle school classes, and teachers did not feel that he had the academic competencies to perform adequately in the regular curriculum. In addition, his teachers noted that his behavior was immature for his age, and he was considered to be a social outcast. He had difficulty sitting still in class and paying adequate attention to lectures. His parents noted deteriorating behavior at home and an increasingly negative attitude toward schooling.

Ivan was found to have significant impairments in cognitive development and adaptive behavior that warrant a diagnosis of mild mental retardation. This diagnosis also triggered a thorough social-emotional assessment consistent with AAMR guidelines. As a result of further diagnostic work, Ivan was found to meet and exceed diagnostic criteria for ADHD–combined type. The presence of ADHD had previously been overlooked, and his behavior problems were erroneously attributed to global developmental delay (American Association on Mental Retardation, 1992). Consequently, Ivan responded favorably to pharmacological treatment with methylphenidate, which resulted in better adaptation in the classroom and improved work output.

These sample cases are intended to show that diagnostic systems exist for several reasons, such as identifying service needs, enhancing communication among professionals, and basing practice on research findings. There are also financial, administrative, advocacy, and other reasons for diagnostic systems. Apparently, there are enough incentives to use diagnostic systems that they continue to propagate and change form. Psychologists in training should use diagnostic systems with adequate understanding of the objectives that they are trying to achieve.

## DIAGNOSTIC SYSTEMS

There are a number of diagnostic and pseudodiagnostic systems, including Section 504 of the Rehabilitation Act of 1974 and the American Association on Mental Retardation's (1992) publication *Mental Retardation: Definition, Classification, and Systems of Support*, among others. The classification systems (essentially diagnostic) associated with the 1990 implementation of the Individuals with Disabilities Education Act (PL 101–475) and the *Diagnostic and Statistical Manual of Mental Disorders* (American Psychiatric Association, 1994) have had the most substantial influence on the daily diagnostic work of the psychologist who practices with school-aged children.

## The Diagnostic and Statistical Manual of Mental Disorders

The modern practice of diagnosis traces its roots to European physicians of the 1600s. The work of Sydenham, Griesenger, and Kraepelin provided the foundation for the development of current diagnostic systems (Kamphaus, Morgan, Cox, & Powell, 1995). Before this era, mental disorders were often thought to be the result of supernatural phenomena, and the mentally ill were accordingly treated with scorn, fear, and

**TABLE 12.1  Summary of DSM-IV Axes I and II Diagnoses Relevant to Children and Adolescents**

| | |
|---|---|
| Intellectual | Mental retardation |
| Learning | Mathematics disorder |
| | Disorder of written expression |
| | Reading disorder |
| Language and speech | Expressive language disorder |
| | Mixed receptive-expressive |
| | Language disorder |
| | Phonological disorder |
| | Stuttering |
| | Selective mutism |
| Motor skills | Developmental coordination disorder |
| Pervasive developmental | Autistic disorder |
| | Rhett's disorder |
| | Childhood disintegrative disorder |
| | Asperger's disorder |
| Behavioral | Attention-deficit hyperactivity Disorder |
| | Oppositional defiant disorder |
| | Conduct disorder |
| | Adjustment disorder with disturbance of conduct[a] |
| Emotional (anxiety) | Separation anxiety disorder |
| | Generalized anxiety disorder[a] |
| | Panic disorder[a] |
| | Agoraphobia[a] |
| | Social phobia[a] |
| | Obsessive compulsive disorder[a] |
| | Posttraumatic stress disorder[a] |
| | Adjustment disorder with anxious mood[a] |

torture. An early function of diagnosis was to disabuse society of such notions by linking diagnoses to specific natural (disease) phenomena.

The ancestor of the well-known modern version of the DSM–IV (American Psychiatric Association, 1994) was published in 1893. This publication was intended to serve the medical community worldwide; hence, it was entitled the *International Classification of Causes of Death* (Kamphaus et al., 1995). This manual was the foundation for the modern *International Statistical Classification of Diseases, Injuries, and Causes of Death* (ICD). Despite efforts to create a medical classification system that could be used internationally, differing diagnostic systems (although many of them have some similarity to the ICD) have been used in Egypt, China, and France, among other countries. The ICD system, however, does include an extensive compilation of mental disorders.

The DSM-IV fills the gaps in the ICD by providing a comprehensive classification of mental disorders (Kamphaus et al., 1995). Moreover, the latest version of the DSM attempted, for the first time, to provide scientific support for its diagnostic criteria. Much of the work in previous editions was based on "expert" judgment and other rational (nonempirical) methods. The DSM-IV used the following methods to develop many of its classifications (Widiger, Frances, Pincus, Davis, & First, 1991):

*Literature reviews.* Comprehensive reviews of psychopathology and related research literatures were sought or created in order to advise the work of committees. This process is more systematic than depending on the memories of committee members for a "review of the literature."

*Data reanalyses.* Some existing large data sets were reanalyzed in order to refine diagnostic criteria. These data sets were used in an iterative fashion for testing the applicability of proposed new diagnostic criteria.

**TABLE 12.1**    *(Continued)*

| | |
|---|---|
| Emotional (mood) | Major depression[a] |
| | Dysthymia[a] |
| | Bipolar disorders (I & II)[a] |
| | Cyclothymia[a] |
| | Adjustment disorder with depressed mood[a] |
| Identity | Gender identity disorder of childhood |
| | Reactive attachment disorder of infancy or early childhood |
| Physical (eating) | Anorexia nervosa[a] |
| | Bulimia nervosa[a] |
| | Pica |
| | Rumination disorder |
| Physical (motor) | Tourette's disorder |
| | Chronic motor or vocal tic disorder |
| | Transient tic disorder |
| | Stereotypic movement disorder |
| Physical (elimination) | Encopresis |
| | Enuresis |
| Physical (somatic) | Somatization disorder[a] |
| | Conversion disorder[a] |
| | Pain disorder[a] |
| | Hypochondriasis[a] |
| | Body dysmorphic disorder[a] |
| | Adjustment disorder with physical complaints[a] |
| Psychosis | Schizophrenia[a] |
| Substance-related disorders | Alcohol (amphetamine, cannabis, etc.) dependence[a] |

[a]Denotes disorders that have the same criteria for children and adults.

We are responsible, not DSM-IV, for the selection of disorders "most relevant" to children and adolescents and the way in which they are grouped.

Adapted from Box 3.3 of Kamphaus & Frick (1996), with permission.

*Field trials.* These data collection efforts were used for testing the reliability and validity of proposed diagnostic categories. A substantial field trial was conducted in order to develop diagnostic criteria for ADHD and the so-called disruptive behavior disorders (Lahey et al., 1996).

Diagnostic criteria for children and adolescents first appeared in the second revision of the DSM (DSM-II) in a short section entitled Disorders of Childhood and Adolescence (Kamphaus & Frick, 1996). The DSM-III expanded this section further under the heading Disorders Usually Evident in Infancy, Childhood, or Adolescence. This edition provided an expanded number of diagnoses with more descriptive information for each category (Kamphaus & Frick, 1996). Subsequently, the third, revised edition (DSM-III-R) placed ADHD and conduct disorder under the heading of Disruptive Behavior Disorders, and this version provided some research evidence for their differentiation (see Table 12.1).

## DSM-IV Diagnostic Criteria for ADHD

The ADHD criteria of the DSM-IV provide a useful example of the modern status of the DSM system because they are based on extensive research (Lahey et al., 1996). The minimum age for the onset of behaviors for ADHD to be diagnosed is seven years old; impairment must be observed in two or more settings that affect the person's life functioning in some manner for a minimum of six months. In the DSM-IV, two symptom lists yield three subtypes relative to hyperactive symptomatology.

The first type—attention deficit/hyperactivity disorder, predominantly inattentive type—refers to difficulty in sustaining attention, following and completing instructions, ignoring unimportant stimuli, organizing, and remembering. Furthermore, inattention is marked by frequent forgetfulness, loss of necessary items to complete tasks, and failure to give adequate attention to detail. The problems of attention are isolated from hyperactive or impulsive symptoms.

The second type—attention deficit/hyperactivity disorder, predominantly hyperactive-impulsive type—focuses on the presence of hyperactive and/or impulsive behaviors without problems of inattention. The associated behaviors include fidgeting, inappropriate movement in the classroom or other settings, excessive talking, constant energy, and difficulty in participating in quiet activities. The impulsive symptoms focus on behaviors that exhibit poor impulse control and impatience, especially in activities that require taking turns.

The third type is a combination of the two previous types, with the expression of at least six symptoms identified as being representative of inattention and hyperactivity-impulsivity; it is referred to as attention deficit/hyperactivity disorder, combined type.

Modern research has allowed the DSM system to make great strides in its psychometric sophistication (Kamphaus & Frick, 1996). At the same time, even the best diagnostic system is characterized by unwanted imperfections, much in the same way that psychological tests cannot avoid some amount of error variance. Moreover, even the most sophisticated diagnostic systems, like psychological tests, are prone to misapplication by poorly trained professionals (Cantwell, 1996; Reynolds, 1992).

## The Individuals with Disabilities Education Act

It would be simplistic to suggest that the exclusive purpose of the Individuals with Disabilities Education Act (PL 101-476) was to promulgate a new diagnostic nosology. The purpose of the act was to serve children with special needs in the public school rather than in residential or other settings. The development of the equivalent of a diagnostic system, however, has resulted, although it can readily be seen that the IDEA classification system has not benefited from continuous improvement.

Nevertheless, this classification system remains the most popular in U.S. school systems (Kamphaus & Frick, 1996). The categories for severe emotional disturbance, specific learning disabilities, and other conditions (see Table 12.2) are used to determine eligibility for special education and related services. Because of this use, the IDEA classification scheme is more widely used in schools than the DSM.

Unfortunately, the public schools are using this classification system (in sometimes slightly varied form) in the absence of empirical support. The IDEA diagnostic system has been roundly criticized for its limited conceptualization of severe emotional disturbance (Bower, 1982; Forness & Knitzer, 1992). A quick review of Table 12.2 gives the immediate impression that the IDEA nosology is not so well developed as the most recent edition of the DSM. It appears that researchers in child psychopathology have devoted most of their energies to improving the DSM, leaving the IDEA to suffer continuing neglect. In fact, newer multivariate approaches to child classification are currently receiving more research attention than the IDEA nosology. The IDEA did not undergo significant revision when recently reauthorized.

The IDEA nosology, more concerned with establishing eligibility for services, does not seek the diagnostic specificity of the ICD-9 or DSM-IV that is required to link specific interventions to diagnosis. The IDEA's only links are to categories of placement in special education, requiring a comprehensive assessment that leads to the development of the IEP (individualized educational plan), where interventions are specified. A more detailed diagnosis, such as suggested in the DSM-IV and like systems, is required at the IEP stage, whereas a more limited diagnostic decision (i.e., eligible or not eligible for services in the schools) is all that is required in the initial stage of diagnosis in the schools. The failure to understand the simple distinction between diagnosis as an eligibility decision and a more refined, detailed diagnosis for developing treatment plans has led some (most prominently Gresham & Gansle, 1992) to the simplistic conclusion that detailed diagnostic systems such as the DSM-IV are irrelevant to practice in school psychology. Obviously, we disagree, for reasons noted throughout this chapter and elsewhere (e.g., Reynolds, 1992).

**TABLE 12.2  Sample Special Education Eligibility Classifications from the Individuals with Disabilities Education Act**

(1) The term "children with disabilities" means children—with mental retardation, hearing impairments including deafness, speech or language impairments, visual impairments including blindness, serious emotional disturbance, orthopedic impairments, autism, traumatic brain injury, other health impairments, or specific learning disabilities.

(2) The term "children with specific learning disabilities" means those children who have a disorder in one or more of the basic psychological processes involved in understanding or in using language, spoken or written, which disorder may manifest itself in imperfect ability to listen, think, speak, read, write, spell, or do mathematical calculations. Such disorders include such conditions as perceptual disabilities, brain injury, minimal brain dysfunction, dyslexia, and developmental aphasia. Such term does not include children who have learning problems which are primarily the result of visual, hearing, or motor disabilities, of mental retardation, of emotional disturbance, or of environmental, cultural, or economic disadvantage. (Section 5[b][4])

(3) The term "seriously emotionally disturbed" means a condition exhibiting one or more of the following characteristics over a long period of time and to a marked degree, which adversely affects educational performance:

    (A) An inability to learn which cannot be explained by intellectual, sensory, or health factors;

    (B) An inability to build or maintain satisfactory relationships with peers and teachers;

    (C) Inappropriate types of behavior or feelings under normal circumstances;

    (D) A general pervasive mood of unhappiness/depression; or

    (E) A tendency to develop physical symptoms or fears associated with personal or school problems.

The term includes children who are schizophrenic (or autistic). The term does not include children who are socially maladjusted, unless it is determined that they are socially disturbed. (U.S. Department of Health, Education, and Welfare, 1977, p. 42478)

(4) The term "autism" means a developmental disability significantly affecting verbal and nonverbal communication and social interaction, generally evident before age three, that adversely affects educational performance. Characteristics of autism—irregularities and impairments in communication, engagement in repetitive activities and stereotyped movements, resistance to environmental change or change in daily routines, and unusual responses to sensory experiences. (U.S. Department of Education, 1991, p. 41271)

## Dimensional and Categorical Methods of Diagnosis

A dimensional approach to the classification of child behavior problems differs significantly from the categorical approaches discussed previously. Categorical systems such as the DSM and IDEA are essentially dichotomous in nature: A child is classified as either having a disability (IDEA) or a mental disorder (DSM) or not. A parent may legitimately ask classification-related questions that cannot be answered by using categorical systems. For example, a parent may ask, "I was told that my child may have a mild case of ADHD; is that true?" This question is difficult to answer because most categorical systems do not classify disorders on a continuum (although there are exceptions, such as the classification of levels of depression). Similarly, ranking along a continuum on a particular construct is inherently more informative. Height provides yet another example of the desirability of dimensional approaches to classification. When we are told that someone is tall, we are likely to have a follow-up question: "How tall?"

Grouping behaviors by constructs (or dimensions) allows for the classification of all children on a particular dimension or several dimensions of behavior (Meehl, 1995). A dimensional approach allows the clinician to classify the full range of behavior for all children evaluated, much in the way we measure the constructs of height, weight, intelligence, anxiety, and so on, both in and out of the school. Dimensional approaches can have greater predictive validity than categorical methods (Fergusson & Horwood, 1995), measure comorbidity more precisely (Caron & Rutter, 1991), and represent categorical disorders like borderline personality disorder with greater accuracy (Garb, 1996).

Cluster analytic and factor analytic methods have been used most frequently in efforts to develop dimensional (sometimes called multivariate) classification schemes for behavior, often to subtype clinical, referral, and national samples of children. The early work of Edelbrock and Achenbach (1980) reflects an attempt to develop a dimensional classification system. Their initial cluster study produced groups of children who were assigned such labels as depressed, somatic complaints, schizoid, hyperactive, delinquent, aggressive, and so on. Curry and Thompson (1985) used the Missouri Children's Behavior Checklist (MCBC) to cluster-analyze small clinical and referral samples. The identified seven clusters in this study are inhibited-nonaggressive, low social skills, behavior problem-free, mildly aggressive, aggressive-active, aggressive-inhibited, and undifferentiated disturbance. Achenbach, Howell, McConaughy, and Stanger (1995) identified new clusters for a national sample—including strange, irresponsible, and shows off—when using the Young Adult Behavior Checklist and Young Adult Self-Report.

McDermott and Weiss (1995) studied classroom behavioral "styles" for a representative national sample. Their study of teachers' ratings of behavior (i.e., the Adjustment Scales for Children and Adolescents) produced 22 clusters (styles) of behavior that ranged from absence of behavior problems to clinical (presumably diagnosable) significance. The obtained clusters were labeled good adjustment, adequate adjustment, adequate adjustment with disruptiveness, adequate adjustment with apprehension, adequate adjustment with indifference, marginal adjustment with withdrawal, marginal adjustment with motivational deficits, marginal adjustment with avoidance, marginal adjustment with attention seeking, marginal adjustment with moodiness, marginal adjustment with nonparticipation, marginal adjustment with dependency, undersocialized aggressive, oppositional, provocative, attention seeking, manipulative, impulsive aggressive, attention-deficit hyperactive, instrumental aggressive, defiant aggressive, avoidant, and schizoid with depressed mood. McDermott and Weiss classified 77% of the sample as either well or marginally adjusted. Approximately 21% were classified as at risk or seriously maladjusted.

Finally, Kamphaus, Huberty, DiStefano, and Petoskey (1997) completed a cluster analysis of the national norming sample for the Teacher Rating Scales–Child (TRS-C) of the Behavior Assessment System for Children (BASC; Reynolds & Kamphaus, 1992). They also identified seven clusters as a viable solution based on the BASC TRS-C dimensions (see Table 12.3).

Theoretically, dimensional assessment studies offer practitioners a classification choice. They may choose among classifications based on comparison, categorically based diagnostic criteria, or an empirically derived syndrome of behaviors based on dimensional methods. Dimensional methods, however, have not yet emerged as serious alternatives for diagnostic practice. At the present time they serve primarily as research tools that may eventually affect child classification.

Moreover, Cantwell (1996) notes some problems with dimensional studies. Cluster analytic methods, for example, are more likely to identify relatively common forms of maladjustment. Rare disorders will probably go undetected. In addition, dimensional approaches do not easily allow the application of etiology or other qualitative considerations to the diagnostic process. Accordingly, Cantwell suggests that eventually some combination of categorical and dimensional approaches to classification will best capture the full range of children's behavior.

Meehl (e.g., 1954) has argued convincingly, supported by decades of research (e.g., Dawes, 1988), that actuarial rules applied to diagnosis—such as in the development of clusters of syndromes that depict diagnostic entities—are more accurate than clinical impressions or single logical approaches. Although psychologists have been remarkably resistant to actuarial modeling of diagnosis and the use of empirical classification systems, we are moving ever so slowly in this direction (e.g., Faust & Ackley, 1988; Kleinmuntz, 1990; Reynolds, 1998).

## EFFECTS OF DIAGNOSIS

The inherent error in diagnosis has led some to recoil at the perceived hegemony of the DSM-IV. Critics assail the scientific evidence that supports some or all of the diagnostic categories as dubious. For example, Kovacs (1996) recently concluded, "The DSM-IV is not an enumeration of scientifically validated 'nervous and mental disorders' (whatever those are), but is in reality a disguised set of moral, highly culture bound descriptions about those behaviors that are to be

**TABLE 12.3    Mean *T* Scores by Scale for the Seven Cluster Solution (Total *N* = 1227)**

| Cluster and % of Sample | Behavior Problems | Adaptive Skills, Assets | Adaptive Skills, Deficits |
| --- | --- | --- | --- |
| Well adapted, 34% | None | Adaptability<br>Leadership<br>Social skills<br>Study skills | None |
| Average, 19% | None | None | None |
| Disruptive behavior problems, 8% | Aggression<br>Hyperactivity<br>Conduct problems<br>Depression<br>Attention problems<br>Learning problems<br>Attention problems | | Adaptability<br>Study skills<br><br><br><br><br>Leadership |
| Learning problems, 12% | Learning problems | | Social skills<br>Study skills |
| Physical complaints and worry, 11% | Somatization | | |
| Severe psychopathology, 4% | Aggression<br>Hyperactivity<br>Conduct problems<br>Anxiety<br>Depression<br>Somatization<br>Attention problems<br>Learning problems<br>Atypicality<br>Withdrawal | | Adaptability<br>Study skills |
| Mildly disruptive, 12% | Aggression<br>Hyperactivity | | |

Adapted from Kamphaus, Huberty, DiStefano, & Petoskey (in press).

tolerated and those that are to be stigmatized and extinguished" (p. 19).

Helmchen (1994) also took issue with the value of current medical diagnostic systems, concluding that they are of limited utility:

> At best, they currently may (1) serve to organize epidemiological data for administrative use in service planning as a framework for specific treatment; (2) regulate in some cases the financing of treatment, care and service use (e.g., in Alzheimer's disease); and (3) be used for each specific diagnosis as a key to knowledge, an instrument to organize and document the individual evaluation, and a challenge for decision making (p. 224).

Yet another criticism has been leveled by Beutler and Harwood (1995), who suggest that medical diagnostic systems are typically not linked to treatment. It is probably often the case, they argue, that a diagnosis merely indicates that there is a need for treatment or intervention, nothing more and nothing less, and this is particularly true of the IDEA system for classifying a child with a disability.

The rejection of formal logical-deductive diagnostic systems has led some to propose what they deem functional classification systems. However, these systems to date have been simplistic and ignore the many different presentations seen by clinicians in the schools and elsewhere. Gresham and Gansle (1992), in their vitriolic arguments (Hynd, 1992) against the relevance of the DSM series, propose a four-group classification scheme for all of childhood psychopathology, which they argue would be more related to treatment. Such systems do not lead to specific interventions, despite claims of their advocators, and they lack even heuristic value in such simplified forms (Reynolds, 1992). The clinician often must follow the diagnostic process by using other quantitative and qualitative assessment procedures to design interventions. Low incidence disorders and other matters related to the tremendously disproportionate incidence of various disorders, as well as resulting statistical compromises, prevent the development of purely empirical classification systems. We are bound to use a combination of clinical, logical-deductive, and actuarial methods in developing and applying diagnostic schemes (e.g., Reynolds, 1998).

Other problems are associated with any classification system. The DSM and other diagnostic systems are categorical at their essence, which leads unerringly to an oversimplification of psychological phenomena. Psychological constructs are often best represented as dimensional (anxiety, hyperactivity, etc.) rather than categorical (Kamphaus et al., 1997).

Categorical classification has many effects, not the least of which is the potential to overlook children with significant problems who nearly meet diagnostic criteria. These cases of subclinical problems are sometimes associated with significant adjustment difficulties (Cantwell, 1996). The diagnoses of mental retardation or of being gifted represent this problem of categorical classification well. If, to oversimplify for the purpose of explication, a child with an overall intelligence composite of 130 is admitted to a gifted enrichment program, and a child with a composite of 124 is not, it is not likely that the first child has a substantially better academic trajectory than the second child.

Categorical classification can also pose problems in behavioral assessment or in any other area of assessment in which decisions are made about who receives treatment, for what duration, and so on. Clinicians may, for example, use behavioral assessment to determine when to cease a treatment, such as social skills training. This decision can be made inappropriately by using rigid cut scores. Children with identical behavioral measures of social skills may have very different levels of adaptation, depending on their familial or school milieu. Hence, categorical special education or mental health diagnostic systems are often accompanied by the problem of forcing dimensional phenomena into a categorical framework. Other than not making decisions about treatment, eligibility for services, or other important decisions, the only option is to avoid inappropriately rigid uses of categorical systems. This objective can be accomplished in part by merging dimensional and categorical approaches as much as possible (Kamphaus & Frick, 1996).

## ASSESSMENT VERSUS DIAGNOSIS AND CLASSIFICATION

Diagnosis is only one of the objectives of assessment. Others may include treatment planning, political advocacy, program evaluation, and research (Keough, 1994). The objectives of the evaluation must be delineated at the outset of the assessment protocol since this decision affects test (assessment method) selection, scheduling, and virtually all other aspects of the assessment process.

Referral questions may be more or less suited to various objectives and assessment procedures. Some sample assessment questions and objectives may include the following:

| Question | Assessment Objective |
| --- | --- |
| 1. Does my child have ADHD? | Diagnosis |
| 2. Will my child outgrow his depression? | Diagnosis and prognosis |
| 3. Is my daughter getting better? | Treatment evaluation |
| 4. What can I do to help her stop avoiding school? | Treatment planning |
| 5. Will schizophrenia keep her from going to college? | Prognosis |
| 6. Can he get extra time when taking the SAT? | Diagnosis and eligibility |
| 7. Did he get his anxiety problems from me? | Etiology |
| 8. Why is his behavior management program not working? | Treatment evaluation |
| 9. Does she also have a reading disability? | Diagnosis and comorbidity |

The adept psychologist will be mindful of the multiple purposes of the assessment to ensure that the primary questions of interest can be answered by the battery of tests and procedures utilized. Moreover, diagnosis is only one assessment purpose, and it should not be reified as the ultimate one. On the one hand, diagnosis may in some cases actually be orthogonal to the assessment process that is necessary for treatment planning or other objectives. On the other hand, diagnosis may have implications for treatment, depending on the results of research related to particular diagnoses.

# DIAGNOSIS AND TREATMENT

Reynolds (1988), for example, extending Kaufman's (1979) model of intelligence testing, suggests that psychological testing and diagnosis may be used to develop individual aptitude by treatment interactions as part of the treatment planning process in the schools. He observed with regard to academic disabilities;

> In the context of the assessment process, effective school psychologists and other assessment staff attempt to delineate individual ATIs. There are three central components of the "Individual ATI," each corresponding to the following questions:
>
> 1. What content is the child to be taught?
> 2. How is the child to be instructed?
> 3. Why will the child acquire the information? What will provide the student with motivation for learning?

Each component must be addressed, and each seems best suited to a different set of psychological and educational tests and perhaps even different models of human behavior. Well-designed, technically adequate tests of all types may be useful in the process, including tests of intelligence, achievement, and special aptitudes. Any one test or approach is most likely to be incomplete, and complementary tests and models should be chosen.

## What

*What* represents the content of education and is determined by an analysis of academic skills that should include at least a good norm-referenced evaluation of achievement (to determine actual deficiencies relative to age and to intel-

lectual level, as well as to pinpoint weakly developed areas of function) and more detailed diagnostic forms of achievement testing. The latter might include criterion-referenced tests, task analysis, informal assessment, or diagnostic achievement tests. Determining what to teach should entail specification of the child's relative academic strengths and weaknesses in a general area (reading, math, spelling, etc.) and a detailed description of specific skills (e.g., phoneme recognition, sound blending, addition of two digit numbers that use carrying, or even more specific subskills). Several models may be useful in designating what to teach, such as behavioral, psychoeducational, and direct-instruction models.

## How

*How* refers to the way in which the content is to be organized and presented so that the child has the best possible opportunity to acquire the information. This process requires differentiated instruction, and at this point the individual (I) is added to the ATI, creating the IATI. Students' characteristics should drive the process at this stage—which clearly is not the case. In determining the *how* of instruction, processing models—cognitive, neuropsychological, or even traditional ability models—have the most to offer. They do not tell us what to teach, however. This is another point of confusion in the National Academy of Sciences report, which alludes to approval of cognitive, dynamic assessment models that encourage the teaching of processes, not content. Dynamic assessment may be helpful with the *how* but not with the *what*.

## Why

Children must have a motive for learning. Most are intrinsically motivated by the time they start school, but many special education children are already discouraged and do not believe they can learn. Behavioral models, particularly positive-reinforcement models, seem best suited for developing motivation. Other models may be useful, but children must be given a reason to acquire knowledge.

Much of the developmental psychopathology research to date is aimed at measuring psychological constructs with increased validity (Kamphaus & Frick, 1996). A diagnosis, therefore, may also serve as a construct in that it represents a tool for classification. Research on children who fit the diagnosis may, in turn, produce implications for treatment, prevention, prediction of outcomes, and so on. This form of psychopathology research, however, differs from research aimed exclusively at establishing an inextricable link between classification and treatment. In other words, child psychopathology research is similar to medical research in that the creation of a diagnosis does not lead inextricably to cures, as is the case for acquired immune deficiency syndrome (AIDS). The creation of an accurate AIDS diagnosis (construct) simply allowed research of the disorder to progress at a faster rate, including research into treatment.

In similar fashion, the delineation of ADHD subtypes in the DSM-III and DSM-IV simply provided diagnostic categories that could be studied in a more effective manner. As a consequence, we now know that children with ADHD, combined type, tend to be more socially rejected, impulsive, and at greater risk for conduct problems. Children with ADHD, primary inattentive type, are quite different: they may be more reticent, perhaps drowsy, and respond well to low doses of stimulant medication (Kamphaus & Frick, 1996). None of these treatment-relevant findings, however, would be available to clinicians without the initial creation of the constructs of subtypes.

It is probably true that child psychopathology research that is based on diagnostic groups is not ideally suited to the development of specific treatment regimens for each diagnosis. Even well-refined diagnostic categories are useful only for stating probabilities (Helmchen, 1994). It is not true that *all* children with ADHD, primary inattentive type, will respond well to low doses of stimulant medication. This treatment suggestion is merely a probability statement, which suggests to the physician a promising intervention. As Helmchen notes, "In other words, the more individualized the treatment goal, the less useful the psychiatric diagnosis is, and vice versa" (p. 218).

The process of classification is helpful to the extent that the classification itself has some validity. It then allows us to think like psychologists. Specifically, classification schemes, whether psychiatric, educational, or behavioral in origin, give psychologists ready access to a burgeoning research literature. It is by accessing this literature that we have the opportunity to apply science to practice, as psychologists are trained to do (Stricker, 1997).

# FUTURE OF DIAGNOSTIC PRACTICE AND SCHOOL PSYCHOLOGY

It is likely that continual progress will be made to improve current diagnostic systems. Furthermore, future innovations in diagnostic systems will probably be more incremental than radical. In the interim, the astute clinician has to deal with the problems of using categorical systems for determining eligibility for specialized treatments by teaching others how to use these systems in an enlightened fashion.

Problems in psychological classification research may be solved by combining current categorical methods with dimensional approaches (Kamphaus & Frick, 1996) and extending the results through logical-deductive methods for disorders of very low incidence (Aicardi syndrome, Soto's syndrome, and the like). Most current diagnostic systems have been based on a medical, often nonempirical tradition. Psychologists are still in the early stages of building dimensional assessment systems that are based on multivariate statistical models. These models may push the field forward, although other problems in determining the role of etiology in diagnosis remain (Cantwell, 1996).

We would also do well to remember that diagnoses per se are not likely to inform our important treatment decisions. Accurate diagnoses can only provide the foundation necessary for research, which in turn may reveal treatment-related findings that can be applied only by highly trained professionals. Just as an inept automobile mechanic prevents an accurate diagnosis of a car's problems, so, too, the most valid diagnostic system is of dubious value in the hands of the unskilled clinician.

# REFERENCES

Achenbach, T. M., Howell, C. T., McConaughy, S. H., & Stanger, C. (1995). Six-year predictors of problems in a national sample: III. Transitions to young adult syndromes. *Journal of the American Academy of Child and Adolescent Psychiatry, 34,* 658–669.

American Association on Mental Retardation (1992). *Mental retardation: Definition, classification, and systems of support* (rev. 9th ed.). Washington, DC: Author.

American Psychiatric Association (1994). *Diagnostic and statistical manual of mental disorders* (4th ed.). Washington, DC: Author.

Beutler, L. E., & Harwood, T. M. (1995). How to assess clients in pretreatment planning. In J. N. Butcher (Ed.), *Clinical personality assessment practical approaches* (pp. 59–77). New York: Oxford University Press.

Bower, E. M. (1982). Severe emotional disturbance: Public policy and research. *Psychology in the Schools, 19,* 55–60.

Cantwell, D. P. (1996). Classification of child and adolescent psychopathology. *Journal of Child Psychology and Psychiatry, 37,* 3–12.

Caron, C., & Rutter, M. (1991). Comorbidity in child psychopathology: Concepts, issues, and research strategies. *Journal of Child Psychology and Psychiatry, 32,* 1063–1080.

Curry, J. F., & Thompson, R. J. (1985). Patterns of behavioral disturbance in developmentally disabled and psychiatrically referred children: A cluster analytic approach. *Journal of Pediatric Psychology, 10,* 151–167.

Dawes, R. M. (1988). *Rational choice in an uncertain world.* San Diego: Harcourt Brace.

Edelbrock, C., & Achenbach, T. M. (1980). A typology of child behavior profile patterns: Distribution and correlates for disturbed children. *Journal of Abnormal Child Psychology, 8,* 441–470.

Faust, D., & Ackley, M. (1998). Did you think it was gonna be easy? Some methodological suggestions for the investigation and development of malingering detection techniques. In C. R. Reynolds (Ed.), *Detection of malingering during head injury litigation.* New York: Plenum.

Fergusson, D. M., & Horwood, J. (1995). Predictive validity of categorically and dimensionally scored measures of disruptive childhood behaviors. *American Academy of Child and Adolescent Psychiatry, 34,* 477–487.

Forness, S. R., & Knitzer, J. (1992). A new proposed definition and terminology to replace "serious emotional disturbance" in the individuals with disabilities act. *School Psychology Review, 21,* 12–20.

Garb, H. N. (1996). Taxometrics and the revision of diagnostic criteria. *American Psychologist, 51,* 553–554.

Gresham, F. M., & Gansle, K. A. (1992). Misguided assumptions of DSM-III-R: Implications for school psychological practice. *School Psychology Quarterly, 7,* 79–95.

Helmchen, H. H. (1994). The validity of diagnostic systems for treatment. In J. E. Mezzich, Y. Honda, M. C. Kastrup (Eds.), *Psychiatric diagnosis, a world perspective* (217–227). New York: Springer-Verlag.

Hynd, G. W. (1992). Misrepresentative or simply misinformed? Comment on Gresham and Gansle's vitriolic diatribe regarding the DSM. *School Psychology Quarterly, 7,* 100–103.

Kamphaus, R. W., & Frick, J. P. (1996). *Clinical assessment of child and adolescent personality and behavior.* Needham Heights, MA: Allyn & Bacon.

Kamphaus, R. W., Huberty, C. J., DiStefano, C., & Petoskey, M. D. (1997). A typology of child behavior in U.S. classrooms. *Journal of Abnormal Child Psychology, 25,* 453–463.

Kamphaus, R. W., Morgan, A. W., Cox, M. R., & Powell, R. M. (1995). Personality and intelligence in the psychodiagnostic process: The emergence of diagnostic schedules. In D. H. Saklofske and M. Zeidner (Eds.), *International handbook of personality and intelligence* (525–544). New York: Plenum.

Kaufman, A. S. (1979). *Intelligent testing with the WISC-R.* New York: Wiley-Interscience.

Keough, B. K. (1994). A matrix of decision points in the measurement of learning disabilities. In G. R. Lyon (Ed.), *Frames of reference for the assessment of learning disabilities: New views on measurement issues* (15–26). Baltimore, MD: Paul H. Brookes.

Kleinmuntz, B. (1990). Why we still use our heads instead of the formulas: Toward an integrative approach. *Psychological Bulletin, 107,* 296–310.

Kovacs, A. L. (1996, Winter). We have met the enemy and he is us! *AAP Advance, 6,* 18.

Lahey, B. B., Applegate, B., McBurnett, K., Biederman, J., Greenhill, L., Hynd, G. W., Barkley, R. A., Newcorn, J., Jensen, P., Richters, J., Garfinkel, B., Kerdyck, L., Frick, P. J., Ollendick, T., Perez, D., Hart, E. L., Waldman, I., & Shaffer, D. (1996). DSM-IV field trials for attention-deficit hyperactivity disorder in children and adolescents. *American Journal of Psychiatry.*

Last, C. G. (1993). *Conclusions and future directions.* In C. G. Last (Ed.), *Anxiety across the lifespan: A developmental perspective* (204–213). New York: Springer.

McDermott, P. A., & Weiss, R. V. (1995). A normative typology of healthy, subclinical, and clinical behavior styles among American children and adolescents. *Psychological Assessment, 7,* 162–170.

Meehl, P. E. (1954). *Clinical versus statistical prediction.* Minneapolis: University of Minnesota Press.

Meehl, P. E. (1995). Bootstraps taxometrics: Solving the classification problem in psychopathology. *American Psychologist, 50,* 266–275.

Ollendick, T., Perez, D., Hart, E. L., Waldman, I., & Shaffer, D. (1994). DSM-IV field trials for attention-deficit hyperactivity disorder in children and adolescents. *American Journal of Psychiatry, 151,* 11.

Reynolds, C. R. (1979). Should we screen preschoolers? *Contemporary Educational Psychology, 4,* 175–181.

Reynolds, C. R. (1988). Putting the individual into aptitude-treatment interaction. *Exceptional Children, 54,* 324–331.

Reynolds, C. R. (1992). Misguided epistemological

shifting, misdirected misology, and dogma in diagnosis. *School Psychology Quarterly, 7,* 96–99.

Reynolds, C. R. (1998). Common sense, clinicians, and actuarialism in the detection of malingering during head injury litigation. In C. R. Reynolds (Ed.), *Detection of malingering during head injury litigation.* New York: Plenum.

Reynolds, C. R., & Kamphaus, R. W. (1992). *Behavior assessment system for children: Manual.* Circle Pines, MN: American Guidance Service.

Stricker, G. (1997). Are science and practice commensurable? *American Psychologist, 52,* 442–448.

Widiger, T. A., Frances, A. J., Pincus, H. A., Davis, W. W., & First, M. B. (1991). Toward an empirical classification for the DSM IV. *Journal of Abnormal Psychology, 100,* 280–288.

Witmer, L. (1907). Clinical psychology. *The Psychological Clinic, 1,* 1–9.

## CHAPTER 13

# INTELLIGENCE TESTING IN THE SCHOOLS

**ALAN S. KAUFMAN**[1]
*Yale University*

**ELIZABETH O. LICHTENBERGER**
*The Salk Institute*

**JACK A. NAGLIERI**
*Ohio State University*

## INTRODUCTION

This chapter provides a context in which to understand children's intelligence by discussing popular intelligence measures and the comprehensive approach necessary in intelligence testing. A brief review of the controversy surrounding intelligence tests is presented, as well as a response to critics of IQ testing that includes a discussion of an "intelligent" testing approach (Kaufman, 1979; 1994a). Selected tests currently available to measure children's intelligence (preschool through adolescence) are described, and detail is provided on the following intelligence tests: Wechsler Intelligence Scale for Children–Third Edition (WISC-III; Wechsler, 1974), Kaufman Assessment Battery for Children (K-ABC; Kaufman & Kaufman, 1983), Kaufman Adolescent and Adult Intelligence Test (KAIT; Kaufman & Kaufman, 1993), Cognitive Assessment System (CAS; Naglieri & Das, 1997b), Woodcock-Johnson Psycho-Educational Battery–Revised: Tests of Cognitive Ability (WJ-R; Woodcock & Johnson, 1989), Differential Abili-

ties Scale (DAS; Elliott, 1990), Stanford-Binet, Fourth Edition (Binet IV; Thorndike, Hagen, & Sattler, 1986), Wechsler Primary and Preschool Intelligence Scale–Revised (WPPSI-R; Wechsler, 1989), and Detroit Tests of Learning Aptitude (DTLA-3; Hammill, 1991). These instruments are then integrated with the WISC-III, focusing on a combined use. The final part of this chapter is a sample case report that combines a number of different measures in the assessment of a 10-year-old male with academic and attentional difficulties.

## CONTROVERSY OVER INTELLIGENCE TESTING

The measurement of intelligence has long been the center of debate. In the past, critics have spoken of IQ tests as "biased," "unfair," and "discriminatory." Today the critics' arguments center more around what the IQ tests truly measure, as well as how or if they should be interpreted, their relevance to intervention, and their scope. Despite the controversy, there is great interest and need for measurement of intelligence, especially in education. Amid the criticisms and limitations of IQ testing, these instruments remain a

---

[1]The authors would like to thank Dr. Kristee A. Beres for her contribution to this chapter.

most technologically advanced and sophisticated tool for providing essential and unique information to school psychologists so they may best serve the needs of children. When used with consideration of the American Psychological Associations (APA) Ethical Principles of Psychologists (American Psychological Association, 1990), Principle 2—Competence, which encourages clinicians to recognize differences among people (age, gender, and socioeconomic and ethnic backgrounds) and to understand test research into the validity and the limitations of their assessment tools, we believe these tests can be beneficial, despite the controversy.

Three current controversial themes associated with IQ testing were recently noted by Kaufman (1994). The first involves opposition to the common practice of subtest interpretation, advocated by Wechsler (1958) and Kaufman (1979, 1994a). The second includes those who would abandon the practice together. Finally, the third group suggests that the concept of intelligence testing is sound, but more contemporary instrumentation could improve the effectiveness of the approach.

The first group of psychologists has encouraged practitioners to "just say 'no' to subtest analysis" (McDermott, Fantuzzo, & Glutting, 1990, p. 299; see also Glutting, McDermott, Prifitera, and McGrath, 1994, and Watkins and Kush, 1994). McDermott and his colleagues argue that interpreting a subtest profile is in violation of the principles of valid test interpretation because the ipsative method fails to improve prediction (McDermott, Fantuzzo, Glutting, Watkins, & Baggaley, 1992) and therefore does not augment the utility of the test. We agree that the results of studies conducted by McDermott et al., (1992) do suggest that using the WISC-III in isolation has limitations, but using the ipsative approach in conjunction with other relevant information such as achievement test results and pertinent background information may be beneficial. Kaufman (1994a) further suggests that by shifting to the child's midpoint score, a more equally balanced set of hypotheses can be developed, which can be integrated with other findings to either strengthen or disconfirm hypotheses. When the ipsative assessment approach is used to create a base from which to search for additional information to evaluate hypothesized strengths and weaknesses in the child's subtest profile, its validity is extended beyond that which

can be obtained by using the Wechsler subtests alone. If support is found for the hypotheses, such a strength or weakness can be viewed as reliable because of its cross validation (Kaufman, 1994). When considering this position and that represented by McDermott et al. (1992), as well as Glutting et al. and Watkins and Kush, it is important to recognize that these authors are against subtest profile analysis, not the use of IQ tests in general. This is in contrast to others, who hold a more extreme negative view of IQ testing.

One extremist group that opposes IQ testing includes those who advocate throwing away Verbal and Performance IQs, along with the subtest profile interpretation, and the Full Scale IQ because, they insist, Wechsler scales measure only $g$ (general intelligence) (MacMann & Barnett, 1994). They argue that differences between the Verbal and Performance Scales on Wechsler tests hold no meaning, that conventional intelligence tests measure only $g$ (and a measure of $g$ is not enough to warrant the administration of such an instrument), and that Wechsler scale data do not have instructional value. However, any clinician who is using intelligence tests cannot ignore the numerous studies that point to significant Verbal-Performance differences in patients with right-hemisphere damage (Kaufman, 1990, Chap. 9), in Hispanic and Navajo children (McShane & Cook, 1985; McShane & Plas, 1984; Naglieri, 1984), and in normal adults (Kaufman, 1990, Chap. 7). If only the Full Scale IQ is interpreted, following MacMann and Barnett's advisement that the Verbal and Performance Scales are meaningless, it prevents the fair use of these tests with those groups who have inconsistent verbal-performance discrepancies. Moreover, it is clear that when a child earns very poor verbal and average performance scores, there are obvious implications for instruction and a high probability that these results will be reflected in poor verbal achievement (Naglieri, 1984).

Another extremist group opposed to IQ testing is Witt and Gresham (1985): "The WISC-R lacks treatment validity in that its use does not enhance remedial interventions for children who show specific academic skill deficiencies" (p. 1717). It is their belief that the Wechsler test should be replaced with assessment procedures that have more treatment validity. However, as Kaufman (1994b) points out, Witt and Gresham do not provide evidence for their statements. Another pair of researchers (Reschly & Tilly, 1993) agree with Witt and Gresham about the lack of treatment validity but only provide references not specific to the Wechsler scales. Thus, the Wechsler scales appear to have been rejected by these researchers without ample relevant data.

Witt and Gresham (1985) also complain that the WISC-R (as well as the WISC-III) yields only a score and does not give school psychologists direct strategies of what to do with and for children, which are what teachers are requesting. As Kaufman (1994a) points out, however, it is not the instrument's responsibility to provide direct treatment information: "It is the examiner's responsibility . . . to provide recommendations for intervention" (p. 35). The examiner should not just look at the bottom-line IQ scores or standard scores but should provide statements about a child's strengths and weaknesses that have been cross-validated through the observations of behavior, background information, and standardized intelligence and achievement tests.

Finally, a group of professionals have suggested that the Wechsler has limits that could be addressed by alternative methods rather than abandoning intelligence testing altogether. Some have argued for a move toward alternative conceptualizations of intelligence and methods to measure new constructs that are based on factor analytic research (e.g., Woodcock, 1990), whereas others have used neuropsychology and cognitive psychology as a starting point (e.g., Naglieri & Das, 1997).

The main goal of this chapter is to use Kaufman's (1994a) philosophy of "intelligent" testing to address some of the concerns about Wechsler interpretation through a careful analysis of the results and integration with other measures. We base much of this discussion on the principles of IQ testing as outlined by Kaufman, which focus on the view that "WISC-III assessment is of the individual, by the individual, and for the individual" (p. 14). Through research knowledge, theoretical sophistication, and clinical ability, examiners must generate hypotheses about an individual's assets and deficits and then confirm or deny these hypotheses by exploring multiple sources of evidence. Well-validated hypotheses must then be translated into meaningful, practical recommendations. A brief description of those five principles of intelligent testing follows.

As clinician-scientists we must come well equipped with state-of-the-art instrumentation, good judgment, knowledge of psychology, and clinical training to move beyond the obtained IQ scores (Kaufman, 1994a). Integration of information from many sources and different tests is very important because it is impossible to fully describe a person just by presenting a few numbers from the Wechsler protocol or those obtained from a computer program. Each adult and child who comes for an assessment has unique characteristics, has a particular way of approaching test items, and may be affected differently by the testing situation. Through an integrated interpretation approach the various dimensions that influence a child can become apparent.

# PRINCIPLES OF THE INTELLIGENT TESTING PHILOSOPHY

The first principle of intelligent testing is that "the WISC-III subtests measure what the individual has learned" (Kaufman, 1994a, p. 6). The WISC-III is like an achievement test, in that it is a measure of past accomplishments and is predictive of success in traditional school subjects. Research indicates that intelligence tests consistently prove to be good predictors of conventional school achievement. The WISC-III manual (Wechsler, 1991, pp. 206–209) gives many such correlations between the WISC-III IQs, or Factor Indexes, and achievement measures. Although this connection is well documented empirically, it should not be ultimately accepted as a statement of fate—that if a child scores poorly on the WISC-III, he or she will do poorly in school (Kaufman, 1994a). Instead, constructive interpretation of a test battery can lead to recommendations that may alter a child's development.

The second principle is that WISC-III subtests are samples of behavior and are not exhaustive. Because the subtests offer only a brief glimpse into a child's overall level of functioning, examiners must be cautious in generalizing the results to performance and behaviors in other circumstances. The Full Scale "should not be interpreted as an estimate of a child's global or total intellectual functioning; and the WISC-III should be administered along with other measures, and the IQ interpreted in the context of other test scores" (Kaufman, 1994a, p. 7). It is important that the actual scores are not emphasized; rather, it is more beneficial to elaborate on what children can do well, relative to their own level of ability. This information can be used to create an individualized education program, which will tap a child's strengths and help improve deficits.

The third principle states, "The WISC-III assesses mental functioning under fixed experimental conditions" (Kaufman, 1994a, p. 8). Rigid adherence to the standardized procedures for administration and scoring, outlined in the WISC-III manual (Wechsler, 1991), helps to ensure that all children are measured in an objective manner. However, parts of the standardized procedure make the testing situation very different from a natural setting. For example, it isn't very often in children's everyday lives that someone is transcribing virtually every word they say or timing them with a stopwatch. The standardization procedures are important to follow but must be recognized as limitations when one is interpreting the scores, which are obtained in an artificial situation. The value of the intelligence test is enhanced when the examiner can meaningfully relate observations of the child's behaviors in the testing situation to the profile of scores.

The fourth principle is that "the WISC-III is optimally useful when it is interpreted from an information-processing model" (Kaufman, 1994a, p. 10). This is especially beneficial in hypothesizing functional areas of strength and dysfunction. This model examines how information enters the brain from the sense organs (input), how it is interpreted and processed (integration), how it is stored for later retrieval (storage), and how it is expressed linguistically or motorically (output). Through this model, examiners can organize the test data, including fluctuations in subtest scores, into meaningful, underlying areas of asset and deficit.

The fifth and very important principle of intelligent testing is that "hypotheses generated from WISC-III profiles should be supported with data from multiple sources" (Kaufman, 1994a, p. 13). Although good hypotheses can be raised from the initial WISC-III test scores, they do not hold water unless verified by diverse pieces of data. Such supporting evidence may come from careful observation of a child's behavior during test administration; from the pattern of responses across various subtests; from background information obtained from parents, teachers, or other referral sources; from previous test data; and from the administration of supplemental subtests. The integration of data from all these different sources is critical in obtaining the best and most meaningful clinical interpretation of a test battery.

# CURRENT MEASURES OF INTELLIGENCE

Intelligence tests are administered for a variety of reasons, including identification (of mental retardation, learning disabilities, other cognitive disorders, and giftedness), placement (gifted and other specialized programs), and as a cognitive adjunct to a clinical evaluation. The following comprehensive intelligence tests are discussed in the next sections: WISC-III, K-ABC, KAIT, CAS, WJ-R Tests of Cognitive Ability, DAS, Binet-IV, WPPSI-R, and DTLA-3.

## Wechsler Intelligence Scale for Children–Third Edition (WISC-III)

### Theory

Wechsler (1974) defines intelligence as "the overall capacity of an individual to understand and cope with the world around him" (p. 5). His tests, however, were not predicated on this definition. The tasks developed were not designed from well-researched concepts that exemplified his definition. In fact, as previously noted, virtually all of his tasks were adapted from other existing tests.

Like Binet, Wechsler's (1974) definition of intelligence also includes an overall global entity. He believed that intelligence cannot be tested directly but can only be inferred from how an individual thinks, talks, moves, and reacts to different stimuli. Therefore, he did not put one task above another but believed that this global entity called intelligence could be ferreted out by probing a person with as many different kinds of mental tasks as possible. Wechsler did not believe in a cognitive hierarchy for his tasks, and he did not believe that each task was equally effective. He did feel that each task was necessary for the fuller appraisal of intelligence.

### Standardization and Properties of the Scale

The WISC-III was standardized on 2,200 children, ranging in age from 6 through 16 years. The children were divided into 11 age groups, 1 group for each year. The median age for each age group was the sixth month (e.g., 7 years, 6 months). The standardization procedures followed the 1980 U.S. Census Bureau data, and the manual provides information by age, gender, race and ethnicity, geographic region, and parent education. "Overall, the standardization of the WISC-III is immaculate . . . a better-standardized intelligence test does not exist (Kaufman, 1993, p. 351).

The WISC-III yields three IQ scores, a Verbal Scale IQ, a Performance Scale IQ, and a Full Scale IQ. All three are standard scores—mean of 100 and standard deviation (SD) of 15—obtained by comparing an individual's score with those earned by the representative sample of age peers. There are 10 mandatory and 3 supplementary subtests in the WISC-III, all of which span the age range of 6 through 16 years. The Verbal Scale's 5 mandatory subtests are Information, Similarities, Arithmetic, Vocabulary, and Comprehension. The supplementary subtest on the Verbal Scale is Digit Span. Digit Span is not calculated into the Verbal IQ unless it has been substituted for another verbal subtest because one of those subtests has been spoiled (Kamphaus, 1993; Wechsler, 1991).

The five mandatory Performance Scale's subtests are Picture Completion, Picture Arrangement, Block Design, Object Assembly, and Coding. The two supplementary subtests on the Performance Scale are Mazes and Symbol Search. The Mazes subtest may be substituted for any Performance Scale subtest; however, Symbol Search may only be substituted for the Coding subtest (Kamphaus, 1993; Wechsler, 1991). "Symbol Search is an excellent task that should have been included among the five regular Performance subtests instead of Coding. Mazes is an awful task that should have been dropped completely from the WISC-III" (Kaufman, 1994a, p. 58). Moreover, "there's no rational reason for the publisher to have rigidly clung to Coding as a regular part of the WISC-III when the new Symbol Search task is clearly a better choice for psychometric reasons" (p. 59). Therefore, for all general purposes, Symbol Search should be routinely substituted for coding as part of the regular battery and Symbol Search used to compute the Performance IQ and Full Scale IQ. The manual does not tell one to do this, but neither does it prohibit it.

The reliability of each subtest except Coding and Symbol Search was estimated by the split-half method. Stability coefficients were used as reliability estimates for the Coding and Symbol Search subtests because of their speeded nature. Across the age groups, the reliability coefficients range from .69 to .87 for the individual subtests. The average reliability, across the age groups, for the IQs and indexes are .95 for the Verbal IQ, .91 for the Performance IQ, .96 for the Full Scale IQ, .94 for the Verbal Comprehension Index, .90 for the Perceptual Organization Index, .87 for the Freedom from Distractibility Index, and .85 for the Processing Speed Index (Wechsler, 1991).

Factor analytic studies of the WISC-III standardization data (Wechsler, 1991) were performed for four age groups: ages 6–7 ($N = 400$), ages 8–10 ($N = 600$), ages 11–13 ($N = 600$), ages 14–16 ($N = 600$). By compiling the results of the analysis, a four-factor solution was found for the WISC-III. Like the WISC-R, Verbal Comprehension and Perceptual Organization remain the first two factors. The former involves verbal knowledge and its expression; the latter, a nonverbal dimension, involves the ability to interpret and organize visually presented material. The third factor is the Arithmetic and Digit Span subtests. This factor has been labeled Freedom from Distractibility because a common element among tasks is the ability to focus, to concentrate, and to remain attentive. Other interpretations have included facility with numbers, short-term memory, and sequencing because the three tasks that make up the factor all involve a linear process in which numbers are manipulated. Success is either facilitated by or wholly dependent on memory (Kaufman, 1979). The fourth factor is Coding and Symbol Search and is referred to as the Processing Speed factor. Taken together, the Verbal Comprehension and Perceptual Organization factors offer strong support for the construct validity of the Verbal and Performance IQs; substantial loadings on the large, unrotated first factor ($g$) supports the construct underlying Wechsler's Full Scale IQ.

## Analyzing the WISC-III Data

To obtain the most information from the WISC-III, one should be more than familiar with each of the subtests individually, as well as with the potential information that they can provide when integrated or combined. The WISC-III is maximally useful when tasks are grouped and regrouped to uncover a child's strong and weak areas of functioning, as long as these hypothesized assets and deficits are verified by multiple sources of information.

As indicated previously, the WISC-III provides a set of four factor indexes in addition to the set of three IQs. The front page of the WISC-III record form lists the seven standard scores in a box on the top right. The record form is quite uniform and is laid out nicely;

however, it is difficult to know just what to do with all of the scores. Kaufman (1994a) has developed seven steps to interpretation that allow the clinician to organize and integrate the test results in a stepwise fashion. The seven steps (see Table 13.1) provide an empirical framework for profile attack while organizing the profile information into hierarchies.

A modification of the seven steps is described by Kaufman (1994a), following Naglieri's (1993) index-level analysis. This approach adds emphasis to the four WISC-III scale indexes, with the assumption that they have adequate validity, and allows for the simultaneous evaluation of the profile at the scale level. The result is a five-step procedure in which the index-level analyses are combined into one set of analyses. In this approach, shown in Figure 13.1, the analysis begins with the same step 1 just described; then steps 2, 3, and 5 are omitted in favor of an ipsative analysis of the four scale indexes. This is followed by steps 4, 6, and 7. This alternative

## TABLE 13.1  Summary of Seven Steps for Interpreting WISC-III Profiles

**Step 1.  Interpret the Full Scale IQ.**

Convert it to an ability level and percentile rank and band it with error, preferably a 90% confidence interval (about ±5 points).

**Step 2.  Determine if the Verbal-Performance (V-P) IQ discrepancy is statistically significant.**

Overall values for V-P discrepancies are *11 points* at the .05 level and *15 points* at the .01 level. For most testing purposes, the .05 level is adequate.

**Step 3.  Determine if the V-P IQ discrepancy is interpretable, or if the Verbal Comprehension (VC) and Perceptual Organization (PO) factor indexes should be interpreted instead.**

Ask four questions about the Verbal and Performance Scales.

*Verbal Scale*

1.  Is there a significant difference ($p < .05$) between the child's standard scores in the VC and the Freedom from Distractibility Index (FD)? **Size needed for significant (VC-FD) = 13+ points.**

2.  Is there abnormal scatter (highest minus lowest scaled score) among the five verbal subtests used to compute V IQ?
    **Size needed for abnormal verbal scatter = 7+ points.**

*Performance Scale*

3.  Is there a significant difference ($p < .05$) between the child's standard scores on the PO and the Processing Speed Index (PS)?
    **Size needed for significant (PO-PS) = 15+ points.**

4.  Is there abnormal scatter (highest minus lowest scaled scored) among the five Performance subtest used to compute P IQ?
    **Size needed for abnormal performance scatter = 7+ points.**
    If all answers are no, the V-P IQ discrepancy is interpretable. If the answer to one or more questions is yes, the V-P IQ discrepancy may not be interpretable. Examine the VC-PO discrepancy. Overall values for VC-PO discrepancies are *12 points* at the .05 level and *16 points* at the .01 level.
    Determine if the VC and PO Indexes are unitary dimensions:
    1.  Is there abnormal scatter among the four VC subtests?
    **Size needed for abnormal performance scatter = 9+ points.**
    2.  Is there abnormal scatter among the four PO subtests?
    **Size needed for abnormal PO scatter = 8+ points.**
       If the answer to either question is yes, you probably shouldn't interpret the VC-PO index discrepancy unless it is too big to ignore (see step 4). If both answers are no, interpret the VC-PO differences as meaningful.

**TABLE 13.1** *(Continued)*

**Step 4. Determine if the V-P IQ discrepancy (or VC-PO discrepancy) is abnormally large.**

Differences of at least *19 points* are unusually large for both the V-P and VC-PO discrepancies. Enter with the IQs or indexes, whichever was identified by the questions and answers in Step 3.

If neither set of scores was found to be interpretable in Step 3, they may be interpreted anyway if the magnitude of the discrepancy is unusually large (19+ points).

**Step 5. Interpret the meaning of the global verbal and nonverbal dimensions and the meaning of the small factors.**

Study the information and procedures in Kaufman (1994a, Chap. 4) for verbal and nonverbal and FD and PS factors (Chap. 5). When the FD and PS factors have too much scatter to permit meaningful interpretation of their respective indexes, the following rules pertain (Chap. 5):

  1. Do not interpret the FD Index if the Arithmetic and Digit Span scaled scores differ by *4 or more points*.
  2. Do not interpret the PO Index if the Symbol Search and Coding scaled scores differ by *4 or more points*.

**Step 6. Interpret significant strengths and weaknesses in the WISC-III subtest profile.**

If the V-P IQ discrepancy is less than 19 points, use the child's mean of all WISC-III subtests administered as the child's midpoint.

If the V-P IQ discrepancy is 19 or more points, use the child's mean of all Verbal subtests as the midpoint for determining strengths and weaknesses on Verbal subtests, and use the Performance mean for determining significant deviations on Performance subtests.

Use either the specific values in Table 3.3 of *Intelligent Testing with the WISC-III* (Kaufman, 1994a), rounded to the nearest whole number, or the following summary information for determining significant deviations:

  **±3 points:** Information, Similarities, Arithmetic, Vocabulary
  **±4 points:** Comprehension, Digit Span, Picture Completion, Picture Arrangement, Block Design, Object Assembly, Symbol Search
  **±5 points:** Coding

**Step 7. Generate hypotheses about the fluctuations in the WISC-III subtest profile.**

Consult Kaufman (1994a), (Chap. 6) for the systematic reorganization of subtest profiles to generate hypotheses about strengths and weaknesses.

From Kaufman (1994a, Table 3.4). Reprinted by permission of John Wiley & Sons, Inc.

shifts the examination from the IQ-level analysis to the four indexes.

## Critique

Professionals in the field of intelligence testing have described the third edition of the Wechsler Intelligence Scale for Children in a number of different ways. Some critics feel that the WISC-III reports continuity, the status quo, but makes little progress in the evolution of the assessment of intelligence. Such critics note that despite more than 50 years of advancement in theories of intelligence, the Wechsler philosophy of intelligence (not actually a formal theory) written in 1939, remains the guiding principle of the WISC-III (Shaw, Swerdlik, & Laurent, 1993). One of the principal goals for developing the WISC-III, stated in the manual, was merely to update the norms, which is "hardly a revision at all" (Sternberg, 1993). If one had chosen to use the WISC-III because one is looking for a test of new constructs in intelligence or merely a new test, one should look elsewhere (Sternberg, 1993).

In contrast to these fairly negative evaluations, Kaufman reports that the WISC-III is a substantial revision of the WISC-R and that the changes that have been made are considerable and well done: "The normative sample is exemplary, and the entire psychometric approach to

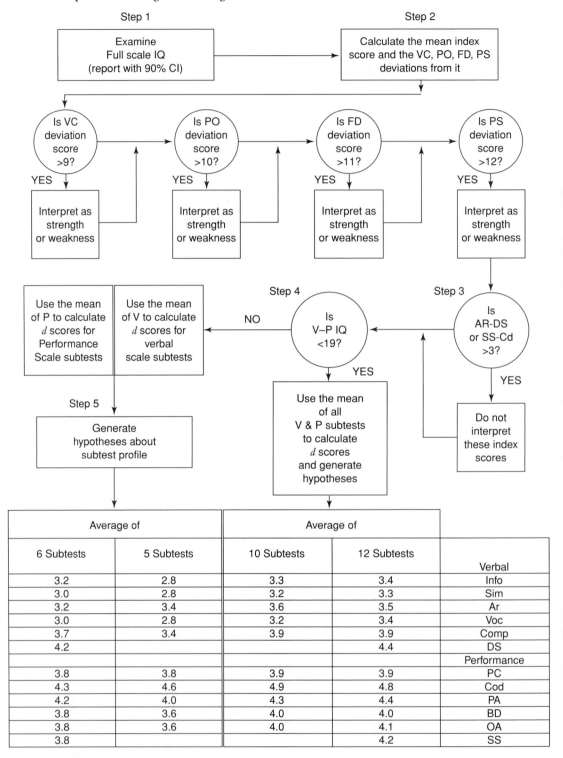

**FIGURE 13.1   WISC-III Flowchart.**
*Source:* Kaufman (1994a).

test development, validation, and interpretation reflects sophisticated, state-of-the-art knowledge and competence" (Kaufman, 1993, p. 345). For Kaufman, the WISC-III is not without its flaws but his overall review of the test is quite positive. Although the WISC-III has clearly had mixed reviews, it is one of the most frequently used tests in the field of children's intelligence testing.

## Kaufman Assessment Battery for Children (K-ABC)

The K-ABC is a battery of tests that measures intelligence and achievement of normal and exceptional children 2½ through 12½ years old. It yields four scales: Sequential Processing, Simultaneous Processing, Mental Processing Composite (Sequential and Simultaneous), and Achievement.

This is becoming a frequently used test in intelligence and achievement assessment, used by both clinical and school psychologists (Kamphaus, Beres, Kaufman, & Kaufman, 1995). In a nationwide survey of school psychologists conducted in 1987 by Obringer (1988), respondents were asked to rank the following instruments in order of their usage: Wechsler's scales, the K-ABC, and both the old and new Stanford-Binets. The Wechsler scales earned a mean rank of 2.69; followed closely by the K-ABC, with a mean of 2.55; the L-M version of the Stanford-Binet, 1.98; and the Stanford-Binet, Fourth Edition, 1.26. Similarly Bracken (1985) surveyed school psychologists and found that for ages 5 to 11 the WISC-R was endorsed by 82%, the K-ABC by 57%, and the Binet IV by 39% of the practitioners. These results suggest that clinicians who work with children should have some familiarity with the K-ABC (Kamphaus et al., 1995).

The K-ABC has been the subject of controversy from the outset, as evident in the strongly pro and con articles written for a special issue of the *Journal of Special Education* devoted to the K-ABC (Miller & Reynolds, 1984). Much of the controversy, especially regarding the validity of the K-ABC theory, will probably be unresolved for some time (Kamphaus et al., 1995). Fortunately, the apparent controversy linked to the K-ABC has resulted in numerous research studies and papers that provide more insight into the test's strengths and weaknesses.

## *Theory*

The K-ABC intelligence scales are based on a theoretical framework of sequential and simulta-neous information processing, which relates to *how* children solve problems rather than *what* type of problems they must solve (e.g., verbal or nonverbal). In stark contrast is Wechsler's theoretical framework of the assessment of *g*, a conception of intelligence as an overall global entity. As a result, Wechsler used the Verbal and Performance Scales as a means to an end, which is the assessment of general intelligence. In comparison, the Kaufmans emphasize the individual importance of the Sequential and Simultaneous Scales in interpretation, rather than the overall Mental Processing Composite (MPC) score (Kamphaus et al., 1995).

The sequential and simultaneous framework for the K-ABC stems from an updated version of a variety of theories (Kamphaus et al., 1995). The foundation lies in a wealth of research in clinical and experimental neuropsychology and cognitive psychology. The sequential and simultaneous theory was primarily developed from two lines of thought: the information-processing approach of Luria (e.g., 1966a) and the cerebral specialization work of Bogen (1975); Kinsbourne (1978); Sperry (1968, 1974); and Wada, Clarke, and Hamm (1975).

The neuropsychological processing model—which originated with the neurophysiological observations of Alexander Luria (1966a, 1973, 1980) and Roger Sperry (1968), the psychoeducational research of J. P. Das (1973; Das, Kirby, & Jarman, 1975, 1979; Naglieri & Das, 1988, 1990), and the psychometric research of A. S. Kaufman and N. L. Kaufman (1983)—has several strengths relative to previous models: (1) provides a unified framework for interpreting a wide range of important individual difference variables; (2) rests on a well-researched theoretical base in clinical neuropsychology and psychobiology; (3) presents a processing, rather than a product-oriented explanation for behavior; and (4) lends itself readily to remedial strategies based on relatively uncomplicated assessment procedures (Kaufman & Kaufman, 1983; McCallum & Merritt, 1983; Perlman, 1986).

This neuropsychological processing model describes two very distinct types of processes that individuals use to organize and process information received to solve problems successfully: successive or sequential, analytic-linear processing and holistic-simultaneous processing (Levy & Trevarthen, 1976; Luria, 1966a). These processes have been identified by numerous researchers in diverse areas of neuropsychology and cognitive psychology (Perlman, 1986). From Sperry's (1968) cerebral specialization perspective, these processes represent the problem-solving strategies of the left hemisphere (analytic-sequential) and the right hemisphere (Gestalt-holistic). From Luria's theoretical approach, successive and simultaneous processes reflect the "coding" processes that characterize "Block 2" functions.

Regardless of theoretical model, successive processing refers to the processing of information in a sequential, serial order. The essential nature of this mode of processing is that the system is not totally surveyable at any point in time. Simultaneous processing refers to the synthesis of separate elements into groups. The essential nature of this mode of processing is that any portion of the result is, at once, surveyable without dependence on its position in the whole. The model assumes that the two modes of processing information are available to the individual. The selection of either or both modes of processing depends on two conditions: (1) the individual's habitual mode of processing information as determined by social-cultural and genetic factors and (2) the demands of the task (Das et al., 1975).

In reference to the K-ABC, simultaneous processing refers to the mental ability to integrate information all at once to solve a problem correctly. Simultaneous processing frequently involves spatial, analogic, or organizational abilities (Kamphaus & Reynolds, 1987; Kaufman & Kaufman, 1983). There is often a visual aspect to the problem, and visual imagery is used to solve it. A prototypical example of a Simultaneous subtest is the Triangles subtest on the K-ABC, which is similar to Wechsler's Block Design. To solve both of these subtests, children must be able to see the whole picture in their mind and then integrate the individual pieces to create the whole.

In comparison, sequential processing emphasizes the ability to place or arrange stimuli in sequential or serial order. The stimuli are all linearly or temporally related to one another, creating a form of serial interdependence (Kaufman & Kaufman, 1983). The K-ABC subtests assess the child's sequential processing *abilities* in a variety of modes. For example, Hand Movements involves visual input and a motor response, Number Recall involves auditory input with a vocal response, and Word Order involves auditory input and visual response. These different modes of input and output allow the examiner to assess the child's sequential abilities in a variety of ways. The Sequential subtests also provide information on the child's short-term memory and attentional abilities.

According to Kamphaus et al. (1995), one of the controversial aspects of the K-ABC was the fact that it took the equivalent of Wechsler's Verbal Scale and redefined it as "achievement." The Kaufmans' analogues of tests, such as Information (Faces and Places), Vocabulary (Riddles and Expressive Vocabulary), and Arithmetic (Arithmetic), are included on the K-ABC as achievement tests and viewed as tasks that are united by the demands they place on children to extract and assimilate information from their cultural and school environment. The K-ABC is predicated on the distinction between problem solving and knowledge of facts. The former *set of skills* is interpreted as intelligence; the latter is defined as achievement. This definition is a distinction from other intelligence tests, in which a person's acquired factual information and applied skills greatly influence the obtained IQ (Kaufman & Kaufman, 1983).

## Standardization and Properties of the Scale

Stratification of the K-ABC standardization sample closely matched the 1980 U.S. Census Bureau data on the variables of age, gender, geographic region, community size, socioeconomic status, race or ethnic group, and parental occupation and education. Also, unlike most other intelligence measures for children (excluding the CAS and DAS), stratification variables also included educational placement of the child (see Table 13.2).

Reliability and validity data provide considerable support for the psychometric aspects of the K-ABC. A test-retest reliability study was conducted with 246 children after a 2- to 4-week interval (mean interval = 17 days). The coefficients for the Mental Processing Composite were .83 for age 2 years and 6 months through 4 years and 11 months; .88 for ages 5 through 8 years and 11 months; and .93 for ages 9 to 12 years and 5 months. Test-retest reliabilities for the Achievement Scale Composite for the same age groups were .95, .95, and .97, respectively (Kamphaus et al., 1995). The test-retest reliability research reveals that there is a clear developmental trend, with coefficients for the preschool ages being smaller than those for the school-age range. This trend is consistent with the known

**TABLE 13.2    Representation of the Standardized Sample by Educational Placement (N = 2,000)**

| Educational Placement | K-ABC Standardization Sample | | U.S. School-Age Population[a] |
| --- | --- | --- | --- |
| | N | % | % |
| Regular classroom | 1,862 | 93.1 | 91.1 |
| Speech impaired | 28 | 1.4 | 2.0 |
| Learning disabled | 23 | 1.2 | 2.3 |
| Mentally retarded | 37 | 1.8 | 1.7 |
| Emotionally disturbed | 5 | 0.2 | 0.3 |
| Other[b] | 15 | 0.8 | 0.7 |
| Gifted and talented | 30 | 1.5 | 1.9[c] |
| Total K-ABC sample | 2,000 | 100.0 | 100.0 |

[a]Data from U.S. Department of Education, National Center for Education Statistics, *The Condition of Education* (Washington, DC: U.S. Government Printing Office, 1980), Table 2.7.

[b]Includes other health-impaired, orthopedically handicapped, and hard-of-hearing subjects.

[c]Data from U.S. Office for Civil Rights, *State, Regional, and National Summaries of Data from the 1978 Child Rights Survey of Elementary and Secondary Schools* (Alexandria, VA: Killalea Associates, 1980), p. 5.

variability over time that characterizes preschool children's standardization test performance in general (Kamphaus & Reynolds, 1987). Split-half reliability coefficients for the K-ABC global scales range from 0.86 to 0.93 (mean = 0.90) for preschool children and from 0.89 to 0.97 (mean = 0.93) for children aged 5 to 12½ (Kamphaus et al., 1995).

There has been a considerable amount of research into the validity of the K-ABC. The *K-ABC Interpretive Manual* (Kaufman & Kaufman, 1983) includes the results of 43 such studies. Construct validity was established by looking at five separate topics: developmental changes, internal consistency, factor analysis (principal factor, principal components, and confirmatory), convergent and discriminant analysis, and correlations with other tests. Factor analysis of the Mental Processing Scales offered clear empirical support for the existence of two, and only two, factors at each age level and for the placement of each preschool and school-age subtest on its respective scale. Analyses of the combined processing and achievement subtests also offered good construct validation of the K-ABC's three-scale structure (Kaufman & Kamphaus, 1984).

Although the K-ABC and the WISC-III differ from each other in a number of ways, there is strong evidence that the two measures correlate substantially (Kamphaus & Reynolds, 1987). In a study of 182 children enrolled in regular classrooms, the Mental Processing Composite (MPC) correlated .70 with the WISC-R Full Scale IQ (FSIQ), thus, sharing a 49% overlap in variance (Kamphaus et al., 1995; Kaufman & Kaufman, 1983). Numerous correlational studies have also been conducted with handicapped and exceptional populations, which may be found in the *Interpretative Manual*. The overall correlation between the K-ABC and the WISC-R ranges from .57 to .74, indicating that the two tests overlap a good deal yet also show some independence (Kamphaus et al., 1995).

### Critique

Although the K-ABC has been the subject of past controversy, it appears that it has held its own and is used often by professionals. The test is well designed, with easy to use easels and manuals. The information in the manuals is presented in a straightforward, clear fashion, making use and interpretation relatively easy (Merz, 1985). The reporting of the reliability and validity data in the manual is complete and understandable. However, not enough information is presented on the content validity of the test. The various tasks in the subtests are based on clinical, neuropsychological, and/or other research-based validity; however, a much clearer explication of the rationale behind some of the novel subtests would have been quite helpful (Merz, 1985). The K-ABC measures intelligence from a strong theoretical and research basis, evident in the amount of research data in the manual.

The K-ABC was designed to measure the intelligence and achievement of children 2½ to 12½ years old, and the research done to date suggests that in fact the test does just that. The nonverbal scale significantly contributes to the effort to address the diverse needs of minority groups and language-handicapped children. Overall, it appears that the authors of the K-ABC have met the goals listed in the interpretive manual and that this battery is a valuable assessment tool (Merz, 1985).

Keith and Dunbar (1984) present an alternate means of interpreting the K-ABC, based on exploratory and confirmatory factor analytic data. The two K-ABC reading subtests are eliminated in this alternate analysis, and factors labeled verbal memory, nonverbal reasoning, and verbal reasoning are presented. For school-aged children whose Achievement Scale splits in half, this model may help interpret their profile. A problem with the Keith and Dunbar labels is that they do not offer evidence to support their verbal memory and nonverbal reasoning labels. Nonetheless, the research results suggest that the precise nature of the constructs underlying K-ABC standard scores should be interpreted cautiously.

## Kaufman Adolescent and Adult Intelligence Test (KAIT)

The Kaufman Adolescent and Adult Intelligence Test (KAIT) is an individually administered intelligence test for individuals between the ages of 11 and more than 85 (Kaufman & Kaufman, 1993). It provides Fluid, Crystallized, and Composite IQs, each a standard score with a mean of 100 and SD of 15.

### *Theory*

The Horn-Cattell (1967) theory forms the foundation of the KAIT and defines the constructs believed to be measured by the separate IQs; however, other theories guided the development process, specifically the construction of the subtests. Tasks were developed from the models of Piaget's formal operations (Inhelder & Piaget, 1958; Piaget, 1972) and Luria's (1973, 1980) planning ability in an attempt to include high-level, decision-making, more developmentally advanced tasks. Luria's notion of planning ability involves decision making, evaluation of hypotheses, and flexibility, and it "represents the highest levels of development of the mammalian brain" (Golden, 1981, p. 285).

Raymond B. Cattell and John Horn (Cattell, 1963; Horn & Cattell, 1966, 1967) postulated a structural model that separates fluid from crystallized intelligence. Fluid intelligence traditionally involves relatively culture-fair, novel tasks and taps problem-solving skills and the ability to learn. Crystallized intelligence refers to acquired skills, knowledge, and judgments that have been systematically taught or learned through acculturation. The latter type of intelligence is highly influenced by formal and informal education and often reflects cultural assimilation. Tasks that measure fluid ability often involve more concentration and problem solving than crystallized tasks, which tend to measure the retrieval and application of general knowledge.

Piaget's formal operations depict a hypothetical-deductive abstract-reasoning system that has as its featured capabilities the generation and evaluation of hypotheses and the testing of propositions. The prefrontal areas of the brain associated with planning ability mature at about ages 11 to 12 (Golden, 1981), the same ages that characterize the onset of formal operational thought (Piaget, 1972). The convergence of the Luria and Piaget theories about the ability to deal with abstractions is striking; this convergence provided the rationale for having age 11 as the lower bound on the KAIT and for attempting to measure decision making and abstract thinking with virtually every task on the test (Kaufman & Kaufman, 1993).

Within the KAIT framework (Kaufman & Kaufman, 1993), crystallized intelligence "measures the acquisition of facts and problem solving ability using stimuli that are dependent on formal schooling, cultural experiences, and verbal conceptual development" (p. 7). Fluid intelligence "measures a person's adaptability and flexibility when faced with new problems, using both verbal and nonverbal stimuli" (p. 7). It is important to note that this crystallized-fluid construct is not the same as Wechsler's (1974, 1981, 1991) verbal-nonverbal split. The results of a factor analysis of the WISC-R and the KAIT showed that the KAIT Crystallized subtests loaded highly on the crystallized-verbal factor (.47–.78), Fluid subtests loaded .51–.88 on the fluid factor, and Memory for Block Designs loaded .41 on the perceptual organization factor (Kaufman & Kaufman, 1993; Kaufman, Ishikuma, & Kaufman, 1994). The KAIT Fluid subtests stress reasoning rather than visual-spatial ability, include verbal comprehension or expression as key aspects of some tasks, and minimize the role played by visual-motor speed for correct responding. In addition, the KAIT scales measure what Horn (1989) refers to as broad fluid and broad crystallized abilities rather than the purer and more specific skill areas that have emerged in Horn's expansion and elaboration of the original Horn-Cattell (1966) Fluid-Crystallized (Gf-Gc) theory.

The Core Battery of the KAIT is made up of three Crystallized and three Fluid subtests, and these six subtests are used to compute the IQs. The Expanded Battery also includes two supplementary subtests and two measures of delayed recall that evaluate the individual's ability to retain information that was learned previously in the evaluation during two of the Core subtests. The Core Battery of the KAIT consists of subtests 1 through 6, and subtests 1 through 10 make up the Expanded Battery. Each subtest except the supplementary Mental Status task yields age-based scaled scores with a mean of 10 and SD of 3. Sample and teaching items are included for most subtests to ensure that examinees understand what is expected of them.

The delayed recall subtests are administered, without prior warning, about 25 and 45 minutes after the administration of the original, related subtests. The two delayed recall subtests provide a good measure of the ability that Horn (1985, 1989) calls TSR (long-term storage and retrieval), which "involves the storage of information and the fluency of retrieving it later through association" (Woodcock, 1990. p. 234).

The Mental Status subtest is made up of 10 simple questions that assess attention and orientation to the world. Most normal adolescents and adults pass at least 9 of the 10 items, but the task has a special use with retarded and neurologically impaired populations. The Mental Status subtest may be used as a screener to determine if the KAIT can be validly administered.

## Standardization and Properties of the Scale

The KAIT normative sample, comprising 2,000 adolescents and adults between the ages of 11 and 94, was stratified on the variables of gender, racial-ethnic group, geographic region, and socioeconomic status. Mean split-half reliability coefficients for the total normative sample were .95 for Crystallized IQ, .95 for Fluid IQ, and .97 for Composite IQ. Mean test-retest reliability coefficients, based on 153 identified normal individuals in three age groups (11–19, 20–54, 55–85+), retested after a one-month interval, were .94 for Crystallized IQ, .87 for Fluid IQ, and .94 for Composite IQ. Mean split-half reliabilities of the four Crystallized subtests ranged from .89 to .92 (median = .90). Mean values for the four Fluid subtests ranged from .79 to .93 (median = .88). Median test-retest reliabilities for the eight subtests, based on the 153 people indicated previously, ranged from .72 to .95 (median = .78). Rebus Delayed Recall had an average split-half reliability of .91, and Auditory Delayed Recall had an average value of .71; their respective stability coefficients were .80 and .63 (Kaufman & Kaufman, 1993).

Factor analysis, both exploratory and confirmatory, gave strong construct validity support for the Fluid and Crystallized Scales and for the placement of each subtest on its designated scale. Crystallized IQs correlated .72 with Fluid IQs for the total standardization sample of 2,000 (Kaufman & Kaufman, 1993).

Table 13.3 summarizes the results of correlational studies of the KAIT and other well-known intelligence tests. The values shown in the table support the construct and criterion-related validity of the three KAIT IQs.

The KAIT benefits from an integration of theories that unite developmental (Piaget, 1972), neuropsychological (Luria, 1973), and experimental-cognitive (Horn-Cattell, 1966) models of intellectual functioning. The theories work well together and do not compete with one another. Together, the theories give the KAIT a solid theoretical foundation that facilitates test interpretation across the broad 11–94 age range on which the battery was normed.

## Critique

The KAIT represents a reconceptualization of the measurement of intelligence that is more consistent with current theories of intellectual development (Brown, 1994). The fluid-crystallized dichotomy, the theory underlying the KAIT, is based on the original Horn-Cattell (1966) theory of intelligence, thus offering a firm and well-researched theoretical framework (Flanagan, Alfonso & Flanagan, 1994) and enhancing the richness of the clinical interpretations that can be drawn from this instrument (Brown, 1994). The test materials are well constructed and attractive, and the manual is well organized and helpful (Dumont & Hagberg, 1994; Flanagan et al., 1984). Furthermore, the test materials are easy to use and stimulating to

TABLE 13.3  Correlations of the Three KAIT IQs with Standard Scores and IQs Yielded by Other Major Intelligence Tests

| | Age | Sample Size | KAIT Crystallized | KAIT Fluid | KAIT Composite |
|---|---|---|---|---|---|
| **WAIS-R IQ Scale** | | | | | |
| Verbal | 16–19 | 71 | .85 | .74 | .86 |
| | 20–34 | 90 | .78 | .66 | .78 |
| | 35–49 | 108 | .79 | .74 | .85 |
| | 50–83 | 74 | .85 | .70 | .86 |
| Performance | 16–19 | 71 | .64 | .70 | .72 |
| | 20–34 | 90 | .60 | .74 | .73 |
| | 35–49 | 108 | .57 | .73 | .73 |
| | 50–83 | 74 | .74 | .66 | .77 |
| Full Scale | 16–19 | 71 | .84 | .79 | .88 |
| | 20–34 | 90 | .77 | .76 | .83 |
| | 35–49 | 108 | .74 | .78 | .85 |
| | 50–83 | 74 | .84 | .70 | .85 |
| **WISC-R IQ Scale** | | | | | |
| Verbal | 11–16 | 118 | .79 | .74 | .83 |
| Performance | 11–16 | 118 | .67 | .67 | .72 |
| Full Scale | 11–16 | 118 | .78 | .75 | .82 |
| **K-ABC** | | | | | |
| Sequential | 11–12 | 124 | .46 | .44 | .50 |
| Simultaneous | 11–12 | 124 | .53 | .62 | .63 |
| Mental Processing Composite | 11–12 | 124 | .57 | .62 | .66 |
| Achievement | 11–12 | 124 | .81 | .64 | .82 |
| **Standford-Binet-IV** | | | | | |
| Composite Intelligence | 11–42 | 79 | .81 | .84 | .87 |

examinees (Flanagan, et al., 1994). The measurement techniques used in the KAIT have been noted to be state-of-the-art (Brown, 1994). The psychometric properties for standardization and reliability are excellent, and the construct validity evidence that is reported in the manual provides a good foundation for its theoretical underpinnings (Flanagan et al., 1994).

The theoretical assumption that formal operations is reached by early adolescence limits that application of the KAIT with certain adolescent and adult populations (Brown, 1994). If an individual has not achieved formal operations, many of the subtests will be too difficult and perhaps frustrating and overwhelming. Examiners should be aware of this limitation when working with such individuals in order to maintain rapport. The KAIT can be a useful assessment tool when working with high-functioning, intelligent individuals; however, it can be difficult to use with borderline individuals and some elderly clients. Elderly clients' scores on some of the subtests may be negatively affected by poor reading, poor hearing, and poor memory (Dumont & Hagberg, 1994). Flanagan et al. (1994) report that the inclusion of only three subtests per scale may limit or interfere with the calculation of IQs if a subtest is spoiled. The usefulness of the Expanded Battery and Mental Status subtest of clinical populations is questionable, given the reliability and validity data presented in the manual, suggesting that interpretations should be made with caution.

Although there clearly are some limitations

in the use of the KAIT with some populations, overall the test appears to be well thought out and validated (Dumont & Hagberg, 1994). The KAIT represents an advancement in the field of intellectual assessment because of its ability to measure fluid and crystallized intelligence from a theoretical perspective and, at the same time, maintain a solid psychometric quality (Flanagan et al., 1994).

## Cognitive Assessment System (CAS)

### Theory

The Cognitive Assessment System (Naglieri & Das, 1997a, 1997b) is based on, and developed according to, the planning, attention, simultaneous, and successive (PASS) theory of intelligence. The PASS theory is a multidimensional view of ability that is the result of the merging of contemporary theoretical and applied psychology recently summarized by Das, Naglieri, and Kirby (1994) and Naglieri and Das (1997a, 1997b). Naglieri and Das linked the work of Luria (1966, 1973, 1980) with the field of intelligence when they suggested that PASS processes are the essential elements of human cognitive functioning. That is, human cognitive functioning includes four components: **planning** processes that provide cognitive control, utilization of processes and knowledge, and intentionality and self-regulation to achieve a desired goal; **attentional** processes that provide focused, selective cognitive activity over time; and **simultaneous and successive** information processes that are the two forms of operating on information. These are described in more detail as follows.

### Planning

"Planning is a mental process by which the individual determines, selects, applies, and evaluates solutions to problems" (Naglieri & Das, 1997a, p. 2). Planning is a way to solve problems for which no solution is apparent. It applies to tasks that may involve attention, simultaneous and successive processes, and acquired knowledge. Success on planning tests should require the child to develop a plan of action or strategy, evaluate its value, monitor its effectiveness, revise or reject an old plan as the task demands change, and control the impulse to act without careful consideration.

### Attention

"Attention is a mental process by which the individual selectively focuses on particular stimuli while inhibiting responses to competing stimuli presented over time" (Naglieri & Das, 1997a, p. 3). An attention task requires focused, selective, sustained, and effortful performance. Focused attention involves concentration directed toward a particular activity. Selective attention requires the inhibition of responses to some stimuli over others, which may be hard to ignore. Sustained attention refers to the performance over time, which can be influenced by the varying amounts of effort required. In other words, attention tests should present children with competing demands and require sustained focus over time.

### Simultaneous Processing

"Simultaneous processing is a mental process by which the individual integrates separate stimuli into a single whole or group" (Naglieri & Das, 1997a, p. 4). The essence of simultaneous processing is that it allows for the interrelation of elements into a conceptual whole. It has strong spatial components in nonverbal tasks and in language tasks that involve logical-grammatical relationships. The spatial aspect involves both the perception of stimuli as a group and the internalized formation of complex visual images. The logical-grammatical dimension allows for the integration of words into ideas through the comprehension of word relationships to obtain meaning. Thus, simultaneous processes can be important to both nonverbal spatial and verbal tasks.

### Successive Processing

"Successive processing is a mental process by which the individual integrates stimuli into a specific serial order that forms a chain-like progression" (Neglieri & Das, 1997a, p. 5). Successive processing is involved when parts must follow one another in a specific order so that each element is related only to those that precede it. Successive processing is most important in tasks with serial and syntactic components. The serial aspect involves both the perception of stimuli in sequence and the formation of sounds and movements in order. The syntactic aspect of successive processing allows for the comprehension of narrative speech, especially when the "individual elements of the whole narrative always behave as if organized in certain successive series" (Luria, 1966, p. 78). Successive processing activities require perception and reproduction of the serial nature of stimuli, the understanding of sentences based on syntactic relationships, and the articulation of separate sounds in a consecutive series.

The CAS was designed to mirror the PASS theory, with subtests organized into four scales to provide an effective measure of each of the PASS cognitive processes. Planning subtests require the child to devise, select, and use efficient plans of action to solve the test problems, regulate the effectiveness of the plans, and self-correct when necessary. Attention subtests require the child to selectively attend to a particular stimulus and inhibit attention to distracting stimuli. Simultaneous Processing subtests require the child to integrate stimuli into groups to form an interrelated whole, and Successive Processing subtests require the child to integrate stimuli in their specific serial order or appreciate the linearity of stimuli with little opportunity for interrelating the parts.

The CAS yields scores for Planning, Attention, Simultaneous, Successive, and Full Scales that are normalized standard scores with a normative mean of 100 and SD of 15. The Planning Scale's subtests include Matching Numbers, Planned Codes, Planned Connections, and Planned Search; the Attention Scale subtests include Number Detection, Receptive Attention, and Expressive Attention; the Simultaneous Scale subtests are Nonverbal Matrices, Verbal-Spatial Relations, and Figure Memory; and the Successive Scale subtests are Word Series, Sentence Repetition, Sentence Questions, and Successive Speech Rate. All subtests are set at a normative mean of 10 and SD of 3.

The interpretation of CAS also follows closely from the PASS theory, with emphasis on the scale rather than subtest-level analyses. The *Interpretive Handbook* includes ample directions for the evaluation of test results; integration of information about the strategies used during planning tests; comparison of PASS scores, using the ipsative method described earlier in this chapter for the WISC-III; and methods for comparing the PASS scores to achievement, using simple and predicted difference models. Illustrative case reports and a summary of relevant intervention research and their implications for treatment are also provided.

### Standardization and Properties of the Scale

The CAS was standardized on 2,200 children, ranging in age from 5 through 17 and stratified by age, gender, race, ethnicity, geographic region, educational placement, and parent education, according to recent U.S. Census Bureau reports, and closely matches the U.S. population on the variables used. A representative sample of 1,600 in the standardization sample was also administered achievement tests from the Woodcock-Johnson Tests of Achievement (Woodcock & Johnson, 1989). This provided a rich source of validity evidence (e.g., the analysis of the relationships between PASS and achievement) and predictive difference values needed for interpretation of ability achievement discrepancies. Finally, 872 children from special populations, for example, attention deficit, mentally retarded, and learning disabled, were tested for validity and reliability studies.

The internal consistency reliability estimates for the CAS Full Scale are comparable with other tests of its type. The average scale reliability coefficients for the CAS Standard Battery (12 subtests) for the entire standardization sample of children aged 5 to 17 are as follows: Full Scale, .96; Planning, .88; Simultaneous, .93; Attention, .88; and Successive, .93. The average reliability coefficients for all ages in the standardization sample for the 12 subtests range from .75 to .89 (median = .82). The test-retest reliability for the Full Scale—for 215 children aged 5 to 17 who were administered the CAS over an interval that ranged from 9 to 73 days (median = 21 days)—is .91; Planning .85; Simultaneous, .81; Attention, .82; and Successive, .86.

In the CAS *Interpretive Handbook*, Naglieri and Das (1997a) provide a substantial amount of validity research. Construct validity was supported by evidence of developmental changes, high internal consistency, results of confirmatory factor analyses, and utilization of strategies for completion of planning tests. Criterion-related validity was shown by the strong relationships between CAS scores and WJ-R achievement tests; correlations with achievement for special populations; and PASS profiles for children with attention-deficit and hyperactivity disorders, traumatic brain injury, and reading disability. Test fairness was demonstrated by a series of studies of the prediction of achievement for whites and blacks, Hispanic and non-Hispanic, and males and females. The utility of the PASS scores for treatment and educational planning was also demonstrated.

### Critique

Carroll (1995) had two main criticisms of the PASS theory. First, he suggested that the planning is better described as a perceptual speed factor; second, he argued that there was insufficient factorial support for the PASS as a measure of the constructs. Since the publication of Carroll's review, both of these criticisms have been amply addressed by data in the CAS *Interpretive Handbook* (Naglieri & Das, 1997a), some of which are summarized here. Naglieri and Das give strong evidence from confirmatory factor analytic investigations, using the CAS standardization data, that a four-factor PASS configuration of the 12 subtests provided the best fit to the data. The one-, two-, and three-factor solutions were inadequate, and the four-factor model was a significant improvement over the competing three-factor solutions. The four-factor PASS model resulted in the lowest chi-square values, highest adjusted goodness-of-fit index, and lowest mean squared root residual. Thus, it appears that Carroll's reanalyses of old experimental test data (some of the tests are not in the final version of the CAS) and smaller sample sizes led to the inconsistencies between his results and those in the manual. Carroll's second criticism, that the Planning subtests really measure speed, is also inconsistent with two sources of data.

Naglieri and Das (1997a) provide convincing data that, overall, approximately 90% of the entire standardization sample used strategies to solve the Planning tests. These strategies show developmental changes and are differentially related to success on the subtests. Clearly, tests that have been shown to demand the generation, use, and monitoring of plans of action cannot be described as simple perceptual speed measures. More evidence that planning is not better described as perceptual speed is apparent when the relationship between planning and achievement is considered.

Naglieri and Das (1997a) provide considerable information about the relationships between PASS and achievement for a large representative sample of children who were administered the WJ-R. For example, they show that for children aged 5–7, 8–10, 11–13, and 14–17 (total $N = 1,600$), the correlations between Planning and Broad Mathematics and Mathematics Reasoning (see Table 13.4) were substantial. In contrast, McGrew and Hessler (1995) provide correlations between the WJ-R Cognitive Gs (Gs = Processing Speed) for the WJ-R standardization sample ($N$ = approximately 5,930) that when similarly described for ages 5–7, 8–10, 11–13, and 14–17, are considerably lower for both Broad Math and

**TABLE 13.4** **Correlations Between the CAS Planning Scale and WJ-R Perceptual Speed Factor with Math Achievement**

| Age Groups | CAS Planning | | WJ-R Gs (Perceptual Speed) | |
|---|---|---|---|---|
| | BdMt | MtR | BdMt | MtR |
| 5–7 | .53 | .44 | .37 | .28 |
| 8–10 | .57 | .51 | .28 | .22 |
| 11–13 | .60 | .61 | .20 | .18 |
| 14–17 | .59 | .53 | .26 | .18 |

Mathematics Reasoning (see Table 13.4). Not only does Gs account for considerably less variance than Planning, but also the correlations decline over the course of ages 5 to 17. The evidence for the use of strategies on Planning tests and the strong and consistent correlations between CAS and math achievement do not support Carroll's (1995) reinterpretation of planning as speed. Moreover, Naglieri (1997) provided evidence that the overall CAS Full Scale correlated substantially (.77) with the Skills Cluster of the WJ-R, and the WJ-R Tests of Cognitive Ability Extended Battery score, like the results in Table 13.4, correlated lower (.71) with Skills. Thus, the strong relationships between the PASS scales and achievement are not limited to a comparison between planning and perceptual speed. The arguments presented here suggest that the CAS Planning Scale measures planning processes that do not seem to be, as Carroll has stated, just measures of perceptual speed. Future research should explore the relationships between pure perceptual speed tasks that involve minimal decision making, as well as other related tests such as the Piagetian formal operations measures found on the KAIT.

Finally, Esters, Ittenbach, and Han (1997) state that "attempts to establish the treatment validity of . . . the CAS have met with little success" (p. 217). This statement is inconsistent with evidence summarized by Naglieri and Das (1997a) and especially the papers published by Naglieri and Gottling (1995, in press), who showed the relevance of PASS to math instruction. Naglieri and Gottling demonstrated that children who are poor in planning improved considerably (80% over baseline) in math calculation taken directly from the classroom curriculum when given instruction that encouraged their use of strategies or plans. In contrast, children who were good in planning showed modest improvement (about 40% over baseline) when given exactly the same instruction. No similar relationships were found between Attention, Simultaneous, Successive, or Wechsler IQ scores. These results are contrary to Esters et al's suggestions and also consistent with earlier research by Cormier, Carlson, and Das (1990) and Kar, Dash, Das, and Carlson (1993) that an interaction between planning and performance can be shown.

## Woodcock-Johnson Psycho-Educational Battery–Revised: Tests of Cognitive Ability (WJ-R)

The WJ-R is one of the most comprehensive test batteries for the clinical assessment of children and adolescents (Kamphaus, 1993). It is a battery of tests for individuals from age 2 to 90+ and is made up of two sections, Cognitive and Achievement. The focus of this discussion is the Cognitive portion of the WJ-R battery.

### Theory

The WJ-R Cognitive battery is based on Horn's expansion of the fluid-crystallized model of intelligence. The standard and supplemental subtests of the WJ-R are aligned with eight of the cognitive abilities isolated by Horn (1985, 1989; Kamphaus, 1993; Kaufman, 1990). The cognitive battery measures seven Horn abilities: long-term retrieval, short-term memory, processing speed, auditory processing, visual processing, comprehension-knowledge, and fluid reasoning. An eighth ability, quantitative ability, is measured by several Achievement subtests on the WJ-R.

The four subtests that measure long-term retrieval (Memory for Names, Visual-Auditory Learning, Delayed Recall/Memory for Names, and Delayed Recall/Visual-Auditory Learning), require the subject to retrieve information stored minutes or a few days earlier. In contrast, the subtests that measure short-term memory (Memory for Sentences, Memory for Words, and Numbers Reversed) require the subject to store information and retrieve it immediately or within a few seconds. The two processing speed subtests (Visual Matching and Cross Out) assess the subject's ability to work quickly, particularly under pressure to maintain focused attention.

In the auditory processing domain, three subtests (Incomplete Words, Sound Blending, and Sound Patterns) assess the subject's ability to fluently perceive patterns among auditory stimuli. The three visual processing subtests (Visual Closure, Picture Recognition, and Spatial Relations) assess the subject's ability to fluently manipulate stimuli that are in the visual domain.

Picture Vocabulary, Oral Vocabulary, Listening Comprehension, and Verbal Analogies are the four subtests linked to the comprehension-knowledge factor, also known as crystallized intelligence in Horn's (1985) theoretical model. These subtests require the subject to demonstrate the breadth and depth of his or her knowledge of a culture. Analysis-Synthesis, Concept Formation, Spatial Relations, and Verbal Analogies (which also loads on the comprehension-knowledge factor) assess the subject's fluid reasoning, or "new" problem-solving ability. Finally, from the Achievement portion of the WJ-R, both the Calculation and Applied Problems subtests assess the individual's quantitative ability.

The Cognitive Battery comprises 21 subtests, 7 of which make up the Standard Battery; the remaining 14 are part of the supplemental battery, one per ability as described by Horn (1985, 1989). Two composite scores, Broad Cognitive Ability and Early Development (for preschoolers), are both comparable to an overall IQ score. The individual subtest scores, as well as the composite scores, have a mean of 100 and SD of 15.

Computer software is available for scoring the WJ-R and is essential if one is to obtain all of the information that the WJ-R is capable of providing. The test provides percentile ranks, grade-based scores, age-based scores, and the Relative Mastery Index (RMI). The RMI is a unique kind of ratio, the second part being set at a value of 90. The denominator of the ratio means that children in the norm sample can perform the intellectual task with 90% accuracy. The numerator of the ratio refers to that child or adolescent's proficiency on that subtest (Kamphaus, 1993). For example, if a child obtains an RMI of 60/90, it would mean that the child's proficiency on the subtest is at a 60% level, whereas the typical child of his or her age (or grade) mastered the material at a 90% level of accuracy.

The entire battery is quite lengthy and therefore can require quite a lot of time to administer. The seven-subtest Standard Battery takes approximately 40 minutes; however, all the clinician will obtain from it is, essentially, a measure of *g*. To obtain all of the information that the WJ-R is capable of providing, a clinician should administer most of the subtests in both the Cognitive and Achievement Batteries. Administration of a thorough cognitive and achievement assessment with the WJ-R would take approximately three and one-half to five hours, depending on the subject's age, abilities, and speed. However, individual subtests may be used to test specific hypothesis without administering the entire battery. The WJ-R tests also provide measures of differential scholastic aptitudes, including reading, mathematics, written language, and knowledge. An aptitude-achievement comparison may be made if the WJ-R Tests of Achievement are also given. Such a discrepancy reflects the amount of disparity between certain intellectual capabilities of an individual and his or her actual academic performance.

## Standardization and Properties of the Scale

The WJ-R was normed on a reasonably representative sample of 6,359 individuals selected to provide a cross section of the U.S. population from age 2 to 90+ (Woodcock & Mather, 1989). The sample included 705 preschool children, 3,245 students in grades K–12, 916 college or university students, and 1,493 individuals aged 14 to 90+ who were not enrolled in school. Stratification variables included gender, geographic region, community size, and race. However, Kaufman (1990) reports that although representation on important background variables was adequate, it was necessary to use a weighing procedure to adjust the data that were collected so they would match U.S. population statistics.

The internal consistency estimates for the standard and supplemental battery subtests are good, with median scores from ages 2 to 79 ranging from .69 to .93. The Broad Cognitive Ability composite score for the seven Standard Battery subtests yields a median internal consistency coefficient of .94, and the Broad Cognitive Ability Early Development Scale yields a coefficient of .96 at ages 2 and 4 (Kamphaus, 1993).

## Critique

The WJ-R Cognitive Battery was based on Horn's (1985) expansion of the Horn and Cattell (1967) fluid-crystallized model of intelligence. This theoretical rationale allows for further empirical analysis of both the WJ-R and the theory (Webster, 1994). The standardization of the battery appears to be sound, and the various age groups are adequately represented.

The Cognitive Battery is quite thorough and, when administered in its entirety, can provide the examiner with a wealth of information about an individual's intellectual functioning and abilities. The test materials and manuals are easy to use and well designed. The administration is fairly simple; however, scoring the test, especially when the Achievement Battery is administered as well, can be quite a lengthy and, initially, a difficult process. The scoring can be done by hand but is more efficient with the computer scoring program. This program is easy to use and provides the individual's raw scores, standard scores, percentile ranks, and age and grade equivalents for each subtest (Webster, 1994).

The WJ-R Cognitive Battery is a well-standardized test developed on a "factorially" based theory of intelligence. However, the test is not without shortcomings. Webster (1994) raises issues with the specific psychometric procedures used in developing test items. Data are lacking that show the efficacy of the WJ-R to predict, from a time-based perspective, actual functional levels of academic achievement and to identify children at risk for failure early in the educational process. Kaufman (1990) points to another shortcoming, the small number of tests that make up each scale. The Standard Scale measures each of the seven scales with one subtest apiece. Finally, McGrew, Flanagan, Keith, and Vanderwood (1997) note that the Gf-Gc theory is "largely a product of linear equations (viz., factor analysis) . . . and "is most likely not a good indication of the organization of actual human abilities" (p. 194).

Several standardization procedures used in the WJ-R are not typical of those used to create norms for the intelligence tests described in this chapter. First, while the sample was stratified on most of the usual variables (see WJ-R *Technical Manual*, p. 64), the individual child's parental educational level or socioeconomic status was not directly determined. Instead, children in the standardization sample were given an SES level based on the characteristics of the school they attended, not a level reported by their parent(s) or guardian(s). Although sampling at the school level is a reasonable approach, the reliance on data from those subjects who agree to be tested (e.g., the higher SES ones) is problematic because it could have excluded the hard-to-get cases. Unfortunately, the data at the individual child level are not available to evaluate precisely the SES level of the children in the WJ-R normative sample. Second, examiners who collected standardization data were mostly "substitute teachers [and] paraprofessionals . . . [who were] not required to have had prior professional training" (McGrew, Werder, & Woodcock, 1991, p. 77). This could create an important difference between the conditions during standardization and those created by a certified school psychologist, for example. Third, unlike the K-ABC or CAS, the WJ-R standardization sample did not include handicapped students unless they happened to attend those regular classes that were sampled.

The *Woodcock-Johnson Psycho-Educational Battery: Revised Examiner's Manual* reports that "Items included in the various tests were selected using item validity studies as well as expert opinion" (Woodcock & Mather, 1989, p. 7). Kamphaus (1993) states that the manual should have included more information on the results of the experts' judgments or some information on the methods and results of the studies that were used to assess validity.

It is clear that the WJ-R Cognitive Battery is quite comprehensive, providing a wealth of information. The standardization sample is large, the factor loadings reveal generally strong factor analytic support for the construct validity for the battery for adolescents and adults, and the reliability coefficients are excellent (Kaufman, 1990).

## Differential Abilities Scales (DAS)
### Theory

The DAS was developed by Elliott (1990) and is an individually administered battery of 17 cognitive and achievement tests for use with individuals aged 2½ through 17. The DAS Cognitive Battery has a preschool level and a school-age level. The latter includes reading, mathematics, and spelling achievement tests that are referred to as "screeners." The same sample of subjects was used to develop the norms for the Cognitive and Achievement Batteries; therefore, intra- and intercomparisons of the two domains are possible.

The DAS is not based on a specific theory of intelligence. Instead, the test's structure is based on tradition and statistical analysis. Nonetheless, the test is not theory free, and in fact is based in part on *g* and the view of intelligence as hierarchical in nature (McGhee, 1993). Elliott (1990)

described his approach to the development of the DAS as "eclectic" and cited such researchers as Cattell, Horn, Das, Jensen, Thurstone, Vernon, and Spearman. Indeed, there are some clear-cut relationships between several DAS scales and theoretical constructs. For example, Horn's (1985, 1989) concepts of fluid and crystallized intelligence are measured quite well by the Nonverbal Reasoning and Verbal Ability scales, respectively. Elliott endorses Thurstone's ideas that the emphasis in intellectual assessment should be on the assessment and interpretation of distinct abilities (Kamphaus, 1993). He also stresses that in the assessment of children with learning and developmental disabilities, clinicians need more fine detail than is provided by a global IQ score (Elliott, in press). Therefore, subtests were constructed to emphasize their unique variance, which should translate into unique abilities.

The cognitive portion of the DAS consists of "core" and "diagnostic" subtests designed to assess intelligence at the preschool and the school-age level. The core subtests measure complex processing and conceptual ability, which is strongly *g*-related. The diagnostic subtests measure less cognitively complex functions, such as short-term memory and processing speed, thereby having less of a *g* saturation (Elliott, in press). The achievement portion measures skills in the areas of word reading, spelling, and basic number skills. The core subtests are averaged to obtain the General Conceptual Ability (GCA) score, and depending on the age of the individual, additional composite scores are calculated, which are referred to as Cluster scores.

The individual cognitive subtests have a mean of 50 and an SD of 10. The GCA scores, Cluster scores, and Achievement scores, have a mean of 100 and SD of 15. Percentile ranks, age equivalents, and score comparisons are also available in the examiner's manual. Score comparisons provide a profile analysis and allow the examiner to ascertain information about aptitude-achievement discrepancies.

Interpretation of the DAS subtests and composites is facilitated by the framework provided in the handbook. One positive aspect of interpreting the DAS is that the "design of scoring procedures on the Record Form enables statistically significant high and low scores to be identified immediately" (Elliott, in press, p. 37). Significant discrepancies between subtests, cluster scores, and ability and achievement can be obtained immediately. Like Kaufman's (1994a) approach in interpreting the WISC-III, an ipsative approach is used to examine differences between subtests, requiring the examiner to compare the child's mean score on core subtests to his or her individual subtest scores. Discrepancy between ability and achievement is analyzed by examining the GCA (or Special Nonverbal Composite) and each of the achievement tests.

## *Standardization and Properties of the Scale*

Elliott (in press) notes that exceptionally careful and effective standardization and data-analytic procedures were used in the development of the DAS, which was standardized on 3,475 children tested between 1987 and 1989. The normative sample included 200 cases for each age level between the ages of 5 and 17. The younger part of the sample consisted of 350 children between the ages of 2 years and 6 months and 4 years and 11 months. Exceptional children were also included in the standardization sample. Gender, race, geographic region, community size, and enrollment (for ages 2–5 through 5–11) in an educational program were controlled. Socioeconomic status was estimated by using the average educational level of the parent or parents living with the child (Kamphaus, 1993).

Over and above the requirements of the norm sample, 600 cases of black and Hispanic children were collected in order to perform statistical analysis for item bias and prediction bias. The test developers wanted to ensure that the rules for scoring would be sensitive to the responses of minority children (Elliott, in press). Only a small number of items were deleted because of item bias, and there was "no evidence" that the DAS is biased against either blacks or Hispanics (Elliott, 1990).

The DAS has a median reliability estimate of .95 for the GCA. Internal consistency reliability estimates for the cluster scores range from .83 for Nonverbal Reasoning at age 5 to .94 for Spatial at several ages (Kamphaus, 1993). The test-retest reliability coefficients for the preschool composite scores are .84 for Verbal Ability and .79 for Nonverbal Ability. The individual subtests' reliabilities vary with an average coefficient of .78.

Correlational research has shown good evidence of concurrent validity for the DAS (Kamphaus, 1993). With a sample of 27 children aged 7 to 14, the WISC-III Full Scale IQ correlated very highly with the DAS GCA score (.92), and the WISC-III Verbal IQ score correlated highly with the DAS Verbal Ability score (.87). The WISC-III Performance IQ correlated .78 with Nonverbal Reasoning and .82 with Spatial Ability. Additionally, the DAS Speed of Information Processing subtest score correlated .67 with the WISC-III Processing Speed Index score. The Binet IV Composite IQ correlated .88 with the DAS GCA for 9- and 10-year-olds and .85 with the DAS GCA for a sample of gifted children. The K-ABC Mental Processing Composite correlated .75 with the DAS GCA for 5- to 7-year-olds (Kamphaus, 1993).

Elliott presents three validity studies not published in the DAS manual. One of these included a confirmatory factor analysis of the DAS by Keith (1990), which concluded that "the constructs measured by the DAS are remarkably consistent across overlapping age levels of the test" (Elliott, in press, p. 20). Elliott also discusses a joint factor analysis of the DAS and WISC-R. In a reanalysis of data, Elliott reports the emergence of five factors: crystallized intelligence (including DAS Verbal and WISC-R Verbal subtests), spatial or broad visualization (including DAS spatial and four of the five major WISC-R Performance subtests), nonverbal reasoning or fluid intelligence (defined only by DAS Nonverbal Reasoning subtests), auditory short-term memory, and speed of processing.

## *Critique*

In general, the professional reviews of the DAS seem to be quite positive. Sandoval reports that it is one of the least biased tests available today. It appears to be a relatively culture-fair measure; however, its use with linguistically different children needs to be explored further (Sandoval, 1992). The group differences typically found on traditional IQ tests are also found on the DAS. For example, African-American and Hispanic children score between half and two-thirds of a standard deviation below white children, and Asian children score above white children on all but verbal areas of the test. Caution is necessary when assessing Hispanic children because the DAS overpredicts achievement for this group (Bain, 1991). The author of the DAS suggests that children who are not proficient in English be given the nonverbal tests on the Special Nonverbal scale in the primary language. However, this can be problematic, as the test developers did not provide directions in other common languages, such as Spanish. In addition, the utility of the English norms for assessing a child who is administered the test in Spanish or another non-English language has not been explored.

The DAS manual has recommendations for administering the test to deaf children or to children with limited English; however, these recommendations are lacking in a couple of areas. Braden (1992) notes, "The recommendations that age equivalents be used to represent the performance of a retarded person is common, but it is potentially misleading" (p. 93). Another problem is that no mention is made of the use of interpreters for hearing-impaired and nonverbal children, which may have a detrimental effect on deaf children's test scores.

According to Braden (1992), the *Technical Manual* includes extensive research data that suggest that the DAS is a psychometric improvement over existing techniques for measuring intellectual abilities and for determining intra-cognitive and aptitude-achievement discrepancies. The GCA of the DAS is largely independent of tasks known to be difficult for learning-disabled children and is able to assist in the identification of learning disabilities or processing deficits.

The DAS can be a useful tool in assessing intelligence and achievement in both children and adolescents. However, a few of its characteristics do not promote ease of administration, especially for novices (Braden, 1992); for example, one has to apply two rules for subtest discontinuation, and it is necessary to convert raw scores to ability scores before obtaining subtest scaled scores. The DAS *Examiner's Manual* provides interpretive information and a framework for interpretation for the composite scores and subtests. The level and/or depth of information that the interpretative portion of the manual provides is quite thorough and is easy to use, making interpretation of the profiles and individual and composite scores much easier.

## The Stanford-Binet, Fourth Edition
### Theory

Like its predecessors, the Stanford-Binet, Fourth Edition (Binet IV), is based on the principal of a general ability factor, *g*, rather than on a connection of separate functions. This edition has maintained, although to a much lesser degree, its adaptive testing format. No examinee takes all the items on the scale, nor do all examinees of the same chronological age respond to the same tasks. Like its predecessors, the scale provides a

continuous appraisal of cognitive development from ages two through young adult.

One of the criticisms in the previous versions is that they tended to underestimate the intelligence of examinees whose strongest abilities did not lie in verbal skills (or overestimate the intelligence of those whose did). Therefore, consideration when developing the Binet IV was to give equal credence to several areas of cognitive functioning. The authors set out to appraise verbal reasoning, quantitative reasoning, abstract and visual reasoning, and short-term memory (in addition to a composite score representing *g*).

This model is based on a three-level hierarchical model of the structure of cognitive abilities. A general reasoning factor is at the top level (*g*). The next level consists of three broad factors: crystallized abilities, fluid analytic abilities, and short-term memory. The Horn-Cattell (1967) theory forms a foundation for the test; measures of Gc are Verbal and Quantitative, and Abstract-Visual is a Gf scale. The third level consists of more specific factors, similar to some of Thurstone's eight primary mental factors: verbal reasoning, quantitative reasoning, and also abstract and visual reasoning. The selection of these four areas came from the authors' research and clinical experience of the kinds of cognitive abilities that correlate with school progress.

The Binet IV contains previous tasks, combining old with new items, and some completely new tasks. In general, test items were accepted if (1) they proved to be acceptable measurements of the construct, (2) they could be reliably administered and scored, (3) they were relatively free of ethnic and/or gender bias, and (4) they functioned adequately over a wide range of age groups.

### Standardization and Properties of the Scale

Standardization procedures followed 1980 U.S. Census Bureau data. There appears to be an accurate sample representation from geographic region, size of community, race and ethnic group, and gender. The standardization falls short, however, in terms of age, parental occupation, and parental education. The total sample size was large (5,013), with age representation extending from 2 years to 23 years and 11 months. The concentration of the sample is on children 4 to 9 years old (41%). Not only were adults 24 years and older not represented, but also representation beyond age 17 years and 11 months was negligible (4%).

To assess SES characteristics, information about parental occupation and education was obtained. A review of Table 13.5 demonstrates that children whose parents came from managerial or professional occupations or who were college graduates and beyond were grossly overrepresented in the sample. In other words, the norms are based on a large percentage of individuals from upper socioeconomic classes. To adjust for this discrepancy, a weighting procedure was applied. Although weighting is a legitimate statistical technique, it is more desirable for a standardization sample to include proportionate representation on all key background variables. The problem is that in those instances when the number of individuals in a "cell" is small, the limited sampling must be used to estimate the test performance of many. For example, the Binet IV standardization sample contained only 10.6% of children whose parents had educational levels less than high school, yet the percentage in the U.S. population is 29.2. Weighting procedures count those same 10.6% children nearly three times to obtain a more representative proportion for calibration of the normative scores. Reliance on the weighting of data from relatively few subjects introduces unwanted error into the standardization data, which is what standardization procedures for most major tests are designed to avoid. Furthermore, the critical importance of SES as a stratification variable for IQ tests has been demonstrated in many studies (Kaufman, 1990, Chap. 6; Kaufman & Doppelt, 1976), making the use of a weighting procedure in the IV ill advised at best.

Internal consistency estimates for the Binet IV Composite Scale are excellent, ranging from .95 to .99 (median = .97) across the age groups (Sattler, 1988). The internal reliabilities are also high for the Verbal Reasoning, Abstract/Visual Reasoning, Quantitative Reasoning, and Short-Term Memory Area scores (typically in the upper .80s to .90s). Subtest reliabilities are also good, with the exception of Memory for Objects, which had a median of .73 (Thorndike, Hagen, & Sattler, 1986b). Test-retest reliability estimates are also good for preschool (Composite coefficient = .91) and elementary school (Composite coefficient = .90) samples (Thorndike et al., 1986b). From an internal reliability perspective, this measure is generally good.

Construct validity for $g$ and for the four factors was studied by using a variant of confirmatory factor analysis. The subtests had impressive high to substantial loadings on $g$ (.51–.79). Unfortunately, the four factors were given weak support by the confirmatory procedure. Also, exploratory factor analysis gave even less justification for the four Binet scales; only *one* or *two* factors were identified by Reynolds, Kamphaus, and

**TABLE 13.5    Representation of the Stanford-Binet, Fourth Edition**

| | Sample Percentage | U.S. Population Percentage |
|---|---|---|
| **By Parental Occupation** | | |
| Managerial/professional | 45.9 | 21.8 |
| Technical sales | 26.2 | 29.7 |
| Service occupations | 9.7 | 13.1 |
| Farming/forestry | 3.2 | 2.9 |
| Precision production | 6.7 | 13.0 |
| Operators, fabricators, other | 8.3 | 9.5 |
| Total | 100.0 | 100.0 |
| **By Parental Education** | | |
| College graduate or beyond | 43.7 | 19.0 |
| 1 to 3 years of college | 18.2 | 15.3 |
| High school graduate | 27.5 | 36.5 |
| Less than high school | 10.6 | 29.2 |
| Total | 100.0 | 100.0 |

Rosenthal (1988) for 16 of the 17 age groups studied. Clearly, the factor analytic structure does not conform to the theoretical framework used to construct the test. Therefore, once again one is left with the Composite score as the only clearly valid representation of a child's cognitive abilities.

Correlational studies, using nonexceptional children, between the Binet IV and the Stanford-Binet (Form L-M), WISC-R, WAIS-R, WPPSI, and K-ABC have ranged from .80 to .91 (comparing full-scale composites). Correlational studies, using exceptional children (gifted, learning impaired, and mentally retarded), produced generally lower correlations, probably because of restricted variability in the test scores. For example, for gifted students the mean composite score on the Binet IV correlated .69 with the WISC-R Full Scale IQ. These data and data from similar validity investigations are presented more extensively in the *Technical Manual* for the Binet IV (Thorndike et al., 1986b). Despite the presentation of ample evidence of concurrent validity, the substantial problems with construct validity, the data collection method, and other difficulties with the Binet IV have led at least one reviewer to recommend that the battery be laid to rest: "To the S-B IV, *Requiescat in pace*" (Reynolds, 1987, p. 141).

## *Critique*

The Binet IV was developed in an attempt to increase the popularity of the test, as well as to address some of the negative reviews that had plagued the previous edition. The test authors attempted to make the new edition significantly different from the previous L-M Edition; however, it appears that this goal has achieved only limited success. Canter (1990) describes the new edition of the Binet as causing complication and confusion to users of intelligence tests. Another reviewer describes the Binet IV as "in most respects, a completely new version of a very old test" (Spruill, 1987). This author also questioned whether or not the weighting procedure that was used to correct for sample bias was not outweighed by the large size of the standardization sample. Finally, it is not clear why a test described as for individuals aged 2 to adult does not include persons over the age of 23 in the standardization sample.

Although there appears to be a number of difficulties with the Binet IV, the test is still used and it is not without its strengths. The administration of some of the subtests allows the examiner flexibility, and young children seem to find the items challenging and fun. The scale has excellent internal reliability and provides a flexible administration format. Despite its shortcomings, Binet IV continues to be a very good assessment of cognitive skills related to academic progress (Spruill, 1987). It also includes several excellent, well-constructed tasks that offer valuable information when they are administered along with the Weschsler scales (Kaufman, 1990, 1994a).

## Wechsler Primary and Preschool Intelligence Scale–Revised (WPPSI-R)

### *Theory*

The WPPSI-R (Wechsler, 1989) is an intelligence test for children aged three years through seven years and three months. The original version of the WPPSI was developed in 1967 for ages four to six and one-half, and the WPPSI-R was revised in 1989. Several changes were made to the revised version: the norms were updated, the appeal of the content to young children was improved, and the age range was expanded.

The WPPSI-R is based on the same Wechsler-Bellevue theory of intelligence, emphasizing intelligence as a global capacity but having Verbal and Performance Scales as two methods of assessing this global capacity (Kamphaus, 1993). The Verbal Scale subtests include Information, Comprehension, Arithmetic, Vocabulary, Similarities, and Sentences (optional subtest). The Performance Scale subtests include Object Assembly, Block Design, Mazes, Picture Completion, and Animal Pegs (optional subtest).

Like the K-ABC and the DAS, the WPPSI-R allows the examiner to "help" or "teach" the examinees on early items of the subtests to ensure that the children understand what is expected of them. This extra help is essential when working with reticent preschoolers (Kamphaus, 1993).

Subtest scores have a mean of 10 and SD of 3. The overall Verbal, Performance, and Full Scale IQs have a mean of 100 and SD of 15. The examiner's manual provides interpretive tables that allow the examiner to determine individual strengths and weaknesses, as well as the statistical significance and clinical rarity of Verbal and Performance score differences.

The WPPSI-R was standardized on 1,700 children from age three through seven years and three months. The standardization procedures followed the 1986 U.S. Census Bureau estimates. Stratification variables included gender, race, geographic region, parental occupation, and parental education.

The WPPSI-R appears to be a highly reliable measure. The internal consistency coefficients across age groups for the Verbal, Performance, and Full Scale IQs are .95, .92, and .96, respectively. For the seven-year-old age group, the reliability coefficients are somewhat lower. The internal consistency coefficients for the individual Performance subtests vary from .63 for Object Assembly to .85 for Block Design, with a median coefficient of .79. The internal consistency coefficients for the individual Verbal subtests vary from .80 for Arithmetic to .86 for Similarities, with a median coefficient of .84. The test-retest coefficient for the Full Scale IQ is .91.

The manual provides some information on validity; however, it has no information on the predictive validity of the test. Various studies have shown that concurrent validity between the WPPSI-R and other tests is adequate. The correlation between the WPPSI and the WPPSI-R Full Scale IQs was reported at .87, and the correlation between WPPSI-R and WISC-III Performance, Verbal, and Full Scale IQs for a sample of 188 children was .73, .85, and .85, respectively. The correlations between the WPPSI-R and other well-known cognitive measures are, on the average, much lower. The WPPSI-R Full Scale IQ correlated .55 with the K-ABC Mental Processing Composite (Kamphaus, 1993). In general, the validity coefficients provide strong evidence for the construct validity of the WPPSI-R (Kamphaus, 1993).

## Critique

The WPPSI-R is a thorough revision of the 1967 WPPSI, with an expanded age range; new, colorful materials; new item types for very young children; new icebreaker subtests (Object Assembly); and a comprehensive manual (Kaufman, 1990). The revision of the test has resulted in an instrument that is more attractive, is more engaging, and has materials that are easier to use (Buckhalt, 1991; Delugach, 1991).

The normative sample is large, provides recent norms, and is representative of the 1986 U.S. Census data. The split-half reliability of the IQs and most subtests are exceptional, the factor analytic results for all age groups are excellent, and the concurrent validity of the battery is well supported by several excellent correlational studies (Delugach, 1991; Kaufman, 1990). The manual provides a number of validity studies, factor analytic results, research overviews, and state-of-the-art interpretive tables, which provide a wealth of information. Kaufman noted that the WPPSI-R has a solid psychometric foundation.

In spite of its reported strengths, the WPPSI-R has flaws. It has an insufficient floor at the lowest age levels, which limits the test's ability to diagnose intellectual deficiency in young preschoolers (Delugach, 1991). The directions on some of the Performance subtests are not suitable for young children because they are not developmentally appropriate, and the heavy emphasis on response speed on some nonverbal tests is inappropriate for young children who have not yet internalized the importance of working very quickly (Kaufman, 1990). However, Delugach reports that if the directions are too difficult, the test provides procedures to ensure that the child understands the demands of the task.

The WPPSI-R is a useful assessment tool, but like all the others it has certain weaknesses that limit its usefulness (Delugach, 1991). Examiners should be aware of its inherent strengths and weaknesses and keep them in mind during administration, scoring, and interpretation. The WPPSI-R may give the examiner useful information; however, "it does little to advance our basic understanding of the development and differentiation of intelligence or our understanding of the nature of individual differences in intelligence" (Buckhalt, 1991).

## Detroit Tests of Learning Aptitude (DTLA-3)

### Theory

The DTLA-3 was developed by Hammill (1991) and was designed to measure different but interrelated mental abilities for ages 6 years through 17 years and 11 months. It is a battery of 11 subtests and yields 16 composites that measure both general intelligence and discrete ability areas. Hammill and Bryant (1991) report that the DTLA-3 was greatly influenced by Spearman's (1927) two-factor theory. This theory of "aptitude" consists of a general factor $g$, which is present in all intellectual pursuits, and specific factors that vary from task to task (McGhee, 1993).

The 11 subtests are used to form the 16 composite scores. The subtests are grouped into different combinations according to various hypothetical constructs that exist in current theories of intelligence and information processing.

In general, the composite scores estimate general mental ability; however, they all do so in a somewhat different manner. The General Mental Ability Composite is formed by combining the standard scores of all 11 subtests and, thus, has been referred to as the best estimate of g. The Optimal Level Composite is made up of the four largest standard scores that the individual earns. This individualized score is often referred to as the best estimate of a person's overall "potential." The Domain Composites may be divided into three areas: Linguistic, Attentional, and Motoric. Furthermore, there is a Verbal and Nonverbal Composite in the Linguistic domain, an Attention-Enhanced and an Attention-Reduced Composite in the Attentional Domain, and a Motor Enhanced and a Motor-Reduced Composite in the Motoric Domain. Finally, there are the Theoretical Composites of the DTLA-3, on which the battery's subtests are constructed. The major theories that the subtests were developed from include Horn and Cattell's (1966) fluid and crystallized intelligences, Das's (1973) simultaneous and successive processes, Jensen's (1980) associative and cognitive levels, and Wechsler's (1974, 1989, 1991) verbal and performance scales.

The DTLA-3 yields five types of scores: raw scores, subtest standard scores, composite quotients, percentiles, and age equivalents. Standard scores for the individual subtests have a mean of 10 and SD of 3, and the Composite Quotients have a mean of 100 and SD of 15.

The individual subtest reliabilities range from .77 to .94, with a median of .87, and the averaged alphas for the composites range from .89 to .96, with a median of .94. To assess the DTLA-3's stability over time, the test-retest method was used with a sample of 34 children, residing in Austin, Texas. The children, ages 6 through 16, were tested twice, with a two-week period between testings (Hammill, 1991). The results of this test-retest analysis indicate that individual subtest reliabilities range from .75 to .96, with a median of .84, and Composite reliabilities range from .81 to .96, with a median of .90.

## Critique

The DTLA-3 was designed to measure both general intelligence and discrete abilities for children aged 6 years to 17 years and 11 months. The DTLA-3 is not grounded in one specific theory but rather can be linked to a number of different theorists and their views on intelligence and achievement. This "eclectic" theorizing has

resulted in the DTLA-3's numerous subtests, composites, and various combinations of the two that yield potentially important information about an individual's abilities.

Reliability and validity studies are encouraging but are based on specific and limited samples (VanLeirsburg, 1994). Additional research in this area would be beneficial. Furthermore, test-retest reliability data were collapsed across age levels, which makes it impossible to determine the stability of scores of the various age levels (Schmidt, 1994). The standardization sample was representative of the U.S. population, but more information on socioeconomic level is needed (Schmidt, 1994). Also, no normative data are reported for subjects with handicapping conditions, and sample stratification for age was not equalized (VanLeirsburg, 1994).

The testing manual suggests that individual testing time may vary but that on average it takes 50 minutes to 2 hours to administer. Scoring and interpretation of the results are easy, yet it can be quite time-consuming without the aid of the computer program (VanLeirsburg, 1994). Despite apparent shortcomings, the DTLA-3 may be useful for eligibility or placement purposes, as well as for research (Schmidt, 1994).

## INSTRUMENT INTEGRATION

It is to the advantage of clinical and school psychologists to have so many instruments available to assess a child's or adolescent's intellectual functioning. Often when one instrument is administered, such as the WISC-III, and then analyzed, the examiner will find that questions and hypotheses are raised about specific areas. One has to be creative and do a bit of detective work to uncover exactly where a child's true deficits and strengths lie. Part of the detective work in this process involves the integration of information from various instruments to support or clarify hypotheses raised as initial results are examined. Thus, examiners ultimately have to be able to integrate data from multiple instruments. As suggested by Kaufman (1994a), "Crucial educational decisions are sometimes made on the basis of a psychological evaluation, and these decisions should be supported by ample evidence" (p. 326) so that initial hypotheses are verified. This section describes and discusses the value of several cognitive tests when integrated with WISC-III results.

## K-ABC Integration with WISC-III

The K-ABC measures some of the same abilities as the WISC-III, but also in ways that are different, and it therefore contributes unique information about a child's cognitive functioning. The K-ABC Simultaneous Processing Scale is believed by some researchers to involve the same cognitive requirements as Wechsler's Performance Scale (Das et al., 1994) and by others to be a measure of Visual Processing (Gv) (Horn, 1991). However, two Simultaneous subtests (Matrix Analogies and Photo Series), involve more reasoning—and load on two of Woodcock's (1990) factors: Fluid Reasoning (Gf) and Visual Processing (Gv)—than Wechsler's Performance subtests. The Sequential Processing Scale of the K-ABC is an excellent addition to the Wechsler because it measures sequential processing more efficiently than any Wechsler subtest. That is, the only Wechsler test that can measure sequential processing is Digit Span Forward (Das et al., 1994), but this subtest score includes Backwards Span, which involves more than sequential processing (Schofield & Ashman, 1986); thus there is no efficient measure of sequential processing on the Wechsler. In addition, the K-ABC Achievement Scales are highly related to the Wechsler Verbal IQ and crystallized abilities (Kaufman & Kaufman, 1983).

Give these characteristics of the K-ABC, examiners may note that the entire Simultaneous Processing Scale serves as a good measure for children with motor and/or speed problems who earn low WISC-III Performance IQs because it minimizes both of these variables. From the Horn (1991) view, the K-ABC offers good supplemental subtests to measure Gc, including Faces and Places and Riddles, in the Achievement Scale. These tasks measure the range of general knowledge by identifying visual stimuli (Faces and Places) and require the child to use verbal reasoning to demonstrate word knowledge (Riddles). This is unlike many tests, such as WISC-III Vocabulary and similar Binet IV and DAS tasks, which measure word knowledge by requiring a child to retrieve word definitions from long-term storage. Like the WJ-R crystallized subtests, Riddles requires a one-word response; it is, therefore, a good WISC-III supplement to help discern whether a low Verbal IQ is due more to conceptual problems or to expressive difficulties. The K-ABC offers some alternative modalities of receiving input and expression of response to supplement WISC-III subtests

that mainly use the auditory-vocal and visual motor channels of communication. The K-ABC has three subtests that call for use of the visual and vocal modalities (Magic Window, Faces and Places, and Gestalt Closure) and one that uses the auditory-motor channel (Word Order).

## Integration of KAIT and WISC-III

The KAIT was developed from the Horn-Cattell (1967) theory and yields both a Crystallized IQ and Fluid IQ. The three subtests in the KAIT Fluid Scale are very good additions to the WISC-III. As noted previously, there is controversy over how well the WISC-III measures fluid abilities; thus it is wise to administer supplemental tests to tap an individual's fluid reasoning ability and learning ability. Assessment of planning ability, formal operational thought, and learning ability may be obtained through KAIT Mystery Codes and Logical Steps. Problem solving through verbal reasoning and verbal comprehension is required in Logical Steps, and Rebus Learning demands vocal responding; therefore, the KAIT Fluid Scale measures an ability that is quite different from the Wechsler Performance IQ. To supplement the WISC-III Verbal Scale, KAIT Crystallized subtests may be used. To assess an individual's base of general factual knowledge, Famous Faces may be administered to supplement WISC-III Information. Famous Faces uses pictorial stimuli integrated with verbal clues about famous people. Formal operational thought in the crystallized domain can be assessed through Double Meanings. Auditory Comprehension can be used for questions about an individual's memory and comprehension ability. This subtest mimics a real-life situation, requiring an individual to listen to a mock news broadcast and answer questions about it. The two delayed recall (TSR) KAIT subtests are also very good WISC-III supplements.

## Integration of CAS with WISC-III

Like the other tests in this chapter, the CAS has some overlap with the WISC-III, but because its conceptualization is based on the PASS theory, unique information about a child's cognitive functioning can be obtained. The CAS Planning and Attention Scales require processes that cannot be effectively assessed by the Wechsler Scales (Das et al., 1994). To adequately measure planning, tests that evaluate the child's ability to decide *how* to solve problems and determine their effectiveness are required. This means that the child must be given the opportunity to complete tasks by planning, unencumbered by rules imposed by the test. Also, items that are influenced by the child's plan rather than other factors (e.g., spatial or verbal skills) are needed. Tests of this type are not found on WISC-III. Attention tests should demand the focus of cognitive activity and selective attention to particular information while avoiding distraction. Carefully constructed measures of attentional processes are not included on the Wechsler, yet these, as well as planning processes, are important when evaluating children, especially those with, say, attention deficits. The measurement of planning and attention offer important cognitive functions that extend beyond the WISC-III and therefore offer additional information for diagnosis, as well as intervention (Naglieri & Das, 1997b).

The CAS, like the K-ABC, provides a measure of simultaneous processing that is similar to the demands of Wechsler's Performance Scale (Das et al., 1994), but there are important distinctions. The CAS offers a verbal test of simultaneous processing (Verbal-Spatial Relations), one that involves memory (Figure Memory), and one with complex demands (Nonverbal Matrices). The addition of the Verbal-Spatial Relations subtest is important because it integrates both nonverbal and verbal stimuli for the comprehension of logical grammatical sentences. Similarly, the Successive Processing Scale of the CAS provides tests that demand the immediate recall of information (Word Series) and the comprehension of syntax (Sentence Repetition and Sentence Questions), as well as those in which the involvement of immediate memory is markedly reduced (Successive Speech Rate).

The CAS offers a view of ability that reduces the influence of language and achievement and, therefore, provides information not available from the WISC-III to evaluate the performance of children who are bilingual or whose educational history is problematic. Because the CAS does not have achievement or language-based tests like the Wechsler (e.g., Arithmetic or Vocabulary), the reduction in the involvement of acquired knowledge provides an opportunity to evaluate children whose poor school history or language difference may have lowered their WISC-III scores. In this situation the CAS scores can help the psychologist determine the extent to which low Wechsler scores may reflect language and achievement issues rather than low intellectual ability.

## Integration of WJ-R and WISC-III

The WISC-III Verbal IQ can be viewed primarily as a measure of crystallized intelligence and short-term memory; Performance IQ as a blend of fluid reasoning, visual processing, and processing speed (Kaufman, 1994a). However, some researchers view Wechsler's Perceptual Organization as a measure of visual processing (McGrew & Flanagan, in press; Woodcock, 1990). Long-term retrieval is not specifically measured by the WISC-III, nor is auditory processing. And if Woodcock and others are correct, fluid reasoning is also not measured very well by the WISC-III. Therefore, the WJ-R extends assessment from the WISC-III by using the Cognitive subtests that were developed to reflect Horn's (1991) pure factors. The WJ-R provides subtests that are controlled learning tasks, allowing the assessment of learning ability. Conventional intelligence tests, including the WISC-III, do not typically measure this ability. The controlled learning subtests include the following: Memory for Names and Visual-Auditory Learning (both long-term retrieval tasks), and Analysis-Synthesis and Concept Formation (both fluid reasoning tasks). Whereas the WISC-III performance subtests emphasize visual-motor coordination and speed of response, Analysis-Synthesis and Concept Formation involve no motor coordination at all, and speed of response is not a major variable in determining performance level.

The WJ-R has several subtests from which to choose in answering questions about Wechsler's Perceptual Organization construct (including visual processing and fluid abilities, as noted). The different aspects of the information-processing model are measured by four WJ-R factors, including Gv (input), Gf (integration), Glr (storage), and Gs (output). A high or low score on the WISC-III Performance Scale should be further explored to determine what aspects of an individual's information processing may have affected this asset or deficit. If an individual is suspected of having a deficit or strength in nonverbal visual-spatial ability, requiring further testing for clarification, the WJ-R Spatial Relations is a useful tool. The other Fluid Reasoning subtests, previously mentioned, have a heavy verbal component and do not assess visual-spatial skills, although they do use figural material. One precaution to note is that cognitive tests in the WJ-R battery are heavily entrenched in the tradition of measuring intelligence through predominantly verbal means (Kaufman, 1990).

For assessing strengths or weaknesses in the auditory-vocal channel, the following WJ-R factors may be used: Ga (input), Gc (integration), and Gsm (storage). These factors can be helpful in clarifying questions raised in the Verbal Scale of the Wechsler test. On the WJ-R, two Gc tasks require one-word responses, which is helpful when you don't know if a low Verbal score reflects poor concepts or poor expression. Auditory-perceptual tasks on the Ga scale assess whether a child can perceive words in isolation (by filling in the gaps or by blending sounds). However, for assessing a processing deficit of longer auditory input, additional subtests may be needed (such as the Cognitive Assessment System subtests Verbal-Spatial Relations, Sentence Repetition, and Sentence Questions).

The WISC-III does not assess long-term memory over the period of a few minutes, although it does measure short-term memory with Digit Span and remote memory with Picture Completion and Information. The Long-term Retrieval subtests of the WJ-R provide a good assessment of the long-term memory function; therefore, these tasks complement the WISC-III subtests for supplementary analysis. In addition, the WJ-R tests Auditory Processing and Visual Processing have strong perceptual components. These perceptual processes are not typically evaluated in most tests of intelligence but need to be assessed in cases with possible neuropsychological difficulties.

## Integration of DAS and WISC-III

The six Core subtests of the DAS create three separate scales for children: Verbal, Spatial, and Nonverbal Reasoning. The WISC-III Verbal Comprehension subtests (specifically Vocabulary and Similarities) are quite similar to the DAS Verbal Scale (Kaufman, 1994a). The DAS Verbal, Spatial, and Nonverbal Reasoning scales correspond to the Woodcock-Johnson–Revised factors of Gc, Gv, and Gf, respectfully (McGhee, 1993).

The two subtests in the DAS Nonverbal Reasoning Scale are an excellent addition to the WISC-III because they are quite different from WISC-III subtests. The Nonverbal Reasoning subtests (Matrices and Sequential and Quantitative Reasoning) measure nonverbal reasoning without time limits, but they do require visual-motor coordination and minimize visualization. Thus, they can provide good measures of an individual's pure fluid ability. The DAS subtests that require visual-motor coordination but place minimal demands on speeded performance include Recall of Designs and Pattern Construction (when the latter is administered through special procedures). Thus, these subtests can be useful in following up hypotheses generated from WISC-III Performance subtests, which reward quick performance.

## Integration of Binet IV and WISC-III

As noted in the discussion of the Binet IV, there is controversial and weak factor analytic support for the four Binet IV area scores (Verbal, Abstract-Visual, Quantitative, and Short-term Memory). The relationship between Wechsler's Verbal and Performance IQs and the Binet IV area scores is not clear-cut. In a correlational analysis with the WISC-R and Binet IV (Thorndike, Hagen, & Sattler, 1986b), both Verbal scales were found to relate substantially to each other. However, Kaufman (1994a) notes that the Absurdities subtest probably lowered the relationship with the Verbal IQ and increased the correlation with the Performance IQ because it uses visual stimuli. In Woodcock's (1990) factor analysis, the Binet IV Quantitative subtests loaded on a separate quantitative factor (Gq), which also included Wechsler Arithmetic and WJ-R Math Achievement subtests. The Binet IV Abstract-Visual subtests, except Matrices, were on the Gv factor, along with most Wechsler Perceptual Organization subtests. Matrices, however, had a substantial loading on the Gf factor; it is, therefore, an excellent addition to the WISC-III Performance Scale.

The Binet IV can be integrated with WISC-III results and can be especially helpful in assessing young children and mentally retarded individuals because of the extension of its norms down to age two. Response time is relatively unimportant on the Binet IV; therefore, it provides several subtests to further evaluate hypotheses regarding a low score on the WISC-III Performance IQ or PO Index. If poor fluid intelligence is suspected, Pattern Analysis, Paper Folding and Cutting, Matrices, and Number Series can be administered. To further assess comprehension knowledge ability measured by the WISC-III, without requiring verbal comprehension, Absurdities is especially good because the stimulus is visual and minimally verbal. To see if a child's fluid reasoning ability generalizes to number manipulation activities, the two Binet IV

Quantitative subtests are useful. The tasks not included on the Wechsler, such as Matrices, Equation Building, Number Series, and Verbal Relations, can be used to further explore an individual's reasoning abilities.

## DTLA-3 Subtests as WISC-III Supplements

The DTLA-3 has several theoretical underpinnings, including such models as fluid and crystallized intelligence, simultaneous and successive processes, and verbal and performance abilities. The DTLA-3 subtests may be used to augment the WISC-III in several instances. To further assess perceptual organization ability, fluid ability, and simultaneous processing, Design Reproduction or Symbolic Relations may be administered. For hypotheses about similar fluid abilities but also tapping sequential processing, examiners may administer Design Sequences. Design Reproduction is also a good supplement to the WISC-III Performance subtests if there is a question about a person's ability being hampered

by response speed tests. This test does require visual-motor coordination but places minimal demands on speeded performance. Like the K-ABC, the DTLA-3 offers some alternative modalities of receiving input and expression of response to supplement WISC-III subtests that mainly use the auditory-vocal and visual motor channels of communication. The DTLA-3 has two subtests that call for use of the visual and vocal modalities (Story Construction and Picture Fragments) and one that uses the auditory-motor channel (Reversed Letters).

# SAMPLE CASE REPORT

## Referral and Background Information[2]

Chris A. is a 10-year-old fourth-grader. Chris's parents were referred to the clinic by a family friend because of concern that Chris was not performing at a level commensurate with his full potential. His parents noted that he is unable to complete all of the tasks assigned to him by his

---

SAMPLE CASE REPORT    Chris A., Age 10
Attentional Difficulty, Language Disorder
Weschler Intelligence Scale for Children–Third Edition
(WISC-III) Profile

| Scale | IQ 90% Confidence Interval | Percentile Rank | Factor | Index 90% Confidence Interval | Percentile Rank |
|---|---|---|---|---|---|
| Verbal Scale | 108 ± 5 | 70 | Verbal Comprehension | 104 ± 5 | 61 |
| Performance Scale | 121 ± 5 | 92 | Perceptual Organization | 128 ± 6 | 97 |
| Full Scale | 116 ± 4 | 86 | Freedom from Distractibility | 98 ± 8 | 45 |
|  |  |  | Processing Speed | 96 ± 7 | 39 |

| Subtest | Scaled Score | Strength/ Weakness | Percentile Rank | Subtest | Scaled Score | Strength/ Weakness | Percentile Rank |
|---|---|---|---|---|---|---|---|
| Information | 12 |  | 75 | Picture Completion | 14 |  | 91 |
| Similarities | 14 | S | 91 | Coding | 8 | W | 25 |
| Arithmetic | 14 | S | 91 | Picture Arrangement | 10 |  | 50 |
| Vocabulary | 10 |  | 50 | Block Design | 18 | S | 99 |
| Comprehension | 7 |  | 16 | Object Assembly | 16 |  | 98 |
| Digit Span | 5 | W | 5 | Symbol Search | 10 |  | 50 |

Kaufman Assessment Battery for Children (K-ABC) Profile

| Global Scales | Standard Score 90% Confidence Interval | Percentile Rank |
|---|---|---|
| Sequential Processing | 95 ± 9 | 37 |
| Simultaneous Processing | 126 ± 6 | 96 |
| Mental Processing Composite | 115 ± 6 | 84 |
| Achievement | 105 ± 5 | 63 |

---

[2]Examiner: Liz Lichtenberger, Ph.D.
  Supervisor: Nadeen Kaufman, Ed.D.

## SAMPLE CASE REPORT *(Continued)*

### Mental Processing Subtests Scaled Scores

| Subtest | Scaled Score | Strength/ Weakness | Percentile Rank | Simultaneous Subtest | Scaled Score | Strength/ Weakness | Percentile Rank |
|---|---|---|---|---|---|---|---|
| Hand Movements | 11 | | 63 | Gestalt Closure | 15 | | 95 |
| Number Recall | 9 | W | 37 | Triangles | 16 | S | 98 |
| Word Order | 8 | W | 25 | Matrix Analogies | 14 | | 91 |
| | | | | Spatial Memory | 9 | W | 37 |
| | | | | Photo Series | 14 | | 91 |

| K-ABC Achievement Subtests | Standard Score | Strength/Weakness | Percentile Rank |
|---|---|---|---|
| Faces and Places | 108 ± 9 | | 70 |
| Arithmetic | 118 ± 9 | S | 88 |
| Riddles | 101 ± 9 | | 53 |
| Reading Decoding | 94 ± 7 | W | 34 |
| Reading/Understanding | 104 ± 7 | | 61 |

### Woodcock-Johnson–Revised Tests of Cognitive Ability (WJ-R) Profile

| Subtest | Standard Score | Percentile Rank (Age) | Grade Equivalent |
|---|---|---|---|
| *Long-term Retrieval* | *100* | *50* | *4.4* |
| Memory for Names | 97 | 42 | 3.2 |
| Visual-Auditory Learning | 102 | 55 | 5.7 |
| *Short-term Memory* | *89* | *24* | *2.0* |
| Memory for Sentences | 93 | 32 | 2.7 |
| Memory for Words | 86 | 18 | 1.0 |
| *Processing Speed* | *90* | *26* | *3.5* |
| Visual Matching | 84 | 15 | 3.0 |
| Cross Out | 102 | 56 | 4.7 |
| *Auditory Processing* | *109* | *72* | *7.2* |
| Incomplete Words | 89 | 23 | 1.7 |
| Sound Blending | 122 | 93 | 16.8 |
| *Fluid Reasoning* | *113* | *81* | *7.9* |
| Analysis-Synthesis | 118 | 89 | 10.0 |
| Concept Formation | 108 | 70 | 6.2 |
| Oral Vocabulary | 101 | 54 | 4.7 |
| Delayed Recall—Memory for Names | 98 | 46 | 2.9 |
| Delayed Recall—Visual-Auditory Learning | 97 | 41 | 1.2 |
| *Differential Aptitudes* | | | |
| Reading Aptitude | 99 | 47 | — |
| Mathematics Aptitude | 103 | 59 | — |
| Written Language Aptitude | 102 | 56 | — |

### Woodcock-Johnson–Revised: Tests of Achievement (WJ-R) Profile

| | Standard Score | Percentile Rank |
|---|---|---|
| *Broad Reading* | *89* | *24* |
| Letter Word Identification | 91 | 27 |
| Passage Comprehension | 89 | 22 |

## SAMPLE CASE REPORT  *(Continued)*

### Woodcock-Johnson–Revised: Tests of Achievement (WJ-R) Profile

|  | Standard Score | Percentile Rank |
|---|---|---|
| *Broad Mathematics* | *100* | *50* |
| Calculation | 114 | 83 |
| Applied Problems | 92 | 30 |
| *Broad Written Language* | *93* | *33* |
| Dictation | 95 | 36 |
| Writing Samples | 94 | 34 |
| *Broad Knowledge* | *103* | *58* |
| Science | 112 | 78 |
| Social Studies | 94 | 34 |
| Humanities | 108 | 69 |

### Woodcock-Johnson–Revised: Aptitude-Achievement Comparisons

| Area | Aptitude | Achievement | SD Differences |
|---|---|---|---|
| Broad Reading | 99 | 89 | −1.03 |
| Broad Mathematics | 103 | 100 | −0.20 |
| Broad Written Language | 102 | 93 | −0.71 |
| Mathematics Reasoning | 103 | 92 | −0.98 |

### Intermediate Auditory and Visual Continuous Performance Test (IVA)

| Off Ritalin | | Percentile Rank | On Ritalin | | Percentile Rank |
|---|---|---|---|---|---|
| Full Scale Response | | | Full Scale Response | | |
| Control Quotient | 88 | 21 | Control Quotient | 89 | 18 |
| Auditory Response | | | Auditory Response | | |
| Control Quotient | 100 | 50 | Control Quotient | 87 | 19 |
| Visual Response Control Quotient | 79 | 8 | Visual Response Control Quotient | 93 | 32 |
| Full Scale Attention Quotient | 90 | 25 | Full Scale Attention Quotient | 100 | 50 |
| Auditory Attention Quotient | 97 | 42 | Auditory Attention Quotient | 98 | 45 |
| Visual Attention Quotient | 86 | 18 | Visual Attention Quotient | 101 | 53 |
| Auditory Prudence Quotient | 85 | 16 | Auditory Prudence Quotient | 100[a] | 50 |
| Visual Prudence Quotient | 91 | 27 | Visual Prudence Quotient | 108[a] | 70 |
| Auditory Consistency Quotient | 99 | 47 | Auditory Consistency Quotient | 97 | 42 |
| Visual Consistency Quotient | 66 | 1 | Visual Consistency Quotient | 97[a] | 42 |
| Auditory Stamina Quotient | 117 | 87 | Auditory Stamina Quotient | 77[a] | 6 |
| Visual Stamina Quotient | 99 | 47 | Visual Stamina Quotient | 81[a] | 10 |
| Auditory Vigilance Quotient | 103 | 58 | Auditory Vigilance Quotient | 103 | 58 |
| Visual Vigilance Quotient | 97 | 42 | Visual Vigilance Quotient | 97 | 42 |
| Auditory Focus Quotient | 78 | 7 | Auditory Focus Quotient | 85 | 16 |
| Visual Focus Quotient | 67 | 1 | Visual Focus Quotient | 103[a] | 58 |
| Auditory Speed Quotient | 114 | 82 | Auditory Speed Quotient | 108 | 70 |
| Visual Speed Quotient | 106 | 66 | Visual Speed Quotient | 103 | 58 |

[a]Indicates a significantly different score on Ritalin than off Ritalin.

teachers, he has difficulty in transcribing writing off the blackboard, and he is reading at the third-grade level. Mr. and Mrs. A. have sought extra help for Chris academically through private tutoring since kindergarten. They have also received interventions through the school system and psychopharmaceutical treatment for Chris's attentional difficulties. His parents hope to learn what is underlying Chris's learning difficulties and to determine what school environment and teaching methods would be best suited for his unique abilities.

Chris lives at home with his parents and his 8-year-old sister, Susie. Mrs. A. reported that she had a normal and healthy pregnancy with Chris. During the birth, Mrs. A. was administered an epidural, and he was delivered by caesarean section one week early because he was in the breech position. Chris weighed 7 pounds and 4 ounces at birth, and his Apgar score was 10. His parents reported that he was a good baby, who ate and slept well.

Chris's parents noted that all of his developmental milestones were within the normally expected time frame. He sat up at four months, stood at eight months, and walked at about one year of age. He spoke at an age-appropriate time and was toilet trained at around age two. He has been evaluated by a psychiatrist because of his difficulties in school with reading, spelling, writing, and mathematics. In this evaluation (almost a year ago), the psychiatrist noted Chris's "impulsivity, distractibility, and a short attention span." He was diagnosed with Attention Deficit Disorder and a mild generalized anxiety disorder by this psychiatrist. Recommendations were given to his parents for a remedial teaching program and medication, Ritalin (5 mg, three times a day), for about eight months. Chris continues to see his psychiatrist every two months to monitor his progress with the medication.

Chris's educational history began when he entered preschool at age two. He completed an extra year of preschool and then started kindergarten the next year. His kindergarten teacher reported that his language arts skills, phonics, and reading were "very weak." Because of these difficulties, Mr. and Mrs. A. took Chris to a private tutor during the latter half of his kindergarten year.

Chris started first grade at age six. His teacher noted in progress reports that although "he made steady progress, he had not completed the work expected" at that point in first grade.

His teacher also noted that he had good attention and interest in subjects like math and science but had trouble focusing on tasks that were less interesting to him. After one semester of first grade, Chris's mother requested that a psychoeducational evaluation be completed by the school. The school psychologist administered a battery of psychoeducational tests to Chris at age seven. The cognitive tests indicated that he was functioning in the average to superior range of intelligence. On the WPPSI-R he performed significantly better on the Performance Scale (standard score 127, 96th percentile) than on the Verbal Scale (standard score 110, 75th percentile). This difference in functioning was considered to be due to well-developed perceptual organizational skills rather than to a psycholinguistic deficiency. He also obtained a Full Scale IQ score of $120 \pm 4$ (91st percentile).

The school psychologist also administered the Wechsler Individual Achievement Test (WIAT). On this measure, Chris performed better overall in mathematics (50th percentile) than in reading (23rd percentile). His reading comprehension appeared weaker than his listening comprehension (23rd versus 63rd percentiles). His spelling ability was also quite poor, scoring only at the nineteenth percentile. The school psychologist noted in her evaluation that his "achievement test grade equivalents in the low to mid-first grade range are commensurate with teacher reports of class functioning"; he had a "significant discrepancy between his intellectual functioning and academic reasoning in the areas of Reading and Written Language, and this discrepancy is due to short term auditory memory processing deficit." Because of possible deficits in attention and concentration, Mr. and Mrs. A. and his teacher were asked to fill out an Attention Deficit Disorders Evaluation Scale to measure Chris's behavior. The test findings and parents' and teacher's reports were all examined in combination at an Individualized Educational Plan (IEP) meeting.

The IEP team found that Chris qualified for special education. The findings stated, "Although Chris' ability and achievement scores range from average to superior, his ability to function independently in the classroom seems to be below the range of the classroom. Chris has difficulty maintaining his attentional focus on independent activities which involve reading and written language." Thus, Chris began to receive assistance from the school's resource specialist.

His second-grade teacher stated in a progress report that she had observed improvement in his reading and work habits since he had received help from the resource specialist. His third-grade teacher noted similar improvements after Ritalin was prescribed. She reported that he seems "more sure of himself, more attentive and happier."

Chris's parents reported that they each had some academic difficulty when they were younger. Mr. A. said that he "battled—did what he had to do" and that he had difficulty with reading. Mrs. A. said she initially loved school and then, after fifth grade, "just plodded along." She reported that she and Chris "fight like cats and dogs," especially about his homework. Chris is easily distracted and can have temper tantrums when he doesn't get his own way. When he does this, Mrs. A. disciplines him by grabbing his arm because he does not like that type of touch. For serious misbehavior, Chris is occasionally spanked. Mr. A. also mentioned that when time can be found, it is effective to talk through a problem with Chris. His parents reported that Chris has no problem in forming friendships and that he "is happy not to mix with others and likes doing things on his own." Mr. and Mrs. A. described Chris as self-confident, imaginative, and independent. They noted that he is the type of child who would just "go to the store manager if he needs something." Chris is involved in karate as an extracurricular activity, although his parents thought that he would rather watch television than participate. He reportedly had a new-found interest in karate when his younger sister earned more advanced belts.

## Appearance and Behavioral Characteristics

Chris is a small, thin, 10-year-old boy with blue eyes and short brown hair, worn in a tousled manner. He was appropriately dressed in a casual style for the evaluation but appeared somewhat disorganized, with one of his shoes untied and his hair a bit messy. Chris was tested on three separate occasions. During the first and third sessions, he took his normal daily dose of Ritalin; however, for the second testing session he was asked not take his usual dose to enable examiners to note any differences in his behavior and performance. Chris indicated to the examiner during the second testing that he had to get up at 5:00 A.M. that morning and was tired, which may have affected his ability to pay attention. How-

ever, during the testing, he appeared to be only mildly inattentive and distractible. In between some items and subtests, he played with his fingers on the edge of the table. During one auditorily presented task, he appeared to "space out" momentarily and completely missed an item, until the examiner called his name and redirected him back to the test. After the second testing session, Chris was asked how he felt he performed without the Ritalin. He stated that he tried his best but felt he could have concentrated even more and possibly performed better with the medication. Based on his behavior and attitude toward testing for the three evaluations, the results of this assessment are a valid measure of Chris's functioning.

Throughout the testing, Chris demonstrated politeness, cooperation, and a serious approach to each task. He seemed comfortable in engaging in casual conversation with the examiner. He talked with ease about his hobbies and about flying model, remote-control airplanes that he makes. Although his parents had noted that Chris likes to draw, when asked to draw a picture of his family doing something together, he was quite hesitant to respond. He did not begin to draw even after encouragement from the examiner, stating that he could not draw people; he said, "My sister likes doing things opposite from me." He appeared to become increasingly anxious about having to draw people but finally agreed to draw a cartoon picture of a "fuzzy gut guy." Chris worked quietly and was quite focused while drawing and shading with his left hand.

Chris also concentrated very intently on tests that required him to remember visual or auditory information. He stared straight ahead with a slightly unhappy look on his face when a string of numbers was presented. It appeared as though he became overloaded with the information when required to remember too many things. The strategies that Chris attempted to use to help him remember a series of words presented auditorally were not consistently effective. He would silently mouth each word to rehearse and would also count how many words were presented. However, these strategies seemed only to get in his way of remembering all the information, and he again became overloaded. At times the strategies of rehearsing would not enable him to attend to the next word or number, again hindering his ability to recall the stimuli. Frequently, Chris's attention to detail, sometimes irrelevant detail, also adversely affected his performance. For example, on a task requiring him to memorize a series of names and drawings of space creature cartoons, he pointed to one creature several times and said, "this one should be a monkey on wheels," rather than attending to the names of the creatures he was being asked about. He also did this on a task that required him to arrange a series of photos in a sensible order. He examined the cards and focused on details that he couldn't figure out and had difficulty in discriminating the small, important visual differences among the cards.

Chris frequently asked for repetition of test items. On an arithmetic task that was presented orally and with additional visual pictures, he tended to ask for verbal repetition. He also asked for further clarification from the examiner after verbal directions were given. Chris was uncomfortable unless he knew exactly what was expected of him. For example, when asked to repeat a series of numbers, he said, "Should I say them just like you, or just the numbers?" He tried to respond to all of the items correctly and exactly as the examiner asked him to. He also asked for clarification on concepts he was unsure of; for example, when he was asked to "round to the nearest hundred," he responded, "hundred or thousand, I don't get it."

The approach that Chris took on most tasks demonstrated his concrete and careful way of working. He had a tendency to self-correct, which is positive. On one novel task, requiring him to determine the underlying pattern of boxes, Chris would reflect just long enough to come up with an answer but then would often quickly correct his answer because he had made a mistake. Similarly, on a task that required him to make a design out of rubber triangles, Chris worked quickly and steadily but needed to correct himself after recognizing that he had not quite gotten it right. His ability to correct himself was noted to be effective in many instances.

## Tests Administered

Wechsler Intelligence Scale for Children–Third Edition (WISC-III)
Kaufman Assessment Battery for Children (K-ABC)
Woodcock-Johnson–Revised (WJ-R): Tests of Achievement
Woodcock-Johnson–Revised (WJ-R): Tests of Cognitive Ability: Selected Subtests
Intermediate Visual and Auditory Continu-

ous Performance Test (IVA)
Kinetic Family Drawing
Behavior Assessment System for Children—Student Observation System

## Test Results and Interpretation

Chris took a series of cognitive tests to assess his information-processing abilities. According to the WISC-III, he is currently functioning in the Average to Superior range of intelligence. He obtained a Verbal IQ score of $108 \pm 5$ (70th percentile), Performance IQ score of $121 \pm 5$ (92nd percentile), and Full Scale IQ score of $116 \pm 4$ (86th percentile). He also obtained a Verbal Comprehension Index of $104 \pm 5$ and a Freedom from Distractibility Index of $98 \pm 8$. Chris's Perceptual Organization Index of $128 \pm 6$ was significantly higher than his Processing Speed Index of $96 \pm 7$, indicating that he performed better on tests of nonverbal reasoning than on tests of visual processing speed.

It is important to note that Chris's Verbal subtest scores and Performance subtest scores both exhibit a significant amount of scatter, suggesting that none of the IQ scales or factor indexes (except the Processing Speed Index), provide a meaningful picture of his abilities. The variance in his Verbal and Performance Scales indicates that some of his abilities are more developed than others. The difference between his verbal and nonverbal abilities, as reflected by his factor indexes, is unusually large and statistically significant. Because there is a 24-point difference in favor of his Perceptual Organization Index over his Verbal Comprehension Index (occurring in less than 10% of normal children), his Full Scale IQ should not be used as an indication of his overall ability. A fuller and clearer picture of Chris's abilities can be found by looking at his performance in individual areas rather than considering the statistical average of these various abilities.

The Kaufman Assessment Battery for Children (K-ABC) is a cognitive test based on the neuropsychological theory of information processing. The theoretical framework of the K-ABC asserts that there are two kinds of problem-solving styles, one that takes information all at once and another that arranges information in a sequential or serial order. On the K-ABC, Chris earned a Sequential Processing standard score of $95 \pm 9$, a Simultaneous Processing standard score of $126 \pm 6$, and a Mental Processing Composite standard score (IQ equivalent) of $115 \pm 6$.

Similar to the WISC-III, these global scores classify his cognitive abilities in the average to well above average level of intelligence. The 31-point difference between his Sequential Processing and his Simultaneous Processing standard scores is statistically significant, indicating that he performs much better when integrating many stimuli at once than when solving problems in a linear, step-by-step fashion. Chris's performance on the K-ABC Achievement subtests was overall significantly lower than his Mental Processing Composite and Simultaneous Processing Scale. He obtained a standard score of 105 ± 4 on the Global Achievement Scale, placing him in the sixty-third percentile. The results on the K-ABC are mirrored by his index scores on the WISC-III. His simultaneous strength and sequential weakness are reflected in the 30-point discrepancy between his Perceptual Organization and Freedom from Distractibility Indexes (128 and 98). His relatively low achievement is denoted by his Verbal Comprehension Index of 104.

Chris's individual subtest scores on the Simultaneous and Sequential Processing Scales further point to this strength in processing information in a holistic manner and his difficulty in processing information sequentially, a profile that is not uncommon in children with attentional or learning difficulties. His significant weakness in tasks that required him to recall auditorily presented lists of numbers (5th percentile on the WISC-III and 37th percentile on the K-ABC) clearly indicates his difficulty in processing information presented in a sequential manner. His difficulty with sequential tasks was also evidenced on subtests that used a visual modality, including remembering a list of auditorially presented words and pointing to pictures of the words, as well as a visual-motor WISC-III task of copying symbols in sequence. His poor performance on subtests that required sequential ability, in combination with the thirty-seventh percentile achieved on a subtest that required him to remember the locations of visually presented stimuli, also points to his difficulty with short-term memory. Additional cognitive testing also supported his poor sequential and memory skills, including his low scores on Woodcock-Johnson Revised Tests of Cognitive Ability (WJ-R) that measure sequencing and short-term memory. Chris scored overall at the twenty-fourth percentile on WJ-R tasks that required him to recall sentences and sequences of unrelated words.

It is interesting that Chris's ability to retain information and retrieve it over extended periods of time is not as weak as his short-term memory. This was evident when he obtained scores in the Average range on WJ-R tests of long-term retrieval (50th percentile). On WISC-III tasks that required Chris to call on his long-term memory to recall acquired information, he scored in the Average to Superior range. For example, he scored at the seventy-fifth percentile on a task measuring his range of general factual knowledge, at the fiftieth percentile on a vocabulary task, and at the ninety-first percentile on a task of mathematical skill. Chris also demonstrated strong ability when he was able to use his knowledge of verbal concepts in a task that required him to reason how two things are alike (91st percentile on this WISC-III task). His long-term memory is probably better than his short-term memory because for the former, one must attach meaning; Chris does much better when context and meaning can be utilized.

Chris used his strong reasoning ability, perceptual organization, trial-and-error learning, and ability to analyze part-whole relationships to excel on WISC-III Performance subtests and K-ABC Simultaneous subtests. He obtained a very high score (99th percentile) on a task of arranging blocks to reproduce an abstract design. He also scored well above most children his age in examining a picture to determine the missing part and to synthesize puzzle pieces to make a whole object (91st and 98th percentiles, respectively). On the Simultaneous Processing subtests of the K-ABC, Chris scored at least 1 SD above the norm for children his age on all tests, except the one, mentioned previously that required short-term memory. He had one significant strength among all of the Simultaneous subtests—scoring at the ninety-eighth percentile and not missing a single item—that is, copying a visually presented two-dimensional design by using rubber triangles; this is similar to his strong ability on the WISC-III task of arranging blocks to reproduce an abstract design.

To objectively assess Chris's ability to attend, he was administered the Intermediate Auditory and Visual Continuous Performance Test (IVA). This is a computerized test specifically designed to help in the identification and diagnosis of Attention Deficit Hyperactivity Disorder (ADHD). It is a relatively short task, developed to create conditions that require sustained attention to a repetitive, mildly boring task, which requires inhibition of responses after a response set has been established. Chris was required to watch and listen for a target stimulus (the number 1) and to click a mouse whenever he heard or saw it. He was also required not to click the mouse whenever he saw or heard the nontarget stimulus (the number 2). Chris took this test both on and off Ritalin, on two different days. On both testings, his scores did not support a diagnosis of ADHD. However, there were some significant differences between his performance on and off medication. When on, he demonstrated a moderately better ability to consistently focus on visual stimuli. He also demonstrated a mildly better ability to remain alert and to respond as quickly as possible but not to overreact and "jump the gun." Chris's reaction time was also mildly to moderately slower when on medication than when not.

Supporting the findings on the IVA, Chris's differing performance on and off his medication was also noted on the WJ-R in two broad areas: auditory processing and processing speed. One auditory-processing task was administered to Chris on medication, on which he scored at the ninety-third percentile. However, on a related auditory-processing task while off medication, he only obtained a score at the twenty-third percentile. As noted in the behavioral observations, Chris momentarily lost complete concentration during this task of identifying an auditorally presented word with one or more missing phonemes. Therefore, his low performance was not due to difficulty with phonics. On tests of processing speed, which also required him to maintain focused attention, Chris performed much better (55th percentile) on medication than off (15th percentile). It should be noted that he performed equally well on and off Ritalin on two separate tasks that involved reasoning in novel situations. His strong ability to reason and analyze stimuli in a controlled-learning situation was not affected by difficulty in attending, as he scored at the seventieth and eighty-ninth percentiles on these tasks.

Chris was administered the WJ-R Tests of Achievement to assess his performance on tasks that measured traditional school-based abilities. His scores from the Achievement portion of the K-ABC were compared to those obtained on the WJ-R. As noted in the background information section of this report, Chris demonstrated stronger ability on K-ABC Arithmetic (88th percentile)

than on Reading Decoding (34th percentile). Although his performance on the WJ-R demonstrated variable performance on Mathematics (30th to 83rd percentile), he generally scored higher on these subtests than on Written Language and Reading (24th and 33rd percentiles). This pattern in achievement is further supported by his performance on the WISC-III, where he scored at the ninety-first percentile on Arithmetic and the fiftieth percentile on Vocabulary. Furthermore, on the previously administered WIAT, he obtained a higher Mathematics Composite (50th percentile) than Reading Composite (23rd percentile).

The significant discrepancy on the K-ABC between Chris's cognitive abilities and achievement, differences between the WISC-III and WJ-R Tests of Achievement, and aptitude-achievement discrepancies on the WJ-R suggest that Chris has a learning disability in the language area (in Basic Reading, in Reading Comprehension, and marginally in writing). Chris scored more than 1 SD lower on WJ-R tests of Broad Reading (which include a test of reading comprehension and word identification) than on his cognitive abilities in the WISC-III Verbal Scale. On the WJ-R, he also scored 1 SD below expectations, given his performance on his cognitive Reading Aptitude. Chris's struggle to attain grade-level competency in reading and spelling is hindered by this learning disability. His tendency to get overloaded when presented with too much information and his short-term memory difficulties make the attainment of reading decoding, comprehension, and writing skills quite difficult. Chris's variable performance on mathematics over time indicates that his attention may not be consistent, and his ability to use compensatory strategies, such as asking for a question to be repeated and correcting himself, is effective for these types of mathematical problems. Math also calls more on fluid reasoning skills, at which Chris excels.

## Summary and Diagnostic Impressions

Chris is a cute, 10-year-old, fourth-grade boy who was referred to the clinic because of his parents' concern about his continued poor academic performance in reading, spelling, and writing. This evaluation was performed to assess the underlying reasons for his academic difficulties and to answer his parents' questions about the best school placement. This evaluation will also provide remedial suggestions to help Chris with these problems. Cognitive and achievement tests were administered over the course of three mornings. One of the three sessions was conducted with Chris not on his normal dose of Ritalin to observe his behaviors clinically. Detailed behavioral observations of the testing and of Chris at school, as well as information provided by his teachers, tutors, previous psychoeducational testing reports, academic records, and Mr. and Mrs. A. during a clinical interview, gave further insight into Chris's strengths and weaknesses.

On the WISC-III, Chris performed in the Average to Superior range of intellectual functioning, which was similar to his performance on the K-ABC, where he performed in the average to Well Above Average range. Although his performance on the WISC-III was variable across the different subtests, he scored significantly better on the Performance subtests than on the Verbal, and he performed better on tests of nonverbal reasoning than on tests of visual processing speed. He scored significantly higher on the K-ABC Simultaneous Processing Scale than the Sequential Processing Scale, demonstrating a stronger ability to process information in a holistic manner when presented all at once, rather than solving problems in a step-by-step approach; this processing preference was also observed on the WISC-III. His difficulty on specific sequential subtests also suggested a short-term memory deficit, which was supported by other cognitive tests. His cognitive strength lies in the area of reasoning and perceptual visualization, which was supported by cognitive testing on the WISC-III and K-ABC.

Chris was diagnosed with Attention Deficit Disorder by a psychiatrist earlier this year and was prescribed 5 mg of Ritalin, three times a day. His scores on the IVA Continuous Performance Test are not indicative of a child with an attentional deficit; however, continuous performance tests rarely identify false positives but are known occasionally to indicate a false negative. Furthermore, his performance was significantly better in several areas when he was on Ritalin than when he was not. Several behavioral reports of Chris's problematic inattention have been obtained from his parents, teachers, and tutors. Taken together, a DSM-IV diagnosis (314.00) Attention Deficit Hyperactivity Disorder, predominantly inattentive type, is warranted. Many of his attentional problems, as noted by teachers, tutors, and his parents, are also confounded with his low sequential processing abilities, difficulty with short-term

auditory and visual memory, and learning problems. However, it is clear from Chris's statements about his performance without medication that he feels more confident and secure about his abilities when he has taken the Ritalin. Based on a review of past and present achievement and cognitive tests, Chris appears to have a learning disability in basic reading, in reading comprehension, and marginally in writing.

## Recommendations

The following recommendations have been made to assist Chris, his parents, and his teachers with his learning difficulties and attentional problems.

1. The overall findings from this evaluation indicate that Chris is able to focus and attend mildly to moderately better, and therefore perform better, when he is taking the prescribed dose of Ritalin. It is recommended that Chris continue to take Ritalin as prescribed by his psychiatrist and that he continue with his follow-up appointments with her to monitor his progress and dosage of medication.

2. During the evaluation, Chris stated that he felt much more confident in his abilities and that his performance was optimal only when he took his medication. This reflected his sense that his behavior was in large part due only to the medication. It is important to help Chris realize that although the medication is helpful, it is only part of what makes him successful. He needs to understand that his behaviors are greatly affected by his many strengths, including his strong intellectual abilities, his caring for others, and his ability to compensate for difficulties. Chris will feel more in control and better about himself when he realizes that he does not have to depend on the medication to make him successful.

3. At home and at school, Chris will function better in a structured, predictable setting and when he knows what is expected of him. He is more at ease with a structured task, and he is able to perform at his best when the assignments and rules are clearly laid out. Mr. and Mrs. A. may want to write a contract with Chris that states what behaviors are expected and what reinforcement will be provided when he follows through. His teachers might also use a contract to

clearly state what is expected of him during class and for assignments. Chris will greatly benefit from having assignments written out in a checklist form. The teachers may help by rewarding his on-task behavior and not reinforcing his behavior when he is not attending in class. A reinforcement system can include tangible rewards or just praise, a smile, or a pat on the back. Rewards given frequently and immediately tend to be most effective.

4. Chris responded positively to one-on-one testing and demonstrated increased on-task behavior in school with more direct attention from the teacher. Thus, it is suggested that small groups or one-on-one settings should be used whenever possible to instruct Chris rather than to risk daydreaming in a large group. The help from his resource specialist is probably beneficial and should be continued and perhaps increased. Also, peer tutors may be quite effective. They should be upper-grade students, to reduce the loss of status that Chris already experiences. He is likely to get more positive feedback if participating in such a setting, and therefore he may be more motivated to do well.

5. Chris is able to work to the best of his ability when he is able to focus on just one activity at a time. He tends to become overloaded when too much information is presented to him, either auditorally or visually. Therefore, structuring his work environment to reduce unnecessary distractions will also be beneficial. But having Chris sit in a carrel or in a setting with little visual or auditory distraction may isolate him too much and underscore his feelings of inadequacy. Directions should be given to Chris in a short, simple written list, which he can cross off as he follows each step.

6. To help increase Chris's motivation to do schoolwork, teachers may try to include assignments that are interesting to him and refine problem-solving detective work. For example, instead of a reading assignment from his normal English book, which he may find uninteresting, a story of scientific exploration or the mechanism for making something work could be substituted. Chris's strong reasoning and perceptual organizational skills can be used in planning interesting lessons that will require him to manipu-

late objects or figure out the relationship between objects. Inclusion of such tasks will provide Chris with positive, successful experiences on a daily basis.

7. To help improve Chris's vocabulary and reading decoding ability, teachers and parents should include more amusing reading for homework and free time or create vocabulary games that will stimulate Chris to further expand his word knowledge base. Board games such as Scrabble or Boggle Junior and various computer games are good and entertaining ways to help increase a child's vocabulary. Interspersing pictures and words to create a story may be one way to entice Chris to write. This is accomplished by cutting out pictures and inserting them instead of words to vary the task.

8. To help Chris improve his short-term memory, it is suggested that demands for practicing new skills should be spread out to avoid fatigue and boredom and to develop automatic skills. For example, homework should be broken up into smaller time periods, such as three 10-minute sessions if a half hour of work is needed. In addition, learning sets that relate his previous abilities and knowledge to the present task can be quite useful for Chris because they will enhance his short-term memory by using his stronger long-term memory, for example, lessons that require Chris to use thinking rather than rote memory of isolated facts.

9. Chris, like many children with reading disabilities, has difficulty with cognitive tasks that demand sequential processing. Because his ability to process information in a holistic, simultaneous manner is stronger, he will benefit from being taught reading decoding and comprehension through remedial strategies that emphasize simultaneous processing. Attached to this report is a copy of reading remediation techniques from the K-ABC *Interpretive Manual*.

10. As Chris and his sister often fight or are in competition with each other, it may be useful to find an extracurricular activity for Chris that is completely different from anything his sister does. This approach would decrease competition and may include more opportunities for cooperation. For example, perhaps karate should be replaced with an activity that would be more enjoyable for

Chris. If he has an interest in music, say, his parents may want to consider a computerized keyboard that he could make musical arrangements on by incorporating the sounds of different musical instruments.

11. To increase positive time spent with Chris and also to make learning to read a more pleasurable experience for him, his mother and father may each implement individual quiet time to read to Chris. To further promote positive time spent together, Chris and his parents will probably benefit if his parents do not engage Chris when a power struggle is beginning. For example, if Chris is beginning to struggle and argue with his parents about doing a particular homework assignment, it would be useful to discuss with Chris how they could all cooperate and work out a plan or resolve the conflict.

# REFERENCES

American Psychological Association. (1990). *Standards for educational and psychological tests and manuals.* Washington, DC: Author.

Bain, S. K. (1991). Test reviews: Differential ability scales. *Journal of Psychoeducational Assessment, 9,* 372–378.

Bogen, J. E. (1975). Some educational aspects of hemispheric specialization. *UCLA Educator, 17,* 24–32.

Bracken, B. A. (1985). A critical review of the Kaufman Assessment Battery for Children (K-ABC). *School Psychology Review, 14,* 21–36.

Braden, J. P. (1992). Test reviews: The differential ability scales and special education. *Journal of Psychoeducational Assessment, 10,* 92–98.

Brown, D. T. (1994). Review of the Kaufman Adolescent and Adult Intelligence Test (KAIT). *Journal of School Psychology, 32,* 85–99.

Buckhalt, J. A. (1991). A critical review of the Wechsler Preschool and Primary Scale of Intelligence Revised (WPPSI-R). *Journal of Psychoeducational Assessment, 9,* 271–279.

Canter, A. (1990). A new Binet, an old premise: A mismatch between technology and evolving practice. *Journal of Psychoeducational Assessment, 8,* 443–450.

Carroll, J. B. (1995). Review of the book *Assessment of cognitive processes: The PASS theory of intelligence. Journal of Psychoeducational Assessment, 13,* 397–409.

Cattell, R. B. (1963). Theory of fluid and crystallized intelligence: A critical experiment. *Journal of Educational Psychology, 54,* 1–22.

Cormier, P., Carlson, J. S., & Das, J. P. (1990). Planning ability and cognitive performance: The compensatory effects of a dynamic assessment. *Learning and Individual Differences, 2,* 437–449.

Das, J. P. (1973). Structure of cognitive abilities: Evidence for simultaneous and successive processing. *Journal of Educational Psychology, 65,* 103–108.

Das, J. P., Kirby, J. R., & Jarman, R. F. (1975). Simultaneous and successive synthesis: An alternative model for cognitive abilities. *Psychological Bulletin, 82,* 87–103.

Das, J. P., Kirby, J., & Jarman, R. F. (1979). *Simultaneous and successive cognitive processes.* New York: Academic Press.

Das, J. P., Naglieri, J. A. & Kirby, J. (1994). *Assessment of cognitive processes.* Boston, MA: Allyn & Bacon.

Delugach, R. (1991). Test review: Wechsler Preschool and Primary Scale of Intelligence–Revised. *Journal of Psychoeducational Assessment, 9,* 280–290.

Dumont, R., & Hagberg, C. (1994). Test reviews: Kaufman Adolescent and Adult Intelligence Test (KAIT). *Journal of Psychoeducational Assessment, 12,* 190–196.

Elliott, C. D. (1990). *Differential Ability Scales (DAS) administration and scoring manual.* San Antonio, TX: Psychological Corporation.

Elliott, C. D. (in press). The Differential Ability Scales (DAS). In D. P. Flanagan, J. L. Gensaft, & P. L. Harrison (Eds.). *Beyond traditional intellectual assessments: Contemporary and emerging theories, tests, and issues.* New York: Guilford.

Esters, I. G., Ittenbach, R. F., Han, K. (1997). Today's IQ tests: Are they really better than their historical predecessors? *School Psychology Review, 26,* 211–223.

Flanagan, D. P., Alfonso, V. C., & Flanagan, R. (1994). A review of the Kaufman Adolescent and Adult Intelligence Test: An advancement in cognitive assessment? *School Psychology Review, 23,* 512–525.

Glutting, J. J., McDermott, P. A., Prifitera, A., & McGrath, E. A. (1994). *School Psychology Review, 23,* 619–639.

Golden, C. J. (1981). The Luria-Nebraska Children's Battery: Theory and formulation. In G. W. Hund and J. E. Obrzut (Eds.), *Neuropsychological assessment of the school-age child.* New York: Grune & Stratton.

Hammill, D. D. (1991). *Interpretive manual for Detroit Tests of Learning Aptitude: Third edition.* Austin, TX: PRO-ED.

Hammill, D. D., & Bryant, B. R. (1991). *Interpretive manual for Detroit Tests of Learning Aptitude–primary: Second edition.* Austin, TX: PRO-ED.

Horn, J. L. (1985). Remodeling old model in intelligence. In B. B. Wolman (Ed.), *Handbook of intelligence: Theories, measurements, and applications* (pp. 267–300). New York: Wiley.

Horn, J. L. (1989). Cognitive diversity: A framework of learning. In P. L. Ackerman, R. J. Sternberg, &

R. Glaser (Eds.), *Learning and individual differences* (pp. 61–116). New York: Freeman.

Horn, J. L. (1991). Measurement of intellectual capabilities: A review of theory. In K. S. McGrew, J. K. Werder, & R. W. Woodcock (Eds.), *Woodcock-Johnson technical manual: A reference on theory; and current research* (pp. 197–246). Allen, TX: DLM Teaching Resources.

Horn, J. L., & Cattell, R. B. (1966). Refinement and test of the theory of fluid and crystallized intelligence. *Journal of Educational Psychology, 57,* 253–270.

Horn, J. L., & Cattell, R. B. (1967). Age difference in fluid and crystallized intelligence. *Acta Psychologica, 26,* 107–129.

Inhelder, B., & Piaget, J. (1958). *The growth of logical thinking from childhood to adolescence.* New York: Basic Books.

Jensen, A. R. (1980). *Bias in mental testing.* New York: Free Press.

Kamphaus, R. W. (1993). *Clinical assessment of children's intelligence.* Boston: Allyn & Bacon.

Kamphaus, R. W., Beres, K. A., Kaufman, A. S., & Kaufman, N. L. (1995). (in press). The Kaufman Assessment Battery for Children (K-ABC). In C. S. Newmark (Ed.), *Major psychological assessment instruments* (2nd ed.). Boston: Allyn & Bacon.

Kamphaus, R. W., & Reynolds, C. R. (1987). *Clinical and research applications of the K-ABC.* Circle Pines, MN: American Guidance Service.

Kar, B. C., Dash, U. N., Das, J. P., & Carlson, J. (1993). Two experiments of the dynamic assessment of planning. *Learning and Individual Differences, 5,* 13–29.

Kaufman, A. S. (1979). *Intelligent testing with the WISC-R.* New York: Wiley.

Kaufman, A. S. (1990). *Assessing adolescent and adult intelligence.* Boston: Allyn & Bacon.

Kaufman, A. S. (1993). King WISC the Third assumes the throne. *Journal of School Psychology, 31,* 345–354.

Kaufman, A. S. (1994a). *Intelligent testing with the WISC-III.* New York: Wiley.

Kaufman, A. S. (1994b). A reply to Macmann and Barnett: Lessons from the blind men and the elephant. *School Psychology Quarterly, 9,* 199–207.

Kaufman, A. S., Ishikuma, T., & Kaufman, N. L. (1994). A Horn analysis of the factors measured by the WAIS-R, Kaufman Adolescent and Adult Intelligence Test (KAIT), and two new brief cognitive measures for normal adolescents and adults. *Assessment, 1,* 353–366.

Kaufman, A. S., & Kamphaus, R. W. (1984). Factor analysis of the Kaufman Assessment Battery for Children (K-ABC) for ages 2½ through 12½ years. *Journal of Educational Psychology, 76,* 623–637.

Kaufman, A. S., & Kaufman, N. L. (1983). *Interpretive Manual for The Kaufman Assessment Battery for Children.* Circle Pines, MN: American Guidance Service.

Kaufman, A. S., & Kaufman, N. L. (1994). *Interpretive Manual for the Kaufman Adolescent and Adult Intelligence Test.* Circle Pines, MN: American Guidance Service.

Keith, T. Z. (1990). Confirmatory and hierarchical confirmatory analysis of the Differential Ability Scales. *Journal of Psychoeducational Assessment, 8,* 391–405.

Keith, T. Z. (1991). Questioning the K-ABC: What does it measure? *Journal of Psychoeducational Assessment, 8,* 391–405.

Keith, T. Z., & Dunbar, S. B. (1984). Hierarchical factor analysis of the K-ABC: Testing alternate models. *Journal of Special Education, 18*(3), 367–375.

Kinsbourne, M. (Ed.). (1978). *Asymmetrical function of the brain.* Cambridge, MA: Cambridge University Press.

Levy, J., & Trevarthen, C. (1976). Metacontrol of hemispheric function in human split-brain patients. *Journal of Experimental Psychology: Human Perception and Performance, 2,* 299–312.

Luria, A. R. (1966). *Higher cortical functions in man.* New York: Basic Books.

Luria, A. R. (1973). *The working brain: An introduction to neuro-psychology.* London: Penguin.

Luria, A. R. (1980). *Higher cortical functions in man.* (2nd ed.). New York: Basic Books.

Macmann, G. M., & Barnett, D. W. (1994). Structural analysis of correlated factors: Lessons from the verbal-performance dichotomy of the Wechsler scales. *School Psychology Quarterly, 9,* 161–197.

McCallum, R. S. (1990). Determining the factor structure of the Stanford-Binet: Fourth Edition— The right choice. *Journal of Psychoeducational Assessment, 8,* 436–442.

McCallum, R. S., & Merritt, F. M. (1983). Simultaneous-successive processing among college students. *Journal of Psychoeducational Assessment, 1,* 85–93.

McDermott, P. A., Fantuzzo, J. W., & Glutting, J. J. (1990). Just say no to subtest analysis: A critique on Wechsler theory and practice. *Journal of Psychoeducational Assessment, 8,* 290–302.

McDermott, P. A., Fantuzzo, J. W., Glutting, J. J., Watkins, M. W., & Baggaley, A. R. (1992). Illusions of meaning in the ipsative assessment of children's ability. *Journal of Special Education, 25,* 504–526.

McGhee, R. (1993). Fluid and crystallized intelligence: Confirmatory factor analysis of the Differential Ability Scales, Detroit Tests of Learning Aptitude–3, and Woodcock-Johnson Psycho-Educational Battery–Revised. In B. A. Bracken & R. S. McCallum (Eds.), *Journal of Psychoeducational/Assessment monograph series, advances in psychoeducational assessment: Woodcock-Johnson Psycho-Educational Battery–Revised* (pp. 39–53). Germantown, TN: Psychoeducational Corp.

McGrew, K. S., & Hessler, G. L. (1995). The relationship between the WJ-R Gf-Gc cognitive clusters and mathematics achievement across the life-span. *Journal of Psychoeducational Assessment, 13*, 21–38.

McGrew, K. S., Werder, J., & Woodcock, R. (1991). *WJ-R technical manual.* Chicago, IL: Riverside.

McGrew, K. S., & Flanagan, D. P. (in press). The Wechsler Performance Scale debate: Fluid intelligence (Gf) or visual processing. Manuscript accepted for publication.

McGrew, K. S., Flanagan, D. P., Keith, T. Z., & Vanderwood, M. (1997). Beyond g: The impact of Gf-Gc specific cognitive abilities research on the future use and interpretation of intelligence test batteries in the schools. *School Psychology Review, 26*, 189–210.

McShane, D., & Cook, V. (1985). Transcultural intellectual assessment: Performance by Hispanics on the Wechsler scales. In B. B. Wolman (Ed.), *Handbook of intelligence* (pp. 385–426). New York: Wiley.

McShane, D. A., & Plas, J. M. (1984). The cognitive functioning of American Indian children: Moving from the WISC to the WISC-R. *School Psychology Review, 13*, 61–73.

Merz, W. R. (1985). Test review of Kaufman Assessment Battery for Children. In D. J. Keyser & R. C. Sweetland (Eds.), *Test critiques* (pp. 393–405). Austin, TX: Test Corporation of America.

Miller, T. L., & Reynolds, C. R. (1984). Special issue. The K-ABC. *Journal of Special Education, 8*, 207–448.

Naglieri, J. A. (1984). Concurrent and predictive validity of the Kaufman Assessment Battery for Children with a Navajo sample. *Journal of School Psychology, 22*, 373–380.

Naglieri, J. A. (1997, August). Relationships Between Achievement and the Cognitive Assessment System. Paper presented at the annual convention of the American Psychological Association, Chicago.

Naglieri, J. A., & Das, J. P. (1988). Planning-arousal-simultaneous-successive (PASS): A model for assessment. *Journal of School Psychology, 26*, 35–48.

Naglieri, J. A., & Das, J. P. (1990). Planning, attention, simultaneous, and successive (PASS) cognitive processes as a model for intelligence. *Journal of Psychoeducational Assessment, 8*, 303–337.

Naglieri, J. A. (1993). Pairwise and ipsative comparisons of the WISC-III IQ and Index scores. *Psychological Assessment, 5*, 113–116.

Naglieri, J. A., & Das, J. P. (1997a). *Cognitive Assessment System Interpretive Handbook.* Chicago: Riverside.

Naglieri, J. A., & Das, J. P. (1997b). *Das Naglieri Cognitive Assessment System.* Chicago: Riverside.

Naglieri, J. A., & Gottling, S. H. (1995). A study of planning and mathematics instruction for students with learning disabilities. *Psychological Reports, 76*, 1343–1354.

Naglieri, J. A., & Gottling, S. H. (in press). Mathematics instruction and PASS cognitive processes. *Journal of Learning Disabilities.*

Obringer, S. J. (1988, November). A survey of perceptions by school psychologists of the Stanford-Binet IV. Paper presented at the meeting of the Mid-South Educational Research Association, Louisville, KY.

Perlman, M. D. (1986). Toward an integration of a cognitive-dynamic view of personality: The relationship between defense mechanisms, cognitive style, attentional focus, and neuropsychological processing. Doctoral dissertation, California School of Professional Psychology, San Diego.

Piaget, J. (1972). Intellectual evolution from adolescence to adulthood. *Human Development, 15*, 1–12.

Reschly, D. J., & Tilly, W. D. (1993, September). The WHY of system reform. *Communique*, pp. 1, 4–6.

Reynolds, C. R. (1987). Playing IQ roulette with the Stanford-Binet, 4th edition. *Measurement and Evaluation in Counseling and Development, 20*, 139–141.

Reynolds, C. R., Kamphaus, R. W., & Rosenthal, B. L. (1988). Factor analysis of the Stanford-Binet Fourth Edition for ages 2 years through 23 years. *Measurement and Evaluation in Counseling and Development, 21*, 52–63.

Sandoval, J. (1992). Test reviews: Using the DAS with multicultural populations: Issues of test bias. *Journal of Psychoeducational Assessment, 10*, 88–91.

Sattler, J. M. (1988). *Assessment of children* (3rd ed.). San Diego, CA: Author.

Schaw, S. R., Swerdlik, M. E., & Laurent, J. (1993). Review of the WISC-III. In B. A. Bracken & R. S. McCallum (Eds.), *Journal of Psychoeducational Assessment monograph series, advances in psychoeducational assessment: Wechsler Intelligence Scale for Children–Third Edition* (pp. 151–160). Germantown, TN: Psychoeducational Corp.

Schmidt, K. L. (1994). Review of Detroit Tests of Learning Aptitude–Third Edition. *Journal of Psychoeducational Assessment, 12*, 87–91.

Schofield, N. J., & Ashman, A. F. (1986). The relationship between Digit Span and cognitive processing across ability groups. Intelligence, 10, 59–73.

Spearman, C. E. (1927). *The abilities of man.* New York: Macmillan.

Sperry, R. W. (1968). Hemisphere deconnection and unity in conscious awareness. *American Psychologist, 23*, 723–733.

Sperry, R. W. (1974). Lateral specialization in the surgically separated hemispheres. In F. O. Schmitt & F. G. Worden (Eds.), *The neurosciences: Third study program.* Cambridge, MA: MIT Press.

Spruill, J. (1987). Review of Stanford-Binet Intelligence Scale, Fourth Edition. In D. J. Keyser & R. C. Sweetland (Eds.), *Test critiques* (pp. 544–559). Austin, TX: Test Corporation of America.

Sternberg, R. J. (1993). Rocky's back again: A review of the WISC-III. In B. A. Bracken & R. S. McCallum (Eds.), *Journal of Psychoeducational Assessment monograph series, advances in psychoeducational assessment: Wechsler Intelligence Scale for Children–Third Edition* (pp. 161–164). Germantown, TN: Psychoeducational Corp.

Thorndike, R. L., Hagen, E. P., & Sattler, J. M. (1986a). *Stanford-Binet Intelligence Scale: Fourth Edition.* Chicago: Riverside.

Thorndike, R. L., Hagen, E. P., & Sattler, J. M. (1986b). *Technical manual for the Stanford-Binet Intelligence Scale–Fourth Edition.* Chicago: Riverside.

VanLeirsburg, P. (1994). Review of Detroit Tests of Learning Aptitude–3. In D. J. Keyser & R. C. Sweetland (Eds.), *Test critiques* (pp. 219–225). Austin, TX: Test Corporation of America.

Wada, J., Clarke, R., & Hamm, A. (1975). Cerebral hemisphere asymmetry in humans. *Archives of Neurology, 37,* 234–246.

Watkins, M. W., & Kush, J. C. (1994). Wechsler subtest analysis: The right way, the wrong way, or no way? *School Psychology Review, 23,* 640–651.

Webster, R. E. (1994). Review of Woodcock-Johnson Psycho-Educational Battery–Revised. In D. J. Keyser & R. C. Sweetland (Eds.), *Test critiques* (pp. 804–815). Austin, TX: Test Corporation of America.

Wechsler, D. (1958). *Measurement and appraisal of adult intelligence* (4th ed.). Baltimore: Williams & Wilkens.

Wechsler, D. (1974). *Manual for the Wechsler Intelligence Scale for Children–Revised.* San Antonio, TX: Psychological Corp.

Wechsler, D. (1989). *Manual for the Wechsler Preschool and Primary Scale of Intelligence–Revised (WPPSI-R).* San Antonio, TX: Psychological Corp.

Wechsler, D. (1991). *Manual for the Wechsler Intelligence Scale for Children–Third Edition (WISC-III).* San Antonio, TX: Psychological Corp.

Witt, J. C., & Gresham, F. M. (1985). Review of the Wechsler Intelligence Scale for Children–Revised. In J. V. Mitchell (Ed.), *Ninth mental measurements yearbook* (pp. 1716–1719). Lincoln: University of Nebraska Press.

Woodcock, R. W. (1990). Theoretical foundations of the WJ-R measures of cognitive ability. *Journal of Psychoeducational Assessment, 8,* 231–258.

Woodcock, R. W., & Johnson, M. B. (1989). Woodcock-Johnson Tests of Cognitive Ability: Standard and Supplemental Batteries. Chicago: Riverside.

Woodcock, R. W., & Mather, N. (1989). *WJ-R Tests of Cognitive Ability–Standard and Supplemental Batteries: Examiner's Manual.* In R. W. Woodcock & M. B. Johnson, *Woodcock-Johnson Psycho-Educational Battery–Revised.* Allen, TX: DLM Teaching Resources.

## CHAPTER 14

# ADVANCES

# IN

# BEHAVIORAL

# ASSESSMENT[1]

THOMAS R. KRATOCHWILL
*University of Wisconsin–Madison*

SUSAN M. SHERIDAN
*University of Nebraska–Lincoln*

JOHN CARLSON
*University of Wisconsin–Madison*

KIM L. LASECKI
*University of Utah*

Interest in behavioral assessment continues to grow since the first chapter on this topic was written for the *Handbook of School Psychology* (Kratochwill, 1982). Although traditionally there were relatively few works that focused on behavioral assessment of children, this picture has changed recently. Several books and chapters (e.g., Mash & Lee, 1993; Mash & Terdal, 1981, 1988b, 1990; Shapiro, 1987a; Shapiro & Kratochwill, 1988b) are now specifically devoted to the topic of behavioral assessment with children in schools and applied settings.

A number of factors account for this growing interest in behavioral assessment. Certainly the continuing success of behavior therapy across diverse settings, child populations, and target problems account for increased interest in applications in the schools (e.g., Kratochwill & Morris, 1991; Morris & Kratochwill, 1984). Moreover, with the increasing diversity of behavior therapy, researchers and clinicians have found it necessary to clarify methodological and conceptual aspects of assessment. Indeed, it has never been easy to speak of commonality in the domain of behavior therapy, and in contemporary practice and theory it is no longer possible to speak of one unifying characteristic. Debates over terminology and the areas of practice to be included in the general rubric of behavior therapy and assessment have existed for some time (e.g., Deitz, 1978; Greenspoon & Lamal, 1978). In this chapter we present an overview of behavioral assessment, focusing on its applications in the domain of academic and social problems in school psychology. We elucidate features of the behavioral approach to assessment and discuss its use in the diagnosis and treatment of learning and behavior disorders.

## SCOPE OF BEHAVIORAL ASSESSMENT

There is currently no single definition of behavioral assessment, but it generally refers to "the identification of meaningful response units and their controlling variables for the purposes of understanding and altering behavior" (Hayes,

[1]The authors express appreciation to Karen O'Connell for her assistance in word processing.

Nelson, & Jarrett, 1986, p. 464). Some writers characterize behavioral assessment of children as a set of problem-solving strategies for understanding behavior and its determinants (Mash & Lee, 1993; Mash & Terdal, 1988a). There is no single element that characterizes a particular assessment as behavioral. However, certain concepts, methods, and purposes can be identified that characterize behavioral assessment as an *approach* (as opposed to a set of techniques), with its own set of assumptions and goals (Barrios, 1988; Nelson, 1985).

Several different models of behavior therapy have developed, including applied behavior analysis, the neobehavioristic mediational S-R model, cognitive behavior modification, and social learning theory. Because each particular model differs in what is to be included in *behavior* (Kazdin, 1978), the focus of assessment varies considerably among the different models. For example, recent developments in behavioral assessment have occurred in the applied behavior analysis field, such as in refinements and extension of functional analysis. A review of each of the various models in behavior therapy is beyond the scope of this chapter. The reader is referred to some other sources for a more detailed presentation (O'Donohue & Krasner, 1995; Wilson & Franks, 1982).

## Common Characteristics

A number of characteristics are associated with what can be described as a prototypical view of behavioral assessment (Mash & Terdal, 1988a, pp. 9–11):

1. Behavioral assessment approaches follow a conceptualization of human behavior that focuses on the client's feelings, thoughts, and behaviors as they occur in specific situations, rather than manifestations of underlying global personality dimensions.

2. Behavioral assessment tends to be predominantly idiographic and individualized.

3. Behavioral assessments emphasize the role of situational influences on behavior.

4. Behavioral approaches have emphasized the instability of behavior over time.

5. Behavioral assessments are by their nature systems-oriented.

6. Behavioral approaches generally emphasize contemporaneous controlling variables rather than historical causes.

7. Behavioral approaches are more often concerned with behaviors, cognitions, and affect

as direct samples of the assessment domains rather than a sign of underlying cause.

8. Behavioral approaches focus on obtaining data that are relevant to treatment.

9. Behavioral approaches rely on multimethod assessment strategies (i.e., emphasizing different informants and methodologies).

10. Behavioral approaches generally embrace a low level of inference in the assessment process.

11. Behavioral approaches typically involve ongoing or repeated measurement in the assessment process.

12. Behavioral assessments should be empirically based (i.e., derived from knowledge in the area focused on in assessment and treatment).[2]

Readers will note that features of behavioral assessment do not differ from more traditional procedures used in psychological and psychoeducational assessment. In fact, many measures that were once considered traditional are now used routinely in behavioral assessment (see Shapiro & Kratochwill, 1988b). Although traditionally, there are numerous conceptual and methodological differences between behavioral and traditional assessment, the major differences emanate from the underlying *assumptions* that each approach adheres to in characterizing human functioning (Nelson & Hayes, 1979). Generally, assessment in both traditional and behavioral assessment leads to hypotheses. Traditional measurement suggests hypotheses about underlying "structures" or "causes," whereas behavioral assessment suggests hypotheses about the environment or person-environment events that become the primary focus of assessment and intervention efforts.

---

[2]There has always been considerable disagreement over the assumption that behavior therapy and assessment always rely on basic research in psychology as a source of hypotheses about treatment and assessment. For example, in applied behavior analysis, there was a trend away from emphasizing research on various social problems toward emphasizing solutions (cf. Dietz, 1978 for an overview). With this has come a trend toward technology (e.g., Azrin, 1977) rather than an applied science. Yet, some empirical data may not be available to support such a technology. Similarly, in the area of behavior assessment, empirical data that support certain assumptions and practices are not always available, as is the case in treatment utility research (cf. Hartmann, Roper, & Bradford, 1979).

# Phases of Behavioral Assessment

Traditionally, and especially in school psychology, assessment has been thought of as something that occurs prior to and perhaps following termination of a treatment program. We again emphasize that assessment procedures should be used to design an intervention and then repeated over various phases of an intervention. In this regard, assessment can be conceptualized as a number of stages or phases (e.g., Bergan & Kratochwill, 1990; Cone & Hawkins, 1977a, Hawkins, 1986). Various names have been applied to phases of behavioral assessment. We use the phases developed for behavioral consultation that integrate both assessment and treatment which include problem identification, problem analysis, plan implementation, plan evaluation, generalization, and follow-up. These six phases are certainly not discrete and often overlap in practice. The clinician may also go back to previous phases to clarity further the nature of the problem. Different assessment procedures and devices can be used during different phases of assessment and therapy.

## Problem Identification

The primary focus of assessment during problem identification is a definition of the scope and nature of the problems. Assessment at this phase could involve traditional diagnosis (e.g., *Diagnostic and Statistical Manual of Mental Disorders*–Fourth Edition, or DSM-IV); multiaxial, empirically based assessment; and/or behavioral assessment that includes keystone target behavior selection, template matching, and functional analysis (Kratochwill & McGivern, 1996). The clinician may be interested in knowing if the referral problem is indeed the primary target for intervention. For example, a teacher may refer a child for a reading problem. Based on the administration of a rating scale such as the Child Behavior Checklist (Achenbach & Edelbrock, 1983), the school psychologist and teacher may determine that the child is also quite withdrawn socially, and this may be related to the reading problem. Thus, both identified problems become the focus of further assessment.

## Problem Analysis

During problem analysis, assessment is focused primarily on an analysis of the target behaviors identified during problem identification. In this phase, an emphasis is placed on determining controlling events in the environment (broadly conceived). For example, setting events (events that are functionally related but temporally or contextually distal to the target behavior), ecological conditions, and cross-setting variables are more carefully reviewed. More direct assessment procedures such as self-monitoring, analogue assessment, and direct observation can be helpful in establishing a baseline level of the target responses. The psychologist may request that the child record the incidence of reading assignments completed (i.e., self-monitor) and that the teacher record (observationally) the frequency of social interaction. In addition to the baseline levels of the target behaviors, the psychologist focuses on the analysis of these events (overt and covert) that may be related to the maintenance of the problem (e.g., skill deficits in reading, attention from the teacher for social behaviors, etc.). Such an assessment may be conducted through functional analysis strategies (discussed later in the chapter). The outcome of this assessment phase may yield hypotheses related to the occurrence or function of the target behavior, which will lead to the development of appropriate interventions.

## Treatment Implementation

Given that previous phases have yielded information useful in the conceptualization of a treatment, an intervention program is implemented during this phase. Assessment procedures can be used to monitor "treatment integrity" (i.e., to determine that it is being implemented as intended). Treatment procedures may be "packaged" and implemented to maximize therapeutic change.

## Treatment Evaluation

Once a treatment plan has been implemented, it should be monitored to evaluate its effectiveness. Direct observational measures can be used to evaluate the treatment (process and outcome), and a high priority is usually placed on these "direct" samples. Indirect measures may also be used to corroborate findings from direct measures and assess the perceptions of significant others. For example, the psychologist can request that the teacher complete various behavior checklists or rating scales.

## Generalization

In behavioral research and treatment, generalization refers to the transfer of behavior change across situations, behaviors, and individuals. Typically, the psychologist is interested in documenting (i.e., assessing) the transfer of behavior improvement on dimensions of clinical interest. For example, an increase in social interaction in the classroom may also be displayed on the playground and in other social settings. Moreover, an intervention program that results in positive change in a significant target behavior may also result in changes in other behaviors. In this example, the positive effects of increasing social interactions may also transfer to improved academic behavior. Finally, it is also possible for the treatment effects to transfer to other individuals in the environment. For example, improving social skills in the target client may also result in improved social skills of others with whom he or she comes in contact.

Historically, it has been argued that generalization must be programmed specifically (cf. Drabman, Hammer, & Rosenbaum, 1979, and Stokes & Baer, 1977, for a review of procedures used to program generalization). Drabman et al. (1979) provided a conceptual framework on which various generalized effects of treatment programs may be categorized into 16 different classes for further analyses. Since the treatment may have effects beyond the target behavior and/or client, these aspects should be assessed.

### Follow-up

Follow-up on the intervention program and client is an extremely important assessment phase. Follow-up assessment is typically aimed at evaluating generalization or maintenance of behavior across time. It is most informative when direct measures of the target behaviors are gathered. However, realizing that time and cost considerations will be a primary factor in follow-up assessment, brief indirect measures (e.g., self-report) are often used. When possible, it is desirable to gather social validation data on both the intervention and the target client. Furthermore, "consumer satisfaction" indexes can be obtained from rating scales completed by the client and various socialization agents (cf. Kazdin, 1977b; Wolf, 1978). For example, the socialization agents may provide positive ratings on client improvement but report that the treatment procedure was time-consuming and costly. Such feedback to the psychologist should be considered in the design of further intervention programs.

### A Conceptual Framework for Behavioral Assessment

Cone (1977, 1978) and Cone and Hawkins (1977) proposed a conceptual framework for classifying behavioral measures. The Behavioral Assessment Grid (BAG) is a taxonomy based on the simultaneous consideration of three aspects of the assessment process: (1) the contents assessed (i.e., motor, physiological, or cognitive); (2) the methods used to assess them (i.e., on a continuum from direct to indirect; see discussion later in chapter); and (3) the types of generalizability (i.e., reliability and validity) established for scores on the measure being classified (i.e., scorer, item, time, setting, method, and dimension). Complete discussions of this conceptual framework are provided in the first two editions of this chapter (Kratochwill, 1982; Kratochwill & Sheridan, 1990), and interested readers are referred to these comprehensive sources for more detail.

## METHODS OF BEHAVIORAL ASSESSMENT

Assessment methods used to gather data in behavioral assessment can be categorized on a continuum from direct to indirect assessment, depending on the degree to which they measure some behavior of clinical relevance and some behavior at the time and place of its natural occurrence (Cone, 1977, 1978). Interview and self-report methods are at the indirect end of the continuum because the behavior is considered a verbal representation of clinically relevant activities that are taking place at some other time and place. Similarly, ratings by others are considered indirect because they typically involve retrospective descriptions of behavior. In contrast to direct observation, a rating of an event occurs subsequent to the behavior; that is, the time of rating is removed from the actual behavioral occurrence. Included in direct assessment methods are self-monitoring, direct observations, and analogue assessment. We now review the most common methods of behavioral assessment; (1) behavioral interviews; (2) self-report, checklists, and rating scales; (3) self-monitoring; (4) analogue measures; and (5) direct observation procedures.[3]

---

[3]We have chosen to organize our presentation by *method* of assessment. Readers interested in the application of various assessment methods to *disorders* should review Mash and Terdal (1988b). The indirect-direct dimensions of behavioral assessment presented here are not to be confused with the indirect-direct distinctions commonly made between traditional and behavioral assessment (see, e.g., Hersen & Barlow, 1976; pp. 114–120).

# Behavioral Interviews

Interview assessment methods are perhaps the most ubiquitous procedures for gathering clinical data (Burke & DeMers, 1979). They have been used widely in psychotherapy and education and may, in fact, be the most frequently used assessment method in clinics and schools (Gresham, 1984). Behavior therapists have also regarded the interview as an important clinical assessment technique (Gresham & Davis, 1988).

Relative to other areas of behavioral assessment there is still a paucity of research on behavioral interviewing (Ciminero & Drabman, 1977; Gresham & Davis, 1988; Hay, Hay, Angle, & Nelson, 1979; Linehan, 1977). Traditionally, major concerns were raised over the reliability and validity of the technique (Haynes & Jensen, 1979). Moreover, although some authors presented conceptual frameworks for the behavioral interview (e.g., Holland, 1970; Kanfer & Grimm, 1977; Kanfer & Saslow, 1969), few formal standardized protocols were provided for the specific questions that should be asked at various points during the intervention process.

One major behavioral system for interviewing clients and consultees is the behavioral consultation model, developed by Bergan, Kratochwill, and their associates (Bergan, 1977; Bergan & Kratochwill, 1990; Kratochwill & Bergan, 1990; Sheridan, Kratochwill, & Bergan, 1996). The behavioral consultation model provides a systematic format to operationalize the verbal interactions during the interviewing. The problem-solving model is designed to assist consultees (e.g., teachers and parents) in defining various problems (e.g., academic and social), to formulate and implement plans to solve problems (i.e., behavior therapy programs), and to evaluate various treatment goals (target of the interventions) and the effectiveness of therapeutic programs. Thus, the major characteristics of the behavioral interview are the specification and definition of target behaviors; the identification and analysis of environmental conditions; and the use of interview data to plan, implement, and evaluate the outcomes of an intervention. Behavioral consultation is procedurally operationalized through formal interviews in the problem identification, problem analysis, and treatment evaluation stages. A recent advance is conjoint behavioral consultation (Sheridan & Kratochwill, 1992; Sheridan et al., 1996), wherein a consultant works with a parent and teacher together to identify, assess, and address target behaviors that occur across contexts and settings.

The consultation model represents an interview assessment strategy within behavior therapy that links assessment to treatment. Since consultation involves a verbal interchange between a consultant and consultee, emphasis has been placed on the analysis of verbal behavior. Consultant control of verbal behavior during consultation necessitates not only recognition of the types of verbal utterances that occur during interviews but also the ability to produce different kinds of verbalizations to meet specific interviewing objectives (Bergan, 1977). If a consultant seeks to obtain information about conditions that control client behavior, he or she must be able to elicit verbal responses most appropriate for that particular goal. In other words, the consultant must use questions and statements strategically so that relevant clinical information is obtained. For example, a consultant might ask for specific behavioral examples that pertain to a general concern to help in operationalizing a target behavior. In this model, a coding system has been developed to analyze verbal interactions during interviews (Bergan & Tombari, 1975). Gutkin and Curtis (Chapter 23 in this book) provide a further account of the behavioral consultation model.

In reviews of behavioral interviews, Gresham (1984) and Gresham and Davis (1988) reviewed psychometric information on interraters' reliability (scorer generality), criterion-related validity (method generality), and content validity. More problem-specific interview formats will probably be developed in the future. The merits of this direction in interview development may be increasingly systematic data-gathering techniques that increase reliability and validity (Mash & Terdal, 1988a). An example of such an interview format is the Semistructured Clinical Interview for Children and Adolescents (SCICA; see McConaughy & Achenbach, 1994). This interview, which is designed for children aged 6 to 18, utilizes a protocol that parallels content found on the other Achenbach (1991a, 1991b, 1991c) scales.

Despite the recognized limitations of current interview procedures, several advantages over other assessment approaches can be identified (Linehan, 1977). First, the interview is a flexible system of obtaining data in that it can be used to gather both general information, covering many areas of the client's functioning, and detailed information in specific areas. Second, variations in the client's nonverbal and verbal behavior can be examined in relation to the assessor's questions, thereby allowing analyses of responses and lines of further inquiry. Third, the interview provides an option for the development of a personal relationship between the therapist and the client (in contrast to such methods as direct observation, in which there may be no interaction between therapist and client). An exception to this advantage occurs when the therapist interviews a consultee rather than the client. Currently, there is little research into children's abilities to accurately report their own behaviors or the situational conditions surrounding their behaviors (including antecedents, consequences, and frequency or duration). It is assumed that several intellectual, developmental, and environmental variables may interact with a child's ability to verbalize accurate behavioral data in an interview, but this assumption has not been investigated extensively. Fourth, the interview allows for potentially greater confidentiality than do some other assessment procedures (e.g., paper-and-pencil methods and direct observation). Fifth, interview assessment is an important method of gathering information from individuals who are unable to provide data through other means (e.g., persons with developmental disabilities or mental retardation). Finally, the interview allows the clinician to modify his or her questions and responses to fit the person's conceptual system and affords an opportunity for modification of the interviewee's verbal description. This advantage must be balanced against the potential disadvantage of a nonstandardized script, which may promote subjective interpretations.

## Self-Report, Behavior Checklists, and Rating Scales

### Self-Report

A self-report is classified as an indirect assessment procedure because it, like the interview, represents a verbal description of clinically relevant behavior that occurred at another time and place. At times, self-report assessment is based on unreliable verbalizations in response to unstructured, open-ended questions. However, a variety of self-report inventories can be used to structure the assessment situation (Bellack & Hersen, 1977a, 1977b). Examples of self-report assessment with parents and children are presented in Mash and Terdal (1988a), and a specific discussion of their use in schools is found in Witt, Heffer, and Pfeiffer (1990). Self-report inventories are potentially useful for at least two functions (Bellack & Hersen, 1977a). First, they can be useful in gathering data on motoric responses, physiological activity, and cognitions. For example, one might ask a child the following questions, which tap different contents: "How many math problems did you complete?" (motoric); "Do your palms sweat when you approach school?" (physiological); "Do you have negative thoughts about your teacher?" (cognitive). Assuming that an accurate assessment is provided, two of these questions, with the exception of cognitions, can be verified independently. A second function of self-report measures is to gather data about a client's subjective experiences. For example, one might ask a child, "Do you like math?" or "Are you afraid of school?" or "Do you dislike your teacher?" This second set of questions includes subjective components that are not objectively verifiable.

A number of variables may influence the type of data one obtains from self-report assessment and their correspondence to the actual criterion measure. Such issues as the source of the data (e.g., written or verbal report by the client), the form of the questions asked, the content of the questions, situational factors, and operational specification of terms will be important (Bellack & Hersen, 1977b; Hayes, 1978; Tasto, 1977). For example, during consultation interviews, a major tool for obtaining objective information is the verbal elicitor. The elicitor is a verbalization that calls for objective information and/or action from a listener (e.g., child or teacher). Thus, a question such as "What are some examples of the things you would have to do to complete your math assignment?" typically yields specific information about the problem.

Self-report measures are widely used in screening and identification procedures, commonly referred to as multiple-gating methods of assessment (Walker et al., 1988). These procedures provide a systematic and comprehensive approach to screening and evaluating childrens' behavioral and emotional problems. Moreover, "gates," or normative-cutoff criteria, are established to help identify children who may benefit from "pereferral" interventions or referral for intervention. Reynolds (1986b), for example, outlined the following three gates when screening children and adolescents for depression: (1) screen a large group with a self-report measure; (2) those who meet cutoff criteria will complete the self-report measure a second time; and (3) diagnostic interviews will be completed with those who score at or above cutoff criteria on the second self-report administration. A specific application of this procedure is available in Kahn, Kehle, Jenson, and Clark (1990). Similar procedures have also been outlined for anxiety disorders (Laurent, Hadler, & Stark, 1994).

## Behavior Checklists and Rating Scales

Behavior checklists and rating scales are conceptually similar assessment strategies. In these methods, an individual is asked to rate others (usually the client,) based on past observations of the other's behavior. Because of the diversity of items that are typically included, the target behavior of actual clinical interest (such as social withdrawal) may or may not be involved. Moreover, teachers or parents may be asked to rate a series of behaviors in addition to the target problem (e.g., fear, aggression, and academic work). Presumably, other relevant clinical problems may emerge from this assessment. Nevertheless, the identifying feature of checklist and rating scale assessment strategies is that the rating occurs subsequent to the actual behavior of clinical interest (Cone, 1977; Wiggins, 1973). A comprehensive review of checklists and rating scales can be found in several sources (e.g., Barkley, 1988; Edelbrock, 1988; Hoge, 1983; see specific chapters in Mash & Terdal, 1988a).

A common device used in behavioral assessment is the Child Behavior Checklist (CBCL) (Achenbach, 1991a, 1991b, 1991c; Achenbach & Edelbrock, 1983), which has been used extensively to assess a wide range of children's behavior problems and adaptive behaviors (see Daugherty & Shapiro, 1994, and McConaughy, 1993, for recent reviews). Rating scales for specific childhood disorders are also available, for example, those for social skills assessment (Gresham & Elliott, 1990; Merrell, 1993; Walker & McConnell, 1988), depression (Reynolds, 1986a, 1989), and anxiety (Reynolds & Richmond, 1985).

Several positive features of checklists and rating scales have been identified (Ciminero & Drabman, 1977; Edelbrock, 1988; Witt et al., 1990). First, checklists are typically more economical in cost, effort, and time than other assessment strategies such as direct observation. Second, many checklists are structured so that a relatively comprehensive picture of the problem can be obtained. Third, because of the diverse range of questions typically asked, the clinician may be able to identify problems that were overlooked by other assessment methods like direct observation and interviewing. In fact, these measures have been applied to a wide range of clinical disorders (Witt et al., 1990). Fourth, data obtained from checklists and rating scales are usually relatively "easy" to quantify (through factor analysis and multidimensional scaling). In this regard, they have been useful for classification of behavior disorders (cf. Kazdin, 1985). Fifth, checklists and rating scales frequently provide a useful measure for pre- and posttest evaluation of an intervention program. Sixth, they are frequently a convenient means of obtaining social validity data on therapeutic outcomes (Kazdin, 1977b; Wolf, 1978). Social validation refers broadly to the external evaluation of the goals, procedures, and results of therapeutic outcome. Finally, when populations of clients can be described accurately in terms of their response to checklist items, this information may assist in identifying the types of clients that were treated and how they responded to treatment. For example, general psychopathology scales are used extensively in the evaluation of children's responses to medication and in the general area of childhood psychopharmacology for participant selection and sample description (see Aman, 1993, for a review of commonly used scales).

Several precautionary considerations are important when using and interpreting data derived from behavioral checklists. First, ratings are simply summaries of observations of the relative frequency of specific behaviors and not completely objective accounts. Second, ratings are judgments affected by the environment and a rater's standard for performance. Third, the social validity of the behaviors being assessed and treated are important. Fourth, ratings of the child's behavior should be solicited from multiple assessors (i.e., sources), but they may agree only to a moderate degree. Fifth, among the many characteristics that may influence behavior, a student's gender is particularly salient (Elliott, Busse, & Gresham, 1993). The usefulness of rating scales should also be based on their practical utility, reliability, and internal and external validity (Elliott et al., 1993; Martens, 1993).

Conceptual and methodological issues have been raised for many years over the use of rating scales and checklists in both research and practice (e.g., Anastasi, 1976; Ciminero & Drabman, 1977; Evans & Nelson, 1977; Spivack & Swift, 1973; Walls, Werner, Bacon, & Zane, 1977).

One major problem with these procedures is that they represent an indirect dimension of assessment. Since data are gathered retrospectively, their relation to actual occurrences of target behaviors in the natural environment is less than perfect. A second issue relates to item selection. Although rating scale developers have some criteria for generating items in the scale, the rationale may not always be evident. Furthermore, an empirical analysis of any item's meaning is not always conducted. Third, the conditions under which the scale should be administered is frequently unclear. Fourth, a clear description or rationale for determining the presence or absence of a particular behavior is often lacking. Fifth, the format of the rating scale differs considerably among the various published scales. Sixth, there is often considerable variation within particular scales about the kinds of judgments required. Seventh, a large number of rating scales are constructed to detect the presence of negative behaviors (i.e., behavioral excesses and deficits) and less frequently focus on positive behaviors (i.e., assets). Finally, published scales vary widely on standards for reliability, validity, and standardization.

A number of these limitations can be adequately addressed when standardized behavioral rating scales are used within a multiple-method or multidimensional assessment framework. McConaughy and Achenbach (1989) highlighted the important role of rating scales in a multiaxial, empirically based assessment of behavior problems. Their five axes include (1) parents' reports, (2) teachers' reports, (3) cognitive assessment, (4) physical assessment, and (5) direct assessment of the child. This method allows for parents', teachers', and children's perceptions or ratings of competencies and behaviors to be obtained systematically to help assess and treat childhood behavioral problems. Procedures for using multiple methods of assessment have been described for a number of specific childhood problems including, for example; (1) social skill deficits (Elliott, Sheridan & Gresham, 1989), (2) severe emotional or behavioral disorders (McConaughy & Ritter, 1995), (3) attention deficit hyperactivity disorder (ADHD; Guevremont, DuPaul, & Barkley, 1990), (4) depression (Landau & Burcham, 1995), and (5) anxiety disorders (Kendall, Cantwell, & Kazdin, 1989).

Rating scales and checklists will probably continue to be used extensively in assessment in schools and other applied settings. One reason for their popularity is to the general ease with which such devices are administered (but not necessarily interpreted). Nevertheless, the previously discussed conceptual and methodological considerations should be considered when using rating scales and checklists in behavioral assessment.

## Self-Monitoring

Self-monitoring (SM) is an assessment technique in which an individual observes and records his or her own behavior at the time of its occurrence. This procedure is regarded as a direct assessment procedure and is distinguished from self-report methods already described. Whereas self-reports report events that occurred at other times and/or places, SM is an observation of the clinically relevant behavior at the time of its occurrence (Cone, 1977). Several authors have reviewed the applications of SM (e.g., Gardner & Cole, 1988; Haynes, 1978; Mahoney, 1977; Nelson, 1977a, 1977b), and the interested reader should consult these seminal sources for greater detail. Self-monitoring can be used for both assessment and treatment of various target behaviors, such as on-task or academic behaviors. In some cases, SM has been used as one component of a more complete system of behavioral self-control (e.g., Coates & Thoresen, 1979; Kanfer, 1979; Mace & West, 1986b; Mahoney & Arnkoff, 1978; O'Leary & Dubey, 1979; Rosenbaum & Drabman, 1979; Thoresen & Mahoney, 1974).

### Self-Monitoring Assessment

When SM assessment is used, the client presents data on his or her own behavior for at least two general reasons. First, SM may be used during the initial stages of assessment to help identify specific problems. Baseline response levels help verify the existence of a problem, as well as specific environmental variables related to the problem. Second, SM may be used to gather information on the success of an intervention program. The range of applications of SM to various target behaviors has been quite extensive, including teachers' classroom behavior, academic behaviors (e.g., assignment completion; study activities; math, reading, and spelling performance; and engaged time), dating behaviors, hand gestures, nail biting, respiration, sleep patterns, speech dysfluencies, face touching, swimming practice, lip and mouth biting, and a variety of unwanted repetitive behaviors.

Many different recording devices and methods have been used for SM assessment. Among the more common are record booklets, check-lists, forms, counters, timers, meters, measures, scales, residual records (e.g., empty soda bottles), archival records (e.g., telephone bills), and di-aries. Figure 14.1 is an example of a SM form, used for a child to record the number of assign-ments completed to a specified criterion over a two-week period.

When used for assessment, a number of variables may influence the quality of self-monitoring. Both *accuracy* and *reactivity* affect the data. Reactivity is a problem when unin-tended or unwanted influences are the result of self-recording, and the data are not repre-sentative of data that would have occurred had SM not been used. Factors that affect the ac-curacy and reactivity of SM assessment are presented in Table 14.1 (McFall, 1977, pp. 200–201).

### Positive Features of SM

Despite some potential methodological limita-tions, SM is very advantageous for assessment. First, it is more cost-efficient than such tech-niques as analogue and direct observational as-sessment. Second, it may be the only assess-ment option, as in the measurement of private events (thoughts). Third, SM can minimize the potentially obtrusive effects of assessment that occur with other assessment procedures (e.g., interview and direct observation). Fourth, it can help verify the existence of a problem in combination with other assessment methods. The accuracy and reactivity variables may emerge in assessment. When SM is used as an intervention, somewhat different concerns must be considered (see Gardner & Cole, 1988, for a review).

## Analogue Assessment

An increasingly popular direct assessment proce-dure requires clients to respond to stimuli that simulate those found in the natural environment. In such assessment analogues, the client is usu-ally requested to role-play or perform as if he or she were in the natural environment. The most common analogue assessment strategies used in school practice are intellectual and psychoeduca-tional tests. Analogue procedures have been used for many years in behavioral assessment, but it is only recently that systematic features have been outlined and advantages and disadvantages eluci-dated (Gettinger, 1988; Haynes, 1978; McFall, 1977; Nay, 1977; Shapiro & Kratochwill 1988a).

|  | M | T | W | T | F | M | T | W | T | F |
|---|---|---|---|---|---|---|---|---|---|---|
| Total number assigned |  |  |  |  |  |  |  |  |  |  |
| Total completed |  |  |  |  |  |  |  |  |  |  |
| Percentage completed |  |  |  |  |  |  |  |  |  |  |

This is to be completed by the clinician

**FIGURE 14.1    Examples of a SM Form used by a 10-Year-Old Boy to Record Assignment Completion over a 2 week period.**

Analogue methods offer several more positive contributions than direct naturalistic observa-tional assessment. First, especially in research, these measures permit increased opportunities for controlling the situation. This feature may also emerge when analogue assessment is being used for clinical and applied purposes. Many variables in the natural environment contaminate assessment efforts, and analogue procedures may reduce or eliminate these influences. Second analogue strategies may allow assessment of be-haviors that are impossible to monitor in natural-istic settings (e.g., low-frequency events). Third, analogue strategies may be less costly than direct observational assessment procedures. Fourth, analogue assessment may help simplify and reduce complex constructs (e.g., intelligence). Through analogue assessment, clinicians may be able to control extraneous influences, isolate and manipulate specific variables, and reliably mea-sure their effects. Finally, analogue assessment procedures may help clinicians avoid certain eth-ical problems that emerge in naturalistic observa-tion. For example, the clinician may be able to test a procedure to learn about its characteristics before implementing it in the natural environ-ment.

### Domains of Analogue Assessment

Five general categories of analogue methods have been identified (Nay, 1977): paper-and-pen-cil, audiotape, videotape, enactment, and role-play analogues. Paper-and-pencil analogues re-quire the client to note how he or she would respond to a stimulus situation presented in writ-ten form. For example, teachers or parents may be asked to respond to a series of multiple-choice questions that depict different options to follow in implementing behavior management proce-dures. In paper-and-pencil analogues of this

**TABLE 14.1    Factors that Affect Self-Monitoring Accuracy and Reactivity**

| Factor | Consideration |
|---|---|
| 1. Training | Clients should be trained in the use of SM. Training a child in SM will generally result in better accuracy (see Mahoney, 1977, for an example of training). |
| 2. Systematic methods | Systematic SM methods, such as using the record form in Figure 14.1, will typically result in more reliable and accurate data than those methods that are more informal and nonsystematic. |
| 3. Characteristics of the SM device | A SM device that is easy to use, allows simple data collection, and does not depend on the client's memory (e.g., wrist counter) usually provides more accurate data than when such a tool is not used. |
| 4. Timing | Generally, a short time interval between the actual SM act and the occurrence of the target behavior is desirable for obtaining accurate data. In the previous example, the child should be directed to make a check each time an assignment is completed rather than, for example, at the end of the day (see Fig. 14.1). Reactivity may also vary as a function of the timing of SM. For example, recording before a behavior may be more reactive than recording after its occurrence. |
| 5. Response competition | When a client is required to monitor concurrent responses, his or her attention is divided. This situation may cause interference and thereby reduce the accuracy of the SM data. In the example provided, the child has been instructed to record only one behavior—that of assignment completion—to reduce response competition. |
| 6. Response effort | The more time and energy the client must spend on the SM activity, the less accurate the data may be. Thus, dimensions of "time" and "energy" may prove to be aversive. |
| 7. Reinforcement | Contingent positive reinforcement for accurate recording tends to increase accuracy. Some external criterion is usually established for accuracy. In the previous example, a teacher may be able to establish the accuracy of the SM assessment data as assignments are completed. |

type, the stimulus situations are presented in a written mode, with written, verbal, and/or physical response options. The client is usually presented with the stimulus, and a cue for a response is made. The response may be verbal and/or physical; that is, the client is asked to describe what he or she would do and/or physically respond as he or she typically would. Although a major advantage of these procedures is that they can be administered to large numbers of clients at the same time and are easily quantified, their predictive utility is largely unknown. Moreover, this type of measure is limited because the clini-

cian does not observe overt behavior in response to the actual stimulus.

Audiotape analogue involves presentation of the stimulus items in an auditory format. These procedures include a set of instructions to the client and a series of audio situations presented by the clinician. The client is typically required to make a verbal or physical response. For example, the clinician may present an audiotape of a teacher giving information to a class of school-aged children. The child (client) may be requested to respond through role-play or free behavior. Although the audio procedure has many of the advantages of the paper-and-pencil analogue, it still may not approach realistic stimulus conditions.

The videotape analogue uses video technology to present a realistic scene for the client, which is one of its major advantages. In this regard it may approximate closely the naturalistic setting. Most often, both audio and visual components are used. Video analogues can also be used for training intervention, as in the teaching of social skills, but cost and availability of the video equipment may represent major limitations of the procedure. Moreover, some child clients may have difficulty "getting into" the presentation.

Enactment analogues require the client to interact within the clinically contrived situation with relevant stimulus persons (or objects) typically present in the natural environment. Sometimes the therapist may bring relevant stimulus persons (e.g., peers or teachers) into the assessment setting to observe clients' responses. A major advantage of this approach is that stimuli can be arranged to be nearly identical to the natural environment. Of course, a limitation of this procedure is that the situation may still not duplicate the natural environment.

The final analogue type, role-play, can be used in any of the analogue assessment procedures. Flexibility in format and option for direct measurement of the behavioral response are major advantages of this procedure. For example, a script may be presented to the client, who is asked to rehearse covertly or enact overtly certain behaviors under various stimulus situations. To assess various dating skills, a psychologist may ask a high school student to role-play asking someone for a date. The client may play himself or herself or another person, and specific instructions may be present or absent. As is true of other analogue assessment procedures, a major disadvantage is the potential lack of a match between the analogue and the natural environment.

## Criterion-Referenced Measurement

Criterion-referenced measures are a special form of analogue assessment that has been aligned closely with, but not limited to, the behavioral paradigm (Bijou, 1976; Cancelli & Kratochwill, 1981). Since criterion-referenced tests were first introduced (Glaser & Klaus, 1962), continued clarification of the term, as well as issues that must be addressed in their use, have proliferated (Hambleton, Swaminathan, Algina, & Coulson, 1978). In the early literature, criterion-referenced tests were considered precise measures of highly specific, discrete behavior capabilities. Such behaviors were purported to be hierarchically sequenced, as derived through task analysis procedures (cf. Gagne, 1962, 1968; Resnick & Ford, 1978; Resnick, Wang, & Kaplan, 1973). Glaser (1971) provided the following definition: "A criterion-referenced test is one that is deliberately constructed to yield measurements that are directly interpretable in terms of specified performance standards. Performance standards are generally specified by defining a class or domain of tasks that should be performed by the individual. Measurements are taken as representative samples of tasks drawn from the domain and such measurements are referenced directly to this domain for each individual" (p. 41).

Within this conceptualization, the term domain-referenced test has evolved. Thus, whether one prefers the term *criterion-referenced* (Hambleton, Swaminathan, Algina, & Coulson, 1978) or *domain-referenced* (Subkoviak & Baker, 1977), the concept of domain is generally implied. Nevertheless, these notions have evolved outside of behavioral assessment. It appears not useful to consider performance on a criterion-referenced test as a function of the immediate test situation and the previous interactions that make up the history of the child (Bijou, 1976). Thus, specific responses to items on a criterion-referenced test are due to the nature of the test items and the settings factors in taking the test.

It should be noted that criterion- and domain-referenced tests are improved with an empirical validation of homogeneous item domains (e.g., Bergan, 1981, 1986), for which procedures are available (e.g., latent structure analysis). Path-referenced assessment was developed with the onset of procedures for empirically validating the scope and sequence of domains of homogeneous items (Bergan, 1981). This assessment procedure provides information about the learner that allows specific identification of skill and/or domain deficiencies, as well as the sequence (i.e., "path") of curriculum instruction that will lead most efficaciously to mastery of the identified task.

## Curriculum-Based Measurement

Curriculum-based measurement (CBM) has grown in popularity since the mid-1970s and is affiliated with several approaches, including the resource/consulting teaching model (e.g., Idol-Maestas, 1981), Vermont consulting teaching models (Christie, McKenzie, & Burdett, 1972), directive teaching (Stephens, 1977), exceptional teaching (White & Haring, 1980), precision teaching (Lindsley, 1964), and data-based program modification (Deno, Marston, & Tindal, 1986, Deno & Mirkin, 1977). A common characteristic of all these approaches is that they involve direct and repeated measurement of a child's performance in the classroom curriculum. Depending on how this form of assessment is used, it might better be represented as a direct observational assessment method. The measure also typically involves a structured instructional program. Considerable work has been done on curriculum-based assessment in recent years, and the range and scope of what is to be assessed has been expanded (see Lentz, 1988; Marston, 1989).

A number of important characteristics of curriculum-based measures make them desirable for monitoring students' progress. The measures are generally meaningful to the student because they: (1) are tied to the curricula; (2) are of short duration to allow for frequent administration and to monitor progress, (3) focus on direct, repeated measurement of performance, using production (rather than selection) types of responses; (4) are capable of having many forms; and (5) are sensitive to improvements in a student's achievement over time. Another important component of CBM procedures is that they are considered to be experimental. The data collected are graphed in a time-series fashion to allow for systematic monitoring of students' progress and to facilitate instructional decision making. As such, the primary unit of analysis of effect is slope, which depicts a student's rate of improvement (Marston, 1989). Readers are referred to Shapiro and Elliott (Chapter 15 of this book) and Marston (1989) for excellent reviews of curriculum-based measurement.

Criterion- and domain-referenced tests and curriculum-based measures have generally been used in applied settings for three purposes: (1) to diagnose problem behavior, (2) to monitor learning, and (3) to assess readiness for placement in a prescribed educational program. A central theme is that they allow measurement of a client's competence in a particular area of the curriculum and assist in the design of a specific instructional program. Yet, several criticisms of these assessments are related to the lack of normative data—a characteristic deemed desirable by many professionals.

In response to this issue, one must consider that norm-referenced and criterion- and do-

main-referenced tests are designed for different purposes. Items in the former are randomly selected from each domain during test construction. However, psychometric theory (governing item selection for norm-referenced devices) suggests that to discriminate between good and poor learners, items that are passed by half of a sample of the population are desirable (Subkoviak & Baker, 1977).

Individuals who want normative information might consider the use of social validation (Kazdin, 1977b; Wolf, 1978) or template matching (e.g., Cone, Bourland, & Wood-Shuman, 1986) as an alternative to psychometrically established norms. *Social validation* procedures have been developed to evaluate treatment outcomes in therapy research. Their use in assessment can occur in several ways. For example, the behavior of a client (e.g., addition skills) can be compared with that of his or her peers who are or are not experiencing difficulties in the target skill. Also, subjective evaluations of the target behavior can be gathered from individuals in the natural environment (e.g., teachers). Although this information may be useful in establishing the degree of deviance among peers, it may not necessarily help design a better instructional program.

*Template matching* is a specific technique for identifying target behaviors that are socially valid, based on normative information. In template matching, behavioral descriptors that represent highly preferred or exemplary performance (e.g., a socially competent peer) are elicited from a client's significant others (e.g., teacher and peer). The descriptors from several individuals are then combined to produce a template of the behavior in question (e.g., social competence). A behavioral profile of the client is obtained in a similar fashion, and differences between the two profiles are evaluated. Discrepancies between the preferred template and the client's description suggest targets for intervention (Hoier & Cone, 1987).

## Authentic and Performance Assessment

Educators have demonstrated increased interest in authentic or performance assessment in recent years. Archbald and Newmann (1988) suggest that "a valid assessment system provides information about particular tasks on which students succeed or fail, but more important, it also presents tasks that are worthwhile, significant, and meaningful—in short, authentic" (p. 1). Performance assessment is often considered to be a subset of authentic assessment (Elliott, 1992) and is defined as "assessments in which the teacher observes and makes a judgment about a pupil's skill in carrying out an activity or producing a product" (Airasian, 1991, p. 252). Authentic and performance assessment methods require students to apply knowledge and skills that result directly in some type of demonstration or product (Sizer, 1990). The overriding goals of this form of assessment are to provide accountability for teaching and learning, to facilitate the link between assessment and direct intervention, and to integrate curriculum and assessment and tailor formal academic assessment to individual needs and interests (Archbald, 1992).

At least five techniques are characteristic of authentic assessment approaches: portfolios, exhibitions, performances or demonstrations, performance-based grading benchmarks, and self-assessment. *Portfolios* are collections of a student's work that a teacher and/or student consider to be important and reliable evidence of the student's learning (Paulson, Paulson, & Meyer, 1991). *Exhibitions* require students to demonstrate a broad range of competencies and include student-initiated tasks that "demonstrate the integration and application of knowledge and skills in targeted areas of outcome competencies" (Elliott, 1992, p. 275). *Performances or demonstrations* are events in which a student can be observed using acquired skills, such as musical recitals or oral reports. *Performance-based grading benchmarks* replace traditional grades and provide the standards by which students' accomplishments are evaluated (i.e., students' skills and competencies are compared to a predetermined criterion to determine mastery rather than to a peer group). *Self-assessment* is a final aspect of authentic assessment, in which explicit learning outcomes are given to students, who are responsible for reviewing and analyzing their own work.

In many ways, authentic assessment represents an educational philosophy (Archbald, 1992) rather than simply a set of assessment methods. It can be a promising technique for behavioral assessors if the data obtained through these methods are reliable and valid indexes of important academic behaviors. Furthermore, techniques such as portfolios and performances can provide useful data about a student's skill level if analyzed functionally. However, limitations of the approach are also apparent. First, operational and standardized procedures for conducting many authentic assessments are not available. Second, its use has not

been evaluated empirically, and its psychometric qualities are unknown. Third, extensive training should be provided to use the procedures appropriately and reliably. Fourth, the treatment utility of the procedures has not been demonstrated. Although authentic assessment may offer a promising direction in behavioral academic assessment, further research is needed before widespread adoption of the procedures.

### *General Considerations*

The analogue assessment procedure presents many assessment options in school. Nevertheless, both reliability and validity issues need to be addressed (Nay, 1977). Individuals who are using these procedures should assess reliability data on target responses. A check on the validity of the analogue is made by comparing the contrived assessment with the target behaviors that are occurring in the natural environment. This check is usually accomplished through direct observation of the behaviors of concern. As is true of other assessment procedures, analogue assessment may best be used as one of several techniques (Shapiro & Kratochwill, 1988a).

## Direct Observational Assessment

Direct observational assessment is one of the most widely used procedures in behavior therapy research and practice. Jones, Reid, and Patterson (1974) summarized three major characteristics of a "naturalistic observational system" that remain the hallmark of this approach: "recording of behavioral events in their natural settings at the time they occur, not retrospectively; the use of trained impartial observer-coders; and descriptions of behaviors which require little if any inference by observers to code the events" (p. 46). Such observations can occur in role playing or free (naturally varying) conditions.

Although observational assessment strategies are commonly affiliated with behavioral approaches (e.g., Johnson & Bolstad, 1973; Jones et al., 1974; Kent & Foster, 1977; Lipinski & Nelson, 1974), they are clearly not limited to this orientation. The rather extensive literature in this area and the numerous methodological and conceptual issues militate against a thorough presentation here (see Hartmann, 1982, for more detailed coverage).

One issue in the use of direct observations in clinical assessment is the distinction between *observational procedures* and *observational instruments* (Kratochwill, Alper, & Cancelli, 1980). Most school psychologists have used some type of observational procedure in their assessment work. This assessment usually takes the form of directly observing a child in a classroom or having a parent or teacher record the occurrence of a child's behavior for some specified period of time. Although observational measurement may vary considerably on a number of dimensions (e.g., the person observing, the target response, or the sophistication of the form), it is most commonly used as part of an assessment battery by school psychologists.

In contrast to such ubiquitous observational procedures, there are relatively few specific observational instruments in use in behavioral assessment. This paucity of instruments may be due to a lack of attention, as well as to typical requirements in applied settings to design situation-specific assessment forms.

Most instruments that have been developed focus on a rather specific range of behaviors (e.g., Alevizos, DeRisi, Liberman, Eckman, & Callahan, 1978; O'Leary, Romanzyk, Kass, Dietz, & Santogrossi, 1979; Patterson, Ray, Shaw, & Cobb, 1969; Wahler, House, and Stambaugh, 1976). These coding systems are used in different settings, for example, institutional program evaluation (Alevizos et al., 1978),[4] home (Patterson et al., 1969),[5] school (O'Leary et al., 1971; Saudargas, 1983),[6] and home and school (Wahler et al., 1976).[7] Each of these systems represents a promising observational instrument for assessment in research and practice (see Saudargas & Lentz, 1986, for a brief overview).

A recently developed system is the Ecobehavioral Assessment System (EBASS), (Greenwood, Carta, Kamps, Terry, & Delquadri, 1994).[8] The EBASS involves a software system for sepa-

rate instruments, including the Ecobehavioral System for Complex Assessments of Preschool Environments (ESCAPE), Code for Instructional Structure and Student Academic Response (CISSAR), and the mainstream version of CISSAR (MS-CISSAR). The EBASS can be used by school psychologists to assess individual students on instructional programs or for intervention outcomes; it can also be used to conduct a functional analysis, evaluate system change, and evaluate teachers.

Several specific codes have been used in school psychology research and practice. One system, designed by Alessi and Kaye (1983), gives the assessor operational procedures to define and measure target behaviors. The assessment system is linked to a consultation model and is quite useful in focusing on specific problems. As another alternative, Saudargas and his associates, 1983; Saudargas & Lentz, 1986) developed the State-Event Classroom Observation System (SECOS), which can be used for assessing multibehavior targets in schools.[9] The system allows the assessor to gather data simultaneously on multiple behaviors in classrooms for various research applications. Saudargas and Lentz (1986) provided a review of the SECOS, decision rules and procedures for constructing standardized multiple observation systems, and procedures for obtaining reliability and validity data, as well as procedures for training observers to use the code. The code is relevant in educational and psychological assessment generally, and it can be used to assess a wide range of teacher and child behaviors (see Shapiro, 1987a; and Shapiro & Lentz, 1986, for further discussion of the scale).

A number of methodological issues have been raised in the use of direct observational assessment (see Hartmann, 1984). Some recommendations have emerged from the research literature to increase the reliability and validity of this form of assessment. First, individuals who are functioning as observers should be trained before participation in observational sessions. Training should include samples of behavioral sequences and environmental settings that closely resemble the behaviors and settings in which data collection will occur. Training through videotaped samples of behaviors in the observation setting may serve as an initial training tool; however, ob-

---

[4]The (BOI) is available from Dr. Peter N. Aleviazas, Department of Psychology, Straub Hall, University of Oregon, Eugene, OR 97403.

[5]The (BCS) is available through Research Press, Box 317741, Champaign, IL 61820.

[6]The O'Leary code is available from Dr. K. Daniel O'Leary, Department of Psychology, State University of New York at Stony Brook, NY 11794.

[7]The Wahler code is available from Dr. Robert G. Wahler, Child Behavior Institute, University of Tennessee, Knoxville, TN 37916.

[8]The EBASS is available from Dr. Charles R. Greenwood, Director, Juniper Gardens Children's Project, 1614 Washington Blvd., Kansas City, KS 66102.

[9]The SECOS is available from Dr. Richard A. Saudargas, Department of Psychology, University of Tennessee, Knoxville, TN 37996-0990.

servers' performance in the criterion environment should also be included in formal training procedures. Performance should be monitored closely, and retraining should be conducted systematically to minimize observer drift from original behavioral definitions.

Second, two or more observers should be involved in assessment efforts to establish interobserver agreement. Observers should be trained together, scores should be compared with a single formal criterion, and training should be long enough to ensure that there is agreement to a specified criterion for each code. Assessment of reliability is an important component of direct observational assessment and is recommended strongly for obtaining credible data. Third, the conditions for assessing observer agreement should be maintained to ensure consistent levels of agreement. Continuous overt and covert monitoring may help generate stable levels of agreement. Fourth, withholding information about the specific treatment plan to the observer(s) may reduce observer bias. Explicit instructions to the observer, indicating that the specific outcomes are unknown, may be preferable to ignoring the topic. Fifth, standardized observational codes should be used when possible (such as those just presented). In the absence of instruments or coding sheets for a target problem, specific observational codes should be developed so that behaviors can be scored easily. The clinician should typically be conservative in the number of codes that are to be rated at any one time (e.g., five or fewer).

Sixth, observations should be conducted in an unobtrusive fashion. To assist in the examination of obtrusiveness, data should be monitored for evidence of reactivity or bias. Seventh, measurement of the generality of observational data across different settings should be conducted. Although direct observations should occur in settings in which the target behavior has been identified, multiple assessment across behaviors and settings will further elucidate the extent of the problem and help monitor therapeutic effects. Finally, normative data are quite desirable in many cases and should be considered in observational assessment, given adequate time and resources. Local normative data may help identity objectively behavioral excesses and deficits in a given client (Hartmann et al., 1979; Nelson & Bowles, 1975). For example, behavioral assessors can record the behavior of both the target child and a "normal" or "typical" peer to compare

their behavior. Such normative information may also be useful to socially validate a problem and help establish a successful treatment, as judged by peers or other socialization agents.

Although direct observational assessment will probably remain an important measurement procedure in school psychology, much work still remains to make this form of assessment less expensive, less time-consuming, and more versatile. Development of problem- disorder-specific instruments will be a high priority in the future. Fortunately, the increasing development of microcomputer technology may make this technology more useful in applied settings (see Kratochwill, Doll, & Dickson, 1991). Because observational assessment can involve less inference about a particular behavior than many traditional assessment practices, and because repeated assessment of the client across various phases of treatment is possible with the procedure, it should be used whenever possible.

# GENERAL ISSUES IN BEHAVIORAL ASSESSMENT

Behavioral assessment represents a growing and diverse range of procedures and techniques. The following general issues provide some perspectives on advances in behavioral assessment as used in school psychology.

## Selection of Target Behaviors

Selection of specific behavior(s) in assessment and treatment received much attention during the past decade (e.g., Barnett & Macmann, 1992; Kratochwill, 1985; Kratochwill & McGivern, 1996; Weist, Ollendick, & Finney, 1991). Of primary consideration are identifying the variables that are operative in selecting and defining target behaviors and delineating how they contribute to an adequate and complete representation of clinical problems (Weist et al., 1991). Several additional factors contribute to the selection of target behaviors, including the assessor's own theoretical and philosophical orientation, the manner in which adjustment or maladjustment is defined, and professional preferences for the enhancement of new, appropriate behaviors versus the elimination of dysfunctional, inappropriate behaviors. Hawkins (1986) advocated a flexible approach in target selection, in which clients' behavioral repertoires are expanded rather than limited. Table 14.2 identifies additional guidelines for selecting target behaviors.

**TABLE 14.2   Guidelines for Selecting Target Behaviors**

1. Change behaviors that are physically dangerous to the client or others.
2. Target behaviors that are aversive by virtue of their deviance or unpredictability.
3. Select behaviors that will maximize the client's flexibility or the client's long-term social or individual good.
4. Select constructive rather than reductive targets.
5. Modify behavior that the environment will continue to maintain.
6. Select targets within the clinician's repertoire.
7. Use normative data to determine behaviors that deviate from a norm group.
8. Ask significant others to identify behaviors that are most important in the situational context.
9. Identify important criterion situations or environments, evaluate the importance of behaviors in the criterion environment, and target the most important behaviors.
10. Select a target behavior that leads to the best treatment outcomes (i.e., have treatment validity).
11. Change behaviors that are the most irritating to or preferred by treatment agents or significant others.
12. Change the behavior with the greatest potential for success.
13. Select behaviors with a high likelihood for therapeutic response generalization.
14. Identify a response chain and target the first behavior of the chain, which may serve as a discriminative stimulus for subsequent behaviors in the chain.
15. Modify behaviors low in a skill hierarchy (i.e., keystone behaviors).
16. Give priority to behaviors that have general utility.
17. Focus on building clients' skill repertoires rather than simply extinguishing behaviors.

Regardless of the approach selected by the assessor, a first step in behavioral assessment is specifying and operationalizing the problems. In this process, specific procedures by which behaviors will be assessed are identified. Recent attention has focused on the extent to which the behaviors, as defined operationally, relate to the actual problems experienced by the client (Weist et al., 1991). Difficulties arise when the specific behaviors and the conditions under which they are assessed bear little relation to the problems identified by the client and instead are selected for purposes of standardization, convenience, and "face validity" and may be inadequate and incomplete (Kazdin, 1985; Mash, 1985; Weist et al., 1991). Preassessment biases also contribute to the identification of behaviors that have a history of being addressed in child behavior therapy. The actual relation of the target behaviors to the client's statement of the problem or to functioning in everyday life is not typically established (Evans & Nelson, 1986).

Second, when selecting target behaviors in behavioral assessment, the possibility that a response may be part of a larger constellation of behaviors must be acknowledged. A constellation (or syndrome) refers to multiple characteristics that occur and encompasses different behaviors,

affect, cognitions, and psychophysiological responses (Kazdin, 1983). Assessment of only one area may fail to consider the complexity of the symptoms and their overall effect on an individual's functioning. Clinical problems may be oversimplified by selecting one or two target behaviors, narrowing the definition so that objective components can be assessed and delineating the conditions under which assessment will occur (Kazdin, 1985).

A third issue in target selection is the degree of correspondence between the targets for treatment and the overall goals. Mash (1985) distinguishes between ultimate, instrumental, and intermediate treatment outcomes. Ultimate outcomes refer to the criteria for treatment success (e.g., goals). Instrumental outcomes are sufficient for the attainment of other outcomes without further intervention (e.g., targets). Intermediate outcomes refer to treatment targets that facilitate continued treatment or are preconditions for a particular intervention. Unfortunately, insufficient attention is often given to conceptualizing and developing measures of ultimate outcome and examine the relations between instrumental and ultimate outcomes (Mash, 1985).

There is still a need in behavioral assessment research for establishing empirically the current and predictive validity of specific target behaviors (Kazdin, 1985; Weist et al., 1991). Of particular concern are studies that show a relation between the target behavior as defined and assessed and other measures of the client's problem. For example, Hoge and Andrews (1987) found validity for selecting academic performance targets but not classroom behavior targets to facilitate academic achievement. If part of a syndrome, the target behaviors should correlate with other facets of the syndrome or with measures of the child's daily functioning. The target focus should also be examined in relation to general functioning in everyday life. Furthermore, it is important to show that change in a target behavior is associated with change in related behaviors. A validational assessment model as presented by Kazdin (1985) can help address these and other research needs and serve as a basis for justifying the selection of target behaviors for treatment. Mash (1985) also suggests that target selection should be validated in relation to the resultant treatment. An appropriate selection is one that leads to generalizable and relevant therapeutic outcomes.

In a discussion of target selection in behavioral consultation, Kratochwill (1985) identified practical and operational constraints and offered a conceptual framework for assessment of target behaviors. Among the constraints identified are the verbal behaviors of the consultant and the verbal behavior in problem description by the consultee. The degree to which target behaviors are identified adequately depends partly on certain types of standardized questions asked by the consultant that elicit certain responses from the consultee. Although a standardized approach to consultation is desirable to enhance treatment validity and permit replication, certain limitations are apparent. For example, standardization may reduce the range and type of targets identified and may support the identification and treatment of isolated behaviors. Also, reliable identification of target behavior does not address the issue of whether the behaviors are important to the client.

## Response Covariation

Advances are being made in the investigation of *response covariation* and interactions among behaviors. Response covariation refers to the correlations among several different responses. Behaviors may be organized into a pattern of "clusters," consisting of a variety of behaviors that covary

systematically. This pattern is identified by concurrently assessing multiple behaviors and evaluating their relation and pattern of change over time.

Several important conditions have been suggested in the development of clusters of behaviors. Interactive, situational, or environmental variables are relevant and may partially explain their development. Different situational cues may constitute a stimulus class, based on their functional equivalence, and serve as discriminative stimuli for particular response classes. For example, various situations that require prolonged attention to academic tasks (such as numerous math problems or a lengthy silent reading assignment) may cause distractable and restless behaviors (such as daydreaming or walking around a classroom) in a child who has ADHD. Likewise, responses may form a single class of behavior because they serve similar functional purposes rather than simply because they are topographically related to environmental events. For example, screaming, pouting, and kicking one's feet may all serve to elicit attention from adults (Evans & Nelson, 1986; see also our discussion of functional analysis). Modeling may also serve as an environmental influence in that it contributes to the organization of behavior in large segments or clusters (Kazdin, 1982).

Wahler (1975) suggested the concept of a *keystone behavior* in which a variety of different behaviors, while not related formally to one another, are all extensions of one or more basic responses. A given behavior might be the central response for a variety of different manifestations. For example, a child may turn red with anger, pound his fist on a desk, scream obscenities, and throw a book when emotionally aroused. However, it is often difficult to distinguish between a keystone behavior that is causal (the behavior structurally supports other behaviors) and one that is simply descriptive (Evans & Nelson, 1986).

Conceptualizing responses as covarying and interrelated has implications for assessment. Evans and Nelson (1986) suggest that the reciprocal interactions among behaviors necessitates a type of systems mapping as an appropriate assessment goal. They present Kanfer and Saslow's (1969) SORC model and Herbert's (1981) assessment procedures to obtain useful summaries of variables that surround the behavior. Kazdin (1982) also suggests an interactional model to examine the impact of person and situational variables and to provide a useful framework for systematic inquiry into response covariation patterns. An interactional approach can identify responses that covary within a given situation, variations in clusters of behaviors across situations, and unifying themes that account for such covariations. For example, a socially withdrawn child may put her head on her desk and refrain from responding to a teacher's questions in the classroom, as well as withdraw physically from peer interactions on the playground. Unifying themes that account for such behaviors may be environmental expectations for social exchange, interacting with the child's depressive affect. If the relations among situations and responses can be identified before treatment, they may serve as a basis for predicting the extent of the effect of change in specific aspects of behavior. Although clusters of responses may appear to be related by a central factor, this dimension does not provide information about the manner in which behaviors initially become organized. Indeed, this dimension and other aspects of response covariation await further research.

## Contextual and Setting Events

Traditionally, behavioral assessment has focused primarily on contemporaneous behavior and controlling conditions. Behavioral influences were seen as proximal in time and in respect to the situation in which it occurred. Likewise, behavioral assessment of children tended to ignore some of the broader contextual variables that might be related to ongoing behaviors (e.g., the family environment). Recently, however, behavioral assessors have recognized the importance of situationally and temporally remote variables as determinants of both child and family behavior and treatment outcomes (Mash & Terdal, 1988b).

As an example of work in the family intervention area, Wahler and his colleagues (e.g., Wahler, 1975; Wahler & Fox, 1981; Wahler & Graves, 1983) discussed the need to expand applied behavioral analysis to include the investigation of distal setting events. Defined as "environmental events that are temporally distant from the child behaviors and their stimulus contingencies" (Wahler & Graves, 1983, p. 19), setting events appear to exert control over stimulus-response interactions. Wahler and Fox suggest that "setting events may occur wholly separate in space and time from the other, succeeding stimulus-response relationships which they influence" (p. 329). Therefore, they may be temporally or contextually distal to the target behavior, yet still bear a functional relationship to its occurrence.

## Functional Analysis Methodology

Historically, the field of applied behavior analysis used a methodology that was variously labeled but typically called functional analysis. Functional analysis, as the name implies, involves analysis of the functions of behavior within the context of the environment. Although most applications of functional analysis have been based on examining functions within observable events (especially in applied behavior analysis), more recent applications have been linked to analyzing cognition or affect (e.g., Kohlenberg, Tsai, & Kohlenberg, 1995).

Early work in applied behavior analysis involved observing behavior in natural settings and specifying antecedent, sequential, and consequent conditions. This form of assessment was conducted in a descriptive observational framework in which antecedents and consequences were identified to form hypotheses about how an intervention program might be implemented (e.g., Bijou, Peterson, & Ault, 1968; Bijou, Peterson, Harris, Allen, & Johnson, 1969). Information was generally obtained through direct observation methods collected by trained observers in natural settings. Although checklists, rating scales, and other assessment formats were often used by practitioners to establish the functions of behavior, researchers developed observational codes that were specific for the target behaviors under consideration.

Over the years functional analysis seemed to fall out of use in favor of a more technological approach to implementing treatments. This approach essentially involved applying treatment, such as reinforcement and punishment, and examining the effects of various outcome targets. Occasionally functional analysis was featured in the development of treatments, but it was an article by Iwata, Dorsey, Slifer, Bauman, and Richman (1982) that again established the importance of functional analysis in the field of behavior modification and spawned a new generation of research. Developments in the field have been extensive in the past few years, as seen by the expanding literature and a recent special miniseries devoted to the topic (Neef & Iwata, 1994). Likewise, functional diagnosis has been featured as an alternative to the DSM (Hayes & Follette, 1992). Methodological, conceptual, and research issues pertaining to functional analysis have been described in great depth by Haynes and O'Brien (1990). In this regard, the authors note the various ways in which functional analysis has been used in the professional literature and the diversity of ways it can be defined. Table 14.3 provides an overview of seven different ways in which functional relationships among environmental events and various target behaviors have been identified (Haynes & O'Brien, 1990). It can be observed that functional relationships represent useful but complex analysis methods for the development of intervention programs.

At the practical level, school psychologists have available several different methodologies for conducting a functional analysis. It is useful to describe the general ways in which functional analysis has been conducted, including variations on the descriptive versus experimental tactics and methods of assessment, as well as analogue and naturalistic or less contrived methodologies. Comprehensive systems for conducting functional analysis have also been presented by O'Neill and his associates, including a set of pro-

## TABLE 14.3    Characteristics of Functional Analysis

1. Functional relationships *always* imply covariance among variables; however, there are different types or forms. First, functional relationships may be *causal* or *correlational*. For example, the level of a student's attention-seeking classroom behavior may correlate with the time of day (e.g., the behavior is more frequent after recess) but be causally related to another factor, such as the level of social reinforcement provided by classmates. Second, functional relationships may be *controllable* (e.g., aggressive behavior) or *uncontrollable* (e.g., developmental level or intellectual ability). Third, functional relationships may be either *important* or *trivial*, depending on the amount of variance accounted for. For example, analysis of a student's achievement problem may reveal that his or her off-task classroom behavior is an important variable, whereas the slight nearsightedness is trivial.

2. Functional relationships are probabilistic rather than exactly deterministic because of the existence of unmeasured functional variables and measurement error. Through functional assessment practitioners support and refute hypotheses about functional relationships, rather than "proving" them.

3. Functional relationships are not exclusive: the existence of a functional relationship between a dependent variable and certain independent variables does not mean that other important functional relationships involving the dependent variable do not exist. For instance, a demonstrated functional relationship between adult attention and a child's noncompliant behavior does not preclude a coexisting functional relationship between noncompliance and escape from task demands. Both functional relationships may be present for a given child in a given situation.

4. Functional relationships can vary over time and must be considered transient. The independent variables that are functionally related to a dependent variable, as well as the strength of the functional relationships, may change over time. For example, reduced social initiation may initially be functionally related to a child's depression, but over time environmental events may become reponsible for maintaining low social initiation rates (e.g., peers neglect or reject a student's attempts at interaction).

5. The role of the independent variable in a functional relationship varies. It may be *necessary* (the dependent variable never changes unless the independent variable changes first), *sufficient* (the dependent variable always changes when the independent variable changes), *necessary and sufficient*, or *neither necessary nor sufficient* (e.g., correlational).

6. Functional relationships are conditional and operate within boundaries. When describing functional relationships, boundary conditions must be specified. For example, a functional relationship between a teacher's praise and increased rates of academic work may be valid only when the academic tasks are within a particular range of difficulty.

7. There are two important characteristics of causal functional relationships. First, causal relationships can be reciprocal or bidirectional. For instance, a child's noncompliance in response to a parental command may lead to removal of the command; at the same time, removal of parental commands in response to noncompliance may lead to subsequent noncompliance. Second, causal functional relationships require the causal variable to precede the event it causes. For example, to state that a time-out caused a student's decrease in tantrum behavior, the time-out procedure must have occurred before the behavior decreased.

*Source:* Adopted from Haynes and O'Brien (1990).

cedures for initially developing descriptions of behavioral targets in operational terms; predictions of behavior variation across environments; and a definition of such functions of behavior as maintaining variables, including reinforcement and punishment (see O'Neill, Horner, Albin, Storey, & Sprague, 1990). The early work of Bijou et al. (1968, 1969) is an example of the descriptive methodology that can be used in applied settings. An extensive discussion of the use of this methodology, as well as others, can be found in Mace, Lalli, and Pinter (1991). At the descriptive level, target behaviors are typically observed in applied settings, and particular antecedent and consequent events are analyzed in terms of presumed functional relationships. However, because the approach is descriptive, variables are not manipulated experimentally to examine their controlling influence on behavior.

A variety of tactics other than direct observation have also been used for conducting a functional analysis, based on practical and logistical rationales. For example, Durand and Crimmins (1992) developed a Motivational Assessment Scale that allows analysis of motivational functions of behavior through checklists and ratings. Likewise, the Problem Behavior Questionnaire (Lewis, Scott, & Sugai, 1994) is a 15-item questionnaire designed to assess functional hypotheses of problem behaviors in three response classes: gain peer/teacher attention, avoid or escape peer/teacher attention, and the influence of setting events. Functional analysis methodology has also been applied to a variety of behavior disorders within the context of the rating scale technology, for example, the School Refusal Assessment Scale, developed by Kearney and Silverman (1990, 1993). Again, these methodologies allow one to develop hypotheses about potential controlling variables. Once the variables are identified, they can be manipulated in either naturalistic or analogue settings to test their influence in a more empirical manner.

Typically, analogues have been used for cost-efficient assessments in applied behavior analysis. A variety of analogue situations have been established with the distinct purpose of creating naturalistic-like behaviors, and they included the manipulation of events to examine functional relationships. For example, Schill, Kratochwill, and Gardner (1996a) developed an analogue assessment framework for children with selective mutism. A child was brought into a clinic, and various environmental conditions were structured and then actively manipulated while observing changes in the child's behavior. In this process, different functional relationships could be established to examine their controlling effect. For example, negative reinforcement was found to be a controlling variable in selective mutism. However, this study, like many others in the area, has not always examined the generalizability of the functional analysis conducted in the analogue or clinical environment to the natural setting.

As an example of functional analysis methodology in a natural environment, Mace and West (1986a) conducted a functional analysis of a child in a preschool classroom. The four-year-old male child was exposed to five analogue conditions that were constructed to assess situations in which he would talk to an adult (i.e., easy task demand–supply answer, hard demand–supply answer, hard demand–allow preferral activity, easy demand–prompt, ignore, praise, and hard demand–prompt, ignore, praise). In a design that used phases that assessed demand conditions; replication of the prompt, ignore, and praise conditions; and classroom generalization probes, the authors found that conditions that permitted escape from demands produced lower rates of speech in contrast to no-escape conditions. Generally, the results suggested that for this child, mute behavior was a function of negative reinforcement contingencies. That is, the child spoke less under conditions that allowed avoidance of academic and social performance. Other examples of functional analysis in natural settings are found in Repp and Karsh (1994) and Repp, Felce, and Barton (1988).

To date, functional analysis methodology has required a sophisticated knowledge base in applied behavior analysis and could best be characterized as an "art form" in the assessment process. More recent applications of the assessment methodology have involved mediators, such as parents and teachers (e.g., Cooper, Wacker, Sasso, Reimers, & Donn, 1990; Harding, Wacker, Cooper, Millard, & Jensen-Kovalin, 1994; Sasso et al., 1992). In such cases, parents and teachers are carefully trained to analyze various functions of behavior and generalize the treatment into settings in which they typically function. However, standardized formats for conducting the functional analysis have been lacking. More recent developments of functional analysis methodology involve standardized formats for either a general assessment (e.g., Durand & Crimmins, 1992) or a combination of descriptive and experimental methodologies (e.g., O'Neill et al., 1990). The development of specific and standardized methods of assessment for functional analysis will facilitate its application in settings in which it has not routinely been applied. Again, the major benefit of functional analysis is the potential linkage of the functions of behavior to experimental manipulations or treatments that can be implemented to change behavior. Hence, at the conceptual level and, more recently, at the empirical level, functional analysis has demonstrated treatment validity.

## Computer Applications

Major technological advances continue to evolve as computer applications become more prominent in behavioral assessment. Literature and research bases began to delineate the uses of computer technology in the 1980s. Historically, behavioral assessment texts included little discussion of computer applications (Mash and Terdel, 1988a, discuss computer developments briefly in their seminal text). In psychology and education, issues of journals have been devoted to computer applications in assessment and treatment (e.g., Bennett & Maher, 1984; McCullough & Wenck, 1984), and these include some descriptions of applications in the behavioral field.

Until recently, the use of computer technology was generally slow to develop in practice (Kratochwill, Doll, & Dickson, 1986; Romanczyk, 1986). Previously, paper-and-pencil tests were the only methods of data collection used in direct observation (Noldus, Van de Loo, & Timmers, 1989), and such methods continued to be popular because they were simple to use and the cost of required materials was not prohibitive. Although these advantages exist, partially dictating the continued use of paper-and-pencil methods, the techniques tend to be cumbersome and expensive. According to Eiler, Nelson, Jensen, and Johnson (1989), administrative costs can be high and staff members are sometimes removed from other important functions. High error rates, entry of false data, failure to record behaviors when they occur, and inaccurate or incomplete data collection are often cited as problems associated with paper-and-pencil tests.

As a result, mechanical chart-recording devices were introduced in the 1960s (Noldus et al., 1989). These methods enabled observers to better measure behaviors that were rapid, complex, and greater in number. However, this technique, like paper-and-pencil methods, involved considerable manual-processing time, which has lead to reduction in their use.

Programmable recording devices came into use with the advent of affordable computers in the 1970s (Noldus et al., 1989). Because of continued declining costs, the widespread use of computer technology to collect assessment data continues to grow. Since the late 1980s, computer technology has begun to supplant traditional paper-and-pencil and mechanical methods of collecting direct and indirect behavioral data, particularly in schools. Among the most recent developments in computer-assisted behavioral assessment are programmable data collection devices, such as personal and laptop computers, and bar code data collection devices that utilize optical scanning technology.

An example of a well-studied computer hardware and software system is the Epson HX-20 used by Repp, Karsh, Van Acker, Felce, and Harman (1989). Because of advancements in technology, many other IBM-PC compatible laptops are also useful for data collection and analysis (for examples of uses, see Repp et al.).

Many programs are widely available for collecting and analyzing data on laptop and desktop computers, which allow data to be entered directly. Typically, software used for behavioral data collection have two functions: data collection and data analysis (Repp & Karsh, 1994). One drawback of laptops is that they tend to analyze data more slowly than desktop computers, but both are capable of output data that provide identifying features like the individual's name, date, and session. Furthermore, data can be entered and analyzed in the order in which they were observed, and their duration and frequency can be coded with the computer's built-in timer (Repp & Karsh, 1994).

Although computer technology has advanced psychologists' ability to gather and analyze behavior information, some shortcomings exist. The need to learn some technical information about computers is an obvious obstacle for some. Also, the limited portability of some computers make them less feasible and practical if continuous observational data must be collected from various locations.

In the area of computer optical-scanning technology, well-documented and studied bar code devices used for data collection are the TimeWand I and TimeWand II Scanners. These bar coders are portable (i.e., they are similar in size to a credit card or calculator) and have the capacity to store between 16 and 320 kilobytes in memory. The TimeWand scanners contain a light-sensing scanning lens that projects from the corner of the card and a control button mounted on its side. This device permits data to be recorded by a single pass over a bar code. Saunders et al. (1994) reported a first-scan success rate of 90% to 95% for observers after two hours of training. Moreover, according to Harmon and Adams (1984), data are recorded more accurately by a bar code scanner than by the keyboard entry methods that are required for direct input into computers. Their research found error rates for bar code readers to be 1 error in 2,700,000 characters, whereas those for computer keyboards yielded errors in every 108 to 230 characters typed. Upon completion of data collection, the information is uploaded to a computer (see Saunders, Saunders, & Saunders, 1994, for details about the application and use of the Time-Wand scanners).

Overall, computer technology may offer many benefits to psychologists. Psychologists may enhance their services because of the time- and cost-efficient nature of this method. Computer technology may also reduce errors in collecting and/or transcribing behavioral data. According to Eiler et al. (1989), when comparisons were made to paper-and-pencil methods of behavior data collection, automated bar-coding systems reduced the routine of behavior analysis by 33 hours per month. Also, Saunders et al. (1994) reported a 45-minute reduction in time per week. Given that surveys of practitioners who have used behavioral assessment have suggested that time and cost are salient limitations, such evidence is encouraging for the continued and increased use of computer technology.

Kratochwill et al. (1986) noted that developments in computer technology are important in behavioral assessment for other reasons. First, many current applications of computer technology in psychology and education have focused on traditional testing (i.e., test administration, test scoring, and report generation). More specifically, psychologists are able to score analogue assessment tools such as the Wechsler Intelligence Scale for Children–Third Edition (WISC-III; Wechsler, 1991) and generate a standard report based on the computer's interpretation of the scores. As discussed earlier in this chapter, computer-assisted observational packages like EBASS have also been developed to assess relationships between classroom instructional processes and learning outcomes for students (see Greenwood et al., 1994, for more information).

Second, there is also potential for the application of computer technology across the wide range of measures of various adult and childhood behavior disorders (Reynolds, McNamara, Marion, & Tobin, 1985). Applications reviewed by Kratochwill et al. (1986) include interviews, checklists and rating scales, direct observation, self-monitoring, and psychophysiological measures.

Third, computer technology may help standardize behavioral assessment on procedural and psychometric dimensions. As noted in this chapter, behavioral assessment has not been highly standardized, even though a movement in this direction could be positive (e.g., Cone & Hawkins, 1977; Kratochwill, 1985; Mash & Terdal, 1988a). Computer programming requires researchers and clinicians to operationalize measures that previously remained only at the conceptual level. Thus, this standardization could occur in both psychometric (accuracy, reliability, validity, and norming) and procedural dimensions (protocol, instructions, and coding) of various behavioral assessment computer strategies.

Fourth, microcomputer software programs can facilitate the dissemination of behavioral assessment strategies into diverse areas of practice. The range of applications, from the least to the most influence of the psychologist in decision making and client care, include the following (Hartmann, 1984): (1) storage and retrieval of clinical records, (2) administration and storage of tests, (3) automated interviewing, (4) automated test interpretation, (5) integrated report writing and evaluations, and (6) treatment programming. Since increasing numbers of practitioners have access to microcomputers, the software programs provide a vehicle for assessment and treatment procedures, encouraging use in diverse settings.

Finally, computers in behavioral assessment may facilitate the link between assessment and treatment. Microcomputers have been used for both assessment and treatment of developmentally disabled children (e.g., Romanczyk, 1984, 1986) and may supplement conventional self-help or bibliotherapy formats in treatment (Reynolds et al., 1985). "Expert systems" may also facilitate the assessment-treatment link (Kramer, 1985).

## Treatment Utility of Assessment

Behavior therapists have argued that their assessment methods are directly relevant to treatment

**TABLE 14.4  Types of Treatment Utility Studies, Questions Asked, and Methods Used**

| Type of Study | Question | Typical Group Comparison | Time Series (Single Case) Main Question Between Subject | Time Series (Single Case) Main Question Within Subject |
|---|---|---|---|---|
| | | **Post Hoc Studies** | | |
| | What is the relation between client characteristics and treatment outcome? | Pre-post correlational. | Time-series design, then correlational. | Not applicable. |
| | | **A Priori Single-Dimension Studies** | | |
| Manipulated assessment | What is the effect of the administration of, or data from, different assessment devices or methods on treatment outcome? | Two or more groups randomly assigned. Assessment taken or made available differs. Use of information in treatment stays the same. | Two or more groups randomly assigned. Assessment taken or made available differs. Use of information in treatment stays the same. Treatment assessed in series of time-series designs. | Assessment taken or made available differs. Use of information in treatment stays the same. Treatments compared within subject using time-series designs. |
| Manipulated use | What is the effect of different uses of available assessment data on treatment outcome? | Two or more groups randomly assigned. Assessment the same. Use of assessment in treatment differs. | Two or more groups randomly assigned. Assessment the same. Use of assessment in treatment differs. Treatment assessed in series of time-series designs. | Assessment the same. Use of assessment in treatment differs. Treatments compared within subject, using time-series designs. |
| Obtained differences | What is the relation between distinct patient types and treatment outcome? | Two or more known groups based on pretreatment differences. Same treatment. | Two or more known groups based on pretreatment differences. Treatment assessed in series of time-series designs. | Not applicable. |

## Time Series (Single Case)

| Type of Study | Question | Typical Group Comparison | Main Question Between Subject | Main Question Within Subject |
|---|---|---|---|---|
| **A Priori Multiple-Dimension Studies** | | | | |
| Manipulated assessment/ manipulated use | What is the effect of different assessment devices or methods when the information from them is used in different ways to design treatment? | Factorial groups randomly assigned. Assessment taken or made available differs. Use of assessment data in treatment differs. | Factorial groups randomly assigned. Assessment taken or made available differs. Use of assessment data in treatment differs. Treatment assessed in series of time-series designs. | Assessment taken or made available differs. Use of assessment data in treatment differs. Treatments based on different combinations of [assessment] compared within subject using time-series designs. |
| Manipulated assessment/ obtained differences | What is the effect of different assessment devices or methods on treatment outcome for two or more distinct patient types? | Groups randomly assigned within known groups. Assessment taken or made available differs. Use of data in treatment stays the same. | Groups randomly assigned within known groups. Assessment taken or made available differs. Use of data in treatment stays the same. Treatment assessed in series of time-series designs. | Assessment taken or made available differs. Use of data in treatment stays the same. Treatments compared within subject using time-series designs in each of two or more known groups. |
| Manipulated use/obtained differences | What is the effect of different uses of available assessment data on treatment outcome for two or more distinct patients types? | Groups randomly assigned within known groups. Use of assessment data differs. Assessment taken or made available stays the same. | Groups randomly assigned within known groups. Use of assessment data differs. Treatment assessed in series of time-series designs. | Use of assessment data differs. Treatments compared within subject using time-series designs in each of two or more known groups. |

*(Continued)*

**TABLE 14.4** *(Continued)*

| | | | Time Series (Single Case) | |
|---|---|---|---|---|
| Type of Study | Question | Typical Group Comparison | Main Question Between Subject | Main Question Within Subject |
| Manipulated assessment/ manipulated use/obtained differences | What is the effect of different types and uses of available assessment data on treatment outcome for two or more distinct patient types? | Groups randomly assigned within known groups. Use of assessment data differs. Assessment taken or made available differs. | Groups randomly assigned within known groups. Use of assessment data differs. Assessment taken or made available differs. Treatment assessed in series of time-series designs. | Nature and use of assessment data differs. Treatments compared within subject using time-series designs in each of two or more known groups. |
| Obtained differences/two or more treatments | What is the effect of different treatments on outcome for two or more distinct patient types? | Two or more known groups of subjects randomly assigned to two or more treatments. | Two or more known groups of subjects randomly assigned to two or more treatments. Treatment assessed in series of time-series designs. Each subject receives one type of treatment. | Two or more known groups of subjects. Two or more treatments compared within subject using time-series designs. |

*Source:* From S. C. Hayes, R. O. Nelson, and R. B. Garrett. The treatment utility of assessment: A functional approach to evaluating assessment quality. *American Psychologist, 42* (1987), 963–974. Copyright 1987 by the American Psychologist Association. Reprinted by permission.

design and monitoring. Nevertheless, historically, few *empiricial* efforts were devoted to this assessment-treatment link. Behavioral assessors could document that certain behavioral assessment methods were used to evaluate treatment; but because documenting how assessment actually led to useful treatment planning remained unclear, conceptual and methodological guidelines for defining treatment validity or treatment utility were proposed (Hayes et al., 1986; Hayes, Nelson, & Jarrett, 1987; Nelson & Hayes, 1979). The term *treatment utility* is preferred and refers to "the degree to which assessment is shown to contribute to beneficial treatment outcome. An assessment device, distinction, or strategy has this kind of utility if it can be shown that the treatment outcome is positively influenced by this device, distinction, or strategy. The treatment utility of assessment deserves to be termed a type of utility because it relates closely to the functional thrust of that psychometric term" (Hayes et al., 1987, pp. 963–964).

The authors note that several different types of research questions can be addressed through treatment utility, including those related to target behaviors and classification, the utility of various assessment device (e.g., functional analyses), and the usefulness of general assessment strategies (e.g., self-monitoring and projective tests). Hayes et al. (1987) developed a methodological topology for researchers interested in treatment utility (see Table 14.4). Each row in the table describes a specific kind of study, and the last three columns present methods appropriate to each research question. Of course, studies on treatment utility extend beyond those of interest to behavioral assessors. Nevertheless, the methodology for treatment utility studies was and is an important conceptual advance.

one of the theoretical areas of behavioral therapy. Since the field of behavior therapy has become extraordinary diverse, there is likely to be high similarity among the various problem-solving approaches that were once traditionally affiliated only with behavioral assessment.

One area of behavior therapy has remained relatively consistent and has made major advances in assessment. This area, which is commonly called applied behavior analysis, has remained relatively homogeneous in theoretical and methodological paradigms. An important advance in this field has been the development of functional assessment, or functional analysis. We consider advances in this area to be one of the most noteworthy achievements in behavioral assessment. Nevertheless, as noted, there are still a number of questions pertaining to the treatment utility of this approach and its application across diverse settings, target problems, and disorders. For a further review of some of the issues in functional analysis, see Schill et al. (1996b).

Finally, we note that the development of the treatment utility of assessment was a major achievement when we were writing this chapter for the previous edition. Nevertheless, there still needs to be considerable attention devoted to the use of this conceptual framework for application to a variety of behavioral assessment techniques. Moreover, comparative analysis of the various techniques along utility dimensions seems to be a very worthwhile endeavor for future research.

The major advances in behavioral assessment stand as important achievements in the application of assessment technology in schools. As we move into the next century, it is hoped that behavioral assessment will continue to achieve its empirical agenda, established many years ago when the field was first launched.

## SUMMARY

In this chapter we have provided an overview of advances in behavioral assessment. The field of behavioral assessment continues to grow in certain areas; in other areas, there has been expansion to the point where many of the techniques and procedures clearly identified as behavioral assessment can be affiliated with a variety of theoretical frameworks. Given that behavioral assessment represents a theoretical orientation to the development, implementation, and use of assessment techniques, one must assume that to define a behavioral assessor one must embrace

## REFERENCES

Achenbach, T. M. (1991a). *Integrative guide for the 1991 DBCL/4–18, YSR, and TRF Profiles.* Burlington: Department of Psychiatry, University of Vermont.

Achenbach, T. M. (1991b). *Manual for the Child Behavior Checklist/4–18, YSR, and TRF Profiles.* Burlington: Department of Psychiatry, University of Vermont.

Achenbach, T. M. (1991c). *Manual for the Teacher's Report Form and 1991 Profile.* Burlington: Department of Psychiatry, University of Vermont.

Achenbach, T. M., & Edelbrock, C. S. (1983). *Manual*

*for the Child Behavior Checklist and Revised Child Behavior Profile.* Burlington: Department of Psychiatry, University of Vermont.

Airasian, P. W. (1991). *Classroom assessment.* New York: McGraw-Hill.

Alessi, G. J., & Kaye, J. H. (1983). *Behavior assessment for school psychologists.* Kent, OH: National Association of School Psychologists Professional Development Publications.

Alevizos, R., DeRisi, W., Liberman, R., Eckman, T., & Callahan, E. (1978). The behavior observation instrument: A method of direct observation for program evaluation. *Journal of Applied Behavior Analysis, 11,* 243–257.

Aman, M. G. (1993). Monitoring and measuring drug effects. II. Behavioral, emotional, and cognitive effects. In J. S. Werry & M. G. Aman (Eds.), *Practitioner's guide to psychoactive drugs in children and adolescents* (pp. 99–159). New York: Plenum.

American Psychiatric Association. (1994). *Diagnostic and statistical manual of mental disorders* (DSM-IV). Washington, DC: Author.

Anastasi, A. (1976). *Psychological testing* (4th ed.). New York: Macmillan.

Archbald, D. A. (1992). Authentic assessment: Principles, practices, and issues. *School Psychology Quarterly, 7,* 279–293.

Archbald, D., & Newmann, F. (1988). *Beyond standardized testing: Assessing authentic academic achievement in the secondary school.* Reston, VA: National Association of Secondary School Principals.

Atwater, J. B., & Morris, E. K. (1988). Teacher's instructions and children's compliance in preschool classrooms: A descriptive analysis. *Journal of Applied Behavior Analysis, 21,* 157–167.

Azrin, N. H. (1977). A strategy for applied research: Learning based but outcome oriented. *American Psychologist, 32,* 17–29.

Baer, D. M., Wolf, M. M., & Risley, T. R. (1968). Some current dimensions of applied behavior analysis. *Journal of Applied Behavior Analysis, 1,* 91–97.

Barkley, R. A. (1988). Child behavior rating scales and checklists. In M. Rutter, A. H. Tuma, & I. S. Lann (Eds.), *Assessment and diagnosis in child psychopathology* (pp. 113–155). New York: Guilford.

Barnett, D. W., & Macmann, G. M. (1992). Decision reliability and validity: Contributions and limitations of alternative assessment strategies. *The Journal of Special Education, 25,* 431–452.

Barrios, B. A. (1988). On the changing nature of behavioral assessment. In A. S. Bellack & M. Hersen (Eds.), *Behavioral assessment: A practical handbook* (3rd ed., pp. 3–41). New York: Pergamon.

Barrios, B. A., & Shigetomi, C. C. (1985). Assessment of children's fears: A critical review.

In T. R. Kratochwill (Ed.), *Advances in school psychology* (Vol. 4, pp. 89–132). Hillsdale, NJ: Erlbaum.

Bellack, A. S., & Hersen, M. (1977a). *Behavior modification: An introductory textbook.* Baltimore, MD: Williams & Wilkins.

Bellack, A. S., & Hersen, M. (1977b). The use of self-report inventories in behavioral assessment. In J. D. Cone & R. P. Hawkins (Eds), *Behavioral assessment: New directions in clinical psychology* (pp. 52–76). New York: Brunner/Mazel.

Bennett, R. E., & Maher, C. A. (Eds.) (1984). Microcomputers and exceptional children: An overview. *Special Services in the Schools, 1,* 3–5.

Bergan, J. R. (1977). *Behavioral consultation.* Columbus, OH: Merrill.

Bergan, J. R. (1981). Path-referenced assessment. In T. R. Kratochwill (Ed.), *Advances in school psychology* (pp. 255–280). Hillsdale, NJ: Erlbaum.

Bergan, J. R. (1986). Path-referenced assessment: A guide for instructional management. *Special Services in the Schools, 2,* 29–41.

Bergan, J. R., & Kratochwill, T. R. (1990a). *Behavioral consultation and therapy.* New York: Plenum.

Bergan, T. R., & Tombari, M. L. (1975). The analysis of verbal interactions occurring during consultation. *Journal of School Psychology, 13,* 109–226.

Bijou, S. (1976). *Child development: The basic stage of early childhood.* Englewood Cliffs, NJ: Prentice Hall.

Bijou, S. W., Peterson, R. F., & Ault, M. H. (1968). A method to integrate descriptive and experimental field studies at the level of data and empirical concepts. *Journal of Applied Behavior Analysis, 1,* 175–191.

Bijou, S. W., Peterson, R. F., Harris, F. R., Allen, K. E., & Johnson, M. S. (1969). Methodology for experimental studies of young children in natural settings. *Psychological Record, 19,* 177–210.

Burke, J. P., & DeMers, S. T. (1979). A paradigm for evaluating assessment interviewing techniques. *Psychology in the Schools, 16,* 51–60.

Christie, L., McKenzie, H., & Burdett, C. (1972). The consulting teacher approach to special education: Inservice training for regular classroom teachers. *Focus on Exceptional Children, 5,* 1–10.

Ciminero, A. R., & Drabman, R. S. (1977). Current developments in the behavioral assessment of children. In B. B. Lahey & A. E. Kazdin (Eds.), *Advances in clinical child psychology* (Vol. I, pp. 47–82). New York: Plenum.

Coates, T. J., & Thoresen, C. E. (1979). Behavioral self-control and educational practice, or do we really need self control? In D. C. Berliner (Ed.), *Review of educational research* (Vol. 7, pp. 3–45). New York: American Educational Research Associates.

Cone, J. D. (1977). The relevance of reliability and

validity for behavioral assessment. *Behavior Therapy, 8,* 411–426.

Cone, J. D. (1978). The behavioral assessment grid (BAG): A conceptual framework and a taxonomy. *Behavior Therapy, 9,* 882–888.

Cone, J. D., Bourland, G., & Wood-Shuman, S. (1986). Template matching: An objective approach to placing clients in appropriate residential services. *The Journal of the Association of Persons with Severe Handicaps, 11,* 110–117.

Cone, J. D., & Hawkins, R. P. (Eds.). (1977a). Current status and future directions in behavioral assessment. In J. D. Cone & R. P. Hawkins (Eds.), *Behavioral assessment: New directions in clinical psychology* (pp. 381–392). New York: Brunner/Mazel.

Cooper, L. J., Wacker, D. P., Sasso, G. M., Reimers, T. M., & Donn, L. K. (1990). Using parents as therapists to evaluate appropriate behavior of their children: Application to a tertiary diagnostic clinic. *Journal of Applied Behavioral Analysis, 23,* 285–296.

Daugherty, T. K., & Shapiro, S. K. (1994). Behavior checklists and rating forms. In T. H. Ollendick, N. J. King, & W. Yule (Eds.), *International handbook of phobic and anxiety disorders in children and adolescents* (pp. 331–348). New York: Plenum.

Deitz, S. M. (1978). Current status of applied behavior analysis: Science versus technology. *American Psychologist, 33,* 805–814.

Deno, S. L., Marston, D., & Tindal, G. (1986). Direct and frequent curriculum-based measurement: An alternative for educational decision-making. *Special Services in the Schools, 2,* 5–27.

Deno, S. L., & Mirkin, P. (1977). *Data-based program modification: A manual.* Minneapolis: Leadership Training Institute/Special Education, University of Minnesota.

Drabman, R. S., Hammer, D., & Rosenbaum, M. S. (1979). Assessing generalization in behavior modification with children: The generalization map. *Behavioral Assessment, 1,* 203–219.

Durand, V. M., & Crimmins, D. B. (1992). *The motivation assessment scale (MAS).* Topeka, KS: Monaco.

Edelbrock, C. (1988). Informant reports. In E. S. Shapiro & T. R. Kratochwill (Eds.), *Behavioral assessment in the schools* (pp. 351–383). New York: Guilford.

Eiler, J. M., Nelson, W. W., Jensen, C. C., & Johnson, S. P. (1989). Automated data collection using bar code. *Behavior Research Methods, Instruments, & Computers, 21*(1), 53–58.

Elliott, S. N. (1992). Authentic assessment: An introduction to a neobehavioral approach to classroom assessment. *School Psychology Quarterly, 7,* 273–278.

Elliott, S. N., Busse, R. T., & Gresham, F. M. (1993). Behavior rating scales: Issues of use and

development. *School Psychology Review, 22,* 313–321.

Elliott, S. N., Sheridan, S. M., & Gresham, F. M. (1989). Assessing and treating social skills deficits: A case study for the scientist-practitioner. *Journal of School Psychology, 27,* 197–222.

Evans, I. M., & Nelson, R. O. (1977). Assessment of child behavior problems. In A. R. Ciminero, K. S. Calhoun, & H. E. Adams (Eds.), *Handbook of behavioral assessment* (pp. 603–681). New York: Wiley.

Evans, I. M., & Nelson, R. O. (1986). Assessment of children. In A. R. Ciminero, K. S. Calhoun, & H. E. Adams (Eds.), *Handbook of behavioral assessment* (2nd ed., pp. 603–681). New York: Wiley.

Gagne, R. M. (1962). The acquisition of knowledge. *Psychological Review, 69,* 355–365.

Gagne, R. M. (1968). Learning hierarchies. *Educational Psychologists, 6,* 1–9.

Gardner, W. I., & Cole, C. (1988). Self-monitoring. In E. S. Shapiro & T. R. Kratochwill (Eds.), *Behavioral assessment in the schools* (pp. 206–246). New York: Guilford.

Gettinger, M. (1988). Analogue measures. In E. S. Shapiro & T. R. Kratochwill (Eds.), *Behavioral assessment in the schools* (pp. 247–289). Hillsdale, NJ: Erlbaum.

Glaser, R. (1971). A criterion-referenced test. In W. J. Popham (Ed.), *Criterion-referenced measurement: An introduction* (pp. 32–64). Englewood Cliffs, NJ: Educational Psychology Publications.

Greenspoon, J., & Lamal, P. A. (1978). Cognitive behavior modification—Who needs it? *The Psychological Record, 28,* 343–351.

Greenwood, C. R., Carta, J. J., Kamps, D., Terry B., & Delquadri, J. (1994). Development and validation of standard classroom observation systems for school practitioners: Ecobehavioral assessment systems software (EBASS). *Exceptional Children, 61,* 197–210.

Gresham, F. M. (1984). Behavioral interviews in school psychology: Issues in psychometric adequacy and research. *School Psychology Review, 13,* 17–25.

Gresham, F. M., & Davis, C. J. (1988). Behavioral interviews with teachers and parents. In E. S. Shapiro & T. R. Kratochwill (Eds.), *Behavioral assessment in schools* (pp. 455–493). New York: Guilford.

Gresham, F. M., & Elliott, S. N. (1990). *The Social Skills Rating System.* Circle Pines, MN: American Guidance Services.

Guevremont, D. C., DuPaul, G. J., & Barkley, R. A. (1990). Diagnosis and assessment of attention-deficit hyperactivity disorder in children. *Journal of School Psychology, 28,* 51–78.

Hambleton, R. K., Swaminathan, H., Algina, J., & Coulson, D. B. (1978). Criterion-referenced testing and measurement: A review of technical issues and developments. *Review of Educational Research, 48,* 1–48.

Harding, J., Wacker, D. P., Cooper, L. J., Millard, T., & Jensen-Kovalan, P. (1994). Brief hierarchical assessment of potential treatment components with children in an out-patient clinic. *Journal of Applied Behavior Analysis, 27,* 291–300.

Harmon, C. K., & Adams, R. (1984). *Reading between the lines: An introduction to bar code technology.* Petersborough, NH: Helmers Publishing.

Hartman, D. E. (1986). Artificial intelligence or artificial psychologist? Conceptual issues in clinical micro-computer use. *Professional Psychology: Research and Practice, 17,* 528–534.

Hartmann, D. P. (Ed.). (1982). *Using observers to study behavior: New directions for methodology of social and behavioral sciences.* San Francisco: Jossey-Bass.

Hartmann, D. P. (1984). Assessment strategies. In D. H. Barlow & M. Hersen (Eds.), *Single case experimental designs: Strategies for studying behavior change* (2nd ed., pp. 107–139). New York: Pergamon.

Hartmann, D. P., Roper, B. L., & Bradford, D. C. (1979). Some relationships between behavioral and traditional assessment. *Journal of Behavioral Assessment, 1,* 3–21.

Hawkins, R. P. (1986). Selection of target behaviors. In R. O. Nelson & S. C. Hayes (Eds.), *Conceptual foundations of behavioral assessment* (pp. 331–385). New York: Guilford.

Hay, W. H., Hay, L. R., Angle, H. V., & Nelson, R. O. (1979). The reliability of problem identification in the behavioral interview. *Behavioral Assessment, 1,* 107–118.

Hayes, S. C., & Follette, W. C. (1992). Can functional analysis provide a substitute for syndromal classification? *Behavioral Assessment, 14,* 345–365.

Hayes, S. C., Nelson, R. O., & Jarrett, R. B. (1986). Evaluating the quality of behavioral assessment. In R. O. Nelson & S. C. Hayes (Eds.), *Conceptual foundations of behavioral assessment* (pp. 463–503). New York: Guilford.

Hayes, S. C., Nelson, R. O., & Jarrett, R. B. (1987). The treatment utility of assessment: A functional approach to evaluating assessment qualify. *American Psychologist, 42,* 963–974.

Haynes, S. N. (1978). *Principles of behavioral assessment.* New York: Gardner Press.

Haynes, S. N., & Jensen, B. J. (1979). The interview as a behavioral assessment instrument. *Behavioral Assessment, 1,* 97–106.

Haynes, S. N., & O'Brien, W. H. (1990). Functional analysis in behavior therapy. *Clinical Psychology Review, 10,* 649–668.

Herbert, M. (1981). *Behavioral treatment of problem children: A practical manual.* London: Academic Press.

Hersen, M., & Barlow, D. H. (1976). *Single case experimental designs: Strategies for studying behavior change.* New York: Pergamon.

Hoge, R. D. (1983). Psychometric properties of teacher-judgment measures of pupil aptitudes, classroom behaviors, and achievement levels. *The Journal of Special Education, 17,* 401–429.

Hoge, R. D., & Andrews, D. A. (1987). Enhancing academic performance: Issues in target selection. *School Psychology Review, 16,* 228–238.

Hoier, T. S., & Cone, J. D. (1987). Target selection of social skills for children: The template-matching procedure. *Behavior Modification, 11,* 137–163.

Holland, C. (1970). An interview guide for behavioral counseling with parents. *Behavior Therapy, 1,* 70–79.

Idol-Maestas, L. (1981). A teacher training model: The resource consulting teacher. *Behavioral Disorders, 6,* 108–121.

Iwata, B. A., Dorsey, M. F., Slifer, K. J., Bauman, K. & Richman, G. S. (1982). Toward a functional analysis of self-injury. *Analysis and Intervention in Developmental Disabilities, 2,* 3–20.

Johnson, S. M., & Bolstad O. D. (1973). Methodological issues in naturalistic observation: Some problems and solutions for field research. In L. A. Hamerlynch, L. C. Handy, & E. J. Mash (Eds.), *Behavior change: Methodology, concepts, and practice* (pp. 7–67). Champaign, IL: Research Press.

Jones, R. R., Reid, J. B., & Patterson, G. B. (1974). Naturalistic observation in clinical assessment. In P. McReynolds (Ed.), *Advances in psychological assessment* (Vol. 3, pp. 42–95). San Francisco: Jossey-Bass.

Kahn, J. S., Kehle, T. J., Jenson, W. R., & Clark, E. (1990). Comparison of cognitive-behavioral, relaxation, and self-modeling interventions for depression among middle-school students. *School Psychology Review, 19,* 196–211.

Kanfer, F. H. (1979). Personal control, social control, and altruism. Can society survive the age of individualism? *American Psychologist, 34,* 231–239.

Kanfer, F. H., & Grimm, L. G. (1977). Behavior analysis: Selecting target behaviors in the interview. *Behavior Modification, 1,* 7–28.

Kanfer, F. H., & Saslow, G. (1969). Behavioral diagnosis. In C. Franks (Ed.), *Behavior therapy: Appraisal status* (pp. 417–444). New York: McGraw-Hill.

Kazdin, A. E. (1977b). Assessing the clinical or applied significance of behavior change through social validation. *Behavior Modification, 1,* 427–452.

Kazdin, A. E. (1982). Symptom substitution, generalization, and response covariation: Implications for psychotherapy outcome. *Psychological Bulletin, 91,* 349–365.

Kazdin, A. E. (1983). Psychiatric diagnosis, dimensions of dysfunction, and child behavior therapy. *Behavior Therapy, 14,* 73–99.

Kazdin, A. E. (1985). Selection of target behaviors. The relationship of the treatment focus to clinical dysfunction. *Behavioral Assessment, 7,* 33–47.

Kearney, C. A., & Silverman, W. K. (1990). A preliminary analysis of a functional model of assessment and treatment for school refusal behavior. *Behavior Modification, 14,* 340–366.

Kearney, C. A., & Silverman, W. K. (1993). Measuring the function of school refusal behavior: The School Refusal Assessment Scale. *Journal of Clinical Child Psychology, 22,* 85–96.

Kendall, P. C., Cantwell, D. P., & Kazdin, A. E. (1989). Depression in children and adolescents: Assessment issues and recommendations. *Cognitive Therapy and Research, 13,* 109–146.

Kent, R. N., & Foster, S. L. (1977). Direct observational procedures: Methodological issues in naturalistic settings. In A. R. Ciminero, K. S. Calhoun, & H. E. Adams (Eds.), *Handbook of behavioral assessment* (pp. 279–328). New York: Wiley.

Kohlenberg, R. J., Tsai, M., & Kohlenberg, B. S. (1995). Functional analysis in behavior therapy. In M. Hersen, R. M. Eisler, & P. M. Miller (Eds.), *Progress in behavior modification* (Vol. 30, pp. 1–24). Pacific Grove, CA: Brooks/Cole.

Kramer, J. J. (1985, August 27). Computer-based test interpretation in psychoeducational assessment. Paper presented at the Ninety-third Annual Convention of the American Psycholgical Association, Los Angeles.

Kratochwill, T. R. (1982). Advances in behavioral assessment. In C. R. Reynolds & R. B. Gutkin (Eds.), *Handbook of school psychology* (pp. 314–350). New York: Wiley.

Kratochwill, T. R. (1985). Selection of target behaviors in behavioral consultation. *Behavioral Assessment, 7,* 59–61.

Kratochwill, T. R., Alper, S., & Cancelli, A. A. (1980). Nondiscriminatory assessment in psychology and education. In L. Mann & D. A. Sabatino (Eds.), *Fourth review of special education* (pp. 229–286). New York: Grune & Stratton.

Kratochwill, T. R., & Bergan, R. (1990). *Behavioral consultation in applied settings: An individual guide.* New York: Plenum.

Kratochwill, T. R., Doll, E. J., & Dickson, W. P. (1986). Microcomputers in behavioral assessment: Recent advances and remaining issues. *Computers in Human Behavior, 1,* 277–291.

Kratochwill, T. R., Doll, E. J., & Dickson, P. (1991). Use of computer technology in behavioral assessments. In J. C. Conoley, S. Wise, & T. B. Gutkin (Eds.), *Buros-Nebraska series on measurement and testing* (pp. 125–154). Hillsdale, NJ: Erlbaum.

Kratochwill, T. M., & McGivern, J. (1996). Enhancing treatment validity in DSDM-IV; Applications in consultation problem solving. *School Psychology Review, 25,* 342–355.

Kratochwill, T. R., & Morris R. J. (1991). *The practice of child therapy* (2nd ed.). New York: Pergamon.

Kratochwill, T. R., & Sheridan, S. M. (1990). Advances in behavioral assessment. In T. B. Gutkin & C. R. Reynolds (Eds.), *The handbook of school psychology* (2nd ed., pp. 328–364). New York: Wiley.

Landau, S., & Burcham, B. G. (1995). Assessment of children with attention disorders. In A. Thomas & J. Grimes (Eds.), *Best Practices in School Psychology III* (pp. 817–830). Washington, DC: National Association of School Psychologists.

Laurent, J., Hadler, J. R., & Stark, K. D. (1994). A multiple-stage screening procedure for the identification of childhood anxiety disorders. *School Psychology Quarterly, 9,* 239–255.

Lentz, F. E., Jr. (1988). Direct observation and measurement of academic skills: A conceptual review. In E. S. Shapiro & T. R. Kratochwill (Eds.), *Behavioral assessment in schools* (pp. 76–120). New York: Guilford.

Lewis, T. J., Scott, T. M., & Sugai, G. (1994). The Problem Behavior Questionnaire: A teacher-based instrument to develop functional hypotheses of problem behavior in general education classrooms. *Diagnostique, 19,* 103–115.

Lindsley, O. R. (1964). Direct measurement and prosthesis of retarded behavior. *Journal of Education, 147,* 62–81.

Linehan, M. M. (1977). Issues in behavioral interviewing. In J. D. Cone & R. P. Hawkins (Eds.), *Behavioral assessment: New directions in clinical psychology* (pp. 30–51). New York: Brunner/Mazel.

Lipinski, D. P., & Nelson, R. O. (1974). Problems in the use of naturalistic observation as a means of behavioral assessment. *Behavioral Therapy, 5,* 341–351.

Mace, F. C., Lalli, J. S., & Pinter Lalli, E. (1991). Functional analysis and treatment of aberrant behavior. *Research in Developmental Disabilities, 12,* 155–180.

Mace, F. C., & West, B. J. (1986a). Analysis of demand conditions associated with reluctant speech. *Journal of Behavior Therapy and Experimental Psychiatry, 17,* 285–294.

Mace, F. C., & West, B. J. (1986b). Unresolved theoretical issues in self-management: Implications for research and practice. *Professional School Psychology, 1,* 149–163.

Mahoney, M. J. (1977). Some applied issues in self-monitoring. In J. D. Cone & R. P. Hawkins (Eds.), *Behavioral assessment. New directions in clinical psychology* (pp. 241–254). New York: Brunner/Mazel.

Mahoney, M. J., & Arnkoff, D. (1978). Cognitive and self-control therapies. In S. L. Garfield & A. E. Bergin (Eds.), *Handbook of psychotherapy and behavior change: An empirical analysis* (2nd ed., pp. 689–722). New York: Wiley.

Marston, D. B. (1989). A curriculum-based measurement approach to assessing academic performance: What it is and why do it. In M. R. Shinn (Ed.), *Curriculum-based measurement: Assessing special children* (pp. 18–78). New York: Guilford.

Martens, B. K. (1993). Social labeling, precision of measurement, and problem solving: Key issues in the assessment of children's emotional problems. *School Psychology Review, 22,* 308–312.

Mash, E. J. (1985). Some comments on target selection in behavior therapy. *Behavioral Assessment, 7,* 63–78.

Mash, E. J., & Lee, C. M. (1993). Behavioral assessment with children. In R. T. Ammerman & M. Hersen (Eds.), *Handbook of behavior therapy with children and adults* (pp. 13–31). Needham Heights, MA: Allyn & Bacon.

Mash, E. J., & Terdal, L. (Eds.). (1981). *Behavioral assessment of childhood disorders.* New York: Guilford.

Mash, E. J., & Terdal, L. G. (1988a). Behavioral assessment of child and family disturbance. In E. J. Mash & L. G. Terdal (Eds.), *Behavioral assessment of childhood disorders* (2nd ed.) (pp. 3–65). New York: Guilford.

Mash, E. J., & Terdal, L. G. (1988b). *Behavioral assessment of childhood disorders* (2nd ed.). New York: Guilford.

Mash, E. J., & Terdal, L. G. (1990). Assessment strategies in clinical behavioral pediatrics. In A. M. Gross & R. Drabman (Eds.), *Handbook of clinical behavioral pediatrics* (pp. 49–79). New York: Plenum.

McConaughy, S. H. (1993). Advances in empirically based assessment of children's behavioral and emotional problems. *School Psychology Review, 22,* 285–307.

McConaughy, S. H., & Achenbach, T. M. (1989). Empirically-based assessment of serious emotional disturbance. *Journal of School Psychology, 27,* 91–117.

McConaughy, S. H., & Achenbach, T. M. (1994). *Manual for the Semistructured Clinical Interview for Children and Adolescents.* Burlington: Department of Psychiatry, University of Vermont.

McConaughy, S. H., & Ritter, D. R. (1995). Multidimensional assessment of emotional and behavioral disorders. In A. Thomas & J. Grimes (Eds.), *Best Practices in School Psychology III.* (pp. 865–878). Washington, DC: National Association of School Psychologists.

McCullough, C. S., & Wenck, L. S. (Eds.) (1984a). Computers in school psychology. *School Psychology Review, 13,* 421.

McFall, R. M. (1977). Parameters of self-monitoring. In R. B. Stuart (Ed.), *Behavioral self-management: Strategies, techniques, and outcomes* (pp. 196–214). New York: Brunner/Mazel.

Merrell, K. W. (1993). *School Social Behavior Scales.* Bradon, VT: Clinical Psychology Publishing.

Morris, R. J., & Kratochwill, T. R. (Eds.). (1984). *The practice of child therapy.* Elmsford, NY: Pergamon.

Nay, W. R. (1977). Analogue measures. In A. R. Ciminero, K. S. Calhoun, & H. E. Adams (Eds.), *Handbook of behavioral assessment* (pp. 233–277). New York: Wiley.

Neef, N. A., & Iwata, B. A. (1994). Current research on functional analysis methodologies: An introduction. *Journal of Applied Behavior Analysis, 27,* 211–214.

Nelson, R. O. (1977a). Assessment and therapeutic functions of self-monitoring. In M. Hersen, R. M. Eisler, & P. M. Miller (Eds.), *Progress in behavior modification* (Vol. 5, pp. 263–308). New York: Academic Press.

Nelson, R. O. (1977b). Methodological issues in assessment via self-monitoring. In J. D. Cone & R. P. Hawkins (Eds.), *Behavioral assessment: New directions in clinical psychology* (pp. 217–240). New York: Brunner/Mazel.

Nelson, R. O. (1985). Behavioral assessment in school psychology. In T. R. Kratochwill (Ed.), *Advances in school psychology* (Vol. 4, pp. 45–87). Hillsdale, NJ: Erlbaum.

Nelson, R. O., & Bowles, P. E. (1975). The best of two worlds—Observation with norms. *Journal of School Psychology, 13,* 3–9.

Nelson, R. O., & Hayes, S. C. (1979). Some current dimensions of behavioral assessment. *Behavioral Assessment, 1,* 1–16.

Noldus, L. P. J. J., Van de Loo, E. L. A. M., & Timmers, P. H. A. (1989). Computers in behavioral research. *Nature, 341*(6244), 767–768.

O'Leary, K. D., Romanzyk, R. G., Kass, R. E., Dietz, A., & Santogrossi, D. (1979). *Procedures for classroom observation of teachers and children.* Stony Brook: Psychology Department, State University of New York.

O'Leary, S. G., & Dubey, D. R. (1979). Applications of self-control procedures for children: A review. *Journal of Applied Behavior Analysis, 43,* 24–30.

O'Neill, R. E., Horner, R. H., Albin, R. W., Storey, K., & Sprague, J. R. (1990). *Functional analysis of problem behavior: A practical assessment guide.* Sycamore, IL: Sycamore Publishing.

Patterson, G. R., Ray, R. W., Shaw, D. A., & Cobb, J. A. (1969). *A manual for coding family interactions* (6th rev.). CCM Information Services, Document No. 01234. New York: ASIS National Auxiliary Publications Service.

Paulson, F. L., Paulson, P. R., & Meyer, C. A. (1991, February). What makes a portfolio a portfolio? *Educational Leadership,* pp. 60–63.

Repp, A. C., Felce, D., & Barton, L. E. (1988). Basing the treatment of stereotypic and self-injurious behaviors on hypotheses of their causes. *Journal of Applied Behavior Analysis, 21,* 281–289.

Repp, A. C., & Karsh, K. G. (1994). Laptop computer system for data recording and contextual analyses. In T. Thompson & D. B. Gray (Eds.), *Destructive behavior in developmental disabilities: Diagnosis and treatment* (pp. 83–101). Thousand Oaks, CA: Sage.

Repp, A. C., Karsh, K. G., Van Acker, R., Felce, D., & Harman, M. (1989). A computer-based system for collecting and analyzing observational data. *Journal of Special Education Technology, 9*(4), 207–217.

Resnick, L. B., & Ford, W. W. (1978). The analysis of tasks for instruction: An information-processing approach. In A. C. Catania & T. A. Brigham (Eds.), *Handbook of applied behavior analysis: Social and instructional processes* (pp. 378–409). New York: Irvington.

Resnick, L. D., Wang, M. C., & Kaplan, J. (1973). Task analysis in curriculum. *Journal of Applied Behavior Analysis, 6*, 679–710.

Reynolds, C. R., & Richmond, B. O. (1985). *The Revised Children's Manifest Anxiety Scale (RCMAS): What I think and feel.* Los Angeles: Western Psychological Services.

Reynolds, R. V. C., McNamara, J. R., Marion, R. J., & Tobin, D. L. (1985). Computerized service delivery in clinical psychology. *Professional Psychology: Research and Practice, 16*, 339–353.

Reynolds, W. (1986). *Reynolds Adolescent Depression Scale: Professional manual.* Odessa, FL: Psychological Assessment Resources.

Reynolds, W. M. (1989). *Reynolds Child Depression Scale: Professional manual.* Odessa, FL: Psychological Assessment Resources.

Romanczyk, R. G. (1984). Microcomputers and behavior therapy: A powerful alliance. *Behavior Therapist, 7*, 59–64.

Romanczyk, R. G. (1986). *Clinical utilization of microcomputer technology.* New York: Pergamon.

Rosenbaum, M. S., & Drabman, R. S. (1979). Self-control training in the classroom: A review and critique. *Journal of Applied Behavior Analysis, 12*, 467–485.

Sasso, G. M., Reimers, T. M., Cooper, L. J., Wacker, D., Berg, W., Steege, M., Kelly, L., & Allaire, A. (1992). Use of descriptive and experimental analysis to identify the functional properties of aberrant behavior in school settings. *Journal of Applied Behavior Analysis, 25*, 809–821.

Saudargas, R. A. (1983). *State-event classroom observation code.* Knoxville: Department of Psychology, University of Tennessee. (Available from author.)

Saudargas, R. A., & Lentz, F. E. (1986). Estimating percent of time and rate via direct observation: A suggested observational procedure and format. *School Psychology Review, 15*, 36–48.

Saunders, R. R., Saunders, M. D., & Saunders, J. L. (1994). Data collection with bar code technology.

In Travis Thompson & David B. Gray (Eds.), *Destructive behavior in developmental disabilities: Diagnosis and treatment* (pp. 102–116). Thousand Oaks, CA: Sage.

Schill, M. A., Kratochwill, T. R., & Gardner, W. I. (1996a). *An assessment protocol for elective mutism: Analogue assessment using parents as facilitators. Journal of School Psychology, 34*, 1–21.

Schill, M. A., Kratochwill, T. R., & Gardner, W. I. (1996b). Conducting a functional analysis of behavior. In M. J. Breen & C. Fiedler (Eds.) *Behavioral approach to assessment of youth with emotional/behavioral disorders* (pp. 83–179). Austin, TX: Pro-Ed.

Shapiro, E. S. (1987a). *Behavioral assessment in school psychology.* Hillsdale, NJ: Erlbaum.

Shapiro, E. S., & Kratochwill, T. R. (1988a). Analogue assessment: Methods for assessing emotional and behavioral problems. In E. S. Shapiro & T. R. Kratochwill (Eds.), *Behavioral assessment in schools* (pp. 290–321). New York: Guilford.

Shapiro, E. S., & Kratochwill, T. R. (Eds.). (1988b). *Behavioral assessment in schools: Conceptual foundations and practical applications.* New York: Guilford.

Shapiro, E. S., & Lentz, F. (1986). Behavioral assessment of academic skills. In T. R. Kratochwill (Ed.), *Advances in school psychology* (Vol. 5, pp. 87–139). Hillsdale, NJ: Erlbaum.

Sheridan, S. M., & Kratochwill, T. R. (1992). Behavioral parent-teacher consultation: Conceptual and research considerations. *Journal of School Psychology, 30*, 117–139.

Sheridan, S. M., Kratochwill, T. R., & Bergan, J. R. (1996). *Conjoint behavioral consultation: A procedural manual.* New York: Plenum.

Sizer, T. (1990). Performances and exhibitions: The demonstration of mastery. *Horace, 6*, 1–12.

Spivack, G., & Swift, M. (1973). The classroom behavior of children: A critical review of teacher-administered rating scale. *Journal of Special Education, 7*, 55–89.

Stephens, T. (1977). *Teaching skills to children with learning and behavior disorders.* Columbus, OH: Merrill.

Stokes, T. F., & Baer, D. M. (1977). An implicit technology of generalization. *Journal of Applied Behavior Analysis, 10*, 349–473.

Subkoviak, M., & Baker, F. B. (1977). Test theory. In L. S. Shulman (Ed.), *Review of research in education* (pp. 275–317). Itasca, IL: Peacock.

Tasto, D. L. (1977). Self-report schedules and inventories. In A. R. Ciminero, K. S. Calhoun, & H. E. Adams (Eds.), *Handbook of behavioral assessment* (pp. 153–193). New York: Wiley.

Thoresen, C. E., & Mahoney, M. J. (1974). *Behavioral self-control.* New York: Holt, Rinehart & Winston.

Wahler, R. G. (1975). Some structural aspects of

deviant child behavior. *Journal of Applied Behavior Analysis, 8,* 27–42.

Wahler, R. G., & Fox, J. J. (1981). Setting events in applied behavior analysis: Toward a conceptual and methodological expansion. *Journal of Applied Behavior Analysis, 14,* 327–338.

Wahler, R. G., & Graves, M. G. (1983). Setting events in social networks: Ally or enemy in child behavior therapy? *Behavior Therapy, 14,* 19–36.

Wahler, R. G., House, A. E., & Stambaugh, E. E. (1976). *Ecological assessment of child problem behavior: A clinical package for home, school, and institutional setting.* New York: Pergamon.

Walker, H. M., & McConnell, S. R. (1988). *The Walker-McConnell Scale of Social Competence and School Adjustment.* Austin, TX: Pro-Ed.

Walker, H. M., Severson, H., Stiller, B., Williams, G., Haring, N., Shinn, M., & Todis, B. (1988). Systematic screening of pupils in the elementary age range at risk for behavior disorders: Development and trial testing of a multiple gating model. *Remedial and Special Education, 9,* 8–20.

Walls, R. T., Werner, T. J., Bacon, A., & Zane, T. (1977). Behavior checklists. In J. D. Cone & R. P. Hawkins (Eds.), *Behavioral assessment: New directions in clinical psychology* (pp. 77–146). New York: Brunner/Mazel.

Wechsler, D. (1991). *Manual for the Wechsler Intelligence Scale for Children–Third Edition (WISC-III).* San Antonio, TX: Psychological Corp.

Weist, M. D., Ollendick, T. H., & Finney, J. W. (1991). Toward the empirical validation of treatment targets in children. *Clinical Psychology Review, 11,* 515–538.

White, O., & Haring, N. (1980). *Exceptional reading.* Columbus, OH: Merrill.

Wiggins, J. S. (1973). *Personality and prediction: Principles of personality assessment.* Reading MA: Addison-Wesley.

Wilson, G. T., & Franks, C. M. (Eds). (1982). *Contemporary behavioral therapy: Conceptual and empirical foundations.* New York: Guilford.

Witt, J. C., Heffern, R. W., & Pfeiffer, J. (1990) Structured rating scales: A review of self-report and informant rating processes, procedures, and issues. In C. R. Reynolds & R. W. Kamphaus (Eds.), *Handbook of psychological & educational assessment of children: Personality, behavior, & context* (pp. 364–394). New York: Guilford.

Wolf, M. M. (1978). Social validity: The case for subjective measurement or how applied behavior analysis is findings its heart. *Journal of Applied Behavior Analysis, 11,* 203–214.

## CHAPTER 15

# CURRICULUM-BASED ASSESSMENT AND OTHER PERFORMANCE-BASED ASSESSMENT STRATEGIES

EDWARD S. SHAPIRO
*Lehigh University*
STEPHEN N. ELLIOTT
*University of Wisconsin–Madison*

Over the past 10 years, the methods of assessing problems in academic skills have been an increasing concern of educational professionals. In particular, methods that can link assessment and intervention effectively have been preferred to techniques that provide only the relative standing of individuals among same-age or same-grade peers. Conceptualized as "treatment validity," educators have emphasized the need for assessment methods to inform, foster, and document the effectiveness of interventions designed to affect academic skills problems (e.g., Reschly & Grimes, 1995; Witt & Gresham, 1985). Two types of methods that have emerged to address these concerns are curriculum-based assessment (CBA) and performance-based assessment (PA).

Curriculum-based assessment is defined as a methodology whereby (1) assessment is linked to the curriculum and instruction, (2) educational success is evaluated by students' progress across key indicators taken from the curriculum, and (3) the primary purpose is to determine students' instructional needs (Shapiro & Derr, 1990). The instructional needs of students are determined from their performance in existing course content. Interventions are focused on alterations and adaptations in curriculum to maximize the student's ability to succeed.

Performance assessment is defined as "test-ing methods that require students to create an answer or product that demonstrates their knowledge or skills" (p. 16) and can take many forms, including conducting experiments, writing an extended essay, or doing mathematical computations (Office of Technology Assessment, 1992). These measures are designed to be authentic analogues of solving real-life problems and to demonstrate the overall outcomes of the teaching process. Common features of PAs are (1) students' construction rather than selection of responses, (2) objective criteria to communicate clearly how students' work will be scored, (3) direct observation of students' behavior on tasks resembling those commonly required for functioning in the world outside of school, and (4) illumination of students' learning and thinking processes. The primary purpose of PA has been instructional intervention, although many states have developed large-scale PAs for school-wide and system accountability.

Both CBA and PA can be viewed as alternative assessment methods, to more traditional, published norm-referenced tests (PNRTs). Indeed, Eckert (1996); Eckert, Shapiro, and Lutz (1995); Elliott & Fuchs, 1997 and Shapiro and Eckert (1994) have demonstrated that CBA is a more acceptable methodology than PNRTs for assessing academic skills problems, as judged by school psychologists and general and special education teachers.

Curriculum-based assessment and performance-based assessment are similar but complementary methods. That is, both CBA and PA are concerned about the alignment between what is taught in a curriculum and what is assessed; however, CBA focuses on the mastery of discrete skills in core content areas, whereas PA focuses on the application of skills to complex, authentic tasks, which often require integration of knowledge and skills from several areas. Figure 15.1 highlights the performance and authenticity dimensions of the emerging conceptualization of educational assessment tasks (Elliott, 1994). It also indicates that a common third dimension of a valid assessment task is that the content assessed represents the content taught. Thus, Figure 15.1 synthesizes three key dimensions educators want to manipulate in their assessments of students' achievement: *students' response, nature of the task,* and *relevance to instruction.* As indicated in the figure, assessment tasks can vary in the degree to which they are performances in nature, authentic, and aligned with curriculum outcomes. Many educators are searching for assessments that are relatively high on all three dimensions. That is, they want highly authentic or "real-world" tasks that are clearly connected to their instructional curriculum and require students to produce, rather than select, a response. Conceptually, such tasks

would lie within the HIGH circle in Figure 15.1. Many standardized tests of achievement cannot offer tasks that fit into this circle.

This chapter presents a brief overview of CBA and PA. After examining some basic assumptions and outcomes for assessing academic skills, we describe various models of CBA, with some attention given to one particular approach (i.e., Shapiro, 1996a; Shapiro & Lentz, 1985). Next, we describe details of PA, along with illustrations of its use to enhance the development of academic skills and applications. Finally, we discuss the relationships between CBA and PA and the limitations inherent in both models.

## ACADEMIC ASSESSMENT: OVERVIEW AND RATIONALE

Lentz and Shapiro (1986) identified a set of assumptions that are key ingredients in defining the methodologies needed to assess academic skills problems effectively.

1. *An assessment of academic skills must reflect how the behavior appears in the natural environment:* An evaluation of academic skills problems must help the evaluator understand the nature of the problem that is occurring in the classroom under typical instructional processes. If the child is removed from the classroom and evaluated in a small, quiet, nondistracting room (as might be typical during an individual psychoeducational assessment) and the child's behavior in that setting differs from the behavior in the typical instructional environment, the teacher will probably not consider the results of the evaluation useful for instructional programming. Also, if the conditions of the assessment process introduce formats that differ greatly from the way in which teachers typically conduct evaluations of academic behavior (e.g., multiple-choice tests on computer-based scan sheets), the outcomes of the assessment may partially reflect the format for assessment rather than the student's skills themselves. The methods used for conducting the assessment need to be a direct and immediate reflection of the behaviors commonly seen in the classroom.

2. *What is tested should be what is taught:* A problem often noted in the use of PNRTs is the distinct lack of overlap between what is being taught in the curriculum and the con-

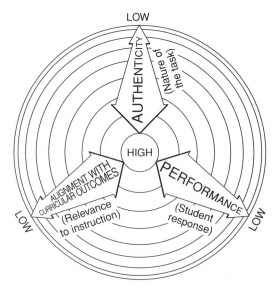

**FIGURE 15.1** The relationship among performance, authenticity, and the classroom curriculum in an assessment task.

tent of the items on the tests (Bell, Lentz, & Graden, 1992; Good & Salvia, 1988; Jenkins & Pany, 1978; Martens, Steele, Massie, & Diskin, 1995; Shapiro & Derr, 1987). A critical component in a more authentic and content-valid assessment is that the assessment process must indicate to an evaluator exactly what has and has not been learned from the instructional process.

3. *The primary purpose of an assessment is to develop interventions to solve problems:* Although assessments of academic skills can serve multiple purposes, the primary reason for an individual evaluation must be to develop more effective interventions to remediate deficient skill areas. Assessment methods that are designed specifically to inform the evaluator of potential remediation strategies should therefore be the primary methods used to conduct evaluations of academic skills problems.

4. *Assessment should be capable of providing ongoing evaluation of progress:* It is not enough for assessment methods to inform evaluators of the current status of students' progress. Because the assessments are designed to assist in the development of instructional strategies, evaluation of the effectiveness of these strategies must be a critical component of the assessment process. Methods selected to evaluate academic progress must be capable of reflecting change in the student's performance of academic skills. Thus measures must be sensitive to small units of change, must be able to be repeated frequently, and must have high degrees of acceptability to teachers.

5. *Measures should be primarily idiographic rather than nomothetic:* If the primary purpose of the assessment process is to develop and monitor intervention strategies, the measurement tools must be idiographic. Such idiographic assessment is critical if one is to determine whether the student is progressing, as shown by his or her own past performance. Nomothetic measures, those whose primary interest is cross-student comparisons, are important but can only reflect outcomes at a static moment in time.

6. *Assessment methods should reflect both skill and performance problems:* Academic skills problems are not simply a reflection of the inner learning capacities of students. The structure of the academic environment can play a significant role in shaping the success or failure of the student's performance (Heller, Holzman, & Messick, 1982; Lentz & Shapiro, 1986; Ysseldyke & Christenson, 1993). Any assessment of academic skills problems must be able to divide the problems between those that are primarily skills and those that are performance deficiencies.

7. *Measures should be capable of a wide range of uses, including screening, determining eligibility for special education, setting goals, evaluating programs, and developing interventions:* Although the primary purpose for an academic assessment should be to help inform modifications in instruction, the measures need to be cost-efficient. As such, the same measures need to serve multiple outcomes.

Standardized, norm-referenced measures of academic achievement fall short in meeting several of these assumptions. Among the important assumptions that have been questioned is whether what is tested in published norm-referenced tests is what is actually taught in the curriculum. Jenkins and Pany (1978) and Shapiro and Derr (1987) examined the degree of overlap between reading curriculum materials and reading subtests of widely used individual achievement tests across grades 1 through 5. These studies determined the scores that would be obtained by hypothetical students if all the words in each grade level of the curriculum series were mastered. The results showed very little overlap between what is taught and what appears on tests. Furthermore, the degree of overlap varied considerably across tests and curricula, indicating that decisions based on these instruments may be related to which measure is given rather than a reflection of the student's knowledge. Although the Jenkins and Pany and Shapiro and Derr studies can be criticized for using data based on hypothetical cases and did not directly assess children, Good and Salvia (1988) and Bell, et al. (1992) found similar outcomes with students who were actually assessed.

In the Good and Salvia (1988) study, a total of 65 third- and fourth-grade students who were being instructed in the same basal reading series (Allyn & Bacon, 1978) were given four reading subtests from different PNRTs. Results showed that differences in test performance for the same students could be predicted by the test's overlap with the curriculum series. Bell et al. (1992), using a similar methodology, examined the impact of different reading subtests across the performance of first- and second-grade students in two different districts that used the same reading series. Results again showed significant and substantial differences in performance across measures. Indeed, students in one district obtained an average standard score on the Woodcock Reading Mastery Test–Revised (Woodcock, 1987) that was a full standard deviation larger than the score obtained on the Wide Range Achievement Test–Revised (Wilkinson, 1993).

Others have found similar problems in other areas. For example, Shriner and Salvia (1988) found a significant lack of overlap between the Key Math (Connolly, Nachtman, & Pritchett, 1976) and Iowa Tests of Basic Skills (Hieronymous, Hoover, & Linquist, 1986) across two elementary mathematics curricula. Martens et al. (1995) found similar outcomes when overlap between tests of decoding and curriculum materials was examined. What published, norm-referenced achievement tests may actually be assessing is not the knowledge acquired by students but, instead, their ability to generalize from taught to untaught stimuli that are similar. For example, a student may be taught the words *sat* and *bat* but *cat* appears on the test. Whether the students can transfer their learned knowledge, based on common principles, to an untaught stimulus may be a more accurate depiction of what the test is measuring. Although this is an important and crucial skill, the test cannot be viewed as a valid measure of the material acquired and certainly not a measure to assess progress in the curriculum across time.

First, however, CBA and PA partially overcome the problems of test-text overlap because the student is tested directly on material that he or she is expected to learn. Because the measures are derived from curriculum, failure by the student to master specific skills as evidenced on the assessment measures reflects true deficits in performance rather than lack of exposure to materials. Certainly, test performance may be influenced by other variables, such as measurement error and setting events (e.g., Derr & Shapiro, 1980; Derr-Minneci & Shapiro, 1992); however, outcomes from CBA and PA measures provide increased assurance to the evaluator that the student's skills reflect failure to master what was actually taught.

Second, outcomes of CBA and PA are linked directly to instruction. Diagnosing failure on these measures suggest directly the potential target areas for instructional design. In a study of 50 teachers who used CBA measures for four months, 90% stated that the measures were helpful in developing IEP (individualized educational plan) objectives and goals and in deciding when to change instructional techniques (Mirkin, Deno, Tindal, & Kuehnle, 1982).

Third, CBA and PA have been shown to provide reliable and valid measures of students' performance in reading (Deno, 1985; Deno, Mirkin, & Chiang, 1982), spelling (Deno, Mirkin, Lowry, & Kuehnle, 1980; Olson, 1995), and writing (Deno et al., 1982). Indeed, Shinn (1989), summarizing CBA research, noted that the data base that supports the relationships between CBA and standardized achievement tests illustrates the strength of these measures. Fuchs and colleagues (e.g., Elliott & Fuchs, in press; Fuchs, Fuchs, Hamlett, & Allinder, 1991a, 1991b; Fuchs, Fuchs, Hamlet, & Stecker, 1991) have also established that CBA and PA measures can be used effectively in designing and planning instructional interventions.

Fourth, by virtue of their ease in application and mode of development, CBA measures in particular may be repeated frequently without practice effects and are highly sensitive to short-term and long-term changes in performance (Deno, 1985; Shinn, 1989). The method has been especially useful in assisting the decision-making process in IEP goal development. For example, Fuchs, Fuchs, Hamlett, and Whinnery (1991) found that providing differing types of feedback about students' progress toward goals resulted in differential improvement in performance. With an ongoing measure of students' progress, teachers are able to judge quickly whether current instructional processes are positive and can make swift changes in the instructional program as soon as the data indicate they are needed. Performance assessments typically have not usually been used to measure short-term academic progress; they are by design more complex and time-consuming to administer and score. In addition, some PAs are subject to practice effects, thus requiring the development of equivalent forms of tasks.

Fifth, CBA and PA can be used for a wide range of decisions. Not only can the measures be used on an idiographic basis for evaluating the progress of individual students across time, but also they can be used effectively for more wide-scale, program-based evaluation. Substantial attention has been given to the development and use of local norms in CBA (Hasbrouck & Tindal, 1992; Shinn, 1988). Data collected at the local level can assist schools in setting district-wide goals and individual student goals, in making between-school comparisons within districts, and in facilitating eligibility decisions (Elliott & Fuchs, 1997; Shinn, Habedank, Rodden-Nord, & Knutson, 1993). Performance assessments have become one of the methods of choice in current revisions of many states' accountability efforts concerning students' progress toward major learning outcomes.

Sixth, the emphasis in CBA and PA on curriculum performance and the development of instructional interventions makes them potentially more racially and culturally neutral than PNRTs (Galagan, 1985). For example, Baker and Good (1995) found that the development of local CBA norms for reading among Hispanic students was helpful in providing a clearer prediction of the outcomes for these students.

In sum, the many advantages of CBA and PA over PNRTs for assessing academic skills strongly suggest that they are feasible and desirable alternatives to more traditional methods of academic assessment. Indeed, CBA and PA can collectively provide a means for preplacement evaluation, determine the accuracy of students' placement within curriculum material, assist in the development of strategies for academic problem remediation, provide a means for setting IEP short- and long-term goals, provide a method for monitoring students' progress and performance across time, provide an empirical method for determining intervention effectiveness, provide a potential strategy for screening, and offer accountability for teachers and psychologists in making eligibility decisions. These methods appear to be highly acceptable to school personnel (Eckert, 1996; Eckert et al., 1995; Shapiro & Eckert, 1994), and CBA measures have been increasingly used by school psychologists over the past decade (Shapiro & Eckert, 1993).

It is important to emphasize, however, that CBA and PA are used for different purposes than PNRTs and thus are not designed to replace them. Traditional academic assessment methods offer excellent, psychometrically sound measures to make between-student and other nomothetic comparisons. Indeed, although CBA and PA measures can also be used in this way, they do not offer the psychometric sophistication of more traditional tests. However, CBA and PA measures can provide clear and direct links to instructional processes, something not typical of PNRTs.

# MODELS OF CBA

Although *curriculum-based assessment* has been recognized as a universal term for assessment methods, in reality many different models fall under this rubric. Fuchs and Deno (1991) classified models of CBA into two categories: general outcome measurement and specific subskill mastery models.

## General Outcome Measurement

General outcome measurement models use standardized measurements across skill areas. Each measure is derived, administered, and scored in a prescribed way. The measures remain the same across the instructional process, thus indexing the student's progress in a standardized manner. For example, in math, students might be asked to complete twice each week a sheet of computational problems taken from all objectives for that grade. Early in a school year, before certain objectives are taught, students are unlikely to get all of these items correct. As each objective is taught and measurement is repeated, students should show improved performance. If results of these repeated measures are displayed graphically, their progress would be reflected by the slope of improvement denoted by the graphed data. If progress no longer moves along an expected line, it indicates that current instructional procedures may need to be altered. Thus, the measures are designed to show long-term progress across curriculum materials and a wide range of skills.

Although this method is not specifically designed to suggest the type of instructional modification needed, attempts to use students' responses on the measures to diagnose instruction have been successful (e.g., Fuchs, Fuchs, Hamlett, & Allinder, 1991a, 1991b; Fuchs, Fuchs, Hamlett, & Ferguson, 1992; Fuchs, Fuchs, Hamlett, & Stecker, 1991; Fuchs, Fuchs, Phillips, Hamlett, & Karns, 1995). Measures derived from a general outcome measurement model may or may not use the curriculum of instruction. However, even when a curriculum not specifically used for teaching the students is used for measurement, results over time reflect students' progress (e.g., Fuchs & Deno, 1992, 1994; Hintze & Shapiro, 1997; Hintze, Shapiro, & Daly, 1996; Hintze, Shapiro, & Lutz, 1994). The most well-known and well-developed general outcome measurement model is Curriculum-Based Measurement (CBM), developed by Deno (1985) and colleagues.

The CBM uses a standardized format. Each area of basic skills (reading, math computation, spelling, and written language) has an empirically derived measure that has been shown to reflect students' outcome in curriculum over time. Material is usually controlled for grade-level difficulty so that material within each grade is equivalent. Measures are always brief and timed, using the rate of performance as the dependent variable. The material selected for assessment is based on a determination of long-term objectives and is viewed as an index of long-term growth.

The advantages of CBM include a large data base to support its reliability and validity, simple and time-efficient methods for data collection, easily interpretable results, and inexpensive materials. Substantial research supports high correlations between CBM measures and standardized, norm-referenced tests, with correlations ranging from .70 to .95 (e.g., Deno, Marston, & Mirkin, 1982; Deno, Mirkin, & Chiang, 1982). Also, these measures frequently discriminate between students who were in special education programs and those who were not eligible (e.g., Deno, 1985; Shinn, 1989).

The CBM provides a clear and precise method of communicating outcomes by using graphic displays. These data are easily understood by teachers, students, parents, and related school personnel. Judgments about changes in instructional programming can be discerned easily from these data.

The collected data have been shown to be very sensitive to growth in students' performance over short periods of time. For example, Marston, Fuchs, and Deno (1986), using PNRTs, failed to show any student growth over a 16-week period. Because CBM data can show change within a short-time frame (days or weeks), teachers can act quickly to remediate potential problems more efficiently. Because these data require only brief periods of measurement, minimal reductions in instructional time are needed to collect them. The resulting statistic (slope data) reflects the dynamic impact of the instructional process rather than just the static picture available through more typical measurement tools.

The collection of local norms and the use of individuals other than the teacher to collect the data are possible. Norms can be obtained for individual classes, schools, or entire school districts (Shinn, 1988), providing a reliable peer-reference comparison for setting goals and evaluating programs. Peer- or self-monitoring procedures to collect the data have also been shown to result in reli-able and valid outcomes (McCurdy & Shapiro, 1992).

The CBM procedures are cost-effective in that they neither require the purchase of additional test materials nor take substantial time. Most measures require approximately 1 to 3 minutes of actual testing per day and are repeated about twice per week. The measures are derived from curriculum and do require copying, but once developed they can easily be used from year to year. In contrast, standardized achievement tests are far more expensive and time-consuming, requiring approximately 60 to 90 minutes for administration. More important, the integrity of these measures is compromised if they are frequently repeated.

## Specific Subskill Mastery

Specific subskill mastery models of CBA involve nonstandardized measures. The measurements are criterion-referenced and are designed to determine the student's acquisition of specifically identified curriculum objectives. Each measure is developed to match the objective being taught. The measures are usually teacher-made and will change as each curriculum objective is taught. Measurement from this model is focused much more on the short-term objectives of instruction and aim at evaluating how well students have learned a very specific skill rather than on more long-term, end-of-year goals. Two of the better known specific subskill models of CBA have been described by Howell, Fox, and Morehead (1993) and Gickling and his colleagues (Gickling & Havertape, 1981; Gickling & Rosenfield, 1995; Gickling & Thompson, 1985; Rosenfield & Kuralt, 1990).

### Curriculum-Based Evaluation

Howell et al.'s (1993) model, entitled curriculum-based evaluation, divides the process into four steps: survey-level assessment, specific-level assessment, instructional planning, and monitoring. The purpose of survey assessment is to get information about the students' academic problems. Usually, this includes informal and multiple measures such as interviews, observations, examination of students' products, and results of existing tests. Hypotheses are derived from these data about the potential causes underlying the student's difficulties. With these hypotheses, more specific assessment procedures are generated to determine which, if any, of the hypotheses derived from survey testing are valid. An error analysis of student performance on measures is typically conducted to complete this level of assessment.

Based on these two steps, strategies to alter instructional planning are derived. The strategies are directly linked to the outcomes of the specific assessment and are intended to improve the specific skills targeted. Howell et al (1993) offer extensive recommendations for instruction in each of the basic skills areas. The final step in their model is monitoring of the student's progress. This step is met by readministering many of the same specific assessment instruments that were used to test the various instructional hypotheses.

Outcomes of Howell et al.'s (1993) model are well designed to provide feedback on the acquisition of short-term instructional objectives. As students move from one objective to the next, new assessment strategies are developed. Thus, the measurement process is not standardized across the curriculum. The degree to which students are moving toward the long-term, end-of-year objectives are determined by the cumulative acquisition of individual objectives and are not based directly on the desired end-of-year behavior.

The model described by Howell et al. (1993) can offer extensive assistance to teachers and other educational professionals in adapting and altering the instructional process on the basis of the assessment. The model makes extensive use of task analysis and error analysis procedures, carefully examining both outcomes and process. Thus, individuals using this approach can fine-tune and plan instruction, based carefully on individual needs. The model does require a fair amount of time in evaluation, and its nonstandardized nature can make it more of an art than a science in administration. In contrast to other general outcome measurement models, however, this one is very focused on the instructional process and its modification, offering evaluators substantial suggestions on what to do rather than just informing teachers that a change in instruction is needed.

## Curriculum-based Assessment: Gickling and Colleagues

Another subskill mastery model of CBA, described by Gickling and his colleagues (Gickling & Havertape, 1981; Gickling & Rosenfield, 1995; Gickling & Thompson, 1985; Rosenfield & Kuralt, 1990), emphasizes the selection of instructional objectives and content based on assessment. The model tries to control the level of instructional delivery carefully so that success is maximized. To accomplish this task, academic skills are evaluated in terms of students' "knowns" and "unknowns" at the point of entry, and adjustments are made in the instructional process to maintain the student at an "instructional" rather than an "independent" or "frustrational" level. Gickling and Havertape note that in their model (1) there is a curriculum scope and sequence for each area to be assessed; (2) perceptual and processing tasks are not prerequisites to academic tasks; (3) curricular materials can be assets or deterrents to learning; (4) assessment should be accurate, continuous, and lead to instructional improvement; and (5) assessment activities should be directly related to teaching activities. They note that many students who are failing academically can be viewed as "curriculum causalities." In other words, the curriculum has produced the problems of these students by demanding that they progress at the pace determined by the curriculum. Expected progress in curriculum does not differ across students and does not adapt to individual needs. As the curriculum demands more and more from students who cannot maintain the pace, they fall further and further behind. Uncorrected difficulties compound themselves as students lack prerequisite skills for later development. Gickling's approach to CBA is to enable teachers to gain control over curriculum by matching it more effectively to students' needs.

Gickling and colleagues have conceptualized the CBA as a process, linking data collection and instructional modification. Control over the curriculum is achieved by eliminating the instructional mismatch between the skills of students and demands placed on them by curricular assignments. The process begins by first determining the instructional level of the student relative to the demands of the task. Each task is examined on three essential components: type, number of items, and the student's familiarity with the items.

There are two types of task requirements: comprehension and drill. In comprehension, meaning is obtained from print. Drill includes all other assignments, for example, math, writing, spelling, and even subskill areas of reading like word attack. Each type of task contains two types of items: known and unknown or challenging items. Known items are those for which students can make an immediate and definitive correct response. All other items, including those for which students are hesitant but correct, are considered to be unknown. A key to this model is understanding the optimal ratio between known and unknown items for facilitating the learning process. These ratios translate into instructional, independent, and frustrational performance levels. For comprehension tasks, the instructional level contains between 93% and 97% known material and 3% to 7% challenging items. For drill tasks, the instructional level is set at 70% to 85% known items with 15% to 30% challenging items. Independent levels are anything higher than instructional level, and frustrational level anything lower. This model states that students will learn most successfully when curriculum materials are maintained at instructional levels.

Some researchers have examined the impact of teaching at these instructional ratios. For example, Roberts, Turco, and Shapiro (1991) used an interspersal technique to teach unknown vocabulary words to first- and second-grade students. Known as the "folding-in" technique, words were presented in a sequence designed to result in high numbers of repetitions. The numbers of known and unknown words were controlled to compare the impact on the acquisition and retention process when instructional ratios varied from 90% known to 10% unknown through 50% known to 50% unknown. Based on the predictions of Gickling (Gickling & Thompson, 1985), it was expected that the best student performance would be evident for the 80% known to 20% unknown condition. After eight weeks of instruction, results surprisingly showed that students acquired the most new words under the most frustrating condition (50% known, 50% unknown). However, retention of words taught, tested at the end of the eight weeks, was highest in the condition predicted by Gickling. In a second study, Roberts and Shapiro (1996) stretched the instructional ratio by comparing 80% known to 20% unknown, 50% known to 50% unknown, and 90% unknown to 10% known. Results again indicated that although students' acquisition of new information was best in the frustrating 90% unknown condition, they retained the information best when they were taught within the ratios recommended by Gickling. Other, more clinical reports have substantiated the potential value of teaching students within the recommended instructional ratios (Shapiro, 1992).

The use of this approach to CBA requires the task difficulty of various curriculum assignments to be identified. Teachers need to examine the suitability of students' assignments within the recommended instructional ratios and make modifications as needed. The preassessment of assignments helps to maintain an instructional level for the student who is struggling, maintaining an instructional match between his or her capacities and assigned materials. Gickling and Thompson (1985) provide six basic rules to facilitate the application of their model: (1) maintain a high percentage of knowns to provide built-in reinforcement for the student; (2) keep new materials within the margin of challenge, to decrease the probability of creating a frustrational task and an overload of instruction; (3) treat items of undetermined status as unknowns to decrease the probability of jeopardizing an appropriate instructional-level ratio; (4) examine the planned content of the lesson before designing the drill work, so that the two tasks become coordinated and enhance the learning situation; (5) present the drill activities before the content of the lesson to prepare the student for the task; and (6) take every task to a mastery level, which requires both independent performance and comprehension, so that no tasks are left at a submastery level.

The translation of the approach to practice involves the development and administration of measures (commonly called probes) to assess each individual objective that is being taught. Typically, teachers are closely involved in this process and use teacher-made tests to identify the initial points where students are failing. From these materials, individual probes similar to specific-level assessment are developed. These are given to students with careful attention to the process by which students complete the measures. Often, informal interviewing and evaluation identify potential strategies that may be successful in modifying the instructional process. Following teaching, the student is reassessed on similar measures to determine progress, albeit unstandardized.

In sum, Gickling's model of CBA gives teachers specific details about where to begin instruction and an instructional strategy for teaching specific children. The model provides a format for assessing the demands of learning tasks, as well as a gauge for controlling the level of difficulty. The expected outcome is that the learning process will be optimized.

## An Integrated Approach Across Models

Although each of these models offers important alternatives to PNRTs for the assessment of academic skills, any single model in itself may lack key components that are crucial in a comprehensive evaluation of academic skills problems. Shapiro and Lentz (1985, 1986) offered a four-step model to bring multiple models into a coherent system for conducting assessments of academic skills problems by using a curriculum-based assessment focus, drawing on the principles used for assessing social-emotional problems (Mash & Terdal, 1981, 1986; Ollendick & Hersen, 1984; Shapiro & Kratochwill, 1988).

As revised by Shapiro (1989, 1996a), the model contains four steps (see Figure 15.2). Beginning with a thorough evaluation of the academic environment as described by Lentz and Shapiro (1986), this portion of the process uses multiple measures, including teachers' and students' interviews, systematic direct observation, and a review of students' permanent products to determine the contributions the instructional environment may be making to their success or failure. Next, a determination is made about the student's current placement within the materials used for instruction. The purpose here is to establish an instructional match between the student's curriculum and his or her current learning level. Often it is found that students are being instructed in materials far beyond their current learning levels, thus accounting partially for their failure. This process is based on the models described originally by Deno and Mirkin (1977), as well as Shapiro and Lentz (1985, 1986).

After these two steps are completed, recommendations for instructional modification can be made. These recommendations are based on the data collected through the first step and are consistent with the subskill mastery models of Gickling and Rosenfield (1995) and Howell et al. (1993). By using the types of academic skill probes and diagnosing the instructional process, instructional modifications are implemented, altered, and revised throughout this stage. The final step in the process is progress monitoring, both short- and long-term. Deno's (1985) CBM methodology is a significant process for conducting the evaluation and is combined with the short-term monitoring procedures described by Gickling and Rosenfeld (1995) and Howell and Morehead (1993).

The approach suggested by Shapiro (1996a) can be likened to a type of functional assessment of academic skills. In a functional analysis, one uses descriptive and observational methods to establish hypotheses that are potential explanations for the target behavior. These hypotheses are then systematically examined through interventions, and evaluated to determine whether the hypotheses are confirmed. Daly, Witt, Martens, and Dool (1997) have provided a superb framework for applying functional analysis to academic performance problems. The model described here by Shapiro (1996a) uses the same elements and problem-solving process, and is consistent with the burgeoning literature in functional analysis of non-academic skills. Additionally, Shinn (1998) has pointed out how the problem-solving model is the keystone of effective use of curriculum-based measurement which is the primary procedure used in the fourth step of Shapiro's (1996a) model.

## CONDUCTING A CURRICULUM-BASED ASSESSMENT WITH THE INTEGRATED MODEL

For purposes of illustration, the details of conducting a CBA by following Shapiro's (1996a) model are described. Because this model incorporates elements to assess both the instructional environment and the child's individual academic skills, it may serve as a useful method for illustrating both general outcome and subskill mastery models of CBA.

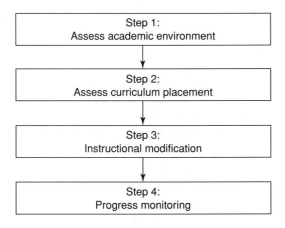

**FIGURE 15.2    Integrated CBA model.**

## Step 1: Assessment of Academic Environment
### Importance and Overview

Academic behavior occurs in an instructional environment. Successful learning requires a student to have certain levels of skill development and a teacher to carefully construct instruction. For example, how teachers present materials, the frequency and type of feedback given for students' responses, the physical arrangement and structure of the classroom, the type and level of prompts provided for questions, and the amount of time devoted to a particular subject, as well as many other ecological variables, can have a significant impact on the outcome of a student's performance (Lentz & Shapiro, 1986; Ysseldyke & Christenson, 1993). A thorough evaluation of academic skills problems must begin with a full understanding of the many variables that could be affecting the student's learning process.

Evaluating the academic environment does not involve a single method. Consistent with a behavioral assessment methodology, the assessment requires understanding the operations of the classroom from multiple perspectives. It is critical to know what the teacher expects of the students, what the specifics of the instructional process are for the classroom, and what types of feedback contingencies are routinely used. Understanding the teacher's perception of the student's problems is also crucial. At the same time, the perceptions held by the student about the classroom expectations are important to understand. A key question that must be addressed in the assessment process is whether the student lacks a clear knowledge of the goals, instructions, and outcomes of his or her academic behavior.

Although obtaining information about the perceptions of behavior as reported by teachers and students is important, such data may not correlate strongly with the actual behavior of students. Therefore, another key component in the assessment of the academic environment is to collect direct, systematic observations of students' behavior during academic assignments. In particular, it is important to determine how often and in which ways students are engaged in academic responding. Considerable research has determined that the amount and types of academic-engaged time are key factors in predicting academic success (e.g., Denham & Lieberman, 1980; Gettinger, 1986; Muyskens & Yesseldyke, 1998). Evidence suggests strongly that students

at risk for academic failure who spend the largest portion of their time actively engaged in academic behavior (i.e., raising their hands, answering academic questions, engaged in academic discussion, and writing academic responses) are more likely to have higher levels of achievement (e.g., Greenwood, Delquadri, & Hall, 1984).

Although systematic observational data are important for determining a student's level of academic-engaged time, collecting such data throughout long periods of instructional time is almost impossible. However, it is important to examine outcomes of academic performance across instructional processes. Thus, a final method for assessing the academic environment is to examine students' permanent products. Throughout the instructional process, students are frequently asked to produce worksheets and other products that reflect outcomes of the learning process. These materials can offer significant windows into academic behavior when systematic observation is not possible.

After each type of data is collected, the information is examined for consistencies and discrepancies. It may be found that in some cases, the teachers' perceptions of problems are consistently noted across all of the data. In other cases, the teachers' reported information may not be verified. These data also provide indications of potential points for intervention, as well as possible strategies. For example, it may be found that current feedback mechanisms for independently completed work are weak and far removed from the actual completion of academic assignments. The use of peer-checkers or a grading table where students can obtain more immediate feedback on performance may improve significantly a student's academic outcomes. Indeed, the literature notes hundreds of studies in which such manipulations of environmental variables have lead to substantial changes in student behavior (Shapiro, 1996a).

### Methods: Teacher Interview

The assessment of the academic environment begins with an interview of the teacher. Questions are asked about the specific curriculum being used for instruction, the student's current level of placement in the curriculum, the expected level of performance of "typical" students in the classroom, the types of instructional techniques used by the teacher, monitoring procedures to evaluate progress, specific contingencies for performance, feedback mechanisms for students, and some global indicators of the student's behavior during the instructional process. In particular, questions are raised about on-task level, homework completion, class participation, and competing events that affect academic performance. An important question in the interview is how time is allotted and divided since this information will help shape the structure of the next step in the process. These types of questions are asked for each of the basic skills under investigation. Shapiro (1996a, 1996b) provides a useful format for conducting this interview.

Based on the interview, the assessor begins to plan the remainder of the assessment process. He or she must determine where and when it would be appropriate to conduct direct observations, the critical variables that may have to be observed directly, the specific questions that may have to be asked of students about the requirements of the academic environment, the permanent products data that should be examined, the most important academic areas in which skill deficiencies may be present, and the expected levels of performance for typical students based on the teacher's report.

## Direct Systematic Observation

Classroom observations yield direct information about the child's academic and academic-related behaviors and how they may be affected by the environment. There are many direct observational codes, and almost any would be applicable for a curriculum-based assessment. A few codes, however, may be more useful when the concern is primarily academic rather than nonacademic (e.g., Alessi & Kaye, 1983; O'Leary, Romanczyk, Kass, Kietz, & Santogrossi, 1979).

The State-Event Classroom Observation System (SECOS), developed by Saudargas (Saudargas, 1997), is an observational code that has been under ongoing development and revision for the past 15 years. The code is designed to assess classroom-based behavior, primarily under academic instruction, and provides extensive information on students' behavior, teachers' behavior, and student-teacher interactions. Normative data have been collected on the code and are reported in Saudargas (1997). Shapiro and Lentz (1986) developed a somewhat abbreviated version.

The SECOS uses a 15-second time-sampling technique, alternating between states and events. State behaviors are those without discrete beginning and/or ending points and are recorded as momentary time samples at the start of each 15-second interval. Behaviors such as school-

work, looking around, and social interaction with another child are examples of these categories. Events are behaviors that have discrete beginning and ending points and are recorded by counting the occurrence of each event within the 15-second intervals. Both student- and teacher-directed behaviors are included, such as a student's hand raising, calling out, and out-of-seat activity and a teacher's approach to the targeted student, approval, and disapproval. Each behavioral category has an extensive operational definition. (Interested readers are encouraged to obtain a copy of the SECOS manual from Richard A. Saudargas, Department of Psychology, University of Tennessee, Knoxville, TN 37916.)

Observations are conducted by alternating between state and event categories. When each interval begins, observers record any states evident at that moment. For the remainder of the 15-second interval, any events that occur are recorded. The procedure continues until the observation is completed.

States and events are scored differently. State behaviors are scored by calculating the percentage of intervals within which the behavior was found to occur. These data represent an estimate of the amount of time during which a particular behavior may be occurring. It is important to realize that these data represent estimates and are not actual percentage time measures. Events are converted into rate data by dividing the frequencies of each behavior by the total time the behavior was observed.

To interpret the data collected on the SECOS, data across different categories must be compared. The state behavior SW (schoolwork) is viewed as an estimate of the rate of engaged time. The SW levels are examined against the teacher-reported allocated time for instruction to obtain an estimate of the amount of time students spend in academic tasks. For example, if a student is found to have an SW level of 50% during reading, and reading is allocated for a total of 60 minutes per day, one may conclude that the observed student was spending about 30 minutes per day in reading. Likewise, one may compare the worksheets or writing samples that were assigned during the observation against the SW data. A student may show high levels of SW, suggesting good levels of on-task behavior, but examination of the accuracy and completion rates on the assignment reveal poor performance. Types and levels of non-SW behavior are also examined to determine how the student spends his or her nonengaged time.

Events are interpreted in terms of the type and level of interactions in the classroom. How the student contacts the teacher, how the students contact one another, and how teachers contact students can all play an important part in the academic performance of students. These data are also examined to establish the types of contingencies that compete with academic performance in the classroom.

Although the SECOS can provide a rich set of data on students' behavior and interactions in the classroom, practitioners may view the code as complex and difficult to master. Gaining competence in the administration of the code requires many hours of instruction and practice. Also, while the SECOS offers extensive information on teacher-student behaviors, it does not clearly put on-task behavior into subcategories. As noted previously, the way in which students are on-task (i.e., active or passive) can be a significant predictor in students' academic outcomes.

As an alternative to the SECOS, Shapiro (1996a, 1996b) developed a simple observational code designed specifically for classroom use during instructional processes. The code necessarily compromises the complexity of student-teacher interaction evident in the SECOS but offers a more detailed analysis of a student's on- and off-task behavior.

The BOSS (Behavioral Observation of Students in Schools) contains two categories of engagement and three of nonengagement. An additional category, which examines the types of instruction in the classroom, is also included. The code uses a 15-second time-sampling technique, alternating between momentary and partial interval recording. Figure 15.3 shows a completed observation from the BOSS. A complete description of the code is included in Shapiro (1996b).

Academic engagement is coded at the moment each interval begins as either present or absent. If present, the behavior is judged as either active engaged time (AET) or passive engaged time (PET). Active engagement is defined as those activities in which students are actively and visibly attending to their assigned work. Such responses as writing, reading aloud, raising hands, and discussing responses with peers in a cooperative group are coded as active. Passive responses include listening to a lecture, looking at an academic worksheet, reading silently, or listening to a peer respond to a question.

Nonengaged behavior is coded as either occurring or not occurring at some time within the 15-second interval. This partial recording procedure allows for any single instance of the behavior to be recorded but does not permit notation of multiple occurrences of the same behavior within the same interval. If a student is not engaged, one of three types of behaviors is recorded: off-task motor, off-task verbal, or off-task passive. Off-task motor behavior requires an instance of motor activity not directly associated with an assigned academic activity and would include such behaviors as out-of-seat activity, aimlessly flipping pages of a book, or drawing or writing that is unrelated to an assigned academic activity. Verbal off-task behavior is defined as audible verbalizations that are not permitted and/or not related to an assigned academic activity. Some behaviors included in this category are calling out when not asked for a response, forced burping, whistling, or other such noises. Passive off-task behaviors are those instances when students are not attending to the required work, such as sitting quietly in unassigned activity, looking around the room, or staring out the window.

Every fifth interval, data are recorded on the teacher's behavior to obtain an estimate of teacher-directed instruction. During this interval, any instance of instructing the whole class as a group, demonstrating assignments at a blackboard, or working individually with a student is recorded.

Systematic observations of classroom behavior can be more meaningful if the behavior of the targeted student is compared to the expected levels of behavior of nontargeted peers. For the BOSS data must be collected on both the target and nontarget peers in the same classroom by examining a randomly selected student every fifth interval, as shown in the shaded intervals on Figure 15.3. In each of these intervals, a different nontargeted student is observed. Data across these intervals are aggregated to provide a peer comparison, which helps in interpreting the outcomes for the targeted student.

Data collected on the BOSS provide estimates of the occurrence rates of behaviors. For each behavioral category, the percentage of intervals in which the behavior occurred are calculated to indicate the nature of a student's on- and off-task behavior. Although the measure is less complex than the outcomes of the SECOS, the data obtained from the BOSS are very helpful in

Child Observed: ___Justin___  Academic Subject: ____ Math ____
Date: ___9/15/95___  Setting: ISW:TPsnt  SmGp:TPsnt
Observer: ___JGL___  ISW:TSmGp  LgGp:TPsnt
Time of Observation: ___10:30 A.M.___  Other: _____

| Moment | 1 | 2 | 3 | 4 | 5* | 6 | 7 | 8 | 9 | 10* | 11 | 12 | 13 | 14 | 15* | S | P | T |
|---|---|---|---|---|---|---|---|---|---|---|---|---|---|---|---|---|---|---|
| AET | \ | | \ | | \ | \ | \ | | | \ | | \ | | | | 5 | 2 | |
| PET | | \ | | | | | | \ | \ | | \ | | | \ | \ | 5 | 1 | |
| Partial | | | | | | | | | | | | | | | | | | |
| OFT-M | \ | | | | | | | | \ | | | | | | \ | 2 | 1 | |
| OFT-V | | | | | | \ | \ | | | \ | \ | | | | | 3 | 1 | |
| OFT-P | \ | | \ | | \ | | | | | | | | | | | 3 | 1 | |
| TDI | | | | | | | | | | | | | | | \ | | | 1 |

| Moment | 16 | 17 | 18 | 19 | 20* | 21 | 22 | 23 | 24 | 25* | 26 | 27 | 28 | 29 | 30* | S | P | T |
|---|---|---|---|---|---|---|---|---|---|---|---|---|---|---|---|---|---|---|
| AET | \ | | | \ | | | | | | | \ | | | | \ | 3 | 1 | |
| PET | | | \ | | \ | \ | | | | | | \ | \ | | | 4 | 1 | |
| Partial | | | | | | | | | | | | | | | | | | |
| OFT-M | | \ | | | | | | | | | | | | | | 1 | 0 | |
| OFT-V | | \ | | | | | | | | \ | | | | | | 1 | 1 | |
| OFT-P | | | | | | | \ | \ | \ | | | | \ | \ | | 5 | 0 | |
| TDI | | | | \ | | | | | | \ | | | | | \ | | | 3 |

| Moment | 31 | 32 | 33 | 34 | 35* | 36 | 37 | 38 | 39 | 40* | 41 | 42 | 43 | 44 | 45* | S | P | T |
|---|---|---|---|---|---|---|---|---|---|---|---|---|---|---|---|---|---|---|
| AET | | \ | | | \ | | | | | | | | | | | 1 | 1 | |
| PET | \ | | \ | \ | | | | | | | \ | \ | \ | \ | | 7 | 0 | |
| Partial | | | | | | | | | | | | | | | | | | |
| OFT-M | | | | | | | \ | \ | | | | | | | \ | 2 | 1 | |
| OFT-V | | | | | | \ | \ | | | | | | | | | 2 | 0 | |
| OFT-P | | | | | | | | | | \ | | | | | | 0 | 1 | |
| TDI | | | | | | | | | | \ | | | | | \ | | | 2 |

| Moment | 46 | 47 | 48 | 49 | 50* | 51 | 52 | 53 | 54 | 55* | 56 | 57 | 58 | 59 | 60* | S | P | T |
|---|---|---|---|---|---|---|---|---|---|---|---|---|---|---|---|---|---|---|
| AET | | | | | \ | | | | | | | | | | | 0 | 1 | |
| PET | | \ | \ | \ | | | | | | \ | | | | | \ | 3 | 2 | |
| Partial | | | | | | | | | | | | | | | | | | |
| OFT-M | | | | | | | | | | | \ | | | | | 1 | 0 | |
| OFT-V | | | | | | | | | | | \ | \ | | | | 2 | 0 | |
| OFT-P | | | | | | \ | \ | \ | \ | | | | | \ | | 5 | 0 | |
| TDI | | | | | | | | | | | | | | | \ | | | 1 |

| | Target Student | | | Peer Comparison | | | Teacher | |
|---|---|---|---|---|---|---|---|---|
| | S AET _9_ | % AET _18.8_ | | S AET _5_ | % AET _41.7_ | | S TDI __7_ | |
| | S PET 19_ | % PET _40.0_ | | S PET _4_ | % PET _33.3_ | | % TDI _58.3_ | |
| Total Intervals | S OFT-M _6_ | % OFT-M _12.5_ | | S OFT-M _2_ | % OFT-M _16.7_ | | Total Intervals | |
| Observed | S OFT-V _8_ | % OFT-V _16.7_ | | S OFT-V _2_ | % OFT-V _16.7_ | | Observed | |
| _48__ | S OFT-P 13_ | % OFT-P _27.1_ | | S OFT-P _2_ | % OFT-P _16.7_ | | __12__ | |

**FIGURE 15.3   Behavioral observations of students in schools (BOSS).**

determining whether academic time is being used efficiently in the classroom.

## Student Interview

Another important aspect in the assessment of the academic environment is gaining the perspective of the student on instructions given by the teacher, the student's knowledge of how to get help when difficulties arise, and whether the student understands classroom rules. Students may also indicate areas of confusion and difficulties that could be sources for remediation.

To help understanding the student's perspective, an informal, semistructured interview is conducted with the student. The interview is done in conjunction with the completion of an academic assignment, usually one in which a systematic, direct observation was conducted. Questions are asked to determine if the student can articulate the specific instructions required for the assignment, knows the expectations of the teacher, and feels self-confident about completing the assignment. Students are also asked whether they feel they are given sufficient time to complete the assignment and the degree to which they are included in classroom discussions.

Numerous forms are available as guides to conduct this interview, such as The Instructional Environment Scale, or TIES (Ysseldyke & Christenson, 1987), the TIES-II (Ysseldyke & Christenson, 1993), and Shapiro (1996a, 1996b).

## Review of Permanent Products

The final step in the assessment of the academic environment is a review of materials that students have produced under normal classroom instruction. These may be worksheets from workbooks, duplicated worksheets developed by the teacher, writing assignments, tests and quizzes, reports, and other such academic activities. Analysis of these materials can offer valuable information about a student's performance under typical instructional demands. They can reflect strengths and weaknesses in specific skill areas, as well as particulars about behavior. For example, one may find that a student does very poorly on a multiple-choice test but much better with free-choice responses. This observation may be very useful in making recommendations and constructing interventions to affect a student's academic performance. The evolving research on performance assessment and portfolio systems indicates that these methods also provide rich work samples and are particularly useful for understanding students' performances when a priori criteria are provided for judging the quality of the work.

Combining a permanent product review with systematic, direct observation is also very useful. For example, a systematic observation, using the BOSS, during which a student was asked to complete a page of math problems may show that the student was passively engaged for over 90% of the intervals. However, examination of the math sheet may reveal that the student completed only 5 of 20 problems, although the answers were all correct. Thus, the contrast between the two outcomes shows a student who is on-task but likely to be failing because of his or her rate of performance.

## Step 2: Assess Curriculum Placement

### Importance and Purpose

The purpose of step 2 in the academic assessment process is to determine the instructional level in curriculum materials for each area of basic skills. Instructional level is that point in the curriculum where students are capable of achieving maximum learning. Material presented at that level is neither too difficult nor too easy. Unfortunately, it is sometimes discovered that students are being instructed in levels of curriculum that are far beyond their own current level. These students will struggle and be unlikely to achieve sufficient acquisition or retention of the material. As part of the assessment process, it is important to determine where in a curriculum the students' current acquisition of skills would place them.

The process for determining instructional level varies for each of the different basic skills. Here we give only a brief overview of the process. Interested readers can find a more detailed discussion in Shapiro (1996a, 1996b).

### Reading

The assessment of reading skills involves the administration of short, oral, graded reading passages taken from the curriculum materials. In some cases, the material is taken directly from the curriculum in which the student is being instructed. In other cases, when material is not well controlled for readability across grades, generic graded passages can be used. Fuchs and Deno (1992, 1994) determined that it was not always necessary to use the curriculum of instruction to obtain valid estimates of reading performance.

Reading passages (commonly called probes) are constructed by selecting three passages from each book of the reading series (one each from the beginning, middle, and end) at each grade level and having students read the passages aloud. Approximately five to eight comprehension questions are developed for each passage. The child is told to stop reading the passages after one minute. The number of words read correctly per minute and words read incorrectly are used as the primary metrics to determine the student's reading performance. For one of the three probes at each level, students are instructed to read the entire passage (usually 150–200 words) and answer the comprehension questions. The percentage of questions answered correctly is used as an outcome measure.

From the median number of correct and incorrect words across the three passages, the student is given a score at each level of the reading series. This score is compared to criteria established district-wide through local norms or by using standards established through research (Fuchs & Deno, 1982). With these data, performance can be judged to be at frustration, instructional, or mastery levels. The process is repeated for all three passages at the next level of the series until the highest level of instructional performance is determined. The optimal pattern would look like this:

Level 7: Frustration
Level 6: Instructional
Level 5: Instructional (where assessment was started)
Level 4: Mastery.

In this example, the student started at level 5 (where the students were being instructed, according to the teacher), was then tested at level 6 (since the students were instructional at level 5), was tested at level 7 (since the students were instructional at level 6), and finally tested at level 4 (where mastery was established). These data indicate that this student's instructional level was level 6 in the curriculum, a level higher than where the students were currently being taught. Often, this exact pattern will not emerge. Some children never reach a mastery level and will have a series of instructional levels. After three consecutive instructional levels, it is unnecessary to continue further.

There is significant controversy about using only the oral reading rate to determine performance (e.g., Foorman, 1995; Stahl & Kuhn, 1995), despite the evidence that high correlations clearly exist between these metrics. The problem with administering a set of comprehension measures after each reading passage is the significant time it would add to the evaluation process. One way to handle this problem is to administer a comprehension check only once across the three probes at each level of the reading series. As a screening measure, this should address the potential of falsely identifying a student as an adequate reader when the significant problem lies in the retention and recall of information. At the same time, it is critical to note that students who have significant comprehension problems but at the same time can read orally very well (often known as word callers) require more in-depth reading evaluation than that described here.

## Math

Assessing mathematics begins by obtaining the sequence of instruction for computation skills in the student's curriculum. If this is not readily available, an evaluator may use a generic list of objectives, available in Shapiro (1996a). Although there has been a significant shift in the instruction of mathematics toward problem-solving skills while deemphasizing computational competencies, CBA still considers computational objectives as the foundation on which other aspects of mathematics are built. Thus, the assessment of mathematics focuses on the acquisition of computation skills.

In determining curriculum placement in math, the evaluator is interested in determining where in the computation sequence the student has achieved instructional level. This is done by constructing and administering a series of math probes, consisting of sheets of problems that assess a specific set of computation objectives. The assessment starts at the current level of classroom instruction according to the teacher, and students are given two to three minutes to complete the assigned probes. The scoring is based on counting the separate digits in an answer. For example, there is a possibility of three correct digits in this problem:

$$\begin{array}{r} 38 \\ + \phantom{0}65 \\ \hline 103 \end{array}$$

This method of scoring allows students to receive partial credit for incomplete answers. Readers interested in the complexities and further details of this scoring method should see Shapiro (1996b).

Typically, only one or two probes are administered for each objective assessed. The objectives selected for assessment usually indicate key shifts in the instructional process. For example, a teacher indicates that a student currently has difficulties when regrouping (borrowing) is added to addition problems but can do problems without regrouping. The teacher notes that the student cannot do problems in subtraction that involve double digits, even without regrouping. In this case, the examiner would begin with probes that involve double-digit addition with regrouping. If the student's performance, when compared to the local district or to research-based criteria, is at a frustration level, probes that involve addition without regrouping would be administered next. Should the student still show frustration-level performance, the next step would be to administer probes that involve addition facts between 10 and 18, followed by facts from 1–9. The same type of sequence would be followed for subtraction, again beginning where the student is currently being instructed and working forward or backward through the curriculum sequence until an instructional level is identified.

The outcomes of this assessment process will identify the specific objectives in math computation in which the student is currently instructional. This information may be especially crucial in constructing math interventions and may help to explain a student's current failure since the technique will have identified potential prerequisite skills that are missing in the student's academic repertoire.

## Spelling

Assessment of spelling is similar to that of reading. From materials for spelling instruction (either spelling curriculum or teacher-generated lists), three sets of 20 randomly selected words are developed for each level of the spelling program. Beginning at the level where the student is being instructed, words are dictated to the students every seven seconds. All three lists at each grade level of the curriculum are administered, and the median score for each level is used to determine the student's instructional level. Testing across levels continues either upward or downward until the student scores 20–39 letter sequences correct per minute in grades 1–2 and 40–50 letter sequences per minute in grades 3 and up.

Two measures are obtained for spelling. One

uses letters in a sequence that are correct. Similar to math, the procedure provides for partial credit for responses. (Readers interested in more detail on this scoring technique are again referred to Shapiro, 1996b.) Students are credited for two-letter sequences that are correct in each word. Although this metric is very sensitive to small changes in performance, it is still important to obtain a measure of the percentage of words spelled correctly since some students who show substantial improvements in letters in a sequence still failed to improve their overall scores on spelling tests.

## Written Language

Unlike reading, math, and spelling, few schools have particular curricula for written language. Assessment of written language does not specifically derive from curriculum materials but can be a good indicator of specific problem areas, like grammar, spelling in context, handwriting, and so on. Written language is assessed by having students write a series of short stories in response to a topic sentence (called a story starter). After hearing the story starter, students are given a minute to think of what they will write and then three minutes to write as much as they can.

The words that are written correctly are counted and serve as the outcome measure. Local norms can be easily collected by having groups of students in the class write similar stories. This can be a more useful technique for interpreting the data than trying to identify an instructional level. Also, the stories can be scored for many other components of the writing process.

## Step 3: Instructional Modification

Step 3 of the assessment process involves the delivery of instruction that has been modified as suggested by the results of steps 1 and 2. The interventions can be focused on changes in the way the academic environment is structured, the way specific skills are being taught, or combinations of these approaches. Most important, the interventions are tied to the outcomes of the assessment process and are conceptualized in a problem-solving process.

The types of interventions can vary widely. Some may be applicable across areas of academic skills. For example, initial assessment procedures might reveal that the student consistently makes errors in the sequence of steps used to solve problems. One strategy that might be recommended is the use of self-instruction training, in which students are required to talk though the stepwise procedure aloud to themselves. This technique has resulted in successful outcomes for some students in math (e.g., Johnston, Whitman, & Johnson, 1980) and other academic skill areas (Fox & Kendall, 1983). In another case, the student may have difficulty in seeking out assistance when errors are made during independent assignments and mistakes are perpetuated throughout the work. The use of peer-mediated interventions like peer tutoring (e.g., Greenwood, Delquadri, & Hall, 1989) or cooperative learning (Slavin, Madden, & Leavey, 1984) might be recommended for this problem. Other cases may show that the feedback and contingencies for academic responding have not been maximized. Indeed, there is substantial literature on changing the type and frequency of rewards following completion of required academic work (e.g., McLaughlin, 1981; Skinner, Bamberg, Smith, & Powell, 1993; Skinner, Ford, & Yunker, 1991).

Other strategies may be specific to a skill area. For example, the assessment may reveal that a student has a problem with reading fluency, and numerous strategies can be designed for this area. For instance, previewing reading materials prior to class assignments often results in substantial improvements in reading fluency (e.g., Rose & Beatty, 1986; Skinner, Adamson, Woodward, Jackson, Atchison, & Mimms, 1993). Having students read material along with a tape-recorded version of a passage played at speeds faster than the students' current rate of reading has also been effective (Freeman & McLaughlin, 1984; Shapiro & McCurdy, 1989), as has frequently repeated reading of the same material (Skinner & Shapiro, 1989). Indeed, research strongly indicates that high numbers of repetitions over a short period of time can be very helpful in improving the reading of students with mild handicaps (e.g., Hargis, Terhaar-Yonker, Williams, & Reed, 1988; Shapiro, 1996a).

Another assessment may show that a student has problems in reading comprehension, for which many studies have suggested successful techniques. For example, Idol (1987) and Idol and Croll (1987) have described a procedure called story mapping to teach comprehension skills. The reader's attention is directed to important and interrelated parts of the passage, and an organizational framework is provided for reporting story information. Significant improvements among students with learning disabilities

have been seen from this technique (Baumann & Bergeron, 1993; Billingsley & Ferro-Almeida, 1993; Davis, 1994; Idol, 1987; Idol & Croll, 1987). Graham and Wong (1993) examined the use of mnemonic strategies plus self-instruction in teaching comprehension skills among average and poor readers. Results showed significant improvement for both groups of students over more traditional, didactic teaching methods.

A number of investigations have demonstrated the potential success of self-instruction in problem solving in mathematics. For example, Cullinan, Lloyd, and Epstein (1981) and Johnston et al. (1980) have demonstrated that self-instruction training can effectively improve the ability of students with mild disabilities to accurately complete addition, subtraction, and multiplication problems that involve regrouping.

Similar types of interventions have been reported for language arts such as spelling and written language. For example, Graham, Harris, and their colleagues (Graham, Harris, MacArthur, & Schwartz, 1991; Harris & Graham, 1994) developed strategies designed to assist students with learning disabilities in writing better compositions. Specifically, students were taught problem-solving strategies like brainstorming to increase the number of action words, action helpers, and description words used in compositions. They also developed strategies specifically to teach students how to frame, pose, and answer questions to improve content. Others have focused on strategies to improve the revision process by using peer editors (e.g., MacArthur, Schwartz, & Graham, 1991; Stoddard & MacArthur, 1993) or to develop a story by using webbing skills (Zipprich, 1995).

In sum, there are literally hundreds of strategies in the literature that have been developed, documented, and empirically validated. Although there is no particular strategy that is guaranteed to improve a student's academic skills problems, it is critical that the strategies chosen for implementation match the outcomes of the assessment process. At times, these strategies will involve only simple, easily manipulated changes in the academic environment. Increasing the amount and type of teacher feedback, altering the way instructions are given, and altering the format for responding could all be successful in some cases. However, for other cases, more involved alterations of the entire instructional process are needed—strategies to facilitate learning by altering the level and complexity of instructional materials or presenting "vital signs" of academic progress. Just as a physician will use the metrics of blood pressure, heart rate, and respiration to reflect the overall quality of a person's health, the educational evaluator will use metrics to determine the academic health of the student. These metrics represent the ability of the student to acquire the instructional goals of the curriculum.

In reading, the use of a one-minute oral reading passage randomly selected from goal-level material is typically employed. Students are assessed twice per week, and the number of words correctly read per minute are graphically displayed. Normative data collected locally or nationally can be used to establish expected rates of improvement over an academic year (Fuchs, Fuchs, Hamlett, Walz, & Germann, 1993; Hasbrouck & Tindal, 1992; Shinn, 1988). In math, students complete sheets of computational problems that were generated by randomly selected problems from across the year's curriculum objectives. Students are given between two and five minutes to complete the problems, which are usually done once or twice per week. Results are graphically displayed, using correct digits per minute, and expected progress is again plotted by using normative data. In spelling, students write the responses to a list of 20 words generated from the year-long curriculum. Words are dictated at the rate of 1 every seven seconds, and the number of correct letters in a sequence is used to reflect performance. Long-term progress in written language is monitored in the same way as it was in step 2; however, only a single sample is collected, usually once per week.

Data collected through CBM are analyzed in several ways, and teachers can begin to see if students are making less than the expected levels of progress. First, when the data suggest that the student is no longer moving along the expected line of progress, a change in the teaching process can be implemented. Second, the CBM tests themselves can be examined for suggestions on what specific skills should be targeted for change. Third, the CBM data can help teachers determine the overall effectiveness of the instructional program. Fuchs and colleagues have developed computerized versions of the CBM system to assist teachers in making these types of instructional decisions (Fuchs, Hamlett, & Fuchs, 1990a, 1990b, 1990c; Fuchs, Fuchs, Hamlett, & Ferguson, 1992).

## Step 4: Progress in Monitoring Short- and Long-term Goals

In monitoring short-term goals, an assessment measure must be developed for each objective. Consistent with subskill mastery models of CBA, the purpose of these measures is to determine specifically if students are learning exactly what is being taught. For example, in reading, one type of short-term assessment measure might be a miscue analysis of oral reading fluency (Parker, Hasbrouck, & Tindal, 1992), in which the specific errors made by the student while reading a passage are examined. Repeated use of the analysis would reflect areas where the student may benefit from instruction. Another technique for reading comprehension problems might be a reading-retell technique. This assessment measure would ask students to read a passage and retell the story in their own words. Responses would be scored by using a standard measure that could reflect the acquisition of various skills, such as understanding the story, setting, characters, events, and so forth (for example, see Shapiro, 1996a, 1996b).

In short-term monitoring for math, an error analysis of a student's responses might be conducted. For example, examination of a probe that evaluates addition with regrouping may show that a student does not understand the algorithm for borrowing. Repeated measures of this same skill, following instruction, would demonstrate whether the instructional strategy was effective. Similar types of error analysis procedures would be used for spelling and written language assessments.

In general, the process of progress monitoring is a key element in the assessment of academic skills. Interventions derived from the data collected at steps 1 and 2 must be evaluated to determine their effectiveness. It is important to recognize that improvement in both the acquisition of the specific skills being taught (short-term goals) and how those skills are reflected in the overall growth expected across the entire year-long curriculum (long-term goals) are critical in evaluating the impact of the intervention process. Strategies that show gains in the skills being taught (short-term growth) may not necessarily be reflected in long-term goals. Gains in long-term goals may not necessarily be displayed in the specific skills being taught. To provide a clear picture of the process, impacts on both the short- and long-term goals need to be seen.

## Summary: Integration of Results

Conducting a CBA, using the approach recommended by Shapiro (1996a), offers a comprehensive picture of a student's academic skills problems. Difficulties that are due to performance rather than skill deficiencies are detected by the multiple behavioral assessment measures of the academic environment. Areas where the academic ecology can be maximized to improve performance are also evident. Assessment of a student's individual academic skills is determined from curriculum materials, both those currently being taught and the possible generic curriculum for that grade. Most important, all of the data collected lead the evaluator to a suggested set of intervention strategies that are likely to improve the problem areas. The outcomes of these interventions are analyzed carefully for both the gains in specific skills and their reflection across the year-long curriculum. Changes needed in the intervention are reflected in the data collection process.

As one can see, the entire process is quite dynamic and fluid. Determination of a student's performance in academic skills is based on change over time rather than the more traditional method of a cross-peer, nomothetic comparison. Such dynamism suggests substantial flexibility and a need for effective training in problem-solving skills among evaluators. Indeed, Shapiro and Eckert (1993), in a national survey of school psychologists on the use of curriculum-based assessment, found that while CBA strategies were increasingly being used in the assessment process, only a small percentage of psychologists had actually received any formal training in the process. Several statewide efforts to offer this training have been initiated (e.g., Iowa and Pennsylvania).

## PERFORMANCE ASSESSMENT

Performance assessment of students' achievement is not new to many educators. For example, those in physical education, art, music, and vocational and technological arts all use, to a large extent, students' products or performances to determine whether the learning objectives have been met. Performance assessments also have a long history in organizational psychology, the workplace, and the military. New aspects of performance assessment in schools are (1) its use in the core curricular of math, science, language arts, and social studies, (2) the use of scoring criteria to influence and interpret performances; and (3) the encouragement of students to conduct self-assessments. Thus, many educators already use some weak forms of performance assessment; that is, they ask students to apply their knowledge and skills by producing a product, and they provide feedback about performances in the form of grades. Besides these two traditional elements of performance assessment, the new, pedagogically stronger forms influence students' performances by (1) selecting assessment tasks that are clearly aligned or connected to what has been taught, (2) revealing the scoring criteria for the assessment task to the students before they begin, (3) providing clear statements of standards and/or several models of acceptable and exemplary performances before the task, (4) encouraging students to complete self-assessments of their performances, and (5) interpreting students' performances by comparing them to consensus standards that are developmentally appropriate and possibly to other students' performances (Elliott, 1994).

The stronger forms of performance assessment interact in visible ways with instruction that precedes *and* follows an assessment task. This approach to performance assessment in its strongest form emphasizes the point that the central purposes of most educational assessments are to guide instruction and to facilitate communication among primary educational stakeholders—teachers, students, and parents—about valued educational accomplishments.

## Comparison of Performance Assessment to Traditional Assessment

The potential for using performance assessments is perhaps best understood by a comparison with traditional assessments. Table 15.1 provides a comparison of these two approaches on 10 common characteristics or dimensions. In this table, traditional assessment is characterized as predominately norm-referenced, focusing on right or wrong answers, privately scored, often standardized, and primarily pencil and paper. Performance assessment is characterized as criterion-referenced; focusing on both process and products in an answer; scored by multiple raters, possibly including the students themselves; often individualized; and often with a range of responding modes (e.g., pencil and paper, videotape, group reports, and graphic materials).

TABLE 15.1   Traditional Assessment vs. Performance Assessment—Some Key
Differences in Practice

| Traditional Assessment | Performance Assessment |
|---|---|
| Information assessed often does not overlap with what was taught. | Information assessed overlaps with what was taught. |
| Comparisons are norm-referenced. | Comparisons are criterion-referenced. |
| It occurs after teaching when *teacher* is ready. | It occurs concurrent with or after teaching when *student* is ready. |
| Does not teach to the test. | Teaches to the test. |
| Assessment focuses on right or wrong products. | Assessment focuses on process and products. |
| Assessment yields a score and global feedback. | Assessment yields qualitative and quantitative feedback about process and products. |
| Scoring criteria are usually private. | Scoring criteria are often public. |
| Assessment tasks provide a good sampling of the domain of knowledge skills. | Assessment tasks provide a limited sampling of the domain of knowledge or skills. |
| Assessment conditions are standardized and involve pencil-and-paper tasks. | Assessment conditions are more individualized and can involve a range of response modes. |

The characteristics of performance assessment considered to be an advantage in the daily classroom-based assessment of a student may be a disadvantage in classifying a student for possible inclusion in a special program. Thus, a thorough understanding of the qualities of the various assessment methods is needed when considering the purpose of any assessment activity. Clearly, in some situations, especially those that require a norm-referenced interpretation and interval scales of measurement, traditional assessments may fit the needs of an assessor better than performance assessments. In others, especially those with a priori competence criteria and low-inference analyses of the application of knowledge and skills by professional judges, performance assessment may be more appropriate.

Performance assessments reportedly are used frequently by regular classroom teachers with individual students and recently by many state departments of education to monitor the status of learning at the school, district, and statewide levels. Although numerous special educators have supported its use in the assessment of students with disabilities because of its perceived flexibility and alignment with curriculum (Choate & Evans, 1992; Coutinho & Malouf, 1992; Taylor, Tindal, Fuchs, & Bryant, 1993), we have not located any published, data-based reports of use by psychoeducational personnel to assess students formally for special education classification or placement. A review of the research literature on performance assessment in education indicates that fewer

than 5% of the articles were based on empirical data (Baker, 1990). Dominating the data-base studies have been accounts of the reliability of scoring procedures, although several researchers have been investigating variables like race and gender and topics concerning equity and test validity. In addition, some recently completed work directed by Elliott and Kratochwill (1996) provides a comparative analysis of mildly disabled and nondisabled students on a large-scale performance assessment in mathematics and language arts.

## Performance Spelling: An Example of Performance Assessment

Performance spelling was designed to increase students' use of spelling words to communicate and to advance their writing skills (Elliott & Bischoff-Werner, 1995). This approach is individualized to each student, encourages active parental involvement in selecting words and studying, has public scoring criteria that all students know and use, and has a scoring and monitoring system that students manage. This system, which has been used by many elementary and early middle school teachers (Olson, 1995), requires students to select 5 target words and teachers to select 5 target words, for a total of 10 words per week. The selected words should be ones the student is interested in using in written communications and for school-work assignments. Students study these words from Friday until the next Thursday, when they are tested, at which time they are required to write each spelling word and a sentence that correctly uses it.

All students have a copy of the scoring requirements, which focus on four areas of spelling and writing (see Figure 15.4). As indicated in Figure 15.4, students' spelling tests focus on accuracy, usage, punctuation, and legibility of writing. Each of these areas has a set of prespecified scoring criteria, which in turn are used to establish performance standards. For example, in usage, students are required to compose a sentence

that uses the target word appropriately. Usage is evaluated on a three-point scale, where 0 = not used or used incorrectly, 1 = acceptable basic use, and 2 = elaborative use (i.e., enriched vocabulary and language use, adjectives, etc.). After each of 10 sentences are scored, an overall usage score can be determined and characterized by the following performance standards: exemplary = 90%–100%, satisfactory = 50%–89%, and inadequate = 0%–49%. A similar logic, employing varying criteria and scales, is used to score the accuracy, punctuation, and legibility areas. Stu-

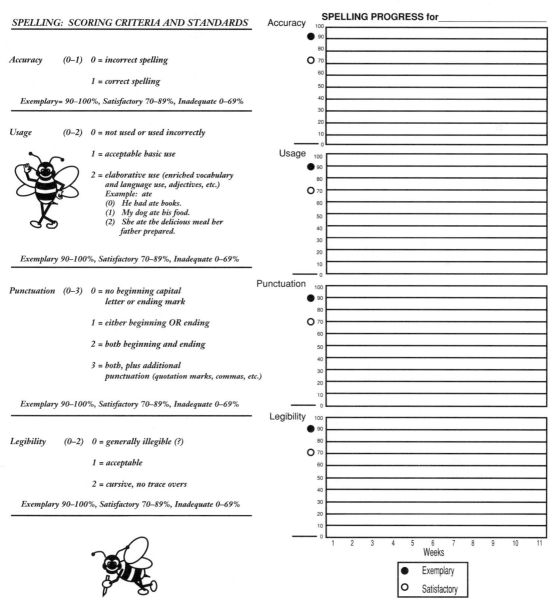

FIGURE 15.4 **An example of performance spelling.**

dents use a monitoring graph to record their own scores for each week in each of the four areas (see Figure 15.4).

Over the course of a year, students progress from writing 10 separate sentences to writing a paragraph with the 5 words they have chosen and another paragraph with the 5 words selected by the teacher. Olson (1995) reported that students at all skill levels could participate successfully in performance spelling; when compared to students in other spelling programs (such as basal series), those in the performance spelling program, on the average, actually spelled more words and more difficult words and wrote much more on a weekly basis. Teachers familiar with this approach see it as more than a weekly spelling test. They commonly characterize it as a language arts program.

This example of performance spelling is intended to summarize and highlight several important characteristics of strong performance assessments. First, the performances are connected to the curriculum and are authentic for the work they require students to create. Second, a priori scoring criteria are available and understood by students before the task. Third, the scoring criteria can be used to build performance standards that communicate to students their level of proficiency in a skill or content area. Finally, teachers can use the results of the test to plan next week's instructional focus.

## CBA AND PA: SUMMARY AND CONCLUSIONS

Curriculum-based assessment and PA have in common several conceptual and practical features. They both require students to construct rather than select responses and to demonstrate a range of skills on a single assessment, and they both correspond closely to the classroom curriculum. Nevertheless, Elliott and Fuchs (in press) point out that CBA and PA also differ in fundamental ways. First, CBA emphasizes administration and scoring efficiency so that assessments can occur on a routine basis—and for purposes of treatment validity, frequent assessment is essential for the measurement of learning over time. In contrast, most PAs require longer administrations and time-consuming, teacher-directed scoring methods, both of which reduce the feasibility of frequent assessment. Second, CBA offers a validated set of procedures for indexing academic competence and growth,

whereas PA has taken several forms and lacks a substantial amount of psychometric research. Both distinctions highlight important technical advantages of CBA. However, these forms of assessment supplement and enhance each other in that CBA indexes the acquisition of basic skills and PA measures the application of those skills to authentic or real-life dilemmas.

By combining the use of CBA and PA, practitioners may enhance the richness of the data available for instructional decision making. As noted by Elliott and Fuchs (in press), "Practitioners potentially can identify whether, and if so when, an instructional adaptation is required in a student's instructional program. They can monitor student growth not only in terms of skills acquisition but also with respect to knowledge application to determine whether acquisition or transfer are indicated. In conclusion, they can broaden their assessment focus to include skill acquisition as well as skills application and integration within rich, authentic contexts and can increase their range of instructional options."

## REFERENCES

Alessi, G., & Kaye, J. H. (1983). *Behavior assessment for school psychologists.* Kent, OH: National Association of School Psychologists.

Allyn & Bacon (1978). *Pathfinder—Allyn and Bacon reading program.* Boston: Author.

Baker, E. L. (1990, October). Assessment and public policy: Does validity matter? Paper presented at the annual meeting of the American Evaluation Association, Washington, DC.

Baker, S. K., & Good, R. H. (1995). Curriculum-based measurement of English reading with bilingual Hispanic students: A validation study with second-grade students. *School Psychology Review, 24,* 561–578.

Baumann, J. F., & Bergeron, B. S. (1993). Story map instruction using children's literature: Effects on first graders' comprehension of central narrative elements. *Journal of Reading Behavior, 25,* 407–437.

Bell, P. F., Lentz, F. E., & Graden, J. L. (1992). Effects of curriculum-test overlap on standardized test scores: Identifying systematic confounds in educational decision making. *School Psychology Review, 21,* 644–655.

Billingsley, B. S., & Ferro-Almeida, S. C. (1993). Strategies to facilitate reading comprehension in students with learning disabilities. *Reading and Writing Quarterly: Overcoming Learning Difficulties, 9,* 263–278.

Choate, J. S., & Evans, S. S. (1992). Authentic

assessment of special learners: Problem or promise? *Preventing School Failure, 37,* 6–9.

Connolly, A., Nachtman, W., & Pritchett, E. (1976). *Manual for the KeyMath Diagnostic Arithmetic Test.* Circle Pines, MN: American Guidance Service.

Coutinho, M., & Malouf, D. (1992, November). *Performance assessment and children with disabilities: Issues and possibilities.* Washington, DC: Division of Innovation and Development, U.S. Department of Education.

Cullinan, D., Lloyd, J., & Epstein, M. H. (1981). Strategy training: A structured approach to arithmetic instruction. *Exceptional Education Quarterly, 2,* 41–49.

Daly, E. J., III, Witt, J. C., Martens, B. K., & Dool, E. J. (1997). A model for conducting a functional analysis of academic performance problems. *School Psychology Review, 26,* 554–574.

Davis, Z. (1994). Effects of prereading story mapping on elementary readers' comprehension. *Journal of Educational Research, 87,* 353–360.

Denham, C., & Lieberman, P. (1980). *Time to learn.* Washington, DC: National Institute of Education.

Deno, S. L. (1985). Curriculum-based measurement: The emerging alternative. *Exceptional Children, 52,* 219–232.

Deno, S. L., Marston, D., & Mirkin, P. K. (1982). Valid measurement procedures for continuous evaluation of written expression. *Exceptional Children, 48,* 368–371.

Deno, S. L., & Mirkin, P. K. (1977). *Data-based program modification: A manual.* Reston, VA: Council for Exceptional Children.

Deno, S. L., Mirkin, P. K., & Chiang, B. (1982). Identifying valid measures of reading. *Exceptional Children, 49,* 36–47.

Deno, S. L., Mirkin, P. K., Lowry, L., & Kuehnle, K. (1980). *Relationships among simple measures of spelling and performance on standardized achievement tests.* Research report No. 21. ERIC Document reproduction service No. ED 197 508. Minneapolis: University of Minnesota, Institute for Research on Learning Disabilities.

Derr, T. F., & Shapiro, E. S. (1989). A behavioral evaluation of curriculum-based assessment of reading. *Journal of Psychoeducational Assessment, 7,* 148–160.

Derr-Minneci, T. F., & Shapiro, E. S. (1992) Validating curriculum-based measurement in reading from a behavioral perspective. *School Psychology Quarterly, 7,* 2–16.

Eckert, T. L. (1996). Teachers' acceptability ratings of psychoeducational assessment methods: A comparison of within-subject versus between-subjects group designs. Doctoral dissertation, Lehigh University, Bethlehem, PA.

Eckert, T. L., Shapiro, E. S., & Lutz, J. G. (1995). Teachers' ratings of the acceptability of

curriculum-based assessment methods. *School Psychology Review, 24,* 499–510.

Elliott, S. N. (1994). *Creating meaningful performance assessments: Fundamental concepts.* Reston, VA: Council for Exceptional Children.

Elliott, S. N. (in press). *Performance assessment of students' achievement: Research and practice.* Washington, DC: National Research Council.

Elliott, S. N., & Bischoff-Werner, K. (1995). Performance spelling. Unpublished manual. University of Wisconsin, Madison.

Elliott, S. N., & Fuchs, L. S. (1997). The utility of curriculum-based measurement and performance assessment as alternatives to intelligence tests. *School Psychology Review, 26,* 224–233.

Elliott, S. N., & Kratochwill, T. R. (1996). *Performance assessment and students with disabilities: Procedures and outcomes in a statewide assessment system.* Madison: Wisconsin Center for Education Research.

Foorman, B. R. (1995). Research on "The Great Debate": Code-oriented versus whole language approaches to reading instruction. *School Psychology Review, 24,* 376–392.

Fox, D. E. C., & Kendall, P. C. (1983). Thinking through academic problems: Applications of cognitive behavior therapy to learning. In T. R. Kratochwill (Ed.), *Advances in school psychology* (Vol. III, pp. 269–301). Hillsdale, NJ: Erlbaum.

Freeman, T. J., & McLaughlin, T. F. (1984). Effects of a taped-words treatment procedure on learning disabled students' sight-word reading. *Learning Disability Quarterly, 7,* 49–54.

Fuchs, L. S., & Deno, S. L. (1982). *Developing goals and objectives for educational programs.* (Teaching guide). Minneapolis: Institute for Research in Learning Disabilities, University of Minnesota.

Fuchs, L. S., & Deno, S. L. (1991). Paradigmatic distinctions between instructionally relevant measurement models. *Exceptional Children, 57,* 488–500.

Fuchs, L. S., & Deno, S. L. (1992). Effects of curriculum within curriculum-based measurement. *Exceptional Children, 58,* 232–243.

Fuchs, L. S., & Deno, S. L. (1994). Must instructionally useful performance assessment be based in the curriculum? *Exceptional Children, 61,* 15–24.

Fuchs, L. S., Fuchs, D., Hamlett, C. L., & Allinder, R. M. (1991a). The contribution of skills analysis within curriculum-based measurement in spelling. *Exceptional Children, 57,* 443–452.

Fuchs, L. S., Fuchs, D., Hamlett, C. L., & Allinder, R. M. (1991b). Effects of expert system advice within curriculum-based measurement on teacher planning and student achievement in spelling. *School Psychology Review, 20,* 49–66.

Fuchs, L. S., Fuchs, D., Hamlett, C. L., & Ferguson, C. (1992). Effects of expert system consultation within curriculum-based measurement using a reading maze task. *Exceptional Children, 58,* 536–450.

Fuchs, L. S., Fuchs, D., Hamlett, C. L., & Stecker, P. M. (1991). Effects of curriculum-based measurement and consultation on teacher planning and student achievement in mathematics operations. *American Educational Research Journal, 28,* 617–641.

Fuchs, L. S., Fuchs, D., Hamlett, C. L., Walz, L., & Germann, G. (1993). Formative evaluation of academic progress: How much growth can we expect? *School Psychology Review, 22,* 27–48.

Fuchs, L. S., Fuchs, D., Hamlett, C. L., & Whinnery, K. (1991). Effects of goal line feedback on level, slope, and stability of performance within curriculum-based measurement. *Learning Disabilities Research and Practice, 6*(2), 66–74.

Fuchs, L. S., Fuchs, D., Phillips, N. B., Hamlett, C. L., & Karns, K. (1995). Acquistion and transfer effects of classwide peer-assisted learning strategies in mathematics for students with varying learning histories. *School Psychology Review, 24,* 604–630.

Fuchs, L. S., Hamlett, C. L., & Fuchs, D. (1990a). Monitoring basic skills progress: Basic math. (Computer program). Austin, TX: Pro-Ed.

Fuchs, L. S., Hamlett, C. L., & Fuchs, D. (1990b). Monitoring basic skills progress: Basic reading. (Computer program). Austin, TX: Pro-Ed.

Fuchs, L. S., Hamlett, C. L., & Fuchs, D. (1990c). Monitoring basic skills progress: Basic spelling. (Computer program). Austin, TX: Pro-Ed.

Galagan, J. E. (1985). Psychoeducational testing: Turn out the lights, the party's over. *Exceptional Children, 52,* 288–299.

Gettinger, M. (1986). Issues and trends in academic engaged time of students. *Special Services in the Schools, 2,* 1–17.

Gickling, E., & Havertape, J. (1981). *Curriculum-based assessment.* Minneapolis, MN: National School Psychology Inservice Training Network.

Gickling, E. E., & Rosenfield, S. (1995). Best practices in curriculum-based assessment. In A. Thomas & J. Grimes (Eds.), *Best practices in school psychology* (Vol. 3, pp. 587–595). Washington, DC: National Association of School Psychologists.

Gickling, E. E., & Thompson, V. P. (1985). A personal view of curriculum-based assessment. *Exceptional Children, 52,* 205–218.

Good, R. H., III, & Salvia, J. (1988). Curriculum bias in published, norm-referenced reading tests: Demonstrable effects. *School Psychology Review, 17,* 51–60.

Graham, L., & Wong, B. Y. (1993). Comparing two modes of teaching a question-answering strategy for enhancing reading comprehension: Didactic and self-instructional training. *Journal of Learning Disabilities, 26,* 270–279.

Graham, S., Harris, K. R., MacArthur, C. A., & Schwartz, S. (1991). Writing and writing instruction for students with learning disabilities: Review of a research program. *Learning Disabilities Quarterly, 14,* 89–114.

Greenwood, C. R., Delquadri, J. C., & Hall, R. V. (1984). Opportunity to respond and student academic performance. In U. L. Heward, T. E. Heron, D. S. Hill, & J. Trap-Porter (Eds.), *Focus on behavior analysis in education* (pp. 58–88). Columbus, OH: Merrill.

Greenwood, C. R., Delquadri, J., & Hall, R. V. (1989). Longitudinal effects of classwide peer tutoring. *Journal of Educational Psychology, 81,* 371–383.

Hargis, C. H., Terhaar-Yonker, M., Williams, P. C., & Reed, M. T. (1988). Repetition requirements for word recognition. *Journal of Reading, 31,* 320–327.

Harris, K. R., & Graham, S. (1994). Constructivism: Principles, paradigms, and integration. *The Journal of Special Education, 28,* 233–247.

Hasbrouck, J. E., & Tindal, G. (1992). Curriculum-based oral reading fluency norms for students in grades 2 through 5. *Teaching Exceptional Children, 24*(3), 41–44.

Heller, K. A., Holtzman, W. H., & Messick, S. (Eds.). (1982). *Placing children in special education: A strategy for equity.* Washington, DC: National Academy Press.

Hieronymus, A. N., Hoover, H. D., & Linquist, E. F. (1986). *Iowa Tests of Basic Skills.* Chicago: Riverside.

Hintze, J. M., & Shapiro, E. S. (1997). Curriculum-based measurement and literature-based reading: Is curriculum-based measurement meeting the needs of changing reading curricula? *Journal of School Psychology, 35,* 351–376.

Hintze, J. M., Shapiro, E. S. Daly, E. J., III (1996). Challenging- versus instructional-level material using curriculum-based measures of oral reading fluency: A comparison of approaches to selecting materials for progress monitoring. Manuscript submitted for publication.

Hintze, J. M., Shapiro, E. S., & Lutz, J. G. (1994). The effects of curriculum on the sensitivity of curriculum-based measurement in reading. *The Journal of Special Education, 28,* 188–202.

Howell, K. W., Fox, S. L., & Moorhead, M. K. (1993). *Curriculum-based evaluation: Teaching and decision making* (2nd ed.). Pacific Grove, CA: Brooks/Cole.

Idol, L. (1987). Group story mapping: A comprehension strategy for both skilled and unskilled readers. *Journal of Learning Disabilities, 20,* 196–205.

Idol, L., & Croll, V. J. (1987). The effects of training in story mapping procedures on the reading comprehension of poor readers. *Learning Disability Quarterly, 10,* 214–229.

Jenkins, J. R., & Pany, D. (1978). Standardized achievement tests: How useful for special education? *Exceptional Children, 44,* 448–453.

Johnston, M. B., Whitman, T. L., & Johnson, M. (1980). Teaching addition and subtraction to mentally retarded children: A self-instructional program. *Applied Research in Mental Retardation, 1,* 141–160.

Lentz, F. E., Jr., & Shapiro, E. S. (1986). Functional assessment of the academic environment. *School Psychology Review, 15,* 346–357.

MacArthur, C. A., Schwartz, S. S., & Graham, S. (1991). Effects of a reciprocal peer revision strategy in special education classrooms. *Learning Disabilities Research and Practice, 6,* 201–210.

Marston, D., Fuchs, L. S., & Deno, S. L. (1986). Measuring pupil progress: A comparison of standardized achievement tests and curriculum-related measures. *Diagnostique, 11,* 77–90.

Martens, B. K., Steele, E. S., Massie, D. R., & Diskin, M. J. (1995). Curriculum bias in standardized tests of reading recoding. *Journal of School Psychology, 33,* 287–296.

Mash, E., & Terdal, L. (1981). *Behavioral assessment of childhood disorders.* New York: Guilford.

Mash, E., & Terdal, L. (1986). *Behavioral assessment of childhood disorders* (2nd ed.). New York: Guilford.

McCurdy, B. L., & Shapiro, E. S. (1992). A comparison of teacher-, peer-, and self-monitoring with curriculum-based measurement in reading among students with learning disabilities. *The Journal of Special Education, 26,* 162–180.

McLaughlin, T. F. (1981). The effects of a classroom token economy on math performance in an intermediate grade class. *Education and Treatment of Children, 4,* 139–147.

Mirkin, P., Deno, S. L., Tindal, G., & Kuehnle, K. (1982). Frequency of measurement and data utilization as factors in standardized behavioral assessment of academic skill. *Journal of Behavioral Assessment, 4,* 361–370.

Muyskens, P., & Ysseldyke, J. E. (1998). Student academic responding time as a function of classroom ecology and time of day. *The Journal of Special Education, 31,* 411–424.

Office of Technology Assessment. (1992, February). *Testing in American Schools: Asking the right questions.* (OTA-SET-519). Washington, DC: U.S. Government Printing Office.

O'Leary, K. D., Romancyzk, R., Kass, R. E., Dietz, A., & Santogrossi, D. A. (1979). *Procedures for classroom observation of teachers and children.* Stony Brook: Psychology Department, State University of New York.

Ollendick, T. H., & Hersen, M. (1984). *Child behavioral assessment: Principles and procedures.* New York: Pergamon.

Olson, A. E. (1995). Evaluation of an alternative approach to teaching and assessing spelling performance. Master's thesis, University of Wisconsin, Madison.

Parker, R., Hasbrouck, J. E., & Tindal, G. (1992). Greater validity for oral reading fluency? Can miscues help? *Journal of Special Education, 25,* 492–503.

Reschly, D. J., & Grimes, J. P. (1995). Best practices in intellectual assessment. In A. Thomas & J. Grimes (Eds.), *Best practices in school psychology* (Vol. 3, pp. 763–773). Washington, DC: National Association of School Psychologists.

Roberts, M. L., & Shapiro, E. S. (1996). The effects of instructional ratios on students' reading performance in a regular education program. *Journal of School Psychology, 34,* 73–92.

Roberts, M. L., Turco, T., & Shapiro, E. S. (1991). Differential effects of fixed instructional ratios on student's progress in reading. *Journal of Psychoeducational Assessment, 9,* 308–318.

Rose, T. L., & Beattie, J. R. (1986). Relative effects of teacher-directed and taped previewing on oral reading. *Learning Disability Quarterly, 9,* 193–199.

Rosenfield, S., & Kuralt, S. (1990). Best practices in curriculum-based assessment. In A. Thomas & J. Grimes (Eds.), *Best practices in school psychology,* (Vol. 2, pp. 275–286). Washington, DC: National Association of School Psychologists.

Saudargas, R. A. (1997). State-Event Classroom Observation System (SECOS). Knoxville: Department of Psychology, University of Tennessee.

Shapiro, E. S. (1989). *Academic skills problems: Direct assessment and intervention.* New York: Guilford.

Shapiro, E. S. (1990). An integrated model for curriculum-based assessment. *School Psychology Review, 19,* 331–349.

Shapiro, E. S. (1992). Gickling's model of curriculum-based assessment to improve reading in elementary age students. *School Psychology Review, 21,* 168–176.

Shapiro, E. S. (1996a). *Academic skills problems: Direct assessment and intervention* (2nd ed.). New York: Guilford.

Shapiro, E. S. (1996b). *Academic skills problems workbook.* New York: Guilford.

Shapiro, E. S., & Derr, T. F. (1987). An examination of overlap between reading curricula and standardized achievement tests. *The Journal of Special Education, 21,* 59–67.

Shapiro, E. S., & Derr, T. F. (1990). Curriculum-based assessment. In T. B. Gutkin & C. R. Reynolds (Eds.), *The handbook of school psychology* (2nd ed., pp. 365–387). New York: Wiley.

Shapiro, E. S., & Eckert, T. L. (1993). Curriculum-based assessment among school psychologists: Knowledge, attitudes, and use. *Journal of School Psychology, 31,* 375–384.

Shapiro, E. S., & Eckert, T. L. (1994). Acceptability of

curriculum-based assessment by school psychologists. *Journal of School Psychology, 32,* 167–184.

Shapiro, E. S., & Kratochwill, T. R. (Eds.). (1988). *Behavioral assessment in schools: Conceptual foundations and practical applications.* New York: Guilford.

Shapiro, E. S., & Lentz, F. E. (1985). Assessing academic behavior: A behavioral approach. *School Psychology Review, 14,* 325–338.

Shapiro, E. S., & Lentz, F. E. (1986). Behavioral assessment of academic behavior. In T. R. Kratochwill (Ed.), *Advances in school psychology* (Vol. 5, pp. 87–139). Hillsdale, NJ: Erlbaum.

Shapiro, E. S., & McCurdy, B. L. (1989). Direct and generalized effects of a taped-words treatment on reading proficiency. *Exceptional Children, 55,* 321–326.

Shinn, M. R. (1988). Development of curriculum-based local norms for use in special education decision-making. *School Psychology Review, 17,* 61–80.

Shinn, M. R. (Ed.). (1989). *Curriculum-based measurement: Assessing special children.* New York: Guilford.

Shinn, M. R. (Ed.). (1998). *Advances in curriculum-based measurement.* New York: Guilford.

Shinn, M. R., Habedank, L., Rodden-Nord, L., & Knutson, N. (1993). Using curriculum-based measurement to identify potential candidates for reintegration into general education. *The Journal of Special Education, 27,* 202–221.

Shriner, J., & Salvia, J. (1988). Chronic noncorrespondence between elementary math curricula and arithmetic tests. *Exceptional Children, 55,* 240–248.

Skinner, C. H., Adamson, K. L., Woodward, J. R., Jackson, R., Atchison, L. A., & Mimms, J. W. (1993). A comparison of fast-rate, slow-rate, and solent previewing interventions on reading performance. *Journal of Learning Disabilities, 26,* 674–681.

Skinner, C. H., Bamberg, H. W., Smith, E. S., & Powell, S. S. (1993). Cognitive cover, copy, and compare: Subvocal responding to increase rates of accurate division responding. *RASE: Remedial and Special Education, 14*(1), 49–56.

Skinner, C. H., Ford, J. M., & Yunker, B. D. (1991). A comparison of instructional response requirements on the multiplication performance of behaviorally disordered students. *Behavioral Disorders, 17,* 56–65.

Skinner, C. H., & Shapiro, E. S. (1989). A comparison of taped-words and drill interventions on reading fluency in adolescents with behavior disorders. *Education and Treatment of Children, 12,* 123–133.

Slavin, R. E., Madden, N. A., & Leavey, M. (1984). Effects of cooperative learning and individualized instruction on mainstreamed students. *Exceptional Children, 50,* 434–443.

Stahl, S. A., & Kuhn, M. R. (1995). Does whole language or instruction matched to learning styles help children learn to read. *School Psychology Review, 25,* 393–404.

Stoddard, B., & MacArthur, C. A. (1993). A peer editor strategy: Guiding learning-disabled students in response and revision. *Research in the Teaching of English, 27,* 76–103.

Taylor, R. L., Tindal, G., Fuchs, L., & Bryant, B. R. (1993). Assessment in the nineties: A possible glance into the future. *Diagnostique, 18,* 113–122.

Wilkinson, G. S. (1993). Wide Range Achievement Test 3 (3rd ed.). Wilmington, DE: Wide Range.

Witt, J. C., & Gresham, F. M. (1985). Review of the Wechlser Intelligence Scale for Children–Revised. In J. Mitchell (Ed.), *Ninth mental measurements yearbook,* (pp. 1716–1719). Lincoln, NE: Buros Institute of Mental Measurements.

Woodcock, R. W. (1987). *Woodcock Reading Mastery Tests–Revised.* Circle Pines, MN: American Guidance Service.

Ysseldyke, J. E., & Christenson, S. (1987). *The Instructional Environment Scale.* Austin, TX: Pro-Ed.

Ysseldyke, J. E., & Christenson, S. (1993). *TIES-II, The Instructional Environment System II.* Longmont, CO: Sopris West.

Zipprich, M. A. (1995). Teaching web making as a guided planning tool to improve student narrative writing. *RASE: Remedial and Special Education, 16,* 3–15.

## CHAPTER 16

# CRITERION-REFERENCED TESTING PRINCIPLES, TECHNICAL ADVANCES, AND EVALUATION GUIDELINES

RONALD K. HAMBLETON
*University of Massachusetts–Amherst*

Criterion-referenced tests are well suited for many of the assessment needs of schools today—monitoring students' progress through a curriculum, diagnosing learning problems, awarding high school diplomas, and evaluating new educational programs. In fact, many school districts are using criterion-referenced tests, and nearly all states have mandated criterion-referenced testing programs (Jaeger, 1989). Criterion-referenced tests, however, go by many names today: domain-referenced tests, objectives-referenced tests, mastery tests, competency tests, minimum competency tests, skills-based tests, outcomes-based assessment, and the currently popular, authentic assessments and performance assessments. Regardless of the name, these tests, when used in schools, are intended to provide information about the knowledge and skill levels of students and to facilitate test score interpretations in absolute levels of performance or performance standards.

This chapter provides school psychologists and others who work with tests in schools with up-to-date information about criterion-referenced testing methods and practices. Definitions, uses, and test score interpretations; differences between norm-referenced and criterion-referenced tests; steps in test development; major advances in testing technology; and guidelines for selecting and evaluating criterion-referenced tests—all are addressed in this chapter.

## DEFINITIONS, USES, AND TEST SCORE INTERPRETATIONS

The first reference to criterion-referenced testing in the research literature appeared in a three-page paper by Robert Glaser in the *American Psychologist* in 1963. Hambleton (1994) reported that he found 3,865 criterion-referenced testing papers in the literature between 1970 and 1991. Clearly, criterion-referenced testing has become an important part of educational testing practices in this country. This testing, however, has changed over the years—not so much in concept but in practice. Until the middle 1980s, criterion-referenced testing tended to be used to assess basic cognitive skills with multiple-choice test items. In recent years, it is more often called performance assessment or authentic assessment and is used to assess higher-level cognitive skills; the range of item formats is very wide—everything from true-false and multiple-choice test items to performance tasks and portfolios.

Glaser (1963) and Popham and Husek (1969) were key studies in introducing the concept of criterion-referenced measurement and steps for developing tests. These authors were interested in an approach to testing that would provide essential information for making a variety of individual and programmatic decisions in connection with specific educational outcomes, sometimes called objectives, skills, or competencies. Norm-referenced achievement tests were seen as limited, in the main, because they provided information about the relative standing of students on fairly broad outcomes of education (e.g., vocabulary and reading comprehension). For example, knowing that a student is performing at the sixtieth percentile on a reading comprehension test provides little or no information about what that student actually knows or can be expected to do.

Standard procedures for constructing and evaluating tests within a norm-referenced framework are well known to educators, but these procedures are less appropriate when the question of interest concerns what students can and cannot do (Glaser, 1963; Hambleton & Novick, 1973; Popham & Husek, 1969). Norm-referenced tests are constructed, principally, to facilitate the comparison of individuals (or groups) with one another or to a norm group on the trait or construct measured by the test (e.g., verbal reasoning). Content considerations are important, but ensuring substantial score variability is also a major consideration in choosing assessment materials for a norm-referenced test.

In contrast, criterion-referenced tests are constructed to permit the interpretation of individual (and group) test scores in relation to a well-defined and clearly articulated domain of content. For this reason, clear descriptions of intended educational outcomes and content validity considerations are especially important in the test development process.

Many definitions of criterion-referenced tests have been proposed in the literature (see, e.g., Nitko, 1980; Popham, 1978a). Gray (1978), for example, reported the existence of 57 different definitions. The one adopted in this chapter is a modification of a definition offered by Popham:

> A criterion-referenced test is constructed to assess the performance levels of examinees in relation to a well-defined domain of content. Sometimes a test might measure a single domain of content, and other times, especially when diagnostic information is valued, a criterion-referenced test might measure several domains of content, with each domain of content representing an objective, skill, or competency of interest.

Four points about the definition require explanation. First, terms such as *objectives*, *skills*, and *competencies* are used interchangeably in the testing literature. Second, each objective measured in a criterion-referenced test must be well defined. This means that there should be sufficient details for test developers to agree on the content or behaviors that can be assessed to measure the objective and that they can draw representative samples of assessment material. Well-defined objectives facilitate the process of developing assessment materials because they provide a framework within which developers and reviewers can work. The validity of test score interpretations is enhanced because of the clarity of the content or behavior domains to which test scores are referenced.

The breadth and complexity of each domain of content or behaviors that define an objective can (and usually does) vary, but the domain must be clearly defined. The purpose of the test will influence the appropriate breadth of domains. For example, on the one hand, diagnostic tests are typically organized around narrowly defined objectives (e.g., the student can solve single-digit sums). Year-end assessments, on the other hand, will normally be carried out with more broadly defined objectives (e.g., the student can apply geometric and algebraic properties and relationships to solve basic problems).

Third, when more than one objective is measured in a criterion-referenced test, the assessment material matched to each objective can be organized into non-overlapping subtests, corresponding to the objectives, and the examinee's performance can be reported on each objective.

Fourth, the definition of a criterion-referenced test does not include a reference to performance standards for classifying students into performance categories (e.g., masters and nonmasters or below basic, basic, proficient, and advanced). It is common to set at least one standard of performance on a criterion-referenced test and interpret the examinee's performance in relation to that standard. But descriptive interpretations of scores—such as "The student answered correctly 70% of the sample of assessment material in the domain of content, which addressed knowledge of capital cities of states"—are also made, and performance standards are not used in this type of interpretation.

That a performance standard need not be set on a criterion-referenced test will come as a surprise to persons who have mistakenly assumed that the word *criterion* in "criterion-referenced test" refers to a performance standard or cutoff score. In fact, *criterion* is the word used by both Glaser (1963) and Popham and Husek (1969) to refer to the domain of content or behavior to which test scores are referenced.

A diagram of a typical criterion-referenced test, examinee's test scores, performance standards, and associated binary mastery decisions is shown in Figure 16.1. The diagram can be used to describe several diverse applications: (1) the classroom teacher who wishes to make a diagnostic assessment of student performance, (2) a school district interested in year-end assessments, or (3) schools that must certify that students are qualified to receive high school diplomas. The differences among the three applications (and other applications as well) occur in the choice, breadth, and complexity of objectives; in the number of objectives included in the test; in the nature and amount of assessment materials used to assess each objective; and in the standards used to interpret examinees' performance.

Figure 16.1 highlights three additional points about criterion-referenced tests:

1. The number of objectives measured in a criterion-referenced test will (in general) vary from one test to the next.
2. The number of test items, or the amount of assessment material that measures each objective, and the performance standards will (in general) vary from one objective to the next.

| Criterion-referenced Test (6 Objectives) | | | | | | |
|---|---|---|---|---|---|---|
| Objective | 0–1 | 0–2 | 0–3 | 0–4 | 0–5 | 0–6 |
| Number of test items | 5 | 5 | 10 | 8 | 3 | 3 |
| Performance standard | 80% | 100% | 80% | 75% | 67% | 100% |
| Examinee's test score | 3 | 5 | 9 | 4 | 2 | 0 |
| Examinee's percentage score | 60% | 100% | 90% | 50% | 67% | 0% |
| Decision | NM | M | M | NM | M | NM |

**FIGURE 16.1   A typical criterion-referenced test—multiple objectives, variable numbers of score points and performance standards for objectives, and simple binary performance classifications.**

3. One method for making a mastery-nonmastery decision involves the comparison of an examinee's percentage (or proportion correct) score on the objective with the corresponding performance standard. If an examinee's score is equal to or greater than the performance standard, the examinee is described as a master, qualified, or certifiable. But, there are many psychometric models for scoring criterion-referenced tests and for assigning examinees to performance categories (Mellenbergh & van der Linden, 1979). Figure 16.1 highlights only the simplest and most common scoring and decision-making model.

Norm-referenced tests and criterion-referenced tests are constructed to achieve different purposes. At the same time, can both norm-referenced and criterion-referenced interpretations of scores be made from each type of test? Certainly norm-referenced interpretations may be drawn from scores on a criterion-referenced test (Linn, 1994). Probably norms from any test could be produced and used in score interpretations (Popham, 1976). Also, weak criterion-referenced interpretations (interpretations limited to the particular items on the test) can certainly be made with item scores from a norm-referenced test. But a criterion-referenced test is not built to produce a heterogeneous distribution of test scores, and therefore norm-referenced interpretations from a criterion-referenced test will be less informative than norm-referenced interpretations from a norm-referenced test because the percentile bands will be considerably wider (that is, include a greater percentage of the students in the test score distribution). Also, a norm-referenced test is not built around objectives that are as carefully defined as those in criterion-referenced tests. This means that the assessment material cannot be assumed to be representative of the domains of content of interest, and therefore inferences from item-level performance must be limited. Also, item-level data are likely to be of modest reliability, which limits their usefulness.

In summary, criterion-referenced tests can be used to make norm-referenced interpretations and vice versa, but neither use will be completely satisfactory. Norm-referenced and criterion-referenced interpretations are best made from tests constructed specifically to facilitate the desired kind of interpretation, that is, norm-referenced tests and criterion-referenced tests, respectively.

## COMPARISON OF NORM-REFERENCED AND CRITERION-REFERENCED ACHIEVEMENT TESTS

Two points about the comparison are important to highlight: (1) both criterion-referenced tests and norm-referenced tests have important roles to play in providing data for educational decision making; (2) what differences do exist are significant, but the two kinds of tests have many common features. On the latter point, it would be a rare person who could correctly label tests as criterion-referenced or norm-referenced from a review of the tests themselves. They use the same item formats (e.g., multiple choice, true-false, matching, essay, and performance task), the directions look similar; both can be administered via paper and pencil or computer; and both kinds of tests can be standardized (i.e., the conditions under which the tests are administered and scored can be tightly controlled).

Still, several important differences exist, even if they cannot be seen from a review of the tests themselves. First, a norm-referenced achievement test consists of assessment materials from the content areas in the proportions defined in a test blueprint *and* that contribute substantially to test score variability. Test scores are interpreted by comparing the examinee's performance to the performance of examinees in a well-defined norm group. A criterion-referenced test, in contrast, consists of assessment materials that sample, in a representative way, well-defined domains of content. The examinee's performance (often on an objective-by-objective basis) is interpreted in relation to the two end points on the percentage scale (0% and 100%) or, more commonly, in relation to performance standards on the test score scale or on a transformed scale—which is often introduced to facilitate the linking of multiple forms of a criterion-referenced test or to simplify score reporting. Sometimes, too, criterion-referenced test scores may be interpreted as stages on a continuum of proficiency. A good example would be the stages of writing proficiency represented by the score points used in grading writing samples.

Second, both norm-referenced and criterion-referenced test developers prepare clear test blueprints. It is common, also, for developers of both tests to prepare objectives to further define the content area of interest. But it is also true that the objectives assessed by criterion-referenced tests must meet higher standards of clarity. Thus, in content specifications, the difference between norm-referenced tests and criterion-referenced tests is in the degree to which the content is clarified.

Third, item statistics are used differently in test construction. Norm-referenced test developers construct tests to be content-valid, but they also select assessment materials (e.g., multiple-choice items and performance tasks) because of their desirable statistical characteristics. Assessment materials of moderate difficulty and high discriminating power are needed to produce heterogeneous score distributions. A heterogeneous distribution of test scores is essential if a norm-referenced test is to serve its purpose, that is, produce reliable and valid norm-referenced score information. The criterion-referenced test developer, in contrast, uses item statistics mainly in the test development process to detect flawed assessment material. (For example, assessment material may be flawed if higher-ability students do less well on the material than lower-ability students.) Also, item statistics may be used in selecting assessment material when parallel forms of a test are being built or if a test is being constructed to discriminate optimally at the performance standards used in test score interpretations. In the latter case, a more effective test is obtained when assessment materials maximally discriminate in the regions on the test score scale where the performance standards are located (see Hambleton, 1989).

## TEST DEVELOPMENT

Steps for constructing criterion-referenced tests are presented in Figure 16.2. The care and attention with which each step is carried out will depend on the purpose of the test. For example, it would be unreasonable to expect a group of classroom teachers who are preparing a test for their own use to pursue each of the steps in depth. However, when a test is to be used for determining high school graduation, the steps should be carried out in considerable depth, and the total process may take a year or more to complete properly.

Brief descriptions of the 12 steps follow:

*Step 1.* Test planning includes specifying test purposes; test content; groups to be assessed; time, money, and expertise available to construct the test; and a list of activities or steps for constructing the test.

**FIGURE 16.2    Steps in Constructing a Criterion-referenced Test**

1. Preliminary activities in constructing the test
   a. State the purpose of the test.
   b. Specify content areas (in the form of a test blueprint).
   c. Identify the groups to be assessed. (Which accommodations need to be made for special populations?)
   d. Make preliminary decisions about assessment formats (selected response versus constructed response).
   e. Specify the amount of time, money, and expertise necessary to construct and validate the test.
   f. Prepare a list of test development activities, with a time schedule, and assign staff.
2. Preparation and review of objectives
   Prepare and review detailed specifications for measuring the objectives of interest.
3. Additional test planning
   a. Select objectives to be included in the test.
   b. Determine the approximate test length and the amount of assessment material per objective (e.g., five multiple-choice items or perhaps one performance task).
   c. Identify item writers.
4. Preparation of assessment material to measure the objectives and initial editing
   a. Conduct training for developers of the assessment materials, if necessary.
   b. Prepare first drafts of the assessment materials. Include scoring rubrics for any performance material.
   c. Conduct self-reviews to identify flaws.
5. Assessment of content validity and score reliability
   a. Use content and measurement specialists to evaluate the assessment materials:
      i. Congruence with the objectives
      ii. Technical quality
      iii. Representativeness
      iv. Potential bias
   b. Field-test the assessment materials on an appropriately sized sample of examinees (for the intended purpose of the test—an important purpose dictates a larger sample):
      i. Detect flawed items.
      ii. Check for bias, using statistical procedures.
      iii. Determine difficulty levels and discrimination indexes.
      iv. Determine consistency of scores and/or decisions.
   c. Choose an appropriate "linking design" if multiple test forms are used.
6. Revisions to the assessment materials
   a. Revise assessment materials as necessary to be consistent with accepted technical standards.
   b. Revise or correct scoring rubrics (if available) to increase the validity of scoring.
7. Assembly of the test
   a. Finalize the test length and amount of assessment material per objective.
   b. Select assessment materials to match the content specifications.
   c. Ensure content representativeness.
   d. Select anchor items, if needed. (This is assessment materials from another form of the test that can be used in linking or equating the test forms.)
   e. Prepare test directions and practice questions, if necessary.
   f. Prepare test layouts and test booklets.
   g. Finalize scoring keys and/or scoring rubrics, test booklets, and/or answer sheets.
   h. Prepare test administrator's manual.
8. Selection and implementation of a standard-setting method
   a. Choose a standard-setting method and design the training material.
   b. Conduct a field test of the method and revise the method, if necessary. (This activity is usually helpful and is especially important with high-stakes assessments such as high school graduation tests.)

FIGURE 16.2 *(Continued)*

    c. Determine the composition of the panel and identify the panelists.

    d. Implement the standard-setting method.

    e. Recommend the resulting performance standards.

    f. Document the process and provide evidence of validity (e.g., panelists' level of confidence in the process; consistency of the performance standards across panelists).

9. Test administration and reporting

    a. Administer and score the test. (Sometimes at this step, some assessment material may be dropped because of bias or other technical flaws.)

    b. Report the test scores and related decisions.

10. Assessment of test score reliability and validity

    Design the studies and compile reliability and validity information.

11. Preparation of a technical manual

    Prepare a manual that includes information addressing content specifications, steps taken in test development, results of field testing, approach to standard-setting, item statistics, and reliability and validity information, as well as the names and qualifications of assessment developers, reviewers, standard-setting panelists, and others who played significant roles in the test development and validation process.

12. Ongoing collection of technical information and technical manual updates

    Compile and write up the technical data.

---

*Step 2.* Individuals (or a committee), working from the general content guidelines prepared in step 1, must prepare a set of well-defined objectives. Each objective description must clearly define the content or behavior domain if it is to be of help to item writers and (later) test score users. After the objectives are drafted, they must be reviewed for clarity and completeness.

*Step 3.* If more objectives are available from step 2 than can be accommodated in the test, a selection process must be implemented. Alternatively, and for some test purposes, some of the objectives can be combined to produce fewer, more broadly defined objectives. Also, an estimate is needed of the amount of assessment material that should be written to measure each objective, and item writers must be located and trained. Assessment material includes multiple-choice, true-false, and matching test items; performance tasks; short and extended essays; and many newer forms of assessment, several of which are being designed specifically for computer-administered tests (Bennett & Ward, 1993).

*Step 4.* Assessment material is prepared to measure the objectives. One important change in recent years has been the assessment of more higher-level cognitive objectives and the expansion of the number of item formats. Before sending the assessment

material on for a formal review, it is useful for item writers to edit their own work.

*Step 5.* A systematic review of the assessment material and any scoring rubrics by content and measurement specialists is carried out, and the material is piloted with groups similar in characteristics to populations for whom the test is intended. A review of the assessment materials for ethnic, racial, and sex bias and stereotyping is also carried out at this step (see Holland & Wainer, 1993).

If multiple forms of the test are prepared for field testing (and this is common), a method is needed to ensure that the item and test statistics across forms are comparable. One way to accomplish this is to distribute the available test forms to students on a random basis (referred to as a randomly equivalent groups equating design). When this can't be done (often because of the nature of the assessments or other logistical reasons), another popular design is to include some common assessment material in each form (called common anchor equating). This design allows for statistical adjustments in the item and test statistics if the students assigned to each test form are not statistically equivalent.

*Step 6.* Based on the data from step 5, additional assessment development work may be carried out, and irreparably flawed material can be discarded.

*Step 7.* The test is assembled (or tests, if parallel forms are needed).

*Step 8.* Normally, a method for setting performance standards is selected and implemented.

*Step 9.* The test is ready for administration and, later, score reporting.

*Step 10.* Reliability and validity information should be collected, and test score norms (if desired) are compiled on appropriately selected samples of examinees.

*Step 11.* Administration and technical manuals should be prepared for the more important tests. In the case of commercially available, standardized criterion-referenced tests, the manuals are of considerable value in assessing quality and usefulness in particular settings.

*Step 12.* The psychometric properties of a test are not static, and therefore it is important over time to continue to assess the technical characteristics of the test and the scores derived from it with groups of examinees for whom the test is intended.

Berk (1984) and Popham (1978a, 1991) provide additional information about constructing criterion-referenced tests. Technical advances associated with several of the steps are considered in the next section.

## TECHNICAL ADVANCES

Six advances in criterion-referenced testing technology are considered in this section: writing objectives, assessing content validity, establishing reliability, selecting assessment material, setting performance standards, and investigating construct validity.

## Writing Objectives

Mager's (1962) classic book on preparing behavioral objectives had a tremendous impact on education in the 1960s and 1970s. Teachers were trained to write the objectives, curricula were defined by them, and tests were constructed to measure them. Behavioral objectives are relatively easy to write and have contributed substantially to the organization of curricula, but they do *not* lead to unequivocal determination of the domains of content or behaviors that describe the objectives. For example, consider the following: "The student will identify the main ideas in passages at the second-grade level." Are passages on any topic acceptable? How long should the passages be? Should the passages be narrative, descriptive, or expository in nature? What should be the readability level of the passages? Should the main idea be stated in the passage or inferred from a careful reading? Which of many item formats should be used?

Consider another objective: "The student will identify the tone or emotion expressed in a paragraph." Whether the objective is to be taught or whether assessment material to measure the objective is needed, several points need to be clarified first. Which tones or emotions are of interest? How long should the paragraphs be? At what readability level should the paragraphs be written? Also, a test item writer might wonder about the "fineness" of discriminations that are to be required of a student and which test item format should be used.

Popham (1974) referred to tests constructed from behavioral objectives as "cloud-referenced tests." The production of assessment material to measure objectives cannot be handled efficiently when the content domains are unclearly defined. Also, when the domains of content are unclear, it is not possible to ensure that representative samples of assessment materials from each item domain are drawn.

Domain specifications are one important development in criterion-referenced testing to address the problem of unclear domains of content (Popham, 1978a, 1991). A domain specification is prepared to clarify the intended content or behaviors specified by an objective. Test users find domain specifications helpful because the domains of content or behaviors to which test scores are referenced are more clear. For the item writer, domain specifications provide much needed clarification on the appropriate content for preparing assessment material.

Domains come in at least two varieties (Gray, 1978; Nitko, 1980). In an *ordered domain*, the subskills that describe an objective are arranged in some meaningful way, such as in a learning hierarchy. One of the advantages of an ordered domain is that statements of examinees' performance in relation to the domain can be made from a test that may measure only a few of the subskills. In an *unordered domain*, and this is the more common of the two, the content or behaviors defining the domain are specified but relationships among the component parts are not.

Popham (1978a, 1991) suggested four steps for the preparation of a domain specification. The first is the general description, which can be a behavioral objective, a detailed description of the objective, or a short cryptic descriptor. Second, sample assessment material is prepared. This material will reveal the desired assessment format and help to clarify appropriate approaches for assessment. The third step is usually the most difficult. It is necessary to specify the content or behaviors included in a domain. Occasionally, for the purpose of clarification, it is also desirable to indicate which content or behaviors are *not* included in a domain specification. Characteristics of response alternatives or response limits and/or the scoring rubric are specified in the final, fourth step.

Domain specifications of a high quality can be prepared in a variety of subject areas for different grade levels by groups of individuals with varying degrees of content and technical expertise. Additional guidelines for preparing domain specifications and a variety of examples are given by Popham (1978a, 1991).

More recently, it has become popular to limit the domain specification to a statement of the skill or skills and offer sample assessment items, with a scoring rubric, if a performance task is used (see, e.g., Popham, 1994). Perhaps the main advantage of this simplified format is that it is less constraining on assessment developers since they have the option of choosing the best format to assess the desired domain of content in a given situation. Also, a full explication of the domain of content matched to a higher-level cognitive objective is very difficult to do. Perhaps a few good examples of how the assessment of the objective might be carried out is sufficient to guide sound criterion-referenced test development. Finally, the domain specification format promoted the concept that there was a best way or perhaps only one way to define and assess the objective, which sometimes led to a narrowing of instruction and approaches used in assessment. The consequence, ultimately, is the limit on the generalizability of inferences from test scores to actual students' performance on educational tasks.

Popham (1994) offered this example for preparing specifications for materials in criterion-referenced assessments to match the desired educational outcome or objective:

*General Description.* Items can be phrased in a variety of ways, but they all must *require*

*the student to have recognized or inferred the central message of the selection or designated part of the selection.* Items may call for students to create or choose the most accurate summary of the selection or part of the selection, to identify or state the topic of all or a part of the selection, or to identify or state the main idea or central point of a selection or part of that selection. Items may or may not require the student to make an inference in order to select or construct the appropriate answer.

Illustrative, Nonexhaustive Items:

a. What is this selection mainly about?
b. Write a brief paragraph describing the theme of this passage.
c. Describe, in one sentence, the passage's central message.
d. What is the main point of this essay?
e. Orally, indicate what the main idea is of the passage's fourth paragraph.
f. Select the best statement of the essay's central message about human development:
   A. Nature is much more important than nurture.
   B. Nurture is much more important than nature.
   C. Nature and nurture are equally important.
   D. Neither nature nor nurture are all that important.

In these revised specifications, the desired objective, skill, or competency is described (or in Popham's words, "the score-based inference we desire to make" is described), and a variety of potentially valid assessment options are delineated. Popham believes that these revised specifications for describing educational objectives will be valuable to both educators and test developers without narrowing the curriculum or suggesting that there is a single best approach to assessment. They will also be easier to write, especially for higher-level cognitive objectives, which have become an integral part of curricula in the 1990s. Popham then calls for a major emphasis on validity studies to ensure that the assessments actually measure the desired outcomes. Two approaches to validation of score inferences from criterion-referenced tests follow.

## Assessing Content Validity

Assessment material is written after the domain specifications, in some form, have been prepared (see, e.g., Roid & Haladyna, 1982). Assessing content validity involves a consideration of three features of the assessment materials: (1) item validities (i.e., the extent to which each item or task measures some aspect of the content in the domain of interest), (2) technical quality, and (3) balance or representativeness (see, e.g., Crocker, 1997). Crocker, in fact, offers an eight-step plan for assessing content validity:

1. Defining the content domain. (This is an essential step in criterion-referenced development.)
2. Identifying criteria for evaluating the assessment material. (These are match to the desired content domain, technical quality, and representativeness.)
3. Structuring the review task for the expert judges.
4. Developing forms for judges to record their ratings. (See Hambleton, 1984, for examples.)
5. Specifying the qualifications of judges and recruiting them. (Desirable qualifications of judges often include years of teaching experience and subject matter expertise.)
6. Determining the minimum number of judges needed. (For important tests, such as high school graduation tests, a panel of 8 to 10 persons is common.)
7. Assessing the reliability of the judges' ratings. (Are judges consistent in their ratings? This is important in evaluating the information from judges.)
8. Summarizing and reporting the judges' ratings in a form understandable to the test developers.

The details for implementing several of the steps follow.

## Item Validity

The quality of criterion-referenced test materials can be determined, in part, by the extent to which they reflect, in terms of content, the domains from which they were derived. Unless one can say with a high degree of confidence that the assessment material in a criterion-referenced test measures the intended content domains, any use of the test score information will be questionable.

One approach to investigating item validity requires content experts to provide judgments of assessment materials. Several procedures have been suggested for obtaining judgmental data (Hambleton, 1984). For example, consider this set of directions:

> First, read carefully through the lists of domain specifications and assessment material. Next, please indicate how well you feel the material reflects the domain specification it was written to measure. Judge the assessment material solely on the basis of the match between its content and the content defined by the domain specification that the material was prepared to measure. Use the five-point rating scale shown below:

| Poor | Fair | Good | Very Good | Excellent |
|------|------|------|-----------|-----------|
| 1 | 2 | 3 | 4 | 5 |

Hambleton (1984) described a second procedure for conducting an item validity study. In this procedure (slightly edited from the original), reviewers are not told which domain specifications the assessment material was written to measure:

> Read carefully through the lists of domain specifications and assessment material. Your task is to indicate whether or not you feel the assessment material measures one of the domain specifications. It is, if you feel examinee performance on the assessment material would provide an indication of an examinee's level of performance measuring the domain specification. Beside each domain specification, write in the assessment material numbers or codes which you feel measure or could be used to assess the domain specification. In some instances, you may feel that the assessment material does not measure any of the available domain specifications. Indicate this on the rating form (p. 116).

With either procedure, a measure of the perceived match between assessment material and the objectives they were written to measure can be obtained, along with an indication of the agreement among the judges' ratings.

A second approach requires items to be pilot-tested on a group of examinees similar in characteristics to those for whom the test is intended. The item response data are analyzed to determine difficulty levels and discrimination indexes. An item or task that has a difficulty level that varies substantially from the difficulty levels of other items or tasks measuring the same domain specification should be studied carefully to determine if the variation is the result of a content or technical flaw. Items with very low or negative-valued discrimination indexes should also be studied carefully for flaws. Readers are referred to Berk (1984), Hambleton (1985), and Popham (1978a) for a discussion of additional item statistics and their usefulness in constructing criterion-referenced tests.

The use of item analysis techniques is important in the content-validation process. In situations in which at least a moderate-sized sample of examinees is available and the test constructor is interested in identifying aberrant items, not necessarily for elimination but for correction, the use of an empirical approach to item validation will provide important information about the assessment of item validity.

In sum, obtaining content experts' ratings is the method to use for assessing item validities; empirical procedures should be used for the detection of aberrant items in need of correction. An excellent review of item statistics for use with criterion-referenced tests was prepared by Berk (1984) and Downing and Haladyna (1997).

## *Technical Adequacy of Test Items*

The technical adequacy of assessment material can be established at the same time as this material is reviewed for the appropriateness of its content. Measurement specialists can be asked to review the material to identify flaws, such as poorly worded item stems and other violations of standard item preparation rules, and incomplete scoring rubrics. Technical review forms for sample items were presented by Hambleton (1984). Other technical flaws can be identified from the item analysis. Freedom from bias and stereotyping is also important and can be identified through judgmental reviews and statistical methods (see, e.g., Holland & Wainer, 1993).

## *Representativeness of the Test Items*

Content experts can be asked to evaluate the representativeness of the assessment material that is measuring the objectives. From a grid developed to describe the content or behaviors in a domain specification, content experts can evaluate the degree of item representativeness. For example, a group of judges can be asked, "How well does the assessment material sample the domain of content or behaviors defining the objective?" When representativeness has not been achieved

to some desired level, new assessment material should be added and/or material deleted to obtain the desired level of representativeness.

## Establishing Reliability

Criterion-referenced test scores are used, principally, in two ways: to describe examinees' levels of performance and to make performance-level classifications. In the first use, the precision with which domain scores are estimated is of interest.[1] Of interest in the second use is the test-retest decision consistency or parallel-form decision consistency. It is clear that the usual approaches to assessing test score reliability (test-retest reliability, parallel-form reliability, and corrected split-half reliability) do not address directly either use, and therefore they are of limited value in the context of criterion-referenced measurement (Hambleton & Novick, 1973).

It has been argued that classical reliability indexes are less useful with criterion-referenced tests because the scores are often fairly homogeneous, so these indexes will be low. But if low reliability indexes were the problem, it could be resolved by interpreting the indexes more cautiously in light of homogeneous test score distributions, adjusting reliability statistics for group homogeneity, or designing reliability studies to ensure more heterogeneous score distributions. In fact, classical reliability indexes are limited because they do not provide information that relates to either use of criterion-referenced test scores.

What follows are several practical approaches for addressing the reliability of criterion-referenced test scores and decisions.

## *Reliability of Domain Score Estimates*

The standard error of measurement or estimates of error associated with domain score estimates can easily be calculated. These are useful in setting up confidence bands for examinees' domain scores. Fortunately, they are not influenced by the homogeneity of the domain scores (Lord & Novick, 1968).

Another approach for determining the consistency of domain score estimates with *dichotomously scored* test items or tasks was reported by Millman (1974) and by Hambleton, Swami-

---

[1]An examinee's domain score is the proportion of items in an item domain that he or she can answer correctly. For performance tasks, domain score is an examinee's expected score over the domain of relevant tasks.

nathan, Algina, and Coulson (1978). They suggested that the standard error of estimation derived from the binomial test model given by the expression $\sqrt{\hat{\Pi}(1 - \hat{\Pi})/n}$ can be used to set up confidence bands around domain score estimates. Here, $n$ is the number of items measuring an objective and $\hat{\Pi}$ is the proportion-correct score for an examinee. For example, if an examinee answers 8 out of 10 binary-scored test items correctly, $n = 10$, $\hat{\Pi} = .80$, and the error associated with the domain score estimate is .13. Therefore, there is (approximately) a 68% chance that the examinee's domain score is somewhere in the interval .67–.93 (i.e., .8 ± .13). The main advantage of the binomial error model is that individual error estimates are obtained. But other estimates of error are possible, too.

## *Reliability of Performance-level Classifications*

Hambleton and Novick (1973) suggested that the reliability of performance-level classification decisions should be defined in terms of the consistency of decisions from two administrations of the same test or parallel forms of a test. Suppose that examinees are to be classified into $m$ performance levels. Hambleton and Novick suggested the following formula to measure the proportion of examinees who are consistently classified on the two administrations:

$$p_o = \sum_{j=1}^{m} p_{jj}$$

where $p_{jj}$ is the proportion of the examinees classified in the $j$th performance category on the two administrations, and $m$ is the number of performance categories. In practice, $m$ is usually equal to a value between 2 and 5. The index $p_o$ is the observed proportion of decisions that are in agreement. Among the factors that affect the value of $p_o$ are test length, quality of the assessment material, choice of performance standards,

test score heterogeneity, and the closeness of the group mean performance to particular performance standards. The $p_o$ statistic has considerable appeal and is easy to calculate.

In the sample data reported in Table 16.1 for a test designed to make a binary decision (i.e., $m = 2$), the proportion of examinees classified in the same way on the two administrations is .82 ($p_o = .16 + .66$). In other words, in the sample of examinees who were administered the test, 82% were classified in the same way (either as masters or nonmasters on both administrations) on the basis of their performance on the two administrations.

Swaminathan, Hambleton, and Algina (1974) argued that the statistic $p_o$ has one limitation: it does not take into account the proportion of agreement that occurs by chance alone. For example, suppose that examinees were assigned to one of two performance categories according to coin flips. Heads are "passers" and tails are "failures." By chance alone, 50% of the examinees will be classified into the same performance categories on "two administrations." Decision consistency is assessed to be 50%, and this is due to chance factors only. In assessing the consistency of decisions that result from the use of a test, it would seem desirable to account in some way for the agreement due to chance. Therefore, Swaminathan et al. suggested using coefficient $k$ (Cohen, 1960) as an index of decision consistency that is corrected for the agreement due to chance alone. This coefficient is

$$k = \frac{p_o - p_c}{1 - p_c}$$

where

$$p_c = \sum_{j=1}^{m} p_{j.} \, p_{.j}$$

The symbols $p_{j.}$ and $p_{.j}$ represent the proportions of examinees assigned to performance category $j$ on the first and second administrations,

---

**TABLE 16.1** **Mastery Classifications for a Group of Examinees on Two Parallel-Form Test Administrations**

| | Form B | | |
| Form A | Pass | Fail | Marginal Proportion |
|---|---|---|---|
| Pass | .66 | .14 | .80 |
| Fail | .04 | .16 | .20 |
| Marginal Proportion | .70 | .30 | |

respectively. The symbol $p_c$ represents the proportion of agreement that would occur even if the classifications based on the two administrations were totally independent events. The statistic $k$ can be thought of as a measure of decision consistency that is over and above the decision consistency due to chance alone.

When the formula is applied to the results in Table 16.1,

$$p_o = .66 + .16$$
$$= .82$$
$$p_c = (.80 \times .70) + (.20 \times .30)$$
$$= .62$$
$$k = \frac{.82 - .62}{1 - .62}$$
$$= .53$$

The properties of $k$ have been discussed in detail by Cohen (1960). The upper limit is +1 and can occur only when the marginal proportions for different administrations are equal. (This condition is met when the two forms of the test are strictly parallel.) The maximum lower limit is close to −1 and depends on a number of factors. The precise maximum lower limit of $k$ is unimportant in the context of criterion-referenced testing, however, because any negative values indicate considerable inconsistency and, therefore, highly unreliable decisions. Negative values are unacceptable, regardless of how close they are to the maximum lower limit.

The coefficient $k$ depends on all factors that affect the decision-making procedure: the performance standards, the heterogeneity of the group of examinees, and the method of assigning examinees to performance categories. Therefore, it is useful to report all of these factors when reporting $k$ since this information contributes to its interpretation. It is common for decision consistency, $k$, the score distributions on each administration, scoring model, and performance standards to appear in a technical manual, to aid in the interpretation of the reliability results.

The concept of decision consistency is a useful one in the context of criterion-referenced measurement, but the approaches described require the administration of a single test twice or the administration of parallel forms of a test. In either case, testing time is doubled. These approaches are often difficult or impossible to implement in practice because of limited testing time. With norm-referenced tests, one way to avoid the extra testing time in assessing reliability is to use the split-half method to determine

the reliability of scores from a test that is one-half as long as the one of interest. Next, the Spearman-Brown formula is used, along with the split-half reliability estimate, to predict the reliability of scores with the test of interest. Unfortunately, the approach used with norm-referenced test scores cannot be applied to the problem of assessing consistency of decisions that emanate from a single administration of a criterion-referenced test because the Spearman-Brown formula is not applicable. A rather different approach for estimating decision consistency from a single administration of a criterion-referenced test was developed by Subkoviak (1976). Although the mathematical development of the formula is not comparable, Subkoviak's formula is the analogue of the corrected split-half reliability index that is used with norm-referenced tests to estimate parallel-form reliability from a single test administration.

It is also possible to obtain an estimate of $k$ by using Subkoviak's (1976) method. The only additional information needed is the proportion of examinees assigned to each performance category on the single test administration. By making the reasonable assumption that these proportions would be the same on a retest or a parallel-form administration, the proportion of agreement expected by change ($p_c$) can be obtained by the method introduced earlier.

Recently, extensions of Subkoviak's (1976) work have been reported for polytomously scored items or tasks. Livingston and Lewis (1995) have produced a straightforward set of calculations for estimating decision consistency from a single administration of a criterion-referenced test in which the items and/or tasks are polytomously scored. This work is a major step forward for assessing criterion-referenced test reliability since single administration estimates are preferred, and polytomously scored data are now common.

Brown (1990) has provided a useful summary of easy-to-calculate criterion-referenced test reliability statistics, and Berk (1980) and Traub and Rowley (1980) have included useful reviews of approaches for estimating the reliability of criterion-referenced test scores and decisions.

## Selecting Assessment Material

The item selection process is straightforward, provided that the criterion-referenced test developer has been careful in defining objectives and in constructing assessment materials. Larger domains require special attention to ensure that representative samples of assessment materials are drawn. With large domains especially, it helps to prepare a grid to organize the relevant content or behaviors. A test is usually constructed by taking either a random or a stratified random sample of assessment material from each domain of interest.

The consistency and validity of performance category decisions can be increased by, in general, increasing the amount of assessment material. But this approach has practical limits because of the time available for assessment. When the primary purpose of a testing program is to make performance category classifications, a better test will result if the assessment material is selected from the available pool of items measuring each objective on the basis of statistical properties.

For example, suppose that a single performance standard is set at 80% correct in the domain of test items measuring an objective. Test items that discriminate effectively in the region of the performance standard on the test score scale will contribute most to decision consistency and validity (see, Hambleton, Swaminathan, & Rogers, 1991). A test constructed in this way will have maximum discriminating power in the region of the score scale where decisions are to be made; therefore, more reliable and valid classification decisions will result.

One possible drawback of this approach to optimal test construction, as it is called, is that scores produced by the test cannot be used directly to make descriptive statements about examinees' levels of performance because the assessment material measuring each objective would not necessarily constitute a representative sample. There is at least one way to make descriptive statements about examinees' level of performance when nonrandom or nonrepresentative samples of assessment materials are selected: By introducing concepts, assumptions, and models from the field of item response theory (Hambleton, 1989; Hambleton et al., 1991), it is possible to make statistical adjustments in the test scores for the nonrepresentative set of assessment material and obtain unbiased estimates of domain scores.

## Setting Performance Standards

One of the primary purposes of criterion-referenced testing in schools is to make decisions about students. This requires performance standards. Sometimes one performance standard is needed, as with high school graduation tests. Recently, it has become popular to sort students into many performance categories, such as below basic, basic, proficient, and advanced (see, e.g., Hambleton, 1996). In these situations, multiple performance standards must be set.

At the outset it is essential to stress that *all* standard-setting methods involve judgment and are arbitrary. Some researchers have argued that arbitrary standards are not defensible (Glass, 1978). Popham (1978a) countered with the following response:

> Webster's Dictionary offers us two definitions of arbitrary. The first of these is positive, describing arbitrary as an adjective reflecting choice or discretion, that is, "determinable by a judge or tribunal." The second definition, pejorative in nature, describes arbitrary as an adjective denoting capriciousness, that is, "selected at random and without reason." In my estimate, when people start knocking the standard-setting game as arbitrary, they are clearly employing Webster's second, negatively loaded, definition.
>
> But the first definition is more accurately reflective of serious standard-setting efforts. They represent genuine attempts to do a good job in deciding what kinds of standards we ought to employ. That they are judgmental is inescapable. But to malign all judgmental operations as capricious is absurd. (p. 168)

Today it seems to be well recognized that errors in student placement or classification will result from the use of performance standards, regardless of how well they are set. At the same time, if the test is well constructed and appropriate steps in setting performance standards are followed, the student performance classifications can be defended.

Perhaps the best way to defend a particular set of performance standards on a criterion-referenced test is to demonstrate that a reasonable process was followed in arriving at the final standards (Hambleton, Jaeger, Plake, & Mills, in press; Hambleton & Powell, 1983). If the process reflects careful attention to the (1) selection of panelists, (2) training of panelists, (3) aggregation of data into a final set of standards, (4) validation of the performance standards, and (5) careful documentation of the process, the defensibility of the resulting standards is considerably increased.

We now discuss 11 steps in the setting of performance standards.

1. Choose a panel (large and representative of the stakeholders).

   *Discussion:* Who are the stakeholders in the decisions that will be made in educational assessments? These are the persons who should be involved in the standard-setting process. With important criterion-referenced tests, such as high school graduation tests, 15 to 20 persons are often placed on a panel to provide the diversity that is needed (geographical, cultural, gender, age, technical background, and educational responsibilities) and to provide stable estimates of the performance standards (Hambleton et al., in press; Jaeger, 1991).

2. Choose one of the standard-setting methods, prepare training materials, and set the meeting agenda.

   *Discussion:* There are many acceptable methods for setting performance standards (Jaeger, 1989). Some of them focus panelists' attention on the items and tasks in the assessment, and others on the students and their work on the items and tasks in the assessment (Hambleton et al., in press; Livingston & Zieky, 1982; Popham, 1978b).

3. Prepare descriptions of the performance categories (e.g., advanced, proficient, and partially proficient).

   *Discussion:* In recent years, time spent on defining the performance-level descriptions has increased considerably in recognition of their importance. In setting performance standards on the National Assessment of Educational Progress, for example, more than two full days are spent on descriptions. Recently, Mills and Jaeger (1997) produced the first published set of steps for producing test-based descriptions of performance levels.

   The following are descriptions used recently in the setting of grade 4 performance standards in reading on the National Assessment of Educational Progress. They provide a good idea of the detail that is needed.

   *Basic.* Demonstrates an understanding of the overall meaning of what they read. When reading text appropriate for fourth graders, they should be able to make relatively obvious connections between the text and their own experiences, and extend the ideas in the text by making simple inferences.

   *Proficient.* Demonstrates an overall understanding of the text, providing inferential as well as literal information. When reading text appropriate to fourth grade, they should be able to extend the ideas in the text by making inferences, drawing conclusions, and making connections to their own experiences. The connection between the text and what the student infers should be clear.

   *Advanced.* Generalizes about topics in the reading selection and demonstrates an awareness of how authors compose and use literary devices. When reading text appropriate to fourth grade, they should be able to judge texts critically and, in general, give thorough answers that indicate careful thought.

4. Train the panelists to use the method (including practice in providing ratings).

   *Discussion:* Effective training for panelists would include (a) explaining and modeling the steps to follow in setting standards, (b) showing the scoring keys and/or scoring rubrics and ensuring they are understood, (c) completing rating forms, (d) giving practice in providing ratings, (e) explaining any normative data that will be used in the process, and so on.

5. Compile item ratings or other data from the panelists (e.g., panelists specify *expected performance* of borderline basic students).

   *Discussion:* This step is straightforward if the training has been effective. A summary of the panelists' ratings can be prepared. For example, suppose panelists are asked to judge the minimum expected performance of proficient students on a task with a five-point scoring rubric (e.g., 0 to 4). The median or typical rating and the range of ratings of the panelists could be calculated. Later (step 6), this information can be given to the panelists and used to initiate discussion about the performance standard for proficient students.

6. Conduct a panel discussion: consider actual performance data (e.g., item difficulty values).

   *Discussion:* It is common to ask panelists to work through the method and set preliminary performance standards, and then to participate in a discussion of these initial standards and actual performances of the students on the test. The purpose of the discussion and feedback is to provide the opportunity for panelists to reconsider their initial ratings and to identify errors or any misconceptions or misunderstandings that may be present.

7. Compile item ratings a second time (could be followed by more discussion, feedback, etc.).

   *Discussion:* Following the discussion phase of the process, panelists are instructed to provide a second set of ratings. It is not necessary for panelists to change any of their initial ratings, but they are given the opportunity to do so (for an example, see Hambleton & Plake, 1997).

8. Compile panelists' ratings and average to obtain the performance standards.

   *Discussion:* At this step, panelists' ratings are compiled to arrive at the performance standards. Often, this is simply an average of the performance standards set by each panelist.

9. Present consequences data to the panel (e.g., passing rate).

   *Discussion:* One step that is sometimes inserted into the process is the presentation of consequential data to panelists. Panelists are informed about the percentage of students who would be located in each performance category. If these findings are not consistent with the panelists' experiences and sense of reasonableness, they could be given the opportunity to revise their performance standards.

10. Revise, if necessary, and finalize the standard(s); conduct an evaluation of the process itself, and determine the panelists' level of confidence in the standards.

    *Discussion:* Again, panelists are given the opportunity to revise their ratings to increase or decrease their performance standards. In addition, an evaluation of the process should be conducted.

11. Compile technical documentation to support the validity of the standards.

    *Discussion:* Not only is it important to be systematic and thoughtful in designing and carrying out a performance standard-setting project, but it is also necessary to document the work that was done and by whom (Kane, 1994). A good example of documentation is seen in the report by Hambleton and Bourque (1991).

Many standard-setting methods have been described, compared, and critiqued in the criterion-referenced testing literature (Berk, 1986; Cizek, 1996a, 1996b; Glass, 1978; Hambleton, Jaeger, Plake, & Mills, 1998; Hambleton et al., in press). These methods can be organized into two main categories: methods in which panelists are focused on a review of test content, called test-based methods, and methods that are focused on the students themselves, called student-based methods. A brief description of these methods follows. In the measurement literature, nearly all of them have been applied to setting a *single* performance standard on a total test score. Many of these methods can be extended to multiple standards. Also, they may be applied to individual objectives or groups of objectives that make up a criterion-referenced test.

Brief descriptions of several of the popular methods follow.

## Test-based Methods

With the test-based methods, individual items are studied to judge how well a borderline student will perform. The borderline student is someone who is judged to have a proficiency score located at the performance standard. With some criterion-referenced tests, there may be several borderline students of interest; for example, one at basic, one at proficient, and one at advanced. The ratings process described next is repeated for each borderline student.

Panelists are asked to assess how or to what degree a student who could be described as borderline would perform on each item or task. The choice of method is inserted into steps 2 and 4 in the standard-setting process.

### Ebel's Method

With the Ebel (1972) method, panelists rate assessment material along two dimensions: relevance and difficulty. There are four levels of relevance in Ebel's method: essential, important, acceptable, and questionable. These levels are often edited or collapsed into two or three levels when the method is used in practice. Ebel used three levels of item or task difficulty: easy, medium, and hard. These levels of *relevance or importance* and *difficulty* can be used to form a 4-by-3 grid for sorting the assessment material. The panelists are asked to do two things:

1. Locate each assessment item or task in the proper cell, based on its perceived relevance and difficulty

2. Assign a percentage to each cell that represents the percentage of score points in the cell that the borderline student should be able to obtain

The number of score points in each cell is multiplied by the percentage assigned by the panelist; the sum of these products, when divided by the total number of score points on the test, yields the performance standard. As with all of the judgmental methods, the standards set by the individual panelists are averaged to obtain a final standard. The process can be repeated for each borderline student of interest to arrive at other performance standards.

### Angoff's Method

When using Angoff's (1971) method with multiple-choice test items, panelists are asked to assign a probability to each test item directly, thus circumventing the analysis of a grid or the analysis of answer choices. Each probability is to be an estimate of whether the borderline student will answer the test item correctly (e.g., the borderline basic student). Assigned probabilities by individual panelists for items in the test can be summed to obtain a standard, and then the panelists' standards can be averaged to obtain a final standard. This process is repeated for each performance standard of interest. The performance standard descriptions are especially useful in operationalizing the borderline students.

Here is one example, from the *Handbook for Panelists*, of the Angoff (1971) method's instructions to panelists who set the 1990 performance standards on the NAEP Mathematics Test (Hambleton & Bourque, 1991):

> For the *Borderline Basic* student, your task is to specify the probability that this borderline student should answer each item in the assessment correctly. This chance or probability for each test item can range from zero (where you would be specifying that the borderline student should have no chance of giving a correct answer) to 1.00 (where you would be specifying that the borderline student should, without a doubt, answer the item correctly). After specifying the performance level for the Borderline Basic student on an item, you should provide estimates on the same item for the *Borderline Proficient* and *Borderline Advanced* students.

As with the other judgmental methods, common practice is to repeat the probability specification process following a discussion among the panelists about their assigned probabilities. Often, too, panelists are given item statistics or information that addresses the consequences (i.e., passing and failing rates) of various performance standards to help them in the standard-setting process.

### Student-based Methods

With student-based methods, judgments are made by panelists about the mastery status of a sample group of students from the population of interest. For example, suppose the goal is to classify students into one of four performance categories: below basic, basic, proficient, and advanced. In a school, these judgments would come from the teachers. The choice of method determines the nature of the required judgments. Next, the groups for whom mastery determinations have been made are given the test. Details are offered next for analyzing the judgmental data and the test scores.

### Contrasting Groups Method

Working with the descriptions of each performance category, teachers are asked to classify their students. The test is administered to the students, and the score distributions for the students assigned to each performance category are compared. The point of intersection is often taken as the initial performance standard. An example from Hambleton, et al. (in press) is given in Figure 16.3. With four groups, first the point of intersection of the advanced (A) and proficient (P) distributions is determined to select the advanced performance standard. Then the proficient and partially proficient (PP) score distributions are compared to determine the proficient standard, and so on.

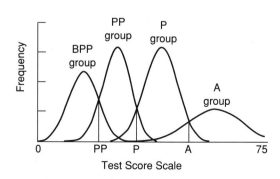

**FIGURE 16.3 Application of the contrasting groups standard-setting method.**

The validity of this approach depends, in part, on the appropriateness of the panelists' classifications of students. On the one hand, if the teachers tend to err in their classifications by assigning students to higher groups than those to which they truly belong, the result is that standards from the contrasting groups method are lower than they should be. On the other hand, the standards tend to be higher if teachers err by assigning students to lower performance groups than those to which they truly belong.

## New Approaches to Standard-setting

Standard-setting has always been the Achilles heel of criterion-referenced testing. At the best of times there has been a concern for both the most suitable method for setting performance standards and validity evidence to support them. Now, there is a new challenge for setting standards: performance assessments. For example, the Kentucky Department of Education has moved to a total performance-based assessment system for school accountability. Most other states are using performance assessments in student accountability with criterion-referenced tests.

Performance assessments are often associated with complex and polytomous (i.e., more than two score points per task) scoring rubrics, multidimensionality in the response data (i.e., the tasks require multiple skills for successful completion), interdependencies in the scoring rubrics (sometimes, if students miss one part of a task, they are unable to complete the remainder because of the absence of a key piece of information), and low score generalizability at the task or exercise level (students who perform well on one group of tasks cannot be assumed to be high performers on another group).

These features of performance-based criterion-referenced tests create special problems for standard-setting methods. For example, several of the popular standard-setting methods, such as the Angoff (1971), Ebel (1972), and Nedelsky (1954) methods, are not even applicable with performance assessments, which are polytomously scored. The challenge is to adapt old standard-setting methods or develop new methods to meet the current characteristics of performance assessments and the existing standards of quality and defensibility. Descriptions of two promising methods follow. Others are considered by Hambleton et al. (1998, in press).

### *Extended Angoff*

Consistent with the traditional Angoff (1971) methodology, panelists estimate the performance of borderline (or minimally competent) students. Panelists are trained to estimate the number of score points that probably would be obtained by borderline students. Also, with this variation of the Angoff method, panelists can set weights for exercises for the total assessment to use in computing the composite performance standard. Exercises judged as more important can be assigned higher weights. Recent research with this method has produced promising results (Hambleton & Plake, 1995).

### *Paper Selection*

When using the paper selection approach, panelists are instructed to select actual products (papers, projects, etc.) that they believe are associated with borderline students who took the assessment (Hambleton & Plake, 1997; Jaeger & Mills, 1997). After some discussion among panel members about their selections, revised selections can be made. The average score associated with the papers identified as borderline is one way to arrive at the performance standard (other ways are described by Jaeger & Mills). This method is being used, on an experimental basis, by some state departments of education, by the National Board of Medical Examiners, and the Educational Commission for Foreign Medical Graduates.

One major advantage of this method is that panelists are required to look at the work products of students. Often, they find this activity to be very interesting and meaningful. A major disadvantage is that the method can be very time-consuming and difficult to implement in practice. For example, when the students' work involves videotapes, reports, projects, and so on, sorting through for examples of borderline work can be very tedious, if not totally impractical.

## Investigating Construct Validity

It is essential to establish the validity of the descriptions and decisions made from the criterion-referenced test scores (Messick, 1989; Popham, 1994). Content validity evidence is easy to obtain and highly relevant; however, this evidence is not sufficient since it pertains to the content of the test, whereas descriptions of examinees' level of performance and classification decisions are based on examinees' *responses* to the assessment material. For example, a set of test items, on the basis of content considerations, may appear to be measuring "understanding," whereas they are actually measuring "recall of factual information."

It is essential to establish the content representativeness of a set of test items, but the usefulness of a set of criterion-referenced test scores (or, for that matter, scores obtained from any test) must be determined by a carefully designed series of construct validation investigations. This point was brought to the attention of criterion-referenced test developers by Messick (1975, 1989) and more recently by Popham (1994). Messick wrote,

> The major problem . . . is that content validity . . . is focused upon test forms rather than measurements. Inferences in educational and psychological measurement are made from scores, and scores are a function of subject responses. Any concept of validity of measurement must include reference to empirical consistency. Content coverage is an important consideration in test construction and interpretation, to be sure, but in itself it does not provide validity. (pp. 960–961)

Messick also offered a useful definition of construct validation: "Construct validation is the process of marshaling evidence in the form of theoretically relevant empirical relations to support the inference that an observed response consistency has a particular meaning" (p. 955).

Fortunately, a wide assortment of methods (intratest, intertest, experimental, prediction) can be used to provide validity evidence for intended uses of a set of test scores (Hambleton, 1984; Kane, 1994; Popham, 1994). Of course, accumulating construct validation evidence is a never-ending process. The amount of time and effort given to construct validation efforts should be consistent with the importance of the testing program. Criterion-referenced tests that are being used to monitor students' progress in the curriculum on a day-to-day basis should demand less time, obviously, than tests that will be used to determine whether or not students will graduate from high school.

Construct validation studies should begin with a statement of the purpose of the test scores. A clearly stated use will provide direction for the kind of evidence that is worth collecting. Later, when all of the data are collected and analyzed, a final conclusion about the validity of the intended use (or uses) of the test scores can be offered. Several types of construct validation investigations are briefly considered here.

## Factor Analysis

Factor analysis is a commonly employed procedure for the dimensional analysis of items in a norm-referenced test or of scores derived from different norm-referenced tests, but it has been used less often in construct validation studies of criterion-referenced test scores. One reason for its more limited use is that the usual input for factor analytic studies are correlations, and correlations are often low between items on a criterion-referenced test or between criterion-referenced test scores and other variables because score variability is often not very great. The problem can be resolved by choosing samples of examinees with a wide range of ability, for example, groups of students at different performance levels.

Domain scores from a criterion-referenced test (or multiple tests, if available) can be factor-analyzed, and the resulting factor structure can be compared to a structure based on theoretical considerations. Similar empirical and theoretical structures provide evidence of construct validity of the domain scores.

## Sources of Invalidity

Many sources of error can reduce the validity of an intended use of a set of criterion-referenced test scores. Suppose, for example, that an examinee was estimated to have an 80% level of performance on a test measuring "ability to identify the main idea in paragraphs." Is the test score valid for the intended interpretation? The answer depends on the answers to several other questions:

1. Were the test directions unclear to the student?
2. Did the student have a problem in using the answer sheet?
3. Was the test administered under speeded conditions?
4. Was the student unmotivated to perform to the best of his or her ability?
5. Was the vocabulary in the passage at a suitable readability level?
6. Did test-taking skills play any role in the student's test performance?

The usefulness or validity of the test scores and associated performance classifications is reduced if any of these (and many other) irrelevant factors influenced examinee's performances.

Experimental studies of potential sources of error to determine their effect on test scores are another important way to assess the construct validity of a set of test scores. Logical analyses and observations of testing methods and procedures can also be used to detect sources of invalidity in a set of test scores.

## Criterion-related Validity

Even if scores derived from criterion-referenced tests are descriptive of the objectives they are supposed to reflect, the usefulness of the scores as predictors of (say) "job success" or "success in the next unit of instruction" cannot be assured. Criterion-related validity studies of criterion-referenced test scores are no different in procedure from studies conducted with norm-referenced tests. Correlational, group-separation, and decision-accuracy methods are commonly used (Messick, 1989).

## Decision Validity

Instructional decisions based on criterion-referenced test scores can be validated by comparing the test performance, in relation to a standard of performance, of two criterion groups—those who have received instruction and those who have not. In an alternative design, two groups might be formed by asking teachers to identify students whom they are certain have an excellent grasp of the skills measured by the test under study and those who do not—and often this is a stronger research design. Decision validity on each objective may be assessed by summing the number of instructed examinees who exceed the performance standard and the number of uninstructed examinees who do not. The assumption is that these are the students who are correctly classified by the testing procedure. If these numbers are high, compared to the total number of students, decision validity has been demonstrated. Of course, this type of study is not without criticism because some of the uninstructed students will have knowledge of the content covered by the test, and some of the students in the instructed group will not. It is for this reason that the second design may be preferable since the classification of students to performance categories by teachers may provide a more satisfactory criterion for addressing criterion-referenced test score validity. Decision validity studies can easily be extended to handle the assignment of students to multiple performance categories.

The findings from decision validity studies are reported in a readily understandable way (percentage of correct decisions resulting from the use of the test and associated performance standard). Alternatively, the correlation between two dichotomous variables (group membership and the mastery decision) can be reported and used as an index of decision validity. Other possible statistics are reported by Berk (1976) and Popham (1978a).

Decision validity will depend on several important factors: (1) the quality of the criterion-referenced test under investigation, (2) the appropriateness of the criterion groups, and (3) the performance standards. Therefore, when decisions that result from the test are not consistent with decisions based on the criterion, there may be many explanations, each of which can be explored to determine its validity.

# SUGGESTIONS FOR SELECTING AND EVALUATING CRITERION-REFERENCED TESTS

A study of the major test publishers' catalogues and/or a review of the *Mental Measurement Yearbooks* reveals the existence of a large number of commercially available criterion-referenced tests. These tests range considerably in the content they cover, the grade levels for which they are appropriate, their special options, and technical quality.

A number of suggestions for selecting and evaluating criterion-referenced tests for use in schools are offered: preliminary, practical, content, and technical considerations. Professional standards for evaluating criterion-referenced tests are given in the *Standards for Educational and Psychological Tests* (American Educational Research Association, American Psychological Association, & National Council on Measurement in Education, 1985), in Hambleton and Eignor (1978), and in the soon to be published edition (expected in 1999) of the *Standards*.

## Preliminary Considerations

Before initiating a search for a criterion-referenced test, a clear statement of the intended uses of the test score information is needed. Information about the match between a test's purposes and the proposed uses is helpful in deciding whether to reject a test outright or retain it for additional review. Also, there are other preliminary considerations that can be used to reduce the pool of suitable tests: specification of the variables of interest (e.g., prereading skills) or the curriculum areas is a basis for excluding many tests from further consideration. Also, tests can be rejected if they are not suitable for administration to the populations of interest. For example, some tests will be unsuitable for examinees with handicaps. Tests that remain after a screening, using these three preliminary considerations, can be reviewed further in relation to the practical, content, and technical requirements.

## Practical Considerations

### Cost

There is little point in reviewing a test for adoption if the cost of test booklets, answer sheets, and scoring exceeds the budget. Scoring of performance assessments can be especially costly and may delay the process of obtaining score reports. Money can sometimes be saved by scoring tests locally, but if the scoring is complicated or if a variety of summary reports are required (e.g., class, grade, school, and district test score summary reports), local test scoring will not usually be practical.

### Availability and Number of Levels

When tests are to be used to monitor examinees' progress over a number of years, a criterion-referenced test battery that includes a sequenced set of tests (varying in difficulty) is preferable to a test from a different test publisher at each grade level. Within a particular test battery, there is uniformity of test directions, answer sheets, terminology, reporting scales, and norm groups, which greatly enhances the validity and usefulness of test score information.

### Parallel Forms

The importance of this feature will depend on the intended uses of the test scores. Often teachers want to monitor students' progress over short periods of time (two weeks, for example). It is better to pretest and posttest with parallel forms (rather than use the same form twice) to reduce the influence of memory on test performance. The impact of memory effects on test performance is reduced when the time between test administrations is increased, but memory remains a factor; thus whenever a test is to be used to monitor a student's growth or development, tests with parallel forms are preferable.

### Item Formats

Item format is an important consideration because it influences the objectivity and speed of test scoring and the skills that can be measured.

### Mode of Administration

Paper-and-pencil test administrations are common, but tests administered at a computer are becoming feasible and increasingly popular. Computer-administered tests are often more expensive, but the advantages include (1) flexibility in scheduling test administrations, (2) immediate feedback (at least on objectively scorable components of the test), (3) adapting test difficulty to the ability level of examinees (this feature can shorten testing time, lower test anxiety levels, and increase test motivation), and (4) using novel item formats to enhance test validity (Bennett & Ward, 1993).

### Administration Time

A test should not be adopted simply because it can be administered in a class period or a time period of interest. But to disregard time considerations completely would be a mistake. For example, tests that are very short require less time to administer, but reliability and validity of test scores will, in general, be lower. Some tests are of a length that would make them administratively inconvenient.

### Qualifications of Administrators

Some tests can only be administered by people with special training. One must ensure that a suitably trained administrator is available (or can be trained).

### Types of Reports and Scores

It is essential to match the types of reports and test information needed with what is available with each test under consideration. For example, a district may want student, parent, teacher, building, and district reports of a student's performance or may need special reports for Title I. Another common request is for grade-level and out-of-level norms with criterion-referenced tests. Not all publishers provide the same types and amounts of test score information, so there is need to consider this very important area carefully.

## Content and Technical Considerations

Following are 23 questions that address important content and technical considerations in evaluating criterion-referenced tests. Many of the questions are self-explanatory. For those that are not, brief comments are provided.

1. Do the content specifications for the test cover the content domain of interest?

   When a curriculum is clearly described, a measure of overlap between the curriculum and the test content specifications can be determined. This is referred to as the curriculum relevance of the test.

2. Are the content specifications clear?

   One of the differences between norm-referenced tests and criterion-referenced tests is the clarity of the content specifications. Content specifications for criterion-referenced tests must be clearer to permit valid score interpretations and evaluation of assessment materials.

3. Is it possible to tailor the test to meet local needs? (Sometimes, this feature is desired.)

4. Are the persons who prepared the test content and statistical specifications, objectives, and assessment materials qualified?

5. Does the test appear to have content validity?

6. Are the assessment materials technically sound?

7. Are the assessment materials free of bias and stereotyping?

   Assessment material that is disadvantageous to a group of examinees because of sex, ethnic background, or race is inappropriate in any kind of test. It is common practice to seek the views of appropriate reviewers about item bias. Also, item bias can be identified by comparing the performance levels of contrasting groups matched on ability, for example, males and females (see, e.g., Hambleton, Clauser, Mazor, & Jones, 1993; Holland & Wainer, 1993).

8. Was a suitable sample of examinees used to pilot-test the items?

   A suitable sample is one that is not too small to produce stable item statistics and is representative of the populations in which the test will be used. Sometimes nonrepresentative samples can be justified when the oversampling of one segment of the population is done to ensure sufficiently large numbers of people from special populations to facilitate item bias analyses.

9. Were item statistics used correctly in constructing the test?

   Some test publishers use item statistics as they would if they were constructing a norm-referenced test. This is incorrect. Item statistics with criterion-referenced tests are especially helpful in the following situations: (a) detecting flawed items, (b) constructing parallel tests, and (c) conducting post hoc reliability studies. Item statistics should not be used in item selection except when a test is being built to optimally discriminate at a particular point (or points) on a test score scale.

10. Do the directions inform examinees about the test's purpose, time limits, marking answer sheets (or booklets), and scoring? Are sample questions available?

11. Are the answer sheets easy for examinees to use?

12. Are the test administrator's directions complete? (Do they provide step-by-step activities for the administrator? Do they provide answers to typical student questions? Do they address matters pertaining to testing conditions, such as lighting and ventilation?)

13. How appropriate is the print size, quality of printing and pictures, and page layouts for the examinees?

14. Are the samples of examinees included in any reliability studies of a suitable size and representative of the populations in which the test will be used?

15. Are the correct kinds of reliability indexes reported?

    The kinds of reliability indexes that are valuable are tied directly to the intended uses of the test scores. When scores are used for descriptive purposes, reliability indexes that reflect the degree of score precision (e.g., the standard error of measurement) are useful. When scores are used to assign examinees to performance categories, an estimate of test-retest or parallel-form decision consistency will be informative. When average group performance is of central interest, some indication of the error associated with each mean is desirable.

16. Are the appropriate reliability indexes high enough to justify the use of the test in the intended situation?

    There are no established minimally acceptable reliability levels. But they should be reported for potential users to make their own determinations of acceptability.

17. Is a discussion of the factors that influence reliability indexes in the technical manual?

18. Is there an explanation in the technical manual for the setting of performance standards?

(Alternatively, is a process described in the technical manual to help users select and apply a standard-setting method?)

19. Is evidence offered for the validity of the uses of the criterion-referenced test scores and performance classifications?

    No matter how carefully performance standards are set, evidence for the validity of the resulting classifications is needed. For example, if a suitable external criterion measure (e.g., teacher evaluations) can be found, the extent of agreement in decisions from the test and the criterion measure is very useful information.

20. Does the technical manual include a discussion of factors that might influence the validity of test scores and decisions?

21. Are details provided in the technical manual for interpreting test scores?

22. Do the score report forms address the specific needs of users?

    A criterion-referenced testing program is of limited value if the test score information is not reported in ways that meet the needs of users. For example, it is common to want student, teacher, building, and district reports. Are these reports available? Can test scores be summarized for special groups of students, such as Title I students?

23. Are the score report forms convenient and understandable?

    Our impression is that there is considerable room for improvement in the communication of test results. It is important to carefully review the reports to ensure their clarity and understandability to the intended audiences. Try-outs of the report forms with appropriate audiences can be very helpful.

These questions should be helpful in the evaluation and selection of commercially available criterion-referenced tests, or they may serve as considerations in the development of criterion-referenced tests by a school district or a state department of education.

## Summary

Following is a set of steps for evaluating and selecting a criterion-referenced test:

1. Select a committee to carry out the review process.

2. Specify the intended uses of the test, content areas of interest, and groups to be assessed.

3. Identify a set of tests that satisfy the preliminary considerations. The *Mental Measurements Yearbook*, measurement textbooks, and test catalogues will be helpful in locating tests.

4. Prepare test reviews by considering practical, content, and technical matters.

5. Specify both the essential and the most important characteristics of the desired test.

6. With the test reviews from step 4 and the information from step 5, identify the most suitable test.

7. Periodically review the suitability of the chosen test by interviewing users of the test and by conducting psychometric investigations of test scores.

## CONCLUSIONS

Testing practices have changed considerably since Robert Glaser introduced criterion-referenced testing to the educational measurement field in 1963. According to Linn (1994), "Glaser's concept of criterion-referenced measurement ranks high among a small list of seminal ideas that have had a lasting impact on the thinking and practice of educational measurement" (p. 12).

Several of the changes brought about by criterion-referenced testing were discussed by Hambleton (1994) in a tribute to Glaser in a special issue of *Educational Measurement: Issues and Practice* in honor of the thirtieth anniversary of his seminal paper.

1. *Clarification in specifying performance outcomes:* Educational tests are more useful today because of the focus on defining what it is that tests actually measure. This emphasis has resulted in more attention to test validation and to content-referenced score interpretations. Tests, today, are capable of addressing such questions as "What do students know and what can they do?"

2. *Progress in item writing and increased emphasis on content validity:* With a focus on defining what tests measure, there has been an expanded concern for the development of content-valid assessments. This expanded concern for content validity in educational assessment has resulted in the development of a wide array of new item formats to enhance the validity of criterion-referenced tests (see, e.g., Hambleton, 1996).

3. *New approaches for reliability and validity assessment and proficiency estimation:* Al-

though decision theoretic models, Bayesian estimation procedures, and other psychometric techniques were developed to address technical matters associated with criterion-referenced testing, many of these advances are now being applied widely in the field of educational and psychological measurement.

4. *New standard-setting methods and improved implementation:* This topic has seen major advances since the introduction of criterion-referenced testing in 1963. Today, there are multiple methods for standard setting on paper-and-pencil and performance assessments, and many related issues in setting standards have been carefully researched and resolved; the consequence is more defensible performance standards (see, e.g., Cizek, 1996a, 1996b; Hambleton et al., 1998, in press).

5. *Increased emphasis on diagnosis, decision making, and criterion-referenced interpretations:* Criterion-referenced testing provides valuable information to teachers that can improve educational experiences for students. Norm-referenced test scores such as percentile scores and grade-equivalent scores cannot affect day-to-day classroom instruction or the diagnosis of students' strengths and weaknesses. Criterion-referenced tests can be beneficial in day-to-day management of classroom instruction, assist in the diagnosis of learning problems, and provide a basis for judging students' progress in the curriculum.

6. *Improved training of teachers in the area of assessment:* With the introduction of criterion-referenced testing, teachers have been required to learn more about the specification of objectives, approaches to measuring objectives, new item formats, test construction, and so on. All of these new skills have made them more effective in the classroom.

The implementation of criterion-referenced testing programs in schools has reached substantial proportions. Furthermore, the establishment of criterion-referenced testing programs at district and state levels ensures that many school-children will be affected by criterion-referenced test score results in the coming years.

In this chapter, current methods for constructing and evaluating criterion-referenced tests were discussed, along with a comparison of norm- and criterion-referenced tests. Criterion-referenced testing has changed over the years.

Today, (1) more tests are used to assess higher-level cognitive outcomes of instruction, (2) item formats are not limited to multiple-choice test items, (3) computers are being used to administer and score criterion-referenced tests, and (4) more attention is being given to test accommodations of students with special needs. In the coming years, school psychologists might expect to see these same four trends continued and expanded, with cognitive science having more influence on the nature of the variables assessed.

# REFERENCES

American Educational Research Association, American Psychological Association, & National Council on Measurement in Education. (1985). *Standards for Educational and Psychological Tests.* Washington, DC: American Psychological Association.

Angoff, W. H. (1971). Scales, norms, and equivalent scores. In R. L. Thorndike (Ed.), *Educational measurement* (2nd ed.). Washington, DC: American Council on Education.

Bennett, R. E., & Ward, W. C. (Eds.). (1993). *Construction versus choice in cognitive measurement issues in constructed response, performance testing, and portfolio assessment.* Hillsdale, NJ: Erlbaum.

Berk, R. A. (1976). Determination of optimal cutting scores in criterion-referenced measurement. *Journal of Experimental Education, 45,* 4–9.

Berk, R. A. (1980). A consumer's guide to criterion-referenced test reliability. *Journal of Educational Measurement, 17,* 323–349.

Berk, R. A. (Ed.). (1984). *A guide to criterion-referenced test development.* Baltimore, MD: Johns Hopkins University Press.

Berk, R. A. (1986). A consumer's guide to setting performance standards on criterion-referenced tests. *Review of Educational Research, 56,* 137–172.

Brown, J. D. (1990). Short-cut estimators of criterion-referenced test consistency. *Language Testing, 7*(1), 77–97.

Cizek, G. J. (1996a). Setting passing scores. *Educational Measurement: Issues and Practice, 15,* 20–31.

Cizek, G. J. (1996b). Standard-setting guidelines. *Educational Measurement: Issues and Practice, 15,* 28–31.

Cohen, J. (1960). A coefficient of agreement for nominal scales. *Educational and Psychological Measurement, 20,* 37–46.

Crocker, L. (1997). Assessing content representativeness of performance assessment exercises. *Applied Measurement in Education, 10*(1), 83–95.

Downing, S. M., & Haladyna, T. M. (1997). Test item development: Validity evidence from quality assurance procedures. *Applied Measurement in Education, 10*(1), 61–82.

Ebel, R. L. (1972). *Essentials of educational measurement.* Englewood Cliffs, NJ: Prentice Hall.

Glaser, R. (1963). Instructional technology and the measurement of learning outcomes. *American Psychologist, 18,* 519–521.

Glass, G. V. (1978). Standards and criteria. *Journal of Educational Measurement, 15,* 237–261.

Gray, W. M. (1978). A comparison of Piagetian theory and criterion-referenced measurement. *Review of Educational Research, 48,* 223–249.

Hambleton, R. K. (1984). Validating the test scores. In R. A. Berk (Ed.), *A guide to criterion-referenced test construction.* Baltimore, MD: Johns Hopkins University Press.

Hambleton, R. K. (1985). Criterion-referenced assessment of individual differences. In C. Reynolds & V. L. Wilson (Eds.), *Methodologies and statistical advances in the study of individual differences.* New York: Plenum.

Hambleton, R. K. (1989). Principles and selected applications of item response theory. In R. L. Linn (Ed.), *Educational measurement* (3rd ed.). New York: Macmillan.

Hambleton, R. K. (1994). The rise and fall of criterion-referenced measurement? *Educational Measurement: Issues and Practice, 13,* 21–26.

Hambleton, R. K. (1996). Advances in assessment models, methods, and practices. In D. C. Berliner & R. C. Calfee (Eds.), *Handbook of educational psychology* (pp. 899–925). New York: Simon & Schuster.

Hambleton, R. K., & Bourque, M. L. (1991). *The levels of mathematics achievement: Initial performance standards for the 1990 NAEP Mathematics Assessment* (Technical Report, Vol. 3). Washington, DC: National Assessment Governing Board.

Hambleton, R. K., Clauser, B. E., Mazor, K. M., & Jones, R. W. (1993). Advances in the detection of differentially functioning test items. *European Journal of Psychological Assessment, 9*(1), 1–18.

Hambleton, R. K., & Eignor, D. R. (1978). Guidelines for evaluating criterion-referenced tests and test manuals. *Journal of Educational Measurement, 15,* 321–327.

Hambleton, R. K., Jaeger, R. M., Plake, B. S., & Mills, C. N. (1998). *Handbook for setting standards on performance assessments.* Washington, DC: Council of Chief State School Officers.

Hambleton, R. K., Jaeger, R. M., Plake, B. S., & Mills, C. N. (in press). Setting standards on performance assessments: Advances, issues, and remaining problems. *Applied Psychological Measurement.*

Hambleton, R. K., & Novick, M. R. (1973). Toward an integration of theory and method for criterion-referenced tests. *Journal of Educational Measurement, 10,* 159–170.

Hambleton, R. K., & Plake, B. S. (1995). Using an extended Angoff procedure to set standards on complex performance assessments. *Applied Measurement in Education, 8,* 41–56.

Hambleton, R. K., & Plake, B. S. (1997, March). An anchor-based procedure for setting standards on performance assessments. Paper presented at the meeting of the American Educational Research Association, Chicago.

Hambleton, R. K., & Powell, S. (1983). A framework for viewing the process of standard-setting. *Evaluation and the Health Professions, 6,* 3–24.

Hambleton, R. K., Swaminathan, H., Algina, J., & Coulson, D. B. (1978). Criterion-referenced testing and measurement: A review of technical issues and developments. *Review of Educational Research, 48,* 1–47.

Hambleton, R. K., Swaminathan, & Rogers, H. J. (1991). *Fundamentals of item response theory.* Newbury Park, CA: Sage.

Holland, P. W., & Wainer, H. (Eds.). (1993). *Differential item functioning.* Hillsdale, NJ: Erlbaum.

Jaeger, R. M. (1989). Certification of student competence. In R. L. Linn (Ed.), *Educational measurement* (3rd ed., pp. 485–514). New York: Macmillan.

Jaeger, R. M. (1991). Selection of judges for standard setting. *Educational Measurement: Issues and Practice, 10,* 3–6, 10.

Jaeger, R. M., & Mills, C. (1997, March). A holistic procedure for setting performance standards on complex large-scale assessments. Paper presented at the meeting of the American Educational Research Association, Chicago.

Kane, M. (1994). Validating the performance standards associated with passing scores. *Review of Educational Research, 64,* 425–462.

Linn, R. L. (1994). Criterion-referenced measurement: A valuable perspective clouded by surplus meaning. *Educational Measurement: Issues and Practice, 14*(4), 12–14.

Livingston, S. A., & Lewis, C. (1995). Estimating the consistency and accuracy of classifications based on test scores. *Journal of Educational Measurement, 32*(2), 179–197.

Livingston, S. A., & Zieky, M. J. (1982). *Passing scores: A manual for setting standards of performance on educational and occupation tests.* Princeton, NJ: Educational Testing Service.

Lord, F. M., & Novick, M. R. (1968). *Statistical theories of mental test scores.* Reading, MA: Addison-Wesley.

Mager, R. F. (1962). *Preparing instructional objectives.* San Francisco: Fearon.

Mellenbergh, G. J., & van der Linden, W. J. (1979). The internal and external optimality of decisions based on tests. *Applied Psychological Measurement, 3*(2), 257–273.

Messick, S. A. (1975). The standard problem: Meaning and values in measurement and evaluation. *American Psychologist, 30,* 955–966.

Messick, S. A. (1989). Validity. In R. L. Linn (Ed.), *Educational measurement* (3rd ed., pp. 13–103). New York: Macmillan.

Millman, J. (1974). Criterion-referenced measurement. In W. J. Popham (Ed.), *Evaluation in education: Current applications.* Berkeley, CA: McCutchan.

Mills, C. N., & Jaeger, R. J. (1997). Creating descriptions of desired student achievement when setting performance standards. In L. Hansche (Ed.), *Handbook for setting performance standards.* Washington: Council of Chief State School Officers.

Nedelsky, L. (1954). Absolute grading standards for objective tests. *Educational and Psychological Measurement, 14,* 3–19.

Nitko, A. J. (1980). Distinguishing the many varieties of criterion-referenced tests. *Review of Educational Research, 50,* 461–485.

Popham, W. J. (1974). An approaching peril: Cloud-referenced tests. *Phi Delta Kappan, 56,* 614–615.

Popham, W. J. (1976). Normative data for criterion-referenced tests. *Phi Delta Kappan, 58,* 593–594.

Popham, W. J. (1978a). *Criterion-referenced measurement.* Englewood Cliffs, NJ: Prentice Hall.

Popham, W. J. (1978b). *Setting performance standards.* Los Angeles: Instructional Objectives Exchange.

Popham, W. J. (1991). *Modern educational measurement: A practitioner's perspective.* Englewood Cliffs, NJ: Prentice Hall.

Popham, W. J. (1994). The instructional consequences of criterion-referenced clarity. *Educational Measurement: Issues and Practice, 13*(4), 15–18, 30.

Popham, W. J., & Husek, T. R. (1969). Implications of criterion-referenced measurement. *Journal of Educational Measurement, 6,* 1–9.

Roid, G. H., & Haladyna, T. M. (1982). *A technology for test-item writing.* New York: Academic Press.

Subkoviak, M. (1976). Estimating reliability from a single administration of a criterion-referenced test. *Journal of Educational Measurement, 13,* 265–275.

Swaminathan, H., Hambleton, R. K., & Algina, J. (1974). Reliability of criterion-referenced tests: A decision-theoretic formulation. *Journal of Educational Measurement, 11,* 263–268.

Traub, R. E., & Rowley, G. L. (1980). Reliability of test scores and decisions. *Applied Psychological Measurement, 4,* 517–546.

## CHAPTER 17

# PERSONALITY ASSESSMENT IN THE SCHOOLS

**FRANCES F. PREVATT**[1]
*Texas A & M University*

Changes in public policy, federal legislation, and the social and economic climate have spearheaded a call for reforms in service delivery models of school psychologists (Bradley-Johnson, Johnson, & Jacob-Timm, 1995; Conoley & Gutkin, 1995; Tapasak & Keller, 1995). Bradley-Johnson et al. contend that school psychologists will suffer if they continue to serve as test-oriented gatekeepers whose primary function is to engage in cost-ineffective assessments that lead to placements in empirically untested programs. It is estimated that school psychologists spend an average of 50% of their time in assessment activities (Stinett, Harvey, & Oehler-Stinett, 1994).

Several aspects of current training and service delivery models are criticized by both Bradley-Johnson et al. (1995) and Conoley and Gutkin (1995). First, school psychologists are too busy testing to be involved in inclusion, despite the fact that numerous political, educational, economic, and social forces are intensifying the trend toward inclusion. Second, training in assessment continues to focus on individual approaches, labeling of pathology, and utilization of techniques with poor psychometric standards. Again, the field is ignoring a move toward ecological approaches, which emphasize multiple factors that affect the child, such as classroom, instructional, home, and family

variables. Third, assessments are not outcome-oriented and do not lead to interventions that are empirically validated. For example, Bradley-Johnson et al. cite studies showing that the average estimated cost of an assessment for special education eligibility is $1,230 per student, with the resulting evaluation providing little of value in instructional interventions. Many personality assessments remain oriented toward the primary objective of determining eligibility for special education services. Bradley-Johnson et al. cite a sixfold increase in enrollments in special education classes from 1953 to 1963, despite no substantial body of data to demonstrate their effectiveness.

This chapter is intended to be consistent with a model for effective personality assessment that considers new trends in service delivery. Several current issues in personality assessment are first presented: adherence to special education law, multimodal assessment, prereferral issues, and projective techniques. Next, a model for effective personality assessment is presented, followed by several specific assessment techniques.

## CURRENT ISSUES IN PERSONALITY ASSESSMENT

### Adherence to Special Education Law

In 1975 Congress passed the Education of All Handicapped Children Act (PL 94-142). This was amended in 1990 and is now known as the Individ-

---

[1]This chapter was written in November, 1995. Dr. Prevatt is currently affiliated with Florida State University

uals with Disabilities Act (IDEA). Several components of IDEA must be taken into consideration when conducting school-based assessments of social and emotional functioning. Initially, assessments require prior consent of parents. Informed consent documents must be in the parents' native language and must include the reasons for the evaluation, the types of procedures to be used, what the assessment results will be used for, and who will have access to the results (Jacob-Timm & Hartshorne, 1994). Other regulations specific to personality assessment require the evaluation to be nondiscriminatory: tests should be standardized and have normative data consistent with the characteristics of the examinees for whom they are used, tests should be validated for the specific purpose for which they are going to be used, and tests should be given in a child's native language only if the test has been validated for that purpose. If the test cannot be administered in the child's native language, an interpreter should be used who has specific credentialing in nonbiased assessment of minority language students. The evaluator must be trained to administer all tests in conformance with the instructions provided by the test developer. No single assessment procedure may be used to make a sole determination of eligibility. Also, IDEA requires a family assessment, based on a face-to-face interview with the child's parents or guardians.

Other federal regulations require that a distinction be made between social maladjustment (SM) and serious emotional disturbance (SED). This regulation has created a great deal of controversy about whether the exclusionary clause for SM should be utilized and, if so, how it should be defined and implemented. Unfortunately, nowhere in PL 94-142 or IDEA is SM defined. Furthermore, there is no commonly accepted definition of SM among professionals (Clarzio, 1992). Skiba, Grizzle, and Minke (1994) have determined that only 34 states (67%) include the exclusionary SM clause in their definition of SED. Of these 34 states, only 7 include a published definition of SM. Three states actually provide guidelines for differential diagnosis or suggestions for screening techniques. For example, Texas gives brief descriptions of the differences between SM and SED students in emotional reactions, thoughts, social support, self-control, social relationships, self-esteem, self-awareness, and responsiveness to treatment (Texas Education Agency, 1990). Clearly, there is a need for practitioners to be aware of individual state mandates and definitions of social maladjustment before they attempt to assess a child for SED.

## Multimodal Assessment

It has been consistently argued that a valid assessment of a child's behavioral and emotional problems requires gathering information from multiple sources (Achenbach, 1993; Greenbaum, Dedrick, Prange, & Friedman, 1994). For school psychologists, these would probably include the child, his or her parents, one or more teachers, and possibly a counselor. Unfortunately, it is also well documented that information from multiple sources tends to be very poorly correlated. A meta-analysis of 119 studies reported an average correlation between parents' and teachers' reports of childhood adjustment as .27 and between parents' and childrens' reports as .25 (Achenbach, McConaughy, & Howell, 1987). Several investigators have attempted to explore this phenomena. Stanger and Lewis (1993) found that when parents, teachers, and children gave ratings on internalizing and externalizing problems, children generally reported the most problems and teachers the fewest. Ritter (1989) found that for a sample of emotionally disturbed adolescents, regular education teachers reported more behavior problems and poorer school adaptive functioning than did special education teachers. Frick, Silverthorne, and Evans (1994) found that teachers disagreed with both parents and children on ratings of children's anxiety and that mothers tended to overreport anxiety, depending on their own symptomatology.

In a study specifically dealing with the assessment of depression, it was found that a self-report, a peer report, and teachers' reports of depression were measuring generally uncorrelated, independent constructs (Crowley, Worchel, & Ash, 1992). It was hypothesized that the difference in reporting was due to the fact that the three tests contained very different items. However, further analysis showed that all three tests contained items that were very similar in content, however, when this subset of similar items was evaluated, low correlations across tests were still evident. It was concluded that low convergence across multiple sources is *not* due to different test items, rather, different respondents evaluate symptomatology differentially. This finding was supported in a recent meta-analysis of 137 studies of childhood depression. Thomas (1995) found consistently low correlations between children's and teachers' reports and between parents' and children's reports, even when different raters were given the same test.

Piacentini, Cohen, and Cohen (1992) note a general agreement in the literature that adults are better informants than children for observable or objective phenomena and children are better reporters for subjective states. Thus, the dilemma for the evaluator is to determine the usefulness of the information collected. When children, teachers, and parents provide discrepant information, whose viewpoint should be treated as the "truth?" If a child relates no symptoms of depression, yet parents and teachers report significant concerns in this area, do we assume that the child is using denial? Does the validity of the information depend on the age of the child, the symptom being observed, gender, or personal characteristics of the other raters? These and other concerns have become so prevalent that in 1990, the National Institute of Mental Health invited 100 eminent scientists and researchers to discuss critical issues in children's mental health. On this topic, the consensus was that "no approach has been able to provide a persuasive rationale and method for combining information about children from multiple informants and sources of data . . . the issue . . . bedevils most child and adolescent psychopathology researchers who rely on multi-informant assessment approaches," (Jensen et al., 1993, p. 551).

Many explanations have been offered for *why* information from different sources may be incongruent. Elliot, Busse, and Gresham (1993) conclude that many rating scales attempt to quantify behaviors that vary widely in frequency, intensity, and duration. Greenbaum et al., (1994) place some of the blame on method effects, such as social desirability, the halo effect, or acquiescence of the rater. Each of these might cause a rater to consciously or unconsciously give responses that are biased in some way by external circumstances or demand characteristics of the testing situation. Of course, it is also possible that the instruments used in data collection are psychometrically unstable.

Several solutions to the problem have been offered. Foremost, one would attempt to use assessment techniques with adequate norms, standardization, and well-documented validity and reliability characteristics. Some investigators have suggested using decision rules for weighing information based on rater and diagnosis. Other possibilities include assuming that the rater who reports a given symptom is "correct;" for example, if a child denies a symptom and a teacher reports that same symptom, assume that the symptom is actually there (Loeber, Green, Lahey, & Stout-Loeber, 1989). Stanger and Lewis (1993) consider establishing different cutoff or criterion scores for different raters. Alternately, the evaluator could merely treat variability as a source of valuable information (Verhulst, Koot, & van der Ende (1994). Using this logic, discrepancies are treated as valid indications that behavior is different in different settings or across time. When one does reach high levels of consensus across raters, one can have greater confidence in the generality of the behavior problems, which would imply the need for more intensive special education interventions (Martens, 1993).

In summary, it appears clear that a comprehensive personality assessment must include data from multiple sources. Integrating these data will take considerable skill and requires awareness of current research on convergence of data from various reports. The evaluator must be careful not to automatically rule out a diagnosis because there is no agreement across sources.

## The Referral Process

As noted, there is a consensus that future service delivery models need to change the current system under which many school psychologists spend a majority of their time engaged in assessment and placement of children in special education classes. One problem with the current system is that it has led to an inappropriate number of placements of minority children. The U.S. Department of Education (1992) has concluded that the proportion of minority youths in special education programs is much larger than their representation in the school population. Robles-Pina (1996) contends that inappropriate referrals and evaluations are especially likely for language minority children because their inability to acquire communication skills can be seen in a variety of difficulties, including increased behavioral problems.

A second problem with the current system is that once referred, students who are tested are highly likely to be placed in special education classes (Robles-Pina, 1996). If a student is referred for an evaluation, the probability is 92% that the student will be tested, and if tested, the probability is about 73% that the student will be declared eligible for special education services (Algozzine, Christenson, & Ysseldyke, 1982). Although this might be appropriate if special education placements were the best alternative for all children referred, research has shown that this is not the case. Consultation with regular education teachers and in-class early interventions may be more effective for many children.

One solution to the current referral-assessment-placement model involves prereferral systems. Numerous investigations have supported the use of prereferral interventions in regular classrooms as an alternative to assessment and placement (Graden, Casey, & Christenson, 1985; Rosenfeld, 1992). According to Bradley-Johnson et al. (1995), prereferral systems can reduce referrals by as much as one-half. It is clear that current models of personality assessment must begin *before* the actual assessment. School psychologists can be the impetus for innovative systems that result in formal personality assessments only as a final process in an outcome-oriented service delivery model.

## Projective Techniques

There has been a great deal of debate in recent years about the validity of projective techniques for school-based assessments. Projective techniques are typically defined as measures that involve an ambiguous stimulus, thus allowing a response that integrates both past experience and current psychological concerns (Worchel & Dupree, 1990). Traditionally, such tests as the Rorschach, thematic storytelling techniques, and human figure drawings have been classified as projective. These techniques have been widely criticized as being psychometrically untenable (Anastasi, 1981; Dean, 1984; Lanyon, 1984). In fact, some authors have asserted that projective techniques are not even tests and therefore should not be subjected to the constraints normally applied to psychometric devices (cited in Chandler, 1990).

A distinction needs to be made, however, between the nature of the test stimuli and the psychometric properties of a test. The Rorschach, which is reviewed later in this chapter, can be used for illustrative purposes. Historically, the Rorschach clearly met the criteria for a projective test. The test stimuli, ink blots, were ambiguous in nature. There was no right or wrong answer to the question "What might this be?" In fact, one might assert that the only "right" answer was that they were splotches of ink. Also, the original scoring of the Rorschach relied heavily on the content of the responses as interpreted from a psychoanalytic perspective. As one might expect, interrater reliability of scoring was low. For example, one clinician's interpretation of the response "a scary dark man coming to get me" might be very different from another's interpretation.

Whereas the ambiguity of the test stimuli have not changed in 50 years, the scoring systems developed for the Rorschach have changed dramatically. The Exner (1993) system views the Rorschach technique as a measure of cognitive, perceptual problem solving. Scoring is based on an empirically derived system, with extensive evidence relating to reliability, validity, and development of the normative sample. Does this mean that the Rorschach, using the Exner system, no longer qualifies as a projective technique? Does the label *projective* apply only to the test stimuli or also to the way in which the scoring system is developed and utilized? The reviews in this chapter are predicated on the belief that the term *projective* should be used with caution and that personality assessment techniques should not be discarded simply because of a possibly misleading label. Rather, one should evaluate individual techniques according to their psychometric qualities, cost effectiveness, and suitability for a particular child and situation.

## A MODEL FOR EFFECTIVE PERSONALITY ASSESSMENTS

Clearly, there is a need for personality assessments to keep pace with calls for reform in the roles and functions of school psychologists. Figure 17.1 presents a model of effective assessment based on current trends in service delivery models. This figure is based on an ecological approach to personality assessment. The ecological approach considers the multiple factors that might affect behavior: the individual child, the home and family, the social and cultural environment, the classroom, and the teacher. Prereferral interventions, which might preclude the need for assessment, should be considered initially. Once a valid referral is received, the school psychologist must pay careful attention to current state and federal guidelines for consent, assessment, and decision making. There should be a careful evaluation, based on technical adequacy, of the techniques utilized, including evidence for the reliability, validity, and adequacy of the standardization norms. Multimodal assessments should be employed. Since so many of the children evaluated are minorities, the evaluator should have

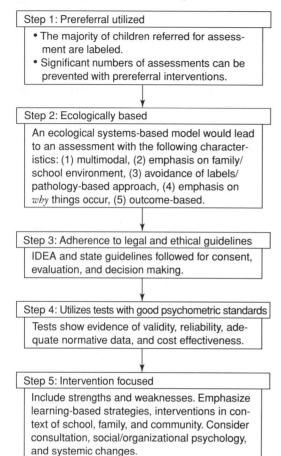

Step 1: Prereferral utilized

- The majority of children referred for assessment are labeled.
- Significant numbers of assessments can be prevented with prereferral interventions.

Step 2: Ecologically based

An ecological systems-based model would lead to an assessment with the following characteristics: (1) multimodal, (2) emphasis on family/school environment, (3) avoidance of labels/pathology-based approach, (4) emphasis on *why* things occur, (5) outcome-based.

Step 3: Adherence to legal and ethical guidelines

IDEA and state guidelines followed for consent, evaluation, and decision making.

Step 4: Utilizes tests with good psychometric standards

Tests show evidence of validity, reliability, adequate normative data, and cost effectiveness.

Step 5: Intervention focused

Include strengths and weaknesses. Emphasize learning-based strategies, interventions in context of school, family, and community. Consider consultation, social/organizational psychology, and systemic changes.

**FIGURE 17.1   A model for effective personality assessment.**

special training in nonbiased assessment practices. The evaluation should be outcome-based, the end point being effective interventions rather than mere labeling. Interventions should incorporate both the strengths and weaknesses of the child and the system within which the child lives.

The entire process should consider the most recent scientific research in assessment processes, tests utilized, and interventions recommended. For example, recent research suggests that children with serious emotional disturbances have a graduation rate of about 36%, compared to 71% for all students. What might be the most effective intervention for these children: inclusion, self-contained classes, alternative schools, related services like counseling or family therapy? Does research support a particular approach for children with similar characteristics in a similar environment? The evaluator must also be aware of recent trends in educational processes, effective

instruction, social and organizational change models, and family-school collaboration projects. Would consultation with teachers on instructional techniques be more suitable than child-based interventions? Might the psychologist use theories of organizational or social psychology to implement changes at the school or district level? A model that considers multiple levels and interacting spheres of functioning is more likely to result in an assessment that leads to positive outcomes.

## ASSESSMENT TECHNIQUES

In selecting techniques to review, I used three criteria: (1) classic techniques that retain high ratings for test usage and for which there have been new research investigations or significant changes in the tests in the past five years; (2) new tests that have not been reviewed previously but are consistent with current guidelines for test development and psychometric standards; and (3) a selection of tests that results in a reasonable range of different types. Since relatively few tests are able to be reviewed in depth, references or further readings for additional tests are also included.

### Multimodal Assessment Techniques
#### Child Behavior Checklist

The Child Behavior Checklist (CBCL) is a multimodal, empirically based assessment technique for children aged 2 to 18 (Achenbach, 1991a, 1991b, 1991c, 1991d). Depending on the age of the child, this technique includes parent-, self-, and teacher-report measures, as well as a semi-structured clinical interview and a direct observation form. Since the early 1990s, several revisions have been made to the CBCL. With well over 1,500 published reports on its usage and translations in 41 languages, the CBCL appears to be one of the most widely used and documented instruments of its kind for children and adolescents.

The CBCL/2–3 and CBCL/4–18 are parent-report forms, which include syndrome scales, broadband Internalizing and Externalizing Scales, and total problem scales. The CBCL/4–18 also includes three competence scales: School, Activities, and Social. The Youth Self Report (YSF), is suitable for ages 11 to 18, with scales similar to the CBCL/4–18. In addition, the YSF includes socially desirable items. The Teacher's Report

Form (TRF), for ages 5 to 18, obtains teachers' ratings of behavior problems, academic performance, and adaptive functioning, with scales similar to the CBCL/4–18. The CBCL/4–18, the YSF, and the TRF are combined to produce eight cross-informant scales: Aggressive Behavior, Anxious/Depressed, Attention Problems, Delinquent Behavior, Social Problems, Somatic Complaints, Thought Problems, and Withdrawn. These scales measure problem dimensions that are similar for both sexes, for all ages, and for each informant and show promising cross-cultural generalizability (DeGroot, Koot, & Verhulst, 1994).

Other new or revised additions to the CBCL include a Semistructured Interview for Children and Adolescents (SCICA) and the Direct Observation Form (DOF). The SCICA employs open-ended questions during a 90-minute clinical interview, addressing activities, school, friends, family relations, fantasies, self-perceptions, and problems reported by parents or teachers. It also includes brief tests of academic achievement and screens for fine and gross motor skills. The DOF is designed to record and rate direct observations of the child's problems during 10-minute time samples in classrooms or other group situations. The observer writes a narrative description and then rates the child on each of 96 items. A training cassette and manual are available to assist in scoring the DOF.

Since 1991, new profiles, manuals, and computer software for the CBCL/4–18, CBCL/2–3, TRF, YSR, and SCICA have been produced, as well as a cross-informant computer program that enables the user to enter up to five informants. Separate publications by the authors detail the use and integration of the information derived from the CBCL/4–18, TRF and YSR. The 1991 revisions of the CBCL, TRF, and YSR have been renormed on a national sample of 4 to 18-year-olds. These profiles provide normalized $T$ scores and percentiles, with cutoffs for borderline and clinical ranges for problem and competence scales. These cutoffs differ from the pre-1991 system in that they are based on the ability to discriminate matched referred from nonreferred children by utilizing analyses of relative operating characteristics (ROC) (Swets & Pickett, 1982).

Psychometric information on the 1991 revisions continues to be produced, with documentation of good reliability and validity. Information from the test manuals show problems only for the TRF interrater reliabilities, and it is suggested that TRFs should be obtained from more than one teacher whenever possible (McConoughly, 1993). Reviews of the CBCL changes have been largely positive (e.g., Elliot et al., 1993; Martens, 1993). Minor difficulties have been noted in both reviews, including problems with the new factor structure of the Internalizing and Externalizing Scales to remove overlap, continued problems with within-source variance (e.g., content, time, and informants), and questionable reliabilities of the clinical and borderline ranges.

Achenbach and McConaughy (1987) have continued to refine a system of empirically based, multiaxial assessment, based on the components just described, in conjunction with other procedures like historical records, medical exams, and standardized psychological and educational tests. This model utilizes five axes, labeled Parent Report, Teacher Report, Cognitive Assessment, Physical Assessment, and Direct Assessment.

In summary, the revised CBCL components have been reworked extensively to balance the benefits of an integrated system with the difficulties inherent in utilizing multiple informants. The revisions to the CBCL, in particular the new norms, attention to issues of interpretation and integration, development of the cross-informant syndromes, and refinement of the multiaxial-axial model, are all impressive. Although there are criticisms of some of the statistical decisions made in revising the test (e.g., eliminating the overlap in the Internalizing and Externalizing Scales or using ROC analyses to arrive at critical score cutoffs), there will be tradeoffs in many decisions of this nature, and it appears that Achenbach and colleagues have used logical and sophisticated techniques to address many of the problems of the older CBCL. Finally, the wealth of published studies on the CBCL provide ample opportunity for the practitioner or researcher to carefully evaluate the usefulness of this technique for his or her own purposes.

## Behavior Assessment System for Children

The Behavior Assessment System for children (BASC) is an integrated assessment technique specifically designed to conduct school-based assessments of emotional and behavioral disorders (Reynolds & Kamphaus, 1992). Designed for ages 4 to 18, the BASC has five components: parents', teachers', and self-ratings; developmental history; and classroom observation.

The Self-Report of Personality (SRP) has separate forms for children 8 to 11 and for adolescents aged 12 to 18. The Teacher Rating Scales (TRS) and the Parent Report Scales (PRS) each have three separate age forms: 4 to 5, 6 to 11, and 12 to 18. All three forms include adaptive and clinical scales. Scales vary by age and form. The SRP includes Anxiety, Atypicality, Locus of Control, Social Stress, Attitudes to School, Attitudes to Teachers, Depression, Sense of Inadequacy, Relations with Parents, Interpersonal Relations, Self-Esteem, and Self-Reliance. The SRP adolescent form adds Sensation Seeking and Somatization. The Emotional Symptoms Index is a composite score, indicating serious emotional disturbance. The TRS includes Aggression, Hyperactivity, Conduct Problems, Anxiety, Depression, Somatization, Attention Problems, Learning Problems, Atypicality, Withdrawal, Adaptability, Leadership, Social Skills, and Study Skills, which are further grouped into one adaptive and three clinical composite scores and a Behavioral Symptoms Index. The PRS scales and composite scores are similar to those in the TRS, deleting Learning Skills and Study Skills. All three scales have a "faking bad" scale. The SRP has a random responding check, and the adolescent SRP has a "faking good" scale.

The Structured Developmental History (SDH) can be written by the respondent or conducted as an interview (both are typically completed by the parent). It includes developmental history, psychosocial, and medical information. The Student Observation System (SOS) is intended for 15-minute observations and has three components: a behavior checklist, a time-sampling record, and space for anecdotal observations. Neither the SDH nor the SOS has norms, formal scores, or specific information about interpretation.

The BASC data from the TRS, PRS, and SRP are converted to linear $T$ scores, percentiles, and confidence intervals, as well as strengths and weaknesses across composites. The $T$ score is used to establish cutoffs for the clinically significant (based on discrepancy of 2 standard deviations) and those at risk (based on discrepancy of 1 standard deviation). A computer scoring program is available. Three separate norms are provided: (1) general, (2) by gender, and (3) compared to a clinical population.

The psychometric data to date are provided by the test developers. Reliability (internal consistency, test-retest, and interrater) is judged to

be acceptable, with the exception of interrater reliability for the TRS preschool form (Flanagan, 1995). Validity is established in comparison to a number of instruments: the CBCL parent and teacher forms (Achenbach, 1991b, 1991c), the Revised Behavior Problem Checklist (Quay & Peterson, 1983), the Conners Parent Scales (Conners, 1989), and the Minnesota Multiphasic Personality Inventory (MMPI; Hathaway & McKinley, 1943), as well as in relation to groups of children with diagnosed personality disorders. Overall validity studies support the use of the test (Sandoval & Echandia, 1994). As would be expected, correlations are variable because of different scaling of instruments.

Two recent reviews of the BASC were generally quite positive. Flanagan (1995) predicts that it will become "a mainstay in school psychology practice." Flanagan is particularly impressed with the BASC's conformity to requirements imposed by the Individuals with Disabilities Act (IDEA) in evaluating personality, social history, and classroom observations, as well as the inclusion of norms for seriously emotionally disturbed children. She further praises the BASC's usefulness in reconciling data from multiple instruments with different scaling. Sandoval and Echandia (1994) refer to the BASC as "one of the most useful and sophisticated of all the new measures available" and are generally positive about its psychometric properties. Concerns about the BASC include the lack of minority norms, low teacher-interrater reliability on some of the preschool forms, lack of norms and guidance in interpreting the SDH and SOS, and difficulty in comparing multiple forms without the computer program.

The BASC has a much shorter history than the CBCL, and more time is needed to investigate its psychometric properties. However, it appears to be a promising system, geared specifically to the needs of school psychologists. In particular, the test is extremely well designed, user friendly, adheres to sound practices of test development, and provides an integrated battery for making placement and treatment decisions consistent with federal law on special education.

## Interviews and Observations

Clearly, interviews and observations will be a cornerstone of any comprehensive evaluation. As these two techniques are now included as components of both the BASC and the CBCL, they will not be described further. Several excellent sources for independent interviewing and observational skills are available. The reader is referred to the following sources for further information: Barrios (1993), Greenspan (1981), Hodges and Zeman (1993), and Hughes and Baker (1990).

## Picture Drawings

In a 1983 survey, picture drawings were rated as the third-most frequently used personality assessment technique, falling behind only the interview and classroom observations (Prout, 1983). More than a decade later, a sample from the National Association of School Psychologists (NASP) rated human figure drawings (HFDs) as *the* most popular test of social-emotional functioning (Kennedy, Faust, Willis, & Piotrowski, 1994), and a separate survey (Stinnett et al., 1994) revealed that over 50% of school psychologists routinely use draw-a-person techniques, giving it a frequency-of-use ranking that is second only to sentence completions. This popularity continues despite the fact that during the same time period, empirical studies of picture drawings can only be described as rare.

A distinct polarization has ensued among scholars in the field, who either vehemently denounce the use of drawings or support its continued usage. This debate is interesting for two reasons. First, it presents comprehensive and cogent arguments from some of the most noted researchers in school psychology about drawing techniques. Second, it exemplifies a dilemma that pervades the field of personality assessment: that is, are projective techniques valid and useful in making determinations about emotional disturbance in school children? After a brief introduction of figure drawings, this debate is discussed, followed by a summary of the most notable and recent research on drawings. (For a more comprehensive review and history of drawings, the reader is referred to one of the following sources: Finch & Belter, 1993; Knoff, 1990; Worchel, 1990.)

The first drawing tests to gain widespread usage as clinical tools were Machover's (1949) Draw-a-Person and Buck's (1948) House-Tree-Person. Since that time, one of the most widely used interpretive systems for figure drawings has been that developed by Koppitz (1968, 1982, 1983). Although Koppitz's system involves a structured scoring technique, she clearly emphasizes the subjective nature of the test. Koppitz (1983) maintains that individual, family, and school drawings reflect four important percep-

tions of the school-aged child: the child's own personality and self-concept, the child's family and his or her place within the family, attitudes about teachers and school, and attitudes toward social and cultural groups. Koppitz also stresses the importance of behavioral observations, such as what aspects the child draws first, and queries after the drawing is completed, such as what the figure might be doing or thinking. This information is used to make a general, global assessment of the drawing (assuming that the evaluator has had sufficient experience with drawings to have a frame of reference for making global inferences.)

Finally, the drawing is analyzed in terms of Koppitz's (1982) 30 emotional indicators (EIs). The EIs are grouped into five categories: impulsivity, insecurity, feelings of inadequacy, anxiety, shyness/timidity, and anger/aggressiveness. Included are such signs as a big figure, no hands, omission of eyes, short arms, or a nude figure. Three or more EIs are believed to suggest the possibility of emotional problems. Koppitz stresses that EIs are not scores; they merely occur more frequently on drawings of emotionally disturbed children than those of normal children. A review of studies in this area led Cummings (1986) to conclude that one should analyze the total number of emotional indicators rather than attempt to relate specific indicators to specific characteristics. He concludes that the greatest interpretive value of picture drawings is gained by analyzing the child's verbalizations and test-taking behaviors.

In recent years, the debate about the usefulness of human figure drawings for school psychologists has continued. In 1993, the *School Psychology Quarterly* devoted the better part of an issue to this debate, soliciting viewpoints from seven different scholars or research teams. So vehemently polarized were the resulting commentaries that the editor published an introduction in defense of controversy! Because of the relevance of this debate to personality assessment in general, a summary of the articles is presented here.

Motta, Little, and Tobin (1993) review data-based studies on HFDs and conclude that evidence supporting their use for predicting or describing behavior, emotions, or personality is weak, at best. They claim that there is virtually no empirical support for the oft-made assertion that examiners with accumulated knowledge of HFDs are competent to make accurate descriptions of personality and behavioral functioning. They also refute the defense that HFDs can be helpful in supporting other test instruments or hypotheses. According to Motta et al., an instrument that is weak psychometrically cannot logically add to the findings of other measures that are psychometrically stronger. They conclude that HFDs are "superfluous" and remain popular largely because of their ease of administration and anecdotal reports of their success.

In support of these conclusions, Knoff (1993) concurs that (1) the majority of research on HFDs is methodological and/or statistically flawed, (2) hypotheses generated from HFDs are largely inferential, and (3) HFDs make little contribution to other instruments in regard to interventions. Knoff concludes by asserting that HFDs are "inefficient, unnecessary, and potentially damaging." Gresham (1993) also criticizes HFDs and provides three possible explanations for their continued popularity. The first is the illusory correlation, in this case the faulty perception that predictions made by experts are more accurate and valid than predictions made by laypersons. Simply stated, if experts interpret an HFD, they must know what they are doing. Second, Gresham repeats Motta et al's (1993) explanation of incremental validity refuting that HFDs add to the findings provided by other measures. Third, Gresham suggests that one cannot "prove" the null hypothesis. By chance some interpretations will be consistent with behavior, and these occurrences serve as partial reinforcement to confirm the validity of the technique. Gresham concludes by suggesting that HFDs should be eliminated from the repertoire of assessment tools in school psychology.

In defense of HFDs, Holtzman (1993) asserts that Motta et al's (1993) selective review ignores strong positive evidence, which suggests that narrowly prescribed uses of the HFD are valid for assessing certain aspects of personality. As evidence, Holtzman cites Koppitz's (1968) work on emotional indicators as highly significant predictors of maladjustment. Naglieri (1993) is also strongly supportive of HFDs. In particular, he describes his own work (Naglieri, McNeish, & Bardos, 1991) with a recent scoring system, the Draw-a-Person: Procedure for Emotional Disturbance (DAP:SPED). This 55-item scoring system is applied to drawings of a man, woman, and oneself, yielding a total score that is converted to a *T* score. The system includes such items as figure dimensions (e.g., large or small figures and placement) and frequency of content (shading, crossed eyes, frowning mouth, era-

sures, etc.). It has been standardized on 2,355 6- to 17-year-olds. In recent research with this system, Naglieri and Pfeiffer (1992) compared 54 normal students with 54 students with conduct or oppositional disorders. The mean *T* score for their clinical sample was significantly higher than that of the normal students and could be used to increase diagnostic accuracy by 25%. Naglieri (1993) maintains that the DAP:SPED offers a significant improvement in the use of the draw-a-person technique to evaluate the presence of emotional problems.

Before closing this area, it is important to cite one additional study not previously mentioned, an attempt to evaluate empirically the feasibility of an HFD scoring system based on actual clinical practice. Tharinger and Stark (1990) postulated that many practitioners use the overall gestalt of a drawing in a holistic way. Thus, they devised a qualitative scoring system that mimicked this approach. Raters were trained to score HFDs according to four characteristics: inhumanness of the drawing; lack of agency (interaction with the world); lack of well-being (facial expressions); and the presence of a hollow, vacant, or stilted sense in the drawing. A similar system was developed for kinetic family drawings (KFDs). Using a sample of normal controls, children with mood disorders and anxiety disorders, and a mixed mood and anxiety group, HFDs and KFDs were scored by using Koppitz's (1968) emotional indicators and the qualitative scoring system. The Koppitz scores and the qualitative scores were not significantly correlated, indicating that these two methods were tapping into different constructs. Furthermore, the Koppitz scores did not differentiate the normal children from those with emotional disturbances. However, the qualitative systems for both the HFDs and KFDs could be used to discriminate the mood disorders from the controls and the mood and anxiety disorders from the controls. These scores were also significantly related to a self-esteem measure and other aspects of family functioning.

In summary, HFDs remain immensely popular in clinical practice. Practitioners use them with great regularity, often utilizing a qualitative, holistic approach to scoring that emphasizes observing and questioning the child, and basing interpretations on a personal store of knowledge about content. Scholars who criticize the use of HFDs point to an inadequate base of research, a lack of psychometric studies of the reliability and validity of scoring systems, and a lack of empirically based scoring systems. Recent attempts to produce standardized scoring systems are encouraging; however, these systems cannot be properly evaluated without further research. This particular debate could and has been applied to other assessment techniques, most often projectives or techniques without standardized scoring systems. The issues raised are clearly important to consider in evaluating any assessment technique.

## Kinetic Family Drawing

The KFD (Burns & Kaufman, 1972) is generally considered a projective technique, designed to gather information about a child's perceptions of his or her family and the relationships within the family. The child is instructed to draw a picture of his or her family doing something together. The drawing is generally evaluated through a qualitative interpretation of content. It is often utilized with children whose parents have undergone divorce or separation to gather information about the child's current perceptions. For example, if one or both parents are remarried, does the child continue to include only his or her natural parents in the drawing? In a recent review of the KFD, Handler and Habenicht (1994) identified several problems. First, it is difficult to determine whether a drawing represents realistic family structure or a child's wishes. Second, there are insufficient normative data to fully evaluate the test. Third, most research with the KFD uses a single interpretation for each sign or variable scored, rather than looking at meaningful patterns in the data. Fourth, many studies use children's behavior (e.g., aggression) as a criterion. However, given that projective tests are generally assumed to portray perceptions, one would not expect to find a relationship between the test and subsequent behaviors and thus much of the research is difficult to evaluate. Overall, it appears that the KFD maintains a position similar to that of HFDs in general; it is frequently used without a sound underlying psychometric basis.

## Thematic Storytelling Techniques

In thematic storytelling techniques, a child is shown a set of pictures and asked to make up a story about them. These are generally considered projective techniques, in that there is no right or wrong answer and the stories vary in level of ambiguity. The child's stories are assumed to be based on events, feelings, and important needs in the child's own life (Worchel & Dupree, 1990). The stories produced are fantasies, combining both past experiences and current psychological concerns. The fantasy should be bound by the reality constraints of the picture. A child who gives concrete, factual descriptions of the pictures may be inhibited, defensive, or lacking in creativity. Alternately, a child who gives consistent themes unrelated to the content of the pictures is more likely to be engaging in a projection of his or her needs or psychological concerns.

Although there is general agreement that projection is the cornerstone of most thematic storytelling techniques, they have been constantly criticized for being psychometrically untenable (Worchel & Dupree, 1990). Although some of the classic techniques continue to be employed, newer methods are being developed that attempt to use standardized scoring systems. This chapter briefly reviews the Thematic Apperception Test (TAT) and the Roberts Apperception Test for Children (RATC), as they have been extensively surveyed elsewhere (for reviews, see Worchel & Dupree, 1990). More attention is given here to reviews of two newer techniques, designed specifically for children or adolescents, the Tell Me a Story (TEMAS) and the Apperceptive Personality Test (APT).

### Thematic Apperception Test

The TAT was first developed by Murray (1938, 1943) and was assumed to measure a person's needs and concerns. Ten cards are selected for presentation, and the cards are labeled as being more suitable for males, boys, females, girls, or either. Subjects are instructed to make up stories about what is happening now, what happened previously, what the people are feeling and thinking, and how the story ends. Numerous scoring systems have been devised, some comprehensive, others for specific characteristics like hostility or aggression. Overall, there does not appear to be a comprehensive, structured technique that is feasible in complexity or time. Many scholars agree that the best scoring technique involves inspection of the stories and observations of the subject's behaviors during the test administration (Worchel & Dupree, 1990).

There has been little recent research of the TAT with children or adolescents. McGrew and Teglasi (1990) created a somewhat complex scoring system, using formal characteristics of story structure. They combined elements of several scoring techniques to evaluate such characteristics as perceptual organization, internal logic, perceptual personalization, story content, judgment, action, and outcome. Using 9 cards, they compared 40 well-adjusted and 40 emotionally disturbed (ED) 6- to 12-year-old males. With this system, they could correctly classify 95% of the ED children and 85% of the normal controls. Stovall and Craig (1990) examined the mental representations of 20 sexually abused, 20 physically abused, and 20 nonabused but distressed 7- to 12-year-old females. They used a combination of two scoring systems (Aaron, 1949; Taylor & Franzen, 1986). No differences were found between the two abused groups; however, the TAT could discriminate between abused and nonabused children. Using Fine's (1955) scoring technique, Pistole and Ornduff (1994) evaluated 6- to 16-year-old sexually abused and normal females. They found between-group differences in sexual preoccupation and guilt. Also using Fine's scoring technique, Worchel, Aaron, and Yates (1990) evaluated whether the male and female cards on the TAT "pull" for specific content. By administering the female cards to males and the male cards to females, as well as a standard administration, they determined that the female cards elicited more responses indicative of psychological distress than did the male cards.

In summary, although there continues to be limited research of the TAT, it is inconsistent in the administration, cards used, and scoring system. Although studies do find significant results with specific characteristics of various scoring systems, the current state of the TAT appears similar to that of the Rorschach in the 1950s and early 1960s: numerous scoring systems, a heavy reliance on subjective clinical interpretations, and inconsistent research results. Fortunately, there have been attempts to use the theoretical foundations of the TAT to pursue storytelling techniques with a stronger psychometric base.

## Roberts Apperception Test for Children

The Roberts Apperception Test for Children (RATC) is a storytelling technique designed specifically for children and adolescents (McArthur & Roberts, 1982). It was very positively reviewed after its publication (Sines, 1985; Worchel, 1990; Worchel & Dupree, 1990) as a promising test that needed further psychometric validation. The author (G. Roberts, personal communication, October 1995) reports that a new handbook has been published and that the RATC has been the subject of several dissertations. Since no further empirical studies have been published in the past five years, it will not be reviewed further here.

## Tell Me a Story Test

The TEMAS (Constantino, Malgady, & Rogler, 1988) was designed as a culturally sensitive projection test. There are two parallel forms: one depicts Black and Hispanic youngsters; the other depicts Anglo children. The two sets each contain 23 colorful drawings of lower-middle-class, urban scenes. Eleven of the cards are gender-specific, and 12 are used with both girls and boys. The TEMAS is intended to be administered in the child's dominant language. Many cards clearly depict conflict and problem-solving dilemmas. For example, one card involves a choice between obeying one's parents and playing with friends. In another, the main character chooses between putting money in a piggy bank and buying ice cream. Both positive and negative mood states are portrayed, as well as frequent action and interaction among individuals. The examiner may choose between a full administration of 23 cards, which takes up to 2 hours, or a short administration of 9 cards, taking about 45 minutes.

The TEMAS scoring yields 18 cognitive functions, 9 personality functions, and 7 affective functions. The 9 personality functions, plus subsets of the cognitive and affective functions, are converted into normalized $T$ scores and make up the Quantitative Scales. The remainder of the cognitive and affective functions make up the Qualitative Indicators. These are used as raw scores, converted to percentile ranks, with specific cutoff levels that indicate the presence of pathology.

The TEMAS was standardized on 642 5- to 13-year-olds from New York City public schools. Norms are provided for three age groups, 5 to 7, 8 to 10, and 11 to 13, and for Hispanics, Blacks, and Anglos. The Hispanic norms are divided into Puerto Rican and non–Puerto Rican; the latter category includes Dominican Republic, South American, and Mexican-American respondents. According to Ritzler (1993), more subjects are needed in the normative sample, as some cells are quite small when broken down by age and ethnicity.

Recent reviews by Ritzler (1993) and Cambias, Killian, and Faust (1992) describe the psychometric properties of the TEMAS. The majority of reliability and validity studies have been conducted by the authors; nonetheless, there is an impressive amount of work in print or in progress. Ritzler concludes that evidence of interrater reliability is quite good, and internal consistency is variable, which would be expected because of the difference in card "pull." Test-retest reliability is less than desirable over an 18-week period, and caution should be used in evaluating changes over time with the TEMAS. Cambias et al. review validity studies and conclude that there is promising support for content, construct, criterion, related, and predictive validity. Several studies that document construct validity distinguish between clinical and nonclinical groups. The test's authors, however, warn that profiling specific diagnostic categories at this point is premature. Studies of concurrent validity show correlations of .32 to .51 with various measures, including ego development, teachers' and mothers' behavior ratings, self-concept, delay of gratification, disruptiveness, and aggression.

Critiques of the TEMAS include the fact that many of the standardization studies involved a bilingual examiner who was testing children in their dominant language. It is unclear, for example, whether a non–Spanish-speaking examiner who is testing a bilingual child will obtain the same results in a nondominant language (Worchel & Dupree, 1990). The norms, which are based on urban, low-SES children, should be used with caution on rural or higher-SES children. Also, independent norms for the short form need to be developed.

Overall, the TEMAS deserves praise for its attention to minority cultures; theory-driven development; well-designed cards; specific administration procedures; comprehensive scoring system; and low-inference, score-based interpretation. Although psychometric work remains to be done, the authors are impressive in their continuing efforts in this area. Work in progress (G. Costantino, personal communication, August 1995) includes normative data for adolescents and piloting of an Asian-American version of the TEMAS.

## The Apperceptive Personality Test

The Apperceptive Personality Test (APT) was specifically designed to overcome criticisms of the TAT (Karp, Holstrom, & Silber, 1989). It can be used with adolescents aged 12 through adulthood. Specifically, the APT developers felt that the TAT did not have a reliable and valid scoring system, there was no one uniform set of pictures, the cards were dated and negatively

toned, and there was an absence of minority figures (Holstrom, Silber, & Karp, 1990). With these concerns in mind, an eight-card test was produced with moderate ambiguity with male and female and young and old subjects, with identifiable minority figures, and with contemporary settings. A broad range of social and interpersonal themes was intended: aggression, guilt, sexuality, authority, conformity, depression, self-evaluation, and confrontation. After producing the stories, the subject completes the APT questionnaire, which contains a series of questions about the characters in the story and their relationships, feelings, actions, outcomes, and affects. The APT questionnaire is then subjected to standardized scoring of over 400 variables. Of these, only about 200 occur with relative frequency, and 22 primary variables have been identified for research and clinical interpretation. A computerized scoring program is available.

Several preliminary studies have evaluated the psychometric properties of the test. Test-retest coefficients range from the low .20s for some variables to an acceptable .70s to .80s for a number of variables (Holstrom et al., 1990). Evidence of criterion-related validity has included comparisons with the MMPI, the TAT, and Rotter's Internal-External Locus of Control (Holstrom, Karp, & Silber, 1992; Karp, Silber, Holstrom, Banks, & Karp, 1992; Karp, Silber, Holstrom, & Kellert, 1992). Predictive validity has been established by positive correlations with the Beck Depression Inventory (Holstrom, Karp, & Silber, 1994).

Recently, a Children's APT has been developed for children aged 4 to 12. This version uses four stimulus pictures and a questionnaire similar to that in the adult and adolescent form. The objective scoring system provides 16 personality measures. Norms are based on 267 children, with separate norms provided by gender and age (two levels). Although African Americans, Hispanics, and Asian Americans are included in the normative sample, small cell sizes preclude separate norms by race. In addition to the children's version, two other versions have recently been developed (Silber, personal communication, November 1995): the APT-Brief Adult and the APT/MR (for mentally retarded subjects). The research on the APT has primarily involved adults and college students, thus its usefulness for school assessments may be limited to older adolescents, pending further psychometric studies. Overall, the APT is impressive in that it appears to have successfully remedied common drawbacks to the TAT, and the authors are continuing to produce evidence of psychometric stability.

## The Rorschach

The Rorschach remains a controversial personality assessment technique for school-based use. Administration, scoring, and interpretation require advanced training, as well as a significant investment in time and effort. However, based on the extensive psychometric work published as the Rorschach comprehensive system (Exner, 1978, 1993; Exner & Weiner, 1982); it certainly deserves coverage in any chapter on personality assessment. The comprehensive system evolved as an integration of five disparate systems and has become the most frequently used system in the United States (Finch & Belter, 1994).

In the Exner system, the Rorschach is considered primarily a cognitive-perceptual task; that is, responses are believed to measure the way in which individuals normally react in problem-solving situations. Administration involves showing subjects 10 inkblots, with these instructions: "Tell me what this might be." An extremely complex scoring system allows for close to 100 possible scores per response, divided into the following major categories: location, determinants (e.g., color, shading, and movement), organization of the response, frequency of the response by the normative group, content, and special scores (e.g., unusual, illogical, and aggressive characteristics of responses). These scores are then transformed into frequency counts, ratios, percentages, and constellations. The constellations are especially important because they utilize discriminant analysis to combine scores into meaningful patterns. The current constellations, termed indexes, provide information about schizophrenia, depression, suicide potential, hypervigilent style, obsessive style, and interpersonal coping style.

Recent work on the comprehensive system has involved attempts to increase the interrater reliability of the scoring categories, as well as refinement of the scoring and interpretation process. Interpretive search strategies allow a more structured approach to integrating the vast amount of data available. Scores are combined to form seven variable clusters, based on the frequency counts, ratios, percentages, and special scores. These variable clusters involve the following personality component or functions: af-fective features, capacity for control and stress tolerance, cognitive mediation, ideation, information processing, interpersonal perception and relations, self-perceptions, and situationally related stress. Interpreting the Rorschach means identifying which key variables are positive for a particular protocol, which then directs the interpreter to consider the seven variable clusters in a specified manner. For example, if a protocol is positive on the Depression Index, the interpretation would begin with the affective cluster. Alternately, if a protocol had a positive Schizophrenia Index, the interpretation would start with the cognitive clusters: ideation, mediation, and processing.

The Exner (1993) system presents normative data based on 700 nonpatient adults; 1,390 nonpatient children (with separate norms by age, from 5 to 16); and four groups of adult psychiatric subjects: 320 inpatient schizophrenics, 315 inpatient depressives, 440 outpatients beginning treatment for the first time, and 180 outpatients with character disorders. The normative data include statistics for 33 different structural variables. Subject distributions are presented by gender, race, SES, and geographic location.

Weiner (1986) reports interrater reliabilities of .85 or more for all the scoring codes, when trained examiners are used. Test-retest reliability is fairly good for adults, with all but 2 of 19 variables showing three-year correlations of .75 or higher. The two variables with low reliabilities are both measures of situational stress and thus are expected to be quite low. For children, particularly those 6 to 9 years old, test-retest reliabilities are substantially lower. Weiner believes this is expected, given that the Rorschach measures cognitive perceptual abilities and patterns of coping, both of which should show developmental changes. When children are retested after short intervals (three weeks), test-retest reliabilities are adequate.

Validity studies on use of the comprehensive system with children have not been extensively published. Spigelman and Spigelman (1991) evaluated 108 10- to 12-year-old children, half from divorced and half from intact homes. Overall, the children from divorced homes scored higher on the Depression Index. An interaction by gender revealed that girls from divorced homes scored highest on a measure of self-esteem, whereas boys from divorced homes scored lowest. Acklin (1990) studied two groups of LD children, one with predominant spatial disorders and the other with predominant language disorders. The Rorschach did not discriminate between the two groups; however, comparison to a control group showed significant differences in cognitive style, perceptual accuracy, conventionality, organizational style, and self-esteem. Abraham, Lovegrove, Lepisto, Lewis, Schultz, and Finkelberg (1994) tested 50 hospitalized adolescents at admission and after two years. They found evidence of good interrater reliability. In addition, there were several expected changes in measures of adjustment (e.g., stress tolerance, reality testing, and modulation of affect); however, other anticipated changes, such as self-esteem, depression, and emotional reactivity, were not found. It is unclear whether this was due to the lack of treatment effects or the Rorschach's inability to measure these constructs. Ball, Archer, Gordon, and French (1991) compared the Rorschach Depression Index (DEPI) to the Depression Scale of the Personality Inventory for Children (PIC; Wirt, Lachar, Klinedinst, & Seat, 1984) on both inpatient and outpatient samples of 5- to 18-year-olds. They found the DEPI to be unrelated to the PIC depression score or to treatment team diagnoses (for inpatients).

Given the complexity of the scoring system, there is legitimate concern that this technique is too time-consuming to be useful for the school psychologist. Administration of the test averages about 45 minutes, and all but the most skilled clinician will require 1 to 2 hours to score and interpret the test. Exner has developed a computer-scoring package that cuts down interpretive time substantially. Concerns about the validity of many of the scores remains, particularly for younger children. Clearly, more empirical work is needed in this area.

Although the Rorschach was not designed with IDEA criteria in mind, many aspects of the system can be useful for school-based assessments of emotional functioning. For example, under IDEA, three of the six criteria for *serious emotional disturbance* include difficulties in the interpersonal realm, pervasive depression, or symptoms of schizophrenia. The Rorschach yields clusters of variables that evaluate affect, self- and interpersonal perception, and cognitive perceptual functioning. In addition, specific empirically derived constellations evaluate patterns of responding found in individuals with symptoms of schizophrenia and depression. The Exner (1993) system can be useful in an outcome-based assessment in that it provides

information about the child's cognitive perceptual abilities, which can be directly related to interventions concerning instructional styles.

## CONCLUSIONS

Based on the information reviewed in this chapter, it is hoped that several changes will be seen in the future. Surveys of test usage among school psychologists continue to reflect assessment practices apparently biased much more by practicality than by empirical support of test instruments. Several new instruments are based on theory; utilize a multimodal approach; and provide evidence about normative samples, cultural diversity, reliability, and validity. In particular, both the CBCL and the BASC appear to be leaders in the field of comprehensive, integrated, empirically based assessment techniques for children and adolescents. Both techniques are particularly well suited to IDEA requirements and allow multiple information to be used.

It is hoped that new surveys of assessment practices will mirror advances in test development. It is unlikely that this will occur unless university training programs change. An emphasis on test construction and the psychometric properties of tests must rival the emphasis on test administration. Tests should be carefully critiqued for evidence of validity, reliability, adequate normative and standardization data, and sensitivity to culturally diverse populations. Similarly, teaching models that are cookbook-oriented need to be supplemented with training in the *process* of assessment. The ecological model for personality assessment is one such process-oriented approach. Rather than focus on administering and interpreting specific techniques, training in assessment should encompass changes in service delivery systems. Evaluators need to be aware of current issues in school psychology, including ethical and legal mandates and their relevance to assessment. The assessment must be outcome-based, with an emphasis on effective interventions that consider the child, the school, the family, and the community. It is hoped that such an approach to personality assessment will allow school psychologists to discard their label of test-oriented gatekeepers.

## REFERENCES

Aaron, B. (1949). *A manual for analysis of the Thematic Apperception Test: A method and technique for personality research.* Berkeley, CA: Berg.

Abraham, P. P., Lovegrove Lepisto, B., Lewis, M. G., Schultz, L., & Finkelberg, S. (1994). An outcome study: Changes in Rorschach variables of adolescents in residential treatment. *Journal of Personality Assessment, 62,* 505–514.

Achenbach, T. M. (1991a). *Integrative guide to the 1991 CBCL, YSR, and TRF profiles.* Burlington: University of Vermont, Department of Psychiatry.

Achenbach, T. M. (1991b). *Manual for the Child Behavior Checklist/4–18 and 1991 profile.* Burlington: University of Vermont, Department of Psychiatry.

Achenbach, T. M. (1991c). *Manual for the Teacher's Report Form and 1991 profile.* Burlington: University of Vermont, Department of Psychiatry.

Achenbach, T. M. (1991d). *Manual for the Youth Self-Report and 1991 profile.* Burlington: University of Vermont, Department of Psychiatry.

Achenbach, T. M. (1993). Implications of multiaxial empirically based assessment for behavior therapy with children. *Behavior Therapy, 24,* 91–116.

Achenbach, T. M. & McConaughy, S. H. (1987). *Empirically based assessment of child and adolescent psychopathology: Practical applications.* Newbury Park, CA: Sage.

Achenbach, T. M., McConaughy, S. H., & Howell, C. T. (1987). Child/adolescent behavioral and emotional problems: Implications of cross-informant correlations for situational specificity. *Psychological Bulletin, 101,* 214–232.

Acklin, M. W. (1990). Personality dimensions in two types of learning disabled children: A Rorschach study. *Journal of Personality Assessment, 54,* 67–77.

Algozzine, B., Christenson, S., & Ysseldyke, J. (1982). Probabilities associated with the referral to placement process. *Teacher education and special education, 5,* 19–23.

Anastasi, A. (1981). *Psychological testing (5th ed.).* New York: Macmillan.

Ball, J. D., Archer, R. P., Gordon, R. A., & French, J. (1991). Rorschach depression indices with children and adolescents: Concurrent validity findings. *Journal of Personality Assessment, 57,* 465–476.

Barrios, B. A. (1993). Direct observation. In T. H. Ollendick & M. Herson (Eds.), *Handbook of child and adolescent assessment* (pp. 65–81). Boston: Allyn & Bacon.

Bradley-Johnson, S., Johnson, C. M., & Jacob-Timm, S. (1995). Where will—and where should—changes in education leave school psychology? *Journal of School Psychology, 33,* 187–200.

Buck, N. J. (1948). The H-T-P Technique, a qualitative and quantitative method. *Journal of Clinical Psychology, 4,* 317–396.

Burns, R. C., & Kaufman, S. H. (1972). *Kinetic Family Drawing System (K-F-D): An introduction to understanding children through kinetic drawings.* NY: Bruner/Mazel.

Cambias, R. D., Killian, G. A., & Faust, J. (1992). Review of the TEMAS. *Test Critiques* (Vol. 19). Austin, TX: Pro-Ed.

Chandler, L. A. (1990). The projective hypothesis and the development of projective techniques for children. In C. R. Reynolds & R. W. Kamphous, (Eds.), *Handbook of psychological and educational assessment of children.* New York: Guilford.

Clarzio, H. F. (1992). Social maladjustment and emotional disturbance: Problems and position. I. *Psychology in the Schools, 29,* 131–140.

Conners, C. K. (1989). *Manual for Conner's Rating Scales.* North Tonawanda, NY: Multi-Health Systems.

Conoley, J. C., & Gutkin, T. B. (1995). Why didn't—why doesn't—school psychology realize its promise? *Journal of School Psychology, 33,* 209–217.

Constantino, G., Malgady, R., & Rogler, L. (1988). *TEMAS (Tell-Me-a-Story).* Los Angeles: Western Psychological Services.

Crowley, S., Worchel, F., & Ash, M. (1992). Self-report, peer-report, and teacher-report measures of childhood depression: An analysis by item. *Journal of Personality Assessment, 59,* 189–203.

Cummings, J. A. (1986). Projective drawings. In H. Knoff (Ed.), *The assessment of child and adolescent personality* (pp. 199–244). New York: Guilford Press.

Dean, R. S. (1984). Commentary on "Personality assessment in the schools: The special issue." *School Psychology Review, 13,* 95–98.

De Groot, A., Koot, H. M., & Verhulst, F. C. (1994). Cross-cultural generalizability of the Child Behavior Checklist cross-informant syndromes. *Psychological Assessment, 6,* 225–230.

Elliot, S. N., Busse, R. T., & Gresham, F. M. (1993). Behavior rating scales: Issues of use and development. *School Psychology Review, 22,* 313–321.

Exner, J. E. (1978). *The Rorschach: A comprehensive system: Vol. 2: Current research and advanced interpretation.* New York: Wiley.

Exner, J. E. (1993). *The Rorschach: A comprehensive system: Vol. 1 (3rd ed.).* New York: Wiley.

Exner, J. E., & Weiner, I. B. (1982). *The Rorschach: A Comprehensive system: Vol. 3: Assessment of children and adolescents.* New York: Wiley.

Finch, A. J., & Belter, R. W. (1993). Projective techniques. In T. H. Ollendick & M. Hersen (Eds.), *Handbook of child and adolescent assessment* (224–236). Boston: Allyn & Bacon.

Fine, R. (1955). Manual for a scoring scheme for verbal projective techniques (TAT, MAPS, stories and the like). *Journal of Projective Techniques, 19,* 310–316.

Flanagan, R. (1995). A review of the Behavior Assessment System for Children (BASC):

Assessment consistent with the requirements of the Individuals with Disabilities Act (IDEA). *Journal of School Psychology, 33,* 177–186.

Frick, P. J., Silverthorne, P., & Evans, C. (1994). Assessment of childhood anxiety using structured interviews: Patterns of agreement among informants and association with maternal anxiety. *Psychological Assessment, 6,* 372–379.

Graden, J. L., Casey, A., & Christenson, S. L. (1985). Implementing a prereferral intervention system: Part I. The model. *Exceptional Children, 51,* 377–384.

Greenbaum, P. E., Dedrick, R. F., Prange, M. E., & Friedman, R. M. (1994). Parent, teacher, and child ratings of youngsters with serious emotional disturbance. *Psychological Assessment, 6,* 141–148.

Greenspan, S. I. (1981). *The clinical interview of the child.* New York: McGraw-Hill.

Gresham, F. M. (1993). "What's wrong in this picture?": Response to Motta et al.'s review of Human Figure Drawings. *School Psychology Quarterly, 8,* 182–186.

Handler, L., & Habenicht, D. (1994). The Kinetic Family Drawing Technique: A review of the literature. *Journal of Personality Assessment, 62,* 440–464.

Hathaway, S. R., & McKinley, J. C. (1943). *Manual for Minnesota Multiphasic Personality Inventory* (pp. 252–264). Minneapolis: University of Minnesota Press.

Hodges, K., & Zeman, J. (1993). Interviewing. In T. H. Ollendick & M. Herson (Eds.), *Handbook of child and adolescent assessment* (pp. 65–81). Boston: Allyn & Bacon.

Holstrom, R. W., Karp, S. A., & Silber, D. E. (1992). Factor structure of the Apperceptive Personality Test (APT). *Journal of Clinical Psychology, 48,* 207–210.

Holstrom, R. W., Karp, S. A. & Silber, D. E. (1994). Prediction of depression with the Apperceptive Personality Test. *Journal of Clinical Psychology, 50,* 234–237.

Holstrom, R. W., Silber, D. E., & Karp, S. A. (1990). Development of the Apperceptive Personality Test. *Journal of Personality Assessment, 54,* 252–264.

Holtzman, W. H. (1993). An unjustified, sweeping indictment by Motta et al. of HFD's for assessing psychological functioning. *School Psychology Quarterly, 8,* 189–190.

Hughes, J. N., & Baker, D. B. (1990). *The clinical child interview.* New York: Guilford.

Jacob-Timm, S., & Harshorne, T. (1994). *Ethics and law for school psychologists* (2nd ed.). Brandon, VT: Clinical Psychology Publishing.

Jensen, P. S., Koretz, D., Locke, B. Z., Schneider, S., Radke-Yarrow, M., Richters, J. E., & Rumsey, J. M. (1993). Child and adolescent psychopathology research: Problems and prospects for the 1990's. *Journal of Abnormal Child Psychology, 21,* 551–580.

Karp, S. A., Holstrom, R. W., & Silber, D. E. (1989). *Apperceptive Personality Test manual (APT).* Worthington, OH: International Diagnostics Systems.

Karp, S. A., Silber, D. E., Holstrom, R. W., Banks, V., & Karp, J. (1992). Outcomes of Thematic Apperception Test and Apperceptive Personality Test stories. *Perceptual and Motor Skills, 74,* 479–482.

Karp, S. A., Silber, D. E., Holstrom, R. W., & Kellert, H. (1992). Prediction of MMPI clinical scores from the Apperceptive Personality Test. *Perceptual and Motor Skills, 74,* 779–786.

Kennedy, M. L., Faust, D., Willis, W. G., & Piotrowski, C. (1994). Social emotional assessment practices in school psychology. *Journal of Psychoeducational Assessment, 12,* 228–240.

Knoff, H. M. (1990). Evaluation of projective drawings. In C. R. Reynolds & R. K. Kamphaus (Eds.), *Handbook of psychological and educational assessment of children: Personality, behavior, and context* (pp. 89–146). New York: Guilford.

Knoff, H. M. (1993). The utility of Human Figure Drawings in personality and intellectual assessment: Why ask why? *School Psychology Quarterly, 8,* 191–196.

Koppitz, E. M. (1968). *Psychological evaluation of children's Human Figure Drawings.* New York: Grune & Stratton.

Koppitz, E. M. (1982). Personality assessment in the schools. In C. R. Reynolds & T. B. Gutkin (Eds.), *The handbook of school psychology* (pp. 245–271). New York: Wiley.

Koppitz, E. M. (1983). Projective drawings with children and adolescents. *School Psychology Review, 12,* 421–427.

Lanyon, R. I. (1984). Personality assessment. *Annual Review of Psychology, 35,* 667–701.

Loeber, R., Green, S. M., Lahey, B. B., & Stouthamer-Loeber, M. (1989). Differences and similarities between children, mothers and teachers as informants on disruptive behavior disorders. *Journal of Abnormal Child Psychology, 19,* 75–95.

Machover, K. (1949). *Personality projection in the drawing of the human figure.* Springfield, IL: Thomas.

Martens, B. K. (1993). Social labeling, precision of measurement, and problem solving: Key issues in the assessment of children's emotional problems. *School Psychology Review, 22,* 308–312.

McArthur, D. S., & Roberts, G. E. (1982). *Roberts Apperception Test for Children: Manual.* Los Angeles: Western Psychological Services.

McConaughy, S. (1993). Advances in empirically based assessment of children's behavioral and emotional problems. *School Psychology Review, 22,* 285–307.

McGrew, M. W., & Teglasi, H. (1990). Formal

characteristics of Thematic Apperception Test stories as indices of emotional disturbance in children. *Journal of Personality Assessment, 54,* 639–655.

Motta, R. W., Little, S. G., & Tobin, M. I. (1993). The use and abuse of Human Figure Drawings. *School Psychology Quarterly, 8,* 162–169.

Murray, H. A. (1938). *Explorations in personality.* New York: Oxford University Press.

Murray, H. A. (1943). *Thematic Apperception Test Manual.* Boston: Harvard College.

Naglieri, J. A. (1993). Human figure drawings in perspective. *School Psychology Quarterly, 8,* 170–176.

Naglieri, J. A., McNeish, T. J., & Bardos, A. N. (1991). *Draw a Person: Procedure for emotional disturbance.* Austin, TX: Pro-Ed.

Naglieri, J. A., & Pfeiffer, S. I. (1992). Performance of disruptive behavior on the Draw a Person: Screening procedure for emotional disturbance. *Psychological Assessment, 4,* 156–159.

Piacentini, J. C., Cohen, P., & Cohen, J. (1992). Combining discrepant diagnostic information from multiple sources: Are complex algorithms better than simple ones? *Journal of Abnormal Child Psychology, 20,* 51–63.

Pistole, D. R., & Ornduff, S. R. (1994). TAT assessment of sexually abused girls: An analysis of manifest content. *Journal of Personality Assessment, 63,* 211–222.

Prout, H. (1983). School psychologists and social-emotional assessment techniques: Patterns in training and use. *School Psychology Review, 12,* 377–383.

Quay, H. C., & Peterson, D. R. (1983). *Manual for the Revised Behavior Problem Checklist.* Coral Gables, FL: University of Miami, Department of Psychology.

Reynolds, C. R., & Kamphaus, R. W. (1992). *Manual for BASC: Behavior Assessment System for Children.* Circle Pines, MN: American Guidance Service.

Ritter, D. (1989). Teacher's perceptions of problem behavior and adaptive functioning in general and special education settings. *Exceptional Children, 55,* 559–564.

Ritzler, B. (1993). Review of the TEMAS. *Journal of Personality Assessment, 11,* 381–389.

Robles-Pina, R. A. (1996). Factors that influence the decision-making process about language minority children on prereferral committees. Doctoral dissertation, Texas A & M University, College Station.

Rosenfeld, S. (1992). Developing school-based consultation teams: A design for organizational change. *School Psychology Quarterly, 7,* 27–46.

Sandoval, J., & Echandia, A. (1994). Behavior Assessment System for Children. *Journal of School Psychology, 32,* 419–425.

Sines, J. O. (1985). Review of the Roberts Apperception Test for Children. In J. Mitchell (Ed.). *The ninth mental measurement yearbook,* Lincoln, NE: Buros Institute.

Skiba, R., Grizzle, K., & Minke, K. M. (1994). Opening the floodgates? The social maladjustment exclusion and state SED prevalence rates. *Journal of School Psychology, 32,* 267–282.

Spigelman, A., & Spigelman, G. (1991). Indications of depression and distress in divorce and nondivorce children reflected by the Rorschach Test. *Journal of Personality Assessment, 57,* 120–129.

Stanger, C., & Lewis, M. (1993). Agreement among parents, teachers, and children on internalizing and externalizing behavior problems. *Journal of Clinical Child Psychology, 22,* 107–115.

Stinnett, T. A., Harvey, J. M., & Oehler-Stinnett, J. (1994). Current test useage by practicing school psychologists: A national survey. *Journal of Psychoeducational Assessment, 12,* 331–350.

Stovall, G., & Craig, R. J. (1990). Mental representations of physically and sexually abused latency-aged females. *Child Abuse and Neglect, 14,* 233–242.

Swets, J. E., & Pickett, R. M. (1982). *Evaluation of diagnostic systems: Methods from signal detection theory.* New York: Academic Press.

Tapasak, R. C., & Keller, H. R. (1995). A reaction to "Where will . . . ?" and suggestions for "How to": The need to address systems-level variables in school psychology role/function change efforts. *Journal of School Psychology, 33,* 201–208.

Taylor, B., & Franzen, S. B. (1986). *The internalized object relations scale.* Unpublished manuscript, University of Chicago.

Texas Education Agency & Texas Department of Mental Health and Mental Retardation. (1990). *Guidelines for assessment of emotional disturbance.* Austin: Texas Education Agency.

Tharinger, D. J., & Stark, K. (1990). A qualitative vs. quantitative approach to evaluating the Draw-a-Person and Kinetic Family Drawings: A study of mood- and anxiety-disorder children. *Psychological Assessment, 2,* 365–375.

Thomas, L. D. (1995). *Corroborative diagnostic evidence of depression in children and adolescents: A meta-analysis.* Doctoral dissertation, Texas A & M University, College Station.

U.S. Department of Education. (1992). *Fourteenth annual report to Congress on the implementation of the individuals with disabilities education act.* Washington, DC: Author.

Verhulst, F. C., Koot, H. M., & van der Ende, J. (1994). Differential predictive value of parent's and teachers' reports of children's problem behaviors: A longitudinal study. *Journal of Abnormal Child Psychology, 22,* 531–546.

Weiner, I. B. (1986). Assessing children and adolescents with the Rorschach. In H. Knoff (Ed.), *The assessment of child and adolescent personality* (pp. 141–170). New York: Guilford.

Wirt, R. D., Lachar, D., Klinedinst, J. K., & Seat, R. D. (1984). *Multidimensional description of child personality: A manual for the Personality Inventory for Children.* Los Angeles: Western Psychological Services.

Worchel, F. F. (1990). Personality assessment. In C. R. Reynolds & T. Gutkin (Eds.), *The handbook of school psychology* (pp. 416–430). New York: Wiley.

Worchel, F. F., Aaron, L. L., & Yates, D. F. (1990). Gender bias on the Thematic Apperception Test. *Journal of Personality Assessment, 55,* 593–602.

Worchel, F. F., & Dupree, J. (1990). Projective storytelling techniques. In C. R. Reynolds & R. Kamphous (Eds.), *Handbook of psychological and educational assessment of children.* (pp. 70–80). New York: Guilford.

## CHAPTER 18

# NEUROPSYCHOLOGICAL ASSESSMENT FOR INTERVENTION

RIK CARL D'AMATO
*University of Northern Colorado*
BARBARA A. ROTHLISBERG
*Ball State University*
PATRICIA H. LEU WORK
*University of South Dakota*

Attention, perception, memory, problem-solving—these are representative constructs of the type that school psychologists must work with each day in the diagnosis and treatment of children's learning difficulties. Yet, all have defied simple explanation and manipulation. Children can be identified when they are not learning easily and/or lag behind their age-mates in basic skills, but the exact interrelations among children's different capacities in areas like attention, reading comprehension, and planning still elude educational specialists. More complex still is finding the key element in fostering behavioral change and educational improvement. The inroads being made by psychology in understanding the learning process and subsequent development of corrective or adaptive programs for children with learning disorders are dwarfed by the burgeoning numbers of learners diagnosed as having special needs. Consequently, school psychologists must build hypotheses about diagnosis and intervention with students by using imprecise views of learning and development based on research findings and theoretical conjecture. Given the state of the art and science of teaching, learning, and cognition, there continue to be large disparities among professionals in the identification and treatment of children's learning differences.

One theoretical approach that holds great promise for the understanding of children's learning and the full range of their behavioral repertoire (e.g., academic achievement, adaptation, and social-emotional growth) is that based on a neuropsychological paradigm (D'Amato, 1990). Grounded in the biological bases of behavior, a neuropsychological perspective can give practitioners added breadth and depth to their understanding of the thinking processes underlying behavior without compromising the value of other perspectives in explaining what has been observed (Gaddes & Edgell, 1994). A neuropsychological approach also integrates the traditional views of looking for the internal causes of behavior (e.g., psychoanalysis) with the external antecedents and consequences of observable behavior (e.g., behaviorism) to fully understand each learner (Whitten, D'Amato, & Chittooran, 1992). It is the intent of this chapter to provide an overview of neuropsychological knowledge about assessment for intervention and suggest how such knowledge can improve the practice of school psychology.

# ASSUMPTIONS THAT ARE SHAPING CURRENT PRACTICE

Interest in the inner workings of the mind and the way in which people process information has intrigued researchers for centuries. Whereas early philosophers contemplated the seat of intellect and emotion, the functioning of the central nervous system was largely unexplored until the eighteenth century, when relatively sophisticated anatomic study of the brain began (Luria, 1980; Whitten, et al., 1992). Early researchers in neurology debated the way in which the brain was organized. Some supported the idea that specific regions mediated particular mental functions, whereas other investigators viewed cerebral structures as related and interdependent; that is, damage to an area did not necessarily mean that a specific ability was impaired. Behavioral consequences of brain damage seemed more related to lesion size than to site (for a full discussion of this issue, see Chapman & Wolff, 1959; Luria, 1980; Meier, 1992; Thatcher & John, 1977; Walsh, 1978). Indeed, the degree of the localization of function in the brain is still open for debate, although complex models, such as Luria's pluripotentialism (i.e., the brain as an interconnecting web of function), attempt to explain the brain's structure and function.

## Differences in Brain Function Between Adults and Children

Advances in neurology and neuropsychology initially were made with adults. For example, the classic findings of Broca and Wernicke about the localization of language involved mature individuals (Lezak, 1995). Continued studies of brain trauma and its consequences for behavior in adults led to suppositions of brain-behavior relations and to an awareness of the way in which complex cognitive behaviors could be organized (Gray & Dean, 1990; Taylor & Fletcher, 1990). In the last several decades, information about brain-behavior relations gleaned from adult models of brain function has been transposed on children. Unfortunately, although knowledge of adult brain functioning has offered direction to the study of the developing brain, the notion of continuity between these functional systems (child and adult) is less clear. In other words, hypotheses about the way behavioral competencies relate to one another in the mature system must be reevaluated when applied to children (Fletcher & Taylor, 1984; Gaddes & Edgell, 1994; Gray & Dean, 1990; Hynd & Willis, 1988).

Fletcher and Taylor (1984) are among researchers who have pointedly contrasted the neuropsychology of adults with that of children. They cautioned that the association of brain disease and behavior in adults does not mean that the same relation exists in childhood or that tests that successfully measure abilities in adults relate to those same abilities in children. Because children are being studied during their developmental period and experience different types of disease or trauma than adults, their patterns of abilities may differ greatly from those of mature individuals. In essence, then, the expectations for a neuropsychological model for children must be modified to account for the developmental diversity observed (Dean, 1986; Gaddes & Edgell, 1994).

Initial assumptions of brain function in children based on preexisting adult models have led to enduring perceptions about the organization of children's abilities. In the 1940s, Strauss and associates applied the label of minimal brain injury or dysfunction to children who had no demonstrable brain damage when it was observed that their specific cognitive and/or behavioral difficulties resembled those of children who had established brain disease (Taylor & Fletcher, 1990). From this point, the recognition that children's observed performance could have a neurological basis changed the way in which learning disorders were defined. Suddenly, learning differences were not environmentally induced but the result of intrinsic variations in the individual's capacity for processing information.

## Codification of Neuropsychological Processes

Gaddes and Edgell (1994) acknowledge that the use of a neuropsychological model for educational problems has been contested as being too medical, too tied into the idea of pathology, and too damning of the child's potential for growth. Certainly, assuming that educational failure rests totally on presumed neurological dysfunction alleviates the responsibility of educators and parents to acknowledge their own roles in learning. Fortunately, the purpose of neuropsychology is not to simply assign diagnoses to children but to provide a base of information from which better treatment options are available (D'Amato & Rothlisberg, 1996; Dean, 1985a, 1986; Hartlage & Telzrow, 1983).

The relevancy of neuropsychological knowledge for educators is obvious (Clark & Hostetter, 1995). If one wishes to understand learning and the learner, one must recognize that "all behavior is mediated by the brain and central nervous system" (Gaddes & Edgell, 1994, p. 5). No two children's central nervous systems are the same in terms of make-up because of the enormous complexity of the system and the infinite possibilities for differences in the ways in which damage and recovery can occur (Gaddes & Edgell, 1994). The importance of accepting underlying psychological processes in learning difficulties has been seen by the fact that educational definitions for children with learning differences include reference to the intrinsic nature of the learning process (Taylor, 1988a, 1988b). For example, the neurological basis of severe learning disability has always been presumed and integrated into its definition (Hynd, 1989). Similarly, dyslexia is seen as a consequence of brain dysfunction (Kinsbourne, 1989). A neuropsychological perspective seems to be quite useful, even with children experiencing severe neurodevelopmental disorders (i.e., mental retardation), because of the qualitative and quantitative differences in performance within groups (Fletcher, 1988; Hooper, Boyd, Hynd, & Rubin, 1993).

The basis of neuropsychological knowledge is closely intertwined with assessment. Investigation of the observed disability or behavioral difference, as well as the individual's relative pattern of strengths and weaknesses in performance, is dependent on the neuropsychologist's clinical skills and assessment acumen. Because of its association with neurology, neuropsychological assessment could easily be characterized as having a predisposition to the medical model. In fact, before the development of sophisticated diagnostic techniques, neuropsychology was used for its ability to predict and localize the site of cortical damage in adults (Gray & Dean, 1990; Lezak, 1995). As diagnosis has evolved, so, too, has the utility of neuropsychological assessment (Gaddes, 1985; Hynd & Obrzut, 1981b). Kosslyn and Intriligator (1992) believe that cognitive neuropsychology offers constraints on theories of cognition and is a source of information about normal thinking. Neuropsychologists obviously look for brain-behavior relations, but they also consider the associations and dissociations between behaviors in their efforts to explain and intervene with behavior (Fletcher, 1988; Rutter, 1981). Neuropsychologists attempt to take what

is known about the central nervous system and use it as a tool to understand and anticipate the child's response to learning situations and to the general environment. Consequently, comprehensive data collection and evaluation are methods used strategically to address the learning question.

## Interest and Training in Neuropsychology

It has been documented that psychologists of all specialties (e.g., school, counseling, and clinical) are exceptionally interested in a neuropsychological approach (Haak, 1989; Hynd & Obrzut, 1981a; Larson & Agresti, 1992; Leavell & Lewandowski, 1988). Most recently, D'Amato, Hammons, Terminie, and Dean (1992) surveyed school psychology doctoral programs to determine if students or faculty were interested in or offered training in neuropsychology. They found that 59% of the American Psychological Association (APA) accredited programs and 53% of the nonaccredited programs offered at least some training in neuropsychology. It was also noted that students reported a greater interest in neuropsychology than did faculty members. This interest is not surprising when one considers the fact that neuropsychological data offer additional information to that obtainable by using traditional school psychology instruments (Chittooran, D'Amato, Lassiter, & Dean, 1993). For example, traditional intelligence tests have been found to overlap only some 10% with common neuropsychological batteries (D'Amato, Gray, & Dean, 1988). Concomitantly, neuropsychology-related employment options continue to grow each year, offering new opportunities for school psychologists who want to leave the traditional public school (D'Amato & Dean, 1988; D'Amato, Dean, & Holloway, 1987).

Training in neuropsychology for school psychologists varies greatly. At the low end, it consists of a unit in a single course or attendance at a workshop that features a neuropsychological approach; at the high end, training involves the completion of a specialization in neuropsychology within a school psychology doctoral degree and includes related internship and/or postdoctoral study. While there are guidelines for the level of preparation required to call oneself a neuropsychologist (Meier, 1981; Reynolds & Fletcher-Janzen, 1989; Stone, Gray & Dean, 1989), the National Association of School Psychologists (NASP) has taken the position that the practice of school psychology should be generic in nature. That is, school psychologists should be trained to work with all or at least the majority of students in the public schools. This seems to dictate that training in neuropsychology should be required by all school psychology programs since so many learning difficulties include a neuropsychological component (e.g., mental disability, learning disability, and traumatic brain injury). So, too, training guides or courses are available for entire school systems (e.g., see Clark & Hostetter, 1995).

# NEUROPSYCHOLOGICAL ASSESSMENT: A PROCEDURAL CONTINUUM

As noted, much has been learned about the structure and function of the brain in the last century. Although the cerebral hemispheres act in concert, the right hemisphere seems to be specialized for holistic, spatial, and/or nonverbal reasoning, whereas the left shows a preference for verbal, serial, and/or analytic-type tasks (Reynolds, 1981; Walsh, 1978). Similarly, models of cognitive processing have been proposed that agree with the specialization of brain structure. For example, simultaneous processing ability has

been affiliated with the right hemisphere because of its holistic nature; it deals with the synthesis of parts into wholes and is often implicitly spatial (Das, Kirby, & Jarman, 1975). In contrast, the left hemisphere processes information by using a more successive and sequential method—considering the serial or temporal order of input (Dean, 1984, 1986).

Aside from knowledge of hemispheric processing abilities, models of brain organization have been proposed that attempt to explain the diversity and complexity of behavior. Some representative disorders with a neuropsychological component can be found in Table 18.1. One model that has guided theory and research is that of Luria (1980), who proposed three basic blocks of function that are connected with brain structures. Block 1 involves subcortical areas and governs such operations as arousal, wakefulness, and attention. Block 2 is located in temporal, parietal, and occipital cortical regions and addresses the individual's need to analyze, code, and store information. Block 3 regulates intentional behavior and planned response and resides in the frontal cortical region. The elegance of Luria's system lies in its capacity to characterize the brain as an interconnected system of attention, information processing, and action, allowing researchers to

**TABLE 18.1   Disorders Found to Have Neuropsychological Underpinnings**

| | |
|---|---|
| ADD and ADHD | Language disorders |
| Alcoholism | Learning disorders: reading, mathematics, written expression |
| Alzheimer's disease | |
| Asthma | Malnutrition |
| Aphasia | Migraines-headaches |
| Attention deficit disorder | Motor skill disorders |
| Behavioral-personality disorders | Multiple sclerosis |
| Cancer | Muscular dystrophy |
| Dementia not otherwise specified | Parkinson's disease |
| Diabetes | Perceptual disorders |
| Eating disorders | Pervasive developmental disorders |
| Epilepsy | Pick's disease |
| Fetal alcohol syndrome | Prematurity |
| Genetic and chromosomal disorders: phenylketonuria (PKU), Down syndrome | Seizure disorders |
| | Traumatic brain injuries as a result of motor vehicle accidents, pedestrian vehicle accidents, contact/noncontact sports, accidental injuries, abuse, assault |
| Hearing-auditory disorders | |
| HIV/AIDS | |
| Huntington's disease | |
| Hypertension | Vascular disorders |
| Infants exposed to prenatal toxins | Vision problems/disorders |

visualize the integrated and reciprocal nature of the brain's organization. What is observed after damage or as a result of dysfunction is not the deficit per se but how the remaining intact areas and subsystems deal with the task or information presented (Morris, 1989). Basic knowledge of how behaviors seem to be interrelated and the areas of the brain purportedly involved in the behavior-behavior association gives practitioners an additional way of investigating learning.

The thrust of the neuropsychological approach to assessment and later to intervention is to systematically integrate information collected about the individual's neurological integrity with that obtained from a comprehensive review of the environmental systems that are influencing the child. The argument that neuropsychological models look only at the intrinsic aspects of an individual's performance misrepresents the true nature of practice (Gaddes, 1985; Gaddes & Edgell, 1994). It is much more likely that the practitioner who is using a neuropsychological model of inquiry will be more complete in the review of information on the child than one who neglects the internal components of behavior. Far from ignoring environmental controls on performance, the practitioner with a neuropsychological background will try to consolidate environmental and biological aspects that are impinging on the issue or problem under study (Taylor & Fletcher, 1990). Figure 18.1 represents the interactional nature of a neuropsychological approach. Not

only are intraindividual differences in behavior noted but the reciprocal relation of contextual factors to behavioral outcomes are considered as well.

Learners should be evaluated in the four major areas of *content, task, method,* and *context.* Figure 18.2 displays the dynamic interaction of learning, with these four areas merging within the learner.

*Content* refers to the subject area to be covered (e.g., math calculation).

*Task* refers to the knowledge base needed to begin learning the content area.

*Method* considers the instructional approach needed for the learner to be successful.

*Context-Individual* refers to the unique characteristics of the learner (e.g., motivation, interests, family relationships, and peer relationships).

*Context-Instructional* refers to the classroom learning environment.

Data collection within a neuropsychological framework is *not* a set procedure but is governed by the particular orientation of the practitioner. Just as different school psychologists express preferences for the types of data included in

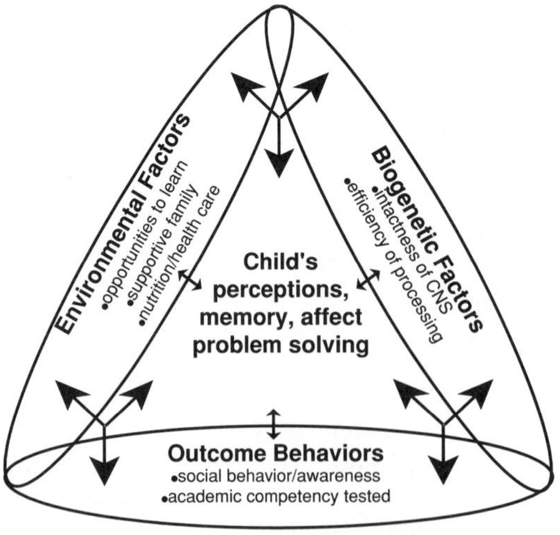

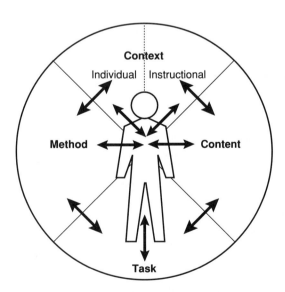

**FIGURE 18.2 Domains to be considered when conducting a neuropsychological evaluation.**

Adapted from Colorado Consortium of Trainers in School Psychology. Figure developed by A. Bardos, R. D'Amato, B. Doll, K. Brehm, S. Kalamaros, M. Lyon, and M. Tombari.

**FIGURE 18.1 Factors to be assessed when working from a neuropsychological perspective.**

their evaluation and intervention plans, neuropsychologists can vary in the degree to which they include quantitative and/or qualitative aspects of performance for the individual being evaluated. In fact, it could be said that distinct "camps" exist within neuropsychology that differ in the types of assessment information deemed most useful. This most obvious dimension, quantitative versus qualitative assessment procedures, helps to define the breadth of information included in a neuropsychological approach. The quantitative-qualitative dimension might also be likened to the purposes of child neuropsychological assessment forwarded by Taylor and Schatschneider (1992). These researchers described the primary aims of assessment as, first, to obtain information on central nervous system integrity based on the extent to which tests are capable of detecting brain status, that is, neuropsychological validity; and second, to use instruments and other sources of information to determine the child's strengths and weaknesses and shed light on the reasons for disabilities, that is, psychological validity. Depending on the position that individuals take on the quantitative-qualitative continuum, these issues of validity will have greater or lesser merit (Retzlaff, Butler, & Vanderploeg, 1992).

## Quantitative Approach

A quantitative or product approach to neuropsychology uses standard performance data to assess individuals within and across all the functional domains to be measured (D'Amato, Rothlisberg & Rhodes, 1997; Dean, 1985b; Lezak, 1995) by comparing the findings to a normative group. This detects whether the individual's skills show a discrepancy when they are compared to other children who are performing within the normal range. Patterns of performance can also be carefully analyzed to determine an individual student's strengths and weaknesses. Data are usually considered in four ways (Jarvis & Barth, 1994; Reitan & Wolfson, 1985; Selz, 1981): (1) level of performance (compared to normative standards), (2) pattern of performance (uniqueness of strengths and weaknesses), (3) right-left differences (comparing tests that evaluate both hemispheres, including both sides of the body), and (4) pathognomic signs (indications of abnormal signs or brain damage). It is interesting that practicing school psychologists may use similar methods or markers to interpret standardized tests but stop short of relating their findings to the brain.

Most proponents of a quantitative neuropsychological approach recommend a standard or fixed battery of tests. A fixed battery, such as the Halstead-Reitan Neuropsychological Test Battery (Reitan & Wolfson, 1985) or the Luria-Nebraska Neuropsychological Battery (Golden, 1981, 1989; Golden & Maruish, 1986), involves the same set of instruments for each individual tested (Hynd & Semrud-Clikeman, 1990; Hynd & Willis, 1988). A standard battery format ensures that *always appropriate tools* are used to cover all significant domains and therefore provide documented results that may be interpreted with ease. In fact, a standard battery approach may be the best choice when and if potential litigation is an issue because this method offers a normative data base to which clients' profiles can be compared and contrasted (Reitan & Wolfson, 1995).

The Halstead-Reitan Neuropsychological Test Battery (HRNB) is the most popular battery used today. It includes tests that were chosen according to their ability to predict brain dysfunction. The entire battery, as proposed by Reitan and Wolfson (1985, 1995), consists of some unique tests, as well as the age-appropriate Wechsler Scale, an achievement test (e.g., Woodcock-Johnson Achievement Battery), a laterality measure (e.g., Lateral Preference Schedule), and an objective personality measure (most often the Minnesota Multiphasic Personality Inventory when older children or adults are evaluated). A comprehensive review of the HRNB can be found in Jarvis & Barth (1994), Lezak (1995), or Reitan and Wolfson (1985, 1995). Component tests of the HRNB are the following:

- The Category Test is useful in measuring problem solving, nonverbal abstract reasoning, and concept formation (Lezak, 1983, 1995; Reitan & Wolfson, 1985; Selz, 1981). The test requires individuals to select colors or numbers that correspond to some abstract problem-solving criteria (i.e., discover the underlying rule). If the person's answer is correct, a bell tone sounds; a buzzing sound indicates an error in reasoning. The immediate feedback is important since the test assesses the person's ability to solve novel problems. This task is used to predict general neuropsychological impairment.

- The Tactile Performance Test (TPT) uses a form board and requires the blindfolded individual to place blocks in their appropriate slots. The task is performed with the dominant hand alone, the nondominant hand alone, and then both hands together. The TPT offers five separate scores—three for time, one for location, and one for memory. This test provides information on tactual discrimination, sensory recognition, and spatial memory (Dean, 1985a; Jarvis & Barth, 1994; Selz, 1981).

- The Speech-Sounds Perception Test is a measure of verbal-auditory discrimination, integration, and attention (Dean, 1985a; Lezak, 1995). A tape-recorded voice presents a sequence of nonsense words. The individual must select the correct word each time from an array of four written possibilities.

- The Seashore Rhythm Test is a measure of nonverbal, auditory discrimination and perception; it can be contrasted with the Speech-Sounds Perception Test, which measures verbal-auditory discrimination (Lezak, 1995; Selz, 1981). In the Seashore Rhythm Test, the individual attempts to match pre-recorded patterns of tones and indicate whether they are the same or different. Success depends on concentration, attention, and nonverbal auditory discrimination.

- The Trail Making Test is made up of two unique but related tracking tasks, which conjointly measure conceptual flexibility, symbolic recognition, and visual tracking under time restraints (Dean, 1985a; Selz, 1981). Reitan and Wolfson (1985) suggest that the Trail Making Tests measure overall functioning because symbolic recognition is a left-hemisphere function, whereas the visual-scanning component more clearly represents right-hemisphere functioning.

- The Finger Oscillation Test requires the person to depress a lever as quickly as possible with the index finger of each hand. This measures gross motor speed and manual dexterity (Selz, 1981). Differences in speed between hands are considered indicative of differences in hemispheric processing.

- The Aphasia Screening Test is a broadband measure of both language and nonverbal functions. Items assess language and provide an overview of general achievement tasks such as naming, copying, spelling, reading, and writing (Lezak, 1995).

- The Reitan-Klove Sensory-Perceptual Examination evaluates bilateral simultaneous sensory stimulation after unilateral stimulation is found to be intact. The auditory, visual, and kinesthetic sensory modalities are each tested separately (Lezak, 1995; Selz, 1981). The examination usually measures auditory-sensory perception, visual-sensory perception, and kinesthetic-sensory perception.

- The Reitan-Klove Tactile Form Recognition Test asks the individual to identify plastic shapes (cross, square, triangle, and circle) when they are placed in one of the person's hands behind a vertical board. The person then uses his or her other free hand to identify the shape, also represented on the corresponding vertical board (Jarvis & Barth, 1994).

- The Grip Strength Test (using a hand dynamometer) evaluates the motor strength of both of the upper extremities (Jarvis & Barth, 1994).

Most quantitative measures like the HRNB are used because they have been found to document the existence of cerebral impairment. Contrary to the belief of many, localization of brain damage is viewed not as determining the specific site of a lesion but rather as offering a better understanding of the systems that remain functional or dysfunctional (D'Amato & Rothlisberg, 1996; Dean, 1985b). It is only after understanding each child's competencies and looking at them within their social contexts that appropriate rehabilitation can be established.

## Qualitative Approach

A qualitative approach to neuropsychological assessment does not deny the power of available quantitative procedures but sees the scope and purpose of assessment in a different light. Practitioners recognize the range of diversity in individual performance on neuropsychological and common psychological tests and techniques and use that individuality to guide assessment. A classic proponent of the qualitative approach, Luria (1980), viewed neuropsychological assessment from a case study perspective. Informal as well as formal assessment procedures could be used to analyze the unique patterns and processes seen in patients. In the pursuit of case analysis, the normative, standardized procedures associated with the quantitative approach were viewed as too rigid to really understand the intricacies of the individual's performance. Instead, unique and individualized sets of procedures, questions, or tasks shaped the evaluation process (for an outline of Luria's method, see Hynd & Semrud-Clikeman, 1990). Luria was interested in how brain damage could disrupt or alter the functional system of organization he had proposed, and he used his process-oriented techniques to direct his hypotheses about his patients (Luria, 1973, 1980).

Although many neuropsychologists identify themselves as using a process-qualitative orientation toward practice (see Guilmette, Faust, Hart, & Arkes, 1990, for survey results), it is difficult to know exactly what that means. Neuropsychologists who value the norm-referenced, quantitative approach to assessment would be hard-pressed to ignore the valuable contribution made by qualitative methods. Indeed, any time examiners note an examinee's reaction to a task, the response time involved, or any problem-solving strategies employed (e.g., rehearsal or verbal cueing), they are inferring the underlying processes being used (Taylor, 1988ab; Taylor & Fletcher, 1990). Thus, it is expected that most practitioners are eclectic in their assessment practices, making use of qualitative procedures and observations to enrich their views of their clients once norm-referenced comparisons have been made.

If a goal of a neuropsychological orientation is to develop hypotheses to better understand why children are having learning or behavior problems, it may be necessary to integrate qualitative methods into the assessment regimen. Taylor and Fletcher (1990) maintain that neuropsychological knowledge and practice are constantly evolving. Informal and experimental procedures are therefore necessary to address the myriad of ways in which individuals can vary in their performance (Fletcher, 1988). Because a child can show a distinctive pattern of learning and behavioral characteristics, it is improbable that any given test, or even battery of tests, in isolation, can capture the range of skills exhibited by that individual. The use of qualitative methods to explore the process of learning or behavior may be better suited than a purely quantitative or prod-

uct-oriented position to suggest intervention options.

Regardless of whether a procedure is promoted as neuropsychologically based or not, the way in which the performance is interpreted can have neuropsychological implications for diagnosis and treatment (Taylor, 1988b). Knowledge of the brain and theories governing information processing can determine the types of data collected during the assessment phase. For example, instead of simply observing whether the learner was successful at a task or set of measures, the practitioner looks beyond the product to see if the influence of neuropsychologically related factors can be discerned. These factors can include the nature of the stimuli (visual, verbal, tactile, etc.), the method of presentation (visual, verbal, concrete, or social), the type of response desired (verbal, motor, or constructional), and the response time allowed (timed or untimed) (Cooley & Morris, 1990). Qualitative procedures can also be used to help analyze tasks into their component parts and help to determine under what sets of conditions performance is optimized (Taylor, 1988a).

There are times when a purely quantitative approach to assessment, used in isolation, may cloud attempts to understand a disability and get at an individual's strengths and weaknesses (Waaland & Kreutzer, 1988). A standardized test procedure often presents information in a prescribed format, with close monitoring of responses and suggested cues to obtain a score. Therefore, it may not be the best method to see how the individual reacts to multiple information inputs (including extraneous information) or selects from a host of problem-solving strategies. Here, the addition of qualitative techniques can be very useful to enhance the practitioner's depth of understanding of learning and behavior. Clark and Hostetter (1995), Harrington (1990), and Ylvisaker et al. (1990) provide excellent advice for using neuropsychological principles for how to look at the process of learning. Their suggestions for detecting learning differences include the following:

- Modification of instructions to involve more or fewer cues to test learning efficiency
- Adjustment of the rate at which information or instruction is given to determine if speed of presentation affects performance
- Modification of the modality of presentation

or response to detect processing differences among receptive and expressive systems

- Variation of environmental stressors (i.e., timing tasks, competitive instead of cooperative learning settings, and demanding an answer) with the difficulty of the task
- Measurement of frustration tolerance when task demands are changed
- Assessment of changes in performance when type of response is changed (i.e., recall versus recognition or verbal versus written)
- Adjustment of task complexity from concrete to abstract to judge the level of understanding

These methods of qualitative assessment give the practitioner insight into what could be processing differences or preferences on the part of the learner. If verbal instruction with verbal response is strongest for the learner, a preference for left-hemisphere processing might be entertained as the reason, and interventions with academic or behavioral difficulties would be tailored with that hypothesis in mind. Similarly, if a learner showed a strength or preference for nonverbal problem-solving situations, instruction could more strongly emphasize pictorial or visual aspects of the content area and downplay verbal explanations. The intent is to use what is learned about the individual's competencies to fashion the most congruent approach to educational programming.

Certainly, one difficulty with a qualitative approach to neuropsychological assessment is its dependence on the clinical skills of the examiner to select and interpret informal or nonstandard test situations. Because process approaches cannot be easily normed, an inexperienced practitioner should be wary of allotting too much power to a purported behavior-brain relation. However, careful review of qualitative data in conjunction with quantitative information could offer useful interpretive options.

When neuropsychologists choose a qualitative approach to assessment they may elect to use a flexible or mixed battery of instruments to measure skills and abilities. Instead of sampling from a standard set of procedures, proponents of a flexible battery would select instruments that address only a subset of the domains possible. Techniques would be geared to exploring hypotheses in a fluid way. Within a mixed battery, a core set of subsets is uniformly administered with

others that are included to measure specific areas of concern.

## Domain Areas or Systems to Be Evaluated

Regardless of the position of the examiner along the quantitative-qualitative continuum, neuropsychological principles aid the practitioner by providing a theoretical base for understanding development and brain functions. In a neuropsychological approach, evaluation for interventions is related to domains or systems. Since the brain serves as a system to produce ideas and behaviors, and given that damage to the brain affects entire systems, it is helpful to conceptualize an evaluation from domain areas rather than from tests or specific problem behaviors. The following domains are offered because of their usefulness to intervention development in educational settings (D'Amato & Rothlisberg, 1992; D'Amato, Rothlisberg, & Rhodes, 1997). These domains or areas include sensory and perceptual systems; motor functions; intelligence/cognitive abilities; memory/learning/processing; communication/language skills; academic achievement; personality/behavior/family; and environmental fit. Each domain can be divided into the subareas in Table 18.2.

Data on the functioning of these domains provide useful information for the school psychologist. Therefore, measures used to evaluate them are listed in Table 18.3. It should be noted that different authors have suggested various subsets of domains for analysis, as well as recommending literally hundreds of other measures appropriate for children and youths (Hynd & Willis, 1988; Lezak, 1995). Thus, the instruments categorized in Table 18.3 represent only a sampling of available measures.

## Purpose of an Assessment

Neuropsychological assessment occurs because questions raised about an individual's performance have defied standard analysis. These questions should drive the focus of the evaluation. The following are types of questions that family members or school personnel commonly ask: Why is the learner suddenly failing? Why does the child want only to be alone? Why has he or she begun to fight? What methods can we use to help? Parents and school personnel are often baffled by academic, behavioral, and

**TABLE 18.2** **Systems to Be Formally and Informally Assessed in Neuropsychological Evaluations**

**Sensory and Perceptual**

Visual
Auditory
Tactile-kinesthetic
Integrated

**Motor Functions**

Strength
Speed
Coordination
Lateral preference

**Intelligence/Cognitive Abilities**

Verbal functions
    Language skills
    Concepts-reasoning
    Numerical abilities
    Integrative functioning
Nonverbal functions
    Receptive perception
    Expressive perception
    Abstract reasoning
    Spatial manipulation
    Construction
    Visual
    Integrative functions

**Memory/Learning/Processing**

Visual processing
Motoric processing
Auditory processing
Spatial processing
Linguistic-verbal processing
Simultaneous processing
Sequential processing
Memory-learning

**Communication/Language Skills**

Receptive vocabulary
Expressive vocabulary
Speech-language
Written language

**Academic Achievement**

Preacademic skills
Academic skills
    Reading decoding
    Reading comprehension
    Arithmetic facts
    Arithmetic calculation
    Social studies
    Language arts
    Science

**Personality/Behavior/Family**

Adaptive behavior
    Daily living
    Development
    Play-leisure
Environmental-social
    Parental-siblings
    Family-community
Learner coping and tolerance
Interpersonal style

**Environmental Fit**

Learning environment
Peer and community reactions
Teacher-staff knowledge
Learner competencies
Teacher-staff reactions

Adapted from D'Amato & Rothlisberg (1996) and D'Amato, Rothlisberg, & Rhodes (1997).

## TABLE 18.3 Common Instruments and Procedures to Evaluate Neuropsychological Functions

### Sensory and Perceptual

Child and classroom observations
Developmental history
Mental status examination
Motor-free Visual Perception Test
Reitan-Klove Sensory-Perception Examination (Halstead-Reitan Battery)
Reitan-Klove Tactile Form Recognition Test (Halstead-Reitan Battery)
Tactile-visual (Luria-Nebraska Battery)
Vision and hearing screening

### Motor (fine and gross)

Bender Visual-Motor Gestalt Test
Detroit Test of Learning Aptitude–3 (Motoric Composite)
Developmental Test of Visual-Motor Integration
Finger Oscillation Test (Halstead-Reitan Battery)
Grip Strength Test (Halstead-Reitan Battery)
K-ABC Nonverbal Scale (e.g., Hand Movements subtest)
McCarthy Scales of Children's Abilities (Motor Scale)
Motor skills (Luria-Nebraska Battery)
Tactile Performance Test (Halstead-Reitan Battery)
WISC-III (Block Design, Object Assembly, Coding subtests)

### Intelligence/Cognitive

Battelle Developmental Inventory
Bayley Scales of Infant Development (2nd. ed.)
Category test (Halstead-Reitan Battery)
Das-Naglieri Cognitive Assessment System
Differential Ability Scales
Intelligence (Luria-Nebraska Battery)
Kaufman Adolescent and Adult Intelligence Test
Kaufman Assessment Battery for Children
Wechsler Adult Intelligence Scale–Revised
Wechsler Intelligence Scale for Children (3rd ed.)

### Academic Achievement

Differential Ability Scales
Kaufman Test of Educational Achievement
Key Math Diagnostic Arithmetic Test–Revised
Peabody Individual Achievement Test–Revised
Reading, writing, arithmetic (Luria-Nebraska Battery)
Wechsler Individual Achievement Test
Woodcock Reading Mastery Test–Revised
Woodcock-Johnson Psycho-Educational Battery–Revised: Achievement

### Communication/Language Skills

Aphasia Screening Test (Halstead-Reitan Battery)
Bracken Basic Concept Scale
Peabody Picture Vocabulary Test–Revised
Receptive/expressive language (Luria-Nebraska Battery)

**TABLE 18.3** (*Continued*)

| Communication/Language Skills |
|---|
| Revised Token Test |
| Test of Adolescent Language |
| Test of Language Development |
| Test of Written Language |

| Attention/Learning/Processing |
|---|
| Children's Auditory Verbal Learning Test |
| Detroit Tests of Learning Ability–3 |
| Rhythm Test (Halstead-Reitan Battery) |
| Speech-Sounds Perception Test (Halstead-Reitan Battery) |
| Tactile Performance Test (Halstead-Reitan Battery) |
| Tests of Memory and Learning |
| Trail Making Test (Halstead Reitan Battery) |
| Wechsler Memory Scale–Revised |
| Wide Range Assessment of Memory and Learning |
| Wisconsin Card Sort |

| Personality/Behavior/Family |
|---|
| Behavioral Assessment System for Children |
|     Parent Rating Scales |
|     Self-report of Personality |
|     Teacher Rating Scales |
| Burk's Behavior Rating Scales |
| Clinical interview with child or adolescent |
| Home visit and family-parent interview |
| Minnesota Multiphasic Personality Inventory–2 |
| Personality Inventory for Children |
| Revised Children's Manifest Anxiety Scale |
| Thematic Apperception Test |
| Vineland Adaptive Behavior Scales |

Adapted from D'Amato, Rothlisberg, & Rhodes (1997).

personality changes, and thus the referral question becomes extremely important.

After the areas of behavioral concern have been identified, hypothesis generation is conducted by the practitioner. A goal of the evaluation is always to refute or confirm a hypothesis based on assessment findings, information collected from interviews, and behavioral observations. Hypotheses should be recorded, and supporting or disputing data should be listed as the evaluation progresses. Based on the pertinent hypotheses, the choice of a neuropsychological approach is made (e.g., fixed or flexible).

## NEUROPSYCHOLOGICAL APPROACHES TO INDIVIDUALIZED INTERVENTIONS

Providing effective interventions should be the cornerstone of any evaluation. In fact, it could be argued that an evaluation is only as effective as the interventions or treatments that flow from it (Bigler, 1990; Cullum, Kuck, & Ruff, 1990). Unfortunately, interventions are often neglected or downplayed in an evaluation because of difficulties in determining their effectiveness. It may be helpful to conceptualize the application of interventions as a process. In this process, an intervention is based on a careful and comprehensive evaluation, which has included information from all desired domains. Then, the intervention is applied and its success monitored and adjusted. Last, the effectiveness of the intervention is ascertained and adjustments made as needed. This approach to the application of treatments is especially important because a typical or characteristic neuropsychological pattern of recovery after injury does not exist (Telzrow, 1985). Two children with similar damage from a blow to the head may demonstrate differing abilities and strengths. Whereas one learner can exhibit difficulties with attention and long-range planning, the other learner may exhibit motoric problems and reading difficulties but have strength in mathematics. Because neuropsychology considers the way in which behaviors relate to one another, as well as the neurological underpinnings of competencies, it should provide a range of treatment options beyond a study of an individual's weaknesses. Instead, the focus shifts to what the brain *can* do and how it *does* effectively process information (D'Amato, 1990; Morris, 1989; Reynolds, 1986).

### Strength-based Focus

Psychology in general, and education specifically, have maintained a long-standing focus on individual performance *deficits* (Bigler, 1990; Reynolds, 1986). That is, learners' weaknesses were identified and intervention programs that emphasized the remediation of problem areas were designed (e.g., visual-motor training and modality training). Unfortunately, a deficit focus was not found to be effective in either discipline (Hartlage & Telzrow, 1983). For example, special education resource rooms have been seen as ineffective because many interventions only address children's weaknesses (D'Amato, 1990; Reynolds, 1981). As shown in Figure 18.2, the academic content to be taught is a small part of the instructional paradigm (D'Amato & Dean, 1987).

A strength-based approach becomes particularly important when working with children who have suffered a trauma, such as a head injury. When parts of the brain are permanently damaged, the learner will experience only greater frustration if the focus of the intervention depends on rehabilitation of the injured areas of the brain. For example, if a learner has sustained

a frontal lobe injury and has difficulty with planning and mental flexibility, it is of little assistance to either the family or the school merely to verify this information. However, determining what the learner can do allows interventions to be formulated that are likely to be effective and provide valuable information (Dean, 1985a; Hartlage & Telzrow, 1985). Moreover, children are often more willing to comply with interventions if the required tasks do not emphasize a weakness but, instead, utilize an area of strength. Similarly, family members may be more willing to assist in interventions if they understand that the learner does have capacities from which to build. Thus, information about the strengths of each learner should be sought throughout the evaluation process.

Intervention may be further conceptualized by using one of three approaches: remediation, compensation, or a combination of both (D'Amato & Rothlisberg, 1996). Each of these approaches is described to illustrate their utility.

### Remedial Approaches

Remediation is the direct teaching of a particular concept to an individual. It can be useful if the needed skill is age-appropriate and the child has never been given the opportunity to learn that specific skill. For example, a second-grade student, who has recently arrived from a rural area, may never have been taught reading. A remedial approach could be used to teach the skills and strategies needed for reading, the goal being to gain a level of expertise similar to his or her classmates. Generally, a remedial approach is deemed effective if the learner makes documented progress. If no progress is made, compensatory strategies may be in order (Gaddes & Edgell, 1994).

### Compensatory Methods

Compensatory teaching methods are used when the child has either lost or lacks the ability to acquire a concept or skill. Different instructional methods, styles, or types of responses can be used to help a child process information. A compensatory approach is useful with children who have been permanently impaired or lack the ability to gain a skill or concept. Just as a child in a wheelchair compensates for the lack of mobility by using wheels, a learner with reading difficulties could compensate by using books on tape.

The learner gains the information without failing in his or her attempt to read. Compensatory methods acknowledge the presence of *roadblocks* in the learning process and seek detours or alternate routes for the learner to accomplish the same goals.

## Integrating Remediation and Compensation

A combined approach to intervention uses both compensation and remediation to facilitate the attainment of skills and concepts. The combination of remediation and compensation is often useful with children since their brains are developing and the impact of neuropsychological damage may be unknown or could fluctuate. In other words, a combined approach is used when the evidence supporting the use of remediation or compensation remains unclear and it is not known whether the child has had the opportunity to gain a skill or is unable to learn the required task. In essence, it allows the learner a choice of strategies when handling a problematic situation. For example, a child with reading-decoding problems might still be made aware of the sound-letter relationship (remediation) but would receive more intensive instruction in sight-word or contextual cue strategies for reading if visual processing and language usage are strengths (compensation). Or if a child has social skill deficits, attempts at remediation (placing the child in social situations) would be supplemented by compensatory aids (providing feedback and cues on performance).

## S.O.S. for Educational Interventions

To clarify the process of providing interventions in an educational setting, the acronym S.O.S.—which stands for *structure, organization,* and *strategies*—is a useful tool. Initially devised for learners who had suffered traumatic brain injury, it is also helpful for those with a variety of neuropsychological needs (D'Amato & Rothlisberg, 1996). This conceptual aid simplifies the levels involved in the intervention process and helps staff members understand the ongoing nature of rehabilitation.

## Structure

Structure refers to the aid gained from the *physical setting*. Children with neuropsychological difficulties often exhibit problems in organizing themselves in space and time. Providing a structured environment that is predictable and consistent allows the learner to function effectively. Specific components of the structure might include creating a home-school partnership, increasing consistency of teachers across the years (e.g., providing the same teacher or group of teachers), providing clear and constant behavioral expectations in the classroom, utilizing a life skill focus, offering vocational education, controlling environmental stimulation, and considering the endurance and stamina of the child.

## Organization

Organization, which is closely related to structure, provides cues and aides that allow the child to gain new learning, as well as access to prior learning. Organizational tactics include teaching the child *how* to learn rather than *what* to learn (Cohen, 1986). Methods might include using compensatory aids such as assignment notebooks, copying notes or tape-recording class lectures, using role models, and teaching social skills.

## Strategies

Strategies refers to the selection of methods that help students control the *process* of learning. Not surprisingly, schools are almost always able to accommodate the academic content areas. However, children with information-processing differences may need assistance in developing cognitive strategies to help them acquire and integrate information. For example, memory-building techniques might be needed to aid in recall of information. Problem-solving strategies would also be included under this mnemonic, providing systematic methods that could aid a learner in determining a course of action and deriving a solution.

## INTERVENTIONS APPLIED TO DOMAINS AND SYSTEMS

To this point, interventions have been discussed in procedural terms, with emphasis given to the general types and levels of adaptation possible. However, just as assessment considers a range of behaviors, so, too, do interventions. Because neuropsychological difficulties are more likely to influence behavioral domains than the performance of isolated tasks, intervention strategies can be conceptualized by brain-related systemic areas. These performance systems may respond differentially when brain impairment or processing differences are present (Clark & Hostetter, 1995). To illustrate the ways in which change might be facilitated in the various systems, representative treatment techniques are offered.

## Sensory-Perceptual Skills

Sensory-perceptual skills are vital to children's understanding and response to the environment because they form the basis of each child's interaction with the world (D'Amato, Rothlisberg, & Rhodes, 1997; Lezak, 1983). Difficulties may show themselves in the individual's inability to use information gained through the senses. For example, a child may be able to hear sounds well but have trouble understanding what is heard (auditory processing). Likewise, a child may be able to see words clearly but have problems in reproducing them when writing (visual-motor difficulties). If children have difficulty in comprehending what they hear, visual or nonverbal cues may be needed to inform them of assignments and directions instead of oral instructions. Other skills influenced by sensory-perceptual problems might include understanding the written word in texts or on the chalkboard. Sensory-perceptual adaptations might include exposing the learner to a variety of experiences that stimulate other sense systems like smell, sight, touch, or taste. Thus, it is evident that sensory-perceptual tasks often form the foundation for the later performance of higher-order cognitive skills. Without the ability to accurately sense and perceive cues from the environment, the learner is placed in the position of trying to decode a message when the code is scrambled and often changing.

Interventions for the sensory-perceptual system include the following:

- Providing the learner with additional cues based on touch rather than depending solely on written or verbal messages
- Providing a young child with clay or sand to feel the letters rather than relying on sight alone
- Giving the learner strategies to check his or her own perceptions (e.g., using the position of the thumbs in left to right sequence to tell if a letter is a *b* or a *d*)
- Providing instruction through a variety of sensory channels (e.g., using overheads or writing on the board while speaking)

## Motor Functions

The motor domain involves a range of both fine and gross motor movements. Fine motor skills are commonly thought of as movements that do not involve the entire body, for example, writing, opening a letter, or tying a shoe. Gross motor movements involve large extremities and often the entire body, such as walking or sitting down. Intentional movements, using both fine and gross motor skills, involve a series of brain-based systems. These movements are learned with repetition. With repetition the movement becomes rote or, as Luria (1973) described it, a kinesthetic melody. Movement can also consist of both discrete and continuous patterns. Movements that are discrete might involve something as simple as lifting a finger, whereas continuous movements include an integrated set of skills like skipping. Movements may be disrupted if there is damage to the premotor cortex, where the kinesthetic melody is believed to be formed. If this occurs, the learner may not be able to perform serial-continuous movements but may be able to demonstrate individual discrete movements. Because of the complexity of motor patterns, the learner's posture, movement in isolation, and movement in serial order should be assessed for possible intervention. This can be accomplished by observing learners completing tasks, such as writing their names (uses one hand), tying their shoes (uses both hands), and performing novel tasks like repeated tapping or clapping patterns. It should be noted whether there is difficulty in integrating the use of both hands. Both fine and gross motor skills should always be evaluated.

Interventions for motoric impairments may include the following:

- Modifying instructions to compensate for motor difficulties (e.g., letting the child point to the correct choice rather than being required to write a response)
- Providing frequent rest periods because the expenditure of energy required to perform such tasks as walking or writing is greater for children with impairment than children who demonstrate no motoric difficulties
- Allowing children to tape-record notes or copy them from others
- Providing environmental adaptations that allow the motorically impaired learner to join in cooperative projects (e.g., a child with motor integration difficulties may be

able to contribute ideas during group work if another child records responses)

- Playing games like "operation," which provide auditory feedback about performance in a fine motor task.

## Intelligence and Cognitive Abilities

Cognitive rehabilitation is an emerging discipline that includes the retraining or use of compensatory strategies in thinking and problem-solving skills (Wedding, Horton, & Webster, 1986). Cognitive retraining can include assistance in strategy development for attention and concentration, memory, language, perceptual and cognitive deficits, and social behavior. Thus, the term *cognitive retraining* encompasses all areas of functioning that may have been affected by neuropsychological difficulties.

Assisting learners with cognitive remediation or compensation often includes the use of metacognitive strategies. Metacognition includes analyzing the processes an individual uses to generate an idea or thought. By assisting children in breaking down problems and understanding the processes needed to solve them, children may learn how to generalize the process to many problem types and improve their overall learning. Although cognitive training is time-consuming, the generalizability of the strategies to many settings has been seen by some researchers (Gray & Dean, 1989; Kavale, Forness, & Bender, 1988). Cognitive rehabilitation is the cumulative goal in any rehabilitation program because all domains and aspects of functioning could be included.

## Memory, Learning, and Processing Areas

Neuropsychological difficulties have been associated with attentional problems like impulsivity, distractibility, and poor social judgment. Problems in the learning process may reflect an uncertainty about whether a concept has been learned or not (Cohen, 1991). The processing area is more difficult to evaluate and is often subsumed in intelligence or achievement domains. Sometimes, specialized measures of processing, learning, or memory (e.g., Test of Memory and Learning) are utilized to evaluate students' abilities.

Memory skills are certainly associated with learning ability but are a difficult area to address because of their variety of levels (e.g., working, short term, and long term) and the potential ramifications of deficits. Therefore, interventions in the memory domain may be divided several ways:

those that involve language; those that are nonverbal; those that require long, short, or intermediate memory; and those that use a combined approach to aid in retention (Gaddes & Edgell, 1994; Lezak, 1995). Strategy selection depends on accessing those parts of the brain that have been the least affected by injury. For example, learners who have difficulty with nonverbal memory tasks but have retained verbal skills may benefit from memory interventions that use language. Mnemonic devices may assist in the recall of information if a series of problem-solving steps is required. For example, each step in the series could be paired with a name that works as a trigger for information recall. Names could be linked together in a silly sentence, such as "Anna's blueberry pies taste excellent," each word representing a step to be recalled: *a*nalyze the problem, *b*rainstorm solutions, *p*ick a solution, *t*ry it, and *e*valuate.

Other organizational interventions can also help with recall. A tape recorder may help students recall the assignments or reinforce instruction. Or children may be helped if the teacher provides written guidelines on how the work is to be completed. Another option is a memory book or a notebook for those students who have the ability to write. In a memory book, assignments may be recorded, as well as the names of teachers, friends, locker combinations, or whatever information is needed for successful daily functioning. Some have argued that memory aids are difficult to implement because they require training and extensive practice (Gouvier, Webster, & Blanton, 1986). At the very least, daily routines should be simple and repetitive to facilitate encoding into memory; for example, instructions should be repeated several times (Blosser & DePompei, 1991).

Visual imagery has been suggested as a strategy to facilitate the recall of words. Techniques such as peg-word systems incorporate paired associate learning to link numbers or words with vivid mental images. This ordered imagery is then associated with unknown material to construct a fanciful mental picture that is easy to recall. When recall is needed, the mental image is decoded through the peg-word (Gouvier, Webster, & Blanton, 1986).

Additional interventions in the memory, learning, and processing area include the following:

- Using a colored line on the wall to mark the way into a building or to a specific classroom

- Using nonverbal signs or sounds as cues for severely impaired learners
- Visualizing an object to pair with a task, for example, representing the daily schedule in symbols or simple pictures rather than words (Gouvier, Webster, & Blanton, 1986)
- Making work periods shorter and limiting distractions
- Simplifying the presentation of materials
- Maintaining a routine in daily activities
- Using a timer so that the learner knows the specific amount of time he or she is expected to attend
- Modifying response requirements to those more appropriate for the student (pointing and recognition rather than recall)

## Communication and Language Skills

Language should be viewed as a key neuropsychological skill because it serves as a primary means of conveying information from the learner to others and from others to the learner. Thus, communication difficulties have the power to affect all areas of life. Assessment must evaluate both receptive and expressive verbal and nonverbal abilities to determine if adaptations to instruction are needed to enhance the learner's understanding of academic and social situations. Word-finding errors are also common and should be assessed.

Interventions in the communication and language system include the following:

- Modifying verbal instructions (shortening them or presenting them in steps)
- Providing repetition of verbal instructions on an intermittent basis and allowing the learner to repeat and explain the instructions back to the teacher to check for understanding
- Pairing verbal instructions with nonverbal cues (e.g., pointing to the reading table while asking the student to take out a book)
- Using nonverbal cues such as sign language, pictures, simple signs, or language boards
- Employing communication devices like voice synthesizers for children with severely impaired language skills

## Academic Achievement

Interventions in the academic arena should be closely linked to the needs of learners when interacting within the family, school, and community. Often learners with neuropsychological im-

pairments need classroom adaptations that have been specifically individualized to meet their difficulties. Development of instructional modifications that capitalize on teachers' strengths are also important. Placement decisions, as well as the learner-teacher match, must be closely monitored (Leu & D'Amato, 1994). The practitioner is advised to use texts that provide specific interventions in individual academic areas, such as reading or mathematics (e.g., see Polloway, Patton, Payne, & Payne, 1991), or to review guides that are geared for serving specific disability areas, such as traumatic brain injuries (TBI) (e.g., Clark & Hostetter, 1985; D'Amato & Rothlisberg, 1996; Savage & Wolcott, 1994).

Specific interventions in the academic achievement area include the following:

- Slowing down the pace of instruction
- Repeating instructions for the student
- Teaching specifically *how* to complete a task, for example, helping children to find the classroom or to understand how to place responses correctly on the paper
- Providing organizational skills and systems for the learner (Cohen, 1991)
- Assisting students through study skills programs or techniques like the SQ3R technique (Cheek & Cheek, 1983)
- Modifying test-taking requirements (e.g. more time to respond, use of tests on tape, oral rather than written responses, or a multiple-choice format

## Personality, Behavior, and Family

The practitioner must understand the importance of the learner's personality and behavior in the intervention process. These factors drastically influence the success or failure of learning, as well as affect every interaction the individual has with others in his or her world. Personality and behavior interact with the students' many social and academic challenges. For example, students with learning disabilities often seem to lose their motivation to learn as they grow older because their efforts have met with repeated failure and frustration. Interventions in the personality and behavioral area need to be fully incorporated across all settings in an ongoing, dynamic manner. This approach is fully expressed in milieu therapy (Prigatano, 1990). For example, if the child is distressed by placement in lower-level courses, the distress might be addressed in a therapy session later in the same day. This approach is immediate and addresses the child's individual needs.

The family system must also be evaluated when conceptualizing the relationship between the family and child. When a child experiences neuropsychological trauma, the family often has difficulty in adapting to the physical, emotional, and intellectual changes that may occur (Sachs, 1991). Particularly with injury, it is important for the practitioner to understand that the family members may be going through a grieving process. Unfortunately, the time when interventions should be initiated is often the very same time that the family may be denying the extent of the child's trauma (Slaikeu, 1990). Working with the family as a system may provide the best opportunity for family members to express their grief and loss (Martin, 1990; Sachs, 1991), as well as adjust to the child's new needs. The focus of therapy or intervention should be on helping the family to adapt, access support networks, and tolerate stress. Adaptation should be viewed as a process that is fluid and changing over time (Martin, 1990). Support for both professionals and the family may be garnered through national foundations (e.g., the National Head Injury Foundation, which is a nationwide self-help group). State-run groups with national or regional affiliations are also available, and many communities have support groups for head-injured survivors and their families.

Interventions in the personality and behavioral system include the following:

- Assisting the teacher, school, and family with behavioral management approaches that are consistent across settings
- Helping the school and family to understand the changes that may have occurred in the child's personality as a result of an illness or injury
- Providing individual counseling for the child, peers, school personnel, and family as needed to cope with changes related to behavior
- Offering appropriate groups for the child-youth and/or parents-family (such as peer support, friendship development, and social skills training)
- Helping children and youths learn to control behavior through such interventions as hypnosis or biofeedback (Wenck, D'Amato, & Leu, 1996)

## Environmental Fit

Educational and home environments must be carefully considered when the learner plans to reenter or continue in school after neuropsychological impairment. Environmental factors can interact with the learner's characteristics and affect the degree of adjustment to an adapted setting (Leu & D'Amato, 1994). Dunst, McWilliams, and Holbert (1986) have outlined a five-step approach to environmental assessment. First, a self-assessment is conducted by all the adults involved in the child's environments. Second, an outside evaluation is made by an unbiased party. Third, the self and outside evaluations are combined and analyzed. Fourth, a plan that capitalizes on the strengths of the various environments is formulated and implemented. The idea is to provide the greatest degree of consistency across behavior settings so that the learner can concentrate his or her efforts on acquiring necessary skills. Fifth, the behavior and academic successes of the learner are monitored to determine if changes in environmental placement are needed. This process can aid in the often overwhelming task of environmental assessment, as well as suggest methods to provide a comfortable child-environment fit. It also allows persons in the environment to participate, making the process multidisciplinary.

Interventions in the environmental fit area include the following:

- Tutoring at home or in the hospital for individuals who need long-term care
- Providing sheltered living or specially trained foster care if the family is not able to care for an individual with a disability
- Placing an individual in a residential treatment facility if home and school environments cannot insure safety for the child or youth or others
- Selecting a teacher, as well as a class, according to the match with a learner's needs
- Using trained management aides in the classroom
- Coordinating a consistent behavior program between home and school or community
- Providing the learner with breaks during the day if needed for fatigue, which can lead to behavioral problems
- Giving the learner a snack if needed to replenish energy in the midmorning and afternoon
- Offering supportive career education, vocational training, and field placements for older learners

# SUMMARY

Neuropsychologists are interested in identifying the behavioral consequences of a suspected disorder—a behavioral-behavioral association—and how it affects future functioning (Fletcher, 1988). The advantage of the evolving neuropsychological approach is the attention given to *layers* or systems of factors that impinge on the child—from underlying biological determinants to the mediating influences of social systems (parents and family and the schools). Consequently, the underlying disability may not be as critical to future adaptability as the environmental responses to it. Children may be able to compensate well even with severe disabilities if the support systems of family, school, and community are able to accommodate differential learning styles. Unfortunately, the reverse can also be true: children with no demonstrable problems or minor disabilities may be unable to adjust to educational expectations if the support systems are unavailable or inconsistent. A neuropsychological view can consider the reciprocal nature of all systems that influence the child.

School psychologists will not automatically be able to call themselves neuropsychologists on the basis of interest or even training in the area. However, a neuropsychological frame of reference will enrich practice because it includes a consideration of the biological underpinnings of behavior without the loss of other perspectives on cognitive, emotional, and social development. The addition of the neuropsychological perspective acknowledges the presence of individual variation without eliminating the impact of the greater environment on the person's ability to function. Indeed, weaknesses do not become such unless some outside standard declares a level of acceptable performance. The strength of considering the unique aspects of the individual from a neuropsychological perspective is that it need not judge the learner from a limited, and unfortunately, negative focus. Because of its interest in function and behavior-to-behavior and behavior-to-brain relationships, neuropsychology helps psychologists to fully understand the mechanisms that drive behavior. As our knowledge of the nervous system is expanded and we begin to understand the intricacies of the brain's organization, we can begin to see how perceptions are formed, information stored and integrated, and action taken. Until that time, the explanation for behavior and certain learning difficulties can only be inferred.

# ILLUSTRATIVE CASE REPORTS

Two case reports illustrate how quantitative and qualitative neuropsychological data, stemming from individual and systemic views of brain functioning, can be integrated to provide realistic interventions.

# THE CASE OF STAN

Stan, age 12, was referred in seventh grade by his school district for an evaluation at a university neuropsychological laboratory because of a severe learning disability. He had been evaluated twice in a local school district and received special education in the form of resource room assistance and speech therapy, but he did not demonstrate reasonable academic progress. He was a quiet individual who was often thought to be mentally retarded by those in his school because of his awkward movements, limited vocabulary, and hesitancy to speak. Stan's parents reported that he had always been much quieter than the other children and that he was like an uncle who was now in prison. They stated that at home he enjoyed playing video games and putting bikes together from spare parts.

Stan was a nonreader and received consistently low grades. In second grade he had some success by using a phonetic approach to reading words in isolation but had difficulty when attempting to use words in context. Several teachers insisted that Stan was mentally retarded and in fact had previously refused to sign a multidisciplinary report stating that Stan had a learning disability.

Stan was evaluated by the Halstead-Reitan Neuropsychological Test Battery for Children, the Test of Memory and Learning, the Woodcock-Johnson Tests of Achievement–Revised, the Vineland Adaptive Behavior Scales, several personality tests including the Behavioral Assessment Scale for Children and the Wechsler Intelligence Scale for Children–III, and several qualitative techniques such as work samples and classroom observations. The results of a recent medical evaluation indicated that Stan was in excellent health with generally good vision and hearing. Inadequate medical care after an earlier accident had resulted in a slight limp, and a defect from birth, which shortened the tendons in his left hand, accounted for his generally awkward movements.

After the evaluation, it was determined that Stan demonstrated significant differences between his abilities to solve problems through verbal solutions and nonverbal or performance solutions. His ability to solve novel problems or deal with nonverbal tasks was in the average range. Conversely, his ability to solve problems by using language, depending on knowledge learned over time, was in the moderately retarded range. Although Stan demonstrated nonverbal concept formation (synthesis) in the superior range, other test scores (e.g., Block Design) indicated that he had difficulty in solving whole-to-part (analysis) nonverbal problems. His performance also indicated average mental flexibility. Stan was able to differentiate sounds that were not related to words but had great difficulty in distinguishing between similar words. Stan's personality characteristics indicated that he was an isolated, passive person who followed others and did little to demonstrate his own independence at home or at school. Adaptive behavior was average in most areas with the exception of socialization skills, which were extremely low.

Whereas Stan's parents were happy to hear that he was not mentally retarded, some school personnel continued to be reluctant to accept the findings of the report. Stan's strengths in solving problems by using part-to-whole nonverbal solutions was stressed. His average functioning in solving nonverbal tasks was also accentuated in the team meeting that followed the report. Stan's mother had recently procured a job for him at a local bicycle shop, helping to assemble new bicycles. It was recommended that Stan be allowed to use some visual cues (similar to sign language) to supplement his communication skills. His resource teacher agreed to allow him to use visual cues paired with words to help him in reading and spelling simple words about bicycles. The team agreed to reconvene in a month to assess the success of the interventions and to formulate additional interventions. One month later, Stan displayed much progress when taught to his strengths and also did extremely well in the bicycle shop.

## THE CASE OF BECKY

Becky, an 18-year-old high school senior, was referred for an evaluation after an automobile accident, which had occurred at age 14, in her freshman year. During her hospitalization, Becky was unconscious for five hours and, when awakened, had no memory of the day before the accident. After her release, Becky's parents noted a marked difference from her preaccident behavior (e.g., she now sat alone in her room for several hours each day and was depressed). In addition, her consumption of alcohol increased dramatically after the accident, and old friends who were initially supportive began to lose interest and no longer invited her to social functions. When school began, Becky was placed in special education classes for academic support. After the first year, she was treated for alcoholism, and some of her behaviors became less problematic. After the accident, both Becky's teachers and parents reported that her attention seemed limited, her memory seemed impaired, and that she displayed significant difficulty in locating herself in space (e.g., getting lost in the school hallways). Becky refused special transportation provided by the school (because it was embarrassing); instead she risked becoming lost while walking. Finally, Becky's family asked the university clinic to conduct a neuropsychological evaluation and provide recommendations for Becky's vocational transition and suggest options of employment.

Becky was given the Halstead-Reitan Neuropsychological Test Battery, tests of personality, a test of memory, and several qualitative procedures including work samples and observations in different settings. The results of the neuropsychological evaluation indicated that Becky's intellectual functioning was in the low average range. She had difficulty with short-term memory but was able to retain material once it was learned. Mental flexibility was problematic for her, but she was able to sequence items rapidly and accurately. Becky appeared to be able to integrate information more successfully if she did not use visual cues. Instead, she was able to solve problems tactually, with a focus on using intact auditory-processing abilities. Her awareness of her body in space was limited, and she had no perception in the upper right quadrant of the visual field in both of her eyes. She remained aware of proper behavior in social situations and wanted to be viewed as normal by her peers. Becky also exhibited a drive toward independence and a wish to live on her own.

It was recommended that the transition team help Becky attend a special course for independent living offered at the local community college. The school offered to provide transportation, but Becky stated that she preferred to take the city bus. Another student who was also attending a transition course at the community college offered to accompany Becky to the campus. One successful modification to her new school environment was a green line taped to the wall to allow Becky to follow it to her classroom and out again after class so she could locate her bus. She also completed a vocational evaluation that emphasized her personal strengths of tactile problem solving and sequential processing.

As a result of the evaluations and with appropriate interventions, Becky now lives in an apartment complex designed for head-injured adults. She has a data entry job and types information she hears from a Dictaphone into a computer. As a hobby, she takes a course in photography at a local community college. Her long-term goal is to be able to live in an apartment by herself and be financially self-supporting.

# REFERENCES

Bigler, E. D. (1990). *Traumatic brain injury: Mechanisms of damage, assessment, intervention, and outcome.* Austin, TX: Pro-Ed.

Blosser, J. L., & DePompei, R. (1991). Preparing educational professionals for meeting the needs of students with traumatic brain injury. *Journal of Head Trauma Rehabilitation, 6,* 73–82.

Chapman, L. F., & Wolff, H. G. (1959). The cerebral hemispheres and the highest integrative functions of man. *A.M.A. Archives of Neurology, 1,* 357–424.

Cheek, E. H., & Cheek, M. C. (1983). *Reading instruction through content teaching.* Columbus, OH: Merrill.

Chittooran, M. M., D'Amato, R. C., Lassiter, K. S., & Dean, R. S. (1993). Factor structure of psychoeducational and neuropsychological measures with learning disabled children. *Psychology in the Schools, 30,* 109–118.

Clark, E., & Hostetter, C. (1995). *Traumatic brain injury: Training manual for school personnel.* Longmont, CO: Sopris West.

Cohen, S. B. (1986). Educational reintegration and programming for children with head injuries. *Journal of Head Trauma Rehabilitation, 1*(4), 22–29.

Cohen, S. B. (1991). Adapting educational programs for students with head injuries. *Journal of Head Trauma Rehabilitation, 6,* 56–63.

Cooley, E. L., & Mooris, R. D. (1990). Attention in children: A neuropsychology based model for assessment. *Developmental Neuropsychology, 6,* 239–274.

Cullum, C. M., Kuck, J., & Ruff, R. M. (1990). Neuropsychological assessment of traumatic brain injury in adults. In E. D. Bigler (Ed.),

*Traumatic brain injury: Mechanisms of damage, assessment, intervention and outcome* (pp. 129–163). Austin, TX: Pro-Ed.

D'Amato, R. C. (1990). A neuropsychological approach to school psychology. *School Psychology Quarterly, 5,* 141–160.

D'Amato, R. C., & Dean, R. S. (1987). Psychological assessment reports, individual education plans, and daily lesson plans: Are they related? *Professional School Psychology, 2,* 93–101.

D'Amato, R. C., & Dean, R. S. (1988). School psychology practice in a department of neurology. *School Psychology Review, 17,* 416–420.

D'Amato, R. C., Dean, R. S., & Holloway, A. F. (1987). A decade of employment trends in neuropsychology. *Professional Psychology: Research and Practice, 18,* 653–655.

D'Amato, R. C., Gray, J. W., & Dean, R. S. (1988). A comparison between intelligence and neuropsychological functioning. *Journal of School Psychology, 26,* 282–292.

D'Amato, R. C., Hammons, P. F., Terminie, T. J., & Dean, R. S. (1992). Neuropsychological training in American Psychological Association–accredited and nonaccredited school psychology programs. *Journal of School Psychology, 30,* 175–183.

D'Amato, R. C., & Rothlisberg, B. A. (1992). *Psychological perspectives on intervention: A case study approach to prescriptions for change.* White Plains, NY: Longman. Reissued by Waveland, Prospect Heights, IL.

D'Amato, R. C., & Rothlisberg, B. A. (1996). How education should respond to students with traumatic brain injuries. *Journal of Learning Disabilities, 29,* 670–683.

D'Amato, R. C., Rothlisberg, B. A., & Rhodes, R. L. (1997). Utilizing a neuropsychological paradigm for understanding common educational and psychological tests. In C. R. Reynolds & E. Fletcher-Janzen (Eds.), *Handbook of clinical child neuropsychology* (2nd ed. pp. 270–295). New York: Plenum.

Das, J. P., Kirby, J., & Jarman, R. F. (1975). *Simultaneous and successive processes.* New York: Academic Press.

Dean, R. S. (1984). Functional lateralization of the brain. *Journal of Special Education, 18,* 239–256.

Dean, R. S. (1985a). Foundation and rationale for neuropsychological bases of individual differences. In L. C. Hartlage & C. F. Telzrow (Eds.), *The Neuropsychology of individual differences: A developmental perspective* (pp. 7–39). New York: Plenum.

Dean, R. S. (1985b). Neuropsychological assessment. In J. D. Cavenar, R. Michels, H. K. H. Brodie, A. M. Cooper, S. B. Guze, L. L. Judd, G. L. Klerman, & A. J. Solnit (Eds.), *Psychiatry* (pp. 1–16). Philadelphia: Lippincott.

Dean, R. S. (1986). Perspectives on the future of

neuropsychological assessment. In B. S. Plake & J. C. Witt (Eds.), *Buros-Nebraska series on measurement and testing: Future of testing and measurement* (pp. 203–241). Hillside, NJ: Erlbaum.

Dunst, C. J., McWilliam, R. A., & Holbert, K. (1986). Assessment of preschool classroom environments. *Diagnostique, 11,* 212–232.

Fletcher, J. M. (1988). Brain-injured children. In E. J. Mash & L. G. Terdal (Eds.), *Behavioral assessment of childhood disorders* (2nd ed., pp. 451–488). New York: Guilford.

Fletcher, J. M., & Taylor, H. G. (1984). Neuropsychological approaches to children: Towards a developmental neuropsychology. *Journal of Clinical Neuropsychology, 6,* 39–56.

Gaddes, W. H. (1985). *Learning disabilities and brain function: A neuropsychological approach* (2nd ed.). New York: Springer-Verlag.

Gaddes, W. H., & Edgell, D. (1994). *Learning disabilities and brain function: A neuropsychological approach* (3rd ed.). New York: Springer-Verlag.

Golden, C. J. (1981). The Luria-Nebraska Children's Battery: Theory and formulation. In G. W. Hynd & J. E. Obrzut (Eds.), *Neuropsychological assessment and the school-age child: Issues and procedures* (pp. 277–302). New York: Grune & Stratton.

Golden, C. J. (1989). The Nebraska Neuropsychological Children's Battery. In C. R. Reynolds & E. Fletcher-Janzen (Eds.), *Handbook of clinical child neuropsychology* (pp. 193–204). New York: Plenum.

Golden, C. J., & Maruish, M. (1986). The Luria-Nebraska Neuropsychological Battery. In D. Wedding, A. M. Horton, Jr., & J. Webster (Eds.), *The neuropsychology handbook: Behavioral and clinical perspectives* (pp. 161–193). New York: Springer.

Gouvier, D., Webster, J. S., & Blanton, P. D. (1986). Cognitive retraining with brain-damaged patients. In D. Wedding, A. M. Horton, & J. S. Webster (Eds.), *The neuropsychology handbook: Behavioral and clinical perspectives* (pp. 278–324). New York: Springer.

Gray, J. W., & Dean, R. S. (1989). Approaches to the cognitive rehabilitation of children with neuropsychological impairment. In C. R. Reynolds & E. Fletcher-Janzen (Eds.), *Handbook of clinical child neuropsychology* (pp. 397–408). New York: Plenum.

Gray, J. W., & Dean, R. S. (1990). Implications of neuropsychological research for school psychology. In T. B. Gutkin & C. R. Reynolds (Eds.), *The handbook of school psychology* (2nd ed., pp. 269–286). New York: Wiley.

Guilmette, T. J., Faust, D., Hart, K., & Arkes, H. R. (1990). A national survey of psychologists who offer neuropsychological services. *Archives of Clinical Neuropsychology, 5,* 373–392.

Haak, R. A. (1989). Establishing neuropsychology in a school setting: Organizations, problems, and benefits. In C. R. Reynolds & E. Fletcher-Janzen (Eds.), *Handbook of clinical child neuropsychology* (pp. 489–502). New York: Plenum.

Harrington, D. E. (1990). Educational strategies. In M. Rosenthal, E. R. Griffith, M. R. Bond, & J. D. Miller (Eds.), *Rehabilitation of the adult and child with traumatic brain injury* (2nd ed., pp. 476–492). Philadelphia: Davis.

Hartlage, L. C., & Telzrow, C. F. (1983). The neuropsychological basis of educational intervention. *Journal of Learning Disabilities, 16,* 521–528.

Hartlage, L. C., & Telzrow, C. F. (1985). *The neuropsychology of individual differences: A developmental perspective.* New York: Plenum.

Hooper, S. R., Boyd, T. A., Hynd, G. W., & Rubin, J. (1993). Definitional issues and neurobiological foundations of selected severe neurodevelopmental disorders. *Archives of Clinical Neuropsychology, 8,* 279–307.

Hynd, G. W. (1989). Learning disabilities and neuropsychological correlates: Relationship to neurobiological theory. In D. J. Bakker & H. Van der Vlugt (Eds.), *Learning disabilities: Neuropsychological correlates and treatment* (Vol. 1, pp. 123–147). Amsterdam: Swets & Zeitlinger.

Hynd, G. W., & Obrzut, J. E. (1981a). *Neuropsychological assessment and the school-age child: Issues and procedures.* New York: Grune & Stratton.

Hynd, G. W., & Obrzut, J. E. (1981b). School neuropsychology. *Journal of School Psychology, 19,* 45–50.

Hynd, G. W., & Semrud-Clikeman, M. (1990). Neuropsychological assessment. In A. S. Kaufman (Ed.), *Assessing adolescent and adult intelligence* (pp. 638–695). Boston: Allyn & Bacon.

Hynd, G. W., & Willis, W. G. (1988). *Pediatric neuropsychology.* Orlando, FL: Grune & Stratton.

Jarvis, P. E., & Barth, J. B. (1994). *The Halstead-Reitan Neuropsychological Battery: A guide to interpretation and clinical applications.* Odessa, FL: Psychological Assessment Resources.

Kavale, K. A., Forness, R. F., & Bender, M. (1988). *Handbook of learning disabilities: Volume II: Methods and interventions.* Boston: College-Hill Press.

Kinsbourne, M. (1989). Neuroanatomy of dyslexia. In D. J. Bakker & H. Van der Vlugt (Eds.), *Learning disabilities: Neuropsychological correlates and treatment* (Vol. 1, pp. 105–122). Amsterdam: Swets & Zeitlinger.

Kosslyn, S. M., & Intriligator, J. M. (1992). Is cognitive neuropsychology plausible? Perils of sitting on a one-legged stool. *Journal of Cognitive Neuroscience, 4,* 96–106.

Larson, P. C., & Agresti, A. A. (Eds.). (1992). Counseling psychology and neuropsychology: An overview. *The Counseling Psychologist, 20,* (Special issue).

Leavell, C., & Lewandowski, L. (1988). Neuropsychology in the schools: A survey report. *School Psychology Review, 17,* 147–155.

Leu, P. W., & D'Amato, R. C. (1994). Right children, wrong teachers? Using an ecological evaluation for placement decisions. Poster presented at the Twenty-sixth Annual Convention of the National Association of School Psychologists, Seattle.

Lezak, M. D. (1983). *Neuropsychological assessment* (2nd. ed.) New York: Oxford University Press.

Lezak, M. D. (1995). *Neuropsychological assessment* (3rd ed.). New York: Oxford University Press.

Luria, A. R. (1973). *The working brain.* London: Penguin.

Luria, A. R. (1980). *Higher cortical functions in man* (2nd ed.). New York: Basic Books.

Martin, D. A. (1990). Family issues in traumatic brain injury. In E. D. Bigler (Ed.), *Traumatic brain injury: Mechanisms of damage, assessment, intervention and outcome* (pp. 381–394). Austin, TX: Pro-Ed.

Meier, M. J. (1981). Education for competency assurance in human neuropsychology: Antecedents, models, and directions. In S. B. Filskov & T. J. Boll (Eds.), *Handbook of clinical neuropsychology* (pp. 754–781). New York: Wiley.

Meier, M. J. (1992). Modern clinical neuropsychology in historical perspective. *American Psychologist, 47,* 550–558.

Morris, R. (1989). Treatment of learning disabilities from a neuropsychological framework. In D. J. Bakker & H. Van der Vlugt (Eds.), *Learning disabilities: Neuropsychological correlates and treatment* (Vol. 1, pp. 183–190). Amsterdam: Swets & Zeitlinger.

Polloway, E. A., Patton, J. R., Payne, J. S., & Payne, R. A. (1991). *Strategies for teaching learners with special needs* (4th ed.). Columbus, OH: Merrill.

Prigatano, G. (1990). Recovery and cognitive retraining after cognitive brain injury. In E. D. Bigler (Ed.), *Traumatic brain injury: Mechanisms of damage, assessment, intervention and outcome* (pp. 297–311). Austin, TX: Pro-Ed.

Reitan, R. M., & Wolfson, D. (1985). *The Halstead-Reitan Neuropsychological Test Battery: Theory and clinical interpretation.* Tucson, AZ: Neuropsychology Press.

Reitan, R. M., & Wolfson, D. (1995, October). Cognitive and emotional consequences of mild head injury. Paper presented at the Fall Conference of the Colorado Neuropsychological Society, Colorado Springs.

Retzlaff, P., Butler, M., & Vanderploeg, R. D. (1992). Neuropsychological battery choice and theoretical orientation: A multivariate analysis. *Journal of Clinical Psychology, 48,* 666–672.

Reynolds, C. R. (1981). The neuropsychological basis of intelligence. In G. W. Hynd & J. E. Obrzut (Eds.), *Neuropsychological assessment and the school-aged child: Issues and procedures* (pp. 87–124). New York: Grune & Stratton.

Reynolds, C. R. (1986). Transactional models of intellectual development, yes. Deficit models of process remediation, no. *School Psychology Review, 15,* 256–260.

Reynolds, C. R., & Fletcher-Janzen, E. (1989). *Handbook of clinical child neuropsychology.* New York: Plenum.

Rutter, M. (1981). Psychological sequelae of brain damage in children. *The American Journal of Psychiatry, 138,* 1533–1541.

Sachs, P. R. (1991). *Treating families of brain-injury survivors.* New York: Springer.

Savage, R. C., & Wolcott, G. F. (1994). *Educational dimensions of acquired brain injury.* Austin, TX: Pro-Ed.

Selz, M. (1981). Halstead-Reitan Neuropsychological Test Batteries for Children. In G. W. Hynd & J. E. Obrzut (Eds.), *Neuropsychological assessment and the school-age child: Issues and procedures* (pp. 195–235). New York: Grune & Stratton.

Slaikeu, K. A. (Ed.). (1990). *Crisis intervention: A handbook for practice and research.* Boston: Allyn & Bacon.

Stone, B. J., Gray, J. W., & Dean, R. S. (1989). School psychologists in neurologic settings. In R. C. D'Amato & R. S. Dean (Eds.), *The school psychologist in nontraditional settings: Integrating clients, services, and settings* (pp. 139–157). Hillsdale, NJ: Erlbaum.

Taylor, H. G. (1988a). Learning disabilities. In E. J. Mash & L. G. Terdal (Eds.), *Behavioral assessment of childhood disorders* (2nd ed., pp. 402–450). New York: Guilford.

Taylor, H. G. (1988b). Neuropsychological testing: Relevance for assessing children's learning disabilities. *Journal of Consulting and Clinical Psychology, 56,* 795–800.

Taylor, H. G., & Fletcher, J. M. (1990). Neuropsychological assessment of children. In G. Goldstein & M. Hersen (Eds.), *Handbook of psychological assessment* (2nd ed., pp. 228–255).

Taylor, H. G., & Schatschneider, C. (1992). Child neuropsychological assessment: A test of basic assumptions. *The Clinical Neuropsychologist, 6,* 259–275.

Telzrow, C. F. (1985). The science and speculation of rehabilitation in developmental neuropsychological disorders. In L. C. Hartlage & C. F. Telzrow (Eds.), *The neuropsychology of individual differences: A developmental perspective* (pp. 271–307).

Thatcher, R. W., & John, E. R. (1977). *Functional neuroscience* (Vol. 1). Hillsdale, NJ: Erlbaum.

Waaland, P. K., & Kreutzer, J. S. (1988). Family response to childhood trauma brain injury.

*Journal of Head Trauma Rehabilitation, 3*(4), 51–63.

Walsh, K. W. (1978). *Neuropsychology: A clinical approach*. New York: Churchill Livingstone.

Wedding, D., Horton, A. M., & Webster, J. S. (1986). *The neuropsychology handbook: Behavioral and clinical perspectives*. New York: Springer.

Wenck, S. L., D'Amato, R. C., & Leu, P. H. (1996). Reducing children's anxiety with a school-based biofeedback intervention. *Journal of Clinical Psychology, 52*, 469–473.

Whitten, J. C., D'Amato, R. C., & Chittooran, M. M. (1992). A neuropsychological approach to intervention. In R. C. D'Amato & B. A. Rothlisberg (Eds.), *Psychological perspectives on intervention: A case study approach to prescriptions for change* (pp. 112–136). White Plains, NY: Longman.

Ylvisaker, M., Chorazy, A. J. L., Cohen, S. B., Mastrilli, J. P., Molitor, C. B., Nelson, J., Szekeres, S. F., Valko, A. S., & Jaffe, K. M. (1990). Rehabilitative assessment following head injury in children. In M. Rosenthal, E. R. Griffith, M. R. Bond, & J. D. Miller (Eds.), *Rehabilitation of the adult and child with traumatic brain injury* (2nd ed., pp. 521–538). Philadelphia: Davis.

## CHAPTER 19

# TEN YEARS LATER: TRENDS IN THE ASSESSMENT OF INFANTS, TODDLERS, PRESCHOOLERS, AND THEIR FAMILIES

**KATHLEEN D. PAGET**
*University of South Carolina*

The proliferation of information pertaining to the assessment of young children is a true late twentieth-century phenomenon. Since the publication of the second edition of this book, advances in technology, graphic production, marketing, and dissemination have created a vast array of methods for increasing professional competence in assessing children from birth through five years of age. If all available measures, including computerized versions and Spanish translations, were displayed in one room, the effect would be very colorful and reassuring. At the same time that young children's needs are the focus of an expanding body of knowledge, however, the information growth can be likened to a weed garden, which propagates wildly after a rainstorm. Entangling the weedlike information flow in the field of early intervention are controversies and complexities that will continue well into the twenty-first century. As the next century approaches, the need to make sense of a vast amount of information is evident.

The importance of simple human judgment supersedes that which numbers and technology can offer as the controversies and intricacies of the referral problems presented to professionals are influenced by the increasing complexity of such social problems as family violence and dissolution, child abuse and neglect, and the effects of chemical dependency and Human Immunodeficiency Virus/Acquired Immunodeficiency Syndrome (HIV/AIDS) during pregnancy. When a young infant is referred for neuromotor difficulties or failure to thrive, or a four-year-old is acting out sexually inappropriate behaviors, the purpose of the assessment, the best assessment strategies for meeting that purpose, and the best way to adapt the strategies over time are not always evident. Thus, the pathways an early developmental assessment follows are likely to change with time and, according to Mayes (1991), to expand to an examination of disturbances in self-regulatory capacities and self-stimulatory behaviors, disturbances in the social development and/or the care-giving environment, psychophysiological disturbances, and delays in specific areas of development. As stated best by Meisels (1996), "Infant/toddler assessment is a moving target that changes as it is implemented" (p. 44).

The proliferation of information about early developmental assessment is largely the result of three key pieces of legislation, authorizing early intervention for infants and toddlers from birth through two years and preschool programming for children three through five years. The Education of the Handicapped Act Amendments (Public Law 99-457) in 1986, its reauthorization as the Individuals with Disabilities Education Act (IDEA, Public Law 102-119) in 1991, and the IDEA Amendments in 1997 (Public Law 105-17) were the culmination of the collective wisdom of policymakers, researchers, and practitioners. Reflected in the legislation were major shifts in fundamental premises and definitions related to assessment and intervention and a broadening of the age range of children for whom services are appropriate. The parameters of assessment became very clear: that assessment is an ongoing process that takes place during intervention and becomes synonymous with program evaluation. Bagnato and Neisworth (1991) defined it as follows: "Assessment for early intervention is not a test-based process. Early childhood assessment is a flexible, collaborative process in which teams of parents and professionals formatively revise their collective judgments and decisions about the changing developmental, educational, mental health, and medical needs of young children and their families" (p. xi).

In addition, the curriculum and assessment guidelines published by the National Association for the Education of Young Children (NAEYC) stated, "Curriculum and assessment are integrated throughout the program; assessment is congruent with and relevant to the goals, objectives, and content of the program. Assessment results in benefits to the child such as needed adjustments in the curriculum or more individualized instruction and improvements in the program" (Bredekamp, 1991, p. 32). Moreover, the interplay among assessment, intervention, and evaluation focused attention on the need for continuity of services offered before and after first grade and resulted in a widening of the age parameters for early intervention services. The Division of Early Childhood (DEC) within the Council for Exceptional Children (CEC) defined young children in need of early intervention services as those between birth and age eight who have disabilities or developmental delays or are at risk for future developmental problems (DEC Task Force, 1993), and the IDEA Amendments of 1997 provide for the application of the term developmentally delayed to children from three through nine years of age.

Because more than a decade has passed since the original authorizing legislation, it is appropriate in this chapter to look at the events that have occurred during the ensuing years. To this end, information is synthesized into 10 trends, each of which is broad enough in scope to be the focus of entire books and courses of study in early intervention and early childhood special education. Specific measures are described to illustrate each of the trends rather than to provide the reader with particular details. Thus, readers must bear in mind the need to supplement this chapter with test reviews in the *Buros Mental*

*Measurements Yearbook* (Conoley & Impara, 1997) and discussions in the sources of additional information at the end of the chapter.

Figure 19.1 illustrates the 10 key trends that serve as a framework for organizing the explosion of professional activity in early assessment and intervention during the past decade. The trends synthesize the activity in politics, research, and practice that resulted from the three key pieces of legislation. For clarity, the trends are shown to the right of the legislation, although each trend actually exists on a continuum that precedes the legislation.

## LESSONS FROM POLICY

When Public Law 99-457 was passed in 1986, there were many predictions about its significant challenges, especially in implementing Part H, the Early Intervention Program for Infants, Toddlers, and their Families. (Part H became Part C of the IDEA Amendments.) Identifying the eligible population, defining case management, determining appropriate services, and understanding just what family-centered meant were among the most significant challenges. In addition, the complex collaborative funding and service delivery expected by Part H had little precedent. Harbin, Gallagher, and Lillie (1989) warned planners, "It appears the components affecting multiple agencies, multiple branches of government and multiple levels of government are going to be most difficult for obtaining consensus and acceptance" (p. iii).

All of these predictions have come true during the past decade. Physicians, teachers, parents, administrators, government officials, social workers, therapists, child-care workers, and anyone else involved with infants and toddlers have faced a paradigm shift. For families, this shift meant the realization that the *special* in specialized services and education resided within themselves, that they had the capability to help their children reach their fullest potential; for professionals, the shift meant a willingness to share expertise with one another and with families and to incorporate their knowledge into a child's daily life (Apter, 1994). Part H also required that the *new* be built on the strength of the already existing, experienced providers and professionals. There was clear intent and direction to policy developers not to reinvent the wheel—not to duplicate what already existed and not to use government funding to replace existing services.

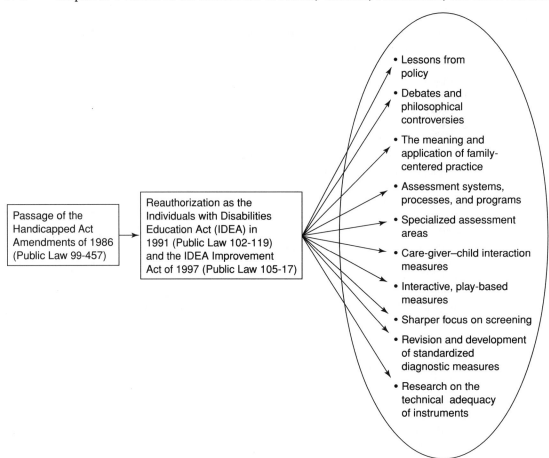

**FIGURE 19.1** **Major trends in early developmental assessment since the passage of Public Law 99-457 in 1986.**

The complexities of interagency coordination and pooled funding have proven to be among the most difficult challenges. Providing early intervention in a new family-centered and coordinated manner, in naturalized settings, without replacing the old extensive, well-funded early intervention programs has caused conflict in many states. As Peterson (1991) reported, "Few are clear how state and local officials can best move from talking about collaborations to fully operating collaborative systems" (p. 101). Many of the key provider constituencies, or stakeholders, were not initially represented on state interagency coordinating councils (ICCs), and consumer (family) participation was difficult to maintain. A good summary was offered by Hausslein, Kaufmann, & Hurth (1992): "Many parents, professionals, and policy-makers had 'Cadillac dreams,' hoping that their interagency planning would create quickly a Part H system

that fulfilled every possibility of this incredibly innovative law. More recently, planners . . . had to limit their dreams in order to make any movement forward" (p. 10). In other words, the translation of policy into systems of financial, human, and agency coordination has brought numerous lessons in modesty and persistence. Even as knowledge is currently compiled and disseminated to the professional community about the complexities of innovation (cf., Rosin, Whitehead, Tuchman, Jesien, Begun, Irwin, 1996), there are questions about how interagency coordination, pooled funding, and community-based planning will work during the next century.

In implementing Part B, the Preschool Program for children three through five years of age, the key assessment issues have been eligibility determination and its accompanying controversies about criteria for classification. Public law 99-457 encouraged states to serve all eligible children with disabilities from age three and relieved states of reporting to the U.S. Department of Education the numbers of three- to five-year-olds served by the disability category. Reauthorization as Public Law 102-119 allowed states, at their option, to incorporate an additional disability category for children ages three though five who had developmental delays. This preschool-specific category was created because of concerns that (1) among preschoolers, some developmental domains are so interrelated (e.g., cognition and language) that the disability that results in a developmental delay or dysfunction is not readily determined; and (2) the need to identify a disability to provide access to services may result in hasty diagnoses and, perhaps, inappropriate services (Danaher, 1996).

Despite efforts to establish parameters for the preschool-specific category (cf. McLean, Smith, McCormick, Schakel, & McEvoy, 1991), there continues to be concern about the self-fulfilling prophecy and the possibility of unfairly stigmatizing children who, with early intervention, may not continue to need special education. No consensus exists about the best way to respond to the concern, as reflected by the four classification systems used nationwide: (1) Part B categories only; (2) Part B categories and a state-defined, preschool-specific category; (3) some, but not all, Part B categories and a preschool-specific category that replaces the omitted Part B categories; and (4) the exclusive use of a preschool-specific or non-Part B category (Danaher, 1996).

Criteria associated with the preschool-specific classifications also vary widely from state to state and include both quantitative and qualitative types of criteria. As summarized by Danaher (1996), for states using standard deviations (SD) below the mean, the range is from 1.0 SD to 3.0 SD in one developmental area and from 1.0 SD to 2.0 SD in two or more areas. The most frequently employed criterion is 2.0 SD in one developmental area or 1.5 SD in two or more developmental areas. Among states using a criterion of delay, expressed as a percentage of chronological age, the range is 25% to 50% delay in one developmental area or 15% to 25% delay in two developmental areas. An increasing number of states are using qualitative criteria, including professional judgment or informed clinical opinion, as an alternative to quantitative criteria or as the sole criterion for eligibility under the preschool-specific category.

Additional data from 49 states and the District of Columbia (Snyder, Bailey, & Auer, 1944) underscore the reality that the preschool eligibility determination under IDEA continues to be fraught with controversy and variability. With specific references to the category of learning disabilities, categorical labeling of preschool children continues to occur and, as predicted by Haring, Lovett, Haney, Algozzine, Smith, and Clarke (1992), developmentally delayed has not universally replaced categorical labeling; in the majority of states it merely has added "one more categorical label into existing categorical systems" (Snyder et Al., 1994, p. 388). A recent study by Keogh, Coots, & Bernheimer (1996) confirmed this statement by documenting the probability that upon school entry, preschool-age children with developmental delays of unknown etiology will move directly into and remain in full-day, self-contained, special education classes. Clearly, more longitudinal research is needed before the causative influences on this situation can be understood. Proposed approaches to eligibility determination that would not require adherence to constructs as specific categories of eligibility must continue to be evaluated in a manner that matches services to individual needs, supports inclusive models of service delivery, and increases consistency among eligibility determination practices across states.

# DEBATE OVER ASSESSMENT APPROACHES AND PHILOSOPHIES

It has become clear that implementation of early intervention policy during the past decade intensified rather than resolved long-standing controversies about early intervention practice in general and specific early assessment practices. The literature is replete with varying contentions concerning the applicability of developmental practice to children with diverse abilities (Carta, Atwater, Schwartz, & McConnell, 1993; Fox, Hanline, Vail, & Galant, 1994; Johnson & McChesney Johnson, 1994), the relationship between general education and special education (Wolery, 1993), and the assessment approaches that should be taken with very young children and their families.

Directly related to the controversy about eligibility determination is the debate about appropriate assessment approaches for very young children. On the defensive end of the debate are norm-referenced measures of intellectual functioning for their failure to be linked to intervention, to reflect change in a child's functioning, and to capture a child's optimal skills. On the offensive end are curriculum-based measures and adapted-to-handicap strategies. Supporters of norm-referenced measures respond by denouncing the sole use of *any* specific measure on which program planning would depend or the futures of children would be decided (Bracken, 1994). Supporters of curriculum-based measurement and adapted-to-handicap approaches advocate the need to use assessment strategies that are directly linked to intervention objectives, provide the means to document a child's progress in meeting these objectives, and prevent false item failure by optimizing chances for success (Bagnato, Neisworth, & Gordon, 1996; Carta et al., 1993; Linder, 1993).

Extensive development of measures directly tied to curriculum objectives (e.g., Bagnato, Neisworth, & Gordon, 1996) and the continued refinement of curriculum packages—for example, the Carolina Curriculum for Infants and Toddlers ( Johnson-Martin, Jens, Attermeier, & Hacker, 1991) and the Carolina Curriculum for Preschoolers (Johnson-Martin, Attermeier, & Hacker, 1990)—are evidence of the continued and intensive effort devoted to curriculum-embedded and curriculum-compatible assessment. Concomitant and equally intensive efforts at developing new standardized measures and refining existing ones are evidence of the health of standardized measures and the continuation of the debate. Outside the norm-referenced versus curriculum-based assessment debate is another vantage point, which states that both types of measures are too product-oriented and do not go far enough in capturing the processes that underlie children's behaviors. Advocates of this view underscore the need for more process-oriented measures that capture children's spontaneous behaviors in naturalistic contexts (Dunst, Holbert, & Wilson, 1990; Johnson & McChesney Johnson, 1994) and the behaviors exhibited when interacting with the assessor in the assessment context (Lidz, 1990).

The importance of continuity between assessment of an individual child and charting that child's progress over time has fueled the debate about appropriate measurement. A clear message from the literature is the need to provide information about children's outcomes as a result of participation in programs. Guidelines from the NAEYC state that scores derived from psycho-metric tests should never be used as the sole criteria for recommending enrolling or retention in a program or placement in special or remedial classes (Bredekamp, 1991). Position statements underscore this view: "Professionals concerned with program accountability should be aware that many conventional measures (e.g., IQ, personality) are not useful for evaluation . . . [they] may not be sensitive enough to detect change because they contain too few items or too wide of differences in scaled intervals." Also, "Tasks found on numerous traditional assessment devices are often not worthwhile as developmental or educational objectives. . . . Parents and teachers must agree that the targets identified through assessment are worthy to include in the child's IFSP or IEP" (DEC Task Force, 1993, pp. 12–13).

Although the intensity of opinion about appropriate assessment approaches is likely to preclude complete resolution of the controversies, the importance of a continuum of early assessment and intervention is very clear. Comprised of a variety of assessment processes, the continuum means that assessment simply cannot be separated from intervention *and* that the relationship is not unidirectional. Characterizing the relationship between assessment and intervention as one of *fusion*, Meisels (1996) states that incorporating evaluation into the continuum is the critical feature that advances assessment beyond a singular process to become periodic and continuous documentation of the reciprocal effect of intervention on the child's progress.

# THE MEANING AND APPLICATION OF FAMILY-CENTERED ASSESSMENT

In the years succeeding the passage of Public Law 99-457, much energy has been directed toward the development of models for family-centered assessment and intervention. The stage was set before the legislation for a paradigm shift and a change in fundamental semantics by extensive research, which demonstrated that family engagement in young children's development is crucial for development to occur optimally and that families must be positioned at the center of assessment, intervention, and evaluation activities. The Dunst (1985) definition of early intervention as the provision of support to families of young children with special needs helped to solidify the focus on families and led to its formalization by the original legislation passed in 1986.

Taken together, legislative provisions for Individualized Family Service Plans (IFSPs), recognition that the relationship between the care-giver and the child is the primary context for early development, issues surrounding the communication of assessment findings to parents, and the effects of a young child's disability on family life combined to create a formal transformation of the "parent involvement" concept of Public Law 94-142 to family support and "family-focused" or "family-centered" practice (Turnbull & Turnbull, 1986).

Continued attempts to clarify meaning have characterized the years following the legislation, with efforts directed toward determining the differences between partnership and collaboration (Dunst & Paget, 1991), the factors that influence collaboration between parents and service coordinators (Dinnebeil & Rule, 1994), the best ways to discuss assessment findings with parents (Murphy, 1990), and the type and amount of information about families that is appropriate on IFSPs (Bricker, 1996). Immediately after the legislation was enacted, the focus of "family assessment" was believed to include a wide range of variables, including coping, stress, marital difficulties, social support, resources, and needs. Concern over intrusiveness into family life, confidentiality of information, the use of deficit models, and an inappropriate search for pathology led to a need to narrow the range of variables included in an assessment, to reexamine the purpose of the information, and to reexamine the ethics of family assessment (Krauss and Jacobs, 1990). Because the specific legislative requirement was to include on the IFSP a statement of the family's strengths and needs in enhancing the development of the family's handicapped infant or toddler, much discussion focused on the aspects of family life directly related to the development of the child and the specific needs of families that arise as a result of specific disabilities of children. Common sense and research both revealed that the issues faced by the family of a child with hearing loss, for example, are very different from those faced by the family of a child with cerebral palsy (Roush & Matkin, 1994).

The discovery of differences between parents and professionals and among family members has been another predominant theme. When models of shared assessment and parents as equal partners were first developed, the unspoken assumption was that professionals and parents would share similar views about a child's

functioning, if not immediately, then eventually. An appreciation of differences has now begun to undergird family-centered assessment to the extent that looking for parent-professional congruence is considered "a misguided practice" and that the focus should be on the reliability of their pooled assessment information (Suen, Logan, & Bagnato, 1995). Extensive documentation of specific differences between families and professionals, among professionals, and among family members has accumulated. Garshelis and McConnell (1993), for example, found that mothers' most frequently cited needs were for more information on present and future services available for their child, more reading material about how other parents cope, more time for themselves, and help in locating a babysitter or respite care provider; they also found that team assessment matched mothers' responses significantly better than did assessment of individual professionals. Specific within-family differences suggest that fathers' needs differ from mothers', with some evidence that more fathers focus on the benefits of learning to be an advocate for their child (Upshur, 1991).

Family-centered practice has come to mean that assessment procedures are *guided* by a professional but *driven* by the family. *Empowerment* has become a term that defines the control families should feel over the process while they identify their needs, strengths, and resources and evaluate the quality of services they receive. In this respect, some professionals have suggested that the IFSP should actually stand for Individualized Family Support Plan rather than Individualized Family Services Plan (Dunst, Trivette, & Deal, 1994). Position statements have been written about case management and parent-professional communication. The policy statements are clear: "DEC believes that the complex needs of each family are best met when each family has access to the services of a single service coordinator whose role it is to support the family in identifying and obtaining the services they want and choose from among the array of available services and who will, to the extent that each family desires, assist the family in obtaining the skills needed for themselves and their child during and beyond the early intervention period" (DEC Task Force, 1993, p. 2).

Instrument development and the application of family assessment strategies to early intervention are in the very early phases of a process that will continue well into the next century (Berman

& Shaw, 1996; Bricker, 1996; Popper, 1996; Rocco, 1996). The next decade will be a time for the conceptual and technical refinement of scales for assessing needs, resources, and strengths, for example, the Family Resource Scale (Dunst & Leet, 1996), the Family Needs Scale (Dunst, Cooper, Weeldreyer, Snyder, & Chase, 1996), and the Family Needs Survey (St. Cloud Community Schools, 1989), as well as for assisting families in evaluating the quality of services they receive, for example, The Family-Centered Program Rating Scale (Murphy, Lee, Turnbull, & Turbiville, 1995).

## ASSESSMENT SYSTEMS, PROCESSES, AND PROGRAMS

The necessity of broadbased, comprehensive assessment systems has emerged because of legislative emphasis on IFSPs, team assessment centered on parents, pooled information and funding, and the assessment-intervention-evaluation continuum. The breadth, depth, and flexibility of these systems are currently viewed as exemplary features for capturing multiple approaches to information gathering, keeping track of children's accomplishments, and including family members in the assessment process.

The Early Assessment System (Meisels, Dichtelmiller, & Marsden, in press) is conceptualized as a "continuous progress assessment" that will facilitate planning, curriculum design, and evaluation across the first three years of life for a range of typically developing children, as well as for children with special needs and children from multirisk families. The system is made up of three elements: Family Portfolio, Developmental Guidelines and Checklists, and Summary Reports. The Family Portfolio is viewed as the pivotal element of the system because it will track family goals for the child, the family's perceptions of the child's strengths and areas in need of development, and parents' objectives for themselves and for their family in relation to specific goals for child services and other interventions. According to the developers, the Family Portfolio will incorporate "some of the features of a journal, scrapbook and purposeful collection of children's work and accomplishments . . . and contain both open-ended and structured opportunities for family members and program staff to record their goals, their accomplishments, and the child's challenges and achievements through

the use of writing, photographs, or other means" (Meisels, 1996, p. 45). The Developmental Guidelines and Checklists are based on developmentally appropriate performance indicators (Lally, Griffin, Fenichel, Segal, Szanton, & Weissbound, 1995) and structure ongoing, focused observations of a child's behavior and development several times a year. The Summary Reports are a tool for structuring formative evaluation of the process of intervention. Completed three or four times per year, a Summary Report represents an overview of the child's and family's challenges, achievements, and accomplishments. The developers of this system emphasize that the intention of the reports is to document both process and outcome rather than to be an "infant report card" or record of achievement (Meisels, 1996, p. 46).

The Assessment, Evaluation, and Programming System for Infants and Children (AEPS) comprises four volumes for interdisciplinary measurement and curricular development and encompasses birth to six years. The first volume (Bricker, 1993) is both criterion-referenced and curriculum-based and is designed to measure the functional skills of infants and children in six key domains: fine motor, gross motor, adaptive, cognitive, social-communication, and social development. It includes teaching objectives and scoring criteria and is intended to be flexible enough to accommodate modifications for children with motor or sensory impairments. It also contains recording forms and progress records for professionals and parents (family self-report of the child's abilities and family interests and priorities that need to be addressed). The second volume (Cripe, Slentz, & Bricker, 1993) is a curriculum for children from birth to three years of age and parallels the AEPS. This curriculum is based on activity-based intervention that emphasizes the integration of activities into children's daily routines and the generalization of new skills. Each curricular activity includes teaching strategies, instructional sequences, and environmental arrangements. The third and fourth volumes (Bricker & Pretti-Frontczak, 1996; Twombly, 1996) are structured similarly to the first two volumes and address the developmental variances that occur as children mature.

The System to Plan Early Childhood Services (SPECS) links four major assessment and intervention objectives: screening, team assessment, program planning, and child's progress or program evaluation (Bagnato et al., 1996). For ages two to six, the system emphasizes assessment as judgment-based decision making, which comprises three basic components: (1) Developmental Specs is a rating scale for each team member to appraise the child's developmental and behavioral status in 19 functional areas organized into 6 domains; (2) Team Specs allows the team to summarize the individual ratings; (3) Program Specs assists the team in creating an individualized service plan and evaluating the child's progress and the intensity of program services. Four stated purposes are to (1) identify children who require early intervention and special education services, (2) evaluate initial status and progress in educational and clinical treatment programs, (3) integrate children with disabilities into regular preschool and kindergarten programs, and (4) evaluate children in transition from kindergarten to first grade.

Infant-Toddler Developmental Assessment (IDA) is another comprehensive, multidisciplinary, family-centered process (Provence, Erikson, Vater, & Palmeri, 1995). The complexity and interdependence of health, family, and emotional-social factors that influence development are considered throughout. Parents are treated as partners during six phases: (1) referral and preinterview data gathering, (2) initial parent interview, (3) health review, (4) developmental observation and assessment, (5) integration and synthesis, (6) giving findings to parents and preparing report. Phase 4 uses the Provence Birth-to-Three Developmental Profile, a standardized measure that employs naturalistic observation and incorporates parents' reports of the child's development in eight developmental domains: gross motor, fine motor, relationship to inanimate objects, language/communication, self-help, relationship to persons, emotions and feeling states, and coping. Emphasized is the use of the Provence Profile as part of the integrated team process rather than as an isolated test.

The Social Skills Rating System (SSRS) is a nationally standardized series of questionnaires that obtains information on the social behaviors of young children and adolescents (ages 3 to 18) from teachers, parents, and students (Gresham & Elliott, 1994). The Social Skills Scale measures positive social behaviors, grouped under five subscales designed to assess behaviors associated with cooperation, assertion, responsibility, empathy, and self-control. The Problem Behaviors Scale measures behaviors that can interfere with the development of positive social skills. These behaviors are grouped into three subscales designed to measure externalizing problems, internalizing problems, and hyperactivity. The Academic Competence Scale is a teachers' rating scale of reading and mathematics performance, general cognitive functioning, motivation, and parental support. The Assessment Information Record (AIR) combines the perspectives of each rater to highlight the behaviors that warrant the most attention when planning intervention strategies. In addition, the SSRS formulates behavioral objectives and suggestions for planning intervention. The preschool component of the SSRS is relevant to this chapter and has strong psychometric integrity (Doll & Elliott, 1994; Powless, & Elliott, 1993).

# SPECIALIZED ASSESSMENT AREAS

The comprehensive systems just described have become necessary because of the reality that within each discipline, assessment has become increasingly specialized. The neurodevelopmental functioning of infants born prematurely or affected by the sequelae of chronic illness or substance abuse best illustrates this trend because of the necessary expertise involved in assessing the intricate behaviors of very young babies. Information-processing measures for infants minimize the need for cooperation and motor skills and are better predictors of later cognitive ability than conventional cognitive measures (Zelazo & Weiss, 1990), and measures for assessing sensorimotor interactive competence—for example, the OBSERVE (Dunst et al., 1990)—have advanced understanding of the complexities of young infants' behaviors. A look at other instruments designed to assess neurodevelopmental functioning in infants further illustrates how specialized and focused infant assessment procedures have become. Readers are encouraged to expand their understanding of additional instruments by reading Samango-Sprouse (1996).

The Infanib (Ellison, 1996) is an instrument designed to measure development in infants born prematurely, treated in neonatal intensive care, affected by illness like meningitis and heart failure, or in general developing slowly. Supporting documentation contains more than 200 photographs that illustrate how to conduct screenings and what results to look for, including examples of infants who are normal, transiently atypical, and atypical. There are 20 assessments, including those for the following areas: supine—scarf sign, heel to ear, leg abduction; prone—head flexation; sitting—sideways parachute, backward parachute; standing—weight bearing, positive support reaction; suspended—forward parachute. The manual includes case studies of a wide range of neuromotor development during the first year of life and suggestions on how and what to tell parents.

Neurobehavioral Assessment of the Preterm Infant (NAPI) is an important tool for evaluating the effects of intervention, monitoring changes in preterm infants over time, and assessing the effects of medical complications on the development of preterm infants (Korner & Thom, 1996). Scores in seven clusters emerge: Scarf Sign, Motor Development and Vigor, Popliteal Angle, Alertness and Orientation, Irritability, Cry Quality, and Percent Asleep Ratings.

The Toddler and Infant Motor Evaluation (T.I.M.E.) is designed for infants from birth to $3\frac{1}{2}$ years and evaluates the overall quality of infant and toddler movements and changes in movement quality over time, rather than isolated skills (Miller & Roid, 1996). Information is elicited from the infant's care-giver to determine the relationships between the child's motor performance and functional level.

## MEASURES OF INTERACTION BETWEEN CARE-GIVER AND CHILD

The specificity required in accurate assessment and intervention practices has combined with recognition of the centrality of the relationship between a care-giver and a young child to spawn the development of measures for assessing interaction patterns. Two aspects of this type of assessment have become clear: first, that observational methods of assessing such interaction provide the assessor with critical information relevant to the prognosis of the child and, second, when the dyadic interaction between a care-giver and a child is dysfunctional, the need for intervention is increased. Thus, assessment and intervention planning within the context of the care-giver and child has assumed central importance in the early intervention literature.

From both conceptual and practical vantage points, the Strange Situation developed by Ainsworth & Bell (1970) is the best-known metric for assessing care-giver and infant attachment. Based on the premise that attachment and exploratory systems are in dynamic interplay, the Strange Situation is an eight-episode structured observation procedure of 22 to 24 minutes, involving the infant and attachment figure, typically the mother, as participants. The interplay between the attachment and exploratory systems becomes particularly evident late in the infant's first year with the emergence of locomotion, person permanence, and cognitive and memory capacities that allow for the development of "working models" of the care-giver and the self. These internal working models have a powerful organizational influence on behavior toward the care-giver and others.

Adaptations of the Strange Situation have been developed and are being refined to assess the quality of attachment between care-givers and children when deviations in the attachment relationship would be expected. Research has indicated that deviations can be detected reliably in relationships in which maltreatment has occurred and when an infant or older child has sensory and physical disabilities (cf. Cicchetti & Barnett, 1992). Although most measures involve the mother in a neutral setting, there is a growing interest in the measurement of attachment between a young child and other care-givers (fathers and grandmothers) in naturalistic environments. The Attachment Q-Set (Waters & Deane, 1985), for example, is a Q-sort measure that is theoretically consistent with the Strange Situation in emphasizing secure base behavior but differs in assessing such behavior in the home. The most recent version contains 90 behavioral descriptors, which pertain to insecurely attached children (e.g., "expects adult to be unresponsive," "is demanding when initiating activities with mother," and "easily becomes angry with mother"), as well as to securely attached children (e.g., "easily comforted by mother," "does not become angry with toys," and "explores objects thoroughly"). Reflecting the diverse ways of describing attachment behaviors, an instrument developed by Greenspan, Lieberman, and Poisson (1981), the Greenspan Lieberman Observation System (GLOS), evaluates not only the quality of goal-corrected attachment behavior but also the early process of attachment formation.

The requirement of frequent and labor-intensive observations of individual families currently mitigates against the broad use of attachment measures. Nevertheless, because of the significance of the attachment construct, continued development, refinement, and application of these measures are occurring and are involving fathers, other care-givers, and siblings. Comprehensive reviews of measures developed thus far (e.g., Greenspan, 1996; Teti & Nakagawa, 1990) are important departure points for future activities.

Moving away from attachment as a construct, The Infant Parent Social Interaction Code (IPSIC) is an example of recent attempts to measure other aspects of these relationships (Baird, Haas, McCormick, Carruth, & Turner, 1992). The IPSIC measures four parental variables (contingent responsivity, directiveness, intrusiveness, and facilitation), four infant variables (initiation, participation, signal clarity, and intentional communicative acts), and one dyadic variable (theme continuity). Mothers (and/or other care-givers) are told, "Play as you normally do when you are not feeding, bathing, or changing your infant," and a 10-minute sample of interaction is videotaped. Each 15-second segment of the videotape is viewed for the presence or absence of each behavioral construct. Behavioral analysis of these interactions leads to the parent-child dyad as the primary context for intervention strategies. For examples of measures that precede instruments such as the IPSIC, the interested reader is referred to Barnard (1997), Barnard and Kelly (1990), and Farran, Clark, and Ray (1990) for comprehensive reviews of interaction measures.

# PLAY-BASED INTERACTIVE APPROACHES

The importance of the relationship between care-giver and child and the significance of play as a context in which young children learn and express skills have combined to create an emphasis on play-based measures of intellectual, social-emotional, and communication competence. Research that supports the effects of different contexts on children's play has been an important influence on the development of these measures. Malone, Stoneman, and Cooper (1994), for example, demonstrated that children's play behaviors vary according to the context in which they occur. Two important variables are toy type and the presence of peers. When observations of children's play were used as an index of children's cognitive and communicative abilities, the observations were more likely to yield maximally valid information when conducted in independent-play sessions than during free-play time in the presence of peers. The authors raised the caveat that young children's abilities are very likely to be underestimated when descriptions are based largely, if not entirely, on classroom data.

Intensive interest in the development and refinement of play-based measures ensures their position as a cornerstone of early assessment and intervention activities. Because of the importance of context in influencing play behaviors, some measures assess peer-to-peer play interactions and others measure adult-child interactions; some are administered in the home and others in a center. A discussion follows of selected examples of play-based measures; readers are encouraged to read Segal and Webber (1996) as a supplement.

Transdisciplinary Play-Based Assessment (TPBA) was developed for children between the developmental ages of six months and six years and is a team process whereby information is gathered from parents about the development status of the child (Linder, 1993). This information is then used to plan a play session, the content and sequence of which are structured to provide observations of the child across four developmental domains: cognitive, social-emotional, language, and sensorimotor. Supporting documentation is very extensive in the form of assessment and intervention manuals, the intensiveness of parental involvement during the assessment process facilitates the translation of results into intervention plans, and functional information translates into specific objectives and activities for Individualized Family Service Plans.

The TPBA is based on principles of arena assessment, which is "the simultaneous assessment of the child by multiple professionals of differing disciplines" (Foley, 1990, p. 277). Emphasis is placed on the expansion of expertise beyond the specific discipline in which each professional was trained so that specific skills, strategies, and techniques can be transferred across disciplines. The transdisciplinary framework and role release across professionals aim for comprehensive and integrated intervention through a primary provider (and parents) and the reduction of multiple individual therapies. Emphasis also is placed on naming one professional on the team as the "primary elicitor" of information from the family.

Developmental Play Assessment (DPA) was designed from procedures of behavioral assessment and parallel procedures for naturalistic assessment of language (Lifter, Sulzer-Azaroff, Anderson, & Cowdery, 1993). These procedures include the collection of a videotaped 30-minute sample of unstructured play, in which the child plays sequentially with four groups of toys in the presence of a teacher. Because a basic premise is that children of different developmental levels play differently with the same group of toys, the emphasis is on what the children do with the toys and not on characteristics specific to the toys.

The Penn Interactive Peer Play Scale (PIPPS) is a teacher-rating instrument of the interactive play behaviors of preschool children three to five years of age (Fantuzzo, Sutton-Smith, Coolahan, Manz, Canning, & Debnam, 1995.) The PIPPS was designed to differentiate children who demonstrate positive play relationships with peers from those who are less successful with peers and to identify play strengths of resilient preschool children in high-risk urban environments. Preliminary factor analyses have begun to support the existence of three underlying dimensions: play interaction, play disruption, and play disconnection.

## SHARPER FOCUS ON SCREENING

Some components of the comprehensive assessment systems already described were designed for screening, as well as diagnostic purposes, and the specialized infant strategies and interaction measures just described may be used to screen children for additional assessment, as well as to supplement diagnostic strategies. Use of these measurement strategies for screening purposes is consistent with provisions of Public Law 99-457 and their reauthorization under Public Law 102-119 to direct early identification efforts not only toward children with established disabilities but also toward children with less well-defined developmental delays and those who are at risk for later developmental delay. In an effort to apply these provisions in a meaningful way, professional attention has focused on the complexity of the term *at risk*, the myriad environmental and biological factors that place children at risk (Dunst, 1993), and the best methods for identifying and screening at-risk children and families.

Major advances in screening have reflected increased validation that information provided by parents is a unique contribution to the accuracy of results (Diamond, 1993; Diamond & Squires, 1993). Bricker and Squires (1989a, 1989b) devised a set of nine Infant Monitoring Questionnaires that parents complete when their child reaches, 4, 8, 12, 16, 20, 24, 30, 36, and 48 months of age. The questionnaire each include 30 items that tap 5 major areas of development: gross motor, fine motor, communication, personal-social, and problem solving. Interrater reliability exceeded 90% in comparisons between parents and professionals, with test-retest reliability recorded at 95%. Validity studies showed that the questionnaires are highly accurate in excluding children who are at risk from further evaluation. These results demonstrated that parents can be included effectively in the screening process and initiated further development of the questionnaires (Bricker, Squires, Mounts, Potter, Nickel, & Farrell, 1995) into the Ages and Stages Questionnaire (ASQ).

Guided by the belief that screening information from parents should be combined with information from other sources, Henderson and Meisels (1994) developed and validated a developmental screening process that combines parental input with direct assessment of the child. The authors investigated the accuracy of an individually administered screening instrument, the Early Screening Inventory (ESI), when combined with its accompanying Parent Questionnaire (Meisels & Wiske, 1983; revised as Meisels, Wiske, Henderson, Marsden, & Browning, 1992). The ESI is a brief assessment designed to identify children between four and six years of age who could benefit from further evaluation. It is divided into three main sections (Visual-Motor/Adaptive, Language and Cognition, and Gross Motor/Body Awareness) and yields a single score that can be categorized into one of three recommendations: (1) refer for further diagnostic evaluation, (2) rescreen in 8 to 10 weeks (because of a marginal score), or (3) OK (i.e., presumed to be developing normally and not in need of further evaluation). The accompanying Parent Questionnaire is a brief survey with 58 items divided into 5 sections that provide basic information about the child's family, school history, medial history, general health, and overall development. The authors concluded that the accuracy with which the ESI correctly excludes children from further diagnostic evaluation increases when the parental measure is included in the identification process. The revised version of the ESI, the ESI-R (Meisels, S. J., Marsden, D. B., Wiske, M. S., & Henderson, L. W. 1998), has recently been published at the same time this chapter goes to press.

Child Development Days (CDD) is a normalized screening approach based on the principles that screening is more than a brief testing of a child, that parents appreciate receiving more than screening results, and that representatives from a variety of community resources need to communicate with one another to identify young children effectively (Wright & Ireton, 1995). In this approach, parents of 2½- to 3½-year-old children are located and identified through a school census and sent an invitation to attend Child Development Days, in which professionals from education, public health, social services, and child care collaborate to provide information about child development and community resources. Early childhood teachers observe children in a play setting, respond to parents' questions and concerns, and talk with parents about the teacher's observations of the child. Parents' concerns and teachers' observations are used to identify children for follow-up assessment for early childhood and special education services or referral to other services.

The Early Screening Profiles (ESP) use multiple domains, settings, and sources to measure cognitive, language, motor self-help, and social development (Harrison et al., 1996). Using a multimethod, multisource format, this measure surveys the child's articulation, home environment, health history, and test behavior. Three basic components, called Profiles (Cognitive/Language, Motor, and Self-Help/Social), are supplemented by four Surveys (Articulation, Home, Health History, and Behavior). There are two scoring systems: Level I to determine which children need further assessment and Level II to set the cutoff point for further assessment. This test can be administered by paraprofessionals and is supported by extensive research during the two-year time period between standardization and publication.

The Bayley Infant Neurodevelopment Screener (BINS) screens infants aged 3 to 24 months in 5 to 10 minutes by assessing basic neurological functions, auditory and visual receptive functions, verbal and motor expressive functions, and cognitive processes (Aylward, 1995). Items were selected from the Bayley Scales of Infant Development, 2nd edition (BSID-II) for their ability to discriminate between a nonclinical and clinical sample of infants. Three classifications of risk status (low, medium, and high) are delimited by two cut scores.

# REVISION AND DEVELOPMENT OF STANDARDIZED DIAGNOSTIC MEASURES

The past 10 years have witnessed the long-awaited revision of two of the most widely used preschool diagnostic instruments and the development of a major alternative to these measures. At the same time that two key measures were revised, others were not. Most notable among this latter group is the McCarthy Scales of Children's Abilities (MCSA; McCarthy, 1972), which continues to enjoy much attention and popularity because of its psychometric strength, its inclusion of gross motor tasks, and its practicality and appropriateness for young children.

The BSID-II (Bayley, 1993) are based on norms developed from a stratified random sample of 1,700 children (850 boys and 850 girls aged 1 to 42 months), closely paralleling the 1988 U.S. Census Bureau statistics on the variables of age, sex, region, race and ethnicity, and parental education. More than 100 new items were added; the Mental Scale and the Motor Scale were retained; and the Infant Behavior Record was revised to become the Behavior Rating Scale, which measures attention-arousal, orientation-engagement, emotional regulation, and motor quality. Data are provided in the manual on a variety of clinical groups, including children who were born prematurely, have the HIV antibody, were prenatally drug exposed, were asphyxiated at birth, are developmentally delayed, have had frequent otitis media, have autism, or have Down syndrome.

In the development of the Wechsler Preschool and Primary Scale of Intelligence–Revised (WPPSI-R), the age range of the original scale was extended downward to three years and upward to seven years and three months (Wechsler, 1989). The upward extension of WPPSI-R provides a one-year overlap with the Wechsler Intelligence Scale of Children-III (WISC-III) to give flexibility in selecting the most appropriate assessment instrument for the transition ages of six to seven years. The revised version contains the original 11 WPPSI subtests with an additional performance subtest, Object Assembly. A design-recognition task was added to the Geometric Design subtest to include two parts: Visual Recognition/Discrimination for younger children and Drawing of Geometric Figures for older children. Optional subtests include Animal Pegs (formerly Animal House) and Sentences.

Norms are based on a standardization sample of 1,700 children, stratified by age, race, sex, geographic region, parents' education, and parents' occupation. Subtest Scaled Scores are expressed as Standard Scores with a mean of 10 and SD of 3. Verbal, Performance, and Full Scale IQ Scores have a mean of 100 and SD of 15.

The Differential Ability Scales (DAS) was designed to assess the multidimensional skills of children and adolescents from 2 years and 6 months to 17 years and 11 months (Elliott, 1990). Scores are obtained in General Conceptual Ability (mean of 100; SD of 15), Verbal Ability, Nonverbal Reasoning, and Spatial Ability. The norm sample included 3,475 children, stratified by age, sex, race and ethnicity, parents' education, geographic region, and educational preschool enrollment to match 1988 census figures. The sample included exceptional children with learning disabilities; speech and language impairments; mental retardation; giftedness; emotional disturbance; and mild visual, hearing, or motor impairment. Bias analysis was applied to the performance of a large sample of African-American and Hispanic children to eliminate biased items. Some items, if failed, require examiner-child interaction around the teaching of items.

## RESEARCH ON THE TECHNICAL ADEQUACY OF MEASUREMENT

The many facets of psychometric integrity that pertain to measurement in general assume even greater significance when applied to infant and preschool measurement because of the increased number of young children being evaluated and the associated developmental challenges. Ten years ago, Bracken (1987) underscored the need for more research into the technical adequacy of preschool measurement tools. In some important ways, this call has been heeded; in some other ways, it has not. Hundreds of research studies have been conducted to verify reliability and validity data in the technical manuals of diagnostic and screening measures for young children. Among diagnostic measures, the focus of the largest number of studies has been the potential for variation in factor structure for preschool-age children when compared with school-age children, differences in factor structure for specific groups of preschool-age children, the discriminant and concurrent validity of scales, and the internal consistency of items (e.g., Bracken, 1991;

Fan, Willson, & Reynolds, 1995; Faust & Hollingsworth, 1991; Molfese, Yaple, Helwig, Harris, & Connell, 1992; Roid & Gyurke, 1991; Snyder, Lawson, Thompson, Stricklin, & Sexton, 1993; Stone, Gridley, & Gyurke, 1991). Despite the importance of developmental variation over time and of measurement stability, less attention has been given to the careful documentation of test-retest reliability of early developmental assessment tools. In addition, the predictive and discriminant strength of most diagnostic instruments remains an elusive concept, except for very young children with the severest disabilities (Snyder et al., 1993). Although some studies have resulted in promising findings (Clemmer, Klifman, & Bradley-Johnson, 1992), others have raised serious questions about the predictive validity of preschool instruments (e.g., Miller & Schouten, 1988). In addition, because too many studies of predictive validity have used a time interval of two years or less, studies are needed that employ longer intervals: "The use of longer intervals would provide assurance that results of preschool tests remain relatively stable over the time period involved in decision making (i.e., until the children in school)" (Clemmer et al., 1992, p. 274).

The sensitivity and specificity of screening tests have received an increased amount of attention from researchers who are studying existing screening measures, developing new ones, and developing short forms of diagnostic measures (e.g., Banerji, 1992b; Glascoe and Byrne, 1993; Prewett, 1992). Because of the importance of such constructs as developmental maturity or "developmental age" under current legislative mandates, the factor structure of screening instruments has also assumed increased importance (Banerji, 1992a).

Although research findings have accumulated to provide increased reassurance that preschool assessment is a process supported by psychometric integrity, some research has raised alarming questions. In examining the internal consistency of the Battelle Developmental Inventory (BDI), for example, Boyd (1989) discovered marked age-related discontinuities when the inventory was used with very young infants. Radically different summary scores were obtained from one day to the next for infants whose chronological age abutted one of the cutoff points between age categories, despite identical performance on the scale. When combined with technical caveats in publications such as the *Buros Mental Measurements Yearbook* (Conoley & Impara, 1997), findings like these continue to provide evidence of the need for meticulous care and immense interpretative judgment from the team of professionals and parents who gather assessment findings on young children.

Considerable concern over the composition of normative samples has led researchers and practitioners to raise questions about the use of instruments with specific disability groups. Some large, nationally stratified samples have not been representative of the U.S. population in racial and ethnic background and disability. Although the normative procedures followed in the development of the BDI set the stage for the inclusion of disability groups in other normative samples (e.g., the DAS) and created opportunities for comparisons of young children with their ability, as well as chronological, peers, currently there is no consistency across instruments in the type and severity of the disability represented. Children with severe disabilities were excluded from the DAS normative sample, for example, and the types of disabilities represented differed from those in the BDI normative group.

Intensive research efforts have also been made into the validity and reliability of preschool measurements for different socioeconomic and racial and ethnic groups. Studies have focused on instruments of intellectual functioning, such as the Griffiths' Mental Development Scales, a measure that was standardized on a non-American population but used rather extensively in this country (McLean, McCormick, & Baird, 1991); the McCarthy Scales of Children's Abilities (Valencia, 1990); and the Kaufman Assessment Battery for Children (Fan et al., 1995; Matazow, Kamphaus, Stanton, & Reynolds, 1991); as well as screening measures (Kaufman & Wang, 1992), checklists in specific domain areas (Alberts, Davis, & Prentice, 1995), and self-report measures of perceived competence (Fantuzzo, McDermott, Manz, Hampton, & Burdick, 1996). Variability in the findings about the validity of instruments for populations other than those on which a given instrument was normed reflects a significant problem that must continue to be addressed in the future. The overall conclusion from studies of a wide variety of instruments is the need for practitioners to examine and understand what bias analysis research indicates about the specific instruments they use most often.

The Fantuzzo et al. (1996) study illustrates increased interest in the social-emotional functioning of young children and the technical adequacy of instruments for measuring such constructs as perceived competence, behavioral style, and adaptive social behavior. Hoge and Wichmann (1994) provided an evaluative review of interview and rating and checklist instruments for assessing social-emotional competence in preschool children and found great variation in the psychometric integrity of the instruments. Low confidence in the technical adequacy of measures of social-emotional functioning has contributed to the dearth of Individualized Education Plan (IEP) goals in the social-emotional arena (cf., Michnowicz, McConnell, Peterson, & Odom, 1995). Some promising advances have been signaled nevertheless by the refinement of existing measures, for example, the Temperament Assessment Battery for Children (TABC; Martin, 1996), and the development of new measures, such as the Adaptive Social Behavior Inventory (ASBI; Hogan, Scott, & Bauer, 1992). Suitable for high-risk three-year-olds, the ASBI was created within the context of a large research study and the discovery that there was no suitable scale of prosocial adaptive behavior to serve as a primary outcome measure. Advances of the inventory were its emphases on (1) wording and content appropriate for mothers of varying education and English fluency; (2) content relevant to home, family, and neighborhood; (3) judgments of parents; (4) affectively negative behaviors in the appropriate developmental context and not necessarily as indexes of clinical problems; and (5) consistency across gender, ethnic, geographic, and birthweight groups.

The technical adequacy of family-level assessment measures has been overshadowed by the attention given to child-level measures, although the situation is beginning to change. With so much attention given to the development of instruments that meet the spirit and word of legislative IFSP provisions, this focus has become imperative. There is little doubt that a significant barrier to effective family assessment has been the lack of technically sound, functional assessment tools. McGrew, Gilman, and Johnson (1992) provided a comprehensive review of family-related assessment measures and concluded, "No individual scale was identified that provides broad coverage of all 17 need categories as well as empirical evidence in all reliability and validity categories" and "no empirical reliability and validity evidence was found for the scale with the broadest coverage of needs" (p. 22). McGrew et al. endorsed goal attainment scaling and open-ended questions as a viable way to augment family assessment beyond what can be attained through existing scales. They also concluded that although existing self-report family inventories are adequate for informal purposes, much more work must be done to understand what kind of information is reliable and valid for documentation on IFSPs. As the twenty-first century approaches, controversy exists over the efficiency of structured scales versus the depth of interviewing when attempting to understand and document family needs. Much more research into the psychometric properties of scales for family needs is required because they are likely to be used as measures of change to evaluate program effectiveness. Larger and broader samples are imperative aspects of this continued process.

# CONCLUSIONS AND FUTURE DIRECTIONS

It is likely that the trends of the past decade are only the first phase of a paradigm shift in early assessment and intervention activities. If the first phase was characterized by "Cadillac dreams," as coined by Hausslein et al. in 1992, then the next phase should feature "Honda realism and fine-tuning." Policymakers, practitioners, researchers, and families involved in early assessment and intervention will continue to be faced with controversies and complexities, but the efforts of the past decade have built an important experiential and informational knowledge base from which to approach the next phase in a realistic way. To sustain this realism and to fine-tune practice, any individual directly or indirectly involved in early developmental assessment, intervention, and evaluation must stay abreast of developments. Active membership in key organizations, such as the Division of Early Childhood (DEC) within the Council for Exceptional Children (CEC), and the National Center for Infants, Toddlers and Families (formerly the National Center for Clinical Infant Programs), is necessary in the process of making sense of the complexities and challenges in the next century. The next decade will see the continuation of existing trends as well as the development of new ones as the IDEA Amendments of 1997 are implemented. As a departure point for understanding this process, families and professionals can anticipate the following:

- Expansive proliferation of information about the assessment of infants, toddlers, and preschoolers and, most importantly, the need to develop ways to manage the information for individual purposes

- Major policy changes in the implementation of early intervention within the context of consolidation of health care delivery plans (i.e., managed care) and changes in the organization and financing of Medicaid and other publicly funded health care

- Vast expansion of technologically driven measures and the concomitant need to use technology and manage information systems in an ethical and judgment-based manner

- Increased emphasis on family-centered service coordination and the development of expertise in families to evaluate progress through adaptations of goal attainment scaling techniques

- Continued vigilance about the ethical limitations of one's practice and the interdependence of professions represented on assessment and intervention teams

- Continued development of standardization procedures that allow for comparisons within cultural, ability, educational, and birthweight groups

- Continued emphasis on the inseparability of assessment, intervention, and progress evaluation and the production and marketing of broadbased, comprehensive assessment systems

- Continued proliferation of specialty areas, especially in the neuromotor assessment of infants, and continued emphasis on infant assessment and intervention as a discipline in its own right

- Increased research into the stability of early assessment measures and the predictive and discriminant power of measurement tools, especially when used with children with nonspecific developmental delays

- Increased research into the reciprocal influences from biology, genetics, and care-giving environments on developmental anomalies and the need to apply these findings to practice

- Continued emphasis on the evaluation of intervention effectiveness and the development of increasingly sophisticated methods for documenting the influence of program factors on an individual child's progress

- Increased focus on accumulated research

findings that create opportunities to pool data bases and conduct meta-analyses

• Continued focus on the development of procedures for easing transitions for toddlers who are entering preschool programs

# REFERENCES

Ainsworth, M. D. S., & Bell, S. M. (1970). Attachment, exploration, and separation: Illustrated by the behavior of one-year-olds in a strange situation. *Child Development, 41*, 49–67.

Alberts, F. M., Davis, B. L., & Prentice, L. (1995). Validity of an observation screening instrument in a multicultural population. *Journal of Early Intervention, 19*, 168–177.

Apter, D. S. (1994). From dream to reality: A participant's view of the implementation of Part H of P.L. 99-457. *Journal of Early Intervention, 18*, 131–140.

Aylward, G. P. (1995). *The Bayley Infant Neurodevelopment Screener (BINS)*. San Antonio, TX: Psychological Corp.

Bagnato, S. J., & Neisworth, J. T. (1991). *Assessment for early intervention: Best practices for professionals*. New York: Guilford.

Bagnato, S. J., Neisworth, J. T., Gordon, J. (1996). *System to Plan Early Childhood Services (SPECS)*. Circle Pines, MN: American Guidance Service.

Baird, S. M., Haas, L., McCormick, K., Carruth, C., & Turner, K. D. (1992). Approaching an objective system for observation and measurement: Infant-Parent Social Interaction Code. *Topics in Early Childhood Special Education, 12*, 544–571.

Banerji, M. (1992a). Factor structure of the Gesell School Readiness Test. *Journal of Psychoeducational Assessment, 10*, 342–354.

Banerji, M. (1992b). An integrated study of the predictive properties of the Gesell School Readiness Screening Test. *Journal of Psychoeducational Assessment, 10*, 240–256.

Barnard, K. E. (1997). Influencing parent-child interactions. In M. J. Guralnick (Ed.), *The effectiveness of early intervention* (pp. 249–268). Baltimore, MD: Paul H. Brookes.

Barnard, K. E., & Kelly, J. F. (1990). Assessment of parent-child interaction. In S. J. Meisels & J. P. Shonkoff (Eds.), *Handbook of early childhood intervention* (pp. 278–301). Cambridge, MA: Cambridge University Press.

Bayley, N. (1993). *Bayley Scales of Infant Development— Second Edition*. San Antonio, TX: Psychological Corp.

Berman, C., & Shaw, E. (1996). Family-directed child evaluation and assessment under the Individuals with Disabilities Education Act (IDEA). In S. J. Meisels & E. Fenichel (Eds.), *New visions for the developmental assessment of infants and young*

*children* (pp. 361–390). Washington, DC: National Center for Infants, Toddlers, and Families.

Boyd, R. D. (1989). What a difference a day makes: Age-related discontinuities and the Battelle Developmental Inventory. *Journal of Early Intervention, 13*, 114–119.

Bracken, B. A. (1987). Limitations of preschool instruments and standards for minimal levels of technical adequacy. *Journal of Psychoeducational Assessment, 5*, 313–326.

Bracken, B. A. (1991). The Wechsler Preschool and Primary Scale of Intelligence (WPPSI-R) *Journal of Psychoeducational Assessment 9*(3) (Special issue).

Bracken, B. A. (1994). Advocating for effective preschool assessment practices: A comment on Bagnato and Neisworth. *School Psychology Quarterly, 9*, 103–108.

Bredekamp, S. (Ed.). (1991). *Developmentally appropriate practice in early childhood programs serving children from birth through age 8*. Washington, DC: National Association for the Education of Young Children.

Bricker, D. (Ed.). (1993). *AEPS Measurement for Birth to Three Years* (Vol. 1). Baltimore, MD: Paul H. Brookes.

Bricker, D. (1996). Assessment for IFSP development and intervention planning. In S. J. Meisels & E. Fenichel (Eds.), *New visions for the developmental assessment of infants and young children* (pp. 169–192). Washington, DC: National Center for Infants, Toddlers, and Families.

Bricker, D., & Pretti-Frontczak, K. (Ed.). (1996). *AEPS Measurement for Three to Six Years* (Vol. 3). Baltimore, MD: Paul H. Brookes.

Bricker, D., & Squires, J. (1989a). The effectiveness of screening at-risk infants: Infant Monitoring Questionnaires. *Topics in Early Childhood Special Education, 9*, 67–85.

Bricker, D., & Squires, J. (1989b). A low-cost system using parents to monitor the development of at-risk infants. *Journal of Early Intervention, 13*, 50–60.

Bricker, D., Squires, J., Mounts, L., Potter, L., Nickel, B., & Farrell, J. (1995). *Ages and Stages Questionnaires (ASQ)*. Baltimore, MD: Paul H. Brookes.

Carta, J. J., Atwater, J. B., Schwartz, I. S., & McConnell, S. R. (1993). Developmentally appropriate practices and early childhood special education: A reaction to Johnson and McChesney Johnson. *Topics in Early Childhood Special Education, 13*, 243–254.

Cicchetti, D., & Barnett, D. (1992). Attachment organization in maltreated preschoolers. *Development and Psychopathology, 3*, 397–411.

Clemmer, S. C., Klifman, T. J., & Bradley-Johnson, D. (1992). Long-term predictive validity of the Cognitive Ability Scales. *Journal of Psychoeducational Assessment, 10*, 265–275.

Conoley, J. C., & Impara, J. C. (Eds.). (1997). *The Buros Mental Measurements Yearbook* (12th ed.). Lincoln, NE: Buros Institute of Mental Measurements.

Cripe, J., Slentz, K., & Bricker, D. (Eds.). (1993). *AEPS Curriculum for Birth to Three Years*, (Vol. 2). Baltimore, MD: Paul H. Brookes.

Danaher, J. (1996, March). Preschool special education eligibility classification and criteria. *Communiqué* insert (pp. 1–5). Washington, DC: National Association of School Psychologists.

DEC Task Force (1993). *DEC recommended practices: Indicators of quality in programs for infants and young children with special needs and their families.* Reston, VA: Council for Exceptional Children.

Diamond, K. E. (1993). The role of parents' observations and concerns in screening for developmental delays in young children. *Topics in Early Childhood Special Education, 13,* 68–81.

Diamond, K. E., & Squires, J. (1993). The role of parental report in the screening and assessment of young children. *Journal of Early Intervention, 17,* 107–115.

Dinnebeil, L. A., & Rule, S. (1994). Variables that influence collaboration between parents and service coordinators. *Journal of Early Intervention, 18,* 349–361.

Doll, B., & Elliott, S. N. (1994). Representativeness of observed preschool social behaviors: How many data are enough? *Journal of Early Intervention, 18,* 227–238.

Dunst, C. J. (1985). Rethinking early intervention. *Analysis and Intervention in Developmental Disabilities, 5,* 161–201.

Dunst, C. J. (1993). Issues related to "at-risk." *Topics in Early Childhood Special Education, 13*(2) (Special issue).

Dunst, C. J., Cooper, C. S., Weeldreyer, J. C., Snyder, K. D., & Chase, J. H. (1996). Family Needs Scale. *Supporting and strengthening families. Vol. II: Empirical findings and outcomes.* Cambridge, MA: Brookline Books.

Dunst, C. J., Holbert, K. A., & Wilson, L. L. (1990). Strategies for assessing infant sensori-motor interactive competencies. In E. D. Gibbs and D. M. Teti (Eds.), *Interdisciplinary assessment of infants: A guide for early intervention professionals* (pp. 91–112). Baltimore, MD: Paul H. Brookes.

Dunst, C. J., & Leet, H. E. (1996). Family Resource Scale. *Supporting and strengthening families. Vol. II: Empirical findings and outcomes.* Cambridge, MA: Brookline Books.

Dunst, C. J., & Paget, K. D. (1991). Parent-professional partnerships and family empowerment. In M. Fine (Eds.), *Collaborative involvement with parents of exceptional children* (pp. 25–44). Brandon, VT: Clinical Psychology Publishing Co.

Dunst, C. J., Trivette, C. M., & Deal, A. G. (1994). *Supporting and strengthening families. Vol. 1: Methods, strategies and practices.* Cambridge, MA: Brookline Books.

Elliott, C. D. (1990). *Differential Ability Scales (DAS).* San Antonio, TX: Psychological Corp.

Ellison, P. H. (1996). *The Infanib.* San Antonio, TX: Psychological Corp.

Fan, X., Willson, V., & Reynolds, C. R. (1995). Assessing the similarity of the factor structure of the K-ABC for African-American and white children. *Journal of Psychoeducational Assessment, 13,* 120–131.

Fantuzzo, J. W., McDermott, P. A., Manz, P. H., Hampton, V. R., & Burdick, N. A. (1996). The Pictorial Scale of Perceived Competence and Social Acceptance: Does it work with low-income urban children? *Children Development, 67,* 1071–1084.

Fantuzzo, J., Sutton-Smith, B., Coolahan, K. C., Manz, P. H., Canning, S., & Debnam, D. (1995). Assessment of preschool play interaction behaviors in young low-income children: Penn Interactive Peer Play Scale. *Early Childhood Research Quarterly, 10,* 105–129.

Farran, D. C., Clark, K. S., Ray, A. R. (1990). Measures of parent-child interaction. In E. D. Gibbs & D. M. Teti (Eds.), *Interdisciplinary assessment of infants: A guide for early intervention professionals* (pp. 227–248). Baltimore, MD: Paul H. Brookes.

Faust, D. S., & Hollingsworth, J. O. (1991). Concurrent validation of the Wechsler Preschool and Primary Scale of Intelligence–Revised (WPPSI-R) with two criteria of cognitive abilities. *Journal of Psychoeducational Assessment, 9,* 224–229.

Foley, G. M. (1990). Portrait of the arena evaluation: Assessment in the transdisciplinary approach. *Interdisciplinary assessment of infants: A guide for early intervention professionals* (pp. 271–286). Baltimore, MD: Paul H. Brookes.

Fox, L., Hanline, M. F., Vail, C. O., & Galant, K. R. (1994). Developmentally appropriate practice: Applications for young children with disabilities. *Journal of Early Intervention, 18,* 243–257.

Garshelis, J. A., & McConnell, S. R. (1993). Comparison of family needs assessed by mothers, individual professionals, and interdisciplinary teams. *Journal of Early Intervention, 16,* 36–49.

Glascoe, F. P., & Byrne, K. E. (1993). The accuracy of three developmental screening tests. *Journal of Early Intervention, 17,* 368–379.

Greenspan, S. I. (1996). Assessing the emotional and social functioning of infants and young children. In S. J. Meisels & E. Fenichel (Eds.), *New visions for the developmental assessment of infants and young children* (pp. 231–266). Washington, DC:

National Center for Infants, Toddlers, and Families.

Greenspan, S. I., Lieberman, A. F., & Poisson, S. S. (1981). *Greenspan-Lieberman observation system for assessment of caregiver-infant interaction during semi-structured play (GLOS)*. Bethesda, MD: Mental Health Study Center, National Institute of Mental Health.

Gresham, F. M., & Elliott, S. N. (1997). *Social Skills Rating System (SSRS)*. Circle Pines, MN: American Guidance Service.

Harbin, G., Gallagher, J., & Lillie, D. (1989). *State's progress related to fourteen components of P.L. 99-457, Part H*. Chapel Hill: University of North Carolina, Carolina Policy Studies Program.

Haring, K. A., Lovett, D. L., Haney, K. F., Algozzine, B., Smith, D. D., & Clarke, J. (1992). Labeling preschoolers as learning disabled: A cautionary position. *Topics in Early Childhood Special Education*, *12*, 151–173.

Harrison, P., Kaufman, A., Kaufman, N., Bruininks, R., Rynders, J., Ilmer, S., Sparrow, S., & Cicchetti, D. (1996). *Early Screening Profiles (ESP)*. Circle Pines, MN: American Guidance Service.

Hausslein, E. B., Kaufmann, R. K., & Hurth, J. (1992). From case management to service coordination: Families, policy making and Part H. *Zero to Three*, *12*(3), 10–12.

Henderson, L. W., & Meisels, S. J. (1994). Parental involvement in the developmental screening of their young children: A multiple-source perspective. *Journal of Early Intervention*, *18*, 141–154.

Hogan, A. E., Scott, K. G., & Bauer, C. R. (1992). The Adaptive Social Behavior Inventory (ASBI): A new assessment for social competence in high-risk three-year-olds. *Journal of Psychoeducational Assessment*, *10*, 230–239.

Hoge, R. D., & Wichmann, C. (1994). An evaluative review of interview and rating/checklist instruments for assessing social/emotional competence in preschool children. Unpublished monograph. Carlton University, Northfield, MN.

Johnson, J. E., & McChesney Johnson, K. (1994). The applicability of developmentally appropriate practice for children with diverse abilities. *Journal of Early Intervention*, *18*, 343–345.

Johnson-Martin, N. M., Attermeier, S. M., & Hacker, B. J. (1990). *The Carolina curriculum for preschoolers with special needs*. Baltimore, MD: Paul H. Brookes.

Johnson-Martin, N. M., Jens, K. G., Attermeier, S. M., & Hacker, B. J. (1991). *The Carolina curriculum for infants and toddlers with special needs* (2nd Ed.). Baltimore, MD: Paul H. Brookes.

Kaufman, A. S., & Wang, J-J. (1992). Gender, race, and education differences on the K-Bit at ages 4 to 90 years. *Journal of Psychoeducational Assessment*, *10*, 219–229.

Keogh, B. K., Coots, J. J., & Bernheimer, L. P. (1996). School placement of children with nonspecific developmental delays. *Journal of Early Intervention*, *20*, 65–97.

Korner, A. F., & Thom, V. A. (1996). *Neurobehavioral Assessment of the Preterm Infant (NAPI)*. San Antonio: Psychological Corp.

Krauss, M. W., & Jacobs, F. (1990). Family assessment and techniques: Purposes and techniques. In S. J. Meisels & J. P. Shonkoff (Eds.), *Handbook of early childhood intervention* (pp. 303–325). Cambridge, MA: Cambridge University Press.

Lally, R., Griffin, A., Fenichel, E., Segal, M., Szanton, E., & Weissbourd, B. (1995). *Caring for infants and toddlers in groups: Developmentally appropriate practice*. Arlington, VA: Zero to Three/National Center for Clinical Infant Programs.

Lidz, C. S. (1990). The Preschool Learning Assessment Device: An approach to the dynamic assessment of young children. Assessments of learning and development potential. *European Journal of Psychology of Education*, *5*(2) (Special issue).

Lifter, K., Sulzer-Azaroff, B., Anderson, S. R., & Cowdery, G. E. (1993). Teaching play activities to preschool children with disabilities: The importance of developmental considerations. *Journal of Early Intervention*, *17*, 139–159.

Linder, T. W. (1993). *Transdisciplinary play-based assessment and intervention*. Baltimore, MD: Paul H. Brookes.

Malone, D. M., Stoneman, Z., & Cooper, A. Y. (1994). Contextual variation of correspondences among measures of play and developmental level of preschool children with cognitive delays. *Journal of Early Intervention*, *18*, 199–215.

Martin, R. P. (1996). *The Temperament Assessment Battery for Children*. Austin, TX: Pro-Ed.

Matazow, G. S., Kamphaus, R. W., Stanton, H. L., & Reynolds, C. R. (1991). Reliability of the Kaufman Assessment Battery for Children for black and white students. *Journal of School Psychology*, *29*, 37–41.

Mayes, L. (1991). Infant assessment. In M. Lewis (Ed.), *Child and adolescent psychiatry*. (pp. 437–447). Baltimore, MD: Williams & Wilkins.

McCarthy, D. (1972). *The McCarthy Scales of Children's Abilities (MSCA)*. San Antonio, TX: Psychological Corp.

McGrew, K. S., Gilman, C. J., & Johnson, S. (1992). A review of scales to assess family needs. *Journal of Psychoeducational Assessment*, *10*, 4–25.

McLean, M. E., McCormick, K., & Baird, S. M. (1991). Concurrent validity of the Griffiths' Mental Development Scales with a population of children under 24 months. *Journal of Early Intervention, 15,* 338–344.

McLean, M., Smith, B. J., McCormick, K., Schakel, J., & McEvoy, M. (1991, December). Developmental delay: Establishing parameters for a preschool category of exceptionality. *DEC position paper.* Reston, VA: Council for Exceptional Children.

Meisels, S. J. (1996). Charting the continuum of assessment and intervention. In S. J. Meisels & E. Fenichel (Eds.), *New visions for the developmental assessment of infants and young children* (pp. 27–52). Washington, DC: National Center for Infants, Toddlers, and Families.

Meisels, S. J., Dichtelmiller, M. L., & Marsden, D. B. (in press). *The Early Assessment System.* Ann Arbor: University of Michigan.

Meisels, S. J., Marsden, D. B., Wiske, M. S., & Henderson, L. W. (1998). *Early Screening Inventory—Revised.* Ann Arbor, MI: Rebus, Inc.

Meisels, S. J., & Shonkoff, J. P. (Eds.). (1990). *Handbook of early intervention.* Cambridge, MA: Cambridge University Press.

Meisels, S. J., & Wiske, M. S. (1983). *The Early Screening Inventory.* New York: Teachers College Press.

Meisels, S. J., Wiske, M. S., Henderson, L. W., Marsden, D. B., & Browning, K. (1992). *The Early Screening Inventory* (rev. ed.). Ann Arbor: University of Michigan.

Michnowicz, L. L., McConnell, S. R., Peterson, C. A., & Odom, S. L. (1995). Social goals and objectives of preschool IEPs: A content analysis. *Journal of Early Intervention, 19,* 273–282.

Miller, L. J., & Roid, G. H. (1996). *The T.I.M.E. Toddler and Infant Motor Evaluation.* San Antonio, TX: Psychological Corp.

Miller, L. J., & Schouten, P. G. W. (1988). Age-related effects on the predictive validity of the Miller Assessment for Preschoolers. *Journal of Psychoeducational Assessment, 6,* 99–106.

Molfese, V., Yaple, K., Helwig, S., Harris, L., & Connell, S. (1992). Stanford-Binet Intelligence Scale (4th ed.): Factor structure and verbal subscale scores for 3-year-olds. *Journal of Psychoeducational Assessment, 10,* 47–58.

Murphy, D. L., Lee, I. M., Turnbull, A. P., & Turbiville, V. (1995). The Family-centered Program Rating Scale: An instrument for program evaluation and change. *Journal of Early Intervention, 19,* 24–42.

Peterson, N. L. (1991). Interagency collaboration under Part H: The key to comprehensive, multidisciplinary, coordinated infant/toddler intervention services: *Journal of Early Interventions, 15,* 89–105.

Popper, B. K. (1996). Achieving change in assessment practices: A parent's perspective. In S. J. Meisels & E. Fenichel (Eds.), *New visions for the developmental assessment of infants and young children* (pp. 59–66). Washington, DC: National Center for Infants, Toddlers, and Families.

Powless, D., & Elliott, S. N. (1993). Assessment of social skills of Native American preschoolers: Teachers' and parents' ratings. *Journal of School Psychology, 31,* 293–307.

Prewett, P. N. (1992). Short forms of the Stanford-Binet Intelligence Scale: Fourth Edition. *Journal of Psychoeducational Assessment, 10,* 257–264.

Provence, S., Erikson, J., Vater, S., & Palmeri, S. (1995). *Infant-Toddler Developmental Assessment (IDA).* Chicago: Riverside.

Rocco, S. (1996). Toward shared commitment and shared responsibility: A parent's vision of developmental assessment. In S. J. Meisels & E. Fenichel (Eds.), *New visions for the developmental assessment of infants and young children* (pp. 55–58). Washington, DC; National Center for Infants, Toddlers, and Families.

Roid, G. H., & Gyurke, J. (1991). General-factor and specific variance on the WPPSI-R. *Journal of Psychoeducational Assessment, 9,* 209–223.

Rosin, P., Whitehead, A. D., Tuchman, L. I., Jesien, G. S., Begun, A. L., & Irwin, L. (1996). *Partnerships in family-centered care.* Baltimore, MD: Brookes.

Roush, J., & Matkin, N. D. (1994). *Infants and toddlers with hearing loss: Family-centered assessment and intervention.* Baltimore, MD: York Press.

Samango-Sprouse, C. (1996). Neurodevelopmental evaluation of newborns and infants with genetic disorders. In S. J. Meisels & E. Fenichel (Eds.), *New visions for the developmental assessment of infants and young children* (pp. 329–344). Washington, DC: National Center for Infants, Toddlers, and Families.

Segal, M., & Webber, N. T. (1996). Nonstructured play observations: Guidelines, benefits, and caveats. In S. J. Meisels & E. Fenichel (Eds.), *New visions for the developmental assessment of infants and young children* (pp. 207–230). Washington, DC: National Center for Infants, Toddlers, and Families.

Snyder, P., Bailey, D. B., & Auer, C. (1994). Preschool eligibility determination of children with known or suspected learning disabilities. *Journal of Early Intervention, 18,* 380–390.

Snyder, P., Lawson, S., Thompson, B., Stricklin, S., & Sexton, D. (1993). Evaluating the psychometric integrity of instruments used in early intervention research: The Battelle Developmental Inventory. *Topics in Early Childhood Special Education, 13,* 216–232.

St. Cloud Community Schools. (1989). *FISC family needs survey.* St. Cloud, MN: Adaptive Living Program.

Stone, B. J., Gridley, B. E., & Gyurke, J. S. (1991). Confirmatory factor analysis of the WPPSI-R at the extreme end of the age range. *Journal of Psychoeducational Assessment, 9*, 263–270.

Suen, H. K., Logan, C. R., & Bagnato, S. (1995). Parent-professional congruence: Is it necessary? *Journal of Early Intervention, 19*, 243–252.

Teti, D. M., & Nakagawa, M. (1900). Assessing attachment in infancy: The Strange Situation and alternate systems. In E. D. Gibbs & D. M. Teti (Eds.), *Interdisciplinary assessment of infants: A guide for early intervention professionals* (pp. 191–214). Baltimore, MD: Paul H. Brookes.

Turnbull, A. P., & Turnbull, H. R. (1986). *Families, professionals, and exceptionality: A special partnership.* Columbus, OH: Merrill.

Twombly, L. (1996). *AEPS curriculum for three to six years* (vol. 4). Baltimore, MD: Paul H. Brookes.

Upshur, C. C. (1991). Mothers' and fathers' ratings of the benefits of early intervention services. *Journal of Early Intervention, 15*, 345–357.

Valencia, R. R. (1990). Clinical assessment of young children with the McCarthy Scales of Children's Abilities. In C. R. Reynolds & R. W. Kamphaus (Eds.), *Handbook of psychological and educational assessment of children: Intelligence and achievement* (pp. 59–67). New York: Guilford.

Waters, E., & Deane, K. E. (1985). Defining and assessing differences in attachment relationships: Q-methodology and the organization of behavior in infancy and early childhood. In I. Bretherton & E. Waters (Eds.), Growing points of attachment theory and research. *Monographs of the Society for Research in Child Development, 50* (Serial No. 209, No. 102), 41–65.

Wechsler, D. (1989). *Wechsler Preschool and Primary Scale of Intelligence–Revised (WPPSI-R).* San Antonio, TX: Psychological Corp.

Wolery, M. (1993). Relationship between general and special early childhood education *Topics in Early Childhood Special Education, 13*(3) (Special issue).

Wright, A., & Ireton, H. (1995). Child development days: A new approach to screening for early intervention. *Journal of Early Intervention, 19*, 253–263.

Zelazo, P. R., & Weiss, M. J. (1990). Infant information processing: An alternative approach. In E. D. Gibbs & D. M. Teti (Eds.), *Interdisciplinary assessment of infants: A guide for early intervention professionals* (pp. 129–144). Baltimore, MD: Paul H. Brookes.

# SOURCES OF ADDITIONAL INFORMATION

Bagnato, S. J., Neisworth, J. T., & Munson, S. M. (1996). *LINKing assessment and early intervention: An authentic, curriculum-based approach.* Baltimore, MD: Paul H. Brookes. This book is a comprehensive discussion of the associated issues and practical application of curriculum-embedded and curriculum-compatible assessment systems. It offers practical guidance concerning the authenticity and effectiveness of assessment practices and their links to intervention strategies and progress evaluation.

Gibbs, E. D., & Teti, D. M. (Eds.). (1990). *Interdisciplinary assessment of infants: A guide for early intervention professionals.* Baltimore, MD: Paul H. Brookes. Despite the publication date, the conceptual discussions in this book make it a classic in the field. The specificity of information reflects the specialized expertise required for proper interpretation of assessment findings for intervention and evaluation.

Guralnick, M. J. (Ed.). (1996). *The effectiveness of early intervention.* Baltimore, MD: Paul H. Brookes. This book is the most comprehensive retrospective review of the major developments in the field of early intervention during the past 10 years. It covers research findings in preventive intervention with children at risk, program factors for children at risk, effects of intervention for children with established disabilities, program factors for children with established disabilities, and general conclusions about the outcomes of early intervention.

Meisels, S. J., & Fenichel, E. (Eds.). (1996). *New visions for the developmental assessment of infants and young children.* Richmond, VA: National Center for Infants, Toddlers, and Families. This book is among the most current and comprehensive compilations of information on the assessment of infants, toddlers, preschoolers, and their families. The various authors discuss assessment from a range of contexts and purposes. Included are the continuum of assessment and interventions; sharing a commitment to assessment and intervention with parents; the value of play-based assessment; tools for measuring very young infants, toddlers, and preschoolers; a values-based model of assessment; and family-directed evaluation and assessment in the twenty-first century.

Meisels, S. J., & Shonkoff, J. P. (1990). *Handbook of early intervention.* Cambridge, MA: Cambridge University Press. When published, this book reflected the most comprehensive and current information on policy, research, and practice in the field of early intervention. Because of its level of discussion, it remains a classic.

Thurman, S. K., Cornwell, J. R., & Gottwald, S. R. (Eds.). (1996). *Contexts of early intervention; Systems and settings.* Baltimore, MD: Paul H. Brookes. This book is the most comprehensive collection of information on the systems, ecologies, and contexts that affect early intervention. Included are sociopolitical factors, funding, culture, the family as a system, neonatal intensive care units, family child-care settings, other child-care settings, early intervention centers, and public schools. Emphasis is placed on the interrelationships among these various systems and contexts in the development of a young child.

AUTHOR'S NOTE    The author would like to acknowledge the assistance of her son, Chris Paget, in the preparation of Figure 19.1.

## CHAPTER 20

# EFFECTIVE INSTRUCTIONAL PRACTICES: IMPLICATIONS FOR ASSESSING EDUCATIONAL ENVIRONMENTS

JIM YSSELDYKE
JUDY ELLIOTT
*University of Minnesota*

Reschly and Ysseldyke (1995) describe a paradigm shift that is occurring at different rates and in different forms in the practice of school psychologists throughout the United States. The shift is from a child deviance or child pathology orientation (Sarason, Doris, 1979) to a problem-solving orientation characterized by a focus on interventions and on changes that can be made in interventions to alter students' outcomes. They talk about the rapid emergence of techniques that involve gathering information in natural environments with frequent, direct measures of behaviors as interventions are implemented. According to Roberts (1995), this shift involves the use of assessment procedures that analyze the functional relationship of academic problems to critical variables in the classroom.

In our discussion of assessment of educational environments, we concentrate on the instructional. We view instructional environments broadly as those contexts in which learning takes place. These include but are not limited to schools. Rather, we like to think of school contexts, home contexts, and home and school contexts. We begin with an analysis of the rationale for assessing instructional environments, describe the ways in which assessors have gathered data on instruction, review evidence on environmental factors that influence instructional outcomes, provide examples of methodologies, and discuss the issues in assessment.

The call for taking environmental factors into account in assessments is not new, but until recently, formal methodologies for assessing educational environments have been limited.

## WHY ASSESS INSTRUCTIONAL ENVIRONMENTS?

For a long time people have talked about the need to assess learning environments or to take context into account when assessing students. Consider the following examples:

> Behavior does not occur in a vacuum. The individual behaves in a particular environmental context, which in part determines the nature of his or her responses. The resulting behavior depends on the interaction of respondent and situational variables. The same individual will respond differently in different situations. Hence, the prediction of criterion performance from test scores or from earlier criterion behavior (such as school grades or performance on a previous job) can be materially improved by taking situational variables into account. (Anastasi, 1976, p. 578)

> In most cases, when a child is observed to be underachieving or acting out in an

inappropriate manner, the major area of evaluative focus is only upon the child. Frequently, the identified student will be referred to a specialist within the school for intensive diagnostic efforts that are designed to isolate inherent disorders or deficits existing within the child that are "responsible" for the learning or behavioral difficulty. Seldom does the educational evaluation attempt to probe those situational factors that may, in fact, have initiated or at least maintained the behavioral patterns that are of concern to the teacher. (Wallace & Larsen, 1978, p. 100)

The assessment of the academic environment requires an evaluation of those variables that may have an impact upon student academic performance. These variables would include behaviors that relate to academic engaged time (e.g., opportunities to respond), teacher instructional procedures (e.g., presentation style, antecedents and consequences of academic responding), competing contingencies (e.g., disruptiveness, student-student contacts), and teacher-student monitoring procedures and expectations . . . the thorough examination of the academic ecology becomes a crucial portion of the evaluation of a student's academic skills. (Shapiro, 1989, p. 33)

A critical component of an instructional assessment process is consideration of the situation in which academic performance occurs. (Fuchs & Fuchs, 1986, p. 322)

An environmental analysis is helpful for each child assessed, regardless of whether the child is ultimately served by a special education program or not. (Helton, Workman & Matuszek, 1982, p. 279)

We believe there are four reasons to assess instructional environments.

## Many Factors Affect Academic Outcomes

If differences in instructional outcomes were a direct result of differences among students, intervention planning would be as straightforward as giving tests to students, profiling their characteristics, grouping students with similar characteristics, and assigning those with different characteristics to different groups. Instructional outcomes differ as a function of complex interactions among many factors. There are many reasons that children do well in school and many reasons that they do less well than we would expect. This point is supported by the results of works by Carroll, Walberg, Christenson, Algozzine, and Ysseldyke.

In 1963, John Carroll proposed a model of school learning in which the degree of learning for an individual student is a function of the amount of time the student spends in learning divided by the amount of time the student needs to learn (see Figure 20.1). Two factors influence the time spent in learning: opportunity to learn and perseverance. Three factors influence the time needed to learn: aptitude, ability to understand instruction, and quality of instruction. In the past, the majority of assessments by school psychologists were of learners' aptitude and personal characteristics like perseverance and ability to understand instruction. More recently, school psychologists have added to their assessment armaments those that look at the aspects of the instructional environment, like opportunity to learn and quality of instruction.

In a quantitative synthesis of about 3,000 studies of causal influences on students' affective behavioral and cognitive outcomes. Walberg (1984) differentiated three causal outcomes: aptitude (ability, development, and motivation), instruction (academically engaged time and quality of instruction), and home environment (home,

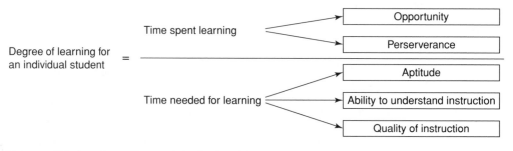

**FIGURE 20.1**  **Carroll's model of school learning.**

peer, classroom climate, and television). Walberg concluded that classroom learning is a multiplicative, diminishing-returns function of four essential factors: student's ability, motivation, quantity of instruction, and quality of instruction. Of special interest to us in this chapter are the quantity and quality of instruction.

Ysseldyke and Christenson (1987) made an extensive list of factors that influence instructional outcomes, grouped into student factors (like cognitive and affective entry behaviors), environmental factors (school district conditions, within-school conditions, and general family characteristics), and instructional factors. They divided the instructional factors into four areas: planning, managing, delivering, and evaluating (see Table 20.1).

## Learning Does Not Occur in a Vacuum

Student assessment cannot be considered complete without an assessment of the student's instructional needs in the context of the classroom. Englemann, Granzin, and Severson (1979) recommend that assessment begin with instructional diagnosis "to determine aspects of instruction that are inadequate, to find out precisely how they are inadequate, and to imply what must be done to correct their inadequacy" (p. 361). While this statement appears to be obvious, in practice most psychoeducational decisions are made without careful systematic analysis of the instructional ecology.

When we talk about instructional ecology, we are referring to the relationships between students and their instructional environments. As early as 1964, Ogden Lindsley introduced the concept of *prosthetic environments* for maximizing the behavioral efficiency of children with disabilities who show deficits when forced to behave in "average" environments. Students' academic performance and behavior are influenced by the environment in which they are taught. Students enter each instructional setting with a set of individual characteristics and learning history. In turn, each student responds differently to educators' instructional efforts.

Ecological theories of learning and behavior have been traditionally based on the interrelationship between behavior and its environment, past and present (Barker, 1963; Brofenbrenner, 1979; Kantor, 1959; Skinner, 1953). The process of learning is influenced by the student, task, and teaching. We focus on alterable variables, or

**TABLE 20.1   Components of Effective Instruction**

| | Component | | |
|---|---|---|---|
| **Planning Instruction** | **Managing Instruction** | **Delivering Instruction** | **Evaluating Instruction** |
| The degree to which teaching goals and teachers' expectations for students' performance and success are stated clearly and are understood by the students | The degree to which classroom management is effective and efficient<br>The degree to which there is a sense of positiveness in the school environment | The degree to which there is an appropriate instructional match<br>The degree to which lessons are presented clearly and follow specific instructional procedures<br>The degree to which instructional support is provided for the individual student<br>The degree to which sufficient time is allocated to academics and instructional time is used inefficiently<br>The degree to which the student's opportunity to respond is high | The degree to which the teacher actively monitors students' progress and understanding<br>The degree to which students' performances are evaluated appropriately and frequently |

those able to be affected by effective instruction and classroom management: skills, perceptions, strategies, expectations, motivation, attention, and memory. All of these are clustered under what Howell, Fox, and Morehead (1993) call "prior knowledge." They point out, based on learning theory, that although not specific enough to provide clues for daily instruction or instruction on specific objectives, prior knowledge does have a relationship to instruction: (1) prior knowledge is the most important variable in learning, (2) special and/or remedial students do not make good use of executive control strategies, and (3) both prior knowledge and the use of strategies are alterable and can be affected through careful evaluation and focused instruction.

The theoretical basis for instructional ecology is derived from Bandura's (1978) concept of reciprocal determinism. He demonstrated how behavior is determined by a continuous reciprocal interaction among behavioral, cognitive, and environmental influences. A student's classroom performance is a function of the student's characteristics interacting with the nature of instructional tasks interacting with what educators do instructionally. As noted by Bijou and Baer (1978), "The interaction between the child and environment is continuous, reciprocal, and interdependent. We cannot analyze a child without reference to an environment, nor is it possible to analyze an environment without reference to a child. The two form an inseparable unit consisting of an interrelated set of variables, or interactional field" (p. 29). Moreover, it is critical to remember that the home influences and is influenced by what occurs in school, and school influences and is influenced by what occurs at home. Brofenbrenner (1986) refers to this link between two microsystems as a mesosystem. A mesosystem can be any connection between any microsystem (e.g., special education and general education, home and school, and family and day care). Factors that occur in the home can support or negate instruction that occurs in the school.

Therefore, students' learning is functionally related to the setting in which it takes place. And learning problems are influenced or triggered by instructional factors in the classroom or school environment, as well as by the degree to which the home-school relationship is collaborative. Therefore, best practice dictates that both the learner and the instructional ecology need to be assessed; they are not mutually exclusive.

## There Are Limits to Assessing the Learner

The majority of assessment practices in schools are focused primarily on the student—what is wrong, missing, deficient, or defective. Attributions for failure are primarily within the student: deficits, deficiencies, dysfunctions, and disabilities. More recently, school psychologists have begun to focus much more extensively on other factors that contribute to school difficulties: instruction, school organization, or classroom. The shift has occurred because of limits in assessing learners. Teachers articulate the limits with statements such as these: "Knowing a student's characteristics tells me nothing about how to teach" "You haven't told me anything I didn't already know; I need to know specifically what to do." There is a long history of the failure to identify interactions between learners' aptitudes and specific treatments (Ysseldyke, 1973). The limited relationships of test behaviors to actual classroom behaviors have long been noted (Howell, 1986).

When assessors gather data both on students' characteristics and on the ways in which students perform in instructional environments, the search for functional relationships between environmental factors and instructional outcomes, assessment, and intervention planning are enhanced. When intervention planning is enhanced, there is a better chance of achieving better outcomes.

## Content Belongs in Consultation and Problem Solving

Consulting has been described as "an act of service in which consultants are expected to help achieve ends that are determined by the client" (Sparks, 1992, p. 12). Much of the consultation and problem solving that go on in today's schools are long on process (e.g., reflective listening) and short on content (i.e., specific information on what to do). The final result of the consultation process should be an outcome statement, a written action plan, and a progress-monitoring system (DeBoer, 1995). A number of different models and theories is associated with consultation. The four basic theoretical models applied to education are the behavioral (Bergen & Kratochwill, 1990; Tharp & Wetzel, 1969), the mental health (Caplan, 1970), the clinical (Conoley, 1981), and the organizational (Schein, 1969). More recent consultation models are the collaborative (Idol, Paolucci-Whitcomb, & Nevin, 1986), the instructional (Alpert & Meyers, 1983), the ecological (Gutkin & Curtis, 1990) and the peer collaboration (Pugach & Johnson, 1988a, 1988b, 1988c). The specific model or approach used should be selected on the basis of the purpose of the consultation and the style or preference of those involved.

Today, schools are moving away from "private classrooms," where teachers work in isolation, to more collaborative partnerships in which knowledge, expertise, and resources are shared (Fullan & Hargreaves, 1991). Very specific intervention programs are now available: *Interventions* (Sprick, Sprick, & Garrison, 1993), *Strategies and Tactics for Effective Instruction* (Algozzine, Ysseldyke, & Elliott, 1997), *TGIF* (Fister & Kemp, 1995), *The Tough Kid Book* (Rhode, Jenson, & Reavis, 1993), *Responding to Individual Differences in Education* (Beck, 1990, 1991, 1993), and *The Teacher's Encyclopedia of Behavior Management* (Sprick & Howard, 1995). These are only a few resources designed to put content into consultation. It is important that assessment activities identify aspects of instruction that are not going as well as they might for individual students, as well as identify interventions to improve instruction and instructional outcomes. To identify aspects of instruction that are in need of improvement necessitates collaboration, consultation, and assessment of instructional environments.

## HOW HAVE WE ASSESSED EDUCATIONAL ENVIRONMENTS IN THE PAST?

Although environmental assessment does not deny the importance of previous learning and other historical factors, the primary emphasis is on the interaction among the student, the task, and the environment in which instruction occurs. Assessment of the educational environment is an important piece of the complex puzzle of exploring what deficits and excesses exist and what role they play in creating the "problem" or concern in the classroom. Traditional psychometry has not provided information about conditions that best facilitate a student's ability to learn, that is, the variables that differentially affect learning (e.g., types of knowledge, levels of proficiency, and reinforcement). There has always been recognition that assessment of the environment is necessary and important, but the focus of most evaluations has been on assessing the student rather than the instructional context. Before there were formalized methods of collecting information on instructional environments, a variety of assessment approaches have been used by school psychologists.

## Observation

Observation, a highly regarded assessment technique (Hargrove & Poteet, 1984), is the most direct approach to data collection in the educational environment. Typically, it involves systematic observation of behavior in the setting where the problem behavior is exhibited (Hintze & Shapiro, 1995). However, in the traditional sense, the main purpose of observation has been to describe the student and to determine correlates, possible causes, and explanations of behavior. There are basically two types of observation: systematic and nonsystematic. In the latter, the observers' purpose is to "take a look" at the child within his or her classroom environment. The product is usually a narrative, often subjective, on what was seen or heard. In systematic observation, the observer sets out to observe one or more behaviors. After specifically operationalizing the behavior, the observer typically counts instances of the behavior or uses other measures such as its frequency, duration, magnitude, or latency. The product is a summary of occurrence or intensity of a select few behaviors (Salvia & Ysseldyke, 1998). An example of such a system is *The Classroom Observer* (Boehm & Weinberg, 1987). Based on the premise that observation skills are an imperative component of an educator's professional repertoire, this is a systematic approach for observing in the learning environment. Highlighted is the role systematic observation in natural settings plays in approaching problems and facilitating educational programs in the classrooms and in other learning environments.

## Teachers' Interviews

Teachers' interviews have been deemed a "conversation with a purpose" (Sundberg, 1977). Teachers have been a primary source of information for a long time; that is, they have been interviewed for their perspective of the problem. Information from interviews has typically rendered what the target behavior is and how it is impeding learning and/or classroom instruction. The product is descriptive data, the quality of which depends heavily on the knowledge of the person being interviewed. Interviews vary in structure and formality, and some familiar ones are the Adaptive Behavior Inventory (Brown & Leigh, 1986) and the AAMR Adaptive Behavior–School 2 (Lambert, Leland, & Nihara, 1992).

## Task Analysis

Task analysis is both an assessment and a teaching tool. First, it allows teachers to develop a system that structures the learning task in a logical teaching sequence. Second, it serves as a method of assessment when it us used to make comparisons between a leaner's progress and specific steps in an instructional sequence. Task analysis allows the teacher to identify exactly where the student is having difficulty and where to begin instruction. As a result, the product of task analysis is a list of task components and of necessary skills stated in teachable terms.

## Checklists

Teachers are often asked to fill out behavior-rating checklists that describe learning and/or behavior deficiencies as witnessed in the classroom. Checklists have been used to describe and prescribe "next steps." Some examples are the Child Behavior Checklist (Achenbach, 1985, 1991), the Behavior Evaluation Scale (McCarney, Leigh, Cornbleet, 1983), and the Systematic Screening for Behavior Disorders (Walker & Severson, 1990). Many checklists and accompanying intervention manuals have been used frequently by teachers and school psychologists and encompass academic behavior, study habits, and social skills, for example, the *Prereferral Intervention Manual* (McCarney & Cummins, 1988), *Study Skills for Students in Our Schools* (McCarney & Tucci, 1991), and *The Learning Disability Intervention Manual* (McCarney & Bauer, 1989).

## Climate Inventories

School climate or classroom climate inventories are used by school personnel to determine ambiance and structure and their effect on the student. The Barclay Classroom Assessment System (BCAS), formerly the Barclay Classroom Climate Inventory, is one such tool (Barclay, 1983). The BCAS provides information from three viewpoints: the child, the child's classmates, and the teacher. Measures are obtained on a broad range of skills, feelings, and attitudes that the student displays in the classroom. Its underlying theory is that students view their own skills and potential in terms of how well or poorly they are treated in their environment. Information is provided about students, their functioning in the classroom, and the reaction of peers and teachers. The BCAS provides alternative strategies that can be used to improve the quality of learning and achievement in the classroom.

## Teacher-Student Interactions

The assessment of teacher-student interaction has been used to identify the quantity and quality of the exchange. The Flanders Interaction Analysis (FIA) provides a framework for analyzing class interactions by observing teacher-student verbal behavior (Flanders, 1970). The FIA focuses on discovering relationships between a teacher's behavior and a student's growth. It allows the observer to draw conclusions about the classroom climate and make inferences about the communication strategies used in the classroom. The FIA has been the forerunner of a wide range of observation techniques (discussed in a later section) for the study of teaching and learning.

## Parent Interview and Social History

Interviewing a parent or guardian is an attempt to uncover family, medical, birth, and developmental milestones that may be contributing to in-school learning and behavior. Parents are often interviewed and/or asked to complete checklists that target their perception of the student's problem in the home. One of the difficulties with this approach is that a parent or guardian's definition or perception of the problem is often different from that of the school or classroom teacher.

# WHAT ARE THE INSTRUCTIONAL FACTORS THAT DETERMINE EDUCATIONAL OUTCOMES?

Most research on effective instruction has been conducted with students in general educational settings, is correlational in nature, reports results of group studies, and uses basic achievement as the central measure of educational results or effectiveness. Several researchers have produced descriptions or lists of components of effective instruction. Sometimes researchers describe effective instruction in general, broad ways (Reith & Evertson, 1988; Stevens & Rosenshine, 1981). In other instances they describe components of effective instruction in specific content areas, such as reading or math (Englert, 1984; Good & Brophy, 1984; Guzzetti & Marzano, 1984).

Rosenshine and his colleagues (Rosenshine, 1983; Rosenshine & Stevens, 1986) identified six components of effective instruction: (1) daily review; (2) presentation of new content and skills;

(3) initial practice, with much teacher-pupil interaction and an 80% success rate; (4) feedback and correctives; (5) independent practice for mastery and automaticity; and (6) weekly and monthly reviews, reteaching concepts and skills if necessary. Rosenshine (1983) indicated that instruction is more effective if it is structured, briskly paced, proceeds in small steps, includes detailed and redundant instructions and many concrete examples, provides students with many opportunities to make overt responses, includes the teacher's monitoring of performance, and emphasizes overlearning.

Good and Brophy (1984), Guzzetti and Marzano (1984), and Blair (1984) identified several general factors related to effective instruction and improved performance. Among these were students' opportunity to learn; active teaching; high rates of students' engagement; efficient use of instructional time; varied and flexible grouping patterns; rapid progress through the curriculum; teaching to mastery; placement of students at appropriate instructional levels; clearly defined goals and objectives; and the presence of a well-organized, academically focused, pleasant learning environment.

Ysseldyke and Christenson (1993) identified common elements of effective teaching programs:

> Teaching approaches that produce relatively greater increases in student achievement are characterized by two factors: structure and interaction. The instructional structure is teacher-directed, academically focused, and follows a demonstrate-prompt-practice instructional sequence. Clear lesson explanations, supervised guided practice, sufficient independent practice (classroom and homework), and evaluation of student performance are provided. Monitoring occurs at all points throughout the instructional sequence. A high degree of teacher-student interaction is maintained by teacher questioning and student responding patterns, and by providing students with informative feedback. Students are provided many opportunities to respond; cues and prompts are provided to increase accuracy of responses. Students work toward mastery of skills. Highly structured, interactive instruction has resulted in greater achievement gains and active participation (academic engaged time) for students. (p. 69)

In describing components of effective instruction, we follow the model of effective instruction developed by Algozzine, Ysseldyke, and Elliott (1992) and used by Ysseldyke and Christenson (1993) in constructing the Instructional Environment System–II. This model, shown in Figure 20.2, includes four components of effective instruction: planning, managing, delivering, and evaluating. Note that for each component there is a set of empirically demonstrated principles of effective instruction. For example, in planning instruction, one must (1) decide what to teach, (2) decide how to teach, and (3) communicate realistic expectations to the student. The components are described in the sections that follow.

## Planning Instruction

Instructional results are better when instruction is planned. Planning involves making decisions about what to teach, the most effective way to teach, and the communication of realistic expectations.

### Deciding What to Teach

In deciding what to teach, teachers must have a good idea of the skills that students do and do not have. It is important to achieve a match between the level of skill development and the level of instruction. Assessors accomplish this by measuring students' entry-level cognitive and affective behaviors. Effective teachers achieve an appropriate match both on initial tasks and on the modifications they make as instruction proceeds. Carpenter and Fennema (1989) showed that teachers who knew what their students did and did not know were more effective.

In deciding what to teach, it is important also to analyze task variables. Engaging in task analysis and examining specifically the psychological demands of classroom tasks assists diagnostic and instructional personnel in designing effective instructional units. In addition, it is important to take into account the ways in which classrooms are organized. Physical space, peer interactions, and instructional grouping arrangements affect a teacher's planning (Squires, Huitt, & Segars, 1983). Those who assess instructional environments experienced by individual students will have to examine the ways in which instruction is planned for the student.

### Deciding How to Teach

Knowing ahead of time how to teach is difficult. Teaching is an experimental process. The best

| Component | Principle | Strategy |
|---|---|---|
| Planning instruction | Decide what to teach | Assess to identify gaps in performance<br>Establish logical sequences of instruction<br>Consider contextual variables |
| | Decide how to teach | Set instructional goals<br>Establish performance standards<br>Choose instructional methods and materials<br>Establish grouping structures<br>Pace instruction appropriately<br>Monitor performance and replan instruction |
| | Communicate realistic expectations | Teach goals, objectives, and standards<br>Teach students to be active, involved learners<br>Teach students consequences of performance |
| Managing instruction | Prepare for instruction | Set classroom rules<br>Communicate and teach classroom rules<br>Communicate consequences of behavior<br>Handle disruptions efficiently<br>Teach students to manage their own behavior |
| | Use time productively | Establish routines and procedures<br>Organize physical space<br>Allocate sufficient time to academic activities |
| | Establish positive classroom environment | Make the classroom a pleasant, friendly place<br>Accept individual differences<br>Establish supportive, cooperative learning environments<br>Create a nonthreatening learning environment |

**FIGURE 20.2** The Algozzine-Ysseldyke model of effective instruction.

way to decide how to teach is to teach and to gather data on the kinds of things that do and do not work. This does not mean that instructional planning is blind; experience provides a basis for knowing what works, and the professional literature is filled with guidelines for instruction (c.f. Wittrock, 1986). Effective teachers make an educated guess about the kinds of instructional activities that will work, then try them and monitor the results. Engleman et al. (1979) describe a process of "instructional diagnosis" that is useful in making decisions about how to teach. There is little evidence to support the contention that test scores or profiles of test scores are useful in these decisions (Ysseldyke, 1973; Ysseldyke & Marston, 1990). In deciding how to teach it is important to set goals, select methods and materials, decide how to pace instruction, monitor performance, and plan subsequent instruction.

### Communicating Realistic Expectations

Good and Brophy (1984), Edmonds (1979), and Kagan (1992) have written about the importance of setting high but realistic expectations for all students. Their research indicates that high academic expectations and students' accountability for meeting them are necessary parts of effective instruction. Students do better when they are expected to perform well and when their performance is monitored and reported on. The work of Anderson (1985) and Kagan indicates that teachers' expectations for success must be communicated clearly to the student. If unstated by the teacher, students' understandings of goals and expectations may be mistaken. Clear communication of high, realistic expectations is an integral part of learning and effective instruction. In assessing students, it is important to consider the expectations that others hold for their performance and the extent to which those expectations are communicated effectively.

### Managing Instruction

Instructional outcomes are enhanced when classrooms and instruction are effectively organized. Few of us are comfortable in unstructured and chaotic situations, particularly in the classroom. Most students function better in or-

| Component | Principle | Strategy |
|---|---|---|
| Delivering instruction | Present information | For presenting content<br>    Gain and maintain attention<br>    Review prior skills or lessons<br>    Provide organized, relevant lessons |
| | | For motivating students<br>    Show enthusiasm and interest<br>    Use rewards effectively<br>    Consider level and student interest |
| | | For teaching thinking skills<br>    Model thinking skills<br>    Teach fact-finding skills<br>    Teach divergent thinking<br>    Teach learning strategies |
| | | For providing relevant practice<br>    Develop automaticity<br>    Vary opportunities for practice<br>    Vary methods of practice<br>    Monitor amount of work assigned |
| | Monitor presentations | For providing feedback<br>    Give immediate, frequent, explicit feedback<br>    Provide specific praise and encouragement<br>    Model correct performance<br>    Provide prompts and cues<br>    Check student understanding |
| | | For keeping students actively involved<br>    Monitor performance regularly<br>    Monitor performance during practice<br>    Use peers to improve instruction<br>    Provide opportunities for success<br>    Limit opportunities for failure<br>    Monitor engagement rates |
| | Adjust presentations | Adapt lessons to meet student needs<br>Provide varied instructional options<br>Alter pace |
| Evaluating instruction | Monitor student understanding | Check understanding of directions<br>Check procedural understanding<br>Monitor student success rate |
| | Monitor engaged time | Check student participation<br>Teach students to monitor their own participation |
| | Keep records of student progress | Teach students to chart their own progress<br>Regularly inform students of performance<br>Maintain records of student performance |
| | Use data to make decisions | Use data to decide if more services are warranted<br>Use student progress to make teaching decisions<br>Use student progress to decide when to discontinue service |

**FIGURE 20.2**  *(continued)*

derly environments and with organized instruction.

Effective classrooms are those in which there is a cooperative, pleasant atmosphere, as well as structure and order, and students are accepted and assisted in completing academic work successfully (Doyle, 1986). There are three principles of effective instructional management: (1) preparing for instruction, (2) using time productively, and (3) establishing a positive classroom environment.

## Preparing for Instruction

Outcomes for students are enhanced when their teachers set rules early in the year, communicate them to the students, teach students the consequences of behavior, handle disruptions effectively (often followed by reteaching), teach consistently, and teach students to manage their own behavior. It is possible to go into classrooms, observe instruction, interview students, or interview teachers to ascertain the extent to which each of these factors is present for an individual student.

## Using Time Productively

The concept of time on task has driven instruction for some time. Grounded in the idea that students need ample opportunities to respond to academic and other classroom tasks, time-management strategies have become central concerns for effective teachers. Ysseldyke and Algozzine (1995) identified six characteristics of a well-managed instructional environment:

- There are well-established routines and procedures.
- The physical space is organized to facilitate learning.
- Transitions between activities are short.
- Few interruptions break the flow of classroom activities.
- The classroom has an academic, task-oriented focus.
- Sufficient time is allocated to academic activities (p. 100). Effective classes are those in which time is conserved by planning activities and tasks to fit learning materials (Evertson & Harris, 1992).

## Establishing a Positive Classroom Environment

Most students perform better and are more motivated when teachers interact positively with them and are supportive and helpful during learning activities. Effective teachers carefully assess the learning atmosphere in their classrooms; they "read" their students and strive to make the classroom a comfortable and supportive environment. Learning outcomes are enhanced when students are required to become involved and to participate (Anderson, Everson, & Brophy, 1979).

## Delivering Instruction

Teaching is the systematic presentation of content assumed necessary for mastery of the subject matter. Good teaching doesn't just happen. It involves strategic planning of what to teach and the effective management of classrooms and instruction. It also involves carefully planned delivery of instruction that is focused on specific academic tasks and content areas of appropriate curricula. Algozzine and Ysseldyke (1992) identified seven principles of effective instructional delivery: (1) instruction is presented in effective ways, (2) thinking skills are taught, (3) students are motivated, (4) feedback is provided, (5) students are given relevant practice, (6) students are actively involved, and (7) instruction is modified on the basis of information on pupils' performance.

## Effectively Presenting Instruction

There are empirically demonstrated effective ways to present instruction: getting students' attention, reviewing earlier lessons or skills, discussing the goals of instruction, making lessons relevant, maintaining students' attention, being enthusiastic, being organized, pacing briskly, interacting positively, communicating instructional goals and intentions, and checking that students understand what they are to do. These characteristics, shown to be effective, have been incorporated into several model teaching programs: (1) active teaching model (Good & Grouws, 1979), (2) the exemplary center for reading instruction (Reid, 1981, 1986), (3) direct instruction (Becker, Engelmann, Carnine, & Rhine, 1981; Gersten, Woodward, & Darch, 1986), and (4) mastery learning (Bloom, 1976).

## Teaching Thinking Skills

An effective way to teach thinking skills is to model thinking skills. Duffy, Roehler, and Rackliffe (1985) underscore the importance of modeling "how to think" when instructing students in reading comprehension.

Thinking skills are also taught by teaching fact-finding skills, divergent thinking skills, and learning strategies. Most studies of effective instruction contend that the thinking skills used in completing assignments should also be explained to students. It is important for teachers to check often the extent to which students understand what it is they are supposed to do.

## Motivating

The importance of motivation for learning is undisputed in the educational and psychological literature. Instructional psychology includes the use of motivational strategies as a principle of learning, and a relationship between achievement and motivation is consistently demonstrated (Brophy, 1983; Newby, 1991). Students learn better when they are motivated. Teachers motivate students by making instruction relevant to the student's background, showing enthusiasm and interest when they present information, rewarding students on an intermittent schedule, and making students believe they can do the work they are assigned.

## Providing Feedback

It is essential that students receive information about the quality of their performance and the extent to which they are performing in accordance with expectations (Bloom, 1985). Good teachers give students immediate, frequent, explicit feedback on their performance and behavior. The most effective feedback gives students increased opportunity to respond. Reid (1986) demonstrate increased reading achievement for elementary students when error-correction procedures were used. These procedures provided feedback in the form of cues and prompts to guide the student to the correct answer. Effective teachers maintain an atmosphere of openness and support when providing feedback, and they strive to minimize the extent to which their responses are viewed as judgmental (Algozzine & Ysseldyke, 1992).

## Providing Relevant Practice

There must be ample amounts of two kinds of practice—controlled (guided) or independent (seatwork or homework)—to optimize students' achievement, and the tasks should be relevant to instructional goals. Variety is important; lack of it increases boredom and potential behavior problems. It is also critical that students be assigned the right amount of work, a judgment made by taking into account students' characteristics and level of skill development.

## Keeping Students Actively Involved

Academically engaged time is a moderate predictor of students' achievement (Ysseldyke & Christenson, 1993). Strategies that teachers use to keep students actively engaged include clear communication of goals, monitoring of students' performance, immediate and academically oriented feedback, carefully sequenced materials and tasks, appropriate pacing, use of reinforcement and praise, allocation of sufficient time to instruction is appropriate for individual students, it is important to look at the extent to which they are actively engaged in responding to instruction. This is usually accomplished by direct observation of behavior in the classroom.

## Modifying or Adapting Instruction

Effective teachers make adjustments in the instructional content and approaches they use with individual students as a result of information gathered on performance. The number of options available for adapting instruction, the teacher's willingness to implement modifications, and the consistency with which modifications are used are all factors that affect adaptive instruction. Effective teachers adapt instruction by changing goals, materials, teaching methods, or task demands.

# Evaluating Instruction

Evaluation is the process by which those responsible for instructing students decide whether the approaches, methods, and materials they are using are effective. It is on this basis that instructional personnel decide to refer students. Two kinds of instructional evaluation are used: (1) formative evaluation, or evaluation that occurs during instruction and is designed to provide data on progress, and (2) summative evaluation, or evaluation that occurs at the end of instruction to see whether pupils have achieved the desired outcomes. Algozzine and Ysseldyke (1992) identified five principles for evaluating instruction: (1) monitoring students' understanding, (2) monitoring engaged time, (3) monitoring students' activity and maintaining their records, and (4) using data to make decisions. Assessors should document the extent to which each of these factors occurs for individual students.

## Monitoring Students' Understanding

Students' perceptions of what they are to do are not always congruent with teachers' expectations and intentions (Winne & Marx, 1982). Teachers' goals must be explicitly stated, as students do not always automatically identify them. Assessors need to examine the extent to which students understand what teachers expect them to do and the process they need to go through to complete classroom assignments, as well as the methods being used by instructors to check students' success rate.

## Monitoring Engaged Time

Students who are actively engaged learn more in school. Engaged time increases when instruction is paced appropriately, goals are communicated, immediate feedback is given, sequencing is appropriate, and so on. In other words, engaged time is directly related to other aspects of effective instruction. Greenwood (1991) demonstrated the importance of engaged time and developed a methodology Code for Instructional Structure and Student Academic Response (CISSAR) for assessing it.

### Monitoring Students' Activity and Maintaining Performance Records

It is important that teachers monitor pupils' performance and success rate rates and keep records of them. Record keeping can be informal or formal, but teachers should be able to indicate the extent to which students are making progress. In addition, assessors can examine the ways in which teachers have taught students to monitor their own progress.

### Using Data to Make Instructional Decisions

Effective teachers use data on students' performance to make decisions about when to refer students for evaluation, to make teaching changes, and to decide when to discontinue provision of special or remedial services. Salvia and Ysseldyke (1998) described the kinds of decisions teachers make and provided detailed information on the ways in which assessment information may be used. Salvia and Hughes (1990, pp. 121–122) offer suggestions for instructional modification, depending on the pattern of a student's performance in relation to the expected performance.

## WHAT ARE THE HOME FACTORS THAT DETERMINE EDUCATIONAL OUTCOME?

Ysseldyke & Christenson (1993) identified five factors in the home support or negate what is occurring instructionally in classrooms: (1) expectations and attributions, (2) discipline orientation, (3) affective environment, (4) parental participation, and (5) structure for learning. Education takes place in both the home and the school, and it is important to take each into account.

### Expectations and Attributions

Academic achievement is consistently correlated with high but realistic parental expectations. For example, we know that when parental expectations and actual performance are at similar levels,

students perform better on cognitive tasks (Scott-Jones, 1984). The effects of parental expectations and attributions can also be indirect. They may influence parental behavior and also affect the extent to which parents participate in schooling. These, in turn, can affect pupils' achievement.

### Discipline Orientation

Researchers have demonstrated that specific parental discipline patterns are correlated with students' high achievement (Dornbusch, Ritter, Leiderman, Roberts, & Fraleigh, 1987; Steinberg, Elmen, & Mounts, 1989). Authoritative discipline is superior to permissive or authoritarian discipline; overcontrol and undercontrol are correlated negatively with academic outcomes.

### Affective Environment

Academic outcomes are usually better in situations in which parents accept children's strengths and weaknesses, nurture children, encourage them, get involved in their activities, and are emotionally responsive to their needs. "In general, a positive parent-child relationship is related to academic success" (Ysseldyke & Christenson, 1993, p. 32).

### Parental Participation

Parental involvement in childrens' schooling at home and in school is correlated highly with positive academic outcomes (Henderson, 1989). Also, students achieve more when there is a match between home and school concerning rules and expectations.

### Structure for Learning

Structure includes both organization of the home environment and manipulation of that environment to support learning. Academic outcomes are better when parents provide opportunities for students to complete homework, give some assistance with schoolwork, and monitor other activities so that students can be involved in learning.

## HOW SHOULD WE ASSESS EDUCATIONAL ENVIRONMENTS?

Psychoeducational testing has been and continues to be a major activity of school psychologists, even though tests hold little or no relevance to the planning and delivery of instructional services (Epps & Tindal, 1987; Reynolds, 1984; Thurlow

& Ysseldyke, 1980; Ysseldyke, 1996). Learning is the product of behavioral interaction with environmental factors such as engaged learning time, activities, teachers' behaviors, and students' active participation (Delquadri, Greenwood, Whorton, Carta, & Hall, 1986). Consequently, it is important to use an ecological perspective to determine the impact that instructional environmental factors have on students' performance (Grade et al., 1986).

We have argued that assessment of instructional environments is important and necessary in designing effective instructional programs for students, and we have shown that there is a solid and extensive knowledge base for effective instruction. In short, we know that we ought to take these factors into account, and we know what to assess. But how do we do so in practice? What methods can be used to assess instructional environments?

There are five primary ways to gather data about instructional environments: (1) direct observation, (2) ratings, (3) self-reports, (4) interviews, and (5) ecobehavioral analysis. An indirect method is through portfolio assessment. We briefly describe each of these data collection methods, and we then conclude this chapter with illustrations of current instrumentation.

**Observation** may be either formal or informal. In formal observation, the factors to be observed are decided ahead of time, and the frequency, duration, or magnitude of their occurrence is recorded. Informal observation, in contrast, involves visiting classrooms and recording behaviors and events as they happen. Observation may be quantitative or qualitative. Quantitative observation is distinguished by five characteristics: "First, the goal of observation is to measure (for example, count) specific behaviors. Second, the behaviors being observed have been defined previously and precisely. Third, before observation, procedures are developed for gathering objective and replicable information about the behavior. Fourth, the times and places for observation are carefully selected and specified. Fifth, the ways in which behavior will be quantified are specified prior to observation" (Salvia & Ysseldyke, 1995, p. 199). Qualitative approaches to observation are characterized by watching or listening and drawing inferences about the presence or absence of known characteristics. An observer could gather data informally on each of the instructional and home components by knowing what to look for and observing classroom and home learning settings.

Observation is the preferred method of assessing social and many academic behaviors.

**Checklists and rating scales** are common tools and differ in their response formats. Checklists often utilize yes-or-no responses. For example a checklist for instructional management techniques might include teacher-directed, guided practice; independent practice; self-monitoring; or cooperative learning formats. Any or all of these could be checked by the respondent. Rating scales are generally qualitative in nature because typically respondents rank opinions or types of behaviors within some range of response. For example, in written expressive language subtests, rating might indicate superior to average, below average, or deficient, based on writing samples of different students.

Another method for collecting data is **self-reports.** Individuals being assessed are asked to reveal common behaviors in which they engage or to identify inner feelings. When applied to assessment of instructional environments, students would be asked to describe or rate the nature of the instruction they receive. Data may also be collected through **interviews:** teachers or parents could be asked to describe the nature of a student's instructional environment.

The use of **portfolios** in schools is one attempt to provide more relevant assessment to enhance instructional decision making and the evaluation of students' progress. Even so, assessment in general has been driven by concerns for measuring and reporting achievement data for outside audiences. Often forgotten is the importance of accountability. That is, what is important for students to know and to be able to demonstrate? How do we provide experiences that give students the opportunity to learn this information? Several different models of portfolio assessment have been introduced, and the profession is far from reaching a consensus about what constitutes a portfolio or how one should be used in assessment.

Portfolios go beyond the simple display of sample products. They are intended to facilitate judgments about performance. For a long time, portfolios have been an integral part of the evaluation process in art, music, photography, journalism, commercial arts, and modeling (Winograd & Gaskins, 1992). Now they are being applied to traditional academic areas and are seen as especially useful alternatives to traditional assessments for students with severe disabilities. They serve several purposes: (1) to document a student's effort, (2) to document growth and achievement, (3) to augment information from other assessment methods, (4) and to provide a public accounting of the quality of educational programs (Salvia & Ysseldyke, 1995, p. 2440.

A rapidly developing area in the field of assessing instructional environments, specifically applied to behavior analysis, is **ecobehavioral analysis,** the observation of functional relationships or interactions between the student's behavior and its ecological contexts. Ecobehavioral assessment takes into consideration the importance of situation or contextual factors. This approach is used to identify interactions among students' behavior, teachers' behavior, time allocated to instruction, physical grouping structures, types of tasks, and instructional content. Ecobehavioral assessment enables educators to identify natural instructional conditions associated with academic success, behavioral competence, or challenging behaviors. It also provides a means to gather data on the opportunity to learn, an important component of Carroll's (1963) model of school learning.

# EXAMPLES OF INSTRUMENTATION

The first version of ecobehavioral assessment was developed by Greenwood, Delquadri, and Hall (1978) and was called the Code for Instructional Structure and Student Academic Response (CISSAR). The taxonomy for the current CISSAR is shown in Figure 20.3. This system allows assessors to categorize ecobehavioral events into students' and teachers' behaviors, as well as to consider the ecology of the classroom. Using momentary time sampling, behaviors are recorded over the entire school day. The frequency of occurrence and the interactions among behaviors and environmental stimuli are analyzed.

Over the past 12 years, two additional ecobehavioral assessments have been developed: Ecobehavioral System for Complex Assessments of Preschool Environments (ESCAPE) and a mainstream version of CISSAR, MS-CISSAR. The three derivative systems (CISSAR, ESCAPE, and MS-CISSAR) have been combined into a software program, Ecobehavioral Assessment System Software (EBASS). The EBASS (Greenwood & Carta, 1994) enables school personnel to conduct systematic classroom observational assessments by using laptops or hand-held computers. Although originally designed specifically for school psychologists, EBASS may be used by other professionals responsible for teacher training and general and special education evaluation activities. The EBASS provides computer-assisted training in instrument use, calibration of reliability checks, instrument modification, simple and complex data analyses, caseload management, and data base capabilities.

The Instructional Priority System (IPS) is a brief but thorough qualitative rating scale that bases students' instructional needs on expectations and demands of the instructional environment (Welch & Link, 1991). Specifically, the IPS gathers information from the special educator, student, and content area teacher to (1) clarify teachers' expectations and classroom demands, (2) determine the degree to which the student is

| BEHAVIOR | | | | | ECOLOGY | | |
|---|---|---|---|---|---|---|---|
| **STUDENT BEHAVIORS** | | | **TEACHER BEHAVIORS** | | | | |
| Academic Responses | Task Management | Competing Responses | Teacher Position | Teacher Behavior | Activity | Task | Structure |
| 1. Writing | 1. AttndTask | 1. Disrupt | 1. InFront | 1. NoResp | 1. Reading | 1. Readers | 1. EntirGrp |
| 2. PlayAca | 2. RaiseHnd | 2. PlayInapp | 2. AtDesk | 2. Teaching | 2. Math | 2. Workbooks | 2. SmallGrp |
| 3. ReadAloud | 3. LookMtrls | 3. TaskInapp | 3. AmongStud | 3. OtherTalk | 3. Spelling | 3. Worksheet | 3. Indiv |
| 4. RdSilent | 4. Moves | 4. TalkInapp | 4. Side | 4. Approval | 4. Hndwrtng | 4. Paper&Pen | |
| 5. TalkAca | 5. PlayApp | 5. LocInapp | 5. Back | 5. Disapprov | 5. Language | 5. LstnLect | |
| 6. AnsAcaQst | | 6. LookArnd | 6. Out | | 6. Science | 6. OthMedia | |
| 7. AskAcaQst | | 7. Self-Stim | | | 7. SocStud | 7. Tch/StDis | |
| | | | | | 8. Arts/Crft | 8. Fetch/Put | |
| | | | | | 9. FreeTime | | |
| | | | | | 10. BusMgmnt | | |
| | | | | | 11. Translt | | |
| | | | | | 12. Cn'tTell | | |

FIGURE 20.3   CISSAR taxonomy.

able to meet identified classroom expectations and demands, (3) identify areas in which students are having problems, and (4) decide which problems to address first.

West (1990) developed the Analysis of Classroom and Instructional Demands (ACID). This inventory identifies and describes the demands of the instructional environment. A teacher or observer rates the target student's ability to meet instructional expectations. The ACID test rates nine areas of students' behavior in the context of the instructional environment: classroom rules, instructional content, presentation, assignment completion, group work, instructional materials, study skills, test taking, and grading procedures.

A comprehensive checklist was developed by Wood (1991) that examines classroom characteristics, including the emotional and social atmosphere, physical layout, teaching techniques, media (e.g., textbooks, chalkboard, audiovisual equipment), content, and evaluation techniques. The checklist also examines the characteristics of related environments, such as the cafeteria, gymnasium, elective settings, and assembly halls.

The one thing these checklists have in common is that none of them specifically examines the components of effective instruction. The Instructional Environment Scale–II (TIES-II) allows systematic data collection on the extent to which components of effective instruction target the student's instructional environment (Ysseldyke & Christenson, 1993). The student's instructional needs are assessed in the context of both the classroom and the home environments. The scale takes into account not only the presence of components of effective instruction in the classroom and home but also their importance to the student's performance in school. The 12 instructional components and 5 home support for learning components, shown in Table 20.2, are nearly identical to the instructional and home components described earlier in this chapter.

Using information gained from interviews with the student, teacher, and parents, TIES-II helps formulate intervention options. In addition, structured classroom observations are preplanned with the teacher and observer, which allows the observer to understand the learning goals and objectives prior to the observation. Thus, the observation can be recorded in the context of classroom expectations.

The TIES-II kit comes with five data collection tools: (1) Observation Record, (2) Teacher Interview Record, (3) Student Interview Record, (4) Parent Interview Record, and (5) Instructional Needs Checklist. In addition, there are three intervention planning forms: (1) Instructional Environment Form, (2) Home Support for Learning Form, and (3) Intervention Planning Form.

The desire to ensure that students graduate with more than basic skills has fueled the interest in performance assessment. **Portfolio assessment systems** have been adapted in varying degrees throughout the country to get a more complete picture of students' abilities. It has been argued that American students are the "most tested" and the "least examined" (Resnick & Resnick, 1985). Performance-based assessment, including portfolios, has provided educators with a means to both measure and tailor instruction to help students meet learning outcomes. Students taking part in performance-based assessment may be asked to write an essay, perform a group experiment, define in writing how they answered a math problem, or keep a portfolio of their best work. Two such systems are being pioneered in Vermont and Kentucky.

Vermont has developed an innovative assessment program in which students' portfolios play a central role. Work is collected by classroom teachers but scored according to criteria that are consistent across the state. The guidelines for the operation of the portfolio program and the criteria for scoring have been developed by committees made up largely of volunteer teachers. The portfolios are complemented by uniform tests that are standardized in content and administrative conditions but not restricted to multiple-choice format. In mathematics, students and teachers are required to construct a portfolio of five to seven "best pieces," which are to be of three types: puzzles, applications, and investigations. The writing system requires students to include six to eight pieces (depending on grade level) from several different categories of work (e.g., poem or short story; personal narration; personal response to a book, event, current issue, mathematical problem, or scientific phenomenon). One piece from each category must be designated as the "best piece."

Under the Kentucky Reform Act (KERA) of 1990, the Instructional Results and Information System (KIRIS) has as its mission the inclusion of all students in the assessment and accountability processes. The KIRIS assessment,

## TABLE 20.2 Components of the TIES-II

| | Component | Definition |
|---|---|---|
| Instructional Environment Components | *Instructional Match* | The student's needs are assessed accurately, and instruction is matched appropriately to the results of the instructional diagnosis. |
| | *Teacher Expectations* | There are realistic, yet high expectations for both the amount and the accuracy of work to be completed by the student, and these are communicated clearly to the student. |
| | *Classroom Environment* | The classroom management techniques used for this student; there is a positive, supportive classroom atmosphere, and time is used productively. |
| | *Instructional Presentation* | Instruction is presented in a clear and effective manner; directions contain sufficient information for this student to understand what kinds of behaviors or skills are to be demonstrated, and the student's understanding is checked. |
| | *Cognitive Emphasis* | Thinking skills and learning strategies for completing assignments are communicated explicitly to the student. |
| | *Motivational Strategies* | Effective strategies for heightening student interest and student efforts are used. |
| | *Relevant Practice* | The student is given adequate opportunity to practice with appropriate materials and to achieve a high success rate. Classroom tasks are clearly important to achieving instructional goals. |
| | *Informed Feedback* | The student receives relatively immediate and specific information on his or her performance or behavior, when the student makes mistakes, correction is provided. |
| | *Academic Engaged Time* | The student is actively engaged in responding to academic content; the teacher monitors the extent to which the student is actively engaged and redirects the student when the student is unengaged. |
| | *Adaptive Instruction* | The curriculum is modified within reason to accommodate the student's unique and specific instructional needs. |

**TABLE 20.2** *(continued)*

| | Component | Definition |
|---|---|---|
| | *Progress Evaluation* | There is direct, frequent measurement of the student's progress toward completion of instructional objectives; data on the student's performance and progress are used to plan future instruction. |
| | *Student Understanding* | The student demonstrates an accurate understanding of what is to be done in the classroom. |
| Home-Support-for-Learning Components | *Expectations and Attributions* | High, realistic expectations about school work are communicated to the child; the value of working hard in school is emphasized. |
| | *Discipline Orientation* | There is an authoritative, not permissive or authoritarian, approach to discipline; the child is monitored and supervised by adults. |
| | *Effective Home Environment* | The parent-child relationship is generally positive and supportive. |
| | *Parent Participation* | There is an educative home environment, and others participate in the child's schooling at home and/or at school. |
| | *Structure for Learning* | Organization and daily routines facilitate the completion of school work, and the child's academic learning is supported. |

From "Identifying students' instructional needs in the context of classroom and home environments" by J. E. Ysseldyke, S. L. Christenson, and J. F. Kovaleski, *Teaching Exceptional Children*, 26 (1994), 37–41. Copyright 1994 by The Council for Exceptional Children. Reprinted with permission.

administered annually, includes each of the three types of assessment tasks:

1. Assessment task involving portfolios—writing and mathematics for grades 4, 8, and 12. These portfolios represent a collection of the student's best work developed over time in conjunction with support from teachers, peers, and parents. The portfolios are scored by local teachers, and the scores are reported to the Kentucky Department of Education for use in the accountability assessment.
2. Assessment tasks involving performance events. Students participate in performance-based assessment tasks that require them to use knowledge and skills learned in school to produce a product or solve a problem. Students are required to apply what they have learned to real situations.
3. Assessment tasks involving open-ended questions. Students respond to open-ended questions that require extended written responses. The focus is on higher-order thinking skills; solving multistep problems; and using reasoning, analytical, and written communication skills.

Students with disabilities must participate in the KIRIS assessments. They may do so in three ways:

1. Full participation in all three components of the assessment program with no adaptations or modifications
2. Full participation in all three components with adaptations and modifications
3. Participation in the Alternative Portfolio Assessment.

A small percentage of students with disabilities (1%–2%), generally those who have moderate to severe cognitive disabilities, participate in the Alternative Portfolio Assessment. This process represents a multidisciplinary approach, as opposed to a single curriculum area. It follows the model of Kentucky mathematics and writing portfolios in using a holistic scoring guide.

# ISSUES AND CONSIDERATIONS IN ASSESSMENT OF INSTRUCTIONAL ENVIRONMENTS

The approaches described in this chapter differ from those currently used by contemporary school psychologists. By design or desire, the practices of school psychologists still consist primarily of assessment of students' skills and abilities for designing instructional interventions (often delivered in special education settings). Practice is changing (Reschly & Ysseldyke, 1995) and is increasingly characterized by greater attention to instructional ecology. Yet there are major issues that arise when this kind of shift takes place. Two that we focus on are time constraints and the fears of teachers in an era of accountability.

Assessment of instructional environments takes time, and for school psychologists time is a precious commodity. They are very busy people, and their caseloads exceed reasonable limits. With no time available to add on functions, we are suggesting substitution instead. Time spent in ecobehavioral analysis, assessment of instructional environments, and portfolio appraisals must take the place of testing. Initially, there will be no time for these activities, and it will need to "come out of the hide" of school psychologists. Moreover, it is critical that data be collected on the merits and limitations of these new activities. Only by documenting the outcomes for students and systems of psychometric activities versus these newer approaches will psychologists be able to justify their implementation and continuation.

Instructional environments are assessed to plan instructional interventions for individual students. Yet realistically, whenever data are gathered on the effectiveness of instruction for individual students, those who teach the students become concerned. We live in an era of educational accountability; teachers, schools, and school systems are increasingly held accountable for academic outcomes (Ysseldyke & Geenen, 1996). From teacher assistance teams all the way up to district-level personnel, intolerance for waiting for a cure has often resulted in many children being needlessly referred and ultimately placed in special education. The desire for a quick fix sometimes dictates the direction a school psychologist must take and often can be considered an unalterable variable. Coupled with today's litigious society, these scenarios can be frustrating to school psychologists. When this is the case and when high stakes are applied to the results of schooling, school personnel become anxious about assessments that look as if they are evaluations. It is necessary and important for assessment personnel to make clear to teachers that they are evaluating the instructional environment and the nature of instruction, not the teacher. The fact that this is very difficult to do led Ysseldyke and Christenson (1993) to develop an Instructional Needs Checklist as part of TIES-II. The form is completed by teachers; assessors observe the student and then compare notes with the teacher.

# SUMMARY

A major shift is taking place in the practice of school psychologists, a shift away from a child-centered deficit model to an ecological model in which as much time and energy are devoted to assessing the instructional environment as to assessing the student. The focus of assessment is on intervention planning, and intervention begins with making changes in the nature of instruction.

This focus on assessing instructional environments is becoming more prevalent for four major reasons: (1) because multiple factors affect academic outcomes, (2) learning does not occur in a vacuum, (3) there are limits to assessing the learner, and (4) to put content into consultation. In the past, assessment of instructional environments has been limited to observation, interaction analyses, and interviews. There is an extensive knowledge base on the instructional factors that influence academic outcomes, as well as on the home factors that also interact to influence outcomes.

Until recently there were no systematic methodologies for assessing instructional environments. Several alternative approaches are now available. We described some recently developed instruments to assess instructional environments. The success of these approaches depends on several alterable variables that are in direct control of those who choose to implement them.

Over the years, education has created the refer-test-place and the dual system monsters. It is now time to tame them. The past practice of assessing students has been not only familiar but also comfortable. Accountability has been minimal or protected by a smoke screen of bureaucracy. Too long we have rested on historical, testimonial, and cash-validated practices. The bandwagons have come and gone, yet many children are not benefiting from the instruction they receive. Now is as good a time as ever to explore proactively, to introduce building-based teams, and to use effective methods of assessing instructional environments for the good of all learners.

# REFERENCES

Achenbach, T. M. (1985). *Assessment and taxonomy of child and adolescent psychopathology*. Beverly Hills, CA: Sage.

Achenbach, T. M. (1991). *Manual for the Child Behavior Checklist/4–18 and 1991 profile*. Burlington: University of Vermont, Department of Psychiatry.

Algozzine, B., & Ysseldyke, J. (1992). *Strategies and factors for effective instruction*. Longmont, CO: Sopris West.

Algozzine, B., Ysseldyke, J. E., & Elliott, J. L. (1997). *Strategies and tactics for effective instruction–II*. Longmont, CO: Sopris West.

Alpert, J. L., & Meyers, J. (Eds). (1983). *Training in consultation: Perspectives from mental health, behavioral, and organizational consultation*. Springfield, IL: Thomas.

Anastasi, A. (1976). *Psychological testing* (4th ed.). New York: Macmillan.

Anderson, L. W. (1985). What are students doing when they do all that seatwork? In C. W. Fisher & D. Berliner (Eds.), *Perspectives on instructional time* (pp. 189–202). New York: Longman.

Anderson, L., Evertson, C., & Brophy, J. (1979). An experimental study of effective teaching in first-grade reading groups. *Elementary School Journal, 79*, 193–223.

Bandura, A. (1978). The self system in reciprocal determinism. *American Psychologist, 33*, 344–358.

Barclay, J. R. (1983). *Barclay Classroom Assessment System (BCAS)*. Los Angeles: Western Psychological Services.

Barker, R. (1963). *The stream of behavior*. New York: Appleton-Century-Crofts.

Beck, R. (1990). *Responding to individual differences in education: Secondary*. Longmont, CO: Sopris West.

Beck, R. (1991). *Responding to individual differences in education: Elementary*. Great Falls: Great Falls, Montana, Public Schools.

Beck, R. (1993). *Responding to individual differences in education: Preschool*. Longmont, CO: Sopris West.

Becker, W. C., Engelmann, S., Carnine, D. W., & Rhine, R. (1981). The direct instruction model. In R. Rhine (Ed.), *Encouraging change in America's schools: A decade of experimentation* (pp. 45–83). New York: Academic Press.

Bergan, J. R., & Kratochwill, T. R. (1990). *Behavioral consultation and therapy*. New York: Plenum.

Bijou, S. W., & Baer, D. M. (1978). *Behavior analysis of child development*. Englewood Cliffs, NJ: Prentice Hall.

Blair, T. R. (1984). Teacher effectiveness: The know-how to improve student learning. *The Reading Teacher, 38*(2), 138–142.

Bloom, B. S. (1976). *Human characteristics and student learning*. New York: McGraw-Hill.

Bloom, B. S. (1985). Learning for mastery. In C. W. Fisher & D. C. Berliner (Eds.), *Perspectives on instructional time* (pp. 73–93). New York: Longman.

Boehm, A. E., & Weinberg, R. A. (1988). *The classroom observer: A guide for developing observation skills* (2nd ed.). New York: Teachers College Press.

Bronfenbrenner, U. (1979). *The ecology of human development*. Cambridge, MA: Harvard University Press.

Bronfenbrenner, U. (1986). Ecology of the family as a context for human development: Research perspectives. *Developmental Psychology, 22*(6), 723–742.

Brophy, J. E. (1983). Classroom organization and management. *Elementary School Journal, 83*, 254–285.

Brown, L., & Leigh, J. (1986). *Adaptive Behavior Inventory*. Austin, TX: Pro-Ed.

Caplan, G. (1970). *The theory and practice of mental health consultation*. New York: Basic Books.

Carpenter, T. P., & Fennema, E. (1989). *Research and cognitively guided instruction*. Madison, WI: National Center for Research in Mathematical Sciences Education.

Carrol, J. B. (1963). A model of school learning. *Teachers College Record, 64*, 723–733.

Conoley, J. C. (1981). Advocacy consultation: Promises and problems. In J. C. Conoley (Ed.), *Consultation in the schools* (pp. 157–178). New York: Academic Press.

DeBoer, A. (1995). *Working together: The art of consulting and communicating*. Longmont, CO: Sopris West.

Delquadri, J., Greenwood, C. R., Whorton, D., Carta, J. J., & Hall, R. V. (1986). Classwide peer tutoring. *Exceptional Children, 52*(6), 535–542.

Dornbusch, S. M., Ritter, P. L., Leiderman, P. H., Roberts, D. F., & Fraleigh, M. J. (1987). The relation of parenting style to adolescent school performance. *Child Development, 58*, 1244–1257.

Doyle, W. (1986). Classroom organization and management. In M. C. Wittrock (Ed.), *Handbook of research on teaching* (3rd ed., pp. 392–431). New York: Macmillan.

Duffy, G. G., Roehler, L. R., & Rackliffe, G. (1985). Qualitative differences in teachers' instructional talk as they influence student awareness of lesson content. Paper presented at the American Educational Research Association, Chicago.

Edmonds, R. R. (1979). Some schools work and more can. *Social Policy, 9*, 28–32.

Englemann, S., Granzin, A., & Severson, H. (1979). Diagnosing instruction. *Journal of Special Education, 13*, 355–365.

Englert, C. (1984). Effective direct instruction practices in special education settings. *Remedial and Special Education, 5*(2), 38–47.

Epps, S., & Tindal, G. (1987). The effectiveness of differential programming in serving students with mild handicaps: Placement options and instructional programming. In M. C. Wang, M. C. Reynolds, & H. J. Walberg (Eds.), *Handbook of special education: Research and Practice—learner characteristics and adaptive education* (Vol. 1, pp. 213–248). New York: Pergamon.

Evertson, C., & Harris, A. H. (1992). What we know about managing classes. *Educational Leadership, 49*(7), 74–78.

Fister, S. L., & Kemp, K. A. (1995). *TGIF: But what will I do on Monday?* Longmont, CO: Sopris West.

Flanders, N. A. (1970). *Analyzing teaching behavior.* Reading, MA: Addison-Wesley.

Fuchs, L. S., & Fuchs, D. (1986). Linking assessment to instructional intervention: An overview. *School Psychology Review, 15*, 318–323.

Fullan, M., & Hargreaves, A. (1991). *What's worth fighting for? Working together for your school.* Toronto: Ontario Public School Teachers' Federation.

Gersten, R., Woodward, J., & Darch, C. (1986). Direct instruction: A research-based approach to curriculum design and teaching. *Exceptional Children, 53*(1), 17–31.

Good, T. L., & Brophy, J. E. (1984). *Looking in classrooms* (3rd ed.). New York: Harper & Row.

Good, T., & Grouws, D. (1979). The Missouri mathematics effectiveness project: An experimental study in fourth-grade classrooms. *Journal of Educational Psychology, 71*, 355–362.

Grade, J. L., Casey, A., & Christenson, S. L. (1986). Implementing a prereferral intervention system: Part I. The model. *Exceptional Children, 51*, 377–384.

Greenwood, C. R. (1991). Longitudinal analysis of time, engagement, and achievement in at-risk and non at-risk students. *Exceptional Children, 57*, 521–535.

Greenwood, C. R., & Carta, J. J. (1994). *Ecobehavioral Assessment Systems Software.* Kansas City, KS: Juniper Gardens Children's Center.

Greenwood, C. R., Delquadri, J., & Hall, V. (1978). *The Code for Instructional Structure and Student Academic Response.* Kansas City, KS: Juniper Gardens Children's Center.

Gutkin, T. B., & Curtis, M. J. (1990). School-based consultation: Theory, techniques, and research. In T. B. Gutkin & C. R. Reynolds (Eds.), *The handbook of school psychology* (2nd ed., pp. 577–611). New York, Wiley.

Guzzetti, B. J., & Marzano, R. J. (1984). Correlates of effective reading instruction. *The Reading Teacher, 37*(8), 754–758.

Hargrove, L. J., & Poteet, J. A. (1984). *Assessment in special education: The education evaluation.* Englewood Cliffs, NJ: Prentice Hall.

Helton, G. B., Workman, E. A., & Matuszek, P. A. (1982). *Psychoeducational assessment: Integrating concepts and techniques.* New York: Grune & Stratton.

Henderson, A. T. (1989). *The evidence continues to grow: Parent involvement improves student achievement.* Columbia, MD: National Committee for Citizens in Education.

Hintze, J. M., & Shapiro, E. S. (1995). Systematic observation of classroom behavior. In A. Thomas & J. Grimes (Eds.), *Best practices in school psychology–III.* Washington, DC: National Association of School Psychologists.

Howell, K. W. (1986). Direct assessment of academic performance. *School Psychology Review, 15*(3), 324–335.

Idol, L., Paolucci-Whitcomb, P., & Nevin, A. (1986). *Collaborative consultation.* Austin, TX: Pro-Ed.

Kagan, D. M. (1992). Implications of research on teacher beliefs. *Educational psychologist, 27*(1), 65–90.

Kantor, J. R. (1959). *Interbehavioral psychology.* Chicago: Principia Press.

Lambert, N., Leland, H., & Nihira, K. (1992). *AAMR Adaptive Behavior Scales–School* (2nd ed.). San Antonio, TX: Psychological Corp., Harcourt, Brace.

Lindsley, O. R. (1964). Direct measurement and prosthesis of retarded behavior. *Journal of Education, 147*, 68–81.

McCarney, S. B., & Bauer, A. M. (1989). *The Learning Disability Intervention manual.* Columbia, MO: Hawthorne Educational Services.

McCarney, S. B., & Cummins, K. K. (1988). *Prereferral Intervention manual.* Columbia, MO: Hawthorne Educational Services.

McCarney, S. B., Leigh, J. E., & Cornbleet, J. (1983). *Behavior Evaluation Scale.* Columbia, MO: Educational Services.

McCarney, S. B., & Tucci, J. K. (1991). *Study skills for students in our schools.* Columbia, MO: Hawthorne Educational Services.

Newby, T. (1991). Classroom motivation: Strategies of first-year teachers. *Educational Psychology, 83,* 195–200.

Pugach, M. C., & Johnson, L. J. (1988a). Peer collaboration: Enhancing teacher problem-solving capabilities for students at risk. (ERIC Document Reproduction Service No. SP 0301140). Paper presented at the Annual Meeting of the American Educational Research Associations, New Orleans.

Pugach, M. C., & Johnson, L. J. (1988b). Peer collaboration: Helping teachers help themselves. *Teaching Exceptional Children, 20*(3), 75–77.

Pugach, M. C., & Johnson, L. J. (1988c). Rethinking the relationship between consultation and collaborative problem-solving. *Focus on Exceptional Children* (Special issue), *21*(4).

Reid, E. R. (1981). *Teaching, scheduling and record keeping.* Salt Lake City, UT: Love Publishers.

Reid, E. R. (1986). Practicing effective instruction: The Exemplary Center for Reading. *Exceptional Children, 52*(6), 510–519.

Reith, H., & Evertson, C. (1988). Variables related to the effective instruction of difficult-to-teach children. *Focus on Exceptional Children, 20,* 2–7.

Reschly, D., & Ysseldyke, J. E. (1995). School psychology paradigm shift. In A. Thomas & J. Grimes (Eds.), *Best practices in school psychology–III* (pp. 17–31). Washington, DC: National Association of School Psychologists.

Resnick, D. P., & Resnick, L. B. (1985). Standards, curriculum, and performance: A historical and comparative perspective. *Educational Researcher, 14,* 5–21.

Reynolds, M. C. (1984). Classification of students with handicaps. In E. W. Gordon (Ed.), *Review of research in education* (Vol. 11, pp. 63–92). Washington, DC: American Educational Research Association.

Rhode, G., Jenson, W. R., & Reavis, H. K. (1993). The tough kid book: Practical classroom management strategies. Longmont, CO: Sopris West.

Roberts, M. L. (1996). Assessing environmental factors that impact student performance. In A. Thomas & J. Grimes (Eds.), *Best practices in school psychology–III* (pp. 679-688). Washington, DC: National Association of School Psychologists.

Rosenshine, B. V. (1983). Teaching functions in instructional programs. *The Elementary School Journal, 83*(4), 335–351.

Rosenshine, B. V., & Stevens, R. (1986). Teaching functions. In M. C. Wittrock (Ed.), *Handbook of research on teaching* (3rd ed., pp. 376–391). New York: Macmillan.

Salvia, J., & Hughes, C. (1990). *Curriculum-based assessment: Testing what is taught.* New York: Macmillan.

Salvia, J., & Ysseldyke, J. E. (1998). *Assessment* (7233 th ed.). Boston; Houghton Mifflin.

Sarason, S., & Doris, J. (1979). *Educational handicap, public policy, and social history.* New York: Free Press.

Schein, E. H. (1969). *Process consultation: Its role in organizational development.* Reading, MA: Addison-Wesley.

Scott-Jones, D. (1984). Family influences on cognitive development and school achievement. *Review of Research in Education, 11,* 259–304.

Shapiro, E. S. (1989). *Academic skill problems: Direct assessment and intervention.* New York: Guilford.

Skinner, B. F. (1953). *Science and human behavior.* New York: Macmillan.

Sparks, D. (1992). Becoming an authentic consultant: An interview with Peter Block. *Staff Development, 13*(2), 12.

Sprick, R. S., & Howard, L. U. (1995). *The teacher's encyclopedia of behavior management: 100 problems/500 plans.* Longmont, CO: Sopris West.

Sprick, R. S., Sprick, U., & Garrison, U. (1993). *Interventions: Establishing positive discipline policies.* Longmont, CO: Sopris West.

Squires, D. A., Huitt, W. G., & Segars, J. (1983). *Effective schools and classrooms: A research-based perspective.* Alexandria, VA: Association for Supervision and Curriculum Development.

Steinberg, L., Elmen, J. D., & Mounts, N. S.. (1989). Authoritative parenting, psychosocial maturity, and academic success among adolescents. *Child Development, 60,* 1424–1436.

Stevens, R., & Rosenshine, B. (1981). Advances in research on teaching. *Exceptional Educational Quarterly, 2*(1), 1–9.

Sunberg, N. D. (1977). *Assessment of persons.* Englewood Cliffs, NJ: Prentice Hall.

Tharp, R. G., & Wetzel, R. J. (1969). *Behavior modification in the natural environment.* New York: Academic Press.

Thurlow, M. L., & Ysseldyke, J. E. (1980). *Instructional planning: Information collected by school psychologists vs. information considered useful by teachers* (Research Report No. 29). Minneapolis: University of Minnesota, Institute for Research on Learning Disabilities.

Walberg, H. J. (1984). Families as partners in educational productivity. *Phi Delta Kappan, 65,* 397–400.

Walker, H. M., & Severson, H. H. (1990). *Systematic screening for behavior disorders (SSBD): A multiple gating procedure.* Longmont, CO: Sopris West.

Wallace, G., & Larsen, S. C. (1979). *Educational assessment of learning problems: Testing for teaching.* Boston: Allyn & Bacon.

Welch, M., & Link, D. P. (1991). The instrumental priority system: A method for assessing the educational environment. *Intervention in School and Clinic, 27*(2), 91–96.

West, J. F. (1990). *Analysis of Classroom and Instructional Demands.* Austin, TX: Institute for Learning and Development.

Winne, P. H., & Marx, R. W. (1982). Students' and teachers' views of thinking processes for classroom learning. *Elementary School Journal, 82,* 493–518.

Winograd, P., & Gaskins, R. (1992). Improving the assessment of literacy: The power of portfolios. *Pennsylvania Reporter, 23*(2), 1–6.

Wittrock, M. C. (1986). Student thought processes. In M. C. Wittrock (Ed.), *Handbook for research on teaching* (3rd ed., pp. 397–414). New York: Macmillan.

Wood, J. W. (1991). *Project SHARE.* Richmond: Virginia Commonwealth University.

Ysseldyke, J. E. (1973). Diagnostic-prescriptive teaching: *The search for aptitude-treatment interactions.* In L. Mann and D. A. Sabatino (Eds.), *The First Review of Special Education.* New York: Grune & Stratton.

Ysseldyke, J. E. (1996). Improving teaching and learning. *British Journal of Special Education, 23*(1), 3–8.

Ysseldyke, J. E., & Algozzine, B. (1995). *Special education: A practical approach for teachers* (3rd ed.). Boston: Houghton Mifflin.

Ysseldyke, J. E., & Christenson, S. L. (1987). Evaluating students' instructional environments. *Remedial and Special Education, 8*(3), 17–24.

Ysseldyke, J. E., & Christenson, S. L. (1993). *The instructional environment system–II.* Longmont, CO: Sopris West.

Ysseldyke, J. E., & Geenen, K. (1996). Integrating the special education and compensatory education systems into the school reform process: A national perspective. *School Psychology Review, 25*(4), 418–430.

Ysseldyke, J. E., & Marston, D. (1990). The need of assessment information to plan instructional interventions: A review of the research. In T. B. Gutkin & C. R. Reynolds (Eds.), *The handbook of school psychology* (2nd ed., pp. 661–682). New York: Wiley.

## CHAPTER 21

# DIAGNOSTIC DECISION MAKING IN SCHOOL PSYCHOLOGY: UNDERSTANDING AND COPING WITH UNCERTAINTY[1]

GREGG M. MACMANN
*University of Kentucky*
DAVID W. BARNETT
*University of Cincinnati*

School psychologists play a vital role in the diagnosis of learning and behavior problems among school-aged children and youths. Yet many of the diagnostic decisions that school psychologists make (e.g., identification of learning disabilities and "strengths" and "weaknesses" in intellectual functioning) are highly vulnerable to error. The errors are both technical and conceptual. They undermine the ability to make confident decisions and place children at risk. Unfortunately, many of the difficulties are inherent in the diagnostic endeavor (reflecting both imperfect assessment technologies and limited understanding of human behavior and development). Because the problems cannot be "solved" in the usual sense, strategies are needed to cope with the difficulties effectively (and thus minimize the risks for children). In this chapter, following a description of sources of error in diagnostic decision making, strong models for coping with diagnostic uncertainty are suggested.

[1]This chapter is partly based on an invited address by Gregg M. Macmann to Division 16 for the Lightner Witmer Award, presented at the Annual Meeting of the American Psychological Association, New York, August 1995.

## DIAGNOSIS OF EDUCATIONAL DISABILITIES

In educational and other human service settings, diagnostic classification systems are intended to organize existing knowledge and facilitate the delivery of needed services, providing a means of communication, treatment planning, legal entitlement, and reimbursement for services. For special education and related services, the identification of school-aged children and youths with educational disabilities (e.g., emotional disorders, learning disabilities, and mental retardation) is guided by the diagnostic categories described in the Individuals with Disabilities Education Act (IDEA; revision and reauthorization of Public Law 94-142). Accordingly, children who have been diagnosed with an educational disability are entitled to a free and appropriate public education, and in turn state and local education agencies may be partly reimbursed for the costs of these services. Although the IDEA legislation has served reasonably well for the purposes of legal entitlement and reimbursement, the contributions have been more vigorously challenged with respect to communication and treatment planning. In the sections that follow, we analyze the controversies through two related themes: what can be said with confidence and what can be said that might be helpful.

# TECHNICAL SOURCES OF ERROR: WHAT CAN BE SAID WITH CONFIDENCE?

The determination of a child's diagnostic status is vulnerable to many sources of error. The technical errors arise from the undependability of measures. Across alternative instruments, times, informants and settings, and examiners, assessment techniques intended to measure the same diagnostic construct are likely to produce different information, thus limiting the reliability and accuracy of diagnostic decisions. As a result, the ability to make confident decisions and communicate meaningfully with others is compromised.

## Decision Reliability

Ordinarily, questions about reliability have been analyzed in terms of the consistency or dependability of *scores*. In contrast, analyses of decision reliability focus on the manner in which scores are actually used in professional practice—that is, the professional *inferences* or *outcomes* of the decision-making process. Professional inferences can take many different forms. For example, it might be inferred that a child has a learning disability or that a child is at risk or that a child has a strength or weakness in verbal comprehension skills. In a decision reliability study, the consistency or dependability of these types of inferences is examined.

Even though the idea for this type of research has been around for about 30 years, the need to evaluate the technical adequacy of assessment in terms of the quality of professional decisions has assumed increasing importance in contemporary measurement theory (e.g., Cronbach, 1988; Kane, 1992; Messick, 1989, 1995; Shepard, 1993). As aptly summarized by Angoff (1988), technical adequacy is not a characteristic of tests per se but of "the interpretations and inferences that the user draws from test scores, and the decisions and actions that flow from those inferences" (p. 24). Decision reliability analyses (*d* studies) have been incorporated in Cronbach's theory of generalizability for scores and profiles (Cronbach, Gleser, Nanda, & Rajaratnam, 1972), but a decision-focused approach in the evaluation of technical adequacy has even broader theoretical and practical implications (e.g., Barnett & Macmann, 1992b; Macmann, Barnett, Allen, Bramlett, Hall, & Ehrhardt, 1996; Peterson & Fishman, 1987).

As indicated by the *Standards for Educational and Psychological Testing* (American Educational Research Association, National Council on Measurement in Education, American Psychological Association, 1985), whenever tests are "used as the primary basis for making dichotomous decisions [e.g., pass-fail or eligible–not eligible] . . . estimates of the consistency of decisions are needed" (p. 20). Because of the "conditional" status of this recommendation, however, the need to provide this kind of information for probable professional decisions (e.g., screening and diagnosis) has rarely been recognized by norm-referenced test developers. Thus, in contrast to the many studies that have examined the reliability of mastery-nonmastery decisions in the context of setting standards for criterion-referenced testing, comparatively little research has been devoted to the reliability of inferences derived through norm-referenced testing. With little more than a caveat emptor on score interpretation and use, professionals have been left with a significant gap in the knowledge base for effective practice.

The *Ethical Principles of Psychologists and Code of Conduct* (American Psychological Association, 1992) indicates that professional psychologists have an obligation to "recognize limits to the certainty with which diagnoses, judgments, or predictions can be made about individuals" (Standard 2.04b) and communicate "any significant reservations they have about the accuracy or limitations of their interpretations" (Standard 2.05). Analyses of decision reliability address these issues. Unfortunately, although published decision reliability data for specific test instruments are typically unavailable, based on general measurement principles, to be described, the degree of uncertainty associated with many common decision-making practices is discouraging; even slight fluctuations in the reliability of scores can have dramatic implications for the reliability of decisions based on them.

### Limits to Professional Confidence

To illustrate, consider the use of IQ (intelligence quotient) in the diagnosis of children with mental retardation. The concept of mental retardation is defined in part by significantly subaverage intellectual functioning. To satisfy that criterion, a child should perform approximately 2 standard deviations below the mean on a measure of general intellectual functioning. The recommended cutoff in many schools corresponds to a Full

Scale IQ of about 70 or below on the Wechsler Scales. Of course, because IQ scores are not perfectly reliable, a child's observed level of test performance may vary on any given day. Consequently, the ability to infer that a child has an IQ score of 68, as opposed to, say, 72 or 75, may be correspondingly limited.

Recognizing the potential for error, professionals have been encouraged to use only the best available diagnostic measures for important individual decisions. In the 1920s, Kelley recommended a reliability coefficient of .98 "for tests used to measure differences among multiple performances by a single individual (Kelley, 1927, p. 11; cited in Hammill, Brown, & Bryant, 1992). Since that time, many have argued without reference to decision outcomes that reliability estimates >.80 represent the minimal acceptable level, and reliabilities >.90 the preferred level, to support the use of tests for important individual decisions (with reliabilities >.70 regarded in some sources as satisfactory for screening). For estimates of internal consistency (e.g., coefficient alpha), these standards imply a fairly strong correlation between how children perform on a test

and how they would be expected to perform on a similar or alternate form of the test (involving similar types of questions and tasks). However, research on the use of norm-referenced tests in professional decision making has shown that Kelley's recommendation may be the most defensible. Even with reliability coefficients above .90, many errors in the classification of children can occur.

The results of a computer simulation are shown in Figure 21.1. In this case, measures A and B are intended to represent parallel or alternate forms of the same test. With a cutoff of 2 standard deviations to identify "low" performers (<70), the scatterplot shows the reliability of classification decisions that might be expected when the correlation across measures is about .95. As indicated by the graph, 73 out of 3,000 cases have scored 2 standard deviations below the mean on measure A (i.e., 52 + 21). Of those 73 cases, however, only 52 have scored 2 standard deviations below the mean on measure B. Thus, even with a conventional reliability coefficient of .95, the reliability of inferring that a particular case is 2 standard deviations below the mean is

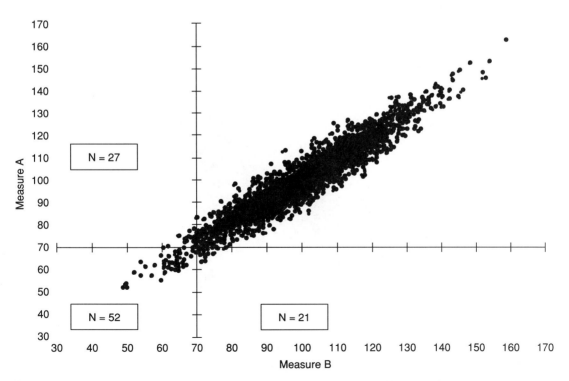

**FIGURE 21.1** **Bivariate plot of agreement for classifications of low performance across two simulated measures with a correlation of $r = .95$ (mean = 100; SD = 15; cut score <70; $N = 3,000$).**

only about 70 percent [52/(52 + 21) = .71]. Similarly, for those cases below the designated cutoff on measure B, the conditional probability of agreement on measure A was .66 [52/(52 + 27)]. Therefore, if measure A had been used instead of measure B to identify "low" performers (or vice versa), a different decision about classification status would have been reached for approximately 3 out of every 10 cases that scored 2 standard deviations below the mean on the other measure.

Unfortunately, the correlations among different tests that are supposed to measure the same construct are generally not in the .95 range. Estimates of internal consistency describe the dependability of scores within a limited domain: *the domain defined by the test developer.* Because these reliability estimates reflect the idiosyncratic emphases of the test developer in content sampling, they *overestimate* the dependability of scores within the larger domain of interest (e.g., reading or intelligence). In essence, because of differences in item content, administration format, and so on, different tests that are supposed to measure the same construct often don't (or do so to a limited degree). For example, although

the estimates of internal consistency for the Stanford-Binet and Wechsler Scales are both above .90, the correlation across these scales is only about .80. Ordinarily, these types of across-scale correlations have been viewed as evidence of validity rather than reliability. However, in diagnosing a child as mentally retarded, for example, the diagnostician's task is to decide whether the child's current level of general intellectual functioning is significantly below average. The particular test used to support that inference is largely irrelevant (when selected from a range of plausible measures); therefore, any difference in performance observed across tests may be legitimately viewed as a source of error or inconsistency in decision making.

The scatterplot in Figure 21.2 shows the reliability of classification decisions when the correlation across measures is in the .80 range. In this example, 80 out of 3,000 cases have been identified as 2 standard deviations below the mean on measure A (i.e., 34 + 46). Of these 80 cases, however, only 34 have scored below the cutoff of 2 standard deviations on measure B. Thus, with a correlation of .80, the reliability of inferring that a particular case is 2 standard devi-

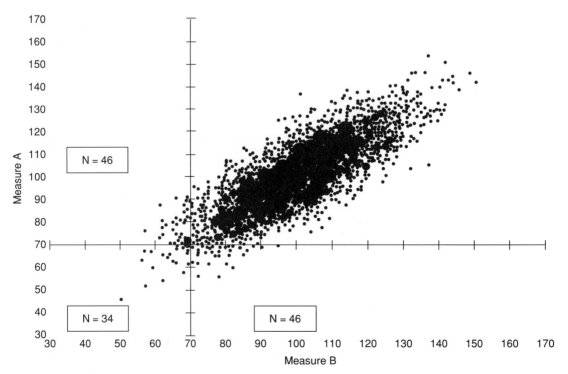

FIGURE 21.2 Bivariate plot of agreement for classifications of low performance across two simulated measures with a correlation of $r = .80$ (mean = 100; SD = 15; cut score <70; N = 3,000).

ations below the mean is only about 42.5 percent [i.e., 34/(34 + 46)]; that is, over half the cases identified as low performers on measure A have not been identified as such on measure B (and vice versa).

## Factors that Affect the Reliability of Decisions

As indicated by Figures 21.1 and 21.2 the reliability of decisions varies according to the reliability of test scores: the stronger the correlation across measures, the higher the reliability of decisions. Another factor that affects the reliability of decisions is the selection rate (the percentage of the population identified by a diagnostic procedure). As a rule, because extreme scores contain more error in an absolute sense than scores closer to the mean (Nunnally, 1978), using a more extreme cut-off score (i.e., resulting in fewer cases classified) will result in less reliable decisions. The effect of these two variables—selection rate and the correlation across measures—has been examined by Sicoly (1992). Figure 21.3 summarizes a selected subset of the data reported in Sicoly's (personal communication, July 10, 1992) expanded tables.

At least three important points can be discerned from the figure. First, it shows that the reliability of decisions varies as a function of the selection rate. The selection rate of .50 represents a median split, corresponding to an IQ cutoff of about 100 (identifying approximately 50 percent of the population). The selection rate of .05 identifies about 5% of the population (roughly equivalent to an IQ cutoff of about 75). As indicated by the graph, the .50 selection rate results in more reliable decisions than the .05 cutoff. Although selection rates <.05 are more typically used in professional practice, the .50 selection rate provides the optimal cut point for maximizing the reliability of decisions (e.g., Subcoviak, 1984).

Second, the graph shows that the relationship between decision reliability and the correlation across measures is not linear. As the correlation across measures (e.g., alternate forms, times, and scorers) drops below $r = 1.00$, the resulting decrease in the reliability of decisions is sharp and dramatic. This means that decision reliability estimates >.90 can be achieved only at the extreme upper limits of conventional reliability—at

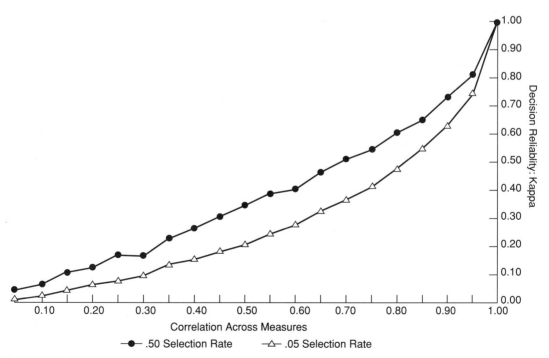

**FIGURE 21.3**   **Decision reliability as a function of selection rate and the correlation across measures.**
*Source:* Adapted from Sicoly (1992).

about $r = .97$ or higher. Although that finding is consistent with Kelley's (1927) recommended criterion of .98, given that different tests intended to measure the same construct are unlikely to do so to such a marked degree, the data are discouraging; that is, reliability estimates of that magnitude cannot realistically be achieved for the diagnostic constructs of interest.

Third, and relatedly, the data suggest that contemporary standards for evaluating the reliability of measures should be viewed with caution. In the case of screening decisions, for example, reliability estimates of about .70–.80 have been recommended in the literature. As shown by the graph, however, the error rates associated with these levels of across-scale correlation are substantial. For the .05 selection rate (again, corresponding to an IQ cutoff of about 75), a conventional reliability estimate of .70 translates into a decision reliability estimate of about .36. This means that about 64% of the children identified by the criterion would be inconsistently classified across measures. Even with a conventional reliability coefficient of .80, the error rates exceed 50%. In sum, although widely disseminated standards for technical adequacy suggest that correlations in the .70–.80 range represent satisfactory levels of scale reliability, with decision reliability estimates well below .90, the resulting error rates do not inspire confidence for professional decision making.

## Diagnostic Accuracy

In contrast to analyses of decision reliability, investigations of diagnostic accuracy assume that the true diagnostic status is known. In a typical study, the diagnoses derived through an experimental procedure are compared with the diagnostic classifications for "known" criterion groups (i.e., those for which the characteristics of interest have already been established as being either present or absent). By cross-classifying the known criterion status with the outcomes of the experimental procedure, the accuracy of decisions may be summarized in a fourfold table (as shown in Figure 21.4). The cells for true positives (TP) and negatives (TN) indicate agreement with criterion status; the cells for false positives (FP) and negatives (FN), diagnostic errors. Although a full discussion of the methodology exceeds the scope of this chapter (e.g., Fleiss, 1981; Swets, 1992; Wiggins, 1973), some key issues and terminology are highlighted in the following paragraphs.

| | | Experimental Procedure | |
|---|---|---|---|
| | | Present | Absent |
| Criterion Status | Present | True positive | False negative |
| | Absent | False positive | True negative |

**FIGURE 21.4 Classic fourfold table for the analysis of diagnostic accuracy.**

### *Measuring Diagnostic Accuracy*

Three basic measures of diagnostic accuracy are specificity, sensitivity, and efficiency. These measures estimate the conditional probability of selected diagnostic outcomes (i.e., the likelihood of A given B). *Specificity* refers to the probability that an individual whose diagnostic status is absent on the criterion will be correctly identified by the experimental procedure [TN/(TN + FP)]; *sensitivity*, to the probability that an individual whose diagnostic status is present on the criterion will be correctly identified by the experimental procedure [TP/(TP + FN)]; and *efficiency* (similar to sensitivity), to the probability that an individual who has been identified as present by the experimental procedure actually has the diagnostic characteristic of interest [TP/(TP + FP)]. The resulting estimates are affected by the base rate and selection rate for the diagnostic procedure. The *base rate* for a diagnostic characteristic is established by the proportion of persons in the sample population identified by the criterion; the *selection rate*, by the proportion of persons identified through the experimental procedure. Whereas base rates presumably are fixed, selection rates can be manipulated to increase the likelihood of specific diagnostic outcomes (e.g., Cronbach & Gleser, 1965; Fleiss, 1981; Swets, 1992).

Most methodologists agree that no single statistical index can adequately summarize the complete 2-by-2 table under all practical circumstances (e.g., Fleiss, 1981). The overall *hit rate* for a diagnostic procedure refers to the sum of true positive and true negative classifications divided by the total number of cases in the sample [(TP + TN)/(TP + TN + FP + FN)]. Analyses of hit rates are generally viewed as problematic, however, because they fail to account for chance agreement. To illustrate, consider a situation in which the base rate and selection rate are each .50. If a diagnostician assigned cases *randomly* to each of the two diagnostic outcomes for the experimental procedure (i.e., present or absent), there is a 50% chance of correct classification. Although an overall hit rate of .50 would not be obtained for all possible random splits of the sample, that is the expected outcome on average across repeated random splits. As discussed by Meehl and Rosen (1955), different base rates produce similar problems. For example, if 95% of the population is schizophrenic, diagnosing every case as schizophrenic (regardless of assessment data) will produce a hit rate of .95. Alternatively, if the base rate is .05, diagnosing every case as *not* schizophrenic will produce the same outcome (hit rate = .95). These examples demonstrate that for many practical situations, it may be difficult to improve the accuracy of diagnostic decisions afforded by base-rate information alone. Clearly, very little can be said about the accuracy of diagnostic decisions independent of the base rate, selection rate, and associated expectations for chance agreement.

In appreciation of these difficulties, Cohen (1960) devised an overall index of diagnostic agreement, called *coefficient kappa*, that includes a correction for chance agreement:

$$\frac{(TP \times TN) - (FP \times FN)}{\sqrt{(TP + FP) \times (TP + FN) \times (FN + TN) \times (FP + TN)}}$$

Although not obvious from the formula, the proportion of agreement expected by chance is defined by the sum of the cross-products for the marginal distributions in the 2-by-2 table (i.e., row and column totals). For example, if both the selection rate and base rate are equal to .50, the proportion of agreement expected by chance equals .50 [(.50 × .50) + (.50 × .50)]. Although the appropriateness of that statistical adjustment has been questioned by some (e.g., Brennan & Prediger, 1981), if the base rate and selection rate are approximately equal, the use of kappa is relatively straightforward because the definition of chance is the same as that used by Pearson for the analysis of simple correlations (e.g., phi). In addition to kappa, the overall probability of agreement can be estimated for specific diagnostic categories (e.g., present or absent) through Dice's (1945) index of specific agreement. Dice's index provides an approximate average of sensitivity and efficiency (uncorrected for chance).

Analyses of diagnostic accuracy also need to consider the purposes and consequences of the selection procedure. For example, in situations in which it is better to be safe than sorry (e.g., early detection of breast cancers), a relatively high percentage of false positive errors may be tolerable (if the number of false negative errors can be either reduced or eliminated). Therefore, although diagnostic errors are generally undesirable, the risks associated with false positive and negative errors may be unequal in some decision-making contexts. To accommodate these circumstances, statistical analyses of diagnostic accuracy may be differentially weighted to reflect the costs and benefits of alternative decision outcomes (e.g., Cronbach & Gleser, 1965; Fleiss, 1981; Swets, 1992).

## The Criterion Problem

Although the statistical issues can be formidable, the most fundamental methodological problem in the analysis of diagnostic accuracy is that known criterion groups may be difficult to establish (e.g., Wiggins, 1973). For some areas of inquiry (e.g., medicine), analyses of diagnostic accuracy can be effectively grounded to relatively unambiguous physical conditions (e.g., cancers) and functional outcomes (e.g., mortality rates). However, that is rarely the case in psychology and education, in which the vast majority of diagnostic constructs are plagued by definitional ambiguities (e.g., mental retardation, learning disabilities, and emotional and behavioral disorders). Given the indefinite nature of the constructs measured, "true" criterion status is known only to God (and even She or He may have questions). When diagnostic status is uncertain, investigations of diagnostic accuracy may be more appropriately viewed as analyses of decision reliability (i.e., examining the consistency of decision outcomes across alternative experimental procedures).

## Implications of Measurement Error for Diagnostic Accuracy

Many sources have observed that measurement error attenuates the strength of the relationship among measures (e.g., Nunnally, 1978). To illustrate the implications of that principle for the accuracy of diagnostic decisions, we developed a simulation to model the accuracy of aptitude-achievement discrepancy scores for the identification of children with learning disabilities (e.g., Reynolds, 1984–1985). To begin, standardized test scores were simulated for two measures of IQ and two measures of achievement (mean = 100; SD = 15) across a computer-generated sample of 3,000 cases. Within each domain (IQ and achievement), the across-scale correlation was set at $r = .80$ (providing estimates of the consistency of scores within each domain). The intercorrelations across the two domains were set at $r = .60$. Regression-prediction discrepancy scores were calculated for each of the two sets of IQ-achievement measures. The correlations among these measures are summarized in Table 21.1.

The representation of "true" criterion status in the simulation was necessarily speculative because relatively little is known about the relationship between IQ-achievement discrepancy scores and the construct of learning disabilities. Some sources have claimed that these discrepancies operationalize the central defining characteristic of a learning disability (i.e., severe underachievement) very well (e.g., Reynolds, 1984–1985), whereas others have argued that the correspondence is negligible (e.g., Fletcher, 1992; Siegel, 1989; Stanovich, 1991). Although the theoretical plausibility of the simulation model remains an open question, simply for the sake of demonstration we used the observed relationships in Table 21.1 to construct a hypothetical representation of "true" criterion status. Specifically, we observed that, consistent with the assumption that learning disabilities can occur at all levels of the IQ distribution (Reynolds, 1984–1985), regression-prediction discrepancy scores (labeled DS 1 and DS 2 in the table) were uncorrelated *with the measure of IQ from which they were derived*. For both discrepancy measures, however, there were small but significant correlations ($r = .15–.16$) with the independent estimate of IQ in the table

(e.g., DS 1 with IQ 2). The discrepancy measures showed a similar pattern of correlations with achievement. They were strongly correlated *with the measure of achievement from which they were derived* ($r = .80–.81$) but only moderately correlated with the independent measure of achievement in the table (i.e., $r = .56$). Based on these observed relationships and the somewhat dubious assumption that the construct of underachievement may exist independently of the particular set of IQ and achievement measures used to define the construct (i.e., uncontaminated by a specific set of measurement procedures), true criterion status was defined by the following pattern of relationships with IQ and achievement: the correlation between true criterion status and IQ was set at $r = .15$; the correlation between true criterion status and achievement, at $r = .56$.

Beyond the mechanics of the simulation, however, the most remarkable finding in Table 21.1 is the correlation between the two regression-prediction discrepancy scores ($r = .58$). Thus, despite fairly strong within-domain correlations for both IQ ($r = .79$) and achievement ($r = .80$), there was only a moderate correlation between the discrepancy scores derived from these two sets of IQ-achievement measures (failing to satisfy even the most lenient standards for the dependability of screening measures). The observed correlation was a predictable function of the reliability of regression prediction discrepancy scores (Thorndike, 1963), where $r_{ACH}$ = the reliability of the achievement measure, $r_{IQ}$ = the reliability of the IQ measure, and $r_{IQ \cdot ACH}$ = the intercorrelation between IQ and achievement:

$$r_{dd} = \frac{r_{ACH} + r_{IQ \cdot ACH}^2 \, r_{IQ} - 2r_{IQ \cdot ACH}^2}{1 - r_{IQ \cdot ACH}^2}$$

**TABLE 21.1  Observed Correlations Among Simulated Measures of IQ, Achievement, and "True" Criterion Status Before the Dichotomization of Scores ($N = 3,000$)**

| Measure | IQ 1 | ACH 1 | IQ 2 | ACH 2 | DS 1 | DS 2 |
|---------|------|-------|------|-------|------|------|
| IQ 1 | 1.00 | | | | | |
| ACH 1 | 0.59 | 1.00 | | | | |
| IQ 2 | 0.79 | 0.58 | 1.00 | | | |
| ACH 2 | 0.60 | 0.80 | 0.59 | 1.00 | | |
| DS 1 | 0.00 | 0.81 | 0.15 | 0.56 | 1.00 | |
| DS 2 | 0.16 | 0.56 | 0.00 | 0.80 | 0.58 | 1.00 |
| Criterion | 0.14 | 0.54 | 0.15 | 0.56 | 0.57 | 0.59 |

IQ = intelligence quotient; ACH = achievement; DS = regression-prediction discrepancy score.

Based on the data reported in Table 21.1 (with $r_{ACH}$ and $r_{IQ} \approx .80$; $r_{IQ \cdot ACH} \approx .60$), a reliability estimate of about .575 was expected. Although the reliability of aptitude-achievement discrepancy scores is a notorious measurement problem, most of the studies that have investigated the issue (e.g., Schulte & Borich, 1984) have been based on *internal consistency* reliability coefficients (that overestimate the generalizability of scores within a construct domain). With few exceptions (e.g., Macmann & Barnett, 1985), the implications of domain sampling have been neglected.

In analyzing the simulation results reported in Table 21.2, the base rate and selection rates need to be considered. On the criterion measure, because definitive estimates of the prevalence of learning disabilities are lacking, the base rate for LD status was arbitrarily set at 5% of the population. Corresponding to that estimate, a $z$-score cutoff of $-1.64$ was used to define a symmetrical selection rate for the discrepancy measures. A *symmetrical selection rate* tends to produce an equivalent proportion of false positive and false negative errors (e.g., Cronbach & Gleser, 1965; Swets, 1992). In comparison, adopting a more *lenient selection rate* would reduce the number of false negative errors (with the specific cutoff score determined by the magnitude of the test-criterion correlation and the number of false negative errors thought to be tolerable), while simultaneously producing an unavoidable increase in false positive errors (because more LD cases would be selected than true LD cases in the population). Similarly, if a more *stringent selection rate* were adopted (compared with the base rate), a decrease in false positive errors for the identification of LD cases would be achieved at the expense of false negative errors.

Although an educational system in which students' instructional needs were identified and met regardless of disability labels would provide the ideal safeguard for both false negative and false positive errors (i.e., no adverse risks associated with either decision outcome), without that system in place we think that the consequences of diagnostic errors should be regarded as equally undesirable. False negative errors suggest that potentially valuable instructional services may be denied; false positive errors, that potentially valuable services may be needlessly diverted. Therefore, a symmetrical decision rule was adopted for the simulation.

Of course, the use of a symmetrical selection rule equalizes but does not eliminate decision errors. As shown by the column subtotals in Table 21.2, the comparison of measure 1 with true criterion status produced a standard fourfold table for the evaluation of diagnostic accuracy. The overall hit rate of .93 [(46 + 2744)/3000] for the diagnostic procedure was slightly below the .95 hit rate that could have been achieved by diagnosing every case as not LD (Meehl & Rosen, 1955). Therefore, although the diagnostic procedure did a very good job of capitalizing on chance in the identification of cases as not LD (specificity = .96), sensitivity and efficiency were fairly low. Of the 149 cases identified as LD by the criterion, only 46 were identified as LD by measure 1 (sensitivity = .31). Similarly, for the 153 cases identified as LD by measure 1, only 46 were identified as LD by the criterion (efficiency = .30).

**TABLE 21.2    Moderating Effect of Measurement Error on the Accuracy of Diagnostic Decisions: Hypothetical Cross-classification of Two Measures of Aptitude-Achievement Discrepancy with True Criterion Status for Children with Learning Disabilities**

| Criterion Status | Measure 2 | Measure 1 | | Row Totals |
|---|---|---|---|---|
| | | **LD** | **Not LD** | |
| LD | LD | 25 | 25 | 50 |
| | NLD | 21 | 78 | 99 |
| | LD Subtotals: | TP = 46 | FN = 103 | 149 |
| Not LD | LD | 24 | 80 | 104 |
| | Not LD | 83 | 2664 | 2747 |
| | Not LD Subtotals: | FP = 107 | TN = 2744 | 2851 |
| | Column Totals: | 153 | 2847 | 30009 |

LD = learning disabled; TP = true positive; FN = false negative; FP = false positive; TN = true negative.

Correcting for chance, the estimate for kappa was .27. Moreover, there were 107 false positive errors (identified as LD by measure 1 but not LD by the criterion) and 103 false negative errors (identified as not LD by measure 1 but LD by the criterion). Consequently, based on the observed ratio of incorrect-to-correct classifications for the identification of children as LD [(107 + 103)/46], the use of discrepancy measure 1 resulted in approximately 4.6 incorrect classifications of LD status for every correct classification. As bleak as those findings may be, the comparison of measure 1 with true criterion status describes only part of the story. As shown by the comparisons with measure 2 (i.e., producing a 2-by-2-by-2 table), of the 46 true positives identified by measure 1, only 25 cases were identified as LD by measure 2. Therefore, across each of the two discrepancy measures, the overall sensitivity of the selection procedure for the identification of true LD cases was only .17 (25/149).

In sum, the simulation results reported in Table 21.2 illustrate the moderating influence of measurement error on the accuracy of diagnostic decisions. Although the findings are hypothetical, reflecting a highly idealized set of assumptions about the nature of the relationship between regression-prediction discrepancies and the construct of learning disabilities, they demonstrate that the correspondence between discrepancy scores and true criterion status is far from satisfactory. Moreover, only one source of variability in construct measurement was represented by the simulation. In addition to content sampling (e.g., different scales intended to measure the same construct), observed scores may vary along many other dimensions (e.g., time or examiners). *The errors are additive;* as each additional source of variability is considered, the number of true positive classifications moves inexorably toward zero.

## Sources of Ambiguity in Construct Measurement: Representative Studies

The technical difficulties associated with the diagnosis of educational disabilities are not confined to simulated data sets. The problems previously outlined have been repeatedly demonstrated in studies involving a wide range of real children and measures (e.g., Barnett & Macmann, 1992b; Barnett, Macmann, & Carey, 1992). The simulation studies have complimented that research by (1) illustrating the basic measurement processes at work, (2) supporting logical generalizations from otherwise sample- or instrument-specific findings, and (3) exploring measurement problems that are too costly or unfeasible to investigate through conventional research methods. The primary drawback is that because of simplifying assumptions reflected in the methodology, the interpretive difficulties tend to be minimized (e.g., Bracken, 1988). In this section, we describe some of the practical contexts in which decision reliability problems have been observed (i.e., across content, time, informants and settings, and examiners).

### Ambiguities Across Content

Across alternative measures of academic achievement, Macmann, Barnett, Lombard, Belton-Kocher, and Sharpe (1989) have examined the reliability of aptitude-achievement discrepancy scores for the identification of severe IQ-achievement discrepancies in a convenience sample of 373 children referred for learning difficulties. Discrepancies were analyzed for the Wechsler Intelligence Scale for Children-Revised (WISC-R; Wechsler, 1974) and selected subtests of the Woodcock-Johnson Psychoeducational Battery (Woodcock, 1978), Wide Range Achievement Test (Jastak & Wilkinson, 1984), and Woodcock Reading Mastery Test (Woodcock, 1973). Chance-corrected estimates of agreement for classifications of severe discrepancy ranged from .19 to .47. Clarizio and Bennett (1987) reported similar findings for a random sample of children referred for psychoeducational evaluation. In that study, the achievement measure (Peabody Individual Achievement Test) was held constant (Dunn & Markwardt, 1970) but IQ scores (WISC-R and Kaufman Assessment Battery for Children) were varied (Kaufman & Kaufman, 1983). Agreement rates for classifications of severe underachievement across measures never exceeded 50% and were less than 25% for half the comparisons. Based on computer simulations across a realistic range of IQ-achievement intercorrelations and severe discrepancy cutoff scores, when both the aptitude and achievement measure are varied the predicted level of chance-corrected agreement is less than 30% (Macmann & Barnett, 1985).

### Ambiguities Across Time

Investigations of the stability of scores over time typically focus on relatively brief retest intervals (usually one or two weeks). By limiting the duration of the retest interval, the effects of true change on test performance (e.g., due to maturation, learning, and practice) are reduced. This produces a more accurate estimate of the robustness of scores to random sources of variation (e.g., fatigue). For diagnostic constructs presumed to be relatively stable or enduring over time, however, true change in performance represents a construct-irrelevant source of variation in diagnostic outcomes. Scores that change over time, for whatever reason, indicate that diagnoses are unstable. Therefore, from a decision-focused perspective, an argument can be made that the duration of the retest interval should be dictated by the "period governed by the decision" (Cronbach & Snow, 1977, p. 161). For example, if test scores will be used to support an educational classification decision that will affect a student's life for three years, the scores used to justify that decision should be sufficiently stable across that three-year span to defend the decision.

As an example of relatively long-term variation in decision outcomes, Shaywitz, Escobar, Shaywitz, Fletcher, and Makuch (1992) conducted a longitudinal analysis of the stability of aptitude-achievement discrepancy scores for a random sample of school-aged children in Connecticut ($N = 414$). The test-retest correlation across grades 1 and 3 was $r = .53$; across grades 3 and 5, $r = .67$. Using a -1.5 standard deviation cutoff for the identification of severe underachievement, only 7 (28%) of the 25 children identified in grade 1 were identified in grade 3. Moreover, only 14 (47%) of the 30 children identified in grade 3 were identified in grade 5.

However, a shorter retest interval does not necessarily eliminate the decision reliability problems. For example, based on the test-retest sample ($N = 303$) for the WISC-R, McDermott, Fantuzzo, Glutting, Watkins, and Baggaley (1992) examined the reliability of interpretations for ipsative strengths and weaknesses on individual subtests. Across a one-month retest interval, the average probability of consistent classification ranged from 42.6% (for strengths) to 34.5% (for weaknesses). Across a three-year retest interval (for a school-identified sample of 159 students with educational disabilities), the average probability of consistent classification ranged from 19.4% (for strengths) to 21.7% (for weaknesses).

Moreover, as shown by Boyd's (1989) analysis of age gradients on the Battelle Developmental Inventory (Newborg, Stock, Wnek, Guidubaldi,

& Svinicki, 1984), even a single day can make a significant difference in decision outcomes on some diagnostic measures. For example, because of a one-day difference in chronological age, standard scores on the communication domain of the Battelle changed from 95 to 120.

## Ambiguities Across Informants and Settings

The errors are not limited to standardized tests but also include behavior ratings and the complicated methods used to combine information across multiple sources (e.g., parents and teachers). Investigations of the reliability of multi-source assessment strategies have been facilitated by multitrait-multimethod (MTMM) analyses (Campbell & Fiske, 1959). Although MTMM analysis was originally developed to investigate convergent and discriminate validity across alternative methods, the logic can be generalized to the analysis of assessment information from multiple sources (Messick, 1989). The degree of convergence across alternative methods and sources of information yields an upper bound of interpretive confidence for the particular construct being assessed (Cronbach et al., 1972; Macmann et al., 1989; Poth & Barnett, 1988). As previously demonstrated (see Figure 21.3), even high degrees of convergence (i.e., correlations in the .8–.9 range) can yield markedly discrepant individual decisions.

Multisource-multifactored assessment strategies produce a profile of scores, and a common professional task is to identify developmental strengths and weaknesses in that profile. Using the multitrait-multisource framework, the following problems have been noted in a series of investigations with common preschool scales (Barnett, Faust, & Sarmir, 1988; Hall & Barnett, 1991; Macmann & Barnett, 1984; Poth & Barnett, 1988). First, the convergent validity coefficients, even when statistically significant, fell within the low to moderate range, suggesting a high probability of error for the classification of individual children. Second, the correlations among scales that purportedly measured different constructs often fell within the low to moderate range as well, making it difficult to establish discriminant validity. Third, the subscales within an instrument (and dependent on a specific source) were often moderately to highly correlated. Thus, the instruments typically functioned as source-specific measures of global developmental attainment rather than a profile of discrete skills.

When scales designed for similar purposes (and credible raters) have been compared, decision reliability analyses have revealed a ratio of about three to five cases of disagreement for every one case of agreement on diagnostic status. For example, Ronka and Barnett (1986) investigated the reliability of decisions associated with adaptive behavior scales and found levels of chance-corrected agreement (coefficient kappa) ranging from .00 to .51 across instruments and raters. Also, a reanalysis of one of the major tools (Child Behavior Checklist) for the evaluation of empirically based syndromes across informants and settings (Achenbach, 1991) has suggested that the discriminant validity of both the broad- and narrow-band scales may be severely limited, contributing to high error rates and low utility of resulting professional decisions (Macmann, Barnett, & Lopez, 1993).

## Ambiguities Across Examiners

The standardization of test administration and scoring procedures is intended to make examiners interchangeable. In reality, although examiner variance has typically been represented as a relatively minor source of error for well-developed tests, complete standardization may be difficult to achieve. As shown by Slate and colleagues (e.g., Slate & Chick, 1989; Slate & Hunnicutt, 1988; Slate, Jones, Coulter, & Covert, 1992), the estimates of interscorer reliability reported in test manuals (based on highly trained examiners and/or preselected cases) may underestimate the effects of scoring errors (e.g., the propensity to "drift" from scoring principles in practice settings). When scoring the *same* Wechsler protocol, differences of as much as 54 IQ points have been documented across examiners (Massey, 1964; Miller & Chansky, 1972).

Even more troubling, however, is the evidence that standardized test scores may vary significantly as a function of familiarity with the examiner—a source of systematic (rather than random) error. Based on a meta-analysis of 22 studies, Fuchs and Fuchs (1986) found that the average effect of familiarity with the examiner was a .28 standard deviation difference in test scores (4.2 points for tests with SD of 15); on IQ tests, the average effect was .43 standard deviations (6.4 points for tests with SD of 15); on IQ tests administered to low SES (socionomic status) children, .51 standard deviations (7.6 points for tests with SD of 15). Thus, as observed by Bronfenbrenner (1979), the effect of answering

strange questions asked by strangers in strange situations may be considerable—suggesting that the sense of rapport experienced by unfamiliar adult examiners is not necessarily shared by the children being tested.

Although assessment information may be fallible, some people may nonetheless believe that well-trained professionals have the ability to know a person with disabilities when they see one. We (Macmann & Barnett, 1993) examined that assumption at a private residential facility where psychiatric and psychological evaluations of the severity of mental retardation were completed independently. Clients were diagnosed as either borderline, mild, moderate, severe, or profound by both a psychiatrist and a psychologist. To evaluate the reliability of the diagnoses, case records were reviewed for 126 persons residing in the facility. Across levels of severity, the proportion of specific agreement ranged from 61% (for borderline and severe levels of functioning) to 50% (for moderate and profound levels of functioning). Corrected for chance, however, the overall proportion of agreement was less than 50% (kappa = .47). In sum, the results suggest that professional diagnoses of the severity of mental retardation may not be as reliable as generally assumed.

## Combined Effect of Measurement Errors

As professionals, we would like to draw inferences that are robust across all sources of construct-irrelevant variation in scores (e.g., content, time, informants and settings, and examiners). Although each source of error reviewed can produce sufficient variability in decision outcomes to raise serious reservations about the likelihood of achieving that goal, in reality the errors act in concert rather than in isolation (Nunnally, 1978). Therefore, the focus on individual sources of error tends to underestimate the decision reliability problems.

For practical purposes, a complete analysis of the combined or additive effect of measurement errors would require an experimental design of nightmarish complexity (e.g., Cronbach et al., 1972); however, the basic concept can be fairly easily grasped in a two-facet design. For example, by administering alternate forms of a test in counterbalanced fashion across a specified retest interval, scores on form A at time 1 can be compared with scores on form B at time 2 to provide an estimate of the combined effect of content and time sampling. Because the two sources of error are independent, the resulting combined effect reliability estimate will be lower than the correlations across either alternate forms or the retest interval (for both form A over time and form B over time).

Although the combined effect of measurement errors has rarely been analyzed for individually administered scales because of cost (e.g., construction of alternate forms) and other practical considerations, the implications for diagnostic error nonetheless remain. To estimate the extent of the problem, a theoretical approximation of the combined effect of measurement errors can be obtained through variance-components analysis (Leonard Feldt, personal communication, September 26, 1991), in which the reliability coefficients for independent sources of variability in scores (e.g., content, time, examiners) are represented by $r_{yy}$ (subscript 1 through $N$):

$$\frac{1}{1 + \left(\frac{1 - r_{yy_1}}{r_{yy_1}}\right) + \left(\frac{1 - r_{yy_2}}{r_{yy_2}}\right) + \cdots \left(\frac{1 - r_{yy_N}}{r_{yy_N}}\right)}$$

For example, the Information subtest of the Wechsler Intelligence Scale for Children–Third Edition (Wechsler, 1991) has an average internal consistency reliability of .84 (indicating the expected correlation across alternate forms) and an average test-retest reliability of .85. Substituting these values into the equation, we see that the predicted correlation across alternate forms ad-

ministered over a three-week retest interval (the average interval for the WISC-III test-retest data) is $r = .73$.

In a recent study, we (Macmann & Barnett, 1997) used the internal consistency and test-retest reliability data reported in the WISC-III manual to develop a computer simulation of the dependability of scores across three sources of variability: content sampling, time sampling, and the combined or additive effect of content and time sampling. Our previous research had suggested that because of the strength of the general factor on the Wechsler Scales, profiles of discrete skills would be difficult to identify with confidence (Macmann & Barnett, 1992, 1994). The simulation provided a means to evaluate that hypothesis and extend McDermott et al.'s (1992) test-retest analyses of the WISC-R to the WISC-III (including statistical control for practice effects and an analysis of the combined effect of measurement errors).

Following the guidelines for profile analysis described by Kaufman (1994), we analyzed the reliability of interpretations for a total of 54 unique combinations of WISC-III subtests. For each profile, conditional probabilities of specific agreement were aggregated across strengths and weaknesses and two independent samples of $N = 5,000$ cases (within each of the three sources of variability). The distribution of reliability estimates for these 54 profile patterns (based on exact calculations of significant subtest deviations) is shown in Figure 21.5 (for each of the three

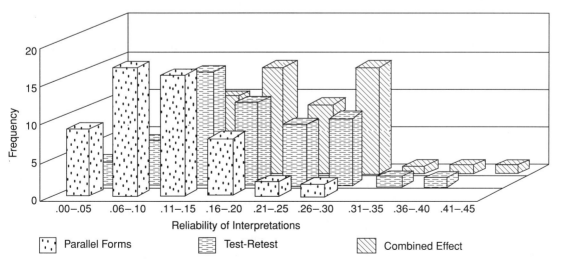

**FIGURE 21.5** **Distribution of decision reliability estimates for 54 ipsative profile patterns on the WISC-III by three types of measurement error.**
*Source:* From Macmann and Barnett (1997).

sources of variability in scores). As indicated by the graph, for the combined effect of measurement errors, the reliability of interpretations for strengths and weaknesses was greater than .20 for only 4 of the 54 profiles; not one profile could be interpreted with a probability of consistent classification greater than .30. Across parallel or alternate forms, the average conditional probability of agreement for the interpretation of relative strengths and weaknesses was .20 (SD = .08); across a three-week retest interval, .18 (SD = .08). However, for the combined effect of measurement errors, the average probability of reliable interpretation was only .11 (SD = .06). The findings suggest that if a parallel form of the WISC-III was administered about three weeks later, only about 1 out of every 10 hypotheses about relative strengths and weaknesses is likely to be confirmed. As hypothetical as these data may be, the findings raise serious concerns about the reliability of interpretations for WISC-III subtest scores and profiles. Statistically significant (i.e., 11-point) Verbal-Performance IQ differences fared marginally better, with a combined effect reliability estimate (kappa) of .32.

Curiously enough, in comparison to McDermott et al.'s (1992) findings for individual WISC-R subtests, the simulation data showed that profiles (involving two or more subtests) were more difficult to interpret than individual subtest scores. Post hoc analysis of our findings revealed that the number of subtests in a profile was negatively correlated with the reliability of interpretations ($r = -.50$). That inverse aggregation effect was primarily due to two factors. First, the ipsatization of subtest scores through comparison with each subject's own mean removed a substantial portion of the shared variance among subtests (McDermott et al., 1992), essentially neutralizing the positive gains in reliability ordinarily associated with aggregation. Second, the way in which subtest scores were combined decreased the selection rate for strength-weakness interpretations (e.g., fewer cases had a weakness on both the Arithmetic and Digit Span subtests than on either of these subtests alone, thus reducing the reliability of interpretations (as shown in Figure 21.3). Overall, the simulation results substantiate McDermott et al.'s WISC-R research, controlling for practice effects and providing further evidence that profiles are not sufficiently reliable to provide a strong foundation for professional decisions.

## Implications for Multisource-Multifactored Assessment

Multisource-multifactored assessments have been described as the sine qua non of full and fair evaluation for children suspected of having educational disabilities, and standardized norm-referenced tests and behavior rating scales have been represented as the primary means through which such unassailable results can be achieved. However, based on the research evidence, what are the likely contributions of multisource-multifactored assessment strategies to the quality of professional decisions? We think the conclusions are necessarily pessimistic. The inconsistencies in decision outcomes are not resolved by adding measures or sources. Indeed, the most likely outcome of comparing assessment information across construct-irrelevant sources of variability (i.e., alternative instruments, informants and settings, examiners, and time) is *indefinite triangulation*—a hopelessly confusing array of findings across multiple measures (Peterson, 1987). In short, if we assume that convergence is necessary to establish confidence for diagnostic decisions, expanding the scope of a diagnostic battery (the foundation of multisource-multifactored assessment) is more likely to create ambiguity than increased clarity. That minuscule proportion of the population consistently identified as needy by such well-intended strategies can be winnowed away by further extending the scope of the analysis (to other measures, informants and settings, etc.) in an infinite regress toward a de facto selection rate of zero (see Table 21.2). Thus, the more rigorous the assessment battery, the more likely that the diagnostic process will inevitably miss the mark and, ultimately, the purpose of assessment.

## CONCEPTUAL SOURCES OF ERROR: WHAT CAN BE SAID THAT MIGHT BE HELPFUL?

Although little can be said with confidence for many diagnostic decisions because of the effects of measurement error, the concept of *assessment error* is much broader (Barnett & Zucker, 1990). Assessments are based on explicit and implicit theories about the nature of human behavior and services delivery. Consequently, assessment plans are vulnerable to many sources of conceptual error, including errors in the understanding or representation of problem situations, inadequate theories about the processes and possibilities for change, and weak professional roles that limit efforts to change problem situations. The conceptual errors represent an additional source of variability in decision outcomes across clinicians; however, the primary threat created by these errors relates to the validity or helpfulness of professional decisions, reducing the likelihood that decisions will result in beneficial client outcomes.

## Decision Validity

Decision validity refers to the appropriateness of using assessment information for a specific decision-making purpose (Messick, 1989, 1995). Analyses of decision validity require consideration of both the *meaning* of the information used to make decisions (based on the degree of theoretical and empirical support for the constructs measured) and the *consequences* of using it (based on the social and educational outcomes of the decision-making process). Although superficially dualistic, Messick's framework is integrative, suggesting that the meaning of assessment information cannot be fully understood independent of the social context in which that information is used. In essence, analyses of decision validity focus on what is measured and where that leads. Decisions that do not contribute to beneficial social and educational outcomes have little value.

The focus on consequences suggests that questions of fairness, acceptability, and usefulness are critical to the evaluation of validity. Other important aspects of validity encompassed by Messick's (1989, 1995) framework include social (Wolf, 1978), ecological (Martens & Witt, 1988), and ethnic validity (Barnett et al., 1995). The concept of treatment utility (Hayes, Nelson, & Jarrett, 1987) addresses a critical subset of consequential validity issues, the functional contributions of assessment information to beneficial treatment outcomes. Decision reliability issues are embedded in the analysis as well. For example, unreliable decisions place limits on the effectiveness of treatment plans (e.g., Kavale, 1990) and are likely to be viewed as capricious or unacceptable by the larger social community.

## Helping is the Goal

Reframing the concept of consequential validity in terms of desirable professional goals, Peterson (1987) has argued that the ultimate purpose of assessment is to help people. Peterson's argument suggests that although assessment information can be used to support many different kinds of professional decisions (e.g., screening, diagnosis, classification, and placement), their quality ultimately must be judged in relation to the goal of helping (e.g., Hawkins, 1979; Messick, 1989, 1995; Reschly, 1988). Although the concept of helping is difficult to define in specific operational terms, it effectively captures the mission of professional psychology and thus provides an organizing set of values for the appraisal of all assessment activities. In our view, "assessment is helpful to the extent that it contributes to meaningful improvements in the quality of instruction (e.g., Heller, Holtzman, & Messick, 1982), or caregiving environments more generally, as shown through the increased functional effectiveness, adaptation, or coping of children and caregivers over long time periods in significant areas of behavior and/or development" (Macmann et al., 1996, p. 139).

## Problem Solving is the Means

In professional practice, helping occurs within the context of a problem-solving process (Allen & Graden, 1995; Deno, 1995; Nezu & Nezu, 1993; Peterson, 1991). Different sources suggest different terminology, but the basic steps in problem solving are aptly summarized by the acronym IDEAL (Bransford & Stein, 1984): identifying (I) the problem, defining (D) and representing the problem, exploring (E) strategies to address the problem, acting (A) on the selected strategies, and looking (L) back to evaluate the effectiveness of the actions. The steps in problem solving represent the cognitive and interpersonal structure "through which assessment information is transformed into professional inferences, actions, and outcomes (and thus ultimately acquires its social meaning)" (Macmann et al., 1996, p. 140).

## Threats to Effective Problem Solving

Given that helping requires problem solving, threats to effective problem solving represent sources of invalidity for professional decisions. A basic premise is that assessments of traditional diagnostic constructs do not address the knowledge base for intervention design and effective problem solving (e.g., Barnett & Zucker, 1990). Although informed by intervention theory and research, our analysis of threats to validity in problem solving is necessarily tentative because relatively little is known about the actual problem solving of successful professionals in real-world situations (Schön, 1983). In principle, similar to Campbell and colleagues' analysis of validity threats in experimental design (Campbell, 1986; Cambell & Stanley 1963; Cook & Campbell, 1979), the framework could be expanded to create a more comprehensive guide. There are many threats to validity in problem solving (Macmann et al., 1996). In addition to measurement errors (which limit the reliability and accuracy of decisions), other technical sources of error in problem solving include the quality of interventions (e.g., strength, acceptability, feasibility, and integrity) and affective and interpersonal dimensions of the helping process (e.g., adequacy of communication skills). The effectiveness of problem solving also may be compromised by a wide range of systems and organizational variables (e.g., system resources and legal regulations). In the remainder of this section, we focus on conceptual sources of invalidity in problem solving.

Central to our analysis is the concept of a *decision frame*, which refers to the decision maker's "conceptions of the acts, outcomes, and contingencies associated with a particular choice" (Tversky & Kahneman, 1984, p. 25). Each step in problem solving requires many different decisions about the questions that need to be asked and the tasks that need to be completed (Allen & Graden, 1995). The decisions made in framing and selecting alternatives at each step in problem solving can lead to enormous differences in the outcomes of the process; thus, the adoption of a particular decision frame is "an ethically significant act" (Tversky & Kahneman, 1984, p. 40). Our analysis focuses on patterns of professional thought and behavior that decrease the likelihood that the goal of helping will be satisfactorily achieved.

## Myth of the Master Detective

The myth of the master detective refers to the erroneous belief that through sheer power of will or intellect, professionals can overcome the limitations of their techniques. The realities are that fallible techniques result in fallible decisions, regardless of the depth of one's clinical wisdom, intuition, or gut feelings (e.g., Dawes, 1994). Indeed, a substantial literature has shown that the exercise of clinical judgment typically decreases rather than increases the accuracy of diagnostic judgments and other types of predictions (e.g., Meehl, 1954, 1986). Although there are some exceptions to the rule (e.g., Dawes, 1994), the outcome is inevitable when diagnostic constructs are ill defined. Without clear decision rules, clinicians invariably will organize and weigh information differently, thus producing variability in decision outcomes (e.g., Macmann & Barnett, 1993). Consequently, the exercise of clinical judgment is unlikely to improve the accuracy of statistical or actuarial rules that, as previously shown, are highly vulnerable to measurement error (e.g., sampling across content, time, informants, and settings).

The diagnostic ambiguities also diminish the benefits that might otherwise be realized through training and experience (e.g., Dawes, 1994). Because true criterion status is unknown, there is no feedback mechanism through which clinicians can evaluate and subsequently improve the accuracy of their decisions over time. Although training and experience may enable clinicians to develop an increased sense of confidence in their idiosyncratic application of diagnostic decision rules, the increased confidence does not improve the accuracy of decisions; in fact, some studies have reported negative correlations between professional confidence and diagnostic accuracy (e.g., Dawes, 1994).

## Information-processing Errors

Another set of errors in problem solving arises through essentially normal aspects of human information processing, referred to as *heuristic biases* (Arkes & Hammond, 1986; Hogarth, 1987; Nisbett & Ross, 1980). Although heuristic biases ordinarily function as adaptive shortcuts, helping to organize otherwise chaotic and overwhelming amounts of information (e.g., reducing demands on short-term memory), in professional practice they lead to predictable errors in decision making (Arkes, 1981; Dawes, 1994; Faust, 1986). As briefly summarized in the paragraphs that follow, Tversky and Kahneman (1984) have identified three heuristic strategies that increase the likelihood of clinical decision errors: representativeness, availability, and anchoring.

The *representativeness* heuristic refers to the tendency for judgments about diagnostic status and causality to be based on estimates of similarity or resemblance. Therefore, in answering certain types of questions (e.g., does child A have disorder B? Is behavior A caused by condition B?), probabilities tend to be based on the degree to which A is perceived to be representative or typical of the decision maker's conception of B. Errors arise when important information is neglected. In the interpretation of WISC-III profile patterns, for example, *small samples* of observed behavior may be perceived as stable or representative (Kaufman, 1994; Sattler, 1992), even though analyses of decision reliability (across content, time, etc.) clearly indicate otherwise (e.g., Macmann & Barnett, 1997). In addition, *base rate* information can be easily neglected. Using Kaufman's recommended procedures for the analysis of 54 profile patterns on the WISC-III, Macmann and Barnett found that 80.7% of the population had at least one significant strength or weakness (with an average of 5.1 significant profiles per case). Given the base rate for these interpretations (which do not include significant verbal-performance differences, small factors, and individual subtest scores), there is an enormous potential for capitalization on chance through comparisons with referral concerns and other sources of assessment information. The end result is a base-rate treasure chest of presumably explanatory hypotheses that, in reality, are likely to reflect only chance fluctuations in performance (e.g., Watkins, Kush, & Glutting, 1997).

Another source of heuristic bias stems from the *availability* of information. Research has shown that information that is more easily accessible to immediate awareness (e.g., because of the recency or vividness of the ideas or events) may exert greater influence on decisions than potentially salient information that is not immediately accessible; consequently, decisions can be based on vivid ideas about "how things are supposed to be" rather than "how things are" (Arkes, 1981). As one possible example, the widespread belief that the analysis of WISC-III profile patterns is a viable means of instructional planning (e.g., Kaufman, 1994), despite repeated failures to demonstrate the utility of that practice (e.g., Cronbach & Snow, 1977; Good, Vollmer, Creek, Katz, & Chowdri, 1993; Gresham & Witt, 1997), may reflect the power of such *preconceived notions* or *illusory correlations*.

Bias also can arise when adjustments to accommodate new information are anchored by previous estimates. The *anchoring* heuristic produces a *confirmatory bias*. First, there is a tendency to search for and accept confirming rather than disconfirming evidence, increasing the likelihood of preserving the initial hypothesis. Second, increases in the quantity of data tend to increase confidence in the initial hypothesis, even though the quality of the information has not been improved. For example, with an average of 5.1 significant strengths and weaknesses per WISC-III profile (Macmann & Barnett, 1997), the initial hypothesis that a child's learning difficulties are due to some kind of intellectual deficit can be easily "confirmed" by using diagnostic information that lacks explanatory power (Watkins et al., 1997).

## Fundamental Attribution Error

The fundamental attribution error (Nisbett & Ross, 1980) refers to the fact that observers are likely to attribute the failure of others to internal factors (stable, dispositional traits), whereas actors are more inclined to attribute their own failures to external factors (e.g., environmental influences). For example, teachers are more likely to attribute the cause of students' learning difficulties to students' characteristics than to either family and home factors or variables related to teaching (e.g., Christenson, Ysseldyke, Wang, & Algozzine, 1983). The diagnostic process reinforces that *within-child focus*, and as a result, important and potentially modifiable aspects of the environment can be easily neglected.

## Asking the Wrong Question, Solving the Wrong Problem

The most basic error in educational diagnosis is inherent to the design of the diagnostic system. In essence, because the diagnostic distinctions lack treatment utility, answers to the diagnostic questions of interest (e.g., is this child learning disabled?) do not provide a sound foundation for instructional planning (e.g., Gresham & Witt, 1997). Proponents of diagnostic classification do not dispute that point; rather, they suggest that the criticism is unfair. For example, Fagan and Bracken (1995) have argued that diagnostic measures should be evaluated in relation to diagnostic rather than treatment goals. Unfortunately, that argument fails to address the larger purpose of diagnosis and classification—the goal of helping. Diagnostic classification systems that do not contribute to the design of effective interventions are not well designed (Blashfield & Draguns, 1976; Cromwell, Blashfield, & Strauss, 1975; Heller et al., 1982).

# SUGGESTED COPING STRATEGIES: STRONG MODELS FOR ASSESSMENT AND DECISION MAKING

Professionals acquire their positions through a series of planned, as well as accidental, events (Bandura, 1982); therefore, from a child's, parent's, or teacher's perspective, a referral initiates an essentially chance encounter with a local service provider (Barnett & Zucker, 1990). The nature of the services received reflect site-specific preferences and regularities that have evolved through many sources of influence (e.g., Gutkin & Curtis, 1990). The developmental implications of that service-delivery encounter may be episodic (e.g., another diagnostic report for the cumulative folder) or far-reaching, producing significant change, either positive or negative, in the developmental trajectories or life paths of any one or more of the parties involved. Because of the wide range of potential outcomes and differences in outcomes that are not necessarily benign, decisions about the organization and delivery of services are ethically significant acts (Tversky & Kahneman, 1984). To cope with these responsibilities and the potential for error, strong models for assessment and decision making are needed.

## Strong Models for Assessment

A strong assessment plan yields the minimal amount of information needed for ethical decision making (Yeaton & Sechrest, 1981). Strong assessment plans have the criteria of (1) achieving confidence in decisions, (2) enabling helpfulness in outcomes, and (3) maintaining frugality in costs for all involved in the process. We review four points of analysis for strong assessments.

### The Purpose of Assessment is Well Defined

To be helpful, the problem-solving process must address the functional concerns of parents, children, and teachers. Although these people request assistance and expect help, professionals often respond through diagnosis or classification. These tactics, using traditional diagnostic instruments designed to identify "strengths and weaknesses" or "significant delays," do not lead to sound intervention-relevant decisions; they add expensive steps and create error-prone (snapshot) diagnostic decisions based on available tests or techniques. In contrast, assessment for intervention design is founded on ecological and behavioral principles, factors facilitative of change, and sequential analyses of change. The probabilities of altering a problem situation, rather than the probabilities associated with a particular diagnostic label, are of interest.

Classification remains a thorny issue because of legal entitlements for children who would be identified as disabled. The model that we advocate is based on the notion of resistance to intervention (Gresham, 1991), which means, simply put, that special service resources are allocated through the analysis of functional needs and the difficulties of actually intervening in specific situations. The focal points for assessment are problem situations (defined in relation to care-givers' goals and concerns) and keystone variables for change (e.g., Barnett, Bauer, Ehrhardt, Lentz, & Stollar, 1996; Barnett, Ehrhardt, Stollar, & Bauer, 1994). *Keystone variables* are those that if changed are likely to positively affect the largest set of other significant behaviors, perceptions, or problem environments to provide most efficiently long-term resolution of problem situations (Evans & Meyers, 1985).

### The Opportunities for Changing Problem Situations are Well Examined

A strong assessment plan produces meaningful and cost-effective information for generating hypotheses or making predictions about interventions that are likely to be helpful in addressing functional goals and concerns. Traditional diagnostic assessment practices result in a disappointing paradox; although tremendous amounts of data are collected, they enable only weak predictions about diagnostic status that frequently miss the questions and concerns of parents and teachers. Parents and teachers expect predictions about change—that change is possible and that interventions are suitable for changing problem situations.

While change is the major characteristic of child development (Bijou, 1995), the course of cognitive and social development is determined through interactions among complex processes (psychological, social, biological, and genetic) and accidental events. Although impressive evidence suggests that cognitive and social behaviors are determined early, there is equally impressive evidence that substantial changes occur throughout the developmental period, including adulthood. Thus, evidence supports the coherence and continuity of human development but also implies that significant change may be possible for individuals.

We do not wish to elevate the status of IQs, but more has been written about IQ and developmental change than any other marker. For many reasons, IQ tests may give misinformation about the possibilities for change. Although they typically predict about half the variation in achievement, they are insensitive to meaningful changes that could be attributable to planned interventions. The variation across time and instruments is one major reason for the need to attend to decision reliability issues. For individuals, IQs may fluctuate considerably, sometimes dramatically, from early childhood to young adulthood, with changes of as much as 50 to 70 IQ points (Wohlwill, 1980). This is true despite the relatively high reliabilities associated with IQ measures and more modest changes for most persons. At approximately age six IQs stabilize to a degree, but important individual changes may be noted later. For individual children, the IQ trajectories may be on an upward or downward trend. The specific reasons for individual changes may never become clear, but evidence suggests a range of possible variables, including personality, accidental, and environmental influences that may function as natural interventions (Wohlwill, 1980).

Evaluations of planned early interventions have provided another context for the analysis of IQ change. Among the most notable of these efforts have been Head Start, Abecedarian, and the Milwaukee Project. Overall, IQ changes based on participation in experimental programs have been more difficult to achieve than originally hoped. Typically, programs have boosted IQ performance immediately following the interventions (the median change is about .5 standard deviations across studies, with a range from 3 to 32 IQ points), but the gains have proven difficult to sustain. More intensive programs have yielded more impressive results, but still the IQ gains seem to fade over time. As summarized by Scarr and Arnett (1987), "Intelligence can be said to be malleable, then, but only within certain limits" (p. 82). The critical question remains: what can be changed and by how much? While the subject of developmental malleability and change has created substantial tensions and significant variation in professional beliefs, for individual children sources of developmental influence cannot be disentangled with any reasonable degree of confidence except in extreme situations. Because studies of intervention design are in their infancy, the limits of change are unknown, especially for individual children.

The practical challenges involve understanding the processes of psychosocial change, helping to identify and modify variables that have the potential for enhancing development and adaptive behaviors and developing resources to support intervention efforts. These variables, related to intervention design and the processes of change, are missed by behavior ratings and traditional measures of IQ and achievement. Even when biological factors are implicated, research shows that environments may rather quickly produce highly significant differences in early skills and behaviors (Hart & Risley, 1995; Patterson & Bank, 1986; Wahler & Dumas, 1986). Caregivers capitalize (or don't) on opportunities to learn, expand, and practice affective, social, cognitive, and language skills in ways that may have a profound cumulative effect. Werner (1986) concluded that basic intervention strategies for children may involve "either . . . decreasing their exposure to biological factors and cumulative life stresses, or . . . increasing the number of protective factors (competencies, sources of support) that they can rely on within themselves or their caregiving environment" (p. 25).

Logical generalizations from well-conducted single-case experimental designs provide a basis for estimating change (e.g., Barnett & Carey, 1992; Edgington, 1967; Haynes, Spain, & Oliveira, 1993). One of the most compelling criteria is evidence of generalization, that is, when behavioral changes lead to improvements in independent functioning in normal settings. Although the current literature reveals many effective interventions for learning and behavior problems (Christenson, Ysseldyke, & Thurlow, 1989; Lentz, Allen, & Ehrhardt, 1996; Sulzer-Azaroff & Mayer, 1991), many uncertainties remain for individual programming. Consequently, single-case designs provide needed methods of accountability to evaluate and to make necessary changes in interventions.

Two overall themes stand out. First, regarding confidence in predictions, many unknowns about individual developmental trajectories are suggested by the empirical research related to change. Second, because of the ambiguities, examining personal models of professional practice and beliefs about change may be critical (e.g., Barnett & Zucker, 1990). Belief systems are direct and indirect sources of decisions about the learning experiences and opportunities provided to children (e.g., Sigel, McGillicuddy-DeLisi, & Goodnow, 1992). For example, the construct of self-efficacy reflects personal beliefs about competency and thus may influence care-givers (and consultants) in making decisions about interventions and carrying them out. Self-efficacy influences the choice of activities, persistence on difficult tasks, thoughts, and emotional reactions

(Bandura, 1986). The self-efficacy of the professional may limit efforts when the research on developmental change is not accurately appraised.

## *Assessments Have a Real-World Basis*

How are assessment plans designed? What aspects of the child's, parents', and teacher's experience should receive attention and to what degree? Strong assessment plans support ongoing problem solving and problem structuring in real-world or naturalistic settings, rather than explicit responses to a set of given questions (Schön, 1983). Situations are defined in terms of physical and social settings, objectives or goals associated with settings, and the observable events that occur within settings (Bijou, Peterson, & Ault, 1968; Bijou, Peterson, Harris, Allen, & Johnston, 1969), including the phenomenological impact of settings and behaviors on all persons in the ecology (Mischel, 1981).

What theoretical guides can professionals use to enter the real world of problem situations? Ecological theory is based on the tenet that problems do not reside within individuals but instead are shared by members in pertinent systems (family, school, peer, and community), and even broader influences as well. Ecobehavioral analysis merges ecological theory with applied behavior analysis (Rogers-Warren, 1984). Ecological consultation describes a model for the delivery of services based on ecological and behavioral principles and collaborative problem solving (Gutkin, 1993; Gutkin & Curtis, 1990). Consultation strategies are used to explore and develop alternatives for resolving problems: (1) modifying the problem behavior, (2) altering or clarifying the expectations of persons encountering the problem behavior, and (3) changing situations or environments. Often, elements of all three alternatives may be used to guide intervention plans. In addition, system strengths; healthy, adaptive coping mechanisms; and coping strategies can be analyzed.

How can professionals know that their assessment plans have a real-world basis? *Ecological validity* has been defined in several ways (Bronfenbrenner, 1977, 1979; Martens & Witt, 1988; Neisser, 1976). Taken together, the basic principles pertinent to intervention efforts include the following: (1) the realities that guide the behaviors of parents, teachers, and children are the place to begin assessment planning; (2) the significant concerns of parents, teachers, and children are addressed; (3) logical generalizations

from intervention research are developed through comparisons to individual children, behaviors, caregivers, settings, resources, and carefully described interventions (Edgington, 1967); (4) intervention outcomes are consonant with setting expectations; and (5) the effects of intervention are evaluated in accord with ecological principles; including the analysis of planned and unplanned outcomes over long time periods (Willems, 1977).

*Social validity* is concerned with defining significant problems for behavioral change and establishing and obtaining goals through procedures acceptable to the immediate social community (Wolf, 1978). Ideally, these judgments inform practice throughout assessment planning, intervention design, and evaluation phases (Schwartz & Baer, 1991). Two general methods stem from social validity appraisals. First, social validity involves subjective evaluations or opinions by others who are able to judge the adequacy of the goals, the methods to achieve goals, and the results. Parents, teachers, and community members can all serve in this capacity. Second, social validity involves social comparisons. For example, peer group (or individual) performance of the target behavior may help differentiate inadequate from adept performance and may suggest behaviors for change. Practical methods for ongoing appraisals of social validity are described by Ehrhardt, Barnett, Lentz, Stollar, and Reifin (1996).

What assessment techniques can professionals use to clarify real-world concerns? Although regarded as a supplementary source of information for educational diagnosis (e.g., Kaufman, 1994), ecobehavioral interviews and observations (e.g., direct observations of academic skills within a well-defined curriculum) provide the foundation for intervention design, addressing a wide range of pertinent issues including settings, problem behaviors and circumstances, key persons, probable change agents, and significant time periods. Interviews and observations are also used to examine intervention alternatives and possible barriers to intervention processes and to help evaluate intervention outcomes. Perhaps the best guideline is that there should be a natural basis for behaviors that are observed and recorded (e.g., Barnett et al., 1994). The natural units should meet at least the following criteria: (1) they should have unequivocal validity for elucidating significant interactions between the child and environment, (2) they should be capable of reflecting planned changes that result from interventions, and (3) they should be countable or repeatable (Johnston & Pennypacker, 1993).

Although interviews and observations are strong techniques for gathering intervention-relevant information, they are vulnerable to both technical and conceptual sources of error (e.g., Barnett & Macmann, 1992b; Macmann et al., 1996). Interviews typically stress the verbal behavior of the teacher or parent and not the actual behavior of the child, teacher, and parent in specific contexts. In addition, caregivers may serve as untrained observers (Kratochwill, 1985), and data may be variable or hard to interpret. Intervention design and evaluation are based on consistent conditions, but real-world situations may change rapidly. Certain types of observations, such as those concerning broad ecological variables, participant-child interactions, and child-child interactions, especially when out of the caregiver's purview, are problematic. Thus, the technical adequacy of intervention decisions warrants ongoing scrutiny.

## *Error Identification is Well Handled*

Assessment techniques contribute both information and error to the understanding of psychological or educational problems. Given that change is the most notable characteristic of childhood, it is not surprising that variability is a notable characteristic of efforts to measure and understand child development. To accommodate changing situations and developmental progressions, assessment for intervention design requires sequential decision making (Bandura, 1969). A key task is to identify problem-solving goals and reasonable steps through which those goals might be achieved (Macmann et al., 1996). The iterative nature of the problem-solving process provides one practical safeguard—facilitating the development of workable plans and reducing errors of judgment because the outcomes of plans are evaluated and adjustments to plans are based on empirical data. Another fundamental way to reduce the likelihood of error is to avoid the use of weak constructs and instead use clearly defined descriptions of behavior, providing functional, real-world referents for problem identification and the evaluation of intervention outcomes.

Professional judgment is a complicated topic, and most studies have been concerned with diagnostic decision making rather than assessment for intervention design. We review several strategies for reducing error (e.g., Barnett, 1988).

1. Consider a range of plausible alternative hypotheses and regard each of them as tenable until it is ruled out. Spend as much energy looking for possible disconfirming information as for confirming information. Although some hypotheses may be difficult to evaluate (e.g., genetic), single-case experimental designs provide the most robust strategy for evaluating competing explanatory hypotheses (Hayes & Follett, 1992; Haynes et al., 1993; Steege & Wacker, 1995; Wacker, Steege, & Berg, 1988).

2. Help parents and teachers establish a range of plausible interventions based on observations of natural interactions that can then be refined through problem solving and experimentation (Barnett & Carey, 1992; Barnett et al., 1994). As professionals, it is tempting to appear quick and ready with suggestions, but doing so also increases the likelihood of error-prone suggestions.

3. Use decision aids to reduce the reliance on memory and increase the likelihood that questions necessary to structure problems will be adequately applied. Examples include the use of structured ecobehavioral interview guides (in contrast to winging it) and graphic data displays from single-case designs for accountability and continuous monitoring of progress.

4. Accept uncertain predictions and offer them as potential patterns of outcomes. Because of countless variables that may alter intervention outcomes, predictions about the behavior of the children, parents, and teachers are limited. Judgmental errors are made when professionals go beyond their data; but even with good data, only descriptive estimates of probable patterns of behavior can be made.

## Strong Models for Decision Making

The most fundamental characteristic of a strong model for professional decision making is a strong model for assessment (e.g., Peterson, 1987). To realize the helpfulness or utility of data, however, assessment information must be integrated and transformed into professional inferences and actions within the context of a problem-solving process (Macmann et al., 1996). Strong models for educational decision making link assessment information and resulting decisions to problem-solving goals (e.g., Reschly & Ysseldyke, 1995).

## Decision-Focused Educational Assessment: A Problem-Solving Model

One strong model for educational decision making has been described by Salvia and Hughes (1990). As shown in Figure 21.6, important educational decisions may be organized (both hierarchically and sequentially) within the context of major tasks or steps in problem solving, that is, problem identification, problem analysis, and plan implementation and evaluation (Bergan & Kratochwill, 1990). For each type of decision, the key questions and sources of assessment information are summarized in Table 21.3.

The process of problem solving and decision making begins and ends with the ongoing evaluation of pupils' progress (Figure 21.6). In evaluating progress, the focal points for assessment include instructional concerns (reframed as curricular goals or expectations) and students' level of proficiency and rate of skill acquisition in relation to those expectations. The data from these analyses are used to develop answers to the following broad question: is the student making satisfactory progress toward instructional goals? The resulting judgments represent hypotheses about the nature and severity of discrepancies between current and needed skills and behaviors.

Based on the analysis of needed skills and behaviors, additional assessment data are collected to generate hypotheses about the instructional modifications needed. These hypotheses are formed through the analysis of current environments in relation to intervention theory and research of relevance to the variables targeted for change (e.g., Barnett et al., 1996; Christenson et al., 1989; Lentz et al., 1996). Instructional planning revolves around the following broad question: should instruction be modified? In formulating an answer, specific decisions are made about what, how, and when students should be taught (e.g., instructional content, methods, and allocated time). For example, for a child who is exhibiting high rates of inappropriate behavior, analyses might indicate an adequate repertoire of social skills but low rates of reinforcement for their application. Based on the hypothesized discrepancy between current and needed environments, an intervention plan might be developed to increase the rate of reinforcement for functional alternative or replacement behaviors (e.g., Sugai & Tindal, 1993). Although the example illustrates a well-conceived or plausible plan, which can be easily justified by behavioral theory and research, it is merely a hypothesis. Almost any theoretical framework can claim utility for planning. The contributions of those plans to beneficial outcomes remain to be demonstrated *for this particular child* (Bandura, 1969).

Hypotheses about needed instructional placements are generated through the analysis of instructional plans (e.g., what needs to be taught) in relation to the specific settings and change agents required to implement plans. The resulting hypotheses may suggest the need to modify either the location of services (e.g., resource room), the personnel responsible for the delivery of services (e.g., trained specialists), or both. Instructional placement decisions are informed by analyses of (1) the modifiability of environments, for example, the effectiveness of efforts to increase the strength, acceptability, and/or integrity of interventions (e.g., Allen & Graden, 1995), and (2) system resources and responsibilities for service delivery, for example, the least restrictive environment where a child's instructional needs are likely to be met. In our opinion, consistent with the concept of resistance to intervention (Gresham, 1991) and service-based delivery models (e.g., Hobbs, 1975), if the need for either special education or related services is implicated by these analyses, the documentation for those decisions should be sufficient to define eligibility or entitlement to the identified services.

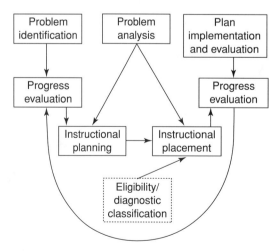

FIGURE 21.6 **Problem-solving model for decision-focused educational assessment.**
*Source:* Adapted from Salvia and Hughes (1990).

**TABLE 21.3    Improving the Quality of Instruction: Decision-focused Educational Assessment**

### Instructionally-Relevant Decisions

I. *Progress evaluation decisions:* Hypotheses based on the analysis of discrepancies between current and *needed skills/behaviors*
   a. Key question: Is the student making satisfactory progress toward instructional goals?
   b. Assessment focus: (i) instructional goals/concerns; (ii) level of proficiency; (iii) rate of skill acquisition

II. *Instructional planning decisions:* Hypotheses based on the analysis of discrepancies between current and *needed environments* to support development
   a. Key question: Should instruction be modified?
      i. *What* should the student be taught (content)?
      ii. *How* and *when* should the student be taught (method, allocated time)?
   b. Assessment focus: (i) pupil progress; (ii) relevant change variables (e.g., instructional environment)

III. *Instructional placement decisions:* A special type of instructional planning decision (based on hypotheses about discrepancies between current and needed environments to support development)
   a. Key question: Should the location of services and personnel responsible for the delivery of services be modified?
      i. *Where* should the student be taught?
      ii. *By whom* should the student be taught?
   b. Assessment focus: (i) instructional plans (i.e., what, how, and when the student should be taught); (ii) progress of change efforts (e.g., effectiveness of efforts to increase the strength, acceptability, and/or integrity of instructional interventions); (iii) system resources and responsibilities for service delivery (e.g., least restrictive environment)

### Surplus/Dysfunctional Decisions

IV. *Eligibility/diagnostic classification decisions:* Instructionally-*ir*relevant hypotheses about *needed disability labels*
   a. Key question: Are decisions about needed instruction (and educational placements needed to provide that instruction) constrained by dysfunctional state or local eligibility criteria?
   b. Assessment focus: (i) diagnostic constructs; (ii) system resources and responsibilities for the provision of functional (i.e., *instructionally relevant*) services

During the next stage of decision making, hypotheses about needed environmental changes to support development (i.e., instructional plans and placements) are empirically tested. The analysis is broadly organized in terms of the key question that initiated the process: is the student making satisfactory progress toward instructional goals? Many other specific questions and tasks are embedded in the analysis (Macmann et al., 1996), including the consideration of intervention integrity, real-world versus anticipated feasibility of plans, and social and ecological validity. Progress evaluation data provide the foundation for ongoing problem solving—redefining instructional concerns and readjusting instructional plans and placements as needed.

## Practical Criteria for Technical Adequacy

In our opinion, important educational decisions should be negotiated within the context of a collaborative, team decision-making process (Barnett & Macmann, 1992a). In contrast, because the understanding of traditional diagnostic constructs is presumed to require specialized expert knowledge, diagnostic decision making relegates nonspecialists, such as parents and teachers, to the role of spectators. Knowledge is power. Parents and teachers can like or dislike the psychologist's recommendation about diagnosis, but they lack the specialized knowledge to participate fully in the decision-making process.

By shifting the focus of team decision making to more pragmatic and functional concerns, the psychologist's expert power and control of the decision-making process is diminished. The types of psychological expertise required in this context relate to the team process and the facilitation of meaningful change through effective intervention design. The hypotheses that emerge from this process, though potentially well informed by instructional theory and research, should be recognized as tentative and be communicated to consumers as such.

For practical purposes, the *reliability of decisions* can be established through agreement among concerned parties about the most reasonable course of action at any particular time. The potential for error is addressed through ongoing analyses of the *validity of decisions*, as determined through the collaborative evaluation of intervention outcomes over time.

### *Surplus and Dysfunctional Decisions*

Diagnostic classification decisions are afforded a tenuous status in the model (see Figure 21.6). For most professionals, the IDEA legislation requires that decisions about eligibility for special education and related services be based on a disability diagnosis. However, because diagnostic classification decisions fail to inform either the identification of functional needs or the design of interventions to address those needs, the decisions are characterized as surplus and dysfunctional in our adaptation of the Salvia and Hughes (1990) model. The decisions serve regulatory mandates, largely divorced from the needs that provided the original impetus for the legislation (e.g., Howard, 1994).

Where state and local eligibility criteria require the analysis of diagnostic constructs to determine eligibility for services, professionals are obligated to divert substantial professional resources to these issues. Although we obviously think that the regulatory guidelines are misdirected, we are encouraged by creative state and local efforts to redirect these dysfunctional diagnostic emphases toward problem-solving goals (Ikeda, Tilly, Stumme, Volmer, & Allison, 1996; Kovaleski, Tucker, & Duffy, 1995; Tilly & Reschly, 1993). Despite the additional burden of regulatory barriers, for those professionals who find themselves in employment situations unsupported by reform initiatives, approximations toward the goal can be realized through school-based organizational change (Curtis & Stollar,

1995; Rosenfield, 1992; Ross, 1995). Even in those settings where regulatory reforms have been initiated, establishing new patterns of professional thought and behavior will require ongoing strategic efforts (e.g., Fullan, 1996; Grimes & Tilly, 1996; Sarason, 1990).

## CONCLUSIONS

Despite the long-awaited arrival of briefer, more accurate, and more scientific diagnostic measures (that presumably will lead to more defensible professional decisions than other assessment alternatives), the use of screening instruments, diagnostic batteries, and ratings is full of promises that have yet to be delivered. The promises and criticisms have become part of the profession. Indeed, it is humbling to consider the monumental challenges raised by luminaries such as Cronbach, Meehl, Messick, Mischel, Peterson, and many others and wonder if any stones have been left unturned.

Seemingly oblivious to the criticisms, recent surveys of assessment practices reveal findings that, depending on one's point of view, may evoke a sense of either comfort or alarm. For example, Stinnett, Havey, and Oehler-Stinnett (1994) found that many traditional diagnostic measures remain "at the top," whereas those relevant to problem solving and intervention design are designated as informal and used sporadically. Although the continued use of traditional diagnostic measures is understandable in light of current special education regulations that exist despite concerted efforts toward reform (e.g., Reschly & Ysseldyke, 1995; Rosenfield & Reynolds, 1990; Ysseldyke & Geenen, 1996), the most remarkable findings from this survey were the positive ratings for "perceived significance of the information . . . for decision making purposes" (Stinnett et al., 1994, p. 334). Many instruments rated highly in this category have been shown to have weak or unknown decision utility. Thus, it appears that many professionals remain unaware of the profound limitations associated with the use of these techniques.

Ultimately, we think that much damage may be done to public confidence in the profession if fundamental questions about the quality of diagnostic assessment practices remain unheeded. The basis for our concern is straightforward. Many converging lines of theory and research lead to the same inescapable conclusion: diagnostic assessment practices result in very little that can be said with confidence that is helpful to intervention design. Our analyses demonstrate that traditional diagnostic measures, even those that meet or exceed established conventions for technical adequacy, may not lead to reliable or valid decisions. The practical implications are truly staggering when projected against the number of school and private sector referrals that result in the administration of diagnostic tests and ratings—suggesting thousands of misinterpretations per day.

It would be wishful thinking, however, to suggest that the strong models for assessment and decision making recommended by our review represent a quick fix or easy remedy for the problems at hand. "The subprocesses of problem solving . . . are easy to delineate but . . . difficult to carry out (Bandura, 1986, p. 464). We do not wish to minimize the difficulties; even when unfettered from the dysfunctional search for diagnostic labels, problem solving is a complex and error-prone task (e.g., Barnett & Macmann, 1992a, 1992b; Macmann et al., 1996). The safeguards against decision errors embedded in the problem-solving process provide the best available means of coping, but they do not eliminate the potential for error.

In closing, however, we are reminded of Kendall's (1959) classic illustration of the distinction between reliability and validity. Although Kendall's Hiawatha could shoot his arrows on the same spot, time after time after time, he eventually had to give up his bow because he was unable to shoot his arrows anywhere near the target. In comparison, diagnostic assessments fall far short of the goal of helping and are no match for Hiawatha in terms of consistency. Thus, like Kendall's Hiawatha, we think it is time for diagnostic classification systems to give up the bow. Problem solving may be error-prone, but it provides an opportunity to aim at the target, which is what professional psychology *should* be about (Peterson, 1987).

# REFERENCES

Achenbach, T. M. (1991). *Manual for the Child Behavior Checklist/4–18 and 1991 profile*. Burlington: University of Vermont, Department of Psychiatry.

Allen, S. J., & Graden, J. L. (1995). Best practices in collaborative problem solving for intervention design. In A. Thomas & J. Grimes (Eds.), *Best practices in school psychology* (3rd ed., pp. 667–678).

Washington, DC: National Association of School Psychologists.

American Educational Research Association, American Psychological Association, National Council on Measurement in Education (1985). *Standards for educational and psychological testing*. Washington, DC: Author.

American Psychological Association (1992). *Ethical principles of psychologists and code of conduct*. Washington, DC: Author.

Angoff, W. H. (1988). Validity: An evolving concept. In H. Wainer & H. I. Braun (Eds.), *Test validity* (pp. 19–32). Hillsdale, NJ: Erlbaum.

Arkes, H. R. (1981). Impediments to accurate clinical judgment and possible ways to minimize their impact. *Journal of Consulting and Clinical Psychology, 49*, 323–330.

Arkes, H. R., & Hammond, K. R. (Eds.). (1986). *Judgment and decision making: An interdisciplinary reader*. New York: Cambridge University Press.

Bandura, A. (1969). *Principles of behavior modification*. New York: Holt, Rinehart & Winston.

Bandura, A. (1982). The psychology of chance encounters and life paths. *American Psychologist, 37*, 122–147.

Bandura, A. (1986). *Social foundations of thought and action: A social-cognitive theory*. Englewood Cliffs, NJ: Prentice Hall.

Barnett, D. W. (1988). Professional judgment: A critical appraisal. *School Psychology Review, 17*, 656–670.

Barnett, D. W., Bauer, A., Ehrhardt, K., Lentz, E., & Stollar, S. (1996). Keystone targets for change: Planning for widespread positive consequences. *School Psychology Quarterly, 11*, 95–117.

Barnett, D. W., & Carey, K. T. (1992). *Designing interventions for preschool learning and behavior problems*. San Francisco: Jossey-Bass.

Barnett, D. W., Collins, R., Coulter, C., Curtis, M. J., Ehrhardt, K., Glaser, A., Reyes, C., Stollar, S., & Winston, M. (1995). Ethnic validity and school psychology: Concepts and practices associated with cross-cultural professional competence. *Journal of School Psychology, 33*, 219–234.

Barnett, D. W., Ehrhardt, K. E., Stollar, S. A., & Bauer, A. M. (1994). PASSKey: A model for naturalistic assessment and intervention design. *Topics in Early Childhood Special Education, 14*, 350–373.

Barnett, D. W., Faust, J. A., & Sarmir, M. A. (1988). A validity study of two preschool instruments: The LAP-D and DIAL-R. *Contemporary Educational Psychology, 13*, 26–31.

Barnett, D. W., & Macmann, G. M. (1992a). Aptitude-achievement discrepancy scores: Accuracy in analysis misdirected. *School Psychology Review, 21*, 494–508.

Barnett, D. W., & Macmann, G. M. (1992b). Decision reliability and validity: Contributions and limitations of alternative assessment strategies. *The Journal of Special Education, 25*, 431–452.

Barnett, D. W., Macmann, G. M., & Carey, K. T. (1992). Early intervention and the assessment of developmental skills: Challenges and directions. *Topics in Early Childhood Special Education, 12*, 21–43.

Barnett, D. W., & Zucker, K. B. (1990). *The personal and social assessment of children: Current status and professional practice issues.* Boston: Allyn & Bacon.

Bergan, J. R., & Kratochwill, T. R. (1990). *Behavioral consultation and therapy.* New York: Plenum.

Bijou, S. W. (1995). *Behavior analysis of child development* (2nd ed.). Reno, NV: Context Press.

Bijou, S. W., Peterson, R. F., & Ault, M. H. (1968). A method to integrate descriptive and experimental fields at the level of data and empirical concepts. *Journal of Applied Behavior Analysis, 1*, 175–191.

Bijou, S. W., Peterson, R. F., Harris, F. R., Allen, K. E., & Johnston, M. S. (1969). Methodology for experimental studies of young children in natural settings. *The Psychological Record, 19*, 177–210.

Blashfield, R. K., & Draguns, J. G. (1976). Evaluative criteria for psychiatric classification. *Journal of Abnormal Psychology, 85*, 140–150.

Boyd, R. D. (1989). What a difference a day makes: Age-related discontinuities and the Battelle Developmental Inventory. *Journal of Early Intervention, 13*, 114–119.

Bracken, B. A. (1988). Ten psychometric reasons why similar tests produce different results. *Journal of School Psychology, 26*, 155–166.

Bransford, J. D., & Stein, B. S. (1984). *The IDEAL problem solver.* New York: Freeman.

Brennan, R. L., & Prediger, D. J. (1981). Coefficient kappa: Some uses, misuses, and alternatives. *Educational and Psychological Measurement, 41*, 687–699.

Bronfenbrenner, U. (1977). Toward an experimental ecology of human development. *American Psychologist, 32*, 513–531.

Bronfenbrenner, U. (1979). *The experimental ecology of human development.* Cambridge, MA: Harvard University Press.

Campbell, D. T. (1986). Relabeling internal and external validity for applied social scientists. In W. M. K. Trochim (Ed.), *Advances in quasi-experimental design and analysis.* New directions for program evaluation (No. 31, pp. 67–77). San Francisco: Jossey-Bass.

Cambell, D. T., & Fiske, D. W. (1959). Convergent and discriminant validation by the multitrait-multimethod matrix. *Psychological Bulletin, 56*, 81–105.

Campbell, D. T., & Stanley, J. C. (1963). *Experimental and quasi-experimental designs for research.* Boston: Houghton Mifflin.

Christenson, S. L., Ysseldyke, J. E., & Thurlow, M. L. (1989). Critical instructional factors for students with mild handicaps: An integrative review. *Remedial and Special Education, 10*, 21–31.

Christenson, S. L., Ysseldyke, J. E., Wang, J. J., & Algozzine, B. (1983). Teachers' attributions for problems that result in referral for psychoeducational evaluation. *Journal of Teacher Education, 76*, 174–180.

Clarizio, H. E., & Bennett, D. E. (1987). Diagnostic utility of the K-ABC and WISC-R/PIAT in determining severe discrepancy. *Psychology in the Schools, 24*, 309–315.

Cohen, J. (1960). A coefficient of agreement for nominal scales. *Educational and Psychological Measurement, 20*, 37–46.

Cook, T. D., & Campbell, D. T. (1979). *Quasi-experimentation: Design and analysis issues for field settings.* Boston: Houghton Mifflin.

Cromwell, R. L., Blashfield, R. K., & Strauss, J. S. (1975). Criteria for classification systems. In N. Hobbs (Ed.), *Issues in the classification of children* (Vol. 1, pp. 4–25). San Francisco: Jossey-Bass.

Cronbach, L. J. (1988). Five perspectives on validation argument. In H. Wainer & H. I. Braun (Eds.), *Test validity* (pp. 3–17). Hillsdale, NJ: Erlbaum.

Cronbach, L. J., & Gleser, G. C. (1965). *Psychological tests and personnel decisions* (2nd ed.). Urbana: University of Illinois.

Cronbach, L. J., Gleser, G. C., Nanda, N., and Rajaratnam, N. (1972). *The dependability of behavioral measurements: Theory of generalizability for scores and profiles.* New York: Wiley.

Cronbach, L. J., & Snow, R. E. (1977). *Aptitudes and instructional methods: A handbook for research on interactions.* New York: Irvington.

Curtis, M. J., & Stollar, S. A. (1995). Best practices in system-level consultation and organizational change. In A. Thomas & J. Grimes (Eds.), *Best practices in school psychology* (3rd ed., pp. 51–58). Washington, DC: National Association of School Psychologists.

Dawes, R. M. (1994). *House of cards: Psychology and psychotherapy built on myth.* New York: Free Press.

Deno, S. L. (1995). School psychologist as problem solver. In A. Thomas & J. Grimes (Eds.), *Best practices in school psychology* (3rd ed., pp. 471–484). Washington, DC: National Association of School Psychologists.

Dice, L. R. (1945). Measures of ecologic association between species. *Ecology, 26*, 297–302.

Dunn, L. M., & Markwardt, F. C., Jr. (1970). *Peabody Individual Achievement Test.* Circle Pines, MN: American Guidance Service.

Edgington, E. S. (1967). Statistical inferences from N = 1 experiments. *Journal of Psychology, 65*, 195–199.

Ehrhardt, K. E., Barnett, D. W., Lentz, F. E., Stollar, S. A., & Reifin, L. H. (1996). Innovative methodology in ecological consultation: Use of scripts to promote treatment acceptability and integrity. *School Psychology Quarterly, 11,* 149–168.

Evans, I. M., & Meyers, L. H. (1985). *An educative approach to behavior problems: A practical decision model for interventions with severely handicapped learners.* Baltimore: Brookes.

Fagan, T., & Bracken, B. (1995). Reaction to Naglieri's "role of intelligence assessment." *The School Psychologist, 47,* 6–7.

Faust, D. (1986). Research on human judgment and its application to clinical practice. *Professional Psychology: Research and Practice, 17,* 420–430.

Fleiss, J. L. (1981). *Statistical methods for rates and proportions* (2nd ed.). New York: Wiley.

Fletcher, J. M. (1992). The validity of distinguishing children with language and learning disabilities according to discrepancies with IQ: Introduction to the special series. *Journal of Learning Disabilities, 25,* 546–548.

Fuchs, D., & Fuchs, L. S. (1986). Test procedure bias: A meta-analysis of examiner familiarity effects. *Review of Educational Research, 56,* 243–262.

Fullan, M. (1996). Professional culture and organizational change. *School Psychology Review, 25,* 496–500.

Good, R. H., Vollmer, M., Creek, R. J., Katz, L., & Chowdri, S. (1993). Treatment utility of the Kaufman Assessment Battery for Children: Effects of matching instruction and student processing strength. *School Psychology Review, 22,* 8–26.

Gresham, F. M. (1991). Conceptualizing behavior disorders in terms of resistance to intervention. *School Psychology Review, 20,* 23–36.

Gresham, F. M., & Witt, J. C. (1997). Utility of intelligence tests for treatment planning, classification, and placement decisions: Recent empirical findings and future directions. *School Psychology Quarterly, 12,* 249–267.

Grimes, J., & Tilly, W. D., III (1996). Policy and process: Means to lasting organizational change. *School Psychology Review, 25,* 465–476.

Gutkin, T. B. (1993). Moving from behavioral to ecobehavioral consultation: What's in a name? *Journal of Educational and Psychological Consultation, 4,* 95–99.

Gutkin, T. B., & Curtis, M. J. (1990). School-based consultation: Theory, techniques, and research. In C. R. Reynolds & T. B. Gutkin (Eds.), *Handbook of school psychology* (pp. 577–611). New York: Wiley.

Hall, J. D., & Barnett, D. W. (1991). Classification of risk status in preschool screening: A comparison of alternative measures. *Journal of Psychoeducational Assessment, 9,* 152–159.

Hammill, D. D., Brown, L., & Bryant, B. R. (1992). *A consumer's guide to tests in print* (2nd ed.). Austin, TX: Pro-ed.

Hart, B., & Risley, T. R. (1995). *Meaningful differences in the everyday experience of young American children.* Baltimore: Brookes.

Hawkins, R. P. (1979). The functions of assessment: Implications for the selection and development of devices for assessing repertoires in clinical, educational, and other settings. *Journal of Applied Behavior Analysis, 12,* 501–516.

Hayes, S. C., & Follette, W. C. (1992). Can functional analysis provide a substitute for syndromal classification? *Behavioral Assessment, 14,* 345–365.

Hayes, S. C., Nelson, R. O., & Jarrett, R. B. (1987). The treatment utility of assessment: A functional approach to evaluating assessment quality. *American Psychologist, 42,* 963–974.

Haynes, S. N., Spain, E. H., & Oliveira, J. (1993). Identifying causal relationships in clinical assessment. *Psychological Assessment, 5,* 281–291.

Heller, K. A., Holtzman, W. H., & Messick, S. (1982). *Placing children in special education: A strategy for equity.* Washington, DC: National Academy Press.

Hobbs, N. (1975). *The future of children: Categories, labels, and their consequences.* San Francisco: Jossey-Bass.

Hogarth, R. (1987). *Judgment and choice* (2nd ed.). New York: Wiley.

Howard, P. K. (1994). *Death of common sense: How law is suffocating America.* New York: Random House.

Ikeda, M. J., Tilly, D. W., III, Stumme, J., Volmer, L., & Allison, R. (1996). Agency-wide implementation of problem-solving consultation: Foundations, current implementation, and future directions. *School Psychology Quarterly, 11,* 228–243.

Jastak, S., & Wilkinson, G. S. (1984). *Wide Range Achievement Test–Revised.* Wilmington, DE: Jastak.

Johnston, J. M., & Pennypacker, H. S. (1993). *Strategies and tactics of behavioral research* (2nd ed.). Hillsdale, NJ: Erlbaum.

Kane, M. T. (1992). An argument-based approach to validity. *Psychological Bulletin, 122,* 527–535.

Kaufman, A. S. (1994). *Intelligent testing with the WISC-III.* New York: Wiley.

Kaufman, A. S., & Kaufman, N. L. (1983). *K-ABC: Kaufman Assessment Battery for Children.* Circle Pines, MN: American Guidance Service.

Kavale, K. (1990). Effectiveness of special education. In T. B. Gutkin & C. R. Reynolds (Eds.), *The handbook of school psychology* (2nd ed., pp. 870–900). New York: Wiley.

Kelley, T. L. (1927). *Interpretations of educational measurements.* Yonkers, NY: World Book.

Kendall, M. G. (1959). Hiawatha designs an experiment. *American Statistician, 13,* 23–24.

Kovaleski, J. F., Tucker, J. A., & Duffy, D. J. (1995). School reform through instructional support: The Pennsylvania initiative. *NASP Communique, 23*(8).

Kratochwill, T. R. (1985). Selection of target behaviors in behavioral consultation. *Behavior Assessment, 7,* 49–61.

Lentz, F. E., Allen, S. J., & Ehrhardt, K. E. (1996).

The conceptual elements of strong interventions in school settings. *School Psychology Quarterly, 11,* 118–136.

Macmann, G. M., and Barnett, D. W. (1984). An analysis of the construct validity of two measures of adaptive behavior. *Journal of Psychoeducational Assessment, 2,* 239–247.

Macmann, G. M., & Barnett, D. W. (1985). Discrepancy score analysis: A computer simulation of classification stability. *Journal of Psychoeducational Assessment, 4,* 363–375.

Macmann, G. M., & Barnett, D. W. (1992). Redefining the WISC-R: Implications for professional practice and public policy. *The Journal of Special Education, 26,* 139–161.

Macmann, G. M., & Barnett, D. W. (1993). Reliability of psychiatric and psychological diagnoses of mental retardation severity: Judgments under naturally occurring conditions. *American Journal on Mental Retardation, 97,* 559–567.

Macmann, G. M., & Barnett, D. W. (1994). Structural analysis of correlated factors: Lessons from the verbal-performance dichotomy of the Wechsler Scales. *School Psychology Quarterly, 9,* 161–197.

Macmann, G. M., & Barnett, D. W. (1997). Myth of the master detective: Reliability of interpretations for Kaufman's "Intelligent Testing" approach to the WISC-III. *School Psychology Quarterly, 12,* 197–234.

Macmann, G. M., Barnett, D. W., Allen, S. J., Bramlett, R. K., Hall, J. D., & Ehrhardt, K. E. (1996). Problem solving and intervention design: Guidelines for the evaluation of technical adequacy. *School Psychology Quarterly, 11,* 137–148.

Macmann, G. M., Barnett, D. W., Lombard, T. J., Belton-Kocher, E., & Sharpe, M. N. (1989). On the actuarial classification of children: Fundamental studies of classification agreement. *The Journal of Special Education, 23,* 127–149.

Macmann, G. M., Barnett, D. W., & Lopez, E. J. (1993). The Child Behavior Checklist/4–18 and related materials: Reliability and validity of syndromal assessment. *School Psychology Review, 22,* 322–333.

Martens, B. K., & Witt, J. C. (1988). On the ecological validity of behavior modification. In J. C. Witt, S. N. Elliott, & F. M. Gresham (Eds.), *Handbook of behavior therapy in education* (pp. 325–341). New York: Plenum.

Massey, J. O. (1964). *WISC scoring criteria.* Palo Alto, CA: Consulting Psychologists Press.

McDermott, P. A., Fantuzzo, J. W., Glutting, J. J., Watkins, M. W., & Baggaley, A. R. (1992). Illusions of meaning in the ipsative assessment of children's ability. *The Journal of Special Education, 25,* 504–526.

Meehl, P. E. (1954). *Clinical versus statistical prediction.* Minneapolis: University of Minnesota Press.

Meehl, P. E. (1986). Causes and effects of my disturb-ing little book. *Journal of Personality Assessment, 50,* 370–375.

Meehl, P. E., & Rosen, A. (1955). Antecedent probability and the efficiency of psychometric signs, patterns, or cutting scores. *Psychological Bulletin, 52,* 194–216.

Messick, S. (1989). Validity. In R. Linn (Ed.), *Educational measurement* (3rd ed., pp. 13–103). New York: Macmillan.

Messick, S. (1995). Validity of psychological assessment: Validation of inferences from persons' responses and performances as scientific inquiry into score meaning. *American Psychologist, 50,* 741–749.

Miller, C. K., & Chansky, N. M. (1972). Psychologists' scoring of WISC protocols. *Psychology in the Schools, 9,* 144–152.

Mischel, W. (1981). A cognitive-social learning approach to assessment. In T. V. Merluzzi, C. R. Glass, & M. Genest (Eds.), *Cognitive assessment* (pp. 479–502). New York: Guilford.

Neisser, U. (1976). *Cognition and reality: Principles and implications of cognitive psychology.* San Francisco: Freeman.

Newborg, J., Stock, J., Wnek, L., Guidubaldi, J., & Svinicki, J. (1984). *Battelle Developmental Inventory: Examiner's manual.* Dallas, TX: DLM/Teaching Resources.

Nezu, A. M., & Nezu, C. M. (1993). Identifying and selecting target problems for clinical interventions: A problem-solving model. *Psychological Assessment, 5,* 254–263.

Nisbett, R., & Ross, L. (1980). *Human inference: Strategies and shortcomings of social judgments.* Englewood Cliffs, NJ: Prentice Hall.

Nunnally, J. C. (1978). *Psychometric theory* (2nd ed.). New York: McGraw-Hill.

Patterson, G. R., & Bank, L. (1986). Bootstrapping your way in the nomological thicket. *Behavioral Assessment, 8,* 49–73.

Peterson, D. R. (1987). The role of assessment in professional psychology. In D. R. Peterson and D. B. Fishman (Eds.), *Assessment for decision* (pp. 5–43). New Brunswick, NJ: Rutgers University Press.

Peterson, D. R. (1991). Connection and disconnection of research and practice in the education of professional psychologists. *American Psychologist, 46,* 422–429.

Peterson, D. R., and Fishman, D. B. (Eds.). (1987). *Assessment for decision.* New Brunswick, NJ: Rutgers University Press.

Poth, R. L., & Barnett, D. W. (1988). Establishing the limits of interpretive confidence: A validity study of two preschool developmental scales. *School Psychology Review, 17,* 322–330.

Reschly, D. J. (1988). Special education reform: School psychology revolution. *School Psychology Review, 17,* 459–475.

Reschly, D. J., & Ysseldyke, J. E. (1995). School psychology paradigm shift. In A. Thomas & J. Grimes (Eds.), *Best practices in school psychology* (3rd ed., pp. 17–31). Washington, DC: National Association of School Psychologists.

Reynolds, C. R. (1984–1985). Critical measurement issues in learning disabilities. *The Journal of Special Education, 18,* 451–476.

Rogers-Warren, A. (1984). Ecobehavioral analysis. *Education and Treatment of Children, 7,* 283–303.

Ronka, C. S., & Barnett, D. W. (1986). A comparison of adaptive behavior ratings: Revised Vineland and AAMD ABS-SE. *Special Services in the Schools, 2,* 87–96.

Rosenfield, S. (1992). Developing school-based consultation teams: A design for organizational change. *School Psychology Quarterly, 7,* 27–46.

Rosenfield, S., & Reynolds, M. C. (1990). Mainstreaming school psychology: A proposal to develop and evaluate alternative methods and intervention strategies. *School Psychology Quarterly, 5,* 55–65.

Ross, R. P. (1995). Best practices in implementing intervention assistance teams. In A. Thomas & J. Grimes (Eds.), *Best practices in school psychology* (3rd ed., pp. 227–237). Washington, DC: National Association of School Psychologists.

Salvia, J., & Hughes, C. (1990). *Curriculum-based assessment: Testing what is taught.* New York: Macmillan.

Sarason, S. B. (1990). *The predictable failure of educational reform: Can we change before it's too late?* San Francisco: Jossey-Bass.

Sattler, J. M. (1992). *Assessment of children* (rev. 3rd ed.). San Diego: Author.

Scarr, S., & Arnett, J. (1987). Lessons from intervention and family studies. In J. J. Gallagher & Craig T. Ramey (Eds.), *The malleability of children* (pp. 71–84). Baltimore, MD: Brookes.

Schön, D. A. (1983). *The reflective practitioner: How professionals think in action.* New York: Basic Books.

Schulte, A., & Borich, G. D. (1984). Considerations in the use of difference scores to identity learning-disabled children. *Journal of School Psychology, 22,* 381–390.

Schwartz, I. S., & Baer, D. M. (1991). Social validity assessments: Is current practice state of the art? *Journal of Applied Behavior Analysis, 24,* 189–204.

Shaywitz, S. E., Escobar, M. D., Shaywitz, B. A., Fletcher, J. M., & Makuch, R. (1992). Evidence that dyslexia may represent the lower tail of a normal distribution of reading ability. *New England Journal of Medicine, 326,* 145–150.

Shepard, L. A. (1993). Evaluating test validity. *Review of Research in Education, 19,* 405–450.

Sicoly, F. (1992). Estimating the accuracy of decisions based on cutting scores. *Journal of Psychoeducational Assessment, 10,* 26–36.

Siegel, L. S. (1989). IQ is irrelevant to the definition of learning disabilities. *Journal of Learning Disabilities, 22,* 469–478.

Sigel, I. E., McGillicuddy-DeLisi, A. V., & Goodnow, J. J. (1992). *Parental belief systems: The psychological consequences for children* (2nd ed.). Hillsdale, NJ: Erlbaum.

Slate, J. R., & Chick, D. (1989). WISC-R examiner errors: Cause for concern. *Psychology in the Schools, 26,* 78–84.

Slate, J. R., & Hunnicutt, L. C., Jr. (1988). Examiner errors on the Wechsler Scales. *Journal of Psychoeducational Assessment, 6,* 280–288.

Slate, J. R., Jones, C. H., Coulter, C., & Covert, T. L. (1992). Practitioner's administration and scoring errors of the WISC-R: Evidence that we do err. *Journal of School Psychology, 30,* 77–82.

Stanovich, K. E. (1991). Conceptual and empirical problems with discrepancy definitions of reading disability. *Learning Disability Quaterly, 14,* 269–280.

Steege, M. W., & Wacker, D. P. (1995). Best practices in evaluating the effectiveness of applied interventions. In A. Thomas & J. Grimes (Eds.), *Best practices in school psychology* (3rd ed., pp. 625–636). Washington, DC: National Association of School Psychologists.

Stinnett, T. A., Havey, J. A., & Oehler-Stinnett, J. (1994). Current test usage by practicing school psychologists: A national survey. *Journal of Psychoeducational Assessment, 12,* 331–350.

Subcoviak, M. J. (1984). Estimating the reliability of mastery-nonmastery classifications. In R. A. Berk (Ed.), *A guide to criterion-referenced test construction* (pp. 267–291). Baltimore, MD: Johns Hopkins University Press.

Sugai, G. M., & Tindal, G. A. (1993). *Effective school consultation: An interactive approach.* Pacific Grove, CA: Brooks/Cole.

Sulzer-Azaroff, B., & Mayer, G. R. (1991). *Behavior analysis for lasting change.* Fort Worth, TX: Holt, Rinehart & Winston.

Swets, J. A. (1992). The science of choosing the right decision threshold in high-stakes diagnostics. *American Psychologist, 47,* 522–532.

Thorndike, R. L. (1963). *The concepts of over- and underachievement.* New York: Bureau of Publications, Teachers College, Columbia University.

Tilly, W. D., III, & Reschly, D. J. (1993, September). Special education system reform: The Iowa story. *NASP Communique, 22* (1).

Tversky, A., & Kahneman, D. (1984). The framing of decisions and the psychology of choice. In G. Wright (Ed.), *Behavioral decision making* (pp. 25–41). New York: Plenum.

Wacker, D., Steege, M., & Berg, W. (1988). Use of single-case designs to evaluate manipulable influences on school performance. *School Psychology Review, 17,* 949–956.

Wahler, R. G., & Dumas, J. E. (1986). "A chip off the

old block": Interpersonal characteristics of coercive children across generations. In P. S. Strain, M. J. Guralnick, & H. M. Walker (Eds.), *Children's social behavior: Development, assessment, modification* (pp. 49–91). Orlando, FL: Academic Press.

Watkins, M. W., Kush, J. C., & Glutting, J. J. (1997). Prevalence and diagnostic utility of the WISC-III SCAD profile among children with disabilities. *School Psychology Quarterly, 12,* 235–248.

Wechsler, D. (1974). *Manual for the Wechsler Intelligence Scale for Children–Revised (WISC-R).* San Antonio, TX: Psychological Corp.

Wechsler, D. (1991). *Manual for the Wechsler Intelligence Scale for Children–Third Edition (WISC-III).* San Antonio, TX: Psychological Corp.

Werner, E. E. (1986). A longitudinal study of perinatal risk. In D. C. Farran & J. D. McKinney (Eds.), *Risk in intellectual and psychosocial development* (pp. 3–27). San Diego: Academic Press.

Wiggins, J. S. (1973). *Personality and prediction: Principles of personality assessment.* Reading, MA: Addison-Wesley.

Willems, E. P. (1977) Steps toward an ecobehavioral technology. In A. Rogers-Warren & S. F. Warren (Eds.), *Ecological perspectives in behavior analysis* (pp. 39–61). Baltimore, MD: University Park Press.

Wohlwill, J. (1980). Cognitive development in childhood. In O. G. Brim, Jr., & J. Kagan (Eds.), *Constancy and change in human development* (pp. 359–444). Cambridge, MA: Harvard University Press.

Wolf, M. M. (1978). Social validity: The case for subjective measurement or how applied behavior analysis is finding its heart. *Journal of Applied Behavior Analysis, 11,* 203–214.

Woodcock, R. W. (1973). *Woodcock Reading Mastery Test.* Circle Pines, MN: American Guidance Service.

Woodcock, R. W. (1978). *Woodcock-Johnson Psychoeducational Battery.* Boston: Teaching Resources.

Yeaton, W. H., & Sechrest, L. (1981). Critical dimensions in the choice and maintenance of successful treatments: Strength, integrity, and effectiveness. *Journal of Consulting and Clinical Psychology, 49,* 156–167.

Ysseldyke, J., & Geenen, K. (1996). Integrating the special education and compensatory education systems into the school reform process: A national perspective. *School Psychology Review, 25,* 418–430.

## CHAPTER 22

# THE PROBLEM
# OF BIAS IN
# PSYCHOLOGICAL
# ASSESSMENT[1]

CECIL R. REYNOLDS
PATRICIA A. LOWE
ADAM L. SAENZ
*Texas A&M University*

*In God we trust,*
*all others must*
*have data.*

*Unknown*

The issues of bias in psychological testing have been a source of intense and recurring social controversy throughout the history of mental measurement. In England, Burt (1921) raised the issue early in this century. The first investigation into cultural bias, however, can be traced to Binet, originating around 1910 in France (Binet & Simon, 1916) and to Stern (1914), shortly thereafter. Discussions pertaining to test bias are frequently accompanied by polemic debate, decrying the use of mental tests with any minority group members since ethnic minorities have not been exposed to the cultural and environmental circumstances and values of the so-called white middle class. Intertwined within the general issues of bias in tests, one finds the more specific question of whether intelligence tests should be used for educational purposes. Although scientific and societal discussions about differences

among groups on measures of cognitive or intellectual functioning in no way fully encompass the broader topic of bias in mental measurement, there is little doubt that the so-called IQ controversy has received the lion's share of public scrutiny over the years. It has been the subject of numerous publications in the more popular press (see Gould, 1981; Herrnstein & Murray, 1994; or Jensen, 1980, Chap. 1), and court actions and legislation have addressed the use of IQ tests in schools and industry. Court challenges to the use of tests with minorities in educational and vocational settings alike, based on claims of cultural bias, are a common occurrence, despite their limited success.

From Binet to Jensen, many professionals have addressed the problem, with varying and inconsistent outcomes. Unlike the pervasive and polemical nature-nurture argument, the bias issue was until the 1970s largely restricted to the professional literature, except for a few early discussions in the popular press (e.g., Freeman, 1923; Lippmann, 1923a, 1923b). Of some interest is the fact that one of the psychologists who initially raised the question was Cyril Burt (1921), who even in the 1920s was concerned about the extent to which environmental and motivational factors affected performance on intelligence tests. Within the last

[1]Portions of this chapter are based in part on a variety of previous works, including Reynolds (1982a, 1982b, 1983, 1995, in press a), Reynolds and Brown (1984), and Reynolds and Kaiser (1990).

30 years, however, the questions of cultural test bias have burst forth as a major problem far beyond the bounds of scholarly academic debate. The debate over bias has raged in both the professional and the popular press for several decades (e.g., Editorial, *Austin-American Statesman*, October 15, 1997; Fine, 1975). Entangled in the larger issues of individual liberties, civil rights, and social justice, the bias issue has become a focal point for psychologists, sociologists, politicians, and the public. Increasingly, the issue has become a political and legal one, as reflected in numerous court cases and passage in the state of New York (and consideration elsewhere) of what is popularly known as truth-in-testing legislation. The magnitude—and the uncertainty—of the controversy and its outcome are shown in two highly publicized federal district court cases. The answer in trial courts to the question "Are the tests used for pupil assignment to classes for the educable mentally retarded biased against cultural and ethnic minorities?" was yes in California (*Larry P. et al.* v. *Wilson Riles et al.* 1979) and no in Illinois (PASE, 1980), although the *Larry P.* finding has now been overturned by a federal appeals court, giving a consistent nature to these legal outcomes.

The word *bias* has several meanings, not all of which are kept distinct, and researchers and the public do not always know which meaning is being professed. In relation to the present issue, *bias* defined as "partiality toward a point of view or prejudice" and *bias* defined as "a statistical term referring to a constant error in the estimation of some value" (direction as opposed to random error) frequently become coalesced. If the latter meaning did not have the excess baggage of the former, the issue of bias in mental testing would be far less controversial and emotional. However, as indicated in the *Oxford English Dictionary*, *bias* defined as "partiality or prejudice" can be traced at least to the sixteenth century and clearly antedates the statistical meaning. Nevertheless, the discussion of bias in psychological testing as a *scientific* issue should concern only the statistical meaning: whether or not there is systematic error in the measurement of a psychological attribute as a function of membership in one or another cultural or racial subgroup (Reynolds, 1982a, 1982b). This definition, elaborated more technically as required later, will be followed throughout this chapter.

# THE CONTROVERSY OVER BIAS IN PSYCHOLOGICAL TESTING: WHAT IT IS AND WHAT IT IS NOT

Systematic group differences on standardized intelligence and aptitude tests occur as a function of socioeconomic level, race or ethnic background, and other demographic variables throughout the various countries of the world. Black-white differences on IQ measures in the United States have received extensive investigation over the past 50 or 60 years. Jensen (1980), Shuey (1966), Tyler (1965), and Willerman (1979) have reviewed the preponderance of these studies. Results have not changed fundamentally in the last century. Although the results occasionally differ slightly, depending on the age groups under consideration, random samples of blacks and whites show a mean difference of about 1 standard deviation, with the mean score of the whites consistently exceeding that of the black groups. The differences have persisted at relatively constant levels for quite some time and under a variety of methods of investigation. The exception to this is the reduction of the black-white IQ (intelligence quotient) difference on the Kaufman Assessment Battery for Children (K-ABC; Kaufman & Kaufman, 1983) to about .5 standard deviations on the intelligence portion of the scale, a controversial and poorly understood finding (see Kamphaus & Reynolds, 1987, for a discussion). These findings are consistent only for the American black population, however, and other, quite diverse findings appear for African and other black populations (e.g., see Jensen, 1980).

When a number of demographic variables are taken into account (most notably socioeconomic status), the size of the mean black-white difference in the United States reduces to .5 to .7 standard deviations (e.g., Jensen, 1980; Kaufman, 1973; Kaufman & Kaufman, 1973; Reynolds & Gutkin, 1981) but is robust in its appearance. However, not all studies of racial and ethnic group differences on ability tests show higher levels of performance by whites. Although not as thoroughly researched as black-white groups, Asian groups have been shown to perform consistently as well as or better than white groups (Pintner, 1931; Tyler, 1965; Willerman, 1979). Depending on the specific aspect of intelligence under investigation, other racial and ethnic groups show performance at or above the performance level of white groups. There have been arguments over whether any racial differences in intelligence are real or even researchable (e.g., Schoenfeld, 1974), but the reliability across studies is very high, even when relying on self-identification of race, and the existence of the differences is now generally accepted. It should always be kept in mind, however, that the overlap among the distributions of intelligence test scores for the different races is much greater than the degree of differences between the various groups. There is always more within-group variability than between-group variability in performance on psychological tests whether one considers race, ethnicity, gender, or socioeconomic status (SES). The differences are, nevertheless, real ones and are unquestionably complex (e.g., Reynolds & Jensen, 1983).

The issue at hand is the explanation of these group differences. It should be emphasized that both the lower scores of some groups and the higher scores of others need to be explained, although not necessarily, of course, in the same way. The problem was clearly stated by Eells in his classic study of cultural differences (Eells, Davis, Havighurst, Herrick, & Tyler, 1951): "Do the higher test scores of the children from high socioeconomic backgrounds reflect genuine superiority in inherited, or genetic, equipment? Or do the high scores result from a superior environment which has brought about real superiority of the child's 'intelligence'? Or do they reflect a bias in the test materials and not any important differences in the children at all?" (p. 4). Eells et al. also concisely summarized cultural test bias as it applied to differences in SES:

> If (a) the children from different social-status levels have different kinds of experiences and have experiences with different types of material, and if (b) the intelligence tests contain a disproportionate amount of material drawn from the cultural experiences with which pupils from the higher social-status levels are more familiar, one would expect (c) that children from the higher social-status levels would show higher IQs than those from the lower levels. This argument tends to conclude that the observed differences in pupil IQs are artifacts dependent upon the specific content of the test items and do not reflect accurately any important underlying ability in the pupils. (p. 4)

Eells was aware that his descriptions were oversimplifications and that it was unlikely that any one of the three factors alone could explain all of the observed group differences. Loehlin, Lindzey, and Spuhler (1975) concluded that all three factors were probably involved in racial differences in intelligence, as have a myriad of other researchers (e.g., Bouchard & Segal, 1985; Flynn, 1991). In its present, more complex form, the hypothesis of test bias itself considers factors other than culture-loaded items. But the basics of Eells's summary of the hypothesis still hold: group differences stem from characteristics of the test or from aspects of test administration; that is, because mental tests are based largely on middle-class, white values and knowledge, standard interpretations are more valid for those groups and are biased against other groups to the extent that they deviate from those values and knowledge bases.

This position has been reframed slightly over the years, principally by Mercer (1979), who argues that the lower scores of ethnic minorities on aptitude measures can be traced to the Anglocentrism (degree of adherence to white, middle-class value systems) of aptitude measures. Mercer developed an entire system of assessments designed to provide complex demographic corrections to IQs obtained by ethnic minorities that had the effect of equating these groups' IQ mean scores. (This system, known as the SOMPA, had quite a bit of popularity for several years, but it is rarely used today because of its conceptual and psychometric inadequacies.) Lonner (1985) discusses similar issues under the rubric of cultural isomorphism in testing and assessment. Helms (1994) makes similar criticisms of ability tests, rejects most psychometric research on these issues, and posits (quite similar to Mercer's position) that it is the Eurocentric nature of aptitude tests that produce artifactual differences in mean levels of performance across ethnic lines, focusing especially on the performance of black Americans. Helms (1992) asserts that implicit biological or environmental philosophical perspectives used to explain differences in cognitive ability in test performance across racial and ethnic groups are based on deficient conceptualizations of culture and that neither perspective provides useful information about the cultural equivalence (meaning) of test scores across racial or ethnic groups. Racial and ethnic groups are culturally, socially, and cognitively different from members of the dominant culture. Therefore, the examination of cultural equivalence in standard cognitive ability tests is needed. In all of these conceptual models, which are essentially contemporaneous (most even with arguments of Burt as early as 1921), ethnic and other group differences in mean levels of performance on aptitude measures are seen to result from flawed psychometric methodology and not from actual differences in aptitude (see also Harrington, 1975, 1976).

Harrington (1975, 1976) has taken a quite different, experimentally oriented approach to the issue of test bias. In earlier research, Harrington (1968a, 1968b) raised the issue of representation in the test development sample from a slightly different perspective. The small actual number of minority children in the standardization sample is unable to exert any significant impact on the item analysis data, and the content of the test subsequently becomes biased against groups with less than minority representation. Although this argument is not now new, Harrington's (1975, 1976) subsequent approach was quite interesting and innovative. He began by creating experimental populations with varying proportions of minority composition (group membership was defined on a genetic basis). For his experimental populations, he used six species of rats from genetically homogeneous groups. He then set out to develop six intelligence tests, using black and/or white Hebb-Williams types of mazes. Items that showed the greatest item-total correlations within each population were retained for the "IQ" test for that population.

Significant positive correlations occurred between the group mean on any individual test and the degree of group representation in the population used to develop the test. Harrington (1975, 1976) concluded that the greater the proportional representation of a homogeneous group in the test base population (the test development sample), the higher the mean score of the group on the test derived on that population. From further analysis of the data set, Harrington concluded that it is not possible for a test that was developed and normed on a white majority to have equivalent predictive validity with blacks or any other minority group. Harrington's comments on predictive validity are particularly crucial since, as will be seen, most definitions of test bias rely heavily on the differential prediction of some specific criterion (e.g., Anastasi, 1976; Bartlett & O'Leary, 1969; Reynolds, 1995).

While Harrington's (1975, 1976) results are impressive and seem to call into question certain

of the basic psychometric assumptions underlying test construction (particularly as they apply to the development of intelligence tests), his generalizations fail on three major points. First, intelligence and other aptitude tests have most often been shown to have equivalent predictive validity across racial groupings in a variety of circumstances with a rather diverse set of criterion measures. Second, well-documented findings that Japanese Americans, Chinese Americans, and Jewish Americans typically score as well or better than whites on traditional intelligence tests and tests of some specific aptitudes (Gross, 1967; Majoribanks, 1972; Tyler, 1965; Willerman, 1979) are entirely contradictory to Harrington's (1975, 1976) results, given their proportionately small representation in the test development population of such instruments. Third, Harrington's theory of minority-majority group score differences cannot account for different patterns of cognitive performance between minority groups (Bogen, DeZure, Tenhouten, & March, 1972; Dean, 1979; Dershowitz & Frankel, 1975; Reynolds, McBride, & Gibson, 1979; Vance, Hankins, & McGee, 1979; Willerman, 1979).

As described, this hypothesis reduces to one of differential validity. The hypothesis of differential validity for mental tests states that tests measure intelligence more accurately and make valid predictions about the level of intellectual functioning for individuals from the groups on which the tests are mainly based than for those from other groups. Artifactually low scores on an aptitude test could lead to pupils' misassignment to educational programs and unfair denial of admission to college, graduate school, or other programs or occupations in which such test scores are an important decision-making component. This is the issue over which most legal cases have been fought. Furthermore, there would be dramatic implications for whole areas of psychological research and practice if, on the one hand, the test-bias hypothesis is correct: the principal research of the last century in the psychology of human differences would have to be dismissed as confounded and largely artifactual because much of the work is based on standard psychometric theory and testing technology. The result would be major upheavals in the practice of applied psychology, as the foundations of clinical, school, counseling, and industrial psychology are strongly tied to the basic academic field of individual differences. The issue, then, is crucial not only to the science of psychology but also to practice (Lonner, 1985; Reynolds, 1980c). On the other hand, if the test-bias hypothesis is incorrect, group differences are not attributable to the tests and must be due to one or to some combination of factors mentioned by Eells et al. (1951). That group differences in test scores reflect real group differences in ability should be admitted as a possibility, and one that calls for scientific study.

The controversy over test bias should not be confused with that over the etiology (beyond the test itself) of any obtained group differences in test scores (see Reynolds & Kaiser, 1990, for a review). Unfortunately, it has often been inferred that measured differences themselves indicate genetic differences and, therefore, the genetically based intellectual inferiority of some groups. Jensen has consistently argued since 1969 that mental tests measure, to a greater or lesser extent, the intellectual factor *g*, which has a large genetic component, and that group differences in mental test scores may then reflect group differences in *g*. Unless one reads Jensen's statements carefully, it is easy to overlook the many qualifications that he makes regarding these differences and conclusions and his contention that other factors do make significant contributions, albeit lesser ones, to intellectual development.

Jensen or anyone else's position on the genetic basis of actual group differences should be seen as irrelevant to the issue of test bias. However controversial, etiology is a separate issue. It would be tragic to accept the test-bias hypothesis as true if it is, in fact, false. In that case, measured differences would be seen as not real, and children might be denied access to compensatory or remedial programs or to another educational environment best suited to them. Furthermore, research on the basis of group differences would be stifled, as would implementation of programs designed to remediate any deficiencies. The most advantageous position for the true white racist and bigot would be to *favor* the test-bias hypothesis. Acceptance of it *inappropriately* would eventually result in inappropriate pupil assignment, less adaptive education for some groups, and less implementation of long-range programs to raise intellectual performance. Inappropriate confirmation of the test-bias hypothesis would appear to maintain, not break down, the poverty cycle (Birch & Gussow, 1970).

The controversy also does not involve the blatantly inappropriate administration and use of mental tests. The administration of a test in English to an individual for whom English is a second language and whose English language skills are poor is inexcusable, regardless of any bias in the tests themselves. It is of obvious importance that tests are administered by skilled and sensitive professionals who are aware of the factors that may artifactually lower an individual's scores. Considering the use of tests to assign pupils to special education classes or other programs, a question needs to be asked: what would one use instead? Teachers' recommendations are notoriously less reliable and less valid than standardized test scores. Whether special education programs are of adequate quality to meet the needs of children is an important educational question but distinct from the test-bias one.

The controversy over the use of mental tests is complicated further by the fact that resolution of the test-bias question in either direction will not resolve the problem of the role of nonintellective factors that may influence the test scores of *individuals* from any ethnic group. Regardless of any group differences, it is individuals who are tested and whose scores may or may not be accurate. Similarly, it is individuals who are assigned to classes, chosen for universities, placed in jobs or vocations, and accepted or rejected. As indicated by Wechsler (1975) and others, nonintellectual factors, informational content, and emotional-motivational conditions may be reflected in performance on mental tests. The extent to which these factors influence individual as opposed to group performance is difficult to determine. Perhaps with more sophisticated multivariate designs, we will be better able to identify individuals with characteristics that are likely to have an adverse effect on their performance on mental tests. Outside of the major thrust of the issue of bias against groups, potential bias against individuals is a serious problem itself and merits research and analysis. Sternberg (1980), also concerned about individual performance, observed that research on bias has concentrated on "status variables" such as ethnicity rather than on "functional variables" such as cognitive styles and motivation.

## THE NATURE OF PSYCHOLOGICAL TESTING ADDS TO THE CONTROVERSY

The question of bias in mental testing arises largely because of the nature of psychological processes and their measurement (Reynolds & Brown, 1984). Psychological processes, by definition internal and not directly subject to observation or measurement, must be inferred from behavior. Theoretically, in the classic discussion by MacCorquodale and Meehl (1948), a psychological process has the status of an intervening variable if it is used only as a component of a system that has no properties beyond those that operationally define it, but it has the status of a hypothetical construct if it is thought actually to exist and have properties beyond the defining ones. A historical example of a hypothetical construct is a *gene*, which has meaning beyond its use to describe the cross-generational transmission of characteristics. Intelligence, from its treatment in the professional literature, has the status of a hypothetical construct, as does personality.

It is difficult to determine one-to-one relationships among observable events in the environment, the behavior of an organism, and the hypothesized underlying mediational processes. Many classic controversies over theories of learning have revolved around constructs such as expectancy, habit, and inhibition (Goldstein, Krantz, & Rains, 1965; Hilgard & Bower, 1975; Kimble, 1961). Disputes among different camps in learning have been polemical and of long duration. Indeed, there are still disputes about the nature and the number of processes such as emotion and motivation (Bolles, 1975; Mandler, 1975). One of the major areas of disagreement has been over the measurement of psychological processes. It should be expected that intelligence, as one of the most complex psychological processes, involves definitional and measurement disputes that are difficult to resolve.

Assessment of intelligence, like that of many other psychological processes in humans, is accomplished by standard psychometric procedures that are the focus of the bias issue. These procedures, described in detail in general assessment texts (e.g., Anastasi, 1982; Linn, 1989), are only briefly summarized here in relation to the issue of bias. The problems specific to validity are discussed in a separate section.

Similar procedures are used in the development of any standardized psychological test. First, a large number of items are developed that for theoretical or practical reasons are thought to measure the construct of interest. Through a series of statistical steps, those items that best measure the construct in a unitary manner are selected for inclusion in the final test battery. The test is then administered to a sample, which should be chosen to represent all aspects of the population on whom the test will be used. Normative scales based on the scores of the standardization sample then serve as the reference for the interpretation of scores of individuals tested thereafter. Thus, as has been pointed out numerous times, an individual's score is meaningful only in relation to the norms and is a relative, not an absolute, measure. Charges of bias frequently arise from the position that the test is more appropriate for the groups heavily represented in the standardization sample. Whether bias does, in fact, result from this procedure is one of the specific questions that must be empirically addressed.

Intelligence is measured by psychological tests on an interval scale of measurement. Interval scales of measurement have no true zero point and are thus entirely relativistic. To define an interval scale, one begins at the midpoint (usually the mean) of a distribution and measures toward the two ends of the score distribution. Interval scales derived from one test are not directly comparable to interval scales derived from another test and must be compared through regression methods. These added levels of complexity in how the hypothetical construct of intelligence must be measured and compared across tests, and their abstruseness to the media and even most of the intelligencia, increases the level of controversy over bias. The issues surrounding scales of measurement and their implications for score interpretation are not well understood by most clinicians or other psychologists outside of the measurement field.

There are few charges of bias of any kind for physical measures that are on absolute scales, especially ratio scales. Group differences in height, as an extreme example, are not attributed by anyone we know of to any kind of cultural test bias. There is no question about the validity of measures of the height or weight of anyone in any culture. Nor is there any question about one's ability to make cross-cultural comparisons of these absolute measures, even though many of these variables, such as height, weight, and blood pressure, are clearly subject to genetic and environmental interactions.

The whole issue of cultural bias arises because of the procedures involved in the development and application of psychological tests. Psychological tests measure traits that are not directly observable, that are subject to differences in definition, and that are measurable only on a relative scale. From this perspective, the question of cultural bias in mental testing is a subset—obviously of major importance—of the problems of uncertainty and of other possible biases in psychological testing in general. Bias may exist not only in mental tests but in other types of psychological tests as well, including personality, vocational, and psychopathological tests. Making the problem of bias in mental testing even more complex is the fact that not all tests are of the same quality: like Orwell's pigs, some may be more equal than others. There is a tendency for critics and defenders alike to overgeneralize across tests, lumping virtually all tests together under the heading "mental tests" or "intelligence tests." As reflected in the *Mental Measurements Yearbook* (Buros, 1978), professional opinions of mental tests vary considerably, and some of the most used tests are not well respected by psychometricians. Thus, unfortunately, the question of bias must eventually be answered on a virtually test-by-test basis.

# MINORITY OBJECTIONS TO STANDARDIZED PSYCHOLOGICAL TESTING

In 1969, the Association of Black Psychologists (ABP) adopted the following official policy on educational and psychological testing:

> The Association of Black psychologists fully supports those parents who have chosen to defend their rights by refusing to allow their children and themselves to be subjected to achievement, intelligence, aptitude and performance tests which have been and are being used to a) label Black people as uneducable, b) place Black children in "special" classes and schools, c) perpetuate inferior education in Blacks, d) assign Black children to educational tracts, e) deny Black students higher education opportunities, and f) destroy positive growth and development of Black people.

Since 1968, the ABP has sought a moratorium on the use of all psychological and educational tests with the culturally different (Samuda, 1975, and Williams, Dotson, Dow, & Williams, 1980, have provided a more detailed history of these efforts). The ABP carried its call for a moratorium to other professional organizations in psychology and education. In direct response, the

Board of Directors of the American Psychological Association (APA) requested its Board of Scientific Affairs to appoint a group to study the use of psychological and educational tests with disadvantaged students. The committee's report (Cleary, Humphreys, Kendrick, & Wesman, 1975) was subsequently published in an official journal of the APA, *American Psychologist.*

Subsequent to the ABP's policy statement, other groups have adopted policy statements on testing: the National Association for the Advancement of Colored People (NAACP), The National Education Association (NEA), the National Association of Elementary School Principals (NAESP), the American Personnel and Guidance Association (APGA), and others (Williams et al., 1980). The APGA called for the Association for Measurement and Evaluation in Guidance (AMEG), a sister organization, to develop a position paper as well.

The NAACP, at its annual meeting in 1974, adopted a more detailed resolution, demanded a moratorium on standardized testing of minority groups, and called on the ABP to assert leadership in aiding the College Entrance Examination Board (CEEB) to develop standardized tests that have been corrected for cultural bias and fairly measure the amount of knowledge retained by students regardless of his or her individual background. Later that year, the Committee on Testing of the ABP issued a position paper on the testing of blacks that described their intent as well as their position:

1. To encourage, support and to bring action against *all* institutions, organizations and agencies who continue to use present psychometric instruments in the psychological assessment of Black people;

2. To continue efforts to bring about a cessation of the use of standard psychometric instruments on Black people until culturally specific tests are made available;

3. To establish a national policy that in effect gives Black folks and other minorities the right to demand that psychological assessment be administered, interpreted, and supervised by competent psychological assessors of their own ethnic background;

4. To work toward and encourage efforts to remove from the records of all Black students and Black employees that data obtained from performance on past and currently used standard psychometric, achievement,

employment, general aptitude and mental ability tests;

5. To establish a national policy that demands the appropriate proportional representation of competent Black psychologists on all committees and agencies responsible for the evaluation and selection of tests used in the assessment of Black folks;

6. To establish a national policy that demands that all persons engaged in the evaluation, selection and placement of Black folks undergo extensive training so they may better relate to the Black experience;

7. To demand that all Black students improperly diagnosed and placed into special education classes be returned to regular class programs;

8. To encourage and support all suits against any public or private agency for the exclusion, improper classification, and the denial of advancement opportunities to Black people based on performance tests.

The statements by these various organizations *assume* that bias is present in tests and that what is needed is its removal. These assumptions continue in the work of Helms (1992), Mercer (1979), Padilla (1988), and others (e.g., Guilford Press, 1997).

## WHAT ARE POSSIBLE SOURCES OF BIAS?

Black and other minority psychologists have raised many potentially legitimate objections to the use of educational and psychological tests with minorities. Unfortunately, these objections are frequently stated as facts on rational rather than empirical grounds (Chambers, Barron, & Sprecher, 1980; Council for Exceptional Children, 1978; Dana, 1996; Helms, 1992; Hilliard, 1979). The most frequently stated problems fall into one of the following categories:

1. *Inappropriate content.* Black and other minorities have not been exposed to the material in the test questions or other stimulus materials. The tests are geared primarily toward the majority class's homes, vocabulary, and values. Different value systems among cultures may produce cognitively equivalent answers, which are scored as incorrect because of prejudicial value judgments, not differences in ability (Bond, 1987; Butler-

Omololu, Doster, & Lahey, 1984; Weiss, 1987).

2. *Inappropriate standardization samples.* Ethnic minorities are underrepresented in standardization samples used in the collection of normative reference data. Proportionate sampling with stratification by ethnicity is the herald for standardization samples for tests and is done to enhance the accuracy of parameter estimations for scaling purposes. Thus, although represented proportionately, ethnic minorities may appear in test standardization samples in small absolute numbers, and this may bias item selection (e.g., Harrington, 1975, 1976) and also fails to have any impact of significance from these ethnic groups on the tests themselves (Greenlaw & Jensen, 1996). In earlier years, it was not unusual for standardization samples to be all white (e.g., the 1937 Binet and 1949 WISC).

3. *Examiners' and language bias.* Since most psychologists in the United States are white and speak only standard English, they may intimidate black and other ethnic minorities. They are also unable to communicate accurately with minority children—to the point of being intimidating and insensitive to ethnic pronunciation of words on the test. Lower test scores for minorities, then, may reflect only this intimidation and difficulty in the communication process, not lower ability (Clarizio, 1982; Emerling, 1990; Isern, 1986).

4. *Inequitable social consequences.* As a result of bias in educational and psychological tests, minority group members, already at a disadvantage in the educational and vocational markets because of past discrimination and being thought unable to learn, are disproportionately relegated to dead-end educational tracks. Labeling effects also fall under this category (Chipman, Marshall, & Scott, 1991; Payne & Payne, 1991).

5. *Measurement of different constructs.* Related to point 1, this position asserts the tests measure different attributes when used with children from other than the majority culture, the culture on which the tests are largely based, and thus are not valid measures of minority intelligence or personality.

6. *Differential predictive validity.* Although tests may accurately predict a variety of out-

comes for members of the majority culture, they do not predict successfully any relevant behavior for minority group members. Furthermore, there are objections to the use of the standard criteria against which tests are validated with minority cultural groups. For example, scholastic or academic attainment levels in white, middle-class schools are themselves considered by a variety of black psychologists to be biased as criteria (see discussion in Reynolds, 1982a, pp. 179–180).

7. ***Qualitatively distinct minority and majority aptitude and personality.*** Championed by Helms (1992), this position would lead to the conclusion that ethnic minorities and the majority culture are so different as to require different conceptualizations of ability and of personality. Helms, for example, argues the potential existence of a "White g" factor that is separate from "African g" (p. 1090), which would necessitate separate tests for these groups.

Contrary to the situation of the late 1960s and 1970s, when the current controversies resurfaced after some decades of simmering, research has examined these areas of potential bias in assessment. Except for the still unresolved issue of labeling effects, the least amount of research is available on the long-term social consequences of testing, although there are some limited but aging data (e.g., Lambert, 1979). Both of these problems are aspects of testing in general and are not limited to minorities. The problem of the social consequences of educational tracking is frequently lumped with the issue of test bias. Those issues, however, are separate. Educational tracking and special education should be treated as problems of education, not assessment. These are going to become more heavily contested areas for psychologists in the future. The revision of the *Joint Technical Standards for Educational and Psychological Tests and Manuals*, now underway, is likely to add the issue of consequential validity to considerations of test use, reflecting concerns by minority groups over its consequences.

## MEAN SCORE DIFFERENCES AS TEST BIAS

A popular lay view has been that differences in mean levels of scoring on cognitive, achievement, or personality tests among groups constitute bias in tests; however, such differences alone

are clearly not evidence of bias. A number of writers in the professional literature have also taken this position (Adebimpe, Gigandet, & Harris, 1979; Alley & Foster, 1978; Chinn, 1979; Guilford Press, 1997; Hilliard, 1979; G. D. Jackson, 1975; Mercer, 1976; Padilla, 1988; Williams, 1974; Wright & Isenstein, 1977). Those who support this definition of test bias correctly state that there is no valid a priori scientific reason to believe that intellectual or other cognitive performance levels should differ across race. It is the inference that tests that demonstrate such differences are inherently biased, because there can, in reality, be no differences, that is fallacious. Just as there is no a priori basis for deciding that differences exist, there is no a priori basis for deciding that differences do not exist. From the standpoint of the objective methods of science, a priori or premature acceptance of either hypothesis (differences exist vs. differences do not exist) is untenable. As stated by Thorndike (1971), "The presence (or absence) of differences in mean score between groups, or of differences in variability, tells us nothing directly about fairness" (p. 64). Some adherents of the "mean score differences as bias" viewpoint also require that the distribution of test scores in each population or subgroup be identical before one can assume that the test is fair: "Regardless of the purpose of a test or its validity for that purpose, a test should result in distributions that are statistically equivalent across the groups tested in order for it to be considered nondiscriminatory for those groups" (Alley & Foster, 1978, p. 2). Portraying a test as biased regardless of its purpose or validity is psychometrically naive. Mean score differences and unequivalent distributions have been the most uniformly rejected of all criteria examined by sophisticated psychometricians in investigating the problems of bias in assessment. Ethnic group differences in mental test scores are among the best-documented phenomena in psychology, and they have persisted over time at relatively constant levels (Reynolds & Gutkin, 1980, 1981).

Jensen (1980) sees the mean-score-differences-as-bias position as exemplary of the egalitarian fallacy, which contends that all human populations are in fact identical on all mental traits or abilities, i.e., any differences in any aspect of the distribution of mental test scores indicate that something is wrong with the test itself. Such an assumption is totally scientifically unwarranted. There are simply too many examples of specific abilities and even sensory capacities that have been shown to differ unmistakably across human populations. The result of the egalitarian assumption, then, is to remove the investigation of population differences in ability from the realm of scientific inquiry. Logically followed, this fallacy leads to other untenable conclusions as well. Torrance (1980), an adherent of the cultural-bias hypothesis, pointed out that disadvantaged black children in the United States occasionally earn higher scores on creativity tests—and therefore have more creative ability—than many white children because their environment has forced them to learn to "make do" with less and with simpler objects. The egalitarian assumption would hold that this is not true, rather that the content of creativity tests is biased against white or high SES children. At its extreme, the egalitarian fallacy would argue against any genetic influence on intelligence even within groups, seeing all variation as environmental, in the tradition of tabula rasa (see also Nichols, 1978).

The attachment of minorities to the mean-score-differences-as-bias definition is probably related to the nature-nurture controversy at some level. Certainly, data that reflect racial differences on various aptitude measures have been interpreted to indicate support for a hypothesis of genetic differences in intelligence and to imply that one race is superior to another. However, as discussed previously, the so-called nature-nurture issue is not an inextricable component of bias investigation. Assertions about the relative impact of genetic factors on group ability levels step into a separate arena of scientific inquiry, with differing bodies of knowledge and methods of research. It is enough to say that in the arena of bias investigation, mean differences on aptitude, achievement, or personality measures among selected groups are not evidence per se that the measures are biased.

## Culture-free Tests, Culture Loading, and Culture Bias

A third area of bias investigation that has been confusing in both the professional (e.g., Alley & Foster, 1978; Chin, 1979) and the lay literature has been the interpretation of culture loading and culture bias. A test can be culture-loaded without being culturally biased. Culture loading refers to the degree of cultural specificity present in the test or individual items of the test. Certainly, the greater the cultural specificity of a test item, the greater the likelihood of the item's being biased when it is used with individuals from

other cultures. The test item "Who was the first president of the United States?" is a culture-loaded item. However, the item is general enough to be considered useful with school-aged children who have been attending school since first grade in the United States. The cultural specificity of the item is too great, however, to allow the item to be used on an aptitude measure of 10-year-old children from other countries (although it might qualify as an appropriate item on a test of achievement in American history). Virtually all tests in current use are bound in some way by their cultural specificity. Culture loading must be viewed on a continuum from general (defining a culture in a broad, liberal sense) to specific (defining a culture in narrow, highly distinctive terms).

A variety of attempts have been made to develop a culture-free (sometimes referred to as culture-fair) intelligence test (Cattell, 1979). However, the reliability and validity of these tests are uniformly inadequate from a psychometric perspective (Anastasi, 1982; Ebel, 1979). The difficulty in developing a culture-free measure of intelligence lies in making the test irrelevant to intellectual behavior in the culture under study. Intelligent behavior is defined in large part on the basis of behavior judged to be of value to the survival and improvement of the culture and the individuals in it. A test that is culture-blind, then, cannot be expected to predict intelligent behavior in a variety of cultural settings. Once a test has been developed in a culture (a culture-loaded test), generalizability to other cultures or subcultures within the dominant societal framework becomes a matter for empirical investigation; and tests should not be interpreted consistently across cultures without demonstrative evidence for the validity of inferences to be drawn from them.

Jensen (1980) admonishes that when one is investigating the psychometric properties of culture-loaded tests across differing societies or cultures, one cannot assume that simple inspection of the content will determine which tests or items are biased against those cultures or societies not represented in the tests or item content. Tests or items that exhibit characteristics of being culturally loaded cannot be determined to be biased with any degree of certainty unless objective statistical inspection is completed. Jensen refers to the mistaken notion that anyone can judge tests and/or items as being "culturally unfair" on superficial inspection as the "culture-bound fallacy." The issue of item bias is revisited in some detail later in this chapter.

## The Examiner-Examinee Relationship

A view held by many individuals is that white examiners impair the test performance of minority children (Sattler, 1988). Despite empirical evidence to the contrary, this view has become one of the leading myths in psychology (Sattler & Gwynne, 1982). Many psychologists have uncritically accepted this myth as fact and have allowed it to guide their thinking and practice.

The research literature refutes the myth that racial differences in the examiner-examinee relationship contribute substantially to the lowered scores of minority children (Sattler, 1988). Sattler and Gwynne (1982) reviewed 27 published studies on the effects of the examiner's race on children and youths' test scores on individual intelligence tests and other cognitive measures. Preschoolers through twelfth-graders from largely urban cities throughout the United States were administered a wide range of commonly used tests, including the Wechsler Scales, Stanford-Binet: Form L-M, Peabody Picture Vocabulary Test, Draw-a-Man, and Iowa Test of Preschool Development, as well as other tests of cognitive ability. In 23 of the 27 published studies, no significant relationship was found between the race of the examiner (i.e., black or white) and black and white examinees' test scores. The four studies that reported significant differences in the examiner-examinee relationship were found to be lacking in methodological rigor, including inappropriate statistical designs—such as the exclusion of comparison groups and external criteria to evaluate the validity of various procedures—and statistical tests. These findings suggest that Anglo-American examiners have little or no influence on the test score performance of African-American children and youth.

Likewise, if minority children exhibit behaviors during the assessment process that interfere with optimal test performance because of the racial differences between the examiner and examinee, such as fear and/or anxiety, lower test performance would be expected on subtests that are influenced by these behaviors. Research has found that this is not the case. For example, black populations obtain their highest scores on subtests most sensitive to the anxiety levels exhibited by the examinees (Kaufman, 1994).

Moreover, the belief that white examiners are not as effective as Hispanic-American examiners in testing Hispanic-American children and adolescents has received little support (Sattler, 1988). Gerken (1978) found that the examiner's ethnicity (i.e., Anglo-American or Hispanic-American) and linguistic facility (being monolingual or bilingual) did not have a significant effect on four-, five-, and six-year-olds' IQ test scores on the Weschler Preschool and Primary Scale of Intelligence or Leiter International Performance Scale. In addition, Morales and George (1976) reported higher WISC-R (Weschler Intelligence Scale for Children–Revised) Performance IQs for bilingual Hispanic children in grades 1–3 when tested by monolingual non-Hispanic examiners than by bilingual Hispanic examiners, who administered the test in both English and Spanish. Research has not supported the notion that racial differences in the examiner-examinee relationship contributes substantially to the lowered scores of minority children (Sattler, 1988).

Although substantial contributions to the lowered test scores of minority children by this factor is not likely, examiners need to keep in mind the ethnicity of the examinees. Examiners need to be *competent* in the administration and interpretation of test results with minority children. Language and dialectical differences need to be addressed, and selection of appropriate tests and proper test administration are required. During the assessment process, examiners, whether working with children and youths from the dominant or minority culture, must establish rapport and identify *any* nuances in the testing situation that may invalidate performance (Suzuki, Meller, & Ponterotto, 1996). The examiner's competency is the critical issue in test administration and interpretation, not racial differences in examiner-examinee relationships, and is best addressed by rigorous academic and clinical training.

## The Question of Labeling Effects

The relative impact of placing a label on a person's behavior or developmental status has also been a hotly discussed issue in the field of psychometrics in general and bias investigation in particular. The issue undoubtedly has been a byproduct of the practice of using intellectual measures for the determination of mental retardation. Although the question of labeling effects is a viable and important one, it requires consideration in bias research only in much the same way as does the ongoing debate of the nature-nurture question. As the concept of consequential validity grows, this issue will likewise grow in importance. However, there are some important considerations concerning bias in referral for services, diagnosis, and labeling that no interested student of the diagnostic process in psychology can afford to ignore.

Rosenthal (1976) is the researcher most closely associated with the influence of labeling on teachers' and parents' perceptions of a child's ability and potential. Even though his early studies had many methodological and statistical difficulties, labeling effects have been shown in some subsequent experimental studies (Critchley, 1979; Foster & Ysseldyke, 1976; Jacobs, 1978) but not in others (MacMillan, Jones, & Aloia, 1974; McCoy, 1976). However, these studies have generally been of a short-term nature and have usually been conducted under quite artificial circumstances. Typically, participants are asked to rate the behavior or degree of pathology of a child seen on videotape. Categorical labels for the child are systematically varied while the observed behaviors remain constant. The demand characteristics of such a design are substantial. Long-term effects of labeling and special education placement in real-life situations have been examined less vigorously. Comparisons of the effects of formal diagnostic labels with the informal, often cursory, personal labeling process that occurs between teachers and children over the course of a school year, and which is subsequently passed on to the next grade in the teachers' lounge (Dworkin & Dworkin, 1979), need to be made. Although Reynolds (1982b) called for this research in the last decade, this important question has not been addressed. The strict behaviorist position (Ross, 1974, 1976) also contends that formal diagnostic procedures are unnecessary and potentially harmful because of labeling effects. However, whether or not the application of formal labels has detrimental effects remains an open question now, much as it did at the conclusion of a monumental effort to address these important questions throughout the United States in the mid-1970s (Hobbs, 1975).

Even without the application of formal, codified labels by psychologists or psychiatrists, the mental labeling, classification, and appraisal of individuals by people with whom they come into contact are common, constant occurrences (Reynolds, 1979). Auerbach (1971) found that adults often interpret early learning difficulties as primarily emotional disturbances, unrelated to learning problems. According to Bower (1974), children who start the first grade below the mean age of their classmates and are below average in the development of school readiness skills or have behavior problems are more likely to be regarded as emotionally disturbed by the school's staff and are more likely to be referred to residential placement than are their peers. The American Psychological Association (1970) acknowledges that such constant appraisal of individuals occurs at the informal level and in an official position statement takes the stance that specialized, standardized psychological techniques have been developed to supersede our informal, often casual approach to the appraisal of others. The specialized psychological techniques available to the trained examiner add validity and utility to the results of such appraisals. The quantification of behavior permits systematic comparisons of individuals' characteristics with those of a selected reference or norm group. It is not unreasonable to anticipate that the informal labeling of children so often indulged in by teachers and parents is substantially more harmful than accurate psychoeducational diagnostics intended to accrue beneficial activity toward the child. Should noncategorical funding for services to exceptional children become a reality or should the use of normative assessment ultimately be banned, the informal labeling process will continue and, in all likelihood, will exacerbate children's problems.

From the standpoint of cultural *test* bias, the question of labeling children or not labeling children is moot. Cultural test bias is concerned with the accuracy of such labels across some nominal grouping system (typically, race, sex, and SES have been the variables of interest). It is a question of whether race, sex, or any other demographic variable influences the diagnostic process or the placement of a child in special programs, independent of the child's cognitive, emotional, and behavioral status. Several well-designed studies have investigated the influences of race and SES on the class placement recommendations of school and clinical psychologists (i.e., bias in test interpretation). One of the studies investigated teachers' bias as well.

Frame (1979), in what is still one of the best conducted studies to date, investigated the accuracy of school psychologists' diagnoses and consistency of treatment plans in the United States, in light of bias effects associated specifically with race and SES. In Fame's study, 24 school psychologists from a number of school districts diagnostically rated and provided treatment plans for hypothetical cases in which all information except race, SES, and the achievement level of the child's school was held constant. No differences in the accuracy of diagnosis (as defined by interrater reliability) occurred as a function of race or SES. Differences did occur with regard to treatment recommendations, however. With all other data held constant, lower-SES black children were less likely to be recommended for special education placement than their white counterparts or higher-SES black children. A more general trend was for higher-SES children to be recommended for special class placement more often than children of lower SES.

In a similar vein, Matuszek and Oakland (1979) asked whether SES and race influenced teachers' or psychologists' placement recommendations, independent of other characteristics such as adaptive behavior, IQ, and classroom achievement levels. This study included 76 teachers, 53 psychologists, and 106 child studies. Matuszek and Oakland concluded, "The data from this study clearly indicate that they [psychologists] did not make different recommendations on the basis of race." Consistent with the results of Frame (1979), psychologists were more likely to recommend special class placement for high-SES children than for low-SES children when other variables were held constant. Teachers showed no bias in regard to special education placement recommendations on the basis of race or SES. Tomlinson, Acker, Canter, and Lindborg (1977) reported that psychologists recommended special education resource services more frequently for minority (black, Native American, or Asian), than for white children. Placement in a special education class, however, was recommended more frequently for white than minority children. A rather extensive study of placement in classes for the educable mentally retarded (EMR) in California also failed to find any racist intent in the placement of minority children (Meyers, MacMillan, & Yoshida, 1978). In fact, the tendency was *not* to place black children in special education classes, even though they might be failing in the regular classroom. An even earlier study by Mercer (1971), one of the major critics of IQ testing with minorities, reached the same conclusion.

The general tendency not to label black children also extends to community mental health settings. Lewis, Balla, and Shanok (1979) reported that when black adolescents were seen in mental health settings, behaviors symptomatic of schizophrenia, paranoia, and a variety of psychoneurotic disorders were frequently dismissed as only "cultural aberrations," appropriate for coping with the frustrations created by the antagonistic white culture. They further noted that white adolescents who exhibited similar behaviors were given psychiatric diagnoses and referred for therapy and/or residential placement. Lewis et al. contended that this failure to diagnose mental illness in the black population acts as bias in the denial of appropriate services. A tendency for psychologists to regard depressed performance on cognitive tasks by blacks and low-SES groups as a "cultural aberration" has also been shown. An early empirical study by Nalven, Hofmann, and Bierbryer (1969) demonstrated that psychologists generally rated the "true intelligence" of black and lower-SES children higher than that of white and middle-class children with the same WISC IQ. This tendency to overrate the intellectual potential of black and low-SES children probably accounts, at least in part, for psychologists' reluctance to recommend special education placement for these children; it could also be viewed as a discriminatory denial of services, depending on whether the provision of services is considered beneficial or harmful to the individual.

Ethnicity bias in the diagnosis of specific forms of affective disturbance has been the subject of fewer examinations in the literature. However, there is little evidence to suggest that race or ethnicity independently influences a clinical diagnosis, such as autistic disorders or attention deficit hyperactivity disorders (e.g., Cuccaro, Wright, Rownd, Abramson, Waller, & Fender, 1996). In contrast, Cuccaro et al. found that professional perceptions of developmental difficulties suggestive of autism in young children differed as a function of SES. Young children from high-SES backgrounds were more likely to receive a diagnosis of autism than were children from low-SES backgrounds. This result stands in contrast to current knowledge about the relationship between autism and SES. The role of SES as an etiologically relevant factor for autism or the notion that autism is associated with high social class has not been supported in the literature (Gillberg, Steffenburg, & Schaumann, 1991; Steffenburg & Gillberg, 1986; Tsai, Stewart, Faust, & Shook, 1982).

These studies clearly indicate that the demographic variables of race and SES do not, independent of other pupil characteristics, influence or bias psychologists' diagnostic or placement behavior in a manner that would cause blacks or lower-SES children to be labeled inaccurately or placed inappropriately or in disproportionate numbers in special education programs. The empirical evidence, rather, argues in the opposite direction. In the United States, black and low-SES children are *less* likely to be recommended for special education classes than their white or higher-SES peers with similar cognitive, behavioral, and emotional characteristics. The data simply do not support Williams's (1970) and others' (e.g., Guilford Press, 1997; Padilla, 1988) charges that ethnic minority children are placed in special education programs on the basis of race or test bias against blacks. When referrals for placement in gifted and talented programs are considered separately from referrals in general, the disproportionate representation of minorities in special education programs historically can be accounted for by the disproportionately higher incidence of referrals among minority student populations (Tomlinson et al., 1977; Waits & Richmond, 1978).

## The Nature-Nurture Issue

While Bond (1981) observes that there has been a strong pull by professionals and the lay public alike to formulate conclusions regarding the relative impact of genetic and environmental factors on test performance, determining which conclusions are most acceptable can be more a matter of doctrine than of science (Gottfredson, 1994). Bond points out that one reason bias research and intelligence testing has remained so vital a social issue is the pervasive discussions pertaining to race differences and intelligence. He asks the reader to consider this statement: "Test results indicate that White students, on average, achieve higher levels of competence in most academic subjects than Black students, on average" (p. 56). The statement, viewed objectively, merely addresses a presumed result of past academic achievement and does not provide an etiology for observed differences. However, consider this: "Test results indicate that White students as a group possess greater aptitude for academic work than Black students as a group" (p. 56). The seemingly minor change in language quickly elevates the statement into the realm of genetic or innate superiority of one group and, understandably, triggers a decidedly emotional response.

The investigation of test bias can proceed unabated without paying attention to the nature-nurture question. That is not to say that the relative impact of endowment and experience on human intellectual development is not a viable issue in the scientific arena. It is, but it is also burdened with inadequate methodology at present for convincing conclusions to be made. Jensen (1980) notes that data obtained from all test scores are measures of phenotypic and not genotypic expression. The idea of phenotype in scientific terminology refers to the detectable expression of the interaction of both genotype and the environment, which ultimately constitute the characteristics of an organism. Consequently, investigation of test bias is, by nature, investigation of possible bias in the measure of phenotypes. If bias is not found in a purely statistical sense in a test, conclusions drawn about genetic differences between and among groups using the "nonbiased" measure are, simply put, another issue with a plethora of complicating factors.

## THE PROBLEM OF DEFINITION

The definition of test bias has produced considerable continuing debate among measurement and assessment experts (Angoff, 1976; Bass, 1976; Bernal, 1975; Cleary et al., 1975; Cole & Moss, 1989; Cronbach, 1976; Darlington, 1978; Einhorn & Bass, 1971; Flaugher, 1978; Gordon, 1984; Gross & Su, 1975; Helms, 1992; Humphreys, 1973; Hunter & Schmidt, 1976; 1978; Linn, 1976; McNemar, 1975; Moreland, 1995; Novick & Petersen, 1976; Reschly, 1980a; Reynolds, 1978, 1982b, 1995; Reynolds & Brown, 1984; Sawyer, Cole, & Cole, 1976; Schmidt & Hunter, 1974; Thorndike, 1971). Although the resulting debate has generated a number of selection models with which to examine bias, they focus on the decision-making system and not on the test itself. The various selection models are discussed at some length in Hunter and Schmidt (1976), Hunter, Schmidt, and Rauschenberger (1984), Jensen (1980), and Ramsay (1979). The choice of a decision-making system (especially a system for educational decision making) must ultimately be a societal one; as such, it will depend to a large extent on the value systems and goals of the society. Thus, before a model for test use in selection can be chosen, it must be decided whether the ultimate goal is equality of opportunity, equality of outcome, or representative equality (these concepts are discussed in more detail in Nichols, 1978).

Equality of opportunity is a competitive model in which selection is based on ability. As more eloquently stated by Lewontin (1970), under equality of opportunity "true merit . . . will be the criterion of men's earthly reward" (p. 92). Equality of outcome is a selection model based on ability deficits. Compensatory and remedial programs are typically constructed on the basis of the equality-of-outcome model. Children of low ability or children believed to be at high risk for academic failure are selected for remedial, compensatory, or other special educational programs. In a strictly predictive sense, tests are used in a similar manner in both of these models. However, in equality of opportunity, selection is based on the prediction of a high level of criterion performance; in equality of outcome, selection is determined by the prediction of failure or a preselected low level of criterion performance. Interestingly, it is the failure of compensatory and remedial education, bilingual education, and similar special programs to bring the disadvantaged learner to "average" levels of performance that has continued the charges of test bias now in vogue.

The model of representative equality also relies on selection, but selection that is proportionate to numerical representation of subgroups in the population under consideration. Representative equality is typically thought to be independent of the level of ability in each group; however, models can be constructed that select from each subgroup the desired proportion of individuals (1) according to the relative ability level of the group, (2) independent of group ability, or (3) according to some decision rule between these two positions. Even under the conditions of representative equality, it is imperative to employ a selection device (test) that will rank-order individuals within groups in a reliable and valid manner. The best way to ensure fair selection in any of these models is to employ tests that are equally reliable and equally valid for all groups concerned. The tests should also be the most reliable and most valid for all groups under consideration. The question of test bias per se, then, becomes a question of test validity. Test use (i.e., fairness) may be defined as biased or nonbiased only by the societal value system; at present,

this value system in the United States is leaning strongly toward some variant of the representative equality selection model. As noted, all models are facilitated by the use of a nonbiased test. That is, the use of a test with equivalent cross-group validities allows the most parsimonious selection model, greatly simplifying the creation and application of the selection model that has been chosen.

This leads to the essential definitional component of test bias. Test bias refers in a global sense to *systematic* error in the estimation of some "true" value for a group of individuals. The key word here is *systematic;* all measures contain error and in all cultural settings, but this error is assumed to be random unless shown to be otherwise. Bias investigation is a statistical inquiry that does not concern itself with culture loading, labeling effects, or test use or test fairness. Concerning the last of these, Jensen (1980) comments, "Unbiased tests can be used unfairly and biased tests can be used fairly. Therefore, the concepts of bias and unfairness should be kept distinct . . . [A] number of different, and often mutually contradictory, criteria for fairness have been proposed, and no amount of statistical or psychometric reasoning per se can possibly settle any arguments as to which is best" (pp. 375–376).

There are three types of validity as traditionally conceived: content, construct, and predictive (or criterion-related). Test bias may exist in any or all of these categories of validity. Although no category is completely independent of any other category, each is discussed separately here for clarity and convenience. (All true evidence of validity is as likely as not to be construct validity, and other, more detailed divisions, including this one, are for convenience of discussion). Frequently encountered in bias research are the terms *differential validity* and *single-group validity*. The latter refers to the phenomenon of a score interpretation being valid for one group but not another. Differential validity refers to a condition in which an interpretation is valid for all groups concerned, but the degree of validity varies as a function of group membership. Although these terms have been most often applied to predictive or criterion-related validity (validity coefficients are then examined for significance and compared across groups), the concepts of single-group and differential validity are equally applicable to content and construct validity.

# RESEARCH STRATEGIES AND RESULTS

The methodologies available for research into bias in mental tests have grown rapidly in numbers and sophistication over the last two decades. Extensive reviews of the questions to be addressed in such research and their corresponding methodologies are available in Camilli and Shepard (1994), Jensen (1980), Reynolds (1982b; 1995), and Reynolds and Brown (1984). We review the most popular methods, along with a summary of findings from each area of inquiry. The sections are organized primarily by methodology in each content area of research (i.e., research into content, construct, and predictive validity).

## Bias in Content Validity

Bias in the item content of intelligence tests is one of the favorite topics of those who decry the use of standardized tests with minorities (e.g., Hilliard, 1979; Jackson, 1975; Williams, 1974; Wright & Isenstein, 1977). The earliest work in cultural test bias centered on content. Typically, critics review the items of a test and single out specific items as being biased because (1) the items ask for information that an ethnic minority or a disadvantaged person has not had equal opportunity to learn; (2) the scoring of the items is improper since the test's author has arbitrarily decided on the only correct answer, and ethnic minorities are inappropriately penalized for giving answers that would be correct in their own culture but not that of the author; and/or (3) the working of the questions is unfamiliar, and an ethnic minority who may "know" the correct answer may not be able to respond because he or she does not understand the question. Each of these and related criticisms, when accurate, have the same basic empirical result: the item becomes relatively more difficult for ethnic minority group members than for the majority population; for example, an ethnic minority and a member of the majority culture with the same standing on the construct in question will respond differently to such biased items. This leads directly to a definition of content bias for aptitude tests that allows empirical assessment of the phenomenon:

> An item or subscale of a test is considered to be biased in content when it is demonstrated to be relatively more difficult for members of one group than for members of another when the general ability level of the groups

being compared is held constant and no reasonable theoretical rationale exists to explain group differences on the item (or subscale) in question.

With regard to achievement tests, the issue of content bias is considerably more complex. Exposure to instruction, the general ability level of the group, and the accuracy and specificity of the sampling of the domain of items are important variables in determining whether the content is biased (see Schmidt, 1983). Research into item (or content) bias with achievement tests has typically, and perhaps mistakenly, relied on methodology appropriate for determining item bias in aptitude tests. Nevertheless, research that examines both types of instruments for content bias has yielded quite comparable results. Items on personality tests may be perceived differently across cultures as well, or appropriate responses may vary dramatically and quite properly deserve different interpretations cross-culturally. If so, the items will behave differently across groups for individuals with the same relative standing. This, too, is detectable through analyses of item response data across groups.

One method of locating "suspicious" test items requires item difficulties to be determined separately for each group under consideration. if any individual item or series of items appears to be exceptionally difficult relative to other items on the test for the members of any group, the item is considered potentially biased and removed from the test. A once thought to be more exacting and widespread approach to identifying biased items involves analysis of variance (ANOVA) and several closely related procedures, in which the group by item interaction term is of interest (Angoff & Ford, 1973; Cardall & Coffman, 1964); until the late 1980s, ANOVA was the most popular empirical approach (Camilli & Shepard, 1987).

The definition of content bias just presented actually requires that the relative differences in item difficulty between groups be the same for every item on the test. Thus, in the ANOVA procedure, the group by item interaction should not yield a significant result. Whenever the differences in items are not uniform (a significant group by item interaction does exist), one may contend that these are biased items. Earlier in this area of research, it was hoped that the empirical analysis of tests at the item level would result in the identification of a category of items having similar content as biased and that such items could then be avoided in future test development (Flaugher, 1978). Very little similarity among items determined to be biased has been found. No one has been able to identify those characteristics of an item that cause it to be biased. It does seem that poorly written, sloppy, and ambiguous items tend to be identified as biased with greater frequency than those items typically encountered in a well-constructed, standardized instrument. The variable at issue, then, may be the item reliability. Item reliabilities are typically not large, and poorly written or ambiguous test items easily can have reliabilities that are approaching zero. Decreases in reliability have long been known to increase the probability of the occurrence of bias (Linn & Werts, 1971). Informal inventories and locally derived tests are much more likely to be biased than professionally written, standardized tests, which have been scrutinized for bias in the items and whose item characteristics are known.

Once items have been identified as biased under the procedures described, attempts have been made to eliminate "test bias" by eliminating the offending items and rescoring the tests. As pointed out by Flaugher (1978) and Flaugher and Schrader (1978), however, little is gained by this tactic. Mean differences in performance between groups are affected only slightly, and aptitude and achievement tests become more difficult for everyone involved since the eliminated items typically have moderate to low difficulty. When race by item interactions have been found, the interaction typically accounts for a very small proportion of variance. For example, in analyzing items on the WISC-R, Jensen (1976), Miele (1979), and Sandoval (1979) found the interaction accounted for only 2% to 5% of the variance in performance. Using a similar technique with the Wonderlic Personnel Test, Jensen (1977) found the interaction to account for only about 5% of the test score variance. Thus, the elimination of the offending items can be expected to have little if any significant effect. These analyses have been of a post hoc nature (i.e., after the tests have been standardized), however, and the use of empirical methods for determining item bias during the test development phase (as with the K-ABC is to be encouraged.

The ANOVA methodology is appealing conceptually but has some significant problems, even though it was the dominant methodological approach to the issue of item bias through the 1980s. Camilli and Shepard (1987) have provided convincing examples, although using contrived data, that ANOVA methods often miss biased items, in both directions, and identify some items as biased that are not. An algebraic demonstration of the reasons for this is provided in Camilli and Shepard (1994), who conclude that ANOVA should no longer be used.

Based on their thorough and compelling analyses of methods for detecting biased items, Camilli and Shepard (1994) recommend methods derived from item response theory to detect what has come to be known as differential item functioning (DIF). The DIF statistics work by identifying all items in a test that function differently from the standards for different groups. Ideally, once these items are identified, a logical analysis is conducted to determine why they are relatively more difficult for one or more groups. Based on the analysis, a subset of DIF items are identified as biased and are eliminated from the test. Therefore, DIF indexes are merely raw or uninterpretable indexes that detect multidimensionality of an item set in a test or subtest. Significant DIFs do not necessarily mean that particular items are biased. Biased items are determined according to the *interpretation* of the items within a coherent and substantive framework about their relevancy to the construct being measured. In other words, if items tap traits irrelevant to the intended construct, as determined through careful judgment and additional empirical investigation, these items are considered to be biased. For example, if baseball is the topic of a reading passage on the reading comprehension section of the verbal portion of the Graduate Record Examination (GRE), and items relating to baseball on the reading comprehension section produce significant DIFs when comparing males and females, further analyses would need to be conducted to determine if these items were measuring reading comprehension or tapping some other trait, such as prior knowledge about baseball. Through careful deliberations and further empirical study, if it is found that these items are tapping the examinees' knowledge about baseball instead of reading comprehension, these items would be labeled as biased and would be removed from the test.

Item response theory (IRT) is primarily concerned with the probability of a particular response to a test item as a function of the examinee's relative position on the latent trait. The IRT's principal conceptual unit, the item characteristic curve (ICC), represents this relationship. The ICC is determined by three parameters, $a$, $b$, and $c$. The *a* parameter represents the discrimination power of an item (i.e., how well an item distinguishes examinees who score high or low on the latent trait). Discrimination corresponds to the slope of the ICC. The *b* parameter represents the difficulty of an item and is measured in the same scale units as the latent trait. The *b* parameter is located along the latent trait scale at the point where the probability of a correct response is equal to $(1 + c)/2$. The *c* parameter, the guessing parameter, represents the probability of examinees who score low on the latent trait answering a test item correctly. The *c* parameter is the lower asymptote of the ICC. These three parameters determine the shape of the ICC. Diagrammatic representation of one group's ICC for one item is depicted in Figure 22.1.

Different IRT models are derived from estimates of these three different parameters. The three-parameter (3P) model is made up of the three parameter estimates and is the most commonly used and recommended IRT model, especially with multiple-choice items because of the complexity of the data (Camilli & Shepard, 1994). A two-parameter (2P) model and one-parameter (1P), or Rasch, model also exist. Camilli and Shepard and Hambleton, Swaminathan, and Rogers (1991) describe these models more extensively. The selection of an appropriate IRT model is critical, as failure to use an adequate model will lead to inaccurate estimates of item parameters and decrease the utility of IRT techniques. Computer programs are available for estimating item and latent parameters, such as LOGIST and BILOG, using joint maximum likelihood (JML) or marginal maximum likelihood (MML) techniques, respectively.

In applying IRT to DIF, the ICCs of the two different groups (group A and group B) are compared on the same item. Conceptually, the ICCs for the two groups are plotted on the same scale, and the area between the two ICCs is measured to determine the degree of DIF. The area between the two ICCs, for group A and group B, DIF, is depicted in Figure 22.2. The DIF procedure requires not only equating item and latent parameter estimates for the the two different groups but also selecting appropriate IRT measures and tests for DIF. If the DIF index is significant, further analysis of this item and all the other items with significant DIFs are needed to determine if they are biased.

To plot the two ICCs on the same scale, the parameters or estimates of the item and latent pa-

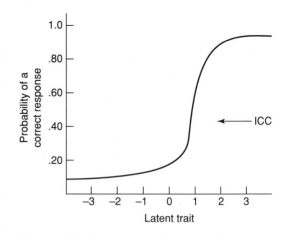

**FIGURE 22.1    An item characteristic curve.**

rameters must be equated or scaled in the same metric. There are two techniques for equating the item parameter estimates, the anchor test method and separate sample method. The latter requires running the IRT analyses separately for each group and then transforming the parameter estimates so they can be placed on a common scale. This method involves explicit equating. A more implicit equating approach, recommended by Camilli and Shepard (1994), is the anchor test method, which requires that estimated parameters for both groups be simultaneously equated during a single computer estimation run by using MML. During the computer run, all items except the item of interest, known as the anchor items, are constrained. This procedure is repeated for each item on the test so that biased items will not spoil the estimation of the examinee's latent trait.

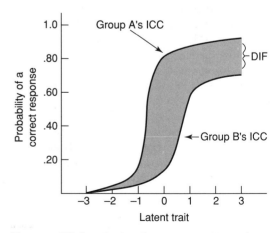

**FIGURE 22.2    A visual representation of DIF. DIF is the shaded region between group A and group B's item characteristic curves.**

To determine the degree of DIF, an IRT method for measuring the size of the area or differential performance of the two groups on a test is needed. The IRT measures of DIF include simple area indexes, *b* parameter difference indexes, pseudo-IRT indexes, and probability difference indexes. In the probability difference indexes, the area between the ICCs is weighted. The probability difference statistics, signed probability difference controlling for the latent trait (SPD-Θ) and unsigned probability difference controlling for the latent trait (UPD-Θ), are calculated for uncrossed or crossed ICCs, respectively, to determine the degree of DIF. According to Camilli and Shepard (1944), probability difference indexes have more stability and power and are the preferred methods for determining the degree of DIF because they have outperformed the other measures of DIF.

Once the degree of DIF is measured, an IRT statistical test is used to determine if DIF is statistically significantly different from the null hypothesis. The IRT statistical tests include the test of *b* differences, item drift method, Lord's chi-square, bootstrap and jackknife methods, and model comparison measures. Descriptions of these IRT statistical tests are found in Camilli and Shepard (1994).

Model comparison procedures are the recommended approaches to test for significance of DIF, according to numerous researchers and psychometricians (Camilli & Shepard, 1994; Judd & McClelland, 1989; Thissen, Steinberg, & Wainer, 1993). In this approach, the relative fit of the compact model and augmented model are compared. The compact model is a model in which all of the estimated parameters of an item, *a*, *b*, and *c*, for all of the groups are identical, yielding a single ICC for all groups. In contrast, the augmented model allows one, two, or all three of the estimated parameters to vary, yielding different ICCs for the different groups. To determine which model provides a better fit of the data, an inferential test statistic based on a natural log transformation of a likelihood ratio that is approximately distributed as a chi-square is calculated. If the inferential test statistic is significant, significant DIF exists for that one item. This procedure is repeated for all items on a test. Once this procedure is completed, those items with significant DIFs undergo further empirical study and deliberation to determine if they are biased. If the items are biased, they are removed from the test.

The IRT methods provide the most sensitive tests for DIF when the models accurately describe the data. These are the preferred approaches in research to obtain generalizable results; however, these methods are computer-intensive and require large samples for testing the model fit. As a result, contingency table (CT) approaches, using nonparametric methods, are often utilized for detecting DIF in applied settings during test development when sample size, resources, time, and programmatic experience are limited.

In comparison to the IRT methods, CT approaches correspond closely to the visual inspection of the area between the ICC curves (Camilli & Shepard, 1994). In addition, these approaches use observed scores rather than measures of latent traits in statistical analyses (Ackerman, 1991). Contingency table methods for testing DIF include summed chi-square, Mantel-Haenszel chi-square, and logistic regression. Camilli and Shepard provide a detailed description of these CT methods for testing DIF. Both CT and IRT methods have their advantages; however, the decision whether to use one or the other often boils down to sample size.

A CT approach, the Mantel-Haenszel technique, was used to examine possible racial, ethnic, and gender bias on the Guide to the Assessment of Test Session Behavior (GATSB). The subjects were 534 boys and 528 girls, ranging in age from 6 to 16, of Anglo-American, black, or Hispanic ethnicity. Only 10 out of 80 items were found to have significant DIFs, and the 10 significant DIF items barely exceeded the chance rate. This result lends support to the notion that the GATSB shows no signs of item bias across gender and ethnicity (Nandakumar, Glutting, & Oakland, 1993).

The IRT models, such as those to detect DIF, are conceptually similar to other models, such as ANOVA. The IRT models to detect DIF are primarily superior to previous methods because they are less sample-dependent, and they allow one to estimate multiple item statistics more precisely than a technique like ANOVA. Using the item characteristic curves, DIF more accurately and readily detects when the probability of a particular response changes as a function of some nominal variable (e.g., ethnicity or gender) for individuals with the same relative standing on the latent trait being assessed.

Early studies, using a partial correlation procedure developed independently by Stricker

(1982) and Reynolds, Willson, and Chatman (1984), have found no systematic bias in measures of intelligence and related aptitudes. In very large N studies, Reynolds et al. found no systematic bias against American blacks or against women on measures of English vocabulary. Willson, Nolan, Reynolds, and Kamphaus (1989), using the same partialling methodology, examined DIF on the mental processing scales of the Kaufman Assessment Battery for Children, concluding that "there appears to be little evidence of systematic race or gender bias" (p. 289).

With multiple-choice tests, another level of complexity is added to the examination of content bias. With a multiple-choice question, three or four distractors are typically given, in addition to the correct response. Distractors may be examined for their attractiveness (the relative frequency with which they are chosen) across groups. When distractors are found to be disproportionately attractive for members of any particular group, the item may be defined as biased. When items are constructed to have an equal distribution of responses to each distractor for the total test population, chi-square can be used to examine the distribution of choices for each distractor for each group (Burrill, 1975).

Jensen (1976) investigated the distribution of wrong responses for two multiple-choice intelligence tests, the Peabody Picture Vocabulary Test (PPVT) and Raven's Progressive Matrices (the Raven). These two tests were individually administered to 600 white and 400 black children between the ages of 6 and 12. The analysis of incorrect responses for the PPVT indicated that the errors were distributed in a nonrandom fashion over the distractors for a large number of items. However, no racial bias in response patterns occurred since the disproportionate choice of distractors followed the same pattern for blacks and whites. On the Raven, blacks made different types of errors than whites, but only on a small number of items. Jensen followed up these items and compared the black response pattern to the response pattern of white children at a variety of age levels. For every item showing differences in black-white response patterns, the black response patterns could be duplicated by the response patterns of whites approximately two years younger than blacks.

Veale and Foreman (1983) have advocated inspecting multiple-choice tests for bias in distractor or "foil" response distribution as a means of refining tests *before* they are finalized for the marketplace. They note that there are many instances in which unbiased external criteria (such as achievement or ability) or culturally valid tests are not readily accessible for detecting bias in the measure under study. They add that inspection of incorrect responses to distractor items can often lead to greater insight into cultural bias in any given question than would inspection of the percentage of correct responses across groups. Veale and Foreman provide the statistical analyses for their "overpull probability model," along with the procedures for measuring cultural variation and diagramming the source of bias in any given item.

Investigation of item bias during test development is certainly not restricted to multiple-choice items and methods such as those outlined by Veale and Foreman (1983). The possibilities are numerous (see Jensen, 1980, Chap. 9). For example, Scheuneman (1987) used the results of linear methodology on GRE item data to show interesting influences on black-white performance when item characteristics (vocabulary content, one true or one false answer to be selected, diagrams to be used or not used, antonym items, etc.) are uniformly investigated. Although Scheuneman indicates that future research of this type should reduce the number of variables to address (there were 16 hypotheses), the results nonetheless suggest that bias or content research across groups is a viable way in which to determine whether differential effects can "be demonstrated through the manipulation of relatively stable characteristics of test items" (p. 116). Scheuneman presented pairs of items, with the designated characteristic of a question format under study present in one item and absent or modified in the other. Paired experimental items were administered in the experimental section of the GRE General Test, given in December 1982. Results indicated that certain "item elements"— common in general form to a variety of questions—appeared to have a differential impact on black and white performance. For example, significant group by version interactions were seen for one correct true versus one correct false response and for adding or modifying prefixes and suffixes to the stimulus word in antonym items. The question is thus raised as to whether the items showing differential impact are measuring the content domain (e.g., verbal, quantitative, or analytical thinking) or, to some degree, an aspect of an "element" in the presentation.

Jensen (1976) has pursued another approach

TABLE 22.1    **Cross-racial Analysis of Content Bias for Five Major**
**Intelligence Scales**

| | Cross-racial Correlation of Rank Order of Item Difficulties[a] | |
|---|---|---|
| Scale | Black-white Correlations[b] | White and Mexican-American Correlations[b] |
| Peabody Picture Vocabulary Test (Jensen, 1974) | .99 (.79), .98 (.65) | .98 (.78), .98 (.66) |
| Raven's Progressive Matrices (Jensen, 1974) | .99 (.98), .99 (.96) | .99 (.99), .99 (.97) |
| Stanford-Binet Intelligence Scale (Jensen, 1976) | .96 | |
| Wechsler Intelligence Scale for Children–Revised (Jensen, 1976) | .95 | |
| (Sandoval, 1979)[c] | .98 (.87) | .99 (.91) |
| (Miele, 1979) (1949 WISC) | .96, .95 | |
| Wonderlic Personnel Test (Jensen, 1977) | .94 (.81) | |

[a]Correlation of *P* decrements across race is included in parentheses if reported.

[b]Where two sets of correlations are presented, data were reported separately for males and females and males are listed first. The presence of a single correlation indicates that data were pooled across gender.

[c]Median values for the 10 WISC-R subtests, excluding Digit Span and Coding.

to the identification of biased items. According to Jensen, if a test contains items that are disproportionately more difficult for one group of examinees than another, the correlation of *P* decrements between adjacent items will be low for the two groups. (*P* decrement is the difference in the difficulty index, *P*, from one item of a test to the next item. Typically, ability test items are arranged in ascending order of difficulty.) Jensen (1974, 1976) also contends that if a test contains biased items, the correlation between the rank order of item difficulties for one race with another will also be low. Jensen (1974, 1976, 1977) calculated cross-racial correlations of item difficulties for large samples of black and white children on five major intelligence tests: PPVT, Raven, Revised Stanford-Binet Intelligence Scale Form L-M, WISC-R, and Wonderlic Personnel Test. Cross-racial correlations of *P* decrements were reported for several of the scales. Jensen's results are summarized in Table 22.1, along with the results of several other investigators who also used Jensen's methodology.

As is readily apparent in Table 22.1, little evidence to support any consistent content bias in any of the scales was found. The consistently large magnitude of the cross-racial correlations of *P* decrements is impressive and indicates a general lack of content bias in the instruments as a whole. As previously noted, however, some individual items were identified as biased; yet they collectively accounted for only 2% to 5% of the variance in performance differences and showed no detectable pattern in content.

This method has proved popular with some test publishers who want to look at the items on a test as a group, despite the fact that this approach may be overly sensitive. Using the Detroit Tests of Learning Aptitude (DTLA-3), Hammill (1991) reported correlations of *P* decrements exceeding .90 for all subtests, with most exceeding .95. Similar results have been reported for other aptitude measures. On the 14 subtests of the Test of Memory and Learning (TOMAL), Reynolds and Bigler (1994) report correlations across *P* decrements by gender and ethnicity that all exceed .90, with most again above .95.

Another approach is to use the partial correlation between a demographic or other nominal variable and item score, where the correlation between total test score and the variable of interest has been removed from the relationship. If a significant partial correlation exists, say, between race and an item score after the race–total test score relationship has been partialed, the item is performing differentially across race within ability level. Bias has been demonstrated at this point under the definition just offered. The use of the partial correlation (typically a partial point-biserial $r$) is the simplest and perhaps the most powerful of the item bias detection approaches, but its development is relatively recent and its use not yet common. An example of its application may be found in Reynolds et al. (1984).

A common practice in recent times has been a return to the expert judgment of professionals and members of minority groups in the item selection for new psychological and educational tests. This approach was used in development of the K-ABC, the revision of the Wechsler Preschool and Primary Scale of Intelligence (WPPSI-R), the PPVT-R, and a number of other contemporary tests. The practice typically asks for an "armchair" inspection of individual items as a means of locating and expurgating biased components in the measure under development. Since, as previously noted, no detectable pattern or common characteristic of individual items statistically shown to be biased has been observed (given reasonable care in the item-writing stage), it seems reasonable to question this approach. The bulk of scientific data since the pioneering work of McGurk (1951) has not supported the position that anyone can—upon surface inspection—detect the degree to which any given item will function differentially across groups. Several researchers since McGurk's time have identified items as being disproportionately more difficult for minority group members than for members of the majority culture and have subsequently compared their results with a panel of expert judges. The data have provided some interesting results.

Although examples of the failure of judges to identify biased items now abound (Camilli & Shepard, 1994) and show that judges are as right about an item almost as often as they are wrong, two studies demonstrate this failure most clearly. After identifying the eight least and eight most racially discriminating items on the Wonderlic Personnel Test, Jensen (1976) asked panels of five black psychologists and five white psychologists to sort out the eight most and eight least discriminating items when only these 16 items were presented to them. The judges sorted the items at a level no better than chance. Sandoval and Mille (1979) conducted a more extensive analysis, using items from the WISC-R. These researchers had 38 black, 22 Mexican-American, and 40 white

university students from Spanish, history, and education classes identify items from the WISC-R that would be more difficult for a minority child than a white child and items that would be equally difficult for each group. A total of 45 WISC-R items were presented to each judge, including the 15 most difficult items for blacks as compared to whites, the 15 most difficult items for Mexican Americans as compared to whites, and the 15 items with the most nearly identical difficulty indexes for minority and white children. The judges were asked to read each question and determine whether they thought the item was (1) easier for minority than for white children, (2) easier for white than for minority children, or (3) of equal difficulty for white and minority children. Sandoval and Mille's results indicated that the judges were not able to differentiate accurately between items that were more difficult for minorities and items that were of equal difficulty across groups. The effects of the judges' ethnic background on the accuracy of their judgments were also considered. Minority and nonminority judges did not differ in their ability to identify accurately biased items, nor did they differ with regard to the type of incorrect identification they tended to make. Sandoval and Mille's two major conclusions were that "(1) judges are not able to detect items which are more difficult for a minority child than an Anglo child, and (2) the ethnic background of the judge makes no difference in accuracy of item selection for minority children" (p. 6). In each of these studies, the most extreme items were used, which should have given the judges an advantage.

Anecdotal evidence is also available to refute the assumption that armchair analyses of test bias in item content are accurate. By far, the most widely cited example of a biased intelligence test item is item 6 of the WISC-R Comprehension subtest: "What is the thing to do if a boy (girl) much smaller than yourself starts to fight with you?" This item is generally considered to be biased against black children in particular because of the scoring criteria. According to the item's critics, the most logical response for a black child is to "fight back," yet this is a zero-point response. The correct (two-point) response is to walk away and avoid fighting with the child—a response that critics claim invites disaster in the black culture, where children are taught to fight back and would not know the correct white response. Black responses to this item have been investigated empirically in several studies, with the same basic results: the item is relatively easier for black children than for white children. When all items on the WISC-R are ranked separately according to the difficulty level for blacks and whites, this item is the forty-second least difficult item (where one represents the easiest item) for black children and the forty-seventh least difficult item for white children (Jensen, 1976). Miele (1979), in a large $N$ study of bias, reached a similar conclusion, stating that this item "is relatively easier for Blacks than it is for Whites" (p. 163). The results of these empirical studies with large samples of black and white children in the United States are unequivocal: when matched for overall general intellectual skill, more black than white children will answer this item correctly—the very item most often singled out as blatant example of the inherent bias of intelligence test against blacks (see also Reynolds & Brown, 1984).

Even without empirical support for its accuracy, a number of prestigious writers support the "face validity" approach of using a panel of minority judges to identify "biased" test items (Anastasi, 1982; Kaufman, 1979; Sandoval & Mille, 1979). Those who support the continued use of this technique see it as a method of gaining greater rapport with the public. As pointed out by Sandoval and Mille, "Public opinion, whether it is supported by empirical findings, or based on emotion, can serve as an obstacle to the use of a measurement instrument" (p. 7). The elimination of items that are offensive or otherwise objectionable to any substantive segment of the population for whom the test is intended seems an appropriate action that may aid in the public's acceptance of new and better psychological assessment tools. However, the subjective judgment approach should not be allowed to supplant the use of more sophisticated analyses in the determination of biased items. The subjective approach should serve as a supplemental procedure, and items identified through this method (provided that some interrater agreement can be obtained, an aspect of the subjective method yet to be demonstrated) can be eliminated when a psychometrically equivalent (or better) item can be obtained as a replacement and the intent of the item is kept intact (e.g., with a criterion-referenced measure, the new item must be designed to measure the same objective).

It is remarkable how difficult it is to call such research to the attention of practitioners and the public. Used to identify and delete offensive or objectionable content, judgmental review has much to offer. As a method of detecting biased items, it has nothing to offer. Nevertheless, the myth of the method persists. Responding during a television interview (in Austin, Texas, on October 14, 1997) to a recent lawsuit against the Texas Education Agency (TEA), alleging that the TEA competency test, which must be passed to receive a high school diploma, is biased against minorities (these claims, incidentally, being based on the mean differences definition of test bias), a ranking TEA testing official defended the test by stating, essentially, that it could not be biased because members of different minority groups are asked to read the items prior to their use and identify those biased against minorities, which are then deleted from the test. While this procedure may identify offensive items, it is irrelevant to the question of bias and cannot substitute for DIF statistics.

Considerably less work has been conducted in all areas of bias in personality testing, where there would appear to be greater opportunity for cultural, social, and ethnic factors to produce bias. Research on item bias of personality measures, though less extensive than with aptitude measures, has produced results similar to those with aptitude measures (Moran, 1990; Reynolds, in press b; Reynolds & Harding, 1983).

Evaluations of behavior rating scales are also meager but at present support the use of parental ratings in the diagnosis of childhood psychopathology independent of the child's ethnic background (e.g., see Mayfield & Reynolds, in press). A common set of items seems to measure consistently a variety of personality and behavioral traits for whites, blacks, and various Hispanic and Latin populations residing in the United States (James, 1995; Mayfield & Reynolds, in press; Reynolds & Kamphaus, 1992).

Thus far, this section has focused on the identification of biased items. Several studies that evaluate other hypotheses have provided data relevant to the issue of content bias of psychological tests, specifically the WISC-R; although now largely superseded in practice by WISC-III, little data about bias is specifically available for this new scale.

Jensen and Figueroa (1975) investigated black-white differences in mental test scores as a function of differences in Level I (rote learning and memory) and Level II (complex cognitive processing) abilities. These researchers tested a large number of blacks and whites on the WISC-R Digit Span and then analyzed the data separately for digits forward and digits backward. On the one hand, the content of the procedures is the same. Thus, if score differences are due only to bias in content validity, score differences across race should remain constant for the two tasks. On the other hand, since the information-processing demands of the two tasks are quite different (Reynolds, 1997), the relative level of performance on the two tasks should not be the same for blacks and whites who differ in their ability to process information according to the demands of the two tasks. Jensen and Figueroa found the latter to be the case. The black-white score difference on digits backward was more than twice the magnitude of the difference for digits forward. Granted, this methodology can provide only indirect evidence about the content validity of an instrument; however, its importance is in providing a different view of the issues and an alternative research strategy. Since these results do not indicate any content bias in the Digit Span subtest, they add to a growing body of literature that strongly suggests the lack of cultural bias in well-constructed, standardized tests, such as the WISC-R.

Another study (Reynolds & Jensen, 1983) examined each of the 12 WISC-R subtests for cultural bias against blacks, using a variation of the group by item ANOVA methodology. Reynolds and Jensen matched 270 black children with 270 white children from the WISC-R standardization sample on the basis of gender and WISC-R Full Scale IQ. The IQs were required to match within 1 standard error of measurement (about three points). When multiple matching cases were encountered, children were matched on the basis of SES. Matching the two groups of children on the bases of the Full Scale IQ essentially equated the two groups for g. Therefore, examining black-white differences in performance on each subtest of the WISC-R made it possible to determine which, if any, of the subtests were disproportionately difficult for blacks or whites. A significant F ratio in the multivariate analysis of variance (MANOVA) for the 12 WISC-R subtests was followed with univariate F tests between black and white means on each of the 12 WISC-R subtests. A summary of the Reynolds and Jensen results is presented in Table 22.2. Blacks exceeded whites in performance on two subtests: Digit Span and Coding. Whites exceeded blacks in performance on three subtests: Comprehension, Object Assembly, and Mazes. A trend was apparent for blacks to perform at a higher level on the Arithmetic subtest, whereas

TABLE 22.2 **Means, Standard Deviations, and Univariate Fs for Comparison of Performance on Specific WISC-R Subtests by Groups of Blacks and Whites Matched for WISC-R Full Scale IQ**

| WISC-R variable | Blacks | | Whites | | $D^a$ | $F^b$ | $\rho$ |
| --- | --- | --- | --- | --- | --- | --- | --- |
| | $\overline{X}$ | SD | $\overline{X}$ | SD | | | |
| Information | 8.40 | 2.53 | 8.24 | 2.62 | −.16 | 0.54 | NS[c] |
| Similarities | 8.24 | 2.78 | 8.13 | 2.78 | −.11 | 0.22 | NS |
| Arithmetic | 8.98 | 2.62 | 8.62 | 2.58 | −.36 | 2.52 | .10 |
| Vocabulary | 8.21 | 2.61 | 8.27 | 2.58 | +.06 | 0.06 | NS |
| Comprehension | 8.14 | 2.40 | 8.58 | 2.47 | +.44 | 4.27 | .05 |
| Digit Span | 9.51 | 3.09 | 8.89 | 2.83 | +.62 | 6.03 | .01 |
| Picture Completion | 8.49 | 2.88 | 8.60 | 2.58 | +.11 | 0.18 | NS |
| Picture Arrangement | 8.45 | 2.92 | 8.79 | 2.89 | +.34 | 1.78 | .01 |
| Block Design | 8.06 | 2.54 | 8.33 | 2.76 | +.27 | 1.36 | NS |
| Object Assembly | 8.17 | 2.90 | 8.68 | 2.70 | +.51 | 4.41 | .05 |
| Coding | 9.14 | 2.81 | 8.65 | 2.80 | −.49 | 4.30 | .05 |
| Mazes | 8.69 | 3.14 | 9.19 | 2.98 | +.50 | 3.60 | .05 |
| Verbal IQ | 89.63 | 12.13 | 89.61 | 12.07 | −.02 | 0.04 | NS |
| Performance IQ | 89.29 | 12.22 | 90.16 | 11.67 | +.87 | 0.72 | NS |
| Full Scale IQ | 88.61 | 11.48 | 88.96 | 11.35 | +.35 | 0.13 | NS |

[a]White-black difference.

[b]Degrees of freedom = 1,538.

[c]Not significant.

whites tended to exceed blacks on the Picture Arrangement subtest. Although these results can be interpreted to indicate bias in several of the WISC-R subtests, the actual differences were very small (typically on the order of 0.10–0.15 standard deviations), and the amount of variance in performance associated with ethnic group membership was less than 5% in each case. The results are also reasonably consistent with Jensen's theory on mental test score differences and their relationship to Level I and Level II abilities. The Digit Span and Coding subtests are clearly the best measures of Level I abilities on the WISC-R, whereas Comprehension, Object Assembly, and Mazes are more closely associated with Level II abilities.

From a large number of studies, employing a wide range of methodology, a relatively clear picture emerges: content bias in well-prepared, standardized tests is irregular in its occurrence, and no common characteristics of items that are found to be biased can be ascertained by expert judges (minority and nonminority). The variance in group score differences on mental tests associated with ethnic group membership when content bias has been found is relatively small (typically ranging from 2% to 5%). Even this small amount of bias may be seriously questioned as basically methodological artifacts. Although the search for common "biased" item characteristics will continue, and psychologists must pursue the public relations issues of face validity, armchair claims of cultural bias in aptitude tests have found no empirical support in a large number of actuarial studies that contrast the performance of a variety of racial groups on items and subscales of the most widely employed intelligence scales in the United States; neither differential for single-group validity has been demonstrated. These results, however, apply only to groups in which there is a common language among examiners. Test translations are a different issue and require a different line of study altogether.

## Bias in Construct Validity

There is no single method for the accurate determination of the construct validity of educational and psychological tests. Defining bias in construct validity thus requires a general statement that can be researched from a variety of viewpoints with a broad range of methodologies. The following, rather parsimonious definition is proffered:

Bias exists in regard to construct validity when a test is shown to measure different hypothetical traits (psychological constructs) for different groups; that is, differing interpretations of a common performance are shown to be appropriate as a function of ethnicity, gender, or another variable of interest.

As befits the concept of construct validity, many different methods have been employed to examine existing tests for potential bias. One of the most popular and necessary empirical approaches to investigating construct validity is factor analysis (Anastasi, 1982; Cronbach, 1970). Factor analysis, as a procedure, identifies clusters of test items or clusters of subtests of psychological or educational tests that correlate highly with one another and less so or not at all with other subtests or items. It thus allows one to determine patterns of interrelationships of performance among groups of individuals. For example, if several subtests of an intelligence scale load highly on (are members of) the same factor and if a group of individuals scores high on one of these subtests, it would be expected to score at a high level on other subtests that load highly on that factor. Psychologists attempt to determine, through a review of the test content and correlates of performance on the factor in question, what psychological trait underlies performance; or, in a more hypothesis-testing approach, they will make predictions concerning the pattern of factor loadings. Hilliard (1979), one of the more vocal critics of IQ tests on the basis of cultural bias, has pointed out one of the potential areas of bias in comparisons of the factor-analytic results of tests across races: "If the IQ test is a valid and reliable test of 'innate' ability or abilities, then the factors which emerge on a given test should be the same from one population to another, since 'intelligence' is asserted to be a set of mental processes. Therefore, while the configuration of scores of a particular group on the factor profile would be expected to differ, logic would dictate that the factors themselves would remain the same" (p. 53).

Although researchers do not necessarily agree that identical factor analyses of an instrument speak to the innateness of the abilities being measured, consistent factor-analytic results across populations do provide strong evidence that whatever is being measured by the instrument is being measured in the same manner and is, in fact, the same construct within each group. The information derived from comparative factor analysis across populations is directly relevant to the use of educational and psychological tests in diagnosis and other decision-making functions. Psychologists, to make consistent interpretations of test score data, must be certain that a test measures the same variable across populations.

Two basic approaches, each with a number of variations, have been employed to compare factor-analytic results across populations. The first and more popular approach asks how similar the results are for each group; the second and less popular approach asks whether the results show a statistically significant difference between groups. However, little has been done with the latter approach in the context of test bias research.

A number of techniques have been developed to measure the similarity of factors across groups. The two most common methods of determining factorial similarity or factorial invariance involve the direct comparison of factor loadings across groups. The two primary techniques for this comparison are (1) the calculation of a coefficient of congruence (Harman, 1976) between the loadings of corresponding factors for two groups and (2) the simple calculation of a Pearson product-moment coefficient of correlation between the factor loadings of the corresponding factors. The latter technique, although used with some frequency, is less satisfactory than the coefficient of congruence since in the comparison of factor loadings certain assumptions that underlie the Pearson $r$ may be violated. When one is determining the degree of similarity of factors, a value of .90 or greater is typically, though arbitrarily, indicative of equivalent factors (factorial invariance). However, the most popular methods of calculating factorial similarity produce quite similar results (Reynolds & Harding, 1983), at least in large $N$ studies. In contrast to Hilliard's (1979) strong statement that studies of factorial similarity across race have not been reported in the technical literature, many such studies have dealt with a number of different tests.

Because the WISC and its successor, the WISC-R—now superseded by the WISC-III, although as yet no such bias research is available on the latter—have been the most widely employed individual intelligence tests with school-aged children, it is appropriate that the cross-race structure of these two instruments has received extensive investigation for both normal and referral populations of children. Using a large, random sample, Reschly (1978) compared the factor structure of the WISC-R across four racially identifiable groups: whites, blacks, Mexican Americans, and Native American Papagos, all from the southwestern United States. Consistent with the findings of previous researchers with the 1949 WISC, Reschly (1978) reported substantial congruency of factors across races when the two-factor solutions were compared (the two-factor solution typically iterated Wechsler's a priori grouping of the subtests into a Verbal Scale and a Performance, or Nonverbal, Scale). The 12 coefficients of congruence for comparisons of the two-factor solution across all combinations of racial groupings ranged only from .97 to .99, denoting factorial equivalence of the solution across groups. Reschly also compared three-factor solutions (three-factor solutions typically include Verbal Comprehension, Perceptual Organization, and Freedom from Distractibility factors), finding congruence only between whites and Mexican Americans. These findings are also consistent with previous research into the WISC. The $g$ factor in the WISC-R was shown to be congruent across race, as was also demonstrated by Miele (1979) for the WISC. Reschly concluded that the usual interpretation of the WISC-R Full Scale IQ as a measure of overall intellectual ability appears to be equally appropriate for whites, blacks, Mexican Americans, and Native American Papagos. Jensen (1985) has presented compelling data, indicating that the black-white discrepancy seen in major tests of aptitude primarily reflects the $g$ factor. Reschly also concluded that the Verbal-Performance distinction on the WISC-R is equally appropriate across race and that there is strong evidence for the integrity of the WISC-R's construct validity for a variety of populations. Support for Reschly's (1978) conclusions is available from a variety of other studies of the WISC and WISC-R.

Several studies that compare the WISC-R factor structure across races for normal and referral populations of children have also provided increased support for the generality of Reschly's (1978) conclusions and those of the other investigators just cited. Oakland and Feigenbaum (1979) factor-analyzed the 12 WISC-R subtests' intercorrelations separately for stratified (race, age, sex, and SES) random samples of normal white, black, and Mexican-American children from an urban school district in the northwestern United States. Pearson $r$'s were calculated between corresponding factors for each group. For the $g$ factor, the black and white correlation between factor loadings was .95, the Mexican-American and white correlation was .97, and the black and Mexican-American correlation was .96. Similar comparisons across all WISC-R variables produced correlations ranging only from .94–.99. Oakland and Feigenbaum concluded that the results of their factor analyses "do not reflect bias with respect to construct validity for these three racial-ethnic . . . groups" (p. 973).

Gutkin and Reynolds (1981) determined the factorial similarity of the WISC-R for groups of black and white children from the WISC-R standardization sample. This study is particularly important in determining the construct validity of the WISC-R across races because of the sample used in the investigation. The sample included 1,868 white and 305 black children obtained in a stratified random sampling procedure designed to mimic the 1970 U.S. Census Bureau data on the basis of age, sex, race, SES, geographic region of residence, and community size. The similarity of the WISC-R factor structure across race was investigated by comparing the black and white groups for the two- and three-factor solutions on (1) the magnitude of unique variances, (2) the pattern of subtest loadings on each factor, (3) the portion of total variance accounted for by common factor variance, and (4) the percentage of common factor variance accounted for by each factor. Coefficients of congruence comparing the unique variances, the *g* factor, the two-factor solutions, and the three-factor solutions across races all achieved a value of .99. The portion of total variance accounted for by each factor was the same in both the two- and three-factor racial groups. Gutkin and Reynolds concluded that for white and for black children, the WISC-R factor structure was essentially invariant and that no evidence of single-group or differential construct validity could be found.

Subsequent studies, comparing the WISC-R factor structure for referral populations of white and Mexican-American children, have also strongly supported the construct validity of the WISC-R across races. Dean (1979) compared three-factor WISC-R solutions across races for whites and Mexican Americans referred because of learning problems in the regular classroom. Analyzing the 10 regular WISC-R subtests, Dean reported coefficients of congruence between corresponding factors of .84 for factor I (Verbal Comprehension), .89 for factor 2 (Perceptual Organization), and .88 for factor 3 (Freedom from Distractibility). Although not quite

reaching the typical value of .90 that is required for indicating equivalent factors, Dean's results do indicate a high degree of similarity. The relative strength of the various factors was also highly consistent across races.

Gutkin and Reynolds (1980) also compared two- and three-factor principal-factor solutions to the WISC-R across race for referral populations of white and Mexican-American children. Gutkin and Reynolds made additional comparisons of the factor solutions derived from their referral sample to solutions derived by Reschly (1978; personal communication, 1979), and also to solutions from the WISC-R standardization sample. Coefficients of congruence for the Gutkin and Reynolds two-factor solutions for whites and Mexican Americans were .98 and .91, respectively. The *g* factor showed a coefficient of congruence value of .99 across races. When Gutkin and Reynolds compared their solutions with those derived by Reschly (1978) for normal white, black, Mexican-American, and Papago children, as well as with results based on the WISC-R standardization sample, the coefficients of congruence all exceeded .90. When three-factor solutions were compared, the results were more varied but also supported the consistent similarity of WISC-R factor-analytic results across race.

DeFries et al. (1974) administered 15 mental tests to large samples of Americans of Japanese ancestry and Chinese ancestry. After examining the pattern of intercorrelations among the 15 tests for each of these two ethnic groups, DeFries et al. concluded that the cognitive organization of the two groups was virtually identical. In reviewing this study, Willerman (1979) concluded, "The similarity in factorial structure [between the two groups] suggests that the manner in which the tests are constructed by the subjects is similar regardless of ethnicity and that the tests are measuring the same mental abilities in the two groups" (p. 468).

At the adult level, Kaiser (1986) and Scholwinski (1985) have analyzed the Wechsler Adult Intelligence Scale–Revised (WAIS-R) and reported substantial similarity between factor structures for black and white samples obtained from the WAIS-R standardization data. Kaiser completed separate hierarchical analyses for all black subjects ($N = 192$) and white subjects ($N = 1,664$) in the WAIS-R standardization sample and calculated coefficients of congruence of .99 for the *g* factor; .98 for the Verbal factor; and .97 for the Performance, or nonverbal, factor.

Scholwinski selected 177 black and 177 white subjects from the standardization sample, closely matched in age, sex, and Full Scale IQ. Separate factor analyses again showed that structures generated from the Wechsler format showed strong similarity across black-white groups beyond childhood and adolescent levels of development. At the preschool level, factor-analytic results also tend to show consistency of construct validity across races (Reynolds, 1982a).

As is appropriate for studies of construct validity, comparative factor analysis has not been the only method of determining whether single-group or differential validity exists. Another method of investigation involves comparing reliability estimates of internal consistency across groups. Internal consistency reliability is determined by the degree to which the items are all measuring a similar construct. To be unbiased in construct validity, internal consistency estimates should be approximately equal across races. This characteristic has been investigated with blacks, whites, and Mexican Americans for a number of popular aptitude tests.

With groups of black and white adults, Jensen (1977) calculated internal consistency estimates (using the Kuder-Richardson 21 formula) for the Wonderlic Personnel Test (a frequently used employment and aptitude test). Kuder-Richardson 21 values of .86 and .88 were found, respectively, for blacks and whites. Using Hoyt's formula, Jensen (1974) determined internal consistency estimates of .96 on the PPVT for each of three groups of children: blacks, whites, and Mexican Americans. When children were categorized by gender in each racial grouping, the values ranged from only .95 to .97. On Raven's Progressive Matrices (colored), internal consistency estimates were also quite similar across race and gender, ranging only from .86 to .91 for the six race-gender groupings. Thus, Jensen's research with three popular aptitude tests shows no signs of differential or single-group validity with regard to the homogeneity of test content or the consistency of measurement across groups.

Sandoval (1979) and Oakland and Feigenbaum (1979) have extensively investigated internal consistency of the various WISC-R subtests (excluding Digit Span and Coding, for which internal consistency analysis is inappropriate) for whites, blacks, and Mexican Americans. Both of these studies included large samples of children, Sandoval's including over 1,000. Sandoval found internal consistency estimates to be within .04 of one another for all subtests except Object Assembly. This subtest was most reliable for blacks (.95), and about equally reliable for whites (.79) and Mexican Americans (.75). Oakland and Feigenbaum reported internal consistency estimates that never differed by more than .06 among the three groups, again with the exception of Object Assembly. In this instance, Object Assembly was most reliable for whites (.76), with about equal reliabilities for blacks (.64) and Mexican Americans (.67). Oakland and Feigenbaum also compared reliabilities across gender, finding highly similar values for males and females. Dean (1979) examined the internal consistency of the WISC-R for Mexican-American children tested by white examiners. He reported internal consistency reliability estimates consistent with, although slightly exceeding, values reported by Wechsler (1974) for the predominantly white standardization sample. The Bender-Gestalt Test has also been reported to have similar internal consistency estimates for whites (.84), blacks (.81), and Mexican Americans (.72) and for males (.81) and females (.80) (Oakland & Feigenbaum, 1979).

Several other methods have also been used to determine the construct validity of popular psychometric instruments across races. Since intelligence is considered a developmental phenomenon, the correlation of raw scores with age has been viewed as one measure of constrict validity for intelligence tests. Jensen (1976) reported that the correlations between raw scores on the PPVT and age were .79 for whites, .73 for blacks, and .67 for Mexican Americans. For Raven's Progressive Matrices (colored), correlations for raw scores with age were .72 for whites, .66 for blacks, and .70 for Mexican Americans. Similar results are apparent for the K-ABC (Kamphaus & Reynolds, 1987). Thus, in regard to increase in scores with age, the tests behave in a highly similar manner for whites, blacks, and Mexican Americans.

In the review work of Moran (1990) and in a search for more recent work, it is apparent that only a few studies of the differential construct validity of personality tests have been undertaken, despite large mean differences across ethnicity and gender on such popular measures as the stalwart MMP. A look at the newer MMPI-2 manual suggests gender difference in construct validity but provides no real evidence either way. A few studies of factorial similarity of such instruments as the Revised Children's Manifest Anxiety Scale show little bias and high degrees of similarity by ethnicity and gender (Moran, 1990; Reynolds & Paget, 1981).

Construct validity of a large number of popular psychometric assessment instruments has been investigated across races and sexes with a variety of minority and white children and with a divergent set of methodologies (see Reynolds, 1982b, for a review of methodologies). All roads have led to Rome: no consistent evidence of bias in construct validity has been found with any of the many tests investigated. This leads to the conclusion that psychological tests (especially aptitude tests) function in essentially the same manner, that test materials are perceived and reacted to in a similar manner, and that tests measure the same construct with equivalent accuracy for blacks, whites, Mexican Americans, and other American minorities of both sexes and at all levels of SES. Single-group validity and differential validity have not been found and probably do not exist in well-constructed and well-standardized psychological and educational tests.

## Bias in Predictive or Criterion-related Validity

Evaluating bias in predictive validity of educational and psychological tests is less closely related to the evaluation of group mental test score differences than to the evaluation of individual test scores in a more absolute sense. This is especially true for aptitude (as opposed to diagnostic) tests, in which the primary purpose of administration is the prediction of some specific future outcome or behavior. Internal analyses of bias (such as in content and construct validity) are less confounded than analyses of bias in predictive validity, however, because of the potential problems in bias in the criterion measure. Predictive validity is also strongly influenced by the reliability of criterion measures, which frequently are poor. The degree of relationship between a predictor and a criterion is restricted as a function of the square root of the product of the reliabilities of the two variables.

Arriving at a consensual definition of bias in predictive validity is also a difficult task, as has already been discussed. Yet, from the standpoint of the practical applications of aptitude and intelligence tests, predictive validity is the most crucial form of validity in relation to test bias. Much of the discussion in professional journals concerning bias in predictive validity has centered on models of selection. These issues have been discussed previously in this chapter and are not repeated here. Since this section is concerned with bias in respect to the test itself and not the social or political justification of any one particular selection model, the Cleary et al. (1975) definition, slightly rephrased here, provides a clear and direct statement of test bias with regard to predictive validity:

> A test is considered biased with respect to predictive validity if the inference drawn from the test score is not made with the smallest feasible random error or if there is constant error in an inference or prediction as a function of membership in a particular group.

This definition is a restatement of previous definitions by Cardall and Coffman (1964), Cleary (1968), and Potthoff (1966) and has been widely accepted, although certainly not without criticism (e.g., Bernal, 1975; Linn & Werts, 1971; Schmidt & Hunter, 1974; Thorndike, 1971).

Oakland and Matuszek (1977) examined procedures for placement in special education classes under a variety of models of bias in prediction and demonstrated that the smallest number of children is misplaced when the Cleary et al. (1975) conditions of fairness are met. However, under "quota" system requirements, Oakland and Matuszek favor the Thorndike (1971) condition of selection. The Cleary et al. definition is also apparently the one used in the U.S. government guidelines on testing and has been held in at least one court decision (*Cortez* v. *Rosen*, 1975) to be the only historically, legally, and logically required condition of test fairness (Ramsay, 1979)—although apparently the judge in the *Larry P. et al.* v. *Wilson Riles et al.* (1979) decision in the U.S. federal court system adopted the mean-score-differences-as-bias approach. A variety of educational and psychological personnel have adopted the Cleary et al. regression approach to bias (Reynolds, 1982b, 1995).

The evaluation of bias in prediction under the Cleary et al. (1975) definition (the regression definition) is quite straightforward. With simple regression, prediction takes the form of $\hat{Y}_i = aX_i + b$, where $a$ is the regression coefficient and $b$ is a constant. When this equation is graphed (forming a regression line), $a$ represents the slope of the regression line and $b$ the $Y$ intercept. Since our definition of fairness in predictive validity requires errors in prediction to be independent of group membership, the regression line formed for any pair of variables must be the same for each group for whom predictions are to be made.

Whenever the slope or the intercept differs significantly across groups, there is bias in prediction if one attempts to use a regression equation based on the combined groups. When the regression equation for two (or more) groups are equivalent, prediction is the same for all groups. This condition is referred to variously as homogeneity of regression across groups, simultaneous regression, or fairness in prediction. Homogeneity of regression across groups is illustrated in Figure 22.3. In this case, the single regression equation is appropriate with all groups, any errors in prediction being random with respect to group membership (i.e., residuals uncorrelated with group membership). When homogeneity of regression does not occur, for fairness in prediction to occur, separate regression equations must be used for each group.

In actual clinical practice, regression equations are seldom generated for the prediction of future performance. Instead, some arbitrary or perhaps statistically derived cutoff score is determined, below which failure is predicted. For school performance, IQs that are 2 or more standard deviations below the test mean are used to infer a high probability of failure in the regular classroom if special assistance is not provided for the student in question. Essentially, then, clinicians are establishing mental prediction equations that are assumed to be equivalent across races, genders, and so on. Although these mental equations cannot be readily tested across groups, the actual form of criterion prediction can be compared across groups in several ways. Errors in prediction must be independent of group membership. If regression equations are equal, this condition is met. To test the hypothesis of simultaneous regression, slopes and intercepts must both be compared. An alternative method is the direct examination of residuals through an ANOVA or similar design (Reynolds, 1980a).

Potthoff (1966) has described a useful technique that allows one to test simultaneously the equivalence of regression coefficients and intercepts across $K$ independent groups with a single $F$ ratio (the Potthoff equations may also be found in Reynolds, 1982b). A cognate analysis may be done, using the general linear model procedure in SAS. If a significant $F$ results, the researcher may then test the slopes and intercepts separately for information about which value differs. When homogeneity of regression does not occur, three basic conditions can result: (1) intercept constants differ,

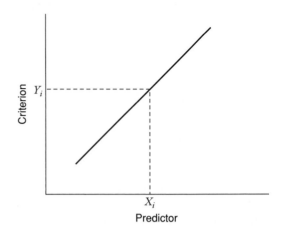

**FIGURE 22.3    Equal slopes and intercepts result in homogeneity of regression that causes the regression lines for group a, group b, and the combined group c to be identical.**

(2) regression coefficients (slopes) differ, or (3) slopes and intercepts differ. These conditions are depicted pictorially in Figures 22.4, 22.5, and 22.6, respectively.

The regression coefficient is related to the correlation coefficient between the two variables and is one measure of the strength of that relationship. When intercepts differ and regression coefficients do not, a situation such as that shown in Figure 22.3 results. Relative accuracy of prediction is the same for the two groups ($a$ and $b$); yet, the use of a regression equation derived by combining the two groups results in bias that works against the group with the higher mean

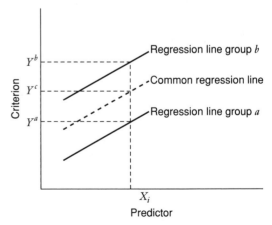

**FIGURE 22.4    Equal slopes with differing intercepts result in parallel regression lines and a constant bias in prediction.**

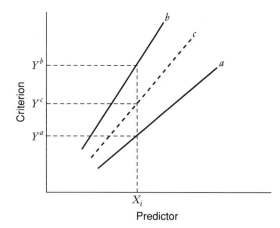

**FIGURE 22.5  Equal intercepts and differing slopes result in nonparallel regression lines with the degree of bias dependent on the distance of the individual's score (x$_i$) from the origin.**

criterion score. Since the slope of the regression line is the same for all groups, the degree of error in prediction remains constant and does not fluctuate as a function of an individual's score on the independent variable. That is, regardless of the group *b* member's score on the predictor, the degree of underprediction in performance on the criterion is the same. As illustrated in Figure 22.4, the use of the common score of $Y^c$ for a score of $X$ overestimates how well members of group *a* will perform and underestimates the criterion performance of members of group *b*.

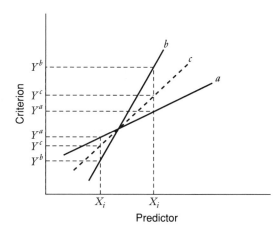

**FIGURE 22.6  Differing slopes and intercepts result in the complex condition where the amount and the direction of the bias are a function of the distance of an individual's score from the origin.**

In Figure 22.5, nonparallel regression lines illustrate the case in which intercepts are constant across groups but the slope of the line is different for each. Here, too, the performance of the group with the higher mean criterion score is typically underpredicted when a common regression equation is applied. The amount of bias in prediction that results from using the common regression line is the distance of the score from the mean. The most difficult, complex case of bias is represented in Figure 22.6. Here we see the result of significant differences in slopes and intercepts. Not only does the amount of bias in prediction accruing from the use of a common equation vary in this instance, but also the actual direction of bias can reverse, depending on the location of the individual's score in the distribution of the independent variable. Only in the case of Figure 22.6 do members of the group with the lower mean criterion score run the risk of having their performance on the criterion variable underpredicted by the application of a common regression equation.

A considerable body of literature has developed about the differential predictive validity of tests across races for employment selection and college admissions. However, virtually nothing appears in this regard with reference to personality tests (Moran, 1990), and this is a major weakness.

In a review of 866 black-white test validity comparisons from 39 studies of test bias in personnel selection, Hunter, Schmidt, and Hunter (1979) concluded that there was no evidence to substantiate hypotheses of differential or single-group validity with regard to the prediction of job performance for blacks and whites. A number of studies have also focused on differential validity of the Scholastic Aptitude Test (SAT) in the prediction of college performance, typically measured by grade point average (GPA). In general, these studies have found either no differences in the prediction of criterion performance for blacks and whites or a bias (underprediction of the criterion) against whites (Cleary, 1968; Cleary et al., 1975). When bias against whites has been found, the differences between actual and predicted criterion scores, although statistically significant, have been quite small.

Reschly and Sabers (1979) evaluated the validity of WISC-R IQs in the prediction of Metropolitan Achievement Tests (MAT) performance (Reading and Math subtests) for whites, blacks,

Mexican Americans, and Native American Papagos. The choice of the MAT as a criterion measure in studies of predictive bias is particularly appropriate since item analysis procedures were employed (as described earlier) to eliminate racial bias in content during the test construction phase. Anastasi (1982) has described the MAT as an excellent model of an achievement test designed to reduce or eliminate cultural bias. Reschly and Sabers's comparison of regression systems indicated bias in the prediction of the various achievement scores. Again, however, the bias produced generally significant underprediction of white performance when a common regression equation was applied. Achievement test performance of the Native American Papago group showed the greatest amount of overprediction of all nonwhite groups. Although some slope bias was evident, Reschly and Sabers typically found that intercept bias resulted in parallel regression lines. Reynolds and Hartlage (1979) investigated the differential validity of Full Scale IQs from the WISC-R and its 1949 predecessor, the WISC, in predicting reading and arithmetic achievement for black and white children who had been referred by their teachers for psychological services in a rural, southern school district. Comparisons of correlations and a Potthoff (1966) analysis to test for identity of regression lines revealed no significant differences in the ability or function of the WISC and WISC-R to predict achievement for these two groups. Reynolds and Gutkin (1980) replicated this study for the WISC-R with large groups of white and Mexican-American children from the Southwest. Reynolds and Gutkin contrasted regression systems among WISC-R Verbal, Performance, and Full Scale IQs and the "academic basics" of reading, spelling, and arithmetic. Only the regression equation between the WISC-R Performance IQ and arithmetic achievement differed for the two groups. The difference in the two equations was due to an intercept bias that resulted in the overprediction of achievement for the Mexican-American children. Reynolds, Gutkin, Dappen, and Wright (1979) also failed to find differential validity in the prediction of achievement for males and females with the WISC-R.

In a related study, Hartlage, Lucas, and Godwin (1976) compared the predictive validity of what they considered to be a relatively culture-free test (Raven's Progressive Matrices) with a more culture-loaded test (the 1940 WISC) for a group of low-SES, disadvantaged, rural children. Hartlage et al. found that the WISC had consistently larger correlations with measures of reading, spelling, and arithmetic than did the Raven's Matrices. Although it did not make the comparison with other groups that is necessary for firm conclusions, the study does support the validity of the WISC, which has been the target of many claims of bias in the prediction of achievement for low-SES, disadvantaged, rural children. Henderson, Butler, and Goffeney (1969) also reported that the WISC and the Bender-Gestalt Test were equally effective in the prediction of reading and arithmetic achievement for white and nonwhite groups, although their study had a number of methodological difficulties, including heterogeneity of the nonwhite comparison group. Reynolds et al. (1985) evaluated the predictive validity of the K-ABC for blacks and for whites. Occasional evidence of bias was found in each direction, but mostly in overprediction of the academic attainment levels of blacks. However, for most of the 56 Potthoff (1966) comparisons of regression lines, no evidence of bias was revealed.

Weiss and Prifitera (1995) examined the differential prediction of the Wechsler Individual Achievement Test (WIAT) scores, based on the Wechsler Intelligence Scale for Children–III (WISC-III) Full Scale IQ in a sample ($N = 1,000$) of black, Hispanic, and white children, ranging in age from 6 to 16. Slopes and intercepts across groups were examined. The results were consistent with previous findings of the WISC-III predecessors (i.e., WISC-R and WISC) in supporting the general absence of bias in predicting achievement from IQ.

Bossard et al. (1980) published a regression analysis of test bias on the 1972 Stanford-Binet Intelligence Scale for separate groups of black and white children. Neither regression systems nor correlations differed at $p < .05$ for the prediction of the basic academic skills of reading, spelling, and arithmetic achievement for these two groups of referred children.

Jensen (1980) and Sattler (1974) have reviewed a series of studies comparing the predictive validity of group IQ measures across races. Typically, regression systems have not been compared in these studies; instead, the researchers have compared only the validity coefficients across races—a practice that tells only whether the test is actually nonbiased. The comparison of validity coefficients is, nevertheless, relevant since equivalence in predictive validities is a first step in evaluating differential validity. That is, if predictive validities differ, regression systems must differ; the reverse is not necessarily true, however, since the correlation between two variables is a measure of the strength or magnitude of a relationship and does not dictate its form. Although the number of studies that evaluated group IQ tests across races is small, they have typically employed extremely large samples. The Lorge-Thorndike Verbal and Nonverbal IQs have been most often investigated. Jensen and Sattler concluded that the few available studies suggest that standard IQ tests in current use have comparable validities for black and white children at the elementary school level.

Guterman (1979) reported on an extensive analysis of the predictive validity of the Ammons and Ammons Quick Test (QT, a measure of verbal IQ) for adolescents of different social classes. Social class was determined by a weighted combination of Duncan's SES index and the number of years of education of each parent. There were three basic measures: (1) the Vocabulary subtest of the General Aptitude Test Battery (GATB), (2) the test of Reading Comprehension from the Gates Reading Survey, and (3) the Arithmetic subtest of the GATB. School grades in academic subjects for ninth, tenth, and twelfth grades were also used to examine bias in prediction. Guterman reached similar conclusions about all criterion measures across all social classes: slopes and intercepts of regression lines did not differ across social class for the prediction of any of the criterion measures by the IQ derived from the QT. Several other social knowledge criterion measures were also examined. Again, slopes were constant across social class, and with the exception of sexual knowledge, intercepts were also constant. Guterman concluded that his data provided strong support for the equivalent validity of IQ measures across social class.

Reynolds (1978) conducted an extensive analysis of predictive bias for seven major preschool tests (the Draw-a-Design and Draw-a-Child subtests of the McCarthy Scales; the Mathematics and Language subtests of the Tests of Basic Experiences; the Preschool Inventory–Revised Edition; and the Lee-Clark Reading Readiness Test) across race and gender for large groups of blacks and whites. For each preschool test, validity coefficients, slopes, and intercepts were compared with prediction of performance on four subtests of the MAT (Word Knowledge, Word Discrimination, Reading, and Arithmetic)

as the criterion measure. The general advantage of the MAT as a criterion in external studies of bias has previously been pointed out. In the Reynolds study, the MAT had the added advantage of being chosen by the teachers in the district. Data were gathered on a large number of early achievement tests, and the teachers selected the MAT as the battery most closely measuring what was taught in their classrooms. Regression systems and validity coefficients were compared for each independent-dependent variable pair for white females (WF) versus white males (WM), black females (BF) versus black males (BM), WF versus BF, and WM versus BM, resulting in 112 comparisons of validity coefficients and 112 comparisons of regression systems. Mean performance on all criterion measures was in the following rank order: $WF > WM > BF > BM$. The mean validity coefficients (by Fisher $Z$ transformations) between the independent and dependent variables across the 12-month period from pre- to posttest were .59 for WF, .50 for WM, .43 for BF, and .30 for BM. Although the mean correlations were lower for blacks, the 112 comparisons of pairs of correlations revealed only 3 significant differences, a less-than-chance occurrence with this number of comparisons. Using the Potthoff (1966) technique for comparing regression lines produced quite different results. Of the 112 comparisons of regression lines, 43 (38.4%) showed differences. For comparisons with race as the major variable (and with gender controlled), 31 (55.2%) of the 56 comparisons showed significantly different regression lines. Clearly, racial bias was significantly more prevalent than gender bias ($p < .01$) in prediction. In comparing the various pretests, bias occurred most often with the Preschool Inventory and the Lee-Clark, whereas none of the comparisons involving the MRT showed bias. Though race clearly influenced homogeneity of regression across groups, the bias in each case acted to overpredict performance of the lower-scoring groups; thus the bias acted against whites and females and in favor of blacks and males. A follow-up study (Reynolds, 1980a) has indicated one potential method for avoiding bias in the prediction of early school achievement with readiness or screening measures.

Brief screening measures, especially at the preschool level, typically do not have the high level of reliability obtained by such instruments as the WISC-R or the Stanford-Binet. As previously discussed, Linn and Werts (1971) have convincingly demonstrated that poor reliability can lead to bias in prediction. Early screening measures, as a rule, also assess a very limited area of functioning rather than allowing the child to demonstrate his or her skills in a variety of areas of cognitive functioning. The one well-researched, reliable, broad-based readiness test, the MRT, has failed to show bias in internal or external criteria. Comprehensive and reliable individual preschool instruments such as the WPPSI and the McCarthy Scales, while showing no internal evidence of test bias, have not been studied for predictive bias across race.

Since the definition of predictive bias noted earlier requires that errors in prediction be independent of group membership, Reynolds (1980a) directly examined residuals (a residual term is the remainder when the predicted score for an individual is subtracted from the individual's obtained score) across races and genders when the seven-test battery was used to predict MAT scores in a multiple-regression formula. Subtests of the seven-test battery were also examined. Results of a race by gender ANOVA of residuals for each of the MAT subtests when the seven-tests were employed revealed no significant differences in residuals across races and genders, and no significant interactions occurred. When a subset of the larger battery was submitted to the same analysis, racial bias in prediction did not occur; however, a significant $F$ resulted for gender effects in the prediction of two of the four MAT subscores (Word Discrimination and Word Knowledge). Examination of the residuals for each group showed that the bias in prediction was again against the group with the higher mean criterion scores: there was a consistent underprediction of performance for females. The magnitude of the effect was small, however, being on the order of 0.13 to 0.16 standard deviation. Thus, at the preschool level, the only convincing evidence of bias in predictive validity is a gender effect, not a race effect. Although females tend to be slightly overidentified through early screening, it is interesting to note that although special education classes are more blatantly sexist than racist in composition, it is boys who outnumber girls at a ratio of about 3.5:1 to 4:1. Few if any would argue that this disproportionate representation of males in special education is inappropriate or due to test bias.

Kamphaus and Reynolds (1987) reviewed the available literature on predictive bias with the K-ABC and concluded that overprediction of black children's performance in school is more common, particularly with the K-ABC Sequential Processing Scale, than with other tests. The effects are small, however, and are mitigated in large part by using the K-ABC Mental Processing Composite. Some bias also occurs against blacks, but when the extensive nature of the bias research with the K-ABC is considered, results are not substantially different from the results of the WISC-R (with the exception of overprediction of black academic performance by the K-ABC Sequential Processing Scale).

Keith and Reynolds (1990) have suggested the use of path analysis as an alternative model for assessing bias in predictive validity. In such a path model, ability would be proposed to predict achievement, and group membership would be assessed as a moderator variable. Diagrammatic representations of biased and unbiased models are shown in Figures 22.7–22.9.

Figure 22.7 shows a path model of nonbias in which the scores on an intelligence test serve as the predictor variable and the scores on an achievement test serve as the criterion. Group membership is the dichotomous bias variable, coded 0 for all individuals who are members of one group (e.g., the minority group or males) and 1 for all members who make up the other group (e.g., the majority group or females). The true ability variable is the latent trait or factor. In the nonbiased model, group membership affects intelligence test scores and achievement test scores only through true ability, the latent trait. In contrast, Figure 22.8 shows a path model of bias in which group membership affects not only true ability but also intelligence test scores independent of true ability. In other words, the path

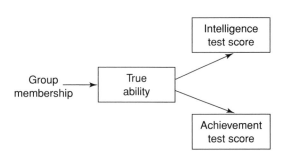

**FIGURE 22.7 A path model of nonbias. Group membership affects intelligence test scores or achievement test scores indirectly through true ability.**

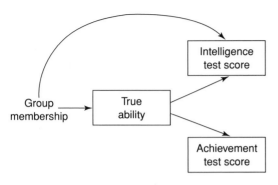

**FIGURE 22.8    A path model of bias. Group membership affects intelligence test scores directly producing a condition in which the intelligence test is biased.**

that connects group membership to intelligence test scores (i.e., the relationship between group membership and intelligence test scores) deviates from 0. The extent that the path deviates from 0, the intelligence test is considered biased and errors of measurement are associated with group membership (Keith & Reynolds, 1990).

The path model of bias depicted in Figure 22.8 is probably not an accurate or a realistic diagrammatic representation, as the direct effect of group membership on true achievement has not been included. That is, group membership affects achievement test scores directly through true achievement, a latent trait variable, or indirectly through true ability. Bias occurs when

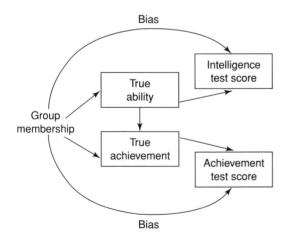

**FIGURE 22.9    A more complete path model of bias. Group membership affects intelligence test scores directly producing conditions in which the intelligence test and achievement test are biased.**

group membership affects intelligence test scores independent of true ability, as well as when group membership affects achievement test scores independent of true achievement. In other words, the path directly connecting group membership to intelligence test scores and/or the path directly linking group membership to achievement test scores deviates from 0. The extent to which these paths deviate from 0 provide evidence that the intelligence test and/or achievement test is biased and the errors of measurement are related to group membership. Figure 22.9 illustrates this more complete path model of bias (Keith & Reynolds, 1990).

An example of a path model of bias that affects achievement test scores occurs when one group of high school students completes more academic coursework than another group of high school students. The coursework variable would affect achievement test scores directly. The direct path between group membership and achievement test scores would deviate from 0, and evidence of bias would be present (Keith & Reynolds, 1990).

As noted, bias in prediction exists when group membership affects measured ability *independent* of true ability and/or when group membership affects measured achievement *independent* of true achievement; that is, errors of measurement in testing of ability and/or achievement would be correlated with group membership.

For bias in predictive validity, the empirical evidence suggests conclusions similar to those for bias in content and construct validity. There is no strong evidence to support contentions of differential or single-group validity. Bias occurs infrequently and with no apparently observable pattern, except when instruments of poor reliability and high specificity of test content are examined. When bias occurs, it is most often in the direction of favoring low-SES, disadvantaged, ethnic minority children or other low-scoring groups. Clearly, bias in predictive validity cannot account for the disproportionate number of minority group children diagnosed and placed in programs for children with disabilities, especially children with mental retardation or emotional disturbance.

# CULTURAL EQUIVALENCE AS A FUTURE APPROACH?

As mentioned earlier in this chapter, Helms (1992) asserted that the implicit biological or environmental philosophical perspectives used to explain differences in cognitive ability test performance across racial and ethnic groups were based on deficient conceptualizations of culture. Neither perspective, according to Helms, provides useful information about cultural equivalence (meaning) of test scores across racial or ethnic groups.

Helms (1992) claims that racial differences in IQ test performance are due to cultural bias in the tests. Although her claim may have some merit and future research in bias assessment will continue, as it has in the past, to address the cultural variable, Helms's underlying logic runs counter to the empirical evidence. She suggests that blacks or other visible racial or ethnic groups are culturally, socially, and cognitively different from members of the dominant culture. However, research shows that IQ tests appear to measure the same psychological characteristics in blacks or other racial or ethnic groups and Anglo-Americans (Rowe, 1994).

Nevertheless, Helms (1992) and Bentancourt and Lopez's (1993) calls to address the cultural variable to a greater extent than has been done in the past may or may not be the wave of the future in bias assessment research. However, if Helms's position prevails, the examination of the cultural equivalence of existing and future standardized cognitive ability tests across seven dimensions will be required (Butcher, 1982): (1) functional equivalence (the extent to which test scores have the same meaning across different cultural groups), (2) conceptual equivalence (whether test items have the same familiarity and meaning in different racial groups), (3) linguistic equivalence (whether the tests have the same linguistic meaning to different groups), (4) psychometric equivalence (the extent to which the tests measure the same thing across groups), (5) testing condition equivalence (whether groups are equally familiar with testing procedures and view testing as a means of assessing ability) (6) contextual equivalence (the extent to which the cognitive ability to be assessed is evaluated similarly in different contexts in which people function), and (7) sampling equivalence (the idea that comparable samples of each cultural group are available at the test development, validation, and interpretation stages).

Helms (1992) believes that diversification in existing tests, development of new standardized tests, and the use of explicit principles, hypotheses, assumptions, and theoretical models for investigating cultural differences will be needed. In addition, the existing frameworks (i.e., biological, environmental, and cultural) need to be operationally defined.

Helms (1992) recommends six areas for future research in test development to address the cultural equivalence issue: (1) development of measures for determining interracial cultural dependence and levels of acculturation and assimilation in test items, (2) modification of existing test content to include items that reflect cultural diversity, (3) examination of wrong answers, (4) incorporation of cognitive psychology into interactive modes of assessment, (5) utilization of theories to examine environmental content of criteria, and (6) separate racial group norms for existing tests. Helms's recommendations to address, investigate, and possibly control the culture of cognitive ability tests may or may not prove to be beneficial. She suggests that the field proceed with caution in the interpretation of test results until psychometricians develop more diverse methodologies to address the culture issue.

Much of this has in fact been done. Virtually every area noted in the preceding paragraph has been addressed in the literature review in this chapter. Psychometricians have been working diligently, but all of the answers are not yet in. If Helms (1992) were calling for continued research into these areas, such a call would have our support, but to dismiss the many studies that are addressing these issues is improper. Helms coins new terms for what she believes needs to be done, but her definitions reveal constructs that have been researched for many years. Cronbach and Drenth (1972) have provided a book-length treatment of many of these issues that is decades old.

# CROSS-CULTURAL TESTING WHEN TRANSLATION IS REQUIRED

When a test is translated from one language to another, the research findings discussed thus far do not hold. It is inappropriate to simply translate a test and apply it in a different linguistic culture. A test basically must be redeveloped from scratch before any such application would be appropriate. New items, new normative data, and new scaling would all be required. This has been known since the early days of psychological assessment and testing. In the early 1900s, when the Binet-Simon tests were brought to the United States from France, approximately 30 different versions of the test were developed by various researchers. However, most of these were mere translations or contained minor modifications to adapt to American culture. The Stanford-Binet Intelligence Scale, in its various incarnations, however, became the standard bearer for measurement of intelligence for nearly 60 years and was even more popular in France at one time than the original French scales. The reason for the domination of the Stanford-Binet series was Lewis Terman's insight and tenacity in redeveloping the test in the United States. After determining that Binet's theory of intelligence applied, new items were written and tried out, and a new scale was devised for norming that was conceptually consistent with the Binet-Simon scales but in practical application was a new and different test.

Beginning with the Binet-Simon Scales (Binet & Simon, 1905), the translation or adaptation of psychological and educational tests from one language or culture to another has become common practice. Despite the long history, few psychologists are familiar with the proper methods for conducting test adaptations and establishing score equivalence (Hambleton & Kanjee, 1995). Judgmental and statistical methods and procedures for adapting tests are available, which focus on identifying nonequivalent items. When these methods and procedures are used, the validity of the adapted tests increases (Hambleton & Kanjee, 1995).

There are many reasons for adapting psychological or educational tests. First, it allows individuals to be assessed in their own language. Second, it facilitates international and national comparative studies in which differences among ethnic and/or cultural groups are of interest. Third, it reduces the time and costs associated with the development of new tests. There are other reasons for adapting tests, but these three are the most common and are at the heart of the cross-cultural testing movement.

Although adapting tests over the last 90 years has been a common practice, the field of cross-cultural and cross-national comparisons is relatively new. Currently its major thrust revolves around the development and use of guidelines for adapting tests (Hambleton, 1994), ways to interpret and use cross-cultural and cross-national data (Hambleton & Kanjee, 1994; Poortinga & Malpass, 1986), and methods and procedures for establishing equivalence of test items and ultimately test scores (Ellis, 1991; Hambleton, 1993; Van de Vijver & Poortinga, 1991), much of which predates Helms's (1992) lament that no such study has been undertaken.

Establishment of the equivalence of test items is the most central issue in cross-cultural or cross-national research (Poortinga, 1983). Test items are considered to be equivalent when members of each group—that is, members from different language and/or cultural groups—with the same score on the construct measured by the test have the same probability of selecting the correct answer on the latent trait item (Hambleton & Kanjee, 1994).

Two methods are used to establish item equivalence, judgmental and statistical designs. Judgmental designs are based on an individual's or group's decision concerning the degree of each item's translation equivalence. Two of the most common judgmental designs are forward translation and back translation (Hambleton & Bollwark, 1991). In forward translation, translators translate or adapt the measure from the original, called the source, to the target language or culture. The source and target versions are then assessed by another individual or group of translators to determine their equivalency. If the versions are not equivalent, changes are made. In back translation, one or more translators translate or adapt the instrument from the source to the target language or culture, and then another translator or a group of translators retranslate the test items back to the source language or culture. The two source versions are then assessed to determine if they are equivalent. Judgmental designs provide good preliminary checks of item translation equivalence, but additional checks are needed, such as statistical methods like DIF.

In addition to judgmental designs, statistical designs are used to establish item equivalency. There are three different statistical designs, which vary according to the characteristics of the sample. In the bilingual examinees' design, both the source and target versions of the test are given to bilingual examinees (Hambleton & Bollwark, 1991). In the source and target language monolinguals' design, source language monolinguals take the original source or back-translated version of the test and the target language monolinguals take the target version (Ellis, 1991). In the third statistical design, the source language monolinguals are administered the original and back-translated versions of the test. Once testing has been completed, specific analytical procedures are selected, for example, factor analysis, item response theory, logistic regression, and Mantel-Haenszel procedure, and performed to detect DIF. If DIF is significant, further analyses of the significant DIF items are needed to determine if the items are biased or language and/or cultural equivalency has not been obtained.

In the field of cross-cultural testing, equivalence of test items has been a major methodological concern as interest in international comparative studies of educational achievement, aptitude, and personality measures and cross-cultural research continue to grow (Hambleton, 1994). Because of this growth, the International Test Commission, a 13-member panel of psychologists who represent a number of international organizations, developed a set of 22 guidelines to assist researchers and practitioners who are adapting educational and psychological tests. The guidelines are organized into four sections: context, instrument development and adaptation, administration, and documentation or score interpretation. The context guidelines address concerns about construct equivalence in the target groups. The instrument development and adaptation category provides a vast array of information about the selection of translators, judgmental and statistical designs, and statistical tests needed to examine score equivalency. The administration guidelines include everything from selecting administrators to setting time limits. The documentation and score interpretation category addresses the need for researchers to document the adaptation process to establish the validity of adapted tests. A review of the 22 guidelines can be found in Hambleton (1994).

The importance of addressing test item and score equivalence and of the set of 22 guidelines for adapting psychological tests is highlighted in a study that examined the relationship between level of acculturation and performance on the Halstead-Reitan neuropsychological test with nonimpaired Hispanics (Arnold, Montgomery, Castaneda, & Longoria, 1994). It was found that the level of acculturation affected several measures, including the Tactual Performance Test, the Seashore Rhythm Test, and the Halstead Category Test. These results raise questions about the validity of existing norms with nonimpaired Hispanics. Arnold et al. suggest that acculturation measures should accompany neuropsychological evaluations of Hispanics until the specificity and sensitivity of existing neuropsychological tests are better understood.

Moreover, the authors suggest greater interpretative caution when assessing nonimpaired Hispanics who have not been acculturated or exhibit low levels of acculturation.

In contrast, the findings from a study of 47 Lao children, ranging in age from 5 to 12, suggested that cognitive and neuropsychological measures can be adapted so that they can effectively tap basic and universal brain-behavior traits (Boivin et al., 1996). The Lao children completed the Kaufman Assessment Battery for Children (K-ABC), the Tactual Performance Test (TPT), and the computerized Tests of Variables of Attention (TOVA). The TPT performance was found to be related to nutritional development; the K-ABC performance was sensitive to parental education and home environment; and the TOVA performance was associated with attention, K-ABC global performance, and TPT memory.

Boivin et al.'s (1996) study suggests that tests can be adapted for use with groups from other cultures; however, the problems in adapting tests across cultures are difficult and present challenges to the field of psychometrics. Contrary to Helms's (1992) view, psychologists have been confronting these issues for many years. Cronbach and Drenth (1972) have provided a book-length treatment of these problems and various experiences with proposed solutions to the cross-cultural adaptation of psychological tests in some 30 nations throughout the world. The various contributors describe both the strengths and limitations of adapting tests cross-culturally, providing perspectives from such diverse disciplines as psychometrics, cognitive and developmental psychology, and anthropology. More recent guidelines can be found in Hambleton (1994) and in Van de Vijver and Hambleton (1996).

## CONCLUSION

There is little question that the issue of bias in mental testing is an important one with strong historical precedence in the social sciences and, ultimately, formidable social consequences. Because the history of mental measurement has been closely wed from the outset to societal needs and expectations, testing in all forms has remained in the limelight, subjected to the crucible of social inspection, review, and (at times) condemnation in various cultures throughout the world. However, the fact that tests and measures of human aptitude and achievement continue to be employed in most modern cultures (and were more than 2000 years ago in some cultures) indicates strongly that the practice has value, despite the recurring storms of criticism over the years. The ongoing controversy related to test bias and the "fair" use of measures undoubtedly will remain with the social sciences for at least as long as we entangle the nature-nurture question with these issues and affirm differences between and among groups in mean performance on standardized tests. Numerous scholars in the field of psychometrics have been attempting to separate the nature-nurture issue and data on mean score differences from the more orderly, empirically driven specialty of bias investigation, but the separation will undoubtedly not be a clean one. A sharp distinction has developed between the popular press and scientific literature about the interpretation of mental measurement research. The former all too often engenders beliefs that biased measures are put into use for socially pernicious purposes (e.g., psychology and education) often accused of courting political, social, and professional ideologies, and it appears to have created confusion in public opinion about the possibility of "fair" testing, to say the least. The latter—reported in this chapter—has been demonstrating through a rather sizable body of data that the contention that tests are culturally biased is not supported at present, at least in cultures with a common language and some degree of common experience. In any event, societal scrutiny and ongoing sentiment about testing have without question forced the psychometric community to refine its definition of bias further, to inspect practices in the construction of nonbiased measures, and to develop statistical procedures to detect bias when it is occurring. We can argue whether the social sciences have from the outset overstepped their bounds in implementing testing for social purposes before adequate data and methods were developed, but the resulting advancements in bias technology in response to ongoing public inspection are undeniable.

Data from the empirical end of bias investigation do suggest several guidelines to ensure equitable assessment: (1) investigation of possible referral source bias, as there is evidence that persons are not always referred for services on the basis of impartial, objective rationales; (2) inspection of test developers' data for evidence that sound statistical analyses for bias across groups to be evaluated with the measure have been completed; (3) assessment with the most reliable measure available; and (4) assessment of multiple abilities with multiple methods. In other words, psychologists need to view multiple sources of accurately derived data before making decisions about individuals. We may hope that this is not too far afield from what has actually been occurring in the practice of psychological assessment, although one continues to hear isolated stories of grossly incompetent diagnostic decisions. This does not mean that psychologists should be blind to a person's environmental background. Information about the home, community, and other environmental circumstances must be evaluated in the individualized decision-making process. Exactly how this may be done is addressed in other chapters and volumes of this work. Neither, however, can the psychologist ignore the fact that low-IQ, disadvantaged children from ethnic minority groups are just as likely to fail academically as are majority, middle-class, low-IQ children, provided that their environmental circumstances remain constant. Indeed, it is the purpose of the assessment process to beat the prediction—to provide insight into hypotheses for environmental interventions that will prevent the predicted failure.

A philosophical perspective that is emerging in the bias literature requires test developers not only to demonstrate whether their measures have differential content, construct, and predictive validity across groups *before* publication but also to incorporate in some form content analyses by interested groups to ensure that offensive materials are omitted. Although there are no sound empirical data to suggest that persons can determine bias upon surface inspection, the synergistic relationship between test use and pure psychometrics must be acknowledged and accommodated in orderly fashion before tests gain greater acceptance in society. Ideally, a clear consensus on fairness (and steps taken to reach this end) is needed between those persons with more subjective concerns and those interested in gathering objective bias data during and after test construction. Accommodation along this line will ultimately ensure that all parties interested in any given test believe that the measure in question is nonbiased and that the steps taken to achieve fairness can be held up to public scrutiny without reservation. Given the significant and reliable methods developed over the last several decades in bias research, it is untenable at this point to abandon statistical analyses in favor of armchair determinations of bias. Test authors and publishers need to demonstrate factorial invariance across all groups for whom the test is designed to make the instrument more readily interpretable. Comparisons of predictive validity across races and genders during the test development phase are also needed. With the exception of some recent achievement tests, this has not been common practice, yet it is at this stage that tests can be altered through a variety of item analysis procedures to eliminate any apparent racial and sexual bias.

Bias research in personality testing must be expanded. Little has been done, and this represents a major weakness in the literature. Only recently (e.g., Reynolds & Kamphaus, 1992) have publishers begun to give appropriate attention to this problem. Researchers in personality and psychodiagnostics must move ahead in this area of concern.

# REFERENCES

Abebimpe, V. R., Gigandet, J., & Harris, E. (1979). MMPI diagnosis of black psychiatric patients. *American Journal of Psychiatry, 136,* 85–87.

Ackerman, T. A. (1991). A didactic explanation of item bias, item impact, and item validity from a multidimensional perspective. *Journal of Educational Measurement, 29*(1), 67–91.

Alley, G., & Foster, C. (1978). Nondiscriminatory testing of minority and exceptional children. *Focus on Exceptional Children, 9,* 1–14.

American Psychological Association (1970). Psychological assessment and public policy. *American psychologist, 31,* 264–266.

Anastasi, A. (1976). *Psychological testing* (4th ed.). New York: Macmillan.

Anastasi, A. (1982). *Psychological testing* (5th ed.). New York: Macmillan.

Angoff, W. H. (1976). Group membership as a predictor variable: A comment on McNemar. *American Psychologist, 31,* 612.

Angoff, W. H., & Ford, S. R. (1973). Item-race interaction on a test of scholastic aptitude. *Journal of Educational Measurement, 10,* 95–106.

Arnold, B., Montgomery, G., Castaneda, I., & Longoria, R. (1994). Acculturation and performance of Hispanics on selected Halstead-Reitan neuropsychological tests. *Assessment, 1*(3), 239–248.

Auerbach, A. G. (1971). The social control of learning disabilities. *Journal of Learning Disabilities, 4,* 25–34.

Bartlett, C. J., & O'Leary, B. S. (1969). A differential prediction model to moderate the effect of heterogeneous groups on personnel selection. *Personnel Psychology, 22,* 1–18.

Bentancourt, H., & Lopez, S. R. (1993). The study of culture, ethnicity, and race in American psychology. *American Psychologist, 48,* 629–637.

Bernal, E. M. (1975). A response to "Educational Uses of Tests with Disadvantaged Students." *American Psychologist, 30,* 93–95.

Binet, A., & Simon, T. (1905). Methods nouvelles pour le diagnositic du nivea intellectual des anormaux. *L'Ann Ce Psychologique, 11,* 191–244.

Binet, A., & Simon, T. (1916/1973). *The development of intelligence in children.* New York: Arno.

Birch, H. G., & Gussow, J. D. (1970). *Disadvantaged children: Health, nutrition, and school failure.* New York: Grune & Stratton.

Blaha, J., Wallbrown, F., & Wherry, R. J. (1975). The hierarchical factor structure of the Wechsler Intelligence Scale for Children. *Psychological Reports, 35,* 771–778.

Bogen, J. E., DeZure, R., Tenhouten, N., & March, J. (1972). The other side of the brain: IV. The A/P ratio. *Bulletin of the Los Angeles Neurological Society, 37,* 49–61.

Boivin, M., Chounramany, C., Giordani, B., Xaisida, S., Choulamountry, L., Pholsena, P., Crist, C., & Olness, K. (1996). Validating a cognitive ability testing protocol with Lao children for community development applications. *Neuropsychology, 10*(4), 1–12.

Bolles, R. C. (1975). *Theory of motivation* (2nd ed.). New York: Harper & Row.

Bond, L. (1981). Bias in mental tests. In B. F. Green (Ed.), *Issues in testing: Coaching, disclosure, and ethnic bias.* San Francisco: Jossey-Bass.

Bond, L. (1987). The golden rule settlement: A minority perspective. *Educational Measurement: Issues and Practice, 6*(2), 23–25.

Bossard, M., Reynolds, C. R., Gutkin, T. B. (1980). A regression analysis of test bias on the Stanford-Binet Intelligence Scale. *Journal of Clinical Child Psychology, 9,* 52–54.

Bouchard, T. J., & Segal, N. L. (1985). Environment and IQ. In B. Wolman (Ed.), *Handbook of intelligence* (pp. 391–464). New York: Wiley-Interscience.

Bower, E. M. (1974). The three-pipe problem: Promotion of competent human beings through a preschool kindergarten program and other sundry matters. G. Williams & S. Gordon (Eds.), *Clinical child psychology.* New York: Behavioral Publications.

Buros, O. K. (Ed.). (1978). *Eighth mental measurements yearbook.* Highland Park, NJ: Gryphon.

Burrill, L. E. (1975). Statistical evidence of potential bias in items and tests assessing current educational status. Paper presented at the Annual Meeting of the Southeastern Conference on Measurement in Education, New Orleans.

Burt, C. (1921). *Mental and scholastic tests.* London: P. S. King.

Butcher, J. N. (1982). Cross-cultural research methods in clinical psychology. In P. C. Kendall & J. N. Butcher (Eds.), *Black children: Social educational and parental environments* (pp. 33–51). Beverly Hills, CA: Sage.

Butler-Omololu, C., Doster, J., & Lahey, B. (1984). Some implications for intelligence test construction and administration with children of different racial groups. *Journal of Black Psychology, 10*(2), 63–75.

Camilli, G., & Shepard, L. A. (1987). The inadequacy of ANOVA for detecting test bias. *Journal of Educational Statistics, 12*, 87–99.

Camilli, G., & Shepard, L. A. (1994). *Methods for identifying biased test items.* Thousand Oaks, CA: Sage.

Cardall, C., & Coffman, W. E. (1964). *A method of comparing the performance of different groups on the items in a test* (RB-64-61). Princeton, NJ: Educational Testing Service.

Cattell, R. B. (1979). Are culture fair intelligence tests possible and necessary? *Journal of Research and Development in Education, 12*, 3–13.

Chambers, J. S., Barron, F., & Sprecher, J. W. (1980). Identifying gifted Mexican-American students. *Gifted Child Quarterly, 24*, 123–128.

Chinn, P. C. (1979). The exceptional minority child: Issues and some answers. *Exceptional Children, 46*, 532–536.

Chipman, S., Marshall, S., & Scott, P. (1991). Content effect on word-problem performance: A possible source of test bias? *American Educational Research Journal, 28*(4), 897–915.

Clarizio, H. (1982). Intellectual assessment of Hispanic children. *Psychology in the Schools, 19*(1), 61–71.

Cleary, T. A. (1968). Test bias: Prediction of grades of negro and white students in integrated universities. *Journal of Educational Measurement, 5*, 118–124.

Cleary, T. A., Humphreys, L. G., Kendrick, S. A., & Wesman, A. (1975). Educational uses of tests with disadvantaged students. *American Psychologist, 30*, 15–41.

Cole, N. S., & Moss, P. (1989). Bias in test use. In R. Linn (Ed.), *Educational measurement* (3rd ed.). New York: Macmillan.

*Cortez v. Rosen.* (1975). U.S. District Court for the No- District of California.

Council for Exceptional Children (1978). Minorities position policy statements. *Exceptional Children, 45*, 57–64.

Critchley, D. L. (1979). The adverse influence of psychiatric diagnostic labels on the observation of child behavior. *American Journal of Orthopsychiatry, 49*, 157–160.

Cronbach, L. J. (1970). *Essentials of psychological testing.* New York: Harper & Row.

Cronbach, L. J. (1976). Equity in selection—where psychometrics and political philosophy meet. *Journal of Educational Measurement, 13*, 31–42.

Cronbach, L. J., & Drenth, P. J. D. (Eds.). (1972). *Mental tests and cultural adaptation.* The Hague: Mouton.

Cuccaro, M. L., Wright, H. H., Rownd, C. V., Abramson R., Waller, J., & Fender, D. (1996). Professional perceptions of children with developmental difficulties: The influence of race and socioeconomic status. *Journal of Autism and Developmental Disorders, 26*, 461–469.

Dana, R. H. (1996). Culturally competent assessment practices in the United States. *Journal of Personality Assessment, 66*, 472–487.

Darlington, R. B. (1978). Cultural test bias: Comments on Hunter and Schmidt. *Psychological Bulletin, 85*, 673–674.

Dean, R. S. (1979, September). WISC-R factor structure for Anglo and Hispanic children. Paper presented at the Annual Meeting of the American Psychological Association, New York.

DeFries, J. C., Vandenberg, S. G., McClearn, G. E., Kuse, A. R., Wilson, J. R., Ashton, G. C., & Johnson, R. C. (1974). Near identity of cognitive structure in two ethnic groups. *Science, 183*, 338–339.

Dershowitz, Z., & Frankel, Y. (1975). Jewish culture and the WISC and WAIS test patterns. *Journal of Consulting and Clinical Psychology, 43*, 126–134.

Dworkin, N., & Dworkin, Y. (1979). The legacy of *Pygmalion in the Classroom. Phi Delta Kappan, 61*, 712–715.

Ebel, R. L. (1979). Intelligence: A skeptical view. *Journal of Research and Development in Education, 12*, 14–21.

Eells, K., Davis, A., Havighurst, R. J., Herrick, V. E., & Tyler, R. W. (1951). *Intelligence and cultural differences: A study of cultural learning and problem-solving.* Chicago: University of Chicago Press.

Einhorn, H. J., & Bass, A. R. (1971). Methodological considerations relevant to discrimination in employment testing. *Psychological Bulletin, 75*, 261–269.

Ellis, B. B. (1991). Item response theory: A tool for assessing the equivalence of translated tests. *Bulletin of the International Test Commission, 18*, 33–51.

Emerling, F. (1990). An investigation of test bias in nonverbal cognitive measures for two ethnic groups, *Journal of Psychoeducational Assessment, 8*(1), 34–41.

Fine, B. (1975). *The stranglehold of the IQ.* Garden City, NY: Doubleday.

Flaugher, R. L. (1978). The many definitions of test bias. *American Psychologist, 33*, 671–679.

Flaugher, R. L., & Schrader, W. B. (1978). *Eliminating differentially difficult items as an approach to test bias* (RB-78-4). Princeton, NJ: Educational Testing Service.

Flynn, J. R. (1991). *Asian-Americans: Achievement beyond IQ.* Hillsdale, NJ: Erlbaum.

Foster, G., & Ysseldyke, J. (1976). Expectancy and

halo effects as a result of artificially induced teacher bias. *Contemporary Educational Psychology, 1*, 37–45.

Frame, R. (1979, September). Diagnoses related to school achievement, client's race, and socioeconomic status. Paper presented at the Annual Meeting of the American Psychological Association, New York.

Freeman, F. N. (1923). A referendum of psychologists. *Century Illustrated Magazine, 107*, 237–245.

Gerkin, K. C. (1978). Performance of Mexican-American children on intelligence test. *Exceptional Children, 44*, 438–443.

Gillberg, C., Steffenburg, S., & Schaumann, H. (1991). Is autism more common now than ten years ago? *British Journal of Psychiatry, 158*, 403–409.

Goldstein, H., Krantz, D. L., & Rains, J. D. (Eds.). (1965). *Controversial issues in learning*. New York: Appleton-Century-Crofts.

Gordon, R. A. (1984). Digits backward and the Mercer-Kamin law: An empirical response to Mercer's treatment of internal validity of IQ tests. In C. R. Reynolds & R. T. Brown (Eds.)), *Perspectives on bias in mental testing*. New York: Plenum.

Gottfredson, L. (1994). Egalitarian fiction and collective fraud. *Society, 31*(3), 53–59.

Gould, S. J. (1981). *The mismeasure of man*. New York: Norton.

Greenlaw, R., & Jensen, S. (1996). Race norming and the Civil Rights Act of 1991. *Public Personnel Management, 25*(1), 13–24.

Gross, A. L., & Su, W. (1975). Defining a "fair" or "unbiased" selection model. *Journal of Applied Psychology, 60*, 345–351.

Gross, M. (1967). *Learning readiness in two Jewish groups*. New York: Center for Urban Education.

Guilford Press. (1997). Culturally sensitive assessment: Paying attention to cultural orientation. *Child Assessment News, 6*, 8–12.

Guterman, S. S. (1979). IQ tests in research on social stratification: The cross-class validity of the test as measures on scholastic aptitude. *Sociology of Education, 52*, 163–173.

Gutkin, T. B., & Reynolds, C. R. (1980). Factorial similarity of the WISC-R for Anglos and Chicanos referred for psychological services. *Journal of School Psychology, 18*, 34–39.

Gutkin, T. B., & Reynolds, C. R. (1981). Factorial similarity of the WISC-R for white and black children from the standardized sample. *Journal of Educational Psychology, 73*, 227–231.

Hambleton, R. K. (1993). Translating achievement tests for use in cross-national studies. *European Journal of Psychological Assessment, 9*, 54–65.

Hambleton, R. K. (1994). Guidelines for adapting educational and psychological tests: A progress report. *European Journal of Psychological Assessment, 10*(3), 229–244.

Hambleton, R. K., & Bollwark, J. (1991). Adapting tests for use in different cultures: Technical issues and methods. *Bulletin of the International Test Commission, 18*, 3–32.

Hambleton, R. K., & Kanjee, A. (1994). Enhancing the validity of cross-cultural studies: Improvements in instrument translation methods. In T. Husen & T. Postlewaite (Eds.), *International encyclopedia of education* (2nd ed.). Oxford: Pergamon.

Hambleton, R. K., & Kanjee, A. (1995). Increasing the validity of cross-cultural assessments: Use of improved methods for adaptations. *European Journal of Psychological Assessment, 11*(3), 147–157.

Hambleton, R. K., Swaminathan, H., & Rogers, H. J. (1991). *Fundamentals of item response theory*. Newbury Park, CA: Sage.

Hammill, D. (1991). *Detroit tests of learning aptitude* (3rd ed.). Austin, TX: Pro-Ed.

Harman, H. (1976). *Modern factor analysis* (2nd ed.). Chicago: University of Chicago Press.

Harrington, G. M. (1968a). Genetic-environmental interaction in "intelligence": I. Biometric genetic analysis of maze performance of Rattus norvegicus. *Developmental Psychobiology, 1*, 211–218.

Harrington, G. M. (1968b). Genetic-environmental interaction in "intelligence": II. Models of behavior, components of variance, and research strategy. *Developmental Psychobiology, 1*, 245–253.

Harrington, G. M. (1975). Intelligence tests may favor the majority groups in a population. *Nature, 258*, 708–709.

Harrington, G. M. (1976, September). Minority test bias as a psychometric artifact: The experimental evidence. Paper presented at the Annual Meeting of the American Psychological Association, Washington, DC.

Hartlage, L. C., Lucas, T., & Godwin, A. (1976). Culturally biased and culturally fair tests correlated with school performance in culturally disadvantaged children. *Journal of Consulting and Clinical Psychology, 32*, 325–327.

Helms, J. E. (1992). Why is there no study of cultural equivalence in standardized cognitive ability testing? *American Psychologist, 47*, 1083–1101.

Helms, J. E. (1994). The conceptualization of racial identity and other "racial" constructs. In E. Trickett, R. Watts, & D. Birman (Eds.), *Human Diversity* (pp. 285–311). San Francisco: Jossey-Bass.

Herrnstein, R. J., & Murray, C. (1994). *The bell curve*. New York: Free Press.

Hilgard, E. R., & Bower, G. H. (1975). *Theories of learning* (4th ed.). Englewood Cliffs, NJ: Prentice Hall.

Hilliard, A. G. (1979). Standardization and cultural bias as impediments to the scientific study and validation of "intelligence." *Journal of Research and Development in Education, 12*, 47–58.

Hobbs, N. (1975). *The futures of children.* San Francisco: Jossey-Bass.

Humphreys, L. G. (1973). Statistical definitions of test validity for minority groups. *Journal of Applied Psychology, 58,* 1–4.

Hunter, J. E., & Schmidt, F. L. (1976). Critical analysis of the statistical and ethnical implications of various definitions of test bias. *Psychological Bulletin, 83,* 1053–1071.

Hunter, J. E., & Schmidt, F. L. (1978). Bias in defining test bias: Reply to Darlington. *Psychological Bulletin, 85,* 675–676.

Hunter, J. E., Schmidt, F. L., & Hunter, R. (1979). Differential validity of employment tests by race: A comprehensive review and analysis. *Psychological Bulletin, 86,* 721–735.

Hunter, J. E., Schmidt, F. L., & Rauschenberger, J. (1984). Methodological, statistical, and ethical issues in the study of bias in psychological tests. In C. R. Reynolds & R. T. Brown (Eds.), *Perspectives on bias in mental testing.* New York: Plenum.

Isern, M. (1986). An investigation of bias in tests of writing ability for bilingual Hispanic college students. Doctoral dissertation, University of Miami. *Dissertation Abstracts International, 47,* 2135A.

Jackson, G. D. (1975). Another psychological view from the Association of Black Psychologists. *American Psychologist, 30,* 88–93.

Jacobs, W. R. (1978). The effect of the learning disability label on classroom teachers' ability objectively to observe and interpret child behaviors. *Learning Disability Quarterly, 1,* 50–55.

James, B. J. (1995). A test of Harrington's experimental model of ethnic bias in testing applies to a measure of emotional functioning in adolescents. Doctoral dissertation, Texas A&M University, College Station.

Jensen, A. R. (1974). How biased are cultural loaded tests? *Genetic Psychology Monographs, 90,* 185–224.

Jensen, A. R. (1976). Test bias and construct validity. *Phi Delta Kappan, 58,* 340–346.

Jensen, A. R. (1977). An examination of culture bias in the Wonderlic Personnel test. *Intelligence, 1,* 51–64.

Jensen, A. R. (1980). Bias in mental testing. New York: Free Press.

Jensen, A. R. (1985). The nature of the black-white differences on various tests: Spearman's hypothesis. *Behavioral and Brain Sciences, 8,* 193–263.

Jensen, A. R., & Figueroa, R. (1975). Forward and backward digit span interaction with race and IQ. *Journal of Education Psychology, 67,* 882–893.

Joreskog, K. (1971). Simultaneous factor analysis in several populations. *Psychometrika, 30,* 409–426.

Judd, C. M., & McClelland, G. H. (1989). *Data analysis: A model comparison approach.* San Diego: Harcourt Brace Jovanovich.

Kaiser, S. (1986). Ability patterns of black and white adults on the WAIS-R independent of general intelligence and as a function of socioeconomic status. Doctoral dissertation, Texas A&M University, College Station.

Kamphaus, R. W., & Reynolds, C. R. (1987). *Clinical and research applications of the K-ABC.* Circle Pines, MN: American Guidance Service.

Kaufman, A. S. (1973). Comparison of the performance of matched groups of black children and white children on the Wechsler Preschool and Primary Scale of Intelligence. *Journal of Consulting and Clinical Psychology, 41,* 186–191.

Kaufman, A. S. (1979). *Intelligent testing with the WISC-R.* New York: Wiley-Interscience.

Kaufman, A. S. (1994). *Intelligence testing with the WISC-III.* New York: Wiley; Pines, MN: American Guidance Service.

Kaufman, A. S., & Kaufman, N. L. (1973). Black-white differences on the McCarthy Scales of Children's Abilities. *Journal of School Psychology, 11,* 196–206.

Kaufman, A. S., & Kaufman, N. L. (1983). *Kaufman Assessment Battery for Children.* Circle Pines, MN: American Guidance Service.

Keith, T. Z., & Reynolds, C. R. (1990). Measurement and design issues in child assessment research. In C. R. Reynolds & R. W. Kamphaus (Eds.), *Handbook of Psychological and Educational Assessment of Children.* New York: Guilford.

Kimble, G. A. (1961). *Hilgard and Marquis' conditioning and learning* (2nd ed.). New York: Appleton-Century-Crofts.

Lambert, N. M. (1979, October). Adaptive behavior assessment and its implications for educational programming. Paper presented to the Fourth Annual Midwestern Conference on Psychology in the Schools, Boys Town, Nebraska.

*Larry P. et al. v. Wilson Riles et al.* (1979, October). C 71 2270. U.S. District Court for the Northern District of California, slip opinion.

Lewis, D. O., Balla, D. A., & Shanok, S. S. (1979). Some evidence of race bias in the diagnosis and treatment of the juvenile offender. *American Journal of Orthopsychiatry, 49,* 53–61.

Lewontin, R. C. (1970). Race and intelligence. *Bulletin of the Atomic Scientists, 26,* 2–8.

Linn, R. L. (1976). In search of fair selection procedures. *Journal of Educational Measurement, 13,* 53–58.

Linn, R. L., & Werts, C. E. (1971). Consideration for studies of test bias. *Journal of Educational Measurement, 8,* 1–4.

Lippmann, W. (1923a). A judgment of the tests. *New Public, 34,* 322–323.

Lippmann, W. (1923b). Mr. Burt and the intelligence tests. *New Republic, 34,* 263–264.

Loehlin, J. C., Lindzey, G., & Spuhler, J. N. (1975). *Race differences in intelligence.* San Francisco: Freeman.

Lonner, W. J. (1985). Issues in testing and assessment in cross-cultural counseling. *The Counseling Psychologist, 13,* 599–614.

MacCorquodale, K., & Meehl, P. E. (1948). On a distinction between hypothetical constructs and intervening variables. *Psychological Review, 55,* 95–107.

MacMillan, D. L., Jones, R. L., & Aloia, G. F. (1974). The mentally retarded label: A theoretical analysis and review of research. *American Journal of Mental Deficiency, 79,* 241–261.

Mandler, G. (1975). *Mind and emotion.* New York: Wiley.

Marjoribanks, K. (1972). Ethnic and environmental influences on mental abilities. *American Journal of Sociology, 78,* 323–337.

Matuszek, P., & Oakland, T. (1979). Factors influencing teachers' and psychologists' recommendations regarding special class placement. *Journal of School Psychology, 17,* 116–125.

Mayfield, J. W., & Reynolds, C. R. (in press). Are ethnic differences in diagnosis of childhood psychopathology an artifact of psychometric methods? An experimental evaluation of Harrington's hypothesis using parent report symptomatology. *Journal of School Psychology.*

McCoy, S. A. (1976). Clinical judgments of normal childhood behaviors. *Journal of Consulting and Clinical Psychology, 44,* 710–714.

McGurk, F. V. J. (1951). *Comparison of the performance of Negro and white high school seniors on cultural and noncultural psychological test questions.* Washington, DC; Catholic University of America Press.

McNemar, Q. (1975). On so-called test bias. *American Psychologist, 30,* 848–851.

Mercer, J. R. (1971). The meaning of mental retardation. In R. Koch & J. Dobson (Eds.), *The mentally retarded child and his family: A multidisciplinary handbook.* New York: Brunner/Mazel.

Mercer, J. R. (1976, August). Cultural diversity, mental retardation, and assessment: The case for nonlabeling. Paper presented to the Fourth International Congress of the International Association for the Scientific Study of Mental Retardation, Washington, DC.

Mercer, J. R. (1979). *System of multicultural pluralistic assessment: Conceptual and technical manual.* San Antonio, TX: Psychological Corp.

Meyers, C. E., MacMillan, D. L., & Yoshida, R. K. (1978). Validity of psychologists' identification of EMR students in the perspective of the California decertification experience. *Journal of School Psychology, 16,* 3–15.

Miele, F. (1979). Cultural bias in the WISC. *Intelligence, 3,* 149–164.

Morales, E. S., & George, C. (1976, September). Examiner effects in the testing of Mexican-

American children. Paper presented at the Annual Meeting of the American Psychological Association, Washington, DC.

Moran, M. P. (1990). The problem of cultural bias in personality assessment. In C. R. Reynolds & R. W. Kamphaus (Eds.), *Handbook of psychological and educational assessment of children, Vol. 2, Personality, behavior and context* (pp. 524–545). New York: Guilford.

Moreland, K. L. (1995). Persistent issues in multicultural assessment of social and emotional functioning. In L. A. Suzuki, P. J. Meller, & J. G. Ponterrotto (Eds.), *Handbook of multicultural assessment: Clinical psychological and educational applications.* San Francisco: Jossey-Bass.

Nalven, F. B., Hoffman, L. J., & Bierbryer, B. (1969). The effects of subject's age, sex, race and socioeconomic status on psychologists' estimates of "true IQ" from WISC scores. *Journal of Clinical Psychology, 25,* 271–274.

Nandakumar, R., Glutting, J. J., & Oakland, T. (1993). Mantel-Haenszel methodology for detecting item bias: An introduction and example using the guide to the assessment of test session behavior. *Journal of Psychoeducational Assessment, 11*(2), 108–119.

Nichols, R. C. (1978). Policy implications of the IQ controversy. In L. S. Schulman (Ed.), *Review of research in education* (Vol. 6). Itasca, IL: Peacock.

Novick, M. R., & Petersen, N. S. (1976). Towards equalizing educational and employment opportunity. *Journal of Educational Measurement, 13,* 77–88.

Oakland, T., & Feigenbaum, D. (1979). Multiple sources of test bias on the WISC-R and the Bender-Gestalt Test. *Journal of Consulting and Clinical Psychology, 47,* 968–974.

Oakland, T., & Matuszek, P. (1977). Using tests in nondiscriminating assessment. In T. Oakland (Ed.), *Psychological and educational assessment of minority group children,* New York: Brunner/Mazel.

Padilla, A. M. (1988). Early psychological assessment of Mexican-American children. *Journal of the History of the Behavioral Sciences, 24,* 113–115.

*PASE* (parents in action on special education) *et al.* v. *Hannon et al.* (1980, July). No. 74 C 3586. U.S. District Court for the Northern District of Illinois, Eastern Division, slip opinion.

Payne, B., & Payne, D. (1991). The ability of teachers to identify academically at-risk elementary students. *Journal of Research in Childhood Education, 5*(2), 116–126.

Pintner, R. (1931). *Intelligence testing.* New York: Holt, Rinehart & Winston.

Poortinga, Y. H. (1983). Psychometric approaches to intergroup comparison: The problem of equivalence. In S. H. Irvine & J. W. Berry (Eds.), *Human assessment and cross-cultural factors* (pp. 237–258). New York: Plenum.

Poortinga, Y. H., & Malpass, R. S. (1986). Making inferences from cross-cultural data. In W. J. Lonner & J. W. Berry (Eds.), *Field methods in cross-cultural psychology* (pp. 17–46). Beverly Hills, CA: Sage.

Potthoff, R. F. (1966). *Statistical aspects of the problem of biases in psychological tests.* Institute of Statistics Mimeo Series No. 479. Chapel Hill: University of North Carolina.

Ramsey, R. T. (1979). *The testing manual: A guide to test administration and use.* Pittsburgh: Author.

Reschly, D. (1978). WISC-R factor structures among Anglos, Blacks, Chicanos, and Native-American Papagos. *Journal of Consulting and Clinical Psychology, 46,* 417–422.

Reschly, D. J. (1980). Concepts of bias in assessment and WISC-R research with minorities. In H. Vance & F. Wallbrown (Eds.), *WISC-R: Research and interpretation.* Washington, DC: National Association of School Psychologists.

Reschly, D., & Sabers, D. (1979). Analysis of test bias in four groups with the regression definition. *Journal of Educational Measurement, 16,* 1–9.

Reynolds, C. R. (1978). Differential validity of several preschool assessment instruments for blacks, whites, males, and females. Doctoral dissertation, University of Georgia, Athens.

Reynolds, C. R. (1979). Should we screen preschoolers? *Contemporary Educational Psychology, 4,* 371–379.

Reynolds, C. R. (1980a). Differential construct validity of intelligence as popularly measured: Correlation of age and raw scores on the WISC-R for blacks, white, males and females. *Intelligence: A Multidisciplinary Journal, 4,* 371–379.

Reynolds, C. R. (1980b). An examination for test bias in a preschool battery across race and sex. *Journal of Educational Measurement, 17,* 137–146.

Reynolds, C. R. (1980c). In support of "Bias in Mental Testing" and scientific inquiry. *The Behavioral and Brain Sciences, 3,* 352.

Reynolds, C. R. (1982a). Construct and predictive bias. In R. A. Berk (Ed.), *Handbook of methods for detecting test bias.* Baltimore, MD: Johns Hopkins University Press.

Reynolds, C. R. (1982b). The problem of bias in psychological assessment. In C. R. Reynolds & T. B. Gutkin (Eds.), *The Handbook of School Psychology,* (pp. 178–208). New York: Wiley.

Reynolds, C. R. (1983). Test bias: In God we trust, all others must have data. *Journal of Special Education, 17,* 214–268.

Reynolds, C. R. (1995). Test bias in the assessment of intelligence and personality. In D. Saklofske & M. Zeidner (Eds.), *International handbook of personality and intelligence* (pp. 545–576). New York: Plenum.

Reynolds, C. R. (1997). Forward and backward memory span should not be combined for clinical analysis. *Archives of Clinical Neuropsychology, 12*(1), 29–40.

Reynolds, C. R. (in press a). Cultural bias in testing of intelligence and personality. In M. Hersen & A. Bellack (Eds.), *Comprehensive clinical psychology, Vol. 8, Cross Cultural Applications.* Cambridge: Elsevier Science.

Reynolds, C. R. (in press b). Need we measure anxiety separately for males and females. *Journal of Personality Assessment.*

Reynolds, C. R., & Bigler, E. D. (1994). *Test of memory and learning.* Austin, TX: Pro-Ed.

Reynolds, C. R., & Brown, R. T. (1984). Bias in mental testing: An introduction to the issues. In C. R. Reynolds & R. T. Brown (Eds.), *Perspectives on bias in mental testing* (pp. 1–39). New York: Plenum.

Reynolds, C. R., & Gutkin, T. B. (1980, September). WISC-R performance of blacks and whites matched on four demographic variables. Paper presented at the Annual Meeting of the American Psychological Association, Montreal.

Reynolds, C. R., & Gutkin, T. B. (1981). A multivariate comparison of the intellectual performance of blacks and whites matched on four demographic variables. *Personality and Individual Differences, 2,* 175–180.

Reynolds, C. R., Gutkin, T. B., Dappen, L., & Wright, D. (1979). Differential validity of the WISC-R for boys and girls referred for psychological services. *Perceptual and Motor Skills, 48,* 868–870.

Reynolds, C. R., & Harding, R. E. (1983). Outcome in two large sample studies of factorial similarity under six methods of comparison. *Educational and Psychological Measurement, 43,* 723–728.

Reynolds, C. R., & Hartlage, L. C. (1979). Comparison of WISC and WISC-R regression lines for academic prediction with black and white referred children. *Journal of Consulting and Clinical Psychology, 47,* 589–591.

Reynolds, C. R., & Jensen, A. R. (1983, September). Patterns of intellectual performance among blacks and whites matched on "g." Paper presented at the Annual Meeting of the American Psychological Association, Montreal.

Reynolds, C. R., & Kaiser, S. (1990). Test bias in psychological assessment. In T. B. Gutkin & C. R. Reynolds (Eds.), *The handbook of school psychology* (2nd ed., pp. 487–525). New York: Wiley.

Reynolds, C. R., & Kamphaus, R. W. (1992). *Behavior Assessment System for Children: Manual.* Circle Pines, MN: American Guidance Service.

Reynolds, C. R., McBride, R. D., & Gibson, L. J. (1979, March). Black-White IQ discrepancies may be related to differences in hemisphericity. Paper presented at the Annual Meeting of the National Association of School Psychologists, San Diego.

Reynolds, C. R., & Paget, K. (1981). Factor analysis of the Revised Manifest Anxiety Scale for blacks, whites, males, and females with a national normative sample. *Journal of Consulting and Clinical Psychology, 49,* 349–352.

Reynolds, C. R., Willson, V. L., & Chatman, S. P. (1984). Item bias on the 1981 revisions of the Peabody Picture Vocabulary Test using a new method of detecting bias. *Journal of Psychoeducational Assessment, 2,* 219–221.

Reynolds, C. R., Willson, V. L., & Chatman, S. P. (1985). Regression analyses of bias on the Kaufman Assessment Battery for Children. *Journal of School Psychology, 23,* 195–204.

Rosenthal, R. (1976). *Experimenter effects in behavioral research.* New York: Halstead.

Ross, A. O. (1974). A clinical child psychologist "examines" retarded children. In G. J. Williams & S. Gordon (Eds.), *Clinical child psychology: Current trends and future perspectives.* New York: Behavioral Publications.

Ross, A. O. (1976). *Psychological aspects of learning abilities and reading disorders.* New York: McGraw-Hill.

Rowe, D. (1994). No more than skin deep. *American Psychologist, 49*(3), 215–216.

Samuda, A. J. (1975). *Psychological testing of American minorities: Issues and consequences.* New York: Dodd, Mead.

Sandoval, J. (1979). The WISC-R and internal evidence of test bias with minority groups. *Journal of Consulting and Clinical Psychology, 47,* 919–927.

Sandoval, J., & Mille, M. (1979). Accuracy judgments of WISC-R item difficulty for minority groups. Paper presented at the Annual Meeting of the American Psychological Association, New York.

Sattler, J. M. (1974). *Assessment of children's intelligence.* Philadelphia: Saunders.

Sattler, J. M. (1988). *Assessment of children* (3rd ed.). San Diego: Author.

Sattler, J. M., & Gwynne, J. (1982). White examiners generally do not impede the intelligence test performance of black children: To debunk a myth. *Journal of Consulting and Clinical Psychology, 50*(2), 196–208.

Sawyer, R. L., Cole, N. S., & Cole, J. W. (1976). Utilities and the issue of fairness in a decision theoretic model for selection. *Journal of Educational Measurement, 13,* 59–76.

Scheuneman, J. D. (1987). An experimental, exploratory study of the causes of bias in test items. *Journal of Educational Measurement, 29,* 97–118.

Schmidt, F. L., & Hunter, J. E. (1974). Racial and ethnic bias in psychological tests: Divergent implications of two definitions of test bias. *American Psychologist, 29,* 1–8.

Schmidt, W. H. (1983). Content biases in achievement tests. *Journal of Educational Measurement, 20,* 165–178.

Schoenfeld, W. N. (1974). Notes on a bit of psychological nonsense: "Race differences in intelligence." *Psychological Record, 24,* 17–32.

Scholwinski, E. (1985). Ability patterns of blacks and whites as determined by the subscales on the Wechsler Adult Intelligence Scale–Revised. Doctoral dissertation, Texas A&M University, College Station.

Shuey, A. M. (1966). *The testing of Negro intelligence* (2nd ed.). New York: Social Science press.

Steffenburg, S., & Gillberg, C. (1986). Autistic and autistic-like conditions in Swedish rural and urban areas: A population study. *British Journal of Psychiatry, 149,* 81–87.

Stern, W. (1914). *The psychological methods of testing intelligence.* Baltimore, MD: Warwick & York.

Sternberg, R. J. (1980). Intelligence and test bias: Art and science. *Behavioral and Brain Sciences, 3,* 353–354.

Stricker, L. J. (1982). Identifying test items that perform differentially in population subgroups: A partial correlation index. *Applied Psychological Measurement, 6,* 261–273.

Suzuki, L. A., Meller, P. J., & Ponterotto, J. G. (1996). Multicultural assessment: Present trends and future directions. In L. A. Suzuki, P. J. Meller, & J. G. Ponterotto (Eds.), *Handbook of multicultural assessment: Clinical, psychological, and educational applications.* San Francisco: Jossey-Bass.

Thissen, D., Steinberg, L., & Wainer, H. (1993). Detection of differential item functioning using the parameters of item response models. In P. W. Holland & H. Wainer (Eds.), *Differential item functioning: Theory and practice* (pp. 67–113). Hillsdale, NJ: Erlbaum.

Thorndike, R. L. (1971). Concepts of culture-fairness. *Journal of Educational Measurement, 8,* 63–70.

Tomlinson, J. R., Acker, N., Canter, A., & Lindborg, S. (1977). Minority status, sex, and school psychological services. *Psychology in the Schools, 14,* 456–460.

Torrance, E. P. (1980). Psychology of gifted children and youth. In W. M. Cruickshank (Ed.), *Psychology of exceptional children and youth.* Englewood Cliffs, NJ: Prentice Hall.

Tsai, L., Stewart, M. A., Faust, M., & Shook S. (1982). Social class distribution of fathers of children enrolled in the Iowa Autism Program. *Journal of Autism and Developmental Disorders, 12,* 211–221.

Tyler, L. E. (1965). *The psychology of human differences.* New York: Appleton-Century-Crofts.

Vance, B., & Sabatino, D. (1991). Identifying sources of bias in the WISC-R. *Diagnostique, 17*(1), 40–48.

Vance, H. B., Hankins, N., & McGee, H. (1979). A preliminary study of black and white differences on the Wechsler Intelligence Scale for Children. *Journal of Clinical Psychology, 35,* 815–819.

Van de Vijver, F., & Hambleton, R. K. (1996). Translating tests: Some practical guidelines. *European Psychologists, 1,* 89–99.

Van de Vijver, F., & Poortinga, Y. H. (1991). Culture-free measurement in the history of cross-cultural psychology. *Bulletin of the International Test Commission, 18,* 72–87.

Veale, J. R., & Foreman, D. F. (1983). Assessing cultural bias using foil response data: Cultural variation. *Journal of Educational Measurement, 20,* 249–258.

Waits, C., & Richmond, B. O. (1978). Special education—who needs it? *Exceptional Children, 44,* 279–280.

Wechsler, D. (1974). *Wechsler Intelligence Scale for Children–Revised.* New York: Psychological Corp.

Wechsler, D. (1975). Intelligence defined and undefined: A relativistic appraisal. *American Psychologist, 30,* 135–139.

Weiss, L. G., & Prifitera, A. (1995). An evaluation of differential prediction of WIAT achievement scores from WISC-III FSIQ across ethnic and gender groups. *Journal of School Psychology, 33*(4), 297–304.

Willerman, L. (1979). *The psychology of individual and group differences.* San Francisco: Freeman.

Williams, R. L. (1970). Danger: Testing and dehumanizing black children. *Clinical Child Psychology Newsletter, 9,* 5–6.

Williams, R. L. (1974). From dehumanization to black intellectual genocide: A rejoinder. In G. J. Williams & S. Gordon (Eds.), *Clinical child psychology: Current practices and future perspectives.* New York: Behavioral Publications.

Williams, R. L., Dotson, W., Dow, P., & Williams, W. S. (1980). The war against testing: A current status report. *Journal of Negro Education, 49,* 263–273.

Willson, V. L., Nolan, R. F., Reynolds, C. R. & Kamphaus, R. W. (1989). Race and gender effects on item functioning on the Kaufman Assessment Battery for Children. *Journal of School Psychology, 27,* 289–296.

Wright, B. J., & Isenstein, V. R. (1977/1978). Psychological tests and minorities. DHEW Publication No. (ADM) 78-482. Rockville, MD: National Institutes of Mental Health.

# SCHOOL PSYCHOLOGICAL INTERVENTIONS: FOCUS ON CHILDREN

●

## CHAPTER 23

# SCHOOL-BASED CONSULTATION THEORY AND PRACTICE: THE ART AND SCIENCE OF INDIRECT SERVICE DELIVERY

**TERRY B. GUTKIN**
*University of Nebraska–Lincoln*
**MICHAEL J. CURTIS**
*University of South Florida*

Over the last several decades, school-based consultation has emerged as one of the professional activities most preferred by school psychologists, often being ranked by practitioners as the most desired role and almost always viewed as a job function in which they would like to engage more often (e.g., Bahr, 1996; Fisher, Jenkins, & Crumbley, 1986; Meacham & Peckham, 1978; Roberts & Rust, 1994). Since the publication of this chapter in the first and second editions of the *Handbook of School Psychology* (Gutkin & Curtis, 1982, 1990), a continuing stream of books, book chapters, and journal miniseries have appeared, attesting to the central role of school-based consultation in the eyes of school psychologists (Bergan & Kratochwill, 1990; Bernard & DiGiuseppe, 1994; Brown, Pryzwansky, & Schulte, 1987; Caplan & Caplan, 1993; Cole & Siegel, 1990; Conoley & Conoley, 1992; Costenbader, Swartz, & Petrix, 1992; Dougherty, 1990; Erchul, 1993a; Erchul & Marten, 1997; Gutkin, 1997b; Kratochwill & Bergan, 1990; Kratochwill, Elliott, & Carrington Rotto, 1990, 1995; Levinson, 1990; Marks, 1995; Noell, 1996; Rosenfield, 1987; Sheridan, Kratochwill, & Bergan, 1996; Zins & Erchul, 1995; Zins, Kratochwill, & Elliott, 1993b; Zins & Ponti, 1990). The initiation of the *Journal of Educational and Psychological Consultation* in 1990, a refereed journal devoted entirely to consultation theory and

research, is further evidence of the expanding interest of school psychologists and other human service professionals in consultation. Consistent with the positive attitudes toward consultation reflected in these and other publications has been a growing number of literature reviews and meta-analyses that indicate that school-based consultation is, in fact, an effective means of service delivery (Kratochwill, Elliott, & Busse, 1995; Mannino & Shore, 1975; Medway, 1979, 1982; Medway & Updyke, 1985; Sheridan, Welch, & Orme, 1996).

Although the remainder of this chapter is devoted primarily to the examination of school-based consultation services from the perspective of school psychologists, it is important to note that school psychologists are not alone in their support for this approach to service delivery in educational, as well as community, settings. For example, special educators (e.g., Idol, Nevin, & Paolucci-Whitcomb, 1994; Zins & Heron, 1996), counseling psychologists (e.g., Randolph & Mitchell, 1995), community psychologists (e.g., O'Hearn & Gatz, 1996), and speech pathologists (Secord, 1990), among others, also appear to view these services as vital. Above and beyond these individual professional groups, there is clear evidence that entire school districts, agencies, and national professional organizations are also moving toward implementing and supporting consultation service delivery (Bush et al., 1989; Canter, 1991; Franklin & Duley, 1991; Givens-Ogle, Christ, & Idol, 1991; House & McInerney, 1996; Ikeda, Tilly, Stumme, Volmer, & Allison, 1996; National Association of School Psychologists, 1994; Tindal, Shinn, Walz, & Germann, 1987; Ysseldyke, Dawson, Lehr, Reschly, Reynolds, & Telzrow, 1997).

## IMPORTANCE OF CONSULTATION FOR SCHOOL PSYCHOLOGICAL SERVICES

The ability of school psychologists to serve children has always been, and probably always will be, mediated to a large extent by their ability to function effectively as consultants. While consultation services have always been valued highly by both school psychologists and the consumers of school psychological services (Gutkin & Curtis, 1982), recent events have served to underscore even further the centrality of this approach. With each passing year, consultation seems to grow in importance as a foundational role for the profession.

The critical importance of consultation for school psychologists lies in what Gutkin and Conoley (1990) termed the "Paradox of School Psychology." That is, "to serve children effectively school psychologists must, first and foremost, concentrate their attention and professional expertise on adults" (p. 212). Although not intuitively obvious, the impact of school psychologists on children is typically a function of actions taken (or not taken) by adults other than school psychologists in the school and home environments of children. In earlier times, many believed that the school psychologist's job was complete after correctly diagnosing a child's problems and/or designing an efficacious intervention for a referred child. Today, such a belief would be considered naive (Witt, 1990b).

Gutkin and Conoley (1990) provide the following example to illustrate the nature of the "Paradox of School Psychology."

> Consider the hypothetical case of a third-grade child who is referred to a school psychologist because of academic difficulties. The school psychologist is highly sophisticated regarding academic dysfunctions of third graders and does a superior job of assessing and diagnosing the

child's difficulties. In addition to isolating and correctly diagnosing the specific psychoeducational deficits exhibited by the referred child, the psychologist also develops a set of insightful treatment recommendations centering around the initiation of a system of contingent positive reinforcement for appropriate academic behavior in the child's regular classroom. The psychologist communicates her or his expertise and ideas for intervention to the classroom teacher via a detailed written report and a multidisciplinary team meeting. Although the stage is set for effective treatment to occur, no such outcome ever comes to pass . . . because the child's teacher, who has to implement the psychologist's plan, believes that behavior modification is tantamount to bribery (a belief that is not uncommon among teachers [Grieger, 1977]). The final results of the school psychologist's efforts in this hypothetical (but not at all unusual) case are: (a) a high-quality assessment of the referred child, (b) an accurate diagnosis of the referred child's problems, (c) the development of an effective treatment plan for the referred child, but (d) no meaningful psychological service provided to the referred child. (pp. 210–211)

In other words, the expertise of the school psychologist was of no benefit to the child. As per the "Paradox of School Psychology," the ability of this school psychologist to deliver meaningful assistance to this student hinged directly on his or her ability to consult effectively with the teacher, going beyond both the diagnosis of the child's problems and written recommendations for intervention.

Given the "Paradox of School Psychology," interpersonal influence with adults should be viewed as a key to successful school psychological services for children (Gutkin, 1997b). And while consultation clearly is not the only means by which school psychologists can exert influence on the lives of children through significant adults, it would seem to hold more promise than either assessment (Andrews & Gutkin, 1994) or child-focused therapy services "given its unique emphasis on long-term, face-to-face, collaborative relationships between school psychologists and relevant third-party adults" (Gutkin & Conoley, 1990, p. 211).

Consultation has become vitally important

to school psychological services for other reasons as well. In particular, recent years have seen a growing emphasis on the inclusion of students with disabilities in mainstream and general education environments. This movement has grown rapidly in response to (1) meta-analyses that indicate that segregated, pull-out placements for children with disabilities are not typically superior to the maintenance of children in mainstream settings (Carlberg & Kavale, 1980; Wang & Baker, 1986); (2) research that indicates that special education placements often provide educational programs that are pedagogically indistinguishable from what is offered in general education (Epps & Tindal, 1987; Ysseldyke, Christenson, Thurlow, & Bakewell, 1989); (3) evidence of rapidly increasing costs of educating children with disabilities in non-mainstream environments (Ysseldyke, Algozzine, & Thurlow, 1992); (4) federal mandates for education in the least restrictive environment, initiated by the Education for All Handicapped Children Act (PL 94-142) and continued in the Individuals with Disabilities Education Act (IDEA, PL 101-476); (5) federal directives such as the Regular Education Initiative (Will, 1988); (6) growing disillusionment by school psychologists (e.g., Gutkin & Tieger, 1979; Reschly, 1988; Ysseldyke, et al., 1984) and other powerful groups of educators (National Association of State Boards of Education, 1992) with categorical approaches to special education services; and (7) preliminary research supportive of inclusive practices for a broad range of children with disabilities (Hollowood, Salisbury, Rainforth, & Palombaro, 1994; Janney, Snell, Beers, & Raynes, 1995; Salisbury, Evans, & Palombaro, 1997; Shinn, Powell-Smith, & Good, 1996).

To effectively include children with disabilities, schools have relied on two primary strategies, both of which are premised on the delivery of consultation services by school psychologists and other educational specialists. First, whenever possible, handicapped children in segregated, special education programs are returned to general education classrooms to the maximum extent possible. Given that many of these children still have significant academic and behavioral problems, the general education teachers who work with them are typically in need of substantial support and assistance (Scruggs & Mastropieri, 1996; Will, 1988; Zins, Curtis, Graden, & Ponti, 1988). School districts that have documented successful programs for reintegrating children with disabilities into general education have relied very heavily on consultation and collaborative services as a primary vehicle for providing this support (e.g., Bush et al., 1989; Canter, 1991; Franklin & Duley, 1991; Givens-Ogle et al., 1991; Janney et al., 1995).

The second major vehicle for achieving inclusion has been what initially was termed *prereferral intervention*. To avoid the belief by many teachers that prereferral intervention represented procedural obstacles that had to be cleared before referring a child for a suspected disability, rather than a system to address the child's problems, the term *intervention assistance* came to be used (Zins, Curtis, Graden, & Ponti, 1988). The latter term tended to convey a message of support for teachers in their attempts to respond to children's needs. As detailed by Graden, Casey, and Christenson (1985) in one of the earlier descriptions of this approach, the process involves joint problem solving by teachers and educational specialists for the purposes of designing and implementing effective educational programs in mainstream settings for children who are experiencing significant academic and behavioral problems. The goal of this approach is to prevent children from being removed unnecessarily from general education environments. At the beginning of the 1990s, a significant majority of states required or strongly encouraged intervention processes prior to special education assessment and/or placement (Carter & Sugai, 1989). This trend has continued to accelerate over time, drawing school psychologists and other school specialists increasingly into consultative roles with both general and special education teachers. To date, outcome research with these intervention-based programs has been quite positive when teams follow appropriate group consultation procedures, showing high levels of acceptance by teachers and substantial decreases in special education referral rates (Fuchs, Fuchs, & Bahr, 1990; Graden, Casey, Bonstrom, 1985; Gutkin, Henning-Stout, & Piersel, 1988; Henning-Stout, Lucas, & McCary, 1993; Nelson, Smith, Taylor, Dodd, & Reavis, 1991; Ponti, Zins, & Graden, 1988; Rosenfield, 1992). Unfortunately, there are also indications that without explicit training efforts, group processes for many intervention teams are inconsistent with consultation principles, thus leading to far less than optimal results (e.g., Flugum & Reschly,

1994; Meyers, Valentino, Meyers, & Boretti, 1996).

Beyond inclusion programs, consultation services provide school psychologists with a mechanism by which they can positively affect the educational and psychological development of all children, rather than just those with disabilities. The opportunity to provide services to *all* children has been articulated as a major goal for the profession since the Thayer Conference in 1954 (Cutts, 1955) and continues to be reflected in our most contemporary statements of professional standards (e.g., National Association of School Psychologists, 1992) and role definitions (e.g., Shinn & McConnell, 1994). To accomplish this goal, school psychologists strive to "give psychology away" (Miller, 1969) through consultation services to those persons who have the most intensive daily contact with the broadest range of children (e.g., teachers). By enhancing the psychological, educational, and mental health skills of consultees such as teachers, school psychologists can indirectly benefit the lives of innumerable children.

Clearly, consultation is a crucial component of the school psychologist's professional role, and this has been recognized in virtually (if not, literally) every major professional document that addresses comprehensive school psychological services (e.g., Ysseldyke et al., 1997). Proceeding within this context, we turn now to a delineation of the core characteristics of consultation services that undergrid the interactions between consultants and consultees. Specifically, we examine those central philosophical and operational components that we perceive to make up the basic foundations of consultation theory and practice.

# CORE CHARACTERISTICS OF SCHOOL-BASED CONSULTATIVE SERVICES

Consultation is a complex and sophisticated set of service delivery methodologies. And although there are numerous consultation models from which the practitioner can choose (three of the most prominent models are described subsequently), these models are bound together by a set of essential characteristics and assumptions that constitute the core of all consultation services. These core elements are the defining features of consultation that serve both to unify the various consultation models and to set them apart from other approaches to service delivery, such as psychotherapy.

The discussion that follows details those core characteristics that have both significant historical roots (e.g., Bergan, 1977; Caplan, 1970; Schein, 1969) and broad contemporary acceptance (e.g., Bergan & Kratochwill, 1990; Caplan & Caplan, 1993; Conoley & Conoley, 1992; Gutkin, 1996a), emerging from theorists who hold diverse orientations. Although widely accepted, these core elements are not without controversy, and many authors have noted the need to continuously reexamine and revise these assumptions in response to emerging theoretical and empirical information (e.g., Gresham & Noell, 1993; Gutkin, 1993b; Noell & Witt, 1996; Witt, 1990a).

## An Overarching Definition

Despite the broad and growing interest in consultative approaches among educators, school psychologists, and other health service providers, there remains considerable confusion regarding what constitutes consultation per se. Part of the problem is the term *consultation* itself, which is used in so many contexts and in reference to so many different types of service relationships that for some it has almost become devoid of meaning. Decades ago Barry (1970) observed, "Today almost everyone is a consultant. Every program has consultants. Sometimes it seems as if there are more consultants than consultees!" (p. 363). This statement remains quite accurate some 25 years after it was made.

Although there is no single definition of consultation with universal support, we continue to find Medway's (1979) to be both succinct and accurate. As such, it is used for the purposes of this chapter. Specifically, Medway defined consultation as a process of "collaborative problem-solving between a mental health specialist (the consultant) and one or more persons (the consultees) who are responsible for providing some form of psychological assistance to another (the client)" (p. 276).

## Indirect Service Delivery

Indirect service is the single most definitive characteristic of consultation. In the more traditional system of direct service delivery, the psychologist's primary contact is with a client (or patient) who receives services directly from the psychologist. Psychotherapy and counseling are common exemplars of direct services. Psychologists who work from an indirect service delivery model, however, interact primarily with other professionals and care-givers (consultees) who work directly with clients. In the indirect model, psychologists do not provide services directly to clients themselves. In school-based consultation, school psychologists frequently function as the consultant, teachers or parents as the consultees, and students as clients. Of course, other alignments are possible. That is, other professionals may serve as either the consultant or consultee, and the client could be anyone associated with the school (e.g., principal, team leaders, and teachers' aides). Regardless of the specific case, however, when functioning as a consultant, psychologists provide indirect services to one or more clients by working through one or more consultees who have direct and continuing contact with clients. These relationships are illustrated in Figure 23.1.

The indirect service concept should not be mistakenly assumed to imply that consultants are prohibited from having any direct contact with clients as they provide consultation services (Noell & Witt, 1996). The crucial issue is not whether consultants interact directly with clients but rather that treatment services that are ultimately delivered to clients as a result of the consultation process are implemented by one or more consultees instead of by the consultant. Seen from this perspective, it is clear that psychologists' assessment activities, be they traditional (e.g., norm-referenced testing) or nontraditional (e.g., curriculum-based assessment) in nature, should not be viewed as antithetical to consultation processes, as long as they facilitate the provision of treatment interventions by consultees (Gutkin & Conoley, 1990).

## Focus of Consultation

The primary focus of consultation interactions is the provision of services to one or more clients.

**Direct Service Delivery Model**

Teacher —*referral*→ Psychologist —*treatment*→ Child

**Indirect Service Delivery Model**

Psychologist ←*referral*— Teacher —*treatment*→ Child

(consultant) ←→ (consultee)
*consultation*

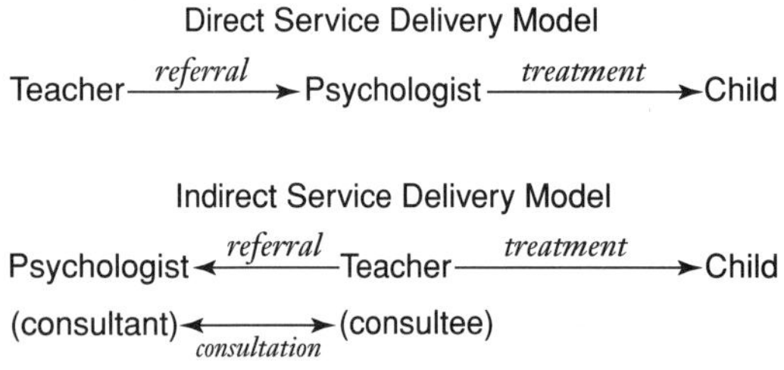

**FIGURE 23.1 Direct and indirect service delivery models.**

That is, consultants interact with consultees to improve the educational and psychological circumstances of clients. Whereas success at improving the lives of clients (e.g., children) will often simultaneously lighten the burden of consultees (e.g., teachers and parents), this is a byproduct (albeit one that is very positive) rather than the central purpose of consultative interactions. In consultation, unlike psychotherapy, the personal needs of the consultee are a legitimate focus only to the extent that these personal needs have an impact on a client. Thus, while it would be entirely appropriate to consult with teachers about methods for controlling their anger toward students, it would be inappropriate to consult with these same teachers about reducing angry outbursts directed toward their spouses. Although circumstances can sometimes make it difficult to distinguish between consultation and psychotherapeutic services, consultants must remain vigilant to avoid dual relationships (i.e., serving as a consultant and a psychotherapist to the same individual) (American Psychological Association, 1992), in accordance with our ethics codes. Consultation should remain focused first and foremost on the provision of services to clients, not on the provision of psychotherapeutic services to consultees.

## Goals of Consultation

All consultation models have a dual set of goals. One goal is to provide remedial services for the presenting problems of clients; another goal is to improve the functioning of consultees so they can prevent and/or respond more effectively to similar problems in the future. The degree of emphasis placed on each of these goals varies across consultation models, but both goals should always be present in the consultant's mind as she or he works with a consultee.

### Remediation

The remedial goals of consultation services are rather straightforward. Typically, children (clients) are referred to school psychologists (consultants) because teachers or parents (consultees) are experiencing academic and/or behavioral difficulties that they have been unable to resolve on their own. The consultant's role is to work with the consultee to develop effective interventions. Success is determined by assessing whether the referred problem is resolved or improved on to everyone's satisfaction.

Most available consultation research addresses remedial rather than preventive goals. That is, the bulk of the consultation literature examines whether consultants were able to bring about behavioral and attitudinal changes in consultees and clients in response to presenting problems. Although this body of research has been, and continues to be, criticized on methodological grounds and for its lack of specific directions for practitioners (Fuchs, Fuchs, Dulan, Roberts, & Fernstrom, 1992; Gresham & Kendell, 1987; Gutkin, 1993b; Hughes, 1994; Medway, 1982; Meyers, Pitt, Gaughan, & Freidman, 1978; Pryzwansky, 1986), there is consensus that school-based consultation services are effective from a remedial perspective. For example, reviewing the recent consultation research literature (from 1985 to 1995), Sheridan, Welch, & Orme (1996) reported positive outcomes in 76% of published studies, which was remarkably similar to the earlier findings of Mannino and Shore (1975) and Medway (1979)—78% and 76% positive outcomes, respectively. Employing meta-analyses, Medway and Updyke (1985) documented effect sizes of .55 for consultees and .39 for clients, indicating that "consultees showed improvements greater than 71% and clients showed improvements greater than 66% of untreated comparable groups" (p. 489). More recently, a meta-analysis by Kratochwill, Elliott, and Busse (1995) of changes in individual clients over time reported an overall effect size of .95, indicating that the average client moved from fiftieth percentile before treatment to roughly the eighty-third percentile following intervention. Parenthetically, this latter finding is equivalent to the effect sizes typically reported in contemporary psychotherapy outcome research (Lambert & Bergin, 1994).

## Prevention

While the prevention goals of consultation are a bit less obvious at first glance, they are every bit as important. In fact, when viewed from a public health perspective, one could make a strong case that the prevention outcomes of consultation are substantially more improvement in the long term than are those related to remediation (Conoley & Gutkin, 1995).

Within the context of consultation services, prevention is most frequently conceptualized as "giving psychology away" (Miller, 1969) to consultees. That is, as consultees learn new ways of remediating presenting problems, it is hoped and expected that they may also be able to apply newly acquired content and process knowledge and skills to clients' problems that arise in the future, thus nipping new problems in the bud (secondary prevention) or preventing them from occurring in the first place (primary prevention).

On the content side, if a teacher learns how to work effectively with a child's acting-out behaviors through consultation with a school psychologist, he or she may be able to apply these same behavior management techniques to other students, either now or in the future, and thus reduce and/or prevent the appearance of other discipline problems. Supportive research findings include the following: (1) dramatic decreases in student referral rates following consultation (Fuchs et al., 1990; Graden, Casey, & Bonstrom, 1985; Gutkin et al., 1988; Henning-Stout et al., 1993; Nelson et al., 1991; Ponti et al., 1988; Rosenfield, 1992), (2) generalization of clients' gains and/or consultee skills to other children in the same class or other settings subsequent to the receipt of consultation services (Jason & Ferone, 1978; Meyers, 1975; Peck, Killen, & Baumgart, 1989), (3) reports of consultees' enhanced professional skills learned through consultation interactions (Carrington Rotto & Kratochwill, 1994; Gutkin, 1980, 1986; Gutkin, Singer, & Brown, 1980), and (4) empirical evaluations of long-standing prevention programs based largely on consultation methodologies (e.g., Cowen & Hightower, 1990; Hightower, Johnson, & Haffey, 1995; Jackson, Cleveland, & Merenda, 1975; Zins & Forman, 1988).

In terms of process, consultation is intended to also help consultees become better problem solvers. With a large body of research suggesting that even young children can be taught problem-solving skills through modeling (e.g., Johnson, Gutkin, & Plake, 1991), it seems quite reasonable to assume that consultation interactions can be utilized by consultants to enhance the problem-solving skills of consultees (Brown & Schulte, 1987; Gutkin, 1993a). To date, a number of studies suggest that consultees' process skills can, in fact, be improved by exposure to consultation, the modeling of consultation, or consultation training (Anderson, Kratochwill, & Bergan 1986; Cleven & Gutkin, 1988; Curtis & Metz, 1986; Curtis & Watson, 1980; Curtis & Zins, 1988; Kratochwill, VanSomeren, & Sheridan, 1989; McDougall, Reschly, & Corkery, 1988; Revels & Gutkin, 1983; Zins & Ponti, 1996). Although some negative findings have been reported (Robbins & Gutkin, 1994) and it is clear that additional research is needed in this area (Noell & Witt, 1996), there appears to be sound empirical reason for cautious optimism (Kratochwill, Bergan, Sheridan, & Elliott, in press).

## Consultant-Consultee Relationship

Much as the therapist-client relationship is thought to be crucial to the process of psychotherapy (Cormier & Cormier, 1991), the consultant-consultee relationship is viewed as pivotal to effective consultation. Although initially given less attention by those who were focused primarily on the technology of a client's behavior change, it is becoming increasingly clear to consultation advocates of all persuasions that the person-to-person relationships established during the course of consultation mediate the effectiveness of consultation services (Conoley & Conoley, 1992; Kratochwill, Elliott, & Carrington Rotto, 1995; Rosenfield, 1991).

The "Paradox of School Psychology" concept (Gutkin & Conoley, 1990) discussed earlier in this chapter and/or a review of Figure 23.1 makes it abundantly clear why the consultant-consultee relationship is so crucial. Quite simply, the consultee always comes between the consultant and the client. Without the cooperation of the consultee, the consultant is powerless to provide assistance to the client. Consequently, consultants will probably be successful only to the extent that they are able to elicit the cooperation of consultees in the execution of treatment programs. While not the sole determinant of this phenomenon, the nature of the consultant-consultee relationship is undoubtedly one major factor influencing whether a consultee adopts a resistant or cooperative approach to the consultation process and the intervention plans that result.

The following dimensions of consultant-consultee relationships are thought to be particularly important to the success of consultation services. Although not an exhaustive list, these factors do communicate collectively the intended "spirit" of the consultation process. They are also quite consistent with theory and research that is emerging from the psychotherapy literature, indicating that therapists are more likely to succeed with their clients when these clients perceive their therapists as high on trustworthiness, attractiveness, and expertness (Beutler, Machado, & Neufeldt, 1994).

### Coordinate Power Status

Perhaps the most common and long-standing assumption about consultant-consultee relationships is that they should be collegial and collaborative rather than hierarchical and coercive (Bergan, 1977; Caplan, 1970; Meyers, 1973). Prior to consultation, the dominant relationship metaphors in psychological services were doctor-patient and superior-subordinate. Neither, however, is believed to be suitable for consultation.

A doctor-patient relationship is clearly not appropriate because the consultee is not the consultant's patient. The consultee is neither sick nor seeking assistance with a personal problem. Rather, consultation is designed to assist consultees as they examine alternative ways to interact with and serve their clients.

Likewise, superior-subordinate relationships are deemed to be inappropriate. First and foremost, they do not reflect the realities that confront school psychologists or other educational professionals who function as consultants. Whereas Captain Piccard may be able to gain cooperation and compliance from his Star Trek crew simply by commanding them to "Make it so," few if any school psychologists will ever find themselves in this position vis-à-vis the consultees with whom they work (e.g., teachers, parents, and principals). Although schools may have a formal organizational chart, implying that some individuals are in superordinate positions, few successful schools function by having those at the top of the organizational chart issue orders and commands to those beneath them (Davis & Thomas, 1989; Schmuck, 1990). Schools are inherently different from either military or corporate environments, and different decision-making and relationship styles are necessary.

Coordinate power status is thought to be the appropriate relationship between consultants and consultees. The most essential element of this relationship is shared and equal power in the decision-making process. That is, neither consultants nor consultees should be making unilateral decisions against the wishes of their consulting partners. This means that a consultee must be allowed to accept or reject ideas put forth by a consulting school psychologist, based on that consultee's perception of the merit of the ideas, rather than being pressured into acceptance because the consultant "ordered" the consultee to "Make it so."

Having noted what is meant by coordinate

power status, we must also note what is not meant by this term, for it is subject to misinterpretation without some further explanation. Coordinate power status does *not* mean, for example, that consultants and consultees have equivalent bodies of knowledge, for they do not. Whereas psychologists, teachers, parents, and others each have knowledge that is important for the success of a consultation interaction, it is not the same knowledge. In fact, it is these very differences that makes the consultation relationship so potentially powerful, as different perspectives and knowledge bases are integrated and synthesized to produce solutions that would not have been evident to either the consultant or consultee working in isolation (Tyler, Pargament, & Gatz, 1983).

Also, coordinate power status does *not* mean that consultants and consultees function in the same way during consultation interactions, for they do not (Sheridan, 1992). Recent research (Erchul, 1987; Erchul & Chewning, 1990; Erchul, Covington, Hughes, & Meyers, 1995; Erchul, Hughes, Meyers, Hickman, & Braden, 1992; Gutkin, 1996b; Martens, Erchul, & Witt, 1992; Witt, Erchul, McKee, Pardue, & Wickstrom, 1991) suggests strongly that consultants and consultees behave quite differently as they consult with each other. The most consistent finding to emerge from this growing body of research is that consultants tend to ask more questions than consultees, whereas consultees tend to talk more than consultants, especially during the problem identification process.

Some have interpreted these data to suggest that the need for consultant-consultee collaboration is little more than a myth in the context of school-based consultation (e.g., Erchul & Martens, 1997; Witt, 1990a). We disagree vigorously with this conclusion (see Gutkin, 1997a, for an extensive review of this body of research). The finding that consultants are, in *some ways*, more directive than consultees during the consultation process does *not* suggest the absence of collaboration. Gutkin (1997a) argues that consultants can be *both* directive and collaborative at the same time, for *directiveness* and *collaboration* are not opposites. The opposite of *collaboration* is *coercion*. Consultants who suggest topics and issues to explore with their consultees while accepting that their consultees may either accept or reject their ideas are, in fact, being both directive and collaborative. There are, in fact, no indications in any of the research conducted to date suggesting that an effective consultant "tells the consultee what to do" (Erchul & Martens, 1997, p. 23; see Deno, 1975, for an interesting case study) or that school psychologists should behave like "Conan the Consultant" (Erchul, 1992, p. 364).

It is precisely this lack of any empirical support for a hierarchical power relationship between the consultant and consultee that leads us to reaffirm the long-standing conclusion that school-based consultation is conducted most effectively within a collaborative context. While other researchers (e.g., Erchul, 1992; Erchul & Martens, 1997) continue to prefer descriptors such as *cooperation* and *teamwork* rather than *collaboration* to describe the consultation enterprise, our primary point is that a "rose by any other name would smell just as sweet." Regardless of what term we use, there appears to be a research-based consensus that noncoercive, coordinate power relationships are most facilitative of effective school-based consultation.

## Voluntary Participation

As might be surmised from the concept of coordinate power relationships, consultation has always been (e.g., Reschly, 1976) and continues to be (Zins, Kratochwill, & Elliott, 1993a) conceptualized as a voluntary activity. Much as is true for involuntary psychotherapy, trying to pressure a consultee into consultation makes it very difficult to achieve a successful outcome. Although school authorities can mandate that a teacher interact with a psychologist about a particular problem, they have few (if any) ways to ensure that this interaction will be productive. Given the nature of consultative activities, it is quite easy for either party to sabotage the effort when he or she has a hidden agenda to do so. When forced to consult, teachers may wish to "prove" the ineffectiveness of the consultant's ideas.

Especially subtle and problematic are those instances in which a teacher is required by his or her principal to work with a psychologist but, to save face, the psychologist is never overtly informed of the mandatory nature of the interaction. In these circumstances, consultants may experience significant reactance and resistance from their consultees, and successful consultation may be difficult to achieve (Hughes & Falk, 1981; Wickstrom & Witt, 1993).

Consistent with the voluntary nature of consultation, its initiation ideally should come from the consultee rather than the consultant. Initiation by the consultee is thought to be beneficial because it suggests that the consultee recognizes the existence of a problem and is motivated to take action. Reality, of course, is not always congruent with theoretical ideals (Harris & Cancelli, 1991). In actual practices school psychologists may find that they must make the initial contact, often at the request of principals, intervention assistance teams, or parents. The critical issue, however, is not so much who initiates the consulting relationship but rather that its continuation is voluntary.

## Confidentiality of Communication

While there is a strong consensus that confidentiality is an essential element of consultation relationships (Conoley & Conoley, 1992; Zins et al., 1993a), there has been virtually no empirical study of this important assumption (see Nowell & Spruill, 1993, and Woods & McNamara, 1980, for exceptions pertaining to psychotherapy). Nevertheless, the logic of maintaining confidentiality with consultees seems compelling and congruent with important standards of professional ethics (American Psychological Association, 1992; Hughes, 1986). To be successful in consultation, consultees have to feel free to communicate with consultants in an open and honest manner. It is highly unlikely that they would do so, exposing their professional weaknesses, personal concerns, and so on, if they perceived that this information might be leaked to other people in the school or community. Without trust in the consultant, consultees would probably feel the need to focus only on safe topics, steering clear of controversial and potentially embarrassing facts and opinions. Doing so, however, could render the consultation process impotent.

Not all information can be or should be kept confidential, however. Consultants frequently have to make subtle judgment calls, balancing the confidentiality rights of consultees with the rights of society, school officials, and parents to be informed about the education and treatment of children. At the extreme are cases of child abuse; threats of violence against a reasonably identifiable victim as per the Tarasoff case (Fischer & Sorenson, 1996; Jacob-Timm & Hartshorne, 1994); and the commission of felonies, in which psychologists have the legal responsibility to report information to the proper authorities (e.g., child protective service agencies and local police) in most states. Even in those states with protections of privileged communication that apply to psychologists, it strikes us as unlikely that a consultee (as opposed to a patient or client) could invoke that privilege. As such, consultants could probably be compelled to break confidentiality in a court of law.

Of course, most consultations are not nearly so dramatic, and the legitimacy of maintaining confidentiality is less problematic. But even in run of the mill cases, not all information should be or can be kept confidential. For example, the fact that a psychologist is consulting with a teacher about a particular child may be part of an intervention assistance plan or an Individual Education Program (IEP). In such instances, both the existence and goals of this consultation relationship would probably be known, in advance, to the intervention assistance or IEP team. Likewise, principals, parents, and others would seem to have a legitimate right to know if a psychologist was consulting with a teacher about a particular child and the nature of the problem being addressed (e.g., the child is having difficulty in adding three-digit numbers and completing homework assignments). Although sharing information such as this would rarely be a problem, it would be important for consultants to maintain confidentiality about sensitive issues that arose during consultation sessions (e.g., personal feelings or professional inadequacies of the consultee).

Given the complexity of confidentiality decisions, it is important for consultants to discuss with consultees and other key members of an organization the nature and limits of confidentiality before entering into any consultation relationships, as per our ethics codes (American Psychological Association, 1992; Hughes, 1986). Of equal importance, there should be a consensus between the consultant and the consultee at all points during a consultation relationship about which aspects of this relationship are public and which are confidential.

## Encouraging Active Participation by Consultees During Consultation

To whatever extent it is possible, consultants should encourage active participation by consultees throughout the consultation process. Consultees' involvement during consultation is thought to (1) facilitate the collection of broadranging assessment data, as consultees typically have a unique and in-depth view of clients' behaviors in relevant environments, for example, school and home (Gresham, MacMillan, & Bocian, 1997; Pyle, 1977); (2) provide consultants with an opportunity to assess and develop treatments in response to the professional perspectives and "biases" of the consultee, which may prove to be crucial information when packaging interventions to make them more attractive and ecologically friendly for the consultee (Conoley, Conoley, Ivey, & Scheel, 1991; Gutkin, 1997b; Martens & Witt, 1988b; Witt & Martens, 1988); (c) enhance consultees "ownership" of interventions, thus increasing the likelihood that they will carry out a treatment as planned (Meichenbaum & Turk, 1987; Reinking, Livesay, & Kohl, 1978; Rosenfield, 1991); (d) generally expand the opportunity for consultants and consultees to provide each other with corrective feedback, helping both members of the consultation dyad stay on track throughout the entire process; and (e) increase the possibility of "giving psychology away" (Miller, 1969) to consultees as more "teachable moments" are created during the consultation process.

Despite the apparent advantages of having consultees actively engaged in the consultative problem-solving process, the extent to which most teachers wish to participate actively remains clouded. On the positive side, there are both long-standing and more contemporary indications that teachers prefer consultation to more traditional and passive forms of service delivery by school psychologists (e.g., Babcock & Pryzwansky, 1983; Gutkin, 1980; Gutkin & Curtis, 1982; Kutsick, Gutkin, & Witt, 1991) and are actively involved during actual consultation sessions (Conoley, Conoley, & Gumm, 1992; Gutkin 1996b, 1997a; Martens et al., 1992). On the negative side, there are both long-standing and more contemporary indications that consultees may sometimes just be going through the motions, particularly in regard to prereferral intervention (e.g., Flugum & Reschly, 1994; Lambert, 1976; Meyers et al., 1996; Wilson, Gutkin, Hagen, & Oats, 1998). As noted above, it has been suggested that the term *prereferral intervention* may have itself contributed to expectations by teachers that this process is merely an administrative hurdle that must be cleared for a child to be considered for a different placement, typically a special education class. As of this date, we are forced to reiterate our conclusion from the previous edition pertaining to this crucial issue. Specifically, "We do not know just how much the 'typical' teacher is predisposed to be an active participant in consultative interactions and . . . such inclinations probably vary with the specifics of particular circumstances" (Gutkin & Curtis, 1990, p. 580).

Perhaps the best tact for contemporary school psychologists is to worry less about whether teachers do or do not wish to be active consultation participants—for it appears that the answer to that question is highly variable—and concentrate more on how we might increase consultees' involvement in working with difficult-to-teach children, in general, and in consultation, in particular. With these goals in mind, Bandura's (1993) work on self-efficacy would seem to be especially important, as persons with high self-efficacy perceptions "set themselves challenging goals and maintain strong commitment to them. They maintain a task-diagnostic focus that guides effective performance. They heighten and sustain their effort in the face of failure. They attribute failure to insufficient effort or deficient knowledge and skills that are acquirable. They quickly recover their sense of efficacy after failures or setbacks. They approach threatening situations with assurance that they can exercise control over then" (pp. 144–145). Research specific to teaching seems to confirm Bandura's hypotheses pertaining to heightened levels of self-efficacy and teachers' persistence in the face of difficult problems (e.g., Gibson & Dembo, 1984; Gorrell & Capron, 1990; Hughes, 1992; Hughes, Barker, Kemenoff, & Hart, 1993; Meijer & Foster, 1988; Podell & Soodak, 1993; Sachs, 1988; Smylie, 1988; Woolfolk & Hoy, 1990).

Building on Bandura's (1993) work and the suggestions of Brown and Schulte (1987), Gutkin and Ajchenbaum (1984) found a substantial positive correlation between teachers' perceptions of control over presenting problems and their preferences for consultative versus referral services. DeForest and Hughes (1992) also reported a positive relationship between teaching self-efficacy, and teachers' ratings of consultants and the acceptability of interventions. However, even in those studies in which heightened self-efficacy was not related to increased preferences for consultation per se (e.g., Hughes et al., 1993), a positive relationship between efficacy and willingness to persist with difficult instructional tasks emerged. As such, increasing teachers' self-efficacy appears to be a worthy goal for school-based consultants (Hughes, Grossman, & Barker, 1990).

Although still few in number, there are some reports of successfully increasing teachers' self-efficacy, and these may provide consultants with useful tools for accomplishing this goal. Ponti and Curtis (1984), for instance, found a significant increase in teachers' generalized expectations for success in dealing with students' problems after only three weeks of interactions with high-skilled consultants. Wehmann, Zins, and Curtis (1989) reported that teachers' expectations for successful problem resolution increased significantly following 10 weeks of school psychological consultation. Likewise, Gutkin et al (1980) discovered that teachers perceived a broad range of common school problems as less severe after receiving 14 weeks of consultation services in comparison to a control group that had no access to consultants. Focusing on enhancing teachers' confidence and knowledge about classroom interventions, Gutkin and Hickman (1988) and Hagen, Gutkin, Wilson, and Oats (in press) were both able to raise in-service and preservice teachers' perceptions of self-efficacy and, in the former study, increase teachers' preferences for consultation versus referral services as well. These studies suggest that increasing the content and process skills of consultees in classroom interventions and consultation interactions, which has been done successfully in the past (Anderson et al., 1986; Carrington Rotto & Kratochwill, 1994; Cleven & Gutkin, 1988; Curtis & Metz, 1986; Curtis & Watson, 1980; Curtis & Zins, 1988; Gutkin, 1980, 1986; Gutkin et al., 1980; Kratochwill et al., 1989; McDougall et al., 1988; Revels & Gutkin, 1983; Zins & Ponti, 1996), might also result in increased efficacy perceptions by teachers. Finally, research by Bergan, Byrnes, and Kratochwill (1979) and Tombari and Bergan (1978) indicates that teachers are more likely to experience a positive sense of efficacy when classroom problems are framed in behavioral rather than medical model terms. These findings are presumably the result of feeling some reasonable sense of control over classroom environmental variables but little control over students' internal pathological traits.

## Intervention Processes and Products

### Assessment

To develop interventions that will benefit clients, it is necessary to conduct a thorough assessment (Taylor & Miller, 1997). That is, interventions should be based on the gathering of relevant information and data, not simply the consultant's or consultee's intuitions and opinions. Given the vast array of assessment techniques that are available, a multitude of approaches could be employed. While it is not possible to specify what

should be done in all circumstances within the limited confines of this chapter, some overarching guidance can be provided.

First, assessment processes should be congruent with one's underlying assumptions about the nature of human behavior. As suggested over a decade ago by Reynolds, Gutkin, Elliott, and Witt (1984), we believe that Bandura's (1978) model of reciprocal determinism provides the most effective conceptual foundation on which to base consultation. From this point of view, a student's individual characteristics, behavior, and surrounding environment are all seen as having continuous, mutual, and reciprocal influences on one another. As such, the assessment of individual, behavioral, and/or environmental characteristics are all viewed as legitimate foci. Beyond this, however, the reciprocal determinism perspective directs us to pay particular attention to the interactions among individual, behavioral, and environmental variables.

In light of this, consultants rely primarily (but not exclusively) on assessments of clients' behavior in the natural environment, where the interaction of individual, behavioral, and environmental variables are easiest to observe. Thus, classroom observations and functional analyses (e.g., Broussard & Northup, 1995; Taylor & Miller, 1997) are employed frequently because they permit consultants and consultees to view directly the interaction among these factors. Likewise, teachers' and parents' interviews are a major source of assessment data. By "living" with their students and children in the natural environment day in and day out, month in and month out, both parents and teachers are in a unique position to analyze individual, behavioral, and environmental interactions over a sustained period of time and under a wide variety of conditions. It is important to note, however, that even in those instances when consultees' observations are less than completely accurate, these data will be critical because the subjective perceptions of consultees will probably influence their future behavior toward clients, as well as their willingness to implement interventions (Conoley et al., 1991).

Recently, curriculum-based (Kramer, 1993; Shapiro, 1990; Shinn, Rosenfield, & Knutson, 1989), performance-based (Aschbacher, 1991; Baker, O'Neill, & Linn, 1993), process (Meyers, 1988), portfolio (Salvia & Ysseldyke, 1995), responsive (Henning-Stout, 1994), and authentic (Elliott, 1991) assessment methodologies have grown rapidly in popularity. As measures of clients' behavior and individual abilities that occur in the natural environment, all are viewed as being highly compatible with the reciprocal determinism perspective. Norm-based assessments that measure individual traits outside the natural environment (e.g., measures of intelligence) generally receive less attention than those that address clients' behavior in the natural environment (e.g., behavior rating scales), although this may vary with specific characteristics of the individual case.

A second useful guideline in conducting assessments is that they should be designed to answer relevant questions. If, as is generally the case, the focus of consultation is on developing a school- or home-based intervention, the assessment process should be such that the information emerging from it will contribute to resolving important issues in intervention and treatment. Data that assist only with the identification of a special education diagnosis (e.g., learning disabilities) are of limited utility within this context. Once again, assessment methods that focus on the intersection of individual characteristics, behavior, and the environment are most likely to shed important new light on how best to develop effective interventions. Thus, for example, learning from direct observation what environmental stimuli lead to appropriate and inappropriate learning behaviors for a child will typically be of much greater significance to consultation processes than will discovering though an intelligence test whether that child is or is not mildly mentally retarded.

Finally, assessments should be conducted in a way that secures useful information without disrupting unnecessarily the natural environment in which the assessment takes place. In classrooms, this means that data-gathering procedures involving teachers should require no more time and training on their part than is absolutely necessary. Observational procedures, for example, should be designed so they are simple to learn and easy to conduct. There are numerous possibilities—for example, having teachers move a coin from their left to their right pockets as a way to conduct frequency courts, engaging children in self-monitoring of problem behaviors, or focusing on permanent products produced by clients whenever possible (Shapiro, 1987). Involving consultees in a thorough discussion of data collection procedures is probably the best way to ensure that assessment processes will provide necessary information in a manner that is acceptable to the consultee, without being unnecessarily cumbersome or disruptive to the natural environment.

## *Interventions*

Subsequent to conducting an assessment, the focus of consultation shifts to the design of interventions. Fortunately, there is nearly a limitless array of intervention strategies from which to choose (e.g., Bear, Minke, & Thomas, 1997; Cohen & fish, 1993; Fine & Carlson, 1992; Jongsma, Peterson, & McInnis, 1996; LeCroy, 1994; Millman, Schaefer, & Cohen, 1980; Stoner, Shinn, & Walker, 1991; Thomas & Grimes, 1995; Wittrock, 1986), and there is likely to be a multitude of approaches that could be used effectively with any given case. Despite this, however, designing a successful consultative intervention is often a complex and difficult task. The following are among the issues to consider when developing an intervention plan within the context of a consultation relationship.

Has the intervention been shown to be effective? Consistent with a scientist-practitioner model for professional practice, empirical knowledge should form the basis for selecting a treatment strategy. The research literature should be consulted to determine the efficacy of an intervention before implementation decisions are made. Doing so will help consultants and consultees avoid treatments for which there is no relevant research or there has been a demonstrated lack of success. Of course, as every practitioner knows, there is usually not a one-to-one correspondence between formal research studies and the specifics of a presenting case (Bardon, 1987; Stoner & Green, 1992). By reading the research literature critically, however, it should be possible to make a reasoned and informed judgment about whether the findings of one or more studies are applicable to the specifics of a particular problem.

Although important, the efficacy of a treatment is not sufficient, in and of itself, to achieve a successful consultation intervention. A number of other critical factors must be considered. Specifically, since the treatment plans developed during consultation will be implemented by the consultee, it is essential to consider those aspects of the treatment plan that might determine whether the intervention is acceptable to the consultee. Efficacy is only one of those factors (Gutkin, 1993c; Martens & Witt, 1988a; Witt, 1990b). Although a comprehensive review of the treatment acceptability literature is beyond the scope of this chapter (the interested reader is referred to Elliott, 1988, and Reimers, Wacker, and Koeppl, 1987), its importance cannot be overstated because it is unlikely that a consultee will implement any treatment that she or he does not find acceptable. As noted by Gutkin and Curtis (1981) nearly two decades ago, "Once the door to the classroom is closed, there is little that any of the educational specialists can do to insure the occurrence of any event that the teacher does not want to occur. . . . We must recognize that if a teacher decides that a remedial program is inappropriate, it is highly unlikely that the plan will ever be implemented. This would be true regardless of the actual quality of the particular program" (pp. 220–221). Thus, to be successful, consultants and consultees must design interventions that satisfy a number of important criteria above and beyond the documented effectiveness of those interventions (Lentz & Daly, 1996).

1. It would seem to be important to develop interventions that consultees believe themselves to be capable of doing. Based on a broad array of self-efficacy research (Bandura, 1993; DeForest & Hughes, 1992; Dunst & Trivette, 1988; Gibson & Dembo, 1984; Gorrell & Capron, 1990; Gutkin & Ajchenbaum, 1984; Gutkin & Hickman, 1988; Hughes, 1992; Hughes et al., 1993; Podell & Soodak, 1993; Sachs, 1988; Smylie, 1988; Woolfolk & Hoy, 1990), consultants should not expect consultees to carry through on interventions that they do not believe they can do. As noted earlier, following the research of Bergan and his associates, it is generally believed that focusing on the behavioral rather than the psychopathological elements of presenting problems will help consultees to achieve a sense of competence and enhanced self-efficacy (Bergan et al., 1979; Tombari & Bergan, 1978).

2. Beyond the perception of competence by consultees, success will hinge to a large extent on whether consultees are, in fact, able to execute a treatment correctly, that is, with high treatment integrity (Gresham, 1989). Although extensive research with a broad array of intervention techniques makes it clear that mental health paraprofessionals (e.g., teachers and parents) are quite capable of implementing educational and psychological treatments effectively (Christensen & Jacobson, 1994; Hattie, Sharpley, & Rogers, 1984;

Sulzer-Azaroff & Mayer, 1991), this capability should not be taken for granted (Robbins & Gutkin, 1994). Horror stories of inappropriately executed interventions are not uncommon, such as one teacher we know who implemented a timeout program by placing a kindergarten child into a small, isolated space for five hours a day for an entire week. Recent work suggests that direct training and feedback and intervention scripts may increase consultees' treatment integrity when implementing various intervention techniques (Ehrhardt, Barnett, Lentz, Stollar, & Reifin, 1996; Watson & Robinson, 1996).

3. Consultees must perceive an intervention to be congruent with their legitimate professional responsibilities before they are likely to carry it through. One of the major sources of resistance to consulting psychologists who strive to implement legal mandates, such as least restrictive environment programming and prereferral interventions (Carter & Sugai, 1989), and professional guidelines, such as mainstreaming, inclusion, and the Regular Education Initiative (Will, 1988) is the perception by many general education teachers that the education of children with disabilities in general education settings is simply not their job (Graden, Zins, Curtis, & Cobb, 1988; Stainback & Stainback, 1988). From their point of view, working with children who have special needs is the responsibility of specialists, such as resource teachers, special educators, school psychologists, counselors, speech therapists, and so on. To consult successfully under these circumstances, consultants must work with consultees to develop interventions that feel legitimate to the consultee. As noted earlier, framing children's problems in environmental rather than pathological terms may help with this dilemma (Bergan et al., 1978; Tombari & Bergan, 1978), as teachers are more likely to perceive manipulations of the educational environment than internal psychological and psychiatric diseases to be within their normal job role.

4. Interventions are most likely to be implemented by a consultee if they are congruent with the consultee's perceptions of the problem. As demonstrated by Witt, Moe, Gutkin, and Andrews (1984), the terms used to describe an intervention to a teacher can

substantively affect his or her evaluation of that intervention. Along similar lines, research by Conoley et al. (1991) indicates that consultants can increase the acceptability of treatment recommendations simply by matching the rationale for them to the perceptions expressed by their consultees. Thus, consultants should attempt to frame interventions that emerge from consultation in terms that are compatible with the worldviews of their consultees. It would appear that the way in which interventions are presented to consultees may prove to be as important as the operational specifics of the interventions themselves.

5. Interventions are more likely to be implemented by a consultee if they fit easily into the natural ecology in which the consultee must carry out the plan (Gutkin 1993c; Lentz, Allen, & Ehrhardt, 1996; Lentz & Daly, 1996). Treatments that are incompatible with the manner in which consultees manage their environments are likely to be rejected or implemented incorrectly. Teachers who depend exclusively on large-group instruction, for example, are unlikely to utilize techniques such as individualized reinforcement contingencies or peer tutoring, even though these treatments have been shown in research studies to be efficacious (Greenwood, Maheady, & Carta, 1991; Sulzer-Azaroff, & Mayer, 1991). To be successful with such consultees, consultants should focus their energies on developing intervention strategies that can be implemented within the context of large-group instruction. Building on existing behavioral regularities and taking advantage of the existing strengths of consultees are effective strategies for enhancing the probabilities for successful consultation outcomes (Martens & Witt, 1988b; Witt & Martens, 1988).

Although not an exhaustive discussion by any means, the foregoing points serve to communicate how important it is for consultants to think more deeply about the interventions they might recommend to consultees than simply assessing whether an intervention has been demonstrated by research to be effective. Interventions must not only have been demonstrated to be efficacious in general but also work well for the particular consultee, client, and environmental context in which the presenting problem occurs.

## Short-term Follow-up

Short-term follow-up (ranging from a day to a few weeks) is an essential element of consultation services. This need stems from the reality that regardless of how thorough and comprehensive our assessment might be, we are unable to know in advance whether our treatment recommendations will resolve presenting problems effectively (e.g., Stoner & Green, 1992). For both children and adults, there are few documented relationships between taxonomies of formal diagnoses and empirically validated interventions (Arter & Jenkins, 1979; Beutler, 1991; Dance & Neufeld, 1988; Good, Vollmer, Creek, Katz, & Chowdhri, 1993; Gresham & Gansle, 1992; National Association of School Psychologists, 1994; Ysseldyke & Christenson, 1988). Thus, mechanisms for corrective feedback must be built into all consultation services. Even those intervention plans in which we are most confident should be implemented with the expectation that follow-up will be required to determine if refinement or replacement of the original treatment program will be necessary. To be effective, school-based consultation must be an iterative process. A meta-analysis by Fuchs and Fuchs (1986) provides empirical support for incorporating systematic formative evaluation procedures into consultation processes.

There are numerous other reasons why follow-up contacts with consultees are thought to be so important. To quote an old and wise adage, "There are many slips twixt the cup and the lip." First, ideas that sound simple during the course of consultation may, in fact, require skills that the consultee does not possess to an adequate degree. Often, the consultee does not become aware of this fact until actually attempting to implement the strategy in question. At this point, it may become painfully clear to the consultee that he or she does not really know how to carry out the treatment that was agreed on. For example, a teacher who has always depended on punishment for class control may agree to institute a program of contingent social reinforcement for a child but have considerable difficulty because it runs counter to already well-ingrained teaching habits. Follow-up is needed in such cases to monitor implementation and either revise the treatment or assist the consultee in acquiring the necessary skills (Ehrhardt et al., 1996; Watson & Robinson, 1996).

Second, the consultee may realize after attempting to implement the program that he or she lacks one or more prerequisite resources. Many psychoeducational interventions are complex and require a variety of materials and support to be administered effectively. Individualized instruction is perhaps one of the best examples. A teacher who attempts to implement such a program may be stymied by a lack of time to carry out the intervention, inadequate access to necessary curricular materials in the building, the absence of teachers' aides, an excessively large number of other children in the classroom (many of whom also need considerable personal attention), or any of a wide variety of other similar problems. Follow-up contacts give the consultant an opportunity to work with the consultee either to secure necessary resources or to redesign the intervention so that it can be carried out effectively without the aid of such supports.

Third, there is evidence to indicate that teachers are often so busy that they are not aware of the nature of their own interactions with children (Martin & Keller, 1976). Jackson (1968), for example, reported that teachers may engage in up to 1,000 interpersonal interchanges per day, a pace at which it is most difficult to recall accurately the details of each interaction. When this is the case, teachers may improperly implement interventions because of a lack of awareness of their own classroom behavior. In these cases, follow-up observations by a consultant, coupled with corrective feedback to the teacher (Ehrhardt et al., 1996; Watson & Robinson, 1996), will be critical to increase treatment integrity and thus the probable success of the intervention (Gresham, 1989).

Fourth, as discussed previously, treatments need to be compatible with the natural ecology of a classroom if they are to succeed over a protracted period of time (Gutkin 1993c; Lentz et al., 1996; Lentz & Daly, 1996; Martens & Witt, 1988b; Witt & Martens, 1988). When trying to implement an agreed-upon treatment plan, teachers may discover that it does not fit easily into the pedagogical structure they have established for their classroom. In these instances, it is unlikely that consultees would modify their instructional or disciplinary approaches for their entire class just to meet the needs of a single, difficult-to-teach child. In all likelihood, these consultees will simply discard the intervention, even though they had agreed to it previously during consultation sessions. Follow-up consultation sessions provide consultants with an opportunity to address this dilemma by either assisting in the refinement of treatments, helping consultees to

be more flexible and individualized in the approaches they take with their class, or perhaps facilitating a broad-based change in a consultee's teaching style.

Fifth, the consultant's reinforcement of the consultee is also critical during that period of time after the intervention has been initiated and before treatment success or failure is evident. In those instances when interventions do not bring about the desired results, the consultant needs to be around to share the responsibility and frustration, provide support, and join the consultee in starting over. Given the lack of clear diagnosis-treatment relationships (e.g., Arter & Jenkins, 1979; Beutler, 1991; Dance & Neufeld, 1988; Good et al., 1993; Gresham & Gansle, 1992; National Association of School Psychologists, 1994; Ysseldyke & Christenson, 1988), unsuccessful outcomes are bound to occur despite everyone's best efforts and intentions. In fact, it may be important for the consultant to alert the consultee beforehand to this reality, to dispel unrealistic expectations for instant cures. Follow-up permits the consultant to help the consultee learn to take failure in stride and to use information resulting from an unsuccessful program as input for the generation of a new intervention.

Sixth, when treatment proves to be successful, someone ought to provide reinforcement to the consultee for a job well done. As Sarason, Levine, Goldenberg, Cherlin, and Bennett (1966) point out, "teaching is a lonely profession" (p. 74) and teachers typically go without overt reinforcement from adults (e.g., colleagues, support specialists, supervisors, and administrators) when everything is going well. This tends to sap consultees' motivation for handling future problems. During follow-up, consultants are in an excellent position to provide reinforcement to consultees for their successes and, perhaps of equal importance, to receive some reinforcement for their own work.

Last, follow-up facilitates the professional growth of both the consultee and the consultant. Recalling that all consultation interactions have both remedial and preventive goals, follow-up contacts give consultants an opportunity to review effective interventions with consultees and to determine the underlying reasons for the program's success. There is considerable potential for learning in this process for both consultees and consultants, and this knowledge can be used by either party for dealing with similar cases encountered in the future.

# Consultant and Consultee Responsibilities

First and foremost, consultants are responsible for the process elements of consultation interactions. As detailed by Dunst and Trivette (1988), the help offered by human service providers such as consultants can be either helpful, leading consultees to increased perceptions of self-efficacy, empowerment, and independence, or harmful, resulting in the opposite outcomes. It is the responsibility of consultants to create a service delivery context that supports and encourages consultees' growth and development as consultative assistance is provided. The relationship elements described earlier are believed to facilitate these outcomes, as are open and supportive styles of communication (e.g., attentive, genuine, empathetic, high in positive regard, and effective listening) with consultees (Cormier & Cormier, 1991; Ivey, 1994; Kurpius & Rozecki, 1993; Maitland, Fine, & Tracy, 1985; Rosenfield, 1991).

Consultants are also responsible for the integrity of the problem-solving processes that are employed during consultation interactions. More often than not, consultees will have little previous training in the art and science of problem solving per se. Thus, consultants must not only be cognizant of the content being discussed during consultation sessions but also monitor the problem-solving process. When the process goes off track (e.g., when a consultee tries to rush ahead with generating solutions before a problem has been defined adequately), it is the responsibility of the consultant to direct the interaction in more productive directions. While historically there has been some sense that focusing solely on consultation processes might be a sufficient contribution by consultants (e.g., Schien, 1969), we believe this is unlikely to be adequate in and of itself in most schools.

In addition to the process obligations of the consultant, both the consultant and consultee are responsible for bringing their content expertise to bear on presenting problems. As professionals, each should draw on the science and practice knowledge of their respective fields (e.g., psychology and education) during consultative interactions. Even parents, who would not be considered to be professionals in the strict sense of the term, have important content expertise to contribute in terms of the dynamics of day-to-day life in their own family and the history of behavior exhibited by the child in the home (Sheridan, Kratochwill, & Bergan, 1996). As noted earlier, it is the mixing, integrating, and synthesizing of these distinct bodies of knowledge and information brought to the consultation relationship by consultants and consultees alike that makes consultation such a powerful tool.

Given the indirect service delivery nature of consultation, consultees are responsible for taking action based on treatment plans that emerge from interactions with consultants. While this does not rule out some intervention strategies that would involve consultants in providing direct service to clients, such instances clearly would be the exception rather than the rule. School psychologists can not move into either the classroom or the home to provide services on a long-term, ongoing basis. The ultimate responsibility for implementing interventions in schools and homes clearly will fall to persons such as teachers and parents, that is, consultees. This underscores further how important it is for the consultee to believe in the treatment plan and to have a sense of ownership of it (Dunst & Trivette, 1988).

That consultees have the primary responsibility for intervention implementation, of course, does not rule out the role of consultants as role models and providers of feedback. Thus, when appropriate, given the specifics of a particular case, and when invited to do so, psychologists should enter the classroom or the home to provide demonstrations for and feedback to consultees (Ehrhardt et al., 1996; Watson & Robinson, 1996). Giving consultees support services such as these should dramatically increase the probability that interventions will be implemented as they were intended, that is, with high treatment integrity (Gresham, 1989).

As noted earlier, consultees also have the primary responsibility for initiating the consultation relationship. Whereas principals or multidisciplinary and intervention assistance teams may sometimes assign a consultant to a consultee, it is thought to be best when consultees approach consultants rather than vice versa. Given the nature of the consultation relationship, it would be easy to get off on the wrong foot if consultees work with a consultant because they have been ordered to do so by some external authority. At the very least, it seems important that ongoing consultation interactions be based on voluntary participation by the consultee, regardless of who initiates the first contact.

Finally, both consultants and consultees are responsible for the successes and failures of the treatments they jointly design for clients. Both parties should share in the "glory" of positive outcomes and both should feel obligated to improve on strategies that produced less than desired results.

## Entry Processes

Given the substantive differences between consultation and the traditional roles of school psychologists (e.g., assessment and psychotherapy/counseling), many consultation theorists (e.g., Conoley & Conoley, 1992; Fullan, Miles, & Taylor, 1980) believe that offering consultation services to a new organization should begin with an entry process. The purposes and goals of such entry processes are numerous.

For example, there is a need for school personnel to develop an understanding of the consultation process. Thus consultants need a way to communicate the core characteristics described in this chapter to potential consultees and persons in influential positions, typically starting with the building principal (Marks, 1995). In some instances, a written contract may be helpful for specifying "fees, obligations, times, acceptable activities, time limits, and so on" (Conoley & Conoley, 1992, p. 81). Subsequent interactions should involve assistant principals, team leaders, specialists, and so on. Eventually, the consultant should have an opportunity to meet with the entire school faculty, again to explain the consultation model. A 15-minute slide-tape package produced by Curtis and Anderson (1976) has been used successfully by many practitioners for this purpose. The goal for all of these meetings is to clarify proactively the nature of consultation services that will be offered and help school personnel see the advantages these services might hold for them and their students.

A second goal for an entry process is to allow potential consultees to get to know the consultant as a person. Given that the success of consultation services will hinge to a considerable degree on the consultant's ability to establish a facilitative relationship with consultees (Maitland et al., 1985; Rosenfield, 1991) and communicate her or his unique process and content skills (Knoff, Hines, & Kromrey, 1995; Stenger, Tollefson, & Fine, 1992), it is important to start building these perceptions at the earliest possible opportunity. As suggested by psychotherapy research (Beutler et al., 1994), consultants should

strive to communicate their expertness, attractiveness, and trustworthiness to potential consultees. By establishing these relationships, consultants can quickly gain the confidence of school personnel and come to be viewed as one of "us" rather than one of "them."

Third, it is very important for the consultant to get to know the individual consultees, their organizational structure, and the school climate (Marks, 1995). Before consulting with teachers, for example, it is helpful if consultants can get a feel for how the teachers in a particular building teach and how they conceptualize their role as teachers. In this way, consultants are able to present ideas and concepts that match and mesh easily with the natural ecologies in a school building (Conoley et al., 1991; Martens & Witt, 1988b; Witt & Martens, 1988). Also, it is important to identify political hot spots in a school as quickly as possible to avoid being caught unintentionally in a crossfire among school personnel.

With all of this information in hand, consultants and consultees can jointly determine exactly how consultation services should be provided in their building. Referred to in the research literature as mutual adaptation (McLaughlin, 1976), this is an empirically validated way to increase the adoption of innovations by school organizations. Rather than informing schools that they must implement the consultation model in one particular way (i.e., the consultant's way), it is much more effective to negotiate implementation procedures with the host organization, even if this means less than full implementation of the model initially.

Despite broad support among theorists for an entry process, there has been precious little research specifically focused on this topic (see Martens, Lewandowski, & Houk, 1989, and Robinson, Cameron, & Raethel, 1985, for exceptions). And while it is reasonable to extrapolate conclusions from other bodies of work (e.g., the adoption of innovations and treatment acceptability literatures), this is a poor substitute indeed for research on the entry process per se. As noted by Gutkin (1993b), empirical work in this area is among the most pressing contemporary agendas for school-based consultants.

## MODELS OF SCHOOL-BASED CONSULTATION

Over the last half century or so, a considerable number of differing consultation models have emerged in the school psychology literature (Reschly, 1976). Although each of these models shares the core characteristics detailed earlier in this chapter, each is also different enough in orientation and operation to warrant independent examination. What follows is a brief review of the three major consultation models employed by school psychologists: (1) ecobehavioral consultation, (2) mental health consultation, and (3) organizational consultation.

## Ecobehavioral Consultation
### A Word About Terminology

With each new version of this chapter, our thinking has evolved somewhat about how best to name this form of consultation. In our original work (Gutkin & Curtis, 1982), we distinguished between problem-solving and behavioral consultation and treated them as two separate models. Eight years later (Gutkin & Curtis, 1990), we shifted our terminology after becoming convinced that there were many commonalities between the problem-solving and behavioral approaches and neither title captured the essence of the model being discussed. Thus, we renamed and integrated these two approaches into one model and called it ecological consultation. Today, as we go through our third edition of this caper, our thoughts along these lines have continued to change, and we are suggesting yet a new title, namely, ecobehaviorial consultation. We realize, of course, that by making this change we risk adding confusion to an already confusing situation (i.e., there are already too many different names for consultation models that are essentially the same). Nonetheless, we are willing to run this risk because we believe that the name of an approach matters substantially because it sets a metaphorical context in which the specifics of a methodology come to be understood (Gutkin, 1993c).

Our choice of ecobehavioral consultation is explained more fully elsewhere (Gutkin, 1993c) but summarized very briefly here. Although the name behavioral consultation is used most frequently in the literature and is probably the name best understood among practitioners and researchers alike, we perceive it as unintentionally limiting the scope and breadth of problem solving to proximal environmental variables that surrounding a client's behavior. Although behavioral concepts such as setting events (Wahler & Fox, 1981) could be employed to expand on this relatively limited frame of analysis, it is our perception that, unfortunately, this is usually not the case. An examination of the major texts on behavioral consultation (e.g., Bergan, 1977; Bergan & Kratochwill, 1990), for example, reveals a near exclusive focus on proximal (i.e., immediate antecedents and consequences) environmental variables, with little or no consideration of distal events. As discussed by Gutkin (1993c), however, distal environmental events—for example, teachers' tolerance for particular behaviors, parental pressures on school personnel to either secure or avoid special education placement for their child, school building or district procedures for initiating special education referrals, school board directives regarding professional practices such as inclusion, family disruptions like divorce or parental substance abuse, and the interaction among all of these and other related variables—can often have a greater impact on why children behave as they do than immediate (proximal) antecedents and consequences. Our earlier shift to the title of ecological consultation (Gutkin & Curtis, 1990) was intended to address this problem by calling consultants' and consultees' attention to a systems orientation that considered seriously both proximal and distal environmental variables, as well as interactions among them (Morse, 1993).

Using the name ecobehavioral consultation is an attempt to avoid throwing out the proverbial baby with the bathwater:

> [While] an ecological perspective can improve on a narrow view of behavioral psychology for school-based consultants, there can be little doubt that the reverse is also true. The behavioral model brings to the "marriage" methodological rigor, experimental precision, and a long track record of successful intervention and practice in school settings, all of which are essential ingredients to the future success of any consultation approach. The hard-nosed empiricism and extensive knowledge base that have developed under the behavioral "umbrella" must not be lost. (Gutkin, 1993c, p. 97)

In short we are arguing that traditional behavioral consultation must be expanded to incorporate systemic, ecological thinking, while maintaining the well-documented advantages of behavioral approaches to school-based problems. Given that behavioral and ecological conceptualizations of human behavior and service delivery have long been recognized as highly compatible (e.g., Rogers-Warren & Warren, 1977; Willems, 1974), we believe that an ecobehavioral orientation toward consultation allows us to have our cake and eat it too.

## Operationalizing the Ecobehavioral Consultation Model

Drawing on behavioral (Baldwin & Baldwin, 1998; Skinner, 1953; Sulzer-Azaroff & Mayer, 1991), ecological (Barker, 1965; Christenson, Abery, & Weinberg, 1986; Minor, 1972; Morse, 1993), and ecobehavioral (Greenwood, Carta, & Atwater, 1991; Morris & Midgley, 1990; Rogers-Warren & Warren, 1977; Willems, 1974) theory and research, ecobehavioral consultants work with their consultees to identify and manipulate relevant person-environment relationships to improve, eliminate, and/or prevent identified problems (Zins & Erchul, 1995). For school psychologists who are using this approach, presenting problems typically center around academic and/or behavioral difficulties that result from dysfunctional interactions among children, teachers, peers, parents, siblings, school administrators, and others in school, home, and community environments.

To develop effective interventions for identified problems, the ecobehavioral consultant leads the consultee through one or more forms of structured problem solving. While there are many different problem-solving processes from which to choose, most are highly similar to one another (Gutkin & Curtis, 1990). Bergan's (1977) four-step sequence has received the most attention in the school psychology literature, and very detailed operational descriptions have been presented in a number of recent books, book chapters, and training manuals (Bergan & Kratochwill, 1990; Kratochwill & Bergan, 1990; Kratochwill, Elliott, & Carrington Rotto, 1995; Sheridan, Kratochwill, & Bergan, 1996). A highly congruent seven-step model proposed by Gutkin and Curtis (1982, 1990), based on the work of Osborn (1963) and D'Zurilla and Goldfried (1971), has also been used frequently in both school psychology research and practice (Bush et al., 1989, Henning-Stout & Conoley, 1988), as have other variations on these problem-solving sequences (e.g., Goodwin & Coates, 1976; Jayanthi & Friend, 1992; Maitland et al., 1985).

Step 1 of Bergan's (1977) problem-solving process is *problem identification*, in which the consultant and consultee delineate a clearly defined statement of the presenting problem. Although to the novice this may sound like the easiest step of the process, experienced consultants recognize that problem definition is usually complicated by the fact that problems occur in interconnected clusters rather than in isolation and may be clouded by consultees' affective reactions (e.g., frustration, anger, and anxiety). Teasing out the central problem from the background noise can be quite complex. Some criteria for selecting and isolating target behaviors are deciding which are (1) most important to address, (2) easiest to fix, (3) most distressing to the consultee or other relevant people in the client's ecosystem, or (4) most impactful in that resolving this one behavior may result in the muting or disappearance of other problem behaviors. Early research suggests that successful completion of the problem identification stage is closely related to the efficacy of the entire consultation process (Bergan & Tombari, 1976).

A useful problem definition is one that is stated in concrete, descriptive, behavioral terms so that it is both directly observable and amenable to quantification. Lambert's (1976) study of elementary school teachers, however, led her to conclude that teachers experience considerable difficulty when trying to specify pupils' problems in this manner. She found that teachers tended to report students' problems with general and vague statements (e.g. the child is poorly motivated or the student has low ability) rather than in terms that have clear implications for "operational changes in classroom practice" (p. 516). Recent research by Wilson et al. (1998) reinforces this perception. Coolahan (1991) also found that teachers may make many "inferential" statements in describing students' problems, although consultants' verbalizations resulted in increased numbers of validation and specification statements by these same consultees. Other research also suggests that teachers exposed to highly skilled consultants through direct interaction or modeling significantly improve in their problem clarification skills (Cleven & Gutkin, 1988; Curtis & Watson, 1980).

One of the consultant's first tasks, therefore, is to help consultees arrive at a concrete, behavioral definition of a problem. One means for doing this is simply to ask for further specification of vague problem statements. For example, if a consultee states that Johnny has "a bad attitude toward school," the consultant could ask, "Can you be more specific?" or "What behaviors lead you to say that he has a bad attitude?" or "The last time you found yourself realizing that Johnny had a bad attitude toward school, what was he actually doing at that moment?" Often a series of questions such as these can lead to a useful clarification of the problem. Giving the consultee sufficient space to express her or his thoughts may be another effective vehicle. It is hoped that as a consultee expresses his or her perceptions, more and more operational specificity will arise.

Often consultees are unable to provide a clear behavioral definition of a problem because they are trying to describe too many problems at once. Both experience and research (Caron & Rutter, 1991; Mash & Dozois, 1996; Saxe, Cross, & Silverman, 1988) tell us that children typically have multiple rather than singular difficulties. Social adjustment problems, for example, often occur concomitantly with academic difficulties and family dysfunction. The range of difficulties with children is often so broad that a specific behavioral definition of the problem may be very difficult to develop. In such instances, the consultant should help the consultee divide the overall problem into its component parts, rank each of the specific components, and work toward a behavioral definition for the most important one. This procedure should help consultees reduce the complexity of presenting problems so that they can avoid being overwhelmed and work more effectively toward the development of a useful problem statement.

A frequent error made by consulting psychologists during problem identification is to assume that a consultee's first verbalization of a problem statement corresponds to the consultee's major concern. Although never researched directly, it is our experience that initial problem statements by consultees often serve, either intentionally or unintentionally, to mask their real concern. In some instances, they may need to establish a strong sense of trust in a consultant before revealing highly sensitive information. In presenting a safe problem, consultees may be testing the consultant. The consultant's ability to execute an effective entry process and maintain a nonevaluative stance should increase the probability that the consultees will eventually reveal problems that are both more substantive and more sensitive. In other instances, consultees may be experiencing so many problems that they are genuinely confused about what constitutes the essential versus the peripheral elements of

the situation. In these cases, the consultant's listening skills and ability to help consultees discuss and establish priorities for the component parts of the problem situation will be important.

Once an effective problem definition has been agreed on, it is important to focus on the collection of baseline data and the development of realistic, short-term (three-to-six week) goals. This will allow the consultant and consultee to judge accurately whether their treatment plans are working satisfactorily soon after they are implemented.

Step 2 is *problem analysis*. This is the assessment and treatment generation phase of the consultation process. The primary goals are to develop and assess hypothesis pertaining to why the target behaviors are occurring and work up a set of intervention plans that are likely to produce desired outcomes.

Proximal environmental antecedents and consequences that surround target behaviors are typically analyzed in great detail at this point. Interactions among the behaviors, distal environments, and individual characteristics of all involved must also be considered to understand more fully the client's ecosystem (Gutkin, 1993c). When conducting problem analysis assessments, it is important to identify client and ecosystem resources that might be incorporated into treatment plans (e.g., the student is highly motivated to improve and has strong peer relationships; the parents have a positive history with the teacher and are highly motivated to support treatment plans in whatever way they can; the school and community have relevant after-school programs), as well as focusing on problematic phenomena.

The generation of intervention plans should flow naturally from the problem definition process and the ecobehavioral assessment data that have been collected. Brainstorming is thought to be an effective mechanism for these purposes. Specifically, the consultant and consultee should engage in a freewheeling generation of as many potential intervention strategies as possible, while refraining at this point from criticizing or praising each other's ideas. Research (e.g., D'Zurilla & Goldfried, 1971; Heppner, 1978; Jayanthi & Friend, 1992) suggests that criticism (either positive or negative) will reduce the number of ideas, and that the larger the number of brainstormed ideas there are to choose among the higher the probability of finding optimal and high quality solutions. Once a sufficient number of potential ideas have arisen, the consultant and consultee should review the list of alternatives to determine which are acceptable to the consultee and most likely to meet the needs of the client.

Step 3 is *plan implementation*. Treatments and interventions designed in step 2 are now put into action by the consultee (and others, when appropriate), and data are collected an analyzed (Shinn, 1995) to determine their impact. Given the complexity of relationships between attitudes and behaviors (e.g., Petty, Heesacker, & Hughes, 1997) and the subtleties of treatment compliance and integrity (Gresham, 1989; Gutkin & Conoley, 1990; Meichenbaum & Turk, 1987; Witt, 1990b), consultants should never assume that a consultee's good intentions and verbal agreements to implement a particular treatment program necessarily ensure that the program will be carried out or that it will be carried out as intended. As discussed earlier, follow-up contact is crucial.

To increase the probabilities that appropriate action will be taken by consultees, consultants should design interventions that are highly compatible with the natural ecosystems in which they are to be implemented (Martens & Witt, 1988a, 1988b; Witt & Martens, 1988). Thus, for example, proposed consultative interventions should build on the existing strengths of consultees, rather than focusing on the remediation of deficits, and take advantage of existing resources, rather than depending on the intrusion of new resources into an ecosystem.

When consultees fail to implement agreed-upon intervention plans, consultants should assume (at least initially) that there are legitimate reasons for this decision rather than leaping to the conclusion that the consultee is resistant, incompetent, or a "three-toed sloth" (Witt, 1990a, p. 368). The ecologies in which most consultees function are complex, unpredictable, uncontrollable, in many ways, and often pressure-packed. Implementing treatment plans for difficult-to-teach children may often be secondary to meeting the needs of other children in the classroom, principal's demands, parental pressures, excessive numbers of team meetings, a demanding (and, perhaps, unreasonable) team leader, unexpected emergencies, and so on. In our opinion, attributing a consultee's failure to act on treatment recommendations to resistance is less likely to result in meaningful and positive change in consultee behavior than attempting to understand and as-

sist with the demands and pressures placed on a consultee by the ecosystem in which she or he functions (Conoley, 1994).

The fourth and final step is *treatment evaluation*. At this point the consultant and consultee determine jointly whether the implemented intervention was successful. Baseline data and short-term goals developed during problem identification, assessment data collected during problem analysis, and treatment data collected during plan implementation are crucial in making this judgment. At the extremes, the consultant and consultee may conclude that the intervention was (1) a resounding success and that the consultation relationship for this particular problem can now be terminated, or (2) a total failure and that the consultation relationship should either be continued or terminated, according to the perceptions of both participants that subsequent interactions will lead to more substantive and positive outcomes. More often than not, however, the outcome falls somewhere between these two extremes, and the consultant and consultee both perceive the need for additional refinements and adjustments in the intervention program. Returning to the problem identification, problem analysis, and/or plan implementation steps should facilitate the attainment of this goal.

## Mental Health Consultation

As the first consultation model to be articulated in detail, the term *mental health consultation* has sometimes been taken as a generic phase for all consultation models (Meyers, Parsons, & Martin, 1979). Our use of this term is much more restricted and reflects primarily the work of Gerald Caplan (Caplan, 1970; Caplan & Caplan, 1993). Caplan's impact on mental health consultation has been so significant, in fact, that recently others have begun to publish books and chapters focusing solely on the history of his work (Erchul, 1993a).

Although Caplan's mental health consultation has a great deal in common with the ecobehavioral approach (most of the core characteristics of school-based consultation were first articulated by him in 1970), there are enough unique aspects to warrant its presentation as a distinct model. In particular, since Caplan and many of the earlier theoreticians were psychoanalytically oriented psychiatrists, the early literature often focuses on such topics as ego states, pre- and subconscious motivations, penis envy, castration fears, and so forth. In this regard, mental health consultation is quite disparate from the more extrapersonal, situationally oriented perspectives of ecobehavioral approaches.

In both his early and contemporary writings, Caplan (1970; Caplan & Caplan, 1993) discusses four overlapping types of mental health consultation: (1) client-centered case consultation, (2) consultee-centered case consultation, (3) program-centered administrative consultation, and (4) consultee-centered administrative consultation. These approaches differ according to whether the primary goal of consultation is prevention or remediation and whether the focus of consultation is on individual cases or programs. Most school psychologists consider consultee-centered case consultation to be the centerpiece of Caplan's and thus it receives more detailed analysis here.

Consultee-centered case consultation, in which the primary goal is prevention and the focus is on individual cases, is described by Caplan and Caplan (1993) as follows:

> The consultant's primary focus is on elucidating and remedying the shortcomings in the consultee's professional functioning. The discussion is mainly restricted to clarifying the details of the client's situation to increase the consultee's cognitive grasp and emotional mastery of the issues involved in caring for him. This is likely to lead to an improvement in the consultee's professional planning and action, and hopefully to improvement in the client. But in consultee-centered consultation, improvement in the client is a side effect, welcome though it may be; the primary goal is to improve the consultee's capacity to function effectively in this category of case, in order to benefit many similar clients in the future. Because of the educational emphasis, the consultant uses the discussion of the current case situation not primarily to understand the client but to understand and remedy the consultee's work difficulties. (p. 101)

There are several subtle but significant differences between ecobehavioral consultation, on the one hand, and consultee-centered case consultation, on the other. In the former, the consultant works with the consultee to delineate the causes of a client's presenting problem, as well as potential solutions. In the latter, a consultant is only indirectly interested in the causes for and solutions of the client's presenting problem. Instead, the primary focus is on determining why the consultee is having difficulties with a particular case and resolving these difficulties so that he or she can handle the client's problem independently. For example, under the ecobehavioral consultation methodology, a consultant might work with a consultee to determine why a particular child is continuously hostile to his or her teacher and peers. The outcome would typically be a series of planned interventions designed to reduce the occurrence of the child's problem behaviors. In consultee-centered case consultation, however, the consultant's main concern would be neither on the causes of the child's behavior nor on potential solutions for this problem. Rather, the consultant would be interested in determining why the consultee cannot handle this particular problem more effectively and implementing strategies to improve the consultee's professional functioning in such situations.

Throughout his writings, Caplan (1970; Caplan & Caplan, 1993) has postulated four reasons for consultee-centered case consultation. First, consultees might lack professional knowledge pertaining to a particular problem. Second, consultees might lack necessary professional skills. That is, even though they know what they need to do for a client, they lack the ability to carry it out. Third, consultees might lack sufficient self-confidence. In these instances, consultees would not be lacking either knowledge or skills but would be held back because they didn't fully trust themselves to intervene with the client effectively. Fourth, consultees might lack sufficient professional objectivity. That is, they find themselves unable to resolve a presenting problem because they have become emotionally involved in a case and have lost their professional distance. Caplan and Caplan describe this lack of professional objectivity as follows.

> The consultee is either too close or too distant from actors in the client's life drama, and is not able to perceive them accurately enough to carry out his task. Personal subjective factors in the consultee cloud his judgment, so that in this current case he behaves less effectively than is usual for him and thus is not able to utilize his existing knowledge and skills. By the time he comes for consultation, this situation is usually aggravated by his feelings of frustration at the impasse in the case, by a feeling of

professional failure, and a consequent lowering of self-esteem, all of which add to his loss of professional poise. (p. 107)

In early writings, Caplan (1970) discounts the relative importance of consultees' lack of knowledge, skill, and self-confidence, assuming that most consultees in need of consultee-centered case consultation were experiencing a lack of objectivity: "in a well-organized institution or agency in which there is an effective personnel system, administrative control, and a well-developed supervisory network, most cases that present themselves . . . fall into this fourth [lack of objectivity] category" (p. 131). In the preceding edition (Gutkin & Curtis, 1990), we questioned the logic of this assumption in reference to schools, wondering whether they are typically characterized by "an effective personnel system, administrative control, and a well-developed supervisory network," and also noting that existing empirical evidence (Gutkin, 1981) was not consistent with Caplan's assumptions. More recently, Caplan appears to be ambivalent about this issue, indicating in an interview with Erchul (1993b) that "most of the cases that come for consultation are cases where the consultee has difficulties because of lack of knowledge or lack of skill" (p. 65) and, in Caplan and Caplan (1993), that "most cases of consultee-centered case consultation fall into this last [lack of objectivity] category" (p. 107).

It is clear that Caplan's work in this area (Caplan, 1970; Caplan & Caplan, 1993), has been a major contribution to the consultation literature. In his writings he details five reasons why a consultee might suffer from a lack of objectivity: (1) direct personal involvement of the consultee with the client, (2) simple identification of the consultee with the client, (3) transference of consultee experiences and psychic difficulties onto the client's case, (4) characterological distortions of perception and behavior on the part of the consultee in regard to the client, and (5) theme interference. Because the last of these causes is a concept that Caplan stresses so heavily and one with which most school psychologists are not familiar, theme interference requires some additional explanation:

The theme is a continuing representation of an unsolved problem or a defeat, it carries a negative emotional tone of rankling failure. It also has a quality of repetition compulsion. This usually takes a syllogistic form, involving an inevitable link between two items or statements. Statement A denotes a particular situation or condition that was characteristic of the original unsolved problem. Statement B denotes the unpleasant outcome. The syllogism takes the form "All A inevitably leads to B." The implication is that whenever the person finds himself involved in situation or condition A, he is fated to suffer B; also, that this generalization applies universally, that everyone who is involved in A inevitably suffers B. . . . For instance, if Statement A (initial category) is "A person who masturbates excessively" and Statement B (inevitable outcome) is "His nervous system will be damaged and his intelligence will be blunted," the syllogism takes the form of "*All* people who masturbate excessively damage their nervous systems and blunt their intelligence." This theme may be a sequel to guilt-ridden conflicts over masturbation in the professional worker's childhood or adolescence, and represents a foreboding that one day in the future a punishing nemesis will inevitably strike. When, for whatever reason, the defenses against this old conflict weaken, the situation is ripe. . . . The consultee unconsciously selects a client from his caseload and fits him into the initial category of "a person who masturbates excessively." This then arouses the expectations that "his nervous system will inevitably be damaged and his intelligence blunted." The worker becomes very upset by this foreboding and attempts to stave off the expected doom. . . . These preventive efforts are usually panicky and inconsistent, and a realization of their obvious ineffectiveness confirms the consultee's certainty that the expected doom cannot be prevented despite all his efforts. Unconsciously, his consolation is that this time the catastrophe will occur to a client and not to himself. (Caplan & Caplan, 1993, pp. 122–124)

Caplan (1970; Caplan & Caplan, 1993) proposes several techniques to reduce theme interference. One strategy is to unlink the presenting problem from the theme by convincing the consultee that the client does not fit into the initial category. For example, if the theme is "All children who are not sufficiency disciplined by their parents will grow up without self-control and thus lead unproductive lives as adults," the consultant could attempt to show the consultee that in the current case the client is adequately disciplined by his or her parents. If successful with this intervention, the consultee will unlink the client from the theme and will return to his or her normal professional efficiency. Although unlinking may resolve the presenting problem, Caplan argues against using this tactic because it leaves the consultee's theme intact. The situation has been resolved for a specific client, but the generalized bias remains. In place of unlinking, Caplan proposes strategies for the reduction of theme interference, all of which are intended to weaken a consultee's theme and thus enable the consultee to cope effectively with the presenting problem and future problems of a similar nature.

> The goal of the consultant's intervention is to invalidate the obligatory link between the two categories that express the theme. The consultant accepts and supports the displacement of the theme onto the client's case and the definition of it as a test case by concurring with the initial category in all its details that are personally meaningful to the consultee. The consultant then engages the consultee in a joint examination of the link between the initial category and the outcome category and helps the consultee realize that this outcome is not inevitable. Since the syllogism says that the connection is invariable, if we can demonstrate that on even one occasion *in an authentic test case* that meets all the consultee's unconscious requirements the connection between the categories does not hold, we will dissipate or weaken the theme. (Caplan & Caplan, 1993, pp. 139–140)

Caplan suggests four specific theme interference reduction techniques, all of which reflect his general approach. The first of these strategies is called "verbal focus on the client." In this approach, the consultant verbally examines the presenting problem with the consultee and "demonstrates that although the inevitable outcome is one logical possibility, there are other possibilities too; and the evidence indicates that one or more of these is more probable than the doom that the consultee envisages" (Caplan & Caplan, 1993, p. 140). The second approach is called "verbal focus on an alternate object—the parable," in which the consultant directs discussion

away from the client's situation and onto a case that is superficially as different as possible from the presenting case but which retains the essential elements of the theme. The third tactic is termed "nonverbal focus on the case." The essence of this technique is for the consultant to remain calm and relaxed, thus nonverbally signaling that the expected inevitable outcome and the negative consequences associated with it are rather unlikely. Caplan hypothesizes that this method will work only if the consultant successfully communicates to the consultee that she or he "truly understands the danger in the case [so that the consultee will not] believe that the consultant's relaxed behavior means that he does not understand what is likely to happen to the client, or does not care" (pp. 152–153). Caplan's fourth intervention is "nonverbal focus on the consultation relationship." He hypothesizes that consultees will often express themes in the way they relate to the consultant and that the consultant can invalidate these themes by purposefully acting in ways that are congruent with the initial category but then failing to behave in a manner that is consistent with the inevitable outcome.

Building on Caplan's (1970; Caplan & Caplan, 1993) work, Bernard and DiGiuseppe (1994) have recently proposed a model they call rational-emotive consultation (REC). Like Caplan, they suggest that irrational thinking by consultees may play a major factor in many consultation problems. Unlike Caplan, however, they employ a rational-emotive (Ellis, 1963) rather than a psychodynamic framework to understand and intervene with this phenomenon. Whereas Caplan recommends dealing indirectly with inappropriate emotionality through theme interference reduction, Bernard and DiGiuseppe suggest a more confrontational approach, in which the irrational thoughts of a consultee are challenged directly.

To date, although mental health consultation has been a long-standing tool for school-based consultants and REC seems quite promising, there has been a paucity of empirical research into these models. In 1987, Gresham and Kendell concluded after reviewing the consultation literature that "there is no empirical support for the hypothesis that theme interference (Caplan, 1970) seriously impedes consultees' professional objectivity nor is there empirical support for the techniques suggested by Caplan (1970) to reduce theme interference" (p. 311). Unfortunately, little seems to have changed in this regard, and it is clear that a focused and systematic program of empirical research is needed to advance the theory and practice of these approaches.

## Organizational and Systems Consultation

Unlike either ecobehavioral or mental health consultation, both of which focus primarily on the problems of individuals, the client in organizational and systems consultation is typically a group within an organization or an entire organizational system itself. In discussing system-level consultation, Curtis and Stollar (1995) provide examples in which school psychologists could be engaged in such efforts at the classroom, grade, building, district, or county level. Going a step further, Grimes and Tilly (1996) discuss their experiences in working toward systemic changes on a statewide basis. Given that school psychologists frequently practice within groups (e.g., intervention assistance, IEP, and multidisciplinary teams) and are typically situated in community organizational settings (e.g., schools, community mental health centers, hospitals, and residential facilities), the ability to address group, organizational, and system problems would seem to be crucial to the profession (Curtis & Stollar, 1995; Gutkin & Conoley, 1990; Gutkin & Nemeth, 1997). The working assumption underlying school-based organizational and systems consultation is that "healthy" educational and psychological experiences for children and teachers alike are more likely to occur in "healthy" organizations and systemic contexts (Davis & Thomas, 1989; Schmuck, 1990; Snapp, Hickman, & Conoley, 1990).

Historically, changing schools at the organizational and systems level has been a major goal for school psychologists (Reynolds et al., 1984). In Bardon and Bennett's (1974) classic book, entitled *School Psychology*, for example, serving as a systems change agent was conceptualized as the highest level of functioning. Likewise, consultation pertaining to organizational issues has long been recognized as a major role for school-based consultants (e.g., Meyers, 1973). With recent growing emphases on school reform and innovation, contemporary schools psychologists appear to be more interested than ever in focusing on consultation services that promote organizational and system-wide change (Elliott & Witt, 1986; Graden, Zins, & Curtis, 1988; Henning-Stout & Conoley, 1988; Illback & Zins, 1993; Knoff,

1995; Knoff & Curtis, 1996; Kruger, 1988; Lennox, Hyman, & Hughes, 1988; Plas, 1986; Ponti et al., 1988; Schmuck, 1990; Snapp et al., 1990; Zins & Ponti, 1990).

## *Theoretical Bases and Empirically Validated Approaches*

To provide organizational and systems consultation services, school psychologists draw on a broad array of theoretical perspectives, ranging from those that are widely applicable to all organizational systems, for example, force field analysis (Lewin, 1951) and general systems theory (von Bertalanffy, 1968), to those that were developed specifically for human service organizations like schools, for example, domain theory (Dappen & Gutkin, 1986; Kouzes & Mico, 1979). Although a considerable number of specific operational models have been articulated (e.g., Knoff, 1995; Maher, & Illback, 1985), four interrelated elements seem to emerge as crucial components of successful organizational/systems consultation.

First, mutual adaptation emerged from a comprehensive Rand Corporation review of 293 local organizational change projects carried out under four federal programs in 18 different states (McLaughlin, 1976, 1990). Specifically, it was found that implementation success in schools hinged to a substantial degree on the extent to which local school personnel were able to shape and mold innovations to make them fit into the local ecology of their communities, school districts, and classrooms. McLaughlin (1990) reported that for effective change programs, "local variability is the rule; uniformity is the exception" (p. 13). Parenthetically, these findings appear to be contrary to the research and theory reported earlier regarding the use of scripts and direct consultation methods, in which highly prescriptive behaviors by consultants were deemed to facilitate treatment implementation (Ehrhardt et al., 1996; Watson & Robinson, 1996). In light of the findings, however, it is our suspicion that scripts would probably be most effective when consultees are given sufficient elbow room to adapt them to local conditions as necessary. This is, of course, an empirical question and one that should be addressed through research rather than armchair theorizing. Nevertheless, based on contemporary empirical analyses, it does appear that mutual adaptation is an essential ingredient of consultation at the organizational and systems level. Consultants must learn how to work collaboratively with local school personnel in shaping and reformulating systemic change efforts rather than expecting to dictate the wholesale adoption of prefabricated packages. This point is reinforced by Curtis and Stollar (1995), who emphasize the need to design change strategies that respond to the uniqueness of each system. Janney et al. (1995) provide an example of these processes in action, as five school districts in Virginia set out to increase the integration of students with moderate and severe handicaps into general education classes.

The second concept is the involvement of all primary stakeholders in all aspects of the change process. The literature identifies this principle as fundamental to any successful change program. Curtis and Stollar (1995) see the failure to involve classroom teachers as a major reason that efforts to implement intervention assistance programs encounter resistance and are often unsuccessful:

> Typically, the discussions, planning, and even implementation have involved seemingly everyone *but* classroom teachers. Principals, special education personnel, school psychologists, and other related services professionals then "inform" teachers about the new procedures. Confusion and frustration result when teachers do not participate regardless of the good intentions of the change agents. . . . They [teachers] should be meaningfully involved in every aspect of such change efforts, beginning with initial discussions regarding *potential* change and continuing through implementation. (p. 55)

Needless to say, parents represent another primary stakeholder group that is largely ignored in many school-based change efforts.

The third element is the endorsement of change efforts by relevant system administrators. Although bottom-up planning, such as mutual adaptation, seems to be crucial in organizational change, it is widely believed that there is a simultaneous need for top-down sanctioning and support (e.g., Curtis & Stollar, 1996; Henning-Stout & Conoley, 1988; Knoff, 1995; Schrag, 1996; Villa, Thousand, Meyers, & Nevin, 1996). Studies by Broughton and Hester (1993), Ponti et al. (1988), Janney et al. (1995), and McLaughlin (1990), among others, support this assumption. Although it would appear that administrative and upper-management support for change in no way ensures its suc-

cess, its absence may substantially increase the chances for failure.

Finally, the literature has long suggested the need for a coherent system of collaborative problem solving (e.g., Schmuck, Runkel, Arends, & Arends, 1977). Given the complexity and multivariate nature of organizational and systems consultation, it would be very easy for consultants and consultees alike to get overwhelmed and confused without a structured road map for approaching target problems. Exemplifying one such road map is the model recently proposed by Curtis and Stollar (1996).

1. Describe the problem or concern as concretely and as specifically as possible. Once the problem has been defined, identify the desired outcome of your planning and problem-solving efforts, again using concrete, descriptive terms.

2. Analyze the specific problem chosen in terms of the factors that might help to address it (i.e., the resources needed and the factors that serve as obstacles to its resolution).

3. Select one obstacle that is significant in terms of its hindrance to resolving the specific problem identified in Step 1.

4. Focus only on the one obstacle selected in Step 3 and brainstorm resources and activities that might be used to reduce or eliminate that obstacle.

5. Design a concrete plan of action that builds in accountability for its completion (i.e., who, what, when).

6. Establish a procedure for follow-up and review. (pp. 414–415)

Note that although the words differ from the problem-solving steps described earlier for ecobehavioral consultation, which is employed primarily with individual cases, this suggested sequence is really quite similar from a functional point of view.

## Targets for Organizational and Systems Consultation

Without doubt, an enormous range of important issues can be addressed by organizational and systems consultation, for example, program evaluation, diffusion of innovations, organizational conflict, group norms, group process, role expectations, leadership, group decision making, intra- and intergroup communication, group problem solving, and school-community relationships (Knoff & Curtis, 1996; Owens, 1987; Romualdi & Sandoval, 1995; Sarason, 1982; Schein, 1969; Schmuck, Runkel, Arends, & Arends, 1977; Snapp et al., 1990; Thomas & Grimes, 1995). Several case studies have already been presented in the research literature, such as Ponti et al. (1988), Rosenfield (1992), Curtis and Metz (1986), Hertz-Lazarowitz and Od-Cohen (1992), and Snapp et al. (1990).

Beyond these published reports, however, the need for increased organizational consultation activities by school psychologists seems clear. Consider, for example, the growing epidemic of violence in our nation's schools (Goldstein, Harootunian, & Conoley, 1994). There seems to be little or no attention to this issue until children commit serious acts of violence. Then schools respond by (1) assessing the offenders to determine if they are seriously emotionally disturbed, (2) consulting with the individual teachers and parents of the offenders to develop remedial programs for them, and/or (3) placing the offending student into psychotherapy. A superior alternative to any of these approaches might be to initiate a proactive organizational consultation process with school administrators, teachers, and community leaders to develop violence prevention programs (Hyman, 1997).

Along similar lines, one of us worked as a psychologist in a school in which over 80% of the students were reading below grade level. Once becoming aware of these dismal data, the principal suggested that the school psychologist begin testing a very long list of students who were below grade level to determine who was handicapped. The school psychologist suggested to the principal that instead he would like to start an organizational consultation project with the school's team leaders and the district's reading specialists to redesign the reading curriculum.

A final example centers around the fact that although virtually all important special education decisions are made in team meetings of one sort or another, relatively few school personnel ever receive formal training of any kind in group processes, dynamics, or problem-solving methodologies. The result is that many team meetings are dysfunctional, and something less than the best decisions often are made for difficult-to teach and referred children (Flugum & Reschly, 1994; Gutkin & Nemeth, 1997; Meyers et al., 1996; Wilson et al., 1998; Ysseldyke, 1987).

Obviously, working with or consulting about individual students will not lead to effective solutions for this type of problem. Intervention at the organizational and systems level will be required. It is also important to note that until systemic impediments such as these are removed, it will be difficult for school personnel to make high-quality decisions for the students who are in need of school psychological or related support services.

# SELECTED FUTURE RESEARCH DIRECTIONS

We believe that the research base in consultation reflects a great deal of progress, despite continuing methodological criticism to the contrary (e.g., Fuchs et al., 1992; Gresham & Noell, 1993; Gutkin, 1993b; Hughes, 1994). Most salient in our opinion are the meta-analyses and literature reviews, which document the effectiveness of consultative approaches (Kratochwill, Elliott, & Busse, 1995; Mannino & Shore, 1975; Medway, 1979, 1982; Medway & Updyke, 1985; Sheridan, Welch, & Orme, 1996). Still, it is clear that the empirical base for consultation services has a long way to go, and there is no shortage of important research agendas for the future. A few of the most significant issues identified in the literature have already been discussed at earlier points in this chapter (e.g., interpersonal influence with adults, entry processes, prevention, enhancing teachers' self-efficacy with difficult-to-teach children, assumptions of mental health consultation in general and theme interference in particular), and others can be highlighted very briefly.

Consultation methodologies for working with groups and teams is one area that seems to demand substantially more research. Beginning with the passage of PL 94-142 (Education of All Handicapped Children Act) in 1975, school psychologists spend much of their time in group settings (e.g., intervention assistance, IEP, and multidisciplinary team meetings). Despite this, the bulk of the scholarly literature on consultation services involves one-to-one relationships (see Gutkin & Nemeth, 1997, and Rosenfield, 1992, for some recent exceptions). Groups are, of course, more complex interpersonally than are dyads, and as noted by Gutkin (1993b), "Generalizing research knowledge gained from interactions involving single consultees to consultations conducted in group settings seems risky, at best" (p. 240). As a starting point, consulting school psychologists should consider the group dynamics literature developed by clinical and counseling (e.g., Corey, 1990; Napier & Gershenfeld, 1989; Yalom, 1985) and industrial and organizational (e.g., Sundstrom, De Meuse, & Futrell, 1990) psychologists, translating concepts whenever possible to a school-based context. Without a substantial increase in school-based, group-oriented consultation research, school psychologists will be unprepared to deal with the increasing trend to deliver psychological and consultation services in group environments.

Resistance is another area of consultation that is in great need of additional research. Although, as stated earlier, we believe that the resistance construct is flawed, because it implies that consultants' failures are somehow the fault of consultees, it is clear nonetheless that consultees often resist the efforts of consultants to bring about change (readers are once again referred to Deno, 1975, for a fascinating case study). Despite a broad range of conceptual approaches, including those derived from behavioral (Piersel & Gutkin, 1983), social psychological (Hughes & Falk, 1981), psychodynamic (Caplan, 1970), and ecological points of view (Wickstrom & Witt, 1993), little is known empirically about either the nature or prevalence of this phenomenon. And while Gutkin and Hickman (1990) determined that consultants perceive consultant, consultee, and organizational components to this problem, there is virtually no body of direct research evidence that provides guidance to practitioners regarding how they can cope successfully with it. The urgency of addressing this agenda seems obvious, and it calls our attention back to the need for a more sophisticated understanding of interpersonal influence with our consultees (Gutkin, 1997b; Gutkin & Conoley, 1990).

In both of the previous editions of this chapter (Gutkin & Curtis, 1982, 1990), we focused on the importance of developing a better technology of communication and argued the following: "At its most basic level, consultation is an interpersonal exchange. As such, the consultant's success if going to hinge largely on his or her communication . . . skills" (Gutkin & Curtis, 1982, p. 822). We continue to consider this a truism. Although the pace of research in this area has accelerated dramatically in recent years (e.g., Benes, Gutkin, & Kramer, 1991; Erchul, 1987; Erchul & Chewning, 1990; Erchul et al., 1992, 1995; Erchul & Schulte, 1990; Gutkin, 1996b, 1997a; Houk & Lewandowski, 1996; Hughes &

DeForest, 1993; Martens, Deery, & Gherardi, 1991; Martens et al., 1989, 1992; Safran, 1991; Witt et al., 1991), we remain a long way from understanding precisely how the verbal and nonverbal behaviors of consultants and consultees affect each other. In addition to needing more research along these lines, we must also strengthen our design methodologies. In particular, virtually all of the studies to date have been descriptive and correlational rather than experimental (see Martens et al., 1991, for an important exception). Thus, while we are beginning to understand some rudimentary relationships between naturally occurring communication behaviors, we have virtually no empirical basis on which to predict how changing one's own verbal and/or nonverbal behavior might influence one's consultation partner. Ultimately, however, it will be crucial for us not only to understand descriptively how consultants and consultees communicate with each other but also to develop methods for modifying the nature of communication when it is not proceeding effectively.

Finally, we perceive conjoint behavioral consultation, in which consultants work simultaneously with both teachers and parents, as one of the most important areas of contemporary and future research in consultation. Developed primarily by Susan Sheridan and her colleagues (e.g., Sheridan, 1993, 1997; Sheridan & Kratochwill, 1992; Sheridan, Kratochwill, & Bergan, 1996), conjoint behavioral consultation provides school psychologists with a rich theoretical and a growing empirical framework on which to build current and future practice. By articulating the interaction among ecological, systems, and behavioral psychology, conjoint behavioral consultation is one of the very best examples of the ecobehavioral approach to consultation described. It succeeds in bringing a rigorous behavioral methodology to bear on a complex and important ecological phenomenon, namely the facilitation of home-school collaboration. Given that home and school are the two dominant social systems in the lives of children, improving coordination and collaboration between them is clearly among our most pivotal challenges as we move into the next century (e.g., Christenson & Conoley, 1992). As a result of the operational specificity with which the conjoint behavioral consultation model has been explicated, it has also lent itself very nicely to meaningful empirical investigation. To date, a small but well-executed body of research has been quite supportive, indicating that this technique is effective and produces outcomes that exceed those found by consultants who work with either the home or school alone (e.g., Sheridan & Colton, 1994; Sheridan, & Kratochwill, & Elliott, 1990). Conjoint behavioral consultation is an exciting approach to practice and one that is, without doubt, deserving of additional empirical attention. Given the nature and significance of this model, we are optimistic that such research will appear in growing quantities in the not-too-distant future.

# CONCLUDING COMMENTS

Consultation has always been viewed as a major role for school psychologists (Bardon & Bennett, 1974), and based on contemporary thinking it would appear that its centrality to school psychology is increasing rapidly (e.g., Gutkin & Conoley, 1990). Above and beyond its own independent benefits, the consultation role undergirds and strengthens the impact of other professional activities performed by school psychologists (Ysseldyke et al., 1997). Assessment results in and of themselves, for example, are unlikely to produce positive educational and psychological changes for children unless they are followed up by effective consultative interactions between psychologists and the significant adults in children's lives, such as teachers and parents. Likewise, the impact of individual therapy with children can be enhanced through coordination of services with those adults who populate the daily worlds of children. Finally, consultation holds unique potential for achieving prevention by "giving psychology away" (Miller, 1969) to those nonpsychologists who are in a position to use psychological information for the benefit of children (Christensen & Jacobson, 1994). Given today's grim national statistics on violence, pregnancy, illiteracy, drug abuse, and so on, few priorities would seem to be more important.

# REFERENCES

American Psychological Association. (1992). Ethical principles of psychologists and code of conduct. *American Psychologist, 47,* 1597–1611.

Anderson, T. K. Kratochwill, T. R., Bergan, J. R. (1986). Training teachers in behavioral consultation and therapy: An analysis of verbal behaviors. *Journal of School Psychology, 24,* 229–241.

Andrews, L. W., & Gutkin, T. B. (1994). Influencing attitudes regarding special class placement via a psychoeducational report: An investigation of the elaboration likelihood model. *Journal of School Psychology, 32,* 321–337.

Arter, J. A., & Jenkins, J. R. (1979). Differential diagnosis—prescriptive teaching: A critical appraisal. *Review of Educational Research, 49,* 517–555.

Aschbacher, P. R. (1991). Performance assessment: State activity, interest and concerns. *Applied Measurement in Education, 4,* 275–288.

Babcock, N. L., & Pryzwansky, W. B. (1983). Models of consultation: Preferences of educational professionals at five stages of service. *Journal of School Psychology, 21,* 359–366.

Bahr, M. W. (1996). Are school psychologists reform-minded? *Psychology in the Schools, 33,* 295–307.

Baker, E. L., O'Neil, H. F., Jr., & Linn, R. L. (1993). Policy and validity prospects for performance-based assessment. *American Psychologist, 48,* 1210–1218.

Baldwin, J. D., & Baldwin, J. I. (1998). *Behavior principles in everyday life* (3rd ed.). Upper Saddle River, NJ: Prentice Hall.

Bandura, A. (1978). The self-system in reciprocal determinism. *American Psychologist, 33,* 344–358.

Bandura, A. (1993). Perceived self-efficacy in cognitive development and functioning. *Educational Psychologist, 28,* 117–148.

Bardon, J. I. (1987). The translation of research into practice into school psychology. *School Psychology Review, 16,* 317–328.

Bardon, J. I., & Bennett, V. C. (1974). *School psychology.* Englewood Cliffs, NJ: Prentice Hall.

Barker, R. G. (1965). Explorations in ecological psychology. *American Psychologist, 20,* 1–14.

Barry, J. R. (1970). Criteria in the evaluation of consultation. *Professional Psychology, 1,* 363–366.

Bear, G. G., Minke, K. M., & Thomas, A. (1997). *Children's needs II; Development problems and alternatives.* Bethesda, MD: National Association of School Psychologists.

Benes, K. M., Gutkin, T. B., & Kramer, J. J. (1991). Micro-analysis of consultant and consultee verbal and nonverbal behaviors. *Journal of Educational and Psychological Consultation, 2,* 133–149.

Bergan, J. R. (1977). *Behavioral consultation.* Columbus, OH: Merrill.

Bergan, J. R., Byrnes, I. M., & Kratochwill, T. R. (1979). Effects of behavioral and medical models of consultation on teacher expectancies and instruction of a hypothetical child. *Journal of School Psychology, 17,* 306–316.

Bergan, J. R., & Kratochwill, T. R. (1990). *Behavioral consultation and therapy.* New York: Plenum.

Bergan, J. R., & Tombari, M. L. (1976). Consultant skill and efficiency and the implementation and outcomes of consultation. *Journal of School Psychology, 14,* 3–14.

Bernard, M. E., & DiGiuseppe, R. (Eds.). (1994).

*Rational-emotive consultation in applied settings.* Hillsdale, NJ: Erlbaum.

Beutler, L. E. (1991). Have all won and must all have prizes? Revisiting Luborsky et al.'s verdict. *Journal of Consulting and Clinical Psychology, 59,* 226–232.

Beutler, L. E., Machado, P. P. P., & Neufeldt, S. A. (1994). Therapist variables. In A. E. Bergin & S. L. Garfield (Eds.), *Handbook of psychotherapy and behavior change* (4th ed.), pp. 229–269). New York: Wiley.

Broughton, S. F., & Hester, J. R. (1993). Effects of administrative and community support on teacher acceptance of classroom interventions. *Journal of Educational and Psychological Consultation, 4,* 169–177.

Broussard, C. D., & Northup, J. (1995). An approach to functional assessment and analysis of disruptive behavior in regular education classrooms. *School Psychology Quarterly, 10,* 151–164.

Brown, D., Pryzwansky, W. B., & Schulte, A. C. (1987). *Psychological consultation: Introduction to theory and practice.* Boston: Allyn & Bacon.

Brown, D., & Schulte, A. C. (1987). A social learning model of consultation. *Professional Psychology: Research and Practice, 18,* 283–287.

Bush, K. J., Carter, D. W., Dickerson, C., Evans, G., Martin, F., Raskind, L. T., & Thomas, A. (1989). Gwinnett County: Changing its service delivery in response to population growth. *Professional School Psychology, 4,* 189–200.

Canter, A. S. (1991). Effective psychological services for all students: A data-based model of service delivery. In G. Stoner, M. R. Shinn, & H. M. Walker (Eds.), *Interventions for achievement and behavior problems* (pp. 49–78). Silver Spring, MD: National Association of School Psychologists.

Caplan, G. (1970). *The theory and practice of mental health consultation.* New York: Basic Books.

Caplan, G., & Caplan, R. B. (1983). *Mental health consultation and collaboration.* San Francisco: Jossey-Bass.

Carlberg, C., & Kavale, K. (1980). The efficacy of special versus regular class placement for exceptional children: A meta-analysis. *Journal of Special Education, 14,* 295–309.

Caron, C., & Rutter, M. (1991). Comorbidity in child psychopathology: Concepts, issues, and research strategies. *Journal of Child Psychology and Psychiatry, 32,* 1063–1080.

Carrington Rotto, P., & Kratochwill, T. R. (1994). Behavioral consultation with parents: Using competency-based training to modify child noncompliance. *School Psychology Review, 23,* 669–693.

Carter, J., & Sugai, G. (1989). Survey on prereferral practices: Responses from state departments of education. *Exceptional Children, 55,* 298–302.

Christensen, A., & Jacobson, N. S. (1994). Who (or what) can do psychotherapy: The status and challenge of nonprofessional therapies. *Psychological Science, 5,* 8–14.

Christenson, S., Abery, B., & Weinberg, R. A. (1986). An alternative model for the delivery of psychological services in the school community. In S. N. Elliott & J. C. Witt (Eds.), *The delivery of psychological services in schools: Concepts, processes, and issues* (pp. 349–391). Hillsdale, NJ: Erlbaum.

Christenson, S. L., & Conoley, J. C. (1992). *Home-school collaboration: Enhancing children's academic and social competence.* Silver Spring, MD: National Association of School Psychologists.

Cleven, C. A., & Gutkin, T. B. (1988). Cognitive modeling of consultation processes: A means for improving consultees' problem definition skills. *Journal of School Psychology, 26,* 379–389.

Cohen, J. J., & Fish, M. C. (1993). *Handbook of school-based interventions: Resolving student problems and promoting health educational environments.* San Francisco: Jossey–Bass.

Cole, E., & Siegel, J. A. (Eds.). (1990). *Effective consultation in school psychology.* Toronto: Hogrefe & Huber.

Conoley, C. W., Conoley, J. C., & Gumm, W. B., II. (1992). Effects of consultee problem presentation and consultant training on consultant problem definition. *Journal of Counseling and Development, 71,* 60–62.

Conoley, C. W., Conoley, J. C., Ivey, D. C., & Scheel, M. J. (1991). Enhancing consultation by matching the consultee's perspectives. *Journal of Counseling and Development, 69,* 546–549.

Conoley, J. C. (1994, December). Resistance to consultation. *Communiqué,* pp. 26–28.

Conoley, J. C., & Conoley, C. W. (1992). *School consultation: Practice and training* (2nd ed.). New York: Pergamon.

Conoley, J. C., & Gutkin, T. B. (1995). Why didn't—Why Doesn't—school psychology realize its promise? *Journal of School Psychology, 33,* 209–217.

Coolahan, S. M. (1991). An analysis of consultation verbal behavior during problem identification interviews. Unpublished doctoral dissertation, University of Cincinnati.

Corey, G. (1990). *Theory and practice of group counseling* (3rd ed.). Pacific Grove, CA: Brooks/Cole.

Cormier, W. H., & Cormier, L. S. (1991). *Interviewing strategies for helpers: Fundamental skills and cognitive behavioral interventions* (3rd ed.). Pacific Grove, CA: Brooks/Cole.

Costenbader, V., Swartz, J., & Petrix, L. (1992). Consultation in the schools: The relationship between preservice training, perception of consultative skills, and actual time spent in consultation. *School Psychology Review, 21,* 95–108.

Cowen, E. L., & Hightower, A. D. (1990). The Primary Mental Health Project: Alternative approaches in school-based preventive intervention. In T. B. Gutkin & C. R. Reynolds (Eds.), *The handbook of school psychology* (2nd ed., pp. 775–795). New York: Wiley.

Curtis, M. J., & Anderson, T. E. (1976). *Consulting in educational settings: A collaborative approach* (slide/tape). Cincinnati: Faculty Resource Center, University of Cincinnati.

Curtis, M. J., & Metz, L. W. (1986). System level intervention in a school for handicapped children. *School Psychology Review, 15,* 510–518.

Curtis, M. J., & Stollar, S. A. (1995). Best practices in system-level consultation and organizational change. In A. Thomas & J. Grimes (Eds.), *Best practices in school psychology—III* (pp. 51–58). Washington, DC: National Association of School Psychologists.

Curtis, M. J., & Stollar, S. A. (1996). Applying principles and practices of organizational change to school reform. *School Psychology Review, 25,* 409–417.

Curtis, M. J., & Watson, K. L. (1980). Changes in consultee problem clarification skills following consultation. *Journal of School Psychology, 18,* 210–221.

Curtis, M. J., & Zins, J. E. (1988). Effects of training in consultation and instructor feedback on acquisition of consultation skills. *Journal of School Psychology, 26,* 185–190.

Cutts, N. E. (Ed.). (1955). *School psychologists at mid-century.* Washington, DC: American Psychological Association.

Dance, K. A., & Neufeld, R. W. J. (1988). Aptitude-treatment interaction research in the clinical setting: A review of attempts to dispel the "patient uniformity" myth. *Psychological Bulletin, 104,* 192–213.

Dappen, L. D., & Gutkin, T. B. (1986). Domain theory: Examining the validity of an organizational theory with public school personnel. *Professional School Psychology, 1,* 257–265.

Davis, G. A., & Thomas, M. A. (1989). *Effective schools and effective teachers.* Boston: Allyn & Bacon.

DeForest, P. A., & Hughes, J. N. (1992). Effect of teacher involvement and teacher self-efficacy on ratings of consultant effectiveness and intervention acceptability. *Journal of Educational and Psychological Consultation, 3,* 301–316.

Deno, S. (1975). Brad and Mrs. E.: A consulting problem in which student behavior change is the focus. In C. A. Parker (Ed.). *Psychological consultation: Helping teachers meet special needs* (pp. 11–16). Reston, VA: Council for Exceptional Children.

Dougherty, A. N. (1990). *Consultation: Practice and perspectives.* Pacific Grove, CA: Brooks/Cole.

Dunst, C. J., & Trivette, C. M. (1988). Helping, helpfulness, and harm. In J. C. Witt, S. N. Elliott, & F. M. Gresham (Eds.), *The handbook of behavior*

*therapy in education* (pp. 343–376). New York: Plenum.

D'Zurilla, T. J., & Goldfried, M. R. (1971). Problem solving and behavior modification. *Journal of Abnormal Psychology, 78,* 107–126.

Ehrhardt, K. E., Barnett, D. W., Lentz, F. E., Jr., Stollar, S. A., & Reifin, L. H. (1996). Innovative methodology in ecological consultation: Use of scripts to promote treatment acceptability and integrity. *School Psychology Quarterly, 11,* 149–168.

Elliott, S. N. (1988). Acceptability of behavioral treatments: Review of variables that influence treatment selection. *Professional Psychology: Research and Practice, 19,* 68–80.

Elliott, S. N. (1991). Authentic assessment: An introduction to a neobehavioral approach to classroom assessment. *School Psychology Quarterly, 6,* 273–278.

Elliott, S. N., & Witt, J. C. (Eds.). (1986). *The delivery of psychological services in schools: Concepts, processes, and issues.* Hillsdale, NJ: Erlbaum.

Ellis, A. (1963, *Rational-emotive psychotherapy.* New York: Institute for Rational-Emotive Therapy.

Epps, S., & Tindal, G. (1987). The effectiveness of differential programming in serving students with mild handicaps: Placement options and instructional programming. In M. C. Wang, M. Reynolds, & H. J. Walberg (Eds.), *Handbook of special education: Research & practice* (Vol. 1, pp. 213–248). New York: Pergamon.

Erchul, W. P. (1987). A relational communication analysis of control in school consultation. *Professional School Psychology, 2,* 113–124.

Erchul, W. P. (1992). On dominance, cooperation, teamwork, and collaboration in school-based consultation. *Journal of Educational and Psychological Consultation, 3,* 363–366.

Erchul, W. P. (Ed.). (1993a). *Consultation in community, school, and organizational practice: Gerald Caplan's contributions to professional psychology.* Washington, DC: Taylor & Francis.

Erchul, W. P. (1993b). Reflections on mental health consultation: An interview with Gerald Caplan. In W. P. Erchul (Ed.), *Consultation in community, school, and organizational practice: Gerald Caplan's contributions to professional psychology* (pp. 57–72). Washington, DC: Taylor & Francis.

Erchul, W. P., & Chewning, T. G. (1990). Behavioral consultation from a request-centered relational communication perspective. *School Psychology Quarterly, 5,* 1–20.

Erchul, W. P., Covington, C. G., Hughes, J. N., & Meyers, J. (1995). Further explorations of request-centered relational communication within school consultation. *School Psychology Review, 24,* 621–632.

Erchul, W. P., Hughes, J. N., Meyers, J., Hickman, J. A., & Braden, J. P. (1992). Dyadic agreement concerning the consultation process and its relationship to outcome. *Journal of Educational and Psychological Consultation, 3,* 119–132.

Erchul, W. P., & Martens, B. K. (1997). *School consultation: Conceptual and empirical bases of practice.* New York: Plenum.

Erchul, W. P., & Schulte, A. C. (1990). The coding of consultation verbalizations: How much is enough? *School Psychology Quarterly, 5,* 256–264.

Fine, M. J., & Carlson, C. (Eds.). (1992). *The handbook of family-school intervention: A systems perspective.* Boston: Allyn & Bacon.

Fischer, L., & Sorenson, G. P. (1996). *School law for counselors, psychologists, and social workers* (3rd ed.). White Plains, NY: Longman.

Fisher, G. L., Jenkins, S. J., & Crumbley, J. D. (1986). A replication of a survey of school psychologists: Congruence between training, practice, preferred role, and competence. *Psychology in the Schools, 23,* 271–279.

Flugum, K. R., & Reschly, D. J. (1994). Prereferral interventions: Quality indices and outcomes. *Journal of School Psychology, 32,* 1–14.

Franklin, M. R., Jr., & Duley, S. M. (1991). Psychological services in Amphitheater School District. *School Psychology Quarterly, 6,* 66–80.

Fuchs, D., Fuchs, L. S., & Bahr, M. W. (1990). Mainstream assistance teams: A scientific basis for the art of consultation. *Exceptional Children, 57,* 128–139.

Fuchs, D., Fuchs, L. S., Dulan, J. Roberts, H., & Fernstrom, P. (1992). Where is the research on consultation effectiveness? *Journal of Educational and Psychological Consultation, 3,* 151–174.

Fuchs, L. S., & Fuchs, D. (1986). Effects of systematic formative evaluation: A meta-analysis. *Exceptional Children, 53,* 199–208.

Fullan, M., Miles, M. B., & Taylor, G. (1980). Organization development in schools: The state of the art. *Review of Educational Research, 50,* 121–183.

Gibson, S., & Dembo, M. H. (1984). Teacher efficacy: A construct validation. *Journal of Educational Psychology, 76,* 569–582.

Givens-Ogle, L., Christ, B. A., & Idol, L. (1991). Collaborative consultation: The San Juan Unified School District Project. *Journal of Educational and Psychological Consultation, 2,* 267–284.

Goldstein, A. P., Harootunian, B., & Conoley, J. C. (1994). *Student aggression: Prevention, management, and replacement training.* New York: Guilford.

Good, R. H., III, Vollmer, M., Creek, R. J., Katz, L., & Chowdhri, S. (1993). Treatment utility of the Kaufman Assessment Battery for Children: Effects of matching instruction and student processing strength. *School Psychology Review, 22,* 8–26.

Goodwin, D. L., & Coates, T. J. (1976). *Helping students help themselves.* Englewood Cliffs, NJ: Prentice Hall.

Gorrell, J., & Capron, E. (1990). Cognitive modeling and self-efficacy: Effects on preservice teachers' learning of teaching strategies. *Journal of Teacher Education, 41,* 15–22.

Graden, J. L., Casey, A., & Bonstrom, O. (1985). Implementing a prereferral intervention system: Part II. The data. *Exceptional Children, 51,* 487–496.

Graden, J. L., Casey, A., & Christenson, S. L. (1985). Implementing a prereferral intervention system: Part I. The model. *Exceptional Children, 51,* 377–384.

Graden, J. L., Zins, J. E., & Curtis, M. J. (1988). *Alternative educational delivery systems: Enhancing instructional options for all students.* Washington, DC: National Association of School Psychologists.

Graden, J. L., Zins, J. E., Curtis, M. J., & Cobb, C. T. (1988). The need for alternatives in educational services. In J. L. Graden, J. E. Zins, & M. J. Curtis (Eds.), *Alternative educational delivery systems: Enhancing instructional options for all students* (pp. 3–15). Washington, DC: National Association of School Psychologists.

Greenwood, C. R., Carta, J. J., & Atwater, J. (1991). Ecobehavioral analysis in the classroom: Review and implications. *Journal of Behavioral Education, 1,* 59–77.

Greenwood, C. R., Maheady, L., & Carta, J. J. (1991). Peer tutoring programs in the regular education classroom. In G. Stoner, M. R. Shinn, & H. M. Walker (Eds.), *Interventions for achievement and behavior problems* (pp. 179–200). Silver Spring, MD: National Association of School Psychologists.

Gresham, F. M. (1989). Assessment of treatment integrity in school consultation and prereferral intervention. *School Psychology Review, 18,* 37–50.

Gresham, F. M., & Gansle, K. A. (1992). Misguided assumptions of DSM-III-R: Implications for school psychological practice. *School Psychology Quarterly, 7,* 79–95.

Gresham, F. M., & Kendell, G. K. (1987). School consultation research: Methodological critique and future research directions. *School Psychology Review, 16,* 306–316.

Gresham, F. M., MacMillan, D. L., & Bocian, K. M. (1997). Teachers as "tests": Differential validity of teacher judgments in identifying students at-risk for learning difficulties. *School Psychology Review, 26,* 47–60.

Gresham, F. M., Noell, G. H. (1993). Methods for documenting the effectiveness of consultation: A critical analysis. In J. E. Zins, T. R. Kratochwill, & S. N. Elliott (Eds.), *The handbook of consultation services for children* (pp. 249–273). San Francisco: Jossey-Bass.

Gieger, R. M. (1977). Teacher attitudes as a variable in behavior modification consultation. In J. Meyers,

R. Martin, & I. Hyman (Eds.), *School consultation: Readings about preventive techniques for pupil personnel workers* (pp. 137–148). Springfield, IL: Thomas.

Grimes, J., & Tilly, W. D., III. (1996). Policy and process: Means to lasting educational change. *School Psychology Review, 25,* 465–476.

Gutkin, T. B. (1980). Teacher perceptions of consultation services provided by school psychologists. *Professional Psychology, 11,* 637–642.

Gutkin, T. B. (1981). Relative frequency of consultee lack of knowledge, skill, confidence, and objectivity in school settings. *Journal of School Psychology, 19,* 57–61.

Gutkin, T. B. (1986). Consultees' perceptions of variables relating to the outcomes of school-based consultation interactions. *School Psychology Review, 15,* 375–382.

Gutkin, T. B. (1993a). Cognitive modeling: A means for achieving prevention in school-based consultation. *Journal of Educational and Psychological Consultation, 4,* 179–183.

Gutkin, T. B. (1993b). Conducting consultation research. In J. E. Zins, T. R. Kratochwill, & S. N. Elliott (Eds.), *Handbook of consultation for children: Applications in educational and clinical settings* (pp. 227–248). San Francisco: Jossey-Bass.

Gutkin, T. B. (1993c). Moving from behavioral to ecobehavioral consultation: What's in a name. *Journal of Educational and Psychological Consultation, 4,* 95–99.

Gutkin, T. B. (1996a). Core elements of consultation service delivery for special service personnel. *Remedial and Special Education, 17,* 333–340.

Gutkin, T. B. (1996b). Patterns of consultant and consultee verbalizations: Examining communication leadership during initial consultation interviews. *Journal of School Psychology, 34,* 199–219.

Gutkin, T. B. (1997a, August). Collaborative versus directive/expert school-based consultation: Reviewing and resolving a false dichotomy. Paper presented at the Annual Convention of the American Psychological Association, Chicago.

Gutkin, T. B. (Ed) (1997b). Social psychology and consultation. *Journal of School Psychology* (Special section) *35*(2).

Gutkin, T. B., & Ajchenbaum, M. (1984). Teachers' perceptions of control and preferences for consultative services. *Professional Psychology: Research and Practice, 15,* 565–570.

Gutkin, T. B., & Conoley, J. C. (1990). Reconceptualizing school psychology from a service delivery perspective: Implications for practice, training, and research. *Journal of School Psychology, 28,* 203–223.

Gutkin, T. B., & Curtis, M. J. (1981). School-based consultation: The indirect service delivery concept. In M. J. Curtis & J. E. Zins (Eds.), *The theory and practice of school consultation* (pp. 219–226). Springfield, IL: Thomas.

Gutkin, T. B., & Curtis, M. J. (1982). School-based consultation: Theory and techniques. In C. R. Reynolds & T. B. Gutkin (Eds.), *The handbook of school psychology* (pp. 796–828). New York: Wiley.

Gutkin, T. B., & Curtis, M. J. (1990). School-based consultation: Theory, techniques, and research. In T. B. Gutkin & C. R. Reynolds (Eds.), *The handbook of school psychology* (2nd ed. pp. 577–611). New York: Wiley.

Gutkin, T. B., Henning-Stout, M., & Piersel, W. C. (1988). Impact of a district-wide behavioral consultation prereferral intervention service on patterns of school psychological service delivery. *Professional School Psychology, 3,* 301–308.

Gutkin, T. B., & Hickman, J. A. (1988). Teachers' perceptions of control over presenting problems and resulting preferences for consultation versus referral services. *Journal of School Psychology, 26,* 395–398.

Gutkin, T. B., & Hickman, J. A. (1990). Relationship of consultant, consultee, and organizational characteristics to consultee resistance to school-based consultation: An empirical analysis. *Journal of Educational and Psychological Consultation, 1,* 111–122.

Gutkin, T. B., & Nemeth, C. (1997). Selected factors impacting decision making in prereferral intervention and other school-based teams: Exploring the intersection between school and social psychology. *Journal of School Psychology, 35,* 195–216.

Gutkin, T. B., Singer, J. H., & Brown, R. (1980). Teacher reactions to school based consultation services: A multivariate analysis. *Journal of School Psychology, 18,* 126–134.

Gutkin, T. B., & Tieger, A. G. (1979). Funding patterns for exceptional children: Current approaches and suggested alternatives. *Professional Psychology, 10,* 670–680.

Hagen, K. M., Gutkin, T. B., Wilson, C. P., & Oats, R. B. (in press). Using vicarious experience and verbal persuasion to enhance self-efficacy in pre-service teachers: "Priming the pump" for consultation. *School Psychology Quarterly.*

Harris, A. M., & Cancelli, A. A. (1991). Teachers as volunteer consultees: Enthusiastic, willing, or resistant participants? *Journal of Educational and Psychological Consultation, 2,* 217–238.

Hattie, J. A., Sharpley, C. F., & Rogers, H. J. (1984). Comparative effectiveness of professional and paraprofessional helpers. *Psychological Bulletin, 95,* 534–541.

Henning-Stout, M. (1994). *Responsive assessment.* San Francisco: Jossey-Bass.

Henning-Stout, M., & Conoley, J. C. (1988). Influencing program change at the district level. In J. L. Graden, J. E. Zins, & M. J. Curtis (Eds.),

*Alternative educational delivery systems: Enhancing instructional options for all students* (pp. 471–490). Washington, DC: National Association of School Psychologists.

Henning-Stout, M., Lucas, D. A. & McCary, V. L. (1993). Alternative instruction in the regular classroom: A case illustration and evaluation. *School Psychology Review, 22,* 81–97.

Heppner, P. P. (1978). A review of the problem-solving literature and its relationship to the counseling process. *Journal of Counseling Psychology, 25,* 366–375.

Hertz-Lazarowitz, R., Od-Cohen, M. (1992). The school psychologist as a facilitator of a community-wide project to enhance positive learning climate in elementary schools. *Psychology in the Schools, 29,* 348–358.

Hightower, A. D., Johnson, D., & Haffey, W. G. (1995). Best practices in adopting a prevention program. In A. Thomas & J. Grimes (Eds.), *Best practices in school psychology–III* (pp. 311–323). Washington, DC: National Association of School Psychologists.

Hollowood, T. M., Salisbury, C. L., Rainforth, B., & Palombaro, M. M. (1994). Use of instructional time in classrooms serving students with and without severe disabilities. *Exceptional Children, 61,* 242–253.

Houk, J. L., & Lewandowski, L. J. (1996). Consultant verbal control and consultee perceptions. *Journal of Educational and Psychological Consultation, 7,* 107–118.

House, J. E., & McInerney, W. F. (1996). The school assistance center: An alternative model for the delivery of school psychological services. *School Psychology International, 17,* 115–124.

Hughes, J. N. (1986). Ethical issues in school consultation. *School Psychology Review, 15,* 489–499.

Hughes, J. N. (1992). Social psychology foundations of consultation. In F. J. Medway & T. P. Cafferty (Eds.), *School psychology: A social psychological perspective* (pp. 269–303). Hillsdale, NJ: Erlbaum.

Hughes, J. N. (1994). Back to basics: Does consultation work? *Journal of Educational and Psychological Consultation, 5,* 77–84.

Hughes, J. N., Barker, D., Kemenoff, S., & Hart, M. (1993). Problem ownership, causal attributions, and self-efficacy as predictors of teachers' referral decisions. *Journal of Educational and Psychological Consultation, 4,* 369–384.

Hughes, J. N., & DeForest. (1993). Consultant directiveness and support as predictors of consultation outcomes. *Journal of School Psychology, 31,* 355–372.

Hughes, J. N., & Falk, R. S. (1981). Resistance, reactance, and consultation. *Journal of School Psychology, 19,* 134–142.

Hughes, J. N., Grossman, P., & Barker, D. (1990). Teachers' expectancies, participation in consultation, and perceptions of consultant helpfulness. *School Psychology Quarterly, 5,* 167–179.

Hyman, I. A. (1997). *School discipline and school violence: The teacher variance approach.* Boston: Allyn & Bacon.

Idol, L., Nevin, A., & Paolucci-Whitcomb, P. (1994). *Collaborative consultation* (2nd ed.). Austin, TX: Pro-Ed.

Ikeda, M. J., Tilly, W. D., III, Stumme, J., Volmer, L., & Allison, R. (1996). Agency-wide implementation of problem solving consultation: Foundations, current implementation, and future directions. *School Psychology Quarterly, 11,* 228–243.

Illback, R. J., & Zins, J. E. (1993). Organizational perspectives in child consultation. In J. E. Zins, T. R. Kratochwill, & S. N. Elliott (Eds.), *Handbook of consultation services for children: Applications in educational and clinical settings* (pp. 87–109). San Francisco: Jossey-Bass.

Ivey, A. E. (1994). *Intentional interviewing and counseling: Facilitating client development in a multicultural society* (3rd ed.). Pacific Grove, CA: Brooks/Cole.

Jackson, P. W. (1968). *Life in classrooms.* New York: Holt, Rinehart & Winston.

Jackson, R. M., Cleveland, J. C., & Merenda, P. F. (1975). The longitudinal effects of early identification and counseling of underachievers. *Journal of School Psychology, 13,* 119–128.

Jacob-Timm, S., & Hartshorne, T. (1994). *Ethics and law for school psychologists* (2nd ed.). Brandon, VT: Clinical Psychology Publishing.

Janney, R. E., Snell, M. E., Beers, M. K., & Raynes, M. (1995). Integrating students with moderate and severe disabilities into general education classes. *Exceptional Children, 61,* 425–439.

Jason, L. A., & Ferone, L. (1978). Behavioral versus process consultation interventions in school settings. *American Journal of Community Psychology, 6,* 531–543.

Jayanthi, M., & Friend, M. (1992). Interpersonal problem solving: A selective literature review to guide practice. *Journal of Educational and Psychological Consultation, 3,* 39–53.

Johnson, K. M., Gutkin, T. B., & Plake, B. S. (1992). The use of modeling to enhance children's interrogative strategies. *Journal of School Psychology, 29,* 81–88.

Jongsma, A. E., Jr., Peterson, L. M., & McInnis, W. P. (1996). *The child and adolescent psychotherapy treatment planner.* New York: Wiley.

Knoff, H. M. (1995). Best practices in facilitating school-based organizational change and strategic planning. In A. Thomas & J. Grimes (Eds.), *Best practices in school psychology–III* (pp. 239–252). Washington, DC: National Association of School Psychologists.

Knoff, H. M., & Curtis, M. J. (Eds.). (1996). Organizational change and school reform. *School Psychology Review* (Special series), *25*(4).

Knoff, H. M., Hines, C. V., & Kromrey, J. D. (1995). Finalizing the consultant effectiveness scale: An analysis and validation of the characteristics of effective consultants. *School Psychology Review, 24*, 480–496.

Kouzes, J., & Mico, P. (1979). Domain theory: An introduction to organizational behavior in human services organizations. *Journal of Applied Behavioral Science, 15*, 449–469.

Kramer, J. J. (Ed.). (1993). *Curriculum-based measurement.* Lincoln, NE: Buros Institute of Mental Measurements.

Kratochwill, T. R., & Bergan, J. R. (1990). *Behavioral consultation in applied settings: an individual guide.* New York: Plenum.

Kratochwill, T. R., Bergan, J. R., Sheridan, S. M., & Elliott, S. N. (in press). Assumptions of behavioral consultation: After all is said and done more has been done than said. *School Psychology Quarterly.*

Kratochwill, T. R., Elliott, S. N., & Busse, R. T. (1995). Behavior consultation: A five-year evaluation of consultant and client outcomes. *School Psychology Quarterly, 10*, 87–117.

Kratochwill, T. R., Elliott, S. N., & Carrington Rotto, P. (1990). Best practices in behavioral consultation. In A. Thomas & J. Grimes (Eds.), *Best practices in school psychology–II,* (pp. 147–169). Washington, DC: The National Association of School Psychologists.

Kratochwill, T. R., Elliott, S. N., & Carrington Rotto, P. (1995). Best practices in school-based behavioral consultation. In A. Thomas & J. Grimes (Eds.), *Best practices in school psychology–III* (pp. 519–537). Washington, DC: National Association of School Psychologists.

Kratochwill, T. R., VanSomeren, K. R., & Sheridan, S. M. (1989). Training behavioral consultants: A competency-based model to teach interview skills. *Professional School Psychology, 4*, 41–58.

Kruger, L. J. (1988). Programming change strategies at the building level. In J. L. Graden, J. E. Zins, & M. J. Curtis (Eds.), *Alternative educational delivery systems: Enhancing instructional options for all students* (pp. 491–511). Washington, DC: National Association of School Psychologists.

Kurpius, D. J., & Rozecki, T. G. (1993). Strategies for improving interpersonal communication. In J. E. Zins, T. R. Kratochwill, & S. N. Elliott (Eds.), *Handbook of consultation services for children: Applications in educational and clinical settings* (pp. 137–158). San Francisco: Jossey-Bass.

Kutsick, K. A., Gutkin, T. B., & Witt, J. C. (1991). The impact of treatment development process, intervention type, and problem severity on treatment acceptability as judged by classroom teachers. *Psychology in the Schools, 28*, 325–331.

Lambert, M. J., & Bergin, A. E. (1994). The effectiveness of psychotherapy. In A. E. Bergin & S. L. Garfield (Eds.), *Handbook of psychotherapy and behavior change* (4th ed., pp. 143–189). New York: Wiley.

Lambert, N. M. (1976). Children's problems and classroom interventions from the perspective of classroom teachers. *Professional Psychology, 7*, 507–517.

LeCroy, C. W. (1994). *Handbook of child and adolescent treatment manuals.* New York: Lexington Books.

Lennox, N., Hyman, I. A., & Hughes, C. A. (1988). Institutionalization of a consultation-based service delivery system. In J. L. Graden, J. E. Zins, & M. J. Curtis (Eds.), *Alternative educational delivery systems: Enhancing instructional options for all students* (pp. 71–89). Washington, DC: National Association of School Psychologists.

Lentz, F. E., Allen, S. J., & Ehrhardt, K. E. (1996). The conceptual elements of strong interventions in school settings. *School Psychology Quarterly, 11*, 118–136.

Lentz, F. E., Jr., & Daly, E. J., III. (1996). Is the behavior of academic change agents controlled metaphysically? An analysis of the behavior of those who change behavior. *School Psychology Quarterly, 11*, 337–352.

Levinson, E. M. (1990). Actual/desired role functioning, perceived control over role functioning, and job satisfaction among school psychologists. *Psychology in the Schools, 27*, 64–74.

Lewin, K. (1951). *Field theory in social science: Selected theoretical papers.* New York: Harper.

Maher, C. A., & Illback, R. J. (1985). Implementing school psychological service programs: Description and application of the DURABLE approach. *Journal of School Psychology, 23*, 81–89.

Maitland, R. E., Fine, M. J., & Tracy, D. B. (1985). The effects of an interpersonally based problem-solving process on consultation outcomes. *Journal of School Psychology, 23*, 337–345.

Mannino, F., & Shore, M. (1975). The effects of consultation: A review of empirical studies. *American Journal of Community Psychology, 3*, 1–21.

Marks, E. S. (1995). *Entry strategies for school consultation.* New York: Guilford.

Martens, B. K., Deery, K. S., & Gherardi, J. P. (1991). An experimental analysis of reflected affect versus reflected content in consultation interactions. *Journal of Educational and Psychological Consultation, 2*, 117–132.

Martens, B. K., Erchul, W. P., & Witt, J. C. (1992). Quantifying verbal interactions in school-based consultation: A comparison of four coding schemes. *School Psychology Review, 21*, 109–124.

Martens, B. K., Lewandowski, L. J., & Houk, J. L. (1989). The effects of entry information on the consultation process. *School Psychology Review, 18*, 225–234.

Martens, B. K., & Witt, J. C. (1988a). On the ecological validity of behavior modification. In J. C. Witt, S. N. Elliott, & F. M. Gresham (Eds.), *Handbook of behavior therapy in education* (pp. 325–341). New York: Plenum.

Martens, B. K., & Witt, J. C. (1988b). Expanding to the scope of behavioral consultation: A systems approach to classroom behavior change. *Professional School Psychology, 3,* 271–281.

Martin, R. P., & Keller, A. (1976). Teacher awareness of classroom dyadic interactions. *Journal of School Psychology, 14,* 47–55.

Mash, E. J., & Dozois, D. J. A. (1996). Child psychopathology: A developmental-systems perspective. In E. J. Mash & R. A. Barley (Eds.), *Child Psychopathology* (pp. 3–60). New York: Guilford.

McDougall, L. M., Reschly, D. J., & Corkery, J. M. (1988). Changes in referral interviews with teachers after behavioral consultation training. *Journal of School Psychology, 26,* 225–232.

McLaughlin, M. W. (1976). Implementation as mutual adaptation: Change in classroom organization. *Teachers College Record, 77,* 339–351.

McLaughlin, M. W. (1990). The Rand change agent study revisited: Macro perspectives and micro realities. *Educational Researcher, 18*(9), 11–16.

Meacham, M. L., & Peckham, P. D. (1978). School psychologists at three-quarters century: Congruence between training, practice, preferred role and competence. *Journal of School Psychology, 16,* 195–206.

Medway, F. J. (1979). How effective is school consultation: A review of recent research. *Journal of School Psychology, 17,* 275–282.

Medway, F. J. (1982). School consultation research: Past trends and future directions. *Professional Psychology, 13,* 422–430.

Medway, F. J., & Updyke, J. F. (1985). Meta-analysis of consultation outcome studies. *American Journal of Community Psychology, 13,* 489–504.

Meichenbaum, D., & Turk, D. C. (1987). *Facilitating treatment adherence: A practitioner's guidebook.* New York: Plenum.

Meijer, C. J. W., & Foster, S. F. (1988). The effect of teacher self-efficacy on referral chance. *The Journal of Special Education, 22,* 378–385.

Meyers, B., Valentino, C. T., Meyers, J., & Boretti, B. (1996). Implementing prereferral intervention teams as an approach to school-based consultation in an urban school system. *Journal of Educational and Psychological Consultation, 7,* 119–149.

Meyers, J. (1973). A consultation model for school psychological services. *Journal of School Psychology, 11,* 5–15.

Meyers, J. (1975). Consultee-centered consultation with a teacher as a technique in behavior management. *American Journal of Community Psychology, 3,* 111–121.

Meyers, J. (1988). Diagnosis diagnosed: Twenty years after. *Professional School Psychology, 3,* 123–134.

Meyers, J., Parsons, R. D., & Martin, R. (1979). *Mental health consultation in the schools.* San Francisco: Jossey-Bass.

Meyers, J., Pitt, N. W., Gaughan, E. J., & Friedman, M. P. (1978). A research model for consultation with teachers. *Journal of School Psychology, 16,* 137–145.

Miller, G. A. (1969). Psychology as a means of promoting human welfare. *American Psychologist, 24,* 1063–1075.

Millman, H. L., Schaefer, C. E., & Cohen, J. J. (1980). *Therapies for school behavior problems: A handbook of practical interventions.* San Francisco: Jossey-Bass.

Minor, M. W. (1972). Systems analysis and school psychology. *Journal of School Psychology, 10,* 227–232.

Morris, E. K., & Midgley, B. D. (1990). Some historical and conceptual foundations of ecobehavioral analysis. In S. Schroeder (Ed.), *Ecobehavioral analysis and developmental disabilities: The twenty-first century* (pp. 1–32). New York: Springer-Verlag.

Morse, W. C. (1993). Ecological approaches. In T. R. Kratochwill & R. J. Morris (Eds.), *Handbook of psychotherapy with children and adolescents* (pp. 320–355). Boston: Longwood.

Napier, R. W., & Gershenfeld, M. K. (1989). *Groups: theory and experience* (4th ed.). Boston: Houghton Mifflin.

National Association of School Psychologists (1992). National Association of School Psychologists standards for the provision of school psychological services. In *Professional conduct manual* (pp. 31–48). Silver Springs, MD: Author.

National Association of School Psychologists. (1994). *Assessment and eligibility in special education: An examination of policy and practice with proposals for change.* Alexandria, VA: National Association of State Directors of Special Education.

National Association of State Boards of Education. (1992). *Winners all: A call for inclusive schools.* Alexandria, VA: Author.

Nelson, J. R., Smith, D. J., Taylor, L., Dodd, J. M., & Reavis, K. (1991). Prereferral intervention: A review of the research. *Education and Treatment of Children, 14,* 243–253.

Noell, G. H. (Ed.). (1996). New directions in behavioral consultation. *School Psychology Quarterly* (Special issue), *11*(3).

Noell, G. H., & Witt, J. C. (1996). A critical evaluation of five fundamental assumptions underlying behavioral consultation. *School Psychology Quarterly, 11,* 189–203.

Nowell, D., & Spruill, J. (1993). If it's not absolutely confidential, will information be disclosed? *Professional Psychology: Research and Practice, 24,* 367–369.

Osborn, A. F. (1963). *Applied imagination* (3rd ed.). New York: Scribner.

O'Hearn, T. C., & Gatz, M. (1996). The educational pyramid: A model for community intervention. *Applied & Preventive Psychology, 5*, 127–134.

Owens, R. G. (1987). *Organizational behavior in education* (3rd ed.). Englewood Cliffs, NJ: Prentice Hall.

Peck, C. A., Killen, C. C., & Baumgart, D. (1989). Increasing implementation of special education instruction in mainstream preschools: Direct and generalized effects of nondirective consultation. *Journal of Applied Behavior Analysis, 22*, 197–210.

Petty, R. E., Heesacker, M., & Hughes, J. N. (1997). The Elaboration Likelihood Model: Implications for the practice of school psychology. *Journal of School Psychology, 35*, 107–136.

Piersel, W. C., & Gutkin, T. B. (1983). Resistance to school-based consultation: A behavioral analysis of the problem. *Psychology in the Schools, 20*, 311–320.

Plas, J. M. (1986). *Systems psychology in the schools*. New York: Pergamon.

Podell, D. M., & Soodak, L. C. (1993). Teacher efficacy and bias in special education referrals. *Journal of Educational Research, 86*, 247–253.

Ponti, C. R., & Curtis, M. J. (1984, August). Effects of consultation on teachers' attributions for children's school problems. Paper presented at the Annual Meeting of the American Psychological Association, Toronto.

Ponti, C. R., Zins, J. E., & Graden, J. L. (1988). Implementing a consultation-based service delivery system to decrease referrals for special education: A case study of organizational considerations. *School Psychology Review, 17*, 89–100.

Pryzwansky, W. B. (1986). Indirect service delivery: Considerations for future research in consultation. *School Psychology Review, 15*, 479–488.

Pyle, R. R. (1977). Mental health consultation: Helping teachers help themselves. *Professional Psychology, 8*, 192–198.

Randolph, D. L., & Mitchell, M. M. (1995). A survey of consultation articles in key counseling journals, 1967–1991. *Journal of Educational and Psychological Consultation, 6*, 83–94.

Reimers, T. M., Wacker, D. P., & Koeppl, G. (1987). Acceptability of behavioral interventions: A review of the literature. *School Psychology Review, 16*, 212–227.

Reinking, R. H., Livesay, G., & Kohl, M. (1978). The effects of consultation style on consultee productivity. *American Journal of Community Psychology, 6*, 283–290.

Reschly, D. J. (1976). School psychology consultation: "Frenzied, faddish, or fundamental?" *Journal of School Psychology, 14*, 105–113.

Reschly, D. J. (1988). Special education reform: School psychology reform. *School Psychology Review, 17*, 459–475.

Revels, O. H., & Gutkin, T. B. (1983). Effects of symbolic modeling procedures and model status on brainstorming behavior. *Journal of School Psychology, 21*, 311–318.

Reynolds, C. R., Gutkin, T. B., Elliott, S. N., & Witt, W. C. (1984). *School psychology: Essentials of theory and practice*. New York: Wiley.

Robbins, J. R., & Gutkin, T. B. (1994). Consultee and client remedial and preventive outcomes following consultation: Some mixed empirical results and directions for future research. *Journal of Educational and Psychological Consultation, 5*, 149–167.

Roberts, A. H., & Rust, J. O. (1994). Role and function of school psychologists, 1992–93: a comparative study. *Psychology in the Schools, 31*, 113–119.

Robinson, V. M. J., Cameron, M. M., & Raethel, A. M. (1985). Negotiation of a consultative role for school psychologists: A case study. *Journal of School Psychology, 23*, 43–49.

Rogers-Warren, A., & Warren, S. F. (Eds.). (1977). *Ecological perspectives in behavior analysis*. Baltimore, MD: University Park Press.

Romualdi, V., & Sandoval, J. (1995). Comprehensive school-linked services. Implications for school psychologists. *Psychology in the Schools, 32*, 306–317.

Rosenfield, S. A. (1987). *Instructional consultation*. Hillsdale, NJ: Erlbaum.

Rosenfield, S. A. (1991). The relationship variable in behavioral consultation. *Journal of Behavioral Education, 1*, 329–336.

Rosenfield, S. A. (1992). Developing school-based consultation teams: A design for organizational change. *School Psychology Quarterly, 7*, 27–46.

Sachs, J. (1988). Teacher preparation, teacher self-efficacy and the regular education initiative. *Education and Training in Mental Retardation, 23*, 327–332.

Safran, S. P. (1991). The communication process and school-based consultation: What does the research say? *Journal of Educational and Psychological Consultation, 2*, 343–370.

Salisbury, C. L., Evans, I. M., & Palombaro, M. M. (1997). Collaborative problem-solving to promote the inclusion of young children with significant disabilities in primary grades. *Exceptional Children, 63*, 195–209.

Salvia, J., & Ysseldyke, J. E. (1995). *Assessment* (6th ed.). Boston: Houghton Mifflin.

Sarason, S. B. (1982). *The culture of the school and the problem of change* (2nd ed.). Boston: Allyn & Bacon.

Sarason, S. B., Levine, M., Goldenberg, I. I., Cherlin, D. L., & Bennett, E. (1966). *Psychology in community settings*. New York: Wiley.

Saxe, L., Cross, T., & Silverman, N. (1988). Children's

mental health: The gap between what we know and what we do. *American Psychologist, 43,* 800–807.

Schein, E. H. (1969). *Process consultation: Its role in organization development.* Reading, MA: Addison-Wesley.

Schmuck, R. (1990). Organization development in schools: Contemporary concepts and practices. In T. B. Gutkin & C. R. Reynolds (Eds.), *The handbook of school psychology* (2nd ed., pp. 899–919). New York: Wiley.

Schmuck, R. A., Runkel, P. J. Arends, J. H., & Arends, R. I. (1977). *The second handbook of organization development in schools.* Palo Alto, CA: Mayfield.

Schrag, J. A. (1996). Systems change leading to better integration of services for students with special needs. *School Psychology Review, 25,* 489–495.

Scruggs, T. E., & Mastropieri, M. A. (1996). Teacher perceptions of mainstreaming/inclusion, 1958–1995: A research synthesis. *Exceptional Children, 63,* 59–74.

Secord, W. A. (Ed.). (1990). *Best practices in school speech-language pathology—Collaborative programs in the schools: Concepts, models, and procedures.* San Antonio, TX: Psychological Corp.

Shapiro, E. S. (1987). *Behavioral assessment in school psychology.* Hillsdale, NJ: Erlbaum.

Shapiro, E. S. (1990). An integrated model for curriculum-based assessment. *School Psychology Review, 19,* 331–349.

Sheridan, S. M. (1992). What do we mean when we say "collaboration"? *Journal of Educational and Psychological Consultation, 3,* 89–92.

Sheridan, S. M. (1993). Models for working with parents. In J. E. Zins, T. R. Kratochwill, & S. N. Elliott (Eds.), *Handbook of consultation for children: Applications in educational and clinical settings* (pp. 110–133). San Francisco: Jossey-Bass.

Sheridan, S. M. (1997). Conceptual and empirical bases of conjoint behavioral consultation. *School Psychology Quarterly, 12,* 119–133.

Sheridan, S. M., & Colton, D. L. (1994). Conjoint behavioral consultation: A review and case study. *Journal of Educational and Psychological Consultation, 5,* 211–228.

Sheridan, S. M., & Kratochwill, T. R. (1992). Behavioral parent-teacher consultation: conceptual and research considerations. *Journal of School Psychology, 30,* 117–139.

Sheridan, S. M., Kratochwill, T. R., & Bergan, J. R. (1996). *Conjoint behavioral consultation.* New York: Plenum.

Sheridan, S. M., Kratochwill, T. R., & Elliott, S. N. (1990). Behavioral consultation with parents and teachers: Delivering treatment for socially withdrawn children at home and school. *School Psychology Review, 19,* 33–52.

Sheridan, S. M., Welch, M., & Orme, S. F. (1996). Is consultation effective? A review of outcome research. *Remedial and Special Education, 17,* 341–354.

Shinn, M. R. (1995). Best practices in curriculum-based measurement and its use in a problem-solving model. In A. Thomas & J. Grimes (Eds.), *Best practices in school psychology–III* (pp. 547–567). Washington, DC: National Association of School Psychologists.

Shinn, M. R., & McConnell, S. (1994). Improving general education instruction: Relevance to school psychologists. *School Psychology Review, 23,* 351–371.

Shinn M. R., Powell-Smith, K. A., & Good, R. H., III (1996). Evaluating the effects of responsible reintegration into general education for students with mild disabilities on a case-by-case basis. *School Psychology Review, 25,* 519–539.

Shinn, M. R., Rosenfield, S., & Knutson, N. (1989). Curriculum-based assessment: A comparison of models. *School Psychology Review, 18,* 299–316.

Skinner, B. F. (1953). *Science and human behavior.* New York: Macmillan.

Smylie, M. A. (1988). The enhancement function of staff development: Organizational and psychological antecedents to individual teacher change. *American Educational Research Journal, 25,* 1–30.

Snapp, M., Hickman, J. A., & Conoley, J. C. (1990). Systems interventions in school settings: Case studies. In T. B. Gutkin & C. R. Reynolds (Eds.), *The handbook of school psychology* (2nd ed., pp. 920–934). New York: Wiley.

Stainback, S., & Stainback, W. (1988). Changes needed to strengthen regular education. In J. L. Graden, J. E. Zins, & M. J. Curtis (Eds.), *Alternative educational delivery systems: Enhancing instructional options for all students* (pp. 17–32). Washington, DC: National Association of School Psychologists.

Stenger, M. K., Tollefson, N., & Fine, M. J. (1992). Variables that distinguish elementary teachers who participate in school-based consultation from those who do not. *School Psychology Quarterly, 7,* 271–284.

Stoner, G., & Green, S. K. (1992). Reconsidering the scientist-practitioner model for school psychology practice. *School Psychology Review, 21,* 155–166.

Stoner, G., Shinn, M. R., & Walker, H. M. (1991). *Interventions for achievement and behavior problems.* Silver Spring, MD: National Association of School Psychologists.

Sulzer-Azaroff, B., & Mayer, G. R. (1991). *Behavior analysis for lasting change.* Fort Worth, TX: Holt, Rinehart & Winston.

Sundstrom, E., De Meuse, K. P., & Futrell, D. (1990). Work teams: Applications and effectiveness. *American Psychologist, 45,* 120–133.

Taylor, J., & Miller, M. (1997). When timeout works some of the time: The importance of treatment integrity and functional assessment. *School Psychology Quarterly, 12,* 4–22.

Thomas, A., & Grimes, J. (Eds.). (1955). *Best practices in school psychology–III.* Washington, DC: National Association of School Psychologists.

Tindal, G., Shinn, M., Walz, L., & Germann, G. (1987). Mainstream consultation in secondary settings: The Pine County model. *The Journal of Special Education, 21,* 94–106.

Tombari, M. L., & Bergan, J. R. (1978). Consultant cues and teacher verbalizations, judgments, and expectancies concerning children's adjustment problems. *Journal of School Psychology, 16,* 212–219.

Tyler, F. B., Pargament, K. I., & Gatz, M. (1983). The resource collaborator role: A model for interactions involving psychologists. *American Psychologist, 38,* 388–398.

Villa, R. A., Thousand, J. S., Meyers, H., & Nevin, A. (1996). Teacher and administrator perceptions of heterogeneous education. *Exceptional Children, 63,* 29–45.

von Bertalanffy, L. (1968). *General systems theory.* New York: Braziller.

Wahler, R. G., & Fox, J. J. (1981). Setting events in applied behavior analysis: Toward a conceptual and methodological expansion. *Journal of Applied Behavior Analysis, 14,* 327–338.

Wang, M. C., & Baker, E. T. (1986). Mainstreaming programs: Design features and effects. *Journal of Special Education, 19,* 503–523.

Watson, T. S., & Robinson, S. L. (1996). Direct behavioral consultation: An alternative to traditional behavioral consultation. *School Psychology Quarterly, 11,* 267–278.

Wehmann, B., Zins, J. E., & Curtis, M. J. (1989, March). Effects of consultation on teachers' perceptions of children's problems. Paper presented at the Annual Meeting of the National Association of School Psychologists, Boston.

Wickstrom, K. F., & Witt, J. C. (1993). In J. E. Zins, T. R. Kratochwill, & S. N. Elliott (Eds.), *Handbook of consultation services for children: Applications in educational and clinical settings* (pp. 159–178). San Francisco: Jossey-Bass.

Will, M. (1988). Educating students with learning problems and the changing role of the school psychologist. *School Psychology Review, 17,* 476–478.

Willems, E. P. (1974). Behavioral technology and behavioral ecology. *Journal of Applied Behavior Analysis, 7,* 151–165.

Wilson, C. P., Gutkin, T. B., Hagen, K. M., & Oats, R. G. (1998). General education teachers' knowledge and self-reported use of classroom interventions for working with difficult-to-teach students: Implications for consultation, prereferral intervention and inclusive services. *School Psychology Quarterly, 13,* 45–62.

Witt, J. C. (1990a). Collaboration in school-based consultation: Myth in need of data. *Journal of Educational and Psychological Consultation, 1,* 367–370.

Witt, J. C. (1990b). Complaining, precopernican thought and the univariate linear mind: Questions for school-based behavioral consultation research. *School Psychology Review, 19,* 367–377.

Witt, J. C., Erchul, W. P., McKee, W. T., Pardue, M. M., & Wickstrom, K. F. (1991). Conversational control in school-based consultation: The relationship between consultant and consultee topic determination and consultation outcome. *Journal of Educational and Psychological Consultation, 2,* 101–116.

Witt, J. C. & Martens, B. K. (1988). Problems with problem-solving consultation: A re-analysis of assumptions, methods, and goals. *School Psychology Review, 17,* 211–226.

Witt, J. C., Moe, G., Gutkin, T. B., & Andrews, L. (1984). The effect of saying the same thing in different ways: The problem of language and jargon in school-based consultation. *Journal of School Psychology, 22,* 361–367.

Wittrock, M. C. (Ed.). (1986). *Handbook of research on teaching* (3rd ed.). New York: Macmillan.

Woolfolk, A. E., & Hoy, W. K. (1990). Prospective teachers' sense of efficacy and beliefs about control. *Journal of Educational Psychology, 82,* 81–91.

Woods, K. M., & McNamara, J. R. (1980). Confidentiality: Its effect on interviewee behavior. *Professional Psychology, 11,* 714–721.

Yalom, I. D. (1985). *The theory and practice of group psychotherapy* (3rd. ed.). New York: Basic Books.

Ysseldyke, J. E. (1987). Classification of handicapped students. In M. C. Wang, M. Reynolds, & H. J. Walberg (Eds.), *Handbook of special education: Research & practice* (Vol. 1, pp. 253–271). New York: Pergamon.

Ysseldyke, J. E., Algozzine, B., & Thurlow, M. L. (1992). *Critical issues in special education* (2nd ed.). Boston: Houghton Mifflin.

Ysseldyke, J. E., & Christenson, S. L. (1988). Linking assessment to intervention. In J. L. Graden, J. E. Zins, & M. J. Curtis (Eds.), *Alternative educational delivery systems: Enhancing instructional options for all students* (pp. 91–109). Washington DC: National Association of School Psychologists.

Ysseldyke, J. E., Christenson, S. L., Thurlow, M. L., & Bakewell, D. (1989). Are different kinds of instructional tasks used by different categories of students in different settings? *School Psychology Review, 18,* 98–111.

Ysseldyke, J., Dawson, P., Lehr, C., Reschly, D., Reynolds, M., & Telzrow, C. (1997). *School psychology: A blueprint for training and practice–II.* Bethesda, MD: National Association of School Psychologists.

Ysseldyke, J. E., Reynolds, M. C., Weinberg, R. A., Bardon H, Heaston, P., Hines, L., Ramage, J., Rosenfield, S., Schakel, J., & Taylor, J. (1984). *School psychology: A blueprint for training and practice*. Minneapolis, MN: National School Psychology Inservice Training Network.

Zins, J. E., Curtis, M. J., Graden, J. L., & Ponti, C. R. (1988). *Helping students succeed in the regular classroom: A guide for developing intervention assistance programs*. San Francisco: Jossey-Bass.

Zins, J. E., & Erchul, W. P. (1995). School consultation. In A. Thomas & J. Grimes (Eds.), *Best practices in school psychology–III* (pp. 609–623). Washington, DC: National Association of School Psychologists.

Zins, J. E., & Forman, S. G. (1988). Primary prevention: From theory to practice. *School Psychology Review* (Special series), *17*(4).

Zins, J. E., & Heron, T. E. (Eds.). (1996). Current practices, unresolved issues, and future directions in consultation. *Remedial and Special Education* (Special issue), *17*(6).

Zins, J. E., Kratochwill, T. R., & Elliott, S. N. (1993a). Current status of the field. In J. E. Zins, T. R. Kratochwill, & S. N. Elliott (Eds.), *Handbook of consultation services for children: Applications in educational and clinical settings* (pp. 1–12). San Francisco: Jossey-Bass.

Zins, J. E., Kratochwill, T. R., & Elliott, S. N. (1993b). *Handbook of consultation services for children: Applications in educational and clinical settings*. San Francisco: Jossey-Bass.

Zins, J. E., & Ponti, C. R. (1990). Strategies to facilitate the implementation, organization, and operation of system-wide consultation programs. *Journal of Educational and Psychological Consultation, 1*, 205–218.

Zins, J. E., & Ponti, C. R. (1996). The influence of direct training in problem solving on consultee problem clarification skills and attributions. *Remedial and Special Education, 17*, 370–376.

## CHAPTER 24

# BEHAVIOR ANALYSIS:
# THEORY AND
# PRACTICE IN
# EDUCATIONAL SETTINGS

**BRIAN K. MARTENS**
*Syracuse University*

**JOSEPH C. WITT**
*Louisiana State University*

**EDWARD J. DALY III**
*University of Cincinnati*

**TIMOTHY R. VOLLMER**
*University of Pennsylvania School of Medicine*

## INTRODUCTION

Behavior analysis refers to a set of strategies for selecting, implementing, and evaluating intervention programs based on the lawful principles of behavior. Although the strategies of applied behavior analysis are continuing to evolve, as discussed throughout this chapter, the principles underlying behavioral treatment programs were examined in basic laboratory research dating back to the 1930s (Skinner, 1932). Using the now familiar "Skinner box," consequences were programmed for a single subject while the animal's behavior was recorded mechanically over periods of days or weeks (Ferster & Skinner, 1957). This approach was used in the decades that followed to examine systematically how behavior could be altered by varying its effects on the environment. By the late 1960s, the methods used to program consequences and record behavior in laboratories became known as the *experimental operant paradigm*, whereas the consequences that were programmed and their effects on responding became known as the *principles of operant conditioning*.

In the late 1960s and 1970s, researchers began applying the principles of operant conditioning to clinically relevant and socially significant problems (e.g., Azrin & Foxx, 1974), and many of these applications occurred in educational settings (Broden, Bruce, Mitchell, Carter, & Hall, 1970; Hall, Lund, & Jackson, 1968; Kazdin & Klock, 1973; Madsen, Becker, & Thomas, 1968). For such applications to take place, methods for programming consequences in the laboratory (e.g., ratio schedules of food reinforcement) had to be replaced with procedures that could be used in schools and other child-related settings. Similarly, in the absence of mechanical recording devices, systematic observation became the standard means of reliably detecting changes in children's behavior, and single-case experimental designs were used to relate these changes with confidence to the procedures being implemented.

The strategies and tactics of applied behavior analysis and many of the behavioral treatment protocols in use today were developed during the 1970s and early 1980s (Johnston & Pennypacker, 1980; Sulzer-Azaroff & Mayer, 1977). Not coincidentally, it was during this period that the term *behavior modification* was coined. In many ways this term reflected the characteristics of early behavior analytic research (Hayes, 1991; Martens & Witt, 1988; Pierce & Epling, 1980), and we believe that these characteristics offer a useful contrast to contemporary behavior analysis in the schools.

First, because behavior modification procedures were effective, they were often implemented with little concern over the factors that maintained problem behaviors at baseline. Rather, it was assumed that the procedure being implemented would override these factors by requiring teachers to engage in new behaviors (e.g., removing slips of paper that represent recess time or escorting a child to time out). In contrast, recent advances in functional analysis and functional assessment technology have shown that assessing the environmental determinants of problem behavior can facilitate treatment selection and greatly enhance treatment effectiveness (e.g., Iwata et al., 1994; Lalli, Browder, Mace, & Brown, 1993).

Second, behavior modification tended to emphasize the basic principle of positive reinforcement, and did so by using procedures that were uncommon in typical classrooms (Pierce & Epling, 1980; Witt & Martens, 1988). Although such approaches often produced large initial gains, these tended to dissipate as adherence to the procedure waned over time. In recent years, a variety of conditioning principles have been brought to bear on children's learning and adjustment problems, ranging from negative reinforcement to more complex processes like momentum and choice (e.g., Mace & Belfiore, 1990; Marcus & Vollmer, 1995; Martens, Lochner, & Kelly, 1992). In addition, the procedures that invoke these principles are being designed to approximate existing classroom conditions more closely than many earlier, standardized protocols (e.g., Kern, Childs, Dunlap, Clarke, & Falk, 1994).

Third, whereas emphasis was placed on the development of specific intervention procedures in the 1970s, contemporary behavior analysis is concerned both with treatment programs and the methods by which these programs are implemented and evaluated. Wolery, Bailey, and Sugai (1988) indicated that the behavior analytic approach to instruction combined the principles of behavior with the principles of measurement. In line with this view, issues surrounding program implementation such as goal setting, treatment integrity, and systematic formative evaluation have been shown to contribute significantly to the effectiveness of behavior analysis in educational settings (e.g., Fuchs & Fuchs, 1986; Gresham, Gansle, & Noell, 1993; Martens, Hirallal, & Bradley, 1997).

Behavior analysis has been adopted as standard practice in many areas of psychology and education, including institutional and out-patient programs for individuals with developmental disabilities; direct instruction and remediation of academic skills; child behavior therapy for learning, elimination, and disruptive behavior disorders; and adult behavior therapy for weight loss, as well as substance-related and anxiety disorders (Baker & Kirschenbaum, 1993; Carnine, 1994; Iwata et al., 1994; Kazdin, 1994; Matson & Coe, 1992; Shinn, 1989; Sturmey, 1995; Witt, Elliott, & Gresham, 1988; Wolery, Bailey, and Sugai, 1988). The goal of this chapter is to describe the theory and practice of behavior analysis as it applies to educational settings. We begin by discussing the causes of classroom problems from a behavior analytic perspective and within the context of teacher-student interactions. The key elements of behavior analysis as an explicit approach to teaching and management are also described. Next, behavior analytic approaches to classroom management are discussed, including the functional assessment of classroom behavior problems and the use of this information to select appropriate intervention strategies. The section that follows discusses the behavioral principles that underlie effective classroom instruction and reviews intervention programs based on these principles: In this section, the instructional hierarchy is described as a theoretical framework for basing instructional interventions on the level of skill proficiency. The chapter concludes with a discussion of issues pertaining to the implementation and use of behavioral interventions by teachers. Barriers to successful implementation and elements that make up a technology of implementation are described.

# FOUNDATIONS OF APPLIED BEHAVIOR ANALYSIS

## Principles of Operant Learning

Applied behavior analysis is rooted in the philosophical positions of empiricism, contextualism, and determinism, which assume that many problem behaviors are learned, that learning occurs through interactions with others, and that these interactions can be described and then altered to produce desired changes in behavior (Nelson & Hayes, 1986; Neuringer, 1991). When we speak of learned behaviors, we refer to behaviors that occur (or fail to occur) because of how they are responded to by significant others in the child's environment. In classrooms, these consequences for behavior may take a variety of forms (e.g., posting an A paper on the bulletin board or ignoring a child who is working quietly), may occur with varying degrees of consistency ("As a teacher, I should catch children being good whenever I can"), and may provide information to children in explicit or subtle ways (e.g., discussing class rules or feigning hurt feelings to induce guilt).

Like all learned behaviors, learned problem behaviors are lawful. In this respect, Skinner (1987) compared natural selection at a species level to operant selection at a behavioral level. Just as species adapt to their physical environment through the processes of variation and selection, Skinner proposed that humans adjust to their social environment through basic behavioral processes like reinforcement and extinction. In both cases, behaviors come to predominate because they are selected and strengthened by the natural environment in which they occur.

The notion of operant selection carries several important implications for the practice of behavior analysis in schools and other child-related settings. First, many chronic behavior problems may actually be appropriate (i.e., lawfully related) to events that surround their occurrence (Donnellan, Mirenda, Mesaros, & Fassbender, 1984; Durand & Crimmins, 1988). This means that either wittingly or unwittingly, teachers and other significant adults may play a role in supporting the very problems for which they seek assistance (Baer, 1988). For example, Carr, Newsom, and Binkoff (1980) examined the causes of severe aggressive behavior in a 14-year-old boy with mental retardation and autism. Teachers complained that the child would hit, kick, and bite them when even small demands were placed on him. During test conditions, the aggressive behavior occurred at high rates when it allowed the child to escape from demands, indicating that it had been strengthened by similar contingencies in the past. Significant decreases in the aggressive behavior were observed when escape from demands was made contingent on a more appropriate, alternative response.

If inappropriate classroom behaviors are strengthened through interactions with adults, under what conditions do these learned behaviors become viewed as problem behaviors? Sturmey (1995) discussed the conditions under which psychiatric disorders in adults with developmental disabilities are identified, suggesting that similar process may be involved in identifying behavior disorders in children. Behaviors are likely to be viewed as problems when children enter a new environment such as attending school for the first time or passing to the next grade. Teachers in the new setting may hold differing goals for children's behavior or differing attitudes about what is developmentally appropriate. Similarly, when new adults enter the child's environment, they may perceive behaviors that had been tolerated in the past as significant problems. The tolerance levels of teachers themselves may change over time as a result of stressful life events, leading them to refer a child for behaviors that had previously been viewed as minor irritants. Moreover, teachers may be encouraged at the building or administrative levels to identify certain types of behavior problems. For example, the recent popularity of attention deficit hyperactivity disorder (ADHD) as a diagnostic category may reflect increasing concern by teachers and parents over the level of violence in our public schools (Frick & Lahey, 1991; Furlong & Morrison, 1994).

Second, the notion of operant selection suggests that problem behaviors develop over time according to the same principles that would be used in behavioral treatment programs. Although teachers interact differently with each student in each classroom, the effects of these interactions on behavior can be described by the principles of operant conditioning. Viewed as causes of learned problem behaviors, these principles are limited in number and occur whether teachers and other care-givers are aware of them or not. Table 24.1 lists the possible causes of classroom behavior problems and the operant-conditioning principle that underlies each.

It is necessary to understand these principles in designing effective behavioral intervention programs for three reasons. First, behavioral treatment programs are more effective if the principles they invoke counteract or weaken the contingencies that maintain problem behavior at baseline (e.g., Iwata et al., 1994). Procedures for matching treatment programs to their hypothesized causes are generally referred to as the functional analysis

**TABLE 24.1    Operant Principles That Underlie Classroom Behavior Problems**

| Cause | Operant Principle |
|---|---|
| The child has not learned a more appropriate behavior that leads to the same consequence. | Skill deficit |
| More appropriate behaviors are ignored. | Extinction |
| More appropriate behaviors lead to undesired consequences. | Punishment |
| The problem behavior is followed by desired sensory, edible, tangible, social, or activity consequences. | Positive reinforcement |
| The problem behavior allows the child to stop or avoid undesired situations. | Negative reinforcement |
| The problem behavior occurs when it is likely to be reinforced. | Stimulus control |
| The problem behavior occurs when it is initiated by other individuals. | Prompting |
| The problem behavior occurs because the child observed someone else doing it. | Modeling |

of behavior (discussed in detail in the next section). Second, although basic behavioral principles are always operating during teacher-student interactions, teachers are not always aware of the effects their behavior has on that of children. Behavioral treatment programs are designed to help teachers achieve greater consistency in encouraging desired or appropriate behavior while discouraging undesired or inappropriate behavior (Martens & Kelly, 1993). Third, problem behaviors often develop over long periods of time, resulting in patterns of teacher-student interaction that may be resistant to change. In this respect, behavior analytic procedures can be viewed as explicit approaches to instruction and management (Carnine, 1994; Erchul & Martens, 1997). By setting goals, specifying procedures, and monitoring outcomes, behavioral treatment programs offer explicit guidance to teachers in their efforts to change children's behavior. The key features of behavior analysis as an explicit approach to instruction and management follow.

## Key Methodological Features
### Setting Goals

Establishing explicit standards for performance and comparing them to current performance levels is a form of self-monitoring known as goal setting (Bandura, 1977; Miller & Kelley, 1994). Goal setting and systematic performance monitoring are defining features of behavior analysis (Sulzer-Azaroff & Mayer, 1977) and have been used successfully in response to a variety of children's learning and adjustment problems (e.g., Brownell, Colletti, Ersner-Hershfield, Hershfield, & Wilson, 1977; McLaughlin, 1982; Schunk,

1984). For example, Miller and Kelley (1994) taught four parent-child dyads to divide daily homework assignments into challenging yet attainable goals and negotiate time periods during which each goal was to be completed. At the end of each period, parents determined if the goal had been met, and the children were given daily and weekly rewards as specified in a contract. The goal-setting plus contingency-contracting procedure was effective at increasing both homework accuracy and time on-task during evening homework periods. Moreover, the intervention was judged by parents as being highly useful and easy to implement.

More recently, Martens, Hiralall, and Bradley (1997) examined the effects of goal setting and feedback as applied to teachers' behavior as a means of producing desired changes in students' behavior during consultation. The participants were two 6-year-old male students enrolled full time in a classroom for children with emotional disturbances. Using a multiple-baseline-across-subjects design, the classroom teacher (1) identified up to four desired behaviors that should be increased for each student; (2) set a goal for the number of times she was to praise each student during a daily activity period; and (3) was given a feedback note each day that listed the identified target behaviors as prompts and indicated whether, based on classroom observation, she did or did not meet her self-imposed goal. The intervention was effective in increasing appropriate student behavior and was judged by the teacher to be acceptable.

### Restructuring Contingencies

A variety of intervention protocols have been reported in the literature for invoking the principles listed in Table 24.1. One important distinction is the degree of structure the protocols place on the nature and frequency of teacher-student interactions. For example, verbal praise and behavioral contracts are both designed to invoke the principle of positive reinforcement to increase a behavior. Verbal praise requires teachers to reward children whenever possible by stating the desired behavior together with some form of positive evaluation. Behavioral contracts require the teacher and child to specify in writing the desired behavior and its required level of performance, as well as any rewards that will be given for failing to meet, meeting, or exceeding the performance criterion. Although both procedures can be effective in increasing the desired behavior, some teachers may require the extra guidance and structure of behavioral contracts to change their own behavior successfully.

When selecting among intervention procedures, it is important to keep the following points in mind. First, whenever possible, it is better to select less intrusive, less structured interventions over those that require more time, energy, and resources or that constrain teacher-student interactions. Not only is this practice consistent with the least-restrictive-environment mandate of federal legislation, but also less complicated procedures can be implemented more quickly and teachers are more likely to use them for extended periods of time. Second, procedures that reinforce appropriate behavior should be emphasized over those that punish inappropriate behavior. On the one hand, consistently administered reinforcement encourages children to choose certain behaviors over others, and these choices extend through time (Martens, 1992). Punishment, on the other hand, merely informs children about what not to do, leaving the choice up the child's discretion. Third, the overall quality of teacher-student interactions should be taken into consideration before suggesting any behavioral treatment program (Wolery, Bailey, & Sugai, 1988). Are the teacher's instructional practices based on an adopted curriculum? Is the difficulty of assigned work appropriate for students' skill levels? Are interactions between the teacher and students generally positive and enjoyable or tense and punitive? Without a foundation of positive teacher-student interactions, many interventions may not have their intended effects or may be too much for teachers to handle, given their regular duties (Witt & Martens, 1988). For example, the effectiveness of time-out as a behavior reduction technique is based on a discrepancy between the reinforcing properties of time-in, that is, time spent in ongoing classroom activities, and time-out (that is, time spent being excluded from such activities (Harris, 1985). If students do not find ongoing classroom activities enjoyable, time away from these activities, contingent on misbehavior, is not likely to be perceived as aversive.

## Monitoring Progress

A key feature of any behavioral treatment program should be efforts to monitor systematically its effects on students' performance. Fuchs and Fuchs (1986) refer to the ongoing evaluation of program outcomes that lead to revisions in program procedures as *systematic formative evaluation*, which is based on the assumption that outcomes of school-based interventions cannot be predicted with certainty but instead represent hypotheses that must be tested empirically (Ysseldyke & Marston, 1990). This view can be contrasted with the ability-training approach, which emphasizes the diagnosis of one or more correlates of achievement by using standardized tests (i.e., student aptitudes) and basing instructional programs on these inferred traits (Shinn, 1989). Once the appropriate aptitude and treatment interaction has been identified, program effectiveness is assumed. However, data currently do not support this approach to school-based intervention because of poor psychometric properties of many existing aptitude measures and uncertainty over the extent to which various instructional programs actually address the aptitudes being targeted (Good, Vollmer, Creek, Katz, & Chowdhri, 1993; Ysseldyke, 1979).

Although federal law requires individual education programs for children who are receiving special services to be reviewed at least annually, monthly or even weekly monitoring of progress has been shown to increase students' achievement significantly. For example, Fuchs and Fuchs (1986) conducted a meta-analysis of the effects of systematic formative evaluation on students' achievement. Evaluation was defined as twice-weekly monitoring of students' progress, using materials taken from the curriculum, depicting these data in a figure or graph, and using data evaluation rules to guide decision making. Results indicated that monitoring progress and graphing the data were associated with an average effective size (ES) of .70, regardless of the instructional procedure used, and using data evaluation rules increased the average ES to .91. These findings indicate that students' achievement test scores improved by nearly 1 standard deviation over controls simply as a function of how the instructional program was monitored. In a more recent study, Fuchs, Fuchs, Hamlett, and Allinder (1991) compared the effects of weekly progress monitoring on students' achievement in spelling. Teachers who monitored students' progress, graphed the results, and used data evaluation rules averaged 3.7 instructional adjustments over an 18-week period. Teachers in the control group averaged only .17 changes in instruction during the same time period. Not surprisingly, the students of teachers who monitored progress frequently learned three times more spelling words by the end of the study.

To be useful in evaluating intervention outcomes, measures of students' performance must have certain characteristics. When monitoring academic performance, measures must be directly related to the skills taught, sensitive to short-term improvements, capable of repeated administration, and time- and cost-efficient, in addition to being reliable and valid (Fuchs & Fuchs, 1986). One assessment method that has these characteristics is known as *curriculum-based measurement (CBM)*. The CBM probes are brief samples of production-type responses obtained by using materials from the local curriculum (Shinn, 1989). Administered in standardized format, the CBM probes involve one minute of passage reading, two minutes of spelling from dictation, two minutes of math computation, and three minutes of writing from a story starter. Different materials are selected at each grade level and scored for fluency, or the number of correct responses in the time allocated (e.g., correctly read words per minute). Not only are these measures psychometrically sound, but also they have been used to monitor the effects of a variety of instructional programs, including special class placement (Shinn, 1989), instructional intervention (Daly & Martens, 1994), and stimulant medication (Stoner, Carey, Ikeda, & Shinn, 1994).

When monitoring intervention effects on classroom behavior, it is important that the measures selected assess the actual behavior of interest at the actual time and place of its occurrence (Cone, 1978; Hayes, Nelson, & Jarrett, 1986). *Direct observation* is one of the few assessment methods that accomplishes this goal, and as a result it is commonly used to evaluate the effects of school-based interventions (Alessi, 1980).

Several approaches have been reported in the literature for collecting direct observational data, including continuous event recording, duration recording, discrete categorization, and time sampling (Kazdin, 1994). Continuous event recording is simply tallying the number of times a behavior occurs during an observation session, and it is most appropriate for behaviors with brief durations (Saudargas & Lentz, 1986). Duration recording involves the use of a stopwatch to record the cumulative duration of behaviors that extend in time, whereas discrete categorization involves the use of a checklist to record the occurrence of behaviors that have several discrete steps. Time sampling refers to a set of procedures for observing behavior in which occurrence or nonoccurrence is recorded during brief, consecutive intervals, for example, 15 seconds (Powell, Martindale, & Kulp, 1975). Time-sampled data are summarized as the percentage of intervals in which a behavior occurred during any part of an interval (partial interval time sampling), during an entire interval (whole interval time sampling), or at the end of an interval when the observer looks up (momentary time sampling).

# BEHAVIOR ANALYSIS APPLIED TO CLASSROOM MANAGEMENT

## Functional Assessment of Classroom Behavior Problems

A primary goal of functional assessment is to identify the operant function(s) of a behavior problem. That is, a functional assessment asks this question: what features of the environment are responsible for evoking and/or reinforcing the behavior? Functional assessments usually incorporate data from various sources to develop specific hypotheses about why a problem behavior occurs (Horner, 1994), including descriptive analysis (such as interviews and naturalistic observation) and functional analysis (such as experimental manipulation of hypothesized antecedents and consequences). The results of a functional assessment may allow the researcher or practitioner to develop more effective classroom management procedures for at least three reasons.

1. The contingencies of reinforcement for problem behavior can be eliminated (Mace, 1994). For example, if a functional assessment shows that a child engages in disruptive behavior because it intermittently

evokes the teacher's attention (positive reinforcement), an intervention may include planned ignoring to ensure that the contingency between disruption and attention is eliminated.

2. The contingencies that maintain or support problem behavior can be reversed to support more desired behavior (Carr & Durand, 1985). For example, if disruptive behavior is maintained by escape from instructional activity (e.g., time out), an intervention may allow the student to earn break time by engaging in instructional activity.

3. Situational features of the environment can be modified to make problem behavior less likely (Dunlap, Kern-Dunlap, Clarke, & Robbins, 1991). For example, if disruptive behavior is maintained because of escape from instructional activity, it may be important to evaluate the contents or presentation of the instruction to find out why it is aversive for a given student. It may be that the work is outside of the student's skill level (too difficult), the student may be bored with the work (too easy), or perhaps the student is experiencing health problems (e.g., headaches or sore eyes). In any event, stimulus properties of the instructional material may be modified to make problem behavior less likely.

One potential criticism of functional assessment is that the information-gathering process (data collection and experimental analysis) is labor-intensive and cumbersome (Northup et al., 1991). Furthermore, given the possible success of behavior modification procedures in the absence of a true behavioral analysis, the necessity of a functional assessment may not be obvious at first glance. However, apart from the three benefits of a functional assessment already described (eliminating, reversing, and modifying contingencies of reinforcement), failure to conduct one in favor of traditional behavior modification procedures may result in the prescription of interventions that either have no effect on behavior or, worse, strengthen the behavior through inadvertent reinforcement. Also, many behavior modification procedures do not explicitly provide sources of reinforcement for alternative behavior. Each of these limitations of traditional behavior modification approaches is briefly discussed.

Many behavior modification procedures can have little or no effect on a child's behavior if behavioral function is not addressed. In other words, some interventions may be "functionally irrelevant" (Vollmer & Northup, 1996). The intervention known as planned ignoring is commonly applied in classrooms (e.g., Madsen, Becker, Thomas, Koser, & Plager, 1968). The premise of planned ignoring is that the teacher's attention is a reinforcing consequence, and ignoring will eliminate the relevant contingency. However, a child may be engaging in disruptive behavior for reasons unrelated to the teacher's attention, such as when peer reactions serve as positive reinforcement (Northup, Broussard, Jones, George, Vollmer, & Herring, 1995; Solomon & Wahler, 1973). If peer attention is serving as reinforcement, ignoring by the teacher does not eliminate the contingency between problem behavior and the relevant reinforcer.

Many common behavior modification procedures can actually strengthen problem behavior through inadvertent reinforcement, for example, teachers' reprimands (White, 1975) and time-out (Plummer, Baer, & LeBlanc, 1977). Although these procedures can be effective punishments for some behavior problems in some circumstances (e.g., Porterfield, Hebert-Jackson, & Risley, 1976; Rosen, Gabardi, & Miller, 1990), teachers' reprimands can also act as positive reinforcement by providing attention (e.g., Broussard & Northup, 1995) and time-out can act as negative reinforcement by permitting escape (e.g., Plummer et al., 1977).

Finally, many common behavior modification procedures do not explicitly allow development of alternative replacement behaviors. Punitive procedures such as suspension, detention, or time-out, are not explicitly paired with reinforcement schedules for alternative behavior (Vollmer & Northup, 1996). Again, without knowing why the problem behavior occurs to begin with, the development of reinforcement contingencies to support desired alternative behavior becomes guesswork.

Given the benefits of identifying behavioral functions and the potential limitations of traditional behavior modification, we now discuss general components of a functional assessment, including descriptive analysis and functional analysis.

## Descriptive Analysis of Behavior

As it relates to functional assessment, descriptive analysis involves observing and recording instances of behavior or gathering information about behavior without making any experimental manipulations (Lerman & Iwata, 1993). It is designed to develop hypotheses about the operant function of a behavior problem (Lalli et al., 1993) and thus may take the form of observations, interviews, or questionnaires.

A functional assessment typically begins with a parent, teacher, or staff interview (O'Neill, Horner, Albin, Storey, & Sprague, 1990). The interview is designed to serve some of the same purposes as other types of behavioral interviews, such as problem identification, information gathering about the child, information gathering about frequency and intensity of the behavior, and so on. Interviews may also involve more directed questions about operant behavioral function (e.g., Durand & Crimmins, 1988). For example, the interviewer may ask a teacher directly, "Does the child seem to disrupt in order to get your attention?" Interview and questionnaire formats are particularly useful in generating initial hypotheses about the behavior, and it may be the only option available when a behavior occurs at extremely low rates. For example, a child may engage in escape-maintained aggression, but the aggression may occur only once per week. Infrequent aggression may be severe enough to warrant intervention, but the person conducting the assessment would be unlikely to see the behavior during naturalistic observations or during analogue functional analysis sessions.

Descriptive analysis through naturalistic observation is often used to identify typical antecedent and consequent conditions without relying on the verbal report of others. It can also provide information about idiosyncratic schedules of reinforcement (Mace & Lalli, 1991) and idiosyncratic sources of reinforcement. For example, a child may display aggression only when a particular toy is taken by another child, and the aggression may intermittently produce the return of the toy (Patterson, Littman, & Bricker, 1967). Finally, naturalistic observation can be used to promote better data collection either from the evaluator or from the teacher, parent, or staff. For example, baseline data during the normal classroom routine can be collected by using a scatter plot chart (Touchette, MacDonald, & Langer, 1985), which provides an estimate of the frequency and duration of behavioral episodes and shows how they are distributed across the day or week. Thus, specific problem times and/or locations can be identified, and the

frequency of problem behavior during intervention can be compared to baseline (preintervention) levels.

The primary limitation of any descriptive analysis is that functional relations between environmental events and problem behavior cannot be established because all information obtained is correlational. For example, a teacher may scold a child for disruption every time the behavior occurs ($p = 1.0$) and may send a child to the hallway for time-out once every 20 times the behavior occurs ($p = .05$). It is possible that the teacher's attention is functionally irrelevant to the disruption, which is actually maintained on a variable ratio (VR) schedule of negative reinforcement (VR 20 for escape). Thus, a functional (experimental) *analysis* may be required to evaluate the independent role of each hypothesized source of reinforcement for the problem behavior.

## Functional Analysis of Behavior

Functional analysis refers to the experimental manipulation of environmental variables to identify factors that are maintaining or suppressing a target behavior. In the most general sense, a functional analysis is any experimental analysis of the effects of an independent variable on a dependent variable (Baer, Wolf, & Risley, 1968; Skinner, 1953). The distinction between a functional analysis and a descriptive analysis, in relation to the assessment and treatment of behavior problems, is that the former involves intentionally manipulating antecedent and consequent events to observe when the behavior occurs at the highest rate.

In general, the purpose of a functional analysis is to identify operant reinforcement contingencies that are maintaining problem behavior (e.g., Iwata, Dorsey, Slifer, Bauman, & Richman, 1982/1994). Many of the initial methods were evaluated as assessment components for severe behavior problems in developmental disabilities. For example, one severe class of behavior displayed by some people with developmental disabilities is self-injurious behavior (SIB), such as head banging, hand biting, or self-scratching. Even though SIB can look very similar in two different individuals, the behavior can be maintained by very different reinforcement contingencies. Some SIB is maintained by adult attention that serves as positive reinforcement (Carr, 1977); other SIB is maintained by escape from instructional tasks that results in negative reinforcement (e.g., Steege et al., 1990). Although SIB is a relatively rare disorder among a relatively low-incidence group of individuals with disabilities (most often, individuals with severe and profound mental retardation or autism), the assessment of SIB is a good model for functional analysis. Therefore, SIB is used here to draw parallels with more common classroom behavior management.

Because the behavior is so dangerous that it almost naturally results in social attention of some sort, SIB can be maintained by socially mediated positive reinforcement. Care providers are compelled to reprimand, physically intervene, comfort, and/or provide the individual with preferred items in an effort to stop the behavior. Without intending to, these care providers may be giving positive reinforcement to children and adults who often have few appropriate means of obtaining attention (e.g., Carr & Durand, 1985). Just as the child with developmental disabilities learn that SIB is an effective means of drawing attention or access to tangible reinforcers, other children may learn that common disruptive behaviors reliably result in some sort of attention (e.g., laughter from other children or reprimands from the teacher).

Because SIB occurs at high rates when instructional sessions begin, it can be maintained by socially mediated negative reinforcement (escape or avoidance) if care providers are compelled to discontinue ongoing instruction. For example, if an individual is asked to dress himself or herself (but finds dressing difficult or otherwise aversive) he or she may begin to engage in self-injury because it reliably stops or delays the instructional activity. That is, the individual learns that SIB results in the termination or delay of instructions (e.g., Iwata, Pace, Cowdery, Kalsher, & Cataldo, 1990). Similarly, common disruptive behaviors often result in temporary escape from instructional activity, for example, when time-out is made contingent on behavior problems or when instructional activity is aborted or delayed to redirect a child.

Not all SIB is maintained by social reinforcement contingencies. It can produce its own source of reinforcing stimulation (often called self-stimulation), which is a process known as automatic reinforcement (Vaughn & Michael, 1982). The reinforcement contingency is automatic in the sense that no social mediation is required. Many common positive or negative behaviors can be reinforced independent of the social environment (e.g., reading a novel, drinking alcohol, watching television, and smoking cigarettes). Similarly, common disruptive behaviors in the classroom can produce reinforcement independent of the social environment. For example, a child may climb on a table "to see outside" or to "be higher." Also, there is empirical evidence that being allowed simply to run or walk about the classroom is reinforcing for some children (e.g., Osborne, 1969).

Because problem behavior may serve various functions, Iwata et al. (1982/1994) arranged an analogue environment and observed the SIB of developmentally disabled participants under four distinct experimental conditions presented in a multielement, single-subject experimental design: reprimand, demand, alone, and play. Fifteen-minute sessions were alternated randomly until clear patterns of differential responding were observed. In the reprimand condition, participants were allowed to play with toys but were otherwise ignored unless SIB occurred. When SIB occurred, the experimenter reprimanded the child and provided other response-contingent attention. The reprimand condition was a test for behavioral sensitivity to adult attention as a positive reinforcer for SIB. In the demand condition, the children were presented with academic demands and instructions but were allowed brief escape periods (time-out), contingent on SIB. The demand condition was a test for behavioral sensitivity to escape from instruction as a reinforcer for SIB. In the alone condition, the children were observed with no toys and no adult interaction. The alone condition was a test to see if SIB persisted in the absence of social consequences. The play condition was a control.

Results showed that the behavioral function of SIB was idiosyncratic across individuals. For example, some participants showed high rates of SIB during the reprimand condition only (suggesting a positive reinforcement function). Others showed high rates of SIB in the demand condition only (suggesting a negative reinforcement function). Finally, some subjects showed high levels of SIB even when no social contingencies were in effect. Iwata et al.'s (1982/1994) findings are important conceptually, because more is known about why self-injurious behavior occurs, but are equally important practically because knowledge of the operant function of self-injury can lead to effective intervention.

Similar approaches are now emerging in the assessment of more common classroom behavior problems. For example, Broussard and Northup

(1995) intentionally arranged teachers' attention, peers' attention, and escape contingencies to demonstrate that common behavioral consequences can act as reinforcers for problem behavior. Furthermore, they demonstrated that by making attention and escape contingent on alternative behavior, problem behavior was markedly reduced. Northup and colleagues have replicated and extended these findings in recent work, showing the effects of peer attention as reinforcement for children diagnosed with ADHD (e.g., Northup et al., 1995). The peer attention condition was arranged by using peer "confederates," who were asked to respond verbally to specific disruptive behaviors (talking out, being out of seat, etc.). Essentially, the logic of functional analysis in classrooms is similar to the logic proposed by Iwata et al. (1982/1994). The effects of specific consequences as reinforcement can be evaluated by isolating those events and presenting them during experimental test conditions. If the problem behavior occurs at a relatively higher rate in one condition than in other test conditions, it suggests that the consequence being evaluated may serve as reinforcement for a particular child's problem behavior. This information is then used to develop interventions.

## Interventions Based on Functional Analysis

Much of human behavior is choice behavior. When an alarm rings in the morning we choose to stay in bed or get up and go to work. When viewing television, we choose which program to watch. Presumably, the choices we make are controlled in part by contingencies of positive and negative reinforcement, relative response effort, delay to reinforcement, magnitude of reinforcement, and so on (e.g., Neef, Shade, & Miller, 1994). Similarly, classroom behavior is choice behavior (Martens, 1992). A student may choose to complete work or to engage in disruptive behavior, to stand up or to sit down, to participate in discussions or to sleep, and so on. At any given moment, behavior problems may arise or desired alternatives may occur. The goal of behavior analysis is to make the desired alternative a more attractive option.

By using the information obtained in a functional analysis, shifting response allocation to the desired alternative is an easier task. Because the reinforcer for problem behavior is known, it can be withheld, contingent on problem behavior (extinction), or presented, contingent on the desired alternative (differential reinforcement). Thus, the concurrent schedules of reinforcement in effect (extinction for problem behavior and reinforcement for the alternative) make problem behavior less likely and desired alternatives more likely. Some general strategies for shifting response allocation away from problem behavior and toward the desired alternative are briefly presented.

### Differential Reinforcement

The most common classroom applications are differential reinforcement of alternative behavior (DRA) and differential reinforcement of other behavior (DRO). When positive reinforcement is applied, the procedures are typically described as DRA and DRO; when negative reinforcement is applied (such as to intervene in escape behavior), the terms *differential negative reinforcement of alternative behavior* (DNRA) and *differential negative reinforcement of other behavior* (DNRO) are suitable (Vollmer & Iwata, 1992).

As an example of DRA, suppose a behavior problem is maintained by the teacher's attention. An intervention might involve ignoring the problem behavior to the extent possible and providing praise and/or points for work completion or positive social interactions that can be traded for time to play with or work with the teacher. It is important to note that the ignoring and differential reinforcement package would be unlikely to have an effect if the problem behavior was maintained by, say, peer attention (because the teachers' attention would be functionally irrelevant). In that case, a different intervention, involving differential peer attention, would be more suitable. Similarly, if problem behavior is maintained by escape contingencies, a DNRA procedure could be arranged so that a student would earn a break from work that was contingent on progressively longer intervals of academic engagement or work completion (while ensuring that the problem behavior no longer produces escape).

The DRO procedures are very similar to the DRA, but rather than providing reinforcement that is contingent on some specific alternative response, reinforcement is provided for intervals of time without the problem behavior. For example, a teacher may note that an attention-maintained or escape-maintained problem behavior occurs approximately once every 30 minutes during baseline observations. Thus, the teacher may set an initial DRO or DNRO interval at around 30 minutes (to ensure at least some contact with the reinforcer). If the student completes the 30-minute interval without the problem behavior, the reinforcer (such as interaction with the teacher or a break) is presented. If the student engages in the problem behavior, the interval is either reset or the reinforcer for that 30-minute time block is lost (Poling & Ryan, 1982).

An important component in differential reinforcement packages is extinction. In these examples, it is unlikely that the child would engage in appropriate behavior if reinforcers are still available for the problem behavior. In fact, research on the matching equation (e.g., McDowell, 1982) suggests that differential reinforcement would not be effective without an extinction component because the delay to reinforcement for the desired alternative is often greater. In other words, if a student can obtain the teacher's attention immediately through disruption or later through cooperation, the more immediate source of reinforcement will probably win out (assuming both types of attention are qualitatively equivalent). The necessity of an extinction component raises a special issue in the case of behavior maintained either by peer attention or automatic reinforcement because the teacher does not have direct control over those sources of reinforcement. In such cases, some negative consequence (i.e., punishment) may be necessary to compete with the reinforcement for the problem behavior, while reinforcement remains available for the desired alternative. Punishment as an adjunct procedure is discussed shortly.

A variation of differential reinforcement that is emerging in the intervention literature is noncontingent reinforcement (NCR). Although NCR procedures have not been well evaluated in classrooms, preliminary research in developmental disabilities suggests that, in principle, it may be a viable classroom intervention. Noncontingent reinforcement refers to the response-independent delivery of reinforcers on a fixed time schedule (Vollmer, Iwata, Zarcone, Smith, & Mazaleski, 1993). If a child is engaging in attention-maintained problem behavior, for example, a teacher may provide noncontingent attention at set points throughout the school day. Similarly, to intervene in escape-maintained behavior, a teacher may provide noncontingent breaks at prespecified time intervals. Thus, NCR may serve two purposes: (1) it reduces the motivation to engage in problem behavior; if the student is already getting attention and escape, why engage in problem behavior to get it? (2) It disrupts the contingency between problem behavior and the reinforcing consequences; the problem behavior no longer produces the reinforcing consequence, and the reinforcing event is often delivered independently of the behavior.

Furthermore, NCR may have several advantages over differential reinforcement procedures: (1) the schedule is easier to follow because it is a fixed time schedule that is not influenced by the student's behavior (i.e., no resetting requirement). Teachers in a busy classroom may be unable to notice every instance of the problem behavior and therefore may not be able to reset an interval timer correctly as prescribed by a DRO schedule. By using a fixed time schedule, the reinforcer is always delivered at the same time, regardless of the student's behavior during the preceding time interval. (2) Extinction-induced behavior, such as extinction bursts, aggression, disruption, or response variation, may be less likely to occur because the reinforcer is freely available on a rich schedule. (3) The relative rate of reinforcement can be adjusted according to the student's needs. Presumably, a student who engages in problem behavior that is reinforced by attention or escape may *require* a lot of attention or escape. A straightforward extinction or differential reinforcement schedule may prescribe low levels of reinforcement, whereas NCR schedules can be arranged to generate high levels of positive or negative reinforcement (Vollmer et al., 1993).

## *Punishment*

Punishment is a behavioral process. At times, members of our culture tend to view punishment as an act of retribution or revenge; but it should be clear that in this chapter *punishment* refers to a process or procedure in which behavior becomes less likely to occur in the future as a result of its consequences. Thus, even a reprimand or facial expression can function as punishment if the result is a decreased likelihood of the behavior that precedes it (Van Houten, Nau, MacKenzie-Keating, Sameoto, & Colavecchia, 1982). Although some have argued that functional analysis methods render punishment obsolete (e.g., Donnellan & LaVigna, 1990), there may be circumstances when punishment is a useful adjunct to reinforcement-based procedures. In this section we focus on punishment procedures based on the result of a functional assessment.

If a behavior is maintained by teachers' or peers' attention, *time-out* may be an effective punisher because, if conducted correctly, it temporarily eliminates the opportunity to obtain attention. Thus, time-out is a procedure that can be derived logically from a functional assessment and used in conjunction with reinforcement-based procedures (such as making attention or peer interaction contingent on work completion). To reiterate, however, time-out can also represent reinforcement in the form of escape, so it would be contraindicated for those students who engage in escape-maintained disruptive behaviors. Time-out, then, is a perfect example of a procedure that requires knowledge about behavioral function to be implemented correctly.

If a behavior problem is maintained by escape from or avoidance of instructional activity, *contingent effort* may be an appropriate punishment-based intervention that is logically derived from functional analysis. For example, suppose a student has learned that disruptive behavior produces a time-out during spelling (temporary escape). If a functional assessment reveals escape as the functional reinforcer, one prescribed intervention might involve reversing the contingency so that disruption now leads to additional work or effort (e.g., more spelling words). Based on the logic of differential reinforcement, appropriate participation should then lead to a reduced work load or temporary breaks.

Another circumstance in which punishment may be prescribed by the results of functional assessment is when the sources of reinforcement are uncontrolled or difficult to identify. For example, if a behavior problem is reinforced by peer attention, it may be difficult to induce peers to ignore the behavior, and therefore the necessary extinction component is not possible during differential reinforcement. If our conceptualization of human behavior as choice behavior is true, the student is then faced with a choice between problem behavior, which produces immediate peer reinforcement, and desired behavior, which produces relatively delayed reinforcement. By incorporating a punishment component, the matching equation is now shifted away from the problem behavior because it produces immediate contact with aversive events. Indeed, basic behavioral research on choice between two alternatives suggests that introducing a punishment contingency will result in choice behavior toward an alternative that is not punished—even when both alternatives produce reinforcement (Deluty, 1976).

Token or point systems may also mesh well with the logic of functional analysis if the backup reinforcers include the relevant events identified during functional assessment (time spent with a favorite peer, extra time with the teacher, time away from work, etc.). Using these functionally relevant reinforcers, *response cost* is a viable intervention because point or token loss that is contingent on problem behavior is a form of punishment that addresses the operant function of the behavior. For example, if a student engages in escape-maintained disruption, intervention may involve points for appropriate participation, which can be traded for breaks, and loss of points for disruptive behavior, which equates to a loss of break time. Similarly, if a student engages in disruption maintained by peer attention, points or tokens could be equated with peer interaction time (game playing, extra recess, etc.). In that case, the contingent loss of points or tokens (response cost) should function as punishment.

## BEHAVIOR ANALYSIS APPLIED TO CLASSROOM INSTRUCTION

In a behavior analytic framework, the purpose of instruction is to promote task engagement in curricular materials and elicit frequent, accurate responses to academic tasks (i.e., the stimulus materials). The intended end product of instruction is to bring the students' behavior under the stimulus control of curricular materials so that students can respond to diverse tasks with sufficient accuracy and fluency to meet educational demands (Martens & Kelly, 1993). We infer that we have "taught" a student and that the student has "learned" when she or he is able to respond accordingly, no longer requiring explicit manipulation of environmental events by the teacher. Fortunately, there is a finite number of behavioral principles that can be implemented to increase students' learning.

In reading instruction, there are two instructional programs in particular whose procedures embody these core principles of learning—the Exemplary Center for Reading Instruction (ECRI) and Direct Instruction (Becker, Engelmann, Carnine, & Rhine, 1981). The ECRI (Reid, 1986) embraces five guiding principles: reading instruction is effective when (1) there is sufficient explicit, basic skill instruction; (2) teachers positively reinforce oral reading accuracy and fluency; (3) it elicits overt, accurate, and rapid responses; (4) teachers expect all students to obtain high levels of accurate and fluent responding; and (5) instructional time is maximized and response latency is minimized through such teaching behaviors as redundant directives, succinct questions, and praise of accurate responding. Significant reading improvements following ECRI instruction have been found for regular education, Chapter I, and special education students (Reid, 1986).

Like the ECRI, Direct Instruction is grounded in the explicit manipulation of instructional events to improve students' learning (Englemann, Granzin, & Severson, 1979). Direct Instruction, published as DISTAR, is technologically based, ensuring the clarity and precision of teachers' presentation through empirically generated, scripted, teacher-student interactions and carefully constructed curricular materials (Becker et al., 1981). Teacher-student interactions are designed to promote sequential mastery at each level of the learning process. The initial portion of the instructional sequence involves modeling and guided student practice to promote accuracy of responding. The teacher then provides opportunities to practice in materials directly related to the skill that was taught. According to Gersten (1985), direct instruction is based on "a belief in the utility of structured curricular materials, a concern with reinforcement of appropriate responses, the modeling and shaping of correct responses, the use of task analysis, and the continuous assessment of student performance" (p. 42). Direct Instruction has been highly effective with those students who are most at risk for academic failure—low-income students, disabled students, and low-IQ (intelligence quotient) students (Gersten, Woodward, & Darch, 1986). The success of these programs is due to the systematic implementation of behavioral principles such as modeling, specific teachers' behaviors that promote high rates of accurate responding (directives, questions, etc.), frequent monitoring of performance, corrective feedback, positive reinforcement, and practice in materials directly related to the skill objectives.

## Instructional Interventions for Reading

There is a growing data base of specific behavior analytic reading interventions to improve learning rates of students who are having academic difficulty. There are generally three kinds of behavior analytic reading interventions: (1) phonics and word reading in isolation (e.g., word list training), (2) error correction procedures, and (3) previewing passage reading (either by the student

or by an instructor). As we review the literature in this area, we examine the treatment components of each intervention. An instructional intervention may include any of the following behavioral treatment components: modeling, prompting, drill and opportunities to respond, reinforcement, or generalization strategies (training across instructional materials, training reading fluency to improve comprehension, etc.). We also discuss whether each intervention is designed to promote responding *in isolation* from natural conditions (e.g., word list reading) or *in the context* of natural conditions (e.g., reading words in passages). Finally, we examine the target level of students' responding: error rate (number of errors made), accuracy (percentage correct or number of words mastered), fluency (rate of correctly read words per minute), and generalization (across time, to natural conditions, to other texts or stimulus materials, or to comprehension).

## Word List Training

Numerous attempts have been made to increase students' reading competence by training them to read words in isolation on word lists. The advantage of this type of training is that the instructor can carefully control the presentation of learning materials, reducing potential sources of ambiguity in the instructional process that may hinder students from discriminating words carefully. In this manner, the teacher facilitates the transfer of stimulus control from prompting to the printed words themselves (Browder & D'Huyvetters, 1988). One such intervention procedure is referred to as Taped Words (Freeman & McLaughlin, 1984), in which students listen to an audiotape of word lists before reading the word lists (the outcome measure). Freeman and McLaughlin and Skinner and Shapiro (1989) found Taped Words to be effective in improving word list reading fluency. The latter researchers also found, however, that a drill condition, in which students practiced reading the word lists before assessment, was equally as effective at improving fluency. In both studies, instructional lists contained many words students were already able to read accurately. Skinner and Shapiro concluded, therefore, that drill was the active treatment component in the Taped Words intervention.

Cuvo, Ashley, Marso, Zhang, and Fry (1995) examined the effects of different parameters of practice (i.e., more versus less and different forms such as oral versus written) on word list reading accuracy. Based on their results, they recommended limiting the amount of response practice. One issue that will be discussed in greater detail later is the effect of drill or practice on accuracy versus its effect on fluency. According to the instructional hierarchy (Haring, Lovitt, Eaton, & Hansen, 1978), drill is effective in improving response fluency but not necessarily response accuracy. This consideration may explain the limited effects obtained by Cuvo et al., who were measuring only accuracy.

The strength of word list training is also its weakness. Responding on word lists can be improved efficiently with modeling and/or drill procedures; however, the goal of reading instruction is to read words in the natural context of passages. With one notable exception (Tan, Moore, Dixon, & Nicholson, 1994), the data suggest that students do not generalize reading fluency to passages following word list training (Roberts, Turco, & Shapiro, 1991; Shapiro & McCurdy, 1989).

## Error Correction Procedures

Error correction procedures have the advantage of being implemented in the context of reading passages and therefore increase the likelihood that students will read text better following intervention. Instructors can therefore diagnose words that are not mastered and train correct reading in context. The error correction procedures investigated empirically have employed a variety of behavioral strategies, including modeling, prompting, phonetic analysis, drill, positive practice overcorrection, and positive reinforcement for corrected responding. In an analysis of various types of corrective feedback, Perkins (1988) found that feedback was better than no feedback, that modeling (saying the misread word correctly) and sounding out error words was better than general (nonspecific) feedback, and that modeling was generally more effective than sounding out. Modeling also appears to be more effective than prompting for improving reading accuracy (Espin & Deno, 1989). Pany and McCoy (1988) found that corrective feedback on every oral reading error is more effective in increasing accuracy and comprehension than corrective feedback on errors involving the meaning of words only.

Modeling the accurate reading of a misread word has been referred to as word supply (Jenkins, Larson, & Fleisher, 1983; Rose, McEntire, & Dowdy, 1982), which is efficient and simple (Rose, McEntire, & Dowdy, 1982). It has not, however, been found to be as effective as other error correction procedures at decreasing reading errors and increasing oral reading fluency. When Jenkins et al. compared word supply to word drill (word supply plus having the student repeat the error word several times), they found that word drill increased the accuracy of word recognition and the comprehension of target sentences. Rosenberg (1986) found word drill to be more effective than word supply or phonic analysis (sounding out for students and having students subsequently sound out the words) in reducing errors in isolation and increasing oral reading fluency.

A variation of word drill is overcorrection (Singh & Singh, 1986b, 1988). In overcorrection procedures, the student repeats the misread word five times after the instructor models the accurate response. Overcorrection has been shown to be more effective than phonetic analysis at reducing errors (Singh & Singh, 1988) and is adaptable to group instruction formats, which may provide opportunities for incidental learning by all group members (Singh, 1987). Word drill as a strategy has been further improved by having students reread any entire sentence (sentence repeat) that contains a misread word (Singh, 1990) and incorporating repetitions of the entire phrase (phrase drill). Phrase drill has been found to improve oral reading fluency in isolation and in passage reading more than word drill and word supply (O'Shea, Munson, & O'Shea, 1984). Combining drill (i.e., accurate repetitions of the misread word) with modeling of the correct reading of misread words in context is a powerful error correction strategy.

Even further refinements of error correction strategies have been made. For instance, overcorrection plus positive reinforcement has been effective in reducing error rates (Singh, Singh, & Winton, 1984). Also, Singh, Winton, and Singh (1985) found that delayed error correction reduced the error rate in reading passages more than did immediate error correction. Singh and Singh (1986a) have developed a behavior remediation program that incorporates previewing, delayed attention to oral reading errors, positive practice overcorrection, and positive reinforcement for self-correction. Following implementation of the program, Singh and Singh found that students reduced their error rates and increased their comprehension. The nature of error correction is remedial, however, being implemented after inaccurate responding has already occurred. Even though it is essential to have effective error correction strategies, it is even more critical to shape responding in a manner that reduces the likelihood of errors and increases accuracy.

## *Passage Previewing*

Previewing is one commonly used antecedent technique for increasing oral reading accuracy and fluency (Rose & Beattie, 1986) and decreasing oral reading errors (Singh & Singh, 1984). Previewing generally involves one of three strategies: (1) having the student practice reading a passage prior to assessment (done either silently or aloud), (2) having the instructor read the passage to the student prior to assessment, or (3) having the student listen to an audiotape recording of the passage prior to assessment (Rose & Beattie, 1986). Previewing contains a relatively larger number of treatment components than the other interventions reviewed (Daly & Martens, 1994). Depending on the nature of previewing, it may include drill, modeling, and generalization (to the natural context of passage reading). Student previewing is essentially a drill condition in which students practice reading the words they have already acquired in the passage. Previewing by the instructor or taped previewing (often referred to as listening previewing and taped previewing, respectively) add a modeling component in which the instructor or audiotape models accurate reading of words that the student may not yet have acquired. Presumably, there will be some words already acquired in the passage, so listening previewing and taped previewing also contain a drill component. Finally, there is an implicit generalization strategy—training under the criterion stimulus conditions of passage reading.

Listening previewing (containing modeling, drill, and generalization components) has been found to be effective in increasing oral reading fluency rates in reading passages (Rose 1984a, 1984b, 1984c; Rose & Beattie, 1986; Rose & Sherry, 1984; Singh & Singh, 1984). Listening previewing has also been found to be more effective than student previewing, both silently (Rose, 1984a, 1984b, 1984c; Rose & Sherry, 1984) and orally (Daly & Martens, 1994). There is also substantial support for the effectiveness of having peers preview texts for students (Greenwood, 1991; Salend, 1988). Rousseau and colleagues

(Rousseau & Tam, 1991; Rousseau, Tam, & Ramnarain, 1993) further improved listening previewing by adding a component called discussion of key words, in which the teacher models accurate reading of important words in the text and discusses their meaning with the students. Rousseau and Tam found that listening previewing and discussion of key words was more effective in increasing students' oral reading accuracy than no previewing or student previewing with discussion of key words. Rousseau et al. extended these findings by demonstrating that listening previewing and discussion of key words also increased reading comprehension. It is interesting that these researchers found that discussion of key words increased students' oral reading accuracy better than listening previewing. In the absence of fluency measures, however, it was not possible to compare the effectiveness of the two treatments in improving reading fluency. Given the drill component of listening previewing that is lacking in discussion of key words, it would be expected that the former would be more effective in increasing oral reading fluency.

Some work has been done on the effects of varying students' fluency and modeling fluency rates. Using a group design, Braznitz (1987) found that having students read at their maximal normal reading rates decreased errors and increased comprehension more than did self-paced reading. Braznitz also found that having students read at their slowest normal reading rates increased accuracy but decreased comprehension. More recently, Skinner, Adamson, Woodward, Jackson, Atchison, and Mims (1993) examined fast and slow listening previewing reading rates and student silent previewing. They found that the slower rate and student silent previewing were equally effective and that both were more effective than the fast-rate listening previewing, suggesting that there are probably upper limits on the effectiveness of such treatments.

## The Instructional Hierarchy

Some studies have attempted to assess the broader or long-term effects of similar instructional interventions to those discussed here. Most of these interventions contain multiple treatment components. As a result, it is not possible to delineate the precise components responsible for obtained generalization effects (Yeaton & Sechrest, 1981). Nonetheless, the method of repeated readings has proven effective in improving reading fluency when there is explicit generalization programming (Rashotte & Torgesen, 1985). A similar reading intervention that has improved passage comprehension is the oral recitation lesson (Reutzal & Hollingsworth, 1993). All of the interventions discussed here contain varying types and amounts of active treatment elements (modeling, drill, etc.), and each varies in its ability to promote generalization of accurate and fluent reading. What is needed is a conceptual framework for describing how different treatment components interact with levels of responding (i.e., accuracy versus fluency versus generalization). If there are systematic relationships between treatment components (modeling, drill, reinforcement, etc.) and levels of responding, it may be possible to identify which treatment components will be more effective in improving different levels of responding.

The instructional hierarchy (Haring et al., 1978) is one such conceptual framework that attempts to describe the relationship between treatment components and different levels of responding (i.e., stages of skill mastery). It has two basic premises: (1) students progress through a learning hierarchy before they achieve skill mastery, and (2) there are different instructional procedures that promote mastery at each stage. According to the learning hierarchy, students first *acquire* a skill, increasing their accuracy of responding. They then become *fluent* in the skill, increasing their rate and speed of responding. Next, students are able to *generalize* their acquired and fluent skill use to novel situations or stimulus materials that differ from those used in training. Finally, students *adapt* or modify the skill to fit into more complex repertoires of behavior. Instruction at each level, however, involves different procedures. Modeling, prompting, and cueing improve accuracy of responding (i.e., acquisition), whereas drill and reinforcement improve fluency of responding. Generalization training requires discrimination training, training across stimulus items, and training across time.

One benefit of the instructional hierarchy is that it can be used to clarify the effects observed for various instructional interventions that have been reported in the literature. For instance, in the case of the taped words procedure, Freeman and McLaughlin (1984) attributed its effectiveness in increasing fluency of responding to modeling. The instructional hierarchy suggests that modeling increases accuracy and that drill in-

creased fluency. Skinner and Shapiro (1989) found that a drill condition was just as effective as the taped words procedure, confirming that drill may have been the active treatment element in improving fluency rates. As another example, Cuvo et al. (1995) found limited effects of varying the amounts of drill on accuracy of responding. Once again, however, drill is primarily effective in promoting fluency of responding, a stage not examined by Cuvo et al. These examples help us to see the utility of carefully examining the relationship between the response target of the intervention (e.g., accuracy versus fluency) and the active treatment components.

To date, there has been one direct experimental investigation of the instructional hierarchy. In a comparison of three reading interventions, Daly and Martens (1994) specified the active treatment components and accurately predicted treatment outcomes for each of the interventions. They found that the intervention that had the largest number of treatment elements (modeling, drill, and implicit generalization programming) produced the largest intervention gains for accurate and fluent reading. The utility of this approach is that pretreatment assessment of important dimensions of students' responding, together with knowledge of the corresponding learning principle, can facilitate treatment selection, much like functional analysis for aberrant social behaviors (Iwata et al., 1994). Finally, because of the sequential nature of learning, treatments need to be varied sequentially as students progress through the learning hierarchy. As discussed earlier, an effective performance monitoring system is a requirement for knowing when to change treatments and which treatments are most appropriate (Fuchs & Fuchs, 1986).

## ISSUES IN TREATMENT IMPLEMENTATION

This section describes issues in the implementation and use of behaviorally based procedures. Well-designed procedures will not have their intended effects if they are not implemented properly (Baer et al., 1968). In most educational settings, it is assumed that behavioral procedures will be designed with at least the input of a psychologist who is knowledgeable about the fundamentals of behavior analysis but implemented by a teacher. Typically this type of service delivery is referred to as consultation, in which a school psychologist consults with a teacher in the design and implementation of an intervention (Bergan & Kratochwill, 1990).

In behavior analysis, implementation is the neglected stepchild of a highly evolved set of procedures for behavior change. Although behavior analysis has made great strides in such areas as functional assessment and intervention design, the technology for implementation is much weaker. Gresham, Gausle, and Noell (1993) noted that intervention studies published in the *Journal of Applied Behavior Analysis*, which is considered to be the flagship journal for behavior analysts, reported the measurement of implementation (i.e., treatment integrity) only 15.8% of the time. If researchers are not reporting treatment integrity data, it follows that the issue might also be problematic for practitioners.

This section begins with an examination of some of the many barriers to a technology of implementation. We then discuss some elements of a technology for the implementation of behavior analytic interventions in educational settings.

## Some Barriers to a Technology of Implementation

Given that implementation issues have been of concern to behavior analysts for some time (Baer et al., 1968) and given that implementation of behavioral procedures remains a vexing question, especially to practitioners, why is our implementation technology so poorly developed? Why have there been so few studies published on how to achieve optimal implementation? Why are there so few studies in the *Journal of Applied Behavior Analysis* that measure implementation of the independent variable?

### *The Collaboration Barrier*

It has been generally assumed that for implementation to occur, a consultant must interact with the teacher in a collaborative manner (Allen & Graden, 1995; Bergan & Kratochwill, 1990). The collaborative ethic calls for the consultant and teacher to be coequal partners in the development of the intervention, and the teacher has the freedom to accept or reject the consultant's suggestions.

While collaboration has considerable face validity, taken too far it may interfere with implementation. Whether collaboration improves the quality of the intervention is an empirical question that has yet to be answered. A crucial question for those who advocate collaboration, however, is to demonstrate that consultation

conducted collaboratively is superior in effect to consultation conducted noncollaboratively. Currently there is no empirical basis to suggest that collaboration results in greater treatment integrity than other interpersonal styles. Some teachers are not as competent in curriculum, classroom management, or behavior management as the consultant and can benefit from this expertise. The collaborative egalitarian ethic is so strong in educational settings, however, that "now, it has become anathema to think that a speech clinician should behave as if he knew more about language pathology than a teacher, or that a principal should behave as if she knew more about personnel management than a custodian. Instead, each opinion is afforded equal rather than due consideration" (Barone, 1995).

Working collaboratively with teachers is obviously the preference of most of us, and some of the time we can operate in this way and the teacher will be satisfied. However, the job of making changes so a child can survive (if not thrive) in the general education setting needs to be taken seriously by both special and general educators. There will be situations in which the relationship will not be collaborative because a special educator with expertise will have to tell an inexperienced teacher what to do. And the general education teacher will be expected to make the modifications even though he or she may not like them. The teacher who does not make the modifications will be held accountable. The alternative is that we don't demand very much from the teacher, we don't hold the teacher accountable for making modifications (i.e., the teacher is trusted to do the job), and we either accept the teacher's self-report that the modifications were conducted with fidelity or we *excuse* the teacher because he or she claims personal hardship or competing concerns (e.g., "What about the other children? I don't have the time"). In other words, either we don't know whether the modifications were made or we dismiss their absence. We do know that the child will remain a problem if modifications are not made, and we may have to provide the child with the more intensive and costly services available through special education.

As is discussed later, behavior analysis has procedures that would allow the teacher's behavior to be monitored. However, the collaborative and egalitarian ethic is such that monitoring teachers' behavior is not correct or acceptable. The teacher is assumed, by those who hold this view, to be a professional who does not require monitoring or feedback. Such procedures would be demeaning and inconsistent with professional-to-professional collaboration. Perhaps, however, we must begin to separate a political and social process from a scientifically supported practice. The egalitarian ethic, which is at this juncture both popular and politically correct, may not directly help the children.

## The Measurement Barrier

Implementation of a relatively simple intervention in a classroom for several hours a day can present complex problems of measurement. For example, consider the situation in which the intervention requires the teacher to reduce talking-out behavior for a particular student with a combination of DRO and response cost for talking. At issue is how to measure implementation of this intervention.

Several measurement options are available, all of them with distinct advantages and disadvantages. First, one could conduct direct observation, which has the advantage of providing direct evidence about whether the intervention was implemented. A major disadvantage is reactivity. That is, the teacher will be more likely to use the intervention when being observed. Also, many researchers, much less practitioners, do not have the resources to station an observer in the classroom for several hours a day. In our experience, some teachers wait until just before the self-report data form is to be reviewed by the consultant to complete the form for previous days rather than document implementation behaviors as they occur.

A second measurement option is a self-report on intervention usage. However there is no evidence that teachers will reliably report on their own usage. Wickstrom (1995) found, in fact, that teachers' self-report measures of implementation were always very high and did not correlate at all with direct observation or permanent product measures of implementation.

A third measurement option is to videotape the classroom and then use the tapes to code implementation. This procedure is sometimes unacceptable to teachers, to teachers' unions, and to parents who may not want their children videotaped. Also, it requires someone to review the tapes and accurately code the data. This process does yield accurate data, however.

A fourth option is to use children in the classroom, including the target child, for measurement of implementation. Children could be trained to keep data on implementation, the target child could be taught to self-monitor, or students could be interviewed periodically. The disadvantages of this option are the teacher's acceptance of the monitoring by students and calibrating the accuracy of the data.

A final measurement option is to use permanent products, which although appropriate for some interventions, are not usable in other. In a situation in which the teacher must observe a child who is exhibiting a behavior such as talking out, which leaves no permanent product, and then respond appropriately to the behavior with some consequence such as a reprimand, which also leaves no permanent product, permanent product measurement may not apply.

## The Contingencies Barrier

Teachers' implementation of an intervention can be viewed as a series of responses. The teacher either chooses to engage or to not engage in these implementation responses. Although it is likely that placing contingencies on these behaviors would increase the probability that teachers would implement an intervention, this strategy is not usually considered. That consultants are seemingly reluctant to use contingencies with teachers is attributable to several factors. First, consultants, such as school psychologists, do not typically have control over important contingencies because they are not responsible for supervising or evaluating the teacher. If the teacher chooses not to implement or resists the measurement of implementation, there is often very little the school-based consultant can do. Second, in traditional behavioral consultation, it has been assumed that contingencies on teachers' behavior are not necessary. Rather, the modus operandi has been to *talk* to teachers and *hope* that they will change. This is an aspect of the collaborative and egalitarian ethic already discussed. That is, the teacher is considered to be a professional who will change in the face of a good idea that will help the child. Third, the use of contingencies requires that implementation be measured, and as noted, this entails problems.

## The Hypothetical Constructs Barrier

Another factor that has impeded research and practice in implementation has been the importance ascribed to hypothetical constructs in comparison to functional relations. Does the intervention have *treatment acceptability?* To what extent is the teacher *resistant?* Did the consultant maintain a *collaborative* relationship? Is the teacher's *attribution* system such that he or she feels that factors out of his or her immediate control are influencing the child (Elliott, Witt, & Kratochwill, 1993). While use of these constructs is believed to increase our understanding, they have not been shown to significantly influence actual implementation. Their use may have led to conceptual dead ends because, like all constructs, they lead into a tautological system. When the teacher does not implement the intervention, we call the teacher resistant or say that the treatment was unacceptable. How do we know the teacher is resistant? Because he or she did not implement the intervention.

A more direct and epistemologically sound assumption is that when a teacher does not implement the intervention, environmental conditions were not favorable for implementation. It does not contribute to our understanding of teachers to say that they are resistant. Perhaps they didn't understand the intervention well enough to use it. Alternatively, perhaps they simply preferred to do other things. Acceptability, resistance, and other constructs used in the literature are indirect measures of the true outcome, which is implementation. Given that such explanations are indirect, circular, and represent pseudoexplanations, they are barriers to an empirically based technology of implementation. This technology must be built on an understanding of the conditions under which teachers will and will not implement an intervention and not on an understanding of hypothetical constructs.

## Toward a Technology of Implementation

In this section, we discuss elements of a technology of implementation that derive from the work of Noell and Witt (1998). This model is based on the assumption that a technology of implementation should build on the existing technology in behavior analysis. That is, teachers' implementation of interventions is not a special situation that requires different laws of behavior. Instead, general principles of human behavior can be applied to specific implementation skills. Implementation skills of the teacher are learned behaviors that cannot be assumed to be part of the teacher's behavioral repertoire. Instead, the skills required to implement an intervention must be systematically *taught*, using procedures such as modeling, coaching, guided practice, and

feedback. Once learned, the new behaviors must be generalized so that they can be applied correctly by the teacher to additional behaviors and/or settings.

While these methods will seem quite familiar to behavior analysts, who routinely use them for teaching new skills in a variety of settings, the process may seem fundamentally different to those who have been operating under a collaborative consultation model like behavioral consultation (Bergan & Kratochwill, 1990). Here, we assume that modifications in a general education classroom are needed or wanted. Such modifications are routinely *required* by IDEA and Section 504. In a case in which interventions are not formally required by law, it is assumed that a teacher who is requesting assistance is unable to resolve the problem. By requesting assistance, the teacher has tacitly entered into an agreement to change his or her behavior in order to change that of the child. This should be made explicit by the consultant. Teachers ask for consultation for various reasons, including the need to talk to an understanding person (Witt & Martens, 1988). However, given the very limited personnel resources, there must be some understanding on the part of teachers that to continue they must be willing to commit to behavior change for both themselves and the child.

A behavior analytic model of implementation also represents a shift from traditional consultation to a model in which the consultant essentially teaches the intervention to the teacher and ensures that the teacher can and does carry out the implementation with integrity. In traditional consultation, the following is assumed:

1. The teacher who is *talking* about the problem will provide the consultant enough information to design an intervention.

2. The consultant who is *talking* to the teacher will provide the teacher with enough information to properly implement the intervention.

3. The teacher who is *talking* to the consultant about the effects of the intervention will provide data that are sufficient and valid enough to evaluate the quality of implementation and the effects of the intervention on the child.

These assumptions are antithetical to the philosophy and practice of behavior analysis, where it has been shown repeatedly that behavior change occurs reliably only when the controlling variables are understood (Johnston & Penny-packer, 1993). Talking has not been shown to be a reliable means for assessing the problem (Cone, 1981) or for obtaining the desired performance from direct service personnel (Duncan & Bruwelheide, 1986). In behavior analysis, those behaviors connected to the implementation of an intervention are considered to be similar to other behaviors. Hence, the consultant can rely on the same *teaching* processes for the behaviors in intervention implementation as have been used to establish other behaviors. The three phases of an implementation process that is consistent with behavior analysis are teaching, monitoring, and providing feedback.

## Teaching New Intervention Skills

In traditional consultation, information about how to use an intervention is transmitted to the teacher through *discussion*. In behavioral analysis, this is viewed as a necessary but not sufficient condition for ensuring that the teacher has the skill to implement the intervention. In addition to describing the intervention, the behavior analyst might also model the appropriate skills; the teacher might practice the intervention with prompting and coaching from the consultant and then independently use the intervention, with observation and feedback by the consultant. These represent standard procedures for teaching any new behavior. More specifically, a consultant might utilize the following process:

1. *The consultant engages in a tell, show, and do sequence outside the classroom.* That is, the consultant first describes the procedures. Next, the consultant models the procedures, including how to talk to the child, tone of voice, and so on. The consultant then engages in role-playing the procedure, with the teacher being expected to correctly perform the behavior *outside* the classroom.
2. *The teacher receives coaching and prompting until correct implementation occurs inside the classroom.* When the teacher can correctly perform the behavior outside the classroom, the consultant follows a similar pattern of training inside the classroom. It is not assumed that because the teacher can role-play the intervention outside the classroom that the skills automatically generalize to the classroom. Hence, the consultant would observe implementation of the procedure *inside* the classroom. As mistakes are

made, the consultant provides feedback about proper procedures. This continues until the teacher can perform the intervention in the classroom with 100% accuracy. The goal is to ensure that the teacher does not have a skill deficit for any behavior necessary for implementation.

## Monitoring

Once the consultant is sure that the teacher has the necessary skills, it is necessary to monitor implementation. A teacher's self-report is unacceptable; instead, some combination of permanent products, direct observation, and spot checking will yield more accurate evidence of implementation.

## Providing Feedback

That the teacher implemented the intervention with 100% integrity *with the consultant present* does not ensure that the teacher will continue implementation with the consultant absent. Hence, it may be necessary to provide performance feedback, a set of procedures for providing information on past performance (Arco, 1991; Balcazar, Hopkins, & Suarez, 1985–1986; Peterson, 1982). In industry, feedback typically has been delivered by supervisors to workers. In human service agencies, it has been delivered primarily by supervisors or professionals to direct care staff. Feedback enhances performance by helping the learner to identify correct versus incorrect responding. In addition, feedback from supervisors or professionals serves effectively as a positive or negative reinforcer. As with all forms of reinforcement, feedback is also a discriminative stimulus, which sets the occasion for behaviors likely to be reinforced (Duncan & Bruwelheide, 1986). Although performance feedback has been used successfully in other settings to improve performance, there are no reports of its application with teachers in schools. Its use depends on accurate measurement of teachers' implementation and, ideally, accurate measurement of students' performance in response to the intervention. Graphically presented performance feedback shows that the child improves as a function of the intervention (Arco, 1991). Feedback also provides information about which parts of the intervention were not implemented.

## A Final Note on Implementation

The procedures advocated here to enhance implementation derive from standard procedures long available in behavior analysis. However, only recently have they been receiving attention in educational settings (Noell, 1996; Noell & Witt, 1998), so at this point it is not possible to state conclusively that procedures such as coaching and performance feedback can be used successfully by a school psychologist with a teacher in a school.

Certainly these procedures rest on a stronger research foundation than the collaborative consultation approaches that are so prevalent in the current literature. Behavioral consultation (Bergan & Kratochwill, 1990), for example, since its inception in the mid-1970s, has failed to produce studies that show conclusively that consultant behaviors, which are defined by behavioral consultation, are related to teachers' implementation of an intervention. In other words, *talking* to teachers via the methods described by Bergan and Kratochwill or others advocating collaborative methods (e.g., Allen & Graden, 1995; Friend & Cook, 1992) has not been shown to be related to behavior change. From a behavior analytic perspective, it is highly improbable that talking, in the absence of teaching, practice, and contingencies, will in fact change behavior.

# REFERENCES

Alessi, G. J. (1980). Behavioral observation for the school psychologist: Responsive-discrepancy model. *School Psychology Review, 9,* 31–45.

Allen, S. J., & Graden, J. L. (1995). Best practices in collaborative problem solving for intervention design. In A. Thomas & J. Grimes (Eds.), *Best practices in school psychology–III* (pp. 667–700). Washington, DC: National Association of School Psychologists.

Arco, L. (1991). Effects of outcome performance feedback on maintenance of client and staff behavior in a residential setting. *Behavioral Residential Treatment, 6,* 4, 231–247.

Azrin, N. H., & Foxx, R. M. (1974). *Toilet training in less than a day.* New York: Pocket Books.

Baer, D. M. (1988). If you know why you're changing a behavior, you'll know when you've changed it enough. *Behavioral Assessment, 10,* 219–223.

Baer, D. M., Wolf, M. M., & Risley, T. (1968). Some current dimensions of applied behavior analysis. *Journal of Applied Behavior Analysis, 1,* 91–97.

Baker, R. C., & Kirschenbaum, D. S. (1993). Self-monitoring may be necessary for successful weight control. *Behavior Therapy, 24,* 377–394.

Balcazar, F., Hopkins, B. L., & Suarez, Y. (1985–1986).

A critical objective review of performance feedback. *Journal of Organizational Behavior Management, 7*(3/4), 65–87.

Bandura, A. (1977). *Social learning theory.* Englewood Cliffs, NJ: Prentice Hall.

Barone, S. G. (1995). The egalitarian virus. *Education Week,* March 1.

Becker, H. J., Engelmann, S., Carnine, D. W., & Rhine, R. (1981). The direct instruction model. In R. Rhine (Ed.), *Encouraging change in America's schools: A decade of experimentation* (pp. 45–83). New York: Academic Press.

Bergan, J. R., & Kratochwill, T. R. (1990). *Behavioral consultation and therapy.* New York: Plenum.

Braznitz, Z. (1987). Increasing first graders' reading accuracy and comprehension by accelerating their reading rates. *Journal of Educational Psychology, 79*(3), 236–242.

Broden, M., Bruce, C., Mitchell, M. A., Carter, V., & Hall, R. V. (1970). Effects of teacher attention on attending behavior of two boys at adjacent desks. *Journal of Applied Behavior Analysis, 3,* 199–203.

Broussard, C. D., & Northup, J. N. (1995). An approach to functional assessment and analysis of disruptive behavior in regular education classrooms. *School Psychology Quarterly, 10,* 151–164.

Browder, D. M., & D'Huyvetters, K. K. (1988). An evaluation of transfer of stimulus control and of comprehension in sight word reading for children with mental retardation and emotional disturbance. *School Psychology Review, 17*(2), 331–342.

Brownell, K., Colletti, G., Ersner-Hershfield, R., Hershfield, S. M., & Wilson, T. (1977). Self-control in school children: Stringency and leniency in self-determined and externally imposed performance standards. *Behavior Therapy, 8,* 442–455.

Carnine, D. (1994). Introduction to the mini-series: Diverse learners and prevailing, emerging, and research-based educational approaches and their tools. *School Psychology Review, 23,* 341–350.

Carr, E. G. (1977). The motivation of self-injurious behavior: A review of some hypotheses. *Psychological Bulletin, 84,* 800–816.

Carr, E. G., & Durand, V. M. (1985). Reducing behavior problems through functional communication training. *Journal of Applied Behavior Analysis, 18,* 111–126.

Carr, E. G., Newsom, C. D., & Binkoff, J. A. (1980). Escape as a factor in the aggressive behavior of two retarded children. *Journal of Applied Behavior Analysis, 13,* 101–117.

Cone, J. D. (1978). The behavioral assessment grid (BAG): A conceptual framework and a taxonomy. *Behavior Therapy, 9,* 882–888.

Cone, J. D. (1981). Psychometric considerations. In M. Hersen & A. Bellack (Eds.), *Behavioral*

*Assessment: A Practical Handbook* (pp. 38–70). New York: Pergamon.

Cuvo, A. J., Ashley, K. M., Marso, K. J., Zhang, B. L., & Fry, T. A. (1995). Effects of response practice variables on learning spelling and sight vocabulary. *Journal of Applied Behavior Analysis, 28,* 155–173.

Daly, E. J., III, & Martens, B. K. (1994). A comparison of three interventions for increasing oral reading performance: Application of the instructional hierarchy. *Journal of Applied Behavior Analysis, 27,* 459–469.

Deluty, M. Z. (1976). Choice and the rate of punishment in concurrent schedules. *Journal of the Experimental Analysis of Behavior, 25,* 75–80.

Donnellan, A. M., & LaVigna, G. W. (1990). Myths about punishment. In A. C. Repp and N. N. Singh (Eds.), *Perspectives on the use of nonaversive and aversive interventions for persons with developmental disabilities* (pp. 33–57). Sycamore, IL: Sycamore Publishing.

Donnellan, A. M., Mirenda, P. L., Mesaros, R. A., & Fassbender, L. L. (1984). Analyzing the communicative functions of aberrant behavior. *Journal of the Association for Persons with Severe Handicaps, 9,* 201–212.

Duncan, P. K., & Bruwelheide, L. R. (1986). Feedback: Use and possible behavioral functions. *Journal of Organizational Behavior Management, 7*(3/4), 91–114.

Dunlap, G., Kern-Dunlap, L., Clarke, S., & Robbins, F. R. (1991). Functional assessment, curricular revision, and severe behavior problems. *Journal of Applied Behavior Analysis, 24,* 387–397.

Durand, V. M., & Crimmins, D. B. (1988). Identifying the variables maintaining self-injurious behavior. *Journal of Autism and Developmental Disorders, 18,* 99–117.

Elliott, S. N., Witt, J. C., & Kratochwill, T. R. (1988). Selecting, implementing and evaluating classroom interventions. In G. Stoner, M. Shinn, & H. Walker (Eds.), *Interventions for achievement and behavior problems* (pp. 99–135). Silver Spring, MD: National Association of School Psychologists.

Englemann, S., Granzin, A., & Severson, H. (1979). Diagnosing instruction. *Special Education, 13*(4), 335–363.

Erchul, W. P., & Martens, B. K. (1997). *School-based consultation: Conceptual and empirical bases of practice.* New York: Plenum.

Espin, C. A., & Deno, S. L. (1989). The effects of modeling and prompting feedback strategies on sight word reading of students labeled learning disabled. *Education and Treatment of Children, 12,* 219–231.

Ferster, C. B., & Skinner, B. F. (1957). *Schedules of reinforcement.* Englewood Cliffs, NJ: Prentice Hall.

Freeman, T. J., & McLaughlin, T. F. (1984). Effects of a taped-words treatment procedure on learning disabled students' sight-word reading. *Learning Disability Quarterly, 7,* 49–54.

Frick, P. J., & Lahey, B. B. (1991). The nature and characteristics of attention-deficit hyperactivity disorder. *School Psychology Review, 20,* 163–173.

Friend, M., & Cook, L. (1992). *Interactions: Collaboration skills for school professionals.* New York: Longman.

Fuchs, L. S., & Fuchs, D. (1986). Effects of systematic formative evaluation: A meta-analysis. *Exceptional Children, 53*(3), 199–208.

Fuchs, L. S., Fuchs, D., Hamlett, C. L., & Allinder, R. M. (1991). Effects of expert system advice within curriculum-based measurement on teacher planning and student achievement in spelling. *School Psychology Review, 20,* 49–66.

Furlong, M. J., & Morrison, G. M. (1994). School violence and safety in perspective. *School Psychology Review, 23,* 139–150.

Gersten, R. (1985). Direct instruction with special education students: A review of evaluation research. *The Journal of Special Education, 19,* 41–58.

Gersten, R., Woodward, J., & Darch, C. (1986). Direct-instruction: A research-based approach to curriculum design and teaching. *Exceptional Children, 53,* 17–31.

Good, R. H., Vollmer, M., Creek, R. J., Katz, L., & Chowdhri, S. (1993). Treatment utility of the Kaufman Assessment Battery for Children: Effects of matching instruction and student processing strength. *School Psychology Review, 22,* 8–26.

Greenwood, C. R. (1991). Classwide peer tutoring: Longitudinal effects on the reading, language, and mathematics achievement of at-risk students. *Reading, Writing, and Learning Disabilities International, 7,* 105–123.

Gresham, F. M., Gansle, K. A., & Noell, G. H. (1993). Treatment integrity in applied behavior analysis with children. *Journal of Applied Behavior Analysis, 26,* 257–263.

Hall, R. V., Lund, D., & Jackson, D. (1968). Effects of teacher attention on study behavior. *Journal of Applied Behavior Analysis, 1,* 1–12.

Haring, N. G., Lovitt, T. C., Eaton, M. D., & Hansen, C. L. (1978). *The Fourth R: Research in the classroom.* Columbus, OH: Merrill.

Harris, K. R. (1985). Definitional, parametric, and procedural considerations in timeout interventions and research. *Exceptional Children, 51,* 279–288.

Hayes, S. C. (1991). The limits of technological talk. *Journal of Applied Behavior Analysis, 24,* 417–420.

Hayes, S. C., Nelson, R. O., & Jarrett, R. B. (1986). Evaluating the quality of behavioral assessment. In R. O. Nelson & S. C. Hayes (Eds.), *Conceptual foundations of behavioral assessment* (pp. 463–503). New York: Guilford.

Horner, R. H. (1994). Functional assessment:

contributions and future direction. *Journal of Applied Behavior Analysis, 28*, 401–404.

Iwata, B. A., Dorsey, M. F., Slifer, K. J., Bauman, K. E., & Richman, G. S. (1982/1994). Toward a functional analysis of self-injury. *Journal of Applied Behavior Analysis, 27*, 215–240 (reprinted from *Analysis and Intervention in Developmental Disabilities, 2*, 1–20).

Iwata, B. A., Pace, G. M., Cowdery, G. E., Kalsher, M. J., & Cataldo, M. F. (1990). Experimental analysis and extinction of self-injurious escape behavior. *Journal of Applied Behavior Analysis, 23*, 11–27.

Iwata, B. A., Pace, G. M., Dorsey, M. F., Zarcone, J. R., Vollmer, T. R., Smith, R. G., Rodgers, T. A., Lerman, D. C., Shore, B. A., Mazaleski, J. L., Goh, H., Cowdery, G. E., Kalsher, M. J., McCosh, K. C., & Willis, K. D. (1994). The functions of self-injurious behavior: An experimental-epidemiological analysis. *Journal of Applied Behavior Analysis, 27*, 215–240.

Jenkins, J. R., Larson, K., & Fleisher, L. S. (1983). Effects of error correction on word recognition and reading comprehension. *Learning Disability Quarterly, 6*(2), 139–145.

Johnston, J. M., & Pennypacker, H. S. (1980). *Strategies and tactics of human behavioral research.* Hillsdale, NJ: Erlbaum.

Johnston, J. M., & Pennypacker, H. S. (1993). *Readings for strategies and tactics of behavioral research.* Hillsdale, NJ: Erlbaum.

Kazdin, A. E. (1994). *Behavior modification in applied settings.* Pacific Grove, CA: Brooks/Cole.

Kazdin, A. E., & Klock, J. (1973). The effect of nonverbal teacher approval on student attentive behavior. *Journal of Applied Behavior Analysis, 6*, 643–654.

Kern, L., Childs, K. E., Dunlap, G., Clarke, S., & Falk, G. D. (1994). Using assessment-based curricular intervention to improve the classroom behavior of a student with emotional and behavioral challenges. *Journal of Applied Behavior Analysis, 27*, 7–19.

Lalli, J. S., Browder, D. M., Mace, F. C., & Brown, D. K. (1993). Teacher use of descriptive analysis data to implement interventions to decrease students' problem behaviors. *Journal of Applied Behavior Analysis, 26*, 227–238.

Lerman, D. C., & Iwata, B. A. (1993). Descriptive and experimental analyses of variables maintaining self-injurious behavior. *Journal of Applied Behavior Analysis, 26*, 293–319.

Mace, F. C. (1994). The significance and future of functional analysis methodologies. *Journal of Applied Behavior Analysis, 27*, 385–392.

Mace, F. C., & Belfiore, P. (1990). Behavioral momentum in the treatment of escape-motivated stereotypy. *Journal of Applied Behavior Analysis, 23*, 507–514.

Mace, F. C., & Lalli, J. S. (1991). Linking descriptive and experimental analyses in the treatment of bizarre speech. *Journal of Applied Behavior Analysis, 24*, 553–562.

Madsen, C. H., Becker, W. C., & Thomas, D. R. (1968). Rules, praise, and ignoring: Elements of elementary classroom control. *Journal of Applied Behavior Analysis, 1*, 139–150.

Madsen, C. H., Becker, W. C., Thomas, D. R., Koser, L., & Plager, E. (1968). An analysis of the reinforcing function of "sit-down" commands. In R. K. Parker (Ed.), *Readings in educational psychology* (pp. 265–278). Boston: Allyn & Bacon.

Marcus, B. A., & Vollmer, T. R. (1995). Effects of differential negative reinforcement on disruption and compliance. *Journal of Applied Behavior Analysis, 28*, 229–230.

Martens, B. K. (1992). Contingency and choice: The implications of matching theory for classroom instruction. *Journal of Behavioral Education, 2*, 121–137.

Martens, B. K., Hiralall, A. S., & Bradley, T. A. (1997). A note to teacher: Improving student behavior through goal setting and feedback. *School Psychology Quarterly, 12*, 33–41.

Martens, B. K., & Kelly, S. Q. (1993). A behavioral analysis of effective teaching. *School Psychology Quarterly, 8*(1), 10–26.

Martens, B. K., Lochner, D. G., & Kelly, S. Q. (1992). The effects of variable-interval reinforcement on academic engagement: A demonstration of matching theory. *Journal of Applied Behavior Analysis, 25*, 143–151.

Martens, B. K., & Witt, J. C. (1988). Ecological behavior analysis. In M. Hersen, R. M. Eisler, & P. M. Miller (Eds.), *Progress in behavior modification* (Vol. 22, pp. 115–140). Beverly Hills, CA: Sage.

Matson, J. L., & Coe, D. A. (1992). Applied behavior analysis: Its impact on the treatment of mentally retarded emotionally disturbed people. *Research in Developmental Disabilities, 13*, 171–189.

McDowell, J. J. (1982). The importance of Herrnstein's mathematical statement of the law of effect for behavior therapy. *American Psychologist, 37*, 771–779.

McLaughlin, T. F. (1982). Effects of self-determined and high performance standards on spelling performance: A multi-element baseline analysis. *Child and Family Behavior Therapy, 4*, 55–61.

Miller, D. L., & Kelley, M. L. (1994). The use of goal setting and contingency contracting for improving children's homework performance. *Journal of Applied Behavior Analysis, 27*, 73–84.

Neef, N. A., Shade, D., & Miller, M. S. (1994). Assessing influential dimensions of reinforcers on choice in students with serious emotional disturbance. *Journal of Applied Behavior Analysis, 27*, 575–583.

Nelson, R. O., & Hayes, S. C. (1986). *Conceptual foundations of behavioral assessment.* New York: Guilford.

Neuringer, A. (1991). Humble behaviorism. *The Behavior Analyst, 14,* 1–13.

Noell, G. (1996). New directions in behavioral consultation. *School Psychology Quarterly, 11,* 187–188.

Noell, G. H., & Witt, J. C. (1998). Toward a behavior analytic approach to consultation. In T. S. Watson and F. M. Gresham (Eds) *Handbook of child behavior therapy* (pp. 41–57). New York: Plenum.

Northup, J., Broussard, C., Jones, K., George, T., Vollmer, T. R., & Herring, M. (1995). The differential effects of teacher and peer attention on the disruptive classroom behavior of three children with a diagnosis of attention deficit hyperactivity disorder. *Journal of Applied Behavior Analysis, 28,* 227–228.

Northup, J., Wacker, D. P., Sasso, G., Steege, M., Cigrand, C., Cook, J., & DeRaad, A. (1991). A brief functional analysis of aggressive and alternative behavior in an outclinic setting. *Journal of Applied Behavior Analysis, 24,* 509–521.

O'Neill, R. E., Horner, R. H., Albin, R. W., Storey, K., & Sprague, J. R. (1990). *Functional analysis of problem behavior: A practical assessment guide.* Pacific Grove, CA: Brooks/Cole.

Osborne, J. G. (1969). Free-time as a reinforcer in the management of classroom behavior. *Journal of Applied Behavior Analysis, 2,* 113–118.

O'Shea, L. J., Munson, S. M., & O'Shea, D. J. (1984). Error correction in oral reading: Evaluating the effectiveness of three procedures. *Education and Treatment of Children, 7,* 203–214.

Pany, D., & McCoy, K. M. (1988). Effects of corrective feedback on word accuracy and reading comprehension of readers with learning disabilities. *Journal of Learning Disabilities, 21*(9), 546–550.

Patterson, G. R., Littman, R. A., & Bricker, W. (1967). Assertive behavior in children: A step toward a theory of aggression. *Monographs of the Society for Research in Child Development, 32*(5).

Perkins, V. L. (1988). Feedback effects on oral reading errors of children with learning disabilities. *Journal of Learning Disabilities, 21*(4), 244–248.

Peterson, N. (1982). Feedback is not a new principal of behavior. *The Behavior Analyst, 5,* 101–102.

Pierce, W. D., & Epling, F. W. (1980). What happened to analysis in applied behavior analysis? *The Behavior Analyst, 3,* 1–9.

Plummer, S., Baer, D. M., & LeBlanc, J. M. (1977). Functional considerations in the use of procedural timeout and an effective alternative. *Journal of Applied Behavior Analysis, 10,* 689–705.

Poling, A., & Ryan, C. (1982). Differential reinforcement of other behavior schedules:

Therapeutic applications. *Behavior Modification, 6,* 3–21.

Porterfield, J. K., Herbert-Jackson, E., & Risley, T. R. (1976). Contingent observation: An effective and acceptable procedure for reducing disruptive behavior of young children in a group setting. *Journal of Applied Behavior Analysis, 9,* 55–64.

Powell, R. A., Martindale, B., & Kulp, S. (1975). An evaluation of time-sampling measures of behavior. *Journal of Applied Behavior Analysis, 8,* 463–469.

Rashotte, C. A., & Torgesen, J. K. (1985). Repeated reading and reading fluency in learning disabled children. *Reading Research Quarterly, 20,* 180–188.

Reid, E. R. (1986). Practicing effective instruction: The exemplary center for reading instruction approach. *Exceptional Children, 52,* 510–519.

Reutzal, D. R., & Hollingsworth, P. M. (1993). Effects of fluency training on second graders' reading comprehension. *Journal of Educational Research, 86*(6), 325–331.

Roberts, M. L., Turco, T. L., & Shapiro, E. S. (1991). Differential effects of fixed instructional ratios on students' progress in reading. *Journal of Psychoeducational Assessment, 9*(4), 308–318.

Rose, T. L. (1984a). The effects of previewing on retarded learners' oral reading. *Education and Treatment of the Mentally Retarded, 19,* 49–52.

Rose, T. L. (1984b). Effects of previewing on the oral reading of mainstreamed behaviorally disordered students. *Behavioral Disorders, 10,* 33–39.

Rose, T. L. (1984c). The effects of twp prepractice procedures on oral reading. *Journal of Learning Disabilities, 17,* 544–548.

Rose, T. L., & Beattie, J. R. (1986). Relative effects of teacher-directed and taped previewing on oral reading. *Learning Disability Quarterly, 9,* 193–199.

Rose, T. L., McEntire, E., & Dowdy, C. (1982). Effects of two error correction procedures on oral reading. *Learning Disability Quarterly, 5,* 100–105.

Rose, T. L., & Sherry, L. (1984). Relative effects of two previewing procedures on LD adolescents' oral reading performance. *Learning Disability Quarterly, 7,* 39–44.

Rosen, L. A., Gabardi, L., & Miller, C. D. (1990). Home-based treatment of disruptive junior high school students: An analysis of the differential effects of positive and negative consequences. *Behavioral Disorders, 15,* 227–232.

Rosenberg, M. S. (1986). Error-correction during oral reading: A comparison of three techniques. *Learning Disability Quarterly, 9*(3), 182–192.

Rousseau, M. K., & Tam, B. K. (1991). The efficacy of previewing and discussion of key words on the oral reading proficiency of bilingual learners with speech and language impairments. *Education and Treatment of Children, 14,* 199–209.

Rousseau, M. K., Tam, B. K., & Ramnarain, R. (1993). Increasing reading proficiency of language-minority students with speech and language impairments. *Education and Treatment of Children, 16*, 254–271.

Salend, S. J. (1988). Effects of peer-previewing on LD students' oral reading skills. *Learning Disability Quarterly, 11*(1), 47–53.

Saudargas, R. A., & Lentz, F. E. (1986). Estimating percent of time and rate via direct observation: A suggested observational procedure and format. *School Psychology Review, 15*, 36–48.

Schunk, D. (1984). Enhancing self-efficacy and achievement through rewards and goals: Motivational and informational effects. *Journal of Educational Research, 78*, 29–34.

Shapiro, E. S., & McCurdy, B. L. (1989). Direct and generalized effects of a taped-words treatment on reading proficiency. *Exceptional Children, 55*, 321–325.

Shinn, M. R. (1989). *Curriculum-based measurement: Assessing special children.* New York: Guilford.

Sindelar, P. T., Rosenberg, M. S., & Wilson, R. J. (1985). An adapted alternating treatments design for instructional research. *Education and Treatment of Children, 8*, 67–76.

Singh, N. N. (1987). Overcorrection of oral reading errors: A comparison of individual- and group-training formats. *Behavior Modification, 11*(2), 165–181.

Singh, N. N. (1990). Effects of two error-correction procedures on oral reading errors: Word supply versus sentence repeat. *Behavior Modification, 14*, 188–199.

Singh, N. N., & Singh, J. (1984). Antecedent control of oral reading errors and self-corrections by mentally retarded children. *Journal of Applied Behavior Analysis, 17*, 111–119.

Singh, N. N., & Singh, J. (1986a). A behavioural remediation program for oral reading: Effects on errors and comprehension. *Educational Psychology, 6*(2), 105–114.

Singh, N. N., & Singh, J. (1986b). Increasing oral reading proficiency: A comparative analysis of drill and positive practice overcorrection procedures. *Behavior Modification, 10*(1), 115–130.

Singh, N. N. & Singh, J. (1988). Increasing oral reading proficiency through overcorrection and phonic analysis. *American Journal of Mental Retardation, 93*(3), 312–319.

Singh, N. N., Singh, J., & Winton, A. S. (1984). Positive practice overcorrection of oral reading errors. *Behavior Modification, 8*(1), 23–37.

Singh, N. N., Winton, A. S., & Singh N. N. (1985). Effects of delayed versus immediate attention to oral reading errors on the reading proficiency of mentally retarded children. *Applied Research in Mental Retardation, 6*(3), 283–293.

Skinner, B. F. (1932). Drive and reflex strength: II. *Journal of Genetic Psychology, 6*, 38–48.

Skinner, B. F. (1953). *Science and human behavior.* New York: Macmillan.

Skinner, B. F. (1987). Whatever happened to psychology as the science of behavior. *American Psychologist, 42*, 780–786.

Skinner, C. H., Adamson, K. L., Woodward, J. R., Jackson, R. R., Atchison, L. A., Jr., & Mims, J. W. (1993). A comparison of fast-rate, slow-rate, and silent previewing interventions on reading performance. *Journal of Learning Disabilities, 26*(10), 674–681.

Skinner, C. H., & Shapiro, E. S. (1989). A comparison of taped-words and drill interventions on reading fluency in adolescents with behavior disorders. *Education and Treatment of Children, 12*, 123–133.

Solomon, R. W., & Wahler, R. G. (1973). Peer reinforcement control of classroom problem behavior. *Journal of Applied Behavior Analysis, 6*, 49–56.

Steege, M. W., Wacker, D. P., Cigrand, K. C., Berg, W. K., Novak, C. G., Reimers, T. M., Sasso, G. M., & DeRaad, A. (1990). The use of negative reinforcement in the treatment of self-injurious behavior. *Journal of Applied Behavior Analysis, 22*, 23–33.

Stoner, G., Carey, S. P., Ikeda, M. J., & Shinn, M. R. (1994). The utility of curriculum-based measurement for evaluating the effects of methylphenidate on academic performance. *Journal of Applied Behavior Analysis, 27*, 101–113.

Sturmey, P. (1995). Diagnostic-based pharmacological treatment of behavior disorders in persons with developmental disabilties: A review and a decision-making typology. *Research in Developmental Disabilities, 16*, 235–252.

Sulzer-Azaroff, B., & Mayer, G. R. (1977). *Applying behavior-analysis procedures with children and youth.* New York: Holt, Rinehart & Winston.

Tan, A., Moore, D. W., Dixon, R. S., & Nicholson, T. (1994). Effects of training in rapid decoding on the reading comprehension of adult ESL learners. *Journal of Behavioral Education, 4*(2), 177–189.

Touchette, P. E., MacDonald, R. F., & Langer, S. N. (1985). A scatter plot for identifying stimulus control of problem behavior. *Journal of Applied Behavior Analysis, 18*, 343–351.

VanHouten, R., Nau, P. A., MacKenzie-Keating, S. E., Sameotot, D., & Colavecchia, B. (1982). An analysis of some variables influencing the effectiveness of reprimands. *Journal of Applied Behavior Analysis, 15*, 65–83.

Vaughn, M. E., & Michael, J. L. (1982). Automatic reinforcement: An important but ignored concept. *Behaviorism, 10*, 217–228.

Vollmer, T. R., & Iwata, B. A. (1992). Differential reinforcement as treatment for behavior disorders: Procedural and functional variations. *Research in Developmental Disabilities, 13*, 393–417.

Vollmer, T. R., Iwata, B. A., Zarcone, J. R., Smith, R. G., & Mazaleski, J. L. (1993). The role of attention in the treatment of attention-maintained self-injurious behavior: Noncontingent reinforcement (NCR) and differential reinforcement of other behavior (DRO). *Journal of Applied Behavior Analysis, 26,* 9–21.

Vollmer, T. R., & Northup, J. (1996). Some implications of functional analysis for school psychology. *School Psychology Quarterly, 11,* 76–92.

White, M. A. (1975). Natural rates of teacher approval and disapproval in the classroom. *Journal of Applied Behavior Analysis, 8,* 367–372.

Wickstrom, K. (1995). A study of the relationship among teacher, process and outcome variables within school-based consultation. Doctoral dissertation, Louisiana State University, Baton Rouge.

Witt, J. C. (1995). Project ON-TASC: A direct intervention model for intervention implementation (Applied Research Grant, 107-75-4106, Louisiana Department of Education).

Witt, J. C., Elliott, S. N., & Gresham, F. M. (1988). *Handbook of behavior therapy in education.* New York: Plenum.

Witt, J. C., & Martens, B. K. (1988). Problems with problem-solving consultation: A re-analysis of assumptions, methods and goals. *School Psychology Review, 17,* 211–226.

Wolery, M., Bailey, D. B., & Sugai, G. M. (1988). *Effective teaching: Principles and procedures of applied behavior analysis with exceptional students.* Boston: Allyn & Bacon.

Yeaton, W. H., & Sechrest, L. (1981). Critical dimensions in the choice and maintenance of successful treatments: Strength, integrity, and effectiveness. *Journal of Consulting and Clinical Psychology, 49*(2), 156–167.

Ysseldyke, J. E. (1979). Issues in psychoeducational assessment. In G. D. Phye & D. J. Reschly (Eds.), *School psychology: Perspectives and issues* (pp. 87–121). New York: Academic Press.

Ysseldyke, J. E., & Marston, D. (1990). The use of assessment information to plan instructional interventions: A review of the research. In T. B. Gutkin & C. R. Reynolds (Eds.), *The handbook of school psychology* (2nd ed., pp. 661–682). New York: Wiley.

## CHAPTER 25

# INTERVENTION TECHNIQUES FOR ACADEMIC PERFORMANCE PROBLEMS

**STEPHEN N. ELLIOTT**
*University of Wisconsin–Madison*

**R. T. BUSSE**
*University of Wisconsin–Whitewater*

**EDWARD S. SHAPIRO**
*Lehigh University*

**Authors' Note** *We wish to thank Mary Ann Godlewski for her assistance in the preparation of this chapter.*

Many children experience significant academic difficulties in the course of their journey through school. These difficulties take many forms (e.g., word recognition, reading comprehension, mathematical reasoning, written communications, and spelling) and can be influenced by an array of personal and environmental variables. In this chapter, as in the second edition of this book, we are interested in focusing on *alterable variables* that are operating in the classroom. These primarily include students' learning behaviors, teachers' instructional behaviors, and instructional materials and practices. These variables admittedly are only part of the educational context aptly characterized by Centra and Potter (1980) and other educational researchers interested in the effects of a wide range of variables (socioeconomic status, race, or school size) on students' achievement (Reynolds & Walberg, 1991). Once we have identified key alterable variables that influence students' academic performance, we examine an array of interventions designed to affect them. Finally, we conclude with the presentation of an intervention imple-

mentation model, which integrates our discussion of alterable variables and effective intervention tactics.

## A PERFORMANCE-BASED MODEL FOR UNDERSTANDING ALTERABLE VARIABLES

As B. F. Skinner (1968) observed, "Influencing student learning in the classroom is a matter of changing the classroom environment in certain, specific ways. . . . Understanding how to improve student academic performance . . . is a matter of understanding how changing the environment leads to changed behavior" (p. 34). Following from this deceptively simple observation, Greenwood and colleagues (Greenwood & Delquadri, 1995; Greenwood, Delquadri, & Hall, 1989; Greenwood, Terry Utley, Montagna, & Walker, 1993) and others (e.g., Gersten, Keating, & Becker, 1988) have researched the effects of alterable instructional variables on directly measured indexes of student performance. As a result, Greenwood (1996) posited a *performance-based instructional model* in which *instruction* affects *engagement*, but only *engagement* directly affects school outcomes. Thus, instruction indirectly affects learning or is mediated by students' academic behavior as operationalized by engagement (see Figure 25.1). This model is a useful heuristic that highlights alterable variables that interventionists should consider as a first line of offense for academic performance problems. Indirect support for the model can be found in both behavioral and educational research (e.g., Brophy, 1979; Cobb, 1972; Gersten, Becker, Heiry, & White, 1984; Greenwood et al., 1992). A brief review of research on academic engagement and instruction provides a strong foundation for understanding learning difficulties and for conceptualizing interventions to improve academic functioning (i.e., work completion, accuracy, and rate of responding).

## Opportunity to Learn

The opportunity to learn academic subjects and to practice what is earned is critical to a performance-based instructional model. Several researchers have demonstrated that the time available to learn a subject is a significant variable in predicting students' achievement (e.g., Denham & Lieberman, 1980; Kane, 1994); however, there

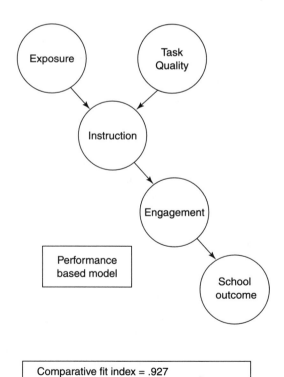

Comparative fit index = .927
chi-square (54) = 70.1 $p < .069$ $R^2 = 27\%$

**FIGURE 25.1 Performance-based instruction model.**

is wide variation in time devoted to subject matter instruction across students and classrooms. For example, Greenwood (1991) found that in a 7-hour school day, elementary students in Chapter 1 schools were taught basic academic subjects for only 2.6 hours, compared to 2.7 hours for students in non-Chapter 1 schools. This finding indicates that about 37% of the time in a typical school day is spent on academics and that students from lower socioeconomic strata (SES) spend about 6 minutes per day less on academic subjects than students from middle to high SES. Other researchers' estimates of this daily difference between low-SES students and middle- or high-SES students and students with learning disabilities (LD) versus students without disability have ranged from 10 to 15 minutes (Greenwood, Arreaga-Mayer, & Carta, 1994; Walker, Greenwood, Hart, & Carta, 1994).

The reasons for these small, but important, differences in time taught are unclear. The management of instructional time is a critical aspect of any academic intervention; instructional time must be increased, not decreased. Recent research by Skinner, Fletcher, and Henington (1996), which is examined later, has identified ways in which educators can increase learning rates and time allocated for instruction without extending school days or terms.

## Academic Responding

The construct of engagement has evolved out of research on students' attention and academically relevant responses, described as academic survival skills (Hoge, 1985), academic learning time (Berliner, 1988), and academic responding composite (Greenwood, Delquadri, & Hall, 1984). Engagement can be directly observed and often involves low-inference behaviors such as writing, drawing, reading aloud, playing academic games, asking or answering academic questions, and calculating with pencil and paper or calculator. These academic behaviors can be altered as a function of change in instructional materials or teachers' behavior. Students who spend less instruction time engaged in academic tasks over a period of years will generally learn less and consequently are more likely to experience academic difficulties. Hence, Greenwood (1996) emphasized engagement in academic responding as a sensitive indicator of the effects of instruction and has made it is the central element in his performance-based instructional model.

## Instructional Materials and Practices

Students' engagement in academic tasks is influenced by the instructional materials and teaching practices. For example, researchers have documented that teachers who frequently use overhead projectors and lectures as their primary instructional method can actually reduce students' engagement in academic responding (Greenwood, Delquadri, & Hall, 1984). In contrast, the same researchers found that students increased their academic responding when teachers used worksheets, pencils, and textbooks in small- and large-group instruction and such practices as classwide peer tutoring. This study suggests that many students need to be involved actively (i.e., handling materials, physically responding, and generating their own responses) in learning to stay engaged.

Instructional activities have also been found to play a significant role in reducing or preventing problem behaviors in the classroom (Dunlap & Kern, 1996). Thus, instructional activities play a significant role as antecedents to more academically oriented behaviors. Key instructional activities or tactics include pacing, student preferences, and choice making.

In summary, there are many variables in the instructional environment (see Ysseldyke & Christenson, 1987) and aspects of individual learners that we have not mentioned in this introduction to academic interventions. Instead, we have chosen to emphasize as a starting point a parsimonious performance-based model of instruction and learning that features alterable variables found in any classroom. Before examining more variables and related intervention tactics for students exhibiting academic performance difficulties, that is, poor rates of work completion, accuracy, or responding, we present a framework for understanding the nature of a student's academic problem and for hypothesizing about potential treatment.

## Performance Considerations and Intervention Impact Points

Academic difficulties can result from multiple variables, including a student's environment, cognition, and behaviors. In general, academic problems can be seen as difficulties in response acquisition or response performance, and thus students may exhibit either skill deficits or performance deficits. The major difference between these difficulties is that students with skill deficits typically require the acquisition of new behaviors before progress can occur; that is, they must learn a skill that is not in their academic repertoire. Rather than lacking skills, students with performance deficits fail to exhibit those skills consistently or fail to build on skills for further learning. Performance problems are often related to teachers' or students' behaviors during the prelearning (antecedent) and/or postlearning (consequent) phases of a learning event. Thus, these phases of learning should be targets for assessment and intervention.

Witt, Elliott, Daly, Gresham, and Kramer (1998) noted several common explanations for reduced academic engagement and subsequent poor achievement in a given subject matter: (a) the student is not motivated to respond, (b) the student needs more time to work on the task, (c) the student needs more help or support to complete the task, and (d) the task is too hard for the student. These explanations can be systematically investigated in the order presented. That is, the first concern an interventionist has when confronted with an academic performance problem is a student's motivation. If motivation is low, solutions are likely to include reinforcement or choice tactics. If motivation does not appear to be a concern, time engaged in work should be examined. If this is inadequate, possible solutions may involve task modifications or pacing strategies that increase allocated time, as well as time to work. If time to work is not a major concern, direct helping strategies should be the focus of intervention. Direct instruction or peer tutoring, which provides support and practice, may be appropriate. Finally, if these direct helping strategies fail to increase engagement and the quality of learning outcomes, changes in the difficulty level of the task should be considered.

The performance-based instructional model (see Figure 25.1) fits well into this conceptualization of academic performance difficulties and related interventions. The model was derived from data gathered over a two-year study by Greenwood et al. (1989) on the effects of classwide peer tutoring with 53 second- and third-grade students. Classroom and student variables were observed through the Code for Instructional Structure and Student Academic Response (CISSAR) (Stanley & Greenwood, 1981) to define the constructs of task exposure, task quality, and student engagement. School outcome was assessed with the Metropolitan Achievement Test (MAT), subtests of reading, language, and mathematics

(Prescott, Balow, Hogan, & Farr, 1987). Greenwood, Terry, Marquis, and Walker (1994) subjected these data to a series of structural, equation-modeling procedures. Model estimates indicated that the performance-based instructional model showed the best fit with the data and accounted for 27% of the variance in school outcome. Thus, the structural model indicated that exposure and task quality were second-order variables that did not directly affect students' outcomes. Rather, exposure and task quality make up the variable of instruction. The final model indicated that only engagement was a first-order variable; that is, only engagement directly affected school outcomes.

Several limitations are evident in the data from which the model was derived. First, the data were gathered on second- and third-grade students, and therefore the model may not generalize to other age groups. Second, the sample size was relatively small, which constricts the generalizability and power of the analyses. Third, the use of the MAT as the measure of school outcome is potentially limiting. Finally, the model failed to account for 73% of the variance in outcomes. Further validation of the performance-based model is clearly needed; however, it is a promising heuristic for conceptualizing *alterable* academic performance difficulties. For example, although the model accounted for only 27% of the outcome variance, this may be an indicator of the amount of variance over which one has reasonable control. The total accounted variance could be increased by the inclusion of such variables as SES; however, because these variables are typically outside an interventionist's control, their inclusion would be superfluous. Perhaps the most compelling reason for using the model rests with its simplicity and its similarity to a behavioral model of performance. From this perspective, instruction serves as the stimulus or antecedent-setting event for engagement. Engagement, in turn, is the behavior that is targeted for reinforcement.

Taken together, concerns about performance and other potential explanations for performance difficulties can be organized under the S-O-R-C model, made popular among behavioral psychologists by Kanfer and Goldstein (1986). The basic elements of this model are a stimulus (the people or events that precede an action and are thought to stimulate the action), an organism (the student and his or her mediational processes, involving emotions and thoughts), a response (the overt reactions of the organism to a perceived stimulus), and a consequence (the reactions to the response perceived by the organism).

The S-O-R-C model is compatible with Greenwood's (1996) performance-based instructional model and helps organize information about a particular behavior episode. From the coupling of these two models, it is hypothesized that academic performance can be altered by addressing antecedent stimuli (instruction) to affect organism variables (cognitions) and subsequent responses (engagement) or by addressing consequent conditions (e.g., reinforcement) to affect responses. In short, what the S-O-R-C and performance-based instructional models provide is a useful framework for conceptualizing target behaviors and points for intervention. For example, imagine that a teacher is giving directions about a mathematics assignment and the target student is still working on her social studies. The teacher asks if anyone has questions; nobody responds, so he says, "Get to work and please hand in your assignment by the end of the hour." The target student looks up, hearing something about handing in an assignment, and is surprised to see everyone around her working on math rather than social studies. She yells, "Hey, what are we supposed to be doing in math. I didn't hear the instructions." The teacher responds by asking the student to come to his desk.

The S-O-R-C model offers four potential impact points for intervening to change a student's behavior (see Figure 25.2). Thus, to change an undesirable or unproductive behavior, a change must occur in the stimulus or antecedent event, the organism's mediational processing of the stimulus, the organism's response, or the consequences the organism experiences. As an example and precursor to the next section on effective intervention techniques, we offer a simple classification scheme for conceptualizing target behaviors and interventions based on performance or acquisition deficits. As shown in Figure 25.2, this scheme distinguishes performance and skill deficits with interventions that have been found effective for the various problem types. In this scheme, instructional interventions are hypothesized to have the most robust effect at the point of instruction, whereas consequent-oriented interventions are directed at engagement. This model certainly is not inclusive of all the potential interventions that could be used at each point, nor is it intended to be. Rather, the model is presented as a starting point

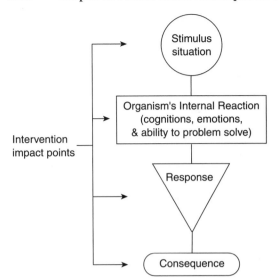

**FIGURE 25.2** **The Stimulus-Organism-Response-Consequence (S-O-R-C) model of behavior with intervention impact points.**

for conceptualizing practice and research on intervention techniques for academic performance problems.

Two of the intervention impact points, the organism's mediational processes and response, require interventions that directly involve changes in a student. The other two impact points, the stimulus and the consequence, generally require interventions that involve persons other than the student or those in the situations surrounding the student. Of course, students can also be involved in antecedents and consequences. Many factors influence decisions about which components to target for change. Knowing which interventions are generally *acceptable* to teachers and students and which are *effective* is perhaps the best place to start in conceptualizing an intervention pathway. We have found the performance-based instructional model and the S-O-R-C model to be very useful tools for focusing and organizing our knowledge of classroom learning events and interventions that might be effective.

## EFFECTIVE INTERVENTION TECHNIQUES

The performance-based instructional model provides a parsimonious framework for conceptualizing targets for academic interventions. In this section, we discuss a few of the interventions that

can be used to target instruction and engagement, with the bulk of the section devoted to interventions targeted at engagement. Instructional practices obviously are important antecedents to academic engagement and can be deterrents for performance problems. Our coverage is brief for three reasons. First, in working from a performance-based model, engagement most directly affects school outcomes. Second, academic difficulties can remain, even in classrooms with strong instructional practices. Third, the focus of this chapter is on performance problems rather than skill deficits. Thus, we follow the work that addressed academic interventions in the previous editions of this book by emphasizing interventions that are more consequence-oriented.

## Instructional Interventions

Many instructional variables are potentially related to academic performance, which of course indicates that there are many potential interventions. Ysseldyke and Christenson (1993), for their work on The Instructional Environment Scale, reviewed the literature on instructional variables and identified eight correlates of academic achievement: (a) time allocation and engagement, (b) student-instructional match, (c) teachers' expectations, (d) lesson presentation, (e) assigned tasks, (f) practice, (g) classroom management, and (h) opportunity to learn. Each of these variables has been related to students' achievement, although the preponderance of research has resulted in low to moderate correlations (Ysseldyke & Christenson, 1993). As these authors aptly noted, recognizing important correlates of academic performance is an important step, but recognition does not necessarily lead to effective intervention.

Skinner et al. (1996) gave a useful review of instructional variables and methods for increasing students' response rates within the time required to learn. One avenue involves increasing the quality of learning trials, that is, the amount of learning that occurs per learning trial, so that qualitatively stronger trials require fewer trials to meet a given criterion. Reinforcement of correct responding is often used to increase the quality of learning rates. Another avenue involves increasing the quantity of learning rates through allocated time (see Berliner, 1988, and Gettinger, 1995). Allocated learning time (ALT) is time in which students are actively and successfully engaged in their learning. Careful observation of classroom ALT can lead to more effective time management. One method for increasing allocated learning time is to engage in proactive classroom management that minimizes disruptions to instruction (see Gettinger, 1988).

Several instructional variables in the literature have been altered to decrease disruptions and increase the quantity of learning rates. For example, reducing intertrial intervals has been shown to result in increased learning rates and on-task behavior (Carnine, 1976). An intertrial interval is the time elapsed between the end of one trial and the beginning of another (Skinner et al., 1996) or, in other words, the packing of instruction. Faster pacing also tends to minimize potential problem behaviors that can interfere with learning for students with and without disabilities (Carnine, 1976; Munk & Repp, 1994; West & Sloan, 1986). Relatedly, increasing wait times or intervals can result in an increased rate of responding and opportunity to learn. For example, research reviewed by Skinner et al. indicated that when teachers increased the time they waited for responses from one to three seconds, students' accuracy and rates of responding increased. Problems can arise, however, if wait times interfere with the pace of instruction.

Skinner et al. (1996) identified several other instructional strategies for increasing learning rates during independent seat-work: timed performance, reducing the amount of time allocated for assignments, and task modifications such as altering response topography (e.g., written versus verbal responding). Finally, students' preferences or choices can be a component of an instructional intervention. Investigators have found that when a learning outcome was meaningful and valued by students, their engagement in the activity to produce the outcome was characterized as more focused with few problem behaviors (Horner, Sprague, & Flannery, 1993). An area of research closely related to preferences is choice making (Guess, Benson, & Siegel-Causey, 1985). Providing students with choices allows them some control over their instruction and has been shown to increase academic performance and decrease disruptive behaviors (Dunlap & Kern, 1996; Munk & Repp, 1994). Dunlap and Kern summarized much of the research on the ability of persons with disabilities to make valid choices, as well as the motivational and performance benefits that are often associated with choice-making procedures. Choice making seems to be an important antecedent to increased task engagement

for most learners and thus should be strongly considered when planning interventions.

Many instructional variables and interventions can be implemented to increase academic performance. They involve teacher training; curricular modifications; and target antecedents, or setting events for behavior. Most successful instructional interventions, however, include some form of consequent condition such as feedback or praise.

## Academic Performance Interventions

A large body of research focuses on positive (e.g., on-task behavior and work completion) and negative (e.g., off-task behavior and inattention) behaviors related to academic performance problems (Hoge & Andrews, 1987). The literature is also replete with behavioral and cognitive-behavioral techniques for remediating academic difficulties. We focus on several general strategies with substantial empirical support that can be used with a variety of students and academic problems. The intervention techniques are presented in an order, albeit somewhat arbitrary, that represents the level of intrusiveness into school ecologies.

### School-Home Notes

School-home notes—such as daily report cards or progress reports—are a rather easily administered intervention technique that can enhance academic performance through communication between school and parents or guardians. Kelley (1990) provided a review of the efficacy of school-home notes and offered practical applications of the method. Variants of the method have been used to enhance math performance of elementary school students (Blechman, Taylor, & Shrader, 1981; Karraker, 1972), adolescents' classroom behavior (Schumaker, Hovell, & Sherman, 1977), and on-task behavior of children with attention deficit hyperactivity disorder, or ADHD (see Kelley, 1990, for case studies). The general procedure for constructing a school-home note program begins with a parent-teacher conference at which target behaviors are specified and goals are defined. Next, the school-home note is designed, along with responsibilities for the parents, teacher, and child, and agreed-upon reinforcers. Once the procedure is implemented, frequent verbal feedback and praise should occur, and if behavior improves, the note should be *faded* gradually and discontinued.

There are several advantages to using school-home notes. They can engender conjoint problem solving between teachers and parents, they can provide parents with frequent feedback to facilitate home-school communication, and the small time commitment required for implementation enhances the probability for treatment acceptability and integrity. Furthermore, because most school-home note procedures emphasize positive behaviors, their use may increase parental praise and attention, which may enhance children's self-esteem and self-efficacy. Finally, increased parental involvement may enhance treatment maintenance and generalization. School-home notes may be inappropriate for children with severe behavior problems and/or academic deficits or for children who live in highly dysfunctional families (Kelley, 1990). Care must also be taken to ensure that parents or guardians are not excessively punitive if the child brings home a "bad" note.

Blechman, Taylor, and Shrader (1981) examined the effects of school-home notes with second- through sixth-grade students in 17 classrooms. Children from each classroom who did inconsistent math work were assigned randomly to one of three conditions: (a) note home ($N = 27$), (b) "family problem solving" ($N = 26$), and (c) control ($N = 16$). An additional 51 students with consistent math performance were selected as a comparison group. The home-note intervention consisted of a "Good News Note" for which the children received praise or reinforcers when their accuracy on math assignments equaled or surpassed their baseline means. For the note-only condition, parents received a brief letter describing the procedure. The family problem-solving intervention was a one-hour training session in which parents were guided through the process of contingency contracting and providing reinforcers for the Good News Note. Participants in the problem-solving condition also received weekly phone calls to discuss compliance with the procedures. In each of the conditions, no note was sent home if a child did not reach criterion, and a No Work Assigned note was sent if the class did not have math work on a given day.

The results indicated that both experimental conditions were effective in decreasing the variability of math performance compared to the control and comparison conditions. Math accuracy increased only in the problem-solving condition and decreased for the other three conditions. These results indicate that school-home notes were effective in stabilizing math perform-ance but not math accuracy, whereas the problem-solving intervention was effective in stabilizing and enhancing math performance. These results, however, should be interpreted with caution because of the design of the study. Specifically, it is unknown which components of the problem-solving intervention affected math performance, and only the problem-solving condition used treatment integrity and plan implementation checks. Finally, although the results were statistically significant, the actual mean percentages of change in scatter and accuracy were somewhat small ($<10\%$).

These cautions highlight issues with the research base and use of school-home notes. There are few well-controlled studies that have used this technique, and only a handful of studies have examined the maintenance or generalization of treatment effects (Kelley, 1990). Furthermore, whereas school-home notes can effect substantial increases in performance (e.g., Karraker, 1972), student (e.g., problem severity) and environment variables need to be considered, which may minimize the treatment strength of the notes. Thus, although school-home notes can be used alone, typically they are integrated into a treatment package to serve as communication devices (e.g., Forgatch & Ramsey, 1994).

### Performance Feedback

Performance feedback is another rather easily administered technique for improving a variety of academic behaviors. It simply involves giving students response-contingent feedback about their performance. The underlying premise is that students may be motivated when they can view their progress or when their progress is available for public view. There are several systems for providing contingent feedback to students. The general method is to create a chart to monitor progress in a target area. These charts can vary from a simple recording of scores (e.g., homework and tests) to more elaborate methods like bar graphs. The choice of chart may depend on the age of the students and their ability to comprehend the data that will be charted or graphed. For example, a simple bar graph with a rocket ship to indicate score position is suitable for elementary-aged students. Students' progress can be individualized and personal or publicly posted for group interventions. If the data are posted publicly, it is important to convey the scores in a positive and constructive manner.

One method for offsetting potentially negative effects of public posting is to use code names or numbers (e.g., Bourque, Dupuis, & Van Houten, 1986). The most obvious advantages of this technique are its simplicity, lack of intrusiveness, and common use as a feedback mechanism for teachers. The major disadvantages are that the procedure can result in negative attention, such as public humiliation, and may lack treatment strength when used alone.

In a two-part study, Van Houten and Lai Fatt (1981) examined the effects of public posting of weekly biology test scores of twelfth-grade students. Results from the first study revealed its effects coupled with immediate feedback and praise, increased test accuracy from 56% to 73% across the 47 students in the study. In a within-study replication with 106 students, public posting, with biweekly feedback, increased test performance. These results were consistent with earlier studies that examined the use of explicit timing and public posting in increasing math and composition skills of elementary school students (Van Houten, Hill, & Parsons, 1975; Van Houten & Thompson, 1976). Other investigations have provided supportive evidence for the use of performance feedback with task completion in reading (Kastelen, Nickel, & McLaughlin, 1984) and with test scores in spelling (Bourque et al., 1986). These studies indicate that feedback systems and public recognition can sufficiently motivate students to enhance their academic performance.

## Self-management

Self-management techniques are often cost-efficient, effective interventions that have inherent advantages over more externally controlled interventions. *Self-management* typically refers to actions designed to change or maintain one's own behavior (Shapiro, 1994). Thus, in self-management interventions, children are taught to apply specified contingencies on their own behavior. Reviewers of self-management research have found it to be an effective mechanism for behavior change (Roberts & Dick, 1982; Shapiro & Cole, 1994). Applications of self-management can be found for a wide variety of problems with a wide variety of populations, including children and adults with cognitive disabilities (e.g., Ackerman & Shapiro, 1984), and children with multiple disabilities (e.g., Lam, Cole, Shapiro, & Bambara, 1994), learning disabilities (e.g., Hallahan, Lloyd, Kosiewicz, Kauffman, &

Graves, 1979), and emotional difficulties (Sheridan, Kratochwill, & Elliott, 1990).

Kanfer (1971) provided a useful tripartite model—self-monitoring, self-evaluation, and self-reinforcement—for understanding self-management processes. *Self-monitoring* involves self-observation and self-recording of behavior. The process of self-monitoring alone may have an added advantage of reactivity, which can result in behavior change (e.g., Nelson, 1977). Once behavior is monitored, the individual evaluates her or his behavior against a set criterion. If *self-evaluation* indicates that the behavior is progressing in the desired direction, the student decides if the criterion for *self-reinforcement* is satisfied and applies the appropriate consequences.

Self-management procedures are typically divided into two categories (Roberts & Dick, 1982; Shapiro & Cole, 1994). The first category is contingency management. These procedures generally focus on self-monitoring of behaviors and subsequent consequences (e.g., rewards) for attaining desired behaviors. Thus, behavioral control in contingency management is established through the use of consequent conditions. The other type of self-management procedures focuses on the manipulation of cognitive variables. These procedures typically use a verbal mediation strategy to control antecedents to problem behavior. The most commonly used cognitive mediation strategies for academic performance problems are variations of self-instructional training (SIT) in which students problem-solve aloud as they perform a task (Meichenbaum & Goodman, 1971).

The two major categories of self-management use similar methods to deploy a selected strategy. These methods typically follow some or all parts of a general three-step procedure. The first step is agreeing on a specified behavior for change. Although little is known about the relation between target behavior selection in self-management and subsequent treatment outcomes, problem identification is an important aspect of behavior change (Witt & Elliott, 1983). Behavior specification is also important in operationalizing a behavior to allow for accurate self-observation. The second step involves teaching the components of self-monitoring. It is often necessary to collect interrater reliability data to ascertain whether the child is accurately observing her or his behavior. The final step involves selecting and dispersing agree-upon rewards or other self-reinforcement like self-praise.

Self-management has a number of advantages over externally controlled behavior interventions. First, it places the responsibility for treatment management and behavior change on the student, which may increase a student's responsibility for her or his own behavior. Second, because the targeted individual controls the contingency, there is a higher probability for treatment generality (e.g., Holman & Baer, 1979). Third, self-management can be an efficient intervention because teachers or other adults are less involved in treatment implementation. Thus, teachers and other care-givers may find self-management strategies more acceptable than adult-mediated interventions, which require more time, energy, and resources (Elliott, 1988).

Self-management obviously may be contraindicated for some individuals. For example, some children lack the prerequisite cognitive skills or emotional control necessary for implementing self-management strategies. In these cases, individuals may be unresponsive to part or all of the self-management training procedures (Browder & Shapiro, 1985). Self-management also may be nonadvantageous when the focus is solely on the child as the target for behavior change, but the environment (e.g., classroom, family) requires more ecological, systemic intervention. We present examples of a contingency management procedure and a cognitive-based procedure to demonstrate the use and effectiveness of self-management strategies in remediating academic problems. For a more comprehensive review and understanding of self-management interventions, see Shapiro and Cole (1994).

### Contingency Management Interventions

Contingency management interventions have been used to treat a variety of academic behaviors, including on-task behavior (Hughes & Hendrickson, 1987; Prater, Hogan, & Miller, 1992), work completion and accuracy (Piersel & Kratochwill, 1979), and productivity in spelling (Reid & Harris, 1993) and arithmetic (Loyd, Bateman, Landrum, & Hallahan, 1989). Applications of contingency-based self-management most often have used self-monitoring as the intervention strategy. For example, Lam et al. (1994) examined the effects of self-monitoring on three adolescent boys who attended a university-affiliated school for students with severe behavior disorders. The dependent measures were on-task behavior, academic accuracy, and disruptive behavior. On-task behavior was defined as

keeping one's eyes on worksheets or writing on worksheets. Academic accuracy was the percentage of accurate math computation movements. Disruptive behavior was defined by a variety of behaviors, such as out-of-seat, noise-making, and aggressive behavior. The three students were trained individually to self-monitor behavior in one to three sessions of approximately 20-minutes duration. The training procedures were standardized through the use of scripts to facilitate experimental control. For on-task and disruptive behaviors, the students were given color-coded self-monitoring sheets and were trained to self-monitor for 10 minutes at the sound of a recorded tone set at a variable-interval schedule of 1 minute. The students were trained to differentiate on-task from off-task behavior with a yellow, color-coded self-observation sheet with the words "Was I paying attention?" Math accuracy was self-monitored through a green worksheet, on which the students were trained to check their answers at the tone. Finally, the students were trained to monitor their disruptive behaviors on a pink sheet with the words "Was I disruptive?" During the self-monitoring conditions, the teacher cued the students to self-monitor at the sound of the tone. The students were assigned randomly to each self-monitoring condition within a counterbalanced treatment withdrawal design.

Average interobserver agreements were high for both on-task behavior (95%) and disruptive behavior (98%). Self-monitoring accuracy checks revealed that two of the students accurately monitored (80%–100% agreement) their behaviors, whereas one student was consistently inaccurate (40%–60% agreement) despite an apparent understanding of the procedures during training sessions. Treatment integrity checklists completed by trained observers indicated that the teacher adhered (i.e., prepared specific materials) to the treatment protocol. Results indicated overall improvement compared to baseline for each student across the three self-monitoring conditions. Collateral effects were also demonstrated. Specifically, improvements in one behavior were seen when another was self-monitored. Thus, it appears that the improvements in behavior generalized from one treatment phase to another. The greatest generalization effects occurred during the academic accuracy self-monitoring condition for all three students. These conclusions, however, must be interpreted with caution. Four of the withdrawal phases did not show a return to baseline levels of behaviors; therefore, control over behavior was not established during these phases.

This study provides a useful illustration of the general components and issues in the implementation of self-management strategies. First, the target behaviors were operationalized and interobserver agreement data were gathered. Second, training in self-monitoring occurred and was assessed for integrity. In this study, self-reinforcement was not a specific component of the treatment; therefore, it appears that the observed improvements were reactive to the self-monitoring procedure, although, as noted by the authors, performance feedback may have served as a reinforcer.

One issue that arose during the Lam et al. (1994) study was the low self-monitoring accuracy displayed by one of the students. It may be that resistance or oppositional behavior interfered with accuracy despite the student's demonstrated ability to engage in the self-monitoring procedure. The difficulty noted with this student underscores the potential drawback of self-management procedures for students who lack prerequisite skills or who show resistant behavior. It may have been fruitful to employ a specific contingency such as praise or a reward to offset the student's interfering behaviors. Another issue that arose relates to the generalization of effects across behaviors. One of the underlying, potentially positive aspects of self-management procedures is generality of behavior. The results from this study indicate that effects did generalize across the three behaviors, which, of course, is a desirable outcome. It is interesting that, the effects were strongest for the academic accuracy condition, a finding that lends additional support for the selection of academic performance as a target behavior rather than on-task or disruptive behaviors (Lentz, 1988).

### Cognitive-based Interventions

Self-instruction training (SIT) was first directed toward reducing children's impulsive behavior; however, it has been used with other behaviors such as increasing on-task behavior (Bornstein & Quevillon, 1976), social skills (Cartledge & Milburn, 1983), and academic skills (Fox & Kendall, 1983; Roberts, Nelson, & Olson, 1987). In Johnston, Whitman, and Johnson (1980), a self-instruction program was implemented for three children with mild cognitive disabilities. These students performed addition and subtraction by regrouping. The SIT involved a 20- to 30-minute session, during which students were taught to engage in self-statements related to task performance. The instructor modeled self-instruction by overtly asking and responding to a series of verbal mediation questions such as "What kind of problem is this? It's an add problem. I can tell by the sign. Now what do I do? I start with the top number in. . . . How do I check it? I got it right so I'm doing well!"

This method of SIT followed the typical sequence established by Meichenbaum and Goodman (1971) and involved (a) overt modeling in which the trainer first solved the problems by using self-instructions while the students observed, (b) overt instruction in which the students performed the task while the trainer instructed aloud, (c) overt guidance in which the students performed the task with the help of the trainer, (d) overt performance in which the students performed the self-instructions aloud without trainer prompting, and (e) covert performance in which the students performed the task by using private speech. Results indicated that the students demonstrated substantial increases in math performance, although they did not automatically transfer the self-instruction to the related task of subtraction. Whitman and Johnston (1983) found similar outcomes in a related study. These findings indicate that SIT may require generality enhancers to facilitate its use in nontraining areas or subjects.

### Peer Tutoring

The incorporation of peers as agents of academic change is a frequently used method for increasing academic performance and remediating skill deficits. The rationale for this intervention strategy is typically based on the premise that it can increase students' involvement in learning activities, thereby increasing academic engagement (Hawryluk & Smallwood, 1988). Peer tutoring can assume several forms, including single dyad situations in which an older and/or more compete peer serves as the tutor, single dyads in which reciprocal teaching or tutoring occurs, and class-wide or schoolwide peer tutoring. Variants of peer tutoring have been successful in increasing academic performance in math (Fuchs, Fuchs, Phillips, Hamlett, & Karns, 1995; Heller & Fantuzzo, 1993), reading (see Mathes & Fuchs, 1994), and overall achievement (Greenwood, Terry, Utley, Montagna, & Walker, 1993). Peer tutoring offers several advantages as an instructional strategy. For example, it can increase opportunities for students to respond while giving teachers more time to facilitate and remediate responses. Thus, peer tutoring can be a cost-effective method of instruction. Furthermore, students typically receive and observe repeated practice and exposure to academic materials. The initial implementation of a peer-tutoring system can be time-consuming, however, which may limit its use. Also, although it can be relatively simple to implement, it requires a skilled teacher-facilitator.

In a well-delineated series of studies, Greenwood and colleagues (Greenwood, 1991; Greenwood, et al., 1989; Greenwood, Terry, Utley, Montagna, & Walker, 1993) provided longitudinal data on the effects of classwide peer tutoring (CWPT). A group comparison design included two at-risk, low-SES samples—a control group and an experimental CWPT group—and an index sample of nonrisk, high-SES students. Students from nine elementary schools were tracked from first to third grade (Greenwood, 1991) and to fourth grade (Greenwood et al., 1989). A standardized procedure for peer tutoring (Greenwood, Delquadri, & Carta, 1988) included (1) weekly assignment to competing teams, (2) assignment of tutor-tutee pairs within teams, (3) points earned for correct responding, (4) tutor-modeled error correction, (5) teacher-mediated point dispersal for correct tutor behavior, (6) switching of tutor-tutee roles midway through 20-minute sessions, (7) daily tabulation and public posting of points on a team chart, (8) recognition of the "winning" team through applause, and (9) teachers' curriculum-based assessments of students' performance.

Findings based on direct observations revealed significant increases in the experimental groups' use of academic materials and academic engaged time. Significant differences that favored the CWPT group over the control group were found on the Reading, Language, and Mathematics subscales of the MAT (Prescott et al., 1987). Finally, the enhanced performance shown by the CWPT group was comparable to the nonrisk index group's performance. These results were consistent with those of previous researchers (Greenwood, Dinwiddie, Terry, Wade, Stanley, Thibadeau, & Delquadri, 1984). Greenwood, Terry, Utley, Montagna, and Walker (1993) extended this work by examining academic outcomes of these students after the peer-tutoring procedure was discontinued. Of the original sample of 416 students, 303 (73%) were followed to sixth grade. In follow-up results, the CWPT group maintained higher scores on achievement tests than the control group, although the difference were less pronounced for reading and language. The CWPT group's math scores were enhanced, although the difference between the two groups was not significant. A major limitation of this study was the use of a different achievement test (Comprehensive Test of Basic Skills) (CTB/McGraw-Hill, 1995) during follow-up. It is also unfortunate that the authors did not include curriculum-based measures, nor did they provide follow-up on academic engagement.

## Group Contingencies

Interventions that use group contingencies are often acceptable (see Elliott, 1988) and successful (e.g., Chadwick & Day, 1971; Shapiro & Goldberg, 1986; Turco & Elliott, 1990) treatments for a variety of academic performance problems. In a typical group contingency program, a desired behavior is defined and a criterion for reward is based on the performance of an entire group, subgroup, or individuals. There are three major types of group contingencies (Litlow & Pumroy, 1975), each with varying strengths and limitations. *Dependent* group contingencies base the group's attainment of a reward on the performance of a target students. *Interdependent* group contingencies require the group to attain a specified criterion that is based on a measure of overall group performance (e.g., average performance). Finally, *independent* group contingencies focus on individual performance toward a specified criterion.

Group contingencies offer several advantages that facilitate their use (Gresham & Gresham, 1982). For example, because students are organized in a group, less of the teacher's time and attention are required for procedural aspects of the intervention (e.g., monitoring and charting behavior). Thus, group contingencies are implemented in a time-efficient manner, which facilitates treatment acceptability (Elliott, 1988). Furthermore, because students in dependent and interdependent group contingencies are working toward a group goal, peers may act as behavior change agents by modeling appropriate behavior and/or exerting pressure on group members to work toward specified criteria. The advantage of peer pressure can also be a major disadvantage of the technique in that a low-achieving student may be criticized by other members of the group. Another potential disadvantage may occur when group members perceive they have lost the reinforcer for a particular day and are no longer motivated to maintain academic effort. In addition, group contingencies may deemphasize individualization of instruction, which may be necessary in some specific instances.

Fantuzzo, King, and Heller (1992; see also Fantuzzo & Rohrbeck, 1992) conducted an interesting study in which an interdependent group contingency technique was incorporated with and compared to reciprocal peer tutoring (RPT). In this study, 64 fourth- and fifth-grade students were assigned randomly to four groups, each consisting of eight same-sex dyads: (1) peer tutoring plus group contingency, (2) group contingency only, (3) peer tutoring only, and (4) control group. An additional 16 students made up an inactive comparison group. Dependent measures were rate of correct math computations, teacher's ratings of classroom behavior, and students' ratings on the Self-Perception Profile for Children (Harter, 1985) of global self-worth and subscales of scholastic competency, behavioral conduct, and social acceptance. The group contingency procedure allowed students to select from a menu of rewards and to choose team goals for math performance beyond baseline levels.

Results from the dyad teams revealed a significant main effect for the rate of accurate math computations only for the reward condition, with a significant interaction for the peer-tutoring plus group contingency condition. Student dyads in the tutoring plus reward condition showed the highest rates of correct computations. Students in the two group contingency conditions received higher teacher's ratings for classroom behavior than the students in the no contingency conditions. Students in the peer-tutoring conditions reported higher perceptions of scholastic competence, behavioral conduct, and global self-worth. Finally, active participation in the intervention enhanced math performance but did not enhance perceived competencies compared to the inactive group. These results provide support for the use of group contingencies for increasing academic performance.

The researchers noted the use of aspects of self-management as integral components in the intervention (Fantuzzo & Rohrbeck, 1992). Specifically, they noted that tutoring dyads corrected each other's responses (self-observation), self-recorded the number of correct responses, self-evaluated whether the team goal was attained, and self-reinforced for goal attainment. Furthermore, the study included students' choice in selecting rewards and setting performance goals.

## Cooperative Learning

The final technique comprises a variety of related interventions, all falling under the rubric of cooperative learning. In cooperative learning, students typically work together in teams or small groups to accomplish academic tasks. In traditional classrooms, individual achievement and competition are emphasized rather than group cooperation. Competitive goal structures have been criticized for discouraging students from helping each other learn (Johnson & Johnson, 1975) and for establishing classroom situations in which lower-achieving students have little chance of success (Slavin, 1977). Cooperative learning techniques are based on the premise that cooperation is conducive to academic achievement and social development (Slavin, 1991). Reviews of research on cooperative learning (e.g., Nastasi & Clements, 1991; Slavin, 1983, 1991) indicate that it has been used effectively across (1) a variety of content areas and skill levels, including reading, language arts, mathematics, social studies, and science; (2) all school-age groups and skill levels, including college students; and (3) a variety of disabilities. Cooperative learning also appears to help students from diverse cultures (e.g., Haynes & Gebreysus, 1992).

Several cooperative learning methods are identified in the literature. Nastasi and Clements (1991) divided the various cooperative learning strategies into four categories that are focused on defining characteristics and implementation of the methods. In *team learning*, students learn and assist each other. Four major types of team learning have been developed by Slavin and colleagues (see Slavin, 1991, for an overview). In Student Teams–Achievement Divisions (STAD), the teacher presents a lesson, and teams of four or five mixed (e.g., sex, ethnicity, performance/skill level) students work to master it. Then each student is quizzed on the material. The scores each student contributes to the team are based on the degree to which the students have met or improved on their individual past performance. Teams-Games-Tournament (TGT) is similar to STAD except that instead of being quizzed, students compete in academic tournaments against others with similar performance scores. Thus, TGT emphasizes more individual competition than STAD. These two cooperative learning strategies are most appropriate for participants with well-defined objectives and single correct responses, such as math computations and science facts.

The third type of team-learning technique combines the methods used in STAD and TGT with individualized instruction. Team Assisted Indivualization (TAI) uses an individualized learning pace based on baseline performance levels. Teams check one another's work and help when difficulties arise in mastering the material. This method is designed specifically for math instruction in grades 3 through 6 or for older children who are not engaged in more advanced mathematics such as algebra. The final team-learning technique focuses on reading and writing in upper elementary grades. In Cooperative Integrated Reading and Composition (CIRC) students are assigned to teams of two pairs of students from two different reading levels. Students engage in a series of activities such as reading to one another, predicting outcomes of stories, summarizing, and decoding. During writing instruction, they engage in such activities as revising and editing members' work and preparing team writings for classroom publication.

Each of the team-learning techniques has three central components (Slavin, 1991): (1) team rewards, (2) individual accountability, and (3) equal opportunities for success. Team rewards are achieved when performance meets or exceeds a given criterion. Rewards are not competitive across teams; rather they are contingent only on a single team's performance. Individual accountability is accomplished by assessing performance on tests without help from one's teammates. Finally, there is equal opportunity for success because students contribute to their teams by improving their own past performance. Thus, team-learning techniques involve a group task structure and reward components that are akin to an interdependent group contingency.

Another set of cooperative learning techniques are *expert groups*, in which each student develops expertise in a component of a topic and teaches the material to peers. One of the earliest expert group strategies is Jigsaw (Aronson, 1978). Topics are divided into components for individual study; for example, a social studies Jigsaw activity for China may be divided into sections related to the country's culture, history, languages,

political structure, religion, economics, and so on. After students learn about or become expert in their unique components, they meet with their counterparts from other groups to discuss the information. They then return to their respective teams and teach what they have learned to their teammates. Students are tested individually, and rewards are provided according to individual performance. A related method, Jigsaw II (Slavin, 1986), uses expert groups but begins by having students read a common narrative on a topic before breaking into expert sections. Thus, students have previous exposure to all aspects of the topic before engaging in expert groups. Jigsaw II also differs from the original method by using rewards for individual *and* group performance.

In the third set of methods, the *collaborative task completion* approach, students work together on a task for which the group is rewarded on the basis of the product or performance of the group. This type of cooperative learning is exemplified by Johnson and Johnson's (1975) Learning Together model. Students work together in small groups to complete assignments that, depending on the task and level of the teacher's direction, may involve student responsibilities for task assignments and goal attainment procedures. Thus, collaborative task completion methods stress group study and group product incentives.

Nastasi and Clements (1991) referred to the final set of cooperative learning methods as *collaborative problem solving or investigation*. In these approaches, students bear the responsibility for their own learning. Sharan and Sharan (1976) developed a fairly complicated collaborative problem-solving method called Group Investigation. In this model, small groups of students take responsibility for deciding what they will learn, how they will organize themselves to learn, how they will present what they have learned, and how they will be evaluated. Because extrinsic reward is not emphasized, this method has the least in common with the other cooperative strategies. Furthermore, unlike the other cooperative strategies, collaborative problem-solving methods have not been shown to enhance basic academic performance.

The advantages of cooperative learning strategies relate to issues of social and academic engagement. Similar in many respects to peer tutoring with group contingencies, cooperative learning uses peers as instructional mediators, which gives teachers time to facilitate responses.

Peers also serve as coaches and models, which can enhance academic and social behaviors. The disadvantages are also similar to those of peer tutoring with group contingencies. First, although at first blush the strategy appears simple to implement, it requires considerable time and energy to facilitate appropriately the cooperative group process. Second, low-achieving students in heterogeneous teams may have little to contribute, which can result in negative interactions; students may feel that they are forced to compensate for their low-achieving teammate, whom they may belittle. Similarly, students who are not motivated to perform academically may choose not to engage in the group process.

Dugan, Kamps, Leonard, Watkins, Rheinberger, and Stackhaus (1995) compared the effects of cooperative learning groups and teachers' lectures on social studies performance, academic engagement, social skills, and students' interactions with two students with autism and a fourth-grade class. The cooperative learning groups occurred for 40 minutes, four times a week, across a three-week period. Each group had four or five students, with one student of high academic functioning, two peers with moderate academic skills, and one peer at a low level of functioning. The two students with autism were the low-functioning students in two of the groups. Students were assigned to a team role, that is, materials manager, recorder, checker, or organizer. All students were responsible for answering questions from the teacher at the end of each session. Reinforcement for the use of social skills (e.g., sharing ideas, encouraging, and praising) was provided through stickers that were dispensed by teachers and aides whenever they observed a social skill being used by the students. The dependent measures included weekly quizzes, academic engagement probes with the CISSAR observational system (Stanley & Greenwood, 1981), and observations of the time spent in appropriate social interactions. Results from an ABAB treatment withdrawal design indicated that the students' quiz scores increased two to four times from baseline to posttest for each treatment phase. The percentage of time in academic engagement was increased from baseline ranges of 2%–25% to treatment ranges of 72%–90%. Finally, substantial increases for all the students were seen in the duration of social interactions.

The results from the Dugan et al. (1995) study provide further evidence for the already large empirical base that supports the effectiveness of cooperative learning strategies in enhancing academic and social behaviors. As these authors posited, cooperative learning groups appear to act as instructional setting events for academic engagement and performance and peer interactions among students with and without disabilities.

## Summary

The techniques and research reviewed in this section provide evidence that academic performance can be enhanced through different avenues of intervention. These interventions, although not always explicitly described as such, focus on alterable variables over which intervention mediators can exert control. The various interventions have been used successfully to target students' motivation and engagement. One underlying component of each of these procedures is differential contingent reinforcement. Each of the methods includes some form of reinforcer, such as tangible rewards, social and/or self-praise, attention and feedback, and points for correct responding. As we concluded in the previous edition, reinforcement is probably a critical variable in any intervention for improving academic behavior.

## IMPLEMENTATION OF INTERVENTIONS

In this final section, we present a framework for conceptualizing the selection and implementation of academic performance interventions. The beginning general framework is described by the acronym DATE (define-assess-treat-evaluate), which is drawn from Gresham and Elliott's (1990) work on social skills assessment and intervention. First, behaviors are operationalized, and antecedent and consequent conditons surrounding the target behavior are defined. Second, behaviors are assessed with multiple methods, including academic assessments and observations of the instructional environment and academic engaged time. Third, treatment strategies are prescribed to fit the student's needs as determined by the assessment results and the classification that best chararacterizes the academic deficit. Fourth, the effects of the treatment are evaluated empirically with the assessment methods used to measure the target behavior.

There are several considerations to which interventionists must attend in each of these general steps. Target behaviors should be alterable and clearly defined in behavioral terms. In addition, goals for behavior improvement should be explicit and attainable. Subsequent assessment should be functionally related to target behaviors and linked to intervention. Assessment should incude teachers' and students' interviews, direct classroom observations, permanent product review, and curriculum-based assessment of academic skills.

A useful procedure for assessing the learning environment is the Instructional Environment System–II (TIES-II; Ysseldyke & Christensen, 1993), which is made up of student, teacher, and parent interviews; a supplemental instructional needs checklist; and a set of observation forms that identify components of 17 instructional and home variables for planning interventions. The instructional environment form contains 12 components that are related to academic performance: (a) instructional match, (b) teachers' expectations, (c) classroom environment, (d) instructional presentation, (e) cognitive emphasis, (f) motivational strategies, (g) relevant practice, (h) informed feedback, (i) academic engaged time, (j) adaptive instruction, (k) progress evaluation, and (l) students' understanding. Like its predecessor, TIES (Ysseldyke & Christensen, 1987), TIES-II appears to have solid psychometric properties, which, together with its strong conceptual base, make it a useful system for assessing instructional variables linked to intervention.

Another useful assessment procedure also focuses on instructional variables and academic engaged time. The Code for Instructional Structure and Student Academic Response (CISSAR; Stanley & Greenwood, 1981) is a 53-item observational system designed to measure 6 instructional categories (academic activities, nonacademic activities, tasks, structure, teachers' position, and teachers' behavior) and three categories of students' behavior (academic responding, task management behavior, and competing behaviors). The CISSAR specifically examines academic engagement in general education by focusing on opportunities to respond, a concept that incorporates antecedent-behavior relationships in the instructional process and environment. Engagement is viewed as active responding (e.g., asking questions and writing) to opportunities in the instructional environment rather than the more passive definitions of on-task behavior (e.g., listening and in seat) typified in many direct observation systems. Greenwood and colleagues have

also developed systems for assessing children with disabilities in mainstream settings, that is, MS-CISSAR (Carta, Greenwood, Schulte, Arreaga-Mayer, & Terry, 1988), and children in kindergarten and preschool, that is, Ecobehavioral System for Complex Assessments of Preschool Environments, or ESCAPE (Carta, Greenwood, & Atwater, 1985). These codes have been configured into a computer program for data collection and analysis in a system called the Ecobehavioral Assessment Systems Software, or E-Bass (Greenwood, Carta, Kamps, & Delquadri, 1993). The CISSAR and its derivatives have adequate psychometric characteristics and have demonstrated treatment validity. One issue that arises with the CISSAR is that it may be too complex for most schools.

Saudargas and Creed (1980) developed an observation code designed by school psychologists that is useful for classroom observation. The State-Event Classroom Observation System, or SECOS (Saudargas, 1992; Saudargas & Creed, 1980) measures 15 student behaviors, which are divided into states and events, and 6 teacher behaviors. A state is a behavior in which a student can engage for different lengths of time (e.g., schoolwork, and looking around), whereas an event is a discrete occurrence of behavior, such as raising a hand or calling out.

In the direct assessment of academic skills, academic behaviors that represent the responses required in a student's curriculum should be measured. Much of the current research has used standardized achievement measures to assess outcomes. Although standardized tests serve as one form of dependent variable, they often are not strongly correlated with curricula and thus lack treatment utility and validity. Other dependent variables typically used in research also warrant reconsideration. One example is academic accuracy. Although accuracy obviously is an important variable, it is a weak measure if not coupled with response rate. Consider the student who is 100% accurate on a simple, 10-problem subtraction worksheet but takes five hours to complete it. As we continue to reconceptualize academic problems, we must also refine and redefine our outcome measures.

Curriculum-based assessment (CBA) is designed to provide reliable, direct measurement of academic performance. Because CBA draws from the curriculum and uses repeated measures, it's sensitive to students' progress and can assist in deriving appropriate intervention strategies.

Thus, CBA procedures often demonstrate content and treatment validity. Several related methods of CBA have these characteristics, with differing foci (for reviews, see Shapiro, 1990; Shinn, 1989, Tindal, 1988). Fuchs and Deno (1991) classified these methods as either general outcome measurement or specific subskill mastery models. Among the former, the curriculum-based measurement (CBM) model of Deno and colleagues (e.g., Deno, 1985) has the most substantial research base. The CBM uses standardized measures to monitor progress rather than to develop interventions. In contrast, subskill mastery models are criterion-referenced and typically are based on the development of a skill hierarchy. Examples of these models are Blankenship's (1985) and Gickling's (e.g., Gickling & Havertape, 1981) models of CBA and Howell's curriculum-based evaluation, or CBE (Howell, Fox, & Morehead, 1993).

Shapiro (1990) provided a four-part integrated model of curriculum-based assessment that draws from each of the methods already described. From this integrated model, Shapiro (1996a) developed a series of interviews and an observation system to assess the instructional environment and described CBA procedures to measure a variety of academic behaviors. A unique feature of this model is that it includes interviews, direct observation, and permanent product review as the first step in assessment (Shapiro & Lentz, 1985, 1986). The observation system, Behavioral Observation of Students in Schools (B.O.S.S.) is designed to measure on-task behavior through two components that assess active and passive engaged time (Shaprio, 1996b). Although the B.O.S.S. has not yet been subjected to empirical scrutiny, it does have a solid conceptual base and is a practitioner-friendly observation system. The second step in the integrated CBA model involves assessment of rate-based skill probes to assess curriculum placement. The third step assesses instructional modication through accuracy-based skill probes. Thus, accuracy and rate of academic responding are assessed in the model. Finally, the fourth step involves progress-monitoring procedures to assess short- and long-term goals.

The next step in the DATE framework is selection and implementation of an intervention. There are several important variables to consider when selecting an intervention (see Elliott, Witt, & Kratochwill, 1991). Chief among these are treatment effectiveness, treatment acceptability, treatment integrity, and treatment generality.

Two obvious aspects of treatment selection are whether a treatment is likely to be effective and whether it has been empirically demonstrated to be effective. Although much has been written about treatment effectiveness, questions remain about such issues as potential side effects and treatment strength (Yeaton & Sechrest, 1981). Given the limited knowledge base, it appears prudent to first consider treatments that are less complicated and invasive, particularly for less severe academic difficulties. In general, treatments that are socially positive (e.g., differential reinforcement and token economy) are more acceptable than reductive or negative procedures like time-out. Furthermore, research on treatment acceptability has indicated that treatments that are less time-consuming are more acceptable, although the acceptable time tends to increase as problem severity increases (see Elliott, 1988). A particularly important rationale for determining treatment acceptability is that if consumers or treatment agents do not find a treatment acceptable, they may be resistant; therefore it is unlikely that the treatment will be implemented as intended. Thus treatment integrity is related to acceptability. Treatment integrity raises the probability of successful outcomes and provides internal validity control for evaluating the variables that influence outcomes. Gresham (1989) identified several factors that appear to be related to the integrity of treatment implementation. For example, more complex, time-consuming treatments tend to result in lower integrity; multiple treatment agents may lower integrity; and the motivation of the treatment agent is related to treatment integrity. It can be enhanced through integrity checks and reminders, clearly delineated treatment protocols, and the selection of acceptable procedures.

For treatments to be effective and valid, the level of change produced must be maintained over time and generalized to nontraining conditions. Although maintenance is often subsumed under the rubric of generalization, the two concepts are different aspects of treatment generality (Cooper, Heron, & Heward, 1987). Treatment generality is often evaluated as a passive collateral effect; however, maintenance and generalization should be explicit, systematic facets of treatment programing (Stokes & Baer, 1977). Generality programming, which should occur for both teachers' and students' behaviors, can be facilitated by targeting behaviors that will be maintained in the environment by natural reinforcement contingencies, including examples for behavioral change across settings, self-management techniques, and systematic withdrawal of intervention procedures to approximate the natural environment (Stokes & Osnes, 1989).

The final leg of the treatment journey invariably ends with the deceptively simple question, "Was the treatment effective?" Although treatment effectiveness is assessed as a matter of course, methodologically sound measurement is often overlooked in evaluation. The methods used during assessment should continue to be employed for evaluation. The particular assess-

ment methods already described are useful for measuring short- and long-term outcomes in single-case designs. Thus, progress monitoring and treatment evaluation are based on behavioral assessment and use direct observations of the outcome response, repeated curriculum-based measurements, and time-series analysis. Beyond assessing behavioral change, treatment evaluation should include the ongoing assessments of acceptability, integrity, and generality.

We conclude this section with a practical set of "think rules" as a guide to formulating academic interventions, summarized by the acronym PASSED. We suggest that interventionists think *positive* interventions that focus on increasing ap-

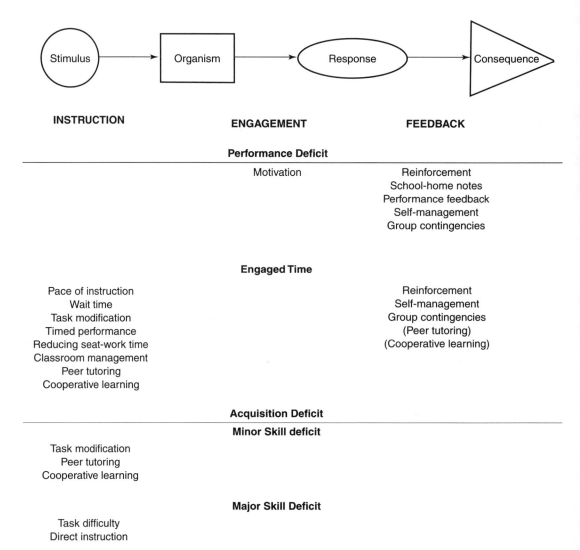

FIGURE 25.3   Hypothesized treatment impact points and selected intervention procedures for academic performance and acquisition deficits.

propriate behaviors and use socially positive procedures, *acceptable* interventions to increase social validity and enhance treatment integrity, *simple* procedures that are parsimonious and cost- and time-efficient, *strong* interventions with empirical support for effectiveness, *ecological* assessment and intervention that fit into and are linked with the natural instructional environment, and *doable* strategies that are feasible to implement.

## CONCLUSIONS

We have examined several aspects and issues related to intervention techniques for academic performance problems. We focused on the performance-based instructional model and the SORC model because they provide useful heuristics for conceptualizing alterable target behaviors and treatment impact points that can be addressed through well-founded behavioral principles (see Figure 25.3). The intervention techniques we reviewed have been shown to enhance academic performance through antecedent instructional modification and consequence-oriented behavioral interventions. The treatment selection and implementation framework was offered to provide a more comprehensive view of the multiple processes involved in effective intervention. This framework can be applied equally to direct and indirect intervention. Indeed, many performance problems can be addressed through teacher-mediated interventions, and interventions for academic performance are often delivered effectively through a consultation method. Behavioral consultation (Bergan, 1977; Bergan & Kratochwill, 1990; Kratochwill & Bergan, 1990) in particular has been shown to be an effective means for delivering interventions to remediate a variety of academic problems (Elliott & Busse, 1993), and it is often used in the delivery of instructional consultation (e.g., Rosenfield, 1987).

As research on academic intervention continues, more needs to be done to link treatment implementation to actual curricular outcomes and performance. Curriculum-based assessment and direct measures of academic engagement should be included in all academic intervention studies. As Greenwood (1996) recommended, it is fruitful to conceptualize target behaviors and the variables involved in academic performance with a concerted effort toward alterable variables. Intervention techniques such as those described in this chapter and their variants for remediating academic problems have been avail-able for many years. As our knowledge and use of valid target and outcome variables continue to evolve, our intervention procedures need to be examined within this paradigm.

## REFERENCES

Ackerman, A. M., & Shapiro, E. S. (1984). Self-monitoring and work productivity with mentally retarded adults. *Journal of Applied Behavior Analysis, 17,* 403–407.

Aronson, E. (1978). *The jigsaw classroom.* Beverly Hills, CA: Sage.

Bergan, J. R. (1977). *Behavioral consultation.* Columbus, OH: Merrill.

Bergan, J. R., & Kratochwill, T. R. (1990). *Behavioral consultation and therapy.* New York. Plenum.

Berliner, D. C. (1988). Effective classroom management and instruction: A knowledge base for consultation. In J. L. Graden, J. E. Zins, & M. J. Curtis (Eds.), *Alternative educational delivery systems: Enhancing instructional options for all students* (pp. 309–326). Washington, DC: National Association of School Psychologists.

Blankenship, C. S. (1985). Using curriculum-based assessment data to make instructional management decisions. *Exceptional Children, 42,* 233–238.

Blechman, E. A., Taylor, C. J., & Schrader, S. M. (1981). Family problem solving versus home notes as early intervention with high-risk children. *Journal of Consulting and Clinical Psychology, 49,* 919–926.

Bornstein, P. H., & Quevillon, R. P. (1976). The effects of a self-instructional package on overactive preschool boys. *Journal of Applied Behavior Analysis, 9,* 179–188.

Bourque, P., Dupuis, N., & Van Houten, R. (1986). Public posting in the classroom: Comparison of posting names and coded numbers of individual students. *Psychological Reports, 59,* 295–298.

Brophy, J. E. (1979). Teacher behavior and its effects. *Journal of Educational Psychology, 71,* 733–750.

Browder, D. M., & Shapiro, E. S. (1985). Applications of self-management to individuals with severe handicaps: A review. *Journal of the Association for Persons with Severe Handicaps, 10,* 200–208.

Carnine, D. (1976). Effects of two teacher presentation rates on off-task behavior, answering correctly, and participation. *Journal of Applied Behavior Analysis, 9,* 199–206.

Carta, J. J., Greenwood, C. R., & Atwater, J. (1985). *Ecobehavioral system for complex assessments of preschool environments (ESCAPE).* Kansas City: Juniper Gardens Children's Project, Bureau of Child Research, University of Kansas.

Carta, J. J., Greenwood, C. R., Schulte, D. Arreaga-Mayer, C., & Terry, B. (1988). *The mainstream* code for instructional structure and student academic response (MS-CISSAR). Kansas City: Juniper Gardens Children's Project, Bureau of Child Research, University of Kansas.

Cartledge, G., & Milburn, J. F. (1983). Social skill assessment and teaching in the schools. In T. R. Kratochwill (Ed.), *Advances in school psychology* (Vol. 3, pp. 175–236). Hillsdale, NJ: Erlbaum.

Centra, J. A., & Potter, D. A. (1980). School and teacher effects: An interrelation model. *Review of Education Research, 50,* 273–291.

Chadwick, B. A., & Day, R. C. (1971). Systematic reinforcement: Academic performance or underachieving students. *Journal of Applied Behavior Analysis, 4,* 311–319.

Cobb, J. A., (1972). Relationship of discrete classroom behaviors to fourth-grade academic achievement. *Journal of Educational Psychology, 63,* 74–80.

Cooper, J. O., Heron, T. E., & Heward, W. I. (1987). *Applied behavior analysis.* Columbus, OH: Merrill.

CTB/McGraw-Hill (1995). *Comprehensive Test of Basic Skill.* Palo Alto, CA: Author.

Denham, C., & Lieberman, A. (1980). *Time to learn.* Washington, DC: National Institute of Education, U.S. Department of Education.

Deno, S. L., (1985). Curriculum-based measurement: An emerging alternative. *Exceptional Children, 52,* 219–232.

Dugan, E., Kamps, D., Leonard, B., Watkins, N., Rheinberger, A., & Stackhaus, J. (1995). Effects of cooperative learning groups during social studies for students with autism and fourth-grade peers. *Journal of Applied Behavior Analysis, 28,* 175–188.

Dunlap, G., & Kern, L. (1996). Modifying instructional activities to promote desirable behavior: A conceptual and practical framework. *School Psychology Quarterly, 11,* 297–312.

Elliott, S. N. (1988). Acceptability of behavioral treatments in educational settings. In J. C. Witt, S. N. Elliott, & F. M. Gresham (Eds.), *Handbook of behavior therapy in education* (pp. 121–150). New York: Plenum.

Elliott, S. N., & Busse, R. T. (1993). Effective treatments with behavioral consultation. In J. E. Zins, T. R. Kratochwill, & S. N. Elliott (Eds.), *Handbook of consultation services for children* (pp. 179–203). San Francisco: Jossey Bass.

Elliott, S. N., Witt, J. C., & Kratochwill, T. R. (1991). Selecting, implementing, and evaluating classroom interventions. In. G. Stoner, M. R. Shinn, & H. M. Walker (Eds.), *Interventions for achievement and behavior problems* (pp. 99–135). Silver Spring, MD: National Association of School Psychologists.

Fantuzzo, J. W., King, J. A., & Heller, L. R. (1992). Effects of reciprocal peer tutoring on mathematics and school adjustment: A component analysis. *Journal of Educational Psychology, 84,* 331–339.

Fantuzzo, J. W., & Rohrbeck, C. A. (1992). Self-managed groups: Fitting self-management approaches into classroom systems. *School Psychology Review, 21,* 255–263.

Forgatch, M. S., & Ramsey, E. (1994). Boosting homework: A videotape link between families and schools. *School Psychology Review, 23,* 472–484.

Fox, D. E. C., & Kendall, P. C. (1983). Thinking through academic problems: Applications of cognitive behavior therapy to learning. In T. R. Kratochwill (Ed.), *Advances in school psychology* (Vol. 3, pp. 269–301). Hillsdale, NJ: Erlbaum.

Fuchs, L. S., & Deno, S. L. (1991). Paradigmatic distinctions between instructionally relevant measurement models. *Exceptional Children, 57,* 488–500.

Fuchs, L. S., Fuchs, D., Phillips, N. B., Hamlett, C. L., & Karns, K. (1995).Acquisition and transfer effects of classwide peer-assisted learning strategies in mathematics for students with varying learning histories. *School Psychology Review, 24,* 604–620.

Gersten, R., Becker, W. C., Heiry, T. J., & White, W. A. (1984). Entry IQ and yearly academic growth of children in direct instruction programs: A longitudinal study of low SES children. *Educational Evaluation and Policy Analysis, 6,* 109–121.

Gersten, R. Keating, T., & Becker, W. C. (1988). The continued impact of the direct instruction model: Longitudinal studies of follow through students. *Education and Treatment of Children, 11,* 318–327.

Gettinger, M. (1988). Methods of proactive classroom management. *School Psychology Review, 17,* 227–242.

Gettinger, M. (1995). Best practices for increasing academic learning time. In A. Thomas & J. Grimes (Eds.), *Best practices in school psychology–III* (pp. 943–954). Washington, DC: National Association of School Psychologists.

Gickling, E., & Havertape, J. (1981). *Curriculum-based assessment.* Minneapolis, MN: National School Psychology Inservice Training Network.

Greenwood, C. R. (1991). Longitudinal analysis of time, engagement, and achievement in at-risk versus non-risk students. *Exceptional Children, 57,* 521–535.

Greenwood, C. R. (1996). The case for performance-based instructional models. *School Psychology Quarterly, 11,* 283–296.

Greenwood, C. R., Arreaga-Mayer, C., & Carta, J. J. (1994). Identification and translation of effective, teacher-developed instructional procedures for general practice. *Remedial and Special Education, 15*(3), 140–151.

Greenwood, C. R., Carta, J. J., Hart, B., Kamps, D., Terry, B., Arreaga-Mayer, C., Atwater, J., Walker, D., Risley, T., & Delquadri, J. (1992). Out of the laboratory and into the community: 26 years of applied behavior analysis at the Juniper Gardens Children's Project. *American Psychologists, 47,* 1464–1474.

Greenwood, C. R., Carta, J. J., Kamps, D., & Delquadri, J. (1993). *Ecobehavioral assessment systems software (EBASS): Observational instrumentation for school psychologists.* Kansas City: Juniper Gardens Children's Project, University of Kansas.

Greenwood, C. R., & Delquadri, J. C. (1995). Class Wide Peer Tutoring and the prevention of school failure. *Preventing School Failure, 39*(4), 21–25.

Greenwood, C. R., Delquadri, J. C., & Carta, J. J. (1988). *Class Wide Peer Tutoring (CWPT): Programs for spelling, math, and reading* (Training manual). Delray Beach, FL: Educational Achievement Systems.

Greenwood, C. R., Delquadri, J. C., & Hall, R. V. (1984). Opportunity to respond and student academic performance. In W. L. Heward, T. E. Heron, J. Trap-Porter, & D. S. Hill (Eds.), *Focus on behavior analysis in education* (pp. 55–88). Columbus, OH: Merrill.

Greenwood, C.R., Delquadri, J. C., & Hall, R. V. (1989). Longitudinal effects of classwide peer tutoring. *Journal of Educational Psychology, 81,* 371–383.

Greenwood, C. R., Dinwiddie, G., Terry, B., Wade, L., Stanley, S. O., Thibadeau, S., & Delquadri, J. C. (1984). Teacher versus peer-mediated instruction: An ecobehavioral analysis of achievement outcomes. *Journal of Applied Behavior Analysis, 17,* 521–538.

Greenwood, C. R., Terry, B. Marquis, J., & Walker, D. (1994). Confirming a performance-based instructional model. *School Psychology Review, 23,* 652–668.

Greenwood, C. R.,Terry, B., Utley, C. A., Montagna, D., & Walker, D. (1993). Achievement, placement, and services: Middle school benefits of Classwide Peer Tutoring used at the elementary school. *School Psychology Review, 22,* 497–516.

Gresham, F. M. (1989). Assessment of treatment integrity in school consultation and prereferral intervention. *School Psychology Review, 18,* 37–50.

Gresham, F. M., & Elliott, S. N. (1990). *Social Skills Rating System.* Circle Pines, MN: American Guidance Service.

Gresham, F. M., & Gresham, G. N. (1982). Interdependent, dependent, and independent group contingencies for controlling disruptive behavior. *Journal of Special Education, 16,* 101–110.

Guess, D., Benson, H. S., & Siegel-Causey, E. (1985). Concepts and issues related to choice-making and autonomy among persons with severe disabilities. *Journal of the Association for Persons with Severe Handicaps, 10,* 79–86.

Hallahan, D., Lloyd, J., Kosiewicz, M., Kauffman, J., & Graves, A. (1979). Self-monitoring of attention as a treatment for a learning disabled boys' off task behavior. *Learning Disability Quarterly, 2,* 24–32.

Harter, S. (1985). *Manual for the Self-perception Profile for Children.* Denver, CO: University of Denver.

Hawryluk, M. K., & Smallwood, D. L. (1988). Using peers as instructional agents: Peer tutoring and cooperative learning. In J. L. Graden, J. E. Zins, & M. J. Curtis (Eds.), *Alternative educational delivery systems: Enhancing instructional options for all students* (pp. 371–389). Washington, DC: National Association of School Psychologists.

Haynes, N. M., & Gebreyesus, S. (1992). Cooperative learning: A case for African-American students. *School Psychology Review, 21,* 577–585.

Heler, L. R.,& Fantuzzo, J. W. (1993). Reciprocal peer tutoring and parent partnership: Does parent involvement make a difference? *School Psychology Review, 22,* 517–534.

Hoge, R. D. (1985). The validity of direct observation measures of pupil classroom behavior. *Review of Educational Research, 55,* 469–483.

Hoge, R. D., & Andrews, D. A. (1987). Enhancing academic performance: Issues in target selection. *School Psychology Review, 16,* 228–238.

Holman, J., & Baer, D. M. (1979). Facilitating generalization of on-task behavior through self-monitoring of academic tasks. *Journal of Autism and Development Disabilities, 9,* 429–446.

Horner, R. H., Sprague, J. R., & Flannery, B. (1993). Building functional curricula for students with severe intellectual disabilities and severe behavior problems. In R. Nan Houten & S. Axelrod (Eds.), *Effective behavioral treatment: Issues and implementation* (pp. 47–71). New York: Plenum.

Howell, K. W., Fox, D. L., & Morehead, M. K. (1993). *Curriculum-based evaluation: Teaching and decision making* (2nd ed.). Pacific Grove, CA: Brooks/Cole.

Hughes, C. A., & Hendrickson, J. M. (1987). Self-monitoring with at-risk students in the regular class setting. *Education and Treatment of Children, 10,* 236–250.

Johnson, D. W., & Johnson, R. T. (1975). *Learning together and alone.* Englewood Cliffs, NJ: Prentice Hall.

Johnston, M. B., Whitman, T. L., & Johnson, M. (1980). Teaching addition and subtraction to mentally retarded children: A self-instructional program. *Applied Research in Mental Retardation, 1,* 141–160.

Kane, C. M. (1994). *Prisoners of time: Research.* Report of the National Education Commission on Time and Learning. Washington, DC: U. S. Government Printing Office.

Kanfer, F. H. (1971). The maintenance of behavior by self-generated stimuli and reinforcement. In A. Jacobs & L. B. Sachs (Eds.), *The psychology of private events* (pp. 39–58). New York: Academic Press.

Kanfer, F., & Goldstein, A. P. (Eds.). (1986). *Helping people change: A textbook of methods.* New York: Pergamon.

Karraker, R. J. (1972). Increasing academic performance through home-managed contingency programs. *Journal of School Psychology, 10,* 173–179.

Kastelen, L., Nickel, M., & McLaughlin, T. F. (1984). A performance feedback system: Generalization of effects across tasks and time with eighth-grade English students. *Education and Treatment of Children, 7,* 141–155.

Kelley, M. L. (1990). *School-home notes: Promoting children's classroom success.* New York: Guilford.

Kratochwill, T. R.,& Bergan, J. R. (1990). *Behavioral consultation in applied settings: An individual guide.* New York: Plenum.

Lam, A., Cole, C. L., Shapiro, E. S., & Bambara, L. M. (1994). Relative effects of self-monitoring on-task behavior, academic accuracy, and disruptive behavior in students with behavior disorders. *School Psychology Review, 23,* 44–58.

Litlow, L., & Pumroy, D. K. (1975). A brief review of classroom group-orientated contingencies. *Journal of Applied Behavior Analysis, 8,* 341–347.

Lloyd, J. W., Bateman, D. F., Landrum, T. J., & Hallahan, D. P. (1989). Self-monitoring of attention versus productivity. *Journal of Applied Behavior Analysis, 22,* 315–323.

Mathes, P. G., & Fuchs, L. S. (1994). The efficacy of peer tutoring in reading for students with mild disabilities: A best-evidence synthesis. *School Psychology Review, 23,* 59–80.

Meichenbaum, D., & Goodman, J. (1971). Training impulsive children to talk to themselves: A means of developing self-control. *Journal of Abnormal Psychology, 77,* 115–126.

Munk, D. D., & Repp, A. C. (1994). The relationship between instructional variables and problem behavior: A review. *Exceptional Children, 60,* 390–401.

Nastasi, B. K., & Clements, D. H. (1991). Research on cooperative learning: Implications for practice. *School Psychology Review, 20,* 110–131.

Nelson, R. O. (1977). Assessment and therapeutic functions of self-monitoring. In M. Hersen, R. M. Eisler, & P. M. Miller (Eds.), *Progress in behavior modification* (Vol. 5, pp. 263–308). New York: Academic Press.

Piersel, W. C., & Kratochwill, T. R. (1979). Self-observation and behavior change: Applications to academic and adjustment problems through behavioral consultation. *Journal of School Psychology, 17,* 151–161.

Prater, M. A., Hogan, S., & Miller, S. R. (1992). Using self-monitoring to improve on-task behavior and academic skills of an adolescent with mild handicaps across special and regular education settings. *Education and Treatment of Children, 15,* 43–55.

Prescott, G. A., Balow, I. H., Hogan, T. P., & Farr, R. C. (1987). *Metropolitan Achievement Tests.* San Antonio, TX: Psychological Corp.

Reid, R., & Harris, K. R. (1993). Self-monitoring of attention versus self-monitoring of performance: Effects on attention and academic performance. *Exceptional Children, 60,* 29–40.

Reynolds, A.J., & Walberg, H. J. (1991). A structural model of science achievement. *Journal of Educational Psychology, 83,* 97–107.

Roberts, R. N., & Dick, M. L. (1982). Self-control in the classroom: Theoretical issues and practical applications. In T. R. Kratochwill (Ed.), *Advances in school psychology* (Vol. 2, pp. 275–314). Hillsdale, NJ: Erlbaum.

Roberts, R. N., Nelson, R. O., & Olsen, T. W. (1987). Self-instruction: An analysis of the differential effects of instruction and reinforcement. *Journal of Applied Behavior Analysis, 20,* 235–242.

Rosenfield, S. A. (1987). *Instructional consultation.* Hillsdale, NJ: Erlbaum.

Saudargas, R. A. (1992). *State-Event Classroom Observation System (SECOS).* Knoxville: Department of Psychology, University of Tennessee.

Saudargas, R. A., & Creed, V. (1980). *State-Event Classroom Observation System.* Knoxville: Department of Psychology, University of Tennessee.

Schumaker, J. B., Hovell, M. F., & Sherman, J. A. (1977). An analysis of daily report cards and parent-managed privileges in the improvement of adolescents' classroom performance. *Journal of Applied Behavior Analysis, 10,* 449–464.

Shaprio, E. S., (1990). An integrated model for curriculum-based assessment. *School Psychology Review, 19,* 331–349.

Shapiro, E. S. (1996a). *Academic skills problems: Direct assessment and intervention* (2nd ed.). New York: Guilford.

Shapiro, E. S. (1996b). *Workbook for academic skills problems.* New York: Guilford.

Shapiro, E. S., & Cole, C. L. (1994). *Behavior change in the classroom: Self-management interventions.* New York: Guilford.

Shapiro, E. S., & Goldberg, R. (1986). A comparison of group contingencies in increased spelling performances among sixth grade students. *School Psychology Review, 15,* 546–559.

Shapiro, E. S., & Lentz, F. E. (1985). Assessing academic behavior: A behavioral approach. *School Psychology Review, 14,* 325–338.

Shapiro, E. S., & Lentz, F. E. (1986). Behavioral assessment of academic behavior. In T. R. Kratochwill (Ed.), *Advances in school psychology* (Vol. 5, pp. 87–139). Hillsdale, NJ: Erlbaum.

Sharan, S., & Sharan, Y. (1976). *Small-group teaching.* Englewood Cliffs, NJ: Educational Technology.

Sheridan, S. M., Kratochwill, T. R., & Elliott, S. N.

(1990). Behavioral consultation with parents and teachers: Delivering treatment for socially withdrawn children at home and school. *School Psychology Review, 19*, 33–52.

Shinn, M. R. (Ed.). (1989). *Curriculum-based measurement: Assessing special children.* New York: Guilford.

Skinner, B. F. (1968). *The technology of teaching.* New York: Meredith.

Skinner, C. H., Fletcher, P. A., & Henington, C. (1996). Increasing learning rates by increasing student response rates: A summary of research. *School Psychology Quarterly, 11*, 326–336.

Slavin, R. E. (1977). Classroom reward structure: An analytic and practical review. *Review of Educational Research, 47*, 633–650.

Slavin, R. E. (1983). Team-assisted individualization: A cooperative learning solution for adaptive instruction in mathematics. In M. C. Wang & H. J. Walberg (Eds.), *Adapting instruction to individual differences* (pp. 236–253). Berkeley, CA: McCutchan.

Slavin, R E. (1986). Cooperative learning: Engineering social psychology in the classroom. In R. S. Feldman (Ed.), *The social psychology of education: Current research and theory* (pp. 153–171). Cambridge, MA: Cambridge Press.

Slavin, R. E. (1991). Synthesis of research on cooperative learning. *Educational Leadership, 49*, 71–77.

Stanley, S. O., & Greenwood, C. R. (1981). *Code for instructional structure and student academic response: CISSAR.* Kansas City: Juniper Garden's Children's Project, Bureau of Child Research, University of Kansas.

Stokes, T. F., & Baer, D. M. (1977). An implicit technology of generalization. *Journal of Applied Behavior Analysis, 10*, 349–367.

Stokes, T. F., & Osnes, P. (1989). An operant pursuit of generalization. *Behavior Therapy, 20*, 337–355.

Tindal, G. (1988). Curriculum-based measurement. In J. L. Graden, J. E. Zins, & M. J. Curtis (Eds.), *Alternative educational delivery systems: Enhancing instructional options for all students* (pp. 111–135). Washington, DC: National Association of School Psychologists.

Turco, T. L., & Elliott, S. N. (1990). Acceptability and effectiveness of group contingencies for improving spelling achievement. *Journal of School Psychology, 28*, 27–37.

Van Houten, R., Hill, S., & Parson, M. (1975). An analysis of a performance feedback system: The effects of timing and feedback, public posting, and praise upon academic performance and peer interaction. *Journal of Applied Behavior Analysis, 8*, 449–457.

Van Houten, R., & Lai Fatt, D. (1981). The effects of public posting on high school biology test performance. *Education and Treatment of Children, 4*, 217–226.

Van Houten, R., Thompson, C. (1976). The effects of explicit timing on math performance. *Journal of Applied Behavior Analysis, 9*, 227–230.

Walker, D., Greenwood, C. R., Hart, B., & Carta, J. J. (1994). Improving the prediction of early school academic outcomes using socioeconomic status and early language production. *Child Development, 65*, 606–621.

West, R. P., & Sloan, H. N. (1986). Teacher presentation rate and point delivery rate. *Behavior Modification, 10*, 267–286.

Whitman, T., & Johnston, M. B. (1983). Teaching addition and subtraction with regrouping to educable mentally retarded children: A group self-instructional training program. *Behavior Therapy, 14*, 127–143.

Witt, J. C., Elliott, S. N. (1983). Assessment in behavioral consultation: The initial interview. *School Psychology Review, 12*, 42–49.

Witt, J. C., Elliott, S. N., Daly, E., Gresham, F. M., & Kramer, J. (1998). *Assessing special children.* Boston: McGraw-Hill.

Yeaton, W. H., & Sechrest, L. (1981). Critical dimensions in the choice and maintenance of successful treatments. Strength, integrity, and effectiveness. *Journal of Consulting and Clinical Psychology, 49*, 156–167.

Ysseldyke, J. E., & Christenson, S. (1987). *The Instructional Environment Scale.* Austin, TX: Pro-Ed.

Ysseldyke, J. E., & Christenson, S. (1993). *TIES-II, The Instructional Environment System II.* Longmont, CO: Sopris West.

## CHAPTER 26

# SOCIAL SKILLS IN CONTEXT: CONSIDERATIONS FOR ASSESSMENT, INTERVENTION, AND GENERALIZATION

**SUSAN M. SHERIDAN**
*University of Nebraska–Lincoln*
**DORLENE WALKER**
*University of Utah*

*Can social competence be defined merely in the scientific tradition of breaking it down atomistically into smaller and smaller subunits, or is something lost when the whole is broken into parts?*

*Haring (1992, p. 307)*

The ability to interact effectively with others in social relationships is among the most important tasks an individual must master. When interacting with others, children have opportunities to learn basic foundations for successful functioning as adults, such as cooperation, compromising, making decisions, and solving problems. Prosocial behaviors like sharing, communicating, and helping are often modeled and imitated in peer groups. Social play can enhance the development of abstract concepts such as reciprocity, rule formation, and divergent thinking (Hops & Greenwood, 1988). For many students, behaviors that are considered socially skillful are learned easily and early in the normal course of development. For others, direct efforts are required to help them establish skills and behaviors that will promote effective social relationships across various environments.

In this chapter, we (1) provide a conceptual overview and contextualized definition of social skills and social skillfulness; (2) discuss a broad-based, ecological approach to assessing social skills; (3) review various social skills interventions; and (4) explore issues surrounding social skills generalization from a ecological-contextual perspective. Of primary importance is the consideration of social skills within an ecological framework. As such, specific behaviors in a child's repertoire are important prerequisites to social competence and skillfulness. Beyond these behaviors, however, are the significant others with whom the child interacts and the situations or contexts within which the behaviors must be performed. The reciprocal interaction among the child, others, and settings are all considered central in our conceptualization of skillful social behaviors and their assessment, intervention, and generalization.

## TRADITIONAL CONCEPTIONS OF SOCIAL SKILLS

The term *social skills* has been defined in numerous ways. Typically, a distinction is made between social skills and social competence. *Social skills*, on the one hand, are discrete, learned behaviors exhibited by an individual for the purpose of performing a task. For example, if a child wants to play with another, he or she may use the skill of "asking to play." The behavior is observable, measurable, and concrete.

A difficulty with traditional conceptions of social skills is that they are often considered outside of the context in which they must be performed. In other words, defining social skills in terms of discrete behaviors that are performed by a child precludes consideration of the appropriateness of those behaviors in a given situation, their meaningfulness to the child and others, and the reciprocal nature of social interactions. The primary consideration in assessing and treating social skills in this manner is the child per se. Skills are assessed as discrete behaviors (often in terms of prerequisite subskills), identified as deficient in the absence of important components, and trained through a series of steps in contrived settings (i.e., outside of the criterion setting). Social behaviors, however, do not occur in a vacuum. By definition, they occur in an interactive relationship that subsumes interpersonal and environmental considerations; that is, they occur in relation to a particular setting, as well as to others in the setting. Therefore, behaviors that are appropriate and reinforced in some relationships (both person-person and person-environment relationships) are not necessarily the same as those that are appropriate and reinforced in others.

*Social competence*, on the other hand, is concerned primarily with the evaluative judgments of others (Gresham, 1986). It is typically conceptualized in terms of the opinions of others as recipients of social overtures made by students. Rather than emphasizing discrete social behaviors, social competence often focuses on the impact of those behaviors on others. Social competence is typically determined by the opinions of significant others with whom a student interacts, by comparisons to explicit criteria of skillfulness, or by comparisons to others (Gresham, 1986). Thus, it is usually defined by using standards of social validity (i.e., the degree to which the social behavior is meaningful to the child in a particular context).

We believe that social skillfulness is best conceptualized as a combination of traditional conceptions of social skills and social competence. Neither alone fully explains the development and demonstration of social behaviors. In our framework of social skillfulness, children must master at least two interrelated tasks. First, they must learn a range of important social skills that will be necessary in a variety of situations. In other words, they must "master" social behaviors that will be necessary and useful as they interact with others. Second, they must learn to relate in a way that is acceptable to others in a range of social situations. The effectiveness with which they are able to use learned behaviors in acceptable ways depends in large part on the context which the interaction oc-

curs and their understanding of it. To be effective socially, children must be aware of reciprocity in relationships and interactions, including the impact their behaviors have on others and the ability to take the perspective of another person. They must be able to read social situations, have a range of alternative social responses, know what is appropriate in a particular situation, and respond in a way that others find acceptable. They must have in their behavioral repertoire skills that allow them to discriminate and generalize from one social situation to another.

# DEFINITION OF SOCIAL SKILLS IN CONTEXT

With these considerations in mind, we offer a definition of social skills that encompasses intrapersonal, interpersonal, and ecological considerations. Specifically, we define social skills as *goal-directed, learned behaviors that allow one to interact and function effectively in a variety of social contexts*. Central to this definition is the notion that the behaviors are goal-directed, learned, interactive, functional, and context-specific.

First, we believe that social skills begin as cognitive events internal to the child, who has in mind specific desired outcomes (i.e., goals). Thus, social skills are seen as purposeful behaviors driven by desired outcomes that a child has for his or her behaviors. The goals can be relational (e.g., "I want to play hopscotch with the other kids") or needs-driven (e.g., "I need help completing this assignment"), and they are mediated by a child's language abilities and developmental levels. Children of differing language and developmental levels have varying capacities to articulate personal goals they have for their actions.

Second, and consistent with many definitions, we believe that the behaviors that constitute social skills are learned. An important mechanism for learning is through observation and imitation of others (Bandura, 1977). The child is surrounded by opportunities to learn from the social behaviors of adults and peers in a variety of situations. For learning to occur, however, individuals must recognize and attend to salient cues that determine social efficacy. Difficulties in learning arise when events or factors interfere with the attention that is necessary for observation and imitation to occur, for example, impulsivity and distractibility (Gresham & Elliott, 1984). Also, children who are not engaged in social interactions in a regular or meaningful way (e.g., withdrawn or rejected children) may miss out on opportunities to learn important behaviors from others. Direct instruction can facilitate the acquisition of important social behaviors, but these behaviors cannot be considered in isolation of the cognitive events that precede behavioral execution, the others in the social interaction, or the ecological context (i.e., environment and situation) in which the behavior is exhibited.

A third consideration central to our definition of social skills is that they are interactive in nature. That is, they do not occur in a vacuum but rather in a bidirectional, reciprocal human relationship. Thus, social skillfulness requires one to engage in various social-cognitive actions, such as perspective taking (Selman, 1980) or compromising. Furthermore, the effect that social behaviors have on others is of importance in skillful social behavior. The notion of social validity is central to this discussion. Specifically, it might be considered that social behaviors are appropriate only if the criterion group perceives them to be. These perceptions are affected by the functional utility of prosocial behaviors in one's repertoire. Because no one individual can predict with certainty the behaviors of others in any social interaction, a range of alternative functional responses that can be used in social interactions is necessary for social skillfulness.

Finally, the ecological setting in which the behaviors occur must be considered in the determination of social skillfulness. To be socially skilled, a child must selectively choose behaviors that are appropriate in a particular context. For example, play behaviors (including physical activity and voice tone) that are appropriate for a game of flag football in the park are quite different than those for a game of checkers in the classroom. Also, context-specific behaviors encompass characteristics of the setting and variables related to the task at hand (e.g., nature of the task and goals for interaction), as well as rules in force and behavioral norms in different situations.

In summary, we view social skillfulness in an ecological-behavioral paradigm. Thus, skillful social behavior is a function of the interaction among a child (including cognitive events and discrete behaviors), others (including their perceptions of a child's social behaviors and their own responses in a social situation), and the context (setting or situation) in which a behavior occurs. A conceptual framework is presented in Figure 26.1. As can be seen in the figure, social

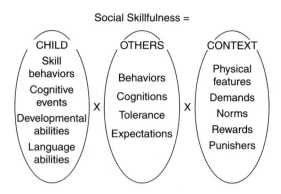

**FIGURE 26.1  Conceptual schemata representing social skillfulness as the interaction of three variables (child, others, and context) and examples of components of each variable.**

skillfulness is a function of the interaction of the child with others in a certain context.

Characteristics of the *child* include his or her specific behaviors (including topographical features), cognitive events (such as goals, attributions, interpretations, perspective taking, and social information-processing skills[1]), and developmental abilities (including language development). *Others* include those with whom a person interacts in a social situation. This may include a child's peer group, immediate and extended family members, teachers, and additional significant adults and children. Behaviors (e.g., initiations and responses), cognitions (e.g., perceptions, beliefs, and attitudes), and tolerance levels are among the characteristics of others that are important to consider. *Contextual* characteristics include features of the physical setting in which the social behaviors occur (e.g., place, space, arrangement, and equipment), demands of the criterion environment (e.g., rules and behavioral

---

[1]Research by Dodge and his colleagues has demonstrated that aggressive children have specific deficits in the way that they process social cues in ambiguous and challenging situations, in their ability to generate and evaluate responses to these situations, and in their enactment of effective solutions (Dodge, 1980; Dodge & Coie, 1987; Dodge, Coie, & Brakke, 1982; Dodge, Coie, Pettit, & Price, 1990; Dodge & Frame, 1982; Dodge, Pettit, McClaskey, & Brown, 1986). A complete review of the cognitive and information-processing deficits of children with specific social difficulties is beyond the scope of this chapter. Interested readers are referred to Pepler and Rubin (1991) for a comprehensive account.

expectations), and rewards and punishers for certain actions.

In the following pages, we discuss assessment, intervention, and generalization of social skills. In each of these discussions, we present techniques and procedures that address the three relevant dimensions of our schematic conceptualization: child, other, and context. Consideration of each dimension separately and in relation to one another is important in understanding and treating social problems in children and adolescents.

# ECOLOGICAL ASSESSMENT OF SOCIAL SKILLS

Traditionally, social skills assessment was considered to have two functions: identification of general and specific social difficulties and evaluation of treatment outcomes. Extending this traditional approach to an ecological-contextual perspective, we believe that a functional approach to assessment is central. An assessment approach is considered functionally useful (i.e., has functional utility) to the extent that (1) accurately identifies general and specific social difficulties that are important in a meaningful social context, (2) leads to effective social interventions, and (3) measures outcomes in terms of their meaningfulness to the individual in relevant social situations.

Central to this assessment approach is consideration of social behaviors and their interrelationships in the social environment. It follows, then, that a standard procedure for assessment is not generally recognized (Gresham & Reschly, 1988). A multisource, multisetting, multimethod model is recognized as "best practice" (Gresham, 1995), and is implicit in a contextual social skills definition. Subsequently we discuss assessment methods within an ecological framework of child, other, and context variables. It should be noted that some overlap exists across these domains, and they are presented in this manner primarily for heuristic purposes.

## Assessment of Child Variables

From an ecological/contextual perspective, a number of characteristics (e.g., behavioral skill level, cognitive events, language abilities, developmental status, gender, age, and culture) interact to define the child in a social context. Although all of these characteristics will not be included in social skills assessments, it is imperative that practitioners and researchers consider

their influence when conceptualizing a child's effectiveness in a social arena.

The identification and definition of specific and observable social behaviors or skills provide the basis of individual social skills assessment. Informant reports (e.g., rating scales), self-reports, skill-based direct or analogue observations, and child interviews are methods for assessing the child's social skillfulness. Assessment also considers whether the child is lacking the critical information or behavioral ability to apply a particular skill (skill deficit) or simply does not successfully render the skill in appropriate contexts or with sufficient frequency (performance deficit).

## Informant reports

Informant reports (e.g., rating scales and behavioral checklists) are most frequently used for identification and classification. They provide estimates of the frequency of behaviors, appraisals of skills or performance deficits, and indications of problem areas to investigate when gathering information by interviews or direct observations. Rating scales can also give normative information, thus providing a general developmental perspective. Sources for rating scales are typically teachers or parents. Several rating scales are briefly reviewed here, but interested readers are referred to Demaray et al. (1995) for more extensive coverage.

The Social Skills Rating Systems (SSRS; Gresham & Elliott, 1990) is a multisource rating scale that requests information on both the frequency and importance of important prosocial behaviors. Separate forms are available for parents, teachers, and students at the preschool, elementary, and secondary school levels. The SSRS-Parent Form is a 70-item questionnaire designed to measure the behavior of children and adolescents in two broad areas: social skills and problem behaviors. Factor analysis of the SSRS-P Social Skills Scale revealed four factors: cooperation, assertion, responsibility, and self-control. The SSRS-Teacher Form is a 57-item questionnaire designed to measure the behavior of children in three broad areas: social skills, problem behaviors, and academic competence. Factor analysis of the SSRS-T Social Skills Scale revealed three factors: cooperation, assertion, and self-control. The Problem Behavior Scale of both the Parent and Teacher Forms comprises three factors: externalizing, internalizing, and hyperactivity. Overall SSRS results are reported as standard scores with a mean of 100 and a standard deviation (SD) of 15. Psychometric properties such as test-retest reliability, internal consistency, and validity are well supported (Gresham & Elliott, 1990). An advantage of the SSRS is the degree of specificity it provides in identifying skills. With this system, links to interventions are readily created (Elliott & Gresham, 1992).

The Walker-McConnell Scale of Social Competence and School Adjustment (WMS; Walker & McConnell, 1988) is a five-point, 43-item checklist, designed to assess teacher's perceptions of students' social competence. The WMS provides the examiner with the ability to discriminate between teachers' preferred social behaviors, such as cooperation, consideration for others, acceptance of constructive criticism, and peer-preferred social behaviors, such as flexibility in activities, compromising, and maintaining interactions. Standard scores are available for the total scale (mean = 100; SD = 15) and the three subscales (mean = 10; SD = 3). The WMS was standardized on 1,812 children from four major U.S. census zones. Factor analysis indicates three scales that measure school adjustment, peer-preferred social behavior, and teacher-preferred social behavior. Children's and adolescent versions of this scale are available, and the adolescent version includes an additional empathy subscale (Walker, Stieber, & Eisert, 1991). There is good evidence for the reliability of both versions of this measure, and concurrent and construct validity are established. The scale provides a simple and reliable measure of social competence (Demaray et al., 1995).

The School Social Behavior Scales (SSBS; Merrell, 1993) is a 65-item rating scale assessing perceptions of students' social skills (grades K–12) from teachers or other school personnel. The scale was standardized on 1,858 children, primarily form the western United States. Two major scales make up the instrument: social competence (Scale A) and antisocial behavior (Scale B), each with three subscales (interpersonal skills, self-management, and academic skills on Scale A; hostile-irritable, antisocial-aggressive, and disruptive-demanding on Scale B). Each item is rated on a five-point Likert scale. Total SSBS scores are reported as standard scores with a mean of 100 and SD of 15. The SSBS manual reports evidence of internal consistency, test-retest, and interrater reliability. Evidence of content, criterion-related, construct, and factorial validity is also presented (Merrell, 1993). The scale appears to be a useful measure of social competence and antisocial behavior in schools (Demaray et al., 1995).

The Social Behavior Assessment Inventory (SBAI; T. M. Stephens, 1981; Stephens & Arnold, 1992) provides a list of 135 social skills and asks the teacher to rate the identified child on a three-point scale (acceptable level, less than acceptable level, or never). Four domains of behavior can be identified from these items—interpersonal, environmental, task-related, and self-related behaviors. Psychometric properties of reliability and validity have been shown to be satisfactory; however, the SBAI lacks group norms (i.e., it is a criterion-referenced rather than a norm-referenced scale) so comparisons with other children cannot be obtained. The primary uses of the SBAI are to measure discrepancies between observed and expected behaviors and to select target behaviors for individual training.

The Taxonomy of Problematic Social Situations for Children (TOPS; (Dodge, McClaskey, & Feldman, 1985) is a rating scale that can be used by teachers or clinicians to identify the situations and tasks most likely to present social difficulties for a child. The utility of this instrument is the information it provides in describing the contexts of social difficulties and the factors that influence a child's response. Forty-four situations are presented. The adult is asked to respond on a five-point Likert scale, indicating how much of a problem each situation might pose for the identified child. The following factors can be identified across situations: (1) peer group entry, (2) response to provocation, (3) response to failure, (4) response to success, (5) social expectations, and (6) teachers' expectations. Total and factor scores have been shown to be stable, with high internal consistency. Item and factor replicability and convergent validity are well established.

## Self-reports

Self-reports provide unique information about the child's subjective interpretations of social status or skill level. They are best used to assess important cognitive events, such as a child's thoughts and opinions about her or his social behaviors and relationships. It should be recognized that self-reports are inherently subjective, lack criterion-related validity, and fail to predict performance on other measures, such as teachers' and parents' rating scales, sociometrics measures, or direct observations of actual social behavior. Therefore, self-report measures are not recommended as selection or outcome measures (Gesham, 1986).

The Social Skills Rating System–Self Report (SSRS-S; Gresham & Elliott, 1990) is a standardized measure of a child's self-perceptions of social skills. The SSRS-S contains 34 items that assess four factors: cooperation, assertion, empathy, and self-control. As with the other SSRS scales, this instrument has a mean of 100 and SD of 15. The information provided on the SSRS-S allows normative comparisons; however clear indexes for the development of interventions cannot be inferred from the information gained in a self-report. Also, self-report measures do not predict performance on parents' or teachers' rating scales, sociometric placement, or even actual behavior (Gresham, 1986). Thus self-reports should not be used as selection or outcome measures because of a lack of criterion-related validity and the variability of subjective responses; their chief utility lies in obtaining self-perceptions of social behaviors.

## Skill-based Direct Observations

Direct observations of children's social behavior are key in understanding peer relationships; they provide information about the frequency of interactions with other children, as well as the range of behaviors in the child's repertoire. La Greca and Stark (1986) provide an excellent overview of naturalistic behavioral observations. In this section we narrow the focus to skill-based direct observations as a tool of assessment. Focusing on specific skills provides information about the nature of the problem and directions for skill-based interventions.

Skill-based observations combine observational recording methods (e.g., narrative, interval, event, and ratings) with an observational coding system that specifies the categories used in recording. By assessing a behavior at the time and place of its actual occurrence, information about frequency, antecedent, consequent, and sequential conditions can be identified. When conducted with specific, operational definitions of target behaviors, observations can minimize the subjectivity inherent in many forms of indirect assessment (La Greca & Stark, 1986). Likewise, they are useful for identification, analysis, and evaluation. Specifically, they are conducive to repeated measurements over time, demonstrate sensitivity to treatment effects, and effectively differentiate situational specificity of behaviors.

Although there are several desirable features of direct observations in natural settings, they are not without their drawbacks. They are costly and time-consuming, and they may not provide sufficient information about the nature of social difficulties or the social validity of certain behaviors. Also, there is not a great deal of empirical data attesting to the predictive validity of various observation codes (La Greca & Stark, 1986).

Many observational measures are available (e.g., Hops, Walker, & Greenwood, 1988; Kahn & Hoge, 1983; Rubin & Daniels-Beirness, 1983). A commonly cited procedure is the Consultant Social Interaction Code (CSIC), developed by Hops et al. (1988) as part of an intensive intervention package for withdrawn students—Procedures for Establishing Effective Relationship Skills (PEERS). This code was designed for recording social behavior on playgrounds. A five-second interval recording procedure is used to collect data on (1) percentage of positive social behavior, (2) percentage of talk, (3) rate of starts (initiations by the child), (4) rate of answers (student's responses to peer initiations), (5) rate of interaction, and (6) ratio of starts to answers (a sociability ratio). The primary codes for use as baseline (and potentially outcome) assessment data are positive social behavior (PS; includes all forms of positive social behavior) and negative/alone (NA; includes all instances of nonsocial or inappropriate social behavior). Norms are available to identify socially withdrawn, primary-grade children on the playground (Hops et al., 1988).

Observation systems like the CSIC focus on topographical features of social behaviors, such as rate. However, other aspects of peer interactions, such as quality of behaviors and duration of social exchanges, are generally preferable because they can provide specific information about the nature of social difficulties, the importance of certain skills, and the impact of interventions on social contacts. As with other assessment methods, direct observations should occur across settings.

## Analogue Observations

Performance in analogue situations (e.g., behavioral role playing) is another means of assessing actual behavioral skills. Analogue settings for direct observations are useful when naturalistic observations are not practical (e.g., extremely low-frequency behaviors). In role-play assessments, the individual conducting the assessment sets the stage for the target child to demonstrate certain behaviors. For example, a hypothetical social problem may be posed to a child (e.g., being teased by a peer), who is asked to provide a response or act out what he or she would do if that situation were experienced personally. Serious concerns have been raised about the lack of ecological validity of analogue role playing. Several studies indicate a lack of correspondence among role-play assessments, behavior in the naturalistic setting, and sociometric status (see Gresham, 1986, for a review). They are useful, however, in assessing low-frequency behaviors or behaviors that occur in very restricted settings (Shapiro & Kratochwill, 1988).

### Child Interviews

There are two approaches for using child interviews as an assessment tool. A nonstructured interview will provide information about children's perceptions of their strengths and weaknesses in social situations. Important directions for investigation and intervention can be brought to light by obtaining impressions about antecedent and consequent conditions related to social skills and the perceived effects of one's behavior. A structured behavioral interview can help identify and delineate specific target behaviors for intervention. In both cases, reliability and validity are difficult to document because of the diversity inherent in interview conditions (interviewer bias, interviewee response, and type and situation of interview).

## Assessment of Others

To understand the social skillfulness of a child, it is important to recognize his or her relation to others in the natural setting. One way this can be conceptualized is in terms of relative status or place within a group. Assessment instruments have been selected here because they provide an indication of the relative status of the child in relation to a significant peer group or perceptions of a child's behaviors in a social context. Perceptions of relative status can be obtained from peer group members, immediate and extended family members, teachers, and additional significant adults and children.

### Teachers' Nominations and Rankings

Teachers' nominations and rankings provide a relative assessment of a child on target behaviors (e.g., "interacts the most," "cooperates the least," or "is the most disruptive") in comparison to other children. In nomination techniques, teach-

ers are asked to list a certain number of students who demonstrate a behavioral characteristic to the greatest or least extent compared to other classmates. The primary utility of nomination or ranking methods lies in their ability to identify children who are considered to demonstrate excessive problems in relation to local standards and for social validation purposes. Walker, Greenwood, Hops, & Todd, (1979) found that teachers' rankings of verbal frequency could reliably identify the least socially responsible child in a classroom. Also, teachers' ratings of popularity can reliably predict positive interactive behavior (Landau, Milich, & Whitten, 1984). Rankings are cost- and time-efficient in identifying children who act out but do not provide information about the specific nature of a problem or determine goals for treatment.

### Sociometric Techniques

Informant reports, adult rating scales, and teachers' nominations are based on the assumption that adults who know the child well are able to interpret and understand the child's social interactions with peers in the social context in which they occur. However, a large portion of the peer culture is not accessible to adults, and adults' assessments may be biased by the child's academic performance or behaviors toward themselves (Rubin, 1985). Sociometric methods (e.g., peer ratings or nominations) provide important contextual information about the child's relative standing in his or her social group.

Sociometric methods are used to obtain information on the social impact and preference of a child. They also allow for the classification of his or her sociometric status (i.e., popular, rejected, neglected, or controversial) and are based on the assumption that the peer group may be a reliable source concerning a child's social acceptability and impact. Indeed, the peer group is most often the primary recipient of the child's social overtures and is most familiar with the social context in which social behaviors occur. Sociometric assessment is also used at times to monitor the effects of social skills training (McConnell & Odom, 1986) and may be the best available measure of social competence in children and the criterion against which other measures of social behavior should be compared (Asher, Markell, & Hymel, 1981).

The psychometric properties of sociometric measures have been established and can be used to identify accepted, rejected, and/or neglected students in the classroom (Gresham & Reschly, 1988). Concurrent validity of these measures has also been established. For example, Landau et al. (1984) found that teachers' and peer acceptance scores were significantly better at predicting observed social behaviors than teachers' popularity ratings. Interested readers are referred to the extensive review by McConnell and Odom (1986) for additional discussion of research on the validity of sociometric measures.

There are several important considerations when using sociometric instruments and interpreting sociometric data. First, sociometric status is multidimensional. A variety of factors that are not social in nature (e.g., attractiveness) may affect the status measure (McConnell & Odom, 1986). Second, these techniques require adaptations based on the developmental level of children with whom they are being used. For example, use with preschool children requires adapting to the memory requirement of each task, as well as for expectations of reading and verbal skills. Third, some individuals question the appropriateness of asking children for expressions of social rejection or acceptance. This is based on the undocumented fear that the procedure itself may reinforce negative perceptions of rejected or isolated children.

Sociometric techniques take several forms, including peer nominations, social comparisons (paired comparisons), and peer ratings. The various techniques in sociometry have at least one characteristic in common: they measure social acceptance among members of a specific group. Sociometric techniques are useful as screening devices for children; however, they do not provide information about specific behavioral deficits or excesses. They are also useful in documenting concomitant increases in positive, reinforcing, and prosocial behaviors in the social environment as a means of assessing the effects of interventions (Gresham & Reschly, 1988).

*Peer nominations* are one form of sociometric technique. Similar to teachers' nominations, peer nominations require children to identify three to five members of their social group or class according to some criterion. Both positive nominations (e.g., "Circle the names of three children whom you like the best") and negative nominations (e.g., "Circle the names of three children you like the least") are used. As a rule, scores are obtained by summing the nominations a child receives. Separate scores are obtained for positive and negative nominations. Children who receive several positive nominations but few negative

nominations are considered, popular, and those who receive several negative and few positive are classified as rejected. Some children are not named by anyone in the peer group; these children are considered neglected. Finally, those who receive a great deal of both positive and negative nominations are classified as controversial. Early research by Coie, Dodge, and Coppotelli (1982) indicated that approximately 55% of the children in any classroom will be classified in one of these categories.

Another form of sociometry involves *social (paired group) comparisons*. In paired comparisons, all possible pairs of children in a group are presented, and one from each pair is chosen according to some criterion. Positive or negative criteria may be used. For example, students may be asked to select the child who is most likely to share their toys or to select the child who is most likely to argue about rules in a game. An advantage of this procedure is that children give equal consideration to all members of the group. A disadvantage is that it may be time-consuming to prepare and score (McConnell & Odom, 1986).

Because there is some controversy about negative nomination techniques, *peer ratings* can also be used. Peer ratings consist of a list of the names of every child in the class, with a three-option response (positive, neutral, and negative) following each name. Scoring involves averaging the rating of each student; a negative response is given one point, a neutral response two, and a positive response three. When used in conjunction with a positive nomination measure (Asher & Dodge, 1986), this method has been found to be especially reliable in identifying rejected children, although there are some problems in classifying neglected children. Because this procedure produces more data points than nomination and peer comparison methods, it may be among the most reliable of the sociometric procedures.

## Assessment of the Social Context

A third element of assessing social skillfulness requires an evaluation of the criterion environment or setting (i.e., context). Haring (1992) argued that a task analytic approach to social skills training may provide a sense of "decontextualized" social behavior and actually create problems of generalization and maintenance by artificially separating antecedents and responses from the contexts that give them meaning.

Embedded within this level of assessment are attempts to identify ecological conditions in the criterion setting (contextual analysis) and to discern the function of certain behaviors in the natural environment (functional analysis). Specific objectives of assessing the environmental context include (1) determing the expectations, demands, and norms for behavior in the criterion environment; (2) determining conditions in the environment that precipitate, reinforce, discourage, or extinguish specific behaviors; (3) analyzing functions that target behaviors serve in naturalistic settings; and (4) identifying behaviors and skills that have practical and meaningful significance in the natural setting (i.e., are socially valid). Common assessment approaches include contextual analyses and ecological observations, functional analyses, performance-based direct observations and interviews. Issues surrounding social validity are also discussed.

## Contextual Analysis and Ecological Observations

Central to an assessment of the social context is a careful analysis of its important features. Careful ecological observations in the criterion setting will allow for a greater understanding of normative behaviors and possible identification of specific skills or behaviors that are likely to be reinforced. Important tasks that are central to success in that environment and task-related variables (e.g., task demands) that should be mastered might also be identified. Various behavioral norms can be discerned, as can implicit and explicit rules for behavior that may reinforce or extinguish certain social behaviors. For example, it may be standard procedure for a child to continue playing successive games of tetherball until defeated by another child. In this case, it would be inappropriate for the target child to approach the game and ask the winner to have the next turn.

Unfortunately, there is currently a dearth of standardized procedures available by which reliable and valid contextual analyses can be conducted. There is a need to develop contextually sensitive strategies to assess behavioral expectations, demands, and norms in natural social situations. Likewise, standard and objective procedures for pinpointing environmental conditions that promote, maintain, or reinforce certain actions in various social contexts would be useful.

## Functional Analysis

Functional analysis integrally related to contextual analysis, is conceptualized as an assessment process used to understand the function (or pur-

pose) of specific social behaviors, as well as to explore environmental events that may be encouraging or reinforcing them. Functional analyses are particularly useful for intervention because they pinpoint manipulable environmental stimuli (i.e., antecedents and consequences) that maintain behaviors. They also have a great amount of face validity because they allow behavioral analyses at the time and setting in which social behaviors occur (Gresham, 1986).

Differential functional analyses are important in assessing social context. First, similar social behaviors (e.g., arguing about a task) can serve different functions across settings (e.g., attention on the playground or escape in a classroom). Second, different social behaviors (e.g., sharing toys or helping with toys) can serve similar functions across settings (e.g., positive reinforcement at home and at school). Assessment of the antecedents, consequences, and situational events through a careful A-B-C analysis is central. A discussion of the procedural details for conducting functional analyses is beyond the scope of this chapter, and interested readers are referred to Kratochwill, Sheridan, Carlson, and Lasecki (Chapter 14) for a more thorough review.

A useful framework for conducting a functional analysis is presented by O'Neill, Horner, Albin, Sprague, Storey, and Newton (1997). With functional analysis techniques like observations and interviews, environmental variables that are hypothesized to bear a functional relation to target social behaviors can be manipulated directly. This allows one to test hypotheses through the observation of actual behavior change.

## Performance-based Direct Observations

Performance-based direct observations are useful for assessing children with known skills in their repertoire who demonstrate performance problems in the natural environment. The primary consideration of these observations concerns assessing the criterion setting to determine environmental or ecological factors that may be promoting specific performance problems. A child with performance deficits may exhibit alternative behaviors (e.g., aggressive outbursts) rather than prosocial ones (e.g., talking calmly to solve a problem), even though he or she has shown a capability to perform the skill in other settings or at other times. The objective of this form of observation is to identify environmental factors that discourage skill use or reinforce the use of socially incompetent behaviors. It is particularly important to identify the conditions under which undesirable, competing behaviors occur and assess their reliability and efficiency relative to the reliability and efficiency of the socially skilled alternative behaviors that are the target of intervention (Gresham, 1986).

## *Interviews*

Interviews across sources allow the specific identification and delineation of behaviors that are considered important in the criterion setting, as well as functional analyses of social behaviors in specific situations. The structured behavioral consultation model of Bergan, Kratochwill, and their associates provides useful interview formats for social skills assessment (Kratochwill & Bergan, 1990; Sheridan, Kratochwill, & Bergan, 1996). This format is structured to help consultants identify specific problems, environmental conditions, and skill or performance deficits. It extends beyond defining the problem to designing and evaluating interventions to address the identified concerns. Thus, it is useful for the three primary objectives of social skills assessment: identification, analysis, and evaluation. Also, information gleaned from consultation interviews cuts across the important domains of child, other, and context.

## Social Validity

Social validity refers to the demonstration that therapeutic changes are socially important to the client (Kazdin, 1977). There are several ways in which social validity assessments can be incorporated meaningfully into the assessment process.

Traditionally, social validation has been assessed through subjective evaluation or social comparison procedures. *Subjective evaluation* involves global and overall appraisals of the child's social functioning and performance. This method of social validation addresses the question of whether behavior changes have led to qualitative differences in how the child is viewed by significant others. For example, teachers can be asked to provide general perceptions of the child's social behavior changes, and global checklists and sociometric ratings can provide a data-based method of subjective evaluation.

*Social comparison* is a normative comparison with others who are considered socially average or appropriate. It is assessed through the identification of "average" peers in the criterion environment, and the level of their behavior serves as

the criterion by which the clinical importance of treatment is evaluated. In this method of social validity, it is determined whether the child's behavior following treatment is similar to the behaviors of peers (Kazdin, 1977). Direct observations of matched peers are typically conducted in the same setting to determine comparability of the target child's social behaviors with those of the peers.

Subjective evaluation and social comparison procedures are useful when considering the social validity of particular social behaviors; however, they suffer from some important limitations. Subjective evaluations are typically collected from adults in the child's environment, such as parents and teachers. As alluded to previously, these respondents are removed from and only indirectly related to the social circle in which validity should be measured. Although social comparison procedures address this limitation, it has been suggested that the normative standard may underestimate the degree of change required for children with disabilities, based on the hypothesis that the less competent an individual, the less deviance is tolerated by the peer group.

An alternative model to conceptualize social validity is based on "context relevance theory" (Sailor, Goetz, Anderson, Hunt, & Gee, 1988). According to this theory, a skill should have immediate utility and be desirable for the child; that is it should produce something that the child would probably choose if the opportunity arose. The skill should be acquired in the actual physical context in which it is used (in the case of social skills, in a social context), it should have practical relevance, and it should be adaptable to various social situations (it should be flexible). Assessment of social validity based on this model may be obtained by eliciting the reactions of others who are part of the individual's stable social network (Haring, Breen, Lee, Pitts-Conway, & Gaylord-Ross, 1987).

*Template matching* is a related approach that identifies relevant social behavior based on input from peers in natural social contexts. It is a specific technique for identifying socially valid behaviors based on normative information. In template matching, peers identify behaviors that are most important to them, in a particular context. For example, behavioral descriptors that represent highly preferred or exemplary performance (e.g., a well-liked peer) are elicited from a child's significant others (in this case, peers in a social network). The descriptors from several individuals are then combined to produce a template of the behavior in question (e.g., social competence). A behavioral profile of the child is obtained in a similar fashion, and differences between the two profiles are evaluated. Discrepancies between the preferred template and the child's description suggest targets for intervention (Hoier & Cone, 1987).

# CONTEXTUALIZED SOCIAL SKILLS INTERVENTIONS

Interventions for children who demonstrate social difficulties can be characterized along the same dimensions of social skillfulness presented throughout this chapter (i.e., child, other, and context). A contextualized social skills intervention is a series of multidimensional tactics aimed at improving conditions for a child. Both internal (e.g., child-related) and external (e.g., environmental) conditions must be considered in the development of contextualized interventions. For example, teaching children discrete steps for a specific skill, such as solving problems, is important to ensure that they have the necessary behaviors in their repertoire. However, variables of the other students with whom problem solving will occur (including their goals and behaviors), the task or event from which the problem arose, and the setting in which it occurs all interact to define appropriateness and effectiveness of specific social behaviors. In contrast, in a traditional treatment perspective, a strategy is imposed on a child to address presumed internal deficiencies in isolation from broader ecological contexts. Indeed, attention to each level is necessary in effective social skills programs.

## Child-focused Interventions

In general, there are at least two social skills treatment strategies that focus almost exclusively on the child: social learning procedures and cognitive-based strategies. These approaches address the specific discrete behaviors of students, teach them alternative methods of interacting with others, and address the internal events of the child or adolescent (such as attributions for social events and means-end thinking).

### Social Learning Procedures

According to social learning theory, social behaviors are acquired through observation and reinforcement (Bandura, 1977). *Modeling*, an effective type of social learning procedure often used in social skills training (Gresham, 1985; Wandless & Prinz, 1982), uses films, audiotapes, videotapes, or live demonstrations of skills to be acquired. It can play a major role in learning and performing new social behaviors, especially when the model is similar to the target child and is reinforced for prosocial behaviors.

Modeling is typically carried out in three steps. The first step is *skill instruction*, a procedure in which the essential skill components for successful behavioral performance are identified, a rationale for the behavior is presented, and information on skill performance is disseminated. In this first step, participants are provided with a verbal behavioral sequence (step-by-step process) in which a skill is performed. Second, the behavior is modeled by a social skills trainer, teacher, peer, or videotaped demonstration. In live modeling, the target child observes the social behaviors of models in naturalistic settings like the classroom. Symbolic modeling requires the child to observe the social behaviors of a model in a film or videotape. The third step in modeling is *skill performance*. After social skills are presented and modeled, participants are required to perform the skill (i.e., behavioral enactment) through role-play procedures. From a social learning perspective, this can occur through guided practice, involving covert responding (the child uses visual imagery to imagine a social situation and think through appropriate social responses), verbal responding (the child extends his or her cognitive thoughts by verbalizing possible resolutions), or motor responding (the child acts out the responses that have been observed, visualized, and verbalized). Active attempts at skill performance are typically responded to with constructive feedback from social skills trainers (Cartlege & Milburn, 1995).

Research on the effects of modeling has yielded generally positive results. For example, modeling has been shown to effectively increase the amount of social interaction of withdrawn children (O'Connor, 1969, 1972), affect problem-solving behavior (Debus, 1970), and improve sociometric status (Gresham & Nagle, 1980). Both live and symbolic modeling have been shown to be effective; however, most of the empirical studies have used symbolic modeling to allow increased control in the experimental procedures (e.g., Gresham, 1981).

An interesting form of modeling, self-modeling, has received empirical support in areas related to social skills (e.g., selective mutism and behavior disorders). For example, Kehle, Clark,

Jenson, and Wampold (1986) used a self-modeling videotape technique to decrease disruptive behaviors of three boys with behavioral disorders. The children were instructed to behave appropriately and were then videotaped in live classroom interactions. All disruptive behaviors depicted on the videotape were then edited out, and the boys were shown an 11-minute segment of only their appropriate behaviors. The disruptive behaviors decreased substantially from baseline during the treatment condition, and the improved behaviors were maintained when the treatment was withdrawn and at a six-week follow up. A wait-list control condition was used, in which a fourth child was shown an unedited tape of his inappropriate behaviors. During this condition, his disruptive classroom behaviors increased. After viewing an edited tape of only appropriate social behaviors, the wait-list control child also demonstrated improvements in his natural classroom behaviors.

To learn new skills through modeling, the child must attend to and understand salient components of the model's behaviors, code and retain these for future use, and demonstrate adequate motivation to perform the desired behavior. Therefore, modeling is often coupled with cognitive-based strategies and operant techniques in social skills training programs.

## Cognitive-behavioral procedures

Cognitive behavioral intervention procedures emphasize a child's internal cognitions (thoughts and self-statements) and problem-solving abilities. Two common procedures include coaching and social problem solving.

*Coaching* procedures involve direct verbal instructions and discussion as the major media of intervention. A coach (e.g., social skills trainer, teacher, or parent) first provides the child with specific rules or steps for a behavior. The coach and child then rehearse the steps, and the coach provides feedback about the child's performance. Coaching is often paired with other social skill intervention methods (such as modeling and positive reinforcement) to enhance its efficacy.

The efficacy of coaching has been studied empirically, with generally favorable results (e.g., Gottman, Gonso, & Schuler, 1976; Gresham & Nagle, 1980; Ladd, 1981; Mize, 1995; Oden & Asher, 1977). For example, Oden and Asher (1977) used coaching to teach participation, communication, cooperation, and peer reinforcement. The procedure resulted in increased

demonstration of the target social skills and improved sociometric status of the participants.

Gresham and Nagle (1980) conducted a study in which coaching was compared to modeling procedures. Participants in this study were exposed to one of four conditions: coaching, modeling, a coaching-modeling combination, and attention control. The three treatment conditions were equally effective in increasing the frequency of positive social interactions and in improving the sociometric status of the students. The treatments with coaching alone or in combination with modeling were more effective than modeling alone in decreasing rates of negative social interactions.

Mize (1995) reported the results of a coaching intervention with preschool children. Twenty-nine children were randomly assigned to a skills-training or attention-control condition. Instruction in the former focused on specific social skills (i.e., leading, supporting, questioning, and commenting) and the underlying components of social competence (social knowledge, performance proficiency, and monitoring and self-evaluation). Children who participated in the coaching condition more than doubled the frequency with which they used the target skills with peers from pretest to posttest. The largest improvements were seen in the skills of commenting and leading, with smaller improvements in questioning and supporting skills. Children in the control condition showed a slight decrease in their use of social skills. Furthermore, children who received skills training showed increases in positive sociometric nominations and overall sociometric ratings (assessing overall group acceptance). Control group children showed declines at follow-up in both measures of group acceptance.

*Social problem-solving* (SPS) interventions focus on the interaction of cognitive, emotional, and behavioral factors associated with social competence. These approaches teach children the process of solving social problems by logically evaluating interpersonal problems and considering alternative, adaptive solutions (Spivack & Shure, 1982; Weissberg, 1985). A set of at least six steps are often incorporated into a comprehensive SPS model, which attempts to teach target students (1) that they *can* resolve most problematic social situations; (2) how to recognize when problems exist; (3) how to generate various alternative solutions to reach social goals and to consider their consequences; (4) how to select a strategy and develop a plan of action; (5) how to carry out the strategy competently; and (6) how to use self-monitoring behaviors, evaluate their effectiveness, and modify plans (Weissberg, 1985). The procedures typically teach children to analyze problems by asking a series of questions, such as "What is the problem?" "What are my choices?" "What are the consequences?" "What is my best choice?" and "How did I do?" They are common components of several classroom-based social skills curricula. However, when used in isolation, they generally do not teach discrete social behaviors and may be ineffective with individuals who exhibit skill deficits.

Research on cognitive-based social problem-solving procedures has yielded equivocal results. Several reviewers report the overall findings from social problem-solving interventions to be positive (e.g., Spivack & Shure, 1982; Urbain & Kendall, 1980), and others interpret the general outcomes as negative (e.g., Abikoff & Gittleman, 1985; Durlak, 1983; Kirschenbaum & Ordman, 1984). It should be noted that many of the studies on the efficacy of cognitive-based social problem-solving procedures assess cognitive thoughts or ideas as the primary outcome measures, without attention to behavioral change as a function of training.

## Other-focused Interventions

Several interventions focus on individuals or groups other than the target child or adolescent. These include parent training, peer-based interventions, and classroom and school-wide programs.

### *Parent Training*

Parents play essential roles in a child's socialization experiences. Therefore, it is often deemed feasible and desirable to involve them in the intervention process (Budd, 1985). It has been demonstrated empirically that parents can be trained to effectively manage overt behavioral problems and noncompliance in children (see Wright, Stroud, & Keenan, 1993, for a review). However, few social skills programs have articulated a clear role for parents. Although it may be unrealistic to expect them to provide direct and primary social skills training to their children (Budd, 1985), they are often in ideal positions to provide supplemental (i.e., adjunct) training in natural settings, for example, helping children's problem-solving efforts directly in the social en-

vironment and prompting, monitoring, and reinforcing skill use immediately.

Budd and Itzkowitz (1990) evaluated the effects of a four-week training session on parents' conceptual knowledge of social skills and perceptions of their children's social competence and psychosocial adjustment. They also investigated the relationship between parents' and peers' sociometric measures of acceptance in the peer group. The researchers found that parent training produced a significant effect in parents' conceptual knowledge and perceptions of children's social skills over time. Although they suggested that their findings supported the value of parents as trainers of their children's social skills, specific behavioral effects on parents and their children were not measured.

Sheridan, Dee, Morgan, McCormick, and Walker (1996) included parents as meaningful treatment agents in a social skills intervention program for boys with attention deficit hyperactivity disorder (ADHD). The child-based intervention involved 10 weekly sessions, focusing on target skills in social entry, maintaining interactions, and solving problems. Training modalities included skill instruction, modeling, role playing, homework, and reinforcement. A parent group met separately but simultaneously with the children's group to teach parents skills to help their children with their social problems. Parents were taught the skills of debriefing/active listening, problem solving, and goal setting. A multiple baseline design across behaviors was used for the participants. The children demonstrated substantial positive changes in their social initiation and maintenance skills as assessed in analogue role plays. Positive changes also were noted in participants' problem-solving skills; however, more variability in performance was noted in these behaviors during treatment. Parents' skills in debriefing, problem solving, and goal setting also improved, as demonstrated on home-based audiotape assessments. All participants reported improvements of at least 1 standard deviation on self-report social skills rating scales, and parents' and teachers' reports also suggested general improvement for most participants. Positive changes also were evident in some aspects of the participants' cognitive problem-solving abilities. In general, behavioral changes were considered to be socially valid, and all participants viewed the social skills interventions very positively. Unfortunately, a components analysis was not conducted, so no information is available on the differential or unique contribution of parents as adjunct facilitators of their children's social skillfulness.

## Peer-based Interventions

In peer-based interventions, peers play a central role as informal or formal change agents. Examples include cooperative learning, structured peer contact (cooperative interactions), peer-initiated contact, and peer reinforcement.

*Cooperative learning* is a technique in which small groups of students work together toward some academic goal. Various cooperative learning models have been described, including those by Aronson (1978), Johnson and Johnson (1975), Sharan and Sharan (1976), and Slavin (1980). They vary in terms of the (1) degree of structure provided, (2) nature and type of reinforcers dispensed, and (3) extent of individual accountability and group interdependence required. Typically, each student in a cooperative learning group has a distinct role or task, which emphasizes individual accountability; however, praise or rewards are generally based on group performance, which emphasizes interdependence.

The overall goals of cooperative learning are enhancing personal growth, peer relations, interracial relations, classroom climates, and academic achievement (Furman & Gavin, 1989). Research in each of these areas yields generally positive results. Although methodological flaws are apparent in some of the empirically based outcome research, cooperative learning has been found to have a positive impact on self-esteem (Blaney, Stephan, Rosenfield, Aronson, & Sikes, 1977), interpersonal cooperation and altruism (Hertz-Lazarowitz, Sharan, & Steinberg, 1980), locus of control (Johnson, Johnson, & Scott, 1978), role taking (Bridgeman, 1981), sociometric status (Slavin & Karweit, 1981), interracial relations (DeVries, Edwards, & Slavin, 1978; Slavin, 1983a), classroom environment (DeVries & Slavin, 1978), and students' achievement (Johnson, Maruyama, Johnson, Nelson, & Skon, 1981; Sharan, 1980; Slavin, 1983b).

Interventions designed in the realm of *structured peer contact* typically involve the formation of cooperative, goal-oriented interactions between target children and members of their peer group. Studies in this area have suggested that simply placing children together in play situations is not sufficient to increase positive influences among them. Rather, the contact must be designed to elicit cooperative, rewarding, and otherwise positive interactions to enhance positive or alter negative perceptions (Furman & Gavin, 1989).

An important social skills intervention method involves *peer-initiated contact*, in which confederate peers initiate social interactions with target children. Strain and his colleagues have conducted a great deal of research in this area, particularly withdrawn children and children with disabilities. The research has produced convincing evidence that children can foster socially interactive behavior in one another (e.g., Hendrickson, Strain, Tremblay, & Shores, 1982; Sisson, Van Hasselt, Hersen, & Strain, 1985; Strain, Kerr, & Ragland, 1979; Strain, Shores, & Timm, 1977).

## Classroom and Schoolwide Programs

Classroom and schoolwide programs are often implemented from a preventive framework to provide important intervention experiences to large groups of students, only some of whom may be identified as needing direct training. These programs are developed and implemented in large groups of students to ensure that target children and peers alike possess important knowledge and skills. Such programs can be considered other-focused in that many children other than those identified as socially deficient are part of the intervention. They can also be conceptualized as ecologically based interventions when accompanied by operant systems such as group contingencies, schoolwide token and back-up reinforcement programs, structured recess experiences, and staff prompting. Examples are available in Gamble and Strain (1979); Jones, Sheridan, and Binns (1993); and Sheridan (1995).

Jones et al. (1993) described a schoolwide social skills training model for students at risk. The model was developed as a secondary prevention program, with the goal of addressing identified problems early and reducing future, more serious problems. Among the rationales for this program was the importance of generalization of skills in the natural environment, with individuals in students' primary ecological settings (i.e., teachers, aides, administrators, support staff, and office personnel) included in the training and generalization activities.

The model described by Jones et al. (1993) was a four-tiered program with a multigate assessment procedure, classroom-based skills training, small-group training for high-risk students, and standardized cuing and reinforcement procedures to facilitate generalization. The entire school was involved in the training, with classroom teachers and school psychologists responsible for skill instruction, discussion, modeling, and role playing. Small-group sessions were conducted for students who were considered at highest risk of developing serious social or interpersonal problems. These sessions involved structured opportunities in the natural environment (e.g., playground) for students to practice skills learned in classroom instruction (similar to the structured peer contact procedures already described). Generalization was programmed by training all school staff in structured cuing procedures (i.e., delivering in vivo prompts to students to use appropriate and relevant social skills in natural school settings when opportunities arose); providing concrete reinforcers (i.e., tokens) to students who were observed using appropriate social skills; and running a "school store," where students could redeem their tokens for a variety of backup reinforcers. Although this program appears promising, empirical data to support its efficacy are not currently available in the published literature.

## Ecological and Contextual Interventions

Interventions aimed at social context attempt to maximize environmental support for the development and maintenance of effective social relationships. These include manipulation of environmental contingencies, contextual enhancement strategies, and systemic interventions.

### Manipulating antecedents and consequences

Antecedent events are those that precede desired social behaviors and increase their likelihood of occurrence. *Manipulation of social antecedents* can set the stage for positive interactions and are thus important in promoting successful relations. Methods of manipulating antecedent events include prompting, cuing, peer initiation strategies, and cooperative learning. Although the latter two procedures were discussed earlier (see discussion on other-based intervention procedures), they can also be conceptualized as methods for manipulating conditions antecedent to social interactions.

*Manipulation of consequences* includes procedures designed to reinforce positive social behaviors. In general, three reinforcement techniques are used: contingent social reinforcement, group contingencies, and differential reinforcement. Although these procedures may be considered child-focused, we discuss them here because of their emphasis on maximizing the environmental support for the development and demonstration of relevant social skills.

*Contingent social reinforcement* focuses on overt, discrete behaviors in the natural setting. A prerequisite to using operant intervention procedures is the possession of appropriate skills in a child's repertoire. The goal of these procedures is to increase their effective use in desirable situations. Thus, they are especially appropriate for children with performance deficits or as training components for children with skill deficits (i.e., following active training to ensure competence in specific social behaviors).

In contingent social reinforcement, a teacher, parent, or other significant person reinforces appropriate social behavior socially and/or concretely. A variety of methods can be used, such as contracts, spinners, tokens, or point systems (Rhode, Jenson, & Reavis, 1994; Sheridan, 1995). These procedures successfully increase rates of positive social behaviors; however, they require moderate levels of involvement and monitoring by teachers, parents, or treatment agents (Elliott & Busse, 1991).

Research on contingent social reinforcement has yielded generally consistent, positive results. Sheridan, Kratochwill, and Elliott (1990) described a consultation study in which four socially withdrawn children were assigned to one of two behavioral consultation conditions: teacher-only consultation, or parent and teacher (conjoint) consultation. Treatment goals were to increase the social initiation behaviors of withdrawn children in the home and the school. The social skills intervention in both conditions included self-monitoring and positive reinforcement of social initiation behaviors. In the teacher-only consultation condition, treatments were delivered in the school only. In the conjoint consultation condition, treatments were delivered in both settings. Behavioral observations indicated that participants in both conditions demonstrated increases in social initiations at school, with greater increases for participants in the conjoint consultation condition. Increases were also demonstrated in the home for participants in the conjoint condition (the social skills intervention was implemented across settings); however, home behaviors remained at baseline levels for participants in the teacher-only condition (the treatment was not in place in that setting). Follow-up data were limited but suggested that school behaviors maintained after the treatment were no longer in effect for participants in the conjoint condition only. This study suggested the importance of implementing social skills interventions across relevant settings to maximize treatment effects, and it demonstrated the role that parents and teachers can play in delivering direct social skills interventions.

*Group contingencies* involve the application of consequences for behaviors of group members (e.g., classmates) and can be applied in various ways. For example, reinforcement can be based on the behavior of selected children rather than an entire group (dependent group contingency), based on individual behavior regardless of the behavior of others (independent group contingency), or based on the collective behavior of the group (interdependent´ group contingency). These procedures have been found to be effective for teaching social skills in classrooms (Crouch, Gresham, & Wright, 1985; Gamble & Strain, 1979). Because children serve as behavior managers for themselves, group contingencies are also efficient in teacher time and effort.

*Differential reinforcement procedures* are used to decrease the rate of undesired target behaviors (such as socially aggressive behaviors) and can also be applied in a variety of ways. With differential reinforcement of other behaviors (DRO), reinforcement follows any behavior except the target behavior. This has the effect of increasing the frequency of positive social behaviors and decreasing aggressive behaviors. For example, Pinkston, Reese, LeBlanc, and Baer (1973) used a DRO procedure to decrease a young boy's aggressive behavior, along with a contingent social reinforcement procedure to increase his positive social interactions.

Differential reinforcement of low rates of behavior (DRL) involves the delivery of reinforcement for reduced rates of the undesired target behavior. Dietz and Repp (1973) used a DRL schedule to reduce the inappropriate talking of an entire classroom (see also Zwald & Gresham, 1982). Although differential reinforcement procedures can decrease the frequency of undesired behaviors, they fail to actively train more appropriate social behaviors. They may be most useful as adjuncts to other interventions that teach the child appropriate interaction skills with which to replace their inappropriate social behaviors.

Repp and Karsh (1994) used differential reinforcement for alternative behaviors (DRA) to decrease the disruptive social behaviors (i.e., tantrums) of two students with developmental disabilities. Through a careful functional analysis, these authors identified the function of the disruptive behaviors in their participants as gaining the teacher's attention under different demand conditions. Based on this hypothesis, they developed an intervention that included (1) withholding attention, (2) providing frequent reinforcement for task engagement in the form of high fives and pats on the back, and (3) increasing the opportunities for social interaction between each student and the teacher and teaching assistant. Results of a multiple baseline design across participants demonstrated a substantial reduction in the percentage and frequency of disruptive tantrums for each child, with maintenance of the behavioral improvements at a one-year follow-up. This study illustrated a very useful approach based on the outcomes of functional analysis, in developing hypothesis-driven interventions for negative social behaviors.

## Contextual Enhancement Strategies

Contextual enhancement interventions are concerned with maximizing environmental support for the development and maintenance of social relationships. Examples include manipulation of the physical parameters of the environment and supported social relationships. The physical layout or parameters of a social setting may facilitate or impede social interactions. Careful attention to the arrangement of the physical setting can contribute to contextual interventions. For example, class schedules, seating arrangements, or the availability of appropriate objects can be altered to facilitate interaction. Horner (1980) provided an example of the power of manipulating contextual variables on the behavior of children with profound disabilities. By increasing the number of toys in the training setting, the number of appropriate adaptive behaviors of target students were doubled and the level of maladaptive behaviors were reduced.

Supported social relationships promote meaningful peer relationships in natural settings by structuring interactions among children, for example, structured recess, "circles of friends" (Forest, 1987), and "special friends" (Meyers, 1985). Forest described a program in which a network ("circle") of friends was established as a resource for a student with disabilities to increase opportunities in age- and context-appropriate activities. The "special friends" program described by Meyer identified social and leisure opportunities that were important in natural settings and taught students the necessary social interaction and game-playing skills to engage effectively in these activities.

## Systemic Manipulations

A systemic orientation considers the interaction of several systems or domains as relevant in the development and demonstration of child behaviors. Programs that consider a systems approach often involve a hybrid of programs or elements of programs that permeate the various intervention targets already mentioned (i.e., child, others, and environment).

The importance of systemic programs in addressing social problems is apparent in the gang intervention literature (Goldstein, Harootunian, & Conoley, 1994). R. D. Stephens emphasized the importance of effective interventions that cut across various systems, including school, home, police, and community resources. Specifically, intervention programming includes a number of components: an in-school gang prevention curriculum (e.g., problem-solving training, gang resistance techniques, and enhancing self-esteem and gang awareness), a model dress code, enhanced understanding of graffiti, a gang crime-reporting hotline, support and protection of gang crime victims, in-service teacher training, a visitor-screening policy, parental notification, community networking, and a strong extracurricular program (R. D. Stephens, 1993).

In a comprehensive text on gangs and school violence, Goldstein et al. (1994) provide a multidimensional intervention strategy that includes goals and treatment modalities at the community, school, teacher, and individuals student levels. Specific environmental manipulations to reduce aggressive behaviors include reducing class sizes, invoking a "vandalism watch" program, ensuring that the school is well lit, clearing graffiti immediately, using personal alarm systems, hiring security personnel, providing aggression management and interpersonal skills training, using skilled conflict negotiators, and educating school staff about the student climate and ethnic milieu.

# GENERALIZATION OF SOCIAL SKILLS

From an ecological contextual perspective, social skills interventions are effective only to the extent that they encourage generalization to the natural, criterion environment. In other words, generalization is an essential, not desirable, component of social skills intervention programs. It can be considered from two perspectives (Gresham, 1994). A traditional approach considers the occurrence of relevant behaviors under different, nontraining conditions. In this conceptualization, generalization can occur across settings/situations, time, and behaviors. Unfortunately, the generalization of the effects of social skills training programs is the exception rather than the rule (DuPaul & Eckert, 1994). There are a number of possible reasons to account for the lack of observed generalization. First, there is often a lack of functional equivalence between trained skills and skills that have importance (i.e., social validity) in the criterion setting (Gresham, 1994). For example, a decontextualized approach to social skills training may teach a child to state how he or she feels when being teased by a peer, when in fact that behavior may be met with further teasing or ridicule in the natural setting. Second, training conditions are often too far-removed from natural contingencies. For example, training in controlled clinics fails to approximate conditions in classrooms or on playgrounds in terms of their physical, social, and affective features. Competing behaviors such as impulsivity or distractibility may also interfere with the use of appropriate social skills in the natural setting (Gresham & Elliott, 1984; Horner & Billingsley, 1988).

An alternative, functional approach to generalization is concerned with the occurrence of similar behaviors under various stimulus conditions or the occurrence of multiple behaviors in response to the same stimulus. Procedures involve exploiting functional contingencies, training diversely, and incorporating functional mediators (Stokes & Osnes, 1989). It is important that the behaviors taught in the first place have social validity (Moore, 1994). As discussed previously, it is critical to demonstrate that social skills interventions produce behaviors that are empirically linked to critical social outcomes.

A number of generalization strategies have been documented, including the "train and hope" method, the modification of consequences, and the training of sufficient exemplars. In the first procedure, an intervention is employed in a training setting, and generalization across responses, settings, therapists, and/or time is examined without any active treatment. Not surprisingly, this is the least effective strategy (DuPaul & Eckert, 1994). When consequences are modified in the natural setting, contingencies are put into place to alter the environmental control of social behaviors. For example, Lewis and Sugai (1993) used a multiple baseline design across participants to ascertain treatment-related changes, and they provided a strong demonstration of the value of alterations in environmental contingencies to promote maintenance and generalization. Finally, when sufficient exemplars are used, training occurs across stimuli (e.g., persons and settings) that are common to the natural environment. For example, significant peers might be included in training sessions to increase the similarity between the training and criterion environments. Additional means of promoting generalization include teaching relevant behaviors that are likely to be maintained by naturally occurring contingencies, communities of reinforcement, or entrapment such as turn taking or sharing toys (McConnell, 1987); gradually withdrawing response contingencies to approximate naturally occurring consequences; and offering booster sessions at regular intervals (Elliott & Busse, 1991). Examples of empirical studies that have effectively incorporated generalization strategies into social skills interventions include Bierman, Miller, and Stabb (1987); Foxx, Faw, and Weber (1991); Gunter, Fox, Brady, Shores, and Cavanaugh (1988); Hansen, St. Lawrence, and Christoff (1989); Rhode, Morgan, and Young (1983); and Smith, Young, West, Morgan, and Rhode (1988). Interested readers are referred to Landrum and Lloyd (1992) for a review of these and other studies.

The difficulty some social skills trainers experience in establishing generalization of treatment effects may stem from the traditional manner in which generalization is promoted. As suggested by Haring (1992), a sequence of responses for engaging in appropriate social behavior in a particular setting is easier to specify than those characteristics that promote behaviors to generalize across circumstances. Accordingly, generalization may be enhanced by training important social behaviors in multiple, naturally occurring contexts. For example, a child could talk to peers while waiting for class to begin, or a child could be prompted to ask a peer a question during teacher-organized group activities.

General case programming is a unique procedure for teaching generalized skills. Although originally used to teach functional academic skills (Becker, Engelmann, & Thomas, 1975), it has also been used with students with severe handicaps (Horner, Sprague, & Wilcox, 1982) and may

provide a useful conceptualization of social skills generalization. General case instruction (Horner, McDonnell, & Bellamy, 1986) emphasizes the selection and sequencing of teaching examples to help students generalize and discriminate the use of learned skills across stimulus conditions. In other words, students are taught not only the appropriate skills but also the contexts for which they are appropriate and inappropriate.

Five steps in general case instruction are necessary in social skills interventions. First, the instructional universe is defined. The instructional universe is made up of stimulus conditions across which the target skills should be performed; that is, the environmental and situational conditions to which students are exposed can control or cue a new behavior, much like discriminative stimuli. This universe might include the various social settings in which behaviors are expected, such as classrooms, playgrounds, and hallways. It also requires attention to situational conditions such as the persons present (e.g., certain groups of children and adults), task demands (e.g., cooperation and competition), and other environmental stimuli (e.g., equipment, space). The key to generalization is to define the set of stimulus conditions in instructional universes that are functional for a child and to identify the skills that are necessary to perform competently in those stimulus conditions.

The second step to general case programming is to select teaching examples that will maximize the chance that the student will generalize from stimulus conditions to the larger universe. This involves teaching with multiple examples that sample a range of relevant situations and stimuli. Third, these teaching examples are sequenced in meaningful and practical segments (much like direct instructional approaches to social skills training). Fourth, teaching sessions are implemented through prompting, fading, shaping, reinforcing, and effective pacing. Finally, testing (e.g., probing) the child with a new set of examples is necessary to ensure that a generalized skill has been learned. To the greatest extent possible, these tests may occur in the stimulus conditions in which generalization is desired (Horner et al., 1986).

# CONCLUSIONS

We started this chapter with a compelling quote by Haring (1992), who asked if social competence can be defined in terms of its subunits.

Throughout the subsequent pages, we emphasized the importance of conceptualizing social skills within the interactive framework of child, other, and context. Each of these variables must be considered independently and together when considering the broad and comprehensive construct of social skillfulness. Each is a necessary piece of a complex social puzzle, and no one variable is sufficient in understanding the various subtleties and dynamics of social interactions.

In response to Haring's (1992) question, then, we believe that although information about social competence may be lost (or missed) when "the whole is broken into parts" (p. 307), the converse must also be acknowledged. That is, the smaller subunits provide the basis on which advanced social behaviors are predicated.

We draw an analogy to the construction of a house. Before building begins, blueprints are drawn to give a sense of the entire plan; a gestalt that includes a framework for how the rooms will be organized (internal characteristics), how the exterior will complement the interior (interactive characteristics), and how the structure will be situated in relation to the neighborhood and environment (contextual characteristics). These characteristics form the whole and describe the ecology of the house. Yet, the process of building the house cannot be understood by reading the plan. The physical acts of building the house begins by laying a foundation that supports other substructures, such as the frame, roof, and plumbing. This is analogous to the development of specific social skills; prerequisite prosocial skills serve as the foundation for the structure of social competence and sometimes must be taught by using basic intervention tools. Through reciprocal interaction with others and experience in various social contexts, a child builds the skills necessary for the complex architecture known as social skillfulness.

# REFERENCES

Abikoff, H., & Gittleman, R. (1985). Hyperactive children treated with stimulants: Is cognitive training a useful adjunct? *Archives of General Psychiatry, 42*, 953–961.

Aronson, E. (1978). *The Jigsaw classroom*. Beverly Hills, CA: Sage.

Asher, R., & Dodge, R. A. (1986). Identifying children who are rejected by their peers. *Developmental Psychology, 22*, 444–449.

Asher, S. R., Markell, R. A., & Hymel, S. (1981). Identifying children at risk in peer relations: A critique

of the rate-of-interaction approach to assessment. *Child Development, 52*, 1239–1245.

Bandura, A. (1977). *Social learning theory*. Englewood Cliffs, NJ: Prentice Hall.

Becker, W., Englemann, S., & Thomas, D. (1975). *Teaching 2: Cognitive learning and instruction*. Chicago: Science Research Associates.

Bierman, K. L., Miller, C. L., & Stabb, S. D. (1987). Improving the social behavior and peer acceptance of rejected boys: Effects of social skill training with instructions and prohibitions. *Journal of Consulting and Clinical Psychology, 55*, 194–200.

Blaney, N. T., Stephan, S., Rosenfield, D., Aronson, E., & Sikes, J. (1977). Interdependence in the classroom: A field study. *Journal of Educational Psychology, 69*, 121–128.

Bridgeman, D. L. (1981). Enhanced role-taking through cooperative interdependence: A field study. *Child Development, 52*, 1231–1238.

Budd, K. S. (1985). Parents as mediators in the social skills training of children. In L. L'Abate & M. A. Milan (Eds.), *Handbook of social skills training and research* (pp. 245–262). New York: Wiley.

Budd, K. S., & Itzkowitz, J. S. (1990). Parents as social skills trainers and evaluators of children. *Child and Family Behavior Therapy, 12*(3), 13–30.

Cartlege, G., & Milburn, J. F. (1995). *Teaching social skills to children and youth: Innovative approaches* (3rd ed.). Boston: Allyn & Bacon.

Coie, J. D., Dodge, K. A., & Coppotelli, H. (1982). Dimensions and types of social status: A cross-age perspective. *Developmental Psychology, 18*, 557–570.

Crouch, P. L., Gresham, F. M., & Wright, W. R. (1985). Interdependent and independent contingencies with immediate and delayed reinforcement for controlling classroom behavior. *Journal of School Psychology, 23*, 177–188.

Debus, R. L. (1970). Effects of brief observation of model behavior on conceptual tempo of impulsive children. *Developmental Psychology, 2*, 22–32.

Demaray, M. K., Ruffalo, S. L., Carlson, J., Busse, R. T., Olson, A. E., McManus, S. M., & Leventhal, A. (1995). Social skills assessment: A comparative evaluation of six published rating scales. *School Psychology Review, 24*, 648–671.

DeVries, D. L., Edwards, K. J., & Slavin, R. E. (1978). Biracial learning teams and race relations in the classroom: Four filed experiments on Teams-Games-Tournaments. *Journal of Educational Psychology, 70*, 356–362.

DeVries, D. L., & Slavin, R. E. (1978). Teams-Games-Tournament: Review of term classroom experiments. *Journal of Research and Development in Education, 12*, 28–38.

Dietz, S., & Repp, A. (1973). Decreasing classroom misbehavior through the use of DRL schedules of reinforcement. *Journal of Applied Behavior Analysis, 6*, 457–463.

Dodge, K. A. (1980). Social cognition and children's

aggressive behavior. *Child Development, 51,* 162–170.

Dodge, K. A., & Coie, J. D. (1987). Social-information processing factors in reactive and proactive aggression in children's peer groups. *Journal of Personality and Social Psychology, 53,* 1146–1158.

Dodge, K. A., Coie, J. D., & Brakke, N. P. (1982). Behavior problems of socially rejected and neglected preadolescents: The roles of social approach and aggression. *Journal of Abnormal Child Psychology, 10,* 389–409.

Dodge, K. A., Coie, J. D., Pettit, G. S., & Price, J. M. (1990). Peer status and aggression in boys' groups: Developmental and contextual analyses. *Child Development, 61,* 1289–1309.

Dodge, K. A., & Frame, C. L. (1982). Social cognitive biases and deficits in aggressive boys. *Child Development, 53,* 620–635.

Dodge, K. A., McClaskey, C. L., & Feldman, E. (1985). Situational approach to the assessment of social competence in children. *Journal of Consulting and Clinical Psychology, 53,* 344–353.

Dodge, K. A., Pettit, G. S., McClaskey, C. L., & Brown, M. M. (1986). Social competence in children. *Monographs of the Society for Research in Child Development, 51*(2; Serial No. 213).

DuPaul, G. J., & Eckert, T. L. (1994). The effects of social skills curricula: Now you see them, now you don't. *School Psychology Quarterly, 9,* 113–132.

Durlak, J. A. (1983). Social problem-solving as a primary prevention strategy. In R. D. Felner, L. A. Jason, J. N. Moritsugu, & S. S. Fanber (Eds.), *Preventive psychology* (pp. 31–48). New York: Pergamon.

Elliott, S. N., & Busse, R. T. (1991). Social skills assessment and intervention with children and adolescents: Guidelines for assessment and training procedures. *School Psychology International, 12,* 63–83.

Elliott, S. N., & Gresham, F. M. (1992). *Social skills intervention guide.* Circle Pines, MN: American Guidance Services.

Forest, M. (Ed.). (1987). *More education integration.* Downsview, Ont.: G. Allan Roehler Institute.

Foxx, R. M., Faw, G. D., & Weber, G. (1991). Producing generalization of inpatient adolescents' social skills with significant adults in a natural environment. *Behavior Therapy, 22,* 85–99.

Furman, W., & Gavin, L. A. (1989). Peers' influence on adjustment and development: A view from the intervention literature. In T. T. J. Berndt & G. W. Ladd (Eds.), *Peer relationships in child development* (pp. 319–340). New York: Wiley.

Gamble, R., & Strain, P. S. (1979). The effects of dependent and interdependent group contingencies on socially appropriate responses in classes for emotionally handicapped children. *Psychology in the Schools, 16,* 253–260.

Goldstein, A. P., Harootunian, B., & Conoley, J. C. (1994). *Student aggression: Prevention, management, and replacement training.* New York: Guilford.

Gottman, J. M., Gonso, J., & Schuler, P. (1976). Teaching social skills to isolated children. *Journal of Abnormal Child Psychology, 4,* 179–197.

Gresham, F. M. (1981). Social skills training with handicapped children: A review. *Review of Educational Research, 51,* 139–176.

Gresham, F. M. (1985). Utility of cognitive-behavioral procedures for social skills training with children: A review. *Journal of Abnormal Child Psychology, 13,* 411–423.

Gresham, F. M. (1986). Conceptual issues in the assessment of social competence in children. In P. S. Strain, M. J. Guralnick, & H. M. Walker (Eds.), *Children's social behavior: Development, assessment, and modification* (pp. 143–179). New York: Academic Press.

Gresham, F. M. (1994). Generalization of social skills: Risks of choosing form over function. *School Psychology Quarterly, 9,* 142–144.

Gresham, F. M. (1995). Best practices in social skills assessment. In A. Thomas & J. Grimes (Eds.), *Best practices in school psychology–III* (pp. 1021–1030). Washington D.C.: National Association of School Psychologists.

Gresham, F. M., & Elliott, S. N. (1984). Assessment and classification of children's social skills: A review of methods and issues. *School Psychology Review, 13,* 292–301.

Gresham, F. M., & Elliott, S. N. (1990). *Social Skills Rating System: Manual.* Circle Pines, MN: American Guidance Services.

Gresham, F. M., & Nagle, R. J. (1980). Social skills training with children: Responsiveness to modeling and coaching as a function of peer orientation. *Journal of Consulting and Clinical Psychology, 48,* 718–729.

Gresham, F. M., & Reschly, D. J. (1988). Issues in the conceptualization, classification, and assessment of social skills in the mildly handicapped. In T. R. Kratochwill (Ed.), *Advances in school psychology* (Vol. 6; pp. 203–247). Hillsdale, NJ: Erlbaum.

Gunter, P., Fox, J. J., Brady, M. P., Shores, R. E., & Cavanaugh, K. (1988). Nonhandicapped peers as multiple exemplars: A generalization tactic for promoting autistic students' social skills. *Behavioral Disorders, 13,* 116–126.

Hansen, D. J., St. Lawrence, J. S., & Christoff, K. A. (1989). Group conversational-skills training with inpatient children and adolescents: Social validation, generalization, and maintenance. *Behavior Modification, 13,* 4–31.

Haring, T. G (1992). The context of social competence: Relations, relationships, and generalization. In S. L. Odom, S. R. McConnell, & M. A. McEvoy (Eds.), *Social competence of young children with disabilities: Issues and strategies for intervention* (pp. 307–320). Baltimore, MD: Brookes.

Haring, T. G., Breen, C. G., Lee, N., Pitts-Conway, V., & Gaylord-Ross, R. J. (1987). Adolescent peer tutoring and special friend experiences. *Journal of the Association for Persons with Severe Handicaps, 12,* 280–286.

Hendrickson, J. M., Strain, P. S., Tremblay, A., & Shores, R. E. (1982). Interactions of behaviorally handicapped children: Functional effects of peer social interactions. Behavior Modification, 6, 323–353.

Hertz-Lazarowitz, R., Sharan, S., & Steinberg, R. (1980). Classroom learning style and cooperative behavior of elementary school children. *Journal of Educational Psychology, 72,* 99–106.

Hoier, T., & Cone, J. D. (1987). Target selection of social skills for children: The template-matching procedure. *Behavior Modification, 11,* 137–163.

Hops, H., & Greenwood, C. R. (1988). Social skill deficits. In E. J. Mash & L. G. Terdal (Eds.), *Behavioral assessment of childhood disorders* (2nd ed., pp. 263–313). New York: Guilford.

Hops, H., Walker, H. M., & Greenwood, C. R. (1988). *Procedures for Establishing Effective Relationship Skills (PEERS): Manual for consultants.* Delray, FL: Educational Achievement Systems.

Horner, R. H. (1980). The effects of an environmental "enrichment" program on the behavior of institutionalized profoundly retarded children. *Journal of Applied Behavior Analysis, 13,* 473–493.

Horner, R. H., & Billingsley, F. F. (1988). The effect of competing behavior on the generalization and maintenance of adaptive behavior in applied settings. In R. Horner, G. Dunlap, & R. Koegel (Eds.), *Generalization and maintenance: Life-style changes in applied settings* (pp. 197–220). Baltimore, MD: Paul H. Brookes.

Horner, R. H., McDonnell, J. J., & Bellamy, G. T. (1986). Teaching generalized skills: General case instruction in simulation and community settings. In R. H. Horner, L. H. Meyer, & H. D. B. Fredericks (Eds.), *Education of learners with severe handicaps: Exemplary service strategies* (pp. 289–314). Baltimore, MD: Brookes.

Horner, R. H., Sprague, J., & Wilcox, B. (1982). General case programming for community activities. In B. Wilcox & G. T. Bellamy (Eds.), *Design of high school programs for severely handicapped students* (pp. 61–98). Baltimore, MD: Paul H. Brookes.

Johnson, D. W., & Johnson, R. T. (1975). *Learning together and alone.* Englewood Cliffs, NJ: Prentice Hall.

Johnson, D. W., Maruyama, G., Johnson, R., Nelson, D., & Skon, L. (1981). Effects of cooperative, competitive, and individualistic goal structures on achievement: A meta-analysis. *Psychological Bulletin, 89,* 47–62.

Johnson, R. T., Johnson, D. W., & Scott, L. (1978). The effects of cooperative and individualized instruction on student attitudes and achievement. *The Journal of Social Psychology, 104,* 207–216.

Jones, R. N., Sheridan, S. M., & Binns, W. R. (1993). Schoolwide social skills training: Providing preventive services to students at-risk. *School Psychology Quarterly, 8,* 57–80.

Kahn, N. A., & Hoge, R. D. (1983). A teacher-judgment measure of social competence: Validity data. *Journal of Consulting and Clinical Psychology, 51,* 809–814.

Kazdin, A. E. (1977). Assessing the clinical or applied importance of behavior change through social validation. *Behavior Therapy, 12,* 493–506.

Kehle, T. J., Clark, E., Jenson, W. R., & Wampold, B. E. (1986). Effectiveness of self-observation with behavior-disordered elementary school children. *School Psychology Review, 15,* 289–295.

Krischenbaum, D., & Ordman, A. M. (1984). Preventive intervention for children: Cognitive behavioral perspective. In A. W. Meyers & W. E. Craighead (Eds.), *Cognitive behavior therapy for children* (pp. 397–409). New York: Plenum.

Kratochwill, T. R., & Bergan, J. R. (1990). *Behavioral consultation in applied settings: An individual guide.* New York: Plenum.

Ladd, G. W. (1981). Effectiveness of a social learning method for enhancing children's social interaction and peer acceptance. *Child Development, 52,* 171–178.

La Greca, A. M., & Stark, P. (1986). Naturalistic observations of children's social behavior. In P. S. Strain, M. J. Guralnick, & H. M. Walker (Eds.), *Children's social behavior: Development, assessment, and modification* (pp. 181–213). New York: Academic Press.

Landau, S., Milich, R., & Whitten, P. (1984). A comparison of teacher and peer assessments of social status. *Journal of Clinical Child Psychology, 13,* 44–49.

Landrum, T. J., & Lloyd, J. W. (1992). Generalization in social behavior research with children and youth who have emotional or behavioral disorders. *Behavior Modification, 16,* 593–616.

Lewis, T. J., & Sugai, G. (1993). Teaching communicative alternatives to socially withdrawn behavior: An investigation in maintaining treatment effects. *Journal of Behavioral Education, 3,* 61–75.

Martin, R. P. (1988). *Assessment of personality and behavior problems: Infancy through adolescence.* New York: Guilford.

McConnell, S. R., & Odom, S. L. (1986). Sociometrics: Peer referenced measures and the assessment of social competence. In P. S. Strain, M. J. Guralnick, & H. M. Walker (Eds.), *Children's social behavior: Development, assessment, and modification* (pp. 215–284). New York: Academic Press.

Merrell, K. W. (1993). *School Social Behavior Scales.* Brandon, VT: Clinical Psychology Publishing.

Meyer, L. (1985, December). Friendships, or why nonhandicapped children should be friends rather than peer tutors. Paper presented at the Twelfth Annual The Association for Persons with Severe Handicaps (TASH) Conference, Boston.

Mize, J. (1995). Coaching preschool children in social skills: A cognitive-social learning curriculum. In G. Cartledge & J. F. Milburn (Eds.), *Teaching social skills to children and youth: Innovative approaches* (3rd ed., pp. 237–261). Boston: Allyn & Bacon.

Moore, L. A. (1994). The effects of social skills curricula: Were they apparent initially? *School Psychology Quarterly, 9,* 133–136.

O'Connor, R. D. (1969). Modification of social withdrawal through symbolic modeling. *Journal of Applied Behavior Analysis, 2,* 15–22.

O'Connor, R. D. (1972). Relative efficacy of modeling, shaping, and the combined procedures of the modification of social withdrawal. *Journal of Abnormal Psychology, 79,* 327–334.

Oden, S. L., & Asher, S. R. (1977). Coaching children in social skills for friendship making. *Child Development, 48,* 495–506.

O'Neill, R. E., Horner, R. H., Albin, R. W., Sprague, J. R., Storey, K., & Newton, J. S. (1997). *Functional assessment and program development for problem behavior: A practical handbook* (2nd ed.). Pacific Grove, CA: Brooks/Cole.

Pepler, D. J., & Rubin, K. H. (Eds.). (1991). *The development and treatment of childhood aggression.* Hillsdale, NJ: Erlbaum.

Pinkston, E. M., Reese, N. M., LeBlanc, J. M., & Baer, D. M. (1973). Independent control of a preschool child's aggression and peer interaction by contingent teacher attention. *Journal of Applied Behavior Analysis, 6,* 223–224.

Repp, A. C., & Karsh, K. G. (1994). Hypothesis-based interventions for tantrum behaviors of persons with developmental disabilities in school settings. *Journal of Applied Behavioral Analysis, 27,* 21–31.

Rhode, G., Jenson, W. R., & Reavis, H. K. (1994). *The tough kid book.* Longmont, CO: Sopris West.

Rhode, G., Morgan, D. P., & Young, K. R. (1983). Generalization and maintenance of treatment gains of behaviorally handicapped students from resource rooms to regular classrooms using self-evaluation procedures. *Journal of Applied Behavior Analysis, 16,* 171–188.

Rubin, K. H. (1985). Socially withdrawn children: An "at risk" population. In B. H. Schneider, K. H. Rubin, & J. E. Ledingham (Eds.), *Children's peer relations: Issues in assessment and intervention* (pp. 125–139). New York: Springer-Verlag.

Rubin, K. H., & Daniels-Bierness, T. (1983). Concurrent and predictive correlates of sociometric status in kindergarten and grade 1 children. *Merrill Palmer Quarterly, 29,* 337–351.

Sailor, W., Goetz, L., Anderson, J., Hunt, P., & Gee, K. (1988). Research on community intensive instruction as a model for building functional, generalized skills. In R. H. Horner, G. Dunlap, & R. L. Koegel (Eds.), *Generalization and maintenance: Life-style changes in applied settings* (pp. 67–98). Baltimore, MD: Paul H. Brookes.

Selman, R. L. (1980). *The growth of interpersonal understanding: Developmental and clinical analyses.* New York: Academic Press.

Shapiro, E. S., & Kratochwill, T. R. (1988). Analogue assessment: Methods for assessing emotional and behavioral problems. In E. S. Shapiro & T. R. Kratochwill (Eds.), *Behavioral assessment in the schools: Conceptual foundations and practical applications* (pp. 290–321). New York: Guilford.

Sharan, S. (1980). Cooperative learning in small groups: Recent methods and effects on achievement, attitudes, and ethnic relation. *Review of Educational Research, 50,* 241–271.

Sharan, S., & Sharan, Y. (1976). *Small group teaching.* Englewood Cliffs, NJ: Educational Technologies Publications.

Sheridan, S. M. (1995). *The tough kid social skills book.* Longmont, CO: Sopris West.

Sheridan, S. M., Dee, C. C., Morgan, J., McCormick, M., & Walker. D. (1996). A multimethod intervention for social skills deficits in children with ADHD and their parents. *School Psychology Review, 25,* 57–76.

Sheridan, S. M., Kratochwill, T. R., & Bergan, J. R. (1996). *Conjoint behavioral consultation: A procedural manual.* New York: Plenum.

Sheridan, S. M., Kratochwill, T. R., & Elliott, S. N. (1990). Behavioral consultation with parents and teachers: Delivering treatment for socially withdrawn children. *School Psychology Review, 19,* 33–52.

Sisson, L. A., Van Hasselt, V. B., Hersen, M., & Strain, P. S. (1985). Peer interventions: increasing social behaviors in multihandicapped children. *Behavior Modification, 9,* 293–321.

Slavin, R. E. (1980). *Using student learning.* Baltimore, MD: Johns Hopkins University, Center for Social Organization of Schools.

Slavin, R. E. (1983a). *Cooperative learning.* New York: Longman.

Slavin, R. E. (1983b). When does cooperative learning increase student achievement? *Psychological Bulletin, 94,* 429–445.

Slavin, R. E., Karweit, N. (1981). Cognitive and affective outcomes of an intensive student team learning experience. *Journal of Experimental Education, 50,* 29–35.

Smith, D. J., Young, K. R., West, R. P., Morgan, D. P., & Rhode, G. (1988). Reducing the disruptive behavior of junior high school students: A classroom of self-management procedures. *Behavioral Disorders, 13,* 231–239.

Spivack, G., & Shure, M. B. (1982). The cognition of social adjustment: Interpersonal cognitive problem-solving thinking. In B. B. Lahey & A. E.

Kazdin (Eds.), *Advances in clinical child psychology* (Vol 5, pp. 323–372). New York: Plenum.

Stephens, R. D. (1993). School-based interventions: Safety and security. In A. P. Goldstein & C. R. Huff (Eds.), *The gang intervention handbook.* Champaign, IL: Research Press.

Stephens, T. M. (1981). *Technical manual: Social Behavior Assessment.* Columbus, OH: Cedars Press.

Stephens, T. M., & Arnold, K. D. (1992). *Social Behavior Assessment Inventory: Professional manual.* Odessa, FL: Psychological Assessment Resources.

Stokes, T. F., & Osnes, P. G. (1989). An operant pursuit of generalization. *Behavior Therapy, 20,* 337–355.

Strain, P. S., Kerr, M. A., & Ragland, E. U. (1979). Effects of peer-mediated social initiations and prompting/reinforcement procedures on the social behavior of autistic children. *Journal of Autism and Developmental Disabilities, 9,* 41–54.

Strain, P. S., Shores, R. E., & Timm, M. A. (1977). Effects of peer social initiations on the behavior of withdrawn preschool children. *Journal of Applied Behavior Analysis, 10,* 289–298.

Urbain, E. S., & Kendall, P. C. (1980). Review of social-cognitive problem-solving interventions with children. *Psychological Bulletin, 88,* 109–143.

Walker, H. M., Greenwood, C. R., Hops, H., & Todd, N. M. (1979). Differential effects of reinforcing topographic components of social interaction: Analysis and direct replication. *Behavior Modification, 3,* 291–321.

Walker, H., & McConnell, S. (1988). *Walker-McConnell Scale of Social Competence.* Austin, TX: Pro-Ed.

Walker, H. M., Steiber, S., & Eisert, D. (1991). Teacher ratings of adolescent social skills: Psychometric characteristics and factorial replicability across age-grade ranges. *School Psychology Review, 20,* 301–314.

Wandless, R. L., & Prinz, R. J. (1982). Methodological issues in conceptualizing and treating childhood social isolation. *Psychological Bulletin, 92,* 39–55.

Weissberg, R. P. (1985). Designing effective social problem-solving programs for the classroom. In B. H. Schneider, K. H. Rubin, & J. E. Ledingham (Eds.), *Children's peer relations: Issues in assessment and intervention* (pp. 225–242). New York: Springer-Verlag.

Wright, L., Stroud, R., & Keenan, M. (1993). Indirect treatment of children via parent training: A burgeoning form of secondary prevention. *Applied and Preventive Psychology, 2,* 191–200.

Zwald, L., & Gresham, F. M. (1982). Behavioral consultation in a secondary class: Using DRL to decrease negative verbal interactions. *School Psychology Review, 11,* 428–432.

# Families as Educational Partners for Children's School Success: Suggestions for School Psychologists

Sandra L. Christenson
Karla Buerkle
*University of Minnesota*

*To use a chemical analogy, parent intervention functions as a kind of fixative, which stabilizes effects produced by other processes.*

*Bronfenbrenner (1974, p. 34)*

The home environment is a powerful predictor of school learning for students—their level of achievement, their interest in learning, and the number of years of schooling they will attain (Christenson, Rounds, & Gorney, 1992; Henderson & Berla, 1994; Sloane, 1991). As a consequence, there has been an increase in the development of family participation in education. Three reasons for this activity were advanced by Kellaghan, Sloane, Alvarez, and Bloom (1993): (1) the cumulative impact of research findings that underscore the importance of the home in contributing to children's educational and developmental progress; (2) reform efforts that focus only on one microsystem—the school or classroom—have not been as successful in increasing achievement as anticipated; and (3) the dramatic changes in the structure and function of families, which has given rise to concern about the family's ability to foster, without support, children's scholastic development.

In this chapter, we provide empirical evidence and theoretical support for school personnel working with families as educational partners. We argue that families are essential to the optimal success of students in schools. In doing

so, we introduce the concept of two curricula and the importance of the home-school partnership in promoting academic, social, and behavioral competence for students. First, we provide a rationale for family involvement in education. Second, we review the contributions of four theorists. Next we review the empirical basis for the effect of family influences on a child's competence, as well as specific findings on the curriculum of the home. We end with suggestions for school psychology practice.

## Rationale for Family Involvement

### Empirical Foundation

The cumulative impact of research findings that underscore the importance of the home environment in contributing to children's educational and developmental progress provides a basis of support for family involvement in education. Based on a review of 66 studies, reviews, reports, and books, Henderson and Berla (1994) conclude that "the family makes critical contributions to student achievement, from earliest childhood through high school. Efforts to improve children's outcomes are much more effective if they encompass their families" (p. 14). For example, when parents are involved in the educational lives of their children, we know that students show improvement in grades (Dornbusch, Ritter, Leiderman, Roberts, & Fraleigh, 1987; Ferhmann, Keith, & Reimers, 1987), test scores including reading achievement (Comer, 1988; Epstein, 1991) and math achievement (Epstein, 1986; Mullen, 1989), attitude toward schoolwork (Kellaghan et al., 1993), behavior (Comer & Haynes, 1992; Steinberg, Mounts, Lamborn, & Dornbusch, 1989), self-esteem (Collins, Moles, & Cross, 1982), completion of homework (Clark, 1993), academic perseverance (Estrada, Arsenio, Hess, & Holloway, 1987), and participation in classroom learning activities (Sattes, 1985). In addition, benefits for students include fewer placements in special education (Lazar & Darlington, 1978), greater enrollment in postsecondary education (Baker & Stevenson, 1986; Eagle, 1989), higher attendance rates (Collins et al., 1982; Sattes, 1985), lower dropout rates (National Center for Educational Statistics, 1992), fewer suspensions (Comer & Haynes, 1992), and realization of exceptional talents (Bloom, 1985). What is most impressive about these findings is that students' outcomes are congruent with educators' goals.

In addition to positive outcomes for students, we also know that there are benefits for families and schools (Davies, 1993). For parents, teachers hold higher opinions of their capabilities, they develop more confidence about helping their children learn at home, and they have more self-efficacy and comfort with educational issues. Benefits for schools include increased confidence in the school, enhanced teachers' morale, and a better reputation in the community. Three other relevant findings are (1) the predictive power of family process variables, (2) consistency across socializing environments as a contributing factor in educational outcomes, and (3) evidence that a comprehensive partnership approach is necessary to reduce the achievement gap between children from low- and middle-income families.

First, there is evidence that family process variables, the specific things families do to support students' learning, are considered more important than family status variables, the descriptive characteristics of families, for enhancing positive outcomes. Based on the review of numerous studies, Kellaghan et al. (1993) report that social class or family configuration predicts up to 25% of the variance in achievement, whereas family process variables such as discussing homework or consistent routines for study predict up to 60% of this variance. Fur-

thermore, the considerable variation in families learning environments within social class has led to the conclusion that what parents do vis-à-vis their children's education is more important than who they are. In sum, in the family process versus status debate, what matters most for student achievement is the degree to which parents are able to provide positive educational experiences for their children (Milne, 1989). Across several studies of families with varying income and ethnic backgrounds, the presence of three factors in homes was strongly associated with positive academic outcomes: strong, consistent values about the importance of education; willingness to help children and to intervene at school; and ability to become involved (Mitrsomwang & Hawley, 1993). Milne states, "Family structures are not inherently good or evil per se; what is important is the ability of the parent to provide pro-educational resources for children—be they financial, material, or experiential" (p. 58).

We know that some children learn attitudes, skills, and behaviors at home that prepare them well for the tasks and demands at school. We know that some children do not, and therefore, the issue of equity is apparent. Given that our data base on home learning influences and child outcomes is replete with correlational studies, to attribute a causal link between home environments and educational performance would be unfounded. However, we do know that families are potential facilitators (not determinants) of their children's educational and developmental success (Grolnick & Ryan, 1992) and that parents, regardless of education, income, or ethnic background, want their children to be successful in school, are uncertain about how to help their children with schoolwork or what their role should be with their children's school, and desire information on how schools function and consultation from school psychologists on child and adolescent development and behavior (Christenson, Hurley, Sheridan, & Fenstermacher, 1997; Epstein, 1991).

Second, consistency across socializing environments is often ignored in intervention efforts. After reviewing the family's effect on cognitive, social, and motivational aspects of students' behavioral and their relationship to classroom performance, Hess and Holloway (1984) concluded that consensus between home and school about the goals of education is essential to counter information from competing sources, such as television and peers, and that discontinuities between families and educators compromise the effectiveness of either parents or educators as socializing agents. Their conclusion is consistent with the findings from *Running in Place* (Zill & Nord, 1994), a research report of the challenges to families in the 1990s. The authors describe three challenges—making ends meet in a changing economy, combating negative peer influences, and maintaining parental control as children grow older—and provide data to support two conclusions: family processes are a more important indicator of family health and well-being than family structure, and families need the support and cooperation of other institutions to function well, particularly to combat negative peer influences. In addition, Hansen (1986) demonstrated achievement gains from third to fifth grades for those students who experienced congruence in rules and interaction styles across home and school environments. He found the greater the discontinuity between home and school, the more students' academic grades declined. He also found that there was no preferred classroom or home type; rather, the match in the message received by students from home and school about rules and expectations was the critical factor for children's academic success.

With respect to behavioral outcomes for students, the extensive work of Reid and Patterson (1989) with aggressive children and youths illustrates the generalization of children's behavior across home, peer, and school contexts and the absolute necessity to intervene across contexts for behavior change. In an interview study with 55 ethnically and academically diverse youths in four urban high schools, Phelan, Yu, and Davidson (1994) found that all students—even those who describe their home, peer, and school contexts as congruent for academic expectations—report psychosocial pressure and stress. However, students whose peer, school, and family worlds are different experience greater adversity in navigating across borders because of divergent messages. Students in this group reported a low probability of graduating from high school and perceived their personal futures as bleak. Collectively, these results challenge current communication practices between families and educators, such as the limited time available for meaningful dialogue and information sharing. It is important to examine the degree to which a weak match or no match between home and school is a contributing factor to the mean level of national educational outcomes in Amer-

ica's schools and to differential outcomes for subgroups of students.

Third, successful home-school partnership programs are comprehensive; well planned; and provide options for family involvement, which allows schools to be responsive to the diversity of families. Studies that correlate levels of parent involvement with gains in students' achievement invariably find that the more extensive the involvement, the greater the achievement (Henderson & Berla, 1994). In programs that are designed to be full partnerships, students' achievement not only improves, but also reaches levels that are standard for middle-class children (Comer, 1995; Comer & Haynes, 1992). Furthermore, children who are farthest behind make the greatest gains (Henderson & Berla, 1994). The effect of family processes, continuity across socializing environments, and partnerships on children's educational performance has led to the inclusion of families in school restructuring (e.g., Levin, 1987).

## Essential Issues for Family Involvement

Although our knowledge of the importance of the home environment in promoting educational outcomes is growing, "our understanding of the home-school interface in relation to children's learning is still limited" (Kellaghan et al., 1993, p. 83). We believe three issues are missing or are far less salient than desirable in discussions about working with families as educational partners: (1) differences between a traditional and partnership approach to family involvement in education; (2) recognition of students' out-of-school time as a differentiating factor on their educational outcomes; and (3) limited recognition by educators for what families do to promote competence—academic, social, and behavioral, in children and youth.

### *Defining Features*

Educators value family involvement in education, and there is much evidence that parents and educators agree that both are important for children's success in school (Christenson, 1995b; Olson, 1990; Williams & Stallworth, 1984). However, we estimate that 90% of relationships between schools and families would be characterized as traditional and conventional. In this section, we provide a description of the defining features of the traditional and partnership approaches to family involvement (Berger, 1992; Epstein, 1995; Henderson, Marburger, & Ooms,

1986), which we argue are both viable approaches but qualitatively different. The differences are worthy of examination because successful family-school relationships depend on site-specific development (National Association of State Boards of Education, 1992).

First, an underlying assumption in the traditional approach to family involvement is that families and educators have separate roles and responsibilities in educating and socializing children and youths. One defining feature of the traditional approach is physical and social distance between home and school. For example, there tends to be limited contact between parents and educators, and often the contact tends to be at prescribed times, such as parent-teacher conferences or back-to-school nights, or precipitated by a concern or crisis. Thus, the stimulus for the contact at unusual times is negatively oriented—something is wrong. In addition, one-way communication is the norm; the direction of the communication is mostly from schools to home, which Swap (1993) has described as the school-to-home transmission model. Parent-teacher conferences with an emphasis on the evaluation of a student's progress or setting school policy without asking for parental input are common events in this model.

Second, in a traditional approach, much emphasis is placed on parent involvement in ways that address the school's agenda. Schools designate prescribed roles for parents, which are often traditional roles like volunteering or fundraising. These roles are found in the context that parents' help is needed to accomplish something—a task—for the school; therefore, parents are seen as desirable in specific situations.

Third, there is a high frequency of school-determined recommendations to families. For example, educators may recommend to families that they need to monitor students' homework. This recommendation is not inherently bad; however, it is often made without understanding other family demands or the need for family resources to comply successfully with the recommendation. Another relatively common example is educators who refer families to parent education when their children are exhibiting behavior problems. There is an assumption that families are part of the problem and need to learn new management strategies. In this approach, families are viewed as clients to whom the school needs to deliver services; family deficits can be corrected by professional services or what Seeley

(1985) has referred to as the delegation of services model. There is little recognition that the family can personally identify resources or supports that would be helpful in resolving the concern.

Fourth, the traditional approach has been characterized by legal mandates to involve parents, for example, Special education, Even Start, and Title I. These mandates have increased the opportunity for families and educators to have a dialogue, although many parents continue to be passive recipients.

Finally, it is helpful to examine who is involved when a traditional approach is used. Generally, parents of primary-grade children or those for whom there is a match between the approach of the school and the family tend to be most involved. Thus, the dramatic decline in parent involvement at fourth grade and the uninvolvement of minority and lower-income families may, in part, be explained by features of a traditional approach. In this approach, educators measure success in terms of the number of parents or which parents attend school functions and participate at school; the emphasis tends to be on parent involvement.

The partnership approach to family involvement is characterized by a belief in shared responsibility for educating and socializing children and youth, a broad definition of home and school contributions, and collaborative interactions among participants. First, the goal of a partnership approach to family involvement is to enhance the success of all children in school, that is to improve the educational experiences and educational outcomes for students. To do so, families and educators recognize the need to share information and resources across home and school contexts. Both are viewed as essential for children's optimal progress in school. There is a recognition that two systems working together can accomplish more than either system can accomplish separately and that both parents and educators have legitimate roles and responsibilities in the partnership. However, the emphasis is not on roles, particularly on the roles families can play. Rather, the emphasis is on relationships, specifically, how families and educators work together to promote the academic and social development of students. As a result, the attitude between partners is integral to the success of the relationship.

Second, in a partnership approach, the systems of home and school are conceptualized broadly. Home does not refer to the biological parent but rather to the primary care-giver or individual in the child's home who can serve as a school contact and partner. Home may include the contributions of parents, older siblings, grandparents, other relatives, and mentoring adults. School refers to all school personnel (e.g., administrators and support personnel), not only teachers. Therefore, home-school partnerships for children's success in the school are not synonymous with parent-teacher relationships, although these are the linchpin in a successful program. There are many opportunities for all individuals to contribute to children's competence, and the contributions of individuals are valued, even when they are not perceived as directly meeting a present need of the school or home.

Third, families and educators interact differently. They model collaboration by listening to each other's perspective and viewing differences as a strength; sharing information to coconstruct the big picture about children's behavior; respecting the skills and knowledge of each other; and planning together and making decisions that address parents', educators', and students' needs. Interactions are based on a problem-solving and no-fault orientation; the partners are uninterested in who is to blame for the problem and interested in who is responsible for a solution.

In sum, a partnership approach (a) focuses the goal of family involvement on enhanced success for students, (b) develops a relationship based on shared decision making and contributions toward a common goal, and (c) strives to provide students with a consistent message about their schoolwork and behavior. Although home and school are two systems that are still primarily used to operating autonomously, there has been an increase in partnership programs in schools. These programs share school governance (Comer, 1995) and often use action teams to develop a partnership program (Epstein, (1995). Researchers have found that the partnership approach tends to result in greater levels of family participation for previously uninvolved families (Palanki & Burch, 1995; Rioux & Berla, 1993). Table 27.1 shows the defining features of the traditional and partnership approaches to family involvement in education. The qualitative differences and ramifications for program implementation, we contend, are vital to the successful involvement of different families under varying situations in education.

## Out-of-school Time

In debates about national educational performance in our country, we believe the failure to recognize the use of out-of-school time as an educational opportunity is a mistake. Varied statistics about the ratio of in- to out-of-school time appear in the literature. In 1984, Walberg reported that 87% of students' time from birth to age 18 was spent outside of school; therefore, he concluded that educational productivity in American schools would be enhanced by paying attention to what he referred to as the "curriculum of the home." In 1991, Usdan, president of the Institute for Educational Leadership, pointed out that "although 91% of the time kids spend between birth and age 18 is spent outside the schools, the new America 2000 thrust pays too little attention to this reality and assumes that just changing academic requirements alone will improve the life chances of millions of poverty-ridden youngsters" (cited in Ooms & Hara, 1991, p. ii). Usdan argued for new incentives for collaborations between schools and other institutions in the public

## TABLE 27.1    Defining Features of Traditional and Partnership Approaches

| Variable | Traditional | Partnership |
|---|---|---|
| Goal | Involve parents | Children's school success |
| Focus | Roles | Relationships |
| Contact | Greater physical and social distance | More contact and dialogue |
| Rationale for program | Deficit-oriented view of families | Strength, empowerment view of families |
| Intervention focus | Single setting (home or school) | Multiple contexts (home, school, community) |
| Who is involved | Families interested | Greater involvement by more families |

sector to address some root causes of educational failure, such as nutritional deficiencies and health and mental health needs. The central role of the home is illustrated by the mere quantity of time spent outside of school; equally relevant is the quality of time so spent.

In his study of the use of out-of-school time for African-American twelfth-graders in Chicago and Hispanic, Asian, African-American, and Anglo students in elementary, middle, and high schools in Los Angeles, Clark (1990) found that high-achieving students from low-income backgrounds spend, on average, 20 hours a week in constructive learning activities. Clark hypothesized that the term *disadvantaged* should not be restricted to the particular circumstances of low income or unhealthy living environments but must consider the necessary conditions for educational and occupational success. He believed that some children from low-income environments perform well in school and in later life because specific behaviors and attitudes that allow them to achieve mediate their social circumstances. In particular, Clark showed that the difference between high- and low-achieving students from similar backgrounds was explained, in part, by how and with whom they spend their time—particularly the 70% of their waking hours outside of school in grades K–12.

Clark (1990) concluded that (1) supportive guidance from adults is a critical factor, and (2) constructive learning activities that allow students to engage in mental workouts include deliberate, out-of-school learning and work activities (homework, lessons, practice, and volunteer work); high-yield leisure activities (reading, writing, conversation, problem solving, and visiting museums); recreational activities (sports, movies, biking, and talking on the phone); and health maintenance activities (exercising, going to church, grooming, and meditating). Whether an activity promotes students' learning and development depends on the time spent; degree of thinking involved; extent of supportive input by knowledgeable adults and peers; and standards, expectations, and goals for the activity.

## Competence Enhancement

The construct of competence has its earliest roots in the writing of White (1959), who defined competence as "an organism's capacity to interact effectively with its environment" (p. 297). Typically, competence is viewed as an outcome variable that concisely summarizes the quality of an individual's functioning in a particular situation. Waters and Sroufe (1983) defined the competent individual as "one who is able to make use of environmental and personal resources to achieve a good developmental outcome" (p. 81). Ford (1982) defined competence in terms of two outcomes: behavioral effectiveness in achieving personal goals and a sense of personal well-being. Similarly, Strayhorn (1988) referred to competence as specific skills, beliefs, and/or behaviors that are useful in responding to environmental demands.

The competence enhancement model proposed by August, Anderson, and Bloomquist (1992) assumes that children's responses to specific environmental demands are determined by risk and protective factors that children bring to meet the challenges. Risk factors, which include biological and genetic deficiencies, family and community environmental factors, and life events, weaken children's capacity to cope with crises and transitions. In contrast, protective factors provide children with the necessary resources to mitigate developmental challenges. Protective factors include personal resources, such as intrinsic attributes of the child (e.g., problem-solving ability and self-regulation), and ecological resources, which include environmental supports (e.g., family cohesiveness, adequate rule setting, and facilitative interpersonal interactions). In this scheme, competence represents "an outcome of the interaction of risk and protective factors in the face of challenge" (p. 178). We support the authors' contention that the development of academic, social, and behavioral competence in students requires parents and educators to identify personal and ecological resources during different developmental periods. Thus, a goal for parents and educators who adopt a competence perspective is to provide children and youth with the personal and ecological resources needed for them to confront challenges imposed on them as they develop (August et al., 1992). This approach is consistent with the notion that home and school are vital contexts for children's development (Bronfenbrenner, 1986; Coleman, 1987) and that parents and educators must view their roles as facilitators of children's development (Christenson, 1995a).

The competence enhancement perspective is reflected in National Educational Goal 8: "By the year 2000, every school will promote partnerships that will increase parent involvement and participation in promoting the social, emotional, and academic growth of children" (*National Educational Goal Report*, 1994, p. 11). Working with parents as educational partners is both a preventive and health promotion activity. While there is no question that forming partnerships with families helps educators work in problem-preventing ways (Rich, 1987), we assert that the value of working with families as educational partners is the promotion of health. Our goal, as partners, should be to promote the healthy development of children. In our experience, educators agree with this statement philosophically; however, in practice, they often find themselves trapped in blaming families or viewing "the home as auxiliary, merely providing supplemental support for the work of the school" (Kellaghan et al., 1993, p. 135).

## Two Curricula

In this chapter, we explicitly introduce the idea that there are two curricula for students' optimal school success. Furthermore, we contend that the essential message schools must provide is that a shared responsibility between home and school—or the curriculum of the home and the curriculum of school—is necessary for positive educational outcomes. The message addresses two points: support from a child's home is essential, not merely desirable, if children are to be optimally successful in school; and schools on their own are not likely to be totally successful in meeting all of society's expectations for students' outcomes.

The essential message is based on several assumptions: (a) educators are interested in increasing opportunities for students to learn and in creating conditions for optimal learning; (b) students' success is dependent on multiple influences, including student, teacher, instruction, peer, and home; and (c) out-of-school time provides a learning opportunity for students. Because we know that both in- and out-of-school time is correlated with performance outcomes for students, both families and educators are facilitators of children's educational performance.

There are two curricula for students: the curriculum of the school and the curriculum of the home. Students' outcomes, unquestionably, depend on what teachers do. The curriculum of the school is strongly supported by the effective instructional literature (see Gettinger and Stoiber, Chapter 35; Ysseldyke & Christenson, 1993). The curriculum of the home, which reemphasizes the educative role of the family and is the degree to which the home functions as an effective learning environment, includes such variables as parental expectations, structured time for study, modeling of learning and a positive attitude toward schooling, and amount of support for students' learning. There are many ways in which teachers implement the principles of effective instruction in classrooms. Similarly, there are many ways for families to create a positive home learning environment. Students' optimal performance depends on the active involvement with learning in both the school and the home.

The essential message supports the notions that both schools and homes are contexts for development, families and educators are behavior change agents, and working with families as educational partners holds the greatest promise for promoting all children's success and progress and is based on new principles and beliefs about families (Liontos, 1992). These principles include a no-fault, problem-solving approach; an ecological perspective; and a commitment to collaboration. The new beliefs are that all families have strengths, parents can learn new techniques, and parents have important perspectives about their children. In sum, the emphasis since 1990 on working with families as educational partners is based on the empowerment philosophy: Thus, our role as school psychologists has changed. We now strive to deliver content that is responsive to families' needs, invite parents to be active participants in their children's schooling, and provide opportunities for parents to contribute significantly to their children's educational and developmental progress. The purpose of this chapter is to provide theoretical support, empirical evidence, and implications for practice for working with families as educational partners. We recognize the seminal role of the curriculum of the school; however, the content in this chapter is directed to the curriculum of the home.

## THEORETICAL CONTRIBUTIONS

Four theorists make somewhat mutually exclusive contributions that support the curriculum of the home and shared responsibility for educational outcomes. First, Bronfenbrenner (1986) is well known for his theory of child development and description of the ecology of children. His theory contributes the notion that children and families are members of multiple environments and that "nested connections" exist between children, families, and other organizations like schools and social service agencies. Therefore, Bronfenbrenner clearly articulates the multiple influences on children's development, as well as the fact that the relationship between the environments (home and school) is the major contributing factor.

Coleman (1987) contends that home and school provide different inputs for the socialization of children and youth. In his theory, the home provides the base for teaching children a positive attitude toward school, an effort related to outcome, and a positive sense of self. The inputs from school give the child new learning opportunities, place demands on the child and reward the child for performance. He contends that the interaction between the resources provided by the home and the school result in differential socialization outcomes. Because there is greater variation in the resources provided by the home, schools need to reach out to families to help them address ways to increase their inputs for children's socialization. Coleman also offers the concept of social capital for children's development. There has been an erosion in the availability of social capital; for example, the amount of time for interaction between children and adults about academics and personal matters has declined because of changing demographics, both results of the divorce rate and dual working parents. Social capital at the community level refers to consistency in values, attitudes, and norms for acceptable behavior. The impact of the erosion of social capital is that a growing number of children are unprepared to perform successfully in schools. Because of this situation, Barton and Coley (1992) have suggested that "policies that deal with family resources, welfare dependency, and poverty among children are also educational policies to the extent that they make the home a better school" (p. 3). Therefore, partnerships to support children's development is seen as vital to the optimal socialization of children and youth.

Comer (1995), the developer of the School Development Program, demonstrated that a partnership approach resulted in increasing the achievement levels of black, poor, inner-city children to the standards expected for white, middle-class students and reducing disciplinary problems and behavioral referrals. His approach is based on problem solving between parents and educators to establish academic and social goals for students and to implement comprehensive school plans based on mutual input and shared decision making. Comer contends that family involvement in education is most successful when the initiative is a component of a focused school improvement process that creates positive relationships among adults that support children's total development. His theory and application has shown us that for many children, particularly those from low-income, working-class, or non-English-speaking families, there is a big cultural gap between home and school. However, when parents and educators help children adjust to the world of school, children from all backgrounds tend to do well. Finally, Comer emphasizes relationships, stating that children learn from people with whom they bond. When parents and teachers understand and respect each other, share similar expectations, and stay in touch, children feel comfortable about whom they are and can more easily reconcile their experiences at school and home.

Epstein (1995) builds on the theoretical work of Bronfenbrenner (1986) and other ecologically oriented models (Leichter, 1974; Litwak & Meyer, 1974) as she describes her theory of overlapping spheres of influence. Because families and educators can have separate or shared responsibilities for students, the spheres of influence across home and school can be pushed closer together to enable educators and families to increase their interactions and share responsibilities or pulled apart to separate responsibilities and reduce interactions. A separate responsibility approach tends to create a division of labor between home and school, whereas a shared responsibility approach creates a combination of labor. Epstein contends that the nature of the overlap in practices and interactions between partners will change across the grades as children, families, and schools change. Her perspective is particularly important to school psychologists. Epstein argues that a 13-year contract between home and school is important for students' performance, although the nature of the contract will differ. In the spheres of influence model, she states that there is no pure school or pure family time; children and adolescents transfer concerns, attitudes, and behaviors across settings.

Walberg's (1984) meta-analytic synthesis of 2,575 empirical studies of academic learning found that parents directly or indirectly influence eight determinants of cognitive, affective, and behavioral learning: students' ability, students' motivation, quality of instruction, amount of instruction, psychological climate of the classroom, academic stimulation in the home environment, peer group, and television. Social and economic factors—class size, socioeconomic status (SES), and financial expenditures per student—influence school learning but to a lesser degree. Altering home conditions for academic learning and the relations between home and school should produce large effects on learning. According to Walberg (1984), "the curriculum of the home predicts academic learning twice as well as the socioeconomic status of families" (p. 400).

## EMPIRICAL EVIDENCE

It is apparent we need to explore more systematically the available empirical evidence. Has empirical research provided support for these conceptualized influences? The data-based section of this paper is divided into three sections. The first section illustrates the ways in which family competence affects children's functioning. Next, we present studies on the impact of family stress and support. The final section begins with a summary of the curriculum of the home data base and describes the impact of the family on children's learning in three areas; academic, behavioral, and social.

### Family Competence and Children's Functioning

Family competence can be viewed in a number of ways. Researchers have focused on parenting styles (Baumrind, 1991; Dornbusch et al., 1987; McCord, 1991; Pratt, Hunsberger, Pancer, Roth, & Santolupo, 1993; Steinberg et al., 1989), parenting behaviors and family health (Ellwood & Stolberg, 1993; Trickett, 1993), parental personal competence (Fischer, Barkley, Fletcher, & Smallish, 1993), communication and balanced and warm family interaction (Greenwald, 1990; Greenwald & Harder, 1994), and parent-child relationships (Neighbors, Forehand, & McVicar, 1993).

Children's competence is also construed in a variety of ways. McCord (1991) explored the competence construct longitudinally, differentiating competence as a form of achievement from adjustment. She defined achievement as abilities or attitudes leading to academic and occupational success and adjustment as the converse of antisocial, disruptive behavior, a dimension of social adjustment. Participants were 225 males raised in inner-city, high-crime neighborhoods. In her follow-up study, men, now between 45 and 53 years of age, with good family interactions in their childhood exhibited both forms of competence. Processes varied; maternal self-confidence was associated with an increase in offspring's achievement, whereas the extent to which maternal affection, parental conflict, and family expectations were present had an impact on subjects' adjustment. McCord's study provided evidence for the long-range effects of childhood socialization, as well as stylistic differences in parenting, on competence outcomes for offspring.

According to Darling and Steinberg (1993), parenting style is "a constellation of attitudes toward the child that are communicated to the child and that, taken together, create an emotional climate in which the parents' behaviors are expressed" (p. 493). Research on parenting styles has shown that, in general, an authoritative approach to parenting is preferred. Diana Baumrind (1991), an authority on parenting styles, examined the effects of parents' behaviors on adolescent competence. She found that authoritative parenting, a style she defines as highly demanding and highly responsive, not only predicated adolescent competence but also served as a protective factor against substance abuse. Unfortunately, Baumrind's sample was homogeneous—white, middle-class, and educationally advantaged—so her results are limited in application. However, researchers who studied more diverse samples concur with Baumrind's results. Eight thousand high school students in Wisconsin and California were surveyed to determine the relationship of authoritative parenting characteristics to children's educational outcomes (Steinberg et al., 1989). Participants were from low-income families and were ethnically diverse: 9% African American, 12% Hispanic, 14% Asian American, and 60% Anglo American. Based on two self-report questionnaires, findings showed a strong association between authoritative parenting characteristics (e.g., accepting, firm, and democratic) and positive students' outcomes (e.g., higher grades and self-reliance; lower anxiety, depression, and delinquent behavior). The authors state that this relationship "appears to transcend ethnicity, socioeconomic status, and family structure" (p. 15).

Parenting style is associated with increased parental competence in understanding children's development, resulting in positive effects on their learning (Pratt et al., 1993). The quality of parents' tutoring behavior was investigated in a sample of 28 fifth-graders and their parents (Pratt, Green, McVicar, & Bountrogianni, 1992; described in Pratt et al., 1993). The researchers hypothesized that parents with a better understanding of their child's developmental level would provide more effective tutoring and that this effectiveness would be reflected in higher scores on Baumrind's responsiveness and demandingness parenting dimensions, as well as a math posttest. Findings concurred in that parents' level of reasoning about development was related to greater sensitivity in tutoring style, which also was related to improved learning for children. Parents with higher developmental reasoning were also more responsive to and supportive of their children, although they did not exhibit high demandingness (e.g., consistent structure and high expectations).

Dornbusch et al. (1987) have also investigated the effect of parenting styles on children's learning. An authoritative parenting style appears to help mediate children's competence through discussion of schoolwork and everyday events, the modeling of problem-solving and negotiation skills, and support and expectations for success. Based on questionnaires distributed to 7,836 high school students and their parents in the San Francisco Bay area, the study showed that authoritative parenting is strongly associated with adolescents' school performance. An authoritative parenting style was a more powerful predictor of students' grades than were family status variables such as parents' educational level, ethnicity, or family structure.

Research has highlighted the stronger effects of family competence (what families do) and the weaker effects of family composition (what families are) on children's competence-related outcomes (Christenson et al., 1992; Ellwood & Stolberg, 1993; Kellaghan et al., 1993). What parents do to support their children's learning (i.e., consistent routines and communication about school) predicts up to 60% of variance in achievement, whereas family structure characteristics (e.g., size and sibling spacing) and social class predict up to 25% of achievement variance (Kellaghan et al., 1993). Ellwood and Stolberg (1993) propose a family competence model for understanding differences in children's adjustment and resulting psychosocial competence following divorce. Participants were 81 middle-income families with an 8- to 11-year-old child. Data supported the authors' hypotheses that family competence, comprising parenting behaviors and family health variables (e.g., discipline, cohesion, and communication), would be better predictors of children's adjustment than family composition (e.g., intact or separated). They found that higher levels of family functioning and children's positive adjustment were associated with low parental hostility and rejecting behaviors, combined with the practice of consistent and appropriate discipline. Results show that 21% of the variance in children's adjustment was explained by these family competence behaviors in contrast to 8% explained by family composition.

Prospective studies also provide evidence for the importance of family competence for children's outcomes. Fischer et al. (1993) studied hyperactive children over an eight-year period to delineate predictors of adolescents' competence. Although no single predictor cut across all domains of competence, results suggested that promoting family competence and early treatment of defiance and aggression may improve adolescents' outcomes. Specifically, personal parental competence (greater maternal education and fewer antisocial acts by fathers) predicted higher levels of children's social competence, and early intervention for aggression had a similar effect on behavioral competence.

Parental competence in high-risk families is a subject frequently investigated. Greenwald (1990) examined interactions in families in which one parent had been hospitalized previously for psychiatric illness. Participants were 94 Caucasian, middle-income families with sons aged 4, 7, and 10 at baseline. Findings at a three-year follow-up showed a significant positive impact of communication, balance, warmth, and activity in family interactions on children's cognitive, social, and emotional functioning. Greenwald and Harder (1994) investigated outcome predictor variables in this same high-risk sample. Two groups of the best-functioning and worst-functioning boys were chosen according to these variables: class-wide ratings by peers and teachers, parent-reported adaptive behavior scores, parent and child interviews, and the Wechsler Intelligence Scale for Children (WISC) IQ. Following the classification of 17 high-functioning and 13 low-functioning boys, $t$ tests were performed on potential predictor variables: parental communication; activity, balance, and warmth in family interaction; chronicity and level of parental psychopathology; and SES. As expected, most of the potential predictors significantly differentiated the highest-functioning from the lowest-functioning boys. The strongest predictors were process variables—measures of activity, balance, and warmth in family interactions and levels of communication deviance among family members—followed by the status variable of socioeconomic class.

As shown in Greenwald's work (Greenwald & Harder, 1994), family interaction variables play a key role in overall family competence and its impact on children's competence. Interparental conflict is a negative variable, although research demonstrates a differential effect for adolescents. Neighbors et al. (1993) studied the effects of high interparental conflict on two groups of adolescents. Participants differed by competence level, defined as cognitive competence as assessed by the Teacher's Rating Scale. Adolescents high in competence were considered resilient; those low in competence were nonresilient. The researchers used a stress-buffering model to explain the differential findings. Resilient teens ($N = 24$) were characterized by high self-esteem and a positive relationship with their mothers, whereas nonresilient teenagers ($N = 34$) did not have a positive, stable relationship with a parent.

There is also evidence in the literature that parents have the capacity to negatively affect the development of their children's competence. Trickett (1993) investigated the child-rearing contexts of abusive versus nonabusive homes. Participants were 29 physically abused children, ages 4 to 11, and a comparison group matched on SES, age, race, and gender. Children raised in abusive homes had significantly lower cognitive and social skills and more problem behaviors than comparison children. Findings pointed to aspects of a negative child-rearing context (e.g., conflict-ridden and rejecting) as significant influences on the development of children's competencies.

## External Stress and Support

Stress, whether chronic or transient, negatively affects families in a variety of ways. A stressful event is often seen as a temporary crisis; coping requires a marshaling of the family's capabilities, and differences in competencies help explain differential adjustment (Shaw, 1987). The presence or absence of chronic stress (e.g., poverty) or child-rearing support (e.g., extended family) may help or hinder the development of children's competencies.

Researchers frequently study the impact of stressors such as poverty, conflict and violence, and single parenting on families. Not surprisingly, the effect of poverty is usually negative and significant (Brody, Stoneman, Flor, McCrary, Hastings, & Conyers, 1994; Gersten, 1992; Minnesota Extension Service, 1993). Socioeconomic status is a very powerful predictor of children's competence because of the high-risk variables (Gersten, 1992). When reviewing multiple-risk studies of families in poverty, Gersten stated that "impaired social, emotional, and cognitive functioning of children is rooted in multiple, cumulative inadequacies of the child-rearing or caretaking environment" (p. 145). Although sometimes indirect and mediated through its impact on parent functioning and care-giving, financial strain drains family resources. Brody and colleagues studied rural, two-parent, African-American families with 9- to 12-year-old children and found that a lack of adequate finances led to parental depression, conflict, and lowered support. These outcomes, in turn, negatively influenced children's academic competence and socioemotional adjustment. The authors propose a family process model in which external stresses disrupt parent functioning and the development of youths' self-regulation and, subsequently, negatively affecting children's competencies.

In a similar vein, Wierson and Forehand (1992) propose that the disruption caused by family stressors interferes with adolescents' sense of security and stability rooted in their home environment and the parent-adolescent relationship, thus negatively affecting their adjustment and competencies. In their study of 184 11- to 15-year-olds, findings showed that for early adolescents, perception of the mother-adolescent relationship was a significant mediator between interparental conflict and cognitive competence, whereas for middle adolescents, parent communication skills had a direct relationship to cognitive competence. The authors' hypothesized that as parenting becomes less authoritarian, older children perceive relationships with their parents as reflected by their communication. The presence of stressors such as interparental conflict have a negative impact since the adolescent perceives insecurity in the relationship with his or her mother because of the instability of the home. Thus, subjective experience and perception is a key mechanism in the development of adolescents' competencies.

Verbal and physical conflict, as forms of violence, affect children both directly and indirectly. Methodological problems abound in studies of the effects of violence on children, largely because of confounding environmental variables and differences in the type of violence experienced. To control for such factors, researchers divided families with preschool children in Head Start into four groups: home and shelter-residing groups exposed to either verbal or physical conflict, a home group exposed to verbal conflict only, and a home control group (Fantuzzo, De-Paola, Lambert, Martino, Anderson, & Sutton, 1991). Participants were 107 preschoolers and their mothers. All families were characterized as low income, 55% had both biological parents present, and 41% represented minority groups (29% Hispanic, 5% black, 4% Asian, 4% Native American, and 2% mixed).

Results illustrated the additive nature of the negative effects of violence and an unstable home. Preschoolers exposed to verbal interparental conflict only exhibited a moderate level of conduct problems; those living with verbal and physical conflict showed clinical levels of behavior problems and moderate levels of emotional problems; and the addition of a family disruption, like temporary shelter residence, was associated with clinical levels of conduct problems, higher levels of emotional problems, and lower levels of social functioning and perceived maternal acceptance. Cumulative family stressors often increase children's risk of negative outcomes, as was seen in this study. Children witnessing verbal conflict had behavior problems; those exposed to verbal and physical interparental violence had increased levels of behavior problems and emotional problems; and those experiencing interparental violence and residing in shelters had even lower levels of behavioral, social, and emotional competence and perceived less acceptance from their mothers.

Another common stressor studied in the literature is the difficulty of raising children as a single parent. Research findings point to the stress inherent in finding adequate time and resources for children as a single parent rather than characteristics of single-parent adults per se (Belle, 1989; Cross, 1990; Gunnarsson & Cochran, 1990; Kamerman, 1985). Gringlas and Weinraub (1995) provide empirical support for this observation in a follow-up longitudinal study of 42 mother-child pairs. At a young age, children from single-parent homes did not look different, but by adolescence these children were showing decreased behavioral, social, and academic competence and more adjustment problems than children from two-parent homes. Maternal stress and a lower number of social supports for single mothers were hypothesized as significant mediators in negative outcomes.

Support is viewed as an important protective factor (Cochran, 1991; Dunst, Trivette, & Deal, 1988) when dealing with the negative effects of stress. The differential effects of family versus school support were investigated in a study of 120 middle-school students (Cauce, Hannan, & Sargeant, 1992). Sixth- and eighth-graders were assessed for life stress, social support, locus of control, psychological adjustment, and school performance. Outcome data highlighted family support and internal locus of control as key to the adolescents' competence in general, whereas school and peer support affected only cognitive and interpersonal competence, respectively. Findings were limited, however, since participants were predominantly white and middle class in private suburban schools. Chen and Rubin (1994) studied 476 fourth- and sixth-graders in China—two-thirds from workers' or peasants' homes and one-third from professional families—and found that parental support (i.e., acceptance) and parental resources (e.g., education, occupation, and psychological functioning) were strongly associated with children's social competence and low aggression. Thus, empirical data lend credence to informal beliefs about the important of family support for children's competence-related outcomes.

## The Family Influence on Children's Learning

Empirical studies have demonstrated the significant impact of general family competence, as well as external stress, on children's functioning. More specific to our role as school psychologists, the empirical literature also provides clear evidence of the family's significant impact on children's learning. This evidence lays the groundwork for our central tenet in this chapter. We believe it is critical to view families as educational partners for children's school and, even more broadly, life success. The data base on the curriculum of the home is summarized, followed by summaries of research.

### Curriculum of the Home

Based on his meta-analyses of over 2,500 empirical studies, Walberg (1984) further explicated parents' strong influence on academic learning. He identified eight major determinants of cognitive, affective, and behavioral learning for students. The first four—students' ability and motivation and quality and amount of instruction—directly affect students' achievement. The others—the psychological climate of a classroom; an academically stimulating home environment; exposure to a peer group with academic goals, interests, and activities; and minimum TV exposure—are considered supportive factors and benefit learning indirectly. Parents' influences on educational learning in these eight areas are variable yet substantial. For example, parents directly influence children's motivation by communicating their belief in the importance of education and by providing structure for discussions about schoolwork and enforcing homework. Termed the curriculum of the home, Walberg described the ways in which families promote children's learning: informed parent-child conversations daily, encouragement and discussion of reading materials, monitoring and analysis of TV programs, deferral of immediate gratification for long-term benefits, expressions of affection, and interest in children's academic and personal growth. Walberg points out that 87% of children's waking hours are spent outside of school in the nominal control of their parents. Therefore, he contended that partnering with parents to use this out-of-school time more efficiently and altering home conditions to support learning should produce large positive effects on children's competence.

Table 27.2 lists factors that have been identi-

## TABLE 27.2    Five Categorizations of Curriculum of the Home Factors

### Walberg (1984)

Informed parent-child conversations about everyday events
Encouragement and discussion of leisure reading
Monitoring and joint analysis of television viewing
Expression of affection
Interest in children's academic and personal growth
Delay of immediate gratifications to accomplish long-term goals

### Clark (1983)

Frequent dialogues between parents and children
Strong parent encouragement of academic pursuits
Warm and nurturing interactions
Clear and consistent limits
Consistent monitoring of how time is spent
Parental responsibility for assisting children with literacy and to gain knowledge
Communicating regularly with school personnel
Involvement in school functions
Expecting postsecondary outcomes

### Hess & Holloway (1984)

Much verbal interaction
Parental expectations for child success or press for achievement
Parental warmth and nurturance toward child
Parental control
Parental beliefs and attributions
Fostering children's interest and skill in reading and math
Providing quality reading material and math experiences
Modeling learning by reading and using math in the home
Reading with children
Engaging in discussions about reading with children
Expecting children to learn math and to read
Requesting verbal responses from their children
Believing children's effort, not luck, will result in learning
Developing a reflective problem-solving style
Orienting student's attention to learning opportunities

**TABLE 27.2** *(Continued)*

---

### Christenson, Rounds, & Gorney (1992)

---

High, realistic parental expectations for school performance
Parents' use of effort attributions for school performance
Parents' structure and support for learning in the home
Positive emotional interaction between parents and children or parents' emotional responsiveness to children's developmental needs
Parents' use of an authoritative parenting style

---

### Kellaghan, Sloane, Alvarez, & Bloom (1993)

---

Work habits of the family
    Degree of structure, sharing, and punctuality in home activities (work and play, chores, routine in management of home)
    Emphasis on regularity in the use of time and space in the home (balance of sleep, eat, study, read, play)
    Priority given to schoolwork, reading, and other educative activities over television and other recreation (schoolwork before play)
Academic guidance and support
    Frequent encouragement of children for their schoolwork (praise, approval)
    Parental knowledge of strengths and weaknesses in children's school learning and supportive help when they really need it (knowledge of strengths & weaknesses so supervision of homework is smoother)
    Availability of a quiet place for study with appropriate books, reference materials, and other learning materials
Stimulation to explore and discuss ideas and events (opportunities for good language habits)
    Family interest in hobbies and games and other activities of educative value
    Family use and discussion of books, newspapers, magazines, and TV programs
    Frequent use of libraries and museums and engagement in cultural activities
Language environment (opportunities for good language habits)
    Family concern and help for correct and effective use of language
    Opportunities for the enlargement of vocabulary and sentence patterns
Academic aspirations and expectations
    Parental knowledge of children's current schoolwork and school activities
    Parental standards and expectations for children's schoolwork
    Parental education and vocational aspirations for children

---

fied by researchers who have extended Walberg's (1984) original work. In his intensive observational study of the home environments of 10 high-achieving and 10 low-achieving secondary-level students, all of whom were African American in low-income families, Clark (1983) identified home variables that differentiated the achievement of students. Clark referred to the style of parenting for high achievers as "sponsored independence" and pointed out that it is also referred to as authoritative. Hess and Holloway's (1984) list is based on an extensive, integrative review of the developmental literature for children. Similarly, in their review of over 100 data-based manuscripts, Christenson et al. (1992)

concluded that five family factors were amenable to change and thus could serve as the basis of interventions to promote students' school success. Finally, Kellaghan et al. (1993) delineated a model for intervention on what they refer to as the home process approach. They advocate direct teaching of specific family behaviors that are correlated with positive academic outcomes for students.

Recent research has examined which family process variables are most critical for enhancing academic outcomes. Using data for eighth-grade students from the National Educational Longitudinal Study (NELS), Peng and Lee (1992) identified parental educational expectations, talking with students about school, providing learning materials, and providing learning opportunities outside of school as the variables that showed the strongest relationship with students' achievement. Parental aspirations for children's education have been shown to have a powerful influence on eighth-grade students' achievement (Singh, Bickley, Trivette, Keith, Keith, & Anderson, 1995) and the academic and social adjustment of low-income, minority children in sixth grade (Reynolds, Mavrogenes, Hagemann, & Bezuczko, 1993). Eight indicators of the home as an educative environment were used to predict the mean achievement of students in 37 states and the District of Columbia on the National Assessment of Educational Progress (NAEP). Barton and Coley (1992) found that three factors—students' absenteeism, variety of reading materials, and amount of television watching—fall under the control of the family and explain nearly 90% of the difference in performance between high- and low-achieving states. Fortunately, the three variables are amenable to change.

In contrast to these studies, Clark (1983) argued that "it is the overall quality of the family's lifestyle, not the composition, or status, or some subset of family process dynamics, that determines whether children are prepared for academically competent performance in the classroom (p. 1). In his study, parents of high-achieving students held common attitudes toward education that were accompanied by specific behaviors. In general, these parents put their children's growth and development before their personal needs, felt responsible for helping their children acquire basic literacy skills, believed that their children were responsible as learners, pursued postsecondary options, visited school periodically, and initiated contacts with teachers. The parenting style of the less successful children was termed "unsponsored independence," which was characterized by loose social connections and less parental vigilance. Low-achieving students reported that teachers provided less encouragement for their efforts and held lower expectations for their success. Their parents seldom visited the school or initiated contact with teachers, except in response to a negative report or crisis, and there was no mutually reinforcing pattern of home-school encouragement.

The notion of a generalized parenting style is also supported by the work of Dornbusch et al. (1987), who have shown that authoritative parents (1) encourage family discussions, specifically for children to examine both sides of an issue and for parents to be open to learning from their children; (2) respond to good grades with praise; and (3) react to bad grades with some structure in the form of restrictions, offers for help, and overall encouragement. They found that parenting style is a more powerful predictor of students' achievement than parental education, ethnicity, or family structure and that students who reside in authoritative homes perform better in school than similar students whose parents are authoritarian or permissive. Similarly, Eagle (1989) found that a family climate characterized by talking together, planning for postsecondary school activities, and monitoring schoolwork influenced the degree to which students from varied social class backgrounds pursued postsecondary education.

Mitrsomwang and Hawley (1993) examined the connection between family attitudes toward education and intervention behaviors in the home. Indo-Chinese high school students whose academic performance was well above average came from families who held strong values about education and were involved in their children's education. Students with average performance came from two types of families: those who held strong values about education but did not follow through on intervention behaviors, such as contacting the school or helping children learn at home, or those who had weaker values but were actively involved in their children's education. Students' performance was lowest when families held weak values and were uninvolved in education. Across all studies, both parents' attitudes (e.g., "I expect you to do well in school") and behavior (e.g., "I will communicate with school and support your learning") are evident in homes of high achievers.

## Family Influences on Academic and Cognitive Competence

In a meta-analytic synthesis of 29 programs designed to increase the educationally stimulating qualities of the home, Graue, Weinstein, and Walberg (1983) concluded that significant positive effects on children's learning were the result of (1) closer family relations, (2) extended learning time, (3) educationally stimulating home environments, (4) motivating influences, and (5) reduced television watching. In this investigation of the effects of school-based home instruction programs on children's academic learning, the authors found consistently favorable, and often large, effects.

Kellaghan et al. (1993) stress that "it is what parents do in the home rather than their status that is important" (p. 145). In their book, *The Home Environment and School Learning*, they describe the powerful impact of the home on children's cognitive competence, stating that when the home and school have a similar emphasis on motivation and learning, children are likely to do well. They present evidence that family structure and status characteristics (e.g., family size and SES) generally show modest (.20–.50) correlation with students' achievement, whereas family process variables (e.g., high expectations and academic support and guidance) explain up to 60% of the variance in achievement. Although causal links have not been proven, strong associations between family processes and students' achievement provide direction for intervention programs. The authors conclude that "schools are likely to find rewarding any efforts they make to link home and school, not only in terms of improved student behavior and achievement but also in the support network that a close home-school partnership can provide for their work" (p. 153).

Parent involvement in the early years provides a strong basis for children's healthy development. Cochran and Henderson (1986) found positive effects in achievement two years after families participated in the Family Matters program, an intensive, family-oriented, early childhood intervention program. Families were empowered to support their children's development through home visits by paraprofessionals who provided child-rearing information and demonstrated examples of parent-child learning activities. The authors concluded that schools can empower parents through communication; feedback; and ideas, information, and materials to help them work with their children at home. Parents as Teachers (PAT), another well-known parent education and support program for families with young children, has also been successful in promoting children's cognitive competence (Pfannensteil, Lambson, & Yarnell, 1991). The PAT program is aimed at strengthening the skills parents need to support their children's development in the first three years of life. Evaluation research on a diverse group of families (26% minority, 23% single parent, and 8% on public assistance) showed that more than half the children

with observed developmental delays overcame them by age three; PAT children scored above the national average on the K-ABC Achievement Scale (Kaufman & Kaufman, 1983); and the most frequent family risk, difficulty in coping and family stress, was lessened or resolved for half the families within three years.

In their review of 66 studies, Henderson and Berla (1994) describe the synergistic effect of parents as partners in children's learning. When parents are involved, children do better, children stay in school longer, and schools are better. The synergistic nature is illustrated by increases in children's achievement when parents are involved as teachers, supporters, advocates, and decision makers. Leler (1983) reviewed 48 studies of educational programs with parent involvement and found that the more parents participated, the more effective were the results. When parents are involved in a variety of roles (e.g., home tutoring, volunteering, decision making, and program management), highly positive results are seen in students' achievement. For example, Gillum (1977) compared three Michigan school districts' parent involvement programs, which implemented performance contracts to improve reading skills. Nearly 2,000 low-income second- through six-grade children were given achievement tests at the beginning and end of the school year. In all three school districts, students achieved higher scores in reading than was expected, but in the district in which parent involvement was the highest and most intensive, students scored considerably higher than those in the two districts with lower levels of parental involvement. Similarly, home-school contracts were implemented by Walberg, Bole, and Waxman (1980) as part of a citywide program to improve academic support in the home. Participants were 826 first- through sixth-grade students in inner-city schools. Contracts, signed by the superintendent, principal, teacher, parents, and student, outlined parents' roles in the home: provide a special place in the home for study, encourage the child daily through discussion, attend to the child's progress in school and compliment any gains, and cooperate with the teacher (i.e., by providing these elements). Students whose parents were more intensely involved gained .5 to .6 more grade equivalents in reading comprehension than those with less parent involvement.

Tizard, Schofield, and Hewison (1982) studied the effects of a collaboration between teachers and parents in assisting children's reading. They divided 1,900 elementary-age students into three groups, chosen at random. The first group read aloud to their parents several times a week from books sent home with them from school, and parents received teacher-generated tips on good practice ideas. The second group received extra reading help about twice a week at school from a reading teacher who listened to students read and offered additional help. The control group received no additional reading help. Students were administered several reading achievement tests at the end of the school year. There was highly significant improvement by children who received parental support and help at home but not by children who received help at school or who had not received extra help. In addition, those children who received help at home attained a mean level of achievement consistent with the national standard, whereas before the intervention over 80% of the children were reading below age level. The authors concluded that parental involvement was more powerful than extracurricular involvement of teachers.

Heller and Fantuzzo (1993) investigated the effects of parent involvement when combined with peer tutoring in mathematics. Participants were 80 fourth- and fifth-grade African-American students having difficulties in mathematics, assigned randomly to one of three conditions: reciprocal peer tutoring (RPT) plus parent involvement (PI), RPT only, or control. Students in the RPT plus PI group showed the greatest achievement in math scores, had better work habits and higher levels of motivation, were more task-oriented and less disruptive and more interpersonally confident as rated by their teachers, and perceived themselves as more socially confident in peer interactions. In addition, parents, teachers, and children were highly satisfied with the intervention. Treatment integrity was excellent; 100% of the parents who were involved followed through with the home reward program across the eight-month intervention period. It is interesting that the most frequently selected reward category was parent-child interaction activities, suggesting that students preferred their parents' time over material rewards. Parents were asked to determine ways in which they were willing and able to participate consistently. The authors encourage school psychologists to design mesosystemic interventions to achieve the most beneficial effects for children.

Clark (1993) elicited characteristics of high achievers in his study of 460 third-graders from 71 Los Angeles schools. With a participant pool of mainly minority children, Clark sent questionnaires to parents of low and high achievers to learn about their perceptions of and practices toward homework, how their children handle homework, and family background. Differences were seen between the two groups. Parents of high achievers were more involved in home-learning activities; their children spent more time on homework and used the dictionary more. Parents' emphasis on their children's academic success and family circumstances and resources for achievement were significantly related to higher achievement, explaining 47% and 42% of the variance in achievement, respectively. Scott-Jones (1987) found similar results in her study of low-income black mothers of 24 high- and low-achieving first-graders. Family process variables, mirroring the curriculum of the home factors described by Walberg (1984), set the tone for the high achievers' stimulating environment in that mothers clearly expressed high academic goals for their children, were supportive and responsive (nondirective) to their children's initiations, kept more books in their homes, and had children who took active roles.

Thus, research has shown that parents, regardless of ethnicity, social class, or educational level, want to help their children but often lack the knowledge or feel unsure of their abilities to make a difference (Christenson, 1995b). The evidence is now clear regarding the indisputable nature of families' primary roles in student's educational success; we, as school psychologists, should heed our mandate to involve parents as partners in children's education at home and at school.

Redding (1991) describes an action plan for the educator-parent partnership called Alliance for Achievement. Although the key players are children's parents and teachers, the focus is on building a school community based on educational values. Headed by a message of shared responsibility for children's educational success, the plan exhorts all community members to contribute to strengthening social capital (as described by Coleman, 1987). Redding suggests 11 steps in building a school community. Representation includes (1) establishing a school council of the principal, parents, and teachers and (2) developing a school constitution. Establishing a value base requires (3) adopting school community values; (4) restating the values as student goals; and (5) developing expectations for teachers, parents, and students. Communication entails (6) preparing a school community report and (7) integrating values and expectations into two-way school-home communication. The education should include educational programs for (8) teachers and (9) parents around school community values, expectations, and support and (10) planning a common experience (e.g., curriculum and event) for each value. Finally, (11) planning an association (e.g., program and activity) related to each value strengthens the school community.

Intertwined in his plan is Walberg's (1984) call for home-school partnerships to enhance factors that have the greatest impact on children's learning—attitudes, values, and habits. Development of the curriculum of the home, the expectations, learning, and support, is part of the Alliance for Achievement. Program evaluation data consisted of surveys sent to parents and teachers after three years of participation with the Alliance for Achievement project. Although no changes in students' school achievement were found, parents reported significant increases in their implementation of curriculum of the home strategies, for example, discussions of schoolwork at home and consistent structure (S. Redding, personal communication, December 1, 1995). Parental perceptions and satisfaction with the program were also uniformly favorable.

## Family Influences on Behavioral Competence

The strong effect of the family on children's behavior is rarely disputed; in fact, parents are often given either praise or censure, depending on how their children behave. Unfortunately, parents' roles often end there, without teaching or expanding on their abilities to be problem solvers or guides in modeling positive behavior. Sheridan and her colleagues have developed and tested a conjoint behavioral consultation (CBC) model, teaching problem-solving methods of goal setting, rewards, and children's self-monitoring to parents of children who are exhibiting behavioral difficulties. The CBC model is collaborative problem solving by parents and teachers, facilitated by a consultant. It is defined as "a systematic, indirect form of service-delivery, in which parents and teachers are joined to work together to address the academic, social, or behavioral needs of an individual for whom both parties bear some responsibility" (Sheridan &

Kratochwill, 1992, p. 122). In one study, four 9- to 13-year-old socially withdrawn children were given identical treatments; two had teacher-only consultation and two had joint teacher and mother consultation (Sheridan, Kratochwill, & Elliott, 1990). Children who received the joint consultation services improved their social initiations both at home and at school, whereas teacher-only children improved only at school. Despite the small number of participants, the authors' work provides a basis for a feasible and effective partnership between parents and teachers in solving problems across contexts.

Galloway and Sheridan (1994) compared CBC plus a home-note intervention with home note only for three primary-age students who had low motivation to complete math assignments. The CBC consisted of a series of behavioral interviews with both the teacher and the parents, based on problem identification, problem analysis, and treatment evaluation. The student was also involved in the interview at the problem analysis and treatment evaluation stages. In both conditions (CBC plus home note and home note only), a home reward system was put in place to reward improved math performance. Findings highlighted the greater efficacy of the CBC plus home-note condition; all students demonstrated gains in mean accuracy scores of 50% to 149% over baseline, which raised their math performance from a failing level to one considered by teachers to designate "a good math student." Thus, a behavioral reward system implemented by parents at home can increase children's academic performance. The authors suggest that for those students who have failed to respond to more traditional intervention strategies, CBC may be imperative for school success.

Vosier and Proctor (1990) found evidence, through a multivariate analysis procedure, that children's social environment and family stressors are strong predictors of behavioral competence. Using scores from the Behavior Problems Scales of the Child Behavior Checklist (Achenbach & Edelbrock, 1983) and a variety of parent-reported family and environment variables, they analyzed data from 226 children, ages 1 to 18, from diverse racial, economic, and family structure backgrounds, seen in a Midwest child guidance agency. Using an ecological framework, they proposed a model that incorporates stressors, resources, and competencies at three systems levels (individual child, family, and larger social environment) to help predict, and thus intervene in, children's behavior problems. Their findings lend credence to the importance of multisystem, method, and source behavioral intervention.

One successful family-focused intervention, a popular parent-training program in Ireland, aims to teach skills necessary to deal with children's conduct problems and to meet the parents' own personal and psychological needs as a precursor to being effective parents (Mullin, Quigley, & Glanville, 1994). Participants were 36 mothers in the parent-training program and a matched control group of mothers on the waiting list. Results showed a significant positive impact of the training problem, with targeted children (aged 3 months to 14 years) exhibiting fewer and less intense behavior problems and mothers reporting fewer psychological symptoms and increased self-esteem and social competence. Benefits were also seen at a mesosystemic level; mothers developed better relationships with others and actively initiated and developed a variety of community-based activities.

Family interventions for specific behavior problems have also been successful. Barkley and colleagues are well known for their work with children who have attention deficit and hyperactivity disorder (ADHD). They compare the effectiveness of three widely used family therapy programs for handling conflicts in families with ADHD (Barkley, Guevremont, Anastopoulos, & Fletcher, 1992). All three family-based treatments (behavior management training, problem-solving and communication training, and structural family therapy) led to significantly less negative communication, conflicts, and anger, as well as improvements in school adjustment and decreased levels of children's (internalizing and externalizing) and maternal (depression) symptoms. At a three month follow-up, families reported that improvements were maintained and rated themselves highly satisfied. Despite clinical assessment of limited improvement in children's ADHD-related behaviors, the authors stress that family-based interventions help parents and children cope with the disorder.

One of the best-known and exemplary parent-training programs was developed by Patterson, Reid, and colleagues in Oregon. Parents of children with conduct disorder (CD) were taught a step-by-step approach in family management:

naming a specific behavior problem, tracking it, implementing first tangible and then social reinforcements, learning discipline procedures, monitoring children's behavior, and finally problem solving and negotiation skill building. Evaluations of these programs have been favorable; parents reported 20% to 60% reductions in children's levels of aggression (Patterson, 1982; cited in Webster-Stratton, 1993), yet improvements do not always generalize from home to school. Kazdin (1987) describes structured family intervention based on behavioral social learning principles as the most promising treatment for antisocial behavior in children. Conduct problems are assumed to have been acquired and maintained through social learning within the family; therefore implementing parents as behavior change agents is most effective.

Carolyn Webster-Stratton (1993) speaks to the importance of home-school partnerships when intervening with children with behavior disorders such as CD and oppositional defiant disorder (ODD). The most effective interventions have supported parents' roles in facilitating children's social competence and conflict resolution skills and have provided parent training for children's management skills. It is extremely important to intervene with children who exhibit conduct problems since their noncompliant, disruptive behavior often leads to poor relationships with peers and teachers, with the result of receiving less support and nurturing in school (Webster-Stratton, 1993). This cycle can be devastating. Research has shown a strong tie between academic performance and CD (Kazdin, 1987), so early intervention in the cycle, when parents and teachers are still primary socialization influences, offers the best chance of preventing the negative trajectory on which many children with ODD and CD seem to find themselves. Webster-Stratton and colleagues (Webster-Stratton, 1989; Webster-Stratton & Hammond, 1990; Wester-Stratton, Kolpacoff, & Hollinsworth, 1988) have developed a successful intervention, using videotapes for parent training; evaluations have shown its effectiveness, particularly in parent satisfaction, when combined with group discussion treatment. Unfortunately, these children still have problems in the school, as generalization is frequently not successful. Webster-Stratton has identified this lack of focus on school-related issues as a missing link in developing behavioral interventions. Successful behavioral intervention programs, again, are targeted across risk factors, settings, and agents.

Miller and Prinz (1990) go one step further to address the missing link identified by Webster-Stratton (1993); they advocate a multisystems model of intervention that incorporates agents across a child's primary contexts. The authors support extending social learning theory into a mesosystemic arena since the most effective interventions address children's problems within a systems framework. Consistency in reinforcing socially appropriate behavior and providing consequences for negative behavior by multiple players is identified as effective intervention (Miller & Prinz, 1990). Behavioral intervention for high-risk children should be carried out across home and school; a "dual-focus treatment involving parents and schools may foster greater between-environment consistency in the behavioral consequences a child receives for both prosocial and antisocial behavior" (Blechman, 1987; Blechman, Kotanchik, & Taylor, 1981, as cited in Miller & Prinz, 1990, p. 298).

Schoolwide programs that emphasize partnerships with parents to develop children's behavioral, as well as academic and social, competence have been effective (Comer & Haynes, 1992; Johnson, 1990; Schweinhart & Weikart, 1992). The School Development Program (SDP) was developed by James Comer in response to the ineffectiveness of many schools in educating poor, minority children. Comer believes that educational improvement encompasses behavioral and social, as well as academic, growth. The program, implemented in elementary and middle schools in three counties in Connecticut, was aimed at increasing parental involvement in the schools for effective problem solving, cooperation among all adults concerned with children's educational success, decision by consensus, and regular meetings that represent the entire school community. Results showed astounding success: children improved their behavior (e.g., less suspensions, punishments, and absences), attitudes, participation, and achievement. Also there were increases in students' self-concepts and significantly more positive assessments by students and their parents of their classroom and school climate (Comer & Haynes, 1992).

The Perry Preschool Study, a longitudinal design following 123 people living in Michigan from age 4 to age 28, has demonstrated similar positive findings on behavioral, academic, and social variables (Schweinhart & Weikart, 1992).

The Perry program implemented curriculum focused on enhancing children's competence by pairing teachers with parents for weekly classes and home visits to discuss progress and model parent-child activities. Parents were treated as partners and were involved with the program for two years. Based on parent and participant interviews; standardized tests; and school, police, and social services records, the participants' behavior, academic, and social outcomes were striking. As compared with no-program controls, fewer Perry program participants were on welfare or had ever been arrested at age 19; and significantly more were employed, completed homework at age 15, were high school graduates, and had fewer years in special education. Thus, high-quality early childhood programs seem to produce long-term benefits on behavioral, as well as social and academic, outcomes for children by involving parents in promoting competencies necessary for educational success.

## Family Influences on Social and Interpersonal Competence

Children's successful adaptation and functioning is largely dependent on the development of social competence skills, defined broadly as behavioral effectiveness of one's transactions with the environment or a sense of efficacy when encountering social situations across domains (Weissberg, Caplan, & Sivo, 1989). Social competence is believed to be necessary for school success, enabling children to become part of the culture of literacy. Even a cursory review of the literature reveals the substantial impact of the family on the development of social competence. The home environment consists of specific cultural beliefs, parental values, and parenting practices, all influencing the development of children's interaction and coping styles, beliefs and behaviors, and competencies (Coleman, 1987; Saunders & Green, 1993). Several problems may arise, one being the difficulty of dissimilar environments for children. If the home and the school have different expectations and rules, children may feel lost in a new setting. Similarly, differences in social competence definitions, values, and methods of evaluation may cause difficulties for children without continued support and partnerships across settings (Comer, 1984; Saunders & Green, 1993).

Empirical research focuses on the affective nature of socialization practices (Garner, Jones, & Miner, 1994), family relations and nurturance

(Henggeler, Edwards, Cohen, & Summerville, 1991; Portes, Howell, Brown, Eichenberger, & Mas, 1992), stressful family events (MacKinnon-Lewis, Volling, Lamb, Dechman, Rabiner, & Curtner, 1994), parental protectiveness (Scott, Scott, & McCabe, 1991), and maternal depression (Goodman, Brogan, Lynch, & Fielding, 1993). School-based research has also been done, although it is more rare and frequently looks at social competence outcomes as secondary or more peripheral to educational success (Kellaghan et al., 1993; Reynolds, 1989). This view is changing: as school reform efforts take root and schools look to families for support in their mission to educate children, the importance of social competence outcomes becomes clearer (Comer & Haynes, 1992; Reynolds et al., 1993).

Psychological literature frequently presupposes a chronic negative relationship between the relatively high levels of distress evident in low-income families and affective parenting practices. These socialization practices are the basis for children's emotional understanding, which research has shown predicts their social competence (Denham, McKinley, Couchoud, & Holt, 1990, as cited in Garner et al., 1994). Garner and colleagues studied low-income preschoolers' social competence and defined negative emotion socialization practices by conflict level, maternal anger directed toward children, and maternal discouragement of the expression of children's negative emotion. The authors hypothesized that these relationships among socialization practices, children's emotional knowledge, and social competence would hold true. Results showed that elevated levels of negative, submissive emotion within families predicted less prosocial behavior by children, providing additional empirical support for the importance of positive affect between parents and children. However, the dysregulation and disorganization of participants' homes predicted lower social competence and emotional knowledge. Because participants came from low-income homes, the authors suggested that unpredictability of the home environment rather than low-income status may be the key variable.

When studying children's postdivorce socioemotional adjustment, Portes et al. (1992) found that families in which nurturance, mutual support, and some family rituals are maintained yielded the best outcomes for children. Family process variables (e.g., affect, involvement, behavior control, and family roles) were significant.

Family relations also have a positive effect on children's interpersonal competence, specifically in peer popularity (Henggeler et al., 1991). Participants were 24 third-graders studied over the school year. Even when their social and academic competencies were statistically controlled, children's perceptions of family relations, combined with researcher-observed paternal receptivity to children's problem solving, were associated with increased peer acceptance.

Patterson and colleagues in Oregon have provided theoretical and empirical groundwork for understanding the family's influence on children's social learning. The cyclic nature of children's development and learning in social and behavioral arenas is illustrated by their conceptualization of the family as a training ground for children's aggression, which leads to rejection in other contexts, particularly with peers (Patterson, 1982; cited in MacKinnon-Lewis et al., 1994). Seven- to nine-year-old boys' ($N = 104$) social competence was analyzed across home and school contexts (MacKinnon-Lewis et al., 1994). Boys who suffered stressful events behaved more coercively with their mothers and were also more aggressive and less competent with their peers. Mothers' hostile attributions and sons' increased aggressiveness were associated with less acceptance by peers. The critical nature of these findings are underscored by researchers, who cite evidence that peer rejection, a frequent occurrence among socially incompetent school-age children, is associated with many later adjustment problems (Garner et al., 1994; MacKinnon-Lewis et al., 1994; Portes et al., 1992).

Parental protectiveness is among family variables shown to have an effect on children's competence. Researchers assessed 2,699 children, ages 11 to 20, from eight cultures on measures of self-esteem, anxiety, interpersonal competence, and hostility (Scott et al., 1991). Findings provided support for previous research and showed uniformity across cultures; children's poor interpersonal competence was associated with high parental protectiveness and increased hostility and punitiveness, whereas positive self-esteem and low anxiety were associated with family harmony and nurturance. Children's and parents' ratings of competence and family characteristics were different, with the children's appearing to be more valid on the basis of independent assessment. This speaks to the importance of multisource validity data.

Similarly, parental characteristics such as depression and psychopathology have an effect on children's social competence. Five- to ten-year-old children with depressed mothers were lower in peer popularity as rated by teachers, and children who also had fathers with a psychiatric disorder had additional decreased levels of social and emotional competence, based on self-ratings (Goodman et al., 1993). The authors propose a multiple-risk model to account for the additive nature of parental depression and psychopathology. These parents may be unable to provide an adequate model for healthy social relationships or teach the social skills necessary for interpersonal success. Negative family relations may be a cause or effect of parental characteristics; again, correlational findings connote a complex relationship. The evidence merely provides additional support for the important influences of parents and the home on the development of children's competencies.

School-based research illustrates an even broader impact on children's educational outcomes. Reynolds (1989) tested a model to explore the impact of child, school, and home variables on first-grade outcomes for urban, low-income, African-American students. He found that parent involvement, a key variable in children's overall educational success, had the most significant direct effect on children's social-emotional maturity (e.g., is ready to learn, completes work, follows rules, and works well with others) and mediated the effect of motivation on outcomes. Since parent involvement in schools is an educationally alterable variable, Reynolds advocated its increase. Nearly half a decade later, Reynolds teamed with colleagues on investigating results from the Longitudinal Study of Children at Risk (LSCAR) and again found that family variables are consistent predictors of children's academic and social competence (Reynolds et al., 1993). The LSCAR project focuses on low-income, minority children in the Chicago public schools; participants in this study were 1,235 sixth-graders, 95% African American and 5% Hispanic. Based on observations; standardized tests; interviews; and surveys by teachers, parents, and students, the authors concluded that parents' satisfaction with their child's school and expectations for their child's success are highly related to children's social and academic competence.

The practice of developing partnerships requires an understanding of family abilities and strengths, as well as resources for their support. Johnson (1990) describes a project aimed at enhancing the strengths of at-risk Mexican-American families to foster children's social and academic competence. Cultural sensitivity and responsiveness to family needs were identified as integral components. The Houston Parent-Child Development Center (H-PCDC) project hires and trains Mexican-American mothers in similar environmental contexts as participants, many of whom were graduates of the program themselves, to conduct home visits, family workshops, and ESL classes and to connect families to community services. Program participants also attended center-based classes (e.g., child care and management and home management), participated in activities, and were active in program planning as members of the parent advisory committee. Participants were approximately 100 families, each with a two-year-old child, who took part in the program for one year. Results highlighted the program's effectiveness. Mothers were more affectionate and encouraging, less critical, more responsive, and provided more educationally stimulating environments for their children. Positive outcomes were seen across social, behavioral, and cognitive variables. Children were rated as engaging in more socially desirable behaviors and significantly reducing their behavior problems, as well as increasing their academic competence based on Stanford-Binet (Thorndike, Hagen & Sattler, 1986) scores. These results, obtained five to eight years after program completion, are especially impressive because of their long-term benefits for children's school success.

## Summary

Families enhance children's educational success by influencing their academic; behavioral, and social competence. Henderson and Berla (1994) cite evidence of family influences: when families are involved in children's education, the results are (1) higher grades and test scores, (2) improved long-term academic achievement, (3) positive attitudes and behavior, (4) more successful education programs, and (5) more effective schools. In fact, Coleman and Hoffer (1987) state that the quality of a school's relationship with the families it serves is key; highly effective schools see themselves as extensions of the families they serve. Swap (1993) promotes a partnership model, and Ziegler (1987) provides a concise, telling summary of the importance of home-school links: "The influence of the home on children's success at school is profound. Whether indirectly, as models, or directly, as readers, audience, or homework helpers, parents' learning-related and school-related activities at home are a very strong influence on children's long term academic success" (p. 5).

Based on our review of the literature, we believe school psychologists must ask themselves, "To what degree has efficacy of interventions designed for academic, social, or behavioral referrals been reduced because implementation has occurred in only one environmental context—home or school?" A follow-up question is this: "Is there evidence for a positive effect of mesosystemic interventions on children's outcomes?" The answer, supported by literature, yes; although the data base is small, it is not insignificant. We believe that students show greater gains in academic, social, and behavioral performance when a mesosystemic intervention is implemented (Galloway & Sheridan, 1994; Heller & Fantuzzo, 1993; Sheridan et al., 1990). Furthermore, the generalization of children's skills across environments, most noticeably from parent training to school settings, is generally poor (Webster-Stratton, 1993). We also recognize that much more research on the effect of mesosystemic interventions with varied populations is necessary to conclude that students' academic, social, and behavioral competence is best attained under these conditions. Creating partnerships with families is a promising practice for enhancing children's competence. In the next section, we describe strategies for school psychologists.

# SUGGESTIONS FOR SCHOOL PSYCHOLOGISTS

School psychologists are encouraged to be leaders in forming and supporting productive home-school-community partnerships to enhance the competence of children and youths. Partnership connotes a highly interactive relationship—working together to best support and challenge children in their quest to become competent and successful adults in today's society. The rhetoric on developing effective family-school partnerships is plentiful and seemingly well thought out. Unfortunately, partnerships are neither plentiful nor planned. All too often partnership in process becomes more expert-driven and less collaborative, more prescriptive and less flexible, more "this is what I need from you" and less "what do

you need from me?" Families come in a variety of forms and are influenced by diverse experiences. The diversity inherent in families is often viewed as a barrier rather than as an opportunity to share disparate messages and to enhance ways of fostering children's development. We know that successful partnership programs are based on (1) site-specific development, (2) shared governance and decision making, (3) direct invitations to families to become involved, and (4) opportunities to improve trust between families and educators and for ongoing dialogue about attaining goals for students (Christenson, 1995b).

A partnership approach requires educators to admit that help is needed to resolve some school-based concerns; to change their beliefs about parents described as at risk or uninvolved; and to reconceptualize roles and responsibilities for parents, educators, and students. Swap (1993) suggests three paths to partnership: (1) limited (e.g., workshops for parents of first-graders); (2) comprehensive, involving networks of mutual support (e.g., parent center and school-parent council); and (3) restructured for partnership and students' achievement [e.g., shared governance across contexts of development, for example, Comer's (1995) model]. We describe three specific suggestions for school psychologists to help facilitate partnerships, regardless of the path chosen.

## Disseminate Information

Our first suggestion is to disseminate information to educators and parents on the notion of two curricula, the curriculum of the school and the curriculum of the home. We strongly contend that the missing link is an overemphasis on traditional approaches to parent involvement and an underemphasis on developing partnership approaches, approaches based on delivering the message about the essentiality (not merely desirability) of both contexts for children's development. A shared responsibility recognizes the predictive power of both out-of-school time and consistency across socializing environments, as well as the need to emphasize competence enhancement. A solution-oriented focus reframes educators' and parents' goals in a way that is motivating to each partner and has been found to be helpful when distrust has permeated the previous home-school relationship (e.g., Carlson, Hickman, & Horton, 1992; Swap, 1993).

Maintaining effective communication between home and school depends on both the quantity and quality of the message (McAfee, 1993). With respect to quantity, the development of a regular and reliable home-school communication system that fosters two-way communication and reaches all families is necessary. Regarding quality, educators should examine whether the right message is being communicated about students. Educators should communicate that "the mutual respect and interdependence of the home, school, and community are essential to children's development" (McAfee, 1993 p. 21). Therefore, we believe school psychologists should disseminate information on the two curricula in print and nonprint forms, attend to idiosyncratic needs of families in understanding how to apply the curriculum of the home, and provide ongoing support for families through successful workshop formats (Goodman, Sutton, & Harkavy, 1995) and parent-support-parent formats. According to Kellaghan et al. (1993), we need to raise awareness in parents of their own capabilities to enhance their children's educational progress and to assist in developing life-relevant skills.

Family processes that are strongly associated with positive outcomes for students—authoritative parenting, family interaction variables like communication and cohesion, discipline and alternatives to physical punishment, and home support for learning—should be communicated to parents. Sharing the curriculum of the home provides an opportunity for school psychologists to work with families and to address discontinuities in messages received by students across home and school.

Information about family influences that are associated with negative outcomes for students, must also be available to parents, albeit less emphasized than family processes that promote positive outcomes. Community resources available to families need to be communicated routinely. In a recent interview sponsored by the National Association of School Psychologists (NASP), parents indicated a strong desire for schools to provide this information (Christenson et al., 1997).

We believe school psychologists should plan a coordinated, comprehensive way to disseminate information on the two curricula, using, for example, newsletters, curriculum nights, workshops attended by parents and educators, home visits, electronic technology, and home-school partnership contracts. Communication between home and school will be improved in general and the dissemination of the information in particu-

lar if the following guidelines are followed: adopt a positive orientation rather than a deficit-based or crisis orientation, develop a regular and reliable home-school communication system that increases the potential for two-way communication, focus communication and dialogue between parents and educators on children's performance and attainment of mutually established goals, ensure that parents understand the language of schooling (e.g., homework policy and grading practices), and ensure that all communications underscore a shared responsibility for educational outcomes (Christenson & Hirsch, in press). Shared responsibility is well articulated by Seeley (1985), who reminds us that the product of education—learning—is not produced by schools but by the active involvement of students, with the help and support of schools, parents, peers, and other community resources.

There is evidence for the need to intervene mesosystemically in both home and school contexts. Three problem-solving approaches that create a mesosystemic orientation have been developed. Inherent in each approach is ongoing support for families as they learn how to apply the curriculum of the home in their home environment.

## Parent-Educator Problem Solving

The purposes of Parent-Educator Problem Solving (PEPS) are to create a partnership between parents and educators and to use the partnership as a vehicle for fostering an educative home environment, one in which congruence between home and school environments in achieved (Christenson, 1995b). A modification of the family-school meeting described by Weiss and Edwards (1992), PEPS was developed with parents' and educators' input and has been implemented in both suburban elementary and urban middle-schools. The four steps in PEPS are introduction, identification, selection, and implementation. Although a structured sequence is followed by the facilitator, a relaxed conversational tone between parents and educators is sought. In the introduction stage, the facilitator of the meeting (e.g., school psychologist) builds rapport with parents, educators, and the student by discussing a positive school, school district, or community event and offering a positive comment that has been stated by an educator about the student. The school-based concern is described in specific, observable, behavioral language and reframed as a learning goal (i.e., what the student needs to earn or educators want to teach the student). Parents are told that they are important partners in school-based interventions and that students' achievement is enhanced through family-school partnerships. If parents decide not to be active participants, the intervention to be employed by school personnel is described, parental input is sought, and parents' questions are answered. A way to maintain ongoing contact, usually through the phone or home-school notes, is established. If parents agree to participate and become contributors to the solution, the remaining three stages are followed.

In the identification stage, concerns and perceptions of the participants are identified. Other concerns described by parents are reframed and listed as learning goals and recorded so they can be addressed. Mutual learning goals are identified and ranked, and parents and educators select one to work on collaboratively. It is possible that parents and educators will work independently to address other goals. Sharing information about efforts to address these goals is encouraged and facilitated by establishing a contact system between home and school. The school psychologist, as facilitator, checks for the understanding of participants by restating the learning goal as a discrepancy between the student's actual and desired behavior. The goal of the partnership is described as a common effort toward closing this discrepancy. The facilitator also asks whether there are other contributing factors in the child's life that must be known to enhance success.

In the selection stage, possibilities for solution are generated by brainstorming, listing all suggestions, and eliminating any evaluation of suggestions. The emphasis is on what parents, educators, and the student can do to enhance the probability that the learning goal will be achieved. Next, participants indicate their choice of intervention. The facilitator helps parents and educators identify necessary information or resources (such as the need for ongoing consultation) to support their implementation efforts. In the implementation stage, the solution plan is described by clearly stating the roles and responsibilities of participants and determining a time line for implementation and evaluation. The generated plan is implemented, during which time dialogue between home and school focuses on whether the plan is enhancing the student's performance. Modifications to the plan may be made as a result of this ongoing contact. The plan is considered successful if the discrepancy between actual and desired behavior is closed. In these cases, all participants celebrate. If the plan is unsuccessful, no one is to blame, and replanning occurs.

In the PEPS approach, parents are directly invited to be partners and they overwhelmingly agree; however, without active follow-up by a designated case manager, implementation of the plan is low. It has been found that parents need information and support to follow through. The approach has been successful in addressing attendance and homework problems for elementary and middle-school students. Although no gains in students' achievement have been attributed to PEPS, parents and teachers rated home-school communication and interactions more favorably.

## Solution-oriented Family-school Meetings

Carlson et al. (1992) have adopted the solution-oriented brief therapy approach (DeShazer, 1982) for use in schools through what they refer to as solution-oriented family-school meetings. The hallmark of the solution-oriented framework is a shift from problem resolution, that is, analyzing the problem in detail, to solution identification through an active search for solutions. The terminology of solution-oriented brief therapy is different: *difficulty* is used to replace problem, and *complaint* is used to signal that repeated efforts to resolve a difficulty have been unsuccessful because individuals become mired in how they view the difficulty and, subsequently, how they respond to it. At solution-oriented family-school meetings, the facilitator (e.g., school psychologist) helps parents and educators construct solutions that fit personal constraints of the situation. Thus, the facilitator blocks blame, encourages experimentation with different interventions, and maintains a positive orientation.

An assumption underlying solution-oriented family-school meetings is that individuals have gotten stuck in their view of the child's problem and in their efforts to change the child's behavior. As a result, the behavior appears to be stable, internal, and uncontrollable; parents and educators are frustrated and defeated; and blaming is often used to alleviate adults' emotions. To resolve the complaint, 10 phases are followed by a facilitator during the family-school meeting in which the child is present.

***Phase 1: Introduction*** The facilitator (usually a school psychologist, counselor, or principal) introduces the participants and acknowledges the importance of multiple perspectives and active participation by all. In addition, a collaborative tone is set by noting the expertise of both parents and teachers and the good fortune of the student to have adults interested in his or her growth and development.

*Phase 2: Explanation of the solution-oriented approach.* The benefit of advance cognitive organizers, according to the authors, is to set the expectation that complaints are "dissolvable" and solutions are possible. The authors have found that the "norms for blaming and complaining in schools are so strong that some advance cognitive organizers are helpful" (Carlson et al., 1992, p. 201).

*Phase 3: Joining.* Joining is a necessary step toward building rapport and involves acknowledging each person's point of view through active listening and responding by mirroring a person's language. For example, if parents discuss an "attitude problem," the facilitator uses the word "attitude" in subsequent questions or reflective statements.

*Phase 4: Negotiating a solvable complaint.* In this phase the facilitator looks for similarities and differences across participants in their complaint and view of the problem. Participants are asked to provide a "video" description of their complaint (i.e., other participants can see the complaint in action as in a video recording) and to identify the strengths of the child and past solutions to the complaint. Exceptions to the difficulty or visualization of the future without the problem by parents and educators often point to possible solutions.

*Phase 5: Establish a solution goal.* After a mutually agreed-upon complaint is identified, participants identify an initial, positively oriented goal for change.

*Phase 6: Gain agreement on the smallest change in the direction of the goal.* According to the authors, "Working toward the smallest change is an important shift in both the viewing and doing of the complaint within the social contexts of the child such that lasting change, which generally occurs in small increments, can be rewarded" (Carlson et al., 1992, p. 203). For example, the goal of taking a 10-minute walk each day will be more noticeable than will be the goal of losing 10 pounds.

*Phase 7: Elicit multiple solutions toward accomplishing the smallest change.* Brainstorming is used. The facilitator both elicits positive solutions to the complaint from participants and offers positive solutions by noting exceptions to the complaint pattern and resources and strengths within the complaint system.

*Phase 8: Clarify individual responsibilities and task assignments.* The facilitator elicits participants' understanding of their roles in the solution plan generated and serves as a consultant to parents, teachers, and student during the implementation phase.

*Phase 9: Follow-up.* Follow-up occurs in either a scheduled meeting or in individual meetings with participants and the designated coordinator. A focus on what is different, what has changed, or what parents and educators want to keep happening is encouraged. The purpose is to show that participants made a small change in the agreed-upon direction toward the goal, even if the change is different from that articulated at the initial meeting. The authors have found that parents or educators who report no change often desire complete alleviation of the difficulty and must be reminded of the importance of small changes in the direction of the desired goal.

*Phase 10: Evaluate and recycle if necessary.* Parents and educators are reminded of the long-term advantages of gradual change. A new set of solutions may be identified by revisiting phases 1 through 9.

In closing, Carlson et al. (1992) report that this strategy has been a particularly positive experience for the identified children and their parents. They hypothesize that it is "likely that the unexpected focus on 'what is working' within the meeting allowed the child and parent, both of whom were expecting to hear about blame and failure, to relax defenses and become involved in the collaboration" (p. 209). We speculate that this strategy, as do other approaches that emphasize a partnership between home and school, changes participants from cocomplainers to cocontributors.

## Conjoint Behavioral Consultation

As noted earlier, conjoint behavioral consultation (CBC) is defined as "a systematic, indirect form of service delivery, in which parents and teachers are joined to work together to address the academic, social, or behavioral needs of an individual for whom both parties bear some responsibility" (Sheridan & Kratochwill, 1992, p. 122). Process goals of CBC are to (1) improve the relationship among student, family, and school personnel; (2) promote shared ownership for problem identification and resolution; and (3) address problems as occurring across home *and* school, rather than within home *or* school. Relevant outcome goals are to (1) facilitate parent-teacher communication and a philosophy of shared decision making to promote future conjoint problem solving between home and school, (2) establish consistency in intervention programs across settings, and (3) enhance generalization and maintenance of intervention effects through consistent programming. The CBC model is designed to engage parents and teachers in a collaborative problem-solving process that involves four stages: problem identification, problem analysis, treatment implementation, and treatment evaluation.

In the first stage of CBC, problem identification, the target problem, which may be exhibited across settings or only in one setting, is identified and defined behaviorally by parents and teachers with the assistance of the consultant. Contextual conditions that affect the behavior are discussed. Parents and teachers reach consensus on a goal for behavior change and establish data collection procedures for baseline assessment. Problem analysis, the second stage, is initiated when baseline data confirm the existence of a problem. Factors contributing to the occurrence of the target problem, including cross-setting antecedents and consequences, as well as setting events, are specified. The simultaneous involvement of parents and teachers in problem analysis facilitates a thorough delineation of ecological conditions and setting events. An intervention plan that includes the responsibilities of all parties is developed. Resources in home and school settings that may contribute to intervention effectiveness are identified. The intervention plan designed during the previous stage is put into action in stage three. A home-school intervention is warranted if the target behavior is evident across settings. The consultant monitors implementation of the plan, provides necessary training and support, assesses for intervention contrast effects (i.e., unintended side effects in which the controls exerted in one setting enhance the problem in other settings),

and facilitates plan modifications. In the final stage, treatment evaluation, the consultant, parents, and teachers examine data on the target behavior that were collected during the implementation phase and compare it to baseline data to determine whether consultation goals were attained. Parents' and teachers' satisfaction about the procedures and outcomes are determined.

Consultation with parents and teachers simultaneously has enhanced treatment outcomes for students with social (Sheridan et al., 1990) and academic (Galloway & Sheridan, 1994) problems. Maintenance and treatment gains tend to be stronger when parents are actively involved in the collaborative problem-solving process. Sheridan and Colton (1994) attribute the improvement for students to the "nature of the relationship that develops among participants in the CBC process" (p. 219). Finally, Sheridan and Kratochwill (1992) suggest that the use of conjoint behavioral consultation is inappropriate when there is significant teacher resistance, family dysfunction, or home-school conflict.

## Develop Family-School Teams

Team approaches hold great promise for improving educational outcomes for students and are the foundation of successful family-school partnership efforts (Comer, 1995). Team approaches address the three barriers identified by Weiss and Edwards (1992) to positive family-school relationships: (1) schools and families fail to establish an ongoing, routine vehicle for sharing information and planning in a two-way dialogue; (2) differences between school personnel and families—whether racial, cultural, or economic—create either assumed or real barriers to communication and partnership; and (3) school personnel have a restricted conception of the roles families could play in schools. Two different approaches, action team and action research team, have been developed.

According to Epstein (1995), "The action team guides the development of a comprehensive program of partnership, including all six types of involvement, and the integration of all family and community connections within a single, unified plan and program" (p. 708). A comprehensive partnership program includes six types of family involvement: parenting, communicating, volunteering, learning at home, decision making, and collaborating with community groups. Each type of involvement has benefits for students, parents, and teachers. For example, when parents are actively involved in decision making, students are aware of family representation in school decisions and, as a result, receive a congruent message about school behavior. Feeling of ownership of school and shared experiences and connections with other families were identified as some of the parental benefits. Teachers' benefits include awareness of parental perspectives in policy development and school practices, a benefit that can be used to prevent misunderstandings.

Based on work with families and schools since 1987, Epstein (1995) describes five important steps schools can take to develop positive school-family connections. Step 1 is to create an action team of three teachers from different grade levels, three parents with children in different grade levels, one administrator, possibly a member from the community at large, and others central to the school's work with families (e.g., school psychologist). The goal of the team is to organize, implement, and evaluate options for new partnerships until a coordinated program, with the six types of involvement, is established. Step 2 is to obtain some funds and other support, such as release time for the team to accomplish its work. In step 3, the action team identifies starting points. Epstein suggests collecting information about present strengths (e.g., "What practices of school-family-community partnerships are now working well for the school?"), needed changes (e.g., "How do we want school-family-community partnerships to work in three years?"), expectations (e.g., "What do teachers expect of families? What do families expect of school personnel?"), sense of community (e.g., "Which families are we reaching? Which families have we yet to reach?"), and links to goals (e.g., "How might family-community connections assist the school in helping more students perform with greater success?"). Generated from the data collected, the action team develops in step 4 a three-year outline that specifies how subcommittees will begin to develop desired partnership activities to reach all families, as well as a one-year plan that is shared with parents, teachers, and students. Step 5 is ongoing planning and working. Epstein suggests that it is important to reflect on both problems and successes as the team works toward achieving the three-year outline. The team needs to address two questions: "How can it ensure that the program of school-family-community partnership will continue to improve its structure, processes, and practices in order to increase the number of families who are partners with the school in their children's education? and What opportunities will teachers, parents, and students have to share information on successful practices and to strengthen and maintain their efforts?" (p. 710).

The approach recommended by Epstein (1995) is successful in building partnerships for many reasons; however, three are particularly noteworthy: the identification of benefits for all key stakeholders in education, input from the many voices represented in the school community, and the dynamic quality of developing stronger partnerships between families and schools. Epstein has found that the structure and work of action teams is most successful when teams work to develop many types of involvement simultaneously and weave activities into an integrated program.

Parent-teacher action research is a process that helps school communities identify the strategies that build family-school-community collaboration (Davies, Palanki, & Burch, 1993). As part of the process, parents and teachers address a meaningful school problem, create a model for ongoing problem solving in the school, and generate support for creativity and innovation in the schools. With this approach, parents and teachers become program developers and evaluators. Together they design, implement, and evaluate a program. Schools in the League of Schools Reaching Out Project followed 10 steps: getting a group together, choosing a facilitator, picking a researchable topic, finding out what colleagues already know, finding out what others have written about the topic, designing and implementing an action plan, gathering data, compiling and discussing data, writing about what happened and what was learned, and sharing findings. Davies et al. recommend that team membership be based on parents' and teachers' interest. The team should select a focused topic or question and then use structured interviews with school personnel and parents to gather data on current practices and attitudes about the topic. The major goal of the action research team is to create systemic change. Implemented in elementary and middle schools, a variety of topics have been studied and addressed through this approach. For example, the Atenville Elementary School action research team learned "that increasing parent involvement is a sum of personal connections to families, whose ties to the school are nurtured over time. To help them make the connections between individual parents' increased involvement and changes in children, the action research team designed a three-part portfolio (collection of materials compiled over time) approach" (p. 17). The school's strategies are documented in the school portfolio. Families' attendance at school events, contacts with schools, and resources and skills are documented in the family portfolio. The contents of the student portfolio are jointly determined by parents and teachers and provide a picture of students' progress over time. Parent-teacher action research is a structured way for parents and educators to study and intervene on a concern that is relevant to a specific school.

Parents and Teachers Heading to Success, (PATHS), is another example of an action research team (Sinclair, Lam, Christenson, & Evelo, 1993). Implemented at an urban middle school, PATHS designed changes in home-school communications, sex education curricula, and homework policies that were mutually agree upon by parents and educators. The purpose of PATHS was to share information and resources, to address concerns of mutual interest, and find ways to enhance students' learning. Unlike the action team, this team did not focus on developing an integrated, coordinated partnership program.

Based on the experience of implementing this team for two-and-one-half years, we learned seven lessons. First, a team should be made up of many parents with diverse backgrounds. Various voices in the school need to be represented; therefore, parents from different ethnic and social class backgrounds, parents with different educational and skill levels, parents whose children are performing with varied academic success, and parents who are more and less involved at school should be represented. Also, our decision to overrepresent parents was wise because there was always a critical mass of parents available to attend PATHS meetings.

Second, an honest but positive orientation during team discussions is important and should be maintained. We selected our use of language carefully. For example, we did not focus on problematic individuals; we did focus on problematic situations between home and school (e.g., lack of communication). We facilitated conversations between home and school so that others' perspectives were seen. It was important to elicit parents' and teachers' feelings and desires about a situation. It was also important for each party to think about the other's feelings and desires.

We reinforced the team goal, to enhance students' academic and behavioral success in school. We reviewed ground rules at each PATHS meeting. For example, when PATHS was working on promoting home-school communication, the ground rules were as follows: (1) every participant is a consultant or coach for both parents and teachers; (2) this is a brainstorming session, and participants share what they think, (3) this is also a planning session for action, and participants will follow up on activities; and (4) the focus of our discussion is on solutions that benefit all students rather than on problems of a specific student.

Third, it is important to share information between home and school, but sharing resources to resolve the problematic situation is the primary goal. We were action-oriented; team members completed activities between meetings.

Fourth, meetings need to be organized and semistructured; beliefs and ground rules for working together must be shared and reiterated. Some of these for PATHS were as follows: (1) differences of opinion are helpful; (2) conflict is natural and can be managed; (3) a good action plan satisfies parents', teachers', and students' needs; (4) both parents and teachers are important for students' success in school; and (5) parents and teachers have inadequate information about youths because they see them in only one context.

Fifth, issues and concerns that affect home or school can be team-generated or referred to the team. At our first meeting, the team members generated a list of home-school concerns, which included home-school communication, homework, study skills for students, discipline, use of out-of-school time, ways to promote self-esteem, and ways parents and teachers contribute to students' success in school. The list, which was continuously reviewed and modified, serves as the basis for team actions. While problem solving provided the structure for discussion and action, it was employed flexibly. Because the facilitator emphasized understanding the issue, she asked team members to consider the following: what is the issue? What do I need to say about the issue? What do I need to understand from others about the issue? How can we develop a better action plan?

Sixth, the importance of nonblaming interactions was apparent. In general, parents and teachers did not engage in blaming the other system, perhaps because of the clearly focused purpose of the team, skill of the facilitator (e.g., school psychologist), or the structure provided by problem solving. However, team members were known to slip into the world of blame. Even after two years of operation, team members found themselves engaged in finger-pointing behavior when a new issue was discussed. The encouraging news is that they quickly identified their unproductive behavior and focused common efforts toward a shared goal. They learned to listen; understand that different perspectives were acceptable; and create a plan that addressed the needs of students, families, and schools.

The final lesson, and perhaps the most important, was that the partnership notion had to be salient. The group facilitator was very persistent about ensuring that the goal of PATHS—partnerships for students' learning—was dominant.

Parent-teacher action research teams, a tool for collective social problem solving, are considered especially relevant for schools and communities who are coping with complex social and educational problems (Palanki & Burch, 1995). A successful team process was characterized by negotiation and compromise and by shifting discussion from complex rhetoric to specific and solvable problems. Among the identified benefits was the development of a constructive two-way communication process between families and school staff.

## Clarify Roles and Responsibilities

Third, we suggest that school psychologists clarify roles and responsibilities for the partners—parents and educators—in promoting educational success for students. To this end, we view consultation, staff development, and serving as a liaison between home and school as vital roles for school psychologists, who provide the leadership needed for family-school partnership programs (Epstein, 1992). The majority of school personnel are most familiar with the traditional approach to parent involvement and parent-education avenues. A partnership philosophy and many family outreach strategies are alien to educators. Therefore, opportunities for educators to be trained in approaches for building family-school partnerships are necessary; fortunately, training materials are available (e.g., Moles, 1993). We also suggest that school personnel need to have a dialogue about the qualitative differences between traditional and partnership approaches to family involvement. Finally, we believe that the partnership principles identified by

the League of Schools Project (cited in Ooms & Hara, 1991, pp. 13–16) should guide educators' efforts in working with families as educational partners.

1. Every aspect of the school building and general climate is open, helpful, and friendly to parents.
2. Communications with parents—whether about school policies and programs or about their own children—are frequent, clear, and two-way processes.
3. Parents are treated by teachers as collaborators in the educational process.
4. Parents' own knowledge, expertise, and resources are seen as essential to their child's success in school.
5. The school recognizes its responsibility to forge a partnership with all families in the school, not simply those most easily available.
6. The school principal and other administrators actively express in words and deeds the philosophy of partnership with all families.
7. The school encourages volunteer support and help from all parents by providing a wide variety of volunteer opportunities, including those that can be done from home and during nonworking hours.
8. The school provides opportunities for parents to meet their own needs for information, advice, and peer support.
9. Parents' views and expertise are sought in developing policies and solving schoolwide problems; in some schools parents are given important decision-making responsibilities at a policy level.
10. Schools recognize that they can best help parents provide a home environment conducive to learning if they facilitate their access to basic and supportive services.

## CONCLUDING REMARKS

As indicated in the opening quotation for this chapter, Bronfenbrenner (1974) suggested that parent intervention was necessary for fostering children's development because it functioned as a kind of fixative or stabilizer of important influences. In this chapter we have described the theoretical support and empirical evidence for conducting mesosystemic interventions across home and school. Translation of theory and research into practice suggests to us that schools need to expect family involvement in education and focus on working with families as educational partners in enhancing the development of children and youths. We offer an approach based on the notion of two curricula. The curriculum of the home illustrates the predictive power of home influences (out-of-school time) on children's academic, social, and behavioral development. The curriculum of the home needs to be shared with families. Although educators need to expect family involvement in education, caution must be taken against mandating how families will be involved. Family responsibilities for supporting children's learning must be flexible and negotiated. We suggest that a focus on competence enhancement and solutions for concerns about students serve as the basis for the partnership. A commonsense understanding of families' needs is important. No parent wants to hear about his or her child's deficits. Although parents want to know about problematic situations, such as normative delays in behavior or performance and a mismatch between the student's needs or skills and the demands of the environment, they want to hear an optimistic message about their children. Finally, parents are motivated by being asked to be partners and by understanding the role they can realistically play in assisting their children's progress.

Working with families as educational partners appears to be a promising avenue to travel, although it is not a panacea. In 1996, over two decades after Bronfenbrenner's suggestion, we have begun to design mesosystemic intervention studies in academic, social, and behavioral areas. The results of the studies lend credence to the importance of both in- (curriculum of the school) and out-of-school time (curriculum of the home) for promoting optimal outcomes. Finn (1990) has suggested that the premier policy question for the 1990s is how to create social capital for children and youths where it is not naturally occurring. Working with families as educational partners may be one way.

# REFERENCES

Achenbach, T. M., & Edelbrock, C. (1983). *Manual for the Child Behavior Checklist and Revised Child Behavior Profile.* Burlington: University of Vermont, Department of Psychiatry.

August, G. J., Anderson, D., & Bloomquist, M. L. (1992). Competence enhancement training for children: An integrated child, parent, and school approach. In S. L. Christenson & J. C. Conoley (Eds.), *Home-school collaboration: Enhancing children's academic and social competence* (pp. 175–193). Silver Spring, MD: National Association of School Psychologists.

Baker, D. P., & Stevenson, D. L. (1986). Mothers' strategies for children's school achievement: Managing the transition to high school. *Sociology of Education, 59,* 156–166.

Barkley, R. A., Guevremont, D. C., Anastopoulos, A. D., & Fletcher, K. E. (1992). A comparison of three family therapy programs for treating family conflicts in adolescents with attention-deficit hyperactivity disorder. *Journal of Consulting and Clinical Psychology, 60*(3), 450–462.

Barton, P. E., & Coley, R. J. (1992). *American's smallest school: The family.* Princeton, NJ: Educational Testing Service, Policy Information Report.

Baumrind, D. (1991). The influence of parenting style on adolescent competence and substance use. *Journal of Early Adolescence, 11*(1), 56–95.

Belle, D. (Ed.). (1989). *Children's social networks and social supports.* New York: Wiley.

Berger, E. A. (1992). Parent involvement: Yesterday and today. *The Elementary School Journal, 91*(3), 209–220.

Blechman, E. A. (1987). *Solving child behavior problems at home and at school.* Champaign, IL: Research Press.

Blechman, E. A., Kotanchik, N. l., & Taylor, C. J. (1981). Families and schools together: Early behavioral intervention with high risk children. *Behavior Therapy, 132,* 308–319.

Bloom, B. S. (1985). *Developing talents in young people.* New York: Ballantine Books.

Brody, G. H., Stoneman, Z., Flor, D., McCrary, C., Hastings, L., & Conyers, O. (1994). Financial resources, parent psychological functioning, parent co-caregiving, and early adolescent competence in rural two-parent African-American families. *Child Development, 65,* 590–605.

Bronfenbrenner, U. (1986). Alienation & the four worlds of childhood. *Phi Delta Kappan,* pp. 430–436.

Bronfenbrenner, U. (1974). *Is early intervention effective? A report on longitudinal evaluations of preschool programs* (Vol. 2). Washington, DC: U.S. Department of Health, Education, and Welfare.

Carlson, C. I., Hickman, J., & Horton, C. B. (1992). From blame to solutions: Solution-oriented family-school consultation. In S. L. Christenson & J. C. Conoley (Eds.), *Home-school collaboration: Enhancing children's academic and social competence* (pp. 193–213). Silver Spring, MD: National Association of School Psychologists.

Cauce, A. M., Hannan, K., & Sargeant, M. (1992). Life stress, social support, and locus of control during early adolescence: Interactive effects. *American Journal of Community Psychology, 20*(6), 787–798.

Chen, X., & Rubin, K. (1994). Family conditions, parental acceptance, and social competence and aggression in Chinese children. *Social Development, 3*(3), 269–290.

Christenson, S. L. (1995a). Families and schools: What is the role of the school psychologist? *School Psychology Quarterly, 10*(2), 118–132.

Christenson, S. L. (1995b). Supporting home-school collaboration. In A. Thomas & J. Grimes (Eds.), *Best practices in school psychology–III* (pp. 253–267). Silver Spring, MD: National Association of School Psychologists.

Christenson, S. L., & Hirsch J. A. (in press). Facilitating partnerships and conflict resolution between families and schools. In K. C. Stoiber & T. Kratochwill (Eds.), *Group interventions in the school and community.* Boston: Allyn & Bacon.

Christenson, S. L., Hurley, C. M. Sheridan S. M. & Fenstermacher, K. (1977). Parents' and school psychologists' perspectives on parent involvement activities. *School Psychology Review, 26*(1), 111–130.

Christenson, S. L., Rounds, T., & Gorney, D. (1992). Family factors and student achievement: An avenue to increase students' success. *School Psychology Quarterly, 7*(3), 178–206.

Clark, R. M. (1983). *Family life and school achievement.* Chicago: University of Chicago Press.

Clark, R. M. (1990). Why disadvantaged students succeed: What happens outside school is critical. *Public Welfare,* pp. 17–23.

Clark, R. M. (1993). Homework-focused parenting practices that positively affect student achievement. In N. F. Chavkin (Ed.), *Families and schools in a pluralistic society* (pp. 85–105). Albany: State University of New York Press.

Cochran, M. (1991). Personal social networks as a focus of support. In D. G. Unger & D. R. Powell (Eds.), *Families as nurturing systems: Support across the life span.* (pp. 45–67). New York: Haworth.

Cochran M., & Henderson, C. R., Jr. (1986). *Family matters: Evaluation of the parental empowerment program.* Ithaca, NY: Cornell University Press.

Coleman, J. S. (1987, August). Families and schools. *Educational Researcher,* pp. 32–38.

Coleman, J. S., & Hoffer, R. (1987). *Public and private high schools: The impact of communities.* New York: Basic Books.

Collins, C. H., Moles, O., & Cross, M. (1982). *The home-school connection: Selected partnership programs in large cities.* Boston: Institute for Responsive Education.

Comer, J. P. (1984). Home-school relationships as they affect the academic success of children. *Education and Urban Society, 16*(3), 323–337.

Comer, J. P. (1988). Educating poor minority children. *Scientific American, 259*(5), 2–8.

Comer, J. P. (1995). *School power: Implications of an intervention project.* New York: Free Press.

Comer, J. P., & Haynes, N. M. (1992). *Summary of School Development Program effects.* New Haven, CT: Yale Child Study Center.

Cross, W. E. (1990). Race and ethnicity: Effects on social networks. In M. Cochran, M. Larner, D. Riley, L. Gunnarsson, & C. R. Henderson (Eds.), *Extending families: The social networks of parents and their children* (pp. 67–85). Cambridge: Cambridge University Press.

Darling, N., & Steinberg, L. (1993). Parenting style as context: An integrative model. *Psychological Bulletin, 113*(3), 487–496.

Davies, D. (1993). Benefits and barriers to parent involvement: From Portugal to Boston to Liverpool. In N. F. Chavkin (Ed.), *Families and schools in a pluralistic society* (pp. 205–216). Albany: State University of New York Press.

Davies, D., Palanki, A., & Burch, P. (1993). *Getting started: Action research in family-school-community partnerships* (Center Report 30). Baltimore MD: Center on Families, Communities, Schools, and Children's Learning. Johns Hopkins University.

Denham, S. A., McKinley, M., Couchoud, E. A., & Holt, R. (1990). Emotional and behavioral predictors of preschool peer ratings. *Child Development, 61*, 1145–1152.

DeShazer, S. (1982). *Patterns of brief family therapy.* New York: Norton.

Dornbusch, S., Ritter, P., Leiderman, P. H., Roberts, D. F., & Fraleigh, M. (1987). The relation of parenting style to adolescent school performance. *Child Development, 58*(5), 1244–1257.

Dunst, C. J., Trivette, C. M., & Deal, A. G. (1988). *Enabling and empowering families: Principles and guidelines for practice.* Cambridge, MA: Brookline Books.

Eagle, E. (1989). Socioeconomic status, family structure, and parental involvement: The correlates of achievement. (ERIC: Reproduction Document Service ED 307 332.) Paper presented at the Annual Meeting of the American Educational Research Association, San Francisco.

Ellwood, M. S., & Stolberg, A. L. (1993). The effects of family composition, family health, parenting behavior and environmental stress on children's divorce adjustment. *Journal of Child and Family Studies, 2*(1), 23–36.

Epstein, J. L. (1986). Parents reactions to teacher practices of parent involvement. *The Elementary School Journal, 86*, 277–294.

Epstein, J. L. (1991). Effects on student achievement of teachers' practices of parent involvement. In S. B. Silvern (Ed.), *Advances in reading/language research: Vol. 5. Literacy through family, community, and school interaction* (pp. 261–276). Greenwich, CT: JAI Press.

Epstein, J. L. (1992). School and family partnerships:

Leadership roles for school psychologists. In S. L. Christenson & J. C. Conoley (Eds.), *Home-school collaboration: Enhancing children's academic and social competence* (pp. 499–515). Silver Spring, MD: National Association of School Psychologists.

Epstein, J. L. (1995, May). School/family/community partnerships: Caring for the children we share. *Phi Delta Kappan*, pp. 701–712.

Estrada, P., Arsenio, W. F., Hess, R. D., & Holloway, S. (1987). Affective quality of the mother-child relationship: Longitudinal consequences for children's school-relevant cognitive functioning. *Developmental Psychology, 23,* 210–215.

Fantuzzo, J. W., DePaola, L. M., Lambert, L., Martino, T., Anderson, G., & Sutton, S. (1991). Effects of interparental violence on the psychological adjustment and competencies of young children. *Journal of Consulting and Clinical Psychology, 59*(2), 258–265.

Fehrmann, P. G., Keith, T. Z., & Reimers, T. M. (1987). Home influences on school learning: Direct and indirect effects of parent involvement on high school grades. *Journal of Educational Research, 80,* 330–337.

Finn, C. E. (1990, April). Ten tentative truths. Paper presented at the Center of the American Experiment Inaugural Conference, St. Paul, MN.

Fischer, M., Barkley, R. A., Fletcher, K. E., & Smallish, L. (1993). The adolescent outcome of hyperactive children: Predictors of psychiatric, academic, social, and emotional adjustment. *Journal of the American Academy of Child and Adolescent Psychiatry, 32*(2), 324–332.

Ford, M. E. (1982). Social cognition and social competence in adolescence. *Developmental Psychology, 18,* 323–340.

Galloway, J., & Sheridan, S. M. (1994). Implementing scientific practices through case studies: Examples using home-school interventions and consultation. *Journal of School Psychology, 32*(4), 385–413.

Garner, P. W., Jones, D. C., & Miner, J. L. (1994). Social competence among low-income preschoolers: Emotion socialization practices and social cognitive correlates. *Child Development, 65,* 622–637.

Gersten, J. C. (1992). Families in poverty. In M. E. Procidano & C. B. Fisher (Eds.), *Contemporary families. A handbook for school professionals* (pp. 137–158). New York: Teachers College Press, Columbia University.

Gillum, R. M. (1977). The effects of parent involvement on student achievement in three Michigan performance contracting programs (ERIC: Reproduction Document Service). Paper presented at the Annual Meeting of the American Educational Research Association, New York.

Goodman, S. H., Brogan, D., Lynch, M. E., & Fielding, B. (1993). Social and emotional competence in children of depressed mothers. *Child Development, 64,* 516–531.

Goodman, J. F., Sutton, V., & Harkavy, I. (1995). The effectiveness of family workshops in a middle school setting: Respect and caring make the difference. *Phi Delta Kappan, 76*(9), 694–700.

Graue, M. E., Weinstein, T., & Walberg, H. J. (1983). School-based home instruction and learning: A quantitative synthesis. *Journal of Educational Research, 76*(6), 351–360.

Greenwald, D. F. (1990). Family interaction and child outcome in a high-risk sample. *Psychological Reports, 66*(2), 675–688.

Greenwald, D. F., & Harder, D. W. (1994). Outcome predictors in a longitudinal study of high-risk boys. *Journal of Clinical Psychology, 50*(4), 638–643.

Gringlas, M., & Weinraub, M. (1995). The more things change. . . . Single parenting revisited. *Journal of Family Issues, 16*(1), 29–52.

Grolnick, W. S., & Ryan, R. M. (1992). Parental resources and the developing child in school. In M. E. Prociadano & C. B. Fisher (Eds.), *Contemporary families: A handbook for school professionals* (pp. 275–291). New York: Teachers College Press.

Gunnarsson, L., & Cochran, M. (1990). The support networks of single parents: Sweden and the United States. In M. Cochran, M. Larner, D. Riley, L. Gunnarsson, & C. R. Henderson (Eds.), *Extending families: The social networks of parents and their children* (pp. 105–116). Cambridge: Cambridge University Press.

Hansen, D. A. (1986). *Family-school articulations: The effects of interaction rule mismatch. American Educational Research Journal, 23*(4), 643–659.

Heller, L. R., & Fantuzzo, J. W. (1993). Reciprocal peer tutoring and parent partnership: Does parent involvement make a difference? *School Psychology Review, 22*(3), 517–534.

Henderson, A. T., & Berla, N. (Eds.). (1994). *A new generation of evidence: The family is critical to student achievement.* Columbia, MD: National Committee for Citizens in Education.

Henderson, A., Marburger, C., & Ooms, T. (1986). *Beyond the bake sale: An educator's guide to working with parents.* Columbia, MD: National Committee for Citizens in Education.

Henggeler, S. W., Edwards, J. J., Cohen, R., & Summerville, M. B. (1991). Predicting changes in children's popularity: The role of family relations. *Journal of Applied Developmental Psychology, 12,* 205–318.

Hess, R. D., & Holloway, S. D. (1984). Family and schools as educational institutions. In R. D. Parke, R. M. Emde, H. P. McAdoo, & G. P. Sackett (Eds.), *Review of Child Development Research: Volume 7. The Family* (pp. 179–222). Chicago: University of Chicago Press.

Johnson, D. L. (1990). The Houston parent-child

development center project: Disseminating a viable program for enhancing at-risk families. In H. W. Johnson (Ed.), *Prevention in human services* (pp. 89–108). New York: Haworth.

Kamerman, S. B. (1985). Young, poor, and a mother along: Problems and possible solutions. In H. McAdoo & T. M. J. Parham (Eds.), *Services to young families: Program review and policy recommendations.* Washington, DC: American Public Welfare Association.

Kaufman, A., & Kaufman, N. (1983). *Kaufman Assessment Battery for Children.* Circle Pines, MN: American Guidance Services.

Kazdin, A. E. (1987). Treatment of antisocial behavior in children: Current status and future directions. *Psychological Bulletin, 102*(2), 187–203.

Kellaghan, T., Sloane, K., Alvarez, B., & Bloom, B. S. (1993). *The home environment and school learning: Promoting parental involvement in the education of children.* San Francisco: Jossey-Bass.

Lazar, I., & Darlington, R. B. (1978). *Summary: Lasting effects after preschool* (ERIC: Reproduction Document Services ED 175 523). Ithaca, NY: Consortium for Longitudinal Studies, Cornell University.

Leichter, H. J. (1974). *The family as educator.* New York: Teachers College Press.

Leler, H. (1983). Parent education and involvement in relation to the schools and to parents of school-aged children. In R. Haskins & D. Adamson (Eds.), *Parent education and public policy* (pp. 141–180). Norwood, NJ: Ablex.

Levin, H. (1987). Accelerated school for disadvantaged students. *Educational Leadership, 44*(6), 19–21.

Liontos, S. B. (1992). *At risk families and schools: Becoming partners.* Eugene: ERIC Clearinghouse on Educational Management, College of Education, University of Oregon.

Litwak, E., & Meyer, H. (1974). *School, family, and neighborhood: The theory and practice of school-community relations.* New York: Columbia University Press.

MacKinnon-Lewis, C., Volling, B. L., Lamb, M. E., Dechman, K., Rabiner, D. & Curtner, M. E. (1994). A cross-contextual analysis of boys' social competence: From family to school. *Developmental Psychology, 30*(3), 325–333.

McAfee, O. (1993). Communication: The key to effective partnerships. In R. C. Burns (Ed.), *Parent and schools: From visitors to partners* (pp. 21–34). Washington, DC: National Education Association.

McCord, J. (1991). Competence in long-term perspective. *Psychiatry, 54,* 227–237.

Miller, G. E., & Prinz, R. J. (1990). Enhancement of social learning family interventions for childhood conduct disorder. *Psychological Bulletin, 108*(2), 291–307.

Milne, A. M. (1989). Family structure and the achievement of children. In W. J. Weston (Ed.), *Education and the American Family* (pp. 32–65). New York: New York University Press.

Minnesota Extension Service (1993). *Minnesota families and poverty.* M. A. Sutherland & J. W. Bauer, Eds. St. Paul: Children Youth and Family Consortium Electronic Clearinghouse, University of Minnesota.

Mitrsomwang, S., & Hawley, W. (1993). Cultural adaptation and the effects of family values and behavior on the academic achievement and persistence of Indochinese students. Final report (#R117E00045) to U.S. Department of Education, Office of Educational Research and Improvement.

Moles, O. C. (1993). *Building home-school partnerships for learning: Workshops for urban educators.* Washington, DC: U.S. Department of Education, Office of Educational Research and Improvement.

Mullen, B. L. (1989, April). Implementation of parent involvement in math program in Creve Couer Schools, Creve Couer, Illinois. Paper presented at the Annual Meeting of the American Educational Research Association, San Francisco.

Mullin, E., Quigley, K., & Glanville, B. (1994). A controlled evaluation of the impact of a parent training programme on child behavior and mothers' general well-being. *Counselling Psychology Quarterly, 7*(2), 167–179.

National Association of State Boards of Education (1992). *Partners in educational improvement: Schools parents, and the community.* Alexandria, VA: Author.

National Center for Educational Statistics (1992). *Characteristics of At-risk Students in NELS 1988.* Technical Report No. NCES 92-042. Washington, DC: U.S. Government Printing Office.

*National Educational Goals Report* (1994). Washington, DC: U.S. Government Printing Office.

Neighbors, B., Forehand, R., & McVicar, D. (1993). Resilient adolescents and interparental conflict. *American Journal of Orthopsychiatry, 63*(3), 462–471.

Olson, L. (1990, April). Parents as partners: Redefining the social contract between parents and schools *Education Week* (Special issue), *9*(28, 17–24.

Ooms, T., & Hara, S. (1991). *The family-school partnership: A critical component of school reform.* Washington, DC: Family Impact Seminar.

Palanki, A., & Burch, P. (1995, July). *In our hands: A multi-site parent teacher action research project* (Research Report No. 30). Baltimore, MD: Center on Families, Communication, Schools, and Children's Learning.

Patterson, G. R. (1982). *Coercive family process.* Eugene, OR: Castalia.

Peng, S. S., & Lee, R. M. (1992, April). Home variables, parent-child activities, and academic achievement: A study of 1988 eighth graders. Paper presented at the Annual Meeting of the American Educational Research Association, San Francisco.

Pfannensteil, J., Lambson, T., & Yarnell, V. (1991). *Second wave study of the Parents as Teachers program.* St. Louis, MO: Parents as Teachers National Center.

Phelan, P., Yu, H. C., & Davidson, A. L. (1994). Navigating the psychosocial pressures of adolescence: The voices and experiences of high school youth. *American Educational Research Journal, 31*(2), 415–447.

Portes, P. R., Howell, S. C., Brown, J. H., Eichenberger, S., & Mas, C. A. (1992). Family functions and children's postdivorce adjustment. *American Journal of Orthopsychiatry, 62*(4), 613–617.

Pratt, M., Green, D., MacVicar, J., & Bountrogianni, M. (1992). The mathematical parent: Parental scaffolding, parenting style, and learning outcomes in long-division mathematics homework. *Journal of Applied Developmental Psychology, 13*, 17–34.

Pratt, M. W., Hunsberger, B., Pancer, S. M., Roth, D., & Santolupo, S. (1993). Thinking about parenting: Reasoning about developmental issues across the lifespan. *Developmental Psychology, 29*(3), 585–595.

Redding, S. (1991). Alliance for achievement: An action plan for educators and parents. *International Journal of Educational Research, 15*, 147–162.

Reid, J. B., & Patterson, G. R. (1989). Early prevention and intervention with conduct problems: A social interactional model for the integration of research and practice. In G. Stoner, M. R. Shinn, & H. M. Walker (Eds.), *Interventions for achievement and behavior problems* (pp. 715–739). Silver Spring, MD: National Association of School Psychologists.

Reynolds, A. J. (1989). A structural model of first-grade outcomes for an urban, low socioeconomic black population (ERIC: Reproduction Document Service). Paper presented at the Annual Meeting of the American Educational Research Association, San Francisco.

Reynolds, A. J., Mavrogenes, N. A., Hagemann, M., & Bezruczko, N. (1993). *Schools, families, and children: Sixth year results from the Longitudinal Study of Children at Risk.* Chicago: Chicago Public Schools, Department of Research, Evaluation, and Planning.

Rich, D. (1987). *Schools and families: Issues and actions.* Washington, DC: National Education Association.

Rioux, J. W., & Berla, N. (1993). *Innovations in parent and family involvement.* Princeton, NJ: Eye on Education.

Sattes, B. (1985). *Parent involvement: A review of the literature* (Report No. 21). Charleston, WV: Appalachia Educational Laboratory.

Saunders, S. A. & Green, V. (1993). Evaluating the social competence of young children: A review of the literature. *Early Child Development and Care, 87*, 39–46.

Schweinhart, L. J., & Weikart, D. P. (1992). The High/Scope Perry Preschool Study, similar studies, and their implications for public policy in the U.S. In D. A. Stegelin (Ed.), *Early childhood education: Policy issues for the 1990s.* Norwood, NJ: Ablex.

Scott, W. A., Scott, R., & McCabe, M. (1991). Family relationships and children's personality: A cross-cultural, cross-source comparison. *British Journal of Social Psychology, 30*, 1–20.

Scott-Jones, D. (1987). Mother-as-teacher in the families of high- and low-achieving low-income black first-graders. *Journal of Negro Education, 56*(1), 21–34.

Seeley, D. S. (1985). *Education through partnership.* Washington, DC: American Enterprise Institute for Public Policy Research.

Shaw, J. A. (1987). Children in the military. *Psychiatric Annals, 17*(8), 539, 543–544.

Sheridan, S. M., & Colton, D. L. (1994). Conjoint behavioral consultation: A review and case study. *Journal of Educational and Psychological Consultation, 5*(3), 211–228.

Sheridan, S. M., & Kratochwill, T. R. (1992). Behavioral parent-teacher consultation: Conceptual and research considerations. *Journal of School Psychology, 30*, 117–139.

Sheridan, S. M., Kratochwill, T. R., & Elliott, S. N. (1990). Behavioral consultation with parents and teachers: Delivering treatment for socially withdrawn children at home and school. *School Psychology Review, 19*(1), 33–52.

Sinclair, M., Lam, S. F., Christenson, S. L. & Evelo, D. (1993). Action research in middle schools. *Equity and Choice, 10*(1), 23–24.

Singh, K., Bickley, P., Trivette, P., Keith, T. Z., Keith, P., & Anderson, E. (1995). The effects of four components of parental involvement on eighth-grade student achievement: Structural analysis of NELS-88 data. *School Psychology Review, 24*(2), 299–317.

Sloane, K. D. (1991). Home-support for successful learning. In S. B. Silvern (Ed.), *Advances in reading language research: Vol. 5. Literacy through family, community, and school interaction* (pp. 153–172). Greenwich, CT: JAI Press.

Steinberg, L., Mounts, N. S., Lamborn, S. D., & Dornbusch, S. (1989). Authoritative parenting and adolescent adjustment across varied ecological niches (ERIC: Reproduction

Document Service). Paper presented at the Annual Meeting of the Society for Research in Child Development, Kansas City, MO.

Strayhorn, J. M. (1988). *The competent child: An approach to psychotherapy and preventive mental health*. New York: Guilford.

Swap, S. M. (1993). *Developing home-school partnerships: From concepts to practice*. New York: Teachers College Press, Columbia University.

Thorndike, R. L., Hagen, E., & Sattler, J. (1986). *Stanford-Binet Intelligence Scale: Fourth Edition*. Chicago: Riverside.

Tizard, J., Schofield, W. N., & Hewison, J. (1982). Collaboration between teachers and parents in assisting children's reading. *British Journal of Educational Psychology, 52*(1), 1–11.

Trickett, P. K. (1993). Maladaptive development of school-aged, physically abused children: Relationships with the child-rearing context. *Journal of Family Psychology, 7*(1), 134–147.

Vosier, N. R. & Proctor, E. K. (1990). Stress and competence as predictors of child behavior problems. *Social Work Research and Abstracts, 26*(2), 3–9.

Walberg, H. J. (1984). Families as partners in educational productivity. *Phi Delta Kappan, 65*, 397–400.

Walberg, H. J., Bole, R. E., & Waxman, H. C. (1980). School-based family socialization and reading achievement in the inner-city. *Psychology in the Schools, 17*, 509–514.

Waters, E., & Sroufe, L. A. (1983). Social competence as a developmental construct. *Developmental Review, 3*, 79–97.

Webster-Stratton, C. (1989). Systematic comparison of consumer satisfaction of three cost-effective parent training programs for conduct problem children. *Behavior Therapy, 20*, 103–115.

Webster-Stratton, C. (1993). Strategies for helping early school-aged children with oppositional defiant and conduct disorders: The importance of home-school partnerships. *School Psychology Review, 22*(3), 437–457.

Webster-Stratton, C., & Hammond, M. (1990).

Predictors of treatment outcome in parent training for families with conduct problem children. *Behavior Therapy, 21*, 319–337.

Webster-Stratton, C., Kolpacoff, M., & Hollinsworth, T. (1988). Self-administered videotape therapy for families with conduct-problem children: Comparison with two cost-effective treatments and a control group. *Journal of Consulting and Clinical Psychology, 56*(4), 558–566.

Weiss, H. M., & Edwards, M. E. (1992). The family-school collaboration project: Systemic interventions for school improvement. In S. L. Christenson & J. C. Conoley (Eds.), *Home-school collaboration: Enhancing children's academic and social competence* (pp. 215–243). Silver Spring, MD: National Association of School Psychologists.

Weissberg, R. P., Caplan, M. Z., & Sivo, P. J. (1989). A new conceptual framework for establishing school-based social competence promotion programs. In L. A. Bond & B. E. Compas (Eds.), *Primary prevention and promotion in the schools* (pp. 255–296). New York: Sage.

White, R. W. (1959). Motivation reconsidered: The concept of competence. *Psychological Review, 66*, 297–333.

Wierson, M., & Forehand, R. (1992). Family stressors and adolescent functioning: A consideration of models for early and middle adolescents. *Behavior Therapy, 23*, 671–688.

Williams, D. L., & Stallworth, J. T. (1984). *Parent involvement in education: What a survey reveals* (ERIC Document Reproduction Service No. ED 253 327). Austin, TX: Southwest Regional Educational Development Lab: Parent Involvement in Education Project.

Ysseldyke, J. E., & Christenson, S. L. (1993). *TIES-II: The Instructional Environment System*. Longmont, CO: Sopris West.

Ziegler, S. (1987). *The effects of parent involvement on children's achievement: The significance of home/school links*. Toronto: Toronto Board of Education.

Zill, N., & Nord, C. W. (1994). *Running in place*. Washington, DC: Child Trends.

## CHAPTER 28

# CHILD PSYCHOTHERAPY

**JAN N. HUGHES**
*Texas A&M University*

Writing a chapter on child psychotherapy is a daunting task. The published literature describes over 230 psychosocial approaches to treating children's dysfunctions (Kazdin 1990), and recent meta-analyses of the field include over 300 studies evaluating the effectiveness of child psychotherapy (Weisz, Donenberg, Han, & Weiss, 1995). Literally hundreds of books on the subject have appeared within the past 10 years. Given the fact that child psychotherapy was a stepchild in therapy literature even 10 years ago, the rapid growth of both the theoretical and the empirical literature is a welcome development.

The breadth and depth of the subject requires a highly selective approach. The primary purpose of this chapter is to describe an integrative approach to child therapy rather than an overview of the field. The approach described in this chapter is based on the assumption that children's problems are multidetermined and require interventions that address not only children's characteristics but also important contextual factors, as well as the interaction among child, family, and broader contextual influences. Furthermore, components of a multimodal intervention are based on a constructed model of the child's problems.

The construction of such a model is guided by knowledge of the etiology of the disorder (including precursors of the disorder and risk and protective factors in the development of the disorder that may be a treatment focus), extant literature on the effectiveness of different interventions, and assessment of the particular child's assets and limitations (including contextual supports and stressors). Clearly, developing such an integrated approach to children's problems requires a firm basis in developmental psychopathology, knowledge of diverse theoretical perspectives, and knowledge of and skill in a range of intervention modalities.

To accomplish the chapter's purpose, it is divided into the following sections. First, child psychotherapy is defined, and issues specific to psychotherapy with children are discussed. Second, key assumptions underlying integrated child psychotherapy are discussed. This section includes a discussion of models for the delivery of child psychotherapy. Third, evidence of the efficacy of child psychotherapy is reviewed. This overview of outcome literature is followed by a section on proven and promising approaches to the treatment of problems that are frequently the focus of treatment. Selected approaches are consistent with the chapter's emphasis on multimodal and empirically supported treatment.

## DEFINITION OF CHILD PSYCHOTHERAPY

Psychotherapy has been defined as a special interaction between a client who has sought help for a particular problem and a therapist who provides conditions to alleviate the client's (or patient's) distress and to improve functioning in everyday life (Garfield, 1980). "The interaction is designed to alter the feelings, thoughts, attitudes, or actions of the person who has sought or has been brought to treatment" (Kazdin, 1988, p.1). This broad definition may describe most of what occurs in adult psychotherapy, but it is an inadequate definition of child psychotherapy. Although the child may be the "identified patient," the child rarely has sought help from the therapist, and the distress may be experienced as much by the child's parents or teachers as by the child. Furthermore, the interactions in child psychotherapy usually involve not only the patient (the child) but also other significant persons in the child's life, including parents, siblings, and teachers. Because children depend on adult care-givers for most of their needs, adults' thoughts, feelings, and behaviors may be the focus of child psychotherapy. Whereas one-on-one child ther-apy was the prevalent model 20 years ago, our current understanding of the nature of children's disorders and of the importance of mobilizing developmental mechanisms for healthy growth and development requires more ecologically ori-ented approaches.

A useful approach in the definition of child psychotherapy defines its goals and methods and establishes its boundaries (i.e., defining what is outside its scope). The goals of child psychother-apy include the alleviation of children's disorder of behavior, feeling, and thinking and the pro-motion of healthy growth and development. These goals are construed broadly and include improved functioning in both the intrapersonal and interpersonal spheres, reduction of maladap-tive behaviors, and reduction of psychological (and often physical) complaints (Kazdin, 1988). These goals are achieved through psychosocial interventions, which are based on psychological principles of learning, development, and behav-ior. The therapist uses talking, instruction, and other influencing strategies to bring about im-proved functioning.

In adult psychotherapy, a usual script charac-terizes therapy. The patient describes his or her problem; the therapist asks questions to obtain necessary detail and uses interpersonal sources of influence such as teaching, persuasion, and dis-cussion to accomplish therapy goals. In child therapy, adults usually initiate therapy and are ac-tive agents in the therapeutic enterprise. There-fore, the therapist directs his or her influence at-tempts to parents and other adults to bring about the child's improved functioning. Thus, the defi-nition of child psychotherapy includes interac-tions in which the therapist attempts to change the child's functioning by working directly with the child, as well as interactions in which the therapist works through other agents, which may include parents, teachers, or peers, to accomplish the goals of psychotherapy.

The definition of child therapy excludes bio-logically based interventions, such as medication therapy or diet. (However, the child therapist plays important consultative and coordinating roles in such treatment.) It also excludes academic interventions, such as tutoring or instructional

consultation, although educational interventions, defined in terms of enhancing children's compe-tence, are included in our definition. Equipping the child and the child's caretakers with skills, knowledge, and beliefs that enable the child to successfully meet developmental challenges is a primary goal of child psychotherapy. An educa-tional framework to accomplishing its goals has several advantages: (1) emphasizes the develop-ment of competence, (2) reduces the stigmatizing aspects of therapy, (3) encourages incorporating the child's strengths into the intervention ap-proach, and (4) underscores the preventive aspect of all child psychotherapy in the sense that reso-lution of current problems affects developmental pathways.

## ASSUMPTIONS THAT UNDERLIE INTEGRATIVE CHILD PSYCHOTHERAPY

The approach to integrative child psychotherapy in this chapter is based on a few underlying as-sumptions, which serve as an organizing frame-work for developing interventions. Approaching child therapy with such conceptual frameworks give coherence to one's work, allowing the thera-pist to develop an integrative (versus an eclectic) approach that draws from a wide array of poten-tial therapeutic approaches.

*First, children's problems that are the focus of psychotherapy are usually multidetermined.* Children are embedded in multiple systems that exert both direct and indirect influences on their behavior. Furthermore, these systems (e.g., peer group, family, school, and community) interact with one another and with the child's characteristics, in-cluding developmental status. Thus, effective in-terventions are multimodal and match the com-plexity of children's problems. The day of single-focused therapies for such complex prob-lems as aggressiveness or depression is over. The therapist's task is to assess the interplay of child, family, and broader contextual factors and to se-lect an intervention approach that maximizes the child's positive transactions with the environ-ment. The following vignette illustrates this multisystemic approach to child psychotherapy.

Rick is a nine-year-old boy who was referred for therapy by his school assistance team because of aggressiveness and disruptiveness. His individ-ual strengths include above-average intelligence and good athletic abilities. His parents separated when he was three years old, after more than a year of high marital conflict, leading to physical abuse of the mother. Rick has one sibling, age seven. Rick has not seen his father in three years. His mother works as a clerk in a grocery store and often is unavailable to supervise Rick after school, and he has begun hanging out with a couple of older boys who have reputations at school for conduct problems and have been arrested for shoplifting. Rick and his mother are emotionally close, but she has difficulty in enforcing limits and relies on Rick for her own emotional support. Rick has adequate social problem-solving skills but believes aggression is a legitimate way to obtain his goals ("You either get used or you use others" or "If you show any weakness, people will stomp on you"). In developing an integrative intervention, the therapist was influenced by the knowledge that association with antisocial peers is an important precursor to delinquency and substance use. Furthermore, the mother's insularity enhances her dependence on Rick, which undermines her ability to set and reinforce behavioral limits. Rick endorses antisocial norms and beliefs, and his aggression is more purposeful than impulsive and out of control. The intervention included his mother's participation in a small parenting skills group (which provides social support and teaches such parenting skills as establishing and enforcing limits, handling misbehavior, and providing structure and consistency) and enrolling Rick in an after-school basketball program (which provides an opportunity for developing a network of prosocial peers) and a school-based social competence group, made up of an equal number of aggressive and socially competent peers, in which prosocial skills and beliefs are modeled and practiced.

*A second assumption is that a given therapeutic approach that is derived from a specific theoretical perspective, such as social learning theory or family systems theory, is best understood from multiple theoretical perspectives.* In other words, a given intervention is likely to affect multiple areas of child and family functioning. For example, behavioral parent training is based on social learning theory (Patterson, Reid, & Dishion, 1992), but improving parents' ability to set and enforce behavioral limits is likely to affect the overall parent-child relationship, as well as the family system. For example, as parents agree on parenting approaches, their alliance is strengthened, and the child's intrusion into the parental subsystem is blocked. As the parents begin to experience the child as less demanding, they are more positive to and accepting of the child. The child, feeling more accepted and less angry, is more cooperative and affectionate. The indirect effects of a given intervention are illustrated by research that documents that training of parents of conduct-disordered children results in decreases in parental depression and anger and overall family stress (Webster-Stratton, 1994). A psychodynamically oriented intervention, such as individual play therapy, may foster a child's sense of self-worth, leading to changes in his or her level of positivity at home, which changes the quality of parent-child interactions. Of course, indirect effects can also be negative. For example, providing social skills training with groups of conduct-disordered adolescent boys may both enhance social skills and foster the adoption of antisocial beliefs and values through increased association with antisocial peers (Andrews & Dishion, 1995). In developing interventions, the therapist has to consider potential direct and indirect effects.

*Third, psychotherapy is an applied science.* More succinctly, child psychotherapy is applied developmental psychology. The child therapist must know a great deal about normal and abnormal development to identify aberrations that suggest that a child is on a deviant developmental pathway. The therapist must understand how socialization experiences, such as peer group involvement, the parent-child relationship, and school adaptation, affect the child's developmental course at different ages, as well as know how to influence these experiences to enhance the child's competence and prevent future psychopathology. The effective child therapist is well versed in data-driven theories of childhood disorders and in empirically supported interventions for different disorders.

To speak of the therapist as applied scientist does not suggest that interpersonal skills and clinical intuition are unimportant ingredients of successful therapy. Therapists' characteristics are clearly important to such critical aspects of child therapy as establishing the therapeutic alliance with parents and children and accurately interpreting clients' verbal and nonverbal behavior. Appreciating elements of art in psychotherapy does not eliminate the requirement that psychotherapeutic approaches be supported by empirical evidence of their efficacy (Weisz, Donenberg, Han, & Weiss, 1995). Rather, psychotherapy as applied science underscores the premise that it is informed by a broad body of theoretical and empirical literature.

Effective psychotherapy requires a conceptual understanding of the disorder one is treating and knowledge of those factors that contribute to its development, maintenance, and prognosis.

Some authors have suggested that research on psychotherapy is largely irrelevant to psychotherapy practice: "Because therapy is so individualized and the therapist is making decisions about intervention on a moment-to-moment basis, specific treatment prescriptions based on research findings are few" (Tuma & Ross, 1993, p. 155). This view minimizes the lessons that psychotherapy research has to offer. Critical reviews of the empirical literature that identify therapeutic approaches (e.g., cognitive behavior therapy, parent training, and social skills training) for which there is evidence of effectiveness. Of course, a given intervention should be delivered in a flexible manner, tailored to the client's particular characteristics and situation. Moment-to-moment decisions are inevitable. However, these decisions are made within a framework that specifies intervention foci, goals, and general methods for achieving those goals. This framework gives coherence to the therapy process.

Adherence to empirically supported intervention approaches does not mean that the therapist rigidly adheres to prescribed procedures. Some circumscribed problems, such as a child's enuresis, respond well to standardized behavioral treatment protocols. However, most problems require a more flexible and individualized approach. This flexibility is not incompatible with reliance on empirically supported therapies. In implementing cognitive therapy with a depressed adolescent, say, the therapist selects treatment goals, intervention foci, and therapy procedures that are consistent with the approach but matched to an individual assessment of the adolescent and the adolescent's transactions with his or her environment. For example, the amount and type of homework assigned is based on the therapist's assessment of the adolescent's energy and motivation, and decisions about parental involvement depend on such characteristics of the family as the level of stress experienced by the parents.

## ISSUES SPECIFIC TO PSYCHOTHERAPY WITH CHILDREN

The developmental status of children has many implications for providing psychotherapy.

*First, children are not in control of those factors that have the greatest impact on their growth and development.* The quality of the home environment, including parental nurturance and provision of cognitive stimulation, is primarily determined by adults in children's environments. This statement does not deny the importance of children's effects on the home environment but acknowledges that parents have more control over the environment than do children. The child's relationship with teachers and classmates has important implications for learning and adjustment, and teachers have the primary responsibility for creating a classroom climate that is accepting or rejecting, competitive or cooperative, and so on. Thus, the inclusion of parents, teachers, and other care-givers in therapy is usually recommended.

An obvious corollary to the fact that parents are in control of their children's environments is that adults, not children, seek treatment for children's problems. Parents initiate treatment and are responsible for the child's continuation in treatment. This simple fact has enormous implications for child psychotherapy. Approximately 50% to 75% of children referred for therapy either do not initiate therapy or terminate early if they do begin (Pekarik & Stephenson, 1988). Clearly, engaging parents in therapy and maintaining their support are crucial to the success of child psychotherapy. The therapist must develop a consensus with parents about the goals of therapy, as well as support for the method of achieving these goals. When parent training is a component of treatment, attending to the parent's own personal issues increases the probability that parents will complete training (Prinz & Miller, 1994). Several family characteristics, for example, maternal insularity, depression, antisocial history, stress, and socioeconomic disadvantage, predict who terminates from therapy, as well as who benefits from it (Dumas & Wahler, 1983; Kazdin, Mazurick, & Bass, 1993). An effective therapy approach with mothers who are isolated or depressed will probably need to address the mother's social isolation and resources for coping with stressors. An emotionally supportive relationship between the therapist and the child's mother may be a prerequisite for the child's continuation in therapy. Improvement in the mother's coping resources and social support not only improve the likelihood that the parent will remain in therapy but also is expected to have beneficial effects on the child's adjustment.

Because children do not seek treatment,

they may not see the need for treatment and have little motivation for cooperating with the tasks of therapy. The effective child therapist uses developmentally sensitive interviewing to help children feel respected, accepted, and safe in the relationship. Hughes and Baker (1990) emphasize the importance of explaining the purpose of therapy to children in ways that they can understand and that address their concern of being blamed for problems.

*Second, what is developmentally appropriate treatment for a 6-year-old child is not appropriate for a 12-year-old child.* For example, parent training is most appropriate for younger children, who are more amenable to parental influence. Cognitive therapy, which requires clients to reflect on their own thinking processes, is more effective with adolescents than with younger children (Durlak, Fuhrman, & Lampman, 1991). Presumably, adolescents have the cognitive abilities necessary to evaluate the logic of their thinking. In a meta-analytic study of social competence training, Beelman, Pfingsten, and Losel (1994) found that age moderated effectiveness. Specifically, children between the ages of 3 and 8 who are experiencing social problems benefit more from single-focus social competence programs than from multimodal programs, whereas 9- to 11-year-old children benefit more from multimodal programs (Beelmann, et al., 1994). The researchers suggest that the interaction between age and complexity of the intervention may be due to the increasingly complex nature of social interaction as children mature. Also, simple behavioral skill-training programs for young children may equip them with skills they need to transact more successfully with their environment, contributing to improved transactions with others, which promote the development of social competence. In other words, a relatively small positive change in the early years may set in motion positive child-environment transactions that deflect a child from a deviant developmental pathway. At later ages, similar problems may require a more comprehensive intervention because they are embedded in a broader context.

*Third, some childhood problems are defined in terms of a deviation from what is typical for one's age.* For example, children's attention span, ability to delay gratification, motor activity, ability to follow directions, and ability to wait one's turn all improve with increasing age. Only when a child's development in these areas departs significantly from developmental expectancies is the child considered to have a condition for which psychotherapy and, perhaps, medication may be recommended. Similarly, night-time enuresis is common in children, especially boys, up to six years of age and is likely to improve with the passage of time. Childhood fears (e.g., of the dark, of thunder, and of monsters) are common at young ages and are also likely to remit with time. Unless fears interfere significantly with the child's accomplishment of other developmental tasks (independence and sense of mastery), treatment is not necessary.

*Fourth, knowledge of precursors of later childhood problems is important in determining whether or not to treat a specific problem.* The therapist needs to know what early problems are indicative of a deviant developmental pathway. "A pathway is identified when a group of individuals experience a behavioral development that is distinct from the behavioral development of another group of individuals. A key feature of the concept of a pathway is that it takes into account the stability of problem behavior by focusing on different manifestations of each problem behavior, particularly when the problem behavior increases in seriousness over time" (Loeber & Farrington, 1994, p. 890). Even problems that may be fairly common, such as childhood aggression and noncompliance, may warrant intervention because of their association with subsequent dysfunction. These problems affect later functioning through a variety of mechanisms. The problem may be an early manifestation of an underlying condition that, if left untreated, will become manifest. Similarly, the fact that shy children often become anxious adults may reflect a common disorder that is manifested differently at different developmental stages. Early problems may also alter the child's transactions with the environment in a negative direction, increasing the child's risk for subsequent dysfunction. Noncompliant children elicit more controlling and critical behaviors from parents and teachers (Walker & Buckley, 1973), which contribute to a less accepting environment. That is, the child's characteristics influence the child's environment, which subsequently influences the child's behavior. These reciprocal and dynamic influences may lead to a deviant developmental pathway.

The concept of developmental pathways is useful in identifying, at an early stage, children who appears at highest risk for subsequent maladjustment. Early intervention, before dysfunction is serious or when the child and family are more amenable to intervention, may prevent subsequent dysfunction. The knowledge of developmental pathways can aid in the identification of protective factors, or factors that account for why some youths who show early risk signs do not develop serious problems. The therapist can attempt to strengthen these protective factors (e.g., social support, self-esteem, social problem-solving skills, and a sense of school belonginess) and thereby prevent subsequent dysfunction. Conversely, some problems, such as enuresis, do not place the child at risk for subsequent maladjustment and therefore do not require intervention.

*Fifth, a child's developmental status interacts with environmental events, such as divorce, loss of a parent, or the experience of sexual abuse.* That is, the same event is likely to affect children of differing ages differently.

## MODELS FOR DELIVERING PSYCHOTHERAPY TO CHILDREN

Friedman (1994) makes the case that changes in the way things were (or were thought to be) when psychotherapy for children was forming is very different from the way things are. Psychotherapy services were based on the assumption that few children would require psychotherapy, that therapy would be provided for discrete problems, and that children in therapy would have two parents who gave stability and support. These assumptions clash with existing realities:

> Between 14% and 22% of children and adolescents experience significant emotional and mental disorders (Brandenburg, Friedman, & Silver, 1990), and disorders are being seen in children at younger ages (Earls, 1989).
>
> Twenty-five% of children (a threefold increase between 1960 and 1991) live with only one parent, and 50% will live in a single-parent home.
>
> One in four children live in poverty, and increasing numbers are exposed to violence (Jones, 1990).
>
> Families with children are the fastest increasing homeless group and in 1987 made up nearly 38% of all homeless persons in the United States (U.S. Congress, House Select Committee on Children, Youth and Families, 1987).
>
> The interrelatedness of problems such as

child abuse, violence, emotional and behavioral disorders, substance abuse, delinquency, and school difficulty is becoming increasingly apparent (Friedman, 1994; Shorr, 1988).

The school-aged population is increasingly linguistically and ethnically diverse. By the year 2030, there will be 32 million post-1986 immigrants and their descendants, or 1% of the population (Spencer, 1988). These new immigrants are more likely to have experienced traumatic backgrounds in their countries of origin (Culbertson, 1993).

The response of the mental health system to children's needs has been far from adequate. Only 70% to 80% of children in need of mental health services receive appropriate care (Tuma, 1989). When services are available, they are fragmented and overutilize restrictive interventions, such as residential placement, despite the lack of evidence of the effectiveness of these restrictive (and costly) interventions. Fewer than 1% of school-aged children are identified as seriously emotionally disturbed, far under prevalence rates for serious emotional and behavioral disturbance, and only a small percentage receive psychotherapy (Duchnowski, 1994).

These current realities underscore the need for dramatic changes in how psychotherapy services are delivered to children. It is unlikely that any treatment delivered once a week for 50 minutes in a therapist's office will be successful in treating a conduct-disordered 10-year-old boy who struggles academically and whose mother is addicted to crack cocaine and lives in a violent neighborhood.

Another indication of the inadequacies of traditional, clinic-based models is the fact that between 50% and 75% of children and families referred for outpatient treatment do not initiate treatment or terminate early if they do begin (Pekarik & Stephenson, 1988). Furthermore, children most in need of treatment, based on problem severity, comorbidity, and antisocial behaviors and additional risk factors (e.g., family stress, socioeconomic disadvantage, harsh and inconsistent parenting, parents' antisocial history, and minority status), are least likely to initiate or complete treatment (Kazdin et al., 1993).

A consensus has been achieved about needed changes in models for the delivery of mental health services (Henggeler, 1994): within a revised system of care, psychotherapy is most likely to be effective when it is coordinated with other services, accessible, provided in clients' natural environments, individualized, culturally competent, and consistent with the multidetermined nature of children's disorders. Multisystemic therapy (MST; Henggeler & Borduin, 1990) is a excellent example of the type of therapy needed to address today's current realities. It has been found to produce long-term improvements in seriously delinquent adolescents, one of the most difficult-to-treat populations. The MST therapist provides therapy in the adolescent's school, home, or neighborhood; targets multiple systems and their interrelationships; and employs multiple methods based on an individual assessment of the adolescent's and family's strengths and weaknesses. Thus, MST is a flexible approach that considers the individual child's or adolescent's characteristics, parent-child variables, peer factors, and school performance. Treatment focuses on one or some combination of these four systems and their interrelationships.

The success of MST is especially noteworthy, given the fact that it is provided in community settings with referred clients with serious and complex problems. The effectiveness of such community-based therapy has been questioned by recent meta-analyses of psychotherapy (Weisz, Weiss, & Donenberg, 1992). Henggeler attributes the success of MST in treating delinquent inner-city youths and maltreating families to its ecological methods:

Fundamental principles of MST interventions pertain to understanding how identified problems fit within the youth's social ecology (i.e., family, peers, school, neighborhood) and designing interventions to directly address difficulties within and between systems. . . . Consistent with the causal modeling literature on delinquency and substance abuse . . . all serious problems are viewed as multidetermined. Consequently, interventions targeting such problems must consider the interrelations of individuals and systems to optimize the probability of successful outcomes. Clearly, for example, improved parental monitoring and discipline will not affect lasting change in antisocial adolescents who remain attached to deviant peers and disengaged from educational or vocational pursuits. Thus, MST interventions are implemented simultaneously in multiple systems in

anticipation of synergistic effects (Henggeler, Schoenwald, & Pickrel, 1995, pp. 713–714).

Effective psychotherapy must be family-focused. The majority of child clinicians actively involve parents in the child's treatment (Kazdin, Siegle, & Bass, 1990). One of the most consistent findings in developmental psychopathology is the influence of the home environment on children's growth and development. The child's home environment can buffer or exacerbate the level of risk associated with such characteristics as hyperactivity and directly influence the development of problems such as conduct disorder and school underachievement. Many aspects of the home environment are amenable to treatment. For example, parenting practices and the level of academic stimulation predict changes in academic and behavioral adjustment of poor, elementary school–age children (Dubow & Ippolito, 1994). Both of these aspects of the home environment can be positively affected through interventions (Christenson, Rounds, & Franklin, 1992; Webster-Stratton, 1984). Patterson et al. (1992) have built a convincing case for their view that childhood antisocial behavior is a family concern and that children learn aggression through coercive family processes. The few studies that have compared treatments that involve parents and child-only treatments consistently support the inclusion of parents in their children's therapy (Dishion & Andrews, 1995; Kazdin, Siegel, & Bass, 1992).

# IS CHILD PSYCHOTHERAPY EFFECTIVE?

Clinical researchers have attempted to answer the question of child psychotherapy's effectiveness in a variety of ways, including meta-analysis, comparative evaluation studies, and the systematic investigation of the effects of a given therapeutic approach. Each approach makes an important but unique contribution to our understanding of the effectiveness of child psychotherapy.

## Meta-analytic Studies

Meta-analyses address the "ultimate" question of the degree of benefit experienced by treated children, relative to control children, on treatment outcome measures. In meta-analysis, the results of multiple studies are analyzed in such a way as to permit the combination and comparison of results from different studies. Meta-analysis provides an "analysis of analyses" (Smith, Glass, & Miller, 1980, p. 809). Although there are variations on quantitative procedures, most methods involve computation of an effect size (ES) for a given study. An effect size is calculated as the difference in means between treatment and control subjects at posttreatment, divided by the standard deviation of the control treatment (or by the standard deviation of the pooled control and treatment conditions). The ES becomes the dependent measure for the meta-analysis. For studies reporting multiple outcomes, an ES for the study is obtained by averaging effect sizes across each of the individual measures. Thus, an ES is a common metric for the impact of treatment. An ES of .50 means that at posttreatment treated children performed on outcomes measures, on average, .50 standard deviations higher than control children. An ES indicates the percentile standing of the average treated child on the outcome measures, if that child were placed in the control group after treatment. Cohen (1992) classifies effect sizes into qualitative ranges. Thus, an ES of .50 (moderate ES) means that the typical treated child performed better than 69% percent of the untreated children. An ES of .20 (small effect) corresponds to the fifty-eighth percentile, and an ES of .80 (large effect) means that a typical treated child performed better than 79% of untreated children. When questions about the differential impact of treatment on different outcome measures is of interest (e.g., on teachers' ratings of adjustment or on self-concept), an ES for each study is computed only on the measures of interest.

In an early and influential meta-analysis of child psychotherapy, Casey and Berman (1985) reviewed 75 studies of children between the ages of 3 and 15, which included a control group, published between 1952 and 1983. The ES for these studies was .71, indicating that the average treated child performed better than 76% of untreated children. Subsequent meta-analyses (involving more than 300 studies in all) have found similar results (e.g., Kazdin, Bass, Ayers, & Rodgers, 1990; Weisz, Weiss, Alicke, & Klotz, 1987; Weisz, Weiss, Han, Granger, & Morton, 1995).

Although meta-analysis provides an index of benefits that accrue from participating in therapy, results of meta-analytic studies offer little information to guide clinical practice. One cannot translate an ES for psychotherapy in general

to treatment planning for an individual client. All outcomes are considered equal in meta-analysis, but studies differ in their methodological rigor, and study measures vary in their clinical meaningfulness or social validity. For example, social skills training results in large gains, relative to control conditions, on measures of discrete skills taught but very limited gains on measures of social functioning, such as peer sociometric or teachers' reports (Beelman et al., 1994).

The types of interventions and client populations vary too much to permit translation to particular types of therapy with particular populations. Even meta-analyses that attempt to draw comparisons between different treatment approaches, such as between behavioral versus psychodynamic approaches, as Casey and Berman (1985) do, are insufficient guides to clinical practice. Groupings such as "behavioral" and "psychodynamic" put together interventions that vary widely in methods.

Recent meta-analytic studies have addressed some limitations of these general studies by focusing on the effectiveness of a specific therapeutic approach. For example, Durlak et al., (1991) reported an effect size of .56 in a review of 64 studies of cognitive behavior therapy (CBT) with children aged 4 to 13. These authors were interested in identifying variables that moderate the outcomes of CBT with maladapting children. They demonstrated that the overall ES of .56 obscures important differences in the effectiveness of CBT between children who had achieved formal operational thinking and children at less advanced cognitive stages. The ES (.92, large) for children aged 11 to 13 (who presumably are in the formal operational stage) was nearly twice that for younger children (aged 5 to 7: ES = .57; aged 8 to 11: ES = .55). Despite the usefulness of these more focused meta-analyses, the diversity of treatments subsumed under the designated treatment approaches (e.g., CBT or family therapy) and the diversity of problems treated (from nonreferred samples with mild symptoms to clinic-referred children with severe problems) limit their usefulness to the individual clinician faced with developing a treatment plan for a particular client.

The more informative meta-analyses evaluate a given treatment approach with a given problem and investigate those client and treatment factors associated with larger effects. Beelman, et al. (1994) include 49 studies that employ social competence training. They report an ES of .83 on social-cognitive tests but only .13 for sociometric and .10 for parents' and teachers' reports of functioning. Furthermore, they report that interventions are more successful with some clients than with others. For example, older children and children with externalizing problems respond better to multimodal interventions that combine problem-solving skills and self-control training, whereas withdrawn children and younger children respond best to single-modality treatments (e.g., behavioral social-skills training). The authors conclude, "This study emphasizes the need to discuss the effectiveness of social cognitive training under very specific aspects. Global effect sizes can quickly lead to inappropriate conclusions. The variability of effects found here is a complex function of types of intervention, client characteristics, outcome ratings, and specific interactions among these variables" (p. 268).

Several researchers have questioned the relevance of the studies in meta-analytic analyses because they involve "children interventions, and treatment conditions that were relatively unrepresentative of conventional clinical practice" (Weisz et al., 1992, p. 1580). They argue that the majority of children in these studies were recruited by researchers rather than referred for treatment and that treatment departed from typical clinical practice in several ways: the selections were based on specific characteristics, resulting in more homogeneous samples; therapy addressed the focal problem primarily or exclusively; therapists were trained immediately before therapy in the particular techniques they would use and therapy involved an exclusive or primary reliance on those techniques; therapists followed a structured manual; and the therapy was monitored regularly for its adherence to the treatment plan. Furthermore, treatments were often delivered at school and involved group rather than individual treatments (Weisz et al., 1992). The types of intervention studies in meta-analyses overrepresent behavioral and cognitive behavioral methods, and those methods reported as most common in clinical practice (i.e., psychodynamic, eclectic, and family therapy) are generally not represented in published studies.

Kazdin, Bass, Ayers, and Rodgers (1990) conclude that meta-analysis informs us about the effectiveness of *research therapy* but not about therapy as typically provided in clinical practice, or *clinic therapy*. The extant limited research on the effectiveness of clinic therapy suggests much smaller effects than those obtained in research therapy (Weisz et al., 1992).

Even though most of the studies in meta-analyses of child psychotherapy represent cases, treatments, and conditions that are not representative of therapy as practiced in community settings, these studies help us identify the conditions under which child therapy can be successful (Kaxdin, Bars, Ayers, & Rodgers, 1990). Many of the conditions that characterize research therapy (e.g., adherence to a treatment protocol, therapists well trained in the procedures used, inclusion of behavioral strategies, and problem-focused therapy) can be replicated in clinic settings.

Weisz, Donenberg, Han, and Weiss (1995) systematically investigated each of eight differences between clinic therapy and research therapy, using subsets of a large meta-analysis, to determine why research therapy is more effective. The strongest evidence pointed to the superiority of behavioral versus nonbehavioral interventions: "If behavioral methods truly generate more positive effects than nonbehavioral methods, the fact that behavioral methods are so commonly used in research therapy, and so infrequently used in clinic therapy, may help explain the superior outcomes of research therapy" (p. 695).

## Individual Comparative Studies

The question of most relevance to the clinician is this: "What approach with what problems for which clients, under what conditions will result in what effects?" (Kazdin, 1995). Individual studies that compare different approaches with the same population and problem are particularly informative because many factors that influence treatment outcome, other than the particular treatment approaches being evaluated, are the same across treatment conditions because of random assignment of individuals to the various treatment approaches.

Studies that systematically manipulate specific treatment parameters are highly relevant to clinical practice. These studies address how to provide a particular therapeutic approach, such as cognitive-behavioral therapy, parent training, or family therapy. For example, parent training for parents of conduct-disordered children often focus on both parent-child relationship enhancement skills (primarily nondirective play skills) and control skills (e.g., limit setting and using time-out). Some clinicians begin with play skills, believing that a relationship characterized by warmth, acceptance, and reciprocity is a prerequisite for gaining a child's compliance, whereas other clinicians believe that parents must first be given skills for managing disruptive behavior before being able to engage the child in mutually rewarding interaction. Eisenstadt, Eyberg, McNeil, Newcomb, and Funderburk (1993) randomly assigned parents of conduct-disordered children to one of two sequences of skill training. One-half of the parents received instruction and practice in play skills first, followed by instruction and practice in control skills, and one half of the parents received these components in reverse order. Although the treatment resulted in benefits for children in both conditions, those parents who received the control skills training first reported greater improvement and a higher degree of posttreatment satisfaction. The authors state the implications of their findings for clinical practice: "In clinical practice, it may be advisable to present the discipline stage before the play therapy stage for certain types of children and presenting problems. For example, for children whose behavior is seriously out of control and potentially dangerous (e.g., extreme aggression toward younger siblings), the more rapid decrease in conduct-problem behaviors produced by starting with [control skills] may be decisive" (p.49).

Recent experimental studies have also documented the effectiveness of parent training for parents of conduct-disordered children through a focus on parents' concerns that were not directly connected to parent-child interactions. Attention in therapy to parents' own concerns (e.g., job stress, health problems, personal worries, and family disputes) both reduces treatment attrition (Prinz & Miller, 1994) and enhances children's outcomes (Webster-Stratton, 1994).

A recent study on the effectiveness of different treatment procedures for children of divorced parents provides yet another illustration of the relevance of clinical research to practice (Stolberg & Mahler, 1994). Each treatment condition involved a school-based intervention, either focusing exclusively on provision of support to the child or a combined focus on provision of support and teaching coping skills. One treatment condition involved a parent component, in which parents and children completed a workbook at home that encouraged parent-child communication about divorce-related issues. Treated children were between the ages of 8 and 12, and 42% were diagnosed with a clinical disorder.

Contrary to expectations, inclusion of a parent component did not enhance treatment gains. Particularly for children whose parents were more stressed and unavailable, the parent component may have reduced children's benefits from the school-based intervention. Additional comparisons documented that children with the greatest adjustment difficulties improved more from the support-only group than from the support-plus-skills-training group. These findings underscore the importance of selecting intervention components based on an individual assessment of the child's and family's characteristics. Emotionally needy children may require support-oriented therapy prior to, or in lieu of, skill training. Also, children from high-functioning homes are likely to benefit from assignments, but children from low-functioning homes may require a more intensive parent-focused intervention that addresses the parents' own concerns before requiring their assistance with their child's therapy.

Studies of the effectiveness of brief versus long-term therapy have challenged the assumption that the latter is superior to short-term therapy. Smyrnios and Kirkby (1993) randomly assigned clients in a community-based clinic to one of three conditions: minimal contact (a child and parent intake session followed by therapist feedback), time-limited therapy (averaging 10 child visits and 6 parent visits after the two intake sessions), or time-unlimited therapy (averaging 28 child visits and 10 parent visits). All conditions resulted in improvement, with the minimal contact and time-limited conditions producing nonsignificantly greater improvement than the time-unlimited treatment. The results of this and other studies (e.g., Fisher, 1980; Weisz, Walter, Weiss, Fernandez, & Mikow, 1990) suggest that brief therapy may be as effective or more effective than long-term therapy. Brief approaches have certain characteristics that may account for their positive impact. Specifically, they are more goal-focused, rely on informational approaches, and rely on parents as agents of change.

## SAMPLE OF PROVEN AND PROMISING TREATMENTS

Three proven or promising intervention approaches for children and adolescents are described and evidence of their effectiveness summarized. Selected approaches have been the subject of systematic research. Thus, evidence of an approach's effectiveness comes not from a single study but from an accumulation of knowledge about a well-defined approach with a specific problem and population. These approaches are merely illustrative of the genre of empirically supported psychotherapies for children, and several comprehensive reviews of psychotherapies for different problems are available. The most informative of these texts (Ammermann, Last, & Hersen, 1993; Kendall, 1991; Kratochwill & Morris, 1991) critically evaluate evidence of the effectiveness of different approaches, including a discussion of client and treatment factors. LeCroy (1994) has published a book of treatment manuals for child and adolescent therapy that provides specific treatment procedures.

## Parent Training with Conduct Problems

The efficacy of parent training (PT) with parents of children with conduct disorders is supported by research spanning three decades (for a review, see Kazdin, 1985, or McMahon & Forehand, 1984). Gerald Patterson and his colleagues were pioneers in developing and evaluating parent-training programs (Patterson, Chamberlain, & Reid, 1982; Patterson & Fleischman, 1979). Their approach to PT was based on social learning principles, especially on altering parent-delivered contingencies for antisocial and prosocial behaviors. Other researchers have made modifications to this approach and contributed to the systematic evaluation of PT approaches with parents of conduct-disordered children (e.g., McMahon, Forehand, & Griest, 1981; Webster-Stratton, 1984). These programs of research have greatly increased the knowledge of who responds to PT, mechanisms responsible for improved child functioning, and the impact of modifications in treatment procedures on client outcomes.

Parent training is based on the well-documented finding that parents of conduct-disordered children are deficient in parenting skills. These deficiencies include overreliance on critical and punitive approaches, inconsistency in implementing consequences for negative behavior, permissiveness, and low rates of praise and positive reinforcement for prosocial behavior (Hughes & Cavell, 1994). Parent training is based on social learning theory, and parents are taught how to alter reinforcement contingencies that support antisocial behavior. That is, they are taught how to give clear commands, establish rules, reinforce compliance, follow rule infractions with mild punishment, and use specific strategies such as token economies and time-out. Parents are also instructed in how to specify undesirable and desirable behaviors and to recognize and modify coercive processes in family interactions. Coercion occurs when a child's aggressive or antisocial behavior directed toward a parent is reinforced by the parent. For example, a parent instructs a child to turn off the television, and the child begins to scream and throw things. The parent withdraws the demand, thereby reinforcing the child's defiant behavior. The parent's acquiescence is reinforced when the child stops the defiant behavior. However, the short-term benefit is offset by the long-term increased likelihood of noncompliance (Patterson et al., 1992).

In recent years, training in parent management skills has been combined with training in positive parent-child interactional skills, especially nondirective play skills (Eyberg & Robinson, 1982). The emphasis on parental acceptance and positive parenting skills is based on findings that a combination of parental warmth and appropriate behavioral controls results in best child outcomes (Parke & Slaby, 1983) and that parents of conduct-disordered children are overly controlling and provide lower levels of acceptance (Greenberg, Speltz, & DeKlyen, 1993). Thus, current programs represent a merger of behavioral management approaches and relationship enhancement approaches (Eyberg & Robinson 1982). More recent approaches also emphasize the establishment of cooperative parent-child interactions through problem-solving and communication skills (Webster-Stratton, 1987).

Both individual and group formats of PT have been found to be effective, and therapist, or leader, manuals are available for both formats (Barkley, 1987, Webster-Stratton, 1987). Although individual and group formats have not been directly compared, a comparison of training with videotaped materials and parent workbooks with and without group discussion found that only those who received group discussion maintained gains three years after treatment (Webster-Stratton, Holinsworth, & Kolpacoff, 1989). Despite variations, all programs in this genre include instruction, modeling, and rehearsal of targeted parenting skills; homework assignments to promote generalization of skills to home settings; and discussion of homework assignments to identify obstacles and modifications needed in strategies.

Several studies have documented marked improvements for children and parents in PT relative to treatment control conditions (see

McMahon & Forehand, 1984, for a review). These benefits are evident on measures of parental and children's behavior and parents' perceptions of children's adjustment. Training results in significant decreases in aggressive and noncompliance behaviors, and those parents who demonstrate the greatest understanding of social learning principles show the greatest generalization and maintenance of effects (McMahon & Forehand, 1984). It is important that the majority of children are within the normal range at the end of treatment. Furthermore, follow-up assessments conducted between one and four years after treatment document continued benefits. Fourteen years after treatment, treated children continue to show the benefits of their parents' participation (Long, Forehand, Wierson, & Morgan, 1994). These children performed in the normal range of measures of internalizing and externalizing problems, social competence, emotional adjustment, and relationship with parents. Thus PT appears to alter the developmental trajectory of young, aggressive children, presumably by influencing family functioning. Indeed, indirect effects of PT include improved compliance from siblings who were not a focus of treatment and lessened levels of maternal depression (Patterson & Fleishman, 1979; Webster-Stratton, 1990).

Despite the overall effectiveness of PT, 30% to 40% of treated parents report that children's problems remain in clinical range after treatment, and 25% to 50% of teachers report that children's externalizing problems are within the clinical range (Webster-Stratton, 1990). Parents who are least likely to respond positively to PT are those who are experiencing significant stress. Mothers who are socially isolated, with few sources of social support outside the family; socioeconomically disadvantaged families; children whose problems are more severe; and parents who evince psychopathology are less likely to benefit from PT (Webster-Stratton, 1985). These same characteristics predict attrition (Kazdin, 1990). Multiple demands interfere with commitment to learning and practicing the skills taught. With such parents, attention to family stress and parents' personal issues and worries may be a necessary adjunct to PT. When the scope of PT is broadened to include family problems characteristic of families with conduct-disordered children, its effects are increased (Dadds, 1987). A supportive and positive alliance with parents may also be especially important in working with parents who experience high levels

of stress and few sources of support. Families with more severe problems may also require more than the typical 10 to 12 sessions. Kazdin (1985) provided between 50 and 60 hours of training with parents of children with severe problems. Combining PT with other therapies, such as problem-solving skills training for children, enhances the effects of PT alone (Kazdin et al., 1992).

Parent training is less successful with adolescents (Henggeler & Borduin, 1990). Whereas parenting factors loom as the most significant influence on the development of aggression and conduct problems in the preschool years, other systems become increasingly important after children enter school. By adolescence, the peer group is the preeminent influence on conduct disorders. Adolescents need multisystemic approaches that recognize the influence of additional systems, peers and school.

Helping parents change their interactions with their children requires more than knowledge of parenting skills. Webster-Stratton and Herbert (1993) provide practical wisdom to therapists that goes beyond the technology of PT to the science and art of helping parents change. They define the relationship between therapist and parents as collaborative, "a nonblaming, supportive, reciprocal relationship based on using equally the therapists' knowledge and the parents' unique strengths and perspectives" (p. 410).

Parenting is a very personal endeavor, and parents bring to this important relationship long-standing and deeply felt beliefs about children in general, their child, parenting, and their competence as parents. These beliefs guide moment-to-moment interactions with children and must be processed in therapy for parents to make significant and durable changes in their behavior. A mother who sees the child's aggressive behavior as being "just like her father—a bad seed" needs to view the child's behavior as a result, in part, of having learned that aggression is rewarded, at least in the short term. A father who believes he is doomed to repeat the mistakes of his own parents needs to see himself as capable of making changes and gaining control. Changes in beliefs, attitudes, and affective reactions often require a supportive and nonblaming relationship with a therapist.

Traditional skills of listening, genuiness, acceptance, empathy, concreteness, immediacy, and confrontation are essential to the therapist. The parent-therapist relationship is characterized by shared understanding of the child and of goals, mutual respect, trust, open communication, and shared responsibility for the process and the outcome. The therapist is not an "expert" who prescribes particular parenting strategies; rather the therapist engages the parent in a collaborative problem-solving process that has as its goals improved parent-child interaction, decreased aggression and oppositional behavior, and improved competence. The therapist presents information and alternatives but engages parents as active participants in evaluating the usefulness of suggested alternatives in their particular situation. "The therapist's role, then, as collaborator is to understand the parents' perspectives, to clarify issues, to summarize important ideas and themes raised by the parents, to teach and interpret in a way that is culturally sensitive, and finally, to teach and suggest possible alternative approaches or choices when parents requires assistance and when misunderstandings occur" (Webster-Stratton & Herbert, 1993, p. 410).

The therapist-parent relationship becomes a model for the parent-child relationship. The therapist treats parents with respect, acceptance, and patience and attempts to see the situation from their point of view. The therapist is quick to encourage and praise efforts and views mistakes as normal. The therapist recognizes that parents are likely to have experienced critical, inconsistent parenting and feel guilty and incompetent. Thus, enhancing parents' self-efficacy and sense of self-worth is one of the latent goals of PT.

Parent training requires key skills in client-centered therapy (genuiness, positive regard and empathy), behavior therapy (application of social learning principles and specification of behaviors), cognitive therapy (e.g., identifying, challenging, and modifying maladaptive thoughts), and family therapy (teaching parents how to support each other and to "refuel" themselves and how to work through disagreements over children). Thus, it illustrates the value of multiple theoretical perspectives and a broad array of strategies. The elements in PT work synergistically to improve parent-child interactions and to establish behaviors and attitudes that lead to maintenance of treatment effects.

## Cognitive Therapy with Depressed Children and Adolescents

Cognitive and behavioral strategies have been used successfully in the treatment of adult depression (Rush, Beck, Kovacs, & Hollon, 1977).

These same strategies have been modified for children and adolescents, and several studies have investigated their effectiveness. Cognitive behavior therapy with children and adolescents attempts to remediate skill deficits and cognitive distortions characteristic of depressed individuals. These skill deficits, which include coping skills, self-control skills, and interpersonal skills, are presumed to be both the product and the initiator of distorted patterns of thinking. Furthermore, the deficits and cognitive distortions are a result of the interaction of child factors (e.g., temperament and biological predisposition for depression) and family interactional patterns. Thus, treatment attempts to alter the child's self-defeating thinking, improve the child's social skills, and improve family interactional patterns.

The dysfunctional thinking of depressed individuals is dominated by the "negative triad" (Beck, 1967) of a negative view of the self, the world, and the future. This negative bias in thinking affects the individual's behavior. If children believe that they lack skills for successfully interacting with peers (negative view of self), they will tend to avoid social interaction, which further limits their opportunity to develop social skills, experience rewarding social interaction, and alter their self-view. Cognitive distortions reflect underlying maladaptive cognitive schemata, that is, core beliefs about one's worth and competence and others' availability as sources of support. These schemata affect what a person attends to, perceives, and recalls. Thus, they provide the guidelines for moment-to-moment processing of self-relevant information (Kendall, 1991).

Beck (1967) identified a number of cognitive errors that characterize the thinking of depressed adults and that presumably are an expression of maladaptive schemata: (1) magnification and minimization, (2) overgeneralization, (3) selective abstraction, (4) arbitrary inference, and (4) dichotomous thinking. Selective attention to and recall of negative self-relevant information and minimization of positive self-relevant information are products of a core belief that one is unworthy, a belief maintained by these distortions in processing information.

Depressed individuals also have deficits in social skills knowledge and behaviors (Stark, Rouse, & Livingston, 1991). Thus, treatment targets depressogenic thinking and social skills:

> The cognitive-behavioral treatment
> consisted of training in self-control skills

social skills, and cognitive restructuring. More specifically, the self-control training consisted of teaching the children more adaptive self-consequation (self-reinforce more and self-punish less), self-monitoring (pay attention to positive thoughts, good things that happen, and enjoyable things that you do), and self-evaluation (set less perfectionistic standards). Assertiveness training focused on interactions with significant others, including asking someone to do something fun, giving positive feedback, and telling someone to stop doing something that is annoying. Social skills training emphasized initiating interactions, maintaining interactions, and handling conflict. Relaxation training and imagery were used to help prepare the children for using their skills. (pp. 178–179)

Children were also taught to identify and challenge distorted thinking, such as "The teacher is always on my case," by examining the evidence and substituting more accurate self-statements.

These skills are taught through games, stories, role playing, homework (described as experiments), and group discussion. Because some symptoms of depression (e.g., hopelessness and social withdrawal) pose obstacles to compliance with treatment activities, the therapist devotes considerable attention to providing an emotionally supportive relationship with the child and a cohesive and supportive group climate, to encourage active involvement with the tasks of therapy.

Several school-based studies have evaluated CBT with children identified as depressed (Butler, Miezitis, Friedman, & Cole, 1980; Reynolds & Coats, 1986; Stark, Reynolds, & Kaslow, 1987). These studies demonstrated that children with symptoms of depression accrue short-term benefits from participation in relatively brief (10 to 12 sessions) group therapy that combines behavioral skills training, self-control training, and cognitive restructuring.

In a subsequent study, Stark et al. (1991) modified training to include three to four family sessions that focused on teaching parents to encourage their children to use new skills and to engage in more pleasant family activities. In a randomized controlled treatment study, CBT was compared with traditional counseling in the treatment of 24 children from grades 4 to 7 who were first screened as part of a schoolwide identi-

fication process and who met diagnostic criteria for a depressive disorder, based on a semistructured interview. Treatment consisted of 24 to 26 sessions, lasting 45 to 50 minutes, conducted over 3½ months. Although children who received CBT reported on an interview measure at posttreatment less depression, than children in a counseling condition, there were no group differences at the 7-month follow-up (Startk et al., 1991). However, children in both treatment conditions maintained their gains from posttreatment to follow-up.

The use of CBT with adolescents (Lewinsohn Clarke, Hops, & Andrews 1990) utilizes similar treatment procedures and achieves results comparable to those with children. In the coping with depression course, adolescents participate in 14 two-hour sessions in which self-control skills (relaxation, increased pleasant events, and self-reinforcing), cognitive restructuring, and social skills are taught. Adolescents are also taught conflict resolution skills for dealing with parent-adolescent conflict. Between 52% and 57% of adolescents completing the treatment program no longer met diagnostic criteria for a depressive disorder, whereas 95% of wait-list control youths did. The treated youths also reported fewer depressed symptoms at posttreatment. The addition of a parent component, emphasizing parental reinforcement of skills the children were learning and skills for resolving conflicts without fighting, provided minimal additional benefits, perhaps because of the limited nature of the parental involvement.

The use of CBT with depressed children and adolescents appears to reduce symptoms of depression. However, more research is needed before conclusions about its long-term effectiveness can be made. The use of CBT with children has been investigated with nonreferred populations, and long-term effects of treatment have not been investigated. The critical question of the effect of treatment on the course of childhood depression from childhood to adolescence and adulthood has not been addressed. Also, the specific mechanisms of treatment benefits are not known. Because various treatment procedures produce similar levels of benefits relative to no-treatment control groups, benefits could be a result of nonspecific treatment factors. Studies that investigate clients' characteristics that predict responsiveness (e.g., age and level of severity) and the impact of variations in treatment procedures on treatment outcomes (e.g., duration and inclusion of parents) and that include follow-up assessment of the impact of treatment on clinically significant measures, such as depressive disorder in adolescence or adulthood, are necessary before conclusions about CBT's efficacy can be reached.

## Anxiety Disorders and CBT

Anxiety disorders may be the most prevalent psychological disorder of children and adults (Anderson, 1994). It negatively affects academic work (Dweck & Wortman, 1982) and social adjustment (Strauss, Lease, Kazdin, Dulcan, & Last, 1989). Children who experience anxiety problems are at significantly increased risk for anxiety and depressive disorders as adults (Last, 1988).

Behavioral techniques have proven effective in alleviating specific fears and phobias (for a reviews, see Hughes, 1988, and Kendall et al., 1992). These techniques include desensitization, role playing, contingency management, in vivo exposure, and self-statement modifications. Although results of these laboratory-based studies suggest the potential value of behavioral techniques in the treatment of childhood fears, the specific fears that are the focus of treatment are not representative of the anxiety disorders that are most prevalent and that are the reason for referral. Dental fears, nighttime fears, and test anxiety are well represented in laboratory studies but are not common in clinical practice (Ollendick & Francis, 1988).

Children referred for treatment generally experience fearful, anxious behavior that causes significant psychological distress and interferes with such normal activities as going to school, participating in social activities, and gaining independence skills. These early demonstrations of the efficacy of behavioral techniques may have limited relevance to clinical practice because of their reliance on highly structured, single-modality intervention; nonclinical, recruited samples; short-term nature of the intervention; and limited outcome assessment (i.e., limited to the specific fear rather than to general anxiety).

Recently, Kendall and his colleagues (Kendall, 1994; Kendall & Southam-Gerow, 1995) have attempted to develop and evaluate interventions that have more relevance for clinic-based treatment of children who are experiencing significant anxiety problems. Kendall's multimodal treatment approach is based on documentation that thoughts related to fear of the threat or evaluation by others are more common

in anxious persons (Kendall, Howard, & Epps, 1988; Prins, 1986), who engage in more negative self-evaluation, focus more on their own performance, and anticipate others' negative judgments. Anxious children also tend to avoid anxiety-provoking situations.

However, CBT has shown promise as a treatment for generally anxious children and adolescents. Kendall's (1994) manualized treatment program for anxious children involves between 16 to 20 individual sessions. Although treatment is delivered in a flexible format, four sets of skills are emphasized: (1) recognition of anxious feelings and corresponding bodily reactions, (2) identification of maladaptive cognitions in anxiety-producing situations, (3) formulations of plans to cope by engaging in coping self-talk or taking some overt actions, and (4) self-evaluation and self-reinforcement. Children are also instructed in self-relaxation. Behavioral training strategies include modeling, in vivo exposure, role playing, relaxation training, and contingent reinforcement. Homework assignments include applying the taught skills in increasingly anxiety-provoking situations. Parental involvement in the treatment program is rather minimal—teaching the parents the goals and methods of therapy and encouraging them to reinforce children's new coping skills.

Evidence of the effectiveness of this treatment was provided in a study with a multiple baseline design of four socially anxious children between the ages of 9 and 13 (Kane & Kendall, 1989). Treated children experienced fewer internalizing symptoms and showed fewer targeted fears (e.g., difficulty in sleeping or fearful of walking home from school alone). These goals were maintained at the six-month follow-up assessment. These initial positive results were replicated and extended in a randomized clinical trial with children diagnosed as having a childhood anxiety disorder (Kendall, 1994). These children were representative of clinical samples both in severity of symptoms and in the prevalence of comorbidity (e.g., 32% were comorbid with depression, 16% with attention deficit hyperactivity disorder, and 60% with simple phobia). Treated children improved more than children in a wait-list control condition at posttreatment on self-reported and parent-reported signs of anxiety and were rated as less anxious in a contrived observational setting. It is important that 64% of the treated subjects (compared to 5% of controls) no longer met criteria for a diagnosis of anxiety at posttreatment, based on semistructured parent and child interviews. These gains were maintained at one-year (Kendall, 1994) and three-year (Kendall & Southam-Gerow, 1995) follow-ups. Given the stability of anxiety disorders (Last, 1988), the percentage of treated children no longer exhibiting clinically significant anxiety problems suggest that treatment interrupts the pathological pathway to adult distress. Presumably, children learn skills for coping with stressful situations that they carry with them to new situations and challenges; thus, their future interactions with the environment are more positive and contribute to the further development of confidence and competence. Because a wait-list control was used, benefits may be the result of nonspecific aspects of treatment, such as a supportive relationship with a therapist, rather than to the specific components of the cognitive behavioral treatment. Thus it is important to compare CBT with anxious children to a credible alternative treatment, such as client-centered counseling, and to dismantle this multimodal treatment to determine what components contribute to its effectiveness.

## CONCLUSION

The explosion of empirically derived knowledge of developmental psychopathology and of effective psychotherapies for children and adolescents in the past 10 years has made it possible to rely on the empirical literature in providing child psychotherapy. However, there is still a large gap between therapy as practiced under the auspices of university researchers and therapy as typically practiced in schools and other community settings. Considerable evidence supports the conclusion that research therapy is more effective than clinic therapy. This gap in effectiveness is unlikely to lessen until practitioners rely more on the empirical literature in developing interventions. The fact is, research is not much used by practitioners (Cohen, Sargent, & Sechrest, 1986). Psychologists who are trained in the scientist-practitioner model and are responsible for the provision of mental health services to children and adolescents can have a tremendous impact on the quality of these services if they make a commitment to empirically supported interventions. Also, clinical researchers must evaluate their interventions in settings and with populations that more closely parallel the settings and populations in which therapy is provided to children and adolescents.

## REFERENCES

Ammermann, R. T., Last, C. G., & Hersen, M. (Eds.). (1993). *Handbook of prescriptive treatments for children and adolescents*. Boston: Allyn & Bacon.

Anderson, J. C. (1994). Epidemiological issues. In T. H. Ollendick, N. J. King, & W. Yule (Eds), *International handbook of phobic and anxiety disorders in children and adolescents* (pp. 43–66). New York: Plenum.

Barkley, R. A. (1987). *Defiant children: A clinician's manual for parent training*. New York: Guilford.

Beck, A. T. (1967). *Depression: Causes and treatment*. Philadelphia: University of Pennsylvania Press.

Beelman, A., Pfingsten, U., & Losel, F. (1994). Effects of training social competence in children: A meta-analysis of recent evaluation studies. *Journal of Clinical Child Psychology, 23*, 260–271.

Brandenburg, N. A., Friedman, R. M., & Silver, S. E. (1990). The epidemiology of childhood psychiatric disorders: Prevalence findings from recent studies. *Journal of the American Academy of Child and Adolescent Psychiatry, 29*, 76–83.

Butler, L., Miezitis, S., Friedman, R., & Cole, E. (1980) The effect of two school-based intervention programs on depressive symptoms in preadolescents. *American Educational Research Journal, 17*, 111–119.

Casey, R. J., & Berman, J. S. (1985). The outcome of psychotherapy with children. *Psychological Bulletin, 98*, 388–400.

Christenson, S. L., Rounds, T., & Franklin, M. J. (1992). Home-school collaboration: Effects, issues, and opportunities. In S. L. Christenson & J. C. Conoley (Eds.), *Home-school collaboration*. Silver Springs, MD: National Association of School Psychologists.

Cohen, J. (1992). A power primer. *Psychological Bulletin, 112*, 155–159.

Cohen, L. H., Sargent, M. M., & Sechrest, L. B. (1986). Use of psychotherapy research by professional psychologists. *American Psychologist, 41*, 198–206.

Culbertson, J. L. (1993). Clinical child psychology in the 1990s: Broadening our scope. *Journal of Clinical Child Psychology, 22*, 116–122.

Dadds, M. R. (1987). Marital discord and child behavior problems: A description of family interactions during treatment. *Journal of clinical child psychology, 16*, 192–203.

Deblinger, E., McLeer, S. V., & Henry, D. (1990) Cognitive behavioral treatment for sexually abused children suffering post-traumatic stress: Preliminary findings. *Journal of the American Academy of Child and Adolescent Psychiatry, 29*, 747–752.

Dishion, T. J., & Andrews, D. W. (1995). Preventing escalation in problem behaviors with high-risk young adolescents: Immediate and 1-year outcomes. *Journal of Consulting and Clinical Psychology, 63,* 538–548.

Dubow, E. F., & Ippolito, M. F. (1994). Effects of poverty and quality of the home environment on changes in the academic and behavioral adjustment of elementary school-age children. *Journal of Clinical Child Psychology, 23,* 401–412.

Dubow, E. F., & Tisak, J. (1989). The relations between stressful life events and adjustment in elementary school children: The role of social support and social problem-solving skills. *Child Development, 60,* 1412–1423.

Dubow, E. F., Tisak, J., Causey, D., Hryshko, A., & Reid, G. (1991). A two-year longitudinal study of stressful life events, social support, and social problem-solving skills: Contributions to children's behavioral and academic adjustment. *Child Development, 62,* 583–599.

Duchnowski, A. J. (1994). Innovative service models: Education. *Journal of Clinical Child Psychology, 23,* 19–25.

Dumas, J. E., & Wahler, R. G. (1983). Predictors of treatment outcome in parent training: Mother insularity and socioeconomic disadvantage. *Behavioral Assessment, 5,* 301–313.

Durlak, J. A., Fuhrman, T., & Lampman, C. (1991). Effectiveness of cognitive-behavioral therapy for maladaptive children: A meta-analysis. *Psychological Bulletin, 110,* 204–214.

Dweck, C., & Wortman, C. (1982). Learned helplessness, anxiety, and achievement. In H. Krone & L. Laux (Eds.), *Achievement, stress and anxiety* (pp. 93–125). New York: Hemisphere.

Earls, F. (1989). Epidemiological strategies in child mental health. In P. E. Greenbaum, R. M. Friedman, A. J. Duchnowski, K. Kutash, & S. Silver (Eds.), *Children's mental health services and policy: Building a research base—Conference proceedings.* Tampa: University of South Florida, Florida Mental Health Institute.

Eisenstadt, T. H., Eyberg, S., McNeil, C. B., Newcomb, K., & Funderburk, B. (1993). Parent-child interaction therapy with behavior problem children: Relative effectiveness of two stages and overall treatment outcome. *Journal of Clinical Child Psychology, 22,* 42–51.

Eyberg, S. M., & Robinson E. A. (1982). Parent-child interaction training: Effects on family functioning. *Journal of Clinical Child Psychology, 11,* 137–139.

Fisher, S. G. (1980). The use of time-limits in brief psychotherapy: A comparison of six-sessions, twelve-sessions and unlimited treatment with families. *Family Process, 19,* 377–392.

Friedman, R. B. (1994). Restructuring of systems to emphasize prevention and family support. *Journal of Clinical Child Psychology, 23,* 40–47.

Garfield, S. L. (1980). *Psychotherapy: An eclectic approach.* New York: Wiley.

Greenberg, M. T., Speltz, M. L., & DeKlyen, M. (1993). The role of attachment in the early development of disruptive behavior problems. *Development and Psychopathology, 5,* 191–214.

Henggeler, S. W. (1994). A consensus: Conclusions of the APA task force report on innovative models of mental health services for children, adolescents, and their families. *Journal of Clinical Child Psychology, 23* (Supplement). 3–6.

Henggeler, S. W., & Borduin, C. M. (1990). *Family therapy and beyond: A multisystemic approach to treating the behavior problems of children and adolescents.* Pacific Grove, CA: Brooks/Cole.

Henggeler, S. W., Schoenwald, S. K., & Pickrel, S. G. (1995). Multisystemic therapy: Bridging the gap between university- and community-based treatment. *Journal of Consulting and Clinical Psychology, 63,* 709–717.

Hughes, J. N., & Baker, D. B. (1990). *The clinical child interview.* New York: Guilford.

Hughes, J. N., & Cavell, T. A. (1994). Enhancing competence in aggressive children. In G. Cartledge & J. F. Milburn (Eds.), *Teaching social skills to children: Innovative approaches* (3rd ed.; pp. 199–236). New York: Pergamon.

Jones, J. E. (1990). *Report from the National Center for Children in Poverty.* New York: Columbia University School of Public Health.

Kane, M. T., & Kendall, P. C. (1989). Anxiety disorders in children: A multiple-baseline evaluation of a cognitive-behavioral treatment. *Behavior Therapy, 20,* 499–508.

Kazdin, A. E. (1985). *Treatment of antisocial behavior in children and adolescents.* Homewood, Il: Dorsey Press.

Kazdin, A. E. (1988). *Child psychotherapy: Developing and identifying effective treatments.* New York: Pergamon.

Kazdin, A. E. (1990). Premature termination from treatment among children referred for antisocial behavior. *Journal of Consulting and Clinical Psychology, 60,* 733–747.

Kazdin, A. E. (1995). Scope of child and adolescent psychotherapy research: Limited sampling of dysfunctions treatments, and client characteristics. *Journal of Clinical Child Psychology, 24,* 125–140.

Kazdin, A. E., Bass, D., Ayers, W. A. & Rodgers, A. (1990). Empirical and clinical focus of child and adolescent psychotherapy research. *Journal of Consulting and Clinical Psychology, 58,* 729–740.

Kazdin, A. E., Mazurick, J., & Bass, D. (1993). Risk for attrition in treatment of antisocial children and families. *Journal of Clinical Child Psychology, 22,* 2–16.

Kazdin, A. E., Siegel, T. C., & Bass, D. (1990). Drawing upon clinical practice to inform research on child and adolescent psychotherapy: A survey of practitioners. *Professional Psychology: Research and Practice, 21,* 189–198.

Kazdin, A. E., Siegel, T. C., & Bass, D. (1992). Cognitive problem-solving skills training and parent management training in the treatment of antisocial behavior in children. *Journal of Consulting and Clinical Psychology, 60,* 733–747.

Kendall, P. C. (Ed.). (1991). *Child and adolescent therapy: Cognitive-behavioral procedures.* New York: Guilford.

Kendall, P. C. (1994). Treating anxiety disorders in children: Results of a randomized clinical trial. *Journal of Consulting and Clinical Psychology, 62,* 100–110.

Kendall, P. C., Chansky, T. E., Kane, M. T., Kim, R. S., Kortlander, E., Ronan K. R., Sessa, F. M., & Siqueland, L. (1992). *Anxiety disorders in youth: Cognitive-behavioral interventions.* Needham Heights, MA: Allyn & Bacon.

Kendall, P. C., Howard, B., & Epps, J. (1988). The anxious child: Cognitive-behavioral treatment strategies. *Behavior Modification, 12,* 181–310.

Kendall, P. C., & Southam-Gerow, M. A. (1995). Issues in the transportability of treatment: The case of anxiety disorders in youths. *Journal of Consulting and Clinical Psychology, 63,* 702–708.

Kratochwill, T. R., & Morris, R. J. (1991). *The practice of child therapy* (2nd ed.). New York: Pergamon.

Last, C. (1988). Anxiety disorder in childhood and adolescence. In C. Last & M. Hersen (Eds.), *Handbook of anxiety disorders.* New York: Plenum.

LeCroy, C. W. (1994). *Handbook of child and adolescent treatment manuals.* New York: Macmillan.

Lewinsohn, P. M., Clarke, G. N., Hops, H., & Andrews, J. (1990). Cognitive-behavioral treatment for depressed adolescents. *Behavior Therapy, 21,* 385–401.

Loeber, R., & Farrington, D. P. (1994). Problems and solutions in longitudinal and experimental treatment studies of child psychopathology and delinquency. *Journal of Consulting and Clinical Psychology, 62,* 887–900.

Long P., Forehand, R., Wierson, M., & Morgan, A. (1994). Does parent training with young noncompliant children have long term effects? *Behaviour Research and Therapy, 32,* 101–107.

McMahon, R. J., & Forehand, R. (1984). Parent training for the noncompliant child: Treatment outcome, generalization, and adjunctive therapy procedures. In R. F. Dangel & R. A. Polster (Eds.), *Parent training: Foundations of research and practice* (pp. 298–328). New York: Guilford.

McMahon, R. J., Forehand, R., & Griest, D. L. (1981). Effects of knowledge of social learning principles on enhancing treatment outcome and generalization in a parent training program. *Journal of Consulting and Clinical Psychology, 49,* 526–532.

O'Donohue, W. T., & Elliott, A. N. (1992). Treatment of the sexually abused child: A review. *Journal of Clinical Child Psychology, 21,* 218–228.

Ollendick, T., & Francis, G. (1988). Behavioral assessment and treatment of childhood phobias. *Behavior Modification, 12,* 165–204.

Parke, R. D., & Slaby, R. G. (1983). The development of aggression, In E. M. Hetherington (Ed.), *Handbook of child psychology: Vol. 4. Socialization, personality and social development* (pp. 547–641). New York: Wiley.

Patterson, G. R., Chamberlain, P., & Reid, J. B. (1982). A comparative evaluation of a parent-training program. *Behavior Therapy, 13,* 638–650.

Patterson, G. R., & Fleischman, M. J. (1979). Maintenance of treatment effects. Some considerations concerning family system and follow-up data. *Behavior Therapy, 10,* 168–185.

Patterson, G. R., Reid, J. B., & Dishion, T. J. (1992). *Antisocial boys.* Eugene, OR: Castalia Publishing.

Pekarik, G., & Stephenson, L. A. (1988). Adult and child client differences in therapy dropout research. *Journal of Clinical Child Psychology, 17,* 316–321.

Prins, P. J. M. (1986). Children's self-speech and self-regulation during a fear provoking behavioral test. *Behavior Research and Therapy, 24,* 181–191.

Prinz, R. J., & Miller, G. E. (1994). Family-based treatment for childhood antisocial behavior: Experimental influences on dropout and engagement. *Journal of Consulting and Clinical Psychology, 62,* 645–650.

Reynolds, W. M., & Coats, K. I. (1986). A comparison of cognitive-behavioral therapy and relaxation training for the treatment of depression in adolescents. *Journal of Consulting and Clinical Psychology, 54,* 653–660.

Rush, A. J., Beck, A. T., Kovacs, M., & Hollon, S. (1977). Comparative efficacy of cognitive therapy and pharmacotherapy in the treatment of depressed outpatients. *Cognitive Theory and Research, 1,* 17–37.

Shorr, L. B. (1988). *Within our reach: Breaking the cycle of disadvantage.* New York: Anchor Books.

Smith, M. L., Glass, G. V., & Miller, T. L. (1980). *Benefits of psychotherapy.* Baltimore, MD: Johns Hopkins University Press.

Smyrnios, K. X., & Kirkby, R. J. (1993). Long-term comparison of brief versus unlimited psychodynamic treatments with children and their parents. *Journal of Consulting and Clinical Psychology, 61,* 1020–1027.

Spencer, G. (1988). Projections of the population of the United States, by age, sex, and race, 1988–2080. In U.S. Bureau of the Census (Ed), *Population estimates and projections* (Series P-25, No. 1018). Washington, DC: U.S. Government Printing Office.

Stark, K. D., Reynolds, W. M., & Kaslow, N. J. (1987). A comparison of the relative efficacy of self-control therapy and a behavioral problem-solving therapy for depression in children. *Journal of Abnormal Child Psychology, 15*, 91–113.

Stark, K. D., Rouse L. W., & Livingston, R. (1991). Treatment of depression during childhood and adolescence: Cognitive-behavioral procedures for the individual and family. In P. C. Kendall (Ed.), *Child and adolescent therapy.* (pp. 165–206). New York: Guilford.

Stolberg, A. L., & Mahler, J. (1994). Enhancing treatment gains in a school-based intervention for children of divorce through skill training, parental involvement, and transfer procedures. *Journal of Consulting and Clinical Psychology, 62*, 147–156.

Strauss, C., Lease, C., Kazdin, A., Dulcan, M., & Last, C. (1989). Multimethod assessment of the social competence of anxiety disordered children. *Journal of Clinical Child Psychology, 18*, 184–190.

Tuma, J. M. (1989). Mental health services for children: The state of the art. *American Psychologist, 44*, 188–199.

Tuma, J. M., & Russ, S. W. (1993). Psychoanalytic psychotherapy with children. In T. R. Kratochwill and R. J. Morris (Eds.), *Handbook of psychotherapy with children and adolescents* (pp. 131–161). Boston: Allyn & Bacon.

U.S. Congress, House Select Committee on Children, Youth and Families. (1987). *The crisis in homelessness: Effects on children and families.* Washington, DC: U.S. Government Printing Office.

Walker, H. M., & Buckley, N. K. (1973). Teacher attention to appropriate and inappropriate classroom behavior: An individual case study. *Focus on Exceptional Children, 5*, 5–11.

Webster-Stratton, C. (1984). Randomized trial of two parent-training programs for families with conduct-disordered children. *Journal of Consulting and Clinical Psychology, 52*, 666–678.

Webster-Stratton, C. (1985). Predictors of treatment outcome in parent training for conduct disordered children. *Behavior Therapy, 16*, 223–242.

Webster-Stratton, C. (1987). *The parents and children series.* Eugene, OR: Castalia Publishing.

Webster-Stratton, C. (1990). Long-term follow up of families with young conduct problem children: From preschool to grade school. *Journal of Clinical Child Psychology, 19*, 144–149.

Webster-Stratton, C. (1994). Advancing videotape parent training: A comparison study. *Journal of Consulting and Clinical Psychology, 62*, 583–593.

Webster-Stratton, C. & Herbert, M. (1993). What really happens in parent training? *Behavior Modification, 17*, 407–456.

Webster-Stratton, C., Hollinsworth, T., & Kolpacoff, M. (1989). The long-term effectiveness and clinical significance of three cost-effective training programs for families with conduct-problem children. *Journal of Consulting and Clinical Psychology, 57*, 550–553.

Weisz, J. R., Donenberg, G. R., Han, S. S., & Weiss, B. (1995). Bridging the gap between laboratory and clinic in child and adolescent psychotherapy. *Journal of Consulting and Clinical Psychology, 63*, 688–701.

Weisz, J. R., Walter, B. R., Weiss, B., Fernandez, G., & Mikow, V. (1990). Arrests among emotionally disturbed violent and assaultive individuals following minimal versus lengthly intervention through North Carolina's Willie M Program. *Journal of Consulting and Clinical Psychology, 58*, 720–728.

Weisz, J. R., Weiss, B., Alicke, M. D., & Klotz, M. L. (1987). Effectiveness of psychotherapy with children and adolescents: Meta-analytic findings for clinicians. *Journal of Consulting and Clinical Psychology, 55*, 542–549.

Weisz, J. R., Weiss, B., & Donenberg, G. R. (1992). The lab versus the clinic: Effects of child and adolescent psychotherapy: *American Psychologist, 47*, 1578–1585.

Weisz, J. R., Weiss, B., Han, S., Granger D. A., & Morton, T. (1995). Effects of psychotherapy with children and adolescents revisited: A meta-analysis of treatment outcome studies. *Psychological Bulletin, 117*, 450–468.

***Received November 1995.***

## CHAPTER 29

# PRIMARY PREVENTION IN SCHOOL SETTINGS

JOEL MEYERS
*Georgia State University*
BONNIE K. NASTASI
*The University at Albany*
*State University of New York*

Anyone who has spent time in today's schools recognizes the range of problems that are confronted by children and that can have implications for their health, learning, and adjustment. These include alcohol abuse, AIDS, behavioral problems, child abuse, divorce and other family problems, drug abuse, gangs and violence, latchkey children, malnutrition, obesity, poverty, pregnancy, psychopathology, sex-related problems, smoking, suicide, and stress-related diseases like headaches and ulcers. Although these problems may be exacerbated in large urban centers, they present significant challenges in rural and suburban schools as well. The negative effects on children are painfully obvious to school professionals, and a major concern is long-term effects, which can influence some students' lives as adults in profound ways (e.g., Cicchetti & Carlson, 1989; Guidubaldi, Perry, & Nastasi, 1987b; Schweinhart & Weikart, 1989). Children who have AIDS eventually die. Those who smoke are at great risk of cancer and heart disease. Those who abuse drugs are at risk of premature death, as well as incarceration for various criminal behaviors. Those who get pregnant are less likely to finish school, are likely to wind up with less adequate jobs, and are more likely to have children who get pregnant early. Finally, those with behavioral and learning problems in school are less

likely to finish school, are more likely to face limitations in an increasingly technological job market, and are more likely to develop serious emotional difficulties later in life. Primary prevention offers an orientation that may allow schools to develop effective approaches to responding to these types of problems.

A recent Gallup poll indicated that parents believe that a range of social and emotional issues are considered to be priorities in today's schools (Elam & Rose, 1995). For example, 91% of respondents indicated that "serving the emotional and health needs of students" is important (only 3% rated this role as unimportant). Violence, drug abuse, and lack of discipline were three of the four most frequently cited problems in schools, and family problems were viewed as an important factor in school violence. A final point from this Gallup poll is relevant to the possible support from parents for prevention programs (Elam & Rose, 1995). Eighty-nine percent of the respondents indicated they would be willing to sign a contract that would specify responsibilities in promoting their child's growth and development (i.e., the school's, the child's, and the parent's responsibilities).

It has been estimated that between 12% and 20% of children experience social and emotional problems that require intervention (Carlson, Paavola, & Talley, 1995; Costello, 1989). However, few of these children receive services; for example, less than one-third of the children with emotional and behavior disorders receive appropriate services in the community (Costello, Burns, Angold, & Leaf, 1993; Knitzer, 1993), and this creates a substantial gap between those needing and those receiving mental health services (see Carlson, Paavola, & Talley, 1995). In this context, Alpert (1985) estimated that about 6.2 million children with learning and adjustment problems received absolutely no services at all. Serious questions can be raised about the actual psychological and/or educational services that are received by needy children.

This difficulty in providing educational and mental health interventions to the large numbers of people in need of them was predicted four decades ago by George Albee (1968), who suggested that we will never have a sufficient number of professionals to treat all those in need of services by using individual treatment models. Albee studied the number of people in need of mental health services and the number of trained professionals available to provide such services in the 1950s. At that time it was clear that there was an insufficient number of professionals. He then projected the increased number of mental health professionals that could be predicted, based on the growing number of training programs, while simultaneously projecting the increased numbers of people with mental health needs over time. Although the number of mental health professionals was increasing dramatically, the number of people in need of services was increasing to such an extent that the gap between needs and available services was expanding. As an alternative to individually based, direct treatment models, Albee (1968, 1982, 1990) posited that approaches to prevention provided the only realistic way to offer services with the hope of reaching a reasonable number of those in need of help.

Although there is a serious need for research into primary prevention, some emerging data bases indicate that school-based prevention efforts do have the potential to counteract these problems by facilitating the learning, health, and mental health of children (Tharinger, 1995). The result of such programs might be adults who are healthy, physically and mentally, and who contribute productively to society. For example, the reported effects of one early education model on school behavior include fewer grade retentions, fewer children placed in special education, re-

duced expenditures on special education, and fewer school dropouts. Postschool outcomes of this early education model include higher earnings, fewer court convictions, and a lower birthrate (Schweinhart & Weikart, 1989; Weikart, 1984).

While these outcomes are appealing, preventive approaches represent a radical change for educators and school psychologists who are more inclined to be concerned with remediation than prevention. It can be difficult to convince educators that preventive mental health services are needed before a problem is apparent, and it can be even more difficult to convince the community to pay for preventive services when it doesn't see the need. This problem was expressed clearly by a school principal, who asked, "How can we fix what ain't broke?" (Lorion, Work, & Hightower, 1984).

Emory Cowen (1977) has argued that difficulties with the research on primary prevention have contributed to resistance to this construct. It is hard to demonstrate the efficacy of preventive techniques when prevention is not clearly defined in the literature, and it is difficult to demonstrate the efficacy of an approach when the goal is to prevent something from happening. This is compounded by the fact that preventive efforts require an extension of the purposes of schooling beyond the traditional 3Rs. One goal of this chapter is to provide suggestions for preventive approaches that are realistic for implementation in a range of school settings and to provide a framework and method that can be implemented readily by school psychologists and school-based researchers.

This chapter suggests that primary prevention would be most effective if (1) school psychologists developed and used their understanding of the school culture; (2) they made a serious effort to work collaboratively with school professionals to develop preventive efforts rather than importing prevention programs to the schools; and (3) they took advantage of the ongoing ways in which prevention can be implemented in the normal school curriculum and instructional process rather than being limited to external primary prevention programs, which are often costly and incompatible with school culture. This viewpoint does not imply that formal prevention programs are necessarily ineffective or that they should not be implemented. In fact, reference will be made to various prevention programs that have a promising data base in support of their use, and a model will be presented for implementing comprehensive prevention programs. However, a preoccupation with externally developed and imposed programs frequently misses important opportunities for primary prevention in the schools, may ignore the local school culture, and may fail to consider some of the steps associated with collaborative consultation that are needed to facilitate a sense of ownership of prevention programs implemented by educators.

The primary purpose of this chapter is to provide a framework for implementing prevention programs in schools that will be useful to school psychologists and other professionals working in schools. In an effort to accomplish this purpose, this chapter provides an overview of the field of prevention with an emphasis on primary prevention, discusses practical approaches in implementing primary prevention within the context of existing roles, and presents a model for that maximizes the potential for effectiveness. This chapter is divided into three sections. The first section presents a conceptual framework for school-based prevention programs that includes definitions and a rationale. The second section presents practical approaches within the context of the normal school routine. The last section presents a model for implementing comprehensive prevention programs, which often require substantial changes in school routine and are able to produce a marked impact on a range of needy children.

# CONCEPTUAL FRAMEWORK FOR SCHOOL-BASED PREVENTION

Conceptual models can help educators develop an awareness of the range of methods that can be used in schools to promote learning and adjustment and to prevent health and mental health problems. Conceptual models that focus particularly on primary prevention are proposed and provide a basis for a conceptual shift in educational philosophy and the delivery of psychological services in schools. This section addresses the following issues: definitions of the types of prevention that are relevant for schools; empowerment theory, which provides a foundation for our approaches to prevention; research on resilience, which provides some of the rationale for primary prevention; and a prevention formula, which provides a framework for conceptualizing preventive interventions. In addition, this section discusses a range of preventive interventions by analyzing those that are focused on (1) modifying the environment to reduce stress, (2) modifying the individual to promote competence, and (3) considering the individual and the environment simultaneously. Each approach is illustrated by discussions of preventive programs designed to promote social competence, to reduce problems associated with divorce, and to prevent substance abuse.

## A Definition of Primary Prevention

Gerald Caplan (1964) developed a framework of preventive services that is the foundation for much of the work on the prevention of learning, adjustment, and mental health problems in schools (Meyers, Brent, Faherty, & Modafferi, 1993). This framework defined primary prevention, secondary prevention, and tertiary prevention approaches. Primary prevention refers to those methods that are designed to prevent the entire population (or a particular subgroup) from developing a disorder and are implemented before individuals show signs of the disorder. Secondary prevention refers to those methods that are designed to prevent the development of more serious problems after beginning signs of the disorder appear. These procedures are often implemented through early screening and the use of prompt, effective treatment with populations showing early signs of the disorder. Tertiary prevention refers to those methods that are designed to remediate established cases of disorder, to reduce their duration, and to minimize their effects on the targeted individual(s) and others in the community. An important goal of this approach is to reduce the prevalence of the targeted problems in the community.

Caplan's (1964) distinction among primary, secondary and tertiary prevention has influenced research and practice in the field of prevention for over three decades. However, there are some ambiguities in the definitions of primary and secondary prevention that require clarification. For example, some groups of children are known to be at risk because they are exposed systematically to serious sources of stress. It can be important to work with these children before they show signs of disorder. At-risk groups do not fit clearly into the definitions of either primary or secondary prevention. They do not fit clearly into the definition of primary prevention, which emphasizes the goal of reaching all children instead of at-risk groups. Similarly, at-risk groups do not fit into the definition of secondary prevention because members of at-risk groups may not yet show early signs of problems resulting from stress. We prefer to use four categories of preventive intervention by differentiating between primary prevention and risk reduction, as noted in the following definitions of prevention types, which are suggested as a basis for conceptualizing research and practice in the field of prevention (see Nastasi, 1995a, for additional discussion of these four approaches).

*Primary prevention* refers to strategies that are designed to prevent the entire population (e.g., all students in a community, school district, or school) from developing a disorder. Prevention is implemented without identifying individual members of the population who may be at risk of developing a disorder and before the group members are identified as showing signs of disorder. Typical goals include fostering individual development and creating supportive social environments for all students. As a result, primary prevention programs are focused on intact groups such as the school or the classroom, and these programs are often implemented by teachers, paraprofessionals, and even peer educators, all supported by professional staff. Professional staff relevant to prevention programs can include mental health professionals, health professionals, or educators, depending on the focus of the prevention program.

*Risk reduction* refers to strategies that are designed for members of a subgroup from the general population that is identified as being at risk of developing a disorder. Risk reduction is implemented before group members are identified as showing signs of disorder. For example, risk reduction is appropriate for groups that are at risk, such as children of divorce, children of alcoholic parents, children whose parent dies, and children of poverty. While the goals of risk reduction can overlap with primary prevention (e.g., both can be focused on building competence), risk reduction programs are typically focused on skills and competence that are directly relevant to the area of risk. Thus, for example, in addition to promoting general social competence, children of divorce would be taught coping skills specific to divorce (e.g., how to talk to other people about the divorce, how to talk with one parent about the other parent, and how to deal with parental jealousies). Risk reduction programs are often implemented with small groups that include the at-risk population, and these programs can be implemented by the mental health staff or by teachers or paraprofessionals who are supported by professional staff.

*Early intervention* refers to those methods that are designed to prevent the development of more serious problems after beginning signs of the disorder appear. These procedures are often implemented through early screening and the use of prompt effective treatment with populations showing early signs of the disorder. This is similar to approaches described as secondary prevention in previous literature (e.g., Caplan, 1964). The goals of early intervention are to treat mild adjustment problems and to reduce the risk of more severe problems, and these programs are often implemented by using small groups or individual treatment modalities. Early intervention programs can be implemented by mental health staff and/or by teachers or paraprofessionals supported by professional staff.

*Treatment* refers to those methods that are designed to remediate established cases of disorder, to reduce their duration, and to reduce their effects on others, thereby reducing their prevalence in the community. This is similar to approaches described as tertiary prevention in previous literature on prevention (e.g., Caplan, 1964). Treatment is usually implemented by using small groups or individual treatment modalities and would be staffed by mental health professionals.

There is substantial overlap between Caplan's (1964) early definition of primary prevention and our definitions of primary prevention and "risk reduction." Therefore, this chapter focuses on techniques that are classified as either primary prevention or risk reduction since these are targeted toward the whole population or a vulnerable subgroup prior to the identification of emergent or diagnosable problems. By targeting children before symptoms emerge, these approaches have the greatest potential to influence large numbers of people. Thus, preventive approaches are considered in this chapter if they are applicable to the population as a whole (e.g., the community, school district, or school) or to a vulnerable subgroup (e.g., children of divorce, children of poverty, children whose parents have AIDS, or children of alcoholics).

## Empowerment and Prevention in Schools

Empowerment theory (Rappaport, 1981) provides a useful conceptual foundation for the primary prevention and risk reduction methods that are discussed in this chapter. Rappaport (1981) has argued that an empowerment model may be more comprehensive and powerful than other models of primary prevention. He suggests that primary prevention derives from a needs-based model in which people are viewed as dependent on others to solve their problems and society (rather than the individual) is responsible to meet their needs. Effective approaches to prevention can be viewed as potentially efficient since the needs that are identified economically by professionals can be prevented from occurring. Traditional prevention approaches do not encompass advocacy, which is 'a rights-based rather than a needs-based model of social services. As Rappaport suggests, advocacy derives from a legalistic and due process view of people as citizens. A model that views people as citizens with rights who can solve their own problems has very different implications than traditional preventive models, which view people as depending on society (and perventionists) to meet their needs.

Rappaport (1981) argues that a social change theory based on empowerment is more comprehensive than either prevention or advocacy models because empowerment considers both the needs and the rights of people.

> Empowerment implies that many competencies are already present or at least possible. . . . Prevention implies experts fixing the independent variables to make the dependent variables come out right. Empowerment implies that what you see as poor functioning is a result of social structure and lack of resources which make it impossible for the existing competencies to operate. It implies that in those cases where new competencies need to be learned, they are best learned in a context of living life rather than in artificial programs where everyone, including the person learning, knows that it is really the expert who is in charge. (p. 16)

Empowerment suggests that people be given the opportunity to control their own lives, and this is substantially different from preventive philosophy, which suggests that the professional solve the problem before it occurs. This new theory implies a dramatic restructuring of the relationship between professionals and those they serve so that community values (and the clients' values), rather than professionals' values, dictate professional intervention (Alpert, 1985). A variety of social science research suggests that control over one's own life can be a potent variable (Rappaport, 1981), including work focused on locus of control, learned

helplessness, ascribed versus achieved status, attributions, the impact of perceived labels, beliefs about powerful others, group cohesiveness, and self-help groups and other community organizations. The concept of empowerment has some parallels with much of the recent work on school reform that seeks to involve teachers, community members, parents, and even students in determining policy about the educational process (e.g., Comer, 1993; Meyers, Meyers, Gelzheiser, Munoff, Kelly, & Muller, 1995; Weiss, 1993). It is suggested that the construct of empowerment can be a useful component of any framework for conceptualizing preventive interventions. Using this construct may increase the probability that preventive interventions will be implemented consistently; will be acceptable to both interventionists and the participants in the intervention; and will have long-term, generalizable effects.

## Resilient Children

Research on the impact of stress on children who appear to be resilient or invulnerable to such stress provides important theoretically and empirically based rationales for prevention. Cowen, Wyman, Work, and Parker (1990) provide a useful summary of a substantial body of research into the effects of stress, illustrating that stress has generally negative effects on children's adjustment, including adverse physical, as well as psychological, outcomes (e.g., Compas, 1987; Elias, Gara, & Ubriaco, 1985; Garmezy & Rutter, 1983). This research has differentiated between acute and chronic stressors (Compas, 1987; Compas, Phares, & LeDoux, 1989; Compas, Howell, & LeDoux, 1989). Chronic stressors, such as a child's maltreatment (Cicchetti & Carlson, 1989), family discord (Rutter, Cox, Tupling, Berger & Yule, 1975), and poverty (Broussard, 1976), have all been documented to have negative effects on children. Specific life events, which serve as acute stressors that are time-limited (e.g., moving to a new community and a new school and loss of a key friend or family member), have been shown to have more negative and enduring effects when they occur in the context of a chronically stressful environment (Cowen et al., 1990).

Of particular relevance to the prevention literature has been the finding that certain children are resilient (Cowen et al., 1990) or invulnerable to stress (e.g., Garmezy, 1983; Rutter, 1979). This issue has been studied by a range of researchers, who have concluded that several factors appear to account for resilience (Cowen et al., 1990; Garmezy & Devine, 1985; Rutter, 1979; Werner, 1989; Werner & Smith, 1982). This has important implications for research on prevention because it suggests variables that might profitably be considered as the focus of preventive interventions. For example, Cowen et al. have suggested that the following variables are associated with stress-resilient children: (1) an easy temperament in infancy through the school years; (2) personal qualities like self-esteem, problem-solving skills and social competence; (3) absence of substantial separations of an infant from his or her care-giver; (4) availability of child-care support and involvement of a father figure; (5) warm and secure parent-child relationships during preschool and school years; (6) parental efficacy and reasoned discipline practices; and (7) availability of extrafamilial adult models for identification and support. These factors provide a useful basis for developing preventive interventions, and the prevention formula in the next section provides a framework for conceptualizing preventive interventions based on factors associated with stress and resilience.

## The Prevention Formula

George Albee (1988) has developed a formula for psychological dysfunction that can be used as a framework to understand the research on resiliency and can be a vehicle for applying concepts derived from resiliency research to the development of interventions consistent with primary prevention and risk-reduction models. Albee's formula, which was developed with a focus on mental health problems, can be modified to provide a meaningful basis for conceptualizing methods designed to prevent difficulties in adjustment, education, health, and mental health. This adapted formula is presented in the equation at the bottom of the page.

*Educational and health disorder* refers to any health, mental health or educational disorder. If the impact of the factors in the numerator of this formula are reduced, it may be possible to prevent some educational/health disorders. *Individual predisposition* refers to the physical, cognitive, or emotional characteristics that make the individual vulnerable to a particular disorder. These might include factors such as high anxiety, external locus of control, or difficult temperament. *Stress* is defined as an environmental condition that requires substantial energy devoted to adaptation and that increases the probability that an individual will develop an educational or health disorder. As noted in the previous discussion of resiliency, models of stress have been developed along with theory and research about negative behavioral, emotional, and physical outcomes that can result from stress (e.g., Compas et al., 1989; Garmezy, 1983; Lazarus & Folkman, 1984; Rutter, 1981). *Exploitation* is a form of environmental stress considered by Albee (1988) that results from the existing social order, which favors certain groups in society (e.g., wealthy, Caucasian, male, and middle class) over other groups (e.g., poor, female, and minority group members). Although it may be difficult to design interventions to eliminate or minimize exploitation, Albee (1988) argues that exploitation has substantial stressful effects and that it should be a focus of preventive interventions. Furthermore, Cummins (1986) suggests that empowerment of exploited (disempowered) groups can be accomplished through preventive systemic efforts such as changing the relationships between educators and disempowered (e.g., minority) students and between schools and minority communities.

The denominator of the prevention formula includes variables that can inhibit the development of educational and health disorders. Prevention programs should be designed to increase the power of variables in the denominator. *Competence* refers to the individual's ability to cope with environmental stressors. It can include variables in multiple domains such as academic competence, intellectual competence, social competence, and personal decision-making competencies. Social problem-solving skills (e.g., Elias, Gara, Ubriaco, Rothbaum, Clabby, & Schuyler, 1986; Shure, 1988) provide an example of competence that is frequently considered in the prevention literature. *Self-esteem* refers to the individual's feelings of self-confidence and self-worth, which can help make a child more resistant to stress (e.g., Bandura, 1993; Bandura & Cervone, 1983; Garmezy, 1983; Rutter, 1981). Finally, *educational/medical/social support* refers to those supportive factors in the environment that reduce stress and/or help the child to cope more effectively when experiencing stress. Environmental supports can be provided through supportive adults (e.g., coaches, teachers, parents,

## Albee's Formula

$$\text{Educational and health disorder} = \frac{\text{Individual predisposition} + \text{stress} + \text{exploitation}}{\text{Competence} + \text{self-esteem} + \text{educational/social/medical support}}$$

and mentors) or peers (e.g., peer counseling, peer tutoring, student-run hot lines, and peer-run conflict resolution programs). In addition, support groups can be used to enable children to cope with divorce, death, obesity, inadequate nutrition, AIDS, and test anxiety (e.g., Katz & Hermalin, 1987).

The prevention formula implies that to prevent a particular health disorder from occurring, it is important to find ways to reduce the numerator and/or increase the denominator of this formula. Prevention strategies that effectively attack multiple components of the formula have the greatest chance to succeed. Techniques are considered for a particular disorder that have the potential to reduce stress, reduce exploitation, and/or modify the characteristics that make the individual vulnerable to the disorder. At the same time, methods are sought that have the potential to increase competence, self-esteem, and/or social supports. Two basic approaches to primary prevention in schools have been conceptualized in the literature and are related to the above formula: modifying the individual to promote competence and modifying the environment to reduce stress (i.e., Albee, 1982; Alpert, 1985; Cowen, 1985; Elias & Branden, 1988; Meyers & Parsons, 1987).

## Modifying the Environment to Reduce Stress

There is a growing body of evidence indicating that social environments have a profound impact (e.g., Bonfenbrenner, 1989; Moos, 1979; Trickett, 1984; Trickett & Berman, 1989). Environmental modifications such as provision of educational, social, and health supports and promotion of positive school climate have the potential to reduce stress (e.g., Albee, 1988; Cowen, 1977, 1983, 1985; Meyers & Parsons, 1987).

The key feature of this approach is that it seeks to modify the environment to prevent learning, health, or mental health problems. A frequent goal of these environmental modifications is to reduce or eliminate unnecessary stress. For example, when a child has a memory deficit, instructional strategies that provide memory supports to facilitate the child's learning can reduce stress and facilitate learning (Phillips, Martin, & Meyers, 1972). Stress can also be reduced in social situations by providing social support. This can be accomplished in schools by using techniques like cooperative learning, which encourages children to work together by teaching the

skills needed for productive cooperation, and by structuring group projects that facilitate cooperative efforts (Deutsch, 1993; Johnson & Johnson, 1983; Johnson, Johnson, Buckman & Richards, 1985; Nastasi & Clements, 1991, 1993).

Other forms of social support can be provided in schools by developing various networks designed to provide support for students. These can include after-school activities in which students from different classes and grades work together on an area of joint interest (e.g., the student newspaper, students against drunk driving, and students concerned with weight and weight loss), so that they can find out about each other's strengths and use them for support. In addition, it is possible that mentors can provide support for students that can reduce stress and promote successful coping (e.g., Rhodes, Ebert, & Fischer, 1992). However, research is needed to document the methods and efficacy of these approaches.

Formal, cross-age networks can be a helpful form of social support for both old and young children. Bower (1964) presented the idea of children at one developmental level (e.g., junior high school students) serving as tutors for those from another developmental level (e.g., young children in elementary school). In this way, young children benefit from the experience of older children who are willing to help, and this can provide support that the young child can call on outside of the formal tutoring relationship. The emerging adolescent who faces his or her own social and personal problems can learn to deal more effectively with these issues by helping another child. In addition to such cross-age networks, peer tutoring can be used as a vehicle to provide social support, reduce stress, and facilitate academic growth in both members of the tutorial relationship (e.g., Fantuzzo, King, & Heller, 1992; Greenwood, Carta, & Maheady, 1991).

Since stress is associated with school transitions (Elias et al., 1985; Felner, Primavera, & Cauce, 1981), modifying the school environment can facilitate transitions from one school to another. The School Transition Project is an example of a program designed to facilitate transition to high school for at-risk students (Felner, Ginter, & Primavera, 1982). This program restructures the role of homeroom teachers so that these teachers, who have daily contact with the students, serve many of the functions traditionally associated with school guidance counselors by advising students in class selection, contacting the family following students' absences, and counseling students about personal difficulties. This increases students' access to an educator in the role of a guidance counselor. Another element of this program is to assign students to academic classes from the same small pool of students in the school, thereby reorganizing the social system. This provides greater stability to the peer group and is designed to increase the support provided from peers while reducing the constant change and social stress traditionally associated with the new social environment of the high school (Felner et al., 1982). The increased emotional support provided by the teaching staff and the more stable environment that is established in this program was associated with students' feelings of accountability, knowledge of school rules and expectations, regular school attendance, and positive school performance (Felner et al., 1982).

One approach to modifying the school environment has been developed by James Comer (1993). This approach seeks to make parents active participants in low socioeconomic status (SES) schools. Parents work as aides in classrooms, attend various school meetings, bring other parents to meetings with them, and play a role in school governance. Comer argues that this reduces the cultural gap between low-SES children and their schools and increases the belief that they can control their own school performance. He presents some data suggesting improved behavior and academic performance associated with this environmental intervention.

Alpert (1985) has described community-based prevention efforts in which the school serves as a center for the family, school, and community as they work together to promote goals that are consistent with prevention. She suggests, for example, that the school could serve as an information and referral registry for the community and as a resource for a variety of innovative programs for parents and preparents. Ross, Saavedra, Shur, Winters, and Felner (1992) give an example of an after-school community prevention program for urban latchkey children. Schools and teachers provided a context in which students could do supervised homework and participate in a drug education program focused on self-esteem and decision making, creative dramatics, and field trips. This program not only provided environmental supports through after-school care and supervised homework but also focused on the development of personal competencies. The results indicated that participation

in homework activities alone was insufficient to improve academic achievement.

## Modifying the Individual to Promote Competence

Approaches in modifying the individual seek to promote competence, increase self-esteem, and reduce individual vulnerability to particular disorders; as noted earlier, this is the second major approach to primary prevention that has been frequently discussed in the literature (e.g., Albee, 1982; Alpert, 1985; Cowen, 1985). Examples of this approach include strategies designed to increase interpersonal skills (Shure & Spivack, 1988), to foster self-esteem (Schunk & Swartz, 1993), to develop social-emotional coping skills (Shure & Spivack, 1988), to develop study skills (Carns & Carns, 1991; Cavallaro & Meyers, 1986), to increase important academic and cognitive skills (Adey & Shayer, 1993; Borkowski & Muthukrishna, 1992; Paris & Winograd, 1990), and to increase knowledge about health and mental health practices while generating behaviors that promote physical and mental health (Tharinger, 1995). Children need to develop skills in these areas. For example, children need decision-making skills so that they are able to make their own decisions about smoking, drugs, alcohol, and sex (Botvin & Dusebury, 1989). Children also need good habits in nutrition and exercise. As a result they may be better able to maintain a nutritional diet and keep active physically so that they avoid future health problems such as high blood pressure, high cholesterol, obesity, and heart disease (Pflaum, 1991). In addition, children need study skills to promote maximum educational performance and to prevent educational failure. Finally, children need social skills to cope effectively with the range of social situations that confront them throughout their development and later in adulthood (Shure, 1988). Research into prevention programs focused on building social competence, children's adjustment to divorce, and preventing substance abuse are discussed as examples of this approach.

### *Social Competence*

Several researchers have developed curricula and teaching procedures designed to promote the development of social skills (Elias et al., 1986; Gesten, DeApodaca, Rains, Weissberg, & Cowen, 1979; Goldstein, 1988; Goldstein, Reagles, & Amann, 1990; Lochman, 1992; Shure, 1988; Shure & Spivack, 1988; Weissberg, Caplan, & Harwood,

1991). For example, an approach has been developed to teach children such skills as sensitivity to others, awareness of the causal effects of one's behavior on others, perception of feelings, development and use of alternative plans, and awareness of means-end relationships (Shure, 1988; Shure & Spivack, 1988). In this framework, means-end relationships refer to the ability to conceptualize the specific sequence of steps necessary to achieve a particular end. These researchers have worked carefully to develop curricular materials designed to teach these skills to four-year-old, inner-city children (Shure, 1988; Shure & Spivack, 1988). Their research suggests that two particular cognitive skills consistently relate to behavioral adjustment: the ability to generate alternative action plans and the ability to anticipate consequences of behavior. They have demonstrated that these cognitive problem-solving skills are highest in well-adjusted children, that training with curricular materials can result in increased problem-solving skills, and that improved interpersonal cognitive problem-solving skills are related to improved behavioral adjustment.

## Divorce Adjustment

Clearly, divorce is one stressor that has an impact on large numbers of schoolchildren. Divorce rates have increased dramatically to the point where it is estimated that 60% of those getting married today are likely to get divorced, 50% of children born today will have divorced parents before they reach the age of 18, and about 3 million people annually are affected by divorce. There is considerable evidence that divorce can have negative effects on children's social and academic adjustment (Forehand, Armistead, & Klein, 1995; Guidubaldi, Cleminshaw, Perry, & McLoughlin, 1983; Guidubaldi, Perry, & Nastasi, 1987a; Hetherington, Cox, & Cox, 1982; Wallerstein, 1983). This body of research suggests that a child's response to divorce varies with age, with younger children (e.g., between 6 and 8 years of age) showing grief and sadness and older children (e.g., between 9 and 10 years of age) displaying anger, loneliness, and embarrassment (Pedro-Carroll & Cowen, 1985). While short-term effects have been demonstrated more convincingly than long-term effects, the latter have been related to such factors as the quality of the parent-child relationship, a stable home environment, effective parenting, and the extent to which both parents can contain their conflict and negotiate solutions on behalf of their children

(e.g., Guidubaldi, Cleminshaw, Perry, Nastasi, & Lightel, 1986). This research needs to be considered in any effort to develop preventive interventions focused on children of divorce.

There has been some research on the efficacy of intervention programs focused on children of divorce (Grynch & Fincham, 1992). One approach that has been implemented for over 10 years is the Children of Divorce Intervention Program (Pedro-Carroll & Cowen, 1985). Several studies provide empirical support for the efficacy of this program when implemented with elementary school-age children (Pedro-Carroll, Alpert-Gillis, & Cowen, 1992; Pedro-Carroll & Cowen, 1985; Pedro-Carroll, Cowen, Hightower, & Guare, 1986). This program uses a range of approaches based on developing children's coping skills. Skill building is focused in the area of social problem solving, communication, and self-control (Pedro-Carroll et al., 1992).

## Substance Abuse

School-based prevention of substance abuse has become particularly important since the adoption of the National Education Goals in 1989 (National Education Goals Panel, 1992). Goal 6, in particular, calls for the provision of safe, disciplined, and drug-free schools and the development of comprehensive K–12 drug and alcohol preventive programs as part of the health curriculum. Despite suggestions that both ecological and personal factors contribute to abuse of alcohol and other drugs (Hawkins, Catalano, & Miller, 1992), school-based substance abuse prevention programs are most frequently directed at enhancing individuals' knowledge, attitudes, and practices about alcohol and other drugs (particularly, tobacco and marijuana). Reviews of research on program efficacy suggest that early programs (in the 1960s and 1970s), directed toward changing knowledge and attitudes without specific focus on behavioral change, had negligible effects on drug use (Bangert-Drowns, 1988; Schinke, Botvin, & Orlandi, 1991; Tobler, 1986, 1992).

In contrast to these earlier prevention efforts, more recent efforts (1980s and 1990s) have focused on developing resistance skills (i.e., resistance to social influences) and general personal-social competence as protective factors against substance abuse. (For reviews of this work, see Botvin & Dusenbury, 1989; Botvin & Wills, 1985; Nastasi & DeZolt, 1994; Rhodes & Jason, 1988; Schinke et al., 1991.) In general, research supports the efficacy of resistance skills programs for preparing youths to resist dangerous drug-related situations and for reducing drug use or preventing initiation of substance use. In addition, some studies have documented enhanced knowledge, self-efficacy regarding ability to resist, and interpersonal skills (e.g., communication, assertiveness) related to resistance. Programs focused on personal-social competence (e.g., self-efficacy, problem solving or decision making, coping, and interpersonal or group interactive skills) have also been shown to be effective. Research has consistently documented short-term effects on targeted personal-social competencies, drug-related knowledge and attitudes, and self-reported drug use. However, drug-use effects were not always maintained, and in some cases treatment groups showed negative effects; that is, participants reported higher use rates compared to nonparticipants. These variations can be attributed to variations in program design or implementation. For example, Botvin, Baker, Filazzola, and Botvin (1990) and Pentz (1985) report maintenance of program effects following intervention for one and two years, respectively. The unique features of their programs were consistent involvement of program developers in the implementation (e.g., as cofacilitators or consultants), the use of peer leaders as cofacilitators, and booster or follow-up sessions (the last specific to Botvin et al.).

These program descriptions do not do enough to consider the ecological context of behavior, as the school and home environments are not systematic components of these interventions. However, methods designed to promote individual competence, to facilitate adjustment to divorce, and to prevent alcohol and drug abuse are implemented most effectively by using the ecological context in a systematic manner. The following framework provides a conceptual basis for implementing prevention programs in an ecological context. After this framework is presented, the previous examples of person-centered prevention programs are discussed in relationship to it (i.e., social competence, divorce adjustment, and substance abuse prevention).

## Preventive Interventions as Interactions Between Environmental and Person-centered Approaches, Using an Ecological Framework

### An Ecological Perspective

Trickett (1984) has indicated that preventive approaches to modify the individual to promote competence have limited effects unless they take an ecological perspective. This viewpoint suggests that efforts to modify the individual must use the ecological context to advantage to reinforce and maintain any modifications that are obtained.

The intersection of environment- and person-centered models can be represented by an ecological-developmental perspective that assumes a progressive, mutual accommodation throughout the life span between the individual and the environment, taking into account the social-cultural and historical contexts (Bronfenbrenner, 1989). Consideration must be given not only to the immediate ecological context in which the individual is functioning (microsystem: e.g., classroom) but also to other contexts that influence the individual's functioning or development (exosystems: e.g., school and family) or that interact with the microsystem (mecosystems: e.g., school-family relationships). In addition, sociocultural and historical influences (macrosystem) must be considered. The combination of these various systems—microsystems, exosystem, mesosystem, and macrosystem—constitute what Bronfenbrenner refers to as the *ecosystem*.

Bronfenbrenner's (1989) theory is also developmental, as he contends that early experiences influence later experiences in the same or similar environments though the instigative characteristics of the individual. That is, the individual, through inherent personal qualities or behavior patterns learned in earlier contexts, engenders certain interactions in new environments. In effect, earlier experiences provide the individual with a frame of reference for interpreting social environments and for guiding social interactions across multiple contexts. As the individual seeks or elicits similar experiences across contexts, the cognitions and behaviors initially learned are reinforced and become characteristic patterns for interpreting and interacting in social contexts. Unless other frames of reference and interpersonal experiences are provided in new contexts, early experiences (e.g., within the family) are expected to have long-term influences on the individual's adjustment. Thus, for example, the adult is likely to re-create ecological systems (e.g., friendships and family relationships) analogous to the family system of origin that maintain the cognitions and behaviors learned during childhood. In this manner, characteristic family dynamics are transmitted across generations, for example, intergenerational patterns of families affected by alcohol (see Nastasi & DeZolt, 1994).

A full understanding of the individual's functioning in a microsystem (e.g., classroom) requires that we consider the wider contexts in which the microsystem is embedded (school system) and other contexts that influence the microsystem (family, peer group, society, culture, and history). To do this, for example, one might ask the following questions: what is the history of the school system regarding mental health intervention? What are the cultural mores and taboos regarding mental illness? What behaviors and social interaction patterns are promoted in the school, family, peer group, and community? Are they consistent across contexts? To what extent does the school system communicate with the family regarding children's mental health? What are the societal values and norms that shape the school's role in promotion of children's mental health? In addition, we must consider the consistency across systems in which the child operates and the interactions among these systems. Specifically, how consistent are school values and norms with those of the peer group, family, community, and society at large? And to what extent do schools, families, and community work together to promote the emotional well-being of children?

In summary, the ecological development framework reflects a synergistic interaction between the person and the environment. The person and the environment are in a constant state of negotiation, and it is difficult to understand one separate from the other. The notion of synergism implies that person-environment interaction is qualitatively different from the person plus the environment. To understand the individual, one must consider the person within the context. Likewise, to understand the context, one must consider the individuals within it. Thus, assessment or intervention requires attention to the dynamic quality of the person-environment interaction; as a result, it is important to consider these sorts of person-environment interactions when designing any prevention program that seeks to modify the individual.

The prevention formula presented earlier provides a useful framework for developing programs based on this interactive perspective. Many preventive interventions can be based on this framework, and in fact, many of the approaches to prevention already described are most appropriately considered as illustrations of this approach. For example, Comer's (1993) approach, which does use substantial modifications of the environment as discussed, also uses social skills training (a person-centered approach) as a component of its preventively oriented approach to school reform. The previously discussed approaches to modifying the individual can be used to illustrate the importance of developing prevention programs based on interaction between the person and environment (i.e., social competence, divorce adjustment, and alcohol and drug abuse prevention).

## Social Competence Programs: Ecological Context

The preventive potential of Shure and Spivack's (1988) cognitive, social, problem-solving skills program has been demonstrated over time as a function of ecological factors. Teacher-trained four-year old children are less likely than controls to show evidence of problems in kindergarten, and these gains have been maintained in second grade without further intervention. Moreover, children trained by mothers have demonstrated changes in problem-solving skills (Shure, 1988). These results have particular preventive implications in that changes in the child may be reinforced on an ongoing basis by changes in the teacher's approaches to classroom management and/or the mother's parenting style because the child's behavior reinforces changes in the teacher's and/or the mother's behavior. This could also result in improved behavior of siblings or classmates, which would add further to a more positive climate in the classroom and/or the family. It is reasonable to assume that these changes in the classroom and/or family would result in improved problem-solving skills by children that would last years beyond the training program, presumably because of changes in teacher-pupil, mother-child, sibling, and peer interactions.

This type of environmental support has been a key component of the successful research conducted by Shure and Spivack, who use "dialoguing" to provide environmental support for formal instruction in their approach to social skills training (Shure, 1988; Shure & Spivack, 1988). Dialoguing is an approach to child management by the teacher and/or parent to supplement the formal cognitive training in the curricular materials. The teacher (or parent) uses instances of problem behavior as opportunities to reinforce concepts and to try out relevant skills from the curriculum. For example, during a real social conflict, dialoguing can be used to help the child identify the problem, to conceptualize a variety of alternative responses, to conceptualize the potential consequences of these alternatives, and to try out at least one of the alternatives. This provides an opportunity for learning that extends beyond the deliberate instruction and promotes generalization to real situations of what has been learned. It is noteworthy that many unsuccessful efforts to replicate Shure and Spivack's findings have failed to use this procedure.

Despite the positive findings associated with the research conducted by Shure and Spivack (1988), other researchers have failed to replicate these findings consistently, and this has resulted in questions about the efficacy of social skills training (Durlak, 1983). One possible reason for these inconsistent findings may be that the necessary environmental supports were not included in the replication efforts. It is likely that the positive effects of social skills training programs may require additional supportive intervention in the classroom and/or home environment to reinforce the learning that occurs during formal instruction. This viewpoint is consistent with the arguments presented by Trickett (1984; Trickett & Berman, 1989) concerning the importance of integrating ecological theory with person-centered interventions.

The focus on ecological context exemplifies a multiyear, classroom-based program designed to foster prosocial behavior (Solomon, Watson, Delucchi, Schaps, & Battistich, 1988). Prosocial interactions characterized by such behaviors as helping sharing, comforting, and cooperation were promoted through the creation of a classroom environment that included modeling and discussion of prosocial behavior, opportunities to engage in prosocial behaviors, student participation in rule setting and decision making, cooperative learning, and supportive teacher-student relationships. The classroom environment was designed both to encourage prosocial reasoning and behavior and to provide adult and peer support of prosocial interactions. Students who participated in this program for five years (grades K–4) exhibited more frequent prosocial interactions than those in comparison groups; in addition, findings were replicated in a two-year program.

## Divorce Adjustment: Ecological Context

Pedro-Carroll's approach to divorce adjustment emphasizes skills training focused on the child. It also provides social support, but this is done by meeting with groups of children to share feelings, clarify misconceptions, and reduce feelings of isolation. This is designed to facilitate social-emotional growth and divorce adjustment skills (Pedro-Carroll et al., 1992). Despite the promising effects of this program, there would be greater potential for generalized and long-lasting effects with meaningful program components focused on relevant factors in the child's ecology. Based on research into the role of contextual (school and family) factors in facilitating children's adjustment to divorce, Guidubaldi et al. (1987a) suggest an ecological approach to interventions, including parent and teacher education, modifications of school policy and curriculum, and coordination of school and community services.

Another approach with potential to strengthen divorce adjustment programs is to target the home setting in addition to the child. Research on the impact of divorce suggests that chronic parental conflict plays an important role as a stressor with negative effects on children (Forehand et al., 1995; Rutter et al., 1975). Naturally, parental conflict can occur after a divorce or separation, and depending on how this is handled by the parents it can have continued stressful impact on the child long after a divorce. In addition, there is evidence that a positive parent-child relationship, a parent's sense of efficacy, and the use of reasoned disciplinary practices contribute to children's adaptive responses to stress (Cowen, Wyman et al., 1990; Guidubaldi et al., 1986). These are all aspects of parental functioning that can be impaired as a function of divorce, and preventive interventions focused on divorce adjustment can be strengthened by dealing with this important component of the child's environment.

The divorce adjustment program developed by Stolberg (1988; Stolberg & Garrison, 1985) is an example of one that does pay some systematic attention to the home environment. This program includes groups for children that have similar goals and are structured in a manner that resembles Pedro-Carroll's (Pedro-Carroll & Cowen, 1985) program. However, Stolberg's model also includes a parent-support group designed to promote the parent's adjustment to divorce and to facilitate effective parent-child interactions. There has been research on the efficacy of this program, with some positive effects being noted (Stolberg, 1988; Stolberg & Garrison, 1985).

### Substance Abuse: Ecological Context

Based on a review of research, Hawkins et al. (1992) identified a number of contextual factors that contribute to substance abuse among adolescents and young adults. These include variables that warrant intervention at the societal or community level, such as norms and laws that promote drug use, availability, and illegal trafficking. In addition, they identified family and peer environment factors, such as family conflict, parent-child relationships, consistency of parenting, and family or peer norms (e.g., attitudes and behaviors) that support substance use and abuse. For example, familial and peer use of drugs predict drug abuse. In particular, association with peers who use drugs was consistently one of the strongest predictors of substance abuse across all ethnic groups (Caucasian, African American, Asian American, and Hispanic American). In this section are examples of substance abuse prevention programs that focus on these contextual factors in addition to individual competencies.

A community-based intervention program designed for high-risk urban youths aged 11 to 17 was successful in improving family functioning and parent-child communication about drugs and reducing drug use by participating youths (Bruce & Emshoff, 1992). This program included separate and joint groups for youths and parents focused on providing information about drugs, developing communication skills, and telling parents how to discuss drugs with their children. The program also used peer leaders, identified by Botvin et al. (1990) as a critical factor in promoting maintenance of program effects.

Pentz, Alexander, Cormach, and Light (1989) describe a community-based program that extends prevention efforts beyond schools and peers to include parents and family, community organizations, health policy, and mass media. While mass media efforts are conducted throughout the project, the other components are introduced in an order that reflects proximal to distal community influence; that is, intervention efforts begin with schools and peers, and each year a new component is added (i.e., parents and family in year 2, community organizations in year 3, and health policy in year 4).

## PRACTICAL APPROACHES IN IMPLEMENTING PRIMARY PREVENTION AND RISK REDUCTION BY SCHOOL PSYCHOLOGISTS

The future of primary prevention in schools depends on the development of pragmatic approaches that may overcome resistance and have a realistic chance of being implemented and institutionalized as a routine component of school practice. Preventive efforts will have a maximum opportunity for success to the extent that they are considered to be a regular component of the ongoing educational process (Meyers, 1989). Another factor that can promote the efficacy of preventive interventions is to focus on goals and interventions that meet the perceived needs of key members of the organization (Meyers, 1989). In this context, it is important to consider empowerment (Rappaport, 1981) and social acceptability (Elliott, Witt, & Kratochwill, 1991) by developing and implementing prevention programs that facilitate feelings of ownership by school professionals, students, and their families and that can be effective in resolving problems that are viewed as important by the organization and the community (the topic of program acceptability is discussed in more detail later in this chapter, in the section on program evaluation). The following are examples of practical approaches that school psychologists can use to increase acceptability, empowerment of educators, and long-term implementation of preventive interventions. These examples each derive from Albee's (1988) prevention formula described earlier and are relevant to at least one of the four types of prevention (i.e., primary prevention, risk reduction, early intervention, and treatment). These include using the school routine to accomplish goals associated with primary prevention and risk reduction, using early intervention and treatment to build support for risk reduction and primary prevention, and using school-based consultation strategies to facilitate prevention.

### Using the School Routine

Modifications of both curriculum and instruction can be used to implement primary prevention and risk reduction programs (Meyers, 1989; Meyers & Parson, 1987; Nastasi & DeZolt,

1994). For example, it has been suggested that if the curriculum were changed to include social problem-solving skills, this could have an impact on developing social competence and preventing the development of various social and emotional difficulties (Weissberg, Caplan, & Sivo, 1989). This is a realistic goal as there are well-developed curricular materials for teaching social skills and social problem solving from a range of perspectives (e.g., Elias et al., 1986; Shure & Spivack, 1988; Weissberg et al., 1991). Similarly, the earlier discussion of dialoguing as an approach to social problem solving suggests that instructional modifications such as this could facilitate the development of social competence and prevent the development of some social-emotional problems.

A range of preventive goals could be accomplished through other changes in curriculum and instruction. For example, it has been argued elsewhere that changes in the language arts curriculum, incorporating such goals as morality, empathy, and understanding feelings, as well as social problem-solving skills, could have important effects (Meyers, 1989; Nastasi & DeZolt, 1994). This could be accomplished by using reading materials that focus on themes directly related to these issues, a range of instructional practices designed to maximize learning in these areas from such readings, and testing and assessment to determine outcomes in areas such as those that are related closely to important preventive goals (Meyers, 1989).

Curriculum materials also can be developed to facilitate children's active involvement in learning by stressing metacognitive theory and the cognitive strategies children use in a variety of academic, cognitive, and social problem-solving situations (Nastasi & DeZolt, 1994). This concept can be applied in a meaningful manner to instruction in math, in which children's problem-solving strategies and the use of logic are particularly important in successful performance, and to science, in which the scientific method represents a problem-solving sequence that is similar to the strategic behavior invoked in a variety of problem-solving situations. Effective instruction in cognitive strategies requires this to be viewed as a major educational goal, and one way to accomplish this would be for schools to use assessments that evaluate these types of outcomes. One approach toward this goal has been recent work focused on authentic assessment (Wiggins, 1989, 1993). However, standardized tests of cognitive problem-solving approaches

are also needed in various content areas if these are to have a long-term role as important educational outcome measures.

It has also been suggested that schools can help children build resistance to stress by taking advantage of routine experiences associated with loss, conflict, and developmental crises (Meyers, 1989; Meyers & Parsons, 1987; Phillips et al., 1972). For example, loss is experienced by the school-aged child in many different ways, which vary in terms of severity. Exposure to loss can include instances when the child loses some parental support and comfort upon entering school; loses friends in school after moving to other schools and locations; loses a classroom pet or mascot who has died; loses contact with a particular teacher during the transition that occurs following promotion; loses contact with a parent as a function of divorce; loses a relative or friend through death. The school experience has great preventive potential because it provides repeated exposure to each type of stress, and teachers can work effectively to help children develop coping skills for each of these issues. Examples of such approaches to prevention have been presented elsewhere (Meyers, 1989; Meyers & Parsons, 1987). This chapter describes preventive approaches in dealing with conflict through the use of training in social problem-solving skills and dialoguing. Also, the section of this chapter on modifying the environment describes the School Transition Project (Felner et al., 1982), which is focused on one important developmental crisis period (i.e., the transition to high school).

Preventive approaches focused on children's exposure to loss are based on the assumption that each exposure, while acting as a source of stress, simultaneously serves as an opportunity to teach the child coping skills. These situations (e.g., the death of a pet, a classmate, or a relative) can always provide teaching opportunities, and the potential benefits of these teachable moments can be maximized when they are used in conjunction with ongoing efforts to provide instruction in coping and social competence. If appropriate reading materials are included in the curriculum, the classroom can provide opportunities to deal with feelings about bereavement by assigning relevant literature, encouraging class discussions, and using written assignments on related topics. If children can better adapt to the stress associated with loss, they may become more competent and adaptive in later life when confronted with other intensive stressors like separation, divorce, or death (Meyers, 1989; Meyers & Parsons, 1987; Nastasi & DeZolt, 1994).

## Using Early Intervention (Secondary Prevention)

It has been suggested that one potentially effective strategy to implement primary prevention (i.e., primary prevention and risk reduction) is to establish effective secondary prevention programs first, that is, early intervention, as defined in this chapter (Meyers, 1989). This can be effective to the extent that early intervention may be accepted more readily in some schools.

Emory Cowen's (1980) primary mental health project is an example of an effective early intervention program that has wide acceptability, given that it has been implemented in many school districts across the country (Cowen, Gesten, & Wilson, 1979; Weissberg, Cowen, Lotyczewski, & Gesten, 1983). This program uses screening to identify children with early signs of emotional difficulty, and paraprofessionals are trained to provide preventive treatment. Other approaches also use screening, assessment, and intervention (Barclay, 1983; Hagin, 1980). Mental health consultation is another commonly used procedure that is viewed by some as being consistent with early intervention (Jason & Ferone, 1981; Meyers, 1989).

Initiating prevention efforts with early intervention is a useful guideline in those circumstances in which early intervention programs are more readily accepted than primary prevention and risk reduction programs. However, professionals should also recognize those situations in which the need for primary prevention and risk reduction is expressed from the outset (Meyers, 1989). For example, it is likely that educators in some schools will view serious school problems such as disruptive youths, drug abuse, school dropouts, and teen pregnancy as appropriate for primary prevention and risk reduction interventions. The perceived importance of various intervention approaches can be determined in a particular school or school district by using needs assessment procedures consistent with the discussions of program design (e.g., Nastasi & DeZolt, 1994) and organizational consultation (Parsons & Meyers, 1994) (presented later in this chapter). This can result in preventive interventions that have the greatest potential to be accepted and effective.

## School-based Consultation

Even though school-based consultation is not often considered in this context, it offers a practical approach for school psychologists in implementing preventive interventions that are consistent with primary prevention and risk reduction (Meyers, 1989; Meyers et al., 1990; Parsons & Meyers, 1984). A variety of approaches to school-based consultation focus on the teacher, the classroom, and the school system and have clear implications for primary prevention or risk reduction. School-based consultation is an approach to service delivery that provides a unique opportunity to promote primary prevention and risk reduction because it is a well-accepted procedure and frequently an ongoing component of the school routine (Meyers, 1989).

Many school personnel have provided school-based consultation services, including school psychologists, special education teachers, speech and language pathologists, counselors, and others (e.g., see Curtis & Meyers, 1985). School consultation procedures have been described in some detail (e.g., see Chapter 23 by Gutkin & Curtis). Research evaluating the process and outcome of consultation supports the relative efficacy of this approach, including a number of preventive outcomes (e.g., Curtis & Meyers, 1985).

Consultation services focused on the teacher, classroom, school, or school system offer opportunities for primary prevention, as well as risk reduction, that have been discussed elsewhere (e.g., see Meyers, 1989). In this context, organizational consultation provides a set of methods that can be useful to school psychologists, including surveys, interviews, and extant records to gather information about the system. Feedback is then given to key elements of the organization, based on this information, and these data are used by members of the organization to develop intervention plans designed to strengthen the organization. See Parsons and Meyers (1984) for more details on this approach. There is considerable overlap between the methods used in organizational consultation and the collaborative action research models discussed next.

### Collaborative Action Research

Collaborative action research approaches based on applied anthropology and ethnography (the study of culture as represented in the behavior, knowledge, and artifacts of its members; Spradley, 1980) provide a useful framework for conducting organizational consultation and prevention programming. Action research is an interactive model of theory, research, and action-practice that guides applied social science (S. Schensul, 1985) and is consistent with the scientific-practitioner model of school psychology (for a full discussion, see Nastasi, 1994). S. Schensul describes the theory-research-action paradigm as follows. Theory guides the generation of applied research questions and data collection (e.g., pre-assessment data). These data provide the basis for reformulating the theory (to fit the specific context and population) and for developing interventions (practice). Intervention outcomes, documented through data collection (research), then influence the development of the theory and subsequent interventions, and so on. Collaborative action research refers to the the collaborative implementation of ethnographic research in an action (intervention) setting, typically used to effect social change, policy formulation, and program and community development (J. Schensul, 1985). The partners in collaborative action research are representatives from constituent groups with vested interests in the target social issue and/or those who can contribute necessary resources. Collaborators participate in the various phases of action research. In the case of program design, they participate in intervention design, implementation, and evaluation. The active engagement of program participants in the program development process is likely to facilitate their empowerment (Anderson, 1989), thus increasing the likelihood of acceptability, ownership, and continuation of the program after outside consultants leave.

Given the goal of strengthening the organization as a whole, organizational development and action research models have great potential for preventive outcomes. The following pragmatic example illustrates how school psychologists can use organizational consultation procedures to facilitate preventive goals through involvement with the prereferral intervention process.

## A Case Example of Organizational Consultation

Prereferral intervention teams are an approach to primary prevention and risk reduction that schools can use to help nonidentified children, prevent unnecessary referrals to special educa-

tion, accomplish systemic school changes, and facilitate professional development of teachers (e.g., Graden, Casey, & Christenson, 1985; Meyers, Valentino, Meyers, Boretti, & Brent, in press). The example reported here took place in a large urban school district that had recently begun to use this method (Meyers, et al., in press). These teams typically consisted of a guidance counselor, social worker, school administrator, drug counselor, resource room teacher, remedial educator, and various representatives from the committee on special education (e.g., education evaluators and school psychologists).

After a model for implementing prereferral intervention teams was adopted by the district, organizational consultation was offered to provide support and staff development. The first step was a meeting that solicited input from the principals in the eight participating schools, and based on their input the following organizational consultation procedures were selected. Surveys were distributed to team members and teachers from each of the schools. The survey, designed to obtain perceptions, used an open-ended format in which respondents were asked about the goals, strengths, weaknesses, and recommendations to improve the teams. After the surveys were completed, each team was observed for approximately one hour, at least once, as it reviewed cases that had been referred. The purpose of these observations was to learn about the procedures typically used by each prereferral intervention team and to gather data about the collaborative problem solving process used by each team. During the same time period as the observations, interviews were conducted with many of the members of the teams and a sample of teachers from each school. These interviews and the observations were conducted after the surveys were completed to follow up on key findings concerning the goals, strengths, weaknesses, and recommended changes for these teams.

Two types of follow-up visits were conducted with each team to share results, develop plans for team improvement, and gather additional information to ensure that an accurate description of these teams was obtained. The first follow-up meeting gave the consultants an opportunity to discuss the results of the surveys, interviews, and observations and to facilitate an open team discussion. These discussions provided additional data, used by each team in future meetings held on its own, to develop a specific set of goals unique to each team. Once the teams had developed their goals, a written outline of the goals and projected time lines were submitted to the consultants. Some teams requested specific information and services from the researchers on such topics as discipline, self-esteem programs, social skills training, bibliotherapy, and a reporting format for referring teachers. The district provided training on these alternative educational approaches and gave the teams an opportunity to meet together to discuss problems and successful strategies. The second set of follow-up meetings was held to give each team a forum to articulate proposed team changes, to discuss the progress that had been made in attaining these goals, and to refine goals for the following fall.

Consistent with the action research model, data were analyzed by qualitative procedures to develop and refine categories reflecting the essential properties of each of these three data sources (surveys, observations, and interviews), using a continuous process of comparison and clarification (e.g., Bogdan & Biklen, 1982; Lincoln & Guba, 1985; Spradley, 1979, 1980; Strauss & Corbin, 1990). Final decisions about whether to use information from the surveys, observations, and interviews in the summary of the data depend on whether the criteria for triangulation were met, that is, support for each finding being sought in multiple data sources and from multiple data collectors (Bogdan & Biklen, 1982; Lincoln & Guba, 1985; Spradley, 1979; 1980; Strauss & Corbin, 1990). The consultants sought confirmation of these categories to establish that they accurately represented respondents' perspectives by using "member checking" (Lincoln & Guba, 1985) to obtain feedback from the prereferral intervention teams about the findings.

The information gathered from the surveys, interviews, and observations revealed a great deal of satisfaction with these teams. It is noteworthy that this positive feeling about their competence helped to facilitate positive morale for the staff in these urban schools, where it can be easy for educators to feel overwhelmed by the difficult and seemingly unending problems faced on a daily basis. Overcoming poor school morale has a range of potential preventive outcomes associated with more effective staff functioning, which should be a special incentive for school systems that are thinking of implementing prereferral intervention teams.

Implementation varied from school to school on a number of important factors such as frequency of meetings, involvement of teachers, use of the problem-solving stages, systematic data collection, use of data, and implementation of consultation. Knowledge and perceptions of team functioning also varied among teachers from the same school. These findings resulted in several recommendations to increase the consistency and effectiveness of the teams (e.g., increase frequency of meetings, increase teachers' involvement, use the problem definition stage, gather data as a basis for developing interventions, consistently implement consultation, and provide training to team members and teachers). A summary of the key findings and suggestions has been presented elsewhere (Meyers et al., in press).

It is noted that this process was based on principles of empowerment, because the primary recommendations came from the educators in these schools rather than the consultants. As a result, many of these suggestions were implemented as appropriate to each team during the year that followed this consultation project. This facilitated more effective and consistent team implementation.

Some of the interventions developed by these teams had possibly powerful preventive effects because they sought to create change based on teacher-centered and system-centered interventions (Parsons & Meyers, 1984), which have the potential to prevent the development of learning and adjustment problems in some at-risk groups (e.g., children from Caribbean countries with no previous formal education) and in the school population as a whole. Some of these teacher-centered and system-centered interventions may be attributable to the organizational consultation that was provided, as in the following examples.

As a result of the training provided on collaborative consultation, the counselor on one team offered consultation by observing certain teachers, coteaching an affective education curriculum with these teachers to model effective teaching procedures, and providing suggestions for these teachers at their request. An example of a system-centered intervention that occurred after training in one school was the development of special programming for Caribbean children who had no formal schooling and were ineligible for special education. Another example was the establishment of a teacher mentor system for students at risk of failing sixth grade. The result was that all at-risk students passed for the year and were able to go on to junior high school.

Despite the use of teacher-centered and system-centered interventions, child-centered interventions (e.g., counseling, special class placement, and tutoring outside of school) were recommended more frequently. One reason for this may be lack of knowledge about effective school-based interventions on the part of team members and teaching staff. In this context, the team members consistently felt a need for greater access to ideas about alternative intervention strategies. This seems particularly important in schools that have a high concentration of serious educational and behavioral difficulties and where many educators feel that it is not possible to intervene effectively in the regular classroom. Relevant resources with pragmatic ideas about interventions (e.g., bibliotherapy, cooperative learning, self-esteem and social skills training, and alternative approaches to instruction) should be investigated and made available to such teams, and this was a major focus in much of the professional development.

This organizational consultation effort found that professional development was a key to success, as training was provided in consultation skills (Meyers, 1995; Meyers et al., 1993), problem-solving stages (Flugum & Reschly, 1994; Fuchs & Fuchs, 1989), curriculum-based assessment (Rosenfield, 1987), alternative approaches to intervention (Stoner, Shinn, & Walker, 1991), and group processes (Schmuck & Schmuck, 1988). The extensive in-service training and staff development activities in this district were viewed by respondents as a necessary ingredient to implementing these teams, and this finding supports researchers who have suggested that training is a key ingredient in implementing pre-referral intervention teams (e.g., Flugum & Reschly, 1994; Fuchs & Fuchs, 1989).

It is not sufficient to offer training at the beginning of such a project. Ongoing training should be provided throughout its life. This can help teams continue to improve over time. In this project, all participating schools received training at the onset of the project, with additional in-service presentations presented twice per year for the first three years of the project. The observations, surveys, and interviews conducted through this investigation provided further training to the participating teams.

# MODEL FOR IMPLEMENTING COMPREHENSIVE PREVENTION PROGRAMS

Comprehensive school-based programs include and/or facilitate access to programs at all levels of prevention (primary prevention, risk reduction, early intervention, and treatment). Within a comprehensive service model, access to group or individual therapeutic interventions (e.g., counseling, therapy, and support groups) is ensured for at-risk individuals who self-identify and/or who are identified as currently experiencing mild to severe adjustment difficulties. Such services may be provided by health or mental health professionals in schools or community agencies. In the latter case, school personnel are in a critical position to facilitate referral and access to community services for children, adolescents, and their families.

This section presents a model for program design that can be used to develop comprehensive prevention programs. This model reflects many of the frameworks presented earlier, including ecological-developmental (Bronfenbrenner, 1989), empowerment (Rappaport, 1981), and action research perspectives (Anderson, 1989; J. Schensul, 1985; S. Schensul, 1985; Spradley, 1980). In addition, it uses research on resiliency and the prevention formula as a partial basis for program design. Consistent with action research models and organizational consultation, a collaborative, participatory approach is emphasized in which program developers and recipients collaborate in all aspects of program development (Nastasi & DeZolt, 1994; Parsons & Meyers, 1984). While the ideas presented in this section are used to formulate comprehensive prevention programs, they are applicable and can facilitate the efficacy of any prevention program, whether or not it is comprehensive in focus.

We use a collaborative, participatory model of program development, which is consistent with empowerment (Anderson, 1989; Rappaport, 1981), as a framework for the preventive approaches discussed in this chapter. Drawing from the evaluation framework presented by Elliott et al. (1991), it is proposed that effective program development must address acceptability (consumer satisfaction), integrity (adherence to program design), and efficacy (program outcomes) throughout the process of program design, implementation, and evaluation. Since program participants play an active role in planning and monitoring, they become partners in collaborative program development rather than recipients of a prescribed program. In this manner, participants can take an active role in ensuring program acceptability, integrity, and efficacy.

For example, in an ongoing community-based AIDS prevention program (Eisenberg, Nastasi, & Silva, 1995; Ratnayake et al., 1995; Silva et al., 1995), young adults from the target population assist in the data collection used to develop the intervention program in which these same individuals serve as peer educators (i.e., implementors of the intervention). The peer educators also initially serve as recipients of the intervention (as part of staff training) and subsequently provide feedback about its acceptability and perceived efficacy. Furthermore, the peer educators are fully informed of the program philosophy, goals and objectives, and the critical nature of program activities and intervention techniques. They are also involved in monitoring program implementation (to ensure integrity) as part of ongoing consultation with research and clinical staff. Thus, they are full participants in the three phases of program design, implementation, and evaluation. In subsequent sections, we discuss considerations relevant to these phases of program development.

In designing and implementing prevention programs in the school, program developers should address several practical and ethical issues: (1) ecological (contextual) considerations, (2) levels of intervention within a continuum of services, (3) program goals and objectives, (4) intervention methods and content, (5) selection of participants, (6) staff selection and development, (7) promotion of generalization, and (8) program evaluation. Table 29.1 presents a series of questions to guide program development (adapted from Nastasi & DeZolt, 1994). As suggested earlier, consideration must be given to program acceptability, integrity, and effectiveness throughout the process.

## Considering the Ecology (Context)

*What are the ecological (contextual) considerations?* As suggested by an ecological-developmental perspective, it is critical to consider the various components of the ecological system in which the proposed intervention is to occur. Using Bronfenbrenner's (1989) model, it is important to consider not only the immediate context (microsystem) but also the multiple contexts (exosystem, mesosystem, and macrosystem) that influence the person-environment interactions in the microsystem. Thus, a comprehensive needs assessment can be used to address the needs and competencies of students, teachers, school-based support staff, administrators, parents, and community when designing classroom-based preventive interventions. Ideally, needs assessment involves collaboration from representatives of each of these constituencies. Furthermore, a comprehensive needs assessment attends to sociocultural and historical factors such as the history of prevention and treatment in the school and community; participants' values and beliefs; and school, family, and community norms. Attention to norms of relevant contexts also helps to ensure the ecological validity of the intervention (i.e., the degree to which the intervention is appropriate for, and effective in, the particular ecological setting in which it is implemented). The goal of needs assessment is threefold: (1) to guide program design, (2) to promote acceptability, and (3) to ensure ecological validity. Furthermore, an ecological focus is applied to program design; that is, through the process of needs assessment, relevant contexts for program implementation and generalization are identified. For example, one needs assessment in a community-based prevention program suggested that certain community centers represented natural contexts for young adults (i.e., they regularly gathered in these settings). Such settings thus provide the locus for implementation of a community-based program and generalization for a school-based program. Without involvement of representatives from the community, program developers would have been unaware of the potential value of these community centers as intervention sites.

Examples from school-based programs suggest the importance of considering contexts outside of the classroom. For example, one middle school adopted cooperative learning as part of an overall effort to promote a community of learners in which teachers and students collaborated in the teaching-learning process. Cooperative learning as an instructional strategy was generally acceptable to teachers throughout the school, and the administration provided needed support and resources. However, parental objections threatened the viability of the community of learners. In particular, parents of high-achieving students objected to their children working cooperatively with lower-achieving students, and some parents requested alternatives, such as

## TABLE 29.1   Program Development Guide

### Considering the Ecology (Context)

What are the ecological considerations?
What systems factors are likely to facilitate or inhibit program development?

### Choosing Levels of Intervention Within a Continuum of Services

What levels of intervention does the program include?

### Identifying Intervention Methods and Content

How are program content and activities selected?
What is the theoretical-empirical basis for program design?
What are the program goals and objectives?
What target skills does the program address?
What instructional or therapeutic techniques and strategies are consistent with program goals and
     objectives?
What content and activities are consistent with program goals and objectives?
How do we integrate program goals, objectives, and content into existing school curricula?
How do we distinguish preventive education from therapeutic intervention?

### Selecting Participants

How are participants identified?
How do characteristics of the participants influence program development?
How can diverse populations be best served in prevention programs?

### Selecting and Preparing Staff

Who will be involved in program design, implementation, and evaluation?
What are the necessary qualifications of program staff?
What are the respective roles and responsibilities of staff?
What types of services can existing program staff provide?
How do we secure additional staff?
What makes up staff development?

### Promoting Generalization

How do we ensure generalization and maintenance of program outcomes?
How do we extend the program beyond the school system? How do we involve families and
     communities?
How do we create a school culture consonant with prevention?

### Evaluating the Program

What are the critical components of program evaluation?
How do we link assessment and intervention?
How will we assess program acceptability?
How will we assess program integrity?
How will we assess program effectiveness and generalization of program outcomes?

individual tutoring of their children during co-operative learning activities. Some parents even suggested they might come into the school, re-move their children from the classroom, and tu-tor their own children during these periods. This example suggests the critical nature of in-volving parents in the design of innovative school programs.

The second school-based example comes from a program designed to promote the inclu-sion of special education students. The focus of the project was to enhance the social and behav-ioral skills of students classified as behaviorally disordered to facilitate inclusion in regular class-room contexts. The intervention program was conducted in the special education resource classroom, a natural context that provided op-portunities for peer interaction and thus practice of target skills. Generalization was promoted by a system in which the students monitored their own social and behavioral skills. To ensure that students' use of self-monitoring was accurate, this process was checked intermittently by the teacher. Despite changes in the social-behavioral skills of the target students in the special educa-tion setting (suggesting learning of more accept-able behavior), effective inclusion was hindered by rejection of the target students by regular classroom teachers and non–special education peers. Although consideration had been given to ecologically valid competencies (i.e., social-behavioral skills necessary for success in the reg-ular class), program developers neglected to con-sider the attitudes of regular classroom teachers toward students with behavior disorders and the history of peer rejection, which impeded accep-tance despite behavior changes. This example in-dicates the potential importance of the next question.

*What systems factors are likely to facilitate or in-hibit program development?* To ensure program ac-ceptability and efficacy, identifying ecological factors that are likely to facilitate or inhibit pro-gram implementation is crucial. Factors that warrant consideration include values, needs, competencies, resources, sources of support, and resistance. As suggested by a collaborative, par-ticipatory model, program success is contingent on active involvement of participants and repre-sentatives from other contexts relevant to the ecosystem. Otherwise, even empirically validated programs may prove to be ineffective. Nastasi and DeZolt (1994) provide one such example in which program failure occurred when the district

administration was not considered during the initial steps of planning a drug abuse prevention program.

> Pupil support personnel in one school district identified and documented the need for a substance abuse prevention program, based on the prevalence of drug abuse among adolescents in the district. With money from a parent organization, they purchased a program that had been implemented successfully in other schools. Teachers and counselors received training in program implementation. Prior to program initiation, the district superintendent at a school board meeting denied the existence of drug problems in the district and advised against implementation of the program. As a result, the program was not adopted. The superintendent subsequently was asked to resign because of his own alcohol-related problems. The following year the district successfully instituted the program with administrative and community support. (pp. 130, 132)

Steps can be taken throughout the process of program development to monitor and ensure acceptance and to minimize resistance (for more detail, see Meyers & Parsons, 1987; Nastasi & DeZolt, 1994). Attention should be given to the match between the proposed program and the school context. Nastasi and DeZolt (1994) sug-gest assessing the system's history and current re-ceptivity to change in general and to change that is specific to the goals of the prevention pro-gram. It is suggested that this assessment con-sider potential sources of power, support, and resistance to the prevention program (e.g., per-sonnel whose endorsement will be critical to suc-cess). The potential for system-wide acceptance of the prevention program can be further en-hanced by establishing a system of clear and open communication in the design phase of the program. This might include initial meetings with the staff to obtain input regarding the pre-vention program and regular meetings to discuss and monitor implementation.

During program design, information gather-ing from an involvement of representatives from relevant ecological contexts are critical to accep-tance and success. These might include represen-tatives from important components of the school environment (e.g., grade-level academic teachers; special area teachers such as in art and physical education; and personnel workers such as guidance counselors, key administrators, aides, secretaries, and bus drivers) and of related environments (e.g., church, community recreation, and family). Methods for collecting data about values, beliefs, competencies, resources, and needs include focus groups (Stewart and Shamdasani, 1990), individual interviews with key informants (Spradley, 1979), participant observations (Spradley, 1980), surveys, and collaborative consultation (Parsons & Meyers, 1984).

Program acceptability can also be maximized by involving school staff in identifying and securing the necessary resources for implementation and evaluation. For example, it can be helpful to solicit teachers' input regarding necessary program materials and staff training. In addition, it can be important to spend time working with administrators to ensure that the necessary resources can be secured. It may be necessary to negotiate with the school principal, to obtain staff time for training and consultation, money for program materials, and additional staff for evaluation.

To ensure that the program is implemented as planned (i.e., program integrity), it is critical that program participants are involved in determining goals and objectives, program activities, and intervention strategies. In addition, program participants should be consulted about the ecological validity of techniques, activities, and materials. For example, in a substance abuse prevention program for adolescents, real-life dilemmas of drug use were identified through preintervention focus groups. These dilemmas were used later as content for simulated decision-making activities in the drug abuse prevention program. Furthermore, it is advisable to include participants in the ongoing monitoring and modification of program activities and techniques (while maintaining acceptability).

In summary, a collaborative approach to program design and implementation can help to foster acceptability and offset resistance. Comprehensive prevention programs should be conceived as multiyear efforts. Often it is necessary to devote at least one year to needs assessment, planning, and staff preparation. To maximize the potential success of such comprehensive programs, it is often advisable to conduct a pilot project with a few highly motivated staff members and to monitor program implementation closely to demonstrate the efficacy of the program while identifying factors that contribute to

or impede its integrity and efficacy. In addition to considering the developmental needs of the system, it can be critically important to consider those of program participants.

## Choosing Levels of Intervention Within a Continuum of Services

*What levels of intervention does the program include?* A comprehensive prevention program provides services at all four levels, that is, primary prevention, risk reduction, early intervention, and treatment. Providing a continuum of services requires collaboration among mental health professionals in the school and local community. The range of services provided in the school system is influenced by a multitude of factors such as staff qualifications, availability of staff with expertise in issues related to health and mental health, specific system needs and resources, and acceptability by relevant constituents. As with other aspects of program design, decisions about levels of intervention should be made in collaboration with program participants, staff, administrators, and community agents.

## Identifying Intervention Methods and Content

*How are program content and activities selected?* Decisions about program-specific content and activities should be grounded in a theoretical-empirical base, that is, a generative base (Cowen, 1984; Meyers & Parsons, 1987) and closely linked to program goals and objectives. Ideally, program developers integrate context-specific needs and resources with a sound generative base. This requires that one or more members of the program development team take responsibility for researching literature on prevention (i.e., risk and protective factors and efficacy of specific programs or techniques). Depending on the nature of the existing literature and the problem being considered, it may be necessary to gather local data to add to the generative data base. The goal then becomes the application of the generative base to the existing context.

Once the theoretical-empirical base is determined, program goals and objectives are selected that are grounded in this base and specific to the target population. Furthermore, consideration of both the generative base and the target context (i.e., the target population in the ecosystem) guides the selection of target skills, intervention techniques and strategies, and program content and activities. It is advisable to examine existing prevention programs (e.g., social skills and drug education) and relevant school curricula (e.g., health education and social studies) and consider using them with appropriate modifications. Before adopting even the most empirically sound program, it is critical to ask questions such as these: does the intervention address the preventive goals of the program? Is it appropriate to the target population? Program developers should also consider how best to integrate the proposed program into the existing school culture and curricula in order to facilitate acceptability (e.g., by using existing resources and minimizing interference with academic activities) and generalization (e.g., by implementing the program in natural contexts). Some of the ideas mentioned earlier about use of the school routine to implement prevention may be relevant in this context.

Decision making about program content and activities is best conducted as a collaborative endeavor, involving school and community mental health professionals, teaching staff, students, parents, and administrators. The following set of questions should be addressed during this decision-making process. What is the theoretical-empirical basis for program design? What are the program goals and objectives? What target skills does the program address? What instructional or therapeutic techniques and strategies are consistent with program goals and objectives? What content and activities are consistent with program goals and objectives? How do we integrate program goals, objectives, and content into existing school programs?

*How is preventive education distinguished from therapeutic intervention?* School-based prevention programs integrate educational and therapeutic interventions. A collaborative approach requires participation of educational (e.g., teachers and administrators), health (e.g., school nurse and physician), and mental health (e.g., school psychologists, counselors, and social workers) specialists in all aspects of program development. Program developers are well advised to make clear distinctions between educational and therapeutic techniques, activities, and content and to delineate clearly the roles of educators and professionals from the fields of health and mental health. It is critical that program staff have requisite knowledge and skills and are aware of the limitations of their respective roles. In addition, appropriate procedures for consultation and referral regarding health and mental health issues should be developed. For example, the mental

health staff should be available to the educational staff to discuss mental health concerns expressed by students and to assist in referral for treatment when necessary. Similar approaches are needed for health problems. Particularly when program goals include the identification of students who need more intensive services, program developers should have a mechanism in place to handle referrals. When program content is focused on specific issues related to health and/or mental health (e.g., how to identify signs of depression and risk for suicide), it is critical that program implementors be advised of warning signs and appropriate referral procedures.

## Selecting Participants

*How are participants identified?* All of the potential levels of programming (i.e., primary prevention, risk reduction, early intervention, and treatment) are relevant to comprehensive prevention programs, and this variety of levels influences the selection of program participants. Thus, comprehensive prevention programs will often focus on the entire population and on an at-risk group that is a key target population. In addition, there are individuals with some degree of symptomatology who are targeted for more intensive services, such as early intervention and treatment. Identification should be guided in part by ecological considerations in the given context. In this section we describe a set of identification and selection procedures. The process of choosing program participants should consider the unique features of the target system and should be negotiated with representatives from relevant contexts.

The multitude of risk and protective factors that have been identified by prevention researchers (e.g., Cowen et al., 1990; Garmezy, 1983; Hawkins et al., 1992; Rutter, 1981; Werner, 1989) and summarized in the prevention formula presented earlier support a multifactored approach to the identification of program goals and participants. In a comprehensive prevention program, both personal factors (e.g., personal-social competencies and personal predispositions to respond to certain stressors) and environmental factors (e.g., socialization practices, stressors, and supports) guide the selection of goals at all levels (i.e., primary prevention, risk reduction, and early intervention) and the identification of individuals for the more intensive preventive interventions (risk reduction, early intervention, and treatment). For example, a schoolwide substance abuse prevention program could also include procedures for identifying the at-risk population of children of alcoholics (Nastasi, 1995a). Such identification procedures can be critical to risk reduction programs for students who are not easily identified through routine screening procedures such as teachers' referral. It is suggested that comprehensive prevention programs require multiple opportunities for identification of students experiencing serious adjustment difficulties or early signs of such difficulties, as well as those who are at-risk of experiencing these problems. These approaches to identification might include the following.

1. Primary prevention programs offered to all students provide access to knowledge and competence building without requisite identification. One way to provide access to more intensive interventions can be through topic-specific programs that permit self-selection without self-identification of being at risk. For example, the school psychologist could offer a group counseling or educational program focused on such topics as anxiety, conflict resolution, family alcoholism, and/or sibling relationships.

2. Classroom-based primary prevention programs provide contexts for self-identification, both formally and informally. Informal identification can occur when students express concerns during class discussion, and formal identification can occur through self-report measures related to program content. Self-identification is likely to be enhanced through a specific educational focus on topics such as risk and protective factors, mental health, and psychopathology. In addition, the long-term nature of prevention programs allow participants to become comfortable with sharing personal information and therefore may be critical to self-identification (J. Schensul, 1994).

3. Another way to identify those in need of more intensive services is by conducting school- or classroom-wide screenings focused on personal-social competence, internalized emotional difficulties (e.g., depression), and family concerns (e.g., alcoholism, parental divorce, and family conflict), using multiple data sources like students' self-reports, teachers' ratings, and observations by school personnel.

4. A multiple-stage procedure might be used to identify students in need of intervention at varying levels. In this type of procedure, students participate in multiple levels of screenings, with all students participating in a general screening and progressively fewer students receiving more intensive assessment. Such procedures have been shown to be valid for identifying students with internalized disorders like depression (Reynolds, 1986) and anxiety (Laurent, Hadler, & Stark, 1994).

5. Education of school psychologists and other school personnel can enhance identification efforts and, moreover, may be necessary for accurate and complete identification of at-risk students.

*How do characteristics of the participants influence program development?* Nastasi and DeZolt (1994) suggest that the affective, cognitive, and behavioral competencies of the target population should guide the development of program goals, objectives, content, activities, and assessment techniques. In addition to normative developmental considerations, it can be important to assess the competencies of individual participants to facilitate individualization of interventions. Thus, program design should include assessment activities geared toward the general target population to facilitate program development and toward individuals in the target population to facilitate individualization of the program.

In addition to considering characteristics of the target group, effective program design requires careful consideration of the program staff's characteristics. It can be helpful to assess knowledge and competencies relative to the proposed prevention program and to develop appropriate development activities to augment knowledge and competence in relevant areas. However, such efforts to assess the staff must be done carefully, to avoid engendering resistance.

*How can diverse populations be best served in prevention programs?* The American Psychological Association (1993) recommends that psychological service providers possess a sociocultural framework and the knowledge and skills relevant to assessment and intervention with ethnic, linguistic, and culturally diverse populations, including the ability to "recognize cultural diversity; understand the role that culture and ethnicity/race play in the sociopsychological and economic development of ethnic and culturally diverse populations; understand that socioeconomic and political factors significantly impact the psychosocial, political, and economic development of ethnic and culturally diverse groups; help clients to understand/maintain/resolve their own sociocultural identification; and understand the interaction of culture, gender, and sexual orientation on behavior and needs" (p. 45).

"Program developers are responsible for insuring that all aspects of the program embrace the diversity of the target population" (Nastasi & DeZolt, 1994, p. 140). Specifically, Nastasi and DeZolt recommend that (1) program foci include appreciation of diversity and peaceful functioning among individuals with diverse perspectives; (2) program content reflects both common and unique characteristics of participants, particularly their sociocultural experiences; and (3) program activities provide opportunities for social construction of norms that integrate diverse beliefs and attitudes. In addition, program developers and staff need to examine their own attitudes and competencies in the context of the APA guidelines, and staff training should address diversity issues directly.

Prevention researchers in the field of substance abuse call for cultural competence or sophistication among researchers and practitioners who work with racially and ethnically diverse populations (Orlandi, Weston, & Epstein, 1992). Such sophistication requires attention to the knowledge, attitudes, and skills of those who work with diverse populations. The publication edited by Orlandi et al. discusses cultural competencies relative to working with African-American, Asian-American, Hispanic, and Native-American populations.

An example of a program addressing diversity is the bicultural competence program for preventing substance abuse among Native-American youths, developed by Schinke, Botvin, Trimble, Orlandi, Gilchrist, & Locklear (1988). Program goals included enhancing bicultural competencies (relevant to Native-American and non–Native-American contexts) such as assertiveness skills, and developing resistance skills such as communication, coping, and decision making. Program content was culturally relevant (e.g., hypothetical situations for decision making reflected participants' cultural experiences), the program was implemented in the local community (on reservation sites), and program facilitators were Native-American counselors. The program yielded positive effects on drug-related knowledge and attitudes, interactive skills, and drug use.

## Selecting and Preparing Staff

*Who will be involved in program design, implementation, and evaluation?* Decisions about staffing are critical to program viability and effectiveness. During the collaborative program design process, participants need to address issues related to staff qualification, roles and responsibilities, and staff resources. The following questions can guide discussion, which should consider ecological factors, as well as program goals and objectives. What are the necessary qualifications of program staff? What are the respective roles and responsibilities of staff? What types of services can existing program staff provide? How can additional staff be secured?

*What is included in staff development?* Once decisions have been made about staff needs and qualifications, program developers can plan staff development, which should be tailored to program goals and objectives, as well as specific needs of selected or anticipated staff. Staff development has been shown to be a crucial factor in educational innovations (Weiss, 1993), and it has been argued that ongoing staff development can be an important factor as well (Meyers et al., in press). Support for this latter idea can be found in the concepts of program acceptability and integrity. That is, staff development goes beyond initial training to include ongoing monitoring and consultation concerning the knowledge and skills of the staff. Providing consultation and monitoring for the prevention program in a collaborative manner helps to ensure that staff members are full participants in program development and that the program is implemented with integrity and has high acceptability.

Decisions about staff development also involve consideration of resources in the school and community. The following questions need to be addressed: who will conduct training? Who will conduct ongoing consultation? Do certain aspects of the program require specialized expertise not available in the school? If so, how can the services of individuals with such expertise be obtained (e.g., through community agencies)? How will time and money be secured for conducting staff training and consultation? How can existing staff be used to facilitate training for other professionals in the school or district?

## Promoting Generalization

*How can generalization and maintenance of program outcomes be ensured?* Generalization and maintenance of effects is a frequently cited problem in educational and psychological interventions. For example, despite the high level of social skill acquisition (by more than 90% of participants) from the cognitive-behaviorally based Skill-streaming programs, transfer to real-life situations was shown in only 45% to 50% of the participants (Goldstein et al., 1990). Furthermore, mixed findings in the long-term effects of prevention programming (e.g., substance abuse prevention programs) may reflect variations in program design and implementation (Nastasi & DeZolt, 1994). Without specific attention to generalization, preventive effects are likely to be limited.

Specific program features have been identified by intervention researchers as critical to generalization over time and context: (1) development of self-regulatory, cognitive strategies such as cognitive mediators, self-monitoring and self-reinforcement, and efficacy expectation (Bandura, 1986; Shure, 1988); (2) extended training through prolonged programming or intermittent "booster" or review sessions (Botvin et al., 1990; Lochman, 1992; Solomon et al., 1988; Weissberg et al. 1991); (3) prompting by agents (e.g., teachers and parents) in natural contexts to apply new skills in the real-life context, using methods similar to dialoguing (Shure & Spivack, 1988); (4) using peers as educators or mediators (Botvin et al., 1990; Johnson, Johnson, Dudley, & Acikgoz, 1991; Pentz, 1985); and (5) prolonged involvement of program developers in implementation through cofacilitation, consultation, and/or monitoring (Botvin et al., 1990; Pentz, 1985). Program developers should build such features into the program's design to ensure generalization of target skills. Planning for generalization is likely to be facilitated by attention to ecological variables and collaboration with key individuals from the real-life contexts of the target population. In addition, attention to the culture of the target ecology is critical.

*How can prevention programs be extended beyond the school system to involve families and communities?* A collaborative approach to program development implies establishment of effective school-family-community partnerships. These partnerships can also be effective mechanisms for promoting generalization (Nastasi & DeZolt, 1994). For example, parent education programs consonant with school-based programs facilitate collaboration between schools and families and promote generalization of target skills. Similarly, extending classroom activities to home and com-

munity can both foster school-family-community collaboration and facilitate generalization. In the ESCAPE program (see Nastasi and DeZolt, 1994), students interview family and community members about their experiences related to program content, invite community representatives to participate in program activities, and conduct community service projects. Such activities facilitate students' communication with family and community, thereby establishing links that support program goals and outcomes. Similarly, in one community-based substance abuse prevention program, mothers and their adolescent daughters participated in the prevention program and then developed and implemented community projects to extend program goals to other community members.

*How can a school culture be created that is consonant with prevention?* An ecological perspective mandates attention to the entire ecosystem of the program participants, and sociocultural features like norms and values. Thus, the design of prevention programs in schools should include plans for creating a school culture that will support program goals. Ideally, decisions about critical features for establishing a school culture that is congruent with prevention goals should be grounded in the program's theoretical-empirical base and focused on extending program outcomes. For example, Nastasi and DeZolt (1994) describe a school culture that fosters personal-social development, provides a safe environment for self-identification of at-risk students, and advocates measures for the protection of children and youths. As Table 29.2 indicates, the key components of the culture include valuing and appreciating diverse competencies and perspectives; diverse role models; effective communication and conflict resolution; opportunities for success, positive feedback, and social support; and a sense of social responsibility for the well-being of all members. The essential characteristics of this culture are embodied in the prevention curriculum they devised and are grounded in relevant research and theory.

Research on school-based prevention programming supports systemic modifications in promoting personal-social and academic competence, compliance with school regulations, positive attitudes toward school, and reduced substance use (Felner & Adan, 1988; Fry & Addington, 1984; Graves & Graves, 1985; Hawkins et al., 1992; Solomon et al., 1988). These systemic modifications require programming that is focused at all

**TABLE 29.2    Creating a School Culture to Enhance Social Competence and Personal Efficacy**

- *Multiple perspectives and competencies are mutually valued and encouraged.* Individuals are encouraged to express opinions, consider multiple perspectives, appreciate common characteristics, and respect unique qualities. Individuals are provided opportunities and support to develop unique competencies. Collaborative activities reflect the contributions of multiple competencies within and beyond the academic domain.

- *Social support from peers and adults is the norm.* Individuals are encouraged to provide mutual emotional support and practical assistance. Specifically, prosocial behaviors such as empathy, caring, helping, and sharing are cultivated. Opportunities for social support beyond the school community are available.

- *Peaceful conflict resolution is customary.* Individuals are encouraged to confront and reconcile discrepancies without fear of reproach or retaliation. Negotiation, compromise, mediation, and cooperative problem solving are common.

- *Communication is characterized by* perspective taking, active listening, reciprocal sense-making, seeking clarification, providing explanations, and giving informational feedback and social reinforcement.

- *Success is fostered through* realistic goal setting and self-appraisal, performance-contingent feedback, and emphasis on progress rather than mastery. Coping through persistence and optimistic thinking is advocated.

- *Diverse role models who embody personal-social competencies are manifest.* Models include school personnel, older students, peers, family and community members, and story characters.

- *Social responsibility* for the mutual enhancement of personal-social competencies exists within and extends beyond the school. Members of the school and community at-large collaborate to create a culture that fosters social competence and personal efficacy of all constituents.

B. K. Nastasi, and D. M. DeZolt, *School Interventions for Children of Alcoholics* New York: Guilford, 1994. Reprinted with permission.

levels of the school environment to support the goals of instructional prevention programs (e.g., social competence training, drug abuse prevention, prevention of teen pregnancy, violence prevention). Examples of systemic modifications that can support preventive goals include using cooperative learning in academic subject areas, preparing school personnel to provide support and guidance to students, involving students in setting classroom and school regulations, modeling of prosocial behavior by school personnel, and altering the school's organization through shared decision making or home-school collaboration.

## Evaluating the Program

In applied settings, evaluation is often a neglected aspect of program development. In this section we discuss a model for program evaluation that (1) focuses on acceptability, integrity, and effectiveness; (2) incorporates both formative and summative evaluation; (3) adheres to a multisource, multimethod approach; and (4) is easily integrated into a collaborative consultation approach.

*What are the critical components of program evaluation?* In contrast to the limited traditional emphasis on program outcomes, we advocate evaluation of program acceptability and integrity, as well as effectiveness. Elliott et al. (1991) have suggested that acceptability and integrity are essential to the evaluation of program efficacy. (In later sections, we examine these evaluation components separately.) They contend that efficacy is dependent on integrity of program implementation, which in turn is influenced by acceptability of the program by participants and staff. Furthermore, failure to conduct formative (ongoing) evaluation of acceptability and integrity not only makes it difficult to explain program outcomes and foster replication but also may contribute to program failure. In a collaborative consultation framework, monitoring of acceptability, integrity, and effectiveness provides content for consultation and program development.

Ideally, program evaluation is both formative and summative (Scriven, 1980), with data collection at multiple points, including preintervention, throughout program implementation, postintervention, and specific follow-up bench marks (e.g., six months and one year). Furthermore, data collection is multimethod and multisource. Nastasi and DeZolt (1994), for example, suggest the use of both *qualitative* and *quantitative* measures such as observations, interviews, personal journals, behavior-rating scales, and other standardized measures collected from student participants, parents, teachers, and other school staff.

> The combined use of qualitative and quantitative methods capitalizes on the benefits of both approaches. Quantification objectifies and standardizes the measurements of program goals and objectives, thus facilitating replicability and generalizability. The sole use of quantitative methods, however, does not capture the complex dynamics inherent in program acceptability, implementation, and efficacy. Qualitative techniques provide the means for examining (a) the meaning of program-specific constructs; (b) the individual and contextual variability in manifestations (i.e., operational definitions) of constructs; (c) the construction and co-construction of knowledge, behavior, and norms; and (d) individual and contextual factors that facilitate or inhibit the change process. Furthermore, the integration of quantitative and qualitative methods not only enhances our understanding of these complex variables, but facilitates the application of theory and research to practice. (Nastasi & DeZolt, 1994, p. 125)

Program evaluation also requires documentation of demographic characteristics of program participants and staff, staff-training requirements, management of program activities, logistics of data collection, procedures for accessing resources, and monetary and time costs. Such data facilitate thorough program description, provide accountability, allow cost-benefit analysis, and facilitate program replication.

*How are assessment and intervention linked?* Effective evaluation requires assessment procedures that are clearly linked to program goals and objectives and measure constructs consistent with target skills and program content. Assessment and intervention should be integrated in such a way that preassessment and formative assessment inform the construction and modification of the intervention, and postassessments (immediate and follow-up) accurately measure program outcomes and their generalization over time and context. Accurate assessment of generalization depends on the ecological validity of assessment and intervention procedures.

*How is program acceptability assessed?* Acceptability refers to the degree to which program participants (developers, implementers, evaluators, and recipients) embrace program philosophy, goals and objectives, and procedures. In particular, do they find the program useful, feasible, and effective? (For a full discussion, see Elliott et al., 1991). Formative assessment of acceptability is advisable to foster continued involvement in program activities and ensure program integrity (Nastasi & DeZolt, 1994.) Furthermore, collaboration of representatives from relevant constituencies throughout the program development process serves to encourage and monitor acceptability. Identification of informants should be guided by ecological considerations. That is, representatives should be chosen from systems that will directly or indirectly affect program success (e.g., students, teachers, administrators, parents, community agencies, and local citizens).

Standardized rating scales such as those designed to assess teachers' and students' perceptions of the acceptability of behavioral interventions provide quantitative measures (Elliott et al., 1991). Program developers may find these measures, adapted to reflect program goals and objectives, to be useful. In addition, Nastasi and DeZolt (1994) suggest the use of qualitative techniques such as focus groups, interviews, journals, and logs. For example, focus groups of representative program recipients and providers conducted prior to program implementation can be used to assess the initial acceptability of program techniques and content. In addition, periodic interviews with recipients and providers throughout implementation provides in-depth qualitative data about program acceptability. (For information on focus group and ethnographic interviewing techniques, see Stewart and Shamdasani, 1990, and Spradley, 1979; respectively.) Facilitator (provider) journals and logs can serve multiple purposes, such as promoting reflective practice, providing content for consultation sessions, and monitoring acceptability. Content analysis and coding of interviews and journals provide both qualitative and quantitative measures of program acceptability. In addition, particularly in multiyear projects, data from these qualitative measures can be used to develop program-specific standardized measures of acceptability.

*How is program integrity assessed?* Integrity (e.g., Elliott et al., 1991) has been referred to as the degree to which the program is implemented as prescribed or planned. We define integrity as the manner in which the program is implemented. We can assume that even well-validated programs will require some modification to fit the needs of a specific setting, and program evaluators should document implementation in a given setting through the use of thick description, that is, detailed, thorough description of the program, the setting, and the conditions (Guba & Lincoln, 1981). Such detailed description promotes generalizability or "applicability," that is, the extrapolation of findings to other contexts (Guba & Lincoln, 1981). Assessment of program implementation can serve multiple purposes (Nastasi & DeZolt, 1994): (1) to document program implementation (i.e., integrity); (2) to guide professional development and collaborative consultation; (3) to facilitate identification of program variables that contribute to program efficacy (i.e., process evaluation); and (4) to guide the development of program-specific standardized measures of integrity.

To provide thick description, the evaluation of program implementation needs to focus on instructional or facilitation techniques, participant behaviors, use of target skills, program content and activities, and the interaction of these variables. For example, in a program focused on facilitation of group processes that are theoretically and empirically linked to program outcomes, observers can record the occurrence of targeted facilitation and interactive behaviors in specific program activities (Nastasi, 1995b). Such data permit the examination of the interactions among facilitator behaviors, participant behaviors, and program activities and content. In addition to observations, integrity measures could include facilitator logs of program activities and content, program artifacts, and the content of discussions during periodic consultation sessions.

*How can program effectiveness and generalization of program outcomes be assessed?* Effective evaluation of program efficacy (i.e., the extent to which the program met intended goals) and generalization (extension of program outcomes across time and context) requires the selection of measures consistent with program goals and objectives. For example, prevention programs (e.g., substance abuse programs) that target knowledge, attitudes, and practices and behaviors need to include outcome measures of these factors. In addition, competencies (e.g., decision-making skills) proposed as mediators of target behaviors (e.g., substance use) should be included as outcome measures to examine their mediating role (i.e., the change in the mediator is linked to the change in the target behavior) and to assess the effectiveness of the program in changing both mediating and target variables. Furthermore, the evaluation of generalization requires assessment of ecologically valid indexes in natural contexts. The use of a multimethod, multisource approach implies the use of a combination of measures. For example, measures of knowledge, attitudes, and practices and behaviors could include self-report (interviews, journals, and rating scales), informants' reports (e.g., teachers and parents), analogue assessment (use of decision-making skills in a role-play context), and direct observation in and outside of the intervention context.

## CONCLUSIONS

This chapter has considered a range of ideas for implementing prevention programming in schools with a particular focus on primary prevention and risk reduction. Prevention is a revolutionary construct in education and psychology, as the focus is on preventing the development of future problems rather than remediating them. It also requires a radical shift in the way school psychologists and other educators think about the process of schooling and the delivery of school psychological services because as the focus is on the interaction between the person and the environment to prevent problems rather than conceptualizing existing problems as residing within the child (Albee, 1982; Alpert, 1985). Prevention is linked to ecological theory, consultation models, and research on stress, as well as research on children who are invulnerable to stress. This chapter presents an approach to the design, implementation, and evaluation of comprehensive prevention programs, with a focus on primary prevention and risk reduction, while also providing opportunities for children in need of early intervention or treatment related to the topic of the prevention program. However, in addition to such formal approaches to prevention programming, this chapter has emphasized pragmatic approaches in implementing primary prevention (and risk reduction) with minimal resources by using the school routine. The ultimate growth and development of children and the prevention of learning and adjustment problems suggest that schools implement a range of approaches to prevention.

Research is needed to establish the generative base for and the efficacy of preventive approaches to various problems, and this chapter addresses a number of issues that can be considered as targets for research designed to establish this data base (e.g., conceptual framework for school-based prevention, practical approaches to implementing prevention, and comprehensive prevention programs). Such research on the generative base for the efficacy of prevention programs should be interdisciplinary, including, for example, anthropology, economics, education, epidemiology, medicine, psychology and public health, as this would maximize the utility of information that is developed. Data on the long-term economic effects of the Perry Preschool Project is one example of a productive interdisciplinary analysis of prevention data (Schweinhart & Weikart, 1989). Although multiple research models can be appropriate, including quantitative and qualitative approaches, we believe that a particularly promising model for future research involves an integration of research and practice through the use of collaborative action research models (e.g., J. Schensul, 1985; S. Schensul, 1985). This model facilitates intensive case studies of implementation within specific contexts, incorporating thick description to promote transferability to other contexts (e.g., Lincoln & Guba, 1985). This approach is potentially productive because of its emphasis on implementing potentially effective approaches to prevention in different settings, and on documenting the efficacy of these efforts, and because it is an approach that can be implemented readily by practitioners. At this early stage in the development of preventive approaches, we believe that it is critical for research to emphasize methods of implementation. A focus on methodology is potentially more productive than quantitative designs that use mean differences to measure the overall effectiveness of programs because it will help to develop a knowledge base about how theoretically and empirically sound programs are implemented and/or modified with maximum effectiveness across multiple settings. There are several priorities for research that merit consideration. Research concerning

prevention programs must consider the links among acceptability, integrity, and effectiveness; ecological variables that contribute to program success and failure; the role of collaborative consultation and its use of formative evaluation; the efficacy of various approaches to ongoing staff development (within a collaborative consultation model); and the implementation of comprehensive service delivery models that require collaborations within the school and among the school, family, and community.

# REFERENCES

Adey, P., & Shayer, M. (1993). An exploration of long-term transfer effects following an extended intervention program in the high school science curriculum. *Cognition and Instruction, 11*, 1–29.

Albee, G. W. (1968). Conceptual models and manpower requirements in psychology. *American Psychologist, 23*, 317–320.

Albee, G. W. (1982). Preventing psychopathology and promoting human potential. *American Psychologist, 37*, 1043–1050.

Albee, G. W. (1988). A model for classifying prevention programs. In G. W. Albee, J. M. Joffe, & L. A. Dusenbury (Eds.), *Prevention, powerlessness, and politics: Readings on social change* (pp. 13–22). Newbury Park, CA: Sage.

Albee, G. W. (1990). The futility of psychotherapy. *Journal of Mind and Behavior, 11*, 369–384.

Alpert, J. L. (1985). Change within a profession: Change, future, prevention, and school psychology. *American Psychologist, 40*, 1112–1121.

Alpert, J. L., & Meyers, J. (Eds.). (1983). *Training in consultation*. Springfield, IL: Thomas.

American Psychological Association. (1993). Guidelines for providers of psychological services to ethnic, linguistic, and culturally diverse populations. *American Psychologist, 48*, 45–48.

Anderson, G. L. (1989). Critical ethnography in education: Origins, current status, and new directions. *Review of Educational Research, 59*, 249–270.

Bandura, A. (1986). *Social foundations of thought and action: A social cognitive theory*. Englewood Cliffs, NJ: Prentice Hall.

Bandura, A. (1993). Perceived self-efficacy in cognitive development and functioning. *Educational Psychologist, 28*, 117–148.

Bandura, A., & Cervone, D. (1983). Self-evaluative and self-efficacy mechanisms governing the motivational effects of goal systems. *Journal of Personality and Social Psychology, 45*, 1017–1028.

Bangert-Drowns, R. L. (1988). The effects of school-based substance abuse education a meta-analysis. *Journal of Drug Education, 18*(3), 243–265.

Barclay, J. R. (1983). Moving toward a technology of

prevention: A model and some tentative findings. *School Psychology Review*, *12*, 228–239.

Bogdan, R., & Biklen, D. K. (1982). *Qualitative research for education: An introduction to theory and methods.* Boston: Allyn & Bacon.

Borkowski, J. G., & Muthukrishna, N. (1992). Moving metacognition into the classroom: "Working models" and effective strategy teaching. In M. Pressley, K. R. Harris, & J. T. Guthrie (Eds.), *Promoting academic competence and literacy in school* (pp. 478–501). San Diego: Academic Press.

Botvin, G. J., Baker, E., Filazzola, A. D., & Botvin, E. M. (1990). A cognitive-behavioral approach to substance abuse prevention: One-year follow-up. *Addictive Behaviors*, *15*, 47–63.

Botvin, G. J., & Dusenbury, L. (1989). Substance abuse prevention and the promotion of competence. In L. A. Bond & B. E. Compas (Eds.), *Primary prevention and promotion in the schools* (pp. 147–178). Newbury Park, CA: Sage.

Botvin, G. J., & Wills, T. A. (1985). Personal and social skills training: Cognitive behavioral approaches to substance abuse prevention. In C. Bell & R. Battjes (Eds.), *Prevention research: Deterring drug abuse among children and adolescents* (pp. 8–49). Washington, DC: National Institute on Drug Abuse (NIDA) Research Monograph.

Bower, E. M. (1964). The modification, mediation and utilization of stress during the school years. *American Journal of Orthopsychiatry*, *34*, 667–674.

Bronfenbrenner, U. (1989). Ecological systems theory. In R. Vasta (Ed.), *Annals of Child Development* (Vol. 6, pp. 187–249). Greenwich, CT: JAI Press.

Broussard, E. R. (1976). Neonatal predictions and outcome at 10/11 years. *Child Psychiatry and Human Development*, *7*, 85–93.

Brown, D., Pryzwansky, W. B., and Schulte, A. C. (1987). *Psychological consultation: Introduction to theory and practice.* Boston: Allyn & Bacon.

Bruce, C., & Emshoff, J. (1992). The SUPER II program: An early intervention program. In R. P. Lorion & J. G. Ross (Eds.), *Journal of Community Psychology. Programs for Change: Office for Substance Abuse Prevention Demonstration Models* (OSAP special issue) (pp. 10–21). Brandon, VT: Clinical Psychology Publishing.

Caplan, G. (1964). *Principles of preventive psychology.* New York: Basic Books.

Carlson, C. I., Paavola, J., & Talley, R. (1995). Historical, current, and future models of schools as health care delivery settings. *School Psychology Quarterly*, *10*, 184–202.

Carns, A. W., & Carns, M. R. (1991). Teaching study skills, metacognitive strategies, and metacognitive skills through self-diagnosed learning styles. *The School Counselor*, *38*, 341–346.

Cavallaro, D. M., & Meyers, J. (1986). Effects of study habits on cognitive restructuring and study skills training in the treatment of test anxiety with girls.

*Techniques: Journal for Remedial Education and Counseling*, *2*, 145–155.

Cicchetti, D., & Carlson, V. (Eds.). (1989). *Child maltreatment: Theory and research on the causes and consequences of child abuse and neglect.* New York: Cambridge University Press.

Comer, J. P. (1993). *School power: Implications of an intervention project.* New York: Free Press.

Compas, B. E. (1987). Coping with stress during childhood and adolescence. *Psychological Bulletin*, *101*, 393–403.

Compas, B. E., Howell, D. C., & LeDoux, N. (1989). Parent and child stress and symptoms: An integrative analysis. *Developmental Psychology*, *25*, 550–559.

Compas, B. E., Phares, V., & LeDoux, N. (1989). Stress and coping preventive interventions for children and adolescents. In L. A. Bond & B. E. Compas (Eds.), *Primary prevention and promotion in the schools* (pp. 319–340). Newbury Park, CA: Sage.

Costello, E. J. (1989). Developments in child psychiatric epidemiology. *Journal of the American Academy of Child and Adolescent Psychiatry*, *28*, 836–841.

Costello, E. J., Burns, B. J., Angold, A., & Leaf, P. J. (1993). How can epidemiology improve mental health services for children and adolescents? *Journal of the American Academy of Child and Adolescent Psychiatry*, *32*, 1106–1114.

Cowen, E. L. (1977). Baby steps toward primary prevention. *American Journal of Community Psychology*, *5*, 1–22.

Cowen, E. L. (1980). The Primary Mental Health Project: Yesterday, today and tomorrow. *Journal of Special Education*, *14*, 133–154.

Cowen, E. L. (1983). Primary prevention in mental health: Past, present, and future. In R. Felner, L. Jason, J. Moritsugu, & S. Farber (Eds.), *Preventive psychology: Theory, Research and Practice* (pp. 11–30). New York: Pergamon.

Cowen, E. L. (1984). A general structure model for primary prevention program development in mental health. *The Personnel and Guidance Journal*, *62*, 485–490.

Cowen, E. L. (1985). Person-centered approaches to primary prevention in mental health: Situation-focused and competence enhancement. *American Journal of Community Psychology*, *13*, 31–48.

Cowen, E. L., Gesten, E. L., & Wilson, A. B. (1979). The primary mental health project (PMHP): Evaluation of current program effectiveness. *American Journal of Community Psychology*, *7*, 293–303.

Cowen, E. L., Wyman, P. A., Work, W. C., & Parker, G. R. (1990). The Rochester child resilience project: Overview and summary of first year findings. *Development and Psychopathology*, *2*, 193–212.

Cummins, J. (1986). Empowering minority students: A

framework for intervention. *Harvard Educational Review, 56,* 18–36.

Curtis, M. J., & Meyers, J. (1985). Best practices in school-based consultation. In A. Thomas & J. Grimes (Eds.), *Best practices in school psychology* (pp. 74–94). Kent, OH: National Association of School Psychologists.

Deutsch, M. (1993). Educating for a peaceful world. *American Psychologist, 48,* 510–517.

Durlak, J. A. (1983). Social problem-solving as a primary prevention strategy. In R. Felner, L. Jason, J. Moritsugu, & S. Farber (Eds.), *Preventive psychology: Theory, research and practice* (pp. 31–48). New York: Pergamon.

Eisenberg, M., Nastasi, B. K., & Silva, T. U. (1995, August). *Socialization into sex in Sri Lanka.* Paper presented at the Fifth Sri Lanka Conference, University of New Hampshire, Durham.

Elam S. M., & Rose, L. C. (1995, September). The 27th Annual Phi Delta Kappa/Gallup Poll of the Public's Attitudes toward the public schools. *Phi Delta Kappan,* pp. 41–56.

Elias, M. J., & Branden, L. R. (1988). Primary prevention of behavioral and emotional problems in school-aged populations. *School Psychology Review, 17,* 581–592.

Elias, M. J., Gara, M., & Ubriaco, M. (1985). Sources of stress and support in children's transition to middle school: an empirical analysis. *Journal of Child Clinical Psychology, 14,* 112–118.

Elias, M. J., Gara, M., Ubriaco, M., Rothbaum, P. A., Clabby, J. F., & Schuyler, T. (1986). Impact of a preventive social problem solving intervention on children's coping with middle-school stressors. *American Journal of Community Psychology, 14,* 259–276.

Elliott, S. N., Witt, J. C., & Kratochwill, T. R. (1991). Selecting, implementing, and evaluating classroom interventions. In G. Stoner, M. R. Shinn, & H. M. Walker (Eds.), *Interventions for achievement and behavior problems* (pp. 99–136). Silver Spring, MD: National Association of School Psychologists.

Fantuzzo, J. W., King, J. A., & Heller, L. R. (1992). The effects of reciprocal peer tutoring on mathematics and school adjustment: A component analysis. *Journal of Educational Psychology, 84,* 331–339.

Felner, R. D., & Adan, A. M. (1988). The school transitional environment project: An ecological intervention and evaluation. In R. H. Price, E. L. Cowen, R. P. Lorion, & J. Ramos-McKay (Eds.), *14 ounces of prevention: A casebook for practitioners* (pp. 111–122). Washington, DC: American Psychological Association.

Felner, R. D., Ginter, M., & Primavera, J. (1982). Primary prevention during school transitions: Social support and environmental structure. *American Journal of Community Psychology, 10,* 277–290.

Felner, R. D., Primavera, J., & Cauce, A. M. (1981). *American Journal of Community Psychology, 9,* 449–459.

Flugum, K. R., & Reschly, D. J. (1994). Pre-referral interventions: Quality indices and outcomes. *Journal of School Psychology, 32,* 1–14.

Forehand, R., Armistead, L., & Klein, K. (1995). Children's school performance: The roles of interpersonal conflict and divorce. In B. A. Ryan, G. R. Adams, T. P. Gullota, R. P. Weissberg, & R. L. Hampton (Eds.), *The family-school connection* (pp. 250–269). Thousand Oaks, CA: Sage.

Fry, P. S., & Addington, J. (1984). Comparison of social problem solving of children from open and traditional classrooms: A two-year longitudinal study. *Journal of Educational Psychology, 76,* 318–329.

Fuchs, D., & Fuchs, L. S. (1989). Exploring effective and efficient pre-referral interventions: A component analysis of behavioral consultation. *School Psychology Review, 18,* 260–279.

Garmezy, N. (1983). Stressors of childhood. In N. Garmezy & M. Rutter (Eds.), *Stress, coping, and development in children* (pp. 73–84). New York: McGraw-Hill.

Garmezy, N., & Devine, V. (1985). Project competence: The Minnesota studies of children vulnerable to psychopathology. In N. Watt, E. J. Anthony, L. C. Wynne, & J. E. Rolf (Eds.), *Children at risk for schizophrenia* (pp. 289–232). Cambridge: Cambridge University Press.

Garmezy, N., & Rutter, M. (1983). *Stress, coping, and development in children.* New York: McGraw-Hill.

Gesten, E. L., DeApodaca, R. F., Rains, M., Weissberg, R. P., & Cowen, E. L. (1979). Promoting peer-related social competence in schools. In M. W. Kent & J. E. Rolf (Eds.), *Primary prevention of psychopathology. Vol. 3: Social competence in children* (pp. 220–247). Hanover, NH: University Press of New England.

Goldstein, A. P. (1988). *The prepare curriculum: Teaching pro-social competencies.* Champaign, IL: Research Press.

Goldstein, A. P., Reagles, K. W., & Amann, L. L. (1990). *Refusal skills: Preventing drug use in adolescents.* Champaign, IL: Research Press.

Graden, J. L., Casey, A., & Christenson, S. L. (1985). Implementing a prereferral intervention system: Part I. The model. *Exceptional Children, 51,* 377–384.

Graves, N. B., & Graves, T. D. (1985). Creating a cooperative learning environment: An ecological approach. In R. Slavin, S. Sharan, S. Kagan, R. H. Lazarowitz, C. Webb, & R. Schmuck (Eds.), *Learning to cooperate, cooperating to learn* (pp. 403–436). New York: Plenum.

Greenwood, C. R., Carta, J. J., & Maheady, L. (1991). Peer tutoring programs in the regular education classroom. In G. Stoner, M. R. Shinn, & H. M.

Walker (Eds.), *Interventions for achievement and behavior problems* (pp. 179–200). Silver Spring, MD: National Association of School Psychologists.

Grynch, J. H., & Fincham, F. D. (1992). Interventions for children of divorce: Toward greater integration of research and action. *Psychological Bulletin, 111*, 434–454.

Guba, E. G., & Lincoln, Y. S. (1981). *Effective evaluation: Improving usefulness of evaluation results through responsive and naturalistic approaches.* San Francisco: Jossey-Bass.

Guidubaldi, J., Cleminshaw, A. K., Perry, J. D., & McLoughlin, C. S. (1983). The impact of parental divorce on children: Report of the nationwide NASP study. *School Psychology Review, 12*, 300–323.

Guidubaldi, J., Cleminshaw, H. K., Perry, J. D., Nastasi, B. K., & Lightel, J. (1986). The role of selected family environment factors in children's post-divorce adjustment. *Family Relations, 35*, 141–151.

Guidubaldi, J., Perry, J. D., & Nastasi, B. K. (1987a). Assessment and intervention for children of divorce: Implications of the NASP-KSU nationwide study. In J. P. Vincent (Ed.), *Advances in family intervention, assessment and theory: A research annual* (Vol. 4, pp. 33–69). Greenwich, CT: JAI Press.

Guidubaldi, J., Perry, J. D., & Nastasi, B. K. (1987b). Growing up in a divorced family: Initial and long-term perspectives on children's adjustment. In S. Oskamp (Ed.), *Applied social psychology annual* Vol. 7, pp. 202–237. Beverly Hills, CA: Sage.

Hagin, R. A. (August, 1980). *Prediction, prevention, presumption.* Division 16 distinguished service award address presented at the Annual Meeting of the American Psychological Association, Montreal.

Hawkins, J. D., Catalano, R. F., & Miller, J. Y. (1992). Risk and protective factors for alcohol and other drug problems in adolescence and early adulthood: Implications for substance abuse prevention. *Psychological Bulletin, 112*, 64–105.

Hetherington, E., Cox, M., & Cox, R. (1982). Effects of divorce on parents and young children. In M. Lamb (Ed.), *Nontraditional families: Parenting and child development* (pp. 233–288). Hillsdale, NJ: Erlbaum.

Jason, L. A. & Ferone, L. (1981). From early secondary to primary preventive interventions in schools. *Journal of Prevention, 1*, 156–173.

Johnson, D. W., & Johnson, R. T. (1983). The socialization and achievement crisis: Are cooperative learning experiences the solution? *Applied Social Psychology Annual, 4*, 119–164.

Johnson, D. W., Johnson, R. T., Buckman, L. A., & Richards, P. S. (1985). The effect of prolonged implementation of cooperative learning on social support within the classroom. *The Journal of Psychology, 119*, 405–411.

Johnson, D. W., Johnson, R., Dudley, B., & Acikgoz, K. (1991). *Peer mediation: Effects of conflict resolution training on elementary schools students.* Minneapolis, MN: Cooperative Learning Center.

Katz, A. H., & Hermalin, J. (1987). Self-help and prevention. In J. Hermalin & J. A. Morell (Eds.), *Prevention planning in mental health* (pp. 151–190). Beverly Hills, CA: Sage.

Knitzer, J. (1993). Children's mental health policy: Challenging the future. *Journal of Emotional and Behavioral Disorders, 1*, 8–16.

Laurent, J., Hadler, J. R., & Stark, K. D. (1994). A multiple-stage screening procedure for the identification of childhood anxiety disorders. *School Psychology Quarterly, 9*(4), 239–255.

Lazarus, R. S., & Folkman, S. (1984). *Stress, appraisal and coping.* New York: Springer.

Lincoln, Y. S., & Guba, E. G. (1985)., *Naturalistic inquiry.* Newbury Park, CA: Sage.

Lochman, J. E. (1992). Cognitive-behavioral intervention with aggressive boys: Three-year follow-up and preventive effects. *Journal of Consulting and Clinical Psychology, 60*, 426–432.

Lorion, R. P., Work, W. C., & Hightower, A. D. (1984). A school-based multilevel preventive intervention: Issues in program development and evaluation. *The Personnel and Guidance Journal, 62*, 479–484.

Meyers, B., Meyers, J., Gelzheiser, L. M., Muhoff, I., Kelly, E., & Muller, C. (April, 1995). Observing a role in transition: Principal voices, shared decision making, and Goals 2000. Paper presented at the Annual Meeting of the American Educational Research Association, San Francisco.

Meyers, J. (1989). The practice of psychology in the schools for the primary prevention of learning and adjustment problems in children: A perspective from the field of education. In L. A. Bond & B. E. Compas (Eds.), *Primary prevention and promotion in the schools* (pp. 391–422). Newbury Park, CA: Sage.

Meyers, J. (1995). A consultation model for school psychological services: 20 years later. *Journal of Educational and Psychological Consultation, 6*, 59–71.

Meyers, J., Brent, D., Faherty, E., & Modafferi, C. (1993). Caplan's contributions to the practice of psychology in schools. In W. P. Erchul (Ed.), *Consultation in community, school and organizational practice: Gerald Caplan's contributions to professional psychology* (pp. 99–122). Washington, DC: Taylor & Francis.

Meyers, J., & Parsons, R. D. (1987). Prevention planning in the school system. In J. Hermalin & J. Morell (Eds.), *Prevention planning in mental health* (pp. 111–150). Beverly Hills, CA: Sage.

Meyers, J., Parsons, R. D. & Martin, R. (1979). *Mental health consultation in the schools.* San Francisco: Jossey-Bass.

Meyers, J., Valentino, C., Meyers, J., Boretti, M., &

Brent, D. (in press). *Journal of Educational and Psychological Consultation.*

Moos, R. H. (1979). *Evaluating educational environments.* San Francisco: Jossey-Bass.

Nastasi, B. K. (1994, March). The relevance of ethnography to school psychology research and practice. Paper presented at the Annual Meeting of the National Association of School Psychologists, Seattle, WA.

Nastasi, B. K. (1995a). Is early identification of children of alcoholics necessary for preventive intervention? Reaction to Havey & Dodd. *Journal of School Psychology, 33,* 327–345.

Nastasi, B. K. (1995b), *UWASA Project Coding Scheme.* Albany: State University of New York.

Nastasi, B. K., & Clements, D. H. (1991). Research on cooperative learning: Implications for practice. *School Psychology Review, 20,* 110–131.

Nastasi, B. K., & Clements, D. H. (1993). Motivational and social outcomes of cooperative computer education environments. *Journal of Computing in Childhood Education, 4*(1), 15–43.

Nastasi, B. K., & DeZolt, D. M. (1994), *School interventions for children of alcoholics.* New York: Guilford.

National Education Goals Panel. (1992). *The national education goals report: Building a nation of learners.* Washington, DC: U.S. Government Printing Office.

Neel, R. S. (1981). How to put the consultant to work in consulting teaching. *Behavioral Disorders, 6,* 78–81.

Orlandi, M. A., Weston, R., & Epstein, L. G. (Eds.). (1992). *Cultural competence for evaluators: A guide for alcohol and other drug abuse prevention practitioners working with ethnic/racial communities* (Vol. OSAP Cultural Competence Series 1). Rockville, MD: U.S. Office of Substance Abuse Prevention.

Paris, S. G., & Winograd, P. (1990). How metacognition can promote academic learning and instruction. In B. F. Jones & L. Idol (Eds.), *Dimensions of thinking and cognitive instruction* (pp. 15–51). Hillsdale, NJ: Erlbaum.

Parsons, R. D. & Meyers, J. (1984). *Developing consultation skills: A guide to training, development and assessment for human services professionals.* San Francisco: Jossey-Bass.

Pedro-Carroll, J. L., Alpert-Gillis, L. J., & Cowen, E. L. (1992). An evaluation of the efficacy of a preventive intervention for 4th–6th grade urban children of divorce. *Journal of Primary Prevention, 13,* 115–130.

Pedro-Carroll, J. L., & Cowen, E. L. (1985). The children of divorce intervention project: An investigation of the efficacy of a school-based prevention program. *Journal of Consulting and Clinical Psychology, 53,* 603–611.

Pedro-Carroll, J. L., Cowen, E. L., Hightower, A. D., & Guare, J. C. (1986). Preventive interventions with latency-aged children of divorce: A replication study. *American Journal of Community Psychology, 14,* 277–290.

Pentz, M. A. (1985). Social competence and self-efficacy as determinants of substance abuse in adolescence. In S. Shiffman & T. A. Wills (Eds.), *Coping and substance use* (pp. 117–142). Orlando, FL: Academic Press.

Pentz, M. A., Alexander, P. S., Cormach, C. C., & Light, J. (1989). Issues in the development and process of community-based alcohol and drug prevention: The Midwestern Prevention Project (MPP). In N. Giesbrecht, P. Conley, R. W. Denniston, L. Gliksman, H. Holder, A. Pederson, R. Room, & M. Shain (Eds.), *Research, action, and the community: Experiences in the prevention of alcohol and other drug problems,* (OSAP Monograph 4, pp. 136–143). Rockville, MD: U.S. Office of Substance Abuse Prevention.

Pflaum, S. W. (1991). (Ed.). *Health education: Health educators and teacher educators collaborate.* Albany: New York State Education Department.

Phillips, B. N., Martin, R. P., & Meyers, J. (1972). Interventions in relation to anxiety in school. In C. D. Spielberger (Ed.), *Anxiety: Current trends in theory and research* (pp. 409–464). New York: Academic Press.

Rappaport, J. (1981). In praise of paradox: A social policy of empowerment over prevention. *American Journal of Community Psychology, 9,* 1–25.

Ratnayake, P. U., Silva, T. U., de Silva, M. W. A., Schensul, S., Schensul, J., Eisenberg, M., Lewis, J., & Nastasi, B. (1995, August). Attitudes toward virginity and its effects on sexual behavior in a sample of Sri Lankan youth. Paper presented at the Third USAID HIV/AIDS Prevention Conference, Washington, DC.

Reynolds, W. M. (1986). A model for the screening and identification of depressed children and adolescents in school settings. *Professional School Psychology, 1,* 117–129.

Rhodes, J. E., Ebert, L., & Fischer, K. (1992). Natural mentors: An overlooked resource in the social networks of young African-American mothers. *American Journal of Community Psychology, 20,* 445–461.

Rhodes, J. E., & Jason, L. A. (1988). *Preventing substance abuse among children and adolescents.* Elmsford, NY: Pergamon.

Rosenfield, S. A. (1987). *Instructional consultation.* Hillsdale, NJ: Erlbaum.

Ross, J. G., Saavedra, P. J., Shur, G. H., Winters, F., & Felner, R. D. (1992). The effectiveness of after-school program for primary grade latchkey students on precursors of substance abuse. In R. P. Lorion & J. G. Ross (Eds.), *Journal of Community Psychology. Programs for Change: Office for Substance Abuse Prevention Demonstration Models*

(OSAP Special Issue, pp. 22–38). Brandon, VT: Clinical Psychology Publishing.

Rutter, M. (1979). Protective factors in children's responses to stress and disadvantage. In M. W. Kent, & J. E. Rolf (Eds.), *Primary prevention of psychopathology: Social competence in children* (Vol. 3, pp. 49–74). Hanover, NH: University Press of New England.

Rutter, M. (1981). Stress, coping, and development: Some issues and some questions. *Journal of Child Psychology and Psychiatry, 126,* 493–509.

Rutter, M., Cox, A., Tupling, C., Berger, M., & Yule, W. (1975). Attainment and adjustment in two geographical areas: I. The prevalence of psychiatric disorder. *British Journal of Psychiatry, 126,* 493–509.

Schensul, J. J. (1985). Systems consistency in field research, dissemination, and social change. *American Behavioral Scientist, 29,* 186–204.

Schensul, J. J. (1994). *Teen action research project.* Unpublished data, Institute for Community Research, Hartford, CT.

Schensul, S. L. (1985). Science, theory, and application in anthropology. *American Behavioral Scientist, 29,* 164–185.

Schinke, S. P., Botvin, G. J., & Orlandi, M. A. (1991). *Substance abuse in children and adolescents: Evaluation and intervention* (Vol. 22). Newbury Park, CA: Sage.

Schinke, S. P., Botvin, G. J., Trimble, J. E., Orlandi, M. A., Gilchrist, L. D., & Locklear, V. S. (1988). Preventing substance abuse among American-Indian adolescents: A bicultural competence skills approach. *Journal of Counseling Psychology, 35*(1), 87–90.

Schmuck, R. A. & Schmuck, P. A. (1988). *Group processes in the classroom* (5th ed.). Dubuque, IA: W. C. Brown.

Schunk, D. H. & Swartz, C. W. (1993). Goals and process feedback: Effects on self-efficacy and writing achievement. *Contemporary Educational Psychology, 18,* 337–354.

Schweinhart, L. J., & Weikart, D. P. (1989). Early childhood experience and its effects. In L. A. Bond & B. E. Compas (Eds.), *Primary prevention and promotion in the schools* (pp. 81–105). Newbury Park, CA: Sage.

Scriven, M. (1980). Self-referent research I. *Educational Researcher, 9,* 7–11.

Shure, M. B. (1988). How to think, not what to think: A cognitive approach to prevention. In L. A. Bond & B. M. Wagner (Eds.), *Families in transition: Primary prevention programs that work.* Newbury Park, CA: Sage.

Shure, M. B., & Spivack, G. (1988). Interpersonal cognitive problem solving. In R. H. Price, E. L. Cowen, R. P. Lorion, & J. Ramos-McKay (Eds.), *14 ounces of prevention: A casebook for practitioners* (pp. 69–82). Washington, DC: American Psychological Association.

Silva, T. U., Ratnayake, P. U., Schensul, S., Schensul, J., de Silva, M. W. A., Eisenberg, M., Lewis, J., & Nastasi, B. (1995). Youth and sexual risk in Sri Lanka. Research in progress. University of Peradeniya, Sri Lanka; University of Connecticut; Institute for Community Research, Hartford, CT; State University of New York–Albany.

Solomon, D., Watson, M. S., Delucchi, K. L., Schaps, E., & Battistich, V. (1988). Enhancing children's prosocial behavior in the classroom. *American Educational Research Journal, 25,* 527–554.

Spradley, J. P. (1979). *Ethnographic interview.* New York: Holt, Rhinehart & Winston.

Spradley, J. P. (1980). *Participant observation.* New York: Holt Rhinehart & Winston.

Stewart, D. W., & Shamdasani, P. N. (1990). *Focus groups: Theory and practice.* Newbury Park, CA: Sage.

Stolberg, A. L. (1988). Prevention programs for divorcing families. In L. A. Bond, & B. M. Wagner (Eds.), *Families in transition: Primary prevention programs that work* (pp. 225–251). Newbury Park, CA: Sage.

Stolberg, A. L., & Garrison, K. M. (1985). Evaluating a primary prevention program for children of divorce: The divorce adjustment project. *American Journal of Community Psychology, 13,* 111–124.

Stoner, G., Shinn, M. R., & Walker, H. M. (Eds.). (1991). *Interventions for achievement and behavior problems.* Washington, DC: National Association of School Psychologists.

Strauss, A. & Corbin, J. (1990). *Basis of qualitative research.* Newbury Park, CA: Sage.

Tharinger, D. (1995). Roles for psychologists in emerging models of school-related health and mental health services. *School Psychology Quarterly, 10,* 203–216.

Tobler, N. S. (1986). Meta-analysis of 143 adolescent drug prevention programs: Quantitative outcome results of program participants compared to a control or comparison group. *The Journal of Drug Issues, 16*(4), 537–567.

Tobler, N. S. (1992). Drug prevention programs can work: Research findings. *Journal of Addictive Diseases, 11*(3), 1–28.

Tricket, E. J. (1984). Toward a distinctive community psychology: An ecological metaphor for the conduct of community research and the nature of training. *American Journal of Community Psychology, 12,* 261–280.

Trickett, E. J., & Berman, D. (1989). Taking ecology seriously: A community development approach to individually based preventive interventions in schools. In L. A. Bond & B. E. Compas (Eds.), *Primary prevention and promotion in the schools.* Newbury Park, CA: Sage.

Wallerstein, J. S. (1983). Children of divorce: The psychological tasks of the child. *American Journal of Orthopsychiatry, 53,* 230–243.

Weikart, D. P. (1984). Early childhood education: Lessons for the prevention of mental health problems in children. Address presented to the Fourth Annual Delaware Valley Conference on the Future of Psychology in the Schools, sponsored by the Department of School Psychology, Temple University, Philadelphia.

Weiss, C. H. (1993). Shared decision making about what? A comparison of schools with and without teacher participation. *Teachers College Record*, *95*, 69–92.

Weissberg, R. P., Caplan, M., & Harwood, R. L. (1991). Promoting competent young people in competence-enhancing environments: A systems-based perspective on primary prevention. *Journal of Consulting and Clinical Psychology*, *59*, 830–841.

Weissberg, R. P., Caplan, M., & Sivo, P. J. (1989). A new conceptual framework for establishing school-based social competence promotion programs. In L. A. Bond & B. E. Compas (Eds.), *Primary prevention and promotion in the schools* (pp. 255–296). Newbury Park, CA: Sage.

Weissberg, R. P., Cowen, E. L., Lotyczewski, B. S., & Gesten, E. L. (1983). The Primary Mental Health Project: Seven consecutive years of program outcome research. *Journal of Consulting and Clinical Psychology*, *51*, 100–107.

Werner, E. E. (1989). High-risk children in young adulthood: A longitudinal study from birth to 32 years. *American Journal of Orthopsychiatry*, *59*, 72–81.

Werner, E. E., & Smith, R. S. (1982). *Vulnerable but invincible: A study of resilient children*. New York: McGraw-Hill.

Wiggins, G. (1989). Teaching to the (authentic) test. *Educational Leadership*, *46*, 41–49.

Wiggins, G. (1993, November). Assessment, authenticity, context, and validity. *Phi Delta Kappan*, pp. 200–214.

## CHAPTER 30

# SECONDARY PREVENTION: APPLICATIONS THROUGH INTERVENTION ASSISTANCE PROGRAMS AND INCLUSIVE EDUCATION

JOSEPH E. ZINS
*University of Cincinnati*
TIMOTHY E. HERON
*The Ohio State University*
YVONNE L. GODDARD
*The Ohio State University*

Most readers will probably agree that it is more cost-effective and efficient to require children to wear bicycle safety helmets than to treat their head injuries, to keep first-time offenders out of the juvenile justice system than to rehabilitate them, or to enable families to avoid poverty than to help them out of it. Similarly in education, it might reasonably be assumed that it is better to prevent academic failure or to intervene with students who are at risk than to provide costly remedial programs later. Such fields as community psychology, epidemiology, and public health regularly have advocated for preventive approaches, but educators and school psychologists have not been proactive in addressing antecedent conditions associated with failure (Simeonsson, 1994; Zins & Forman, 1988).

Today, there continues to be a reliance on rehabilitative and treatment approaches in educational settings to solve the vast majority of the problems that arise. Students, in essence, too often are "required" to fail if they are to receive assistance or have their instructional programs modified. Even when interventions are provided, they tend to be directed toward individual students, with little attention devoted to the broader ecological conditions that may be associated with failure or to systemic changes that could benefit large numbers of students. For the most part the educational establishment in general and the educational reform movement in particular have

been remarkably quiet about prevention, and programs for students in special education who are at particular risk are especially underdeveloped (Zins, Travis, & Freppon, 1997).

The major thesis of this chapter is that prevention should be an integral component of any effort to improve our nation's educational system, that more resources need to be devoted toward such endeavors, and that school psychologists should be leaders in this movement. No single approach can provide the type of support and the range of assistance necessary to meet the needs of all students, teachers, and families, but rather a network and continuum of integrated, cohesive service delivery options is needed. In this chapter we discuss one component of a comprehensive service delivery system, that is, secondary prevention. We begin our discussion by examining the need for prevention and different approaches to it. Next we provide detailed reviews of two applications of secondary prevention: intervention assistance programs and strategies for inclusive educational settings. We conclude by offering some observations about school-based secondary prevention based on this review.

## NEED FOR PREVENTIVE INTERVENTIONS

This section briefly outlines the need for school-based prevention services. Interested readers are referred to the more extensive discussions of the rationale for providing these services in schools (e.g., Bond & Compas, 1989; Dryfoos, 1990; Durlak, 1995; Weissberg & Greenberg, 1997), as well as of the need for school psychologists to be involved in these efforts (e.g., Zins, Conyne, & Ponti, 1988; Zins & Wagner, 1997). These sources provide sound arguments for preventive interventions, but most of their focus is on primary rather than secondary prevention.

It should come as no surprise to school psychologists that one of the most compelling reasons for prevention services has to do with the overwhelming number of students who experience mental health and educational problems and the limited resources available to address their needs. As most readers are aware, there even has been criticism from some segments of the public that too large a percentage of our educational dollars are spent on too few students (i.e., those in special education), which they perceive as detrimental to regular education students. Yet, epidemiological data indicate that 15% to 22% of children and adolescents have mental health problems severe enough to warrant treatment (Costello, 1990; Tuma, 1989). Moreover, there is evidence that 25% of those aged 10 to 17 are extremely vulnerable to the negative consequences of engaging in multiple high-risk social and health behaviors (e.g., violence, pregnancy, drug abuse, and AIDS), with another 25% being moderately vulnerable (Dryfoos, 1990). However, fewer than 20% of these young people with mental health problems currently receive appropriate services (Tuma, 1989). Academic problems similarly affect large numbers of students and pose great challenges to those responsible for their education. All of these factors point to an increasing need for additional special education services and other forms of remedial assistance, *if* we continue to rely on current service delivery models that focus on treatment and remediation. Unless changes are instituted, it is easy to project that our educational system will become inundated with greater demands for special education and related services.

In contrast to this scenario, there is mounting evidence that many students who are served within a special education context could be successful in a less restrictive setting (e.g., Lipsky & Gartner, 1989). Too often, students are placed in special education because they were caught in the refer-test-place service delivery model. That is, they experienced some type of difficulty, and consequently their teachers or parents sought assistance by asking for a special education evaluation. Most of these students subsequently were identified as eligible for special education and then placed in a special education program. Yet, there is considerable evidence that instructional, environmental, or other modifications and adequate support services from special services staff may have enabled them to succeed in the general education setting. Clearly, school psychologists, who typically spend a considerable amount of their time in this identification and placement process (Reschly & Wilson, 1995), could instead provide supportive assistance to these students and their teachers and families.

Interest in prevention also has been stimulated by a variety of federal-level initiatives. For example, 20 years ago the President's Commission on Mental Health (1978) declared that we should "undertake a concerted national effort to prevent mental disabilities" (p. 10). More recently the U.S. Surgeon General's *Healthy People 2000* report (U.S. Department of Health and Human Services, 1995) called for increased national efforts for health promotion and disease prevention. A parallel set of national educational goals was developed by state governors and the U.S. Department of Education. Among its major goals are the promotion of school readiness and the assurance of adequate environments for learning, for example, one free of drugs (America 2000: An Educational Strategy, 1991), which are both prevention-oriented. Weissberg and Greenberg (1997) present a more extensive account of these events at the federal level.

More recently, the work of Howard Gardner (1993) on multiple intelligences and Daniel Goleman (1995) on emotional intelligence have exerted some relevant influence. There is a growing awareness that when schools attend to students' social and emotional education, as is done in most prevention programs, problem behaviors decrease, academic achievement increases, and the quality of the relationships surrounding students are enhanced (Elias et al., 1997). These findings provide additional support for prevention and competence-enhancement programs.

For all of these reasons, we have concluded that preventively oriented services must become more widely available in schools if the needs of more students are to be met. Further, we strongly believe that school psychologists should take a leadership role in this movement.

## APPROACHES TO PREVENTION

In this section we begin by reviewing the definitions of three widely recognized approaches to prevention—primary, secondary, and tertiary—which were introduced in the public health and epidemiological fields in the 1950s (Clark & Leavell, 1953, 1958) and adapted by Caplan (1961) for the mental health field shortly thereafter. This review is followed by a discussion of an alternative approach to classifying preventive interventions that has been proposed by a number of individuals in the prevention field.

When most people think of prevention, they probably have in mind *primary prevention*. This approach has a dual focus: to stop the development of problems and to enhance well-being. Accordingly, primary prevention efforts are designed to reduce the occurrence of disorders and to strengthen individuals' competencies so that they do not develop maladaptive behaviors (Cowen, 1983; Weissberg & Greenberg, 1997). Examples include social problem-solving programs in elementary schools, smoking prevention programs in the junior high, and community service projects for high school students to promote bonding and attachment.

Distinctions have been made between primary prevention, and health promotion and competence enhancement (e.g., Mrazek & Haggerty, 1994). Health promotion focuses on the enhancement of well-being and competence rather than interventions for preventing psychological, social, and educational problems. In other words, there is an emphasis on health rather than illness. However, others argue that a synthesis of approaches and a broad conceptualization that incorporates risk reduction and enhancement of protective factors is needed (Carnegie Corporation on Adolescent Development, 1995; Consortium on the School-Based Promotion of Social Competence, 1994).

*Secondary prevention* is directed toward early intervention and treatment of problems, keeping less severe problems from becoming more debilitating, shortening the duration of problems, or lowering the prevalence of problematic behaviors (Cowen, 1983; Weissberg & Greenberg, 1997). In this approach, there is usually some type of screening to identify those who show early signs of maladaptive behavior, and interventions are provided promptly so that more serious consequences are averted. Examples include support groups for children whose families are experiencing a recent divorce, after-school cross-age tutoring for students who have begun to fall behind academically, and early intervention preschool programs. Consultative services provided to teachers who were experiencing difficulties managing the behavior of children in their classes could be another example.

Strategies focused on the treatment of individuals who have "established" or entrenched disabilities or disorders and that seek to reduce the adverse consequences of these problems are considered *tertiary prevention*. These interventions are necessary for many students and are the most prevalent in the schools. Traditional special education resource rooms or self-contained classes, special schools for students who have engaged in serious disruptive or violent behaviors, and treatment programs for those who abuse drugs are examples of tertiary prevention. These approaches more appropriately are classified as rehabilitation than prevention (Mrazek & Haggerty, 1994; Weissberg & Greenberg, 1997).

In real-world applications it is often difficult to differentiate between primary and secondary prevention efforts. These programs are often overlapping, as both are proactive, usually population- or large-group oriented, and delivered before the onset of a full-blown disorder (Durlak, 1995). Also, both are antecedent interventions in the sense that they help preclude engagement in seriously maladaptive behaviors and influence the probability of more appropriate behavior. For these reasons, it has been suggested that the "term *prevention* be reserved for only those interventions that occur before the initial onset of a clinically diagnosable disorder" (Munoz, Mrazek, & Haggerty, 1996, p. 1118). Thereafter, interventions that focus on a disorder would be considered in the realm of treatment, and those designed to reduce relapses viewed as maintenance interventions. From this perspective, prevention is reconceptualized to include universal, selective, and indicated preventive interventions (Gordon, 1983, 1987; Mrazek & Haggery, 1994).

Interventions that target the "general public or a whole population group that has not been identified on the basis of individual risk" (Mrazek & Haggerty, 1994, pp. 24–25) are included as *universal preventive interventions* (e.g., directed toward all elementary school students). Weissberg and Greenberg (1997) suggested that "because these programs are positive, proactive, and provided independent of risk status, their potential for stigmatizing participants is minimized and they may be more readily accepted and adopted (p. 890)." *Selective prevention interventions* are directed toward "individuals or a subgroup of the population whose risk of developing mental disorders is significantly higher than average. Risk groups may be identified on the basis of biological, psychological, or social risk factors that are known to be associated with the onset of a mental [or educational] disorder" (Mrazek & Haggerty, 1994, p. 25). For example, students making the transition from elementary to junior high school are at risk for academic failure. *Indicated prevention strategies* focus on "high-risk individuals who are identified as having minimal but detectable signs or symptoms foreshadowing mental disorder [educational failure] or biological markers indicating a predisposition for mental disorder, but who do not meet DSM-III-R [*Diagnostic and Statistical Manual, Third Edition, Revised*] diagnostic levels at the current time" (p. 25). Students who have failed several courses, for instance, are at risk for grade retention and then for dropping out of school.

Although this alternative classification scheme emphasizes the importance of considering risk and protective factors in developing prevention programs and thereby advances the field, additional clarification of the terms is needed (Weissberg & Greenberg, 1997). Furthermore, there is concern that this perspective is unnecessarily limiting because it does not emphasize health promotion efforts, which are not driven by a focus on disorders as part of the overall prevention strategy (Albee, 1996). A number of concrete applications of this taxonomy has been provided by Simeonsson (1994).

Prevention traditionally has been used to refer to interventions with groups or populations, and it is most cost-effective and efficient when delivered in this manner. However, similar types of efforts that alter antecedent conditions to set the occasion for appropriate performance can be extended to individual students, as we illustrate later in the chapter.

# EXAMPLES OF SECONDARY PREVENTION: INTERVENTION ASSISTANCE PROGRAMS AND INCLUSIVE EDUCATION STRATEGIES

In this section two examples of secondary preventive interventions are examined in terms of what these services are, how they are delivered, and their outcomes. These approaches could also be considered selective or indicated prevention strategies.

Each year increasing numbers of students are referred for special education services (Office of Special Education, 1993). This trend, which has continued since the implementation of Public Law 94-142, prompted Secretary of the Department of Education M. Will (1986) to call for alternative models of service delivery, so that general education teachers can receive support from special services personnel, and for additional efforts in meeting individual needs in the general education classroom. Rather than simply referring students who experience difficulty for a psychoeducational evaluation, usually numerous interventions can be provided that may alleviate the problems (Zins, Curtis, Graden, & Ponti, 1988). For instance, early intervention preschool programs can be established, the reading curriculum changed, teacher's instructional approaches altered, peer tutoring provided, disciplinary policies modified, staff development programs introduced, or smoking cessation efforts instituted, to assist students who are beginning to experience academic, social, or health problems. Some of these approaches focus on children, whereas others are directed toward elements in the environment or system that influence children's learning and behavior. Both primary and secondary prevention interventions may be appropriate for addressing these concerns.

In this chapter we focus our review on two specific approaches to service delivery to illustrate the range of possible secondary prevention efforts. Both *intervention assistance programs* and *inclusive education* are services delivery options that represent mechanisms of providing additional assistance to students at risk and are means of bridging the gap between general and special education. They are not, however, interventions in and of themselves in the sense of directly changing students' behavior. They have the goals of keeping students in the least restrictive placements, creating learning environments that can better accommodate children's needs, and increasing the success of students in the mainstream setting. They are also components of a comprehensive continuum of educational services that should be available to all students.

## Intervention Assistance Programs

A variety of terms have been applied to programs that are implemented proactively to support students and their teachers in the general education setting. Although each approach has its unique aspects, they also have a great deal in common. That is, through application of a joint, systematic problem-solving process, appropriate interventions are developed after it is recognized that a student is experiencing learning, behavioral, and/or social problems and before making a referral for special education assessment and subsequent decision making. The individual needs and diversity of students are acknowledged, and it is hoped that teachers' skills are also improved through this process. In contrast to traditional supportive assistance, services provided through this orientation are available to all students without the necessity of attaching potentially stigmatizing labels; are provided on a more timely basis; and can include a wide variety of interventions, ranging from those focused on an individual student to those with a systemic focus. Programs within this general framework include intervention assistance programs, prereferral intervention, student support teams, and so forth. As explained later, however, the most accurate term for these consultation-based procedures is *intervention assistance programs* (Zins, Curtis, Graden, & Ponti, 1988). The process is illustrated in Figure 30.1 and is described in Zins and Johnson (1994).

Most descriptions of the intervention assistance process were introduced in the mid- to later 1980s. However, school consultation, the foundation on which these activities are based, has a much longer history, particularly in school psychology (see Erchul, 1993; Gutkin & Curtis, 1982). Accordingly, these approaches are not entirely new in most respects but rather describe methods in which consultation services are provided somewhat differently than traditionally was done in the individual case-centered approach. As Christenson, Ysseldyke, and Algozzine (1982) observed, "If intervention within the classroom through consultation with the classroom teacher occurred before referral,

instructional planning might improve for students" (p. 344).

Several advances in service delivery are reflected in the intervention assistance process. A primary step forward is that these programs represent formalized sanction (or legitimization) for providing consultation services in a coordinated manner on a system-wide basis. They also make such assistance another option along the continuum of services for students experiencing school-related difficulties, which is consistent with Individuals with Disabilities Education Act (IDEA) mandates and a preventive focus. An additional contribution is that these programs introduced the notion of a team approach that is not associated with special education (e.g., multidisciplinary teams for assessment and placement purposes). Moreover, these procedures have spread well beyond school psychology and have captured the interest of a wide range of support personnel, including special educators, speech and language pathologists, school social workers, and guidance counselors, as well as general education teachers and educational administrators. Consequently, consultative services are now more broadly recognized and utilized in schools (see Chapter 23, by Gutkin and Curtis, for a discussion of consultation), and they are a major means of facilitating the delivery of many secondary prevention programs (see, however, cautions about the preventive benefits of consultation discussed in Zins, 1995).

*Prereferral intervention* appears to be the most commonly used term for this process, with *Teacher Assistance Teams, Intervention Assistance Teams, Teacher Support Teams, Student Assistance or Support Teams*, and *Mainstream Assistance Teams* being among the others most widely used. Each of these terms, while usually referring to procedures similar to the intervention assistance process, is problematic and has led to much confusion, as has been articulated elsewhere (e.g., Zins, Curtis, Graden, & Ponti, 1988). Briefly, *prereferral* suggests that the process ultimately results in a special education assessment referral (e.g., Sindelar, Griffin, Smith, & Watanabe, 1992), an outcome contrary to a primary goal of the process. The confusion associated with this term apparently even led the Department of Public Instruction in one state in the mid-1980s to refer to the process as "preassessment activities." Use of *team* suggests that a group (team) of individuals is always involved (e.g., Graebner & Dobbs, 1984; Hayek, 1987), when in fact the

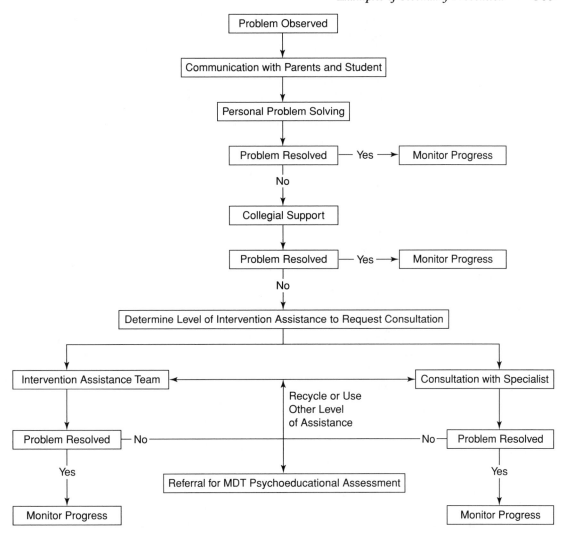

**FIGURE 30.1** **Flow chart for the intervention assistance process.**
Reprinted from J. E. Zins & L. J. Johnson, Prereferral intervention for students with special needs. In T. Husén & T. N. Postleth-waite (Eds.), *The international encyclopedia of education: Vol. 8. Research and studies* (2nd ed.). Copyright 1994, p. 4660, with kind permission from Elsevier Science Ltd., The Boulevard, Langford Lane, Kidlington 0X5 1GB, UK.

majority of interventions do not require the involvement of a team but rather only a single consultant and consultees. The words *teacher* and *student* suggest that these individuals are the focus, when in fact either or both could be. A final problem is that different authors use the same term to refer to procedures that are not necessarily similar. For example, Bay, Bryan, and O'Connor (1994) and Sindelar et al. both discuss prereferral intervention. The first authors view the process as an alternative to special education referral, whereas the second group notes that "it is clear that prereferral intervention ends

with referral for special education assessment" (p. 245).

## Intervention Assistance Services

Although there may be general agreement that intervention assistance programs are a method of providing secondary prevention interventions (Zins & Ponti, 1987), there are many differences, and often substantial ones, in how such programs are organized, implemented, and delivered. The intervention assistance process discussed in Zins, Curtis, Graden, and Ponti (1988) is, we believe, the most complete description available, as the other approaches often do not contain adequate descriptions of their theoretical foundations or of their procedural components. Thus, most truly cannot be considered "models." For these reasons, replication of these approaches is difficult, and generalizations and implications that can be drawn are limited. Nevertheless, our discussion covers many of the different approaches because of the commonalities among them. Readers are cautioned, however, that some inaccuracy inevitably results when these variations are discussed together, and conclusions about their effectiveness therefore must be considered carefully.

In general, the programs selected for inclusions in this section (a) are implemented proactively to support students and/or teachers, (b) involve application of a problem-solving process, (c) result in the development of interventions for students before a referral for special education assessment and decision making, and (d) are provided on a schoolwide basis. Only brief summaries are included here; readers are referred to the original sources for additional information.

One of the earliest descriptions of a team approach was provided in a brief article by Chalfant, Pysh, and Moultrie (1979). The Teacher Assistance Team (TAT) consists of a three-member group of teacher-peers and often parents, who help the referring teacher obtain assistance for children who are experiencing difficulties. Special services staff and administrators sometimes serve on the team. Hayek (1986) expanded on their discussion, addressing such issues as the need for staff training, staff attitudes toward the process, and facilitating adoption of TATs. Later, Chalfant and Pysh (1989) described the process as "a forum where classroom teachers can meet and engage in a positive, productive, collaborative, problem-solving process to help students indirectly, that is, through teacher consultation" (p. 50), and they emphasized a teacher- rather than a student-orientation. The School Consultation Committee (McGlothlin, 1981) is similar to the TAT.

Prereferral intervention programs, which have been described by a variety of authors (e.g., Bay et al., 1994; Graden, Casey, & Christenson, 1985; Meyers, Valentino, Meyers, Boretti, & Brent, 1996; Nelson, Smith, Taylor, Dodd, & Reavis, 1991), represent a consultation-based approach in which a teacher requests assistance informally from a consultant (school psychologist, special education teacher, school social worker,

etc.), formally from a building team, or from some combination of these individuals. The goals are to "reduce inappropriate referrals for testing, reduce inappropriate placements in special education, and provide relevant, needed intervention assistance to students and teachers in the least restrictive educational environment" (Graden, Casey, & Christenson, 1985, p. 384). The approach consists of four prereferral stages (request for consultation, consultation, observation, and conference) and two formal referral, assessment, and decision-making process stages. Although the last two stages occur only if appropriate, their inclusion in the initial description of the approach, as well as the word *prereferral*, have been construed by some to indicate that the process ultimately results in a referral for assessment (e.g., Sindelar et al., 1992).

The Mainstream Assistance Team (MAT) model (e.g., D. Fuchs & L. Fuchs, 1988; D. Fuchs, L. Fuchs, Bahr, Fernstrom, & Stecker, 1990) was based on a strong research orientation, and it has been modified systematically according to implementation experiences. Its goals are similar to prereferral intervention, and it takes an ecological perspective in providing behavioral consultation as a means of developing interventions for students at risk for referral and failure. Consultants follow written scripts that guide their verbal behavior to increase the fidelity of the process. There is a strong emphasis on drawing special and general educators together to engage in collaborative problem solving and on obtaining measurable outcomes for the process. Despite the terminology, assistance through this model can be provided by individual consultants, as well as by a team of consultants. More research has been conducted on this model than on any other.

Zins and colleagues (e.g., Curtis, Zins, & Graden, 1987; Zins, Curtis, Graden, & Ponti, 1988; Zins & Johnson, 1994) developed the intervention assistance program model, which they defined as "a systemwide consultation-based model of services delivery intended to meet the special needs of individual students through the systematic and collaborative provision, evaluation, and documentation of problem-solving strategies in the least restrictive setting prior to referral for consideration of a more restrictive placement" (Zins, Curtis, Graden, & Ponti, 1988, pp. 6–7). Of particular note is that the model recognizes and sanctions the personal problem solving that usually occurs before a request for assistance, as well as the collegial support that frequently is provided by teacher-peers. In addition, formal individual consultation and/or team problem solving may be used to resolve the concerns experienced by students, teachers, and/or parents (Zins & Johnson, 1994; see Figure 30.1). The process is applicable to all students and to all problems. Extensive discussions of consultation, implementation issues, and evaluation procedures are included in the descriptions of the model.

Other approaches, such as peer collaboration, a process in which general educators engage in a reflective process to assist one another in rethinking classroom problems (Johnson & Pugach, 1991; Pugach & Johnson, 1990), and Intervention Assistance Teams (e.g., Ohio Department of Education, 1985; Whitten & Dieker, 1995), which rely on a group of individuals to provide problem-solving assistance, are similar to the other procedures described. Some of the research reviewed is based on these approaches.

## Outcomes

There is a surprisingly small amount of research on the intervention assistance process, even though it has been either required or recommended since the late 1980s by nearly 70% of the nation's state departments of education (Carter & Sugai, 1989; Wood, Lazzari, Davis, Sugai, & Carter, 1990). Also, much of the research tends to be of a nonexperimental nature.

Before examining studies specific to intervention assistance programs, we want to point out that there have been many reviews of the consultation research literature. This information is relevant to the discussion because consultation is the foundation on which virtually all intervention assistance programs rest. Although several research limitations are found consistently (e.g., D. Fuchs, L. Fuchs, Dulan, Roberts, & Fernstrom, 1992; Gresham & Kendell, 1987; Gutkin, 1993), overall positive changes were reported in each of the reviews (Kratochwill, Sheridan, & VanSomeren, 1988; Mannino & Shore, 1975; Medway, 1979, 1982; Medway & Updyke, 1985). Sheridan, Welch, and Orme (1996), in their review of outcome studies published between 1985 and 1995, stated, "In general, consultation was found to produce at least some positive results in 76% of the studies reviewed. Thirty-three percent of the studies reported some neutral results . . . and 4% of the studies reported negative results. When considering all of the outcomes reported across studies . . . 67% were positive, 28% were neutral, and 5% were negative" (p. 344).

In our examination of selected outcomes of intervention assistance programs, we focus on factors that may be related to the effectiveness of the process. The review is not exhaustive but rather is representative of the types of reports and evaluation studies available.

### Performance of Students

The ultimate beneficiaries of intervention assistance programs, or of any educational intervention, are the students. Although it might be expected that most investigations would focus on student-related outcomes, that has not been the case. However, studies that have examined the performance of students have found generally positive results.

A series of carefully designed studies was conducted by D. Fuchs and L. Fuchs and colleagues on MATs. They found that the interventions used were quite effective, and many did not require modification (D. Fuchs, L. Fuchs, Bahr, Fernstrom, & Stecker, 1990). They attributed this outcome at least partially to the high integrity with which the interventions were implemented and to the prescriptive nature of the MAT scripts used. In another report they found that MAT pupils' target behaviors decreased in frequency, relative to the level of their peers, although the behavior of controls did also. This finding may have been related to the use of two rating systems that addressed different aspects of behavior (D. Fuchs, L. Fuchs, & Bahr, 1990). It should be noted, however, that although D. Fuchs, L. Fuchs, Harris, and Roberts (1996) consistently have reported measurable gains, they also noted that there was no continuity once the university team departed, despite the competence of field personnel and the availability of a comprehensive resource manual. Reimbursement that favors more restrictive placements was hypothesized by the authors as one explanation, although others have raised questions about original ownership of the MAT process and how that issue may have affected its durability (Safran & Safran, 1997).

Zins, Graden, and Ponti (1988) reported a case study of prereferral interventions with a first-grade student. Disruptive and noncompliant behaviors were targeted, and the intervention resulted in noticeable improvements in both areas at school, although the intervention effects did not generalize to the home. Maher (1986) had teacher resource teams use goal attainment scaling (see Chapter 34, by Illback, Zins, & Maher, or Kiresuk, Smith, & Cardillo, 1994) to establish goals for students and/or teachers. He found that students' goal attainment occurred in 75% of the cases and that teachers' improvement goals, such as changing teaching methods, were achieved in 85% of the cases.

A study of proposed and actual interventions for students experiencing behavioral problems prior to a referral was conducted by Sevcik and Ysseldyke (1986). In both situations, the types of interventions primarily involved teacher-directed actions, such as specific behavioral interventions and structural changes, but their efforts were generally not successful because the students were referred for evaluation. Of particular interest was the fact that few participants sought consultative assistance in developing the interventions.

The success or failure of the approach in specific situations is highly dependent on the quality of the intervention, as well as on the integrity with which it is implemented. Flugum and Reschley (1994), for example, found that prereferral interventions varied dramatically in quality and often were implemented improperly, which resulted in less successful outcomes. Most of the studies reported in the literature, however, have not monitored treatment integrity, which significantly decreases the confidence we have in their outcomes (D. Fuchs & L. Fuchs, 1989; D. Fuchs, L. Fuchs, Bahr, Fernstrom, & Stecker, 1990; and Maher, 1986, are exceptions). The durability of the interventions has also not received sufficient attention. Follow-up periods have been short, so it is unclear whether these students have long-term success in the mainstream or if they simply have been delayed from entering the special education system.

### Teachers' Behaviors and Attitudes

Teachers are significant mediators of students' environments, and consequently their behaviors and attitudes are important aspects of the intervention assistance program. Several studies have included a focus on this aspect of the process.

Bay et al. (1994) implemented a prereferral model in an urban school in which teachers assisted other teachers (special services staff were not involved). The process included three components: information-sharing sessions, peer exchange sessions, and peer-coaching teams. Ten teachers participated in the prereferral approach and 10 in a comparison group, although it was not clear whether the participants were randomly assigned to their groups. At the conclusion of the program open-ended interviews with participants were conducted. Those who participated in the prereferral program reported offering more categories of teaching strategies than nonparticipants.

Additional support for the process was provided by B. Meyers et al. (1996), who found that general education teachers and prereferral team members expressed general satisfaction with the teams. Although the teams provided some support to participating teachers, team members were more likely to recognize such benefits in the process than were teachers. The researchers also found that these positive feelings about the competence of the teams helped to build staff morale.

Several studies examined teachers' attitudes and tolerance for problem behaviors. Among the outcomes for Mainstream Assistance Teams reported by D. Fuchs, L. Fuchs, Bahr, Fernstrom, and Stecker (1990) was that teachers viewed problems as less severe, although their tolerance for such behaviors was not affected. Teachers who engaged in the peer collaboration process were more tolerant of the cognitive functioning of children and changed their attributions for problems from a student-centered focus to a teacher-centered one (Johnson & Pugach, 1991). Participating teachers indicated that they were better able to plan for individual student needs McGlothlin (1981), and a teacher (Zins, Graden, & Ponti, 1988) was able to adjust her teaching in a general education classroom to successfully accommodate a student who was exhibiting very challenging, disruptive behaviors.

One shortcoming associated with many of these programs is that participants are expected to engage in consultation and develop effective interventions, even though many do not have the necessary training and expertise. Wood et al. (1990), for example, found that in most of the states that required or recommended intervention assistance procedures, very few of the general education teachers had preservice training in the various intervention strategies, even though they are primarily responsible for implementing them. A larger number had inservice training, but the authors questioned the adequacy of this preparation. There are also substantial numbers of educators who participate in intervention assistance programs who have not received training in consultation and collaboration. As Safran and Safran (1996) noted, there are significant implications for university training programs for intervention assistance programs.

### Special and General Education Service Delivery Practices

Of all the intervention assistance program outcomes examined, the primary ones have been related to service delivery. Changes in referrals for assessment and subsequent placements in special education, and in the amount of time devoted to the consultative role, have been studied by a number of investigators. Consistent reports have indicated that intervention assistance programs result in a reduction in the number of students tested for special education (e.g., Gutkin, Henning-Stout, & Piersel, 1988; D. Fuchs, L. Fuchs, & Bahr, 1990; Ponti, Zins, & Graden, 1988; Zins, 1992), with these reductions often being in the 40% to 60% range. Along with the decrease in referrals, there usually is an increase in the amount of time spent in consultation.

An early case study by McGlothlin (1981), using a School Consultation Committee, for instance, found that there was up to a 50% reduction in referrals for testing in most schools and that almost all of the teachers in schools with such assistance sought help from the committee. Specific data were not reported, and comparison schools were not used. In a case study that evaluated data over a five-year period, Ponti et al. (1988) found that referrals for assessment decreased by 40% and that far more consultative assistance was provided when a prereferral intervention model in which the school psychologist served as the primary consultant was employed. Studies by Gutkin et al. (1988) and D. Fuchs, L. Fuchs, and Bahr (1990) also found substantial reductions (40% to 60%) in special education testing and placement following the introduction of prereferral consultation services. Graden, Casey, and Bonstrom (1985) reported that in four of the six schools in which the program was implemented, there was a high demand for consultation and a concomitant decline in testing and placement.

Others have found similar results. Maher (1986), for example, implemented Teacher Resource Teams in two high schools. They discussed five or six students each week in meetings that lasted about 1 ½ hours, which was associated

with a statistically significant decrease in the number of referrals for special education. Participating teachers in the program developed by Bay et al. (1994) referred significantly fewer students than nonparticipants, and MAT teachers in the D. Fuchs, L. Fuchs, and Bahr (1990) project were statistically less likely to refer pupils than those in their control group. Only one study (Flugum & Reschly, 1994) found little influence on the number of students identified for special education.

Finally, programs in which teachers assist other teachers with problem solving, as through peer coaching and peer collaboration, have shown some evidence of being effective (e.g., Bay et al., 1994; Johnson & Pugach, 1991). Indeed, we now include peer collaboration as part of the intervention assistance process (see Figure 30.1). School psychologists could play a significant role in introducing such programs, providing training in the collaborative problem-solving process, and serving as a "consultant to the consultants" when the need arises.

### Team Effectiveness

Many of the approaches described earlier rely exclusively on a team to provide assistance. Although we believe that a team is not necessary for the majority of cases, teams are important in many instances, for example, with more complex issues or when communication among a number of staff members is vital (Zins, Curtis, Graden, & Ponti, 1988). Thus, although examination of team effectiveness is clearly important, most reports do not contain detailed descriptions of the teams and there has been very little research on them (Gutkin & Nemeth, 1997).

One of the few studies in this area examined educators' perceptions of teams, their strengths and weaknesses, and the nature of the consultation provided in a large urban district (B. Meyers et al., 1996). Although the teams provided support to participants, as noted earlier, there were also a number of problem areas. Teachers often were not actively involved in the teams, and teams sometimes were unclear about teachers' roles. Consistent with the experiences of others (e.g., Zins, Curtis, Graden, & Ponti, 1988), scheduling was a significant logistical hurdle. The teams also tended to rush into developing solutions too quickly, before the problem was clarified. Finally, although school psychologists and other special services staff were supposed to be team members, their participation was inconsistent.

## Consumer Satisfaction

The reactions of participants in the intervention assistance process is also important to examine because if they do not like it or find it acceptable, it is less likely that they will use it (Witt & Elliot, 1985). A similar statement could be made about the strategies developed.

Participants in the MAT program conducted by D. Fuchs, L. Fuchs, Bahr, Fernstrom, and Stecker (1990) reflected "generally positive sentiments about the project's effectiveness, value, feasibility, and fairness" (p. 510). Bay et al. (1994) had participants in their program provide a written evaluation of the various components. Respondents indicated that the process helped them work with children whom they perceived to be at risk for referral, and they most highly valued the peer-coaching component. All desired to continue their participation. Zins (1992) also found substantial support from consumers for consultation services over the five years of his program. An anecdotal report by Graebner and Dobbs (1984) found that teachers were satisfied with the solutions generated through their Teacher Assistance Team. And, as noted earlier, B. Meyers et al. (1996) reported that teachers were satisfied with the prereferral intervention team used in their schools and had higher morale.

A survey of preassessment team experiences by Harrington and Gibson (1986) found that the vast majority of the general education teachers reported that the team did not give them new intervention ideas, that few options were explored, that those provided were unsuccessful, and that they did not implement the interventions recommended. Surprisingly, three-quarters indicated that they wanted the preassessment process continued, suggesting that some other unassessed positive benefits had accrued.

## Conclusions About Intervention Assistance Programs

The question remains, do intervention assistance programs work? As this review suggests, the answer is not a simple one. The methodological rigor of the research, differences in definitions of what constitutes intervention assistance programs, and the quality of the interventions implemented are confounding variables. A number of positive outcomes are reported for most dependent variables, but there are also some indications that the process does not necessarily lead to all of the outcomes proponents suggest. It is unfortunate that more high-quality research has not

been conducted to provide clearer evidence of the efficacy of the process.

Bearing these significant caveats in mind, we are led to conclude that intervention assistance programs are a promising method for delivering preventively oriented school psychological and educational services. This statement is based on the assumption that through the process, jointly developed quality interventions are delivered with high fidelity by adequately trained personnel within a supportive organization. In other words, we believe that the process will be successful overall when implemented correctly. Unless those criteria are met, however, the process ultimately may become one more failure on the educational bandwagon. Clearly, it merits further attention through research, theory development, and practice.

## Secondary Prevention Strategies in Inclusive Settings

The other example of secondary prevention we address in some detail is inclusive education. In this section inclusive education is used as the services delivery mechanism for a variety of interventions.

> Despite their current dominance in special and remedial education, pull-out programs are inconsistent with a preventive orientation since they do not maximize the opportunity for the special education teacher to provide instruction to or influence the instruction of ineligible students who are educated in the regular classroom, many of whom may be at risk of developing learning and adjustment problems. These ineligible students do not have access to the special attention that might prevent the development of these problems. Structural changes that reduce the tendency to categorize and remove children from the mainstream must be developed to achieve goals associated with the prevention of learning and adjustment problems. (Will, 1986; cited in J. Meyers, 1989, p. 396)

For these and many of the reasons cited earlier, inclusive education has become an important method of providing educational services.

Although inclusion can be viewed as a secondary prevention strategy, there is little evidence that by itself it can benefit learners with mild disabilities (Kauffman, & Hallahan, 1995; Stainback, Stainback, East, & Sapon-Shevin, 1994). However, when specific interventions and evaluations are undertaken in the inclusive setting, students' performance is enhanced (L. Fuchs & D. Fuchs, 1986; Walker, McConnell, Holmes, Todis, Walker, & Golden, 1983). This section describes several specific interventions that practitioners can use to improve the likelihood of success.

There are several distinguishing features of the inclusive secondary prevention programs that we propose. First, the strategies are designed at the micro level of application. That is, professionals such as school psychologists can apply these tactics in an individual classroom or in the home. They are not necessarily designed for universal and wholesale application across a school building or district. We take the view that secondary prevention programs can be extended to the individual level. Given the range of strategies that we propose, it is conceivable—even desirable—that students in classrooms in the same building will have individualized programs based on their needs. Also, students attending multiple classes—as they might in an inclusive setting—can be exposed to multiple strategies, each designed as a secondary prevention strategy to address a different facet of the overall problem (i.e., social, academic, and behavioral).

Second, whereas local dollars are usually required to implement macro-level programs, the tactics that we propose are designed as low- or no-cost interventions that school psychologists can develop with teachers or parents. Furthermore, they meet the litmus test for acceptability. That it, they are judged "by lay persons, clients, and others [as] appropriate, fair and reasonable for the problem or client" (Kazdin, 1981, p. 493).

Finally, the secondary prevention strategies that we propose meet the spirit of "best practice" (Peters & Heron, 1993). That is, they have a sound theoretical base, they are backed by compelling and convincing efficacy literature, they are based on solid research methodology, they generate product outcomes, and they are socially valid. Applying these criteria to secondary prevention strategies enhances their efficacy, overall appeal, and utility.

## *Inclusive Education Strategies*

Secondary prevention programs in inclusive general education classrooms can be conceptualized across several dimensions. The functional approach that we take is to use the three-term contingency as a basis for our discussion. Briefly, the three-term contingency examines and manipulates antecedents and consequences as the principle way to change behavior. Using this metric allows practitioners to (1) focus attention on secondary prevention tactics that set the occasion for appropriate student performance and (2) reinforce instances in which, at the point that the teacher or parent notices at-risk behavior, an appropriate secondary prevention countermeasure can be used to teach a new or incompatible behavior, or to reduce an inappropriate behavior in students' repertoires. We agree with Hightower, Johnson, and Haffey (1990) that "the essence of secondary prevention is the early detection of problems during their earliest stages and intervention before the problems become more severe. By identifying problems in their initial stages, interventions are designed to shorten their duration and minimize the intensity, thus reducing the prevalence of disorders" (p. 63).

The strategies discussed next present a representative, but not exhaustive, sampling of tactics that school psychologists can suggest to general education teachers when students' academic or social behavior is dysfunctional or counterproductive.

## *Antecedent Strategies*

Students in inclusive classrooms face challenges in several discrete areas, including academics, social skills, and organizational skills. The expectations for skill acquisition in these areas may vary by grade level and by individual.

### *Improving Academic Skills*

*Active student responding* (ASR), which occurs when students make detectable responses to ongoing instruction (Heward, 1994), is included in the broader concepts of the opportunity to respond (OTR) literature. Greenwood, Delquadri, and Hall (1984) define OTR as "the interaction between: (a) teacher formulated instructional antecedent stimuli (the materials presented, prompts, questions asked, signals to respond, etc.), and (b) their success in establishing the academic responding desired or implied by the materials" (p. 64). Because ASR measures student responding directly, it is a response-based measure; OTR is a time-based measure (Heward, 1994).

According to Heward (1994), ASR generates more learning for students, and the observation of students' responses provides important feedback to the teacher about students' comprehension. Finally, ASR is correlated with increased levels of on-task behavior. Barbetta, Heron, and Heward (1993) found that ASR resulted in higher academic performance during instruction, as well as on same-day, next-day, and generality tests. Other studies (Greenwood, Delquadri, & Hall, 1984; Sainato, Strain, & Lyon, 1987) have shown comparable results.

Three types of ASR are relevant for our discussion: choral responding, response cards, and guided notes. In choral responding, groups of students (or the entire class) verbally respond in unison to a teacher-posed question. Because of the high level of attention required, choral-responding sessions should be short (5 to 10 minutes). Choral responding is best suited to a curriculum that lends itself to brief responses, and questions and items that can be presented at a fast, lively pace (Heward, Courson, & Narayan, 1989). Carnine (1976) showed that a fast rate of presentation by teachers resulted in more frequent participation, more correct answers, and less off-task behavior than slow presentation rates. Replications of this study (Cashman, 1990; Morgan, 1987; Williams, 1993) produced similar results.

When using response cards (Heward, 1994), students collectively hold up preprinted or write-on cards to indicate their response to a question presented by the teacher. Every student in the classroom has the opportunity to respond to teacher-presented trials, as well as to view the response cards of other students in the classroom. Response cards also allow the teacher to view individual responses. During the instructional phase of a study conducted by Narayan, Heward, Gardner, Courson, and Omness (1990), the rate of ASR was much higher with response cards than with hand raising, and most students scored higher on quizzes of material covered in response card sessions than in hand-raising sessions. Also, 19 of the 20 students in the class preferred response cards over hand raising. Other studies have shown similar positive effects in favor of response cards across generality, social validity, and maintenance measures (Gardner, Heward, & Grossi, 1994; Narayan, 1988; Wheatly, 1986).

Guided notes are teacher-prepared handouts that follow the sequence of a lecture, providing cues and spaces for the students to complete as the teacher progresses through the lesson. Kline (1986) demonstrated that at-risk high school students performed at higher levels on end-of-session and unit tests under guided notes conditions

than they did with a conventional lecture-take-notes procedure. Essentially, Kline showed that students' performance improved when the students had an identical copy of the information that the teacher was presenting so that they could write key information directly on this form. Social validity data showed that the high school students preferred the preprinted guided notes to taking their own notes without the supplement.

Accuracy of note taking is an important skill in regular education classrooms. Baker and Lombardi (1985) found a strong relationship between thorough, accurate note taking and test performance. Carrier (1983) concluded that recording and reviewing notes increases learning for students and that some students may need additional assistance from the instructor to obtain helpful notes. Guided notes can fulfill this role. Students who are at risk for academic difficulties often find note taking a frustrating experience.

### Tutoring Systems

Tutoring can occur in at least five formats: class-wide, cross-age, small-group, one-to-one, and home-based (Miller, Barbetta, & Heron, 1994). The one-to-one and small-group formats are most suitable as secondary prevention strategies in inclusive settings because they target select students in an inclusive class for remedial or specialized practice while simultaneously not affecting other programs being conducted in the classroom.

Tutoring systems have many benefits (Cooke, Heron, & Heward, 1983; Miller et al., 1994). Students are in direct contact with individualized academic materials, and they work at their own pace and level, which helps to reduce frustration. Additionally, immediate feedback is provided in a nonthreatening manner; tutors' responses to errors are scripted; and tutors are trained, monitored, and reinforced for appropriate responses to errors. As with the ASR strategies, students are actively engaged during tutoring sessions. Another important benefit, especially for students who are potentially at risk for behavior problems, is socialization with peers who are more academically and socially adept. Efficacy studies of tutoring in inclusive classrooms have been well documented in the literature (Barbetta & Heron, 1991; Barbetta et al., 1993; Harper, Maheady, & Mallette, 1997; Pigott, Fantuzzo, & Clement, 1986).

## Improving Social Skills

General educators value social skills in their classrooms (Walker et al., 1983), although Cartledge and Milburn (1995) suggest that social skills instruction is often a "hidden curriculum." Yet, there are many instances in inclusive settings in which groups of students require secondary prevention strategies to teach specific social skills.

Social skills programs can be implemented in three ways: (1) the entire class can participate; (2) small groups can participate in a classroom; or (3) students can be pulled out of the classroom, either individually or in small groups (Strain, Odom, & McConnell, 1984). Teaching small groups in a classroom sometimes is best, for example, when a particular group of children experiences problems. The main focus of social skills instruction, however, usually involves the entire class.

School psychologists and other consultants could encourage teachers to use a direct instruction format when providing social skills instruction to students. In this approach, the social skill is illustrated by the teacher, examples and counterexamples are provided, and students practice the skills under first controlled and then uncontrolled situations.

## Improving Organizational Skills

Shields and Heron (1989) discuss several strategies that school psychologists can use with teachers who have students who are unable to organize themselves, their time, or their materials. Antecedent strategies include assignment logs and charts, work stations, color-coded materials, timers, and guided notes. These strategies can be implemented as secondary prevention measures for either large or small groups of at-risk students.

## Consequence Strategies

Two major secondary prevention consequence strategies that teachers can use in the classroom are reinforcement and feedback. Within reinforcement are individual and group contingencies.

### Reinforcement

According to Cooper, Heron, and Heward (1987), ". . . the most basic and pervasive principle of behavior is that of operant reinforcement" (p. 25). Reinforcement occurs when a behavior is followed by a stimulus, and as a consequence, the future probability of occur-

rences of that response class of behavior increases. Although Ferster and Skinner (1957) articulated the principle of reinforcement, the relevant schedules, and the fundamental effect on increasing behavior, practitioners have been slow to implement it on a systematic or consistent basis. Furthermore, despite evidence that shows the effects of reinforcement, punishment continues to be the major method that teachers, administrators, and parents use to manage behavior (Cooper et al., 1987).

There are at least two principle ways in which teachers and parents can operationalize reinforcement: individual and group applications, and positive and reductive approaches.

Literally scores of studies could be cited to show the effects of contingent reinforcement on student-improved performance (an *individual application of reinforcement*). The classic study, conducted by Hall, Lund, and Jackson (1968), examined the effects of the teacher's attention on the study and disruptive behavior of six elementary-aged students in a general education classroom in an impoverished neighborhood. Essentially, the procedures were conducted with a systematic reversal design: baseline ($A_1$), reinforcement ($B_1$), baseline ($A_2$) and reinforcement ($B_2$). During baseline, students' study and disruptive behavior were observed during a 30-minute period. When reinforcement was applied, the teacher attended to students contingently, moved to student's desks, and/or provided proximal or physical attention (e.g., pat on the shoulder). Nonstudy or disruptive behavior was ignored. Results showed a marked effect in favor of the teacher's attention. That is, when attention was in effect, study behavior increased and disruptive behavior decreased. When attention was not in effect, these behaviors reverted to their previously high levels.

The authors made several observations subsequent to the study that are relevant and prescriptive for those implementing secondary prevention programs. The first relates to the power of teachers' attention and praise: "Effective teachers have known that casually praising desired behaviors and generally ignoring disruptive ones can be useful procedures for helping maintain good classroom discipline. What may appear surprising to school personnel, however, is the degree to which student behavior responds to thoroughly systematic teacher attention" (Hall et al., 1968, p. 10). Second, the teachers in the study were largely unfamiliar with applying reinforcement procedures in classrooms. Even so, they were able to carry out the study in crowded, noisy, inner-city classrooms, where high levels of nonstudy and disruptive behavior previously prevailed. Third, reinforcement procedures did not interfere with any other teacher's duty in the classroom. In fact, a collateral benefit may have been enjoyed; that is, with less disruptive and more study behavior occurring, teachers were free to engage in other behaviors (e.g., more one-to-one instruction) that had been limited previously. Finally, the authors warn that although these procedures can be effective, using them does not relieve teachers of providing students with age- and skill-appropriate instructional materials. In their view, it would be unlikely that reinforcement alone, in the absence of appropriate materials, would produce the academic or social gains found in this study. Vargas (1982) confirms this position, stating that teachers must pay particular attention to the curriculum materials in classrooms, not just reinforcement contingencies.

There are essentially three ways that *group-oriented contingencies* can be implemented in inclusive classrooms as secondary prevention techniques. Litow and Pumroy (1975) outline these approaches as dependent, independent, and interdependent group-oriented contingencies.

Allen, Gottselig, and Boylan (1982) conducted a study of *dependent group-oriented contingencies* in what could be described as an inclusive setting, where secondary prevention was clearly the intent of the investigation. Essentially, the study involved 8 disruptive third-graders in a class of 29 students whose behavior affected the teacher, the other students, and their own chances of success at that grade level. The students were placed on a contingency in which decreased levels of disruptive behavior during math and language arts produced one minute of extra free time for the class. During baseline conditions across both subject areas, disruptive behavior ranged from approximately 40% to 55% of observed intervals. When the dependent group-oriented contingency was in effect, disruptive behavior was reduced to between 5% and 10% of observed intervals. Stern, Fowler, and Kohler (1988) report similar positive results of a dependent group-oriented contingency for reducing high levels of disruptive behavior when two fifth-grade students were working together. The students were either point monitors or point earners, and earned points were exchangeable for a class movie. Both conditions were equally effective in reducing high levels of disruptive behavior. The authors noted that this group contingency was effective, cost-efficient, applicable for students with chronic histories of disruptive behavior, and useful when a teacher's direct supervision was not possible.

An *independent group-oriented contingency* outlines the requirements to all members in the group, but reinforcement is delivered only to those members who meet the conditions of the contingency successfully. According to Cooper et al. (1987), contingency contracting and token reinforcement arrangements are the two most popular applications of this type. Readers interested in their methodological variations might consult Dardig and Heward (1981) and Zwald and Gresham (1982).

In an *interdependent group-oriented contingency*, reinforcement is delivered only when all members of the group—individuals, as well as the total group—meet the conditions of the contingency. Cooper et al. (1987) indicate that this group arrangement is probably the most conservative of the three contingencies, and that four methodological variations are available: total group meets the criterion, group averaging, randomly selected students meet the criterion, and the Good Behavior Game (Barrish, Saunders, & Wolf, 1969). Briefly, in the Good Behavior Game, the class is divided into two or more groups. Each group is told that the team with the fewest points registered against it wins, a mark being recorded if a class rule is broken. Students are yoked together, and reinforcement is based on average performance.

## Feedback

Feedback differs from reinforcement in a fundamental way. Feedback is a behavioral procedure or application, whereas reinforcement is a behavioral principle. The distinction is important because there are only a few behavioral principles (e.g., reinforcement, punishment, and extinction), but scores of applications of these principles in applied settings (feedback, time-out, response cost, etc.).

Feedback essentially refers to the stimuli that are presented subsequent to a response that provide the learner with information relative to some aspect of that response (e.g., its frequency, magnitude, duration, or topography). According to Van Houten (1980, 1984), feedback can serve as a reinforcer, increasing the likelihood of future occurrences of the behavior, and as a discriminative stimulus that sets the occasion for the behavior to occur. Depending on the student's stage of learning (i.e., acquisition or practice), the form of the feedback could vary.

Barbetta, Heward, Bradley, and Miller (1994) and Drevno, Kimball, Possi, Heward, Gardner, and Barbetta (1994) demonstrated the beneficial effects of feedback with special and general education students. For instance, Barbetta et al. (1994) compared immediate and delayed error correction (feedback) during reading instruction with five students with developmental disabilities. Feedback on response accuracy was provided to students immediately after an error or at the end of the session. For all students, immediate feedback provided higher levels of response on same-day and next-day tests. Also, all students maintained higher levels of performance at one- and two-week intervals.

Drevno et al. (1994) compared active student response (ASR) error correction with a no-response (NR) error correction procedure when teaching science to elementary students. During ASR error correction, if a student erred, the teacher modeled the correct response and the student imitated the teacher. During the no-response condition, if an error occurred, the student merely looked at the teacher's model but did not say the correct answer. All students improved during ASR feedback on instructional and postinstructional tasks, demonstrating that the ASR feedback can be beneficial.

Overall, the combined results of these studies have significant implications for secondary prevention-oriented practice: feedback should be direct (copy the model) and immediate (completed immediately after the error is detected), and the student should supply the correct response.

### Conclusions About Inclusive Education

Although there can be many benefits to learners in an inclusive setting as discussed throughout this section of the chapter, readers are certain to realize that it is not likely that a single type of inclusionary intervention strategy such as a dependent group-oriented contingency will meet the majority of the needs of special education students in general education classrooms. After all, by definition, special education is defined as specially designed instruction to meet unique needs. Still, when school psychologists, teachers, and parents recognize early on that a student's performance is deteriorating, sufficient secondary prevention resources can be rallied to intervene effectively. Using sensitive measurement tactics like curriculum-based measurement (Shinn, Nolet, & Knutson, 1990), coupled with the inclusionary-based educational intervention strategies that meet the spirit of best practices (i.e., have a sound theoretical base, are backed by strong efficacy literature, are based on solid research methodology, generate product outcomes, and are socially valid), can help enormously in problem prevention. Consequently, the likelihood that the inclusionary setting will be successful in meeting students' needs will be increased.

## CONCLUDING COMMENTS

Remarkably, the field of school psychology, with notable exceptions such as Phillips (1990), Zins and Forman (1988), and a few others, has been slow to embrace a preventive orientation, even though training and practice standards list prevention as one of the comprehensive services that should be provided (e.g., National Association of School Psychologists, 1994). However, surveys of practitioners and training programs suggest that there generally has been little emphasis on prevention (Fagan, 1990; Reschly & Wilson, 1995). In addition to becoming more involved in secondary prevention through intervention assistance and inclusive education programs, there are many other ways in which school psychologists could become involved, for example, by initiating programs, collaborating with colleagues, conducting program evaluations, and so forth. Schools greatly need to prevent interpersonal violence, drug abuse, AIDs, and suicide, as well as to promote social and emotional learning (see Elias et al., 1997). Indeed, prevention is highly consistent with the comprehensive school health movement that has captured the interest of many psychologists (see Kolbe, Collins, & Cortese, 1997). However, if school psychologists choose not to take up these challenges, they likely will continue to serve as gatekeepers to special education, a role that may not have a bright future.

Despite the possibilities offered, there are many difficulties and challenges in working within a preventive mode. "Prevention is not easy work. In many ways it is frustrating, since it involves coordinating more persons and constituents than does the 'diagnose and remediate' model. . . . Training in prevention, screening, and early classroom intervention can promote our participation in all levels of school programming and, in the end, ensure a broader context for our role" (Severson & Zoref, 1991, p. 554).

Therefore, we would like to remind readers of the words spoken by President John F. Kennedy (1963), who called for a bold new approach in dealing with mental health and related problems:

> ". . . an ounce of prevention is worth more than a pound of cure." For prevention is far more desirable for all concerned. It is far more economical and it is far more likely to be successful. Prevention will require both selected specific programs directed especially at known causes, and the strengthening of our fundamental community, social welfare, and vocational programs which can do much to eliminate or correct the harsh environmental conditions which often are associated with mental retardation and mental illness. (p. 127)

His words ring true today. But now that nearly 40 years have passed and prevention continues to remain elusive in educational settings, we once again must ask, "What are we waiting for?" (Zins & Forman, 1988, p. 539).

# REFERENCES

Albee, G. W. (1996). Revolutions and counterrevolutions in prevention. *American Psychologist, 51*, 1130–1133.

Allen, L. D., Gottselig, M., & Boylan, S. (1982). A practical mechanism for using free time as a reinforcer in the classroom. *Education and Treatment of Children, 5*, 347–353.

*America 2000: An Education Strategy*. (1991). Washington, DC: U.S. Department of Education.

Baer, D. M. (1987). Weak contingencies, strong contingencies, and many behaviors to change. *Journal of Applied Behavior Analysis, 20*(4), 335–337.

Baker, L., & Lombardi, B. (1985). Students' lecture notes and their relation to test performance. *Teaching of Psychology, 12*, 28–32.

Barbetta, P. M., & Heron, T. E. (1991). Project SHINE: Summer home instruction and evaluation. *Intervention in School and Clinic, 26*, 276–281.

Barbetta, P. M., Heron, T. E., & Heward, W. L. (1993). Effects of active response during error correction on the acquisition, maintenance, and generalization of sight words by students with developmental disabilities. *Journal of Applied Behavior Analysis, 26*(1), 111–119.

Barbetta, P. M., Heward, W. L., Bradley, D. M., & Miller, A. D. (1994). Effects of immediate and delayed error correction on the acquisition and maintenance of sight words by students with developmental disabilities. *Journal of Applied Behavior Analysis, 27*(1), 177–178.

Barrish, H. H., Saunders, M., & Wolf, M. (1969). The Good Behavior Games: Effects of individual contingencies for group consequences on disruptive behavior in the classroom. *Journal of Applied Behavior Analysis, 2*, 119–124.

Bay, M., Bryan, T., & O'Connor, R. (1994). Teachers assisting teachers: A prereferral model for urban educators. *Teacher Education and Special Education, 17*, 10–21.

Bond, L. A., & Compas, B. E. (Eds.). (1989). *Primary prevention and promotion in the schools*. Newbury Park, CA: Sage.

Caplan, G. (1961). *Principles of preventive psychiatry*. New York: Grune & Stratton.

Carnegie Corporation on Adolescent Development. (1995). *Great transitions: Preparing adolescents for a new century/Concluding report of the Carnegie Council on Adolescent Development*. New York: Carnegie Corporation of New York.

Carnine, D. W. (1976). Effects of two teachers' presentation rates on off-task behavior, answering correctly, and participation. *Journal of Applied Behavior Analysis, 9*, 199–206.

Carrier, C. A. (1983). Notetaking research: Implications for the classroom. *Journal of Instructional Development, 6*(3), 19–26.

Carter, J., & Sugai, G. (1989). Survey on prereferral practices: Responses from state departments of education. *Exceptional Children, 55*, 298–302.

Cartledge, G., & Milburn, J. F. (1995). *Teaching social skills to children and youth: Innovative approaches* (3rd ed.). Boston: Allyn & Bacon.

Cashman, C. T. (1990). *The effect of fast- versus slow-paced instruction during choral responding*. Unpublished senior honors thesis, The Ohio State University, Columbus.

Chalfant, J. C., & Pysh, M. V. (1989). Teacher assistance teams: Five descriptive studies on 96 teams. *Remedial and Special Education, 10*, 49–58.

Chalfant, J. C., Pysh, M. V., & Moultrie, R. (1979). Teacher assistance teams: A model for within-building problem solving. *Learning Disabilities Quarterly, 2*, 85–96.

Christenson, S., Ysseldyke, J., & Algozzine, B. (1982). Institutional constraints and external pressures influencing referral decisions. *Psychology in the Schools, 19*, 341–345.

Clark, E. G., & Leavell, H. R. (1953). Levels of application of preventive medicine. In E. G. Clark & H. R. Leavell (Eds.), *Textbook of preventive medicine* (pp. 7–27). New York: McGraw-Hill.

Clark, E. G., & Leavell, H. R. (1958). Levels of

application of preventive medicine. In E. G. Clark & H. R. Leavell (Eds.), *Preventive medicine for the doctor in his community* (2nd ed., pp. 13–39). New York: McGraw-Hill.

Consortium on the School-based Promotion of Social Competence [Elias, M. J., Weissberg, R. P., Hawkins, J. D., Perry, C. L., Zins, J. E., Dodge, K. A., Kendall, P. C., Gottfredson, D., Rotheram-Borus, M. J., Jason, L. A., & Wilson-Brewer, R. J.]. (1994). The school-based promotion of social competence: Theory, research, practice, and policy. In R. J. Haggerty, L. Sherrod, N. Garmezy, & M. Rutter (Eds.), *Stress, risk, and resilience in children and adolescents: Processes, mechanisms, and interaction* (pp. 268–316). New York: Cambridge University Press.

Cooke, N. L., Heron, T. E., & Heward, W. L. (1983). *Peer tutoring: Implementing classwide programs in the primary grades*. Columbus OH: Special Press.

Cooper, J. O., Heron, T. E., & Heward, W. L. (1987). *Applied behavior analysis*. Columbus, OH: Merrill.

Costello, E. J. (1990). Child psychiatric epidemiology: Implications for clinical research and practice. In B. B. Lahey & A. E. Kazdin (Eds.), *Advances in clinical child psychiatry* (Vol. 13, pp. 53–90). New York: Plenum.

Cowen, E. L. (1983). Primary prevention in mental health. In R. D. Felner, L. A. Jason, J. N. Moritsugu, & S. S. Farber (Eds.), *Preventive psychology: Theory, research, and practice* (pp. 11–25). New York: Pergamon.

Curtis, M. J., Zins, J. E., & Graden, J. (1987). Prereferral intervention programs: Enhancing student performance in regular education settings. In C. A. Maher & J. E. Zins (Eds.), *Psychoeducational interventions in the schools* (pp. 7–25). Elmsford, NY: Pergamon.

Dardig, J., & Heward, W. L. (1981). *Sign here: A contracting book for children and their parents* (2nd ed.). Bridgewater, NJ: Fournies.

Drevno, G. E., Kimball, J. W., Possi, M. K., Heward, W. L., Gardner, R., III, & Barbetta, P. (1994). Effects of active student response during error correction on the acquisition, maintenance, and generalization of science vocabulary by elementary students: A systematic replication. *Journal of Applied Behavior Analysis, 27*(1), 179–180.

Dryfoos, J. (1990). *Adolescents at risk*. New York: Oxford University Press.

Durlak, J. A. (1995). *School-based prevention programs for children and adolescents*. Thousand Oaks, CA: Sage.

Elias, M. J., Zins, J. E., Weissberg, R. P., Frey, K. S., Greenberg, M. T., Haynes, N. M., Kessler, R., Schwab-Stone, M. E., & Shriver, T. P. (1997). *Promoting social and emotional learning: Guidelines for educators*. Alexandria, VA: Association for Supervision and Curriculum Development.

Erchul, W. (Ed.). (1993). *Consultation in community, school, and organizational practice*. Washington, DC: Taylor & Francis.

Fagan, T. K. (1990). Best practices in the training of school psychologists. In A. Thomas & J. Grimes (Eds.), *Best practices in school psychology–II* (pp. 723–742). Washington, DC: National Association of School Psychologists.

Ferster, C. B., & Skinner, B. F. (1957). *Schedules of reinforcement*. Englewood Cliffs, NJ: Prentice Hall.

Fowler, R., & Tisdale, P. C. (1992). Special education students as a high risk group for substance abuse: Teacher perspectives. *School Counselor, 40*, 103–108.

Flugum, K. R., & Reschly, D. J. (1994). Prereferral interventions: Quality indices and outcomes. *Journal of School Psychology, 32*, 1–14.

Fuchs, D., & Fuchs, L. S. (1988). Mainstream assistance teams to accommodate difficult-to-teach students in general education. In J. Graden, J. E. Zins, & M. J. Curtis (Eds.), *Alternative educational delivery systems* (pp. 49–70). Washington, DC: National Association of School Psychologists.

Fuchs, D., & Fuchs, L. S. (1989). Exploring effective and efficient prereferral interventions: A component analysis of behavioral consultation. *School Psychology Review, 18*, 260–279.

Fuchs, D., Fuchs, L. S., & Bahr, M. W. (1990). Mainstream assistance teams: A scientific basis for the art of consultation. *Exceptional Children, 57*, 128–139.

Fuchs, D., Fuchs, L. S., Bahr, M. W., Fernstrom, P., & Stecker, P. M. (1990). Prereferral intervention: A prescriptive approach. *Exceptional Children, 56*, 493–513.

Fuchs, D., Fuchs, L. S., Dulan, J., Roberts, H., & Fernstrom, P. (1992). Where is the research on consultation effectiveness? *Journal of Educational and Psychological Consultation, 3*, 151–174.

Fuchs, D., Fuchs, L. S., Harris, A. H., & Roberts, P. H. (1996). Bridging the research-to-practice gap with mainstream assistance teams: A cautionary tale. *School Psychology Quarterly, 11*, 244–266.

Fuchs, L. S., & Fuchs, D. (1986). Effects of systematic formative evaluation: A meta-evaluation. *Exceptional Children, 53*, 199–208.

Gager, P. J., Kress, J. S., & Elias, M. J. (1996). Prevention programs and special education: Considerations related to risk, social competence, and multiculturalism. *Journal of Primary Prevention, 16*, 395–412.

Gardner, H. (1993). *Multiple intelligences: The theory in practice*. New York: Basic Books.

Gardner, R., III, Heward, W. L., & Grossi, T. A. (1994). Effects of response cards on student participation and academic achievement: A systematic replication with inner-city students during whole-class science instruction. *Journal of Applied Behavior Analysis, 27* (1), 63–71.

Goleman, D. (1995). *Emotional intelligence.* New York: Bantam.

Gordon, R. S. (1983). An operational definition of disease prevention. *Public Health Reports, 98,* 107–109.

Gordon, R. S. (1987). An operational definition of disease prevention. In J. A. Sternberg & M. M. Silverman (Eds.), *Preventing mental disorders: A research perspective* (pp. 20–26). (DHHS Publication No. ADM 87-1492). Washington, DC: U. S. Government Printing Office.

Graden, J., Casey, A., & Bonstrom, O. (1985). Implementing a prereferral intervention system: Part II. The data. *Exceptional Children, 51,* 461–487.

Graden, J., Casey, A., & Christenson, S. L. (1985). Implementing a prereferral intervention system: Part I. The model. *Exceptional Children, 51,* 4377–4384.

Graebner, J., & Dodds, S. (1984). A team approach to problem solving in the classroom. *Phi Delta Kappan, 66,* 138–141.

Greenwood, C. R., Delquadri, J., & Hall, R. V. (1984). Opportunity to respond and student academic achievement. In W. L. Heward, T. E. Heron, D. S. Hill, & J. Trap-Porter (Eds.), *Focus on behavior analysis in education* (pp. 58–88). Columbus, OH: Merrill.

Gresham, F. M., & Kendell, G. K. (1987). School consultation research: Methodological critique and future research directions. *School Psychology Review, 16,* 306–316.

Gutkin, T. B. (1993). Conducting consultation research. In J. E. Zins, T. R. Kratochwill, & S. N. Elliott (Eds.), *Handbook of consultation services for children* (pp. 227–248). San Francisco: Jossey-Bass.

Gutkin, T. B., & Curtis, M. J. (1982). School-based consultation: Theory and techniques. In C. R. Reynolds & T. B. Gutkin (Eds.), *The handbook of school psychology* (pp. 796–828). New York: Wiley.

Gutkin, T. B., Henning-Stout, M., & Piersel, W. (1988). Impact of a district-wide behavioral consultation prereferral intervention service on patterns of school psychological service delivery. *Professional School Psychology, 3,* 301–308.

Gutkin, T. B., & Nemeth, C. (1997). Selected factors impacting decision making in prereferral intervention and other school-based teams: Exploring the intersection between school and social psychology. *Journal of School Psychology, 35,* 195–216.

Hall, R. V., Lund, D., & Jackson, D. (1968). Effects of teacher attention on study behavior. *Journal of Applied Behavior Analysis, 1,* 1–12.

Harper, G. F., Maheady, L., & Mallette, B. (1997, May). *Classwide student tutoring teams: A hybrid cooperative learning and peer-tutoring program.* Paper presented at the annual meeting of the Association for Behavior Analysis, Chicago.

Harrington, R., & Gibson, E. (1986). Preassessment procedures for learning disabled children. *Journal of Learning Disabilities, 19,* 538–541.

Hayek, R. A. (1987). The teacher assistance team: A pre-referral support system. *Focus on Exceptional Children, 20,* 1–7.

Heward, W. L. (1994). Three "low-tech" strategies for increasing the frequency of active student response during group instruction. In R. Gardner, III, D. M. Sainato, J. O. Cooper, T. E. Heron, W. L. Heward, J. Eshleman, & T. A. Grossi (Eds.), *Behavior analysis in education: Focus on measurably superior instruction* (pp. 283–320). Pacific Grove, CA: Brooks/Cole.

Heward, W. L., Courson, F. H., & Narayan, J. S. (1989). Using choral responding to increase active student response. *Teaching Exceptional Children, 21,* 72–75.

Heward, W. L., Heron, T. E., Ellis, D., & Cooke, N. L. (1986). Teaching first grade peer tutors to use praise on an intermittent schedule. *Education and Treatment of Children, 9,* 5–15.

Hightower, A. D., Johnson, D., & Haffey, W. G. (1990). Best practices in adopting a prevention program. In A. Thomas & J. Grimes (Ed.), *Best practices in school psychology–II* (pp. 63–79). Washington, DC: National Association of School Psychologists.

Johnson, L. J., & Pugach, M. (1991). Peer collaboration: Accommodating students with mild learning and behavior problems. *Exceptional Children, 57,* 454–461.

Kaufman, J. M., & Hallahan, D. P. (1995). *The illusion of full inclusion: A comprehensive critique of a current special education bandwagon.* Austin, TX: Pro-Ed.

Kazdin, A. E. (1981). Acceptability of child treatment techniques: The influence of treatment efficacy and adverse side effects. *Behavior Therapy, 12,* 493–506.

Kennedy, J. F. (1963). *Message from the President of the United States relative to mental illness and mental retardation.* 88th Congress, First Session, U.S. House of Representatives Document No. 58. Washington, DC: U.S. Government Printing Office.

Kiewra, K. A. (1984). Acquiring effective notetaking skills: An alternative to professional notetaking. *Journal of Reading, 27,* 299–302.

Kiresuk, T., Smith, A., & Cardillo, J. (Eds.). (1994). *Goal attainment scaling.* Hillsdale, NJ: Erlbaum.

Kline, C. (1986). *Effects of guided notes on academic achievement of learning disabled high school students.* Unpublished master's thesis, The Ohio State University, Columbus.

Kolbe, L. J., Collins, J., & Cortese, P. (1997). Building the capacity of schools to improve the health of the nation: A call for assistance from psychologists. *American Psychologist, 52,* 256–265.

Kratochwill, T. R., Sheridan, S. M., & VanSomeren, K. R. (1988). Research in behavioral consultation: Current status and future directions. In J. F. West (Ed.), *School consultation: Interdisciplinary perspectives on theory, research, training, and practice* (pp. 77–102). Austin, TX: Association for Educational and Psychological Consultants.

Lipsky, D. K., & Gartner, A. (Eds.). (1989). *Beyond separate education: Quality education for all.* Baltimore, MD: Paul H. Brookes.

Litow, L., & Pumroy, D. K. (1975). A brief review of classroom group-oriented contingencies. *Journal of Applied Behavior Analysis, 8,* 341–347.

Lovitt, T. C. (1991). *Preventing school dropouts: Tactics for at-risk, remedial, and mildly handicapped adolescents.* Austin, TX: Pro-Ed.

Maher, C. A. (1986). *Providing prereferral support services to regular classroom teachers: The teacher resource team.* Unpublished manuscript, Rutgers University, Piscataway, NJ.

Mannino, F. V., & Shore, M. F. (1975). The effects of consultation: A review of the literature. *American Journal of Community Psychology, 3,* 1–21.

McGlothlin, J. E. (1981). The school consultation committee: An approach to implementing a teacher consultation model. *Behavior Disorders, 6,* 101–107.

Medway, F. J. (1979). How effective is school consultation? A review of recent research. *Journal of School Psychology, 17,* 275–282.

Medway, F. J. (1982). School consultation research: Past trends and future directions. *Professional Psychology, 13,* 422–430.

Medway, F. J., & Updyke, J. F. (1985). Meta-analysis of consultation outcome studies. *American Journal of Community Psychology, 13,* 489–505.

Meyers, B., Valentino, C. T., Meyers, J., Boretti, M., & Brent, D. (1996). Implementing prereferral intervention teams as an approach to school-based consultation in an urban school system. *Journal of Educational and Psychological Consultation, 7,* 119–149.

Meyers, J. (1989). The practice of psychology in the schools for the primary prevention of learning and adjustment problems in children: A perspective from the field of education. In L. A. Bond & B. E. Compas (Eds.), *Primary prevention and promotion in the schools* (pp. 391–422). Newbury Park, CA: Sage.

Miller, A. D., Barbetta, P. M., & Heron, T. E. (1994). START tutoring: Designing, training, implementing, adapting, and evaluating tutoring programs for school and home settings. In R. Garner, III, D. M. Sainato, J. O. Cooper, T. E. Heron, W. L. Heward, J. Eshleman, & T. A. Grossi (Eds.), *Behavior analysis in education: Focus on measurably superior instruction* (pp. 265–282). Pacific Grove, CA: Brooks/Cole.

Morgan, D. (1987). *Effects of fast and slow teacher presentation rates on the academic performance of special education students during small-group reading instruction.* Unpublished master's thesis, The Ohio State University, Columbus.

Mrazek, P. J., & Haggerty, R. J. (Eds.). (1994). *Reducing risks for mental disorders: Frontiers for preventive intervention research.* Washington, DC: National Academy Press.

Munoz, R. F., Mrazek, P. J., & Haggerty, R. J. (1996). Institute of Medicine report of prevention of mental disorders: Summary and commentary. *American Psychologist, 51,* 1116–1122.

Narayan, J. S. (1988). *Comparison of hand raising and response card methods of group instruction on fourth-grade students' opportunity to respond and academic achievement.* Unpublished master's thesis, The Ohio State University, Columbus.

Narayan, J. S., Heward, W. L., Gardner, R., III, Courson, F. H., & Omness, C. K. (1990). Using response cards to increase student participation in an elementary classroom. *Journal of Applied Behavior Analysis, 23*(4), 483–490.

National Association of School Psychologists. (1994). *Standards for the provision of school psychological services.* Washington, DC: Author.

Nelson, J. R., Smith, D. J., Taylor, L., Dodd, J. M., & Reavis, K. (1991). Prereferral intervention: A review of the research. *Education and Treatment of Children, 14,* 243–253.

Office of Special Education. (1993). *Fifteenth annual report to Congress.* Washington, DC: U.S. Government Printing Office.

Ohio Department of Education. (1985). *Intervention assistance teams.* Columbus, OH: Author.

Peters, M., & Heron, T. E. (1993). When the best is not good enough: An examination of best practice. *Journal of Special Education, 26*(4), 371–385.

Phillips, B. N. (1990). *School psychology at a turning point.* San Francisco: Jossey-Bass.

Pigott, H. E., Fantuzzo, J. W., & Clement, P. W. (1986). The effects of reciprocal peer tutoring and group contingencies on the academic performance of elementary school children. *Journal of Applied Behavior Analysis, 19,* 93–98.

Ponti, C. R., Zins, J. E., & Graden, J. (1988). Implementing a consultation-based service delivery system to decrease referrals for special education: A case study of organizational considerations. *School Psychology Review, 17*(1), 89–100.

President's Commission on Mental Health. (1978). *Report to the President from the President's Commission on Mental Health* (Vol. 1). Washington, DC: U.S. Government Printing Office.

Pugach, M., & Johnson, L. J. (1990). Meeting diverse needs through professional peer collaboration. In W. Stainback & S. Stainback (Eds.), *Support networks for inclusive schools* (pp. 123–151). Baltimore, MD: Brookes.

Reschly, D. J., & Wilson, M. S. (1995). School psychology practitioners and faculty: 1986 to 1991–2–Trends in demographics, roles, satisfaction, and system reform. *School Psychology Review, 24,* 62–80.

Safran, S. P., & Safran, J. (1997). Prereferral consultation and intervention assistance teams revisited: Some new food for thought. *Journal of Educational and Psychological Consultation, 8*(1), 93–100.

Sainato, D. M., Strain, P. S., & Lyon, S. L. (1987). Increasing academic responding of handicapped preschool children during group instruction. *Journal of the Division of Early Childhood Special Education, 12,* 23–30.

Sevcik, B., & Ysseldyke, J. (1986). An analysis of teachers' prereferral interventions for students exhibiting behavioral problems. *Behavior Disorders, 11,* 109–117.

Severson, H., & Zoref, L. (1991). Prevention and early interventions for addictive behaviors: Health promotion in schools. In G. Stoner, M. R. Shinn, & H. M. Walker (Eds.), *Interventions for achievement and behavior problems* (pp. 539–557). Washington, DC: National Association of School Psychologists.

Sheridan, S. M., Welch, M., & Orme, S. F. (1996). Is consultation effective? A review of outcome research. *Remedial and Special Education, 16,* 341–354.

Shields, J. M., & Heron, T. E. (1989). Teaching organizational skills to students with learning disabilities. *Teaching Exceptional Children, 21,* 8–13.

Shinn, M. R., Nolet, V., & Knutson, N. (1990). Best practices in curriculum-based measurement. In A. Thomas & J. Grimes (Ed.), *Best practices in school psychology–II* (pp. 287–307). Washington, DC: National Association of School Psychologists.

Simeonsson, R. J. (Ed.). (1994). *Risk, resilience, and prevention: Promoting the well-being of all children.* Baltimore, MD: Brookes.

Sindelar, P. T., Griffin, C. C., Smith, S. W., & Wantanabe, A. K. (1992). Prereferral intervention: Encouraging notes on preliminary findings. *The Elementary School Journal, 92,* 245–259.

Stern, G. W., Fowler, S. A., & Kohler, F. W. (1988). A comparison of two intervention roles: Peer monitor and point earner. *Journal of Applied Behavior Analysis, 21,* 103–109.

Stainback, S., Stainback, W., East, K., & Sapon-Shevin, M. (1994). A commentary on inclusion and the development of a positive self-identity by people with disabilities. *Exceptional Children, 60,* 486–490.

Strain, P. S., Odom, S. L., & McConnell, S. (1984). Promoting social reciprocity of exceptional children: Identification, target behavior selection, and intervention. *Remedial and Special Education, 5*(1), 21–28.

Tuma, J. (1989). Mental health services for children: The state of the art. *American Psychologists, 44,* 188–199.

U.S. Department of Health and Human Services. (1995). *Healthy people 2000: Midcourse review and 1995 revisions.* Washington, DC: U.S. Government Printing Office.

Van Houten, R. (1980). *Learning through feedback.* New York: Human Sciences Press.

Van Houten, R. (1984). Setting up performance feedback systems in the classroom. In W. L. Heward, T. E. Heron, D. S. Hill, & J. Trap-Porter (Eds.), *Focus on behavior analysis in education* (pp. 114–125). Columbus, OH: Merrill.

Vargas, J. (1982). What are your exercises teaching? An analysis of stimulus control in instructional materials. In W. L. Heward, T. E. Heron, D. Hill, & J. Trap-Porter (Eds.), *Focus on behavior analysis in education* (pp. 126–141). Columbus, OH: Merrill.

Walker, H., McConnell, S., Holmes, D., Todis, B., Walker, J., & Golden, N. (1983). *The Walker social skills curriculum: The ACCEPTS program.* Austin, TX: Pro-Ed.

Weissberg, R. P., & Greenberg, M. T. (1997). Social and community competence-enhancement and prevention programs. In W. Damon (Series Ed.) & I. Sigel & K. A. Renninger (Vol. Eds.), *Handbook of child psychology: Vol. 4, Child psychology in practice* (5th ed., pp 877–954). New York: Wiley.

Wheatly, R. K. (1986). *The effects of hand raising and response card conditions on nine intermediate developmentally handicapped students during and after money instruction.* Unpublished master's thesis, The Ohio State University, Columbus.

Whitten, E., & Dicker, L. (1995). Intervention assistance teams: A broader vision. *Preventing School Failure, 40,* 41–45.

Will, M. (1986). Educating children with learning

problems: A shared responsibility. *Exceptional Children, 52,* 411–416.

Williams, V. I. (1993). *Effects of two teacher presentation rates on student participation and academic achievement during small group instruction by students with severe behavior disorders.* Unpublished master's thesis, The Ohio State University, Columbus.

Witt, J. C., & Elliott, S. N. (1985). Acceptability of classroom intervention strategies. In T. R. Kratochwill (Ed.), *Advances in school psychology* (Vol. 6, pp. 142–158). Hillsdale, NJ: Erlbaum.

Wood, J., Lazzari, A., Davis, E., Sugai, G., & Carter, J. (1990). National status of the prereferral process: An issue for regular education. *Action in Teacher Education, 12,* 50–56.

Zins, J. E. (1992). Implementing school-based consultation services: An analysis of five years of practice. In R. K. Conyne & J. M. O'Neil (Eds.), *Organizational consultation: A casebook* (pp. 50–79). Newbury Park, CA: Sage.

Zins, J. E. (1995). Has consultation achieved its primary prevention potential? *Journal of Primary Prevention, 15*(3), 285–301.

Zins, J. E., Conyne, R. K., & Ponti, C. R. (1988). Primary prevention: Expanding the impact of psychological services in schools. *School Psychology Review, 17*(4), 540–547.

Zins, J. E., Curtis, M. J., Graden, J., & Ponti, C. R. (1988). *Helping students succeed in the regular classroom: A guide for developing intervention assistance programs.* San Francisco: Jossey-Bass.

Zins, J. E., & Forman, S. G. (Eds.). (1988). Primary prevention: From theory to practice [Special issue]. *School Psychology Review, 17*(4).

Zins, J. E., Graden, J., & Ponti, C. R. (1988). Prereferral intervention to improve special services delivery. *Special Services in the Schools, 4*(3/4), 109–130.

Zins, J. E., & Johnson, L. J. (1994). Prereferral intervention for students with special needs. In T. Husén & T. N. Postlethwaite (Eds.), *The international encyclopedia of education: Vol. 8. Research and studies* (2nd ed., pp. 4657–4662). Oxford, England: Elsevier Science.

Zins, J. E., & Ponti, C. R. (1987). Prereferral consultation: A system to decrease special education referral and placement. *The Community Psychologist, 20*(2), 10–12.

Zins, J. E., Travis, L. F., III, & Freppon, P. A. (1997). Linking research and educational programming to promote social and emotional learning. In P. Salovey & D. Sluyter (Eds.), *Emotional development and emotional intelligence: Implications for educators* (pp. 257–274). New York: Basic Books.

Zins, J. E., & Wagner, D. I. (1997). Health promotion. In G. G. Bear, K. M. Minke, & A. Thomas (Eds.), *Children's needs–II: Development, problems, and alternatives* (pp. 945–954). Bethesda, MD: National Association of School Psychologists.

Zwald, L., & Gresham, F. M. (1982). Behavioral consultation in a secondary class: Using DRL to decrease negative verbal interactions. *School Psychology Review, 11,* 533–544.

CHAPTER **31**

# PSYCHOPHARMACOTHERAPY WITH SCHOOL-AGED CHILDREN

RONALD T. BROWN
*Medical University of South Carolina*
DOUGLAS LEE
JOAN E. DONEGAN
*Emory University School of Medicine*

## INTRODUCTION

Over the past several years, there has been a burgeoning interest in the biological components of many learning and psychiatric disorders (Brown & Donegan, 1996). Whereas new technological developments in the field of neural sciences have spawned an impressive body of research in the adult psychopharmacology literature, only recently have studies begun to focus on the biological etiology of learning and psychiatric disorders in children (Brown & Donegan, 1996). The advancement of diagnostic techniques with children has allowed the systematic investigation of the role of the central nervous system (CNS), particularly the brain, in studying various psychiatric and developmental disorders. In fact, the past decade is frequently referred to as "the age of the brain." Although this program of research is still in its infancy, significant advancements have been made in understanding the role of neurotransmitters, structural differences in the brains of children with psychopathology and/or learning disabilities compared to those of their normally developing peers, and the influence of hormones in psychiatric and learning disorders in children (Brown & Donegan, 1996).

Coupled with the technological advances that have made possible a more precise understanding of the biological factors in psychiatric and developmental disorders that are manifested across the life span, there has been a growth of new pharmaceuticals to manage these disorders. In fact, for a number of adult psychiatric disorders, medication has become the primary treatment modality, supplemented by other modes of therapy (Brown, Dingle, & Landau, 1994). In the field of child psychiatry, there has also been a tremendous increase in the use of psychotropic medication, although with this age group chemical agents are still more often prescribed as an adjunct to other, more traditional psychotherapies. In part, this revolution in pediatric pharmacotherapy has developed because of the now more commonly accepted notion that many disorders in school-aged children have a biological component (Brown & Donegan, 1996; Kruesi et al., 1990), as well as the development of a number of pharmaceutical agents that have been shown to directly improve behavior and cognitive functioning in children (Gadow, 1992). Despite the exciting advancements in pediatric psychopharmacology, research in psychoactive medications for children has progressed at a much slower rate than that for adults. Moreover, the efficacy and safety of various psychotropic agents prescribed for children have yet to be demonstrated through empirical investigation (Brown et al., 1994).

School psychologists should have a solid understanding of the behavioral, cognitive, and physiological effects of psychotropic medication for a number of compelling reasons. As Brown et al. (1994) have suggested, children spend a significant portion of their lives at school, and learning and psychiatric disorders significantly affect their academic achievement and behavior. Thus, the key role of school officials in the reporting and monitoring of the psychological and physiological symptoms in their students is apparent. Numerous investigations have disclosed that certain drug effects may improve classroom behavior and enhance a child's attention, so that improved academic performance may take place. Conversely, some psychotropic medications in sufficiently high doses may compromise learning and inhibit behavior. A careful evaluation of the effects of various medications on children's learning and behavior is therefore not only necessary but also a basic part of the standard of care for physicians who prescribe these medications. Whereas this obligation of the prescribing physician is undisputed, it is interesting that much of the empirical contribution about the effects of psychotropic medication on learning and behavior has been made by either clinical or school psychologists (Brown, Dingle, & Dreelin, 1997; DuPaul & Kyle, 1995; Pelham, 1993; Shelton & Barkley, 1995; Whalen & Henker, 1991).

Brown et al. (1994) have noted that school psychologists have expertise in the assessment of children's learning and behavior, as well as in the development of intervention programs designed to assist children with difficulties in these areas. For this reason, a valuable asset may be underutilized if training in the fundamental aspects of psychotropics, including the indications for use, as well as potential benefits and untoward side effects, is not provided to psychologists. School personnel need to be familiar with the various psychotropics used with school-aged children so they may communicate effectively with health care providers about the selection of appropriate medication to treat specific symptoms, the adjustment of doses, and the documentation of untoward side effects (DuPaul & Kyle, 1995; Forness & Kavale, 1988). The importance of this issue has been underscored in recent surveys of practicing psychologists, most of whom state that they work with children who receive some type of psychotropic medication (Barkley, McMurray, Edelbrock, & Robbins, 1990; Kubiszyn & Carlson, 1995).

Although the use of psychotropic medication for school-aged children has continued at a high pitch, there has been a dearth of empirical data to document their efficacy and safety. In fact, as Werry (1993) has suggested, much of the knowledge of pediatric psychopharmacology has been derived from the principles of adult psychopharmacology. Brown et al. (1994), however, have noted that the school provides an ideal, ecologically sound laboratory in which to examine the effects of medication on cognition, learning, and behavior in the pediatric population. Moreover, there is a natural affinity between the skills that result from the training of school psychologists and the expertise required to conduct research in pediatric psychopharmacology. School psychologists with a sound knowledge of the principles of learning, assessment, and rigorous research methodology are in a prime position to design and participate in research studies in this area. Furthermore, until only recently, pediatric psychopharmacology research has been primarily at a descriptive level, without a great deal of scientific theory to drive this research. Again, the training and expertise provided by psychologists across all disciplines will enhance the development of a more theoretically driven research model.

The emerging role for school psychologists in the delivery of mental and general health services in the schools is coming to fruition (DeMers, 1995; Gutkin, 1995). In part, this role has been dictated by the high cost of health care in the private sector and the scarcity of available health care services in outpatient clinics in the public sector. Moreover, there is a shortage of mental health care providers who have been adequately trained to work with children and adolescents. In response to these issues, Carlson, Paavola, and Talley (1995) have reviewed a model of a full service school in which the provision of mental health services would be part of the job description of most school psychologists. Thus, the future training of school psychologists in this important area is a high priority for the next decade.

The purpose of this chapter is to provide an overview of pediatric psychopharmacology, particularly as it relates to the learning and behavior of children and adolescents. The role of school psychologists in pharmacotherapy is also discussed. The specific classes of psychopharmacological agents are reviewed, with particular attention to pediatric populations. The effects of medication on children's cognition and behavior are a specific focus, as is the training of school psychologists in pediatric psychopharmacology.

# CLASSIFICATION OF PSYCHOTROPIC DRUGS AND CLINICAL INDICATIONS

Psychotropic drugs for children and adolescents have been classified in this chapter primarily by their drug type and/or the specific symptoms to be modified. The drug type classification scheme includes antidepressants and lithium, antipsychotics or neuroleptics, stimulants, anxiolytics, sedatives and hypnotics, and anticonvulsants, as well as the newer medications clonidine, propranolol, and desmopressin (DDAVP). Table 31.1 presents an overview of the psychopharmacologic agents commonly administered to children and ado-

**TABLE 31.1** **Classification of Psychotropic Medications for Children and Adolescents**

| Class of Psychotropic | Generic Name of Medication | Target Symptoms for Class of Psychotropic | Possible Side Effects for Class of Psychotropic |
|---|---|---|---|
| Anticonvulsants | Carbamazepine Ethosuximide Felbamate Gabapentin Phenobarbital Phenytoin Primidone Valproic acid | Seizures, aggression, emotional lability, irritability, mania | Memory and attention disturbance, hyperactivity, irritability, aggression, depressed mood, drowsiness, nausea, rashes, eye problems, gastrointestinal distress, weight gain, tremor, reversible bone marrow effects, agitation, mania |
| Antidepressants Tricyclics | Amitriptyline Desipramine Imipramine | Enuresis, depressive symptoms (i.e., neuro-vegetative symptoms, anhedonia, hopelessness, sadness), ADHD symptoms, particularly with lability of mood | Sedation, dry mouth, constipation, urinary retention, blurred vision, cardiac conduction slowing, mild tachycardia, elevated blood pressure, weight gain, orthostatic hypotension |
| Heterocyclics | Clomipramine Nortriptyline | | |
| Selective serotonin reuptake inhibitors | Fluoxetine Sertraline Paroxetine | Depressive symptoms, obsessive-compulsive disorder | Anxiety, nervousness, insomnia, drowsiness, fatigue, tremor, sweating, gastrointestinal complaints including nausea and diarrhea, dizziness |
| Atypical antidepressants | Bupropion Trazodone | Depressive symptoms | Agitation, dry mouth, insomnia, headache/migraine, nausea/vomiting, constipation, tremor |
| Antidiuretic hormones | Desmopressin acetate | Enuresis | Nasal congestion, rhinitis, mild abdominal cramps, nosebleed, sore throat, cough, upper respiratory infections, hypertension |
| Antihistamines | Diphenhydramine Hydroxyzine | Anxiety, sleep induction, agitation | Dizziness, oversedation, agitation, incoordination, abdominal pain, blurred vision, dry mouth |
| Antihypertensives | Clonidine | Aggression, | Dry mouth, photosensitivity, hypo- |

lescents, with indications, potential benefits, and possible untoward side effects.

## Antidepressants

Antidepressant medications are traditionally that classification of psychotropics used to treat

symptoms of depression. The parameters of the antidepressant classification have been expanded since the 1980s, however, to include a new category that treats not only major depressive disorder and dysthymia (see review by Ambrosini, Mianchi, Rabinovich, & Elia, 1993a,

## TABLE 31.1  (*Continued*)

| Class of Psychotropic | Generic Name of Medication | Target Symptoms for Class of Psychotropic | Possible Side Effects for Class of Psychotropic |
|---|---|---|---|
| | Propranolol | Tourette's disorder, panic attacks, hypertension | tension, dizziness, depression |
| Antimanics | Lithium carbonate | Bipolar disorders, aggression | Gastrointestinal upset, tremor, headache, polyuria/polydipsia, possible renal injury, thyroid dysfunction, toxicity, ataxia, slurred speech, dizziness, sedation, weakness, leukocytosis |
| Anxiolytics, sedatives, hypnotics benzodiazepines | Diazepam Clonazepam Lorazepam Pimozide Buspirone | Seizures, anxiety | Substance abuse, sedation, diminished cognitive performance, ataxia, confusion, emotional lability |
| Neuroleptics Phenothiazines | Chlorpromazine Fluphenazine Thioridazine Trifluoperazine Trifluoperazine | Acute psychotie states, autism, pervasive developmental disorder, Tourette's disorder, dyskinetic movement | Sedation, orthostatic hypotension Anesthesia motor restlessness, Parkinson's symptoms, cognitive blunting, photosensitivity, hypotension, headache, gastrointestinal upset, anticholinergic effects, insomnia, tardive dyskinesia, neuroleptic malignant syndrome, seizures, elevated liver enzymes, Agranulocytosis, acute dystonic reaction, seizures, eye changes (retinopathy), rebound hypertension, depression, cardiac arrhythmia |
| Thioxanthenes | Navane | | |
| Butyrophenes | Haldol | | |
| Stimulants | Dextroamphetamine Methylphenidate Pemoline | Attention and concentration problems impulsivity, distractibility | Insomnia, dysphoria, behavioral rebound, impaired cognitive performance, anorexia, weight loss or failure to gain, depression, tachycardia, growth retardation, tics |

1993b; Pliszka, 1991; Steingard, DeMaso, Goldman, Shorrock, & Bucci, 1995) but also many other psychiatric disorders in children and adolescents.

Antidepressants are now also used to treat several childhood disorders such as attention deficit hyperactivity disorder (ADHD; Biederman, Baldessarini, Wright, Knee, & Harmatz, 1989; Rapoport, Quinn, Bradbard, Riddle, & Brooks, 1974), separation anxiety disorder (school phobia; Gittelman-Klein & Klein, 1971, 1973), overanxious disorder (Birmaher et al., 1994), obsessive-compulsive disorder (De-Veaugh-Geiss, Moroz, Biederman et al., 1992; Flament et al., 1985; Liebowitz, Hollander, Fairbanks, & Campeas, 1990), enuresis (Blackwell, & Currah, 1973), sleep disorders (Pliszka, 1991), and bulimia nervosa (Fava, Herzog, Hamburg, Reiss, Anfang, & Rosenbaum, 1990; Pope, Hudson, Jonas, & Yurgelun-Todd, 1983). Notwithstanding the new and widely varied uses for antidepressants in children and adolescents, these medications are still primarily employed in the treatment of major depression. Before the 1970s, it was widely held that children did not experience depression, but we now appreciate that children experience depressive symptoms that are phenomenologically similar to those of adults (Kaslow, Brown, & Mee, 1995; Kovacs & Goldston, 1991; Ryan et al., 1987). The symptoms of major depressive disorder as presented in the *Diagnostic and Statistical Manual, Fourth Edition* (DSM-IV; American Psychiatric Association, 1994) include depressed mood, appetite change (a substantial increase or decrease in body weight), anhedonia, anergia (lack of energy), decreased concentration, changes in psychomotor activity or sleep patterns, and recurrent thoughts of death. Because depression only recently has been recognized as a diagnostic entity applicable to children (Kaslow et al., 1995), the empirical data about the efficacy of antidepressant medication in this population remain inconclusive (Gadow, 1992; Pliszka, 1991). Despite the scant empirical data, however, the clinical use of these agents is widespread, with substantial anecdotal and clinical support for their efficacy (Puig-Antich et al., 1987).

Since the first use of antidepressants, several descriptive classes have been introduced, including tricyclic antidepressants, selective serotonin reuptake inhibitors, and monoamine oxidase inhibitors, as well as the category of atypical antidepressants. The tricyclics were the first class of

antidepressants to be introduced and have been the most widely used, particularly among British child psychiatrists (Bramble, 1995). Because of the long track record of these psychotropic agents, we have the most experience with this class of antidepressants. However, because of a more favorable side effect profile than tricyclic antidepressants and the increasing recognition of efficacy, specific serotonin reuptake inhibitors have been gaining favor quickly since their relatively recent introduction. In contrast, monoamine oxidase inhibitors have been prescribed significantly less frequently because of potential deleterious side effects due to dietary restrictions, the higher potential of life-threatening drug interactions, and potentially more frequent lethal overdoses. Also, other medications, including lithium carbonate or thyroid hormone (triiodothyronine), are occasionally prescribed to augment the actions of antidepressants when treatment-resistant depression is encountered.

## Tricyclic Antidepressants

The most commonly used tricyclics include amitriptyline (Elavil), nortriptyline (Pamelor), imipramine (Tofranil), desipramine (Norpramin), and clomipramine (Anafranil). Although tricyclics were initially used in the pediatric population to treat enuresis, today the common indications also include major depressive disorder, ADHD, and anxiety disorder.

Tricyclic antidepressants are used to treat major depressive disorders, especially in the presence of the neurovegetative signs and symptoms that typically accompany major depression, such as changes in sleep and appetite, diurnal variations in mood, alterations in attention and concentration, anhedonia, and sadness. The efficacy of tricyclic antidepressant treatment of children and adolescents with major depressive disorder as reported in the literature is interpreted differently, depending on the design of the trial (for a review, see Steingard et al., 1995). Six open trials (trials in which the investigators and the patients are not blind to the medication condition) that used tricyclics for children with a diagnosis of depression found that 46% to 100% of the subjects responded favorably to treatment, and seven open trials in adolescents reported a response rate ranging from 30% to 73% (see the review by Steingard et al., 1995). In contrast to these encouraging findings, four placebo-controlled studies of children diagnosed with depression reported favorable response rates of 31% to 67%, although the placebo response rate was up to 68%. Three placebo-controlled studies of adolescents with the same diagnosis demonstrated response rates of 8% to 50%, with a placebo response rate of 21% to 33%. Essentially, the efficacy of tricyclic antidepressants for depressed children and adolescents in these trials was broadly comparable to that of the placebo. Similarly, in a recent clinical trial of desipramine prescribed for adolescents diagnosed with major depressive disorder, Kutcher et al. (1994) found no significant differences in treatment outcome between desipramine and placebo-treated groups. These findings must be interpreted in the context of the relatively small total number of subjects in these investigations, the diagnostic issues raised not only by comorbidity but also by the response to placebo, the therapeutic effects of the periodic clinical contact, and the brief length of the trials.

Whereas tricyclics had been used historically as a first-line treatment for depression, following the development of selective serotonin reuptake inhibitors, with their favorable side effect profiles, these psychotropic agents are now often prescribed only after other antidepressants have failed. A particular tricyclic is frequently chosen for a specific individual, depending on the characteristic properties of the medication and the likelihood of the individual to tolerate them. Specifically, the tricyclics like desipramine or nortriptyline tend to have less untoward side effects than amitriptyline or imipramine.

Tricyclic management of ADHD was initially reported in the 1970s (Waizer, Hoffman, Pulizos, & Englehardt, 1974). Subsequent double-blind placebo-controlled studies (Biederman et al., 1989; Gualtieri, Keenan, & Chandler, 1991) have found significantly decreased hyperactivity with the use of tricyclic antidepressants. However, studies comparing tricyclics with stimulant medication found the stimulants to be superior in the management of ADHD-related symptoms (Garfinkel, Wender, Sloman & O'Neill, 1983; Rapoport et al., 1974). Some investigators report that tricyclics improve hyperactivity and mood symptoms more than attention and concentration (Wender, 1988). The tricyclics have been found to be particularly beneficial for children with ADHD, who have comorbid mood or anxiety disorders, as well as for those children with comorbid tic disorders and/or Tourette's disorder and for those who have encountered a number of untoward side effects with stimulant medications (Brown et al., 1994; Pliszka, 1991;

Spencer, Biederman, Kerman, Steingard, & Wilens, 1993; Steingard, Biederman, Spencer, Wilens, & Gonzalez, 1993). Tricyclics are considered the second-line choice of treatment for ADHD after stimulants have failed to control the symptoms. Since this occurs in about one-third of the cases, the tricyclics offer some promise of alleviating ADHD symptoms when children are refractory to stimulant medication (Rapoport & Zametkin, 1980).

In addition to treating major depressive disorder and ADHD, tricyclics have frequently been used for other psychiatric conditions. Clomipramine, a tricyclic antidepressant and potent inhibitor of the reuptake of the neurotransmitter serotonin, has been the standard of treatment for obsessive-compulsive disorder in adults. In children and adolescents with obsessive-compulsive disorder, clomipramine has been found to be effective in placebo-controlled and crossover-designed studies (DeVeaugh-Geiss et al., 1992; Flament et al., 1985; Leonard et al., 1989). Also, tricyclic antidepressants have been reported to successfully treat separation anxiety disorder, also referred to as school phobia (Gittelman-Klein & Klein, 1971), although other studies have not replicated these findings (Bernstein, Garfinkel, & Borchardt, 1990). Some recent research from the National Institute of Mental Health has suggested that clomipramine may be clinically useful for developmental stuttering disorders, thus suggesting that stuttering may have a biological etiology (Gordon, Cotelingam, Stager, Ludlow, Hamburger, & Rapoport, 1995).

Most tricyclics are effective in rapidly reducing nocturnal enuresis. The psychotropic agent that is most widely used to treat this disorder is imipramine. Fritz, Rockney, and Yeung (1994) examined the efficacy of imipramine compared to a placebo for children diagnosed with nocturnal enuresis. They found that imipramine was superior to a placebo and that efficacy was positively associated with the dose of imipramine. The dose required to manage enuresis is usually less than that needed to effectively treat major depressive disorder. The drawback of using a tricyclic to manage enuresis is that once the medication is discontinued, a relapse of enuresis often occurs within days to months (Shaffer, Costello, & Hill, 1968).

Although tricyclics may improve behavior and concentration, a wide constellation of untoward side effects may hinder a child's functioning at school. Sedation is a common side effect, especially with amitriptyline and imipramine, hereas nortriptyline and desipramine tend to cause less sedation. Anticholinergic side effects are blurred vision, dry mouth, and constipation; the severity of these complications tends to increase proportionately with the level of tricyclic serum (blood) concentration.

Several less common but nonetheless clinically significant conditions associated with tricyclics may affect a child's clinical presentation. An example is CNS toxicity, which may manifest itself in a variety of ways, including a worsening of mood symptoms, psychotic symptoms, and organic symptoms like disturbed memory, disorientation, confusion, and agitation (Preskorn & Jerkovich, 1990). Often this condition develops within the first two weeks of treatment (Davies, Tucker, Harrow, & Detre, 1971), is associated with elevated tricyclic levels, and can affect approximately 4% of the recipients (Preskorn, Jerkovich, Beber, & Widener, 1989; Preskorn, Weller, Jerkovich, Hughes, & Weller, 1988). Tricyclics can also precipitate hypomania or mania (Siegel, 1989), may contribute to cardiovascular changes (Leonard et al., 1995; Puig-Antich et al., 1987), and may even produce fatal reactions (Riddle, Geller, & Ryan, 1993). For this reason, some experts have recommended against the use of tricyclic antidepressants for children (Werry, 1995), although others have been more positive about their beneficial effects and less concerned about cardiac changes (Biederman, Thisted, Greenhill, & Ryan, 1995). Nonetheless, if tricyclics are used for children, careful monitoring of serum tricyclic levels and electrocardiograph changes is imperative.

Tricyclic antidepressant treatment is usually initiated with low doses so that the child's sensitivity to untoward side effects and the ability to tolerate the medication can be carefully evaluated. Thereafter, tricyclic antidepressants are titrated slowly until they reach therapeutic range. The monitoring of tricyclics must include a careful evaluation of their optimal effects, as well as untoward side effects, with the understanding that clinical improvement may not be appreciated for weeks, until after reaching therapeutic serum levels. The range of effective doses will vary across medications, dosages, and individual differences, including the child's size and metabolism (Brown et al., 1994).

## Selective Serotonin Reuptake Inhibitors

Since their introduction in the 1980s, selective serotonin reuptake inhibitors (SSRIs) have quickly become widely prescribed in the United States be-

cause of their relative safety and favorable side effect profile. The currently available SSRIs include fluoxetine (Prozac), sertraline (Zoloft), paroxetine (Paxil), and fluvoxamine (Luvox), each of which has slightly different pharmacologic properties but similar indications. The psychopharmacology literature has generally supported the efficacy and therapeutic advantage of SSRIs relative to tricyclic antidepressants for treating depression in adults (Stokes, 1993).

Although the indications for SSRIs in children have mirrored those in adults, the experience is still limited. Preliminary reports of fluoxetine (Como & Kurlan, 1991; Geller, Biederman, Reed, Spencer, & Wilens, 1995; Liebowitz et al., 1990; Riddle, Hardin, King, Scahill, & Woolston, 1990; Riddle, Scahill, King, Hardin, Anderson, Ort, Smith, Leckman, & Cohen, 1992) and fluvoxamine (Apter et al., 1994) have shown promising efficacy in managing obsessive-compulsive disorder in prepubertal children and sustaining the benefits over time (Geller et al., 1995). Other initial investigations have found SSRIs to be promising in the management of symptoms of ADHD (Barrickman, Noyes, Kuperman, Schumacher, & Verda, 1991), elective mutism (Black & Uhde, 1994; Black, Uhde, & Tancer, 1992; Wright, Cuccaro, Leonhardt, Kendall, & Anderson, 1995) and acquired head injuries (Jain, Birmaher, Garcia, Al-Shabbout, & Ryan, 1993; Simeon, Diniala, Ferguson, & Copping, 1990). One recent trial of fluoxetine in children with overanxious disorder, social phobia, or separation anxiety disorder demonstrated that these children showed marked improvement with minimal untoward side effects (Birmaher et al., 1994). Nevertheless, despite the promising clinical efficacy of SSRIs with pediatric populations, more studies are required to fully evaluate the efficacy and safety of this class of medications.

Notwithstanding the relatively favorable side effect profile of these psychoactive substances, some potential untoward side effects of SSRIs can be of concern. Motoric activation, anxiety, agitation, insomnia, somnolence, and decreased appetite have been reported, at times necessitating discontinuation of the SSRI (Geller et al., 1995; Riddle, King, Hardin, Scahill, Ort, Chappell, Rasmusson, & Leckman, 1990). Also, as with most antidepressants, SSRIs can precipitate mania and hypomania (Rosenburg, Johnson, & Sahl, 1992). One case study has even suggested the possibility of fluoxetine-induced cognitive and memory disturbances (Bangs, Petti, & Mark-David, 1994). Consequently, as with many other psychotropic agents, SSRIs are usually started at low doses to assess the presence of possible adverse reactions and, in their absence, are then titrated upward to therapeutic doses.

## Atypical Antidepressants

Alternative antidepressants with more limited experience with children may be prescribed when tricyclic antidepressants and SSRIs have not been clinically effective. One such medication is trazodone, which primarily has been used to treat depression and occasionally chronic pain in adults and at times is prescribed to treat similar conditions in children. Even though the clinical experience of trazodone with children is very limited, it has been determined that sedation is a common side effect.

Bupropion is another antidepressant that has had limited use with children but has shown particular promise in attenuating attentional problems from either ADHD or major depressive disorder. Preliminary results have revealed the potential of bupropion in treating ADHD (Barrickman et al., 1995; Simeon, Ferguson, & Fleet, 1986). In fact, bupropion was as effective as stimulant medication in treating ADHD in a double-blind crossover study. However, even though it may improve memory performance in children with ADHD (Casat, Pleasants, Schroeder, & Parler, 1988), agitation, confusion, and irritability may prove to be side effects (Dager & Herich, 1990). Clearly, additional studies are required for bupropion as well as other atypical antidepressants for children.

## Lithium

Lithium has been endorsed in the child psychiatric literature as an effective treatment of bipolar disorder (manic depressive illness), depression, and severe impulsive aggression (Bukstien, 1992). Lithium is a naturally occurring salt, which comes in two forms: lithium carbonate and lithium citrate. Lithium carbonate, which comes in pill form, is more commonly used than lithium citrate, which is a liquid. Lithium carbonate is available in regular, as well as slow-release, forms. The latter has the advantage of requiring fewer daily doses and characteristically has less severe untoward side effects.

The use of lithium for children and adolescents over a period of years has expanded our knowledge of its properties and indications (Alessi, Naylor, Ghaziuddin, & Zubieta, 1994). Most pediatric indications for lithium involve mood disorders in adolescents and severe aggression and disruptive behavior disorders in children (Alessi, et al., 1994). In adults, lithium has been the medication of choice for bipolar disorder. Manic signs and symptoms such as racing thoughts, pressured speech, grandiosity, and increased activity often respond to therapeutic lithium serum levels. Despite the paucity of large-scale studies involving children with bipolar disorder, several reports have suggested the efficacy of lithium in treating this disorder (Carlson, Rapport, Pataki, & Kelly, 1992; Varanka, Weller, Weller, & Fristad, 1988). Open trials have demonstrated lithium to be effective for children (DeLong & Aldershof, 1987) and adolescents (Strober, Morrell, Burroughs, Lampert, Danforth, & Freeman, 1988). The efficacy of lithium has been demonstrated for bipolar disorder (Strober, Morrell, Lampert, & Burroughs, 1990), treatment-resistant depression, and severe impulsive aggression (Campbell, Small, Green Jennings, & Anderson, 1984; Ryan, Meyer, Dachille, Mazzie, & Puig-Antich, 1988; Strober et al., 1990). However, large placebo-controlled studies have yet to be conducted with children.

Children usually tolerate lithium without many adverse reactions (Lena, 1979; Varanka et al., 1988). The more common untoward side effects, which resolve with dose reduction or discontinuation of the medication, include fatigue, tremor, vomiting, diarrhea, headache, and weight gain. Younger children tend to experience untoward side effects more often than do their older peers, and the side effects tend to be significantly associated with the severity of the diagnosis (Campbell et al., 1991). Lithium toxicity, which may occur when the serum levels are elevated, may be seen in such symptoms as slurred speech, delirium, hallucinations, drowsiness, vomiting, and diarrhea (Campbell, et al., 1991). Because of a relatively low therapeutic index, lithium doses are increased slowly, and serum levels need meticulous monitoring. It should be cautioned that lithium may have significant adverse physiological effects such as toxicity that may not be evident except through laboratory tests. For this reason, dosing, compliance, and a routine medical examination of the child or adolescent are imperative.

In summary, the effectiveness of antidepressant medications for depressed children and adolescents has yet to be empirically substantiated.

While the use of antidepressant medications for the management of the symptoms of other psychiatric disorders, such as those relating to anxiety and ADHD, has demonstrated some promise, there has been little diagnostic specificity for the benefits of the drug; rather, antidepressants are probably most appropriately viewed as a broad-spectrum pharmacotherapy, in which the potential therapeutic effects for a child must be considered individually. The only means of confidentially predicting a positive response is to conduct a trial. Ambrosini et al. (1993a) have raised some methodological issues characteristic of this research that may obscure differences across clinical drug trials. These issues include clinical trials of antidepressants characterized by heterogeneous samples in the types of depression and comorbidity patterns, sex differences, and sample heterogeneity across ages. Clearly, many more studies of the clinical efficacy of antidepressant medications need to include ratings of behavior, cognitive effects, and biological markers.

## Antipsychotics

Antipsychotic medications, sometimes also referred to as neuroleptics or major tranquilizers, are the medications of choice in the treatment of psychotic disorders like schizophrenia, as well as in the developmental disorders like autism and, in some cases, severe aggression (Campbell, Gonzalez, Silva, & Werry, 1993). Target symptoms for which antipsychotics have been clinically demonstrated to be effective are overactivity, aggression, hallucinations, delusions, stereotypies, and agitation (Campbell et al., 1993). Again, as with many other psychotropics, there has been a limited number of drug trials of these medications, particularly investigations of a double-blind nature. Nonetheless, the limited empirical data that are available suggest generally modest effects for psychotic symptoms. It has been found that younger children tend to have less response than their older peers; children frequently require higher doses of neuroleptics than adults because of the relatively high metabolism rates of younger persons (DuPaul & Kyle, 1995).

The neuroleptics are classified according to chemical structure and potency. The most frequently employed classes for pediatric populations are the phenothiazines, the thioxanthenes, and the butyrophenones (Gelenberg, 1991). Examples of the phenothiazines include chlorpromazine (Thorazine), thioridazine (Mellaril), trifluoperazine (Stelazine), and fluphenazine (Prolixin). Thiothixene (Navane) is a commonly used agent in the tioxanthene class, and haloperidol (Haldol) is one of the neuroleptics in the butyrophenone class. Neuroleptics are typically ranked by their potency in comparison with chlorpromazine (Thorazine). High-potency agents include haloperidol and trifluoperazine, and low-potency medications include chlorpromazine and thioridazine (Brown et al., 1994).

Haloperidol has been demonstrated to be effective for children in reducing the target symptoms associated with schizophrenia in both open and double-blind trials, whereas some other neuroleptic drugs have been investigated only in open drug trials (for review, see DuPaul & Kyle, 1995). Although a number of neuroleptics have shown promise in alleviating some of the symptoms of pervasive developmental disorder, including aggression, stereotypies, and social withdrawal, as well as in enhancing communication skills (Campbell, et al., 1993), none has been demonstrated to be effective in completely abating symptoms (Gadow, 1986). Haloperidol has also been demonstrated to be effective in eliminating symptoms of tic disorders, particularly in low doses (Gadow, 1986; Shapiro & Shapiro, 1988), although there has been some concern about the effect of the drug on children's learning, as well as the behavioral effects on withdrawal of the medication (Campbell et al., 1993). For this reason, the benefits of haloperidol in temporarily eliminating the behaviors associated with tic disorders must be weighed carefully against its potentially adverse side effects.

Frequently occurring untoward side effects of antipsychotic medications include sedation, weight gain, hypotension, anticholinergic effects (i.e., dry mouth and constipation), and—more seriously—cardiovascular toxicity (Campbell et al., 1993). These particular symptoms are more likely to be manifested with the low-potency neuroleptics. Other deleterious side effects of the neuroleptics include extrapyramidal symptoms and neuroleptic malignant syndrome. Extrapyramidal symptoms may include acute dystonic reactions (involuntary muscle contractions that are acute, episodic, and recurrent), akathisia (motoric restlessness), Parkinson syndrome (tremor, rigidity, and akinesia-decreased movement), and tardive dyskinesia (abnormal involuntary movements). Neuroleptic malignant syndrome, a very serious and potentially fatal disorder, consists of fever, muscular rigidity, and stupor. These untoward side effects are more frequently associated with high-potency neuroleptics (Brown et al., 1994). Since these side effects are typically correlated with dose and length of treatment, Gadow (1986) has recommended that the minimum effective dose should be used to diminish their likelihood. Finally, given the higher incidence of deleterious side effects, it is evident that careful monitoring of children and adolescents is mandatory.

One neuroleptic that shows particular promise in the treatment of childhood schizophrenia is clozapine; this medication has had widespread appeal among the psychiatric community, in part because it has minimal extrapyramidal side effects (Meltzer, 1992). Mozes et al. (1994) have reported several cases in which clozapine was successfully used for children who had been diagnosed with schizophrenia and who were refractory to other neuroleptic drugs. While research with clozapine is still in its infancy, the potential of this medication to effectively manage psychotic disorders in children is encouraging, particularly for those with childhood-onset schizophrenia who have not shown any improvement with other neuroleptics.

## Stimulants

Stimulants are drugs that produce excitation of the CNS (for a review, see Brown, 1996). These psychotropics have been used since the 1930s in the management of certain psychiatric disorders of children and adolescents (Bradley, 1937). Since that time, there has been an ongoing clinical and research interest in stimulants, which has been the most meticulously studied treatment modality in child and adolescent psychiatry (Brown et al., 1997). This phenomenon is a result of the fact that management of specific attentional and behavioral problems in children has increased significantly over the past two decades (Wilens & Biederman, 1992), and the rate of written prescriptions has doubled every four to seven years (Safer & Krager, 1988).

The most commonly administered stimulants in the United States are dextroamphetamine (Dexedrine), methylphenidate (Ritalin), and pemoline (Cylert). Dextroamphetamine and methylphenidate alter the availability of neurotransmitters, primarily dopamine and norepinephrine, by stimulating the release of dopamine into the synapses and thereby preventing the presynaptic reuptake of these neurotransmitters (Levy & Hobbes, 1988; Wilens & Biederman,

1992). Despite the plethora of research into the effects of stimulants on the CNS, no definitive conceptualization of the specific mechanism of their action is available (Pelham, 1993). Nonetheless, as Pelham has argued, an understanding of the neurophysiology of stimulants is not necessary for appropriate and effective clinical application. In fact, the most illuminating information about stimulant drug application has come from the clinical and pediatric psychology literature, which has examined the effects of stimulants on learning, cognition, and behavior (Brown et al., in press). Stimulants influence the regulation of arousal, attention, and reactivity (Douglas & Peters, 1979).

The most commonly used stimulants, their indications, and their adverse effects are presented in Table 31.2.

The stimulants are typically administered orally several times a day and are quickly eliminated from the body within 24 hours (Brown et al., 1997). Both dextroamphetamine and methylphenidate are available in regular and in long-acting forms (Dexedrine-Spansules and Ritalin-SR), and recently published empirical evidence attests to the equivalent efficacy and minimal side effects of both the sustained release (SR) and standard forms (Fitzpatrick, Klorman, Brumaghim, & Borgstedt, 1992; Pelham et al., 1990). A decided advantage of the long-acting forms is that administration may not be required during the school day.

Some well-controlled clinical trials have examined the comparative efficacy of dextroamphetamine and methylphenidate to manage the symptoms of ADHD and have demonstrated similar benefits, as well as untoward side effects (for a review, see Brown et al., 1997). However, clinical experience clearly suggests that response is idiosyncratic and that the failure to respond to one of these medications warrants a trial of the other (Barkley, DuPaul, & Costello, 1993). Pelham, Swanson, Bender-Furman, and Schwindt (1995) have provided encouraging data to support the efficacy of pemoline in a series of behavioral and academic measures during the course of a school day. Nonetheless, because of the need to carefully monitor liver functioning (Goodman & Gilman, 1980), pemoline is used less frequently than the other stimulants.

Typically, stimulants are administered on a twice daily schedule, with a third dose in the afternoon if this is deemed to be necessary. Pemoline is administered only once a day because of its

**TABLE 31.2  Commonly Used Stimulants for Children and Adolescents**

| | Dextroamphetamine (Dexedrine) | Methylphenidate (Ritalin) | Pemoline (Cylert) |
|---|---|---|---|
| Indications | Overactivity, Impulsivity, Inattention | | |
| How supplied (mg) | 5, 5, 10, 15-spansule | 5, 10, 20, SR-20 | 18.75, 37.5, 75 |
| Single-dose range (mg/kg) | .15 to .5 | .3 to .7 | .5 to 2.5 |
| Daily dose range | | | |
|   mg/kg/day | .3 to 1.25 | .6 to 2.0 | .5 to 3.0 |
|   mg/day | 5 to 40 | 10 to 60 | 18.75 to 112.5 |
| Initial dosage | 2.5 mg, 2 to 3 times/day | 5 mg, 2 to 3 times/day | 18.75 mg each morning |
| Peak plasma level | 2 to 3 hours | 1.5 to 2.5 hours | 2 to 4 hours |
| Plasma half-life | 4 to 6 hours | 2 to 3 hours | 7 to 8 hours (children) |
| Peak clinical effect | 1 to 2 hours | 1 to 3 hours | If prescribed as indicated, several weeks after treatment begins therapeutic effect is generally sustained over several hours |
| Onset of behavioral effect | 30 to 60 minutes | 30 to 60 minutes | Variable |
| Duration of behavioral effect | 4 to 6 hours | 3 to 5 hours | 6 to 8 hours |
| Common adverse reactions | Difficulty in falling asleep and mild elevation of pulse and blood pressure | | |
| Less frequent adverse reactions | Decreased appetite (temporary), crying and dysphoria, growth retardation (ht. and wt., mild), drowsiness, anxiety, and irritability | | |
| Serious but unusual adverse reactions | Psychotic thoughts, lowering seizure threshold, worsening of tic disorder or dyskinesia, potential for medication abuse, and hypertension | | Psychotic thoughts, lowering seizure threshold, worsening of tic disorder or dyskinesia, potential for medication abuse, hypertension, hepatocellular injury, elevated serum glutamic pyruvic transaminase |

longer half-life. Over the past two decades, there has been significant interest in empirically determining doses of stimulants that target the management of specific behaviors, including learning (Sprague & Sleator, 1977) and cognition (Brown & Sleator, 1979). However, more recently, specific dose-response relationships have been seriously questioned (Douglas, Barr, Desilets, & Sherman, 1995; Rapport & Kelly, 1991). A consensus of the clinical literature is that stimulant effects are interactive and interdependent on a number of variables, including duration of the ef-

fect, task and performance characteristics, individual differences, and the prevailing social and environmental conditions.

## Iatrogenic and Emanative Effects
### Short Term

Although six decades of research have consistently found the stimulants to be one of the safest classes of psychotropics, as with all medications, these psychotropics have both positive and negative effects. The most common untoward side effects include insomnia and decreased appetite, although irritability, weight loss, headaches, and abdominal pain are also frequently reported (Werry & Aman, 1993). Other less common untoward side effects include negative mood changes, tics and other nervous movements, dizziness, drowsiness, nail biting, anxiety, social withdrawal, euphoria, nightmares, and staring (DuPaul & Barkley, 1990). Barkley et al. (1990) found that over one-half of their sample, who had been diagnosed with ADHD, demonstrated decreased appetite, insomnia, anxiousness, irritability, or proneness to crying. However, many of these untoward side effects were also evident in the placebo condition, leading the investigators to conclude that many of these symptoms may be associated with ADHD rather than untoward side effects of stimulants. Most importantly, the frequency and severity of side effects were found to be related to the dose, with greater untoward side effects being associated with higher doses (Brown & Sexson, 1988; DuPaul & Barkley, 1990).

One particular untoward side effect that has been noted with methylphenidate is the rebound phenomenon, which has been described as a deterioration of behavior (worse than baseline) that occurs in the late afternoon or early evening following day-time stimulant drug therapy (Johnston, Pelham, Hoza, & Sturges, 1988). While such rebound effects are quite variable across children, alterations in dosing and scheduling can be helpful in either eliminating or lessening the problem.

One potentially serious untoward side effect from stimulants is the development of abnormal motor movements, that is, tics (DuPaul & Barkley, 1990). While it is unclear whether stimulants can induce Tourette's or other tic disorders in children who did not previously exhibit the symptoms, screening for a family history of Tourette's before prescribing stimulant medication is, in any case, important. Other rare side effects of the stimulants are allergic skin reactions, lip licking and biting, and picking of the finger tips (Brown et al., 1997). Some clinical reports have also found a decrease in social interactions in response to stimulant drug treatment, and other studies have noted dysphoric symptoms during the period of treatment (DuPaul & Barkley, 1990). Finally, tactile and visual hallucinations have been reported, although the origins of these symptoms are frequently found in the presence of previously existing thought disturbances. Fortunately, many of these deleterious effects are resolved by either stopping or lowering the dose of the medication.

Aside from the more serious side effects of the stimulants, the clinical literature indicates that the less serious side effects are frequently transitory, with some dissipation following the administration of a lower dose. Also, side effects encountered with one stimulant may not necessarily be encountered with another in the same class. Finally, although stimulants are effective for the majority of children and adolescents for whom they are prescribed, youths who receive these agents must be carefully monitored, with the clinician balancing the possible benefits of the medication with the potential adverse side effects.

## Long Term

Despite the plethora of studies on the short-term effects of stimulants, few studies have addressed the potential long-term effects of this class of drugs (DuPaul & Barkley, 1990; Rapport & Kelly, 1991) because of the systematic difficulties encountered in attempting to conduct longitudinal studies, as well as the ethical issues involved in placing children in a no-medication or in a placebo-control group for extensive periods of time. Generally, the results of these investigations have suggested that children with ADHD who were treated with stimulants for at least five years did not differ in any meaningful way from children who had never received pharmacotherapy for the disorder (Hechtman, Weiss, & Perlman, 1984). It should be noted, however, that many of the children participating in these investigations were not on the medication at the time of follow-up, which may, in part, have contributed to the negative results (Brown, Borden, Wynne, Schleser, & Clingerman, 1986). Clearly, additional research is sorely needed in this area.

The most informative follow-up studies that are available on the long-term effects of stimulants have focused on their potential deleterious effects. Gittelman-Klein and associates (Gittelman-Klein, Landa, Mattes, & Klein, 1988; Gittelman-Klein & Mannuzza, 1988) have carefully addressed the issue of growth suppression in children treated with stimulant medication over the course of several years. They assessed the effects of methylphenidate withdrawal on the growth of children with ADHD and found that the children who were taken off this medication during the summer months realized a positive effect on height but not on weight. In a follow-up investigation, Gittelman-Klein and Mannuzza compared the heights of young adults who had been treated with stimulants to a nonmedicated control group with a history of behavior problems. No differences were found between the treated patients and the controls, and both groups were comparable with the national norm for stature. Based on their findings, Gittelman-Klein and associates conclude that a compensatory growth rate, or growth rebound, occurs after the discontinuation of stimulant drug therapy.

Questions have long been raised about the long-term effects of stimulant medication on the cardiovascular system, given the short-term effects of increased heart rate, respiration, and blood pressure (Barkley et al., 1993; Brown & Sexson, 1988). A consensus of the clinical research is that the cardiovascular effects are transitory and dissipate when the medication is eliminated from the body. Unfortunately, there have been no longitudinal follow-up studies to systematically address this issue, an area that remains ripe for future investigation.

One concern frequently raised by the parents of children who are administered stimulants is the possible addiction of their children to the medication or perhaps the increased risk of abuse of other drugs at adolescence. The few available studies that have examined this issue have failed to confirm that children medicated with stimulants are at more risk for addiction than their peers who were not treated with medication (Gadow, 1981; Henker, Whalen, Bugenthal, & Barker, 1981). In fact, some research has suggested that a positive response to stimulants may be associated with a lower probability of alcohol and drug abuse later in life than would generally be expected in the population free of psychopathology (Blouin, Bornstein, & Trites, 1978; Loney, Kramer, Milich, 1981). It should also be noted that many older children frequently resist taking medication and wish to discontinue its use prematurely (Brown, Borden, Wynne, Clingerman, & Spunt, 1987). As Gittelman and Wender (1995) have argued, in spite of the widespread application of stimulant drug therapy in children and adolescents, very few cases of abuse have been reported in the literature. Nonetheless, despite these encouraging data and given the frequent comorbidity of ADHD with conduct disorders, which place children and adolescents at a significantly higher risk for substance abuse, careful monitoring should be the rule.

## Clinical Indications

Stimulants are primarily indicated for the clinical management of ADHD, although there has been a burgeoning of research to study their efficacy with other disorders, both of a psychiatric and physical nature. In the following section, we review the particular disorders for which stimulants have been effective, as well as those disorders for which the relevant research to date has demonstrated some promising clinical uses for these agents.

### Attention Deficit Hyperactivity Disorder (ADHD)

It has been estimated that up to 6% of elementary school–aged children are receiving stimulant medication for the management of overactivity and inattention (Jacobvitz, Sroufe, Steward, & Leffert, 1990), and stimulants continue to be the most pervasive treatment of ADHD (Henker & Whalen, 1989). The results of a number of studies have consistently attested to the efficacy of stimulants in enhancing the performance of children with this disorder for laboratory tasks of cognitive performance, more efficient search strategies (Rapport & Kelly, 1991), long- and short-term recall tasks (Douglas, Barr, Amin, O'Neill, & Britton, 1988), improved paired associate learning (Dalby, Kinsbourne, & Swanson, 1989), flexible thinking, and tasks related to perceptual and motoric functioning (Douglas et al., 1988, 1995).

Despite the impressive track record of stimulants in the short term, a major unresolved issue is their influence on academic performance and learning. Although classroom behavior has shown a positive effect from stimulants (DuPaul & Rapport, 1993; Gadow, 1993; Rapport, Denney, DuPaul, & Gardner, 1994), several investigations have failed to demonstrate an association between these impressive behavioral effects in the classroom and academic achievement on standardized tests. Recent studies have been more encouraging on this issue (Balthazor, Wagner & Pelham, 1991; Tannock, Schachar, Carr, & Logan, 1989; Vyse & Rapport, 1989), and although they have been more methodologically rigorous than previous studies in this area, they are still somewhat limited because they have not used standardized instruments of academic achievement.

Elia, Welsh, Gullotta, and Rapoport (1993) recently studied the effects of methylphenidate on the performance of children with ADHD on standardized achievement tests of reading and mathematics. When receiving either methylphenidate or dextroamphetamine, children attempted more reading and mathematics tasks, with an increased percentage correct on the reading series. In contrast to these rather encouraging findings, Forness, Cantwell, Swanson, Hanna, and Youpa (1991) evaluated the effects of methylphenidate on standardized academic achievement for children who were diagnosed with ADHD, some of whom also had comorbid conduct disorder. Only the comorbid group demonstrated enhanced reading comprehension as a function of stimulant drug therapy, although a six-week follow-up evaluation yielded more encouraging findings for the modestly long-term effects of stimulant treatment. Finally, although the effects of stimulants have not been particularly positive in raising achievement scores, academic efficiency has been enhanced (Pelham, Bender, Caddell, Booth, & Moorer, 1985).

Another major issue has been whether or not stimulants exert their effects on learning through the development of dependent states. The majority of studies examining the effects of state-dependent learning, or the failure to transfer learning in a medicated state to an unmedicated state, have not found support for this development (for a review, see Brown & Borden, 1989). Nonetheless, practitioners still need to carefully monitor the effects of stimulants on learning and the overall academic performance of the children who are receiving these agents, as well as any other type of psychotropic medication that may affect the CNS.

There is a voluminous literature, which parallels the cognition literature, on the effects of stimulant medication on the behaviors of children with ADHD. Generally, stimulant drugs exert beneficial influences on rule-governed behavior and compliance with commands (Pelham, Carlson, Sams, Vallano, Dixon, & Hoza, 1993), parent-child interactions (for a review, see Barkley, DuPaul, & McMurray, 1991), and physical and verbal aggression (Hinshaw, 1991). The results of these studies have unequivocally demonstrated the efficacy of stimulants in decreasing classroom disruption, increasing time on-task in completing assignments, and improving adherence to classroom rules (Pelham, Val-

lano, Hoza, Greiner, & Gnagy, 1992). In fact, in a recent investigation, DuPaul and Rapport (1993) indicate that methylphenidate exerted a significant positive effect on classroom measures of attention and academic efficiency for children with ADHD, to the point that, as a group, the scores for these children were no longer deviant from those obtained by normally developing children.

Pelham, Vallano, Hoza, Greiner, and Gnagy (1992) have employed the techniques of behavioral observations and controlled trials of stimulant medication in a summer camp, in a classroom type of program at the University of Pittsburgh. In one particularly interesting study, Pelham et al. (1990) evaluated the efficacy of methylphenidate on children's attention while playing baseball. These children were on-task twice as often while medicated, although methylphenidate did not improve their baseball skills.

Over the years, there has been considerable interest in pharmacological interventions for children with severely aggressive behaviors. Hinshaw (1991) has reviewed the empirical evidence regarding the efficacy of stimulants in treating aggressive and antisocial behaviors in children with ADHD. These studies have been conducted primarily in both laboratory and large-group natural settings; there is a clear discrepancy between the effects of stimulants in the laboratory, which have been generally nonsignificant, and the rather large effects of stimulants in the naturalistic setting, including the classroom or play setting.

Because of the myriad difficulties that children with ADHD often encounter in social relationships, a natural direction for investigation has been the effects of stimulants on social behaviors. Whereas these studies generally have cast doubt on the efficacy of stimulants in increasing prosocial behaviors, they have been found to influence compliance and level of intrusiveness (Pelham, 1993). Pelham has recommended that in order to use stimulants most effectively to increase prosocial behaviors, multimodal therapies, including behavioral interventions, should be simultaneously employed.

In summary, for children with ADHD the beneficial effects of stimulants are well documented in the areas of cognitive functioning, behavioral and motoric effects, and aggression. However, the efficacy of this psychotropic medication on prosocial behaviors is less well demonstrated. Clearly, additional studies are needed in naturalistic settings, as well as others that examine the efficacy of various behavioral therapies in combination with stimulant medication.

## Learning Disabilities

Significant numbers of children with ADHD also have concomitant learning disabilities (Brown & Donegan, 1996). Thus, a logical question that emerges from the relevant research to date is the effect of stimulants on children with specific learning disabilities. The few studies that have examined the use of stimulants to treat basic learning disabilities have been conducted primarily with children who had reading disabilities (Kupietz, Winsberg, Richardson, Maitinsky, & Mendell, 1988; Richardson, Kupietz, Winsberg, Maitinsky, & Mendell, 1992), and stimulants demonstrated little or no beneficial effects on reading performance. The majority of the research in this area has examined children with both ADHD and learning disabilities, finding that the benefits of stimulants for this group are specific to attention rather than to enhanced academic processing. In short, although stimulants may have an adjunct role in the treatment of learning disabled children who also have attentional problems, there is little substitution for educational remediation.

## Conduct Disorders

There has been a dearth of studies on the effects of stimulants for children with conduct disorders, despite the encouraging support for their use in managing disruptive and aggressive behaviors (Gadow, 1992), which are the core symptoms found in children and adolescents diagnosed with these conduct disorders. As Rapoport (1983) has pointed out, many of the participants in the earlier stimulant drug trials were delinquent youths (Eisenberg, Lachman, Molling, Lockner, Mizelle, & Conners, 1963), thus lending some support to the hypothesis that conduct-disordered youths would respond to these agents. Current research suggests the potential efficacy of stimulants for conduct-disordered adolescents with or without ADHD (Brown, Jaffe, Silverstein, & McGee, 1991; Kaplan, Busner, Kupietz, Wasserman, & Segal, 1990). Nonetheless, despite the tentative empirical support, judicious prescribing of stimulants for conduct-disordered youths is warranted, given the high comorbidity

of substance abuse disorders. Until further research on the use of stimulants for these youths is forthcoming, careful and systematic monitoring of the use of stimulants with this population seems prudent (Brown et al., 1997).

## Mental Retardation

Whereas the efficacy of stimulants for the mentally retarded had been questioned several years ago (Aman, 1982), the more recent literature indicates similar efficacy of stimulants with children who are mentally retarded and with those who are not but who have ADHD (Handen, Breaux, Gosling, Ploof, & Feldman, 1990; Handen, Feldman, Gosling, Breaux, & McAuliffe, 1991). In 2 other studies, findings revealed a significant relationship between intelligence test scores and positive response to stimulants; children exhibit higher cognitive functioning, evidencing a better response to stimulants (Aman, Kern, McGee, & Arnold, 1993).

## Acquired Neurological Conditions

Fletcher and Levin (1988) have meticulously reviewed the studies of pediatric acquired brain injuries and have concluded that the children with these injuries demonstrate a chronic pattern of poor inhibitory control and sustained attention. The high frequency of attentional deficits in children with acquired brain injuries, including brain tumors (Fletcher, Levin, & Landry, 1984) and sustained hypoxic ischemic events (Morris, Krawiecki, Wright, & Walters, 1993), suggests that stimulants may represent an appropriate treatment of the target behaviors most often associated with these conditions. For this reason, Gualtieri (1991) has suggested that stimulants should prove efficacious in the clinical management of children with acquired brain injuries. Also, the stimulants may prove particularly useful for those patients with acquired brain injuries whose deficits are attributable to frontal lobe or frontal-subcortical system injuries (more typical of closed-head injuries). In support of this notion, Gualtieri and Evans (1988) have suggested that stimulants exert their effects by influencing transmission to the frontal cortex. The effects of stimulants in this population are accordingly of particular theoretical importance, as additional research in this area may further elucidate the specific CNS actions of these drugs.

Although anecdotal reports of stimulant drug effects are available in the neuropsychiatric literature (Weinstein & Wells, 1981), few double-blind trials are available, with the exception of two that have examined these drug effects in adolescents and adults with acquired brain injuries (Evans, Gualtieri, & Amara, 1986; Gualtieri & Evans, 1988). The data have generally suggested some improvement in attention, memory, verbal fluency, and emotional lability, with specific target behaviors responding differentially to high and low doses of methylphenidate. While the findings indeed offer encouraging support for the use of stimulants for children with acquired brain injuries, much more research is needed before endorsing their efficacy.

## Tourette's Syndrome

Tourette's syndrome is a hereditary neurobehavioral disorder characterized by multiple motor and verbal tics. Prevalence rates of ADHD in children with Tourette's exceeds 70% (Gadow & Sverd, 1990). Over the years, there has been some clinical evidence to suggest that stimulant medication may precipitate motoric tics and stereotypies or perhaps exacerbate the symptoms associated with Tourette's syndrome. Recent studies have provided encouraging evidence to suggest that methylphenidate may decrease the frequency of vocal tics exhibited at school (Sverd, Gadow, Nolan, Sprafkin, & Ezor, 1992). Gadow, Sverd, Sprafkin, Nolan, and Ezor (1995) found no evidence that methylphenidate exacerbated tic disorders, thus leading these investigators to conclude that methylphenidate is a safe and effective pharmacotherapy for the majority of children with ADHD who have comorbid tic disorders. Moreover, this study indicated that methylphenidate effectively suppressed overactive, disruptive, and aggressive behaviors. Although the recent studies by the Gadow group are encouraging, more clinical trials are necessary to definitively determine the efficacy and safety of stimulants for children who have comorbid Tourette's disorder with ADHD. After warning parents and children of the potential risks of stimulant medication, careful monitoring should always be the rule.

## Depression

An emerging body of research has posited the efficacy of stimulant medications with chronically ill adults who are also depressed, for whom traditional antidepressant therapy may be contraindicated (Stoudemire, Morau, & Fogel, 1991). Based on this clinical literature, there has been some interest in applying the findings from the corresponding research to the treatment of children and adolescents who have been diagnosed with depression. Only one pediatric case study can be found, a 15-year-old adolescent with hemophilia, AIDS, and major depressive disorder who manifested a number of untoward side effects with traditional antidepressant medications, whereas methylphenidate was found to improve his levels of energy, appetite, and mood (Walling & Pfefferbaum, 1990). Although these findings are too premature for clinical applicability, the potential use of stimulants to treat depression in youths who are refractory to traditional antidepressant medications underscores the importance of additional research in this area.

## Developmental Issues

Stimulants have been used primarily with elementary school–aged populations, although there has been an increasing recognition that attentional problems span the course of development. The appropriateness of stimulants for other age groups, therefore, has been recently studied. There has been scant research on the efficacy of stimulants with preschoolers, although the little data that are available have generally suggested a minimal effect on preschoolers who are less than three years of age (Brown et al., 1997). Barkley et al. (1990) also have indicated that an adequate response to stimulants may not be present until children reach the age of three years. These investigators hypothesize that the maturation of the prefrontal cortex and its connections to the limbic system occur between the age of four and five. Thus, before the age of three, this substrate may not be sufficiently developed for stimulants to achieve a positive behavioral response (Barkley et al., 1990). Although research indicates that older preschoolers may benefit from stimulants (Pelham, 1993), caution in their use has been recommended because of the lack of studies to adequately assess the potential of untoward and possibly deleterious effects on this special population (Brown et al., in press).

Over the years, research has indicated that as children with attentional problems grow older, they continue to have significant problems with attention and impulsivity. The few available studies that have assessed the efficacy of stimulants during adolescence have generally paralleled the data for their elementary school–aged counterparts. These data have generally attested to the efficacy of stimulants for adolescents in cognitive functioning (Brown et al., 1991), impulse control

(Brown et al., 1991), academic efficiency (Brown et al., 1991), and diminished aggression (Kaplan et al., 1990). Pelham and Evans (1991) have provided compelling evidence to suggest a comparable efficacy of methylphenidate and pemoline in the management of attentional and behavioral problems, although a lower response rate in adolescents than in prepubertal boys (Pelham, Vodde-Hamilton, Murphy, Greenstein, & Vallano, 1991). Clearly additional research must be mounted to determine optimal dosing, possible untoward side effects, and the long-term effects of stimulants administered during the course of adolescence into early adulthood.

Recently, there has been increased recognition that ADHD persists well into adulthood (Wilens, Biederman, Spencer, & Prince, 1995), and this understanding has stimulated significant interest in the treatment of adult ADHD. Thus, there has been a growing effort to study the effects of stimulants on the cognitive functioning and behavior of adults who have had a history of ADHD. While some preliminary data are rather encouraging (Spencer, Wilens, Biederman, Faraone, Ablon, & Lapey, 1995; Wilens et al., 1995), much more research is needed to determine the viability and suitability of stimulant pharmacotherapy for adults.

## Anxiolytics, Sedatives, and Hypnotics

Anxiolytics used for the treatment of anxiety-related disorders include the benzodiazepines—diazepam (Valium), lorazepam (Ativan), and clonazepam (Klonopin)—and antihistamines—diphenhydramine (Benadryl), hydroxyzine (Atarax), and buspirone (BuSpar). To date, few data are available regarding the efficacy and safety of these medications to treat pediatric populations, and accordingly they are best reserved for therapeutic use when other behavioral and/or psychotropic interventions are insufficient or inadequate (Brown et al., 1994).

In a very comprehensive and meticulous review of pharmacological trials for childhood anxiety disorder, Allen, Leonard, and Swedo (1995) located a total of only 13 controlled studies, a surprisingly low number given that nearly 10% of the pediatric population is believed to have some type of anxiety disorder. The pharmacological management of obsessive-compulsive disorder has been studied most systematically, together with separation anxiety and social phobia. Clearly, research on pharmacological treatments for anxiety disorders remains in its infancy, and

future studies employing double-blind trials will be an important next direction.

## Benzodiazepines

Benzodiazepines are used rarely in the management of childhood psychiatric disorders. However, there are preliminary data to suggest that these drugs are useful in the treatment of severe anticipatory anxiety, panic disorder, night terrors, insomnia, and sleepwalking (Biederman, 1987). Specifically, recent evidence has attested to the efficacy of clonazepam in the treatment of obsessive-compulsive disorder, although untoward side effects, which include drowsiness and disinhibition, proved to be problematic (Leonard et al., 1995). Substance abuse is a significant risk with the use of these drugs since psychological and/or physical dependence is not uncommon (Brown et al., 1994). Other untoward side effects may include sedation, motor incoordination, ataxia, confusion, and emotional lability. Because benzodiazapines may also diminish cognitive functioning, their use may result in possible impairment of learning (Waterman & Ryan, 1993; Werry & Aman, 1993). These agents can also disinhibit behavior and can produce adverse symptoms like excitation, irritability, increased anxiety, hallucinations, increased aggression and hostility, rage, insomnia, euphoria, and/or incoordination (Coffey, Shader, & Greenblat, 1983). Thus, their use for children and adolescents with ADHD and/or associated symptoms is particularly discouraged.

## Antihistamines

Antihistamines are sometimes used to manage insomnia, as well as to treat the extrapyramidal reactions produced by neuroleptics. Although antihistamines have also been employed with some children and adolescents for behavioral control, recent research has cast doubt on their efficacy for this purpose (Vitiello, Hill, & Elia, 1991). Diphenhydramine (Benadryl) is a specific antihistamine that has had some limited success in mitigating some of the severe symptoms of pervasive developmental disorder (Gadow, 1986), although no controlled trials have clearly attested to the efficacy of antihistamines for this disorder. The possible untoward side effects include dizziness, oversedation, agitation, incoordination, abdominal pain, blurred vision, and dry mouth (Brown et al., 1994).

# Anticonvulsants

Anticonvulsants, also referred to as antiepileptic drugs, have been used for many years for children and adolescents, mainly in the management of seizure disorders (Behrman & Vaughan, 1983). For numerous years, the available anticonvulsants were phenobarbital, phenytoin (Dilantin), carbamazepine (Tegretol), valproic acid (Depakote and Depakene), and benzodiazepines. However, several new anticonvulsants, such as felbamate (Felbatol) and gabapentin (Neurontin), have recently been developed and introduced into the pharmaceutical market. It should be noted that anticonvulsants also have been used to manage the symptoms associated with behavior disorders, although they are not the first-line drugs of choice for behavior disorders and, rather, are typically used when children have not responded to other psychotropic agents that are conventionally prescribed.

The two anticonvulsants most frequently encountered in the treatment of psychiatric conditions are valproic acid and carbamazepine, both of which have similar indications. Much of the clinical experience with these medications is derived from the treatment of adults. Valproic acid and carbamazepine have demonstrated antimanic and antidepressant effects in adults with bipolar disorder, especially when lithium has not been totally effective in treating these individuals (McElroy, Deck, Pope, & Hudson, 1988; Pope, McElroy, Keck, & Brown, 1991; Post & Uhde, 1985; Post, Uhde, Roy-Byrne, & Joffe, 1987). These medications have also been used to augment the antimanic effect of lithium, to treat rapid-cycling bipolar disorder, and to treat lithium-resistant bipolar disorder. Also, the efficacy of these medications in combination with lithium has been demonstrated in adolescents with bipolar disorder (Garfinkel, Garfinkel, Himmelhoch, & McHugh, 1985; West et al., 1994).

As the promise of treatment efficacy and overall experience with anticonvulsants increases for adults, more interest has emerged in their use with pediatric populations. There is little information about the efficacy of the anticonvulsants in treating bipolar disorder in children, a condition that only recently has been recognized in this population (Akiskal, 1995). As with adults, carbamazepine and valproic acid are often used to treat preadolescents when lithium has been ineffective. Moreover, carbamazepine has been effective in reducing aggression in children with conduct disorder (Kafantaris, Campbell, Padrol-Gayol, Small, Locasio, & Rosenburg, 1992). Carbamazepine has also been used to treat ADHD (Evans, Clary, & Gualtieri, 1987), although usually only when all of the standard treatments have been exhausted.

Anticonvulsants have a wide range of untoward side effects, which vary significantly in intensity and frequency. Untoward side effects are usually more severe in younger children, and for this reason, preschoolers are typically treated with relatively low doses. Behavioral side effects of anticonvulsants are well documented (Corbett, Trimble, & Nichol, 1985; Rivinus, 1982). Of all anticonvulsants, phenobarbital is most frequently associated with behavioral changes, especially overactivity, which may occur in as many as 80% of the children who are given this psychotropic agent (Wolf & Forsythe, 1978). Phenobarbital can also impair memory and attention and may produce irritability, aggression, and a depressed mood. In contrast, behavioral side effects are less commonly exhibited with the use of carbamazepine or valproic acid (Herranz, Armijo, & Arteaga, 1988; Rivinus, 1982). As with most anticonvulsants, drowsiness, irritability, and hyperactivity have been reported as untoward side effects for valproic acid and carbamazepine, with a frequency of occurrence of up to nearly one-fifth of the children for whom they have been prescribed (Herranz et al., 1988).

Additional adverse side effects of valproic acid and carbamazepine include complications of the gastrointestinal, hematological (blood), and neurological systems (Herranz et al., 1988). Appetite loss, nausea, and vomiting occur relatively frequently, although carbamazepine and valproic acid are typically titrated carefully to reduce untoward side effects. Also, diplopia or nystagmus may be more common with the administration of carbamazepine, whereas tremors may be more characteristic of valproic acid (Trimble, 1990). Because of the potential hematological and hepatic effects, as well as the possible toxic effects of carbamazepine and valproic acid, careful monitoring of serum levels is required. Overall, despite the possibility of these deleterious side effects, most individuals tolerate carbamazapine and valproic acid relatively well when they are carefully monitored for any untoward reactions.

# Other Psychotropics

Over the past several years, other medications that have been used for various medical disorders have been found to have psychotropic effects and thus have been used successfully to treat childhood psychiatric disorders. As with many medications, much information about the newly introduced psychotropics has been gained from studies and clinical experience involving adults. Thus, clonidine, propranolol, and buspirone remain relatively new agents in child psychopharmacology.

## Clonidine

Clonidine (Catapres) was originally developed and introduced as an antihypertensive drug and was subsequently discovered to have several uses in psychiatry. This medication, which is dispensed in tablets and in the form of a transdermal patch for gradual and extended release, is used to treat Tourette's disorder and ADHD in children and adolescents. The effectiveness of clonidine to manage the symptoms of Tourette's disorder has been demonstrated in many studies (Leckman, Hardin, Riddle, Stevenson, Art, & Cohen, 1991), although it has been found to be less effective than antipsychotic medication (Troung, Bressman, Shale, & Fahn, 1988). However, when augmenting antipsychotics to treat Tourette's disorder, clonidine has been sufficiently effective to allow a reduction in the dose of antipsychotic medication (Bruun, 1984).

Clonidine is also being increasingly used to treat ADHD. Placebo-crossover studies (Hunt, Minderaa, & Cohen, 1985) have supported the efficacy of clonidine in the treatment of ADHD (for a review, see Hunt, Capperl, & O'Connel, 1990). One recent report has suggested the efficacy of clonidine for sleep disturbances associated with ADHD because of its sedative properties (Wilens, Biederman, & Spencer, 1994). However, when compared to stimulants, clonidine has been found to decrease the symptoms of overactivity more effectively than those problems associated with attention or distractibility. For this reason, clonidine is frequently most beneficial when it is used as an adjunct to stimulants (Dulcan, in press).

In one recent investigation, Kemph, Lindsay-DeVane, Levin, Jarecke, and Miller (1993) evaluated the efficacy and safety of clonidine in 17 children who were classified as aggressive. Concomitant changes were assessed in the neurotransmitter believed to inhibit aggression, namely, gamma aminobutyric acid (GABA). Aggression decreased in the majority of subjects, with few untoward side effects. A reduction in the plasma levels of GABA also was found, suggesting the potential importance of this neurotransmitter in the monitoring of drug response. Some preliminary research has attested to the efficacy of clonidine in the treatment of stuttering in children, although one double-blind crossover study has recently cast doubt on its success in ameliorating stuttering.

Clonidine is usually well tolerated, but untoward side effects can be problematic for the school-age child. Sedation is the most frequently encountered side effect, which usually arises within one hour after ingestion, lasts up to one hour, and is most prominent in the first month of therapy (Hunt et al., 1985, 1990). After the initial month of treatment, the incidence and level of sedation may diminish. Dizziness, headaches, and/or stomachaches may also be frequently experienced early in treatment. However, when dosing is started at low levels and increased gradually, untoward side effects can be minimized. Vital signs, including pulse rate, temperature, and blood pressure, are usually monitored periodically while children are receiving this medication.

## Propranolol

For several years, propranolol (Inderal) has been prescribed predominantly to control hypertension, but its applications in psychiatry have gradually increased. The most common psychiatric conditions for which propranolol are used are aggression and anxiety. Propranolol has been effective in treating stage fright (performance anxiety) in adults, but its effective use for performance anxiety in children has yet to be demonstrated conclusively. Only a few empirical reports have been published to date involving propranolol and anxiety in children. One anxiety disorder for which propranolol has been used and has shown promise for pediatric populations is posttraumatic stress disorder (PTSD), although there has been only one study of this use (Famularo, Kinscherff, & Fenton, 1988). Other investigators, however, have demonstrated the efficacy of propranolol in treating hyperventilation (Joorabchi, 1977) and the anxiety associated with test performance (Faigel, 1991). Additional research data attest to its efficacy in reducing rage, aggression, impulsivity, and self-injurious behavior in children with mental retardation (Kuperman & Stewart, 1987; Williams, Hehl, Yudofsky, Adams, & Roseman, 1982).

In general, children tolerate propranolol without experiencing significant untoward side effects. However, it may occasionally cause fatigue, weakness, and/or depressed mood. For this reason, it must be used judiciously in the management of behavior problems, particularly for those children with severely handicapping conditions who may not be able to accurately report troublesome side effects.

## Buspirone

Buspirone (BuSpar) was introduced as an antianxiety agent for adults, and it has been effective in reducing the symptoms of anxiety associated with generalized anxiety disorder. In children and adolescents, however, the clinical experience with buspirone is limited. Nevertheless, preliminary studies have suggested its application for children with autism (Realmuto, August, & Garfinkel, 1989), overanxious disorder (Kranzler, 1988), and ADHD (Quaison, Ward, & Kitchen, 1991). In one encouraging case study, Zwier and Rao (1994) presented a summary of an open trial of buspirone in a 16-year-old male with a social phobia disorder for which buspirone was found to be effective. However, the paucity of investigations with this agent and the limited number of children who have been studied have made it difficult to draw definitive conclusions about the efficacy and safety of buspirone. Most pediatric clinical studies of buspirone have involved treating aggression in children who have acquired brain injuries. In addition, several clinical reports and open drug trials for adults have found the medication to also be effective in reducing aggression and anxiety in children with mental retardation (Ratey, Sovner, Mikkelsen, & Chmielinski, 1989; Ratey, Sovner, Parks, & Rogentine, 1991). Buspirone commonly produces few adverse reactions, although its therapeutic effects may not be appreciated for at least three weeks after its initiation. The more frequent untoward side effects are dizziness, drowsiness, nausea, headache, insomnia, and light-headedness.

## Desmopressin

Desmopressin (DDAVP) is a newly developed agent that is administered as a nasal spray for the management of nocturnal enuresis, and DDAVP is an analogue of a hormone that regulates fluid balance of the body (Thompson & Rey, 1995). The onset of therapeutic effect is quite rapid, and untoward side effects, which may primarily include a dry nose and headaches, are minimal (Houts, 1991). One of the major limitations of DDAVP is its high cost. Also, although it has shown some promise in the management of enuresis, many children continue to exhibit symptoms after the drug has been discontinued (Thompson & Rey, 1995). For this reason, coupled with the fact that additional research is needed to address its long-term effectiveness and potential untoward side effects, DuPaul and Kyle (1995) have recommended that the use of any medication to treat enuresis be implemented adjunctly with behavior therapy, rather than simply as a substitution for behavioral modification techniques.

## THE ROLE OF THE SCHOOL PSYCHOLOGIST IN PSYCHOPHARMACOTHERAPY

When considering whether medication should be used as an adjunct to other, more traditional therapies for children and adolescents, unique issues emerge. Developmental issues that pertain to children in particular are frequently involved, and school psychologists must consult with both parents and physicians in evaluating a child's response to medication. DuPaul and Kyle (1995) have reviewed principles set forth by Werry (1993) to guide the practitioner in deciding whether pharmacotherapy will probably be useful. First, the clinician must weigh the potential benefits of other available psychotherapies or interventions along with the possible deleterious side effects of a specific medication. Werry has suggested that when a traditional psychotherapy offers promise in treating a particular disorder, it should be the first line of treatment prior to medication. Second, given the myriad pharmacotherapies that are available to the physician, a thorough knowledge of both the clinical and empirical literature must guide the practice of prescribing medication. Third, pharmacotherapy must be part of an integrated treatment program, which may include special education, psychotherapy, and other types of psychoeducational intervention. Fourth, given that children are frequently involved in a number of activities during the day and that medication administration must be either supervised by their parents or school personnel, Werry and others have recommended that administration be kept simple to enhance compliance with treatment (LaGreca & Schuman, 1995). Fifth, it is important that effective communication take place among the health-care provider, the child, and the child's family. This includes addressing concerns about behavioral and attributional effects, as well as untoward side effects of the medication (DuPaul & Kyle, 1995). Sixth, all treatment alternatives should be weighed, and an adequate period for assessment should be a core component of any clinical drug trial. Furthermore, pharmacotherapy should always be in the best interest of the child and not used to punish a child for inappropriate behavior. Finally, the potential benefits and risks of pharmacotherapy should always be evaluated carefully in all cases, and empirical data should always guide clinical practice.

## Developmental Issues in Pharmacotherapy with Children

As noted previously, the clinical practice of psychopharmacology with children and adolescents has been based primarily on basic tenets from the adult psychopharmacology literature (DuPaul & Kyle, 1995). Unfortunately, there is a dearth of studies on the effects of various psychotropic agents on pediatric populations. In fact, much of the practice of psychopharmacology with children, with the exception of stimulants, is based primarily on adult clinical case studies and pharmacology literature. Given their training and expertise in developmental issues and research, school psychologists can play an important role in both the development of research and the practice of pediatric psychopharmacology. Specifically, DuPaul and Kyle have recommended that psychologists be involved in programs of research that investigate dose-response associations of various psychotropics used for children and adolescents and that developmental variables be examined as they interact with the response of psychotropics in this population.

DuPaul and Kyle (1995) have also suggested that additional research efforts be focused on both the preschool and adolescent years. Because of the number of untoward side effects of many psychotropic agents when administered to preschoolers, coupled with the scant empirical data for this age group, most practitioners are reluctant to treat younger children with psychotropic medication. Moreover, there is increasing evidence that significant development of the CNS continues in young preschool children (Brown & Donegan, 1996), thereby posing additional concern about the deleterious side effects that could result from the use of psychotropic medication for this age group. For this reason, most psychotropic medications are used for chil-

dren under the age of five years, and only for developmental disorders that are refractory to other behavioral interventions or when the target behaviors may be considered to be injurious or life-threatening to the child.

Adolescence is another stage of development that has received increasing research and clinical attention in psychopharmacology. Many of these investigations have begun in response to the research that has documented the fact that many children with various disruptive behavior disorders continue to have problems well into adolescence (Brown & Borden, 1989). Thus, for these youths there has been an active search to provide therapies that may enhance learning and cognition and reduce maladaptive behavior. Although there has been a burgeoning of promising research with adolescents (Brown et al., 1991; Pelham et al., 1991), DuPaul and Kyle (1995) have urged careful evaluation and ongoing monitoring of these youths, as well as judicious administration of psychotropic medications, particularly for those who are at risk for substance abuse and overdoses.

In their recent review of developmental perspectives in pediatric psychopharmacology, Vitello and Jensen (1995) have noted the many achievements in this area, although there is much research yet to be accomplished in the study of pharmacokinetic differences between children and adults. Many of the short- and long-term effects on the CNS, particularly for children, are unknown. Future research that uses newly developed technology, such as nuclear magnetic resonance spectroscopy, will undoubtedly result in significant advances in the field. Furthering our understanding of pediatric psychopharmacology will probably also have an impact on adult pharmacology (Vitiello & Jensen, 1995).

## Assessment of Drug Response

School psychologists have available a great many assessment techniques to evaluate the behavioral and affective responses of medication. Werry and Aman (1993) have recommended that medication responses be evaluated across physiological, behavioral, and affective domains. Despite the existence of an ideal prototype for a thorough medication evaluation, many pediatricians do not necessarily employ objective data systematically to guide decisions about titration of doses and treatment efficacy (Wolraich, Lindgren, Stromquist, Milich, Davis, & Watson, 1990).

## Physiological

Over the past several years, there has been an increasing interest in the anatomical, biochemical, and physiological processes of the brains of children with various types of learning disorders and psychopathology (for a review, see Brown & Donegan, 1996). Although far from conclusive, this body of research has generally suggested differences in structure, metabolism, and activity in the CNS, specifically in the brain, as a function of psychopathology. The few studies that have been conducted in this area have primarily investigated stimulants and suggest that there is a normalizing of nervous system variables as a function of pharmacotherapy (Brown & Donegan, 1996). Research has demonstrated, for example, that these medications have a normalizing effect on the electroencephalograms and evoked related potentials for children with ADHD (for a review, see Brown & Donegan, 1996). Other biochemical and physiological processes have demonstrated the possibility of being good barometers of the CNS effects of various psychotropic medications. New technology in this area continues to increase at exponential rates, making exciting new developments likely to emerge in the near future.

## Behavioral

Behavioral assessment is the major means by which children are evaluated for medication and by which they are monitored. A variety of techniques is available for the assessment of behavior, including direct observation, rating scales, and sociometric ratings. Direct observations provide clearly delineated measures, minimizing interference on the part of these observers and thereby decreasing the subjectivity of responses (Atkins & Pelham, 1991). These observations are conducted in a classroom or playroom, where the observers are blind to the diagnostic or medication status of the participants, and have been especially successful in documenting stimulant drug effects (Gadow, 1993). Rating scales provide a summary of behavior and have a number of advantages, including simplicity, cost effectiveness, and reduced subjectivity (Gadow, 1993). Perhaps the best model of assessment of the efficacy and management of psychotropic medication may be derived from the voluminous studies of stimulant medication frequently conducted with children with ADHD. Nevertheless, direct observations of behavior or behavioral assessment techniques

have been hailed as the assessments of choice in evaluating the response of children to psychotropic medication cross a number of areas of functioning. They also have the distinct advantage of evaluating behavioral domains with significant ecological validity (DuPaul & Kyle, 1995).

In support of behavioral assessment methodologies, DuPaul and Kyle (1995) have noted that medication-related changes in a specific behavioral domain may vary by dose and that separate behaviors may be affected differentially by a specific medication at differential doses. For example, with stimulant medication for children diagnosed with ADHD, it was demonstrated that cognition is best enhanced with a lower dose of medication and that behavior is improved with a relatively higher dose of the same medication (Brown & Sleator, 1979; Sprague & Sleator, 1977). Moreover, some investigators have provided convincing evidence that children may vary idiosyncratically in their behavior as a function of the dose of a medication (Rapport, DuPaul, Stoner, & Jones, 1986), and for this reason, DuPaul and Kyle have recommended that behavior change be evaluated across doses on an individual basis by single-subject methodologies.

## Psychological Testing

The development of psychological tests for the assessment of drug responses has been an enterprising endeavor among test publishers. It should be noted, however, that psychological testing is merely one facet of a comprehensive test battery used to evaluate a child for the possibility of a trial of medication. Psychological tests should always be employed simultaneously with behavioral observations, teachers' and parents' ratings of behavior, and sociometric ratings. In a recent investigation, Barkley and Grodinsky (1994) evaluated the predictive power of a number of psychological instruments assessing frontal lobe functioning to identify children in whom ADHD had been clinically diagnosed. The level of sensitivity for the ADHD group was low; that is, the measures did not adequately discriminate children with ADHD from their normal peers. Moreover, having a score that falls within the normal range does not necessarily suggest the absence of psychopathology or learning problems. In fact, the behavioral and cognitive functioning of children and adolescents may differ in one-to-one testing from a traditional classroom setting. Since the administration of these tests is often labor-intensive and costly, their appropriateness for evaluating a drug response must be carefully evaluated. Thus, psychological instruments are apt to be most helpful when considered simultaneously with behavioral observations in the home (Barkley et al, 1991; Fischer & Newby, 1991), in the classroom (Gadow, 1993; Nolan & Gadow, 1994), and from peers (Pelham & Hoza, 1987).

## Model Assessment Approach

Atkins and Pelham (1991) have recommended that a multivariate approach be employed in assessing a drug response. Thus, it would be necessary to obtain behavioral observations from teachers, parents, peers, and the children themselves across a variety of situations so that information from various sources can be obtained.

The excellent model developed for psychostimulants seems appropriate for evaluating all psychoactive medications. Barkley, Fischer, Newby, and Breen (1988) and Gadow, Nolan, Paolicelli, and Sprafkin (1991) have delineated procedures for evaluating medications in the laboratory, and these procedures seem fitting in the clinical setting as well: (1) using placebo controls and double-blind trials to mitigate the possibility of biases in both parents' and teachers' reports of behavior; (2) randomizing the order of the dose across children to control for order effects; (3) using multiple assessment measures, including laboratory measures, teachers' and parents' ratings of behavioral symptoms, performance on academic tasks, and evaluation within social domains; (4) assessing functioning during peak drug response; (5) systematically evaluating untoward side effects during active medication and placebo administration. In fact, some experts have recommended that a double-blind trial of medication be the prototype of assessment in the clinical setting, thereby allowing an objective evaluation of medication and adequate assessment of untoward effects at home and at school (Barkley et al., 1993; Varley & Trupin, 1982).

In deciding whether a trial of medication is successful and whether one particular dose is more effective than another in an unstructured or a structured activity, the school psychologist and the pediatrician should collaborate. This may be accomplished by systematic data collection from each party involved. The end result will be a rather cost-effective evaluation that is guided by a reliable assessment process, which will enhance the treatment decision, as well as document the efficacy of a particular medication.

## Predicting Response

There has been a continued search for the identification of measures and rating instruments that may accurately predict a response to a particular psychotropic medication. Most of these investigations involving children and adolescents have been conducted with the stimulants. Some recent research (DuPaul, Barkley, & McMurray, 1994; Tannock, Ickowicz, & Schachar, 1995) has found that children with ADHD and comorbid internalizing behavioral symptoms, including anxiety, exhibit a poorer response to stimulants. These studies are significant because they underscore the importance of diagnostic subtypes of ADHD. Buitelaar, Van der Gaag, Swaab-Barneveld, and Kuiper (1995) have recently examined factors that predict a favorable stimulant drug response in children diagnosed with ADHD. Their findings indicate that favorable responses to stimulants are best predicted by high IQ, inattentiveness, young age, low rates of anxiety, and low severity of ADHD.

Some investigators have found that children who were high in disinhibition (i.e., similar to the DSM-IV hyperactive-impulsive type) display a particularly favorable response to methylphenidate on measures of cognition, behavior, and compliance with adult directives (Beery, Quay, & Pelham, 1995; Wilkison, Kircher, McMahon, & Sloane, 1995). Children who were classified as low in disinhibition (i.e., similar to the DSM-IV inattentive type) responded favorably to operant techniques without the use of stimulant medication (Beery et al., 1995). Again, these investigations are important because they support the differential response to stimulants on the basis of ADHD subtyping. Certainly, additional investigation is needed in this area so that stimulants can be more precisely prescribed for specific subtypes of ADHD. Unfortunately, there are few studies that predict children's response to psychotropic medications. Until more definitive research is forthcoming, the use of a systematic drug trial, taking care to match the specific class of psychotropic to the child's target symptoms, is the most appropriate means of assessment.

# MANAGEMENT ISSUES OF PSYCHOTROPIC MEDICATION

## Multimodal or Adjunctive Therapies

In this time of health-care reform, managed care, budget constraints, and biological psychiatry, the use of medication alone has been hailed as a cost-effective treatment strategy for managing children with psychopathology and those with some types of learning problems. First, it should be noted that not all children respond positively to pharmacotherapy and that the beneficial effects of medication may be circumscribed in duration and in the extent of response (Whalen & Henker, 1991). Second, psychotropic medication merely manages symptoms and does not cure a disorder, in contrast to other medications used in pediatrics such as antibiotics (Brown et al., 1994). Coupled with the recognition that most psychiatric disorders in children are lifelong and may persist well into adulthood, many experts agree that even when pharmacotherapy is beneficial, appropriate psychoeducational and psychotherapeutic interventions should be adjunctly employed (Pelham, 1993). There has been some hope raised and empirical corroboration from studies undertaken with adult populations to support the notion that a combination of psychotherapy and pharmacotherapy will prove more efficacious than either one alone (Broen et al., 1994).

Based on the intuitive belief that combined therapies of medication and other techniques, including operant and cognitive approaches, will result in more effective treatments than either therapy used alone, there has been a series of investigations into the effects of combined or multimodal therapies, particularly for children with ADHD. The effects of stimulant medication alone compared to behavior therapy, or pharmacotherapy and behavioral therapy combined, has been studied in the Pelham laboratory at the University of Pittsburgh. These studies have generally shown methylphenidate to be superior to behavior modification alone; the combination of the two therapies was only slightly better than medication alone (Carlson, Pelham, Milich, & Hoza, 1993; Pelham et al., 1988, 1993). These findings were reiterated in an investigation examining the effects of parent training compared to stimulant medication combined with parent training (Horn et al., 1991; Ialongo et al., 1993). Similar findings emerged in examining the effects of cognitive therapy with those of stimulant

medication in the treatment of ADHD, with medication alone producing superior effects to the combination of cognitive therapy and medication (Abikoff, Ganeles, Reiter, Blum, Foley, & Klein, 1988; Abikoff & Gittelman, 1985; Brown, 1980; Brown, Borden, Wynne, Schleser, & Clingerman, 1986; Brown, Wynne, & Medenis, 1985).

Carlson et al. (1993), however, offer a glimmer of hope on the empirical horizon. This group found significantly improved classroom behavior when a combination of behavior therapy and low-dose stimulant medication was employed simultaneously. Behavior therapy was found to be as effective on classroom behavior as a relatively higher dose of methylphenidate. The results of this investigation are important since they indicate that behavioral therapies may have an augmenting effect on stimulant medication. Future studies will need to be conducted with the aim of replicating this finding. The potential importance of multimodal therapies in the treatment of psychiatric illnesses in children and adolescents has been supported by the National Institute of Mental Health's funding of a multicenter research program designed to investigate combinations of treatments for ADHD (Richters et al., 1995). The multisite investigation specifically proposes to address the circumstances and children's characteristics that specific treatments affect in various domains of children's functioning. While data from this intensive investigation are still mounting, the findings will have important implications for the treatment of schoolchildren across the United States.

# INFORMED CONSENT, TREATMENT ACCEPTABILITY, COMPLIANCE, AND SATISFACTION WITH MEDICATION

The pediatric psychopharmacology literature has generally suggested that many parents and children are hesitant about medication treatment and perceive pharmacotherapy as less acceptable or desirable than behavioral therapy (Kazdin, 1984; Summers & Caplan, 1987). These findings are reminiscent of the behavioral medicine literature, in which parents and caretakers are more accepting of behavioral modalities for managing pain than they are of pain management with analgesia (Tarnowski, Gavaghan, & Wisniewski, 1989).

When parents are ambivalent about specific interventions, treatment compliance and satisfaction are at jeopardy (Cross-Calvert & Johnston, 1990; Johnston & Fine, 1993; Tarnowski, Kelly, & Mendlowitz, 1987). Parents' concerns may suggest that pharmacotherapy is underutilized despite some of the compelling empirical evidence that some medications represent the most beneficial treatment approach in the symptom management of several disorders. More importantly, there has been some research to suggest that children and parents may actually fail to adhere to prescribed medical regimens and may even prematurely discontinue treatment (Brown et al., 1987; Firestone, 1982; Kaufman, Smith-Wright, Reese, Simpson, & Fowler, 1981).

Firestone (1982) reports that nearly one-fifth of his sample discontinued methylphenidate administration prematurely and that fewer than 10% of the families participating in this project consulted with project staff before discontinuing treatment. The parents cited discomfort with the medication as their primary reason for premature discontinuation. The more numerous the untoward side effects, the more likely the noncompliance (DuPaul & Kyle, 1995; LaGreca & Schuman, 1995). Similarly, Brown et al. (1987), in a short-term drug trial involving stimulants, found that nearly one-quarter of the prescribed doses were missed, as verified by pharmacists' counts. Brown et al. also noted that social class and intelligence were significantly associated with adherence, with lower social class and intelligence being significant predictors of nonadherence. Kauffman et al. (1981) support these findings by showing that one-third of their sample did not adhere to prescribed drug regimens, as verified by urine screens. In fact, Zametkin and Yamada (1993) have argued that noncompliance with treatment is a major reason for children's failure to respond to a particular medication treatment program.

In turn, Johnston and Fine (1993) have posited that the problems of acceptability, satisfaction, and compliance with treatment are intricately related. To investigate this relationship, Johnston and Fine compared two methods, one of which included a double-blind drug trial and the other a standard evaluation of drug efficacy. Ratings of treatment satisfaction were higher in the double-blind drug trial. Thus, the study supports the use of careful assessment in the evaluation of drug efficacy in enhancing treatment satisfaction. The study is important because it supports the use of patient education, including the review of potential benefits and untoward side effects with parents and children. Consent and assent should always be obtained, and the practitioner must be sensitive to the cultural factors that influence values, expectations, and norms among various social classes and cultural groups (Westmeyer, 1987).

The importance of family support for children's treatment adherence has been underscored in the pediatric psychology literature (LaGreca & Schuman, 1995). Moreover, many psychotropic medications must be administered during the course of the school day, and school staff attitudes and personnel availability may also affect compliance and treatment acceptability (Brown et al., 1994). School personnel can be actively involved in facilitating parents' and children's medication compliance regardless of whether the medication is administered at school or at home. Finally, other factors that have been associated with positive medication adherence include peer support, simplifying treatment regimens, structuring the medication administration, and providing rewards for appropriate adherence. Although adherence to medication regimens is a complex issue, the studies reviewed support the need for careful assessment of compliance before evaluating either the short- or long-term efficacy of any psychotropic drug.

## Attitudes and Beliefs About Medication

An important consideration in medicating children for behavioral difficulties is the notion of treatment acceptability (Kazdin, 1980, 1981, 1984) and satisfaction by the child, the family, and other individuals who are involved in the child's daily life. As Kazdin (1980) has suggested, attitudes of consumers are apt to influence their willingness to accept treatment and ultimately the integrity with which the treatment is delivered. As Barkley, Conners, Barclay, Gadow, Gittleman, Sprague, & Swanson (1990) have pointed out, environmental management for behavioral difficulties among schoolchildren may be far more preferable to society than only medical management. Specifically, drugs may be viewed as less acceptable, particularly for children, who are unable to assert their rights, or when behavioral therapies have been shown to be effective. This issue is particularly relevant for school psychologists, who work with children and may be in the position to offer alternative treatments.

Much of the treatment acceptability research with pediatric populations has focused on the relative merits of operant techniques in comparison to stimulant drug therapy for children who have symptoms of ADHD. There is scant research on the treatment acceptability of other psychotropic medications. In previous literature (Kazdin, 1980, 1981, 1984), the use of medication has always been rated as less preferable to behavioral techniques, including response cost and time-out, although medication has been more acceptable than severe punishment, such as electric shocks by cattle prods (Kazdin, 1980, 1981). The severity of symptoms from the behavior disorder coupled with the frequency of untoward side effects has been a determinant of medication acceptability (Kazdin, 1980, 1981, 1984). Several studies have indicated that the acceptability of treatments frequently varies across raters (parents, teachers, and peers), suggesting that practitioners carefully assess both the child and the parents when developing a treatment program.

## Societal Attitudes

Society's concerns about inappropriate, illegal, and prescribed drug use have had a significant impact on decisions to medicate schoolchildren for learning and behavioral problems. For example, Summers and Caplan (1987) conducted surveys of laypeople regarding their beliefs about psychotropic medications for schoolchildren; their findings indicate that the use of medication was endorsed as being justified primarily for disorders that had an organic etiology. Moreover, psychotropic medication was believed by many to exacerbate psychological symptoms. Similarly, Mittl and Robin (1987) found that undergraduates rated medication as less effective than problem-solving communication and behavioral contracting in parent-adolescent conflict; medication was rated above only paradoxical therapy, which was found to be the least acceptable treatment modality. Kazdin (1980, 1981, 1984) has also pointed out that medication is never rated as the most acceptable treatment when compared to other therapies, including behavior management.

## Parental Attitudes

The experience of parents with the treatments available for various disorders has been found to significantly affect their acceptability of medication to control school-related behavioral and learning problems. For example, Liu, Robbin, Brenner, and Eastman (1991) surveyed mothers of children diagnosed with ADHD and those of nonreferred children about the relative acceptability of medication, behavior modification, and their combination in the treatment of ADHD. Both groups of parents rated behavior modification as the most acceptable treatment and stimulant medication as the least acceptable, although the mothers' knowledge of the disorder was associated with greater acceptability of pharmacotherapy. Similarly, Tarnowski, Simonian, Bekeny, and Park (1992), in their evaluation of mothers of children referred by pediatricians, found that for both mild and severe depression, pharmacotherapy was rated as less acceptable than all other available treatments, a finding consistent with that of Liu et al. (1991).

To address parental concerns about the use of stimulant medication for the treatment of ADHD, Slimmer and Brown (1985) evaluated the efficacy of a decision-making conference on the treatment acceptance process. The mothers' decisions to elect a trial of medication were enhanced when they were encouraged to express guilt about the disorder and when they were encouraged to consider treatment alternatives. Borden and Brown (1989) examined the attributional effects of combining medication with psychotherapy in the treatment of children with externalizing behavior disorders. All of the children received an intensive treatment program in cognitive therapy that focused on self-control. The children were also randomly assigned to a methylphenidate, placebo, and no-pill condition. Parents in the no-pill condition believed most strongly that their children were capable of solving their own problems, whereas parents in the methylphenidate and placebo groups endorsed the efficacy of medication.

In a recent survey designed to assess the social importance and personal benefits of participation in drug trials, Aman and Wolford (1995) surveyed parents of children with mental retardation who participated in several drug trials. The majority of parents reported being satisfied with the individual conclusions reached for their children regarding pharmacotherapy. Moreover, the parents reported that the research experience was of practical benefit to them. The study is important because it underscores the benefits of double-blind drug trials in both determining drug efficacy and promoting consumer satisfaction among parents.

## Teachers

Because most children who receive medication for learning and behavioral problems receive at least one dose during the school day, treatment acceptability of pharmacotherapy among teachers and special education personnel are likely to have an impact on children and their parents. Epstein, Matson, Repp, and Helsel (1986) requested special education and regular teachers to rate the acceptability of various treatments for modifying the behavioral symptoms of a first-grade boy described in a case study. The various treatments included medication, behavior modification, counseling psychotherapy, special education, and affective education. Consistent with the Liu et al (1991) investigation with parents, both groups of teachers endorsed special education as the most appropriate treatment modality and pharmacotherapy as the least appropriate intervention. Consistent with these findings, Kasten, Coury, and Heron (1992) found that over 40% of special education teachers believed that too many children receive stimulants and that they are prescribed far too often for children diagnosed with ADHD. Similarly, Power, Hess and Bennett (1995) report that elementary and middle school teachers rated behavioral interventions as more acceptable than stimulant drug therapy. Stimulant medication was more acceptable when used in combination with behavior therapy than when used in isolation.

One possible explanation for these findings may be that as teachers frequently report, they are often unaware of the medication status of their students because of a lack of communication between the teachers and physician (Gadow, 1981). Empirical data indicate that special education teachers who serve both learning-disabled (Epstein, Singh, Luebke, & Stout, 1991) and emotionally handicapped youths (Singh, Epstein, Luebke, & Singh, 1990) have little influence on whether children are medicated to treat disorders that affect their academic performance or behavior at school. Moreover, most of the teachers surveyed indicate that they needed additional training in issues related to drug therapy for schoolchildren.

In an investigation that compared medication beliefs among mainstream educators, school psychologists, and special educators, Malyn, Jensen, and Clark (1993) asked these school personnel whether they would recommend stimulant medication to the parents of the children with whom they worked. Whereas 82% of the school psychologists endorsed the efficacy of stimulant medication for children with ADHD, only one-third of the psychologists indicated that they would inform parents of this option.

## Children and Peers

Paralleling the interest in the attitudes of society, including those of parents and teachers, a burgeoning body of research has evolved on children's attitudes and expectations regarding pharmacotherapy. Because many psychotropic medications typically require multiple doses throughout the day, children are frequently medicated while at school and often in front of their peers. Research has found that other children's knowledge of the use of psychoactive medication may affect their social relations with children who are receiving medication for learning or behavioral problems (Whalen & Henker, 1991). In support of this notion, Sigelman and Shorokey (1986) investigated children's attributions and the relative likability of a hypothetical child who was receiving medication or was exerting personal efforts to control his or her behavioral problems in the classroom; this child was perceived as more likable in the effort situation. These findings are important because they underscore the possibility that children's medication may affect their social standing with peers.

Another line of research has suggested that pharmacological treatment may have cognitive and affective consequences, or *emanative effects*, for the child because the need for medication may convey an undesirable message to the child about self-competence and personal control (Whalen & Henker, 1976; Whalen, Henker, Hinshaw, Heller, & Huber-Dressler, 1991). Henker and Whalen (1989), for example, have argued that stimulant treatment for ADHD may convey an undesirable message to the child about these attributes. A concern is that children may ascribe the benefits of the medication to external causes, considering their efforts and capabilities to be irrelevant and thereby further impeding academic achievement.

This issue was addressed in a number of investigations conducted by Milich and associates (Carlson et al., 1993; Milich, Carlson, Pelham, & Licht, 1991; Pelham, Murphy, Vannatta, Milich,

Licht, Gnagy, Greenslade, Greiner, Vodde-Hamilton, 1992). In a series of well-controlled studies, boys with ADHD were exposed to success and failure conditions in a counterbalanced methylphenidate trial. Medication was found to enhance persistence, but only in the face of failure. When attributions for success and failure were examined, however, boys receiving active medication, versus those who were not, did not differ in their attributions when exposed to solvable tasks. However, following failure, boys were found to make more external (i.e., task difficulty) and fewer internal (i.e., effort) attributions concerning medication versus placebo. This investigation was replicated, with the addition of a no-pill condition. The children receiving medication attributed success to their ability or effort and attributed failure to the medication or program staff (Pelham, Murphy, Vannatta, Milich, Licht, Gnagy, Greenslade, Greiner, & Vodde-Hamilton, 1992). Thus, the medication diminished the boys' sense of personal responsibility following failure, a pattern that is consistent with a more adaptive and healthy attributional response style.

In a more recent investigation, Ialongo, Lopez, Horn, Pascoe, and Greenberg (1994) evaluated the effects of stimulant medication on children's ratings of self-competence and found no adverse change in mood or diminished perceptions of competence. Similarly, Milich, Licht, Murphy, and Pelham (1989) found boys with ADHD who were receiving stimulant medication to be more accurate in assessing the quality of their vigilance on a task of sustained attention. Thus, children who received stimulant medication behaved in a mastery-oriented fashion, whereas their unmedicated peers with ADHD displayed helplessness.

For psychotropic medications other than stimulants, it is clear that much more research needs to be conducted into treatment acceptability. In fact, the literature pertaining to child and peer attitudes toward pharmacotherapy has been limited almost entirely to those children with ADHD who are being treated with stimulants. The emanative effects of other psychotropic medications as they influence children's treatment acceptability are fertile areas for future investigation.

## ISSUES RELATED TO TRAINING

As noted, various psychopharmacologic agents have been demonstrated to be effective in managing many disorders frequently encountered among school-aged children. The beneficial effects of these medications, at times in combination with psychosocial and/or psychoeducational interventions, have been seen in the learning and cognitive abilities of some children and adolescents. As providers of mental health services to this population, school psychologists are called on to understand the short- and long-term effects of these medications. In addition, as practitioners, they must understand the interaction of the effects of these drugs with various forms of psychoeducational and psychosocial therapies.

There has been significant momentum in the American Psychological Association (APA) to study the training needs of psychologists who provide mental health services to children and adolescents. Accordingly, an ad hoc task force was developed several years ago by the APA to systematically explore these needs, particularly those pertaining to pediatric psychology (Smyer et al., 1993). The rationale has been that as our understanding of the role of neurobiology in human behavior increases, there is a concomitant need to incorporate biological approaches to manage behavior in the years to come. The reality is that many school psychologists already participate in decisions to medicate school-aged children. Thus, there is an obvious need for them to have a clear understanding of the actions of these medications, as well as of the professional, ethical, and social issues pertaining to pharmacotherapy for children. Some experts have argued that a psychologist who works with children must have specific training in pediatric psychopharmacology through formal course work. It has also been suggested that some of the traditional courses required in the training of school psychologists, including assessment and consultation, should encompass the study of the appropriate pharmacotherapies for specific childhood disorders, as well the assessment of medication response (Barkley, Conners, Barclay, Gadow, Gittleman, Sprague, & Swanson, 1990).

Smyer et al. (1993) have argued for psychopharmacotherapy training for doctoral-level psychologists that proceeds in three sequential levels: (1) basic psychopharmacology education, (2) training needs for collaborative practice with physicians, and (3) prescription privileges. The first level of training would encompass a fundamental course in psychopharmacology, which would be offered in the form of continuing education classes for those psychologists who are already engaged in professional practice. Building on the first level of training, the second level would require a combination of didactic education and direct experience with health-care providers in learning to collaborate with these professionals in the decision-making process regarding medication. This second level of training would require greater in-depth knowledge of psychodiagnosis, pathophysiology, therapeutics, emergency treatment, substance abuse treatment, developmental psychopharmacology, psychopharmacology research, and supervised clinical experience (Smyer et al., 1993). Finally, the third level of training would provide the school psychologist with independent prescription privileges, limited by the scope of the practice. The required training could be accomplished by formal postdoctoral training or retraining of currently practicing school psychologists through continuing education workshops.

This additional training of school psychologists in psychopharmacology would give practitioners not only a greater knowledge base from which to work collaboratively with the physicians who may be prescribing medication but also opportunities for greater involvement in psychopharmacology research (Smyer et al., 1993). Given their scientist-practitioner training, school psychologists would bring new discipline and experience to this field that is not always available from other providers of mental health services (Smyer et al., 1993). A new effect that will arise from these developments is the employment of additional faculty who have expertise in pediatric psychopharmacology. These experts will be called on to teach courses in this area, supervise graduate students in research, and be mentors to other faculty members. In addition, school psychologists who are employed in academic institutions will probably be asked to play a role in the continuing education efforts of their colleagues already engaged in clinical practice. Finally, the financial resources necessary for conducting psychopharmacology research with children and adolescents, which is greatly needed, must be addressed. Traditional funding vehicles, such as the National Institute of Mental Health and the Office of Education, as well as pharmaceutical firms and other private sources, must continue to be explored. The support of various federal agencies in the funding of research on the effects of pediatric psychotropic medication on learning and behavior will no doubt remain important.

Finally, and of equal significance, as psychologists participate further in the decision-making process with physicians and parents to medicate children and adolescents, school psychologists must wrestle with the ethical issues that arise. Barkley, Conners, Barclay, Gadow, Gittelman, Sprague, & Swanson (1990), in summarizing the research in this area, raise a number of critical points: (1) since the long-term effects of psychotropic medications in children are unknown and because children are experiencing rapid brain growth and development in these early years, should these medications be employed on a widespread basis, as they currently are? (2) Given the expertise of psychologists in the area of environmental effects on behavior, might an increased emphasis on medication therapies convey the impression of an exclusive focus on biologically based foundations of behavior? (3) Might psychotropic medications affect attributional bases of behavior that are important correlates of behaviors in parents and their children? (4) Because medication is often a less costly option than special education or psychotherapy, might medication be overprescribed? (5) Because children are limited in their capacity to self-report, might medication simply lead to the reduction of overt behaviors that are distressing to teachers, parents, and other caretakers but mask other important symptoms or issues with which children and adolescents might be struggling? (6) Is there a double standard in instructing children not to turn to certain illicit drug substances but to use prescription drugs to solve their problems? (7) Will children who are economically deprived be more apt to receive medication because other psychotherapies might be unavailable to them because of their higher cost, and conversely, are more affluent children apt to be unnecessarily medicated because their families are more likely to be able to afford these treatments? (9) Given the dearth of scientific literature about the efficacy and potential untoward side effects of most psychotropic drugs, is their widespread use justified for this special and perhaps most vulnerable population? There are no easy answers to these issues, but they must be considered by psychologists when participating in the decision to medicate children.

The issue of initiating prescription privileges for psychologists has received widespread attention, particularly in the recent literature, from those researchers and practitioners training psychologists in a wide range of specializations (Smyer et al., 1993), including those who train clinical child psychologists (Barkley, Conners,

Barclay, Gadow, Gittelman, Sprague, & Swanson, 1990) and school psychologists (Carlson & Kubiszyn, 1994). We are well aware of the opposition to this notion from many psychologists and closely allied professionals, as well as of the sentiment among some other psychologists that this new privilege may contribute to their financial well-being. In the end, we believe that the ultimate decision should be based on the benefits to be derived by the children and families whom we serve.

# CONCLUSIONS AND RECOMMENDATIONS FOR FUTURE RESEARCH

There have been significant advances in the study of psychopharmacology in children and adolescents. In part these achievements have been due to greater diagnostic precision in both the internalizing and the externalizing behavior disorders, coupled with a greater understanding of the CNS and biological etiologies of various disorders. Clearly, much of the research has been conducted with adults, and more recently greater efforts have been devoted to adolescent populations. Nonetheless, with the exception of the stimulants, there is a dearth of studies with children. This is indeed surprising, as a significant number of schoolchildren receive some type of medication to manage their behavior and enhance their learning in the classroom. It is indeed alarming that so many medications are being used clinically when there is an insufficient empirical base to justify their treatment efficacy and long-term safety.

In more recent years, greater attention has been devoted to the assessment of drug response and efficacy, as well as careful measurement of untoward side effects. Nonetheless, there have been insufficient clinical trials with antidepressant medications and neuroleptic agents. For example, little is known about how these drugs affect cognition and behavior in the long term. Moreover, the research with antidepressant medication is somewhat conflicting and decidedly inconclusive. Because of their strong training in assessment and research design, psychologists are in a prime position to contribute to the psychopharmacology literature. This contribution, it is hoped, will involve the design of more methodologically rigorous studies with dependent measures that will devote greater attention to the effects of these medications on classroom learning.

Some progress has been made in the treatment of comorbid disorders, particularly those that co-occur with ADHD. Unfortunately, there has been little systematic study of comorbid disorders that occur with other externalizing and internalizing behavioral disturbances, including children's conduct disorders. Again, school psychologists, who are carefully trained in assessment procedures and diagnosis, may make a substantial contribution to this area.

With the burgeoning interest in consumer satisfaction with medical treatments and the recent changes in health-care delivery in this country, there has been a parallel interest in issues related to treatment acceptability and emanative effects of psychotropics, particularly stimulants. Parents' and teachers' acceptability of stimulant medication has been meticulously researched, although the effect of medication on peers' acceptance and rejection is ripe for investigation. Further study is also needed into teacher, parent, and peer acceptability issues with other classes of medication. With their expertise in the assessment of peer sociometry, school psychologists especially can contribute to this area.

The effects of medication on family functioning is another area that requires more rigorous study. In particular, the effect of various psychotropic medications on parental management strategies, as well as siblings' response, is an important direction for research. The interplay of medication as it affects both family involvement and school functioning is an appropriate domain for the expanding role of the school psychologist.

With the increased use of psychopharmacotherapy to manage children's learning and behavior, there has been a growing recognition of the importance of training school psychologists in the actions and effects of these medications in the classroom. This training mandate will probably require additional didactic experiences in graduate programs, as well as internship and postdoctoral programs. Greater training in the biological bases of behavior will serve as a foundation for basic training in psychopharmacology. In addition, practicing school psychologists will need continuing education that prepares them to monitor drug effects and systematically assess untoward side effects. Finally, clinical experiences that involve consultation with health-care providers in monitoring psychotropic drug responses will need to be a core component of the practicum training of school psychologists.

Important ethical considerations confront school psychologists as they consider an expansion of their role in consultation with health-care providers on psychopharmacotherapy with children and adolescents. Issues include the appropriate integration of psychotherapies, including parents' intervention programs, individual and group psychotherapy, and psychoeducational treatment programs. As the availability of financial resources become more of a challenge, medication may be seen as a panacea for treating behavioral and learning disorders. It is hoped that school psychologists may educate the health-care community about the importance of psychological interventions.

In the spirit of the Boulder scientist-practitioner model, it is hoped that there can be an integration of research and practice as professional school psychologists embark on their understanding, research, and training efforts in the use of various psychotropic medications. In this way, it is hoped that there will be greater precision in evaluating the efficacy of medication in both the laboratory and the classroom. It is hoped that the end result will be the enhancement of the quality of life for the children whom we serve.

# REFERENCES

Abikoff, H., Ganeles, D., Reiter, G., Blum, C., Foley, C., & Klein, R. G. (1988). Cognitive training in academically deficient ADHD boys receiving stimulant medication. *Journal of Abnormal Child Psychology, 16*, 411–432.

Abikoff, H., & Gittelman, R. (1985). Hyperactive children treated with stimulants: Is cognitive training a useful adjunct? *Archives of General Psychiatry, 42*, 953–961.

Akiskal, H. S. (1995). Developmental pathways to bipolarity: Are juvenile onset depressions pre-bipolar? *Journal of the American Academy of Child and Adolescent Psychiatry, 34*, 754–763.

Alessi, N., Naylor, M. W., Ghaziuddin, M., & Zubieta, J. K. (1994). Update on lithium carbonate therapy in children and adolescents. *Journal of the American Academy of Child and Adolescent Psychiatry, 33*, 291–304.

Allen, A. J., Leonard, H., & Swedo, S. (1995). Current knowledge of medications for the treatment of childhood anxiety disorders. *Journal of the American Academy of Child and Adolescent Psychiatry, 34*, 976–986.

Aman, M. G. (1982). Stimulant drug effects in developmental disorders and hyperactivity— Toward a resolution of disparate findings. *Journal of Autism and Developmental Disorders, 12*, 851–859.

Aman, M. G., Kern, R. A., McGee, D. E., & Arnold, L. E. (1993). Fenfluramine and methylphenidate in children with mental retardation and ADHD: Clinical and side effects. *Journal of the American Academy of Child and Adolescent Psychiatry, 32*, 851–859.

Aman, M. G., & Wolford, P. L. (1995). Consumer satisfaction with involvement in drug research: A social validity study. *Journal of the American Academy of Child and Adolescent Psychiatry, 34*, 940–945.

Ambrosini, P. J., Mianchi, M. D., Rabinovich, H., & Elia, J. (1993a). Antidepressant treatments in children and adolescents I. Affective disorders. *Journal of the American Academy of Child and Adolescent Psychiatry, 32*, 1–6.

Ambrosini, P. J., Mianchi, M. D., Rabinovich, H., & Elia, J. (1993b). Antidepressant treatments in children and adolescents I. Anxiety, physical, and behavioral disorders. *Journal of the American Academy of Child and Adolescent Psychiatry, 32*, 483–493.

American Psychiatric Association. (1994). *Diagnostic and statistical manual of mental disorders* (4th ed.). Washington, DC: Author.

Apter, A., Ratzoni, G., King, R. A., Weizman, A., Iancu, I., Binder, M., & Riddle, M. (1994). *Fluvoxamine open label treatment of adolescent inpatients with obsessive-compulsive disorder or depression, 33*, 342–348.

Atkins, M. S., & Pelham, W. E. (1991). School-based assessment of attention deficit-hyperactivity disorder. *Journal of Learning Disabilities, 24*, 197–204.

Balthazor, M. J., Wagner, R. K., & Pelham, W. E. (1991). The specificity of the effects of stimulant medication on classroom learning-related measures of cognitive processing for attention deficit disorder children. *Journal of Abnormal Child Psychology, 19*, 35–52.

Bangs, M. E., Petti, T. A., & Mark-David, J. (1994). Fluoxetine-induced memory impairment in an adolescent. *Journal of the American Academy of Child and Adolescent Psychiatry, 33*, 1303–1306.

Barkley, R. A., Conners, C. K., Barclay, A., Gadow, K., Gittelman, R., Sprague, R., & Swanson, J. (1990). Task force report: The appropriate role of clinical child psychologists in the prescribing of psychoactive medication for children. *Journal of Clinical Child Psychology, 19* (Supplement), 1–38.

Barkley, R. A., DuPaul, G. J., & Costello, A. (1993). Stimulants. In J. S. Werry & M. G. Aman (Eds.), *Practioners' guide to psychoactive drugs for children and adolescents* (pp. 205–237). New York: Plenum.

Barkley, R. A., DuPaul, G. J., & McMurray, M. B. (1991). Attention deficit disorder with and without hyperactivity: Clinical response to three dose levels of methylphenidate. *Pediatrics, 88*, 519–531.

Barkley, R. A., Fischer, M., Newby, R. F., & Breen, M. J. (1988). Development of a multimethod clinical protocol for assessing stimulant drug response in children with attention deficit disorder. *Journal of Clinical Child Psychology, 17,* 14–24.

Barkley, R. A., & Grodinsky, G. M. (1994). Are tests of frontal lobe functions used in the diagnosis of attention deficit disorders? *The Clinical Neuropsychologist, 8,* 121–139.

Barkley, R. A., McMurray, M. B., Edelbrock, C. S., & Robbins, K. (1990). Side effects of methylphenidate in children with attention deficit hyperactivity disorder: A systemic, placebo-controlled evaluation. *Pediatrics, 86,* 184–192.

Barrickman, L., Noyes, R., Kuperman, S., Schumacher, E., & Verda, M. (1991). Treatment of ADHD with fluoxetine: A preliminary trial. *Journal of the American Academy of Child and Adolescent Psychiatry, 30,* 762–767.

Barrickman, L., Perry, P. J., Allen, A. J., Kuperman, S., Arndt, S. V., Herrmann, K. J., & Schumacher, E. (1995). Bupropion versus methylphenidate in the treatment of attention-deficit hyperactivity disorder. *Journal of the American Academy of Child and Adolescent Psychiatry, 34,* 649–657.

Behrman, R. E., & Vaughan, V. C. (1983). *Nelson Textbook of Pediatrics* (12th ed.). Philadelphia: Saunders.

Bernstein, G. A., Garfinkel, B. D., & Borchardt, C. M. (1990). Comparative studies of pharmacotherapy for school refusal. *Journal of the American Academy of Child and Adolescent Psychiatry, 29,* 773–781.

Berry, S. H., Quay, H. C., & Pelham, W. E. (1995, August). Behavioral disinhibition and response to methylphenidate in children with attention deficit hyperactivity disorder. Paper presented at the Annual Meeting of the American Psychological Association, New York.

Biederman, J. (1987). Clonazepam in the treatment of prepubertal children with paniclike symptoms. *Journal of Clinical Psychiatry, 48,* 38–41.

Biederman, J., Baldessarini, R. J., Wright, V., Knee, D., & Harmatz, J. S. (1989). A double-blind placebo controlled study of desipramine in the treatment of ADD: I. Efficacy. *Journal of the American Academy of Child and Adolescent Psychiatry, 28,* 777–784.

Biederman, J., Thisted, R., Greenhill, L., & Ryan, N. (1995). Resolved: Cardiac arrhythmias make desipramine an unacceptable choice in children (negative). *Journal of the American Academy of Child and Adolescent Psychiatry, 34,* 1241–1245.

Birmaher, B., Waterman, S., Ryan, N., Cully, M., Balach, L., Ingram, J., & Brodsky, M. (1994). Fluoxetine for childhood anxiety disorders. *Journal of the American Academy of Child and Adolescent Psychiatry, 33,* 993–999.

Black, B., & Uhde, T. W. (1994). Treatment of elective mutism with fluoxetine: A double-blind, placebo-controlled study. *Journal of the American Academy of Child and Adolescent Psychiatry, 33,* 1000–1006.

Black, B., Uhde, T. W., & Tancer, M. E. (1992). Fluoxetine for the treatment of social phobia. *Journal of Clinical Psychopharmacology, 12,* 293–295.

Blackwell, B., & Currah, J. (1973). The psycho-pharmacology of nocturnal enuresis. In I. Kelvin, R. MacKeith, & S. R. Meadow (Eds.), *Bladder control and enuresis* (pp. 231–257). Philadelphia: Lippincott.

Blouin, A. G. A., Bornstein, R. A., & Trites, R. L. (1978). Teenage alcohol use among hyperactive children: A five-year follow-up study. *Journal of Pediatric Psychology, 3,* 188–194.

Borden, K. A., & Brown, R. T. (1989). Attributional outcomes: The subtle messages of treatments for attention deficit disorder. *Cognitive Therapy and Research, 13,* 147–160.

Bradley, C. (1937). The behavior of children receiving Benzedrine. *American Journal of Psychiatry, 94,* 577–585.

Bramble, D. J. (1995). Antidepressant prescription by British child psychiatrists: Practice and safety issues. *Journal of the American Academy of Child and Adolescent Psychiatry, 34,* 327–331.

Brown, R. T. (1980). Impulsivity and psychoeducational intervention in hyperactive children. *Journal of Learning Disabilities, 13,* 249–254.

Brown, R. T., & Borden, K. A. (1989). Neuropsychological effects of stimulant medication on children's learning and behavior. In C. R. Reynolds & E. Fletcher-Janzen (Eds.), *Handbook of clinical child neuropsychology* (pp. 443–474). New York: Plenum.

Brown, R. T., Borden, K. A., Wynne, M. E., Clingerman, S. R., & Spunt, A. L. (1987). Compliance with pharmacological and cognitive treatments for attention deficit disorder. *Journal of the American Academy of Child and Adolescent Psychiatry, 26,* 521–526.

Brown, R. T., Borden, K. A., Wynne, M. E., Schleser, R., & Clingerman, S. R. (1986). Methylphenidate and cognitive therapy with ADD children: A methodological reconsideration. *Journal of Abnormal Child Psychology, 14,* 481–497.

Brown, R. T., Dingle, A., & Dreelin, B. (1997). Neuropsychological effects of stimulant medication on children's learning and behavior. In C. R. Reynolds & E. Fletcher-Janzen (Eds.), *Handbook of clinical child neuropsychology.* New York: Plenum Press.

Brown, R. T., Dingle, A., & Landau, S. (1994). Overview of psychopharmacology in children and adolescents. *School Psychology Quarterly, 9,* 4–25.

Brown, R. T., & Donegan, J. E. (1996). The growing impact of neurology. In D. K. Reid, W. P. Hresko,

& H. L. Swanson (Eds.), *Cognitive approaches to learning disabilities* (3rd ed.). Austin, TX: PRO-ED.

Brown, R. T., Jaffe, S., Silverstein, J., & McGee, H. (1991). Methylphenidate and adolescents hospitalized with conduct disorder: Dose effects on classroom behavior, academic performance, and impulsivity. *Journal of Clinical Child Psychology, 20*, 282–292.

Brown, R. T., & Sexson, S. B. (1988). A controlled trial of methylphenidate in black adolescents: Attentional, behavioral, and physiological effects. *Clinical Pediatrics, 27*, 74–81.

Brown, R. T., & Sleator, E. K. (1979). Methylphenidate in hyperkinetic children: Differences in dose effects on impulsive behavior. *Pediatrics, 64*, 408–411.

Brown, R. T., Wynne, M. E., & Medenis, R. (1985). Methylphenidate and cognitive therapy: A comparison of treatment approaches with hyperactive boys. *Journal of Abnormal Child Psychology, 13*, 69–87.

Bruun, R. D. (1984). Gilles de la Tourette's syndrome: An overview of clinical experience. *Journal of the American Academy of Child and Adolescent Psychiatry, 23*, 126–133.

Buitelaar, J. K., Van der Gaag, R. J., Swaab-Barneveld, H., & Kuiper, M. (1995). Prediction of clinical response to methylphenidate in children with attention-deficit hyperactivity disorder. *Journal of the American Academy of Child and Adolescent Psychiatry, 34*, 1025–1032.

Bukstein, O. (1992). Overview of pharmacological treatment. In V. B. Van Hasselt & M. Hersen (Eds.), *Handbook of behavior therapy and pharmacotherapy for children* (pp. 213–232). Boston: Allyn & Bacon.

Campbell, M., Gonzalez, N. M., Silva, R. R., & Werry, J. S. (1993). Antipsychotics (neuroleptics). In J. S. Werry & M. G. Aman (Eds.), *Practitioner's guide to psychoactive drugs for children and adolescents* (pp. 269–296). New York: Plenum.

Campbell, M., Silva, R. R., Kafantaris, V., Locascio, J. J., Gonzalez, N. M., Lee, D., & Lynch, N. S. (1991). Predictors of side effects associated with lithium administration in children. *Psychopharmacology Bulletin, 27*, 373–380.

Campbell, M., Small, A. M., Green, W. H., Jennings, W. G., & Anderson, L. (1984). Behavioral efficacy of haloperidol and lithium carbonate. *Archives of General Psychiatry, 41*, 650–656.

Carlson, C. L., & Kubiszyn, T. (1994). Psycho-pharmacology in schools: Introduction to the issues. *School Psychology Quarterly, 9*, 1–4.

Carlson, C. L., Paavola, J., & Talley, R. (1995). Historical, current, and future models of schools as health care delivery settings. *School Psychology Quarterly, 10*, 184–202.

Carlson, C. L., Pelham, W. E., Milich, R., & Hoza, B.

(1993). ADHD boys' performance and attributions following success and failure: Drug effects and individual differences. *Cognitive Therapy and Research, 17*, 269–287.

Carlson, G. A., Rapport, M. D., Pataki, C. S., & Kelly, K. L. (1992). Lithium in hospitalized children at 4 and 8 weeks: Mood, behavioral, and cognitive effect. *Journal of Child Psychology and Psychiatry, 33*, 411–425.

Casat, C. D., Pleasants, D. Z., Schroeder, D. H., & Parler, D. W. (1989). Buprorion in children with attention deficit disorder. *Psychopharmacology Bulletin, 25*, 198–201.

Coffey, B., Shader, R. I., & Greenblatt, D. J. (1983). Pharmacokinetics of benzodiazepines and psychostimulants in children. *Journal of Clinical Psychopharmacology, 3*, 217–225.

Como, P. G., & Kurlan, R. (1991). An open label trial of fluoxetine for obsessive compulsive in Gilles de la Tourette's syndrome. *Neurology, 41*, 872–874.

Corbett, J. A., Trimble, M. R., & Nichol, T. C. (1985). Behavioral and cognitive impairments in children with epilepsy: The long-term effects of anticonvulsant therapy. *Journal of the American Academy of Child and Adolescent Psychiatry, 24*, 17–23.

Cross-Calvert, S., & Johnston, C. (1990). Acceptability of treatments for child behavior problems: Issues and implications for future research. *Journal of Clinical Child Psychology, 19*, 61–74.

Dager, S. R., & Herich, A. J. (1990). A case of bupropion-associated delirium. *Journal of Clinical Psychiatry, 51*, 307–308.

Dalby, J. T., Kinsbourne, M., & Swanson, J. M. (1989). Self-paced learning in children with attention deficit disorder with hyperactivity. *Journal of Abnormal Child Psychology, 17*, 269–275.

Davies, R. K., Tucker, G. J., Harrow, M., & Detre, T. P. (1971). Confusional states and antidepressant medication. *American Journal of Psychiatry, 128*, 127–131.

DeLong, G. R., & Aldershof, A. L. (1987). Long-term experience with lithium treatment in childhood: Correlation with clinical diagnosis. *Journal of the American Academy of Child and Adolescent Psychiatry, 26*, 389–394.

DeMers, S. T. (1995). Emerging perspectives on the role of psychologists in the delivery of health and mental health services in schools. *School Psychology Quarterly, 10*, 179–183.

DeVeaugh-Geiss, J., Moroz, G., Biederman, J., Cantwell D., Fontaine, R., Greist, J. H., Reichler, R., Katz R., & Landau P. (1992). Clomipramine hydrochloride in childhood and adolescent obsessive-compulsive disorder—a multicenter trial. *Journal of the American Academy of Child and Adolescent Psychiatry, 31*, 45–49.

Douglas, V. I., Barr, R. G., Amin, K., O'Neill, M. E., & Britton, B. G. (1988). Dosage effects and individual responsivity to methylphenidate in attention deficit disorder. *Journal of Child Psychology and Psychiatry, 29,* 453–475.

Douglas, V. I., Barr, R. G., Desilets, J., & Sherman, E. (1995). Do high doses of stimulants impair flexible thinking in attention-deficit hyperactivity disorder? *Journal of the American Academy of Child and Adolescent Psychiatry, 34,* 877–885.

Douglas, V. I., & Peters, K. (1979). Toward a clearer definition of the attention deficit of hyperactive children. In G. A. Hale & M. Lewis (Eds.), *Attentional and cognitive development* (pp. 173–247). New York: Plenum.

Dulcan, M. K. (in press). Treatment of children and adolescents. In R. E. Hales, S. C. Yudofsky, & J. A. Talbott (Eds.), *American psychiatric press textbook of psychiatry* (2nd ed.). Washington, DC: American Psychiatric Association.

DuPaul, G. J., & Barkley, R. A. (1990). Medication therapy. In R. A. Barkley (Ed.), *Attention deficit hyperactivity disorder: A handbook for diagnosis and treatment* (pp. 573–612). New York: Guilford.

DuPaul, G. J., Barkley, R. A., & McMurray, M. B. (1994). Response of children with ADHD to methylphenidate: Interaction with internalizing symptoms. *Journal of the American Academy of Child and Adolescent Psychiatry, 33,* 894–903.

DuPaul, G. J., & Kyle, K. E. (1995). Pediatric pharmacology and psychopharmacology. In M. C. Roberts (Ed.), *Handbook of Pediatric Psychology* (2nd ed., pp. 741–758). New York: Guilford.

DuPaul, G. J., & Rapport, M. D. (1993). Does methylphenidate normalize the classroom performance of children with attention deficit disorder? *Journal of the American Academy of Child and Adolescent Psychiatry, 32,* 190–198.

Eisenberg, L., Lachman, R., Molling, P. A. Lockner, A., Mizelle, J. D., & Conners, C. K. (1963). A psychopharmacological experiment in a training school for delinquent boys: Methods, problems, findings. *American Journal of Orthopsychiatry, 33,* 431–447.

Elia, J., Welsh, P. A., Gullotta, C. S., & Rapoport, J. L. (1993). Classroom academic performance: Improvement with both methylphenidate and dextroamphetamine in ADHD boys. *Journal of Child Psychology and Psychiatry, 34,* 785–804.

Epstein, M. H., Matson, J. L., Repp, A., & Helsel, W. J. (1986). Acceptability of treatment alternative as a function of teacher status and student level. *School Psychology Review, 15,* 84–90.

Epstein, L., Singh, N. N., Luebke, J., & Stout, C. E. (1991). Psychopharmacological intervention. II. Teacher perceptions of psychotropic medication for students with learning disabilities. *Journal of Learning Disabilities, 24,* 477–483.

Evans, R. W., Clary, T. H., & Gualtieri, C. T. (1987). Carbamazepine in pediatric psychiatry. *Journal of the American Academy of Child and Adolescent Psychiatry, 26,* 2–8.

Evans, R. W., Gualtieri, C. T., & Amara, I. (1986). Methylphenidate and memory: Dissociated effects on hyperactive children. *Psychopharmacology, 90,* 211–216.

Faigel, H. C. (1991). The effect of beta blockade on stress-induced cognitive dysfunction in adolescents. *Clinical Pediatrics, 30,* 441–445.

Famularo, R. A., Kinscherff, R., & Fenton, T. (1988). Propranolol treatments for childhood past traumatic stress disorder, acute type. *American Journal of Diseases of Children, 142,* 1244–1247.

Fava, M., Herzog, D. B., Hamburg, P., Reiss, H., Anfang, S., & Rosenbaum, J. F. (1990, April). A retrospective study of long-term use of fluoxetine in bulimia nervosa. Abstract presented at the Fourth International Conference on Eating Disorders, New York.

Firestone, P. (1982). Factors associated with children's adherence to stimulant medication. *American Journal of Orthopsychiatry, 52,* 447–457.

Fischer, M., & Newby, R. F. (1991). Assessment of stimulant response in ADHD children using a refined multimethod clinical protocol. *Journal of Clinical Child Psychology, 20,* 232–244.

Fitzpatrick, P. A., Klorman, R., Brumaghim, J. T., & Borgstedt, A. D. (1992). Effects of sustained-release and standard preparations of methylphenidate on attention deficit disorder. *Journal of the American Academy of Child and Adolescent Psychiatry, 31,* 226–234.

Flament, M. F., Rapoport, J. L., Berg, C. J., Sceery, W., Kilts, C., Mellstrom, B., Linnoila, M. (1985). Clomipramine treatment of childhood obsessive-compulsive disorder. *Archives of General Psychiatry, 42,* 977–979.

Fletcher, J. M., & Levin, H. (1988). Neurobehavioral effects of brain injury in children. In D. K. Routh (Ed.), *Handbook of pediatric psychology* (pp. 258–295). New York: Guilford.

Fletcher, J. M., Levin, H., & Landry, S. H. (1984). Behavioral consequences of cerebral insult in children. In C. R. Amli & S. Finger (Eds.), *Early brain damage* (Vol. 1). New York: Academic Press.

Forness, S. R., Cantwell, D. P., Swanson, J. M., Hanna, G. L., & Youpa, D. (1991). Differential effects of stimulant medication on reading performance of boys with hyperactivity with and without conduct disorder. *Journal of Learning Disabilities, 24,* 304–310.

Forness, S. R., & Kavale, K. A. (1988). Psychopharmacological medication: A note on classroom effects. *Journal of Learning Disabilities, 21,* 144–147.

Fritz, G. K., Rockney, R. M., & Yeung, A. (1994). Plasma levels and efficacy of imipramine treatment for enuresis. *Journal of the American Academy of Child and Adolescent Psychiatry, 33,* 60–64.

Gadow, K. D. (1981). Drug therapy for hyperactivity: Treatment procedures in actual settings. In K. D. Gadow & J. Loney (Eds.), *Psychosocial aspects of drug treatment for hyperactivity* (pp. 325–378). Boulder, CO: Westview.

Gadow, K. D. (1986). Stimulant side effects checklist. State University of New York, Department of Psychiatry, Stony Brook. (Available from author.)

Gadow, K. D. (1992). Pediatric psychopharmacotherapy: A review of recent research. *Journal of Child Psychology and Psychiatry, 33,* 153–195.

Gadow, K. D. (1993). A school-based medication evaluation program. In J. L. Matson (Ed.), *Handbook of hyperactivity in children* (pp. 186–219). Needham Heights, MA: Allyn & Bacon.

Gadow, K. D., Nolan, E. E., Paolicelli, L. M., & Sprafkin, J. (1991). A procedure for assessing the effects of methylphenidate on hyperactive children in public school settings. *Journal of Clinical Child Psychology, 20,* 268–276.

Gadow, K. D., & Sverd, J. (1990). Stimulants for ADHD in child patients with Tourette's syndrome: The issue of relative risk. *Developmental and Behavioral Pediatrics, 11,* 269–271.

Gadow, K. D., Sverd, J., Sprafkin, J., Nolan, E. E., & Ezor, S. N. (1996). Efficacy of methylphenidate for attention-deficit hyperactivity disorder in children with tic disorder. *Archives of General Psychiatry, 52,* 444–455.

Garfinkel, M., Garfinkel, L., Himmelhoch, J., & McHugh, T. (1985). Lithium carbonate and carbamazepine: An effective treatment for adolescent manic or mixed bipolar patients. Unpublished manuscript, Scientific proceedings, Annual Meeting of the American Academy of Child and Adolescent Psychiatry, held in San Antonio, TX.

Garfinkel, B. D., Wender, P. H., Sloman, L., & O'Neill, I. (1983). Tricyclic antidepressants and methylphenidate treatment of ADD in children. *Journal of the American Academy of Child and Adolescent Psychiatry, 22,* 343–348.

Gelenberg, A. J. (1991). Psychoses. In A. J. Gelenberg, E. L. Bassuk, & S. C. Schoonover (Eds.), *The practitioner's guide to psychoactive drugs* (pp. 125–178). New York: Plenum.

Geller, D. A., Biederman, J., Reed, E. D., Spencer, T., & Wilens, T. E. (1995). Similarities in response to fluoxetine in the treatment of children and adolescents with obsessive-compulsive disorder. *Journal of the American Academy of Child and Adolescent Psychiatry, 34,* 36–44.

Gittelman, R., & Wender, P. (1995). The role of methylphenidate in psychiatry. *Archives of General Psychiatry, 52,* 429–433.

Gittelman-Klein, R., & Klein, D. F. (1971). Controlled imipramine treatment of school phobia. *Archives of General Psychiatry, 25,* 204–207.

Gittelman-Klein, R., & Klein, D. F. (1973). School phobia: Diagnostic considerations in the light of imipramine effects. *Journal of Nervous and Mental Disorders, 156,* 199–215.

Gittelman-Klein, R., Landa, B., Mattes, J., & Klein, D. F. (1988). Methylphenidate and growth in hyperactive children: A controlled withdrawal study. *Archives of General Psychiatry, 45,* 1127–1130.

Gittelman-Klein, R., & Mannuzza, S. (1988). Hyperactive boys almost grown up: III. Methylphenidate effects on ultimate height. *Archives of General Psychiatry, 45,* 1131–1134.

Goodman, A., & Gilman, L. S. (1980). *The pharmacological basis of therapeutics.* New York: Macmillan.

Gordon, C. T., Cotelingam, M., Stager, S., Ludlow, C., Hamburger, S. D., & Rapoport, J. L. (1995). A double-blind comparison of clomipramine and desipramine in the treatment of developmental stuttering. *Journal of Clinical Psychiatry, 56,* 238–242.

Gualtieri, C. T. (1991). Pharmacotherapy and the neurobehavioral sequelae of traumatic brain injury. Unpublished manuscript, University of North Carolina, Chapel Hill.

Gualtieri, C. T., & Evans, R. W. (1988). Stimulant treatment for the neurobehavioral sequelae of traumatic brain injury. *Brain Injury, 2,* 273–290.

Gualtieri, C. T., Keenan, P. A., & Chandler, M. (1991). Clinical and neuropsychological effects of desipramine in children with attention deficit hyperactivity disorder. *Journal of Clinical Psychopharmacology, 11,* 155–159.

Gutkin, T. B. (1995). School psychology and health care: Moving service delivery into the twenty-first century. *School Psychology Quarterly, 10,* 236–246.

Handen, B. J., Beaux, A. M., Gosling, A., Ploof, D. L., & Feldman, H. (1990). Efficacy of methylphenidate among mentally retarded children with attention deficit hyperactivity disorder. *Pediatrics, 86,* 922–930.

Handen, B. L., Feldman, H., Gosling, A., Breaux, A. M., & McAuliffe, S. (1991). Adverse side effects of methylphenidate among mentally retarded children with ADHD. *Journal of the American Academy of Child and Adolescent Psychiatry, 30,* 241–245.

Hechtman, L., Weiss, G., & Perlman, T. (1984). Young adult outcome of hyperactive children who received long-term stimulant treatment. *Journal of the American Academy of Child and Adolescent Psychiatry, 23,* 261–269.

Henker, B., & Whalen, C. K. (1989). Hyperactivity and attention deficits. *American Psychologist, 44,* 216–223.

Henker, B., Whalen, C., Bugenthal, D. B., & Barker, C. (1981). Licit and illicit drug patterns in stimulant treated children and their peers. In K. D. Gadow & J. Loney (Eds.), *Psychosocial aspects* of drug treatment for hyperactivity (pp. 443–462). Boulder, CO: Westview.

Herranz, J. L., Armijo, J. A., & Arteaga, R. (1988). Clinical side effects of phenobarbital, primidone, phenytoin, carbamazepine, and valproate during monotherapy in children. *Epilepsia, 29,* 794–804.

Hinshaw, S. P. (1991). Stimulant medication and the treatment of aggression in children with attentional deficits. *Journal of Clinical Child Psychology, 20,* 301–312.

Horn, W. F., Ialongo, N. S., Pascoe, J. M., Greenberg, G., Packard, T., Lopez, M., Wagner, A., & Putter, L. (1991). Additive effects of psychostimulants, parent training, and self-control therapy with ADHD children. *Journal of the American Academy of Child and Adolescent Psychiatry, 30,* 233–240.

Houts, A. C. (1991). Nocturnal enuresis as a bio-behavioral problem. *Behavior Therapy, 22,* 133–151.

Hunt, R. D., Capperl, X., & O'Connel, P. (1990). Clonidine in child and adolescent psychiatry. *Journal of Child and Adolescent Psychopharmacology, 1,* 87–102.

Hunt, R. D., Minderaa, R. B., & Cohen, D. J. (1985). Clonidine benefits children with attention deficit disorder and hyperactivity: Report of a double-blind placebo-crossover therapeutic trial. *Journal of the American Academy of Child and Adolescent Psychiatry, 24,* 617–629.

Ialongo, N. S., Horn, W. F., Pascoe, J. M., Greenberg, G., Packard, T., Lopez, M., Wagner, A., & Pyttler, L. (1993). The effects of multimodal intervention with attention deficit hyperactivity disorder children: A 9-month follow-up. *Journal of the American Academy of Child and Adolescent Psychiatry, 32,* 182–189.

Ialongo, N. S., Lopez, M., Horn, W. F., Pascoe, J. M., & Greenberg, G. (1994). Effects of psychostimulant medication on self-perceptions of competence, control, and mood in children with attention deficit hyperactivity disorder. *Journal of Clinical Child Psychology, 23,* 161–173.

Jacobvitz, D., Sroufe, A., Steward, M., & Leffert, N. (1990). Treatment of attentional and hyperactivity problems in children with sympathomimetic drugs; A comprehensive review. *Journal of the American Academy of Child and Adolescent Psychiatry, 29,* 677–688.

Jain, U., Birmaher, B., Garcia, M., Al-Shabbout, M., & Ryan, N. (1993). Fluoxetine: A chart review of efficacy and adverse effects. *Journal of Child and Adolescent Psychopharmacology, 2,* 259–265.

Johnston, C., & Fine, S. (1993). Methods of evaluating methylphenidate in children with attention deficit hyperactivity disorder: Acceptability, satisfaction, and compliance. *Journal of Pediatric Psychology, 18,* 717–730.

Johnston, C., Pelham, W. E., Hoza, J., & Sturges, J. (1988). Psychostimulant rebound in attention deficit disordered boys. *Journal of the American Academy of Child and Adolescent Psychiatry, 27,* 806–810.

Joorabchi, B. (1977). Expressions of the hyperventilation syndrome in childhood. *Clinical Pediatrics, 16,* 1110–1115.

Kafantaris, V., Campbell, M., Padrol-Gayol, M. V., Small, A. M., Locasio, J. J., & Rosenburg, C. R. (1992). Carbamazepine in hospitalized aggressive conduct disorder children: An open pilot study. *Psychopharmacology Bulletin, 28,* 193–199.

Kaplan, S. L., Busner, J., Kupietz, S., Wasserman, E., & Segal, B. (1990). Effects of methylphenidate on adolescents with aggressive conduct disorder and ADHD: A preliminary report. *Journal of the American Academy of Child and Adolescent Psychiatry, 29,* 719–723.

Kaslow, N. J., Brown, R. T., & Mee, L. (1995). Contemporary cognitive-behavioral models for childhood depression. In W. M. Reynolds & H. F. Johnston (Eds.), *Handbook of depression in children and adolescents* (pp. 97–121). New York: Plenum.

Kasten, E. F., Coury, D. L., & Heron, T. E. (1992). Educators' knowledge and attitudes regarding stimulants in the treatment of attention deficit hyperactivity disorder. *Journal of Developmental and Behavioral Pediatrics, 13,* 215–219.

Kauffman, R. E., Smith-Wright, D., Reese, C. A., Simpson, R., & Fowler, J. (1981). Medication compliance in hyperactive children. *Pediatric Psychopharmacology, 1,* 231–237.

Kazdin, A. E. (1980). Acceptability of alternative treatment for deviant behavior. *Journal of Applied Behavior Analysis, 13,* 259–273.

Kazdin, A. E. (1981). Acceptability of child treatment techniques: The influence of treatment efficacy and adverse side affects. *Behavior Therapy, 12,* 493–506.

Kazdin, A. E. (1984). Acceptability of aversive procedures and medication as treatment alternatives for deviant child behavior. *Journal of Abnormal Child Psychology, 12,* 289–302.

Kemph, J. P., Lindsay-DeVane, C., Levin, G. M., Jarecke, R., & Miller, R. L. (1993). Treatment of aggressive children with clonidine: Results of an open pilot study. *Journal of the American Academy of Child and Adolescent Psychiatry, 32,* 577–581.

Kovacs, M., & Goldston, D. (1991). Cognitive and social cognitive development of depressed children and adolescents. *Journal of the American Academy of Child and Adolescent Psychiatry, 30,* 388–392.

Kranzler, H. R. (1988). Use of busipirone in adolescents with overanxious disorder. *Journal of the American Academy of Child and Adolescent Psychiatry, 27,* 789–790.

Kruesi, M. J. P., Rapoport, J. L., Hamburger, S., Hibbs, E., Potter, W. Z., Lenane, M., & Brown, G. L. (1990). Cerebrospinal fluid metabolites, aggression, and impulsivity in disruptive behavior disorders of children and adolescents. *Archives of General Psychiatry, 47,* 419–426.

Kubiszyn, T., & Carlson, C. I. (1996). School psychologists' attitudes toward an expanded health care role: Psychopharmacology and prescription privileges. *School Psychology Quarterly, 10,* 247–270.

Kuperman, S., & Stewart, M. A. (1987). Use of propranolol to decrease aggressive outbursts in younger patients. *Psychosomatics, 28,* 315–319.

Kupietz, S. S., Winsberg, B. G., Richardson, E., Maitinsky, S., & Mendell, N. (1988). Effects of methylphenidate dosage in hyperactive reading-disabled children: I. Behavior and cognitive performance effects. *Journal of the American Academy of Child and Adolescent Psychiatry, 27,* 70–77.

Kutcher, S., Boulos, C., Ward, B., Marton, P., Simeon, J., Ferguson, H. B., Szalai, J., Katic, M., Roberts, N., DuBois, C., & Reed, K. (1994). *Journal of the American Academy of Child and Adolescent Psychiatry, 33,* 686–694.

LaGreca, A., & Schuman, W. (1995). Adherence to prescribed medical regimes. In M. Roberts (Ed.), *Handbook of pediatric psychology* (2nd ed., pp. 55–83). New York: Guilford.

Leckman, J. F., Hardin, M. T., Riddle, M. A., Stevenson, J., Ort, S. I., & Cohen, D. J. (1991). Clonidine treatment of Gilles de la Tourette's syndrome. *Archives of General Psychiatry, 48,* 324–328.

Lena, B. (1979). Lithium in child and adolescent psychiatry. *Archives of General Psychiatry, 36,* 854–855.

Leonard, H. L., Meyer, M. C., Swedo, S. E., Richter, D., Hamburger, S. D., Allen, A. J., Rapoport, J. L., & Tucker, E. (1995). Electrocardiographic changes during desipramine and clomipramine treatment in children and adolescents. *Journal of the American Academy of Child and Adolescent Psychiatry, 34,* 1460–1468.

Leonard, H. L., Swedo, S., Rapoport, J. L., Koby, E. V., Lenane, M. C., Cheslow, D. L. & Hamburger, S. D. (1989). Treatment of obsessive-compulsive disorder with clomipramine and desipramine in children and adolescents. A double-blind crossover comparison. *Archives of General Psychiatry, 46,* 1088–1092.

Levy, F., & Hobbes, G. (1988). The action of stimulant medication in attention deficit disorder with hyperactivity: Dopaminergic, noradrenergic, or both. *Journal of the American Academy of Child and Adolescent Psychiatry, 27,* 802–805.

Liebowitz, M. R., Hollander, E., Fairbanks, J., & Campeas, R. (1990). Fluoxetine for adolescents with obsessive-compulsive disorder. *American Journal of Psychiatry, 147,* 370–371.

Liu, C., Robin, A. L., Brenner, S., & Eastman, J. (1991). Social acceptability of methylphenidate and behavior modification for treating attention deficit hyperactivity disorder. *Pediatrics, 88,* 560–565.

Loney, J., Kramer, J., & Milich, R. (1981). The hyperactive child grows up: Predictors of symptoms, delinquency and achievement at follow-up. In K. D. Gadow & J. Loney (Eds.), *Psychosocial aspects of drug treatment for hyperactivity* (pp. 381–415). Boulder, CO: Westview.

Mayln, D., Jensen, W. R., & Clark, E. (1993). Myths and realities about ADHD: A comprehensive survey of school psychologists and teachers about causes and treatments. Paper presented at the Annual Convention of the National Association of School Psychologists, Washington, DC.

McElroy, S. L., Deck, P. E., Pope, H. G., & Hudson, J. I. (1988). Valproate in the treatment of rapid cycling bipolar disorder. *Journal of Clinical Psychopharmacology, 8,* 275–278.

Meltzer, H. Y. (1992). Dimensions of outcome with clozapine. *British Journal of Psychiatry, 160* (Supplement 17), 46–53.

Milich, R., Carlson, C. L., Pelham, W. E., & Licht, B. G. (1991). Effects of methylphenidate on the persistence of ADHD boys following failure experiences. *Journal of Abnormal Child Psychology, 19,* 519–536.

Milich, R., Licht, B. G., Murphy, D. A., & Pelham, W. E. (1989). Attention-deficit hyperactivity disordered boys' evaluations of attributions for task performance on medication versus placebo. *Journal of Abnormal Child Psychology, 98,* 280–284.

Mittl, V. F., & Robin, A. (1987). Acceptability of alternative interventions for parent-adolescent conflict. *Behavioral Assessment, 9,* 417–428.

Morris, R., Krawiecki, N., Wright, J., & Walters, W. (1993). Neuropsychological, academic, and adaptive functioning in children who survive in-hospital cardiac arrest and resuscitation. *Journal of Learning Disabilities, 26,* 46–51.

Mozes, T., Toren, P., Chernauzan, N., Mester, R., Yoran-Hegesh, R., Blumensohn, R., & Weizman, A. (1994). Clozapine treatment in very early onset schizophrenia. *Journal of the American Academy of Child and Adolescent Psychiatry, 33,* 65–70.

Nolan, E. E., & Gadow, K. D. (1994). Relation between ratings and observations of stimulant drug response in hyperactive children. *Journal of Clinical Child Psychology, 23,* 78–90.

Pelham, W. E. (1993). Pharmacotherapy for children with attention-deficit hyperactivity disorder. *School Psychology Review, 22,* 199–227.

Pelham, W. E., Bender, M. E., Caddell, J., Booth, S., & Moorer, S. H. (1985). Methylphenidate and children with attention deficit disorder. *Archives of General Psychiatry, 42,* 948–952.

Pelham, W. E., Carlson, C., Sams, S. E., Vallano, G., Dixon, M. J., & Hoza, B. (1993). Separate and combined effects of methylphenidate and behavior modification on boys with attention deficit hyperactivity disorder in the classroom. *Journal of Consulting and Clinical Psychology, 61,* 506–515.

Pelham, W. E., & Evans, S. W. (1991). Psychostimulant effects on academic and behavioral measures for junior high school students in a lecture format classroom. *Journal of Abnormal Child Psychology, 19,* 537–552.

Pelham, W. E., Greenslade, K. E., Vodde-Hamilton, M., Murphy, D., Greenstein, J. J., Gnagy, E. M., Guthrie, K. J., Hoover, M. D., & Dahl, R. E. (1990). Relative efficacy of long-acting stimulants on children with attention deficit hyperactivity disorder: A comparison of standard methylphenidate, sustained-release methylphenidate, sustained-release dextroamphetamine, and pemoline. *Pediatrics, 86,* 226–237.

Pelham, W. E., & Hoza, J. (1987). Behavioral assessment of psychostimulant effects on ADD children in a summer day treatment program. In R. Prinz (Ed.), *Advances in behavioral assessment of children and families* (Vol. 3, pp. 3–34). Greenwich, CT: JAI Press.

Pelham, W. E., Murphy, D. A., Vannatta, K., Milich, R., Licht, B. G., Gnagy, E. M., Greenslade, K. E., Greiner, A. R., & Vodde-Hamilton, M. (1992). Methylphenidate and attributions in boys with attention-deficit hyperactivity disorder. *Journal of Consulting and Clinical Psychology, 60,* 282–292.

Pelham, W. E., Schnedler, R. W., Bender, M. E., Miller, J., Nilsson, D., Budlow, M., Ronnei, M., Paluchowski, C., & Marks, D. (1988). The combination of behavior therapy and methylphenidate in the treatment of hyperactivity: A therapy outcome study. In L. Bloomingdale (Ed.), *Attention deficit disorders* (pp. 29–48). London: Pergamon.

Pelham, W. E., Swanson, J. M., Bender-Furman, M., & Schwindt, H. (1995). Pemoline effects on children with ADHD: A time-response by dose-response analysis on classroom measures. *Journal of the American Academy of Child and Adolescent Psychiatry, 34,* 1504–1513.

Pelham, W. E., Vallano, G., Hoza, B., Greiner, A. R., & Gnagy, E. M. (1992). Methylphenidate dose effects on ADHD children: Individual differences across children and domains. Unpublished manuscript, University of Pittsburgh, Pittsburgh, PA.

Pelham, W. E., Vodde-Hamilton, M., Murphy, D. A., Greenstein, J., & Vallano, G. (1991). The effects of methylphenidate on ADHD adolescents in recreational, peer group, and classroom settings. *Journal of Clinical Child Psychology, 20,* 293–300.

Pliszka, S. R. (1991). Antidepressants in the treatment of child and adolescent psychopathology. *Journal of Clinical Child Psychology, 20,* 313–320.

Pope, H. G., Jr., Hudson, J. I., Jonas, J. M., & Yurgelun-Todd, D. (1983). Bulimia treated with imipramine: A placebo-controlled, double-blind study. *American Journal of Psychiatry, 140,* 554–558.

Pope, H. G., McElroy, S. L., Keck, P., & Brown, S. (1991). Valproate in the treatment of acute mania: A placebo controlled study. *Archives of General Psychiatry, 48,* 62–68.

Post, R. M., & Uhde, T. W. (1985). Carbamazepine in bipolar illness. *Psychopharmacology Bulletin, 21,* 10–17.

Post, R. M., Uhde, T. W., Roy-Byrne, P. P., & Joffe, R. T. (1987). Correlates of antimanic response to carbazepine. *Psychiatric Research, 21,* 71–83.

Power, T. J., Hess, L. E., & Bennett, D. S. (1995). The acceptability of interventions for attention deficit disorder among elementary and middle school teachers. *Developmental and Behavioral Pediatrics, 16,* 238–243.

Preskorn, S. H., & Jerkovich, G. (1990). Central nervous system toxicity of tricyclic antidepressants: Phenomenology, course, risk factors, and role of therapeutic drug monitoring. *Journal of Clinical Psychopharmacology, 10,* 88–95.

Preskorn, S. H., Jerkovich, G. S., Beber, J. H., & Widener, P. (1989). Therapeutic drug monitoring of tricyclic antidepressants: A standard of care issue. *Psychopharmacology Bulletin, 25,* 281–284.

Preskorn, S. H., Weller, E. B., Jerkovich, G., Hughes, C. W., & Weller, R. (1988). Depression in children: Concentration dependent CNS toxicity of tricyclic antidepressants. *Psychopharmacology Bulletin, 24,* 140–142.

Puig-Antich, J., Perel, J. M., Lupatkin, W., Chambers, W. J., Tabrizi, M. A., King, J., Goetz, R., Davies, M., & Stiller, R. L. (1987). Imipramine in prepubertal major depressive disorders. *Archives of General Psychiatry, 44,* 81–89.

Quaison, N., Ward, D., & Kitchen, T. (1991). Buspirone for aggression. *Journal of the American Academy of Child and Adolescent Psychiatry, 30,* 1026.

Rapoport, J. L. (1983). The use of drugs: Trends in research. In M. Rutter (Ed.), *Developmental neuropsychiatry* (pp. 385–403). New York: Guilford.

Rapoport, J. L., Quinn, P. O., Bradbard, G., Riddle, D., & Brooks, E. (1974). Imipramine and methylphenidate treatments of hyperactive boys: A double-blind comparison. *Archives of General Psychiatry, 30,* 789–793.

Rapoport, J. L., & Zametkin, A. (1980). ADD. *Psychiatric Clinics of North America, 3,* 425–442.

Rapport, M. D., Denney, C., DuPaul, G. J., & Gardner, M. J. (1994). *Journal of the American Academy of Child and Adolescent Psychiatry, 33,* 882–893.

Rapport, M. D., DuPaul, G. J., Stoner, G., & Jones, J. T. (1986). Comparing classroom and clinical measures of attention deficit disorder: Differential, idiosyncratic and dose-response effects of methylphenidate. *Journal of Consulting and Clinical Psychology*, *54*, 334–341.

Rapport, M. D., & Kelly, K. L. (1991). Psychostimulant effects on learning and cognitive function: Findings and implications for children with attention deficit hyperactivity disorder. *Clinical Psychology Review*, *11*, 61–92.

Ratey, J. J., Sovner, R., Mikkelsen, E., & Chmielinski, H. E. (1989). Buspirone therapy for maladaptive behavior and anxiety in developmentally disabled persons. *Journal of Clinical Psychiatry*, *50*, 382–384.

Ratey, J. J., Sovner, R., Parks, A., & Rogentine, K. (1991). Buspirone treatment of aggression and anxiety in mentally retarded patients: A multiple-baseline, placebo lead-in study. *Journal of Clinical Psychiatry*, *52*, 159–162.

Realmuto, G. M., August, G. J., & Garfinkel, B. D. (1989). Clinical effect of buspirone in autistic children. *Journal of Clinical Psychopharmacology*, *9*, 122–125.

Richardson, E., Kupietz, S. A., Winsberg, B. G., Maitinsky, S., & Mendell, N. (1992). Effects of methylphenidate dosage in hyperactive reading-disabled children. II. Reading achievement. *Journal of the American Academy of Child and Adolescent Psychiatry*, *27*, 78–87.

Richters, J. E., Arnold, L. E., Jensen, P. S., Abikoff, H., Conners, C. K., Greenhill, L. L., Hechtman, L., Hinshaw, S. P., Pelham, W. E., & Swanson, J. M. (1995). NIMH collaborative multisite multimodal treatment study of children with ADHD: I. Background and Rationale. *Journal of the American Academy of Child and Adolescent Psychiatry*, *34*, 987–1000.

Riddle, M. A., Geller, B., & Ryan, N. (1993). Another sudden death in a child treated with desipramine. *Journal of the American Academy of Child and Adolescent Psychiatry*, *32*, 792–797.

Riddle, M. A., Hardin, M. T., King, R., Scahill, L., & Woolston, J. L. (1990). Fluoxetine treatment in children and adolescents with Tourette's and obsessive compulsive disorders: Preliminary clinical experience. *Journal of the American Academy of Child and Adolescent Psychiatry*, *29*, 45–48.

Riddle, M. A., King, R. A., Hardin, M. T., Scahill, L., Ort, S. I., Chappell, P., Rasmusson, A., & Leckman, J. F. (1990). Behavioral side effects of fluoxetine in children and adolescents. *Journal of the Child and Adolescent Psychopharmacology*, *1*, 193–198.

Riddle, M. A., Scahill, L., King, R. A., Hardin, M. T., Anderson, G. M., Ort, S. I., Smith, J. C., Leckman, J. F., Cohen, D. J. (1992). Double-blind, crossover trial of fluoxetine and placebo in children and adolescents with obsessive-compulsive disorder. *Journal of the American Academy of Child and Adolescent Psychiatry*, *31*, 1062–1069.

Rivinus, T. M. (1982). Psychiatric effects of the anticonvulsant regimens. *Journal of Clinical Psychopharmacology*, *2*, 165–192.

Rosenburg, D. R., Johnson, K., & Sahl, R. (1992). Evolution of hypomania and mania in an adolescent treated with low dose fluoxetine. *Journal of Child and Adolescent Psychopharmacology*, *2*, 299–305.

Ryan, N. D., Meyer, V., Dachille, S., Mazzie, D., & Puig-Antich, J. (1988). Lithium antidepressant augmentation of TCA-refractory depression in adolescents. *Journal of the American Academy of Child and Adolescent Psychiatry*, *27*, 371–376.

Ryan, N. D., Puig-Antich, J., Ambrosini, P., Rabinovich, H., Robinson, D., Nelson, B., Lyengar, S., & Twomey, J. (1987). The clinical picture of major depression in children and adolescents. *Archives of General Psychiatry*, *44*, 854–861.

Safer, D. J., & Krager, J. M. (1988). A survey of medication treatment for hyperactive/inattentive students. *Journal of the American Medical Association*, *260*, 2256–2258.

Shaffer, D., Costello, A. J., & Hill, J. D. (1968). Control of enuresis with imipramine. *Archives of Diseases in Children*, *43*, 665–671.

Shapiro, A., & Shapiro, E. (1988). Treatment of tic disorders with haloperidol. In D. J. Cohen, R. D. Bruun, & J. F. Leckman (Eds.), *Tourette's syndrome and tic disorders: Clinical understanding and treatment* (pp. 267–280). New York: Wiley.

Shelton, T., & Barkley, R. A. (1995). The assessment and treatment of attention deficit hyperactivity disorder in children. In M. Roberts (Ed.), *Handbook of pediatric psychology* (2nd ed., pp. 633–654). New York: Guilford.

Siegel, D. M. (1989). Bulimia, tricyclic antidepressant and mania. *Clinical Pediatrics*, *28*, 123–126.

Sigelman, C. K., & Shorokey, J. J. (1986). Effects of treatments and their outcomes on peer perceptions of a hyperactive child. *Journal of Abnormal Child Psychology*, *14*, 397–410.

Simeon, J. D., Diniala, V. F., Ferguson, H. B., & Copping, W. (1990). Adolescent depression: A placebo controlled fluoxetine treatment study and followup. *Progress in Neuropsychopharmacology and Biological Psychiatry*, *14*, 791–795.

Simeon, J. G., Ferguson, H. B., & Fleet, J. W. (1986). Buproprion effects in attention deficit and conduct disorders. *Canadian Journal of Psychiatry*, *31*, 581–585.

Singh, N. N., Epstein, M. H., Luebke, J., & Singh, Y. N. (1990). Psychopharmacological intervention. I: Teacher perceptions of psychotropic medication for students with serious emotional disturbance. *The Journal of Special Education, 24,* 283–295.

Slimmer, L. W., & Brown, R. T. (1985). Parent's decision-making process in medication administration for control of hyperactivity. *Journal of School Health, 55,* 221–225.

Smyer, M. A., Balster, R. L., Egli, D., Johnson, D. L., Kilbey, M. M., Leith, N. J., & Puente, A. E. (1993). Summary of the report of the ad-hoc task force on psychopharmacology of the American Psychological Association. *Professional Psychology: Research and Practice, 24,* 394–403.

Spencer, T., Biederman, J., Kerman, K., Steingard, R., & Wilens, T. (1993). Desipramine treatment of children with attention-deficit hyperactivity disorder and tic disorder or Tourette's syndrome. *Journal of the American Academy of Child and Adolescent Psychiatry, 32,* 354–360.

Spencer, T., Wilens, T., Biederman, J., Faraone, S. V., Ablon, J. S., & Lapey, K. (1995). A double-blind, crossover comparison of methylphenidate and placebo in adults with childhood-onset attention-deficit hyperactivity disorder. *Archives of General Psychiatry, 52,* 434–443.

Sprague, R. L., & Sleator, E. K. (1977). Methylphenidate in hyperkinetic children: Differences in dose effects on learning and social behavior. *Science, 198,* 1274–1276.

Steingard, R. J., Biederman, J., Spencer, T., Wilens, T., & Gonzalez, A. (1993). Comparison of clonidine response in the treatment of attention-deficit hyperactivity disorder with and without comorbid tic disorders. *Journal of the American Academy of Child and Adolescent Psychiatry, 32,* 350–353.

Steingard, R. J., DeMaso, D. R., Goldman, S. J., Shorrock, K. L., & Bucci, J. P. (1995). Current perspectives on the pharmacotherapy of depressive disorders in children and adolescents. *Harvard Review of Psychiatry, 2,* 313–326.

Stokes, P. E. (1993). Fluoxetine: A five-year review. *Clinical Therapeutics, 15,* 216–243.

Stoudemire, A., Morau, M. G., & Fogel, B. S. (1991). Psychotropic drug use in the medically ill: Part II. *Psychosomatics, 32,* 34–36.

Strober, M., Morrell, W., Burroughs, J., Lampert, C., Danforth, H., & Freeman, R. (1988). A family study of bipolar I disorder in adolescence: Early onset of symptoms linked to increased familial loading and lithium resistance. *Journal of Affective Disorders, 15,* 255–268.

Strober, M., Morrell, W., Lampert, C., & Burroughs, J. (1990). Relapse following discontinuation of lithium maintenance therapy in adolescents with bipolar I illness: A naturalistic study. *American Journal of Psychiatry, 28,* 574–579.

Summers, J. A., & Caplan, P. J. (1987). Lay people's attitudes toward drug treatment for behavioral control depend on which disorder and which drug. *Clinical Pediatrics, 26,* 258–263.

Sverd, J., Gadow, K. D., Nolan, E. E., Sprafkin, J., & Ezor, S. N. (1992). Methylphenidate in hyperactive boys with comorbid tic disorder. *Advances in Neurology, 58,* 271–281.

Tannock, R., Ickowicz, A., & Schachar, R. (1995). Differential effects of methylphenidate on working memory in ADHD children with and without comorbid anxiety. *Journal of the American Academy of Child and Adolescent Psychiatry, 34,* 886–896.

Tannock, R., Schachar, R. J., Carr, R. P., & Logan, G. D. (1989). Dose-response effects of methylphenidate on academic performance and overt behavior in hyperactive children. *Pediatrics, 86,* 648–657.

Tarnowski, K. J., Gavaghan, M. P., & Wisniewski, J. J. (1989). Acceptability of interventions for pediatric pain management. *Journal of Pediatric Psychology, 14,* 463–472.

Tarnowski, K. J., Kelly, P. A., & Mendlowitz, D. R. (1987). Acceptability of behavioral pediatric interventions. *Journal of Consulting and Clinical Psychology, 55,* 435–436.

Tarnowski, K. J., Simonian, S. J., Bekeny, P., & Park, A. (1992). Acceptability of interventions for childhood depression. *Behavior Modification, 16,* 103–117.

Thompson, S., & Rey, J. (1995). Functional enureses: Is desmopressin the answer? *Journal of the American Academy of Child and Adolescent Psychiatry, 34,* 266–271.

Trimble, M. R. (1990). Anticonvulsants in children and adolescents. *Journal of Child and Adolescent Psychopharmacology, 1,* X–4.

Troung, D. D., Bressman, S., Shale, H., & Fahn, S. (1988). Clonazepam, haloperidol, and clonidine in tic disorders. *Southern Medical Journal, 81,* 1103–1105.

Varanka, T. M., Weller, R. A., Weller, E. B., & Fristad, M. A. (1988). Lithium treatment of manic episodes with psychotic features in prepubertal children. *American Journal of Psychiatry, 145,* 1557–1559.

Varley, C. K., & Trupin, E. (1982). Double-blind administration of methylphenidate to mentally retarded children with attention deficit disorder: A preliminary study. *American Journal of Mental Deficiency, 86,* 560–566.

Vitiello, B., Hill, J. L., & Elia, J. (1991). P. R. N. medication in child psychiatric patients: A pilot placebo-controlled study. *Journal of Clinical Psychiatry, 52,* 499–501.

Vitello, B., & Jensen, P. (1995). Developing clinical trials in children and adolescents. *Psychopharmacology Bulletin, 31,* 75–81.

Vyse, S. A., & Rapport, M. D. (1989). The effects of methylphenidate on learning in children with

ADHD: The stimulus equivalence paradigm. *Journal of Consulting and Clinical Psychology, 57,* 425–435.

Waizer, J., Hoffman, S. L., Pulizos, P., & Englehardt, D. (1974). Outpatient treatment of hyperactive children with imipramine. *American Journal of Psychiatry, 131,* 587–591.

Walling, V. R., & Pfefferbaum, B. (1990). The use of methylphenidate in a depressed adolescent with AIDS. *Developmental and Behavioral Pediatrics, 11,* 195–197.

Waterman, G. S., & Ryan, N. C. (1993). Pharmacological treatment of depression and anxiety in children and adolescents. *School Psychology Review, 22,* 228–242.

Weinstein, G. S., & Wells, C. E. (1981). Case studies in neuropsychiatry: Post-traumatic psychiatric dysfunction-diagnosis and treatment. *Journal of Clinical Psychiatry, 42,* 120–122.

Werry, J. S. (1993). Introduction: A guide for practitioners, professionals, and public. In J. S. Werry & M. G. Aman (Eds.), *Practitioner's guide to psychoactive drugs for children and adolescents* (pp. 3–21). New York: Plenum.

Werry, J. S. (1995). Resolved: Cardiac arrhythmias make desipramine an unacceptable choice in children. *Journal of the American Academy of Child and Adolescent Psychiatry, 34,* 1239–1241.

Werry, J. S., & Aman, M. G. (1993). *Practitioner's guide to psychoactive drugs for children and adolescents.* New York: Plenum.

West, S. A., Keck, P. E., McElroy, S. L., Strakowski, S. M., Minnery, K. L., McConville, B. J., & Sorter, M. T. (1994). Open trial of valproate in the treatment of adolescent mania. *Journal of Child and Adolescent Psychopharmacology, 4,* 263–267.

Whalen, C. K., & Henker, B. (1976). Psychostimulants and children: A review and analysis. *Psychological Bulletin, 83,* 1113–1130.

Whalen, C. K., & Henker, B. (1991). Therapies for hyperactive children: Comparison, combinations, and compromises. *Journal of Consulting and Clinical Psychology, 59,* 126–137.

Whalen, C. K., Henker, B., Hinshaw, S. P., Heller, T., & Huber-Dressler, A. (1991). Messages of medication: Effects of actual versus informed medication status on hyperactive boys'

expectancies and self-evaluations. *Journal of Consulting and Clinical Psychology, 59,* 602–606.

Wilens, T. E., & Biederman, J. (1992). The stimulants. *Pediatric Psychopharmacology, 15,* 191–222.

Wilens, T. E., Biederman, J., & Spencer, T. J. (1994). Clonidine for sleep disturbances associated with attention-deficit hyperactivity disorder. *Journal of the American Academy of Child and Adolescent Psychiatry, 33,* 424–426.

Wilens, T. E., Biederman, J., Spencer, T. J., & Prince, J. (1995). Pharmacotherapy of adult attention deficit/hyperactivity disorder: A review. *Journal of Clinical Psychopharmacology, 15,* 270–279.

Wilkison, P. C., Kircher, J. C., McMahon, W., & Sloane, H. N. (1995). Effects of methylphenidate on reward strength in boys with attention-deficit hyperactivity disorder. *Journal of the American Academy of Child and Adolescent Psychiatry, 34,* 897–901.

Williams, D. T., Hehl, R., Yudofsky, S., Adams, D., & Roseman, B. (1982). The effect of propranolol on uncontrolled rage outbursts in children and adolescents with organic brain dysfunction. *Journal of the American Academy of Child and Adolescent Psychiatry, 21,* 129–135.

Wolf, S. M., & Forsythe, A. (1978). Behavior disturbance, phenobarbital, and febrile seizures. *Pediatrics, 61,* 728–731.

Wolraich, M. L., Lindgren, S., Stromquist, A., Milich, R., Davis, C., & Watson, D. (1990). Stimulant medication use by primary care physicians in the treatment of attention deficit hyperactivity disorder. *Pediatrics, 86,* 95–101.

Wright, H. H., Cuccaro, M. L., Leonhardt, T. V., Kendall, D. F., & Anderson, J. H. (1995). Case study: Fluoxetine in the multimodal treatment of a preschool child with selective mutism. *Journal of the American Academy of Child and Adolescent Psychiatry, 34,* 857–862.

Zametkin, A., & Yamada, E. M. (1993). Monitoring and measuring drug effects. I. Physical effects. In J. S. Werry & M. G. Aman (Eds.), *Practitioner's guide to psychoactive drugs for children and adolescents* (pp. 75–97). New York: Plenum.

Zwier, K. J., & Rao, U. (1994). Buspirone use in an adolescent with social phobia and mixed personality disorder (Cluster A type). *Journal of the American Academy of Child and Adolescent Psychiatry, 33,* 1007–1011.

## CHAPTER 32

# INTERVENTIONS FOR INTEGRATING CHILDREN WITH TRAUMATIC BRAIN INJURIES INTO THEIR SCHOOLS

DORRIE L. RAPP
*Clinical Neuropsychologist*
*White River Junction, Vermont*

Recent advances in medical research and technology now allow children who acquire severe brain injuries and illnesses not only to survive but also to return to their neighborhood schools. New specializations of neuropsychology and traumatic brain injury (TBI) rehabilitation have grown dramatically during the past decade. Educational philosophy has become more inclusionary, and there are fewer special schools and self-contained classrooms. Public Law 94-142 has been reauthorized as P.L. 101-476 (see Appendix C of this volume), the Individuals with Disabilities Education Act (IDEA), and now includes a specific eligibility category for students with TBI (*Federal Register*, 1992). Traumatic brain injury is not a rare disorder; there are estimates of new TBIs each year (including mild to severe injuries) of approximately 1 in 500 school-aged children and a prevalence (accumulated across all ages and grades, past and recent injuries) of 3% (Mira, Tyler, & Tucker, 1992). The leading cause of death in children (Savage & Wolcott, 1994), TBI occurs five times more often than leukemia (Lehr, 1990). Therefore, school psychologists, school administrators, and classroom teachers will encounter students who have acquired TBI. Psychologists working in schools, whether as an employee or as a contractual consultant, are asked to provide wide-ranging services for the reentry of students after TBI, coordination and translation between medical and neuropsychological specialists and school staff, and crucial monitoring and long-term follow-up of these students. These new roles for school psychologists may include providing information about TBI, in-service training, behavioral and in-class observation and assessment of the student; being a member of the student's individualized educational program (IEP) team; and providing various forms of counseling with the student, family, teachers and peers.

"Normal" child development occurs within the context of home, family, community, and all-important workplace—the school. When any severe injury occurs, children are removed from their usual environment and placed in the very abnormal environment of a hospital filled with strangers, instead of family, and invasive, painful, and bewildering procedures, rather than comfortable routines. The life of the entire family is turned upside down and may never be the same again. When the injury occurs to the brain, children also experience confusion; disruption in behavior, emotions, and coping abilities; and cognitive changes—in addition to physical pain. It is crucial for families, medical staff, neighbors, peers, and school staff to understand all of these factors so that everyone on the child's team can contribute to a real habilitation process (American Cancer Society, 1988; Lash, 1990, 1992; Raines & Waaland, 1992; Rapp, 1986; Singer, Nixon, & Powers, 1991; Williams & Kay, 1991). There is a crucial void that needs to be filled with specific knowledge about TBI if school psychologists, teachers, and other individuals who are interacting with the recovering children are to appropriately guide them during the transition back to their normal daily life and classroom.

This chapter discusses the similarities and differences between students with acquired TBIs and other student populations. Medical, neuropsychological, and educationally relevant information and strategies for practical application in the real-world contexts of the classroom and the student's life are also provided. Given the necessary breadth of information to be presented, essential information and crucial concepts are emphasized, with frequent reference to additional resources for in-depth coverage of each area to allow the readers to select areas of greatest relevance to their practice and ages of children served.

## DEFINITIONS OF TERMS

Many different terms have been and continue to be used interchangeably, producing confusion. *Head injury* was initially used, as in National Head Injury Foundation (NHIF), although external injuries to the head (e.g., lacerations and stitches, hematomas to the face and scalp, or even skull fractures) are not the essential factors nor necessarily relevant to the educational process. What is crucially important is an injury that produces transient or permanent disruption to the functioning of the *brain* within the protective coverings of membranes, fluid, and skull designed to protect it. Brain functioning is the new-learning machine and control center for the entire body, including thinking, emotions, and behavior. This important distinction between the terms *head* and *brain* injury was formally recognized by the Board of Directors of the NHIF in June 1995, when the foundation changed its name to the Brain Injury Association (BIA). *Brain injury* is a clearer term, although if not qualified, it can produce confusion since it has also been applied to birth injuries and congenital malformations and disorders.

*Acquired brain injury* (ABI) has been used increasingly (Savage & Wolcott, 1994) to include any source that produces disruption of brain functioning after a period of relatively normal development, including infections (meningitis or encephalitis), strokes or cerebral vascular accidents (CVAs from nontraumatic sources like aneurysms, secondary to cardiac problems, or arterial-venous malformations, AVMs), and brain tumors and secondary effects from chemotherapy and radiation treatments (Brown and

Madan-Swain, 1993). Other sources of ABI in children are anoxic or hypoxic (reduction in oxygen flow to the brain, causing brain cell death from near drowning, attempted suicide through overdoses or strangulation, and carbon monoxide or other toxic inhalation). Any of these sources can produce brain injury or disruption to brain functioning and may produce serious immediate and long-term effects on the child's cognitive and behavioral neurodevelopment and the ability to socialize, learn, and participate in regular education classes. In all of these cases, the child's continually developing, specializing, and maturing brain system has been affected, reorganized, and compromised. The procedures suggested in this chapter for awareness and in-service presentations, assessment, educational interventions, and integration in the classroom will be applicable and useful for a child with any type of ABI. Its source or cause, however, will affect the *category of eligibility* for special education services and the type of documentation needed to meet the eligibility requirements.

### Federal Definition of Traumatic Brain Injury

A specific subgroup of acquired brain injury is *traumatic brain injury*, frequently abbreviated TBI. Advocacy groups like the NHIF (now BIA) lobbied for the creation of a distinct special education eligibility category for students who acquired a TBI, which adversely affected their educational performance but did not match the criteria of eligibility of the 11 existing categories under Public Law 94-142 (1975). These lobbying efforts were successful, and TBI was specifically included as one of the 13 eligibility categories in the reauthorized Public Law 101-476 (1991), Individuals with Disabilities Education Act (1992). As of 1992, TBI was defined as follows:

> Traumatic brain injury means an acquired injury to the brain caused by an external physical force, resulting in total or partial functional disability or psychosocial impairment, or both, that adversely affects a child's educational performance. The term applies to open or closed head injuries resulting in impairments in one or more areas, such as cognition; language; memory; attention; reasoning; abstract thinking; judgment; problem-solving; sensory, perceptual and motor abilities; psychosocial behavior; physical functions; information

processing; and speech. The term does not apply to brain injuries that are congenital or degenerative, or brain injuries induced by birth trauma. (*Federal Register*, 1992, p. 44802)

The sudden onset of a change in brain functioning produces many crucial differences than do learning difficulties due to congenital problems (e.g., Down's Syndrome, cerebral palsy, or developmental learning disabilities), in which the condition is relatively static, deficits are predictable, and the child has always had the same pattern of learning strengths and weaknesses. The sudden and often diffuse nature of the physiological disruption to the brain in TBI (and secondary to infections and hypoxia), and the accompanying impetus for adaptation, are quite different from that of brain tumors or congenital malformations, which are more localized and more slowly developing, allowing the brain to gradually accommodate and reorganize. When a TBI occurs, the child's cognitive, emotional, and physical abilities and self-perceptions—who they are and how they learn and interact with their peers, family, and school personnel—are all suddenly changed. The child may not be able to perceive or recognize the changes (due to the injury itself), even when they are obvious to everyone else. Thus the child may resist any changes in educational placement, special education, or therapeutic services, or even in how he or she attempts to study and learn. This is compounded when the family and educational staff also do not understand nor immediately recognize the changes in the child and the necessary changes required in their interactions with the child.

## Variations in State Rules and Regulations for TBI

A requirement of the federal definition of TBI under P.L. 101-476 is that the injury has been caused *by an external physical force*. This has produced much controversy. Each state determines its own definition for implementation of the federal rules and is free to *provide more services*, but it cannot choose to provide less than the federal definition requires. Vermont, for example, expanded the definition of TBI to include "an injury to the brain caused by an external physical force *or by an internal occurrence such as stroke or aneurysm*" (Vermont State Board Manual of Rules and Procedures, 1992). Vermont also requires that the opinion as to the existence of a TBI must be given by a *medical doctor*, although

other states allow a neuropsychologist or psychologist to make this determination. Effective January 1993, the Regulations of the New York Commissioner of Education amended the definition of TBI: "Traumatic brain injury means an injury caused by an external physical force or by certain medical conditions such as stroke, encephalitis, aneurysm, anoxia or brain tumors with resulting impairments that adversely affect educational performance."

Whatever the etiology, each child with an acquired brain injury and impairments that adversely affect his or her education deserves and requires individualized evaluation and an IEP designed to meet specific short- and long-term needs. Each school psychologist and school administrator should obtain a copy of the actual definition adopted by their state to determine whether the TBI category of eligibility can be used for a particular student or if the more generic category—Other Health Impaired—should be used. The variations in definition will unfortunately affect counts and obscure prevalence statistics for TBI, complicating the prediction of needs and resources for services.

Throughout this chapter, the term TBI will be used, and emphasis will be placed on traumatic brain injuries caused by external forces (e.g., accidents of various sorts). Because children with mild to moderate TBIs often appear to be physically "normal" and fully recovered when they return to school, they frequently do not receive the evaluations and services they require. Mild to moderate TBIs are frequent occurrences, and all school districts have one or more students with these injuries each year. School psychologists who know about the subtle cognitive and behavioral dysfunctions produced by TBIs can be the first to identify these students to the school team and begin the crucial monitoring process that will allow them to successfully return to school and to prevent unnecessary secondary behavioral and academic problems.

## MAJOR CAUSES AND CONSEQUENCES OF TBI

Children are not miniature adults in any sense. They definitely do not respond to a TBI as an adult would to one of the same type, location, and severity. The brain is a work in progress, from the prenatal environment through late adolescence. Any injury to the brain, no matter how mild, can disrupt the development and growth of this intricate learning machine, and all subsequent development can be altered. When a child sustains a TBI, the process of recovery is superimposed on the underlying process of growth, specialization, and interconnection of brain systems (Ringle-Bartels & Story, 1993). The age of the child at the time of the injury will affect the overall formation of the child's capacity to learn, develop a sense of self, and cope as an adult. In contrast, the rehabilitation of an adult after a TBI concentrates on *regaining previously learned skills* that were lost and learning compensations for disrupted functioning.

Age at the time of the TBI is an important factor because (1) the brain is in different stages of growth and spurts of development at various ages; (2) the functions and skills normally expected vary at different ages; (3) *how* children learn, and from whom, varies with age; and (4) the consequences of the same degree and location of injury will differ according to the developmental stages that were interrupted at the time of the injury (Begali, 1992; Lehr & Savage, 1990; Ylvisaker, Szekeres, & Hartwick, 1994).

For many years it was believed that children recovered from TBI both more quickly and with fewer deficits than adults. It is true that children often show dramatic early improvements. They suddenly emerge from coma, walk, talk, and are quickly discharged from the hospital; in many cases they return directly to the home, without a stay in pediatric rehabilitation units, and reenter school shortly thereafter. Children's brains were considered "plastic" because they were still growing and specializing, and therefore it was thought easier for different parts to reorganize and assume functioning for the damaged areas. However, cumulative research and long-range prospective studies now indicate that children are not spared cognitive and behavioral sequelae after TBI, as was originally assumed (Lehr & Savage, 1990; Michaud, Rivara, Jaffe, Fay, & Dalley, 1993; Mira et al., 1992; Rapp & McIntire, 1993). Reorganization of brain functioning does occur, although at a cost that is seen much later in the development of higher cognitive functioning. Functional deficits may not be apparent until many years after the initial injury (Kaufmann, Fletcher, Levin, Miner, & Ewing-Cobbs, 1993; Lehr & Savage, 1990; Telzrow, 1991; Teuber & Rudel, 1962; Ylvisaker, 1993). A child who appears to have recovered from a TBI, and may not currently require special services at school, is nonetheless at risk for later failure because

of new and previously undetected cognitive-processing problems.

## Infancy Through Preschool

The external forces that produce TBIs vary with the age of the child (Farmer & Peterson, 1995; Goldstein & Levin, 1990). Infants, toddlers, and preschoolers most often acquire TBIs because of accidental dropping and falling, shaken baby syndrome (Bruce & Zimmermann, 1989), physical abuse, and vehicular accidents (including improperly installed car seats). The rate of growth of the brain is extremely accelerated from conception through preschool. After birth, the neurons in the brain begin to form increasingly complex interconnections as the brain organizes and integrates (Savage, 1994). Therefore, injuries during this period of accelerated development and organization of brain functioning can produce significant and widespread cognitive difficulties.

Early injuries may not be reported at the time nor at school entry for a variety of reasons. However, this information is valuable in understanding the student's needs. The school psychologist, coordinating with the school nurse, can be instrumental in developing specific questions about possible TBIs on the school health intake and can play an important role in reducing the number of future TBIs in young children by providing prevention information as part of parenting groups, during parent-teacher days, in health and community living courses for adolescents, and through prevention posters for students and parents (see Resources, Prevention, at the end of this chapter).

## Preadolescent Children

Elementary school children are increasingly involved in vehicular accidents, including pedestrian and bicycle-car collisions, falls, and recreation and sports injuries (Mira et al., 1992). Brain development is continuing throughout this age range, usually in spurts of development followed by periods of slower integration of the cognitive system. A TBI interrupts this process and will produce immediate and long-term effects on development. Children are acquiring and mastering basic academic concepts and skills during elementary school. Impairment to selective attention and ability to acquire new learning will have serious consequences. Adults would have previously mastered these academic skills, and therefore they would be more resistant to disruption.

During childhood, children learn from their peers and develop interpersonal relationships and their sense of self and competence, and TBIs, as well as secondary peer reactions, can disrupt these processes.

School-based prevention programs such as bike helmet and safe-cycling incentives can reduce the incidence of TBIs in this age group (see Resources, Prevention). School psychologists can suggest that the school library obtain entertaining books that foster awareness about TBI at an elementary reading level (e.g., Auch, 1990) and that give peers sensitive and accurate information that can be used in positive "buddy" and peer-tutoring programs (Nisbet, 1992) if a friend or classmate acquires a TBI.

## Adolescents and Young Adults

Adolescents and young adults are at the highest risk of any age group for acquiring TBIs (Savage & Wolcott, 1994), primarily through vehicle accidents but also from sports injuries and assaults. During adolescence, the last brain system completes its development, that is, the frontal system, which controls executive functioning such as independent judgment and problem solving; abstraction and generalization; and inhibitory controls of thought, emotion, and behavior. Functioning of this system is essential to independent adult competence (Mateer & Williams, 1991). Also during this time period, major social developments occur, and important lifelong educational and personal decisions are made and implemented. Any time away from school or any alterations to the academic program disrupt plans for graduation and further education. The adolescent's reactions to the effects of the injury can be as significant as the underlying injury itself. This age group is the most inclined to deny or resist changes or deficits after a TBI, but it is also most likely to need modifications and accommodations, at least during the reentry to school, especially after a "mild" TBI (Fay et al., 1993). There are prevention videos and other materials for this age group; however, given its view that "it won't happen to me," the most effective inservices are provided by students who have already sustained a TBI and can speak directly to other adolescents. Local chapters of the Brain Injury Association (BIA, formerly NHIF) can provide the names of peer advocates who offer such presentations (see Resources). It can be very positive for a student to write a paper or provide another presentation for credit about the personal experience of TBI.

## Hidden Past TBIs

When a student acquires a TBI during the school year, the student is likely to be identified. However, if the injury occurs during a school vacation, prior to moving to a new school or school district, or prior to school age, or before placement in foster care or adoption, the school is not likely to be informed. Unfortunately, current learning and/or behavior problems may be directly related to an earlier TBI and require different evaluation and intervention techniques (Savage & Mishkin, 1994). Results of the injury to the brain may not become apparent until many years after the initial injury, when functioning systems would normally mature and be required to function (Lehr, 1990). Also, a child may have coped in a preschool setting, but demonstrate severe difficulties when asked to sit at a desk and learn to read in first grade. Other students who coped within the clear structure and concrete materials of early elementary grades will have difficulty when they go to junior high school and are expected to generalize learning, organize their work load from various teachers, and produce lengthy projects (Lehr, 1990; Rapp & McIntire, 1993; Savage & Wolcott, 1994). Uncovering past TBIs can be crucial in providing appropriate educational interventions for the student.

## PHYSIOLOGICAL EFFECTS OF TBIs

Our brains float in cerebral spinal fluid (CSF) inside several layers of membranes, all protected by the skull. When the head suddenly runs into something (windshield, floor, or tree) or something hits the head (baseball, fist, or bullet) or the head is shaken vigorously back and forth (shaken baby syndrome or acceleration/deceleration in a car accident), the brain moves back and forth and twists *within the skull* and may hit the rough inside walls of the skull. These movements cause *shearing* (stretching and tearing) of some of the billions of interconnected neurons that make up the brain; blood vessels within and around the brain can also be damaged, causing secondary bleeding; swelling and increased pressure can decrease oxygen to the brain. It is not necessary to have a severe blow to the head nor a skull fracture to cause severe damage and dysfunction. It depends on exactly what tissues, where, and how many are temporarily interrupted or killed. A minor blow or fall can produce serious long-term consequences (Fay et al., 1993; Rapp & McIntire, 1993).

An open TBI means that the skull and brain were penetrated and exposed (e.g., by a bullet or depressed skull fracture, where fragments of bone might be pushed into the membranes and brain tissue). The risks of infection, bleeding, and seizures are all increased with an open TBI, and neurosurgery to raise the bone fragments and stop bleeding is usually necessary. These injuries would be considered severe. A closed TBI is more common, and there may be a cracked line or no skull fracture but disturbed soft brain tissue inside (e.g., swollen, sheared, bruised, bleeding, or changed neurochemistry). Closed TBIs can range from what is commonly called a concussion, or "minor" or "mild" TBI, to very severe injury. A skull fracture is not necessarily a more severe injury than a closed TBI. The skull protects the brain, and by absorbing the impact, the fractured skull can sometimes spare injury to the brain. However, closed TBIs can be fatal if the force of the injury produces severe disturbance to the brain inside.

The brain is often injured in one or more places: (1) directly under the location of the impact and external bruises; (2) directly opposite (contracoup) because the brain bounces away from the blow but hits the inside of the skull on the other side; (3) diffusely throughout the brain, that is, anywhere that twisting or shearing occurred; and (4) secondary effects from swelling, bleeding, and chemical changes, as the brain reacts to the injury. Medical tests such as magnetic resonance image (MRI) and computerized tomography (CT) scans of the brain may indicate where localized injuries or swelling and bleeding occurred, but they will not indicate where microscopic shearing or chemical changes have occurred. These tests do not measure the ability of the brain to function and process information; they show the position of brain structures and the size of lesions and are used to determine the extent of injuries that may require urgent medical interventions. If MRI or CT scan results are within normal limits, that is good news, but it does not exclude disruption of brain functioning nor indicate that the student has the cognitive-processing abilities required to return to school and participate in learning (e.g., attention, memory and new learning, and self-regulation of behavior).

## Medical Severity of the Initial Injury

There are three primary factors that medical personnel use to determine the severity of the initial TBI: (1) level of consciousness (alertness and orientation) and length of loss of consciousness, which is operationally defined by the Glasgow Coma Scale (Teasdale & Jennett, 1974); (2) inability to recall events that occurred immediately before the accident (retrograde amnesia, RA) and the length of time after the accident or injury during which new events and information were not registered (post-traumatic amnesia, PTA); the longer the period of PTA, the more severe the injury and the more likely there will be long-term difficulties with new learning and memory; and (3) the presence of specific localized injuries such as depressed skull fracture, bleeding between the skull and brain (hematomas), and brain tissue bruises (contusions). There is a correlation between the severity of the initial medical injury and the degree and persistence of *cognitive, behavioral, and new learning difficulties*, although there is significant individual variability (Boyer & Edwards, 1991; Dalby & Obrzbut, 1991; Fay et al., 1993; Jaffe et al., 1993).

When a child is discharged from the hospital and medically cleared to return to school, this *does not mean that there are no further problems that will affect the child's performance and learning in school*. The school psychologist has a crucial role in coordinating, collaborating, and translating information among medical, rehabilitation, and school personnel. Any child who has sustained a TBI, even those labeled minor, mild, or concussion, needs to be closely monitored for at least six months after his or her return to school. Children who have sustained more medically severe TBIs (e.g., any neurosurgery, depressed skull fractures, seizures, unconsciousness for more than a few minutes, or confusion and disorientation for more than a day) should have an individualized reintegration plan, close monitoring, and referral to an appropriate school team responsible for determining the degree of evaluation and special accommodations and services that the child requires (see Levels of Educational Teams).

As previously mentioned, a child can appear to make a good adjustment and recovery after the TBI but have TBI-related cognitive or behavioral impairments, which will become apparent only at a later age and/or in a later environment, when a higher level of independent cognitive and behavioral functioning is required. Therefore, it is advisable to ensure that the past history of any TBI is noted in the student's records, not to stigmatize the child but to serve as an early warning, which can be investigated and pursued if any educational difficulties are noted in the future. This is particularly relevant when the child goes to a new school or transitions to a higher level of education.

# PROCEDURES TO FOLLOW FOR NEW TBI

When notified that a student has had a TBI, it is not appropriate to have the child return to class and "see how the child does and if there are any problems." Difficulties may not be obvious immediately because of the allowances initially made for any child who has been ill and missed school and because the child may be able to function for a period of time by utilizing past learning and skills. Teachers and school psychologists already have a wealth of knowledge and intervention techniques that may be quite appropriate for a student with TBI. The *selection* of techniques and when and how to apply them require information provided through collaboration with TBI experts and frequent, flexible, indepth real-world observational evaluation of each individual student.

Teachers and other school personnel commonly react in one of two ways when a student has sustained a significant TBI and is returning to their class or school: (1) panic about their lack of knowledge and preparation, feeling they are not equipped to handle a severely impaired student; or (2) overconfidence about their ability to meet the child's needs, just as before or through existing special education programs, since the student would not be returning to school until stable and the level of need is known. Both reactions are unrealistic and unnecessary (Rapp & McIntire, 1993).

School psychologists, teachers, special educators, and school administrators already have a fund of knowledge and experience in dealing with children of all sorts. Many of these techniques and strategies will be applicable to the student with a TBI (Ylvisaker, Szekeres, & Hartwick, 1994; Ylvisaker, Szekeres, Hartwick, & Tworek, 1994). Direct consultation and in-service training with clinicians who have expertise in TBI is needed to provide support and specific programming suggestions so that the school staff feel confident and prepared to work with the child. It is inappropriate to expect a regular classroom teacher to be able to meet all of the specialized needs of a student without these supports. Proactive preparation is far superior to and more cost-effective than crisis intervention. With sufficient supports and flexible programming, most students with TBI can be successfully returned to their neighborhood school.

An excellent practical, nontechnical discussion of school reentry; ways to avoid unnecessary barriers to successful reintegration of the student; and positive strategies for success is provided in Mira et al., 1992. This book provides practical checklists of specific programming suggestions for schools: (1) how to check out the physical environment of the school, (2) how to make scheduling modifications, (3) how the child's performance in the testing situation is likely to differ from that seen in the classroom, and (4) how to use the classroom teacher's expertise to observe and monitor the child's performance in the classroom.

It is important to realize that the family, peers, and school staff have all been affected by the injury to the child and are coping with the aftermath. The feelings and needs of the peers and staff also have to be addressed for the team to function well for the benefit of the student. If the family, peers, and teachers have a positive attitude and interest, they can be valuable additions to the behavioral and educational program. A "buddy guide" can accompany the student through the maze of hallways and unstructured periods; provide a positive behavioral model; and assist the student by organizing materials, sharing notes, and providing reminders of assignments. This can be a very positive experience for both students. If peers are not informed and involved in the reintegration process, they can easily become part of the problem by reinforcing inappropriate behaviors or by isolating and excluding the returning student.

## Similarities and Differences Between TBI and Learning Disability

Students with learning disabilities, and with TBI have many of the same difficulties. However, students with TBI are *dissimilar* in the following ways:

1. A primary disturbance of attention (inhibiting irrelevant or distracting information)

and limited ability to concentrate, self-organize, and follow multistep procedures

2. Difficulty with the amount and rate of processing, storage, and retrieval of new information and breakdowns in generalization of learning

3. Very uneven and unpredictable strengths and gaps in past learning and previously mastered skills

4. Rapid reacquisition of some skills; struggle with mastery of some skills; and difficulty in retention, recall, and application of new skills

5. Improving and changing pattern of strengths and weaknesses, with the appearance of later "new" deficits and problems after apparent resolution of difficulties

6. Specific difficulty with generalization of learning to other appropriate contexts

7. Resistance to using suggested accommodations and strategies, preferring to use previous, but no longer effective, learning strategies

8. Behavioral difficulties that can be extreme, can be out of proportion to events, and may actually result from specific cognitive deficits; the behaviors may or may not respond to the usual school interventions (e.g., suspensions, behavioral contracts, and talking it through), but may respond to changes in antecedents in the environment (Deaton, 1994)

9. Changing patterns of cognitive functioning, which require dynamic IEPs, using flexible process goals rather than standard product goals, and frequent reevaluations (Blosser & DePompei, 1994; Jaffe et al., 1993; Savage, 1991).

Because of these factors, the process of accommodating, referring, and assessing the student with TBI requires unusual and additional procedures, not commonly employed for students with other types of learning difficulties.

## Levels of Educational Teams

The special education eligibility process under P.L. 101-476 is a time-, paper-, and effort-intensive process, with formal safeguards and regulations. For a student with a TBI to be eligible for special education protections, services, and an individualized educational program (IEP), a referral to the basic staffing team (BST) is required. The BST will convene and prepare a compre-

hensive evaluation plan with the family, gather medical and rehabilitation information (Mira et al., 1992; Tyler, 1990), implement the evaluation plan and collect the results, meet to determine eligibility, and then hold follow-up meetings to develop the IEP for the student. This formal process may be necessary when the student clearly has significant needs that will require long term removal from mainstreamed classes (specialized instruction or change of placement) and/or needs-specialized related services (therapies) that will require extraordinary expenditures (e.g., hiring an individual aide or contracting with outside therapists).

Unfortunately, this lengthy process can delay school reentry or result in the student being placed in a mainstreamed classroom without sufficient support services, often for months, until the process is completed. In the case of a recent TBI, this is particularly inappropriate because the child's needs are greatest immediately, followed by improvements and constant changes; therefore, the accommodations and interventions need to be flexible and updated on a very frequent basis (e.g., weekly or monthly). The costs (time, effort, and money) involved in the special education evaluation process can be used as the reason for adopting the wait and see approach, which results in crisis intervention after the situation is untenable and the child, family, and staff have become thoroughly frustrated. The recommended alternative is to adopt a proactive plan for a success-based reentry process, in which intensive support services and accommodations are provided initially and gradually deleted as the student demonstrates successful functioning.

Many states have developed informal, easily accessible instructional support teams to which a teacher can refer any student in order to brainstorm problems and solutions at a classroom-intervention level with experienced teachers. Vermont's Act 230 (1992) created instructional support teams (ISTs) as an alternative resource. The IST, or its local equivalent, is a logical first step when the teacher learns that a student has sustained a TBI. This may be the only monitoring source necessary in the case of a concussion or mild TBI or when the student's needs are already clearly known (e.g., from evaluations already conducted at a rehabilitation center) and can be appropriately addressed through inservice training, therapist-teacher consultations, environmental modifications (e.g., shortened school day), and accommodations in the classroom (e.g., peer buddy, note-taker, shortened assignments, and multiple-choice or oral exams). These interventions can be immediately available and used as a hypothesis-testing process and as information-gathering tools to determine if a formal referral is necessary and/or while the formal special education determination process is occurring.

Suggested practical accommodations and interventions to be directly applied by school staff encountering difficulties in the following categories can be found in the following resources:

1. Cognitive aspects of attention, memory, and new learning; problem-solving; and organization (Ylvisaker, Szekeres, Hartwick, & Tworek, 1994, pp. 101–115)
2. Cognitive-behavioral (Deaton, 1994)
3. Successful versus unsuccessful school reintegration strategies (Savage & Mishkin, 1994)
4. Creating effective classroom environments and learning strategies (Blosser & DePompei, 1994, pp. 432–450).

## Section 504 of Vocational Rehabilitation Act

For some students with TBI who are not eligible for, nor need, special education protections and services per se (e.g., a student with a mild concussion, requiring a change in schedule because of fatigue, or a student whose TBI occurred several years ago and now needs only specific accommodations for standardized tests and a note-taker in class), the Vocational Rehabilitation Act of 1973, Section 504 can provide sufficient services and protections under civil rights law. Section 504 outlines a school district's responsibility to provide appropriate accommodations to allow the student equal access to all publicly funded programs that are available to the student's nondisabled peers. Through a written plan, the school's 504 team will outline the appropriate educational accommodations and related services necessary for this student to access and benefit from the educational program.

# EVALUATION PROCESS

## Standard Psychoeducational Evaluations

The TBI category of eligibility for special education has the distinct advantage of not specifying arbitrary cutoff scores or discrepancies between intelligence scores and achievement. Students with a recently acquired TBI frequently do not demonstrate below-average intelligence (unless that was also the case before the injury) and usually do not show an immediate discrepancy between intelligence and achievement scores; these problems are seen later because of the relative lack of continued progress (Ewing-Cobbs & Fletcher, 1990; Hanson & Clippard, 1992). Standardized measures of intelligence and achievement are "product" measures, resulting from complex interactions of cognitive systems, and are heavily influenced by past learning. Unless the TBI was severe, the child is likely to score within the average range of both intelligence and achievement (Fletcher & Levin, 1988), unless there were premorbid learning difficulties, and even this pattern can be altered by the TBI.

A serious and unfortunately common mistake is to conduct only a standard psychoeducational evaluation (i.e., intelligence, achievement, and behavior rating scale) of a student returning to school after a TBI. Although measures of intelligence are often used to predict *future learning potential*, this is definitely not appropriate for the child who has sustained a recent TBI. The most common areas of cognitive dysfunction after a TBI are attention and concentration (Kaufmann et al., 1993), new learning retention and retrieval, (Jaffe et al., 1993), organization and problem solving (Levin et al., 1988), and changes in behavior (Deaton, 1994; Levin et al., 1994; Mateer & Williams, 1991).

The standard psychoeducational battery will not detect the child's significant cognitive processing and new learning difficulties, which will negatively affect current and future learning from this point onward. Conducting the standard aspects of a special education evaluation can be appropriate and useful (particularly to determine whether the student has lost any previously learned information, which may require review and remediation) as long as the school psychologist clearly explains to the team that this may be necessary, but it is definitely not sufficient to understand the child's current learning strengths and weaknesses for the development of successful interventions and accommodations for reintegration. The child with a TBI will not be appropriately evaluated by using only standard psychoeducational techniques (Begali, 1992, 1994; Mira et al., 1992; Reitan & Wolfson, 1992; Slomka & Tarter, 1993; Telzrow, 1991). More true residual deficits would be missed than found (Begali,

1992; Ewing-Cobbs & Fletcher, 1990; Rourke, Fisk, & Strang, 1986; Savage & Wolcott, 1994.).

## Ecological Evaluations

Tests of any type are *tools* to help evaluate a student, not the evaluation itself. Detailed, real-world observations are important when evaluating any student but critical when evaluating a student with a TBI (Deaton, 1994; Farmer & Peterson, 1995; Ylvisaker, Hartwick, Ross, & Nussbaum, 1994). Students with TBI frequently have difficulty with self-monitoring, self-regulation of behavior, generalization of skills and abilities, and cognitive organization. The structure of one-on-one standardized testing (e.g., very tight control of the environment, external initiation of tasks, clear instructions and demonstrated examples, brief questions and limited amounts of information presented at one time, and personal interaction and rapport) can obscure many of the student's most significant deficits. Frontal lobe injuries are very common with TBI, and a student with frontal system impairment would commonly have a profile of adequate test performance in such a structured setting but would have serious difficulty in learning and in regulating his or her behavior in the real world (Benton, 1991; Bigler, 1988; Deaton, 1994; Mateer & Williams, 1991; Welsh, Pennington, & Groisser, 1991; Ylvisaker, Hartwick, Ross, & Nussbaum, 1994). The abilities demonstrated during standardized testing represent the student's *optimal functioning* in that particular structure, which unfortunately bears no resemblance to the classroom environment.

A comprehensive evaluation of a child with a TBI should include structured, recorded observations of the child in the following environments: during formal one-on-one assessment; during mainstreamed group classes; while doing independent written work in the classroom; and during unstructured, minimally supervised times with peers, such as at recess, at lunch, on the school bus, and if possible in the totally different environment and social interactions of the home. Equal emphasis should be placed on observations of *environmental variables* surrounding the child. A child with TBI is likely to be much more sensitive to environmental factors, and changes in the environment are usually much quicker and easier to achieve than changes in the child. Crucial environmental variables include the following:

1.  ***Physical plant*** (Mira et al., 1992), for example, sensitivity to lighting; height of seating; visual and auditory distractions from hallways, windows, and sounds in the next classroom; distance, navigation, and crowds between classes; amount and organization of materials needed for each class

2.  ***Task requirements*** (Ylvisaker, Szekeres, Hartwick, & Tworek, 1994), for example, copying from the board, taking notes from lectures, volume and speed of presentation of information, concrete versus abstract information, and how the instructions are given

3.  ***Teacher's style and interactions*** (Blosser & DePompei, 1994; McKee & Witt, 1990), for example, speed, complexity, and amount of auditory-verbal information presented; multisensory presentation; expectations for independent work; provides debriefing and prompts, (or versus) student must ask for assistance; positive reinforcement for on-task behavior or attention for negative behavior; and willingness to provide adapted assignments and tests and teacher-prepared outlines and notes

4.  ***Peer interactions*** (Nisbet, 1992; Ylvisaker, Urbanczyk, & Feeney, 1992; Ylvisaker, Feeney, & Urbanczyk, 1993), for example, peers offer appropriate assistance, such as helping the student locate his or her place in a book, accompany the student to the next class; are willing and appropriate peer buddies or tutors; ignore off-task behavior or reinforce or encourage it; tease or make inappropriate comments

5.  ***Scheduling variables,*** for example, day of the week; time of day; difficulty of subject matter and sequence of classes; nonacademic breaks such as gym, lunch, and nap

Standardized testing supplemented with testing of the limits and process procedures (Kaplan, 1988) and classroom observations by the school psychologist and teacher will provide valuable information for designing appropriate accommodations and interventions. The school psychologist needs to conduct creative detective work and hypothesis testing in natural environments, in addition to formal assessments, to provide more than a static description of isolated deficits. An excellent appendix with specific questions, strategies, and materials that the school psychologist might use to fully understand the functioning of the student with TBI is provided in Ylvisaker, Hartwick, Ross, and Nussbaum (1994, pp. 101–115). These real-world observational assessments can and should be repeated frequently (e.g., weekly or monthly) as a feedback and monitoring tool to assess the appropriateness of the educational program and interventions and the student's progress. The information obtained should then be used to change the short-term goals and strategies in the flexible process goals of the IEP.

## Neuropsychological Evaluation

I commonly meet school staff who are confused by the distinctions between neurological and neuropsychological evaluations, the types of information each will provide, and which evaluations they want for a particular child. My standard explanation is that a neuropsychological evaluation will assess the child's cognitive and behavioral processing, using many different measures of the child's current functioning including intelligence; sensory-perceptual (visual, tactile, and auditory); motor strength, fine motor speed, and dexterity; complex psychomotor skills; temporal, spatial, and sequential abilities; receptive and expressive language (including auditory discrimination in quiet and noisy backgrounds); executive functioning, including independent problem solving, organization and judgment, and mental flexibility; rate of information processing in different modalities; internal inhibition of behavior; memory and the best modalities for new learning; selective attention, concentration, and alertness; and behavioral and adaptive functioning. A neuropsychological evaluation is not a medical evaluation and is not conducted by a medical doctor or neurologist. (See also Chapter 18; Begali, 1994; Telzrow, 1991.)

In contrast, a neurological evaluation is conducted by a medical specialist (optimally a *pediatric* neurologist) and will probably consist of a physical assessment and possibly recommendations for such medical tests as electroencephalogram (EEG), MRI, and so on. Unless conducted by a rare pediatric behavioral neurologist, such an evaluation is not likely to provide detailed functional information useful for developing educational plans for the child. A neurological evaluation is certainly preferable if the questions are about a sudden or progressive deterioration in alertness or possible seizure disorder. Which evaluation is most appropriate at a given time depends on the school staff's specific questions and the student's current level of recovery and residual difficulties.

A neuropsychological evaluation assesses a broader range of brain-behavior relationships, current cognitive processing, and new learning strengths and weaknesses than a traditional psychoeducational evaluation. However, a neuropsychological evaluation will not necessarily provide better or more comprehensive information if conducted in the original medical model (i.e., tests administered by trained testing assistants, with only an interview and review of raw data numbers by a neuropsychologist for the primary purpose of diagnosis) or by a fully qualified neuropsychologist who is not familiar with assessing children or the school's needs for prescriptive information. Large, urban school districts may employ a child neuropsychologist or have an established contractual arrangement with child neuropsychologists at a local children's teaching hospital or pediatric rehabilitation center. However this will be the exception, particularly in rural areas.

A few states separately license neuropsychologists (most have only generic psychology and school psychology licensure); however, board certification (Diplomate status) in neuropsychology is available as a national credential through the American Board of Professional Neuropsychology (ABPN) and the American Board of Clinical Neuropsychology (ABCN). The school psychologist can fulfill important roles by (1) interviewing possible neuropsychological referral sources to ensure that the procedures and report style will be useful for educational purposes, (2) collaborating with a neuropsychologist to cooperatively conduct various aspects of the comprehensive evaluation, and (3) translating the report and recommendations for the family and school team. Table 32.1, a Consumer's Guide to Useful Neuropsychological Evaluations (Rapp & McIntire, 1993), can be used by the school psychologist and team in preparing a referral.

## Timing of Neuropsychological Evaluations

A neuropsychological evaluation should not be thought of as a one-time event for a student with a TBI. It should be a dynamic process to monitor the child's recovery and future development (or lack thereof) in cognitive-processing abilities and changes in the profile of strengths and weaknesses with increasing age and classroom demands. A neuropsychological evaluation should occur before school reentry (for more than visits or limited resource room instruction) to serve as a baseline for individualized accommodations

TABLE 32.1   Consumer's Guide to Useful Neuropsychological Evaluations

1. Clearly define what problems you need more information about and the questions you want answers to before making a referral for an evaluation. Do not just ask for a neuropsychological evaluation (unspecified), or you may get an incomprehensible medical report that does not address your specific educational needs.
2. Call the neuropsychologist directly to discuss what you want and in what time frame. Ask what age groups this neuropsychologist feels competent to evaluate. Ask questions about his or her credentials (e.g., licensed school psychologist, licensed psychologist in your state, whether he or she has board certification in neuropsychology from either American Board of Professional Neuropsychology (ABPN) or American Board of Clinical Neuropsychology/American Board of Professional Psychology (ABCN/ABPP). Ask whether he or she will do the testing personally (to obtain detailed observations of the student's process of succeeding or failing) or whether all or some of the testing will be carried out by a student or technician.
3. Determine whether this neuropsychologist will give you a report with the student's specific learning strengths and weaknesses and provide educationally relevant recommendations.
4. Find out if this neuropsychologist will be available to meet with the team to explain the results, make site visits to observe, and make recommendations for specific problems.
5. Determine what the evaluation will cost and when the report will be available. Ask for a test list in advance of the evaluation to use in developing the school's evaluation plan, as well as to confirm exactly what will be done during the evaluation (to avoid duplication with the school's psychoeducational testing and to ensure comprehensiveness).

The answers you receive to these questions should help you to decide if this neuropsychologist should conduct the evaluation and whether he or she will be able to provide answers to your specific questions.

*Source:* Adapted from Rapp and McIntire (1993), p. 592.

and modifications to the educational program and for special education eligibility. However, the prerequisite skills the student needs to participate in a neuropsychological evaluation include the ability to work for 20 to 30 minutes at a time, maintain attention, and follow directions; the student's rate of recovery should have slowed so that major changes are not seen day to day (otherwise the information is obsolete by the time the report is written). If the student does not currently have these abilities, he or she is clearly not ready to return to mainstreamed classes. However, useful information for home tutoring or other specialized instruction and therapies can be gathered through careful observations and probes with much briefer evaluation tools at the student's present level of functioning (Begali, 1994; Deaton, 1994; Ylvisaker, Szekeres, & Hartwick, 1994).

At least partial if not complete neuropsychological reevaluations should occur frequently during the first year after a TBI and thereafter at all major school transitions, whenever there are concerns about new or different problems, or there is a lack of educational progress. Appropri-

ate neuropsychological information, in conjunction with thorough observations and ecological data, can provide crucial information to use in problem solving and developing program modifications.

## Interpreting Evaluation Reports and Results

The ultimate purpose of a comprehensive evaluation of a child with TBI should be to understand *how* the child currently processes information and *what factors* (within and around the child) increase or decrease learning, as well as to provide a detailed profile of the child's current learning style and relative processing strengths and weaknesses (including problem solving and organization, auditory-verbal and visual performance, and new learning and retrieval). The neuropsychological report for school staff should not be esoteric nor too much like a medical report. It should answer the teacher's specific questions. It should clearly describe the child's current cognitive and behavioral new learning style strengths and weaknesses. Most importantly, it should suggest practical strategies, accommodations, and modification techniques for the teacher's use. Recommendations should include behavioral interventions, changes in the environment, and teachers' and peers' interactions, as well as resources for additional materials and future in-service information for the family, student, and staff.

The school psychologist plays a primary role in translating this valuable information into relevant, understandable, and practical applications for the family and classroom teacher and in follow-up monitoring to ensure that recommendations and accommodations are appropriate, successful, and actually occur on a routine and sustained basis. All recommendations must be dynamic since the student with a TBI will constantly change, causing some recommendations to be obsolete within weeks or months. Informal weekly meetings with the classroom teachers and school psychologist is a useful feedback procedure. Interdisciplinary collaboration is essential for successful reintegration (Harrington, 1990; Lash & Scarpino, 1993; Telzrow, 1991).

## Active Student Involvement

The student with a TBI is a member of the school team whose opinions, suggestions, knowledge, and understanding are crucial to successful intervention but whose input is often not solicited. In my practice, I involve the students in the evaluation process, offer feedback and explanation during testing, and send a private and confidential letter (with parental notification and permission) directly to the students regardless of their age but geared to their level of understanding. The letter explains the results, explains why changes may be made, and tells the students' that I will ask the teachers to make changes to help them succeed. The letter may need to be read to the students by their parents, and thus it also serves as a succinct summary for the parents, who often become overwhelmed by all of the detailed information contained in reports.

This process has been extremely successful in gaining cooperation, understanding, and involvement of the student and family in developing and applying compensations and accepting resource room or other special instruction, and it creates students who will advocate for their needs. For example, a third-grader would raise his hand in class and remind the teacher that he could not copy the homework assignment from the board and that the teacher needed to provide this in written form. Although sometimes the student can go overboard and be demanding, this is far better than being embarrassed, avoiding and resisting accommodations, or feeling "dumb" when removed from the classroom for services. Once students see that an intervention or accommodation allows successful performance, they are more likely to use the strategy.

However, it is important to note that just because students state (and may believe) that they do not have any problems, this should not be taken at face value and definitely should not be used as a reason for not evaluating them or initiating services. Active involvement, explanation, and negotiating priorities for intervention are the key elements. This is especially true of behavioral interventions, which are particularly easy to undermine. The students are in the best position to indicate what is truly reinforcing for them.

## BEHAVIORAL PROBLEMS AFTER TBI: EVALUATION AND INTERVENTIONS

Behavioral and psychosocial problems are extremely common and persistent residuals for both children and adults after TBI. They are often the most distressing and incapacitating deficits (Mateer & Williams, 1991; Wood, 1987). What appears on the surface to be a behavioral problem can frequently be due to the student's underlying cognitive-processing deficits, can be directly produced by brain dysfunction, or is a response to antecedents in the environment (Deaton, 1994). The first step must be careful observation and recording of the antecedents, behaviors, and consequences surrounding the student's behavior *before* implementing a behavioral plan. Behavioral outbursts could result from (1) a seizure (temporal lobe epilepsy, TLE) triggered by environmental events; (2) overload and fatigue from excessive demands on the student or a too long school day; (3) learned behavior to escape frustrating or difficult work; (4) inability to read nonverbal social cues from peers and misunderstanding intentions: (5) inability to understand the requests or instructions given; (6) inability to remember (or generalize) school rules, despite their consistency and repetition.

Clearly, the appropriate method of intervention and the likelihood of success will be quite different, depending on the source of the behavior. The methods selected will come from the school psychologist's established repertoire; additional observation and knowledge about the student's unique processing abilities and situation will be crucial to determine the appropriate type of intervention. Ylvisaker, Szekeres, Hartwick, and Tworek (1994) provide a detailed discussion of the interaction between specific cognitive dysfunctions and apparent behaviors and compensatory techniques. Deaton (1994) presents a practical discussion of case examples and procedures for assessing behaviors after TBI and implementing appropriate interventions.

A student who had behavioral and emotional difficulties before the TBI will probably have exacerbated behavior and additional difficulties, which may not respond to the same techniques or reinforcement contingencies previously implemented (Fletcher, Ewing-Cobbs, Miner, Levin, & Eisenberg, 1990). There are no unique behavioral problems associated with TBI. However, common problems seen include irritability, hypersensitivity, impulsivity and short attention span, poor tolerance for frustration, reduced coping skills and more primitive reactions, and lack of initiation and follow-through. Some of these behaviors will quickly pass as the child's brain recovers. However, they should not be ignored or reinforced because they can quickly become secondary learned behaviors that will be difficult to break at a later time. Changes in the environment and requirements and clear behavioral limits (within the student's abilities to understand and respond) are often the most likely initial intervention methods. Do not assume that the student knows or remembers what behaviors are expected. All behaviors need to be clearly and explicitly defined, reviewed, and practiced. Students may need an individual aide to provide the external structure and cues until they demonstrate that they have relearned, internalized, and generalized these behaviors.

# REMEDIATION, COMPENSATION, ACCOMMODATION

This chapter has been devoted to strategies and procedures for assessing the cognitive abilities and learning style of students with TBI and developing appropriate interventions for reintegration. Although individualized for each student, based on his or her unique profiles and needs, there are different categories of approach that are based on theories of cognition: remediate

isolated specific skills and abilities, provide information-processing system strategies, and apply cognitive-behavior modification. Ylvisaker, Szekeres, and Hartwick (1994) provide an in-depth discussion of cognitive learning theories and empirical support for each of these approaches. In practice, aspects of several or all of these approaches are usually implemented for each student. Working with a student after TBI will involve channeling spontaneous recovery and avoiding unnecessary, secondarily learned maladaptive behaviors; remediating specific lost skills; attempting to retrain specific past-learned cognitive skills; teaching compensatory strategies to circumvent cognitive impairments; and creating and implementing environmental accommodations. It is important to consider the theoretical and empirical bases of each approach, as well as its advantages and pitfalls, and how they apply to a particular student.

## Spontaneous Recovery and Remediation

A TBI is an injury to the child's new learning system, superimposed on normal development and maturation of cognitive processes. Brain tissue and brain-behavior systems will demonstrate the most dramatic improvements during the first year after injury, with a gradual leveling off of the rate of change and improvement. During this period it is most important to frequently reevaluate the child, environment, and appropriateness of the interventions. Continued cognitive and behavioral recovery will continue thereafter, and improved *functioning* can continue forever. Assessing and remediating gaps and lost skills is also appropriate. Significant limitations are inherent in the *specific skills retraining approach* with students who have a TBI. Critical scrutiny and empirical studies have found this approach to be overly simplistic in that it does not consider the dynamic interaction of cognitive systems, it does not teach strategies for future learning, and improvements may not generalize from the specific training setting to functional application in the classroom and in future skills. Remediation of deficit skills alone is inappropriate and not likely to be reinforcing for the student. It is important to prevent unnecessary maladaptive, secondary learned behaviors; frustration due to inability to cope; and progressive falling behind classmates due to impairment in new learning abilities without appropriate accommodations.

# Accommodations and Compensations

Accommodations are modifications in the environment and interactions of others around the child that allow the child to succeed despite cognitive deficits. Accommodations, therefore, are applicable immediately and throughout the child's recovery and future education. They need to be creative, flexible, continually monitored, and changed in response to the child's cognitive changes and to changes in the environmental requirements over time. Accommodations primarily affect the expectations *others* have of the student and therefore impose little new learning on the child.

Compensations, in contrast, are strategies that the child learns (and then learns to generalize and functionally apply in other situations) to perform cognitive and learning tasks in a different way because of the acquired cognitive impairments. This distinction is important because the child with a TBI has difficulty with new learning; generalization of new learning; and recognizing when, how, and why to apply strategies. An error frequently made is to bombard the students with many new strategies and techniques (presumably to enable them to succeed) but simultaneously overwhelm them with new procedures and executive requirements in addition to the classroom assignments. For example, using a laptop word processor to compensate for decreased written language abilities may seem appropriate. However, if the student had not previously learned typing and basic computer skills nor used word-processing skills to complete assignments before the accident, one would be requiring massive amounts of new learning of skills and procedures, generalization to applicable contexts, and memory requirements, on top of the required classroom assignments. An assessment of whether the student is presently able to learn all of these new components (and by what methods) is essential before, and separate from, their application to classroom work.

Explicit learning of *generalization* to desired applied contexts is also essential. For example, after learning how to use a word processor in the resource room, the student will also need to come into the classroom and complete actual assignments by using the equipment in the classroom. Practical problems often arise. Where will the machine be kept? Is the desk large enough? Where is the printer and when will the student have access to it? How will the equipment be moved from class to class? Does the computer remain at school or travel back and forth between home and school? What happens when it is left behind or broken? The same process and problems apply to non-equipment-based compensations, such as using mnemonics to aide retrieval of information; the student will require explicit generalization training to determine if he or she will recognize when this strategy would be helpful and to remember to apply it in the classroom or during a test.

A computer or word processor can be a very useful accommodation and compensation tool for organizing and accomplishing specific tasks when it is appropriately selected, the procedures are taught and generalized, and it is used by a particular student in a particular context. Computer tools can also be totally inappropriate for a particular student (e.g., who has major visual impairments, has difficulty with eye-hand coordination, has severe impairments in attention span, or is currently processing at a mental age of three years). A computer is inappropriate if merely purchased and given to a student without a specifically tailored introduction and learning plan and specific appropriate applied use of the equipment.

## Cognitive Retraining

I am frequently asked, "Does the student need cognitive retraining, and who should provide it?" Often the questioner means specialized computer retraining programs that have been created and marketed for individuals after TBI. Several assumptions underlie this question and require thorough consideration. The idea behind many computerized cognitive-retraining programs is that exercising and practicing a specific cognitive-processing ability (e.g., memory) could restore the functioning of the system, and thereafter the individual could and would spontaneously generalize this skill to functional, real-life tasks. The research support for these assumptions has generally not been good (Sohlberg & Mateer, 1989; Ylvisaker, Szekeres, Hartwick, & Tworek, 1994), although some other authors will disagree with this statement (Lynch, 1986). Individuals may learn specific tasks or procedures through computerized practice (e.g., improve reaction time, relearn math facts, or learn to follow a diary system provided on the computer to organize the day), and they will demonstrate improved performance on the computerized task itself. However research support for *functional generalization of cognitive-processing abilities to other contexts* has been lacking to date. Use of a computer or computerized retraining programs should not be a substitute for individualized special education and carefully created and adjusted specific accommodations and compensation strategies.

Another important point is that the accommodations, compensations, and appropriate learning strategies for the student must occur throughout the student's day and life and be implemented, supported, and monitored by all staff. An unfortunate side effect of having one designated person responsible for cognitive retraining in an isolated setting is that the teachers (and even the student) may feel that they do not have to be actively involved or change their approaches. There is no easy cure for the complex, integrated impairments in cognitive processing after a TBI. However, a dynamic integrated approach, which considers the uniqueness of the student (cognitive, behavioral, and physical) in his or her life context and is fully supported by the educational staff, peers, and family, is feasible.

## CASE STUDY

The following actual case study is presented to demonstrate integration of the preceding information into a situation that one is likely to encounter in a typical elementary or high school.

Terry was 14 years old, in the last week of eighth grade, when he sustained a severe TBI (including depressed right temporal skull fracture, large epidural hematoma requiring two neurosurgical procedures, raised intracranial pressure and ischemic infarct due to herniation, secondary meningitis, and prolonged unresponsiveness) from being punched in the head by another student. Terry was acutely hospitalized for a month and was barely responsive when transferred to a rehabilitation center for an additional month. At discharge, Terry was using a walker and conversing but was confused and responded in an automatic-appropriate manner. He had difficulty with organization and problem solving and became easily fatigued and frustrated when tasks were unstructured or challenging. Terry was taking Dilantin to prevent seizures. He began his freshman year at a new school at this point in his recovery.

Terry had been partially evaluated at the re-

habilitation center (two to three months after the injury) and at school (using IQ, achievement, and speech and language tests). Terry had obtained a Wechsler Intelligence Scale for Children (WISC III) full scale intelligence quotient (FSIQ) of 97 and demonstrated preserved achievement, testing at the eighth-grade level. The school staff were well intentioned and concerned, and Terry had been placed on an IEP and some modifications in his assignments had been made. Before his injury, Terry had been an A-B student; when he returned and was placed in honors courses at the high school level, he received D's and failed math (previously his strength). Terry had previously wanted to be a lawyer; by the end of his freshman year he stated that he did not like school, wanted to work in his father's business as a construction laborer, and was concerned that he had "lost intelligence." His parents noted that Terry did not initiate any activities (eating, calling friends, or getting up from the couch) unless specifically cued to do so; therefore, they felt that he needed to be supervised at all times. Terry's friends had drifted away since he was not able to participate in former activities such as contact sports and riding four-wheelers. Terry seemed depressed and had started seeing a counselor. The family requested an independent neuropsychological evaluation 13 months after the injury, before he began his sophomore year.

## Observations

Terry presented with a flat, expressionless face, which did not express his true emotional state. He was nervous, concerned, obsessively detailed in his performances, and fatigued by midmorning. Terry walked with a slow, robotlike gait; his written output was slow and nonautomatic; and his speech was slow, lacked prosody, and was somewhat unclear. Terry misperceived communications at times. He was cooperative and performed reasonably well within the structure of formal standardized testing (because of external control and initiation by the examiner).

## Neuropsychological Procedures

The WISC-III was not repeated at this time; it had been given recently and would not provide sufficient information about Terry's current new learning and processing abilities to justify the expenditure of time and Terry's energy. Emphasis was placed on assessment of executive functioning (organization and problem solving, mental control and flexibility, selective attention, and initiation and inhibition of thoughts and behaviors); new learning style, memory, and retrieval; sensory, motor, and perceptual functioning; processing speed; auditory processing; adaptive and emotional functioning through observation and interviews with Terry and his family; and review of pre- and postinjury educational records.

## Current Cognitive and Behavior Profile

Although Terry recalled academic skills he had learned before the injury and obtained an average IQ score, these isolated, preserved past abilities were false indicators, overestimating his present learning abilities. One year after the injury, Terry clearly had continuing *cognitive weaknesses* in new learning and retrieval of new memories; initiation, independent organization, and judgment; processing of all types of information; written language (motor output and content); auditory discrimination in noisy settings; physical residuals including visual field deficit, specific left-hand deficits, impairment of gait, side effects of Dilantin, and significant fatigue; and reduced adaptive behavior (below premorbid age level) and emotional difficulties (both reactive and direct brain injury, including physical and verbal disinhibition; difficulty modulating emotional reactions; obsessive-compulsive and perseverative behaviors beyond his control; and poor judgment, leaving him easily lead by others). His *strengths* included preserved right-hand strength and fine motor skills (other than motor planning and written output); unimpaired naming and word retrieval; ability to utilize clear external structure, step-by-step processes, and computer-based presentation; ability to utilize word processing (right hand only because of impairment in timing with the left hand); ability to learn new information through visual and paired visual-verbal presentation; retention of the information he was able to initially register; and supportive family and receptive school staff.

## Educationally Relevant Recommendations

Given this profile, the following recommendations were offered to the school staff for inclusion in a revised IEP:

1. Extensive accommodations were made to limit the amount of both written and word-processed output, with alternatives such as multiple-choice exams; short-answer questions rather than essays, reports, or compositions; copies of notes by high-achieving peers and teachers' prepared outlines; and permission to dictate his responses.

2. Terry is debriefed on his understanding of classroom lecture content, supplemented with instruction in and application of work-study skills [e.g., survey, question, read, review (SQ3R) method, sun diagrams, and outlining and underlining techniques] for actual assignments.

3. Initiation must be provided by the teachers and resource room staff rather than asking Terry to seek assistance as needed. There is a scheduled daily check in with a designated staff person (on arrival and before leaving school) for organization and specific outlining of tasks to be performed that day.

4. Terry is limited in the amount of new information he can register; therefore he should be expected to learn main concepts and how to locate important information by using organization techniques and library resources, rather than memorizing facts or details. Multiple-choice questions should be utilized to cue retrieval.

5. With Terry's and his family's permission, the full report and additional discussion were provided to his psychotherapist. In addition, small-group counseling with selected peers and the school counselor was recommended to address Terry's safety and acceptance at school and for prosocial and role-playing skills, using actual school issues as they arose.

6. Terry is still early in his recovery will continue to improve, and he is now more able than he was during the past school year (ninth grade). Accommodations need to be frequently reviewed and altered to meet his needs.

7. Specific written materials were provided to Terry, his family, and the school staff.

### Student Letter
The following is a shortened version of the letter sent to Terry.

*Thank you for working with me, Terry. I know that it was a long and stressful day. However, by completing the evaluation, I am able to offer a great deal of positive information. This letter is sent only to you. A separate detailed report has been sent to your parents, the school, and Dr. P. Terry, you currently perform at least "average" (normal, like other 15-year-old guys) or better in all of these areas: intelligence, structured problem solving, new visual learning and memory, visual perception and organization, physical strength (stronger than 15 years, at the level of grown men), your sensory abilities, naming ability, and symbolic processing when you can say (rather than write) your answers. The majority of your cognitive (thinking) abilities are at least average. You have shown great improvements since your injury, and you will continue to improve for a long time to come. You may ask, then, why was school so difficult last year? The answer is that you no doubt had far more difficulties with slow processing, new learning and memory, and physical problems when you returned to school. With hindsight, it was probably much too early for you to have returned to school with a full load of honors courses. This new school year should be much better since you are functioning much better and the school will now understand the types of unusual difficulties you have; I have provided suggestions for the teachers about how to present information to you and how to ask you to respond so that you can demonstrate your knowledge.*

*At the present time I detected the following problems, which will need accommodations to allow you to compensate while you continue to improve: slowness in fine motor dexterity, slow written output (with "perseverative" overworking of details), continuing visual problems, difficulty memorizing facts that are not logically connected, difficulty focusing and discriminating relevant voices from background noise, and difficulty initiating (getting started) unless someone else provides a "jump start" and suggestions for how to do something. These problems are residual difficulties from the TBI. These problems can be minimized by both your and the teachers' understanding of them and applying appropriate accommodations to allow you to use all of your other strengths and talents. I have also written to Dr. P, asking that he check on your medications and to do a few more different tests to rule out some problems.*

*Terry, I think that you are a great guy and that you are trying very hard to overcome the complicated difficulties that resulted from the*

*TBI. I assure you that you will continue to improve and that school and life in general will continue to improve. Please call or write to me if you have any questions that I may be able to answer. I will remain in touch with your family and the teachers. Best wishes and enjoy your summer.*

*Dorrie Rapp, Ph.D.*

## Medically Relevant Findings and Recommendations

A copy of the full report was sent to Dr. P with the following cover letter.

*Thank you for referring Terry for a comprehensive neuropsychological evaluation. Although the insurance carrier denied benefits as "not medically necessary" despite your referral, I arranged funding through the school district, and I will continue to work closely with the school staff to develop a more appropriate education program for Terry. In summary, Terry has continued to demonstrate improvements since the early evaluations in the rehabilitation hospital. However, I detected continuing significant brain-behavior difficulties in the following areas:*

1. *Frontal-limbic impairment:* loss of taste and smell; abulic presentation; lack of initiation of all activities including eating and social contact; difficulties with modulation of affect, from generally flat and nonreactive to outbursts of anger and physical aggression; easily lead and does not think before saying or doing; yet some other good higher-cortical abilities, which he can use only after external initiation and within a clear structure.

2. *Physical/physiologic:* slow, nonautomatic gait and fine motor output; flat facial expression, in combination with need for external initiation; history of raised intracranial pressure and herniation syndrome; and early "locked-in" presentation. These problems raise the question of possible thalamic impairment, which appears Parkinsonian-like. I question whether a trial medication such as Sinemet might be useful and possibly allow Terry to be better able to functionally use his preserved abilities. I have also suggested that Terry discuss with you the need for continued anticonvulsant prophylaxis due to side effects and his possible noncompliance. I am

also concerned by Terry's obsessive-compulsive behaviors, which interfere with completion of his daily routines. Dr. T, neuropsychiatrist, is willing to coordinate with you to provide consultations regarding Terry's care.

I would like to reevaluate Terry in one year's time. Please let me know if I can provide any additional information or assistance.

*Dorrie Rapp, Ph.D.*
*Lic. School Psych.; Lic. Psych.*
*Diplomate, ABPN*

## Follow-up

A full-day in-service training presentation was held with Terry's teachers and other school staff. Terry's IEP was substantially modified to incorporate the changes noted in the neuropsychological report. Terry and the family have become involved with a local TBI support group. His medications were changed, with resulting improvements in physical and behavioral presentation. Terry will be allowed to retake several core courses from the ninth grade, and his previous grades will not count in his cumulative average. Terry continues to require accommodations and compensations, as well as close follow-up monitoring and reevaluation.

# RESOURCES

## Catalogue of Educational Materials

A catalogue of materials about TBI is available at no charge from the National Head Injury Foundation (now BIA). This includes professional and nontechnical reading materials, packets of information by topic, videos, public service announcements, and school-based information and prevention programs. Contact Publications Department, NHIF, 1776 Massachusetts Avenue NW, Suite 100, Washington, DC 20036-1904. Fax (202) 296-8850; phone (202) 296-6443.

## Prevention

*Shaken baby syndrome* Posters and other materials for students and parents are available from Casa Colina Children's Service Center, 255 East Bonita Avenue, Pomona, CA 91767. Phone (714) 593-7521.

*Bike helmet safety* Posters and other presentation materials for children and schools are available through SHIPS (Sunnyview Hospital Injury Prevention Services), Attention Ann Burton, 1270 Belmont Avenue, Schenectady, New York 12308. Phone (518) 382-4520.

*Airbags, seat belts, helmets, bike safety* Articles, community guides, video public service announcements, brochures, posters, and children's coloring book are available through the Catalogue of Educational Materials, Brain Injury Foundation.

*Videos* Presentations by and for teenagers on risk-taking behaviors and TBI are available for purchase through the BIA (see preceding entry).

## In-service Training Program for Schools

A complete TBI in-service training module specifically for school personnel (text, overheads, videotape, hand-out, etc.) is available through Janet Tyler, Project Director, Traumatic Brain Injury Project, Department of Special Education, University of Kansas Medical Center, 3901 Rainbow Boulevard, Kansas City, KS 66160. Price approximately $30.

## Guide to Understanding Section 504

A practical guide for school personnel about the implications of Section 504 for students with disabilities is *Student Access, A Resource Guide for Educators, Section 504 of the Rehabilitation Act of 1973*, available from the Council of Administrators of Special Education, Inc. (CASE), 615 Sixteenth Street NW, Albuquerque, NM 87104. Price $5 bound, $3 photocopied.

## Review Publications on TBI for Schools

**Introductory** Mira, M. P., Tucker, B. F., & Tyler, J. S. (1992). *Traumatic brain injury in children and adolescents. A sourcebook for teachers and other school personnel*. Austin, TX: Pro-Ed.

**Intermediate** Farmer, J. E., & Peterson, L. (1995). Pediatric traumatic brain injury: promoting successful school reentry. *School Psychology Review, 2*, 230–243.

**Advanced** Savage, R. C., & Wolcott, G. F. (Eds.). (1994). *Educational dimensions of acquired brain injury*. Austin, TX: Pro-Ed.

## Books for Young Children and Peers

*For Kids Only: A Guide to Brain Injury.* Available from RRTC/STBI, MCV, Box 434, Richmond, VA 23298-0434. Cheryl Thomas (804) 786-7290. Price $5 each (bulk discounts available).

*Kidnapping Kevin Kowalski.* Auch, M. J. (1990). New York: Scholastic, Apple Paperbacks.

*Mom I Have a Staring Problem.* Buckel, M. C., & Buckel, T. (1992). Available from Marion Buckel, P.O. Box 692633, Orlando, FL 32869-2633. Price $3.95.

*The Elephant Who Forgets.* Snyder, H. (1997). L&A Publishing, 22 Keewaydin Road, Wolfeboro, NH 03894. Phone (603) 569-3826. Price $15.

## Books for Families Who Have a Child with a TBI

*When Your Child Is Seriously Injured. The Emotional Impact on Families.* Lash, M. (1990). Price $4.50. Available through Catalog of Educational Materials, BIA.

*HDI Coping Series.* Includes easy-to-understand, practical guides: guide for families, home-based cognitive rehabilitation program, hiring the head-injured, life after head injury, and teaching the head-injured. Price for five-volume set $45. Available through the Catalogue of Educational Materials, NHIF.

*National Head Injury Foundation (Brain Injury Foundation).* Toll-free *family* help-line: 1-800-444-6443.

## National Brain Tumor Foundation

Family and professional information, resource directory, pamphlets and a free booklet "Understanding and coping with your child's brain tumor" (1997), that provides suggestions for return to school. Phone (800) 934-CURE.

# REFERENCES

*Act 230: Regulation or Revolution?* (1992, Spring). (Available through Vermont Department of Education, 120 State Street, Montpelier, VT 05620-2501, (802) 828-3141).

American Cancer Society. (1988). *Back to school. A handbook for teachers of children with cancer.* (Available from 1-800-ACS-2345)

Auch, M. J. (1990). *Kidnapping Kevin Kowalski.* New York: Scholastic, Apple Paperback.

Begali, V. (1992). *Head injury in children and adolescents* (2nd ed.). Brandon, VT: Clinical Psychology Publishing Company.

Begali, V. (1994). The role of the school psychologist. In R. C. Savage & G. F. Wolcott (Eds.), *Educational dimensions of acquired brain injury* (pp. 453–473). Austin, TX: Pro-Ed.

Benton, A. (1991). Prefrontal injury and behavior in children. *Developmental Neuropsychology, 7,* 275–281.

Bigler, E. D. (1988). Frontal lobe damage and neuropsychological assessment. *Archives of Clinical Neuropsychology, 3,* 279–297.

Blosser, J. L., & DePompei, R. (1994). Creating an effective classroom environment. In R. C. Savage & G. F. Wolcott (Eds.), *Educational dimensions of acquired brain injury* (pp. 413–451). Austin, TX: Pro-Ed.

Boyer, M. G., & Edwards, P. (1991). Outcome 1 to 3 years after severe traumatic brain injury in children and adolescents. *Injury, 22,* 315–320.

Brown, R. T., & Madan-Swain, A. (1993). Cognitive, neuropsychological, and academic sequelae in children with leukemia. *Journal of Learning Disabilities, 26,* 74–90.

Bruce, D. A., & Zimmermann, R. A. (1989). Shaken impact syndrome. *Pediatric Annals, 18,* 482–494.

Dalby, P. R., & Obrzut, J. E. (1991). Epidemiological characteristics and sequelae of closed head-injured children and adolescents: A review. *Developmental Neuropsychology, 7,* 35–68.

Deaton, A. V. (1994). Changing the behaviors of students with acquired brain injuries. In R. C. Savage & G. F. Wolcott (Eds.), *Educational dimensions of acquired brain injury* (pp. 257–275). Austin, TX: Pro-Ed.

Ewing-Cobbs, L., & Fletcher, J. M. (1990). Neuropsychological assessment of traumatic brain injury in children. In E. D. Bigler (Ed.), *Traumatic brain injury* (pp. 107–128). San Antonio, TX: Pro-Ed.

Farmer, J. E., & Peterson, L. (1995). Pediatric traumatic brain injury: Promoting successful school reentry. *School Psychology Review, 24,* 230–243.

Fay, G. C., Jaffee, K. M., Polissar, N. L., Liao, S., Martin, K. M., Shurtleff, H. A., Rivara, J. B., & Winn, H. R. (1993). Mild pediatric traumatic brain injury: A cohort study. *Archives of Physical Medicine and Rehabilitation, 74,* 895–901.

*Federal Register.* (1992). Assistance to States for the Education of Children With Disabilities Program and Preschool Grants for Children With Disabilities, Final Rule. 57(189), p. 44802.

Fletcher, J. M., Ewing-Cobbs, L., Miner, M. E., Levin, H. S., & Eisenberg, H. M. (1990). Behavioral changes after closed head injury in children. *Journal of Consulting and Clinical Psychology, 58,* 93–98.

Fletcher, J. M., & Levin, H. S. (1988). Neurobehavioral effects of brain injury in children. In D. K. Routh (Ed.), *Handbook of pediatric psychology* (pp. 258–295). New York: Guilford.

Goldstein, F. C., & Levin, H. S. (1990). Epidemiology of traumatic brain injury: Incidence, clinical characteristics, and risk factors. In E. D. Bigler (Ed.), *Traumatic brain injury* (pp. 51–67). Austin, TX: Pro-Ed.

Hanson, S. L., & Clippard, D. (1992). Assessment of children with traumatic brain injury: Planning for school re-entry. In S. L. Hanson & D. M. Tucker (Eds.), *Physical medicine and rehabilitation state of the art review: Neuropsychological assessment* (pp. 483–494). Philadelphia: Hanley & Belfus.

Harrington, D. (1990). Educational strategies. In M. Rosenthal, E. Griffith, M. Bond, & J. D. Miller (Eds.), *Rehabilitation of the adult and child with traumatic brain injury* (2nd ed., pp. 476–492). Philadelphia: Davis.

Individuals with Disabilities Education Act. (1992, September 29, October 27). Part B Regulations, 34 Code of Federal Regulations, Part 300. *Federal Register* (pp. 44794–44852).

Jaffe, K. M., Fay, G. C., Polissar, N. L., Martin, K. M., Shurtleff, H., Rivara, J. B., & Winn, H. R. (1993). Severity of pediatric traumatic brain injury and neurobehavioral recovery at one year. A cohort study. *Archives of Physical Medicine and Rehabilitation, 74*, 587–595.

Kaplan, E. (1988). A process approach to neuropsychological assessment. In T. Boll & B. K. Bryant (Eds.), *Clinical neuropsychology and brain function: Research, measurement, and practice* (pp. 129–167). Washington, DC: American Psychological Association.

Kaufmann, P. M., Fletcher, J. M., Levin, H. S., Miner, M. E., & Ewing-Cobbs, L. (1993). Attentional disturbance after pediatric closed head injury. *Journal of Child Neurology, 8*, 348–353.

Lash, M. (1990). *When your child is seriously injured. The emotional impact on families.* Boston: Research and Training Center, Tufts–New England Medical Center.

Lash, M. (1992). *When your child goes to school after an injury.* Boston: Research and Training Center, Tufts–New England Medical Center.

Lash, M., & Scarpino, C. (1993). School reintegration for children with traumatic brain injuries. *NeuroRehabilitation, 3*, 13–25.

Lehr, E. (1990). *Psychological management of traumatic brain injuries in children and adolescents.* Rockville, MD: Aspen Publishing.

Lehr, E., & Savage, R. (1990). Community and school integration from a developmental perspective. In J. Kreutzer & P. Wehman (Eds.), *Community integration following traumatic brain injury* (pp. 301–310). Baltimore, MD: Paul H. Brookes.

Levin, H. S., High, W. M., Ewing-Cobbs, L., Fletcher, J. M., Eisenberg, H. M., Miner, M. E., & Goldstein, F. C. (1988). Memory functioning during the first year after closed head injury in children and adolescents. *Neurosurgery, 22*, 1043–1052.

Levin, H. S., Mendelsohn, D., Lilly, M. A., Fletcher, J. M., Culhane, K. A., Chapman, S. B., Harward, H., Kusnerik, L., Bruce, D., & Eisenberg, H. M. (1994). Tower of London performance in relation to magnetic resonance imaging following closed head injury in children. *Neuropsychology, 8*, 171–179.

Lynch, W. J. (1986). An update on software in cognitive rehabilitation. *Cognitive Rehabilitation, 4*(3), 2–6.

Mateer, C. A., & Williams, D. (1991). Effects of frontal lobe injury in childhood. *Developmental Neuropsychology, 7*, 359–376.

McKee, W. T., & Witt, J. C. (1990). Effective teaching: A review of instructional and environmental variables. In T. B. Gutkin & C. R. Reynolds (Eds.), *The handbook of school psychology* (2nd ed., pp. 821–846). New York: Wiley.

Michaud, L. J., Rivara, F. P., Jaffe, K. M., Fay, G., & Dalley, J. L. (1993). Traumatic brain injury as a risk factor for behavioral disorders in children. *Archives of Physical Medicine and Rehabilitation, 74*, 368–375.

Mira, M. P., Tucker, B. F., & Tyler, J. S. (1992). *Traumatic brain injury in children and adolescents: A sourcebook for schools.* Austin, TX: Pro-Ed.

Nisbet, J. (Ed.). (1992). *Natural supports in school, at work, and in the community for people with severe disabilities.* Baltimore, MD: Paul H. Brookes.

Public Law 94-142. (1975). U.S. Congressional and Administrative News, 94th Congress, First Session. *Legislative History, 1*, 773–796. St. Paul, MN: West.

Public Law 101-476. (1991). *Individuals with Disabilities Act.* Washington, DC: U.S. Department of Education, Office of Special Education and Rehabilitative Services.

Raines, S. R., & Waaland, P, K. (1992). *For kids only: A guide to brain injury.* Richmond, VA: Regional Research and Training Center on Severe Traumatic Brain Injury, Medical College of Virginia.

Rapp, D. (1986). *Brain injury casebook. Methods for reintegration into home, school, and community.* Springfield, IL: Thomas.

Rapp, D. L., & McIntire, J. C. (1993). Assessment and educational planning for children with traumatic brain injury. In L. VandeCreek, S. Knapp, & T. L. Jackson (Eds.), *Innovations in clinical practice: A sourcebook* Vol. 12, pp. 581–594.

Regulations of the New York Commissioner of Education (1993). 8 NY C.R.R. 200.1(mm)(12).

Reitan, R. M., & Wolfson, D. (1992). *Neuropsychological*

*evaluation of older children*. South Tucson, AZ: Neuropsychology Press.

Ringle-Bartels, J., & Story, T. B. (1993). Treatment of acquired cognitive-communicative deficits in young children. *NeuroRehabilitation, 3,* 26–43.

Rourke, B. P., Fisk, J. L., & Strang, J. D. (1986). *Neuropsychological assessment of children: A treatment oriented approach.* New York: Guilford.

Savage, R. C. (1991). Identification, classification, and placement issues for students with traumatic brain injuries. *Journal of Head Trauma Rehabilitation, 6*(1), 1–9.

Savage, R. (1994). An educator's guide to brain and brain injury. In R. C. Savage & G. F. Wolcott (Eds.), *Educational dimensions of acquired brain injury* (pp. 13–31). Austin, TX: Pro-Ed.

Savage, R. C., & Mishkin, L. (1994). A neuroeducational model for teaching students with acquired brain injuries. In R. C. Savage & G. F. Wolcott (Eds.), *Educational dimensions of acquired brain injury* (pp. 393–411). Austin, TX: Pro-Ed.

Savage, R. C., & Wolcott, G. F. (Eds.). (1994). *Educational dimensions of acquired brain injury.* Austin, TX: Pro-Ed.

Singer, G. H. S., Nixon, C. D., & Powers, L. (1991). *You can't imagine unless you've been there yourself.* Albany: New York State Head Injury Association.

Slomka, G. T., & Tarter, R. E. (1993). Neuropsychological assessment. In T. H. Ollendick & M. Hersen (Eds.), *Handbook of child and adolescent assessment* (pp. 208–223). Boston; Allyn & Bacon.

Sohlberg, M. M., & Mateer, C. A. (1989). *Introduction to cognitive rehabilitation: Theory and practice.* New York: Guilford.

Teasdale, G., & Jennett, B. (1974). Assessment of coma and impaired consciousness: A practical scale. *Lancet, 2,* 81–84.

Telzrow, C. F. (1991). The school psychologist's perspective on testing students with traumatic brain injury. *Journal of Head Trauma Rehabilitation, 6*(1), 23–34.

Teuber, H. L., & Rudel, R. G. (1962). Behavior after cerebral lesions in children and adults. *Developmental Medicine and Child Neurology, 4,* 3–20.

Tyler, J. S. (1990). *Traumatic head injury in school-aged children: A training manual for educational personnel.* Kansas City: University of Kansas Medical Center, Children's Rehabilitation Unit.

Vermont State Board Manual of Rules and Procedures (1992, October). 2362.1(i). (Available from Vermont Department of Education, 120 State Street, Montpelier, VT 05620-2501).

Vocational Rehabilitation Act of 1973, Section 504. (1977, May 4). 29 U.S. Cong. S 794. 34, Code of Federal Regulations, Part 104, *Federal Register* (pp. 22676–22702).

Welsh, M. C., Pennington, B. F., & Groisser, D. B. (1991). A normative-developmental study of executive function: A window on prefrontal function in children. *Developmental Neuropsychology, 7,* 131–149.

Williams, J. M., & Kay, T. (Eds.). (1991). *Head injury: A family matter.* Baltimore, MD: Paul H. Brookes.

Wood, R. L. (1987). *Brain injury rehabilitation: A neurobehavioral approach.* Rockville, MD: Aspen.

Ylvisaker, M. (1993). Communication outcome in children and adolescents with traumatic brain injury. *Neuropsychological Rehabilitation, 3,* 367–387.

Ylvisaker, M., Feeney, T. J., & Urbanczyk, B. (1993). A social-environmental approach to communication and behavior after traumatic brain injury. *Seminars in Speech and Language, 14,* 74–87.

Ylvisaker, M., Hartwick, P., Ross, B., & Nussbaum, N. (1994). Cognitive assessment. In R. C. Savage & G. F. Wolcott (Eds.), *Educational dimensions of acquired brain injury* (pp. 69–119). Austin, TX: Pro-Ed.

Ylvisaker, M., Szekeres, S. F., & Hartwick, P. (1994). A framework for cognitive intervention. In R. C. Savage & G. F. Wolcott (Eds.), *Educational dimensions of acquired brain injury* (pp. 35–67). Austin, TX: Pro-Ed.

Ylvisaker, M., Szekeres, S. F., Hartwick, P., & Tworek, P. (1994). Cognitive intervention. In R. C. Savage & G. F. Wolcott (Eds.), *Educational dimensions of acquired brain injury* (pp. 121–184). Austin, TX: Pro-Ed.

Ylvisaker, M., Urbanczyk, B., & Feeney, T. J. (1992). Social skills following traumatic brain injury. *Seminars in Speech and Language, 13,* 308–322.

# COMPUTERS IN EDUCATION AND SCHOOL PSYCHOLOGY: THE EXISTING AND EMERGING TECHNOLOGY KNOWLEDGE BASE SUPPORTING INTERVENTIONS WITH CHILDREN

ROBERT D. TENNYSON
DWIGHT MORRISON
*University of Minnesota*

## THEORY, RESEARCH, AND PRACTICE

### Minnesota Practice

Visualize, if you will, two tenth-grade students actively involved in the study of toxins in the St. Louis River in Minnesota. They have spent a week in the library, using the computerized catalogue and the CD ROM periodical index with full text to locate information for a hypothesis for their investigation, "The Cause of Water Pollution of the St. Louis River." They obtain an Excel data-base of River Watch monitoring results from the MPCA (Minnesota Pollution Control Agency). From that data they decide to focus on the topic acid rain. Their data are the raised pH levels collected at all sites over a four-year period. They obtain computerized details on acid rain from the MPCA and then search the Internet for other schools with similar interests. The home page of a southern Minnesota school involved in deformed frog research has some links to information sources. They also find more acid rain background material on the Green Net, the River Net, and GLIN (Great Lakes Information Net). From these sources,

they download pictures and text and proceed to construct a storyboard multimedia presentation, using HyperStudio. This presentation will be the final summary (qualitative and quantitative) of their processes and efforts. As part of their learning activities, they will also analyze the actual water quality by taking samplings at the Indian Point site on the St. Louis River, and they will compare those findings with the established criteria from the MPCA on river-based toxins. The most interesting thing about this whole scenario is that these students are in a special education science class at the high school level.

### Technological Change: Is Technology Outpacing Educational Change?

The preceding scenario is typical of one technologically mature use of computers on a daily basis in one class at the Duluth Central High School in Duluth, Minnesota. Computers have been used for instruction in schools for over 25 years in Minnesota, with some real successes and some definite concerns, which we explore in detail in this chapter (Kulik & Kulik, 1987, 1991). Miniaturization of computer chips in the 1970s has provided a powerful technological tool—the microcomputer. But the concern is that the educational microcomputer does not come with directions for its appropriate use. Educational theory and the resulting research are explored as a possible guide to how computers should be used to support instructional interventions. The paradigm shifts in research in the 1980s and 1990s from scientific reductionism to holistic social constructivism (Salomon, 1993), and in practice from twentieth-century industrialism to today's postindustrial information society, are used to explain the complex and interrelated issues of using computers for instructional interventions in special education.

The existing knowledge base for computers in the state of Minnesota is explored thoroughly in the following pages, as Minnesota has been in the forefront of the adoption of computers in education. It started with mainframe access across Minnesota in the 1970s, was followed by local MECC (Minnesota Educational Computing Consortium) site coordinators and microcomputer efforts in the 1980s, and has been consummated with legislative funding for technology site testing and Internet explorations in the 1990s.

Technological change is driving both the computer industry and education at a frenetic pace, while at the same time schools nationwide are striving to find the most educationally sound applications for the newly emerging computer technologies. We also explore the driving mechanisms of computer use in educational institutions of many kinds (public, private, and distributed) by looking at how miniaturization, networking, artificial intelligence, and business initiatives are driving the change process. At the end of this chapter, we describe some of the *emerging knowledge base* that is supporting computer interventions with children.

## Research and Practice: Can Research Improve Educational Practice?

Schools across the nation have married the computer for better or worse, with wedding expenses in the $30 billion range. Meta-research over the last 10 years (Kulik & Kulik, 1987, 1991) indicates that computers can improve instruction, so the investment has not gone to waste. Properly designed computer instruction is equal to or more effective than traditional large-group or small-group instruction (Tennyson & Breuer, 1993). The research results build an incomplete

picture, but they suggest that certain hardware and software employed with particular populations under competent teachers can meet instructional objectives (Morrison, 1994). Students who use a computer improve their spelling, sentence memory, listening comprehension, vocabulary, and reading comprehension (literacy) skills more than those who do not (Kozma, 1994).

A critical question still persists, though, because of the large amount of school computer hardware and software presently in use. Is the software and hardware used in education based on successful research that can lead to improvement in school practice, or are teachers just going through another educational fad—driven by the media hype of the "information revolution"? Schools cannot stop the worldwide computer revolution and ongoing technological change, but they can willfully put computers into education in ways that are most efficient and effective, based on sound research that is linked to educational theory (Tennyson, 1988, 1990).

## National Center for Improvement of Practice

In 1994, the National Center for the Improvement of Practice (NCIP) collected testimony on the problems associated with putting computer theory and research into educational practice. On one side of the table sat the university professors, with a clear research agenda based on solid theory, and on the other side sat the practitioners, the college, high school, or primary school educators. This was one of the few times that these two groups had come together to focus on the holistic issue—how to move from theory-based research to the practical classroom implementation of computer-based instruction. Most of the practitioners and researchers present recognized that there was a significant problem in moving from closely structured, theory-based research to the complexity of the real classroom.

Many NCIP conference sessions and discussions were held because the problem of moving research into practice appeared to be real and significant to all. Examples were given of the few research projects that had resulted in commercial successes, such as the reading program *Reader Rabbit* and the problem-solving experiences of *Jasper Woodbury*, but most did not. The NCIP discussions came to be directed at the large amount of research that was funded and completed but was not possible to put into practice. Much of computer research is focused on a narrow segment of education (e.g., eighth grade, small-group computer instruction) that would be difficult to replicate at another site or is so theoretical in nature (e.g., the artificial intelligence visual recognition research) that it is not possible to convert it to a practical educational product. Researchers defended their specific research agendas, which were tightly linked to theory and have suffered from shortages of research dollars in recent years. Practitioners positioned themselves as overworked and underfunded but with a clear need to utilize the power of technology and the microcomputer to improve interventions with children.

The NCIP has, since 1984, provided a valued service to both researchers and practitioners by (a) selecting specific research projects that can most easily be put into practice through their funding and development programs, (b) developing video vignettes of viable computer practices, and (c) providing an Internet site to continue the dialogue on the conversion of research to practice. (Note: the NCIP is at http://www.edc.org/FSC/NCIP/ on the World Wide Web for your review and study.) The NCIP has brought our attention to the need for careful analysis of computer-based interventions with children and for sound research that can be put into practice. The important question is, How can theory and research lead to improved educational practice in a time of decreasing budgets and ever-increasing speed of technological change?

The researcher and the practitioner may have to seek a common ground on which the student can benefit, or the future of computer-based education may default to the software salespeople, who are interested in monetary returns instead of educational results.

## Complexity: Can Education Deal With the Large Number of Variables?

The educational classroom application of computer interventions for children is a very complex task. Cognitive factor research has isolated a large number of abilities related to schools and education (e.g., verbal, spatial, perceptual speed, and visual memory). The number of educational research variables that have been investigated individually is well over 100 (Sternberg, 1986) and includes such variables as

> Abstract reasoning, achievement, aptitude, attitude, behavior, calculations, cognitive

style, cooperative learning, deductive reasoning, difficulty, discovery, educability, encoding, experience, failure, feedback, forgetting, general intelligence, genotype, goal-directed, grouping, growth, health, heredity, imagery, individual difference, interest, instructor, instruction, judgment, knowledge base, language, latency, listening, memory, mental age, metacognition, motor, observation, organization, parenting, past performance, personality, problem solving, recognition, reflection, rehearsal, self-regulation, sex differences, social class, spatial, strategy, teaching style, test anxiety, time-on-task, trainability, transfer, underachievement, values, verbal, whole brain, working memory, zone of proximal development, etc. (p. 5).

The complexity of implementing an instructional program is obvious to those instructional designers who are attempting to utilize computers for educational improvement, and it is one of the major roadblocks in the operationalization of research for classroom practice. There is a need to rigorously match the relevant research findings to students' individual needs. We need to plan for computer intervention by linking cognitive theory and research to specific appropriate prescriptions (Tennyson, 1988, 1995). The complexity of computer-human interaction is an added complication to the myriad of variables in the instructional setting, which combine to form a complex environment.

## Research: What Do We Know About Research on Computer-Based Instruction?

Researchers have seen fit to study most of these 100-plus variables in what is basically a laboratory environment to control for intervening and confounding effects during the investigations. Based on the NCIP meetings, the very control of independent variables that leads to quality research does not seem to allow for easy replication in the real world of multicultural schools, with their myriad of social problems, diversity of students, and multiplicity of extraneous variables. Each school has its own unique mix of variables that make implementation in actual school environments so difficult.

Research that looks at a number of studies, meta-analysis, can give us a broader view of the impact of educational research completed in the last 25 years. The 1991 meta-analysis of 254 computer-based instruction (CBI) studies since the 1960s (Kulik & Kulik, 1991) came to the conclusion that CBI usually produces positive instructional effects on students. The studies found that CBI raised the average final exam scores from the fiftieth to the sixty-second percentile (.30 standard deviations) in the typical study. This seems to match a previous study (Kulik & Kulik, 1987) that found a .31 standard deviation increase, and it also matches other studies that show CBI to be at least as effective as live teaching and often saving instructional time. The detailed meta-analysis findings give us some insight into what may be relevant to computer implementation, including the following:

1. Effectiveness. CBI used during four weeks or less improved performance by .42 standard deviations over traditional instruction in a traditional classroom.
2. Teaching. Instructors had a significant effect on instructional outcomes, which addresses the issue of human and social interaction. Good instructors are necessary.
3. Software. Microcomputers are more effective than older mainframe computers because of the growing sophistication of the available software.
4. Efficiency. CBI took only two-thirds the time of conventional instruction but taught as well.
5. Attitudes. CBI improves students' attitudes toward instruction, the content, and the instructor.

## Practice: What Do We Know About Implementing Computer Instruction?

At the NCIP meetings, college, high school, and primary school teachers bemoaned the low quality of available software and the lack of solid research and evaluation support for these interventions. Only since 1990 has the computer hardware and software industry provided the multimedia products that are making data access through the computer such a powerful tool for educators. Yet, many titles are nothing more than computerized books, like encyclopedias, with no research to support their use. Apple Computer has been a leader in funding the area of applied research and has released its findings from a 10-

year study called the Apple Classroom of Tomorrow (ACOT).

Some of the ACOT findings from the long-term effects of using computers in the classroom are as follows (Ringstaff, 1993):

1. Performance: Scores on both mathematics and English were higher than those of control groups, and ACOT keyboard skills averaged 39 words per minute (WPM), compared to the control groups of 18 WPM. Test scores indicated that students were performing well, and some were clearly performing better. Students wrote more effectively, with greater fluidity, and classes finished whole units of study far more quickly than in past years.
2. Collaboration. Researchers found that instead of isolating students, access to technology actually encouraged them to collaborate more than in traditional classrooms. Instead of becoming boring with use, technology became even more interesting.
3. Competencies. Students wrote more and better when they had access to computers, and ACOT students did almost twice as much writing as students in other classes. Students explored and represented information dynamically and in many forms, became socially aware and more confident, communicated effectively about complex processes, used technology routinely and appropriately, became independent learners and self-starters, knew their areas of expertise and shared that expertise spontaneously, worked well collaboratively, and developed a positive orientation to the future.

## Summary

At this point we can unequivocally say that research and practice on computer instruction show positive results. The microcomputer is effective in delivering classroom instruction, does improve students' attitudes about instruction, and is efficient in delivering instruction in less time. Microcomputer software is an improvement over the mainframe instruction of the past, and the instructional skills of the teacher are a significant factor in the success or failure of any use of computers for instructional interventions with children. Students seem to do better academically than in the traditional classroom and feel good about the use of technology in education.

# PARADIGM SHIFTS IN EDUCATIONAL RESEARCH AND PRACTICE

Educational paradigms are the theories and models that support the research and practice of computer-based instruction. In educational theory there have been a number of paradigm shifts over the years, from the behaviorist to the cognitive to the constructivist. Educational systems should and usually do reflect the underlying cultural beliefs, values, and ethics of a given society (Banathy, 1987). Yet, education has been severely criticized in the last 15 years because of its inability to change and meet the needs of the evolving multicultural society of America.

Businesses and industries that count on the schools to provide young minds have been increasingly critical of public education. The ongoing criticism of education suggests that classroom educational experiences that are grounded in the industrial age of the last century are outmoded and do not meet the needs of an information-based society. Business corporations have had to undergo large restructuring to keep up with information-driven demands. Business expects that schools also have to change from the industrial paradigm of large groups and mass production to a customized, education-utilizing technology (Reigeluth, 1992). Education needs to focus on learning and diversity to be realistic in the multicultural world, in place of the conformity of large-class instruction and classification of individuals: "The current paradigm . . . needs to change . . . from 'advancement of the fittest' to the more spiritually and humanistically defensible one of 'advancement of all'" (Reigeluth, 1992, p. 14).

The moving of the educational paradigm to a learning focus requires a shift from the teacher focus of the past. Some of the recommendations are to concentrate on *construction* in place of *instruction*, so that learners can build their own knowledge instead of being fed information by the subject matter expert (Hannafin, 1995). This new type of educational paradigm requires a shift of instruction to active learning, authentic tasks, and allowance of flexible time to achieve success. This is quite a change from the existing paradigm, in which the learners are expected to sit down, be quiet, and do what they are told by the authoritarian teacher.

The rate of change in our postindustrial society is increasing, and many feel that technology is leaving education behind. Scientific knowledge is growing at an increasing rate, but American schools have generally not changed at anywhere near the pace required to disseminate that knowledge. We can see this trend most clearly in the sciences, where the amount of new knowledge is doubling yearly. Many schools are still teaching science in the same laboratory manner that we all grew up with, even though the capabilities exist for the school laboratory to move out into the real world. For example, with a laptop computer and the proper probes placed in real rivers, science labs can analyze water acidity directly. Schools can move from the older analysis of laboratory experiments to the construction of answers to real problems, problems that have social and cultural relevance to students, their lives, and their future.

## Computers, Research, and the Paradigm Shift

The use of the computer is compatible with the paradigm shift that is taking place today in psychology and education. Educators are moving from schools based on a nineteenth-century industrial model to a more postindustrial, information-based approach to lifelong learning. Researchers appear to be moving from the old reductionist view of the study of small pieces of instruction in isolation to a more holistic view of dealing with the complexities of the educational experience (Salomon, 1993). Past educational research has used a reductionist paradigm that studied computer education by breaking down the computer-relevant psychological phenomena into their discrete parts for study (Morrison, 1994). This has allowed for well-controlled studies of specific phenomena but has the ecological limitation of not representing the real educational experience in an authentic way. Once a phenomenon has been breaking down to its constituent parts, such as the graphics and text components, these parts no longer accurately resemble the real-life instructional phenomenon of interest. This lack of ecological realism, due to research reductionism, could explain the difficulty that exists in taking the significant results of a research effort and using them in the classroom (Breuer & Kummer, 1990).

The positive aspect of the new paradigm is that a significant research movement is underway to change from the study of decontextualized processes to the study of computer-based interventions in the context of the real classroom

(Salomon, 1993). There is a move to eliminate the reductionist nature of educational research and to focus on the broader social and environmental context that affects the practice of computer-based education. The psychological theory that supports this research appears to be moving to a more holistic and social view of the learning experience (Salomon, 1993). It is starting to consider the whole ecology of instruction when designing a research study. The concern is for ecological validity by looking to wholes, processes, and networks (Barron & Orwig, 1995).

The shift in computer-based instructional research is away from the search for behavioral effects to internal mental states and external environment variables that affect computer-human interaction. Since the paradigm shift to the convergence of the cognitive viewpoint, the Piagetian constructivist viewpoint, and the social constructionist viewpoint, educational research and practice have started to look at the realistic ecology of computer-based instruction during lifelong learning.

## Is the Existing Research Flawed? Is Type I Error Present?

Part of the motivation for a paradigm shift is probably caused by the media researchers that have been highly critical of past media research (Clark, 1983, 1994). They hold the position that there are *no unique effects* from media like television, the computer, and CD ROM because of type I error—the research error of finding significance where none exists. An example of type I error is research showing that the *ADAM* CD ROM significantly improves medical instruction when the improved efficiency of instruction may be totally due to better teachers, better planning, or the increased content of the CD ROM.

Many media studies that have shown educational gains have utilized a regular classroom group for comparison. These comparison groups have been taught by regular teachers, who taught the usual load of classes and had minimal time for course preparation (Clark, 1994). If we take the average time to prepare 1 hour of CD instruction to be about 228 hours (Barron & Orwig, 1995), it is likely that the argument of type I error with respect to the preparation time is realistic. The CD project usually hires the best teacher they can find to do the presentation, and that teacher is assigned to just the CD project until it is completed—which is not at all compa-

rable to the regular classroom setting. Yes, type I error can surely be present.

Type I error may be a blessing in disguise to the overworked regular classroom teacher. The traditional teacher receives the benefit of the improved teacher and increased preparation time, as well as other benefits of the media effort, for the price of a single CD ROM. Having the CD ROM deliver more content than the traditional teacher may be type I error to the researcher, but to the traditional teacher and student they are benefits of the media and they translate into more learning. The selection of the best teacher for the CD ROM may also be a type I error, but to the computer-using teacher it means improving a portion of the course. The *ADAM* CD is a good example of a type I error and also an example of how the effects of media can make a difference in the medical curriculum. That is, students are learning better and learning more (Barron & Orwig, 1995).

# EXISTING KNOWLEDGE BASE: EDUCATIONAL COMPUTER TECHNOLOGY

The knowledge base in computer technology is the scaffolding that supports all future learning. Our present declarative, procedural, and contextual knowledge about computers in education is the foundation for better instructional designs. Declarative knowledge refers to the stable facts that represent "what" is to be known about computers in education. Procedural knowledge refers to the processes and sequential knowledge that is the "how" of computer use. Contextual knowledge refers to the ecology and context in which the computer is used (Tennyson & Rasch, 1988). The time line in Figure 33.1 provides an initial description of the relationships between the developing knowledge base about computers in education and activities in Minnesota.

## Minnesota Educational Computing Consortium

Minnesota has been in the forefront of computer-based instruction during the 35 years covered by the time line in Figure 33.1. The 1960s was the decade of mainframe development, when Minnesota companies like Control Data, Cray Research, and Honeywell were world leaders in computer growth. The Minnesota legislature in the early 1970s created and funded the organization called the Minnesota Educational Comput-

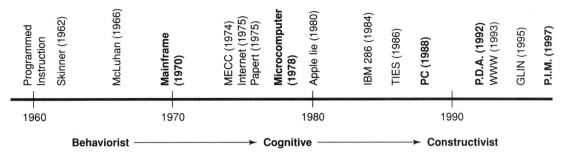

**FIGURE 33.1** Timeline illustrating developments in computer-based instruction.

ing Consortium (MECC) to form technology districts across the state. These districts each had a MECC-based coordinator who would facilitate the integration of instructional computing into the public schools of Minnesota.

The initial MECC efforts involved a statewide educational computer network accessible from individual districts through phone lines that allowed immediate access to computing power for any school. The system was heavily used, although by modern standards it was slow and totally text-based. As the microcomputer became affordable to school districts at the end of the 1970s, more MECC efforts were directed at establishing the districts' computing power, quality software collections, and computer coordinators. The MECC coordinators also conducted a number of regional computer conferences in the early 1980s, which created interest and excitement in the use of the microcomputer in education for both students and teachers. Students and teachers wrote and shared their own programs and participated in instructional sessions on both hardware and software.

Minnesota schools moved into the decade of the 1980s in anticipation of the innovations that the microcomputer could bring. They moved ahead with microcomputer laboratory purchases and with individual machines for business, drafting, and design applications. After Minnesota schools made a significant initial investment in Apple II computers and PCs, they had high expectations for computer-based instruction, which were, however, slow to materialize. Software in the late 1970s and early 1980s was based on the behaviorist paradigm (see the following section) and was usually of low quality and of simplistic nature. There were only a few programs that were successful, such as the word processor tools, CAD and CAM applications,

simulations (e.g., *Oregon Trail*), and simple games (e.g., *Munchers*).

Legislative support for computers and for MECC decreased in the middle 1980s, when open bids were taken for the computer district coordinators and MECC coordinators were replaced by other groups. Then MECC looked to the private sector for ongoing funding, and in 1986 became a public corporation. It is still one of the premiere educational software producers in the 1990s. The original star software of MECC was the *Oregon Trail* simulation that is now known to most educators by the term *Edutainment*. *Oregon Trail*, which is a simulation of the westward movement in the nineteenth century, integrates simple games with historical experiences that illustrate certain conditions and situations that might have occurred on a given trek.

## Behavioral Paradigm: Do Animals and Humans Learn in the Same Way?

Experimental research by Russian physiologists provided much of the foundation for American behavioral psychology. Sechenov (1829–1905), known as the father of Russian physiology, suggested that experimental approaches used in physiology were also applicable to psychology. He is also noted for his work on the role that reflexes and learning play in behavior. Bechterev (1857–1927), credited for developing reflexology, advanced the position that external behavior is the only valid consideration in scientific experimental inquiry. Following in these traditions, the best known of the Russian physiologists, Pavlov (1849–1936), tested the hypothesis that certain reflexes could be conditioned. In his work on glandular secretions and motor movement, Pavlov initially included a reference to mental states in his research with animals but in his later writings excluded such references, resulting in a purely objective stance. Most influential in American behaviorism was his research in classical or Pavlovian conditioning, the process in which an initially neutral stimulus, called the conditioned stimulus, is repeatedly paired with a reinforcer or unconditioned stimulus, replacing the initial response—referred to as the unconditioned response with a conditioned response.

Applying these concepts in America, Watson (1878–1958) purposely intended to establish a new school of psychology in America, one that was to apply a purely objective and experimental approach in the study of behavior, both animal and human. Rejecting the teachings of the American functionalist school, which included concepts of introspection, Watson suggested that the goal of psychology was to predict and control behavior, thus discarding all reference to consciousness. Watson was particularly influenced by the work of Thorndike (1874–1949), whose work advanced the development of comparative (animals as subjects) psychology and culminated in his theories of trial-and-error learning. Reflecting on these advances, Watson applied the method of observation to comparative psychology in his work on fear responses of children and animals. Although pragmatic in practice, Watson's behaviorism was foundational to the work of neo-behaviorists, who further advanced behaviorism to its position of dominance in American psychology.

Beginning in the 1930s and progressing into the 1960s, neo-behaviorism advocated explanatory systems and encouraged increased precision through common methods and terminology. Applying postulates from both moralism and Gestalt theory, Tolman (1866–1959) introduced the concept of purposive behaviorism, which utilized a systematic treatment of the data in his research in learning and cognitive complexity, based on studies done with animals and mazes. Utilizing a more theoretical than empirical approach, Guthrie (1886–1959) based contiguous conditioning on an instrumental conditioning model that suggested that learning occurs through the pairing of a stimulus and a response, and reinforcement is not necessary for learning to occur. Hull (1884–1952) applied concepts of mathematics to learning, resulting in his mathematico-deductive theory of learning, based on classical conditioning, which emphasized habit strength and drive. Hull's theory was quite complex and usually stated in mathematical formulations. The most famous of the neo-behaviorists

was Skinner (1904–1990), developer of operant conditioning and its schedules of reinforcement. Skinner proposed that if the occurrence of an operant or emitted response is followed by a reinforcing stimulus, the rate of responding would increase. Skinner's theory of operant conditioning has been of vital influence to instructional development, particularly in learning, cognition, and artificial intelligence.

The application of the behavioral paradigm in education was promoted by the use of teaching machines in the 1960s and 1970s. Behaviorists treated the computer experience as a black box, where input and output functions were the observable behavior of the student. Similarly, the computer-managed teaching machine was a black box, where an individual student could press a button to indicate which answer was correct—and then receive immediate reinforcement. An example of a teaching machine during this era was a closed-loop filmstrip that the computer would stop so an answer could be selected from the choices given. With the management control provided by a mainframe computer and later with the increasingly powerful microcomputer, these teaching machines became quite sophisticated tools for industrial and military instruction by the late 1970s. However, they never caught on in the public schools because of the initial high cost and because they dealt with only the lowest level of declarative knowledge.

### Behavioral Software

Much of the initial software that was developed for mainframe computers, and later converted to microcomputers, was based on the behavioral paradigm (Enkenberg, 1995). For example, the software developed for the Apple IIe was primarily of a drill and practice nature, like *Math Drill*, which presented a math problem and had the student select the correct answer in a multiple-choice format. Reinforcement was in the form of a word reward, like *correct*; sound and animation were added later as the rewards for correct responses. However, students found the short games that were part of these first math drills, such as the first *Number Munchers*, to be more captivating than the drill software. This is the same time period in which *Pacman* became a best-selling game (which can still be found on most small computer systems today). The *Muncher* programs in the Apple system have since become a standard instructional strategy for many subjects. The goal of the muncher is to eat only the correct answers, thus providing a reward.

## Weaknesses of Behavioral Paradigm in CBI

The weakness of the behavioral approach to CBI design was the structured format of small, incremental steps followed by randomly presented rewards. Humans are capable of going beyond the simple behavioral strategy of learning by reinforcement; they can learn by modifying their actions through the cognitive process of mental reflection—a process largely ignored by the behaviorist. There are some powerful examples of drill and practice software, such as the *SAT Preparation* materials and the latest versions of *Math Munchers*, but these employ the stimulus-response-reinforcement instructional design strategy. They all have the common attributes of restricting the user to a lower level of declarative knowledge learning.

## Special Education

The field of special education has benefited from the ongoing use of the behavioral paradigm because there is a real need for drill and practice and low-level software in which retardation is individually diagnosed. These software programs, which were developed in the late 1970s and early 1980s serve a valuable function for students who are many grades below their age-appropriate developmental level and need a large number of repetitions. Similar programs have been developed to assist in such tasks as teaching the street signs and their meanings to low-functioning students.

The microcomputer has also been useful in special education for monitoring actual behavior in the classroom through data-recording methods and in providing school psychologists with tools for test administration and analysis. An example of the former is the *Mpls. Record*, which allows the observer to record actual student behaviors as they happen on a portable microcomputer. An example of the latter is the *Behavior Evaluation Scale* program, which allows immediate access to behavior assessment data and results.

## Cognitive Paradigm: Can We Understand What Goes on in the Mind?

Contemporary cognitive theories of learning are having a similar effect on current instructional design for computer applications in education as the behavioral theories had on the earlier applications (e.g., Salomon, Perkins, & Globerson, 1991). The concern of cognitive theories with knowledge structures, metacognitive strategies for problem solving, and integration of new and existing knowledge structures by the learner is leading to a number of instructional design changes: (a) the development of a new theoretical basis for the design of learning environments intended to facilitate exploration and reinforce context (e.g., computer "microworlds" and hypertext); (b) significant expansion of learner control coupled with an enriched dialogue between the learner and the learning environment to support individual differences, facilitate integration and enhance motivation (e.g., the "coach" technique in intelligent tutorial systems); and (c) a redefinition of the structural requirements for simulations and games.

In outlining the history of cognitive psychology, Tennyson and Elmore (1997) write that cognitive psychology grew out of a history of behaviorism (e.g., Skinner) and psychoanalysis (e.g., Freud). These two approaches focused on the individual, as did the measurement tools developed in cognitive psychology. To the extent that teachers and school psychologists understand the learner, they can develop more effective instruction, although cognitive psychology has not been primarily concerned with that process. Effective instruction is an implementation of the research findings. That is, experimental psychologists conducting basic research in human learning have not traditionally been responsible for diffusion and dissemination of their findings into the field of education.

That this attitude is changing somewhat is exemplified by Ausubel, Novak, and Hanesian (1978), who emphasize a stronger relationship between theories of learning and theories of teaching, suggesting that they are interdependent and not mutually exclusive. An adequate theory of learning is essential to a theory of teaching because it is unproductive to experiment with varying teaching methods without some basis in learning theory (Tennyson, 1990). Discovering the most effective teaching methods depends on knowing the status of the learner and the variables that affect learning.

Computers have enabled cognitive science theorists to analyze the learning process in new ways, and much of the work in cognitive theory has been done by those familiar with computers

(Bransford, 1979). Computer programs and system flowcharting have made it possible to simulate cognitive procedures and mental models, such as students' problem-solving methods. Mayer (1981) points out that while mental models that children use have been identified, they are rarely taught. Children invent them. Since all the mental models may be different, children may be giving the same answers but using entirely different methods, some more or less effective and efficient than others, to arrive at their conclusions. Rather than focusing on the answers provided by students (basically the methodology paradigm of behaviorism), cognitive methodology focuses on the mental procedure being used (the cognitive model); the outcome is information that may allow the transformation of a learning theory into an instructional theory.

A primary application of computer techniques in describing learning has been the development of information processing (IP). The basic components of the IP model of learning (Figure 33.2) include the following: sensory receptors, perception, short-term (working) memory, and long-term memory. Contemporary IP models, unlike the behavioral models, have two primary sources of knowledge acquisition: external and internal. External information enters the cognitive system through the standard sensory mechanisms, whereas internal information is constructed as a result of the output-input relationship between the three system components. External behavior is exhibited through the output of the sensory receptors.

### Sensory Receptors Component

External information enters and behavior exits the cognitive system through the sensory receptors. Basically, these sensory receptors are the learner's ears (auditory) and eyes (visual). The information in this register decays rapidly and is easily interrupted. External stimuli include those aspects of instructional design referred to as delivery systems, such as text materials, visuals, audio sources, graphics, illustrations, and drawings.

### Perception Component

Information coming from the external receptors or from internal knowledge sources passes through the perception component, which performs the functions of, respectively, being aware of and evaluating the potential value and worth of that information and knowledge. The perception component can be viewed as a filtering device for the cognitive system. Over time, the perception component performs this filtering task in an autonomous or subconscious matter, all within a short time period (0.5–2.0 seconds).

### Short-Term (Working) Memory Component

There is considerable debate about the divisions or architecture of memory, but in a broad sense the exact details are not important in the instructional implications of the various theories. In general, there is agreement that memory comes in two forms, a store for previously learned information and a store for information that is currently being processed. This latter form, short-term (working) memory, is defined with these salient aspects: (a) it is limited in storage capacity and time (approximately 20 seconds); (b) items in working memory are subject to manipulations such as rehearsal, comparison, or matching and reordering by the processes that operate in short-term memory; and (c) items are selected for inclusion in short-term memory either by some consciously active process or by the automatic action of well-developed processes in such activities as reading, processing of verbal discourse, imagery-evoking processes, and so on.

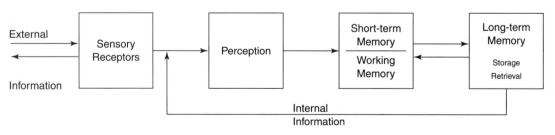

FIGURE 33.2  Illustration of an information processing model.

## Long-Term Memory Component

The acquisition of knowledge and the means to employ it occur within the storage and retrieval subsystems of the long-term memory component. Information is encoded into the knowledge base of the storage subsystem according to various representations (i.e., declarative and procedural knowledge), whereas the retrieval subsystem uses cognitive abilities to employ knowledge (i.e., differentiation and integration).

The storage subsystem is where coded knowledge is assimilated into a learner's existing knowledge base. A knowledge base can be described as an associative network of concepts (or schemas) that varies according to the amount, organization, and accessibility of an individual's knowledge. Amount refers to the actual volume of knowledge coded in memory, organization implies the structural connections and associations of that knowledge, and accessibility refers to the processes used in servicing the knowledge base. The latter two forms of knowledge are those that separate an expert from a novice. That is, a large amount of knowledge is not the key to expert performance, but rather the ability to both find and employ knowledge appropriately.

## Artificial Intelligence

The mind can be viewed as similar to a computer (e.g., the IP model) and vice-versa—the computer can be modeled after our developing understanding of the human mind. Artificial intelligence (AI) is a field in computer science that has been working since the middle 1960s on efforts to model mental processes and has had some reasonable success. It is based on computer logic, and the computer is taught a number of rules to which it adheres in order to make decisions at each step in the analysis-synthesis process. Recent AI-based models of neural functions allows the computer to see edge detail in modeling vision systems and to pick up an egg with a sensitive feedback system similar to the human neurological system.

The well-publicized chess match in 1996 between Big Blue (a mainframed chess software program developed by IBM and associates) and a world-class chess master is an excellent example of AI. It was a close contest until the human adapted his playing style to take advantage of the rigid rules that the computer was using in its game. The human still won the chess match, but by the narrowest margin ever. This may fore-shadow the future progress possible in mental modeling by computer software design.

## Intelligent Tutor Systems

The need for individual diagnoses and prescription has been present for years in American schools and has been given added impetus through the individualizing capabilities of the microcomputer. Intelligent tutor systems (ITS) software design methodology provides a level of intelligence adequate to measure students' achievement level and to prescribe the appropriate remediation to facilitate the student's mastery of instructional content. For those students who lack the self-regulation capability to make accurate instructional decisions, an ITS can be designed to provide a depth of instruction to match their needs and performance level.

An example of a basic ITS tutor for mathematics is the BUGGY program, which is based on the detailed analysis of mathematical mistakes made by students and how to correct them. More than 232 bugs (mistakes) in the subtraction of two- and three-digit numbers can be remediated by the computer-based tutor. The tutor is designed to respond intelligently to the bugs, or mistakes, that are made and to remediate specific problems.

Another ITS is the MAIS system, which can respond accurately to a student's past performance and offer at the moment adaptive instruction. The main decision-making process for the MAIS is provided by Bayesian statistics (Tennyson & Breuer, 1993), which utilize the probability of prior success combined with the probability of present success to predict when the student has had enough instruction on a particular topics to achieve the learning goal. This type of intelligent tutor overcomes the limitations of the novice in making accurate judgments, based on successfully learning the present material, about when to go on to the next section.

## Instructional Learning Systems

The cognitive approach to learning research has resulted in a number of attempts to develop comprehensive instructional learning systems (ILS); for example, the WICAT system. As implemented in Minnesota K–8 programs, WICAT is a large program that delivers the major curricular content of a school. It has a track record of success in providing instruction at a level equal to or better than conventional instruction, with a rather substantial initial investment that is recovered over the years of its use. Although WICAT lacks much in individual flexibility and creativity, it does deliver English, mathematics, and other curricular subjects, on a reasonable level of quality, in place of or in cooperation with the traditional teacher.

## *Weaknesses of Cognitive Paradigm*

The weaknesses of the cognitive paradigm include the assumption that the computer and human mind are similar—in fact they may be two totally unrelated systems serving similar functions, and what goes on in the mind of the learner is of the highest importance to instruction—when in reality the lack of a breakfast may be a much more important environmental concern than any cognitive memory function. The ability of research to deal with the multiple variables that are involved in education go far beyond the limitations of the cognitive paradigm. The investigations of situated cognition that emphasize the contextual aspects of the cognitive experience are recent attempts to consider the ecology of education along with the cognitive and behavioral aspects.

## Constructivism Paradigm: Is the Locus of Learning Primarily in the Mind?

The constructivism paradigm appears to be moving to a dominant position in educational technology research today. In direct contrast to the behavioral paradigm, constructivism holds that learners use their existing mental structures to form or construct a new idea or problem and knowledge. For example, the Piagetian model states that this understanding is accomplished through a process of fitting the new information into the existing knowledge structure (assimilation) and/or by revising the existing knowledge structure (accommodation). The restructuring of existing knowledge structures is the central focus of constructivist thinking, with the educational process changed to match this model. The constructivist emphasis since the 1930s has held that the child, from the youngest age, seeks to make sense of the surrounding world through the process of constructing better and always more complicated mental models of what he or she perceives as reality. Once neurological growth is well along in the womb, the unborn child begins to hear the sounds of the mother and the surrounding world. Touch is also active in unborn infants, as they have already started to explore their world by pushing, moving, and touching the limits of their environment.

Furthermore, constructivists emphasize the role of social interactions (e.g., student to student, teacher to student, and student to media) as influencing what students learn. Educational constructivists differ in the degree to which they ascribe knowledge construction to the student. On the one hand, certain constructivists view mental models as reflective of external realities; on the other hand, some constructivists see no independent reality external to the mental model of the individual. However, for educational purposes, most constructivists agree on the following attributes of instructional design for a learning environment: students are active in constructing their own knowledge, and social interactions are important to knowledge construction.

The Logo computer language is a good example of both the positive and negative aspects of the constructivism paradigm as it is applied to education. Researchers at the Massachusetts Institute of Technology (MIT) in the early 1970s developed Logo as a way for young children to construct mathematical meaning by creating drawings on a computer (Papert, 1980, 1990). In Logo, the student writes a program to direct an imaginary or actual turtle to draw pictures. These pictures are run by typing the words that were their titles, and they could also be made into larger pictures by combining the Logo words in different ways. Logo allows the young child to construct pictures for words and then to creatively combine those pictures to draw even more complex pictures. Research testing the basic constructs of Logo has shown some gains in specific cognitive skills such as mathematical problem solving but not in general transferable skills. Logo is, and remains, a good example of the constructivism paradigm in action.

The latest multimedia tools, such as *Linkway Live* for PCs and *HyperStudio* for Macintoshes, allow the student to construct meaning during the multimedia writing experience. HyperStudio allows the integration of text, still pictures, sound, video, and animation on a page. The student plans a presentation, using a storyboard to show graphics in miniature and a script next to each graphic. Then, the final graphics are constructed on a card (page) by using the integrated paint program. Pictures can be imported directly as paint files and placed on the background, or they can be imported as graphic objects on any level in the foreground. The use of multiple levels, similar to a computer-aided drafting (CAD) program, allows graphic objects to overlay each other and also to be animated where they pass in front of and behind other objects.

The student has to construct information by planning a presentation, collecting the information from diverse sources, and matching still pictures or live video to the text. The final multimedia product can become part of a student's portfolio and is a unique example of the constructivism process. The student has to reorganize new information and integrate it into the thinking process through the use of technology.

Another example of a constructivism-based instructional program is the *Jasper Woodbury* mathematical series, which uses computer-controlled video experiences to provide the contextual information that much math instruction lacks. The learners have to find the relevant information that is embedded in the context, such as the time and distance for a river trip. Once they understand the river scenario, they then solve a multistep math problem, using authentic information from the river. The computer controls the laser disk player and allows immediate access to critical information as the students construct their solution to the distance and time problem.

## *Weaknesses of the Constructivism Paradigm*

The weakness of the constructivism position is that it deals with only one aspect of computer instructional interaction—those interactions that are going on from the viewpoint of the individual who is constructing meaning from the exchange of information. The teacher is considered to be a resource to the instruction, but in many cases the teacher has to become the major information source—not just a guide. From a social perspective, the teacher is pictured as a required mediator of knowledge, when in fact there may be a number of mentor situations to consider. From the Russian social constructivist viewpoint, the teacher is needed to mediate the knowledge and to serve as a mentor and scaffolding assistant to the developing learner, but in reality these functions may be accomplished by other means (programmed instruction, help screens, intelligent tutors, etc.). The expectation that the novice learner can make accurate judgments in his or her learning may also have its limitations.

## CBI System Design: Where Do We Go Now with Technology?

The use of computer technology in all areas of education has expanded immensely since the 1960s. Compared to other educational media, computer technology offers several advantages in an educational environment. The interactive capabilities of computer-based instruction (CBI) are attractive to learners because they allow the individual to become an active partner in the learning process, resulting in increased interest and motivation. Furthermore, instruction and testing can be individualized to meet the needs of the individual learner, and students can pace and manage themselves according to their specific rate of learning. The flexibility offered by CBI makes it an invaluable tool for delivering instruction and administering tests.

The first uses of computers in education began in the late 1950s and early 1960s. As Stolurow (1962) stated, the early applications of CBI involved mainly drill-and-practice lessons with large computers linked to teletype machines and electric typewriters. One such application in schools was an elementary mathematics program developed in 1964 by Patrick Suppes and Richard Atkinson of Stanford University's Institute for Mathematical Studies in the Social Sciences (IMSSS). This program provided daily arithmetic drill-and-practice lessons in the classroom on a teletype machine connected by phone lines to the main computer located at IMSSS (Suppes & Macken, 1978).

Another well-financed CBI project of the 1960s was the PLATO system, a joint effort of the National Science Foundation and Control Data Corporation managed at the University of Illinois under the direction of Donald Bitzer. The use of student terminals with display graphics and symbol capabilities provided a major improvement over earlier CBI systems (Suppes, 1979). The PLATO courseware system is still in use today for applications ranging from library use to role-playing games (Foshay, 1995).

In 1972, with funding from the National Science Foundation, Victor Bunderson at Brigham Young University began work on Time-shared, Interactive Computer-controlled Information Television (TICCIT). This system was designed to use minicomputers and modified televisions to deliver CAI lessons in English and mathematics to community college students (Suppes & Macken, 1978). Further developments in CAI in the 1970s brought continued improvements in students' terminals. Minicomputers helped reduce the high costs of CAI, but problems with communication lines, down-time, and batch-oriented processing often failed to meet the needs of students in a timely manner (Suppes, 1979).

In the later 1970s, the development of microcomputers had a major impact on the CBI movement. By using a microcomputer to deliver instruction, many of the problems associated with CBI on larger computer systems, such as the down-time dilemma, were eliminated. In addition, the devices were much less expensive than previously available computers, making CBI accessible to more students. This growth became evident in the 1980s with the increased presence of microcomputers in the schools.

During the 1980s, advances in technology continued to create increasingly powerful and efficient computers available at reduced costs. There was also a tremendous growth in educational software. According to Barron and Orwig (1995), more than 10,000 packages were produced by 700 educational software publishers providing drill-and-practice programs, tutorials, simulations, and games. Unfortunately, not all of the software available was of high quality. Often, manufacturers and purchasers were more concerned with the attractiveness and availability of the software than the educational effectiveness, suggesting a clear need for improvements in the process of evaluation (Roblyer, Edwards, & Havriluk, 1997).

A technological innovation of the 1980s that had a high level of potential in education was interactive video. When videodisk technology and computers are used together, instructional materials can be presented in a format that maximizes the motivational qualities of visual media. This format also takes advantage of the programmatic characteristics of the computer to individualize instruction and testing, thus meeting the learning needs of students. Interactive video has been successfully used in training, but educational applications are only recently becoming more prevalent.

Advantages of the more advanced and emerging computer capabilities of the 1990s include increased flexibility, greater potential for interactivity, and improved individualization of instruction. In addition, significant advances have occurred in the development of alternative ways to access the computer. Innovations in this area include touch screens, light pens, bar codes, and voice activation, as well as more commonly used joy sticks and mouse technology. In addition to making computer use more efficient and flexible, these adaptations allow persons otherwise unable to use a computer keyboard manually to have computer access through alternative input modes. Adapted switches and keyboards have also made computers accessible to almost anyone, regardless of disability.

Just as the audiovisual arena suffered from an inadequate empirical foundation in the 1960s, educational computer developers in the 1990s have seen the need for supporting technology with research. Specifically addressed was the need to bring contributions from the fields of cognitive psychology and educational research into the design of computer-based instruction. Debate over the educational effectiveness of instructional media and the ability to meaningfully research it continues in the literature (Clark, 1994; Ross, Sullivan, & Tennyson, 1992; Tennyson, 1994). According to Kozma (1994), the presence of modern technology in schools does not guarantee that it will be used wisely. However, he goes on to say that we have the capability to solve the increasing problems in education if we utilize past experience to plan for the future.

As advances in technology continue to shape and promote educational media and methods of delivering instruction, the educational experience will rapidly become more flexible, more interactive, and more individualized. Further exposure of these tools to academic scrutiny will define more clearly the extent of meaningful application and use. Needless to say, and contrary to the opinion of earlier critics of audiovisual media, technology has not replaced teachers. There is no evidence, empirical or otherwise, to support the thought that the future will be any different. Instead, advanced technology has provided teachers and special educators with new methods for delivering effective and efficient instruction and testing to address the unique needs of the individual student.

# EMERGING KNOWLEDGE BASE: INTERACTION INSTRUCTION

Imagine students who are not only capable of regulating their own learning, but who are so enthusiastic about it that they voluntarily explore new bodies of knowledge. (Jonassen, 1995, p. 5)

This quotation describes one of the dreams of teachers—to have students so taken with the educational experience that they freely explore new learning situations without prompting. This occurred during the last two days of the 1995–1996 school year in Duluth, Minnesota, when two special education students came in to explore music on the Internet. This was very unusual because those two days were teacher-only work days, and school was officially closed for the year. The two students who were working so diligently were experiencing education in one of the best ways—through personal involvement with interactive, Internet-based learning. The key component activating these students' excitement for learning was the interactive instruction provided by the Internet. It is most important to look at the requirements of interactive instruction that instill such deep involvement in students—the same students who will not sit still to learn from a teacher who is giving what students call a boring lesson.

## Interactive Instruction: Variables Linking Research and Practice

Key constructs of interactive, Internet-based instruction are learners' control, self-regulation, and continuing motivation. Once defined in measurable form as variables, they give some important insights into interactive instruction.

*Learner control* is the active manipulation of the situation, experience, or effort while under the control of the involved individual. It is based on the premise that each learner will know what is best for oneself. In the Internet example, the students could select the content from a large resource base of music.

In *self-regulation*, the individual actively receives and selects information. It is based on the premise that the more effective individuals feel they are in managing their own instruction, the better they will do.

*Continuing motivation* is the self-involvement of the individual in the activity so that the involvement itself is found to be pleasant and rewarding. The activity itself is the equivalent to the behaviorist's concept of positive reinforcement, and it is recognized cognitively as being an activity that is enjoyable to continue. The Internet was individually satisfying for the two students because finding the music made their personal internal reward system complete.

## Interactive Niches (Internet)

*Niche* is a term from biology that describes the relevant physical, social, emotional, and other characteristics of the ecology that support a living organism. The interactive niche for the two students in our example is a portion of a very potent educational ecology. They are involved in a learner-controlled process of finding new sounds and their creators (musicians, bands, etc.) on this hypermedia form of telecommunication (i.e., Internet niche). Hypermedia allows the linking of one idea (picture or text) to another, so that a person can click on one idea and go immediately to the next. The Internet niche allowed the students to self-regulate their experiences through their decisions, which are made as part of the Internet niche. The combination of control and self-regulation are the motivators that allow the students' natural interest and creativity to lead them into a cycle of continuing motivation. The computer affords these students a unique learning environment (Internet niche) that had never existed before the two students turned on the computer during that Thursday and Friday in June.

This World Wide Web Internet niche is a good example of the combined behaviorist, cognitive, and constructivist experiences that will motivate future learners. The students were in control of the learning experience, but they were using the search techniques that the teacher had provided through previous instruction. The teacher served as a mediator and a resource to the students, but the students determined the direction and content of the instruction. They were in control of their learning and were intrinsically motivated to explore new knowledge on the Web. Students sensed their effectiveness in exploring the Internet environment, and this provided them with continuing motivation to explore further; and the students interpreted their findings and captured the sounds based on their interest to either of the two students. They could also regulate the speed and direction that the net searches took, as well as the choices of topics at each new Web page. The Internet niche is a learning environment that is very responsive to the learners' choices and makes very attractive choices available to the learner. Learner's control can help the student develop the self-regulation necessary to make decisions about the music choices available on the Internet.

## Minnesota Experience: Learner Control/Self-Regulation

Minnesota continues to be in the forefront of the fast-changing integration of computers in education because of legislative support for Internet use across the state. It started with the mainframe access across Minnesota in the 1970s and then MECC site coordinators and microcomputer technology efforts in the 1980s; the 1990s have been a consummating era, with legislative funding for Internet explorations into hypermedia and interactive Internet instruction.

### Minnesota Outcome-Based Learning: Learner Oriented

The state of Minnesota in 1996 released the final document on its multiyear transition process to use outcome measures for state graduation requirements. The move in Minnesota is to update the theories and practices of education throughout the state by moving to outcome-based learning (OBL). Outcome-based learning is an effort to move from a system that measures educational inputs (salaries, time, etc.) to a statewide effort to measure educational outputs (communication, mathematics, problem solving, etc.). Graduates will have to prove their intellectual competency through a process of testing and through the production of a portfolio of work samples that demonstrates their success in such areas as the communication of technical ideas, application of mathematics in authentic situations, written communication, and other academic and intellectual skills.

The goal of Minnesota's form of OBL appears to be to move the state from a single behavioral paradigm, based on what teachers and students do in school, to a mixed model that combines cognitive and behavioral-based testing along with a constructivism portfolio. Graduation requirements for clock hours in class are replaced by measurable outcomes of the learning process. The Minnesota OBL approach is directed toward accountability, access, effectiveness, efficiency, equity, flexibility, and improved quality of education. The change to the new paradigm also resulted from new demands for training and reduced funding (Morrison, 1994). It is interesting that the portfolio will probably end up as a digital summary (computer-based) of the students' experiences. Portfolios will require a high degree of computer literacy to complete adequately.

### Learners' Control and Self-Regulation in Minnesota

The new Minnesota OBL standards for graduation appear to place control of learning more in the hands of the learner because they allow students to meet graduation requirements in a number of different ways. Although they still have to pass some basic competency tests, the Minnesota standards allow flexibility in going beyond requirements. The portfolio graduation requirement also allows students to develop and explore areas of personal interest, where they have control of the choices. Self-regulation is a more sensitive concern because of the developing nature of metacognitive skills. Teachers, peers, and computers will have to provide the cues that are required for self-regulation by the learner, and some learners have limited skills. Still, the combination of the learner's control and self-regulation is a potent mix in Minnesota that should go far in promoting the maximum educational potential of all students

## Schools and Technology: What Technology Is in Use in Minnesota?
### Early Childhood

The young child is a captive audience for the computer and the many software programs currently available. Much of the sales of microcomputers are to homes, and so a large number of software titles available to the young child are prepackaged with computers. The two- or three-year-old can easily master the mouse and can easily add the proper color of a hat to the row of four ducks in one popular program. Software in common use is *Raffi* (music to sing along to), CD books (animal characters like Lamb Chop), early literature (rhymes, naming, identify, and classification), paint programs, games (like *Munchers* and *Reading Maze*), and simple multimedia (e.g., *Story Weaver Picture Writer*).

### Elementary School

The elementary schools of Minnesota are a mixture of the haves and have-nots. Limited teacher training has controlled the speed at which the elementary schools have utilized computers for instruction, but the ease of preparing software for the younger child has made elementary school software commonly available. Some of the popular programs are word processors (e.g., *KidWriter* or *Picture Writer*), spread sheets (e.g., *Cruncher*), encyclopedias (with extensive pictures), simulations (e.g., *SimTown*), multimedia (e.g., *HyperStudio*), and some discovery programs (e.g., *Logo, Lego Logo,* and *What's the Secret?*).

## Secondary Schools

Software is more limited for the upper grades because of the complexity of development, and the multiplicity of curricular offerings. Some of the important applications are the tools like word processors (e.g., *Word* and *Works*), spreadsheets (e.g., *Excel* and *Claris*), and data bases (e.g., *DataPro*). Special software has been developed for mathematics (e.g., *Tessellations* and *Problem Solver*), biology (e.g., *Living Body*), and other specific classes. The advent of the Internet will help improve education activities in homes, as well as in the school. For example, home-based Internet systems can access the same materials as school-based systems. Also, some of the curricular materials available through the Internet are better than those in schools because of the recency of their development (e.g., there are daily cites for science-related topics). With complete home curricula available from University OnLine and courses available on Internet from other national sources, students can further enrich their studies during nonschool hours.

Another example is the Edison Project, which uses the infusion of technology as the catalyst for change in education. The project takes over management of the school system and then adds technology in the form of computers to each classroom. Significant improvements in basic skills have been reported, but the project has been criticized for using computers for drill and practice. High-level computer use and improvement in high-level thinking have yet to be seen.

## Colleges and Universities

Colleges and universities have also seen change from a paradigm shift in the last few years. Higher education is moving away from entrepreneurial-populist principles and moving in the direction of greater emphasis on quality research and instruction (Foshay, 1995). As the change is just taking place, a number of strategies are put forward as ways to influence the process: (1) focus on the customer, (2) demand quality, (3) build from collaboration, (4) utilize technology to the fullest, and (5) recognize the power of accountability measures.

The University of Minnesota has been a leader in the digital revolution in schools since the publishing of the Gopher server and search software. Currently, the university is a center for the development of Web66, an educational Internet access system that allows nontechnical construction of Internet sites; it serves as a valuable training project by providing the expertise for schools to set up their own Internet servers. The university set up the first elementary school in Minnesota to be on the Internet and have the Web66 Internet Cookbook published.

# FUTURE THEORY, RESEARCH, AND PRACTICE WITH COMPUTERS

> Fifteen students are scattered about the room in groups of threes and fours; a dozen of their classmates are doing scientific fieldwork at a nearby state forest, scanning plant samples for a multimedia presentation with a hand held digital camera. The rest of the kids are logged on to school from home or elsewhere. In the classroom, one group of students is exploring a simulated excavation site of an ancient Greek City, while a few others join a group of students from England on a virtual-reality bike expedition to study local flora in the Yucatan in Mexico. The teacher is a guide on their journeys, not just a lecturer. (Winn, 1990, p. 22).

Although this scene represents a technology-based future for education that was described in the early 1990s, such a possibility is readily available in some schools today. Schools like those in Eagan and Edina, Minnesota, have all the technology in place to enact the scene today. Yet, other schools a few miles down the road have only the teacher laptops and some out-dated Apple II computers for drill and practice because of financial limitations. We have pieces of the future already present in our society in schools like those in Eagan and Edina, which are well funded by a combination of public and private sources. What have we seen in these future schools in the way of teaching, learning, and materials that we should be aware of when planning and implementing learning niches today?

## Teaching Beyond 2000: Teachers' Role in Intelligent Mediation

The teachers' role in the 1990s has already been redefined as a mediator within the constructivist learning process, but the future will not be that simple. With the development of information infrastructure across the globe, teachers will mediate a learning niche without the barriers of time and distance (Salomon et al., 1991). With the wide range of students' social, emotional, and intellectual development, the teacher needs to be more intelligent and to utilize artificial intelligence in providing a full range of learning choices as part of curricular planning. Learners with mature capabilities can benefit from the teacher who provides nurturing and cognitive guidance, whereas the immature learner needs a teacher who provides more in the way of direct instructional guidance and direct instruction. Intelligent computer diagnostic tools and tutor programs will allow the teacher to focus on creativity and adaptations in curricula.

## Distributed Learning: Learning from a Variety of Locations and Sources

Distance learning will be transformed into *distributed learning* through the ongoing development of global communications and high-performance computing (Salomon et al., 1991). Distributed learning takes place in the new instructional niches that are available through new forms of expression such as knowledge webs, virtual communities, synthetic environments, and sensory immersion. Knowledge webs use telecommunication to provide distributed access to experts, archival resources, authentic environments, and shared investigations. Virtual communities supplement face-to-face interactions with support from people who share common "joys and trials" and give future learners access to new people and experiences and shared ideas, humor, and fellowship. Synthetic environments are learning niches that do not yet exist but are shared synthetic environments that extend our experiences beyond what we can encounter in the real world. Sensory immersion is an extension of the learning niche created by the computer development of artificial realities, and it allows the learner to see the patterns and relationships in large amounts of information gathered from diverse sources.

Distributed learning through technology will be an accepted instructional method because of the increasing economics of schooling and the need for one teacher to handle an increasing student load to meet efficiencies of scale. Student-teacher ratios of 50 to 1 will be common but will be compensated for by intelligent tools, like computer-based personal assistants, that are designed to match each student's needs. As computers decrease in cost in the future and the simple networked computer for each learner becomes a reality, individualized instruction may become possible in future education. Until that time, we will deal with the small-group and large-group capabilities of the microcomputer, as we presently know it.

## Classes and Schools: What Do Schools and Classes Afford Students?

A physical school building will still exist beyond 2000, but it won't be necessary (Winn, 1990). With computer technology that is cheap and invisible in the future, the classroom can be located where it can have the most impact on the learner. With distance learning the norm, the only limit in the learning experience will be the creativity of the instructor and student: "Classroom walls will become more permeable, boundaries between community and school reduced" (p. 39). In the Ojibwe sense, the whole community will be part of the education of every developing child. The experiential learning of the 1990s will mature into community-based cooperative learning, in which students will, for example, assist the city government in researching development options, such as the GLEAM (Great Lakes Environmental Action Mentors) team of students from Anoka High School. The teacher could be a University of Minnesota professor one day, a computer tutor the next, and the city zoning commissioner the next—with students providing valuable services at all levels.

## Reading, Writing, and Mathematics: Hooks, Zines, Pines, and Vines

Reading, writing, and mathematical skills will become even more important in the time beyond 2000, when intellectual production will exceed manufacturing production in America. The book will take on new hypermedia forms (hooks) that are adaptable to students' choices of plot, characters, settings, and actions—not unlike the game of *Dungeons and Dragons*. Magazines (zines) designed for networks are just starting to take on an Internet form of their own and will mature to integrate learners' control of sound, text, and graphics. Newspapers (pines) will be delivered and printed in the home, with learners' control over subjects, story type, and extent of coverage, but allow hyperlinking to all relevant supportive information through intelligent agents in software form. These agents will provide research and retrieval functions to support any direction of investigation that is interesting to a particular student because of his or her individual differences. A fully accessible video interaction (vine) at each computer will allow access to any and all media forms on demand, with the teachers providing the level of mediation required for development of the individual's intellect and discipline. Mathematics will be integrated into all activities, as it is in real life, with the emphasis on ever-increasing levels of applied mathematics in business, industry, and sports. Computer vines will become three-dimensional through technology, where students can project their presence into any experience and through visual, tactile, and olfactory feedback experience such things as the whales' pod type of family structure.

## Is the Medium the Message: Instructional Design in the Future

The start of the media revolution and the criticism of scientific reductionism can be dated to 1966, when Marshal McLuhan declared, "In a culture like ours, long accustomed to splitting and dividing all things as a means of control, it is sometimes a bit of a shock to be reminded that, in operation and practical fact, the medium is the message" (McLuhan, 1966, p. 23). The use of the computer in education has allowed a true McLuhan type of extension of ourselves, as we come to better use this new and developing digital technology. It has restructured our work and our play and will continue to restructure our schools. We cannot believe that the message brought to us by the computer is the ecological change that this powerful mental tool evokes. McLuhan made us aware of the changes wrought by the technology of his time, but he could not have predicted the effects that were triggered by miniaturization of the silicone chip.

The instructional design industry is also changing, with movement from the behavior paradigm of the past to the cognitive paradigm of the 1980s and the constructivist paradigm of the 1990s (Salomon, 1993). The more complex understanding of mental processes resulting from the cognitive paradigm has led to sophisticated software that can be run on microcomputers. The adoption of constructivist models will make software more user-controlled and allow more creative individual use of software tools.

## Systemic Approach: Theory and Paradigm Considerations

A new systemic approach to research and practice is required, one that considers the educational experience in all of its complexity and keeps intact all of the variables that are involved at each level. We can no longer just look at the behavior that students exhibit their internal mental state, what they construct, or the computer environment in which they are functioning. We must consider the Gestalt of all of the factors that affect the ecology of learning.

The term *niche* has been introduced to help us understand more clearly the new systemic approach to educational paradigms. The educational ecology is made up of a number of niches (activity spaces), which contain the behavioral, cognitive, biological, and constructivism attributes that are relevant to computer-based instruction. Learning experiences are filled with niches in niche spaces, in which the dynamic interactions of using computers take place. Thus new systemic approach will unify the behavioral, cognitive, constructivism, and social viewpoints through the use of multiple, integrated variables that represent more of the realistic educational situation in niche space.

## Technology Tools: Cost Is No Longer a Limitation

The future of technology in education appears to be unlimited, with microcomputers providing a wonderful tool for individual students. The student will be able to utilize the distributed knowledge of the Internet with the touch of a keyboard, a pen, or voice access in the future. For example, the price of the calculator has been reduced from the 1965 high of $799, to the 1975 Texas Instrument for $29, to the 1995 Scientific for $9. This economy of scale has provided the financial incentive to drive the computer revolution of the 1980s and 1990s. By 1978 the cost of the microcomputer was low enough to support efforts by Apple Computer to market the Apple II to the schools in quantity. We will see similar major cost reductions in educational computing. The 200 MHz computer that is capable of running full-frame video will drop to prices that allow their use as a standard teaching computer by the year 2000. Each classroom will be able to afford a computer for the teacher and at least one matching for every four students—in addition to having access to computer labs and digital media centers. The cost of wiring the schools of America seems high now, but in just a few years the network power will pay for itself in better education and in improved national output from our schools.

## Cognitive Prescriptions: Practical Versus Theoretical Research

America is a recognized leader in technology and the creative research that supports that technological success. But the Japanese have far surpassed us in the art of taking an existing idea, whether it is education or the flat-screen display, and developing it into a successful application through applied research. The previous successes that were mentioned, such as *Reader Rabbit* and *Jasper Woodbury*, were accomplished through a conscientious effort to apply research to the application of the computer in the classroom. We may see a resurgence in the applied research effort in America—as manufacturers see the value of the financial return for the research dollars—as it becomes obvious that education can be improved through the use of technology that is carefully researched for specific applications.

Schools cannot stop the information revolution that is changing the face of America. They can, however, willfully put computers into education in ways that are most efficient and effective, based on sound research that is linked to educational theory (Tennyson, 1988, 1995). Each educational application in the classroom has to be studied in its own right, in place of the computer laboratory mentality of the past. Instead of throwing money at the problems of education and purchasing another computer laboratory, schools need to utilize past research to move from theory to practice. We need to move from theory to prescriptions that work in the niche of the individual student. Schools of the future will be improved through the utilization of technology to facilitate the construction of new knowledge. Minnesota is a leader in using WANs (wide area networks) to connect the state's schools and has hosted many conferences and studies of networking. The state has access to the TIES system through its networking from the major universities, and Web66 is designed to be communication-oriented so that students and teachers can use the network interactively. Schools that are members of the system can post a project that they have underway or can participate in any of the ongoing projects that are now running. The legislative and human investment in computers in education will pay off in Minnesota in a few short years with creative increases in intellectual property.

## CONCLUSION

One of the common visions for computer-based instruction is to use the computer to individually prescribe and deliver instruction to meet students' individual differences. While schools have purchased a large number of computers in the decade of the 1980s, financial constraints have kept the numbers at an average of 1 computer for every 10 students (Kulik & Kulik, 1991). The reality of computer use in America is that we will probably have enough machines to facilitate small-group instruction for all students but only be able to individualize in part of the school day, when students have access to a computer lab. Small groups of students working together on one machine will be the norm of school computer use, except for those portions of the day when individual use can be facilitated by the availability of the computer lab, with 30 or more machines for a whole class.

The finding of a 1992 conference on libraries in Australia is that the library is becoming the true learning center of the campus or school. With the move from print media to digital media and from physical research to online research, the library is becoming the digital online source for students from diverse regional, cultural, and educational backgrounds. Although there is no consensus on the direction that libraries need to take, there is consensus that the digital revolution is taking place, leading to Internet access and CD data base library services in order to stay competitive (Barron & Orwig, 1995).

The separation between our libraries and our communication networks are becoming fuzzy as the digital revolution continues. These fuzzy edges change our concept of education to a process of constructing knowledge through library-accessible information. The library's new role is to serve a worldwide user group by becoming a fluid and dynamic source of information through networks and the Internet. Greater freedom of access with electronic networks and cooperative sharing of resources, such as the Fargo-Moorhead library system of Minnesota, can be shown to have great promise. The Minnesota and North Dakota high schools, colleges, and universities have a combined library structure to make access easier. A common catalogue allows access from multiple locations and makes both paper and digital information access a present reality.

School administrators need to meet the demands of the new technologies that are revolutionizing the ways in which students learn. If administrators are going to survive into the next decade, they are going to have to recognize the irrelevance of smokestack (industrial) education and move forward by using information age approaches. Some of the suggestions are to: (1) use Channel 1 to teach visual literacy, (2) use hyper-navigation to learn critical thinking, and (3) design environments for student-centered learning and shared decision making (Roblyer et al., 1997).

The Minnesota OBL efforts should go far in moving most Minnesota schools in the direction of student-centered learning by giving them choices of topics beyond the basics. Shared decision making has support from the Minnesota legislature in the form of putting in-service financing into teachers' hands, but further efforts will require cooperation from school boards, teachers, and their groups.

Finally, teachers have been educated from 5 to 20 years in the past, when the behaviorist paradigm was in place. Schools may have to utilize staff development funds and time to facilitate the transition of staff from the reductionist, behavioral paradigm to the constructivism paradigm. Meeting in small groups to discuss and rethink the nature of the educational enterprise seems to facilitate the transition process. The Minnesota legislature has passed laws that designate a portion of state funds specifically for in-service education. These funds are totally administered by teachers and are used to update staff members on the digital revolution, however slow it may proceed in education.

To help present our topic in this chapter, we have deliberately used the state of Minnesota as our example. Our goal is to blend theory with application. Computer technology is a rapidly changing field that makes certain concrete hardware and software techniques and methods obsolete in a short period of time. Thus, we feel that the use of computers in education and school psychology should be based on learning theory rather than hardware and software. For example, good writing is possible with any tool that records words. A computer may improve the efficiency of writing but not the quality. That is true also for educational uses of computers. The computer is a tool that can enhance existing practice and perhaps even introduce new practices. We are therefore arguing for both theory foundation and experience to help us move ahead in improving education.

# REFERENCES

Ausubel, D. P., Novak, J. D., & Hanesian, H. (1978). *Educational psychology: a cognitive view* (2nd ed). New York: Holt, Rinehart & Winston.

Barron, A. E., & Orwig, G. W. (1995). *Multimedia technologies for training*. Englewood, CO: Libraries Unlimited.

Banathy, B. H. (1987). Instructional systems design. In R. Gagné & R. Glaser (Eds.), *Instructional technology: Foundations* (pp. 85–112). Hillsdale, NJ: Erlbaum.

Bransford, J. D. (1979). *Human cognition*. Belmont, CA: Wadsworth.

Breuer, K., & Kummer, R. (1990). Cognitive effects from process learning with computer-based simulations. *Computers in Human behavior, 6,* 69–81.

Clark, R. E. (1983). Reconsidering research on learning from media. *Review of Educational Research, 53,* 445–459.

Clark, R. E. (1994). Media and method. *Educational Technology Research and Development, 42,* 21–31.

Enkenberg, J. (1995). Complex technology-based learning environment. In R. D. Tennyson & A. E. Barron (Eds.), *Automating instructional design: Computer-based development and delivery tools* (pp. 245–264). Berlin: Springer.

Foshay, W. R. (1995, April). The problem with ISD models. Paper presented at the meeting of the National Society for Performance and Instruction, Chicago.

Hannafin, M. J. (1995). Open-ended learning environments: Foundations, assumptions, and implications for automated design. In R. D. Tennyson & A. E. Barron (Eds.), *Automating instructional design: Computer-based development and delivery tools* (pp. 101–130). Berlin: Springer.

Jonassen, D. H. (1995). *Mindtools for schools*. New York: Macmillan.

Kozma, R. B. (1994). Will media influence learning? Reframing the debate. *Educational Technology Research and Development, 42*(2), 7–19.

Kulik, C. C., & Kulik, J. A. (1987). Review of recent research literature on computer-based instruction. *Contemporary Educational Psychology, 12,* 222–230.

Kulik, C. C., & Kulik, J. A. (1991). Effectiveness of computer-based instruction: An updated analysis. *Computers in Human Behavior, 7,* 75–94.

Mayer, R. E. (1981). *The promise of cognitive psychology*. San Francisco: Freeman.

McLuhan, M. (1966). *Media is the message*. New York: New Books.

Morrison, G. (1994). The media effects question: Unresolvable or asking the right question. *Educational Technology Research and Development*, *42*(2) 41–44.

Papert, S. (1980). *Mindstroms*. New York: Basic Books.

Papert, S. (1990). Introduction by Seymour Papert. In I. Harel (Ed.), *Constructionist learning* (pp. 1–8). Boston: MIT Media Laboratory.

Reigeluth, G. M. (1992). New directions for educational technology. In E. Scanlon & T. O'Shea (Eds.), *New directions in educational technology* (pp. 251–276).

Ringstaff, C. (1993). Trading places: When students become the experts. *Apple Education Review*, *3*.

Roblyer, M. D., Edwards, J., & Havriluk, M. A. (1997). *Integrating educational technology into teaching*. Columbus, OH: Merrill.

Ross, S. M., Sullivan, H., & Tennyson, R. D. (1992). Educational technology: Four decades of research and theory. *Educational Technology Research and Development*, *40*(2), 5–8.

Salomon, G. (1993). No distribution without individuals' cognition. In G. Salomon (Ed.), *Distributed cognitions* (pp. 111–138). New York: Cambridge University Press.

Salomon, G., Perkins, P. N., & Globerson, T. (1991). Partners in cognition: Extending human intelligence with intelligent technologies. *Educational Researcher*, *20*(3), 2–9.

Sternberg, R. J. (1986). *The triarchic mind: A new theory of human intelligence*. New York: Penguin.

Stolurow, L. M. (1962). Implications of current research and future trends. *Journal of Educational Research*, *55*, 519–527.

Suppes, P.. (1979). Current trends in computer-assisted instruction. In M. C. Yovits (Ed.), *Advances in computers* (Vol. 18, pp. 173–229). New York: Academic Press.

Tennyson, R. D. (1988). An instructional strategy planning model to improve learning and cognition. *Computers in Human Behavior*, *4*, 35–45.

Tennyson, R. D. (1990). Cognitive learning theory linked to instructional theory. *Journal of Structural Learning*, *10*, 249–258.

Tennyson, R. D. (1994). Knowledge base for automated instructional system development. In R. D. Tennyson (Ed.), *Automating instructional design, development, and delivery* (pp. 29–60). Berlin: Springer.

Tennyson, R. D. (1995). The impact of the cognitive science movement on instructional design fundamentals. In B. Seels (Ed.), *Instructional design fundamentals: A reconsideration* (pp. 113–136). Englewood Cliffs, NJ: Educational Technology.

Tennyson, R. D., & Breuer, K. (1993). Computer-based training: Advancements from cognitive science. In G. M. Piskurich (Ed.), *The ASTD handbook of instructional technology* (pp. 24.1–24.12). New York: McGraw-Hill.

Tennyson, R. D., & Elmore, R. (1997). Learning theory foundations for instructional design. In R. D. Tennyson, F. Schott, N. Seel, & S. Dijkstra (Eds.), *Instructional design: International perspectives, Vol. I: Theory and research* (pp. 55–78). Hillsdale, NJ: Erlbaum.

Tennyson, R. D., & Rasch, M. (1988). Linking cognitive learning theory to instructional prescriptions. *Instructional Science*, *17*, 369–385.

Winn, W. (1990). Some implications of cognitive theory for instructional design. *Instructional Science*, *19*, 53–69.

SECTION **5**

# SCHOOL
# PSYCHOLOGICAL
# INTERVENTIONS:
# FOCUS ON
# STAFF, PROGRAMS, AND ORGANIZATIONS

•

## CHAPTER 34

# PROGRAM PLANNING AND EVALUATION: PRINCIPLES, PROCEDURES, AND PLANNED CHANGE

ROBERT J. ILLBACK
*R.E.A.C.H. of Louisville, Inc.*
JOSEPH E. ZINS
*University of Cincinnati*
CHARLES A. MAHER
*Rutgers University*

Many school psychologists have become involved in leadership roles in planning and evaluating educational services and programs (Illback & Kalafat, 1997; Maher & Illback, 1984). To perform such functions in a competent manner, practitioners can benefit from knowledge and skills in program planning, evaluation, and planned organizational change (Maher & Illback, 1982). Such knowledge and skill can also enhance the practitioner's ability to function effectively in educational and related work settings by increasing awareness of program management and change processes within these human service organizations (Illback, 1991).

In this chapter we provide an overview of important principles and procedures of program planning and evaluation in the human services arena, with particular reference to educational services, programs, and settings. We emphasize that planning and evaluation activities are related integrally to management and decision-making processes in human service organizations. Information obtained from these activities is useful to the extent that it informs decision making. Thus, central concepts, terminology, strategies, and methods from program planning and evaluation are reviewed, followed by discussion of the relationship of planning and evaluation activities to planned organizational change. We conclude with an examination of the role and function of

school psychologists in planning and evaluation functions and the approaches to overcoming barriers and resistances that may occur when school psychologists try to fulfill this role.

## HISTORICAL DEVELOPMENT OF PROGRAM PLANNING AND EVALUATION

Few scientific and technical fields can trace their exact points of origin, and program evaluation is no exception. Some writers (e.g., Cronbach, 1980) trace the origins of program evaluation to the 1860s, when Thomas Hobbs and his associates were involved in data collection to identify and address social problems of the day, particularly morbidity and mortality. However, it was not until the 1950s that program evaluation, conceived as a systematic method of empirical inquiry, came to the fore in education and human services.

Flaherty and Morrell (1978) propose four reasons for the evolution of program planning and program evaluation: (1) greater requirements for accountability in publicly funded programs, (2) increased interest among social scientists in social relevance, (3) increasing scarcity of resources for social science, and (4) expansion of methods appropriate for applied evaluative research. The field began to grow rapidly during the period following World War II. During the 1950s, federal monies were expended on large-scale projects such as urban and rural renewal, preventive health, housing, delinquency, and family planning. With these expansive social change efforts came demands for knowledge about outcomes and program effectiveness. The emerging technologies of evaluation, including survey research and multivariate statistical analysis techniques, were used to supply data on program efficiency and effectiveness to federal officials (Rossi & Freeman, 1993).

## Social and Health Programs

During the 1960s, a proliferation of social programs occurred in the United States. There was increased emphasis on developing highly specialized programs, targeted toward a broad range of social problems. This decade saw the birth of the categorical approach to funding and service delivery in education and the human services (Hobbs, 1981). In this paradigm, selected, high-risk populations of individuals were identified as needing intervention and categorized or classified in terms of diagnostic constructs or eligibility criteria (e.g., extent of disadvantage). Programs were designed and implemented to address the identified needs of all eligible (entitled) parties. Especially emphasized in categorical programming were the oppressed, disadvantaged, poverty-stricken, and disabled (Attkisson & Broskowski, 1978). It was also during this time that specialized services in community mental health, social services, and education (including school psychological services) became well established (Hobbs, 1981). As human service programs proliferated, program evaluation became a growth industry as a function of increased concerns and demands for data on the part of administrators, funders, and society as a whole. The evolution of program evaluation was therefore tied to contemporary social, political, and financial circumstances.

Unfortunately, large-scale social programs often seemed to exacerbate social problems; questions immediately arose about the wisdom of many of these endeavors. Duplication of effort, overlapping of personnel responsibilities, maldistribution of human and finance resources, ineffective practices, and evaluation findings of nonsignificance called into question the continued expansion of government-mandated entitlement programs. In this context, some evaluative efforts were framed in adversarial terms (Haveman, 1987).

For the most part, however, evaluation focused on understanding the impact of social programs. The pioneering work of Donald Campbell (1969) is an excellent example of this perspective. Campbell's conception of social reforms as experiments and the accompanying technology that he and others promoted, had a profound effect on the shape and evolution of social and educational programs (and their evaluation). Before this work, most programs were evaluated by using restrictive evaluation models in a traditional research perspective (i.e., controlled experimentation). Campbell and his colleagues (Cook & Campbell, 1976) emphasized innovation in design through quasi-experimental models (e.g., time series and single-subject designs, creative use of design elements, and innovative statistical analysis) and the need for relevance in designing evaluations. This perspective fostered experimentation in the service of societal improvement.

Whereas Campbell's work remained tied to the experimental model, the field of evaluation has moved to more broad-based and pragmatic approaches, which may or may not incorporate a high degree of control. Thus Cronbach (1982) states,

> The central purpose of evaluation differs from that of basic social research, and evaluations fit into a different institutional and political context. The strategy of evaluative research therefore requires special consideration. Logic is necessarily the same in all disciplined inquiry, but the translation of logic into procedure should depend upon context, purpose, and expected payoff. Many recommendations appropriate for long-term programs of scientific research are ill suited to evaluation. (pp. 1–2)

With the 1970s, the continued expansion of social programs came under closer scrutiny. There was a continuing commitment on the part of legislators and professionals to strengthen and preserve the integrity of efforts implemented during the 1950s and the 1960s. However, the convergence of social and political pressures (e.g., the Vietnam War), combined with a huge inflationary crisis, emerged as powerful forces for cost containment and the curtailment of large-scale entitlements. Program evaluation and the interrelated area of program planning became tools for the reexamination of programmatic efforts and the identification of new methods for attaining worthy goals. Increased attention was directed toward fiscal responsibility, with the result that programs were designed more modestly. Also, jurisdiction for programmatic efforts was gradually turned over to local and state governments and agencies through block grants (the New Federalism). All of these factors contributed to the recognition of program evaluation as an essential management function (Rossi & Freeman, 1993).

More recently, fiscal responsibility has become the watchword in human services, especially health care (DeMers & Bricklin, 1995; Frank, Sullivan, & DeLeon, 1994). Following a number of years in which health (including mental health) services grew as a percentage of the gross national product and costs appeared to be out of control, numerous cost containment strategies have been implemented or attempted. These include new organizational structures (e.g., health maintenance organizations), credentialing procedures and limitations on eligible providers (e.g., preferred provider networks), standards for practice (e.g., number of eligible units of service), and related strategies (e.g., capitation). All of these methods can be conceived as part of managed care, and all rely on elaborate information systems that seek to relate services to outcomes and cost (especially the latter).

## Educational Programs

Parallel processes have occurred in public education. For example, the curricular reform movement of the late 1960s and early 1970s gave initial impetus to planning and evaluation in education (Borish & Jemelka, 1982). Beginning with the Sputnick launch in 1957, substantial changes were seen in curricular methods and materials across the content areas of education, particularly in mathematics and the sciences. Planning and evaluation of curricular materials became more closely linked, and the strategies used for program planning and evaluation became more available to local school districts (Scriven, 1967).

During the 1970s, a number of educational entitlement programs came into being, such as Title I (now Chapter I) of the Elementary and Secondary Education Act (ESEA) of 1965 and the Education for All Handicapped Children Act of 1975 (Public Law 94-142), now the Individuals with Disabilities Education Act (IDEA). These and similar landmark legislative initiatives mandated that school districts incorporate program planning and evaluation activities into their organizational routines. School professionals, including school psychologists, of necessity became involved in the data collection and analysis process. While initially much of the focus was on establishing the need for services and justifying reimbursement, interest in documenting services and relating them to outcomes has gradually increased.

Beginning with the publication of *A Nation at Risk* in 1983 (National Commission on Excellence in Education), the education community has been inundated with reports documenting public education's shortcomings. Most recently, the National Education Goals Panel (1991) has made numerous broad-scale recommendations for standardization of standards. During this turbulent period, blame for the "education crisis" has been attributed to a wide range of factors: (1) the decline of family and community support systems; (2) the lack of educational standards; (3) inadequate teacher preparation and the changing demographics of the teaching profession; (4) deficient school leadership, especially on the part of school principals; (5) outmoded curricular materials and instructional methods; (6) inappropriate testing and assessment; (7) school size, organization, and governance; and (8) any number of similar dimensions (see Tharinger et. al., 1996, for a more comprehensive discussion of education reform and its relation to psychology).

Proposed remedies for these pervasive ills have also proliferated. A partial list of school reform initiatives over the past 15 years includes (1) revisions to student testing, such as authentic assessment and portfolio approaches (Grace & Shores, 1991; Spady, 1988); (2) major revisions to the curriculum, including more precise and rigorous standards (Gandal, 1995; Lewis, 1995; National Education Standards and Improvement Council, 1993); (3) supports for teachers, including internships, mentoring programs, career ladders, merit pay, more extensive supervisory processes, and performance rewards (Fullan, 1993); (4) changes in the teacher certification process, including alternative paths to certification in subject matter areas and minimum skills testing of prospective teachers (Ball & McDiarmid, 1990); (5) school-based councils, emphasizing shared decision making and accountability (Tirozzi & Uro, 1997); (6) parental involvement programs (Christensen, Rounds, & Gorney, 1992); (7) changes to organizational structure and governance (Elmore, 1990), including such extreme measures as performance contracting with for-profit corporations for school management and the recent advent of Charter Schools (Dranda & Corwin, 1994; U.S. General Accounting Office, 1995); (8) technological innovation, including computer-assisted instruction and Internet utilization (Bell & Elmquist, 1992); and (9) integration of service delivery systems, including the concept of the school as a health service delivery system (DeMers & Bricklin, 1995). These and related reforms have prompted numerous evaluation efforts and rich opportunities for evaluation practitioners (Fullan, 1993; Illback & Kalafat, 1997; Payne, 1996; Rossi, 1995; U.S. General Accounting Office, 1989).

The field of special education is of great concern for school psychologists, who often serve in the role of assessment specialist and consultant to programs for children with disabilities. In the period following the implementation of PL 94-142, there was considerable interest in special education program evaluation (e.g., Maher & Bennett, 1984). However, a recent review by George et al. (1990) surveyed 145 school districts to assess their involvement in special education program evaluation activities. Questions concerned preplanning, who evaluates special education programs, what evaluation activities focus on, evaluative methods, criteria for judging program effectiveness, and perceived benefits of the evaluation. It was found that, beyond monitoring for compliance with state and federal regulations, program evaluation in special education has been minimal (see the example from New York City in a later section).

It is possible that there has been little impetus for evaluation because of the service entitlement that underlies this program, but it also seems likely that this is an area where school psychologists can play a role in improving services or working on special evaluative issues. For example, Fourqurean and LaCourt (1991) designed a program evaluation system to assess outcomes for special education students who had graduated or dropped out of high school. Similarly, for a program serving 84 behaviorally disturbed adolescent males, DeSouza and Sivewright (1993) developed an ecobehavioral strategy to assess the relevance of narrowly focused educational outcomes. Major program challenges that could be formulated in evaluative terms include transitional services, service quality, service integration, collaboration, parental involvement, and the regular education initiative. As traditional

roles for school psychologists such as assessment diminish (Talley & Short, 1996), expanding practice into areas of special education program planning and evaluation may provide welcome opportunities for the profession.

Another major trend in the field of evaluation has been qualitative and case study evaluation strategies (Patton, 1990). Partly as a function of concern for relevance and applicability, and also because evaluators have recognized that outcome findings in the absence of knowledge about context and process are uninterpretable, the field has sought to integrate these designs (Illback & Kalafat, 1997; Kalafat, 1996). A related trend is the increased use of single-subject methodology, with an emphasis on intrasubject (or intraprogram) variability, treatment specification, and repeated measurement. In this paradigm, it is often possible to establish a functional relationship between implementation of the intervention and change, using creative design elements (Shapiro, 1987). Interest in an action research model, which involves an ongoing series of steps following a problem-solving approach (Price & Smith, 1985) is increasing (see, e.g., Kress, Cimring, & Elias, 1997).

Currently, program planning and evaluation activities are broad-based, diverse, and integrally related to management functions. Program evaluations do not focus exclusively on establishing cause-effect relationships between and among variables through controlled experimentation, but rather they try to make judgments about program effort, effectiveness, efficiency, and adequacy, based on systematic data collection and analysis in the service of program planning (Rossi & Freeman, 1993).

## PLANNING AND EVALUATION AS METHODS OF EMPIRICAL INQUIRY

An overview of program planning and evaluation concepts, terminology, strategies, methods, and issues, with special reference to the practice of psychology in schools, is presented in this section. Initially, the concept of program is defined, followed by a discussion of the need to conceptualize and specify services clearly. Program planning approaches and their relationship to program evaluation are then described, leading to the discussion of implementation (process) evaluation. Finally, the task of assessing programmatic outcomes is described, and the section concludes with consideration of standards for school-based program evaluation practice.

## Concept of Program

For a program planning or program evaluation project to have focus, attention must first be given to defining the unit of analysis (i.e., the program to be analyzed). Programs that can be reviewed range from individualized education programs (IEPs) to classroom-, building-, or organizational-level programs. To address questions such as "How effective is the special education resource room program at Sunnyville Elementary School?" or "Do students whose families receive school-linked support services do better in school?" parameters must be established regarding what these programs encompass. Such questions as "What are the distinguishing features of the interventions to be evaluated?" and "How is the program organized?" and "What are its constituent elements?" need to be asked before more specific evaluation questions can be derived.

All human services programs are embedded in complex social and community contexts. The decision to focus on a particular program or aspect of a program must take into account the fact that it is difficult, if not impossible, to separate the program fully from its context. Nonetheless, the essential features of the program under examination must be delineated before evaluative efforts can proceed. For example, in studying the effectiveness of special education services, a question arises about whether the activities of students with disabilities in mainstream classes should be categorized as part of the special or regular education program and if they should be included in the evaluation. Should community awareness, attitudes, and involvement with persons with disabilities be considered in the program evaluation? Many schools (and school psychologists) have recently become involved in the development of school-based and school-linked health, mental health, and social services (Carlson, Tharinger, DeMers, Bricklin, & Paavola, 1996). Clarifying the nature and scope of these services and their relationship to educational processes can be perplexing. These issues need to be clarified before formulating more specific evaluation questions.

Decisions about how to categorize various services and programs in human service settings are aided by conceptual frameworks that organize thinking about programs. Maher and Bennett (1984) provide one such framework that is highly relevant to school psychology practice. Five domains of interrelated educational services are defined in this model: assessment, instructional, support (related), personnel development, and administrative services. *Assessment services* encompass programs such as pupil evaluation (individual or group testing), IEP design, and annual review processes. Essentially they involve information-gathering processes designed to enable parents and professionals to make important decisions (e.g., What needs should be addressed? In what ways? By whom? Has progress been made?). Individual and group interventions (e.g., IEPs and special and remedial programs) that result from these assessment programs are carried out through programs in the instructional services and support services domains.

*Instructional services* in this schema can be seen as the direct interventions carried out by school personnel (teachers, classroom aides, and other staff) to enhance learning, behavior, social interaction, or other child outcome domains. In the most complete sense, instruction occurs in classrooms around specific curricular material, as well as in less formal but intentional ways (e.g., in the halls, on the playground, or in the cafeteria). In addition to learning objectives, schools have (for better or worse) become increasingly responsible for the behavioral, social, and moral development of children.

*Support services* are indirect and ancillary but crucial services that enhance and support direct interventions in schools. These may include counseling and psychological services, physical and occupational therapy, speech and language therapy, special transportation, family resource and youth service centers, and any other specialized approaches designed to support the learning process. *Personnel development services* involve preservice and in-service supports designed to help educational personnel, parents, and others acquire the knowledge, skills, and attitudes that will result in improved learning and adjustment of children. Finally, *administrative services* are the organizational activities that enable schools to deliver services, including planning, budgeting, evaluating, supervising, funding, public relations, and accountability functions. In each of these domains, which serve as heuristics to organize thinking about program parameters, programmatic activity can be delineated, enabling the development of more specific evaluation questions.

Increasingly, program evaluations in schools are likely to involve questions about systems external to school settings in which the educational process is embedded, such as the family, other human service organizations, and the community as a whole (see examples in Zins, 1997). In this regard, H. B. Weiss (1988) provides a useful model for conceptualizing evaluation in the context of ecological theories of human development, highlighting the need to link what is known about family and community processes to programmatic intervention through evaluation. In recognizing the need to include these systems in evaluative efforts, evaluators are challenged by what Crowson and Boyd (1993) describe as "submerged labyrinths of disconnected and often competing organizations, incentives, and allegiances" (p. 141) and "Balkanized" stakeholders (p. 155). These authors further note that "evaluation of integrated services for children shows a history of experimentation colliding with ubiquitous problems of institutional deficiency, professional training differences, resource constraints, communication gaps, authority and turf issues, and legal and leadership problems" (pp. 152–153).

Service delivery programs can thus be seen as distinct but interdependent entities. More specifically, they are organized configurations of resources—human, informational, financial, and technological—that are designed to assist an individual, group, or organization to meet a specific need (Maher & Bennett, 1984). Programs in schools may focus on general developmental needs, prevention of difficulties, promotion of competence, or remediation of problems experienced by one or more groups or systems (e.g., children, families, teachers, and school systems). Notably, the term *problems* as used here includes (1) goals that have not been achieved, (2) opportunities or resources that have not been fully utilized, and, (3) dysfunctional states in client systems. This broadened definition of problems may enable the evaluator to refocus questions to encourage program development and improvement and emphasize the empowering nature of the process (Fetterman, Kaftarian, & Wandersman, 1996).

## Program Specification

The manner in which programmatic resources are configured or organized must be described by the evaluator before the formulation of specific evaluative questions; that is, for a program to be evaluated, it must be described in a form that is capable of being evaluated. Wholey (1979) terms this process "evaluability assessment." Determining program evaluability allows (1) an examination of a program's logic, including whether causal links have been established between program goals and activities; (2) an analysis of program operations, including the plausibility and measurability of expected events (activities); (3) identification of program design options, such as new activities or products; and (4) possible uses of program performance information.

Most fundamentally, evaluability assessment seeks well-defined programs that can be implemented and evaluated in a prescribed manner. C. H. Weiss (1973) notes, "The sins of the program are often visited on the evaluation. When programs are well-conceptualized and developed, with clearly defined goals and consistent methods of work, the lot of evaluation is relatively easy. But when programs are disorganized, beset with disruptions, ineffectively designed, or poorly managed, the evaluation falls heir to the problems of the setting" (p. 54). There are certain characteristics of a well-defined program that are derived from the concept of program described earlier.

### Target Population

Well-conceived programs specify the target audience toward whom the program is directed. The needs of the target population are based on a defensible rationale, and the defining characteristics of the eligible population are described. For example, if the program to be evaluated is teachers' consultation services offered by the school psychologist, the client system for the services would need to be stated (e.g., elementary school teachers, with children experiencing specific types of learning and behavioral problems in the classroom).

### Intended Outcomes

Well-defined programs also state the intended outcomes of the program in the form of goals or objectives. Thus, a particular reading program for students with learning disabilities may focus on goals like phonic analysis, comprehension, reading speed and accuracy, and attitude toward reading. Causal links between program outcomes and program activities can be established only when goals are well conceived and specified.

## Resource Utilization

Another important element of program specification relates to the use of resources: staffing, methods, and materials. Here, the explicit strategies, approaches, concepts, activities, materials, methods, and other resources that make up the program are stated. Elements that are described include (1) number, type, and qualifications of required staff; (2) psychological or educational strategies that are central to the program's conception; (3) materials and equipment necessary for the implementation of the program; (4) financial resources that are required in the form of an operating budget; and (5) other temporal and physical resources (e.g., time, rooms, buildings, and sites).

## Program Plan

A final critical element of program design involves the development of a plan for program operation, to include (1) policies, procedures, and practices that will be used in organizing and operating the program; (2) roles, responsibilities, and relationships of staff members; (3) sequences and timing of programmatic activities; and (4) description of permissible variations of activities.

# Program Planning Strategies

Ideally, professionals with responsibility for program evaluation are asked to become involved in the initial stages of the design of new programs. Sometimes, this request may be in connection with submission of a state or federal grant application to seek funds for a new method or approach. More often, it is in connection with the development of new or reconfigured programs, using local resources, such as preschool education programs; a peer tutoring project; or reorganized support services for students with learning and behavior problems.

A number of strategies to assist in the planning of new programs are available, all of which are aimed toward the development of responsive, evaluable, feasible, and cost-efficient programmatic efforts. This aspect of planning and evaluation can be subdivided into three subareas: (1) contextual analysis and clarification of need, (2) providing initial structure to the intervention plan (program), and (3) preparing for implementation and evaluation of the program.

## Problem Clarification

Presenting problems in service delivery, similar to those arising with an individual client system, can reflect unsatisfactory states of affairs. Problem clarification activities are intended to gather systematic information to place the problems in context and to ensure that appropriate planning is based on a clear understanding of service needs.

Placing the problem in context involves initial data gathering about the nature and scope of the presenting problems. Through preliminary interviews with involved persons, record reviews, direct observation, and similar methods, the evaluator seeks to (1) obtain a general sense of the history and development of the concern, (2) understand what the present state of affairs appears to be, (3) know which individuals perceive the problem, and (4) recognize there are multiple perspectives from which the problem may be viewed. The task in the initial contact is largely heuristic in formulating hypotheses about problems and needs that may exist. Also, sensitivity to limitations of available resources, potential problems or sources of resistance to programmatic intervention, and beliefs and attitudes of key persons is crucial at this stage.

Following the initial contextual analysis, evaluators may construct a more formal *needs assessment*. The term *need* is defined as a discrepancy between an unsatisfactory state of affairs (current) and some desired state (future). Thus, needs assessment is the process of gathering information about actual conditions and comparing them to some desired state. The conduct of a needs assessment involves determining the client or service delivery systems that will be assessed, specifying the aspects (domains) of those systems that will be examined, designing appropriate methods (e.g., procedures and instrumentation) to obtain reliable and valid information about the relevant areas, and planning for data aggregation and analysis (Maher & Illback, 1981).

Many systematic needs assessment methods are available. The *key informant approach* is one in which persons in central positions in the organization (relative to the presumed problem area) are identified and interviewed to obtain estimates of the problem. This approach has the advantage of obtaining essential information from persons who are assumed to be knowledgeable and influential. It can also help form the basis for an effective intervention (program) by establishing the readiness of the organization for change and developing support for new initiatives. The approach has a disadvantage in that these persons have their own built-in biases and interests, which may not be representative of others in the organization. Also, individual key informants may not have full access to crucial information.

Another method for estimating need can be termed *indicator analysis*. Many federal, state, and local agencies, including schools, are required by regulation to maintain a broad base of statistical information on clients and products. For example, schools must collect information about racial balance, family socioeconomic status (for such purposes as free and reduced lunches), average daily attendance, types and severity of handicapping conditions, and the like. Often this information can help formulate the nature and types of needs that may exist in a particular problem. The ultimate utility of indicator analysis rests on the reliability and validity of the descriptive information, the logical and statistical appropriateness of the procedures used in data gathering, and the subjective perception developed about the problem on the basis of the data (Siegel, Attkisson, & Carson, 1978).

Related to indicator analysis approaches are methods involving *analysis of demands for services* (e.g., requests for consultation) and *analysis of service resources* (i.e., compiling, describing, and integrating available services or resources). Both are more passive approaches, using already available data, which is less costly but may not be as valid or reliable as other approaches.

Another needs assessment approach, probably the most common, is the *questionnaire* or *survey*. This approach is the most direct and is usually accurate and representative. A sample of respondents is asked central questions about the problem, and findings are generalized to the target population as a whole. There is a well-developed science to survey construction and administration (e.g., Kosecoff & Fink, 1982; Udinsky, Osterlind, & Lynch, 1981); more sophisticated data analysis and interpretation can often result from the use of these measures.

Perhaps the most active and informative approaches to needs assessment are those that involve people in systematic analysis and/or discussion. In the *nominal group approach*, a broad-based sample is invited to generate in a workshop format ideas about problems, needs, and possible solutions. Clients, external resource people, key administrators and resource controllers, and staff work together in a multistage process to explore problems and knowledge, set priorities, and develop and evaluate programs (Delbecq & Van de Ven, 1971). The *Delphi approach* (Dalkey, 1967) is also structured carefully but focuses more on the use of experts with presumed knowledge about the problem, forecasting needs through a systematic questionnaire process. The *community forum* is an open-ended group discussion similar to town meetings, in which anyone can express his or her opinions or ideas. These groups are often used in federally funded programs to give the public an opportunity to comment without imposing any constraints; this lack of structure is useful from an heuristic perspective but may lead to skewed or misleading findings.

The ultimate goal of problem clarification activities is to obtain a clear statement of the needs that exist in relation to contextual variables. Such a needs description specifies the individual, group, or service delivery system that is experiencing the problem and indicates the specific needs of target systems in the form of discrepancy statements (current versus desired states of affairs). The needs description should also place the identified needs in some priority or logical order. Some needs are of less importance than others, some are subsets of larger problems or issues, and some will not be amenable to direct intervention. The needs description thus forms the basis for program design.

## Initial Program Organization

In this stage, the evaluator is concerned with designing a systematic course of action in response to a clarified problem. Crucial to ultimate success is reaching agreement with key persons about the nature and priority of needs to be addressed by the programmatic intervention. Activities at this level may include presenting the needs description to decision makers, negotiating about the needs that are to be addressed, and facilitation of group decision making. Evaluative methods to accomplish this task range from *informal discussion* to highly formalized means, such as *decision-analytic techniques* and *voting procedures*.

Once needs have been placed in the order of priority, a structure of goals for the prospective program must be established. Goals are statements of intent about what the program will accomplish and are derived directly from the statement of needs described earlier. Goals are specified so that programmatic efforts can be deployed logically and sequentially.

Program goals may be general or specific. Also, goals may be stated in terms of *outcomes* (intrinsically worthy occurrences, such as increased knowledge) or *outputs* (e.g., successful completion of a task at 90% accuracy). Moreover, goals may be primary, in that they are valued for their own sake, or instrumental to some other primary goal. To the extent possible, goals should be stated in terms that are measurable or observable, and it is often useful to attach goals indicators (performance criteria) to goal statements for this purpose.

A final component of program organization relates to intervention planning. For an effective intervention to be planned, a systematic examination of solution requirements and solution alternatives must be employed. The *specification of solution requirements* should delineate the conditions or constraints under which the program must be planned and developed. *Generation of solution alternatives* is characterized initially by an open-ended approach, followed by validation-oriented strategies, resulting in a set of possible methods, materials, and resources for the program. It is thus possible to evaluate critically the advantages and disadvantages of available solution alternatives in light of established program goals. Available methods for this phase include *brainstorming, logical analysis, site visitation, group discussion, literature review,* and *structured group decision making.*

The ultimate intent of the program organization phase is to derive a sequence of logical goals and activities that can focus the program. Once these have been selected, they should be discussed and negotiated with decision makers to ensure their fit with environmental features and constraints.

## *Program Development*

Once the structure of the program has been determined and agreed upon, resources to implement the program must be assembled and packaged. Here, evaluative strategies are used to address questions about resource identification and utilization, packaging, personnel needs and issues, program routines and procedures, organizational readiness for the program, and program evaluation. Evaluative activities in this stage may include (1) writing a policy and procedure manual, (2) conducting training with staff on programmatic activities, (3) delineating permanent products (e.g., reports) of the program, (4) conducting pilot tests and simulations of the program, (5) developing descriptive material for clients and professionals, (6) acquiring materials and supplies, and (7) designing a program information system (programmatic, administrative, and financial information).

Program design can be evaluated in relation to five criteria suggested by Provus (1972). The first, *clarity,* refers to the extent to which the design is understandable and its components objectively measurable. Second, *comprehensiveness* relates to the extent to which the design fully describes the purpose, implementation, and expected outcomes of the effort. Third, the components of the design can be assessed to make certain that they are logically interrelated, or *internally consistent. Compatibility* with the established need, with existing support conditions, and with other programs is a fourth aspect to be evaluated. Finally, *theoretical soundness* in relation to the prevailing literature can be assessed.

A final element of program design involves actual preparations for implementation. Activities in this phase may include *specifying implementation activities* and time lines and developing a *plan for program management and outcome evaluation.*

## Implementation Evaluation

The primary purpose of implementation evaluation is to determine the extent to which the program is operating as planned. This information can be used to document compliance with important legal and ethical mandates, such as state and federal guidelines and regulations, and the ethical and practice codes of professional organizations. Also, implementation evaluation facilitates program development and improvement by identifying problem areas that may require adaptation of program standards or operations. It also highlights program elements that are being effectively implemented. Finally, implementation evaluation increases confidence in the eventual assessment of program outcomes by ensuring that measured effects are attributable to an intervention that has been implemented as planned.

To a large extent, the area of implementation has employed qualitative methods of data gathering and analysis. Patton (1990) describes the emerging area of qualitative inquiry in terms of 10 interconnected themes, as shown in Table 34.1. These themes emphasize the fact that qualitative inquiry is complementary to, but not in competition with, quantitative analysis. Whereas the traditional research paradigm emphasizes pure variables, manipulation and control of processes, experimenters' neutrality, and definitive conclusions, qualitative (or naturalistic) methodology focuses on program process, collaboration between the evaluator and program

TABLE 34.1    Themes of Qualitative Inquiry

| | |
|---|---|
| 1. Naturalistic inquiry | Studying real-world situations as they unfold naturally; non-manipulative, unobtrusive, and noncontrolling; openness to whatever emerges—lack of predetermined constraints on outcomes |
| 2. Inductive analysis | Immersion in the details and specifics of the data to discover important categories, dimensions, and interrelationships; being by exploring genuinely open questions rather than testing theoretically derived (deductive) hypotheses |
| 3. Holistic perspective | The *whole* phenomenon under study is understood as a complex system that is more than the sum of its parts; focus on complex interdependencies not meaningfully reduced to a few discrete variables and linear, cause-effect relationships |
| 4. Qualitative data | Detailed, thick description; inquiry in depth; direct quotations capturing people's personal perspectives and experiences |
| 5. Personal contact and insight | The research has direct contact with and gets close to the people, situation, and phenomenon under study; research's personal experiences and insights are an important part of the inquiry and critical to understanding the phenomenon |
| 6. Dynamic systems | Attention to processes; assumes change is constant and ongoing whether the focus is an individual or an entire culture |
| 7. Unique case orientation | Assumes each case is special and unique; the first level of inquiry is being true to, respecting and capturing the details of the individual cases being studied; cross-case analysis follows from and depends on the quality of individual case studies |
| 8. Context sensitivity | Places findings in a social, historical, and temporal context; dubious of the possibility or meaningfulness of generalizations across time and space |
| 9. Empathetic neutrality | Complete objectivity is impossible; pure subjectivity undermines credibility; the researcher's passion is understanding the world in all its complexity—not proving something, not advocating, not advancing person agendas, but understanding; the researcher includes person experience and empathetic insight as part of the relevant data, while taking a neutral nonjudgmental stance toward whatever content may emerge |
| 10. Design flexibility | Open to adapting inquiry as understanding deepens and/or situations change; avoids betting locked into rigid designs that eliminate responsiveness; pursues new paths of discovery as they emerge |

From M. Q. Patton, *Qualitative Evaluation and Research Methods* (Newbury Park, CA: Sage, 1990). Used with permission.

personnel, incremental clarification of knowledge, and an action orientation (Kalafat & Illback, in press).

For Patton (1990), qualitative inquiry is appropriate when (1) a new field of study where few definable hypotheses are available is to be investigated, (2) a discovery-oriented method will enable judgments to be made about incremental and developmental aspects of program implementation, (3) there is a need to depict program processes that are fluid and dynamic, and (4) understanding of quantitative findings will be enhanced with a more in-depth and detailed analysis of processes ("unlocking the black box"). Most typically, the process of inquiry begins with initial exploration of the issues that surround implementation, resulting in the development of a set of themes. Then, more systematic data are gathered, using the methods of observation, interviewing, and records review. This process is followed by analysis of field notes, documenting the data that were obtained, and ultimately categorization and description of the findings (data reduction and interpretation).

Implementation evaluation is especially crucial to program managers, such as directors of special services, who are concerned with the fidelity and smooth operation of the program and want problems to be identified early so that they can be corrected. Relevant evaluative questions at the implementation phase include the following: (1) in what areas are program staff engaged in programmatic activities and to what extent? (2) How are program participants (client groups) involved in the program? (3) Are appropriate materials and facilities being utilized in the program? (4) What intended and unintended side effects do individuals perceive? (5) What types of services have been delivered to clients? (6) Is there a discrepancy between what was planned and what was actually delivered? (7) What permanent products (e.g., written documents) have resulted from programmatic activities?

Evaluative methods in implementation evaluation can be divided into two areas: retrospective monitoring and naturalistic nmonitoring. In retrospective monitoring, self-report information is obtained from program managers and staff about the extent to which the program has been operationalized. The evaluator may conduct a series of individual or small-group interviews or use paper-and-pencil measures to gather perceptual information about salient process variables. These may include the frequency of program sessions held relative to the number planned, the range of methods and materials used in the sessions, and any noted effects or problems. Record reviews or examination of other permanent products (e.g., staff activity log and written reports) may also be employed.

In naturalistic monitoring, the evaluator observes the programmatic process directly, using formal (e.g., systematic recording of behavior) and less formal means. In addition to systematic observation, checklists and rating scales may be used to obtain information on the nature and scope of the activities being provided and to compare that information to the program design. Retrospective and naturalistic monitoring methods are complementary in that information derived from one approach can supplement and enhance the other.

One of the best-researched approaches to implementation evaluation in education is the concerns-based adoption model (CBAM) promulgated by Hall and Loucks (1977). Relying heavily on structured interviews, CBAM views programs from a developmental perspective and postulates that there are naturally occurring levels of use of any innovation (program). These levels range from nonuse, in which the user has minimal knowledge of or involvement with the innovation, through orientation and preparation stages to mechanical and routine levels of use. Hall and Hord (1987) updated and expanded the CBAM model for an approach they call innovation configuration analysis. Involving extensive discussions with stakeholders and program participants, this strategy seeks to identify the essential features of the innovation, with the ultimate aim of creating an implementation scale for each dimension (called an ICC map). Central to the concept of implementation evaluation as expressed in these strategies is the belief that programs proceed through developmental stages as a function of the nature of the program, characteristics of the adopting unit, and general organizational characteristics (Fullan & Pomfret, 1977).

As with any research approach, there is always concern for rigor. Lincoln and Guba (1985) use the term "going native" for the potential for losing one's objectivity and becoming coopted by the program. This is clearly a danger in qualitative evaluation, and these authors offer a series of methods for enhancing rigor in this style of work: (1) prolonged engagement and persistent observation (less risky than initial impression formation), (2) peer debriefing and review of field notes, (3) member checks (reviewing categories, analysis, and interpretations with stakeholders throughout the process), (4) negative case analysis (identifying cases that do not fit the dominant theme or conclusion), and (5) referential adequacy (retaining a portion of the field data for analysis by another investigator or critic).

## Outcome Assessment

The purpose of outcome assessment is to describe the effects that a program has had. It is critical to the design of an outcome assessment to specify clearly the evaluative questions that are of concern. The results will largely be a function of the general decision area that is under consideration and of the decision maker who is involved. For example, some decisions to be made about the program are in the domain of program managers. These decisions focus on internal program operations and effects, such as judging the effectiveness of the program in addressing the unmet needs of clients, the extent to which client goals are attained, and service recipient and staff perceptions of outcomes and appropriateness of services (consumer satisfaction).

Another level of decision making involves external accountability requirements, such as determining the extent to which the program complies with the intent of state and federal regulations. Evaluative information for external purposes may include cost-efficiency analysis, consumer reaction, and global outcome measures.

Decisions about program effectiveness may also be important by contributing to scholarly knowledge and informing prospective adopting sites (dissemination and diffusion). In this regard, evaluative concerns may focus more on determining cause-effect relationships between independent and dependent variables. In making decisions about program effectiveness in field settings such as schools, it is difficult to determine experimental validity because of problems in establishing adequate experimental control. The use of quasi-experimental designs (Cook & Campbell, 1976) and single-subject methodology (Kratochwill, 1978) is therefore of increased relevance.

A range of evaluation questions may be addressed in the outcome assessment phase. The focus of the evaluation may be on one or more aspects, including (a) degree of goal attainment, (b) related program effects, (c) consumer reaction, (d) cause-effect relationships, (3) cost efficiency, and (f) need for program revision. The specific methods and strategies used to assess outcomes are thus a direct result of such factors as the evaluative question, the decision makers who are seeking the information, the availability of methods and approaches (e.g., instrumentation) to investigate the problem area, and practical design considerations (e.g., cost, ability to randomize, and time requirements).

A fundamental goal for any outcome assessment is to impose the greatest rigor that is practical to achieve increased confidence in obtained findings. A major source of rigor in any experiment is the research design. Whereas traditional research methodology recognizes a rather limited number of designs, program evaluators tend to include a broader range of approaches, implicitly recognizing that the vagaries of conducting research in the "real" world will necessarily lead to weak and incomplete knowledge. Rossi and Freeman (1993) have therefore described a typology of potential research designs: (1) "true"

or randomized experiments, (2) quasi-experiments with nonrandom controls, (3) regression-discontinuity designs, (4) before-and-after studies, (5) retrospective before-and-after studies, (6) panel studies, (7) time-series analysis studies, (8) cross-sectional surveys, and (9) judgmental assessments. These are listed in descending order of control and power, and it remains for the evaluator to determine which design most appropriately fits the particular situation and provides the greatest possible rigor.

Another source of rigor stems from the instrumentation used for measurement. An array of collection alternatives (instruments) such as observations (e.g., standard and time-sampling observations), interviews, performance tests (e.g., achievement), and written self-report measures (e.g., questionnaires, rating scales, ranking scales, semantic differentials, Q-sorts, diaries, and critical incidents) is available (Kosecoff & Fink, 1982). Each has advantages and disadvantages, both psychometrically and practically. Some will have established reliability and validity, but most will not. The evaluator is obligated to develop and employ measurement devices that can be shown to be internally consistent, reliable, valid, and relevant to the problem at hand. (For a summary review of the measurement technology for each of these approaches, see Kosecoff & Fink, 1982).

Rigor can also be enhanced through data collection and data analysis. To obtain accurate information, collectors need to be identified and trained to ensure their proper use of procedures, potential sources of bias must be minimized through various methods of control and cross-checking, collection must be monitored to ensure that information is not lost, and steps must be taken to be certain that clients' rights (e.g., confidentiality) are not violated. In preparing data for analysis, systems for categorizing and coding a range of information can be delineated. The choice of statistical analysis derives from the research design used, the types of data (e.g., ordinal or interval), the purposes of the evaluation (e.g., descriptive or comparative), and the availability of time and resources (e.g., expertise and computer access).

Some outcome assessment methods are specifically designed for program evaluation. Typical of these is Goal Attainment Scaling, a measurement approach formulated by Kiresuk, Smith, and Cardillo (1994), which has been used extensively in mental health, social service, and educational agencies. The centerpiece of Goal Attainment Scaling is the follow-up guide, on which expected outcomes of intervention plans are specified along a five-point continuum of potential outcomes. The actual degree of goal attainment over the predetermined time period is then compared to the predicted levels for each goal area, and results are aggregated across domains. This system allows idiosyncratic assessment of client outcomes in a somewhat standardized approach; relative weighting of goal areas; and data aggregation across domains, clients, and even programs. However, it relies heavily on professional judgment in setting and assessing outcome levels and has a number of design and statistical limitations. Nonetheless, when used appropriately, it can contribute significantly to data-based decision making.

Increasingly, schools and related agencies are utilizing management information systems to track relevant information about clients and programs. The most sophisticated of these systems can conduct periodic outcome assessments that are both descriptive and inferential in nature. The role of the evaluator is crucial in this regard

to ensure that information is properly structured, analyzed, and interpreted.

## Standards for Effective Evaluation

Growing out of the well-established *Standards for Educational and Psychological Tests and Manuals* (American Psychological Association, 1985), a Joint Committee on Standards for Educational Evaluation was formed in 1975 by the American Educational Research Association, the American Psychological Association, and the National Council on Measurement in Education. These were joined by nine other prominent education groups, representing the major constituencies in the field and resulting in the publication of *Standards for Evaluations of Educational Programs, Projects, and Materials* (Joint Committee on Standards for Educational Evaluation, 1981). A subsequent revision to incorporate new developments was published in 1994, entitled *The Program Evaluation Standards* (Joint Committee on Standards for Educational Evaluation, 1994). This document provides a comprehensive conceptual framework for assessing the extent to which a particular evaluative effort is consistent with accepted practice, as shown in Table 34.2.

**TABLE 34.2  Standards of Program Evaluations**

| Utility |
|---|
| The utility standards are intended to ensure that an evaluation will serve the information needs of intended users. |

**U1  Stakeholder Identification:** Persons involved in or affected by the evaluation should be identified, so that their needs can be addressed.

**U2  Evaluator Credibility:** The persons conducting the evaluation should be both trustworthy and competent to perform the evaluation, so that the evaluation findings achieve maximum credibility and acceptance.

**U3  Information Scope and Selection:** Information collected should be broadly selected to address pertinent questions about the program and be responsive to the needs and interests of clients and other specified stakeholders.

**U4  Values Identification:** The perspectives, procedures, and rationale used to interpret the findings should be carefully described, so that the bases for value judgments are clear.

**U5  Report Clarity:** Evaluation reports should clearly describe the program being evaluated, including its context, and the purposes, procedures, and findings of the evaluations, so that essential information is provided and easily understood.

**U6  Report Timeliness and Dissemination:** Significant interim findings and evaluation reports should be disseminated to intended users, so that they can be used in a timely fashion.

**U7  Evaluation Impact:** Evaluations should be planned, conducted, and reported in ways that encourage follow-through by stakeholders, so that the likelihood that the evaluation will be used is increased.

**TABLE 34.2** (*Continued*)

### Feasibility

The feasibility standards are intended to ensure that an evaluation will be realistic, prudent, diplomatic, and frugal.

**F1** **Practical Procedures:** The evaluation procedures should be practical, to keep disruption to a minimum while needed information is obtained.

**F2** **Political Viability:** The evaluation should be planned and conducted with anticipation of the different positions of various interest groups, so that their cooperation may be obtained, and so that possible attempts by any of these groups to curtail evaluation operations or to bias or misapply the results can be averted or counteracted.

**F3** **Cost Effectiveness:** The evaluation should be efficient and produce information of sufficient value, so that the resources expended can be justified.

### Propriety

The propriety standards are intended to ensure that an evaluation will be conducted legally, ethically, and with due regard for the welfare of those involved in the evaluation, as well as those affected by its results.

**P1** **Service Orientation:** Evaluations should be designed to assist organizations to address and effectively serve the needs of the full range of targeted participants.

**P2** **Formal Agreements:** Obligations of the formal parties to an evaluation (what is to be done, how, by whom, when) should be agreed to in writing, so that these parties are obligated to adhere to all conditions of the agreement or formally to renegotiate it.

**P3** **Rights of Human Subjects:** Evaluations should be designed and conducted to respect and protect the rights and welfare of human subjects.

**P4** **Human Interactions:** Evaluations should respect human dignity and worth in their interactions with other persons associated with an evaluation, so that participants are not threatened or harmed.

**P5** **Complete and Fair Assessment:** The evaluation should be complete and fair in its examination and recording of strengths and weaknesses of the program being evaluated, so that strengths can be built upon and problem areas addressed.

**P6** **Disclosure of Findings:** The formal parties to an evaluation should ensure that the full set of evaluation findings along with pertinent limitations are made accessible to the persons affected by the evaluation, and any others with expressed legal rights to receive the results.

**P7** **Conflict of Interest:** Conflict of interest should be dealt with openly and honestly, so that it does not compromise the evaluation processes and results.

**P8** **Fiscal Responsibility:** The evaluator's allocation and expenditure of resources should reflect sound accountability procedures and otherwise be prudent and ethically responsible, so that expenditures are accounted for and appropriate.

### Accuracy

The accuracy standards are intended to ensure that an evaluation will reveal and convey technically adequate information about the features that determine worth of merit of the program being evaluated.

**A1** **Program Documentation:** The program being evaluated should be described and documented clearly and accurately, so that the program is clearly identified.

**A1** **Context Analysis:** The context in which the program exists should be examined in enough detail, so that its likely influences on the program can be identified.

**A3** **Described Purposes and Procedures:** The purposes and procedures of the evaluation should be monitored and described in enough detail, so that they can be identified and assessed.

**TABLE 34.2** (*Continued*)

| Accuracy (*continued*) |
| --- |

**A4 Defensible Information Sources:** The sources of information used in a program evaluation should be described in enough detail, so that the adequacy of the information can be assessed.

**A5 Valid Information:** The information gathering procedures should be chosen or developed and then implemented so that they will assure that the interpretation arrived at is valid for the intended use.

**A6 Reliable Information:** The information gathering procedures should be chosen or developed and then implemented so that they will assure that the information obtained is sufficiently reliable for the intended use.

**A7 Systematic Information:** The information collected, processed, and reported in an evaluation should be systematically reviewed and any errors found should be corrected.

**A8 Analysis of Quantitative Information:** Quantitative information in an evaluation should be appropriately and systematically analyzed so that evaluation questions are effectively answered.

**A9 Analysis of Qualitative Information:** Qualitative information in an evaluation should be appropriately and systematically analyzed so that evaluation questions are effectively answered.

**A10 Justified Conclusions:** The conclusions reached in an evaluation should be explicitly justified, so that stakeholders can assess them.

**A11 Impartial Reporting:** Reporting procedures should guard against distortion caused by personal feelings and biases of any party to the evaluation, so that evaluation reports fairly reflect the evaluation findings.

**A12 Metaevaluation:** The evaluation itself should be formatively and summatively evaluated against these and other pertinent standards, so that its conduct is appropriately guided and on completion, stakeholders can closely examine its strengths and weaknesses.

---

Guidelines and illustrative cases to assist evaluation participants in meeting each of these standards are provided in The Program Standards. . . . The illustrative cases are based in a variety of educational settings that include schools, universities, medical and health care fields, the military, business and industry, the government, and law.

---

From Joint Committee on Standards for Educational Evaluation, *The Program Evaluation Standards*, 2nd ed. (Newbury Park, CA: Sage, 1994). Used with permission.

## USING PROGRAM EVALUATION TO SUPPORT PLANNED ORGANIZATIONAL CHANGE

Most school psychologists might be expected to place great value on program evaluation because of their backgrounds in research and measurement, although we recognize that few have received specific formal training in program evaluation, which has certain implications (as discussed later). However, most other educators do not have such backgrounds and consequently may not share the same enthusiasm for this perspective. These professionals are usually not accustomed to using evaluation data to help them reflect on and guide their practices and decision making. Although they clearly want to know that the programs in which they are involved are effective and worthy of the resources devoted to them, at the same time they are facing significant pressures to address more immediate day-to-day problems and may not want to devote the effort necessary for program evaluation.

Our goals in this section are to describe the uses of evaluation information and, at the same time, to stress the importance of evaluating programs. As should be evident by now, the primary purpose is to facilitate the effective operation of educational services and programs and to educate decision makers and constitutents. Evaluation findings can foster improvement in specific programs, as well as in organizational functioning in general. Moreover, they are also useful for self-evaluation and professional development (Whiston, 1996). Relevant activities might include measuring the attainment of specific outcomes, assessing staff performance, and/or determining the extent to which key components of a program are being implemented, and then disseminating this information in an understandable format. Such information can help educational leaders reduce uncertainties about decisions they must make and thereby increase their ability to predict the outcomes of programmatic activities (Patton, 1978). Accordingly, it is desirable for formative and summative evaluation to be integral, routine components of an organization's operation. Indeed, evaluation should be considered an essential part of any program from the time it is first discussed, rather than an afterthought. Evaluation data help guide organizational change so that it occurs in a planned, systematic manner instead of haphazardly. Directions and goals are not followed rigidly but are continually readjusted according to evaluation results, and this process can assist in making any adaptations necessary (Beer & Walton, 1987). The bottom line is that program evaluation results enable decision makers to make informed judgments about how to maintain, modify, or discontinue programs.

## Organizational Context

A prerequisite to adequate evaluations of educational programs is the support of the school organization. Without such support, attempts to evaluate individual programs may still be undertaken, but these efforts will probably be narrow in scope and the results will have significant limitations. First, if the administration does not support these activities, it probably will not use the data produced, no matter how good they are. Second, access to sources of data may be restricted. Third, resources sufficient for carrying out evaluation activities may not be allocated. Finally, the commitment of organizational members to participation in the evaluation may also be lessened. Thus, the program evaluation is unlikely to accomplish its goals effectively.

A basic ingredient of a supportive organization is a culture that values inquiry and reflection, that advocates a scientist-practitioner approach (Barlow, Hayes, & Nelson, 1984). In addition to being willing to examine current practices, members of such an organization must trust one another, be intellectually curious, provide mutual support, be open to challenge, and be willing to share observations. The administration must ensure that members have the time to engage in relevant activities, support their efforts toward new actions, and model similar behaviors themselves (Elias et al., 1997).

## Systems Perspective

Viewing schools from a systems perspective enables the evaluator to gain a broader understanding of factors that potentially influence the operation of the school. The educational change literature makes it clear that system factors such as administrative support, school environment, community sanction, and constituent opportunity for involvement in the change process are all important to the success of any program (e.g., Fullan, Miles, & Taylor, 1980; Lippitt, Langseth, & Mossop, 1986), and they need to be considered when a program evaluation is conducted. However, school psychologists have traditionally focused their practice on the remediation of problems experienced by individual students, thereby often inadvertently limiting their perspectives and their consideration of the broad range of factors internal and external to the school that may influence any program.

In a systems perspective, schools consist of a variety of subsystems (e.g., administration, school psychological services, special education program, and mathematics department), rather than being a single entity. Furthermore, from this vantage point the school is also recognized as part of larger systems (e.g., community, state, and federal education agencies). Each of these systems and subsystems is interrelated and interdependent of the others. A concept that helps explain these relationships is reciprocal interaction, which means that there is a tendency for a change in any system component to affect other components in the system, as well as the organization itself. Each system, in whole and in part, both influences and is influenced by other systems, and their component parts also continuously interact with one another. To illustrate this point, most readers have observed that a new principal can have dramatic effects on communication patterns in every subsystem in the school, or a school's reputation for excellence or mediocrity can be reflected in neighborhood property values. On a larger level, when the State Department of Education in the Commonwealth of Kentucky adopted new state educational standards (Kentucky Educational Reform Act), public and professional perceptions of the schools were altered. Consequently, to be most effective, evaluators must develop an understanding and appreciation of all the interrelated components of a school organization.

## Relationship to Management of Programs

Program evaluation should be closely linked to the management of school programs by guiding policies, plans, and directions. The results can provide concrete information for decision making. In fact, effective program evaluation can even help to stimulate the identification and clarification of possible problems, thereby helping to prepare the organization to make vital decisions so that fewer of them are made under "crisis" conditions. Although the advantages of operating a school on a data-based foundation seem intuitive, what happens in the real world is somewhat different. The example that follows illustrates how the importance of program evaluation is not always reflected in day-to-day educational practice.

The local newspaper in a midwestern city recently published a story, based in part on the wire services, indicating that a new national study of the popular D.A.R.E. (Drug Abuse Resistance Education) program, which involved 10,000 students in 19 schools over five years, found that it was not as effective as other types of drug prevention programs (Gregg & Bonfield, 1997). The article also reported that several other studies over the years had reached similar conclusions. Despite these findings, a principal who was interviewed for the newspaper article said, "I personally feel it makes a big difference. . . . Just the presence of the officers in the building, talking to the children in a personal way about the dangers of drugs and alcohol, is very powerful" (p. A14). Rather than being an unusual reaction, such incidents are often the rule. Too many educators either choose to ignore evaluation data when making decisions or do not implement program evaluation procedures in the first place.

Another issue related to program management is that once a program is adopted, there is no assurance that it will be implemented as planned. As a result, decision makers are placed in the position of not knowing why a particular result was achieved. For this reason, as part of the program evaluation process, it is essential to focus on the fidelity with which a program was carried out. By fidelity we mean that key program elements must be consistently conducted as they were intended. There are still adaptations of programs, but changes must be planned and made explicitly so that components that led to program outcomes can be identified to the extent possible.

## Assessing Need and Readiness for Change

In any educational organization, there are differential levels of readiness and willingness to attempt or accept change (Goodstein, 1978). Readiness refers to the social, technological, or systemic ability of a school to change or to try new things. Willingness is related to stakeholders' involvement in the change process. We have all seen situations in which change was introduced into a school without adequate examination of constituents' readiness and willingness to change. Inevitably, problems arose. For this reason, evaluation programs need to help schools identify areas where change is possible, so that it is not imposed on a highly resistant or unprepared system (Beer & Walton, 1987). Instead, steps can be taken to increase the likelihood that the change process will be successful or, if necessary, that an informed decision can be made about the feasibility of even undertaking the effort.

As an initial step, it is necessary to assess organizational receptivity to the planned change. Successful change programs are likely to be based on timely, relevant, and technically adequate organizational assessment data (Illback & Zins, 1984). Among the issues that need to be addressed is the congruence in values of the proposed program and those currently in existence. Teachers and parents are unlikely to be receptive to programs whose values appear to be in conflict with those prevailing in the school or community. For example, in the late 1980s we were involved in a discussion with a superintendent of a suburban school district about implementing a violence prevention program. The superintendent recognized that school violence was likely to become a significant issue in the 1990s and thought that efforts should be undertaken to address the issue proactively. However, as the issue was discussed with other school personnel and the community, it became obvious that they were not prepared to acknowledge school violence as an upcoming problem; they viewed it as a concern only for urban schools. As a result, the proposed program was not begun for five more years, and opportunities to influence many students were lost.

The issue of feasibility must also be considered. That is, a program should require reasonable amounts of staff time and other resources and involve only minimal disruption of other programs (Maher & Bennett, 1984) so that the benefits outweigh the costs. Decisions have to be made, as only a finite number of resources and energies can be devoted to any program, no matter how important it is.

Among the most common methods of organizational assessment are (1) an examination of organizational flowcharts (graphic representations of organizational structure and the formal and informal chains of command), (2) record reviews (e.g., minutes of school board meetings, graduation and attendance data, newspaper articles, financial statements, and proficiency test results), (3) direct observation (e.g., of patterns of organizational behavior, gatekeepers, and interactions among staff members and students), (4) questionnaires and surveys (developed to address specific information needs and usually administered anonymously to staff and/or community members), and (5) interviews (usually with a sample of organizational members to provide more in-depth information). A systems perspective remains important when attempting to understand a school's need and readiness for change; because both internal and external factors can exert influence, a multifaceted approach to collecting data is essential.

An important element in program evaluation is the school's organizational climate, particularly the value that is placed on reflection and inquiry (Zins, Travis, & Freppon, 1997). As noted, schools that believe these activities are important may be more likely to engage in program evaluation activities and, equally as important, to use the outcomes of these efforts to improve educational programming. Administrative support is crucial in modeling relevant behaviors and creating a culture in which organizational members are encouraged to be intellectually curious, raise questions, and be supportive. They must also have adequate time and flexibility to try new actions that are based on their inquiry and reflection efforts (Elias et al., 1997).

## Dissemination and Utilization of Evaluation Results

Introduction of a program does not guarantee that it eventually will become a permanent part of the organization. Factors that increase the likelihood that a program will be adopted are discussed in detail elsewhere (e.g., Adelman & Taylor, 1997), but one that we would like to emphasize is communication of evaluation findings.

The content, manner, and form in which evaluation results are disseminated or diffused are the primary factors in utilization. Throughout the evaluation process, open, two-way lines of communication should be maintained and a participatory style of interaction established. The evaluator and organization members must use a team approach to draw on the strengths that each has to offer. Frequent communication that is timely, relevant, and appropriate is preferable to relying on a single summative report at the conclusion of a program. With ongoing communications, formative information is readily provided; as a result, "surprise" findings, which tend not to be utilized or to have little impact if they conflict with and disconfirm decision makers' prevailing beliefs, can be avoided (Legge, 1984). We are not suggesting that a final presentation and report of the findings should be omitted but rather that such communication mechanisms are not usually the most effective ways to ensure utilization of evaluation findings, and therefore should not be relied on exclusively.

When developing summative evaluation reports, decisions need to be made about the methods used to communicate findings to facilitate their utilization. Questions that need to be asked include the following: (1) to what extent should quantitative or qualitative data be included? (2) Is it appropriate to use technical jargon? (3) Is brevity or comprehensiveness more important? (4) Is formality or informality called for? (5) To what audiences should the information be communicated? (Legge, 1984). Clearly, varying approaches are needed to reach different consumer groups, who may have specific needs, and there is no one "right" method.

Utilization is generally considered to have occurred if the findings are used in decision making, although many factors beyond the evaluation data are also considered. However, a frequent concern is that this information results in minimal influence on decision making or that it is even ignored by decision makers (Sproull & Larkey, 1979). Sproull and Larkey referred to this outcome as a problem in delivery, which means that although the evaluation information was produced, it was not delivered in such a way that it was actually used by decision makers. At the same time, the lack of use could be related to the decision makers. For a variety of reasons, they might chose to ignore the data (as with D.A.R.E.). Although they have no obligation to base their decision on only evaluation results, they have a responsibility to at least consider them.

Common reasons for the lack of utilization include the fact that evaluation results may (1) reach the administrators/decision makers after decisions have been made, (2) speak to the wrong issues, or (3) may be incomprehensible to all but the most sophisticated methodologists" (Sproull & Larkey, 1979, p. 90). The extent to which evaluation procedures approach methodological rigor is also a consideration. The results may be equivocal or in some way qualified, thus becoming less persuasive, although methodological rigor does not in itself invariably appear to be strongly related to utilization (Legge, 1984). Among the elements that make an evaluation useful are these: it is directed toward issues users consider important, the data are relevant to their problems, consumers are involved in the evaluation process, and the results do not conflict a great deal with information from other sources (Cousins & Leithwood, 1986).

For all of these reasons, it is important for evaluators to collaborate with potential consumers to clarify the goals and possible uses of the evaluation, thereby increasing the relevance of the results and enhancing the users' commitment to the overall evaluation process. Consumer involvement helps ensure that results are relevant and credible and that they will meet the organization's information needs (Cousins & Leithwood, 1986). Establishing partnerships also fosters positive and productive interactions that are most conducive to effective program evaluation, which may also help avoid or reduce potential conflicts (Zins, 1985). Evaluators, who have more technical competence in this area than do most consumers, are in essence requesting that users develop trust in their judgments. Collaboration fosters this trust and the interest that users have in the evaluation, both of which are predictive of whether the knowledge will be utilized (Beer & Walton, 1987). However, Cousins and Leithwood warn that user involvement can decrease objectivity and threaten the evaluator's integrity, although they also note that these potential costs must be weighted against those associated with nonuse of the results.

# INVOLVING SCHOOL PSYCHOLOGISTS IN PROGRAM EVALUATION

As mentioned several times, many educational leaders do not have a background in research and measurement and the related technical training to conduct program evaluations. Thus, they may not see program evaluation as an essential component of educational programs and, therefore, may not use evaluative data in making educational decisions. As also discussed, school psychologists as evaluators may find themselves in the position of trying to convince educational decision makers of the value of evaluation research. Once administrators recognize the need and potential benefits of program evaluation, however, they often delegate authority for designing and conducting program evaluations to school psychologists because they are the primary (and often only) staff members who have the necessary expertise in research techniques.

## Role and Function Issues

The professional practice standards of the American Psychological Association (1981) and the National Association of School Psychologists (NASP; 1992) both stress that program evaluation is an important role for school psychologists and note the importance of documenting the delivery of effective school psychological services. For example, the NASP standards state, "School psychologists provide program planning and evaluation services to assist in decision-making activities" (p. 45).

Despite the emphasis placed by these professional organizations on the role of the school psychologist in evaluation activities and even though discussions about its importance have appeared in the literature for nearly two decades (e.g., Maher, 1981), significant changes in the functioning of school psychologists in this area have not occurred since the last edition of this volume. In fact, very little new information has been published on this topic in the school psychology literature, and surveys of school psychologists' daily practices over the years consistently suggest that there is minimal involvement in these endeavors. For example, Smith, Clifford, Hesley, and Leifgren (1992) reported that school psychologists they surveyed spent just over 5% of their time in "program development" and less than 1% in "developing and conducting research." A category for program evaluation was not included, but it appears that program evaluation would be subsumed within these categories.

A survey of school psychologists' accountability practices was conducted in 1991 by Fairchild and Zins (1992). They found that only 57.8% reported currently collecting some type of accountability data, which was consistent with the results of their 1984 survey (Zins & Fairchild, 1986). In an international survey of school psychologists that used the same questionnaire as Smith et al., Zins, Johnson, and Thomas (1995) found quite different results. Respondents spent over 6% of their time in program development but 17.5% in research. Most of the difference in the research category, however, was associated with non-U.S. respondents, who engaged in research 21.4% of their time. They also found that those in the United States devoted 5.7% of their time to research, which is much greater than the findings of Smith et al.

It appears as though a vicious cycle is in operation, at least in the United States. Educational leaders may not recognize the value of program evaluations, so they do not ask school psychologists to conduct them; and school psychologists do not perceive the need to pursue such training, as their jobs generally do not require such efforts. Because school psychologists have a limited background in program evaluation, they do not emphasize to administrators the potential contributions that they could make through such actions.

Much of the lack of emphasis in practice may originate from the limited preservice training in this area. Several national surveys have found that about one-third of the respondents had completed university coursework related to program evaluation and accountability (Fairchild & Zins, 1992; Moore & Carlson, 1988), whereas Fagan's (1990) survey of 70 doctoral school psychology programs identified only two in which program evaluation was an area of subspecialization.

For all of these reasons, we once again must conclude, as we did in the previous edition, that program evaluation is still not emphasized in graduate training programs, nor does it represent a major job function for most school psychologists, despite its importance in effective educational and psychological service delivery. Given this state of affairs, the question must be raised, who in the educational system will assume these

responsibilities, or will they become the domain of outside consultants, such as community psychologists, who are willing and able to undertake these evaluation tasks (see examples in Zins, 1997)? Many professionals are available to carry out these evaluations, but most lack the ongoing involvement that may lead to more useful findings.

## Overcoming Barriers and Resistance

Throughout this chapter we have mentioned several factors that appear to be associated with the minimal focus on program evaluation by schools and school psychologists. These barriers need to be addressed so that program evaluation becomes a more routine aspect of school psychological service delivery systems.

### Technical Expertise and Evaluation Design

Because most educators have not received training in program evaluation, it is understandable that they may resist participating in such ventures. A related outcome of having limited expertise is that those who conduct program evaluations may generate data that have limited usefulness for understanding program operation or for effectively determining whether the program should be maintained, modified, or discontinued. School psychologists, therefore, may be required to teach them the importance of program evaluation and how to apply the findings to educational decision making. At the same time, in the capacity of an evaluator, it is important to remember that the major purpose of program evaluation is usually not to discover new knowledge and that it is not generally possible to implement strict experimental designs. An action research paradigm is usually more appropriate.

Contrary to the beliefs of many, evaluation need not be "high science" to be meaningful, significant, or useful. Although our faith in the data gathered through program evaluation efforts can be only as strong as the design and the resulting information, in the real world of the school it is often difficult or impossible to conduct evaluations with direct control over the independent variable (the program), random assignment of participants to different treatment groups, and so on (see Bennett, 1988, for further discussion). In fact, experimental research methods are often inappropriate. Instead, action research and quasi-experimental designs, such as comparison group and time-series designs, are more commonly used in schools. Moreover, an understanding of realistic programmatic improvement relative to the developmental level of implementation is needed. Extraordinary improvements cannot be expected in a new program, and declining outcomes ought to be a concern in a mature program (Fetterman, 1996).

## Perceived Threat

Evaluation activities are often perceived as threatening because educators are concerned that the findings will be less than favorable. Indeed, the Fairchild and Zins (1992) survey on accountability practices found that over 10% expressed concern about the potential negative consequences of such activities. The key to addressing this issue is to have a supportive organizational context in which inquiry and reflection are valued (Zins et al., 1997). Rather than focusing on the darker side of evaluation, a supportive organization emphasizes the professional growth and service delivery improvements that can evolve from the evaluation effort.

The manner in which the evaluation is presented to the organization, therefore, is critical to its acceptance and utilization (Illback & Zins, 1984). Assessment of a program's worth and value cannot be viewed as the end product of the evaluation but instead as part of an ongoing process directed toward program and organizational improvements (Fetterman, 1996). Of course, we must acknowledge that evaluation data can result in the need for change. Sometimes programs do not accomplish their goals as planned and must be modified to improve their effectiveness or to address changing circumstances. At other times programs simply must be discontinued. However, even when a program must be discontinued, the decision to take this action is far more likely to be accepted by all constituents if there are solid data behind it.

## Resource Requirements

Evaluation activities are inherently time- and resource-consuming if done properly. In fact, virtually unlimited amounts of time could be expended on evaluation. Fairchild and Zins (1992) found that about 3% of their respondents did not collect accountability data because the practice was too time-consuming. Therefore, realistic expectations must be established so that the resources allocated correspond to the benefits derived. On the one hand, there are only limited resources that can be directed toward any aspect of an educational program. On the other hand, evaluation can be an exciting avenue that leads to professional growth and development, that establishes and demonstrates a program's value and credibility to consumers and decision makers, and that represents an effective means of managing service delivery options and procedures. Considering the evaluation component when initially planning a program will help to ensure that such a balance is achieved.

## Administrative Support

As alluded to throughout this chapter, administrators must actively support and sanction program evaluation efforts so that they can be carried out satisfactorily. Although sufficient time and resources must be allocated to staff who conduct the evaluation, what is just as important is an organizational climate supportive of inquiry and reflection. The research literature consistently identifies open interactions and dialogue among staff, students, parents, and the community as characteristic of a supportive organizational climate (Elias et al., 1997). Nevertheless, as Bennett (1988) points out, getting school officials to support evaluation is often difficult. For this reason, a strategy that we have found to be successful in such instances is to start with a relatively small-scale evaluation but to do a good job of demonstrating how even a limited amount of information can be useful in decision making and in improving the educational program. Once administrators see the results of this relatively low-cost demonstration, they may be more inclined to expand the evaluation effort. Furthermore, it is far more likely that the administration would support school psychologists' work if they understood the outcomes that resulted. It is also likely that administers would be less inclined to cut back on the psychological services program or replace it with contractual services even in times of financial strain if they were equipped with data about its effectiveness and the benefit to consumers.

## Communicating Results

A key characteristic of effective program evaluation is to communicate the results effectively so that multiple constituents understand them. Reports must be clear, concise, and free of technical jargon. They should also consider the technical sophistication and the needs of the audiences for whom they are written. The challenge is to present an understandable description of what is usually a very complex situation. Thus, as noted earlier, a single report is often not sufficient. Finally, because program evaluation may identify organizational or managerial areas in need of change, the results must be communicated sensitively and tactfully, although still accurately.

## Planning the Evaluation

Educational programs are too often developed without adequate consideration of the evaluation component, even when vast resources are devoted to the program. For example, the New York City school system spends nearly one-fourth of its $7.5 billion budget on special education, a total of $1.7 *billion*. However, according to a report from the city comptroller, the district had no comprehensive policy for measuring the program's effectiveness (Miller, 1994). Students in the program have IEPs, as required by federal law, but schools were not required to keep copies of these plans with the dates students had met the goals. The comptroller also found that it was not possible to use standardized test scores to measure the program's success. Unfortunately, similar situations exist nationwide.

It is also common to find that interest in evaluation emerges because it is required by some external agency or funding source or that consideration is given to program evaluation only at the end of the school year. For example, one of us was recently asked by a school to conduct an evaluation of a new social and emotional education program for a report that was due in six weeks to the state department of education, who funded the initiative. Although there were adequate funds for the evaluation and initial observations suggested that the program was well developed and effectively conducted, at that time it was virtually impossible to assess programmatic outcomes because essential data collection points had passed. We can cite numerous examples of evaluations conducted in such circumstances, but these types of situations almost always preclude a careful, thoughtful approach to designing and carrying out the evaluation.

## Involving Schools in Evaluation Efforts

Among the major challenges facing most school psychologists who want to be active in program evaluation is how to get schools involved in these efforts, ensure that the evaluations are of high quality, and increase the probabilities that the results will be utilized. Bennett (1988) suggested that program evaluation needs to be sold to educational decision makers as being a cost-effective component for improving various programs in the school so that they produce better outcomes. Without knowledge of how effectively a program operates and of how it might be improved, it is difficult to understand how resources can be continually directed toward the program. Evaluation attempts to provide some of this information. Bennett further observed that evaluation can be viewed as a type of insurance policy. That is, it helps determine whether resources are being allocated and used wisely, thereby avoiding costly mistakes for the school. Again using the cost effectiveness frame of reference should make evaluation more palatable to administrators.

The establishment of collaborative partnerships is a critical aspect in developing support for program evaluation. It is necessarily a collaborative activity and as such demands participation in an open forum (Fetterman, 1996). When members of the organization have been involved in developing program evaluation goals and procedures, they are more likely to feel ownership of the process, a commitment to ensuring that it is carried out according to plan, and a vested interest in the outcomes. There also is a higher probability that the results will meet their needs for decision making. For these reasons, school personnel must truly be viewed as partners in the evaluation process if evaluators are to expect them to cooperate with the plan and utilize the results.

## SUMMARY

We have described the historical and conceptual development of program planning and evaluation in human services, including the education system. Salient concepts, terminology, strategies, and methods from this rapidly developing field of empirical inquiry have been delineated in such areas as needs assessment, evaluability assessment, implementation evaluation, and outcome determination. The process of infusing evaluation into the routine of the organization and ensuring that evaluation findings are used to help organizations develop and improve has been discussed, and the need to identify and overcome barriers and resistance in utilization has been emphasized.

There is an increased sense of urgency in education about the importance of effective program planning and evaluation. The desire to establish and monitor the quality of educational programs and practices at individual, classroom, building, and school district levels occurs in part as a function of political and social pressures, as seen in the educational reform movement. However, this emphasis is also attributable to recognition by school professionals of the contributions that systematic program planning and evaluation can make in developing and improving school organizations. It is our expectation that school psychologists will be increasingly asked to participate in planning and evaluation activities and thus need to prepare themselves to fulfill this role.

# REFERENCES

Adelman, H. S., & Taylor, L. (1997). Toward a scale-up model for replicating new approaches to schooling. *Journal of Educational and Psychological Consultation, 8*(2), 197–230.

American Psychological Association. (1985). *Standards for educational and psychological tests and manuals.* Washington, DC: Author.

American Psychological Association. (1981). Specialty guidelines for the delivery of services by school psychologists. *American Psychologist, 36,* 670–681.

Attkisson, C. C., & Broskowski, A. (1978). Evaluation and the emerging human service concept. In C. C. Attkisson, W. A. Hargreaves, M. J. Horowitz, & J. E. Sorensen (Eds.), *Evaluation of human services programs* (p. 523). New York; Academic Press.

Ball, D. L., & McDiarmid, G. W. (1990). The subject-matter preparation of teachers. In W. R. Houston (Ed.), *Handbook of research on teacher education* (pp. 437–449). New York: Macmillan.

Barlow, D. H., Hayes, S. C., & Nelson, R. O. (1984). *The scientist practitioner: Research and accountability in clinical and educational settings.* Elmsford, NY: Pergamon.

Beer, M., & Walton, A. E. (1987). Organization change and development. *Annual Review of Psychology, 36,* 339–367.

Bell, T. H., & Elmquist, D. L. (1992). Technology: A catalyst for restructuring schools. *Electronic learning, 11* (5), 10–11.

Bennett, R. E. (1988). Evaluating the effectiveness of alternative educational delivery systems. In J. L. Graden, J. E. Zins, & M. J. Curtis (Eds.), *Alternative educational delivery systems.* Washington, DC: National Association of School Psychologists.

Borish, G. D., & Jemelka, R. P. (1982). *Programs and systems: An evaluation perspective.* New York: Academic Press.

Campbell, D. T. (1969). Reforms as experiments. *American Psychologist, 24,* 409–429.

Carlson, C. I., Tharinger, D. J., DeMers, S. T., Bricklin, P. M., & Paavola, J. C. (1996). Health care reform and psychological practice in schools. *Professional Psychology: Research and Practice, 27,* 14–23.

Christensen, S. L., Rounds, T., & Gorney, D. (1992). Family factors and student achievement. An avenue to increase students' success. *School Psychology Quarterly, 7,* 178–206.

Cook, T. J., & Campbell, D. T. (1976). The design and conduct of quasi-experiments and true experiments in field settings. In M. D. Dunnette (Ed.), *Handbook of industrial and organizational psychology* (pp. 223–326). Skokie, IL: Rand McNally.

Cousins, J. B., & Leithwood, K. A. (1986). Current empirical research on evaluation utilization. *Review of Educational Research, 56,* 331–364.

Cronbach, L. J. (1980). *Toward reform of program evaluation.* San Francisco: Jossey-Bass.

Cronbach, L. J. (1982). *Designing evaluations of educational and social programs.* San Francisco: Jossey-Bass.

Crowson, R. L., & Boyd, W. L. (1993). Coordinated services for children: Designing arks for storms and seas unknown. *American Journal of Education, 101,* 140–174.

Dalkey, N. C. (1967). *Delphi.* Santa Monica, CA: Rand Corp.

Delbecq, A. L., & Van de Ven, A. H. (1971). A group process model for problem identification and program planning. *Journal of Applied Behavioral Science, 7,* 446–492.

DeMers, S. T. & Bricklin, P. (1995). Legal, professional, and financial constraints on the delivery of health care services in schools. *School Psychology Quarterly, 10*(3), 217–235.

DeSouza, E. R., & Sivewright, D. (1993). An ecological approach to evaluating a special education program. *Adolescence, 28,* 517–525.

Dranda, M. R., & Corwin, R. G. (1994). *Vision and reality: A first-year look at California's charter schools.* Los Alamitos, CA: Southwest Regional Laboratory.

Elias, M. J., Zins, J. E., Weissberg, R. P., Frey, K. S., Greenberg, M. T., Haynes, N. M., Kessler, R., Schwab-Stone, M. E., & Shriver, T. P. (1997). *Promoting social and emotional learning: Guidelines for educators.* Alexandria, VA: Association for Supervision and Curriculum Development.

Elmore, R. F. (Ed.), (1990). *Restructuring schools: The next generation of educational reform.* San Francisco: Jossey-Bass.

Fagan, T. N. (1990). Best practices in the training of school psychologists. In A. Thomas & J. Grimes (Eds.), *Best practices in school psychology–II* (pp. 723–742). Washington, DC: National Association of School Psychologists.

Fairchild, T. N., & Zins, J. E. (1992). Accountability

practices of school psychologists: 1991 national survey. *School Psychology Review, 21*(4), 617–627.

Fetterman, D. M. (1996). Empowerment evaluation: An introduction to theory and practice. In D. M. Fetterman, S. J. Kaftarian, & S. J. Wandersman (Eds.), *Empowerment evaluation* (pp. 3–48). Thousand Oaks, CA: Sage.

Fetterman, D. M., Kaftarian, S. J., & Wandersman, A. (Eds.). (1996). *Empowerment evaluation.* Thousand Oaks, CA: Sage.

Flaherty, E. W., & Morrell, J. A. (1978). Evaluation: Manifestations of a new field. *Evaluation and Program Planning, 1,* 1–10.

Fourqurean, J. M., & LaCourt, T. (1991). A follow-up of former special education students: A model for program evaluation. *Remedial and Special Education, 12,* 16–23.

Frank, R. G., Sullivan, M. J., & DeLeon, P. H. (1994). Health care reform in the states. *American Psychologist, 49,* 855–867.

Fullan, M. G. (1993). *Change forces: Probing the depths of education reform.* Bristol, PA: Falmer.

Fullan, M., Miles, M. B., & Taylor, G. (1980). Organization development in schools: The state of the art. *Review of Educational Research, 50,* 121–183.

Fullan, M., & Pomfret, A. (1977). Research on curriculum and instruction implementation. *Review of Educational Research, 47,* 335–397.

Gandal, M. (1995). *Making standards matter: A fifty-state progress report on efforts to raise academic standards.* Washington, DC: American Federation of Teachers.

George, M. F., et al., (1990). Features of program evaluation in special education. *Remedial and Special Education, 11,* 23–30.

Grace, C., & Shores, E. F. (1991). *The portfolio and its use: Developmentally appropriate assessment of young children.* Little Rock, AR: Southern Early Childhood Assoc.

Gregg, B. G., & Bonfield, T. (1997, February 26). Council questions worth of D.A.R.E.: National study prompts local concerns. *Cincinnati Enquirer,* pp. A1, A14.

Hall, G. E., & Hord, S. M. (1987). *Change in schools: Facilitating the process.* Albany: State University of New York Press.

Hall, G. E., & Loucks, S. F. (1977). A developmental model for determining whether the treatment is actually implemented. *American Educational Research Journal, 14,* 263–276.

Hobbs, N. (1981). *The futures of children.* San Francisco: Jossey-Bass.

Illback, R. J. (1991). Organizational influences and applications in the practice of psychology in the schools. In F. P. Medway and T. P. Cafferty (Eds.), *School psychology: A school psychological perspective.* Hillsdale, NJ: Erlbaum.

Illback, R. J., & Kalafat, J. (1997). Evaluating integrated service programs. In R. J. Illback, C. T. Cobb, & H. M. Joseph, Jr. (Eds.), *Integrated services for children and families: Opportunities for psychological practice.* Washington, DC: APA Books.

Illback, R. J., & Zins, J. E. (1984). Organizational interventions in educational settings. In C. A. Maher, R. J. Illback, & J. E. Zins (Eds.), *Organizational psychology in the schools* (pp. 21–51). Springfield, IL: Thomas.

Joint Committee on Standards for Educational Evaluation. (1981). *Standards for evaluations of educational programs, projects, and materials.* New York: McGraw-Hill.

Joint Committee on Standards for Educational Evaluation. (1994). *The program evaluation standards* (2nd ed.). Thousand Oaks, CA: Sage.

Kalafat, J. (1996). Planning and evaluating integrated school-based services. In R. J. Illback & C. M. Nelson (Eds.), *Emerging school-based approaches for children with emotional and behavioral problems: Research and practice in service integration* (pp. 209–224). New York: Haworth.

Kalafat, J., & Illback, R. (in press). A qualitative evaluation of school-based family resource and youth service centers. *American Journal of Community Psychology.*

Kiresuk, T. J., Smith, A., & Cardillo, J. E. (Eds.). (1994). *Goal attainment scaling.* Hillsdale, NJ: Erlbaum.

Kosecoff, J., & Fink, A. (1982). *Evaluation basics: A practitioner's manual.* Beverly Hills, CA: Sage.

Kratochwill, T. R. (Ed.). (1978). *Single subject research: Strategies for evaluating change.* New York; Academic Press.

Kress, J. S., Cimring, B. R., & Elias, M. J. (1997). Community psychology consultation and the transition to institutional ownership and operation of intervention. *Journal of Educational and Psychological Consultation, 8*(2), 231–253.

Legge, K. (1984). *Evaluating planned organization change.* London: Academic Press.

Lewis, A. C. (1995). An overview of the standards movement. *Phi Delta Kappan, 76*(10), 744–750.

Lincoln, Y. S., & Guba, E. G. (1985). *Naturalistic inquiry.* Beverly Hills, CA: Sage.

Lippitt, G. L., Langseth, P. M., & Mossop, J. (1986). *Implementing organizational change.* San Francisco: Jossey-Bass.

Maher, C. A. (1981). Program evaluation and school psychology: Perspectives, principles, procedures. In T. R. Kratochwill (Ed.), *Advances in School Psychology* (Vol. 1, pp. 169–216). Hillsdale, NJ: Erlbaum.

Maher, C. A., & Bennett, R. E. (1984). *Planning and evaluating special education services.* Englewood Cliffs, NJ: Prentice Hall.

Maher, C. A. & Illback, R. J. (1981). Planning for the delivery of special services in public schools. A multidimensional needs assessment framework. *Evaluation and Program Planning, 4*, 249–259.

Maher, C. A., & Illback, R. J. (1982). Organizational school psychology: Issues and considerations. *Journal of School Psychology, 20*, 244–253.

Maher, C. A., & Illback, R. J. (1984). A team approach to the evaluation of special services in public schools. In C. A. Maher, R. J. Illback, and J. E. Zins (Eds.), *Organizational psychology in the schools: A handbook for professionals.* Springfield, IL: Thomas.

Miller, L. (1994, July 13). Lack of accountability in spec.-ed. program blasted. *Education Week*, p. 5.

Moore, C. M., & Carlsen, D. (1988, April). Accountability: Practices and issues. Paper presented at the Annual Meeting of the National Association of School Psychologists, Chicago.

National Association of School Psychologists. (1992). *Standards for the provision of school psychological services.* Washington, DC: Author.

National Commission on Excellence in Education. (1983). *A nation at risk: The imperative for education reform.* Washington, DC: U.S. Department of Education.

National Education Goals Panel. (1991). *The national education goals report: Building a nation of learners.* Washington, DC: Author.

National Education Standards and Improvement Council. (1993). *Promises to keep: Creating high standards for American students.* Washington, DC: National Goals Panel.

Patton, M. Q. (1978). *Utilization-focused evaluation.* Beverly Hills, CA: Sage.

Patton, M. Q. (1990). *Qualitative evaluation and research methods.* Newbury Park, CA: Sage.

Payne, D. A. (1996). Designing educational project and program evaluations: A practical overview based on research and experience. *Evaluation and Program Planning, 19*, 273–274.

Price, R. D., & Smith, S. (1985). *A guide to evaluating prevention programs in mental health* (DHHS Publ. No. ADM 85-144). Washington, DC: U.S. Government Printing Office.

Provus, M. M. (1972). *Discrepancy evaluation.* Berkeley, CA: McCutchan.

Rossi, R. J. (1995). *Educational reforms and students at risk.* New York: Teachers College Press.

Rossi, P. H., Freeman, H. E. (1993). *Evaluation: A systematic approach* (5th ed.). Beverly Hills, CA: Sage.

Scriven, M. (1967). The methodology of evaluation. In *Perspective on curriculum evaluation* (AERA Monograph Series on Curriculum Evaluation No 1). Skokie, IL: Rand McNally.

Shapiro, E. (1987). Intervention research methodology in school psychology. *School Psychology Review, 16*, 290–305.

Siegel, L. M., Attkisson, C. C., & Carson, L. G. (1978). Need identification and program planning in the community context. In C. C. Attkisson, W. A. Hargreaves, M. J. Horowitz, & J. E. Sorensen (Eds.), *Evaluation of human services programs* (pp. 215–252). New York: Academic Press.

Smith, D. K., Clifford, E. S., Hesley, J., & Leifgren, M. (1992, March). The school psychologist of 1991: A survey of practitioners. Paper presented at the Annual Meeting of the National Association of School Psychologists, Nashville, TN.

Spady, W. G. (1988). Organizing for results. The basis of authentic restructuring and reform. *Educational Leadership, 46*(2), 4–8.

Sproull, L., & Larkey, P. (1979). Managerial behavior and evaluator effectiveness. In H. C. Schulberg & J. M. Jerrell (Eds.), *The evaluator and management* (pp. 89–104). Beverly Hills, CA: Sage.

Talley, R. C., & Short, R. J. (1996). Social reforms and the future of school practice: Implications for American psychology. *Professional Psychology: Research and Practice, 27*, 5–13.

Tharinger, D. J., Bricklin, P. M., Johnson, N. F., Paster, V. S., Lambert, N. M., Feshbach, N., Oakland, T. D., & Sanchez, W. (1996). Education reform: Challenges for psychology and psychologists. *Professional Psychology: Research and Practice, 27*, 24–33.

Tirozzi, G. N., & Uro, G. (1997). Education reform in the United States: National policy in support of local efforts for school improvement. *American Psychologist, 52*, 241–249.

Udinsky, B. F., Osterlind, S. J., & Lynch, S. W. (1981). *Evaluation resource handbook: Gathering, analyzing, reporting data.* San Diego: EdITS.

U.S. General Accounting Office. (1989). *Effective schools programs: Their extent and characteristics.* Gaithersburg, MD: Author.

U.S. General Accounting Office. (1995). *Charter Schools: New models for public schools provide opportunities and challenges.* Washington, DC: Author.

Weiss, C. H. (1973). Between the cup and the lip. *Evaluation, 1*, 49–55.

Weiss, H. B. (1988). Family support and education programs: Working through ecological theories of human development. In H. B. Weiss & F. H. Jacobs (Eds.), *Evaluating family programs* (pp. 3–36), Hawthorne, NY: Aldine.

Whiston, S. C. (1996). Accountability through action research: Research methods for practitioners. *Journal of Counseling and Development, 74*, 616–623.

Wholey, J. S. (1979). Evaluability assessment. In L. Rutman (Ed.), *Evaluation research methods: A basic guide* (pp. 39–56). Beverly Hills, CA: Sage.

Zins, J. E. (1985). Best practices for improving school psychology through accountability. In A. Thomas & J. Grimes (Eds.), *Best practices in school psychology* (pp. 493–503). Washington, DC: National Association of School Psychologists.

Zins, J. E. (Ed.). (1997). Community psychology contributions to consultation. *Journal of Educational and Psychological Consultation* (Special issue), *8*(2).

Zins, J. E., & Fairchild, T. N. (1986). An investigation of the accountability practices of school psychologists. *Professional School Psychology*, *1*(3), 193–204.

Zins, J. E., Johnson, J. R., & Thomas, A. (1995, March). Characteristics and activities of practicing school psychologists: Results of an international survey. Paper presented at the Annual Meeting of the National Association of School Psychologists, Chicago.

Zins, J. E., Travis, L. F., III, & Freppon, P. A. (1997). Linking research and educational programming to promote social and emotional learning. In P. Salovey & D. Sluyter (Eds.), *Emotional development and emotional intelligence: Implications for educators* (pp. 257–274). New York: Basic Books.

# Excellence in Teaching: Review of Instructional and Environmental Variables

Maribeth Gettinger
Karen Callan Stoiber
*University of Wisconsin-Madison*

Over the years, researchers have engaged in numerous studies to identify instructional and environmental variables that contribute to excellence in teaching. Working from a variety of different theoretical orientations, researchers have examined teacher, student, and classroom variables using diverse measurement procedures, including personality tests, attitudinal measures, observations systems, rating scales, videotapes, and qualitative interviews. Despite hundreds of studies on classroom instruction, research has yielded few established facts. There is no yardstick to gauge whether instruction matches a set of professional practices that are synonymous with excellence. Nonetheless, research on teaching has provided a rich and diverse knowledge base that can be a useful tool for school psychologists who consult with teachers to ensure that learning is maximized.

In this chapter, we provide a review of current research on teaching, with an emphasis on instructional and environmental variables that have been shown to enhance students' learning. This chapter is based on the following key assumption: excellence in teaching occurs when there is teaching for understanding, when learners are helped to take an active role in their own learning, and when there is consideration of students' diverse and individual needs. The chapter is divided into three sections. First, we provide a general overview and comparison of two major paradigms that have guided research on teaching for the last two decades. Next, we offer a con-

temporary view of teaching, learning, and thinking, highlighting research that has led to current conceptualizations of the nature of excellence in teaching. Finally, we review research and implications for practice related to six critical variables that influence students' learning. Collectively, these variables represent a profile of excellence in teaching.

## RESEARCH ON TEACHING: PARADIGMS AND PITFALLS

Research on teaching over the last 20 years has been conceptualized within two dominant paradigms. The first is a process-product or process-outcome approach. Using this paradigm, researchers investigate teaching by correlating process variables that depict what occurs during teaching (i.e., teachers' behaviors, teaching methods, or teacher-student interactions) with specific products or learner outcomes, such as performance on paper-and-pencil achievement tests. In this regard, effective teaching means engaging in behaviors that match as closely as possible a list of prescriptions or general principles. The second paradigm, termed an interpretive approach, relies predominantly on qualitative or case study methodology to examine the overall context of teaching and learning. Researchers focus on teachers' thinking and how they accommodate diverse learners or domain-specific content. Effective teaching means adaptive teaching (rather than adherence to a prescribed teaching method) that facilitates students' understanding of academic content and application of knowledge (Brandt, 1992; Cochran-Smith & Lytle, 1990). Collectively, process-product and interpretive paradigms have generated most of the current knowledge about effective teaching.

## Process-Product Research Paradigm

During the 1970s, research on teaching involved a systematic analysis of teachers' behaviors that were related to positive student outcomes, such as good grades on classroom tests, strong performance on standardized achievement tests, and high rates of on-task behavior. Several productive research programs incorporating a process-product perspective were initiated during the 1970s (see Brophy & Good, 1986, for a review). Although some studies provided contradictory results, many identified patterns of classroom interaction that consistently produced desirable student outcomes.

Process-product research typically followed a three-step process. First, researchers observed individuals who were effective versus ineffective classroom teachers. This approach yielded a list of teaching behaviors that were used more frequently by effective teachers and, as hypothesized, accounted for student achievement. Second, correlational studies were conducted to identify positive associations between the use of effective teaching behaviors and student outcomes. Outcomes (such as test performance) were averaged across individual students to represent the collective learning that had occurred in a classroom. Some behaviors were highly correlated with positive outcomes, and others were not. This step in a research program was designed to narrow the list of effective teaching behaviors to those that were used frequently by effective teachers and demonstrated a positive association with student achievement. Finally, studies were conducted in which experimental group teachers received training in effective teaching behaviors, while control group teachers did not. Achievement and classroom behavior of students were compared between experimental and control teachers, with students of experimental teachers exhibiting higher performance (Borich, 1988; Brophy & Good, 1986).

A critical assumption underlying this approach is that teaching is a linear activity whereby processes (teaching behaviors) directly influence the products or outcomes of learning (student achievement). Process-product re-

searchers attempted to identify a set of discrete behaviors and patterns of teacher-student interaction that generalized across all teachers, classrooms, and learning contexts. Marshall (1992) characterized this approach as examining classrooms through "behaviorist lenses." Consistent with a behavioral approach, researchers focused on observable teacher behaviors, correlated observable behaviors with measurable student outcomes, and then compared outcomes across classrooms.

Several criticisms and warnings about the interpretation and use of process-product findings have been articulated over the years. For example, some school districts offer staff development courses based on the results of process-product research and have attempted to translate research findings into instruments for evaluating teachers. Critics are concerned that such efforts tend to enforce a prescriptive set of uniform teaching behaviors with little regard to diverse content, curriculum, or student ability (Darling-Hammond, 1996; Richardson, 1994). Teaching approaches that incorporate structured practice-and-drill routines may lead to high scores on standardized tests but do not help students apply their knowledge, develop critical thinking skills, or acquire competence in more cognitively complex tasks (Darling-Hammond, 1996). In other words, process-product research focuses on basic aspects of teaching, without considering the more complex variables that distinguish true excellence (Ornstein, 1990). Furthermore, because process-product research relies extensively on achievement test performance as the outcome variable, it excludes a focus on other important "products" of classroom instruction, such as application and problem solving (Cochran-Smith & Lytle, 1990).

Eisner (1983) voiced another concern about process-product research. Because critical aspects of effective teaching, such as teachers' decision making, are difficult to measure, process-product researchers have replaced them with behaviors that are less meaningful but comparatively easy to measure. Looking at teaching in a process-product paradigm may result in overlooking the difficult-to-measure but critical aspects of teaching. The problem lies in assuming that teachers who enact principles evolving from process-product research are "effective," while ignoring the other qualities that contribute to effective teaching.

Despite these concerns, process-product research has established some conclusions about teaching that remain important today. First, teachers make a difference in students' learning. Learning occurs, in part, because of exposure to appropriate academic material and opportunities to engage in meaningful learning, both of which are controlled primarily by teachers. Process-product research has also confirmed that teachers who facilitate learning do not simply keep students on-task; rather, they spend time actively interacting with their students. Process-product research is important because it has provided an initial knowledge base for looking at classrooms and teaching practices and because its conclusions remain at the heart of current research on teaching (Brandt, 1992; Brophy, 1992).

In further defense of process-product research, Needels and Gage (1991) argued that most critics have "found fault with many incidental characteristics without realizing that they were attacking nothing essential to the enterprise." For example, process-product research has been criticized because of its focus on simplistic variables that fail to reflect the highly complex nature of teaching. Nothing inherent in a process-product paradigm, however, prevents an analysis of other variables. In other words, more complex aspects of classroom teaching can be studied as process variables. The traditional focus on observable behaviors is what Needels and Gage call an "accident" of process-product research, not the "essence" of the approach. Similarly, the specific methods for measuring process variables are also accidents of process-product research, not the essence. Process variables may be measured through interviews, questionnaires, or in-depth analyses of videotapes, not just standardized achievement tests. In sum, criticisms of process-product research, although legitimate, should not minimize the important contributions researchers have made to our understanding of and improvement in teaching.

## Interpretive Research Paradigm

In the 1980s, research on teaching moved from linking teachers' behaviors with students' achievement to exploring the complexity of the teaching-learning process. This shift away from a process-product paradigm was catalyzed by criticism that lists of "teacher should" behaviors failed to reflect the dynamic nature of classrooms. Specifically, the emphasis on "effective" teaching behaviors ignored critical pedagogical considerations of subject content, diverse learners, and the development of students' critical thinking. Thus, a new paradigm for educational research, known as an interpretive approach, evolved from a different conception of effectiveness. Interpretive researchers are concerned with indicators of classroom effectiveness that are context- and situation-specific, including classroom qualities (e.g., equality of opportunities to participate, teacher-student communication patterns, and interchanges between students with different cultural backgrounds) and highly developed student performances (e.g., independence in learning, problem-solving approaches, and writing coherence).

Embedded in the interpretive paradigm are qualitative approaches to understanding classroom life. Researchers have built a rich, case-based knowledge of teaching that considers learning in different contexts and subject domains and examines the role of planning, actions, and decision making. Shulman (1986) stated that the changes introduced by interpretive researchers have been more than methodological; rather, a conceptual shift in the focus of inquiry is evident. In contrast to the behavior emphasis of process-product researchers, interpretive researchers focus on the personal meaning of classroom life. As pointed out by Shulman, interpretive researchers attempt to capture the situations and contexts in which classroom life is situated:

> While process-product researchers view classrooms as reducible to discrete events and behaviors which can be noted, counted, and aggregated for purposes of generalization across settings and individuals, interpretive scholars view classrooms as socially and culturally organized environments. Individual participants in those environments contribute to the organization and to the definition of meanings. They are actively engaged in "making sense" in the setting. Life in classrooms is understood as a function, not only of jointly produced local meanings of the particular classroom group, but also as influenced by the larger contexts in which the class is embedded—the school, the community, the society, the culture. (p. 20)

An interpretive model of inquiry addresses questions about what educators can do to facilitate academic and social competence among all students. What interpretive researchers have uncovered is that teaching for understanding does not follow a step-by-step, prescriptive package. Rather, teachers require sophisticated knowledge for their work. This finding highlights the importance of being able to understand diverse characteristics of learners and educational contexts (Ladson-Billings, 1995). Interpretive researchers examine how teachers make sense of their students and their classrooms. Insights on decision making, the nature of knowledge in content-specific domains, and teachers' use of practical and personal knowledge are captured through rich case studies of classrooms. For example, teachers are often interviewed about their thinking while engaged in lesson planning. Students are also asked to describe their approaches to solving problems or learning new concepts (Swing, Stoiber, & Peterson, 1988).

Advocates of interpretive research subscribe to more student-centered pedagogy, focusing on how students of diverse abilities and backgrounds have equity in learning (Bereiter & Scardamalia, 1987). Based on interpretive research findings, effective teachers are those who engage students in meaningful tasks that allow them to make choices. They also use students' strengths as a point of entry for enhancing their motivation and interest in learning, while challenging them with projects and concepts about which to think. This conception of teaching as a complex task, a nonlinear process of many overlapping demands, constraints, and opportunities, represents the most important contribution of interpretive research during the 1980s.

# TEACHING, LEARNING, AND THINKING: A CONTEMPORARY VIEW

Since the late 1980s, educational reform has been advocated as researchers and practitioners become aware of the need for innovation in classroom practices (Fullan, 1991). Efforts to ensure learner-responsive teaching have framed research initiatives in the 1990s. Three concepts are fundamental to contemporary views on teaching, learning, and thinking. First, classroom teachers must possess diverse types of knowledge and competencies to be successful in their efforts to teach for understanding. Second, learners' cognitions and perceptions dramatically influence the learning process and mediate and interpret academic content. Third, classroom learning and knowledge acquisition are highly social processes. These concepts have important impli-

cations for transforming the way teaching occurs in classrooms and for shaping contemporary research on teaching.

## Teachers' Knowledge

Current research underscores the importance of teaching to promote understanding among students (Wang, Haertel, & Walberg, 1993). Teachers are being challenged to implement practices that respond to the diverse needs of students, taking advantage of their strengths and their learning readiness and providing instruction that moves all students toward proficiency (Darling-Hammond, 1996). Darling-Hammond states that teachers and administrators must work to "develop settings that are both learning-centered—that is, focused on challenging curriculum goals for all students—and learner-centered—that is, attentive to the needs and interests of individual learners" (p. 9).

Teaching for excellence requires that teachers have diverse types of knowledge and competence on which to draw when making decisions and taking action in classrooms. In their analysis of school-restructuring efforts, Elmore, Peterson, and McCarthey (1996) make a passionate plea that teachers must have access to the kinds of knowledge and skills necessary to improve their classroom practices. Too often, schools assume that teachers know how to involve students in meaningful learning experiences, but teachers should receive ongoing feedback about how to engage students in self-directed learning, how to help students approach problems in a thoughtful way, and how to facilitate students' construction of knowledge. Teaching that promotes students' understanding of content is more complex than simply presenting the subject matter. Given the complexity of teaching, one-shot seminars on a particular instructional approach or brief consultation directed at a single issue lack the potency necessary to promote excellence.

Educational leaders who advocate teaching for understanding assert that most teaching emphasizes rote learning and memorization of facts (Anderson, Blumenfeld, Pintrich, Clark, Marx, & Peterson, 1995; Cohen, McLaughlin, & Talbert, 1993; Darling-Hammond, 1996; Langer, 1993; Peterson, McCarthey, & Elmore, 1996; Richardson, 1994). According to Elmore et al. (1996), teaching is often "devoid of connection to any broad scheme of context for knowledge, or of any application to problems that engage students' interests" (p. 4). In striving toward excellence, teachers must have knowledge about strategies that are responsive to the individual needs of their students. There are many goals in teaching for excellence, including higher expectations for all students, more responsive approaches to cultural and ability differences, better assessment of students' learning, and more explicit links between students' ways of knowing and teachers' ways of teaching.

Several researchers have found that teachers struggle in determining how to teach for understanding (Darling-Hammond, 1996; Peterson et al., 1996). A teacher's success in facilitating students' understanding of content is evidenced when students engage in intentional learning. Intentional learning refers to students' active organization and management of diverse types of knowledge and their flexible use of judgments and decisions. Teachers' capability in creating classroom environments that promote intentional learning depends on their own deployment of a diverse knowledge base. Good teaching is based on accessing different types of knowledge. Kennedy (1988) posited four forms of teachers' knowledge. The first is technical knowledge, such as providing a brief overview of new concepts, using concrete examples, and modeling organizational strategies. Principled or theoretical knowledge is the second form, for example, applying a learning theory or principle, such as advanced organizers, to classroom routines. Kennedy questioned the usefulness of these first types of knowledge as the sole bases for constructing classroom practices. Others have posited a more developmental view, suggesting that these two types of knowledge may serve a useful purpose for novice teachers as they navigate the complexity of classroom life (Anderson et al., 1995). A capacity for critical analysis of classroom situations is the third form of teachers' knowledge. The fourth form incorporates the first three types—technical, principled, and situational analysis—but places a strong emphasis on conscious action. The actions of teachers are guided by a sense of purpose or goals, technical and principled knowledge, and an analysis of the immediate situation. According to Kennedy, teachers must deliberately consider and prioritize their goals for each teaching situation and act on their choices.

Based on their recent analysis of what constitutes good teaching, Elmore et al. (1996) noted that less successful teachers do not differ from more successful teachers in the effort they commit to teaching or in their pedagogical views. Both types of teachers talk similarly about their intentions to achieve excellence. All of the teachers they interviewed espoused aspirations of taking a more active role in constructing curriculum, of being more student-centered in promoting students' active engagement, and of wanting to help students cultivate a deeper understanding of their own learning. Elmore et al. found, however, that good teaching is distinguished by (a) a sophisticated awareness of what students do and how they think as they try to achieve an understanding of academic content, (b) a clear command of the subject domain being taught, and (c) confidence in connecting content to the experience and backgrounds of children. In addition, excellence in teaching is marked by a systematic knowledge of practice, one that embraces both abstract and concrete knowledge. This blending of fundamental knowledge of subject concepts and abstract conceptions about teaching is exemplified in Elmore et al.'s description of the teaching of Dan Rollins (fictitious name) as he discusses praying mantis egg cases with his students: "First, he set out the larger framework of life cycles; then, he let students explore eggs in various forms; and, finally he listened to students talk and ask questions about what they were observing as they focused on the praying mantis egg cases. While his practice looked both spontaneous and seamless, it had a strong undercurrent of careful planning, forethought, and inquisitiveness about students' modes of thought" (p. 228).

This kind of teaching is more complex, requires deeper knowledge of content and student learning, and is more flexible than traditional "knowledge transfer" methods. The instruction of Dan Rollins demonstrates the need for teachers to constantly monitor what and how students are thinking and also demonstrates the use of guided discovery. His lesson contains many elements of discovery learning, in which students learn by doing. In addition, he seems to incorporate elements of structured intervention, or more direct sharing of knowledge, through his use of questioning and didactic techniques.

Recent studies have begun to demonstrate how expert teachers construct forms of teaching that build on students' experiences, interests, and learning approaches, while also promoting understanding and competence. As case studies of teaching excellence accumulate, some common features of practice emerge. Recent discussions emphasize that teachers who succeed in fostering students' understanding focus on both the process of learner development and the content of subject matter (Darling-Hammond, 1996). Darling-Hammond has summarized seven key practices of teachers who are successful at developing students' understanding of challenging content. These teaching strategies highlight the importance of teachers' capacity to vary their practices according to the content being covered, their goals for instruction, and their knowledge about students' learning:

1. They engage students in meaningful work by providing projects and tasks that encompass a whole area of investigation, such as "publishing" a short book or doing historical research.
2. They design tasks that provide opportunities for students to make choices and engage in learning experiences based on their strengths, interests, and goals.
3. They use two-way pedagogical tools to uncover what students are thinking or struggling to solve, such as student presentations, interviews, journals, and learning logs.
4. They use assessment methods to understand their teaching and students' learning. They find ways to monitor student progress, to identify their strengths, and to analyze their learning.
5. They scaffold or mediate students' learning through the use of successive conversations and learning experiences that move students from differing starting points to proficient performance.
6. They build strong relationships with students and their families, blending affective, motivational, and cognitive aspects into their instruction.
7. They develop their students' confidence by attending to their efforts and in attempting to make students feel comfortable and accepted at school.

Teachers have to be able to look at the world of teaching from multiple perspectives. The capacity for an expanded perspective of learning makes it easier for teachers to seek people, ideas, concepts, and strategies that are essential in guiding their practice. This expanded capacity is critical to developing a knowledge base that responds to the multifaceted experiences of students and the multifaceted dimensions of differ-

ent subject domains. School psychologists can play a critical role in building teachers' knowledge. One important approach is to forge a joint experience with teachers to help them observe and document their practice and children's learning. It is critical for school psychologists to expand their own knowledge about excellence in teaching beyond the boundaries that often separate educational professionals. As curriculum and teaching change to reflect a greater emphasis on students' understanding and application of content, school psychologists will need to develop complementary knowledge and skills.

## Learner-Centered Principles

A second contemporary dimension is a focus on students' cognitions and characteristics. Research on teaching has traditionally investigated teachers' behaviors and instructional contexts. Recently, the role of students' thoughts in mediating the teaching-learning process has been emphasized, representing a learner-centered orientation. This orientation stresses the role of the student in stimulating learning; it recognizes that students are not passive recipients of information from teachers but that they actively mediate or interpret content, trying to make sense of it and to relate new knowledge to what they already know. In this perspective, students develop new knowledge through a process of active construction, facilitated in part by the classroom teacher. Focusing on learner-centered principles, researchers view students as important actors and their thought processes as key elements during instruction. Thus, the focus is on covert behaviors of learners during instruction, not the overt behavior of the teacher.

Knight and Waxman (1991) describe the student-mediating focus as a shift from a behaviorist to an information-processing view, in which students are seen as active interpreters or mediators of instruction. Learner-centered characteristics include students' perceptions and expectations, as well as attention, motivation, memory, comprehension, learning strategies, and metacognitive processes. Evidence of this current focus is seen in a recent document developed by the American Psychological Association (APA), Presidential Task Force on Psychology in Education (1995). This document, entitled *Learner-Centered Psychological Principles: A Framework for School Redesign and Reform*, centers attention on students, rather than teaching or curriculum, as a framework for educational reform efforts. Fourteen principles related to cognitive and metacognitive factors, motivational and affective factors, developmental and social factors, and individual differences are described; collectively, these represent critical learner-centered dimensions of teaching.

A focus on the learner parallels the current emphasis in teaching on promoting good thinking among students. Contemporary views of thinking incorporate several descriptors. Specifically, good thinking requires a repertoire of strategies for approaching tasks and solving problems, as well as metacognition, which is knowledge about and awareness of one's own thinking. Good thinking requires that strategies are used in conjunction with self-monitoring and nonstrategic knowledge and in the context of being motivated and having adequate short-term memory. Excellence in teaching means developing good thinking or information-processing skills, not just high achievers.

A final aspect of students that contributes to their learning is prior knowledge. Specifically, the type and amount of knowledge learners bring to a teaching situation affect their learning of new content. Learning outcomes are determined jointly by what is known previously and by the content of instruction. In other words, prior knowledge influences the processing of new information. The recognition that students bring prior knowledge to new learning suggests that teachers must make this knowledge explicit and then attempt to build on it.

## Social Nature of Teaching and Learning

Learning in classrooms is fundamentally a social and interactive process. Clearly, reciprocal interactions and group processes are likely to occur in all classrooms and schools. The design and delivery of curriculum and instruction, therefore, need to focus on the social context of children's learning (Boekaerts, 1993). Integrating social and academic goals has often been regarded as one of the greatest challenges of teaching (Darling-Hammond, 1996). The need to attend to the social component of learning in classrooms was recognized by the Carnegie Council on Adolescent Development (CCAD; 1980) in their call for educational reform. As their first major recommendation, CCAD advocated in-school "communities for learning, where stable, close, mutually respectful relationships with adults and peers are considered fundamental for intellectual development and personal growth" (p. 9).

The importance of social aspects of classrooms has been acknowledged both in theory and in practice. Several theoretical perspectives, areas of research, and bodies of literature can be applied and extended to understand classroom life. Examples include work on the social dynamics of groups, social support and acceptance, social influences on identity development, and affiliative motivation (Goodenow, 1992). Recognition of the social embeddedness of learning is also apparent in research on classroom climate and expectations. For example, classrooms that establish explicit goals for their students to achieve social competence, prosocial behavior, and positive interactions have been linked to academic success across the preschool, elementary, and high school levels (Cohen, 1994; Wentzel, 1991). The importance of social elements of learning has also been demonstrated in the link between students' relationships with peers and academic performance (Steinberg, Dornbusch, & Brown, 1996; Stevens & Slavin, 1995). In addition, students' perceptions of social support while learning and the degree to which they believe their teachers "like them" have been shown to affect academic and social performance (Goodenow, 1992; Wentzel, 1994).

Although there is general agreement that classrooms involve social elements, differing conceptions of their influence on teaching and learning appear in the literature. Some researchers have suggested that a major challenge faced by teachers is to focus students' attention on academic content while being surrounded by many social distractors. Csikszentmihalyi (1991), for example, used a procedure in which high school students were signaled by a paging device and asked to describe their thoughts and emotions. He found that only a small percentage reported they were actually attending to classroom instruction when they were signaled. Various investigations have explored whether achievement-oriented goals or social goals demonstrate a stronger link to learning-related outcomes, suggesting that social and educational goals are distinct, as well as competing, phenomena (Maehr & Pintrich, 1991). Work by Wentzel (1989, 1991) demonstrates that students are motivated as much by social goals as by learning goals, even when academic performance is emphasized.

Social and learning elements do not simply coexist in classrooms; rather, they are so embedded in the matrix of classroom life that one cannot be understood apart from the other

(Boekaerts, 1993; Goodenow, 1992). This emphasis on the social nature of classroom learning is evident in recent work on social constructivist theories, reciprocal and mediational learning approaches, cooperative learning, and social competence. For example, thinking, problem solving, and learning always begin with social origins and cannot be viewed as solely cognitive (Goodenow, 1992). The concept of promoting competence in a "zone of proximal development" makes explicit that an individual "can do with another's help what cannot be achieved alone" (Boekaerts, 1993). Recent attention to social constructivism and the use of the apprenticeship or mentor metaphor also highlight that learning is interactional and occurs among individuals rather than by individuals in isolation.

That social elements are embedded in instruction and exert significant influence on students' learning has been demonstrated in a variety of classroom investigations. Using information gleaned from 61 research experts, 91 meta-analyses, and 179 handbook reviews, Wang et al. (1993) examined which variables exert the greatest influence on school learning. Their investigation provided robust and consistent evidence of an essential link between the "key proximal variable" of classroom interaction and student outcomes. Moreover, they reported that distal variables, such as state or district policies for special education classification and placement, have limited impact on student outcomes. These researchers suggest that there are two types of teacher-student interactions, academic and social. With both types of interaction, the amount and quality of interaction initiated by the teacher has been tied directly to students' performance. Teachers' questioning and interactions related to subject content help make students aware of subject-specific knowledge and help them develop cognitive representations that permit "sensemaking" of challenging material. By engaging students in social interactions, teachers model appropriate behaviors, discourage students' misbehavior, promote their attention, and establish a conducive classroom atmosphere. Positive teacher-student social interactions contribute to students' self-efficacy and intrinsic interest in learning, and they foster a sense of identity as a member of a learning community. Similarly, students' perceptions of support from their teachers are associated with achievement and academic interest (Cohen, 1994; Weiner, 1994).

Additional support for attending to the social dimensions of classrooms emanates from qualitative descriptions of classroom contexts that emphasize teaching for understanding. In such classrooms, the teacher's role is to promote active engagement of students in learning rather than to transmit information or facts. Students, in turn, are expected to generate ideas while working on projects or "authentic" tasks, to solve challenging problems through thoughtful discovery, and to develop explanations to support their approach to knowledge construction. As noted by Elmore et al. (1996), students' learning in these classrooms hinges on active engagement in discussions and problem solving with other students and their teachers. Students initiate much of the interaction and learning in environments that emphasize understanding by using diverse sources of information, looking at issues with other students, and testing their ideas against those of other classmates. A high level of interaction, aimed at solving problems or running experiments, is evident; students do not sit passively at their desks while "receiving" information. Similarly, teachers function flexibly, adapting their instructional style throughout the lesson to maximize students' active participation in their own learning. When instruction is skillfully orchestrated according to this perspective, the social context operates clearly in tandem with learning. No longer are isolated student outcomes the focal point of teaching. Instead, teaching for excellence requires facilitating a variety of socially embedded learning tasks in a variety of ways to produce academic and social outcomes among learners. Based on the accumulated evidence that social dimensions influence education, teachers, school psychologists, and researchers should take responsibility in creating social environments that support learning and development.

# TOWARD EXCELLENCE IN TEACHING: CRITICAL INSTRUCTIONAL AND ENVIRONMENTAL VARIABLES

Building on both process-product and interpretive research paradigms and incorporating fundamental principles governing contemporary views of teaching, research has identified several instructional and environmental variables that contribute to excellence in teaching. In the following sections, we examine six critical aspects of the teaching-learning process, including teachers' behaviors, teachers' beliefs, grouping and classroom organizational variables, students' motivation, self-regulated learning, and critical thinking.

## Teachers' Behaviors

Research over the past 20 years has identified several key elements of teaching that contribute to students' achievement. Working in a process-product paradigm, researchers have documented patterns of classroom teaching that are associated with positive learning outcomes, specifically higher performance on both classroom and standardized achievement tests (Waxman & Walberg, 1991). Our knowledge about characteristics of effective teaching has grown since the 1970s; however, the complexities of the teaching-learning process are such that incorporating research-based practices into classroom teaching will not always lead to positive outcomes (Ornstein, 1990). Many teaching methods that are effective in one situation may not be appropriate in another. The key to excellence rests with teachers' decision making about effective practices within the context of their particular classrooms (Borko, Livingston, & Shavelson, 1990).

Despite the importance of individual decision making, findings from process-product research have provided a starting point for understanding effective teaching. Research has underscored the importance of interactions between teachers and students and the influence of environmental and instructional variables on students' success in school. Four components of classroom instruction have received strong research support, regardless of the context in which teaching occurs: (a) high student engagement in the learning process, (b) strong academic focus and clarity in content coverage, (c) moderate-to-high rates of academic success, and (d) performance monitoring and informative teacher feedback.

One of the most highly researched teaching dimensions is academic learning time (Gettinger, 1995). Student engagement, or the amount of time a student spends actively thinking about and working with academic content, is a strong determinant of achievement. Certain teaching practices have been shown to influence the amount of time students are actively engaged in learning (Jones & Jones, 1990). The relationship between learning time and achievement, how-

ever, is not simple, and many factors, including the type and quality of learning activities, must be considered. Excellence in teaching requires consideration of three interrelated aspects of academic learning time: (a) how much time is provided or allocated for the teaching-learning process; (b) the degree to which students are on-task or actively involved in learning during the allocated time; and, most importantly, (c) how successfully students are engaged, or the amount of high-quality time during which students devote themselves to and succeed on appropriate, meaningful tasks. This last dimension is referred to as academic learning time (Gettinger, 1986).

Maximizing academic learning time is a challenging goal for teachers. Several researchers have identified teaching behaviors that have the potential to increase students' engagement in learning (Goodman, 1990). Gettinger (1995) referred to these behaviors as representing an interactive teaching style. Through interactive teaching, teachers demonstrate continuous interaction and involvement with the lesson and with their students; as a result, they promote high levels of student engagement. These interactive teaching behaviors are (a) moving around a classroom to monitor students' performance at regular intervals and to communicate an awareness of students' behavior and progress, (b) minimizing time spent in noninstructional activities (e.g., changing activities, organizing materials for lessons, and conducting clerical jobs) by relying on written rules and routine classroom procedures, (c) providing appropriate materials in terms of difficulty and interest and incorporating diverse learning activities and instructional formats (e.g., whole-group instruction, small-group learning, and individualized practice), and (d) using proactive classroom management methods to prevent disruptive behaviors that can interfere with classroom instruction and learning (Berliner, 1988; Murphy, 1992).

In addition to specific behaviors, the nature of teaching activities and instructional methods also characterize interactive teaching. Specifically, high-participation formats that encourage active responding among students, such as discussion, group problem solving, cooperative learning, and peer teaching, are more positively related to student engagement than noninteractive activities, such as reading silently, listening to or watching another student, or working alone (Gettinger, 1995). Several implications for enhancing classroom teaching can be drawn from research on student engagement. For example, teachers can help students accrue greater amounts of academic learning time by doing a critical analysis of time use in their classrooms. Focusing on interactive teaching behaviors and incorporating high-participation instructional formats into classroom practices enable teachers to convert allocated time into productive, academic learning time.

The second teaching practice that influences student achievement is clarity and academic focus. Clarity relates to how teachers organize academic content, the questioning strategies they use, their familiarity with the material, and the degree to which expectations and performance standards are communicated to and understood by learners. Clarity of instruction has been shown to vary significantly among teachers, contributing to differences in students' performance on achievement tests (Anderson, 1989). A high degree of clarity is achieved when explanations of content proceed in a step-by-step fashion, illustrations and applications of the content are provided, and questions are posed to gauge and extend students' understanding. Two additional cognitive dimensions also contribute to clarity in teaching. First, clear instruction helps students link or connect ideas both within and across lessons. Lessons in which students perceive linkages among ideas (through the use of advance organizers, signaling connections among ideas, or summarizing key concepts) contribute to higher understanding than those in which these interconnections are not clarified (Kindsvatter, Wilen, & Ishler, 1988). Second, clarity also occurs when students understand what prior knowledge is relevant for learning and are able to activate this knowledge to process new content.

Related to clarity is the concept of academic focus, which refers to the degree to which teaching is oriented toward maximizing students' opportunities to learn. Academic-oriented aspects of teaching include both the amount of time a teacher allocates to instructional activities and the overall degree of cognitive emphasis provided by a teacher, including asking questions and encouraging students to think critically. Classrooms with a strong academic focus incorporate (a) systematic, goal-oriented activities; (b) lessons and content related to attaining specific learning goals; and (c) ready access to a variety of teaching materials (Myers, 1990). In recent years, educators have voiced some concern that a strong academic emphasis may undermine important affective outcomes and learning processes. Despite the importance of making learning enjoyable, researchers agree that achievement is higher in classrooms where teachers place a stronger emphasis on academic content than on affective or procedural issues (Fuchs, Fuchs, & Phillips, 1994). Furthermore, classrooms with a strong academic focus are actually characterized by warmth, friendliness, motivation, and students' positive attitudes toward school and themselves (Berliner, 1988).

A third aspect that integrates both student engagement and academic focus is the level of difficulty of the learning material and the concomitant success rate. Research consistently points out that instruction that produces moderate to high success rates (i.e., when students have a good understanding of the material and make occasional, but few, errors) results in higher motivation for learning and better achievement (Brophy, 1987; Gettinger, 1995). Beyond significant academic gains, instruction that is designed to ensure high success rates also contributes to higher levels of self-esteem, more positive attitudes, and less disruptive behavior among students. Research with students who exhibit challenging classroom behaviors has provided evidence that a relationship between low success (high errors) and problem behaviors exists for the majority of students (Munk & Repp, 1994).

The fourth component is teachers' feedback. Feedback is information given to students about the accuracy and remediation of their performance. Learners perform better and maintain high levels of academic learning time when they are given frequent feedback about their performance. Although feedback is commonly interpreted to mean knowledge of the accuracy of performance, knowing whether a response is right or wrong alone has a limited effect on learning (Waxman & Walberg, 1991). Students also need to be aware of corrective procedures for rethinking or redoing their work. Thus, effective feedback, regardless of its form, incorporates (a) a high degree of specificity, with explicit reference to the standard or objective to be achieved; (b) information about accuracy, or the results achieved in meeting the standard; and (c) steps the student should take to remediate errors, coupled with recommendations about practice (Kindsvatter et al., 1988). Feedback that incorporates these three dimensions has been found to be highly associated with academic learning time. Not only does academic performance improve, but also students' perceptions of themselves are affected because they are able to evaluate their own progress in achieving learning goals (Stipek, 1993).

Two warnings about findings on effective teaching have surfaced in recent years. First, many researchers feel that a process-product perspective may lead to an overly rigid view of teaching (Ornstein, 1993). Because positive learning outcomes are evidenced primarily by scores on achievement tests, the resulting profile of effective teaching may portray "good" teachers as strictly task-oriented, organized, and highly structured. These findings do not consider that many qualities of effective teaching do not directly correlate with students' performance on achievement tests. Teachers' behaviors that correlate with measurable outcomes may lead to rote learning and automatic responding rather than critical thinking and responsive social behavior. Certainly, effective teaching behaviors need to be integrated with other qualities, such as creativity, a problem-solving orientation that requires students to think about answers, or an experiential focus that encourages students to play with ideas and concepts (Ornstein, 1990).

The second issue is that teachers often claim that findings from teacher-effectiveness research are not new and provide nothing more than verification of behaviors and methods that good teachers have been using for years. To address this concern, Wong (1995) examined the perceived obviousness of 12 findings from process-product research on teaching. A total of 1,215 teachers attempted to select an actual finding of effective-teaching research from two possible response choices. For example, the importance of a strong academic focus was reflected in the following item: "Some teachers work hard to create a warm, positive emotional climate in their classes, showing a lot of concern for children's feelings and giving praise frequently. Others maintain a friendly, but more businesslike climate. Achievement is higher when (a) teachers maintain a warm, emotional climate, or (b) teachers maintain a more businesslike climate." Wong found that fewer than 50% of the participants could distinguish the actual findings from their opposites for 8 of the 12 items. Thus, claims that research findings on effective teaching have been "known all along" may not be warranted.

Effective teaching has been shown to have collateral behavioral effects. Specifically, several research studies have documented that fewer be-

havior disruptions occur when effective teaching practices are used on a consistent basis (Munk & Repp, 1994). Research findings also apply to teachers who are able to adapt their teaching to individual differences among learners (Fuchs, Fuchs, Phillips, & Simmons, 1993). Identifying practices that enable teachers to achieve excellence in teaching and to meet the challenge of student diversity is important, given the increasing range of students' abilities in classrooms today. Using case study methodology, for example, Phillips, Fuchs, Fuchs, and Hamlett (1996) found that the four key components of effective teaching also described a teacher who was successful in promoting uniformly high academic growth among all the students, including students with learning disabilities. In sum, effective teachers are able to promote high levels of progress for students at different points on the achievement continuum.

## Teachers' Beliefs and Thinking

Teachers' beliefs also play an essential role in teaching (Chester & Beaudin, 1996; Kagan, 1992; Pajares, 1992). Stated simply, teachers base their teaching on what they understand and believe about learning (Darling-Hammond, 1996). Teachers' beliefs influence their perceptions, which in turn affect classroom decisions and actions (Alexander & Dochy, 1995; Stoiber, 1991). Understanding the belief structures of teachers is essential for improving teaching practices. For example, Pintrich (1990) contends that beliefs should be a primary focus of teacher education. The critical influence of teachers' beliefs on classroom practices was recently summarized by Kagan (1992):

> The more one reads studies of teacher belief, the more strongly one suspects that this piebald form of personal knowledge lies at the very heart of teaching. Teacher belief appears to arise out of the exigencies inherent in classroom teaching, it may be the clearest measure of a teachers' professional growth, and it appears to be instrumental in determining the quality of interaction one finds among the teachers in a given school. As we learn more about the forms and functions of teacher belief, we are likely to come a great deal closer to understanding how good teachers are made. (p. 85)

Although there is agreement that beliefs have an impact on teachers' daily classroom functioning, what is meant by teachers' beliefs remains less clear. An array of terms may refer to beliefs, including *personal knowledge, orientations, perspectives, practical principles, attitudes,* and *action schemas.* Pajares (1992) noted that beliefs encompass a broad category of constructs, including "beliefs about confidence to affect students' performance, about causes of teachers' or students' performance, [and] about perceptions of self and feelings of self-worth." Kagan (1992) defined teachers' beliefs as "tacit, often unconsciously held assumptions about students, classrooms, and the academic material to be taught." Alexander and Dochy (1995) view beliefs as dispositional characteristics that determine one's action and behavior. In general, beliefs include one's values and plans, as well as ideologies about practice that are used to interpret situations and make decisions.

Research has established a connection between teachers' beliefs and their actions (Richardson, 1990; Schommer, 1994). Beliefs can be separated into two categories: beliefs about efficacy and beliefs about teaching and learning. Self-efficacy refers to beliefs about one's instructional effectiveness, ability to influence students' performance, or confidence in the ability to perform certain tasks (Bandura, 1993, 1995). Bandura (1995) states that teachers' efficacy beliefs "affect their general orientation toward the educational process as well as their specific instructional activities" (p. 20). He argued that a complex process of self-appraisal and self-persuasion is involved in developing a sense of self-efficacy, which influences one's personal goals. Hence, individuals with a greater sense of self-efficacy set more challenging goals for themselves and are more committed to attaining them. An efficacious outlook heightens a teacher's interest in instructional activities and sustains his or her efforts when faced with failure or disappointments. Teachers with a low sense of self-efficacy, in contrast, have low aspirations and avoid challenges because these are viewed as a personal threat.

Teachers with high self-efficacy are focused on students' needs, able to accommodate students who have difficulty in learning and to praise students regularly for their accomplishments. In contrast, teachers with low self-efficacy spend less time teaching subject areas in which they feel less competent, devote less time to academic content, are less likely to persevere when students do not grasp concepts readily, and are more prone to criticize students' failures (Enochs

& Riggs, 1990; Gibson & Dembo, 1984). Ashton and Webb (1986) found that teachers with high self-efficacy were able to raise their students' level of achievement in mathematics and literacy over the course of a school year. Woolfolk and Hoy (1990) provide evidence that prospective teachers with low self-efficacy rely more on negative sanctions to motivate their students, whereas teachers with high self-efficacy promote their students' academic interests and self-directedness. A study by Chwalisz, Altmaier, and Russell (1992) indicates that teachers with high-efficacy beliefs are able to direct their efforts toward resolving academic challenges. Teachers who lack a secure sense of efficacy, however, tend to focus more on their own emotional distress and avoid dealing with academic problems. Thus, teachers' efficacious beliefs affect both their instructional approach and their students' level of academic success.

Bandura (1993, 1995) has investigated how the efficacious beliefs of staff members in a school culture affect the school's functioning as a social system. The collective efficacy of a school has particular relevance for understanding how adverse student body characteristics (e.g., low socioeconomic status and low student body stability) can influence students' achievement levels. Student characteristics often alter teacher efficacy. That is, a high proportion of students from low socioeconomic backgrounds and a high rate of student absenteeism contribute to low collective efficacy in a school. However, schools in which staff believe that all students can succeed, regardless of family and economic backgrounds, promote high levels of mathematical and language competencies among students. Hence, collective staff efficacy contributes significantly to a school's level of academic excellence. Hoy and Woolfolk (1993) examined the relation between school climate and personal teaching efficacy. They reported that in school settings where collegial support and teacher morale are high, teachers believe they can reach even the most difficult students. Chester and Beaudin (1996) examined the effects of teachers' characteristics and school practices on efficacy beliefs of newly hired teachers in urban schools. They found that schools that provide opportunities for teachers to discuss teaching practices with their colleagues and to collaborate with administrators and experienced staff foster positive change in novice teachers' efficacy beliefs.

Teachers' beliefs about learning and instruction are seldom influenced by reading research findings but derive mostly from their practice, knowledge, and experience (Kagan, 1992). With regard to content-specific beliefs, researchers have demonstrated that teachers' conceptual understanding is associated with their instruction (Anders & Evans, 1994; Garner & Alexander, 1994). For example, teachers' beliefs about how to teach literacy influences the instructional materials they choose and the nature of the instructional approaches (Borko, Davinroy, Flory, & Hiebert, 1994). Teachers with a cognitive-based understanding of mathematics and science emphasize conceptual understanding among their students, display knowledge of students' problem-solving strategies, and produce students who excel on problem-solving measures (Reynolds, 1989; Swing et al., 1988). Teachers' beliefs are also considered to be situation-specific. For example, a teacher may hold beliefs about problem solving or instruction in a specific content area but have different beliefs about student learning in another subject domain.

Teachers' beliefs about instruction may be most influenced by their conceptions of how students learn. Anderson et al. (1995) warn that teachers' beliefs may limit their practice. More specifically, teachers may view "teaching primarily as transmission of intact bodies of knowledge to students who learn by reception and who differ in their ability to learn depending in large part on their home background" (p. 150). Likewise, teachers' views about the role of intelligence in students' learning can affect whether they attempt new approaches to instruction. When teachers believe a student's failure to learn is due to limited intelligence or poor home environment, they may be less willing to attempt innovative teaching strategies, even when these strategies have been shown to improve learning in low achievers.

Teachers' beliefs about accommodating the diverse needs of students are rooted in their personal and professional experience. In general, beliefs are distinguished from knowledge. Beliefs are based on subjective evaluation and judgment, whereas knowledge has a more objective basis (Pajares, 1992). Together, teachers' knowledge and beliefs frame their problem identification, problem representation, and problem solving, as well as how they respond to classroom situations or the instructional approaches they choose. Even when teachers' decisions are influenced by contextual factors, their beliefs and knowledge

affect their disposition to action and resolution (Pajares, 1992).

The combined influence of teachers' knowledge and beliefs about instruction is perhaps most apparent in the movement toward inclusive education. Successful inclusion of students with disabilities requires classroom teachers to believe that all students can learn and that teachers have the knowledge and capacity to teach every student (Moeller & Ishii-Jordon, 1996). Teachers with administrative support and experience hold more positive beliefs about inclusion than teachers who lack support and experience (Stoiber, Gettinger, & Goetz, in press). Developing inclusive beliefs is critical to seeking educative paths that respond to diversity in students (Darling-Hammond, 1996).

## Grouping and Classroom Organizational Variables

The use of cooperative learning groups represents one of the most pervasive changes in classrooms during the past two decades, and it is included among the critical variables that contribute to excellence in teaching (Cohen, 1994; Stevens & Slavin, 1995). Many school districts, state departments of instruction, and national education organizations are now recommending, or even mandating, instruction that incorporates small groups or cooperative learning (e.g., California State Department of Education, 1992; National Council of Teachers of Mathematics, 1989). Cohen defines cooperative learning "as students working together in a group small enough that everyone can participate on a collective task that has been clearly assigned. Moreover, students are expected to carry out their task without direct and immediate supervision of the teacher" (p. 3). Cohen's definition is intentionally broad, encompassing collaborative learning, cooperative learning, and group work. In general, cooperative groups are characterized by joint goals, shared resources, complementary roles among group members, and mutual rewards. In contrast, competitive situations require that only one or a few students can achieve the goal or reward by outperforming their classmates (Qin, Johnson, & Johnson, 1995).

Students in groups will learn from one another. Students are especially helpful to peers because they often have greater insight into areas of misunderstanding and can explain concepts by using familiar language and terms. Critics of cooperative learning groups suggest, however, that there may be differences in the overall effectiveness of cooperative learning. In a synthesis of cooperative learning in mathematics instruction, Davidson (1985) found favorable benefits for cooperative groups when compared to traditional instruction for one-third of the investigations he reviewed but no significant differences in outcomes for the remaining studies. A study by Solomon, Watson, Schaps, Battistich, and Solomon (1990) in which cooperative learning methods were used over a five-year period found positive effects on prosocial behaviors, social problem solving, and appreciation of democratic values; however, no effects on achievement were obtained. The model of cooperative learning used stressed the production of a group product, although there were no formal group goals. In addition, students were not held accountable for their own learning, and the formulation of a group product did not require each participant to contribute equally.

Work by Webb and others (Webb, 1991; Webb, Troper, & Fall, 1995) demonstrates that the type and quality of interaction during group learning affect students' achievement. For example, although students can benefit from both giving and receiving explanations, there is stronger evidence of achievement gains for students who give explanations. Webb et al. (1995) reported that the level of constructive activity, or the amount of work a student demonstrates in solving problems after receiving explanations, is the best predictor of achievement. That is, the more students are engaged in finding solutions to a problem, the better their achievement. Moreover, constructive activity during group work is a better predictor of performance than previous achievement or the level of help received. Slavin (1994) concluded that the promotion of student learning in groups requires two essential features: group goals and individual responsibility. Furthermore, these two features must be linked in practice; that is, attaining the group goal must depend on successful learning by all participants. For example, when students know that all of them must garner understanding through the group process, individual students are motivated to construct high-quality explanations and are less prone to simply give answers to other group members (Slavin, 1994).

Finally, the nature of the task influences the nature of relationships, group interactions, and achievement outcomes in group learning (Cohen, 1994). The type and amount of interaction vary when the task objective is routine or when rote learning versus learning for understanding. For routine learning situations, students ensure that peers grasp the content by offering one another substantive or procedural information. In contrast, when the objective is learning for understanding, productive interaction is characterized by a mutual sharing and clarifying of ideas and strategy experimentation.

Several studies have shown that cooperative learning influences social outcomes as well. Working collaboratively with others has a positive impact on students' self-esteem, intergroup relations, acceptance of differences in others, and attitudes toward class and school (Qin et al., 1995; Slavin, 1994). Groups also provide opportunities for students to balance different viewpoints and to monitor their control in progressing toward a group-constructed product. It is interesting that these nonacademic outcomes do not depend on the presence of group goals and individual accountability methods, as do academic outcomes.

Experts on cooperative learning emphasize that small-group methods alter classroom organization, increase student engagement, and promote students' responsibility for their learning (Cohen, 1994; Stevens & Slavin, 1995). This shift in classroom organization also permits greater opportunities for teachers to interact with individual students or with groups of students. It also frees teachers from many management demands (e.g., correcting worksheets and keeping students on-task during seat-work).

Several innovative approaches to the organization of classroom teaching also contribute to excellence in teaching and have facilitated the development of classrooms that are able to accommodate diverse learners. One such organizational teaching model is coteaching or team teaching. In a coteaching model, a special educator collaborates and shares in teaching responsibilities for all children in an inclusive classroom, rather than pulling out children with disabilities for remedial work. The coteaching team members meet with each other concerning substantive issues in instructional planning and curricular implementation. The ongoing dialogue that accompanies team teaching fosters the development of classroom and instructional techniques aimed at reaching diverse learners. Peer coaching is another approach that has been shown to facilitate the implementation of inclusive practices (Stevens & Slavin, 1995). The aim of peer coaching is to enhance teachers' opportunities to obtain constructive feedback from one another in a nonthreatening way. Through peer coaching, teachers develop a deeper sense of what is meant by good instruction and increase their commitment to innovative practices. Reporting on the results of a two-year study of an innovative school model, which included cooperative learning across a variety of content areas, full-scale inclusion, peer coaching, and teachers' cooperative planning, Stevens and Slavin (1995) found several important benefits. First, students with disabilities in the cooperative elementary school demonstrated high achievement in reading and mathematics and were socially accepted by their typically developing classmates. In addition, higher achievement was attained by gifted students in heterogeneous cooperative learning classes than by similar ability-level students who received an enrichment program without cooperative learning.

## Student Motivation

Excellence in teaching is also characterized by a high level of interest and motivation for learning among students. When students are motivated to learn, they pay attention to instruction, are actively involved in learning, and demonstrate persistence in trying to achieve academic goals (Stipek, 1993). Questions about motivating students have traditionally been studied apart from questions about effective teaching. In the last decade, however, researchers have documented a critical link between motivation and cognitive engagement (Blumenfeld, Puro, & Mergendoller, 1992). We now understand that effective teaching strategies that press for active learning will not necessarily translate into higher motivation unless teachers also work to enhance students' interest in and value for learning. Similarly, unless teachers act in ways that promote cognitive engagement, student motivation will not necessarily result in thoughtfulness or greater understanding of content (Blumenfeld, Soloway, Marx, Krajcik, Guzdial, & Palincsar, 1991).

Discussions of motivation from a traditional process-product perspective place a great deal of emphasis on factors external to students, focusing on teachers' behaviors that are effective in promoting student motivation. Many aspects of teaching have been shown to contribute to student motivation: (a) relating instruction to students' interests, cultural backgrounds, and lives outside of school; (b) structuring lessons to ensure success; (c) providing specific feedback to students about their performance; (d) projecting enthusiasm and communicating that lessons are meaningful and worthwhile learning experiences; (e) offering praise that is both appropriate and sincere; and (e) introducing content in ways that invoke interest or arouse curiosity (Brophy, 1987; Brophy & Alleman, 1991).

In recent years, researchers have begun to look at motivation from a different perspective. Specifically, research has shifted to a focus on the motivational role of cognitive constructs such as students' thoughts, beliefs, and perceptions (Dweck, 1986; Weiner, 1990). Although this shift in focus has enhanced our understanding of individual differences in motivation, it has also led to a proliferation of several different constructs and theories. A glance at current research reveals the complexity of motivation and explains, in part, why there is no single theory of motivation.

Despite the heterogeneity of theoretical orientations, there appear to be three interrelated cognitive constructs that constitute the primary antecedents of motivation in schools: (a) beliefs about one's own ability to engage in and accomplish tasks; (b) the reasons, purposes, or goals for engaging in tasks; and (c) the extent to which students find classroom tasks to be interesting and valuable. Focusing on these constructs, researchers have concentrated on describing individual differences in motivation. Furthermore, current research has begun to examine how classroom environments and teaching practices may affect student motivation (Meece, 1991). Based on this work, a number of teaching strategies have been identified that are likely to enhance motivation among the majority of students. In particular, classroom practices can be grouped into three areas: (a) those that affect students' perceptions of ability and their expectancies for success, (b) those that help sustain a task focus rather than a performance focus, and (c) those that affect students' interest and perceptions of the value of the material (Maehr & Pintrich, 1991). Research related to each motivational construct and resulting guidelines for enhancing teaching are summarized in the following paragraphs.

A key contribution is Bandura's (1986) social-cognitive theory of motivation. Bandura asserted that students' thoughts play a central role in determining their level of motivation. His research demonstrated that personal evaluation and self-satisfaction function as powerful reinforcers, perhaps more powerful than reinforcers provided by others. According to a social-cognitive perspective, involving students in setting personal goals that are concrete, specific, and realistic, as well as providing frequent opportunities for them to monitor their own progress, is likely to increase student motivation (Pintrich & DeGroot, 1991).

Related to social-cognitive theory is attribution theory, which deals with the perceived causes of success and failure on school tasks, and the concept of self-efficacy, which refers to an individual's expectations that he or she can succeed. When feelings of self-efficacy are high, individuals are more likely to exert effort toward completing tasks because they believe they can be successful. Conversely, when feelings of self-efficacy are low, motivation is diminished (Dweck & Leggert, 1988; Weiner, 1986). According to attribution theory, students' perceptions of *why* they succeed or fail at school tasks also have a direct impact on motivation (Stipek, 1993). There are five general factors to which students are likely to attribute success and failure—ability, effort, task difficulty, luck, and other people such as the teacher. The only factor that can be controlled directly by students is effort. When students attribute success to their own efforts, and failure to a lack of or inappropriate types of effort, they are more likely to be motivated toward additional effort in the future (Weiner, 1990). Students who believe that their personal efforts influence their learning exhibit higher motivation than do students who believe that learning depends on teachers or other factors like task difficulty or luck (Dweck & Leggett, 1988). Students' perceptions of the role of errors can affect their self-perceptions of competence as well. Errors are detrimental to motivation when they are thought to represent failure. When errors are perceived as attempts to derive meaning or to solve challenging problems, they signal cognitive and motivational efforts that are desirable for meaningful learning. In fact, errors are a natural and inevitable consequence of being highly motivated and ambitious in learning (Schunk, 1994).

Many implications for excellence in teaching stem from social-cognitive and attribution theories of motivation. First, students should be assigned tasks that are moderately challenging but within their ability. Second, teachers' statements can encourage students to attribute success or failure to effort rather than to other variables.

When students are successful, teachers can attribute their success directly to effort or appropriate strategies. Finally, children's need for competence is fostered when they experience optimal structure in the classroom. Structure refers to the amount of information provided to students about how to achieve desired outcomes. Teachers provide structure by (a) clearly communicating their expectations, (b) responding predictably to students' performance, (c) offering instrumental help and support, and (d) adjusting strategies to the level of the child (Maehr & Midgley, 1991; Schunk, 1994).

Teachers can also enhance students' perceived abilities and expectancies for success by creating opportunities and support for learning, grouping strategies, and grading practices. Specifically, teachers can offer support for cognitive engagement by scaffolding students' learning and by teaching learning strategies to enable students to accomplish tasks on their own. Teachers who do not group students by ability and do not rely on reporting practices that highlight ability-related information also enhance students' beliefs in their ability to succeed (Brophy, 1987; Maehr & Pintrich, 1991; Pintrich & Schrauben, 1992).

Even if students perceive themselves to be competent in school tasks, they may not be motivated to engage in schoolwork in a manner that promotes understanding and learning when performance, rather than learning, is the most salient goal. Hence, recent research on motivation and achievement had concentrated on the role of goals and purposes in conducting classroom learning activities (Meece, 1991). One of the more prominent developments in motivation research in the past decade has been the emergence of goal theory (Ames, 1992; Elliott & Dweck, 1988). Goal theory is concerned with the role or purpose of learning in determining motivation. According to goal theory, the perceived goal of doing something determines an individual's level and quality of engagement in the task. Research on school motivation has focused primarily on two types of goals: task-focused or mastery goals and ability-focused or performance goals. These types have been differentiated by their link to contrasting patterns of motivational processes. Specifically, students who pursue learning-oriented or task-focused goals try to improve their level of competence or understanding. Learning is valued as an end in itself. Subjective feelings of pride, success, and accomplishment are derived from achieving a sense of mastery or developing one's competence according to self-referenced standards. In contrast, students who pursue performance-oriented or ability-focused goals seek to demonstrate high ability or to gain favorable judgments of their abilities in relation to the efforts and performances of others. These students use norm-referenced standards to judge the adequacy of their performance. A sense of accomplishment is derived from doing well, doing better than others, or meeting some other normatively defined standard of success (Ames & Ames, 1989).

Numerous studies have found that students who adopt task-focused or mastery goals are more likely to engage in deep cognitive processing (e.g., thinking about how new knowledge relates to previous knowledge). In contrast, students who adopt ability-focused or performance goals tend to use surface-level strategies, such as memorization of facts (Blumenfeld, 1992). Students who adopt task-focused goals also use more adaptive help-seeking strategies and show higher levels of creativity (Anderman & Maehr, 1994). Research suggests that a mastery goal orientation promotes a motivation pattern most likely to support long-term and high-quality involvement in learning (Ames, 1990).

Students perceive classrooms as defining the purpose of learning in differing ways, and these perceptions influence the goals that they adopt, thereby influencing their motivation (Maehr & Midgley, 1992; Pintrich & DeGroot, 1991). Simply put, students can and do perceive classrooms as emphasizing task or ability goals, and this perception is associated with the quality and level of motivation they exhibit. Given this conclusion, what orients students toward these different goals? The child's learning environment at school can elicit different goal orientations and affect whether students adopt learning versus performance goals. Learning situations that emphasize self-improvement, discovery of new information, and the usefulness of learning material can influence task or learning goals. Research suggests that a focus on ability is likely to develop when students are given little choice in tasks, competition and social comparison are emphasized, ability grouping is used, public evaluations of performance are common, grading is based on relative ability, and cooperation and interaction among students are discouraged. Conversely, a task focus is likely to occur when students are involved in choice and decision making; there are opportunities for peer interaction and cooperation; grouping is based on interest and needs; and success is defined in terms of effort, progress, and improvement (Blumenfeld et al., 1991; Maehr & Midgley, 1991; Meece, 1994). Finally, teachers' feedback, accountability, and evaluation practices also influence whether students adopt a motivation orientation that stresses learning rather than performance. Students' expectancies for success are increased when teachers (a) hold students accountable for learning and understanding, not just getting the right answers; (b) give students the freedom to take risks and be wrong; (c) stress improvement over time; (d) minimize competition and comparisons with others; and (e) use private rather than public evaluation (Blumenfeld et al., 1992).

Another cognitive construct addressed by motivation researchers is student interest. Students' interest in and perceived value of the material being taught are enhanced when teachers (a) emphasize intrinsic reasons for learning rather than stressing grades or other rewards; (b) relate material to students' lives and experiences or to current events; (c) offer choices about what, where, with whom, or how work is done; (d) assign tasks that are varied and include novel, humorous, fantasy, or gamelike elements; (e) ask students to work on problems that are authentic and challenging; and (f) assign challenging work that involves creating a product or provides some form of closure (Brophy, 1987; Dweck, 1986).

There has been a trend toward focusing on the affective needs of children in classrooms and how they relate to motivation (Pintrich & DeGroot, 1991). The underlying premise of this work is that the source of motivation is internal to the child, and when the classroom environment provides for children's basic psychological needs, motivation is enhanced. According to this perspective, one of the most basic needs among students is to be connected to other people. Researchers have suggested that children's need for belongingness and their connectedness to a community of learners represent a fundamental motivator. In fact, students who are at risk of dropping out of school are often characterized as being disconnected and alienated from school (Wehlage, Rutter, Smith, Lesko, & Fernandez, 1989). A category of teachers' behavior that fulfills children's needs for relatedness is involvement, that is, the quality of the interpersonal relationship between teachers and students. Teachers are involved with their students to the extent that they take time for, express affection toward, enjoy interactions with, are attentive to, and dedicate resources to their students (Ornstein, 1993).

In sum, current research demonstrates that teachers can enhance students' motivation by using practices recommended by several different researchers. Unless teachers act in ways that promote cognitive engagement, however, students' motivation to learn will not necessarily translate into greater learning or understanding of content. Several practices documented in this section contribute to both motivation and cognitive engagement—providing opportunities to learn, enhancing students' interest in and value of content, supporting students' efforts to learn and their expectations for success, and maintaining a task focus by holding students accountable for participation and careful thought. Teachers can create environments that promote motivation to learn and encourage thoughtfulness by minimizing ability-related information and focusing on learning rather than performance.

## Self-Regulated Learning

In recent years, much has been written on self-regulated learning and the role of instructional variables in the development of self-regulatory processes. Research has arrived at two important conclusions relevant to a discussion of excellence in teaching. First, learners who use self-regulated learning strategies tend to be successful in school (Schunk & Zimmerman, 1994; Zimmerman & Schunk, 1989). Models of academic learning that involve self-regulation portray self-regulated students as active participants in their own learning. They set goals for themselves, and they are metacognitively aware of what they are doing and how effective their strategies are in leading to successful goal attainment. Self-regulated students approach tasks with confidence, diligence, and resourcefulness. They are aware when they understand material and when they do not. Furthermore, they are proactive in seeking information when they need it and taking necessary steps to complete a task.

Second, the development of self-regulation is responsive to environmental influences. Researchers agree that self-regulated learning develops incrementally as a learner participates in instructional experiences that incorporate responsive scaffolding and guidance from teachers or peers (e.g., Brown & Pressley, 1994; Henderson & Cunningham, 1994; Zimmerman, Greenberg, & We-

instein, 1994). The development of self-regulation occurs, in part, through interactions with others in a social context. There is strong evidence that school-based interventions that focus on self-regulatory skills are beneficial. Nonetheless, there are important qualifications surrounding this conclusion. Winne (1995) has argued that self-regulation is inherent in the learning process, and to the extent that students' inherent expertise in self-regulation does not match a teacher's objectives, explicit training may not be helpful.

Observations of individuals who are self-regulated learners, as well as teachers who effectively promote self-regulation, have provided guidelines for teaching and instruction. Self-regulated learning and the instructional strategies that promote it have been studied from several different theoretical perspectives. A variety of metacognitive, motivational, and behavioral strategies have been investigated, including self-monitoring, decision making, goal setting, explicit teaching, and collaborative learning. Self-regulation can be supported through appropriate curriculum and explicit teaching (including extensive practice and scaffolding). Self-regulated learning can also be enhanced through implicit prompts and authentic learning experiences, not just controlled delivery of instruction (Corno, 1995). Several important instructional principles follow from research on self-regulated learning, and the following is a brief review.

Students' self-monitoring plays a critical role in self-regulated learning. For example, Harris (1990) found that, when compared to teaching a reading comprehension strategy alone, teaching students to self-monitor the effectiveness of a strategy not only enhanced their reading comprehension but also encouraged them to continue to use the strategy. Monitoring increases students' awareness of whether sufficient and complete learning has occurred, to enable them to perform as expected (Sawyer, Graham, & Harris, 1992). This type of metacognitive self-monitoring differs substantially from behavioral self-monitoring. In the latter, students rely on monitoring actual records or samples of performance (such as the number of pages read or problems completed) without necessarily engaging in active metacognitive monitoring during acquisition or performance. In other words, self-monitoring for self-regulation is directed toward strategic processes and not only learning outcomes (Zimmerman, 1995).

All learners, even those who are highly self-regulated, have the option of not self-regulating. Self-regulated learning requires more than metacognitive skills; it also requires will, or motivation (Boekaerts, 1995; Corno, 1995; McCombs, 1989). When students understand that they are responsible for their own learning, their will provides the motivation for self-regulation. To promote the volitional component of self-regulation, teachers should cultivate in students the belief that learning is challenging, even for capable learners, and that knowledge is rarely absolute; that is, there are several alternative perspectives and ways of accomplishing tasks (Jehng, Johnson, & Anderson, 1993). To promote the development of self-regulated learning, teachers should focus on developing students' awareness that they have the power of choice. This includes designing programs that give students opportunities for choice and for active participation in decision making about their own learning.

Self-regulated learning also involves goal-directed activities. Goals direct learning. They must exist prior to activities in which learners engage, and they must articulate the criteria learners use to monitor what they do. When students set goals for themselves that are specific in content and proximal in time, they perceive their learning progress more readily, which in turn enhances their self-efficacy (Locke & Latham, 1990; Schunk, 1990, 1995; Schunk & Swartz, 1993). Many implications for enhancing goal setting have resulted from the literature. First, goals that incorporate specific performance standards are more likely to enhance learning and activate self-evaluation than are general goals, such as "Do your best." Proximal goals also result in greater motivation than distant goals, in part because it is easier to gauge progress toward a specific and proximal goal. Thus, students should be encouraged to monitor in detail their mastery of each day's lessons and activities. Research also confirms that when comparing goal conditions in which students set their own goals, versus having them established by others, self-set goals lead to higher performance (Schunk, 1990). Finally, self-regulatory skills require that students' goals are realistic, that is, challenging but attainable. With realistic goals, students are able to monitor progress and decide on a different task approach if their present one is ineffective. Realistic goal-setting often requires explicit training. One strategy for enhancing goal setting is to impose upper

and lower limits on students' goals. Limits are gradually removed when students demonstrate an understanding of the nature of the tasks and their immediate capabilities for completing them. Goal-setting conferences have also been recommended to promote self-regulation. By meeting with teachers, students learn to assess goal difficulty relative to their present knowledge and skills. Furthermore, conferencing enables teachers to model and explain mature thoughts about goals. Goal-setting conferences increase the accuracy and appropriateness of individual goal setting (Locke & Latham, 1990).

Teaching students to self-regulate their academic performance may be more complex than initially thought. Initial optimism for training students to use strategies has been tempered by evidence that their use involves more than mere knowledge of a strategy (Schunk & Zimmerman, 1994). For self-regulation to occur, several things must happen. First, the learner must play an active collaborative role in the design, implementation, and evaluation of the strategy used. Second, students should receive extensive practice in using new procedures, even to the point of automatization, before they are expected to use them in a self-regulated fashion. According to Winne (1995), "Self-regulated learning can be automatic and nondeliberate once the learner has automated procedural knowledge that recognizes when to regulate and what to do" (p. 223). Similarly, students should be provided with diverse opportunities to acquire the general understanding that effort pays off through positive learning outcomes; specifically, students should be given diverse tasks in which they experience consistent success by expending effort. Finally, it is recommended that students learn and practice multiple strategies, not just one new procedure. When strategy training resembles the imposition of static routines, there is often failure. Students should be allowed to learn and practice several different procedures, interspersed simultaneously, so that their long-term use of effective procedures is internalized, personalized, and more frequent (Corno, 1995).

Most researchers agree that the capability to self-regulate is developmental. Before the age of seven, children do not self-regulate their learning (Paris & Newman, 1990). They tend to be naive and overly optimistic about their ability to learn. They have only a vague understanding of what is involved in academic tasks, and their strategic knowledge is limited. As children approach adolescence, however, their academic self-perceptions become more accurate. They develop an increasingly differentiated understanding of academic tasks, and their ability to monitor the effectiveness of learning strategies increases. Paris and his colleagues (e.g., Paris & Byrnes, 1989; Paris & Newman, 1990) have hypothesized that these developmental changes in children's use of self-regulation depend, in part, on their building personal theories of self-competence and academic task performance. Explicit teaching of strategies may have immediate effects on performance, but the benefits are not sustained unless students incorporate this information into their own theories about the task. In effect, students must make a personal commitment to the new strategy. Otherwise, change in performance reflects obedience rather than enduring beliefs about self-regulation and achievement. In fact, young children tend to believe that "trying hard" or "doing what the teacher says" is sufficient to ensure academic success. The development of self-regulation relies, to a great extent, on the social context. Therefore, collaborative teaching and peer interactions are examples of instructional methods that promote children's development of effective personal theories to regulate their learning. Discussions allow students to hear the difficulties and solutions encountered by their peers and to enrich their awareness of alternative solutions to problems. Cooperative learning, peer tutoring, brainstorming, and peer conferences facilitate a shift from other-regulated learning to self-regulated learning (Paris & Newman, 1990).

Thus, excellence in teaching involves the implementation of methods that encourage self-regulation. Despite the importance of applying mechanisms and teaching methods discussed in this section to promote self-regulation, Pressley (1995) warns that the development of self-regulation results from "years of experience, years that undoubtedly are filled with histories of reward, with tasks of varying difficulty, transfer opportunities following proceduralization of skills, and occasions when the benefits of using strategies and new concepts have been salient" (p. 209). In other words, single or short-term application of any instructional approach will probably not lead to long-term use of self-regulatory processes. Self-regulated thinking, according to Pressley, is more complex and requires a longer time to develop.

# Thinking Skills and Strategic Learning

Developing critical thinking skills and strategic learning among students is another hallmark of excellence in teaching and is clearly facilitated through consideration of the other variables we have already discussed. Strategic learning refers to students' capacity to accelerate their own learning, to overcome learning blocks or gaps, and to control their own learning styles (Calfee, 1992). Most of the research on strategic learning has been laboratory-based, occurring during narrow time periods and focusing on isolated methods or content areas. This small-scale approach has limited our understanding of strategic learning and the generalizability of its concepts (Stoiber & Peterson, 1992).

In reviewing recent literature on strategic learning (Chan, Burtis, Scardamalia, & Bereiter, 1992; King, 1994; Langer, 1993; McKeachie, 1990; Palincsar, Anderson, & David, 1993; Paris & Winograd, 1990; Stoiber & Peterson, 1992), several assumptions about learners and learning are apparent: (a) students build on the knowledge, skills, competencies, and interests that they already have; (b) students remember information and make it meaningful for them when they have learned through active processing and with enjoyment; (c) students have the will to learn, but their motivation diminishes when they feel incompetent as learners; and (d) students must be given opportunities to practice problem-solving approaches and strategic thinking in a variety of circumstances. In addition, when information or facts are viewed as irrelevant by students, they fail to activate processes that can enhance their learning. Most models of strategic learning emphasize that students who are generally "nonstrategic" can be taught how to use more appropriate strategies.

Reciprocal teaching (Palincsar & Brown, 1984; Palincsar et al., 1993) is one example of a successful approach to strategies. Palincsar and Brown initiated their work with a thorough analysis of trainable, task-appropriate strategies for reading comprehension. They selected four activities that were thought to foster reading comprehension and comprehension monitoring—summarizing, self-directed questioning, clarifying, and predicting. Reciprocal teaching involves a "socio-instructional" approach that immerses students in a natural dyadic exchange of strategy training. Palincsar and Brown's method is designed to capitalize on learners' capabilities while also tailoring instruction to target gaps in strategy use. In their research, reciprocal teaching improved children's independent work with new materials, and at a 3-month follow-up, the reciprocal-teaching group showed an average gain of 15 months in reading comprehension grade level. Palincsar et al. have also trained students successfully to use specific explanation prompts to help them connect scientific ideas. That is, students were given guidelines concerning what to include in their explanations when helping team members solve a problem (e.g., descriptions about what was happening to the substances being tested in an experiment).

Wittrock (1992) proposed a model of generative learning and teaching that has four major thinking processes: attention, motivation, knowledge and preconceptions, and generation. According to Wittrock, the brain is a knowledge builder, and each of these processes is linked to cognitive functions studied in knowledge acquisition. In this framework, one's brain actively controls the processes of generating meaning and planning action. Wittrock's model of generative learning processes differs from cognitive theories that focus on the storage of information. Wittrock's model is a functional model of learning that emphasizes the importance of activating students' deep-level of processing of information. Teachers who apply a model of generative learning develop instruction that is attuned to learning processes (such as attention), motivational processes (such as interest and learner attributions), knowledge-construction activities (such as concept application), and most importantly the process of generation (such as fostering their use of analogies, metaphors, and summarization). An example is the request that students either construct analogies or summaries after reading a chapter of a high-imagery book. Research indicates that Wittrock's model can be applied to diverse content areas, including reading, mathematics, science, and economics. These investigations demonstrate that instruction can produce sizable gains in students' learning and understanding when it explicitly helps students to construct meaning by building relations among learning concepts.

Consistent with Wittrock's (1992) work, other approaches that help students develop active processing through elaboration also facilitate learning. Elaboration can explain the relationship between two concepts, make inferences, associate new material with previously learned knowledge, and generate questions or explanations to questions about material to be learned (King, 1994; Langer, 1993; Webb et al., 1995). In general, elaborations generated by students themselves are most effective because they build on a student's prior learning history and knowledge. To encourage students' strategic questioning (called reciprocal questioning or guided cooperative questioning), King trained students to develop and respond to high-level questions aimed at eliciting elaborate understanding or connecting of ideas. Students learned the most and showed the greatest evidence of knowledge construction when they were prompted to either connect ideas in a lesson or to a prior learning experience.

Although research on strategic learning is promising, any intervention that attempts to improve students' learning should be monitored and adapted to their capabilities and preferences. It should be noted that more research is needed to determine the types of strategy instruction that are most responsive to students' needs, with some interventions likely to be more effective for some than for others. Teachers and school psychologists are cautioned against the use of one-on-one tutoring when it means robbing resources that could be necessary for enhancing the critical thinking of many students.

# CONCLUSIONS AND FUTURE RESEARCH DIRECTIONS

It is clear that teachers and schools can succeed with many students when they follow sound pedagogical principles that contribute to excellence in teaching. Collectively, these relate to (a) encouraging students' active engagement in learning; (b) promoting efficacious beliefs among teachers about teaching and student success; (c) exploring innovative approaches to grouping and organizing classroom instruction; (d) making learning meaningful by keeping it enjoyable, interesting, student-centered, and goal-directed; (e) fostering self-regulated and independent learning; and (f) teaching for understanding. Yet there are still several questions about how to improve pedagogy, classroom organization, and teachers' practices (Darling-Hammond, 1996; Peterson et al., 1996). In facing the dilemma of improving classroom practice, it must be realized that achieving best practices is challenging work.

In Darling-Hammond's words, this work requires "massive learning from all of us" (p. 14).

What are some of the questions that future research on teaching might address? If research is to consider the issue of classroom restructuring uncovered by Elmore et al. (1996), it must explore how teaching for understanding can provide practices that help all children create new ways of knowing and thinking. Research also needs to determine what approaches are necessary to help teachers understand how to achieve the kinds of day-to-day teaching practices they want. In focusing on teaching, researchers can learn what specific school structures and support are necessary to improve pedagogy. Future research might extend the work of Cohen, Slavin, Webb and others on cooperative learning by examining what kinds of student interactions are most useful for different types of tasks and diverse types of learners. Also, what types of guidance or direction seem to influence the quality of students' learning, and how might teachers ensure that peer-directed cooperative groups produce maximum outcomes for all students? As researchers who are concerned about classroom equity, we can try to ensure that instructional conditions are effective for all types of learners. In considering areas related to students' motivation, future research should examine how to keep learning interesting for students, including those with diverse learning needs and educational histories. Research questions in strategic learning, self-regulation, and problem solving might consider under what conditions learners come to generalize these skills, the prerequisites to becoming strategic learners, and the most efficient approach to strategic learning.

These are some of the questions that should provide productive outcomes for teachers and classrooms. As these questions are explored, new issues related to instruction, strategies, students' learning, diversity, and classroom organization are likely to arise. Regardless of the question, partnerships among teachers, parents, school psychologists, and researchers must be forged for developing understandings that are derived and implemented from inside-out and outside-in America's classrooms.

# REFERENCES

Alexander, P. A., & Dochy, F. J. R. C. (1995). Conceptions of knowledge and beliefs: A comparison across varying cultural and educational communities. *American Educational Research Journal, 32,* 413–442.

American Psychological Association, Presidential Task Force on Psychology in Education (1995). *Learner-centered psychological principles: A framework for school redesign and reform.* Washington, DC: Author.

Ames, C. (1990). Motivation: What teachers need to know. *Teachers College Record, 91,* 409–421.

Ames, C. (1992). Classrooms: Goals, structures, and student motivation. *Journal of Educational Psychology, 84,* 261–271.

Ames, C., & Ames, R. (Eds.). (1989). *Research on motivation in education* (Vol. 3). New York: Academic Press.

Anderman, E. M., & Maehr, M. L. (1994). Motivation and schooling in the middle grades. *Review of Educational Research, 64,* 287–309.

Anders, P. L., & Evans, K. S. (1994). Relationship between teachers' beliefs and their instructional practice in reading. In R. Garner & P. A. Alexander (Eds.), *Beliefs about text and instruction with text* (pp. 137–153). Hillsdale, NJ: Erlbaum.

Anderson, L. M. (1989). Classroom instruction. In M. C. Reynolds (Ed.), *Knowledge base for the beginning teacher* (pp. 129–167). New York: Pergamon.

Anderson, L. M., Blumenfeld, P., Pintrich, P. R., Clark, C. M., Marx, R. W., & Peterson, P. (1995). Educational psychology for teachers: Reforming our courses, rethinking our roles. *Educational Psychologist, 30,* 143–157.

Ashton, P. T., & Webb, R. B. (1986). *Making a difference: Teachers' sense of efficacy and student achievement.* New York: Longman.

Bandura, A. (1986). *Social foundations of thought and action: A social cognitive theory.* Englewood Cliffs, NJ: Prentice Hall.

Bandura, A. (1993). Perceived self-efficacy in cognitive development and functioning. *Educational Psychologist, 28,* 117–148.

Bandura, A. (Ed.). (1995). *Self-efficacy in changing societies.* New York: Cambridge University Press.

Bereiter, C., & Scardamalia, M. (1987). An attainable version of high literacy: Approaches to teaching higher-order skills in reading and writing. *Curriculum Inquiry, 17*(1), 9–30.

Berliner, D. C. (1988). Effective classroom management and instruction: A knowledge base for consultation. In J. L. Graden, J. E. Zins, & M. C. Curtis (Eds.), *Alternative educational delivery systems: Enhancing instructional options for all students* (pp. 309–325). Washington, DC: National Association of School Psychologists.

Blumenfeld, P. C. (1992). Classroom learning and motivation: Classifying and expanding goal theory. *Journal of Educational Psychology, 84,* 272–281.

Blumenfeld, P. C., Puro, P., & Mergendoller, J. (1992). Translating motivation into thoughtfulness. In

H. Marshall (Ed.), *Redefining student learning: Roots of educational change* (pp. 207–240). Norwood, NJ: Ablex.

Blumenfeld, P. C., Soloway, E., Marx, R. W., Krajcik, J. S., Guzdial, M., & Palincsar, A. (1991). Motivating project-based learning: Sustaining the doing, supporting the learning. *Educational Psychologist, 26,* 369–398.

Boekaerts, M. (1993). Being concerned with well-being and with learning. *Educational Psychologist, 28,* 149–167.

Boekaerts, M. (1995). Self-regulated learning: Bridging the gap between metacognitive and metamotivation theories. *Educational Psychologist, 30,* 195–200.

Borich, G. (1988). *Effective teaching methods.* Columbus, OH: Merrill.

Borko, H., Davinroy, R. H., Flory, M. D., & Hiebert, E. H. (1994). Teachers' knowledge and beliefs about summary as a component of reading. In R. Garner & P. A. Alexander (Eds.), *Beliefs about text and instruction with text* (pp. 155–182). Hillsdale, NJ: Erlbaum.

Borko, H., Livingston, C., & Shavelson, R. (1990). Teachers' thinking about instruction. *Remedial and Special Education, 11*(6), 40–49, 53.

Brandt, R. (1992). On research on teaching: A conversation with Lee Shulman. *Educational Leadership, 50,* 14–19.

Brophy, J. (1987). Synthesis of research on strategies for motivating students to learn. *Educational Leadership, 45,* 40–48.

Brophy, J. (1992). Probing the subtleties of subject-matter teaching. *Educational Leadership, 50,* 4–8.

Brophy, J., & Alleman, C. (1991). Activities as instructional tools: A framework for instructional analysis and evaluation. *Educational Researcher, 20,* 9–23.

Brophy, J., & Good, T. (1986). Teacher behavior and student achievement. In M. C. Wittrock (Ed.), *Handbook of research on teaching* (Vol. 3, pp. 328–375). New York: Macmillan.

Brown, R., & Pressley, M. (1994). Self-regulating reading and getting meaning from text: The transactional strategies instruction model and its ongoing validation. In D. H. Schunk & B. J. Zimmerman (Eds.), *Self-regulation of learning and performance: Issues and educational applications* (pp. 155–180). Hillsdale, NJ: Erlbaum.

Calfee, R. (1992). Refining educational psychology: The case of the missing links. *Educational Psychologist, 27,* 163–177.

California State Department of Education. (1992). *Mathematics framework for California public schools, kindergarten through grade twelve.* Sacramento, CA: Author.

Carnegie Council on Adolescent Development. (1989). *Turning points: Preparing American youth for the 21st century.* Washington, DC: Author.

Chan, C. K., Burtis, P. J., Scardamalia, M., & Bereiter, C. (1992). Constructive activity in learning from text. *American Educational Research Journal, 29,* 97–118.

Chester, M. D., & Beaudin, B. Q. (1996). Efficacy beliefs of newly hired teachers in urban schools. *American Educational Research Journal, 33,* 233–257.

Chwalisz, K. D., Altmaier, E. M., & Russell, D. W. (1992). Causal attributions, self-efficacy cognitions, and coping with stress. *Journal of Social and Clinical Psychology, 11,* 377–400.

Cochran-Smith, M., & Lytle, S. L. (1990). Research on teaching and teacher research: The issues that divide. *Educational Researcher, 19,* 2–11.

Cohen, D. K., McLaughlin, M. W., & Talbert, J. E. (Eds.). (1993). *Teaching for understanding: Challenges for policy and practice.* San Francisco: Jossey-Bass.

Cohen, E. G. (1994). Restructuring the classroom: Conditions for productive small groups. *Review of Educational Research, 64,* 1–35.

Corno, L. (1995). Comment on Winne: Analytic and systemic research are both needed. *Educational Psychologist, 30,* 201–206.

Csikszentmihalyi, M. (1991, April). Motivation, development, and task engagement. Paper presented at the meeting of the American Educational Research Association, Chicago.

Darling-Hammond, L. (1996). The right to learn and the advancement of teaching: Research, policy, and practice for democratic education. *Educational Researcher, 25,* 5–17.

Davidson, N. (1985). Small group learning and teaching in mathematics: A selective review of the research. In R. Slavin, S. Sharan, S. Kagan, R. Hertz-Lazarowitz, G. Webb, & R. Schmuck (Eds.), *Learning to cooperate, cooperating to learn* (pp. 43–69). New York: Plenum.

Dweck, C. S. (1986). Motivational processes affecting learning. *American Psychologist, 41,* 1040–1048.

Dweck, C. S., & Leggett, E. L. (1988). A social-cognitive approach to motivation and personality. *Psychological Review, 95,* 256–273.

Eisner, E. W. (1983). The art and craft of teaching. *Educational Leadership, 40,* 4–13.

Elliott, E. S., & Dweck, C. S. (1988). Goals: An approach to motivation and achievement. *Journal of Personality and Social Psychology, 54,* 5–12.

Elmore, R. F., Peterson, P. L., & McCarthey, S. J. (1996). *Restructuring in the classroom: Teaching, learning, and school organization.* San Francisco: Jossey-Bass.

Enochs, L. G., & Riggs, I. M. (1990). Further development of an elementary science teaching efficacy belief instrument: A preservice elementary scale. *School Science and Mathematics, 90,* 694–706.

Fuchs, L. S., Fuchs, D., & Phillips, N. B. (1994). The

relation between teachers' beliefs about the importance of good student work habits, teacher planning, and student achievement. *Elementary School Journal, 94*, 331–345.

Fuchs, L. S., Fuchs, D., Phillips, N. B., & Simmons, D. (1993). Contextual variables affecting instructional adaptation for difficult-to-teach students. *School Psychology Review, 22*, 722–740.

Fullan, M. (1991). *The new meaning of educational change* (2nd ed.). London: Cassell.

Garner, R., & Alexander, P. A. (1994). *Beliefs about text and instruction with text.* Hillsdale, NJ: Erlbaum.

Gettinger, M. (1986). Issues and trends in academic engaged time of students. *Special Services in the Schools, 2*(4), 1–17.

Gettinger, M. (1995). Best practices for increasing academic learning time. In A. Thomas & J. Grimes (Eds.), *Best practice in school psychology–III* (pp. 943–954). Washington, DC: National Association of School Psychologists.

Gibson, S., & Dembo, M. (1984). Teacher efficacy: A construct validation. *Journal of Educational Psychology, 76*, 569–582.

Goodenow, C. (1992). Strengthening the links between educational psychology and the study of social contexts. *Educational Psychologist, 27*, 177–196.

Goodman, L. (1990). *Time and learning in the special education classroom.* Albany: State University of New York Press.

Harris, K. T. (1990). Developing self-regulated learners: The role of private speech and self-instructions. *Educational Psychologist, 25*, 35–49.

Henderson, R. W., & Cunningham, L. (1994). Creating interactive sociocultural environments for self-regulated learning. In D. H. Schunk & B. J. Zimmerman (Eds.), *Self-regulation of learning and performance: Issues and educational applications* (pp. 255–281). Hillsdale, NJ: Erlbaum.

Hoy, W. K., & Woolfolk, A. E. (1993). Teachers' sense of efficacy and the organizational health of schools. *The Elementary School Journal, 93*, 355–372.

Jehng, J. C., Johnson, S. D., & Anderson, R. C. (1993). Schooling and students' epistemological beliefs about learning. *Contemporary Educational Psychology, 18*, 23–35.

Jones, V. F., & Jones, L. S. (1990). *Comprehensive classroom management: Motivating and managing students* (3rd ed.). Boston: Allyn & Bacon.

Kagan, D. M. (1992). Implications of research on teacher beliefs. *Educational Psychologist, 27*, 65–90.

Kennedy, M. M. (1988). Inexact sciences. Professional development and the education of expertise. In E. Z. Rothkopf (Ed.), *Review of research in education* (Vol. 14, pp. 133–167). Washington, DC: American Educational Research Association.

Kindsvatter, R., Wilen, W., & Ishler, M. (1988). *Dynamics of effective teaching.* New York: Longman.

King, A. (1994). Guiding knowledge construction in the classroom: Effects of teaching children how to question and how to explain. *American Educational Research Journal, 31*, 338–368.

Knight, S. L., & Waxman, H. C. (1991). Students' cognition and classroom instruction. In H. C. Waxman & H. J. Walberg, *Effective teaching: Current research* (pp. 239–255). Berkeley, CA: McCutchan.

Ladson-Billings, G. (1995). Toward a theory of culturally relevant pedagogy. *American Educational Research Journal, 32*, 465–491.

Langer, E. J. (1993). A mindful education. *Educational Psychologist, 28*, 43–50.

Locke, E. A., & Latham, G. P. (1990). *A theory of goal setting and task performance.* Englewood Cliffs, NJ: Prentice Hall.

Maehr, M., & Midgley, C. (1991). Enhancing student motivation: A schoolwide approach. *Educational Psychologist, 26*, 399–428.

Maehr, M., & Pintrich, P. (Eds.). (1991). *Advances in motivation and achievement* (Vol. 7). Greenwich, CT: JAI Press.

Marshall, H. M. (1992). Seeing, redefining, and supporting student learning. In H. M. Marshall (Ed.), *Redefining student learning: Roots of educational change* (pp. 1–32). Norwood, NJ: Ablex.

McCombs, B. L. (1989). Self-regulated learning and academic achievement. A phenomenological view. In B. J. Zimmerman & D. H. Schunk (Eds.), *Self-regulated learning and academic achievement: Theory, research, and practice* (pp. 51–82). New York: Springer-Verlag.

McKeachie, W. J. (1990). Learning, thinking, and Thorndike. *Educational Psychologist, 25*, 127–142.

Meece, J. (1991). The classroom context and children's motivational goals. In M. Maehr & P. Pintrich (Eds.), *Advances in motivation and achievement* (Vol. 7, pp. 261–286). Greenwich, CT: JAI Press.

Meece, J. L. (1994). The role of motivation in self-regulated learning. In D. H. Schunk & B. J. Zimmerman (Eds.), *Self-regulation of learning and performance: Issues and educational applications* (pp. 25–44). Hillsdale, NJ: Erlbaum.

Moeller, A. J., & Ishii-Jordan, S. (1996). Teacher efficacy: A model for teacher development and inclusion. *Journal of Behavioral Education, 6*, 293–310.

Munk, D. D., & Repp, A. C. (1994). The relationship between instructional variables and problem behavior: A review. *Exceptional Children, 60*, 390–401.

Murphy, J. (1992). Instructional leadership: Focus on time to learn. *NASSP Bulletin, 76*, 19–26.

Myers, S. S. (1990). The management of curriculum

time as it relates to student engaged time. *Educational Review, 42,* 13–23.

National Council of Teachers of Mathematics. (1989). *Curriculum and evaluation standards for school mathematics.* Reston, VA: Author.

Needels, M. C., & Gage, N. L. (1991). Essence and accident in process-product research on teaching. In H. C. Waxman & H. J. Walberg (Eds.), *Effective teaching: Current research* (pp. 3–31). Berkeley, CA: McCutchan.

Ornstein, A. (1990). A look at teacher effectiveness research—Theory and practice. *NASSP Bulletin, 74,* 63–80.

Ornstein, A. (1993). How to recognize good teaching. *American School Board Journal, 13,* 24–27.

Pajares, M. F. (1992). Teachers' beliefs and educational research: Cleaning up a messy construct. *Review of Educational Research, 62,* 307–332.

Palincsar, A. S., Anderson, C., & David, Y. M. (1993). Pursuing scientific literacy in the middle grades through collaborative problem solving. *Elementary School Journal, 93,* 643–658.

Palincsar, A. S., & Brown, A. L. (1984). Reciprocal teaching of comprehension-monitoring activities. *Cognition and Instruction, 1,* 117–175.

Paris, S. G., & Byrnes, J. (1989). The constructivist approach to self-regulation and learning in the classroom. In B. J. Zimmerman & D. H. Schunk (Eds.), *Self-regulated learning and academic achievement: Theory, research, and practice* (pp. 168–200). New York: Springer-Verlag.

Paris, S. G., & Newman, R. S. (1990). Developmental aspects of self-regulated learning. *Educational Psychologist, 25,* 87–102.

Paris, S. G., & Winograd, P. (1990). Dimension of thinking and cognitive instruction. In B. F. Jones & L. Idol (Eds.), *How metacognition can promote academic learning and instruction* (pp. 15–51). Hillsdale, NJ: Erlbaum.

Peterson, P. L., McCarthey, S. J., & Elmore, R. F. (1996). Learning from school restructuring. *American Educational Research Journal, 33,* 119–153.

Phillips, N. B., Fuchs, L. S., Fuchs, D., & Hamlett, C. L. (1996). Instructional variables affecting student achievement: Case studies of two contrasting teachers. *Learning Disabilities Research and Practice, 11*(1), 24–33.

Pintrich, P. R. (1990). Implications of psychological research on student learning and college teaching for teacher education. In W. R. Houston (Ed.), *Handbook of research on teacher education* (pp. 826–857). New York: Macmillan.

Pintrich, P. R. & DeGroot, E. V. (1991). Motivational and self-regulated learning components of classroom academic performance. *Journal of Educational Psychology, 82,* 33–40.

Pintrich, P. R., & Schrauben, B. (1992). Students' motivational beliefs and their cognitive engagement in classroom academic tasks. In D. H. Schunk & J. L. Meece (Eds.), *Student perceptions in the classroom* (pp. 149–183). Hillsdale, NJ: Erlbaum.

Pressley, M. (1995). More about the development of self-regulation: Complex, long-term, and thoroughly social. *Educational Psychologist, 30,* 207–212.

Qin, Z., Johnson, D. W., & Johnson, R. T. (1995). Cooperative versus competitive efforts and problem solving. *Review of Educational Research, 65,* 129–143.

Reynolds, M. C. (Ed.). (1989). *Knowledge base for the beginning teacher.* New York: Pergamon.

Richardson, V. (1990). Significant and worthwhile change in teaching practice. *Educational Research, 19,* 10–18.

Richardson, V. (1994). Conducting research on practice. *Educational Researcher, 23*(5), 5–10.

Sawyer, R. J., Graham, S., & Harris, K. R. (1992). Direct teaching, strategy instruction, and strategy instruction with explicit self-regulation: Effects on the composition skills and self-efficacy of students with learning disabilities. *Journal of Educational Psychology, 84,* 340–352.

Schommer, M. (1994). An emerging conceptualization of epistemological beliefs and their role in learning. In R. Garner & P. A. Alexander (Eds.), *Beliefs about text and instruction with text* (pp. 25–55). Hillsdale, NJ: Erlbaum.

Schunk, D. H. (1990). Goal setting and self-efficacy during self-regulated learning. *Educational Psychologist, 25,* 71–86.

Schunk, D. H. (1994). Self-regulation of self-efficacy and attributions in academic settings. In D. H. Schunk & B. J. Zimmerman (Eds.), *Self-regulation of learning and performance: Issues and educational applications* (pp. 75–99). Hillsdale, NJ: Erlbaum.

Schunk, D. H. (1995). Inherent details of self-regulated learning include student perceptions. *Educational Psychologist, 30,* 213–216.

Schunk, D. H., & Swartz, C. W. (1993). Goals and progress feedback: Effects on self-efficacy and writing achievement. *Contemporary Educational Psychology, 18,* 337–354.

Schunk, D. H., & Zimmerman, B. J. (Eds.) (1994). *Self-regulation and attributions in academic settings: Issues and educational applications.* Hillsdale, NJ: Erlbaum.

Shulman, L. (1986). Paradigms and research programs in research on teaching: A contemporary perspective. In M. C. Wittrock (Ed.), *Handbook of research on teaching* (3rd ed., pp. 3–36). New York: Macmillan.

Slavin, R. (1994). *Cooperative learning: Theory, research, and practice* (2nd ed.). Boston: Allyn & Bacon.

Solomon, D., Watson, M., Schaps, E., Battistich, V., & Solomon, J. (1990). Cooperative learning as a part of a comprehensive classroom program designed to promote prosocial development. In S. Sharan (Ed.), *Recent research on cooperative learning* (pp. 111–139). New York: Praeger.

Steinberg, L., Dornbusch, S., & Brown, B. (1996). *Beyond the classroom: Why school reform has failed and what parents need to do.* Boston: Simon & Schuster.

Stevens, R. J., & Slavin, R. E. (1995). The cooperative elementary school: Effects on students' achievement, attitudes, and social relations. *American Educational Research Journal, 32,* 321–351.

Stipek, D. J. (1993). *Motivation to learn: From theory to practice* (2nd ed.). Needham Heights, MA: Allyn & Bacon.

Stoiber, K. C. (1991). The effect of technical and reflective preservice instruction on pedagogical reasoning and problem solving. *Journal of Teacher Education, 42,* 131–139.

Stoiber, K. C., Gettinger, M., & Goetz, D. (In press). Exploring factors influencing parent and early childhood practitioners' beliefs about inclusion. *Early Childhood Research Quarterly.*

Stoiber, K. C., & Peterson, P. L. (1992). Attention and classroom learning. In M. C. Alkin (Ed.), *Encyclopedia of Educational Research* (6th ed., pp. 102–107). Washington, DC: American Educational Research Association.

Swing, S. R., Stoiber, K. C., & Peterson, P. L. (1988). Thinking skills versus learning time: Effects of alternative classroom-based interventions on students' mathematical problem solving. *Cognition and Instruction, 5*(2), 123–191.

Wang, M. C., Haertel, G. D., & Walberg, H. J. (1993). Toward a knowledge base for school learning. *Review of Educational Research, 63,* 249–294.

Waxman, H. C., & Walberg, H. J. (Eds.). (1991). *Effective teaching: Current research.* Berkeley, CA: McCutchan.

Webb, N. M. (1991). Task-related verbal interaction and mathematics learning in small groups. *Journal for Research in Mathematics Education, 22,* 366–389.

Webb, N. M., Troper, J. D., & Fall, R. (1995). Constructive activity and learning in collaborative small groups. *Journal of Educational Psychology, 87,* 406–423.

Wehlage, G. G., Rutter, R. A., Smith, G. A., Lesko, N., & Fernandez, R. R. (1989). *Reducing the risk: Schools as communities of support.* New York: Falmer.

Weiner, B. (1986). *An attributional theory of motivation and emotion.* New York: Springer-Verlag.

Weiner, B. (1990). History of motivational research in education. *Journal of Educational Psychology, 82,* 616–622.

Weiner, B. (1994). Integrating social and personal theories of achievement striving. *Review of Educational Research, 64,* 557–573.

Wentzel, K. R. (1989). Adolescent classroom goals, standards for performance, and academic achievement: An interactionist perspective. *Journal of Educational Psychology, 81,* 131–142.

Wentzel, K. R. (1991). Social competence at school: Relations between social responsibility and academic achievement. *Review of Educational Psychology, 61,* 1–24.

Wentzel, K. R. (1994). Relations of social goal pursuit to social acceptance, classroom behavior, and perceived social support. *Journal of Educational Psychology, 86,* 173–182.

Winne, P. H. (1995). Inherent details in self-regulated learning. *Educational Psychologist, 30,* 173–188.

Wittrock, M. C. (1992). Generative learning processes of the brain. *Educational Psychologist, 27,* 531–541.

Wong, L. Y. S. (1995). Research on teaching: Process-product research findings and the feeling of obviousness. *Journal of Educational Psychology, 87,* 504–511.

Woolfolk, A. E., & Hoy, W. K. (1990). Prospective teachers' sense of efficacy and belief about control. *Journal of Educational Psychology, 82,* 81–91.

Zimmerman, B. J. (1995). Self-regulation involves more than metacognition: A social cognitive perspective. *Educational Psychologist, 30,* 217–222.

Zimmerman, B. J., Greenberg, D., & Weinstein, C. E. (1994). Self-regulating academic study time: A strategy approach. In D. H. Schunk & B. J. Zimmerman (Eds.), *Self-regulation of learning and performance: Issues and educational applications* (pp. 181–199). Hillsdale, NJ: Erlbaum.

Zimmerman, B. J., & Schunk, D. H. (1989). *Self-regulated learning and academic achievement: Theory, research, and practice.* New York: Springer-Verlag.

## CHAPTER 36

# THE IMPLICATIONS OF THE EFFECTIVE SCHOOLS LITERATURE FOR SCHOOL RESTRUCTURING[1]

WILLIAM E. BICKEL
*University of Pittsburgh*

In 1990 I observed that "there has been a resurgence in interest at national, state, and local levels in the quality of education available in our public schools, and in how current practices can be improved" (Bickel, 1990, p. 847). If anything, the interest in school reform has intensified in recent years with the important caveat that systemic reform or school restructuring has more often than not replaced school improvement as the end in view. It was apparent then, but is not true today, that the "literature on effective schools" had a major impact on the educational policy community's thinking on public schools and how to improve them. By almost any measure, today's reform debates rarely refer to this body of knowledge directly. Although the contemporary topography of reform is enormous and varied in scope, what dominates is a call for the fundamental restructuring of schooling in America.

I begin with a brief description of the basic tenets of the effective schools literature, followed by a more detailed discussion of recent work that can fairly be placed in this stream of research. Next, I provide an overview of school restructuring, its origins and key components. Similarities and differences between the reform philosophies extant in these two approaches to educational change are identified. This is followed by an analysis of implications the effective schools literature has for continuing efforts to improve (re-

structure) the educational experiences of students in our schools.[2]

## THE EFFECTIVE SCHOOLS LITERATURE: HOLDING SCHOOLS RESPONSIBLE FOR STUDENT ACHIEVEMENT

### Guiding Questions

The effective schools research has its origins in the late 1960s and early 1970s, when the efficacy of schooling, especially its capacity to affect populations of at-risk youths, was under serious and sustained attack. Both radical critics on the left (e.g., Kozol, 1967; Silberman, 1970) and researchers from more traditional social science communities (e.g., Coleman et al., 1966) were providing substantial evidence about how public

---

[1]The author gratefully acknowledges the editorial assistance of Rosemary McNelis in the preparation of this manuscript.

[2]In general, a "review of reviews" approach will be used in the discussion of various literatures, given the limitations of space and the breadth of the task. The exception is a more detailed review of recent research on effective schools, specifically, the examination of one study (Teddlie & Springfield, 1993) that is central in understanding where the effective schools research has gone in the past decade.

schools were failing in their mission to educate all children. Schools were seen by many as largely ineffective for poor and minority students and often viewed as the social institution that, as much as any other, was guilty of a kind of "cultural imperialism" (Carnoy, 1974) that helped to replicate social inequities in generations of disadvantaged children.

The effective schools research begins with an acceptance of the seriousness of the problems facing public schools but with a radically different view of their potential role in addressing these issues. In the words of Ron Edmonds in Edmonds and Frederiksen (undated), one of the earliest effective school researchers and its greatest spokesperson in the 1970s and early 1980s,

> For some time before I began this project [research on effective schools] I had been intrigued by three facts. First, reading achievement in the early grades in almost all inner-city schools is both relatively and absolutely low. Second, most laymen and most school people believe that such low achievement is all that can be expected. Third, I have seen for myself one inner-city school and had heard reports of several others in which reading achievement was not relatively low, in which it was, indeed, above the national average or better (Weber, 1971, p. 1). We are surrounded and daily besieged by irrefutable evidence of the social pathology that characterizes much of the life of our major institutions. Schools are no exception. Our national need to know of "things that work" has never been greater. It is at precisely this point in the public policy fray that this discussion seeks to enter. This discussion will describe the authors' efforts to identify and analyze city schools that are instructionally effective for poor and/or minority children. We are pleased to note that we have already developed unusually promising evidence of the thesis we seek to demonstrate in the research under discussion. Our thesis is that all children, excepting only those of certifiable handicap, are eminently educable, and the behavior of the school is critical in determining the quality of that education. (pp. 3–4)

The fundamental questions that effective schools researchers asked were these: can we identify specific schools that are unusually effective in teaching poor and minority children basic academic skills? Do such schools have common characteristics?[3] The affirmative answers to these questions and how the researchers came to these conclusions follow.

## Schools Can Make a Difference

That schools can make a difference to students' achievement in basic skills is an overriding conclusion that emerges from a small but quite diverse body of research conducted since the early 1970s. The effective schools research has been well described and summarized elsewhere (e.g., Armor et al., 1976; Austin, 1979; Bossert, Dwyer, Rowan, & Lee, 1982; Brookover & Lezotte, 1979; Brookover & Schneider, 1975; Edmonds & Frederiksen, 1978; Mackenzie, 1983a, 1983b; Purkey & Smith, 1983; Rutter, Maughan, Mortimore, Ouston, & Smith, 1979; Venezky & Winfield, 1979; Weber, 1971). It is sufficient here to observe that across many studies to varying degrees, and often using quite different methodological approaches, effectiveness measurements and criteria, a rough agreement can be constructed of what Edmonds came to call the "correlates of effectiveness." Bossert (1985) summarizes these characteristics of effective schools for poor and minority children well:

- A school climate conducive to learning—one free of disciplinary problems and vandalism.
- The expectation among teachers that all students can achieve.
- An emphasis on basic skills instruction and high levels of student time-on-task.
- A system of clear instructional objectives for monitoring and assessing student performance.
- A school principal who is a strong programmatic leader and who sets school goals, maintains student discipline, frequently observes classrooms, and creates incentives for learning (p. 39).

The fundamental message emanating from this research is that a number of important characteristics of effective schools is within the reach of educators to manipulate and make a difference for students' achievement. As Edmonds (un-

[3]Eventually, a secondary question was associated with this research, namely, "Can these correlates of effectiveness be used as guides to improving ineffective schools?" The answer to this question was played out in numerous school improvement projects across the country, spawned by the effective schools research.

dated) explains, "We can, whenever we choose, successfully teach all children whose schooling is of interest to us. We already know more than we need to do that. Whether or not we do it must finally depend on how we feel about the fact that we haven't so far" (Edmonds, undated, p. 35). For Edmonds, and for many others, the message of the effective schools research was as much political in its import as educational or technical. That is, for its proponents, the effective schools research refuted the conclusion (rooted in the social sciences as the effective schools judged it) that "family background is the principal cause of pupil acquisition of basic school skills" (p. 35).

As has been discussed extensively elsewhere (e.g., General Accounting Office, 1989; Miles, Farrar, & Neufield, 1983; Odden & Dougherty, 1982), the effective schools research spawned numerous initiatives around the country during the 1980s. By 1989 it is estimated that 51% of the school districts in the nation had or were planning to implement "effective schools programs" (Government Accounting Office, 1989, p. 2). It is not within the scope of this article to review the applications for school improvement emanating from the research.[4] What is important to observe here is that the use of effective schools characteristics as guides for the construction of school improvement programs is at once both a splendid example of how research can be of service to practice and a sobering chapter in educational research development in that the leap to application surely preceded certainty in knowledge. Even its greatest proponents would agree that much work needed to be done to shore up and extend to new contexts the understandings being gleaned from early effective schools research. The limits in the knowledge base provided by this body of research are briefly reviewed.

## What We Know and Don't Know About Schools

The limitations of the early effective school research have been analyzed in considerable detail (e.g., Bickel, 1990; Good & Brophy, 1986; Mackenzie, 1983a; Purkey & Smith, 1983). For our purposes it is enough to note that these limitations roughly sort into philosophical-conceptual and methodological concerns, as well as issues related to gaps in knowledge. For example, a consistent and common theme in effective schools research has been the measure of students' achievement in basic skills, usually through standardized achievement tests as the primary evidence of effectiveness. This emphasis on basic skills ignores many other important areas of intellectual and social growth that should be and are likely to be influenced by schools and that most would agree are essential to a good education. If standardized tests are to be the key measure of effectiveness, what should be the criteria of effectiveness? How stable should we expect the scores of an effective school to be? Most of the studies in the early research were undertaken in urban contexts, primarily in elementary schools.[5] Should we expect that the key variables are free of context (e.g., grade level)?

Another kind of gap in our knowledge concerns how what is being found at the school level intersects with and influences effective instructional practices in the classroom. In 1990, I looked forward to a fruitful interaction between the researchers who were describing effective schools and those who were describing powerful, classroom-level instructional practices.[6] At that time solid examples of this kind of intellectual interaction were beginning to occur (Good & Brophy, 1986; Kyle, 1985; Mackenzie, 1983a, 1983b). In referring to this emergent "connections literature" I wrote optimistically that such efforts "suggest important structures for further research . . . new work can fill in our understanding of how school processes variables can be connected operationally to important within-classroom variables such as time-on-task, direct instruction, grouping practices, curriculum priorities, and so on" (Bickel, 1990, p. 861). Alas, the kind of mutually informative research agenda that knitted findings about school variables with classroom-level analyses of powerful instructional techniques never really came about. Why

---

[4]One can find examples of the results of such applications in the work of Clark and McCarthy, 1983; Rossman, Corbett, and Firestone, 1988; Taylor, 1990; case studies of school improvement programs based on the effective schools research are described in considerable detail.

[5]There are, of course, exceptions; the most notable is the study of effective secondary schools by Rutter et al., 1979.

[6]In some of the other areas (e.g., the nature of sound instructional leadership) where additional research was also needed it has occurred (e.g., Dwyer, Lee, Rowan, & Bossert, 1983; Leithwood & Montgomery, 1982; Murphy, 1988).

is unclear. American educational reform interests are a restless lot. Ten years of significant focus on school-level variables is almost excessive by our historic standards. Professional and methodological predispositions and barriers in the research community surely played a part. Perhaps as important, the nature of the reform need was yet again redefined. More is said about this topic in a subsequent discussion in this chapter of the school restructuring movement.

Although the rapprochement between classroom and school-level researchers was never realized to any great extent, one can point to selected investigations that in very significant ways address a number of the flaws in the original research. The single best example is the work of Teddlie and Stringfield (1993) and the Louisiana School Effectiveness Study (LSES).

## Recent Research on Effective Schools

The authors of LSES (Teddlie & Springfield, 1993) describe the origins of what amounts to the seminal follow-up study to the initial effective schools research: "The LSES was begun in 1980, following the watershed period in school effects research marked by the works of Wilbur Brookover, Michael Rutter, and Ron Edmonds, and proceeding the stern but productive criticism that was to engulf the field in the early to mid-eighties. At that time we assumed that there were many other researchers across the United States busily working to follow up on the leads created by the aforementioned authors" (p. xiii).

Although the initial idea for the LSES preceded the volume of criticism leveled at the early effective schools research, its design and execution in many respects seemed to anticipate some of these critiques. As the study progressed, the LSES explicitly addressed a number of the most important concerns, especially those of a methodological nature. Thus, the four-phased LSES conducted over the better part of a decade is an extremely important source of information on the validity of the central tenets of the early effective schools research.

The overall conclusion to be drawn from the LSES, in the words of the author, is as follows: "The LSES is the fourth major study (Brookover & Lezotte, 1979; Mortimore et al., 1988; Rutter et al., 1979; Teddlie et al., 1989) to clearly identify school effects as important influences on school-level student achievement. These effects occur at a single point in time, but are especially

pronounced over time" (Teddlie & Stringfield, 1993, p. 217). How these researchers came to this conclusion is now briefly described.

The LSES-I consisted of an initial conceptualization of the research and a pilot testing of data collection instruments. The LSES-II collected data in 12 districts across the state of Louisiana. Analyses emphasized

> [a determination of] . . . the amount of variance in student achievement that was attributable to student SES and school climate; and [a comparison of] . . . schools that varied in terms of effectiveness status and student SES characteristics. [An initial] . . . set of analyses utilized both multiple regression and Hierarchical Linear modeling (HLM) techniques. . . . The second set of analyses enabled us to make the following comparisons: 1) differences among effective, typical, and ineffective schools; 2) differences between middle- and low-SES schools; and 3) differences among the six groups of schools generated by the design. (Teddlie & Stringfield, 1993, pp. 12–14).

Both the LSES-III and LSES-IV consisted of case studies of "eight matched pairs of effective and ineffective schools over a seven-year time period" (p. 14). In effect, the LSES-III is "time-one" and the LSES-IV is "time-two" extended over a seven-year period. It is important to observe that the schools were selected in a way that enabled the researchers to test several important contextual variables (e.g., urban-ruralness). Data collection also included "the gathering of quantitative and qualitative classroom observational data on teachers." (p. 14).

In combination, the four components of the LSES allowed the researchers to address some of the limitations in the initial effective schools research, including (1) whether effectiveness is a stable characteristic of schools; (2) the cumulative effects of school climate variables; (3) the relationships among school climate, selected teachers' practice variables, and students' achievement on both norm and criterion-referenced tests; and (4) comparisons of the characteristics of effective and ineffective schools in several different contexts (i.e., rural, suburban, and urban). This study also confirmed several of the original findings in the effective schools literature (e.g., the importance of principal leadership in school effectiveness). Key findings of this important study are summarized in Figure 36.1.

## FIGURE 36.1    Summary Findings on School Effects from the LSES

### *Characteristics Associated with Effectiveness*

1. Clear academic mission and focus;
2. Orderly environment;
3. High academic engaged time-on-task; and,
4. Frequent monitoring of student progress.

### *Stability of School Effects*

5. A significant percentage (approximately 50%) of the LSES-III and -IV schools retained their effectiveness over an eight-year period.

### *Effects of School Context*

6. Context matters. Effective schools implement somewhat different strategies, depending upon the students' SES [socioeconomic status], and whether the school is in an urban, rural, or suburban context[a].

### *School Leadership and Effectiveness*

7. Principal leadership is "pivotal," but must be understood as fulfilling their [the principal's] functions nested within a larger context that involves relationships between central structures and schools as much as between principals and teachers, and between teachers and students.

### *The Relationship Between Teacher and School Effects*

8. The LSES confirms that there are consistent differences in the behaviors of teachers in effective and ineffective schools. More work has to be done to understand how school-level variables and classroom practice interact to encourage effectiveness. (Teddlie & Stringfield, 1993)

### *The Relationship Between District Offices and Effective Schools*

9. Somewhat surprisingly, the researchers were "struck by the lack of meaningful influence from district offices on school effectiveness. In fact, the only influences we saw were negative . . ." (p. 220). These negatives mostly had to do with "the absence of resources" in economically disadvantaged schools.

[a] Teddlie, Kirby, and Stringfield report that Virgilio, Teddlie, and Oescher (1991) found that grade level is also an important context variable in school effectiveness.

The results reported in Figure 36.1 both confirm prior findings in the research on effective schools and extend this work in important ways. Finding 6, concerning context, is an interesting example of the latter. In LSES-II and III, the researchers questioned whether characteristics associated with effective schools differ significantly across school contexts. Figure 36.2, reproduced from the study, pertains to variations in students' SES.

Although indicating that all effective schools shared some "definite similarities," the researchers report that "there are a number of interesting differences" (Teddlie & Stringfield, 1993, p. 36) also. The reader will observe, for example, that the schools differed markedly on such variables as the use of external rewards and curricular emphases. Low-SES schools tended to emphasize external rewards and basic skills more than middle-SES schools, which tended to offer a more expanded curriculum. Similarly, principals across the two sets of schools varied significantly: "Teachers reported that principals in effective low-SES schools observed their classes an average of 2.4 hours per semester, while teachers in effective middle-SES schools were observed only 1.4 hours. Additionally, teachers in effective low-SES schools reported the greatest frequency

FIGURE 36.2    Characteristics Associated with Effectiveness in Middle-
and Low-SES Schools

| *Middle-SES Schools* | *Low-SES Schools* |
|---|---|
| 1. Promote both high present and future educational expectations. | 1. Promote high present educational expectations. Ensure that students believe they can perform well at their current grade level. Allow high future educational goals to develop later. |
| 2. Hire principals with good managerial abilities. Increase teacher responsibility for the ownership of instructional leadership. | 2. Hire principals who are initiators, who want to make changes in the schools. Encourage a more active role for the principal in monitoring classrooms and providing overall instructional leadership. |
| 3. De-emphasize visible external rewards for academic achievement (such rewards should be unnecessary if an adequate orientation is found at home). | 3. Increase the external reward structure for academic achievement. Make high-achieving students feel special. |
| 4. Expand curricular offerings beyond the basic skills. | 4. Focus on basic skills first and foremost, with other offerings after basic skills have been mastered. |
| 5. Increase contact with the community. Encourage parents with high educational expectations to exert pressure for school achievement. | 5. Carefully evaluate the effect of the community on the school. If the community does not exert positive pressure for school achievement, create boundaries to buffer the school from negative influences. |
| 6. Hire more experienced teachers. | 6. Hire younger, possibly more idealist teachers. Give the principal more authority in selecting staff. |

Teddlie & Stringfield, 1993, p. 36.

of principal assistance. . . . Principals in effective middle-SES schools allowed teachers greater responsibility for and ownership of instructional leadership. Principals in effective low-SES schools tended to be initiators regarding academic programs. (Teddlie & Stringfield, 1993, pp. 38–39)[7]. The study of such context variables as the SES of the students represents a very useful addition to the knowledge base from research on the characteristics of effective schools.

Findings on teachers' behaviors and how these vary across effective and ineffective schools is another important domain. In one of the substudies of the LSES-III, two schools, one a positive outlier and one a negative outlier in the same district and with similar SES characteristics, were compared along a number of dimensions related to the organization and delivery of instruction. The researchers found through extensive classroom observations that classrooms in the more effective school exhibited significantly more total and interactive time on-task, and the teachers were rated consistently higher by the observers on the "presentation of new content, teacher expectations, and discipline" (Teddlie & Stringfield, 1993, p. 191). Differences in more general, schoolwide characteristics (beyond the specific classrooms observed by the researchers) were also favorably correlated with those found in the classroom. These included (1) differences in expectations of students, (2) a clearer focus on academic expectations, (3) an active program for removing ineffective teachers, and (4) "related to the third . . . more active, direct monitoring and [the provision of in-service training] to teachers" (p. 193).

---

[7]These researchers report similar findings by Evans (1988) and Hallinger and Murphy (1986).

The results from the two case studies were validated by the researchers in further analyses conducted on all 16 schools in the LSES-III. This study contained both time on-task index and data from field notes gathered from a classroom observation instrument "based on the teaching functions identified in Rosenshine's (1983) synthesis of teacher effectiveness research" (Teddlie & Stringfield, 1993, p. 193). Results of these additional analyses indicated,

> Teachers in more effective schools consistently outscored those from ineffective schools on all effective teaching indices. Teachers in effective schools were consistently more successful in keeping students on task, spent more time presenting new material, provided more independent practice, demonstrated higher expectations for students, provided more positive reinforcement, experienced fewer classroom interruptions, had fewer discipline problems, generated more consistently friendly classroom ambiances, and provided more pleasant classrooms than did their peers in matched ineffective schools. (p. 193)

The researchers also note that the standard deviations on most of these measures were smaller among the effective schools than those of the ineffective ones, implying that "some formal or informal socialization process is ongoing [schoolwide] at effective schools" (p. 194).

The findings of the two analyses of LSES-III data were further substantiated in a study by Virgilio, Teddlie, and Oescher (1991). Teddlie and Stringfield (1993) report that in this study similar questions about teachers' behavior were investigated by using a wider range of "types of schools" (p. 195). That is, these researchers examined "teacher behaviors . . . in typical as well as negative and positive outlier schools" (p. 195). They conclude that "teachers from the different school effectiveness levels behaved quite distinctively. . . . Teachers from more effective schools demonstrated better teaching skills than those from typical schools, who performed better than those from less effective schools. This school effect was more pronounced at the elementary school level, but still persisted at the junior high level on the Virgilio Teacher Behavior Inventory (VTBI) indices" (p. 195). The Virgilio et al. findings also replicated the findings of the LSES-III, showing less school-level variance in

teaching behavior in the more effective schools than in the "typical schools." The latter, in turn, had less school-level variance in teaching behavior than that in the less effective schools.

This represents only the briefest summary of the decade of research encompassed in the LSES. The reader is encouraged to go directly to the work (Teddlie & Stringfield, 1993) and to the substudy reports that have emerged over the years (e.g., Teddlie et al., 1989; Virgilio et al., 1991). For our purposes here there are two fundamental points to be made about the LSES research. First, it represents the kind of followup—the serious, sustained, and methodologically rigorous investigation of the characteristics of effective schools—called for by the critics of the first wave of research (Purkey & Smith, 1983; Rowan, Bossert, & Dwyer, 1983). Several fundamental methodological concerns are directly addressed, and whereas they may not be finally put to rest, there is little doubt from the LSES that the central conclusion of the effective schools research—that identifiable school-level factors influence students' achievement—is indeed accurate.

Second, the results of the LSES begin to weave the school-level and classroom-level research together in crucial ways. The researchers themselves observe both this fact and its implications for future research: "Data from the four studies just described confirm that there are mean and variance differences in the behaviors of teachers from more and less effective schools. These results indicate that the joint study of school/teacher effects can yield consistent, predictable results, which can generate more probing questions about the processes underlying these effects. The next stage of this research should examine more precisely how school-level variables affect teacher-level behavior, which directly affects student learning" (Teddlie & Stringfield, 1993, p. 201). In the LSES the researchers speculate that at least five areas of school-level behavior that can affect teachers' behavior deserve attention in future research:

1. the method and selection of teachers;
2. type of classroom monitoring feedback;
3. the type of support for an individual teacher improvement provided by the administration;
4. instructional leadership provided by the administration, including allocating and protecting academic time; and,

5. instructional leadership to promote a positive academic climate at the school level, which translates to higher expectations and standards at the classroom level. (pp. 200–201).

I believe that the researchers' speculation is exactly right, both in important, fruitful variables for investigation and in the general argument that what is needed is more careful research on how school- and classroom-level variables interact to influence effectiveness. Regrettably, the likelihood of this happening is modest at best. In fact, our national attention on school reform has shifted once again and with it resources for research and educational improvement projects. Indeed, the very concept of school improvement has largely been dismissed for the more ambitious school restructuring. Why this has occurred and how the national push for school restructuring (or systemic change) as defined by its proponents is discussed in the following section.

## SCHOOL RESTRUCTURING: PREPARING STUDENTS FOR THE TWENTY-FIRST CENTURY

### A Working Definition

Restructuring as an organizing concept for reforming education in the United States is a relatively recent phenomenon.[8] Thus, it is perhaps not surprising that the most consistent thing that can be said by way of defining school restructuring is that it defies easy definition. The complexity or ambiguity (depending on whether one is a believer or a skeptic) about what restructuring means, and how one knows it when it exists, is self-consciously apparent in the emergent restructuring literature and among the writers that would describe it. For example, Murphy (1993) writes, "Although there appears to be no shortage of schools that have embraced restructuring throughout the nation and the world there is still a good deal of confusion about exactly what this construct means" (p. 2). Richard Miller, executive director of the American Association of School Administrators (AASA), observes, "Restructuring! It has become a catchword of the

decade. Many people favor it. Some are opposed. Others are merely cautious. However, few actually can describe what it means, especially for schools" (cited in Lewis, 1989, p. iv). Brian Rowan (1991), a researcher very familiar with the literature on effective schools, comments,

> As the proposals to reform the organizational structures of schools grow in number, education analysts are beginning to speak of a new wave of educational reform— the "restructuring" movement. Unlike past reform movements in education that have a certain measure of coherence and unity, a perplexing aspect of this latest reform movement is the lack of common ground among its supporters. Rather than consisting of a set of coherent demands for change, the restructuring movement instead consists of various reform initiatives which, in the aggregate, contain conflicting accounts of what is wrong with schools and conflicting proposals about how school structures should be changed. (cited in Elmore et al., 1991, p. 30)

Shashkin and Egermeier (1993) place restructuring (I think quite usefully) within a larger framework of systemic reform. "Systemic reform is based on and incorporates a change approach called 'restructuring.' The term restructuring seems to have become the watchword of the 1990s. In fact, restructuring is such a popular term that it is in real danger of becoming so widely applied to so many different things as to be meaningless" (p. 13). Although recognizing the ambiguity of the term and noting that even then it must be considered in the larger context of debates about systemic reform, these writers offer their definition of what *restructuring* means at its core: "Restructuring involves changes in roles, rules, and relationships between and among students and teachers, teachers and administrators, and administrators at various levels of the school building to the district office to the state level, all with the aim of improving student outcomes." (p. 14).

Shashkin and Egermeier (1993) offer examples of the recommended changes, and their discussion illustrates the definitional problems confronting any analysis of restructuring. They begin by saying that there are "at least four [specific and concrete components of restructuring] referred to consistently in the recent literature." They go on to identify two, decentralization of

---

[8]Although the precise parentage of restructuring is open to debate, most writers place the Carnegie report *A Nation Prepared: Teachers for the 21st Century* as an early foreshadowing.

authority (described as "most important") and district and state and even national strategies and mechanisms to hold schools accountable. It is interesting that the authors do not go into specifics here but do refer to the establishment of "standards" as an important element in the accountability process; for example, with the establishment of voluntary national standards, states could develop curriculum frameworks based on these standards, which in turn would be a basis for holding schools, and presumably districts, accountable. Having come this far in defining restructuring, the writers shift to a discussion of how "systemic reform [includes] but goes well beyond restructuring." Elements of the more encompassing concept are identified: curriculum restructuring or curriculum alignment ("new and more integrated and cohesive curriculum"), the development of meaningful standards (noted as important to the accountability component of restructuring), modifications in instruction (e.g., "a new emphasis on the student as opposed to the delivery system"), and "new ways of assessing performance and progress." They close by observing that "making all of this work requires teacher empowerment, that is, a substantial increase in the professionalization of teaching" (pp. 14–16).

How much to include under the restructuring umbrella was addressed by Newmann and Clune (1992) in their briefing report entitled "When Restructuring Meets Systemic Curriculum Reform": "Policy makers face a throng of proposals to improve education: chartered schools, school choice, new systems of testing, year round schools to name a few. While the merits of each initiative should be considered, the policy makers must also assess how one reform relates to another. Examining the connections helps to minimize inefficiencies when separate interventions contradict one another or operate in isolation. Educational policy should be crafted to support mutually beneficial reforms," (p. 1). These researchers make some useful distinctions that will be quite important to our quest for a working definition of restructuring. Like Shashkin and Egermeier (1993), Newmann and Clune observe that "school restructuring tends to focus primarily upon process—the roles and rules that govern how educators and students function in schools" (p. 1). The emphasis in restructuring is on fundamentally changing "the roles of teachers, administrators, students, and parents working with schools" (p. 1). Exam-

ples include school-based management, team teaching across grades and disciplines, longer class periods but meeting fewer times per week, heterogenous grouping, and replacing Carnegie units with outcomes-based assessment.

Newmann and Clune (1992) see the development of systemic curriculum reform as a necessary companion to the school restructuring process—in effect, providing the "beef" or "substantive content" for instruction in restructuring schools. "Teachers in restructured schools often consider curriculum guides, published instructional materials, and tests woefully inadequate. . . . Although individual teachers may work hard to develop new curriculum and tests, there is usually not enough time to reach solid consensus about the best curriculum, or to produce materials of sufficient quality to be validated by authorities beyond the school. . . . Ideally, curriculum reform would solve these problems by offering curriculum guides, instructional materials, and assessment tools" (p. 2). With these tools in hand the "school restructuring process could then focus on delivering the content most effectively" (p. 2). Although their hopes for the impact of systemic curriculum are quite interesting, at least in the breadth of the assertion, of primary concern to this discussion is the emphasis placed on process variables, largely seen at the school level, that are at the core of the school restructuring concept. This emphasis on school-level process variables is echoed by others (e.g., Lewis, 1989; Murphy, 1991).

By this point the reader may well be impatient with this discussion of definitions. But there has been a purpose to the telling of this tangled tale. It is my belief that the restructuring movement, almost one decade since its appearance on the educational scene, is still not well defined. It clearly does mean different things to different observers.

What can we say (or are at least willing to assert) for sure about restructuring? First, for the purpose of focusing this discussion, the modifier *school* will be used when discussing restructuring. This is not to say that there are no relationships and mechanisms that seem to go hand-in-hand with most school restructuring descriptions that lie outside the immediate school boundaries (e.g., curriculum frameworks and assessment reforms); nevertheless, I believe that it is still the school that is the essential focus of school restructuring. Much of the school-focused work done to date has essentially concerned how the professionals and adults in the school community relate to one another and, to a lesser extent, how these groups relate to other components in the broader educational system. Second, I examine whether the school restructuring process as discussed in the literature, although it is by no means uniform on this, includes the examination of critical classroom and instructional variables (e.g., pedagogy and curriculum content)—what Murphy (1991) calls the "core technology of schools" (p. 50)—as part of the school restructuring process.[9] These two elements, then—the focus on changing roles, rules, and relationships of those in schools and, as a part of this, the reexamination of instructional practice—for the purposes of this discussion are the central components of school restructuring. Systemic reform is seen as both complementing and encompassing school restructuring. In such a conceptualization, initiatives such as national and state standards, state curriculum frameworks and alignments, and assessment innovations provide contexts and tools that school restructuring participants might fruitfully use to help support and legitimize their own work.

With some semblance of definition in hand, we are now in a position to compare school restructuring and effective schools as reform concepts. Similarities and differences in these important reform conceptualizations are noted. The basic premise here is that both the effective schools literature and the emergent school restructuring theory are important sources of recent and current educational reform initiatives and that the proponents of each and the researchers investigating and analyzing each might learn from the thinking and experiences of the other.

## COMPARING THE EFFECTIVE SCHOOLS AND SCHOOL RESTRUCTURING REFORM AGENDA

In this section the effective schools and the school restructuring literature are compared along several dimensions: basic definitions of the problem, target populations and intended student outcomes, selected recommended solutions to the problem, empirical bases of recommended solutions, their respective engagement with issues of instructional practice (core technology), the educational community's receptivity to the reform agenda, and issues of educational accountability. Several caveats are in order before turning to the comparisons. My purpose here is to compare both reform movements in their essential conceptualizations (as opposed to their applications). School change programs, whether generated by the effective schools literature or the much more recent school restructuring work, are not the focus of this discussion.[10]

## Nature of the Problem

The effective schools research was largely defined in terms of equity concerns for specific populations of students, namely, poor and minority youths. There was a presumption that schools in general were efficacious for most students (at least comparatively so) in basic skills. It was the educational interests of poor and minority populations that were largely not met. The effective schools researchers, Edmonds (1978) included, felt, in effect, that they were providing evidence that this failure was more the result of a lack of political will than of knowledge of what to do. As noted in a previous commentary on this issue,

> The work manifested in the early effective schools literature represents a noteworthy period in American educational research. In what was an extremely short period of time by almost anyone's standards, a new body of knowledge was created about what worked in some schools, and by implication, what could work in other. . . . The relative balance between despair and optimism, between institutional denial and acceptance of responsibility for the education of poor and minority youth, at least has been shifted, if not entirely redressed. The hopeful message of this literature is powerful and overdue. The ways schools are organized can make a difference in the education of students, even if those students happen to be [serving] poor or minority [children]. . . While many . . .

---

[9]The fact that much of the early school restructuring theorizing and rhetoric omits this instructional emphasis has been recognized by others (e.g., Bolin, 1989; Murphy, 1991; Sykes & Elmore, 1989).

[10]Such a comparison would itself be of interest, in my view, with some interesting similarities and contradictions likely to be uncovered as they relate to change philosophies, implementation strategies, and so on.

never lost this sense of hope (and responsibility) some had. (Bickel & Bickel, 1986, p. 491)

In contrast, the roots of restructuring rest with a deep concern for the fate of the nation as a whole. In the last decade, beginning with the National Commission on Excellence in Education (1983) and soon to be followed by such reports as Carnegie's Forum on the Nation and the Economy *A Nation Prepared: Teachers for the Twenty-First Century* (1986) and the Task Force on Education (1990), the "terms of engagement" in the need for educational reform in the United States changed dramatically, if one uses the effective schools literature as the point of comparison. The "E-word" *equity*, was essentially supplanted by the "E-word" *economy*. The educational system was seen to be in general decline by many (a theme in Carnegie's Forum) and, if not in decline, certainly not up to the challenges of the twenty-first century workplace.[11] This latter perspective, dominating the current restructuring movement and seen in Carnegie's report is expressed as follows: "While it was once possible for people to succeed in this society if they were willing to work hard, it is increasingly difficult for the poorly educated to find jobs . . . [coupled with the fact that] the proportion of the population in the prime working years will decline steadily in the years to come . . . this makes it imperative that all those who are able to work make the maximum contribution to the economic well being of the nation" (p. 14).

In a similar vein, Tyack (1974) tells us that reform periods in education are typically times when issues and problems influencing the society or economy become demands for the schools to set things aright. The effective schools research can be seen, if not as generated by the former,[12] at least as being responsive (for some) to it. The restructuring movement is surely a manifestation

of the latter concern namely, economic. Lewis (1989) states the economic case for restructuring rather baldly: "One of the major influences is the consistent, collaborative voice of business leaders . . . [they] hold a consistent and strong view of how and why schools in the United States must change. Part of their reasoning concerns the changes that the American workplace has undergone in order to stay competitive in world markets; part of it stems from the insufficient supply of workers needed to occupy those workplaces. Both are crucial problems to the American business community" (p. 6). Lewis goes on to describe what this means for education, citing the analyses of Sue Berryman (1988), director of the Institute on Education and the Economy at Teachers College, Columbia University: "She [Berryman] explains what this means for schools . . . [in the new workplace] job responsibilities are broadened and increasingly intermeshed, implying the need for teamwork . . . the ability to self-regulate or self direct. . . . But what Berryman and business leaders and others emphasize—particularly in the restructured workplace—is the need for employees with higher order thinking skills" (Lewis, 1989, pp. 6–7).

The arguments presented for restructuring thus far have been purely economic in their origins and essential goals. On the face of it, this contrasts sharply with the explicit equity focus of at least the initial effective schools research and school improvement movement. However, there is a subtext in the economic case made for school restructuring that does, indeed, have implications for disadvantaged populations in the United States. The changes in the workplace are paralleled by disturbing changes in the demographics of the United States. Simply put, "Fewer workers will enter the labor force during the next decade than at any time since World War II" (Lewis, 1989, p. 8). The fundamental issue at stake is how society can educate all of its youths to the highest standards.

Perhaps for the first time in our history, economic forces and equity issues, or quality and equity values/goals . . . are being conjoined . . . in the service of improved education for all students. The rapidly changing demographic picture in schools (and in society) has been amply documented: schools are increasingly populated by less advantaged youth, children of color. . . . These at-risk students, for whom schools

---

[11]It is clear from the literature that there is much made of distinction between "Wave I and Wave II" reports in the 1980s as impetus for subsequent reforms. See, for example, Bondy, Kilgore, Ross, and Webb (1994) for an analysis of the reform approaches in these reports.

[12]The "concerns" of such individuals as Edmonds (1978) and Weber (1971) were, on the one hand, certainly "social" but, on the other hand, focused on what, in today's terms, are the needs of the "underclass" in that society.

have been the least successful historically, will soon constitute fully one third of the student population. . . . At the same time, the number of low-skilled jobs in the economy is declining, the demand for highly skilled workers is increasing, and the surplus of workers is falling as the population ages. These conditions are exerting a tremendous force on schools to be more effective for at-risk youth. (Murphy, 1991, p. 8)

This closer inspection of school restructuring reveals that within the economic argument lies an important rationale for educating poor and minority youths. The effective schools and restructuring agenda at this point appears to be potentially compatible, though hardly similar. The school restructuring interest in at-risk youths is largely economic; the effective schools agenda still, in sharp contrast, is rooted in social justice concerns. In the words of Edmonds (1978),

I want first to say something of the premises from which this discussion [of the effective schools literature] will proceed. . . . Equity is the focus of my discussion. By equity I mean a simple sense of fairness in the distribution of the primary goods and services that characterize our social order. At issue is the efficiency of a minimum level of goods and services to which we are all entitled. Some of us, rightly, have more goods and services than others, and my sense of fairness is not disturbed by that fact. Others of us have almost no goods, and access to only the most wretched services, and that deeply offends my simple sense of fairness. . . . I measure our progress as a social order by our willingness to advance the equity interests of the least among us. . . . This discussion will apply just such a standard to public schooling. Equitable public schooling begins by teaching poor children what their parents want them to know and ends by teaching poor children at least as well as it teaches middle-class children. Inequity in American education derives first and foremost from our failure to educate the children of the poor (pp. 1–2).

Whether in the long run an explicit social justice–equity or the world competition–economic approach will engender greater social commitment and finally be more productive for the youths in question is debatable. Harold

Howe II, former U.S. Commissioner of Education, speaking of both the "excellence movement of the Eighties" and the then (in 1987) nascent school restructuring movement, observed,

[The] economic argument is the engine that is driving the present reform movement. It demands that schools produce excellence among the children of the poor for the sake of the nation's economic health. It wastes little time with concepts of equity or our nation's need for independent-minded citizens to make a democracy and a complex society workable. Lip service has been paid to these latter concepts, but after the appropriate rhetoric has been supplied, school reform is back to the serious business of rescuing our corporations from Japanese competition. I am not sure where this trend of doing the right things for the wrong reasons will take us. It could lead to substantial gains. . . . If, however, the main reason for helping the poverty-stricken to succeed in school is a scarcity which has resulted from the small size of age cohorts for a few years, what will happen when the second generation of baby boomers appears, as it surely will? Will minorities and the poor again be expendable? (cited in Lewis, 1989, pp. 32–33.)

## The Target Population and Envisioned Student Outcomes of the Reforms

The definition of the problem largely signals the target populations implicit in the reform rhetoric. It is clear from earlier discussion in this chapter that proponents of effective school research—with their explicit interest in a more equitable distribution of the social good—have poor and minority students as their primary population of interest. In contrast, the school restructuring platform, rooted in the perception that the nation faces a crisis because of world competition, in effect has all youths in our nation's schools as its target population. Assuming the best of intentions, it is fair to say that at least the expressed goal of the school restructuring movement is to bring all students to higher standards of performance. The effective schools movement, at least its earliest proponents, had a narrower population of interest.

The two reform efforts are also different in the scope and substance of student outcomes emphasized. For the effective schools proponents, especially for the early writers such as Edmonds (1978) and Weber (1971; see Bickel, 1990), the crucial goal is a reduction in the correlation between one's race or economic class and achievement in basic educational skills. This criterion has both a political and educational component.[13] In contrast, the school restructuring movement emphasizes that American students, to compete with their peers around the world, must perform to world-class standards (see National Educational Goals Panel, 1993; Resnick & Nolan, 1995). Depending on who one consults, one gets somewhat different takes on the expressed goals implicit in the standards discussions. For our purposes, the recent Goals 2000 (National Educational Goals Panel, 1993) will serve as a typical expression of the kind of educational goals that undergird the school restructuring movement. Some of the expressed goals and standards go beyond the school walls (e.g., "all children in America will start school ready to learn"). Most, however, are in the direct purview of formal schooling:

- The high school graduation rate will increase to at least 90%
- American students will leave grades 4, 5, and 12 having demonstrated competence in challenging subject matter, including English, mathematics, science, history, and geography; and every school in America will insure that all students use their minds well, so that they may be prepared for responsible citizenship, further learning, and productive employment in our modern economy.
- Every school in America will be free of drugs and violence and will offer a disciplined environment conducive to learning. (National Educational Goals Panel, p. 3)

The content emphasis is on "deeper understanding of substantive knowledge, problem-solving, creativity, and analytical thinking" (as quoted in Lewis, 1989, p. 48)—what others have termed "authentic student achievement" (Newmann, 1991, p. 4).

---

[13]The basic skills emphasis in the effective schools research has been the subject of criticism from its earliest days (e.g., Good & Brophy, 1986; Purkey & Smith, 1983). The essential argument is that such an emphasis in effect reduces the scope of the educational experience too narrowly, especially for students whose lives are already subjected to a number of other intellectual and social privations.

Thus, a comparison of the effective schools and school restructuring movements in terms of student outcomes reveals considerable divergence. The linked basic skills and political criteria in the former are essentially absent in school restructuring rhetoric. Indeed, one could argue from the latter that past emphases on basic skills in education is part of the problem, or at the very least a grossly inadequate standard for "preparing for the twenty-first century."

## Comparing Solutions

The research on effective schools generated a number of implicit change goals that were deemed to be appropriate places to start a school improvement effort. These goals were empirically derived, drawn from researchers' analyses of the characteristics of effective schools. In effect, the change theory was that the correlates of effectiveness one found in effective schools could be used as a sort of blueprint for developing effectiveness in schools.

The correlates of effectiveness have been discussed elsewhere in this chapter and extensively in the literature (e.g., Mackenzie, 1983a). All of the correlates focus on school-level variables (e.g., academic emphasis, the regular monitoring of achievement, instructional leadership, and safe and orderly environment) that could be manipulated by educators. Thus, for example, this research places great emphasis on the importance of strong instructional leadership. As the literature matured, researchers were able to report on what such leadership (almost always in the hands of the principal) entailed (Dwyer et al., 1983; Teddlie & Stringfield, 1993).

First, the portrait of responsible leadership, with the principal exercising significant say over the direction of school educational policy and practices, including the selection and review of teachers, is perhaps the most pervasive image to emerge from the effective schools research. Second, no student is to fall through the cracks. Each student's progress is regularly monitored, and mastery goals are typically set. When a student does not reach mastery, the material is retaught and retested (e.g., Venson, 1981). The tests used are both curriculum-embedded exams and standardized tests. The latter have been the typical measures of overall school effectiveness in this literature, although this is changing somewhat in recent work (e.g., Teddlie & Stringfield, 1993, use both norm-referenced and criterion-referenced tests).

Very little was said in the research about the core technology of education, namely, the processes of teaching and learning. Indeed, this absence of attention to what occurs in the classroom and how school variables affect important classroom-level factors is part of the criticism of the effective schools literature (e.g., Bickel & Bickel, 1986; Mackenzie, 1983a, Purkey & Smith, 1983). Recent effective schools research has in a modest way begun to address this issue (Teddlie & Stringfield, 1993). Most observers recognize the need for more of this linking research.

In sum, the effective schools research identified several key, school-level variables associated with effectiveness. These variables have been used to structure school improvement programs. Presumably, increasing the presence of these characteristics in schools not currently operating in an effective manner would be instrumental in enhancing effectiveness. The effectiveness literature provides clear targets of change but little in the way of advice on how to get there.

School restructuring, in contrast, has tended to define both visions of a changed order and suggested strategies for achieving the restructured school. Proposed solutions to a certain extent vary according to the individual proponent. However, certain fundamental directions are discernible. All advocates of school restructuring agree that it involves fundamental changes in the way schools are organized—the roles, rules, and relationships that guide how those in the school community interact (Newmann, 1991, p. 3).

Newmann (1991) identifies four arenas in which restructuring initiatives, to varying degrees, typically focus their change agenda: (1) students' experiences; (2) the professional life of teachers; (3) school governance, management, and leadership; and (4) coordination of community resources (p. 3). As Newmann points out, school and district plans may include activities in more than one arena (they almost always do in my experience). Newmann provides a very useful set of criteria for evaluating the new structures being created (see Figure 36.3).

The reader will observe that students, for example, in restructured settings are more likely to be in heterogeneous groups, experiencing a range of instructional strategies (from whole group to cooperative to individual) and involved in learning tasks that provide opportunities for in-depth learning. Teachers are likely to be serving in differentiated roles; have opportunities for self-defined, ongoing staff development; and exercise significant control over such areas as curriculum and school

policy. Leadership, management, and governance tends to be school-based and shared among a range of school and community partners. Finally, a restructuring school will probably have significant community and parental involvement, including participation in governance and as resources for teaching and learning processes. The Center on the Organization and Restructuring of Schools indicates that their criteria are likely areas in which restructuring schools will depart from conventional practice. Newmann (1991) is careful to note that not all aspects of this criteria for school restructuring are necessarily recommended for adoption: "The degree of restructuring at a school is far less important than the ends or qualities that the school promotes. It would be foolish for a school to adopt a restructuring plan that attempted to implement the 38 criteria as if adding separate ingredients to a recipe. The school must first build a foundation—by clarifying the educational ends it seeks, assessing its unique needs, and analyzing how it must serve the ends" (p. 4).

Murphy (1991) in his analysis of school restructuring provides a conceptual framework that describes "key actors, strategies, and metaphors." Murphy sees four strategies as being most prevalent in the promulgation of school restructuring: a greater presence of "market philosophy" and customer orientation in the development of school policy ("choice/voice"), a redesign of the power arrangements in the school ("school based management"), an associated growth of the voice of teachers in school decision making ("teacher empowerment"), and the reworking of the work and technology of teaching ("teaching for understanding") (pp. 15–21).

Murphy (1991), like Newman (1991), notes the complexity inherent in the school restructuring phenomenon. Commenting on his framework, he observes, "It should also be obvious that restructuring efforts can begin in a variety of places and employ a number of different strategies depending upon the specific objectives sought. The framework is also designed to convey the message that real educational transformation will require the involvement of all the key players, work on all components of the system and the simultaneous use of four distinct but interrelated restructuring strategies" (p. 17). Murphy admits that the actual experience of school restructuring has fallen far short of this ideal of working simultaneously on four substantive fronts: "To date, most efforts at reformation have emphasized only one or two strategies. Teacher empowerment held the center stage at the outset of the restructuring movement. More re-

## FIGURE 36.3    Criteria for School Restructuring

To study the effects of restructuring, the Center searches for public schools with comprehensive restructuring according to the criteria listed below. The search began in 1990 and will continue through Spring 1993 to identify schools for possible study participation in the School Restructuring Study.

To suggest a possible research site, either complete and send the nomination form or contact: Center on Organization and Restructuring of Schools, 1025 W. Johnson St., Room 659, University of Wisconsin, Madison, WI 53706. Telephone 608-263-7575. Please answer yes (Y), or no (N) to each item, and elaborate if you wish. Further information will be requested from schools that answer "yes" to 12 or more of the questions on the nomination form.

The criteria represent major departures from conventional practice, but the Center does not recommend that all schools adopt all criteria.

### Student Experiences

1. Is learning time more equally distributed among whole class instruction, small group work, and individual study, rather than dominated by whole class instruction?
2. Do students spend most of their time in heterogeneous groups?
3. Do learning and assessment tasks emphasize student production rather than reproduction of knowledge?
4. To complete their work, do students usually speak and write in full sentences and continuous sequences rather than in few-word fragments?
5. Do learning tasks aim for depth of understanding rather than broad exposure?
6. Do learning tasks emphasize "multiple intelligence" and multiple cultures?
7. Are academic disciplines integrated in the curriculum?
8. Is time for school learning flexibly organized rather than in periods of standard length?
9. Do students participate in community-based learning?
10. Do students relate to adult mentors, either teachers or persons outside the school, in a long-term programmatic way?
11. Is student work assisted by extensive use of computer technology?
12. Do students serve as and have access to peer tutors?
13. Do students have substantial influence in the planning, conduct, and evaluation of their work?

### Professional Life of Teachers

1. Do teachers function in differentiated roles such as mentoring of novices, directing curriculum development, and supervision of peers?
2. Do staff function in extended roles with students that involve advising and mentoring?
3. Do staff help to design on-going, on-the-job staff development based on local needs assessment?
4. Do staff participate in collegial planning, curriculum development and peer observation-reflection, with time scheduled for this during the school day?
5. Do teachers teach in teams?
6. Do teachers exercise control over curriculum and school policy?
7. Are there specific organizational incentives for teachers to experiment and to develop new programs and curriculum that respond more effectively to student diversity?
8. Do teachers work with students in flexible time periods?
9. Do teachers work with students as much in small groups and individual study as in whole class instruction?
10. Do teachers work closely with parents and human service professionals to meet student needs?
11. Do teachers receive financial rewards based on student outcomes or evaluation of teaching performance?

### Leadership, Management, and Governance

1. Does the school exercise control over budget, staffing and curriculum?
2. Has the school been divided into schools within schools, divisions, or houses?
3. Is the school run by a council in which teachers and/or parents have control over budget, staffing, and curriculum?

**FIGURE 36.3** *(Continued)*

---

*Leadership, Management, and Governance*

---

4. Does the school receive financial rewards based on student outcomes?
5. Does the school make program decisions based on systematic analysis of student performance data disaggregated by student subgroups (e.g., race, gender, socio-economic status)?
6. Does the district provide special incentives for the principal to participate in restructuring?
7. Do students enroll in the school by choice rather than residential assignment?

---

*Coordination of Community Services*

---

1. Does the school have a systematic program for parent involvement in the academic life of students that goes beyond the normal activities of PTO, parents' night, and attendance at extracurricular events?
2. Does the school have formal mechanisms for coordinating with community agencies offering services dealing with child care, drug and alcohol abuse, family disruption, homelessness, sexual abuse, teen pregnancy, crime and delinquency, economic welfare assistance and parental employment and training?
3. Does the school participate in an external mentoring program, such as "I Have a Dream," which follows students for several years?
4. Does the school have formal arrangements with local employers to place students in career-ladder jobs during the school year, summers and following high school graduation?
5. Does the school have formal arrangements with institutions of higher education to assist students to continue their schooling?
6. Does the school have formal arrangements with institutions of higher education to assist with staff development and curriculum design?
7. Does the school offer adult education programs and recreational opportunities for the community at large?

---

cently, attention has shifted to school based management and choice. Considerably less work has been devoted to teaching for understanding, or redefining the teacher-learning process" (p. 17).

The change theory implicit in the school restructuring movement is that the school restructuring modification being called for will "enhance either the motivation and commitment of students and adult educators to learn and to teach or their technical capacity and competence to do so. These can be considered respectively, the 'will' and 'skill' assumptions behind school restructuring" (Newmann, 1991, p. 3).

## Comparing the Empirical Bases of the Reform Movements

One of the most striking differences between the two reform literatures is the empirical basis of one (the effective schools research) and the essential absence of an empirical base for the other. The empirical basis of the effective schools literature is functionally self-evident. The correlates of effectiveness are derived directly from analyses of existing effective schools. They are grounded in a reality that operates both as a guide to improving schools and as a source of optimism that the work to be done—the improvement of schooling effects for the children of poor and minority households—is achievable. Edmonds (1978) in the early days of this literature, after reviewing the work of Weber (1971), Brookover and Lezotte (1979), and others, would rhetorically pose the following question: "How many effective schools would you have to see to be persuaded of the educability of poor children?" (p. 23). His own answer was instructive here: "If your answer is more than one, then I submit that you have reasons of your own for preferring to believe that basic pupil performance derives from family background instead of school response to family background . . . we can, whenever and wherever we choose, successfully teach all children whose schooling is of interest to us; we already know more than we need to do that; and, whether we do it must finally depend on how we feel about the fact that we haven't so far" (p. 23).

Of course, the assertion of "knowing more than we need to know" about effective schooling for poor children must in retrospect seem overly optimistic given (1) the severe criticism the early effective schools research was to meet on largely methodological grounds and (2) the relative absence of practical insights about how to get there that would be guides to the numerous school improvement efforts generated by this research.[14] These qualifiers notwithstanding, the school improvement movement, which takes its direction from the effective schools research, stands on an impressive empirical base, one, to be sure in need of much expansion, refinement, and verification but one that nevertheless exists and did exist at the initiation point for school improvement projects.[15]

In contrast, the school restructuring movement, at this admittedly early stage in its life, for the most part has no such empirical basis. It is long and, to its proponents, persuasive on the nature of the problem (the need to address world-class competition in the twenty-first century). School restructuring supporters, like the romantic critics of the 1960s (e.g., Holt, 1964; Kozol, 1967; Silberman, 1970),[16] provide extensive critiques of what is wrong in today's schools or is hopelessly inadequate in the context of our changing economic needs as we approach the next millennium.[17] What is starkly absent from these calls to fundamental reform is a coherent appeal to educational or other evidence in support for the actions being suggested and why they should be expected to be successful in student outcomes, which are themselves touted as being at the heart of the change effort. This is especially troubling in light of the rapid promulgation of some of the core restructuring strategies across the educational landscape.

A number of observers of the current reform scene have taken note of the absence of evidence to support restructuring activities: "[The] proposed changes in schools are rarely defended through explicit theories of individual and organizational behavior, and even less frequently by solid research" (Newmann, 1991, p. 3). Shashkin & Egermeier (1993) while asserting that systemic reform (including school restructuring) "holds real promise for successful change in schools . . . [allow that] it is too early to cite definitive research on this approach" (p. 17).[18]

The devolution of authority (from centralized to school-based management structures) and teacher empowerment are two of the most frequently cited elements in school restructuring projects. Yet, as others have observed, there is little that connects the redesign of structural elements to the kinds of student outcomes being called for as the essential measure of school restructuring success. Murphy (1991) quotes D. David Cohen on this very issue: "The relations between policy and practice also are taken for granted. . . . As in most discussions of educational reform, some direct relationship between course structure and practice is assumed . . . they are much less often confirmed by research or experience" (pp. 74–75). Murphy also observes "Despite a good deal of informed opinion about the salutary effects of SBM (site-based management), teacher empowerment, and choice, the empirical evidence is troublesomely thin. Systematic monitoring of current restructuring efforts such as SBM is rare" (p. 75). In addition,

> Structural changes in and of themselves never have and never will predict organizational success (i.e., student learning in this case). It is also instructive to remember that historically, the structural elements that, according to most analysts, form the core of the restructuring movement have been decoupled from the teaching-learning process. . . . Thus, in the absence of . . . micro-level efforts to address the production function itself and concerted efforts to link structural changes with classroom processes, analysts should be cautious in raising suggestions that

---

[14]It is fair to say, however, that open-minded critics of the effective schools research (e.g., Purkey & Smith, 1985) pointed to educational change theory as a viable source for such insights.

[15]It is important to note that the targets of school improvement were known and empirically based. How to get there was not then and is not now well specified, although astute writers such as Purkey and Smith (1985) have illuminated connections to research of organizational change theory that are very useful in this regard.

[16]See Rich (1985) Schrag (1975), and Troost (1973), for more complete discussions of the romantic and radical critics of education prevalent during the late 1960s and early 1970s.

[17]Even the analyses of the problem and the enormity of the crisis are coming under recent attack (Berliner & Biddle, 1995; Bracey, 1991, 1992, 1993).

[18]Although beyond the scope of this discussion, the identical criticism pertains to elements of the more systemic components of the current restructuring scene (e.g., national standards and curriculum alignment). Indeed, what is seemingly a significant body of relevant and potentially cautionary evidence on the effects of the minimum competency movement in the early and mid-1970s, (see Tyack & Cuban, 1995) is largely ignored.

structural changes—even radical ones—will have a dramatic impact on the outcomes of schooling (p. 76)[19]

Murphy notes others who have raised similar questions (Elmore, 1988; Malen et al., 1989).

Important empirical work that has been done on implementation processes related to building communities of empowered teachers in restructuring contexts (e.g., Bondy et al., 1994; Bryk, Easton, Kerbow, Rollow, & Sebring, 1993; Lieberman et al., 1993; Odden & Wohlstetter, 1995; Pristine, 1993). These are sources of valuable insights for understanding "how to get there" when there is attainment of some of the structural reforms being pushed by restructuring advocates.

This is not to say that there is no work that directly links structural changes and student outcomes in the school restructuring rhetoric. For example, Lee and Smith (1994) in their analysis of 820 high schools and data on 11,000 students, report that "it [their study] offers solid evidence that students learn more in restructuring schools" (p. 1).[20] This study analyzed 1988 test results and survey data collected as a part of the National Education Longitudinal Study (NELS). The researchers constructed a variable list of "structural [and organizational] practices" in secondary schools (e.g., departmentalization with chairs, school-within-a-school, and flexible time for classes) that can be used to distinguish "between the practices that were the most significant departures from conventional practice, and those that were more familiar reforms. The 'significant departure' criteria are consistent with criteria developed by the Center on Organization and Restructuring of Schools" (p. 2). Three categories were created: traditional, moderately restruc-

tured along more familiar reform lines, and more nontraditional restructuring practices (the "significant departure" schools). The researchers then classified the 820 high schools, using these sets of practices, associated with a particular secondary school culture. Students' performance measures (gain scores) were then compared for schools classified as traditional to those with moderate and greater (more unconventional) degrees of restructuring practice. The researchers report that "in engagement and every subject area [math, reading, history, and science], students attending schools with [the less conventional] restructuring practices showed greater gains than students" in the schools in the other two sets (p. 4).

Lee and Smith (1994) also ask the question often posed by researchers on effective schools: do restructuring schools differ markedly in relation to equity measures ("the most equitable schools being those in which the gap in achievement between students of high and low socioeconomic status (SES) is the smallest" (p. 4). Here, again, the researchers find progress in the more dramatically restructured schools: "These data show that the gap between highest and lowest SES students was consistently smaller in schools with restructuring practices. Traditionally restructured schools, however, had narrower gaps than schools with no restructuring practices" (p. 4). Lee and Smith fairly observe that "the study has not been able to show how or why these links occur" (p. 1). Nevertheless, their work (and that of Newmann & Wehlege, 1995, for that matter) represents a contribution to the empirical research on school restructuring practices (as they relate to student outcomes) that needs to be greatly expanded if the implementation of school restructuring ideas is to be more than a passionate rejection of current practices and a leap of faith that new practices must be better.[21]

## Focus on Instructional Practice

The research on effective schools and the literature on school restructuring at first glance give rather little attention to matters inside the classroom. The caveat here is that this is true if one compares where much of the early writing and most of the initial implementation in the restructuring arena is used.

---

[19]Newmann (1993) reflects a similar skeptical stance about the theoretical basis for restructuring in his analysis of assumed links between school restructuring and instructional content: "Why should restructuring be expected to improve education for students? The implied theory behind many proposals seems grounded largely on the assumption that the new organizational structures will increase either the commitment or the competence of teachers and students" (p. 4).

[20]It is worth noting that the authors were not able to "show how or why" the association between restructuring characteristics and student performance occurred, and they lacked the ability to identify particularly effective subsets of restructuring practices (see Bryk et al., 1993, in this same document).

---

[21]There is significant empirical evidence on the immediate and intermediate horizon. See Bickel (1995) and Bryk et al., (1993).

The research on effective schools is an explicit attempt to identify schools that are unusually effective in teaching basic skills to poor and minority students. The correlates of effectiveness are school-level variables associated with such schools. As Bickel and Bickel (1986), Mackenzie (1983a), and Teddlie and Stringfield (1993) have noted, the theoretical and actual links between school-level variables and teaching and learning practices that are likely to be casually related to the desired student outcomes have not been well mapped. For example, how does strong instructional leadership in the principal's office manifest itself and how do these behaviors operate either directly or indirectly on teachers and students? Researchers like Bossert et al. (1982) have tried to pursue this line of inquiry to a degree. But it is still fair to say that the links to effective classroom practice have not been well made in the effective schools literature.

School restructuring initiatives in a similar vein have largely focused on such school-level variables as teachers' and parents' empowerment as the primary engines of the change process. Murphy (1991) comments, "Of all the elements of the restructuring agenda (e.g., school-based management, choice, teacher empowerment), the teaching-learning piece was the one receiving the least amount of attention. Worse, the other elements were increasingly being treated as ends in themselves" (p. 254). Fullan (1993) similarly observes, "In reviewing the evidence on site-based management in *The New Meaning of Educational Change*, I concluded that restructuring reforms that devolved decision making to schools may have altered governance procedures but did not affect the teaching-learning core of schools" (pp. 143–144).

To the extent that systemic reform (e.g., with an interest in standards and curriculum frameworks) overlaps and influences school restructuring efforts already underway, attention to the core technology of schools may well be seen to be on the increase. Unlike the effective schools literature and much of the school restructuring literature, one can find direct discussion of instructional issues in the rhetoric supporting systemic reform. These discussions tend to be rooted in recent cognitive research about learning and instruction. The student is seen as worker, constructing knowledge out of the worlds around him or her, with the teacher no longer the transmitter of knowledge but rather a guide (Conley, 1994). In this respect, one might hypothesize that school restructuring, which began largely as a "governance or management reform" (Carnoy & MacDonell, 1990) may over time be transformed. The larger reform context—centered around learner-centered pedagogy, with constructivist (as opposed to behaviorist) principles of learning as its core assumption about how students acquire knowledge (Murphy, 1993), and curriculum frameworks aligned with classroom practice and national standards—may well reshape the school restructuring efforts already in place.

## Educational Community's Receptivity

There is at least a superficial similarity in the experience of the research on effective schools and the general literature on school restructuring in the degree to which they both appear to have been widely accepted (adopted or interpreted are also reasonable characterizations here) as important guides for school change projects. For example, a report by the General Accounting Office (1989) found that "effective schools concepts, in some form and to some extent, have been adopted more or less systematically in over one half of all school districts in the United States (cited in Shashkin & Egermeier, 1993). Remarkably, this adoption occurred within a very short period of time—less than a decade. Bickel (1983), in commenting on reasons for the widespread implementation of school improvement projects grounded in the research on effective schools, observed, "[One] basis for the [rapid growth of] the effective schools movement rests with the psychological climate prevalent among practitioners. . . . Teachers, principals, and administrators were ready to hear a more hopeful message about the ability of schools to educate children. . . . [Another] factor explaining the phenomenal growth . . . is implicit in the findings most publicized by this research. . . . [They] had an intuitive appeal to most individuals knowledgeable about schools" (pp. 3–4).

The rhetoric of school restructuring permeates the current educational landscape. Just to take one simple measure, a review of recent presentations at the 1995 American Educational Research Association (1995) Annual Conference reveals that almost 50 were made directly under the topical headings of "restructuring" or "school restructuring." This doesn't take into account the scores of presentations made on features of school restructuring like site-based management, shared decision making and collaboration, various standards and assessment models, and so on. A similar review of articles in popular professional journals (e.g., *Educational Leadership* and *Kappan*) would yield a plethora of articles about school restructuring and systemic issues.

Although there is much rhetoric and publishing about school restructuring, one can question the extent that the level of discussion reflects actual practice. The Center on the Organization and Restructuring of Schools noted in 1992 that there hasn't been a systematic survey of restructuring in the nation's schools. Using criteria for comprehensive restructuring that includes changes in four areas—(1) students' experiences, (2) professional life of the teacher, (3) school governance, and (4) collaboration between schools and community—these researchers found that in a number of schools that had been nominated for participation in various studies of restructuring schools, "few can boast comprehensive restructuring across all four themes" (p. 1). More recently, Lee and Smith (1994), in a sample of 820 high schools drawn for the NELS data base, found that approximately 46% reported engaging in at least 3 of the 12 restructuring practices designated by the researchers as representing a "significant departure from conventional practice" (p. 5). Comprehensive, systematic data are largely nonexistent on this issue. In their absence, it is probably reasonable to say that some schools (by no means a majority) are probably engaged in some sort of self-declared restructuring. Whether many of these schools would qualify under close inspection in using stringent criteria is doubtful. Nevertheless, the rhetoric and perhaps restructuring reality are likely to be on the increase for a while, as David (1991) observes: "Pressure on school districts to restructure is mounting, as more and more people—from corporate leaders and policy makers to educators and parents—acknowledge that the current system is not working [and perceive] the increasing gap between what schools look like now and what they must look like in the future to meet society's needs" (p. 209).

## Basis for Accountability

One of the most interesting areas for comparisons between the effective schools literature and the current restructuring movement is the emphasis placed on accountability and the targets of accountability. The effective schools researchers believe their work contributes to the empirical basis for expecting schools to take responsibility for the education of children, even if those children happen to be from poor or minority households. This research demonstrates that schools can be effective for such students. As Edmonds (1978) stated, the knowledge exists, and creating more effective schools is a matter of political will. The school, then, is the focus of accountability for the effective schools researchers, and the excuse for nonperformance provided for some educators by the "family background" factor is directly challenged. The research on effective schools both provides insights about how to improve schooling effects and in the same stroke (its proponents would argue) takes away the implicit excuse that poor and minority children can't learn by providing examples of schools that are making a difference for these populations.[22]

The restructuring literature, in contrast to that on effective schools, is far less precise on this issue. Certainly, all of the fuss about restructuring schools implicitly supports a view that schools do have something to do with students' performance. The relatively diminished presence of equity as a philosophical and moral imperative for restructuring does not alone decide the focus of accountability. However, a review of literature calling for restructuring yields little in the way of a clear signal on the accountability question.[23] What is apparent is an extensive commitment to assessing students' performance in the systemic reform models that surround most school restructuring discussions. Like the literature on effective schools, the restructuring literature, writ large, calls for the careful monitoring of students' progress. Little is said, however, about what one is to do with the data. Unlike the competency-based education movement of the 1970s (e.g., Bickel, 1976), writers of restructuring literature do not seem to be suggesting that students

---

[22]It is important here to distinguish between what the researchers were saying and implying about who is accountable and the development and implementation of actual school accountability models. School improvement projects tended to have uneven success in holding schools and educators accountable for student outcomes. See Clark et al. (1983) and Cooley and Bickel (1986) for information on the realities of school improvement implementation.

[23]One does find some evidence of a school accountability logic being followed in specific restructuring implementations (e.g., see Pittsburgh Public Schools, 1996; Steffy, 1993).

should not graduate if they do not reach high standards; neither is a philosophical base being put forward that suggests that schools should be held to task for students' poor performance. Yet, in today's circumstance, the accountability issue is unlikely to go away. Framed by their own rhetoric, the stakes for restructuring are high— no less than being prepared for the twenty-first century.

# IMPLICATIONS OF THE EFFECTIVE SCHOOLS LITERATURE FOR SCHOOL RESTRUCTURING

The research on effective schools has three important implications, lessons if you will, for the current movement to restructure schools. The first is somewhat rhetorical, the simple assertion that this newest round of reformers must learn from past attempts at reform, including the research on effective schools. Although the effective schools movement is the past at play, the first lesson is really larger than that one single movement.

Taking a march from Sarason's (1991) examination of cycles of reform in U. S. education, this question can be asked of the proponents of school restructuring: what is there in this new round of reform that demonstrates evidence of knowledge about the predictable failure of educational reform? One could argue that, to the extent that school restructuring is addressing some of the basic power relationships in the school (e.g., shared decision making) and in the classroom (e.g., a constructivist approach to learning), there is at least an implicit recognition that change must address what exists now. What is not apparent in any of the macro literature on school restructuring is an analysis of how to get there. Or to state the issue another way, there is no evidence in this new reform movement of a careful analysis of why things are the way they are, something I would argue is needed as a precursor to planning how to change things in a fundamental way. This absence of a change analysis seems to risk a faithful repetition of the mistakes made by the school improvement reform movement. Those reformers, like contemporary school restructuring advocates, had much to say about what the vision of the improved school looked like but little on how to get there.

School restructurers, already producing evidence about how difficult it is to change schools,

are learning again what is already known about school change (see e.g., Bondy et al., 1994). Tyack and Tobin (1994), in their analysis of the difficulty of changing the "grammar [read culture] of schooling," observe,

> Reformers believe that their innovations will change schools, but it is important to recognize that schools change reforms. . . . Cultural constructions of schooling have changed over time and can change again. To do this deliberately would require intense public dialog about the ends and means of schooling, including the reexamination of cultural assumptions about what a "real school" is and what sort of improved schooling could realize new aspirations. Shared beliefs could energize a broad social movement to remake the schools. To do so would require reaching beyond a cadre of committed reformers to involve the public in a broad commitment to change. This would require not only questioning what is taken for granted but also preserving what is valuable in existing practice. (p. 478)

Ironically, one can find similar critiques of the effective schools literature and their lack of a change theory to guide the reform effort. For example, Purkey and Smith (1983) more than a decade ago called for linking educational change literature to what was being discovered about the characteristics of effective schools to build more powerful school improvement processes.

A second area in which the restructuring advocates can learn from the effective school research experience is the failure of the literature on effective schools (with a few notable exceptions) to connect what was being learned at the school level with other knowledge bases being generated about sound learning and instruction in the classroom. MacKenzie (1983a), among others, started to make such connections; Teddlie & Stringfield (1993) has done so recently. However these are the exceptions. As Murphy (1992) observes, "The effective schools literature movement, while recognizing and leveling devastating attacks on the existing system of learning and teaching, has been unable in many ways . . . to get beyond these deficiencies . . . reasonable interpretation of this literature is that the changes in the technical core [curriculum, instruction, and assessment] have been on the margins" (p. 99).

Murphy (1992) believes that the school restructuring movement is addressing this problem in fundamental ways: "The school restructuring movement offers the promise of providing schools with a more robust understanding of the educational production function that in turn may generate fairly radical changes in the design and unfolding of learning experiences" (p. 99). Murphy sees these possibilities in what he calls a "newly-forming alternative model of learning" that contains "radical changes in assumptions about intelligence and knowledge" (p. 99), that is, cognitive, constructivist, and sociological perspectives on how learning occurs and on the nature of instruction. Murphy does not discount either the potential connection this "within the classroom work" has to the school restructuring movement nor the implicit breath of change for current instruction. What is troublesome is the enormous amount of energy being spent on organizational and structural reforms like shared decision making, as noted earlier, and far less energy on core technology issues. In part one sees that the two issues are the primary concerns of two different reform communities. The danger here, of course, is that the cross-fertilization that should occur will not, replicating in part the nonconnection to classroom research that characterized the effective school research.

The third implication for school restructuring to be drawn from the effective schools literature is the contrastive empirical bases of the two. As observed, the effective schools work rests on an explicit empirical base—much criticized to be sure but nevertheless apparent. The school restructuring movement has no such base. This is true for both the organizational and structuring reforms and the somewhat distant but associated alternative model for learning. When I say there is no empirical base, what I mean is that there is no meaningful evidence that these reforms will lead to the kind of changes in student outcomes wished for—all students meeting world-class standards, either singly or, especially, in combination.[24] What exists seems to justify important pilot projects, experiments in real settings to test the theory in the school restructuring reforms. But such testing and gathering of empirical evi-

dence is just really occurring only now, well into implementation in numerous states and locales.[25]

Why is such evidence important? There are many reasons to be concerned, but perhaps the most telling involves the implicit stakes in the game as defined by the reformers themselves. Tyack and Cuban (1995) state,

> In a society prone to equating change with progress, it is not surprising that people who promise to reinvent schooling attract followers. Innovators appeal to the faith that Americans have vested in education as an engine of social betterment and to the fear that existing schools cannot fulfill their high hopes. Indeed, the dream of a golden age in the future has often been a central theme in utopian designs to reinvent education in the present. Setting goals is an essential stage in reform, but raising expectations to a level likely to be achieved only by "schools that are light years beyond those of today"[26] can quickly lead to discouragement or disillusionment. Perhaps even more than the average citizen, teachers tend to be allergic to utopian claims for school reform, for they, the agents supposed to carry out the break-the-mold reforms, are often the people blamed when grandiose innovations fail. (p. 132)

One sees signs already that the lack of evidence for the grandiose reform agenda is taking its public toll in the recent comments of Albert Shanker (1995), past president of the American Federation of Teachers, in which he calls many current reforms into question. "Reformers by and large have not been honest with the public about how effective their programs are. They rarely acknowledge that what they are doing is experimental . . . we ought to take the same approach to innovation in education as we do in medicine. . . . They do a considerable amount of testing and refining before they make these innovations publicly available. This caution is part of what creates public confidence" (p. 37).[27]

---

[24]Just to put a fine point on this, the latter might reasonably require evidence that teachers in a shared decision-making context would be inclined to make instructional decisions that might lead, in turn, to the installation of constructivist approaches to learning and instruction, and this in turn would lead to the meeting of high standards across an array of performance domains.

[25]See Newmann & Wehlege (1995).

[26]The authors are referring to the rhetoric surrounding the launching of the New American School Corporation (see p. 170).

[27]The irony here is significant in that Shanker was clearly leading the charge on a number of the innovations recently associated with the school restructuring movement.

What is sobering here is that when contrasted with the effective schools movement, the school restructuring reformers have less evidence and very few working models of what the future portends. Perhaps the answer lies in the words of Tyack and Cuban (1995): "Rather than starting from scratch in reinventing schools, it makes most sense to graft thoughtful reforms onto what is healthy in the present system" (p. 133). If this is so, one of the healthy elements in the current system is the knowledge base provided by the research on effective schools.

# REFERENCES

American Educational Research Association (1995). *Annual Meeting Program, San Francisco, CA.* Washington, DC: Author.

Amor, D. J., Conry-Oseguera, P., Cox, M., King, N., McConnell, L., Pascal, A., Pauly, E., & Zellman, G. (1976). *Analysis of the school referred reading program in selected Los Angeles minority schools* (Report No. R-2007-LAUSD). Santa Monica, CA: Rand Corp.

Austin, G. R. (1979). Exemplary schools and the search for effectiveness. *Educational Leadership, 37,* 10–14.

Beare, H., & Boyd, W. L. (Eds.). (in press). *Restructuring schools: An international perspective.* Berkeley, CA: McCutchan.

Berliner, D. C., & Biddle, B. J. (1995). *Manufactured crisis.* Reading, MA: Addison-Wesley.

Berryman, S. (1988). Education and the economy: What should we teach/to whom? When? How? Paper delivered to the Continuing Conference of Southern Educational Foundation, Atlanta, GA.

Bickel, W. E. (1976). A critical review. In *CBTE: Issues and perspectives.* Pittsburgh: University of Pittsburgh.

Bickel, W. E. (1983). Effective schools: Knowledge, dissemination, inquiry. *Educational Researcher, 12*(4), 3.

Bickel, W. E. (1990). The effective schools literature: Implications for research and practice. In T. B. Gutkin & C. R. Reynolds (Eds.), *The handbook of school psychology* (2nd ed.). New York: Wiley.

Bickel, W. E. (1995). Pittsburgh Public Schools Restructuring Evolution. Pittsburgh: School Restructuring Evaluation Project, University of Pittsburgh.

Bickel, W. E., & Bickel, D. D. (1986). Effective schools, classrooms, and instruction: Implications for special education. *Exceptional Children, 52*(6), 489–500.

Bolin, F. S. (1989, Fall). Empowering leadership. *Teachers College Record, 91*(1), 81–86.

Bondy, E., Kilgore, K., Ross, D., & Webb, R. (1994). *Building blocks and stumbling blocks: Three case studies of shared decision making and school restructuring.* New York: National Center for Restructuring Education, Schools, Teaching.

Bossert, S. T. (1985). Effective elementary schools. In R. M. J. Kyle (Ed.), *Reaching for excellence: An effective schools sourcebook.* Washington, DC: E. H. White.

Bossert, S. T, Dwyer, D. C., Rowan, B., & Lee. G. U. (1982). The instructional management role of the principal. *Educational Administration Quarterly, 18,* 34–64.

Bracey, G. W. (1991, October). Why can't they be like we were? *Phi Delta Kappan,* pp. 104–117.

Bracey, G. W. (1992, October). The second Bracey report on the condition of public education. *Phi Delta Kappan,* pp. 104–117.

Bracey, G. W. (1993, October). The third Bracey report on the condition of public education. *Phi Delta Kappan,* pp. 104–117.

Brookover, W. B., & Lezotte, L. W. (1979). *Changes in school characteristics coincident with changes in student achievement.* East Lansing: Michigan State University, Institute for Research on Teaching.

Brookover, W. B., & Schneider, J. M. (1975). Academic environments and elementary school achievement. *Journal of Research and Development in Education, 9*(1), 82–91.

Bryk, A. S., Easton, J. Q., Kerbow, D., Rollow, S. G., & Sebring, P. A. (1993, July). A view from the elementary schools: The state of reform in Chicago. Paper presented to the Consortium on Chicago School Research, Chicago.

Carnegie Forum on Education and the Economy. (1986, May). *A nation prepared: Teachers for the 21st century.* Washington, DC: Author.

Carnoy, M. (1974). *Education as cultural imperialism.* New York: David McKay.

Carnoy, M., & MacDonell, J. (1990). School district restructuring in Santa Fe, New Mexico. *Educational Policy, 4*(1), 49–64.

Center on the Organization and Restructuring of Schools. (1992). *Brief to policymakers: Estimating the extent of school restructuring.* (Brief 4). Madison, WI: Author.

Clark, T. S., & McCarthy, D. P. (1983). School improvement in New York City: The evolution of a project. *Educational Research, 12*(4), 17–23.

Coleman, J., Cambell, E., Hobson, C., McPartland, J., Mood, A., Weinfield, F., & York, R. (1966). *Equality of educational opportunity.* Washington, DC: U.S. Government Printing Office.

Conley, D. T. (1994). Roadmap to restructuring. *The Eric Review, 3*(2), 12–21.

Cooley, W. W., & Bickel, W. E. (1986). *Decision-oriented educational research.* Boston: Kluwer.

David, J. (1991). Restructuring in progress: Lessons from pioneering districts. In R. E. Elmore & Associates, *Restructuring schools: The next generation of educational reform.* San Francisco: Jossey-Bass.

Dwyer, D. C., Lee G. V., Rowan, B., & Bossert, S. T. (1983). *Five principals in action: Perspectives on instructional management.* San Francisco: Far West Laboratory.

Edmonds, R. R. (1978). A discussion of the literature and issues related to effective schooling. Unpublished manuscript, New York City Public Schools, New York.

Edmonds, R., & Frederiksen, J. R. (undated). *Search for effective schools: The identification and analysis of city schools that are instructionally effective for poor children.* Cambridge, MA: Harvard University, Center for Urban Studies.

Elmore, R. F. (1988). *Early experiences in restructuring schools.* Washington, DC: National Governors' Association.

Elmore, R. E. (1991). *Restructuring schools: The next generation of educational reform.* San Francisco: Jossey-Bass.

Evans, R. L. (1988). Teachers' perceptions of principals' change facilitor styles in schools that differ according to effectiveness and socioeconomic context. Doctoral dissertation, University of New Orleans, New Orleans.

Fullan, M. G. (1993). Coordinating school and district development in restructuring. In J. Murphy & P. Hallinger (Eds.), *Restructuring schools.* Newbury Park: CA: Corwin Press.

Good, T. L., & Brophy, J. E. (1986). School effects. In M. C. Wittrock (Ed.), *Handbook of research on teaching* (3rd ed.). New York: Macmillan.

Government Accounting Office (1989). *Effective schools programs: Their extent and characteristics* (GAO-HRD-89-132BR). Washington, DC: U.S. Government Printing Office.

Hallinger, P., & Murphy, J. (1986). The social context of effective schools. *American Journal of Education, 94,* 328–355.

Holt, J. (1964). *How children fail.* New York: Pitman.

Kozol, J. (1967). *Death at an early age.* Boston: Houghton Mifflin.

Kyle, R. M. J. (Ed.). (1985). *Reaching for excellence: An effective schools sourcebook,* Washington, DC: E. H. White.

Lee, V. E., & Smith, J. B. (1994). *High school restructuring and student achievement: Issues in restructuring schools* (Issue Report No. 7). Madison, WI: Center on Organization and Restructuring of Schools.

Leithwood, K. A., & Montgomery, D. J. (1982). The role of the elementary school principal in program improvement. *Review of Educational Research, 52,* 309–339.

Lewis, A. (1989). *Restructuring America's schools.* Arlington, VA: American Association of School Administrators.

Lieberman, A., Darling-Hammond, L., & Zukerman, D. (1993). *Early lessons in restructuring schools.* New York: National Center for Restructuring

Education, Schools, Teaching, Teachers College, Columbia University.

Mackenzie, D. E. (1983a). Research for school improvement: An appraisal of some recent trends. *Educational Researcher, 12*(4), 5–16.

Mackenzie, D. E. (1983b). School effectiveness research: A synthesis and assessment. In P. C. Duttweiler (Ed.), *Educational productivity and school effectiveness.* Austin, TX: Southwest Educational Development Laboratory.

Malen, B., Ogawa, R. T., & Kranz, J. (1989, May). What do we know about school-based management? Paper presented at the Conference on Choice and Control in American Education. Madison: University of Wisconsin.

Miles, M. B., Farrar, E., & Neufield, B. (1983). *The extent of adoption of effective schools programs.* Cambridge, MA: Huron Institute.

Mortimore, P., Sommons, P., Stoll, L., Lewis, D., & Ecob, R. (1988). School matters: The junior years. *Educational Leadership, 45*(2), 4–8.

Murphy, J. (1988, Summer). Methodological measurement and conceptual problems in the study of instructional leadership. *Educational Evaluation and Policy Analysis, 11*(3), 209–221.

Murphy, J. (1991). *Restructuring schools.* New York: Teachers College Press.

Murphy, J. (1992). School effectiveness and school restructuring: Contributions to educational improvement. *School Effectiveness and School Improvement, 3*(2), 90–109.

Murphy, J. (1993). Restructuring: In search of a movement. In J. Murphy & P. Hallinger (Eds.), *Restructuring schooling: Learning from ongoing efforts.* Newbury Park, CA: Corwin Press.

National Commission on Excellence in Education (1983). *A nation at risk: The imperative for educational reform.* Washington, DC: U.S. Department of Education.

National Educational Goals Panel (1993, November). *Promises to keep: Creating high standards for American students.* Washington, DC: Author.

Newmann, F. M. (1991, Fall). *Hidden supports in school restructuring: Issues in restructuring schools,* Madison: Center on Organization and Restructuring of Schools, University of Wisconsin.

Newmann, F. M. (1993, March). Beyond common sense in educational restructuring, *Educational Researcher, 22*(2), 4–13, 22.

Newmann, F. M., & Clune, W. H. (1992, Summer). *When school restructuring meets systemic curriculum reform.* Madison: Center on Organization and Restructuring of Schools, University of Wisconsin.

Newmann, F. M., & Wehlege, G. G. (1995). *Successful school restructuring.* Madison: University of Wisconsin.

Odden, A, & Dougherty, U. (1982). *State programs of

*school improvement: A 50-state survey*, Denver, CO: Education Commission of the States.

Odden, E., & Wohlstetter, P. (1995). Making school-based management work. *Educational Leadership*, *52*(5), 32–36.

Pittsburgh Public Schools (1996). *Accountability plan*. Pittsburgh, PA: Author.

Pristine, N. A. (1993). Feeling the ripples, riding the waves. In J. Murphy & P. Hallinger (Eds.), *Restructuring schooling: Learning from ongoing efforts*. Newbury Park, CA: Corwin Press.

Purkey, S. C., & Smith, M. S. (1983). Effective Schools: A review. *Elementary School Journal, 83*, 427–452.

Purkey, S. C., & Smith, M. S. (1985). School reform: The district policy implementations of the effective schools literature. *Elementary School Journal, 85*(3), 353–389.

Resnick, L., & Nolan, K. (1995, March). Where in the world are world-class standards? *Educational Leadership, 62*(6), 6–11.

Rich, J. M. (1985). *Innovations in education: Reformers and their critics*. Boston: Allyn & Bacon.

Rosenshine, B. V. (1983). Teaching functions in instructional programs. *Elementary School Journal, 83*, 335–352.

Rossman, G. B., Corbett, H. D., & Firestone, W. A. (1988). *Change and effectiveness in schools*. Albany: State University of New York Press.

Rowan, B. (1991). Applying conceptions of teaching to organizational reform. In R. E. Elmore, & Associates. *Restructuring schools: The next generation of educational reform*. San Francisco: Jossey-Bass.

Rowan, B., Bossert, S. T., & Dwyer, D. C. (1983). Research on effective schools: A cautionary note. *Educational Researcher, 12*(4), 24–31.

Rutter, M., Maughan, B., Mortimore, P., Ouston, J., & Smith, A. (1979). *Fifteen thousand hours: Secondary schools and their effects on children*. Cambridge, MA: Harvard University Press.

Sarason, S. B. (1991). *The predictable failure of educational reform*. San Francisco: Jossey-Bass.

Schrag, P. (1975). Education's "romantic" critics. In S. Dropkin, H. Full, & E. Schwarcz (Eds.), *Contemporary American education*. New York: Macmillan.

Shanker, A. (1995, December 6). Why schools need standards and innovation. *Education Week, 15*(14), 48.

Shashkin, M., & Egermeier, J. (1993). *School change*

models and processes: A review and synthesis of research and practice*. Washington, DC: U.S. Department of Education.

Silberman, C. (1970). *Crisis in the classroom*. New York: Random House.

Steffy, B. E. (1993, September). Top down—bottom up: Systemic change in Kentucky. *Educational Leadership, 51*(1), 42–44.

Sykes, G., & Elmore, R. F. (1989). Making schools more manageable. In J. Hannaway & R. L. Crowson (Eds.), *The politics of reforming school administrations*. New York: Palmer Press.

Task Force on Education (1990). *Educating America: State strategies for achieving national educational goals*. Washington, DC: National Governors Association.

Taylor, B. O. (Ed.). (1990). *Case studies in effective schools research*. Madison, WI: National Center for Effective Schools Research and Development.

Teddlie, C., Kirby, P. C., & Stringfield, S. (1989). Effective versus ineffective schools: Observable differences in the classroom. *American Journal of Education, 97*(3), 221–236.

Teddlie, C., & Stringfield, S. (1993). *Schools make a difference: Lessons learned from a 10-year study of school effects*. New York: Teachers College Press.

Troost, C. J. (1973). *Radical school reform*. Boston: Little, Brown.

Tyack, D. (1974). *One best system*. Cambridge, MA: Harvard University Press.

Tyack, D., & Cuban, L. (1995). *Tinkering toward utopia*. Cambridge, MA: Harvard University Press.

Tyack, D., & Tobin, W. (1994, Fall). The "grammar" of schooling: Why has it been so hard to change? *American Educational Research Journal, 31*(3), 453–479.

Venezky, R. L., & Winfield, L. F. (1979). Schools that succeed beyond expectation in teaching (Studies in Education Technical Report No. 1). Newark: University of Delaware.

Venson, L. (1981). *The Pittsburgh school improvement program*. Pittsburgh, PA: Pittsburgh Public Schools.

Virgilio, I., Teddlie, C., & Oescher, J. (1991). Variance and context differences in teaching a differentially effective school. *School Effectiveness and School Improvement, 2*(2), 152–168.

Weber, G. (1971). *Inner-city children can be taught to read: Four successful schools*. Washington, DC: Council for Basic Education.

CHAPTER **37**

# EFFECTIVENESS OF SPECIAL EDUCATION

**KENNETH A. KAVALE**
*University of Iowa*
**STEVEN R. FORNESS**
*University of California, Los Angeles*

Special education, like other segments of the educational community, is experiencing a wave of reform (Kauffman, 1993). Although the call for change has a variety of sources, one primary vehicle has been the perception that special education has not achieved its desired outcomes. Reynolds, Wang, and Walberg (1987), for example, discuss the fragmented and disjointed nature of special education that limits effectiveness. Such discussions about effectiveness are not really new and can be traced back to the beginnings of special education in Itard's (1806/1962) work with Victor, the "wild boy" of Aveyron. Do special education students attain outcome levels that warrant the continuation of programs and services under the rubric of special education? Depending on your perception, answers may range from a call for the status quo, because of perceived benefits derived from special education, to a call for radical reform through a restructuring that essentially merges general and special education into a single system that serves all students.

## THE MEANING OF SPECIAL EDUCATION

For a domain that has generated so much debate, special education is not well defined. According to federal regulations, special education means "specifically designed instruction, at no cost to the parent, to meet the unique needs of a handicapped child, including classroom instruction in physical education home instruction, and instruction in hospitals and institutions" (U.S. De-

partment of Education, 1992). The key words in the definition are *specifically* and *unique* since they represent the concept of individualization. The essence of special education is instruction matched to particular needs. Although individualization is a fundamental concept, the definition does not address the nature of the instruction to be provided. How should individualization be achieved? How this question is answered provides insight into the philosophical foundations of special education (see Table 37.1).

The first response in the table emphasizes the *special* in special education through the development of methods that are unique and exclusive. The techniques developed would not be routinely used in general education and are associated with special education only. The second response emphasizes the *education* in special education. Rather than developing methods within the context of special education, existing general education techniques are modified for special education. An alternative response is for general education methods to be used intact but fitted to the individual needs of a special education student. In both cases, the emphasis is on education and the use of existing procedures to achieve desired outcomes without relying on techniques that would typically be found only in special education.

Given the different emphases, problems in defining special education can be readily discerned. For example, if the *education* part of special education is stressed, is it proper to term the transaction special education, or is it better viewed as an optimal form of general education?

**TABLE 37.1    The Meaning
of Special Education**

| Special Education |
| --- |
| **SPECIAL** Education |
| Special **EDUCATION** |

To provide a distinct identity and clearly differentiate itself from general education, special education has long opted for an emphasis on the *special*. At one time, special education was essentially defined by its special methods and techniques. Although successful in creating a distinctiveness for special education, the special procedures also introduced a level of separateness that presented a complementary relationship with general education. The separateness has meant that special education has repeatedly been called on to prove itself, particularly because it is more labor-intensive and thus expensive and because general educators are often skeptical of special education programming (Balow & Brinkerhoff, 1983).

The difficulty in separating special and general education is that for a majority of special education students, programming is limited to the goals and objectives of general education. Special education students need to read, write, spell, calculate, solve problems, and perform all basic curricular activities. When dealing with populations that possess essentially intact learning processes, special education can closely parallel general education. For example, students with sensory impairments have learning abilities that are similar to students in general education if the effects of the particular handicap (i.e., hearing or visual loss) are accommodated (e.g., through sound amplification or enlarged print). Because learning processes are not altered, the enhanced stimulus input permits learning processes to operate efficiently. Special education, in these circumstances, becomes basically a process of accommodation.

The situation becomes more complicated when the special education population does not have intact learning processes. For the majority of special education students (e.g., learning disabled, mentally retarded, and behaviorally disordered), learning problems in the form of altered learning processes represent their fundamental disability. A common feature of these conditions is school failure, caused by a variety of learning handicaps. The altered learning functions may result from difficulties with, say, different types of learning (Scruggs, 1988), inactive learning (Torgesen, 1982), or cognitive-motivational problems (Licht, 1983). Regardless of the source, the result is the same: a student who does not learn in the ways expected. In these circumstances, accommodation would be inadequate. Accommodation must be carefully crafted and individually designed, but its effectiveness is readily judged by whether or not the student is then capable of learning in the same way as other students. However, when the learning process is not intact, accommodation is insufficient and a concept like remediation is required. Remediation refers to procedures that correct or reverse something that has gone wrong. Remediation places special education within the context of a medical model—treatment directed at correcting, reversing, or curing what is wrong. Such a framework suggests that learning problems require treatment, rather than simply teaching, if they are to be overcome.

The concept of remediation, with its emphasis on curing, can be in conflict with the goals and objectives of general education instruction. These differences, however, are what has historically defined special education. If a student requires remediation, special education, with its remedial methods and techniques, is best equipped to deal with students whose primary difficulties are found in a variety of learning disorders. In theory, the necessity for special to be *special* through its remedial procedures makes sense, but the effectiveness of these procedures has to be assessed. Has special education demonstrated sufficient efficacy in its unique procedures to warrant continuation?

# RESEARCH IN SPECIAL EDUCATION

Special education has a long history of research, and large quantities of data have been accumulated. In research, special education has closely adhered to the scientific method, which has its roots in logical positivism. The primary idea is that all knowledge can be accounted for by emphasizing empirical and logical components, without resort to metaphysics (Achinstein & Barker, 1969). What counts as evidence is rock-bottom sense experience (i.e., positive knowledge). The hypothetico-deductive model of logical positivism (scientific method) has carried the weight of authority, and it has been assumed that only by following a specified sequence can credible findings be obtained. Special education, like most educational research, has had the credibility of its research judged by the strength of its adherence to the scientific method. Especially for a field viewed as "soft," faithfulness to the scientific method is considered necessary if useful knowledge is to be attained (Kavale & Forness, 1994).

Although logical positivism may no longer be a predominant philosophical view (see Eisner, 1983; Phillips, 1983), its influence on the research process remains in the form of the scientific method, which is the disciplined inquiry that is distinguished from other forms of opinion and belief (Cronbach & Suppes, 1969). In adhering to the scientific method, special education research takes on a numbing sameness, and contributions are judged, not by their content, but rather by the extent they parallel the scientific method (Smart & Elton, 1981). The consequences for special education research is a rigid and narrow system based on a single, sacrosanct, officially approved set of methods. For example, Campbell and Stanley's (1966) classic treatise describes *the* way to do research in special education, and competence is defined only in terms of that research.

The primary difficulty with the scientific method is the emphasis on data collection and analysis at the expense of understanding. The scientific method creates an "empiricism," which includes large quantities of data that are not joined in any theoretical configuration and thus remain isolated and independent elements, without rational connection. The system that is created is not one that aims at building knowledge cumulatively through a logical research program but one that seeks the single "perfect" study, which will be the all-time true and unassailable fact about, for example, the effectiveness of special education (see Lindblom & Cohen, 1979). No single study approaches the desired perfectness and is subjected to any number of criticisms, based on common pitfalls in human research (see Barber, 1976), or the number of judgment calls necessary in research even when based on the hard and fast rules of the scientific method (see McGrath, Martin, & Kulka, 1982).

Besides careful collection of data, the scientific method emphasizes data analysis, but there appears to be an overreliance on statistical probabilities in deciding to accept or to reject hypothe-

ses (Carver, 1978). Statistical inference is useful for eliminating chance findings but not as helpful in deciding subject matter issues. The techniques of statistical analysis were designed for making practical decisions in applied work, which should not be confused with making reliable conclusions (Fisher, 1956). Regardless of the sophistication of the statistical analysis, probabilities neither confirm nor refute research hypotheses but only null hypotheses (e.g., Morrison & Henkel, 1970). Findings may be significant, but that significance should not be confused with importance. The difficulty, however, is that caution regarding subject matter conclusions is quickly abandoned when probabilities are less than .05. The reverse, however, is not true, and studies with probabilities greater than .05 are neither often published nor given serious consideration (Skipper, Guenther, & Nass, 1967).

The consequences are significant. For example, consider the case in which a new special education intervention is compared with an established treatment. Suppose that the new intervention demonstrates a higher mean performance level, but the obtained probability level is .07. The new intervention is probably considered a failure and does not find its way into print. Special education, however, has lost valuable information because evidence that could aid in decision making is not available. Now suppose that one study (even if flawed) finds the established treatment more effective, with a probability level of .001, and is published. Although it might be only a random finding, its publication makes it the standard and also makes it difficult to eliminate. The new intervention, in the meantime, is relegated to the background and considered "experimental" without the benefit of a fair and objective evaluation.

## RESEARCH SYNTHESIS IN SPECIAL EDUCATION

The research tradition in special education makes for a fragile process. The search for a single perfect study to provide *the* answer is a quixotic quest that has not proved fruitful. As an alternative, the findings from many studies may be combined and integrated in an effort to provide a comprehensive picture about "what the research says." Traditionally, research findings have been combined through either a narrative method, a verbal report that synthesizes individual studies, or a numerical method, a "box score" tally based on statistical significance and non-significance. The primary difficulty with these methods is their subjectivity; they lack an explicit, unambiguous, and well-defined context for securing unequivocal outcomes (Jackson, 1980).

Quantitative methods of research synthesis were developed to overcome the perceived theoretical and pragmatic difficulties associated with traditional procedures for summarizing research (Glass, 1976). Quantitative methods, which have come to be termed meta-analysis, have been described (e.g., Glass, McGaw, & Smith, 1981; Rosenthal, 1984; Wolf, 1986) and, while not unequivocally accepted (e.g., Abrami, Cohen, & d'Appolonia, 1988; Slavin, 1984), have become an accepted means of statistically summarizing a research domain. The techniques of meta-analysis have undergone a number of technical advances (e.g., Bangert-Downs, 1986; Hedges & Olkin, 1985) that have enhanced objectivity, verifiability, and replicability (Kavale, 1984).

Meta-analysis is based on a metric called effect size, which transforms study data into standard deviation units (z-scores). The effect size (ES) for studies investigating treatment efficacy is defined by

$$ES = \frac{M_T - M_C}{SD_C}$$

where $M_T$ = mean (average) score of group receiving special intervention, $M_C$ = mean (average) score of comparison (control) group, and $SD_C$ = standard deviation of comparison (control) group.

Individual ES calculations may then be combined and recombined into different aggregations, representing average treatment effects ($\overline{ES}$). The meaning of ES can be translated into notions of overlapping distributions and comparable percentiles. For example, suppose a hypothetical study investigating the efficacy of Temporal Centripetal Therapy revealed an ES of +1.00. The obtained ES of +1.00 indicates an average superiority of 1 standard deviation for the therapy group. If two separate distributions are drawn for those receiving therapy and those in the control condition, the distributions will be separated by 1 standard deviation at their means, as shown in Figure 37.1

The average of the therapy curve is located above 84% of the area under the control group curve. This relationship suggests that the student receiving therapy was better off than 84% of the

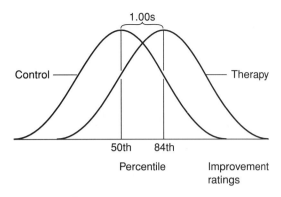

**FIGURE 37.1 Illustration of the findings from a hypothetical study on the efficacy of temporal centripetal therapy.**

control group, whereas only 16% of the control group was left better off than the average child receiving therapy.

In some instances, ESs are meaningful without comparison. For example, a zero ES or negative ES is categorically clear and meaningful. There are several other ways to interpret ES. Comparisons might be made within a single meta-analysis. Suppose two special education interventions are compared with traditional instruction: the ES for comparisons of method A and traditional instruction was .50, favoring method A, whereas method B produced an ES of .25 when compared to traditional instruction. Thus, method A was half again more beneficial than method B.

It is also possible to add meaning to ES by reference to known interventions. It is known, for example, that the average pupil will gain 10 months of achievement in a school year. Thus, the average third-grade pupil will score 3.0 in early September and 4.0 at the end of the school year. With the known standard deviation of 1.0 grade-equivalent units on most elementary achievement tests, the ES for one year's instruction at the elementary school level is +1.00. This ES can then be used as a basis for comparison. Suppose a new technique (intervention X) is introduced and the combined ES from a number of validation studies is .25. This ES is one-fourth as great as the effect of instruction itself (.25 versus 1.00). Hence, intervention X benefits the average treated subject by the equivalent of one-fourth school year of teaching.

# META-ANALYSIS AND SPECIAL EDUCATION

Kavale (1984) described the potential advantages of meta-analysis in terms of understanding and explanation. Meta-analysis, as an empirical and systematic form of applied epistemology, imparts a clarity, explicitness, and openness necessary to make research findings believable. The findings of meta-analyses investigating special education practices are presented to provide a basis for judging the effectiveness of special education.

## Process Training

Process training has a long and glorious history in special education (see Mann, 1979). In fact, process training represents one of the oldest forms of education. The philosophy and precepts of process training appear to possess a powerful appeal that has survived any number of attacks. Mann likened the appearance of processes and process training in special education to rain upon parched land; this "new scientific pedagogy was going to revitalize education, provide individual prescriptive correctives for learning problems, reclaim the cognitively impaired" (p. 538).

Although process training has great intuitive appeal, empirical evidence about its efficacy has been both positive and negative. With the empirical evidence typically providing equivocal interpretation, long-standing debate has surrounded questions about the effectiveness of process training. The findings from three meta-analyses investigating forms of process training follow in an effort to determine if firmer conclusions might be possible.

## Perceptual-Motor Training

The most popular forms of process training are programs that attempt to enhance perceptual-motor abilities. A number of clinical reports attesting to the efficacy of perceptual-motor training have appeared (e.g., Arena, 1969; Barsch, 1967; Van Witsen, 1967). Besides clinical reports, experimental studies have tested the validity of perceptual-motor interventions and have been reviewed selectively (e.g., Balow, 1971; Footlik, 1971; Hammill, Goodman, & Weiderholt, 1974). The conclusions did not favor perceptual-motor training, but some caution was urged because of faulty reporting and questionable methodological practices. In addition, philosophical attacks on perceptual-motor training continued (Mann, 1970, 1971a), although their

**TABLE 37.2  Average Effect Size for Perceptual-Motor Outcome Classes**

| Outcome Class | Mean Effect Size | No. of Effect Sizes |
|---|---|---|
| Perceptual/sensory motor | .166 | 233 |
| Academic achievement | .013 | 283 |
| Cognitive/aptitude | .028 | 95 |
| Adaptive behavior | .267 | 26 |

validity was challenged (Kephart, 1972). Thus, the efficacy of perceptual-motor training was a fertile ground for a quantitative synthesis that could bring together a disparate literature.

Kavale and Mattson (1983) found 180 experiments assessing the efficacy of perceptual-motor training. A total of 637 ES measurements were obtained and represented about 13,000 subjects, who averaged 8 years of age, had an average IQ of 89, and received an average of 65 hours of perceptual-motor training. The $\overline{ES}$ across 637 ES measurements was .082, which in relative terms indicates that a student no better off than average (i.e., at the fiftieth percentile), rises to the fifty-third percentile as a result of perceptual-motor interventions. At the end of treatment, the average trained subject was better off than 53% of control subjects, a gain only slightly better than no treatment at all (50%). Also, of 637 ESs, 48% were negative, suggesting that the probability of obtaining a positive response to training was only slightly better than chance.

The effect of perceptual-motor training appears to be negligible, but a single index may mask particular situations in which perceptual-motor training might be more effective. Consequently, ES data were aggregated into increasingly differentiated outcome groupings, and the findings are shown in Tables 37.2–37.4.

The findings speak for themselves; regardless of how global or discrete the aggregation, the effects of perceptual-motor training provide no evidence of effectiveness. There were few positive effects and no indications of an effective intervention.

Tables 37.5 and 37.6 provide aggregated ES data for diagnostic category and grade level. Interpretation is unencumbered: essentially zero

**TABLE 37.3  Average Effect Size for Perceptual-Motor General Outcome Categories**

| General Outcome Categories | Mean Effect Size | No. of Effect Sizes |
|---|---|---|
| **Perceptual/Sensory Motor** | | |
| Gross motor | .214 | 44 |
| Fine motor | .178 | 28 |
| Visual perception | .149 | 145 |
| Auditory perception | .122 | 16 |
| **Academic Achievement** | | |
| Readiness | .076 | 69 |
| Reading | −.039 | 142 |
| Arithmetic | .095 | 26 |
| Language | .031 | 18 |
| Spelling | .021 | 16 |
| Handwriting | .053 | 12 |
| **Cognitive/Aptitude** | | |
| Verbal IQ | −.007 | 53 |
| Performance IQ | .068 | 34 |

**TABLE 37.4  Average Effect Size for Perceptual-Motor Specific Outcome Categories**

| General Outcome Categories | Mean Effect Size | No. of Effect Sizes |
|---|---|---|
| **Gross Motor Skills** | | |
| Body awareness/image | .256 | 22 |
| Balance/posture | .263 | 14 |
| Locomotor skills | −.017 | 8 |
| **Visual Perceptual Skills** | | |
| Visual discrimination | .146 | 31 |
| Figure-ground discrimination | .173 | 28 |
| Visual-motor ability | .222 | 26 |
| Visual integration | .086 | 17 |
| Visual spatial perception | .144 | 16 |
| Visual memory | .062 | 15 |
| **Reading Achievement** | | |
| Word recognition | −.016 | 36 |
| Comprehension | −.055 | 33 |
| Oral reading | −.037 | 17 |
| Vocabulary | −.012 | 25 |
| Speed/rate | −.038 | 8 |

**TABLE 37.5  Average Effect Size for Subject Groups**

| Subject | Mean Effect Size | No. of Effect Sizes |
|---|---|---|
| General education | .054 | 58 |
| Mildly mentally retarded (IQ = 50–75) | .132 | 143 |
| Moderately mentally retarded (IQ = 25–50) | .147 | 66 |
| Slow learner (IQ = 75–90) | .098 | 14 |
| Disadvantaged | .045 | 85 |
| Learning disabled | .018 | 77 |
| Reading disabled | −.007 | 74 |
| Motor disabled | .121 | 118 |

**TABLE 37.6  Average Effect Size for Grade Level**

| Level | Mean Effect Size | No. of Effect Sizes |
|---|---|---|
| Preschool | .053 | 47 |
| Kindergarten | .099 | 129 |
| Primary elementary (grades 1–3) | .079 | 226 |
| Middle elementary (grades 4–6) | .066 | 74 |
| Junior high school | .085 | 67 |
| High school | .088 | 67 |

effects are seen for all groups and at all grade levels. These data suggest that there are no selected benefits for perceptual-motor training. In no instance was perceptual-motor intervention effective; in fact, among the lowest ESs were those found for students with learning and reading disabilities, for whom perceptual-motor training is a favored treatment.

Perceptual-motor training programs have taken a variety of forms, and the associated names read like the roster from a Special Education Hall of Fame. The $\overline{ES}$s for the various training methods are shown in Table 37.7. The findings are not encouraging: there is no indication of positive effects. Studies investigating the efficacy of individual programs include research performed by both program advocates and independent investigators, and an example will reveal the fragility of such findings. The Delacato program (e.g., Delacato, 1959), based on the concept of neurological patterning, was assessed by both Delacato disciplines (see Delacato, 1966) and more critical investigators (e.g., Cohen, Birch, & Taft, 1970; Glass & Robbins, 1967). The Delacato sources produced an $\overline{ES}$ of .723, whereas the non-Delacato sources revealed an $\overline{ES}$ of −.242. A nonselective and uncritical reading of the literature could thus result in very different interpretations.

The findings from this meta-analysis would support the position statement offered by the Council for Learning Disabilities (1986): "There is little or no empirical support for claims that the training of perceptual and perceptual-motor functions improves either academic performance or perceptual or perceptual-motor functions . . . schools must view the time, money, and other resources devoted to such activities as wasteful, as an obstruction to provision of appropriate services,

and as unwarranted for any purposes other than those of pure research" (p. 247). Yet, there have been suggestions that the available evidence does not permit either a positive or a negative evaluation of perceptual-motor training (e.g., Hallahan & Cruickshank, 1973). The quantitative synthesis presented here found no significant benefits and appears to provide the negative evaluation necessary for questioning the value of perceptual-motor training. The empirical evidence seems unequivocal but must face the challenge presented by the deep historical roots and strong clinical tradition associated with perceptual-motor training.

## Psycholinguistic Training

Psycholinguistic training is another type of process training and at one time was among the most popular special education interventions. Training was based on test results from the Illinois Test of Psycholinguistic Abilities (ITPA), which assessed receptive, integrative, and expressive abilities by presenting stimuli in auditory-vocal and visual-motor channels (Kirk, McCarthy, & Kirk, 1968). Test findings would reveal intraindividual deficits that would then be subjected to treatment through a variety of remedial and developmental programs.

Psycholinguistic training is based on the assumption that discrete psychological and linguistic abilities can be identified and trained. The assumption about training touched off a longstanding and heated debate that represented very different philosophical perspectives about the nature of special education interventions. A number of research studies were undertaken and were reviewed periodically, but interpretation showed significant differences, and decisions about the effectiveness of psycholinguistic training became increasingly difficult.

Hammill and Larsen (1974) offered a review, in which they constructed a table with either a + or 0 for total ITPA score, ITPA subtests, or both, that paralleled the findings from 39 studies on statistical significance or nonsignificance. This vote-counting methodology led Hammill and Larsen to conclude that "researchers have been unsuccessful in developing those skills which would enable their subjects to do well in ITPA . . . [and] . . . the idea that psycholinguistic constructs, as measures by ITPA, can be trained by existing techniques remains nonvalidated" (pp. 10–11).

Minskoff (1975) offered a critique of Hammill and Larsen's (1974) review: "Because of Hammill and Larsen's oversimplified approach,

**TABLE 37.7** **Average Effect Size for Perceptual-Motor Training Programs**

| Training Program | Mean Effect Size | No. of Effect Sizes |
|---|---|---|
| Barsch | .157 | 18 |
| Cratty | .113 | 27 |
| Delacato | .161 | 79 |
| Frostig | .096 | 173 |
| Getman | .124 | 48 |
| Kephart | .064 | 132 |

39 studies with noncomparable subjects and treatments were grouped together. Moreover, for the most part, they reviewed methodologically inadequate studies in which there was short term training using general approaches to treatment primarily with mentally retarded or disadvantaged subjects having no diagnosed learning disabilities" (p. 137). In effect, Minskoff suggested that Hammill and Larsen had compared apples and oranges, and 10 specific methodological errors were described. Minskoff then provided guidelines for research on psycholinguistic training, suggesting that psycholinguistic disabilities can be trained, with a conclusion decrying the skepticism surrounding psycholinguistic training because "it can be dangerous if it leads to the abolition of training methods that may be beneficial to some children with psycholinguistic disabilities" (p. 143).

Immediately following was a response by Newcomer, Larsen, and Hammill (1975), which contested the major points made by Minskoff (1975). It is enough to say that the rhetoric became increasingly confusing and enmeshed in trivial controversy. Nevertheless, Newcomer et al. contended that "the reported literature raises doubts regarding the efficacy of presently available Kirk-Osgood psycholinguistic training programs" (p. 147).

The debate lay dormant for some three years, until Lund, Foster, and McCall-Perez (1978) offered a reevaluation of the 39 studies synthesized by Hammill and Larsen (1974). The studies were reexamined individually to determine the validity of negative conclusions about the effectiveness of psycholinguistic training. Six of the 24 studies clearly showed positive results for psycholinguistic training and "contraindicate the conclusions that such training is nonvalidated" (p. 317). Of 10 studies showing negative results, only 2 were reported accurately; the remaining 8 where either equivocal or showed positive results. Lund et al. reached conclusions markedly at variance with the statement that psycholinguistic training is nonvalidated: "Our analysis indicates that some studies show significant positive results as measured by ITPA, some studies show positive results in the areas remediated, and some do not show results from which any conclusions can be drawn. It is, therefore, not logical to conclude either that all studies in psycholinguistic training are effective or that all studies in psycholinguistic training are not effective" (p. 317).

The special education community did not wait long for the debate to continue. Hammill and Larsen (1978) reaffirmed their original position with the statement that "the cumulative results of the pertinent research have failed to demonstrate that psycholinguistic training has value, at least with the ITPA as the criterion for successful training. It is important to note that, regardless of the reevaluations by propsycholinguistic educators, the current state of the research strongly questions the efficacy of psycholinguistic functioning and needs to be viewed cautiously and monitored with great care" (p. 413).

After some five years of debate, polemics abounded, but a nagging question remained: what is really known about the efficacy of psycholinguistic training? In an effort to bring closure, Kavale (1981) performed a meta-analysis on 34 studies investigating the effectiveness of psycholinguistic training. The 34 studies yielded 240 ESs that produced an overall $\overline{ES}$ of .39. This finding was based on data representing approximately 1,850 subjects who averaged 7.5 years of age with a mean IQ of 82 and who received an average of 50 hours of psycholinguistic training. Thus, the average subject receiving psycholinguistic training stands at approximately the sixty-fifth percentile of subjects receiving no special psycholinguistic training; the latter remain at the fiftieth percentile. Table 37.8 presents ESs classified by ITPA subtest.

**TABLE 37.8  Average Effect Size for ITPA Subtests**

| ITPA Subtest | Mean Effect Size | No. of Effect Sizes |
|---|---|---|
| Auditory reception | .21 | 20 |
| Visual reception | .21 | 20 |
| Auditory association | .44 | 24 |
| Visual association | .39 | 21 |
| Verbal expression | .63 | 24 |
| Manual expression | .54 | 23 |
| Grammatic closure | .30 | 21 |
| Visual closure | .48 | 5 |
| Auditory sequential memory | .32 | 21 |
| Visual sequential memory | .27 | 21 |
| Auditory closure | −.05 | 3 |
| Sound blending | .38 | 3 |

If subtests in which the data are limited (i.e., 5 or fewer ESs) are eliminated, then five of nine subtests show small, but positive, effects. It is questionable, however, whether these psycholinguistic abilities respond to training and whether they should be subjected to training. The case is different for four abilities: auditory and visual association and verbal and manual expression. For these psycholinguistic abilities, training improves functioning from 15 to 23 percentile ranks. Thus, the average trained subject would be better off than approximately 65% to 73% of untrained subjects in associative or expressive abilities.

Subtests of the ITPA were patterned on psycholinguistic constructs derived from Osgood's (1957) model of communication. Table 37.9 presents an analysis of the effects of training on theoretical psycholinguistic dimensions underlying the ITPA. Expressive Processes showed the greatest response to psycholinguistic training, whereas small effects were noted for Receptive Processes and Automatic Level subtests. The analysis offered by Hammill and Larsen (1974) suggest that both Representational Level and the Visual-Motor Modality were not particularly responsive to training, but the obtained $\overline{ES}$s of .40 and .38, respectively, for these abilities belie such an interpretation. Consequently, the 15 and 14 percentile rank improvement shown by trained subjects on Representational Level and Visual-Motor Modalities subtests cannot be easily dismissed.

The ES data were next integrated by approach and method for psycholinguistic training,

and the findings are shown in Table 37.10. Not surprisingly, prescriptive and individualized approaches were found superior to generalized and nonindividualized methods. As with many other educational approaches, individualized instruction proved to be superior. The next finding was surprising: the Peabody Language Development Kits (PLDK); (Dunn & Smith, 1967) demonstrated the largest $\overline{ES}$ when compared to both ITPA related activities and other methods (sensory, perceptual, or motor training activities).

On the surface, the superiority of the PLDK appears contrary to expectation since ITPA-type activities should be most closely related to the criterion measure, the ITPA itself. Upon reflection, these findings are not surprising if viewed in terms of program structure. The PLDK represents a highly structured sequence of lessons designed to increase general verbal ability. Although ITPA training procedures are based on the Osgood-Kirk model (Bush & Giles, 1977; Kirk & Kirk, 1971), they are only suggestions and guidelines for training activities. As such, they do not provide the sequential, structured activities found in the PLDK. Consequently, they do not represent a comprehensive training package but merely examples for psycholinguistic training activities that must be structured and planned by individual teachers (Kavale, 1982b).

The present findings appear to provide a cautious but affirmative answer to the question of the effectiveness of psycholinguistic training. In particular instances, it demonstrated positive outcomes and cast doubt on previous conclusions such as "the overwhelming consensus of research

**TABLE 37.9    Average Effect Size for ITPA Psycholinguistic Constructs**

| Dimension | Construct | No. of Effect Size |
|---|---|---|
| Level | Representational | .40 |
|  | Automatic | .21 |
| Process | Reception | .21 |
|  | Organization | .32 |
|  | Expression | .59 |
| Modalities | Auditory-Verbal | .32 |
|  | Visual-Motor | .38 |

**TABLE 37.10    Average Effect Size for Study Features**

| Feature | Mean Effect Size | No. of Effect Sizes |
|---|---|---|
| **Approach** | | |
| General/nonindividualized | .37 | 38 |
| Prescriptive/individualized | .49 | 6 |
| **Method** | | |
| ITPA | .30 | 12 |
| PDLK | .49 | 14 |
| Other | .35 | 9 |

evidence concerning the effectiveness of psycholinguistic training is that it remains essentially nonvalidated" (Hammill & Larsen, 1978, p. 412). Hammill and Larsen (1974) probably overstated their case when they concluded that "neither the ITPA subtests nor their theoretical constructs are particularly ameliorative" (p. 12). Clearly, the findings regarding the receptiveness to intervention of the expressive constructs, particularly Verbal Expression, and the Representational Level subtests are encouraging since they embody the "linguistic" aspects of the ITPA and, ultimately, productive language behavior.

These findings, however, only fueled the debate over the efficacy of psycholinguistic training. Larsen, Parker, and Hammill (1982), for example, suggested that Kavale (1981) had reviewed a body of literature that was more favorable to psycholinguistic training and was thus different from that used by Hammill and Larsen (1974). The difference, however, was only four studies that would have added 28 ES measurements to the 240 obtained and would have led to a decline in $\overline{ES}$ of .04, on average, across subtests. Overall, the $\overline{ES}$ would decline from .39 to .35, which means that instead of 65% of the students receiving psycholinguistic being better off than a control group, 64% would now be better off. This is an inconsequential decline and does not qualify as an inflated estimate.

For a basic area like language, the average elementary school student gains about 1 standard deviation (ES = +1.00) over the school year and exceeds about 84% of the students' scores on a language achievement measure at the beginning of the school year. The approximately 60% success rate for training in verbal expression is thus substantial. In fact, roughly 50 hours of psycholinguistic training produce benefits on the Verbal Expression subtest ($\overline{ES}$ = .63), exceeding that which would be expected from one-half year of schooling in language ($\overline{ES}$ = .50).

Larsen et al. (1982), as well as Sternberg and Taylor (1982), questioned the findings on a cost-benefit basis since the gains represented only about 15 to 20 items across ITPA subtests. A distinction was made between statistical significance and practical significance, with Sternberg and Taylor pursuing this question: "Does the increase of only two or three items per subtest within this instrument really make a *clinically significant* difference?" (p. 255).

The answer is affirmative, and the example of Verbal Expression demonstrates why. In concrete terms, the obtained ES for Verbal Expression (.63) translates into improvement by perhaps an additional half-dozen correct responses on the ITPA. If these six items are considered proxies for hundreds of language skills and abilities, improvement on these seemingly few items is significant. Consider an analogous situation: a student with an IQ (intelligence quotient) of 130 answers perhaps nine more Information questions or nine more Vocabulary items on the Wechsler Intelligence Scale for Children-Revised (WISC-R) than a student with an IQ of 100. Does this suggest that the difference between an IQ of 100 and one of 130 is nine bits of knowledge? Certainly the abilities involved transcend nine pieces of information or words. Likewise, improvement on the Verbal Expression subtest represents more than the expected increase of six items since it comprises a complex amalgam of language abilities. Thus, for a student deficient in the areas enhanced by psycholinguistic training, remedial programs are likely to provide salutary effects and advantages for the student that probably surpass the abilities themselves.

## Modality Training

The practice of assessing abilities and devising subsequent instruction in accord with assessed modality patterns has a long history and intuitive appeal (e.g., R. S. Dunn, 1979). Arter and Jenkins (1977), for example, found that 99% of teachers surveyed thought that a student's modality strengths and weaknesses should be considered and that a student learned more when instruction was modified to match modality patterns. Whether it is termed the modality model, aptitude × treatment interaction, differential programming, or diagnostic-prescriptive teaching, the benefits are widely believed (e.g., Dunn & Dunn, 1978), even though the weight of the evidence is negative (e.g., Cronbach & Snow, 1977), Yet, the deep historical roots and strong clinical support have prevented the modality model from being dislodged from the repertoire of special education practices (Carbo, 1983).

Kavale and Forness (1987) synthesized data from 39 studies evaluating the modality model. The 39 studies yielded 318 ES measurements and represented about 3,100 subjects whose average age was 8.66 years and average IQ was 98. Because the modality model includes two components, testing and teaching, no substantive insight is provided by a single index.

On the assessment side, the ES measurements indicate the level of differentiation between subjects chosen because of assessed modal preferences and those demonstrating no such preferences. A total of 113 ES measurements were concerned with assessment and are shown in Table 37.11. The first ES column represents the magnitude of group differentiation as originally calculated. The tests used to assess modality preferences have been shown to possess poor reliabilities (Ysseldyke & Salvia, 1980), and this suggests that these ES measurements need to be corrected for the influence of measurement error to provide a "true" level of group differentiation (see Hunter, Schmidt, & Jackson, 1982).

Across the 113 ES measurements, for example, the $\overline{ES}$, after correction, declined from .931 to .512; on average, 70% of subjects demonstrating a modality preference could be differentiated clearly on the basis of their test scores, whereas 30% could not be distinguished unequivocally. With the original $\overline{ES}$ (.931), the 1 standard deviation (SD) difference typically used as a criterion to establish modality groups was approached; but when corrected for measurement error, only 7 out of 10 subjects actually demonstrated a modality preference score different enough to warrant placement in a particular modality preference group, and 3 out of 10 would be misplaced in a modality preference group.

Although modality assessments were presumed to differentiate subjects with respect to modality preferences, there was, in actuality, considerable overlap between preference and nonpreference groups. Much of the difficulty was the result of test unreliability, and when ES was corrected for test unreliability, it was found that measurement error reduced the distinction among modality groups to a level no better than, on average, two out of three correct placement decisions.

Besides assessing modality preferences, the 39 studies also evaluated the effect of matching instruction to preferred modalities. Of the 318 ES measurements, 205 assessed the effectiveness of modality teaching (see Table 37.12). The 205 ES measurements produced an $\overline{ES}$ of .144, which translates into only a 6 percentile rank improvement. This indicates that 56% of the experimental subjects were better off after modality instruction, but this is only slightly above chance (50%) and indicates conversely that 44% of the experimental subjects did not reveal any gain. Furthermore, 72 ES measurements (35%) were negative, indicating that over one-third of the subjects who were receiving instruction that matched with their preferred learning modality actually scored less well than comparison subjects who were receiving no special modality-based instruction.

In the achievement domain, the effects of modality-matched instruction were evaluated in reading. Reading achievement data are displayed in Table 37.13. Across modalities, modality teaching produced gains from 2 (comprehension) to 7 (vocabulary and spelling) percentile ranks; these levels of improvement are modest. Only 57% of the experimental subjects would show benefits, and 43% would not exhibit benefits from modality-based instruction; modality instruction appears to have only modest effects on improving reading abilities. When instructional methods were matched to modality preferences, the positive effects were small. Across reading skills, 50% (6 out of 12) of the comparisons revealed modality teaching effects that were not different from zero (as shown by a 95% confidence interval).

In providing answers to the question "Why teach through modality strengths?" Barbe and Milone (1981) suggested that research supports the contention that modality-based instruction works. Although the presumption that matching

TABLE 37.11    The Effects of Modality Assessments

| Modality | Number of Effect Sizes | Mean Effect Size (Uncorrected) | Mean Effect Size (Corrected) | Percent of Subjects Differentiated from Comparison Group |
|---|---|---|---|---|
| Auditory | 47 | .925 | .552 | 71 |
| Visual | 46 | .899 | .506 | 70 |
| Kinesthetic | 20 | .970 | .430 | 67 |

**TABLE 37.12   The Effects of Modality-Matched Instruction**

| Modality | Number of Effect Sizes | Mean Effect Size | Percentile Status of Experimental Subject in Control Group |
|---|---|---|---|
| Auditory | 80 | .184 | 57 |
| Visual | 81 | .086 | 54 |
| Kinesthetic | 44 | .175 | 57 |

instructional strategies to individual modality preferences will enhance learning efficiency has great intuitive appeal, little empirical support for this proposition was found. It was shown that groups seemingly differentiated on the basis of modality preferences actually revealed considerable overlap, and it was doubtful whether any of the presumed preferences could really be deemed to be so. Also, little (or no) gain in achievement was found when instructional methods were matched to preferred learning modality.

The present negative findings contravene the conventional wisdom found in statements such as these: "All children do not learn the same way. They rely on different sensory modes to help them. Some depend heavily on their sense of sight, others on their sense of hearing, and still others on their sense of touch. The mode they use influences their classroom behavior and achievement" (Barbe & Milone, 1980, p. 45).

The negative evaluation of the modality model by Kavale and Forness (1987) did not go unchallenged. R. S. Dunn (1990) suggested that the conclusions were biased and were based on inappropriate choices. The bias was related to the presumption that the studies chosen suffered

from serious design flaws. Also, the fact that most studies used standardized tests to measure outcomes was considered a liability rather than an asset. It was suggested that Kavale and Forness did not take into account the presumed modality differences between younger and older students; the multiplicity among preferences, which suggested that modalities cannot be studied in isolation; the proper definition and interpretation of the terms *auditory, visual,* and *kinesthetic* with regard to modality; and instrumentation problems that prevented a valid measurement of the constructs.

R. S. Dunn (1990) then challenged the interpretation of ES by suggesting that because the samples studied were students with disabilities, any positive findings should be considered laudatory. In addition, because of the difficulties in attaining achievement gains on standardized tests, even the modest gains demonstrated were excellent and might even be unusual in general education. To remedy the situation, Dunn presented findings from 10 studies that presumably overcame the difficulties cited and revealed significantly higher achievement for students taught through modality preferences.

**TABLE 37.13   The Effects of Modality-Matched Instruction on Reading Skills**

| | Total | | | Auditory | | | Visual | | | Kinesthetic | | |
|---|---|---|---|---|---|---|---|---|---|---|---|---|
| | N | ES | % | N | ES | % | N | ES | % | N | ES | % |
| Word recognition | 75 | .150 | 56 | 28 | .203 | 58 | 33 | .081 | 53 | 14 | .197 | 58 |
| Comprehension | 38 | .046 | 52 | 15 | .062 | 52 | 16 | .034 | 51 | 7 | .041 | 52 |
| Vocabulary | 45 | .174 | 57 | 18 | .194 | 58 | 17 | .141 | 56 | 10 | .185 | 58 |
| Spelling | 47 | .184 | 57 | 19 | .249 | 60 | 15 | .088 | 54 | 13 | .216 | 59 |

*N* = number of effect sizes;  ES = mean effect size;  % = percentile status of experimental (modality-matched) subject in comparison group.

Kavale and Forness (1990) responded to R. S. Dunn's (1990) critique, but the specifics are not important. Of greater importance were the difficulties involved in judging the effectiveness of special education. By its very nature, meta-analysis produces summary statements that are more precise, more dispassionate, and more detached than other review techniques; yet the findings were challenged. The reason for the disagreement surrounds advocacy and the less than disinterested view held by Dunn, who has a vested interest in modality-based instruction. Given the involvement in assessment devices (Dunn, Dunn, & Price, 1979), intervention techniques (Dunn & Dunn, 1978), and a Center for the Study of Learning and Teaching Styles, Dunn has a substantial stake in modality-based instruction.

Although it is appropriate to defend one's interest, it is not appropriate to do so through misinterpretation and misunderstanding. R. S. Dunn provided a Byzantine mixture of interpretation that did little to undermine confidence in the primary conclusion: modality-based instruction is ineffective. However, when such conclusions encounter positive intuitive appeal and strong advocacy, it is difficult to dislodge the method through evidence and reason. The unbridled advocacy pursued by Dunn appears to be an injustice that should be abandoned because learning is really a matter of substance over style.

## Conclusions About Process Training

The question of process training is vexing for special education. For psycholinguistic training, there are selected benefits, especially in basic language skill. Selected benefits mean that psycholinguistic training is not an all-or-none proposition, and caution must be exercised lest the baby gets thrown out with the bath water. The case for perceptual-motor training and modality training appears to be quite different. Here there are no selected benefits, and they can be rightly judged in an all-or-none manner, with the judgment unequivocally clear. Yet, they reveal a stubborn resistance because of the seductive statements found in clinical reports. When conjoined with their intuitive appeal and historical foundation, they remain established practices in the special education repertoire.

The attacks on process training (Mann, 1971b; Mann & Phillips, 1967) have been vigorous but apparently not convincing to a segment of special education practitioners. Why? Because

processes are presumed to possess a reality that then assumes they must be considered in remediation. For a process like language, which is reasonably well understood and readily observed, this assumption is probably true and accounts for the selected benefits of psycholinguistic training. These assumptions, however, were not supported for perceptual-motor training and modality training, where perception, learning style, and the like are not well understood and certainly not obvious. The empirical evaluations of these methods were decidedly negative but yet were not enough to dislodge fundamental belief. This belief sets in motion an attitude of questioning about research findings typically centered around the notion "What if . . . ?" The tension between belief and reality provides a continuing sense of justification for process training. When historical considerations are also included, process training becomes an entrenched element in special education. Debate about its efficacy becomes centered on philosophical issues that are not so easily resolved. Regardless of the weight of research evidence against it, process training, with its established clinical, historical, and philosophical base, has proven remarkably resistant, as suggested by Mann (1979): "Process training has always made the phoenix look like a bedraggled sparrow. You cannot kill it. It simply bides its time in exile after being dislodged by one of history's periodic attacks upon it and then returns, wearing disguises or carrying new *noms de plume*, as it were, but consisting of the same old ideas, doing business much in the same old way" (p. 539).

## MEDICALLY BASED INTERVENTIONS

With roots in medicine, special education has long based its intervention techniques on medical practice. The field of medicine has also shown an interest in schools, and the interaction between medicine and special education has made some special education medically based.

### Stimulant Drugs and Hyperactivity

The practice of treating hyperactivity—presently the preferred terminology is attention deficit hyperactivity disorder (ADHD), but the review was completed when hyperactivity was the more common designation—with stimulant drugs is among the most controversial and emotionally loaded issues in special education. The medical community considers stimulant drugs to be an efficacious treatment for hyperactivity (e.g., American Academy of Pediatrics Committee on Drugs, 1970; American Academy of Pediatrics Council on Health Care, 1975), but this conclusion has been challenged: first, in the form of critical reviews that suggest that no positive interpretation could be drawn from extant literature because of numerous methodological flaws (e.g., Sprague & Werry, 1971; Sroufe, 1975) and, second, in the form of ideological, ethical, and moral attacks on stimulant drug treatment (e.g., Schrag & Divoky, 1975).

Kavale (1982a) found 135 studies that assessed the effectiveness of stimulant drug treatment for hyperactivity. They represented approximately 5,300 subjects, averaging 8.75 years of age, with an average IQ of 102; the subjects received medication for an average of 10 weeks. The $\overline{ES}$ across 984 ES measurements was .578, which indicates that the average drug-treated student moves from the fiftieth to the seventy-second percentile as a result of drug intervention. This 22-percentile rank gain suggests that an average drug-treated student would be expected to be better off than 72% of untreated control students.

The diverse assortment of outcomes measured in drug research makes it difficult to interpret a single index of drug efficacy. Three major outcome classes were identified: behavioral, cognitive, and physiological (see the findings in Table 37.14). This more refined analysis revealed substantial positive effects for behavioral and cognitive outcomes. The negative effect for physiological outcomes indicated that drug intervention produced some negative consequences. (The physiological findings, however, are generally difficulty to interpret and are outside the province of this chapter.)

Note (with the exception of anxiety) the impressive gains on behavioral outcomes. Substantial benefits were found on ratings of behavioral functioning, lowered activity levels, and improved attending skills. Although not of the same magnitude as behavioral improvements, cognitive functioning also exhibited consequential improvement. For cognitive tasks, the present findings were generally in accord with findings from laboratory studies (for reviews, see Cantwell & Carlson, 1978; Gittelman & Kanner, 1986) concerning the salutary effects of stimulants on tasks that tap various aspects of attention and memory. Unlike past reviews (e.g., Aman, 1980; Barkley &

**TABLE 37.14  Average Effect Sizes for Stimulant Medication Research Outcome Classes**

|  | Mean Effect Size | No. of Effect Sizes |
|---|---|---|
| **Behavioral** | | |
| Global improvement ratings | .886 | 192 |
| Rating scales and checklist | .837 | 113 |
| Activity level | .846 | 127 |
| Attention and concentration | .782 | 119 |
| Behavior (social and classroom) | .634 | 92 |
| Anxiety | .118 | 12 |
| **Cognitive** | | |
| Intelligence | .391 | 54 |
| Achievement | .383 | 47 |
| Drawing and copying | .467 | 38 |
| Perceptual, memory and motor | .412 | 91 |
| Learning characteristics | .367 | 41 |
| **Physiological** | | |
| Biochemical | .558 | 7 |
| Psychophysiological | −.275 | 51 |

Cunningham, 1978), the meta-analytic findings also showed stimulant medication to have a positive effect on academic performance. Students on stimulants could, in fact, be expected to gain the equivalent of a 15-percentile rank increase in achievement when compared to nontreated students. To put these gains in perspective, meta-analyses of interventions deemed to be just as controversial as psychopharmacological treatment (e.g., perceptual-motor training and modality instruction) have resulted in gains of only 5 or 6 percentile ranks (Forness & Kavale, 1988).

There appears to be, however, a resistance to acknowledging the positive effects of medication on academic achievement (e.g., Gadow, 1983; O'Leary, 1980). The improved academic performance is usually attributed to improved attention and reduced impulsivity. When the effects of attention were held constant in the meta-analysis (through partial correlation), the positive effect for achievement was reduced by only 20%, suggesting that factors other than attention alone were operating to enhance academic performance.

Pelham (1986) has also questioned the validity of negative findings in these studies. It was suggested that the studies suffered from methodological difficulties, such as (1) insensitivity to the typically short (4–12 weeks) duration of medication studies, (2) lack of attention to dose factors, (3) lack of compliance in administering medication, (4) lack of attention to the time course of stimulant effects, and (5) lack of attention to individual differences. Pelham suggested that the presumed positive effects of behavioral interventions have resulted in an antimedication bias, and different evidential standards were being applied to medication studies. These caveats suggest that previous negative findings should not necessarily be interpreted as evidence that stimulants have no beneficial effect on academic achievement. For example, the $\overline{ES}$s for achievement measures are shown in Table 37.15. With the exception of arithmetic, the gains in academic achievement represent a level of improvement equal to approximately a half-year's worth of schooling (ES = .50); the effects of drug treatment exhibit a similar gain in achievement in only 10 weeks.

Drug research has been criticized on methodological grounds, but no significant differences were found among ESs for the low, medium, and high ratings of internal validity (see Campbell & Stanley, 1966). Design problems thus appeared to play a subordinate role; design considerations accounted for only 1% of the variance in the findings for the behavioral and cognitive classes. Among the more important design procedures is placebo control. The control group is given an inert substance (sugar pill), and if improvement is shown, the gain is attributed to the placebo effect and casts doubt on the observed drug effects. The difference between placebo-controlled studies ($\overline{ES}$ = .562) and studies without placebo control ($\overline{ES}$ = .628) was not significant. The ES difference (.066) can be considered an approximate index of the placebo effect that is well below the standard value (around 35%) and indicates that the placebo effect accounted for only 7% of the improvement shown by drug-treated subjects.

Stimulant drug treatment appears to be an effective intervention for the treatment of hyperactivity. Compare this conclusion with this statement from a narrative review of the drug literature: "Our analysis of the literature in this area indicates that research findings do not indicate the general efficacy and therefore do not support the widespread use of stimulant drugs" (Adelman & Compas, 1977, p. 406). The present findings demonstrate that drug effects produced substantive positive outcomes in which the average drug-treated subject would be better off than 72% of the control subjects. No empirical analysis, however, can hope to elucidate the complex ideological and moral issues associated with drug intervention. The beneficial effects of stimulant drug treatment have been demonstrated, and it is now necessary to debate the ethical issues.

## Diet Treatment and Hyperactivity

In 1975, Dr. Benjamin Feingold suggested that the ingestion of artificial (synthetic) food additives (colors and flavors) contributes to hyperactivity (Feingold, 1976). The recommended treatment was based on the Feingold Kaiser-Permanente (K-P) diet, designed to eliminate all foods containing artificial additives (Feingold & Feingold, 1979).

Feingold (1979) reported that between 40% to 70% of hyperactive subjects demonstrated a marked reduction in hyperactive behavior. The available evidence, based on uncontrolled clinical trials and anecdotal accounts, was challenged, but the diet nevertheless received widespread media attention and a favorable and enthusiastic response from the general public. The question

**TABLE 37.15 Average Effect Sizes for Stimulant Medication Research Achievement Measures**

| Measures | Mean Effect Size | No. of Effect Sizes |
|---|---|---|
| **Wide Range Achievement Test** | | |
| Reading | .322 | 11 |
| Arithmetic | .094 | 10 |
| Spelling | .365 | 7 |
| Iowa Test of Basic Skills | .628 | 6 |
| Gray Oral Reading | .424 | 3 |
| Language | .500 | 6 |
| Handwriting | .437 | 4 |

thus remained: is there any justification for the major dietary changes required by the Feingold K-P diet in terms of reduced hyperactivity?

Kavale and Forness (1983) examined 23 experimental studies assessing the efficacy of the Feingold K-P diet in treating hyperactivity. The 23 studies produced 125 ES measurements and yielded an $\overline{ES}$ of .118 but a median ES of .045, suggesting a skewed distribution in which the $\overline{ES}$ probably overestimated the treatment effect. The average subject was 8.3 years of age, had an IQ of 99, and remained on the Feingold K-P diet for 39 weeks.

In relative terms, the $\overline{ES}$ of .118 indicates that a subject no better off than average (i.e., at the fiftieth percentile), would rise to the fifty-fifth percentile as a result of the diet. When compared to the 22-percentile rank gain for stimulant drug treatment, the 5-percentile rank improvement for diet intervention is less than one-fourth as large. Although the average ages and IQ were similar for drug-treated and diet-treated subjects, the average duration of treatment differed: 39 weeks in a diet study and 10 weeks in a drug study. In relation to the $\overline{ES}$ (.118 vs. 587), these comparisons suggest that when compared to the Feingold K-P diet treatment, stimulant drug treatment is approximately five times as effective in about one-fourth the time. Thus, the diet is cast in an unfavorable light since it produces a substantially lower treatment effect than stimulant drug treatment and approximates the negligible effects of, for example, perceptual-motor training ($\overline{ES}$ = .082).

The ES data were next aggregated into descriptive outcome categories, and the findings are shown in Table 37.16. The effects of the Feingold K-P diet ranged from a loss of 2 percentile ranks (learning ability) to a gain of 11 percentile ranks (Conners Scale–Teachers, and hyperkinesis ratings). Thus, the only obvious effect of diet treatment is on overt behavior, specifically a perceived reduction in hyperactivity. This conclusion, however, must be tempered; global ratings of improvement have two major problems: objectivity in defining improvement and psychometric deficiencies (reliability and validity). These problems influence the reactivity, or subjectivity, of outcome measures; that is, the measures are under the control of observers who have an acknowledged interest in achieving predetermined outcomes (e.g., improvement). Non-reactive measures, in contrast, are not easily influenced in any direction by observers. The

**TABLE 37.16 Average Effect Sizes for Feingold Diet Research Outcome Categories**

| Category | Mean Effect Size | No. of Effect Sizes |
|---|---|---|
| Conners Scale–Parents | .156 | 26 |
| Conners Scale–Teachers | .268 | 9 |
| Global improvement | .128 | 23 |
| Hyperkinesis rating | .293 | 15 |
| Attention | .015 | 36 |
| Disruptive behavior | .052 | 6 |
| Impulsivity | .153 | 5 |
| Learning ability | −.055 | 10 |

correlation of ES and ratings of reactivity ($r = .181$) was significant ($p < .05$), suggesting that larger treatment effects were associated with more reactive measures. Also, aggregations of reactive versus nonreactive measures found an $\overline{ES}$ of .179 and .001, respectively, suggesting that in those instances in which instruments paralleled the valued outcomes of observers, there was a tendency to view more improvement, as revealed in larger treatment effects.

The initial evaluations of diet treatment by Feingold and associates were based on clinical trials and observations. The findings from such quasi-experimental designs are at variance with results from "better" studies, that is, those studies with more rigorous experimental control. Of the 23 studies, 6 were uncontrolled clinical trials, and they yielded an $\overline{ES}$ of .337, compared to the $\overline{ES}$ of .089 for the 17 controlled studies. There was, however, a significant relationship ($r = -.193$) between the ES and ratings of design quality, which indicates that larger ESs were associated with studies rated low on internal validity.

The controlled studies used two primary experimental designs. The first is a diet crossover study that places groups of hyperactive subjects on two experimental diets; one follows the Feingold K-P diet strictly, whereas the other is disguised as the diet but actually contains the substances supposedly eliminated. The second design is a challenge study that selects subjects who appear to respond to the diet and then are divided into experimental and control conditions. Both groups are placed on a strict Feingold

K-P diet, and at the end of the trial the experimental group is given a challenge food (usually a cookie or drink) that contains large doses of the eliminated substances.

Of the 17 controlled studies, 7 used a diet crossover design and 10 were challenge studies. The diet crossover studies exhibited an $\overline{ES}$ of .196, whereas the challenge studies revealed an $\overline{ES}$ of .045. Challenge studies offer a design that permits the attribution of behavioral change to the substances eliminated in the Feingold K-P diet; they can be considered the "best" studies and provide the best evidence for evaluating the efficacy of the diet. The weight of this evidence, however, is decidedly negative ($\overline{ES}$ = .045); at the end of diet treatment, the average treatment subject was better off than 52% of the control subjects, a gain only slightly better than no treatment at all.

These findings offer little support for the Feingold hypothesis. The modest and limited gains suggest a more temperate view of the efficacy of the diet than that asserted by its proponents. Nevertheless, Rimland (1983) questioned the research base on the basis of a "garbage in, garbage out" analysis. It was suggested that (a) most of the studies were essentially irrelevant, (b) dosage levels were too small, (c) there was a failure to recognize different nutritional status among selected subjects, (d) there was a failure to recognize and control relevant variables (e.g., copper ingestion and fluorescent lighting), (e) there were arbitrary negative conclusions because of bias against the Feingold diet, and (f) there was inadequate attention to animal and in vitro studies. The slight improvement shown by some subjects should not interfere with the critical examinations of the Feingold K-P diet since it may postpone more appropriate medical, psychological, or educational intervention (Mattes, 1983; Wender, 1977).

Although the Feingold K-P diet offers an appealing treatment approach for hyperactivity by offering a natural alternative to stimulant medication, it is not without pragmatic difficulties. The implementation of the diet requires an abrupt lifestyle change since increased vigilance is necessary in grocery shopping and food preparation, families generally cannot eat at restaurants, and the student cannot eat school lunches (Sheridan & Meister, 1982). Lew (1977) conducted a four-week trial of the Feingold K-P diet and concluded that "the Feingold Diet is indeed a very different and very difficult diet to maintain

in practice. The deprivations to the participants are real and is not the hyperactive child already set apart from his peers and family enough?" (p. 190). The negative empirical findings call into question the validity of the Feingold K-P diet as a treatment for hyperactivity and suggest a cautious policy toward accepting the Feingold hypothesis.

## Conclusions About Medically Based Interventions

Thus, the fascination with medical interventions by special education is not entirely warranted. The findings related to medically based treatment for hyperactivity (or ADHD) present an inconsistent picture: one (stimulant medication) was effective but the other (diet modification) was not. These results suggest that medicine does not necessarily offer "better" treatments than those based on psychoeducational foundations; they require the same critical examination as any other treatments.

# SOCIAL SKILLS TRAINING

A relatively new intervention that has received much attention is social skills training. Social skill deficits have been associated with special education students (Bryan, 1991; LaGreca & Vaughn, 1992; Pearl, 1992; Schumaker & Hazel, 1988) and range in form from deficits in social cognition (Pearl, 1987) and social behavior (LaGreca, 1987) to peer status (Dudley-Marling & Edmiaston, 1985) and self-concept (Chapman, 1988).

Although it is not clear how social skill deficits develop (e.g., Gresham, 1992), a number of efforts directed at enhancing social skills have been initiated (Vaughn & LaGreca, 1988). Evaluations of social skills training have shown mixed results (e.g., Gresham, 1981; McIntosh, Vaughn, & Zaragoza, 1991; Vaughn, 1991). The difficulties in reaching conclusions about its effectiveness are partially related to problems in outcome assessments (Maag, 1989) and in actually defining such training (Gresham, 1985; Pray, Hall, & Markley, 1992). Most training programs involve observing or modeling the skill to be learned, shaping or approximating skills through verbal cues or reinforcement, and rehearsal or practice activities; some stress cognitive understanding rather than overt social behaviors. Since programs give a different emphasis to these procedures, it is difficult to assess the contribution of specific methods in a particular intervention or across interventions.

Kavale and Forness (1995) synthesized data from 52 studies investigating the effectiveness of social skills training for students with learning disabilities. The studies included 2,113 subjects who averaged 11.5 years of age with an average IQ of 96; the subjects received training for approximately three hours per week for 10 weeks. The 52 studies produced 328 ES measurements with an $\overline{ES}$ of .211; the median ES was .182, suggesting a positive skew. Of the 328 ES measures, 22% were negative, suggesting that in about one in five instances social skills training actually produced better gains in the control than in the experimental group.

In relative terms, the mean ES of .211 suggests that an average special education student (i.e., at the fiftieth percentile) would rise only to the fifty-eighth percentile as a result of social skills training, indicative of only modest gains. With J. Cohen's (1977) classification of ES magnitude, the $\overline{ES}$ of .211 would be called small. There were, however, slight differences in the way that teachers, peers, and students themselves evaluated the outcome of social skills training or intervention.

When special education students evaluated themselves on outcomes of social skills training, the largest ESs were obtained. These findings, which could be aggregated across six dimensions, are shown in Table 37.17. The mean ES across 117 measures in which self-report or self-rating by students was obtained was .244, an effect that would leave the average special education student better off than 59% of the students who received no training. The largest $\overline{ES}$ was found for social status, where 65% of the students perceived that social skills training enhanced their

status. Apparently, special education students, after receiving training, believed that their social status was enhanced, whereas their peers who assessed the effects of the same training perceived no such enhancement. More than 6 out of 10 special education students also perceived benefits from social skills training in self-concept, social problem solving, and social competence, but fewer perceived improvement in social interactions or locus of control.

Peers evaluated the effects of social skills training for their special education classmates somewhat more modestly. The mean ES across seven dimensions was .205, as shown in Table 37.18. Peers found the greatest advantage for social skills training in the area of communicative competence. About 60% of special education students were seen by classmates as improved in their ability to understand the dynamics of communication in social settings. The social status of their classmates was perceived to be the least enhanced, and the five other areas concerned with social integration clustered around the $\overline{ES}$. The overall level of improvement was only slightly above chance, which suggests that general education peers may be somewhat more amenable to integrating special education students but still saw them as having inferior status.

Evaluations of social skills training among teachers could be aggregated across six dimensions and are the least sanguine (see Table 37.19). The mean ES across 73 measures was .163; about 6 out of 10 special education students were perceived by teachers to be slightly better adjusted and less dependent as the result of social interventions. Conduct disorder as a problem was seen as slightly more improved, whereas hyperactivity (i.e., non-goal-directed behavior) was essentially unimproved, at least in the perception

## TABLE 37.17 Self-Assessment of Social Skills Training

| Components | Number of Effect Sizes | Mean Effect Size | Percentile Equivalent |
|---|---|---|---|
| Status | 16 | .379 | 65 |
| Self-concept | 24 | .280 | 61 |
| Social problem solving | 11 | .279 | 61 |
| Social competence | 30 | .265 | 61 |
| Interaction | 17 | .188 | 58 |
| Locus of control | 19 | .079 | 53 |
| Self composite | 117 | .244 | 59 |

TABLE 37.18   Peer Assessment of Social Skills Training

| Components | Number of Effect Sizes | Mean Effect Size | Percentile Equivalent |
|---|---|---|---|
| Communication | 19 | .250 | 60 |
| Acceptance | 25 | .230 | 59 |
| Cooperation | 13 | .222 | 59 |
| Friendship | 13 | .217 | 59 |
| Rejection | 23 | .202 | 58 |
| Interaction | 24 | .198 | 58 |
| Status | 21 | .126 | 55 |
| Peer composite | 138 | .205 | 58 |

of teachers. Both the perception about the lack of academic competence and the amount of social interaction showed little enhancement.

There were no differences in the $\overline{ES}$ among the three groups assessing outcomes: $F(2,325) = 1.81; p > .25$. Although the largest effect of social skills training was found in the evaluations performed by students with learning disabilities themselves, the ES translated into only a modest 9-percentile rank gain. Regardless of who did the evaluation, however, it appears that such training resulted in relatively minimal gains.

Although social skills deficits would seem to be quite characteristic of special education students, these deficits appear to be resistant to treatment. Across more than 50 studies, training effects were modest; in better than 1 in 5 studies, control groups actually responded better. There were some differences among teachers, peers, and special education students themselves in the perception of beneficial effects; but these proved to be insignificant.

Special education students seemed the most

impressed with their social skills after training. Even in those studies, however, general education peers tended to view the same results as significantly less positive. Although special education students ranked their social status as the most improved of all deficits, peers rated their status as least improved. Teachers' impressions of the impact of training on overall social adjustment were quite modest, and almost negligible regarding intervention for such problems as conduct disorders and hyperactivity. Teachers rated academic competence as being virtually untouched by such training. All three groups rated actual social interaction among the least improved skills.

Why did such a widely used intervention prove to be such a disappointment? There are a number of possibilities. The most obvious involves intensity of training. The average amount of social skills training tended to be 30 hours or less (i.e., fewer than 3 hours per week for fewer than 10 weeks). Although no significant correlation emerged overall, there is always the possibility that longer interventions might be needed to

TABLE 37.19   Teacher's Assessment of Social Skills Training

| Components | Number of Effect Sizes | Mean Effect Size | Percentile Equivalent |
|---|---|---|---|
| Adjustment | 15 | .294 | 62 |
| Dependency | 10 | .250 | 60 |
| Conduct disorder | 8 | .218 | 59 |
| Interaction | 17 | .113 | 54 |
| Hyperactivity | 9 | .074 | 53 |
| Academic competence | 14 | .049 | 52 |
| Teacher composite | 73 | .163 | 56 |

produce results. Since the average treated student was in the sixth grade, it is not unreasonable to assume that social skill deficits were relatively long-standing; it should then come as no surprise that 30 hours would prove insufficient to ameliorate the social problems. Even in intensive interventions over a period of years, there may be only modest outcomes with some students, or some students may respond during some periods and not others (Vaughn & Hogan, 1994).

A second possibility concerns measurement issues. A number of criticisms have been directed at assessment of social skills (e.g., Forness & Kavale, 1991; Hughes & Sullivan, 1988; Vaughn & Haager, 1994). The problems include a poor rationale for the inclusion of items, dubious psychometric properties of instruments, failure to account for contextual or social validity variables that influence expression of social skills, and lack of differentiation between skill and performance deficits. These shortcomings become even more problematic when such instruments are used to assess effects over time. Many studies in the meta-analysis did not employ social skills rating scales that have been recently developed to address these issues (e.g., Gresham & Elliott, 1990; Walker & McConnell, 1988). A careful review of studies also revealed either a vagueness in conception or a lack of concordance between dimensions of social skills being assessed and those being trained (Zaragoza, Vaughn, & McIntosh, 1991). Given available dependent measures, it was thus not always clear that if an intervention worked, the outcomes could be demonstrated.

Training packages themselves represented a third possible reason for the lack of significant effects. Almost all studies used a social skills training program specifically designed for research. Such programs usually represent an amalgam of techniques with no clear rationale and little pilot testing beforehand. Several potentially effective social skills training packages are indeed available (e.g., Elliott & Gresham, 1991; Hazel, Schumaker, Sherman, & Sheldon-Wildgen, 1981; McGinnis, Goldstein, Sprafkin, & Gershaw, 1984; Vaughn, Levine, & Ridley, 1986; Walker, Street, Garrett, Crossen, Hops, & Greenwood, 1978; Walker, McConnell, Holmes, Todis, Walker, & Golden, 1983), but these were seldom used in the available studies. It may well be that social skills training works, but this fact could not be demonstrated by the intervention programs used nor could effective components be isolated.

The possibility cannot be entirely dismissed, however, that the ES is a valid indicator of the effectiveness of social skills training for special education students (i.e., it is a very weak intervention or at least one that receives very limited empirical support). Social skill deficits continue to characterize students with learning disabilities as they grow up and seem to be even more devastating than the lack of academic skills on adult outcomes (Vogel & Forness, 1992). Beyond the school years, situations requiring social competence tend to far outnumber those requiring academic skill; competent social presentation may in turn minimize the adverse impact of academic skill deficits. That social skills training or intervention has only limited empirical support is indeed discouraging, but it is premature to abandon this treatment in the absence of further research that might clarify critical factors in treatment intensity, delineation of training, subject selection, and other methodological issues that seem as yet unresolved.

# EVALUATING THE EFFECTIVENESS OF SPECIAL EDUCATION

The meta-analytic evaluation of six prominent interventions does not paint an optimistic picture about the efficacy of special education. If an ES of 1.00 is used as a yardstick, representing the average achievement of the average student at the end of one year's worth of schooling, these interventions are not impressive. Most revealed an $\overline{ES}$ below .50 and thus represent less advantage than one-half year's worth of schooling. It would not be unreasonable to demand that special interventions exceed the gains of regular schooling if special education students are to eliminate the gaps in their educational performance.

The special interventions demonstrated effects that primarily ranged from negligible to small and, at best, *medium*, using J. Cohen's (1977) classification system. None approached the large effects (.80 and above) that would be necessary to enhance performance at a rate that would accelerate grade-level performance. For special interventions, the obtained ESs are not eloquent testimony to the efficacy of practices that have almost come to define special education. To provide perspective, consider that something as simple (setting aside financial considerations) as reducing class size (e.g., from 35 to 25) can enhance achievement with an $\overline{ES}$ of .31 (see

TABLE 37.20 **Summary of Meta-Analyses in Special Education**

| Intervention | Number of Studies | Mean Effect Size | Standard Deviation of Effect Size |
|---|---|---|---|
| Perceptual-motor training | 180 | .08 | .27 |
| Psycholinguistic training | 34 | .39 | .54 |
| Modality instruction | 39 | .15 | .28 |
| Stimulant drugs | 135 | .58 | .61 |
| Diet intervention | 23 | .12 | .42 |
| Psychotropic drugs | 70 | .30 | .75 |
| Early intervention | 74 | .40 | .62 |
| Social skills training | 52 | .21 | .68 |
| Applied behavior analysis | 41 | .93 | 1.16 |

Glass & Smith, 1979). Four of the six interventions discussed did not produce the same magnitude of effect, which suggests that the special practices that are defining special education must be questioned.

In evaluating the effectiveness of special education, another complication arises and is illustrated in Table 37.20, which summarizes the meta-analyses described previously plus three additional meta-analytic efforts. The ES is shown in the second column and the associated standard deviation (SD) in the third column; the SD is a measure of dispersion around the mean and represents an index of variability. When compared to the mean ES, the SD reveals magnitudes two to three times greater; in every case, the intervention exhibits greater variability than effectiveness. If the two statistics are combined, they represent a theoretical expectation (ES ± SD) about the magnitude of an intervention (see Kaplan, 1964). A bit of simple arithmetic reveals that special education practice may vary from negative to zero to positive over a wide range. Although these are merely theoretically possible values, it does demonstrate that special interventions are more variable than beneficial in their effects. This is not a hallmark of effective practice; the variability makes special education essentially indeterminate. In such circumstances, it would be difficult to provide other than an equivocal response about the effectiveness of special education.

As part of the meta-analytic procedure, important study features (e.g., age, gender, IQ, SES, and severity level) are correlated with ES. If some correlations are significant, it is possible to state some relationship. For example, psycholin-

guistic training would be most effective with a particular special education classification, or social skills training would be most effective at a particular age level. In performing the six meta-analyses described, hundreds of correlations were calculated, but very few were significant, suggesting that the relationships were not of a magnitude that permitted useful prediction. The effectiveness of special interventions is thus also unpredictable.

Special education interventions do not operate as "perfect" knowledge (Brodbeck, 1962) that would represent a lawful set of input-output associations (i.e., do A in circumstance X and Y and do B in circumstance Z). Instead, special education should be viewed as imperfect knowledge and should not operate on the basis of prescriptive action, a single course of action over a variety of situations. Imperfect knowledge is also confounded by the fact that generalizations in the behavioral sciences tend to change over time (Gergen, 1973) because of modifications in values underlying perceptions about what is important and desirable (Eisner, 1979). Special education, in the form of special practices, needs to be understood as an enterprise that is variable, indeterminate, unpredictable, unlawful, and value-laden. In these circumstances, it is little wonder that special education has not demonstrated unequivocal efficacy.

## WHY SPECIAL EDUCATION MAY NOT BE EFFECTIVE

The lack of demonstrated effectiveness among special education interventions may be related to the fact that too much emphasis has been placed on the *special* adjective. To define its uniqueness, special education developed *special* interventions, but their very uniqueness cast them in the role of instant and simple solutions for the educational needs of special education students. The difficulty was that the special practices never fulfilled the promise of being *the* solution or *the* answer. The meta-analytic findings presented earlier demonstrate clearly that no such claim could be made.

Special education has also been limited by the way it has viewed a number of conceptual problems that mediate intervention effectiveness. By explicating these conceptual problems, it is possible to explain partially why intervention activities do not often produce expected results.

The first conceptual problem relates to what is believed about certain interventions. The strong clinical tradition and historical roots of many special education interventions strongly influence perceptions about their efficacy. Any negative research evidence is dismissed as inconclusive; questions about efficacy thus never achieve closure, and basic beliefs are not altered. A good example is the modality concept, in which more than 9 out of 10 teachers surveyed believed that modality strengths and weaknesses should be considered and that students learned more when instruction was modified to match modality patterns (Arter & Jenkins, 1977; Kavale & Reese, 1991).

Although the Kavale and Forness (1987) quantitative synthesis offered a negative evaluation of the modality model, it is important to note that many previous reviews (e.g., Larrivee, 1981; Tarver & Dawson, 1978; Ysseldyke, 1973) reached similar conclusions. Nevertheless, because of the strong intuitive appeal of the modality model, the consistent and persistent negative evaluations are discounted in favor of unsubstantiated claims. Unlike old soldiers, the modality model does not fade away, as shown by yet another debate about its efficacy (see Carbo, 1992; Snider, 1992a, 1992b).

The strength of such belief is seen in Swanson's (1984) finding of a significant discrepancy between what teachers say and what they do. Teachers are most comfortable with what they already know, what they have been exposed to, and what the conventional wisdom says. Regardless of how exciting teachers may find new theoretically based strategies, there is a resistance to implementing them in favor of existing practices that they find comfortable (like those described

earlier in the meta-analytic findings). Thus, a strong theoretical rationale does not appear to guide actual teaching practice.

A second problem surrounds the nonproductive ways in which issues have come to be perceived. An example here is the concept of individualized instruction, the cornerstone of most special education models. In its classic sense as diagnostic-prescriptive teaching (see Peter, 1965), nothing is more fundamental to special education intervention than the idea that a student is assessed to determine strengths and weaknesses and then instruction is designed to capitalize on these strengths and remediate these weaknesses. This basic idea, however, has become polarized into diametrically opposed positions (i.e., process, or ability, models versus skill, or behavioral, models) that reflect philosophical differences about special education (Ysseldyke & Salvia, 1974). Neither model is satisfactory by itself (Smead, 1977), but such philosophical debate deflects attention away from actual instructional practice. Lloyd (1984) emphasized this point in an analysis of individualized instruction. Three models of individualization were analyzed (remedial, compensatory, and preferential), but little support was found for any of these aptitude × treatment interaction hypotheses. It was concluded that the assumption that some kinds of instruction are better for some students and other kinds are better for other students may not be valid, and instruction instead should be based on "skills students need to be taught" (p. 14).

Fuchs and Fuchs (1986) followed this suggestion with a call for systematic formative evaluation as the basis for individualization. This focuses on ongoing evaluation and modification of proposed programs to provide a data base on which individualized programs may be developed. Its advantages include the fact that (1) it is an inductive, rather than deductive, approach to individualization, which avoids the pitfalls of formulating a diagnosis before the relationship between learners' characteristics and educational intervention is fully established; (2) it is based on more psychometrically acceptable measurement procedures; and (3) it has more ecological validity because of repeated measurements in the classroom. In a meta-analysis of 21 studies, an $\overline{ES}$ of .70 was found, which suggests that a formative evaluation is a productive procedure for individualizing instruction. Thus, discussion about individualization can be useful if structured in productive ways, rather than obfuscating the concept by the creation of nonproductive issues.

A third conceptual problem surrounds the confounding of issues. The primary example is the long-standing issue of *where* special education students should be educated. Kauffman (1993) referred to this as "keeping place in perspective" (p. 7) because of the paucity of knowledge about how placement determines what is possible and what is probable for instruction and educational outcomes. From neither a historical view (e.g., MacMillan & Hendrick, 1993) nor evaluations of placement effects (e.g., Hallahan, Keller, McKinney, Lloyd, & Bryan, 1988) can it be concluded that location is the primary factor in special education. Of greater importance is what actually occurs instructionally and the types of interactions that take place in the setting (Gottlieb, Alter, & Gottlieb, 1991). The *what* is thus of greater import than the *where*, but special education has argued primarily about placement options at the expense of instructional options.

## THE EFFICACY QUESTION AND PROBLEMS OF SPECIAL EDUCATION

It would be an error to underestimate the magnitude and longevity of the debate on the question of where special education students should be placed. It has been a focus since the 1940s and has escalated into debate about the viability of special education as any kind of place at all (see Fuchs & Fuchs, 1994). What is missing is critical discussion about what occurs, instructionally and socially, in special education settings. This is what Mitroff and Featheringham (1974) termed Type III error, defined as asking the "wrong" question when you should have asked the "right" question. Too much emphasis has been placed on the merits of different settings, when they have relatively little effect per se on whether or not special education is effective.

Efficacy studies of special education placement have a long history. Polloway (1984) identified five historical stages and discussed the major question associated with each, as well as their time span:

1. Would special education students profit from being in school together with non-handicapped peers? (1930s to 1940s)
2. Are the needs of special education students best met in regular—or special—class programs? (1950s to mid-1960s)
3. Are special classes a viable program option for special education students given the increasing legal, sociological, and political concerns as well as the paucity of research documenting their benefits? (late 1960s to early 1970s)
4. Given a variety of placement options within a "cascade" model of services, which alternative is most appropriate for the individual special education student? (early 1970s to 1980s)
5. Can the population of special education students benefit from the more integrated placements common since the passage of the Education for All Handicapped Act (PL 94-142)? (mid-1980s to present)

Although there is a long history of research into these questions, the findings have been difficult to interpret and conclusions have been equivocal (e.g., Guskin & Spiker, 1968; Kirk, 1964; Meyers, MacMillan, & Yoshida, 1980). Nevertheless, legislation and litigation emphasized the "least restrictive environment," and there was a decided trend toward mainstreaming and primary placement in the regular classroom (Kavale, 1979). The advocacy for mainstreaming was built on philosophical (e.g., Christopolos & Renz, 1969; L. M. Dunn, 1968) rather than empirical foundations and was more steadfast than warranted by the empirical evidence (MacMillan, 1971).

Carlberg and Kavale (1980) performed a meta-analysis on 50 studies examining the efficacy question. The studies produced 322 ES measurements and yielded an $\overline{ES}$ of $-.12$. (The ES statistic was arranged so that a positive ES favored the special class, whereas a negative ES favored the regular or mainstreamed class.) These data represented approximately 27,000 students, who averaged 11 years of age with a mean IQ of 74, and who remained in the special class for a little under two years. Approximately 58% of the ESs were negative: in more than half the cases, special classes were less effective than regular classes. Since the average comparison (regular class) subject would be at the fiftieth percentile, the effect of approximately two years of special class placement was to reduce the relative standing of the average special class subject by 5 percentile ranks. Thus, special class students were slightly worse off than if they had remained in regular classes.

Efficacy studies generally measured two outcomes. In the Carlberg and Kavale (1980) analysis, achievement and social-personality variables revealed $\overline{\text{ES}}$s of $-.15$ and $-.11$, respectively. Thus, special class placement was inferior to regular class placement, regardless of outcome measures. Special class subjects declined by 6 and 4 percentile ranks on achievement, as did social and personality measures, respectively. These findings lend support for a significant, although small, negative effect for special class placement. The critics were apparently correct: special education placement produces no tangible benefits.

By the late 1970s, mainstreaming was defined primarily by the resource model of service delivery (e.g., Deno, 1973; Hammill & Weiderholt, 1972; Reger, 1973). A resource program is a school program in which an individual (usually resource teacher) has responsibility for providing supportive, educationally related services to special education students. An integral component is a resource room, a place where students receive specific instruction on a regularly scheduled basis, while receiving the majority of their education in a general education program.

The resource model became the most frequently used alternative to the regular classroom for servicing students with mild disabilities (Friend & McNutt, 1984). Although the model continued to develop (e.g., McLoughlin & Kelly, 1982; Speece & Mandell, 1980; Wiederholt, Hammill, & Brown, 1978), critical evaluations of resource programs showed considerable variability and equivocal outcomes (Sindelar & Deno, 1978; Wiederholt & Chamberlain, 1989).

Wang and Baker (1985–1986) performed a meta-analysis on 50 studies investigating the efficacy of mainstreaming. A total of 3,413 students were included across grades K–12 and across special education categories. The studies produced 455 ES measurements and yielded an $\overline{\text{ES}}$ of .11, about 40% of which was negative. The $\overline{\text{ES}}$ of .11 indicates that 54% of mainstreamed students would be better off than those in the comparison groups. For comparisons involving mainstreamed versus nonmainstreamed special education students, the $\overline{\text{ES}}$ was .43, indicating that 67% of mainstreamed students were better off by about 17 percentile ranks. However, when the comparison group was nonhandicapped peers, the mainstreaming $\overline{\text{ES}}$ was $-.31$, meaning that mainstreamed students lost 12 percentile ranks. There was a positive, although small, effect for mainstreaming; special education students in mainstreaming programs outperformed

those in self-contained settings but performed lower than their nonhandicapped peers.

The findings from these meta-analyses suggest that placement has only a modest effect on outcomes. By any standard (see J. Cohen, 1977), the obtained ESs, in all cases, were quite small. The emphasis on setting brought about by the cascade model (see Deno, 1970) has made it the focus of attention (e.g., Leinhardt & Pallay, 1982); yet, there was very little advantage to any placement, as shown by the rather small ES associated with evaluations of different settings. Two explanations are possible: special education may indeed be ineffective, and the methodology for measuring outcomes may not be appropriate. The analysis of the efficacy research reveals a number of methodological difficulties that threaten the validity of findings (Tindal, 1985):

1. Placement histories: Different placement histories among special education students may interact with current placement; the effect of each successive intervention may then become confounded with its order in the sequence (Cegelka & Tyler, 1970). Such confounded effects may limit the generalizability of findings (Campbell, 1969).

2. Assignment to treatment: When sampling is not random, groups may not be comparable and it is difficult to determine whether outcomes are related to treatment (Cook & Campbell, 1979). Many efficacy studies did not use random assignment and instead used existing groups that were probably not established in a random basis. Thus, group differences may be due to antecedent conditions rather than intervention activities (Kaufman & Alberto, 1976).

3. Appropriateness of measurement: Standardized tests may not be sensitive enough to detect small changes produced by interventions programs (Sheehan & Keogh, 1984). Also, tests, although purporting to measure similar skills, may not be interchangeable because they may sample very different behaviors (Jenkins & Pany, 1978). Finally, most efficacy studies using standardized tests report findings in grade-equivalent scores, which have a number of technical problems that limit their usefulness (Berk, 1984).

4. Variability among definitions: Efficacy studies, although focusing on particular categories of special education, actually investigate heterogeneous groups of students who

have been classified according to diverse and often ambiguous criteria that may vary significantly across settings. Students placed into one category in one setting are likely to be different from those placed in another setting (Hallahan & Kauffman, 1977). The reliance in categorical labels may thus limit the kinds of conclusions that may be drawn from efficacy research (Heller, Holtzman, & Messick, 1982).

Although it is difficult to demonstrate particular conclusions about categories of special education, general conclusions may emerge, as seen in the Carlberg and Kavale (1980) meta-analysis. After calculating overall efficacy ($\overline{ES} = -.12$), ES measurements were aggregated into three categories: mildly mentally retarded (MMR; IQ 50–75), slow learner (SL; IQ 75–90), and learning disabled (LD) or behavior disorder/emotionally disturbed (BD/ED). The findings are shown in Table 37.21.

Special class placement was most disadvantageous for special education students whose problem was lower IQ levels (MMR and SL). In comparison to their regular class counterparts, SLs lost 13 percentile ranks and MMRs declined by 6 percentile ranks. For LD and BD/ED students in special classes, however, an improvement of 11 percentile ranks resulted from their placement. The average LD or BD/ED student in a special class was better off than 61% of those who remained in a regular class.

The ESs for special education classification were thus larger than those found earlier and deserve some attention. The most fundamental question is why some students (e.g., MMR and SL) in special classes were slightly worse off than they would have been had they remained in regular classrooms? The significant variable appears to be intelligence: on the one hand, if a student is placed in a special class because of a low IQ, it may lower the teacher's expectations for performance, which results in less effort on the teacher's part and less learning on the student's (e.g., Rosenthal & Jacobson, 1968; Rosenthal & Rubin, 1978). The lower expectancy, either conscious or unconscious, may divert instructional efforts away from academic pursuits toward a solely maintenance function. Thus, the special class may become an instrument for preserving social order and not necessarily an arrangement for providing better educational opportunities. On the other hand, the average intelligence of LD and BD/ED students (at least, by definition) apparently does not dampen teachers' expectation. Special class teachers apparently take an optimistic view and provide significant efforts to improve academic functioning. Perhaps these efforts represent the "real" special education, not a system seeking the status quo but one focusing on individual learning needs and abilities to design the most effective program of *academic* remediation necessary to overcome *academic* deficits.

In general, these findings suggest that basic questions about the best placement for service delivery to special education students are complex and not easily answered. The efficacy studies included a multitude of different service delivery models under the general rubric of special education placement. Since no service arrangement proved more effective, it appears that the differences were related to indeterminate and imperceptible variables not easily assessed or controlled. As MacMillan (1971) noted, "The real issue is not whether special classes or regular classes are better but rather where the best interests of the students might be" (p. 9). The basic problem is that debate has focused on placement and degree of restrictiveness to such an extent that setting has come to be viewed as treatment itself (Epps & Tindal, 1988). Clearly, setting is not the salient variable that determines instructional success; as an independent variable, setting provides little insight into what constitutes effective instruction (Burstein & Guiton, 1984). The

**TABLE 37.21  Average Effect Size by Special Education Diagnosis for Special Versus Regular Class Placement**

| Diagnosis | Average Effect of Special vs. Regular Placement | Number of Effect Sizes |
|---|---|---|
| MMR (IQ 50–75) | −.14 | 249 |
| SL (IQ 75–90) | −.34 | 38 |
| LD and BD/ED | .29 | 35 |

efficacy findings may, in fact, indicate the lack of differences between special and regular education at the level of instruction. Features of instruction are probably the major influence on outcomes but are not unique to setting. Setting is thus a macro variable; the real question lies in examining what occurs in the setting (Maher & Bennett, 1984).

## SPECIAL EDUCATION AND INSTRUCTION

Although *place* has long held a predominant position in debate about the nature of special education, there has also been an accompanying development of instructional techniques. As suggested earlier, the techniques developed were special in the sense of being associated with only special education and not usually seen in general education. The meta-analytic findings presented earlier demonstrate the limited effectiveness of the practices developed to define special education.

Hagin (1973) reviewed intervention methods over a 15-year period and found a shift in emphasis. Early efforts viewed the problems of special education students from a pathology perspective; academic disability was regarded as a disease entity and interventions (e.g., perceptual-motor training) were aimed at removing the pathology. Before 1965, a majority of intervention reports emphasized the pathology model. After 1965, emphasis shifted to what was termed an educational mismatch model, where failure was viewed as the result of a mismatch between educational methods and a student's developmental level. The educational mismatch model was gradually replaced by a learning process model, which was concerned with substantive aspects of learning, particularly as they related to cognitive, linguistic, and social factors. Special education thus slowly shifted its emphasis from *special* to *education*.

Several special practices that emphasize *education* have been shown to be effective. Any special practice, to be deemed effective, should enhance learning at a level comparable to general education (ES = 1.00 after one year of instruction). The special (i.e., unique and different) interventions reviewed earlier did not achieve this goal, but meta-analyses of two instructional techniques have demonstrated such levels of effectiveness. The first is direct instruction, which involves academically focused, teacher-directed learning with sequenced, structured materials and high levels of student involvement; it produces an $\overline{ES}$ of .84 (White, 1988). Even more impressive are learning strategies that use mnemonic techniques, involving elaboration strategies (e.g., key words and peg words), to teach history and science facts; it produces an $\overline{ES}$ of 1.62 (Mastropieri & Scruggs, 1989). Special education students, for example, receiving mnemonic instruction would be better off than 98% of the students not receiving such instruction, and they would gain over $1\frac{1}{2}$ years of credit on an achievement measure, compared to about one month for modality teaching ($\overline{ES}$ = .14), discussed earlier. Thus, special practices based on sound instructional techniques are anywhere from 5 to 10 times more effective than "special" practices attempting to "cure" special education students by overcoming the pathological effects of unobservable constructs (e.g., perceptual-motor factors).

## CREATING EFFECTIVE SPECIAL EDUCATION

Special education becomes significantly more effective when the *education* aspect is emphasized. It is evident that when the *special* is emphasized, only modest outcomes are achieved. Enhanced effectiveness, however, is possible when special practices are based on sound instructional techniques. The goal becomes one of adapting instructional procedures for the purposes of special education. How is this best accomplished?

The teaching-learning process, whether in special or in general education, is enormously complex; learning is mediated through a whole host of intervening variables (e.g., Dunkin & Biddle, 1974; Joyce & Weil, 1972; Peterson & Walberg, 1979). The past 15 years, however, have brought to the fore factors that influence school performance, and this has come to be termed the *effective school* research (e.g., Mackenzie, 1983; Purkey & Smith, 1983; Squires, 1983). The research in effective teaching has moved from a state of confusion to a point where consistent findings are emerging (Good, 1983).

The myriad findings about effective instruction have been shown to be strong and robust enough to warrant implementation as best practice (e.g., Haertel, Walberg, & Weinstein, 1983; Walberg, 1984; Waxman & Walberg, 1982). Christenson, Ysseldyke, and Thurlow (1989) identified nine critical factors for positive instructional outcomes:

1. Classrooms are managed effectively.
2. There is a sense of positiveness in the school environment.
3. There is an appropriate instructional match.
4. Goals are clear, expectations are explicitly communicated, and lessons are presented clearly.
5. Students receive good instructional support.
6. Sufficient time is allocated to instruction.
7. Opportunity to respond is high.
8. Teachers actively monitor student progress and understanding.
9. Student performance is evaluated appropriately and frequently.

Similarly, Waxman, Wang, Anderson, and Walberg (1985) identified features of successful adaptive instruction in mainstream settings:

1. An instructional match is maintained for each student.
2. Individualized pacing for achieving instructional goals is maintained.
3. Student progress is monitored, and continuous feedback is provided.
4. Students are involved in the planning and monitoring of their learning.
5. A broad range of techniques and materials is used.
6. Students help each other to learn.
7. Students are taught self-management skills.
8. Teachers engage in instructional teaming.

It is evident that much is known about effective instruction. Although usually originating in general education, components of effective instruction have been studied in special education and include factors like motivating students (Alderman, 1990), using classroom management (Wang, 1987), providing success (Reith & Evertson, 1988), establishing goals and expectations (Fuchs, Fuchs, & Deno, 1985), monitoring progress (Slavin & Madden, 1989), providing feedback (Larrivee, 1986), having a positive and supportive environment (Lovitt, 1984), teaching generalization (Ellis, Lenz, & Sabornie, 1987), and teaching independent learning skills (Pressley & Harris, 1990).

In examining the literature, it appears that the most investigated area is teachers' behavior and what factors have a positive influence on students' achievement (e.g., Brophy & Good, 1986; Medley, 1982; Weil & Murphy, 1982). For special education teachers (Reith & Evertson, 1988), these behaviors include the following:

1. Maintaining an academic focus in selecting activities and directing work.
2. Maintaining direction and control in the management of the learning environment.
3. Holding high expectations for academic progress.
4. Holding students accountable for satisfactory completion of work.
5. Having students work together cooperatively rather than competitively.
6. Establishing a positive affective climate.

When implemented, the teaching behaviors create "active teaching" (Brophy & Good, 1986), in which "the teacher carries the content to the students personally rather than depending on the curriculum to do so" (p. 361). The primary task of the teacher is to direct learning experiences, and "students spend most of their time being taught rather than working on their own (or not working at all)" (p. 361). Such active teaching has been related to enhanced achievement; Stevens and Rosenshine (1981) stated, "Teachers who most successfully promoted achievement gain played the role of strong leader; that is, they selected and directed the academic activities, approached the subject matter in a direct, businesslike way, organized learning around questions they posed, and occupied the center of attention" (p. 2).

The use of systematic instructional procedures has been supported in special education (Reynolds, Wang, & Walberg, 1992). Perhaps the most comprehensive form of special education is Direct Instruction (Gersten & Keating, 1987; Gersten, Woodward, & Darch, 1986). In an analysis, Gerstein, Carnine, and Woodward (1987) suggested six critical features for Direct Instruction;

1. An explicit step-by-step strategy.
2. Development of mastery at each step in the process.
3. Strategy (or process) corrections for student errors.
4. Gradual fading from teacher-directed activities toward independent work.
5. Use of adequate systematic practice with a range of examples.
6. Cumulative review of newly learned concepts.

The implementation of direct and systematic approaches creates individualized instruction, which is a cornerstone of special education (Talmage, 1975). Increased opportunity to learn is also created, which in the form of academic learning time (ALT) is a major contributor to learning (Denham & Lieberman, 1980; Wilson, 1987). Such engaged time has been shown to be positively associated with learning (Fisher & Berliner, 1985) and is also a critical factor in special education (Goodman, 1990). Wilson and Wesson (1986) suggest that instructional time, time on-task, and students' success are essential components of ALT in special education. With findings showing that special education students require more time to achieve mastery (e.g., Gettinger, 1991; Greenwood, 1991), Wilson and Wesson offer a number of suggestions to increase actual instructional time, to increase time on-task during teacher-directed instruction, and to increase on-task rates during practice. Thus, effective instruction is predicated on establishing appropriate academic instructional objectives and designing intervention programs that maximize opportunities for the special education student to work successfully on tasks related to the objectives. The overall goal is to achieve "instructional alignment," which fosters congruence among objectives, instructional procedures, and evaluation procedures (Cohen, 1987).

## BARRIERS TO EFFECTIVE SPECIAL EDUCATION

The research on effective schools and instruction has been studied in special education settings, and implications for special education interventions have been described (e.g., Bickel & Bickel, 1986; Samuels, 1986). Essentially, it was suggested that the valuable insights obtained about what makes instruction effective are applicable to special education, and it is necessary to reconceptualize how special education should be conceived and delivered.

A number of investigations, however, have shown that discrepancies exist between the stipulated components of effective instruction and the observation of actual special education practice (Morsink, Soar, Soar, & Thomas, 1986). In examining reading instruction in self-contained classrooms, Leinhardt, Zigmond, and Cooley (1981) found that although full days were allocated to reading, only about one-third of the day was actually spent on that activity. Similarly, Haynes and Jenkins (1986) found significant variability in the time students spent on direct reading; there was almost no relationship between students' need and program offerings. In general, students' characteristics, particularly achievement level, were only weakly linked to scheduling and the amount of reading instruction received. Across content areas, Englert (1983, 1984) demonstrated that there was only a relatively modest amount of time spent on activities that could be considered direct instruction with learners' active involvement and teachers' attention. In general, Ysseldyke, Thurlow, Christenson, and Weiss (1987) reported that the percentage of engaged time in special education classes is about 75% and that engaged time varies across classrooms, as well as among students within a classroom.

It seems safe to conclude that teachers vary widely in implementing components of effective instruction. Good (1983) suggested that many teachers do not actively teach content; instruction consists of brief explanations followed by long periods of seat-work that do not provide sufficient opportunities for meaningful and successful practice. Brophy (1982) further suggested that the content of instruction defined in the curriculum is often the subject of deletions, additions, and incorrect applications when implemented by teachers in classrooms. The distortions due to teachers' misinterpretations are more typical than any indirect distortion resulting from incomplete or inadequate teaching. Consequently, students may be given content that is fragmented, limited, repetitive, and mystifying. What these findings suggest is that although research on effective instruction has provided a basis for improving practice, the generalizations are far from prescriptive. The major problem is the lack of specificity for proper implementation. Thus, the gap between theory and practice requires far more narrowing.

## RESEARCH, EVALUATION, AND EFFECTIVE INSTRUCTION

The research base for describing effective instruction has been predicated on a process-product paradigm shown in Figure 37.2(a). The goal is to search for processes (teachers' behaviors) that predict or cause products (usually achievement outcomes) (Gage, 1963). Although useful in a descriptive sense, the process-product paradigm has been criticized as too narrow since it

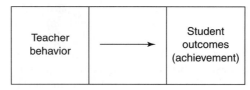

(a) Process-Product Paradigm

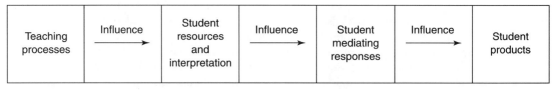

(b) Elaborated Process-Product Paradigm

**FIGURE 37.2    Research designs for effective instruction.**

omits concern with events that intervene between teachers' behavior and learning outcomes (Doyle, 1978). The consequences are limited findings in the form of low correlations and methodological disputes. Further criticism of the process-product paradigm is found in its inherent assumptions about causation (i.e., teachers cause students' achievement), its formulation of rules of pedagogy without a normative base, and its emphasis on teachers' behavior that ignores content (Garrison & Macmillan, 1984).

The findings from research that uses a basic process-product paradigm are often equivocal; it is basically correlational rather than experimental in nature. There is little active manipulation of variables, as in true experimental designs, and it might be better termed a quasi-experimental design (Cook & Campbell, 1979). As such, process-product research is closer in spirit to evaluation rather than research design; there is little control over extraneous variables (Cronbach, 1982).

To overcome many of these difficulties, two additional paradigms have been suggested to expand the basic process-product paradigm (see Doyle, 1978). The first is a mediating-process paradigm that takes into account students' responses and psychological processes governing learning. The second is a classroom-ecology paradigm that focuses on relationships between environmental demands and responses occurring in a natural setting. The elaborated process-product paradigm is shown in Figure 37.2(b). The advantages are found not in a simple comparison of $X$ and $Y$ but rather in the ability to examine a whole range of variables (e.g., degree of structure, allocation of academic time, and teachers' feedback) in a large sample of classrooms using a variety of instructional approaches. Such "impact evaluations" (Gersten & Hauser, 1984) capitalize on the natural variation in teaching procedures, curriculum content, and classroom organization.

The recognition of the complex nature of special education and the variety of interactions that influence effectiveness has resulted in evaluation procedures that emphasize formative procedures concerned with program improvement over summative procedures concerned with the evaluation of static programs. To accommodate what is known about effective schooling and instruction, evaluation efforts must be based on questions that reflect those research findings. An example is found in the following list of questions that may be used to evaluate a special education program (Utah Special Education Consortium Evaluation Task Force, 1986):

**1.0** Are students achieving appropriate outcomes?

    **1.1** Have appropriate student outcomes in academic, vocational/life skills and social/behavioral areas been identified?

    **1.2** Are *all* ongoing monitoring procedures focused on final program outcomes?

    **1.3** Are program change processes directed by student outcome data?

**2.0** Are staff using effective pedagogy?

    **2.1** Are the major instructional and management procedures validated for the target population and the curriculum outcome?

**2.2** Is there a high level of engaged time?

**2.3** Is the total instructional time managed to ensure achievement of the projected outcomes?

**2.4** Are instructional practices congruent with prescribed outcomes?

**2.5** Is at least 50 percent of the instructional time committed to the intense acquisition of new skills?

**2.6** Are daily prescriptive and intervention procedures incorporating prerequisite skills and curriculum sequencing?

**2.7** Are teacher/learner interactions consistent with the research literature on praise and feedback?

**3.0** Are identification and placement procedures facilitative of student growth and consistent with applicable regulations?

**3.1** Do screening procedures identify the high risk students?

**3.2** Have interventions relevant to the presenting problems been implemented and results documented prior to referral for assessment for possible special education services?

**3.3** Are assessment practices appropriate for the problem and facilitative of instruction?

**3.4** Are team classification decisions consistent with available assessment data and applicable regulations?

**3.5** Are IEP goals and objectives team decisions and consistent with assessed student needs?

**3.6** Are special education interventions delivered in the least restrictive environment?

**4.0** Are instructional program coordination practices effective?

**4.1** Are program needs and strengths being assessed for determining priorities for program change?

**4.2** Are staff development activities identified, implemented, and evaluated consistent with priorities?

**4.3** Is there effective coordination of interventions across instructional environments?

**4.4** Are the roles and responsibilities of all system elements defined and clearly communicated to all involved in the education of special students?

**5.0** Are community communication and involvement practices effective?

**5.1** Are there effective procedures in place to allow parent and community comments, suggestions, and concerns to be voiced and responded to at the program level?

**5.2** Are there effective procedures for communicating program activities and rationales to parents and community?

**5.3** Have available community resources been identified and used effectively?

# PHILOSOPHICAL PERSPECTIVES IN THE EFFICACY OF SPECIAL EDUCATION

Although research endeavors in special education reveal a trend toward more dynamic designs, there are still questions about how to study special education. How should the instructional situation be viewed? Should we examine small elements or large units? Answers reveal fundamental differences about the theoretical and philosophical foundations of special education.

Heshusius (1982) suggested that the foundation provided by a predominantly mechanistic (i.e., behavioral) approach only reduces teaching and learning to the subordinate level of rules and instrumentality. The required measurement and quantification of instruction and learning tend not to operate at those levels that are meaningful or worthwhile for the special education student. Heshusius warned that such mechanistic assumptions are too narrow and simplistic, and although recognizing that no one model holds ultimate truth or reality, contended that special education practitioners have been trying to do the impossible—"to force the innately unpredictable into the predictable, the unmeasurable into the measurable, and wholeness into fragmentation" (p. 12).

The basic problem with a mechanistic approach is the demand that teachers become behavioral engineers or technicians, a transformation that only promotes the reduction of complex reality into quantifiable triviality. Optimal intervention requires an understanding of "complexity in its own right and the relationship of the whole to its parts, rather than trying to understand complexity by fragmenting it and reducing it to small, statistically measurable units over which one thinks one has control" (Heshusius, 1986, p. 463). This view did not go unchallenged (see Ulman & Rosenberg, 1986), and mechanistic approaches have been credited with being the primary agents for the efficient evaluation and modification of special education programs (Kimball & Heron, 1988; Nelson & Polsgrove, 1984). This debate has not been restricted to special education but extends to all educational research, as shown by the debate about positivism and its influence (see Phillips, 1983, and the response by Eisner, 1983). The debate led to an examination of the nature of educational research, particularly its philosophical underpinnings (e.g., Garrison, 1986; Macmillan & Garrison, 1984).

The debate continued with Poplin's (1988b) criticism of the reductionistic tendencies found in all special education models, whether medical, process, behavioral, or cognitive, and further suggested that holistic principles should underlie instruction (Poplin, 1988a). Similarly, Iano (1986) suggested that the natural science-technical model failed to capture the complexity of the teaching-learning process and has created an artificial distinction between researchers and practitioners. Researchers tend to reduce classroom behavior to controlled or defensible variables that fail to recognize classroom reality, whereas teachers view these as minor contributors and hence have little confidence in the generalizability of research findings. Iano's view was followed by commentary (e.g., Carnine, 1987; Forness & Kavale, 1987; Lloyd, 1987) either criticizing, expanding, or expanding, or clarifying specific points, to which Iano (1987) responded.

These debates have focused on the increased attention toward model-based practice in special education (Rosenberg & Jackson, 1988). Presently, the validity and worth of any particular model is virtually impossible to determine. For example, holistic principles may differ in effectiveness, depending on whether the task emphasizes the acquisition of basic skills or higher-order learning (Englert, Tarrant, & Mariage, 1992). It may be the case that special education needs to accept the fact that multiple models can be equally productive for studying efficacy (Labouvie, 1975; Licht & Torgesen, 1989). Although different models would lead to different interpretations of observed intervention effects, all would be retained for utilization in classrooms. Nonetheless, this relativism—or belief

that judgments about the adequacy of conflicting models cannot be made—has been challenged (Phillips, 1983). For example, Soltis (1984), while encouraging tolerance for all educational perspectives in an "associated community," emphasized that open-mindedness must not be mistakenly viewed as synonymous with empty-mindedness; special education professionals must exercise judgment when evaluating their interventions. Donmoyer (1985) asserted that relativism has contributed to special education being a "solipsistic morass," where any single conclusion about the effectiveness of an intervention could be judged as positive as any other intervention, even when there are conflicting findings.

Nevertheless, Rosenberg and Jackson (1988) discussed two issues that are of central importance in making choices and are predicated on the assumptions "that (a) changing the behaviors of students is a useful and appropriate educational goal, (b) the behavior changes are the product of specifiable activities that can be employed in other situations with the same or other students, and (c) changes are significant in the practical sense and are enduring either for the specific learners or for other populations of learners" (p. 30).

The first issue involves instructional validity, the degree to which an educational model can be relied on to effect a certain outcome. The two important considerations are internal validity and external validity (Campbell & Stanley, 1966; Cook & Campbell, 1979); internal validity refers to whether or not the intervention in question was responsible for observed behavior changes, and external validity refers to the question of generalizability. From a mechanistic view, variables that might be considered contaminating (and thus may limit internal validity) would be viewed as important determinants of change and studied in their own right from a holistic perspective to ensure external validity. Depending on your theoretical view, threats may not really be threats but rather the independent variables that are producing change. Thus, to ensure a comprehensive perspective, instructional validity should not emphasize either internal or external validity but rather the nature of the independent variables and specific learning outcomes.

The second issue involves outcome validity, which refers to the value of intervention activities in terms of the results being shown to have importance from an educational perspective (Howe, 1985). Outcome validity thus transcends any philosophical perspective by investigating the social utility of interventions, that is, whether they have functional relevance and contribute to explicit educational goals and objectives. For an applied field like special education, the evaluation of social utility should be integral to any assessment of intervention efficacy since it also addresses the question of accountability. Thus, a broader view of efficacy that encompasses the entire process of special education is achieved.

## CONCLUSION

Although research about effective schooling and instruction has produced an impressive set of findings, the generalizations are far from prescriptive. For this reason, special education will remain a system that is variable, indeterminate, unpredictable, unlawful, and value-laden. Thus, multiple models will need to be accepted because what works in one place may not work someplace else. Consequently, general education involves a degree of uncertainty (Glass, 1979) and risk (Kaplan, 1964) because an intervention may or may not work.

The recognition of uncertainty and risk, however, does not preclude rational instructional planning. What these elements do is to make the teacher the central character in the special education process. Success or failure is often the result of uncontrolled (and sometimes unknown) factors. In such a circumstance, a teacher must command options rather than truths in an effort to minimize risk by providing a satisfactory solution in conditions of uncertainty. A satisfactory solution is best achieved when dogmatic beliefs are replaced by rational choices. These rational choices are best gleaned from the research literature, and it is important that teachers gain insight into the best practice. The goal is to narrow the gap between the state of the art (what researchers have demonstrated is possible) and the state of the practice (current ways of providing instruction). Smith and West (1986) posed a series of questions that teachers may use to determine if they are providing state-of-the-art practice.

1. Do you upgrade your services by actively seeking information on new developments in your field?
2. Do you provide daily interactions with non-handicapped same age peers for your students?

3. Is the classroom in which you work within a structure used by the same age non-disabled peers?
4. Is the program, including learning materials, appropriate for the student's chronological age?
5. Do you provide individualized instruction that is tailored for each student's individual needs?
6. Do parents contribute to the design of individualized program plans?
7. Do your students receive community-based instruction that goes beyond a field trip at least twice a week?
8. Does your program provide a planned transition process for students moving from school to community?
9. Do you follow a formal plan in making referrals?
10. Does your program utilize the services of outside consultants to provide technical assistance at least once yearly?
11. Do you consider your program to be comprehensive in meeting all your student's needs?
12. Do you measure program effectiveness in terms of changes in daily performance in instructional, social, residential, and vocational environments?
13. Do you enjoy a high level of interagency cooperation and coordination?
14. Do you serve as a case manager for all the students you serve?
15. Do you offer support to help meet the needs of the student's family?

Although state-of-the-art knowledge is important, its interpretation in a state of practice is the critical element. This interpretation is accomplished by the individual teacher, and how well it is accomplished determines the success or failure of special education. Although the research base of special education may be specified, it can only be specified so much, and then the practitioner's wisdom and experience enter to complete the intricate concatenation of events involved in the special education teaching-learning process.

The effectiveness of special education thus includes elements of both science and art. Science refers to the theoretical and empirical foundation that defines the state of the art, and art refers to the interpretation provided to initiate the state of practice. Gage (1978) argued that practical enterprises in the real world (e.g., special education) have both scientific and artistic components. Gage provided analogies with medicine and engineering, whose scientific basis is unquestioned but where artistic elements also abound: "To practice medicine and engineering requires a knowledge of much science: concepts, or variables, and interrelations in the form of strong or weak laws, generalizations, or trends. But using science to achieve practical ends requires artistry—the artistry that enters into knowing when to follow the implications of the laws, generalizations, and trends, and especially, when *not* to, and how to combine two or more laws or trends in solving a problem" (p. 18).

The movement from the state of the art to the state of the practice has been termed the *is-ought* dichotomy (Phillips, 1980): Research findings take an *is* form (i.e., X is Y) whereas practical implications take an *ought* form (i.e., A ought to do B). The *ought* form thus requires translation of research findings, and the process has been aided significantly by recent methods texts (e.g., Bos & Vaughn, 1994; Kameenui & Simmons, 1990; Mastropieri & Scruggs, 1994); nevertheless, specific application requires the sagacity and perspicacity of the individual special education practitioner, which should not be limited by overspecifying the teaching-learning process. Like doctors and engineers, special education practitioners need to go beyond the scientific basis of their work. A special education student is quite likely to present problems for which scientific generalizations, principles, and suppositions will not apply directly and must be mediated through the teacher's own rendering of best practice. Therefore, the creativity of the individual special education practitioner must not be stifled because quality education for special education students will always be based on the artful application of science.

# REFERENCES

Abrami, P. C., Cohen, P. A., & d'Appolonia, S. (1988). Implementation problems in meta-analysis. *Review of Educational Research, 58*, 151–179.

Achinstein, P., & Barker, F. (1969). *The legacy of logical positivism*. Baltimore, MD: Johns Hopkins University Press.

Adelman, H. S., & Compas, B. E. (1977). Stimulant drugs and learning problems. *Journal of Special Education, 11*, 377–416.

Alderman, M. K. (1990). Motivation for at-risk students. *Educational Leadership, 48*, 27–30.

Aman, M. G. (1980). Psychotropic drugs and learning problems: A selective review. *Journal of Learning Disabilities, 13*, 89–97.

American Academy of Pediatrics Committee on Drugs. (1970). An examination of the pharmacologic approach to learning impediments. *Pediatrics, 46*, 142–144.

American Academy of Pediatrics Council on Child Health. (1975). Medication for hyperkinetic children. *Pediatrics, 55*, 560–562.

Arena, J. I. (Ed.). (1969). *Teaching through sensory-motor experiences*. San Rafael, CA: Academic Therapy Publications.

Arter, J. A., & Jenkins, J. R. (1977). Examining the benefits and prevalence of modality considerations in special education. *Journal of Special Education, 11*, 281–298.

Balow, B. (1971). Perceptual-motor activities in the treatment of severe reading disability. *Reading Teacher, 25*, 513–525.

Balow, B., & Brinkerhoff, R. (1983). Influences on special education evaluation. In R. O. Brinkerhoff, D. Brethower, T. Hluchjy, & J. Nowakowski (Eds.), *Program evaluation: A practitioner's guide for trainers and educators* (pp. xxiii–xxvii). Boston: Kluer-Nijoff.

Bangert-Downs, R. L. (1986). Review of developments in meta-analytic method. *Psychological Bulletin, 99*, 388–399.

Barbe, W. B., & Milone, M. N. (1980). Modality. *Instructor, 89*, 44–47.

Barbe, W. B., & Milone, M. N. (1981). What we know about modality strengths. *Educational Leadership, 38*, 378–380.

Barber, T. X. (1976). *Pitfalls in human research: Ten pivotal points*. New York: Pergamon.

Barkley, R. A., & Cunningham, C. E. (1978). Do stimulant drugs improve the academic performance of hyperactive children? *Clinical Pediatrics, 17*, 85–92.

Barsch, R. H. (1967). *Achieving perceptual-motor efficiency* (Vol. 1). Seattle: Special Child Publications.

Berk, R. A. (1984). An evaluation of procedures for computing an ability-achievement discrepancy score. *Journal of Learning Disabilities, 17*, 262–266.

Bickel, W. E., & Bickel, D. D. (1986). Effective schools, classrooms, and instruction: Implications for special education. *Exceptional Children, 52*(6), 489–500.

Bos, C. S., & Vaughn, S. (1994). *Strategies for teaching students with learning and behavior problems* (3rd ed.). Boston: Allyn & Bacon.

Brodbeck, M. (1962). Explanation, prediction, and "imperfect" knowledge. In H. Feigl and G. Maxwell (Eds.), *Minnesota studies in the philosophy of science* (Vol. 3). Minneapolis: University of Minnesota Press.

Brophy, J. E. (1982). How teachers influence what is taught and learned in classrooms. *The Elementary School Journal, 83,* 1–13.

Brophy, J. E., & Good, T. L. (1986). Teacher behavior and student achievement. In M. C. Wittrock (Ed.), *Handbook of research on teaching* (3rd ed., pp. 328–375). New York: Macmillan.

Bryan, T. (1991). Social problems and learning disabilities. In B. Y. L. Wong (Ed.), *Learning about learning disabilities* (pp. 195–229). San Diego: Academic Press.

Burstein, L., & Guiton, G. W. (1984). Methodological perspectives on documenting program impact. In B. K. Keogh (Ed.), *Advances in special education* (Vol. 4, pp. 21–42). Greenwich, CT: JAI Press.

Bush, W. J., & Giles, M. T. (1977). *Aids to psycholinguistic teaching* (2nd ed.). Columbus, OH: Merrill.

Campbell, D. T. (1969). Reforms as experiments. *American Psychologist, 24,* 409–429.

Campbell, D. T., & Stanley, J. C. (1966). *Experimental and quasi-experimental designs for research.* Chicago: Rand McNally.

Cantwell, D. P., & Carlson, G. A. (1978). Stimulants. In J. S. Werry (Ed.), *Pediatric psychopharmacology: The use of behavior modifying drugs in children* (pp. 171–207). New York: Brunner/Mazel.

Carbo, M. (1983). Research in reading and learning style: Implications for exceptional children. *Exceptional Children, 49,* 486–494.

Carbo, M. (1992). Giving unequal learners an equal chance: A reply to a biased critique of learning styles. *Remedial and Special Education, 13,* 19–29.

Carlberg, C., & Kavale, K. (1980). The efficacy of special versus regular class placement for exceptional children: A meta-analysis. *Journal of Special Education, 14,* 295–309.

Carnine, D. (1987). A response to "False standards, a distorting and disintegrating effect on education, turning away from useful purposes, being inevitably unfulfilled, and remaining unrealistic and irrelevant." *Remedial and Special Education, 8*(1), 42–43.

Carver, R. P. (1978). The case against statistical significant testing. *Harvard Educational Review, 48,* 378–399.

Cegelka, W. J., & Tyler, J. L. (1970). The efficacy of special class placement for the mentally retarded in proper perspective. *Training School Bulletin, 67,* 33–68.

Chapman, J. W. (1988). Learning disabled children's self-concepts. *Review of Educational Research, 58,* 347–371.

Christenson, S. L., Ysseldyke, J. E., & Thurlow, M. L. (1989). Critical instructional factors for students with mild handicaps: An integrative review. *Remedial and Special Education, 10,* 21–31.

Christopolos, F., & Renz, P. (1969). A critical examination of special education programs. *Journal of Special Education, 3,* 371–379.

Cohen, H. J., Birch, H. G., & Taft, L. T. (1970). Some considerations for evaluating the Doman-Delacato "patterning" method. *Pediatrics, 45,* 302–314.

Cohen, J. (1977). *Statistical power analysis for the behavioral sciences* (rev. ed.). New York: Academic Press.

Cohen, S. A. (1987). Instructional alignment: Searching for the magic bullet. *Educational Researcher, 16,* 16–20.

Cook, T. D., & Campbell, D. T. (1979). *Quasi-experimentation: Design and analysis for field settings.* Chicago: Rand McNally.

Council for Learning Disabilities. (1986). Measurement and training of perceptual and perceptual-motor functions: A position statement. *Learning Disability Quarterly, 9,* 247.

Cronbach, L. J. (1982). *Designing evaluations of educational and social programs.* San Francisco: Jossey-Bass.

Cronbach, L. J., & Snow, R. E. (1977). *Aptitudes and instructional methods: A handbook for research on interactions.* New York: Irvington.

Cronbach, L. J., & Suppes, P. (1969). *Research for tomorrow's schools: Disciplined inquiry for education.* New York: Macmillan.

Delacato, C. H. (1959). *The treatment and prevention of reading problems: The neurological approach.* Springfield, IL: Thomas.

Delacato, C. H. (1966). *Neurological organization and reading.* Springfield, IL: Thomas.

Denham, C., & Lieberman, A. (Ed.). (1980). *Time to learn.* Washington, DC: National Institute of Education.

Deno, E. (1970). Special education as developmental capital. *Exceptional Children, 37,* 229–237.

Deno, E. (1973). *Instructional alternatives for exceptional children.* Reston, VA: Council for Exceptional Children.

Donmoyer, R. (1985). The rescue from relativism: Two failed attempts and an alternative strategy. *Educational Researcher, 14,* 13–20.

Doyle, W. (1978). Paradigms for research on teacher effectiveness. In L. S. Shulman (Ed.), *Review of research in education, 5,* 163–197.

Dudley-Marling, C. C., & Edmiaston, R. (1985). Social status of learning disabled children and adolescents: A review. *Learning Disability Quarterly, 8,* 189–204.

Dunkin, M. J., & Biddle, B. J. (1974). *The study of teaching.* New York: Holt, Rinehart & Winston.

Dunn, L. M. (1968). Special education for the mildly retarded—Is much of it justifiable? *Exceptional Children, 35,* 5–22.

Dunn, L. M., & Smith, J. O. (1967). *Peabody Language Development Kits.* Circle Pines, MN: American Guidance Service.

Dunn, R. S. (1979). Learning—A matter of style. *Educational Leadership, 36,* 430–432.

Dunn, R. S. (1990). Bias over substance: A critical analysis of Kavale and Forness' report on modality-based instruction. *Exceptional Children, 56,* 352–356.

Dunn, R. S., & Dunn, K. J. (1978). *Teaching students through their individual learning styles.* Englewood Cliffs, NJ: Prentice-Hall.

Dunn, R. S., Dunn, K. J., & Price, G. E. (1979). *Learning style inventory.* Lawrence, KS: Price Systems.

Eisner, E. W. (1979). *The educational imagination.* New York: Macmillan.

Eisner, E. W. (1983). Anastasia might still be alive, but the monarchy is dead. *Educational Researcher, 12,* 13–24.

Elliott, S. N., & Gresham, E. M. (1991). *Social skills intervention guide.* Circle Pines, MN: American Guidance Service.

Ellis, E. S., Lenz, B. K., & Sabornie, E. J. (1987). Generalization and adaptation of learning strategies to natural environments: Part I: Critical agents. *Remedial and Special Education, 8,* 6–20.

Englert, C. S. (1983). Measuring special education teacher effectiveness. *Exceptional Children, 50*(3), 247–254.

Englert, C. S. (1984). Effective direct instruction practice in special education settings. *Remedial and Special Education, 5,* 38–47.

Englert, C. S., Tarrant, K. L., & Mariage, T. V. (1992). Defining and redefining instructional practice in special education: Perspectives on good teaching. *Teacher Education and Special Education, 15,* 62–87.

Epps, S., & Tindal, G. (1988). The effectiveness of differential programming in serving mildly handicapped students: Placement options and instructional programming. In M. Wang, M. Reynolds, & H. Walberg (Eds.), *Handbook of special education: Research and practice* (Vol. 2, pp. 172–215). Oxford: Pergamon.

Feingold, B. F. (1976). Hyperkinesis and learning disabilities linked to the ingestion of artificial food colors and flavors. *Journal of Learning Disabilities, 9,* 551–559.

Feingold, B. F., & Feingold, H. S. (1979). *The Feingold cookbook for hyperactive children.* New York: Random House.

Fisher, C. W., & Berliner, D. C. (1985). *Perspectives on instructional time.* White Plains, NY: Longman.

Fisher, R. A. (1956). *Statistical methods and scientific inference.* New York: Hafner.

Footlik, S. W. (1971). Perceptual-motor training and cognitive achievement: A survey of the literature. *Journal of Learning Disabilities, 3,* 40–49.

Forness, S. R., & Kavale, K. A. (1987). Holistic inquiry and the scientific challenge in special education: A reply to Iano. *Remedial and Special Education, 8*(1), 47–51.

Forness, S. R., & Kavale, K. A. (1988). Psychopharmacologic treatment: A note on classroom effects. *Journal of Learning Disabilities, 21,* 144–147.

Forness, S. R., & Kavale, K. A. (1991). Social skill deficits as a primary learning disability: A note on problems with the ICLD diagnostic criteria. *Learning Disabilities Research and Practice, 6,* 44–49.

Friend, J., & McNutt, G. (1984). Resource room programs: Where are we now? *Exceptional Children, 51,* 150–155.

Fuchs, D., & Fuchs, L. S. (1994). Inclusive schools movement and the radicalization of special education reform. *Exceptional Children, 60,* 294–309.

Fuchs, L. S., & Fuchs, D. (1986). Effects of systematic formative evaluation: A meta-analysis. *Exceptional Children, 53*(3), 199–208.

Fuchs, L. S., Fuchs, D., & Deno, S. L. (1985). The importance of goal ambitiousness and goal mastery to student achievement. *Exceptional Children, 52,* 63–71.

Gadow, K. D. (1983). Effects of stimulant drugs on academic performance in hyperactive and learning disabled children. *Journal of Learning Disabilities, 16,* 290–299.

Gage, N. L. (1963). Paradigms for research on teaching. In N. L. Gage (Ed.), *Handbook of research on teaching.* Chicago: Rand McNally.

Gage, N. L. (1978). *The scientific basis of the art of teaching.* New York: Teachers College Press, Columbia University.

Garrison, J. W. (1986). Some principles of postpositivistic philosophy of science. *Educational Researcher, 15,* 12–18.

Garrison, J. W., & Macmillan, C. J. B. (1984). A philosophical critique of process-product research on teaching. *Educational Theory, 34,* 255–274.

Gergen, K. J. (1973). Social psychology as history. *Journal of Personality and Social Psychology, 26,* 309–320.

Gersten, R., Carnine, D., & Woodward, J. (1987). Direct instruction research: The third decade. *Remedial and Special Education, 8,* 48–56.

Gersten, R., & Hauser, C. (1984). The case for impact evaluations in special education. *Remedial and Special Education, 5,* 16–24.

Gersten, R., & Keating, T. (1987). Long-term benefits from direct instruction. *Educational Leadership, 44,* 28–31.

Gersten, R., Woodward, J., & Darch, C. (1986). Direct instruction: A research-based approach to curriculum design and teaching. *Exceptional Children, 53,* 17–31.

Gettinger, M. B. (1991). Learning time and retention differences between nondisabled students and students with learning disabilities. *Learning Disability Quarterly, 14,* 179–189.

Gittelman, R., & Kanner, A. (1986). Psychopharmacology. In H. Quay & J. Werry (Eds.), *Psychopathological disorders of childhood* (3rd ed.). New York: Wiley.

Glass, G. V. (1976). Primary, secondary, and meta-analysis of research. *Educational Researcher, 5*, 3–8.

Glass, G. V. (1979). Policy for the unpredictable (uncertainty research and policy). *Educational Researcher, 8*, 12–14.

Glass, G. V., McGaw, B., & Smith, M. L. (1981). *Meta-analysis in social research.* Beverly Hills, CA: Sage.

Glass, G. V., & Robbins, M. P. (1967). A critique of experiments on the role of neurological organization in reading performance. *Reading Research Quarterly, 3*, 5–51.

Glass, G. V., & Smith, M. L. (1979). Meta-analysis of research on class size and achievement. *Educational Evaluation and Policy Analysis, 1*, 2–16.

Good, T. L. (1983). Classroom research: A decade of progress. *Educational Psychologist, 18*, 127–144.

Goodman, L. (1990). *Time and learning in the special education classroom.* Albany: State University of New York Press.

Gottlieb, J., Alter, M., & Gottlieb, B. W. (1991). Mainstreaming academically handicapped children in urban schools. In J. W. Lloyd, N. N. Singh, & A. C. Repp (Eds.), *The regular education initiative: Alternative perspectives on concepts, issues, and models* (pp. 95–112). Sycamore, IL: Sycamore.

Greenwood, C. R. (1991). Longitudinal analysis of time, engagement, and achievement in at-risk versus non-risk students. *Exceptional Children, 57*, 521–534.

Gresham, F. M. (1981). Social skills training with handicapped children: A review. *Review of Educational Research, 51*, 139–176.

Gresham, F. M. (1985). Conceptual and definitional issues in the assessment of social skills: Implications for classification and training. *Journal of Clinical Child Psychology, 15*, 16–25.

Gresham, F. M. (1992). Social skills and learning disabilities: Causal, concomitant, or correlational? *School Psychology Review, 21*, 348–360.

Gresham, F. M., & Elliott, S. N. (1990). *Social skills rating system.* Circle Pines, MN: American Guidance Service.

Guskin, S. L., & Spicker, H. H. (1968). Educational research in mental retardation. In N. R. Ellis (Ed.), *International review of research in mental retardation* (Vol. 3). New York: Academic Press.

Haertel, G. D., Walberg, H. J., & Weinstein, T. (1983). Psychological models of educational performance: A theoretical synthesis of constructs. *Review of Educational Research, 53*, 75–92.

Hagin, R. A. (1973). Models of intervention with learning disabilities: Ephemeral and otherwise. *School Psychology Monograph, 1*, 1–24.

Hallahan, D. P., & Cruickshank, W. M. (1973). *Psychoeducational foundations of learning disabilities.* Englewood Cliffs, NJ: Prentice Hall.

Hallahan, D. P., & Kauffman, J. M. (1977). Labels, categories, behaviors: ED, LD, and EMR reconsidered. *The Journal of Special Education, 11*, 139–149.

Hallahan, D. P., Keller, C. E., McKinney, J. D., Lloyd, J. W., & Bryan, T. (1988). Examining the research base of the regular education initiative: Efficacy studies and the adaptive learning environments model. *Journal of Learning Disabilities, 21*, 29–35.

Hammill, D. D., Goodman, L., & Weiderholt, J. L. (1974). Visual-motor processes: Can we train them? *Reading Teacher, 27*, 469–478.

Hammill, D. D., & Larsen, S. C. (1974). The effectiveness of psycholinguistic training. *Exceptional Children, 41*, 5–14.

Hammill, D. D., & Larsen, S. C. (1978). The effectiveness of psycholinguistic training: A reaffirmation of position. *Exceptional Children, 44*, 402–414.

Hammill, D. D., & Wiederholt, J. L. (1972). *The resource room: Rationale and implementation.* Philadelphia: JSE Press.

Haynes, M. C., & Jenkins, J. R. (1986). Reading instruction in special education resource rooms. *American Educational Research Journal, 23*, 161–190.

Hazel, J. S., Schumaker, J. B., Sherman, J. A., & Sheldon-Wildgen, J. (1981). *ASSET: A social skills program for adolescents.* Champaign, IL: Research Press.

Hedges, L. V., & Olkin, I. (1985). *Statistical methods for meta-analysis.* New York: Academic Press.

Heller, K. A., Holtzman, W. H., & Messick, S. (1982). *Placing children in special education: A strategy for equity.* Washington, DC: National Academy Press.

Heshusius, L. (1982). At the heart of the advocacy dilemma: A mechanistic word view. *Exceptional Children, 49*, 6–13.

Heshusius, L. (1986). Paradigm shifts and special education: A response to Ulman and Rosenberg. *Exceptional Children, 52*, 461–465.

Howe, K. (1985). Two dogmas of educational research. *Educational Researcher, 14*, 10–18.

Hughes, J. N., & Sullivan, K. A. (1988). Outcome assessment in social skills training with children. *Journal of School Psychology, 26*, 167–183.

Hunter, J. E., Schmidt, F. L., & Jackson, G. B. (1982). *Meta-analysis: Cumulating research findings across studies.* Beverly Hills, CA: Sage.

Iano, R. P. (1986). The study and development of teaching: With implications for the advancement of special education. *Remedial and Special Education, 7*(5), 50–61.

Iano, R. P. (1987). Rebuttal: Neither the absolute certainty of prescriptive law nor a surrender to mysticism. *Remedial and Special Education, 8*(1), 52–61.

Itard, J.-M.-G. (1962). *The wild boy of Aveyron.* (G. & M. Humphrey, Trans.). New York: Appleton-Century-Crofts. (Originally published in 1806).

Jackson, G. B. (1980). Methods for integrative reviews. *Review of Educational Research, 50,* 438–460.

Jenkins, J. R., & Pany, D. (1978). Standardized achievement tests: How useful for special education? *Exceptional Children, 44,* 448–453.

Joyce, B., & Weil, M. (1972). *Models of teaching.* Englewood Cliffs, NJ: Prentice Hall.

Kameenui, E. J., & Simmons, D. C. (1990). *Designing instructional strategies: The prevention of academic learning problems.* Columbus, OH: Merrill.

Kaplan, A. (1964). *The conduct of inquiry.* San Francisco: Chandler.

Kauffman, J. M. (1993). How we might achieve the radical reform of special education. *Exceptional Children, 60,* 6–16.

Kaufman, M. E., & Alberto, P. A. (1976). Research on efficacy of special education for the mentally retarded. In N. R. Ellis (Ed.), *International review of research in mental retardation* (Vol. 8, pp. 225–255). New York: Academic Press.

Kavale, K. A. (1979). Mainstreaming: The genesis of an idea. *The Exceptional Child, 26,* 3–21.

Kavale, K. A. (1981). Functions of the Illinois Test of Psycholinguistic Abilities (ITPA): Are they trainable? *Exceptional Children, 47,* 496–510.

Kavale, K. A.. (1982a). The efficacy of stimulant drug treatment for hyperactivity: A meta-analysis. *Journal of Learning Disabilities, 15,* 280–289.

Kavale, K. A. (1982b). Psycholinguistic training programs: Are there differential treatment effects? *The Exceptional Child, 29,* 21–30.

Kavale, K. A. (1984). Potential advantages of the meta-analysis technique for research in special education. *Journal of Special Education, 18,* 61–72.

Kavale, K. A., & Forness, S. R. (1983). Hyperactivity and diet treatment: A meta-analysis of the Feingold hypothesis. *Journal of Learning Disabilities, 16,* 324–330.

Kavale, K. A., & Forness, S. R. (1987). Substance over style: Assessing the efficacy of modality testing and teaching. *Exceptional Children, 54,* 228–234.

Kavale, K. A., & Forness, S. R. (1990). Substance over style: A rejoinder to Dunn's animadversions. *Exceptional Children, 56,* 357–361.

Kavale, K. A., & Forness, S. R. (1994). Models and theories: Their influence on research in learning disabilities. In S. Vaughn & C. Bos (Eds.), *Research issues in learning disabilities: Theory, methodology, assessment, and ethics* (pp. 38–65). New York: Springer-Verlag.

Kavale, K. A., & Forness, S. R. (1995). Social skill deficits and training: A meta-analysis of the research in learning disabilities. In T. E. Scruggs & M. A. Mastropieri (Eds.), *Advances in learning and behavioral disabilities* (Vol. 9, pp. 119–160). Greenwich, CT: JAI Press.

Kavale, K. A., & Mattson, P. D. (1983). One jumped off the balance beam: Meta-analysis of perceptual-motor training. *Journal of Learning Disabilities, 16,* 165–173.

Kavale, K. A., & Reese, J. H. (1991). Teacher beliefs and perceptions about learning disabilities: A survey of Iowa practitioners. *Learning Disability Quarterly, 14,* 141–160.

Kephart, N. C. (1972). On the value of empirical data in learning disability. *Journal of Learning Disabilities, 4,* 393–395.

Kimball, W. H., & Heron, T. E. (1988). A behavioral commentary on Poplin's discussion of reductionistic fallacy and holistic/constructivist principles. *Journal of Learning Disabilities, 21,* 425–428.

Kirk, S. A. (1964). Research in education. In H. A. Stevens & R. Heber (Eds.), *Mental retardation: A review of research.* Chicago: University of Chicago Press.

Kirk, S. A., & Kirk, W. D. (1971). *Psycholinguistic learning disabilities: Diagnosis and remediation.* Urbana: University of Illinois Press.

Kirk, S. A., McCarthy, J. J., & Kirk, W. D. (1968). *The Illinois Test of Psycholinguistic Abilities* (rev. ed.). Urbana: University of Illinois Press.

Labouvie, E. W. (1975). The dialectical nature of measurement activities in the behavioral sciences. *Human Development, 18,* 205–222.

LaGreca, A. M. (1987). Children with learning disabilities: Interpersonal skills and social competence. *Journal of Reading, Writing, and Learning Disabilities International, 3,* 167–185.

LaGreca, A. M., & Vaughn, S. (1992). Social functioning of individuals with learning disabilities. *School Psychology Review, 21,* 340–347.

Larrivee, B. (1981). Modality preference as a model for differentiating beginning reading instruction: A review of the issues. *Learning Disability Quarterly, 4,* 180–188.

Larrivee, B. (1986). Effective teaching for mainstreamed students is effective teaching for all students. *Teacher Education and Special Education, 9,* 173–179.

Larsen, S. C., Parker, R. M., & Hammill, D. D. (1982). Effectiveness of psycholinguistic training: A response to Kavale. *Exceptional Children, 49*(1), 60–66.

Leinhardt, G., & Pallay, A. (1982). Restrictive educational settings: Exile or haven? *Review of Educational Research, 52,* 557–578.

Leinhardt, G., Zigmond, N., & Cooley, W. W. (1981). Reading instruction and its effects. *American Educational Research Journal, 18,* 343–361.

Lew, F. (1977). The Feingold diet, experienced (letter). *Medical Journal of Australia, 1,* 190.

Licht, B. G. (1983). Cognitive-motivational factors

that contribute to the achievement of learning disabled children. *Journal of Learning Disabilities, 16*, 483–490.

Licht, B. G., & Torgesen, J. K. (1989). Natural science approaches to questions of subjectivity. *Journal of Learning Disabilities, 22*, 418–419.

Lindblom, C. E., & Cohen, D. K. (1979). *Usable knowledge: Social science and social problem solving.* New Haven, CT: Yale University Press.

Lloyd, J. W. (1984). How shall we individualize instruction—Or should we? *Remedial and Special Education, 5*(1), 7–15.

Lloyd, J. W. (1987). The art and science of research on teaching. *Remedial and Special Education, 8*(1), 44–46.

Lovitt, T. C. (1984). *Tactics for teaching.* New York: Merrill/Macmillan.

Lund, K. A., Foster, G. E., & McCall-Perez, G. C. (1978). The effectiveness of psycholinguistic training: A reevaluation. *Exceptional Children, 44*, 310–319.

Maag, J. W. (1989). Assessment in social skills training: Methodological and conceptual issues for research and practice. *Remedial and Special Education, 53*, 519–569.

Mackenzie, D. E. (1983). Research for school improvement: An appraisal of some recent trends. *Educational Researcher, 12*(4), 5–17.

Macmillan, C. J. B., & Garrison, J. W. (1984). Using the "new philosophy of science" in criticizing current research traditions in education. *Educational Researcher, 13*, 15–21.

MacMillan, D. L. (1971). Special education for the mildly retarded: Servant or savant? *Focus on Exceptional Children, 2*, 1–11.

MacMillan, D. L., & Hendrick, I. G. (1993). Evolution and legacies. In J. I. Goodlad & T. C. Lovitt (Eds.), *Integrating general and special education* (pp. 23–48). Columbus, OH: Merrill/Macmillan.

Maher, C. A., & Bennett, R. E. (1984). *Planning and evaluating special education services.* Englewood Cliffs, NJ: Prentice Hall.

Mann, L. (1970). Perceptual training: Misdirections and redirections. *American Journal of Orthopsychiatry, 40*, 30–38.

Mann, L. (1971a). Perceptual training revisited: The training of nothing at all. *Rehabilitation Literature, 32*, 322–327, 335.

Mann, L. (1971b). Psychometric phrenology and the new faculty psychology: The case against ability assessment and training. *Journal of Special Education, 5*, 3–14.

Mann, L. (1979). *On the trail of process.* New York: Grune & Stratton.

Mann, L., & Phillips, W. A. (1967). Fractional practices in special education: A critique. *Exceptional Children, 33*(4), 311–317.

Mastropieri, M. A., & Scruggs, T. E. (1989). Constructing more meaningful relationships: Mnemonic instruction for special populations. *Educational Psychology Review, 1*, 83–111.

Mastropieri, M. A., & Scruggs, T. E. (1994). *Effective instruction for special education* (2nd ed.). Austin, TX: Pro-Ed.

Mattes, J. A. (1983). The Feingold diet: A current reappraisal. *Journal of Learning Disabilities, 16*, 319–323.

McGinnis, E., Goldstein, A., Sprafkin, R., & Gershaw, N. (1984). *Skill streaming the elementary school child: A guide for teaching prosocial skills.* Champaign, IL: Research Press.

McGrath, J. E., Martin, J., & Kulka, R. A. (1982). *Judgment calls in research.* Beverly Hills, CA: Sage.

McIntosh, R., Vaughn, S., & Zaragoza, N. (1991). A review of social interventions for students with learning disabilities. *Journal of Learning Disabilities, 24*, 451–458.

McLoughlin, J. A., & Kelly, D. (1982). Issues facing the resource teacher. *Learning Disability Quarterly, 5*, 58–64.

Medley, D. M. (1982). Teacher effectiveness. In H. E. Mitzel (Ed.), *Encyclopedia of educational research* (5th ed., pp. 1894–1903). New York: Free Press.

Meyers, C. E., MacMillan, D. L., & Yoshida, R. K. (1980). Regular class education of EMR students, from efficacy to mainstreaming: A review of issues and research. In J. Gottlieb (Ed.), *Educating mentally retarded persons in the mainstream.* Baltimore, MD: University Park Press.

Minskoff, E. (1975). Research on psycholinguistic training: Critique and guidelines. *Exceptional Children, 42*, 136–144.

Mitroff, I. I., & Featheringham, T. R. (1974). On systematic problem solving and the error of the third kind. *Behavioral Science, 19*, 383–393.

Morrison, D. E., & Henkel, R. E. (Eds.). (1970). *The significance test controversy: A reader.* Chicago: Aldine.

Morsink, C. V., Soar, R. S., Soar, R. M., & Thomas, R. (1986). Research on teaching: Opening the door to special education classrooms. *Exceptional Children, 53*(1), 32–40.

Nelson, C. M., & Polsgrove, L. (1984). Behavior analysis in special education: White rabbit or white elephant. *Remedial and Special Education, 5*, 6–15.

Newcomer, P., Larsen, S., & Hammill, D. (1975). A response. *Exceptional Children, 42*, 144–148.

O'Leary, K. D. (1980). Pills or skills for hyperactive children. *Journal of Applied Behavior Analysis, 13*, 191–204.

Osgood, C. E. (1957). Motivational dynamics of language behavior. In M. R. Jones (Ed.), *Nebraska symposium on motivation.* Lincoln: University of Nebraska Press.

Pearl, R. (1987). Social cognitive factors in learning-disabled children's social problems. In S. J. Ceci (Ed.), *Handbook of cognitive, social, and neuropsychological aspects of learning disabilities* (pp. 273–294). Hillsdale, NJ: Erlbaum.

Pearl, R. (1992). Psychosocial characteristics of learning disabled students. In N. N. Singh & I. L. Beale (Eds.), *Learning disabilities: Nature, theory, and treatment* (pp. 96–125). San Diego: Academic Press.

Pelham, W. E. (1986). The effects of psychostimulant drugs on learning and academic achievement in children with attention-deficit disorders and learning disabilities. In J. Torgesen & B. Wong (Eds.), *Psychological and educational perspectives on learning disabilities* (pp. 160–168). New York: Academic Press.

Peter, L. J. (1965). *Prescriptive teaching*. New York: McGraw-Hill.

Peterson, P. L., & Walberg, H. J. (Eds.). (1979). *Research on teaching: Concepts, findings, and implications*. Berkeley, CA: McCutchan.

Phillips, D. C. (1980). What do the researcher and the practitioner have to offer each other? *Educational Researcher, 9*, 17–20, 24.

Phillips, D. (1983). After the wake: Post positivistic educational thought. *Educational Researcher, 12*, 4–12.

Polloway, E. A. (1984). The integration of mildly retarded students in the schools: A historical review. *Remedial and Special Education, 5*, 18–28.

Poplin, M. S. (1988a). Holistic/constructivist principles of the teaching/learning process: Implications for the field of learning disabilities. *Journal of Learning Disabilities, 21*, 389–400.

Poplin, M. S. (1988b). The reductionistic fallacy in learning disabilities: Replicating the past by reducing the present. *Journal of Learning Disabilities, 21*, 401–416.

Pray, B. S., Hall, C. W., & Markley, R. P. (1992). Social skills training: An analysis of social behaviors selected for individualized education programs. *Remedial and Special Education, 13*, 43–49.

Pressley, M., & Harris, K. R. (1990). What we really know about strategy instruction. *Educational Leadership, 48*, 31–34.

Purkey, S. C., & Smith, M. S. (1983). Effective schools: A review. *Elementary School Journal, 83*, 427–452.

Reger, R. (1973). What is a resource room program? *Journal of Learning Disabilities, 6*, 607–614.

Reith, H. J., & Evertson, C. (1988). Variables related to the effective instruction of difficult-to-teach children. *Focus on Exceptional Children, 20*, 1–8.

Reynolds, M. C., Wang, M. C., & Walberg, H. J. (1987). The necessary restructuring of special and regular education. *Exceptional Children, 53*, 391–398.

Reynolds, M. C., Wang, M. C., & Walberg, H. J. (1992). The knowledge bases for special and general education. *Remedial and Special Education, 13*, 6–10, 33.

Rimland, B. (1983). The Feingold diet: An assessment of the reviews by Mattes, by Kavale and Forness and others. *Journal of Learning Disabilities, 16*, 331–333.

Rosenberg, M. S., & Jackson, L. (1988). Theoretical models and special education: The impact of varying world views on service delivery and research. *Remedial and Special Education, 9*, 26–34.

Rosenthal, R. (1984). *Meta-analytic procedures for social research*. Beverly Hills, CA: Sage.

Rosenthal, R., & Jacobson, L. (1968). *Pygmalion in the classroom*. New York: Holt, Rinehart & Winston.

Rosenthal, R., & Rugin, D. D. (1978). Interpersonal expectancy effects: The first 345 studies. *The Behavioral and Brain Sciences, 3*, 377–415.

Samuels, S. J. (1986). Why children fail to learn and what to do about it. *Exceptional Children, 53*(1), 7–16.

Schrag, P., & Divoky, D. (1975). *The myth of the hyperactive child*. New York: Pantheon.

Schumaker, J. B., & Hazel, J. S. (1988). Social skills and learning disabilities: Current issues and recommendations for future research. In J. Kavanagh & T. Truss (Eds.), *Learning disabilities: Proceedings of the national conference* (pp. 293–344). Parkton, MD: York Press.

Scruggs, T. E. (1988). Nature of learning disabilities. In K. A. Kavale (Ed.), *Learning disabilities: State of the art and practice* (pp. 22–43). Boston: Little, Brown/College-Hill Press.

Sheehan, R., & Keogh, B. K. (1984). Approaches to evaluation in special education. In B. K. Keogh (Ed.), *Advances in special education* (Vol. 4, pp. 1–20). Greenwich, CT: JAI Press.

Sheridan, J. J., & Meister, K. A. (1982). *Food additives and hyperactivity*. New York: American Council on Science and Health.

Sindelar, P. T., & Deno, S. L. (1978). The effectiveness of resource programming. *The Journal of Special Education, 12*, 17–28.

Skipper, J. K., Guenther, A. L., & Nass, G. (1967). The sacredness of .05: A note concerning the uses of statistical levels of significance in social science. *The American Sociologist, 2*, 16–18.

Slavin, R. (1984). Meta-analysis in education. How has it been used? *Educational Researcher, 13*, 6–15.

Slavin, R. E., & Madden, N. A. (1989). What works for students at risk: A research synthesis. *Educational Leadership, 46*, 1–8.

Smart, J. C., & Elton, C. F. (1981). Structural characteristics and citation rates of education journals. *American Educational Research Journal, 18*, 399–414.

Smead, V. S. (1977). Ability training and task analysis in diagnostic-prescriptive teaching. *Journal of Special Education, 11*, 113–125.

Smith, B. C., & West, R. P. (1986). Assessing best practices. *The Special Educator, 7*, 6–8.

Snider, V. E. (1992a). Learning styles and learning to read: A critique. *Remedial and Special Education, 13*, 6–18.

Snider, V. E. (1992b). Unscientific documentation and philosophical issues: A rejoinder to Carbo. *Remedial and Special Education, 13*, 30–33.

Soltis, J. (1984). On the nature of educational research. *Educational Researcher, 13*, 5–10.

Speece, D. L., & Mandell, C. J. (1980). Resource room support services for regular teachers. *Learning Disability Quarterly, 3*, 49–53.

Sprague, R. L., & Werry, J. S. (1971). Methodology of psychopharmacological studies with the retarded. In M. R. Ellis (Ed.), *International review of research in mental retardation* (Vol. 5). New York: Academic Press.

Squires, D. (1983). *Effective schools and classrooms: Research-based perspective.* Alexandria, VA: Association for Supervision and Curriculum Development.

Sroufe, L. A. (1975). Drug treatment of children with behavior problems. In F. J. Horowitz (Ed.), *Review of Child Development Research* (Vol. 4). Chicago: University of Chicago Press.

Sternberg, L., & Taylor, R. L. (1982). The insignificance of psycholinguistic training: A reply to Kavale. *Exceptional Children, 49*(3), 254–256.

Stevens, R., & Rosenshine, B. (1981). Advances in research on teaching. *Exceptional Education Quarterly, 2*, 1–9.

Swanson, H. L. (1984). Does theory guide practice? *Remedial and Special Education, 5*(5), 7–16.

Swanson, H. L. (1988). Toward a metatheory of learning disabilities. *Journal of Learning Disabilities, 21*, 196–209.

Talmage, H. (Ed.). (1975). *Systems of individualized education.* Berkeley, CA: McCutchan.

Tarver, S. G., & Dawson, M. M. (1978). Modality preference and the teaching of reading: A review. *Journal of Learning Disabilities, 11*, 5–17.

Tindal, G. (1985). Investigating the effectiveness of special education: An analysis of methodology. *Journal of Learning Disabilities, 18*(2), 101–112.

Torgesen, J. K. (1982). The learning disabled child as an inactive learner: Educational implications. *Topics in Learning and Learning Disabilities, 2*, 45–52.

Ulman, J. D., & Rosenberg, M. S. (1986). Science and superstition in special education. *Exceptional Children, 52*, 459–460.

U.S. Department of Education. (1992). *IDEA Regulations, 34*, CFR 300.552.

Utah Special Education Consortium Evaluation Task Force. (1986). Critical questions for the evaluation of a special education program. *The Special Educator, 7*, 3–4.

Van Witsen, B. (1967). *Perceptual training activities handbook.* New York: Teachers College Press.

Vaughn, S. (1991). Social skills enhancement in students with learning disabilities. In B. Y. L. Wong (Ed.), *Learning about learning disabilities* (pp. 407–440). San Diego: Academic Press.

Vaughn, S., & Haager, D. (1994). Social assessments of students with learning disabilities: Do they measure up? In S. Vaughn & C. Bos (Eds.), *Research issues in learning disabilities: Theory, methodology, assessment, and ethics* (pp. 276–311). New York: Springer-Verlag.

Vaughn, S. R., & Hogan, A. (1994). The social competence of students with learning disabilities over time: A within-individual examination. *Journal of Learning Disabilities, 27*, 292–303.

Vaughn, S. R., & LaGreca, A. M. (1988). Social interventions for learning disabilities. In K. A. Kavale (Ed.), *Learning disabilities: State of the art and practice* (pp. 123–140). Boston: Little, Brown/College-Hill Press.

Vaughn, S., Levine, L., & Ridley, C. (1986). *PALS: Problem-solving and affective learning strategies.* Chicago: Science Research Associates.

Vogel, S., & Forness, S. R. (1992). Social functioning in adults with learning disabilities. *School Psychology Review, 21*, 375–386.

Walberg, H. J. (1984). Improving the productivity of America's schools. *Educational Leadership, 41*, 19–30.

Walker, H. M., & McConnell, S. (1988). *Walker-McConnell Scale of Social Competence and School Adjustment.* Austin, TX: Pro-Ed.

Walker, H. M., McConnell, S., Holmes, D., Todis, B., Walker, J., & Golden, N. (1983). *The Walker social skills curriculum: The ACCEPTS Program.* Austin, TX: Pro-Ed.

Walker, H. M., Street, A., Garrett, B., Crossen, J., Hops, H., & Greenwood, C. R. (1978). RECESS (Reprogramming environmental contingencies for effective social skills): Manual for consultants. Unpublished manuscript, Center for Behavioral Education of the Handicapped, University of Oregon, Eugene.

Wang, M. C. (1987). Toward achieving educational excellence for all students: Program design and instructional outcomes. *Remedial and Special Education, 8*, 25–34.

Wang, M. C., & Baker, E. T. (1985–1986). Mainstreaming programs: Design features and effects. *The Journal of Special Education, 19*, 503–521.

Waxman, H. C., & Walberg, H. J. (1982). The relation of teaching and learning: A review of reviews of process-product research. *Contemporary Education Review, 1*, 103–120.

Waxman, H. C., Wang, M. C., Anderson, K. A., & Walberg, H. J. (1985). Adaptive education and student outcomes: A quantitative synthesis. *Journal of Educational Research, 78*, 228–236.

Weil, M. L., & Murphy, J. (1982). Instructional processes. In H. E. Mitzel (Ed.), *Encyclopedia of educational research* (5th ed., pp. 890–917). New York: Free Press.

Wender, E. H. (1977). Food additives and hyperkinesis. *American Journal of Diseases of Children, 131*, 1204–1206.

White, W. A. T. (1988). A meta-analysis of effects of direct instruction in special education. *Education and Treatment of Children, 11*, 364–374.

Wiederholt, J. L., & Chamberlain, S. P. (1989). A critical analysis of research programs. *Remedial and Special Education, 10*, 15–37.

Wiederholt, J. L., Hammill, D. D., & Brown, V. (1978). *The resource teacher*. Boston: Allyn & Bacon.

Wilson, R. (1987). Direct observation of academic learning time. *Teaching Exceptional Children, 19*, 13–17.

Wilson, R., & Wesson, C. (1986). Making every minute count: Academic learning time in LD classrooms. *Learning Disabilities Focus, 2*, 13–19.

Wolf, F. M. (1986). *Meta-analysis: Quantitative methods for research synthesis*. Beverly Hills, CA: Sage.

Ysseldyke, J. E. (1973). Diagnostic-prescriptive teaching: The search for aptitude-treatment interactions. In L. Mann & D. Sabatino (Eds.), *The first review of special education*. Philadelphia: JSE Press.

Ysseldyke, J. E., & Salvia, J. (1974). Diagnostic-prescriptive teaching: Two models. *Exceptional Children, 41*, 181–185.

Ysseldyke, J. E., & Salvia, J. (1980). Methodological considerations in aptitude-treatment interaction research with intact groups. *Diagnostique, 6*, 3–9.

Ysseldyke, J. E., Thurlow, M. L., Christenson, S. L., & Weiss, J. (1987). Time allocated to instruction of mentally retarded, learning disabled, emotionally disturbed, and nonhandicapped elementary students. *The Journal of Special Education, 21*, 43–55.

Zaragoza, N., Vaughn, S., McIntosh, R. (1991). Social skills interventions and children with behavior problems: A review. *Behavioral Disorders, 16*, 260–275.

## CHAPTER 38

# WORKING WITH TEAMS IN THE SCHOOL

SYLVIA ROSENFIELD
*University of Maryland, College Park*
TODD A. GRAVOIS
*Howard County (MD) Public Schools*

The educational literature, especially that of the last several years, is replete with innovations, ideas, and advice for educational change and reform. Numerous individual structural changes, many accompanied by a substantial research base, have been presented as potential answers to the ills of education. This is not surprising, given educational reformers' emphasis on restructuring. According to Elmore (1995), structural change occupies a highly visible place in school reform: "It has high symbolic value, it is relatively easy to do, and it is consistent with deeply held beliefs among reformers and practitioners about what people think is wrong with schools" (p. 24). However, the importance of understanding what a structure can and cannot do and how to build quality into any given structure are critical elements of successful change.

One innovation involving structural change has been the increased reliance on teams in schools. However, introducing quality teams into the culture of schools, particularly those in which the norms of isolation and lack of collaboration have been dominant, "requires extensive investment and support—investment in the form of training and facilitation and support as the responsibility of management to remove the barriers to success from the team's path" (Arcaro, 1995, p. vii).

A functional team has at the minimum the following requirements: "(a) a group of two or more people, (b) a shared sense of purpose or purposes among the group members, and (c) interactions among the members that make them able to accomplish more than each would be able to accomplish working individually toward the shared purpose" (Platt, 1994, p. 4). These interactions include both processes that are internal and those that connect the team to the external world. As Platt suggests, these processes require considerable work and the commitment of team members.

Support for the use of teams in schools is not universal, however, and their effectiveness in practice has been questioned. The criticism of teams is captured, in part, in a letter to the *Communique*, the newsletter of the National Association of School Psychologists:

> The concept of the pre-referral team was/is one of the most ill-conceived concepts fostered on public education in the past 15 years. . . . It would be a great service to our profession to expose the massive loss of efficiency . . . being promoted in the public schools.
>
> I would suggest . . . a survey study . . . to find out what is happening in the field versus the glowing reports coming from University researchers. (Book, 1995, p. 19)

This chapter addresses the multiple issues concerning an organizational structure that has been characterized as everything from an important contributor to school problem solving to a colossal waste of time. To explore teaming, we begin with the assumptions underlying the use of teams, followed by a brief historical perspective on the development of teams in educational settings. We describe the factors involved in developing effective teams and the research base supporting one type of team that is becoming more popular with special service providers—the pre-referral or support team. Finally, we discuss the issues involved in implementing teams.

## WHY TEAMS?

Although there are considerable difficulties inherent in building functional teams, there are at least two basic reasons for their creation: (1) they are mandated for certain specified functions, such as the multidisciplinary teams created by special education law and regulation, and/or (2) it is believed that "an issue, problem, function, or situation may be such that a team will work better than an individual or a bunch of individuals" (Platt, 1994, p. 5). Both of these rationales operate in the educational arena, which has, over the latter half of this century, coped with a growing array of problems and populations in an era of increasing professional specialization.

The multiplication of teams has been fueled, thus, by "the acceleration of professional specialization and fragmentation . . . increases in size and complexity of service organizations, and broadened conceptions of the interrelated nature of human problems and the need for comprehensive professional approaches" (Billups, 1987, p. 146). Even within a single school, professional specialization and increased size have created a lack of community. For example, in the large American high school, the primary community is often the subject area department, described as "sturdy, micro-political organizations" (Wasley, 1994, p. 181). Yet in her study of the high school teachers involved in the Coalition of Essential Schools (CES), Wasley found,

> Although the Coalition makes no recommendations about teaming, it is perhaps the single most common strategy adopted by CES schools nationwide. . . . Although . . . individual work may be more creatively compelling, these teachers made choices that suggest that collaborative work provides more benefits for both students and teachers. They indicate that working collaboratively enables teachers to strengthen support for children while fostering their own professional growth. (pp. 182–183)

The high school teachers in Wasley's study indicated that teams help them in a variety of specific ways: reducing isolation, building opportunities for professional development, improving curriculum, and gaining greater flexibility in the use of time.

The issue of specialization has been addressed through differing types of team structures, that is, multidisciplinary, transdisciplinary, and interdisciplinary teams. These terms refer to the composition of a team in which members of a variety of professional roles work collaboratively toward a common goal. In education this may include teams made up of classroom teachers, reading specialists, psychologists and administrators. The rationale for multidisciplinary teams is the idea that professionals from a variety of disciplines can make better decisions than individuals working alone (Fuchs & Fuchs, 1989; Huebner & Hahn, 1990). Multidisciplinary teams consist of members of "more than one profession . . . interested in a particular problem" (Harbaugh, 1994, p. 19), but the type of interaction is not specified. Transprofessional teams are those in which the members, who may differ in profession, are willing to blur the distinctions among their roles to get the work done. However, most often human services professionals try to develop interdisciplinary teams, which involve "intention, mutual respect, and commitment, for the sake of a more adequate response to a human problem" (p. 20), breaking through but not blurring the distinctiveness of the professional roles. The interdisciplinary team, at its best, is intended not only to assist individuals in their needs but also to identify "macro issues that require collaborative strategies for prevention, early detection, or intervention at the systemic or societal level" (p. 20).

But while professional specialization creates an increased need for collaborative structures, it also intensifies the problem of developing functional teams. According to Frank (as cited in Billups, 1987, p. 146) greater attention is required to bring together individuals with differing conceptions "of human nature, of human conduct, with different beliefs, assumptions, expectation about people . . . unable to communicate or collaborate in their practice or even to recognize what other specialists see and do". Teams provoke a number of challenges in the school culture, causing "disruption to the normal order of business" (Wasley, 1994, p. 183), including confronting the norms of teachers' autonomy, time constraints, and resistance to change.

A brief history of the use of teams in the helping professions provides a background for the challenges in developing such structures.

# A Brief Historical Perspective

Julia and Thompson (1994b), in their overview of the development of teams in the helping professions, indicate that the earliest conceptions of teamwork were oriented to single professions and were recommended in the 1920s for medical practice. By the 1940s, there were references to multiprofessional teams in the health, mental health, and rehabilitation fields, and these became more common in the 1960s. During the 1960s the federal government gave incentives for the development of comprehensive diagnostic centers to provide interdisciplinary services for the handicapped (Maher & Yoshida, 1985); school-child study teams were also in operation (Armer & Thomas, 1978), and teaming was used as a strategy in schools, although later it faded. According to Wasley (1994), teachers today seem to be unclear about why teaming had been undertaken in the 1960s and why it went out of fashion.

In the 1970s, the multidisciplinary team (MDT) was written into the special education law, Public Law 94-142. The law mandated that a team using multiple criteria and sources would be the decision-making body. This requirement was initially welcomed as a way to improve educational programming decisions by bringing together "school professionals with different perspectives . . . for evaluating a student and individualizing program plans" (Maher & Yoshida, 1985, p. 14). The inclusion of the MDT also grew out of concern that minority group members were being misclassified as handicapped (Maher & Yoshida, 1985) and the belief that a group decision would safeguard against individual bias and error in judgment.

However, according to Maher and Yoshida (1985), the mandated use of the MDT in special education decision making was based on neither theory nor research specific to that process, but rather research drawn from the behavioral science literature supporting the effectiveness of group decision making. The rationale for utilizing teams made up of multiple professional disciplines is often intuitive and is not based on research. For example, Huebner and Hahn (1990), in their review of the literature on multidisciplinary teams, note that "the rationale for the team approach was based upon the notion that 'two heads are better than one.' That is, representatives from multiple disciplines working together can make better decisions than individuals working alone" (p. 235). Likewise, Fuchs and Fuchs (1989), in describing "an important distinctive feature" of their particular model of multidisciplinary teams, stated, "The team comprised the classroom teacher, a school-based special educator, and either the building-based school psychologist or PPS. The presence of such a group . . . reflects our beliefs that . . . many heads are better than one or two, especially when they collectively present diversity and richness in formal training and professional experience" (pp. 60–61).

Implementation of the MDT was considered problematic from the beginning (e.g., Maher & Pfeiffer, 1983). Although the MDT was mandated, there was little consideration of the type of team or processes that would lead to the desired outcome, and school districts have struggled with their implementation. Research documented a variety of problems, as summarized by Friend and Cook (1992):

> (1) use of unsystematic approaches to collecting and analyzing diagnostic information, (2) minimal parent or regular educator participation on the teams, (3) use of a loosely construed decision-making/planning process, (4) lack of interdisciplinary collaboration and trust, (5) territoriality, (6) ambiguous role definition and accountability, and (7) lack of experience and training for professionals to work together. (p. 26)

Fleming and Fleming (1983) suggested that most MDT team members, although they might recognize the problems in their team functioning, were unable to "organize their perceptions into structured analyses of issues facing teams," blinding them "to their shared responsibilities for successful implementation of the team model" (p. 144). Maher and Yoshida (1985) also questioned the basic underlying assumption of the use of a group problem-solving model in the special education placement process.

> In order to maximize the benefits of team member skills, the group problem-solving situations studied by industrial psychologists required unusual solutions in which there

were few prior constraints upon what alternatives could be considered. However, MDT pre-placement decisions are typically reduced to whether students are eligible for special services and to what programs they should be assigned. . . . With these choice constraints, it is not surprising that MDTs demonstrate similar outcomes as groups in business of no greater effectiveness than individuals when decisions are made routinely and in quantity. (p. 17)

During this period, however, there were also numerous calls for enhancing the MDT's role beyond determining pupil eligibility for special education (Maher & Yoshida, 1985). One outgrowth of the problems with the MDT, and with the special education delivery system in general, was the "development of building-level, problem-solving teams to assist teachers in accommodating students with behavioral or learning difficulties in their classroom" (Friend & Cook, 1992, p. 27). The 1975 special education law stipulated that, before referral for determination of special education eligibility, interventions were to be attempted in the regular classroom. The prominence of school-based teams as an alternative system of service delivery, to provide support services to teachers and students, is evident by the attention devoted to them in the professional literature (Abelson & Woodman 1983; Chalfant & Pysh, 1984, 1989a, 1989b; Chalfant, Pysh & Moultrie, 1979; Cole, Siegel, & Yau, 1990; Fuchs & Fuchs, 1989; Hayek, 1987; Horvath & Baker, 1982; Maher & Yoshida, 1985; McGlothlin, 1981; Ott, 1990; Pryzwansky, 1986; Pryzwansky & Rzepski, 1983; Rosenfield, 1992; Rosenfield & Gravois, 1996; Stokes, 1982; Stokes & Axelrod, 1982; Weinberg, 1989; Wojtusik & Sikorsky, 1991) and in the importance given to team utilization at federal, state, and local levels (Fudell & Dougherty, 1989; Walsh, 1989). In their survey of state and local education districts' use of school-based teams, Fudell and Dougherty discovered that 13% of the states or protectorates had mandated teams, whereas 67% had districts where school-based team models were being developed or were in operation on a voluntary basis.

Although there are discrepancies among team names, stated functions, and compositions, the concept of a school-based team has emerged from the early days of P.L. 94-142 as a powerful service delivery option for educators. Efforts to provide effective prereferral services have included supportive and collaborative consultation services to teachers. These indirect services, traditionally provided by school psychologists (see, e.g., Bergan, 1977; Rosenfield, 1987), special educators (e.g., West & Idol, 1987), and a host of other resource personnel, have increasingly included the use of school-based teams for support. Hence, MDTs acquired a narrowly defined role in the traditional refer-test-place special education structure (Huebner & Hahn, 1990), while a new set of structures arose in the alternative prereferral support models. In many instances, these teams were initially called *prereferral teams*, but this term has been criticized: because "these teams were designed to reduce inappropriate referrals to special education and to prevent the escalation of students' learning and behavior disorders, the implication of subsequent referral and evaluation seems contradictory" (Friend & Cook, 1992, p. 27). Indeed, these support teams were seen as "an underpinning for teachers themselves" (Maeroff, 1993, p. 19).

During the 1970s and 1980s, however, there was also a multitude of calls for educational reform, resulting from reports highlighting the condition of both general and special education in America. One response to the educational reform agenda that arose from these reports has been an increased focus on creating educational environments that are collaborative and problem solving (see, e.g., Fullan, 1991; Maeroff, 1993; Rosenholtz, 1989; Sarason, 1990; Thousand & Villa, 1992) to address the increasing diversity and range of educational problems in today's schools. Although collaboration is not normative in American schools, it has been argued that collaborative teams can be "vehicles for inventing solutions that traditional bureaucratic school structures have failed to conceptualize" (Thousand & Villa, 1992, p. 74). The multidisciplinary school-based team is one innovation that continues to foster collaborative, problem-solving relationships among school personnel.

Miles and Ekholm (1991) refer to such teams as "meta-structures," which assist in the development and maintenance of changes in the school organization. Such teams, typically made up of diverse educational professionals, operate in the school building as a problem-solving entity dealing with building-level concerns. Although the history and structure of such teams are diverse, their basic use in education have focused on assisting students who exhibit special needs or are considered at risk for school failure (e.g., Fuchs & Fuchs, 1989; Rosenfield & Gravois, 1996), as well as addressing a larger array of curriculum, instructional, and management issues, such as site-based decision making, team teaching, grade-level collaboration, and other issues beyond individual student concerns (Arcaro, 1995; Friend & Cook, 1992; Maeroff, 1993).

In sum, since the mid-1970s, the use of school-based teams as an in-building support structure has expanded considerably, and the actual number of teams has proliferated (Fudell & Dougherty, 1989; Hayek, 1987). Major reasons for establishing teams have centered around special education functions, such as the mandated MDT or the various attempts to reduce the flow of referrals for formal psychoeducational evaluations by having these teams function as collaborative and consultative supports to teachers of students at risk for school failure (Fudell & Dougherty, 1989). But there are also other reasons, focused more broadly on using the team structure to assist in schoolwide collaborative problem solving. Unfortunately, the research base for school-based, problem-solving teams remains limited and in many respects has not kept pace with the proliferation of variant school-based team models indicated in the literature (Chalfant & Pysh, 1989a; Gravois, 1995) and practice.

In the remainder of this chapter, we focus on the multidisciplinary, school-based team—the research supporting it and its facilitative role. We review team models that have been discussed in the literature, their usefulness and effectiveness, and the complexity of creating functioning teams in schools.

# CONCEPTUALIZING EFFECTIVE TEAMS

Although the results of most research on school-based teams suggest positive outcomes on such variables as changes in referral patterns for special education services (e.g., Chalfant & Pysh, 1989a, 1989b; Ott, 1990), teachers' satisfaction with the team model (e.g., Chalfant & Pysh, 1989b; Fudell, 1992), and targeted student variables like achievement (Chalfant & Pysh, 1989b; Kuralt, 1990), most of the studies are based on pilot implementations, a small number of schools, and a lack of appropriate research control (Chalfant & Pysh, 1989b). Moreover, because of the enormous expense in labor and time that must be

devoted to implementing this complex structure (Evans, 1990), there is a need for research addressing the developmental processes that school-based teams undergo during implementation and the reciprocal impact of implementing these teams in existing school cultures (Gravois, 1995).

Over time, the concept of the team has evolved from "a group based on likeness that combined similar efforts to obtain a goal" to a group "comprising different parts coming together to achieve a common goal" (Julia & Thompson, 1994b, p. 35). Friend and Cook (1992) further characterize teams as having interdependent membership, in which the actions and events of one member relate to and affect the rest of the team. Likewise, the actions of the team as a whole affect its individual members.

The literatures of business, mental health, and education are in increasing agreement about what constitutes an effective team. Simply bringing professionals together and sitting them around a table does not ensure that a team exists (Arcaro, 1995; Barth, 1991; Huebner & Hahn, 1990); rather understanding how effective teams operate and developing the necessary training are essential. Certainly, the group process literature helps us to understand the functioning of the team, although this literature is beyond the scope of this chapter (see, e.g., Johnson & Johnson, 1991, for a review). According to Julia and Thompson (1994b), the relevance of the following group process assumptions is clear:

> The interprofessional team is a small group subject to the same laws that govern any primary group; the professionals' behavior on an interprofessional team is a product of group process. . . . To be an effective team member, one must have knowledge about and skills in the group processes that underlie the interaction of team members and accept group processes as part of effective interprofessional team functioning . . . appropriate utilization of the interprofessional team approach . . . depend on the cognitive grasp, sensitive understanding, and careful handling of a number of specific dynamics conceptually grouped under the generic label of interprofessional group process. (p. 37)

For example, there is considerable literature on the evolution of effective groups that is helpful in understanding the developmental stages of group life (see Johnson & Johnson, 1991, for a review of the research on this topic; see Julia & Thompson, 1994b, for an application of the developmental stages to interdisciplinary groups).

However, it is also important to differentiate teams from the general run of small groups described in the literature: "Teams are different from small groups in that teams consist of well-defined positions and often tackle a variety of tasks over and above group problem solving exercises" (Baker & Salas, 1992, p. 470). Baker and Salas refer to two categories of behaviors that assist in conceptualizing teams. These are task work, behaviors related to individual team members and the tasks they perform, and team-

work, behaviors that are more related to the interactions among team members. Others have used the terms *task functions* and *maintenance functions* to refer to the same phenomena (Julia & Thompson, 1994b; Rosenfield & Gravois, 1996). Teams need to develop skills to conduct both types of function to be effective. For example, Figure 38.1 illustrates the business and maintenance activities for an intervention assistance team (Rosenfield & Gravois, 1996, p. 121).

Further definitions of what constitutes an effective team have been given. For example, Billups (1987) indicates that there are critical variables common across various team models and organizational structures (e.g., business,

## FIGURE 38.1  Team Functioning Activities

*Team Business Activities*

*Regularly scheduled meetings*—Meetings should be scheduled 1 hour per week at a convenient time for all team members to attend.

*Case review and documentation*—All team members provide regularly scheduled updates of their cases at which time the system manager and other team members ensure that all necessary documentation is being completed.

*Feedback for case managers*—The team meeting provides opportunities for members to give specific feedback to case managers regarding case progress and monitoring activities.

*Problem solving*—Teams engage in creative problem solving to help case managers more effectively manage their cases and offer suggestions as to interventions and resources available. However, team members only offer interventions for well-defined problems.

*New case assignments*—Each team determines procedures by which new cases are assigned.

*Documentation of team meetings*—Minutes of each team meeting document activities and future actions and responsibilities.

*Team Maintenance Activities*

*Temperature taking*—Conducted monthly, temperature-taking sessions provide a structured process by which issues and concerns, as well as celebrations and excitement, are shared and discussed.

*Collaborative communication skills*—Team members model, utilize, and monitor their use of communication during team meetings.

*Giving and receiving feedback*—Team members are trained in appropriate techniques of giving and receiving feedback. Open, honest, and objective feedback is the foundation for continued team and individual member growth and developments.

*Needs assessments*—Teams conduct needs assessments on an ongoing basis to assist in designing and planning necessary training.

*Continued training*—Training is provided based on both active involvement of team members and facilitators and the results of needs assessments.

*Faculty/parental participation*—Team members recognize that the collaborative problem-solving nature of the team requires faculty and parental participation. However, there are times when team meetings provide specific training and feedback for case managers and faculty/parental participation would be unwarranted.

Rosenfield and Gravois (1996). Reprinted with permission.

mental health, and education). Conceptually, according to Billups, a team that functions well has six commonly encountered processes:

- Individual team members, prior to entry on a team, achieve a sound professional identification. That is, individual professionals understand their professional role and functioning within the specific organizational structure prior to becoming a team member.
- Team members recognize the reciprocal impact of the functioning team in its environment.
- Skills of communication and conflict resolution are especially important in promoting an understanding of interprofessional contributions and effective team functioning.
- Functional teams have members who are skilled in and share clearly articulated processes of problem solving.
- Negotiation remains key for the implementation of and follow through with appropriate interventions.
- Teams reflect on their own functioning through intrateam activities and through collection of formalized evaluations.

In the educational literature, Thousand and Villa (1992) view the effective collaborative team as an adult analogue to the effective cooperative-learning group for students, performing at their best under the following conditions: frequent face-to-face interaction among the team members; "mutual 'we are all in this together' feeling of positive interdependence;" development of interpersonal skills "in trust building, communication, leadership, creative problem-solving, decision making, and conflict management;" ongoing "assessment and discussion of the team's functioning and the setting of goals for improving relationships and more effectively accomplishing tasks;" and maintaining accountability for "agreed-upon responsibilities and commitments" (p. 76). A quality team, according to Arcaro (1995), includes the following elements: commitment to the team's mission, which is understood by the team members; objectives consistent with the mission; trust and respect by team members for one another, with the capacity to anticipate and cope with conflict; efficient meetings that produce results; shared responsibility by team members who know their roles and responsibilities; active participation; and shared communication.

# DIVERSITY ISSUES IN PROBLEM-SOLVING TEAMS

Organizational structure and the team process are two central dynamics. The presence of a diverse group of professionals is considered an advantage for overall team functioning in that multiple disciplines provide greater access to diverse expertise, which can be systematically applied to the problem at hand (Fuchs & Fuchs, 1989; Huebner & Hahn, 1990; Maeroff, 1993). In education, multiple disciplines typically serving on school-based, problem-solving teams may include the principal, school psychologist, special and general education teacher, nurse, counselor, and other specialists.

But the concept of different professional specialties of team members is only part of the challenge of diversity. More sophisticated analyses of group structure suggest how complex and multidimensional the concept of diversity is when applied to team functioning. According to McGrath, Berdahl, and Arrow (1995), in their discussion of diversity in work groups, members may be more or less homogeneous or diverse on the following clusters of attributes:

1. Demographic attributes . . . that are socially meaningful in the society in which the organization is embedded (e.g., age, race, ethnicity, gender, sexual orientation, physical status, religion, and education).
2. Task-related knowledge, skills, and abilities. . . .
3. Values, beliefs, and attitudes. . . .
4. Personality and cognitive and behavioral styles. . . .
5. Status in the work group's embedding organization (e.g., organizational rank, occupational specialty, departmental affiliation, and tenure). (p. 23)

Diversity in any of these clusters or in combinations of clusters affects not only the behavior of members of the group, their interaction, and task performance but also how the team members may attempt to modify the effects of diversity (McGrath et al., 1995). McGrath et al. suggest that "a broader array of knowledge, skills, and abilities" presented by group members may facilitate the ability "to tackle technical problems," while diversity on values "may impede goal selection" and "affect the level of attraction and respect among members, ease of communication, and degree of overt conflict in the group" (p. 25). For example, multidisciplinary teams with extensive understanding of adaptive classroom instructional strategies may not be able to utilize those skills most effectively if the value structure of members is not compatible with the inclusive education of students who have challenging instructional needs.

For diverse teams to be effective, however, these types of issues must be managed successfully (Cox, 1995; Rosenfield & Gravois, 1996). According to Cox, successful management means "taking proactive steps to create a climate in which cultural norms, values, work practices, and interpersonal relations reinforce rather than hinder the full participation of all organizational members" (p. 240). Many of the negative consequences of diversity occur when such management is not effective: "The extent to which diversity's potential positive impact is maximized and its negative impact minimized will depend on the extent to which effective interventions are used to proactively address the dynamic of diversity" (p. 242). Knowledge and skill in the process of intergroup dynamics are essential for effective teams.

Multidisciplinary teams have some unique process problems. Process is the flow of transactions that allows free communication, full participation, and sufficient levels of agreement to arrive at a series of collective actions and decisions (Billups, 1987; Ott, 1993). Research findings indicate that a lack of interdisciplinary collaboration and trust, territoriality, mixed participation by differing professional roles (Huebner & Hahn, 1990; Pfeiffer & Heffernan, 1984), and differing conceptualizations of one another's role and function (Cole et al., 1990) are a few of the difficulties found in actual team practices. According to Billups (1987), it is assumed that (a) appropriate and successful utilization of multidisciplinary teams requires a sensitive understanding and cognitive grasp of its process, (b) the formation and conduct of multidisciplinary teams should not threaten competently prepared professionals with the fear that their area of specialization will be belittled or ignored, and (c) "there are no absolute arbiters of the way in which the multidisciplinary team process is shaped" (p. 147). An interactive and interdependent relationship among team members, the people in whose behalf the team functions, and the larger environmental factors is the basis for team development and functioning.

# MODELS OF SCHOOL-BASED PROBLEM-SOLVING TEAMS

The focus of this section of the chapter is on models of school-based, problem-solving teams that have been developed as support structures for teachers. In reviewing the literature, Gravois (1995) indicated that such teams are often similar in name but propose differing functions and underlying assumptions (see Figure 38.2). Stokes (1982) examined school-based teams according to their (a) composition, (b) leadership, (c) focus, and (d) function. The investigation of team models depicted in Figure 38.2 extends Stokes' structure by two additional components: (e) indication of a formal training package and (f) organization of teams' delivery of service.

In reviewing Figure 38.2, there appear to be several distinguishing factors among the presented models. A key area is team composition. For example, some team models, such as Assistance Teams (Stokes, 1982), advocate multidisciplinary team composition, including regular and special education teachers, administrators, and support personnel—whether school-based or not. Other team models, such as Building Teams (Stokes, 1982) and Teacher Assistance Teams (TAT) (Chalfant & Pysh, 1989a, 1989b; Chalfant et al., 1979), propose narrowly composed teams of only school-based personnel, with the TAT model made up primarily of teachers.

Of great interest in investigating the various models of school-based teams are their indicated focus and function. Although an attempt was made in Figure 38.2 to categorize such aspects, most models did not directly specify their primary focus or function. In many cases teams appeared to do a little of everything. Hence, the focus or function that was cited most frequently was recorded first and considered to be primary, and other aspects were secondary. Team models were noted as being focused on the individual student, on the teacher or staff, or on the organization. For example, Assistance Teams (Stokes, 1982), Building Teams (Stokes, 1982) and Local School Teams (Cole et al., 1990) appear to be focused on individual students, and the teams' primary function is to expedite referrals and plan for students' educational needs, typically through special educational services. Teacher Assistance Teams (Chalfant & Pysh, 1989a, 1989b, Chalfant et al., 1979), Staff Support Teams (Stokes & Axelrod, 1982), and Instructional Consultation Teams (IC) Rosenfield & Gravois, 1996) focused

**FIGURE 38.2** Comparison of School-based Teams Across Organization Structures

| Team Name | Team Composition | Leadership | Team Focus | Team Function | Formal Training Package Indicated | Primary Organization of Service Delivery | Principle Investigator/ Reference |
|---|---|---|---|---|---|---|---|
| Assistance teams | Multidisciplinary | Principal | At-risk students | Expedite referral process for the assessment and placement of students | Yes | Whole team | Barrs (cited in Stokes, 1982) |
| Building teams | Multidisciplinary, building-based staff | Principal | Students/teachers | Helping teachers help targeted students; in-service of staff | None indicated | Whole team | W. Mickler (cited in Stokes, 1982) |
| Instructional support teams | Multidisciplinary, building-based staff | Varies | Building issues/ teachers | Support; inservice | None indicated | Whole team/ teacher consultant | Hovath & Baker (1982) |
| Staff support teams | Multidisciplinary | Shared by team members | Staff | Problem-solving forum; expedite referral & evaluation process; inservice | None indicated | Whole team | Stokes & Axelrod (1982) |
| Teacher assistance teams | Primarily teachers | Teacher member | Teachers | Problem-solving unit | Yes | Whole team | Chalfant & Pysh 1989a, 1989b); Chalfant, Pysh, & Moultrie (1979) |
| Local school teams | Multidisciplinary | Principal | Students/teachers | Individual student planning; consultation to school personnel | None indicated | Whole team | Cole, Siegel, & Yau (1990) |
| Teacher support teams | Multidisciplinary, no regular classroom teachers | School psychologist/ special educator | School organization | Collaborative problem solving | Yes | Whole team | Ott (1989) |
| Instructional consultation teams | Multidisciplinary | Designated systems' manager | Teachers/students organization | Collaborative problem solving; instructional improvement | Yes | Case Manager/ consultant; whole team | Rosenfield & Gravois (1996) |

on supporting teachers or staff members through problem-solving processes; their ultimate goal was to help students succeed in their current classrooms through this support. Teacher Support Teams (Ott, 1990) appeared to focus more on issues at the school organizational level than did other teams, while also functioning as a collaborative problem-solving mechanism in the school.

Differences were also noted in the organization of delivery of services and availability of a formal training package. The organization of service delivery refers to the procedures developed by teams in addressing referrals or concerns. As depicted in Figure 38.2, a majority of team developers and researchers advocated a whole-team approach, in which referrals or concerns were addressed at team meetings or through whole-team problem solving. Several teams had follow-up consultations with individual referring teachers by a teacher-consultant who was a team member. However, this was not indicated as the primary mode of team organization. Only the IC-Team (Rosenfield, 1992; Rosenfield & Gravois, 1996) model described the use of a Case Manager/Consultant process that relies on collaboration between dyads of team members and referring teachers as the primary organization for service delivery.

There are clear distinctions among the team models in Figure 38.2 in composition, function, organization, and so forth. However, as Cole et al. (1990) suggest, these differences may be a reflection of an evolutionary process in team development and utilization in schools. Prereferral teams have increasingly moved away from processing referrals for special education services toward problem-solving activities that help to educate all children, ensuring appropriate learning and social development.

This evolution of team development has also resulted in common components across various models. Critical components, such as multidisciplinary team composition; the focus on school, teacher, and student; and comprehensive training opportunities, are seen more frequently. The most recently proposed models appear to incorporate more of these key components. In addition, team developers and researchers are now enumerating the key components that facilitated successful team functioning and implementation of their particular models. For example, Cole et al. (1990) propose three features: (a) multidisciplinary membership; (b) balanced representation

of regular and special educators, specialists, administrators and support services; and (c) team membership indigenous to the building. Pryzwansky and Rzepski (1983) further suggest that teams incorporate "an explicit problem-solving process" (p. 176). Although such key components will be helpful for future development and implementation, research continues to be needed to document the effectiveness of various components, the process of implementing such complex innovations in schools, and the impact of school-based teams on outcomes of interest to educators.

# REVIEW OF RESEARCH ON SCHOOL-BASED TEAMS

In spite of the increased use of school-based teams in educational settings, there remains a limited data base about their effectiveness and efficiency (Chalfant & Pysh, 1989b; Gravois, 1995), perhaps largely because of the complexity of implementing and evaluating teams in applied settings. The research that does exist is often characterized by descriptive reports and is based on few schools (Chalfant & Pysh, 1989b). In addition, research in applied settings often lacks rigorous design and methodology (Chalfant & Pysh, 1989b; Fudell, 1992).

Recent reviews of the literature indicate few comprehensive studies of the process of team functioning or specific elements that are considered important in establishing effective teams (Cole et al., 1990; Fudell, 1992; Gravois, 1995). Most research findings center on school-based teams' impact on various outcome variables, such as the rate of special education referrals, teachers' satisfaction with the team process, and targeted student performance indicators (Gravois, 1995; Rosenfield, 1992).

Chalfant and Pysh (1989b) reviewed nearly 10 years of research pertaining to 96 TATs (Chalfant & Pysh, 1989b; Chalfant et al., 1979) implemented in several states. Information from a questionnaire was gathered over three stages. Descriptive data about the team, school organization, procedures, and available supports were gathered during stage 1. Stage 2 investigated the problems encountered during implementation and reviewed the goals set for students. The impact of the TAT on students' performance, special education referral rates, and teachers' satisfaction and concerns were documented in stage 3. According to Chalfant and Pysh (1989b), the "teams were effective in reducing the total number of students referred to special education found to be ineligible for services and reducing costs for unnecessary testing of students" (p. 56). In addition, results indicated that the TATs were effective in reaching goals set for individual students. These latter results were determined by achieving consensus on three criteria: (a) whether the student actually met the goal set, (b) whether the teacher and the team agreed that the teacher was able to cope satisfactorily with the problem that prompted the referral, and (c) whether team support was withdrawn within six weeks. Consensus on these criteria indicated that team-planned interventions were successful for approximately 89% of the nonhandicapped students referred to the teams and for 100% of the mainstreamed handicapped students. In addition, an open-ended questionnaire was coded to provide an estimate of teachers' satisfaction with the TAT process: 88% of the statements were positive.

In a related study, Talley (cited in Chalfant & Pysh, 1989b) conducted a pretest and posttest comparison of special education referral rates in nine schools with TATs. Reported results indicated a 63.6% (14 students) drop in the number of inappropriate referrals for special education services across all nine schools. The costs saved for the nine participating schools by not evaluating inappropriate referrals was estimated to be approximately $16,000.

Ott (1990) investigated the efficacy of Teacher Support Teams and also found a reduction in the number of referrals for psychoeducational evaluations and a 26% reduction in the tuition costs of special education. In addition, Ott documented an increase in the request for school psychological consultation services and an increase in the delivery of special education services within the mainstream. However, the lack of adequate research control warrants the need for greater systematic evaluations of this model.

Research on the IC-Team model (Rosenfield, 1992; Rosenfield & Gravois, 1996) and similar models, especially the Early Intervention Project and Project Link (Fudell, 1992; Rosenfield, 1992), has also focused on specific outcome measures, such as the impact on students' achievement and behavior (e.g., Green-Resnick & Rosenfield, 1989; Kuralt, 1990), referral rates of students for special education (Rosenfield, 1992; Kuralt, 1990; Wojtusik & Sikorsky, 1991), and the satisfaction and attitudes of teachers (Fudell, 1992). These studies provide support for the positive impact of school-based teams on the specified outcomes. For example, Douville (cited in Rosenfield, 1992) investigated the Early Intervention Project in Connecticut. Pilot schools implementing the model were noted to have, on average, substantially lower referral rates for special education evaluation than control schools. The findings indicated that the school districts' referral rates for special education services varied from 11.6% to 17.5%; the pilot schools' referral rates varied from 0% to 1.7%. Wojtusik and Sikorsky (1991) also documented a reduction in the number of special education placements as a result of implementing teams trained in consultation and curriculum-based assessment in the Early Intervention Project.

Investigating the implementation of the instructional consultation package in one school district, Kuralt (1990) concluded that "through successful implementation of a team-based consultation model, schools can serve [a] greater number of teachers and students; significantly redirect collaborative professional effort toward classroom implementation of effective instructional strategies; and provide a wider range of services" (p. 18). Specifically, students served through the collaborative team model made significant gains in reading comprehension, as assessed through the use of a standardized measure, and referrals for special education evaluation were reduced (Kuralt, 1990).

Fudell's (1992) review of research on school-based teams presents the results of several unpublished reports on local- or state-initiated models. Such teams were found to have positive outcomes in decreasing referrals for special education evaluation and decreasing the number of students actually placed in special education.

## Research on Components of Effective Teams

As has been indicated, "teams do not *automatically* demonstrate greater effectiveness than individuals. Without training in team process skills, some teams are no more effective than individuals" (Huebner & Hahn, 1990, p. 237; emphasis in original). Moreover, greater attention must be given to the developmental processes through which innovations, such as teams, are assimilated and accommodated into existing structures (Fullan, 1991; Rosenfield & Gravois, 1996). Despite the growing use of school-based teams, as indicated in several surveys of state departments (Fudell & Dougherty, 1989), the lack of attention to team development and functioning remains a critical area for future research. Studies of the key structural components and processes of effective teams are limited because of difficulties in measurement and research design in applied settings (Baker & Salas, 1992). However, there have been investigations of several key aspects of effective teams, including multidisciplinary team composition, team problem-solving and collaboration, team communication, and size.

Cole et al. (1990) investigated the functioning of 79 Local School Teams implemented in Canada. This descriptive study investigated team members' perceptions of the teams' roles and documented various team processes. An interesting finding was the discrepant perceptions of the teams' purpose. For example, the researchers found a difference in perceived team goals according to professional role. Psychoeducational consultants and school social workers who served as team members thought they should provide schoolwide programming and planning services, whereas classroom teachers and guidance counselors who served on the teams thought they should be facilitating referrals for specialized services. Even with several years of training and implementation, these discrepant perceptions among team members existed and again highlight the difficulty of creating common goals within the team, much less within the school as a whole. Such findings are related to those reported by Huebner and Hahn (1990), who noted in their review of the research on multidisciplinary teams that lack of interdisciplinary collaboration and trust were frequently cited difficulties.

Ott (1993) investigated school-based, problem-solving teams and their interactions with parents of targeted students. As part of a pilot study, Ott developed the Team Collaboration Scale and Team Development Questionnaire as a way of measuring team members' perceptions of the team's development and engagement in collaborative problem solving. Results indicated a moderate positive link between the level of training that teams received and team collaboration. However, Ott also reported that, in general, training, especially in communication skills, problem solving, and decision making, received significantly less attention than other components of team development. This research represents an initial investigation of school-based team functioning (team development and training) as it relates to specific outcomes (parental involvement).

Kuralt, Hanson, and Rosenfield (1987) investigated the differences between individual psychologists' communication skills and communication skills employed by multidisciplinary teams. The study compared the communication skills of six school psychology graduate students with the communication skills used by five multidisciplinary teams during the problem identification stage of problem solving. Through content analysis of audiotaped interviews, the two groups were compared on their use of specific communication techniques: (a) asking clarifying questions, (b) asking relevant questions, (c) asking irrelevant questions, (d) paraphrasing, (e) perception checking, (f) offering information, (g) offering knowledge, (h) giving case information, (i) suggesting interventions, (j) active attentive listening, (k) using procedural statements, and (l) other responses.

Kuralt et al. (1987) found significant differences across specific skills. Multidisciplinary teams used "offering information" and nondescript "other" statements more frequently than individual psychologists. It was also found that teams rarely employed skills, such as clarifying questions and paraphrasing, that are traditionally associated with collaboration in the consultation literature. Of 460 coded team responses from five teams, the researchers coded only 1 clarifying question, 18 paraphrases, and no perception checks, so that these three types of responses accounted for less than 5% of the total communications.

Gravois (1995) provided additional information on team communication by analyzing the communication skills used by IC-Teams. Utilizing a comprehensive coding procedure, Gravois coded approximately 3,300 communication units into 11 categories from 9 school-based teams: (a) asking relevant questions, (b) asking clarifying questions, (c) asking evaluative or advising questions, (d) paraphrasing, (e) perception checking, (f) summarizing, (g) confirming or acknowledging, (h) offering information, (i) suggesting, (j) minimal encouraging, and (k) uncodable/other.

Content analysis of audiotape-recorded team meetings indicated that the most frequently used communication skills of all team members was offering information, followed by confirming and making suggestions. When communication skills were grouped according to their intentions, that is, whether the team members intended to gather information, provide information, or clarify information, Gravois (1995) found that, in general, teams members typically provided information most frequently (more than 57% of the communications). Approximately 30% of team communications were intended to clarify information, and 11% intended to gather additional information.

The final team component reviewed is size. The recommended team size, anywhere between five and nine members (e.g., Maeroff, 1993; Thousand & Villa, 1992), appears to be related to the suggested size for task groups in the literature. However, teams remain different from groups in the type and variety of tasks addressed (Baker & Salas, 1992) and will probably require different compositions and sizes. In a survey of teams in industry, Wellins et al. (cited in Maeroff, 1993) found that average team sizes ranged from 6 to 12 members, slightly larger than that recommended by traditional group researchers. Furthermore, Gravois (1995) found significant positive differences in team collaboration; that is, larger teams (9–12 members) were found to have significantly higher levels of perceived team collaboration than smaller teams (5–8 members).

It appears that, as indicated by Maeroff (1993), the size of the team should also reflect the purpose and demands placed on it: "A team with too few members is one in which each member may end up with too much to do and too small a network of support. But having too many on a team can impede the team building process by limiting the level of intimacy and bonding that is possible . . . consideration in fixing the size of the team is the size of the school" (p. 32).

## Issues in Team Implementation

A major distinction between IC-Teams (Rosenfield & Gravois, 1996) and other school-based models has been the emphasis on the process of implementation. Utilizing a template of evaluation grounded in the educational change literature (Fullan, 1982, 1991; Hall & Hord, 1987; Miles & Ekholm, 1991), the research on IC-Teams has focused on understanding not only their efficacy but also the issues involved in achieving effective implementation. For example, Kuralt (1990) assessed the degree of utilization of the instructional consultation model through the Concerns-Based Adoption Model (CBAM; Hall & Hord, 1987). In this type of evaluation, attention is given to assessing the concerns expressed by program participants and the degree to which the innovation is utilized. By assessing the degree to which the innovation was implemented, Kuralt was able to make greater connections between the model's positive impact in reducing placements in special education and gains in targeted students' reading comprehension. In a separate study, Green-Resnick and Rosenfield (1989) attempted to monitor students' outcomes. They found that poor training in and implementation of specific techniques for measuring students' progress prohibited a full investigation.

Fudell (1992) examined 13 schools involved in Project Link—a Pennsylvania initiative to train and implement teams. A Level of Implementation Scale was developed and administered to determine the degree of implementation. The degree to which teams implemented the model increased over three administrations of the scale, documenting the growth and development of skill use by team members. Fudell's results also indicated a significant positive correlation between the degree of implementation and utilization of specific team forms. Teams whose members were accurate in their use of forms documenting the problem-solving processes, were assessed to have higher implementation of the critical dimensions of the model. This finding reinforces the need of team developers to develop concurrently appropriate organizing structures that support the process skills team members are attempting to implement.

The role of the team facilitator has received attention by Rosenfield and Gravois (1996), who studied the facilitator skills employed by an on-site IC-Team facilitator. They described the basic tasks for the team facilitator, who was trying to develop the team, including, "good understanding of group functioning and . . . skills in facilitating the team . . . thus building collaborative relationships between the facilitator and participants as well as among the school personnel . . . being able to build the trust of the participants . . . but also the ability to confront . . . when that is needed, and to resolve conflicts . . . provide appropriate support . . . interpersonal ease in relating to others . . . initiative taking . . . and the capacity to organize the work, time, and activities" (p. 75). Rosenfield and Gravois provide a manual for those interested in becoming facilitators of IC-Teams.

## CONCLUSION

There is increasing recognition that effectiveness in innovation design and impact in controlled studies do not easily translate into widespread practice or remain in place for extended periods of time (Fullan, 1991; Hall & Hord, 1987; Miles & Ekholm, 1991). Creating and sustaining school-based teams is no exception. Addressing the issue of creating true reform or change in education, Fullan and Miles (1992) indicated the presence of two underlying problems: "One is that mistaken or superficial solutions are introduced; the other is that, even when the solution is on the right track, hasty implementation leads to failure" (pp. 747–748). The fact remains that selection of a particular model of school-based teams is only the beginning of the change process. Implementing and continuing such teams require complex changes in existing structures and practices, and change is often not easy in educational or any organizational setting (Fullan, 1991; Fullan & Miles, 1992; Hall & Hord, 1987; Miles & Ekholm, 1991).

The practitioner interested in school-based teams, pro or con, should recognize the distinction between well-conceived teams and those that have just been thrown together. Indeed, innovations that are haphazardly conceived and implemented are rarely effective, and school-based teams are no different.

> A school team has to be carefully built if its members are going to be reasonably able to take on roles that are new to them. Not that team building is a panacea. The best a team can do for a school is to lead a rigorous struggle to professional fulfillment. . . . Team building is a means to an end, rather than the end. If it goes well, a team might be a vehicle for changing the climate and practice in the school so that student achievement may prosper. (Maeroff, 1993, p. 16)

# REFERENCES

Abelson, M. A., & Woodman, R. W. (1983). Review of research on team effectiveness: Implications for teams in schools. *School Psychology Review, 12,* 125–136.

Arcaro, J. S. (1995). *Teams in education: Creating an integrated approach.* Delray Beach, FL: St. Lucie Press.

Armer, B., & Thomas, B. (1978). Attitudes toward interdisciplinary collaboration in pupil personnel services teams. *Journal of School Psychology, 16,* 167–176.

Baker, D., & Salas, E. (1992). Principles for measuring teamwork skills. *Human Factors, 34,* 469–475.

Barth, R. (1991). Restructuring schools: Some

questions for teachers and principals. *Phi Delta Kappan, 73,* 123–128.

Bergan, J. R. (1977). *Behavioral consultation.* Columbus, OH: Merrill.

Billups, J. O. (1987). Interpersonal team process. *Theory into Practice, 26,* 146–152.

Book, R. M. (1995, May). Utility of pre-referral teams questioned [Letter to the editor]. *Communiqué,* p. 19.

Chalfant, J., & Pysh, M. (1984). Teacher assistance teams: A model for within-building problem-solving. In L. Liberal (Ed.), *Preventing special education for those who didn't need it* (pp. 16–28). Newtown, MA: Gloworm Publications.

Chalfant, J., & Pysh, M. (1989a). Teacher assistance teams. (Report for the Central Pennsylvania Special Education Resource Center.) Tucson: University of Arizona.

Chalfant, J., & Pysh, M. (1989b). Teacher assistance teams: Five descriptive studies on 96 teams. *Remedial and Special Education, 10*(6), 49–58.

Chalfant, J., Pysh, M., & Moultrie, R. (1979). Teacher assistance teams: A model for within building problem solving. *Learning Disabilities Quarterly, 2,* 85–96.

Cole, E., Siegel, J., & Yau, M. (1990). *The local school team: Goals, roles and functions.* Toronto: Toronto Board of Education, Research Services.

Cox, Jr., T. (1995). The complexity of diversity: Challenges and directions for future research. In S. E. Jackson & M. N. Ruderman (Eds.), *Diversity in work teams: Research paradigms for a changing workplace* (pp. 235–246). Washington, DC: American Psychological Association.

Elmore, R. F. (1995). Structural reform and educational practice. *Educational Researcher, 24*(9), 23–26.

Evans, R. (1990). Making mainstreaming work through prereferral consultation. *Educational Leadership, 47,* 73–77.

Fleming, D. C., & Fleming, E. R. (1983). Problems in implementation of the team approach: A practitioners' perspective. *School Psychology Review, 12,* 144–149.

Friend, M., & Cook, L. (1992). *Interactions: Collaboration skills for school professionals.* New York: Longman.

Fuchs, D., & Fuchs, L. S. (1989). Mainstream assistance teams to accommodate difficult-to-teach students in general education. In J. Graden, J. Zins, & M. Curtis (Eds.), *Alternative educational delivery systems: Enhancing instructional options for all students* (pp. 49–70). Washington, DC: National Association of School Psychologists.

Fudell, R. (1992). Level of implementation of teacher support teams and teachers' attitudes toward special needs students. Doctoral dissertation, Temple University, Philadelphia.

Fudell, R., & Dougherty, K. (1989). Teacher support

teams: State of policy and description of elements. Unpublished manuscript. Temple University, Philadelphia.

Fullan, M. (1982). *The meaning of educational change.* New York: Teachers College Press.

Fullan, M. (1991). *The new meaning of educational change.* New York: Teachers College Press.

Fullan, M., & Miles, M. (1992, June). Getting reform right: What works and what doesn't. *Phi Delta Kappan,* pp. 745–752.

Gravois, T. A. (1995). The relationship between communication use and collaboration of school-based problem-solving teams. Doctoral dissertation, University of Maryland, College Park.

Green-Resnick, B. M., & Rosenfield, S. (1989, March). Monitoring student outcomes of a teacher student team service. Paper presented at the Annual Meeting of the National Association of School Psychologists, Boston.

Hall, G. E., & Hord, S. M. (1987). *Change in schools: Facilitating the process.* New York: State University of New York Press.

Harbaugh, G. L. (1994). Assumptions of interprofessional collaboration: Interrelatedness and wholeness. In Commission on Interprofessional Education and Practice, *Interprofessional care and collaborative practice* (pp. 11–21). Pacific Grove, CA: Brooks/Cole.

Hayek, R. A. (1987). The teacher assistance team: A pre-referral support system. *Focus on Exceptional Children, 20,* 1–7.

Horvath, M. J., & Baker, L. (1982). Instructional support teams: Their initiation in local school buildings. In S. Stokes (Ed.), *School based staff support teams: A blueprint for action* (pp. 40–46). Reston, VA: Council for Exceptional Children.

Huebner, E. S., & Hahn, B. M. (1990). Best practices in coordinating multidisciplinary teams. In A. Thomas & J. Grimes (Eds.), *Best practices in school psychology* (Vol. 2, pp. 235–246). Washington, DC: National Association of School Psychologists.

Johnson, D. W., & Johnson, R. P. (1991). *Joining together: Group theory and group skills* (4th ed.). Englewood Cliffs, NJ: Prentice Hall.

Julia, M. C., & Thompson, A. (1994a). Essential elements of interprofessional teamwork: Task and maintenance functions. In Commission on Interprofessional Education and Practice, *Interprofessional care and collaborative practice* (pp. 43–57). Pacific Grove, CA: Brooks/Cole.

Julia, M. C., & Thompson, A. (1994b). Group process and interprofessional teamwork. In Commission on Interprofessional Education and Practice, *Interprofessional care and collaborative practice* (pp. 35–41). Pacific Grove, CA: Brooks/Cole.

Kuralt, S. (1990, August). Classroom collaboration: Implementing consultation-based interventions in five multidisciplinary teams. Paper presented at the Annual Meeting of the American Psychological Association, Boston.

Kuralt, S., Hanson, J., & Rosenfield, S. (1987, March). A comparison of individual consultant and school team communication skills: The initial problem identification interview. Paper presented at the National Association of School Psychologists, New Orleans.

Maeroff, G. I. (1993). *Team building for school change: Equipping teachers for new roles.* New York: Teachers College Press.

Maher, C. A., & Pfeiffer, S. I. (Eds.). (1983). Multidisciplinary teams in the schools: Perspectives, practice, possibilities. *School Psychology Review* (Special issue), *12,* 123–189.

Maher, C., & Yoshida, R. (1985). Multidisciplinary teams in schools. In T. Kratochwill (Ed.), *Advances in school psychology* (Vol. 4, pp. 13–44). Hillsdale, NJ: Erlbaum.

McGrath, J. E., Berdahl, J. L., & Arrow, H. (1995). Traits, expectations, culture, and clout: The dynamics of diversity in work groups. In S. E. Jackson & M. N. Ruderman (Eds.), *Diversity in work teams: Research paradigms for a changing workplace* (pp. 17–45). Washington, DC: American Psychological Association.

McGlothlin, J. E. (1981). The school consultation committee: An approach to implementing a teacher consultation model. *Behavior Disorders, 6,* 101–107.

Miles, M. B., & Ekholm, M. (1991, April). Will new structures stay restructured? Paper presented at the Annual Meeting of the American Educational Research Association, Chicago.

Ott, C. A. (1990). The teacher support team: An organizational approach to enhancing ecologically valid practices in school psychology. Unpublished manuscript.

Ott, C. A. (1993). Parent involvement with school-based problem-teams. Doctoral dissertation, Indiana University of Pennsylvania, Indiana.

Pfeiffer, S., & Heffernan, L. (1984). Improving multidisciplinary team functions. In C. A. Maher, R. J. Illback, & J. E. Zins (Eds.), *Organizational psychology in the schools: A handbook for professionals* (pp. 283–301). Springfield, IL: Thomas.

Platt, L. J. (1994). Why bother with teams? An overview. In Commission on Interprofessional Education and Practice, *Interprofessional care and collaborative practice* (pp. 3–10). Pacific Grove, CA: Brooks/Cole.

Pryzwansky, W. B. (1986). Indirect service delivery: Considerations for future research in consultation. *School Psychology Review, 15,* 479–488.

Pryzwansky, W. B., & Rzepski, B. (1983). School based teams: An untapped resource for consultation and technical assistance. *School Psychology Review, 12,*

174–179.

Rosenfield, S. (1987). *Instructional consultation.* Hillsdale, NJ: Erlbaum.

Rosenfield, S. (1992). Developing school-based consultation teams: A design for organizational change. *School Psychology Quarterly, 7,* 27–46.

Rosenfield, S., & Gravois, T. (1996). *Instructional consultation teams: Collaborating for change.* New York: Guilford.

Rosenholtz, S. J. (1989). *Teachers' workplace: The social organization of schools.* New York: Teachers College Press.

Sarason, S. B. (1990). *The predictable failure of educational reform.* San Francisco: Jossey-Bass.

Stokes, S. (Ed.). (1982). *School based staff support teams: A blueprint for action.* Reston, VA: Council for Exceptional Children.

Stokes, S., & Axelrod, P. (1982). Staff-support teams: Critical variables. In S. Stokes (Ed.), *School based staff support teams: A blueprint for action.* (pp.35–38). Reston, VA: Council for Exceptional Children.

Thousand, J. S., & Villa, R. A. (1992). Collaborative teams: A powerful tool in school restructuring. In R. Villa, J. Thousand, W. Stainback, & S. Stainback (Eds.), *Restructuring for heterogeneity: An administrative handbook for creating effective schools for everyone* (pp. 73–108). Baltimore, MD: Paul H. Brookes.

Walsh, J. (1989). Prereferral intervention: The state of practice, implementation, and effectiveness. Doctoral dissertation, Columbia University, 1989. *Dissertation Abstracts International, 50,* 2344A.

Wasley, P. A. (1994). *Stirring the chalkdust.* New York: Teachers College Press.

Weinberg, R. B. (1989). Consultation and training with school-based crisis teams. *Professional Psychology: Research and Practice, 20,* 305–308.

West, J. F., & Idol, L. (1987). School consultation (part I): An interdisciplinary perspective on theory, models, and research. *Journal of Learning Disabilities, 20,* 388–408.

Wojtusik, M. L., & Sikorsky, S. (1991, April). Design for the implementation of successful instructional support teams. Paper presented at the Annual Convention of the Council of Exceptional Children, Atlanta, GA.

## CHAPTER 39

# SCHOOL PSYCHOLOGY IN A DIVERSE WORLD: CONSIDERATIONS FOR PRACTICE, RESEARCH, AND TRAINING

MARY HENNING-STOUT
*Lewis & Clark College*
MICHAELANTHONY BROWN-CHEATHAM
*San Diego State University*

*In May 1995, Michaelanthony Brown-Cheatham met an untimely death. He had agreed to coauthor this chapter some months earlier, and we engaged in numerous discussions about its shape and substance. We arrived together at the observation that an inventory of interventions for addressing diversity issues would overlook the primary challenges facing our profession. Two challenges seemed most salient: (1) making overt the influence of diversity and privilege in the practice, research, and training of school psychology and (2) articulating a conceptual base to support our profession's positive contribution to the diverse communities we serve. We came to understand our task in this chapter as one of developing a scholarly reflection on the status of school psychology's engagement with diversity in hopes that such a reflection would aid the development of needed conceptual anchors. The discussion that follows is my elaboration of what I have understood as our mutual goal. Interspersed throughout the narrative are excerpts from Dr. Brown-Cheatham's writings.*

*Mary Henning-Stout*

The stories we live shape the way we know (Greenberg et al., 1992; Solomon, Greenberg, & Pyszczynski, 1991). How we have been raised, fed, clothed, educated, acknowledged, ignored— all carry our culture and teach us who we are. Because this is one of the first and most easily forgotten lessons of diversity, I begin this chapter with two stories. First, from Michaelanthony Brown-Cheatham (1994, March):

> I grew up as a step child of the Kennedy administration. It was hailed as a time of great promise for educational and economic mobility and attainment that would begin to make reparation of generations past. I also grew up in an Afro-Creole household, listening to drums, voodoo chants, and sermons. There I learned to fear God, taunt the devil, appreciate and respect my elders, pour libations, and to be seen and rarely heard. I was reared in an environment where raising children was the communal responsibility of tribeswomen who instilled motherwit. Simply put, motherwit is steeped in folklore, oral history and spirituality. It is a cultural belief predicated on the notion that formal learning begins at home and within the community. As a male child, I received the care of tribeswomen who rubbed a blend of hot corn and walnut oils

on my brow and limbs with hands caked hard by "days work," all to toughen my skin against the piercing winds I would surely meet. These formative experiences would later serve me well in my struggles to negotiate outside my tribe and within the mainstream European American environment with its prominent heritage and traditions. (p. 1)

The second story, parallel in time, is my own:

I was raised a white woman in the southern United States. I lived in the dust of west Texas, the hills of central Texas, and the humidity of Georgia. My father was a Presbyterian minister, a math major, and a Republican. My mother was his wife, the primary caregiver for their four daughters, a sociology major, and a Democrat. I was oldest of the four girls and, as I grew, I was told sketchy stories of my white ancestors going back to before the American Revolution. "Our people," on my mother's side, were teachers and farmers in Georgia. They had immigrated many generations earlier from Scotland and Ireland. Some had owned slaves. On my father's side were journalists and railroad workers, more recent immigrants from Germany and Britain. In the rooms of our homes and the halls of our churches, I learned to listen behind words, to read the hidden language of women and children—words that spoke the stories we could not tell out loud. I learned to watch for certain dangers and for certain privileges made available to well-behaved white girls. And over time in the face of my culture's disapproval, I learned to voice what I saw.

As authors of this chapter, Michaelanthony Brown-Cheatham and I have both acknowledged that our thoughts and observations are filtered through these stories and the many others we have lived. Our individual scholarship and practice have arisen from fundamentally different worldviews—worldviews reflecting our respective enculturations, what we experienced and were taught as we grew. As school psychologists, ours are two of many perspectives on psychology; mental health; and the proper content, process, and goals of education. We share a common knowledge base with others in our discipline (Division 16 Task Force on Specialty Defi-

nition, 1995; National Association of School psychologists, 1995), but our codification and application of that knowledge have been mediated by who we are and how we know.

With these understandings, Dr. Brown-Cheatham and I reviewed the literature and documented practice of school psychology and reached the conclusion that our profession is beginning to engage in the struggle necessary for accommodating diversity, and thus school psychology is greatly in need of a conceptual base for supporting professional thought and action in a diverse world. The purpose of this chapter is to initiate exploration and articulation of such a base.

I begin with broad consideration of the sociopolitical context in which diversity resides. Diversity is not the exclusive concern of any social service or political agenda, and as a human service profession, school psychology should be anchored in the fundamental appreciation of diversity as an ontological reality, which affects all areas of human experience (Amin, 1989; Harding, 1991). To address bias more directly, I follow the opening section with a description of two theoretical explanations for cultural bias. These perspectives provide context for the subsequent survey of encounters with diversity in areas closer to school psychology. This survey leads, in turn, to the articulation of a definition for diversity—a first step in building a conceptual base. With this definition, I focus on describing current practice, research, and training activities in school psychology that link specifically with diversity concerns. Finally, I identify questions that may help the profession move toward establishing the dynamic conceptual foundation needed for school psychology's positive contribution to the diverse communities we serve.

## SPEAKING DIVERSITY

The current conversation on issues of diversity is more than a passing concern; it defines contemporary U.S. culture. In this conversation, personal stories are generally left unheard. We speak of problems and solutions, of tragedies and reparative measures, but rarely do we stop to realize the extent to which participation in this conversation is mediated by the stories that have shaped the way we each understand the world (Greenberg et al., 1992; Solomon et al., 1991). Each person's epistemology, or way of knowing, develops through the complex interplay of personality (individual uniqueness), race, gender, physical ability, sexual orientation, language, religious and spiritual practice, socioeconomic status, ethnic tradition, and geographic setting (Amin, 1989; Harding, 1991; Sampson, 1991). Our ways of knowing are dynamic; they shift as what we know shifts.

Diversity is a concept and a reality that has molded what we know in the United States, as individuals and as a nation. Diversity is at the center of human experience and, arguably, the foundation on which the United States as a political entity was established (Zinn, 1981). At that time, European immigrants sought enduring answers to questions of how people of diverse religious beliefs could live together. The answers they articulated remain at the core of our nation's definition and keep open the dialogue on issues of diversity. Placing this philosophical tradition in the context of many European settlers' overwhelming inhumanity to the indigenous people of these lands, to African slaves, to Chinese railroad laborers, and to Mexican and Latino farmworkers shifts the conversation on diversity from abstract discussion to social mandate. When history is stretched to include the little-told stories of women (lesbian, bisexual, and heterosexual), gay men, people with disabilities, people who are working and poor, people who are in abject poverty, and children, both the urgency and complexity of this conversation are apparent (Amin, 1989; Harding 1991). Diversity is our country's greatest challenge and, potentially, our greatest asset. Diversity is who are.

In this context, the profession and discipline of school psychology are challenged to contribute. Practitioners and researchers of school psychology are faced with developing intercultural competence (Salzman, 1995), recognizing and honoring cultural wisdom (Brown-Cheatham, 1993), and applying these to the delivery of mental health services and the development of research agendas. However, school psychology remains more in a position of naiveté than expertise on issues of diversity, in particular, issues of bias as they are evident in learning environments and as they affect learning success. There is limited literature addressing these issues (Cajigas-Segredo, 1993; Rogers & Bursztyn, 1995a). We stand at the point of identifying how we as individuals and as a profession contribute to problems associated with diversity and how we can move toward improving our competence to address these problems.

# DIVERSITY AND BIAS

Diversity presents a broad array of challenges and possibilities. An all too common response to diversity among humans, however, has been bias. Bias, or any "ism" associated with behaviors that marginalize people, is often attributed to the individual or collection of individuals who perpetrate it. Fine and Wong (1995) have suggested, however, that most of the bias we encounter as psychologists and educators is more appropriately understood as being institutionalized. That is, the bias we see aimed at others or ourselves may be as much a feature of the institution in which the event occurs as a predisposition within the perpetrator. Fine and Wong present evidence from their observations in two social psychological contexts: a southern high school, where a prom was canceled because of interracial dating and where racial segregation is perpetuated through academic tracking, and a northeastern law school, where all women and all men of color enter with skill and self-assurance equal to their white male peers but leave segregated from those peers in both areas. Based on these data, the authors suggest that deeply established systems of bias run through institutions and are absorbed by the people who participate in them. Fine and Wong express their concern "that as social psychologists and educators we traditionally study 'success' and 'failure' as though they were *inherently individualistic* and therefore only *coincidentally* white (or not) and male (or not). By so *deinstitutionalizing* these stories of success and failure, as scholars we deny that these narratives reveal the racial and gendered performances of institutional life" (p. 11; emphasis in original).

The concerns described by Fine and Wong (1995) stand as a call for school psychologists to become aware not only of the systems of bias affecting the people they serve but also those affecting the school psychologists themselves. This institutionalization of bias in schools and other educational settings calls forth the bias within us. Because we, too, are products of institutions, we have not escaped being bathed in these bias systems and cannot avoid carrying internalized beliefs and worldviews that reflect them.

A second theoretical perspective on biased behavior, terror management theory (Greenberg et al., 1992; Solomon et al., 1991), underscores the importance of mental health professionals' increased consciousness of the role culture plays in our own and others' behaviors. An extensive series of studies documenting the links between thoughts of one's own death and biased social behaviors supports the theory that culture provides a protective buffer between each individual and her or his mortality concerns (e.g., Greenberg et al., 1990, 1992; Greenberg, Pyszczynski, Solomon, Simon, and Breus, 1994). As human beings, we have the ability to be aware of our mortality. According to terror management theory, we buffer ourselves from the disabling effects of incessant thoughts of death by embracing the rules, instructions, stories, and other reassurances of culture. Culture teaches us how to live, and living by culture's standards and values gives us self-esteem.

So it happens that when two or more people meet who have noticeable contrasts in culture, their respective buffers are threatened, and both the salience of their mortality and their need for faith in the reliability of their worldviews increase. "Because of the critical role that the cultural worldview and self-esteem play in protecting individuals from anxiety, terror management theory posits that a great deal of social behavior is directed toward their maintenance and defense" (Greenberg et al., 1994, p. 627). This explanation for biased behavior is immediately relevant to our understanding of clashes among people of diverse groups. It also illustrates the depth of existential challenge brought on with unmediated cross-cultural encounters, that is, encounters in which the threats of cultural differences are accentuated by the rigidity of cultural worldviews brought to them. Taken together with Fine and Wong's (1995) observations, these explanations of bias challenge school psychologists to identify and moderate the rigidity of the worldviews that drive professional and institutional functioning.

## ENCOUNTERS WITH DIVERSITY

*Diversity* is the word used to contain and reflect the variation among and within species of living beings and types of inorganic matter. The concept of diversity explains the uniqueness in fingerprints, DNA (deoxyribonucleic acid), and grains of sand. Because it is incontrovertable and everywhere in evidence, diversity can be understood as a natural law. Apparently, however, this law is only a problem for human beings (James, 1890).

## Diversity and Education

Bringing this concept to bear on the cultural phenomena associated with education illustrates the difficulties humans have in living with diversity. These difficulties are evident in matters of curriculum, instruction, personnel, structuring of time, evaluation of the learning progress, and enforced standards of behavior. By and large, schools and other educational institutions are organized to be consistent with the values and goals of the dominant culture. This culture emerges from the numeric and/or political and economic majority, that is, from the people who are either the greatest in number or who have the most political and economic power. For almost 500 years in North America, the dominant culture has been Anglo American, the group that has had both the greatest numbers and the most wealth, the latter increasingly concentrated in fewer hands.

To uncover the implications of diversity for education, the nature of inclusion or exclusion of perspectives at variance with the dominant culture must be considered. This consideration evokes the now familiar list. How and to what extent is schooling adjusted to take into account matters of race, gender, ability, sexual orientation, language, religious and spiritual belief and practice, socioeconomic status, ethnic tradition, and geographic setting?

In the literature on psychology in education, initial attention has been given to some of these issues in discussions of bilingual education (e.g., Lopez, 1995; Palmer, Hughes, & Juarez, 1991; Rosenfield & Esquivel, 1985); school violence (e.g., Soriano, Soriano & Jimenez, 1994); the developmental experiences of adolescent girls (e.g., Gilligan, Lyons, & Hanmer, 1990); the concerns of lesbian, gay, and bisexual youths and families (e.g., Unks, 1994); and the unique issues of rural children and families (e.g., Kramer & Peters, 1985). Some attention has been paid to these issues, as reflected in the visual and narrative representation of people in textbooks (e.g., Bigelow, 1991; Holden, 1987) and in discussions of the possibility of voucher systems that would reimburse wage earners who choose to send their children to private schools (e.g., Kozol, 1992; Miner, 1992).

## Diversity and Assessment

The emergence of special education, especially following the institution of the Education for all Handicapped Children Law (now the Individuals with Disabilities in Education Act, IDEA), led to increased attention to the diverse ways in which people learn (e.g., Collier & Hoover, 1987; Reynolds, 1992; Sigmon, 1990). In spite of revision in the law, interpretations have fallen consistently in line with the culturally prevalent disease model, leaving learners who qualify for special education to be seen by both professionals and laypeople as flawed rather than simply different.

A recent perspective on variation in how people learn has been developed by a group of scholars who point to the inevitable clash between curricula and diverse learners (e.g., Carnine, 1994). This line of research and theory advocates constructing instructional technologies that lead students to produce measurable outcomes (gauged with curriculum-based tests), which researchers then interpret as evidence of learning. This line of inquiry is focused overtly on helping "school psychologists better understand how some student failures can be seen as resulting from a curriculum disability and how the appropriate use of high quality educational tools might reduce the number of curriculum-disabled students" (p. 342). Yet, the goal is clearly to bring the students into line with the curriculum, rather than adjusting the curriculum to represent and build on the knowledge of learners. Research in curriculum-based measurement and direct instruction holds up well under the scrutiny of quantitative behavioral science; yet, the discussion still lacks consideration of fundamental questions about the cultural loading in researchers' operational definitions of learning. Without full exploration of these questions, the fact of diversity as a key variable in learning remains unaddressed and adequate, practical accountability to diverse learners cannot be established (Rogoff & Chavajay, 1995).

In other areas of psychological measurement there have been more substantive, although intermittent, discussions of diversity (e.g., Cummins, 1986; Dana, 1995; Figueroa, 1990; Frisby, 1995; Gould, 1981; Herrnstein & Murray, 1994; Reynolds & Brown, 1984). These discussions have centered variously around justifications of social stratification with the data of intelligence tests (e.g., Jensen, 1980; Herrnstein & Murray, 1994), demonstrations of the psychometric integrity of tests apart from their potential misuse (e.g., Reynolds & Brown, 1984), and calls for careful analyses of tests as artifacts of the cultures of test authors and publishers (e.g., Gould, 1981; Helms, 1992; Henning-Stout, 1994c).

## Defining Diversity

In most of the psychological and educational literature speaking to these concerns, diversity is determined by race, gender, class, and/or speaking a language other than English. For the purposes of this chapter, however, *diversity* refers to all the ways in which humans are diverse; it refers, once again, to the list: race, gender, ability, sexual orientation, language, religious and spiritual belief and practice, socioeconomic status, ethnic tradition, and geographic setting.

This list is lengthy (and probably incomplete) precisely because the diversity with which we work and live is so vast. At the same time, the commonality implied by a listing of diverse groups is controversial. It can be argued convincingly that speaking of people who are marginalized as a whole group dilutes the specific concerns of individual groups. The ability to respect unity and diversity simultaneously is imperative to responsive school psychology. Listing a range of human groupings illustrates diversity as both complex and "the norm," yet the unique concerns of the groups and individuals included must not be erased.

Salzman (1995) elucidates this dilemma in his consideration of potential attributional biases affecting providers of mental health counseling. He suggests that many of the misunderstandings that arise in the midst of human diversity stem from misattributions of behavior to a person's membership in a cultural group. Such misattribution, or sterotyping, by a school psychologist can give rise to incorrect identification of the problem and ineffective (if not destructive) intervention. At the same time, Salzman identifies the attribution of behavior to individual idiosyncrasy as an equally threatening tendency on the part of mental health service providers. Reflecting specifically on an Anglo teacher's misattribution of a cool reception of her greeting by a Navajo coworker, Salzman writes, "The misattribution of unfriendliness and its consequences might have been avoided if the cultural context of the behavior had been salient to the Anglo teacher" (p. 185).

It is vital to know what we are speaking of when we speak of human diversity. We must know that (a) each person has qualities and understandings in common with all other human beings (universal), (b) each person has qualities and understandings that match with some other human beings (cultural), and (c) each person has qualities and understandings that are entirely unique (personal). Furthermore, all three of these aspects of an individual are engaged at all times (Turner, 1990). This poses two particular challenges to school psychologists. First, we must remain open to information that might disprove or refine diagnostic insights and related intervention plans. Second, we must engage the ethical necessity for becoming increasingly conscious of the ways *our own* personal, cultural, and universal qualities and understandings mediate what we can know about the person, group, or system with which we are working.

## DIFFICULTIES WITH DIVERSITY IN SCHOOL PSYCHOLOGY

Where are difficulties with diversity evident in school psychology—in our practice, research, and training? The existing philosophical or empirical literature on this question has focused almost exclusively on practice (e.g., Cummins, 1986; Dana, 1995; Figueroa, 1990; Gopaul-McNicol, 1992; Harris, 1993; Henning-Stout, 1994b, 1994d; Mosley-Howard, 1995). These contributions are important beginnings; yet given the extent of practical issues involving diversity in school psychology, much remains to be done (Cajigas-Segredo, 1993; Rogers & Bursztyn, 1995a). In school psychology research, the discussion of diversity issues in research design, implementation, and publication practices has been virtually nonexistent (cf. Henning-Stout, 1994a). Slightly more scholarship has addressed diversity in training (e.g., Barona, de Barona, Flores, & Gutierrez, 1990). Initial explorations have occurred in the areas of preparing school psychologists to support bilingual education (Lopez, 1995; Palmer et al., 1991), articulating competencies for bilingual school psychologists (Rosenfield & Esquivel, 1985), attending to the experiences of women as graduate students and professional school psychologists (Alpert & Conoley, 1988), and identifying comprehensive cross-cultural training programs (Rogers & Bursztyn, 1995b, 1996; Rogers, Ponterotto, Conoley, & Wiese, 1992). In addition, a few survey research efforts have considered the experiences of women (Conoley & Welch, 1988; Wilson & Reschly, 1995) and people of color (Ingraham, 1992) as students and faculty in academic institutions. Finally, there has been almost no discussion of diversity issues in school psychology research (cf. Henning-Stout, 1994a).

Perhaps the relative lack of attention to questions of diversity in the literature of our profession is due, in part, to the substantial shift in perspective necessary for viewing critically the cultures in which we are involved. We must be willing to entertain the possibility that any of the things we know or do may be inadequate or may be biased. What follows are observations and questions that may encourage this perspective.

## Practice

The practice of school psychology is a product of culture. The tools and ideas used in practice have been developed by people who have had the time and inclination to develop them. These tools and ideas can be assumed to be extensions of the goal of school psychology, that is, to generate and apply knowledge from psychology and education in support of learning and learners in schools and other settings where learning takes place (Division 16 Task Force on Specialty Definition, 1995; National Association of School Psychologists, 1995). When considered in light of diversity, this is a dynamic and generative goal. Inevitably, "knowledge from psychology and education" will be limited in its representation of the diverse social and psychological situations from which learners come. As these limits are reached, the goal of our profession suggests alterations in knowledge and practice should naturally follow.

In keeping with this goal, school psychologists must be continually attuned to the places where our recorded knowledge and sanctioned technology break down. Those inadequacies may be evident on several levels: (a) the level of ethnocentrism, seeing as pathological any behavior inconsistent with sanctioned dominant culture; (b) the level of stereotyping, making overgeneralizations from limited samples, or even normative evidence, to expect all people in an identified group to behave in the same way; and (c) the level of idiosyncracy, seeing behavior as purely indicative of a person's individual character without regard for her or his social context. These three levels are reminiscent of the aspects of shared and unique human behavior described earlier and will illustrate the limitations to practice that occur when the universal, group, and personal sources of a person's behavior are considered in isolation.

For example, in the practice of assessment, prevailing technology almost exclusively allows the application of the dominant culture (i.e., ethnocentrism) through instrumentation derived from that culture (Rogoff & Chavajay, 1995). Translating the content of those instruments may afford accurate assessment of learners who otherwise match with the epistemology represented in the test's content. However, without further translation of the nonverbal and syntactical nuance of an instrument to match an individual's cultural reality, the instrument retains ethnocentric bias, and its sensitivity and validity fall seriously into doubt (Messick, 1980; Tulviste, 1991).

Similar problems occur with overemphasis on cultural affiliation. Brown-Cheatham (1994, March) commented specifically on the problem of sterotyping in a discussion of issues of race in school psychology:

> Recently in our professional journals, several debates have emerged that center on the role culture plays in learning styles and educational achievement among African American children. The history of African Americans is complex and varied. Therefore, a singular or uniform approach to reaching such a diverse group, as we can find in the literature and in our personal and professional experiences, falls short of reality. As long as we ignore the diversity within our group, all African Americans continue to be denied equal access and opportunity to influence decisions that affect the quality of our lives. (p.6)

No assessment or instructional strategy will work with all members of any one cultural group. In our efforts to identify culturally specific values and communication patterns, we must realize that individual behaviors or learning styles are often at variance with group norms. To apply normative expectations to all members of any group (e.g., "All Native-American children learn best in groups;" "All African-American children need structure;" "All European-American children respond best to public praise") is to engage in stereotyping.

Still, there remain tendencies to attribute to idiosyncracy behaviors that are best understood in cultural and social context. This is illustrated by the tendency to locate learning and behavioral problems inside learners (Conoley & Conoley, 1992). This medical-illness model overlooks the social context in which any learner functions. Regardless of the causal proportions attributed to nature and nurture, the personality, cognition, and behavior of each individual are mediated substantially by group affiliation (chosen or assigned). Our predominantly Anglo-American profession requires consistent engagement by school psychologists with learners in a range of settings and from cultural groups widely different from our own. Thus, awareness of the cultural variation across groups and the individual variation within them, as well as the limitations of current practice for accommodating this diversity, is vital for school psychologists.

## Research

Like any human activity, research is culturally bound. What we know is determined by the questions we ask, and what we ask is mediated by the way we know (Amin, 1989; Harding, 1991). These are insights of anthropology, quantum physics, and new philosophies of science (e.g., Keller, 1985). They stand as profound challenges to researchers in school psychology. The tools and ideas of our practice originate and/or are validated through the efforts of the researchers in our field. This research cannot escape its determination, in part, by the cultures of the researchers themselves. The participants chosen, the data collection tools adopted, the research questions, and the data interpretation are all influenced by the way the world already makes sense to the people conducting the research (Hoshmand & Polkinghorn, 1992; Sampson, 1991).

This fact, another fact of diversity, does not invalidate research but makes more salient traditional questions of external validity and the necessary limitation of quantitative descriptions of observed phenomena (Hoshmand & Polkinghorn, 1992; Ponterotto & Casas, 1991; Sampson, 1991). Research carries bias when it is presented as incontrovertible truth and used to justify rigid practices that have no room for human diversity.

## Training

In the preparation of school psychologists for roles in practice and research, issues of diversity are particularly evident in the construction of curricula and in the recruitment of students and faculty from diverse groups. Because curricula reflect accepted knowledge, they are necessarily limited by the reach of that knowledge and, as suggested, knowledge is limited by the worldviews of those articulating it (Harding, 1991; Hoshmand & Polkinghorne, 1992). It is within the capability of practitioners and researchers to learn of cultures other than their own, but this knowledge will always be incomplete. Fuller, more authentic understandings are most possible with the collected perspectives of practitioners and researchers with diverse ways of knowing.

The difficulties faced by school psychology in attracting people of diverse cultural groups into the profession are vast and reflected in similar struggles across higher education. The tendency is to create committees within the academy to consider what can be done to attract more students and faculty from diverse groups. In her writings on scientific practice, Sandra Harding (1991) reveals the limitations of such activity, which is confined to the experiential range of the people present, often an exceedingly homogeneous lot. Harding believes that the real insights on what we do not yet know, on the next edges of knowledge, come from the perspectives of those most marginalized by current constructions on human activities like science, government, and education—and like school psychology.

It follows that school psychology could be best informed about ways of serving people of diverse backgrounds by actively holding central places for the voices and experiences of the people most marginalized by the profession as it currently functions. Brown-Cheatham's (1994, March) extended recollection of experiences in graduate school is an example of the struggles encountered by many people of color who attempt to enter school psychology from the margins:

> Just over a decade ago . . . I applied to a school psychology program in a large metropolitan area. I was excited about the prospect of professional training, and when I was invited for an interview, I believed that I was well on my way to fulfilling a goal. The interview was chaired by two senior members of the program. They entered the small interview room, glanced above my application portfolio and seemed awestruck when they saw a young Black male interviewee. They both quickly excused themselves and returned to the departmental office a short distance down the corridor. . . . One professor shouted to the departmental secretary, "You didn't tell us he was Black!" I had been forewarned by the secretary who handled applications and appointments that she had not told them I was a minority applicant. When I asked her

why, she said, "If I'd told them you were Black, you wouldn't have gotten an interview." She added, "Anyway, they believe that no minority would want to be in school psychology, and that any really qualified minority would apply to another program." . . .

> You may be wondering why I did not leave. You need to know a few things. I was a 21-year-old Black male, of large frame, in a major urban area. My options seemed limited to getting a menial job, going to school, or going to jail. Unlike my grandmother, I was a poor apprentice of any magic that might loose me from this finite list, so school won my internal election. School was where I had shown some of my grandmother's magic. It took at least some magic to get a Black male from the inner-city, a first generation college student, through the prestigious academy where I had earned a B.A. with honors. Some kind of magic gave me the ability to adapt and persevere despite the social and educational apartheid that consumed by contemporaries. (pp. 2–4)

After ultimate admission into graduate school, subsequent completion of a doctoral degree, and successful pursuit of an academic post, Brown-Cheatham (1994, March) reflected on the cost of such career choices, costs that inhibit the engagement of many people with higher education:

> I was like many African Americans who have been socialized early to take pride in our cultural heritage only to find that these significant aspects of our lives are not valued. To be sure, standardized national admissions tests and other traditional college entrance criteria (e.g., SAT, GRE, Grade point average) have not reflected a diversity of cultural perspectives mirroring instead the mainstream Anglo experience. It is important to recognize that this negation of ethnic and cultural groups' most important experiences contributes to their devaluation as scholars, professionals, and human beings.

> Regrettably, mainstream universities and professions are not immune to the tendency to dilute the importance of core cultural beliefs and values of students and faculty of color. Many institutions assume that if minority students survive the

educational gauntlet and continue pursuing graduate studies, then the minority student has triumphed over adversity and serves as an example of having successfully negotiated individual bouts of racism and oppression. Yet, obtaining admission into mainstream educational institutions or professions does not even afford a person from a minority group acceptance within his or her own culture. Rather, such an accomplishment signifies to the individual and his or her cultural group, that person's invitation to join the mainstream culture, embrace its values, and distance from his or her core cultural beliefs, values and traditions. (p. 6)

The struggle for people of nondominant cultural groups to remain true to their values, beliefs, and traditions must be appreciated and addressed if our profession is to include diverse voices. Myriad conditions in the graduate preparation of school psychologists mitigate against understanding of and competence within the realities of diversity. Certainly reviews of curricula and instructional practices are needed, but the absence of diverse people as students and faculty in graduate school psychology programs is perhaps the most glaring weakness.

The argument for including voices like Brown-Cheatham's in the discussion of our responsiveness to diversity is not, however, an argument for tokenism—the practice of bringing individuals of diverse groups into Anglo-dominated systems with no intention of listening or accommodating to the truths they reveal. Instead, this is an argument for graduate programs to become actively open to substantial changes identified and engineered by people who historically have been and continue to be marginalized in higher education and, therefore, in the professions. School psychology must be infused with the diverse and multiple perspectives of the populations the profession is supposed to be serving. This infusion, possible only with diversity among the practitioners and academicians of our profession, is fundamental in meeting the ethical imperative of competence.

# DIRECTIONS FOR SCHOOL PSYCHOLOGY

School psychology is uniquely situated to move decisively into conscious engagement with diversity in the communities we serve. Education, especially in public settings, includes learners from across the human range. Diversity has never been absent from these communities but has only recently been made visible enough to demand the attention of professions like ours. The careful public documentation of dramatic shifts in the population of our country to include increasing numbers of people from linguistically, ethnically, and racially diverse groups (Hill, Soriano, & Chen, 1994) has helped to bring these realities into long-overdue public discussion. For our profession, this documentation makes visible and unavoidable the necessity of accounting for the representativenss of our practices, our research efforts, and the composition of our faculty and graduate students. School psychology must respond.

Three broad initiatives seem necessary. First, the members of our profession must make concerted and substantive efforts to bring people from all groups into our ranks. Our professional and employing organizations must develop specific and immediate plans for achieving and maintaining this goal. Second, we must develop enduring methods for identifying and remaining vigilant to the ways practice, research, and training carry and perpetuate systems of bias. Finally, we must initiate and maintain strategies for learning from and acting on the ceaseless lessons of diversity. Diversity is dynamic and requires the development of processes for engaging variation, and doing so in ways consistent with school psychology's goal of supporting learning. Following, often in the form of enumerated lists, are questions of practice, research, and training that are offered as vehicles for these initiatives.

## Directions for Practice

"Understanding . . . that culture anchors learning allows all learners to have their culture incorporated into every educational and interpersonal experience and enriches all of our lives" (Brown-Cheatham, 1994, March, p. 6). The practice of school psychology must move beyond understanding to action based on that knowledge. That is the point of practice. Practitioners who are aware and respectful of diversity demonstrate intercultural competence (Salzman, 1995) and cultural wisdom (Brown-Cheatham, 1993), both of which involve self-confident understanding of and security within one's own culture. This type of cultural security grounds practitioners' acceptance of and comfort with people of cultures different from their own. Culturally responsive practitioners are open and sensitive to information that may alter their understanding of a person's experience. They continually ask questions such as the following, demanding of themselves awareness and respect and demanding fairness of the techniques they employ.

1. Is the practice sensitive to and respectful of the individuality of the person or people being served?

2. Does the practice take into account the individual's group affiliations and universal characteristics?

3. If the practice has not historically been applied in respectful ways, are there ways to adjust the practice toward accommodation of diverse ways of knowing and being, or should the practice be discarded?

4. Has the service provider looked critically at the biases she or he carries about the culture of the person or people being served?

5. Is the service provider open to the possibility of evidence of her or his bias arising at any time during service?

6. Does the service provider have skills for referring to colleagues those people against whom she or he holds insurmountable bias?

## Directions for Research

"Ethnic identity is an anchor that bonds individuals to a historical reality. The significance of this reality cannot be ignored or understated. It forms the apertures from which we perceive ourselves in relation to the universe" (Brown-Cheatham, 1994, June, p. 20). Along with ethnic identity, our understandings are influenced by any affiliation we have with any group (Rogoff & Chavajay, 1995). This fact stands as the most fundamental challenge to the integrity of our conceptual and knowledge bases. More accurately, this fact stands as the reminder that all research is filtered through the epistemologies of the researchers. All findings are possibilities (James, 1890). They are certainly viable, but they cannot by themselves be the complete or unwavering truths.

Researchers in school psychology who are aware and respectful of diversity grapple with questions like these:

1. Whose reality is represented by the research question posed and the answers sought?

2. Whose experiences are surveyed by the research questions, and how accurate a portrayal of the realities is it possible to develop within the parameters of the research design?

3. What can and cannot be detected with the measures used to collect data?

4. How do researchers' frames of reference mediate their interpretation of data?

5. How is the process of reviewing and publishing scholarly writings influenced by the cultural perspectives of the few scholars selected to serve as editors and on editorial review boards?

6. What can be done to extend the relevance of research findings to people of diverse groups?

7. How can the knowledge base in psychology and education be enhanced with research grounded in diverse perspectives?

Research in school psychology is rarely a vain pursuit. What researchers ask and learn contribute continually to the dynamic story of what we know. It is imperative, however, that research findings be presented as they are, interpretations of data filtered through the cultural lens of the researcher. Such presentation is not only more accurate, but it also makes overt the role of research in pushing at the edges of knowledge as an ongoing process, rather than an ultimately finite accumulation of truths.

## Directions for Training

"Valuing ethnic diversity within the academies is a new and arduous endeavor. Yet, many institutions are taking steps to reach out and bring minority voices and views into the halls of academia" (Brown-Cheatham, 1995, p. 9). The presence or absence of these voices and views in graduate programs influences profoundly the way school psychologists are prepared to respond to diversity. Robinson-Zinartu and Cook-Morales (1994) suggest eight critical features of school psychology programs that would prepare culturally competent graduates. Such programs would (a) employ faculty with cultural competence and multicultural expertise; (b) articulate program philosophies that emphasize engagement with diversity; (c) employ faculty of diverse cultural groups; (d) recruit, admit, and retain students of diverse cultural groups; (e) support faculty and student engagement in cross-cultural research; (f) implement a curriculum infused with attention to diversity that provides both theoretical and practical grounding for students; (g) provide mentors who can support the range of culturally and linguistically diverse students; and (h) be physically located in areas that are accessible to diverse students. To build on this list, the areas of curriculum and mentorship bear special attention.

## Curriculum

"Members of the academy need to be provided with culturally derived methods and strategies to reframe points of reference and challenge their assumptions and expectations as a means of embracing diversity. When such change occurs, all aspects of racial and cultural differences are considered and infused into policies, practices and curriculum" (Brown-Cheatham, 1995, p. 9). Curriculum carries culture, and the curriculum in school psychology is no exception. The cultural loading of curriculum is a problem if it is left covert, with the implication that its interpretations are the best or final word. In preparing graduate students to be school psychologists, it is imperative that the realities of diversity be addressed in every context, that understandings based on these realities be translated into practical competencies, and that the limitations of our knowledge and practice bases be both acknowledged and probed. The curricula of school psychology are based on the best understandings of their authors and purveyors at the time they are written and employed. There is much that is quite useful in existing curricula, yet they remain constrained in scope with the absence of perspectives that reflect the diversity of the people we serve.

In both preservice and in-service training, fundamental questions should be posed to students and faculty that probe the systems of bias we perpetuate as individuals and as a profession. Among these questions are inquiries into the origin of human fear of diversity. What has led us to seeing diversity as a problem to be solved rather than a reality from which to learn? Such philosophical inquiry would take professors and graduate students into considerations of ontology, of how humans and the state of human affairs came to be as they are. Because these are fairly esoteric questions relative to much of the content of school psychology practice, they might seem at odds with typical curricula, yet these are the questions that can lead our profession into generative engagement with the diversity in which we live and work.

## Mentors

Just as I was about to acquiesce and submit a letter of resignation following numerous injustices and indignities, I went to a professional school psychology meeting. There was a woman, a Black woman, a doctor, a Black doctor woman, Dr. Laura Hines. She sat poised and in command, drawing attention and respect from the predominantly White male audience. She was doing the impossible in my eyes. At this moment I realized that I no longer needed magic, I had an image to follow, albeit vicariously. That evening I quietly resolved an internal and external dilemma and decided I would complete my school psychology training. (Brown-Cheatham, 1994, March, p. 4)

The availability of mentors for graduate students of diverse groups is central to the successful retention of those students in graduate programs. Based on his experiences as a mentor for African-American students, Brown-Cheatham (1995) suggested considerations for the provision of mentorship, summarized here:

1. Make overt and available for discussion the historical and current realities of people of color and other marginalized groups.
2. Recognize yourselves (faculty and administration) as holders of the privilege to either obstruct or enact policies and practices that value and enhance diversity. Without institution-wide commitment to such policies and practices, no laudable rhetoric, campaign effort, or recruitment strategy focused on diversity can have positive effects.
3. Ensure that students are not expected to defend, represent, or reflect the views of their group. Intergroup differences are vast.
4. Define, support, and value mentorship for all students and junior faculty in higher education settings. Identify faculty and community leaders who can and will provide mentorship, assist other interested persons in developing mentorship skills, involve students in both defining the mentor role and identifying capable mentors, and establish methods for evaluating mentor relationships.
5. Attend to race and gender matching to promote confidence and fill important gaps in

the educational and professional experiences of both the mentor and the student.

In addition, Brown-Cheatham (1994, June) offered observations on the unique requirements for faculty from marginalized groups, which should be considered by graduate training programs and the institutions housing them. Although he speaks here as an African-American male professor, his experiences have features in common with other faculty: other people of color; all women; lesbians and gay men; people with disabilities; and people from working-class backgrounds, rural settings, or minority religions.

> As an ethnic minority mentor, I have the onerous task of modeling for proteges how to (a) keep one foot in mainstream society and the other in the ancestral culture without losing integrity or balance, (b) become biculturally competent and "whole," (c) find and secure a niche in the academy and in a chosen profession, and (d) share observations and insights majority group faculty are reticent to discuss. This is a demanding and precarious balance, tantamount to walking a "cultural tightrope," that is not factored into tenure and promotion decisions or fully recognized by professional organizations, yet expected from proteges and encouraged by academic institutions and professional organizations. (p. 20)

# CONCLUSION

"The situation before us commands great and immediate attention. Culture is an important factor central to every human life. It cannot be devalued or ignored" (Brown-Cheatham, 1994, March, p. 6). In the work of school psychology, we intend to contribute to the well-being of people who are learning. In the process of fulfilling this intention, we learn as well. The diversity among humans and throughout the Earth's environment is what sustains our lives and communities. Myriad turns of events across the ages have brought us to this place, where we as humans experience diversity as a problem. School psychology, like all professions, is part of the problem and part of the solution.

This chapter is an attempt to initiate a level of dialogue necessary for our profession to move into substantive and positive engagement with the challenges of diversity. Such engagement is best rooted in strong theory—in conceptual ground. Based on the discussions we had as authors and on the logical flow these ideas have taken, it is possible to distill an essential concept. Diversity is a given. If diversity goes, we all go. If diversity is nurtured and engaged, we all thrive.

For school psychologists, philosophically committed to learning and ethically bound to competence in our service delivery, this conceptual base provides direct guidance for our efforts. Both intercultural competence (Salzman, 1995) and cultural wisdom (Brown-Cheatham, 1993) are central to competent school psychology (in practice, research, or training). Competence grows from identification and correction of the bias systems in individual practice; in accepted technology; in the overt and covert standards of our profession; and in the exclusive systems of privilege in institutions, communities, and nations. Competence also grows from recognizing the profound strength inherent in diversity, a variation that sustains and defines the web of life—the social and educational systems that support children, and the economic and community systems that support teachers, parents, and each of us.

This is a conceptual base on which our profession must stand. Practice, research, and training in school psychology must be anchored to the challenge and promise of diversity if the mission of our profession is to be fulfilled. As a profession and as individuals, we must reframe our perspectives, our ways of knowing, with full recognition and regard for our part in a diverse world.

**AUTHOR'S NOTE**   I would like to express my sincere appreciation to the following people for their careful critiques of earlier drafts of this chapter; their generosity with ideas and suggestions strengthened this writing considerably. My thanks to Giselle Esquivel, Patrick Ethel-King, Colette Ingraham, Antoinette Miranda, Hector Ochoa, Margaret Rogers, Michael Salzman, and David Stout.

# REFERENCES

Alpert, J. L., & Conoley, J. C. (Eds). (1988). Women and school psychology: Issues through the professional life cycle. *Professional School Psychology (Miniseries)*, *3*(1).

Amin, S. (1989). *Eurocentrism*. New York: Monthly Review Press.

Barona, A., de Barona, M., Flores, A., & Gutierrez, M. (1990). Critical issues in training school psychologists to serve minority school children. In A. Barona & E. Garcia (Eds.), *Children at risk: Poverty, minority status and other issues in educational equity* (pp. 187–200). Washington, DC: National Association of School Psychologists.

Bigelow, B. (1991). Once upon a genocide . . . Christopher Columbus in children's literature. In B. Bigelow, B. Miner, & B. Peterson (Eds.), *Rethinking Columbus: Teaching about the 500th anniversary of Columbus's arrival in America* (pp. 23–30). Milwaukee, WI: Rethinking Schools.

Brown-Cheatham, M. (1993, February). A paradigm for African American school psychologists. The four "C's." In C. Robinson-Zinartu (Chair), *Developing multicultural emphasis in professional education programs: Federal personnel preparation grants.* Symposium. Los Angeles: National Association for Multicultural Educators.

Brown-Cheatham, M. (1994, March). On the perils of sleepwalking: The importance of cultural wisdom in the provision of psychoeducational services to children of color. In M. Henning-Stout (Chair), Issues of race and ethnicity in school psychology. Symposium conducted at the Annual Meeting of the National Association of School Psychologists, Seattle.

Brown-Cheatham, M. (1994, June). From me to we: Rethinking mentorship and ethnic identity. *Focus: Official Publication of Division 45 of the American Psychological Association, 8*(1), 19–21.

Brown-Cheatham, M. (1995). Mentorship: Increasing opportunities for African-American students in the academy. Unpublished manuscript. San Diego: San Diego State University.

Cajigas-Segredo, N. (1993). Student characteristics and the training of school psychologists. *Spectrum, 8*(3), 3–9.

Carnine, D. (Ed.). (1994). Diverse learners and prevailing, emerging, and research-based educational approaches and their tools. *School Psychology Review (Miniseries), 23*(3).

Collier, C., & Hoover, J. (1987). *Cognitive learning strategies for minority handicapped students.* Lindale, TX: Hamilton.

Conoley, J. C., & Conoley, C. W. (1992). *School consultation: Practice and training* (2nd ed.). New York: Macmillan.

Conoley, J. C., & Welch, K. (1988). The empowerment of women in school psychology: Paradoxes of success and failure. *Professional School Psychology, 3,* 13–19.

Cummins, J. (1986). Empowering minority students: A framework for intervention. *Harvard Educational Review, 56,* 18–36.

Dana, R. H. (1995). Impact of the use of standard psychological assessment in the diagnosis and treatment of ethnic minorities. In J. F. Aponte,

R. R. Rivers, & J. Wohl (Eds.), *Psychological interventions and cultural diversity* (pp. 57–73). Boston: Allyn & Bacon.

Division 16 Task Force on Specialty Definition. (1995, Fall). Definition of the specialty of school psychology. *The School Psychologist, 49,* 95, 98–104.

Figueroa, R. A. (1990). Assessment of linguistic minority group children. In C. R. Reynolds & R. W. Kamphaus (Eds.), *Handbook of psychological and educational assessment of children: Intelligence and achievement* (pp. 671–696). New York: Guilford.

Fine, M., & Wong, L. M. (1995, August). Individual and social resilience in the face of discrimination. Paper presented at the Annual Meeting of the American Psychological Association, New York.

Frisby, C. L. (Ed.). (1995). The bell curve commentaries. *School Psychology Review (Miniseries), 24*(1).

Gilligan, C., Lyons, N. P., & Hanmer, T. J. (Eds.). (1990). *Making connections: The relational worlds of adolescent girls at Emma Willard School.* Cambridge, MA: Harvard University Press.

Gopaul-McNicol, S. (Ed.). (1992). Understanding and meeting the psychological and educational needs of African-American and Spanish-speaking students. *School Psychology Review (Miniseries), 21*(4).

Gould, S. J. (1981). *The mismeasure of man.* New York: Norton.

Greenberg, J., Pyszczynski, T., Solomon, S., Rosenblatt, A., Veeder, M., Kirkland, S., & Lyon, D. (1990). Evidence for terror management theory II: The effects of mortality salience reactions to those who threaten or bolster the cultural worldview. *Journal of Personality and Social Psychology, 58,* 308–318.

Greenberg, J., Pyszczynski, T., Solomon, S., Simon, L., & Breus, M. (1994). Role of consciousness and accessibility of death-related thoughts in mortality salience effects. *Journal of Personality and Social Psychology, 67,* 627–637.

Greenberg, J., Solomon, S., Pyszczynski, T., Rosenblatt, A., Burling, J., Lyon, D., Simon, L., & Pinel, E. (1992). Why do people need self-esteem? Converging evidence that self-esteem serves an anxiety-buffering function. *Journal of Personality and Social Psychology, 63,* 913–922.

Harding, S. (1991). *Whose science? Whose knowledge? Thinking from women's lives.* Ithaca, NY: Cornell University Press.

Harris, K. C. (Ed.). (1993). Culture and consultation. *Journal of Educational and Psychological Consultation (Special issue), 4*(3/4).

Helms, J. E. (1992). Why is there no study of cultural equivalence in standardized cognitive ability testing? *American Psychologist, 47,* 1083–1101.

Henning-Stout, M. (1994a). Consultation and connected knowing: What we know is determined by the questions we ask. *Journal of Educational and Psychological Consultation, 5*, 5–21.

Henning-Stout, M. (Ed.). (1994b). Gender and consultation. *Journal of Educational and Psychological Consultation, (Special issue), 5(1/2)*.

Henning-Stout, M. (1994c). *Responsive assessment: A new way of thinking about learning*. San Francisco: Jossey-Bass.

Henning-Stout, M. (1994d). Thoughts on being a white consultant. *Journal of Educational and Psychological Consultation, 5*, 269–273.

Herrnstein, R. J., & Murray, C. (1994). *The bell curve: Intelligence and class structure in American life*. New York: Free Press.

Hill, H., Soriano, F. I., & Chen, (1994). *Sociocultural factors in youth violence*. Washington, DC: American Psychological Association.

Holden, C. (1987). Textbook controversy intensified nationwide. *Science, 235*, 19–21.

Hoshmand, L. T., & Polkinghorne, D. E. (1992). Redefining the science-practice relationship and professional training. *American Psychologist, 47*, 55–66.

Ingraham, C. L. (1992, January). Attracting a diverse applicant pool to graduate education in school psychology. *Trainers' Forum, 11*(2), 6–8.

James, W. (1890). *Principles of psychology*. New York: Holt, Rinehart, & Winston.

Jensen, A. R. (1980). *Bias in mental testing*. New York: Free Press.

Keller, E. F. (1985). *Reflections on gender and science*. New Haven, CT: Yale University Press.

Kozol, J. (1992). *Savage inequalities*. New York: Crowne Press.

Kramer, J. J., & Peters, G. J. (1985). What we know about rural school psychology: A brief review and analysis. *School Psychology Review, 14*, 452–456.

Lopez, E. C. (1995). Working with bilingual children. In A. Thomas & J. Grimes (Eds.), *Best practices in school psychology–III* (pp. 1111–1122). Washington, DC: National Association of School Psychologists.

Messick, S. (1989). Validity. In R. L. Linn (Ed.), *Educational measurement* 3rd ed., pp. 13–104. New York: Macmillan.

Miner, B. (Ed.). (1992). *False choices: Why school vouchers threaten our children's future*. Milwaukee, WI: Rethinking Schools.

Mosley-Howard, G. S. (1995). Best practices in considering the role of culture. In A. Thomas & J. Grimes (Eds.), *Best practices in school psychology–III* (pp. 337–345). Washington, DC: National Association of School Psychologists.

National Association of School Psychologists. (1995). Standards for the provision of school psychological services. In A. Thomas & J. Grimes (Eds.), *Best practices in school psychology–III* (pp. 1161–1172). Washington, DC: Author.

Palmer, D. J., Hughes, J., & Juarez, L. (1991). School psychology training and the education of minority at-risk youth: The Texas A & M University program emphasis on handicapped Hispanic children and youth. *School Psychology Review, 20*, 472–484.

Ponterotto, J. G., & Casas, J. M. (1991). *Handbook of racial/ethnic minority counseling research*. Springfield, IL: Thomas.

Reynolds, C. R., & Brown, R. T. (Eds.). (1984). *Perspectives on "Bias in mental testing."* New York: Plenum.

Reynolds, M. (1992). Students and programs at the school margins: Disorder and needed repair. *School Psychology Quarterly, 7*, 233–244.

Robinson-Zinartu, C., & Cook-Morales, V. J. (1994, March). Model for systematic change toward equity in education. Paper presented at the Annual Meeting of the National Association of School Psychologists, Seattle.

Rogers, M. R., & Bursztyn, A. (1995a). Cultural diversity in professional awareness: Reaching a critical threshold at 50. In M.R. Rogers & A. Burstyn (Eds.), Multicultural issues in school psychology. *The School Psychologist (Special edition), 49*, 81, 84, 109.

Rogers, M. R., & Bursztyn, A. (Eds.). (1995b, Fall). Multicultural issues in school psychology, Part I. *The School Psychologist (Special edition), 49*(4).

Rogers, M. R., & Bursztyn, A. (Eds.). (1996, Winter). Multicultural issues in school psychology, Part II. *The School Psychologist (Special edition), 50*(1).

Rogers, M. R., Ponterotto, J. G., Conoley, J. C., & Wiese, M. J. (1992). Multicultural training in school psychology: A national survey. *School Psychology Review, 21*, 603–616.

Rogoff, B., & Chavajay, P. (1995). What's become of research on the cultural basis of cognitive development? *American Psychologist, 50*, 859–877.

Rosenfield, S., & Esquivel, G. B. (1985). Educating school psychologists to work with bilingual/bicultural populations. *Professional Psychology: Research and Practice, 16*, 199–208.

Salzman, M. (1995). Attributional discrepancies and bias in cross-cultural interactions. *Journal of Multicultural Counseling and Development, 23*, 181–193.

Sampson, E. E. (1991). The democratization of psychology. *Theory and Psychology, 1*, 275–298.

Sigmon, S. B. (Ed.). (1990). *Critical voices on special education: Problems and progress concerning the mildly handicapped*. Albany: State University of New York Press.

Solomon, S., Greenberg, J., & Pyszczynski, T. (1991). A terror management theory of social behavior: The psychological functions of self esteem and cultural worldviews. In M. E. P. Zanna (Ed.), *Advances in experimental social psychology* (Vol. 23, pp. 91–159). San Diego: Academic Press.

Soriano, M., Soriano, F. I., & Jimenez, E. (1994). School violence among culturally diverse populations: Sociocultural and Institutional considerations. *School Psychology Review, 23,* 216–235.

Tulviste, P. (1991). *The cultural-historical development of verbal thinking.* Commack, NY: Nova Science Publishers.

Turner, F. (1990). Social work practice theory: A transcultural resource for health care. *Social Science and Medicine, 31,* 13–17.

Unks, G. (Ed.). (1994). The gay teenager. *The High School Journal (Special issue),* 77(1/2).

Wilson, M. S., & Reschly, D. J. (1995). Gender and school psychology: Issues, questions, and answers. *School Psychology Review, 24,* 45–61.

Zinn, H. (1981). *A people's history of the United States.* New York: Beacon.

# PSYCHOLOGY IN THE SCHOOLS: SYSTEMS INTERVENTION CASE EXAMPLES

**CHRISTINE E. BORGELT**
*University of Nebraska–Lincoln*
**JANE CLOSE CONOLEY**
*Texas A&M University*

The word *system* is ubiquitous in current parlance. Practitioners and researchers from every field are called on to create linkages, maximize outcomes, and overcome insular and potentially redundant practices. New scholarship combines traditionally separate disciplines of, for example, chemistry and biology, engineering and medicine, meteorology and anthropology, and psychology and neuroscience.

In this information age, the practices used by psychologists in schools to facilitate change have remained largely unaltered for several decades (Reschly & Wilson, 1995; Stinnett, Havey, & Oehler-Stinnett, 1994), perhaps because of a professional identity that has little to do with change and more to do with the measurement of individual status quo. With a guiding principle of accurate individual measurement of individual attributes, the practices of most psychologists in schools are understandably rather fragmented and disconnected from the contexts in which the systems' actors operate.

Although the individualistic test-and-place role of psychologists remains preeminent, compelling theories and many examples of successful systems interventions continue to entice researchers and practitioners to the world of systems or ecological work (e.g., Friedman, 1994; Krovetz & Speck, 1995, Snapp, Hickman, & Conoley, 1990). The actual difference between systems and nonsystems interventions must be constructed to reveal helpful distinctions. Any

intervention could be a systems intervention, but most interventions are not. This seeming paradox occurs because of individual and systemic obstacles, which are discussed later. The objectives of this chapter include the following:

1.  Offer some case studies of systems interventions in schools.
2.  Illustrate theoretical constructs that can guide intervention development.
3.  Outline the obstacles school psychologists face in mounting systems interventions and how these obstacles can be overcome.

## WHAT IS A SYSTEMS INTERVENTION?

Because everything is a system (e.g., brains, human bodies, governments, rocks and trees, school districts, and classrooms), constructing system interventions should be easy. Such is not the case, however. For the purposes of this chapter, a systems intervention is a change effort aimed at making a difference in how a human organization operates. The goals are to either improve performance or enhance the viability or resilience of the system. An array of possible strategies is available (Curtis & Stollar, 1995; Fullan, Miles, & Taylor, 1980; Gutkin & Curtis, 1990).

1.  *Diagnosis:* Systems can be assessed through a large number of strategies, including inter-

views, questionnaires, surveys, focus groups, observations, and analyses of archival data. Organizational diagnosis is always followed by feedback sessions to plan for the use of diagnostic data.

2. *Team Building:* Promoting successful job completions, teaching skills to accomplish tasks, building relationships among team members, and coaching leader skills are possible approaches in improving team performance.

3. *Intergroup Activities:* Arranging for joint work, with the output as a single system product, can break down unhelpful barriers between groups whose collaborations would improve the organization's success.

4. *Education and Training:* Many approaches for training (e.g., workshops, teleconferences, individual readings, group process events, and mentoring relationships) can be used to improve skills, knowledge of leadership dimensions, responsibilities and functions of group members, decision-making approaches, goal setting and planning, problem solving, or technology applications. Education may also increase the organization-specific knowledge members can use to improve effectiveness.

5. *Structural Activities:* Work design can be adjusted to improve productivity or morale by using job enrichment procedures, changes in communication patterns, or adjustments in supervisory practices or reporting lines.

6. *Mediation:* Some groups may benefit from very directed problem-solving experiences that allow productive confrontation, conflict management, compromise, and problem resolution.

7. *Coaching:* Individualized education is a key to improving performance. Expertly done feedback with an accompanying exploration of alternative behaviors can assist leaders and followers to experiment with new behaviors.

8. *Technology Management:* Organizations need content and management expertise to enhance their uses of information technology. Consultation that helps in determining best-fit technology for organizations can be a vital component in improving school organizational effectiveness, staff morale, and students' learning.

System interventions are easily listed, but practitioners have had difficulty in constructing them, for many individual and contextual reasons. One obstacle has been confusion between intervention targets and operational levels.

## TARGETS AND OPERATIONAL LEVELS

The distinction between intervention targets and operational levels at which work is done partly illuminates the meaning of systems work. For example, a child's learning problem is the most common referral issue for a psychologist (Harris, Gray, Rees-McGee, Carroll, & Zaremba, 1987). The target, improving a child's achievement, is clear, but the choice of the operational level of the intervention is not.

Should the child be assisted by in-depth diagnostic testing, followed by an individually adapted curriculum? Will assistance be better aimed at the instructional skills of the teacher, who may be relying too often on unsupervised seat-work to accomplish learning objectives? Or should a team of educators be formed so that a consistent teaching approach can be constructed to assist the child across the curriculum? Would a building- or district-level in-service program to translate the newest findings of brain research into everyday work with youths be the most strategic?

The target of improving a child's achievement can be reached from a number of levels. Even operations that tend to stay on the individual level, however, may create system change. Consider the first option offered, that is, assessment that leads to curriculum change.

If in-depth assessments were translated into unique curriculum tasks for children, then delivered and assessed for success, a major system intervention would be accomplished, even if the people involved numbered only two or three. Routine translation of assessment results into continuously monitored learning objectives would constitute an instructional system. An instructional systems intervention is implemented when the parts of the teaching-learning system interact in information-bearing ways so that adjustments can be made in the instructional tasks or delivery strategies and a purpose accomplished.

In our opinion (and one shared by others, e.g., Gresham & Witt, 1997), most individual testing of children does not lead to system interventions.

This gap occurs because the assessment device is not related to the instruction, the instruction is not modified in any systematic way after assessment, and the results of any instructional changes that are made are rarely evaluated. Consider an alternative scenario described in the following case (B. Cole, personal communication, 1997).

## CASE STUDY: DOES PRACTICE MAKE PERFECT?

Because all the public school districts in Texas are ranked according to the performance of students on a criterion mastery test, many have established programs to assist students who fail to reach this standard. One student with a moderately successful performance on some parts of the test failed the ninth-grade level in math three times. After each failure she was assigned to Saturday school, during which she completed many practice versions of the test. Following the third failure, her parents asked for guidance from the academic counselor, who referred them to the neighboring district's program.

In this program, the girl's test-taking approach was assessed and special instructions developed. The program personnel noticed that the girl's attention flagged as she made her way through the test. As she began to encounter the most difficult parts of the exam, she was highly distracted and made careless errors inconsistent with her knowledge base.

They asked her to do the last part of the exam first and proceed toward the easier beginning problems. She was still less attentive as the test progressed; however, being faced with progressively easier problems reduced both her anxiety and triggers for careless errors. Although on previous administrations she had never scored above 65% (70% is passing), on this fourth administration she scored 95% and graduation was ensured.

The first practice program was not an instructional system. Assessment did not guide intervention for her test-taking difficulties. The second program reflected interacting elements that produced purposeful behavior (see Asayesh, 1993, and Vollmer & Northup, 1997, for other examples of instructional systems.) If the tests given by psychologists in the schools led even to individual interventions, they would be the source of systems interventions.

A systems intervention takes into account the multiple operational levels that can be used

to effect a desired change, and it is organized so that meaningful connections are created. A successful system intervention changes some aspect of interactions and creates valued-added information for the system (e.g., the child makes more errors at the end of the test despite knowing the material; therefore, change the order in which she works on the problems).

## SEEING CONTENT AND PROCESS

Another approach in developing systems intervention skills is to keep distinctions between content and process very clear. The dual existence of the "whats" and the "hows" of life is obvious. What should be done? How is it best accomplished? What must be said? How is it best communicated? What job needs completion? How should people be organized for success?

Often the "what" that must be achieved is painfully obvious, but accomplishment is illusory. The test-and-place job description of many psychologists in schools should be adjusted because it underutilizes their skills and has not resulted in meaningful change for children (Johnson, Malone, & Hightower, 1997; Kavale, 1990). Knowing the "what" is often not enough.

Systems intervention experts rely on powerful content and changed delivery strategies to facilitate change. Change does not occur simply by discussing the need to change or by presenting a good idea. A change in the behavioral regularities of a school is best accomplished by introducing some program that has both meaningful and helpful content and demands an adjustment in existing communication or interactional regularities (Sarason, 1982).

Following is a case that illustrates how a change in one psychologist's behavior facilitated more effective intervention for her clients. Note that the content of the change was behavioral consultation and intervention; the communication adjustments included assuming both a training and a consultation role with many school personnel and a direct role with students.

## CASE STUDY: SCHOOL PSYCHOLOGICAL SERVICE DELIVERY CHANGE

The individual action of a psychologist can have effects on an entire system of psychological service delivery. This case is based on a narrative provided by one of three school psychologists in a midwestern district of about 15,000 students (D. Sabers, 1996, personal communication). Her goal was to reduce the number of referrals for special education placement, increase the use of child data for intervention planning and decision making, and increase the time she spent in consultation with teachers.

What follows is a summary of the insights she gained from eight years of practice in implementing classroom-level interventions for individual students. During that time, she has developed strategies and identified processes that minimize the test-place role in service delivery. Child gains, data collection, and a consultative approach to services are highlighted. Benefits have included (a) greater involvement in children's academic programming, (b) greater job satisfaction for the psychologists, (c) fewer children identified as educationally disabled, and (d) a 90% to 95% success rate in achieving teacher-identified student goals. When she began her work as a school psychologist, referrals for assessment averaged approximately 100 per year. This year she completed only 40 assessments, while serving 30 additional children through behavioral programming.

The psychologist describes her success as a gradual process, with the staff learning to know and trust her. Skillful entry into individual buildings was critical. She had previously taught in the elementary grades and described this as helpful in establishing her expertise and credibility among the teachers. Beyond initial perceptions, however, her availability to building staff was essential. Early on, the psychologist designed many brief in-service offerings and accepted every opportunity to provide input to teachers. She was available to serve on student assistance teams every time she was asked, and she considered high-level communication skills as key in developing and maintaining working relationships with school staff.

Her accessibility and willingness to expand her job responsibilities led initially to longer work hours. Over the course of several years, however, as successful early intervention strategies reduced the testing caseload, the time required for traditional assessment decreased and her overall time commitment to work was reduced to manageable levels.

Systematic, ongoing data collection was the strongest tool for effective communication between the psychologist and individual teachers.

For example, in a recent case involving a behavioral program, the teacher approached the school psychologist to suggest that the child's program should be altered to exclude a particular period of the day because, in the teacher's opinion, "I feel that it's not working." During a follow-up consultation with the teacher, the psychologist pointed to 27 good days (i.e., where the child had met the specified goal) and 9 unsuccessful days. Upon seeing the data and the percentage of the student's successful days, the teacher agreed that a major change in the behavior plan was not warranted. The psychologist relies on the following pattern: (a) listen to the teacher's concerns; (b) present data as information, not as indisputable proof; and (c) request the teacher's input (see Martens, Hiralall, & Bradley, 1997, for research on a closely related technique).

The psychologist's reputation for successful consultations has prompted a process through which referrals for behavior programs are initiated. The teacher or school counselor contacts the psychologist with a concern. The psychologist expects that liaison with parents remains the responsibility of the classroom teacher. Communication with the parents emphasizes that it is the teacher's concern that has generated the request for an individual plan to increase the child's success at school. The teacher also coordinates any parental responsibility in a behavior contract. Generally, there has been no formal procedure for obtaining parental permission for the psychologist's involvement with the child. Verbal agreement is established through the teacher, and parents receive a copy of the behavior contract. If a behavior contract includes a reinforcer that would involve leaving the school grounds (e.g., going out to lunch with the psychologist or going to the yogurt shop), part of the behavior plan includes the student's responsibility for returning a signed permission from the parent to do so.

Every person who is included in the plan, including custodian, lunchroom staff, teacher, child, or parent, receives a personal copy of the behavior contract. This seems to enhance personal investment and involvement in the plan and makes each contributor understand his or her importance in its success.

The socioeconomic status (SES) of the family seems to affect parental involvement. Parental resistance has been greater in higher-SES buildings. The middle- to upper-middle-income parents expressed concern about differential classroom treatment of their children. In addition, these parents were more likely to offer excuses for the child's difficulties. However, once invested in the plans, these parents have played very active roles.

Parents of lower SES have agreed quickly to the behavior plans. It may be that these parents see the additional effort to ensure the child's success as an appropriate role for the school staff. Generally, these parents requested that information be sent to them, and they preferred limited direct involvement in the interventions. Although this limited involvement is a constraint, the parents' willingness to allow behavioral programming is an asset. Others in the school building have been recruited to help in the generalization of the plan's goals.

The role of the psychologist in implementing plans generally includes regular follow-up with the teacher and the child; often the psychologist delivers the reinforcers and meets with the child to discuss the program. In fact, success in some cases has been dependent on the psychologist's coaching of the child on how to remind the teacher to sign a checklist. Many successful interventions have used self-monitoring by the child (Shapiro & Cole, 1994).

Parents, teachers, and children must understand that behaviors do not change quickly. The psychologist establishes an agreement of 15 school days as a minimum initial intervention period. At the end of 15 days, participants decide if the plan has been implemented consistently, as well as what changes may need to occur. Subsequent ongoing revisions are discussed at the teacher's request.

Continuous collection and sharing of data have been the key tools for the success reported in this case. This psychologist provides end-of-the-year feedback to each individual who was involved in any behavioral plan. Ongoing data collection prevents this from being a gargantuan task. A building summary goes to each principal. Teachers and parents each receive individual child summaries.

For school psychologists entering the field and for those expanding and redefining roles in the schools, this case study offers several key reminders. First, credibility is not gained instantly; it requires patience and an ability to offer a clear role definition. Effective communication is critical. Components identified by this psychologist included careful listening, clarifying questions that lead to elaborations of others' contributions, assertive follow-up on decisions, encouragement

of others through positive comments, and congruent nonverbal skills. Communication targets must include teachers, parents, principals, supervisors, and even the other school psychologists in the district.

For this individual psychologist, the process of meeting teachers' and students' needs has been redefined from a test-and-place role to a consultative approach over an eight-year period. What began as a 10-month job of testing 80 to 100 students has evolved into a multidimensional role. She now averages approximately 40 special education evaluations per year, with associated instructional system designs, and addresses the needs of 30 additional students through behavior programs. Overall, the result has been a more effective use of a wider range of her skills and a greater sense of improving academic and social outcomes for children. In addition, this approach enhances the competencies of school staff, yielding long-term benefits to the staff and the children they teach (Christenson, Abery, & Weinberg, 1986; Gutkin, 1995; Kamphaus, 1995; Welch & Sheridan, 1995).

## WHAT IS A HEALTHY SYSTEM?

In addition to identifying the content and process of possible system change targets, it is useful to understand a framework that describes well-functioning human systems. Several such descriptions are extant and can be useful in guiding systems work.

Biologically based systems theory (von Bertalanffy, 1968; 1981) illuminated the meaning of systems by using biological descriptors such as wholism, centralization and differentiation, regulation, and the distinctions between open and closed systems. This work was seminal in linking the development and experience of humans to that of all other living organisms. Such links are heuristic in developing systems interventions. For example, the tendency for systems under stress to turn toward internal developmental tasks and eschew external input is a normal and helpful short-term response to trauma. Extended boundary rigidity toward external resources is, however, dangerous for system viability. Consider the biologically adaptive focus of blood flow and antibodies that occurs when an organism is injured. The marshalling of internal resources is useful but must be followed by a rapid realignment of the biological processes so that the whole organism is preserved.

When a school is injured, there is a tendency for the same internal focus to occur. Consider the dramatic examples of schoolyard or classroom murders that have occurred over the past decade. It is adaptive for schools to convene internal resources to begin healing processes. Long-term safety is determined, however, by connecting the school to community resources such as neighborhood policing, parental involvement, enhanced opportunities and skills for young people, and enriched services for troubled or troubling students or community members (Goldstein & Conoley, 1997).

Ecological psychology (Bronfenbrenner, 1979) provides useful parameters to describe system levels (e.g., micro-, meso-, and macrosystems) and to understand that human behavior is a product of the interaction between the organism and the context. People are powerful actors, but other forces—ranging from individual attributes, such as intelligence, to political systems, which help or hinder educational opportunity—also act on them. Ecological system interventionists seek to bring people into balance with their contexts so that supports are maximized and constraints are minimized.

From an ecological perspective, individuals are seen as matching or being discordant with their systems. Assessment is concerned with the person in transaction with the context. A child who is failing academically is not seen as "learning disabled" but rather as out of balance with the instructional system. What instructional adjustments must be made and what learning skills enhanced for the child to be successful? What adult expectations must be adjusted (Conoley & Carrington Rotto, 1997; Gump, 1980)?

More specific system theories have evolved around families (e.g., DeShazer, 1985; Lusterman, 1985). Olsen and his colleagues have proffered the influential circumplex model (Gorall & Olson, 1995). Key constructs of cohesion, flexibility, and communication are seen as predictive of family success when each exists in a balanced amount within the family system. Too little or too much cohesion (i.e., disengagement or enmeshment), flexibility (i.e., rigid or chaotic), and communication describe families that have great difficulty in coping with normal or extraordinary family crises.

Lusterman (1985) has suggested that schools can be conceptualized along these same dimensions. Interventions planned for children will be successful only if the school system's dynamics are respected. For example, a psychologist who encounters a rigid system that has difficulty in sharing important information across classroom or administrative boundaries may have to be very active in creating communication networks so that an intervention may succeed. Even the most elegant intervention will fail if the system components are not considered in the planning and implementation phases.

Organizational psychology (Argyris, 1987) is another source of theory and practice information useful in designing and evaluating systems interventions. For example, many private and public entities now espouse some version of Deming's (1986) continuous improvement or total quality management model of organizational effectiveness (Bowsher, 1992). The key components of this approach—that is, explication of a mission that outlines core values, identification of critical processes and outcomes for success, and development of valid assessment approaches to guide work—are applicable to human systems of any size.

Defining characteristics of effective schools and classrooms have been identified (Haynes, Comer, & Hamilton-Lee, 1988). For example, strong instructional leadership, a focus on learning, a small number of meaningful rules, high expectations for prosocial behavior, many opportunities for development and learning, informative feedback, and provision of necessary resources are all descriptors of successful educational organizations. In fact, with only minor wording changes, these are descriptors of effective families, businesses, and friendships. Understanding healthy families, communities, or friendships gives significant clues for developing effective system interventions.

Understanding what facilitates healthy systems provides a map to inform work. These descriptors are not, however, ultimate "goods" in their own rights. As illustrated in the circumplex model, balance is critical. More is not always better. For example, excellent communication is a critical component in system success but so is appropriate autonomy. Increasing venues for communication and teaming can be powerful system enhancers, but too many meetings can overwhelm a person's ability to accomplish personal work. Information is power, but too much E-mail every day can reduce rather than enhance productivity.

The following case illustrates that even successful systems work may not result in the anticipated consequence and that overreliance on one intervention strategy may be misplaced confidence. Even valid system interventions must be examined within the larger contexts of organizational processes.

## CASE STUDY: TOO MUCH OF ONE THING?

A psychologist consulted with a school-based day treatment program for six years (Conoley, Oestmann, & Walker, 1995). The primary focus of the work was the interpersonal relations among the teams of teachers, mental health staff, and other specialists. The very disturbed and disturbing clients put stress on the staff, as did the new roles each had to assume to make the program a success. Because of staff turnover, the psychologist planned and implemented many training events for decision-making, conflict management, teamwork, and communication skills.

Evaluation of these efforts indicated success. Staff turnover was reduced, new members were inducted with care, and the overall relationships among staff and program administrators were generally positive. In fact, four years of consultation was credited with a stable teaching force of active problem solvers and creative program developers.

A change in special education directors at the district level, however, created a new demand on the program. The consultation focus on professional development had not been paired with an equal focus on program evaluation, using student outcomes as evidence for success. No outcomes-oriented evaluation plan was in place. Staff believed their program was effective and cited increasing demand by principals for their services as their evidence. The new special education director was not impressed by this evidence and asked for academic outcomes to be the focus of the evaluation.

The consultant refocused energy on assisting the staff to create an evaluation plan and then, after one year, analyzed the data on behavioral and academic outcomes. The findings supported program success, but the delay in providing the information allowed time for the special education director to become convinced that the program required major organizational re-engineering. The director's concerns centered on the high cost of the program and the relatively small number of children who were served.

Following the presentation of the evaluation findings, which highlighted the program's effectiveness in facilitating academic growth for these very severely impaired students—the day treatment program was reorganized, with new leadership, and distributed to new locations. Although the well-tested systems intervention of providing valid information was implemented, the anticipated goal of garnering support for the program as it existed was not reached.

Analysis of the consultation effort suggested the following:

1. The systems work on improving and developing the interpersonal skills of the staff was too narrow. Although the staff did explore and improve their relationships, they did not get experience in identifying other needed sources of data related to program success.

2. The consultant did not involve the special education director in the evaluation plan. The well-established internal focus of her work continued. The evaluation plan was constructed without external input and so did not gather data that the director considered critical.

3. The timing of the evaluation report was unfortunate. It was too late to change the director's mind. The director's need for immediate reassurance that such a novel program was, indeed, effective was unknown and unexamined by a consultant and staff who had grown responsive to each other but not to the central administration.

## FORCES AFFECTING THE USE OF SYSTEM INTERVENTIONS

Persuasive theoretical and empirical evidence can be garnered to support psychologists who are embracing systemic interventions as their treatments of choice. Yet, the daily practice of most psychologists in schools has little to do with improving systems. Why is this happening?

Powerful individual and contextual forces keep psychology working at individual and disconnected levels. Gutkin and Conoley (1990) point out that the professional education of most psychologists does not have enough emphasis on social psychology and organizational change. Rather, current professional psychology programs are focused on individual assessment and medical models of disorders. In addition, economic incentives in independent practice and in schools are based on providing services to individuals who are identified as disordered (Carlson, Paavola, & Talley, 1995; DeMers, 1995; DeMers & Bricklin, 1995; Reschly, 1988; Ronsenfield & Reynolds, 1990; Tharinger, 1995).

Professional training, economic incentives, the press of individual case demands, and the apparent simplicity of individual versus system interventions discourage practitioners from conceptualizing their work from a systems perspective. The crushing problems facing schools, however, are all more amenable to change through systems work.

Consider the problem of school violence. Many schools have resorted to one strategy—expelling acting-out youths. Although this may support short-term improvement in the school environment, it does not represent a change in the school's capacity to increase children's safety at school.

## CASE STUDY: FACING UP TO SCHOOL VIOLENCE

A northeastern school on the outskirts of a major metropolitan area had historically served the children of affluent professionals who commuted to the city center (A. P. Goldstein, personal communication, 1997). Because of metropolitan growth and the location of some industries in the suburbs, many poor children entered the school district in a very short period of time. A number of disquieting issues became apparent. District personnel learned that approaches that had been successful in the past were failing the new population of students. One of the important problems the district identified was the negative publicity caused by a number of gang-related incidents and the dramatic rise in discipline referrals.

At first the district personnel opted to put their energies into alternative learning units (ALUs, i.e., self-contained classrooms) for acting-out youths. These alternative classrooms were expensive, extremely disruptive, and had no effect on increasing the overall safety of the district (i.e., the level of disruption in the regular classrooms remained the same). Following the negative evaluation of the ALUs, the school psychologist, who was the pupil personnel director, suggested a systems approach for increasing school safety. Over the period of five years the following strategies were implemented in the district:

1. **Survey research:** A survey of the types and frequency of violent events and discipline referrals that characterized each school building and the interventions that were used in response was completed. Feedback of results created a plan in which highly disturbing and dangerous situations were identified and analyzed for antecedent and consequent conditions. Surveys also indicated what the high-frequency problems really were, in contrast to the high-visibility concerns. For example, most district discipline referrals were based on verbal insolence or disrespect, not physically intimidating situations.

2. **Identification of priorities:** The highest-priority situations were identified. For example, in one high school, fights were breaking out among students during class changes. The school implemented the following strategies.

   - Assigned more teachers to supervise the corridors
   - Had the police establish a presence in the building
   - Adopted a block scheduling format that resulted in only a few transitions per day
   - Reconfigured freshman classrooms so that teachers moved among a cohort of students instead of students moving from class to class
   - Replaced outdoor recreation with quiet reading times
   - Selected the most frequent instigators of hallway violence and had them stay in class until most of the students had left the hallways
   - Involved fathers in visits to the school building so there were more adult men in the halls as the students changed class
   - Remodeled some of the classroom walls into windows so that hallways were easily observed from the inside of classrooms

3. **Increased human resources:** The establishment of several school safety committees helped the schools make the problem of violence a concern for all community stakeholders.

   - A student group was trained as peer mediators.
   - A student court to hear cases of rule infractions was established. A group of

administrators, teachers, and students analyzed school rules to ensure that all were necessary and none needlessly oppressive. This team also wrote a "Handbook of Student Rights and Responsibilities."

• A community group made up of parent, police, social service, business, and medical representatives was charged with developing strategies to increase safety for young people. It implemented the following: improved lighting around the buildings, more chaperones at social events, more extracurricular activities, extended school hours, implementation of skill-enhancing programs for students concerning drugs and alcohol, increased police presence before and after school in the vicinity of the school, and establishment of a dress code for students.

The five-year evaluation of the plan indicated that despite a rapidly rising district census, there was no concomitant rise in violent incidents. In fact, the costs of repairing vandalism decreased by 30%, fist fights decreased by 80% in the school that targeted that problem as its main priority, and overall district discipline referrals were reduced by 35%.

Each strategy required many school professionals to adopt new roles. For example, school psychologists became very heavily involved in skills-training and parental contacts. Many teachers were required to change their team memberships so that there were grade-level teams in the junior and senior high schools instead of the more traditional content area teams. Coaches and physical education and health teachers created many new programs to involve large numbers of students in extracurricular activities that emphasized safety and positive decision making.

Today, the district continues to grow in diversity. The professionals now see the advantage of arranging for adult-focused system interventions that do not rely solely on changing individual children.

## Additional Cases

We think psychologists' practice in schools would be enriched if practitioners and researchers discussed case information more often. Although no claims for experimental rigor can be made for any of the cases described, each is heuristic (Yin, 1989).

Given how useful we find case examples, the following section reproduces the cases that appeared in the Snapp, Hickman, and Conoley (1990) chapter for the second edition of *The Handbook of School Psychology*. A careful reading of each will illustrate the important organizational dynamics that have been outlined in this chapter.

## Case Study 1

The school superintendent received a request for the long-term suspension of an eighth-grade junior high school student. Consistent with existing school board policy, the school suspended him for a "short term" for marijuana possession and requested that he be suspended for the remainder of the school term with the superintendent's approval. If the request was approved, the student would lose credit for the second half of the eighth grade and would be unable to go on to the ninth grade with his classmates. The school superintendent was new to the district. Upon receipt of the suspension request, he sent a memorandum to the directors of pupil personnel services, the director of secondary education, and other members of the administrative staff including the school psychologist, requesting their opinions and suggestions for possible actions.

This was the first time the school psychologist had been asked to become involved with the administration's handling of a discipline problem. He had been aware of the frustration expressed by counselors that students they were working with might be suspended from school and the counselors had no opportunity to offer suggestions for handling the problem. Seeing an important opportunity in the superintendent's request, the school psychologist quickly investigated the case. He determined that a counselor had developed an excellent relationship with the student in question and with the student's friends. It was also apparent that this was not an isolated incident of drug abuse at the school.

The problem, while not unique to this junior high school, was a great concern to the school's faculty and parents. Few people had much information about drugs and drug abuse, and no one was really sure how to deal with the issue. In similar situations throughout the school district, the typical strategy had been to try to discover any drugs brought to school, identify anyone in possession, and permanently suspend that student. The discipline policy established by the school board stated clearly that possession of marijuana would result in long-term suspension for the remainder of the school terms, as well as a loss of credit for that term.

The psychologist also learned that the suspended boy was one of a group of 8 to 10 eighth-grade students who were thought to be responsible for most of the drugs at the school. The suspended student's peer group enjoyed high status among the other students. Their influence and status seemed to be contributing to other students' interest in experimenting with drugs. Simply enforcing the suspension policy in this case would, at best, punish one student and be a warning to others. It might do little to affect the more general problem of drug abuse in the school. The school psychologist also realized that although the superintendent would be concerned with the handling of this individual suspension request, he would be more concerned with the larger issues of suspension policies and the problem of drugs in the schools.

The school psychologist began to consider possible ways in which the superintendent could reduce the "drug problem" in the student population. In regard to the individual student, the suspension needed only to be examined for appropriateness. Administrators could certainly look to the eighth-grader who was caught with the marijuana to determine what would be the most appropriate punishment and what would bring about the highest possibility for rehabilitation. They could view the punishment as being in the best interest for the overall development of the boy.

A more feasible option was to consider mental health interventions in addition to, or instead of, suspension and ways to affect the group of students associated with the suspended boy. Another consideration was to think of the entire school as a subsystem of the school district and to target that subsystem for intervention. As a whole, the use of illicit drugs by students and how school administrators responded in the district was becoming a more critical problem. The question of primary interest for the school psychologist was how to intervene to reduce the use of drugs at the school; that is, what could be done to change that subsystem in the school that provided status to those students modeling drug abuse to their peers? A feasible alternative seemed to be acceptance of the status of the students and modification of how this status was being used.

The school psychologist presented to the su-perintendent an alternative to suspension: the counselor would bring together the suspended student's friends thought to be responsible for most of the drugs on campus. The psychologist intended to speak very directly to the students and, in effect, offer them a deal. That is, if the students were willing to remove all drugs from the campus through the end of the school year, he would be willing to argue for the reinstatement of their suspended friend. It would be made clear that the superintendent had given no guarantee of reinstatement but that he had agreed to listen to the argument. If the school psychologist could be convinced that the campus would be free of drugs, he would try to convince the superintendent to allow the student to return to school. It was also pointed out that everyone in the school would know that they were responsible for getting their friend readmitted. The students would continue to have high status, but it would be conferred for helping a friend and for "cleaning up the school" rather than for abusing and/or providing drugs. The students would have to develop a plan of action and convince the school psychologist of its efficacy. The superintendent agreed to the plan, seeming quite pleased to have an alternative to suspension and a way to reduce drug use.

With the superintendent's support, the school psychologist had the counselor bring the students to a meeting. At first, their reaction to the psychologist's plan was denial, questions such as "Why us?" and comments such as "We don't know anything about drugs!" Not willing to argue with them, the school psychologist gave them the information they needed for their decision. If the students decided to go along with the plan, they would have to propose a way to convince him that the school would be clean. They were told, "You have 20 minutes; take it or leave it." At the end of the 20 minutes, the school psychologist returned to hear the decision. The students began by saying that some of the seventh-graders were rather "immature," taking pills from home medicine cabinets without knowing what the drugs would do. They would not take responsibility for that. The school psychologist did not agree, reminding them that the seventh-graders looked up to them and that they could convince the younger students to stop using those drugs. They agreed, accepted the terms, and convinced the school psychologist that they would rid the school of all drugs to help their friend return.

The school psychologist then asked the superintendent to reinstate the suspended student. The superintendent agreed, and the boy was allowed to finish the school year, having received only a short-term suspension. During the following months, the counselors closely monitored the campus for drug usage. They believed that drugs were completely absent until the afternoon of the last school day, when one individual got high. The boy graduated with his peers, went to high school, and has since successfully completed his public education.

Chin and Benne's (1976) assertions appear to be upheld by these data. The intervention in this case was not directed at the suspended student. Instead, it involved responding very differently to a general discipline problem by intervening directly with a subsystem within a school system. In this case, the targeted subsystem included all those students directly or indirectly involved in giving status to the eighth-graders who were primarily responsible for using and distributing drugs at that school. If intervention had been aimed only at an individual level, it might have changed the behavior of that one student, perhaps even a few others. The result of the systems intervention was that patterns of drug usage within that subsystem were drastically reduced through the end of that school year. The organization (district) was also involved in the intervention and was affected by the outcome.

What were the results of this intervention? First, it had a significant impact on reducing drug usage in that school at that time. Second, the superintendent later sought the advice of the school psychologist on many other discipline cases. Third, the superintendent developed a reorganization plan for administration, which now included a role for the school psychologist in developing and implementing district discipline policy. This reorganization included the addition of an Office of Student Affairs, which would be charged with ensuring that students' rights were protected, especially the right to due process. The Office of Student Affairs was organized by the school psychologist with the direction of the superintendent. The office would be required to monitor discipline and develop alternatives to punishment.

## Case Study 2

The next case involved an entire school district. It was precipitated by the concerns of four school board members, who constituted a majority of a seven-member board. The four board members approached the administration with their interest in eliminating, or at least severely limiting, the use of both corporal punishment and long-term suspension of students. They asked the administration to report on the different kinds of discipline (e.g., corporal punishment and long- and short-term suspension) and the extent to which they were used. They also wanted information from staff and the community about recommendations for major changes in the school district's policies and procedures for discipline.

Following the board's request, the superintendent asked the school psychologist to design a study of discipline in the district and present it to the superintendent's cabinet. The original design was developed to ensure objectivity and generalizability of results. The school psychologist saw the study as an opportunity to assist in the overall discipline problem and provide a vehicle to distribute techniques presented in a step-by-step fashion.

The superintendent's cabinet was concerned about the reaction of local school administrators to the prospect of losing some of their usual punishment techniques. The school principals might even think that some of their authority would be taken away, particularly in relation to the suspension of students. The cabinet decided to modify the design so that the data would be collected at each campus by the principal. This was avoided in the original design because of the school psychologist's concerns about objectivity. The schools and the community were included to obtain broad-based information about preferences and practices of discipline. The school psychologist pointed out that the evaluation design was no longer objective, that it allowed for a strong "principal" bias. However, the politics of the administration at that time outweighed the need for objectivity. The original design for the survey was modified.

Students, teachers, local school administrators, and parents were the subjects of the survey on current disciplinary practices and preferences for the management of student behavior. The results of the study produced a rather massive document, including the teacher's manual as an appendix. Upon receiving the report, the board reacted to its weaknesses, especially to the fact that principals were prime recipients of the information. The board considered it useless for decision making. The board president in particular indicated that the only thing of value was the appendix, calling the rest of the report a "hodge-podge." The board suggested disseminating the manual to every teacher, as well as staff training in the use of classroom management techniques.

Despite the report's bad reviews, one issue clearly emerged. The survey consistently stated the principals' and teachers' wish to eliminate corporal punishment if they received training in other techniques for maintaining discipline. Following the report and the positive reception given to the teacher's manual, the school psychologist and his staff submitted a proposal to the National Institute of Mental Health (NIMH) for the purpose of funding personnel to be used exclusively for training teachers in classroom management techniques. The grant was obtained, and teams of psychologists and master teachers were hired. The training occurred in large groups, in small groups, and on a one-to-one basis with individual teachers.

Following the hodgepodge discipline study, many changes occurred. There was a drastic reduction in the use of corporal punishment in the school district and a significant reduction in long-term suspension. In-school suspension centers, based on the principles of reality therapy (Glasser, 1969) and involving total faculty and staff development, were designed and used. A significant reduction in the disproportionate representation of black students among the number of disciplined students and a major reduction in suspensions of black students also resulted.

In this case, as far as the school psychologist was concerned, the question of the appropriateness or objectivity of the study dealt only with preferences for punishment. If he had been unyielding in trying to avoid the bias in the study, he would have missed an opportunity to modify the entire system's attitudes and practice. Doing the study provided a means to focus public attention on more positive approaches to discipline and ways to justify extensive staff development in alternatives to punishment.

Fortunately for the district and others concerned, the unscientific survey had beneficial side effects. It provided an opportunity for disseminating ideas about more effective ways to discipline students after infractions occurred. This case gave the school psychologist an opportunity to implement an intervention that could have a major impact on the entire school district's system for managing students' behavior.

## Case Study 3

The school district was about to experience a series of major changes: desegregation, "back to basics," dramatic expansion of due process for students, increases in services with special needs, and so on. Generally, faculty and staff seemed very poorly prepared for these changes. Most of the administration had long histories in the school district, and many changes precipitated the willingness of the old guard to listen to new ideas.

The school psychologist found an opportunity for systemic intervention in the midst of these changes when a group of Mexican Americans, the Concerned Parents for Equal Education, presented the school board with 20 concerns for the education of their children. The superintendent was instructed by the school board to develop a response.

The school psychologist became involved when asked by the superintendent to respond to a question about the poor performance of Mexican-American children on academic achievement tests. The total written responses were developed and given to the Concerned Parents for Equal Education. The response did not satisfy the committee, and the members returned to the board. The superintendent summoned his administrators and asked for additional ideas for rephrasing or redeveloping the responses. However, the school psychologist suggested that a different approach might be advisable. He contended that trying to explain away the identified problems might only increase the frustration and anger of the Mexican-American parents. Furthermore, he believed that the parents were more interested in being heard and understood and that they wanted some voice in attempting to remediate the problems they knew existed in the school district. He suggested that key problems be acknowledged. Even more important, he maintained that the parents' questions should be interpreted not as a criticism of the district but rather as a genuine expression of concern about such vital issues as low achievement scores of Mexican-American students and a disproportionately high incidence of Mexican-American students in special education.

Because the parents' committee included leaders of the Mexican-American community, the school psychologist recommended not writing any more responses. Instead, he proposed that some or all of the committee members attend a series of evening meetings to discuss different topics with representatives from different areas in the administration. For example, one night could be set aside for achievement test scores, another night for proposed bilingual education programs, another for disproportionate participation in special education programs, and so on.

This suggestion was based on certain assumptions that were explained to the superintendent and the other administrators. First, serious problems did exist. Second, the problems would be difficult to solve. Third, ongoing communication was essential. Showing that the administration was aware of the problems and planning changes to alleviate them would require continuing cooperation in examining, defining, and mutually attacking the problems. The suggestions and assumptions were acceptable to the superintendent. The task was delegated to the assistant superintendent, divisional directors, and the school psychologist for scheduling, organizing, and holding the meetings. The parents' committee very much appreciated the response, seeing it as a major positive shift in the attitude of the administration.

The school psychologist saw this crisis as an opportunity to modify the way in which the administration had been responding to demands placed on the school district. The previous approach seemed dysfunctional, destined to keep the district in a mode of reacting to crises generated by groups finding reason to criticize the schools. The intervention contributed to a proactive system that could develop more communication with various interest groups.

Responding directly to the persons involved defused anger and allowed meaningful discussion. Many of the administrators were surprised to find how much the parents understood the educational problems, not only their nature and causes, but also the programs that had been used in other school districts to try to solve them. Parents' thoughts and feelings became an effective resource for the administration and motivated needed changes, especially in regard to minority group interests. Evening meetings were suggested in order to be convenient to the parents and to show willingness on the part of the administration. Effective conflict management involved openly confronting the issues rather than trying to negate or explain them away.

## Case Study 4

The next case focused on a junior high school that was considered to be in "transition." The school was serving a neighborhood that had been all white and was gradually being integrated (Snapp & Sikes, 1977). During this time, the school staff noticed a dramatic increase in physical confrontations between students. The principal and one of the counselors requested a conference with the school psychologist for assistance in planning a program that might help prevent these physical confrontations.

The school staff had already made an assumption. They believed that a systematic group counseling program, emphasizing counselor availability to intervene and induce controlled, verbal confrontation within a group, would be the way to avoid physical confrontations. The staff believed that the school psychologist was needed to train the counselors in small-group techniques. The school's faculty was supportive of the program since they, too, were very concerned about the increase in fighting. The faculty agreed to help free the counselors' time so that they would be able to provide needed services (e.g., they were willing to take over all class-scheduling responsibilities).

The school psychologist agreed to provide training in group skills for the counselors and students and to co-lead a group with each counselor during the school year. The school psychologist would provide supervision, using the group experiences as opportunities to focus on issues that co-leaders could discuss after each group session. He also agreed that beyond the first year, his supervision and/or consultation could be available on request.

In this case there was an opportunity to do more than simply reduce the high incidence of fighting. The school staff might be able to provide a greater sense of pride and togetherness throughout the school if they were to use the resources already being mobilized (i.e., counselors, students, and faculty.). The focus would be on verbal and nonverbal communication as an alternative to physical altercations to settle disputes.

The school psychologist's plan for intervening in the school as a system was to train and supervise the teachers, counselors, and principal by setting up a group in which the adults in the school could participate on a voluntary basis. After each group, the counselors discussed with the school psychologist those issues and techniques that came up during the session. This ongoing group later became a support group for those who would be involved in the training program for students.

The program included the co-leading of an ethnically balanced group of 10 students. Each group of students, co-led by a teacher or an administrator and one of the counselors, focused on the development of communication skills, especially when strong feelings were involved. Students learned to describe their feelings, to state clearly their preferences, and to respond to each other's feelings. The groups had clearly defined socially acceptable ways for group members to behave. Fighting was absolutely not acceptable.

Initially, there were few instructions. However, this remarkable and energetic group of teachers and counselors was available for crisis group work. Any time there was a threat of a fight, any one of the students involved could initiate a contact with the counselor. In turn, the counselor invited any other students who might be involved in the potential fight to participate in small-group discussions in the group room. They would stay in the room and talk it out until there was no longer a threat of violence and until the students made an explicit agreement not to fight.

After the first year of this program, the numbers of actual fights were tabulated and a significant reduction was found. For the first time in four years there had not been an increase in the number of physical altercations. In comparison to the high school that was serving the same transitional area, desegregation in this junior high school progressed more smoothly and with little serious difficulty.

This program was continued for more than eight years. Most of the teachers on the junior high school faculty were trained by the school psychologist during the first three years. Training beyond the first three years was provided to new faculty volunteers by the counselors themselves, with consultation from the psychologist as needed. The program became a regular part of the overall school program.

In addition to the success in reducing fighting at that junior high school, the game plan developed by the counselors and teachers became a manual for group-counseling activities in junior high schools. It was disseminated widely throughout the district and the state and received state and federal commendations for its usefulness in human relations. The manual included both activities for student groups and details for three-day training sessions for interested faculty.

From a broader perspective, this was an ideal opportunity to consult with and intervene in a system. The system was in crisis, and its resources were already being mobilized in an attempt at a solution. The school psychologist needed only to help focus the efforts and identify more of the available resources to affect the system further. The program came to involve a larger segment of the faculty in a way that promoted integration instead of merely diminishing some of the negative effects of desegregation.

## Case Study 5

The following case involves a crisis of great proportions, the most extreme act of violence in the school district's history—the shooting and killing of a teacher by a student. One morning, apparently without provocation, an eighth-grader came to school with a .22-caliber rifle. He walked into the classroom, within 10 feet of his teacher, and fired three shots. The teacher died instantly in front of 32 of the boy's classmates.

The school psychologist had been visiting a nearby high school when a staff member heard about the shooting on a local radio station. Upon confirming the radio report, the school psychologist arrived at the junior high school within 40 minutes of the shooting. He discovered that all the student witnesses had been taken by bus to the police station, where they were giving their accounts of the shooting. He was asked to join them at the station and remain until all of the students had returned to school or were taken home. After the questioning was finished and the students were taken care of, he went back to the junior high school to offer his help to the principal. At that time, the psychologist had not formulated a plan, but it was apparent that follow-up counseling services had to be made available. The principal was in need of additional help. Calls from parents had already begun, asking if the students would receive any help in dealing with the tragedy.

The school staff and the school psychologist designed a plan for intervention in this crisis. A doctoral-level counselor was assigned as a temporary part of the counseling staff at the junior high school. His function was to be available for individual students and teachers who might seek assistance. He was also available to the regular school counselors for supervision, advice, or consultation. The principal was notified that a team of support personnel would be available to meet with parents concerning the services and activities to be provided to the students. In addition, the team would discuss the kinds of reactions that parents might expect from their children immediately following the crisis and thereafter.

The support team was made up of the teacher who had team-taught with the deceased, a specially trained crisis intervention counselor, the school's social worker, and one of the school's counselors. All of them joined the school psychologist in working with the students who had witnessed the violence. The team believed that the students needed to explore their feelings about the shooting, the student who had done the shooting, and the deceased teacher. Many of the students in the class were school leaders who had become a major source of information for the school and community.

The students were told what services would be offered and they were given some options. Group-counseling sessions were available for questions and discussion about death, dying, and grieving. Students were also given opportunities to engage in activities in preparation for the funeral. In addition, some of the students had expressed interest in becoming actively involved in a special project dedicated to the deceased teacher. About half of the students chose to participate in the discussion and counseling group, and most of the rest became involved in tasks related to the funeral and the dedication.

Parents requested a meeting with the school psychologist and the rest of the intervention team. There was open discussion about what had occurred at school and with the students and faculty. The parents asked questions about their own concerns and what they could expect from their sons and daughters. For example, the children's rather dramatic mood swings were puzzling to them. The team helped the parents plan ways to listen to and support their children and to anticipate possible future reactions.

It is hard to evaluate the effectiveness of this intervention except in terms of the human experience. The gratitude of the eighth-graders' classmates, their parents, and the school's faculty confirmed that the strategy met the expressed needs of those individuals, at least at that time. It is, however, an example of how the school psychologist can respond to a crisis and intervene at a systems level.

## Case Study 6

This case concerns the design and implementation of a system for delivering support services to a school district. The city in which this school district was located had a wide variety of mental health services. At the time of the intervention, there were many services in the city and school district but no systematic coordination of them.

As a typical example, a principal called and was very concerned about the behavior of a fifth-grade boy in his school. The boy was described as difficult to control, generally disobedient, and frequently fighting. The boy had been referred at various times to the school counselor, to the school social worker, to the school nurse, and to the psychologist assigned to that building. He had also been referred to the local mental health center for evaluation and treatment.

The supervising school psychologist asked if all people involved in the case had ever met to compare notes, exchange information, and develop a cooperative plan for intervention. Because no such meeting had occurred, one was set up for all the people involved. They identified strengths and weaknesses unique to that child, as well as relatively successful and unsuccessful strategies previously tried. They wanted to start a team effort that could circumvent the cycle of frustration, which in the past had led to the consideration of long-term suspension.

This team effort occurred when the concern about how resources were being utilized in the school paralleled concern that was being expressed by the staffs of mental health agencies. The agencies felt they had little access to the school staff, with whom they needed to work cooperatively. Agency personnel were frustrated in attempts to provide information about what they thought a student might need in an educational setting. Neither could they obtain information or feedback from the school that would help them evaluate the effectiveness of their mental health interventions. Access to a school usually depended on the relationship developed with an individual principal. The agencies wanted to explore ways to coordinate with the school district to develop a better designed delivery system and to mobilize existing resources. The school psychologist met with the superintendent and discussed the possible benefits to the school district. The superintendent responded favorably and committed staff time to the planning and coordination process. The school psychologist then began to develop a delivery system that would better serve the entire school district.

The first step in the process was to list possible representatives from the school district and community agencies who would serve on a planning committee. The School Community Consultation Committee (SCCC) was formed. It included representatives from support services in the school district and from community agencies (e.g., Mental Health-Mental Retardation Center, Child Guidance Center, Family Services Center, Police Department, and Juvenile Court).

Representatives and agency heads were asked to meet and review existing referral procedures in an attempt to strengthen referrals and maximize the utilization of existing resources. Information about agency and interagency referral procedures was exchanged, and the full spectrum of services available from all sources was outlined.

The SCCC held a series of meetings in which a total delivery system was designed. The committee met monthly for two years. During this time the referral procedures between the agencies were revised and refined. Considerable information about problems in the processing of referrals was shared, and decisions were made to enhance the referral system. Consequently, communication and cooperation between the school and various agencies in the community increased. Also, the agencies expressed a desire to aid the school district in one of its major priorities at that time—the desegregation of all schools in the system. The community agencies understood that desegregation of the district would create some disruption and require assistance from mental health and social services agencies.

The SCCC developed an overall service delivery system. The model, the Psychoeducational Services Delivery System (Snapp, Pells, Smith, & Gilmore, 1974), coordinated the services that were available to schools on an itinerant basis. The unit for coordination at the local level was called the Local Support Team (LST). It included a way for community agency personnel to directly serve the schools. A referral to a community agency could originate from the LST. The community agency personnel would first contact the LST and request information about how agency personnel might work further with the school and/or with individual students. This freed agencies from dependence on individual personal relationships with the principals. A

strong positive relationship with the school administrators was helpful, but that was not the only way to gain access to a school.

The school board approved the proposal for the Psychoeducational Services Delivery System, which called for four levels of intervention. The first level was made up of persons within the school itself (i.e., the teacher, the principal, and the parent). The second level incorporated the first and added personnel (LST) assigned on a regular and itinerant basis to the school. There were guidelines to facilitate the operation of the LST and its problem solving and planning for individuals and small groups of students. Also large, campus-wide problems could be brought to the LST for assistance in defining problems and planning solutions. Centrally assigned personnel, on call to the school, made up the third-level intervention.

The fourth level was different. It included a program designed by the SCCC as part of the total delivery system. This level, named the Diagnostic Intervention (D-I) Program, was designed as an additional resource for psychological services in the district. Community agency staff interacted directly with this program, as well as the LST.

The type of mutual planning between school and community agencies became a priority in the community (Pells, Sanford, Haug, & Snapp, 1974). Over a six-year period, the local community mental health center paid the salaries of two staff persons, a psychologist and a master teacher of emotionally disturbed children and youths, who worked full time with students in the school district and promoted interagency communications.

The D-I Program provided a staff of master teachers, under the supervision of a school psychologist, to provide an assessment and planning model that was primarily educationally based. The diagnostic teaching technique was essentially that of developing hypotheses, testing them out with the referred students in an education environment, consulting with teachers about the results of the assessment, and planning ways to work with the students. The school and the community mental health center trained mental health workers in school consultation techniques. This facilitated more effective planning between the two agencies.

The previous case studies all illustrate the positive impact and aspects of systems level interventions. It is possible, and in fact probable, that interventions for individuals can have a negative effect on the system and, in turn, the individuals in the system and the systems themselves. This results in a failed consultation effort, even when change is accomplished at the individual level. The following case illustrates the results of failing to address systems-level issues accurately even though objective data indicated that the behavior of the individual child was significantly improved.

## Case Study 7

Often when a system-level change is attempted, the results may not go as planned or the impact may be even more far-reaching. In this case, the psychologist was working in a public school. As part of her role definition in the district, she was to serve as a member of the multidisciplinary team whose job was to assess and determine a child's best educational plan. In one elementary school, she was also asked to attend special multidisciplinary committee meetings held expressly to determine students' eligibility for retention.

The school retention committee was made up of the principal, the child's teacher and special education teacher, and the psychologist. At the first meeting, two things were obvious: (a) a decision whether or not to retain students was largely dependent on an individual teacher's and administrator's "experience" with such children, and (b) there were no data showing that children below grade level who were retained actually performed better than similar children who were not retained.

Recognizing the opportunity to make a systems-level change in the guise of decision making on an individual student, the psychologist attempted to facilitate change in the team's decision-making processes. She remembered a recent review of the literature on retention of children, and she mentioned to the committee that research reported certain variables that were important to consider when deciding whether or not to retain a student. Generally, the literature suggests that the students who are retained do not perform significantly better academically or behaviorally than students with similar academic problems who are not retained. The committee acknowledged her suggestions but seemed to ignore the information in their final decision for the child under consideration. The psychologist was disheartened that she had not been able to effect change in the subcommittee's decision-making strategies.

The consultant was unaware at that time that the principal of the school had recently been appointed chair of a district-wide committee established by the superintendent to study the problem of retention. Several weeks after the committee meeting, the principal asked the psychologist for more information on the research findings that were mentioned at the earlier meeting. The psychologist answered various questions and offered to bring in the particular research articles on retention for the principal to read. No specific follow-up was planned.

Later in the semester, the principal enthusiastically thanked the psychologist for the retention information and reported that many of the concepts presented directly affected the district committee's policy statements on retention. In this case, what began as an attempt to effect change at the individual level (i.e., a decision on retention) turned into a significant systems-level change. What is important is that the consultant recognized the potential for such a change and was prepared to attempt it. In this case, what began as a microsystems intervention (i.e., the school retention subcommittee) turned into a much higher-level systems change (i.e., district retention policy).

## Case Study 8

The psychologist in this case was an advanced doctoral student in school psychology. A component of her doctoral training program was to serve as a consultant to one special education student teacher. She was asked by the student teacher to consult on a student, hereafter referred to as C, who was currently seen as a major behavior problem and who had a history of behavior problems since entering school. Quickly, the supervising teacher was included in the consultation sessions, as the student teacher had only two more weeks in that classroom. During the initial meeting it was evident that both consultees, but particularly the supervising teacher, felt hopeless about improving C's behavior. The problem of greatest concern to the consultees was C's failure to follow directions and his negative interactions with peers (e.g., hitting, name calling, and shoving), which were most apparent during transition times. The supervising teacher had previously contacted the school counselor, and together they decided to refer the student for placement in a class for the emotionally disturbed. The consultant did not agree that the child was emotionally disturbed. She then suggested to the teacher that she (the consultant) work hard with her (the teacher) to help remediate the student's behavior, at least until more formal referral processes could begin.

The consultant used a collaborative, problem-solving consultation approach with the supervising teacher in which she actively facilitated the consultee's participation in the problem-solving process. One primary goal of the consultant was to restore the consultee's hope that the problem could be solved or at least improved. For several weeks the consultant met with the consultee; problems were defined; baseline data were collected; and interventions were chosen, implemented, evaluated, and revised on two occasions. Throughout a five-week period, the consultee reported feeling much more hopeful about remediation and was consistently cooperative and active in the problem-solving process. The student consultant was reminded by her university supervisor to include the counselor in all problem efforts when possible because she was a very important systems variable. The consultant did meet with the counselor early in the process to elicit her ideas and support for interventions with the child. The counselor volunteered to see the student with a group she had and to be a reinforcer to him when possible.

At the end of the fifth week, the consultant checked to see how the revised interventions were working. She was surprised to hear the consultee express considerable doubt about whether the intervention had been at all successful. The consultant then showed the consultee graphic representation of the data, which showed that the behavior had in fact significantly decreased since the baseline data were gathered. The consultee acknowledged that the undesirable behaviors had decreased, but she still seemed totally unwilling to invest any more time in finding an even more optimal solution to the problem. The consultant was confused and disappointed that what appeared to be such a positive consultation outcome, both in changes in the consultee's attitude and actual client behaviors, had taken such a negative turn. The consultant, however, continued to reinforce the consultee for her hard work and success, although she was puzzled about what had occurred.

The following week the consultant again contacted the consultee just to see what, if anything, had developed. The consultee was polite but very terse. She reported that the school counselor had agreed with her earlier suspicions that this child was a "hopeless" case and needed to be in a class for the emotionally disturbed. The teacher seemed quite relieved with the decision, but the consultant was dumbfounded.

Analysis of the case suggests that possibly the consultant failed to properly involve an important school gatekeeper in the problem-solving process and that this gatekeeper was threatened by what appeared to be the consultant's success, whereas the counselor had failed in the past. The result was a psychological consultation intervention that worked on the individual level but failed to account for other systems variables (i.e., school counselor and in-house psychological intervention subsystems) and thus ultimately failed to maintain the change.

## Case Study 9

When careful retrospective analysis is possible, the signals of possible failure are often recognized as having occurred early in the consultation process. In the midst of implementing a strategy, however, such early-warning signs are often overlooked or misunderstood. This case is one such failed intervention. The school psychologist attempted to improve the skills of special services staff so that children and other school personnel might receive more comprehensive psychological services. A post hoc analysis is offered, but obviously any "explanations" are merely hypotheses.

The special education director of a large metropolitan district was concerned about the functioning of her special services teams. These teams were made up of a psychologist and social workers. Her primary concern was that interactions among the group members were often acrimonious and that certain individuals were performing at very low levels of productivity and expertise.

After a brief consultation with the group about her concerns, the director hired a university-based school psychologist to serve as a conflict management consultant to the entire group. The consultant's name had been suggested by one of the team members (a former student of the consultant). Unknown to the consultant, he had not been the group's unanimous choice; rather, the choice had been very controversial among the group.

The consultant began gathering premeeting assessment data by interviewing the special education director. He learned that the team members were polarized around a number of issues:

some having to do with the personal characteristics of team members, some with recent changes in district policies that increased team accountability, and some with the different training orientations of the team members. In addition, the consultant spoke at length with his former student before the initial meeting with the entire team. Many red flags were raised through these conversations, and the consultant planned accordingly.

The positive goals of the 1 1/2-day consultation with the special services team were conceptualized as follows: (a) improve the communication and problem-solving skills of the team members (e.g., feedback, nondefensive communication, and thorough problem identification and analysis; (b) increase the morale of the team by focusing on its strengths and positive accomplishments; (c) improve the administrative skills of the director though modeling and didactic input.

The consultant's initial contact with the team members indicated that they were unaware of the goals of the consultation and distrustful of the motives and expertise of the consultant. For example, several team members were very late in arriving for the opening meal. At the first session with the consultant, this same group wanted to be "allowed" to drink wine during the meeting (the sessions were held in a nearby conference center, not in a school building). With no rapport built, the consultant worried about disallowing the drinking but did so anyway, using the rationale that a genuine encounter would be compromised if people could later blame the alcohol for what had been said. The dissatisfaction of the team with the consultant's plans was quite evident.

Following a reorientation of the goals of the consultation to meet the wishes of the team, the subsequent meetings proceeded quite smoothly. The team members were amenable and had participated actively in activities and interactions. The consultant felt that the interactions had been difficult at times but had culminated successfully. In particular, the team members had given one another very positive feedback, they had disclosed personal information to one another that made each member feel more trusted and valued by the others, and several had confronted the special education director with their specific concerns about changing school district policy.

The consultant had not implemented all of his plans but was confident the director would see an improvement in the productivity, morale, and professionalism of the group. He was surprised, therefore, to hear from the director three weeks later that nothing had changed for the better and, in fact, her relationship with the staff was more tenuous than ever.

In retrospect it seems clear that the consultant had made errors throughout the consultation in assessment, implementation, and evaluation. For example, he relied on only two sources of information for his intervention planning, each of which was probably unrepresentative of the entire team. The director's insights were necessarily that of an outsider (and evaluator) looking in on the team process. The consultant's former student probably looked at group dynamics through his eyes and perhaps was unable to provide data that would engender innovative interventions. The former student would also be unable to gauge her contribution to the team's difficulties.

The result of the inadequate assessment was that most of the team members were alienated and distrustful of the consultation process. In retrospect, their resistance to consultant-generated activities was predictable. The pressure they put on the consultant to revise the experience completely was successful in keeping the focus off their uncomfortable group dynamics. He facilitated "good feelings" among the group, as well as confrontation of the director (outside of the group and, perhaps, safe to criticize).

The consultant's assessment did not lead to the careful identification of learning or behavioral objectives. He did not develop a mechanism for evaluating the effects of the consultation. This failure to identify short- and long-term goals (and a method to measure attainment) made his work susceptible to washing out very quickly, as nothing specific was brought from the training to the work environment.

## CONCLUSIONS

There are system problems in communication, morale, power distribution, and enrichment needs in every organization at every level. No manual of the one-and-only preferred intervention is available to provide ready-made approaches. The challenge of systems work is in the construction of various approaches to enlist the human resources necessary to solve organizational problems.

# REFERENCES

Argyris, C. (1987). Bridging economics and psychology: The case of the economic theory of the firm. *American Psychologist, 42*, 456–463.

Asayesh, G. (1993). Using systems thinking to change systems. *Journal of Staff Development, 14*(4), 8–12.

Bowsher, J. E. (1992). What can we learn from corporate education about systemic change? *Educational Technology, 32*(11), 51–54.

Bronfenbrenner, U. (1979). The ecology of human development: *Experiments by nature and design.* Cambridge: Harvard University Press.

Carlson, C. I., Paavola, J., & Talley, R. (1995). Historical, current, and future models of schools as health care delivery settings. *School Psychology Quarterly, 10*, 184–202.

Chin, R., & Benne, K. D. (1976). General strategies for effecting changes in human systems. In W. G. Bennis, K. D. Benne, R. Chin, & K. D. Corey (Eds.), The planning of change (3rd ed., pp. 45–63). New York: Holt, Rinehart & Winston.

Christenson, S., Abery, B., & Weinberg, R. A. (1986). An alternative model for the delivery of psychological services in the school community. In S. N. Elliott & J. C. Witt (Eds.), *The delivery of psychological services in schools: Concepts, processes, and issues* (pp. 349–392). Hillsdale, NJ: Erlbaum.

Conoley, J. C., & Carrington Rotto, P. (1997). Ecological interventions with students. In W. E. Martin & J. L. Swartz (Eds.), *Applied ecological psychology in schools within communities: Assessment and intervention* (pp. 145–168). Hillside, NJ: Erlbaum.

Conoley, J. C., Oestmann, J., & Walker, M. (1995). Evaluation of the Lincoln Public School Behavioral Skills Program. Unpublished evaluation report, Lincoln, NE.

Curtis, M. J., & Stollar, S. A. (1995). System-level consultation and organization change. In A. Thomas & J. Grimes (Eds.), *Best practices in school psychology–III* (pp. 51–58). Washington, DC: National Association of School Psychologists.

DeMers, S. T. (1995). Emerging perspectives on the role of psychologists in the delivery of health and mental health services. *School Psychology Quarterly, 10*, 179–183.

DeMers, S. T., & Bricklin, P. (1995). Legal, professional, and financial constraints on psychologists' delivery of health care services in school settings. *School Psychology Quarterly, 10*, 217–235.

Deming, W. E. (1986). *Out of the crisis.* Cambridge, MA: MIT Press.

DeShazer, S. (1985). *Keys to solution in brief therapy.* New York: Norton.

Friedman, M. (1994). Systems philosophy, curriculum integration, and units of joy: Cultivating a new paradigm for an information-intensive world. *Middle School Journal, 25*(4), 11–14.

Fullan, M., Miles, M. B., & Taylor, G. (1980). Organization development in schools: The state of the art. *Review of Educational Research, 50*, 121–183.

Glasser, W. (1969). *Schools without failure.* New York: Harper & Row.

Goldstein, A. P., & Conoley, J. C. (1997). *Interventions for school violence.* New York: Guilford.

Gorall, D. M., & Olson, D. H. (1995). Circumplex model of family systems: Integrating ethnic diversity and other social systems. In R. H. Miskell, D-D. Lusterman, & S. H. McDaniel (Eds.), *Integrating family therapy: Handbook of family psychology and systems theory* (pp. 217–233). Washington, DC: American Psychological Association.

Gresham, F. M., & Witt, J. C. (1997). Utility of intelligence tests for treatment planning, classification, and placement decisions: Recent empirical findings and future directions. *School Psychology Quarterly, 12*, 249–267.

Gump, P. V. (1980). The school as a social situation. *Annual Review of Psychology, 31*, 553–582.

Gutkin, T. B. (1995). School psychology and health care: Moving service delivery into the twenty-first century. *School Psychology Quarterly, 10*(3), 236–246.

Gutkin, T. B., & Conoley, J. C. (1990). Reconceptualizing school psychology from a service delivery perspective: Implications for practice, training, and research. *Journal of School Psychology, 28*, 203–223.

Gutkin, T. B., & Curtis, M. J. (1990). School-based consultation: Theory, techniques, and research. In T. B. Gutkin & C. R. Reynolds (Eds.), *The handbook of school psychology* (2nd ed., pp. 577–613). New York: Wiley.

Harris, J. D., Gray, B. A., Rees-McGee, S., Carroll, J. L., & Zaremba, E. T. (1987). Referrals to school psychologists: A national survey. *Journal of School Psychology, 25*, 343–354.

Haynes, N. M., Comer, J. P., & Hamilton-Lee, M. (1988). The school development program: A model for school improvement. *Journal of Negro Education, 57*, 11–21.

Johnson, D. B., Malone, P. J., & Hightower, A. D. (1997). Barriers to primary prevention efforts in the schools: Are we the biggest obstacle to the transfer of knowledge? *Applied and Preventive Psychology, 6*, 81–90.

Kamphaus, R. W. (1995). Defining ourselves via needs met and competencies provided. *The School Psychologist, 49*(3), 54, 70.

Kavale, K. (1990). The effectiveness of special education. In T. B. Gutkin & C. R. Reynolds (Eds.), *The handbook of school psychology* (2nd ed., pp. 868–898). New York: Wiley.

Krovetz, M., & Speck, M. (1995). Student resiliency: Towards educational equity. *The High School Journal, 78,* 111–114.

Lusterman, D-D. (1985). An ecosystemic approach to family school problems. *The American Journal of Family Therapy, 13,* 22–30.

Martens, B. K., Hiralall, A. S., & Bradley, T. A. (1997). A note to teacher: Improving student behavior through goal setting and feedback. *School Psychology Quarterly, 12,* 33–41.

Pells, B., Sanford, G., Haug, D., & Snapp, M. (1974). A collaborative school mental health program. *International Journal of Mental Health, 3,* 177–194.

Reschly, D. J. (1988). Special education reform: School psychology revolution. *School Psychology Review, 17,* 459–475.

Reschly, D. J., & Wilson, M. S. (1995). School psychology faculty and practitioners: 1986 to 1991 trends in demographic characteristics, roles, satisfaction, and system reform. *School Psychology Review, 24,* 62–80.

Rosenfield, S., & Reynolds, M. C. (1990). Mainstreaming school psychology: A proposal to develop and evaluate alternative methods and intervention strategies. *School Psychology Quarterly, 5,* 55–65.

Sarason, S. B. (1982). *The culture of the school and the problem of change* (2nd ed.). Boston: Allyn & Bacon.

Shapiro, E. S., & Cole, C. L. (1994). *Behavior change in the classroom: Self-management interventions.* New York: Guilford.

Snapp, M., Hickman, J. A., & Conoley, J. C. (1990). Systems interventions in school settings: Case studies. In T. B. Gutkin & C. R. Reynolds (Eds.), *The handbook of school psychology* (2nd ed., pp. 920–934). New York: Wiley.

Snapp, M., Pells, B., Smith, J., & Gilmore, G. A. (1974). A district-wide psychoeducational services delivery system. *Journal of School Psychology, 12,* 60–69.

Snapp, M., & Sikes, J. N. (1977). Preventive counseling for teachers and students. In J. Meyers, R. Martin, & I. Hyman (Eds.), *School consultation.* Springfield, IL: Thomas.

Stinnett, T. A., Havey, J. A., & Oehler-Stinnett, J. (1994). Current test usage by practicing school psychologists: A national survey. *Journal of Psychoeducational Assessment, 12,* 331–350.

Tharinger, D. (1995). Roles for psychologists in emerging models of school-related health and mental health services. *School Psychology Quarterly, 10,* 203–216.

Vollmer, T. R., & Northup, J. (Eds.). (1997). Applied behavior analysis and school psychology. *School Psychology Quarterly, 12*(1).

von Bertalanffy, L. (1968). *General systems theory.* New York: Braziller.

von Bertalanffy, L. (1981). *A systems view of man.* Boulder, CO: Westview.

Welch, M., & Sheridan, S. M. (1995). *Educational partnerships: Serving students at risk.* New York: Harcourt Brace.

Yin, R. K. (1989). *Case study research: Design and methods.* (Applied Social Research Methods Series, Vol. 5). Newbury Park, CA: Sage.

## CHAPTER 41

# LAW AND SCHOOL PSYCHOLOGY

DANIEL J. RESCHLY
*Iowa State University*

DONALD N. BERSOFF
*MCP-Hahnemann University and Villanova University*

The influence of law on school psychology, as well as on other areas of applied psychology, has grown enormously over the past four decades. Indeed, it is nearly impossible to think of any professional activity by school psychologists—from conducting research as a faculty member in a university to choosing assessment procedures for a child's evaluation in a school—that is not influenced by the law. In this chapter we describe the major sources of legal influence and the mechanisms by which they are implemented, followed by a consideration of two kinds of litigation that have profoundly influenced the practice of school psychology. We conclude with discussions of general principles regarding legal influences and the effects of psychology on the law, an often ignored dynamic in the law-psychology relationship. Throughout we emphasize the importance of psychologists' understanding of the law as a means to protect precious rights, as well as a method to resolve disagreements over rights and responsibilities. The better understanding of legal influences is one way to enhance opportunities for implementing the best professional practices.

Although all forms of professional psychology (clinical, counseling, industrial-organizational, and school) are subject to legal influences (Brodsky, 1991; Hess & Weiner, 1987; Levine, Anderson, Ferretti, & Steinberg, 1993), the effect of the law on school psychology is arguably the greatest. Over 80% of school psychologists work in public schools (Fagan & Wise, 1994; Reschly & Wilson, 1995), which are the legal creations of state governments. Thus, as creations of state governments, public schools are subject to key constitutional principles that do

not apply to the same degree to psychologists in private practice or to many other employers of psychologists. Two of the historical trends noted by Fagan (1992) as being crucial influences on the growth of school psychology involve changes in laws that govern access to education—compulsory attendance and mandatory special education. Indeed, the laws that have regulated school psychologists most over the past two decades are the same laws that have led to vastly increased employment opportunities for school psychologists (Fagan, 1988; Goldwasser, Meyers, Christenson, & Graden, 1983; Lund, Reschly, & Martin, 1998). To a very great extent, state and federal laws create the requirements that lead to employment for school psychologists and, with this benefit, comes significant legal regulation over how school psychology will be practiced.

## ORIGINS OF LEGAL INFLUENCES

Legal influences originate in four sources: federal and state constitutional law, federal and state legislation, federal regulations and state rules implementing legislative principles, and case law from federal and state courts. School psychology practice has been affected by legal provisions from all four of these sources. This chapter emphasizes federal constitutional, legislative, regulatory, and court influences, but readers should be knowledgeable about the law in the state in which they practice.

### Constitutional Law

The U.S. Constitution does not mention education, psychology, or school psychology. Education is one of the areas of authority that is considered to be reserved to the states by the Tenth Amendment to the constitution. These circumstances do not isolate school psychologists from the influences of constitutional law, however, because much of what they do "directly and sharply implicates the Constitution" (Bersoff & Hofer, 1990, p. 939). Three principles in constitutional law have enormous implications for school psychologists.

## Equal Protection

First, the equal protection clause of the Fourteenth Amendment restrains states from denying to any person "the equal protection of the laws" unless there is a substantial and legitimate reason to do so. Equal protection means that state governments must treat citizens equally unless there are good reasons for differential treatment.

All states have established public schools. Once established, access to these schools must conform to the equal protection provision of the U.S. Constitution. Judicial interpretation of equal protection has evolved over the course of our history. At one time, restriction of educational access by race was permitted despite the equal protection clause under the legal theory of "separate but equal" (*Plessy v. Ferguson*, 1896). By 1954 equal protection analysis compelled a different conclusion: "separate [but equal] is inherently unequal" (*Brown v. Board of Education*, 1954, p. 495), leading eventually to the elimination of state laws that required racial segregation of schools. Since the mid-1950s the courts have increasingly struck down state laws that provided for or allowed differential treatment in the public schools on the basis of race (*Brown*, 1954), sex, or disability (*Mills v. Board of Education*, 1972; *Pennsylvania Association for Retarded Children v. Commonwealth of Pennsylvania [PARC]* 1972). These latter cases have been an especially important influence on school psychology.

## Due Process

The right to due process, based on the Fifth and Fourteenth Amendments to the Constitution, restricts states (and subdivisions thereof such as school districts) from depriving persons of "life, liberty, or property, without due process of law." Due process is required whenever the state proposes action that affects an individual's life, liberty, or property. Education is viewed as a property right by the U.S. Supreme Court (*Goss v. Lopez*, 1975) that comes under the purview of the due process constitutional protections. *The due process right also protects against the loss of liberty due to a reputational injury that can occur through inaccurate labeling or misdiagnosis of a disability or mental illness.* Once education became compulsory in the early decades of this century, as well as increasingly important to job and career opportunities, there were grounds for equal protection and due process challenges to provisions that restricted or denied access to educational programs because of race, sex, or as the courts came to acknowledge in the early 1970s, disability status.

Due process is a mechanism that is intended to ensure fundamental fairness in decision making. To understand the concept, consider the protections that should exist if a graduate program in a state university were to consider expelling a student because of alleged misbehavior in a practicum setting or if a public school were to consider expulsion of a child because of alleged misconduct. Moreover, assume that these decisions might be incorrect and that the persons affected disputed the allegations. What protections should exist to protect these students from incorrect decisions by a state government agency?

By personalizing decisions that affect educational opportunities (a property right), most persons generate the critical elements of due process. Fundamental to implementing the due process protection are (a) provision of notice to the affected person of the intended action, (b) provision of the rationale for and the evidence that supports the decision, (c) opportunity for the affected person to challenge the action through an impartial procedure such as a hearing, and (d) opportunity to present information and evidence that challenge the state's rationale and evidence.

## Privacy

The degree to which the Constitution protects an individual's privacy has been debated vigorously in the context of abortion rights and other controversial areas. Although privacy, like education, is not mentioned in the Constitution, privacy protections have been inferred from other constitutional principles such as due process and equal protection. Privacy rights have been extended to conduct in "marriage, procreation, contraception, family relationships, child rearing, and education" (Bersoff & Hofer, 1990, p. 940). A right to privacy is part of the basis for laws that restrict access to educational records to persons in the educational system who have a need to use the records. These laws also restrict communication of the content of educational records to other persons or agencies without the permission of the person to whom the records pertain.

## Federal and State Statutes

A second important source of legal influence is legislation enacted at the state and federal levels. Legislation generally establishes broad principles that must be carried out by government agencies, private institutions, or individuals. The three most important federal statutes regarding school psychology are the Individuals with Disabilities Education Act (1990, 1997) (IDEA), the Americans with Disabilities Act (1990), and the Rehabilitation Act of 1973 (1973, 1977).

## Federal Regulations and State Rules

Federal regulations and state rules, a third source of legal influence, provide further details on how legislative principles will be implemented. Their purpose is to carry out the intent of the legislative body, and they are usually far more detailed than the original legislation. An example of the typical relationship between legislation and regulations can be seen in the general principles in the IDEA (1990) statute about assessment of students suspected of meeting the disability eligibility criteria and the regulations implementing these principles. The statute requires

> procedures to assure that testing and evaluation materials and procedures utilized for the purposes of evaluation and placement of children with disabilities will be selected and administered so as not to be racially or culturally discriminatory. Such materials or procedures shall be provided and administered in the child's native language or mode of communication, unless it clearly is not feasible to do so, and no single procedure shall be the sole criterion for determining an appropriate educational program for a child. (U.S.C. Section 1412(5)(c).

The 758-word federal regulations implement the statutory language of 81 words. Even with the considerably greater detail in the regulations, there is still enormous ambiguity in the meaning and interpretation of the legislative principles. For example, the meaning of nondiscrimination is not specified in the IDEA statute or IDEA regulations, leaving the ultimate meaning to executive branch interpretations and the courts (see later discussion).

Regulations are most often developed by the department or agency in the executive branch of government that is responsible for implementing the legislation. The regulations are usually formulated and submitted to the public for review and comment and then reformulated one or more times on that basis. Professional associations such as the National Association of School Psychologists (NASP), Division 16 (School Psychology) of the American Psychological Association (APA), and several headquarters units of APA (e.g., Practice Directorate and Education Directorate) typically attempt to influence federal legislation and regulations through lobbying efforts and contributions to the public comment phase. State psychological associations and school psychology organizations engage in similar activities at the state level. These lobbying activities often represent a significant proportion of the budgets of psychological associations, another indication of the importance of law to psychologists.

## Case Law

Case law is a fourth source of legal influence. Case law at the federal level is established through court decisions by district courts, where trials are conducted; appeals courts in the 13 judicial circuits; and the U.S. Supreme Court. Case law originates when a person or group seeks resolution through litigation of a dispute over the application of constitutional law, state or federal statutes, or federal regulations and state rules. Written decisions stating the outcomes of the proceedings create case law, which has been crucial in all phases of the current legal system governing the practice of school psychology.

It is now commonplace to regard the United States as a litigious society, and indeed, compared to other societies with modern economies, we use courts of law to a far greater extent to resolve social and moral issues. Judicial activism regarding the public schools, however, particularly by federal courts, is relatively new in our national experience. In education cases we often see comments in federal court opinions expressing reluctance to intervene in educational matters (e.g., *Board of Education* v. *Rowley*, 1982; *Coalition to Save Our Children* v. *State Board of Education*, 1995). Despite this reluctance, numerous federal court opinions on educational issues affect the practice of school psychology. Federal court interventions have occurred because of concerns about how precious rights, such as equal protection, due process, and privacy, may be abrogated by the action or inaction of school officials.

Two fundamentally different kinds of cases involving the practice of school psychology have been and continue to be crucial legal influences at all levels, from administrative law hearings in a local school district to cases decided ultimately by the U.S. Supreme Court. On the one hand, there are the right-to-education cases, which originally sought access to an appropriate education for students with disabilities (*Mills*, 1972; *PARC*, 1972). Right-to-education cases continue today, now directed primarily toward refinement of the concepts of appropriate education and least restrictive environment.

The other kind of case with enormous influence on school psychology is based on alleged misclassification of minority students as disabled. These cases established basic due process rights, as well as requirements for nondiscriminatory assessment, use of valid and reliable assessment procedures, multifactored assessment, and group decision making. Early cases established those rights (*Diana v. State Board of Education*, 1970; *Guadalupe Organization v. Tempe Elementary School District No. 3*, 1972); and recent cases have refined their meaning and applications (*Larry P. v. Riles*, 1979, 1992; *Marshall v. Georgia*, 1984, 1985; *S-1 v. Turlington*, 1986).

There is irony here: in the right to education cases, educational agencies were sued for not providing special education; in the disproportionate placement cases, educational agencies were sued for providing too much special education because the students allegedly were not disabled. The work of psychologists was and is scrutinized in both areas.

Case law is evolutionary and often ambiguous. It is the primary means by which the meaning, breadth, and scope of basic principles from various sources of legal influences are defined. For example, culturally and racially nondiscriminatory assessment and decision making in diagnosis and placement of students is a basic principle that was firmly established, first by cases filed under constitutional law and then through federal and state legislation, followed by federal and state regulations. But many ambiguities still have to be clarified. For instance, does *nondiscriminatory* mean a prohibition of IQ (intelligence quotient) tests with certain minority students? The federal district and appeals courts have issued contradictory rulings on that question. Even

with a court ruling, ambiguities nearly always remain because case law always applies specifically to a particular situation or set of facts and only by inference to other situations.

Case law establishes precedents that may be binding on subsequent cases, but there can be enormous differences in impact depending on the level of the legal proceeding and the legal status of the hearing or court. Administrative hearings at the local level typically have no direct influence on other hearings. In contrast, federal district court decisions carry the weight of law within their respective districts; they become law in several court districts if upheld on appeal to a federal appeals court; they become law throughout the country when decided by the U.S. Supreme Court. In considering the progression of broadening influence by successively higher courts, it is sometimes important to recall that the Supreme Court is not supreme because it is best. It is supreme because it is last.

## Changing Legal Provisions

Opportunities to change the four kinds of legal influences vary dramatically. Constitutional law is extremely difficult to change because obviously it requires an amendment to the Constitution. There have been fewer than 30 such changes since 1787. However, interpretation of the Constitution does change through the rather unpredictable mechanism of case law. State and federal legislation are also relatively difficult to change since concurrence of two legislative bodies, as well as approval of the chief executive (president or governor), are usually required. In contrast to constitutional law and federal and state statutes, regulations and rules are relatively easy to change. These changes typically represent the most effective and realistic way to influence the law governing school psychology practice.

## MECHANISMS OF LEGAL INFLUENCE

There are a variety of mechanisms through which the law is implemented. These include several kinds of court proceedings, as well as various executive branch functions such as monitoring compliance and providing financial support.

### Judicial Mechanisms

Judicial mechanisms include injunctions, an order by a judge before a trial (as a temporary or preliminary injunction) or after a trial (permanent injunction), in which current procedures or activities must be changed to comply with the court order. Consent decrees are settlements negotiated by plaintiffs and defendants in a court action and approved by a judge. Judicial opinions, the most important court mechanism, are developed after the presentation of evidence by the parties in the suit, written briefs, and oral or written arguments. Judicial opinions have the effect of law in the area or region within the court's jurisdiction. Judicial opinions appealed to higher courts broaden the applicability of the decision if they are upheld by the higher court.

*Administrative hearings* are a quasi-judicial proceeding established in some statutes as a mechanism to resolve disputes without using the more complex mechanisms of state or federal courts. Administrative hearings, in the context of public education, are designed to resolve disputes between parents and local or state agencies. Hearings can be initiated by students, by representatives of students (usually parents), or by an educational agency. An impartial hearing officer then conducts a hearing in which both sides have the opportunity to present evidence, examine witnesses, and enter oral and written arguments. Hearings allow parents and others to carefully scrutinize the recommendations of school officials, including key decisions about classification, placement, and programming. Disputes decided by hearings can be appealed by either party to the state or federal courts; however, the courts typically require the administrative mechanisms to be used by the parties before submitting their dispute to the courts. Most school psychologists will be required, at some point in their careers, to give testimony under oath in a legal proceeding. Due process hearings under the IDEA provisions are the most likely venue for this testimony.

## Executive Branch Mechanisms

The major mechanisms by which legislation and accompanying regulations and rules are implemented is compliance monitoring and financial incentives. For example, the IDEA provides financial grants to states if they comply with the provisions of the IDEA statute and regulations. Part of the state's compliance involves monitoring and ensuring compliance with IDEA by school districts in the states. Failure to comply with the IDEA legal requirements could result in reductions in or cessation of the federal support for special education and related services for children with disabilities. Compliance monitoring usually involves visits to the service agency (e.g., a local school district), during which information is gathered on policy and practice and compared to regulations and rules. Teachers and parents are interviewed, and a random sample of records is typically reviewed. Inadequacies in policy or practice lead to official citations that require a satisfactory response from the agency. Satisfactory responses may take the form of an appeal of the citation or a description of changes designed to ensure compliance in the future. Financial support can be withdrawn or delayed as a result of noncompliance. The complexity and ambiguity of federal regulations and state rules that have a bearing on school psychology practice lead to at least a few citations in nearly every compliance review of an agency.

## RIGHT-TO-EDUCATION LITIGATION AND LEGISLATION

Landmark litigation and legislation regarding the right of all children to an education were enormous influences on the development of school psychology services over the past two decades. The singular importance of education was emphasized in the 1954 *Brown* decision, which struck down state laws that segregated schools by race. This decision was based on the equal protection principle in the Fourteenth Amendment to the U.S. Constitution, which restrains states from treating persons differently without good reasons for differential treatment. The emphasis in *Brown* on the importance of education for everyone was almost as significant as its monumental conclusion that separate but equal led inevitably to inequality in treatment and opportunities. The conclusion that race was not a permissible basis for differential treatment in educational settings opened the door for other challenges to states' differential treatment of students on other factors, such as sex and disability status. The situation through the 1960s was that most states *permitted* but did not *require* educational services for students with disabilities (Weintraub & Abeson, 1976). Educational rights and opportunities for children and youths with disabilities were inconsistent between and within states. For example, some local districts in a state provided services for students with disabilities whereas others did not. In some instances the services when provided were quite good; in others they were poorly designed and executed with few if any efforts to individualize the services to the needs of the student. Moreover, local schools could and often did exclude children and youths with disabilities without affording their parents fundamental due process rights (Abeson & Ballard, 1976).

Parent advocacy groups and civil rights attorneys in the 1960s increasingly recognized the varying treatment of students with disabilities as a classic question of the equal protection of the law. All states had compulsory attendance laws, and all states established schools for the education of children and youth. These laws, however, did not extend uniformly to children and youth with disabilities. Clearly, the state provided a benefit to some students but not to others. Furthermore, this benefit was often conferred or denied by school officials without any parental recourse. The conditions were ripe for a revolution in the rights of children and youth with disabilities to educational services (Weintraub & Abeson, 1976), a revolution that markedly affected school psychology.

## PARC and Mills Consent Decrees

In the early 1970s, advocacy for persons with disabilities increasingly focused on educational services. Two consent decrees in the early 1970s had profound influences on the provision of services. In 1971, attorneys representing 13 children with moderate to severe mental retardation (MR) went to federal district court in Pennsylvania to secure their rights, and the rights of others similarly situated, to free public schooling (*PARC*, 1972). Although Pennsylvania law provided free public education for children, children with disabilities were typically excluded under the theory that they were not able to benefit from academic instruction. The plaintiffs argued that the exclusion of children with MR violated their Fourteenth amendment rights to equal protection of the laws and due process (Burt, 1975; Gilhool, 1976).

Expert witness testimony from educators and psychologists was crucial to the resolution of *PARC*. Persons with mental retardation were portrayed as capable of learning and benefiting from educational services. This testimony went unchallenged by the state, which agreed in a consent decree to provide appropriate educational services to children with MR. The *PARC* consent decree established crucial principles such as access to educational services at no cost to the parents, individualization of educational services

based on the needs of children with MR, extensive and detailed due process rights, mandated individualized evaluations and reevaluations, and a strong preference for provision of services in as normal an environment as possible (*PARC*, 1972).

The *PARC* consent decree applied only to persons with the disability of MR, not to all children and youth with disabilities. That limitation was rectified almost immediately in *Mills* (1972), a case filed in the District of Columbia on behalf of children with varying disabilities. As in *PARC*, the court agreed with plaintiffs' constitutional arguments and approved a consent decree that required the District of Columbia Schools to (a) advertise the availability of publicly supported educational services for children and youth with disabilities, (b) identify and advise previously excluded children and youth of their rights to educational services, (c) conduct individual evaluations to determine educational needs, and (d) file with the court a plan to provide an appropriate education for each child with a disability.

The *Mills* consent decree forbade financial exigency as a reason for failing to provide a "free and suitable publicly-supported education regardless of the child's mental, physical, or emotional disability or impairment." Like *PARC*, the *Mills* order emphasized the due process rights of parents and the preference for educating students with disabilities in the normal environment. *Mills* also sharply restricted the authority of the school district over suspension and expulsion of students with disabilities. The due process procedures adopted in federal legislation (see next section) were nearly identical to those in *Mills*, an obvious influence of litigation on subsequent legislation.

The *Mills* and *PARC* consent decrees were a powerful impetus in establishing the rights of students with disabilities to educational services in other states. According to Gilhool (1976), court suits similar to *PARC* and *Mills* were filed in the federal courts of most states by 1973. Advocacy groups lobbied legislatures in every state to enact statutes ensuring the rights of students with disabilities to appropriate educational services. Recalcitrant legislators were informed about *PARC* and *Mills* and encouraged to enact legislation. In case the altruism of legislators was not sufficiently mobilized by these precedents, plans were developed by advocacy groups to press federal court suits under the equal protection and due process constitutional principles. As a result, most states mandated educational services for students with disabilities over the 1972–1975 period (Abeson & Ballard, 1976). This period was a golden era of court interventions to secure the rights of persons who previously experienced discrimination in educational settings. Attorneys were highly regarded to a degree not likely to be repeated anytime soon. Psychologist Burton Blatt (1972) commented, "More and more I comprehend the powerful positive influence that lawyers, if not laws themselves, now exert within my field of work. . . . Lawyers are heroes, even now, to some of us today" (pp. 991, 992–993).

## Federal and State Right-to-Education Legislation

The *PARC* and *Mills* consent decrees exerted enormous influence on mandatory special education legislation at the state and federal level. State governors, concerned about possible further litigation, as well as the increased costs of educating students with disabilities, sought federal assistance to pay for special education services. In 1975 Congress passed and President Ford signed the Education of the Handicapped Act (EHA); the name was changed to the Individuals with Disabilities Education Act (IDEA) when the law was reauthorized in 1991.

The EHA was, and now IDEA is, a grant-giving statute that awards financial support to states for providing educational services to students with disabilities *if*, and this is crucial, *if*, the special education services provided by the state meet the requirements of the federal IDEA statute and regulations. The EHA and IDEA created an immense role for the federal government in all aspects of services to students with disabilities, from screening the general student population for disabilities to specifying how a triennial reevaluation of classification and placement was to be conducted. All states comply with the IDEA, and all states receive federal financial support for their special education programs. The original EHA target level of funding was 40% of the additional costs for special education services borne by states and local districts. Actual funding now is less than 10% of those costs, and the federal share has never exceeded 14%.

The clear influence of prior litigation can be seen in the major principles of the EHA/IDEA. Each of these principles appeared earlier in one or more court cases over the educational rights

of students with disabilities, and each principle influenced the development and delivery of school psychological services (see Table 41.1). The right to a free and appropriate education at public expense (FAPE), least restrictive environment (LRE), individualized educational program (IEP), and due process principles were prominent in the *PARC* and *Mills* cases. Virtually all of the protection in evaluation procedures (PEP) components appeared in the *Diana* and *Guadalupe* consent decrees (see later discussion). Thus, the influence of the initial right to education litigation (*PARC* and *Mills*) extended far beyond the situations and facts directly involved in the cases. State and federal legislation reflected the requirements in the consent decrees and extended those requirements to the entire nation, a remarkable development that hardly could have been foreseen by anyone involved directly with the cases in 1970. With the enactment of EHA and the agreements with every state by 1980 to implement the EHA statute and regulations, the entire nation operated under the same general principles for identification, evaluation, provision of special education and related services, annual review, and triennial reevaluation of students with disabilities.

The degree of uniformity among states' legal requirements, however, can be deceiving. There is uniformity at the level of general principles, that is, FAPE, LRE, PEP, but within the general principles there is considerable latitude over such crucial issues as the mandatory components of a multifactored assessment, the categories of disabilities that will be served in the schools, and the classification criteria for categories of disabilities (Mercer, King-Sears, & Mercer, 1990). For example, Patrick and Reschly (1982) reported widely varying terminology for what is referred to as mental retardation (MR) in the federal statute, including mental handicap, mental disability, and significantly limited intellectual capacity. Classification criteria also varied widely concerning the role of adaptive behavior and the level of IQ required to establish the diagnosis. The IQ requirement varied from a low of 68 to a high of 85, meaning that the proportion of persons potentially eligible for the MR diagnosis varied dramatically from state to state. These variations produce anomalies: a student may be classified as mildly MR (MMR) in one state and, following a move across state lines, is reclassified as specific learning disabled (SLD) or, in some more extreme instances, as not disabled.

TABLE 41.1    EHA/IDEA Principles: Effects on Schools and Impact on School Psychology

**1. Right to a free appropriate education at public expense**

Effects: All students with disabilities guaranteed educational rights leading to (a) more students in the existing population of students classified as having mild disabilities such as specific learning disabilities and (b) students with complex multiple disabilities and severe disabilities gain access to public schools.

Impact: More psychologists needed to conduct evaluations and provide other services to students with disabilities; some psychologists needed with highly specialized skills in working with students with low incidence and severe disabilities such as autism.

**2. Least restrictive environment**

Effects: More students with disabilities served in general education environments or in part-time resource teaching programs. Special education is increasingly becoming a range of services brought to children and youth in natural environments rather than a place where educational services are provided.

Impact: More emphasis on psychologists and support services that assist students in general education environments.

**3. Individualized educational program (IEP)**

Effects: Development of detailed plans to guide the provision of special education and related services, including general goals and specific objectives, assessment of progress, and annual review of the IEP.

Impact: More emphasis on identifying specific educational needs during evaluations and on monitoring progress toward goals.

**4. Procedural safeguards**

Effects: Formal procedures to protect rights and to involve parents in decision making through requirements of informed consent, rights to appeal decisions, impartial hearings, and so on.

Impact: Greater scrutiny of psychologists' work, as well as more emphasis on communicating with parents. Increased likelihood of psychologists testifying under oath in administrative hearings in which decisions are challenged.

**5. Protection in evaluation procedures**

Effects: Nondiscrimination in evaluation and decision making; multifactored assessment and decision making by a team that includes various professionals and parents; valid assessment that focuses on educational need, primary language, and triennial reevaluation.

Impact: Some traditional prerogatives of school psychologists were curtailed through placing less emphasis on IQ and greater emphasis on achievement and adaptive behavior; consideration of language differences and sociocultural status, determining educational need and team decision making.

---

Such differences in criteria also produce large differences across the states in the prevalence of disabilities. For example, according to a recent authoritative report, the states' prevalence of the 13 disabilities defined in the IDEA varied from 6.86% in Hawaii to 14.90% in Massachusetts (U.S. Department of Education, 1995, Table AA15, p. A-34).

A second federal law, Section 504 of the Rehabilitation Act of 1973, also established requirements for services to students with disabilities. Section 504 is a civil rights statute that is implemented by the Office for Civil Rights, a unit of the U.S. Department of Education. Section 504 is important because it includes somewhat different enforcement mechanisms and establishes a more liberal definition of a disabled person (Prasse, 1995). It has acquired renewed relevance with the notice to state and local education officials about the rights of students with attention deficit hyperactivity disorder (American Psychiatric Association, 1994) to reasonable accommodations in general education classrooms even if the student is not eligible for special education under the federal and state laws (U.S. Department of Education, 1991). Some of the accommodations in general education listed in the 1991 memorandum are behavior modification, alternative methods to administer tests, and home-school notes with home-based reinforcement. School psychologists are also frequently involved in the development and evaluation of these accommodations, a further example of legal influences on roles.

## Enforcement of Right-to-Education Law

Although federal regulations and state rules have the force of law, they have little effect if not enforced, which is not always an easy task. For example, there is an apocryphal tale that President Andrew Jackson once stated in reference to a U.S. Supreme Court decision, "Chief Justice Marshall made his decision, now let him enforce it" (Hall, 1992, p. 442). However, there are several mechanisms to promote compliance with the IDEA legal principles.

State compliance is monitored by the Office of Special Education Programs (OSEP), a unit of the U.S. Department of Education. State departments of education are also charged by the IDEA with the responsibility of monitoring the compliance of intermediate and local education agencies with state and federal laws. Compliance monitoring typically occurs every three to five years. In virtually every instance, state and local educational agencies are found to fall short of complete implementation of one or more federal regulations, leading to the formulation of corrective action plans that specify how policy and practice will change to ensure compliance with the law. The compliance monitoring process is typically emotionally charged and stressful for those involved. Motives for compliance are complex, probably involving an interaction of (a) educational officials' commitment to comply with the law and to serve students well; (b) the embarrassment that comes from being found out of compliance with the law, particularly if the agency's deficiencies, enumerated in a compliance report (usually a public document), are disseminated through the local media; and (c) the possibility that funds will be reduced or cut off altogether because of inadequate implementation of the law. The last outcome is rare, but that threat, along with the other motives, is usually sufficient to prompt conscientious implementation of the law.

In addition to compliance monitoring, another motivation for local district officials to implement the law is the due process rights of parents, which include the right to seek an impartial hearing to resolve disputes with educational agencies over the implementation of legal requirements. A crucial aspect of this right is the recovery of legal fees from the educational agency if parents prevail in the hearing. In one case, the total costs for the school district's and parents' attorneys for a hearing on the appropriate education for a fifth-grade student with a severe learning disability were over $200,000. The parents prevailed on all the issues, according to the decision rendered by a hearing officer, and the school district had to pay its own and the parents' legal fees.

The requirements that define compliance evolve over time, changing with advances in professional practices, identification of particular problem areas, and court cases that further define the meaning of general principles. Practices that are in full compliance with the law today may not be so at some future date. Because educational agencies must implement certain laws before receiving financial support from the federal or state government, it is exceptionally rare to blatantly refuse to comply with legal requirements. Most agencies are in compliance at the policy level before receiving monies.

Compliance at the level of practice is another matter because there are varying interpretations of what a specific legal principle means. For example, consider the EHA/IDEA requirement, "Testing and evaluation materials and procedures used for the purposes of evaluation and placement of handicapped children must be selected and administered so as not to be racially or culturally discriminatory" [U.S.C. 1412(5)(c) and 34 CFR 300.530]. There is no further definition of nondiscrimination in the law or regulations. Which of the following outcomes is nondiscriminatory: the due process rights of students and parents are carefully implemented regardless of students' race or cultural background? All students receive the same assessment procedures regardless of race? Test interpretation depends on the racial and socioeconomic characteristics of the student? Classification criteria are different for students, depending on race, so that no group is over- or underrepresented in special education programs? In fact, widely varying interpretations of the nondiscrimination principle have appeared in the professional literature (Dent, 1976, 1993; Hilliard, 1980, 1983, 1992; Reschly, 1979, 1996; Reynolds & Kaiser, 1990; Reynolds, Lowe, &

Saenz, Chapter 22). Federal courts have also applied varying standards (see later section) in different cases, and the federal agencies (OCR and OSEP) responsible for ensuring compliance with the nondiscrimination principle have not developed an official interpretation of this crucial standard.

There are many other ambiguities in the implementation of abstract principles such as FAPE, LRE, IEP, PEP, and due process. However, the ambiguities can be reduced in two basic ways: memoranda from the government agency responsible for implementing the law and case law precedents (discussed in the next section). Also, OSEP and OCR answer inquiries about the meaning of statutes and regulations, and state departments of education provide interpretative guidance to local officials.

There are many examples of interpretative guidance from federal and state government units about services to students with disabilities. We have chosen the issue of the availability of test protocols to parents because this matter often involves disputes between psychologists and parents. The confidentiality of information section of the IDEA regulations (34 CFR 300.560 to 34 CFR 300.576), based on the Family Educational Rights and Privacy Act, first enacted in 1974, guarantees parents access to the records of their minor children. Access includes the right to "inspect and review any educational records relating to their children that are collected, maintained, or used by the agency" [34 CFR 562(a)]. In addition to access, parents may challenge the accuracy of records, seek to have the records revised, and establish an impartial hearing to resolve a dispute over the records if the educational agency does not make requested changes.

These rights may seem straightforward, and on a superficial examination, they seem quite easy to interpret. Since the EHA regulations were first implemented in 1977, however, there have been over 115 interpretations of their meaning by OSEP or OCR in response to inquiries from educators, parents, and attorneys. This interpretative guidance typically takes the form of a letter to the person who made the inquiry, or it may be part of a report subsequent to an OCR investigation of a complaint. These letters and reports are printed in the *Education of Individuals with Disabilities Law Report* (before 1991, this publication was called the *Education of the Handicapped Law Report*).

In Table 41.2 portions of the text from an inquiry and excerpts from an OCR investigation report are reprinted from the *Education of the Handicapped Law Report (EHLR)*. In the first inquiry, the issue is whether the parent has access to copyrighted materials, such as the test questions and the test form on which the answers are written. The OSEP answer is unequivocal. Then there is the further issue of whether parents have the right to a copy of the record (protocol and test questions). The regulations state that the educational agency must provide a copy of the record if failure to do so would effectively prevent the parent from reviewing the records (34 CFR 300.562). Also, providing single copies of copyrighted documents probably would fall under the fair use provisions of U.S. copyright law, a position almost certain to be disputed by test publishers if this matter ever goes to court. The dilemma of compliance with two conflicting laws—IDEA, which provides access to virtually all educational records, and U.S. copyright law, which prevents unauthorized copying of materials—is further complicated by ethical considerations (see later discussion).

Some practitioners have reacted arbitrarily and negatively to OSEP and OCR interpretations about the disclosure of records and test materials to parents. For example, some have "hidden" protocols in files maintained in their homes or destroyed the protocols as soon as psychological reports are complete. As noted in Table 41.2, the OCR is sharply critical of that approach. The school district had to go through the expense and stress of an OCR investigation; suffer the embarrassment of being found in noncompliance with federal law; and although the information in *EHLR* did not cover this point, it is almost certain that the district had to pay all of the parents' legal fees. Slick ways to get around legal requirements such as destroying test protocols undermine the intent of the regulations and may place the educational agency at great risk for large legal fees. Moreover, it is hard to see how such destruction of records represents anyone's conception of best professional practices.

## Right-to-Education Case Law

The development of an extensive record of case law was almost inevitable given the abstract and ambiguous nature of key principles such as FAPE, LRE, IEP, and PEP and the extensive procedural safeguards afforded to parents and educational agencies. Both parents and agencies have recourse to due process hearings and to the

**TABLE 41.2   OSEP and OCR Clarifications of the Meaning of Parental Rights to Access to Test Protocols**

### Inquiry

Is it permissible for a school district to refuse to release to parents copies of test protocols and test questions for copyrighted tests such as the Wechsler Intelligence Scale for Children–Revised, in view of the fact that these materials are copyrighted by the publisher?

### OSEP Response

"We believe that, once a test has been given to a student, the test questions become education records of that student if the tests are maintained in personally identifiable form by the education institution or agency. Because these tests are education records, an educational agency or institution must give parents a right to inspect and review the test questions as well as the students response to the questions." (*EHLR*, 1987, pp. 211:420–211:422).

### Issue

An Oak Park, IL, attorney, representing the parents of a school-age child referred for a preplacement evaluation, complained that the school psychologist for an Illinois school district had destroyed the test protocol for the Wechsler Intelligence Scale for Children–Revised as soon as the psychologist report was prepared, which was before the multidisciplinary team meeting with the parents.

### OCR Investigation Report Factual Conclusions

"The investigation established that the District has a policy of destroying test protocols once the school psychologist completes the evaluation report. . . . It is the district's position that the test protocols and scoring sheets are not documents that are to be maintained as part of students' educational records. . . . The parents believed that without the test protocol they could neither successfully challenge the District's recommendation for special education placement nor plan a program that would provide for Student A with an appropriate educational program. . . . This placement recommendation was based, in part, upon the school psychologist's evaluation. The parents refuse to consent to this placement and on May 17, 1990, the District requested a due process hearing."

### OCR Investigation Report Legal Conclusions

The regulations establish procedural safeguards that give parents the right to examine educational records. "The parents and District, in this case, strongly disagree about the intellectual functioning of Student A and his placement in a special education program. The test protocols were relied on by the examining psychologist to prepare his report of Student A's intellectual abilities. . . . These records were relevant and essential to a complete assessment of the findings made by the District's psychologist regarding Student A. Therefore the district was obligated to provide these records to the parents when requested. . . . The District's destruction of these records violated Section 504 and its implementing regulation. . . . The District's categorical destruction of these documents has the effect of denying to parents access to relevant records."

state and federal civil courts if there is no agreement over the identification, evaluation, placement, or provision of FAPE for students with disabilities. (These procedural safeguards appear at 34 CFR 300.500 through 34 CFR 300.514.) Every school psychologist should be intimately familiar with these regulations, which include the following requirements: (a) educational agencies must give prior notice and obtain parental consent before evaluating a child for disability status, need for special education, or placement in a special education program; (b) the agency must hold an impartial hearing if the parties do not agree on decisions relating to referral, diagnosis, special education need, and placement; (c) parents have the right to an independent educational evaluation which must be considered by the agency's multidisciplinary team, and which, under certain circumstances, must be paid for by the agency; and (d) the child must remain in the current educational placement while the due process appeal is being adjudicated unless both sides agree to a change in placement or a federal court orders a change.

Both the parents and the educational agency have the right to initiate a hearing to resolve disputes. Both parties have the right to be accompanied by counsel, to present evidence and to cross-examine witnesses, to obtain an electronic recording of the proceeding and a written decision, and to appeal to a state or federal civil court. As noted previously, parents can recover their legal fees if they prevail in the hearing or the court proceedings. Generally, disputes between parents and educational agencies have to be considered in a due process hearing *before* either party can pursue the case in state or federal courts. Expert witness testimony by school psychologists is most likely to occur in a due process hearing.

## Board of Education *v.* Rowley *(1982)*

The single most important right to education case since the enactment of mandatory federal and state special education legislation is *Rowley*, a case that defined the ambiguous principle of the right to a free and appropriate education at public expense (FAPE) for students with disabilities. *Rowley* began with a disagreement between parents and a local school district in New York over what constituted an appropriate education for Amy Rowley, a kindergarten student with a profound hearing loss who was entering first grade (Martin, 1991). The parents wanted a sign language interpreter because, although Amy Rowley was a bright child, only a portion (59%, according to testimony at the trial) of the verbal discourse in the classroom was available to her through lip reading. The school district's multidisciplinary team refused to provide the interpreter, offering instead "pull out" speech and language therapy for three hours per week, tutoring from a deaf educator for one hour per week, and regular classroom instruction with a few accommodations (e.g., preferential seating). The parents agreed with the provisions of the IEP except that they "insisted that Amy also be provided with a qualified sign language interpreter in all of their academic classes" (*Rowley*, 1982, p. 184). The parents filed a complaint with the New York Department of Education, seeking an impartial due process hearing to resolve the disagreement with the school. While the pro-

ceedings were pending, the child remained in regular education in the program offered by the school, as required by federal law (34 CFR 300.513); that is, a sign language interpreter was *not* provided by the school as this case went through several years of legal proceedings.

The hearing officer upheld the school district's IEP, reasoning that because the testimony and documentary evidence indicated that she was earning average to above average grades, "Amy was achieving educationally, academically, and socially without such assistance" (*Rowley*, 1982, p. 185). The parents then sought resolution of the dispute in federal district court. After a trial in which both sides again presented testimony and documentary evidence, the court ruled that an appropriate education required a sign language interpreter. The court noted that "she understands considerably less of what goes on in class than she would if she were not deaf and thus is not learning as much, or performing as well academically, as she would without her handicap" (p. 185). The court then reasoned that the legal requirement of FAPE meant an education that would provide Amy Rowley with "an opportunity to achieve her full potential commensurate with the opportunity provided to other children" (p. 186). On appeal, the Court of Appeals for the Second Circuit affirmed the trial court's ruling in a divided opinion.

The school district then petitioned the U.S. Supreme Court, which heard arguments in 1991. In 1992 the Court overturned the trial and appeals courts' rulings in a landmark decision that has influenced virtually all special education litigation involving questions of FAPE and LRE. First the court asserted that Congress designed the EHA to ensure "access to specialized instruction and related services which are individually designed to provide educational benefit to the handicapped child" (*Rowley*, 1982, p. 3048). The equal-opportunity-to-learn standard advanced in the lower courts' opinions was rejected as extending the law beyond the intent of Congress. The Court also emphasized that the other provisions of the EHA, including LRE, IEP development with parental involvement, and PEP, were crucial to an appropriate education. The Supreme Court noted that Amy was benefiting from the educational services provided to her, that she was able to advance from grade to grade with her like-age peers, and that the other elements of the law (e.g., PEP, LRE, IEP) were implemented by the school district. The court concluded with an admonition to the lower courts that EHA "is by no means an invitation to the courts to substitute their own notions of sound educational policy for those of the school authorities which they review. . . . Questions of methodology are left to the states" (p. 3051). *Rowley* thus established a characterization of FAPE without establishing any particular standard other than conformance with other aspects of the EHA and the expectation that benefits to students with disabilities will be realized.

Psychologists are involved directly and indirectly in various activities that ensure the rights of children with disabilities to FAPE. First, psychologists must assess students suspected of, or known to have, disabilities (Reschly & Wilson, 1995; Smith, 1984). An individualized evaluation that establishes the child's needs, as well as implementation of the PEP, is an essential component of FAPE. Failure to meet the due process or PEP requirements means that the FAPE requirements were abridged. Second, psychologists must often determine if the student is making progress toward IEP goals, another crucial feature of the *Rowley* conception of FAPE. Failure to make progress, *particularly if the educational agency does not measure progress or if it does not change the IEP when progress is not made*, is a sure way to lose in a due process hearing or in the courts (e.g., *Egg Harbor Township Board of Education* v. *S.O.*, 1992).

Third, psychologists, as related services providers, have direct and indirect treatment responsibilities for many students with disabilities. Some recent court cases have emphasized the responsibility of educational agencies to provide support services in integrating children with disabilities into general education settings. These support services often involve behavior analysis and treatment plans for behaviors that interfere with full integration. Failure to provide these plans is a basis for declaring the FAPE has not been provided in the least restrictive environment. It is important for psychologists to note that related services are an essential component of an appropriate education. In the IDEA regulations, psychological services are defined as a related service that includes "administering psychological and educational tests and other assessment procedures; interpreting assessment results; obtaining, integrating, and interpreting information about child behavior and conditions relating to learning; consulting with other staff members in planning school programs to meet

the special needs of children as indicated by psychological tests, interviews, and behavioral evaluations; planning and managing a program of psychological services, including psychological counseling for children and parents" [34 CFR 300.16(b)(8)].

## Post Rowley Court Decisions

Since 1982 the basic standards for FAPE have not changed; however, the courts have resolved other issues by using the *Rowley* standards and, in doing so, have extended further the meaning of the EHA principles and the right to education. Most of these issues provide further clarification of the rights of students with disabilities (*Honig* v. *Doe*, 1988; *Light* v. *Parkway C-2 School District*, 1994; *Oberti* v. *Board of Education*, 1993). These clarifications have, in many cases, significant implications for school psychological services.

## Summary of Right-to-Education Law

Right-to-education law for students with disabilities has had profound influences on the practice of school psychology: employment opportunities were markedly increased, and as might be expected, the nature of practice was changed was well. The overall effect on school psychology is enormously positive because, in our view, the changes were in the direction of best professional practices and consistent with important obligations that professionals owe to those we wish to serve. Right-to-education law continues to evolve, and further developments with implications for school psychologists should be expected.

## NONDISCRIMINATION IN ASSESSMENT, CLASSIFICATION, AND PLACEMENT

Litigation that addressed alleged discrimination in assessment, disability classification, and special education placement of ethnic or racial minorities was, in retrospect, an almost inevitable outcome of the landmark *Brown* (1954) Supreme Court decision. The landscape for this litigation has changed over time; however, the fundamental issue from the beginning has been overrepresentation of minorities in some educational tracks or programs and underrepresentation in others. The use of tests in educational classification and placement decisions has been controversial; indeed, different courts have, on similar facts, either banned or upheld the use of the same tests. In this section we describe and interpret the history of judicial scrutiny of psychological tests and the legal requirements for testing that were established in federal legislation.

## Judicial Scrutiny of Group-Administered Tests and General Education Tracking

Bersoff (1979a) described the judicial scrutiny of educational tracking and differential placement that used group-administered achievement and ability tests in southern school districts as a way to delay or avoid school desegregation. Initially, these tracking plans, based on group-administered tests, were allowed to exist by the federal courts: "There is no constitutional prohibition against an assignment of individual students to particular schools on the basis of intelligence, achievement or other aptitudes upon a uniformly administered program, but race must not be a factor in making the assignments. However, this is a question for educators and not courts" (*Stell v. Savannah-Chatham*, 1965, p. 93).

The courts in the first decade of the post-*Brown* period allowed disproportionate classification and placement based on the results of tests on which minority students performed more poorly than nonminority students. The differences in test results and classification and placement outcomes were permissible as long as *individual* minority and nonminority children were treated in the same way, for example, the same tracking assignment for the same test score regardless of race (Bersoff, 1979a). During this period there is clear evidence of the judiciary's deference to educators in matters of assessment methodology and classification and placement decision making; however, that deference changed significantly following a landmark case in the nation's capitol.

### Hobson v. Hanson (1967, 1969)

*Hobson* v. *Hanson* was the first direct challenge to the use of standardized tests as part of a tracking system. According to the *Hobson* defendant, the Washington, DC, public schools, tracking was instituted soon after desegregation to improve educational opportunities for black students who exhibited a high incidence of achievement problems. The defendant claimed that the tracking decisions depended on a variety of information, including grades, teachers' recommendations, and various standardized tests of achievement and ability. The effect of the tracking system was

to create disproportionate representation of white and black students in the upper, middle, and lower ability tracks. Although black students constituted about 90% of the total student population, they constituted 95% of the students in the lowest track (Bersoff, 1979, p. 47). Plaintiffs sued the district, alleging violation of the equal protection principle because the tracking led to unequal educational opportunities for black students in the form of poorer facilities, inferior instruction, and limited curriculum or course offerings.

Judge Wright's opinion after a lengthy trial focused almost exclusively on the use of a group-administered ability test, which was viewed as the most important determinant of tracking decisions. He reasoned that the ability measure might meet the legal test of a rational means to carry out a legitimate function if it accurately assessed *innate* ability to learn, but he observed that all the testimony by plaintiffs and defendant experts agreed that presently available tests did not measure innate ability. All witnesses acknowledged the effects of environmental influences on test performance, and all conceded that economically disadvantaged black students probably did not have the same opportunities as middle-class students to learn the information or problem-solving skills required on the test. Judge Wright concluded that the ability measure and the tracking decisions were seriously flawed because they were not based on innate ability. He then enjoined the school from further use of this tracking system because he found it to be inflexible, stigmatizing, and associated with unequal resources with no compensatory educational benefits.

*Hobson* established an extremely important legal precedent for the use of standardized tests when disproportionate placement might result. Judge Wright did not ban disproportionate outcomes as such but rather established a nearly impossible criterion for the acceptance of tests as part of a placement process when disproportionality resulted. He apparently understood tracking to be based on innate ability, and a test acceptable for use in tracking decisions would, likewise, have to reflect innate ability. *Hobson* focused on the classification and placement criteria and procedures, not on outcomes for students or on the alternatives to various tracking systems. The reasoning in *Hobson* was essentially a syllogism: tracking must be based on innate ability; tests are used in tracking students; tests do not measure innate ability; therefore, tracking if based on tests is not acceptable.

## *Marshall* v. *Georgia* (1984, 1985)

*Marshall* v. *Georgia* was a class action suit filed in 1981 on behalf of black students in Georgia who allegedly were improperly tracked in regular education and disproportionately classified as MMR in special education. The defendants in Marshall were 13 poor, rural districts and the state of Georgia. The legal basis for the plaintiffs' challenge to regular education grouping included the equal protection principle and civil rights statutes. The achievement grouping by local districts, a practice implicitly approved by the state, resulted in a disproportionate impact on black students, who were overrepresented in lower tracks and underrepresented in higher tracks. The plaintiffs' case depended heavily on statistical evidence for disproportion and complex statistical analyses relating race, socioeconomic status (SES), and other factors to achievement. The court noted that "some factor correlated with race is influencing the defendants' classroom makeup" (*Marshall*, 1984, p. 97). Experts for the plaintiffs contended that achievement grouping was linked to segregation in southern schools and that different educational experiences were, in all likelihood, provided at the different levels, with higher groups receiving instruction at a faster pace and higher cognitive level, whereas the lower groups received instruction at a slower pace and lower level of reasoning. The remedy advanced by plaintiffs for the alleged harm of grouping was random assignment of students to classroom groups.

The Georgia Department of Education (GDE) and the defendant school districts acknowledged the disproportionate placement of black students across the classroom groups but sharply rejected plaintiffs' inferences and conclusions about its effects. First, the defendant districts argued that a combination of objective and judgmental criteria were used to constitute classroom groups. Although somewhat different procedures were used in the different districts, all districts emphasized the level of achievement—specifically, the skills level in the *basal series*—as the most important influence on achievement grouping. Group-administered aptitude or ability tests, the principal basis for constituting groups, were not used at all or received considerably less emphasis than actual classroom achievement.

The second critical point in the defendants' case was the claim of flexibility in the grouping assignments. The procedures used by several of the districts involved block grouping, which meant that a student's assignment could change by subject area. Furthermore, the Georgia districts were able to present convincing evidence about movement between levels. The defendants' third critical point was that the grouping procedures facilitated greater individualization of instruction, especially for students in the lowest level. The final critical aspect of the defense was the assertion that lower-performing black and white students performed at a higher level on the Georgia Criterion Referenced Test as a result of the achievement grouping.

Judge Edenfield concluded that all claims by the plaintiffs were based largely on supposition, with little or no empirical foundation. In contrast, the court found the defendants' rationale for achievement grouping to be sound and, contrary to plaintiffs' claims, ameliorative of the present effects of past segregation. All the plaintiffs' claims and proposed remedies concerning achievement grouping were rejected by the court. The plaintiffs' appeal of the decision to the eleventh circuit was unanimously rejected (*Georgia State Conference of Branches of NAACP v. State of Georgia*, 1985).

A superficial reading of the trial court decisions in *Marshall* and *Hobson* might suggest that they are markedly different even though similar facts were involved in both. A careful reading of both decisions and examination of the evidence supports a much different conclusion (Reschly, Kicklighter, & McKee, 1988a). Differences in the facts, rather than differing judicial interpretations of the facts or the relevant law, account for the different conclusions.

The first significant difference in *Marshall* and *Hobson* was the conception of the students' characteristics on which grouping decisions were made: *Hobson* focused on innate ability to learn; *Marshall* defendants emphasized achievement and acquired skills. Second, the *Hobson* basis for grouping was an IQ test; in *Marshall*, grouping was based on achievement, as indicated by daily work, classroom tests, and progress through basal curricula. A third difference was the successful effort of the *Marshall* defendants in establishing the direct relevance of grouping to the instruction provided. In contrast, the group-administered ability measure used in *Hobson* had relatively little direct relevance to the curriculum. Assignment to levels were rigid in *Hobson* but flexible in *Marshall*, where the evidence indicated that both black and white students did change levels according to their classroom performance. Educational opportunities in resources and quality of instruction also differed. A major finding in *Hobson* was the diminished resources and lower instructional quality associated with the lower levels, where black students were overrepresented. In *Marshall*, the defendants were able to convince the court that greater, rather than lesser, financial resources; a lower, rather than higher, student-teacher ratio; and greater, rather than lesser, instructional quality were associated with placement in the lower levels, where black students were overrepresented.

Recent litigation regarding tracking has followed the *Marshall* rather than the *Hobson* precedents more closely. Disproportionate representation of minority students in higher and lower tracks and, presumably, the methods to constitute the tracks, such as tests, may still come under the scrutiny of the federal courts if "such assignments are accomplished on the basis of race or for the purpose of racial segregation" (*Coalition*, 1995, p. 37). In this case, Judge Robinson rejected the plaintiffs' claims that differential racial representation in college-bound and noncollege-bound high school curricula constituted impermissible desegregation of students because the course enrollment was clearly related to level of achievement, movement between tracks was relatively easy and largely a matter of parents' and students' choices, differential instruction was provided in the different tracks, and black students with achievement scores above the seventy-fifth percentile on national norms were slightly more likely than white students in the same range to enroll in college preparatory classes.

Although overall achievement among black and white students had not been equalized in the Delaware districts in the *Coalition* litigation, the court refused plaintiffs' efforts to continue the federal court supervision of the districts, a circumstance that began in the mid-1970s as part of a plan to eliminate vestiges of de jure school segregation. In reaching this conclusion, the court cited a recent Supreme Court decision (*Missouri v. Jenkins*, 1995) that overruled a Missouri federal district court's insistence that the Kansas City school district eliminate achievement differences among black and white students as a prerequisite to being relieved of federal district court supervision. The Supreme Court in *Jenkins* also emphasized that "local autonomy of

school districts is a vital national tradition . . . and that a district court must strive to restore state and local authorities to the control of a school system operating in compliance with the Constitution" (p. 2054).

The court ruled that the four Delaware districts in the *Coalition* litigation had complied in good faith with the court orders for desegregation, concluding, "There is no credible evidence demonstrating that the differences between black and white children's success in school can be attributed to the former *de jure* desegregated school system" (p. 104). The court also noted, "One of the fundamental issues implicitly posed by this litigation is whether the time has come to return the focus of the public school system to matters of quality education rather than social policy" (p. 103).

## Summary

The cases in this section established the interests of the courts in testing practices if they were part of the violations of constitutional principles such as equal protection and due process. As these cases illustrate, the use of tests that have a disproportionate impact on minorities may be legally permissible as long as the grouping practice is not a way to establish or continue segregation of educational programs by race and instructional quality and resources are not diminished by the grouping procedures. The overall facts of the situation in which tests are used, such as the allocation of resources to different tracks, rather than tests per se, determine whether or not the testing practices are legally permissible. This will be a recurring theme in the litigation dealing with disproportionate minority representation in special education.

## Nondiscrimination in Special Education: 1970 to 1975 Litigation

Court cases concerning disproportionate classification and placement of minority students in MMR special education programs first appeared around 1970. These cases involved challenges to the use of individually administered tests of general intellectual functioning (hereafter IQ tests) by school psychologists, as well as other aspects of psychological services and special education programming. Litigation involving these issues continues to the present day. Typical facts in these cases were that minority students were overrepresented in special education programs, usually with a diagnosis of MMR and placement in self-contained classes, by a factor of two to three times the rate expected from their numbers in the general population. Unfortunately, these data were, and continue to be, misunderstood— indicating that large percentages of minority students were tested and placed in MMR programs. In fact, the actual percentages have always been quite low (as we now show).

## Diana *and* Guadalupe

Cases in Arizona and California were the first court proceedings in which plaintiffs directly attacked the use of individually administered IQ test (*Diana*, 1970; *Guadalupe*, 1972). *Diana* was a class action suit filed on behalf of nine Mexican-American children in Monterey County Schools, where 18.5% of the student enrollment was Hispanic but one-third of the MMR enrollment was Hispanic. Similar facts were established in *Guadalupe*, a class action case filed on behalf of Hispanic and Native-American children. The plaintiffs claimed that the overrepresentation violated the equal protection principle, as well as civil rights statutes. They also claimed that parents were often not informed that their children were referred, nor given the opportunity to participate in decisions about diagnosis and placement. In addition to the violation of these basic due process rights, the plaintiffs claimed that (1) the classification and placement decisions were made on the basis of verbally loaded IQ tests, which were patently unfair to limited English-proficient (LEP) students; (2) the psychologists were inadequately trained in the evaluation of LEP students; and (3) the special education programs represented limited opportunities that were inadequately funded. The views of the *Diana* and *Guadalupe* plaintiffs were analogous to those of the *PARC* and *Mills* plaintiffs: children were being denied educational opportunities on the basis of some inherent characteristic, here, race or ethnicity, that was not valid.

Both *Diana* and *Guadalupe* were settled by consent decrees; that is, the court approved a settlement negotiated between the parties. In neither case was there a trial, which would have allowed the presentation of the plaintiffs' evidence, as well as an opportunity for the defendants (local school and state department of education officials) to rebut the plaintiffs' claims. It is likely that so many things were wrong in the *Diana* and *Guadalupe* situations that the defendants were well advised to capitulate and agree to the plaintiffs' demands (MacMillan, 1977; Meyers, Sundstrom, & Yoshida, 1974; Reschly, 1979).

The consent agreements focused primarily on the establishment of due process rights for parents regarding referral, classification, and placement decisions and reform in how LEP students were evaluated. Inexplicably, little attention was given to educational programming. Most of the assessment reforms are familiar now and taken for granted, for example, the use of the primary language in assessment; use of nonverbal measures of ability with non-English or bilingual students; procedural safeguards such as informed consent; use of a variety of information (not merely a single IQ score); and from *Guadalupe*, assessment of adaptive behavior through, but not restricted to, a visit to the student's home.

The *Diana* and *Guadalupe* consent decrees focused on the kind of IQ test used with minority LEP students (nonverbal) or the manner in which the test was administered (in the child's primary language). They did not attack testing as such. In fact, these changes in assessment virtually eliminated the overrepresentation of Hispanic or Native-American children in IQ ranges below 75 or 70, the commonly used intellectual criterion to define MMR (Reschly & Jipson, 1976). There appears to be no national trend at this time toward overrepresentation of Hispanic students in any kind of special education program (Finn, 1982; Reschly, 1996; U.S. Department of Education, 1994). The *Diana* and *Guadalupe* consent decrees are also important in the evolution of the legal rights of parents and notions of nondiscrimination in assessment, classification, and placement. The EHA and now the IDEA incorporated verbatim much of the language of the *Diana* and *Guadalupe* consent decrees in the due process, LRE, and PEP sections of their regulations.

## Larry P. *(1972 and 1974)*

*Larry P.*, before the federal courts in one form or another for 25 years, first appeared in November 1971, when it was filed as a class action suit on behalf of black students in the San Francisco Public Schools who were placed in MMR special class programs. The basic facts included overrepresentation data, indicating that although black students constituted 28.5% of the district's overall enrollment, two-thirds of the students in the MMR special classes were black. The *Larry P.* case was developed through the efforts of the Bay Area Association of Black Psychologists (1971), who sought a ban on IQ testing, as well as other changes in general and special education.

In a 1972 preliminary injunction, Judge Peckham ruled that the plaintiffs met their burden of showing disparate treatment (i.e., black students were overrepresented in MMR special classes) and forbade the use of IQ tests in the San Francisco Public Schools, rejecting the defendants' justification for using IQ tests to determine MMR and special education needs. This injunction was appealed by the school district and the California Department of Education (CDE) to the Ninth Circuit Court of Appeals, which in August, 1974 upheld the original injunction. In December 1974, the plaintiffs were awarded an expanded injunction that forbade the use of IQ tests with any black student in the entire state of California if the outcome of its use was classification as MMR.

Judge Peckham was convinced by the plaintiffs' briefs and arguments that MMR special classes offered inferior educational opportunities and subjected students to stigma and humiliation. Of greatest concern was the possibility that students were misidentified as MMR: "This court is thus of the view that for those students who are wrongfully placed in EMR [educable mentally retarded] classes, irreparable harm ensues" (*Larry P.*, 1972, p. 1308).

## IQ Tests and Special Education Treatment on Trial: 1975–1995

Before the late 1970s, none of the cases that challenged individually administered tests actually resulted in a trial in which both the plaintiffs and the defendants could present extensive testimony and documentary evidence. Four trials in different federal district courts between 1977 and 1986 that examined overrepresentation in special education programs for students with MMR because of biases in IQ tests and other evaluation issues (e.g., conception and use of adaptive behavior) resulted in contradictory opinions on all of the basic issues. Further court proceedings in the first and most prominent of these cases, *Larry P.*, were still pending as this chapter went to press. Although the facts in the cases were remarkably similar, the strategies of defendants differed markedly, as did the judicial understanding of the fundamental issues.

### Larry P. *(1979, 1984)*

The previous injunctions in the *Larry P.* case were not satisfactory to the defendants, who vigorously defended the use of IQ tests and overrepresentation of black students in MMR special

education programs in a trial that began in October 1977 and concluded in May 1978. A decision on the merits of the case was issued by Judge Peckham in October 1979. That decision was then appealed to the Ninth Circuit, which on a two-to-one vote, upheld the trial opinion in January 1984.

In many ways, the *Larry P.* trial on IQ testing was for American psychology what the Scopes trial on evolution was for biology in the 1920s. Prominent expert witnesses testified for both sides amid considerable local publicity and in the newsletters and journals of several national associations. Expert witnesses for the plaintiffs included George Albee, Harold Dent, Asa Hilliard, Leon Kamin, and Jane Mercer. Defense experts included Robert Gordon, Lloyd Humphries, Nadine Lambert, Jerome Sattler, and Robert Thorndike. The outcome, a ban on IQ tests with black children under certain conditions, was shocking to mainstream American psychologists (e.g., Elliott, 1987).

The *Larry P.* trial and opinion centered on the issue of bias in IQ tests against black children and youth. These tests were seen by Judge Peckham as the most "pervasive," prominent, and influential element of the process through which children were classified as MMR and placed in special classes. Therefore, the opinion reviewed the extensive testimony on alleged biases in IQ tests, concluding that contemporary IQ tests were related to a pernicious, discriminatory history of standardized testing that tolerated differences between blacks and whites.

Judge Peckham regarded tests as biased if different average scores were obtained by groups; "An unbiased test that measures ability or potential should yield the same pattern of scores when administered to different groups of people" (*Larry P.*, 1979, p. 41). Although group average differences have never been accepted as an appropriate criterion by the vast majority of psychologists, the *Larry P.* opinion cited IQ differences between black and whites, and the acceptance of tests that revealed those differences, as evidence of discriminatory practices. Judge Peckham also found IQ test biased because their content was tailored to the culture of white children and youth and away from the culture and experiences of black children and youths. Finally, in an especially astonishing conclusion to psychologists and assessment specialists, he concluded that the conventional IQ test such as the Wechsler Scales were not correlated with academic achievement to the same extent for black as for white students, a conclusion that goes against the results of considerable research (Jensen, 1980; Reschly, 1996; Reynolds & Kaiser, 1990).

Based on these conclusions, as well as the assertion that the named plaintiffs were not "really" retarded, Judge Peckham then subjected the facts in the case to a legal analysis, using statutory (especially the nondiscrimination principles in Section 504 and EHA) and constitutional law (especially equal protection from the Fourteenth Amendment). He concluded that the defendants had violated the nondiscrimination principle in federal law (34 CFR 300.530), as well as the equal protection principle in the U.S. Constitution. The latter finding was especially surprising in view of the change in equal protection case law from 1972 to 1979, a change that required proof of intent to discriminate (Bersoff & Hofer, 1990). Despite the difficulty of determining intent, Judge Peckham cited several patterns of conduct by the state defendants that he concluded established intent to discriminate against black students, a conclusion that was particularly inappropriate in the view of a school psychologists who was an expert witness in the case (Lambert, 1981). Judge Peckham in his 1979 trial opinion banned IQ tests with black students if the outcome of the test was a diagnosis of MMR and placement in a segregated special education class.

## Parents in Action on Special Education *v.* Joseph P. Hannon [PASE] *(1980)*

*PASE* was a class action suit on behalf of black students in the Chicago Public Schools that alleged misclassification of students as MMR because of biases in IQ tests. A trial was held over a three-week period in 1979, and a decision was rendered in July 1980. Judge Grady ruled in favor of the defendants in a decision that was remarkably contradictory to the *Larry P.* decision. The plaintiffs appealed the decision but withdrew prior to the circuit court decision because the basic issue tried in the case, the use of IQ tests with black students, became moot through the action of the Chicago Public Schools Board of Education that eliminated IQ tests in the Chicago schools. Although *PASE* is an obvious contradiction of *Larry P.*, the fact that the issues in the case are now moot and the absence of an appeals court upholding the decision makes

*PASE* largely irrelevant to the practice of school psychology.

A great deal of analysis concerning *Larry P.* and *PASE* has appeared in the literature (Bersoff, 1982a, 1982b; Elliott, 1987; Lambert, 1981; MacMillan & Meyers, 1980; Prasse & Reschly, 1986; Reschly, 1980, 1996; Reschly, Kicklighter, & McKee, 1988b. 1988c; Sattler, 1981). Both cases made poor use of evidence from psychological theory and research. Bersoff's scathing criticism of both judges is particularly instructive about the poor use of social science evidence, a problem related to the proper use of expert testimony (see later discussion). Sattler provided an excellent contrast of the judges' views in *PASE* and *Larry P.* over the following issues: (a) the function of EMR special classes, (b) how students were selected for EMR special classes, (c) the degree to which the IQ test is the most important information during selection, (d) what intelligence tests measure, (e) the degree to which socioeconomic factors account for black and white differences in average IQ, (f) the degree to which nonstandard English affects the performance of black students, (g) the degree to which cultural differences between black and white students affect performance on IQ tests, and (h) whether specific items on intelligence tests are culturally biased.

## Marshall *and* S-1 *Opinions*

Two trials devoted to overrepresentation of black students in MMR special education programs in the Eleventh Circuit were decided in favor of the defendants (*Marshall*, 1984; *S-1*, 1986). *Marshall*, the most important of these cases in precedent value and possible influence on current school psychology practice, was a class action suit filed by Georgia Legal Services, Inc., and the Georgia State Conference of Branches of NAACP. The class of plaintiffs, all black students in the Georgia public schools, alleged violation of various statutory and constitutional rights.

In the 1983 trial, the plaintiffs alleged that overrepresentation of black students in MMR programs was caused by (a) numerous violations of procedural regulations such as timely reevaluation and participation of appropriate persons in staffing decisions, IEP development, and IEP review and (b) improper interpretation and application of federal and state requirements governing classification and placement of students in MMR programs (particularly IQ cutoff and adaptive behavior assessment). The plaintiffs' expert witnesses provided a statistical analysis of the composition of special education programs in Georgia (especially MMR) and a detailed review of *selected* records of students placed in MMR programs. On the basis of these analyses, the plaintiffs concluded that most Georgia school districts had a statistically significant overrepresentation of black students in MMR programs and, in about half of the districts, underrepresentation of black students in SLD programs. These analyses were the basis for the court's finding of disparate impact and the shifting of the burden to defendants to prove a rational relationship between their procedures and a legitimate state interest.

Based on a review of the special education records of 15 students in the defendant school districts, the plaintiffs' experts testified to multiple violations in what were acknowledged as the worst cases from each of the districts. The alleged violations included (a) several cases in which the global or full scale IQ was slightly above 70 but, apparently, within a standard error of measurement of 70; (b) failure to properly assess adaptive behavior and to exclude students from the MMR diagnosis if the adaptive behavior in any domain was within 2 standard deviations of the mean; (c) some reevaluations older than three years; (d) no documentation of vision and hearing screening in some cases; (e) several cases in which parents did not participate in the development of IEPs, although evidence of parental consent for evaluation and placement was present in all cases; (f) inadequate documentation, such as missing signatures on forms that reflected team members' participation in staffings; (g) inadequate implementation of the LRE principle because most MMR students were in special classes rather than part-time resource programs; (h) occasional improper selection of assessment instruments; (i) achievement scores slightly higher than IQ scores in a few cases; and (j) inadequate consideration of social and cultural background. The plaintiffs claimed that these violations of procedural regulations and the misinterpretation or misapplication of the state IQ guidelines and adaptive behavior requirements caused massive misclassification of black students as MMR.

However, an unintentional, serendipitous event occurred: the records of 3 white students were part of the sample of 15 records selected by the plaintiffs and reviewed by their experts. The same problems existed in the records of white students, undermining the plaintiffs' racial interpretation of the problems in their review.

Although the *Marshall* defendants admitted errors in implementation of some regulations, they sharply disputed the plaintiffs' allegations that these violations were related to race, resulted in misclassification of students, and reflected an intent to discriminate. The defendants argued that their procedures and classification criteria reflected best professional practices and that the same procedures and criteria were applied equally to white and black students. The defendants' case was based on justifying the necessity and benefits of programs for students classified as MMR, as well as rebutting the plaintiffs' recommendations for classification criteria (Reschly et al., 1988b, 1988c). Each of the defendant school districts and representatives of the GDE described the policies for referral, evaluation, classification, and placement. These practices were tied to the best practices described in a recently published National Academy of Sciences Report on equity in special education classification and placement (Heller, Holtzman, & Messick, 1982). The defendants emphasized the use of general education interventions *prior* to referral, which typically occurred after several years of severe and chronic achievement problems in general education.

The defendants also attacked the plaintiffs' interpretation of the statistical evidence for overrepresentation (Reschly et al., 1988b, 1988c). They rejected the assumption that the percentage of black students meeting the MMR criteria should necessarily be proportionate to the number of black students in the total student population. Widely known findings were cited concerning overrepresentation of black students in Chapter I (a federally funded program for low-achieving students) and other compensatory education programs in Georgia and throughout the United States. This overrepresentation was seen as reflecting a higher incidence of learning problems among black students throughout the achievement ranges of low-average, slow learner, borderline, and MMR. The defendants also cited the National Academy Report (Heller et al., p. 42), which indicated that mechanical application of a rigid IQ score in classification, such as that recommended by the plaintiffs, might lead to considerably greater, rather than less, minority overrepresentation.

The defendants admitted violations of procedural regulations: "The local defendants acknowledged that in certain instances they failed to properly document students' files and timely perform reevaluations in violation of the regulations. However, these infractions occurred because of staffing problems and permissible delays rather than any intentional attempts to misclassify students, black or white, for the special education program" (*Marshall*, 1984, p. 62). The critical issue here, according to the court, was whether the procedural violations occurred more frequently with black than with white MMR students, whether the procedural violations led to massive misclassification of black students, and whether the procedural violations reflected intent to discriminate against black students. Repeatedly, Judge Edenfield indicated that evidence for differential treatment of white and black students with achievement problems had to be provided to substantiate the plaintiffs' claims. He concluded that none of the students whose files were reviewed "constituted glaring examples of gross misclassification" (*Marshall*, 1984, p. 141).

The *Marshall* case is important, particularly as elaborated by the appeals court, because of the kind of evidence required to substantiate allegations of discrimination. Clearly, overrepresentation in itself was insufficient. Unequal treatment in decision making appears to be the primary standard, which in the *Marshall* context, required comparisons of black and white referred students who were classified and placed in MMR. Judge Edenfield dismissed all plaintiffs' claims concerning discrimination by race and improper classification.

The *Marshall* decision was appealed to the U.S. Court of Appeals for the Eleventh Circuit in September 1984. A unanimous decision (*Georgia State Conference*, 1985) upheld all of the trial court findings. The appeals court decision was even more explicit and harsher concerning the plaintiffs' approach to proving discrimination, overrepresentation in MMR programs. Specifically, the appeals court suggested that statistical evidence on overrepresentation did not show that practices of local defendants "impacted more harshly on black children than on other students" (p. 36). "Practices which detrimentally affect all groups equally, do not have a discriminatory effect" (p. 38). The appellate tribunal clearly indicated that simple overrepresentation is not sufficient; evidence of differential treatment during referral, evaluation, classification, and placement had to be provided by the plaintiffs to establish the groundwork for discrimination.

## S-1 *v.* Turlington

Another class action trial dealing with overrepresentation of black students in MMR programs was conducted in May-June 1986 in a federal district court in Miami, Florida. The *S-1* plaintiffs alleged violation of numerous EHA principles (nondiscrimination, use of invalid tests, and LRE). The plaintiffs, in contrast to *Marshall* plaintiffs, placed more emphasis on test bias and the interpretation of the sociocultural background portion of federal EHA regulations. The *S-1* defendant, the Florida Department of Education (FDE), used some of the same strategies applied by *Marshall* defendants, along with a strong emphasis on the benefits of MMR programs for students with low general intellectual functioning and severe learning problems. The trial court dismissed the claims of the named plaintiffs "with prejudice" and decertified the class. The court's ruling was quite unequivocal: "Simply stated, plaintiffs failed to satisfy their burden of proof. They did not prove that any black student had been improperly classified and placed into the MMR program. Thus, it is clear that the action must be dismissed and the class decertified" (p. 5). The dismissal with prejudice meant that the plaintiffs did not establish even a prima facie case of discrimination and that reestablishing a similar court suit on these issues in this district would be extremely difficult.

## Larry P. *(1986)*

After prevailing with the Ninth Circuit in 1984, the *Larry P.* plaintiffs sought an expanded injunction against the use of IQ tests because, in their view, school psychologists and special educators were subverting the 1979 trial opinion by using IQ tests as part of the evaluation of the eligibility of African-American students for other disabilities, especially SLD. The MMR classification and MMR programs had been abolished by the CDE as part of a special education master plan in the late 1970s. The *Larry P.* injunction against IQ tests was narrowly drawn: IQ tests were banned "for the identification of black E.M.R. children or their placement into E.M.R. classes . . . or a substantially equivalent category." By 1986 the CDE, the defendant in *Larry P.* in the 1972, 1974, 1979, and 1984 court actions, joined the *Larry P.* plaintiffs to craft an agreement that was acceptable to both parties. The agreement negotiated between the parties was approved by Judge Peckham in an order that required the CDE to inform all school districts of "the complete prohibition against using IQ tests for identifying or placing black pupils in special education . . . an IQ test may not be given to a black pupil even with parental consent. Moreover, when a school district receives records containing test protocols from other agencies . . . IQ scores contained in the records shall not become a part of the pupil's current school record. There are no special education related purposes for which IQ tests shall be administered to black students" (*Larry P.*, 1986, p. 4).

Some might argue that the 1986 injunction appears to be a classic case of violation of equal protection for it meant that the CDE was ordered to establish different rules for the exercise of parental discretion and decision making, depending on the race of the child. If the child was black, one set of rules applied; however, a different set of rules was established if the child was white. It was an astonishing, even stunning, turn of events in a case that had been decided, originally in 1972, on the basis of a school district's violation of the equal protection of the laws.

## Crawford v. Honig *(1988, 1992)*

In May 1988 *Crawford et al.*, v. *Honig* was filed in district court as a class action suit against the CDE on behalf of black students whose parents were prevented by the 1986 *Larry P.* injunction from making decisions about IQ testing in preplacement evaluations of their children, a right exercised by parents of white children. *Crawford* plaintiffs cited the usual legal bases for their assertions of impermissible discrimination, including the U.S. Constitution's due process and equal protection rights, Title VI of the 1964 Civil Rights Act, and the nondiscrimination principle in EHA. The case was recognized immediately as directly relevant to the *Larry P.* issues and then remanded to Judge Peckham.

In 1992 Judge Peckham rescinded the 1986 expanded injunction on due process grounds because the members of the *Crawford* plaintiff class, black children who may be diagnosed as SLD through IQ tests, were not represented in the original *Larry P.* plaintiff class or at the 1986 proceeding that produced the expanded injunction. As noted by Judge Peckham in 1992, the language of the 1979 order in the trial opinion was "clearly limited to the use of IQ tests in the assessment and placement of African-American students in dead-end programs such as MMR" (*Crawford*, 1992; *Larry P.*, 1992, p. 15). The

*Larry P.* plaintiffs and the *Crawford* defendants joined in filing an appeal to the Ninth Circuit Court of Appeals, seeking to overturn the 1992 order that rescinded the 1986 injunction. The appeal was denied, returning the status of the *Larry P.* litigation to the 1979 trial opinion.

The CDE has played a complex and changing role in the quarter century that the *Larry P.* matter has been before the federal courts. From the time of the original filing in 1971, the injunctions in 1972 and 1974, the trial in 1977–1978, court opinion in 1979, and appellate court in 1984, the CDE was a principal in vigorously defending the use of IQ tests and the overrepresentation of African-American children in MMR. By 1986, however, the CDE *joined with* the *Larry P.* plaintiffs in crafting the strongly worded comprehensive ban on IQ tests that was rescinded in 1992. Since 1992, the CDE has disseminated strongly worded directives to school districts, reminding them of the 1979 trial opinion, which it interprets as focusing primarily on the biases in IQ tests against African-American students. In contrast to the recent CDE interpretations of the 1979 *Larry P.* trial opinion as a referendum on IQ tests, Judge Peckham described that opinion in 1992 as "clearly limited to the use of IQ tests in the assessment and placement of African-American students in dead end programs such as MMR" (*Crawford*, 1992; *Larry P.*, 1992, p. 15). "Despite the Defendants' attempts to characterize the court's 1979 order as a referendum on the discriminatory nature of IQ testing, this court's review of the decision reveals that the decision was largely concerned with the harm to African-American children resulting from improper placement in dead-end educational programs" (p. 23).

## Comparisons of *Larry P.*, *Marshall*, and *S-1*

A number of significant differences in *Larry P.*, *Marshall*, and *S-1* were discussed in Reschly et al. (1988c), particularly how basic issues were framed by the defendants. The fundamental differences were as follows: (a) the role of IQ tests, seen as primary in *Larry P.*, were viewed as secondary to severe, chronic achievement problems in *Marshall* and *S-1*; (b) implementation of educational alternatives before referral for possible consideration of special education placement was stressed in *Marshall* and *S-1*, including placement in general education remedial or compensatory education programs; (c) there was greater emphasis on adaptive behavior in *Marshall* and *S-1*, particularly on a conception of adaptive behavior that included practical cognitive skills; (d) there were carefully prepared overrepresentation statistics in *Marshall* and *S-1* so that the court understood clearly the differences between the percentage of a group in a program and the percentage of a program by group statistics (see later discussion); (e) compilation of data in *Marshall* and *S-1* showed that African-American students were much more likely to be placed in other remedial or compensatory education programs than in MMR special education programs (e.g., Head Start, Chapter 1, and LD resource, all of which were used more frequently than MMR special education placement); (f) there was conformance to the American Association on Mental Retardation (AAMR) classification scheme in *Marshall* and *S-1*; (g) an explanation of overrepresentation was provided in *Marshall* and *S-1*, specifically the effects of poverty, as opposed to the "agnostic" position on this issue taken by the California *Larry P.* defendants; and (h) emphasis on the results of the National Academy of Science Panel's analysis (Heller et al., 1982), which accepted overrepresentation if appropriate instruction, among other things, was provided in *Marshall* and *S-1*.

How issues are framed in a case depends on the strategies developed by the plaintiffs and defendants. Both sides in the *Larry P.* case focused on the IQ tests, and the defendants did not spend a great deal of effort in establishing the benefits of the MMR program. Judge Peckham regarded them as dead-end educational programs that conferred few if any benefits and caused much harm, such as stigma and limited academic opportunities, especially if children were misdiagnosed and misplaced. Given the assumptions about the treatment, it is not at all surprising that the court agreed to the solutions proposed by the *Larry P.* plaintiffs, who were, for other reasons, interested primarily in a refutation of the validity of IQ tests for black students. Although Judge Peckham claimed in 1992 that *Larry P.* was not a referendum on IQ, the leadership of the Bay Area Association of Black Psychologists clearly thought otherwise, a view that has not changed (Dent, 1993; Hilliard, 1992; Jones, 1988). The California defendants, because they did not, and perhaps, could not, defend the benefits of the MMR programs, chose instead to focus on IQ tests, unwittingly cooperating with the plaintiffs in making *Larry P.* a referendum on IQ. That

referendum was limited, however, by Judge Peckham's narrow ban that applied only to MMR, a category that the CDE abolished soon after the *Larry P.* trial. Efforts to date to expand the IQ ban to other states or, in California, to other disabilities have been unsuccessful. As noted in Reschly et al. (1988c), as well as in Lerner (1988), the most defensible *Larry P.* outcome, legally and scientifically, would have been a ban on dead-end special education programs for which benefits were undocumented. In retrospect, it is clear now that program benefits were the chief issue in the general education tracking and special education placement litigation. In *Larry P.* and *Hobson*, program benefits were nonexistent, according to Judges Wright and Peckham. In contrast, Judges Edenfield in *Marshall* and Atkins in *S-1* thought that program benefits were sufficient to permit disparate placement. Treatment efficacy, therefore, appears to have been the central issue in disproportionate placement litigation in the past and probably in the future.

## Implicit Issues and Accurate Interpretation of Overrepresentation Data

That more than IQ tests and overrepresentation were involved in the plaintiffs' motives is apparent from a careful analysis of the four cases. For example, consider the *Larry P.* opinion, which reflected the plaintiffs' assertions that (a) IQ tests were biased; (b) IQ and achievement tests "autocorrelate" that is, they were the same; and (c) "the customary uses of achievement tests are not questioned by plaintiff, even though black children also tend not to do well on these tests" (*Larry P.*, 1979, p. 952). That reasoning makes little sense unless factors other than IQ tests were of concern. Furthermore, as noted previously, economically disadvantaged, minority students are overrepresented in a variety of educational programs including Head Start, Chapter 1, and Follow Through. This overrepresentation is well known but, apparently, acceptable. Implicit issues and assumptions provide an explanation for these seemingly inconsistent elements in plaintiffs' positions. Discussions of these implicit issues have appeared at several places in the literature (Reschly, 1979, 1982, 1996) and are mentioned only briefly here. Important implicit issues include (a) the *nature-nurture controversy* and hereditarian views of differences between racial groups (Herrnstein & Murray, 1994; Jensen,

1969) and the efforts of black psychologists to refute these views in the courts (Dent, 1976, 1993; Hilliard, 1980, 1983, 1992; Jones, 1988; Jones & Jones, 1987; Jones & Wilderson, 1976); (b) the *meaning of IQ test results* in the degree to which they are predetermined by genetic factors and whether intelligence is unitary and is measured directly by IQ tests; (c) the *role of tests in placement decisions* (primary determinant of classification or secondary to severe, chronic achievement problems); (d) the *meaning of mild mental retardation* (does "true" MMR require evidence of comprehensive incompetence, permanence, and biological anomaly; (e) the *effectiveness of MMR special classes* (whether they were dead-end programs that provided few opportunities or offered specialized instruction tailored to the abilities of the children placed in them); and (f) the *meaning of bias in testing and assessment.*

A final problem, *exaggerations and distortions of overrepresentation data*, needs further elaboration here. At the time of the *Larry P.* opinion, Judge Peckham reprinted CDE data indicating that black students constituted about 10% of the California student population but 25% of the MMR population. These proportions were apparently stable over a number of years. The question is this: what proportion of black students was in MMR classes?

Many professionals assume from the data just given that a high proportion of black students are in special education programs because they make the mistake of interpreting the percentage of the MMR program by group as the percentage of the group in the MMR program. In fact, the proportion of California black students in MMR special classes at the time of the *Larry P.* trial was only 1.2, an astounding result in view of the heated rhetoric about the effects of ability tests on black students (Reschly, 1996; see Table 41.3). This rather surprising result occurred because the base rate for MMR was low, and in general, whenever the base rates for a particular phenomenon are low, the percentage of the program by group can be markedly different than the percentage of a group in a particular program. Consider this analogy: the gender composition in the career of elementary school teachers is overwhelmingly female, perhaps as high as 95%. The percentage of the career category (elementary school teachers) that is female is 95%. Now consider what percentage of females (group) are elementary school teachers. That percentage is, of course, very low, perhaps about 5%. Although women clearly dominate elementary school teaching, few women are elementary school teachers. An analogous situation occurs with the participation of minority chil-

TABLE 41.3 Comparison of Percentage of Program by Group and Percentage of Group in Program Overrepresentation Statistics Using 1990 OCR School District Survey Data[a]

| Group Category[b] | Black | | Hispanic | | White | |
|---|---|---|---|---|---|---|
| | Group[c] | Program[d] | Group[c] | Program[d] | Group[c] | Program[d] |
| MMR | 2.10% | 34.64% | 0.65% | 7.60% | 0.81% | 55.82% |
| SLD | 4.95% | 16.61% | 4.68% | 11.19% | 4.97% | 69.83% |
| SED | 0.89% | 21.47% | 0.33% | 5.81% | 0.69% | 70.65% |
| Percent of total student population[e] | 16.20% | | 11.54% | | 67.88% | |

[a]These results were derived from data published by the U.S. Department of Education (1994), pp. 198, 201, and 202.

[b]MMR = mild mental retardation, SLD = specific learning disability; and SED = seriously emotionally disturbed.

[c]This column provides the percentage of the group in the disability category; for example, the proportion of black students in MMR was 2.10%.

[d]This column provides the percentage of the disability category by group; for example, black students constituted 34.64% of the students in the category of MMR.

[e]The proportions of black, Hispanic, and white students in the population from which the 1990 Office for Civil Rights sample was drawn were 16.2%, 11.54%, and 67.88%, respectively.

dren in special education. Although the category of MMR by race reveals overrepresentation of African-American students, the actual percentage of African-American students in the MMR category is rather small.

The actual national overrepresentation of black students in special education programs is often exaggerated by giving the percentage of program statistics and implying that a large proportion of black children are in special education programs (e.g., Chinn & Hughes, 1987; Harry, 1994). The percentage of group in special education statistics, that is, the actual proportion of black children in special education, reveals a significantly different perspective: the proportion of black children in special education is relatively small and only slightly larger than the proportions for white students (see Table 41.3). It is also important to note that Hispanic students are not overrepresented in special education programs according to the OCR data.

## Summary

Since 1979 there have been four trials in the federal district courts on issues related to overrepresentation of African-American children in special education programs. The judicial scoreboard is three to one; defendant school districts and state departments of education have prevailed in three of the trials. The only trial in which the plaintiffs prevailed was *Larry P.* Two of the trial opinions were upheld when appealed to circuit courts of appeal (*Larry P.*, 1984; *Marshall, Georgia State Conference*, 1985). The circuit court results are one to one. The Ninth Circuit affirmed the *Larry P.* trial opinion banning IQ tests for the narrow purpose of classifying black children as MMR, whereas the Eleventh Circuit affirmed the *Marshall* trial court opinion that permitted African-American overrepresentation in special education MMR programs. Neither case was appealed to the U.S. Supreme Court; therefore, it is likely that these contradictory circuit court opinions will not be resolved by a higher court opinion. Unlike the legal concept of "appropriate education" that was defined by a Supreme Court opinion, the legal meaning of "nondiscrimination" is likely to remain elusive and ambiguous.

## INTERVENTION AND THERAPY

Interventions delivered to students and teachers through consultation and counseling are governed by complex ethical and legal principles in-

volving parental consent, rights of privacy, and confidentiality of information in professional relationships. In considering these issues, it is important to contemplate a continuum of school psychology services ranging from indirect influences on students, such as in-service training of teachers and administrators about effective ways to improve classroom climate and students' social skills, to very direct services, such as individual counseling with an adolescent about feelings of despair and hopelessness. Across this continuum of influence, the legal obligations of school psychologists vary significantly according to a general principle: the more direct the influence, the greater the need for concerns about (a) informed parental consent, (b) competing claims of privacy rights, (c) limits on protecting the confidentiality of information revealed through the course of treatment, and (d) mandatory reports of child abuse or neglect.

Psychologists who are consulting about instructional approaches with a school staff member or with an individual teacher about a group of students whose personal identities do not become known to the psychologist are providing indirect services, which in most circumstances would not involve informed parental consent, privacy, confidentiality, or concerns about child abuse or neglect laws. These issues become increasingly prominent with interventions for individual students who are personally identifiable and are being treated differently in some way that is apparent to others in the educational setting. These concerns arise in their most difficult form when a student of high school age seeks the aid of a school psychologist but wants the psychologist to promise that the students' parents will not know of the interaction. This situation "surfaces the tension between the right of parents to be informed about and give permission for their children to enter counseling relationships and the right of adolescents to seek professional help when their interest may be adverse to those of their parents" (Bersoff, 1975, p. 370).

The case of *Pesce* v. *Morton High* (1986) illustrates the competing legal interests and professional obligations affecting school psychologists when they provide therapeutic and counseling services to students. Pesce was a school psychologist who was given by C.R., a student at the school, a note written by J.D., another student. The note included possible hints of suicide and expressions of guilt and confusion over J.D.'s sexual identity. C.R. also told Pesce that J.D. said he had visited the home of a faculty member when "something sexual" had occurred. Pesce urged C.R. to have J.D. visit him, and also asked her to pass along the name of a professional therapist. Later that day J.D. visited Pesce in his office at school. Pesce assured him of the confidentiality of any information divulged and questioned him about the issues raised in the letter. J.D. denied suicidal intentions and also that any sexual acts had occurred, but he admitted that the teacher had shown him "pictures" when he visited the teacher's home.

Pesce considered the legal and psychological implications of honoring the confidentiality of the communication with J.D. He consulted with an attorney and another psychologist and considered the relevant state laws, school regulations, and the specialty guidelines of the APA. After due consideration and in good faith, Pesce decided not to notify any school officials nor J.D.'s parents at that time. Ten days later, Pesce learned that after attending two sessions, J.D. had canceled an appointment with his therapist. He met with J.D. and learned that the teacher had in fact engaged in a sexual act with him. He discussed the advantages and disadvantages of disclosing this fact and won J.D.'s agreement that it would be best to reveal the information to school authorities.

Among the state laws in effect at the time was the Illinois Abused and Neglected Child Reporting Act (ILL. Rev. Stat. ch. 23). It requires school personnel having reasonable cause to believe that a child may be abused to report the incident to the Illinois Department of Child and Family Services. Another relevant law was the Mental Health and Development Disabilities Confidentiality Act (ILL. Rev. Stat. ch. 91). It protects confidential disclosures between psychologists and patients, with certain exceptions. Among these are disclosures with the consent of the parent or guardians and either the consent of the minor or a finding by the therapist that disclosure would be in the child's best interest. Also permitted are disclosures required under the reporting act.

There was an arguable ambiguity in the duties imposed by these two laws. The reporting act imposed obligations. The confidentiality act imposed countervailing obligations, with permissible exceptions that would cover the reporting of abuse. Pesce argued that he determined it would be in the best interest of J.D. to maintain his confidential communications.

When school officials learned of the matter and of Pesce's 10-day delay in reporting the incident, they recommended to the school board that Pesce be suspended without pay for 5 days. They notified him of his right to a hearing, at which Pesce and his attorney presented evidence. The school board nevertheless voted to impose a 5-day suspension and to demote Pesce from "School Psychologist" to the "School Psychologist for the Behavior Disorders Program." They cited Pesce's employment contract, which permitted suspension for "misconduct," which was defined to include "any act or failure to act occurring during the course of an employee's duties which jeopardizes the health, safety, and welfare of any . . . student."

Pesce brought suit in federal court for an alleged violation of his constitutional due process and privacy rights. But the judge ruled that it was reasonable for the school board to conclude that Pesce's determination that nondisclosure of the information was in J.D.'s best interest was "misconduct" that jeopardized J.D.'s health. The court refused to interpose its judgment between the school board and its employees.

Clearly, psychologists who act as counselors and therapists in the schools face many of the same problems as adult therapists. But they are further complicated by the special relation of the school to parents and to its students. We must never forget that school psychologists are part of an encompassing institutional structure that affects many aspects of students' lives. The school psychologist is in many ways more similar to a hospital staff psychologist than to a two-hour-a-week counselor. Therapeutic intervention in the schools can be comparable to the design of comprehensive ward treatment plans. Sensitivity to issues of accurate record keeping, conscientious use of punishment or time-out procedures, and great care in designing interventions are required. (See Wherry, 1983, for a discussion of legal considerations in the use of behavior modification in the schools.)

Although the *Pesce* case did not deal with informed parental consent, it is likely that he was vulnerable on those grounds as well. Do children have an independent right to privacy that will enable school psychologists to intervene in their lives without parental knowledge or consent? The question is part of a larger issue: how does the law allocate power among parents, children, and arms of the state like schools? That question has received considerable attention from legal scholars (e.g., Kleinfeld, 1970–1971; Mnookin, 1978; Wald, 1974) and from the courts. In *Tinker v. Des Moines Independent Community School District* (1969), the Supreme Court intimated that at least some rights were evenly distributed among children and adults: "First Amendment rights are available to teachers and students. It can hardly be argued that either students or teachers shed their constitutional rights to freedom of speech or expression at the schoolhouse gate" (p. 506). However, the Court has also made it clear that children do not share equally in all provisions of the Constitution. In *In re Gault* (1967), children in juvenile court proceedings were afforded some but not the entire range of due process protections granted to adult criminals. And although it violates the Eighth Amendment's cruel and inhuman punishment clause to physically discipline adult prisoners, the Court ruled that corporal punishment of schoolchildren was constitutionally permissible (*Ingraham* v. *Wright*, 1977).

The Supreme Court's abortion-related and access to contraception decisions indicate that in some facets of personal life, certain adolescents have privacy rights that will be allowed expression even though to do so may conflict with parental wishes (*Planned Parenthood of Central Missouri* v. *Danforth*, 1976; *Carey* v. *Population Services International Inc.*, 1977; *Bellotti* v. *Baird*, 1979; *City of Akron* v. *Akron Ctr. for Reproductive Health*, 1983). And not all Supreme Court decisions have endorsed the privacy rights of adolescents in the abortion context, for example, *H.L.* v. *Matheson*, 1981.

The courts have struggled with difficult questions of how to distribute decision making among children, parents, and professionals. In addition, we should be cautious about generalizing principles that arise in the abortion context to other domains. For example, the Court in *Parham* v. *J.L.* (1979) was called on to decide the constitutionality of a statute permitting parents to admit their children to mental institutions. When the state seeks to commit adults involuntarily they are afforded a number of procedural safeguards, including a hearing before an impartial decision maker and representation by an attorney. But in almost all states, when parents seek to place their children in mental hospitals it is considered a voluntary admission and children have no due process rights.

In *Parham*, child advocates claimed that such admissions were voluntary in name only, that there was a danger of parents acting adversely to the interest of their children, and that as a result children should be given procedural protections similar to those of adults. The Court found the interests of the parents paramount and ruled that the extensive procedural safeguards governing the admission of adults to mental institutions are not accorded to children. The Court's reasoning was based on its traditional concern for the family unit and of the primacy of the family over the state. While noting the incidence of child neglect and abuse, it relied on what it called "the pages of human experience" to undergird its conclusion that "parents generally do act in [the] child's best interest" (p. 2504).

Most important for our purposes, the Court renewed its belief that children are incompetent to make decisions: "The law's concept of the family rests on a presumption that parents possess what a child lacks in maturity, experience, and capacity for judgment required to making life's difficult decisions" (*Parham*, 1979, p. 2504), and it concluded that "most children, even in adolescence, simply are not able to make sound judgments concerning many decisions, including their need for medical care or treatment" (p. 2505). "Parents," it declared, "can and must make those judgments" (p. 2505). The overall result of this analysis of tripartite interests was to simply hold that a "neutral factfinder" (i.e., a staff physician at the admitting hospital) should review all available sources of information to determine that parental requests for institutionalization were not in error.

The legal system's solicitude for the family unit and the primacy of parental control does not mean, of course, that children are at the mercy of their mothers and fathers. "Parents may be free to become martyrs themselves. But it does not follow they are free . . . to make martyrs of their children (*Prince* v. *Massachusetts*, 1944, p. 170). Courts will override parental prerogatives when parents are unable or refuse to care for their children's physical or emotional needs, when there is an abuse of parental authority, or when protectable property interests of children (e.g., inheritances) conflict with those of their parents. The most clear-cut example of state interference in family life is the passage of child abuse laws in all 50 of the United States (see Katz, Howe, & McGrath, 1975).

In sum, children are generally considered incapable of knowing what is best for themselves. The courts presume that parents, as preferred care-givers, are competent to represent their children's interests and consequently protect the family from unreasonable interference by the state. However, the presumption may be rebutted by evidence of significant harm to the child, and in those instances the courts replace parents—either permanently or for limited purposes—with alternative decision makers.

Furthermore, statutory and case law presently afford adolescents greater freedom to seek medical and psychological help without parental permission, a change advocated by many writers and legal scholars in recent years (Bersoff, 1976–1977; Foster & Freed, 1972; Holt, 1974; Kleinfeld, 1970–1971; Melton, Koocher, & Saks, 1983; Wald, 1974). Many states now have statutes permitting minors to give valid consent to treatment for venereal disease and other sex-related problems. One state permits those 16 years of age or over to consent to treatment for emotional disorders, but potential clients are restricted to receiving this help from medical personnel. Despite these developments, the right of adolescents to seek aid by giving valid consent is far from universal and is presently confined to certain modes of intervention by certain classes of practitioners.

There may be ample justification in the legal literature to support the right of young persons to secure treatment without parental permission, but in the light of the Supreme Court's overriding preference for parental control and its distrust of minors' ability to make mature judgments, it is presently very risky for school psychologists to agree to see children for any kind of therapeutic purpose without their parents' consent. Practitioners must be sensitive to the fact that the minor clients will be talking, in all probability, of family life. In that light, the clinician will be, in a sense, invading the privacy of the student's parents without their consent. Very few states afford school psychologists protection under privileged communications laws (see Bersoff & Jain, 1980; McDermott, 1972), and an unlimited guarantee against revelation is impossible for the practitioner to promise as a matter of law. Indeed, child abuse reporting statutes in all states require psychologists to divulge information concerning violence or sexual abuse, even if given to the psychologist in confidence. Thus, as an ethical and moral matter, it is disingenuous to ensure student clients of confidentiality. Perhaps the best approach is to clearly inform the student of the limits of privacy and confidentiality while at the same time attempting

to secure the agreement of the parents that they will enhance the child's benefit from treatment if they permit the psychologist to see the student without being informed of information revealed during the course of intervention.

## LEGAL INFLUENCES ON RESEARCH

Like assessment and intervention, the role of psychologist-researcher has also been subject to regulation by the legal system. Because of a series of disclosures about the unethical behavior of some researchers in a variety of settings (see Annas, Glantz, & Katz, 1977; Bersoff, 1979b; Katz, 1972), the courts and the federal government began to scrutinize carefully the conduct of biomedical and behavioral research. The year 1974 may be viewed as the watershed in this respect.

In mid-1974 the then-named Department of Health, Education, and Welfare (DHEW), now the Department of Health and Human Services (DHHS), published regulations for the protection of human subjects. These regulations governed the activities of those organizations who receive research funds or are accountable to DHHS. First published in the *Federal Register* (39 *Federal Register* 18917, May 30, 1974) and now codified as federal regulations (45 CFR §46), the rules explicitly declare that the department will not support by DHHS grants or contracts any research unless an institutional review board (IRB) of the organization has reviewed and approved such activity. The most important features of these rules are the establishment of an IRB that is responsible for minimizing risks to subjects, ensuring informed consent by subjects as their representatives, equitable selection of subjects, balancing risks and benefits where risks exist, and maintaining confidentiality of the data on individual subjects.

In certain limited circumstances the requirement of parental permission for children's participation may be waived by the IRB, and other procedures may be implemented with neglected or abused children or with children who are wards of the state. Furthermore, school psychologists doing research may fall under one of the exceptions to the regulations. Certain research does not have to undergo full-scale IRB review, including the use of survey instruments, the observation of public behavior, and the study of documents and records. Perhaps most important, the regulations exempt from review

1. Research conducted in established or commonly accepted educational settings, involving normal, educational practices, such as (i) research on regular and special education instrumental strategies, or (ii) research on the effectiveness or the comparison among instructional techniques, curriculum, or classroom management

2. Research involving the use of educational tests (cognitive, diagnostic, aptitude, or achievement) if information taken from these sources is recorded in such a manner that subjects cannot be identified, directly or through identifiers linked to the subjects (46.101[b]).

An example of the violations of these principles may enhance their importance. *Merriken* v. *Cressman* (1973) is a hybrid case, presenting problems of assessment and research, as well as intervention (Bersoff, 1975, 1978a, 1979a). The case had its origins in 1970 when a survey ordered by the Commissioner of Montgomery County, Pennsylvania, and conducted by a company called Scientific Resources revealed that many children in the county were heavily involved with drugs. Most of the children who used drugs, the study claimed, had some common characteristics (e.g., estrangement from their families). On the basis of these data Scientific Resources proposed to the Montgomery County Drug Commission that they sponsor a drug prevention program, later labeled CPI, for the Critical Period of Intervention. All three of the county school districts agreed to participate.

There were two phases to the study: identification and remediation. In the first phase, questionnaires were to be given to eighth-grade students and their teachers so that certain students, deemed potential drug abusers, could become part of the remediation program. The teachers were asked to identify pupils who most and least fit eight descriptions of antisocial behavior (e.g., "This pupil makes unusual or inappropriate responses during normal school activity"). The student form was to be somewhat lengthier. First, students would be asked to assess their own behavior, for example, to state which of the following statements was most like themselves: (a) someone who will probably be a success in life; (b) someone who gets upset when faced with a difficult school problem; (c) someone who has lost self-confidence; (d) someone who has more problems than other students. In the next part of

the questionnaire, they would be asked questions about their relationships with their parents and the behavior of their parents (e.g., to indicate whether one or both parents "tell me how much they love me" or "make me feel unloved"). Finally, the students would select from their classmates those who fit certain descriptive statements similar in kind to the one given to the teachers.

The second phase of the study was intervention. When the CPI staff had analyzed all the results, they would compile a list of children who would have significant potential for becoming drug abusers. This list would then be given to the school superintendent, who would organize a joint effort among guidance counselors, teachers, school psychologists, and others to provide group therapeutic experiences. One of these experiences, called the Guided Group Interaction, was a program to which the identified students would be involuntarily assigned. One of its stated purposes was to use the peer group as a leveler or equalizer, ensuring that its members do not stray too far from its ranks.

When the program was first developed, the school system did not intend to obtain the consent of the parents for their children to participate. They did plan to send a letter home to each parent as follows:

> Dear Parent:
>
> This letter is to inform you that, this fall, we are initiating a Drug Program called "Critical Period of Intervention" (CPI). The aim of this program is to identify children who may be susceptible to drug abuse and to intervene with concrete measures to help these children. Diagnostic testing will be part of this program and will provide data enabling the prevention program to be specific and positive. . . . We ask your support and cooperation in this program and assure you of the confidentiality of these studies. If you wish to examine or receive further information regarding the program, please feel free to contact the principal in your school. If you do not wish to participate in this program, please notify your principal of this decision. We will assume your cooperation unless otherwise notified by you.

Also, as originally proposed, the study contained no provision for student consent. Sylvia Merriken, the mother of one of the intended participants in the study, who happened to be a therapist in a drug and alcoholic rehabilitation center, complained to the principal of the school where her son was enrolled and to the school board. The American Civil Liberties Union (ACLU) then announced that it would represent Merriken in an attempt to enjoin the school permanently from carrying out its plans. The ACLU began by filing a complaint in federal district court, claiming that the program would violate the constitutional rights of both Merriken and her son. It quickly obtained a temporary injunction that prohibited the county from implementing its proposal until the litigation was completed. At that point, two of the three schools in Montgomery County decided to discontinue their participation, but the Norristown system, which Merriken's son attended, persisted, although it honored the temporary injunction.

When the suit itself began, the school system offered to change the format of its letter so that written parental consent to participate would be required. In another attempt at compromise, the school modified the test so that students who did not want to be included could return an uncompleted protocol. But the proposal contained no provision for student consent and no data were to be provided by which students could make an informed choice about participating.

Of the many constitutional challenges Merriken made, the court entertained only one of them seriously—the right of privacy. The court found that the highly personal nature of the research instrument disrupted family associations and interfered with the right of the mother to rear her child: "There is probably no more private a relationship, excepting marriage, which the Constitution safeguards than that between parent and child. This Court can look upon any invasion of that relationship as a direct violation of one's Constitutional right to privacy" (Merriken, 1973, p. 918). The district court declared that privacy was entitled to as much constitutional protection as free speech. But who possessed this right—the student, the parents, or both? The court seemed ready to answer that question when it declared that "the fact that students are juveniles does not in any way invalidate their right to assert their Constitutional right to privacy" (p. 918). However, the court had not yet reached the essential question of whether the lack of consent by children to the invasion of

their privacy would be sufficient to invalidate the program. Apparently reluctant to provide a definite answer, it found a means to avoid doing so: "In the case at Bar, the children are never given the opportunity to consent to invasion of their privacy; only the opportunity to refuse to consent by returning a blank questionnaire. Whether this procedure is constitutional is questionable, but the Court does not have to face that issue because the facts presented show that the parents could not have been properly informed about the CPI Program and as a result could not have given informed consent for their children to take the CPI Test" (p. 919).

In essence, the court evaded two important issues: whether the failure to secure the child's consent was independently sufficient to discredit the CPI program constitutionally, and whether parents as guardians can waive their children's constitutional rights by consenting for them. Rather, the court concentrated on Merriken's own right of privacy and found that she was unable to give genuinely informed consent to the invasion of her personal life because the parental permission letter was so inadequate. The court deridingly compared the letter to a Book-of-the-Month Club solicitation in which parents' silence would be construed as acquiescence. The letter was also criticized as a selling device in which parents were convinced to allow children to participate. It was not, as it properly should be, an objective document, telling parents of the potentially negative features and dangerous aspects of the program.

Persons may, of course, waive their constitutional rights, but such waivers must be voluntary, knowing, intelligent, and done with sufficient awareness of the relevant consequences. Sylvia Merriken had the right to waive her right of privacy by consenting to the testing and intervention program. But because the request was little more than huckstering, it lacked the necessary substance to afford her the opportunity to consent meaningfully to the exploration of her personal life. There were other infirmities to the program (e.g., no real assurance of confidentiality of the data obtained, lack of psychometric soundness of the instruments themselves, and stigmatization of children inappropriately labeled), but they are relatively irrelevant in this chapter; for a full discussion of these problems, see Bersoff (1978a).

# GENERAL PRINCIPLES IN LEGAL REGULATION OF SCHOOL PSYCHOLOGY

Six major characteristics of legal influences can be identified to summarize the content to this point.

## Reciprocal

The legal system is influenced by various reciprocal forces of two sorts. First, the different legal origins and mechanisms have reciprocal influences. For example, litigation based on constitutional principles has had a profound influence on legislation, which in turn has led to further litigation. The second kind of reciprocal influence is social forces and societal trends. The legal system has an influence on social forces and trends and, in turn, is influenced by them. For example, the changing attitudes toward racial segregation, as well as social science evidence on the influence of segregation on psychological and educational development, had a profound effect on the landmark *Brown* (1954) decision. The *Brown* decision is also credited with influencing the court cases in the early 1970s that established the educational rights of handicapped students. These cases were also strongly influenced by the civil rights movement of the 1960s, as well as the publication of research indicating the educational benefits that could be derived by handicapped students from special education programs.

## Dynamic and Evolutionary

A second characteristic of legal influences is that they are dynamic and evolutionary. Legal influences are rarely static. There is always the possibility of the reinterpretation of a particular legal provision or constitutional protection that would significantly touch on the provision of services to students with special needs. Several such interpretations have been cited in this chapter.

## Relative and Ambiguous

Legal principles are nearly always ambiguous, particularly as they relate to a specific situation, with relative rather than absolute meanings. The LRE principle involves a complex relationship among the particular characteristics of an individual, a set of potential placement options, and the degree to which appropriate services can be provided in various settings. There is no such

thing as a single "least restrictive" placement for all children, and what is regarded at any time as least restrictive can be further influenced by the development of technology or other advances in knowledge about the education of handicapped students. Furthermore, the LRE principle has been interpreted more broadly recently than it was 15 years ago, soon after the EHA was implemented. Then, separate centers of instruction in local school districts for severely handicapped students were generally accepted as being consistent with the LRE principle. Educational services at those centers, coupled with living in the local community, were certainly less restrictive than were the institutional placements that were common prior to EHA implementation. Recently, the LRE has been interpreted as prohibiting the use of separate school attendance centers for disabled students during federal and state compliance monitoring. The literal formulation of the LRE principle in EHA has not been changed since 1975. The *interpretation* of that principle has changed. What was accepted in practice and in the courts as least restrictive is not acceptable now.

## Different Levels of Implementation

In addition to the relative, ambiguous meaning of particular legal principles, there also are different levels of implementation. Bersoff's (1978b) discussion of due process protections gave examples of the different levels of implementation, ranging from surface compliance to full implementation consistent with the spirit and intent of the legislation and, perhaps, even going beyond what might have been contemplated by its authors. There are nearly always different levels of implementation for any legal principle.

## Unanticipated Consequences

The extension of legal principles to new situations or the reinterpretation of legal protections has often unanticipated and far-reaching consequences. An example is the *Armstrong* v. *Kline* (1979, 1980) decision, which ruled that state laws restricting the school year to some arbitrary limit, such as 180 days, were unacceptable limitations on the right to an appropriate education for students with disabilities. This case was filed on behalf of severely handicapped students who were believed to regress significantly in skill performance as a result of summer recess. An unanticipated effect of this court decision was the necessity of developing measures to assess the degree of regression in skills during periods in which the school program was not provided and the time required to recoup these skills when the education program was resumed. Such measures were not developed at that time, and there was very little to apply directly from research. This unanticipated consequence prompted a considerable amount of further effort by special educators, school psychologists, and others (Browder & Lentz, 1985).

## Compliance Through Professional Standards and Best Practices

Because of the nature of legal influences, compliance is often difficult to achieve. This is true even when individuals are making good-faith efforts to conform with both the spirit and the letter of the legal provisions. Perhaps the best way to achieve compliance is not through attempts to follow the exact letter of regulations or to rely on rigid interpretations, but rather to apply best professional practices and to implement authoritative professional standards. Various professional groups have developed best practices and professional standards in recent years, and they were extremely influential in recent court decisions (*Coalition*, 1995; *Marshall*, 1984, 1985; *S-1*, 1986).

## PSYCHOLOGISTS' CONTRIBUTIONS TO LAW AND LEGAL REGULATION

Thus far we have discussed primarily the influence of the law on the practice of psychology but the relationship of law and psychology is reciprocal. Psychology is also an influence on law and on legal regulation, although this chapter does not permit even a cursory discussion of its vast influence.

## EXAMPLES OF PSYCHOLOGY'S INFLUENCE ON LAW

We note in passing several examples of the overlap and reciprocal influences of law and psychology: (a) the existence of several graduate programs that lead to a Ph.D. in psychology and a J.D. in law (Bersoff, 1997); (b) a relatively new APA journal, *Psychology, Public Policy, and Law*; (c) psychological research on eyewitness identification to clarify the usefulness of this evidence in criminal trials; and (d) laboratory and applied studies of the degree of certainty individuals have in false and true memories, as well as the trustworthiness of memories of abuse recovered during therapy, which is, for some families, a genuine matter of life and liberty (Loftus, 1994, 1997). In this section, we restrict our discussion of the influence of psychology on law to expert witness testimony, which is in the experience of virtually every practicing psychologist.

## Expert Witness Testimony

In this final section we wish to comment on the presentation of expert witness testimony and the use and misuse of psychologists and other social scientists in the courts. Although we have served as expert witnesses and, for the second author, conducted direct and cross-examination of experts, we are increasingly aware of the limitations of expert testimony. First, the subjects about which we testify are difficult to explain in the course of a relatively brief trial. Consider, for example, the length of time a typical school psychologist devotes to training in assessment. Then consider the challenge of explaining the most difficult assessment issues so that a federal judge can adequately draw on the knowledge of psychology and other social sciences. It truly is an awesome task.

Based on our experience with litigation, we are increasingly convinced that expert witness testimony as such provides relatively little guidance to the courts. This is true for many reasons, not the least of which is the virtual certainty that other expert witnesses, urging a contradictory point of view or interpretation of the same facts, will appear for the other side. A classic example of disagreement among expert witnesses with impressive credentials occurred in the *Marshall* litigation, where the then current NASP president (W. Alan Coulter) provided evidence for the plaintiffs through a deposition, and the NASP president-elect (Daniel J. Reschly) provided testimony for the defendants. Both of these experts had significant publications on adaptive behavior and both had credibility as national leaders in school psychology. They held very different views. Although the court ultimately adopted the defendants' views, we do not think it was the differences in expert testimony that persuaded the court but rather the creation and effective use of tangible evidence.

We believe that the principles of the social sciences can be best communicated for the benefit of the court through the development of tangible evidence that can be used to further understand expert testimony. In the *Marshall* and *S-1* placement litigation, tangible evidence that was especially useful included a videotaped presentation of average and MMR white and black students performing everyday tasks. This videotape was far more instructive about MMR than even the most erudite and articulate expert witness. Another example was the presentation of the actual items on the Wechsler Intelligence Scale for Children–Revised that would be administered to a 9- or 10-year-old student being considered for a possible classification and placement in an MMR program. The items that have to be missed at this level for a student to meet the requirement of "significantly subaverage" general intellectual functioning mostly involved quite straightforward, everyday sorts of information and quite practical skills or problem-solving processes. Further tangible evidence found useful included actual contrasts of daily classroom work and clear illustrations of difficulties in coping with an out-of-school environment, given various limitations in cognitive skills or educational achievement. In a recent special education hearing, in which the first author served as administrative law judge, least restrictive environment issues were illustrated by the defendant school district by using a videotape of a child with autism engaging in self-injurious behavior to illustrate the frequency and severity of behaviors that were difficult to control in a general education environment. Again, the tangible evidence was far more useful than verbal descriptions ever could have been.

The use of tangible evidence also sharply limits highly inferential psychodynamic or neo-analytic interpretations of behavior, a practice criticized for many years (Faust & Ziskin, 1988; Ziskin & Faust, 1988). These formulations typically have little if any empirical foundation and, by their nature, are virtually impossible to illustrate through tangible evidence in a court or anywhere else. Furthermore, contradiction of that testimony by other experts is a virtual certainty, leading to the rather unsavory spectacle of two "doctors" arguing before the court on underlying dynamics that cannot be observed by ordinary mortals. Such speculative, highly inferential testimony is easily countered by other expert witnesses and can often be easily impeached in cross-examination (Ziskin & Faust, 1988).

# REFERENCES

Abeson, A., & Ballard, J. (1976). State and federal policy for exceptional children. In F. J. Weintraub, A. Abeson, J. Ballard, & M. L. LaVor (Eds.), *Public policy and the education of exceptional children* (pp. 83–95). Reston, VA: Council for Exceptional Children.

*Americans with Disabilities Act* (1990). 42 U.S.C., §§12101–12213.

American Psychiatric Association. (1994). *Diagnostic and statistical manual of mental disorders (4th ed.).* Washington, DC: Author.

Annas, G., Glantz, L., & Katz, B. (1977). *The law of informed consent to human experimentation.* Cambridge, MA: Ballinger.

*Armstrong* v. *Kline*, 476 F. Supp. 583 (E.D. Pa. 1979). Aff'd CA 78-0172 (3rd Cir., July 15, 1980).

Bay Area Association of Black Psychologists (1971). *Position statement on use of IQ and ability tests.* In R. L. Jones (Ed.), *Black psychology* (pp. 92–94). New York: Harper/Row.

*Bellotti* v. *Baird*, 443 U.S. 622 (1979).

Bersoff, D. (1975). Professional ethics and legal responsibilities: On the horns of a dilemma. *Journal of School Psychology, 13,* 359–376.

Bersoff, D. (1976–1977). Representation for children in custody proceedings: All that glitters is not *Gault. Journal of Family Law, 15,* 27–49.

Bersoff, D. (1978a). Legal and ethical concerns in research. In L. Goldman (Ed.), *Research for the counselor.* New York: Wiley.

Bersoff, D. N. (1978b). Procedural safeguards. In L. Morra (Ed.), *Due process: Developing criteria for evaluating the due process procedural safeguards provisions of Public Law 94-142* (pp. 64–142). Washington, DC: U.S. Office of Education, Bureau of Education for the Handicapped.

Bersoff, D. N. (1979a). Regarding psychologists testing: Legal regulation of psychological assessment on public schools. *Maryland Law Review, 39,* 27–120.

Bersoff, D. (1979b). Handicapped persons as research subjects. *Amicus, 4,* 133–140.

Bersoff, D. N. (1982a). The legal regulation of school psychology. In C. R. Reynolds & T. B. Gutkin (Eds.), *The handbook of school psychology* (pp. 1043–1074). New York: Wiley.

Bersoff, D. N. (1982b). *Larry P.* and *PASE:* Judicial report cards of the validity of individual intelligence tests. In T. Kratochwill (Ed.), *Advances in school psychology* (Vol. II, pp. 61–95). Hillsdale, NJ: Erlbaum.

Bersoff, D. N., & Hofer, P. T. (1990). The legal regulation of school psychology. In T. B. Gutkin & C. R. Reynolds (Eds.), *The handbook of school psychology* (pp. 937–961). New York: Wiley.

Bersoff, D. N. (1997). Training in law and psychology. *American Psychologist, 52,* 1301–1310.

Bersoff, D., & Jain, M. (1980). A practical guide to privileged communication for psychologists. In G. Cooke (Ed.), *The role of the forensic psychologist*: Springfield, IL: Thomas.

Blatt, B. (1972). The legal rights of the mentally retarded. *Syracuse Law Review, 23*, 991, 992–993.

*Board of Education v. Rowley*, 458 U.S. 176 (1982).

Brodsky, S. L. (1991). *Testifying in court: Guidelines and maxims for the expert witness*. Washington, DC: American Psychological Association.

Browder, D. M., & Lentz, F. E. (1985). Extended school year services: From litigation to assessment and evaluation. *School Psychology Review, 14*, 188–195.

*Brown v. Board of Education*, 347 U.S. 483 (1954).

Burt, R. A. (1975). Judicial action to aid the retarded. In N. Hobbs (Ed.), *Issues in the classification of children* (Vol. 2, pp. 293–318). San Francisco: Jossey-Bass.

*Carey v. Population Services Int'l. Inc.*, 431 U.S. 6 (1977).

*City of Akron v. Akron Center for Reproductive Health*, 4 U.S. 416 (1983).

Chinn, P. C., & Hughes, S. (1987). Representation of minority students in special education classes. *Remedial and Special Education, 8*(4), 41–46.

*Coalition to Save Our Children v. State Board of Education* 901 F. Supp. 784 (D. Del. 1995).

*Crawford, et al. v. Honig* No. C-89-0014 RFP (N.D. Cal. May 1988) (Complaint for declaratory judgment); (September 29, 1989) (Order) (August 31, 1992) (Memorandum and Order).

Dent, H. (1976). Assessing black children for mainstream placement. In R. Jones (Ed.), *Mainstreaming and the minority child*. Reston, VA: Council for Exceptional Children.

Dent, H. E. (1993). The IQ mythology: A review. *Journal of Black Psychology, 19*(1), 84–88.

*Diana v. State Board of Education*, No. C-70-37 RFP (N.D. Cal. February 3, 1970) (Consent Decree).

*Education of the Handicapped Act* (1975). PL 94-142, 20 U.S.C. 1400–1485, 34 CFR-300.

*Egg Harbor Township Board of Education v. S.O., By His Guardian Ad Litem, R.O.* No. 90-1043 (D.N.J. August 19, 1992).

Elliott, R. (1987). *Litigating intelligence*. Dover, MA: Auburn House.

Fagan, T. K. (1988). The historical improvement of the school psychology service ratio: Implications for future employment. *School Psychology Review, 17*(3), 447–458.

Fagan, T. K. (1992). Compulsory schooling, child study, clinical psychology, and special education: Origins of school psychology. *American Psychologist, 47*, 236–243.

Fagan, T. K., & Wise, P. S. (1994). *School psychology: Past, present, and future*. White Plains, NY: Longmans.

*Family Educational Rights and Privacy Act*, 20 USC §1232g. (1994).

Faust, D., & Ziskin, J. (1988). The expert witness in psychology and psychiatry. *Science, 241*, 31–35.

Foster, H., & Freed, D. (1972). A bill of rights for children. *Family Law Quarterly, 6*, 343–375.

Finn, J. D. (1982). Patterns in special education placement as revealed by OCR surveys. In K. A. Heller, W. H. Holtzman, & S. Messick (Eds.), *Placing children in special education: A strategy for equity* (pp. 322–381). Washington, DC: National Academy Press.

*In re Gault* (1967). 387 U.S. 1.

*Georgia State Conference of Branches of NAACP v. State of Georgia*, 775 F.2d 1403 (11th Cir. 1985).

Gilhool, T. (1976). Education: An inalienable right. In F. Weintraub, A. Abeson, & M. Lavor (Eds.), *Public policy and the education of exceptional children* (pp. 14–21). Reston, VA: Council for Exceptional Children.

Goldwasser, E., Meyers, J., Christenson, S., & Graden, J. (1983). The impact of PL 94-142 on the practice of school psychology: A national survey. *Psychology in the Schools, 20*, 153–165.

*Goss v. Lopez*, 419 U.S. 565 (1975).

*Guadalupe Organization v. Tempe Elementary School District No. 3*, No. 71-435 PHX. (D. Ariz. January 24, 1972) (Consent Decree).

Hall, K. L. (Ed.) (1992). *Oxford companion to the Supreme Court of the United States*. New York: Oxford University Press.

Harry, B. (1994). *The disproportionate representation in special education: Theories and recommendations*. Alexandria, VA: National Association of State Directors of Special Education.

Heller, K., Holtzman, W., & Messick, S. (Eds.). (1982). *Placing children in special education: A strategy for equity*. Washington, DC: National Academy Press.

Herrnstein, R. J., & Murray, C. (1994). *The bell curve*. New York: Free Press.

Hess, A., & Weiner, I. (Eds.) (1987). *Handbook of forensic psychology*. New York: Wiley.

Hilliard, A. G. (1980). Cultural diversity and special education. *Exceptional Children, 46*, 584–588.

Hilliard, A. G. (1983). IQ and the courts: *Larry P. v. Wilson Riles* and *PASE v. Hannon*. *Journal of Black Psychology, 10*, 1–18.

Hilliard, A. G. (1992). The pitfalls and promises of special education practice. *Exceptional Children, 59*, 168–172.

*H.L. v. Matheson*, 450 U.S. 398 (1981).

*Hobson v. Hansen*, 269 F. Supp. 401 (D.D.C. 1967), *cert. dismissed by* 393 U.S. 801 (1969).

*Honig v. Doe*, 484 U.S. 305, 325 (1988).

Holt, J. (1974). *Escape from childhood*. New York: Dutton.

Hunt, J. (1961). *Intelligence and experience*. New York: Ronald Press.

*Individuals with Disabilities Education Act* (1990, 1997).

20 U.S.C. Chapter 33, Sections 1400–1491 (Statute).

*Ingraham* v. *Wright*, 430 U.S. 651 (1977).

Jensen, A. R. (1969). How much can we boost IQ and scholastic achievement? *Harvard Educational Review, 39,* 1–123.

Jensen, A. R. (1980). *Bias in mental testing.* New York: Free Press.

Jones, R. L. (1988). Psychoeducational assessment of minority group children: Issues and perspectives. In R. L. Jones (Ed.), *Psychoeducational assessment of minority group children: A casebook* (pp. 13–35). Berkeley, CA: Cobb & Henry.

Jones, R. L., & Jones, J. M. (1987). Racism as psychological maltreatment. In M. R. Brassard, R. Germain, & S. N. Hart (Eds.), *Psychological maltreatment of children and youth* (pp. 146–158). New York: Pergamon.

Jones, R., & Wilderson, F. (1976). Mainstreaming and the minority child: An overview of issues and a perspective. In R. Jones (Ed.), *Mainstreaming and the minority child.* Reston, VA: Council for Exceptional Children.

Katz, J. (1972). *Experimentation with human beings.* New York: Russell Sage.

Katz, S., Howe, R., & McGrath, M. (1975). Child neglect laws in America. *Family Law Quarterly, 9,* 1–372.

Kleinfeld, A. (1970–1971). Balance of power among infants, their parents, and the state. *Family Law Quarterly, 4, 5,* 320–349, 410–443, 64–107.

Lambert, N. M. (1981). Psychological evidence in *Larry P.* v. *Wilson Riles*: An evaluation by a witness for the defense. *American Psychologist, 36,* 937–952.

*Larry P.* v. *Riles,* 343 F. Supp. 1306 (N.D. Cal. 1972) (Preliminary Injunction), aff'd 502 F. 2d 963 (9th Cir. 1974); 495 F. Supp. 926 (N.D. Cal. 1979) (Decision on merits); *aff'd in part, rev'd in part* 793 F. 2d 969 (9th Cir. 1984); Order modifying judgment, C-71-2270 RFP, September 25, 1986. Memorandum and Order, C-71-2270 RFP, August 31, 1992.

Lerner, B. (1988). Judge's questions versus specialist's questions. (Review of Rogers Elliott's *Litigating intelligence.*) *Contemporary Psychology, 33,* 887–889.

Levine, M., Anderson, E., Ferretti, L., & Steinberg, K. (1993). Legal and ethical issues affecting clinical child psychology. In T. H. Ollendick & R. J. Prinz (Eds.), *Advances in clinical child psychology* (Vol. 15, pp. 81–120).

*Light* v. *Parkway C-2 School District,* 41 F.3d 1223, 1228 (8th Cir. 1994).

Loftus, E. F. (1994). Memories of childhood sexual abuse: Remembering and repressing. *Psychology of Women Quarterly; 18,* 67–84.

Loftus, E. F. (1997). Memory for a past that never was. *Psychological Science, 6,* 60–65.

Lund, A. R., Reschly, D. J., & Martin, L. M. (1998).

School psychology personnel needs: Correlates of current patterns and historical trends. *School Psychology Review, 27,* 106–120.

MacMillan, D. (1977). *Mental retardation in school and society.* Boston: Little, Brown.

MacMillan, D., & Meyers, C. E. (1980). *Larry P.*: An educational interpretation. *School Psychology Review, 9,* 136–148.

*Marshall* v. *Georgia,* No. CV482-233 (S.D. Ga. June 28, 1984), *aff'd sub. nom. Georgia State Conferences of Branches of NAACP* v. *Georgia,* 775 F.2d 1403 (11th Cir. 1985).

Martin, R. (1991). *Extraordinary children: Ordinary lives.* Champaign, IL: Research Press.

McDermott, P. A. (1972). Law, liability, and the school psychologist: Systems of law, privileged communication, and access to records. *Journal of School Psychology, 10,* 299–305.

Melton, G., Koocher, G., & Saks, M. (Eds.) (1983). *Children's competence to consent.* New York: Plenum Press.

Mercer, C. D., King-Sears, P., & Mercer, A. R. (1990). Learning disabilities definitions and criteria used by state education departments. *Learning Disability Quarterly, 13,* 141–152.

*Merriken* v. *Cressman,* 364 F. Supp. 913 (1973).

Meyers, C. E., Sundstrom, P., & Yoshida, R. (1974). The school psychologist and assessment in special education: A report of the Ad Hoc Committee of APA Division 16. *Monographs of Division 16 of the American Psychological Association, 2*(1), 3–57.

*Mills* v. *Board of Education,* 348 F. Supp. 866 (D.D.C. 1972).

*Missouri* v. *Jenkins,* 115 S. Ct. 2038 (1995).

Mnookin, R. (1978). *Child, family, and state.* Boston: Little, Brown.

*Oberti* v. *Board of Education,* 995 F.2d 1357, 18 IDELR 16 (3rd Cir. 1993).

*Parham* v. *J.L.,* 442 U.S. 584 (1979).

*Parents in Action on Special Education* v. *Joseph P. Hannon,* 506 F. Supp. 831 (N.D. IL 1980).

Patrick, J., & Reschly, D. (1982). Relationship of state educational criteria and demographic variables to school-system prevalence of mental retardation. *American Journal of Mental Deficiency, 86,* 351–360.

*Pennsylvania Association for Retarded children* v. *Commonwealth of Pennsylvania,* 343 F. Supp. 279 (E.D. Pa. 1972).

*Pesce* v. *J. Sterling Morton High School District,* 651 F. Supp. 152 (N.D. IL 1986).

*Planned Parenthood of Cent. Mo.* v. *Danforth,* 428 U.S. 52 (1976).

*Plessy* v. *Ferguson,* 163 U.S. 537 (1896).

Prasse, D. P. (1995). School psychology and the law. In A. Thomas & J. Grimes (Eds.), *Best practices in school psychology III* (3rd ed., pp. 41–50). Washington DC: National Association of School Psychologists.

Prasse, D. P., & Reschly, D. J. (1986). *Larry P.*: A case of segregation, testing, or program efficacy? *Exceptional Children, 52*, 333–346.

*Prince* v. *Massachusetts*, 321 U.S. 158 (1944).

*Rehabilitation Act of 1973*, 20 U.S.C. Sec. 794 (Statute).

*Rehabilitation Act of 1973*, 34 C.F.R. 104 (Regulations).

Reschly, D. J. (1979). Nonbiased assessment. In G. Phye & D. Reschly (Eds.), *School psychology: Perspectives and issues* (pp. 215–253). New York: Academic Press.

Reschly, D. J. (1980). Psychological evidence in the *Larry P.* opinion: A case of right problem–wrong solution. *School Psychology Review, 9*, 123–135.

Reschly, D. J. (1982). Assessing mild mental retardation: The influence of adaptive behavior, sociocultural status and prospects for nonbiased assessment. In C. Reynolds & T. Gutkin (Eds.), *A handbook for school psychology* (pp. 209–242). New York: Wiley–Interscience.

Reschly, D. J. (1996). *IQ and special education*. Washington, DC: National Academy of Sciences.

Reschly, D. J., & Jipson, F. J. (1976). Ethnicity, geographic locale, age, sex, and urban–rural residence as variables in the prevalence of mild retardation. *American Journal of Mental Deficiency, 81*, 154–161.

Reschly, D. J., Kicklighter, R. H., & McKee, P. (1988a). Recent placement litigation, Part I: Regular education grouping: Comparison of *Marshall* (1984, 1985) and *Hobson* (1967, 1969). *School Psychology Review, 17*, 7–19.

Reschly, D. J., Kicklighter, R. H., & McKee, P. (1988a). Recent placement litigation, Part II: Minority MMR overrepresentation: Comparison of *Larry P.* (1979, 1984, 1986) with *Marshall* (1984, 1985) and *S-1* (1986). *School Psychology Review, 17*, 20–36.

Reschly, D. J., Kicklighter, R. H., & McKee, P. (1988a). Recent placement litigation, Part III: Analysis of differences in *Larry P.*, *Marshall*, and *S-1* and implications for future practices. *School Psychology Review, 17*, 37–48.

Reschly, D. J., & Wilson, M. S. (1995). School psychology faculty and practitioners: 1986 to 1991 trends in demographic characteristics, roles, satisfaction, and system reform. *School Psychology Review, 24*, 62–80.

Reynolds, C. R., & Kaiser, S. M. (1990). Test bias in psychological assessment. In T. B. Gutkin & C. R. Reynolds (Eds.), *The handbook of school psychology* (2nd ed., pp. 487–525). New York: Wiley.

*S-1* v. *Turlington*, 646 F. Supp. 1179 (S.D. Fla. 1986).

Sattler, J. M. (1981). Intelligence tests on trial: An "interview" with Robert F. Peckham and John F. Grady. *Journal of School Psychology, 19*, 359–369.

Sattler, J. (1982). The psychologist in court: Personal reflections of one expert witness in the case of *Larry P. School Psychology Review, 11*, 306–319.

Smith, D. K. (1984). Practicing school psychologists: Their characteristics, activities, and populations served. *Professional Psychology: Research and Practice, 15*, 798–810.

*Stell* v. *Savannah-Chatham County Board of Education*, 255 F. Supp. 88 (1965).

*Tinker* v. *Des Moines Ind. Comm. Sch. Dist.*, 393 U.S. 503 (1969).

U.S. Department of Education (1991). *Clarification of policy to address the needs of children with attention deficit disorders within general and special education*. Memorandum sent to Chief State School Officers.

U.S. Department of Education (1994). *Sixteenth annual report to Congress on the implementation of the Education of the Individuals with Disabilities Education Act*. (1994). Washington, DC: Office of Special Education and Rehabilitation Services.

U.S. Department of Education (1995). *Seventeenth annual report to Congress on the implementation of the Education of the Individuals with Disabilities Education Act*. Washington, DC: Office of Special Education and Rehabilitation Services.

Wald, P. (1974). Making sense out of the rights of youth. *Human Rights, 4*, 13–29.

Wherry, J. N. (1983). Some legal considerations and implications for the use of behavior modification in the schools. *Psychology in the Schools, 20*, 46–51.

Weintraub, F., & Abeson, A. (1976). New education policies for the handicapped: The quiet revolution. In F. J. Weintraub, A. Abeson, J. Ballard, & M. L. LaVor (Eds.), *Public policy and the education of exceptional children* (pp. 7–13). Reston, VA: Council for Exceptional Children.

Ziskin, J., & Faust, D. (1988). *Coping with psychiatric and psychological testimony* (4th ed., Vols. 1–3). Los Angeles: Law and Psychology Press.

## CHAPTER 42

# THE LEGAL RIGHTS OF STUDENTS

**BRUCE D. SALES**
**DANIEL A. KRAUSS**
*University of Arizona*
**DONAL M. SACKEN**
*Texas Christian University*
**THOMAS D. OVERCAST**
*Attorney at Law, Seattle, WA*

It would be fair to assert that 50 years ago students in elementary and secondary public schools were recognized as having few, if any, legal rights. The teacher and school system were seen as standing in loco parentis to the child. From the time the child left home in the morning until returning in the evening, the school was viewed as the prime source of guidance, discipline, punishment, and control. Many early cases even recognized the right of the school to extend its influence over the child into the home and to the child's behavior during nonschool hours.

However, beginning in the 1960s there was a recognition that the school's control over students should not be so pervasive. The courts have been willing to extend to students many of the legal rights taken for granted by other groups. A large part of the redefinition of the relationship between students and the school arose from school officials' efforts to prohibit certain student activities. As a logical extension of the cases arising out of the civil rights movement, student rights case law initially focused more on racial inequality and the demand by minority groups for equal educational opportunity than it did on the rights of individual students vis-à-vis the school. In addition, most of the earlier cases focusing on individual rights (as opposed to equal opportunity) took place within the context of the college or university. The focus shifted to the individual rights of students in the elementary and secondary schools only at the end of the 1960s. Arguably, by the 1980s, courts had begun to respond to the schools' argument that their authority had been excessively eroded judicially.

In reading the existing case law and legal literature, it is apparent that the issue of student rights arises only in relation to the duties and obligations imposed on the schools by state legislative or constitutional direction, with conflict between the student and the school potentially arising at any of a number of different points:

1. Before a person may be said to have the rights of a student, he or she must obtain access to the school and achieve the status of student. Schools may prescribe rules and regulations controlling access to their facilities. They may attempt to restrict access according to a student's age, race, gender, residence, and physical or mental condition. The school may also attempt to regulate attendance by married students and pregnant females, although less than previously.

2. The school may have regulations for the assignment of students to particular schools or the transfer of students between schools.

3. The school may or may not have a duty to provide transportation for students between their homes and the school. If it does have such a duty, the school may attempt to regulate the eligibility of students to use transportation facilities.

4. Publicly supported schools generally may not charge tuition but may assess incidental or supplemental fees. Special regulations may apply to nonresidents, indigent students, and students in institutions.

5. All states generally require a certain number of years of compulsory education for their citizens. Some students may be excused from compulsory attendance because of religious reasons, and others may be able to take advantage of acceptable alternatives to public schools.

6. Schools have the authority to assign students to particular grades or classes and to establish criteria for promotion and demotion. The school also has control over the course of studies and the content of the curricula at each grade or class level.

7. The school has the general power to regulate the behavior and conduct of students. In varying degrees, this power extends to health regulations and the behavior of students both during and outside school hours. During school hours, the power extends to a wide variety of student behavior, including their freedom of speech and expression and their right to privacy, and justifies a variety of disciplinary actions and punishments for misconduct.

8. For a variety of violations of school rules and regulations, a student may be suspended or expelled from school. The school may provide any of a number of procedural protections to help ensure the justice of such an action.

9. Upon completion of a program of education, students are entitled to a diploma certifying their skills. The school may not be held accountable to the students for the quality of their education.

In this chapter we describe these relationships by reviewing the existing law. No attempt is made to advocate one position over another. The law presented here represents what "is," not necessarily what "ought to be." Because there is little case law in several areas, we have attempted to delineate what seem to be the important issues and to present a brief but balanced exposition of the arguments on both sides.

In this regard, three important points should be kept in mind. First, the legal rights of students do not often have an independent existence. They can only be understood within the framework of the legislative and constitutional authority given to the school. Thus, much of this chapter is phrased in terms of the discretionary authority of the school and the limits of that dis-

cretion, with the legal rights of students often defined by those limits. Second, there may appear to be incongruity in certain areas between the power of the school to regulate student behavior and the school's decision of whether to exercise it. The courts may have bestowed much more power on the school than the school, for many reasons, may choose to exert. Thus, students may appear to have a right when, in fact, it is a privilege extended by the school. Finally, the rights of schools and students will vary between states because state legislatures retain enormous constitutional discretion to shape their educational systems, and state educational codes vary quite broadly. Readers must use this chapter as a guide and not as the definitive answer for particular concerns that they may have.

# ACCESS TO EDUCATION

Generally, the state has broad discretion in determining who may be eligible for a free public education.[1] Thus, to attend a state-supported public school, the student must meet the requirements prescribed by the state constitution and/or statutes and the rules of state and local boards of education.[2] In this section we examine several general requirements affecting students' right of access to the public school system, including regulations relating to age, race, gender, handicapping conditions, and residency.

Minimum and maximum age requirements for attendance at public schools are generally expressly provided for, in either a state's constitution or statutes, and normally have been upheld. However, the West Virginia Supreme Court required a local district to admit a child whose birthday fell only three days after the date for entry into kindergarten, declaring a contrary ruling to be arbitrary and capricious.[3] In the absence of

---

[1] *State* v. *Hershberger*, 144 N.E.2d 693, 103 Ohio App. 188 (1955). But see *White* v. *Linkinogger*, 344 S.E.2d 633 (W. Va. 1986).

[2] *Shuttlesworth* v. *Birmingham Board of Education of Jefferson County*, 162 F. Supp, 372 aff'd, 79 S. Ct. 221, 358 U.S. 101, 3L. Ed. 2d 145 (1958).

[3] *Blessing* v. *Macon County Board of Education*, 34 S.E.2d 407 (W. Va. 1985). Contra, *Hammond* v. *Marx*, 406 F. Supp. 853 (D. Me. 1975).

express constitutional or statutory guidelines, a state-level official (i.e., state board of education) has the authority to establish age requirements for admission to the school system.[4]

It goes without saying that a school district may not withhold access to schooling because of the race of a particular student. It is not certain, however, whether a school may discriminate among applicants on the basis of their gender. The U.S. Supreme Court has affirmed without an opinion the decision of a lower court denying the admission of a female student to an all-male high school in the city of Philadelphia.[5] The lower court emphasized that both sexes were being treated similarly by admissions policies in the female and male high schools and that equal educational opportunities were available to both sexes in terms of the quality of school facilities. In a university-based case, the Supreme Court invalidated a policy of excluding men from a state nursing school at an all-women's university.[6] The Court indicated that gender-based discrimination in admission would require substantial justification. However, separate but equal educational facilities for the two sexes apparently does not infringe per se the Fourteenth Amendment's guarantee of equal protection under the laws.

Although a school district has an affirmative obligation to provide equal educational opportunities to all students in the district,[7] until recently such access was not ensured for handicapped students. Under some states' laws, certain handicapped persons were "exempt" from compulsory schooling based on the belief that they were incapable of benefiting from education.

Now both federal and state laws prohibit a district from denying access to the school system and a free appropriate public education based solely on a student's handicapping condition.[8]

The final requirement that may bar a student's access to the school is residency status. Normally, the expense of providing a free public education is primarily defrayed by a tax imposed on the residents of each school district. As a general rule, the privilege of a free public education in a district's schools is open only to residents of that district. In determining residency, the ordinary rules for legal residency are applied; it is sufficient if the student and his or her parent or guardian actually reside in the district without any present intention of leaving.

In 1982, the Supreme Court narrowly held unconstitutional a Texas statute that prevented children who were illegal aliens from attending public schools. Such a practice violated the equal protection clause because Texas could not demonstrate that its policy furthered a substantial, legitimate goal.[9] In a subsequent case, the Court specified that districts could enforce their normal residency standards (e.g., a requirement that a child reside with parents or legal guardians) without offending the Fourteenth Amendment.[10] Taken in sum, these developments indicate that a district is essentially responsible for providing a public education for any and all children of appropriate ages who happen to reside in that district.[11]

---

[4]*Zweifel v. Joint District No. 1, Belleville*, 251 N.W.2d 822, 76 Wis. 2d 648 (1977).

[5]*Vorchheimer v. School District of Philadelphia*, 532 F.2d 880 (1976), off'd by an equally divided Court, 430 U.S. 703 (1977). But see *Berkelman v. San Francisco Un. Sch. District*, 501 F.2d 1264 (9th Cir. 1974).

[6]*Mississippi University for Women v. Hogan*, 458 U.S. 718, 102 S. Ct. 3331 (1982).

[7]"The constitutional requirements that [the] public school system shall be 'open' to all children . . . means that all children must have equal rights and opportunities to attend the grade or class of school for which they are suited by previous training or development." *Lau v. Nichols*, 414 U.S., 563, 94 S. Ct. 786 (1974).

[8]*Pennsylvania Association for Retarded Children v. Commonwealth of Pennsylvania*, 334 F. Supp. 1257 (E.D. Pa. 1972); Education of All Handicapped Children Act of 1975, P. L. 94-142, 20 U.S.C. §401 (Supp. 1975); Rehabilitation Act of 1973, §504, 20 U.S.C. §794-992 (Supp. 1975); cf. B. D. Sales, D. M. Powell, & R. van Duizend (Eds.), *Disabled Persons and the Law* (New York: Plenum, 1982). For further discussion of the educational rights of handicapped persons, see Chapter 41.

[9]*Pylyer v. Doe*, 457 U.S. 202, 102 S. Ct. 2382 (1982).

[10]*Martinez v. Bynum*, 461 U.S. 321, 103 S. Ct. 1838 (1983). But see *Horton v. Marshall Public Schools*, 769 F.2d 1323 (8th Cir. 1985), which held unconstitutional the exclusion of children who resided with relatives other than parents or legal guardians.

[11]*Delgado v. Freeport Public School District*, 499 N.Y.S.2d 606 (Sup. Ct. 1986).

A public school district normally has no authority to admit nonresident students. Some statutes allow such admissions if it would be more convenient for the student, and other statutes leave it to the discretion of the local district. The student does not, however, acquire any right to admission under these statutes. The local district may accept or reject such admissions at its own discretion.[12]

Similar questions may arise about the residency status of children in public or private institutions or those committed to outside care. In such cases the institution to which the child is committed may be located outside the school district in which the parents reside. The courts have taken two positions on this issue. Some cases have held that such students, for purposes of school admission, are residents of the school district in which the institution is located.[13] Other courts have held that such students are not entitled to a free education in the district; rather, either the institution or the parents must pay a nonresident's tuition fee to offset the cost of the student's schooling. Under Public Law 94-142, handicapped children placed in institutions are ensured a free public education.[14]

As noted, the governing body of a local school district has the inherent power to determine who may be admitted into the schools, subject only to express statutory directives and to a standard of reasonableness in its decision making. Under these standards, children have been refused admission for being morally deficient,[15] having[16] or having been exposed to an infectious disease,[17] or being insufficiently prepared to begin at a particular level in school, although these three criteria would seem to be limited by federal legislation like P.L. 94-142. Federal courts have so held with regard to serum hepatitis carriers

and children with AIDS.[18] Since such decisions are subject to a standard of reasonableness, they are usually not subjected to judicial review if the particular decision was undertaken after fair and considered debate. In cases in which a district's decision is reviewed, a court presumes that the district acted reasonably and properly, and the burden is on the person challenging the decision to affirmatively rebut that presumption. Although the power of the school district to exclude married students and unwed mothers, at least for a reasonable length of time, has been held to be within the discretion of the school district,[19] more courts have taken the position that school districts are never justified in excluding married students or unwed mothers solely on these bases.[20] School officials, after a fair hearing, might be able to show that such a person's presence in the school would significantly disrupt the education of other students.[21] However, efforts to exclude completely would appear to infringe students' constitutional right to privacy, an interest linked with both familial and procreative interests.[22]

## Assignment

Once a student has been admitted to the district, the district has the responsibility of assigning the student to a particular school. Generally, a school district may, at its own discretion, assign a stu-

---

[12]*Frazier* v. *Superintendent of Public Instruction*, 795 P.2d 619 (Wash. 1986).

[13]*University Center, Inc.* v. *Ann Arbor Public Schools*, 191 N.W.2d 302, 386 Mich. 210 (1971).

[14]Because of the high educational costs for some handicapped children, complex financial questions concern the obligation toward children housed in state institutions located in a single district. Cf. Chapter 41.

[15]*Nutt* v. *Board of Education*, 278 P. 1065,128 Kan. 507 (1929).

[16]*Kennedy* v. *Gurley*, 95 So. 34, 208 Ala. 623 (1923).

[17]*Bright* v. *Beard*, 157 N.W. 501, 132 Minn. 375 (1916).

[18]Mentally retarded children who were serum hepatitis carriers could not be excluded from school under §504 of the Rehabilitation Act in *New York Association for Retarded Children* v. *Carey*, 612 F.2d 644 (2d Cir. 1979). Courts sustained a board's policy that children with AIDS would not be excluded automatically but instead reviewed on a case-by-case basis. *District 27 Community School Board* v. *Board of Education*, 502 N.Y.S.2d 325 (Sup. Ct. 1986): *Thomas* v. *Atascadero Unified School District*, 662 F. Supp. 376 (C.D. Cal. 1987).

[19]State ex rel *Thompson* v. *Marion County Board of Education*, 302 S.W.2d 57, 202 Tenn. 29 (1957).

[20]*Anderson* v. *Canyon Independent School District* (Text Civ. App.) 412 S.W.2d 387 (1967); *Board of Education* v. *Bentley*, 383 S.W.2d 677 (1964).

[21]*McLeod* v. *State*, 122 So. 737, 154 Miss. 468 (1929); *Perry* v. *Grenada Municipal Separate School District*, 300 F. Supp. 748 (1969).

[22]See, for example, *Planned Parenthood of Central Missouri* v. *Danforth*, 428 U.S. 52, 96 S. Ct. 2831 (1976); *Zablocki* v. *Redhail*, 434 U.S. 374, 98 S. Ct. 673 (1978).

dent to any school in the district.[23] Of course, the decisions of the district must be reasonable[24] and not in violation of a student's civil rights.[25] The cases arising out of the civil rights arena have affirmed the power of the school district to make such intradistrict assignments. Although under no legal obligation, many school districts have endorsed the neighborhood school concept and have, within the limits imposed by the requirements of the Fourteenth Amendment, attempted to assign students to schools as close to their homes as possible.[26]

As a general rule, students do not have the right to attend a school in a different district at the expense of the district in which they reside. They may have this right, however, if the conditions for such transfer are specified in the state statutes and the student comes within such provisions. These statutory conditions are much the same for both grade school and high school students. To establish a right to transfer outside their residence, grade school pupils must show that there is no school or no adequate school in their home district,[27] that they can be better accommodated by the interdistrict transfer,[28] or that the desired transfer is more conveniently located because of its distance from the students' residence.[29] Generally, interdistrict transfers can be arranged only with the consent of both the receiving and the sending districts.[30]

Under most state statutes, the power to accept or refuse an interdistrict transfer is vested in the local school board or with a county superintendent of schools. Also, some statutes provide that an appeal de novo may be taken to a local court. Under this procedure, the court will hear the same evidence presented to the board or superintendent. The decisions of the board are subject to judicial review and reversal only if it can be shown that the board abused its discretion in refusing a requested transfer.[31]

Interdistrict transfers by high school students are subject to similar restrictions and procedures for judicial review. Within the terms of the controlling status, high school students may be transferred if the transfer is to a more "convenient" school. Convenience in this context has the same meaning as that described for transfers by grade school students.[32]

## Transportation

Provision of transportation to and from school is usually expressly provided for in state statutes, either as a mandatory or a discretionary district duty. In the absence of express authority, school districts may be permitted, but are not usually required, to provide free transportation to students. Where free transportation is authorized, it is usually provided only for students living be-

[23]*U.S. by Wheeler* v. *Choctaw County Board of Education*, 310 F. Supp. 804 (1969); *Wheeler* v. *Durham City Board of Education*, 521 F.2d 1136 (1975).

[24]*Downs* v. *Board of Education of Kansas City*, 336 F.2d 988 (1964): Ex parte *Board of Education of Blount County*, 84 S.2d 653, 264 Ala. 34 (1956).

[25]*Brown* v. *County School Board of Frederick County*, 245 F. Supp. 549 (1965); *Downs* v. *Board of Education of Kansas City*, supra note 24; *Harris* v. *Chrenshaw County Board of Education*, 259 F. Supp. 167 (1966); *Miller* v. *School District No. 2*, 256 F. Supp. 370 (1966).

[26]The neighborhood school concept, under which a student may attend the nearest school, is not in and of itself either constitutionally required nor forbidden, but it cannot be approved where it promotes or preserves de jure racial discrimination. *Diaz* v. *San Jose Unified School District*, 733 F.2d 660 (9th Cir. 1984), cert. denied, 105 S. Ct. 2140 (1985). See also *Hobsen* v. *Hansen*, 269 F. Supp. 401 (1967), and *Smuck* v. *Hobsen*, 408 F.2d 175 (D. C. Cir. 1969), where the court stated that "what appellants seek is assurance that a neighborhood school approach may be maintained by the Board. The decree [in *Hobsen* v. *Hansen*] permits retention of the neighborhood school approach where it does not result in relative overcrowding or other inequality of facilities"; 408 F.2d at 186. Conversely, parents do not normally have a right to demand assignment to a neighborhood school. See *Citizens Against Mandatory Busing* v. *Palmason*, 80 Wash. 2d 445, 495 P.2d 667 (1972).

[27]*School District of Soldier* v. *Moeller*, 73 N.W.2d 43, 247 Iowa 239 (1955); *School District of Mexico* v. *Maple Grove School District*, 324 S.W.2d 369 (Mo. 1959).

[28]*Edwards* v. *State*, 42 N.E. 525, 143 Ind. 84 (1895).

[29]*Otwell* v. *West*, 137 S.E.2d 291, 220 Ga. 95 (1964); In re *Hinze*, 136 N.W.2d 434, 179 Neb. 69 (1965).

[30]*Delta Special School District No. 5* v. *McGehee Special School District No. 17*, 280 Ark. 489, 659 S.W.2d 508 (1983).

[31]*Dove* v. *Parham*, 181 F. Supp. 504 (1960); *Whitley* v. *Wilson City Board of Education*, 457 F.2d 940 (1972); *School Committee* v. *Board of Education*, 287 N.E.2d 438 (Mass. 1972).

[32]State ex rel. *Seidl* v. *Jefferson County Board of Education Appeals*, 548 S.W.2d 853 (1977).

yond a prescribed distance from the school.[33] Students not within the statutory conditions have been unsuccessful in challenging the validity of the statutes.[34] Students may also lose access to transportation through their misconduct.[35]

A statute that requires transportation of students only "to and from" school may not authorize buses for extracurricular activities. Thus, a district may not freely transport students to such outside activities as athletic events, spelling or speech contests, or motion pictures. In some states, districts are authorized or required to transport children to nonpublic schools; such laws have withstood constitutional challenge.[36]

## Tuition and Fees

Generally, students have the right to a free education in the public schools of a district. Thus the district cannot impose a tuition fee on students simply because private money has been used to finance portions of a school.[37] Note, however, that a free public education applies only to the regular course of schoolwork. A district may offer specialized courses, not within the normal curriculum, and require a fee for enrollment in these courses.[38]

Under most statutes, the district is authorized to charge incidental or supplemental fees that are used for purposes other than tuition. Thus, a student may be required to pay a fee for participation in athletics or other social events sponsored by the school and for the use of textbooks,[39] but such fees must be reasonable and must be tied to the actual cost of the books.[40] A requirement that each student pay a registration fee, however, has been held

invalid because it was an attempt to charge tuition, in violation of a state statute.[41]

Nonresidents of a district are ordinarily not entitled to a free education in the district. They may be entitled to such privileges, however, if they are able to pay a nonresident tuition fee. Similarly, most residents of institutions are entitled to an education in the district in which the institution is located. Nearly all states require that the cost of the student's schooling be borne by the district in which he or she resided before coming to the institution.[42] Finally, students who are wards of the court or are otherwise maintained as public charges are considered to be residents of the district in which they live and are entitled to full educational privileges.[43]

## Compulsory Attendance

Compulsory education statutes are commonplace in the United States and everywhere regarded as valid exercises of a state's police power.[44] All statutes, however, allow certain exceptions; generally, the conditions of nonattendance are clearly specified in the statute. For instance, a student may be excused from secondary school attendance if employed. A familiar example is that of the child actor. A less familiar but certainly more widespread example of excused absence occurs in agricultural areas, where children are excused to help with the harvests. In addition, many statutes give the local school district discretionary power to excuse a student's absence due to some hardship based on his or her distance from school and the availability of transportation.[45] In such cases, the statutes provide

---

[33]Transportation may be required for handicapped children regardless of their distance from the school. Section 504 of the Rehabilitation Act imposes duties on schools apart from state transportation law.

[34]*Cross* v. *Fisher*, 177 S.W. 43, 132 Tenn. 31 (1951).

[35]*Rose* v. *Nashua Board of Education*, 679 F.2d 279 (1st Cir. 1982).

[36]*Everson* v. *Board of Education*, 330 U.S.1, 67 S. Ct. 504 (1947). A handicapped child placed in a nonpublic school may well have a right to transportation to that placement.

[37]*State* v. *Wilson*, 297 S.W. 419, 221 Mo. App. 9 (1927).

[38]*Board of Education* v. *Sinclair*, 222 N.W.2d 143, 65 Wis. 2d 179 (1974); *Paulson* v. *Minidoka County School District*, 463 P.2d 935, 93 Idaho 469 (1970).

[39]*Chandler* v. *South Bend Community School Corporation*, 312 N.E.2d 915, 160 Ind. App. 592 (1974).

[40]*Board of Education* v. *Sinclair*, supra note 38; *Bond* v. *Public Schools of Ann Arbor School District*, 178 N.W.2d 484, 383 Mich. 693 (1970).

[41]*Dowell* v. *School District No. 1, Boone County*, 250 S.W.2d 127, 220 Ark. 828 (1952).

[42]*State ex rel. Gibbs* v. *Martin*, 56 N.E.2d 148 Ohio St. 491 (1944). States may assist local districts when the cost of a student's education is extraordinary (e.g., by increasing the state aid for that category of student).

[43]*Brown* v. *Union Free School*, 398 N.Y.S.2d 710, 59 A.D.2d 761 (1977); *Jeter* v. *Ellenville Central School District*, 360 N.E.2d 1086, 392 N.Y.S.2d 403 (1977).

[44]*Hatch* v. *Goerke*, 502 F.2d 1189 (1974); *People* v. *Turner*, 263 P.2d 685, 121 Cal. App. 2d 361, appeal dismissed, 347 U.S. 972 74 S. Ct. 785 (1953); *Snyder* v. *Town of Newton*, 161 A.2d 770, 147 Conn. 374, appeal dismissed, 81 S. Ct. 692, 365 U.S. 299 (1960).

[45]*Berry* v. *Macon County Board of Education*, 380 F. Supp. 1244 (1971); *Roman Catholic Welfare Corporation of San Francisco* v. *City of Piedmont*, 289 P.2d 438, 45 Cal. 2d 325 (1955).

rather strict guidelines that help ensure that the students maintain adequate educational progress.

Under certain conditions, absence from school may also be excused for religious reasons. If authorized by statute, a school district may excuse students from the public school for short periods of time to participate in religious or moral training off the public school grounds.[46] These "released time" programs, in which students are excused from school to obtain religious instruction, withstood an early constitutional challenge, but they cannot be conducted in public schools.[47] However, a child normally may not be excused from school attendance on a certain day of every week because of his or her religious beliefs.[48]

In 1972, the Supreme Court granted to Amish children a partial exemption from compulsory attendance laws in Wisconsin. The Amish argued successfully that requiring their children to attend the last two years of high school would be in sharp conflict with their fundamental religious beliefs, deeply rooted in their way of life. In *Wisconsin* v. *Yoder*,[49] the Court agreed, but in a carefully circumscribed decision. The Court held that the state's interest in compulsory education was not so compelling that the religious practices of the Amish had to give way to it. The Court went to great lengths to detail the specific factors that made the Amish experience unique, referring to long-standing and deeply held religious beliefs that had been incorporated by the Amish into their educational and child-rearing practices. Given the very restrictive nature of the *Yoder*

decision, it seemed unlikely that other groups would come easily under the *Yoder* rule, although that has not prevented many groups and individuals from trying.[50]

Normally, compulsory attendance laws do not require all students to be sent to public schools. Indeed, such a requirement would be an unconstitutional interference with the right of the parent to freely choose a child's educational course.[51] There are several alternatives to public school attendance, the two most important being parochial and private nonsectarian schools. State statutes vary considerably concerning what type of private school attendance fulfills the compulsory education requirement. Generally, however, the private school must receive the sanction of the state educational authorities. State regulation of private schools has generated a substantial volume of litigation, especially during the 1980s.[52]

Where no public or private school satisfies parents, they may engage in home education in most states. State statutes regulate this alternative in a quite divergent manner, and litigation by disappointed parents is a common phenomenon.[53] Court responses have been so varied as to have no discernible pattern. These cases, along with challenges to the regulation of private schools, are largely brought by parents and other groups under the Free Exercise clause of the First Amendment. Thus, these cases represent serious constitutional dilemmas. Generalizations

---

[46]*Dilger* v. *School District*, 352 P.2d 564, 222 Or. 108 (1960); *Perry* v. *School District*, 344 P.2d 1036, 54 Wash. 2d 886 (1959).

[47]Compare *Zorach* v. *Clausen*, 343 U.S. 306, 72 S. Ct. 679 (1952), with *McCollum* v. *Board of Education*, 333 U.S. 203, 68 S. Ct. 461 (1948). Also, there are stringent if inconsistent limits on providing public aid to private school students, particularly in parochial schools. Cf. T. van Geel, *The Courts and American Education* (Buffalo, NY: Prometheus Books, 1987), pp. 31–46.

[48]*Commonwealth* v. *Bey*, 70 A.2d 693, 166 Pa. Super. Ct. 136 (1950); *Commonwealth* v. *Smoker*, 110A.2d 740, 117 Pa. Super. Ct. 435 (1955). In *Bey*, the parents were Mohammedans who refused to send their children to public school on Fridays.

[49]*Wisconsin* v. *Yoder*, 92 S. Ct. 1526, 406 U.S. 205 (1972).

[50]See, for example, *State* v. *Kasuboski*, 275 N.W.2d 101 (Wis. App. 1978); *Duro* v. *District Attorney, Second Judicial District of North Carolina*, 712 F.2d 96 (1983); *Hill* v. *State*, 410 So. 2d 431 (Ala. App. 1981). Most but not all such efforts have been unsuccessful. Cf. R. D. Mawdsley, Compulsory Attendance Laws under Attack, *Education Law Reporter*, 30, 627 (1986). Some states have created statutory "Amish" exemptions, also seeking to limit eligibility. At least one such statute has withstood constitutional attack: *Fellowship Baptist Church* v. *Benton*, 815 F.2d 485 (8th Cir. 1987).

[51]*Pierce* v. *Society of Sisters*, 45 S. Ct. 571, 268 U.S. 510 (1925).

[52]See J. G. Carpenter, State regulation of religious schools, *Journal of Law and Education*, 14, 229 (1985).

[53]Cf. P. M. Lines, Private education alternatives and state regulation, *Journal of Law and Education*, 12, 189 (1983).

are quite difficult, beyond the observation that courts are likely to confront such challenges as long as state statutes prevent access to desired alternatives to public schooling.[54]

## Classifications

Control over the classification of students and curricula is vested in the state and local boards of education. The state normally prescribes the broad outlines of the educational system, leaving control over specified details to individual school districts. Thus the state board of education may prescribe various courses of study for the different grades, but the local school may define the specific content of the courses as long as the coverage is not inconsistent with the intent of the state board.[55]

Implicit in the power to prescribe the necessary rules and regulations for the operation of the school system, local school authorities may require the classification and assignment of students to classes or grades commensurate with their proficiency and ability.[56] To help make such a determination, school authorities may use any reasonable method to test the fitness of a particular student for admission to a class or grade. For instance, the qualifications of a student may be tested by either a written or oral examination, or the school may presume a student's ability from the nature and reputation of his or her previous educational experiences. If such a determination is made fairly and with a sound basis, the school is within the boundaries of its discretion and nei-

ther the parent nor the student may overturn the decision.[57]

During the 1970s, the tradition of using standardized test scores to make educational decisions, including identification and placement of handicapped children, came under judicial scrutiny in a series of highly publicized cases.[58] In large part, these cases were tied to discriminatory effects associated with standardized tests. The best known case, *Larry P. v. Riles*,[59] was actively in litigation for over a decade. The plaintiffs successfully challenged the practice of using IQ (intelligence quota) tests to identify and place students in EMR (educable mentally retarded) classes, winning a statewide ban on such practices. This rather extraordinary outcome has not been duplicated in subsequent litigation.[60] Associated cases also challenged tracking practices,[61]

---

[54]Many state laws have been modified, either in response to a lawsuit or in anticipation of one. Courts have resisted granting exemptions without religious motivations and have attempted to preserve legislative standards, unsurprisingly. For a critical review of statutory and case law, as well as recommendations for a coherent judicial analysis, see D. M. Sacken, Regulating nonpublic education: A search for just law and policy, *American Journal of Education*, *98*, 394 (1988).

[55]As part of the recent educational reform agenda, some state legislatures have become more aggressive and preemptive in regulating local curricular choice. Cf. M. W. Kirst (Ed.), The vanishing *myth* of local control, *Phi Delta Kappan* (November 1984).

[56]*Miller v. School District No. 2, Clarendon County*, 256 F. Supp. 370 (1966).

[57]Of course, classroom assignments of individual students must be made in a racially nondiscriminatory fashion. *Adams v. Rankin County Board of Education*, 524 F.2d 928 (1976); *Moore v. Tangipahoa Parish School Board*, 304 F. Supp. 244, appeal dismissed, 421 F.2d 1407 (1969). In *Hobsen v. Hansen*, 269 F. Supp. 401 (1967), the court also held that "tracking" of students in the District of Columbia as practiced violated their constitutional rights. Students were divided into separate tracks, ranging from "basic" for the slow students to "honors" for gifted students. Such a system was impermissible because disadvantaged children, primarily black, were relegated to lower tracks according to intelligence tests largely standardized on white, middle-class children, where they received reduced and unequal educational opportunity.

[58]Cf. D. N. Bersoff, Regarding psychologists testily: Legal regulation of psychological assessment in the public schools. *Maryland Legal Review*, *39*, 27 (1979).

[59]*Larry P. v. Riles*, 793 F.2d 969 (9th Cir. 1984). This is the last incarnation of a case that produced several voluminous opinions.

[60]See, for example, *PASE v. Hannon*, 506 F. Supp. 831 (N.D. 111. 1980). For a comprehensive discussion of "IQ test" litigation, see R. Elliott, *Litigating Intelligence* (Dover, MA: Aubum House, 1987).

[61]More recently, the Eleventh Circuit held that achievement grouping that remedied disadvantage through better educational opportunities was constitutionally permissible. *Georgia State Conference of Branches of NAACP v. State of Georgia*, 775 F.2d 1403 (11th Cir. 1985). Tracking remains a highly controversial if pervasive educational practice; for a sharp critical analysis of tracking, see J. Oakes, *Keeping Track: How Schools Structure Inequality* (New Haven, CT: Yale University Press, 1985).

as well as testing, classification, and programs for language minorities.[62] It seems clear under both constitutional and statutory law that students have rights to appropriate assessment, as well as programs adequate to their educational needs. Courts have frequently expressed this concept as a right to "meaningful access" to the educational curriculum.[63]

Classification issues, particularly those affecting identifiable student populations, such as racial and ethnic minorities, are likely to continue creating periodic challenges to districts' authority.[64] The local school district has similar powers over the promotion, demotion, and retention of students. As long as they are reasonable, the school district may prescribe rules governing tests and examinations and standards for promotion.[65] Even given the results of tests and examinations, promotion and demotion are largely at the discretion of the school authorities, and in the absence of evidence of abuse the courts generally will not intervene. This discretion is given to the schools to allow them to take account of factors other than academic performance in the decision to promote, demote, or retain a student. For instance, a student's level of physical and psychological maturity may play an important role in determining how well he or she will perform in a higher or lower grade. Such factors are not as easily quantifiable as academic skills; thus, there is reluctance to insist on a strictly objective set of standards for promotion.[66]

As noted, control over the curricula in the public schools is often vested jointly in both the state and local educational authorities. In the absence of specific directions from the state, the local schools have the authority to provide such content as they deem in the best interests of the students.[67] The local school district has no discretion, however, where a state constitutional provision or statute requires the adoption of a uniform statewide curriculum for the public school system. In such a uniform system, usually neither the local districts nor parents and students may require the courts to intervene in altering the established course of study.

A persistent controversy over control of public school curricula, however, has forced courts to play a role. The problem is not new[68] and centers on the teaching of competing theories of the origin of human life. Recent cases have challenged the theories of both divine creation[69] and general evolution.[70] The issues really are twofold: science instruction and freedom of religion and the right of parents to have their child excused from religiously or morally objectionable curriculum material.

In addition to court actions, state and local boards of education have been deluged with complaints from both parents and students protesting the content of a particular course on

---

[62]The seminal case here is *Lau v. Nichols*, 414 U.S. 563, 94 S. Ct. 786 (1974), where the Supreme Court required that schools "open" their curriculum to language minorities. Since that time, both assessment and appropriate programs for language minorities have become complex, disputatious issues. For a case that captures both these qualities, see *Casteneda v. Pickard*, 648 F.2d 989 (5th Cir. 1981). One federal court has treated speakers of "black English" as a linguistic minority: *Martin Luther King, Jr., Elementary School Children v. Michigan Board of Education*, 451 F. Supp. 1324 (E.D. Mich, 1978), and 473 F. Supp. 1371 (E.D. Mich. 1979).

[63]See *Lau v. Nichols* id.; *Board of Education v. Rowley*, 458 U.S. 176 (1982).

[64]Assessment practices in classifying students for educational placement are significantly affected by federal statues. A good example is P. L. 94-142, which requires evaluation of children both in their native language and by using multiple procedures. See 34 C.F.R. §300.532 (1985). Cf. K. Heller, W. Holtzman, & S. Messick, *Placing Children in Special Education: A Strategy for Equity* (Washington, DC: National Academy Press, 1982).

[65]*Morgan v. Board of Education, Trico Community School Unit School District No. 176*, 317 N.E.2d 393, 22 Ill. App. 3d 241 (1974).

[66]*Board of Curators v. Horowitz*, 98 S. Ct. 948 (1978). Courts are also reluctant to scrutinize carefully or second-guess these educational judgments.

[67]*Bright v. Isenbarger*, 314 F. Supp. 1382, *aff 'd*. 445 F.2d 412 (1971). Cf. D. Shelton, Legislative control over public school curriculum, *Williamette Law Review*, 15, 473 (1979).

[68]*Scopes v. State*, 289 S.W. 363, 154 Tenn. 105 (1927); *Epperson v. Arkansas*, 393 U.S. 97 (1968).

[69]*Daniel v. Walters*, 515 F.2d 485 (1975).

[70]*Willoughby v. Stever*, 504 F.2d 271, cert. denied, 420 U.S. 927 (1975); *Wright v. Houston Independent School District*, 366 F. Supp. 1208, cert. denied, 417 U.S. 969 (1974).

the origin of life.[71] In response to lawsuits and public pressure, state legislatures have adopted various procedures for dealing with the problem. For instance, some states have prohibited the teaching of the theory of divine creation. Others have required schools to present a balanced exposure of both viewpoints, couched in terms of competing theories. Balanced treatment statutes or policies are constitutionally vulnerable, however, if a court concludes that the policy constitutes an effort to inject sectarian beliefs into public schools. In 1987, the Supreme Court declared a Louisiana statute unconstitutional under this rationale.[72] These cases can be interpreted as protecting students' rights not to be subjected to religious indoctrination by the state while being a "captive audience."[73]

More generally, the courts have also become involved in litigating the right of a parent to have some control over the content of educational offerings available to the student.[74] For example, recently parents have asserted their right to object to the nature of the values being taught by the school. Such protests have come from both ends of the political spectrum, raising claims of anti-American, anti-Christian, and obscene curricula and objecting to the "conservative" orientation of the schools that results in the teaching of gender bias, racism, and other stereotypes.[75]

The conflict is between the power and interest of the state, expressed through curriculum requirements, and the right of parents to direct the education of their child. On the one hand, there is little question that the state, through curriculum requirements, is engaged in the process of inculcating values, and the state legislature, as the representative of its citizens, may have an affirmative duty to engage in this process. On the other hand, parents may have a considerable stake in the moral and value training given to their children. The Supreme Court has long recognized the constitutional importance of this parental interest and now describes it as a component of fundamental "privacy" rights.[76] Parents may have a legal right to protest a course that perpetuates or advocates a position morally reprehensible to them.[77] Recently, this issue has erupted in two cases in which parents are seeking some judicial protection from "secular humanism" in public schools. In both instances, the parents won at trial, but the verdicts were reversed by federal appellate courts. The parents claimed that the public curriculum was, in effect, indoctrination in a religion of secularism. It is likely that conflicts over school curricula are ineradicable as long as the "common schools" serve the distinctly heterogeneous clientele in this country.[78]

The Supreme Court also generated another ground for raising curricular objections, namely, the student's right to receive information. In a case involving censorship of a public school library, the Court recognized that students have this First Amendment protection against unrea-

---

[71]J. Hefley, *Textbooks on Trial* (Wheaton, IL: Victor Books, 1976).

[72]*Edwards* v. *Aguillard*, 107 S. Ct. 2573 (1987); accord, *McLean* v. *Arkansas Board of Education*, 529 F. Supp. 1255 (E.D. Ark. 1982). In both these cases, the key finding by the court was the improper motivation of the decision makers.

[73]The Supreme Court articulated this interest in *Abington School District* v. *Schempp*, 374 U.S. 203 (1963), which prohibited the pervasive practice of school-initiated religious instruction. Such practices were held to violate the establishment clause of the First Amendment. Parenthetically, teachers who introduce religious activities into public school classrooms are subject to dismissal. See, for example, *Lynch* v. *Indiana State University Board of Trustees*, 378 N.E.2d 900 (Inc. App. 1978).

[74]*Mercer* v. *Michigan State Board of Education*, 379 F. Supp. 580 aff'd., 95 S. Ct. 673, 419 U.S. 1081 (1974).

[75]*Cornwell* v. *State Board of Education*, 314 F. Supp. 340, cert. denied, 400 U.S. 942 (1970); *Todd* v. *Rochester Community Schools*, 200 N.W.2d 90, 14 Mich. App. 320 (1970); *Williams* v. *Board of Education*, 388 F. Supp. 93, aff'd., 530 F.2d 972 (1975).

[76]The Supreme Court recognized the constitutional quality of those parental interests over 60 years ago. See *Pierce* v. *Society of Sisters*, 268 U.S. 510 (1925). The Court currently describes this interest as a type of "highly personal relationship" that warrants "a substantial measure of sanctuary from unjustified interference by the State." *Roberts* v. *United States Jaycees*, 104 S. Ct. 3244, 3250 (1984).

[77]See M. Hirschoof, Parents and the public school curriculum: Is there a right to have one's child excused from objectionable instruction? *Southern California Law Review*, *50*, 871 (1977).

[78]The two "secular humanism" cases are *Mozert* v. *Hawkins County Board of Education*, 827 F.2d 1058 (6th Cir. 1987), reversing, 647 F. Supp. 1194 (E.D. Tenn. 1986), and *Smith* v. *Board of School Commissioners*, 827 F.2d 684 (11th Cir. 1987), reversing 655 F. Supp. 939 (S.D. Ala. 1987). See also *Grove* v. *Mead School District No. 354*, 753 F.2d 1528 (9th Cir. 1985).

sonable or improperly motivated censorship.[79] However, among an otherwise divided Court, there was agreement that students' rights were subordinate in formal curricular matters to the discretion and authority of the legislature or local board. In sum, official authority over the curriculum still firmly resides in the legislature, or its delegatee, the local boards, and parents or students who object have relatively little hope for obtaining judicial assistance.

# SCHOOL REGULATION OF STUDENTS

The courts have recognized that the establishment of an educational system requires the formation of rules and regulations to ensure an orderly learning process. Generally, in formulating rules and regulations, school authorities have broad discretion and courts are deferential toward educators' decisions. They are, however, bound by the requirement that their rules and regulations be reasonable.[80] Courts have adopted a general guideline for determining whether regulations are reasonable: school regulations must be within the authority of the school and reasonably related to the goal of maintaining order and discipline in the educational system.[81] Moreover, other constraints limit school authorities' discretion. The Supreme Court has noted that the vigilant protection of constitutional freedoms is nowhere more vital than in the schools. Thus the state may not impose and enforce unconstitutional conditions on the right of a student to attend a public school. Students in the public schools are "persons" within the meaning of the Constitution and have certain fundamental rights that the state and the schools must respect.[82]

The law does not require that every school regulation be formally adopted and publicized by school authorities before it may be enforced.[83] In addition, school officials are not prohibited from taking appropriate disciplinary action in confronting a problem simply because there is no preexisting rule on the books.[84] Some cases have held, however, that a regulation governing the conduct of high school students must be sufficiently clear to provide meaningful notice to students that they must conform their conduct to its requirements.[85] This concern is heightened if the regulation involves students' basic personal freedoms (e.g., free speech or association).[86] In any event, the enforcement of school rules and regulations must be reasonable, giving due regard to all the circumstances surrounding the nature of each event and the age, health, and mental condition of the student.

Although the local board is the policymaking body for schools, the control and discipline of students is effectively in the hands of teachers, principals, and superintendents of the local schools,[87] with rule-making power given to each. In a sense, then, students may confront multiple-rule systems in the school that should be congruent but distinctive. In exercising authority to control and maintain class discipline, a teacher may adopt reasonable rules and regulations if they are not inconsistent with other school or district rules and regulations. Each teacher's classroom rules nominally will be supplemented by those of the principal, superintendent, and school board.[88] In the following subsections we examine the range of school regulations over students' behavior.

## Health Regulations

Nearly all states delegate the power to prescribe health regulations to the schools as a condition of school attendance. It has generally been held

[79]*Board of Education* v. *Pico*, 457 U.S. 853 (1982). See also *Seyfried* v. *Walton*, 668 F.2d 214 (3d Cir. 1981). The school officials' decision to cancel a student performance of *Pippin* was upheld because the production was an integral part of the educational program.

[80]*Baker* v. *Board of Education*, 307 F. Supp. 517 (1969); *Bumside* v. *Byars*, 363 F.2d 744 (1966).

[81]*Johnson* v. *Joint School District No. 60*, 508 P.2d 547 (Idaho 1973). Cf. S. Goldstein, The scope of school board authority to regulate student status and conduct: A nonconstructional analysis, *University of Pennsylvania Law Review*, 117, 403 (1969).

[82]*Tinker* v. *Des Moines Community School District*, 89 S. Ct. 733, 393 U.S. 503 (1969).

[83]*Leonard* v. *School Committee of Attleboro*, 212 N.E.2d 468, 349 Mass. 704 (1965).

[84]*Richards* v. *Thurston*, 424 F.2d 1281 (1970).

[85]*Sullivan* v. *Houston Independent School District*, 475 F.2d 1071, cert. denied, 94 S. Ct. 461, 414 U.S. 1032 (1973).

[86]*Eisner* v. *Stanford Board of Education*, 440 F.2d 803 (2nd Cir. 1971).

[87]*Melton* v. *Young*, 328 F. Supp. 88, cert. denied, 93 S. Ct. 1926, 411 U.S. 951 (1973).

[88]*Citizens Against Mandatory Busing* v. *Palmason*, 495 P.2d 657, 80 Wash. 2d 445 (1972).

that health measures prescribed by local school systems do not conflict either with compulsory attendance laws or with statutory provisions permitting attendance at a particular age. For example, some school districts have adopted regulations that require students to receive physical examinations as a condition of their admission. The courts have ruled that such regulations are within the police power delegated to the schools by the state.[89] The school has the same power over the formulation of regulations to control the introduction and spread of infectious or contagious diseases. Thus the school may prevent a student from attending if he or she has been exposed to such diseases.[90] As a general rule, a state may require the vaccination of all students before they enroll in school. Such statutes are a valid exercise of the police power and have been generally upheld.[91] It is uncertain, however, whether in the absence of a state statute the local school district may legally require vaccination as a condition for school attendance. It is clear that when threatened by an epidemic, the local school district may require proof of vaccination before admitting a student. Many statutory provisions, however, provide for exemptions from the vaccination requirement, for instance, on medical grounds[92] or based on religious beliefs,[93] although the latter are discretionary. Children are not constitutionally entitled to an exemption from uniform vaccination requirements.[94]

# Behavior Outside of School

Ordinarily, school officials have no right of control over students outside of school, but when the acts or behavior of a student affects the school, officials may be able to regulate it. To penalize a student for such off-school behavior, however, there must be a direct and immediate connection between the prohibited behavior and the welfare of the school.[95] Thus, students may be punished for acts done outside of school if their behavior (1) could directly influence the conduct of other students in the classroom, (2) sets a bad disciplinary example for other students, or (3) impairs the authority of teachers. Although broad discretion is granted to the school in determining when out-of-school behaviors can be regulated, the courts require such regulations to be linked with a direct need of the local school.[96]

In addition to these general guidelines, the courts have also addressed some specific issues. For instance, school regulations relating to policies toward homework have long been upheld,[97] although a school may not require that certain hours of the evening be set aside exclusively for the completion of homework assignments.[98]

Courts have also upheld state statutes and regulations concerning students' school-related, extracurricular recreational and social activities, especially when such rules are used to promote discipline in the school. In evaluating these rules, courts consider whether they are a reasonable exercise of the power and discretion of the school, not whether they are wise or expedient.[99] Older cases intimated that a school could rightly prohibit any kind of outside social or recreational activities if they too greatly diverted students from school and schoolwork. Today, it is probably very difficult for school authorities to intrude

---

[89]*Streich* v. *Board of Education*, 147 N.W. 779, 34 S.D. 169 (1915).

[90]*Breese* v. *Smith*. 501 P.2d 159 (1972). Such a policy necessarily involves interference with the child's right to an education. It may also have implications under the Rehabilitation Act. See M. Welker, The impact of AIDS upon public schools: A problem for jurisprudence, *Education Law Reporter, 33*, 603 (1986).

[91]*Hanzel* v. *Arter*, 625 F. Supp. 1259 (S.D. Ohio 1985); *Mannis* v. *State* ex rel DeWitt School District No. 1, 398 S.W.2d 206, 240 Ark. 42, *cert. denied*, 86 S. Ct. 1864, 384 U.S. 972 (1966).

[92]*Barber* v. *Rochester School Board*, 135 A. 159, 82 N.H. 135 (1926).

[93]In re *Elwell*, 284 N.Y.S.2d 924, 55 Misc. 2d 252 (1967); *Maier* v. *Besser*, 341 N.Y.S.2d 411, 73 Misc. 2d 241 (1972).

[94]*United States* v. *Ballard*, 322 U.S. 78 (1944); *Dalli* v. *Board of Education*, 267 N.E.2d 219 (Mass. 1971).

[95]*Fenton* v. *Stear*, 423 F. Supp. 767 (1976).

[96]For instance, a court held that a student could not be disciplined for an obscene gesture to a teacher off school grounds and after school hours. *Klein* v. *Smith* 635 F. Supp. 1440 (D. Me. 1986).

[97]*Bolding* v. *State*, 4 S.W. 579, 23 Tex. App. 172 (1887).

[98]*Hobbs* v. *Germany*, 49 So. 515, 94 Miss. 469 (1909).

[99]*Coggins* v. *Board of Education*, 28 S.E.2d 527, 223 N.C. 763 (1944); *Gentry* v. *Memphis Federation of Musicians*, 151 S.W.2d 1081, 177 Tenn. 566 (1941); *Starkey* v. *Board of Education*, 381 P.2d 718, 14 Utah 2d 227 (1963).

into any aspect of a student's out-of-school life unless there is some very direct and immediate impact on the school.

School regulation of interscholastic athletics has raised two important issues in students' participation rights. First, the courts have held that participation in school-sponsored sports is not a right but a privilege, subject to any number of different conditions. The power of the school to regulate interscholastic athletics must be exercised reasonably, and the privilege of participation may not be arbitrarily extended or withheld.[100] Under this power, the school may prescribe rules for the eligibility of students who transfer into the district,[101] although, litigation over eligibility questions is persistent.[102] Students who were transferred involuntarily under a court-ordered desegregation plan may not be subject to such interdistrict transfer rules. A recent controversy has been the adoption of increased academic standards as a condition of participation. A "no pass, no play" statute was upheld by the Texas Supreme Court as being rationally related to the state's legitimate educational interests.[103]

Second, a great deal of controversy involves sex discrimination in the availability of athletic programs and the opportunity to participate in existing programs. Although still a litigated matter, these issues are substantially regulated by Title IX and its administrative regulations.[104] Title IX permits sex separation as long as team selection is based on competitive skill or the sport involves substantial contact. The overall statutory demand is that both sexes have comparable opportunities to enjoy athletics.[105] There has been recurrent litigation, however, focusing particularly on the right of girls to play on boys' teams.[106] The results are quite uneven, but girls have won a substantial number of victories, even in contact sports.[107] Apart from Title IX, these cases have turned on equal protection and state civil rights or equal rights laws.[108]

Under its authority to prescribe rules and regulations for the well-being of the school, a school may prohibit students from affiliating with a fraternal society without the permission of school authorities.[109] This is true even though students have the consent of their parents and all of the meetings of the organization are held after school hours and off school grounds.[110] To exercise this power validly, however, the school must show that such organizations have a tendency to destroy good order, discipline, and scholarship among the students. In the absence of such evidence, the school may not prohibit membership.

Regulating students' non-school-based associations will always be problematic because these efforts directly affect students' associational rights, protected by the First Amendment. Decisions that

---

[100]*Florida High School Activities Association* v. *Bryant,* 313 So. 2d 57 (1975); *Marino* v. *Waters,* 220 So. 2d 802 (1969); State ex rel *Missouri State High School Activities Association* v. *Schoenlaub,* 507 S.W.2d 354 (1974); *Wright* v. *Arkansas Athletic Association,* 501 F.2d (1974).

[101]State ex rel *Ohio High School Athletics Association* v. *Judges of the Court of Common Pleas,* 181 N.E.2d 261, 173 Ohio St. 239 (1962); *Kampmeier* v. *Nyquist,* 553 F.2d 296 (1977).

[102]Although schools normally win such cases, the costs cannot be insignificant. Cf. C. Nolte, Judicial intervention in school athletics: The changing scene, *Education Law Reporter,* 8, 1 (1983).

[103]*Spring Branch Independent District* v. *Stamos,* 695 S.W.2d 556 (1985), appeal dismissed, 106 S. Ct. 1170 (1986).

[104]Title IX is 20 U.S.C. §1681 et seq. (1976); its implementing regulations are found at 34 C.F.R. §106 (1985).

[105]34 CFR §106.41 (1985). The demand that schools provide comparable opportunities has not been translated into a requirement of equal expenditure levels.

[106]See, for example, *Yellow Springs* v. *Ohio High School Athletic Association,* 647 F.2d 651 (6th Cir. 1981); *O'Connor* v. *Board of Education District No. 23,* 545 F. Supp. 376 (N.D. Ill. 1982). Parenthetically, boys seeking access to girls' teams have fared less well. *Clark* v. *Arizona Interscholastic Association,* 695 F.2d 1126 (9th Cir. 1982), cert. denied, 464 U.S. 818 (1983).

[107]*Hoover* v. *Meiklejohn,* 430 F. Supp. 164 (D. Colo 1977).

[108]A school's success or failure may depend on the availability of a single-gender team for that sport (i.e., a boys' and girls' basketball team) or the overall range of alternatives for both sexes. Also, state law may be important; schools in states with an equal rights amendment may have less discretion.

[109]*Holroyd* v. *Eibling,* 188 N.E.2d 797, 116 Ohio App. 440 (1963); *Satan Fraternity* v. *Board of Public Instruction,* 22 So. 2d 892, 156 Fla. 222 (1945).

[110]*Passel* v. *Fort Worth Independent School District,* 453 S.W.2d 888, cert. denied, 91 S. Ct. 1667, 402 U.S. 968 (1970).

permit the regulation of students' social organizations came, for the most part, before judicial recognition of students' constitutional rights. The current viability of these older decisions may be suspect. An effort to prevent students' participation that is based on the ideas promoted by an association would be especially dangerous.

## Behavior During School

Generally, school officials have wide latitude in regulating the conduct, behavior, and appearance of students during school hours. Any number of such rules and regulations has been challenged and upheld by the courts. For instance, the school generally may require late students to report to the principal's office or to wait in the hall until the opening exercises of the school are completed,[111] require financially able students to pay a deposit to ensure the proper care of free textbooks,[112] require students to return report cards with a parent's or guardian's signature,[113] prohibit students from wearing metal heel plates on their shoes,[114] and prevent students from obtaining lunches except from home or the school lunch program.[115] Generally, the rules and regulations of the school must be reasonable exercises of its discretion and must have a rational relationship to the orderly conduct of the educational process. There is a legal presumption in favor of the validity of school regulations, and as long as they are reasonable and proper, they will not be disturbed. However, certain areas of school regulation have received much attention and are examined here in detail.

### Clothing and Hairstyles

School regulation of hair and clothing styles is certainly not as important an issue as it was during the 1960s. Then the school's authority to regulate the personal appearance of students was the subject of much litigation, which has diminished because school officials largely acquiesce to changing fashion trends. Cases involving students' appearances will occasionally erupt, but they now appear to be resolved largely outside of the judicial system.[116] However, as a function of the schools' authority to reasonably regulate the conduct of students, schools can prescribe and enforce dress codes,[117] although school officials do not have unlimited discretion in prescribing standards of personal appearance. For example, a dress code may violate a student's right to equal protection under the Fourteenth Amendment if it unduly restricts what clothing is acceptable in the school. This is especially likely if the dress code does not bear some rational relationship to orderly conduct of the school.[118] When the school could not show that wearing blue dungarees disrupted the educational system, a dress code provision prohibiting them was held to be unconstitutional.[119] Also, clearly discriminatory rules, such as one prohibiting only females from wearing slacks, have been found invalid. The court noted that such a regulation was an attempt to control the style and taste of students and did not bear on their safety, order, or discipline.[120]

The authority of the school to regulate hairstyles and lengths is not so clearly established. Courts again have come down on both sides of the issue. For instance, some cases have held that the right to wear one's hair at any length or in any fashion is an ingredient of personal freedom protected by the U.S. Constitution.[121] Other courts have held that a student's hair length is not a form of symbolic expression, and constitutional protections do not attach. Therefore, the school may validly regulate hairstyles.[122]

Restrictions on hairstyles have usually been upheld when the school can show that a legiti-

[111]*Fertich* v. *Michener*, 11 N.E. 605, 111 Ind. 472 (1887).

[112]*Segar* v. *Rockford School District Board of Education*, 148 N.E. 289, 317 Ill. 418 (1925).

[113]*Boume* v. *State*, 52 N.W. 710, 35 Neb. 1 (1892).

[114]*Stromberg* v. *French*, 236 N.W. 477, 60 N.D. 750 (1931).

[115]*Bishop* v. *Houston Independent School District*, 29 S.W. 2d 312, 119 Tex. 403 (1930).

[116]Cf. L. Bartlett, Hair and dress codes revisited, *Education Law Reporter*, 33, 7 (1986).

[117]*Jones* v. *Day*, 89 So. 906, 127 Miss. 136 (1921); *Pugsley* v. *Sellmeyer*, 250 S.W. 538, 158 Ark. 247 (1923).

[118]*Miller* v. *Gillis*, 315 F. Supp. 94 (1969).

[119]*Bannister* v. *Paradis*, 316 F. Supp. 185 (1970).

[120]*Scott* v. *Board of Education*, 305 N.Y.S.2d 601, 61 Misc. 333 (1969).

[121]*Breen* v. *Kahl*, 419 F.2d 1034, cert. denied, 90 S. Ct. 1836, 398 U.S. 937 (1969).

[122]*Brownlee* v. *Bradley County Tennessee Board of Education*, 311 F. Supp. 1360 (1970); *Richards* v. *Thurston*, 424 F.2d 1281 (1970); *Jackson* v. *Dorrier*, 424 F.2d 213, cert. denied, 91 S. Ct. 55, 400 U.S. 850 (1970).

mate interest was served by the rule, such as preventing the distraction of other students or the disruption of a proper classroom atmosphere.[123] Schools have cited incidents of harassment and violence toward male students with long hair,[124] and they have argued that excessive hair length interfered with certain sports or that the enforcement of hair length regulations was a legitimate means of building team morale, discipline, and spirit.[125] When such restrictions have been held invalid, it is usually because the school failed to show that long hair would disrupt the educational process.[126]

## Flag Salute and Pledge of Allegiance

School boards do not have the power to require all students to stand and recite the pledge of allegiance while saluting the flag. The U.S. Supreme Court held that such a requirement went beyond the bounds of the protections of the First Amendment.[127] The Court noted that students' nonparticipation in the flag ceremony did not interfere with or deny the rights of others and did not disrupt the orderly conduct of the classroom. In addition to the right not to participate, students cannot be forced to stand quietly while others do so.[128]

## Married and Pregnant Students

The courts are split over the question of how much control the school may exercise over married students. Some older cases generally upheld the right of the school to prohibit married students from participating in any extracurricular activities. These decisions were generally based on the power of the school to maintain discipline and regulate school activities.[129] In support of such restrictions, schools argued successfully that the policy both discourages students' marriages and helps preserve existing marriages by avoiding time-consuming and distracting activities.[130]

Rules interfering with married students are inherently problematic, however, because marriage is constitutionally protected as a "fundamental right."[131] Courts have ruled more recently that the school has no power to prevent married students from participating in either interscholastic sports or other school-related activities.[132] In *Sturrup* v. *Maban*,[133] the court stated that to justify such a rule, the school must demonstrate some compelling interest. As with other regulations, the court required the school to show that the presence of married students would have a disruptive impact on the conduct of classes in the school. The school officials' desire to discourage students' marriages or to show disapproval of such marriages was not sufficient to outweigh the infringement on the students. Finally, one court has simply held that such a rule denies married students equal protection of the laws under the Fourteenth Amendment[134] and that a school would never be justified in prohibiting married students from participating in any activity available to any other student.

School officials also have less regulatory power now over pregnant students. Title IX regulations no longer permit schools to uniformly exclude pregnant students or those who have had an abortion.[135] To maintain discipline and to help ensure the orderly conduct of learning in the school, however, schools may make reasonable rules concerning such students. In addition, separate schools are permissible but must be voluntary.

---

[123]*Akin* v. *Board of Education*, 262 Cal. App. 2d 161, 68 Cal. Rptr. 557, cert. denied, 89 S. Ct. 668, 393 U.S. 1041 (1968); *Leonard* v. *School Committee of Atteboro*, supra note 83; *Mercer* v. *Board of Trustees*, 538 S.W.2d 201 (1976).

[124]*Brick* v. *Board of Education*, 305 F. Supp. 1316 (1969).

[125]*Nehaus* v. *Torrey*, 310 F. Supp. 192 (1970).

[126]*Black* v. *Cothren*, 316 F. Supp. 468 (1970); *Breen* v. *Kahl*, supra note 121; *Laine* v. *Dittman*, 259 N.E.2d 824, 125 Ill. App. 2d 136 (1974).

[127]*West Virginia State Board of Education* v. *Barnette*, 63 S. Ct. 1178, 319 U.S. 624 (1942).

[128]*Banks* v. *Board of Public Instruction*, 314 F. Supp. 285, S.D. Fla. (1970).

[129]*Board of Directors* v. *Green*, 147 N.W.2d 854, 259 Iowa 1260 (1967); *Estay* v. *Lafourche Parish School Board*, 230 So. 2d 443 (1969).

[130]*Kissick* v. *Garland Independent School District*, 330 S. W.2d 708 (1959); *State ex rel Baker* v. *Stevenson*, 189 N.E.2d 181, 27 Ohio App. 2d 223 (1962).

[131]*Zablocki* v. *Redhail*, 434 U.S. 374 (1978).

[132]*Holt* v. *Shelton*, 341 F. Supp. 821 (1972).

[133]*Sturrup* v. *Maban*, 305 N.E.2d 877, 261 Ind. 463 (1974).

[134]*Indiana High School Athletic Association* v. *Raike*, 329 N.E.2d 66 (1975).

[135]45 CFR §83.37 (1988).

## Leaving School Grounds

Questions about the right of school officials to operate "open" or "closed" campuses often arise, normally over whether students may leave the school grounds during the lunch hour or other blocks of time during which they are not in class. Schools again have substantial discretion in operating the school and may prohibit students from leaving the grounds during school hours. Such rules may validly prevent some students from having their noon meals with their parents[136] or cause them difficulty in transacting legitimate business away from the school.[137] Similarly, the school can validly prevent students who drive to school from using their automobiles during the lunch hour unless they receive special permission.[138] Even if students are permitted to leave the grounds at that time, school officials may validly prohibit them from patronizing restaurants near the school.[139] Relevant to this issue are those of school liability for students. Schools have been found potentially liable for a student's injury when school was left without permission.[140] California now has a constitutional amendment creating a right for all students to a "safe, secure and peaceful" school.[141] School officials have supervisory responsibilities, then, that involve protecting students from injuries caused by other students or outsiders. School policies on leaving campus will very likely be influenced by its possible liability and increasing attention to students' rights to safety.[142]

## Search and Seizure

The legality of a search and seizure in the school usually arises when school officials search a student, or his or her locker, and find drugs or other contraband. The legal issue is whether the search was legally conducted so that evidence found during the search may be used against the student either in criminal or school disciplinary proceedings. Under criminal procedures, if the search was illegal, the evidence is typically excluded. To show an illegal search and seizure, the person (defendant) must show both that the search was conducted by government action and that it was unreasonable. It is less clear that illegally seized evidence must be excluded in school disciplinary hearings.[143]

After substantial confusion and contrary judicial rulings had reigned for many years, the Supreme Court finally entered this arena with the 1985 *New Jersey* v. *T.L.O.* decision.[144] The facts of the case were unextraordinary, involving a student turned over to the police after a school administrator's search found drugs and associated paraphernalia. The Supreme Court held that although students are protected by the Fourth Amendment, searches by school officials would not require a warrant nor would the "probable cause to search" standard apply. Instead, school personnel may rely on a "reasonable suspicion" to justify a search to discover violations of school rules or the law.

The *T.L.O.* decision resolves much of the prior confusion but still makes discretionary judgments quite important at the school level.[145] For instance, some courts have been hostile to schoolwide searches with dogs and to strip searches of students.[146] Any search involves invasion of the student's privacy; thus, the justification for a particular search and the degree of invasiveness will be crucial in determining its reasonableness. A highly unreasonable search

---

[136]*Ambroggio* v. *Board of Education*, 427 N.E.2d 1027 (Ill. App. 1981).

[137]*Christian* v. *Jones*, 100 So. 99, 211 Ala. 161 (1924).

[138]*McLean Independent School District* v. *Andres*, 333 S.W.2d 886 (1960).

[139]*Casey County Board of Education* v. *Luster*, 282 S.W.2d 333 (1955).

[140]*Hoyem* v. *Manhattan Beach City School District*, 585 P.2d 851 (Cal. 1978).

[141]Cal. Const. art. 1, §28(C).

[142]See, generally, G. Nicholson, J. Rapp, & F. Carrington, Campus safety: A legal imperative, *Education Law Reporter*, *33*, 981 (1986).

---

[143]Compare *Jones* v. *Latexo Independent School District*, 499 F. Supp. 223 (E.D. Tex. 1980), applying the exclusionary rule, with *Morale* v. *Griegel*, 422 F. Supp. 988 (D.N.H. 1976).

[144]*New Jersey* v. *T.L.O.*, 195 S. Ct. 733 (1985).

[145]For a thorough discussion of the complexities of school searches, see T. van Geel, *The Courts and American Education Law* (Buffalo, NY: Prometheus Books, 1987), pp. 327–336.

[146]See, for example, *Jones* v. *Latexo Independent School District*, supra note 143; *Doe* v. *Renfrow*, 475 F. Supp. 1012 (N.D. 1979), aff'd in part, 631 F.2d 91 (7th Cir. 1980), *cert. denied*, 451 U.S. 1022 (1981).

could well lead to individual and school liability.[147]

A new aspect of efforts to control drug-related behavior in schools is demanding urine samples from students, as well as employees. Courts have seen such cases as a potential invasion of privacy. When schools have sought urine samples, the standards of *T.L.O.* must be nominally satisfied.[148]

## Freedom of Speech

In *Tinker* v. *Des Moines Community School District*,[149] the U.S. Supreme Court spoke directly to the issue of the relationship between the school's right to regulate students' conduct and the student's constitutionally protected freedom of speech and expression.[150] The Court specifically affirmed that such protections did extend to students in the public schools. Students may not be regarded by the schools as "closed circuit" receptors of only that information to which the school wishes to expose them, nor may students be prohibited from expressing viewpoints other than those accepted by the school. The Court noted that the principle of the vigilant protection of constitutional freedom is nowhere more vital than in the schools, and it is applicable both to

orderly discussions in the classrooms and to communications among students Finally, the right of free expression attaches beyond the classroom to other activities that occur during the school day. At any time, the student has a right to free expression as long as it does not materially and substantially interfere with the orderly conduct of the educational process.

The school can prohibit student expression only when it may materially and substantially disrupt discipline in the school. The school must show that its action was motivated by more than an undifferentiated fear or apprehension that such expression would disrupt the school or a mere desire to avoid the discomfort and unpleasantness that accompanies the expression of an unpopular opinion. The school may, however, prohibit or punish any conduct by a student, in class or out, that materially disrupts classwork or involves substantial disorder of the school or an invasion of the rights of other students. *Tinker* has been an enormously important case, in part because it clearly accords constitutional protections to students; consequently, it has spawned a huge volume of cases. Two important concepts arose out of *Tinker* and its myriad progeny concerning students' freedom of speech and expression. First, the burden of proof concerning the reasonableness of school regulations is on school officials. Thus, if a student chooses to litigate the validity of such a regulation, the court will require school officials to demonstrate a reasonable basis for their interference with the student's life. In addition, the courts will not accept the bare testimony of school officials that students' expressions would be disruptive.[151] Second, if a student is subject to disciplinary action because of a violation of such a regulation, the school must proceed carefully to ensure that justice is done. Because such actions involve the infringement of a basic constitutional right, disciplinary action must be considered on a case-by-case basis, taking into account the particular and often unique facts of each case.

In applying the principles of *Tinker* to specific activities of students in the schools, several distinctions arise in how the courts treat particu-

---

[147]*Doe* v. *Renfrow*, id. Justice Brennan, in dissenting to denial of certiorari, commented that a strip search of the 13-year-old female plaintiff violated not only her constitutional rights but also "any known standard of human decency." 451 U.S. 1022 (Brennan, J., dissenting).

[148]*Odenheim* v. *Carlstadt-East Rutherford Regional School District*, 510 A.2d 709 (N.J. App. 1985); *Anable* v. *Ford*, 653 F. Supp. 22 (W.D. Ark, 1985).

[149]*Tinker* v. *Des Moines Independent Community School District*, 89 S. Ct. 733, 393 U.S. 503 (1968). High school students, however, may be treated differently than students in elementary schools or in college. Thus, high school students are seen as more adolescent and in a more immature stage of life and less able than college students to screen fact from propaganda. *Baker* v. *Board of Education*, 307 F. Supp. 517 (1969); *Widmar* v. *Vincent*, 454 U.S. 263 (1981).

[150]In discussing students' expressive activities, the courts have included under the First Amendment's protection direct speech acts, both written and oral, and "symbolic" speech acts, such as Tinker's black armband, buttons, and other emblems, and even remaining silent as a communicative act.

[151]*Burnside* v. *Byars*, 363 F.2d 744 (1966); *Eisner* v. *Stamford Board of Education*, 440 F.2d 803 (1971); *Tinker* v. *Des Moines Community School District*, supra note 82.

lar forms of expression. For instance, the courts have applied different standards to the production and distribution of printed material by students and the distribution of material not produced in the school. The latter may occur freely as long as it does not unreasonably disrupt normal school activities. However, school officials can lawfully regulate the times when and places where material may be distributed on the school grounds.[152] Thus, it has been held that the publication of off-campus newspapers and their disruption on or near school grounds cannot be prohibited if the school could show no disruptive influence on other students.[153] It has also been held that school officials may prohibit such material when its content goes beyond the bounds of decency, regardless of whether it is produced on or off school grounds.[154] School authority to regulate the use of facilities for non-school-related expressive activities will be influenced by previous conduct and current motives. That is, if a school generally encourages community use of the building, denying any group that use will raise the issue of improper motivation on the part of school officials (e.g., a desire to avoid controversial topics).[155] If the school does not create an "open forum" in school facilities, regulation can be more extensive.

For school-produced materials, it has been held that the school may validly establish a system of prior inspection and approval of material to be published by students.[156] The court did note, however, that such a procedure of prior restraint would be subject to very strict standards to guarantee the protection of students' rights. The school could prohibit distribution of material if it could show that either the material itself or the manner of its distribution would interfere with the operation of the school, cause violence or disorder, or constitute an invasion of the rights of others. To be constitutionally permissible, however, the school must have a formal procedure through which students can submit their material to school officials for prior approval. Specifically, the court noted that such a procedure would require (1) specification of the persons to whom such material would be submitted, (2) criteria by which school officials must make their decision, and (3) a stated period of time in which a decision would be made. In addition, the court required the regulation to define *distribution* and distinguish between public distribution or dissemination and the simple passing of information between friends and acquaintances.[157]

In *Trachtman* v. *Anker*[158] the Court upheld the decision of the school to prohibit the distribution of a questionnaire to students in the school. The project had been undertaken by the student newspaper to prepare an article on the sexual attitudes and practices of high school students. After reviewing the testimony of various witnesses (including several psychologists, acting as expert witnesses), the *Trachtman* court agreed that the questionnaire should not be distributed because of the probability that it would result in psychological harm to some students. As with many other similar cases, the court balanced the infringement of the students' rights of expression against the potential harm that might arise as a result of the exercise of that right, particularly given the "captive audience" of the students.

*Trachtman* suggests two other points concerning students' right of expression. First, in regard to student-produced school newspapers, the school may not exert arbitrary control over the content of the publications. Courts have keyed the degree of permissible regulation to a preliminary determination of whether the paper is intended to be an open forum for student opinion.[159] If it is, substantially less regulation is permissible than for papers described as integrally part of the school's curriculum and subject

---

[152]*Fujishima* v. *Board of Education*, 460 F.2d 1355 (1972); *Nitzberg* v. *Parks*, 525 F.2d 378 (1975); *Peterson* v. *Board of Education*, 370 F. Supp. 1208 (1973), *Sullivan* v. *Houston Independent School District*, 333 F. Supp. 1149 (1971). The court noted that the school may lawfully prohibit students from reading such material during class periods.

[153]*Scoville* v. *Board of Education*, 425 F.2d 10, cert. denied, 91 5. Ct. 51, 400 U.S. 826 (1970).

[154]*Baker* v. *Board of Education*, supra note 149.

[155]*Zuker* v. *Panitz*, 299 F. Supp. 102 (1969).

[156]*Eisner* v. *Stamford Board of Education*, supra note 151.

[157]Given such broad principles, case outcomes are necessarily inconsistent and are driven by contextual circumstances. Prior restraint is possible in schools, but a reviewing court must be persuaded that school officials acted in good faith and from proper motivations (i.e., to protect the education or safety of students).

[158]*Trachtman* v. *Anker*, 563 F.2d 512 (1977).

[159]*Gambino* v. *Fairfax County School*, 429 F. Supp. 731 (E.D. Va.), aff'd, 564 F.2d 157 (4th Cir. 1977).

to the school's comprehensive control of curriculum.[160] Unfortunately, there is an absence of clear-cut standards for determining the character of the newspaper. Second, censorship justified by a motive to protect students must take into account the students' age. In a recent case, censorship of articles about divorce and students' pregnancy on the grounds that the topics were inappropriate and that some students' privacy would be invaded was held unconstitutional, in part because the students were in high school.[161] The protective arguments of school officials were simply unpersuasive to the court.

That courts are still concerned about the special environment of the school and maintaining the authority of school officials is illustrated by the Supreme Court's 1986 decision, *Bethel School District* v. *Fraser*.[162] The Court upheld the school's decision to discipline a student whose speech at a school assembly was made up of unsubtle sexual innuendo. The Court emphasized the school's responsibility for inculcating norms of civility, as well as the disruption and invasion of other students' rights by the speech. These students were viewed as a "captive audience" to the student speaker, a concept that has earned judicial solicitude when the expressive conduct might be viewed as offensive or intrusive to other students. The decision can be interpreted as an application of the long-established principle that schools may reasonably enforce time, place, and manner restrictions on students' expression.[163]

One final area of students' speech activities ties into the multifaceted conflicts over religious activities in public schools. On the one hand, although the Supreme Court invalidated an Alabama statute that required a daily moment of "meditation or prayer," the decision in no way implied that students are prohibited from engaging individually in voluntary prayer during the school day.[164] On the other hand, as with other expressive acts, the prayer may not disrupt the educational process (e.g., an audible prayer during an examination).

A more complicated, unresolved issue is posed by groups of students who request school recognition as an organization or the use of school facilities for religious activities. The Supreme Court reviewed a federal appellate court's decision that such groups should be denied recognition and other privileges accorded to student groups by the school to preserve church-state separation values. Unfortunately, the Supreme Court's decision was on procedural matters only, leaving conflicts among lower court decisions.[165] It is enough to say that the regulation of students' prayers (when no adult participation or school sponsorship is involved) raises very delicate constitutional concerns.[166]

In sum, *Tinker* might be seen as loosing a cacophony of voices in the school by legitimizing students' speech under the First Amendment. It certainly precipitated a flood of interpretive cases, as new speech rights and new roles were renegotiated at the school level. Much remains tentative (and perhaps always will) in students' expressive rights. Most recently, in *Bethel School District* v. *Fraser*, the Supreme Court apparently settled that the texture of speech, if not the ideational content, can largely be determined as a school prerogative. For example, a school could punish a student's vulgarity in protesting a school policy as unfair, but without vulgarity the protest might be constitutionally protected. Decisions also tend to indicate that mechanisms (or fo-

---

[160]Id. Even if a school newspaper is explicitly curricular and subject to substantial school regulation, a school would still be subject to the restrained standard that it cannot act in a wholly arbitrary and capricious manner.

[161]*Hazelwood School District v. Kuhlmeier*, 484 U.S. 260 (1988). This does not imply that there are no limits; some material or expression is unsuitable to a student at any level of public school.

[162]*Fraser v. Bethel School District*, 106 S. Ct. 3159 (1986).

[163]See, for example, *Sullivan* v. *School District*, 307 F. Supp. 1328 (S.D. Tex. 1969).

[164]*Wallace* v. *Jaffee*, 105 S. Ct. 2479 (1985). Any effort to regulate a student's prayers should be subject to free speech analysis under *Tinker* v. *Des Moines*. Cf. *Widmar* v. *Vincent*, supra note 149, applying free speech analysis in a college.

[165]106 S. Ct. 1326 (1986). The Court reversed the prohibition of the student group, but on the ground that the school board member who appealed the trial court's decision did not have standing to appeal. The substantive question of school-recognized religious groups remains unanswered.

[166]In 1984, Congress passed the Equal Access Act, ensuring the right of student groups and others to hold religious, political, and philosophical meetings in public schools. 20 U.S.C. §4071 (1984). See R. Brandley & F. Delon, Influence of the Equal Access Act on school facilities usage policies, *Education Law Reporter*, *34*, 653 (1987).

rums) for students' speech, once created, may still be partially controllable but rarely can be wholly constrained by the wishes and sensibilities of school authorities.

## Privacy

A student's right to privacy involves two related topics. The first has to do with the files compiled on students throughout their academic careers. Of concern here is who is allowed access to these files and to whom information contained in them is released. The second topic is the confidentiality of students' actions when dealing with particular school officials. The rights that are accorded to students under these categories help define the relationship between the student and the school.

Traditionally, a student's academic files were closed to both the student and the parent. The policy of keeping such information at least partly confidential was based on custom, not law. Many other individuals associated with the school were allowed to inspect students' files at their convenience, even if they were not teaching the students or had no other close and direct contact with them. In addition, the schools often permitted outside organizations open access to students' files, even organizations interested only for commercial or business purposes.

There were at least two very real problems with such a procedure. First, fundamental educational decisions were often made for the student on the basis of information contained in his or her file. Because parents had no access to the file, they were unable to participate in informed choices for their children's future. Also, parents had no way of knowing what information the school keep in the file and its accuracy. Second, parents had absolutely no control over the dissemination of information from their children's educational files. They could not prohibit the school from releasing information about them and their children, and they did not know what individuals or organizations had obtained access and what information they had obtained.

These and other associated problems were finally addressed by the Family Educational Rights and Privacy Act (FERPA) of 1974, sometimes known as the Buckley Amendments. The purpose of this act was to give parents access to the educational records of their children, and it applies to all schools that receive federal financial assistance from the U.S. Department of Educa-

tion.[167] The FERPA requirements include the adoption of school policies for (a) informing parents or eligible students of their rights under FERPA; (b) facilitating access to educational records by parents or eligible students, as well as providing information on the types of data kept in the records and procedures for gaining access to them; (c) permitting parents or eligible students to review education records, request changes in the records, and schedule a hearing if the proposed changes are disallowed; and (d) ensuring that institutions do not give out personally identifiable information to outside bodies without the express written consent of the parents or eligible student.[168]

In its most general sense, FERPA allows parents access to all the educational records of their children. There has, however, been some dispute about what information constitutes an educational record. This dilemma has been particularly contested in the area of school psychology therapy and testing. According to the act, some records are not subject to disclosure to parents if they are the personal files of psychologists or teachers, and the information contained in these files is not available to any other school personnel.[169] Consequently, parental access to therapy and testing information hinges on the level of exclusivity accorded to these records by school professionals.

The act also dictates who may request access to students' educational records. Although FERPA allows for "eligible students" to have access to their own records, eligible students are only those individuals over 18 years of age or who are attending postsecondary school.[170] This does not mean that school officials cannot release these records to students if they think it is appropriate but rather that school administrators have no legal obligation to disseminate this information to students. Unlike the case for students, FERPA grants noncustodial parents access to their children's educational records.[171] When FERPA does not apply to a specific case (i.e., the private and exclusive files of a school psycholo-

---

[167]L. Fischer and G. Sorenson, *School Law for Counselors, Psychologists, and Social Workers* (3rd ed.) (New York: Longman 1996), p. 89.

[168]CRF 99.5.

[169]Supra note 167 at 90.

[170]34 CRF 99.31.

[171]34 CRF 99.3.

gist), it is not currently clear under what situations a school may refrain from divulging this information to a custodial or noncustodial parent. This decision will probably depend on the express policies for the dissemination of records that are adopted by a particular school.[172]

In the course of an educational career, a student may have many opportunities to interact with teachers and other school personnel on a basis other than that of student and teacher. For instance, a student may take advantage of a variety of counseling services offered by the school, may consult medical practitioners employed by the state, or may relate personal problems to a teacher. A question that often arises in these circumstances concerns the degree of confidentiality a student may expect for various communications with school personnel.

The first issue is the confused, frequently mistaken use of the terms *confidential* or *privileged*. These terms are often incorrectly employed as synonyms to generally describe the nature of communications between a therapist and a client or patient. In fact, the confidentiality of a communication refers only to the therapist's ethical and/or legal duty to keep secret the information obtained from a client in the course of a professional relationship. A breach of this duty may be grounds for a civil lawsuit against the therapist. The therapist may, however, be forced to divulge confidential communications in the course of a legal proceeding unless these communications are privileged. Confidential communications become privileged only if a law provides that such information cannot be disclosed in a legal proceeding without the client's express consent. Obviously there would be no liability for information divulged during the course of a legal proceeding if the therapist was requested to testify and if the information was not privileged. In addition, if the information is not privileged according to state law, assurances of confidentiality made by the professional to the client will not provide privileged protection.[173]

The degree of confidentiality may depend on the content of the communication, the profession or occupation of the individual to whom the communication was made, the particular ethical standards of the professional to whom the communication was made, the relationship of the two parties involved in the communication, and the extent to which the communication was shared with other persons.[174] If a communication involves information that may bear on the commission of a felony, nearly all states now require recipients to report it to law enforcement officials. Thus, if a student relates violations of drug laws to school officials, he or she should have no expectation that the information will be confidential. Even for attorneys and clients there is no confidentiality or privilege for information that may further a crime. Similarly, all states require all public officials, including school personnel, to report incidents of suspected child abuse. If students communicate such information to school authorities, they cannot expect it to remain confidential.[175]

Students' communications with a school counselor or psychologist may fall within a state's recognized privilege, yet this would not alter the rule concerning the reporting of felonies or the physical or sexual abuse of a child. A word of caution is in order here about the coverage extended by such statutes. Although all 50 states and the federal courts recognize some form of the psychotherapist-parent privilege, these statutes rarely explicitly cover student–school psychologist and student-counselor interactions. Yet, unlike most privileges, the trend has been for courts to increase rather than decrease the types of communications and types of professionals afforded the psychotherapist-patient privilege. Most recently, in *Redmond v. Jaffee*, the U.S. Supreme Court recognized the psychotherapist-parent privilege for the first time and extended it to therapy conducted by social workers, as well as by psychiatrists and psychologists. In this ruling the Supreme Court did not explicitly address the privilege of school counselors or school psychologists, but it did leave the door open for the expansion of the psychotherapist-patient privilege to other pro-

---

[172]Supra note 1 at 25.

[173]See K. Hogan, A look at the psychotherapist-patient privilege, *Family Advocacy Journal*, *14*, 31 (1991).

[174]For a more detailed description of confidentiality concerns with school-age children, see M. Dekraai, B. Sales, & S. Hall. (1998). Informed consent, confidentiality, and duty to report laws in the conduct of child therapy. In T. R. Kratochwill, & R. J. Morris (Eds.), *The practice of child therapy* (3rd Ed.) (pp. 540–559). Boston, MA: Allyn and Bacon.

[175]Interest in controlling child abuse has made those statutes a pervasive reality in educators' lives. There is little research that evaluates the statutes' effects. Cf. F. Lombard, M. Michlak, & T. Pearlman, Identifying the abused child: A study of reporting practices of teachers, *University of Detroit Law Review*, *63*, 657 (1986).

fessionals. In contrast to the federal court standard, some state statutes cover only physicians and surgeons; others include licensed clinical psychologists; still others include counselors and psychometrists. A student would be well advised to consider the legal status of the individual he or she intends to confide in if the information is potentially damaging. Also, states vary in the extent of the privilege extended by their statutes. Most states extend the privilege only when the information was communicated in the course of a professional relationship to treat or diagnose a person's mental or emotional problems.[176] Other states specifically extend the privilege to counselors, psychologists, and psychological examiners in the schools and thus protect communications made to them by students.

Yet even if a court recognizes that a privilege exists for specific types of communications between a student and a counselor or a student and a school psychologist, this does not necessarily mean that the school professional will be protected from divulging the privileged information. The great majority of privilege statutes do not act as absolute bars to the disclosure of the privileged communication to the court or other parties in court proceedings.[177] Most jurisdictions use a balancing test to determine whether privileged communications should be disclosed in court. The balancing tests vary from jurisdiction to jurisdiction but generally mandate disclosure "if in the interests of justice, the evidentiary need for disclosure outweighs the patient's privacy interest."[178] The exact factors used to make this balancing determination are also subject to wide variation according to jurisdiction, as are the procedures (hearing, in camera review by the judge, etc.) used by the court to decide this issue.[179]

In addition, even if a privilege statute protects a communication between a student and a counselor and the court determines that the interests of justice protect this communication from disclosure, a client always has the right to waive the privilege and divulge the information. In child and adolescent counseling this is an extremely tricky issue because it is not clear who holds the privilege, the adolescent or the parent. Most courts recognize that for young children, parents make their treatment and counseling decisions and therefore hold the privilege of determining whether certain information should be disclosed. Traditionally, the courts also gave the parents of any child that was under the age of majority (age 18 in most jurisdictions) the right to waive or evoke the child's rights. More recently, however, there is a growing trend that allows adolescents to make their own treatment decisions.[180] A few jurisdictions have enacted "mature minor" laws, which allows adolescents who are near the age of majority and are able to understand the nature and effect of their decisions to make their own treatment decisions. Likewise, other jurisdictions have promulgated or recognized rules that allow "emancipated minors," minors who have become independent from their parents by living on their own, marrying, or joining the armed forces, the right to make their own treatment decisions.[181] Unfortunately, it is currently unclear how far this movement will reach. Consequently, a therapist or school counselor who treats adolescents must pay special attention to the statutes and court decisions that control this issue in his or her jurisdiction. It should also be noted, however, that a counselor or psychologist may also have an independent duty to warn others if he or she feels that a client may be dangerous to some other person.[182]

---

[176]Under such a statute, it is unclear whether a communication between a student and a school psychologist or counselor would be protected.

[177]A. Pettolina, Defining the standard for abrogating the psychotherapist-patient privilege, *Maryland Law Review*, 695 55, (1996). But see *Redmond* v. *Jaffee* 116 S. Ct. 1923, in which the U.S. Supreme Court treats the psychotherapist-patient privilege as an absolute bar to the disclosure of privileged information for the federal courts.

[178]This was the standard used by the Seventh Circuit court decision of *Redmond* v. *Jaffee*. The lower court determined that the interest of justice did outweigh the patient's privacy interest, and consequently, the social worker was compelled by the court to divulge her privileged communications with her client. This balancing test for federal courts was later overturned by the U.S. Supreme Court in favor of an absolute bar to disclosure.

[179]Supra note 175 at 701.

[180]A full analysis of this area of law is well beyond the scope of this chapter. For a more detailed recitation of issues relevant to child therapy decisions, see M. DeKraii, B. Sales, & S. Hall, *Informed Consent, Confidentiality, and Duty to Report Laws in the Conduct of Child Therapy*, supra note 174.

[181]Id. at 5.

[182]*Tarasoff* v. *Regents of the University of California*, 33 Cal. App. 3d 275 (1973).

In summary,[183] it is simply not clear how much confidentiality a student may expect in dealings with school personnel. It depends on the nature of the communication, to whom the communication is directed, and the particular status of state law. It is important that school personnel explain the limits of confidentiality clearly to students before a potentially damaging revelation occurs. As noted, some information must be divulged by a school official, even though a parent or other nonschool person could keep silent. It is unlikely that most students will be cognizant of such distinctions.[184]

# DISCIPLINE AND PUNISHMENT

Under the general mandate to operate the public school, school officials may exercise the necessary disciplinary authority to ensure that the school's educational purposes are achieved. In doing so, the school may delegate to teachers as much disciplinary power as necessary to ensure order in the classroom. It is also generally held that teachers may reasonably exercise their disciplinary power without seeking formal approval or sanction from school officials.[185] The authority of the school to discipline students certainly exists during school hours. There is also authority, although much older, to exercise control over students between their homes and the school and to discipline or punish students for acts of misconduct occurring on the way to or from school.[186]

The justification for the school to discipline students for misconduct occurring outside of school hours is not clear. On the one hand, some cases have suggested that the school may discipline a student for such behavior if it directly affects the reputation, order, and welfare of the school.[187] On the other hand, it has also been argued that it does not make sense to extend the authority of the school to such lengths if it is based on the theory that such behavior interferes with the orderly process of education.[188] In *Sullivan* the Court noted that school officials did not have the authority to judge students' behavior either in their own homes or on the street corner. The student is subject to the same civil and criminal sanctions as other citizens, and a person's status as a student should not subject him or her to a higher standard of behavior than is applied to other citizens.

During school hours a teacher has the authority to punish a student for any behavior that is detrimental to the order and best interests of the school and for the breach of any rule or regulation that is within the power of the school to adopt. It is not necessary for the school to formally adopt and publish rules and regulations. In addition, a student may be punished for conduct that is technically not a violation of any explicit or recognized school rule. It is only necessary that the school have the power to adopt such a rule, not that the school has exercised its power.[189] Students cannot, however, be disciplined for the breach of an unreasonable regulation or one that was beyond their power of compliance. Nor should students be disciplined for a breach of school rules committed at the request of their parents. For example, a student may refuse to participate in certain required school activities because of the directives of a parent. In such cases, disciplinary actions against the student are not appropriate.[190] What method school officials or teachers choose to discipline students is largely a matter of discretion. Students may be required to perform extra

---

[183]A relatively recent federal law attempts to protect students' and parents' privacy by regulating school use of psychological and psychiatric testing and requiring parental access to curricular materials. 20 U.S.C. §1232h (1985).

[184]Cf. L. Fischer & G. Sorensen, *School Law for Counselors, Psychologists, and Social Workers* (New York: Longman, 1985).

[185]*Leonard v. School Committee of Attleboro*, supra note 83; *People v. Jackson*, 319 N.Y.S.2d 731 (1971).

[186]*Kinzer v. Independent School District*, 105 N.W. 686, 129 Iowa 441 (1906); *Jones v. Cody*, 92 N.W. 495, 132 Mich. 13 (1902).

[187]*R.R. v. Board of Education*, 263 A.2d 180, 109 N.J. Super. 337 (1970).

[188]*Sullivan v. Houston Independent School District*, supra note 152.

[189]*Sims v. Board of Education*, 329 F. Supp. 678 (1971). Of course, most school policies will contain some broadly phrased language, such as prohibiting "behavior detrimental to the order of the school." A wide variety of behavior can be punished under such language.

[190]It is not clear, however, that in such circumstances, the student cannot legally be punished. If the misconduct is by the parent, the child may not be punished for parental actions. *St. Ann v. Palisi*, 495 F.2d 423 (5th Cir. 1974).

schoolwork, to consult with a principal or other school official about their misconduct, or to have their parents come to the school for a disciplinary conference. A student may be excluded from attending a particular class or may be detained after class. Students may also be subjected to corporal punishment administered by the teacher or other school official.[191] Subject to a general standard of reasonableness, the form of discipline or punishment is left to the discretion and creativity of the teacher or school official. Because discipline involves the invasion of various student interests (e.g., liberty and privacy), there is always a possibility that a particular disciplinary decision can be successfully challenged. By and large, however, courts remain quite deferential to schools' decisions,[192] although three particular forms of discipline have been the subject of concern: detention, corporal punishment, and the use of drugs to control in-school behavior.

Detention after the dismissal of the other students, as a penalty for misconduct, has long been an accepted and generally recognized method of enforcing school rules and regulations. If detention is imposed in good faith, without malicious motives, it does not constitute "false imprisonment" or "unlawful detention." This is true even though the teacher and school officials were completely mistaken about the correctness of their decision.[193]

The use of corporal punishment as a means of enforcing discipline and punishing students' misconduct has increasingly been a special concern. It has long been held that corporal punishment was a legitimate tool for a teacher or school official to employ. To allow the school to ensure order, the courts have held that corporal punishment was necessary for the prompt enforcement of the teacher's orders.[194] However, the power of the school to use corporal punishment has come under attack. Lawsuits questioned whether the use of corporal punishment usurped a right belonging only to the parent. There were questions about what procedural rights must be afforded to students and their parents before corporal punishment could be imposed (e.g., was the school required to give notice to both and to provide an opportunity to be represented at a hearing before corporal punishment could be used?). Finally, teachers and school officials were concerned about their own personal civil liability (i.e., for assault and battery for the wrongful imposition of corporal punishment).

The U.S. Supreme Court, in *Ingraham* v. *Wright*,[195] affirmed the right of public school teachers and officials to use corporal punishment. The Court noted that the paddling of students as a means of maintaining school discipline does not constitute cruel and unusual punishment under the Eighth Amendment to the U.S. Constitution because that amendment was designed to protect persons convicted of crimes. Extension of Eighth Amendment protections to ban corporal punishment in the schools was unwarranted because the schools are open to public scrutiny and are supervised by the community through local boards of education. In addition, the acts and behavior of teachers and school officials are subject to the same legal constraints as all other citizens. Thus, if they exceed their authority, they are subject to civil or criminal liability.[196]

In deciding *Ingraham*, the Court also resolved many of the questions posed about the use of corporal punishment. The Court ruled that procedural safeguards, including notice to parents or a hearing, are not constitutionally required.[197] While the schools do have the authority to impose corporal punishment, it must be reasonable and within the bounds of moderation. It must not be cruel or excessive, and the teacher or school official must not act wantonly

---

[191]Discipline should not be excessive or humiliating. School officials are subject to liability for assault and battery or for intentional infliction of emotional distress. *Mott* v. *Endicott School District*, 713 P.2d 98 (Wash. 1986); *Jefferson* v. *Ysleta Independent School District*, 817 F.2d 303 (5th Cir. 1987).

[192]*Board of Education of Rogers, Arkansas* v. *McCluskey*, 102 S. Ct. 3469 (1982); *Petry* v. *Flaughter*, 505 F. Supp. 1087 (E.D. Ky. 1981).

[193]*Fertich* v. *Michener*, supra note 111.

[194]*Carr* v. *Wright*, 423 S.W.2d 521 (1968); *Drum* v. *Miller*, 47 S.E. 421, 135 N.C. 204 (1904); *Marlar* v. *Bill*, 178 S.W.2d 634, 181 Tenn. 100 (1944).

[195]*Ingraham* v. *Wright*, 97 S. Ct. 1401, 430 U.S. 651 (1976).

[196]They are also subject to dismissal. *Mott* v. *Endicott School District*, supra note 191.

[197]The court took judicial notice that the purposes to be served by corporal punishment would be long past if formal notice, hearings, and representation were required, and due process interests were protected by the availability of state law remedies (i.e., civil liability).

or from malice or passion.[198] The punishment, in each case, should be proportional to the seriousness of the offense,[199] the apparent motive and disposition of the student,[200] and the degree of his or her influence on the conduct of other students. Consideration must also be given to the age, size, sex, and physical strength of the student.[201]

The Court recognized the common law right of a student not to be subjected to excessive punishment in school. Teachers and school officials must exercise prudence and restraint in the initial decision to use corporal punishment. Corporal punishment must have appeared to be reasonably necessary in the circumstances of each incident. If the punishment inflicted is later found by a court to have been excessive (i.e., not reasonably believed at the time to be necessary for the student's discipline or training), the teacher or school officials responsible for administering the punishment may be held liable for damages to the student.[202] Finally, if malice on the part of school officials or teachers can be shown, they may be subject to criminal penalties.[203]

In general, issues created by corporal punishment are state law matters.[204] One exception, after *Ingraham*, has been litigation brought in federal courts seeking relief under the Fourteenth Amendment's due process clause for particularly brutal or harmful acts. Students have occasionally claimed that an act of corporal punishment was so brutal and inhumane that it deprived them of liberty without due process of law. Federal courts have split in resolving that question.[205] Otherwise, whether corporal punishment will be used is resolved usually by state legislatures. If corporal punishment is permitted, parental objections are not a barrier;[206] conversely where prohibited, teachers have no right to use it for classroom control.[207]

A problematic disciplinary method employed with some students is the use of stimulant drugs, particularly Ritalin (methylphenidate). These amphetamines do not have the same effect on all people. For certain individuals, proponents claim, instead of accelerating their behavioral activity, the drug slows them down and makes them more controllable. This kind of drug therapy is claimed to work especially well for children who have been diagnosed as hyperactive-hyperkinetic or minimally brain damaged.

The truly hyperkinetic child presents a serious disciplinary problem for the teacher and the school. In class, the child seems incapable of sitting still for the normal course of instruction. Such children are often singled out for their inability to cope with a structured classroom, and the school often recommends to the parents that some form of treatment be sought. Frequently, school officials recommend some form of drug therapy to help the child conform to the expectations of the school. The problem arises when parents resist or refuse to have such drugs administered to their children, and the school refuses to allow them to attend classes until something is done to control their misbehavior. The issue is whether the school can lawfully refuse to allow children in classes until or unless their parents seek some form of drug or other therapy for them. To our knowledge, the courts have not de-

---

[198]*Carr* v. *Wright*, supra note 194; *Houeye* v. *St. Helena Parish School Board*, 67 So. 2d 553, La. 966 (1953); *Suits* v. *Glover*, 71 So. 2d 49, 260 Ala. 449 (1954); *Tinkham* v. *Kole*, 110 N.W.2d 258, 252 Iowa 1303 (1961).

[199]*Lander* v. *Seaver*, 32 Vt. 114 (1859); *State* v. *Mizner*, 50 Iowa 145 (1878).

[200]*Calway* v. *Williamson*, 36 A.2d 377, 130 Conn. 575 (1944); *Patterson* v. *Nutter*, 7 A. 273, 78 Me. 509 (1886).

[201]*Boyd* v. *State*, 7 So. 268, 88 Ala. 169 (1890); *Calaway* v. *Williamson*, supra note 200: *Melen* v. *McLaughlin*, 176 A. 297, 107 Vt. 111 (1935); *Suits* v. *Glover*, supra note 198.

[202]*Wood* v. *Strickland*, 95 S. Ct. 992, 420 U.S. 308 (1975).

[203]*People* v. *Wehmeyer*, 509 N.E.2d 605, 108 Ill. Dec. 909, 605 (111. App. 1987).

[204]A few state legislatures have prohibited corporal punishment in all public schools. See, for example, Mass. Gen. Laws Ann., c. 71 §37G (1985); N. J. Stat. Ann. 18A:6-1 (1968). Most states permit local boards to decide whether their schools will use corporal punishment.

---

[205]The Fifth Circuit has decided that *all* such cases will be handled under state law. *Ingraham* v. *Wright*, 498 F.2d 248 (5th Cir. 1974). The Fourth and Tenth Circuits will allow federal courts to hear claims involving school acts that "shock the conscience." *Hall* v. *Tawney*, 621 F.2d 607 (4th Cir. 1980); *Garcia* v. *Miera*, 817 F.2d 650 (10th Cir. 1987).

[206]*Baker* v. *Owen*, 395 F. Supp. 294 (M.D.N.C.), aff'd mem., 423 U.S. 907 (1975).

[207]*Belasco* v. *Board of Education*, 486 A.2d 538 (Pa. Commw. Ct. 1985).

cided a case based on this issue, and it is difficult to predict how such a case would be decided.[208]

Certainly, the school has the authority to exercise those powers of control, restraint, and correction necessary to accomplish the purposes of education, including maintaining discipline and order in the classroom. To accomplish these purposes, as seen in the following section, the school may lawfully suspend or expel a student for violations of school rules and regulations. It seems likely, then, that a school could take whatever steps were necessary to control the behavior of a persistently misbehaving student. On the one hand, if the student's behavior could be shown to be a disruptive influence on other students, so that a teacher could not teach, the school would be within its right to exclude this student from classes until the behavior was under control. On the other hand, it seems unclear how the school would justify excluding a student until he or she obtained one particular kind of treatment (e.g., Ritalin therapy). This certainly seems like an usurpation of a parental right. One legal commentator has argued at length that the school has absolutely no right to coerce the use of Ritalin as a behavior control method.[209]

## Suspension and Expulsion

Generally, the right to attend a public school is conditioned on compliance with the reasonable rules and regulations established by school officials. Unless a student is willing to adhere to these requirements, the school may legally suspend or expel the student.[210] In most states local school officials are given the authority to determine which offenses merit suspension or expulsion and whether such offenses have occurred. The school is limited, however, by the restriction that its actions in both instances be reasonable. The power of school officials to suspend or expel a student is not limited to those cases in which a formally adopted rule has been violated. Subject to the restriction that they not be arbitrary, school officials may suspend or expel a student any time it is required by the best interests of the school as a whole.[211] Since teachers and principals also have a duty to maintain discipline and order in the classroom and school, they may have the power to suspend a student. In most cases, however, a teacher's recommendation to suspend or expel a student is subject to review by the principal or the local board of education. A principal may usually take some actions involving suspension without review by other school authorities.

As noted, subject to a limitation of reasonableness, a student may be suspended or expelled for violating any rule or regulation or for any other misconduct that disrupts the school's purpose. Several specific grounds for suspension and expulsion have received the attention of the courts more frequently than others. For instance, the courts have consistently held that a student may be suspended or expelled for the use of profane or obscene language, particularly if directed at school personnel. Courts have held that "fighting" words and words that are lewd, obscene, profane, and libelous are not safeguarded by the constitution in a public school.[212]

---

[208]*Cole* v. *Greenfield-Central Community Schools*, 657 F. Supp. 56 (S.D. Ind. 1986), might be suggestive of some courts' attitude. There, the conduct of a nine-year old, hyperactive, emotionally disturbed child was controlled by a variety of techniques, including paddling, isolation in the classroom, denial of field trips, and taping the child's mouth shut. All but the last were approved by the court, which observed that a school "cannot be subjugated by the tyrannical behavior of a nine-year-old child." 657 F. Supp. at 63. Normally, such a child will now be protected by the procedures of P.L. 94-142.

[209]J. E. Jackson, The coerced use of Ritalin for behavior control in public schools: Legal challenges, *Clearinghouse Review*, pp. 181–193 (1976). This chapter does not cover the legal limitations placed on the use of other intervention techniques since that topic is covered in Chapter 41. To the extent that a child was protected under P.L. 94-142, the school's discretion to exclude would be significantly reduced.

[210]*Board of Education* v. *Bentley*, 383 S.W.2d 677 (1964); *Flory* v. *Smith*, 134 S.E. 360, 145 Va. 164 (1926); *Nicholls* v. *Lynn*, 7 N.E.2d 577, 297 Mass. 65 (1973); *Texarkana Independent School District* v. *Lewis*, 470 S.W.2d 727 (1971).

[211]*Board of Education* v. *Booth*, 62 S.W. 872, 110 Ky. 807 (1901); *Douglass* v. *Campbell*, 116 S.W. 211, 89 Ark. 254 (1909): State ex rel *Dresser* v. *District Board*, 116 N.W. 232, 135 Wis. 619 (1908). The age of these cases should be noted. Suspension of students in the absence of their knowledge of the particular rule would raise procedural due process concerns today.

[212]*Fenton* v. *Stear*, supra note 95; *Fraser* v. *Bethel School District*, supra note 162.

It is unclear whether a school may legally suspend or expel a student for failing to maintain a prescribed grade-point average, however; given a student's interests in education, a court might well be skeptical of such a policy. It is also uncertain whether the school may reduce grades to punish misconduct.[213] It is clear, however, that the school may refuse to promote a student to the next grade or may demote the student to a lower grade. The best reasoning appears to be that it is the school's duty to attempt to educate a student, but the student's failure to achieve acceptable results is not grounds for suspension or expulsion.

Suspension or expulsion has been held proper in a variety of other circumstances. For instance, schools may take such action against a student because of excessive absence or tardiness without a satisfactory excuse,[214] gross disrespect and contempt for school officials, and being infested with head lice.[215] The most accurate generalization is that rule making is still largely a local function. Boards may regulate student conduct that they believe is harmful to the school. They may also establish the magnitude of punishment for violence. Given appropriate procedures of application, these decisions will rarely be dislodged by a court, even if harsh or ultimately injurious to the punished student.[216]

An important element of the suspension and expulsion process is the provision of adequate procedural due process rights to the student.

The U.S. Supreme Court, in *Goss* v. *Lopez*,[217] directly addressed this issue. In connection with a short suspension of a student (i.e., a five-day suspension), due process requires that the student be given oral or written notice of the charges, an explanation of the evidence, and an opportunity to explain his or her side of the story. The Court noted that at least these rudimentary protections are necessary to guard against unfair or mistaken charges of misconduct and arbitrary exclusion from school. To clarify its decision, the Court elaborated on the conditions appropriate to short suspensions: (1) there need be no time delay between giving "notice" to the student and holding the hearing—in the majority of cases, the school official may informally discuss the alleged violation with the student only moments after it has occurred; (2) in being given an opportunity to explain his or her version of events, a student must first be told the nature and basis of the accusation; and (3) since the hearing may occur almost immediately after the incident, the notice and hearing should normally precede removal of the student from school. The Court recognized that there were situations in which a student's continued presence in the school posed a danger to that student or to others, or constituted an ongoing threat to the school process; if so, the student may be immediately removed from the school. In such cases, the necessary notice and rudimentary hearing should follow as soon as possible.

Many states now have statutes or administrative regulations that provide more extensive procedural protections for students subject to suspension or expulsion. These procedures will vary, but at the most formal level they include the right to a preliminary hearing, notice of the charges, and a formal hearing at which the student may be represented by counsel and may confront and cross-examine witnesses. It has been held, however, that a student may be suspended without these hearings if there is a clear and present danger to the student's physical or emotional safety and well-being or it is necessary for the safety of others. A student may also waive a required hearing and accept the suspension or expulsion. In these cases the school should require a written waiver signed by both the student and a parent or guardian.

---

[213]Courts have split on this issue. Compare *New Braunfels Independent School District* v. *Armke*, 658 S.W.2d 330 (Text Civ. App. 1983), upholding reduction, with *Gutierrez* v. *School District 4-1*, 585 P.2d 935 (Col. App. 1978), disallowing.

[214]Courts have tolerated both suspensions and expulsions, as well as grade reductions based on absences and truancy, but not with consistency. *Raymon* v. *Alvord Independent School District*, 639 F.2d 257 (5th Cir. 1981); *Dorsey* v. *Bale*, 521 S.W.2d 76 (Ky. 1975).

[215]*Holman* v. *School District No. 5*, 43 N.W. 996, 71 Mich. 605 (1889).

[216]In *Board of Education of Rogers, Arkansas* v. *McCluskey*, supra note 192, the Supreme Court reminded lower federal courts to grant broad discretion to local boards in determining the needs of individual students and schools. When a board expels a child, called "academic capital punishment" by Mark Yudof, it is hardly acting on the "best interest of the child."

---

[217]*Goss* v. *Lopez*, 95 S. Ct. 729, 419 U.S. 565 (1974).

If the school decides to seek a longer suspension or an expulsion, the student should be given a formal notice of the charges. Although it need not be drawn as precisely as a legal document, the notice should contain a statement of the specific charges and the grounds on which suspension or expulsion will be based. Parents should be kept very closely informed of the proceedings against their children and given copies of all documents relating to the school's action.

Ample time should be allowed so that the student may examine the charges and prepare a defense by gathering evidence and witnesses. The time between notice and the formal hearing may be shortened at the request of the student.[218] When a hearing is required, there is no agreement about the exact format it must follow to satisfy constitutional requirements. Some courts have imposed close adherence to a judicial model; others have not. At a minimum, however, the student should have an adequate opportunity to present his or her own version of the incident. Many schools also require witnesses against the student to be present at the hearing and subject themselves to cross-examination.[219]

Issues arising from challenges to the adequacy of student hearings have generated persistent litigation. Given the enormous variability of factual contexts and the relative fluidity of due process concepts, it is very difficult to propose a generalization about judicial outcomes. Perhaps the best criterion to adopt as a guidepost is that students should have an opportunity to avoid unfair or erroneous deprivations of their educational interests. At bottom, procedures should comport with fundamental fairness.

In summary, although the school is required to provide due process under *Goss*, the nature of the hearing may vary as a function of the loss confronting the student. As the hearing moves from the principal's office to the district's board room, the degree of formality will increase commensurately. One issue yet to be resolved is whether "in-house" suspensions trigger due process requirements. If a loss of educational opportunity accompanies the in-house suspension, due process logically would be required.

When it can be shown that a student was wrongfully suspended or expelled from school, the teacher and school officials responsible for the action can be civilly liable for damages.[220] Alternatively, a student may seek a court order requiring readmission.[221] In all such cases, there is a presumption that the school officials acted reasonably and in good faith, and the student will have the burden of showing that the school acted maliciously or unreasonably.[222]

## GRADUATION AND DIPLOMA

When students have completed the prescribed course of studies in a public school system, they are entitled to a diploma or certificate of graduation.[223] What the diploma or certificate indicates about the students, however, depends on whether they live in a state that has adopted a "minimum competency testing" (MCT) program for the public school system. In a very general sense, competency testing involves the measurement (usually by test) of the degree of mastery of certain basic skills and satisfactory performance in functional literacy as designated by the state legislature or the state board of education. Upon completion of schooling and based on the results of competency tests, students would be awarded differentiated diplomas or certificates of atten-

---

[218]*Texarkana Independent School District* v. *Lewis*, supra note 210.

[219]*Tibbs* v. *Board of Education*, 276 A.2d 165, 114 N.J. Super. 287 (1971), although the court noted that questioning should be carefully controlled by the person in charge of the hearing to prevent abuse of the witnesses.

[220]Such liability would nominally occur in a suit involving a claim of civil rights violation. See *Carey* v. *Piphus*, 98 S. Ct. 1042 (1978). Such litigation involves substantial complexities.

[221]*Cooley* v. *Board of School Commissioners of Mobile County*, 341 F. Supp. 1375 (1972); *R.R.* v. *Board of Education of Shore Regional High School District*, 263 A.2d 180, 109 N.J. Super. 37 (1970).

[222]Presumptions of good faith are powerful protections for local boards, but certain factual components can erode favorable presumptions. An example might be an extensive pattern of discriminatory outcomes. *Hawkins* v. *Coleman*, 376 F. Supp. 1330 (N.D. Tex. 1974).

[223]*Board of Elementary and Secondary Education* v. *Nix*, 347 So. 2d 147 (1977); *Clark* v. *Board of Education*, 367 N.E.2d 69, 51 Ohio Misc. 71 (1977); *U.S. by Marshall* v. *Choctaw County Board of Education*, 310 F. Supp. 804 (1969).

dance to correspond with their various achievement levels and competencies.[224]

The initial surge of statutorily mandated competency tests may have peaked, and the accompanying response of litigative challenges has also largely ended.[225] The grounds for legally attacking MCTs were myriad.[226] For instance, such programs nominally create racially discriminatory effects by virtue of the nature of the testing devices.[227] Those effects undergird a Fourteenth Amendment equal protection claim. Unless adequate phase-in periods are provided, students also do not have adequate notice of the change in educational requirements, which may give rise to a Fourteenth Amendment due process claim. The tests are difficult to properly validate, and it is challenging to prove that school programs provide an appropriate match between the instruction and the knowledge demanded by the tests. Finally, plaintiffs could argue that the schools would not be able to provide adequate remedial instruction for those who failed to achieve the highest level of competency. Whatever the format of a competency testing program for a school, the students had reasonable grounds for mounting a legal assault.

Predictably, new MCT requirements were followed in virtually every instance by legal challenges. Although winning some partial victories, the challengers discovered that the courts were unwilling to resolve fully what was essentially a social or educational policy dispute, and finally the keystone case arose in Florida.[228] The plaintiffs did win an initial five-year moratorium on the implementation of the MCT, based partially on due process and partially on the remaining effects of former de jure segregation. Moreover, the appellate court demanded that the state demonstrate "curricular validity" for its test (i.e., that the test covered subjects in the curriculum of Florida's public schools). This burden proved to be costly but not particularly difficult,[229] and in the last analysis the court would not ban the MCT, as the plaintiffs requested.

The more essential societal dilemma is the racial effects associated with MCT programs. Although the number of students who fail to pass the MCT has nominally dropped off after a time, minority students still fail in disproportionate numbers.[230] If the state can demonstrate curricular validity, however, this outcome has not led to judicial declarations that the examination is unconstitutional. When the state can demonstrate that students who fail receive adequate "remediation" opportunities, some judges have been positively predisposed to a program that prevents the high school diploma from being a "hollow certification."[231] As long as a court is persuaded that an MCT is fairly derived from the schools' curriculum and that all students have fair notice and access to the material covered by the test, racially discriminatory outcome data are not a sufficient basis for a court to prohibit a test.

A related problem that may arise after a student has graduated also concerns the basic competency level of the student. Several cases have been filed on behalf of students who have successfully completed all the requirements of a particular school but are found to be functionally illiterate after graduation. Students with educational deficiencies have charged their teachers

---

[224]For a description of the prevalence of state-enacted competency testing programs, see M. McClung, Competency testing: Legal and educational issues, *Fordham Law Review*, 47, 651 (1979).

[225]Cf. A. Logar, Minimum competency testing in schools: Legislative action and judicial review, *Journal of Legal Education*, 13, 35 (1984).

[226]See M. McCarthy, Minimum competency testing for students: Educational and legal issues, *Educational Horizons*, pp. 103–110 (1983).

[227]*McNeal v. Tate County School District*, 508 F.2d 1017 (1975); *Moses v. Washington Parish School Board*, 456 F.2d 1285 (1972).

[228]*Debra P. v. Turlington*, 474 F. Supp. 244 (M.D. Fla. 1979), aff'd in paRt, vacated in paRt and remanded, 644 F.2d 397 (5th Cir. 1981), on remand, 564 F. Supp. 177 (M.D. Fla. 1983), aff'd, 730 F.2d 1405 (11th Cir. 1984). See also *Anderson v. Banks*, 520 F. Supp. 472 (S.D. Ga. 1981).

[229]Florida hired a consulting firm, IOX Associates, to conduct the validity study. They pursued an elaborate, wide-ranging survey process that ultimately satisfied the courts. For a description of that process, see *Debra P. v. Turlington*, 564 F. Supp. 177 et seq.

[230]See *Debra P. v. Turlington*, supra note 228; *Anderson v. Banks*, supra note 228; cf. *McClung*, supra note 224.

[231]This observation was made by a Fifth Circuit judge in an exchange of opinions over the equal educational opportunity implications of MCTs. He argued that to compel Florida to issue diplomas to students who failed its MCT was to "perpetuate the hollow certification that accompanied graduation pre-*Brown*." *Debra P. v. Turlington*, 654 F.2d 1079, 1985 (5th Cir. 1981), denying a petition for rehearing.

and school officials with educational malpractice—the failure of the teachers and the school officials to demonstrate the skill, knowledge, and performance of a reasonable educator or administrator under similar circumstances. Educational malpractice is intended to redress the injuries suffered by students who have made a legitimate effort to meet the demands of coursework and the expectations of school officials, and who have been led by annual promotions and graduation to believe that they have performed in a satisfactory manner, but who are, in fact, inadequately prepared to succeed in society.[232]

The best-known case directly addressing the issue of educational malpractice is *Peter W.* v. *San Francisco Unified School District.*[233] The plaintiff was an otherwise unremarkable student of normal intelligence. Upon his graduation, however, it was discovered that he could read at only the fifth-grade level despite the state statutory requirement of eighth-grade reading level for graduation. Upon appeal, the court dismissed the suit. The court ruled that teachers and school officials owed no duty of care to their students to ensure that they learn even minimal academic skills. The court also dismissed the claims that the school had breached a statutory duty for failing to require an eighth-grade reading level and for misrepresenting that *Peter W.* could read at the eighth-grade level by issuing him a diploma.

The *Peter W.* decision has proven prophetic of courts' reactions to such law suits. Even in cases involving factual situations harshly unfavorable to the school, courts have resisted taking jurisdiction in these disputes.[234] Among professional groups, then, educators alone avoid the prospect of litigation based on unsatisfactory outcomes from professional efforts and judgment.[235] The argument for malpractice cases remains alluring to legal scholars, who have continued to propose bases for judicial review.[236] Thus far, in public schools, although a student may have an enforceable right to appropriate care and supervision to prevent physical (and perhaps emotional) injuries, educational harm remains essentially noncompensable in legal forums.

## CONCLUSION

When the legal rights of students in the public schools are viewed as a whole, contradictory patterns and trends emerge. There are indications that the courts are, at the same time, both expanding students' rights in particular areas and restricting them in others.

The expansion of rights can be seen in three particular areas. First, access to a free public education has been expanded by those cases and statutes that remove barriers based on race, ethnicity, or handicapping condition. For all these groups, the schools have been given an affirmative mandate to ensure that students are given meaningful access to educational opportunities. Also, the courts are unlikely to uphold regulations that restrict full participation in educational activities by married or pregnant students. The courts have recognized that these students, along with all others, have a right to enjoy the full benefits of an education, including participation in extracurricular, school-related activities.[237]

A second area of expansion can be seen in the regulation of a student's right of expression.

---

[232]For a presentation of the logic of the legal cause of action for educational malpractice, see Note, Educational malpractice: Can the judiciary remedy the growing problem of functional illiteracy? *Suffolk University Law Review, 13,* 27 (1979).

[233]*Peter W.* v. *San Francisco Unified School District,* 60 Cal. App. 3d 814, 131 Cal. Rptr. 854 (1976).

[234]See *Hoffman v. Board of Education,* 400 N. E.2d 317, 424 N.Y.S.2d 376 (1979). The plaintiff was able to win a $750,000 jury verdict for injuries caused by misdiagnosis and misplacement that was undiscovered for 12 years. An appellate court reversed the jury verdict, refusing to permit the cause of action.

[235]Because educators operate solely in a "corporate environment" over many years, finding the "guilty party" would be quite difficult, especially as the standard of minimally adequate professional instruction is unclear. See *Peter W.,* supra note 233.

[236]See, for example, G. Ratner, A new legal duty for urban public schools: Effective education in basic skills, *Texas Law Review, 63,* 777 (1985); L. Rothstein, Accountability for professional misconduct in providing education to handicapped children, *Journal of Law and Education, 14,* 349 (1985).

[237]Although nondiscriminatory enjoyment of all school opportunities is required, extracurricular activities are not considered a "right." This distinction has procedural due process consequences. See text at notes 99–103.

The *Tinker* case was a dramatic affirmation of a student's right to hold and express a personal opinion, no matter how offensive it may be to school officials. *Tinker* placed an affirmative burden on the school to show that student expression would probably result in a serious disruption of school activities. Without such a showing, the school may not suppress a student's right of speech or expression. It is important to note, however, that when school officials can show a strong likelihood of disruption or harm to other students (i.e., *Trachtman*),[238] courts are not reluctant to affirm such restrictions. *Bethel School District v. Fraser* also emphasizes that schools may more extensively regulate the mode of a student's expression (i.e., time, place, and manner) than the idea or content.

The students' right to some measure of privacy while in school has also been acknowledged. Reflected in the protection of married and pregnant students, this interest was focal in *T.L.O.*, in which the Court imposed some limits on schools' authority to search students and their possessions. These limits must be put into perspective, however. Because of the school's interest in maintaining a safe and orderly environment, the Court granted more authority to school officials to search than the police enjoy.

Finally, in a very limited sense, *Yoder* may be seen as an expansion of students' rights in state-mandated compulsory attendance. At least for the Amish, the state's interest in compulsory attendance gave way to a small degree to deeply held and long-practiced religious and cultural practices. The *Yoder* opinion was narrowly written, however, and the precedent has not grown, despite the pressures of insistent litigation by parents and private schools. The state's interest in regulating the child's educational experience remains a powerful defense to constitutional challenges.

Just as these areas can be seen as expansions of students' rights, there are others in which courts have refused to enhance the degree of freedom a student (or parent) may exercise. First, when separate but equal facilities are available, the courts have refused to require equal access to the same educational opportunities for both sexes. It is highly likely that these issues will continue to evolve as a function of social change rather than legal mandate. Second, courts have been reluctant to intrude in curricula selection. The legal system (and legislatures) are in a quandary over how to resolve parents' and students' objections about the nature and content of the courses offered by the school. The majority of cases have upheld the right of the school to select an appropriate curriculum. Objections have been heard with both increasing frequency and intensity, but to no avail. Courts have been unresponsive to parental claims rooted in religious beliefs and to students' claims cast as a "right to learn."[239] This area continues to yield a significant number of bitterly contested lawsuits, but there is no evidence that courts will become more receptive to arbitrating these disputes.

Third, the legal rights of students are significantly limited concerning school discipline, particularly in the use of corporal punishment by school officials. Whereas *Goss* ensured procedural protections for students confronting suspension or dismissal, courts have been loath to intrude on substantive concerns involving the type or degree of punishment meted out. *Ingraham* not only upheld the right of school officials to use corporal methods but also eliminated any due process procedures that must precede its use. School authorities' fidelity to minimally appropriate standards will nominally insulate disciplinary judgment from judicial review.

In summary, the area of student rights is in a state of tension. The courts are recurrently faced with a variety of issues, many of which they are clearly uncomfortable in resolving. School officials, students, and parents are each asserting their rights within the educational system.

---

[238]It will be recalled that the *Trachtman* court was willing to limit student speech that interfered with the privacy rights of other students. The *Kuhlmeier* court took a quite different tack, substantially limiting a school's paternalistic authority, at least for secondary students. The Supreme Court justified its decision to permit restriction of "lewd" speech in *Bethel School District*, in part, on the school's paternalistic powers to protect other students' sensibilities. See text *supra* at note 162 et seq.

[239]*Board of Education Island Trees Union Free School District v. Steven, Education Law Reporter. 4*, 1013 (1982). *Pico* approached the identification of "learning" or "inquiry" rights for students, but only in a noncurricular context. Courts have been completely resistant to compensating students who have finished school and are disappointed with their aggregate learning.

Courts are more receptive to requests to ensure fair procedures than to review outcomes for fairness or adequacy. However, a legacy of the 1960s and 1970s is the recognition that students have rights against school officials independent of their parents. These rights are not as comprehensive as those of adults nor as extensive in schools as out of them. In addition, the individual freedoms of each student are subordinate to the larger interests of society and the school in creating and maintaining a safe and efficient educational process. Thus it is not surprising that the balance between the rights of students and those of school officials inherent in a system of "ordered liberty" is constantly in a state of tension.

## CHAPTER 43

# ACCREDITATION AND CREDENTIALING SYSTEMS IN SCHOOL PSYCHOLOGY

WALTER B. PRYZWANSKY
*University of North Carolina–Chapel Hill*

Juxtaposing the topics of *training* and *credentialing* in one chapter may seem somewhat unusual to the casual reader. However, regulatory mechanisms provide accountability for a profession, so that both training programs and individual professionals are affected. At their optimum then, individual credentialing options, when coupled with program training reviews, can form an integrative regulatory system for a profession and/or specialties of a particular profession. Relatively young professions are likely to be characterized by the starts and stops in progress that are made in both the training and the credentialing regulatory arenas; similarly, changes in one arena may not be made in concert with the other. Thus, in the "developing" professions, those connections will not appear as clear-cut as might be expected. Such is the case in professional psychology, which represents both a science and a profession and, as a natural extension of its developmental path, specialties like school psychology. However, school psychology represents a unique case in that its evolution has been shaped by the two dominant conceptual positions that define its mission. That is, school psychology has been claimed by those who would have it represent a specialty in the psychology profession, as well as by those who argue that its uniqueness qualifies it as a separate profession with roots primarily in psychology and education (Pryzwansky, 1993). Although the end result of these two positions yields training and credentialing guidelines that are not dramatically different along many major dimensions, these divergent frameworks have nonetheless resulted in a complex quilt of regulation.

A summary of the current regulatory mechanisms and their sequential relationship to one another are shown in Figure 43.1. Ideally, education and training standards would be reflected in the curriculum of training programs; therefore, licensing and certification examinations would serve an accountability function not only for the knowledge and competencies of the individual school psychologists applying for the credential but for the "qualification rates" of individual training-program graduates as well. This latter measure would be one important source of feedback to training programs. Although there are certain connections among these regulatory bodies, as will be explained, a considerable degree of flexibility still characterizes the specialty of school psychology. One of the factors contributing to this quilted pattern of regulation is the bifurcated visions of school psychology, that is, the specialty dimension, as noted, and the entry level (specialist vs. doctoral degree) dimension (Pryzwansky, 1993). Certainly, *within* those two related perspectives there is growing congruence among the respective accreditation and credentialing bodies. Also, it might be argued that as a result of collaborations such as the Interorganizational Committee on School Psychology, in which the American Psychological Association (APA) Division of School Psychology and the National Association of School Psychologists (NASP) policies are reviewed and collaborations and consensus goals are pursued, there is more overlap than difference in the various regulatory systems. Nevertheless, Fagan and Wise (1994) conclude that the credentialing of school psy-

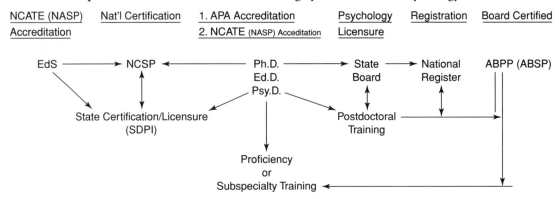

FIGURE 43.1 Regulatory system in school psychology.
Adapted from Brantley & Pryzwansky (1995).

chologists may be the most complex area of professional regulation, with employment setting expectations further complicating regulatory objectives.

The system of accreditation and credentialing, then, is considered more as a congruent unit within each of the two perspectives than as one that applies to both. Consequently, the demands are greater on doctoral-trained school psychologists if they wish to straddle the demands of both, and there is every indication, unfortunately, that they would be ill advised if they were to make choices between them. In the perspective that school psychology is a separate profession, with its entry level at the specialist degree, the National Council for Accreditation of Teacher Education (NCATE) has historically accredited education programs through its relationship with NASP. The National Certificate in School Psychology (NCSP) offers a knowledge-based examination premised on NASP standards for training and credentialing. The NCATE and NASP accreditation review includes both educational specialist and doctoral school psychology training programs. Thus, the fit between these training standards and this practice credential is a relatively good one. A few state departments of public instruction (SDPI) have now begun to use the NCSP credential and/or examination in their certification-licensure for school psychology practice in the schools. National certification from the NCSP and in most instances SDPI certification and licensure typically require continuing education documentation as part of a certificate renewal process. It is important to note that only one level of NCSP certification exists, so this credential is keyed to the specialist degree entry level.

In the psychological community, the APA accredits doctoral-level programs in a number of psychology specialties, including school psychology. It should also be noted that the APA will begin accepting applications from postdoctoral training programs and, where specialty training is specified, will rely on guidelines promulgated by the specialty. Independent psychological practice requires licensure as a psychologist from a state psychology board. The psychology boards require the Examination for Professional Practice in Psychology (EPPP) and usually one year of postdoctoral supervision. Since state psychology licensure is usually generic, not differentiating between applied or academic-research psychologists, some states have used a "health service provider" designation in their acts. It was for this reason and others that the National Register of Health Service Providers in Psychology (hereafter referred to as the National Register) was formed in 1974. A voluntary listing of doctoral-level psychologists, it thus identifies those psychologists with such training, school psychologists among them. Finally, board certification in school psychology has been available since 1968 from the American Board of Professional Psychology (ABPP), which also certifies ten other specialties in psychology.

In summary, then, there is a somewhat integrated regulation system within education for school psychologists trained at the specialist degree level. Although the NCSP credential may not be required for SDPI certification-licensure, the fact that it is oriented to the specialist degree, is a national credential (with potential reciprocity benefits), and is specific to the specialty of school psychology attests to its acceptance by school psychologists regardless of training. For doctorally trained psychologists, state psychology licensure and, to a certain extent, inclusion in the National Register have emerged as a cohesive unit of credentialing. Also, given the increasing interest in a board-specialty certification for the psychology profession, school psychologists can turn to a competency-based examination in their specialty provided by the ABPP. The NCSP is still an alternative specialty credential, but it will hold less meaning in the psychological community because of its emphasis on the specialist-knowledge level. Finally, graduation from an accredited APA program can facilitate the processing of certain regulatory applications in psychology (e.g., licensure and National Register).

As specialty practice has taken hold in psychology, the conceptual challenge of characterizing the field along specialty dimensions has raised the question of whether the so-called de facto specialties, such as clinical, counseling, and school psychology, are indeed specialties, subspecialties, or "emphases" within a generic specialty of health service providers; the relationship of subspecialties to specialties will then need to be addressed, along with questions of what constitutes a "proficiency" and/or "added qualification." School psychology has yet to resolve such a definitional task and incorporate the conclusions into a regulatory system. The APA Division of School Psychology addressed these questions through a task force, charged to prepare a definition of the specialty for submission to the APA Commission for the Recognition of Specialties and Proficiencies in Psychology (CRSPP; Hughes & Conoley, 1995). All of the de facto specialties have been granted formal recognition by CRSPP until 2002, when they will be required to apply for formal recognition. The task force definition is based on broad input from organizations representing the breadth of the doctoral specialty of school psychology and forms the basis of the application made to CRSPP for recognition. It was approved by APA in 1998.

The summary of the accreditation and credentialing system for school psychology (see Figure 43.1) reflects the complexity facing doctoral-level school psychologists in particular. Although formal ties among training and credentialing bodies in each of the two represented training emphases (i.e., doctoral- versus specialist-level school psychology) are much closer to reality than has ever been the case, the interrelationship among the two systems will probably remain tenuous at best for the immediate future. Current

and future collaborative efforts in the school psychology community could prevent future duplication and complexity and move school psychology toward an even more integrated system than exists today.

The remainder of this chapter addresses the current components and regulatory developments (both training-program accreditation and individual practitioner credentials) in school psychology. Minimal attention is paid to background and history since several publications can provide such information (Brown, 1990; Fagan & Wise, 1994; Prasse, 1988; Pryzwansky, 1993).

# LEVELS AND MODELS OF TRAINING

Recent surveys of school psychology training programs find that training continues to be offered toward three levels (i.e., master's, specialist, and doctoral), with the preponderance of graduates completing a 60-credit-hour program, culminating in a master's or specialist degree or some combination of both (Brown, 1990; Fagan & Wise, 1994; Reschly, 1995; Smith & Fagan, 1995). The number and proportion of programs at each level seems to have remained relatively constant in recent years, with 65% emphasizing only predoctoral-level training. Approximately 200 school psychology programs have been graduating an estimated 1,800 students per year. Among school psychology practitioners, approximately one-fifth hold a doctoral degree in school psychology or in a closely related field (Graden & Curtis, 1991). Although the standards and length of preparation have increased, Fagan and Wise (1994) indicate that school psychologists continue to be trained primarily at the predoctoral level, and growth at the doctoral level seems to be less pronounced than had been anticipated. In fact, it has been concluded that there is no reason to believe that the largely nondoctoral character of school psychology is changing now or is likely to change in the future (Reschly, 1995). Clearly, then, what has increasingly been referred to as the specialist level remains the most attractive training option, as does the school system for employment. Indeed, although "specialist level training appears to be sufficient for school practice, additional competencies are surely afforded by doctoral training and may be more significant to effective practice in nonschool settings" (Fagan & Wise, 1994, p. 167). However, the specialty has yet to address such conclusions.

At the present time, school psychology training programs, for the most part, seem to embrace the scientist-practitioner model of training (Pryzwansky & Wendt, 1987). This model was recommended by the Boulder Conference, which was held to examine the training of the professional psychologist (Raimy, 1950). Training in both science and practice is emphasized, so that one area informs the other and the practice of professional psychologists represents an integration of science with professional skills (Lambert, 1993). A professionally oriented model of training was later advocated at the Vail Conference (Korman, 1974), emphasizing applied coursework and culminating in the award of the doctor of psychology degree (Psy.D.). The Vail Conference participants reasoned that when the "primary emphasis in training is on the direct delivery of professional services, and evaluation and improvement of those services, the Psy.D. degree is appropriate" (p. 443). Typically, this training model is found among programs housed in professional schools of psychology and tends to have a clinical psychology specialty orientation. Not many school psychology programs currently offer the Psy.D. degree, although with the growing interest in it (Shapiro & Wiggins, 1994), possibly reflecting growing acceptance of this training orientation in psychology, that situation may not endure for long. Although it might be argued that the doctor of education (Ed.D.) may serve that purpose, training programs offering both the Ph.D. and Ed.D. have not usually offered a sharply differentiating curriculum for each degree. Nevertheless, in universities, where the development of the Psy.D. is not an option, the Ed.D. could serve as the locus for a practitioner-oriented training program. Finally, it should also be noted that 84% of accredited school and counseling programs are located in colleges of education (Reschly, 1995), making such an evolution a relatively easy option to consider.

# TRAINING STANDARDS AND ACCREDITATION

## Training Standards

Both the APA and the NASP have developed training guidelines that serve as the standard for their respective (but separate) accreditation processes. Even though the APA standards and accreditation are limited to doctoral training, one would expect to find, and one does, considerable agreement between both groups, if for no

other reason than the fact that NASP standards emphasize a specialist-level program that includes three years of full-time graduate study (including an internship or the equivalent). Most doctoral programs require only one additional year of education. As early as 1983, the complementary nature of both organizations' accreditation documents was noted (Reilly & Fagan, 1983), although it should be recognized that many doctoral programs do not subscribe to an "add-on" model of training. Nevertheless, each set of standards and associated accreditation procedures will be presented separately, given the fact that they function independently of each other. That is, there is no mechanism for recognition of one by the other, nor is there a procedure by which joint accreditation could take place; in fact, some might argue that the timing is still premature for such efforts, as was the case in the mid-1980s when such efforts occurred. However, Fagan and Wise (1994) report that for APA-accredited doctoral programs seeking NCATE accreditation, NASP will conduct a streamlined review process.

## NASP Training Standards

The National Association for School Psychologists (1994b) standards represent a revision and update of the 1984 standards. These standards were written to guide school psychology training, to serve as a basis for program evaluation, and to be used in the program approval process (i.e., NCATE accreditation). There are six standards. *Standard I, Values as a Program Foundation*, begins with a definition of school psychology as a specialty in the profession of psychology: "founded in respect for the dignity and worth of each individual and in a commitment to further the understanding of human behavior for the purpose of promoting human welfare" (p. 8). The standard calls for a commitment to understanding and responding to human diversity, as well as to enhancing the strengths of critical socialization institutions like families and schools. *Standard II, Knowledge Base, Training Philosophy, Goals and Objectives*, stresses the need for an integrated and sequential program of study and practice. Content is required in the areas of psychological and educational foundations, interventions and problem solving, statistics and research methodologies, and professional school psychology.

*Standard III, Practica*, stresses the centrality of supervised practice and the nature of its training activities as preparatory to the internship. An internship of one academic year, at or near the end of a formal training period, is specified in *Standard IV, Internship*, along with specific features that should characterize this component of training. A systematic evaluation plan is encouraged in *Standard V, Performance-Based Program Accountability*, which focuses on both measures of program elements and student outcomes. Although the NASP standards do not distinguish between doctoral and nondoctoral programs in curriculum, the final standard, *Standard VI, Program Level, and Structural Requirements*, in part, differentiates specialist-level programs from doctoral-level programs in total credit hours (60 vs. 90) and length of internship (1,200 clock hours vs. 1,500 clock hours). Standard VI also includes criteria for students; standards for institutional resources and facilities; and evaluation of graduates, program, and planning.

In addition to guiding curriculum development and revision activities, these standards are used in folio reviews for accreditation. These standards represent a significant shift in emphasis from process requirements to performance-based accountability for training programs. Also, it is important to note that the first five standards refer to both the doctoral and specialist-level programs, whereas a portion of Standard VI provides different criteria for each. Differences between both levels of preparation involve minimum total graduate hours, the nature and length of the internship, and the composition of the faculty.

## APA Training Standards

Although no APA specialty, and thus no APA school psychology training standards exist per se, the American Psychological Association (1981) Specialty Guidelines for the Delivery of Services by School Psychologists specify that APA-accredited school psychology programs must meet the definition of a school psychology program included in that document. In addition to being primarily psychological in nature and recognized by the institution as a school psychology program with an identifiable body of students, there must be an identifiable psychology faculty and a psychologist responsible for the program. The following description is provided:

> Patterns of education and training in school psychology[4] are consistent with the functions to be performed and the services to be provided, in accordance with the ages, populations, and problems found in the various schools and other settings in which school psychologists are employed. The program of study includes a core of academic experience, both didactic and experiential, in basic areas of psychology, includes education related to the practice of the specialty, and provides training in assessment, intervention, consultation, research, program development, and supervision, with special emphasis on school-related problems or school settings.[5] (p. 672)

Footnotes 4 and 5 in the quotation tie the guidelines to earlier APA training and accreditation documents, as well as to a consensus description of education and training components for specialty training in school psychology. The current revisions of the specialty definition of school psychology, which have been spearheaded by the APA Division of School Psychology Task Force (Hughes & Conoley, 1995), were approved in 1998. This revision deals with the structures and levels of training in school psychology and the content of the core scientific and practice foundations for the specialty.

## Accreditation

A description of both the APA and the NCATE (NASP) accreditation process is provided in this section. The reader should note that the APA accredits psychology doctoral-training programs and doctoral internship sites, as well as postdoctoral residencies, which are either generic or specialty-declared in their training orientation. The NCATE (NASP) accreditation process is a unit or specialization recognition system, with no separate accreditation process for internship sites.

## APA Doctoral and Postdoctoral Accreditation

Recognized nationally as accrediting doctoral psychology programs in professional psychology, the APA accredits those programs that self-declare a specialization in primarily clinical, counseling, and school psychology; in addition, only seven "combined professional-scientific psychology programs" are recognized (it is interesting that school psychology is a component of those five programs). More than 300 doctoral programs are presently accredited, 44 of which are school psychology programs (American Psychological Association, 1996a).

In 1995 the APA accreditation structure, process, and criteria underwent rather extensive revisions. First, the Committee on Accreditation (CoA) was reconstituted to include seats for representatives from a number of external organizations (e.g., Council of Graduate Departments of Psychology) so that there is now wider representation of the psychological community; the specialty of school psychology holds 2 seats on the 21-member CoA (Sheridan, Matarazzo, & Nelson, 1995). Also, the CoA was structured to function in a more independent fashion from its parent organization, the APA, than was formerly the case. Similarly, the scope of accreditation has expanded at the doctoral level, and postdoctoral residency training accreditation has been added. At the doctoral training-program level, programs in clinical, counseling, and school psychology will continue to be accredited, along with combinations of these programs, but applications will now also be accepted from emerging, substantive areas of professional psychology. In addition, postdoctoral training programs in specialized fields of professional psychology will also be accepted. This last development is moving forward because of the collaboration of the CoA with an Interorganization Council (IOC) made up of regulatory bodies in psychology and the specialty boards of the American Board of Professional Psychology. Further significant changes in the APA accreditation of training programs include an emphasis on the substantive assessment of the breadth and coherence of program philosophy, resources, and outcomes. The last area of emphasis, an outcome-oriented evaluation focus, reviews the measurable outcomes or products of a program's training efforts as they are defined by the program. This change in turn, will require increased emphasis on the self-study process.

Although school psychology is considered to be a doctoral psychology specialty, no doubt there will emerge postdoctoral school psychology residency programs, which will in turn seek postdoctoral residency program accreditation. More than likely, these programs will continue to provide breadth of training in this specialty, with some emphasis on a proficiency or subspecialty area of practice like supervision; however, it is equally conceivable that there will be postdoctoral programs that emphasize in-depth training in service to a particular population (e.g., early childhood or adolescence), intervention strategy (e.g., prevention), or some other component of school psychological practice (e.g., health service delivery). The IOC and CoA collaboration has resulted currently in an accreditation criteria document, which requires that applications for APA postdoctoral accreditation of a residency program in a specialty must meet the education and training "standards of the specialty practice area in which the program provides its training" (American Psychological Association, 1996c, p. 17). Consequently, an ad hoc task force of school psychology's organizations and regulatory bodies has been organized and is in the process of considering the development of such standards for that specialty.

The APA accreditation model is based on three principles that rest at the core of the profession. First, doctoral education and training is conceptualized as being broad and professional in preparation for entry-level professional psychology practice. Second, the science and practice knowledge base should be relied on by the training programs in the preparation of professional psychologists; together, the science and practice orientations are considered to contribute equally to this objective. Third, considerable latitude is afforded each program to define its own philosophy, model of training, and mission, provided they are consistent with those generally accepted as appropriate to the profession and the CoA. The American Psychological Association (1995) accreditation guidelines state that a program should have "a clear, coherent, and well-articulated description of the philosophy or set of principles underlying its training model, as well as a clear description of its training mission (i.e., its goals, objectives, and the resources, methods and process by which it proposes to attain its desired training outcomes)" (p. 3). Finally, it is important to note that this revised APA process will increasingly emphasize outcomes or products of a program's training efforts and the likelihood that such outcomes can be maintained.

Doctoral graduate programs will be judged specifically for their success in documenting the degree to which they meet domain characteristics considered essential for successful training in professional psychology. The accreditation domains include *Domain A*—Eligibility; *Domain B*—Program Philosophy, Objectives, and Curriculum Plan; *Domain C*—Program Resources; *Domain D*—Cultural and Individual Difference and Diversity; *Domain E*—Student-Faculty Relations: *Domain F*—Program Self-assessment and Quality Enhancement; *Domain G*—Public Disclosure. Specific curriculum areas are mentioned in Domain B. For example, it is expected that "students shall be exposed to the current body of knowledge in at least the following areas: biological aspects of behavior; cognitive and affective aspects of behavior, social aspects of behavior, history and systems of psychology, psychological measurement, research methodology, and techniques of data analysis" (American Psychological Association, 1996c, p. 6). Scientific, theoretical, and methodical foundations of practice in the substantive areas of the training program are also expected, so the curriculum includes exposure to individual differences in behavior, human development, dysfunctional behavior or psychopathology, and professional standards and ethics. A third area involves "diagnosing or re-defining problems through psychological assessment and measurement, formulating and implementing intervention strategies" (p. 7). Finally, it is expected that cultural and individual diversity issues that are relevant to these three curriculum areas will be included.

## APA Accreditation of Doctoral Internship Programs

In addition to doctoral program accreditation, the APA has also accredited doctoral internships, although it no longer distinguishes among them by specialty; approximately 434 doctoral internship programs are accredited (American Psychological Association, 1996b). The APA-accredited internships in school systems have been a recent phenomena, no doubt due in part to the cost involved for the districts in meeting internship accreditation standards and the questioned relevance of a psychological training experience in an organization dominated by the education profession. Currently, there are six accredited school system doctoral internships although several are under review. Three of the internship sites involve only public schools: Cypress Fairbanks Independent School District (Texas), Dallas Public Schools (Texas), and Houston Independent School District (Texas). The remaining three represent consortiums, which include public schools and mental health facilities: University of Tennessee, Memphis Consortium, and Nebraska Internship Consortium in Professional Psychology. However, a number of the other APA-accredited internships, as well as the Association of Psychology Postdoctoral and Internship Centers (APPIC) internship members, will offer training to school psychology applicants (APPIC, 1995).

The internship program that is eligible for APA accreditation must be the equivalent of one full-time year and must be completed in no less than 12 months (10 months for school psychology internships) or no more than 24 months.

Again, accreditation opportunities have been extended to emerging substantive areas, whereas previously only clinical, counseling, and school psychology areas had been accredited. Also, the program will now be required to ensure that its psychology and model of training are consistent with the science and practice of professional psychology. Finally, as in the accreditation of doctoral programs, objectives need to be operationalized into measurable outcomes so that the staff and interns are engaged in an ongoing, regular program review (American Psychological Association, 1996c).

The American Psychological Association (1981) specialty guidelines contain a stipulation that the training of school psychologists must include a supervised internship experience, beyond practicum and fieldwork, equivalent to at least one academic school year (no fewer than 1,200 hours), with a minimum of 600 hours of internship in a school. Since then, the National Register of Health Service Providers in Psychology (1996) has published Guidelines for Defining an Internship or Organized Health Service Training in Psychology (pp. I: 6–7), which are used in their criteria for defining eligibility as a health service provider in psychology. Subsequently, APPIC (1995) listings incorporated a similar definition of an internship. Both of these criteria require a 1,500-hour minimum time period to be completed within a period of no more than 24 months. The Joint Committee on Internships for the Council of Directors of School Psychology (1993) also drew up definitional criteria for school psychology internships that included the 1,500-hour time period. As a result of this action, the National Register and APPIC have agreed to accept those school psychology internships listed by the Joint Committee as meeting their criteria for training in a health service program. In reviewing the APPIC, Joint Committee, and National Register internship criteria, Meyers (1993) noted how little *research* had been done on school psychology internships and, as a result, called for the development of well-conceptualized models of the internship in school psychology and the development of a supporting data base.

## NCATE (NASP) Accreditation

The nationally recognized accrediting body for education specialties is the National Council for Accreditation of Teacher Education (NCATE). It accredits teacher education programs, as well as educational training programs, at a *basic* (entry level) and *advanced* level. As a member of NCATE, NASP's training standards are reinforced through the NCATE accreditation process. "NASP standards were initially approved by the National Council for Accreditation of Teacher Education (NCATE) in 1982 for the review and accreditation of school psychology programs at the sixth year/specialist and doctoral levels" (National Association for School Psychologists, 1994a, p. 2).

Current school psychology training programs can request that NASP conduct a folio review, in which the various components of the program are validated through a review of application materials submitted for documentation. The program folio is first submitted to NCATE, who then forwards it to NASP for evaluation. It is assumed that the program uses systematic evaluation procedures, such as observation of students' skills, performance portfolios, instructional evaluation, and perceptions of students and supervisors. The NCATE's accreditation now involves unit recognition (i.e., department and school) versus program recognition, although since 1988 its listing of departments or schools that have been accredited includes a notation of individual specialty programs that have undergone a positive folio review by the authorized professional organization affiliated with NCATE. In this way, compliance with standards has a significant impact on training. Also, NASP publishes a list of all NASP-approved programs twice each year in the organization's newsletter, *Communiqué*. There may also be a state-mandated program accreditation or approval process conducted by the SDPI of the state in which the program is located, so that NCATE accreditation may be recognized through that system. The NASP folio evaluation teams use the NASP standards for Training and Field Placement to judge programmatic consistency with a given standard. A Program Approval Board receives these judgments in formulating a final decision regarding approval, which is then forwarded to the program and NCATE. Subsequently, interim 5-year reviews are conducted so that submission of a full folio is due only every 10 years.

A second mechanism for NASP approval is available to programs in institutions not affiliated with NCATE or when programs wish to undergo reviews outside the normal NCATE time lines. Finally, APA-accredited doctoral programs in school psychology are not required to submit a folio.

## *NASP Doctoral Internship Standards*

Included as Standard IV of the NASP standards, the internship is presented as a comprehensive, culminating experience for graduate preparation. The settings must be appropriate to the goals and objectives of the program, although the students are expected to complete at least one-half of their internship in a school. The completion of an internship in a nonschool setting is seen as appropriate for doctoral students with a specialist-level internship. Specifically, internships must be full time or half time over a period of two consecutive academic years, with a minimum of 1,500 clock hours. However, NASP does not accredit internship sites, as does the APA; rather, the regulation of field training is done through the program folio review, which is part of the NCATE accreditation process.

## CREDENTIALING FOR THE INDIVIDUAL SCHOOL PSYCHOLOGIST

The monitoring of members through an evaluation of their training, knowledge, and skills has been one hallmark of any group claiming to be a profession. The monitoring process can use a voluntary system of review and/or examination conducted by the profession itself or a state action such as a mechanism to protect its consuming public. It has become axiomatic that state governments need to go beyond the advice of "buyer beware" in protecting its citizens, so state statutes governing the practice of professionals and other services are quite common today. Such regulatory action on the part of states has not been without its critics, particularly in the regulation of a profession. For example, the ideas expressed by Hogan (1979) in this regard continue to garner support and are often behind the "sunset" notion built into many states regulatory systems.

State regulation of professions is typically reflected in statutes or acts that restrict the use of the *title* to those individuals who qualify according to the criteria of the statute, restrict *practice* activities to one group, or sanction the practice activities of a group. These statutes, or acts, have been referred to as certification (title) or licensure (practice and title) acts, although such nuances of definition may not be reflected in all states' nomenclature. One important feature of these acts is that their state origin will account for the variation observed from state to state in the regulation of particular professions, a frustrating reality to professionals who seek consistency for their field, especially the mobile practitioner. Once again, because of school psychologists' dual origin and the fact that their primary employment is in the public schools, two state credentials are salient for practitioners. First, state departments of public instruction (SDPI) have been recognized as the bodies that regulate professional practice in the public schools and, as a result, typically offer *certification* for school psychologists, although some have now begun to use the term *licensure*. At the same time, the independent practice of psychology (and often psychological practice in general, with the exception of school employment) has been regulated by state psychology boards. Consequently, school psychologists who wish to practice or to be recognized as a psychologist in those jurisdictions must seek what has usually been a *license* from the psychology board. To further complicate this description, some state legislatures have recently expressed interest in shifting the credentialing of noneducation professionals (e.g., school psychologists, school counselors, and social workers) from the SDPI credentialing system to the respective credentialing state body that exists for that professional group.

Most professions offer voluntary certification options in addition to those available under state regulation. These credentials tend to have national endorsements within the profession and could represent a more rigorous review than that which is found at the comparable state level. However, they often have a different objective than the state act. In school psychology, the National Certificate in School Psychology (NCSP) is one example of such a credential. Similarly, specialty board certification from the American Board of Professional Psychology exists for psychologists whose practice reflects the activities associated with a specialty within the broader domain of professional psychology. In addition, the APA has recently established the College of Professional Psychology to award certificates that acknowledge knowledge competencies in proficiency areas (American Psychological Association, 1993).

Each of the credentials available to the practicing school psychologist is further described in the following sections. Although there are seldom formal ties among the credentialing bodies, the informal connections are cited where appropriate. Likewise, within both types of statutory credentials, there is usually no reciprocity option, so that professionals must apply to the appropriate state body in the state in which they wish to practice.

## Certification-Licensure (SDPI)

The credential available from the SDPI needs to be recognized as one for *education*, given the fact that it stems from the statutory power of departments of public instruction to set standards for practice in the public schools for many professionals (e.g., teachers, administrators, and counselors). Consequently, it has included among its criteria a review of the degree awarded and the training experiences. For in-state graduates, the latter may require some type of local program-approval process. Thus, applicants from such programs, usually upon the recommendation of the program, are automatically eligible for SDPI credentialing. Otherwise, an equivalence review process is available for out-of-state applicants who have graduated from out-of-state school psychology programs. In addition, there may be an examination requirement. For example, graduates in teacher education may be required to take and pass, at a specified criterion, the relevant specialty examination offered by the Educational Testing Service (ETS). Currently, nine states use the ETS/NASP examination (to be discussed later) as part of their credentialing process for school psychologists, and five others require the NCSP certificate.

A credential from the state department of public instruction was one of the first state credentials available to psychologists. Pennsylvania adopted such a credential in 1933, and by 1963, 32 states were certifying school psychologists (Gray, 1963). By 1976, all SDPIs certified personnel were employing some form of title for school psychologists (Sewell & Brown, 1976). While the overwhelming number of states now use the title *school psychologist*, there is still some variability. Thirty-seven states have the master's degree as the highest level of required training (although some of these require 60 credit hours), and six states accept the bachelor's degree (Prus, Draper, Curtis, & Hunley, 1995). Prus et al. also found that 24 states certified one or more levels of school psychology. Brown (1990) reported that the NCATE/NASP accreditation has provided a mechanism for reciprocity, and 24 states are involved in such an agreement.

## National Certification (NCSP)

In the mid-1980s NASP established the National Certificate in School Psychology (NCSP), which was based on its standards for training and practice. In addition to documentation that training and internship criteria were met, the applicant must take and achieve a passing score on the School Psychology Specialty Area Test of the National Teachers Examination (part of the Praxis Series Professional Assessments for Beginning Teachers), a test administered by the Educational Testing Service (ETS). This knowledge-based objective format deals exclusively with school psychology content; there is only one qualifying score for the certificate, regardless of degree level. The holder of a certificate must be recertified every three years, a decision based on documentation of 75 contact hours of continuing professional development. Although this is a voluntary national credential that validates training and general knowledge in the specialty, over 16,000 school psychologists hold the NCSP (National Association of School Psychologists, 1991). The credential has the potential to facilitate reciprocity among states where SDPI credentialing is involved.

In addition to passing the ETS-administered examination, various entry-level training requirements must be met to qualify for the NCSP; these requirements are based on *Standards for the Credentialing of School Psychologists* (National Association of School Psychologists, 1994a). They include the completion of a sixth-year specialist or higher degree program, including a 60-hour minimum of coursework, practica, and internship. Course preparation in the foundation areas of psychological, educational, and school psychology must be documented, along with preparation in assessment, intervention, and research methods. Successful completion of a supervised 1,200-hour school psychology internship must also be validated.

It is apparent, then, there is a quasi-integrated regulatory system for school psychologists in which standards are related to an individual credential through the various sets of NASP documents. Although not fully operational in all states and targeted at the *non*doctoral entry level, it nevertheless represents a potentially cohesive system because it is tied to training standards.

## Listing as a Health Service Provider

Established in 1974, the *National Register of Health Service Providers in Psychology* (NR) lists 16,000 doctoral psychologists identified as health service providers. A "health service provider in psychology" is defined as "a psychologist, licensed/certified/registered at the independent practice level in a jurisdiction, who is trained and experienced in the delivery of direct, preventative, assessment and therapeutic intervention services to individuals whose growth, adjustment or functioning is impaired or to individuals who otherwise seek services" (Council for the National Register of Health Service Providers in Psychology, 1995, pp. 1–3). A voluntary listing organization, the NR review process consists of a *verification* of education and training of the applicant. The current criteria for listing include the following.

1.  be currently licensed, certified or registered by a State/Provincial Board of Examiners of Psychology at the independent practice level of psychology, and
2.  have completed a doctoral degree in psychology from a regionally-accredited educational institution; and, experience in health services in psychology, of which one year (1500 hours) is in an organized health service training program or internship and one year (1500 hours) is at the postdoctoral level. (pp.1–2)

Psychologists trained in a variety of specialties (e.g., school, clinical, counseling, and health) have obtained this listing.

It is interesting to note that the criteria used by the NR for designating a doctoral program in psychology came about as a result of two conferences in which the NR, the APA, and the American Association of State Psychology Boards and other professional organizations participated. That definition of a professional psychology program includes APA accreditation or satisfaction of nine criteria. Subsequently, the NR has adopted guidelines for defining an internship as an organized health service training program in psychology. These guidelines were later adopted by the APA and the Association of Psychology Internship Centers (APIC); most significantly, the guidelines for school psychology internships (Internships for the Council of Directors of School Psychology, 1997) meet this internship definition. Consequently, for those doctoral school psychologists who identify with the health service provider role and whose education, training and internship meet the criteria, this is a viable verification system. The NR verification is important for health care organizations, for staff privileges in hospitals and other facilities, and for identification as a qualified provider by state and federal government health plans.

## Licensure as a Psychologist

Psychology licensure or certification is usually processed by a state psychology board. Licensure as a psychologist for independent practice is available in all 50 states, the territories of Puerto Rico and Guam, the District of Columbia, and 9 provinces of Canada. According to DeMers (1995), 6 states allow autonomous practice by nondoctoral providers, and 17 other states allow *supervised* practice by nondoctoral providers. Consequently, licensure as a psychologist from psychology boards, in most instances, requires a doctoral degree in psychology. Typical requirements also involve education, experience, examinations, and administrative criteria such as citizenship or age limits.

The license is generic for the most part, that is, without reference to the specialty of the psychologist. Consequently, whereas some individuals with a doctoral degree in psychology are exempt from licensure in some states, provided they do not offer psychological services to the public (e.g., college professors), psychologists from research and applied training programs may be eligible. Incorporation of the APA code of ethics, with its requirement that psychologists practice within their area of competence, governs what services licensed psychologists can offer. The desire to assure the public that psychologists have been trained in an applied area of practice, plus the growing recognition of psychology specialties, have increased the interest in specialty licensure. However, given the impetus for clarifying the type of licensed psychologist (i.e., specialty) for the public and the complexity involved in both recognizing and credentialing specialties, it seems that an added certification to the psychology license, such as "health service provider," has begun to receive attention in some states as an alternative to specialty licensing.

The Association of State and Provincial Psychology Board (ASPPB) was formed to serve the needs of psychology boards, particularly in evaluating applicants for licensure and certification. Consequently, the ASPPB, along with the Professional Examination service, has developed the Examination for Professional Practice in Psychology (EPPP), which is used in all jurisdictions. The EPPP is a standardized, objective examination with 200 multiple-choice questions that is administered semiannually to applicants. Its content is designed to cover knowledge relevant to generic, entry-level practice in psychology. There are five dimensions of content: (a) problem definition or diagnosis; (b) design, implementation, and assessment of intervention; (c) research; (d) professional, ethical, and legal issues; (e) applications to social systems. Whereas ASPPB has recommended a passing score, the cutoff is determined locally by each state; in some states, two levels of psychology licensure are available.

## Specialty Board Certification (ABPP)

Established in 1947 as a way to certify psychologists, in view of the fact that only a few states regulated psychological practice, the American Board of Professional Psychology (ABPP) originally awarded its diplomate certificate in three specialty areas of psychology: clinical, counseling, and industrial or organizational. However, as states passed laws to govern the practice of psychology, the ABPP certificate evolved into a credential designed to recognize practitioner excellence in these applied areas of practice. School psychology was added as a fourth specialty in 1968, at the same time that APA accreditation of school psychology programs became available. In the 1980s, ABPP experienced a second evolutionary change as more specialty practice areas sought formal recognition and the concomitant opportunity to be board-certified in their specialty. Consequently, the ABPP assumed the responsibility for the psychology profession to recognize practice specialties; there are now seven additional specialties—behavioral, health, clinical neuropsychology, forensics, family, psychoanalysis, and rehabilitation—and one additional group within one of three stages of ABPP affiliation prior to full recognition (group). Each of the specialties was eventually incorporated as a specialty board with the responsibility to develop and maintain its credential review and examination process according to minimum ABPP standards, as agreed to by its affiliation. Thus, an American Board of School Psychology was incorporated in 1992.

Board certification is the only *competency*-based credential available in psychology and school psychology. The examination of clinical professional judgment varies according to the specialty. Following a credentials review, candidates must submit representative work samples and undergo an oral examination conducted by diplomates from their specialty. The examination typically deals not only with their work samples but also case-centered segments, ethical content, and substantive content from their specialty. Applications are accepted following three years of practice, one of which may be the doctoral internship.

Clearly, board certification has the highest value for those specialists working in medical or health-related settings, so that as school psychologists identify themselves increasingly as health service providers, either in a school or other related setting, the relevance of this credential becomes obvious. However, for doctoral school psychologists its importance is even more apparent because ABPP board certification is the *only* doctoral-level psychology credential designed specifically for and available in their specialty. It has been noted elsewhere that the majority of doctoral school psychologists enter public rather than private practice, and therefore a justification for seeking licensure is to ascertain evidence of their competence (Brown, 1990). It would seem that they will need to continue seeking such a recognition but increasingly add board certification as a substantive indicator of their competence in the psychology specialty. The recent trend of associating health services with the public schools will enhance the value of such a credential. Board-certified school psychologists are fellows in the American Academy of School Psychology.

## CONCLUSION

The complexity of the regulatory system in school psychology has been increasingly recognized by the specialty, and it may be time, finally, to strive toward a more sequential, integrated system that is relevant to practice and maximizes consumer information. The content and mechanisms for achieving such a goal are in place and, indeed, could have a significant effect on the advancement of roles and functions for school psychologists if trainers and practitioners can come together in a committed and coordinated effort. Whereas training and credentialing have moved forward in a manner that is cognizant of the demands in each arena, an intentionally coordinated system with endorsements from all elements of the school psychology community would be a welcome advance. If nothing else, such a plan could ensure that any future duplica-

tion or unnecessary regulatory system would not develop. As noted, doctoral school psychologists may have already reached a point in which credentialing is overburdensome because of the dual influences from the fields of education and psychology. Some attempt to determine whether a coordinated regulatory system at this level could be realized would seem a prudent consideration for the specialty. Also, it might mitigate the drift of doctoral school psychology to school-related settings or diverse settings (i.e., nonschool practice) and the tendency of trainers to seek only the minimum practice credential.

This presentation would seem to support Fagan's (1995) challenge that a "Thayer-like" conference (Cutts, 1955) would be a timely exercise for the specialty trainers to entertain; at the minimum, an end-of-century review seems to be called for, at which some weighty issues could be entertained. For example, what will happen to the market for school psychologists as the specialty's first retirement phase comes about (Fagan, 1988), especially at the university level. Is this the time that doctoral school psychologists (and other psychology specialists) will begin to constitute 30% to 50% of the school psychology work force, and are they prepared to contribute to the needs of the students, parents, and educational personnel? To what extent does specialist-level education and training needs influence doctoral-level preparation, and what should be the characteristics of that relationship? Are there, and can there be, two levels of training, as envisioned by the Thayer Conference? Is the professional psychology training model overdue in development, or will school psychology emerge only as a subspecialty within a generic professional psychology program? Has our current emphasis on the scientific-practitioner model of training actually held back advancement in psychological interventions? Brown (1990) concluded that there was a trend toward the applied professional psychologist model, but primarily at the specialist level of training. Finally, Fagan and Wise (1994) have identified three potential challenges to training programs: (a) strained program curricula because of dual training standards, (b) weakened ties to schools of education because of the professional psychology model of training in clinical psychology, and (c) pressure on programs in schools of education to identify more with an educational than a psychological orientation.

This sample of questions and potential trends has obvious implications for the future of the specialty, let alone the regulatory system as it attempts to ensure some common review standards. Just as the recent past may have seen significant developments in the regulatory arena, the coming years may see an equal emphasis on education and training. In any event, trainers would seem to have a number of opportunities to affect practice and research if they wish to seize them. Otherwise, the opportunity for affecting schools through psychology, once envisioned by this specialty, may increasingly be incorporated by other psychologists or educational specialists.

# REFERENCES

American Psychological Association (1981). Specialty guidelines for the delivery of services by school psychologists. *American Psychologist, 36*(6), 670–681.

American Psychological Association. (1993). Council debates college, health reform and budget. *APA Monitor, 24*(1), 1, 8.

American Psychological Association. (1995). *Guidelines and principles for accreditation of programs in professional psychology.* Washington, DC: Author.

American Psychological Association (1996a). APA-accredited doctoral programs in professional psychology: 1996. *American Psychology, 51,* 1306–1319.

American Psychological Association (1996b). APA-accredited predoctoral internships for doctoral training in psychology: 1996. *American Psychologist, 51,* 1287–1305.

American Psychological Association (1996c). *Book 1: Guideline and principles for accreditation of programs in professional psychology.* Washington, DC: Author.

APPIC (Association of Psychology Postdoctoral and Internship Centers). (1995). *APPIC Directory* (24th ed.). Washington, DC: Author.

Brantley, J., & Pryzwansky, W. B. (1995, August). Implications of the redefinition of school psychology for credentialing and post-doctoral training. Paper presented at the Second Annual School Psychology Training Conference: Redefining the Doctoral Specialty of School for the 21st Century, New York.

Brown, D. T. (1990). Professional regulation and training in school psychology. In T. B. Gutkin & C. R. Reynolds, *The Handbook of School Psychology* (2nd ed., pp. 991–1009). New York: Wiley.

Council for the National Register of Health Service Providers in Psychology. (1995). *National register of health services providers in psychology* (3rd ed.). Washington, DC: Author.

Cutts, N. E. (Ed.). (1955). *School psychology at mid-century.* Washington, DC: American Psychological Association.

DeMers, S. T. (1995, April). The regulation of school psychology around the world. Paper presented at the First International Congress on Licensure, Certification, and Credentialing of Psychologists, New Orleans, LA.

Fagan, T. K. (1988). The historical improvement of the school psychology service ratio: Implications for future employment. *School Psychology Review, 17,* 447–458.

Fagan, T. K. (1995, August). Architects of change: The special role of trainers in defining or redefining the future of school psychology. Paper presented at the Second Annual School Psychology Training Conference: Redefining the Doctoral Specialty of School for the 21st Century, New York.

Fagan, T. K., & Wise, P. S. (1994). *School psychology.* New York: Longman.

Graden, J., & Curtis, M. (1991, September). *A demographic profile of school psychology: A report to the Delegate Assembly of the National Association of School Psychologists.* Washington, DC: National Association of School Psychologists.

Gray, S. W. (1963). *The psychologist in the schools.* New York: Holt, Rinehart & Winston.

Hogan, D. B. (1979). *The regulation of psychotherapists* (Vols. 1–4). Cambridge, MA: Ballinger.

Hughes, J. N., & Conoley, J. C. (1995, Fall). Request for membership reactions to draft specialty definitions. *The School Psychologist, 49*(4), 95.

Joint Committee on Internships for the Council of Directors of School Psychology; Division of School Psychology, American Psychological Association, and National Association of School Psychologists. (1997). *Directory of internships for doctoral students in school psychology.* University Park, PA: School Psychology Clinic, Pennsylvania State University.

Korman, M. (1974). National conference on levels and patterns of professional training in psychology. *American Psychologist, 29,* 441–449.

Lambert, N. M. (1993). Historical perspective on school psychology as a scientist-practitioner specialization in school psychology. *Journal of School Psychology, 31*(1), 163–193.

Meyers, J. (1993, August). Comparison of CDSPP internship guidelines to those of APPIC. Presentation made to the Council of Directors of School Psychology Programs at the Annual Meeting of the American Psychological Association, Toronto.

National Association of School Psychologists. (1991, November). Recertification deadline draws near. *NASP Communiqué,* pp. 1, 10.

National Association of School Psychologists. (1994a). *Standards for the credentialing of school psychologists.* Washington, DC: Author.

National Association of School Psychologists. (1994b). *Standards for the training and field placement programs in school psychology*. Washington, DC: Author.

National Register of Health Service Providers in Psychology. (1996). *Guidelines for defining an internship or organized health service training in psychology* (14th ed.). Washington, DC: Author.

Prasse, D. P. (1988). Licensing, school psychology, and independent practice. In T. R. Kratochwill (Ed.), *Advances in school psychology* (Vol. 6, pp. 49–80). Hillsdale, NJ: Erlbaum.

Prus, J., Curtis, M. J., Draper, A., & Hunley, S. (1995). A summary of credentialing requirements for school psychologists in public school settings. In A. Thomas & J. Grimes (Eds.), *Best Practices in School Psychology–III* (pp. 1237–1247). Washington, DC: National Association of School Psychologists.

Pryzwansky, W. B. (1993). The regulation of school psychology: A historical perspective on certification, licensure and accreditation. *Journal of School Psychology, 31*, 219–235.

Pryzwansky, W. B., & Wendt, R. N. (1987). *Psychology as a profession*. New York: Pergamon.

Raimy, V. E. (1950). *Training in clinical psychology*. Englewood Cliffs, NJ: Prentice Hall.

Reilly, D., & Fagan, T. (1983). *Final report of the APA/NASP joint accreditation in school psychology*. Washington, DC: American Psychological Association and National Association of School Psychologists.

Reschly, D. J. (1995, August). Characteristics of school psychology graduate education and school-based practice: Implication for doctoral specialty definition. Paper presented at the Second Annual School Psychology Training Conference: Redefining the Doctoral Specialty of School for the 21st Century, New York.

Sewell, T. J., & Brown, D. T. (1976). *Handbook for certification/licensure requirements for school psychologists*. Washington, DC: National Association of School Psychologists.

Shapiro, A. E., & Wiggins, J. G. (1994). A Psy.D. degree for every practitioner: Truth in labeling. *American Psychologist, 49*(3), 183–186.

Sheridan, E. P., Matarazzo, J. D., & Nelson, P. D. (1995). Accreditation of psychology's graduate professional education and training programs: A historical perspective. *Professional Psychology: Research and Practice, 26*(4), 386–392.

Smith, D. K., & Fagan, T. K. (1995). Resources on the training of school psychologists. In A. Thomas & J. Grimes (Eds.), *Best Practices in School Psychology—III* (pp. 1257–1258). Washington, DC: National Association of School Psychologists.

# NAME INDEX

Page references followed by italic *n* indicate material in footnotes. Page references have been conflated to conserve space. A range of page numbers may not necessarily indicate a continuous discussion over the whole range, just that the name was mentioned at least once on each page of the range.

Metalsky, G. I., 206, 217
Metfessel, J. R., 128, 133
Metz, L. W., 603, 608, 624, 628
Meyer, A., 257, 269
Meyer, C. A., 362, 380
Meyer, H., 716–717, 742
Meyer, L., 701–702, 706–707
Meyer, M. C., 827, 838, 858
Meyer, V., 829, 860
Meyers, B., 600–601, 607, 624, 633, 768, 796, 806, 808–810, 819
Meyers, C. E., 561, 592, 1006, 1021, 1093, 1095, 1111
Meyers, H., 623, 636
Meyers, J., 111, 128, 133, 500, 515, 600–601, 603–605, 607–608, 618, 622, 624–625, 628–629, 633, 766, 770–771, 776–781, 784–785, 788, 794–797, 806, 808–810, 819, 1077, 1110, 1151, 1157
Meyers, L. H., 536, 545
Mianchi, M. D., 824, 829, 852
Michael, E. G., 110, 132–133
Michael, J. L., 646, 662
Michael, W. B., 128, 133
Michaels, C. R., 257, 269–270
Michaud, L. J., 866, 883
Michlak, M., 1133n
Michnowicz, L. L., 489, 494
Mick, E., 281, 286
Mico, P., 622, 632
Middleton, D., 60, 77
Middleton, H., 209, 220
Midgley, B. D., 616, 633
Midgley, C., 948–949, 956
Miele, F., 565, 570–571, 574, 592
Miezitis, S., 758, 760
Migeon, B. R., 280, 288
Mikkelsen, E., 841, 859
Milberger, S., 281, 286
Milburn, J. F., 673, 682, 696, 704, 813, 816
Miles, M. B., 109, 120–121, 134–135, 614, 629, 922, 930, 961, 982, 1028–1029, 1037, 1039, 1056, 1075
Milgram, N., 210, 219
Milich, R., 283, 288, 692–693, 706, 834, 842, 845, 848, 854, 858, 862
Millard, T., 369, 378
Mille, M., 570–571, 594
Miller, A. D., 812, 815–816, 819
Miller, C. D., 644, 661
Miller, C. K., 530, 546
Miller, C. L., 703–704
Miller, D. L., 641, 660
Miller, D. T., 195, 220
Miller, G. A., 601, 603, 607, 626, 633
Miller, G. E., 728, 742, 748, 754, 762
Miller, J., 845, 858–859
Miller, J. G., 112, 134
Miller, J. Y., 772, 776, 786, 789, 796
Miller, L., 928, 931
Miller, L. J., 484, 488, 494
Miller, M., 608, 636
Miller, M. S., 647, 660
Miller, N. E., 144, 148, 164, 213, 220
Miller, P., 145–146, 148, 165
Miller, R. L., 840, 857
Miller, S. I., 60, 77
Miller, S. R., 672, 684
Miller, T. L., 315, 348, 752, 762
Miller-Jones, D., 122, 134
Millman, H. L., 609, 633
Millman, J., 418, 433
Millroy, W. L., 109–110, 133
Mills, C. N., 410, 419, 421–425, 431–433
Millstein, S. G., 160, 165
Milne, A. M., 710, 742

Milofsky, E. S., 271–272, 290
Milone, M. N., 994–995, 1016
Mimms, J. W., 399, 408
Mims, J. W., 652, 662
Minderaa, R. B., 840, 856
Miner, B., 1047, 1054
Miner, J. L., 728–729, 741
Miner, M. E., 866, 871, 876, 882–883
Minke, K. M., 2, 29, 256, 270, 435, 450, 609, 626
Minnery, K. L., 839, 861–862
Minnesota Extension Service, 719, 742
Minogue, K., 58, 77
Minor, M. W., 616, 633
Minskoff, E., 990–991, 1021
Minton, H. L., 34, 52, 223–224, 244
Mira, M. P., 863, 866, 869–872, 883
Mirenda, P. L., 640, 659
Mirkin, P. K., 360–361, 377, 386, 388, 391, 405, 407
Mischel, W., 208, 218, 538, 546
Mishkin, L., 867, 871, 884
Mishler, E. G., 119, 134
Misiak, H., 46, 53
Mitchell, M. A., 638, 658
Mitchell, M. M., 598, 634
Mitroff, I. I., 1006, 1021
Mitrsomwang, S., 710, 723, 742
Mittl, V. F., 847, 858
Mize, J., 697, 707
Mizelle, J. D., 836, 855
Mnookin, R., 1103, 1111
Mo, A., 278, 289
Modafferi, C., 766, 781, 796
Moe, G., 610–611, 636
Moeller, A. J., 945, 956
Moffitt, T. E., 161, 164
Moghaddam, F. M., 36, 52
Moles, O., 710, 738, 740, 742
Molfese, V., 488, 494
Molitor, C. B., 460, 475
Moll, L., 127, 134
Molling, P. A., 836, 855
Monk, D., 66, 77
Montagna, D., 664, 673–674, 683
Montesi, M. P., 272, 289
Montgomery, D. J., 961n, 982
Montgomery, G., 586, 588
Mool, L. C., 129, 131
Moore, C. M., 926, 931
Moore, D. W., 651, 662
Moore, J. L., 178, 189
Moore, L. A., 702, 707
Moorer, S. H., 834, 858
Moorhead, M. K., 388–389, 391, 406
Mooris, R. D., 459, 472
Moos, R. H., 770, 797
Morales, E. S., 559, 592
Morales, J., 256, 269
Moran, M. P., 77, 571, 579, 592
Morau, M. G., 837, 861
Morehead, M. K., 499–500, 516, 679, 683
Moreland, K. L., 562, 592
Moreno, J. L., 198, 209, 220
Morgan, A., 295–296, 305, 756, 762
Morgan, D. P., 703, 707, 812, 819
Morgan, J., 698, 707
Moroz, G., 824, 827, 854
Morrell, J. A., 907, 930
Morrell, W., 829, 861
Morris, E. K., 616, 633
Morris, L. L., 128, 134
Morris, R. J., 350, 380, 455, 464, 474, 755, 762, 836, 858
Morrison, D. E., 986, 1021
Morrison, G., 886, 889, 900, 906

Morrison, G. M., 104, 107, 214, 219–222, 640, 659
Morrison, J. A., 124, 127, 134
Morrison, J. E., 62, 77
Morrison, R. L., 214, 220–222
Morrow, M., 213, 217
Morrow, W. R., 11–13, 31
Morse, J. M., 109, 134
Morse, W. C., 615–616, 633
Morsink, C. V., 1011, 1021
Mortimore, P., 960, 961n, 962, 982–983
Mosley-Howard, G. S., 1046, 1054
Moss, P., 562, 589
Moss, P. A., 124, 134
Mossop, J., 922, 930
Motta, R. W., 441–442, 450
Moultrie, R., 806, 816, 1028, 1032, 1034–1035, 1038
Mounts, L., 486, 491
Mounts, N. S., 508, 517, 710, 717, 743–744
Mowrer, O. H., 144, 148, 164
Mozes, T., 830, 858
Mrazek, D. A., 239, 245
Mrazek, P. J., 802–803, 819
Mueller, D. J., 201, 221
Mueser, K. T., 210, 221
Muhoff, I., 768, 796
Muir, S., 258, 269
Mulaik, S. A., 100, 106
Mulick, J. A., 58, 76
Mullen, B. L., 710, 742
Mullen, F. A., 17, 31
Muller, C., 768, 796
Mullin, E., 727, 742
Munk, D. D., 669, 684, 942–943, 956
Munoz, R. F., 802, 819
Munsinger, H., 235, 244
Munson, R. G., 254, 270
Munson, S. M., 651, 661
Munsterberg, H., 10–11, 31
Murphy, D. A., 831, 835, 837, 842, 848, 858–859
Murphy, D. L., 482, 494
Murphy, J., 941, 956, 961n, 964n, 966–967, 968n, 970, 972–973, 975, 977, 979–980, 982, 1010, 1023–1024
Murphy, P. A., 172, 186
Murphy, P. K., 168–172, 175, 178, 181, 186, 189–190, 192
Murray, C., 58, 76, 104, 106, 223, 244, 272, 287–288, 549, 590, 1045, 1054, 1099, 1110
Murray, H. A., 110–111, 134, 443, 450
Murray, R., 239, 244
Muthukrishna, N., 771, 794
Muyskens, P., 392, 407
Myers, S. S., 942, 956

**N**

Nachtman, W., 386, 405
Nagle, R. J., 696–697, 705
Naglieri, J. A., 259, 270, 307–309, 315, 321–324, 333–334, 346, 348, 442, 450
Naidu, S., 280, 288
Nakagawa, M., 485, 495
Nakib, Y., 66, 77
Nalven, F. B., 561, 592
Nanda, N., 520, 529–530, 544
Nandakumar, R., 567, 592
Nantwi, K. D., 275, 288
Napier, R. W., 624–625, 633
Narayan, J. S., 812, 818–819
Nash, W. R., 176, 186
Nass, G., 986, 1022
Nastasi, B. K., 212, 221, 675–676, 684, 764, 767, 770, 772, 774–779, 781–782, 784, 787–792, 795–798

# SUBJECT INDEX

Page references followed by italic *table* indicate material in tables. Page references followed by italic *n* indicate material in footnotes. Additional references for the professional organizations can be found in the Name Index.